HOLMAN
Illustrated
Bible
Dictionary

HOLMAN
Illustrated
Bible
Dictionary

General Editors
Chad Brand, Charles Draper, Archie England

Associate Editors
Steve Bond, E. Ray Clendenen

General Editor, Holman Bible Dictionary
Trent C. Butler

Biblical Reconstructions by
Bill Latta

HOLMAN
REFERENCE

Nashville, Tennessee

Dewey Decimal Classification: 220.3
Subject Heading: BIBLE—DICTIONARIES

ISBN 13: 978-0-8054-2836-0

Printed in China
11 12 13 14 15 • 10 09 08 07

Editorial Foreword

Since the inception of the Christian church, believers have found both the center and circumference of divine revelation in the sacred Scriptures. The day the church was born she had a fully authoritative Bible, the Old Testament. The need for more Scripture was recognized in due time and the authority of the books that constitute the New Testament was affirmed through a centuries-long process of canonization. The historic faith of the church is that authoritative inscribed (that is, written) revelation begins and ends with the Bible. These are fundamental theological affirmations central to this project. We declare unequivocally our commitment, and the commitment of the other editors, to the total trustworthiness, truthfulness, sufficiency, inerrancy, and infallibility of the Bible.

Further, nothing is more basic to progress in the Christian life and to ministry of every kind than a working knowledge of Scripture. Our sincere hope is that this book will serve multiple purposes, such as facilitating acquisition of knowledge about the Bible, understanding the Bible's meaning and message, and providing an entree into the wider world of biblical scholarship.

We stand on the shoulders of others, the editors and writers who produced the *Holman Bible Dictionary* (HBD). Interestingly, that project consumed six years, as has this revision and expansion. Neither edition would have been possible without the Herculean effort of general editor Trent Butler and the contributing editors of the HBD. Trent also encouraged the publisher to prepare a new edition, incorporating the best of recent biblical scholarship.

We are deeply grateful for the opportunity to collaborate with so many gifted people in the completion of the *Holman Illustrated Bible Dictionary* (HIBD). Without the active and aggressive leadership, participation, patience, and support of Ray Clendenen, Steve Bond, Vicki Lee, Dean Richardson, and others at B&H this project could not have been completed. In addition, we have received invaluable assistance from secretarial assistants, especially Lisa Taylor, Lindi Fowler, and Tina Brand. The institutions where we have taught over these years have been very gracious and supportive of the project. We extend thanks to our deans, presidents, and colleagues at North Greenville College, Boyce College, The Southern Baptist Theological Seminary, and New Orleans Baptist Theological Seminary for support, advice, and encouragement along the way. We are indebted also to hundreds of gifted writers.

While our editorial design is to serve a broad audience, from lay people to students and ministers, we believe the HIBD is useful also to professors and scholars. For twelve years prior to the writing of this foreword, the HBD has been among the best-selling Bible dictionaries. We commend the HIBD to you, and we hope and pray that it proves as durable and useful and finds as wide a constituency as its predecessor.

General Editors,

Chad Owen Brand, Ph.D.
Charles W. Draper, Ph.D.
Archie W. England, Ph.D.

Table of Contents

Special Internal Features

INTERNAL MAPS

Key to Pronunciation

MARK	EXAMPLE	SIGN
ā	dāy, lāy	ay
ă	hăt, căt	a
ä	äre, fär	ah
â	câre, fâre	e, eh
a	(unmarked) call	aw
à	àfraid	u, uh
ah	(unmarked) Elijah	uh
âi	âisle	ī
am	(unmarked) adam's apple	uhm
an	(unmarked) roman	uhn
c, k	cord, chorus	k
ç	çity	s, ss
ē	mēte, Crēte	ee
ĕ	mĕt, lĕt	e, eh (uh)
ẽ	tẽrm	u, uh
ə	əlastic	i, ih
g	(unmarked) get	g
ġ	ġerm	gh, j
ī	pīne, fīne	ī
ĭ	hĭm, pĭn	ih
î	machîne	cc
ĩ	firm	u, uh (uhr)
ō	nōte, rōde	o, oh
ŏ	nŏt, rŏt	ah
o	(unmarked) amok	uh
ô	ôr, fôr	aw
ph	(unmarked) alpha	f
ş	hiş, muşe	z
s	(unmarked) kiss	ss
ū	tūne, mūte	yoo, ew
ŭ	ŭp, tŭb	uh
û	hûrl, fûrl	u, uh
ü	trüth	oo, ew
th	thyme	t
ti, ci, si	attraction	sh
y	city	i, ih

Seldom Used Marks

ao	(unmarked) pharaoh (ant)	oh
au	(unmarked) author	aw
on	(unmarked) onion	uhn
ou	(unmarked) out	ow

Transliteration of Hebrew, Greek, & Aramaic

Hebrew			Greek	
א	ʾ		α	a
ב בּ	b		β	b
ג גּ	g		γ	g
ד דּ	d		δ	d
ה	h		ε	e
ו	w		ζ	z
ז	z		η	e
ח	ch		θ	th
ט	t		ι	i
י	y		κ	k
כ כּ	k		λ	l
ל	l		μ	m
מ	m		ν	n
נ	n		ξ	x
ס	s		ο	o
ע	ʿ		π	p
פ פּ	p ph		ρ	r
צ	ts		σ	s
ק	q		τ	t
ר	r		υ	u
שׂ	s		φ	ph
שׁ	sh		χ	ch
ת	t		ψ	ps
			ω	o

vocal shewa	ə
patach	a
qamets	a
qamets chatuph	o
tsere	e (full and defective)
segol	e
chireq	i (short and long)
cholem	o (full and defective)
qibbuts	u
shureq	u

Contributors

Akin, Daniel L. Dean of the School of Theology; VP of Academic Admin.; Prof. of Christian Preaching. The Southern Baptist Theological Seminary, Louisville, Kentucky

Albright, Jimmy Pastor, Wyatt Park Baptist Church, St. Joseph, Missouri

Allen, Leslie C. Prof. of OT. Fuller Theological Seminary, Pasedena, California

Anderson, Douglas Exec. Dir., St. Luke's Community House, Nashville, Tennessee

Andrews, Stephen J. Prof. of OT & Hebrew; Dir. of Morton-Seats Institute of Archaeology & Anthropology. Midwestern Baptist Theological Seminary, Kansas City, Missouri

Arnold, Steve*

Baldwin, Gary D. Pastor, First Baptist Church, Pineville, Louisiana

Baskin, Joe Adjunct Prof. of Davis Center for Ministry Education. Shorter College, Rome, Georgia

Batson, Jerry W. Associate Dean for Academic Affairs; Associate Prof. of Divinity, Beeson Divinity School. Samford University, Birmingham, Alabama

Bean, Albert F. Associate Prof. of OT & Hebrew. Midwestern Baptist Theological Seminary, Kansas City, Missouri

Beck, David R. Associate Prof. of NT & Greek. Southeastern Baptist Theological Seminary, Wake Forest, North Carolina

Beitzel, Barry J. Exec. VP. Trinity International University, Deerfield, Illinois

Bellinger, W. H., Jr. Dir. of Graduate Studies in Religion. Baylor University, Waco, Texas

Berry, Donald K. Prof. of Religion. University of Mobile, Mobile, Alabama

Berry, Everett Pastor, Utica Baptist Church, Utica, Kentucky

Betts, Terry J. Assistant Prof. of OT Interpretation, Boyce College. The Southern Baptist Theological Seminary, Louisville, Kentucky

Bishop, Ronald E. Prof. Jones County Junior College, Ellisville, Mississippi

Blaising, Craig Exec. VP; Provost; Dean of the School of Theology. Southwestern Baptist Theological Seminary, Fort Worth, Texas

Blevins, James L. Retired. Former Prof. of NT Interpretation. The Southern Baptist Theological Seminary, Louisville, Kentucky

Block, Daniel I. Associate Dean, Scripture & Interpretation; Prof. of OT Interpretation. The Southern Baptist Theological Seminary, Louisville, Kentucky

Blount, Douglas Assistant Dean for Ethics & Philosophical Studies; Assistant Prof. of Philosophy of Religion. Southwestern Baptist Theological Seminary, Fort Worth, Texas

Bond, Steve Editor, Bibles and Reference Books. Broadman & Holman Publishers, Nashville, Tennessee

Bonner, Gary*

Borchert, Gerald L. Prof. of NT. Northern Baptist Theological Seminary, Lombard, Illinois

Brand, Chad Owen Associate Prof. of Christian Theology. The Southern Baptist Theological Seminary/Associate Prof. of Christian Theology; Coordinator, Dept. of Bible & Theology. Boyce College, Louisville, Kentucky

Brangenberg, John H., III VP & Academic Dean; Associate Prof. of Bible & Biblical Languages. Pacific Rim Bible College, Honolulu, Hawaii

Bridges, Linda McKinnish Associate Dean of the College of Wake Forest. Wake-Forest University, Winston-Salem, North Carolina

Brisco, Thomas V. Prof. of OT. Baylor University, Waco, Texas

Brooks, James A. Prof. Emeritus of NT. Bethel Seminary, St. Paul, Minnesota

Brooks, Oscar S. Sr. Prof. of NT Studies. Golden Gate Baptist Theological Seminary, Mill Valley, California

Browning, Daniel C., Jr. Prof. of Religion. William Carrey College, Hattiesburg, Mississippi

Bruce, Barbara J. Freelance writer, Ridgecrest, North Carolina

Bruce, Larry Freelance writer, Fort Worth, Texas

Burris, Kevin*

Butler, Bradley S. Pastor, Warren Woods Baptist Church, Warren, Michigan

Butler, Trent C. Editor, Bibles & Reference Books. Broadman & Holman Publishers, Nashville, Tennessee

Byrd, Robert O. Prof. of Religion. Belmont University, Nashville, Tennessee

Cabal, Theodore J. Prof. of Christian Philosophy. The Southern Baptist Theological Seminary, Louisville, Kentucky

Carlson, Stephen W. Leadership & Adult Publishing, Lifeway Christian Resources, Nashville, Tennessee

Cate, Robert L. Phoebe Young Prof. of Religious Studies. Oklahoma State University, Stillwater, Oklahoma

Cathey, Joe Adjunct Prof. of Religion. Dallas Baptist University, Dallas, Texas

Chance, Bradley Chair & Prof. of Religion; Dir. of Academic Advising. William Jewell College, Liberty, Missouri

Chandler, William T., III Minister of Education, Valley Station Baptist Church, Louisville, Kentucky

Choi, Kyoungwon Doctoral candidate. The Southern Baptist Theological Seminary, Louisville, Kentucky

Church, Christopher Prof. of Philosophy & Religion. Baptist College of Health Sciences, Memphis, Tennessee

Clendenen, E. Ray Executive Editor, Bibles & Reference Books. Broadman & Holman Publishers, Nashville, Tennessee

Coats, George W. Prof. Emeritus. Lexington Theological Seminary, Lexington, Kentucky

Cole, R. Dennis Chairperson of the Division of Biblical Studies; Prof. of OT & Archaeology. New Orleans Baptist Theological Seminary, New Orleans, Louisiana

Coleson, Joseph*

Collins, Alvin O.† Former Chairman of Dept. of Religion. Houston Baptist University, Houston, Texas

Compton, Bob Roseboro, North Carolina

Conyers, A. J., III Prof. of Theology, Truett Theological Seminary. Baylor University, Waco, Texas

Cook, Donald E.*

Cook, William F. Associate Prof. of NT Interpretation. The Southern Baptist Theological Seminary, Louisville, Kentucky

Cooper, C. Kenny President-Treasurer, Tennessee Baptist Adult Homes, Inc., Brentwood, Tennessee

Cornett, Daryl C. Assistant Prof. of Church History. Mid-America Baptist Theological Seminary, Germantown, Tennessee

Cowan, Steven B. Associate Director, Apologetics Resource Center, Birmingham, Alabama

Cowen, Gerald P. Dean of Southeastern College at Wake Forest; Prof. of NT & Greek. Southeastern Baptist Theological Seminary, Wake Forest, North Carolina

Cox, Steven L. Associate Prof. of NT & Greek. Mid-America Baptist Theological Seminary, Germantown, Tennessee

Craig, Kenneth M., Jr. Associate Prof. Lees-McRae College, Banner Elk, North Carolina

Cranford, Jeff*

Cranford, Lorin L. Prof. of Religion. Gardner-Webb University, Boiling Springs, North Carolina

Creech, R. Robert Sr. Pastor, University Baptist Church, Houston, Texas

Creed, Brad Provost. Samford University, Birmingham, Alabama

Cresson, Bruce C. Dir., Institute of Biblical Languages. Baylor University, Waco, Texas

Crook, Roger Retired, Prof. of Religion. Meredith College, Raleigh, North Carolina

Cross, Diane*

Culpepper, R. Alan Dean, McAfee School of Theology. Mercer University, Macon, Georgia

Davis, Earl C.*

Davis, John J. Prof. of OT Studies. Grace Theological Seminary, Winona Lake, Indiana

Davis, M. Stephen*

Dean, Robert J. Retired, Sr. Editorial & Curriculum Specialist. Lifeway Christian Resources, Nashville, Tennessee

Dehoney, Wayne Retired pastor, Walnut Street Baptist Church, Louisville, Kentucky

Depp, David Freelance writer, Taylors, South Carolina

DeVries, LaMoine Prof. of NT, OT, & Biblical Archaeology. Southwest Missouri State University, Springfield, Missouri

DeVries, Simon J. Retired, Prof. of OT. Methodist Theological School, Delaware, Ohio

Dockery, David S. President; Prof. of Christian Studies. Union University, Jackson, Tennessee

Dollar, Stephen E. Vidor, Texas

Dominy, Bert B. Prof. of Christian Theology, Truett Theological Seminary. Baylor University, Waco, Texas

Drakeford, John W. Prof. Emeritus of Psychology & Counseling. Southwestern Baptist Theological Seminary, Fort Worth, Texas

Draper, Charles W. Associate Prof. of Biblical Studies, Boyce College. The Southern Baptist Theological Seminary, Louisville, Kentucky

Draughon, Walter D., III Pastor, St. Petersburg First Baptist Church, St. Petersburg, Florida

Drayer, John R.*

Drinkard, Joel F., Jr. Prof. of OT Interpretation; Dir., Joseph A. Callaway Museum. The Southern Baptist Theological Seminary, Louisville, Kentucky

Drumm, C. Scott Assistant Prof. of Theological & Historical Studies, Leavell College. New Orleans Baptist Theological Seminary, New Orleans, Louisiana

Duke, Barrett, Jr. Ethics & Religious Liberty Commission, VP for Public Policy, Southern Baptist Convention, Washington, D.C.

Duke, David Nelson† Former Prof. of Religion. William Jewell College, Liberty, Missouri

Duvall, J. Scott Dean & Fuller Prof. of Biblical Studies. Ouachita Baptist University, Arkadelphia, Arkansas

Eakin, Frank E., Jr. Prof. of Jewish & Christian Studies. University of Richmond, Richmond, Virginia

Eakins, J. Kenneth Dir., Marian Eakins Archaeological Collection. Golden Gate Baptist Theological Seminary, Mill Valley, California

Easley, Kendell Chairman of NT Dept., Prof. of NT & Greek. Mid-America Baptist Theological Seminary, Germantown, Tennessee

Echols, Steve Associate Dean of Professional Doctoral Studies, Associate Prof. of Leadership. New Orleans Baptist Theological Seminary, New Orleans, Louisiana

Edwards, W. T., Jr. Prof. Emeritus of Religion. Samford University, Birmingham, Alabama

Ellenburg, Dale Pastor, Ellendale Baptist Church, Bartlett, Tennessee

Ellis, Bob R. Prof. of OT & Hebrew, Logsdon School of Theology. Hardin-Simmons University, Abilene, Texas

Ellis, Terence B. Pastor, Spring Hill Baptist Church, Mobile, Alabama

England, Archie W. Associate Prof. of OT & Hebrew. New Orleans Baptist Theological Seminary, New Orleans, Louisiana

Enns, Paul P. Adjunct Prof. of Theology. Southeastern Baptist Theological Seminary, Tampa, Florida

Fallis, William J. Retired, Sr. Editor, Broadman Press, Nashville, Tennessee

Feinburg, Charles Lee† Founding Dean & Dean Emeritus, Talbot School of Theology. Biola University, LaMirada, California

Field, Taylor Dir., East Seventh Baptist Ministry, New York, New York

Fink, Michael Knowledge & Channel Management. Lifeway Christian Resources, Nashville, Tennessee

Fisher, Fred L.† Former Prof. of NT. Golden Gate Baptist Theological Seminary, Mill Valley, California

Fleming, David M.*

Fountain, Mark Freelance writer, Louisville, Kentucky

Fredericks, Daniel C. Sr. VP & Provost. Belhaven College, Jackson, Mississippi

Freeman, C. Hal, Jr. Associate Prof. of Christian Studies, Dir. for Christian Emphasis in Academics. North Greenville College, Tigerville, South Carolina

Fricke, Robert Retired Dir., Baptist Seminary, Costa Rica

Fuller, Russell T. Associate Prof. of OT Interpretation. The Southern Baptist Theological Seminary, Louisville, Kentucky

Galeotti, Gary A. Sr. Prof. of OT. Southeastern Baptist Theological Seminary, Wake Forest, North Carolina

Gautsch, Darlene R. Adjunct Prof. of OT & Hebrew. Golden Gate Baptist Theological Seminary, Mill Valley, California

Gentry, Peter J. Associate Prof. of OT Interpretation. The Southern Baptist Theological Seminary, Louisville, Kentucky

George, Timothy Founding Dean of Beeson Divinity School; Prof. of Church History, Historical Theology; Samford University, Birmingham, Alabama. Exec. Editor for *Christianity Today*.

Glaze, Joseph E. First Baptist Church, Hamilton, New York

Glaze, R. E., Jr. Prof. Emeritus of NT. New Orleans Baptist Theological Seminary, New Orleans, Louisiana

Gloer, William Hulitt Prof. of Preaching & Christian Scripture, Truett Theological Seminary. Baylor University, Waco, Texas

Gower, Ralph*

Graham, Charles E. Prof. Emeritus of OT. New Orleans Baptist Theological Seminary, New Orleans, Louisiana

Gray, Elmer L.† Former Editor of *California Southern Baptist,* Fresno, California

Grissom, Fred A. Prof. of Religious Studies. North Carolina Wesleyan College, Rocky Mount, North Carolina

Haag, Joe Dir., Program Planning & Special Moral Concerns, Christian Life Commission. Baptist General Convention of Texas, Dallas, Texas

Halbrook, Gary K. Dir., Center for Care & Counseling, Lufkin, Texas

Hancock, Omer J., Jr. Prof. of OT, Church Ministry, & Field Education, Logsdon School of Theology. Hardin-Simmons University, Abilene, Texas

Hardin, Gary Pastor, Packard Road Baptist Church, Ann Arbor, Michigan

Harris, R. Laird† Former Prof. Emeritus of OT. Covenant Theological Seminary, St. Louis, Missouri

Harrison, R. K.† Prof. Emeritus of OT, Wycliffe College. University of Toronto, Toronto, Canada

Harrop, Clayton† Former Academic VP & Dean of Faculty. Golden Gate Baptist Theological Seminary, Mill Valley, California

Hatchett, Randy L. Associate Prof. of Christianity & Philosophy. Houston Baptist University, Houston, Texas

Hatfield, Lawson G.*

Haygood, B. Spencer Sr. Pastor, Orange Hill Baptist Church, Atlanta, Georgia

Hemer, Colin J.† Former Research Fellow, Tyndale House, Cambridge, England

Henderson, Gene† Former Design Editor, *Adult Bible Teacher.* Lifeway Christian Resources, Nashville, Tennessee

Henry, Jerry M. Pastor, First Baptist Church, Fairhope, Alabama

Hepper, F. Nigel Formerly of the Royal Botanic Gardens, Kew, England

Hill, C. Dale Sr. Pastor, Grand Parkway Baptist Church, Richmond, Texas

Hockenhull, Brenda R.*

Honeycutt, Roy L. Former President, The Southern Baptist Theological Seminary, Louisville, Kentucky

Horton, Fred L., Jr. John Thomas Albritton Professor. Wake Forest University, Winston-Salem, North Carolina

House, Paul R. Dean of Christian Studies; Prof. of OT. Wheaton College, Wheaton, Illinois

Howe, Claude L., Jr. Prof. Emeritus of Church History. New Orleans Baptist Theological Seminary, New Orleans, Louisiana

Hubbard, Kenneth Pastor Emeritus, First Baptist Church, Smyrna, Tennessee

Huckabay, Gary C. Sr. Pastor, Calvary Baptist Church, Las Cruces, New Mexico

Humphries-Brooks, Stephenson Associate Prof. of Religious Studies. Hamilton College, Clinton, New York

Hunt, Harry B., Jr. Retired, Prof. of OT. Southwestern Baptist Theological Seminary, Fort Worth, Texas

Ireland, William J., Jr. Pastor, Ardmore Baptist Church, Winston-Salem, North Carolina

Jackson, Paul Associate Prof. of Christian Studies. Union University, Jackson, Tennessee

Jackson, Thomas A. Pastor, Wake Forest Baptist Church, Wake Forest, North Carolina

Johnson, Jerry A. Dean, Boyce College. The Southern Baptist Theological Seminary, Louisville, Kentucky

Johnson, Ricky L. Former Prof. of OT. Southwestern Baptist Theological Seminary, Fort Worth, Texas

Johnson, Walter Associate Prof. of Philosophy & Christian Studies. North Greenville College, Tigerville, South Carolina

Joines, Karen R. Prof. of Religion. Samford University, Birmingham, Alabama

Jones, Lynn Pastor, First Baptist Church, Booneville, Mississippi

Jones, Peter Rhea Prof. of Preaching & Theology, McAfee School of Theology. Mercer University, Macon, Georgia

Kaiser, Walter C., Jr. President; Prof. of Christian Studies. Gordon-Conwell Theological Seminary, South Hamilton, Massachusetts

Keathley, Naymond Dir. of Undergraduate Studies in Religion. Baylor University, Waco, Texas

Kelly, Brent R. Adjunct Prof. Indiana Wesleyan University, Louisville, Kentucky

Kelm, George L. Retired, Prof. of Biblical Backgrounds & Archaeology. Southwestern Baptist Theological Seminary, Fort Worth, Texas

Kent, Dan Gentry Retired, Prof. of OT. Southwestern Baptist Theological Seminary, Fort Worth, Texas

Kilpatrick, R. Kirk Assistant Prof. of OT & Hebrew. Mid-America Baptist Theological Seminary, Germantown, Tennessee

Kimmitt, Francis X. Associate Dean, Leavell College; Associate Prof. of OT & Hebrew. New Orleans Baptist Theological Seminary, New Orleans, Louisiana

Knight, George W. Prof. of NT, Greek, & Biblical Theology, Logsdon School of Theology. Hardin-Simmons University, Abilene, Texas

Koester, Helmut Research Prof. of NT Studies. Harvard Divinity School, Cambridge, Massachusetts

Laing, John Assistant Prof. of Philosophy and Theology. Southwestern Baptist Theological Seminary, Fort Worth, Texas

Laing, Stefana Dan Adjunct Instructor in Divinity Beeson Divinity School. Samford University, Birmingham, Alabama

Langston, Scott Associate Prof. of Biblical Studies. Southwest Baptist University, Bolivar, Missouri

Lanier, David E. Prof. of NT; Editor, *Faith & Mission.* Southeastern Baptist Theological Seminary, Wake Forest, North Carolina

Laughlin, John C. H. Chairman of the Religion Dept.; Prof. of OT, Hebrew, & Philosophy. Averett University, Danville, Virginia

Lea, Thomas D.† Former Academic Dean. Southwestern Baptist Theological Seminary, Fort Worth, Texas

Lee, H. Page*

Lee, Philip New Orleans, Louisiana

Lemke, Steve W. Provost; Prof. of Philosophy. New Orleans Baptist Theological Seminary, New Orleans, Louisiana

Leonard, Bill J. Dean of the Divinity School & Prof. of Church History. Wake Forest University, Winston-Salem, North Carolina

Lewis, Floyd† Former pastor, First Baptist Church, Eldorado, Arizona

Lewis, Jack P. Prof. of Bible. Harding University Graduate School of Religion, Memphis, Tennessee

Lewis, Joe O. Retired, Provost. Samford University, Birmingham, Alabama

Livingston, George Herbert† Prof. Emeritus of OT. Asbury Theological Seminary, Wilmore, Kentucky

Logan, Phil*

Lorenzen, Thorwald Sr. Lecturer. St. Mark's National Theological Center, Canberra, Australia

Lunceford, Joe E. Prof. of Religion. Georgetown College, Georgetown, Kentucky

MacRae, Allan A.† Chancellor & Emeritus Prof. of OT. Biblical Seminary, Hatfield, Pennsylvania

Mallau, Hans-Harold*

Maltsberger, David C. Sr. Pastor, Westlynn Baptist Church, North Vancouver, British Columbia

Mapes, David Assistant Prof. of Theology. Luther Rice Bible College and Seminary, Lithonia, Georgia

Mariottini, Claude F. Prof. of OT. Northern Baptist Theological Seminary, Lombard, Illinois

Marsh, C. Robert*

Martin, D. C.† Former Chairman & Prof., Dept. of Christian Studies. Grand Canyon, College. Phoenix, Arizona.

Martin, D. Michael Dir. of Online Education; Prof. of NT. Golden Gate Baptist Theological Seminary, Mill Valley, California

Martin, Ralph P. Distinguished Scholar in Residence. Fuller Theological Seminary, Pasadena, California

Martin, Tony M. Prof. of Religion. University of Mary Hardin Baylor, Belton, Texas

Massey, Ken Sr. Pastor, First Baptist Church, Greensboro, North Carolina

Matheney, M. Pierce, Jr. Retired, Prof. of OT & Hebrew. Midwestern Baptist Theological Seminary, Kansas City, Missouri

Matheson, Mark E. Pastor, First Baptist Church, Windermere, Florida

Mathis, Donny R., II Adjunct Prof. of NT, Boyce College. The Southern Baptist Theological Seminary, Louisville, Kentucky

Matthews, E. LeBron Pastor, Eastern Heights Baptist Church, Columbus, Georgia

Matthews, Victor H. Associate Dean of the College of Humanities & Public Affairs; Prof. of Religious Studies; Coordinator of the Antiquities Program. Southwest Missouri State University, Springfield, Missouri

McCoy, Glenn Retired, Bible Chair. Eastern New Mexico University, Portales, New Mexico

McGee, Daniel B. Prof. of Religion. Baylor University, Waco, Texas

McGraw, Larry R. Prof. of NT, OT, & Biblical Backgrounds, Associate Dean for Undergraduate Studies, Logsdon School of Theology. Hardin-Simmons University, Abilene, Texas

McKinney, Larry Dir. of Communications, Baptist Foundation of Kansas City, Overland Park, Kansas

McNeal, T. R. Dir., Leadership Development Team, South Carolina Baptist Convention, Columbia, South Carolina

McRay, John Prof. Emeritus of NT & Archaeology. Wheaton College Graduate School, Wheaton, Illinois

McWilliams, Warren Auguie Henry Prof. of Bible. Oklahoma Baptist University, Shawnee, Oklahoma

Meier, Janice Leadership & Adult Publishing. Lifeway Christian Resources, Nashville, Tennessee

Merkle, Ben L. Gelugor, Penang Malaysia

Michaels, J. Ramsey Prof. Emeritus of Religious Studies, Southwest Missouri State University/Adjunct Prof. of NT. Bangor Theological University, Springfield, Missouri & Madbury, New Hampshire

Mickelsen, A. Berkeley† Prof. of NT Emeritus, Bethel Theological Seminary, St. Paul, Minnesota

Miller, J. Maxwell Prof. Emeritus, Candler School of Theology. Emory University, Atlanta, Georgia

Miller, Stephen R. Chairman of the Doctor of Philosophy Committee; Chairman, Dept. of OT & Hebrew; Prof. of OT & Hebrew. Mid-America Baptist Theological Seminary, Germantown, Tennessee

Millikin, Jimmy A. Dir., Masters & Associates Programs; Chairman, Dept. of Theology; Acting Chairman, Dept. of Church History; Prof. of Theology. Mid-America Baptist Theological Seminary, Germantown, Tennessee

Mitchell, Eric Alan Assistant Prof. of Biblical Backgrounds & Archaeology. Southwestern Baptist Theological Seminary, Fort Worth, Texas

Mitchell, Michael J. VP of Mitchell Oil Company, Fort Payne, Alabama

Mohler, R. Albert, Jr. President; Prof. of Christian Theology. The Southern Baptist Theological Seminary, Louisville, Kentucky

Mooney, D. Jeffrey Doctoral candidate. The Southern Baptist Theological Seminary, Louisville, Kentucky

Moore, Russell D. Assistant Prof. of Christian Theology; Exec. Dir., Carl F. H. Henry Institute for Evangelical Engagement. The Southern Baptist Theological Seminary, Louisville, Kentucky

Morgan, Barry Prof. of NT & Greek. Hannibal-LaGrange College, Hannibal, Missouri

Morris, Leon† Former Principal. Ridley College, Melbourne, Australia

Morris, Wilda W. Adjunct Faculty Member. Garrett Evangelical Theological Seminary, Evanston, Illinois

Mosley, Harold R. Associate Prof. of OT & Hebrew. New Orleans Baptist Theological Seminary, New Orleans, Louisiana

Mott, Stephen Charles Pastor, Cochesett United Methodist Church, West Bridgewater, Massachusetts

Moyer, James C. Dept. Head of Religious Studies. Southwest Missouri State University, Springfield, Missouri

Murrell, Rich Network Specialist, Church Resources Division. Lifeway Christian Resources, Nashville, Tennessee

Music, David W. Prof. of Church Music, School of Music. Southwestern Baptist Theological Seminary, Fort Worth, Texas

Nelson, David P. Assistant Prof. of Systematic Theology. Southeastern Baptist Theological Seminary, Wake Forest, North Carolina

Newell, James Pastor, First Baptist Church, Jasper, Alabama

Newman, Carey C. Academic Book Editor, Westminster/John Knox Press, Louisville, Kentucky

Ngan, Lai Ling Elizabeth Associate Prof. of Christian Scriptures, OT & Hebrews, Truett Theological Seminary. Baylor University, Waco, Texas

Norman, Robert Stanton Associate Prof. of Theology, occupying the McFarland Chair of Theology. New Orleans Baptist Theological Seminary, New Orleans, Louisiana

O'Brien, J. Randall Chair & Prof. of Religion Dept. Baylor University, Waco, Texas

Omanson, Roger L. American Bible Society, New York, New York

Orrick, Jim Scott Prof. of Literature & Culture, Boyce College. The Southern Baptist Theological Seminary, Louisville, Kentucky

Ortiz, Steven Assistant Prof. of Archaeology. New Orleans Baptist Theological Seminary, New Orleans, Louisiana

Osborne, Grant R. Prof. of NT. Trinity Evangelical Divinity School, Deerfield, Illinois

Overstreet, Mark M. Adjunct Prof. of Preaching, Boyce College. The Southern Baptist Theological Seminary, Louisville, Kentucky

Owens, J. J.† Former Sr. Prof. of OT & Hebrew. The Southern Baptist Theological Seminary, Louisville, Kentucky

Palmer, Clark Intentional interim pastor/ Freelance writer, Pineville, Louisana

Parker, W. Dan Dir. of Undergraduate Extension Center System; Associate Prof. of Pastoral Ministry, North Georgia Campus. Leavell College, New Orleans Baptist Theological Seminary, New Orleans, Louisiana

Parkman, Joel*

Parks, D. Mark Adjunct Prof. of Religion. Dallas Baptist University, Dallas, Texas

Parsons, Mikeal C. Associate Prof. of Religion. Baylor University, Waco, Texas

Patterson, Dorothy Prof. of Women's Studies. Southeastern Baptist Theological Seminary, Wake Forest, North Carolina

Patterson, L. Paige President; Sr. Prof. of Theology. Southeastern Baptist Theological Seminary, Wake Forest, North Carolina

Pearce, T. Preston Theological Consultant, International Mission Board, Richmond, Virginia

Plummer, Robert L. Assistant Prof. of NT Interpretation. The Southern Baptist Theological Seminary, Louisville, Kentucky

Polhill, John B. James Buchanan Harrison Prof. of NT Interpretation. The Southern Baptist Theological Seminary, Louisville, Kentucky

Potts, Donald R. Retired, Chairman of the Religion Dept. East Texas Baptist University, Marshall, Texas

Poulton, Gary President Emeritus & Prof. of History. Virginia Intermont College, Bristol, Virginia

Powell, Paul Dean, Truett Theological Seminary. Baylor University, Waco, Texas

Price, Nelson Pastor Emeritus, Roswell Street Baptist Church, Marietta, Georgia

Prince, Robert William, III Vernon, Texas

Quarles, Charles L. Associate Prof. of NT & Greek. New Orleans Baptist Theological Seminary, New Orleans, Louisiana

Queen-Sutherland, Kandy Prof. of Religious Studies. Stetson University, DeLand, Florida

Rainey, Joel Church Starter Strategist, North American Mission Board. Southern Baptist Convention, Richmond, Virginia

Ray, Charles A., Jr. Associate Dean of Research Doctoral Programs; Prof. of NT & Greek. New Orleans Baptist Theological Seminary, New Orleans, Louisiana

Reddish, Mitchell G. Prof. of Religious Studies. Stetson University, DeLand, Florida

Redditt, Paul L. Chair of Religion Dept.; Prof. of OT, NT, & Non-Western Traditions. Georgetown College, Georgetown, Kentucky

Reeves, Rodney Prof. of NT. Southwest Baptist University, Bolivar, Missouri

Register, R. Dean Pastor, Temple Baptist Church, Hattiesburg, Mississippi

Ridge, Donna R. Freelance writer, Kimberly, Wisconsin

Robbins, Ray Frank Prof. Emeritus of NT & Greek. New Orleans Baptist Theological Seminary, St. Joseph, Louisiana

Robertson, Paul E. New Orleans, Louisiana

Robinson, Darrell W. President, Total Church Life Ministries, Inc. & Minister of Evangelism. Roswell Street Baptist Church, Marietta, Georgia

Rogers, Max† Former Prof. of OT. Southeastern Baptist Theological Seminary, Wake Forest, North Carolina

Rooker, Mark Prof. of OT & Hebrew. Southeastern Baptist Theological Seminary, Wake Forest, North Carolina

Ruffle, John University of Durham, Durham, England

Russell, Jeremiah H. Doctoral student. Baylor University, Waco, Texas

Sandlin, Bryce Levelland, Texas

Saul, D. Glenn VP for Academic Services & Graduate Studies. Wayland Baptist University, Plainview, Texas

Sawyer, W. Thomas Prof. Emeritus of NT & Greek. Mars Hill College, Mars Hill, North Carolina

Scalise, Pamela J. Associate Prof. of OT. Fuller Theological Seminary, Pasedena, California

Schemm, Peter R., Jr. Assistant Prof. of Theology. Southeastern Baptist Theological Seminary, Wake Forest, North Carolina

Schreiner, Thomas R. Prof. of NT Interpretation; Editor, *The Southern Baptist Journal of Theology.* The Southern Baptist Theological Seminary, Louisville, Kentucky

Schweer, G. William Sr. Prof. of Evangelism. Golden Gate Baptist Theological Seminary, Mill Valley, California

Sexton, James Cordele, Georgia

Shackleford, David G. Prof. of NT & Greek. Mid-America Baptist Theological Seminary, Germantown, Tennessee

Sheffield, Bob Pastoral Ministries. Lifeway Christian Resources, Nashville, Tennessee

Simmons, Billy E. Prof. Emeritus of NT & Greek. New Orleans Baptist Theological Seminary, Gulfport, Mississippi

Skinner, Craig Former Prof. of Preaching. Golden Gate Baptist Theological Seminary, Mill Valley, California

Sloan, Robert B., Jr. President, CEO, & Prof. of Religion. Baylor University, Waco, Texas

Smith, A. J. Doctoral candidate. The Southern Baptist Theological Seminary, Louisville, Kentucky

Smith, Billy K.† Former Academic Dean & Prof. Emeritus of OT & Greek. New Orleans Baptist Theological Seminary, New Orleans, Louisiana

Smith, Fred Theology Student Advisor & Adjunct Teacher of Philosophy of Religion. Southwestern Baptist Theological Seminary/Adjunct Prof. of Philosophy of Religion, The Criswell College, Dallas, Texas

Smith, Gary V. Prof. of OT & Hebrew. Midwestern Baptist Theological Seminary, Kansas City, Missouri

Smith, Marsha A. Ellis Associate VP for Institutional Research. The Southern Baptist Theological Seminary, Louisville, Kentucky

Smith, Ralph L. Retired, Prof. of OT & Hebrew. Southwestern Baptist Theological Seminary, Fort Worth, Texas

Smothers, Thomas Retired, Prof. of OT & Hebrew. The Southern Baptist Theological Seminary, Louisville, Kentucky

Snider, P. Joel Pastor, First Baptist Church, Rome, Georgia

Songer, Harold S. Retired, Prof. of NT. The Southern Baptist Theological Seminary, Louisville, Kentucky

Spradlin, Michael R. President; Chairman of Dept. of Evangelism; Prof. of OT & Hebrew, Evangelism, Practical Theology, & Church History. Mid-America Baptist Theological Seminary, Germantown, Tennessee

Stabnow, David K. Bible Translation Editor. Broadman & Holman Publishers, Nashville, Tennessee

Stagg, Robert Prof. Emeritus of Bible. Ouachita Baptist University, Arkadelphia, Arkansas

Stein, Robert H. Mildred and Ernest Hogan Prof. of NT Interpretation. The Southern Baptist Theological Seminary, Louisville, Kentucky

Stephens, Shirley Freelance writer/editor, Nashville, Tennessee

Stevens, Gerald L. Prof. of NT & Greek. New Orleans Baptist Theological Seminary, New Orleans, Louisiana

Stewart, Don H. Prof. of NT & Greek. New Orleans Baptist Theological Seminary, New Orleans, Louisiana

Stewart, Robert B. Assistant Prof. of Philosophy & Theology. New Orleans Baptist Theological Seminary, New Orleans, Louisiana

Stinson, Randy Exec. Dir., Council on Biblical Manhood & Womanhood, Louisville, Kentucky

Strange, James F. Prof. of Religious Studies & Dir. of Graduate Studies. University of South Florida, Tampa, Florida

Street, Robert Anderson, Jr. Prof. of OT. Campbellsville University, Campbellsville, Kentucky

Strong, L. Thomas III Dean, Leavell College; Associate Prof. of NT & Greek, Leavell College. New Orleans Baptist Theological Seminary, New Orleans, Louisiana

Summers, Ray† Former Prof. of NT & Greek. Southwestern Baptist Theological Seminary, Fort Worth, Texas

Sutherland, Dixon*

Swanson, Phillip J. Pastor, Colts Neck Baptist Church, Colts Neck, New Jersey

Talbert, Charles H. Distinguished Prof. of Religion. Baylor University, Waco, Texas

Tan, Randall K. J. Doctoral candidate. The Southern Baptist Theological Seminary, Louisville, Kentucky

Tang, Samuel Yau-Chi Sr. Prof. of OT & Hebrew. Golden Gate Baptist Theological Seminary, Mill Valley, California

Tankersley, Bruce Prof. of Religion. East Texas Baptist University, Marshall, Texas

Taulman, James Assistant to the Exec. Dir., Baptist History & Heritage Society, Brentwood, Tennessee

Thompson, J. William Retired, Sr. Design Editor. Lifeway Christian Resources, Nashville, Tennessee

Tobias, Hugh*

Trammell, Timothy Associate Dean, Mary Crowley College of Christian Faith. Dallas Baptist University, Dallas, Texas

Travis, James L. Prof. Emeritus. Blue Mountain College, Blue Mountain, Mississippi

Traylor, John H., Jr. Retired pastor. Monroe, Louisiana

Tullock, John H. Prof. Emeritus of OT & Hebrew. Belmont University, Nashville, Tennessee

Turnham, Tim Pastor, Luther Rice Memorial Baptist Church, Silver Spring, Maryland

Van Leeuwen, Raymond C. Prof. of Biblical Studies. Calvin Theological Seminary, Grand Rapids, Michigan

Vermillion, William H.*

Vickers, Bryan J. Associate Editor, *The Southern Baptist Journal of Theology;* Doctoral candidate, The Southern Baptist Theological Seminary, Louisville, Kentucky

Wade, Charles R. Exec. Dir., Baptist General Convention of Texas, Dallas, Texas

Walker, Douglas C. Sr. VP for Institutional Relations. The Southern Baptist Theological Seminary, Louisville, Kentucky

Walker, Larry Retired, Prof. of OT & Hebrew. Mid-America Baptist Theological Seminary, Germantown, Tennessee

Warren, William F., Jr. Dir., Center for NT Textual Studies; Coordinator, Baptist College Partnership Program; Prof. of NT & Greek. New Orleans Baptist Theological Seminary, New Orleans, Louisiana

Wellum, Stephen J. Associate Prof. of Christian Theology. The Southern Baptist Theological Seminary, Louisville, Kentucky

White, James Dir., Alpha & Omega Ministries, Phoenix, Arizona

Wilbanks, Pete Assistant Prof. of Christian Studies. North Greenville College, Tigerville, South Carolina

Wilder, Terry Prof. of NT & Greek. Midwestern Baptist Theological Seminary, Kansas City, Missouri

Wilson, Douglas K., Jr. Pastor, First Baptist Church, Orchard Park, New York

Wilson, Kimberly P. Orchard Park, New York

Wolf, Christian*

Wooldridge, Judith Sr. Product Development Specialist, Lifeway Church Resources. Lifeway Chirstian Resources, Nashville, Tennessee

Wright, G. Al, Jr. Pastor, First Baptist Church, Waynesboro, Georgia

Wright, Paul H. Dir. of Jerusalem University College, Coordinator of Academic Programs; Biblical History & Geography. Jerusalem University College, Jerusalem, Israel

Wyrick, Stephen Von Prof. of Religion. University of Mary Hardin Baylor, Belton, Texas

Yamauchi, Edwin Prof. of History. Miami University, Oxford, Ohio

Yarnell, Malcolm B., III Assistant Dean for Theological Studies; Associate Prof. of Theology. Southwestern Baptist Theological Seminary, Fort Worth, Texas

York, Hershael W. Lester Prof. of Christian Preaching; Associate Dean of Ministry & Proclamation. The Southern Baptist Theological Seminary, Louisville, Kentucky

Youngblood, Kevin J. Doctoral candidate. The Southern Baptist Theological Seminary, Louisville, Kentucky

Zachariades, Doros Doctoral candidate. The Southern Baptist Theological Seminary/Pastor, Woodstock Baptist Church, Somerset, Kentucky

Time Line

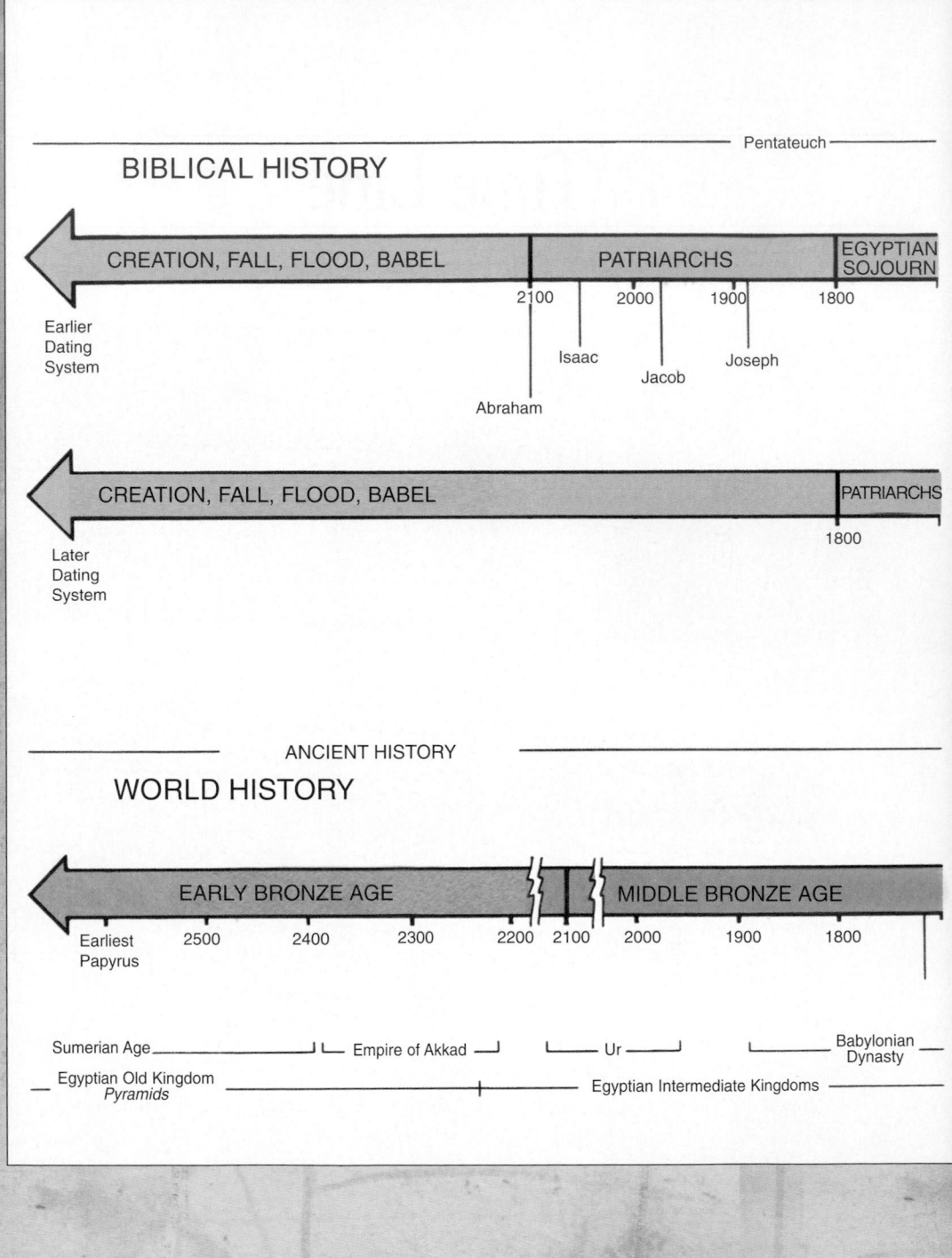

BIBLICAL HISTORY

Pentateuch

CREATION, FALL, FLOOD, BABEL | PATRIARCHS | EGYPTIAN SOJOURN

2100   2000   1900   1800

Earlier
Dating
System

Isaac

Jacob

Joseph

Abraham

CREATION, FALL, FLOOD, BABEL | PATRIARCHS

1800

Later
Dating
System

WORLD HISTORY

ANCIENT HISTORY

EARLY BRONZE AGE | MIDDLE BRONZE AGE

2500   2400   2300   2200 2100   2000   1900   1800

Earliest
Papyrus

Sumerian Age ——————— Empire of Akkad —— —— Ur —— Babylonian Dynasty

Egyptian Old Kingdom ———————————— Egyptian Intermediate Kingdoms ————
Pyramids

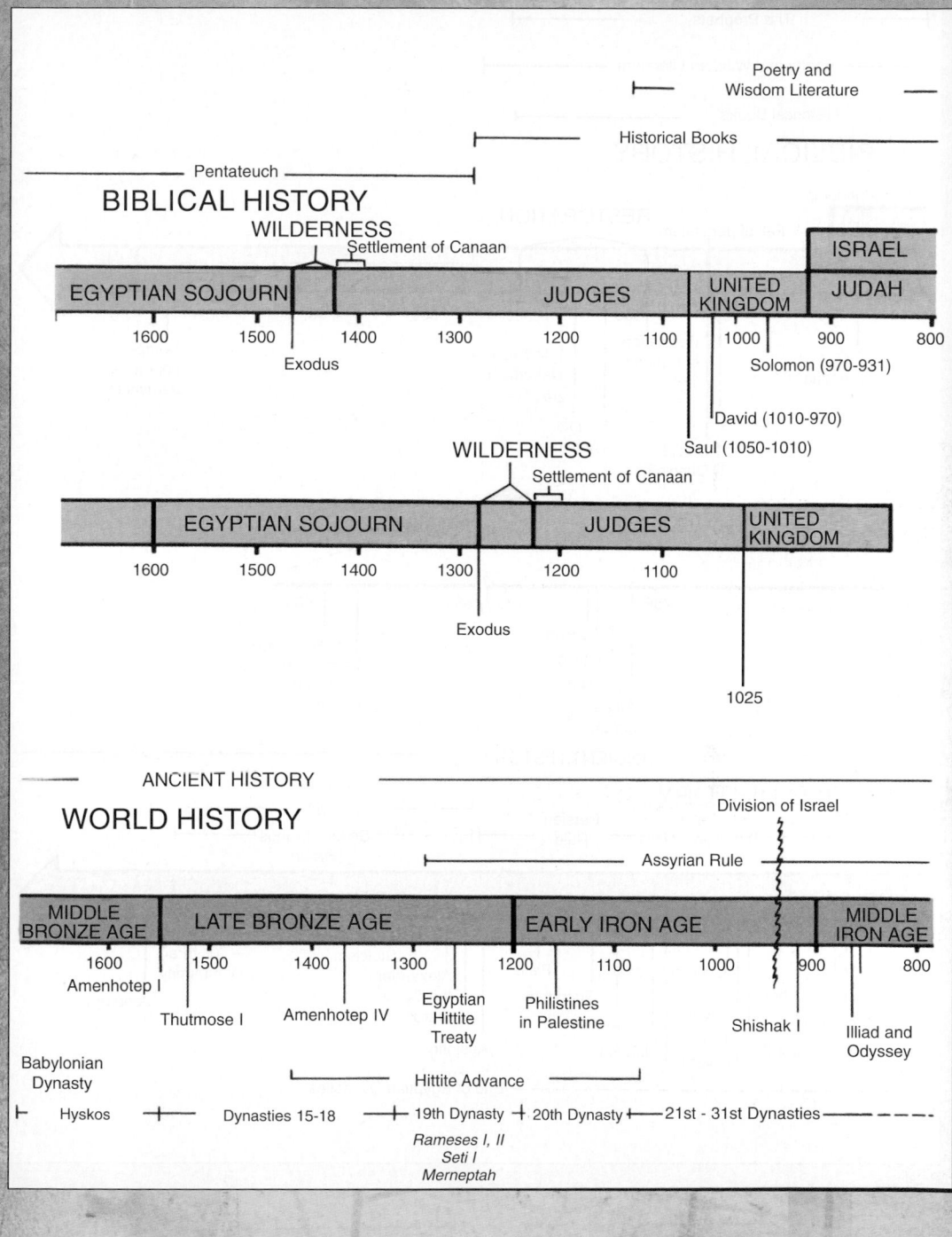

Poetry and
Wisdom Literature

Historical Books

Pentateuch

BIBLICAL HISTORY

WILDERNESS
Settlement of Canaan

ISRAEL

| EGYPTIAN SOJOURN | JUDGES | UNITED KINGDOM | JUDAH |

1600 1500 1400 1300 1200 1100 1000 900 800

Exodus

Solomon (970-931)

David (1010-970)

Saul (1050-1010)

WILDERNESS
Settlement of Canaan

| EGYPTIAN SOJOURN | JUDGES | UNITED KINGDOM |

1600 1500 1400 1300 1200 1100

Exodus

1025

ANCIENT HISTORY

WORLD HISTORY

Division of Israel

Assyrian Rule

| MIDDLE BRONZE AGE | LATE BRONZE AGE | EARLY IRON AGE | MIDDLE IRON AGE |

1600 1500 1400 1300 1200 1100 1000 900 800

Amenhotep I

Thutmose I

Amenhotep IV

Egyptian
Hittite
Treaty

Philistines
in Palestine

Shishak I

Illiad and
Odyssey

Babylonian
Dynasty

Hyskos Dynasties 15-18 19th Dynasty 20th Dynasty 21st - 31st Dynasties

Rameses I, II
Seti I
Merneptah

Hittite Advance

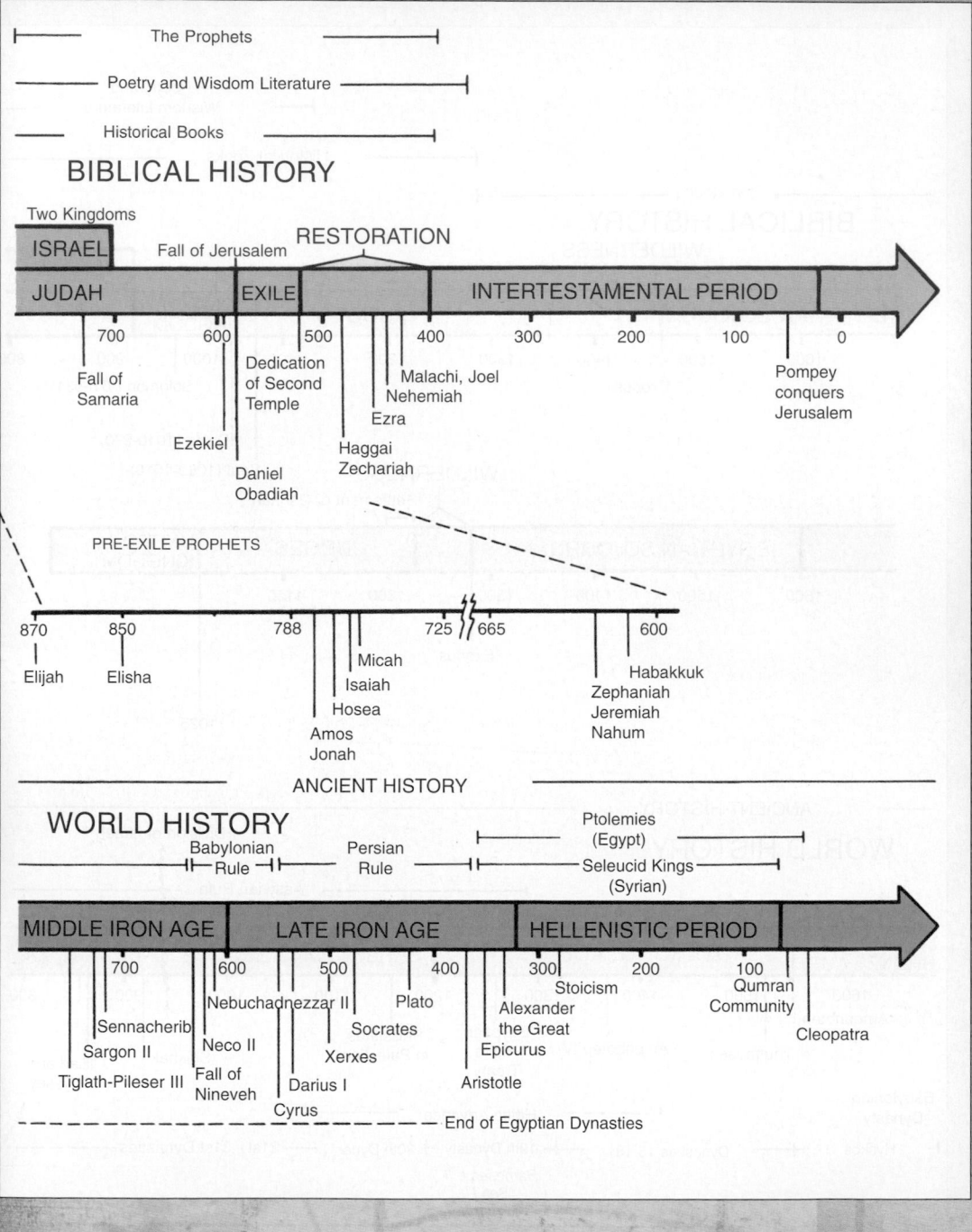

The Prophets

Poetry and Wisdom Literature

Historical Books

BIBLICAL HISTORY

Two Kingdoms

ISRAEL

JUDAH

Fall of Jerusalem

RESTORATION

EXILE

INTERTESTAMENTAL PERIOD

| 700 | 600 | 500 | 400 | 300 | 200 | 100 | 0 |

Fall of Samaria

Dedication of Second Temple

Malachi, Joel
Nehemiah

Ezra

Pompey conquers Jerusalem

Ezekiel

Daniel
Obadiah

Haggai
Zechariah

PRE-EXILE PROPHETS

| 870 | 850 | 788 | 725 // 665 | 600 |

Elijah

Elisha

Micah

Isaiah

Hosea

Amos
Jonah

Habakkuk
Zephaniah
Jeremiah
Nahum

ANCIENT HISTORY

WORLD HISTORY

Babylonian
Rule

Persian
Rule

Ptolemies
(Egypt)

Seleucid Kings
(Syrian)

MIDDLE IRON AGE

LATE IRON AGE

HELLENISTIC PERIOD

| 700 | 600 | 500 | 400 | 300 | 200 | 100 |

Nebuchadnezzar II

Plato

Stoicism

Qumran
Community

Sennacherib

Socrates

Alexander
the Great

Sargon II

Neco II

Xerxes

Epicurus

Cleopatra

Tiglath-Pileser III

Fall of
Nineveh

Darius I

Aristotle

Cyrus

End of Egyptian Dynasties

CHURCH HISTORY

EASTERN EVENTS

0   100

Council of Jerusalem

Events of
Significance to
East and West

Ministry
of
Jesus   Gnosticism — —

WESTERN EVENTS   CHRISTIANITY

0   100

BIBLICAL HISTORY

Clement   NEW TESTAMENT PERIOD

1,2 Thessalonians
Galatians
1,2 Corinthians
James
1,2 Timothy, Titus
Hebrews
Mark
Matthew
Luke, Acts
Jude John   Epistles of John, Revelation

100   0   100

Approximate Dates

Pompey   Titus

50   60   70   80   90   100
1 Peter, 2 Peter
Ephesians, Phillippians, Colossians, Philemon
Romans

Lifetime of Jesus   Crucifixion and Resurrection

Approximate Dates

4   0   10   20   30   40   50   60   70
                                              Conversion   Titus
Jesus'   of Paul   conquers
Birth   Baptism   Jerusalem
                                   of Jesus   Death
                                                                      of Paul

45 46 47 48 49 50 51 52 53 54 55 56 57

Paul's First Paul's Second   Paul's Third
Missionary   Journey   Journey
Journey

———————————————   ANCIENT HISTORY   ———————————————

WORLD HISTORY

ROMAN PERIOD

0   100
Pontius
Pilate

Jerusalem
Destroyed

Lifetime of Jesus

Palestinian   Augustus   Tiberius   Caligula, Claudius   Nero
Rulers   Roman Emperors ⊢   27-14   +   14-37   ⊢ + 37-54 + 54-68 ⊣
                                                                 Herod Agrippa I
⊢   Hasmoneans   +   Herod   37-44   Agrippa II ⊣
    (Maccabeans)   The   Archelaus   44-100
    152-37   Great   4-6   Herod Antipas
                     37-4   4-39
                              Philip
                              4-34

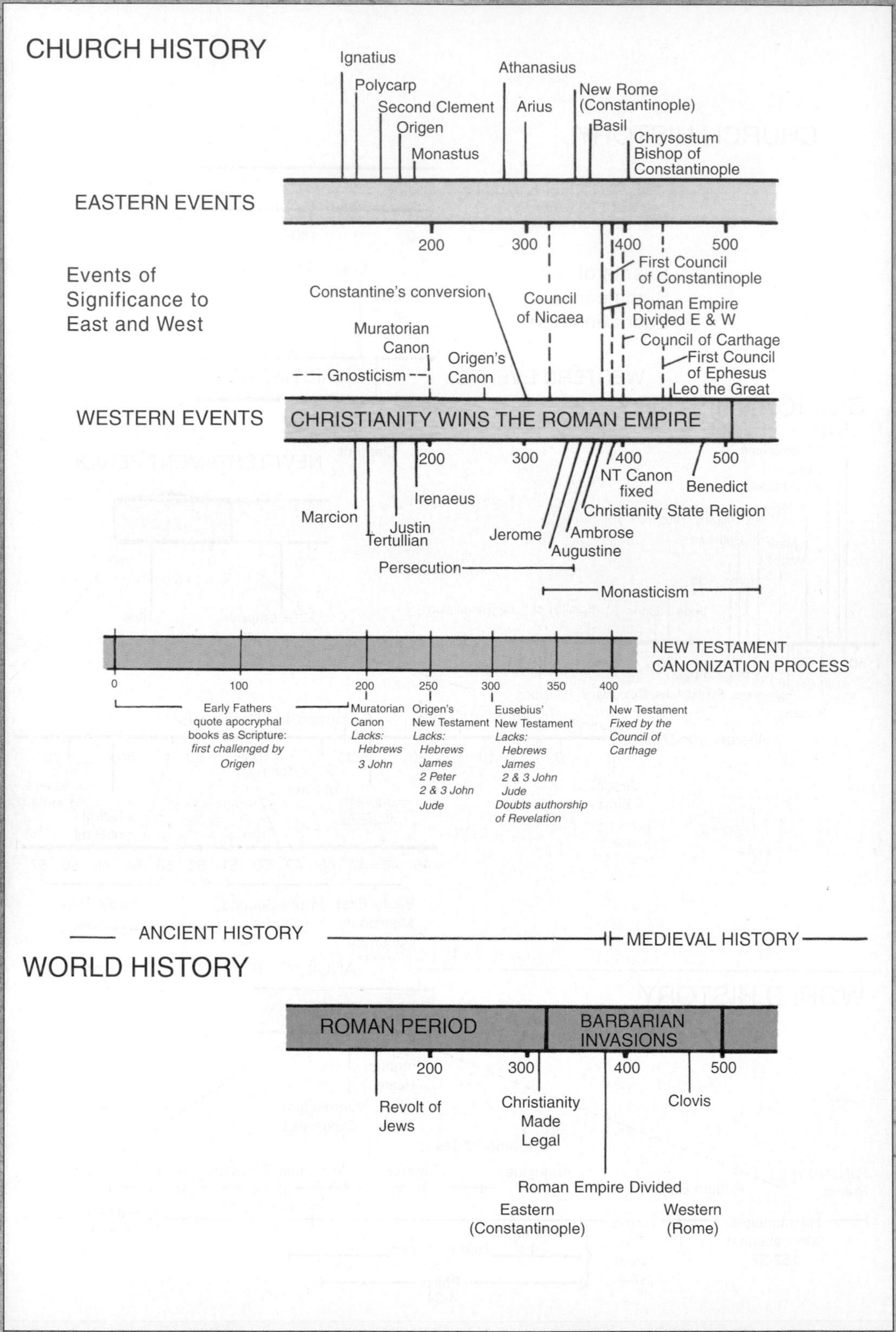

CHURCH HISTORY

Ignatius
Polycarp
Second Clement
Origen
Monastus

Athanasius
Arius

New Rome
(Constantinople)
Basil
Chrysostum
Bishop of
Constantinople

EASTERN EVENTS

200   300   400   500

First Council
of Constantinople

Events of Significance to East and West

Constantine's conversion
Muratorian Canon
Origen's Canon
- - Gnosticism - -

Council
of Nicaea

Roman Empire
Divided E & W
Council of Carthage
First Council
of Ephesus
Leo the Great

WESTERN EVENTS

CHRISTIANITY WINS THE ROMAN EMPIRE

200   300   400   500

NT Canon
fixed
Benedict

Christianity State Religion

Marcion
Irenaeus
Justin
Tertullian
Jerome
Ambrose
Augustine

Persecution ————

Monasticism ————

0   100   200   250   300   350   400

NEW TESTAMENT
CANONIZATION PROCESS

Early Fathers
quote apocryphal
books as Scripture:
*first challenged by
Origen*

Muratorian
Canon
Lacks:
Hebrews
3 John

Origen's
New Testament
Lacks:
Hebrews
James
2 Peter
2 & 3 John
Jude

Eusebius'
New Testament
Lacks:
Hebrews
James
2 & 3 John
Jude
Doubts authorship
of Revelation

New Testament
Fixed by the
Council of
Carthage

──── ANCIENT HISTORY ──────────────────────────┤├─MEDIEVAL HISTORY────

WORLD HISTORY

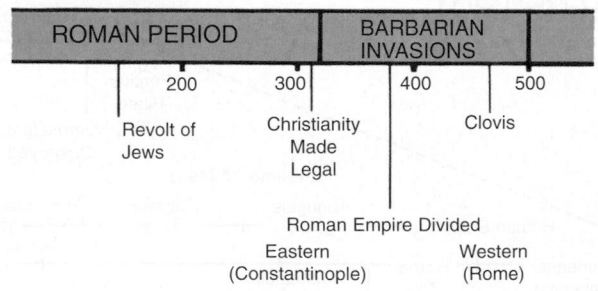

ROMAN PERIOD

BARBARIAN INVASIONS

200   300   400   500

Revolt of
Jews

Christianity
Made
Legal

Clovis

Roman Empire Divided

Eastern
(Constantinople)

Western
(Rome)

CHURCH HISTORY

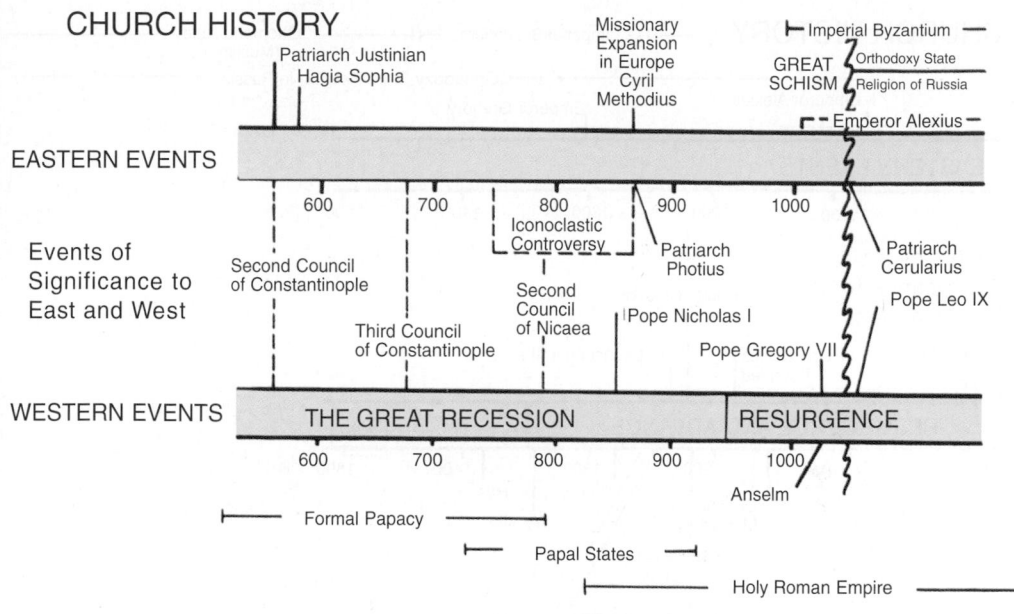

Patriarch Justinian
Hagia Sophia

Missionary
Expansion
in Europe
Cyril
Methodius

Imperial Byzantium

GREAT
SCHISM
Orthodoxy State
Religion of Russia

Emperor Alexius

EASTERN EVENTS

600   700   800   900   1000

Events of
Significance to
East and West

Second Council
of Constantinople

Iconoclastic
Controversy

Patriarch
Photius

Patriarch
Cerularius

Pope Nicholas I

Pope Leo IX

Third Council
of Constantinople

Second
Council
of Nicaea

Pope Gregory VII

WESTERN EVENTS

THE GREAT RECESSION   RESURGENCE

600   700   800   900   1000

Anselm

Formal Papacy

Papal States

Holy Roman Empire

Doctrines Addressed by the Early Church Councils

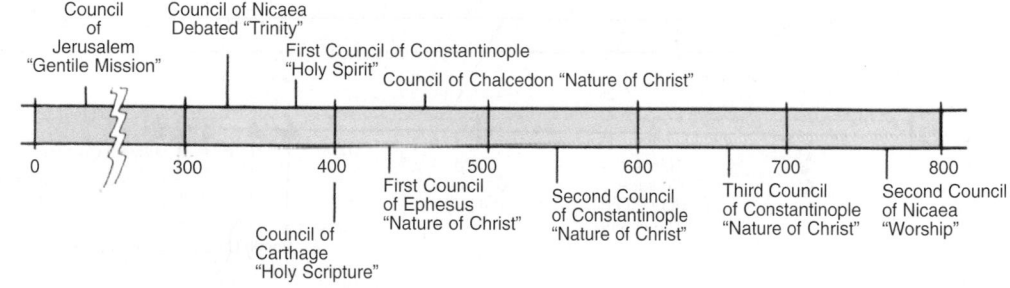

Council
of
Jerusalem
"Gentile Mission"

Council of Nicaea
Debated "Trinity"

First Council of Constantinople
"Holy Spirit"

Council of Chalcedon "Nature of Christ"

0   300   400   500   600   700   800

First Council
of Ephesus
"Nature of Christ"

Second Council
of Constantinople
"Nature of Christ"

Third Council
of Constantinople
"Nature of Christ"

Second Council
of Nicaea
"Worship"

Council of
Carthage
"Holy Scripture"

MEDIEVAL HISTORY

WORLD HISTORY

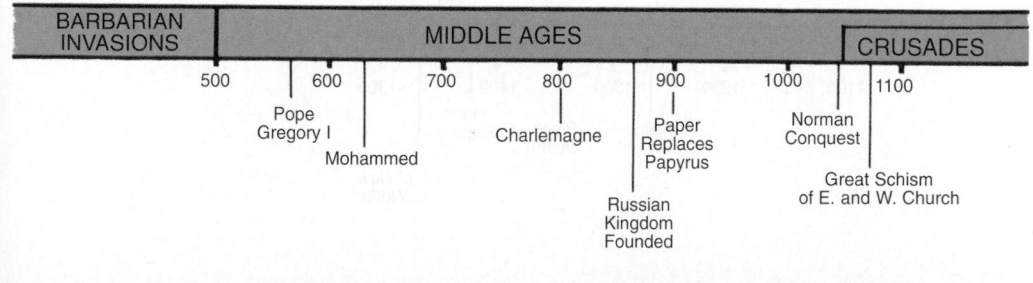

BARBARIAN
INVASIONS

MIDDLE AGES

CRUSADES

500   600   700   800   900   1000   1100

Pope
Gregory I

Mohammed

Charlemagne

Paper
Replaces
Papyrus

Norman
Conquest

Great Schism
of E. and W. Church

Russian
Kingdom
Founded

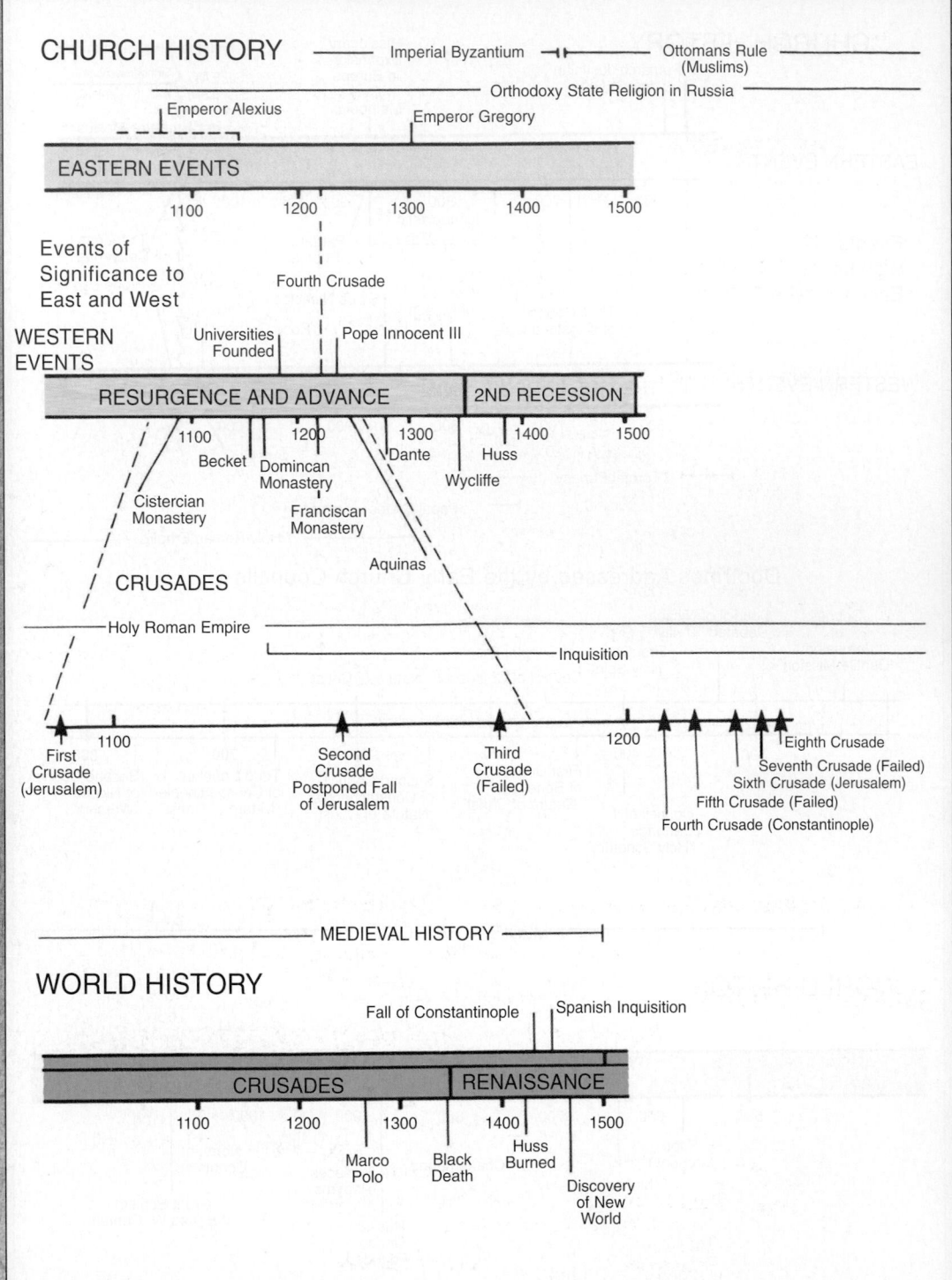

CHURCH HISTORY — Imperial Byzantium — Ottomans Rule (Muslims) —

Orthodoxy State Religion in Russia

Emperor Alexius

Emperor Gregory

EASTERN EVENTS

1100   1200   1300   1400   1500

Events of
Significance to
East and West

Fourth Crusade

WESTERN
EVENTS

Universities Founded   Pope Innocent III

RESURGENCE AND ADVANCE   2ND RECESSION

1100   1200   1300   1400   1500

Becket   Dominican Monastery   Dante   Huss

Wycliffe

Cistercian Monastery   Franciscan Monastery

Aquinas

CRUSADES

Holy Roman Empire

Inquisition

1100   1200   1750

First Crusade (Jerusalem)

Second Crusade Postponed Fall of Jerusalem

Third Crusade (Failed)

Eighth Crusade

Seventh Crusade (Failed)

Sixth Crusade (Jerusalem)

Fifth Crusade (Failed)

Fourth Crusade (Constantinople)

MEDIEVAL HISTORY

WORLD HISTORY

Fall of Constantinople   Spanish Inquisition

CRUSADES   RENAISSANCE

1100   1200   1300   1400   1500

Marco Polo   Black Death   Huss Burned

Discovery of New World

CHURCH HISTORY

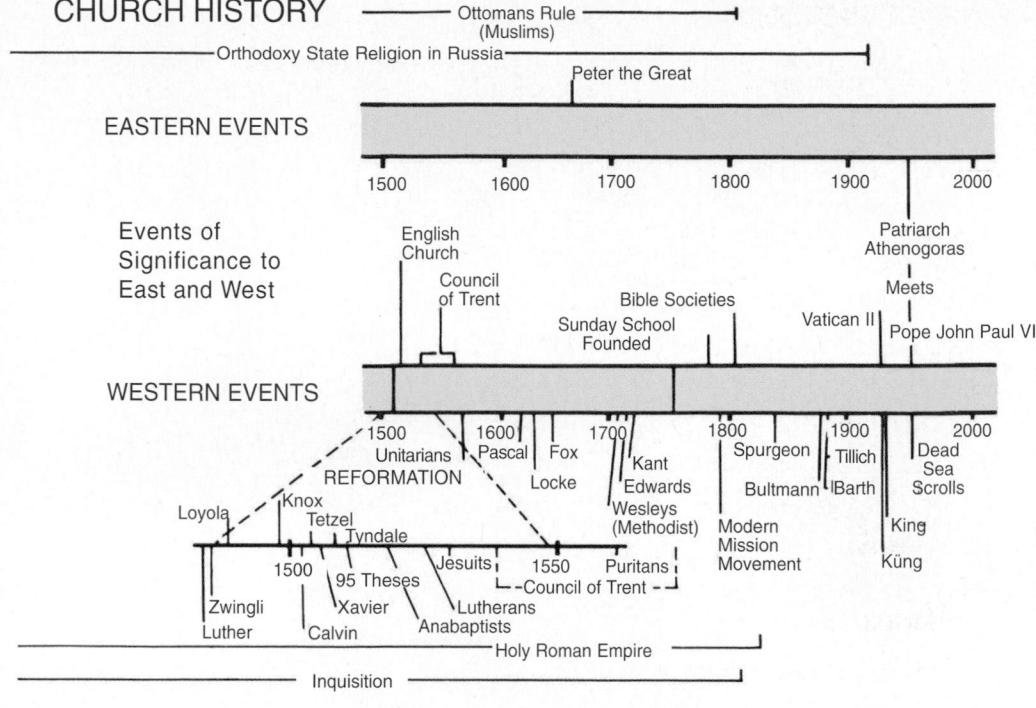

Ottomans Rule (Muslims)

Orthodoxy State Religion in Russia

Peter the Great

EASTERN EVENTS

1500   1600   1700   1800   1900   2000

Events of Significance to East and West

English Church

Council of Trent

Bible Societies

Sunday School Founded

Patriarch Athenogoras

Meets

Vatican II

Pope John Paul VI

WESTERN EVENTS

1500   1600   1700   1800   1900   2000

Unitarians   Pascal   Fox   Kant   Spurgeon   Tillich   Dead Sea Scrolls

REFORMATION   Locke   Edwards   Bultmann   Barth

Loyola   Knox   Wesleys (Methodist)   King

Tetzel   Tyndale   Modern Mission Movement   Küng

1500   Jesuits   1550   Puritans

95 Theses   Council of Trent

Zwingli   Xavier   Lutherans

Luther   Calvin   Anabaptists

Holy Roman Empire

Inquisition

WORLD HISTORY

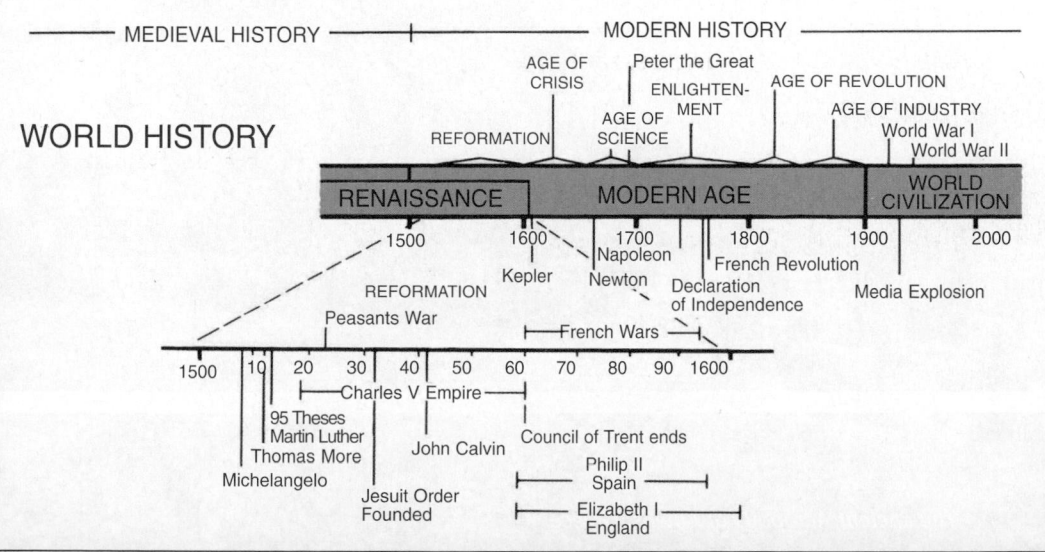

MEDIEVAL HISTORY   MODERN HISTORY

AGE OF CRISIS   Peter the Great

ENLIGHTEN-MENT   AGE OF REVOLUTION

REFORMATION   AGE OF SCIENCE   AGE OF INDUSTRY

World War I
World War II

RENAISSANCE   MODERN AGE   WORLD CIVILIZATION

1500   1600   1700   1800   1900   2000

Napoleon

Kepler   Newton   French Revolution

REFORMATION   Declaration of Independence   Media Explosion

Peasants War   French Wars

1500   10   20   30   40   50   60   70   80   90   1600

Charles V Empire

95 Theses
Martin Luther   John Calvin   Council of Trent ends
Thomas More

Michelangelo   Philip II Spain

Jesuit Order Founded   Elizabeth I England

The ancient Acropolis of Athens, Greece.

A

AARON (Âr´ on) Moses' brother; Israel's first high priest. His parents Amram and Jochebed were from the tribe of Levi, Israel's tribe of priests (Exod. 6:16-26). Miriam was his sister. With his wife Elisheba, Aaron had four sons: Nadab, Abihu, Eleazar, and Ithamar. The first two perished when they offered sacrifices with fire that God had not commanded them to make (Lev. 10:1-2; 16:1-2). Two priestly lines developed from the remaining sons: Ithamar through Eli to Abiathar and Eleazar to Zadok (1 Sam. 14:3; 22:20; 1 Kings 2:26-27; 1 Chron. 6:50-53).

Aaron experienced the joy of starting Israel's formal priesthood, being consecrated to the office (Exod. 28–29; Lev. 8–9), wearing the first priestly garments, and initiating the sacrificial system (Lev. 1–7). He also bore the burdens of his office as his sons were killed for their disobedience (Lev. 10:1-2), and he could not mourn for them (Lev. 10:6-7). He also bore the special rules of conduct, clothing, and ritual cleanness (Lev. 21–22).

He could not live up to such high standards perfectly. Thus he had to offer sacrifices for his own sins (Lev. 16:11). Then in his cleansed, holy office, he offered sacrifices for others. In his imperfection Aaron still served as a symbol or type of the perfect priest as seen in Ps. 110:4, where the future king was described as eternal priest. Zechariah 6:11-15 also speaks of a priest—Joshua—in typical terms. Thus the imperfect Aaron established an office full of symbolic meaning for Israel.

With all his faults Aaron was a man chosen by God. We do not know what Aaron did during Moses' 40-year exile from Egypt, but he maintained the faith, kept contact with Israel's leaders, and did not forget his brother (Exod. 4:27-31). Ready of speech, he served nobly as Moses' spokesman before Pharaoh. More than once he stretched out Moses' staff to bring God's plagues on the land (Exod. 7:9,19). In the wilderness Aaron and Hur helped Moses hold up the staff, the symbol of God's power, so that Israel would prevail over Amalek (Exod. 17:12).

At Sinai Aaron and his two older sons, Nadab and Abihu, were called to go up the mountain with Moses and 70 elders (Exod. 24:9). There they worshiped and ate and drank in heavenly fellowship. As Moses and Joshua went farther up, Moses left Aaron and Hur in charge (Exod. 24:14). When Moses delayed on the mountain, the people asked Aaron for action. They cried, "Make gods for us" (Exod. 32:1 NRSV). Their sin was polytheism (worship of many gods) as well as idolatry. Aaron all too easily obliged and made a calf and apparently led in its worship.

On another occasion Aaron appeared in a bad light. In Num. 12 he and Miriam spoke against Moses' marriage to the Cushite (Ethiopian) woman. (Cush was an old name for Upper Egypt—approximately modern Sudan.) The relationship of the Cushite woman to Zipporah is not clear. Numerous explanations have been offered. Some believe Zipporah had died. Others maintain Moses' relationship with her was severed when he sent her away (Exod. 18:2). Possibly both Zipporah and the Cushite woman may have been Moses' wives at the same time. Some have even suggested that Zipporah was the Cushite woman. Even though Zipporah was a Midianite, at least one side of her family may have been from Cush. Anyway, Aaron and Miriam were jealous of their younger brother. In reality, their murmuring was against God (Num. 12).

Though Miriam was severely judged, Aaron was not, perhaps because he was not the instigator but the accomplice. He confessed his sin and pleaded for mercy for Miriam. When Korah, Dathan, and Abiram opposed Moses and Aaron, Aaron's intercession stopped the plague (Num. 16). God vindicated Aaron's leadership in the miraculous blossoming of his staff (Num. 17). When the people cried for water at Kadesh in the desert of Zin, Aaron joined in Moses' sin as they seized the power of the Lord for themselves (Num. 20:7-13). In consequence, Aaron, like Moses, was not to enter the promised land. Nearby on the border of Edom after 40 years of his priesthood, Moses took Aaron up Mount Hor and transferred his garments to his son, Eleazar. Aaron died there at the age of 123 years (Num. 20:23-28). Israel mourned for their first high priest 30 days (Num. 20:29), as they soon would mourn for Moses (Deut. 34:8).   *R. Laird Harris*

AARONITE (Âr´ on īt) Term used only in the KJV to translate the name Aaron where it refers to the descendants of Aaron (1 Chron. 12:27; 27:17). Equivalent to the phrases "sons of Aaron," "descendants of Aaron," and "house of Aaron" used often in the OT.

AARON'S ROD Aaron used a rod to demonstrate to the Pharaoh that the God of the Hebrews was Lord. It became a snake when cast down (Exod. 7:8-13) and brought about the first three plagues (Exod. 7:19-20; 8:5-7,16-19). This rod was the same one used to strike the rocks at Horeb and Kadesh to bring forth water (Exod. 17:1-7; Num. 20:7-11).

The rebellion of Korah (Num. 16:1-50) made it necessary to determine who would be eligible to come before God in the tabernacle as priests. The head of each tribe was to inscribe his name on an almond rod representing his tribe, and each rod was placed in the tabernacle. The next morning Aaron's rod had blossomed and bore almonds. This was taken as a sign from God that the house of Aaron had the right to serve Him in the tabernacle. The rod was placed inside the tabernacle (Num. 17:1-11). According to Heb. 9:4, the rod was kept in the ark of the covenant. See *Korah.*

AB Name for the fifth month in the Jewish religious calendar corresponding to the eleventh month in the Hebrew civic calendar. It usually covered parts of July and August. The name does not appear in the Bible.

ABADDON (À ·băd´ dŏn) Name meaning "to perish." In the KJV Abaddon appears only in Rev. 9:11 as the Hebrew name of the angel of the bottomless pit whose Greek name was Apollyon. Abaddon occurs six times in the Hebrew Bible (Job 26:6; 28:22; 31:12; Prov. 15:11; 27:20; Ps. 88:11). The KJV and NIV translate Abaddon as "destruction," while the NASB and RSV retain the word "Abaddon." See *Hell.*

ABAGTHA (À băg´ thà) One of seven eunuchs on the staff of Ahasuerus or Xerxes (486–465 B.C.), King of Persia (Esther 1:10). See *Eunuch.*

ABANA (Ăb´ à-nà) or **ABANAH** (NASB) River in Damascus in Syria. In his anger Naaman wanted to wash here rather than in the dirty Jordan (2 Kings 5:12). Many Hebrew manuscripts, the Septuagint, and Targums call the river the Amana (Song 4:8). Its modern name is Barada, and it travels swiftly from snow-capped Mount Hermon through Damascus to end in a marsh.

ABARIM (Ăb à-rĭm) Mountain range including Mount Nebo from which Moses viewed the promised land (Num. 27:12; 33:47-48; Deut.

The Abana River (modern Barad River) flows through the country of Syria.

32:49). The mountain range is in Moab, east of the Dead Sea, west of Heshbon, and slightly southeast of Jericho. Jeremiah called Jerusalem to cross to Abarim and lament because her allies had been defeated (Jer. 22:20). Iye-abarim (Num. 21:11; 33:44) was a different location perhaps south of the Dead Sea. See *Iye-abarim.*

ABASE Word applies to lowering one's office, rank, or esteem. See *Humility; Meekness.*

ABBA (Ăb´ bà) Aramaic word for "father" used by Jesus to speak of His own intimate relationship with God, a relationship that others can enter through faith. It may also refer to an ancestor, grandfather, founder (of something), protector, or even used as an honorary title for an elder.
Old Testament Although *abba* does not occur in the OT, its Hebrew associate *ab* occurs frequently. *Ab* usually refers to a human father. On occasion the OT speaks of God in the role of Father to Israel (Exod. 4:22; Deut. 32:6; Isa. 45:9-11; Mal. 2:10) or to Israel's king (2 Sam. 7:14; Pss. 2:7; 89:26-27).
New Testament The idea of God's intimate relationship to humanity is a distinct feature of Jesus' teaching. God relates to believers as a father relates to his child. Some would translate *Abba* as "Daddy" to convey the close, personal meaning of the word. Even when "Father" in the NT translates the more formal Greek word *pater*, the idea of *Abba* is certainly in the background. Jesus addressed God as *Abba* in prayer (Mark 14:36) and taught His disciples to pray in the same terms (Luke 11:1-2, pater). Jesus' claim of intimate relationship with God offended many of His opponents because they considered *Abba* to be overly familiar in addressing God. Nevertheless, Jesus' usage established the

pattern for the church's view of God and each believer's relationship with Him. Paul used *Abba* to describe God's adoption of believers as His children (Rom. 8:15) and the change in the believer's status with God that results (Gal. 4:6-7).   *Michael Fink*

ABDA (Ăb´ dä) Name meaning "servant" for two men. **1.** Father of Adoniram, whom Solomon entrusted with his labor force (1 Kings 4:6). **2.** Levite living in Jerusalem rather than in one of the Levitical cities (Neh. 11:17). He is also called Obadiah, the son of Shemaiah (1 Chron. 9:16).

ABDEEL (Ăb´ də·ĕl) Name meaning "servant of God." Abdeel's son Shelemiah was one of three attendants whom Jehoiakim (609–597 B.C.) commanded to arrest Baruch, Jeremiah's scribe, and Jeremiah (Jer. 36:26). God hid His servants from the king's servants.

ABDI (Ăb´ dī) Name meaning "my servant," though it is probably an abbreviation for "servant of the Lord." **1.** Levite whose grandson Ethan was one of the temple musicians David appointed (1 Chron. 6:44). **2.** Levite whose son Kish followed King Hezekiah's wishes and helped cleanse the temple (2 Chron. 29:12). **3.** Israelite with a foreign wife in the time of Ezra (Ezra 10:26).

ABDIEL (Ăb´ dĭ·ĕl) Name meaning "servant of God." His son Ahi was a leader in the tribe of Gad (1 Chron. 5:15).

ABDON (Ăb´ dŏn) Geographical and personal name meaning "service" or "servile." **1.** City from the tribe of Asher given the Levites (Josh. 21:30; 1 Chron. 6:74). Its modern name is Khirbet Abdeh. It lies about three miles from the Mediterranean coast between Tyre and Acco. **2.** Judge of Israel from the town of Pirathon in the tribe of Ephraim. He had a large family (40 sons, 30 grandsons) and personal wealth (70 donkeys) (Judg. 12:13-15). **3.** Two men of the tribe of Benjamin (1 Chron. 8:23,30; 9:36). The second of these was an ancestor of King Saul. **4.** Member of the team named by King Josiah to seek God's guidance as to the meaning of the book that Hilkiah, the priest, found in the temple (2 Chron. 34:20). Known in 2 Kings 22:12 as Achbor or Acbor (NIV).

ABEDNEGO (Á·bĕd´ nə·ḡō) In Dan. 1:7 the Babylonian name given to Azariah, one of the three Hebrew youths who were conscripted along with Daniel to serve in the king's court. God delivered them from the fiery furnace (Dan. 2:48–3:30). The precise meaning of the Babylonian name Abednego is disputed. Abed means "servant." Nego may be an intentional corruption of the well-known Babylonian deity Nebo (or Nabu). See *Azariah; Daniel; Daniel, Book of; Meshach; Shadrach.*

ABEL (Ā´ bĕl) Though best known as the name of the second son of Adam and Eve, the Hebrew word *abel* also occurs frequently meaning "vanity, breath, or vapor." See *Ecclesiastes, Book of.*

Perhaps as a personal name, Abel alludes to the shortness of life. Such was the case with Abel (Gen. 4:8). Having offered "by faith … a better sacrifice than Cain" (Heb. 11:4 HCSB), he was murdered by Cain. Why Abel's sacrifice as a keeper of flocks was better than Cain's, whose sacrifice came from harvested fruits, is not directly stated in Gen. 4:4. No ancient evidence for that period yet exists to suggest that animal sacrifice was better than crops, fruits, or precious metals or gems. Two conditions in 4:7, fortunately, provide a partial answer: Cain had not done what was right; Abel had. However, how Abel did right is left unanswered by the historians, prophets, and sages of Israel. Heb. 11:4 offers one further reason: the faith of Abel. His faith relationship with the Lord led him to present a better sacrifice (the fat of the animals); to live as a better person, one who is righteous before God; and to testify eternally, even in death. Identified as the first righteous martyr among the prophets and the ones sent to Israel (Matt. 23:35; Luke 11:51), Abel's blood cried out for God's vengeance against the unrighteous (Gen. 4:10; Rev. 6:9-10). In contrast, the blood of Christ satisfied that cry for the vengeance of God against unrighteousness, accomplishing the forgiveness of sins and making possible the reconciliation of sinners to God. Abel's death, then, is a prototype of Christ's death (Heb. 12:24).

Archie W. England

ABEL (Ā´ bĕl) Place-name used alone and as the first part of other place names as seen below. The Hebrew *'Abel* is a distinct word with a different spelling from the personal name Abel (Hb. *hebel*). The precise meaning of the place name is uncertain. It may mean "brook" or "meadow near a brook." Standing alone, Abel appears in 2 Sam. 20:14-18, probably being the same place as Abel-beth-maachah.

ABEL-BETH-MAACAH or **ABEL-BETH-MAACHAH** (KJV, NKJV) (Ā´ bĕl-bĕth mā´ à-kah) City with a strong Israelite tradition, known for its wise people. Joab besieged the city when Sheba fled there after seeking to lead a rebellion against David. A wise woman delivered the city by getting the citizens to execute Sheba (2 Sam. 20:1-22). Ben-hadad, king of Syria, answered the call for help of Asa, king of Judah (913–873 B.C.) and conquered Abel-beth-maachah from Baasha, king of Israel (1 Kings 15:20). Tiglath-pileser, king of Assyria, captured the city from Pekah, king of Israel (2 Kings 15:29). Abel-beth-maachah is identified with the modern Abil el-Oamh, 12 miles north of Lake Huleh near Dan. Its name indicates it was once part of the city-state of Maachah controlled by Arameans (2 Sam. 10:6). See *Abel.*

ABEL-CHERAMIM (Ā´ bĕl-kĕr´ à-mĭm) or **ABEL-KERAMIM** (NASB, NIV, RSV, TEV) Place-name meaning "brook of the vineyards." Jephthah, the judge, extended his victory over the Ammonites as far as Abel-cheramim (Judg. 11:33), whose location east of the Jordan is not known precisely.

ABEL-MAIM (Ā´ bĕl-mă´ ĭm) Place-name meaning "brook of the waters." Used in 2 Chron. 16:4 for place called Abel-beth-maachah in 1 Kings 15:20. If Abel-maim is a different city, its precise location east of the Jordan is not known.

ABEL-MEHOLAH (Ā´ bĕl-mĕ·hō´ lăh) Place-name meaning "brook of the round dancing." A border town or towns whose location(s) is uncertain. Gideon fought the Midianites in the territory of Issachar west of the Jordan (Judg. 7:22). Solomon places Abel-meholah in a district including Taanach, Megiddo, and Beth-shean (1 Kings 4:12). This was Elisha's home (1 Kings 19:16).

ABEL-MIZRAIM (Ā´ bĕl-mĭz´ rā´ ĭm) Place-name meaning either "brook of Egypt," or, if derived from a different Hebrew word with similar spelling, "mourning of the Egyptians." Jacob's children mourned him there east of the Jordan (Gen. 50:11). In giving the name, the Canaanites identified Jacob's sons as Egyptians.

ABEL-SHITTIM (Ā´ bĕl-shĭt´ tĭm) Place-name meaning "brook of the acacias." The last stop of Israel before crossing the Jordan (Num. 33:49). See *Shittim.*

ABEZ (Ā´ bĕz) or **EBEZ** (NASB, NIV, RSV, TEV) Place-name with unknown meaning. Town allotted to Issachar (Josh. 19:20).

ABI (Ā´ bī) or **ABIJAH** (NIV) Personal name meaning "my father." Mother of King Hezekiah (2 Kings 18:2). "Abi" was shortened from "Abijah."

ABIA (Á·bī´ à) (KJV, 1 Chron. 3:10; Matt. 1:7; Luke 1:5) See *Abijah.*

ABIAH (A·bī´ áh) (KJV, 1 Sam. 8:2; 1 Chron. 2:24; 6:28; 7:8) See *Abijah.*

ABI-ALBON (Ā´ bī-ăl´ bŏn) Personal name meaning "my father is overpowering." One of David's 30 heroes (2 Sam. 23:31). Called Abiel in 1 Chron. 11:32. Original name in 2 Samuel may have been Abi-baal, whose letters were then transposed to a new name to avoid the idolatrous name. See *Abiel.*

ABIASAPH (Á·bī´ à·săph) Personal name meaning "my father has gathered" or "harvested." A Levitical priest in the line of Korah (Exod. 6:24) who rebelled against the leadership of Moses (Num. 16). See *Ebiasaph.*

ABIATHAR (Á·bī´ à·thär) Personal name meaning "father of abundance." The son of Ahimelech and the 11th high priest in succession from Aaron through the line of Eli. He survived the slaughter of the priests at Nob and fled to David, hiding in the cave of Adullam from King Saul (1 Sam. 22). Having escaped with the ephod, Abiathar became the high priest and chief counselor for David (1 Sam. 23:6-12; 30:7). Abiathar shared with Zadok the responsibility of taking the ark to Jerusalem (1 Chron. 15:11-12; 2 Sam. 15:24). While Abiathar remained faithful to David during Absalom's rebellion (2 Sam. 15), he later supported Adonijah as successor of King David instead of Solomon (1 Kings 1:7). Solomon deposed him from the priesthood and banished him to

Anathoth, his hometown, fulfilling the prophecy to Eli. Only because of his faithful service to Solomon's father, King David, was he spared the death penalty (1 Kings 2:26-35).

Mark 2:26 records Jesus' statement that David took the showbread from the place of worship when Abiathar was high priest at Nob. First Samuel 21:1 reports that this happened when Ahimelech, the father of Abiathar, was still the high priest. However, a few days after this incident Abiathar did become high priest (1 Sam. 22:19-20). Some NT Greek manuscripts omit "when Abiathar was high priest." It may be that Abiathar was co-priest with his father, or a copyist of the Gospel of Mark may have copied the text wrong. See *Levites; Priests.*

Donald R. Potts

ABIB (Ā´ bĭb) Month of the exodus deliverance from Egypt (Exod. 13:4) and thus of the Passover festival (Exod. 23:15; 34:18; Deut. 16:1). A harvest month covering parts of March and April, Abib means "ears of grain." Later the month was called Nisan (Esther 3:7). See *Calendar.*

ABIDA or **ABIDAH** (Á·bī´ dȧ) Personal name meaning "my father knows." As the fourth son of Midian, he was the grandson of Abraham by his wife Keturah (Gen. 25:4; 1 Chron. 1:33).

ABIDAN (Ăb´ ĭ·dăn) Personal name meaning "my father judged." Early leader of the tribe of Benjamin who helped Moses and Aaron number the people in the wilderness (Num. 1:11) and captain of the tribe in the wilderness marches (Num. 2:22; 7:60-65; 10:24). He and his family had fallen from leadership by the time of the 12 spies (Num. 13:9), long before the reorganization for entry into Canaan (Num. 26).

ABIEL (Á·bī´ ĕl) Personal name meaning "my Father is God." **1.** Grandfather of King Saul (1 Sam. 9:1) or at least closely related to him (1 Sam. 14:50-51), the meaning of the texts not being absolutely clear. See *Jehiel.* **2.** One of David's mighty men (1 Chron. 11:32); known also as Abi-alban (2 Sam. 23:31), the Arbathite. See *Abi-albon.*

ABIEZER (Ā´ bī-ē´ zēr) Personal and place-name meaning "my Father is help." **1.** Descendant of Manasseh (his father was Gilead, son of Machir) and grandson of Joseph (Josh. 17:2;

1 Chron. 7:18). **2.** Territory belonging to clan of Abiezer of tribe of Manasseh located in southwest part of Manasseh's territory and including towns of Elmattan, Ophrah, and Tetel. The territory was famous for grape production (Judg. 8:2) and was home of the judge Gideon (Judg. 6:11,24,34; 8:32). **3.** Member of David's 30 heroes (2 Sam. 23:27; 1 Chron. 11:28) and an administrator of David's forces in the ninth month (1 Chron. 27:12). See *Jeezer.*

ABIEZRITE (Ā´ bī-ĕz´ rīt) Descendants of Abiezer (Judg. 6:11,24; 8:32). See *Abiezer.*

ABIGAIL (Ăb´ ĭ·gāl) Personal name meaning "my father rejoiced." **1.** Wife of David after being wife of Nabal. She was praised for wisdom in contrast to Nabal, her arrogant and overbearing husband, who was a large landowner and successful shepherd. Nabal held a feast for his sheepshearers while David was hiding from Saul in the wilderness of Paran. David and his 600 men were camped near the town of Maon. He heard about Nabal's feast and requested some food. Nabal, in a drunken state, refused the request and insulted David's 10 messengers. In anger David determined to kill Nabal's entire household. Abigail anticipated David's reaction and loaded a convoy of donkeys with food to feed all of David's men. As soon as she met David, she impressed him with her beauty, humility, praise, and advice (1 Sam. 25:32-35). After Nabal became sober and heard about David's plans to kill him, he had a heart attack. Following Nabal's death, David married Abigail, the second of his eight wives. They lived first at Gath and then at Hebron, where Abigail gave birth to Chileab, who is also called Daniel. Later Abigail was taken captive by the Amalekites when they captured Ziklag, but David rescued her (1 Sam. 30:1-18). **2.** Sister of David and the mother of Amasa (1 Chron. 2:16-17), married to Jether, an Ishmaelite (also called Ithra). Amasa, her son, was at one time the commander of David's army (2 Sam. 17:25). Abigail was the daughter of Nahash who, because of textual uncertainties, has been described as another name for Jesse. See *David.* *Donald R. Potts*

ABIHAIL (Ăb´ ĭ·hāl) Personal name meaning "my father is a terror." **1.** Woman in family list of Judah (1 Chron. 2:29), wife of Abishur. **2.** Wife of King Rehoboam (2 Chron. 11:18).

Personal name with different Hebrew spelling meaning "my father is powerful." **3.** Father of Zuriel, a leading Levite under Moses (Num. 3:35). **4.** Father of Esther and uncle of Mordecai (Esther 2:15). **5.** Member of the tribe of Gad (1 Chron. 5:14).

ABIHU (Ȧ·bī´ hū) Personal name meaning "my father is he." The second son of Aaron; one of Israel's first priests (Exod. 6:23; 28:1). He saw God along with Moses, Aaron, his brother, and 70 elders (Exod. 24:9-10). He and his brother Nadab offered "strange fire" before God (Lev. 10:1-22). The exact nature of their sin is not known. They simply did what God had not commanded. Perhaps they offered sacrifice at the wrong time or with coals or materials not properly sanctified (cp. Lev. 16:12). The result is clear: God's fire consumed them. See *Priests*.

ABIHUD (Ȧ·bī´ hŭd) Personal name meaning "my father is glorious." Grandson of Benjamin (1 Chron. 8:3).

ABIJAH (Ȧ·bī´ jäh) or **ABIJAM** Personal name meaning "Yahweh is my Father." **1.** Second son of Samuel whose crooked acts as judge led Israel to demand a king (1 Sam. 8:2-5). **2.** Son of Jeroboam, first king of the Northern Kingdom Israel. Abijah died according to prophecy of Ahijah (1 Kings 14:1-18). **3.** Son of Rehoboam and second king of divided Southern Kingdom of Judah (915–913 B.C.), called Abijam in 1 Kings 15, a name meaning "my father is Yam" (or sea), possibly a reference to Canaanite god. Abijah was his father's favorite son (2 Chron. 11:22). Abijah followed the sins of Rehoboam (1 Kings 15:3) but still maintained proper worship in Jerusalem (2 Chron. 13:10), and God gave him victory over Jeroboam of Israel (2 Chron. 13:15-20). Abijah was remembered for his large family (2 Chron. 13:21). He is listed in the ancestors of Jesus (Matt. 1:7). **4.** Wife of Hezron connected with genealogy of Caleb in a text whose meaning is not clear (1 Chron. 2:24). **5.** Grandson of Benjamin (1 Chron. 7:8). **6.** Priestly descendant of Aaron (1 Chron. 24:10). He led the eighth (of 24) division of the priests serving in the temple. **7.** Priest under Nehemiah who signed a covenant to obey God's law (Neh. 10:7). **8.** A leading priest in the days of the return from exile (Neh. 12:4), and then a priestly line (Neh. 12:17) to which Zechariah, father of John the

Baptist, belonged (Luke 1:5). **9.** Mother of King Hezekiah (2 Chron. 29:1) and thus a powerful political influence.

ABILENE (Ăb·ĭ·lē´ nē) Small mountainous region ruled by the tetrarch Lysanias at the time that John the Baptist began his public ministry (Luke 3:1-3). Abilene was located about 18 miles northwest of Damascus in the Anti-Lebanon mountain range. Its capital was Abila. In A.D. 37 Abilene came under the administrative control of Herod Agrippa I. Later it was part of the kingdom of his son, Agrippa II.

ABIMAEL (Ă·bĭm´ ā·ĕl) Personal name meaning "El (God) is my father." Ancestor of the Israelites as a descendant of Shem and Eber (Gen. 10:28).

ABIMELECH (Ȧ·bĭm´ ĕ·lĕk) Personal name meaning "My father is king." **1.** King of Gerar, who took Sarah for himself, thinking she was Abraham's sister rather than his wife (Gen. 20). He restored her to Abraham after a nighttime dream of God. **2.** Probably the same as 1., a king who disputed the ownership of a well at Beersheba with Abraham and then made a covenant of peace with him (Gen. 21:22-34). **3.** King of Philistines at Gerar related to or identical with 1. Isaac lived under his protection and fearfully passed Rebekah, his wife, off as his sister. Abimelech scolded Isaac and warned his people not to touch Rebekah. A dispute over water wells led to Isaac's leaving but finally to a treaty of peace (Gen. 26) at Beer-sheba. **4.** Son of Gideon, the judge of Israel (Judg. 8:31). Abimelech seized power after his father's death by murdering his brothers and having himself named king by his relatives at Shechem. This provoked Jotham's famous fable (Judg. 9:7-21). God provoked Shechem against Abimelech, who defeated an army under Gaal and then recaptured Shechem. When he tried to repeat his tactics against Thebez, a woman threw a stone down on his head and killed him (Judg. 9:23-57). Abimelech's fate served as an illustration Joab used to protect himself from David (2 Sam. 11:21). **5.** Priest under David with Zadok (1 Chron. 18:16), but correct reading of text here is probably Ahimelech as in 2 Sam. 8:17. **6.** Person mentioned in title of Ps. 34, which apparently refers to 1 Sam. 21:10-15, where Achish is David's opponent.

Abimelech may have been an official title for Philistine kings.

ABINADAB (Á·bĭn´ á dăb) Personal name meaning "my father is generous." **1.** Resident of Kiriath-jearim whose house was the resting place of the ark of the covenant for 20 years after the Philistines returned it. His son Eleazar served as priest (1 Sam. 7:1-2). Abinadab's other sons Uzzah and Ahio led the cart on which the ark of God was being carried from Kiriath-jearim to the city of David (2 Sam. 6:3-4). **2.** Son of Jesse passed over when David was selected as king (1 Sam. 16:8; 17:13). **3.** Son of King Saul killed by Philistines in battle of Mount Gilboa (1 Sam. 31:2). **4.** Solomon's son-in-law and official over Dor, the Mediterranean seaport below Mount Carmel, was the son of Abinadab or Ben-abinadab (1 Kings 4:11).

ABINOAM (Á·bĭn´ ō·ăm) Personal name meaning "my father is gracious." Father of Barak, army commander with Deborah (Judg. 4–5).

ABIRAM (Á·bī´ răm) Personal name meaning "my father is exalted." **1.** Leader of rebellion against Moses and Aaron, seeking priestly authority. He died when God caused the earth to open and swallow the rebels (Num. 16; 26:9-11). **2.** Son of Hiel sacrificed in foundation of rebuilt Jericho, fulfilling Joshua's warning (1 Kings 16:34).

ABISHAG (Ăb´ ĭ·shăg) Personal name meaning "my father strayed" or "is a wanderer." A young virgin or "maiden" (RSV) brought to David's bed in his last days to keep him warm (1 Kings 1:1-4). They had no sexual relations, but Solomon considered her David's wife when his brother Adonijah asked to marry her after David's death (1 Kings 2:17). Solomon interpreted the request as a step toward becoming king and had Adonijah executed (1 Kings 2:23-25). Abishag was from Shunem, a city guarding the Jezreel Valley.

ABISHAI (Ăb´ ĭ·shā·ī) Personal name meaning "father exists." Son of David's sister Zeruiah and brother of Joab, David's general (1 Sam 26:6; 1 Chron. 2:15-16). He was with David when he spared Abner (1 Sam. 26:7) and with Joab pursuing Abner (2 Sam. 2:24) and killing Abner (2 Sam. 3:30). He commanded troops against Ammon (2 Sam. 10). He sought to kill Shimei for cursing David, but the king restrained him

(2 Sam. 16; 19:21). He led a third of David's troops against David's son Absalom (2 Sam. 18). He commanded forces against Sheba, who led a northern rebellion against David (2 Sam. 20). He killed Isbi-benob, the Philistine giant who threatened David (2 Sam. 21:15-17). A mighty captain, he was still not among David's elite three (2 Sam. 23:18-19). He was famed for killing 18,000 Edomites (1 Chron. 18:12).

ABISHALOM (Áb´ ĭ·shá·lōm) Personal name meaning "my father is peace." Another spelling for Absalom (1 Kings 15:2,10). See *Absalom.*

ABISHUA (Á·bĭsh´ ū·á) Personal name meaning "my father is salvation." **1.** Levite, the great-grandson of Aaron (1 Chron. 6:4). **2.** A Benjaminite (1 Chron. 8:4; cp. 1 Chron. 7:7).

ABISHUR (Ā·bī´ shûr) Personal name meaning "my father is a wall." A descendant of Jerahmeel (1 Chron. 2:28-29).

ABITAL (Á·bī´ tăl) Personal name meaning "my father is dew." Wife of David (2 Sam. 3:4).

ABITUB (Ā·bī´ tŭb) Personal name meaning "my father is good." A Benjaminite from Moab (1 Chron. 8:11).

ABIUD (A·bī´ ŭd) Greek spelling of Abihud, ancestor of Jesus (Matt. 1:13). See *Abihud.*

ABLUTIONS Ceremonial washings with water to make oneself pure before worship. The practice of ablutions is one background for NT baptism. The Hebrew term *rachats* is the everyday word for washing with water, rinsing, or bathing (Gen. 18:4; Exod. 2:5; Ruth 3:3). The Greek word *louein* is similar (Acts 9:37; 16:33; 2 Pet. 2:22).

Old Testament Ablutions were performed for cleansing from the impurity of an inferior or undesirable condition to prepare the person for initiation into a higher, more desirable condition. Aaron and his sons were washed before they were clothed with the priestly robes and anointed with oil (Exod. 29:4; 30:19-21; Lev. 8:6). Such washings prepared people to participate in special acts of religious service.

When a person became unclean (Lev. 11–15), becoming clean involved ablution practices. Washing could symbolize a person's claim to be pure and innocent of sin in a particular case (Deut. 21:1-9).

At times ablutions involved a general washing or bathing as when the Hebrews bathed their bodies and washed their clothes (Lev. 14:8; 15:5; Num. 19:7-8). Such washing occurred in various places—running water (Lev. 15:13), a pool (John 9:7), in a river (2 Kings 5:10), or in a courtyard of a home (2 Sam. 11:2).

In some parts of the Hebrew tradition, the ritual importance of washing became a central part of religious practice with minute descriptions of how a person was supposed to wash before various activities. Some of the stricter groups would not enter a house without ablutions. They said one hand had to be washed first so it could be purified and could wash the second hand.

Old Testament teachings do not give such importance and detail to ablutions. Rather, inward, spiritual purity is the goal. Outward washing is only a symbol (Pss. 24:4; 51:7; 73:13).

New Testament In Heb. 6:2 the writer bid Christians to progress beyond discussion of basic matters, among which he lists "teaching about ritual washings" (HCSB). He may be describing discussions about the differences between Christian baptism and other ablutions. Hebrews 9:10 refers to "ritual washings" (HCSB) practiced by the Hebrews under the law but no longer necessary because Christ was "offered once to bear the sins of many" (9:28 HCSB).

Mark 7:4 (HCSB) mentions that among the traditions observed by the Pharisees was the "washing of cups, jugs, copper utensils, and dining couches." They "wash their hands ritually" (v. 3 HCSB) before meals. They did this to keep "the tradition of the elders." Jesus called this the "tradition of men" which meant "disregarding the commandment of God" (v. 8). He cited Isaiah to call for purity of heart rather than strictness of rules (v. 6).

Examples of Jewish practice in Jesus' day have been illustrated by archaeologists in their excavations at Qumran, the Dead Sea Scroll community of the Essenes, a strict Jewish sect. Excavations revealed a vast network of ritual basins and baths used in ablutions.

For the NT the only washing commanded was that of baptism (Acts 22:16; 1 Cor. 6:11). Ephesians 5:26 shows that the washing of baptism is not effective as a ritual in itself but only

as it shows the working of God's Word in the life of the one baptized. Inward cleansing must accompany the outward washing (Heb. 10:22).

Jimmy Albright

A

ABNER (Ăb´ nĕr) Personal name meaning "father is a lamp." The chief military officer for King Saul and Saul's uncle (1 Sam. 14:50). At Saul's death he supported Ish-bosheth, Saul's son (2 Sam. 2:8) until Ish-bosheth accused him of treason for taking one of Saul's concubines (2 Sam. 3:7-8). Abner transferred loyalty to David. Joab, David's general, went into a jealous rage when David welcomed Abner. Joab then killed Abner, who was buried in Hebron (2 Sam. 3). See 1 Sam. 17:55-58; 20:25; 26:5,14-15.

ABODE OF THE DEAD See *Death; Grave; Hades; Hell; Pit; Sheol.*

ABOMINATION, ABOMINATION OF DESOLATION English versions differ in the number of OT Hebrew words translated "abomination/s," but of these *to'ebah* is by far the most common (KJV 117 times, NRSV 96, NASB 105, HCSB 51). NIV renders *to'ebah* as "detestable" in the vast majority of cases. *To'ebah* expresses that which is repulsive, detestable, or offensive. Examples include sexual perversion (Lev. 18:22-26), pride (Prov. 16:5), hypocritical worship (Isa. 1:13), and especially idolatry (e.g., Deut. 7:25-26; 1 Kgs. 14:24; Ezek. 7:20).

Shiqquts, a "detested thing," is the second most common Hebrew term for "abomination" in English versions. All 28 instances of *shiqquts* in the OT are associated with idolatry, and usually the term describes the idols themselves as disgusting and offensive to God. Other Hebrew words rendered "abomination" or "abominable" in some translations are *piggul* (ceremonially unacceptable foods; Lev. 7:18; 19:7; Isa. 65:4; Ezek. 4:14) and *ba'ash* (literally "stench," but figurative for that which is offensive, odious, or hated; 1 Sam. 13:4).

Bdelugma, "a detestable thing," appears six times in the NT and is the usual Greek word rendered "abomination." Unquestionably the word refers to idolatry in Matt. 24:15; Mark 13:14; and Rev. 17:4,5—possibly in Rev. 21:27.

The abomination of desolation is mentioned five times (Dan. 9:27; 11:31; 12:11; Matt. 24:15; Mark 13:14). The Hebrew varies slightly, but all three Daniel references include a form of *shiqquts* ("abomination") and *shamem* ("be desolated, appalled"). The abomination of desolation is an idolatrous act, object, or person that makes the temple desolate of worshippers.

The "abomination" in Dan. 11:31 was fulfilled in the altar or pagan image of Zeus (Jupiter) erected by Antiochus IV in the Jerusalem temple in December, 167 B.C. (1 Macc. 1:47, 54, 59; 2 Macc. 6:4-5; Josephus *Antiquities* 12.5.4; cf. Dan. 8:13). Interpreters who date the composition of Daniel to the reign of Antiochus IV often suggest the Hebrew for "abomination of desolation" (*shiqquts shomem*) is a contemptuous corruption of Ba'al Shamem ("lord of heaven"), the Syrian equivalent to Zeus. Critics also take Dan. 9:27 and 12:11 to refer to Antiochus's blasphemy, whereas evangelical scholars usually associate these passages with the Roman destruction of A.D. 70 or with a sacrilege of the eschatological Antichrist.

"Abomination of desolation" appears twice in the NT (Matt. 24:15=Mark 13:14). In His Olivet Discourse, Jesus attributed the saying to the prophet Daniel and indicated that its fulfillment was yet future. Accepting Jesus' testimony as authentic, all references to "the abomination of desolation" in Daniel were not fulfilled during the time of Antiochus IV. Granting that Dan. 11:31 refers to Antiochus's blasphemy, Christ's words must point to the "abomination of desolation" of Dan. 9:27 and/or 12:11. Jesus, then, is identifying the "abomination" of these passages with a future sacrilege in the Jerusalem temple.

Most scholars associate this NT "abomination of desolation" with (1) the destruction of the temple, (2) the eschatological antichrist, or (3) both. It could refer to any of several aspects of the Jewish revolt and Roman destruction of Jerusalem and the temple in A.D. 70, including Titus's entering the holy of holies (Josephus, *Wars* 6.4.7; 7.5.5), the Roman army itself (cp. Luke 21:20), specifically the military ensigns with their idolatrous images (Josephus, *Wars* 6.6.1), or the profaning of the temple in A.D. 67-68 by Jewish Zealots (Josephus, *Wars* 4.3.7-10). The

sacrilege of the eschatological Antichrist is mentioned in 2 Thess. 2:3-12. Those who appeal to both events argue that it has a dual application. Since elements of Jesus' prophecy reach beyond the Roman destruction of A.D. 70 to His return (Matt. 24:29-30, 36-44), views 2 or 3 appear to be the best options.

See *Antiochus; Daniel, Book of; Intertestamental History and Literature; Josephus, Flavius.* *Stephen R. Miller*

ABORTION The Bible places a high value on all human life, including that of the unborn. Biblical teaching declares that life is a sacred, God-given gift (Gen. 1:26-27; 2:7; Deut. 30:15-19; Job 1:21; Ps. 8:5; 1 Cor. 15:26), especially the life of children (Ps. 127:3-5; Luke 18:15-16), and condemns those who take it away (Exod. 20:13; 2 Kings 1:13; Amos 1:13-14). The development of unborn life is controlled by God (Job 31:15; Ps. 139:13-16; Eccles. 11:5; Isa. 44:2; 46:3; 49:5; Jer. 1:5; Luke 1:15; Gal. 1:15). The personhood of the fetus is clearly taught in Exod. 21:22 where the unborn is called a "child" (*yeled*) rather than a "fetus" (*nephel* or *golem*). Hos. 9:11 implies that life begins at conception, while Luke 1:41,44 recognizes the consciousness of an unborn child.

The high value placed on unborn human life in the Bible is consistent with the Mosaic law regarding negligent miscarriage (Exod. 21:22-25). This law can be compared to similar statutes in the Code of Hammurabi (nos. 209–214) in which the punishment exacted for acts of negligence that resulted in a woman's miscarriage was dependent on the legal or social status of the mother, not the personhood (or supposed lack thereof) of her unborn child. Middle Assyrian law no. 53 (12th century B.C.) made a self-induced miscarriage (an abortion) a capital offense. *Paul H. Wright*

ABRAHAM (Ā' bră·hăm) Personal name meaning "father of a multitude." The first Hebrew patriarch, he became known as the prime example of faith. He was the son of Terah, a descendant of Noah's son, Shem. (Gen. 11:27). His childhood was spent in Ur of the Chaldees, a prominent Sumerian city. He was known at the

A

Herodian structure built over the Cave of Machpelah, Abraham's burial place for Sarah.

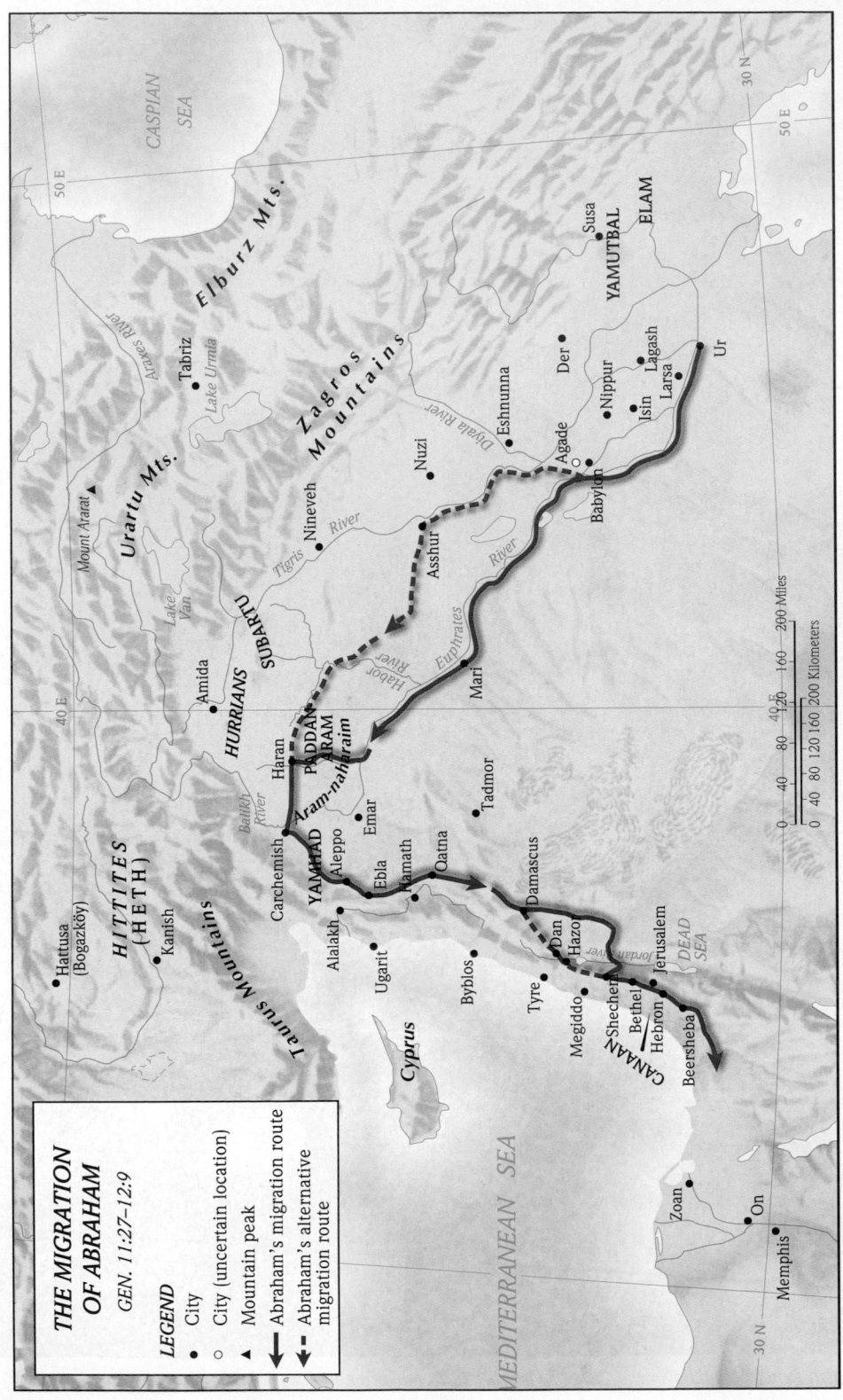

A

THE MIGRATION
OF ABRAHAM
GEN. 11:27–12:9

LEGEND

• City
○ City (uncertain location)
▲ Mountain peak
➡ Abraham's migration route
┅➡ Abraham's alternative
migration route

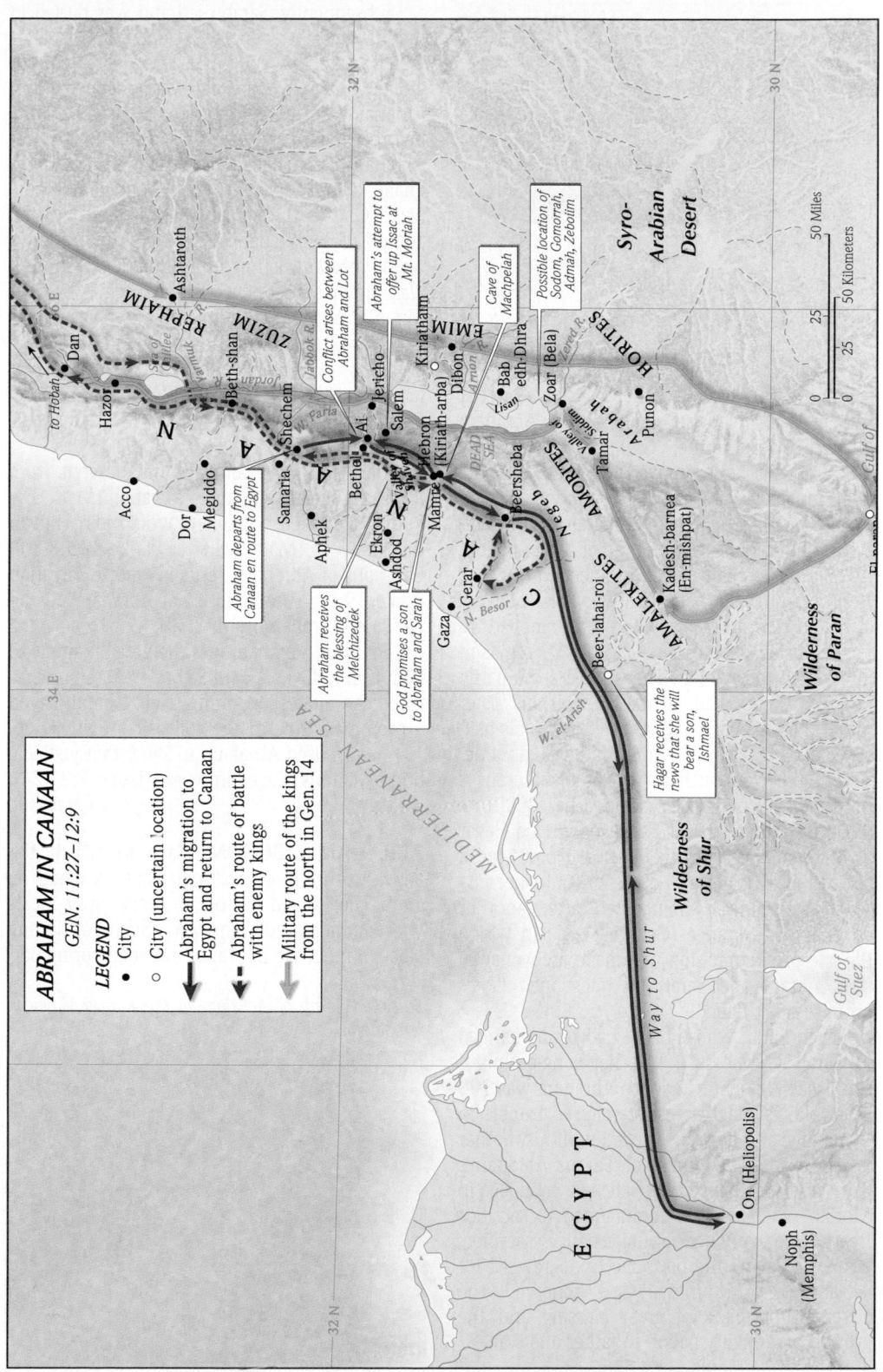

ABRAHAM IN CANAAN

GEN. 11:27–12:9

LEGEND

- City
- ○ City (uncertain location)

→ Abraham's migration to Egypt and return to Canaan

–→ Abraham's route of battle with enemy kings

→ Military route of the kings from the north in Gen. 14

Conflict arises between Abraham and Lot

Abraham's attempt to offer up Isaac at Mt. Moriah

Cave of Machpelah

Possible location of Sodom, Gomorrah, Admah, Zeboiim

Abraham departs from Canaan en route to Egypt

Abraham receives the blessing of Melchizedek

God promises a son to Abraham and Sarah

Hagar receives the news that she will bear a son, Ishmael

Syro-Arabian Desert

HORITES

AMORITES

AMALEKITES

Wilderness of Paran

Wilderness of Shur

EGYPT

On (Heliopolis)

Noph (Memphis)

Way to Shur

W. el-Arish

N. Besor

MEDITERRANEAN SEA

Gulf of Suez

Gulf of

Ashtaroth

Dan

to Hobah

Hazor

REPHAIM

ZUZIM

EMIM

Beth-shan

Shechem

Samaria

Acco

Dor

Megiddo

Aphek

Ekron

Ashdod

Gaza

Gerar

Bethel

Ai

Jericho

Salem

Hebron [Kiriath-arba]

Mamre

Valley of Shaveh

Beersheba

Beer-lahai-roi

Kadesh-barnea (En-mishpat)

Kiriathaim

Dibon

Bab edh-Dhra

Zoar (Bela)

Lisan

Punon

Tamar

Valley of Siddim

Arabah

Negeb

DEAD SEA

El-paran

50 Miles

50 Kilometers

25

25

0

0

A

Well at modern Beersheba thought by some to be Abraham's well.

beginning as Abram ("father is exalted"), but this was changed subsequently to Abraham ("father of a multitude," Gen. 17:5).

Terah, his father, moved to Haran with the family (Gen. 11:31) and after some years died there. God called Abram to migrate to Canaan, assuring him that he would father a vast nation. At different times he lived in Shechem, Bethel, Hebron, and Beer-sheba. His wife Sarai's beauty attracted the pharaoh when they moved to Egypt during a famine (Gen. 12:10), but God intervened to save her. The trouble arose partly because Abram had claimed her as his sister rather than his wife, and in fact she was his half-sister (Gen. 20:12). After returning to Palestine, Abram received further covenantal assurances from God (Gen. 15). He decided he could produce offspring by taking Sarai's handmaid Hagar as a concubine. Though the union produced a son, Ishmael, he was not destined to become Abram's promised heir. Even after another covenantal assurance (Gen. 17:1-21) in which the rite of circumcision was made a covenantal sign, Abram and Sarai still questioned God's promise of an heir.

Then Sarai, whose name had been changed to Sarah ("princess"), had her long-promised son, Isaac ("laughter"), when Abraham was 100 years old. Ishmael's presence caused trouble in the family, and he was expelled with his mother Hagar to the wilderness of Paran. Abraham's faith and obedience were tested by God in Moriah when he was commanded to sacrifice Isaac. God provided an alternative sacrifice, however, saving the boy's life. As a reward for Abraham's faithfulness, God renewed the covenant promises of great blessing and the growth of a mighty nation to father and son.

Subsequently, Sarah died and was buried in the cave of Machpelah (Gen. 23:19), after which Abraham sought a bride for Isaac. A woman named Rebekah was obtained from Abraham's relatives in Mesopotamia, and Isaac married her gladly (Gen. 24:67). In old age Abraham remarried and had further children, finally dying after 175 years. Abraham recognized God as the almighty Lord of all and the author of a covenant by which the Hebrews would become a mighty nation. God Himself was known subsequently as the God of Abraham (Exod. 3:6). Through him God had revealed His plan for human salvation (Exod. 2:24). The promises to Abraham became assurance for future generations (Exod. 32:13; 33:1). Abraham became known as "God's friend forever" (2 Chron. 20:7).

John and Paul showed that descent from Abraham did not guarantee salvation (Matt. 3:9; Rom. 9). Indeed, foreigners would join Him in the kingdom (Matt. 8:11; cp. Luke 16:23-30). Lost sons of Abraham, Jesus invited to salvation (Luke 19:9). True children of Abraham do the works of Abraham (John 8:39).

For Paul, Abraham was the great example of faith (Rom. 4; Gal. 3). In Hebrews Abraham provided the model for tithing (Heb. 7) and played a prominent role in the roll call of faith (Heb. 11). James used Abraham to show that justification by faith is proved in works (James 2:21-24).

R. K. Harrison

ABRAHAM'S BOSOM Place to which the angels carried the poor man Lazarus when he died. The Roman custom of reclining at meals was common among the Jews. Such positioning placed one in the bosom of the neighboring per-

So-called Tomb of Absalom in the Kidron Valley in Jerusalem.

son. To be next to the host, that is to recline in the bosom of the host, was considered the highest honor. Lazarus was comforted after death by being given the place of closest fellowship with the father of the whole Hebrew nation (Luke 16:22-23). See *Heaven*.

ABRAM (Ā´ brăm) Personal name meaning "father is exalted." The name of Abraham ("father of a multitude") in Gen. 11:26–17:4. See *Abraham*.

ABRONAH (Ă·brō´ nah) Place-name meaning "pass" or "passage." Wilderness camp (Num. 33:34). Its location is not known, but it is apparently close to Ezion-geber at the northern tip of the Gulf of Aqaba. KJV spelling is Ebronah.

ABSALOM (Ăb´ sà·lom) Personal name meaning "father of peace." Third son of King David, who rebelled against his father and was murdered by Joab, David's commander (2 Sam. 3:3; 13–19). Absalom apparently resented being ignored by his father and resented his brother Ammon going unpunished for raping Tamar, Absalom's full sister. Being overindulged and ambitious, Absalom became the spokesman for the people (2 Sam. 15:1-6). They, in turn, gladly proclaimed him king in Hebron (15:10), where David was first crowned (2:4). Battle ensued. David left Jerusalem and sent his army to find Absalom, not to hurt him (15:5), but Joab murdered him (18:14). David's lament over Absalom shows the depth of a father's love over the loss of a son as well as regret for personal failures that led to family and national tragedies. See *Abishalom*.   *Robert Fricke*

ABSHAI (NASB) See *Abishai*.

ABSTINENCE Voluntarily refraining from some action, such as eating certain kinds of foods or drinking alcoholic beverages.
Old Testament The most prominent examples of abstinence in the OT relate to the Sabbath (Exod. 31:14-15), food laws (Lev. 11; 19:23-25; Deut. 14), the Nazarite vow (Num. 6), and fasting. While not unique to the Israelites, observance of the Sabbath and food laws became distinguishing characteristics of Israelites in foreign cultures.

The Nazirite vow involved abstinence from fermented products and all produce of the grapevine. On occasion the vow became a life-

long commitment (Judg. 13:5-7). Fasting was practiced as an act of humbling oneself before the Lord. It involved abstinence from food and drink or on occasion only from food or drink. The Day of Atonement was the most prominent fast in Israel. See *Nazirite*.
New Testament Old Testament forms of abstinence continued in the NT period, but the forms themselves frequently were points of controversy between Jesus and the religious leaders (Mark 2:18–3:6). Jesus refocused the prohibitive aspects of the practices by emphasizing internal motive over external observance (Matt. 6:16-18). Paul established the principle of abstaining from any activity that might offend or cause another to stumble (Rom. 14; 1 Cor. 8). This principle often guides the contemporary practice.   *Michael Fink*

ABYSS Transliteration of Greek word *abussos*, literally meaning "without bottom." KJV translates "the deep" or "bottomless" pit. NASB, NIV, RSV use "abyss" to refer to the dark abode of the dead (Rom. 10:7). Abaddon rules the abyss (Rev. 9:11), from which will come the beast of the end time of Revelation (11:7). The beast of the abyss faces ultimate destruction (Rev. 17:8), and Satan will be bound there during the millennium (Rev. 20:1-3). See *Hades; Hell; Sheol*.

ACACIA Hard wood with a beautiful fine grain or close grain, which darkens as it ages. Insects find the taste of acacia wood distasteful, and its density makes it difficult for water or other decaying agents to penetrate. The Israelites pitched their tents by Jordan, from Beth-jesimoth as far as Abel-shittim, translated "meadow of the acacias" (Num. 33:49)

Acacia tree growing in the Sinai Desert.

Moses received the instructions for the building of the tabernacle on Mount Sinai (Exod. 25–35), in the Arabian Desert (Gal. 4:25) where acacia is among the larger of the few timber species to be found. Items constructed for the tabernacle of acacia (shittim) wood include: the ark of the covenant and its poles; the table of showbread and its poles; the brazen altar and its poles; the incense altar and its poles; and all the poles for the hanging of the curtains and the supports (Exod. 36:20,31,36; 37; 38).

The acacia wood was so precious that Exod. 25:5 says that besides the offering of silver and brass, every man who had acacia (shittim) wood brought it for the Lord's offering. In Joel 3:18 Judah will be blessed "in that day" with a spring that will water the valley of Shittim. See *Altar; Ark of the Covenant; Plants; Shittim.*

ACBOR (NIV) See *Achbor.*

ACCAD (Ăk´ ăd) or **AKKAD** (NIV) Place-name of famous city in Mesopotamia ruled by Sargon I about 2350 B.C. (Gen. 10:10). Its exact location is not known. It gave its name to Akkadian language used by Babylon and Assyria.

ACCENT, GALILEAN The peculiarity of Peter's speech that showed he was from Galilee. His peculiar speech made the servant girl suspect that Peter was a follower of Jesus from Nazareth in Galilee (Matt. 26:73; cp. Judg. 12:5-6, where a person's speech betrayed his place of origin. See *Shibboleth.*

ACCEPTANCE Being received with approval or pleasure. In the Bible, things or persons are often said to be acceptable to men or to God. Human acceptance (or rejection) of other humans is affected by many things such as race, class, clan, sex, actions of the individual, prejudice, etc. On a human level Jesus shows us that all human beings are to be accepted, to be loved for their own sake, simply because they are persons created in the image of the loving Father (Gen. 1:26-27; Matt. 5:43-48).

Above all, sin keeps a person from being acceptable to God (Gen. 4:7; Isa. 59:2). From earliest days sacrifices were offered to God in an attempt to make the worshiper acceptable to Him. Later the law revealed more clearly what one needed to do to be acceptable to God. This included ethical actions (Ten Commandments) as well as sacrifices (Leviticus). Israel succumbed

to the temptation of separating sacrifice from ethical action, so the great prophets again and again proclaimed the truth that no sacrifice is acceptable if it is divorced from just treatment of others (Isa. 1:10-17; Amos 5:21-24). Micah summed up the terms of acceptance in 6:6-8, "What does the Lord require of you but to do justice, to love kindness, and to walk humbly with your God?" (NASB). The proper attitude of humility is as important as right action (Ps. 51:16-17; 1 Pet. 5:5-6).

Jesus summarized the law and the prophets in the two great commandments (Matt. 22:37-40) and held them up as the requirements for eternal life (Luke 10:25-28). Paul saw that the law serves two purposes. One, it makes known God's requirements, thus revealing human sinfulness (Rom. 3:20). Two, the moral law as a true expression of God's will remains a goal or guide, even though one no longer thinks God's acceptance is won by the law. The NT proclaims that Jesus has done what is necessary to make one acceptable to God. At the beginning of His ministry, Jesus announced that His mission included proclaiming the acceptable year of the Lord, the time of salvation (Luke 4:19). Jesus revealed the will of God clearer than ever before (Heb. 1:1-2); He destroyed the works of the devil (1 John 3:8); but above all He put away sin "by the sacrifice of Himself" (Heb. 9:26 HCSB). Paul wrote of acceptance before God mainly as justification. People are made acceptable to God because the just requirements of the law have been met by the sacrifice of Jesus (Rom. 3:21-26; 8:3-5). The book of Hebrews presents Jesus as the true High Priest who offers the perfect sacrifice that effectively cleanses or covers sin so that it is no longer a barrier to acceptance by God (Heb. 9:11-14,26). Both Paul and Hebrews taught that for acceptance by God to be effective, one must believe—accept the offer of acceptance from God in Christ and commit oneself to following the way of Jesus, confessing Him as Lord. See *Atonement; Justification; Love.*   *Joe Baskin*

ACCESS Permission and ability to enter into a secured area or into the presence of someone important such as God. In the human realm access usually applied to persons who were permitted to see the king face-to-face (Esther 1:14). Thus they had a place to stand in the king's presence (Zech. 3:7). Each royal court had its own rules. The Persian court which Esther faced set the death penalty for anyone who sought access to the king without royal permission (Esther 4:11). The NT teaches that every person can now have access to God because Jesus' death on the cross has opened the way. Such access is actually experienced by those who express personal trust in Jesus and rely on divine grace. This brings peace and eternal hope (Rom. 5:1-2), but it is always dependent upon the heavenly King's royal favor, not upon entrance requirements established or met by humans. Both Gentiles and Jews have an open door to the Father through Christ's death on the cross and through the work of the Holy Spirit present in the believer's life (Eph. 2:10-18). Access to God through faith in Christ was God's eternal purpose and gives the believer confidence and boldness to approach God (Eph. 3:12). Old Testament religious practices allowed only the high priest to enter the holy of holies and that only once a year (Lev. 16:2,34). Through Christ believers have constant access to the holiest place, where God is (Heb. 10:19-22).

ACCO (Ä´ kō) or **ACCHO** (KJV) Place-name for famous Mediterranean seaport north of Mount Carmel. Territory was assigned to tribe of Asher, but they could not conquer it (Judg. 1:31). The Greeks renamed Acco, Ptolemaïs. On his third missionary voyage, Paul spent one day in Ptolemaïs (Acts 21:7). The city has a long history documented by Near Eastern records reaching back to about 2000 B.C., but it plays a small role in the biblical narrative.

ACCOUNTABILITY, AGE OF Age at which God holds children accountable for their sins. When persons come to this point, they face the inevitability of divine judgment if they fail to repent and believe the gospel.

Scripture speaks plainly of the need for sinful humans to be converted in order to have eternal life, but it does not directly address the matter of the destiny of children who die in infancy or young childhood. Some things are clear, though. Scripture is specific that all persons are sinners, even little ones. "The wicked go astray from the womb; liars err from birth" (Ps. 58:3 HCSB). "Indeed, I was guilty when I was born; I was sinful when my mother conceived me" (Ps. 51:5 HCSB). The psalmist is not saying that only certain persons are sinners from birth, nor is he say-

ing that his mother sinned in conceiving him, but rather that all persons are sinners from their earliest days. Jesus also mades it clear that all who are born are in need of regeneration when He informed Nicodemus, "Whatever is born of the flesh is flesh, and whatever is born of the Spirit is spirit" (John 3:6 HCSB).

Port of Acco from the South.

People are converted when, under the convicting power of the Spirit, they repent of sin and place faith in God who saves through the atoning work of Jesus on the cross (Acts 2:38; Rom. 3:21-26). In order to be saved, one needs to have a basic understanding of the faith and of the relationship between one's sin and Christ's sacrifice (Rom. 10:9-15). This requires, of course, a certain amount of cognitive knowledge and reasoning ability, along with the convicting work of the Spirit. Though there is no specific "age" of accountability technically speaking (for instance, age 12 or 13), there is a "time" in one's life when he or she is accountable for sin.

What hope is there then for little ones who are too young to work out all of these issues mentally and spiritually? Much hope, actually. First, it is clear in the account of judgment against Israel for its failure to trust God at Kadesh-barnea that God held accountable only those who were decision makers—the children were not held responsible (Num. 14:29-31). Though judgment in this case was only temporal and not eternal, it does illustrate a principle of mercy toward those not in a position to make such determinations. It is not that children are innocent, but only that God is merciful, a mercy seemingly applied somewhat differently to infants than to those who are older—that is, universally. Second, when David's child died seven days after being born, the king informed his servants, "I shall go to him, but he will not return to me" (1 Sam. 12:23 NRSV). He clearly was convinced that he would see his child after his own death. This same king wrote in another place that he would spend eternity in the "house of Yahweh" (Ps. 23:6 NJB). It is to that house that he believed his son would go.

If that which is born of the flesh is flesh, and one must be reborn in order to see God, how is it possible for little ones to be saved? Again, Scripture gives no mechanism for this procedure, though it does drop hints. John the Baptist was filled with the Holy Spirit from his mother's womb (Luke 1:15). This makes it clear that the Spirit can have a relationship with someone who has no intellectual understanding of that bond. This ought not to surprise Bible students since Jesus noted that the Spirit moves where He wills (John 3:8).

God's Word does not present an explicit and unequivocal case for infant salvation; it is somewhat silent on the question. Insofar as it does address the relevant issues, however, it seems clearly to imply that those who die before reaching an age of responsibility will not be condemned by God, even though they are sinners by nature and choice, but will instead be received into eternal salvation. See *Family; Regeneration; Salvation.*   *Chad Brand*

ACCURSED Translation of Hebrew *cherem,* a technical term in warfare for items captured from the enemy and devoted to God. TEV demonstrates the difficulty of translating the Hebrew into English, using at various times: "unconditionally dedicate" (Num. 21:2); "put everyone to death" (Deut. 2:34); "completely destroy" (Deut. 20:17); "killed" (Josh. 6:21; 8:26); "become the

Lord's permanent property" (Lev. 27:21); "put a curse on ... destroyed" (Judg. 1:17). REB uses "dedicated" (Lev. 27:21); "devoted" (Lev. 27:28-29); "utterly destroy" (Num. 21:2); "put to death under solemn ban" (Deut. 2:34); "exterminate" (Deut. 7:2); "destroyed" (Josh. 2:10); "put to death" (Judg. 21:11). NRSV consistently uses "devoted" and "utterly destroyed" to translate *cherem,* while NASB uses "set apart" and "utterly destroy." NIV uses "devoted," "totally destroyed," "completely destroyed." Israel's neighbors practiced devoting battle spoils to a god also, as 2 Kings 19:11 shows. "Accursed" appears in KJV for *cherem* only in Joshua and in 1 Chron. 2:7. In Deut. 21:23 and Isa. 65:20 KJV uses "accursed" to translate another Hebrew root, *qalal,* "to make light of, curse."

Paul used a technical Greek term, *anathema,* to call for persons to be put under a holy ban or be accursed (Rom. 9:3; 1 Cor. 12:3; Gal. 1:8-9; cp. 1 Cor. 16:22). Paul used the term in the sense of the Hebrew *cherem.* See *Anathema; Ban; Blessing and Cursing; Devoted Thing.*

ACCUSER Legal term describing a person who claims another is guilty of a crime or a moral offense. The Hebrew word for accuser is *Satan* (cp. Ps. 109:6 in various translations). False accusation called for serious punishment (Deut. 19:15-21). The psalmist prayed for judgment against his accusers (Ps. 109:4,20,29 NASB, NIV, NRSV). False accusers led to Christ's conviction and death (Matt. 27:12). Jewish accusers (Acts 22:30) finally led Paul to appeal to Rome (Acts 25:11). See *Satan.*

ACELDAMA (Á·çĕl´ dá·má) or **AKELDAMA** (KJV) Judas Iscariot purchased this field where he killed himself (Acts 1:19). The name is Aramaic and means "field of blood." *(See picture on next page.)* Evidently it was purchased with the money that had been paid to Judas for betraying Jesus. According to Matt. 27:7 the field purchased with this money was used for the burial of foreigners. See *Judas.*

ACHAIA (Á·kā´ yà) Roman province in which Gallio was deputy, or proconsul, in the time of Paul the apostle (Acts 18:12). It consisted roughly of the southern half of ancient Greece, including the Peloponnesus. Major cities in Achaia included Sparta, Athens, and Corinth, which was the administrative center. Paul

A monastery on Mount Zion marks the traditional site of Judas's suicide overlooking the Field of Blood.

preached successfully in the province (Acts 18:27-28).

ACHAICUS (À chā´ ĭ cŭs) Personal name of messenger who came to Paul from Corinth before he wrote 1 Corinthians (16:17). His presence with Stephanas and Fortunatus encouraged Paul. The three brought news and perhaps a letter (1 Cor. 7:1) to Paul from the church at Corinth. They may have carried 1 Corinthians back to Corinth.

ACHAN (Ā´ kȧn) or **ACHAR** (1 Chron. 2:7). In Josh. 7:1, a Judahite whose theft of a portion of the spoil from Jericho brought divine displeasure and military defeat on the Israelite army. After the battle of Ai, the Lord told Joshua the reason for Israel's defeat was that the ban concerning the spoil of Jericho had been violated (Josh. 7:11). Achan was discovered to be the guilty party, and he and his family were stoned to death (Josh. 7:25). See *Ai; Joshua*.

ACHAZ (KJV, Matt. 1:9). See *Ahaz*.

ACHBOR (Ăk´ bôr) Personal name meaning "mouse." **1.** Father of king in Edom (Gen. 36:38). **2.** Man that King Josiah commissioned to ask God the meaning of the book of the Law found in the temple. He and the others commissioned obtained God's word from Huldah, the prophetess (2 Kings 22:12-14). **3.** Father of Elnathan, whom Jehoiakim sent to bring back the prophet Uriah from Egypt in order to execute him (Jer. 26:22; cp. 36:12).

ACHIM (Ā´ kĭm) Personal name of ancestor of Jesus of whom nothing is known except his name (Matt. 1:14).

ACHISH (Ā´ kĭsh) Philistine personal name. **1.** King of Gath, a Philistine city, to whom David fled in fear of Saul (1 Sam. 21:10). David played as a madman to escape from Achish (21:13). Later David became a soldier for Achish but cunningly expanded his own influence around Ziklag (1 Sam. 27). David joined Achish to fight Saul (28:1-2), but the Philistine leaders forced him to leave without fighting (29:1-11). Saul and his sons, including Jonathan, died in the battle (31:1-6). **2.** King of Gath to whom Shimei went to retrieve his servants but in so doing violated his agreement with Solomon and lost his life (1 Kings 2:36-46).

ACHMETHA (Ăk´ mē-thȧ) or **ECBATANA** (NASB, NIV, RSV, TEV) Capital of the ancient Median empire, located in the Zagros Mountains in western Iran, on two major roads that lead from the south and west to the city of Tehran. Only one reference to the city is found in the canonical books of the Bible (Ezra 6:2), but it is known as Ecbatana in the apocryphal books and is referred to frequently, especially in the books of Judith, Tobit, and 2 Maccabees.

No archeological work has been undertaken at Achmetha for the simple reason that it is now occupied by the modern city of Hamadan. Two surface finds, a gold dagger and a gold tablet written in cuneiform, have been made.

Bryce Sandlin

ACHOR (A´ kôr) Place-name meaning "trouble, affliction," or "taboo." The valley in which Achan and his household were stoned to death (Josh. 7:24-26). Later it formed part of the border of Judah. It is the subject of prophetic promises in Isa. 65:10 and Hos. 2:15. See *Joshua*.

ACHSA (Ak´ sȧ) or **ACHSAH** (NASB, RSV, TEV) or **ACSAH** (NIV) Personal name meaning "bangle" or "ankle ornament." Daughter of Caleb offered as wife to man who conquered Kirjath-sepher (Josh. 15:16). Othniel took the city and the woman (Judg. 1:12-13).

ACHSHAPH (Ăk´ shăph) or **ACSHAPH** (NIV) Place-name meaning "place of sorcery." City-state which joined Jabin, King of Hazor, in opposing Joshua as he invaded northern Israel (Josh. 11:1). Achshaph was a border city for Asher (Josh. 19:25). It was probably located near Acco.

A

ACHZIB (Ăk´ zĭb) or **ACZIB** (NIV) Place-name meaning "deceitful." **1.** Town in southern Judah, perhaps modern Tel el-Beida near Lachish (Josh. 15:44). Micah 1:14 makes a wordplay using Achzib, literally "the houses of deceitfulness will be deceitful." **2.** Border town of Asher (Josh. 19:29) which the Israelite tribe could not conquer (Judg. 1:31). It may be modern Tel Akhziv near Acco.

ACRE Translation of Hebrew *tsemed*, literally a "team" of oxen. As a measure of land, it refers to the land a team can plow in one day (1 Sam. 14:14; Isa. 5:10).

ACROSTIC Literary device by which each section of a literary work begins with the succeeding letter of the alphabet. Thus in Ps. 119 the first eight verses begin with *aleph*, the first letter of the Hebrew alphabet; the next eight with *bet*, the second letter of the Hebrew alphabet, and the pattern is continued through verses 169-176, which each begin with *taw*, the last letter of the Hebrew alphabet. Other examples in the Bible include Pss. 9–10; 25; 34; 37; 111–112; 145; Prov. 31:10-31; Lam. 1–4. The acrostic style helped people memorize the poem and expressed completeness of subject matter from A to Z.

ACSAH (NIV) See *Achsa*.

ACTS, BOOK OF Standing immediately after the four Gospels in the NT, the book of Acts is part two of a work (part one is the Gospel of Luke) beginning with Luke's statement of his purpose for writing and ending with Paul under house arrest in Rome (A.D. 62). Acts is an important source for the history of the earliest church, documenting the accomplishment of the task given to the apostles by the risen Christ in Acts 1:8, "and you will be My witnesses in Jerusalem, in all Judea and Samaria, and to the ends of the earth" (HCSB). The roles of Peter and Paul are featured especially in the spread of the gospel to Rome. The speeches in Acts, which constitute about one third of the book, are rich in solid theology.

Though echoes of Acts may appear as early as 1 Clement (ca. A.D. 95–100) and the Didache (early second century), the earliest identifiable references appear in Justin Martyr (ca. A.D. 130–150), in his *First* and *Second Apologies*. The current title of the book was set by the end of the second century.

By the end of the second century, authorship of both the Gospel of Luke and the book of Acts commonly was attributed to Luke, whom Irenaeus described as a physician and traveling companion of Paul. He noted the occurrences of the second person plural in the later chapters (the so-called "we" passages) of Acts as pointing to the author being a traveling companion of Paul. From Irenaeus forward, patristic opinion is united in support of Lukan authorship and the internal evidence points to common authorship as well. Common style and vocabulary run throughout the two books as do common themes. The prefaces to both books affirm common authorship: both are dedicated to the same person (Theophilus) and the ascension narratives at the end of Luke and the beginning of Acts bind them together.

Many scholars date Luke prior to A.D. 64 because Acts ends abruptly with Paul having been in Rome for two years. The absence of an account of the remainder of Paul's life and ministry would be explained if the book were written at about that point in time (ca. A.D. 62–64). The primitive theology of Peter's speeches and the absence of any reference to the Neronian persecutions of believers in Rome (A.D. 64–67) also support such a date. These arguments are not decisive, however, and perhaps Acts ends as it does because Luke had fulfilled his purpose of describing the extension of the gospel to Rome. Three predictions of the fall of Jerusalem in Luke (19:41-44; 21:20-24; 23:28-31) possibly reflect a knowledge of the fall of the city to the Roman army in A.D. 70. However, they could also reflect authentic predictions by Jesus before the fact. The apparent use of the Gospel of Mark as a source by Luke also suggests a date later than A.D. 62, and most ancient tradition indicates that Mark wrote his gospel based on the memoirs of Peter, after Peter's death (ca. A.D. 67–68). Obviously Acts was written subsequently to Luke but probably not much later. Many scholars also advocate dates between A.D. 70 and 90 for Acts, with most of these falling about midway or about A.D. 80. Though dates between A.D. 95–100 and even as late as A.D. 125–150 have been suggested, they are not tenable.

Opinions vary widely as to the place of writing and the original destination of Acts. Luke and Acts are addressed to Theophilus, possibly a

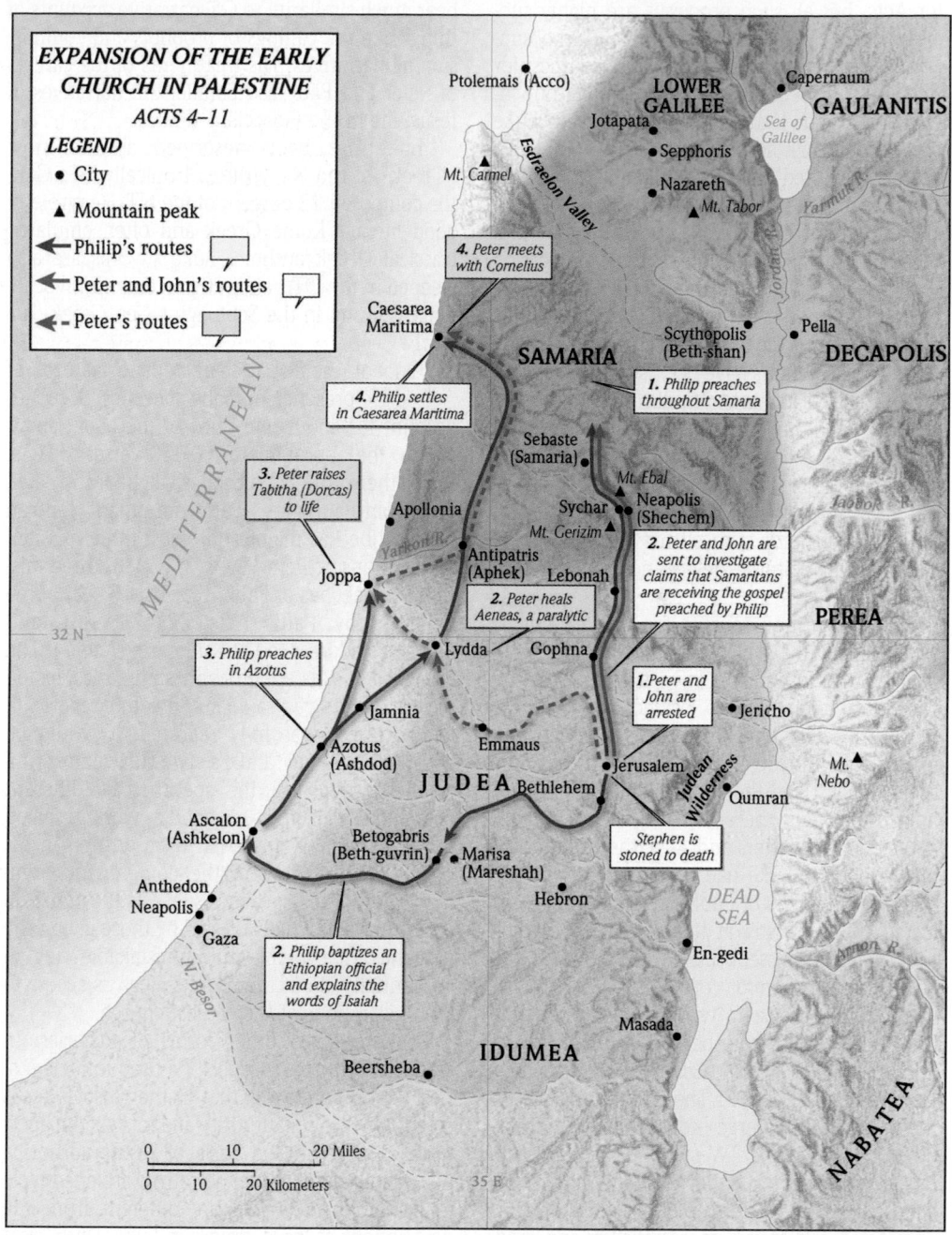

EXPANSION OF THE EARLY CHURCH IN PALESTINE

ACTS 4–11

LEGEND

- • City
- ▲ Mountain peak
- ← Philip's routes
- ← Peter and John's routes
- ←- Peter's routes

4. Peter meets with Cornelius

4. Philip settles in Caesarea Maritima

1. Philip preaches throughout Samaria

3. Peter raises Tabitha (Dorcas) to life

2. Peter and John are sent to investigate claims that Samaritans are receiving the gospel preached by Philip

2. Peter heals Aeneas, a paralytic

3. Philip preaches in Azotus

1.Peter and John are arrested

Stephen is stoned to death

2. Philip baptizes an Ethiopian official and explains the words of Isaiah

Ptolemais (Acco), LOWER GALILEE, Capernaum, GAULANITIS, Jotapata, Sepphoris, Sea of Galilee, Mt. Carmel, Esdraelon Valley, Nazareth, Mt. Tabor, Yarmuk R., Caesarea Maritima, SAMARIA, Scythopolis (Beth-shan), Pella, DECAPOLIS, MEDITERRANEAN, Sebaste (Samaria), Mt. Ebal, Neapolis (Shechem), Sychar, Mt. Gerizim, Apollonia, Yarkon R., Antipatris (Aphek), Lebonah, Joppa, Lydda, Gophna, PEREA, Jamnia, Emmaus, Jericho, Mt. Nebo, Azotus (Ashdod), JUDEA, Bethlehem, Jerusalem, Judean Wilderness, Qumran, Ascalon (Ashkelon), Betogabris (Beth-guvrin), Marisa (Mareshah), Anthedon Neapolis, Hebron, Gaza, En-gedi, DEAD SEA, N. Besor, Masada, Amnon R., IDUMEA, Beersheba, NABATEA

0   10   20 Miles
0   10   20 Kilometers   35 E

A

Roman citizen of some prominence, but all attempts to be more specific are speculative. The content of Acts seems directed at an audience including both Gentile and Jewish believers. Antioch of Syria and Rome are the most common suggestions for the provenance of Acts. Nevertheless, perhaps Luke intended his works for an audience without boundaries, as it was, in fact, widely distributed and appreciated from the beginning.

Luke stated that he used all available sources in his preparation to write his record (Luke 1:1-4). Numerous suggestions have been made as to what documentary sources Luke may have used for Acts, but all such proposals are highly subjective and speculative. A. Harnack, who supported Lukan authorship, posited sources for Acts 1–15 from certain locales such as Antioch, Caesarea, and Jerusalem. He believed Luke drew on his own memory for Acts 16–28. C. C. Torrey suggested an Aramaic language original behind Acts 1–15 because of many "semiticisms" in the text. Others have observed that the data can be accounted for by comparison with the Septuagint, the Greek translation of the Hebrew Old Testament, which was the Bible used by most of the early church.

Several solutions have been suggested for the "we" passages of Acts 16–28. The traditional position, and the most feasible, is that they reflect the presence of Luke when the events occurred. Other suggestions feature the use of the diary of a companion of Paul as a source for a later writer. Some suggest that the use of "we" is simply an editorial device not signifying an eyewitness's presence.

Even if written sources for Acts cannot be established, Luke had access to local traditions of believing communities, eyewitness reports, and cherished reminiscences passed down in the churches. These kinds of sources may account, for instance, for details like the work of Philip the evangelist and the conversions at Cornelius' house. Though there is overlap of content between Paul's letters and Acts, there is no clear indication that Luke had access to the epistles. Perhaps the letters of Paul had not yet been collected and were still at the churches to which they were addressed. Luke evidently did not have access to them or considered them not germane to his purpose in writing Acts: to describe the extension of the gospel to Rome.

The identity of the original text of Acts presents a special problem. The early witnesses for the text of Acts diverge more than those of any other NT book. The "Western" text of Acts differs significantly from the "Alexandrian," being almost 10 percent longer. The Alexandrian is considered earlier and more reliable, and modern Bible translations follow it in Acts. See *Textual Criticism, New Testament.*

As a writer, Luke is among the best in the NT. He wrote with clear intentionality as a historian and theologian. His gospel followed the new genre pioneered by Mark. Acts also has much in common with the genre of Hellenistic historical monograph. The narratives in Acts also bear much similarity to OT narrative accounts of things like the callings of prophets and commissioning narratives. His treatments of the careers of Peter and Paul also parallel the narratives of Jesus' life in the Gospels.

Luke has been described as the most "Greek" of the NT writers. Ironically, this Gentile composed 27 percent of the NT. He wrote in good literary Koine Greek and often emulated classical Greek authors. Luke's works are also steeped in the OT. A full 90 percent of his vocabulary is found in the Septuagint. See *Greek Language.*

One of the most characteristic features of Acts is the presence of many speeches. Speeches account for about one third of the book, about 300 of the approximately 1,000 verses of Acts. In all there are 24 speeches, eight from Peter, nine from Paul, and seven from others. Ten can be described as major addresses: three missionary sermons of Peter (Acts 2; 3; 10), three missionary speeches of Paul (Acts 13; 17; 20), three defenses by Paul (Acts 22; 24; 26), and Stephen's address to the Sanhedrin (Acts 7). The speeches in Acts are probably summaries, examples of what was said, but not full reports. If each address was fully reported, it would be many times longer. Luke's style runs almost uniformly through all the speeches by different characters, indicating his hand at work in selecting the summary material to be written in his book. Sheer variety in the content and argumentation of the speeches suggests they are reliable reports of what was said by those giving the speeches. They have an unmistakable ring of authenticity about them. Acts gives us access to the declarations of the earliest church.

Luke utilized other forms of material. In common with the Gospels, he used miracle stories. The difference is that in the Gospels Jesus acted on His own authority and in Acts the apostles act only on the basis of Jesus' authority, never their own. Travel narratives are effectively employed in Acts and are different from the descriptions of Jesus' travels in Luke. With great intentionality they depict the spread of the gospel from one area to another on each of Paul's missionary journeys. Much of the text consists of short episodes sometimes described as edifying stories. A good example is Acts 19, which is devoted to a series of brief encounters with various people and groups. Luke used these short vignettes to illustrate the success of Paul's missionary endeavors. Luke also uses brief summaries effectively for a variety of purposes. Unlike the episodes, the summaries generalize, giving a broad impression of the main characteristics of the early believing communities.

Luke's personality is reflected in his writings. He was a gifted storyteller, using suspense, irony, and an eye for detail. He described nautical procedures carefully, detailed various lodgings, and shared meals. Luke had great concern for the poor and the needy, the oppressed and downtrodden. Luke showed the prominence of women in the ministry of Jesus and in the life of the early church.

Though many have suggested otherwise, Luke's works have much in common with other works of Hellenistic historiography. He carefully placed the events he wrote about in the broader historical context of the Roman Empire. Through selection, emphasis, and analysis he communicated the significance of the events he described. He especially pointed out how the legitimacy of the earliest church was recognized by Roman observers and authorities at various times.

It would be fair to call Luke a theologian. He viewed early Christian history through the eyes of faith and saw constant traces of divine providence. He retained his reliability as a historian but wrote from within the earliest church, not from a viewpoint of total detachment. Luke's theological concerns have been suggested by various scholars. Hans Conzelmann saw salvation history as Luke's main concern. Ernst Käsemann saw the strong influence of the early institutional church in Acts.

Two observations on the theology of Acts are noteworthy. First, though the Gospel of Luke and Acts are closely related, their theology should be considered separately. Each stands on its own theological feet. Second, the theology of Acts is communicated primarily in its narrative movement by repetition and emphasis of the recurring themes of the narratives. It is a narrative theology. The Christology of Acts is a highly developed messianic Christology, found mostly in addresses to Jewish hearers, based on the witness of the OT. This messianic Christology includes the atonement of Christ's death and the confirmation of messiahship provided by the resurrection. Acts resonates with Pauline soteriology, although it is not presented systematically.

The purpose of Acts is that of volume one (Luke's Gospel) stated in Luke 1:4, "that you may know the certainty of the things about which you have been instructed" (HCSB). He accomplished this goal by careful research and a chronological presentation of events. His immediate audience was Theophilus, but Luke certainly expected the works to be copied and circulated. Some have suggested that Luke wrote to counter some false teaching, such as Gnosticism, but this is highly questionable.

Acts is characterized by a multiplicity of themes. Acts 1:8 states the overarching theme of the spread of the gospel from Jerusalem throughout the earth. That the mission of the church is under the direct control of the providence of God is perhaps the strongest single theme in the theology of Acts. The role of the Holy Spirit is part of the emphasis on God's providence. Much of the book of Acts concerns witnessing to the Jews and the possibility of the restoration of Israel when she embraces her Messiah. If Acts gives a picture of massive Jewish rejection of the gospel and their resulting exclusion from the people of God, it also gives the other side as well—the inclusion of the Gentiles in the people of God. It is not a matter of the exclusion of one and the inclusion of the other. Rather, it is the story of how early Jewish-Christians were led by God to the vision of a more inclusive people of God, a church that transcended all barriers of human discrimination and prejudice.

The concept of faithful witness ties the two halves of Acts together. The last half of Acts emphasizes the relationship of Christians to the Roman political authorities by two recurring patterns: first, the constant note that Paul was innocent of breaking any Roman laws, and that this was recognized and confirmed by Roman officials; and second, Roman officials stepped in to deliver Paul from Jewish threats to his life. Paul modeled how believers should relate to authority, and he utilized his Roman citizenship rights to the advancement of the gospel, all the way to Caesar's tribunal in Rome. Through Paul's example Luke set forth a realistic political agenda for his readers: give no grounds for charges against you, use what legal rights you have, be willing to suffer for your faith, and bear witness wherever and whenever you can. Even Rome could be won for Christ.

The story of Acts can perhaps be summarized in the single phrase "the triumph of the gospel." It is a triumphant story of how the early Christian community in the power of the Spirit saturated their world with the message of God's salvation in Jesus Christ. It was not an easy path. There were internal obstacles and old assumptions were challenged. Opinions had to be revised and prejudices overcome as the Spirit led to an ever more inclusive people of God.

A danger in such triumph is the arrogance of a lopsided "theology of glory." Rightly viewed, there is no room for arrogance here—only humility and openness to God's direction. The witnesses do not triumph—the Word triumphs—and only when the witnesses are faithful servants of the Lord Jesus. The book of Acts is in a real sense a book for renewal, calling the church back to its roots, setting a pattern for faithful discipleship, for witness in the footsteps of the Master, and a wholehearted commitment to sacrifice and suffering. It speaks to us even in times of deep discouragement, reminding us of the reality of the sovereign hand of God bringing His will and purposes for our lives to pass, reassuring us of the reality of the presence of His Spirit in our lives. It challenges us to faithful witness, regardless of what may come our way.

Acts falls naturally into two divisions: the mission of the Jerusalem church (Acts 1–12) and the mission of Paul (Acts 13–28). Each of these may be divided into two main parts. In the Jerusalem portion, Acts 1–5 treats the earliest church in Jerusalem. Acts 6–12 deals with the outreach beyond Jerusalem. In the Pauline portion, Acts 13:1–21:16 relates the three major missionary journeys of Paul. Acts 21:17–28:31 deals with Paul's defense of his ministry.

Outline

   I. The Spirit Empowers the Church for Witness (1:1–2:47)
     A. Literary Prologue (1:1-2)
     B. Instructions Preparatory to Pentecost (1:3-5)
     C. Christ's Legacy: The Call to Witness (1:6-8)
     D. The Ascension of Christ (1:9-11)
     E. Preparation in the Upper Room (1:12-14)
     F. Restoration of the Apostolic Circle (1:15-26)
     G. Miracle at Pentecost (2:1-13)
     H. Peter's Sermon at Pentecost (2:14-41)
     I. The Common Life of the Community (2:42-47)
  II. The Apostles Witness to the Jews in Jerusalem (3:1–5:42)
     A. Peter's Healing a Lame Beggar (3:1-11)
     B. Peter's Sermon from Solomon's Colonnade (3:12-26)
     C. Peter and John before the Sanhedrin (4:1-22)
     D. The Prayer of the Community (4:23-31)
     E. The Common Life of the Community (4:32-37)
     F. A Serious Threat to the Common Life (5:1-11)
     G. The Miracles Worked by the Apostles (5:12-16)
     H. All the Apostles before the Council (5:17-42)
  III. The Hellenists Break through to a Wider Witness (6:1–8:40)
     A. Introduction of the Seven (6:1-7)
     B. Stephen's Arrest and Trial (6:8–7:1)
     C. Stephen's Speech before the Sanhedrin (7:2-53)
     D. Stephen's Martyrdom (7:54–8:1a)
     E. Persecution and Dispersal of the Hellenists (8:1b-3)
     F. The Witness of Philip (8:4-40)
  IV. Peter Joins the Wider Witness (9:1–12:25)
     A. Paul's New Witness to Christ (9:1-31)
     B. Peter's Witness in the Coastal Towns (9:32-43)
     C. Peter's Witness to a Gentile God-fearer (10:1–11:18)
     D. Antioch's Witness to Gentiles (11:19-30)
     E. Persecution Again in Jerusalem (12:1-25)
  V. Paul Turns to the Gentiles (13:1–15:35)
     A. Paul and Barnabas Commissioned (13:1-3)
     B. Sergius Paulus's Conversion on Cyprus (13:4-12)
     C. Paul's Address to the Synagogue at Pisidian Antioch (13:13-52)
     D. Acceptance and Rejection at Iconium (14:1-7)

ADADAH (Ăd´ à·dah) Place-name of city in southeastern Judah (Josh. 15:22).

ADAH (Ā´ dăh) Personal name meaning "adornment, ornament." **1.** Wife of Lamech and mother of Jabal and Jubal (Gen. 4:19-23).

2. Wife of Esau and mother of Edomite officials (Gen. 36:2-16).

ADAIAH (À·dī´ ah) Personal name meaning "Yahweh has adorned." **1.** Grandfather of King Josiah (2 Kings 22:1). **2.** A Levite, one of the family of temple singers (1 Chron. 6:41). **3.** A Benjaminite (1 Chron. 8:21). **4.** Priest who returned to Jerusalem from Babylon after the exile (1 Chron. 9:12). **5.** Father of Maaseiah, who helped make young Joash king instead of Athaliah, the queen mother (2 Chron. 23:1). **6.** Two men with foreign wives in time of Ezra (Ezra 10:29,39). **7.** Member of the tribe of Judah in Jerusalem after the exile (Neh. 11:5). **8.** Priest in the temple after the exile (Neh. 11:12), probably the same as 4.

ADALIA (Ăd·à·lī´ à) Personal name of Persian origin. One of 10 sons of Haman, villain of the book of Esther, who was slain by Jews (Esther 9:8).

ADAM (Ăd´ am) Place-name of city near Jordan River, where waters of Jordan heaped up so Israel could cross over to conquer the land (Josh. 3:16). Its location is probably Tel ed-Damieh near the Jabbok River.

ADAM AND EVE First man and woman created by God from whom all other people are descended.

Old Testament The name *Eve* is related to the Hebrew word for "living," but it occurs only as the name of the first woman. *Adam* means "man," and in many places the Hebrew word refers to mankind in general. Genesis 1:27, for example, says, "So God created man *[adam]* in His own image; He created him in the image of God; He created them male and female" (HCSB; see also Gen. 5:2; 6:1). *Adam* is also used of the first man, either with the article as "the man" (Gen. 2:15-16) or as the name "Adam" (Gen. 4:1,25; 5:3-4). Finally, the term can refer to a member of the human race, "a man" (e.g., Gen. 2:5, "there was no man to work the ground").

New Testament The name Adam also occurs in the NT in reference to the first man. Luke traces Jesus' genealogy back to Adam (Luke 3:38), and Paul refers to Jesus typologically as the last Adam (1 Cor. 15:45). As Adam was the beginning and representative head of humanity, Christ was the beginning and representative head of a new humanity.

A

Eve is mentioned two times in the NT. In 2 Cor. 11:3 she is used as an example of being lured away from the truth by Satan. In 1 Tim. 2:11-15 women are urged to devote themselves to learning in quiet submission rather than pressing for authoritative teaching roles in the church. The reason given is that Adam was created before Eve and that Eve was deceived into sinning. The deception that occurred in the garden that opened the door to sin, death, and corruption was caused in part by Adam passively letting Eve handle Satan by herself rather than his taking his appropriate role according to the created order and dealing with Satan on their behalf. Whether Adam would have been more successful we do not know. We do know that he failed in his responsibility as head of the family and head of the human race, bringing us down with him. So Paul instructs churches not to follow Adam's fatal example by placing women in the front lines in the role of teaching and exercising authority over men.

Theological Concerns The Apostle Paul in his Athens oration based his conviction regarding the unity of the human race on our relation to Adam: "From one man He has made every nation of men to live all over the earth" (Acts 17:26, HCSB).

Although much about the first man and woman was unique, the nature of sin has not changed (see Isa. 53:6), and the goals and strategies of the evil one are essentially the same (see 2 Cor. 11:3). Eve's temptation may be understood as a paradigm of our own, and the sinful corruption that permeates our world and our lives is the direct result of Adam's decision to disobey God. But Adam and Eve were also the first to learn that God had a plan of redemption by which one of their descendants would remove evil from the world (Gen. 3:15).

As the serpent claimed, sin did open their eyes (Gen. 3:5,7), but all that they saw was their own nakedness and alienation from each other. Shame and fear had displaced their innocence, and their first impulse was to cover themselves and hide (v. 10). The second immediate result of their sin was that the man and his wife could no longer walk with God (cp. Lev. 26:12; Ps. 89:15; Mic. 6:8). God's question directed to the man, whom He held primarily responsible, drove this point home. In effect, God asked (Gen. 3:9), "Why are you not walking with Me?"

The penalty suffered by the woman was to be twofold (3:16). First, there would be pain, anxiety, and trouble associated with bearing children. Second, there would be marital conflict.

Adam's sin was not that he listened to his wife but that he listened to her rather than to God (3:17). Like the woman's, the man's penalty would be twofold. First, as the serpent would have conflict with the woman, and the woman with the man, the man would have conflict with the ground, which would produce food for him only through pain, anxiety, and trouble. Second, he would eventually die and return to the dust (3:19), no longer having access to the tree of life (3:22). Although the woman would also die, the penalty was announced to the man because as the representative of the race he was the one responsible (Gen. 2:16-17; Ps. 90:3). Paul explained in Rom. 5:12, "Sin entered the world through one man, and death through sin." Furthermore, "through one trespass there is condemnation for everyone" (3:18). So in Gen. 5 the death knell of "then he died" is sounded eight times. Eve, on the other hand, would be the source of life as the one who would produce the deliverer (3:15). As Paul declared in Rom. 5:15, "If by the one man's trespass the many died, how much more have the grace of God and the gift overflowed to the many by the grace of the one man, Jesus Christ" (also 1 Cor. 15:22).

The consequences of Adam's sin fell not merely on the first family but on all mankind, and even the earth (Gen. 3:17; Rom. 8:19-21). Descent from Adam has resulted not only in physical death but in spiritual and moral corruption—"dead in your trespasses and sins"— and "by nature ... children of wrath" (Eph. 2:1,3). Apart from Christ everyone is "darkened in their understanding, excluded from the life of God, because of the ignorance that is in them and because of the hardness of their hearts" (Eph. 4:18). This can ultimately be traced to Adam from whom all men have inherited a nature inclined toward sin. See *Jesus Christ; Judgment Day; Mercy; Sin; Wrath.*

E. Ray Clendenen

ADAMAH (Ăd´ à·mah) Place-name and common noun meaning "soil, farmland." **1.** The earth or cultivated ground from whose dust God formed mankind, forming the wordplay Adam from dust of *'adamah.* (Gen. 2:7; cp. 2:19).

Pottery was also made from the soil (Isa. 45:9), as were altars (Exod. 20:24). The dead return to the earth (Ps. 146:4), but the soil also produces harvests (Deut. 7:13; 11:7). **2.** City in Naphtali's territory (Josh. 19:36) near where the Jordan River joins the Sea of Tiberias, perhaps modern Hagar ed-Damm.

ADAMANT See *Minerals and Metals.*

ADAMI (Ăd´ a̠·mī) or **ADAMI-NEKEB** (NASB, NIV, RSV, TEV) Place-name meaning "red earth" or "red earth pass." Town in Naphtali's territory (Josh. 19:33), perhaps Khirbet Damiyeh north of Mount Tabor.

ADAR (Ā´ där) Twelfth month of Jewish calendar after the exile, including parts of February and March. Time of Festival of Purim established in Esther (9:21).

ADBEEL (Ăd´ ba̠·ĕl) Personal name meaning "God invites." Son of Ishmael and grandson of Abraham (Gen. 25:13).

ADDAN (Ăd´ dän) Personal name of one who returned from exile but could not prove he was of Israelite parents (Ezra 2:59). Also called Addon (Neh. 7:61).

ADDAR (Ăd´ där) Place-name and personal name meaning "threshing floor." **1.** City on southwest border of Judah (Josh. 15:3). Also called Hazar-addar (Num. 34:4). **2.** Benjamin's grandson (1 Chron. 8:3). Also called Ard (Gen. 46:21; Num. 26:40).

ADDER (Ăd·der) See *Asp; Reptiles.*

ADDI (Ăd´ dī) Personal name meaning "adornment." Hebrew equivalent is *Iddo.* Ancestor of Jesus (Luke 3:28).

ADDON See *Addan.*

ADER (Ā´ dẽr) (KJV) See *Eder.*

ADIEL (Ăd´ ĭ·ĕl) Personal name meaning "an ornament is god." **1.** Important leader of tribe of Simeon (1 Chron. 4:36), a shepherd people. **2.** Father of a priestly family in Jerusalem after the exile (1 Chron. 9:12). **3.** Father of David's treasurer (1 Chron. 27:25).

ADIN (Ā´ dĭn) Personal name meaning "delightful, blissful, luxuriant." **1.** Ancestor of Jews who returned from exile with Zerubbabel and Joshua (Ezra 2:15; Neh. 7:20). **2.** Ancestor of exiles who returned with Ezra (Ezra 8:6). **3.** Signer of the covenant of Nehemiah to obey God's Law (Neh. 10:16).

ADINA (Ăd´ ĭ·na̠) Personal name meaning "delightful, luxuriant." A captain of 30 men in David's army from tribe of Reuben (1 Chron. 11:42).

ADINO (A̠·dī´ nō) Personal name meaning "loving luxury." Chief of David's captains who slew 800 men at one time (2 Sam. 23:8). Name does not appear in Septuagint, earliest Greek translation of this passage, nor in the Hebrew text of the parallel passage in 1 Chron. 11:11. Some modern translators omit it from 2 Sam. 23:8 (NIV, RSV, TEV).

ADITHAIM (Ăd·ĭ·thā´ ĭm) Place-name meaning "elevated place." City Joshua allotted to Judah (Josh. 15:36). Its location is not known.

ADLAI (Ăd´ la·ī) Personal name of father of one of David's chief shepherds (1 Chron. 27:29).

ADMAH (Ăd´ mäh) Place-name meaning "red soil." City connected with Sodom and Gomorrah as border of Canaanite territory (Gen. 10:19). Its king was defeated along with kings of Sodom and Gomorrah by coalition of four eastern kings (Gen. 14). God destroyed Admah, one of "the cities of the plains" (Gen. 19:29), along with Sodom and Gomorrah (Deut. 29:23). God could not stand to treat Israel, the people He loved, like He had treated Admah, even though Israel's behavior resembled Admah's (Hos. 11:8). Admah may have been located under what is now the southern part of the Dead Sea.

ADMATHA (Ăd·mā´ tha̠) Personal name in Persian meaning "unconquered." One of the leading advisors to King Ahasuerus (Xerxes) of Persia (Esther 1:14).

ADMIN (Ăd´ mĭn) Personal name in best Greek manuscripts of Luke 3:33 in the ancestry of Jesus but not in those available to KJV translators. Thus Admin appears in NASB, RSV, TEV, but not in KJV, HCSB, or NIV (see text notes).

ADMINISTRATION Spiritual gift that God gives to some members to build up the church (1 Cor. 12:28 NASB, NIV, RSV; HCSB "managing"), called "governments" in KJV. The Greek word *kubernesis* occurs only here in the Greek NT. It describes the ability to lead or hold a position of leadership.

NASB translates Hebrew idiom "to do justice" as "administer justice" (2 Sam. 8:15; 1 Kings 3:28; 1 Chron. 18:14). Similarly, NASB translates the idiom "to judge justice" as "administer justice" (Jer. 21:12). NIV goes further with other Hebrew and Aramaic idioms translated as "administer." The person called in Hebrew "who is over the house" NIV calls the "palace administrator" (2 Kings 10:5). The OT seeks to lead people in authority to establish a society in which God's law brings fairness and justice to all people without favoritism and prejudice.

KJV speaks of differences of administrations (1 Cor. 12:5), translating the Greek *diakonia*, "services" (NIV, RSV) or "ministries" (NASB, HCSB). Leading a church involves ministering to or serving the needs of its members.

ADNA (Ăd´nà) Aramaic personal name meaning "joy of living." **1.** Postexile Israelite with a foreign wife (Ezra 10:30). **2.** Postexilic priest (Neh. 12:15).

ADNAH (Ăd´näh) Personal name meaning "joy of living." **1.** Military leader from the tribe of Manasseh who joined David at Ziklag (1 Chron. 12:20). **2.** Military leader of Judah stationed in Jerusalem under Jehoshaphat (2 Chron. 17:14).

ADONI-BEZEK (Ăd´ ·ō·nī-bĕ´ zek) Personal name meaning "lord of Bezek," a place-name meaning "lightning" or "fragments." Canaanite king of Bezek. Tribe of Judah defeated him and cut off his thumbs and big toes, a sign of humiliation, before taking him to Jerusalem. There he died (Judg. 1:5-7). See *Bezek.*

ADONIJAH (Ăd·ō·nī´ jäh) Personal name meaning "Yah is Lord." **1.** Fourth son of David. His mother's name was Haggith (2 Sam. 3:4). In David's old age Adonijah maneuvered to succeed his father on the throne of Israel, but his effort failed (1 Kings 1:5-50). After Solomon's accession to the throne, Adonijah gave renewed expression to his regal aspirations by asking for Abishag, David's nurse, as a wife. Solomon's

response to this request was to have Adonijah put to death (1 Kings 2:13-28). Adonijah sought to establish hereditary kingship for Israel in which the eldest son automatically became king. Nathan, the prophet, worked with David and Bathsheba to establish a kingship in which the wishes of the dying monarch and the election by God determined the new king. See *David.* **2.** Levite that Jehoshaphat sent to teach the people of Judah the book of the law (2 Chron. 17:8). **3.** Leader of the Jews after the exile who signed Nehemiah's covenant to obey God's law (Neh. 10:16).

ADONIKAM (Ăd·ō·ni´ kam) Personal name meaning "the Lord has arisen." Family head of 666 persons who returned to Jerusalem with Zerubbabel from Babylon about 537 B.C. (Ezra 2:13). Some members of the family returned with Ezra under Xerxes (Ezra 8:13; cp. 7:18). Some Bible students think Adonikam is the same person as Adonijah in Neh. 10:16.

ADONIRAM (Ăd·ō·ni´ ram) Personal name meaning "the Lord is exalted." Officer in charge of the work gangs Solomon conscripted from Israel (1 Kings 4:6; 5:14). The king forced Israel's citizens to work for the state to secure materials to build the temple and the other projects of Solomon. Apparently the same person continued administering the work force for Rehoboam, though his name is abbreviated to Adoram in 1 Kings 12:18. At that time Israel rebelled against making free citizens work. They stoned Adoniram to death. The name is spelled Hadoram in 2 Chron. 10:18.

ADONIS (À dō´ nĭs) God of vegetation and fertility with Syrian name meaning "lord." Worshiped in Greece and Syria. Rites seem to include the planting of seeds that quickly produced plants and that just as quickly wilted in the sun. These were used to symbolize the dying and rising of the god and to bring blessing upon crops. Similar rites were celebrated for Osiris in Egypt and possibly for Tammuz in Babylon. REB translates Isa. 17:10 as "your gardens in honour of Adonis." The Hebrew term appears only here, being related to the personal name Naaman and to the Hebrew word meaning "lovely, pleasant, agreeable." Other translations read "finest plants" (NIV), "pleasant plants" (KJV), "delightful plants" (NASB), "sacred gardens" (TEV), "pleasant plants" (NRSV).

ADONI-ZEDEK (Ăd´ ō-nī-zē-dĕk) Personal name meaning "the Lord is righteous" or "the god Zedek is lord." King of Jerusalem who gathered coalition of Canaanite kings to fight Gibeon after Joshua made a peace treaty with Gibeon (Josh. 10). Joshua marched to Gibeon's aid and defeated the coalition. Joshua made a public example of the kings before executing them (10:22-26). He exposed their bodies on trees, a further sign of humiliation, since it postponed burial.

ADOPTION Legal process whereby one person receives another into his family and confers upon that person familial privileges and advantages. The "adopter" assumes parental responsibility for the "adoptee." The "adoptee" is thereby considered an actual child, becoming the beneficiary of all the rights, privileges, and responsibilities afforded to all the children of the family.

References to adoption in the OT are rare. Old Testament law did not contain specific legislation concerning the adoption of children. Further, the Hebrew language possesses no technical term for the practice. Its explicit absence among the Israelites may be explained in part by alternatives to infertile marriages. Levirate marriages lessened the need for adoption, and the principle of maintaining property within the tribe (Lev. 25:23-34; Num. 27:8-11; Jer. 32:6-15) allayed some of the fears of childless parents.

Although adoption is not overtly mentioned in the OT, allusions to the concept do exist. Jacob declares to Joseph, "And now your two sons, who were born to you in the land of Egypt before I came to you in Egypt, are mine; Ephraim and Manasseh shall be mine, as Reuben and Simeon are" (Gen. 48:5 NASB). The notion of sonship to Yahweh played a crucial role in the covenantal identity of the nation of Israel. "Then you shall say to Pharaoh, 'Thus says the LORD: "Israel is My son, My first-born. So I said to you, 'Let My son go, that he may serve me'"'" (Exod. 4:22-23 NASB). The idea is also found among the prophets: "When Israel was a youth I loved him, and out of Egypt I called My son" (Hos. 11:1 NASB). Adoption as a covenantal concept was applicable to the Israelites as a corporate

whole; it was not perceived as the adoption of individual Israelites.

The concept of adoption finds its fullest expression in the NT. In Paul's thought it carries various implications. In Rom. 9:4, adoption refers to Israel's unique relationship to Yahweh; in Rom. 8:23, adoption has connotations for future bodily resurrection; and in Rom. 8:15, adoption refers to becoming children of God. Thus, as God's children, the Holy Spirit (1) bears witness in the hearts of believers that they are "God's children" (Rom. 8:16 HCSB); (2) works in the hearts of believers, making possible intimacy with God as Father (Gal. 4:6); and (3) provides personal direction as believers "walk … according to the Spirit" (Rom. 8:4 HCSB). Paul contrasts the unique relationship conferred upon the believer through God's adoptive work to that of the slave who lives, works, and relates in fear (Rom. 8:15). Those adopted by God into His family are "heirs of God" and "joint heirs" with Christ, receiving all the blessings, benefits, and privileges attained by the sacrifice of the Son of God (Rom. 8:17).

Although primarily developed in Paul, certain aspects of adoption are found in other places in the NT. Adoption is implicit in Jesus' teaching concerning God as Father (Matt. 5:16; 6:9; Luke 12:32). The conferral of family benefits upon an adoptee is an expression of the Living Word's authority (John 1:12) and is in keeping with His mission to bring "many sons to glory" (Heb. 2:10 HCSB). Thus, Jesus is not ashamed to call believers "brothers" (Heb. 2:11).

Adoption becomes the primary way that the believers live and relate to God and other believers. Adoption is an action of the Father (Gal. 4:6; Rom. 8:15) and is based on the love of the Father (Eph. 1:5; 1 John 3:1). The basis of this activity of God is the atoning work of Jesus Christ (Gal. 3:26). Adoption involves peacemaking (Matt. 5:9) and compels the believer to become Christlike (1 John 3:2). As an expression of the familial relationship, God as Father disciplines His children (Heb. 12:5-11). Believers are to regard all those who have come to Christ by grace through faith as members of God's family (1 Tim. 5:1-2). See *Regeneration; Salvation.*

Stan Norman

ADORAIM (Ăd-ō-rā´ ĭm) Place-name meaning "double strength." City located at modern Durah, six miles southwest of Hebron.

Rehoboam fortified the city and placed troops and supplies there as part of a massive defense building program (2 Chron. 11:9). See *Rehoboam.*

ADORAM (Á·dō´ răm). See *Adoniram.*

ADRAMMELECH (Á·dräm´ mə·lěk) Divine and personal name meaning "Adra is king." Probably based on earlier form Hadadmelech, "Hadad is king," using name of Canaanite god. **1.** A god of the city of Sepharvaim. The Assyrian king Sargon spread the people of Israel all over his empire and replaced them with settlers from other cities he conquered (2 Kings 17:24). These new settlers tried to worship Yahweh, Israel's God, as the god of the land along with the gods they brought with them. One of these gods was from the city of Sephervaim, possibly in Assyria. His worshipers sacrificed their own children to this Semitic god (17:31-33). **2.** Murderer of Sennacherib, king of Assyria, during the king's worship in the temple of Nisroch (2 Kings 19:37). One reading of the Hebrew manuscripts describes this Adrammelech as Sennacherib's son (KJV, NIV, RSV). Other manuscripts do not have "his sons" (NASB).

ADRAMYTTIUM (Ăd·rà·myt´ tĭ·ŭm) or **ADRAMYTIAN** (NASB) Place-name of a seaport on the northwest coast of modern Turkey in the Roman province of Asia. Paul used a ship whose home port was Adramyttium to make the first leg of his journey from Caesarea to Italy to appeal his case to Caesar (Acts 27:2). The ancient site is near modern-day Edremit.

ADRIA (Ā´ dri·à) or **ADRIATIC SEA** (NASB, NIV) During Paul's time the designated body of water between Crete and Sicily where Paul's ship was battered by gale-force winds and resultant high waves for 14 days as he sailed toward Rome to appeal his case to Caesar (Acts 27:27). Later the Adriatic Sea was extended to cover the waters between Greece and Italy.

ADRIEL (Ā´ drĭ·el) Personal name meaning "God is my help." Saul's daughter Merab was promised as David's wife but then given to Adriel from Meholah, on the northern Jordan River (1 Sam. 18:19). His five sons David gave to the Gibeonites, who hanged them in revenge for unexplained actions Saul had taken against Gibeon (2 Sam. 21:1-9).

ADULLAM (Á·dŭl´ lam) Place-name meaning "sealed off place." City five miles south of Beth-shemesh in Judah, probably modern Tell esh-Sheikh Madkur. Joshua conquered it (Josh. 12:15), though no account of its conquest appears in the Bible. Hirah, a friend of Judah, son of Jacob, was from Adullam (Gen. 38:1,12). He took the sheep Judah had pledged to Tamar and discovered Tamar did not live where they first encountered her (38:20-22). David escaped to the cave at Adullam when he feared Achish, king of Gath (1 Sam. 22:1). There David collected an army from the lower class and outcasts of society. There he assembled an army against the Philistines (2 Sam. 23:13). Micah, the prophet, used David's experience almost 300 years later to warn his people that again their glorious king would have to flee to the caves of Adullam to escape an enemy who would take possession of the country because of Judah's sin (Mic. 1:15). In his build-up of Judah's defenses, King Rehoboam, Solomon's son, rebuilt Adullam's defenses, stationed soldiers, and stored supplies at Adullam (2 Chron. 11:7). After returning from the exile, some members of the tribe of Judah lived at Adullam (Neh. 11:30).

ADULTERY Act of unfaithfulness in marriage that occurs when one of the marriage partners voluntarily engages in sexual intercourse with a person other than the marriage partner.
Old Testament Israel's covenant law prohibited adultery (Exod. 20:14) and thereby made faithfulness to the marriage relationship central in the divine will for human relationships. Many OT regulations deal with adultery as the adulterous man's offense against the husband of the adulterous wife. Yet both the adulterous man and woman were viewed as guilty, and the punishment of death was prescribed for both (Lev. 20:10). The severity of the punishment indicates the serious consequences adultery has for the divine-human relationship (Ps. 51:4) as well as for marriage, family, and community relationships.

Several OT prophets used adultery as a metaphor to describe unfaithfulness to God. Idolatry (Ezek. 23:27) and other pagan religious practices (Jer. 3:6-10) were viewed as adulterous unfaithfulness to the exclusive covenant that God established with His people. To engage in such was to play the harlot (Hos. 4:11-14).

New Testament Jesus' teachings expanded the OT law to address matters of the heart. Adultery has its origins within (Matt. 15:19), and lust is as much a violation of the law's intent as is illicit sexual intercourse (Matt. 5:27-28). Adultery is one of the "works of the flesh" (Gal. 5:19). It creates enmity with God (James 4:4), and adulterers will not inherit the kingdom of God (1 Cor. 6:9).

Adulterers can be forgiven (John 8:3-11); and once sanctified through repentance, faith, and God's grace, they are included among God's people (1 Cor. 6:9-11). See *Divorce; Marriage.*

Michael Fink

ADUMMIM (Å·dum´ mĭm) Place-name meaning "red ones." A rocky pass on the road descending from Jerusalem to Jericho located at modern Tal'at ed-damm. It formed the border of Judah and Benjamin in the tribal allotments Joshua made (Josh. 15:7; 18:17). Today the Inn of the Good Samaritan is there because late traditions locate the Good Samaritan narrative there (Luke 10:30-37).

ADVENT Word with Latin roots, meaning "coming." Christians of earlier generations spoke of "the advent of our Lord" and of "His second advent." The first phrase refers to God's becoming incarnate in Jesus of Nazareth. The latter phrase speaks of Jesus' second coming. In a second sense "advent" designates a period before Christmas when Christians prepare for the celebration of Jesus' birth. This practice may have begun in some churches as early as the late fourth century. Advent began as a time of fasting. Sermons focused on the wonder of the Incarnation. By the Middle Ages four Sundays had become the standard length of the Advent season. Since then, Advent has been considered to be the beginning of the church year. See *Church Year; Parousia; Second Coming.*

Fred A. Grissom and Steve Bond

ADVENTURESS RSV translation of *nokriya,* which is also translated as "strange woman" (KJV), "adulterous woman" (Prov. 23:27 NASB), "wayward wife" (NIV), "adulteress" (NRSV), "forbidden woman" (HCSB), and "immoral women" (TEV) in Prov. 2:16; 5:20; 6:24; 7:5; 23:27. Some see an adventuress as a woman who lives in part by her wits but largely based upon sex. Others describe her as a woman who seeks social advancement or wealth by seduction or other immoral means. Solomon's wives were called *nokriyot*—that is, foreign wives (1 Kings 11:1,8), so the term may refer to women cut off or ostracized from Israelite society and normal social relationships. They are feared as ones that break up marriages.

ADVERSARY Enemy, either human or satanic. Psalmists often prayed for deliverance from adversaries (Pss. 38:20; 69:19; 71:13; 81:14; 109:29). The devil is the greatest adversary and must be resisted (1 Pet. 5:8-9).

ADVOCATE One who intercedes on behalf of another. Used to refer to Christ interceding with the Father on behalf of sinners.

Old Testament While the word "advocate" is not found in the OT, the concept of advocacy is found. Abraham interceded with God on behalf of Sodom (Gen. 18:23-33); Moses interceded with God on behalf of the Israelites (Exod. 32:11-14); Samuel interceded with God on behalf of the children of Israel (1 Sam. 7:8-9). Other examples may be found in Jer. 14:7-9,13,19-22 and Amos 7:2,5-6. Modern translators often use "advocate" to refer to Job's desire for a heavenly attorney to plead his case even though he die (Job 16:19).

New Testament "Advocate" is the translation often given to the Greek *parakletos* in 1 John 2:1, a word found elsewhere only in John's Gospel as a title referring to the Holy Spirit, and there translated "Helper," "Comforter," "Counselor," or "Advocate" (John 14:16,26; 15:26; 16:7). Ancient Greeks used the term for one called in to assist or speak for another, frequently in a court setting. Rabbis transliterated the word into Hebrew, using it to denote an advocate before God. First John portrayed a courtroom scene in which Jesus Christ, the righteous One, interceded with the Father on behalf of sinners. Such a portrayal stands in line with OT ideas of advocacy but supersedes it. In contrast to OT advocates, Jesus is both the one righteous Advocate and the "atoning sacrifice" (NIV) for the world's sins (1 John 2:2). First John 2:1 parallels other NT descriptions of Jesus' intercessory role (Rom. 8:34; Heb. 7:25). See *Helper; High Priest; Intercession; Jesus Christ; Paraclete.*

R. Robert Creech

AENEAS (Ȧ·nē´ ȧs) Personal name of a para-lyzed man Peter healed at Lydda (Acts 9:33-34), resulting in great evangelistic victories in the area.

AENON (Aē´ nŏn) Place-name meaning "double spring." The location where John the Baptist was baptizing during the time that Jesus was baptizing in Judea (John 3:23). The biblical text indicates that Aenon was a place richly endowed with water near Salim, which precise location is unknown. The most likely location of Aenon was in a broad open valley called Wadi-Farah, west of the Jordan and northeast of Nablus.

AFFLICTION Condition of physical or mental distress. While the source and purpose of affliction may vary, the Bible describes the state of affliction with many terms. In the OT the Hebrew language uses as many as 13 words that may be translated "affliction."

Old Testament The OT identifies many forms of affliction, including: national affliction, resulting from the oppression of a political entity (Exod. 1:11; Neh. 9:9); social affliction, resulting from a perversion of the law (Job 5:4; 22:9; Pss. 10:18; 74:21; 94:25; Isa. 3:15); moral affliction, as God's retribution for sin (Job 4:7-9; Ps. 25:16-20; Lam. 3:32-33; Isa. 30:20; Jer. 30:15); natural affliction (Gen. 16:11; 29:32; Ps. 25:18); and spiritual affliction (1 Sam. 16:14; Job 1:6-12).

New Testament Three Greek words may be used for "affliction." "Suffering" is sometimes used interchangeably for the word "affliction," particularly in the KJV. NT reasons for affliction include: God's use to induce humility (2 Cor. 12:7); God's use to promote holiness (1 Pet. 1:6-7; 4:1-2); eschatological endurance (Rom. 5:3-4; James 1:3-4); experience for the instruction of others (2 Cor. 1:3-4); natural causes (James 1:27); persecution because of faithfulness to Christ (2 Cor. 6:4; 1 Thess. 1:6); discipline for the purpose of Christian maturity (Heb. 12:6); and pain resulting from personal sin (Gal. 6:7).

Affliction throughout Scripture serves as a remembrance of God's supreme sovereignty (Job 42:2-4). Affliction can be an individual matter (Phil. 4:14) or a corporate condition (Exod. 3:7; 2 Cor. 8:1-2). One may experience affliction directly (Deut. 16:3) or indirectly (James 1:27). Affliction is sometimes described as overflowing all of life (Pss. 42:7; 69:1; 88:7; 124:4; Isa. 30:20; Jon. 2:5).

Although affliction seems an inevitable fact of human existence, the believer may find comfort in affliction by remembering that God sees and knows the affliction of His people (Gen. 29:32; 31:42; Exod. 3:7; 2 Kings 14:26; Acts 7:34), that affliction will end (2 Cor. 4:17), and that God can deliver from any affliction (Exod. 3:17).

As a response to affliction, the believer should pray to the Lord (Ps. 25:18; Lam. 1:9; James 5:13); comfort others (James 1:27; Phil. 4:14); remain faithful through patient endurance (2 Cor. 6:4; 1 Tim. 4:5; James 1:2,12; 1 Pet. 4:13); cultivate an attitude of joy (James 1:2); and follow the example of Jesus Christ (1 Pet. 2:19-23).

The purpose of affliction is to show the power of Christ (2 Cor. 12:8-9). The discipline of affliction produces strong faith. The end of affliction is the salvation of God's people. Christ's affliction in His atoning sacrifice and the continued affliction of His people will end in the exaltation of God and consummation of His kingdom (Col. 1:24; 2 Tim. 2:10).

Mark M. Overstreet

AFTERBIRTH Placenta and fetal membranes that are expelled after delivery (Deut. 28:57).

AGABUS (Ăḡ´ ȧ·bŭs) Personal name meaning "locust." Prophet in the Jerusalem church who went to visit the church at Antioch and predicted a universal famine. His prophecy was fulfilled about 10 years later in the reign of Claudius Caesar (Acts 11:27-29). His prediction led the church at Antioch to begin a famine relief ministry for the church in Jerusalem. Later Agabus went to Caesarea and predicted that the Jews in Jerusalem would arrest Paul (Acts 21:10-11). Still Paul's friends could not persuade him not to go to Jerusalem.

AGAG (Ā´ ḡăg) Personal name means "fiery one." He was king of the Amalekites, a tribal people living in the Negev and in the Sinai Peninsula. The Amalekites had attacked the Israelites in the wilderness and were therefore cursed (Exod. 17:14). In 1 Sam. 15:8, Saul destroyed all the Amalekites but King Agag. Since the Lord had ordered the complete destruction of the Amalekites, Samuel, Saul's priest, rebuked Saul for his disobedience and reported God's rejection of Saul as king. Then Samuel himself executed Agag.

In Num. 24:7 Agag is used to refer to the Amalekite people. Agag was a common name among Amalekite kings much as Pharaoh among Egyptian rulers.

AGAGITE (Ā´ găg-īt) Apparently, the term means a descendant of Agag. Only Haman, the archvillain in the book of Esther, is called an Agagite (Esther 3:1). Agagite is probably a synonym for Amalekite. See *Agag.*

AGAPE See *Love; Lord's Supper.*

AGAR (KJV, NT) See *Hagar.*

AGATE Translucent quartz with concentric bands, generally white and brown. "Agate" translates three words in the Bible: a stone in the breastpiece of judgment (Exod. 28:19; 39:12), the material in the pinnacles of Jerusalem (Isa. 54:12; Ezek. 27:16), and the third jewel in the foundation wall of the new Jerusalem (Rev. 21:19). See *Jewels, Jewelry; Minerals and Metals.*

AGEE (Ā´ gēē) Personal name, perhaps meaning "camel thorn." Father of one of David's three chief commanders (2 Sam. 23:11).

AGE TO COME The expression "age to come" or "coming age[s]" is found in the Apocrypha (2 Esdras 7:113; 8:52) and several times in the NT (Matt. 12:32; Mark 10:30; Luke 18:30; Eph. 1:21; 2:7; 1 Tim. 6:19; Heb. 6:5). It is usually either explicitly or implicitly considered in opposition to "this age" or "the present age" (Matt. 12:32; Luke 16:8; 20:34-35; 1 Cor. 2:6–8; 2 Cor. 4:4; Gal. 1:4; Eph. 1:21; 2:2; 1 Tim. 6:17; 2 Tim. 4:10; Titus 2:12). The expression "the end of the age" (Matt. 13:39-40,49; 24:3; 28:20) refers to the end of the present age and therefore relates to the age to come.

There is evidence that the biblical writers also viewed this age since the coming of Christ as an era transitional to a time when human history will in some sense come to an end. Thus the present time could also be described as "the end[s] of the ages" (1 Cor. 10:11; Heb. 9:26). In some sense the coming age has already dawned (1 Cor. 10:11; 2 Cor. 5:17), so that being in Christ makes one no longer truly part of the

present age (Luke 16:8; 1 Cor. 1:20; 3:18; Phil. 3:20; Heb. 6:5), although the coming age is not yet fully here (1 Cor. 15:20–28). The distinction, then, between the present age and the coming age is not strictly temporal.

The concept of a former age is implied in which the OT prophets and types announced the present messianic age (Luke 1:70; Acts 3:21; 15:18; Heb. 9:9–10). The expression "before the ages" is also found, referring to eternity past before God created the world and human history began (1 Cor. 2:7).

In the OT a coming age of divine deliverance and blessing is referred to as "that day" or as coming "days" as in Jer. 30:3 ("'For, behold, days are coming,' declares the LORD, 'when I will restore the fortunes of My people Israel and Judah.' The LORD says, 'I will also bring them back to the land that I gave to their forefathers, and they shall possess it'"; cp. Isa. 11:1–12:6; Jer. 23:3–8; 31:27–34; Ezek. 37:21–28; Amos 9:11–15). See also *Eschatology.*

E. Ray Clendenen

AGING Natural process of human beings growing older and, according to the Bible, gaining respect.

Old Testament References to aging persons in the OT stress the physiological changes of aging (1 Kings 14:4; 2 Sam. 19:35; Eccles. 12:1-5; Zech. 8:4), the wisdom of the aging (Deut. 32:7; Job 12:12), the honor due the aging (Exod. 20:12; Lev. 19:32), and the continuing service of the aging (Gen. 12–50, the patriarchs; Josh. 13:1; 14:10; Ps. 92:14; Joel 2:28). Aging is presented as a normal part of the biblical view of the life cycle (Ps. 90:10; Isa. 46:4). See *Elder.*

New Testament References to aging persons in the NT focus on the responsibility of children or the family of faith to care for dependent or disabled aging persons (Mark 7:1-13; Matt. 15:1-6; 1 Tim. 5:4,8; James 1:27). The young are urged to honor the aging (1 Tim. 5:1-2), and the aging are encouraged to be worthy examples (Titus 2:2-3). Christians are expected to care for widows (Acts 6:1-7), and the aging are expected to serve God as did Zechariah, Elizabeth, Simeon, and Anna in Luke 1–2. Such service by the aging can bring blessings to their families, as did Timothy's grandmother and mother (2 Tim. 1:5).

Practical Concerns The biblical view of aging is unequivocally positive, though allowing for the possibility that an older person can be foolish

(Eccles. 4:13). Generally older persons have a reservoir of wisdom and understanding based on past experience (Deut. 32:7). They can experience new family joys, even after many previous sad experiences (Ruth 4:13-17). Both youth and age have their unique worth; they are not in competition (Prov. 20:29). While advancing age results in diminishing strength (Eccles. 12:1-8), God's grace and help are available to persons in each stage of life (Isa. 46:4).

Douglas Anderson

AGRAPHA Unwritten things, used since about 1700 to denote words of Jesus not written in the four canonical Gospels. Some examples are Acts 20:35 and 1 Cor. 11:24-25. More are found in apocryphal writings, Gnostic Gospels, the Talmud, the Islamic sources, Oxyrnchus Papyri, and the church fathers. Some scholars suggest that the canonical gospels may rely in part on these sayings. Scholars regard most sayings as expansions of the gospel tradition or creations by subsequent followers of Jesus, though a few of them may be authentic.

Joe Baskin

AGRICULTURE Cultivating the land to grow food. The people of both the OT and NT periods were essentially agrarian. Even those who lived in towns were close to the country and usually owned gardens or farms. With the seasons as a background to their daily life, the religious calendar was partly based on the agricultural year with several festivals coinciding with significant events such as the Feast of Weeks or first fruits (of wheat, Exod. 32:11 NRSV) and the Feast of Tabernacles or ingathering (of grapes, Lev. 23:34). The primary crops include grain, grapes, and olives (Gen. 27:28; Deut. 7:13; Joel 1:10).

How were grains cultivated? Grain crops were the staple food of rich and poor alike, although the poor may have had to consume barley bread rather than the more palatable wheat. Both were sown by scattering the grains into prepared land usually ploughed by draft animals. The parable of the sower (Matt. 13:3-23; Luke 8:5-15) provides an interesting account of grain sowing and the subsequent fate of the seed. Peasant agriculture, unlike modern farming practices, was unsophisticated with primitive implements often used in harsh conditions where rocky ground and vigorous weeds militated against a good yield. Hence it would be normal for some of the scattered seed to fall on a path of compacted soil where it would not be covered and lie vulnerable to birds. Similarly, some seeds would fall at the margins of the fields

Woman gathering grain.

where thorny thickets and rapidly growing thistles easily suffocated the germinating wheat.
Shallow soil and lack of moisture during the hot
dry summer encouraged the withering of the
seeds that did sprout into young plants on the
field's outer borders. Those seeds that fell on
moist, deep soil grew and matured their ears
ready for harvest.

The book of Ruth provides a vivid picture of
the harvesting scene that was carried out by
whole families and extra hired men, followed by
poor women gleaners picking leftovers. Barley
was harvested first during April and May, followed by wheat a month later. A sickle was used
to cut off the ears which were held with one
hand, and then bundled together in small
sheaves to be carted off to the threshing floor
(1 Chron. 21:22)—a cleared area of stamped
earth or stone. Animals, usually cattle, were
driven over the spread-out stalks to trample out
the grains. Often a cartwheel or a heavy sledge
with small stones inserted in the bottom was
drawn round and round the floor to hasten the
threshing. The grains were swept together and
separated from the useless chaff by winnowing—a process involving the throwing up of the
grain in breezy weather so that the light scaly
chaff is blown away, leaving a pile of clean grain
ready for grinding into flour (Matt. 3:12). A proportion of the crop was always kept aside and
carefully stored in dry conditions for sowing the
following year (Gen. 47:24).

**How did the agriculture of Egypt differ from
that of Canaan?** The essential difference
between Egyptian and Canaanite agriculture
was that Canaan depended on rainfall (Deut.
11:11), while Egypt depended on the Nile River
and its annual flood (Amos 8:8). In other words,
Canaan was a rain-fed agriculture, while Egypt
used irrigation agriculture. In July the Nile rose
following rainfall in Ethiopia and flooded the
land on both sides. (Now the modern Aswan
Dam impounds the water and releases it evenly
throughout the year.) The flood carried silt that
enriched the farmland; and the water level fell
later in the year, leaving behind pools of water
that could be used for irrigation in channels
small enough to be opened and closed by a
farmer's foot (Deut. 11:10). Egypt was
renowned for its rich harvests of wheat and vegetables that were missed by the Israelites fleeing
the country via the desert of Sinai. There the
Israelites longed for the succulent melons,

cucumbers, garlic, leeks, and onions they left
behind (Num. 11:5).

Were vineyards for growing grapevines?
The Bible presents two accounts of vineyards
that describe them in some detail. In Isa. 5:1-7
and Mark 12:1-9 we read how the hillside was
fenced and terraced to provide deep stone-free
soil where the rainfall could water the vines'
roots in winter. Dung and compost nourished
the plants that needed to be trained over rocks
or fences. Constant attention had to be given to
the trailing branches of carefully chosen varieties
in order to yield sweet green or black grapes. As
harvest time approached, the owners of the
vineyards and their families camped near the
vineyards in shelters (booths) or in stone-built
towers (Isa. 1:8) to protect the grapes from animals, such as jackals (foxes) and wild pigs (boar)
(Ps. 80:13) and human thieves. When ripe, the
grapes were picked for eating fresh (Isa. 65:21),
drying in the sun as raisins (1 Sam. 30:12), or
crushed for wine. Most vineyards had a winepress where the grapes were trodden under
human foot (Neh. 13:15; Rev. 19:15), the juice
collected in flagons or skins and fermented
(Matt. 9:17). Fermentation was caused by naturally occurring yeast (*Saccharomyses*) breaking
down the sugars into alcohol and carbon dioxide
gas. During the winter the long shoots of the
previous year's growth had to be pruned away
from the vines to leave a few buds for the next
season (John 15:2).

How long do olive trees live? The huge trees
in the garden of Gethsemane (Matt. 26:36) on
the Mount of Olives in Jerusalem are hundreds
of years old and could potentially stretch back to
NT times. During the siege of Jerusalem in A.D.
70, the Roman forces under Titus felled all the
trees, presumably including the olives which
could have sprouted again (Ps. 123:3) to yield
the aged hollow trees still growing around
Jerusalem.

Olive trees are not raised from seeds because
the seedlings invariably produce very inferior
ones similar to the wild stock. Selected cuttings
are rooted or more often grafted on to the wild
plant that has a better root system. Olive roots
spread widely to gain nourishment on rocky hillsides; hence the trees are often well spaced.
Although flowering begins when the trees are
less than 10 years old, full yield of fruit is not
reached until they are 40 or 50 years old, after
which branches are pruned to encourage new

A

fruitful growth. Olives require a Mediterranean type of climate of moist cool winters and hot dry summers to be economically productive.

Olive groves usually had an oil press nearby where the heavy stone wheel crushed the fruit and its hard kernel. The pulp was placed in a press that extracted the precious yellow oil. This was used for cooking purposes as an essential part of diet (Deut. 7:13, 2 Kings 4:5, 2 Chron. 2:10). Olive oil was rubbed over skin and hair (Pss. 23:5; 133:2; 141:5) and used for anointing guests (Luke 7:46; 1 Kings 1:34). Christ was God's "anointed" one (Ps. 2:2; John 1:41; Acts 4:27), anointing being symbolic of the Holy Spirit (Isa. 61:1; Acts 10:38). Medicinally, olive oil mixed with antiseptic wine healed wounds (Luke 10:34, James 5:14). Taken internally, olive oil soothed gastric disorders and acted as a laxative. Olive oil was used as fuel for lamps with a wick made of flax, producing a bright flame when lit (Exod. 25:6; Matt. 25:34).

What animals were used in agriculture? Mainly cows (oxen) were used to pull carts (1 Sam. 6:7) and simple wooden plows (Job 1:14; 1 Sam. 14:14) tipped with iron, if farmers could afford them (Isa. 2:4). Oxen and donkeys (asses) were driven over the harvested grain to thresh it. The use of horses and camels in agriculture appears to have been limited, presumably because they were more valuable animals, well adapted for carrying heavy loads and for use in time of war. When pairs of animals were used, they were coupled with a wooden yoke across their shoulders (Jer. 28:13; Luke 14:19).

F. Nigel Hepper

AGRIPPA See *Herod*.

AGUE KJV translation of Hebrew word meaning "burning with fever." The Hebrew term appears in Lev. 26:16 and Deut. 28:22, KJV translating "fever" in the second passage.

AGUR (Ā´ gûr) Personal name meaning "hired hand." Author of at least part of Prov. 30.

AHAB (Ā´ hăb) Personal name meaning "father's brother." **1.** The seventh king of Israel's Northern Kingdom, married a foreigner, Jezebel, and incited God's anger more than any of Israel's previous kings. Ahab was the son and successor of Omri. His 22-year reign (874–853 B.C.), while enjoying some political and military success, was

Ahab's palace.

marred by spiritual compromise and failure (1 Kings 16:30).

Ahab's marriage to Jezebel, a Phoenician princess, had both commercial and political benefits. Commercially, it brought desired goods to Samaria and opened the way for expanded sea trade. Politically, it removed any military threat from Phoenicia.

During Ahab's days Israel enjoyed peace with Judah, largely as a result of a marriage he arranged between princess Athaliah and Joram, the crown prince of Judah. The resulting alliance produced cooperative efforts in sea trade (1 Kings 22:48; 2 Chron. 20:35-37) and a joint military campaign to recapture Ramoth-gilead, which had fallen under Aramean control (1 Kings 22:2-40).

Throughout his reign effective control was maintained over Moab, producing revenue extracted by tribute, a tax the Moabite king paid to maintain his position (2 Kings 3:4). The oppression of Moab under Ahab and his father Omri found expression in the famous Moabite Stone.

Ahab was successful in two major campaigns against the Syrian king, Ben-hadad, but was mortally wounded in the third. His participation in the great battle of Qarqar (853 B.C.), though not mentioned in the Bible, is recorded on an inscription of Shalmaneser III of Assyria.

According to Shalmaneser, Ahab committed 2,000 chariots and 10,000 men to the battle.

The days of Ahab in Samaria were days of growing wealth and spiritual apostasy. According to 1 Kings 22:39, he built an "ivory house" for Jezebel, the remains of which were discovered in the Harvard excavations at the site. Rooms and furniture were decorated with ivory inlay that in many cases featured Egyptian deities. His surrender to the influences of idolatry is illustrated by the construction of a temple for Baal (1 Kings 16:32), the massacre of the Lord's prophets (1 Kings 18:4,19), and seizure of an Israelite's property (1 Kings 21).

Ahab appears to have been a worshiper of Yahweh, God of Israel, but probably along with other deities. He frequently consulted with Yahweh's prophets (1 Kings 20:13-14,22,28; 22:8,16), used the divine name in naming his children (Ahaziah, Jehoram, and Athaliah) and did not interfere with the execution of the priests of Baal after the contest on Mount Carmel (1 Kings 18:40). The influence of Jezebel in his life, however, overshadowed any significant influence the prophets of the Lord had in his life. He became a prime example of evil (Mic. 6:16).

2. False prophet living in Babylon who prophesied lies and faced Jeremiah's condemnation (Jer. 29:20-23).   *John J. Davis*

AHARAH (Á·hâr´ ah) Spelling in 1 Chron. 8:1 for Ahiram (Num. 26:38). See *Ahiram*.

AHARHEL (Á·här´ hĕl) Personal name with unknown meaning. Descendant of Judah (1 Chron. 4:8).

AHASAI (Á·hăṣ´ aî) (KJV) See *Ahzai*.

AHASBAI (Á·hăs´ baî) Father of a leader in David's army (2 Sam. 23:34; 1 Chron. 11:35). He apparently came from Maacah.

AHASUERUS (Á·hăs·ū·ē´ rŭs) Hebrew spelling for Xerxes, the king in the book of Esther (NIV, TEV). See *Persia; Xerxes*.

AHAVA (Á·hā´ vá) River in Babylon and town located beside the river where Ezra assembled Jews to return to Jerusalem from exile (Ezra 8:15,21,31). Ahava was probably located near the city of Babylon, but the exact site is not known.

AHAZ (Ā´ hăz) **1.** Evil king of Judah (735–715 B.C.). Ahaz, whose name means "he has grasped," was the son and successor of Jotham as king of Judah and the father of Hezekiah. Ahaz is characterized as an evil man who participated in the most monstrous of idolatrous practices (2 Kings 16:3). His 16-year reign was contemporary with the prophets Isaiah and Micah. Isaiah gave counsel to Ahaz during the Syro-Ephraimitic crisis, when Rezin, king of Syria, and Pekah, king of Israel, joined forces to attack Jerusalem. The prophet Oded rescued some captives from Israel (2 Chron. 28). Ahaz refused the prophet's advice and appealed for help to Tiglath-pileser III of Assyria (Isa. 7). That appeal and the resulting entanglement had unfortunate results religiously and politically in that Ahaz surrendered to Assyrian domination. He even placed an altar made from a Syrian model in the temple (2 Kings 16:11). Ahaz suffered the final humiliation of not being buried in the royal tombs (2 Chron. 28:27). See *Israel; Chronology of the Biblical Period.* **2.** A Benjaminite descended from Saul (1 Chron. 8:35-36; 9:42).

AHAZIAH (Ā·hà·zī´ ah) Name of two OT kings, the king of Israel (850–840 B.C.) and the king of Judah (ca. 842). The name means "Yahweh has grasped." **1.** Son and successor of Ahab as king of Israel (1 Kings 22:40). He reigned two years and died after suffering a fall in his palace at Samaria (2 Kings 1:2-17). The prophet Elijah announced Ahaziah would die because he sent for help from Baal-zebub, the god of Ekron, instead of from Yahweh. **2.** Son and successor of Jehoram as king of Judah (2 Kings 8:25). He reigned for one year and died after being wounded as he fled from Jehu while visiting King Joram of Israel (2 Kings 9:27).

These two kings were related to each other. Athaliah, the mother of Ahaziah of Judah, was the sister of Ahaziah of Israel.

AHBAN (Äh´ băn) Personal name meaning "the brother is wise" or "the brother is creator." A member of the clan of Jerahmeel (1 Chron. 2:29).

AHER (Ā´ hĕr) Personal name meaning "another." A member of tribe of Benjamin (1 Chron. 7:12); may be another spelling for Ahiram (Num. 26:38).

AHI (Ā´ hī) Personal name meaning "my brother." **1.** Member of tribe of Gad (1 Chron. 5:15), who lived in Gilead. **2.** Member of tribe of Asher (1 Chron. 7:34).

AHIAH (Á·hī´ ah) Personal name meaning "Yahweh is my brother." Variant spelling of Ahijah but not used consistently by English translations to reflect Hebrew spellings. See *Ahijah.*

AHIAM (Á·hī´ ăm) Personal name whose meaning is not certain. One of David's 30 heroic soldiers (2 Sam. 23:33).

AHIAN (Á·hī´ ăn) Personal name meaning "little brother." A member of tribe of Manasseh (1 Chron. 7:19).

AHIEZER (Ā·hī·ē´ zĕr) Personal name meaning "my brother is help." **1.** Aide to Moses in the wilderness from the tribe of Dan (Num. 1:12; 2:25). He brought the tribe's offerings (7:66-71) and led the tribe on the march (10:25). **2.** Chief warrior who joined David at Ziklag. He was skilled with both hands and represented Benjamin, the tribe of King Saul, who threatened David (1 Chron. 12:1-3).

AHIHUD (Á·hī´ hŭd) **1.** Personal name meaning "my brother is splendid or majestic" (Hb. *'achihud*). A leader of the tribe of Asher who helped divide the promised land among the tribes (Num. 34:27). **2.** Meaning "my brother is a riddle" (Hb. *'achichud*). A member of tribe of Benjamin (1 Chron. 8:7).

AHIJAH (Á·hī´ jah) Personal name rendered several ways in Hebrew and English meaning "my brother is Yahweh." **1.** Priest of the family of Eli in Shiloh (1 Sam. 14:3-4). He brought the ark of God to Saul (1 Sam. 4:18). **2.** Scribe of Solomon (1 Kings 4:3). **3.** Prophet from Shiloh who tore his clothes in 12 pieces and gave 10 to Jeroboam to signal God's decision to divide the kingdom after Solomon's death (1 Kings 11:29-39). Later when Jeroboam's son fell sick, the blind prophet recognized Jeroboam's wife through God's word. He announced the end of Jeroboam's reign and of his dynasty (1 Kings 14:1-18; 15:29). Second Chronicles 9:29 refers to a prophecy of Ahijah in written form. **4.** Father of King Baasha of Israel from tribe of Issachar (1 Kings 15:27). **5.** Son of Jerahmeel (1 Chron. 2:25). **6.** Son of Ehud in tribe of Benjamin, an official in Geba (1 Chron. 8:7). **7.** One of David's 30 military heroes whose home was Pelon (1 Chron. 11:36). The corresponding list in 2 Sam. 23:34 has Eliam the son of Ahithophel the Gilonite. **8.** Signer of Nehemiah's covenant to obey God's law (Neh. 10:26). **9.** The Hebrew text of 1 Chron. 26:20 says Ahijah, a Levite, had charge of temple treasuries under David (KJV, RSV). The Septuagint or oldest Greek translation suggests reading *'achehem,* "their brothers or relatives" (NASB, NIV, TEV). See *Ahiah.*

AHIKAM (Á·hī´ kăm) Personal name meaning "my brother stood up." Son of Josiah's scribe Shaphan. He took the book of the Law found in the temple to Huldah the prophetess to determine God's will (2 Kings 22:8-20). His son Gedaliah headed the Jews left in Judah after Nebuchadnezzar destroyed Jerusalem (586 B.C.) briefly before rebels killed him (2 Kings 25:22-25). Ahikam protected Jeremiah when King Jehoiakim wanted to kill the prophet (Jer. 26:24). Later his son also protected Jeremiah (Jer. 39:14).

AHILUD (Á·hī´ lŭd) Personal name meaning "a brother is born." The father of Jehoshaphat, David's court recorder (2 Sam. 8:16), who retained the position under Solomon (1 Kings 4:3). Probably the same Ahilud was father of Baana, Solomon's official to get court provisions from the province around Taanach, Megiddo, and Beth-shean (1 Kings 4:12).

AHIMAAZ (Á·hĭm´ á·ăz) Personal name with uncertain meaning, "brother of anger" and "my brother is counselor" being suggestions. **1.** Saul's father-in-law (1 Sam. 14:50). **2.** Son of Zadok, one of David's priests (2 Sam. 15:27). He served as one of David's secret messengers from the court when Absalom rebelled and drove his father from Jerusalem (2 Sam. 15:36; 17:17). Once he had to hide in a well to keep from being found out (17:18-21). He was a swift runner, overtaking Cushi to bring tidings to David (18:19-29), but he did not report Absalom's death. He maintained a reputation as a "good man" (18:27). **3.** One of 12 officers over Solomon's provinces, he had charge of Naphtali. He married Solomon's daughter Basmath. He may be the same as 2. Zadok's son (1 Kings 4:15).

AHIMAN (Á·hī´ man) Personal name with uncertain meaning. **1.** One of the giants of Anak (Num. 13:22). Caleb drove him and his two brothers out of Hebron (cp. Judg. 1:10, where the tribe of Judah killed the three brothers). See *Anak.* **2.** Levite and temple gatekeeper (1 Chron. 9:17).

AHIMELECH (Á·hĭm´ ĕ·lĕk) Personal name meaning "my brother is king." See *High Priest.*

AHIMOTH (Á·hī´ mŏth) Personal name meaning literally "my brother is death" or "my brother is Mot (god of death). A Levite (1 Chron. 6:25).

AHINADAB (Á·hĭn´ á·dăb) Personal name meaning "my brother has devoted himself" or "my brother is noble." One of Solomon's 12 province officials, he provided supplies for the royal court from Mahanaim (1 Kings 4:14).

AHINOAM (Á·hĭn´ ō·ăm) Personal name meaning "my brother is gracious." **1.** King Saul's wife (1 Sam. 14:50). **2.** Wife of David from Jezreel (1 Sam. 25:43) who lived with him under the Philistines at Gath (27:3). When she and Abigail, David's other wife, were captured by the Amalekites, the people threatened to stone David. David followed God's word, defeated the Amalekites, and recovered his wives and the other captives (30:1-20). Ahinoam then moved to Hebron with David, where the people crowned him king (2 Sam. 2:2-4). She gave David his first son, Amnon (3:2).

AHIO (Á·hī´ ō) Personal name meaning "my brother is Yahweh." **1.** Son of Abinadab at whose house the ark of the covenant was stationed (2 Sam. 6:3). He and his brother Uzzah drove an ox and cart carrying the ark. **2.** Member of the tribe of Benjamin (1 Chron. 8:14), but the Septuagint or earliest Greek translation of the OT reads "their brothers" or kinfolk. **3.** Member of Benjamin with connections to Gibeon (1 Chron. 8:31; 9:37). See *Ahiah; Ahijah.*

AHIRA (Á·hī´ rá) Personal name meaning "my brother is a friend." Leader of tribe of Naphtali under Moses (Num. 1:15), who presented the tribe's offerings at the dedication of the altar (7:78-83) and led them in the wilderness marches.

AHIRAM (Á·hī´ ram) Personal name meaning "my brother is exalted." Son of Benjamin who gave his name to a clan in that tribe (Num. 26:38).

AHIRAMITE (Á hī´ rám ĭt) Clan established by Ahiram. See *Ahiram.*

AHISAMACH (Á·hĭş´ á·măk) Personal name meaning "my brother has supported." Father of Oholiab, the artisan who helped Bezaleel create the artwork of the wilderness tabernacle (Exod. 31:6; 35:34; 38:23).

AHISHAHAR (Á·hī´ shā·här) Personal name meaning "brother of the dawn." A member of tribe of Benjamin (1 Chron. 7:10) but not listed in the genealogy of 1 Chron. 8.

AHISHAR (Á·hī´ shär) Personal name meaning "my brother sang." Head of Solomon's palace staff (1 Kings 4:6).

AHITHOPHEL (Á·hĭth´ ō·phĕl) Personal name meaning "brother of folly" if it is not a scribal attempt to hide an original name including a Canaanite god such as Ahibaal. The name of David's counselor who joined Absalom's revolt against King David (2 Sam. 15:12). David prayed that his counsel might be turned to foolishness (15:31) and commissioned the faithful Hushai to help Zadok and Abiathar, the priests, counteract the counsel of Ahithophel. Ahithophel led Absalom to show his rebellion was for real by taking over his father's concubines (16:15-23). Ahithophel's counsel was famous as being equal to the word of God (16:23). Hushai, however, persuaded Absalom not to follow Ahithophel's military advice (chap. 17), this being God's work (17:14). Disgraced, Ahithophel returned home to Giloh, put his house in order, and hanged himself (17:23). He may have been the grandfather of Bathsheba, David's partner in sin and later his wife (2 Sam. 11:3; 23:34).

AHITUB (Á·hī´ tŭb) Personal name meaning "my brother is good." **1.** Priest, son of Phinehas and grandson of Eli ministering in Shiloh (1 Sam. 14:3). He was Ahimelech's father (22:9). **2.** Father of Zadok, the high priest under David and Solomon (2 Sam. 8:17). The name occurs twice in the Chronicler's list of priests (1 Chron. 6:7-8,11-12,52; cp. 9:11). Ezra descended from Ahitub's line (Ezra 7:2).

AHLAB (Âh´ lăb) Place-name meaning "mountain forest" or "fertile." Probably located at Khirbet el-Macalib on the Mediterranean coast four miles above Tyre. The tribe of Asher could not conquer it (Judg. 1:31).

AHLAI (Äh´ lā-ī) Personal name meaning "a brother to me," perhaps an abbreviated form of Ahliya, "the brother is my god." Others interpret as interjection meaning "O would that." **1.** Member of clan of Jerahmeel (1 Chron. 2:31). Ahlai's father was Sheshan. First Chronicles 2:34 says Sheshan had no sons, only daughters. This makes Ahlai either a daughter of Sheshan or part of a Hebrew text that is incomplete due to copying errors. Some would identify Ahlai with Sheshan's grandson Attai (1 Chron. 2:35). Others think Sheshan changed his servant Jarha's name to Ahlai when he made Jarha his son-in-law (v. 35). No certain answer to Ahlai's identity has been offered. **2.** Father of a valiant soldier of David (1 Chron. 11:41).

AHOAH (Á·hō´ ah) Personal name of uncertain meaning. Grandson of Benjamin (1 Chron. 8:4) but lists in 2:25; 8:7; and evidence of early translations may point to Ahijah as the original name.

AHOHITE (Á·hō´ hīt) Clan name. In time of David and Solomon military figures of this clan or place became military leaders (2 Sam. 23:9,28; 1 Chron. 11:12,29; 27:4).

AHOLAH (Á·hō´ lah) (KJV) See *Oholah*.

AHOLIAB (Á·hō´ lĭ·ăb) (KJV) See *Oholiab*.

AHOLIBAH (Á·hō´ lĭ·bah) (KJV) See *Oholibah*.

AHOLIBAMAH (Á·hō·lĭ·bā´ mah) (KJV) See *Oholibamah*.

AHUMAI (Á·hū´ mī) Personal name meaning "a brother is it" or "brother of water." Member of clan of Zorathites of tribe of Judah (1 Chron. 4:2).

AHUZAM (Á·hū´ zăm) or **AHUZZAM** (NASB, NIV, RSV, TEV) Personal name meaning "their grasping" or "their property." A member of the tribe of Judah (1 Chron. 4:6).

AHUZZATH (Á·hŭz´ zăth) Personal name meaning "that grasped" or "property." Official who accompanied Abimelech, king of Philistines, to make covenant of peace with Isaac (Gen. 26:26). Called literally "the friend of the king," he probably held an office as the closest advisor of the king. Compare KJV, NASB, NIV.

AHZAI (Äh´ zī) or **AHASAI** (KJV) Personal name meaning "property" or abbreviated form of Ahzaiah, "Yahweh has grasped." A priest after the return from exile (Neh. 11:13). Sometimes said to be same as Jahzerah (1 Chron. 9:12).

AI (Ā´ ī) Name means "the ruin" in Hebrew. The biblical city of Ai may be a tale of two cities rather than one. In 1924 W. F. Albright first identified Ai with Et Tell, two miles southeast of Beitin (the site originally identified for biblical Bethel by Albright) and 12 miles north of Jerusalem. This site was excavated by John Garstang (1920s), Judith Marquet-Krause and Samuel Yeivin (1930s), and by Joseph Callaway of Southern Seminary (1960s and 1970s). This 27.5-acre walled city of Ai (at Et Tell) flourished from 3000 to 2200 B.C. Et Tell was the Ai of Abraham who pitched his tent between Bethel and Ai on his way to Egypt (Gen. 12:8) and later built his first altar on the same spot when he returned (Gen. 13:3). However, Callaway found no evidence that the site existed as a town in the Late Bronze Age (ca. 1400 B.C.). Later in time, 1220–1050 B.C., Et Tell (Ai) was rebuilt as a small 2.75-acre village without walls. Et Tell's gap in existence has been a problem for anyone holding to the historicity of the biblical conquest account. The debate over Ai has led scholars to discount the biblical account as a legend, to place Ai at Beitin (Bethel), or to relocate Ai (and Bethel) elsewhere. Several sites near Et Tell have been proposed for Ai over time: Deir Dibwan, Haiyan, and Khudriya.

The city name "Ai" of the conquest could have moved to a different site in the 15th century B.C. Albright noted the phenomenon of displacement of place-names "over a considerable local area" (*BASOR*, 74, Apr. 1939, 14). After their 1997 season, Bryant Wood and Gary Byers reported finding a fortified site near the Ai (Et Tell) of Callaway. At the time this article was written, Wood and Byers were excavating Khirbet el-Maqatir that sits on a ridge .9 miles southeast of Beitin and .6 miles west of Et Tell. While Et Tell was in ruins during the 1400's B.C., Fortress I at Khirbet el Maqatir, which was built in the 1400s B.C., covered 1.9 acres with walls 4 meters wide. Byers proposed that this site is Joshua's Ai. Accordingly, Byers followed David Livingston in identifying Bethel with el-Bireh instead of Beitin. Livingston proposed el-Bireh, a city on the north-south road from Jerusalem to Shechem (Nablus), as the best candidate for Bethel. El-Bireh is 1.8 miles west of Khirbet el-Maqatir located on the geographical boundary between Ephraim and Benjamin. El-Bireh is also the correct distance from Jerusalem as coordinated with the Roman mile markers and the correct distance from Gibeon as evidenced by the Onomasticon of Eusebius and Jerome. Livingston identified Ai with Khirbet Nisya and Beitin with Beth-aven, which has never been convincingly located. Josh. 7:2 describes Ai as adjacent to Beth-aven. According to the accounts of Genesis and Joshua, Ai is said to be east of Bethel (Gen. 12:8, Josh. 7:2), Bethel is very near Ai (Josh. 12:9), a mountain is said to

separate Bethel and Ai (Gen. 12:8), and Ai is implied to be a small town (Josh. 7:3). Khirbet el-Maqatir (Ai) was an important military target to Joshua and the Israelites since it guarded the approach to a strategic central crossroads to the central hill country—Bethel. The topography of the account in Joshua fits with this site as does a dating of the conquest in the late Bronze Age (ca. 1400 B.C.). Israel learned at Ai that they cannot prevail without God. The sin of one man, Achan, affected the whole nation's conquest commission. Ai was originally in Ephraimite territory (1 Chron. 7:28) and was later occupied by Benjamites (Neh. 11:31). Isaiah mentions the Assyrians approaching through Ai (Isa. 10:28). The residents of the twin cities of Bethel and Ai who returned from the exile are mentioned together in Ezra 2:28 and Neh. 7:32. Jeremiah also mentions the destruction of a Moabite town of the same name in his prophecy about the Ammonites (Jer. 49:3).   *Eric Alan Mitchell*

AIAH (Ā·ī´ ah) Personal name imitating the cry of a hawk, then meaning "hawk." **1.** Son of Zibeon among the clans of Edom descended from Esau (Gen. 36:24). **2.** Father of Rizpah, Saul's concubine (2 Sam. 3:7) and grandfather of Mephibosheth (2 Sam. 21:8).

AIATH (A·ī´ ăth) Alternate spelling of Ai (Isa. 10:28). See *Ai.*

AIDS (Acquired Immunodeficiency Syndrome) While the Bible does not specifically address AIDS, it does provide principles by which AIDS may be understood and those affected by AIDS may find comfort and hope.

Like all disease, suffering, and death, AIDS is a consequence of the fall (Gen. 2:17; 3:19b; Rom. 1:27). Unlike most other diseases, however, the HIV virus primarily (though not exclusively) infects persons through acts of irresponsible behavior (Hos. 8:7a; Gal. 6:7-8). The Bible enjoins all followers of Christ to cultivate pure lifestyles (Phil. 4:8; Col. 3:1-7; 2 Pet. 1:5-11), thereby minimizing the risk by which they might become infected by the HIV virus and develop AIDS.

Jesus showed compassion to lepers (Mark 1:40-42), social outcasts (Mark 5:1-8; John 4:1-38), and others who were sick and in desperate need (Matt. 9:36; 14:14; Mark 1:32-34) by touching (Matt. 20:34; Mark 1:41) and healing

The ruins of the ancient city of Ai.

all who came to Him. Paul adjures Christians to express active empathy for those in need (Rom. 12:15; Gal. 6:2), declaring that sufferers are comforted by God through the work of Jesus (2 Cor. 1:3-4). In the same way those who are affected by AIDS are able to find comfort and hope through the love of God.

AIJA (Ā·ī´ jȧ) Alternate spelling of Ai (Neh. 11:31). See *Ai.*

AIJALON (Ă´ jȧ·lŏn) Also spelled "Ajalon." Place-name meaning "place of the deer." **1.** Town and nearby valley where moon stood still at Joshua's command (Josh. 10:12). Near the Philistine border, south of Beth-horon, Aijalon belonged to Dan, according to tribal allotments (Josh. 19:42); but Dan did not conquer the territory and moved to the north (Judg. 18:1). It was one city in Dan given the Levites (Josh. 21:24). Amorites gained temporary control, but the Joseph tribes subjected them to pay tribute (Judg. 1:34-35). Saul and Jonathan won a battle between Michmash and Aijalon (1 Sam. 14:31). In postexilic times the Chronicler knew Aijalon as a city of the tribe of Benjamin which defeated Gath (1 Chron. 8:13). Rehoboam, Solomon's son, had fortified Aijalon (2 Chron. 11:10). King Ahaz (735–715 B.C.) asked for Assyrian help because the Philistines had taken Aijalon and other cities. Thus it was an important military location on Judah's western border. Aijalon is located at modern Yalo about 14 miles from Jerusalem. **2.** Elon, a judge of the tribe of Zebulon was buried in a northern Aijalon (Judg. 12:12), whose location may be at Tell et-But-meh.

AIJELETH SHAHAR (Āi´ jĕ·lĕth shā´ här) Musical direction in title of Ps. 22, literally "doe of the dawn." May be name of musical tune.

AIN (Ā´ ĭn) Place meaning "eye" or "water spring." Often used as first part of a place-name indicating the presence of a water source. English often used "En" as first part of such names. See *En-dor,* for example. **1.** Place on eastern border of Canaan (Num. 34:11). Location is uncertain. **2.** City of southern Judah (Josh. 15:32) belonging to Simeon (Josh. 19:7) but assigned as homestead for the Levites, who had no land allotted (Josh. 21:16), if this is not read Ashan as in some manuscripts of Joshua and in 1 Chron. 6:59.

AIR Space beneath the sky according to the human sense description of the universe. English versions translate Hebrew *ruach,* "wind, breath, spirit," as "air" in Job 41:16 to describe empty space between objects on earth (cp. Jer. 14:6 NASB, RSV). The birds fly in the air (Matt. 6:26). Mourners throw dust into the air (Acts 23:23). Inept boxers hit the air instead of opponents (1 Cor. 9:26). Speaking in tongues without an interpreter is vainly speaking in the air with no one understanding (1 Cor. 14:9). More theologically and symbolically Eph. 2:2 (KJV) mentions the "prince of the power of the air," showing Satan's power to tempt and rule people here below but his lack of power in heaven. At the second coming those still alive will be caught up with those being resurrected to meet the Lord Jesus in the air (1 Thess. 4:17). The fifth angel of Revelation opens the bottomless pit, which is so dominated by fire that its smoke darkened the sun and the air (Rev. 9:2). The seventh angel poured destruction into the air, thus on earth, from his vial (Rev. 16:17).

AJAH (Ā´ jah) (KJV, Gen. 36:24). See *Aiah.*

AJALON Variant spelling of Aijalon. See *Aijalon.*

AKAN (Ā´ kan) Personal name of uncertain meaning. An official of Edom of Horite ancestors (Gen. 36:27). Spelled "Jakan" in 1 Chron. 1:42.

AKELDAMA (NIV, RSV, TEV) See *Aceldama.*

AKHENATON (Ăkh·a·nä´ tŏn) Egyptian Pharaoh (1370–1353 B.C.) Originally named Amenhotep IV, he made a radical religious switch from worshiping Amon to serving Aton, the sun disc. Often referred to as the first monotheist, he probably did not go so far as denying the existence of all other gods. Later Egyptian writers called him blasphemer and criminal. He married the famous Nefertiti, known for her beauty, and was succeeded by his son-in-law Tutankhamen, known today as King Tut. He moved his capital northwards from Thebes to Akhenaton at Tell El-Amarna. During his reign he received the reports and requests from city-state rulers in Palestine that archaeologists call the Amarna letters. These show the lack of unity and harmony in Palestine that Joshua found when he entered to conquer Palestine.   *Gary C. Huckabay*

AKIM (NIV) See *Achim.*

AKKAD (NIV) See *Accad.*

AKKADIAN First known Semitic invaders of Mesopotamia and the language they spoke. Also spelled "Accadian." The Akkadians, under Sargon the Great, conquered Mesopotamia and established the first true empire in world history (2360–2180 B.C.). Their ancient capital Akkad (Agade) is mentioned in Gen. 10:10 as one of the cities of Shinar (Mesopotamia).

Akkadian is also the ancient name of the Semitic language used in the cuneiform inscriptions and documents that modern archaeologists have discovered. The earliest inscriptions in Old Akkadian date from about 2400–2000 B.C. Two main dialects evolved, Babylonian and Assyrian. These dialects are conveniently outlined in three phases: Old Babylonian and Old Assyrian, about 2000–1500 B.C., Middle Babylonian and Middle Assyrian, about 1500–1000 B.C., and Neo-Babylonian, about 1000–100 B.C., and Neo-Assyrian, about 1000–600 B.C. After about 600 B.C. Akkadian was increasingly replaced by Aramaic.

Akkadian is commonly classified as East Semitic to distinguish it from Northwest Semitic (Amorite, Ugaritic, Hebrew, etc.) and Southwest Semitic (Arabic, Ethiopic). Akkadian was the international language of diplomacy and commerce in the Near East before 1000 B.C. Consequently, collections of documents written in Akkadian originated among several non-Akkadian-speaking national and ethnic groups. Examples include the Amarna Tablets of Palestinian rulers addressed to Egypt, Akkadian documents from Ugarit in Syria, and the Nuzi Tablets from a Hurrian people.

Akkadian studies have had a profound effect on OT studies in at least four areas. First, the meanings of many Hebrew words have been determined or clarified by Akkadian cognates. Second, the literary (poetic) texts and legal texts have provided a rich source for comparative study of OT poetry and law texts. Third, historical annals and international treaties provide the wider framework for understanding biblical events and sometimes mention events and persons known also from the Bible. Fourth, the Akkadian religious texts have included accounts of creation and flood, as well as prophetic oracles, curses and blessings, and prayers, which

The Treaty of Kadesh, between the Hittites and Egypt, is inscribed on this tablet in Akkadian.

provide a basis for understanding both the common Semitic heritage and the uniqueness of Israel's faith. See *Cuneiform.*

Thomas Smothers

AKKUB (Ăk´ kŭb) Personal name possibly meaning "protector," or "protected one." **1.** Descendant of Solomon in postexilic Judah about 420 B.C. (1 Chron 3:24). **2.** Gatekeeper of the temple after the return from exile (1 Chron. 9:17; Ezra 2:42; Neh. 7:45; 11:19); he was a Levite (Neh. 12:25). Since "the children of Akkub" are mentioned (Neh. 7:45), the family apparently served for several generations, with more than one person in the family line named Akkub. **3.** Levite who helped Ezra teach the Law to God's returned people (Neh. 8:7). He may have been related to 2. **4.** The head of another family of temple staff personnel (Ezra 2:45).

AKRABBIM (Ăk·rab´ bĭm) Place-name meaning "scorpions." The "ascent of Akrabbim" lies southwest of the Dead Sea forming the southern border of Canaan (Num. 34:4; Josh. 15:3; Judg. 1:36). It is a mountain pass on the road southeast of Beersheba, today called Neqb es-Safa. Recent study has found the Scorpion Pass mentioned in other Near Eastern literature.

ALABASTER See *Minerals and Metals.*

Alexander the Great fighting Darius III at the Battle of Issus in 333 B.C. The scene comes from a first-century mosaic found in Pompeii.

ALAMETH (Ălá·mĕth) (KJV, 1 Chron. 7:8). See *Alemeth*.

ALAMMELECH (Ă·lăm´ mĕ·lĕk) (KJV) See *Allammelech*.

ALAMOTH (Ăl´ á·môth) Musical notation meaning literally "upon or according to young woman." This apparently signifies a tune for a high voice, a song for a soprano (1 Chron. 15:20; Ps. 46 title).

ALARM Signal given by shouting or playing an instrument. The Hebrew term (*teru'ah*) literally means a shout, but musical instruments were used as the trumpets of Num. 10:1-10. The alarm called the wilderness community to march (Num. 10:5-6). The alarm was a special, unspecified, sound of the trumpets, for the instruments could be blown without sounding the alarm to march (10:7). Later in Israel the alarm called them to battle (10:9) and reminded them of God's presence with their armies (cp. 31:6). The alarm is sounded against the enemy of God's people (2 Chron. 13:12). Joshua 6 describes a different alarm system. The priests marched with horns, instruments distinct from trumpets, and the people shouted a great shout or alarm (*teru' ah*) before God's miraculous act. The trumpet could also sound the alarm on a great religious day (Lev. 25:9), and Israel would raise a shout of joy (1 Sam. 4:5). The alarm did not always bring joy. The alarm announcing the enemy coming in war brought shock, sadness, and fear (Jer. 4:19; Hos. 5:8). The greatest fear should come, however, when God sounds the alarm for His day (Joel 2:1).

ALDEBARAN Red star of first magnitude in eye of Taurus; brightest star in Hyades; REB, KJV reading for Arcturus (Job 9:9; 38:32).

ALEMETH (Ăl´ á·meth) Place and personal name meaning "concealed" or "dark." **1.** City set aside for the Levites from Benjamin's allotment (1 Chron. 6:60). Known as Almon in Josh. 21:18. **2.** Grandson of Benjamin (1 Chron. 7:8). **3.** Descendant of Saul and Jonathan in tribe of Benjamin (1 Chron. 8:36).

ALEXANDER (Ăl·ĕx·ăn´ dĕr) Five NT men including the son of Simon of Cyrene (Mark 15:21), a relative of Annas (Acts 4:6), a Jew of Ephesus (Acts 19:33), a false teacher (1 Tim. 1:19-20), and a coppersmith (2 Tim. 4:14).

ALEXANDER THE GREAT (Ăl·ĕx·ăn´ dĕr) Succeeded his father as king of Macedonia and quickly conquered the Persian empire. Alexander the Great (356–323 B.C.) was one of the greatest military leaders in history. His father was Phillip of Macedon, king of a region of Greece known as Macedonia.

When Alexander was 20 years old (336 B.C.), his father was killed, and Alexander became king. This ambitious young king immediately began to make plans to conquer Persia. Persia had extended its empire to Asia Minor (modern-day Turkey). In 334 B.C. Alexander led his troops into Asia Minor where they won a series of victories over the Persians.

Alexander the Great continued his victorious military march into Syria and Egypt. From victories there, he led his troops into Persia, Media, and as far east as northern India. He returned to Babylon, where he died in 323 B.C. at the age of 33.

Alexander the Great.

A

Alexander's most lasting legacy was his spread of Greek culture. Everywhere he went he tried to instill that culture. While Alexander is never directly named in the Bible, the culture that he brought to Palestine greatly affected the biblical world, especially during the time between the writing of the OT and NT. His empire is one element of the historical background of Daniel. See *Alexandria; Greece.*

Lynn Jones

ALEXANDRIA (Al·ĕx·ăn´ drĭ·á) Capital of Egypt from 330 B.C., founded by Alexander the Great as an outstanding Greek cultural and academic center.

Alexandria was designed to act as the principal port of Egypt located on the western edge of the Nile Delta. Built on a peninsula, it separated the Mediterranean Sea and Lake Mareotis. A causeway (*Heptastadion,* or "seven stadia") connected the peninsula with Pharos Island and divided the harbor. The Pharos lighthouse was visible for miles at a height of over 400 feet and is remembered today as one of the "Seven Wonders of the World."

The city was divided into sections with a substantial Jewish quarter, the Royal area, the

Lighthouse in the harbor at Alexandria.

Neapolis, and a necropolis to the far west. The city was known for its cultural and academic pursuits. The finest library in the ancient world with over 500,000 volumes attracted many

Well-preserved Roman theater in Alexandria with seating for 800 spectators. It was used for musical performances as well as wrestling matches.

scholars. The Mouseion (Museum) complimented the library as the center of worship for the Muses, goddesses of "music," dancing, and letters. It became the most important center of Judaism outside of Jerusalem. Jewish rabbis gathered in Alexandria to produce the Septuagint (LXX), the Greek translation of the OT. Greek philosophers and mathematicians such as Euclid, Aristarchus, and Eratosthenes worked here. Octavian incorporated it into the Roman Empire about 30 B.C. It quickly became second in importance to Rome. Its importance declined about A.D. 100.

The educated Jews of Alexandria contended with Stephen (Acts 6:9). Apollos, the great Christian orator, came from Alexandria (Acts 18:24), and Paul rode the ships of that port (Acts 27:6; 28:11). Although the Christians suffered persecution there, they produced a school with such notables as Clement and Origen in leadership. The school was noted for its allegorical approach to Scripture.   *Gary C. Huckabay*

ALGUM Rare wood that Solomon imported from Lebanon for the temple (2 Chron. 2:8). The exact type of wood is not known. First Kings 10:11-12 refers to "almug" wood imported from Ophir (cp. 2 Chron. 9:10-11). The rare wood was used for gateways and for musical instruments.

ALIAH (Ă·lī´ ăh) Personal name meaning "height." A leader of Edom (1 Chron. 1:51), known in Gen. 36:40 as Alvah.

ALIAN (Á·lī´ an) Personal name meaning "high one." Descendant of Esau and thus an Edomite (1 Chron. 1:40). Known in Gen. 36:23 as Alvan.

ALIEN Person who is living in a society other than his own. Related terms are "foreigner," "stranger," and "sojourner." Elijah was an alien in the home of the widow of Zarephath (1 Kings 17:20; "to sojourn" is to be an alien). Isaac was an alien with Abimelech, the Philistine king (Gen. 26:3). The patriarchs (Abraham, Isaac, Jacob) were aliens in Canaan but owned large material resources (Gen. 20:1; 26:3; 32:5). Israel had a special place for aliens, because Israel began history in Egypt as aliens (Exod. 23:9). Special laws provided food and clothing for aliens (Deut. 24:19-20; 26:12). Aliens had rights in the courtroom (Deut. 24:17; 27:19).

The ritual expectations of the alien are not always clear (Deut. 14:21; Lev. 17:15). God loves aliens (Deut. 10:19), and the alien could worship God and was supposed to keep the Sabbath (Exod. 23:12; Deut. 31:12). They could observe Passover just as any Israelite (Num. 9:14) and offer sacrifices (Lev. 17:8). They should obey sexual laws (Lev. 18:26).

Unexpectedly, the prophets have little to say about aliens (Jer. 7:6; 22:3; Ezek. 22:7,29). Jeremiah does lament that God appears to be an alien (Jer. 14:8). The psalmist saw all people as aliens on earth (39:12; 119:19). Peter reminded his readers that they were "aliens and temporary residents" on earth (HCSB).

ALLAMMELECH (Ál·lăm´ mĕ·lĕk) Place-name meaning "king's oak" or "royal holy tree." Border town of Asher (Josh. 19:26) whose specific location is not known.

ALLEGORY Literary device in which a story or narrative is used to convey truths about reality. The word "allegory" is taken from two Greek words: *alla* (other) and *agoreuo* (to proclaim). An allegory conveys something other than its literal meaning. Sometimes "allegory" is defined as an extended metaphor. Cicero viewed allegory as a continuous stream of metaphors.

Allegorical interpretation is a reading of a text with a view to finding meanings other than the literal. Such interpretations are legitimate when it is clear that the text is an allegory. For example, John Bunyan wrote *Pilgrim's Progress* as an allegory. Therefore, allegorical interpretation is not only legitimate but is required to understanding Bunyan's work. To bring allegorical interpretation to texts that are not allegories is to misread those texts.

Background Allegorical interpretation can be found among early Greeks who read Homer and other epic tales as allegories. In Book VII of *The Republic*, Plato seeks to convey important truths about human knowledge in the allegory of the cave.

Philo Judaeus of Alexandria (50 B.C.) was a Jewish Platonist who exerted great influence on the course of biblical interpretation. In his commentary of the Pentateuch, Philo employed allegorical exegesis. In addition to the literal meaning, Philo found higher levels of meaning, avoiding unpalatable statements. Others have employed allegorical interpretation to make

Christianity compatible with some other religious form such as Greek philosophy of the New Age movement. Still others employ the method in order to unearth "deeper, spiritual" meanings. Philo's approach was developed around A.D. 200 by Clement of Alexandria and his student Origen.

Old Testament Allegory No entire book of the OT was written as an allegory, but portions of it have been interpreted allegorically. For example, Rabbi Akiba (ca. A.D. 50–132) interpreted the Song of Songs allegorically to refer to God's love of Israel rather than as a collection of romantic love songs. Many Christian scholars have followed that lead and interpreted this OT book as a picture of Christ's love for the church. At least one interpreter has done the same thing with Esther, reading each of the major characters as facets of the spiritual life and interpreting the book as an elaborate allegory of the victorious Christian life.

Philo applied allegorical interpretation to many parts of the OT in order to defend biblical teachings where they seemed to conflict with the philosophical understandings of his day. However, Jewish proponents of allegory, including Philo, never completely abandoned the historical meaning of Scripture. They employed allegorical interpretation alongside lexical, historical, and grammatical interpretations of the text. Whether they were able to retain the historical intent once they detoured into allegorical hermeneutics is questionable.

New Testament Allegory While Jesus never interpreted the OT allegorically, He did give allegorical interpretations to some of His parables. Jesus' interpretation of the parable of the soils (Mark 4:1-20) assigns symbolic meaning to the various elements of the parable: for example, the seed represents the word, and the four kinds of soil symbolize the different ways in which the word is received. Both the parable of the soil and the parable of the tares (Matt. 13:24-30,36-43) were spoken and interpreted by their author as allegories. Most of the parables, however, are not allegorical.

Whether Paul ever used an allegorical hermeneutic in dealing with the OT is debatable. He did employ the term on one occasion (Gal. 4:22-31), and there are two other passages in his writings in which his method of interpretation is not strictly lexical and historical (1 Cor. 9:8-10; 10:1-11). Though Paul used the word

"allegory" in Gal. 4, he did not employ what has come to be known as the allegorical method but rather used typology, seeing the historical Sarah and Hagar as types pointing to later "antitypes." Typological interpretation is a very valid approach that does not remove the historical element from the text, as allegorical interpretation generally does. The texts in 1 Cor. 9 and 10 also feature a typological approach. Paul uses typology in his comparison of Adam and Christ in Rom. 5:12-21 as well. Paul's approach here was similar to Matthew's, citing OT testimonies about Jesus to demonstrate that He was the fulfillment of OT expectations, not to contend for some dehistoricized allegorical interpretation. In the vast majority of Paul's specific interpretations of the OT, he uses a normal, lexical, historical hermeneutic.

Authors are free to use whatever method of communication they wish in order to establish their point. Readers, though, must be careful not to use inappropriate interpretive methods. Allegorical interpretations of nonallegorical passages may seem helpful, "spiritual," and theologically significant. Such approaches, though, eventually distort the meaning of the passage in question and make its "meaning" subject to the interests and prejudices of the interpreter. As Luther once said in allegorical hermeneutics, the text becomes a "nose of wax" which can be formed and manipulated in whatever way the interpreter wishes. In this approach the interpreter no longer is attempting to find the meaning placed in the text by the author but is actually creating his own meaning to replace that of the author. *Chad Brand and Steve Bond*

ALLELUIA (KJV) See *Hallelujah.*

ALLEMETH (Ăl´ lĕ·mĕth) Variant spelling of Alemeth in some English translations (1 Chron. 6:60). See *Alemeth.*

ALLIANCE See *Covenant.*

ALLON (Āl´ lŏn) Personal name meaning "oak." Leader of tribe of Simeon (1 Chron. 4:37).

ALLONBACHUTH (Ăl´ lŏn·băk´ ŭth) or **ALLONBACUTH** Place-name meaning "oak of weeping." Burial place near Bethel of Rebekah's nurse (Gen. 35:8).

ALLOTMENT OT concept of land allocation either by God or by lot. The allotment of the land of Canaan to the tribes of Israel is recorded in Num. 32 and Josh. 13–19. God directed the process through the lot of the priest (Josh. 14:1-2). The tribes of Reuben and Gad, along with half the tribe of Manasseh, requested land east of the Jordan (Num. 32:33). Ezekiel 48 also contains a version of the allotment of the land for the Jews after the exile, revised so that each tribe received an equal share. See *Lots.*

Ronald E. Bishop

ALMIGHTY Title of God, translation of Hebrew *El Shaddai.* The early Greek translation introduced "Almighty" as one of several translations. Recent study has tended to see "The Mountain One" as the most likely original meaning. The name was particularly related to Abraham and the patriarchs (Gen. 17:1; 28:3; 35:11; 49:25). Job is the only book to use *El Shaddai* extensively, 31 times in all. Paul used "Almighty" once at the end of a series of OT quotations to imitate OT style and to underline divine power to bring His word to fulfillment. Revelation refers to God nine times as "Almighty," again giving a feeling of power to the vision of Revelation.

ALMODAD (Ăl·mo´ dăd) Personal name meaning "God is a friend." Grandson of Eber and ancestor of Arabian tribes (Gen. 10:25-26).

ALMON (Ăl´ mŏn) Place-name meaning "darkness," or "hidden," or "small road sign." City given to Levites from tribe of Benjamin, called Alemeth in 1 Chron. 6:60. The site is probably modern Khirbet Almit.

ALMOND Large, nut-bearing tree and the nuts that it bears. Noted as the first tree to bloom (January) and for its pretty white or pink blossoms. Jacob used the almond (KJV, "hazel") as a breeding device to increase his herds (Gen. 30:37). He sent almonds as one of the best fruits of the land to satisfy the Egyptian ruler (Gen. 43:11). The bowls for the tabernacle had almond-shaped decorations (Exod. 25:33-34). Aaron's rod miraculously produced ripe almonds, showing that he and his tribe were the only chosen priests (Num. 17:8). The early-appearing white bloom of the almond apparently serves as a picture of the early graying of a person's hair, pointing the writer of Ecclesiastes to

the certainty of death (Eccles. 12:5). The early blossom meant for Jeremiah that the almond watched for spring and gave the prophet a word-play on the almond (Hb. *shaqed*) and his task to watch (Hb. *shoqed*) (Jer. 1:11).

ALMON-DIBLATHAIM (Ăl´ mŏn-dĭb·là·thä´ ĭm) Place-name meaning "road sign of the two figs." A stopping place near the end of the wilderness wandering near Mount Nebo (Num. 33:46-47). It may be the same as Beth-diblath-aim in Jer. 48:22. Location may be modern Deleilat el-Gharbiyeh that looks over three roadways.

ALMS Gifts for the poor.
Old Testament Although the Hebrew language apparently had no technical term to refer to "alms" or "almsgiving," the practice of charitable giving, especially to the poor, became a very important belief and practice within Judaism. The OT taught the practice of benevolent concern for those in need. Israel's ideal was a time when no one was poor (Deut. 15:4). Every three years, for example, the tithe of the produce of the year was to be brought to the towns and made available to the Levites, the aliens in the land, the orphans, and the widows (Deut. 14:28-29). Every seventh year all debts were to be cancelled among the Israelites (Deut. 15:1-3), and the fields were to lie fallow so that the needy of the people might eat (Exod. 23:10-11). In addition, the law instructed Israel to give generously to the needs of their Hebrew neighbors (Deut. 15:7-11). Such charitable giving was not a grudging chore or a loan for repayment. Failure to comply would be sin (Deut. 15:9-10). Israel showed concern for the needy by not harvesting the corners of fields and by leaving the gleanings so the needy and the stranger might gather what remained (Lev. 19:9-10; 23:22; Deut. 24:19-22).
New Testament The NT regards alms as an expression of a righteous life. The technical term for alms (Gk. *eleemosune*) occurs 13 times in the NT. This does not include Matt. 6:1, where the preferred reading is "righteousness" (NASB, NIV) instead of "alms" (KJV). By the first century A.D. righteousness and alms were synonymous in Judaism. Although Jesus criticized acts of charity done for the notice of men (Matt. 6:2-3), He expected His disciples to perform such deeds (Matt. 6:4) and even commanded them (Luke

11:41; 12:33). Alms could refer to a gift donated to the needy (Acts 3:2-3,10) or to acts of charity in general (Acts 9:36; 10:2,4,31; 24:17).

The principle of deeds of mercy performed in behalf of the needy receives emphatic significance in the NT, since such actions are ultimately performed in behalf of the Lord (Matt. 25:34-45). Early Christians voluntarily sold their possessions and shared all things in common to alleviate suffering and need within the church (Acts 2:44-46; 4:32-35). Much of Paul's later ministry involved the supervision and collection of a contribution for the needy Christians in Jerusalem (Rom. 15:25-28; 1 Cor. 16:1-4; 2 Cor. 8–9). According to James 1:27, pure and undefiled religion consists, at least partially, in assisting orphans and widows in their distress. John also presented charitable giving as evidence of one's relationship to God (1 John 3:17-18). See *Aliens; Hospitality; Mercy, Merciful; Stewardship.*   *Barry Morgan*

ALMUG (1 Kings 10:11) See *Algum.*

ALOE Large tree grown in India and China, producing resin and oil used in making perfumes. Balaam used the beauty of the aloe tree to describe the beauty of Israel's camp as he blessed them (Num. 24:6). The aloe perfume gave aroma to the king's garment as he was married (Ps. 45:8). Aloe also perfumed the harlot's bed (Prov. 7:17). The beloved's garden includes aloe (Song 4:14). Nicodemus brought aloe with myrrh to perfume Jesus' body for burial (John 19:39). See *Plants.*

ALOTH (Ā´ lŏth) Place-name meaning "the height" if not read Bealoth (NASB, RSV), "feminine baals." Center of activity for Baana, one of Solomon's 12 district supervisors (1 Kings 4:16).

ALPHA AND OMEGA First and last letters of the Greek alphabet, used in Revelation to describe God or Christ (Rev. 1:8,17; 21:6; 22:13). "Alpha and omega" refers to God's sovereignty and eternal nature. God and Christ are "the First and the Last, the Beginning and the End" (Rev. 22:13 HCSB).

ALPHAEUS (Ăl·phē´ ŭs) or **ALPHEUS** Personal name. **1.** Father of apostle called James the Less to distinguish him from James, the son of Zebedee and brother of John (Matt. 10:3; Mark 3:18; Luke 6:15; Acts 1:13). Mark 15:40 says James' mother, Mary, was with Jesus' mother at the cross. John 19:25 says Mary the wife of Cleophas was at the cross. This would seem to indicate that Cleophas and Alphaeus are two names for the same person. Some want to equate Alphaeus, Cleophas, and the Cleopas of Luke 24:18. **2.** Father of the Apostle Levi (Mark 2:14). Comparison of Matt. 9:9 and Luke 5:27 would indicate Levi was also called Matthew.

ALTAR Structure used in worship as the place for presenting sacrifices to God or gods.

Old Testament The Hebrew word for altar that is used most frequently in the OT is formed from the verb for "slaughter" and means literally "slaughter place." Altars were used primarily as places of sacrifice, especially animal sacrifice.

While animals were a common sacrifice in the OT, altars were also used to sacrifice grain, fruit, wine, and incense. The grain and fruit sacrifices were offered as a tithe of the harvest or as representative first fruits of the harvest. They were presented in baskets to the priest who set the basket before the altar (Deut. 26:2-4). Wine was offered along with animal and bread sacrifices. Incense was burned on altars to purify after slaughterings and to please God with sweet fragrance.

"Altar" is distinct from "temple." Whereas temple implies a building or roofed structure, altar implies an open structure. Altar and temple were often adjacent, though not all altars had a temple adjacent. The reference to Abraham's sacrifice of Isaac (Gen. 22) may indicate that the animal to be sacrificed was placed on the altar alive but bound and slaughtered on the altar. Such may have been the earliest practice. By the time of the Levitical laws, the animal was slaughtered in front of the altar, dismembered, and only the fatty portions to be burned were placed on the altar (Lev. 1:2-9).

In the OT, altars are distinguished by the material used in their construction. The simplest altars, and perhaps oldest, were the earthen altars (Exod. 20:24). This type altar was made of either mud-brick or a raised roughly shaped mound of dirt. Mud-brick was a common building material in Mesopotamia, so mud-brick altars would have appeared most likely in Mesopotamia. An earthen altar would not have been very practical for permanently settled people, for the rainy season each year would damage or destroy the altar. This type altar might be

Islam's Dome of the Rock, built over the rock said to be the altar of Abraham's near sacrifice of Isaac as well as the site of Solomon's temple.

more indicative of a nomadic people who move regularly and are less concerned with the need for a permanent altar. It might also reflect the Mesopotamian ancestry of the Hebrews, since the mud-brick was the typical building material there.

The stone altar is the most commonly mentioned altar in biblical records and the most frequently found in excavations from Palestine. A single large stone could serve as an altar (Judg. 6:19-23; 13:19-20; 1 Sam. 14:31-35). Similarly, unhewn stones could be carefully stacked to form an altar (Exod. 20:25; 1 Kings 18:30-35). Such stone altars were probably the most common form of altar prior to the building of the Solomonic temple. A number of examples of stone altars have been excavated in Palestine. The sanctuary at Arad, belonging to the period of the Divided Monarchy (900 B.C.–600 B.C.), had such a stone altar. The Hebrew stone altars were not to have steps (Exod. 20:25-26), probably in part to distinguish them from Canaanite altars which did have steps. A striking circular Canaanite altar dating from 2500 B.C. to 1800 B.C. was excavated at Megiddo. It was 25 feet in diameter and 45.5 feet high. Four steps led up to

the top of the altar. Apparently in later times, the requirement forbidding steps on Hebrew altars was not enforced, for in Ezekiel's vision of the restored temple, the altar has three levels and many steps.

Other stone altars have been excavated in Palestine. One from Beersheba, belonging also to the period of the Divided Monarchy, was of large hewn stones and had, when reassembled, horns on the four corners (Exod. 27:2; 1 Kings 1:50). Apparently the Exodus restrictions concerning unhewn stones, like those concerning steps, were not consistently followed throughout the OT period.

The third type altar mentioned in the OT is the bronze altar. The central altar in the court of Solomon's temple was a bronze altar. Its dimensions are given as 20 cubits by 20 cubits by 10 cubits high, about 30 feet square and 15 feet high (2 Chron. 4:1). Yet, it is unclear whether the entire altar was made of bronze or had a bronze overlay on a stone altar. It is also possible that the bronze portion was a grate set on top of the otherwise stone altar (Exod. 27:4). This altar is regularly known as the altar of burnt offering. The earlier tabernacle had a similar altar made of acacia (KJV "shittim") wood overlaid with bronze (Exod. 27:1-2). The tabernacle altar was smaller, only five cubits square and three cubits high. The location of the altar of burnt offering of the tabernacle and Solomon's temple was not given specifically. It was located "at" or "before" the door of the Tent of Meeting, which was also the place that sacrificial animals were slaughtered. Generally reconstructions of the tabernacle and temple locate the altar in the center of the courtyard, but the text seems to favor a location near the entrance of the tabernacle/temple structure. The rationale was probably to locate the altar as close as possible to the focal point of God's presence, near the ark itself.

Ezekiel's vision of the restored temple had the altar of burnt offering located in the center of the courtyard. Although the dimensions are not fully given in the text, it seems that this altar was approximately 18 cubits square and 12 cubits high (Ezek. 43:13-17). Ezekiel's altar had three superimposed levels, each slightly smaller than the preceding, and had steps from the east leading up to the top.

Both the altar of the tabernacle and that of Ezekiel are described as having horns. It is likely that the altar of burnt offering in Solomon's temple also had horns. The stone altar found at Beersheba has such horns preserved. Apparently grasping the horns of the altar was a way of seeking sanctuary or protection when one was charged with a serious offense (1 Kings 1:50-51; 2:28-34; cp. Exod. 21:12-14). More importantly, the horns of the altar were the place where blood from a sacrificial animal was applied for atonement from sin (Exod. 29:12; Lev. 4:7). Jeremiah graphically described the people's sin as being so severe that they were engraved on the horns of the altar (Jer. 17:1). During certain

Canaanite altar at Hazor in Northern Israel.

Fragments of what was probably an altar base unearthed at the high place at Lachish in Israel.

festivals a sacred procession led into the temple and up to the horns of the altar (Ps. 118:27). Probably this procession carried the chosen animal sacrifice to atone for the people's sin and ended at the place of sacrifice.

During the reign of Ahaz, the bronze altar or altar of burnt offering in Solomon's temple was displaced by an altar that Ahaz had built on a Syrian model (2 Kings 16:10-16). This altar was apparently larger than the bronze altar of Solomon and was placed in the central position in the courtyard to be the main altar of sacrifice.

No biblical description exists for the altar of burnt offering from the second temple. However, such an altar was constructed even before the temple was rebuilt (Ezra 3:2). Josephus described the altar in the rebuilt temple of Herod. He wrote that the altar was 50 cubits square and 15 cubits high with a ramp leading to the top. This altar would have been much larger than the earlier ones.

A fourth type of altar is the gold altar or altar of incense. It was located in the inner room of the sanctuary, just outside the holy of holies (1 Kings 7:48-50). The incense altar is described in Exodus as constructed of acacia wood, overlaid with gold, with dimensions one cubit square and two cubits high (Exod. 30:1-6). Like the altar of burnt offering, the altar of incense had horns on the four corners. As its name implies, incense was burned on this altar. The incense served as a means of purification after slaughtering animals, a costly sacrifice, and also as a sweet-smelling offering that would be pleasing to God.

Another Hebrew word for "altar" that is used infrequently in the OT means literally "high place" (Hb. *bamah*). Such "high places" were probably raised platforms at which sacrifices and other rites took place. The "high place" may have been itself a kind of altar, though this is not certain. The circular Canaanite altar mentioned above may be an example of a "high place," an elevated place of sacrifice and worship.

New Testament The Greek word used for altar literally translates "place of sacrifice." New Testament references to altars concern proper worship (Matt. 5:23-24) and hypocrisy in worship (Matt. 23:18-20). The altar of incense described in the OT (Exod. 30:1-6) is mentioned in Luke (Luke 1:11). Several NT references to altars refer back to OT altar events (Rom. 11:3; James 2:21). In Revelation John described a golden altar (Rev. 9:13) that, like the OT bronze altar, had horns.

While direct references to altar and the sacrifice of Jesus Christ are few in the NT (Heb. 13:10), the message that Jesus Christ is the ultimate sacrifice who effects reconciliation with God is the theme of the NT.

Theological Significance Altars were places of sacrifice. Beyond that function, altars also were places of God's presence. The patriarchal narratives regularly record the building of an altar at the site of a theophany, a place where God had appeared to an individual (Gen. 12:7; 26:24-25). It was quite natural to build an altar and commemorate the appearance of God with a sacrifice. If God had once appeared at a site, that would be a good location for Him to appear again. Thus sacrifices would be offered there with the feeling that God was present and would accept the offering. With the building of the Solomonic temple, the presence of God was associated especially with the ark of the covenant. The altar of burnt offering then came to signify more of a sense of reconciliation or mediation. The worshiper brought a sacrifice to the altar where it was burned and thereby given to God. The acceptance of the offerings by the priest symbolized God's acceptance, manifest in blessings (Exod. 20:24) and covenant renewal.

Joel F. Drinkard, Jr.

The summit of Mount Carmel where Elijah's altar to God and the altar of the priests of Baal were built.

ALTASHHETH (Ăl·tăsh´ hĕth) (NASB) or **AL-TASCHITH** (KJV). Word in psalm title (Pss. 57; 58; 59; 75), transliterated letter for letter from Hebrew to English by NASB and KJV, but translated "Do not destroy" by NIV and RSV. This may indicate the tune to which the people sang the psalm.

ALUSH (Ā´ lŭsh) Wilderness camping place not far from Red Sea (Num. 33:13-14).

ALVAH (Ăl´ văh) Personal name of leader of Edom. Spelled Aliah in 1 Chron. 1:51.

ALVAN (Ăl´ văn) Personal name meaning "high" or "tall." A descendant of Seir (Gen. 36:23), spelled Alian in 1 Chron. 1:40.

AMAD (Ā´ măd) Place-name of unknown meaning. City allotted to tribe of Asher (Josh. 19:26).

AMAL (Ā´ măl) Personal name meaning "worker" or "trouble." Leader of tribe of Asher (1 Chron. 7:35).

AMALEKITE (Ă·măl´ ĕ·kit) Nomadic tribe of formidable people that first attacked the Israelites after the exodus at Rephidim. Descendants of Amalek, the grandson of Esau (Gen. 36:12), they inhabited the desolate wasteland of the northeast Sinai Peninsula and the Negev. They were the first to attack Israel after the exodus (Num. 24:20). Israel won the initial battle (Exod. 17:8-16), but later was driven back into the Sinai wilderness by a coalition of Amalekites and Canaanites (Num. 14:39-45). Thereafter the Amalekites waged a barbaric guerrilla war against Israel (Deut. 25:17-19). Fighting continued after Israel settled in Canaan. Because of their atrocities, God commanded Saul to exterminate the Amalekites (1 Sam. 15:2-3). Saul disobeyed and the Amalekites were not defeated completely until late in the eighth century B.C. (1 Chron. 4:43). No archaeological data concerning the Amalekites has been discovered to date. See *Exodus; Negev.*   *LeBron Matthews*

AMAM (Ā´ măm) Place-name in southern Judah (Josh. 15:26).

AMANA (A·mā´ nà) Place-name meaning "trusted." Mountain peak in Anti-Lebanon mountains where lovers met and then descended (Song 4:8).

AMANUENSIS (À·măn·ū·ĕn´ sĭs) One employed to copy manuscripts or write from dictation. Romans 16:22 identifies Tertius as the one "who penned this epistle" (cp. Col. 4:18; 1 Pet. 5:12). See *Scribe.*

AMARIAH (Ăm·à·rī´ äh) Personal name meaning "Yahweh has spoken." Popular name, especially among priests, after the exile. Brief biblical comments make it difficult to distinguish with certainty the number of separate individuals. **1.** Priest in the line of Aaron (1 Chron. 6:7,52; Ezra 7:3). **2.** Priest in the high priestly line after Solomon's day (1 Chron. 6:11). **3.** Priestly son of Hebron in Moses' line (1 Chron. 23:19; 24:23). **4.** Chief priest and highest judge of matters involving religious law under King Jehoshaphat (2 Chron. 19:11). **5.** Priest under Hezekiah responsible for distributing resources from Jerusalem temple to priests in priestly cities outside Jerusalem (2 Chron. 31:15). **6.** Man with foreign wife under Ezra (Ezra 10:42). **7.** Priest who sealed Nehemiah's covenant to obey the law (Neh. 10:3). **8.** Ancestor of a member of tribe of Judah living in Jerusalem during Nehemiah's time (Neh. 11:4). **9.** Priest who returned to Jerusalem from exile in Babylon with Zerubbabel (Neh. 12:2). **10.** Head of a course of priests in Judah after the exile (Neh. 12:13). **11.** Ancestor of Zephaniah, the prophet (Zeph. 1:1).

AMARNA, TELL EL Site approximately 200 miles south of Cairo, Egypt, where, in 1888, 300 clay tablets were found describing the period of history when the Israelites were in bondage in Egypt. Amarna is not mentioned by name in the Bible. Tell el-Amarna lies on the east bank of the Nile River. The name for the area of Tell el-Amarna was apparently coined about 1830 by John Gardner Wilkinson when he combined the name of the village, Et-Till, with the name of the surrounding district, El-Amarna. The use of the word "tell" in the name is misleading. In Arabic, it means "mound," and it would therefore be expected that the site be made up of several levels, indicating successive periods of occupation. There are no such levels, however.

Tell el-Amarna is the present location of the ancient Egyptian city Akhenaton. That city was constructed as the new capital of a young Pharaoh, Amenhotep (or Amenophis) IV, who was in power during the mid-fourteenth century B.C.

The so-called Amarna Letters were written in Akkadian, the international language of that era. These letters were primarily diplomatic communications between Egypt and Egyptian-controlled territories, including Syria and Palestine. Rulers of small Palestinian city-states including Shechem, Jerusalem, and Megiddo complained of mistreatment by other rulers and asked for Egyptian aid. These letters evidence the political unrest, disunity, and instability in the area around the time of the Hebrew conquest. Reference to the *Habiru* in these letters has intrigued scholars, but no definite connection to the Hebrews has been determined.

In recent years archaeologists have done a petrographic analysis of these tablets to determine their chemical composition and where they came from. The letters sent by Canaanite kings of Hazor, Shechem, and Lachish were found to be from those very cities. Other Amarna tablets appear to have been made in Egypt. One explanation of this is the fact that the Egyptians made copies of foreign correspondence. *Hugh Tobias and Steve Bond*

AMASA (Ȧ·mā´ sȧ) Personal name meaning "burden" or "bear a burden." **1.** Captain of Judah's army replacing Joab during Absalom's rebellion against his father David (2 Sam. 17:25). He is related to David, but the texts leave some question as to the exact relationship. Abigail was Amasa's mother. His father was either Ithra an Israelite (2 Sam. 17:25) or Jether the Ishmaelite (1 Chron. 2:17). She was sister of Zeruiah, Joab's mother (2 Sam. 17:25) or sister to David and to Zeruiah, Joab's mother (1 Chron. 2:16). When he defeated the rebel forces and Joab murdered Absalom (2 Sam. 18:14), David made peaceful overtones to Judah by inviting Amasa as his relative to assume command of his army (2 Sam. 19:13). When called to battle, Amasa appeared too late (2 Sam. 20:4-5). Joab marched among David's army and cunningly killed Amasa (2 Sam. 20:10). This served as reason for David to advise Solomon to do away with Joab (1 Kings 2:5) and thus reason for Solomon to kill Joab (1 Kings 2:28-34).

2. Leader in tribe of Ephraim who prevented Israel's soldiers from keeping captives of the army of King Ahaz of Judah, knowing this was a sin (2 Chron. 28:12-14).

AMASAI (Ȧ·mā´ saî) Personal name meaning "burden bearer." **1.** Levite in the line of Kohath (1 Chron. 6:25). **2.** Levite in the line of Kohath and of Heman the singer (1 Chron. 6:35), often identified with 1. **3.** The chief of David's captains, who received prophetic inspiration from the Spirit (1 Chron. 12:18). Note that he does not appear in 2 Sam. 23. **4.** Priest and musician who blew trumpets before the ark of God in David's time (1 Chron. 15:24). **5.** Levite, father of Mahath, who helped purify the temple under Hezekiah (2 Chron. 29:12).

AMASHAI (Ȧ·măsh´ aî) or **AMASHSAI** (NASB, TEV) Personal name of priest after the exile (Neh. 11:13).

AMASIAH (Ăm à sī´ ah) Personal name meaning "Yahweh has borne." One of the captains of Jehoshaphat (2 Chron. 17:16).

AMAW (Ăm´ aw) Place-name meaning "his people." Translated "land of children of his people" (KJV) or "his native land" (NIV) or "land of the sons of his people" (NASB) in Num. 22:5, but translated as place-name in RSV, TEV. Place-name also appears in Idrim Inscription about 1450 B.C. and in an Egyptian tomb inscription. It was located west of Euphrates River south of Carchemish and included Pethor, the hometown of Balaam, the prophet.

AMAZIAH (Ăm·à·zī´ ăh) Personal name meaning "Yahweh is mighty." **1.** A Simeonite (1 Chron. 4:34). **2.** A Levite and a descendant of Merari (1 Chron. 6:45). **3.** Priest at Bethel who sent Amos the prophet home, saying he did not have the right to prophesy against King Jeroboam II of Israel (789–746 B.C.) in the king's place of worship (Amos 7:10-17). **4.** Ninth king of Judah, the son of Joash and father of Uzziah (797–767 B.C.). He was 25 years old when he ascended the throne. He speedily avenged the murder of his father, who had been killed by court servants. Amaziah was uncommonly merciful in his avenging, as he only murdered the guilty servants, not the servants' children (2 Kings 14:5-6).

Among Amaziah's accomplishments, he conscripted an army for Judah, composed of all men age 20 and above. He also hired mercenaries from Israel but declined to use them at the advice of a "man of God" (2 Chron. 25:7). Amaziah led his army to Seir, where he easily defeated the Edomites, making them again subject to Judah. Yet he took Edomite idols back to Jerusalem and worshiped them. He then refused to listen to the rebuke and the forecast of doom brought by God's prophet (2 Chron. 25:11-16).

Encouraged by his victory in Edom, Amaziah challenged Joash, king of Israel, to battle. Though Joash tried to avoid a conflict, Amaziah persisted and was defeated at the hands of Israel. The temple and royal palace were plundered, the wall of Jerusalem was pierced, and Amaziah was taken prisoner. Amaziah survived Joash by 15 years. Because of a conspiracy against him, he fled to Lachish but was murdered there. See *Chronology of the Biblical Period; Jehoaddan; Joash; Uzziah.* *Ronald E. Bishop*

AMBASSADOR Representative of one royal court to another. According to the KJV, NASB, and NIV reading of Josh. 9:4, the Gibeonites pretended to be official ambassadors from a foreign government as they approached Joshua (cp. NRSV). The king of Babylon sent official ambassadors to learn of Hezekiah's power (2 Chron. 32:31). Pharaoh Necho sent ambassadors to prevent King Josiah of Judah (640–609 B.C.) from joining in the battle at Megiddo, but Josiah persisted and died (2 Chron. 35:21-24). Faithful ambassadors bring health to a nation (Prov. 13:17). Isaiah condemned Israel for sending ambassadors to Egypt seeking military aid rather than seeking God's aid (Isa. 30:4). While they suffered before God's announced salvation, the people lamented before God. This included ambassadors who had unsuccessfully worked for peace (Isa. 33:7). Israel consistently relied on ambassadors to foreign lands rather than on Yahweh and His plan (Isa. 57:9). Jeremiah announced that God had prompted an ambassador to call the nations to punish Edom (Jer. 49:14; cp. Obad. 1). Ezekiel condemned King Zedekiah (597–586 B.C.) for sending ambassadors to Egypt seeking help in rebelling against Babylon (Ezek. 17:15).

Paul saw himself even in prison as an ambassador sent by the divine King to proclaim salvation through Christ to the world (Eph. 6:20; cp. 2 Cor. 5:20).

AMBER Yellowish or brownish translucent resin that takes a good polish. Also translated as gleaming bronze in RSV, but amber in NRSV, glowing metal in NASB and NIV, and bronze in TEV (Ezek. 1:4,27; 8:2). Some think that the Greek (Septuagint) and Latin (Vulgate) translations of the OT suggest the substance known as electrum—an amalgam of silver and gold. See *Jewels, Jewelry.*

AMBUSH Military tactic of hiding a unit of troops for surprise attack while carrying on normal battle with the remainder of the troops. Joshua used the tactic against Ai (Josh. 8). The people of Shechem waited in hiding to attack and rob people who crossed the mountain (Judg. 9:25; cp. Hos. 6:9). Abimelech used ambush to defeat Shechem (Judg. 9:43-45). Israel used ambush to attack Gibeah and the rebellious tribe of Benjamin (Judg. 20:29-43). Saul apparently used similar tactics against the Amalekites (1 Sam. 15:5). Jeroboam, king of Israel (926–909 B.C.) tried unsuccessfully to ambush Judah (2 Chron. 13:13). God set ambushes against Moab, Ammon, and Edom to defeat them for King Jehoshaphat (873–848 B.C.). God delivered Ezra from ambush attempts (Ezra 8:31).

The psalmists asked for God's help against wicked persons who sought to ambush them (Pss. 10:8; 59:3; 64:4; cp. Prov. 1:11,18). Jeremiah accused his people of spiritual ambush against one another (Jer. 9:8). He also called for ambushes to defeat Babylon (Jer. 51:12). The people of Jerusalem lamented that the enemy had used ambushes to defeat and destroy the city and nation (Lam. 4:19). Paul's nephew saved him from Jewish plans to ambush him as the Roman authorities transferred him from Jerusalem to Caesarea (Acts 23:12-33; cp. 25:3).

AMEN Transliteration of Hebrew word signifying something as certain, sure and valid, truthful and faithful. It is sometimes translated "so be it." In the OT it is used to show the acceptance of the validity of a curse or an oath (Num. 5:22; Deut. 27:15-26; Jer. 11:5), to indicate acceptance of a good message (Jer. 28:6), and to join in a doxology in a worship setting to affirm what has been said or prayed (1 Chron. 16:36; Neh.

8:6; Ps. 106:48). "Amen" may confirm what already is, or it may indicate a hope for something desired. In Jewish prayer "amen" comes at the end as an affirmative response to a statement or wish made by others, and is so used in the NT epistles (Rom. 1:25; 11:36; 15:33; 1 Cor. 16:24; Gal. 1:5; Eph. 3:21; Phil. 4:20). Paul ended some of his letters with "amen" (Rom. 6:27; Gal. 6:18). Ancient authorities add "amen" in other letters, but translations reflect this only in their notes.

In the Gospels Jesus used "amen" to affirm the truth of His own statements. English translations often use "verily," "truly," "I tell you the truth" to translate Jesus' "amen." He never said it at the end of a statement but always at the beginning: "Amen, I say to you" (Matt. 5:18; 16:28; Mark 8:12; 11:23; Luke 4:24; 21:32; John 1:51; 5:19). In John's Gospel Jesus said "Amen, amen." That Jesus prefaced His own words with "amen" is especially important, for He affirmed that the kingdom of God is bound up with His own person and emphasized the authority of what He said.

Jesus is called "the Amen" in Rev. 3:14, meaning that He Himself is the reliable and true witness of God. Perhaps the writer had in mind Isa. 65:16 where the Hebrew says "God of Amen."   *Roger L. Omanson*

AMETHYST Deep purple variety of stone of the aluminum oxide family. Used in the breastplate of the high priest (Exod. 28:19; 39:12) and the twelfth stone in the foundation wall of the new Jerusalem (Rev. 21:20). See *Jewels, Jewelry; Minerals and Metals.*

AMI (Ā´ mī) Personal name with uncertain meaning. A servant in the temple after the exile belonging to a group called "children of Solomon's servants" (Ezra 2:55-57). Ami is apparently called Amon in Neh. 7:59.

AMINADAB (Á·mĭn´ á·dăb) (KJV, NT) See *Amminadab.*

AMITTAI (Á·mĭt´ taî) Personal name meaning "loyal," "true." Father of the prophet Jonah who lived in Gath-hepher (2 Kings 14:25).

AMIZZABAD (TEV) See *Ammizabad.*

AMMAH (Ăm´ mah) Hill near Giah in the territory of Gibeon between Jerusalem and Bethel.

There Joab and Abishai pursued Abner after he killed Asahel, their brother (2 Sam. 2:24).

AMMI (Ăm´ mī) Name meaning "my people" was given to Israel by Hosea in contrast to the name Lo-ammi (Hos. 1:9) meaning "not my people." The name Lo-ammi was given to the third child of Gomer, the wife of Hosea the prophet, to pronounce God's rejection of Israel. The name "Ammi" was the new name to be given to the restored Israel in the day of redemption.

AMMIEL (Ăm´ mĭ·ĕl) Personal name meaning "people of God" or "God is of my people," that is, God is my relative. **1.** Spy that represented the tribe of Dan whom Moses sent to spy out the promised land. He was one of 10 who brought a bad report and led people to refuse to enter the land (Num. 13:12). **2.** Father of Machir, in whose house Mephibosheth, son of Jonathan and grandson of Saul, lived after the death of his father and grandfather. The family lived in Lo-debar (2 Sam. 9:4; 17:27). **3.** Father of Bathshua, David's wife (1 Chron. 3:5). Second Samuel 11:3 speaks of Bathsheba, daughter of Eliam. Many Bible students think these verses are talking about the same person, whose names have been slightly altered in the process of copying the manuscripts. **4.** Gatekeeper of the temple whom David appointed (1 Chron. 26:5).

AMMIHUD (Ăm·mī´ hŭd) Personal name meaning "my people are splendid." **1.** Father of Elishama, who represented the tribe of Ephraim to help Moses during the wilderness wandering (Num. 1:10). He presented the tribe's offerings at the dedication of the altar (7:48) and led them in marching (10:22). He was Joshua's grandfather (1 Chron. 7:26). **2.** Father of Shemuel of the tribe of Simeon, who helped Moses, Eleazar, and Joshua allot the land to the tribes (Num. 34:20). **3.** Father of Pedahel of the tribe of Naphtali, who helped allot the land (Num. 34:28). **4.** Father of King of Geshur to whom Absalom fled after he killed his brother Amnon (2 Sam. 13:37). **5.** Member of tribe of Judah who returned from exile (1 Chron. 9:4).

AMMINADAB (Ăm·mĭn´ á·dăb) Personal name meaning "my people give freely." **1.** Aaron's father-in-law (Exod. 6:23). Father of Nahshon, who led tribe of Judah in the wilderness (Num. 1:7). Ancestor of David (Ruth 4:19) and Jesus (Matt. 1:4; Luke 3:33). **2.** Son of

Kohath in genealogy of Levites (1 Chron. 6:22), but this may be copyist's change for Izhar (Exod. 6:18,21). **3.** Head of a family of Levites (1 Chron. 15:10). He helped carry the ark of the covenant to Jerusalem (1 Chron. 15:11-29).

AMMI-NADIB (Ăm´ mĭ-nă´ dĭb) KJV takes these words as a personal name in Song 6:12. Most modern versions express uncertainty about the translation of this verse. Some modern translations translate *ammi-nadib* as "my noble people" (NASB, HCSB) or "my people" (NIV), while others translate "my prince" (NRSV) or "chariot driver" (TEV). Some versions (NIV, REB, TEV) take the verse as spoken by the young man. The NRSV takes the words in verse 12 as coming from the maiden who spoke about her fancy (perhaps her imagination) setting her in a chariot beside her prince. Because of the confusion, James Moffatt did not even attempt a translation.

AMMISHADDAI (Ăm´ mĭ·shăd´ daî) Father of Ahiezer, the leader of the tribe of Dan in the wilderness. (Num. 1:12) The name Ammishaddai means "people of the Almighty."

AMMIZABAD (Ăm´ mĭz´ à·băd) Personal name meaning "my people give." Son of Benaiah, one of captains of David's army (1 Chron. 27:6).

AMMON, AMMONITES Territory east of the Jordan roughly equivalent to the modern state of Jordan. The Ammonites were a Semitic people living northeast of the Dead Sea in the area surrounding Rabbah who often battled with the Israelites for possession of the fertile Gilead. Ammon, the kingdom of the Ammonites, was hardly more than a city-state, consisting of the capital city itself, Rabbah or Rabbath-Ammon ("chief city," or "chief city of the Ammonites") and its immediately surrounding territory. Rabbath was located at the headwaters of the Jabbok River, where the southeastern

corner of Gilead gives way to the desert. The agricultural productivity of Gilead, the waters of the Jabbok itself and of associated springs, as well as Rabbah's naturally defendable position, destined Rabbah to be a city of medium importance in ancient times. The proximity of the Ammonites to Gilead likewise destined them to be constant enemies of the Israelites, who made claims to Gilead and actually controlled it during the reigns of certain strong kings such as David, Omri, Ahab, and Jeroboam II.

Most of our information about the Ammonites comes from the OT, although Ammonite kings are mentioned occasionally in the Assyrian records. We know from the latter, for example, that an Ammonite king named Ba'sha, along with Ahab of Israel and other kings of the region, defended Syria-Palestine against

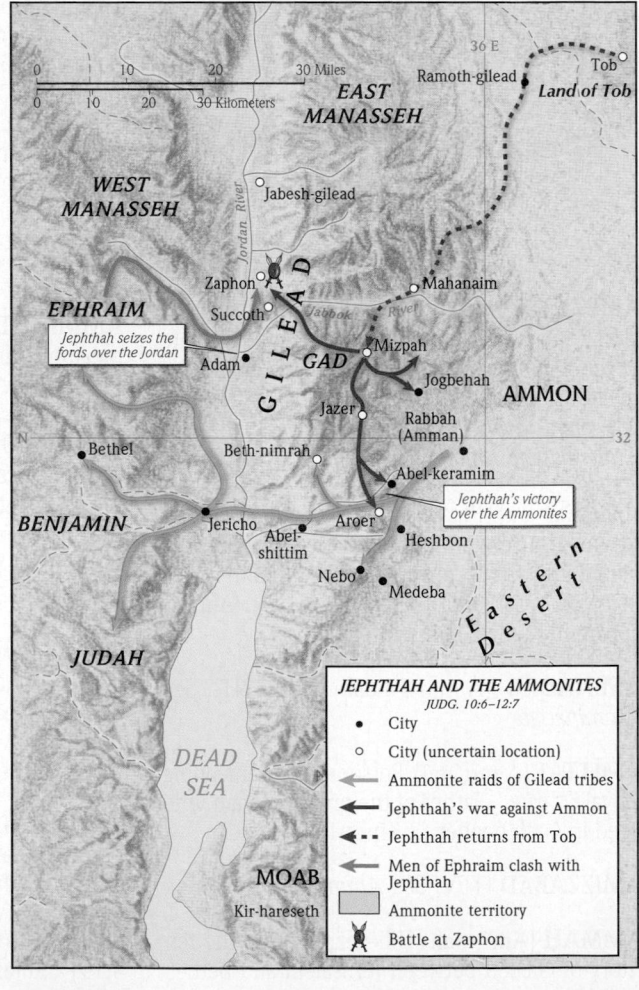

JEPHTHAH AND THE AMMONITES
JUDG. 10:6–12:7

- • City
- ○ City (uncertain location)
- ← Ammonite raids of Gilead tribes
- ← Jephthah's war against Ammon
- ◄·· Jephthah returns from Tob
- ← Men of Ephraim clash with Jephthah
- ▨ Ammonite territory
- ⚔ Battle at Zaphon

Shalmaneser III in 853 B.C. An Ammonite inscription, the so-called Siran Bottle Inscription and several seals/seal impressions have provided additional information about the Ammonites.

Archaeologists have excavated only a small portion of the site of ancient Rabbah (the so-called "citadel" in the heart of the modern city of Amman). The surrounding area remains largely unexplored. In addition to the inscription and seals mentioned above, the bust of an Ammonite warrior (or god) and the remains of round stone towers thought to be Ammonite are significant archaeological discoveries shedding light on the Ammonites.

Conflict broke out between the Ammonites and Israelites as early as the time of the Judges. The Ammonites made war on the Israelites of Gilead, leading the Israelites to appeal to Jephthah, chief of a local band of renegade raiders, to organize and lead their resistance. Jephthah accepted the challenge but only after extracting a promise from the elders of Gilead that, if he indeed succeeded in defeating the Ammonites, they would recognize him as ruler of Gilead. At the same time he vowed to Yahweh, "If you will give the Ammonites into my hand, then whoever comes out of the doors of my house to meet me, when I return victorious from the Ammonites, shall be the LORD's, to be offered up by me as a burnt offering" (Judg. 11:30b-31 NRSV). Jephthah was victorious, and the Gileadites submitted to his rule, but then his little daughter greeted him upon his return (Judg. 10:6–11:40).

On another occasion when the Ammonites were attacking the city of Jabesh in Gilead and the Jabeshites attempted to negotiate terms for surrender, the Ammonites demanded nothing less than to put out the right eye of each man in the city. In desperation the Jabeshites sent messengers to Saul at Gibeah for help. Saul organized an army, hurried to Jabesh, and lifted the siege. Consequently, the Jabeshites were strong supporters of Saul in later years (1 Sam. 11; 31:11-13). The Ammonite king that Saul defeated at Jabesh was Nahash. Presumably this was the same Nahash with whom David had good dealings but whose son, Hanun, renewed hostilities (2 Sam. 10:1–11:1; 12:26-31). The ensuing wars between Israel and Ammon involved warfare between David's troops and those of Hadadezer of Zobah (2 Sam. 10:6-19) and provided the occasion of David's affair with

Bathsheba. Uriah, Bathsheba's husband, was killed while storming the walls of Rabbah (2 Sam. 11–12).

No war with the Ammonites is reported during Solomon's reign. On the contrary, Solomon took one or more Ammonite wives and allowed the worship of Milcom, the Ammonite god, in Jerusalem (1 Kings 11:1-8). Presumably the worship of Milcom continued in Jerusalem until it was stamped out by Josiah many years later (2 Kings 23:13). We know little of relations between the Ammonites and either Israel or Judah during the first half century of the separate kingdoms, probably because neither of the Hebrew kingdoms attempted to exercise influence in the Transjordan. The coalition of Syro-Palestinian kings, which included Ba'sha of Ammon and Ahab of Israel, halted the Assyrian king, Shalmaneser's march in 853 B.C. However, success was only temporary. Later Shalmaneser penetrated the very heart of Syria-Palestine, exacting tribute from the Israelites and, although it is not recorded, probably also from the Ammonites. Eventually, all the petty kingdoms of the region fell to the Assyrians and either were incorporated into the Assyrian province system or controlled as satellites. Ammonite kings paid tribute to Tiglath-pileser III, Sennacherib, and Esarhaddon.

The Israelites recognized the Ammonites as relatives, although somewhat more distant than the Edomites. This relationship was expressed genealogically. Specifically, the Ammonites were descended from an ancestor named Ben-ammi, one of two sons that Lot bore to his two daughters. The Moabites were descended from the other son (Gen. 19:30-38). The Ammonites also are mentioned from time to time in Israel's poetical literature. See, for example, Amos' oracle against the Ammonites in Amos 1:13-15.

Rabbah apparently had dwindled to an insignificant settlement by the third century B.C. when Ptolemy II Philadelphus (285–246) rebuilt the city and renamed it "Philadelphia" after himself. Philadelphia came to be regarded as one of the Decapolis cities, a federation of 10 Greek cities in Palestine (Matt. 4:25), and was annexed with the whole Decapolis region to the Roman Empire in A.D. 90.   *J. Maxwell Miller*

AMNON (Ăm´ nŏn) Personal name meaning "trustworthy, faithful." **1.** Firstborn son of King David (2 Sam. 3:2). He raped his half sister

Tamar. Tamar's brother Absalom avenged this outrage by killing Amnon (2 Sam. 13:1-20). This incident marked the beginning of the decline of David's family following his adulterous relationship with Bathsheba and the murder of Uriah. See *David*. **2.** Member of tribe of Judah (1 Chron. 4:20).

AMOK (Ā´ mŏk) Personal name meaning "deep." A priestly family after the return from exile (Neh. 12:7,20).

AMON (Ā´ mŏn) Personal name meaning "faithful." **1.** Governor of Samaria when Jehoshaphat was king of Judah, who followed orders from the king of Israel and put the prophet Micaiah in prison (1 Kings 22:26). **2.** King of Judah (642 B.C.) following his father Manasseh. He followed the infamous idolatry of his father and was killed in a palace revolt (2 Kings 21:19-23). The people of Judah, in turn, killed the rebels. Good King Josiah, Amon's son, succeeded to his throne. See Matt. 1:10. **3.** Ancestor of temple staff members after the exile (Neh. 7:59), called Ami in Ezra 2:57. **4.** Egyptian god whose worship center at Thebes Jeremiah threatened with divine destruction (Jer. 46:25). KJV translates "the multitude of No."

AMORITES People who occupied part of the promised land and often fought Israel. Their history goes back before 2000 B.C. They took control of the administration of Babylonia for approximately 400 years (2000–1595), their most influential king being Hammurabi (1792–1750). Their descent to Canaan may be traced back to 2100–1800 when their settlement in the hill country helped to set the stage for the revelation of God through Israel.

Abraham assisted Mamre the Amorite in recovering his land from four powerful kings (Gen. 14), but later the Amorites were a formidable obstacle to the Israelites' conquest and settlement of Canaan. They preferred living in the hills and valleys that flank both sides of the Jordan River. Sihon and Og, two Amorite kings, resisted the Israelites' march to Canaan as they approached east of the Jordan (Num. 21:21-35); but after the Israelite victory here, Gad, Reuben and half of Manasseh settled in the conquered area. These two early victories over the Amorites foreshadowed continued success against other Amorites to the west and were often remembered in both history (Deut. 3:8; Josh. 12:2; Judg. 11:19) and poetry (Num. 21:27-30; Pss. 135:10-12; 136:17-22). West of the Jordan the Amorites lived in the hills along with the Hivites, Hittites, and Jebusites (Num. 13:29; Josh. 11:3); but specific identification of Amorite cities cannot be certain since the term "Amorite" is used often as a very general name for all the inhabitants of Canaan, as is "Canaanite" (Gen. 15:16; Josh. 24:15; Judg. 6:10; 1 Kings 21:26). Five city-states in south Canaan formed an alliance instigated by the king of Jerusalem (Jebus, Jebusites) and intimidated an ally of Joshua, Gibeon. These "Amorites," as they are called in the general sense, were defeated by Joshua's army and the Lord's "stones from heaven" (Josh. 10:1-27). Amorites also were among those in the north who unsuccessfully united to repel the Israelites (Josh. 11:1-15). Later two other Amorite cities, Aijalon and Shaalbim, hindered the settlement of Dan near the Philistine border (Judg. 1:34-36).

Amorite culture lay at the root of Jerusalem's decadence, according to Ezekiel (Ezek. 16:3,45); and Amorite idolatry tainted the religion of the Northern and Southern Kingdoms (1 Kings 21:26; 2 Kings 21:11). Despite the Amorite resistance and poor influence, they were subjugated as slaves (Judg. 1:35; 1 Kings 9:20-21; 2 Chron. 8:7-8). Their past hindrance is a subject of derision for the prophet Amos (Amos 2:9-10). See *Babylon; Jebusites; Sihon; Syria.*   *Daniel C. Fredericks*

AMOS (Ā´ mŏs) Personal name meaning "burdened" or, more likely, "one who is supported [by God]." Prophet from Judah who ministered in Israel about 750 B.C.

Amos was a layperson who disclaimed professional status as a prophet: "I am no prophet, nor a prophet's son, but I am a herdsman, and a dresser of sycamore trees, and the Lord took me from following the flock, and the Lord said to me, 'Go, prophesy to my people Israel'" (7:14-15 RSV). Because of God's call, Amos assumed his prophetic responsibilities as a lonely voice prophesying from both the desert and the villages. He indicted both Judah and Israel, challenging the superficial qualities of religious institutions. For Amos, his call and his continuing ministry rested in God's initiative and in His sustaining power: "The lion has roared; who will

3. God's inescapable judgment is on His people (5:10-13,16-20).
4. Practical righteousness is God's ultimate demand of His people (5:21-27).
F. False security in national strength leads to ultimate downfall (6:1-14).
II. The Visions: Seeing God Properly Reveals Both His Judgment and His Mercy (7:1–9:15).
A. God extends mercy in response to serious intercession (7:1-6).
B. Ultimate confrontation with God can never be escaped (7:7-9).
C. A proper view of God brings everything else into perspective (7:10-17).
1. A false view of the nature of God's message leads to wrong decisions (7:10-13).
2. A person transformed by a vision of God sees people and things as they really are (7:14-17).
D. The final consequence of sin offers judgment without hope (8:1–9:4).
1. An overripe, rotten religion is worthless (8:1-3).
2. The empty observance of meaningless ritual leaves our morality unaffected (8:4-6).
3. God's final judgment is a horrible sight (8:7–9:4).
E. God's mercy can be seen beyond His judgment (9:5-15).
1. God is Sovereign over the entire universe (9:5-6).
2. God's mercy still offers hope beyond temporal judgment (9:7-10).
3. God's ultimate purpose of good for His people will be fulfilled (9:11-15).

Roy L. Honeycutt

AMOZ (Ā´ măz) Name means "strong." Father of the prophet Isaiah (2 Kings 19:2).

AMPHIPOLIS (Ăm·phĭp´ o·lĭs) City near the Aegean Gulf between Thessalonica and Philippi. Paul and Silas passed through it on their way to Thessalonica on Paul's second missionary journey (Acts 17:1) as they traveled the famous Egnatian Way.

AMPLIAS (Ăm´ plĭ·ás) or **AMPLIATUS** (Ăm·plĭ·ā´ tus) Christian convert in Rome to whom Paul sent greetings (Rom. 16:8). Amplias was a common name often given to slaves. Paul referred to this individual as "my dear friend in the Lord" (HCSB), which may suggest a particularly warm and affectionate relationship between Amplias and the apostle. Modern translations spell the name "Ampliatus."

AMRAM (Ăm´ răm) Personal name meaning "exalted people." **1.** Father of Moses, Aaron, and Miriam and grandson of Levi (Exod. 6:18-20). Moses' father, Amram, was the father of the Levitical family, the Amramites (Num. 3:27; 1 Chron. 26:23), who served in the wilderness sanctuary and may have served in the temple treasuries in later years. **2.** One of the 12 sons of Bani who was guilty of marrying foreign women (Ezra 10:34). **3.** One of four sons of Dishon in 1 Chron. 1:41. In Gen. 36:26 the four sons of Dishon are also listed; however Amram is listed as Hemdan. Translations other than the KJV list this son of Dishon as Hemdan in Chronicles as well as Genesis.

AMRAPHEL (Ăm´ rá·phĕl) Personal name, probably originally Akkadian, meaning "the God Amurru paid back" or "the mouth of God has spoken." King of Shinar or Babylon who joined a coalition to defeat Sodom and Gomorrah, then other kings in Canaan and the Dead Sea area. The kings captured Lot. Hearing the news, Abraham assembled an army, defeated the coalition, and rescued Lot (Gen. 14:1-16). Amraphel cannot be equated with any other king of whom records are available from the ancient Near East.

AMULETS (Ăm´ ū lĕts) NASB, RSV translation of rare Hebrew word for charms inscribed with oaths, which women wore to ward off evil (Isa. 3:20). NIV translates "charms," KJV, "earrings."

AMZI (Ăm´ zī) Personal name meaning "my strong one," or an abbreviation for Amaziah. **1.** Member of temple singer family (1 Chron. 6:46). **2.** Ancestor of Adaiah, who helped build the second temple (Neh. 11:12).

ANAB (Ā´ năb) Place-name meaning "grape." Joshua eliminated the Anakim from southern Judah including Hebron, Debir, and Anab (Josh. 11:21). Joshua allotted the mountain city to

Judah (Josh. 15:50). Located at modern Khirbet Anab about 15 miles southwest of Hebron.

ANAH (Ā´ näh) Personal name meaning "answer." **1.** Mother of Oholibamah, a wife of Esau (Gen. 36:2), and grandmother of Jeush, Jalam, and Korah (36:14). RSV reads "daughter" as "son." This would allow this Anah to be related to or identified with Anah 2. below. In Gen. 36:24 Anah is noted for having found "mules in the wilderness" (KJV) or "hot springs in the desert" (NIV; cp. NASB, RSV). Here Zibeon is still Anah's father as in 36:2, but this Anah is masculine. In 36:29 Anah is a Horite chief living in Seir. **2.** Son of Seir and brother of Zibeon (Gen. 36:20).

ANAHARATH (Á·nā´ há·răth) Place-name meaning "gorge." City on border of Issachar (Josh. 19:19) located possibly at modern Tell el-Mukharkhash between Mount Tabor and the Jordan.

ANAIAH (Á·naî´ ăh) Personal name meaning "Yahweh answered." Ezra's assistant when Ezra read the law to the postexilic community (Neh. 8:4). He or another man of the same name signed Nehemiah's covenant to obey God's law (Neh. 10:22).

ANAK, ANAKIM (Ā´ năk, Ăn´ á·kĭm), **ANAKITES** (NIV) Personal and clan name meaning "longnecked" or "strongnecked." The ancestor named Anak had three children: Ahiman, Sheshai, Talmai (Num. 13:22). They lived in Hebron and the hill country (Josh. 11:21) before being destroyed by Joshua. Their remnants then lived among the Philistines (Josh. 11:22). These tall giants were part of the Nephilim (Gen. 6:4; Num. 13:33). Arba was a hero of the Anakim (Josh. 14:15). The spelling of "Anakims" puts the English plural "s" on to the Hebrew plural "im." NIV uses "Anakites."

ANAM (Ā´ năm) NASB reading of 1 Chron. 1:11, interpreting Anam as an individual rather than as a tribe or nation. See *Anamim*.

ANAMMELECH (Á·năm´ mĕ·lĕk) Personal name meaning "Anu is king." A god of the Sepharvites who occupied part of Israel after the Northern Kingdom was exiled in 721 B.C. Worshipers sacrificed children to this god (2 Kings 17:31).

ANAMIM (Ăn´ á·mĭm) or **ANAMITES** (NIV) Tribe or nation called "son of Egypt" in Gen. 10:13. No further information is known about these people. See *Anam.*

ANAN (Ā´ năn) Personal name meaning "cloud." Signer of Nehemiah's covenant to obey God (Neh. 10:26).

ANANI (Á·nā´ nī) Personal name meaning "cloudy" or "he heard me." Descendant of David's royal line living after the return from exile (1 Chron. 3:24).

ANANIAH (Ăn·á·nī´ ah) Personal name meaning "Yahweh heard me." **1.** Grandfather of Azariah, who helped Nehemiah repair Jerusalem (Neh. 3:23). **2.** Village where tribe of Benjamin dwelt in time of Nehemiah (Neh. 11:32). It may be located at Bethany, east of Jerusalem.

ANANIAS (Ăn á nī´ ás) Greek form of the Hebrew name Hananiah, which means "Yahweh has dealt graciously." **1.** Husband of Sapphira (Acts 5:1-6). They sold private property, the proceeds of which they were to give to the common fund of the early Jerusalem church (Acts 4:32-34). They did not give all the proceeds from the sale, as they claimed, and both were struck dead for having lied to the Holy Spirit (Acts 5:5,10). **2.** Disciple who lived in the city of Damascus (Acts 9:10-19). In response to a vision he received from the Lord, this Ananias visited Saul (Paul) three days after Saul had his Damascus road experience. Ananias laid his hands on Saul, after which Saul received both the Holy Spirit and his sight. Acts 9:18 may imply that Ananias was the one who baptized Saul. **3.** Jewish high priest from A.D. 47 to 58 (Acts 23:2; 24:1). As high priest, he was president of the Jewish court known as the Sanhedrin which tried Paul in Jerusalem (Acts 23). As was typical of high priests that belonged to the aristocratic Jewish group known as the Sadducees, he was quite concerned to appease Roman authorities and representatives. This desire may have prompted Ananias to take such a personal interest in the case of Paul (Acts 24:1-2), since some Roman authorities suspected the apostle of sedition against Rome (Acts 21:38). Because of Ananias' pro-Roman sentiments, he was assassinated by anti-Roman Jewish revolutionaries at the outbreak of the first great Jewish revolt against Rome in the year A.D. 66. See *Sadducees; Sanhedrin.*

ANATH (Ā´ năth) Personal name meaning "answer," or it was the name of a Canaanite god. Father of Shamgar, a judge of Israel (Judg. 3:31).

ANATHEMA Greek translation of Hebrew *cherem*; booty taken in a holy war that must be thoroughly destroyed (Lev. 27:28; Deut. 20:10-18). The total destruction of this booty showed that it was being completely turned over to God. In the NT, "anathema" has two seemingly opposite meanings. It means gifts dedicated to God (Luke 21:5 HCSB) as well as something cursed. Paul invoked such a curse on those who did not love the Lord (1 Cor. 16:22) as well as one who preached another gospel other than the gospel of grace (Gal. 1:8-9). It is from these uses that anathema has come to mean banned or excommunicated by a religious body. Paul said he was willing to become *anathema*, cursed and cut off from the Messiah for the benefit of his Jewish brothers (Rom. 9:3 HCSB).

ANATHOTH (Ăn´ à·thôth) Personal and place-name. **1.** City assigned to the tribe of Benjamin, located about three miles northeast of Jerusalem (Josh. 21:18). King Solomon sent Abiathar the priest there after removing him as high priest (1 Kings 2:26-27). It was also the home of Jeremiah the prophet, who may have been a priest in the rejected line of Abiathar (Jer. 1:1). Though Jeremiah was opposed and threatened by the citizens of Anathoth (Jer. 11:21-23), he purchased a field there from his cousin Hanameel in obedience to the word of the Lord to symbolize ultimate hope after exile (Jer. 32:6-15). Anathoth was overrun by the Babylonians but resettled following the exile (Neh. 7:27; 11:32). **2.** The eighth of nine sons of Becher, the son of Benjamin (1 Chron. 7:8). **3.** A chief that is a family or clan leader, who along with 84 other priests, Levites, and leaders signed a covenant that the Israelites would obey the law of God given through Moses (Neh. 10:19).

ANCESTORS Those from whom a person is descended both literally and figuratively. Some English versions use the term frequently to translate *'abot* in the OT and *pater* in the NT, both of which are the normal word for "father," "grandfather," etc. When these words are plural and the context deals with the past, the term usually refers to male ancestors or forefathers. Likewise, genealogies normally list male ancestors.

Ancestor Worship Ancestor worship is the adoration or payment of homage to a deceased parent or ancestor. Such worship was usually reserved for deities. Among ancient Israel's neighbors, there are several instances of deification of ancestors (Mesopotamian mythology and Egyptian kings). There may be one instance of ancestor worship recorded in the Bible. Ezekiel 43:7-9 may suggest that the bodies of Israel's dead kings were being worshiped. This practice of ancestor worship was condemned and forbidden.

Cult of the Dead Much like ancestor worship, the cult of the dead involves adoration of the deceased. The cult of the dead goes a step beyond adoration, however, seeking to maintain or manage a relationship with the dead. The cult of the dead involves the beliefs that certain departed spirits must be fed or honored and that they can be channels of information with the spiritual world.

While ancestor worship was not common among Israel or her neighbors, the cult of the dead was widely practiced. The belief in an afterlife was apparently universal in the ancient Near East. The provision of food, drink, and artifacts within tombs is an indication of the belief that the departed spirit would have need of such things.

Though Israel was forbidden to practice the cult of the dead, she often departed from God's injunctions and engaged in the worship of pagan deities. Wayward Israelites were also guilty of practicing the cult of the dead (1 Sam. 28). Israel was specifically warned not to offer to the dead (Deut. 26:14). God warned them through the prophets not to consult the dead in an effort to learn the future (Isa. 8:19; 65:4). Such acts were considered by the prophets to be dangerously at odds with God's will. See *Burial; Divination and Magic; Genealogies; God, Pagan; Medium.*

Larry Bruce and E. Ray Clendenen

ANCHOR Weight held on the end of a cable that when submerged in water holds a ship in place. Anchors were made of stone, iron, and lead during biblical times. The ship on which Paul sailed to Rome let down four anchors as it approached Malta (Acts 27:29-30,40). "Anchor" is used in a figurative sense in Heb. 6:19 where the hope of the gospel is compared to "an anchor of the soul, both sure and steadfast"—that is, a spiritual support in times of trial.

ANCIENT OF DAYS Phrase used in Dan. 7:9,13,22 to describe the everlasting God. Ancient of days literally means "one advanced in (of) days" and may possibly mean "one who forwards time or rules over it."

Several biblical passages are related in terms and ideas with Dan. 7 (Gen. 24:1; Job 36:26; Pss. 50:1-6; 55:19; 1 Kings 22:19-20; Isa. 26:1–27:1; 44:6; Ezek. 1; Joel 3:2). It is impossible to determine the origin or original meaning of this term. However, in ancient Ugaritic literature, the god *El* is designated as "the father of years."

Coupled with the figures of speech in the context of Dan. 7, "Ancient of Days" suggests age, antiquity, dignity, endurance, judgment, and wisdom. It clearly describes Yahweh, the God of Israel.   *J. J. Owens*

ANDREW Disciple of John the Baptist who became one of Jesus' first disciples and led his brother Simon to Jesus. Because of John the Baptist's witness concerning Jesus, Andrew followed Jesus to His overnight lodging and became one of His first disciples. Subsequently Andrew brought his brother Simon to Jesus (John 1:40-41). He was a fisherman by trade (Matt. 4:18). He questioned Jesus about His prophesy concerning the temple (Mark 13:3). Andrew brought the lad with his lunch to Jesus, leading to the feeding of the 5,000 (John 6:8). He and Philip brought some Greeks to see Jesus (John 12:22). He is mentioned for the last time in Acts 1:13. He figures prominently in several early extrabiblical church traditions. He is believed to have been killed on an x-shaped cross. See *Disciple.*

ANDRONICUS (Ăn·drŏn´ ĭ·cŭs) Kinsman of Paul, honored by the church. He had suffered in prison for his faith and had been a Christian longer than Paul (Rom. 16:7). Evidently he lived in Rome when Paul wrote Romans. He is referred to as an "apostle" in the broadest sense, meaning "messenger."

ANEM (Ā´ nĕm) Place-name meaning "fountains." A city given the Levites from the territory of Issachar (1 Chron. 6:73). Joshua 21:29 lists the city as En-gannim.

ANER (Ā´ nēr) Personal and place-name. **1.** Ally of Abraham in the battle against the coalition of kings in Gen. 14. **2.** City from tribe of Manasseh given to Levites (1 Chron. 6:70). In Josh. 21:25 the Levites' city is called Taanach. See *Taanach.*

ANETHOTHITE KJV for Anathothite in 2 Sam. 23:27. See *Anathoth.*

ANGEL Created beings whose primary function is to serve and worship God. Though some interpret the "us" in Gen. 1:26 as inclusive of God and His angelic court, the Bible does not comment as to when they were created. Unlike God they are not eternal or omniscient. The Hebrew word in the OT is *mal'ak,* and the NT Greek word is *angelos.* They both mean "messenger" and occasionally refer to human messengers.

Classification of Angels Angels not only carry messages to people (Gen. 18:9-16; Judg. 13:2-24; Luke 1:13,30; 2:8-15), they also carry out God's will as He directs them (Ps. 148:2-5; Col. 1:16). The Bible offers little description of angelic messengers because the focus is on the message and not the messenger. Angels also performed tasks as mediators (Acts 7:53; Gal. 3:19; Rev. 1:1; 10:1).

Angels also serve God in His heavenly court. Titles such as "sons of God" (Gen. 6:2-4; Job 1:6; 2:1), "holy ones" (Ps. 89:5; Dan. 4:13), and "heavenly hosts" (Luke 2:13) identify angels as celestial beings who worship God (Luke 2:13-15; Rev. 19:1-3), attend His throne (Rev. 5:11; 7:11), and make up God's army (1 Sam. 1:11; 1 Chron. 12:22).

Angels are sometimes identified as winged creatures—the cherubim and seraphim. These angels appear in Ezekiel's visions (1:4-28; 10:1-22) and in Isa. 6:2-6. Cherubim are primarily guards/attendants to God's throne, whereas seraphim attend God's throne and offer praises to Him.

Angelic Appearance The physical appearance of angels varies, based on their categorization. Unlike popular imagery, only cherubim and seraphim have wings. Within biblical texts angels always appear as men and never as women or children. Angels identify with humans on the basis of form, language, and action. Angelic uniqueness is sometimes evidenced in Scripture by their activity or appearing in ways humans do not (Gen. 16:1-11; Exod.

3:2; Num. 22:23; Judg. 6:21; 13:20; John 20:12). The feature of a brilliant white appearance of angels occurs only in the NT (Mark 16:5).

Guardian Angels Though the term "guardian angel" does not occur in the Bible, many people believe angels are assigned to believers for this purpose on a permanent basis. Others hold that angels intervene in human history but in unique situations to assist believers (Pss. 34:7; 91:11-12; Acts 12:6-11,15). Hebrews 1:14 confirms that angels do service to believers but by God's will and under His direction.

Angels are described as heavenly beings in the very presence of God (Matt. 18:10). They cannot be in heaven and on earth simultaneously. A likely interpretation of "their angels" in the presence of God is that they are poised for action at God's command. The angelic guardianship that is apportioned to the faithful appears as a universal phenomenon rather than as an individual one.

Angels at Christ's Return Angels predicted Jesus would personally, bodily, visibly come again to earth (Matt. 25:31; Acts 1:11). In His second advent Christ will descend from heaven (1 Thess. 1:10) with the voice of the archangel and the trump of God (1 Thess. 4:16; 2 Thess. 1:7). According to 2 Thess. 1:7, angels will accompany Him as the executors of His decrees.

Mark 13:26-27 addresses the second coming of "the Son of Man." These verses describe the coming of Jesus with great power and glory and sending His angels to gather His elect. Many scholars assign the fulfillment of prophecy in Mark 13 to A.D. 70 in connection with the Roman destruction of Jerusalem and the temple. It is clear, however, that much of this text refers to His triumphant final return. Verse 27 confirms that the Son of Man will send angels to gather the elect. Angelic appearance often marked a turning point in biblical history (Gen. 18:9-15; Luke 1:13,26-38; 2:8-15). Matthew's parallel passage (24:31) adds that the angels will gather the elect "with a loud trumpet." Angels will gather believers where believers will be like the angels in that they will not die or marry in heaven (Luke 20:35).

By performing this act, angels will assist in vindicating believers in the very presence of their enemies (Rev. 11:12). Angels will worship Christ at His return (Heb. 1:6). Likewise, believ-ers will join the angels in the praise of God in heaven (Rev. 5:13; 19:6).

Angels and the Final Judgment The theme of angelic involvement in divine judgment occurs in both the OT and NT. According to 2 Kings 19:35, the angel of the Lord put to death 185,000 Assyrians, whereas 2 Sam. 24:16 reports that the angel of the Lord brought death to the children of Israel until the Lord told him to stay his hand at Jerusalem (2 Sam. 24:16). Exodus 14:19-20 records that the angel of the Lord stood between the Hebrews and the Egyptians, which resulted in the deliverance of the Hebrews and the subsequent destruction of the Egyptians in the Red Sea.

Some of these references pertained to immediate judgment and some to a final judgment (Gen. 19:12-13; 2 Sam. 24:16-17; 2 Kings 19:35; Ezek. 9:1,5,7). The NT likewise offers several examples of angelic participation in the judgment of evil, including immediate judgment (Acts 12:23) and a futuristic and final judgment (Rev. 8:6–9:21; 16:1-17; 18:1,21; 19:11-14,17-21; 20:1-3). At the crucifixion Jesus could have called upon 12 legions of angels in order to execute immediate judgment on those who crucified and mocked Him (Matt. 26:53).

According to Rev. 14:14-16, "the Son of Man" will gather the grain harvest (the believer), while Rev. 14:17-20 describes angels as gathering the unbelievers for the purpose of judgment. Angels will gather the "wheat" and the "tares" in the name of "the Son of Man" and by His authority (cp. Matt. 13:36-43). Angels will also gather impenitent people for Christ's judgment so that they may be cast into fire (Matt. 13:39-43; 2 Thess. 1:7-10). See *Archangel; Cherub, Cherubim; Seraphim.*

Steven L. Cox

ANGER See *Wrath, Wrath of God.*

ANGLE or **ANGLE OF THE WALL** See *Turning of the Wall.*

ANIAM (A nī´ ăm) Personal name meaning "I am a people," "I am an uncle," or "mourning of the people." A member of the tribe of Manasseh (1 Chron. 7:19).

ANIM (Ā´ nĭm) Place-name meaning "springs." City given tribe of Judah (Josh. 15:50). Located at modern Khirbet Ghuwein at-Tahta, 11 miles south of Hebron.

ANIMAL RIGHTS The Bible provides a clear distinction between animals and people. Though both were created by God (Gen. 1:20-30), people alone were made in His image (Gen. 1:27) and have an immortal soul (Gen. 2:7; 1 Pet. 1:9). Adam's naming of the animals (Gen. 2:19-20) signifies his dominion over them (Gen. 1:26-28; Ps. 8:5-8). This dominion was expanded after the Flood when God gave animals to mankind for food (Gen. 9:3).

Even though Jesus said that people are of greater value than animals (Matt. 6:26), this in no way provides license to mistreat them in any way. Because all animals belong to God (Ps. 50:10), they have great intrinsic worth. People are to care for animals and, when using them, treat them with the utmost dignity.

Just as wild animals are cared for by God (Job 38:39-41; Pss. 104:10-30; 147:7-9; Matt. 6:26), so domesticated animals must be treated well by their human owners (Prov. 12:10; 27:23). The Mosaic law stipulates that animals be fed adequately (Exod. 23:11; Deut. 25:4; cp. 1 Cor. 9:9; 1 Tim. 5:18), helped with their loads (Exod. 23:5), not overworked (Exod. 20:10; Deut. 5:14), and treated fairly (Deut. 22:6-7,10). Ezekiel compared Israel's unjust leaders to shepherds who mistreated their sheep (Ezek. 34:1-6), a situation reversed by Jesus the Good Shepherd (John 10:11; cp. Luke 15:3-6).

Paul H. Wright

ANIMALS In Gen. 1:20-26, on the fifth and sixth days of the creation story, God created the animals. Then He created man to rule over animals. Genesis 2:19-20 indicates that God brought the animals to Adam, the first man, and gave him the task of naming them. Many biblical episodes include the animals as a specific part of their story. As translations have evolved, some of the specific animal names have created confusion because later understandings have given greater knowledge to the general nature of the land and the types of animals existing there. Little is known in some cases what specific animal was actually present or referenced.

Mammals, birds, reptiles, amphibians, fish, and the classification of invertebrates include such a wide range of animals that not all will be found specifically in the Bible, but an attempt has been made to identify those mentioned and to offer some explanation. (Most of the specifically named animals of the Bible will be found under their own alphabetical listing.)

Domestic Generally, the people of Scripture tamed many animals for use in food production, military endeavors, and transportation. Among those found in the biblical text are the ass or donkey, camel, dog, goat, horse, mule, ox, sheep, and swine.

Wild In contrast the wild animals provided food and sport. Frequently biblical people feared them. Some identified in the biblical text are antelope (possibly pygarg [KJV]), ape, badger, bat, bear, behemoth (possibly hippopotamus), boar, coney, deer, dog, dugong, elephant (only referenced in connection with King Solomon and the ivory he imported, 1 Kings 10:22), gazelle, hare, hyena, ibex, jackal, leopard, lion, mole, mouse, ox, porcupine, rat, rodent, weasel, whale, and wolf.

Clean and unclean God established a group of laws specifically for the Israelites concerning clean and unclean animals. He made a stricter distinction for His chosen people than for all the other nations. Whether this distinction was related to idolatry, hygiene, or the ethical and religious nature of the Israelites is debatable. A study of Lev. 11:1-47; 22:4-5; and Deut. 14:1-21 gives the specifics of these regulations. The Apostle Peter had a vision in Acts 10:9-16 indicating that the practice of distinguishing between clean and unclean animals was still taught even in NT times. This distinction has been done away with and is no longer relevant for Christians. See *Clean, Cleanness.*

Amphibians Frogs are the only amphibious animal included in Scripture. They are mentioned prominently in connection with the 10 plagues in Egypt, where frogs were quite common (Exod. 8:2-13). The psalmist reminded the Israelites of that devastating plague in Pss. 78:45 and 105:30. Revelation 16:13 refers to spirits that look like frogs. See *Frogs.*

Birds Mentioned generally and specifically throughout the OT and NT. Some were used for food while others were used for sacrifice. In Luke 9:58 Jesus spoke about the birds having a nest while He had "no place to lay His head." See *Birds.*

Fish Various cold-blooded, aquatic vertebrates with gills (for breathing), fins, and usually scales. Primarily a food source. See *Fish, Fishing.*

Invertebrates Classification of any animal not having a backbone or spinal column. Some have jointed legs, some are legless; some have wings, some have antennae; some even live as parasites. See *Insects; Spiders; Worms.*

Mammals Any class of higher vertebrates including humans and all other animals that nourish their young with milk secreted by mammary glands and have their skin more or less covered with hair. Numerous kinds of mammals can be identified in Scripture with a high degree of certainty even though some in the OT are not as easy to distinguish. (See individual mammal names in the alphabetical dictionary listing.)

Reptiles Members of the class of cold-blooded vertebrates with lungs, bony skeletons, and bodies of scales or horny plates, including the snakes and the dinosaurs. See *Reptiles.*

ANISE KJV translation of the Greek term more properly translated as "dill" in Matt. 23:23. The KJV translates the corresponding Hebrew word as "fitches" in Isa. 28:25,27. Dill is a leafy plant, resembling parsley. It was grown for its seeds, which were aromatic and used in cooking as a seasoning. See *Fitches; Spices.*

ANKLET Ornamental rings worn above the ankles; sometimes called "ankle bracelets." The KJV has "tinkling ornaments about their feet"

(Isa. 3:18; cp. 3:16). Anklets were luxury items worn by the women of Jerusalem during the days of Isaiah. Archaeologists have recovered anklets that date to the biblical period. They were made of bronze, from 2 ½ to 4 ½ inches in diameter and from about $2/10$ to $4/10$ of an inch wide. See *Jewels, Jewelry.*

ANNA Aged prophetess who recognized the Messiah when He was brought to the temple for dedication (Luke 2:36). Anna, whose name means "grace," was the daughter of Phanuel of the tribe of Asher. After seven years of marriage, she was widowed and became an attendant of the temple. She was 84 when she recognized the Messiah, thanked God for Him, and proclaimed to all hope for the redemption of Jerusalem.

ANNAS (Ăn´ nás) Son of Seth; a priest at the time John the Baptist began his public preaching (Luke 3:2). Evidently, Annas, whose name means "merciful," was appointed to the high priesthood about A.D. 6 by Quirinius, governor of Syria. Though he was deposed in A.D. 15 by Gratus, he continued to exercise considerable influence. When Jesus was arrested, He was taken before Annas (John 18:13). After Pentecost,

Church of the Annunciation in Nazareth commemorating Gabriel's unprecedented announcement to Mary.

Annas led other priests in questioning Peter and the other church leaders (Acts 4:6).

ANNUNCIATION In Christian historical tradition, the annunciation refers specifically to the announcement with which the angel Gabriel notified the virgin Mary of the miraculous conception of Christ within her (Luke 1:26-38; Joseph received a similar announcement in Matt. 1:20-25). The births of Isaac (Gen. 17:16-21; 18:9-14), Samson (Judg. 13:3-7), and John the Baptist (Luke 1:13-20) were also announced by divine messengers, but despite a similar format, the news that a "virgin" would conceive by the Holy Spirit was unprecedented; all the other women were married. The Lukan account portrays two main characters, Mary and Gabriel, yet does not omit the work of the "Most High God" and the Holy Spirit in the incarnation of the Son, showing a Trinitarian involvement. Gabriel's announcement points to the Messiah's human (Luke 1:32) and divine (Luke 1:34-35) character and to the eternity of His kingdom (Luke 1:33). In the Christian calendar, March 25 was designated as the feast day of the Annunciation, beginning in about the seventh century.

Stefana Dan Laing

ANOINT, ANOINTED Procedure of rubbing or smearing a person or thing, usually with oil, for the purpose of healing, setting apart, or embalming. A person can anoint himself, be anointed, or anoint another person or thing. While olive oil is the most common element mentioned for use in anointing, oils produced from castor, bay, almond, myrtle, cyprus, cedar, walnut, and fish were also used. In Esther 2:12, for example, the oil of myrrh is used as a cosmetic.

The Hebrew verb *mashach* (noun, *messiah*) and the Greek verb *chrio* (noun, *christos*) are translated "to anoint." From ancient times the priests and kings were ceremonially anointed as a sign of official appointment to office, and as a symbol of God's power upon them. The act was imbued with an element of awe. David would not harm King Saul because of the anointing the king had received (1 Sam. 24:6). Likewise, Israel (Ps. 89:38), and even Cyrus (Isa. 45:1), are called God's anointed because of God's working through them. Israel came to see each succeeding king as God's anointed one, the *messiah*

who would deliver them from their enemies and establish the nation as God's presence on the earth.

In the NT "anoint" is used to speak of daily grooming for hair (Matt. 6:17), for treating injury or illness (Luke 10:34), and for preparing a body for burial (Mark 16:1).

Christians see Jesus as God's Anointed One, the Savior (Acts 10:38). The same symbolism as in the OT is employed in this usage: God's presence and power are resident in the anointing. Likewise, the Christian is anointed by God (2 Cor. 1:21; 1 John 2:27) for the tasks of ministry. *Mike Mitchell*

ANON (Ȧ·nŏn´) Archaic word meaning "immediately."

ANT See *Insects.*

ANTEDILUVIANS Meaning "before the deluge"; refers to those who lived before the flood described in Gen. 6–8. The early chapters of Genesis affirm that the God of Israel is the God who created the world and who guides all of human history. Those chapters connect the history of all humankind to that of God's covenant people, and thus to salvation history.

The genealogy in Gen. 4 is framed by two accounts of violence: (1) the murder of Abel by Cain and God's promise of sevenfold vengeance on anyone who harmed Cain (Gen. 4:8-16), and (2) the war song of Lamech, threatening 77-fold vengeance for any injury (Gen. 4:23-24). In between we are told of the cultural achievements of the antediluvians. Cain is credited with building the first city. The three sons of Lamech are attributed with the origins of cattle raising (Jabal), music (Jubal), and metallurgy (Tubal-cain). Since cultural achievements were often attributed to the gods in the ancient Near East, the Scripture wants to emphasize that they are achievements of human beings created by the one God. The text shows an awareness that development of technology was a mixed blessing then and now. Technology both enhances life and is used for evil purposes.

The longevity attributed to the antediluvians in Gen. 5 is the subject of study and debate. The ages of the antediluvians are reported somewhat differently in the Hebrew Bible (Masoretic Text), the Samaritan Pentateuch, and the Greek OT (Septuagint). One traditional view is that these people lived longer because they were closer to the state in which God created human beings. Others say that their more simple life and vegetarianism (Gen. 2:16-17; 3:18b; and Gen. 9:3) allowed for longer life spans. Some consider the numbers symbolic.

The discovery of lists of Sumerian kings who reigned before the flood has thrown light on the theological significance of the text. The Sumerian kings, who were considered gods, were said to have lived for tens of thousands of years. In contrast, the biblical antediluvians were clearly human. Genesis emphasizes the oneness of God and the distinction between the Creator and human beings who were created. See *Flood.*

Wilda W. Morris

ANTELOPE Fleet-footed mammal with horns, about the size of a donkey. It is a grass-eating deerlike animal which does not appear in the KJV but does in NASB, NIV, NRSV, TEV, translating Hebrew *te'o,* a word translated in different ways by the earliest translations. The references may be to a large white antelope or oryx (*oryx leucoryx*) with striking long horns, black markings, and a tuft of black hair under its neck. It had a divided hoof and chewed the cud and so qualified as a clean animal to be eaten (Deut. 14:5). They were hunted and caught with nets (Isa. 51:20).

The pygarg (KJV), found in a list of animals in Deut. 14:5, has not been identified with certainty but is considered by a number of scholars to be an antelope. Pygarg literally means "white rump" and is the Greek name for a kind of antelope. This animal has been connected with one that is native to North Africa. It has grayish-white hinder parts with a white patch on the forehead and twisted and ringed horns that point upward and backward. It also has been identified with the Arabian Oryx, an antelope of Iraq that has long horns stretching backward.

ANTHOTHIJAH (Ăn·thō·thī´ jäh) Descendant of Benjamin (1 Chron. 8:24). The name may represent connection with city of Anathoth.

ANTHROPOLOGY Biblical anthropology concerns the origin, essential nature, and destiny of human beings. Human beings do not possess a knowledge of their own depraved nature nor a saving knowledge of God apart from the work of

The Rhorr gazelle is one species of antelope found in Palestine.

the Word, both incarnated and inscribed in our hearts and minds.

The OT uses five words for "man." *Adam* may be either individual or collective, may include both men and women (Gen. 5:1-2). Josephus claimed that "adam" means "red" because the first man was formed out of "the red earth." More likely it is related to the same word in Arabic which means "creatures" or "mankind." *Ish* in the OT is most often used for the male gender and is used to refer to man as opposed to God (Num. 23:19), man as opposed to woman (Gen. 2:23), man as opposed to beast (Exod. 11:7), man as husband (Gen. 3:6), man as father (Eccles. 6:3), and man as brave (1 Sam. 4:9). *Enosh* is usually a poetical reference to man individually (Job 5:17), men collectively (Isa. 33:8), or mankind in general (Job 14:19). *Geber* derives from a verb which means to be "strong" or "mighty" and is used poetically to distinguish men from those protected, namely, women and children. *Metim* can refer to males (Deut. 2:34), a quantity of men (Gen. 34:30), or people (Job 11:4).

The NT, likewise, uses about five main words to refer to "man." *Anthropos,* like *Adam,* is used to refer to men as a class (John 16:21), in contrast to other forms of life (plants, animals— Matt. 4:19), as the equivalent of people (Matt. 5:13), and as a physical being (James 5:17) subject to sin (Rom. 5:18) and death (Heb. 9:27). *Anthropos* is used of Christ as representative of all humanity (1 Cor. 15:21). *Aner,* like *Ish,* is used to refer to man as opposed to woman (Matt. 14:21), man as opposed to boy (1 Cor. 13:11), and man as husband (Matt. 1:16). It is also used of Jesus as the Man whom God appointed to be judge of all men (Acts 17:31).

Thnetos refers to man as mortal in reference to flesh (*sarx*, 2 Cor. 4:11), the body (*soma*, Rom. 6:12), and mortal man in general (1 Cor. 15:34). *Psuche* is the soul, the self, or life (John 10:11; cp. *nephesh*, Gen. 2:7). *Arsen* is used to distinguish male from female (Matt. 19:4, cp. LXX; Gen. 1:27; Rom. 1:27).

Creation The Scriptures give no indication that God created humans out of necessity or because He was lonely. Because God is independent, there was no necessity for the creation of humankind (Job 41:11; Acts 17:24-25); He has no need for fulfillment outside of Himself. Therefore, God must have created human beings for His own glory (Isa. 43:6-7; Rom. 11:36; Eph. 1:11-12). Humans, therefore, are to delight in and seek to know their Maker (Pss. 37:4; 42:1-2; Matt. 6:33).

Since humans were created by God for His own glory, then it is logical that humanity reflects His "likeness" or "image" (Gen. 1:26-31; 5:1-3). God's creation of human beings was good (Gen. 1:31), and they were the highest beings in the created order (Gen. 1:26; Ps. 8). As the highest creation, humans were given responsibility over the earth as representatives of God and caretakers of the created order (Gen. 1:26-31). All humans were created equally in His image. While "likeness" does not indicate physical similarity, even the body reflects God's glory and is the means by which humans carry out God's purposes. The image is found particularly in the mind and heart. Being created in the image of God sets humanity apart from the rest of creation. Specifically, it involves the following capacities: moral (original righteousness, Eccles. 7:29), mental (reasoning capacity and knowledge, Isa. 1:18; Rom. 12:2; Col. 1:10; 1 John 5:20), and spiritual (Gen. 2:7; Job 20:3; 1 Cor. 2:12-14; 15:35-50). Yet the purpose for being created with these capacities is that humans might be capable of knowing and being known by their Creator. Hence the relational capacity, in which we glorify, yearn for, and delight in God, encompasses the others. That relationship is for the purpose of glorifying God and taking pleasure in Him forever (Ps. 16:11).

Redemption Because of the fall, the image of God has been damaged. The image was not destroyed but only corrupted (James 3:9). This corruption is universal, affecting everyone, regardless of race, gender, education, or social status (Rom. 3:10-26). Humans are presumed to have some vestiges of God's image because the Bible speaks of its need for restoration (Rom. 8:29; 1 Cor. 3:18; Eph. 4:23-24; Col. 3:10). Because of sin, human beings need redemption, or regeneration, in order that the image might be renovated and the capacity for relationship with God be restored. Sin separates us from our intended purpose of glorifying God (Rom. 3:23). Hence, human beings must depend wholly upon God to reveal His glory as well as our own depravity. When He reveals His glory to us, it has two results: knowledge of God and knowledge of our iniquity (Ezek. 39:21-23; Rom. 3:21-26). In the corrupted nature, humanity rejects the revelation of God's glory. This results in a lack of knowledge both of God and our own condition (Rom. 1:18-32). He has given humankind over to a depraved mind (Rom. 1:28). Having fallen from His glory due to sin, those who do not have the knowledge of God are separated from His glory to eternal destruction (2 Thess. 3:1-3).

Due to the corruption of the image, the only hope for knowledge of God and of our depravity is the special revelation of God's Word, written and incarnate. The means by which human beings are redeemed is by the gracious gift of Christ (John 3:16). It is by His substitutionary atonement on the cross that we may be recreated (Gal. 6:14-15; 2 Cor. 5:14-19). As the Second Adam (1 Cor. 15:45-47), Christ represents the true image of God (John 12:45; Col. 1:15). That likeness can occur in fallen humans only as we are brought into union with Christ (Rom. 12:1-2). The knowledge God gives of Himself by His glory is all that is necessary to escape our corruption and partake of the divine nature (1 Pet. 1:2-4). Through re-creation, the purpose of creation is restored, namely, to glorify and delight in Him. Our redemption serves this purpose of God (Eph. 1:3-5) who purges our sin for His glory (Ps. 79:9). This work of God is a work in process which will be complete at the return of Christ (Phil. 1:6; 1 John 3:2).

Constitution The Bible speaks of humans as a unity of body and soul/spirit (Gen. 2:7). Though there are negative references to the flesh as sinful, others speak of it in relation to the unity of whom we are (Ps. 63:1). Though there is an immaterial part that can exist without the body (1 Cor. 14:14; Rom. 8:16; 2 Cor. 5:8), the body is not the only part infected by sin. Sin involves the understanding and heart (Eph. 4:18). The body can refer to the totality of a person (Rom. 7:18), the flesh (Rom. 8:7-8), the mind and conscience (Titus 1:15), and thought and intent (Gen. 6:5). Hence, body, flesh, soul, spirit, mind, conscience, heart, will, and emotions are not discrete parts of a human being which exist independently, but make up the totality of that person. Spirit, as much as flesh, needs to be rescued from corruption and conformed to the image of Christ (2 Cor. 7:1).

Theological Implications Humans have value because of our creation in the image of God (Gen. 9:6). This value is not based on any merit but is given by God (Ps. 8:4-6). Humans are valued by God more than birds and flowers (Matt. 6:26-29) because we were created with the moral, mental, and spiritual capacity to enjoy and glorify Him. Neither creation nor re-creation is based on merit but upon the basis of His own name's sake (Isa. 48:9-11). Christ gave Himself "to the praise of His glorious grace" (Eph. 1:6 HCSB). Human beings "deserve to die" (Rom. 1:32 HCSB). Only Christ is worthy (Rev. 5:1-14), and only by virtue of His having created (Rev. 4:11) and redeemed us do we have worth. Redemption reflects and manifests God's glory in that, though sinful people were worthless (Matt. 25:30; Titus 1:16), Christ, the Worthy One, died for us.

Humans are fragile and wholly depraved. We are subject to sickness, trouble, and death (Job 5:6; Pss. 103:14-16; 144:3-4). We are conceived in iniquity (Ps. 51:5) and can do nothing to change our nature (Jer. 13:23). Sin is universal to the human race (Rom. 3) and to the constitution of each human (Gen. 6:5).

Humans are created and redeemed for the glory of God and to enjoy Him forever. Human nature was not corrupt as it was created by God but only as it was tainted by Adam. While human beings are wholly depraved due to the fall, God can recreate us and restore our corrupted image through the Second Adam. Only as God reveals Himself to us through Christ and His Word do we unite with Christ and, as a result, know ourselves as depraved and Christ as our sole Redeemer. Once the process of restoration begins, it will be brought to completion. Redeemed men and women will, by the blood of Christ, give glory to His name and enjoy Him forever, thus fulfilling their original purpose (Phil. 2:5-11).

Human beings are held accountable individually and communally. Each person answers for his own deeds, yet we are called not only to love the Lord God with our entire being we are to love our neighbors as ourselves. According to Gen. 5:1-2, part of the image of God is reflected in the creation of male and female. Unlike God humans are interdependent; that is, we need each other. This carries significant implications as to the responsibility of human beings to one another as we live together on this globe to the glory of God and according to His purposes. See *Creation; Death; Eternal Life; Ethics; Humanity; Salvation; Sin.*　　　　　　*David Depp*

ANTHROPOMORPHISM Words which describe God as if He had human features. They occur wherever Scripture mentions God's arm, ear, or other body parts. These descriptions are not to be taken literally because God is Spirit (John 4:24). Scripture uses anthropomorphisms frequently in poetic and prophetic literature, but they may occur elsewhere as well. One common anthropomorphism speaks of God's arm. This is usually related to His power to judge or to save. In Exod. 6:6 God says that He will redeem Israel from the Egyptians "with an outstretched arm and with great judgments" (NKJV). This pictures God reaching out to bring plagues on Egypt. Moses, after the deliverance of the Israelites at the Red Sea, praises God saying that fear of the Lord will fall upon people "because of the greatness of Your arm" (Exod. 15:16 NKJV; cp. Ps. 77:15). Additional passages promise that the arm of the Lord will be strong or victorious (Isa. 40:10; 48:14) and will execute judgment (Isa. 51:5).

Sometimes the Lord's hand is also said to rescue Israel (Exod. 15:16; Deut. 5:15; 11:2-4; 26:8). Psalm 44:1-3 describes how the hand of the Lord and His arm drove the nations out before Israel when they came into the land. Again the words refer to God's actions (breaking down the walls of Jericho, making the sun stand still, etc.) leading to the conquest of Canaan. The hand or arm of the Lord is elsewhere described as having rescued His people or as routing God's enemies (Pss. 89:10; 98:1; 136:11-12).

God's ear is also mentioned often in Scripture. In the Psalms God is implored to incline His ear to the psalmist's prayer (Pss. 17:1,6; 31:2; 39:12; 55:1; 71:2; 86:1,6; 88:2; etc.), meaning He is asked to listen closely. One important passage in Isaiah combines His ear, hand, and face: "The Lord's hand is not shortened that it cannot save; nor is his ear heavy that it cannot hear, but your sins have hidden His face" (Isa. 59:1-2 NKJV).

Anthropomorphism, while rarer in the NT, is found there. There are references to God's "hand" or to His "right hand" (Matt. 26:64; Luke 1:66; 23:46; John 10:29; Acts 2:33; etc.). These refer to divine power or to the place of honor in God's kingdom. First Peter 3:12 speaks of the eyes, ears, and face of the Lord, quoting Ps. 34:15-16.

Scripture also describes God as having human emotions such as joy, anger, and sorrow, as well as having thoughts, will, and plans. These are not anthropomorphisms because God, being a person, has the attributes of personality. Descriptions of His emotions in Scripture are sometimes called anthropopathisms, meaning the attribution of human emotions to God. God, being eternal and unchanging, does not experience emotions in the same way as people, though He certainly has them. Descriptions of His emotions in Scripture are by analogy to emotions as we experience them.

Anthropomorphisms make the language of the Bible more vivid. They help the reader to picture what God does. One may say sin separates us from God, but it evokes a deeper emotional response to say that God hides His face from the sinner (Deut. 31:17). Anthropomorphisms also make the truths of Scripture easier to remember. It is true that God judged Egypt for oppressing Israel, but it is more memorable to picture God "stretching forth His hand" and "touching" Egypt with the plagues. Anthropomorphisms, then, aid one's understanding of who God is and how He acts for His glory in the world.   *Fred Smith*

ANTICHRIST Describes a particular individual or a group of people who oppose God and His purpose.

Old Testament The OT described the antichrist in various ways. Especially in Daniel, there arose the expectation of one who would oppose the Lord and His people Israel. This evil leader was referred to as the king of the north (11:40) who would come with a mighty army to crush the nations, to persecute the righteous (7:25), to bring death (8:10), and to set up his throne in the temple (8:13). This latter event the Jews term the "abomination of desolation." Many Jews viewed the arrival of Antiochus Epiphanes IV as the embodiment of these verses. Yet in the mind of many Jews, the rule of Antiochus did not meet the full expectations of these Scriptures. There evolved a permanent expectation of an antichrist figure in Judaism. In later Jewish history such Roman figures as Pompey and Caligula were identified with the antichrist.

In Daniel one also finds a collective antichrist. In 7:7-28 the Fourth Empire was viewed as a collective antichrist. In later Judaism, the Fourth Kingdom or the collective antichrist was viewed as the Roman Empire (2 Baruch 26-40; 4 Ezra 5:3-4).

New Testament In the NT the only use of the term "antichrist" is in the Johannine epistles. First John 2:18 speaks of the antichrist who is the great enemy of God and, in particular, antichrists who precede that great enemy. These antichrists were human teachers who had left the church. Such antichrists deny the incarnation (1 John 4:3) and Christ's deity (1 John 2:2). In 2 John 7, the antichrists are identified as deceivers who teach that Jesus Christ did not come in the flesh. The concept of the antichrist appears in the term "false Christ" (*pseudo christos*) (Matt. 24:24; Mark 13:22). Mark and Matthew apparently expected a Roman ruler to once again enter the temple as did Antiochus and Pompey. In Rev. 13:3 the beast from the sea is often viewed as an antichrist figure. There, John may have looked for a return of the emperor Nero.

In 2 Thess. 2:1-12, the antichrist figure is armed with satanic power and is fused with Belial, a satanic being (2 Cor. 6:15). In this passage the Roman government is viewed as restraining its power. In Revelation the Roman Caesar is the evil force.

Contemporary Concerns Christians today have differing views of the antichrist figure. Dispensationalists look for a future Roman ruler who will appear during the tribulation and will rule over the earth. Those in the amillennialist school interpret the term symbolically.

James L. Blevins

ANTIMONY (Ăn´ tǐ mō nē) Silvery-white, brittle, metallic chemical element of crystalline structure, found only in combination. It is used in alloys with other metals to harden them and increase their resistance to chemical actions. Compounds of antimony are used in medicines, pigments, matches, and fireproofing. In the NRSV and the NASB "antimony" is used as a translation of the Hebrew terms *'abne-puk* to describe the materials used to build the temple (1 Chron. 29:2; Isa. 54:11; NIV "turquoise"; REB, TEV "stones for mosaic work"; KJV "glistering stones" and "stones with fair colors," respectively). It is likely that *'abne-puk* refers to some sort of cement or mortar used in the creation of mosaics, which it is suggested would make precious stones appear larger and more colorful. In two other passages (2 Kings 9:30; Jer. 4:30), *puk* is consistently translated as eye paint. One of Job's daughters was named Kerenhapuk—that is, "horn of eye paint" (Job 42:14).

ANTINOMIANISM (Ăn tĭ nō´ mĭ ăn ĭsm) False teaching that since faith alone is necessary for salvation, one is free from the moral obligations of the law. The word "antinomianism" is not used in the Bible, but the idea is spoken of. Paul appears to have been accused of being an antinomian (Rom. 3:8; 6:1,15). While it is true that obedience to the law will never earn salvation for anyone (Eph. 2:8-9), it is equally true that those who are saved are expected to live a life full of good works (Matt. 7:16-20; Eph. 2:10; Col. 1:10; James 2:14-26). Since we have been freed from the dominion of sin through faith in Jesus, we have also been freed to practice the righteousness demanded by God (Rom. 6:12-22).

ANTIOCH (Ăn´ tĭ·ŏk) Name of two NT cities, one of which was home to many Diaspora Jews (Jews living outside of Palestine and maintaining their religious faith among the Gentiles), and the place where believers, many of whom were Gentiles, were first called Christians.

One of the cities called Antioch was the third largest city of the Roman Empire after Rome in Italy and Alexandria in Egypt. Because so many ancient cities were called by this name, it is often called Antioch on the Orontes River or Antioch of Syria. Antioch was founded around 300 B.C. by Seleucus Nicator. From the beginning it was a bustling maritime city with its own seaport. It lay about 20 miles inland from the Mediterranean in ancient Syria on the Orontes River nearly 300 miles north of Jerusalem. Many Jews of the Diaspora lived in Antioch and engaged in commerce, enjoying the rights of citizenship in a free city. Many of

Temple of Augustus in Pisidian Antioch.

Antioch's Gentiles were attracted to Judaism. As was the case with many of the Roman cities of the east, Antioch's patron deity was the pagan goddess Tyche or "Fortune."

In the NT only Jerusalem is more closely related to the spread of early Christianity. Luke mentioned Nicholas of Antioch in Acts 6:5 among the Greek-speaking leaders of the church in Jerusalem. The persecution that arose over Stephen resulted in Jewish believers scattering to Cyprus, Cyrene, and Antioch (Acts 11:19). In Antioch the believers were first called Christians (11:26), and it was to Antioch that Barnabas fetched Saul (Paul) from Tarsus so that they could teach this mixed congregation of Jewish and Gentile followers of the Lord. At Antioch the Christian prophet Agabus foretold the famine that would shortly overtake the Roman world (11:28). The disciples responded with the work of famine relief for the church in Jerusalem, directed and carried out from Antioch. The church at Antioch felt the leading of the Holy Spirit to set aside Barnabas and Saul for what was the first organized mission work (13:1-3). Barnabas and Saul left for Seleucia (also known as Pieria, Antioch's Mediterranean seaport) to begin their preaching. The church at Antioch heard the reports of Paul and Barnabas on return from their first missionary journey (14:27) and likely their second missionary journey (18:22). This was a missionary effort to both Jews and Gentiles, about which Paul says in Gal. 2:11 that he had to oppose Peter to his face at Antioch.

Archaeological excavations at Antioch have been very fruitful, revealing a magnificent, walled Roman city of theatres, forums, a circus,

The Cilician Gates through the Taurus Mountains north of Antioch of Syria where Paul would have passed on his second missionary journey.

and other public buildings. The language of the city was Greek, as inscriptions and public records show, but the language of the peasantry around this mighty city was Syriac, a dialect of Aramaic.

Another city called Antioch was in Pisidia, Asia Minor, west of Iconium. Like the Syrian Antioch, this Antioch was founded by Seleucus Nicator. Under Roman rule this city was called Caesarea. Paul preached in a synagogue there on his first missionary journey (Acts 13:14) and was warmly received (13:42-44). Jewish jealousy led to a separate ministry to Gentiles (13:46). Finally, the Jews drove Paul and Barnabas from the city. These Jews from Antioch followed Paul to Lystra and stirred up trouble there (14:19). Despite this, Paul returned to Antioch to strengthen the church (14:21). Paul used the experience to teach Timothy (2 Tim. 3:11).

James F. Strange

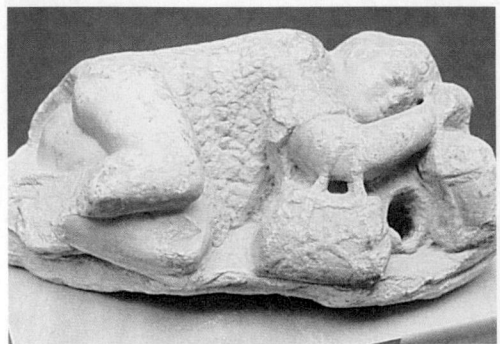

From Antioch of Syria, a small first-century marble statue of a sleeping traveler reminiscent of Paul.

ANTIOCHUS (Ăn tī´ ŏ kŭs) Name of 13 rulers of Syria between 281 B.C and 64 B.C. They were part of the Seleucid dynasty that inherited part of Alexander the Great's kingdom. No Antiochus is

Pisidian Antioch in the mountains of Asia Minor (modern Turkey) north of the Mediterranean Sea.

specifically mentioned in Scripture. Many Bible students think the book of Daniel originally had its attention focused on the Seleucid kings, particularly Antiochus IV (175 to 163 B.C.). The Maccabean revolt and Jewish intertestamental history occurred during the reigns of the Antiochus kings. See *Daniel; Intertestamental History and Literature; Maccabees.*

ANTIPAS (Ăn´ tĭ·pås) Name of a martyr in Revelation and the son of Herod the Great.

1. Tetrarch of Galilee at the time John the Baptist and Jesus began their public ministries (Luke 3:1). Antipas, whose name is an abbreviation of Antipater, ordered John the Baptist beheaded (Matt. 14:3). Pilate sent Jesus to Antipas prior to the crucifixion. On that occasion he treated Jesus with scornful contempt (Luke 23:11). This won the friendship of Pilate. See *Herod.* **2.** According to tradition, the martyr of the church of Pergamum in Rev. 2:13 was roasted in a brazen bowl at Domitian's request.

ANTIPATRIS (Ăn·tĭ·pät´ rĭs) Place-name meaning "in place of father." City that Herod the Great built to honor his father Antipater in 9 B.C. It was 40 miles from Jerusalem and 25 miles from Caesarea on the famous Via Maris, "way of the sea," international highway. Roman soldiers taking Paul from Jerusalem to Caesarea spent the night at Antipatris (Acts 23:31). It is located on the site of OT Aphek. See *Aphek.*

ANTONIA, TOWER OF Fortress near the temple built around A.D. 6 that served as a palace residence for King Herod, barracks for the Roman troops, a safe deposit for the robe of the high priest, and a central courtyard for public

Antonia Fortress (Tower of Antonia) in the model of first-century Jerusalem (Holyland Hotel, Jerusalem)

speaking. The tower of Antonia is not mentioned directly in the Bible. It served various functions between A.D. 6 and A.D. 66, the time of its destruction by Titus. Herod the Great built the tower at the northwest corner of the temple court to replace the Maccabean fort. The tower was 75 feet high and was named for Herod's friend, Mark Antony. Although the name "Antonia" is not used in the Bible, several references from the first-century Jewish historian, Josephus, describe the appearance and function of the tower of Antonia.

Josephus describes the splendor of the tower with spacious apartments, elaborate baths, and beautiful courtyards. The tower served as an official residence for the Roman procurators. Capable of accommodating at least a Roman cohort (500–600 men), the tower housed portions of the Roman army used to guard the Jews inside the temple court. Herod required that the vestments of the high priest be kept in the tower to maintain control over the worship festivals of the Jews.

The pavement beneath the modern convent of Notre Dame de Sion has been thought to be the place of the tower's courtyard, traditionally considered the site of Jesus' trial before Pilate (John 19:13). Recent archaeological evidence, however, has shown that the pavement dates from the second century and not the time of Jesus.   *Linda McKinnish Bridges*

ANTOTHIJAH (Ăn·tō·thī´ jah) (KJV) See *Anthothijah*.

ANTOTHITE (Ăn´ tō·thīt) KJV for person from Anathoth. See *Anathoth*.

ANUB (Ā´ nŭb) Personal name meaning "grape" or "with a mustache." A member of the tribe of Judah (1 Chron. 4:8).

ANXIETY State of mind wherein one is concerned about something or someone. This state of mind may range from genuine concern (Phil. 2:20,28; 2 Cor. 11:28) to obsessions that originate from a distorted perspective of life (Matt. 6:25-34; Mark 4:19; Luke 12:22-31). Jesus did not prohibit genuine concern about food or shelter, but He did teach that we should keep things in their proper perspective. We should make God's kingdom our first priority; everything else will fall in line after we do that (Matt. 6:33).

APE Large, semierect primate, mentioned only twice in the OT and not described. The ape was not native to the Holy Land, but the Israelites were familiar with it. Some types were kept as pets. They were among the gifts that the navy of Hiram brought to Solomon (1 Kings 10:22; 2 Chron. 9:21).

The Hebrew term *qoph* may refer to apes (*papio hamadrias arabicus*), using a loanword from Egyptian, but the exact animal referred to by this term is far from certain, the animal apparently being an imported novelty for the people of Solomon's day.

APELLES (Á·pěl´ lěs) A Christian in Rome whom Paul saluted as "approved in Christ" (Rom. 16:10), which may mean he had been tested by persecution and proved faithful.

APHARSACHITES (Á·phär´ săk·īts) or **APHARSATHCHITES** KJV transliteration of Aramaic terms in Ezra 4:9; 5:6; 6:6. Modern translations translate the term to indicate government officials: governors (RSV); officials (NIV; NASB). The term in 4:9 may represent officials representing the Persian king in the provinces of his kingdom. The term in 5:6 and 6:6 may refer to government investigators or inspectors.

APHARSITES (Á·phär´ sīts) KJV transliteration of Aramaic term in Ezra 4:9 variously translated and interpreted by modern translators and Bible students: men from Persia (NIV); Persians (RSV); secretaries (NASB). The verse is difficult to read in the original language, and no satisfactory interpretation has been offered.

APHEK (Ā´ phěk) Place-name meaning "bed of brook or river" or "fortress." **1.** City whose king Joshua defeated (Josh. 12:18), where Philistine armies formed to face Israel in days of Samuel (1 Sam. 4:1) resulting in Philistine victory and capture of Israel's ark of the covenant. Philistine armies including David and his men gathered in Aphek to fight Saul. The Philistine commanders forced Achish to send David back from battle (1 Sam. 29). Eventually the Philistines defeated Israel, bringing death to Saul and Jonathan. Aphek is located at modern Tell Ras el´ Ain near the source of the Yarkon River in the Sharon plain northeast of Joppa. Egyptian execration texts from about 1900 B.C. apparently refer to Aphek. Aphek became known as Antipatris in the NT era. See *Antipatris*. **2.** Northern border city which Joshua did not conquer (Josh. 13:4). This may be modern Afqa, 15 miles east of ancient Byblos and 23 miles north of Beirut, Lebanon. **3.** City assigned to Asher (Josh. 19:30) but not conquered (Judg. 1:31). This may be modern Tell Kerdanah, three miles from Haifa and six miles southeast of Acco. **4.** City east of Jordan near the Sea of Galilee where Benhadad led Syria against Israel about 860 B.C. but met defeat as a prophet predicted for Israel (1 Kings 20:26-30). A wall of Aphek fell on 27,000 Syrians (1 Kings 20:30). Also Elisha promised Joash victory over the Syrians in Aphek (2 Kings 13:17).

Late Bronze Age palace excavated at Aphek-Antipatris.

APHEKAH (Á·phē´ kăh) City that Joshua assigned to tribe of Judah (Josh. 15:53). Its location is unknown.

APHIAH (Á·phī´ ah) Personal name meaning "forehead." An ancestor of King Saul from the tribe of Benjamin (1 Sam. 9:1).

APHIK (Á·phĭk) Variant Hebrew spelling of Aphek (Judg. 1:31). See *Aphek 3*.

APHRAH (Ăph´ rah) KJV interpretation of place-name in Mic. 1:10, also called Beth Ophrah (NIV) or Beth-le-aphrah (RSV; NASB); or Beth Leaphrah (TEV). The longer name used in modern translations means "house of dust" and is used to make a wordplay by Micah, the meaning of the name being more important than the actual city. The city has not been located. It may be modern Tel et-Taijibe near Hebron.

APHSES (Ăph´ sēs) (KJV) See *Happizzez*.

APIRU See *Habiru*.

APIS (Ā´ pĭs) Sacred bull worshiped in Memphis, Egypt. RSV and TEV divide the words in Jer. 46:15 differently than does printed Hebrew text. They thus translate, "Why has Apis fled?" (RSV) or "Why has your mighty God Apis fallen?" (TEV). Other translations retain the present Hebrew text and read, "Why are thy valiant men swept away?" (KJV)

APOCALYPTIC Occurs 18 times in the NT in the Greek noun form *apokalupsis* and 26 times in the verb form *apokalupto*. These Greek terms derive from the combination of the preposition *apo* and the verb *kalupto*, resulting in the definition "to uncover, unveil, or reveal." Such "uncovering" or "revelation" comes through visions or dreams and refers to the eschatological disclosure of secrets with reference to the last days. The use of the term "apocalyptic" is due to the opening word of Revelation, *apokalupsis*, meaning a revelation. When commentators speak of apocalyptic writings, they mean works written in a similar style to the book of Revelation. Apocalyptic, therefore, refers to writings that employ symbolic or figurative language used to describe a future divine intervention; the doctrinal system explicit in this genre of literature; and the movements that produced such writings and doctrines.

There are some similarities between Zoroastrianism and biblical apocalyptic material, for the eschatological element in apocalyptic thought is combined with a cosmic dualism. In this dualism the future is not an outgrowth of the present, for if it was, humanity would vastly improve, and the present age would not come to an end. The differences between Persian religious ideas and those of the Hebrews are distinct. The apocalypticism of Zoroastrianism is a dualism of two opposing personified forces in the universe, a good god and an evil god. In the Judeo-Christian concept Satan is not equal, but clearly inferior to God and an opponent to God. Satan is the tempter and oppressor of humanity, but even so God is in control with Satan operating at God's pleasure. The Zoroastrian sources from which Jewish apocalyptic supposedly derived occurred later in composition than the biblical materials. Zoroastrianism is indebted to the Bible and not vice versa.

The Nature of Apocalyptic The critical scholars, who accept late dates of apocalyptic literature (including the OT book of Daniel), view apocalyptic merely as a literary method employed by ancient writers to convey a future hope of a better world. The enduring value of apocalyptic is its promise of this better world to those who are overwhelmed by their present circumstances, such as poverty, disease, and persecution. Such is the significance of the canonical apocalyptic book of Daniel and the Revelation. Some hold that the best approach in defining works as apocalyptic is to compare features with those of Revelation. This appears to be the best method. Some typical features of apocalyptic are illustrated from Revelation: the revelation is given by God (Rev. 1:1); the revelation is given through a mediator or an angel (Rev. 1:1; 22:16); the mediator delivers the revelation to a seer/prophet (Rev. 1:1); the revelation is in reference to future events, generally the triumph of good over evil (Rev. 1:1); apocalyptic writings were written during a time of persecution or during a historical crisis (Rev. 1:9); the message is presented in visions (Rev. 1:10); there is much use of symbolism and gematria/numerology (Rev. 1:20; 7:4-8); and the major theme or message is the eschatological triumph of the kingdom of God over the evil kingdoms of the earth (Rev. 19:17-21). Some scholars, however, tend to classify works as apocalyptic that are not of this genre.

Old Testament Critical scholars hold that the genre of apocalyptic is a late development that arose during the postexilic period, though there were earlier influences in this direction. The Jewish people had hoped Israel would regain its former glory and that a Davidic king would rule over them, resulting in the defeat of Israel's enemies. As time passed, the Jews realized that this would not occur without an intervention from God. Gradually, Israel began to place its confidence for the future in a Messiah who would bring in a new era of peace, prosperity, and victory over the nations.

Portions of Joel, Amos, Zechariah, and Isaiah have apocalyptic features, as does Daniel, which many view as most like apocalyptic literature. Though Zech. 1–6 contains many features of this genre, such as visions, gematria, and angels, this material does not appear to emphasize the eschatological themes which are prominent in Daniel and Revelation (e.g. the eschatological

triumph of the kingdom of God over the kingdoms of the earth, the resurrection) and is best not classified as apocalyptic. Zechariah 9–14 is prophecy but does not share the certain features of apocalyptic literature (i.e., angels or visions). Some scholars include Isa. 24–27, Ezek. 38–39, and Joel 3 as apocalyptic, but these passages, though eschatological, lack far too many features of the genre to be classified as apocalyptic.

Apocryphal Works Several apocalyptic works were written between 200 B.C. and A.D. 100, though they were not included in the biblical canon: 1 Enoch (163–80 B.C.), Book of Jubilees (100 B.C.), the Sibylline Oracles (approximately 150 B.C.), the Testaments of the Twelve Patriarchs (140–110 B.C.), the Psalms of Solomon (50 B.C.), the Assumption of Moses (4 B.C.– A.D. 30), the Martyrdom of Isaiah (first century A.D.), 4 Ezra (A.D. 90–100), and 2 Baruch (A.D. 50–100). Differences between canonical and noncanonical apocalyptic literature are numerous: (1) noncanonical apocalypses appeared as imitations of the biblical books; (2) these works were pseudonymous—written under a false name. The people associated with these works had long been deceased, but they were used to lend authority to the books; (3) noncanonical apocalyptic writings claimed to predict future events but were actually prophecies written after the given event occurred; (4) noncanonical apocalypses were written after the OT prophetic message had ceased (approximately 400 B.C.); and (5) noncanonical apocalyptic works were never considered to be inspired in the same way as the biblical books, due to various doctrinal and ethical matters.

New Testament The book of Revelation is the only NT document that is totally apocalyptic. Other sections of the NT classify as true apocalyptic including Matt. 24–25 and Mark 13. Portions of the letters to the Thessalonians, likewise, contain elements that warrant the classification of apocalyptic: the culmination of evil (2 Thess. 2:1-4); Christ will descend from heaven (1 Thess. 1:10) with the voice of the archangel and the trump of God (1 Thess. 4:16; 2 Thess. 1:7); angels will accompany Him as the executors of His decrees (2 Thess. 1:7); vengeance will be taken on the godless among both the Gentiles and Jews (1 Thess. 4:6; 2 Thess. 1:8) and the doom of the wicked is eternal destruction (2 Thess. 1:9). At the climax of evil, Christ will descend from heaven and slay the man of sin with the breath of His mouth and then consume him with the manifestation of His coming (2 Thess. 2:8). See *Daniel, Book of; Eschatology; Revelation, Book of.*

Steven L. Cox

APOCRYPHA, OLD TESTAMENT Jews did not stop writing for centuries between the OT and the NT. The intertestamental period was a time of much literary production. We designate these writings as Apocrypha and Pseudepigrapha. They did not attain canonical status, but some of them were cited by early Christians as almost on a level with the OT writings, and a few were copied in biblical manuscripts. Some NT authors were familiar with various noncanonical works, and the letter from Jude made specific reference to at least one of these books. They were ultimately preserved by the Christians rather than by the Jews.

Meaning "things that are hidden," apocrypha is applied to a collection of 15 books written between about 200 B.C. and A.D. 100. These are not a part of the OT but are valued by some for private study. The word "apocrypha" is not found in the Bible. Although never part of the Hebrew Scriptures, all 15 apocryphal books except 2 Esdras appear in the Greek translation of the OT, the Septuagint. They were made a part of the official Latin Bible, the Vulgate. All except 1 and 2 Esdras and the Prayer of Manasseh are considered canonical (in the Bible) and authoritative by the Roman Catholic Church. From the time of the Reformation, the apocryphal books have been omitted from the canon of the Protestant churches. The Apocrypha represents various types of literature: historical, historical romance, wisdom, devotional, and apocalyptic.

First Esdras is a historical book from the early first century A.D. Paralleling material in the last chapters of 2 Chronicles, Ezra, and Nehemiah, it covers the period from Josiah to the reading of the law by Ezra. In a number of places, it differs from the OT account. It is believed that this writing drew from some of the same sources used by the writers of the canonical OT books. The Three Guardsmen Story, 3:1–5:3, is the one significant passage in 1 Esdras that does not occur in the OT. It tells how Zerubbabel was allowed to lead the exiles back to Palestine.

First Maccabees is the most important historical writing in the Apocrypha. It is the primary source for writing the history of the period that it covers, 180 to 134 B.C. The emphasis is that God worked through Mattathias and his sons to bring deliverance. He did not intervene in divine, supernatural ways. He worked through people to accomplish His purposes. The writer was a staunch patriot. For him nationalism and religious zeal were one and the same. After introductory verses dealing with Alexander the Great, the book gives the causes for the revolt against the Seleucids. Much detail is given about the careers of Judas and Jonathan. Less attention is given to Simon, although emphasis is placed upon his being acclaimed leader and high priest forever. Brief reference to John Hyrcanus at the close suggests that the book was written either late in his life or after his death, probably shortly after 100 B.C.

Second Maccabees also gives the history of the early part of the revolt against the Seleucids, covering the period from 180 to 161 B.C. It is based upon five volumes written by Jason of Cyrene, about which volumes nothing is known. Second Maccabees, written shortly after 100 B.C., is not considered as accurate historically as 1 Maccabees. In places the two books disagree. This book begins with two letters written to Jews in Egypt urging them to celebrate the cleansing of the temple by Judas. In the remainder of the writing, the author insisted that the Jews' trouble came as the result of their sinfulness. He emphasized God's miraculous intervention to protect the temple and His people. Great honor was bestowed upon those who were martyred for their faith. The book includes the story of seven brothers and their mother who were put to death. The book clearly teaches a resurrection of the body, at least for the righteous.

Tobit is a historical romance written about 200 B.C. It is more concerned to teach lessons than to record history. The story is of a family carried into exile in Assyria when Israel was destroyed. The couple, Tobit and Anna, had a son named Tobias. Tobit had left a large sum of money with a man in Media. When Tobit became blind, he sent his son Tobias to collect the money. A man was found to accompany the son Tobias. In reality he was the angel Raphael. Parallel to this is the account of a relative named Sarah. She had married seven husbands, but a demon had slain each of them on the wedding night. Raphael told Tobias that he was eligible to marry Sarah. They had caught a fish and had preserved the heart, liver, and gall. When burned, the heart and liver would drive away a demon. The gall would cure blindness. Thus Tobias was able to marry Sarah without harm. Raphael collected the money that was left in Media, and the blindness of Tobit was cured by means of the fish's gall. The book stresses temple attendance, paying of tithes, giving alms, marrying only within the people of Israel, and the importance of prayer. Obedience to the law is central along with separation of Jews from Gentiles. It introduces the concept of a guardian angel.

The book of *Judith,* from 250 to 150 B.C., shows the importance of obedience to the law. In this book Nebuchadnezzar, the king of the Assyrians, reigned at the time the Jews returned from exile. This shows it is not historically accurate, for Cyrus of Persia was king when the Jews returned from exile (538 B.C.). The story may be based upon some event where a woman played a heroic role in the life of her people. In the story Nebuchadnezzar sent one of his generals, Holofernes, to subjugate the nations in the western part of his empire. The Jews resisted so Holofernes laid siege to the city of Bethulia (unknown except for this reference). Because of a shortage of water, the city decided to surrender in five days if God did not intervene. Judith had been a widow for three years and had been careful to obey all the law. She stated that God was going to act through her to save His people. She went with her maid to the camp of Holofernes, claiming that God was going to destroy the people because of their sin. She promised to show the general how he could capture the city without loss of a life. At a banquet a few days later, when Holofernes had drunk himself into a coma, she cut off his head and took it back to the city. The result was a great victory for the Jews over their enemies. This book places emphasis upon prayer and fasting. Idolatry is denounced, and the God of Israel is glorified. The book shows a strong hatred of pagans. Its moral content is low, for it teaches that the end justifies the means.

The Apocrypha contains additions to the OT book of Esther. The Hebrew text of Esther contains 163 verses, but the Greek contains 270. These additions are in six different places in the Greek text. However, in the Latin Vulgate they are all placed at the end. These sections contain such matters as the dream of Mordecai, the interpretation of that dream, the texts of the letters referred to in the canonical book (Esther 1:22; 3:13; 8:5,10; 9:20,25-30), and the prayers of Esther and Mordecai. The additions give a more obviously religious basis for the book. In the OT book of Esther, God is never named. This omission is remedied by the additions that were probably made between 125 and 75 B.C.

The Song of the Three Young Men is one of three additions to the book of Daniel. It follows Dan. 3:23 in the Greek text. It satisfies curiosity about what went on in the furnace into which the three men were thrown. The final section is a hymn of praise to God. It emphasizes that God acts to deliver His people in response to prayer. This writing, along with the other two additions to Daniel, probably comes from near 100 B.C.

The story of *Susanna* is added at the close of the book of Daniel in the Septuagint. It tells of two judges who were overpowered by the beauty of Susanna and sought to become intimate with her. When she refused, they claimed they had seen her being intimate with a young man. Authorities believed their charges and condemned the young lady to death. Daniel then stated that the judges were lying, and he would prove it. He asked them, separately, under what tree they saw Susanna and the young man. When they identified different kinds of trees, their perjury became apparent. They were condemned to death, and Susanna was vindicated.

The third addition to Daniel is *Bel and the Dragon*, placed before Susanna in the Septuagint. Bel was an idol worshiped in Babylon. Large quantities of food were placed in Bel's temple each night and consumed before the next morning. King Cyrus asked Daniel why he did not worship Bel, and Daniel replied that Bel was only a man-made image. He would prove to the king that Bel was not alive. Daniel had ashes sprinkled on the floor of the temple and food placed on Bel's altar before sealing the temple door. The next morning the seals on the doors were intact, but when the doors were opened the food was gone. However, the ashes sprinkled on the floor revealed footprints of the priests and their families. They had a secret entrance and came at night and ate the food brought to the idol. The second part of the story of Bel and the Dragon concerned a dragon worshiped in Babylon. Daniel killed the dragon by feeding it cakes of pitch, fat, and hair. The people were outraged, and Daniel was thrown into the lions' den for seven days. However, the lions did not harm him. These stories ridicule paganism and the worship of idols.

The next four apocryphal books are examples of Wisdom literature. The *Wisdom of Solomon*, which was not written by Solomon, was probably written about 100 B.C. in Egypt. The first section of the book gave comfort to oppressed Jews and condemned those who had turned from their faith in God. It shows the advantages of wisdom over wickedness. The second section is a hymn of praise to wisdom. Wisdom is identified as a person present with God, although it is not given as much prominence as in some other writings. The final section shows wisdom as helpful to Israel throughout its history. This writing presents the Greek concept of immortality rather than the biblical teaching of resurrection.

The *Wisdom of Jesus the Son of Sirach* is also known as *Ecclesiasticus*. It emphasizes the importance of the law and obedience to it. Written in Hebrew about 180 B.C., it was translated into Greek by the author's grandson shortly after 132 B.C. The book has two main divisions, 1–23 and 24–51, each beginning with a description of wisdom. The writer was a devout Jew, highly educated, with the opportunity to travel outside Palestine. Thus he included in his writing not only traditional Jewish wisdom but material that he found of value from the Greek world. He pictured the ideal scribe as one who had time to devote himself to the study of the law. Chapters 44–50 are a praise of the great fathers of Israel, somewhat similar to Hebrews 11. Wisdom is highly exalted. She is a person made by God. She goes into the earth to seek a dwelling place. After she is rejected by other people, she is established in Zion. Wisdom is identified with the law.

The book of *Baruch* is also in the wisdom category. It is a combination of two or three different writings. The first section is in prose and claims to give a history of the period of Jeremiah and Baruch. However, it differs from the OT account. The second section is poetry and a praise of wisdom. The final section is also poetic and gives a word of hope for the people. As in Sirach, wisdom and law are equated. It was written shortly before 100 B.C.

The *Letter of Jeremiah* is often added to Baruch as chapter 6. As the basis for his work, the author evidently used Jer. 29:1-23, in which Jeremiah did write a letter to the exiles. However, this letter comes from before 100 B.C. It is a strongly worded condemnation of idolatry.

The *Prayer of Manasseh* is a devotional writing. It claims to be the prayer of the repentant king whom the OT pictured as very wicked (2 Kings 21:10-17). Second Kings makes no suggestion that Manasseh repented. However, 2 Chron. 33:11-13,18-19 states that he did repent and that God accepted him. This writing from before 100 B.C. is what such a prayer of repentance might have been.

The final book of the Apocrypha is *2 Esdras*, written too late to be included in the Septuagint. Chapters 1–2 and 15–16 are Christian writings. Chapters 3–14, the significant part of the work, are from about 20 B.C. This writing is an apocalypse, a type of writing popular among the Jews in the intertestamental period and which became popular among Christians. Second Esdras contains seven sections or visions. In the first three, Ezra seeks answers from an angel about human sin and the situation of Israel. The answer he receives is that the situation will change only in the new age that God is about to inaugurate. The third section pictures the Messiah. He will remain 400 years and then die. The next three visions stress God's coming intervention and salvation of His people through the preexistent Messiah. The final section states that the end will be soon and reports that Ezra was inspired to write 94 books. Twenty-four are a rewrite of the canonical OT while the other 70 are to be given to the wise. The last two chapters of 2 Esdras contain material common to the NT. See *Apocalyptic; Pseudepigrapha.*

Clayton Harrop

APOCRYPHA, NEW TESTAMENT Collective term referring to a large body of religious writings dating back to the early Christian centuries that are similar in form to the NT (Gospels, acts, epistles, and apocalypses) but were never included as a part of the canon of Scripture.

Meaning of the Term "Apocrypha" When the term *apokruphos* occurs in the NT, it simply means "hidden things." This original sense does not include the later meanings associated with it. In the formation of the Christian canon of Scripture, "apocrypha" came to mean works that were not divinely inspired and authoritative. The term was also used by certain groups (e.g. Gnostics) to describe their writings as secretive. They believed their writings were written much earlier but kept hidden until the latter days. Such writings were even then only available to the properly initiated. Since the church recognized works that were read openly in services of public worship, the term "apocrypha" came to mean "false" and began to be used to describe heretical material. In contrast to portions of the OT Apocrypha, which have been accepted by some branches of the Christian Church, none of the NT Apocrypha (with the possible exception of the *Apocalypse of Peter* and *the Acts of Paul*) has ever been accepted as Scripture. Though some scholars allow the term to describe writings that are neither a part of the NT nor strictly apocryphal (e.g. apostolic fathers), it seems best to restrict the term to material that was not received into the canon of Scripture yet, by form and content, claimed for itself a status and authority equal to Scripture.

Purpose of the Apocrypha Three general reasons explain the existence of the NT Apocrypha. First, some groups accepted apocryphal writings because they built on the universal desire to preserve the memories of the lives and deaths of important NT figures. Regardless of whether the transmitted traditions were true or false, the desire of later generations to know more detail made the apocryphal writings attractive. The second purpose is closely related to the first. Apocryphal works were intended to supplement the information given in the NT about Jesus or the apostles. This may be the motivation behind the *Third Epistle to the Corinthians* (to provide some of the missing correspondence between Paul and the Corinthian church) and the *Epistle to the Laodiceans* (to supply the letter referred to in Col. 4:16). For the same reason, the apocryphal acts made certain to record the events surrounding the death of the apostles, a matter on which the NT is usually silent. Third, heretical groups produced apocryphal writings in an attempt to gain authority for their own particular views.

Classification of the New Testament Apocrypha These writings parallel, in a superficial way, the literary forms found in the NT: Gospels, acts, epistles or letters, and apocalypses. Although this formal similarity exists, the title of an apocryphal work does not necessarily provide a trustworthy description of its character and contents.

The apocryphal gospels This large group of writings can be further classified into infancy gospels, passion gospels, Jewish-Christian gospels, and gospels originating from heretical groups.

Infancy Gospels is the name given to apocryphal works that in some way deal with the birth or childhood of Jesus or both. Though Matthew and Luke stressed the same basic story line, they emphasized different aspects of the events surrounding the birth of Jesus, primarily because of their audience and their own particular purpose in writing. The writers of these apocryphal infancy gospels attempted to correct what they viewed as deficiencies in the canonical accounts and to fill in the gaps they believed existed. Most of the material is concerned with the silent years of Jesus' childhood. The two earliest infancy gospels, from which most of the later literature developed, are the *Protoevangelium of James* and the *Infancy Gospel of Thomas*. The *Protoevangelium of James* seems to have been written to glorify Mary. It includes the miraculous birth of Mary, her presentation in the temple, her espousal to Joseph (an old man with children), and the miraculous birth of Jesus. This second-century work was extremely popular and undoubtedly had an influence on later views of Mary, the mother of Jesus. The *Infancy Gospel of Thomas* depicts Jesus in a crude manner as a wonder boy, using his miraculous powers as a matter of personal convenience. This work attempts to fill in the silent years of Jesus' childhood but does so in a rather repulsive and exaggerated manner.

As legend continued to expand, many later infancy gospels developed including the *Arabic Gospel of the Infancy*, the *Armenian Gospel of the Infancy*, the *Gospel of Pseudo-Matthew*, the *Latin Infancy Gospel*, the *Life of John According to Serapion*, the *Gospel of the Birth of Mary*, the *Assumption of the Virgin*, and the *History of Joseph the Carpenter*.

Passion Gospels, another class of apocryphal gospel, are concerned with supplementing the canonical accounts by describing events surrounding the crucifixion and resurrection of Jesus. The two most important works in this category are the *Gospel of Peter* and the *Gospel of Nicodemus* (sometimes called the *Acts of Pilate*). The *Gospel of Peter* is a second-century work that downplays Jesus' humanity, heightens the miraculous, and reduces Pilate's guilt, among other things. The *Gospel of Nicodemus* (Acts of Pilate) is another example of an apocryphal passion gospel. The trial and death of Jesus are expanded as Nicodemus, the chief narrator, tells of one witness after another coming forward to testify on Jesus' behalf. Pilate gives in to popular demand and hands Jesus over to be crucified. The *Gospel of Nicodemus* also includes a vivid account of Jesus' "Descent into Hell," much like that of a Greek hero invading the underworld to defy its authorities or rescue its prisoners. Another apocryphal work that might be classified as a passion gospel is the *Book of the Resurrection of Christ by Bartholomew the Apostle.*

Jewish-Christian Gospels are works that originated among Jewish-Christian groups. They include the *Gospel of the Ebionites*, the *Gospel of Hebrews*, and the *Gospel of the Nazorenes.* Although some scholars equate the Gospel of Hebrews and the *Gospel of the Nazorenes*, the evidence is inconclusive. The *Gospel of the Hebrews*, perhaps the most prominent, appears to have been in some ways a paraphrase of the canonical Gospel of Matthew and places a special emphasis on James, the brother of the Lord.

Heretical Gospels cover a wide variety of apocryphal gospels, most of which are considered Gnostic gospels. Gnosticism developed in the second century as a widespread and diverse religious movement with roots in Greek philosophy and folk religion. The *Gospel of Truth* contains no references to the words or actions of Jesus. Some heretical gospels are attributed to all or one of the twelve apostles. These include the *Gospel of the Twelve Apostles* and the gospels of Philip, Thomas, Matthias, Judas, and Bartholomew. Written about A.D. 100, the *Gospel of Thomas* (of no relation to the *Infancy Gospel of Thomas*) is a collection of 114 secret sayings "which Jesus the living one spoke and Didymus Judas Thomas wrote down." This document is one of almost fifty discovered in 1945 near Nag Hammadi in Upper Egypt as a part of what many scholars believe was the library of a Gnostic community. The heretical emphases of the *Gospel of Thomas* are countered in advance by the canonical epistle of 1 John, which emphasizes the gospel of Jesus Christ as the message of life, available for every person to experience. Other gospels in this class include those under the names of Holy Women (for example, the *Questions of Mary* and the *Gospel According to Mary*), and those attributed to chief heretics such as Cerinthus, Basilides, and Marcion.

The apocryphal acts A large number of legendary accounts of the journeys and heroics of NT apostles sought to parallel and supplement the book of Acts. The five major apocryphal acts are second- and third-century stories named after a "Leucius Charinus" and therefore known as the *Leucian Acts.* Even though they show a high regard for the apostles and include some historical fact, much of what they offer is the product of a wild imagination, closely akin to a romantic novel (with talking animals and obedient bugs).

The *Acts of John* is the earliest of the group (A.D. 150–160). It contains miracles and sermons by John of Asia Minor and has a distinct Gnostic orientation. It tells the story of John's journey from Jerusalem to Rome and his imprisonment on the isle of Patmos. After many other travels, John finally dies in Ephesus.

The *Acts of Andrew*, written shortly before A.D. 300, is, like the *Acts of John*, distinctly Gnostic.

The *Acts of Paul* was written before A.D. 200 by an Asian presbyter "out of love for Paul." He was later defrocked for publishing the writing. It is divided into three sections: the Acts of Paul and Thecla, a girl from Iconian who assisted Paul on his missionary travels; correspondence with the Corinthian church; and the martyrdom of Paul.

The *Acts of Peter* is a late second-century writing that tells of Peter defending the church from a heretic named Simon Magus by public preaching. Peter, who is forced to flee, later returns to be crucified upside down. Like the other acts, it is ascetic, that is, it promotes a lifestyle of self-denial and withdrawal from society as a means of combating vice and developing virtue.

The *Acts of Thomas* is a third-century work, thought by most scholars to have originated in Syriac Christianity. It tells how Judas Thomas, "Twin of the Messiah," was given India when the apostles divided the world by casting lots. Thomas, though he went as a slave, was responsible for the conversion of many well-known Indians. The ascetic element is again present in Thomas' emphasis on virginity. In the end he was imprisoned and martyred.

Other later apocryphal acts include: the *Apostolic History of Abdias*, the *Fragmentary Story of Andrew*, the *Ascents of James*, the *Martyrdom of Matthew*, the *Preaching of Peter*, *Slavonic Acts of Peter*, the *Passion of Paul*, *Passion of Peter*, *Passion of Peter and Paul*, the *Acts of Andrew and Matthias*, *Andrew and Paul*, *Paul and Thecla*, *Barnabas*, *James the Great*, *Peter and Andrew*, *Peter and Paul*, *Philip*, and *Thaddaeus*.

The apocryphal epistles We know of a small group of apocryphal epistles or letters, many of which are ascribed to the Apostle Paul. The *Epistle of the Apostles* is a second-century collection of visions communicating postresurrection teachings of Christ. The *Third Epistle to the Corinthians* was purported to be Paul's reply to a letter from Corinth. Though it circulated independently, it is also a part of the *Acts of Paul*. The *Latin Epistle to the Laodiceans* is a gathering of Pauline phrases probably motivated by Col. 4:16.

Other important apocryphal epistles include the *Correspondence of Christ and Abgar*, the *Epistle to the Alexandrians*, the *Epistle of Titus*, of *Peter to James*, of *Peter to Philip*, and of *Mary to Ignatius*.

The apocryphal apocalypses Revelation is the only apocalyptic book in the NT, though there are apocalyptic elements in other books (such as Mark 13 and parallels; 2 Thess. 2:1-12). The term "apocalypse" or "apocalyptic" means "to uncover" and is used to describe a category of writings that seek to unveil the plan of God for the world using symbol and visions. While the NT apocalyptic material emphasizes the return of Christ, the later apocryphal apocalypses focus more on heaven and hell. The most popular of these, the *Apocalypse of Peter*, seems to have enjoyed a degree of canonical status for a time. It presents visions of the resurrected Lord and images of the terror suffered by those in hell. The *Apocalypse of Paul* is probably motivated by Paul's reference in 2 Cor. 12:2 of a man in Christ being caught up to the third heaven. The author is thoroughly convinced this was Paul's personal experience and proceeds to give all the details. Other apocalypses include the *Apocalypse of James*, *of Stephen*, *of Thomas*, *of the Virgin Mary*, and several works discovered at Nag Hammadi.

Other apocryphal works These include the *Agrapha* (a collection of sayings attributed to

Jesus), the *Preachings of Peter*, the *Clementine Homilies* and *Recognitions*, the *Apocryphon of John*, the *Apocryphon of James*, and certain Gnostic writings such as the *Pistis Sophia*, the *Wisdom of Jesus*, and the *Books of Jeu*.

Relevance of the New Testament Apocrypha The NT Apocrypha is significant for those who study church history. Even though these writings were not included in the canon, they are not worthless. They give a sample of the ideas, convictions, and imaginations of a portion of Christian history. The NT Apocrypha also serves as a point of comparison with the writings contained in the canon of the NT. By way of contrast the apocryphal writings demonstrate how the NT places a priority on historical fact rather than human fantasy. While the NT Apocrypha is often interesting and informative, it is usually unreliable historically and always unauthoritative for matters of faith and practice. See *Apocalyptic*. *J. Scott Duvall*

APOLLONIA (Ăp ol lō´ nĭ à) Place-name meaning "belonging to Apollo." Paul visited Apollonia on his second missionary journey, though the Bible reports no activity there (Acts 17:1). The city is in northern Greece or Macedonia on the international highway called Via Egnatia, 30 miles from Amphipolis and 38 miles from Thessalonica.

APOLLOS (Á pŏl´ lŏs) Alexandrian Jew who came to Ephesus following Paul's first visit and was taught Christian doctrine by Priscilla and Aquila. An educated man, Apollos handled the OT Scriptures with forcefulness. However, he was lacking in a full understanding of the way of God, so Priscilla and Aquila took him aside and instructed him (Acts 18:26). Apollos became even more successful in his ministry. He went from Ephesus to Greece with the encouragement of the Asian believers and a letter of introduction (Acts 18:27). He greatly strengthened the believers by using the Scriptures to demonstrate that Jesus was the Christ (Acts 18:28).

Apollos is last mentioned in the book of Acts as being in Corinth (19:1). Paul referred to Apollos frequently, particularly in 1 Corinthians. Here the majority of the references (1 Cor. 1:12; 3:4-6,22) have to do with the schisms in the Corinthian church centering on personalities. Paul noted that some believers championed Paul; some, Apollos; and some, Cephas. What is important is that believers belong to Christ, not to individual leaders. Such references show that Apollos must have been a dynamic figure to be compared with Paul or Peter. In 1 Cor. 4:6 Paul placed Apollos on the same level as himself. They both sought to defeat the arrogance and superiority which comes from being self-centered rather than Christ-centered.

Paul referred to Apollos in 1 Cor. 16:12 as "our brother," showing how much Paul considered him as one of the team. This is also demonstrated in Titus 3:13 where Paul asked Titus to help Apollos on his way. A learned and gifted preacher Apollos was willing to receive more instruction and be part of the team.

Because of Apollos' knowledge of the OT, Luther suggested that Apollos might well be the writer of the letter to the Hebrews. See *Corinth; Corinthians, First Letter to the; Corinthians, Second Letter to the; Ephesus; Priscilla and Aquila.*   *William H. Vermillion*

APOLLYON (Ả·pŏll´ yon) Greek name meaning "destroyer" (Rev. 9:11). See *Abaddon.*

APOSTASY Act of rebelling against, forsaking, abandoning, or falling away from what one has believed.

Old Testament The OT speaks of "falling away" in terms of a person's deserting to a foreign king (2 Kings 25:11; Jer. 37:13-14; 39:9; 52:15). Associated ideas, however, include the concept of religious unfaithfulness: "rebellion" (Josh. 22:22); "cast away" (2 Chron. 29:19); "trespass" (2 Chron. 33:19); and "backslidings" (Jer. 2:19; 8:5). NASB uses "apostasy" in Jer. 8:5 and Hos. 14:4 with the plural in Jer. 2:19; 5:6; 14:7.

The prophets picture Israel's history as the history of turning from God to other gods, from His law to injustice and lawlessness, from His anointed king to foreign kings, and from His word to the word of foreign kings. This is defined simply as forsaking God, not fearing Him (Jer. 2:19). Such action was sin, for which the people had to ask forgiveness (Jer. 14:7-9) and repent (Jer. 8:4-7). The basic narrative of Judges, Samuel, and Kings is that Israel fell away from God, choosing selfish ways rather than His ways. Exile resulted. Still God's fallen people had hope. In freedom God could choose to turn away His anger and heal their "backsliding" (Hos. 14:4).

New Testament The English word "apostasy" is derived from a Greek word (*apostasia*) that means, "to stand away from." The Greek noun occurs twice in the NT (Acts 21:21; 2 Thess. 2:3), though it is not translated as "apostasy" in the KJV. A related noun is used for a divorce (Matt. 5:31; 19:7; Mark 10:4). The corresponding Greek verb occurs nine times.

Acts 21:21 states an accusation made against Paul that he was leading Jews outside Palestine to abandon the law of Moses. Such apostasy was defined as failing to circumcise Jewish children and to observe distinctive Jewish customs.

In 2 Thess. 2:3 Paul addressed those who had been deceived into believing that the day of the Lord had already come. He taught that an apostasy would precede the day of the Lord. The Spirit had explicitly revealed this falling away from the faith (1 Tim. 4:1). Such apostasy in the latter times will involve doctrinal deception, moral insensitivity, and ethical departures from God's truth.

Associated NT concepts include the parable of the soils, in which Jesus spoke of those who believe for a while but "fall away" in time of temptation (Luke 8:13). At the judgment those who work iniquity will be told to "depart" (Luke 13:27). Paul "withdrew" from the synagogue in Ephesus (Acts 19:9) because of the opposition he found there, and he counseled Timothy to "withdraw" from those who advocate a different doctrine (1 Tim. 6:3-5). Hebrews speaks of falling away from the living God because of "an evil heart of unbelief" (3:12). Those who fall away cannot be renewed again to repentance (Heb. 6:6). Yet God is able to keep the believer from falling (Jude 24).

Implications Apostasy certainly is a biblical concept, but the implications of the teaching have been hotly debated. The debate has centered on the issue of apostasy and salvation. Based on the concept of God's sovereign grace, some hold that, though true believers may stray, they will never totally fall away. Others affirm that any who fall away were never really saved. Though they may have "believed" for a while, they never experienced regeneration. Still others argue that the biblical warnings against apostasy are real and that believers maintain the freedom, at least potentially, to reject God's salvation.

Persons worried about apostasy should recognize that conviction of sin in itself is evidence that one has not fallen away. Desire for salvation shows one does not have "an evil heart of unbelief."   *Michael Fink*

APOSTLE Derivation of the Greek word *apostolos,* one who is sent. *Apostolos* was used to refer to a ship or a group of ships. Later it designated a bill, invoice, or passport.

In the NT, "apostle" has three broad uses. First, it referred to the Twelve whom Jesus chose to train for the task of carrying His message to the world. Following His resurrection, Jesus commissioned them for this task. These men had been with Jesus from the beginning of His ministry and were witnesses to His resurrection. Paul was an apostle in this sense because he had seen the risen Christ.

The second designation of apostle is a person authorized by a local congregation with the safe delivery of specific gifts for another Christian church (2 Cor. 8:23; Phil.2:25).

The third sense of apostle is those whom Jesus Christ has sent. Paul refers to a number of people as apostles in this sense (Rom. 16:7; 1 Cor. 9:1,5; 12:28; Gal. 1:17-19). See *Disciple.*
                                                     Steve Bond

APOSTOLIC COUNCIL Meeting in Jerusalem at which the apostles and elders of Jerusalem defended the right of Paul and Barnabas to preach the gospel to the Gentiles without forcing converts to obey the Jewish laws (Acts 15). A "decree" from the council did ask Gentile converts not to eat food that had been sacrificed to idols, not to eat meat with blood in it, not to eat animals which had been strangled, and not to commit sexual immorality (Acts 15:28-29). These requirements may all be taken from Leviticus 17–18, which set up requirements not only on the "house of Israel" but also on "the strangers which sojourn among you" (Lev. 17:8).

In Galatians 2 Paul described the work of the council from his perspective, though some Bible students have long tried to distinguish between the events of Acts 15 and Galatians 2. Paul not only reported the council's decision, he emphasized the fact that the council didn't require Titus, a Gentile, to be circumcised.

APOSTOLIC FATHERS Group of early church writers, some of whom knew the apostles. These writers were not grouped together or called the Apostolic Fathers until the late 17th century. That first collection, entitled the Apostolic Fathers, included the works of Clement, Ignatius, Polycarp, Barnabas, and Hermas. Other works such as the Didache, Diognetus, and Papias often have been included in recent collections. The documents (except for Diognetus, and Papias) were written between approximately between A.D. 96 and 156, yet they were not accepted as part of the NT canon, although Codex Sinaiticus (fourth century) included the Epistle of Barnabas and the Shepherd of Hermas, and Codex Alexandrinus (fifth century) included the two epistles of Clement.

The Apostolic Fathers includes two epistles of Clement who was the third bishop of Rome (following Linus and Anacletus). The first epistle, which dates to 96, was written to the church in Corinth to address internal problems within the church, namely the expulsion of the presbyters by the congregation. Clement called on the congregation to re-instate the expelled presbyters who had been selected by the apostles. The epistle illustrated the continued existence of factions within the Corinthian church, even after Paul had addressed those problems in his own epistles to the church. Clement also provided the seminal idea of apostolic succession when he argued that the elders should be reinstated because they were appointed by the apostles themselves. The second epistle of Clement was in reality a sermon that exhorted the hearers to live a godly life and remain faithful in view of Christ's final coming. Recent scholars have questioned Clement's authorship of the sermon since certain elements may have been directed toward the Gnostics, who did not emerge within the church until the mid-second century.

The Didache, or Teaching of the Twelve Apostles, was an early church handbook that dates between A.D. 100 and 110. Although this anonymous work was not originally grouped with the collection, since its discovery in the late nineteenth century, it has come to be an accepted part of the Apostolic Fathers. The work began by addressing proper conduct, which was discussed as the "way of life" versus the "way of death." The second section of the work provided instructions for church leaders regarding how to conduct services and included instructions to the church leaders should baptize by immersion if at all possible.

The collection contains several epistles from Ignatius, Bishop of Antioch, who was a disciple of the Apostle John. Ignatius wrote these epistles around A.D. 115 as he journeyed to Rome, where he was martyred. Numerous epistles exist, yet scholars have generally only accepted as authentic the epistles to the churches of Ephesus, Magnesia, Tralles, Rome, Philadelphia, Smyrna, and the epistle to Polycarp. Within these epistles Ignatius expressed a desire to be martyred and affirmed Christ's humanity against the heresy of Docetism. Ignatius' epistles made two significant contributions to the development of Roman Catholic theology. The first related to the Eucharist, which Ignatius described as the "flesh of our savior Jesus Christ" (Epistle to Smyrnaens) and the "medicine of immortality, the antidote against death" (Epistle to the Ephesians). These thoughts laid a foundation for the development of the Eucharist as a sacrament and for the doctrine of transubstantiation. The second contribution related to his elevation of the bishop, as he charged, "follow the bishop as Jesus Christ followed the Father" (Epistle to Smyrnaens). This thought helped support the idea of apostolic succession and the elevation of tradition within the church.

The collection contains two documents related to Polycarp, bishop of Smyrna and disciple of the Apostle John. The first document was an epistle written by Polycarp and sent to the church at Philippi. The letter, which may date to around A.D. 116, was essentially an amalgam of quotes from the Pastoral Epistles, although it did include information regarding the debate over whether to celebrate Easter on the actual day of the resurrection or on the closest Sunday. The second document related to Polycarp was an account of his martyrdom. This document, written in 156, detailed the death of Polycarp and described mythical elements surrounding his execution, such as his blood extinguishing the fire which was meant to consume him. It was significant for its encouragement to remain faithful in the face of persecution, for its glorification of martyrdom, and for its use of the term "catholic [i.e., "universal"] church."

The collection also includes the Epistle of Barnabas, which was not written by the biblical Barnabas. The work was most likely written around 135 and was responding to the second Jewish rebellion under Bar Kokhba from 132 to 135. The writing was anti-Jewish in tone, describing OT elements such as animal sacrifice, construction of a temple, and adherence to the law as being mistakes made by the Jews, who did not understand God's will. Barnabas relied upon allegorical interpretation to prove that the OT taught that Christianity was the true religion and Judaism was based upon human misunderstanding.

The Shepherd of Hermas was written by an anonymous writer, probably sometime between A.D. 140 and 150. The work was an allegory that stressed penance. It was significant for its mention of only one forgiveness of sins after baptism, an idea that led many Christians, like Constantine, to postpone baptism until they lay on their deathbed. That practice eventually developed into the sacrament of final unction. In addition, the work also presented the seminal idea of purgatory.

In the 20th century, scholars added several other works to the Apostolic Fathers, although some disagreement over which additions rightly belong does still exist. Among the works added was the Epistle to Diognetus, which was written by an anonymous author to an anonymous recipient. The work is difficult to date, being written sometime during the late second or early third century. This is an apology that argues the merits of Christianity over Judaism and Paganism. Due to the nature of the work, some scholars choose to classify it with the apologetic literature rather than with the Apostolic Fathers. Some scholars consider the works of Papias to be considered to be a part of the collection, even though his works no longer exist. Papias was a disciple of the Apostle John and an associate of Polycarp.

The Apostolic Fathers allow modern scholars to see the issues being dealt with by the early church. They also help scholars trace the development of Roman Catholic doctrines like baptismal regeneration, transubstantiation, and purgatory, which all find their beginnings in the Fathers. In addition, the Apostolic Fathers' quotations of Scripture show not only which Scriptures were being used by the early church but also provide insight into how the early church interpreted and used the Word of God.

Scott Drumm

APOTHECARY (Á pŏth´ ə câr y) KJV translation of a word translated as "perfumer" in modern versions (Exod. 30:25,35; 37:29; 2 Chron. 16:14; Neh. 3:8; Eccles. 10:1). See *Perfume, Perfumer.*

APPAIM (Ăp´ pā·ĭm) Personal name meaning "nostrils." Member of clan of Jerahmeel of tribe of Judah (1 Chron. 2:30-31).

APPEAL TO CAESAR When Paul was brought before Festus for trial on charges made against him by Jews from Jerusalem, Festus asked him if he wanted to return to Jerusalem for trial. Paul, fearing the Jews would kill him, asked that his case be heard by the emperor, as he had done nothing deserving of death (Acts 25:1-12). By all appearances, Paul's Roman citizenship gave him the right to have his case heard by the emperor. There are cases, however, where Roman citizens in Africa were refused the right of appeal and were crucified by Galba, the governor of the province. Paul was granted his appeal, though it was later determined that he need not have appealed his case as he had done nothing wrong (Acts 26:32). We do not know the results of Paul's appeal since Acts ends with Paul still in prison awaiting trial. It is probable that Paul's case was dismissed after two years and he was released from prison.

APPENDAGE OF THE LIVER See *Caul.*

APPHIA (Ăp´ phĭ·à) Christian lady Paul greeted as "beloved" while writing Philemon (v. 2).

Pharaoh's Island in the Gulf of Aqaba.

Early Christian tradition identified her as Philemon's wife, a claim that can be neither proved nor disproved.

APPI FORUM (Ăp´ pĭ fō´ rŭm) KJV translation of Acts 28:15 reference to Forum of Appius or Market of Appius. See *Forum.*

APPIUS (Ăp´ pĭ·ŭs) See *Forum.*

APPLE OF THE EYE English expression that refers to the pupil of the eye and therefore to something very precious. Three different Hebrew words or phrases are rendered as the apple of the eye: (1) the word in Deut. 32:10 and Prov. 7:2 literally means "little man" and evidently refers to the reflection of a person in the eye of another; (2) the word in Ps. 17:8 and Lam. 2:18 (KJV) literally means "the daughter of the eye" with possibly the same significance as (1); and (3) the word in Zech. 2:8 literally means "gate." The reference in Lam. 2:18 is to the pupil of the eye as the source of tears; the other references are metaphorical of something that is precious.

APPLE TREE Known in the OT for its fruit, shade, beauty, and fragrance (Joel 1:12; Prov. 25:11; Song 2:3,5; 7:8; 8:5). Some scholars

doubt that the Hebrew text is referring to the apple tree. They think the common apple tree was only recently introduced to Palestine, and that the wild variety hardly matches the description given to the tree and its fruit in the Bible. The citron, quince, and apricot have been proposed as the tree spoken of in the Bible. Of the three, the apricot seems to have the best support. Having been introduced from China prior to the time of Abraham, the apricot is widespread in Palestine. When conditions for it are right, the apricot tree can grow to a height of about 30 feet with spreading branches, which make it a good shade tree. Hebrew *tappuach* "apple" does appear as a place-name in the Bible and may indicate apple trees were known as unusual occurrences in some Palestinian sites.

APRON Translation of a Hebrew word in the OT otherwise translated as girdle (1 Sam. 18:4; 2 Sam. 18:11; 20:8; 1 Kings 2:5; Isa. 3:24). In Gen. 3:7, the fig leaves sewn together by Adam and Eve are called aprons to hide their nakedness. In the OT the girdle was an inner garment wrapped around the waist. In the NT the girdle was wrapped around the waist of the outer garment. In Acts 19:12 the aprons and handkerchiefs of Paul had healing powers.

AQABA, GULF OF TEV translation in 1 Kings 9:26 to show that the part of the Red Sea meant is the eastern arm below the Dead Sea. Its northern port city is Eloth (or Elath, NIV). See *Elath; Ezion-geber.*

AQUEDUCTS Troughs cut out of rock or soil, or pipes made of stone, leather, or bronze that were used from very early times in the Middle East to transport water from distant places into towns and cities.
Old Testament The simplest aqueducts were troughs cut out of rock or soil and sometimes lined with mortar. These troughs carried water from hillsides to the valleys below. Jerusalem was served by a system of aqueducts which brought mountain spring water first to collecting reservoirs outside the city, and then into the city itself. Hezekiah's tunnel, the Siloam tunnel, was a twisting underground aqueduct that diverted water from the Gihon Spring to the Pool of Siloam (2 Kings 20:20).
Roman Aqueducts The Romans excelled in building aqueducts, and the remains of these sys-

Roman aqueduct at Caesarea Maritima which transported water to the city from the Carmel Mountains.

tems are impressive. Ancient aqueducts, the nonpressure type, carried water downhill by means of gravity. Although most conduits were beneath the ground, lowlands were crossed on high, arched structures, each containing a built-in slope so that water flow was not impeded. Sometimes these elevated sections, while also carrying several channels of water, served as footbridges. The Romans built many aqueducts, the longest of which covered 57 miles.

Diane Cross

AQUILA AND PRISCILLA Married couple who came from Italy to Corinth after the emperor Claudius ordered Jews expelled from Rome, became Christians, and assisted Paul in his ministry. They were tentmakers by trade (2 Tim. 4:19). They came into contact with Paul, who was a tentmaker, in Corinth (Acts 18:2). It is not clear whether they became Christians before or after meeting Paul, but they became workers in the gospel and accompanied Paul to Ephesus (Acts 18:19). There they instructed Apollos in the Christian faith (18:25). A church met in their home, and they joined Paul in writing to the Corinthian church (1 Cor. 16:19).

Aquila and Priscilla were apparently influential among the "Gentile churches" (Rom. 16:3 HCSB). This reference in Romans probably indicates that Priscilla and Aquila moved back to Rome. Some scholars think the church at Ephesus received a copy of the last chapter of Romans. The reference to the couple in 2 Tim. 4:19 may indicate the couple was in Ephesus.

Paul thanked Aquila and Priscilla for risking their own lives for him (Rom. 16:4). The circumstances of this incident are unknown, although it may have occurred during Paul's trouble with Demetrius the silversmith (Acts 19:23-41).   *Taylor Field*

AR (Är) Place-name meaning "city." Town on northern border of Moab on southern bank of Arnon River (Num. 21:15,28). Israel celebrated its defeat with a proverbial taunt song (Num. 21:28). God refused to let Israel occupy Ar, having designated it for Lot's descendants, the Moabites (Deut. 2:9). Israel could only pass through Ar (Deut. 2:18), evidently the region controlled by the city-state. Ar provided provisions for the Israelites as they passed through on the last legs of the wilderness wandering (Deut. 2:29). Isaiah used a threatening situation in Ar to announce a time when Moab would seek protection from Judah (Isa. 15:1). The exact location of the city is not known.

ARA (Ā´ rà) Leader in tribe of Asher (1 Chron. 7:38).

ARAB (Ă´ răb) Place-name meaning "ambush." **1.** City in the hill country of Judah near Hebron (Josh. 15:52). Usually identified with modern er-Rabiyeh. See *Arbite.* **2.** Member of the Semitic people of the Arabian peninsula. See *Arabia.*

ARABAH (Ăr´ á·bāh) Place-name meaning "dry, infertile area" and common Hebrew noun meaning desert with hot climate and sparse rainfall. **1.** Modern usage refers specifically to the rift area below the Dead Sea to the Gulf of Elath or Aqaba, a distance of 110 miles. This was a copper-mining region and was guarded by military fortresses. Control of the Arabah along with control of the Red Sea port on its southern end meant control of valuable trade routes and sea routes connecting to southern Arabia and eastern Africa (Deut. 2:8; 1 Kings 9:26-27). **2.** The wilderness of Judah encompassing the eastern slopes of the mountains of Judah with little rain, deep canyons, and steep cliffs where David hid from Saul (1 Sam. 23:24-25). **3.** The entire Jordan Valley running 70 miles from the Sea of Galilee to the Dead Sea, or more precisely, the desert areas above the actual Zor or lushly fertile areas on the immediate shore of the Jordan (Deut. 3:17 RSV, NIV; Josh. 8:14 TEV, NIV; 11:2,16; 12:8 NASB, NIV; 2 Sam. 2:29 NASB, NIV; Jer. 39:4 NASB, NIV; Ezek. 47:8 NASB, NIV; Zech. 14:10 NIV). **4.** Sea of the Arabah is the Dead Sea (NASB, NIV, RSV of Deut. 3:17;

4:49; Josh. 3:16; 2 Kings 14:25). **5.** Araboth of Moab or plains of Moab includes the eastern shore of the Dead Sea south of the Wadi Nimrim (NEB translation as "lowlands of Moab"; Num. 22:1; 31:12; 36:13; Deut. 34:1; Josh. 13:32). **6.** Desert area or the eastern border of the Jordan River from the Sea of Galilee to the Dead Sea (Josh. 12:1 NASB, NIV, RSV). **7.** Araboth of Jericho or plains of Jericho represent the area near the Jordan once dominated by the city-state of Jericho (Josh. 4:13; 5:10; 2 Kings 25:5; Jer. 39:5). **8.** Brook of the Arabah represents the southern border of Israel (Amos 6:14), possibly the River Zered, the Wadi el-Qelt, or the Wadi Hefren.

ARABIA (Á·rā´ bī·á) Asian peninsula lying between the Red Sea on the west and the Persian Gulf on the east incorporating over 1,200,000 square miles of territory.

Old Testament The Arabian peninsula, together with the adjoining lands which were home to the biblical Arabs, includes all of present-day Saudi Arabia, the two Yemens (San'a' and Aden), Oman, the United Arab Emirates, Qatar, and Kuwait, as well as parts of Iraq, Syria, Jordan, and the Sinai Peninsula. The vast Arabian Peninsula was divided into two distinct economic and social regions. Most biblical references to Arab peoples or territory are to the northern and western parts of this whole but sometimes includes both the northern and southern portions.

In the northern portion of Arabia, the mountains of the Anti-Lebanon, the Transjordanian Highlands, and the mountains of Edom flank the desert on the west. The mountains continue all the way down the western edge of the Arabian Peninsula bordering the Red Sea and are actually much higher and more rugged in the south. The central and northern portions of the peninsula, and extending north into Syria and Iraq, are vast expanses of sandy and rocky desert, including some of the driest climate in the world.

The name "Arab" comes from a Semitic root, which in Hebrew is *arab,* probably meaning "nomad" or Bedouin. This refers to the people of the northwestern parts of the Arabian territory, whom the OT writers knew as nomadic herders of sheep and goats, and later, of camels. Sometimes *arab* simply refers to the economic status of nomads without geographical or ethical reference. Proper understanding of Scripture includes determining the specific meaning of "Arab" in each context.

The Arabs are also called in the Bible "the sons (or children) of the east." Furthermore, many of the names of the OT refer to people or tribes who were ethnically and linguistically Arab. These include the Midianites, the Ishmaelites, the people of Kedar, the Amalekites, the Dedanites, the Temanites, and others. The Israelites recognized their blood relationship with the Arabs. Most of these groups are linked with Abraham through his son Ishmael or through his second wife Keturah (Gen. 25).

The inhabitants of southern Arabia, in the mountains fringing the Red Sea and the Indian Ocean, were town-dwellers with a sophisticated system of irrigation. They possessed considerable wealth from incenses and spices which they grew; from gold, silver, and precious stones, which they mined in their own territory; and from these and other products which they transported and traded to the Mediterranean world, Mesopotamia, and as far away as East Africa, India, and China.

New Testament The NT references to Arabia are fewer and less complex. The territory of the Nabatean Arabs is probably intended in each instance. The Nabateans controlled what is today southern Jordan and the Negev of Israel; for a time they controlled as far north as Damascus. Arabs heard the gospel at Pentecost (Acts 2:11). Paul went to Arabia after his conversion (Gal. 1:17).   *Joseph Coleson*

ARABIM (Är´ à·bĭm) NASB transliteration of name of waterway mentioned in Isa. 15:7. Other translations include: "brook of the willows" (KJV); "Ravine of the Poplars" (NIV); Valley of Willows (TEV); "Wadi of the Willows (NRSV). The water source indicated may be the Wadi el-Chesa at the southern end of the Dead Sea in Moab.

ARAD (Är´ rad) Two towns of significance to the OT and two OT men. One town is referred to in the Bible during the time of Moses, and another was inhabited during the period of the monarchy. Both are located in the dry, semi-desert region known as the Negev in the southern extreme of Judah's territory.

The Arad of Num. 21:1-3 (probably Tel Malhata) was a Canaanite city about 11 miles west southwest of Beersheba. Its king attacked the

The Citadel built by Solomon on the highest point on Arad, a hill about 130 feet high. Arad is some 18.5 miles northeast of Beersheba.

Israelites as they were moving on to Canaan after the wilderness wandering. He was successful temporarily, taking captives; but after vowing to God that they would destroy the city, Israel struck back effectively and renamed the devastated city Hormah. Victory over this king is recorded in Josh. 12:14. Subsequently the Kenites settled in Arad near the tribe of Judah (Judg. 1:16-17).

Another Arad location about 17 miles west northwest of Beersheba is not mentioned in the Bible but was an important fortress for Judah from Solomon's time to Josiah, over 300 years. A temple has been found there with architecture much like the biblical tabernacle and temple, having similar chambers including a holy of holies. Even the names of priestly families of Israel have been found here, Pashhur (Ezra 2:38; 10:22) and Meremoth (Ezra 8:33; Neh. 10:5). The temple may well have been destroyed during Josiah's reforms, which tolerated only the one temple in Jerusalem.

One of the men called "Arad" was one of six sons of Beriah the Benjaminite (1 Chron. 8:15-16), who was one of the major inhabitants of Aijalon.

Reconstruction of the stone altar at Arad.

Another OT "Arad" was a Canaanite king who attacked the Israelites near Mount Hor and was defeated (Num. 21:1). See *Aijalon.*

Daniel C. Fredericks

ARAH (Ā´ răh) Personal name meaning "ox" or "traveler." **1.** Clan of 775 people who returned to Jerusalem with Zerubbabel from Babylonian exile about 537 B.C. (Ezra 2:5). Nehemiah 7:10 gives the number as 652. **2.** Father of Schechaniah, father-in-law of Tobiah, who led opposition to Nehemiah (Neh. 6:18). May be identical with clan head of 1. above. **3.** Member of tribe of Asher (1 Chron. 7:39).

ARAM (Ă´ răm) Personal, ethnic, and geographical name. **1.** Arameans. See *Aramean.* **2.** Original ancestor of Arameans, the son of Shem and grandson of Noah (Gen. 10:22-23). **3.** Grandson of Nahor, Abraham's brother (Gen. 22:21). **4.** Member of tribe of Asher (1 Chron. 7:34). See various compound names with "Aram"; *Beth-rehob; Paddan-aram; Geshur; Maacah; Tob; Zobah.*

ARAMAIC (Ăr·à·mā´ ĭc) North Semitic language similar to Phoenician and Hebrew. It was the language of the Arameans whose presence in northwestern Mesopotamia is known from about 2000 B.C.

Old Testament Although the Aramaeans never founded a great national state or empire, by the eleventh century they had established several small states in Syria, and their language came to be known from Egypt to Persia.

The oldest inscriptions in Old Aramaic are from Syria around 800 B.C. In the ninth century official or Royal Aramaic appeared. This was a

A funerary inscription of the second burial of King Uzziah written in Aramaic during Herod's time.

dialect known from documents from Assyria and known best from documents from the Persian Empire, for which Aramaic had become the official court language. Before 700 B.C. Aramaic had begun to supplant Akkadian as the language of commerce and diplomacy (2 Kings 18:26). Important for biblical history are the fifth-century papyri from Elephantine, the site of a Jewish colony in Egypt. Official Aramaic continued to be used widely throughout the Hellenistic period.

Parts of the OT were written in Aramaic: Ezra 4:8–6:18; 7:12-26; Dan. 2:4b–7:28; Jer. 10:11. Two words in Gen. 31:47, *Jegarsahadutha* (heap of witness) are in Aramaic. A number of Aramaic words came into common Hebrew usage, and several passages in the Hebrew Bible show Aramaic influence.

New Testament The wide diffusion of Aramaic, along with its flexibility and adaptability, resulted in the emergence of various dialects. In Syria-Palestine the western group includes Jewish Palestinian Aramaic, Samaritan, Palmyrene, and Nabataean. Jewish Palestinian Aramaic words and phrases occur in the NT, such as *Abba* (father) (Mark 14:36), *talitha, qumi* (maiden, arise) (Mark 5:41), *lama sabachthani* (why have You forsaken Me?) (Mark 15:34 HCSB). The Palestinian Talmud and the Targums (translations of OT books into Aramaic) also were written in Palestinian Jewish Aramaic. The eastern (Mesopotamian) group includes Babylonian Jewish Aramaic, Mandaean, and Syriac. *Thomas Smothers*

ARAMEAN (Ăr·à·mē´ ăn) or **ARAMAEAN** Loose confederation of towns and settlements spread over what is now called Syria as well as in some parts of Babylon from which Jacob and Abraham came (Deut. 26:5). The Aramaeans were rarely gathered into a cohesive political group; rather they lived as independent towns and tribes settled by nomads prior to 1000 B.C. Although the Aramaeans were quick to form alliances with each one another or with other countries if threatened, once the crisis was ended they disbanded and often fought among themselves and against their former allies.

The OT records interactions between Israel and the Aramaeans on a number of occasions. Deuteronomy 26:5 contains what has become an important confession for Jews—"A wandering Aramean was my father." (RSV)—which claims Aramaean lineage for Jacob and by extension for Abraham. The first mention of Aramaeans outside of the Bible dates from the reign of Tiglath-pileser I of Assyria (1116–1076 B.C.). Thus roughly at the start of Israel's monarchy, the Aramaeans became a potent political force. They were able to seize large portions of Assyrian lands, defeating Tiglath-pileser I and II and Ashur-rabi II. At the same time they suffered losses to David on the western front (2 Sam. 8:9-10). He demanded tribute from Hadadezer, king of Zobah, and married Maacah the daughter of Talmui, king of Geshur. It was Maacah who bore Absalom (2 Sam. 3:3). Both Zobah and Geshur were Aramaean states.

The most important city of the Aramaeans was Damascus. Although the political influence of the Aramaeans was relatively unimportant, they made a lasting contribution with their language. See *Aramaic; Assyria; Damascus.*

Tim Turnham

ARAMITESS (Är´ á·mīt·ĕss) KJV translation in 1 Chron. 7:14 for an unnamed concubine from Aram, thus an Aramaean or Syrian. She was mother of Machir, son of Manasseh.

ARAM-MAACAH (Ā´ răm-Mā´á·căh) Territory in Syria (1 Chron. 19:6), also called Syriamaachah, Maacah, Maachah. In 2 Sam. 10:6 only Aram-Zobah is named. See *Maacah.*

ARAM-NAHARAIM (Ā´ răm-Nā·há·rā´ īm) Country name meaning "Aram of the two rivers." Appears in title of Psalm 60 in KJV. Transliterated from Hebrew also in Gen. 24:10; Deut. 23:4; Judg. 3:8; and 1 Chron. 19:6 by NIV. It refers to the land between the Tigris and Euphrates Rivers. Nahor, Abraham's brother, lived there; and Rebekah, Isaac's wife, came from there. Balaam, the prophet Balak hired to curse Israel as they entered Moab from the wilderness, came from Aram-naharaim. So did Cushan-rishathaim, who oppressed Israel before Othniel delivered them. The Ammonites bought military help from Aram-naharaim to fight David.

ARAM-ZOBAH (Ā´ răm-Zō´ bah) Alternate name for the Aramaean town and kingdom of Zobah found in the superscription of Psalm 60. See *Zobah.*

ARAN (Ā´ răn) Personal name, perhaps meaning "ibex." A Horite descended from Seir (Gen. 36:28).

ARARAT (Âr´ á·răt) Mountainous region in western Asia. **1.** Area where the ark came to rest after the flood (Gen. 8:4). **2.** Region where Sennacherib's sons fled for refuge after murdering their father (2 Kings 19:37). **3.** Jeremiah included in a prophetic call for a war league as

This mountain in modern Turkey may be part of the Mountains of Ararat where Noah's ark came to rest after the flood.

judgment against Babylon (Jer. 51:27). The references in Kings and Isaiah are rendered "Armenia" in KJV, following the Septuagint tradition.

Geography The Errata of the OT is known as the land of Urartu in sources outside the Bible, especially Assyrian sources. The people of the region identified themselves as "children of Haldi" (the national god) and their land as *Biainae*. The country was southeast of the Black Sea and southwest of the Caspian, where the headwaters of the Tigris and Euphrates Rivers were found. Near the center of the land was Lake Van; Lake Sevan lay on its northern border; and Lake Urmia was found in its southeast corner. Modern Turkey, Iran, and Soviet Armenia occupy parts of the ancient land area of Urartu. Mount Ararat is located to the northeast of Lake Van.

Ararat rises from the lowlands of the Aras River to a height of 17,000 feet. Considering the high elevation, the region is remarkably fertile and pasturable. Archaeologists believe that Ararat received more rainfall in biblical times than it does today, an observation which suggests that the area would have been even more productive as farmland in ancient times.

History of Ararat The height of Urartian political prominence was between 900 and 700 B.C. Culturally the Urartians were akin to the earlier Hurrians and to the Assyrians whose empire stretched to the south. From after 1100 until after 800 B.C., Urartu remained independent of Assyria and in many ways was a political rival. The rise of Tiglath-pileser III (745–727 B.C.) in Assyria, followed by Sargon II (721–705 B.C.), crushed any political ambitions Urartu might have had in the region. *See Ark; Flood; Noah.*

A. J. Conyers

ARARITE (Âr´ ā·rīt) NASB spelling of Hararite (2 Sam. 23:33) reflecting distinctive Hebrew spelling of written text, which has already been marked for change by early Hebrew scribes. See *Hararite.*

ARAUNAH (A·raū´ năh) Personal name of unknown meaning. A Jebusite whose threshing floor David purchased as a site for sacrifice, following the prophetic command of God, holding back a divine plague after David disobeyed by taking a census (2 Sam. 24:15-25). Second Chronicles 3:1 and 1 Chron. 21:15-30 refer to Araunah as Ornan.

ARBA (Är´ bä) Personal name meaning "four." Father of Anak for whom Kiriath-arba was named (Josh. 14:15; 15:13). The city became known as Hebron. Arba was the outstanding warrior among the Anakim. See *Anak, Anakim.*

ARBATHITE (Är´ băth·īt) Resident of Beth-arabah (2 Sam. 23:31). See *Beth-arabah.*

ARBITE (Är´ bīt) Native of Arab, a village in Judah near Hebron (Josh. 15:52), identified as modern er-Rabiyeh. One of David's warriors in the 30 was Paarai, an Arbite (2 Sam. 23:35).

ARBITRATOR See *Mediator.*

ARCH KJV rendering of a Hebrew word in Ezek. 40:16-36. The KJV translates the word as "porch" elsewhere (e.g., 1 Kings 6:3; 7:12,19,21). Other versions translate the word as "porch" (NASB), "portico" and "galleries" (NIV), "vestibule" and "walls" (RSV), and "entrance room" and "galleries" (TEV). Aside from 1 Kings 7:6 (where the word describes a covered porch whose roof is supported by columns), the word refers to the entrance room to the main building of the temple just outside the holy place. The entrance was about 30 by 15 feet and 45 feet high (1 Kings 6:2-3; cp. 2 Chron. 3:4). In Ezekiel's vision of the temple, each gate leading into the court of the Gentiles

Greco-Roman arches in the ruins of Gerasa (modern Jerash, Jordan), a city in the Decapolis.

also had a vestibule (40:7-26) as did the gates to the court of the Israelites (40:29-37). See *Hall.*

ARCHAEOLOGY AND BIBLICAL STUDY Archaeology is the study of the past based upon the recovery, examination, and explanation of the material remains of human life, thought, and activity, coordinated with available information concerning the ancient environment. Biblical archaeology, a discipline largely developing since 1800, searches for what can be learned about biblical events, characters, and teachings from sources outside the Bible. Dealing with what ancient civilizations left behind, its goal is to give a better understanding of the Bible itself.

The purpose of excavation is to reconstruct, insofar as is possible, the history and culture of an ancient site. Students of the Bible are particularly interested in the archaeology of ancient Canaan and its adjacent regions. Today this is the land forming the countries of Israel, Lebanon, Syria, and Jordan. In addition, the biblical world included other regions such as Egypt, Greece, Italy, Cyprus, the Arabian Peninsula, and the large areas occupied by present-day Turkey, Iraq, and Iran.

Limitations of Archaeology The student of archaeology must understand its limitations. First, little of what existed in antiquity still remains. Furthermore, the Bible lands have as yet been only partly investigated. Few mounds have been completely excavated, and many remain almost untouched. Thorough publication of archaeological investigations is a very slow process, and the significance of the objects found is often subject to diverse interpretation. Conclusions once held are many times abandoned in favor of new hypotheses. In using archaeological data, biblical students need to take precautions to be current. They also need to be conscious of what archaeology can and cannot do. The basic affirmations of the Bible—that God is, that He is active in history, and that Jesus is His Son raised from the dead—are not subject to archaeological verification. One can demonstrate from archaeological materials that Sennacherib invaded Judah in the time of Hezekiah, but that he was a tool in the hand of the Lord can only be known from biblical assertion.

Brief History of Archaeology The work of archaeologists in the biblical world in general, and in ancient Canaan in particular, can be divided into three overlapping periods.

Stage One In the earliest period, prior to about A.D. 1900, the practice of archaeology was primarily a "treasure hunt" with no organized, systematic way of going about the work. Individuals such as Heinrich Schliemann, Giovanni Belzoni, and A. H. Layard set forth to find spectacular items from the past. Pits and trenches dug into ancient cities often destroyed more than they revealed. Since the area occupied by ancient Israel was relatively poor in "treasure," much of this work was carried out in Egypt and in Mesopotamia, the ancient homeland of the Assyrians and Babylonians (the present site of the country of Iraq).

The beginning of biblical archaeology in Egypt in 1798, under the sponsorship of Napoleon Bonaparte, was for the expressed purpose of disproving the Bible. The assumption was that the biblical record was not historical. The secrets of Egypt began coming to light following the discovery in 1799 of the Rosetta stone and its decipherment by Champollion. The secrets of Mesopotamia began to unfold following the copying and decipherment of the Behistun inscription by Rawlinson begun in 1835 and by the later discovery in 1852 of Ashurbanipal's library by Rassam. Architecture, art, and written sources recovered from numerous ancient sites began to cast light on the Bible, particularly on the OT. About the middle of the nineteenth century, English archaeologists excavated portions of the city of Nineveh, capital of the ancient Assyrian Empire at the height of its power.

Among the discoveries at Nineveh were two great palaces. The huge palace of the Assyrian king Sennacherib (704–681 B.C.) contained hundreds of feet of wall space lined with sculptured reliefs depicting the exploits of the king. Included is a striking picture of the siege of the important biblical fortress-city of Lachish that was captured by the Assyrians in 701 B.C. Also among the discoveries was the Taylor Prism, which contains a written Assyrian version of their invasion of the kingdom of Judah in 701 B.C. The biblical account of the siege of Jerusalem at this time is found in 2 Kings 18:13–19:37. It is interesting to compare the two records. Although Sennacherib does not claim to have captured Jerusalem, he makes no mention of the calamity suffered by his troops as described in the biblical account.

The palace of King Ashurbanipal (668–633 B.C.) was also uncovered. The most significant find here was a great library of written documents that the king had collected from many portions of the empire. These have provided the student of the Bible with much primary source material from this portion of the ancient world. Of particular interest are mythological stories

Overview of the excavations at Tel Arad in Israel, showing the Citadel built by David (right background).

relating traditions of creation and of a great flood.

Numerous other sites such as Ur, Babylon, and Jerusalem were investigated during the first stage of archaeology. Archaeologists gradually learned, however, that they needed to approach their task in a more systematic and disciplined manner in order to extract greater information from ancient civilizations.

Stage Two Near the beginning of the 20th century, significant developments in the discipline of archaeology began to occur. In 1890, Sir Flinders Petrie, an English archaeologist who had done important works in Egypt, began excavations at Tell el-Hesi in southwestern Palestine.

The word "tell" refers to an ancient mound built up over a long period of time by the occupational debris of persons living at the site. In time a site was often abandoned, either briefly or for a long duration, perhaps after being destroyed by an enemy or by a natural catastrophe, such as an earthquake. A town might be deserted because of an epidemic of disease. Another important and probably common reason for people leaving a site was a weather change such as drought. Regardless of why people left, the reasons for settling there in the first place often drew them back. The debris of the earlier occupation was made smooth by leveling off and filling in, and a new village was built on top of the ruins. This process, along with the ordinary accumulation of debris and rebuilding that occurs in any area of human occupation, gradually over the centuries and millennia resulted in the site becoming higher and higher—a "tell" was formed, containing many strata (layers). A large number of these artificially formed mounds dot the biblical landscape.

The work of Petrie and his successor F. J. Bliss was highly significant in two interrelated ways. First, they tried very carefully to excavate Tell el-Hesi layer by layer. Second, they made careful notes of the style of pottery found in each layer. Since the way pottery was made changed through the years, the type found in any one layer permitted the archaeologist to assign an approximate date to that level. Almost a century of study of pottery now enables archaeologists to give almost an absolute date for each strata excavated. Petrie and Bliss's work marks the beginning of a scientific, disciplined approach to archaeology in Palestine. The principles of stratagraphic excavation (isolating each layer) and of pottery analysis are still basic to sound methodology, although many improvements have occurred since the beginning of the twentieth century. See *Pottery.*

Archaeologists attempt to determine when they are leaving one layer and entering another on the basis of such items as changes in the color, consistency, and content of the soil, or, in some cases, the presence of ashes between strata. A stratum may be very thin or quite thick depending on the nature of the occupation and how long it lasted.

During the first half of the 20th century, many archaeological expeditions from numerous countries were sent to the biblical world. Americans, for example, excavated at Megiddo, Beth-shan, and Tell Beit Mirsim, and the British excavated at Jericho and Samaria. Stratigraphic excavation and pottery analysis became more precise and exact. Careful records (written reports, drawings, photographs) were kept.

Samaria was the capital of the Northern Kingdom of ancient Israel. The city was built by the Hebrew kings Omri and his son Ahab in the first half of the ninth century B.C. During the first third of the twentieth century, excavations partially recovered this old capital city of the Northern Kingdom.

Among the many interesting discoveries at Samaria was a group of over 60 ostraca, probably from the time of King Jeroboam II (782–743 B.C.). An ostracon (plural, ostraca) is a piece of broken pottery that has been written upon. Ancient peoples often employed pieces of pottery as a writing surface and used these for records, lists, and letters. The ostraca from

Samaria contain the records of supplies, including grain, oil, and wine, which had been sent for the support of the royal palace by persons living in various towns. From these some information can be deduced about the economy and the political organization of the land. In addition, the presence of names of several persons containing Baal as a component (e.g., Abibaal, Meribaal) reveal the continued influence of Baalism in the land.

A comparison of these ostraca with Amos 6:1-7 also suggests that the "tax" levied on the common people was being used to support a lifestyle of luxury and debauchery on the part of the high officials in the government. The passage in Amos also mentions "beds inlaid with ivory" (v. 4; 3:15; 1 Kings 22:39). Several hundred pieces of ivory were found in the excavations of Samaria. Many of these had been used as inlays in furniture.

Stage Three Whereas many remarkable discoveries were made in the first half of the twentieth century (e.g., the Code of Hammurabi, the Elephantine Papyri, the Hittite monuments at Boghazkoy, the tomb of King Tut, the Ras Shamra texts, the Mari Letters, Lachish ostraca, and the Dead Sea Scrolls), beginning about 1960 a new stage in the history of archaeology in the ancient Near East began to emerge. Archaeologists and others began to realize that it was not enough to make discoveries and to describe those discoveries. They needed synthesis of information and the explanation of data.

This stage of archaeology, sometimes called the "New Archaeology," is characterized by a multidisciplinary team approach to the archaeological task, including botanists, geologists, zoologists, and anthropologists. The approach also emphasizes the use of volunteer help and a strong educational program. In the previous stage much of the labor of digging had been done by persons living in the region who were paid for their services. The third stage of archaeology also is characterized by a growing tendency to think in terms of a regional approach rather than concentrating exclusively on one site. Interest is growing in the investigation of small villages as opposed to an almost total concentration in the past on large, "important" cities.

In Israel, the modern approach was pioneered at Tell Gezer in the 1960s and early 1970s and was continued at numerous sites, such as Tell el-Hesi and Tell Halif in the 1970s and 1980s. The goal of the approach is to derive a complete picture of life in a particular region, in antiquity, and also an understanding of commerce and other cultural contacts between regions.

Contributions of Archaeology to Biblical Study The primary purpose of archaeology is not to prove the Bible true, although it does serve to affirm the accuracy of the Bible's portrayal of the ancient world. Archaeology especially serves to enhance our understanding of the Bible, opening many "windows" into the biblical world.

Archaeology and the Biblical Text Archaeology, through the recovery of ancient Hebrew and Greek copies of the Scripture, plus the discovery of other old literature written in related languages, has helped scholars to determine a more exact text of the Bible than was available previously. It has also demonstrated that the scribes were very careful in their work.

At the end of the last century in a rubbish room (now known as the Cairo Geniza) of an old synagogue in Cairo, Egypt, an invaluable find of Hebrew materials was made. In 1947 the discovery of the Dead Sea Scrolls in 11 caves moved knowledge of Hebrew manuscripts back from the Middle Ages to the period 250 B.C. to A.D. 70. See *Bible Texts and Versions.*

Knowledge of writing has greatly increased. The earliest documents now known from Syria-Palestine would be the Ebla texts (the first of which were found in 1975) dating about 2400 B.C., followed by the Ugaritic texts (found 1929–1937) from Ras Shamra on the coast of Syria and dating about 1400 B.C. Examples of eight different writing scripts in Palestine which antedate the time of Moses have answered the question debated in the last century of whether Moses could have known writing. Examples of decipherable Hebrew found by archaeologists begin at about the time of Solomon with the Gezer calendar.

In 1929 French archaeologists began to excavate the ancient city of Ugarit near the coast of Syria. Many clay tablets containing ancient writing were unearthed. Most of these were written in a previously unknown language, soon called Ugaritic. Ugaritic is a northwest Semitic language closely related to Hebrew. It is the earliest example of a language written in an alphabetical script. A study of Ugaritic has helped OT scholars better understand the nature and development of the Hebrew language, and it has been of particular value in the clarification of some of the ancient Hebrew poetry contained in the Bible.

Earlier scholars defined OT words by comparison with Arabic and by meanings derived from rabbinic tradition. Discovery and decipherment of previously unknown ancient Middle Eastern languages like Sumerian, Akkadian, Hittite, Ugaritic, Aramaic, and Eblite give a wider base for definition of words, making (by the study called Comparative Semitics) for a substantial reorientation of OT vocabulary.

In 1 Samuel 13:21 there is a Hebrew word, *pim,* which occurs nowhere else in the Bible. The meaning of this word was not known to early readers and translators of the Bible. Although the translators of the KJV of 1611 chose the word "file" to translate *pim,* there was no firm basis for the choice. Since that time archaeologists have found several small weights from ancient Israel bearing the word *pim.* A *pim* appears to have weighed a little less than a shekel. Now it is clear that the word *pim* refers to the charge made by the Philistines for working on the Hebrew's iron tools. Recent translations of the Bible reflect this new understanding.

With reference to the NT, during the last one to two centuries, numerous old papyrus manuscripts have been found, mainly in Egypt, which contain portions of the biblical text. At least a small portion of every book in the NT, except 1 and 2 Timothy, has been found in these ancient Greek papyri. The oldest of these is known as the Rylands Papyrus (P52), dated A.D. 100–125. It contains John 18:31-33,37-38. These papyri are useful to scholars involved in the task of determining the best textual base of the NT. The number of Greek manuscripts and fragments known to exist has increased from about 1,500 in 1885 to over 5,700 in 2002. Included are 116 papyrus items that carry knowledge of the text behind the fourth-century codices to the second century for the parts of the text covered. New Greek critical texts are being prepared to make all the material available to students, and already English translations are reflecting the new finds.

The nonbiblical-papyrus find made in Egypt at the end of the last century furnished new insights into everyday Greek usage and vocabulary which have now become the substance of NT language study.

Archaeology and Biblical Geography As late as A.D. 1800, the location of many of the places mentioned in the Bible was unknown. In 1838 an American explorer by the name of Edward Robinson, and his assistant, Eli Smith, made a trip through Palestine on horseback. On the basis of their study of geography and the analysis of place-names, they were able to identify over 100 biblical sites. Robinson returned for further exploration in 1852.

Since the time of Robinson, archaeologists have been able to identify a great many of the sites mentioned in the Bible, including the places visited by the Apostle Paul on his travels. Not only have villages and cities been identified, but entire kingdoms have been located. For example, excavations that began in 1906 by German archaeologists in what is now Turkey recovered the lost empire of the Hittites.

The location of places like Jerusalem and Bethlehem were never forgotten. Other places were destroyed and their location lost. Edward Robinson developed a technique by which literary information and travelers' reports, coupled with local historical memory, could give probable identities. Excavation of the ruins in the areas has helped. Twenty-eight jar handles found in the cistern at El Jib made certain the location of ancient Gibeon; six stone carvings with the name "Gezer" identify that place; and "Arad" seven times scratched on a potsherd confirms its location.

Archaeology and Biblical History Egyptian reports like "The Tale of Sinuhe" show how Palestine appeared to Egyptians about the time of Abraham. The Tell Amarna tablets found by a peasant woman in Egypt are letters from Palestinian rulers to the reigning pharaohs, but they show the unstable conditions in Palestine prior to the Israelite conquest which enabled Israel to conquer the enemy one by one.

The Egyptian Pharaoh Merneptah (1213–1204 B.C.) invaded Syria-Palestine during his brief reign. A monument found in his mortuary chamber at Thebes contains a record of this venture and includes the oldest reference to Israel outside of the Bible. Merneptah claimed to have utterly destroyed them. Here is clear evidence that Israelites were in the land of Canaan by no later than the 13th century B.C.

The discovery of the law code of Hammurabi in 1901 at Susa with its preamble and 282 laws opened the way for interesting comparisons with Israel's laws. Archaeologists now have five law codes that were written in cuneiform before the time of Moses: those of Ur-Nammu, Eshnunna, Lipit-Ishtar, Hammurabi, and the Hittites. Slightly later are the Middle Assyrian laws. Interesting comparisons can be made between these laws and those of Moses. Contrasts include the number of acts for which the accused is subjected to the ordeal (Num. 5) and the punishments of mutilation (Deut. 25:12). While these codes have both similarities and differences from the laws of Moses, the claim of borrowing cannot be established. The varieties of bodily mutilation prescribed by Hammurabi are absent in Israel's laws as are also the unlimited floggings.

A

Continuing archaeological excavations along the southern border of the Temple Mount in Jerusalem.

Interesting sidelights on the general period of the Judges and Kings include the Egyptian custom of counting the victims of a campaign from stacks of severed hands (cp. Judg. 8:6), the putting out of an eye (1 Sam. 11:1-11), or both eyes (2 Kings 25:7), and depiction of circumcised men on a Megiddo ivory (as well as on an Egyptian papyrus) where the subject described his ordeal.

After the death of Solomon (ca. 922 B.C.), the Hebrew kingdom divided into two portions, the Northern Kingdom (Israel) and the Southern Kingdom (Judah). One powerful nation thereby became two weak nations, and the Egyptian ruler Shishak took advantage of the situation by invading the land about 918 B.C. (1 Kings 14:25-28). The biblical account is very brief and only tells of an attack on Jerusalem. Shishak, however, recorded his exploits on a wall in the temple of the god Amun in Karnak, Egypt. He claims to have captured over 150 towns in Palestine, including places in the Northern Kingdom. The probability is that this invasion was a greater blow to the Hebrew kingdoms than is obvious from the brief account in 1 Kings. It is suggested not only by the Egyptian record, which may have been inflated to some degree, but also by the archaeological evidence that several of the cities named were indeed destroyed at about this time. Here is an example of archaeology helping to provide a larger historical context that enriches the study of Scripture.

Mesha, king of Moab, on the Moabite stone gave his account of his servitude to the Israelite kings and his effort to free himself that seems parallel to the record in 2 Kings 3. The names of Omri, of Mesha, of the Lord, of Chemosh, and of numerous Palestinian cities are listed on this stone. The policy of *cherem* by which a place is totally devoted to the deity as Jericho earlier was (Josh. 6:21) is illustrated. Other records enlarge our knowledge of biblical characters. Such are the records of Ahab's participation in the battle of Qarqar in 853 B.C. on a monument set up by Shalmaneser III and of Jehu's tribute to Shalmaneser III recorded on the black obelisk now in the British Museum. Neither episode is mentioned in the Bible.

Omri was king of the Northern Kingdom about 876–869 B.C. During his short reign he moved the capital from Tirzah to the newly built city of Samaria. He was an evil king, and the Bible devotes little space to him (1 Kings 16:15-28). The surrounding nations, however, perceived Omri as a very strong and able ruler. He made such an impression on the Assyrians that for over a hundred years their records continue to refer to Israel as "the House of Omri," even after his dynasty no longer ruled. This reminds one that, from a biblical perspective, faithfulness to God is considered to be much more important than ability in warfare and government.

Assyrian records furnish information on Tiglath-pileser, Sargon, Sennacherib, and Ashurbanipal who are significant in the OT. They also mention the kings of Israel and Judah, chronicling the exchange of the last kings of Israel and the exiling of Samaria. Until the excavation of Sargon's palace by Emil Botta, Sargon was known only from the Bible. Sargon's invasion of Ashdod (Isa. 20) was recorded by Sargon, and a fragment of a stele set up in Ashdod was found there. Sennacherib depicted his siege of Lachish in his palace and told on a cylinder of his bringing Hezekiah to his knees. A water tunnel in Jerusalem is conjectured to be that which Hezekiah built at this time. Its inscription tells of the excavation required to build the tunnel. A record tells of Sennacherib's murder by his son. The Babylonians told of the downfall of Nineveh, of the battle of Carchemish, and of the capture of Jerusalem in a record that establishes March 15/16, 597 B.C., as its date.

The prophetic movement is one of the most distinctive features of OT life. Search for antecedents has looked at Ebla, where an occurrence of the equivalent of the Hebrew word is reported. More than 20 texts from Mari on the Euphrates report prophetic-like figures with visions and spoken messages given to the heads of state. The eleventh-century tale of Wen-Amon's mission to Byblos continues to be the classic example of ecstatic behavior. The eighth-century Zakir inscription from Afis, Syria, has the deity Bacal-sheman speak through his seers (*chozim*). The excavation of Tell Deir Alla yielded Balaam texts in Aramaic from the sixth century, the first prophetic text of any scope outside the OT (cp. Num. 22–24). Even at that date this "seer of the God" was still being revered at some places. None of these areas have a prophetic literature comparable to that of the writing prophets.

Nahum's description of the fall of Nineveh can be better understood by a study of the depiction of ancient warfare on the Assyrian monuments. These picture attacks of cities, war chariot charges, and the exiling of people. Nahum 3:8 compares the date of Nineveh to that of Thebes. The Assyrian records also depict the siege of an Egyptian city plus a description of the capture of Thebes.

The poignant statement in Jer. 34:6-7 that the Babylonian army had captured all the fortified cities in Judah except Jerusalem, Lachish, and Azekah is highlighted by a group of 21 ostraca found by archaeologists at Lachish. These ostraca are rough, draft copies of a letter the Hebrew commander at the doomed city of Lachish was preparing to send to a high official in Jerusalem. Among other things he wrote that signals were no longer being received from Azekah. Apparently he was writing shortly after the time of Jer. 34. Now only two major cities were still resisting the Babylonian onslaught—Azekah had fallen.

The fate of Israelite people in exile is illustrated in a list of rations found in excavations at the Ishtar Gate of Babylon which are for Yaukin (Jehoiachin) and his sons. Banking records found at Nippur show that people of Jewish names were doing business there while in exile. Although there is as yet no known text that

specifically calls Belshazzar a king, this figure once known only from the Bible is abundantly known in texts.

The return from exile was accomplished by means of a decree of Cyrus. Cyrus's cylinder, now in the British Museum, though not mentioning the Jews or their temple, makes clear that such a project was in keeping with Cyrus's general policy. Papyri found at Elephantine Island in Egypt dating about the time of Nehemiah show the condition of Jews in that area but also permit a dating of Nehemiah's work. Sons of Sanballat are mentioned; and these documents together with Samaritan papyri found in a cave northwest of Jericho make clear that a series of figures bore this name.

Archaeology and Ancient Culture A vast gulf separates the cultures of today, especially those found in the Western Hemisphere, from those of the biblical period. One of the greatest contributions of archaeology lies in its ability to break down barriers of time and culture and to move the reader of the Bible back into its ancient context, providing fresh insight and increased understanding of the Scripture.

The list of biblical objects that has been found in excavations, allowing us to know exactly what a word means, is large. Examples

View of Banias palace complex.

Step trench cut into the tel of Old Testament Jericho by archaeologists to uncover levels of destruction.

of weights and measures, plow points, weapons, tools, jewelry, clay jars, seals, and coins are all included. Ancient art depicts clothing styles, weapons, modes of transportation, methods of warfare, and styles of life. Excavated tombs show burial customs that reflect beliefs about life and death. The Beni Hasan tomb in Egypt from around 1900 B.C. shows how Semites coming to Egypt would have been dressed. It is our nearest approach to what a patriarch might have looked like, and it moves students away from the Bedouin analogy previously made.

Archaeology furnishes much knowledge of the cultures of Israel's neighbors—the Canaanites, Egyptians, Hittites, Philistines, Moabites, Assyrians, Arameans, Babylonians, and Persians. Finds reveal the gods they worshiped, their trade, wars, and treaties.

The tables found at Ugarit provide much primary source information about Canaanite faith and practice. They present a fairly clear picture of what life was like in the land where the Israelites settled down. See *Canaan.*

The Ugaritic texts reveal the Canaanite pantheon with the worship practices of the Canaanite people against which the Hebrew prophets like Elijah, Elisha, and Hosea struggled. The Kuntillet Ajrud inscription which speaks of "Yahweh and his Asherah" (female counterpart) reveal the syncretism into which Israel was drawn, confirming the denunciation of such practices by the prophets of Judah and Israel.

Genesis 15:1-6 indicates that Abraham and Sarah had made Eliezer, a member of their household staff, their official heir. They may have adopted him to do so, apparently in response to the long delay in the birth of a promised child. A bit later, as recorded in Gen. 16:1-16, Sarah took the further step of having a child by proxy. At her urging, Abraham fathered a son, Ishmael, by the Egyptian maid, Hagar. What was the stimulus for these actions? Clay tablets have been found at the ancient northeastern Mesopotamian city of Nuzi that cast some light on this question. The tablets came from a time a few centuries after Abraham but contain a record of customs practiced over a long period of time. These tablets reveal that both the adoption of a son and the birth of a son by proxy were common practices for a barren couple. Careful laws were enacted to safeguard the rights of all parties. Abraham's roots were in Mesopotamia (Gen. 11:27-32), and he must have known of these customs. Abraham and Sarah appear to have followed the generally accepted cultural norms of their day.

Genesis 15:7-21 greatly puzzles the modern reader. The passage is difficult to understand. At least partial light has been shed on this passage by the recovery of numerous clay tablets from the northern Mesopotamian city of Mari. The tablets are from the eighteenth century B.C. They indicate that the ceremony used at that time for sealing an agreement or covenant included the cutting of a donkey in half. The persons involved in the contract would then walk between the severed pieces of the animal. One sees that God gave Abraham instructions regarding the ceremony that would have been familiar to the patriarch. God met Abraham in his own cultural context. It is of interest that when people in later OT times made a covenant, they are said, in the Hebrew language, to have "cut a covenant."

New Testament Archaeology confirms at many points the NT account of events and culture in the first-century Greco-Roman world of Palestine and beyond. This includes evidence regarding burial customs, crucifixion, synagogue worship, and the identity of several rulers.

The NT rightly presents Herod the Great as a ruthless and wicked king (Matt. 2:1-23). Very few details of his life are given. A more complete picture of this complex man is now available through the writings of the first-century A.D. Jewish historian, Josephus, and through the work of archaeologists. Herod was one of the greatest builders of the ancient world. A visitor to the Holy Land can now see numerous remains from Herod's building program. These include the temple platform in Jerusalem, the harbor city of Caesarea, the strong fortress of Masada, the striking ruins of Samaria, and the Herodium, the fortress palace where Herod was buried. These, and numerous other sites excavated by archaeologists, remind one that the world in which Jesus lived continued to be dominated to a large degree by Herod—not only through the rule of his sons but also by the monuments of stone that he left behind. In Jerusalem the 35-acre platform on which Herod built his temple still stands, and parts of the tower of David at the Citadel are Herodian. Inscription stones warning the Gentiles not to proceed into the court of Israel have been found.

Alleged relics of NT figures can never be demonstrated to be genuine. Claims for having located the house of Peter at Capernaum and for having located his tomb in Rome are based on pious assumptions. Pilgrims have been going to Palestine since the second century when Melito of Sardis went "to see the places." Many have left records of what they were shown; but sites like the place of Jesus' birth, baptism, and burial have only long veneration to establish their claim.

Most Pauline cities and those of Revelation have been located, and many excavated. Corinth has supplied its inscription "synagogue of the Hebrews" and that of Erastus who laid the pavement at his own expense (cp. Rom. 16:23). Papyrus documents from Egypt contain invitations to pagan dinners that are good illustrations of the Corinthian problem of being invited to a dinner where food has been offered to idols.

Recent Archaeological Discoveries Important archaeological discoveries which enhance our understanding of the Bible occurred late in the 20th century. The discovery and excavation of the city of Sepphoris, a cosmopolitan Roman city which can be seen from Nazareth, changed the perception that Galilee was a strictly rural, unsophisticated area. A fishing boat, dating to the first century A.D., similar to those used by Jesus' disciples was found intact beneath the banks of the Sea of Galilee. The stone ossuary (chest) bearing the name of the high priest Caiaphas and containing his bones was found in Jerusalem. Two small silver amulets bearing a quotation from the book of Numbers were recovered, which predate any other surviving Scripture portion by several centuries. Small clay bullae bearing the impression of the personal seals of Baruch, Jerusalem's scribe, and the kings of Judah, Ahaz and Hezekiah, have been found. A carved ivory pomegranate, which topped a staff and was inscribed as belonging to the service of Solomon's temple, has been authenticated. Recent evaluations of the excavations at Jericho demonstrate that the biblical account of the fall of the city is accurate in many of its particulars. Two inscriptions bear the term "House of David," one discovered in 1993 at Tel Dan and the other, the Mesha Stele, was discovered in 1868 but only translated and published in 1994. These are the only known extrabiblical mentions of the great king.

Conclusion We may expect more significant finds as archaeologists continue to work throughout the lands where biblical events took place. Though the idea that archaeology can prove the Bible is frowned on by many archaeologists, it has nevertheless confirmed biblical accounts in many cases. The main function of archaeology is illumination of past cultures. The great gulf in time, language, and culture between our day and biblical times makes knowledge of archaeological discoveries essential for thorough understanding of the Bible.

J. Kenneth Eakins, Jack P. Lewis,
Charles W. Draper, and E. Ray Clendenen

ARCHANGEL Chief or first angel. The English term "archangel" is a derivative of the Greek word *archangelos,* which occurs only twice in the NT.

Only one archangel is named in the Bible, though it is possible that there are others. In Jude's letter the archangel Michael is depicted as disputing with Satan over the body of Moses (Jude 9, see also *Assumption of Moses*). In the tenth chapter of the book of Daniel, this same Michael is described as *one* of the *chief princes.* This may imply that other chief princes (archangels) exist. Jewish apocalyptic literature of the postexilic period describes seven archangels who stand in the presence of God: Suruel, Raphael, Raguel, Michael, Gabriel, Remiel, and Uriel (Tobit 12:15; 1 Enoch 20:1-7; 9:1; 40:9). Some scholars speculate that these are the same angels who stand before God and blow the trumpets of God's judgment (Rev. 8:2–9:15). Although John does not refer to them as *archangels*, it is interesting to note the association of God's trumpet and the rapture of the Church with the voice of the archangel (1 Thess. 4:16). However, Paul uses the singular form of the noun, and this is probably a reference to the work of Michael at the end of the age (Dan. 12:1).

Archangels seem to command other angels, akin to an army general. Michael and his angels battle the dragon and his angels. It appears that Michael throws Satan down to Earth (Rev. 12:7-9), and it may be Michael who binds Satan for 1,000 years (Rev. 20:1-3), though the text does not say so. It may also be an archangel who holds the scroll which John is instructed to eat (Rev. 10:1). Michael is also described as the protector of God's people (Dan. 12:1).

Two angelic beings named in the Bible which are often thought to be archangels are Gabriel and Satan. The angel Gabriel is called an archangel in some of the apocryphal literature, but the biblical text describes him primarily as a messenger (Dan. 8:16; 9:21; Luke 1:19,26). Yet he also seems to possess some extraordinary powers. Daniel is strengthened by Gabriel on at least one occasion (Dan. 8:18; possibly 10:16, 18-19), and Zechariah loses his ability to speak because he did not believe Gabriel's message (Luke 1:20). Gabriel also seems to have a relationship to Israel similar to that of Michael. Gabriel is described by Daniel as looking like a man (Dan. 8:15-16), and it is likely that the *man* Michael aided in his war with the king of Persia is Gabriel (Dan. 10:13,21). Thus Gabriel may also be a protector of God's people. However, to move from this rather scant evidence to the conclusion that Gabriel is an archangel is to rely too heavily on speculation. See *Gabriel*.

The evidence in favor of the claim that Satan was an archangel is even scarcer. Although Satan is described as leading other angels into war against Michael and his angels (Rev. 12:7) and is referred to as the great dragon (Rev. 12:9), his being cast out of heaven (Rev. 12:8) and over-powered by another angel (Rev. 20:1-2) seem to stand against this claim. See *Angel. John Laing*

ARCHELAUS (Är·chə·lā´ŭs) Son and principal successor of Herod the Great (Matt. 2:22). When Herod died in 4 B.C., his sons Herod Antipas and Philip were named tetrarchs; but his son Archelaus was the principal successor. Aware of the hostility of the Jews toward his family, Archelaus did not attempt to ascend the throne immediately. First, he tried to win the Jews over. His efforts were not successful; as the Jews revolted, Archelaus ordered his army to retaliate.

Archelaus encountered opposition to his reign from his brothers, in particular Herod Antipas, who felt entitled to the throne. The brothers presented their case to the emperor Augustus, who gave Archelaus one-half of his father Herod's land and split the remainder between Antipas and Philip. Archelaus was given the title tetrarch but was promised the title of king if he reigned virtuously.

Archelaus interfered in the high priesthood, married against Jewish law, and oppressed the Samaritans and Jews through brutal treatment. In revolt the people sent deputations to Caesar to have Archelaus denounced. His rule was ended in A.D. 6 when the Roman government banished him to Gaul and added his territory to Syria.

Joseph was warned in a dream to avoid Judea because of Archelaus's rule. He decided to take Mary and the child Jesus to Galilee when they returned from Egypt rather than go to Judea (Matt. 2:22).

ARCHER One who shoots an arrow from a bow. Archery was used in ancient times for the hunting of both small and large game and in warfare. An archer trained from childhood until he could pull a 100-pound bow that would shoot an arrow a distance of 300–400 yards. Several OT passages mention archery in warfare (Gen. 49:23-24; 2 Sam. 11:24). See *Arms and Armor.*

ARCHEVITES (Är´ chə·vīts) Group who joined Rehum the commander in writing a letter to King Artaxerxes of Persia protesting the rebuilding of Jerusalem under Zerubbabel's leadership about 537 B.C. NASB, NIV, NRSV translate

Archevites as people or men of Erech. See *Erech*.

ARCHI (Är´ chī), **ARCHITE** Unknown group of people who gave their name to a border point of the tribes of Ephraim and Benjamin (Josh. 16:2). They may have been a clan of Benjamin or more likely remnants of the ancient "Canaanite" inhabitants. Their only representative in the Bible was David's counselor Hushai. See *Hushai*.

ARCHIPPUS (Är·chĭp pŭs) Personal name meaning "first among horsemen." A Christian whom Paul greeted in Col. 4:17 and Philem. 2, entreating him to fulfill the ministry God gave him. Some have suggested he was the son of Philemon and Appia, but this can be neither proved nor disproved. The nature of his ministry has also been widely discussed without firm conclusions. Paul's use of "fellow soldier" to describe him seems to indicate a strong participation in church leadership. Evidently, he preached in the church at Colossae.

ARCHITECTURE Construction, techniques, and materials used in building the structures of the ancient Near East.

Old Testament The people of the ancient Near East used many types of building materials. Uti-

Reconstruction of a Roman archer's machine from first century A.D.

lizing natural resources, they most often exploited stone, wood, reeds, and mud. Used naturally, mud served as mortar. It also was formed into bricks and then sun dried. Religious or large public buildings used the more expensive lumber that came from cedar, cypress, sandalwood, and olive trees. The sycamore tree served as a less costly lumber. Limestone and basalt were common stones used in construction.

Public Structures As a basic element of city architecture, walls served three general purposes. Protective walls encircled the city to keep out enemy forces. These city walls usually did not support any load. Retaining walls had the purpose of keeping in place any weight that was behind them. In agricultural terracing, they prevented erosion and created a level place for farming on the sides of hills. This type of wall also was placed below city walls to stop any erosion of the soil, which ultimately might weaken the city walls. Lastly, buildings and houses used walls to bear loads or keep out the weather.

Walls were made of several layers or courses of stones placed one on top of the other with mud bricks often set on the stone courses. Composed of large fieldstones, the first few layers served as the foundation of the wall. The placing of the large stones into trenches gave the wall a more stable foundation. In houses and public buildings, the stone courses above the ground may have been given smooth surfaces so as to produce a uniform look, but this was not always done. Large public building projects commonly made use of a technique called headers and stretchers. The builders alternated laying the stones lengthwise and breadthwise to form the wall.

During the time of Solomon, a common type of city wall was the casemate wall. This was composed of two parallel walls with perpendicular walls placed at intervals in between the parallel ones. The empty spaces formed between the walls, called casemates, commonly were filled with stones, earth, or debris. Sometimes the people used the spaces for living quarters, guardrooms, or storehouses. The outer parallel wall averaged about five and one-half feet in width, while the inner parallel wall averaged about four feet. This type of wall had an advantage over a solid wall due to its greater strength and its saving of material and labor. Excavations at Gezer, Megiddo, and Hazor uncovered the remains of casemate walls.

The inset-offset wall came into use as a city wall after the time of Solomon. Its name came from the technique used to build it. After erecting one stretch of the wall, the next stretch was slightly recessed by about one-half yard. The following section then was built slightly forward with the next section placed slightly behind it. Each stretch of the wall was placed alternately, either slightly ahead or slightly behind the previous section. This "insetting" and "offsetting" of the city wall allowed the city's defenders to fire at any attackers from three angles: head on and to the right and left of the attackers. As a solid structure composed of stone or mud bricks placed on a stone foundation, this type of wall contrasts with the casemate wall. The remains of an inset-offset wall, 11 feet in thickness, were excavated at Megiddo.

The city gate was an important part of public architecture because it was the weakest part of the city's defenses. It also served as a meeting place for the various city activities. Remains of Solomonic gates at Megiddo, Gezer, and Hazor show that two square towers flanked the entrance into the gate. The gate complex was composed of three successive chambers or rooms on each side (six chambers in all). A gate

separated each pair of chambers, and the six rooms probably served as guardhouses. At Dan, a later gate had the two towers but only four chambers instead of six. This gate complex measured 58 x 97 feet. The approach to the gate from outside the city usually was placed at an angle. This forced any attackers to expose their flanks to the defenders on the city walls. Should the attackers be able to get inside the gate area, the angle caused the attackers to move at a slower pace.

As a prominent public structure, the temple acted as the house of the god. Two types of temple structures were common in Palestine during the biblical period. The broad-room temple was a rectangular structure with its entrance in the middle of one of the long sides. The plan of the temple, therefore, was oriented around a room that was broader than it was long. The long-room temple likewise was a rectangular structure, but its entrance was in the middle of one of the short sides. This caused the building to be longer than it was broad.

As a long-room temple Solomon's sanctuary in Jerusalem consisted of three main sections. A courtyard with an altar preceded the building. The temple proper actually was one building divided into two parts, the holy place and the

The Pantheon in Rome, built in the first century A.D., was the first large dome ever built.

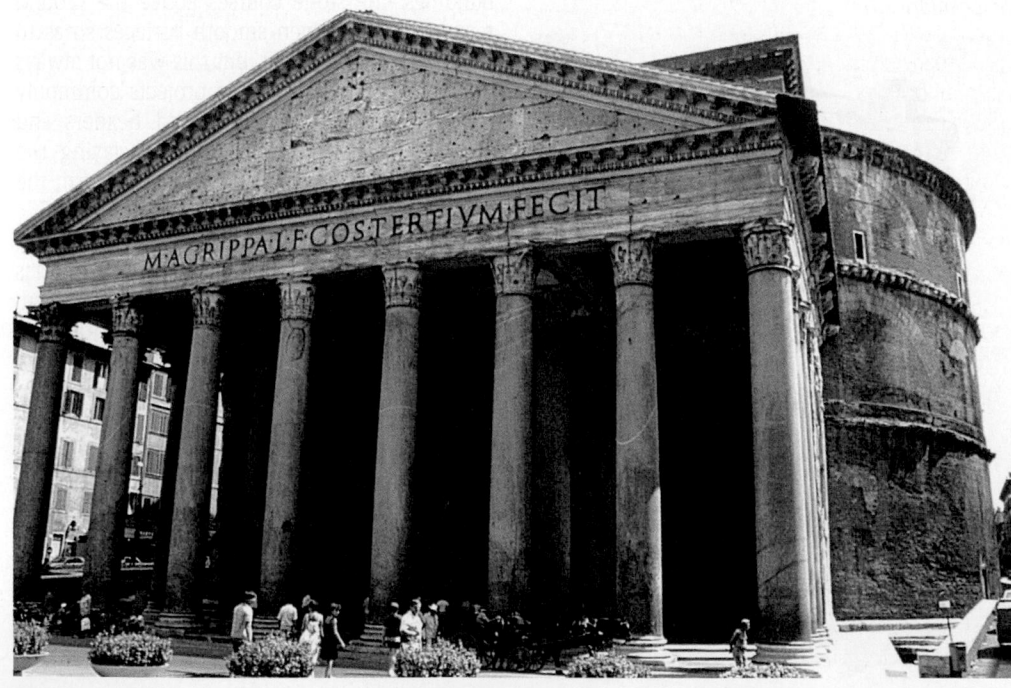

holy of holies. The main room, or the holy place, was entered from the courtyard. A partition separated the holy place from the holy of holies.

Another Israelite temple dating from after 1000 B.C. was uncovered at Arad. It was a broadroom temple entered from the east. The holy of holies was a niche protruding out of the Western Wall opposite the entrance.

Private Structures Houses in the period of the OT usually were built around a central courtyard and entered from the street. They often were two stories high with access to the upper story coming from a staircase or a ladder. The walls of the house consisted of stone foundations with mud bricks placed on the stone layers or courses. They subsequently were plastered. Floors either were paved with small stones or plaster, or they were formed from beaten earth. Large wooden beams laid across the walls composed the supporting structure of the roof. Smaller pieces of wood or reeds were placed in between the beams and then covered with a layer of mud. Rows of columns placed in the house served as supports to the ceiling. Since the roof was flat, people slept on it in the hot seasons and also used it for storage. Sometimes clay or stone pipes that led from the roof to cisterns down below were used to catch rainwater.

The most common type of house was the so-called "four-room" house. This house consisted of a broad room at the rear of the house with three parallel rooms coming out from one side of the broad room. The back room ran the width of the building. Rows of pillars separated the middle parallel room from the other two rooms. This middle room actually was a small, unroofed courtyard and served as the entrance to the house. The courtyard usually contained household items such as silos, cisterns, ovens, and grinding stones and was the place where the cooking was done. The animals could have been kept under a covered section in the courtyard. The other rooms were used for living and storage.

Ovens were constructed with mud bricks and then plastered on the outside. One side of the oven had an air hole. A new oven was created whenever the old one filled up with ashes. By breaking off the top of the old oven and then raising the sides, a new oven was made.

Storage structures were common in the biblical period. Private and public grain silos were round and dug several feet into the ground. The

Atrium of the Roman villa of the poet Menander in Pompeii (destroyed in A.D. 79).

builders usually erected circular mud brick or stone walls around the silo, but sometimes they did nothing to the pit or simply plastered it with mud. Rooms with clay vessels also served as storage space.

While the "four-room" house was the most common plan in Palestine, other arrangements existed. Some homes had a simple plan of a courtyard with one room placed to the side. Other houses had only two or three rooms; still others may have had more than four. The arrangement of the rooms around the open courtyard also varied. The broad room at the rear of the house seems to be common to all plans.

New Testament In this time period architecture in Israel was greatly influenced by Greek and Roman ideas. Some of the primary cities in Israel show this influence in their public buildings.

Public Structures Over 20 Roman theaters were built in Palestine and Jordan. At Caesarea the theater contained two main parts, the auditorium and stage, and the stage building. These two parts formed one building complex. Six vaulted passageways served as entrances. The auditorium was semicircular with upper and lower sections used for seating. The lower tier had six sections of seats, and the upper tier had seven for a total capacity of 4,500 people. A central box was reserved for dignitaries and important guests. The wall of the stage was as high as the auditorium. Other similar theaters were located at Scythopolis (Beth-shan), Pella, Gerasa, Petra, Dor, Hippos, and Gadara.

Arenas for chariot racing, called hippodromes, were long, narrow, and straight with curved ends. Gerasa, Caesarea, Scythopolis, Gadara, and Jerusalem had hippodromes.

Erected in the second century A.D., the one at Caesarea was one-fourth of a mile long and 330 feet wide with a seating capacity of 30,000.

The temple in Jerusalem was destroyed in 586 B.C. and rebuilt in 515 B.C. Herod the Great refurbished it during the first century B.C. As a result, the temple became widely known for its beauty. It retained the same plan as its predecessor, but the area around it was doubled. Retaining walls that marked the boundaries of the temple complex were built, and marble porticos were added all around the temple mount. The stones of the temple mount's retaining walls were about four or five feet high and weighed three to five tons.

Private Structures Houses usually followed a plan that arranged the rooms around a courtyard. A stairway on the outside of the house led to the upper stories. A stone or timber projected out from the wall at intervals and supported the staircase. This architectural technique is known as corbeling. The walls and ceiling were plastered, and arches sometimes supported the roof. Houses at Avdat and Shivta used arches that came out from the walls to form the roof. After placing thin slabs of limestone over the arches, the builders plastered the entire roof. In the lower city of Jerusalem, houses constructed with small stones were crowded closely together. Yet they still maintained small courtyards.

Houses of the rich often had columns placed around a central court that had rooms radiating out from it. Kitchens, cellars, cisterns, and bathing pools may have been located underneath the ground. In Jerusalem one house covered about 650 square feet, a large house by first-century standards. In the courtyard, four ovens were sunk into the ground, and a cistern stored the house's water supply. Inside the house on one of the walls, three niches raised about five feet off the ground served as cabinets for storing the household vessels.   *Scott Langston*

ARCHIVES See *House of the Rolls.*

ARCTURUS (Ärc·tū´ rŭs) Constellation of stars God created (Job 9:9; 38:32) of which exact identification was not clear to the earliest Bible translators and continues to be debated. Modern translations generally use "Bear" (NASB, NIV, NRSV). TEV uses "the Dipper." Some scholars prefer "the lion." Whatever the identification,

the star points to the sovereign greatness of God beyond human understanding.

ARD (Ärd), **ARDITE** Personal name meaning "hunchbacked." **1.** Son of Benjamin and grandson of Jacob (Gen. 46:21). **2.** Grandson and clan father of Benjamin (Num. 26:40). Apparently listed as Addar in 1 Chron. 8:3.

ARDON (Är´ dŏn) Son of Caleb (1 Chron. 2:18).

ARELI (Á·rē´ lī), **ARELITES** Son of Gad (Gen. 46:16) and original ancestor of clan of Arelites (Num. 26:17).

AREOPAGITE (Âr·ə·ŏp´ ȧ·gīte) Member of the highly respected Greek council which met on the Areopagus in Athens. See *Areopagus; Athens; Dionysius.*

AREOPAGUS (Âr·ə·ŏp´ ȧ·gŭs) Site of Paul's speech to the Epicurean and Stoic philosophers of Athens (Acts 17:19). It was a rocky hill about 370 feet high, not far below the Acropolis and overlooked the Agora (marketplace) in Athens, Greece. The word also was used to refer to the council that originally met on this hill. The name probably was derived from Ares, the Greek name for the god of war known to the Romans as Mars. See *Mars Hill.*

ARETAS (Âr´ ĕ·tăs) Personal name meaning "moral excellence, power." The ruler of Damascus in NT times. He sought to arrest Paul after his conversion (2 Cor. 11:32). The name Aretas was borne by several Arabian kings centered in Petra and Damascus. Aretas IV ruled from Petra (9 B.C.–A.D. 40) as a subject of Rome. Herod Antipas married his daughter, then divorced her to marry Herodias (Mark 6:17-18). Aretas joined with a Roman officer to defeat Herod's army in A.D. 36.

ARGOB (Är´ gŏb) Personal and geographical name meaning "mound of earth." **1.** Man who might have joined Pekah (2 Kings 15:25) in murdering Pekahiah, king of Israel (742–740 B.C.), or possibly was killed by Pekah. The Hebrew text is difficult to read at this point. Some scholars omit Argob as a copyist's error duplicating part of verse 29 here (TEV). NIV translation can be interpreted to mean Pekah also killed Argob. **2.** Territory in Bashan in the hill country east of the Jordan River. Argob was probably in the center of the fertile tableland and was famous for its strong cities (Deut. 3:4). Moses gave this land of giants to Manasseh (3:13). Manasseh's son Jair conquered Argob (3:14) and changed the name to Bashan-havoth-jair.

ARIDAI (Ȧ·rĭd´ ā·ī) Persian personal name, perhaps meaning "delight of Hari" (a god). Son of Haman, Esther, and the Jews' archenemy. He died as the Jews reversed Haman's scheme and gained revenge (Esther 9:9).

ARIDATHA (Ăr·ĭ·dā´ thȧ) Persian personal name, perhaps meaning "given by Hari" (a god). Brother of Aridai who shared his fate. See *Aridai.*

ARIEH (Ȧ·rī´ ĕh) Personal name meaning "lion." Paired with Argob in 2 Kings 15:25 with same text problems involved (cp. KJV, NASB, NIV, NRSV). See *Argob.*

ARIEL (Â´ rĭ·ĕl) Personal name meaning "God's lion." **1.** Jewish leader in captivity who acted as Ezra's messenger to the Levites to send people with Ezra to Jerusalem about 458 B.C. (Ezra 8:16). **2.** Code name for Jerusalem in Isaiah 29. Ariel apparently referred to the top of the altar on which the priests burned sacrifices. Jerusalem under Assyrian attack was like the altar. It did not burn but caused everything around it to burn. The sins of Jerusalem had led to the devastation of the rest of Judah in 701 B.C.

ARIMATHEA (Är·ĭ·mȧ·thē´ ȧ) City of Joseph, the disciple who claimed the body of Jesus following the crucifixion and in whose own new tomb the body was placed (Matt. 27:57). The location of Arimathea is not certainly known. In Luke 23:51 Arimathea is described as a Jewish city. See *Joseph 7.*

ARIOCH (Âr´ î·ŏk) Personal, probably Hurrian, name meaning "servant of the moon god." **1.** King of Ellasar, who joined alliance against Sodom and Gomorrah (Gen. 14) but was eventually defeated by Abraham. Parallel names have been found in early Akkadian documents and at Mari and Nuzi, but no other reference to the biblical Arioch can be shown. See *Amraphel; Ellasar.* **2.** Commander of bodyguard of King Nebuchadnezzar (Dan. 2:14-25). He confided in Daniel, who was able to interpret the king's for-

gotten dream and prevent the death of the wise counselors of Babylon.

ARISAI (Ȧ·rĭs´ ī) Persian personal name. Son of Haman (Esther 9:9) who suffered his brothers' fate. See *Aridai.*

ARISTARCHUS (Âr·ĭs·tär´ kŭs) Personal name, perhaps meaning "best ruler." Paul's companion caught by the followers of Artemis in Ephesus (Acts 19:29). Apparently the same person was the Thessalonian who accompanied Paul from Greece to Jerusalem as he returned from his third missionary journey (Acts 20:4). Aristarchus also accompanied Paul when he sailed for Rome (Acts 27:2). Paul sent greetings from Aristarchus, a fellow prisoner and worker, in his letters to the Colossians (4:10) and Philemon (24). Later church tradition said Nero put Aristarchus to death in Rome.

ARISTOBULUS (Ȧ·rĭs·tō·bū´ lŭs) Head of a Christian household in Rome whom Paul greeted (Rom. 16:10).

ARK Boat or water vessel and in particular one built by Noah under God's direction to save Noah, his family, and representatives of all animal life from the flood.

Old Testament God warned Noah of His intentions to destroy the earth because of the wickedness of humanity. Noah was commanded to build an ark to God's specifications to save his family and representatives of all animals from the flood (Gen. 6:18-19). As such, the ark became both a symbol of a faith on the part of Noah and a symbol of grace on the part of God (Gen. 6:8,22).

The shape of the ark was unusual. Although the Bible does not give enough detail to enable a full model to be made, the ark was apparently not shaped like a boat, either ancient or modern. The shape more closely approximates a giant block. The length was 300 cubits (about 450 feet), the width was 50 cubits (about 75 feet), and the height was 30 cubits (about 45 feet), overall dimensions that resemble the dimensions of a giant house (Gen. 6:15). The ark had three floors filled with rooms (Gen. 6:14,16) and one window and one door (Gen. 6:16).

The ark was built of gopher wood (Gen. 6:14) which may have been a variety of cypress. It has also been suggested that gopher wood referred to a particular shape or type of plank or beam, rather than a type of wood. Our limited knowledge makes it impossible to make a final conclusion.

The ark was a testimony of Noah's faith because no large body of water stood nearby on which Noah could have floated such a large boat. Hence people could see no obvious or visible need for such a vessel.

The ark was also a symbol of God's grace. Obviously, the ark was intended by God as an instrument of deliverance to preserve both human and animal life upon the earth (Gen. 6:17-18). As such, it came to be understood as a symbol of His grace and mercy (Heb. 11:7a).

New Testament The Gospel references to the ark are in connection with Jesus' teachings regarding the second coming. The expectancy of some at the second coming is likened to those who were destroyed by the flood. In the book of Hebrews, the preacher lists Noah as a man of faith who prepared an ark even though the danger was at that point unseen. The last NT reference to the ark points to the evil of humanity and God's patient salvation (1 Pet. 3:20).

Extrabiblical Sources The Babylonian flood story, called the Gilgamesh epic, also tells of a large boat by which its hero survived the flood. There, however, the ark was not a symbol of the grace of the gods but of their folly and faulty planning. In the Sumerian and Babylonian traditions, we are given more details concerning the size and shape of the ark. These details may be of interest but are of far less significance than the message of the biblical ark itself as testimony to God's unmerited grace. See *Flood; Noah.*

Robert Cate

ARKITE (Är´ kīt) Canaanite clan listed in the table of nations (Gen. 10:17). They apparently centered around Arqa, modern Tell Arqa in Syria, 80 miles north of Sidon. Thutmose III of Egypt conquered it. It appears in the Amarna letters. Tiglath-pileser III of Assyria conquered it in 738 B.C. Romans called it Caesarea Libani and noted its Astarte worship.

ARK OF BULRUSHES (KJV, Exod. 2:3-5) See *Basket; Bulrush.*

ARK OF THE COVENANT Original container for the Ten Commandments and the central symbol of God's presence with the people of Israel.

Old Testament The ark of ancient Israel is mysterious in its origins, its meanings, and its ultimate fate. Its many names convey the holy sense of God's presence. The Hebrew word for ark (*tebah*) means simply "box, chest, coffin," as is indicated by its use for the coffin of Joseph (Gen. 50:26) and for the temple collection box of King Joash (2 Kings 12:9-10).

The names used for the ark define its meaning by the words that modify it. The word "covenant" in the name defines the ark from its original purpose as a container for the stone tablets upon which the Ten Commandments (sometimes called the "testimony") were inscribed. Sometimes it is identified rather with the name of deity, "the ark of God," or "the ark of the Lord" (Yahweh), or most ornately "the ark of the covenant of the Lord of hosts (Yahweh Sabaoth) who is enthroned on the cherubim" (1 Sam. 4:4).

The origin of the ark goes back to Moses at Sinai. The mysterious origin of the ark is seen by contrasting the two accounts of how it was made in the Pentateuch. The more elaborate account of the manufacture and ornamentation of the ark by the craftsman Bezalel appears in Exod. 25:10-22; 31:2,7; 35:30-35; 37:1-9. It was planned during Moses' first sojourn on Sinai and built after all the tabernacle specifications had been communicated and completed. The other account is found in

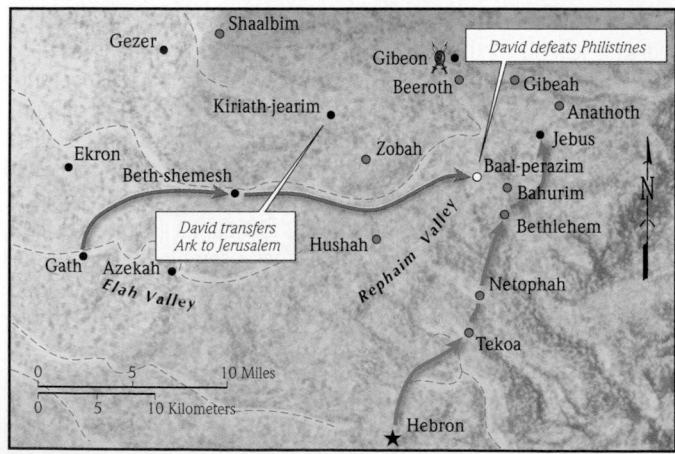

Shaalbim
Gezer
Gibeon · *David defeats Philistines*
Beeroth · · Gibeah
Kiriath-jearim · Anathoth
Jebus
Ekron · Zobah · Baal-perazim
Beth-shemesh · Bahurim
David transfers Ark to Jerusalem · Bethlehem
Gath Azekah · Hushah
Elah Valley · *Rephaim Valley* · Netophah
· Tekoa

0 5 10 Miles
0 5 10 Kilometers

Hebron

Deut. 10:1-5. After the sin of the golden calf and the breaking of the original Decalogue tablets, Moses made a plain box of acacia wood as a container to receive the new tablets of the law.

A very ancient poem, the "Song of the Ark" in Num. 10:35-36, sheds some light on the function of the ark in the wanderings in the wilderness. The ark was the symbol of God's presence to guide the pilgrims and lead them in battle (Num. 10:33,35-36). If they acted in faithlessness, failing to follow this guidance, the consequences could be drastic (Num. 14:39-45). Some passages suggest the ark was also regarded as the throne of the invisible deity, or his footstool (Jer. 3:16-17; Ps. 132:7-8). These various meanings of the ark should be interpreted as complementary rather than contradictory.

The ark was designed for mobility. Its size (about four feet long, two and a half feet wide, and two and a half feet deep) and rectangular shape were appropriate to this feature. Permanent poles were used to carry the ark, since no one was allowed to touch it, and only priestly (Levitical) personnel were allowed to carry it. The ark was the most important object within the tabernacle of the desert period, though its relationship to the tabernacle was discontinued sometime after the conquest of Canaan.

Stone carving of what is thought to be the ark of the covenant in the synagogue ruins at Capernaum.

The ark played a prominent role in the "holy war" narratives of the crossing of the Jordan and the conquest of Jericho (Josh. 3–6). After the conquest, it was variously located at Gilgal, Shechem (Josh. 8:30-35; Deut. 11:26-32; 27:1-26), or Bethel (Judg. 20:26), wherever the people of the Israel were gathered for worship. Finally, it was permanently located at Shiloh, where a temple was built to house it (1 Sam. 1:9; 3:3).

Reconstruction of the ark of the covenant drawn in the Egyptian style, reflecting the 400 years of bondage in Egypt.

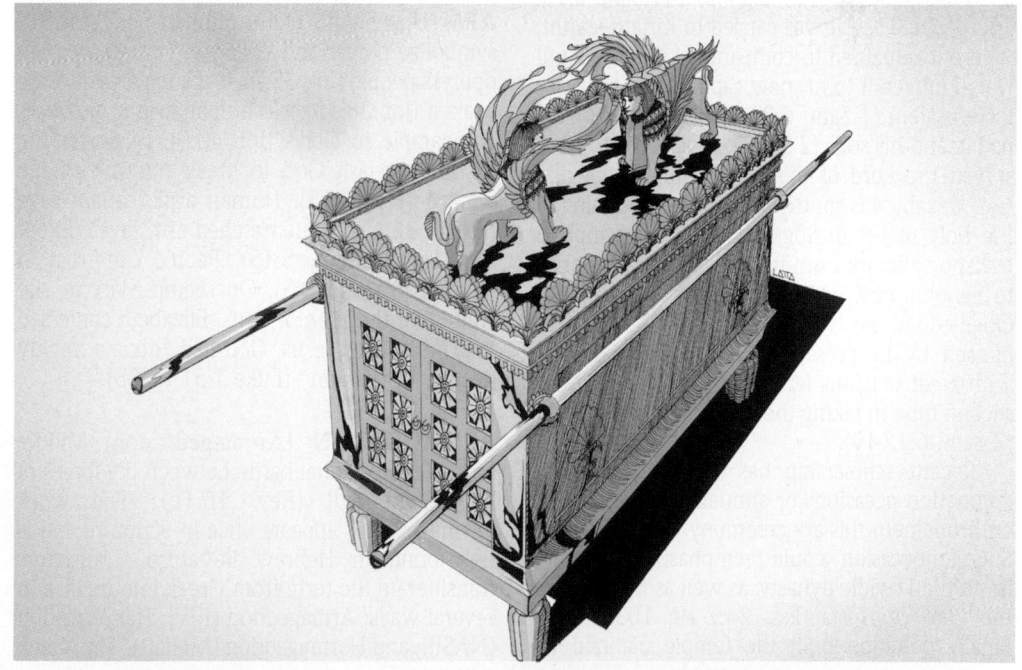

Shiloh, about 30 miles north of Jerusalem, was Israel's religious center for over a century after the conquest of Canaan and the place where the ark of the covenant was kept.

Because of the faithless superstition of the wicked sons of Eli, the Hebrew tribes were defeated in the battle of Ebenezer, and the ark was captured by the Philistines (1 Sam. 4). The adventures of the ark in the cities of Ashdod, Gath, and Ekron are told to magnify the strength and glory of the Lord of the ark. The Lord vanquished Dagon and spread bubonic plagues among the enemy until they propitiated the God of Israel by symbolic guilt offerings and a ritually correct sending away of the dread object (1 Sam. 5:1–6:12). The men of Beth-shemesh welcomed the return of the ark, until they unwisely violated its holiness by looking into it (1 Sam. 6:13-15,19-20). Then it was carried to Kiriath-jearim, where it remained in comparative neglect, until David moved it to his new capital and sanctuary in Jerusalem (1 Sam. 6:21–7:2; 2 Sam. 6). Abinadab and his sons (2 Sam. 6:3) seemed to have served the Lord of the ark faithfully until one son, Uzzah, was smitten for his rash touching of the holy object during David's first attempt to transport the ark from its "hill" at Kiriath-jearim to his own city. In fear David left the ark with Obed-edom the Gittite, whose household was blessed by its presence. More cautiously and with great religious fervor, David succeeded the second time in taking the ark into his capital city (2 Sam. 6:12-19).

Recent scholarship has suggested that on coronation occasions or annually at a festival of enthronement this ark ceremony was reenacted. Such an occasion would reemphasize the promise to the Davidic dynasty, as well as the glory of the Lord of Hosts (Pss. 24:7-10; 103:21-22). Finally Solomon built the temple planned by David, to house the ark, which he then transported into the holy of holies with elaborate festival ceremonies (1 Kings 8; 2 Chron. 5).

The precise time of the theft or destruction of the ark is unknown. Some have suggested Shishak of Egypt plundered the temple of this most holy object (1 Kings 14:25-28), but it seems more likely, from Jer. 3:16-17, that the Babylonians captured or destroyed the ark in 587 B.C. with the fall of Jerusalem and the burning of the temple. As Jeremiah predicted, the ark was never rebuilt for the second temple, the holy of holies remaining empty.

Other mysteries of the ark are its relation to the cherubim, its ornate lid called the "mercy seat," and its precise ritual usage during the time of the monarchy. Because the ark of the covenant was the central symbol of God's presence with His people Israel, its mysteries remain appropriately veiled within the inner sanctuary of the living God. See *Holy of Holies; Mercy Seat; Tabernacle; Temple.*

New Testament Hebrews 9:1-10 shows the ark was a part of the old order with external regulations waiting for the new day of Christ to come with a perfect sacrifice able to cleanse the human conscience. Revelation 11:19 shows the ark of the covenant will be part of the heavenly temple when it is revealed.

M. Pierce Matheney, Jr.

ARM Upper limb of the human body used to symbolize power and strength. Such power can oppress people (Job 35:9), but such arms will be broken (Job 38:15). No human arm or power is comparable to God's (Job 40:9). In prayer the faithful can ask God to break the arm of the wicked (Ps. 10:15). Human arms cannot save (Ps. 44:3). God's outstretched arm saves (Exod. 6:6; 15:16; Deut. 5:15). People can trust in God's arm (Isa. 51:5). On seeing Mary as she waited for the birth of Jesus, Elizabeth confessed that in bringing Jesus, God had "done a mighty deed with His arm" (Luke 1:51 HCSB).

ARMAGEDDON (Är·má·gĕd´ dŏn) Middle East site of the final battle between the forces of good and evil (Rev. 16:16). The word "Armageddon" appears once in Scripture and is not found in Hebrew literature. Translators transliterate the term from Greek into English in several ways: Armageddon (KJV); Har Magedon (NASB); and Harmageddon (Moffatt). The Greek is an approximate transliteration of the Hebrew *har megiddo,* literally, "mountain of Megiddo." Revelation promises that in the face of defeat of God's saints by military forces from the east, south, and the north, the Lord Jesus Christ will return to defeat His enemies and deliver His people. See *Megiddo.*   *Kenneth Hubbard*

ARMENIA (Är·mē´ nĭ·à) KJV translation for land of Ararat (2 Kings 19:37). See *Ararat.*

ARMLET Band or ring worn around the upper arm that should be distinguished from a bracelet worn around the wrist. The Hebrew word is translated as "chain" (Num. 31:50) and "bracelet" (2 Sam. 1:10). A related word is ren-

Gold Persian armlet from the treasury of the Oxus.

dered as "ornaments of the legs" (Isa. 3:20) in the KJV.

ARMONI (Âr·mō´ nī) Personal name meaning "born in Armon." Son of Rizpah and Saul, whom David gave to the Gibeonites in revenge for Saul's earlier killing of Gibeonites (2 Sam. 21:7-9). See *Rizpah.*

ARMOR-BEARER See *Arms and Armor.*

ARMOR OF GOD See *Arms and Armor.*

ARMS AND ARMOR Instruments and body coverings for defense and/or protection.
Old Testament The offensive arms of the OT include long-, medium-, and close-range arms, and the defensive items include shields and armor.

Long-Range Arms The bow and arrow were effective arms from long range (300–400 yards) and were used widely by the nations of the Bible. Israel had expert archers in men from Benjamin (1 Chron. 8:40; 2 Chron. 17:17) and the eastern tribes of Reuben, Gad, and Manasseh (1 Chron. 5:18). Jonathan and Jehu were individual marksmen. At least four Israelite kings were severely or fatally wounded by enemy arrows: Saul (1 Sam. 31:3), Ahab (1 Kings 22:34), Joram (2 Kings 9:24), and Josiah (2 Chron. 35:23). Bows were constructed with single pieces of wood, or more effectively with glued layers of wood, horn, and sinew, and possibly even with added bronze (2 Sam. 22:35; Job 20:24). The size varied from approximately three to six feet in length. Arrows were made of wood shafts or reeds, tipped with metal heads which were forged differently to meet the diverse defenses of the enemy. The arrow was guided by feathers, especially from the eagle, vulture, or kite. A leather quiver strapped to the back or hung over the shoulder carried between 20 and 30 of these arrows, or if strapped to a chariot, perhaps as many as 50. Frequently a leather arm guard was also used on the bow arm to protect it from the gut string that propelled the arrow.

One might be most familiar with the slingshot through reading about David's encounter with Goliath (1 Sam. 17:40-50), without realizing that it was a conventional artillery weapon for deadly long-range use by armies throughout the Middle East. Because of the long-range capabilities, expert slingers were stationed by the hundreds near the archers. It was especially valuable to have those who could sling from the left hand as well as from the right (Judg. 20:16; 1 Chron. 12:2). A patch of cloth or leather with two braided leather cords on either end would hold a smooth stone. The slinger then twirled the pocketed missile above his head. Release of one of the cords would eject the stone towards its victim. The blow would disarm, destabilize, knock out, or even kill the enemy. King Uzziah of Judah developed large catapults that projected arrows and stones long-range to defend Jerusalem (2 Chron. 26:15).

Medium-Range Arms A javelin is a spear thrown obviously a shorter distance than the archers could arch their arrows or slingers could sling their sling stones. However, as a hurled weapon, its medium range is to be differentiated from the close-range thrusting spear of the foot soldier (in a phalanx). David faced the javelin while successfully challenging Goliath (1 Sam. 17:6) and while peacefully attempting to soothe Saul's spirit. Twice the disturbed Saul hurled his javelin at David (1 Sam. 18:10-11; 19:9-10) and even once at his own son Jonathan (1 Sam. 20:33). Usually made of wood or reed, some javelins had one or both of two features that aided its flight: some had a leather cord wrapped around its shaft that caused the released weapon to spin when the cord was retained in the hand, and a counterweight was sometimes fixed on the butt of the shaft. The latter could be even sharp enough to be stuck in the ground to stand the javelin (1 Sam. 26:7) or even used to kill (2 Sam. 2:23). A quiver was used often to aid the soldier in carrying more than one javelin at a time.

Close-Range Arms Hand-to-hand combat brought different weapons to the fore: some sharp, some dull, some long, some short. The thrusting spear was longer and heavier than the javelin and could have been thrown if needed. The soldiers from the tribes of Judah and Naphtali carried spears as a tribal weapon (1 Chron. 12:24,34). Guards protected the temple with these arms (2 Chron. 23:9). Front battle lines often featured foot soldiers equipped with rectangular shields carrying spears jutting out beyond the walls of shields and pressing forward at the expense of the enemy front line.

Two types of swords were used in the biblical times, the single-edged and the two-edged sword (Ps. 149:6; Prov. 5:4). The single-edged was used most effectively by swinging it and hitting the enemy to lacerate the flesh. The blade could be straight or curved to a great degree. In the latter case the sharp edge of the sword was on the outside of the curve. The double-edged sword was used primarily for piercing rather than lacerating, though it could obviously be used either way if necessary. The sword was carried in a sheath attached to the belt. The varieties of the overall width and length of swords in proportion to the hilts were numerous. The difference between a straight sword and the dagger is simply the length. The earliest blades were more daggers than swords. They were lengthened gradually through the ages. Ehud probably used a long dagger in assassinating King Eglon of Moab, since it measured about 18 inches (one cubit, Judg. 3:16-26).

The mace and battle-ax are seldom mentioned in the Bible (Prov. 25:18; Jer. 51:20; Ezek. 9:2), yet they played a significant role in hand-to-hand combat in the biblical lands. The mace was a war club that was used to crush the head of the enemy. The heavy metal or stone head of the weapon would be of various shapes such as round, oval, or pear-shaped. Its wooden handle would fasten by going through the head like a modern hammer or ax. The handle was formed with some flaring at the bottom to keep the weapon from sliding out of the hand. With the pervasive introduction of armor, especially the helmet, the mace gave way in popularity to the piercing edge of the battle-ax. These axes with narrow heads could penetrate more easily a helmet or other armor with their elongated shape. Other blades were designed with wider edges to cut and open the flesh where less or no armor was worn.

Armor-bearers accompanied the military leaders to bring along extra weapons and defensive equipment that would be expended during a battle (arrows, javelins, shields). They sometimes aided the soldier as well by positioning their shields for them, as in the case of Goliath, and at times killing those enemy soldiers who were left helplessly wounded by preceding combatants.

Battering rams, as modeled by Ezekiel in his object lesson for the Israelites (Ezek. 4:2), were actually rolled on wheels and had metal ends attached to wooden shafts to withstand the collision force with city gates or stone walls.

Defensive Arms Defense against all these arms consisted of the shield that was carried or armor that was worn. Shields were made of wicker or of leather stretched over wooden frames with handles on the inside. These were much more maneuverable than heavier metal but obviously less protective. A cross between metal and leather was achieved by attaching metal disks or plates to the leather over a portion of the surface. Two different sizes are referred to in the Bible and in many ancient illustrations (2 Chron. 23:9). One was a round shield used with lighter weapons and covered half the body at most. The tribe of Benjamin preferred these along with the bow and arrow (2 Chron. 14:8). So did Nehemiah when he equipped his men for protection while rebuilding the city walls of Jerusalem (Neh. 4:16). The gold and brass shields made by Solomon and Rehoboam

Roman emperor Trajan in armor (cuirass, kilt, and boots).

respectively were ceremonial and decorative in function (1 Kings 14:25-28) and were of this size. A larger shield was more rectangular and covered nearly, if not all, the body and was so large at times that a special shield bearer was employed to carry it in front of the weapon bearer. Both Goliath and one of these assistants faced David (1 Sam. 17:41). The tribes of Judah (2 Chron. 14:8), Gad (1 Chron. 12:8), and Naphtali (1 Chron. 12:34) used this type of shield with the long thrusting spear or lance as the offensive weapon in the other hand. Bowmen also stood behind standing shields while they flung their arrows.

Armor is essentially a shield that is worn directly on the body. Since the body is most fatally vulnerable in the head and chest regions, it was especially there where armor was worn. Saul and Goliath wore helmets (1 Sam. 17:5,38), as did the entire army of Judah, at least in the time of Uzziah (2 Chron. 26:14). The helmet was usually made of leather or metal and was designed with various shapes depending on the army and even on the unit within an army so that the commander could distinguish one unit from another from a higher vantage point. The differently decorated and constructed helmets helped the soldier tell whether he was near an enemy or comrade in the confusion of tight hand-to-hand combat.

With the rise in popularity of the arrow and with its speed of flight and imperceptible approach on its victim, the mail came to be more and more necessary to cover the torso. Fish scalelike construction of small metal plates sewn to cloth or leather was the breastplate for the ancient soldier. These scales could number as high as 700 to 1000 per "coat." Each coat obviously could be quite heavy and expensive to produce in volume. The distant enemy units of archers who might find themselves firing on each other would wear mail especially, as well as those archers riding in chariots. While in a chariot, Ahab was hit and killed by an arrow exactly where the mail was least protective—at the seam where the sleeve and breast of the coat met (1 Kings 22:34). Leg armor, like the bronze shin protectors of Goliath (1 Sam. 17:6), was not regularly used in the OT times.

New Testament Arms and armor surface on only a few occasions in the NT. Of course, the NT times found Roman imperial soldiers equipped with metal helmets, protective leather and metal vests, leg armor, shields, swords, and spears. Christ accepted a legal, defensive use of the sword (Luke 22:36-38), but he rebuked Peter's illegal and more offensive strike against Malchus at a time of arrest (John 18:10-11). Often the NT uses "arms and armor" symbolically as in the OT poets and prophetic books. The Word of the Lord and its piercing, penetrating effect is referred to as a sword (Eph. 6:17; Heb. 4:12; Rev. 1:16; 2:16; 19:15,21). Paul used both arms and armor of a soldier to express the virtues necessary to defend the believer against Satan (Eph. 6:10-17; cp. Isa. 59:16-17).

Metaphorical Use In the OT the devastating effect of a vicious tongue is compared with the destructive purpose of the sword and arrow (Pss. 57:4; 64:3; Prov. 12:18). However, when weapons are used metaphorically in the OT, it is usually to help convey the supreme sovereignty of God. For instance, one's primary dependence on military arms is considered foolish since they are not the ultimate source of deliverance, whether it be by the bow or sword (Josh. 24:12; Ps. 44:6; Hos. 1:7). This is because God overpowers and shatters the bow and arrow, spear, sword, and shield (Pss. 46:9; 76:3). In other places God's judgment is spoken of as a bow or sword (Ps. 7:12-13; Isa. 66:16; Jer. 12:12). He also uses the literal weapons of conquering nations to judge Israel (Isa. 3:25). Finally, that God is the faithful protector of His people is often expressed by referring to Him as "a shield to those who take refuge in Him" (Prov. 30:5 HCSB), just as He Himself encouraged Abraham, "Do not fear, Abram, I am a shield to you" (Gen. 15:1 NASB).   *Daniel C. Fredericks*

ARMY National military personnel organized for battle. Thus in Egypt, Israel could be referred to as having "armies" even when they did not have a political organization (Exod. 6:26; 7:4; 12:17). Goliath learned that to defy God's people was to defy the "armies of the living God" (1 Sam. 17:26,36), for God was "the God of the armies of Israel" (1 Sam. 17:45 NASB). Face to face with God, humans can only confess, "Is there any number to His troops?" (Job 25:3 NASB). Israel recognized God's anger when God did not go out with their armies (Ps. 44:9). To announce salvation the prophet proclaimed the fury of God upon all armies (Isa. 34:2).

In the NT the writer of Hebrews looked back on the heroes of faith and proclaimed that

A sarcophagus relief depicting a battle scene between Greeks and Galatians.

through faith they "put foreign armies to flight" (Heb. 11:34 HCSB). John's vision of the end time included the armies of heaven following the King of kings to victory over the beast and the false prophet (Rev. 19:11-21).

Armies were organized in different ways during Israel's history. The patriarchs called upon servants and other members of the household (Gen. 14). In the wilderness Joshua led men he had chosen to defend against the Amalekites (Exod. 17:9-10). In the conquest Joshua led the tribes of Israel into battle after being commis-sioned by the "commander of the Lord's army" (Josh. 5:14 HCSB). At times tribes joined together to take territory (Judg. 1:3; 4:6).

Deborah summoned many of the tribes to battle, but some did not answer (Judg. 5). Other judges summoned clans (6:34) and tribes (6:35; 7:2-9). Saul first established a standing, professional army in Israel (1 Sam. 13:2), at first leading it himself with his son but then appointing a professional commander (1 Sam. 17:55). David apparently hired foreign troops loyal to him personally (2 Sam. 15:18). Solomon enhanced the foot soldiers with a chariot corps and calvary (1 Kings 10:26). The army was organized into various units with officers over each, but the precise chain of command cannot be determined (2 Chron. 25:5). Humanitarian laws determined who was excused from military service and how war was conducted (Deut. 20).

ARNAN (Är´ năn) Personal name meaning "quick." Person in messianic line of King David after the return from exile (1 Chron. 3:21).

ARNI (Är´ nī) Ancestor of Jesus in difficult text of Luke 3:33. NASB, NIV read Ram, correlating with list in 1 Chron. 2:10.

The Arnon Valley in southern Jordan where the Israelites passed through, as one of their last barriers, before crossing the Jordan into the promised land.

ARNON (Är´ nŏn) Place-name meaning "rushing river" or "river flooded with berries." River forming border of Moab and Amorites (Num. 21:13). Sihon, the Amorite king, ruled from the Arnon to the Jabbok (Num. 21:24), land which Israel took under Moses. The Arnon then served as the southern limit of territory Israel took east of the Jordan River (Deut. 3:8). It became the southern border of the tribe of Reuben (Josh. 13:16). The king of the Ammonites tried to retake the Arnon in Jephthah's day, but God's Spirit led Jephthah to victory (Judg. 11:12-33). Hazael, king of Damascus, retook the territory from Jehu of Israel (841–814 B.C.). Isaiah pictured Moab as scattered baby birds trying to cross the Arnon (16:2). Jeremiah called for a messenger to announce Moab's defeat by the Arnon (48:20). Near the Dead Sea, the Arnon is large and deep, one of Palestine's impressive sights. The wide river valley rises 1,700 feet to the top of the cliffs above. The modern name is Wadi-el-Mojib.

AROD (Ā´ rŏd) or **ARODI** Personal name meaning "humpbacked." Arodi (Gen. 46:16) or Arod (Num. 26:17) was son of Gad and grandson of Jacob. He was the original ancestor of the Arodite clan.

AROER (Á·rō´ er) Place-name meaning "juniper." **1.** City on north rim of Arnon Gorge east of Dead Sea on southern boundary of territory Israel claimed east of the Jordan River (Josh. 13:9). It figured in territorial claims of Reuben (Josh. 13:16), though the tribe of Gad originally built it (Num. 32:34; cp. Deut. 3:12). Sihon, king of the Amorites, ruled it prior to Israel's conquest (Deut. 4:48; Josh. 12:2). Israel claimed a 300-year history in the area (Judg. 11:26). Jehu's sins brought God's punishment on Israel, including the loss of Aroer to Hazael of Damascus (about 840 B.C.) (2 Kings 10:33; cp. Isa. 17:2). Jeremiah asked Aroer to witness God's coming judgment on Moab (Jer. 48:19). The Moabites had gained control of Aroer under King Mesha, as his inscription on the Moabite Stone witnesses (about 850 B.C.). Spanish excavations show Aroer to have been more of a border fortress than a major city. It is located at Khirbet Arair two-and-one-half miles east of the highway along the Arnon River. **2.** City of the tribe of Gad (Josh. 13:25) near Rabbah, capital of the Ammonites. This may be the Aroer where

Jephthah defeated the Ammonites (Judg. 11:33). **3.** Town in southern Judah about 12 miles southeast of Beersheba with whose leaders David divided the spoil of battle (1 Sam. 30:28). This is located at modern Khirbet Arara. The text of Josh. 15:22 may have originally read "Aroer." Two of David's captains hailed from Aroer (1 Chron. 11:44).

ARPACHSHAD (Är·păk´ shăd) or **ARPHAXAD** (NT) Third son of Shem, son of Noah, and ancestor of the Hebrew people (Gen. 10:22). He was born two years after the flood and was the grandfather of Eber. In the NT the name "Arphaxad" appears in Luke's genealogy of Jesus (Luke 3:36). Luke seems to identify Arphaxad as the great-grandfather, rather than the grandfather, of Eber. This suggests the possibility that the genealogy in Gen. 10 was not intended to be exhaustively complete.

ARPAD (Är´ pad) or **ARPHAD** City-state in northern Syria closely identified with Hamath. The Rabshakeh, representing Sennacherib, Assyria's king, taunted the people of Judah in 701 B.C. (2 Kings 18:17-25; 19:13). He reminded the people walled up in Jerusalem that the gods of Arpad did not save it from Sennacherib. Isaiah mimicked such statements, saying Assyria was only a rod of Yahweh's anger and would soon face punishment for its pride (Isa. 10:5-19). Jeremiah noted Arpad's confusion as he pronounced doom on Damascus (Jer. 49:23). Arpad is modern Tell Erfad, about 25 miles north of Aleppo. Assyrian kings Adad-nirari (806 B.C.), Ashurninari (754 B.C.), Tiglath-pileser (740 B.C.), and Sargon (720 B.C.) all mention victories over Arpad.

ARTAXERXES (Är·tá·zĕrk´ sēz) Persian royal name meaning "kingdom of righteousness," belonging to four Persian rulers and forming a major piece of evidence in dating Ezra and Nehemiah. **1.** Son of Xerxes I, Artaxerxes I ruled Persia from 465 to 424 B.C. He was called Longimanus or "longhanded." Most scholars place Ezra's trip to Jerusalem in the seventh year of his reign or 458 B.C. (Ezra 7:7). He had already received complaints from the inhabitants of Palestine who wanted to stop the returned exiles from rebuilding and had stopped the Jewish builders (Ezra 4:7-24). The temple had been completed under Darius II (522–486) and thus before Artaxerxes (Ezra 6:15). Artaxerxes supported Ezra's work (Ezra 7:6-26). Nehemiah served as cupbearer to Artaxerxes (Neh. 2:1), and the king proved sensitive to Nehemiah's mood (Neh. 2:2). He granted Nehemiah's request to go to Judah (Neh. 2:5-6), making him governor of Judah (Neh. 5:14). **2.** Artaxerxes II ruled Persia 404 to 359 B.C. Some Bible students identify him as ruler under whom Ezra worked. **3.** Artaxerxes III ruled 358–337 B.C. **4.** Name assumed by Arses, who ruled Persia 337–336 B.C. See *Ezra; Nehemiah; Persia.*

ARTEMAS (Är´ tə·màs) Personal name probably shortened from Artemidoros, meaning "gift of Artemis." If this is the case, then the parents worshiped the Greek goddess Artemis. Paul promised to send Artemas or Tychicus to Titus, so Titus could join Paul in Nicopolis (Titus 3:12). Artemas would apparently take over Titus' pastoral duties in Crete. Tradition says Artemas became bishop of Lystra.

ARTEMIS (Är´ tə·mĭs) Name for the Greek goddess of the moon, the daughter of Zeus and Leto, whose worship was threatened by Paul's preaching of the gospel. Artemis was the goddess who watched over nature for both humans and animals. She was the patron deity of wild animals, protecting them from ruthless treatment and at the same time regulating the rules of hunting activities for humans. She was considered the great mother image and gave fertility to humankind. In the Greek homeland she was usually portrayed by the statues as a young, attractive virgin, wearing a short tunic and having her hair pulled back on her head. In Ephesus and western Asia Minor, she was portrayed as a more mature woman. Her robe is draped in such a way as to expose her bosom, which is covered with multiple breasts, depicting her gift of fertility and nurture. Often standing beside her is a fawn or stag on each side representing her relation to the animal world. The official local statue was carefully housed in a temple honoring Artemis.

The most famous statue was located in the city of Ephesus, the official "temple keeper" for Artemis. Artemis was the chief deity of Ephesus, and her temple was one of the Seven Wonders of the ancient world. The temple ceremonies were carried out by priests who were eunuchs and priestesses who were virgins. They conducted the daily ceremonies caring for the deity and for the gifts brought by worshipers, as well as an annual festival on May 25, when numerous statues of the goddess were carried in procession to the amphitheater in Ephesus for a celebration of music, dancing, and drama. This could be the background of the outcry in Acts 19:28: "Great is Artemis of the Ephesians."

The statues of the goddess, often miniature models of the temple with an image of the goddess within, were sold widely. In Acts, a silversmith named Demetrius rallied support against Paul's preaching of the gospel for fear that it might damage his business selling statues.

Diana was a Roman deity somewhat similar to the more popular Artemis. As the Roman and Greek divinities met, she was quickly identified with Artemis. See *Ephesus.*

ARUBBOTH (Ȧ·rūb´ bōth) City name meaning "smoke hole" or "chimney." One of Solomon's provincial officials made headquarters there and administered over Sochoh and the land of Hepher (1 Kings 4:10). This would be territory

Artemis (Diana), patron goddess of Ephesus, covered with eggs (or breasts) as symbols of fertility.

belonging to the clan of Hepher of the tribe of Manasseh in the northern part of the Plain of Sharon, southwest of Megiddo and southeast of Dor. Arubboth is modern Arabbah, nine miles north of Samaria.

ARUMAH (Á·rū´ mäh) Place-name meaning "exalted" or "height." Abimelech, the judge, lived there while he fought to control Shechem (Judg. 9:41). It may be modern Khirbet el-Ormah south of Shechem.

ARVAD (Är´ văd), **ARVADITE** Place-name of unknown meaning and persons from that place. It provided sailors and soldiers for Tyre (Ezek. 27:8,11). It was probably the rocky island called Rouad today, off the coast of Syria. It is related to Canaan in the family of nations (Gen. 10:18).

ARZA (Är´ zȧ) Personal name meaning "wood-worm" or "earthiness." Steward in the house of King Elah (886–885 B.C.) in Tirzah. The king was drunk in Arza's house when Zimri killed Elah (1 Kings 16:8-10).

ASA (Ă´ sȧ) Personal name meaning "doctor" or "healing." **1.** Son and successor of Abijam as king of Judah (1 Kings 15:8). He reigned for 41 years (913–873 B.C.). A pious man, he instituted several reforms to remove foreign gods and foreign religious practices from the land, even removing his mother from political power (1 Kings 15:13). After his death, apparently from natural causes, he was succeeded by his son Jehoshaphat or Josaphat (KJV). The prophet Hanani rebuked Asa (2 Chron. 16:7) for relying on the king of Syria rather than on the Lord (1 Kings 15:17-20). The chronicler further reported that when Asa developed a disease in his feet, he relied on physicians rather than on the Lord (2 Chron. 16:12). Matthew 1:7-8 lists Asa among Jesus' ancestors. See *Chronology of the Biblical Period; Israel.* **2.** Levite who returned from the exile to Jerusalem. He was the head of a family in the villages of the Netophathites near Jerusalem (1 Chron. 9:16).

ASAHEL (Ăs´ ȧ·hĕl) Personal name meaning "God acted" or "God made." **1.** Brother of Joab and Abishai, David's nephew (2 Sam. 2:18). He was a commander in David's army (2 Sam. 23:24). He was a fleet-footed individual who pursued Abner as the latter fled following his defeat at Gibeon. Unable to dissuade Asahel

from pursuing him, Abner slew him. That act led at last to the murder of Abner by Asahel's brother Joab (2 Sam. 3:27-30). **2.** Levite during the reign of Jehoshaphat, Asa's son. Asahel was sent out along with several princes, other Levites, and priests to teach the people of Judah the book of the law of God (2 Chron. 17:8). **3.** A Levite under Hezekiah, the king of Judah following Ahaz. Asahel, along with 10 others, assisted the chief officers in charge of contributions, tithes, and dedicated objects. Asahel's title was that of overseer. **4.** Father of Jonathan who along with Jahaziah opposed Ezra's direction for the men of Judah to separate themselves from the foreign wives they had married. Ezra indicated they had sinned in marrying foreign women (Ezra 10:15).

ASAHIAH (Ăs·ȧ·hī´ ah) or **ASAIAH** (Á·sai´ ăh) Personal name meaning "Yahweh made." **1.** Servant of King Josiah sent with others to Huldah, the prophet, to determine the meaning of the book of the Law found in the temple about 624 B.C. **2.** Leader of the tribe of Simeon who helped drive out the people of Ham from pastures of Gedor when Hezekiah was king of Judah (715–686 B.C.). See *Gedor.* **3.** Musical Levite in line of Merari (1 Chron. 6:30). He is apparently the same as the chief of the sons of Merari, who led 220 of his clan in helping bring the ark of the covenant from the house of Obed-edom to Jerusalem (1 Chron. 15). **4.** Leader of clans from Shiloh who returned from Babylonian exile about 537 B.C. (1 Chron. 9:5).

ASAPH (Ā´ săph) Personal name meaning "he collected." **1.** Father of court official under King Hezekiah (715–686 B.C.), who in sadness reported the threats of Assyria to the king (2 Kings 18). **2.** Levite musician that David appointed to serve in the tabernacle until the temple was completed (1 Chron. 6:39). Asaph was the father of the clan of temple musicians who served through the history of the temple. A member of the clan was among the first to return from exile in 537 B.C. (1 Chron. 9:15). Part of the musical responsibility included sounding the cymbal (1 Chron. 15:19). David established the tradition of delivering psalms to Asaph for the temple singers to sing (1 Chron. 16:7). Asaph and the singers ministered daily (1 Chron. 16:37). Their musical service could be called "prophesying" (1 Chron. 25:1-7). Descendants of Asaph delivered prophetic messages under God's Spirit (2 Chron. 20:14-19). Later generations sang the songs of Asaph "the seer" (2 Chron. 29:30). Psalms 50 and 73-83 are titled "Psalms of Asaph" or similar titles. This may refer to authorship, the singers who used the Psalms in worship, or to a special collection of psalms. See *Psalms, Book of.*

ASAREL (Ă·sā´ rĕl) or **ASAREEL** (KJV) Personal name meaning "God has sworn" or "God rejoiced." A member of tribe of Judah (1 Chron. 4:16).

ASARELAH (Ăs·à·rē´ läh) KJV, NIV, NRSV spelling of Asharelah (NASB, RSV, TEV) in 1 Chron. 25:2. This appears to be a variant of Jesharelah or Jesarelah in 1 Chron. 25:14. The person is a descendant or son of Asaph among the temple singers.

ASCENSION Movement or departure from the lower to the higher with reference to spatial location. Both OT and NT record the events of human ascension in the lives of Enoch (Gen. 5:24), Elijah (2 Kings 2:1-2), and most importantly, Jesus Christ (Acts 1:9). The ascension concluded the earthly ministry of Jesus, allowing eyewitnesses to see both the resurrected Christ on earth and the victorious, eternal Christ returning to heaven to minister at the right hand of the Father.

The concept of ascension is secured in the return of the Son of Man to God (Acts 2:34; Rom. 10:6; Eph. 4:8-10). Christ, the preexistent Logos (John 1:1-5), bridges the gulf between the human and divine in His incarnation, and in the ascension Jesus reveals the Christian's common fatherhood under God and the brotherhood of the Son (John 20:17).

In His ascension Jesus returns to become the believer's advocate at the right hand of the Father (Rom. 8:34; 1 John 2:1; Heb. 7:25). Additionally, the ascension reminds believers of Christ's finished work of sacrifice (Heb. 10:9-18). As the King-Priest of His people, Jesus returns to God's throne fully God and fully man, finished with the work of His substitutionary atonement, and able to exercise His priestly office as the Mediator between God and man.

The return of the Son of Man to heaven (1) secures the resurrection of every believer to God (John 14:2); (2) sends the Holy Spirit to the church (John 16:7); (3) comforts those persecuted unto death (Acts 7:54-60); and (4) grants the strength to persevere for His glory (Col. 3:1-4).

Most importantly, the ascension exalted Christ above all creation (Phil. 2:9), which contrasts with His humbling incarnation and death on the cross (descent). The ascension is God's manifest act of exalting Jesus to the highest position in the universe, declaring Him Lord over everything that exists and all that happens (Phil. 2:9-11). In the ascension Jesus defeated death forever and made eternal life possible (Heb. 6:19-20). Having finished His work, the ascension demonstrates the nature of His authority, thus calling every human to bow in worship and obedience to the sovereign ascended one (Phil. 2:10).   *Mark M. Overstreet*

ASCENTS, SONG OF See *Degrees, Song of.*

ASENATH (Ăs´ ĕ·năth) Egyptian name meaning "Belonging to Neith" (a goddess). Wife of Joseph and daughter of a priest in Egyptian temple at On or Heliopolis. Asenath was Pharaoh's present to Joseph (Gen. 41:45). She was mother of Ephraim and Manasseh (Gen. 41:50-51). See *Potipherah.*

ASER (KJV, Luke 2:36; Rev. 7:6) See *Asher.*

ASH KJV in Isa. 44:14. Some manuscripts of the Hebrew text have the word for cedar, which is very similar to the word found in the text translated by the KJV. Modern versions differ. The word is translated fir (NASB), pine (NIV), cedar (NRSV, REB), and laurel tree (TEV).

ASHAN (Ā´ shăn) Place-name meaning "smoke." City in western hills of tribe of Judah (Josh. 15:42) given to tribe of Simeon (Josh. 19:7). The Aaronic priests claimed Ashan as one of their cities (1 Chron. 6:59; called Ain in Josh. 21:16). Ashan was located at modern Khirbet Asan just northwest of Beersheba. See *Borashan.*

ASHARELAH (Ăsh·à·rē´ läh) See *Asarelah.*

ASHBEA (Ăsh·bē´ à) KJV, TEV translation. NIV, NASB, NRSV read Beth-ashbea. See *Beth-ashbea.*

ASHBEL (Ăsh´ bĕl), **ASHBELITES** Personal name meaning "having a long upper lip." Son of Benjamin, grandson of Jacob, and original ancestor of Ashbelite clan (Gen. 46:21).

ASHCHENAZ (Ăsh´ kə·năz) or **ASHKENAZ** Personal and national name given two spellings in KJV but spelled Ashkenaz in modern translations. A son of Gomer (Gen. 10:3) and original ancestor of people called kingdom of Ashkenaz (Jer. 51:27). Usually identified with Scythians. See *Scythians*.

ASHDOD (Ăsh´ dŏd) One of five principal cities of the Philistines, where the Philistines defeated Israel and captured the ark of the covenant.

Ashdod was 10 miles north of Ashkelon and two and a half miles east of the Mediterranean Sea on the Philistine plain. It was the northernmost city of the Philistine Pentapolis recorded in Josh. 13:3. Ashdod occurs in written history first in the Late Bronze period where it is mentioned in the trade documents of the Ras Shamra tablets discovered at Ugarit (ancient trade center near the Mediterranean coast in northern Syria). Ashdod is described as a manufacturer and exporter of textiles, specifically purple wool. The city name also occurs in the Egyptian list of names, *Onomasticon of Amanope* (263).

Old Testament In the OT Ashdod was a place where some of the Anakim remained during the time of Joshua (Josh. 11:22). As one of the five chief cities of the Philistines, it stood yet to be possessed by Joshua (Josh. 13:3), who allocated it to the tribe of Judah (Josh. 15:46-47). David subdued the Philistines, implicitly including Ashdod (2 Sam. 5:25; 8:1), but it was not described as under Israel's control until Uzziah (783–742 B.C.) captured it (2 Chron. 26:8). Perhaps the most infamous contact between Ashdod and Israel is reported in 1 Sam. 4–6 when the Philistines defeated the army of Israel in battle, killed the two sons of Eli, Hophni and Phinehas, and captured the ark of the covenant. See *Anak, Anakim.*

Although the city was captured by Uzziah, it did not remain long under Judah's control and regained enough strength to revolt from Sargon II in 711 B.C. The Assyrians were able quickly to subdue the Philistines, and they remained under Assyrian control until captured by the Egyptian Pharaoh Psammetichus I (664–610) after a 29-year siege as reported by Herodotus. Under Neb-

uchadnezzar (604–562 B.C.), Babylon soon captured this territory and took the king of Ashdod prisoner.

The prophets of Israel spoke about the city of Ashdod in various military, political and moral contexts (Neh. 13:23-24; Isa. 20:1-6; Jer. 25:20; Amos 1:8; Zech. 9:6). Throughout the Persian period the city remained a threat to Israel.

Extrabiblical Sources In the Greek period Ashdod was known as Azotus and was a flourishing city until being captured by Israel during the Maccabean period. Judas Maccabeus destroyed altars and images in Ashdod (1 Macc. 5:68), and Jonathan later burned the temple of Dagon, those who took refuge there, and ultimately the city itself (1 Macc. 10:84-87).

Josephus reported that Pompey separated Ashdod from Israel after his victory (63 B.C.), Gabinius rebuilt the city, and it was joined to the province of Syria. Augustus granted it to Herod the Great. Herod left it to his sister Salome, who in turn willed it to Julia, the wife of Augustus. Its greatness as a city ended with the Roman destruction of A.D. 67, although it was occupied at least through the sixth century.

Archaeological Evidence The major archaeological work on Ashdod was done from 1962 to 1972 under the direction of D. N. Freedman and others. Some evidence remains from Chalcolithic and Early Bronze times, but the major remains date from Middle Bronze and later including a walled city dating around 1625 B.C. A major destruction of the city was indicated by a three-foot layer of ash and debris dating about 1250 B.C. Two extensive Philistine occupation levels date from the 12th and 11th centuries B.C. The Iron Age showed a flourishing community, and an Iron II temple yielded many cultic artifacts.   *George W. Knight*

ASHDOTH-PISGAH (Ăsh´ dŏth-Pĭs gah) KJV for "slopes of Pisgah" (Deut. 3:17; Josh. 12:3; 13:20). See *Pisgah.*

ASHER (Ăsh´ ēr) or **ASER** (NT Gk.), **ASHERITES** Personal, place, and tribal name meaning "fortune," "happiness." **1.** Eighth son of Jacob, born of Zilpah, the concubine (Gen. 30:13). His four sons and one daughter began the tribe of Asher (Gen. 46:17). Jacob's blessing said Asher would have rich food that he would give a king (Gen. 49:20), perhaps suggesting a period when the tribe would serve a foreign king. **2.** The tribe of Asher numbered 53,400 in the wilderness (Num. 26:47), having grown from 41,500 (Num. 1:41). They formed part of the rear guard in the wilderness marches (Num. 10:25-28). Asher's territorial allotment was in Phoenicia in the far northwest reaching to Tyre and Sidon on the Mediterranean coast (Josh. 19:24-31). They could not drive out the Canaanites and had to live among them (Judg. 1:31-32). When Deborah summoned the tribes to action, Asher did not respond but "continued on the sea shore" (Judg. 5:17 KJV). Apparently Asher was working for the Canaanites in the ports of the Mediterranean. Moses' blessing gives another view of Asher, calling the tribe "most blessed," "favorite of his brothers," and strong (Deut. 33:24-25 NRSV). Asher produced no judge in the book of Judges; nor did it have a tribal leader in the chronicler's list (1 Chron. 27:16-22). Asher did provide troops for Gideon (Judg. 6:35; 7:23) and 40,000 for David at Hebron (1 Chron. 12:36). Some people from Asher made the pilgrimage to Jerusalem to keep Hezekiah's Passover (2 Chron. 30:11). Perhaps Asher's greatest hero was Anna, the prophetess who bore witness to the baby Jesus (Luke 2:36-38). Twelve thousand from Asher are among the 144,000 sealed out of great tribulation to be fed by the Lamb (Rev. 7). **3.** Apparently a border town in Manasseh (Josh. 17:7) but possibly a reference to the border joining the tribal territories of Manasseh and Asher. See *Tribes of Israel.*

ASHERAH (Ă·shē´ răh), **ASHERIM** (pl.) or **ASHEROTH** (pl.) Fertility goddess, the mother of Baal, whose worship was concentrated in Syria and Canaan and the wooden object that represented her. The KJV translated Asherah "grove" and the proper noun "Ashtaroth."

The writers of the OT referred to the image of Asherah as well as to "prophets" belonging to her and to vessels used in her worship (1 Kings 15:13; 18:19; 2 Kings 21:7; 23:4; 2 Chron. 15:16). Over half of the OT references to Asherah can be found in the books of Kings and Chronicles. Deuteronomy 7:5; 12:3 instructed the Israelites to cut down and burn up the Asherim (plural form of Asherah). Deuteronomy 16:21 prohibited the planting of a tree as an "Asherah."

The writers of the OT did not provide an actual description of an "Asherah" or the origin of the worship of Asherah. Other religious writ-

ings from the ancient Near East indicate that "Asherah" was the Hebrew name for an Amorite or Canaanite goddess who was worshiped in various parts of the ancient Near East. The biblical writers sometimes did not make a clear distinction between references to Asherah as a goddess and as an object of worship. According to ancient mythology, Asherah, the mother goddess, was the wife of El and mother of 70 gods, of whom Baal was the most famous. Asherah was the fertility goddess of the Phoenicians and Canaanites. She was called "Lady Asherah of the Sea." See *Canaan; Gods, Pagan.*

Scholars who have studied artwork from the ancient Near East have suggested that some figures in drawings could be representations of the fertility goddess Asherah. Drawings of plain and carved poles, staffs, a cross, a double ax, a tree, a tree stump, a headdress for a priest, and several wooden images could be illustrations of an Asherah. Passages such as 2 Kings 13:6; 17:16; 18:4; 21:3; and 23:6,15 have been interpreted as a definition of an Asherah as a wooden object constructed or destroyed by man. The object stood upright and was used in the worship of a goddess of the same name.

The Asherah existed in both the Southern and Northern Kingdoms of Israel. Jezebel of Tyre apparently installed Asherah worship in the north when she married King Ahab (1 Kings 18:18-19). The principle cities in which the objects were located were Samaria, Bethel, and Jerusalem. According to 1 Kings 14:23 (NASB) the people "built for themselves high places, and sacred pillars and Asherim (plural) on every high hill and beneath every luxuriant tree." See *Baal; Idol.*   *James Newell*

ASHES Often associated with sacrifices, mourning, and fasting. Grief, humiliation, and repentance were expressed by placing ashes on the head or by sitting in ashes. Dirt, sackcloth, fasting, the tearing of clothing, and ashes visibly demonstrated the person's emotions. At times the ashes that remained from a sacrifice were kept and used for ritual purification. They also symbolized the results of divine destruction. The use of ashes to express grief and repentance continued into the NT period. Their use in purification rites is contrasted with the cleansing brought by Christ's blood. They also represent the devastating effect of God's wrath on Sodom and Gomorrah (2 Pet. 2:6).   *Scott Langston*

ASHHUR (Ăsh´ hŭr) Modern translation spelling of Ashur (KJV, TEV). Personal name meaning "to be black," or "belonging to Ishara." Son of Hazron, born after his father's death (1 Chron. 2:24). He had two wives, each of whom bore him children (1 Chron. 4:5-7). His title, "Father of Tekoa," may indicate he founded the city later famous for native son Amos, the prophet. Some Bible students understand Caleb to be Ashhur's father in 1 Chron. 2:24 (TEV, RSV, but not NRSV). See *Tekoa.*

ASHIMA (Á shī´ mà) Syrian god made and worshiped in Hamath (2 Kings 17:30). The Hebrew word *'asham* means "guilt." Hebrew writers may have deliberately written a word associated with guilt instead of the name of the god or goddess. Hamath's goddess may have been Asherah. Amos 8:14 says Israel swore by or made oaths by the "sin" (KJV) "guilt" (NASB) or "shame" of Samaria. REB, CEV, and NRSV read, "Ashimah of Samaria" (NIV footnote). Samaria worshiped falsely. They may have incorporated the god of Hamath into their worship. The exilic Elephantine papyri from a Jewish community in Egypt mention an "Ashim-bethel" who may have been worshiped by Egyptian Jews as a counterpart to Yahweh. See *Asherah; Hamath.*

ASHKELON (Ăsh´ kə lŏn) One of five principal cities of the Philistines (Pentapolis), located on the Mediterranean coast on the trade route, Via Maris, and designated for Judah in the conquest. Ashkelon was a Mediterranean coastal city 12 miles north of Gaza and 10 miles south of Ashdod. It is the only Philistine city directly on the seacoast. Its history extends into the Neolithic Period. The economic importance came from both its port and its location on the trade route, the Via Maris.

The location in southern Palestine put Ashkelon under considerable Egyptian influence throughout much of its history. The first mention of the city was in the nineteenth century B.C. Execration Texts, where a curse on the ruler and his supporters was written on pottery, then smashed, symbolizing breaking his power. A 15th century B.C. papyrus speaks of Ashkelon's loyalty to Egypt, and the 14th century Amarna Letters confirm that relationship with the ruler Widia claiming submission to the Pharaoh, although the ruler of Jerusalem claimed that Ashkelon had given supplies to the 'Apiru. In this period the goddess Astarte was worshiped here by the Canaanites. The city revolted from Egypt and was subsequently sacked by Rameses II (1282 B.C.). Later that same century Pharaoh Merneptah captured the city.

The OT record concerns the city after it had come under Philistine control. It was ruled by a ruler or seren supported by a military aristocracy. Joshua had not taken Ashkelon in the conquest of the land (Josh. 13:3), but it was included in the territory designated for Judah. It appears that Judah did take the city (Judg. 1:18), but it belonged to the Philistines in the Samson account (Judg. 14:19) and under Saul and David (1 Sam. 6:17; 2 Sam. 1:20). Ashkelon subsequently was independent or under the control of Assyria, Egypt, Babylon, and Tyre. Amos 1:8 and Jer. 47:5,7 refer to Ashkelon and her evils. With the coming of the Greeks, Ashkelon became a Hellenistic center of culture and learning. During the Maccabean Period the city flourished and apparently did not have hostilities with the Jews (1 Macc. 10:36; 11:60). In fact, many Jews lived there. Rome granted the status "free allied city" in 104 B.C. A tradition was known in Christian circles that Herod the Great, the son of a temple slave of Apollo, was born in Ashkelon. Herod did have family and friends there and gave the city some beautiful buildings, built a palace there, and left the city to his sister, Salome, at his death. The city was attacked by the Jews in the first Roman Revolt (A.D. 66) but survived and was faithful to Rome.

George W. Knight

ASHKENAZ See *Ashchenaz; Scythians.*

ASHNAH (Ăsh´ näh) Place-name. **1.** City in the valley of the tribe of Judah (Josh. 15:33), possibly modern Aslin. **2.** City in the valley or shephelah of Judah (Josh. 15:43), possibly modern Idna, about eight miles northwest of Hebron.

ASHPENAZ (Ăsh´ pĕn ăz) Chief eunuch guarding the family of Nebuchadnezzar, king of Babylon (605–562 B.C.) (Dan. 1:3). He administered the diet and lifestyle of Daniel and his three friends, giving them new Babylonian names (Dan. 1:7). Daniel developed a close, loving relationship with him.

ASHRIEL (Ăsh´ rĭ ĕl) (KJV) See *Asriel.*

ASHTAROTH (Ăsh′ tărŏth) is the plural form of Ashtoreth, a Canaanite goddess of fertility, love, and war and the daughter of the god El and the goddess Asherah. **1.** OT uses the plural form, Ashtaroth, more than the singular form, Ashtoreth. The only references to Ashtoreth come in 1 Kings 11:5,33; 2 Kings 23:13. The Hebrew scribes replaced the vowels of the name ′*Ashtart* or ′*Ashteret* with the vowels from the Hebrew word for shame, *boshet*, to bring dishonor to the memory of the goddess. This exchanging of vowels formed the word Ashtoreth. The Greek form of the name is *Astarte*.

In Canaanite mythology she appears to be the sister of the goddess Anath and the spouse of the god Baal. Anath also was the spouse of Baal, as well as the goddess of love and war. Some confusion, therefore, exists regarding Ashtaroth's relationship to Anath. Anath and Ashtaroth may have referred to the same goddess, or they may have been two separate deities. Among the people of Palestine Ashtaroth may have taken over Anath's role. The Egyptians gave the title "Lady of Heaven" to Astarte, Anath, and another goddess, Qudshu. In Moab, Astarte was the spouse of the major god, Chemosh. The Babylonians and Assyrians called her Ashtar and worshiped her as goddess of fertility and love. The people of the ancient Near East during the Hellenistic and Roman periods referred to her as Aphrodite-Venus.

Apparently the word "ashtaroth" at one time meant "womb" or "that which comes from the womb." This word, "ashtaroth," appears in Deut. 7:13 and 28:4,18,51 to describe the young of the flock. This use may demonstrate the link between the goddess Ashtaroth and fertility.

The biblical writers often coupled Baal with Ashtaroth as a designation of pagan worship (Judg. 2:13; 10:6; 1 Sam. 7:3-4; 12:10). In addition to her worship by the Canaanites, the OT mentions the people of Sidon (1 Kings 11:5) and the Philistines (1 Sam. 31:10) as reverencing her. At Beth-shan, the Philistines erected a temple to Ashtaroth (1 Sam. 31:10). The reference to the Queen of Heaven (Jer. 7:18) may have Ashtaroth in mind, but this is uncertain. The Israelites worshiped her, and the biblical writers specifically refer to Solomon's leadership in promoting the worship of Ashtaroth (1 Kings 11:5). She was only one of many foreign deities revered by the Israelites. Josiah destroyed the shrines built to her (2 Kings 23:13).

2. Egyptian documents dating from the 18th century B.C. onward refer to a city called Ashtartu or Ashtarot in the region of Bashan. Joshua 21:27 mentions a city with the name Beeshterah in Bashan, while a man named Uzzia is called an Ashterathite (1 Chron. 11:44). Og, king of Bashan, reigned in the city of Ashtaroth (Deut. 1:4; Josh. 9:10; 12:4, 13:12,31). The sons of Machir received it as a part of their inheritance in the land (Josh. 13:31; 1 Chron. 6:71).

Once the city is called Ashteroth-karnaim (Gen. 14:5) or "Ashtaroth of the two horns." A 17th-century B.C. stone mold for making bronze figurines of Astarte was uncovered at Nahariyah. She was represented as a woman with two horns on her head. Many other clay figurines of Astarte have been found at sites throughout Palestine. The city's name, Ashtaroth, may reflect that she was worshiped by the citizens of this settlement.

The city is located at modern Tel Ashtarah about 20 miles east of the Sea of Galilee. It was located on a major branch of the Via Maris, or Way of the Sea and in the King's Highway, the major highway for traffic east of the Jordan.

Scott Langston

ASHTEROTH KARNAIM (Ăsh′ tə·rŏth Kär′ na·ĭm) See *Ashtaroth.*

ASHTORETH (Ăsh′ tō·rĕth) See *Ashtaroth.*

ASHUR (KJV) See *Ashhur.*

ASHURBANIPAL (Ă′ shŭr·băn′ ĭ·păl) Assyria's last great king who is identified in Ezra 4:10 as the king of Assyria who captured Susa, Elam, and other nations and settled their citizens in Samaria.

The son of a king, Esarhaddon, he was the heir apparent from about 673 B.C. He actually ruled from 668 to 629 B.C. Ashurbanipal's legacy is his famous library that contained more than 20,000 clay tablets. The library was located in the Assyrian capital of Nineveh and was discovered in 1853. Ashurbanipal's copyists not only transcribed Assyrian books but also preserved Sumerian and Akkadian literature. Most of what we know about the Assyrian Empire is derived from his library.

Ashurbanipal was also known by the name Osnappar and appears in the KJV as Asnapper.

Ashurbanipal (668–629 B.C.) was ruler of Assyria during its years of decline. This relief is from an earlier period in Assyrian history—the reign of Ashurnasirpal II (883–859).

His name appears only once in the Bible (Ezra 4:10), the only report of such a settlement in Samaria. The Greeks called him Sardanapalus. His reign was contemporary with the reigns of Manasseh, Amon, and Josiah, Kings of Judah. See *Assyria; Osnapper.*   *M. Stephen Davis*

ASHURITE (Ăsh´ ŭr-īt) or **ASHURI** (NIV) Apparently a tribe or clan over which Ishbosheth, Saul's son, ruled (2 Sam. 2:9). The textual tradition among the earliest translations is not clear here with some evidence that the tribe of Asher or the city-state of Geshur is meant. In KJV of Ezek. 27:6 Ashurites made "benches of ivory" for Tyre. Most modern translations use a different division of words in the Hebrew text and see a type of wood used: boxwood (NASB), cypress (NIV), pine (TEV, RSV), cedar (Jerusalem). If people from Ashur are meant in either of the original texts, we know nothing else about them.

ASHVATH (Ăsh´ văth) Personal name meaning "that which has been worked" (as iron). Descendant of Asher (1 Chron. 7:33).

ASIA New Testament refers to a Roman province on the west of Asia Minor whose capital was Ephesus. The Roman province of Asia comprised generally the southwest portion of Anatolia. Its first capital was Pergamum, but the capital was later changed to Ephesus. Asia residents were in Jerusalem at Pentecost (Acts 2:9). Paul the apostle traveled and preached extensively in Asia (Acts 19:10,22), especially in the neighborhood of Ephesus, but God forbade him to preach there prior to his Macedonian call

(Acts 16:6). Men of Asia led to Paul's arrest in Jerusalem (Acts 21:27). The first letter from Peter was addressed to Christians in Asia. Asia was the location of the seven churches to which the book of Revelation was addressed. Asia was known for its worship of Artemis (Acts 19:27). See *Rome and the Roman Empire.*

ASIA MINOR, CITIES OF Cities located on the Anatolian peninsula (modern-day Turkey). Cities of Asia Minor important to the NT accounts included Alexandria, Troas, Assos, Ephesus, Miletus, Patara, Smyrna, Pergamum, Sardis, Thyatira, Philadelphia, Laodicea, Colossae, Attalia, Antioch, Iconium, Lystra, Derbe, and Tarsus. The cities figured prominently in the Apostle Paul's missionary journeys, several of the churches receiving epistles. Among those listed are the "Seven Cities" of the Revelation.

Geography and History The geography of Asia Minor greatly influenced the development of settlements in the area. The region can be described as the point where "East meets West," linking the continent of Europe with the Near East. The peninsula is a high plateau surrounded by steep mountain ranges. The mountains isolate Asia Minor from much of the outside world. Narrow passes through the mountains connect the interior with the Near East. Deep ravines cut by numerous and often navigable rivers linked the cities of the plateau with the western coastline. Cities developed in locales vital to trade and commerce, such as near the mouths of rivers and mountain passes.

The history of Asia Minor reflects the region's unstable position between the east and west. The Hittite Empire thrived in the eastern portion of the peninsula during the second millennium B.C. (before 1000). Exposed on the west to the Aegean Sea, the coastal area became the home to numerous Greek colonies beginning about 1200 B.C. Centered in Sardis, the Lydian Empire began to expand about 600 B.C. but was soon conquered by the Persians. Control passed to Alexander the Great about 333 B.C. Upon his death Asia Minor fell under the rule of the Seleucids. Beginning about 200 B.C., Roman control of the peninsula increased until all of Anatolia was absorbed into the Roman provincial system. At this time "Asia" designated the provinces of only western Anatolia. Galatia, Cappadocia, and Cilicia comprised the eastern provinces, while Bitnia and Pontus bordered the

Black Sea to the north. The Anatolian peninsula was probably first termed "Asia Minor" after A.D. 400.

Coastal Cities The name *Troas* described both the northwest region of Asia Minor as well as the port city. Located 10 miles south of the site of ancient Troy, Alexandria Troas was founded as a Roman colony during the period of Augustus and served as a primary port for trade passing between Asia Minor and Macedonia. Remains of the ruined city wall and a bath complex of the second century A.D. are still visible. As with many ancient ports, the once busy harbor became filled with silt and became unusable. Paul once set sail from Troas to Greece in response to his vision of the "Macedonian Man" (Acts 16:11). On his third journey Paul's companions embarked on a ship sailing toward the port of Assos, 20 miles south (Acts 20:13). A bustling port city surrounded by a wall dating to the fourth century B.C., Assos' temple of Athena sat high on the acropolis overlooking the harbor. At Assos, Paul joined the ship carrying Luke and several others after journeying on foot from Troas.

Ephesus served as the primary trading center of all Asia Minor. The large port facility provided ample anchorage for ships carrying goods east from Greece and Italy, as well as for those which took to Rome the wares brought overland from Asia and the Far East. A well-laid road linked the post facilities at Ephesus with *Tarsus* to the east. The road approached the city from the southeast, entering a monumental gateway near the public baths. Remains of the city's immense theater, capable of seating 24,000 spectators, stand today as a reminder of the great crowd which in protest to Paul filled the seats and for several hours shouted, "Great is Diana of the Ephesians!" (Acts 19:34). The city's temple honoring Diana was one of the Seven Wonders of the World. Known as the Artemision to the Greeks, the temple possessed 127 pillars 60 feet high which held up the roof of the largest all-marble structure in the Hellenistic world. The city's harbor, built around the outlet of the Cayster River, gradually filled with silt; and the site now lies some six miles away from the sea. As the chief port and city of Asia, Paul's choice of Ephesus as a center of ministry provided the perfect base from which the Gospel could be spread throughout the Roman world.

During the early period of Greek colonization, *Miletus* exercised extensive control over

Trajan's Temple in Pergamum. Trajan was Emperor of Rome A.D. 98–117. The Temple was built by his successor Hadrian.

southwestern Anatolia. As a major sea power, the city remained independent throughout the time of Lydian rule in the region. The city was able to withstand attempted incursions by the Persians until 494 B.C. Once a wealthy port for the wool industry, Miletus was a city of little significance during the NT era (Acts 20:15).

Acts 21 recounts how Paul sailed for *Tyre* from Patara. The city served as a popular port for ships traveling eastward during the early autumn months when favorable winds made travel to Egypt and the Phoenician coast easier. The harbor sat near the outlet of the Xanthus River and was the main shipping facility of provincial Lydia.

Smyrna surrounded a well-protected harbor on the Aegean coast at the outlet of the Hermus River. Extensive trade into and out of Asia passed through the city. During the first century A.D. Smyrna reigned as one of the grandest cities of all Asia. A large temple dedicated to the Emperor Tiberius boasted the close alliance of the city with the Empire. Numerous other temples dedicated to a widerange of Roman deities as well as scores of beautifully adorned public buildings decorated the city.

Cities of the Interior Located 15 miles inland overlooking the Caicus River, *Pergamum* contained the first temple in Asia dedicated to a Roman Emperor, Augustus, in 29 B.C. The city possessed a commanding position on a hill high above the valley. Located on the Upper Acropolis were a large theater, library, agora, palace, barracks, and altar of Zeus. The large altar area may be that referred to by John as "Satan's throne" (Rev. 2:13 HCSB). The city was well-known as a center of worship for the gods Asklepios, Zeus, Demeter and Persephone, Serapis, Isis, as well as the cult of the emperor.

The greatest city in Lydia, *Sardis* is remembered as the first municipality to mint coins of silver and gold. Set in the fertile Hermus valley, Sardis served as the capital of the Lydian king Croesus, a name synonymous with wealth. The city fell to the Persian armies of Cyrus in 549 B.C. and to the Romans in 188 B.C. A tremendous earthquake in A.D. 17 struck Sardis, a blow from which it never was able to recover fully.

Following the Hermus River inland from Sardis, one reached *Philadelphia*, the name commemorating the brotherly love between Attalus Philadelphus and Eumenes. Founded during the second century B.C., the city was set amidst vast vineyards and led in the worship of Dionysius. The terrible earthquake of A.D. 17 was followed by dangerous tremors for the next 20 years, each one debilitating the city further. The Apostle John's reference to the giving of a "new name" (Rev. 3:12) may be a wordplay on the proposed dedication of the city as "Neocaesarea" in honor of aid sent by Tiberius.

Journeying inland from Miletus, a traveler followed the course of the Meander River until it joined the Lycus. In the center of the valley sat *Laodicea*. Situated along the major east-west trade route, the city prospered greatly. As the chief city of the wealthy province of Phrygia, Laodicea boasted of a large number of banks. In 51 B.C. Cicero recounted how he stopped to cash drafts at one of the city's banks. The great wealth of Laodicea allowed it to finance its own rebuilding after a destructive earthquake in A.D. 60, refusing help from the Senate of Rome. The city was also known for clothes and carpets woven from the rich, glossy black wool raised in the valley. Laodicea served as home to a medical school renowned for production of collyrium, an eye salve. Revelation mentions the riches of the city, admonishing believers to seek instead spiritual gold of eternal worth, and to anoint their eyes with a spiritual salve. John's description of "white garments" to cover their nakedness contrasts the Laodicean preference for "home-grown" black wool, a symbol of worldly prosperity (Rev. 3:14-18).

Eleven miles south of Laodicea lay *Colossae*. The city was well-known as early as about 450 B.C. as a commercial center, famous for red-dyed wool. The establishment of Laodicea, however, led to the decline of Colossae's prosperity. Several remains are still visible, including a small theater on the city's southeast side. The Apostle Paul never personally evangelized the city. Instead, the church was established by Epaphras during Paul's third missionary journey (Col. 1:7; 4:12-13). Paul wrote to the church during his Roman imprisonment, complementing the work of Philemon's servant Onesimus (Col. 4:9).

Cities of Eastern Asia Minor Much of Paul's Asian ministry centered around the provinces of Galatia and Lycaonia. On his first journey, Paul and Barnabas most likely arrived by sea at *Attalia*, a relatively small and unimportant harbor. Moving northward from the port and crossing Pamphylia, the group arrived at Antioch in the province of Galatia (Acts 13:14). Luke's

"Antioch of Pisidia" carried the title of *Colonia Caesarea Antiocheia*, a colony established in 25 B.C. upon a much earlier Hellenistic city. Antioch had been renovated by Rome to provide for the defense of Galatia. A temple to Augustus dominated the central plaza, and the official inscription telling of his victories and of achievements was displayed in the city. Wagons bearing Anatolian marble passed through Antioch on their way to ships at Ephesus to be used in the decoration of the empire.

Moving southeast from Antioch, Paul and his companions traveled to *Iconium* (Acts 13:51). Located in a fertile, well-watered plain, Iconium supplied large amounts of fruit and grain for the surrounding provinces. Several years after Paul's visit, the Emperor Claudius allowed the town to be renamed Claudiconium in his honor, a reminder of the strong ties it shared with Rome.

Lystra lay 20 miles to the south of Iconium along the *Via Sebaste*. About 6 B.C. Augustus conferred the title of *Julia Felix Gemina Lustra* upon this Roman colony. Connected by a fine road with Antioch to the west, the city honored Zeus and Hermes as patron gods. A statue dedicated to the two was discovered in the 1800s, reminiscent of the city's identification of Paul and Barnabas with the gods (Acts 14). Timothy was a native of Lystra. The ruins of the city are today near the small Turkish town of Katyn Serai.

Derbe was situated 60 miles from Lystra at the present-day site of Kerti Huyuk. Although a large city of Lycaonia, Derbe was relatively unimportant. Paul's decision to visit the city infers a large Jewish population in the region. It is possible that some believers had already advanced the gospel to Derbe, having been earlier expelled from Iconium.

The boyhood home of the Apostle Paul, *Tarsus* of Cilicia lay on the eastern end of the east-west trade route beginning at Ephesus. At Tarsus merchants had the option of going south into Syria and Palestine, or continuing across the mountains on to Zeugma and the East. The Cydnus River provided Tarsus with an outlet to the Mediterranean Sea, 10 miles away. Lumber and linen were the main industries of Tarsus, but the related manufacture of goat's-hair cloth was practiced by many, including Paul. This skill served as his main source of income wherever he traveled. Tarsus also housed a university and school of philosophy, an academic atmosphere

that formed the basis of Paul's latter rabbinic career.   *David C. Maltsberger*

ASIARCHS (Ā′ sī·ärks) Somewhat general term for public patrons and leaders named by cities in the Roman province of Asia. They used their wealth for the public good, especially for supporting worship of the emperor and of Rome. They underwrote expenses of games sponsored in connection with religious festivals. Having served in the position, a person seemed able to continue to use the title. Paul won friends among this elite class (Acts 19:31), and they helped protect him from a religious riot in Ephesus. Note that some versions transliterate Asiarchs from Greek while others translate it to chiefs or officials.

ASIEL (Ăs′ ĭ·ĕl) Personal name meaning "God has made." A descendant of Simeon and clan leader who settled in Gedor in rich pasturelands (1 Chron. 4:35-40).

ASKELON (KJV) See *Ashkelon*.

ASNAH (Ăs′ năh) Proper name possibly with Egyptian origins relating to the god Nah. One of the Nethanims or temple servants who returned to Jerusalem with Zerubbabel from exile about 537 B.C. (Ezra 2:50).

ASNAPPER (Ăs·năpēr) KJV reading in Ezra 4:10. Modern translations read Osnappar (NASB, RSV) or Ashurbanipal (TEV, NIV). See *Ashurbanipal; Osnappar*.

ASP KJV translation for a dangerous, poisonous snake (Deut. 32:33; Job 20:14,16; Isa. 11:8; Rom. 3:13). Other translations use "serpent," "viper," or "cobra" at some or all of these places. The Hebrew term *peten* occurs also in Ps. 58:4, where KJV translates "adder." Some works point to the cobra *naja chaje*, but this identification is not certain. Whatever the specific identification, they serve as symbols of dangerous poison (Deut. 32:33). They can be described as deaf (Ps. 58:4) either as a natural characteristic or as an unusual case. The deafness makes them immune to the snake charmer and thus even more dangerous with their poison. Riches that become the center of life turn out to be as poisonous as asps (Job 20:14,16). The prophetic vision is God's restoration of the world order so that small children can play around the holes of poisonous snakes without fear (Isa. 11:8). Until that day sin continues to dominate humanity, turning speech into poisonous lies (Rom. 3:13). See *Reptiles*.

ASPATHA (Ăs·pā´ thà) Persian personal name. Son of Haman killed by Jews (Esther 9:10).

ASRIEL (Ăs´ rĭ·ĕl), **ASRIELITES** Personal name meaning "God has made happy." A son of Gilead and clan in the tribe of Manasseh (Num. 26:31). They received a land allotment (Josh. 17:2). In 1 Chron. 7:14 KJV spells it Ashriel.

ASS "Beast of burden" and "wild animal" in KJV but translated "donkey" in most modern translations. Six different Hebrew words and two Greek words lie behind the English translations. This animal appears more than 120 times in the Bible.

Aton is a female animal used for riding (Gen. 49:11; Num. 22:21-33; Judg. 5:10; 2 Kings 4:22) and as a beast of burden (Gen. 45:23). Saul's father lost his female asses (1 Sam. 9:3). This indicated loss of pride and prestige, for asses were apparently the riding animals for leaders and for the nobility (cp. Judg. 10:4; 12:14; see below on *ayir*). Warriors rode female asses (Judg. 5:10). Wealthy persons owned numbers of asses (Gen. 12:16; 32:15; 1 Chron. 27:30; Job 1:3). They grazed the grasslands for food (Job 1:14). God used a talking ass to teach the prophet Balaam a lesson in obedience (Num. 22:21-41). Zechariah pictured the Messiah as riding on "a colt the foal of an ass" (*aton*), thus emphasizing the animal was a purebred ass and not a crossbred mule (Zech. 9:9 KJV).

Chamor is the male ass, probably a reddish color according to the basic meaning of the Hebrew term. The original homeland of the ass (*equus asinus*) was probably Africa. It was both a riding animal (Gen. 22:3) and a beast of burden (Gen. 42:26), which could be used for plowing (Deut. 22:10, which forbids yoking an ass with an ox). For his hard work Issachar was pictured as a donkey (Gen. 49:14). An ass was valuable enough that the firstborn ass had to be ritually redeemed through sacrifice of a lamb (Exod. 13:13; 34:20) or by killing the newborn ass. In extreme famine conditions people would go so far as to pay astronomical prices for the head of an ass which they could eat (2 Kings 6:25). The ass was used to illustrate rampant

The donkey, or ass, is still used as a beast of burden and mode of transportation in the Middle East.

sexual lust (Ezek. 23:20). A donkey's burial was an unceremonious dumping on the garbage heap for the vultures and scavengers to eat up (Jer. 22:19). The rich possessed herds of donkeys (Gen. 24:35; 30:43) though the Egyptian farmers suffering under the famine also had asses to bring to Joseph in exchange for food (Gen. 47:17; cp. Exod. 9:3; 20:17). The Messiah would ride on a donkey (Zech. 9:9), the animal of the nobility in days when Israel did not have a king. The animal contrasted to the horse used in the kings' military exploits after Solomon's time (1 Kings 10:26) in violation of Deut. 17:16. The picture in Zech. 9 thus joins the humble suffering servant and the royal Messiah.

Ayir refers to the stallion or young, vigorous male ass. These were apparently riding animals reserved for nobility (Judg. 10:4; 12:14; Zech. 9:9). Isaiah described an unusual caravan on the way to Egypt including young donkeys and camels. The older donkeys would have been the more usual caravan members (Isa. 30:6). Nomads in the desert often led caravans of donkeys and camels loaded with wares to sell. The day of God's salvation would include luxurious food for the donkeys who pulled the plows (Isa. 30:24).

Arod refers to the wild ass (*asinus hemippus*) that God created for freedom in the wilderness rather than to do slave labor for humans (Job 39:5). Such animals explore mountain pastures for food (Job 39:8).

Pere' is a wild donkey or onager which some Bible students identify with the zebra, but no evidence exists for zebras in Palestine. The Hebrew in Gen. 16:12 calls Ishmael "a wild ass of a man" (NRSV, NIV, TEV, NASB), because he would live in opposition to all other people. The wild donkey was known for its braying and for eating grass (Job 6:5). Such a wild animal can never be human (Job 11:12; cp. various translations). It lives in the wilderness searching for food and helpless before the cold and rain (Job 24:5-8; cp. 39:5). Without pastures it breathes its last dying gasp (Jer. 14:6). They ventured into cities only when the cities were forsaken ruins (Isa. 32:14). God had created them to be accustomed to life in the Judean wilderness (Jer. 2:24), where they freely pursued natural instincts and lusts (cp. Hos. 8:9).

Onarion refers to a small donkey and appears only in John 12:14 to show the promise of Zech. 9:9 was being fulfilled.

Onos can refer either to a male or female donkey. John 12:15 sees the ass as the parent of the colt on which Jesus rode, while Matt. 21:2 sees both an ass and a colt involved. These animals were kept in stalls and watered as a natural part of peasant life (Luke 13:15). They could easily get loose and fall into a pit (Luke 14:5). Jesus showed care for the animals, which stricter Jews were prone to let lie in pits in order to obey religious rules.

Hupozugion literally means "one under a yoke." This is Matthew's term for the parent of the "foal of an ass" predicted in Zech. 9:9 (Matt. 21:5). Peter used the term to refer to the animal which spoke to Balaam (2 Pet. 2:16).

The precise difference in meaning of the various words for "ass" is not always evident to modern Bible students, though the differences were surely clear to the original writers and readers.

ASSASSINS Organized Jewish group who attempted to win freedom from the Romans. The word in Greek is derived from the Latin term *Sicarii* and literally means "dagger men." Josephus described them as hiding small daggers in their clothing, which they used in crowded situations to kill their victims. *Sicarii* was used by the Romans to refer to those Jews who engaged in the organized killing of political figures. Perhaps this group should be associated with the Zealots of the NT. The *Sicarii* were often called robbers, and it is likely that the thieves crucified with Jesus were suspected of belonging to this group. In Acts 21:38 Paul was mistaken as a leader of 4,000 *Sicarii*. KJV calls them murderers; REB and TEV, terrorists. See *Zealot.*

ASSAYER One who tests ore for its silver and gold content. According to modern versions of Jer. 6:27, the calling of Jeremiah was to be an assayer of the people. He did not find them to be a precious metal. The KJV takes the word from the Hebrew root for tower, which is spelled the same as the root word for assayer. Modern versions, however, seem to make the best sense of the Hebrew text (Jer. 6:27-30). See *Bellows.*

ASSEMBLY Official gathering of the people of Israel and of the church. See *Congregation.*

ASSHUR (Ăs´ shŭr), **ASSHURIM, ASSHURITES** (NIV) Personal and national name. **1.** Son of Shem and thus a Semite, as were the Hebrew people (Gen. 10:22). **2.** Unknown Arabian tribe (Gen. 25:3). This tribe may also be meant in Balaam's oracle (Num. 24:22-24), but a reference to Assyria is more likely. **3.** The nation Assyria and its inhabitants are generally meant by the Hebrew term *Asshur.* This is the likely meaning in Gen. 10:11; Ezek. 27:23; 32:22; Hos. 14:3. See *Assyria.*

ASSIR (Ăs´ sĭr) Personal name meaning "prisoner." **1.** Son of Korah (Exod. 6:24), the leader of the rebellion against Moses (Num. 16:1-35). **2.** Great grandson of 1. above (1 Chron. 6:23) or grandson of 1. above with Elkanah and Ebiasaph being brothers (cp. 1 Chron. 6:37). **3.** Son of King Jeconiah (or Jehoiachin) in KJV of 1 Chron. 3:17, but this should probably be interpreted as a common noun, "captive," referring to Jehoiachin (NIV, NASB, NRSV).

ASSOS (Ăs´ sŏs) Seaport city on the Gulf of Adramyttium, an offshoot of the east coast of the Aegean Sea. Paul visited there briefly and met Luke and others there as he sailed to Jerusalem from his third missionary journey (Acts 20:13-14).

A

ASSUR (Ăs´ sŭr) (KJV, Ezra 4:2; Ps. 83:8) See *Assyria.*

ASSURANCE See *Security of the Believer.*

ASSURBANIPAL See *Ashurbanipal.*

ASSYRIA (Ăs·sĭr´ ĭ·ä) Nation in northern Mesopotamia in OT times that became a large empire during the period of the Israelite kings. Assyrian expansion into the region of Palestine (about 855–625 B.C.) had enormous impact on the Hebrew kingdoms of Israel and Judah.

History Assyria lay north of the region of Babylonia along the banks of the Tigris River (Gen. 2:14) in northern Mesopotamia. The name Assyria (Hb., *Ashshur*) is from Asshur, its first capital, founded about 2000 B.C. The foundation of other Assyrian cities, notably Calah and Nineveh, appears in Gen. 10:11-12.

The history of Assyria is well documented in royal Assyrian annals, building inscriptions, king lists, correspondence, and other archaeological evidence. By 1900 B.C. these cities were vigorously trading as far away as Cappadocia in eastern Asia Minor. An expanded Assyria warred with the famous King Hammurabi of Babylon

shortly before breaking up into smaller city-states about 1700 B.C.

Beginning about 1300 B.C., a reunited Assyria made rapid territorial advances and soon became an international power. Expanding westward, Tiglath-pileser I (1115–1077 B.C.) became the first Assyrian monarch to march his army to the shores of the Mediterranean. With his murder, however, Assyria entered a 166-year period of decline.

Assyria awoke from its dark ages under Adad-nirari II (911–891 B.C.), who reestablished the nation as a power to be reckoned with in Mesopotamia. His grandson, Ashurnasirpal II (883–859 B.C.) moved Assyria toward the status of an empire. Ashurnasirpal II used a well-deserved reputation for cruelty to extort tribute and taxes from states within the reach of his army in predatory campaigns. He also rebuilt the city of Calah as the new military and administrative capital. Carved stone panels in Ashurnasirpal's palace there show violent scenes of the king's vicious campaigns against unsubmissive enemies.

Ashurnasirpal's son Shalmaneser III (858–824 B.C.) continued a policy of Assyrian expansion through his annual campaigns in all

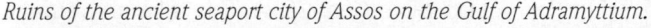

Ruins of the ancient seaport city of Assos on the Gulf of Adramyttium.

These human-faced monumental bulls from Assyria date from the time of Ashurnasirpal II (ninth century B.C.)

directions. These were no longer mere predatory raids. Rather, they demonstrated a systematic economic exploitation of subject states. As always, failure to submit to Assyria brought vicious military action. The results, however, were not always a complete victory for Assyria. In such a context Assyria first encountered the Hebrew kingdoms of the Bible. In 853 B.C. at Qarqar in north Syria, Shalmaneser fought a coalition of 12 kings including Hadad-ezer (Ben-Hadad, 1 Kings 20:26,34) of Aram-Damascus and Ahab of Israel. This confrontation is not mentioned in the Bible, but it may have taken place during a three-year period of peace between Israel and Aram-Damascus (1 Kings 22:1). In his official inscriptions Shalmaneser claims victory, but the battle was inconclusive. In 841 B.C. he finally defeated Hazael of Damascus and on Mount Carmel received tribute from Tyre, Sidon, and King Jehu of Israel. A scene carved in relief on the Black Obelisk of Shalmaneser, unearthed at Calah, shows Jehu groveling before Shalmaneser, the only known depiction of an Israelite king.

With the death of Shalmaneser, Assyria entered another period of decline during which she was occupied with the nearby kingdom of Urartu. For the next century only one Assyrian king seriously affected affairs in Palestine. Adad-nirari III (810–783 B.C.) entered Damascus, taking extensive tribute from Ben-hadad III. He is probably the "savior" of 2 Kings 13:5, who allowed Israel to escape domination by Aram-Damascus. Nevertheless, Adad-nirari also collected tribute from Jehoash of Israel.

Assyrian preoccupation with Urartu ended with the reign of Tiglath-pileser III (744–727 B.C.). The true founder of the Assyrian Empire,

he made changes in the administration of conquered territories. Nations close to the Assyrian homeland were incorporated as provinces. Others were left with native rule, but subject to an Assyrian overseer. Tiglath-pileser also instituted a policy of mass deportations to reduce local nationalistic feelings. He took conquered people into exile to live in lands vacated by other conquered exiles (cp. 2 Kings 17:24).

As Tiglath-pileser, also called Pul, arrived on the coast of Phoenicia, Menahem of Israel (2 Kings 15:19) and Rezin of Aram-Damascus brought tribute and became vassals of Assyria. An anti-Assyrian alliance quickly formed. Israel and Aram-Damascus attacked Jerusalem about 735 B.C. in an attempt to replace King Ahaz of Judah with a man loyal to the anti-Assyrian alliance (2 Kings 16:2-6; Isa. 7:1-6) and thus force Judah's participation. Against the protests of Isaiah (Isa. 7:4,16-17; 8:4-8), Ahaz appealed to Tiglath-pileser for assistance (2 Kings 16:7-9). Tiglath-pileser, in response, campaigned against Philistia (734 B.C.), reduced Israel to the area immediately around Samaria (2 Kings 15:29; 733 B.C.), and annexed Aram-Damascus (732 B.C.), deporting the population. Ahaz, for his part, became an Assyrian vassal (2 Kings 16:10; 2 Chron. 28:16,20-22).

Little is known of the reign of Tiglath-pileser's successor, Shalmaneser V (726–722 B.C.), except that he besieged Samaria for three years in response to Hoshea's failure to pay tribute (2 Kings 17:3-5). The city finally fell to Shalmaneser (2 Kings 17:6; 18:9-12), who apparently died in the same year. His successor, Sargon II (722–705 B.C.), took credit in Assyrian royal inscriptions for deporting 27,290 inhabitants of Samaria.

Sargon campaigned in the region to counter rebellions in Gaza in 720 B.C. and Ashdod in 712 (Isa. 20:1). Hezekiah of Judah was tempted to join in the Ashdod rebellion, but Isaiah warned against such action (Isa. 18). Meanwhile, unrest smoldered in other parts of the empire. A rebellious king of Babylon, Merodach-baladan, found support from Elam, Assyria's enemy to the east. Though forced to flee Babylon in 710 B.C., Merodach-baladan returned some years later to reclaim the throne. He sent emissaries to Hezekiah in Jerusalem (2 Kings 20:12-19; Isa. 39), apparently as part of preparations for a concerted anti-Assyrian revolt.

A colossal stylized bull with human face from the time of Sargon II of Assyria.

News of Sargon's death in battle served as a signal to anti-Assyrian forces. Sennacherib (704–681 B.C.) ascended the throne in the midst of widespread revolt. Merodach-baladan of Babylon, supported by the Elamites, had inspired the rebellion of all southern Mesopotamia. A number of states in Phoenicia and Palestine were also in rebellion, led by Hezekiah of Judah. After subduing Babylon, Sennacherib turned his attentions westward. In 701 B.C., he reasserted control over the city-states of Phoenicia, sacked Joppa and Ashkelon, and invaded Judah where Hezekiah had made considerable military preparations (2 Kings 20:20; 2 Chron. 32:1-8,30; Isa. 22:8b-11). Sennacherib's own account of the invasion provides a remarkable supplement to the biblical version (2 Kings 18:13–19:36). He claims to have destroyed 46 walled cities (2 Kings 18:13) and to have taken 200,150 captives. Sennacherib's conquest of Lachish is shown in graphic detail in carved panels from his palace at Nineveh. During the siege of Lachish, an Assyrian army was sent against Jerusalem where Hezekiah was "made a prisoner ... like a bird in a cage." Three of Sennacherib's dignitaries attempted to negotiate the surrender of Jerusalem (2 Kings 18:17-37), but Hezekiah continued to hold out with the encouragement of Isaiah (2 Kings 19:1-7,20-35). In the end the Assyrian army withdrew, and Hezekiah paid an enormous tribute (2 Kings 18:14-16). The Assyrian account claims a victory over the Egyptian army and mentions Hezekiah's tribute but is rather vague about the end of the campaign. The Bible mentions the approach of the Egyptian army (2 Kings 19:9) and tells of a miraculous defeat of the Assyrians by the angel of the Lord (2 Kings 19:35-36). The fifth century B.C. Greek historian Herodotus relates that the Assyrians

suffered defeat because a plague of field mice destroyed their equipment. It is not certain whether these accounts can be combined to infer an outbreak of the plague. Certainly, Sennacherib suffered a major setback, for Hezekiah was the only ruler of the revolt to keep his throne.

On a more peaceful front, Sennacherib conducted some major building projects in Assyria. The ancient city of Nineveh was rebuilt as the new royal residence and Assyrian capital. War continued, however, with Elam, which also influenced Babylon to rebel again. An enraged Sennacherib razed the sacred city in 689 B.C. His murder, at the hands of his own sons (2 Kings 19:37) in 681 B.C., was interpreted by Babylonians as divine judgment for destroying their city.

Esarhaddon (681–669 B.C.) emerged as the new king and immediately began the rebuilding of Babylon, an act which won the allegiance of the local populace. He warred with nomadic tribes to the north and quelled a rebellion in Phoenicia, while Manasseh of Judah remained a loyal vassal. His greatest military adventure, however, was an invasion of Egypt conducted in 671 B.C. The Pharaoh Taharqa fled south as Memphis fell to the Assyrians but returned and fomented rebellion two years later. Esarhaddon died in 669 B.C. on his way back to subjugate Egypt.

After conducting a brief expedition against eastern tribes, Esarhaddon's son, Ashurbanipal (668–627 B.C.), set out to reconquer Egypt. Assisted by 22 subject kings, including Manasseh of Judah, he invaded in 667 B.C. He defeated Pharaoh Taharqa and took the ancient capital of Thebes. Some 1,300 miles from home, Ashurbanipal had no choice but to reinstall the local rulers his father had appointed in Egypt and hope for the best. Plans for revolt began immediately; but Assyrian officers got wind of the plot, captured the rebels, and sent them to Nineveh. Egypt rebelled again in 665 B.C. This time Ashurbanipal destroyed Thebes, also called No-Amon (Nah. 3:8, NASB). Phoenician attempts at revolt were also crushed.

Ashurbanipal ruled at Assyria's zenith but also saw the beginning of her swift collapse. Ten years after the destruction of Thebes, Egypt rebelled yet again. Assyria could do nothing because of a war with Elam. In 651 B.C. Ashurbanipal's brother, the king of Babylon, organized a widespread revolt. After three years of contin-

A basalt statue of the Assyrian king Shalmaneser III.

ual battles Babylon was subdued but remained filled with seeds of hatred for Assyria. Action against Arab tribes followed, and the war with Elam continued until a final Assyrian victory in 639 B.C. That same year the official annals of Ashurbanipal came to an abrupt end. With Ashurbanipal's death in 627 B.C., unrest escalated. By 626, Babylon had fallen into the hands of the Chaldean Nabopolassar. Outlying states, such as Judah under Josiah, were free to rebel without fear. War continued between Assyria and Babylon until, in 614 B.C., the old Assyrian capital Asshur was sacked by the Medes. Then, in 612 B.C., Calah was destroyed. The combined armies of the Babylonians and the Medes laid siege to Nineveh. After two months the city fell.

An Assyrian general claimed the throne and rallied what was left of the Assyrian army in Haran. An alliance with Egypt brought a few troops to Assyria's aid, but in 610 B.C. the Babylonians approached, and Haran was abandoned. In 605 B.C. the last remnants of the battered Assyrian Empire, along with their recent Egyptian allies, were deferred on The Battle of Carchemish. Assyria was no more.

Religion Assyrian religion, like that of most Near Eastern nations, was polytheistic. Essentially the same as Babylonian religion, official Assyrian religion recognized thousands of gods; but only about 20 were important in actual practice.

Younger gods were usually associated with a newer city or none at all. Adad, the Canaanite Hadad, was the god of storms and thus both beneficial and destructive. Ninurta, the god of war and hunting, became a fitting patron for the Assyrian capital Calah. Most important, however, is the unique figure of Asshur. As patron god and namesake of the original Assyrian capital Asshur and the state itself, Asshur rose in importance to be lord of the universe and the supreme god. Since the god Asshur stood above all others, the Assyrian king was dutybound to show his corresponding dominance on earth. Most Assyrian military campaigns were initiated "at the command of Asshur." See *Babylon*.

Daniel C. Browning, Jr.

ASTAROTH, ASTARTE See *Ashtaroth*.

ASTROLOGER Person who "divided the heavens" (literal translation of Hebrew phrase, Isa. 47:13) to determine the future. Particularly the Babylonians developed sophisticated methods of reading the stars to determine proper times for action. The prophet mocked Babylon's tireless and tiring efforts in astrology. Daniel shows repeatedly that Babylon's well-educated, professional magicians could not match Daniel and his friends. Daniel apparently has magicians and masters of incantations and spells rather than astrologers. The "Chaldeans" of Dan. 2:2; 4:7; 5:7,11 may be the nearest reference to astrologers in the book. The Bible does not seek to describe the skills, tactics, or methods of foreign personnel engaged in various practices to determine the opportune time. Rather the Bible mocks such practices and shows that God's word to the prophets and the wise of Israel far surpasses any foreign skills.

ASUPPIM (Ă·sŭp´ pĭm) KJV interpretation in 1 Chron. 26:15,17. Modern translations read "storehouse."

ASWAN (Ă´ swän) NIV, TEV in Ezek. 29:10; 30:6 for Syene. See *Syene*.

ASYLUM See *Avenger*.

ASYNCRITUS (À·sĭn´ crĭ·tŭs) Personal name meaning "incomparable." Roman Christian whom Paul greeted (Rom. 16:14).

ATAD (Ā´ tăd) Personal name meaning "thorn." Owner of threshing floor, or part of name of Bramble Threshing Floor, east of the Jordan River where Joseph stopped to mourn the death of his father before carrying Jacob's embalmed body across the Jordan to Machpelah for burial. The place was named Abel-mizraim (Gen. 50:10-11). See *Abel-mizraim*.

ATARAH (Ăt´ à·răh) Personal name meaning "crown" or "wreath." Second wife of Jerahmeel and mother of Onam (1 Chron. 2:26).

ATAROTH (Ăt´ à·rôth) Place-name meaning "crowns." **1.** Town desired and built up by tribe of Gad (Num. 32:3,34). Mesha, king of Moab, about 830 B.C. claims he captured Ataroth but admits it belonged to Gad "from of old" and had been built by an Israelite king. It is located at modern Khirbet Attarus, eight miles northwest of Dibon and eight miles east of the Dead Sea. **2.** Village on border of Benjamin and Ephraim (Josh. 16:2,7) It may be modern Khirbet el-Oga in the Jordan Valley.

ATAROTH-ADDAR (Ăt´ à·rôth-ăd´ där) Place-name meaning "crowns of glory." A border town in Ephraim (Josh. 16:5), bordering Benjamin (Josh. 18:13), probably modern Khirbet Attara at the foot of Tell en-Nasbeh or possibly identical with Tell en-Nasbeh and thus with biblical Mizpah.

ATER (Ā´ tēr) Personal name meaning either "crippled" or "left-handed." Clan of which 98 returned from Babylonian exile with Zerubbabel about 537 B.C. (Ezra 2:16). They were temple gatekeepers (Ezra 2:42). The head of the clan signed Nehemiah's covenant to keep God's Law (Neh. 10:17).

ATHACH (Ā´ thăk) Place-name meaning "attack." Town in southern Judah to which David sent spoils of victory while he fled Saul among the Philistines (1 Sam. 30:30). May be the same as Ether (Josh. 15:42), a small copying change causing the difference. See *Ether.*

ATHAIAH (Ă ·thā´ ah) Leader of tribe of Judah who lived in Jerusalem in time of Nehemiah (Neh. 11:4).

ATHALIAH (Ăth·à·lī´ ăh) Personal name meaning "Yahweh has announced His exalted nature"

The Parthenon on the Acropolis at Athens.

A

or "Yahweh is righteous." **1.** Wife of Jehoram, king of Judah, and mother of Ahaziah, king of Judah. She was either the daughter of Ahab and Jezebel of Israel (2 Kings 8:18) or of Omri, king of Israel (2 Kings 8:26; according to a literal reading of text as in KJV; an interpretation of text extends Hebrew word for "daughter" to mean female descendant and thus "granddaughter" as in NASB; NIV; RSV). Some have suggested Omri was her father, but her brother Ahab raised her at court and thus functioned as her father. She brought the northern court's devotion to Baal to the court of Judah. She exercised great political influence during her son's reign of one year (2 Kings 8:27-28). At her son's death from battle wounds, she tried to gain power for herself by having all male heirs killed. She managed to rule Judah for six years (2 Kings 11:1-3), being the only woman to do so. Finally, Jehoiada the priest led a revolt, crowning the child Joash as king and bringing about Athaliah's death (2 Kings 11:5-20). **2.** Son of Jeroham in tribe of Benjamin (1 Chron. 8:26). **3.** Father of Jeshaiah, who led 70 men back to Jerusalem from exile with Ezra (Ezra 8:7).

ATHARIM (Ăth´ à·rĭm) Hebrew word of uncertain meaning. It names a roadway the king of Arad took to attack Israel under Moses. After an initial setback, Israel prayed and found victory under God (Num. 21:1-3). KJV translates "spies" following the Septuagint, the earliest Greek translation. Modern translations simply transliterate the Hebrew. The site may be Tamar a few miles south of the Dead Sea.

ATHENS (Ăth´ əns) Capital of Attica, an ancient district of east central Greece, where Paul preached to the Greek philosophers (Acts 17:15-34). Paul saw that the Athenians were very religious and even had an altar to an unknown God. He based his sermon on this. Though some converts were won to faith in Christ, no biblical record exists of a viable church being established. The city, which probably was named for the wisdom goddess Athene, was already an ancient place by the time Paul visited it. Indeed, human occupation of the area seems to date before 3000 B.C. In the sixth century B.C. Athens became the scene of the world's first great experiment with democratic government. It was destroyed by the Persians early in the fifth century B.C., but during the administra-

tion of Pericles the city was rebuilt into an architectural wonder. The higher part of the city, known as the Acropolis, is where the Parthenon and other temples were built. *(See Reconstruction on pp. 150-51)*

ATHLAI (Ăth´ lī) Personal name meaning "Yahweh is exalted." A man who agreed (Ezra 10:28) under Ezra's leadership to divorce his foreign wife and return to faithfulness to Yahweh.

ATONEMENT (À·tōn´ mĕnt) Biblical doctrine that God has reconciled sinners to Himself through the sacrificial work of Jesus Christ. The concept of atonement spans both Testaments, everywhere pointing to the death, burial, and resurrection of Jesus for the sins of the world.

Atonement as Penal The biblical concept of atonement cannot be understood except in the context of the wrath of God against sin. The need for atonement arises in the earliest stages of the biblical narrative, as the newly created humans rebel against the command of God. For their treasonous disobedience against their Creator, Adam and Eve are told that they face death and have brought the curse of God upon themselves and the entire created order (Gen. 3:13-19).

As a result of this primeval mutiny, the entire world-system stands at enmity with the purposes of God (Eph. 2:2) and is blinded by the deception of Satan (2 Cor. 4:4). Not only did human beings chafe at the command God had given in the garden, they have rebelled against the law He revealed to them within their hearts (Rom. 2:14-16) and in specific revelation (Rom. 3:19-20). As such, each individual human has turned to idolatry (Rom. 1:18-32) and stands guilty before the tribunal of God (Rom. 3:9-18).

The Hebrew prophets warned that the world was kindling the wrath of God against unrighteousness. There would come, they foretold, a great day of cataclysmic judgment against all rebellion. The secrets of human hearts would be exposed, and none would be able to stand against the fury of God's righteous justice (Ps. 1:5; Nah. 1:6; Mal. 3:2). The wrath of God would tear down every citadel of opposition in a fiery revelation of His retribution against sin (Isa. 2:12; 61:2).

The OT prophets, however, also spoke of One who would bear in His own body the condemnation of God against sinners. By His suffer-

First-century Athens, Greece, as it appeared during the time of Paul. The view is from the northwest of the Agora of the lower city, which is in the foreground. The Acropolis (upper city) with the famous Parthenon dedicated to the goddess Athena is in the background. The Areopagus (Mars Hill) where Paul addressed the citizens of Athens is at right.

ing under the wrath of God, the Prophet Isaiah wrote, the coming Servant of God would save many from condemnation (Isa. 53). The NT writings identify these Suffering Servant passages with Jesus' death on a cross outside the gates of Jerusalem (Acts 8:32-35).

Jesus Himself recognized the penal nature of the atonement, speaking of the cross as a fiery "baptism" He was to undergo (Mark 10:38; Luke 12:49-50). He expressed anguish at the prospect of the cross (John 12:27) and even pleaded to be delivered from it, if such were possible (Luke 22:42). The gospels picture vividly the penal nature of the atonement by describing the agony of Jesus on the cross, crying out as One forsaken by God (Matt. 27:46). They describe the crucifixion as accompanied by signs of eschatological judgment—darkness, natural disturbances, and the raising of dead from their graves (Matt. 27:45-54).

The apostles and NT writers spoke of Jesus' atonement as absorbing the wrath of God due to sinners. They described Jesus' death as a propitiation that turns aside the wrath of God (Rom. 3:25; 1 John 4:7). The Apostle Paul wrote to the Corinthians that Jesus was counted as a sinner in order that sinners might be counted as righteous in Him (2 Cor. 5:21). Jesus bore the curse of the law in order to bring the blessings of the Abrahamic covenant to the Gentiles (Gal. 3:10-14). Peter similarly spoke of Jesus bearing sins "in His body on the tree" (1 Pet. 2:24 HCSB).

The sin-bearing work of Christ at *Golgotha* cannot be understood, however, apart from His resurrection. Peter preached to onlookers at Pentecost that Jesus' resurrection is proof God did not abandon Him to the grave but has exalted Him as the triumphant Messiah to whom are due the covenant promises of the OT (Acts 2:22-36). Although Jesus was considered "smitten of God" on the cross (Isa. 53:4), in the resurrection He is "established as the powerful Son of God" (Rom. 1:4 HCSB). Having borne fully the penalty of death due for sin, Jesus is now raised from the dead as the righteous One in whom God is well pleased. Because Jesus has satisfied the penalty for sin, believers wait expectantly for the One who "rescues us from the coming wrath" (1 Thess. 1:10 HCSB).

Atonement as Sacrificial The NT sets the atonement in the context of the OT sacrificial system. The concept of sacrifice emerges in even the earliest passages of the biblical narrative, with the sacrifice of Abel from his flock (Gen. 4:4-5). Sacrifice played a crucial role in the deliverance of the Israelites from Egypt as the sacrifice of the Passover lamb saved the Hebrew children from the dark visitation of the angel of death (Exod. 12:1-32). The Mosaic covenant brought with it a detailed sacrificial system to be followed by the Israelite nation (Lev. 1:1–7:38).

The NT asserts that the animal sacrifices of the old covenant pointed to Jesus' sacrificial offering of Himself at *Golgotha*. In the identification of Jesus with the Suffering Servant of Isaiah, the prophet describes the Messiah as a "guilt offering" (Isa. 53:10), pointing back to the Mosaic sacrificial code (Lev. 5–7). John the Baptist emphasizes the sacrificial nature of the mission of Christ by calling Him the "Lamb of God who takes away the sin of the world" (John 1:29). Jesus Himself speaks of voluntarily "laying down His life" for His sheep as a sacrificial offering to God (John 10:11).

Paul spoke of Christ as "our Passover," directly tying the atoning work of Christ to the sacrifice of the Passover lamb (1 Cor. 5:7). He uses OT sacrificial language to speak of Jesus' atonement as a "sweet-smelling aroma" offered to God (Eph. 5:2). Similarly, Peter uses sacrificial lamb imagery to speak of believers as being purchased by the "precious blood" of Jesus (1 Pet. 1:18-19) who, like the OT sacrificial animals, is "spotless." In his vision on the Isle of Patmos, John sees Jesus being worshiped by the redeemed multitudes because He is the sacrificial Lamb who purchased them with His blood (Rev. 5:1-14).

The sacrificial nature of the atonement is perhaps most clearly explained in the book of Hebrews. For the writer of Hebrews, the crucified Jesus is the ultimate sacrifice, which permanently deals with sin and thus ends the sacrificial system (Heb. 10:11-12). The writer asserts that the blood of animals was never sufficient to take away human sin but merely pointed to the coming sacrifice of Messiah (Heb. 10:4).

Hebrews explains, perhaps to Jewish Christians contemplating a return to the Mosaic sacrificial system, that Jesus is the priest (Heb. 7:23-28) who appears before God to offer His own blood for the sins of the people as a once-for-all sacrifice (Heb. 9:11-28). Alluding to the animals sacrificed "outside the camp" in the old covenant, the writer points to Jesus' suffering outside the gates of Jerusalem (Heb. 11–13). His resurrection from the dead is proof that God has heard the cries of this final Priest and has accepted His sacrifice (Heb. 5:7).

Atonement as Substitutionary The penal and sacrificial language describing the atonement makes clear that Jesus' death was substitutionary. Just as the Israelites of the OT were to offer animals in the place of sinners, so Jesus' death is described as being offered in the place of those who deserved the wrath of God. Jesus spoke of His death as a shepherd laying down His life for His sheep (John 10:11). He describes His mission as offering Himself as a "ransom" for sinners (Mark 10:45). The night before His betrayal Jesus told His disciples that the bread He broke before them represented "My body, which is given for you" (Luke 22:19 HCSB).

After speaking of the universal condemnation deserved by sinners, Paul wrote of Jesus' blood being set forth as a propitiation for sin so that God might remain just in His punishment of sin while justifying those who have faith in Jesus (Rom. 3:2-26). Paul anchors the assurance of God's people that they will not face God's wrath in the fact that God "did not even spare His own Son, but offered Him up for us all" (Rom. 8:31-34 HCSB). The apostle spoke of the substitutionary nature of the atonement as being at the heart of his gospel proclamation (1 Cor. 15:3-4). Jesus' suffering the penalty for sin, Paul asserts, was "on our behalf" (2 Cor. 5:21). He contends that Jesus' bearing the curse of God was "for us" (Gal. 3:13). The apostle employs ransom language to speak of Jesus' mediatorial work (1 Tim. 2:5-6). Similarly, Peter speaks of Jesus' death for sins as being the righteous dying in the place of the unrighteous, thereby accomplishing reconciliation with God (1 Pet. 3:18).

The substitutionary nature of the atonement emphasizes the importance of the humanity of Jesus. As noted above, the Bible points to Jesus' role as a God-appointed Mediator between God and humanity (1 Tim. 2:5). In taking on human nature, Jesus identified Himself with sinful humanity in suffering and ultimately in death. As the second Adam, Jesus represents humanity by overcoming the temptations of the world and the devil (Matt. 4:1-11). He suffers on the cross, not as a detached demigod, but as a human being born under the law (Gal. 4:4-5). In bearing God's wrath in the place of sinful humanity, Jesus is the "forerunner" (Heb. 6:20) who triumphs over death's hold on the human race

(Heb. 2:14). As such, He is able to present to God the redeemed "brothers" for whom He suffered, died, and was resurrected to life (Heb. 2:10-13).

The biblical doctrine of substitutionary atonement causes the biblical writers to marvel at God's love for the world (1 John 2:2), but it also impels them to wonder at the profoundly personal nature of the atonement. The kingdom community is thus reminded that Jesus gave His life because He loves His church (Eph. 5:25-27). The Apostle Paul can proclaim with vigor not only that in the atonement God "was in Christ reconciling the world to Himself" (2 Cor. 5:19) but also that the Lord Jesus "loved me and gave Himself for me" (Gal. 2:20).

Atonement as Cosmic It cannot be said that Jesus died for the "sins" of animals, rocks, or trees. Indeed, the Scripture explicitly notes that Jesus did not die even for angelic beings (Heb. 2:16). He stood in the place of human beings, moral agents who have brought upon themselves the condemnation of God. This does not mean, however, that the atoning work of Jesus' death and resurrection does not have implications for the entire cosmic order.

Paul reminds the church at Rome that because of the Adamic curse the "whole creation has been groaning together with labor pains until now" (Rom. 8:22 HCSB). The curse, which was brought into the cosmos by the sin of humanity, ultimately will be reversed through the atoning work of the Second Adam who accomplishes a cosmic reconciliation through the blood of His cross (Col. 1:20). Because of the atonement, the universe awaits a cosmic renovation into a glorious new heavens and a new earth in which all opposition to God is swept away by the triumphant Messiah (2 Pet. 3:13; Rev. 21:1–22:9).

The Bible reveals that God's original intention for humanity was for the creatures made in His image to rule over the earth (Gen. 1:27-28; Ps. 8:3-8). The fall seemed to derail these purposes. Through the atonement accomplished by Jesus, however, God will place all things under the feet of the triumphant Second Adam (1 Cor. 15:27-28; Heb. 2:5-9).

In Adam's fall the serpent set himself up as the "god of this age" (2 Cor. 4:4), holding humans captive to their own corrupted passions (2 Tim. 3:26). Humanity was given an ancient promise from the Creator, however, of the serpent's impending doom (Gen. 3:15). In Jesus' atoning work, He triumphs over the dark powers (Col. 1:15), destroying the purposes of Satan (1 John 3:8).

Scripture also reveals that God's original purposes for His creation included His dwelling in fellowship with humanity, a situation disrupted by sin (Gen. 3:8). In the atoning work of Jesus, God reclaims a people for Himself (Titus 2:14) and pledges to be with them forever in the redeemed cosmos (Rev. 21:3).

Atonement and the Message of the Gospel The Bible makes clear that the central thrust of the church's proclamation should be the atoning work of God in Christ (1 Cor. 1:22-25). The Scripture presents the truth of the atonement as the gospel itself (1 Cor. 15:3-4), which alone can save a sinner from the wrath of God (Acts 2:13-21).

In the atonement God has revealed to humanity His saving love. He does not wish to condemn the world but to save it through His Son (John 3:17). The sinner must recognize that He is living under a sentence of death, awaiting the coming judgment (John 3:36). The sinner must look to Jesus as bearing the just penalty for sin on the cross (John 3:14-16). The sinner must trust that God has accepted this sacrifice on his behalf by God's raising Jesus from the dead (Rom. 10:9).

When the sinner abandons all hope of his own righteousness before God and trusts in the provision of God in the death and resurrection of Jesus, he finds refuge in Christ (Phil. 3:9). The sinner is now at peace with God (Rom. 5:1). In fact, by the power of the Spirit, he is now a "new creation" awaiting the redemption of the created universe (2 Cor. 5:17). The believer is assured that he no longer faces condemnation because he is united to the One who has already borne and satisfied the wrath of God (Rom. 8:31-39).

The message of the atonement is presented in strikingly universal terms. All are invited to find refuge in the atonement of Christ (Luke 14:16-17). The apostles plead with sinners to trust in the atoning work of Jesus (Acts 2:40; 2 Cor. 5:20). All human beings are not only invited but commanded to believe the gospel (Acts 17:30-31). This does not mean, however, that the objective accomplishment of the atonement brings about universal salvation. Jesus is Himself the One who is the propitiation of God's wrath against the world (1 John 2:2). Those who are redeemed are saved from God's judgment because they are united to Christ through faith (Eph. 1:7). On the final day of judgment, those who are not "in Christ" will bear the eternal penalty for their own sins (2 Cor. 5:10) and for the dread transgression of rejecting God's provision in Christ (John 3:19; Heb. 10:29).

Atonement and the Life of the Church The Bible speaks of the church as itself a visible manifestation of the atoning work of Christ (Acts 20:28). In the sacrifice of Jesus on the cross, God's purposes were not simply to rescue so many units of individual souls. Instead, He purposes to bring forth a new community, the church (Eph. 5:25-27). The NT writers, therefore, constantly anchor their admonitions for church life to the narrative of Jesus' death, burial, and resurrection.

Because Jesus died for the world, the church is not to identify itself in terms of racial, ethnic, or national boundaries (Eph. 2:11-22) but is to reflect in its internal relationships the peace of God in Christ. The makeup and activity of the church should reflect the harmonious end result of the atonement—a vast multinational multitude of redeemed sinners praising the crucified and exalted Messiah (Rev. 5:1-14). Similarly, mature believers are to be careful not to offend weaker believers "for whose sake Christ died" (1 Cor. 8:11). Instead, believers are to bear with one another, forgiving one another "just as God also forgave you in Christ" (Eph. 4:32 HCSB).

The atonement likewise serves to instruct the church on how to relate to the outside world. Jesus instructed His disciples that the cross means both that they will face tribulation from the world and that He has overcome the world through the cross (John 16:33). Jesus' crucifixion is to remind believers to refuse to respond to the world's hostility (Heb. 12:3) by engaging in vengeful counterattacks (1 Pet. 2:21-25). Rather, the cross of Christ reminds believers that God is just (Rom. 3:26) and that vengeance comes not at their hand but at His (Heb. 10:30-31). See *Christ, Christology; Day of Atonement; Expiation; Propitiation; Redeem; Salvation.*   *Russell D. Moore*

ATROTH (KJV) or **ATROTH-BETH-JOAB** (Ăt´ rŏth-bĕth-Jō´ ab) Place-name meaning "crowns of the house of Joab." A "descendant" of Caleb and Hur (1 Chron. 2:54), the name apparently refers to a village near Bethlehem.

ATROTH-SHOPHAN (Ăt´ rŏth·shō´ phăn) Town built by tribe of Gad of unknown location (Num. 32:35). Earliest translations spelled name various ways: Shophar, Shaphim, Shopham, Etroth Shophan.

ATTAI (Ăt´ tī) Personal name meaning "timely." **1.** Member of clan of Jerahmeel in tribe of Judah (1 Chron. 2:35-36). **2.** Warrior of tribe of Gad who served David in the wilderness as he fled from Saul (1 Chron. 12:11). **3.** Son of Maachah (2 Chron. 11:20), the favorite and beloved wife of King Rehoboam of Judah (931–913 B.C.).

ATTALIA (Ăt·tà·lī´ à) Seaport city on northern Mediterranean coast in Asia Minor where Paul stopped briefly on first missionary journey (Acts 14:25). Modern Antalya continues as a small seaport with some ancient ruins.

AUGUSTAN COHORT Unit of the Roman army stationed in Syria from about A.D. 6. The cohort's place among the rest of the Roman army is indicated by the fact that it was named after the emperor. This special unit was given charge of Paul on his way to Rome (Acts 27:1). In Luke's eyes this demonstrated the importance of Paul and, more importantly, the gospel that Paul preached.

AUGUSTUS (Au·gŭs´ tŭs) Title meaning "reverend" that the Roman Senate gave to Emperor Octavian (31 B.C.–A.D. 14) in 27 B.C. He ruled the Roman Empire, including Palestine, when Jesus was born and ordered the taxation that brought Joseph and Mary to Bethlehem (Luke 2:1). He was the adopted son of Julius Caesar. Born in 63 B.C. he first gained power with Antony and Lepidus at Julius Caesar's death in 44 B.C. He gained sole control at the Battle of Actium in 31 B.C., where he defeated Antony and Cleopatra, who both committed suicide. This brought Egypt into the system of Roman provinces. He thus founded the Roman Empire and ruled with popular acclaim. At his death the Senate declared him a god. Herod the Great ruled as appointed by Augustus, even though Herod originally supported Antony. Herod built temples to Augustus as a god in Caesarea and Samaria. The title Augustus passed on to Octa-

Cameo of Augustus Caesar.

vian's successors as emperors of Rome. Thus it is applied to Nero in Acts 25:21,25, when Paul appealed to Caesar. Note the various translations: the Emperor (NIV, NASB, HCSB), his Imperial Majesty (NRSV).

AUTHOR, AUTHOR OF LIFE See *Prince of Life.*

AUTHORITY, DIVINE AUTHORITY Greek term for authority, in both the NT and the Septuagint, is *exousia.* Although sometimes translated "power," *exousia* referred primarily not to physical strength or power (as in *dunamis*), but to the rightful and legitimate exercise of power. A person has authority primarily by virtue of the position one holds, not by physical coercion or might.

All authority could be characterized as either intrinsic or delegated. Intrinsic authority is dominion one exercises because it is innate in that person or inherent in the office held by that person. Because He is God and Creator of the universe, God has sovereignty and dominion over all things. Only the triune God has purely intrinsic authority. Delegated authority is given from one who has intrinsic authority to one serving in an office or carrying out a function. Delegated authority is not in itself innately or inherently authoritative; it is authority derived from one whose authority is intrinsic. All authority is properly God's. All other authority is derived from Him (Matt. 9:8; John 19:11; Rom. 13:1-3; Jude 25).

Jesus possesses the same intrinsic authority as God the Father because He is coequal with the Father (John 1:1; 10:30; 16:15; Phil. 2:6; Col. 1:16; 2:9-10; Rev. 12:10). Because of the unique pattern of relationships within the Trinity, however, especially during Jesus' incarnation, there is also a sense in which His authority is given to Him by the Father (Matt. 9:8; 28:18; John 5:22,27; 17:2; Eph. 1:20-22; Phil. 2:9-10; Rev. 2:27). God has given Jesus authority over all things in heaven and earth (Matt. 28:18). Jesus' authority was manifested in His incarnation by His authority to forgive sin, provide salvation, heal sickness, cast out demons, and judge humanity (Matt. 9:6-8; Mark 2:10-12; Luke 4:36; 5:24-25; John 5:22-27). As Jesus carried out His teaching ministry, He spoke with an authority which was immediately recognized by His hearers as being absent in the teachings of the scribes and Pharisees (Matt. 7:28-29; Mark 1:22; Luke 4:32). Such authority recognized by others on the basis of actions or performance may be called earned authority.

Human Authority Since all authority is derived from God, Christians should submit to the structures of authority that God has established. Submission to authorities ordained by God flows from submission to God Himself. Patterns of authority are necessary in any set of human relationships. Some such authority is positional, in that the authority is by virtue of a position held by an individual, not by any innate authority of the individuals themselves. God ordained civil government to have authority over citizens (Luke 19:17; Rom. 13:1-7; 1 Tim. 2:2; Titus 3:1; 1 Pet. 2:13-14). He established patterns of authority within family relationships (1 Cor. 7:4; Eph. 5:21-25; 6:1-4). Scripture also sanctions a pattern of authority in work and social relationships (Matt. 8:9; Luke 7:8; Eph. 6:5-9; 1 Tim. 2:12).

God established an order of authority in spiritual matters as well. Since the Bible is God's Word, Scripture speaks with divine authority (2 Tim. 3:16; 2 Pet. 1:21-22; 1 Thess. 4:1-2). The Bible affirms the apostolic authority of the first disciples (Matt. 10:1; Mark 3:15; 6:7; Luke 9:1; 2 Cor. 10:8; 13:10; 1 Thess. 2:6) and the authority of other church leaders (Heb. 13:7,17). God also established the authority of certain spiritual beings including angels and Satan and beings in the endtime (Luke 4:6; Eph. 2:2; 3:10; 6:11-12; Col. 1:16; 2:15; Rev. 6:8; 9:3,10,19; 14:18; 16:9; 18:1).

Christians have an obligation to submit to the authority of those whom God has ordained to serve as leaders. To rebel against God's appointed authorities is to rebel against God. Humans who wield authority should do so with humility, cognizant of the fact that all temporary human authority flows from God and will be returned to God (1 Cor. 15:24-28). Christian leaders should not flaunt their authority over others but should practice the servant leadership exemplified by Jesus Christ (Matt. 20:25-28; Mark 10:42-45, Luke 22:25-26; 1 Pet. 5:1-3).

Steve W. Lemke

AVA (Ā´ vȧ) or **AVVA** People that the Assyrians conquered and settled in Israel to replace the people they took into exile (2 Kings 17:24). Their gods did not help them against the Assyrians and could be used as an example to call Jerusalem to surrender (2 Kings 18:34, where Ivvah refers to the same people; cp. 2 Kings 19:13). Avva was apparently in Syria, but their homeland is unknown. Some would suggest Tell Kafr Ayah on the Orontes River. The Avites who made the god Nibhaz (2 Kings 17:31) may refer to these people.

AVEN (Ā´ vĕn) Hebrew noun meaning "wickedness," used in place-names to indicate Israel's understanding of the place as a site of idol worship. **1.** Referred to On or Heliopolis in Egypt (Ezek. 30:17). **2.** Referred to major worship centers of Israel such as Bethel and Dan (Hos. 10:8). **3.** Referred to a valley, perhaps one in place of popularly known names such as Beth-aven for Beth-el (Josh. 7:2; 18:12). See *Beth-aven.*

AVENGER Person with the legal responsibility to protect the rights of an endangered relative. Avenger translates Hebrew *go'el*, which in its verbal form means to redeem. Redemption applies to repossessing things consecrated to God (Lev. 27:13-31) or to God's actions for His people (Exod. 6:6; Job 19:25; Ps. 103:4; Isa. 43:1). Ultimately God is the *go'el* (Isa. 41:14).

The human avenger is tied closely to the institutions of cities of refuge, land ownership, and levirate marriage. Cities of refuge offered people who killed without intention or hatred a place of escape from the avenger of blood (Exod. 21:12-14; Num. 35:6-34; Deut. 4:41-43; 19:1-13; Josh. 20:1-9). The human *go'el* may be a brother, an uncle, a cousin, or another blood relative from the family (Lev. 25:48-49). An established order among these determined the one legally responsible to act as *go'el* (Ruth 3:12-13). The avenger or *go'el* is responsible to take the life of one who killed a family member (Num. 35:12), to receive restitution for crimes against a deceased relative (Num. 5:7-8), buy back property lost to the family (Lev. 25:25), redeem a relative who sold himself into slavery (Lev. 25:48-49), or marry the widow of a relative without sons and perpetuate the family (Deut. 25:5-10). Avenging the death of a relative is placed under strict limits. The murderer must have intentionally waited to kill the relative (Exod. 21:13) or willfully attacked the relative (Exod. 21:14). Vengeance could be exercised only before the murderer reached the city of refuge or after the court either at the victim's hometown or at the murder site judged the case (Num. 35:12). The avenger was free to act if an iron object was used to commit the murder (Num. 35:16) or if a stone or wood object was used (Num. 35:17-18). Pushing a person to death because of hatred made one liable to the avenger (Num. 35:20-21). Unintentional acts could not be punished (Num. 35:22-24).

A killer judged to have committed the crime without hatred or intentional planning was sent to the city of refuge until the death of the high priest. The avenger could not touch the killer in the city of refuge, but if the killer left the city of refuge for any reason, the avenger could reap vengeance even against the unintentional killer (Num. 35:22-28). This shows that even unintentional murder involved sin for which a penalty had to be paid. The law of the avenger thus prevented the shedding of innocent blood while also purging the guilt of murdering the innocent (Deut. 19:11-13). The law maintained the reverence for human life created in the image of God (Gen. 9:5-7).

The NT sets up government to avenge evil doing (Rom. 13:4), while noting God's role in avenging wrong against a brother (1 Thess. 4:6).

AVIM (Ā′ vĭm), **AVIMS, AVITES, AVVIM, AVVITE 1.** People who lived on the Philistine coast before the Philistines invaded about 1200

B.C. (Deut. 2:23). **2.** City in the tribal territory of Benjamin (Josh. 18:23).

AVITH (Ā′ vĭth) City name meaning "ruin." Capital city of Hadad, king of Edom, before Israel had a king (Gen.36:35). Its location is unknown.

AWE, AWESOME Appears in different passages in different English translations as the translation of different Hebrew and Greek words. Of 10 occurrences in the NASB, it translates eight distinct Hebrew and Greek words. It appears only three times in KJV translating three different Hebrew words. NIV uses "awe" 16 times, repeating only six of the NASB usages. The term refers to an emotion combining honor, fear, and respect before someone of superior office or actions (Pss. 4:4; 33:8; 119:161 KJV) (Gen. 28:17; 1 Sam. 12:18; Matt. 9:8; Heb. 12:28 NIV). It most appropriately applies to God. See *Fear; Reverence.*

AWL Instrument or tool made of flint, bone, stone, or metal to bore holes. Biblical references refer to using the awl to pierce a servant's ear (Exod. 21:6; Deut. 15:17). Perhaps a ring or identification tag was placed in the hole. This marked the slave as a permanent slave for life. Excavators in Palestine unearth many such boring tools.

AWNING Usage in Ezek. 27:7 suggests a deck covering to protect the ship's passengers from the sun. It may be similar to the covering of Noah's ark (Gen. 8:13) and the tabernacle (Exod. 26:14).

AX, AX HEAD English translation of several Hebrew terms indicating cutting instruments used in normal small industry and in war. **1.** *Barzel* is the Hebrew term for iron and is used for the iron portion of an ax (Isa. 10:34; 2 Kings 6:5). The ax was used to fell trees. Elisha was able through miraculous power to make the ax head float. **2.** *Garzen* is a hatchet or a tool for cutting stone (Deut. 19:5; 20:19; 1 Kings 6:7; Isa. 10:15). It was made of iron and could be used to cut trees. The iron head was attached to a wooden handle. It was not to be used to destroy a city's trees in war. **3.** *Chereb* is a weapon or tool used to destroy enemies' towers in battle (Ezek. 26:9). The term also is used for flint knives that Joshua used in circumcision (John 5:2), for two-sided daggers (Judg. 3:16), a tool to shape stone (Exod. 20:25), and of battle swords (Judg. 7:20). **4.** *Magzerah* was a tool used in brickwork. David apparently forced the Ammonites to tear down their own city walls and then to produce bricks for Israel (2 Sam. 12:31). **5.** *Ma'atsad* is the craftsman's tool (Jer. 10:3; NIV "chisel") produced by the blacksmith working with iron (Isa. 44:12 NASB, NRSV). It was apparently used to trim or prune trees or lumber. **6.** *Qardom* was an iron tool which has to be sharpened (1 Sam. 13:20) and was used for cutting trees (Judg. 9:48). Skillful use of this tool made a person famous (Ps. 74:5). **7.** *Keylaph* appears only in Ps. 74:6 and is variously translated: hammer (KJV, NASB, NRSV), hatchet (NIV), sledgehammer (TEV), or crowbar (some lexicons). **8.** *Kashshil* appears only in Ps. 74:6 in combination with 7. above. It is variously translated as ax (KJV, NIV, TEV) or hatchet (NASB, NRSV). Whatever the precise nature of these tools, they could be used for destruction as well as construction. **9.** *Axine* was used to chop down trees (Matt. 3:10).

AYYAH (Ăy´ yah) Place-name meaning "ruin." In the unclear Hebrew text of 1 Chron. 7:28, modern translations read Ayyah as a city on the border of Ephraim. Some identify this with Ai. Others follow a Greek text tradition that apparently read Gaza. See *Ai.*

AZAL (Ā´ zăl) (KJV) See *Azel.*

AZALIAH (Ăz·à·lī´ ăh) Personal name meaning "Yahweh has reserved." Father of Shaphan, Josiah's scribe (2 Kings 22:3). See *Shaphan.*

AZANIAH (Ăz·à·nī´ ăh) Personal name meaning "Yahweh listened." Father of Levite who signed Nehemiah's covenant to obey God's law (Neh. 10:9).

AZARAEL (Ăz·à·rā´ ĕl) (KJV, Neh. 13:36), **AZAREEL** (Ăz´ à·rē·ĕl) (KJV), or **AZAREL** (Ăz´ à·rĕl) Personal name meaning "God helped." **1.** David's soldier at Ziklag, skilled with bow and arrow and able to sling stones with either hand (1 Chron. 12:6). **2.** Leader of a course of priests selected by lot under David (1 Chron. 25:18). **3.** Leader of tribe of Dan under David (1 Chron. 27:22). **4.** Priest who had married a foreign wife under Ezra (Ezra 10:41). **5.** Father of Amashai,

head of a priestly family who lived in Jerusalem under Nehemiah (Neh. 11:13). **6.** Priest who played a musical instrument in time of Nehemiah (Neh. 12:36), probably the same as 5. above.

AZARIAH (Ăz·à·rī´ ăh) Personal name meaning "Yahweh has helped." **1.** Son and successor of Amaziah as king of Judah (792–740 B.C.). Also called Uzziah. See *Uzziah.* **2.** High priest under Solomon (1 Kings 4:2) listed as son of Zadok (1 Kings 4:2) or of Ahimaaz (1 Chron. 6:9), the son of Zadok (2 Sam. 15:27). If the latter is accurate, then son in 1 Kings 4:2 means descendant. **3.** Son of Nathan in charge of the system of obtaining provisions for the court from the 12 government provinces (1 Kings 4:5). He would have supervised the persons listed in 1 Kings 4:7-19. **4.** Great grandson of Judah (1 Chron. 2:8). **5.** Member of the clan of Jerahmeel in the tribe of Judah (1 Chron. 2:38-39). **6.** High priest, son of Johanan (1 Chron. 6:10). **7.** High priest, son of Hilkiah (1 Chron. 6:13-14) and father of Seraiah, who is listed as Ezra's father (Ezra 7:1). The list in Ezra is not complete. Apparently some generations have been omitted. **8.** Member of family of Kohath, the temple singers (1 Chron. 6:36). Apparently called Uzziah in 6:24. **9.** A priest, son of Hilkiah (1 Chron. 9:11) may be same as 7. above. **10.** Prophet, son of Oded, whose message gave King Asa (910–869 B.C.) courage to restore proper worship in Judah (2 Chron. 15:1-8). **11.** Two sons of Jehoshaphat, king of Judah (873–848 B.C.) according to 2 Chron. 21:2. Perhaps the boys had different mothers, each of whom gave the son the common name Azariah. **12.** Son of Jehoram, king of Judah (852–841) according to 2 Chron. 22:6, but the correct name is probably Ahaziah as in 2 Kings 8:29. Azariah represents a copyist's error in Chronicles. **13.** Two military commanders of 100 men who helped Jehoiada, the high priest, depose and murder Athaliah as queen of Judah and install Joash as king (835–796). **14.** High priest who led 80 priests to oppose King Uzziah of Judah (792–740) when he tried to burn incense in the temple rather than let the priests. God struck Uzziah with a dreaded skin disease (2 Chron. 26:16-21). **15.** A leader of the tribe of Ephraim under Pekah, king of Israel (752–732 B.C.), who rescued captives Pekah had taken from Judah, cared for their physical needs, and returned them to Jericho (2 Chron. 28:5-15).

16. Levite whose son Joel helped cleanse the temple under Hezekiah, king of Judah (715–686) (2 Chron. 29:12-19). **17.** A Levite who helped cleanse the temple (2 Chron. 29:12-19). See 16. above. **18.** Chief priest under King Hezekiah who rejoiced with the king over the generous tithes and offerings of the people (2 Chron. 31:10-13). **19.** Son of Meraioth in the list of high priests and father of Amariah (Ezra 7:3) Since the list in Ezra is incomplete, this Azariah may be the same as 6. above. **20.** Helper of Nehemiah in rebuilding the wall of Jerusalem (Neh. 3:23). **21.** Man who returned from exile with Zerubbabel (Neh. 7:7) about 537 B.C. He is called Seraiah in Ezra 2:2. **22.** Man who helped Ezra interpret the law to the people in Jerusalem (Neh. 8:7). **23.** Man who put his seal on Nehemiah's covenant to obey God's law (Neh. 10:2). **24.** A leader of Judah, possibly a priest, who marched with Nehemiah and others on the walls of Jerusalem to celebrate the completion of rebuilding the city defense walls (Neh. 12:33). He may be identical with any one or all of 20–23. above. **25.** Friend of Daniel renamed Abednego by Persian officials. God delivered him from the fiery furnace (Dan. 1:7; 4:1-30). See *Abednego; Daniel.* **26.** Son of Hoshaiah and leader of Jewish people who tried to get Jeremiah to give them a word from God directing them to go to Egypt after the Babylonians destroyed Jerusalem. When Jeremiah said not to go, they accused him of lying (Jer. 42:1–43:7). Hebrew text reads Jezaniah in 42:1.

AZARIAHU (Ăz·à·rī´ á·hü) Long form of Azariah used by NASB, NIV in 2 Chron. 21:2 to differentiate two men named Azariah. See *Azariah.*

AZAZ (Ā´ zăz) Personal name meaning "he is strong." A descendant of tribe of Reuben (1 Chron. 5:8).

AZAZEL (À·zà·zĕl) See *Atonement; Scapegoat.*

AZAZIAH (Ăz·à·zī´ ăh) Personal name meaning "Yahweh is strong." **1.** Levite David appointed to play the harp for the temple worship (1 Chron. 15:21). **2.** Father of leader of tribe of Ephraim under David (1 Chron. 27:20). **3.** Overseer among the priests under Hezekiah (715–686 B.C.) (2 Chron. 31:13).

AZBUK (Ăz´ bŭk) Father of a Nehemiah who repaired Jerusalem under the leadership of Nehemiah, son of Hachaliah (Neh. 3:16).

AZEKAH (À·zē´ kăh) Place-name meaning "cultivated ground." City where Joshua defeated southern coalition of kings led by Adonizedek of Jerusalem (Josh. 10:10-11), as God cast hailstones from heaven on the fleeing armies. In the battle Joshua commanded the sun and moon to stand still (Josh. 10:12). Joshua allotted Azekah to Judah (Josh. 15:35). Near it the Philistines lined up their forces for battle against Saul (1 Sam. 17:1), resulting in the David and Goliath confrontation. Rehoboam, king of Judah (931–913 B.C.), built up its fortifications (2 Chron. 11:9). The tribe of Judah occupied it in Nehemiah's day (Neh. 11:30), after it had been one of the last cities to fall to Nebuchadnezzar of Babylon in 588 B.C. (Jer. 34:7). One of the letters found at Lachish tells of searching for signal lights from Azekah but not being able to see them. This can be dated to 588 B.C. An earlier Assyrian inscription, perhaps from 712 B.C. speaks of Azekah's location on a mountain ridge, being inaccessible like an eagle's nest, too strong for siege ramps and battering rams.

Later tradition connected Azekah with the tomb of the prophet Zechariah and then with Zechariah the father of John the Baptist, to whom a large church was dedicated. Thus the Madeba map from about 550 A.D. calls Azekah, "Beth Zechariah," or "house of Zechariah" and pictures a large church there.

Azekah is located at Tell Zakariya five and one-half miles northeast of Beth Govrin above the Valley of Elah. Excavations show the site was occupied before 3000 B.C. and had a strong fortress in the period of the judges.

AZEL (Ā´ zĕl) Personal and place-name meaning "noble." **1.** Descendant of Saul in tribe of Benjamin and father of six sons (1 Chron. 8:37-38). **2.** Unclear word in Hebrew text of Zech. 14:5 which may be a place-name, perhaps near Jerusalem, or a preposition meaning "near to," "beside," or a noun meaning "the side." Translations vary: "Azal" (KJV, NRSV), "the other side" (TEV), "Azel" (NASB, NIV), "the side of it" (RSV).

AZEM (Ā´ zĕm) (KJV) See *Ezem.*

AZGAD (Ăz´ găd) Personal name meaning "Gad is strong." **1.** Clan of which 1,222 (Neh. 7:17 says 2,322) returned from exile in Babylon with Zerubbabel to Jerusalem in 537 B.C. (Ezra 2:12). One hundred ten more returned with Ezra about 458 B.C. (Ezra 8:12). **2.** Levite who signed the covenant Nehemiah made to keep God's law (Neh. 10:15).

AZIEL (Ā·zī´ ĕl) Short form of Jaaziel in 1 Chron. 15:20. See *Jaaziel.*

AZIZA (Ȧ·zī´ zȧ) Personal name meaning "strong one." Israelite who agreed under Ezra's leadership to divorce his foreign wife to help Israel remain true to God (Ezra 10:27).

AZMAVETH (Ăz·mā´ veth) Personal and place-name meaning "strong as death" or "death is strong." **1.** Member of David's elite 30 military heroes (2 Sam. 23:31). He lived in Barhum or perhaps Baharum (NRSV). See *Baharum.* **2.** Descendant of Saul in tribe of Benjamin (1 Chron. 8:36). **3.** Father of two of David's military leaders (1 Chron. 12:3), probably identical with 1. above. **4.** Treasurer of David's kingdom (1 Chron. 27:25). He, too, may be identical with 1. above. **5.** City probably the same as Beth-azmaveth. Forty-two men of the city returned to Jerusalem from exile in Babylon with Zerubbabel in 537 B.C. (Ezra 2:24). Levites on the temple staff as singers lived there. It apparently is near Jerusalem, perhaps modern Hizmeh, five miles northeast of Jerusalem (Neh. 12:29). See *Beth-azmaveth.*

AZMON (Ăz´ mŏn) Place-name meaning "bones." Place on southern border of promised land (Num. 34:4). Joshua assigned it to Judah (Josh. 15:4). It is located near Ain el-Quseimeh, about 60 miles south of Gaza. Some would identify it with Ezem.

AZNOTH-TABOR (Ăz´ nŏth-Tā´ bôr) Place-name meaning "ears of Tabor." A border town of the tribe of Naphtali (Josh. 19:34). It may be modern Umm Jebeil near Mount Tabor.

AZOR (Ā´ zôr) Personal name of an ancestor of Jesus (Matt. 1:13-14).

AZOTUS (Ȧ·zō´ tŭs) See *Ashdod; Philistines.*

AZRIEL (Ăz´ rĭ·ĕl) Personal name meaning "God is my help." **1.** Head of a family of eastern part of tribe of Manasseh (1 Chron. 5:24). **2.** Head of tribe of Naphtali under David (1 Chron. 27:19). **3.** Father of royal officer commanded to arrest Baruch, Jeremiah's scribe (Jer. 36:26).

AZRIKAM (Ăz·rī´ kăm) Personal name meaning "my help stood up." **1.** Descendant of David after the exile (1 Chron. 3:23). **2.** Descendant of Saul of tribe of Benjamin (1 Chron. 8:38). **3.** Father of a Levite who led in resettling Jerusalem after the exile (1 Chron. 9:14). **4.** Officer in charge of palace for Ahaz, king of Judah. Zicri, a soldier in Israel's army, killed him when Israel attacked Judah about 741 B.C. (2 Chron. 28:7).

AZUBAH (Ȧ·zū´ bah) Personal name meaning "forsaken." **1.** Queen mother of Jehoshaphat (1 Kings 22:42), king of Judah (873–848 B.C.). **2.** First wife of Caleb, son of Hezron (1 Chron. 2:18-19).

AZUR (Ā´ zûr) (KJV, Jer. 28:1; Ezek. 11:1) See *Azzur.*

AZZAH (KJV, Deut. 2:23; 1 Kings 4:24; Jer. 25:20). See *Gaza.*

AZZAN (Ăz´ zăn) Personal name meaning "he has proved to be strong." Father of representative of tribe of Issachar in assigning territorial lots to the tribes after God gave Israel the promised land (Num. 34:26).

AZZUR (Ăz´ zur) Personal name meaning "one who has been helped." **1.** Jewish leader who sealed Nehemiah's covenant to obey God's law (Neh. 10:17). **2.** Father of Hananiah, the prophet, in Jeremiah's days (Jer. 28:1). **3.** Father of Jaazaniah, Jewish leader in Jerusalem who plotted evil in Ezekiel's day (Ezek. 11:1).

B

Sea of Galilee from the Church of the Beatitudes.

BAAL (Bā´ ăl) Lord of Canaanite religion and seen in the thunderstorms, Baal was worshiped as the god who provided fertility. He proved a great temptation for Israel. "Baal" occurs in the OT as a noun meaning "lord, owner, possessor, or husband," as a proper noun referring to the supreme god of the Canaanites, and often as the name of a man. According to 1 Chron. 5:5 Baal was a descendant of Reuben, Jacob's firstborn son, and the father of Beerah. Baal was sent into exile by Tiglath-pileser, king of Assyria. The genealogical accounts of Saul's family listed in 1 Chron. 9:35-36 indicates that the fourth son of Jehiel was named Baal.

The noun comes from a verb that means to marry or rule over. The verb form occurs in the Hebrew text 29 times, whereas the noun occurs 166 times. The noun appears in a number of compound forms which are proper names for locations where Canaanite deities were worshiped, such as Baal-peor (Num. 25:5; Deut. 4:3; Ps. 106:28; Hos. 9:10), Baal-hermon (Judg. 3:3; 1 Chron. 5:23), and Baal-gad (Josh. 11:17; 12:7; 13:5). See *Canaan.* *James Newell*

BAALAH (Bā´ ä·lăh) Place-name meaning "wife, lady," or "residence of Baal." **1.** City on northern border of tribe of Judah equated with Kirjath-jearim (Josh. 15:9-11). David kept the ark there before moving it to Jerusalem (1 Chron. 13:6). It is located at modern Deir el-Azar, eight miles west of Jerusalem. It is called Baale of Judah (2 Sam. 6:2) and may be the same as Kirjath-baal (Josh. 15:60). See *Kirjath-jearim.* **2.** Town on southern border of Judah (Josh. 15:29) that may be same as Balah (Josh. 19:3) and as Bilhah (1 Chron. 4:29). Tribe of Simeon occupied it. Its location is unknown. **3.** Mountain on Judah's northern border between Jabneel and Ekron. It may be the same as Mount Jearim.

BAALATH (Bā´ ä·lăth) Place-name meaning "feminine Baal." City in original inheritance of tribe of Dan (Josh. 19:44). Same or different town which Solomon rebuilt (1 Kings 9:18). It may have been near Gezer on the road to Beth-horon and Jerusalem. Some would identify Solomon's town with Simeon's Balah, with Kirjath-jearim, or with Baalath-beer.

Statuette of Baal, the Canaanite weather god, from Minet-el-Beida (15th–14th century B.C.).

BAALATH-BEER (Bā´ ȧ·lăth-bē´ ẽr) Place-name meaning "the baal of the well" or the "lady of the well." A city in the tribal allotment of Simeon (Josh. 19:8), identified with Ramath of the south (KJV) or Ramah of the Negev (NASB, NIV, NRSV). It may be identical with Baal (1 Chron. 4:33) and/or with Bealoth (Josh. 15:24).

BAALBEK See *Heliopolis*.

BAAL-BERITH (Bā´ ȧl-bērĭth) In Judg. 8:33 a Canaanite deity whom the Israelites began to worship following the death of Gideon. The name means "lord of covenant," and the god's temple was located at Shechem. The precise identity of this deity cannot be determined. The designation, "lord of covenant," may mean that a covenant between the Israelites and the She-chemites was agreed to and annually renewed in his shrine. See *Shechem*.

BAALE (KJV), **BAALE-JUDAH** (NASB, NRSV) (Bā´ ȧ·lē-jū´ dăh) Place-name meaning "Baals of Judah" or "lords of Judah." Second Samuel 6:2 may be read as "from the lords of Judah" or as "went from Baale-judah." If the latter reading is correct, then Baale-judah is place-name where the ark of the covenant was before David took it to Jerusalem. First Chronicles 13:6 calls the place Baalah of Judah and identifies it with Kir-jath-jearim. See *Kirjath-jearim*.

BAAL-GAD (Bā´ ȧl·găd) Place-name meaning "Baal of Gad" or "lord of Gad." Town representing northern limit of Joshua's conquests (Josh. 11:17) in Valley of Lebanon at foot of Mount Hermon. It has been variously located at modern Hasbeya and at Baalbek, over 50 miles east of Beirut where imposing ruins of Greek and Roman worship remain.

BAAL-HAMON (Bā´ ȧl-hā´ mōn) Place-name meaning "lord of abundance." Location of Solomon's vineyard according to Song 8:11.

BAAL-HANAN (Bā´ ȧl-hā´ năn) Personal name meaning "Baal was gracious." **1.** King of Edom prior to any king ruling in Israel (Gen. 36:38). **2.** Official under David in charge of olive and sycamore trees growing in Judean plain or Shep-halah (1 Chron. 27:28).

BAAL-HAZOR (Bā´ ȧl-hā´ zôr) Place-name meaning "Baal of Hazor." Village where David's son Absalom held celebration of sheepshearing (2 Sam. 13:23). During festivities Absalom had his employees kill his brother Amnon, who had violated his sister Tamar. The village is modern Jebel Asur, five miles northeast of Bethel.

BAAL-HERMON (Bā´ ȧl-hẽr·mŏn) Place-name meaning "Baal of Hermon" or "lord of Hermon." A mountain and village Israel could not take from the Hivites, whom God left to test Israel (Judg. 3:3). It marked the Hivites' southern border and Manasseh's northern border (1 Chron. 5:23). Its location is unknown. Some would equate it with Baal-gad, others with modern Baneas or Caesarea Philippi.

BAALI (Bā´ ȧl·ī) Form of address meaning "my lord," or "my Baal." Hosea used a play on words to look to a day when Israel would no longer worship Baal (Hos. 2:16). He said Israel, the bride, would refer to Yahweh, her God and husband, as "my man" (Hb. *'ishi*) but not as "my lord" (Hb. *baali*). Even though "baal" was a common word for lord or husband, Israel could not use it because it reminded them too easily of Baal, the Canaanite god. See *Baal; Canaan*.

BAALIM (Bā´ ȧ·lĭm) Hebrew plural of Baal. See *Baal; Canaan*.

BAALIS (Bā´ ȧ·lĭs) Personal name of king of Ammon who sent Ishmael to kill Gedaliah, governor of Judah immediately after Babylon captured Jerusalem and sent most of Judah's citizens into the exile (Jer. 40:14).

BAAL-MEON (Bā´ ȧl-mē´ on) Place-name meaning "lord of the residence" or "Baal of the residence." City tribe of Reuben built east of Jordan (Num. 32:38), probably on the tribe's northern border. Mesha, king of Moab about 830 B.C., claims to have rebuilt Baal-meon, meaning he had captured it from Israel at that date. Ezekiel 25:9 pronounces judgment on Baal-meon as a city of Moab about the time of the exile in 587. Baal-meon is located at modern Main, 10 miles southwest of Heshbon and 10 miles east of the Dead Sea.

BAAL-PEOR (Bā´ ȧl-pē´ ôr) In Num. 25:3 a Moabite deity that the Israelites worshiped when they had illicit sexual relations with

Moabite women. The guilty Israelites were severely punished for this transgression, and the incident became a paradigm of sin and divine judgment for later generations of Israelites (Deut. 4:3; Ps. 106:28; Hos. 9:10). See *Moab; Peor.*

BAAL-PERAZIM (Bā´ ăl-pĕr´ á·zīm) Place-name meaning "Lord of the breakthroughs" or "Baal of the breaches." Place of David's initial victory over the Philistines after he became king of all Israel at Hebron, then captured and moved to Jerusalem (2 Sam. 5:20). The location is not known. It is probably identical with Mount Perazim (Isa. 28:21).

BAAL-SHALISHAH (Bā´ ăl-shăl´ ĭ´ shăh) Place-name meaning "Baal of Shalishah" or "lord of Shalishah." Home of unnamed man who brought firstfruits to Elisha, who used them to feed a hundred men (2 Kings 4:42-44). The "land of Shalishah" was evidently in the tribal territory of Ephraim (1 Sam. 9:4). Baal-shalishah may be modern Kefr Thilth, 20 miles southwest of Shechem. See *Shalishah.*

BAAL-TAMAR (Bā´ ăl-tā´ mär) Place-name meaning "Baal of the palm tree" or "lord of the palm tree." Place where Israelites attacked and defeated tribe of Benjamin for killing concubine of traveling Levite (Judg. 20:33). It must have been near Gibeah. It may be Ras et-Tawil north of Jerusalem.

BAAL-ZEBUB (Bā´ ăl-zē´ bŭb) Deity's name meaning "lord of the flies." In 2 Kings 1:2 a Philistine deity from which the Israelite King Ahaziah sought help after injuring himself in a fall. Though the Philistines themselves may have used this name, it is more probable that it is intentionally used to distort the god's actual name. The problem of identification is further complicated by references in the NT. Jesus is reported to have used the name Beel-zebub in reference to the prince of demons (Matt. 10:25). Beel-zebub is clearly a variation of Baal-zebub. However, the Greek text of the NT has Beelzebul. The meaning of Beelzebul is disputed. One suggestion is "lord of the dwelling." A second and more likely possibility is "lord of dung." Regardless of the exact meaning of the name, Jesus clearly used it in reference to Satan. See *Baal; Philistines; Satan.*

BAAL-ZEPHON (Bā´ ăl-zē´ phôn) Place-name meaning "lord of the north" or "Baal of the north." Place in Egypt near which Israel camped before miracle of crossing the sea (Exod. 14:2,9). The exact location is not known. Some suggest Tell Defenneh known in Egypt as Tahpanhes in the eastern Nile Delta. See *Exodus.*

BAANA (Bā´ á·ná) or **BAANAH** Personal name of uncertain meaning. Some have suggested "son of grief" or "son of Anat." English spelling variations reflect similar Hebrew spelling variations. **1.** One of Solomon's district supervisors to provide food one month a year for the court. His territory encompassed the great central plain with the famous cities of Beth-shean, Taanach, and Megiddo (1 Kings 4:12). **2.** Another district supervisor over Asher, the western slopes of Galilee in the north. His father Hushai may have been "David's friend" (2 Sam. 15:37). **3.** Father of Zadok, who repaired walls of Jerusalem under Nehemiah (Neh. 3:4). **4.** A captain of Ish-bosheth's army after Saul died and Abner deserted to David and was killed by Joab. Baanah and his brother killed Ishbosheth and reported it to David, who had them killed (2 Sam. 4). **5.** Father of Heleb, one of David's 30 heroes (2 Sam. 23:29). **6.** Man who returned with Zerubbabel from Babylonian captivity about 537 B.C. (Ezra 2:2). **7.** One who signed Nehemiah's covenant to obey God's law (Neh. 10:27).

BAARA (Bā´ á·rá) Personal name meaning "burning" or a name intentionally changed from one honoring Baal. Wife of Shaharaim in tribe of Benjamin (1 Chron. 8:8).

BAASEIAH (Bā·á·sē´ ah) Personal name of unknown meaning. A Levite ancestor of Asaph (1 Chron. 6:40).

BAASHA (Bā´ á·shá) King of Israel who was at war against Asa, king of Judah (1 Kings 15:16). Baasha gained the throne of Israel by violence. He conspired against and killed his immediate predecessor Nadab, the son of Jeroboam I (1 Kings 15:27). Furthermore, he exterminated the entire line of Jeroboam (15:29). Baasha reigned over Israel for 24 years (908–886 B.C.). His capital was at Tirzah. He died, apparently from natural causes, and was succeeded by his son Elah. See *Chronology of the Biblical Period; Israel; Tirzah.*

BABBLER Common translation of a derogatory term the Epicureans and Stoics used against Paul in Athens (Acts 17:18). The Greek word literally means "seed picker" and was used of birds (especially crows) that lived by picking up seeds. It was applied to people who lived parasitically by picking up pieces of food off the merchants' carts. In the field of literature and philosophy the term was applied to those who plagiarize without the ability to understand or properly use what they had taken. The philosophers referred to Paul as a babbler because they considered Paul an ignorant plagiarist.

Another Greek word *bebelos* refers to something outside the religious sphere. It appears in 1 Tim. 4:7; 6:20; 2 Tim. 2:16; Heb. 12:16, usually in reference to chatter or babbling talk about worldly things, an activity Christians should avoid. In Hebrews it refers to a godless person.

BABEL (Bā´ bĕl) Hebrew word meaning "confusion," derived from a root which means "to mix." It was the name given to the city that the disobedient descendants of Noah built so they would not be scattered over all the earth (Gen. 11:4,9). Babel is also the Hebrew word for Babylon.

The tower and the city which were built were intended to be a monument of human pride, for they sought to "make a name" for themselves (Gen. 11:4). It was also a monument to mankind's continued disobedience. They had been commanded to fill up the earth but were seeking to avoid being scattered abroad (Gen. 9:1; 11:4). Further, it was a monument to human engineering skills, for the techniques of its building described the use of fired clay bricks as a substitute for stone. Bitumen, found in relative abundance in the Mesopotamian Valley, was used to bind the bricks together.

Ruins of numerous templetowers, called ziggurats, have been found in the region of Babylon. It is possible that ruins of the great templetower to Marduk found in the center of ancient Babylon is the focus of this narrative.

To bring the people's monumental task to an end, God confused their language. The inspired writer apparently considered this to be the basis for the origin of the different human languages. When the builders were no longer able to communicate with one another, they then fled from one another in fear. The city of Babylon became to the OT writers the symbol of utter rebellion against God and remained so even into the NT (Rev. 17:1-5). See *Babylon.*   *Robert L. Cate*

BABOON NIV translation of *tukkiyim* (1 Kings 10:22; 2 Chron. 9:21). TEV and REB translate the same word as "monkeys." KJV, NASB, and NRSV give the translation "peacocks" (but see NRSV margin). There is a similarity between *tukkiyim* and the Egyptian word for "ape" that leads many to accept baboon or monkey as the correct translation.

BABYLON City-state in southern Mesopotamia during OT times, which eventually became a large empire that absorbed the nation of Judah and destroyed Jerusalem.

History The city of Babylon was founded in unknown antiquity on the river Euphrates, about 50 miles south of modern Baghdad. The English names "Babylon" and "Babel" (Gen. 10:10; 11:9) are translated from the same Hebrew word (*babel*). Babylon may have been an important cultural center during the period of

Relief of Nabonidus, king of Babylonia (556–539 B.C.) when Babylon fell to Cyrus. Here Nabonidus stands before emblems of the moon god, sun god, and war/love god.

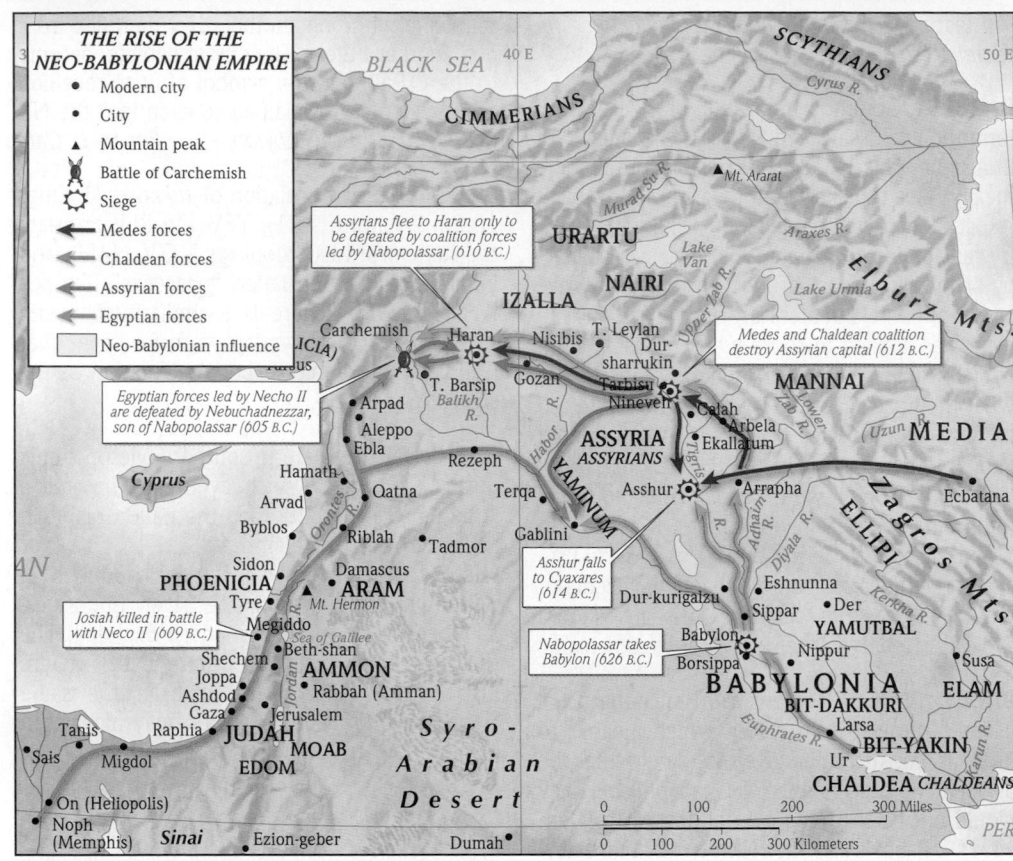

THE RISE OF THE NEO-BABYLONIAN EMPIRE

- Modern city
- City
- ▲ Mountain peak
- Battle of Carchemish
- ☼ Siege
- ← Medes forces
- ← Chaldean forces
- ← Assyrian forces
- ← Egyptian forces
- ☐ Neo-Babylonian influence

Assyrians flee to Haran only to be defeated by coalition forces led by Nabopolassar (610 B.C.)

Medes and Chaldean coalition destroy Assyrian capital (612 B.C.)

Egyptian forces led by Necho II are defeated by Nebuchadnezzar, son of Nabopolassar (605 B.C.)

Asshur falls to Cyaxares (614 B.C.)

Nabopolassar takes Babylon (626 B.C.)

Josiah killed in battle with Neco II (609 B.C.)

the early Sumerian city-states (before 2000 B.C.), but the corresponding archaeological levels of the site are below the present water table and remain unexplored.

Babylon emerged from anonymity shortly after 2000 B.C., a period roughly contemporary with the Hebrew patriarchs. At that time an independent kingdom was established in the city under a dynasty of Semitic westerners, or Amorites. Hammurabi (1792–1750 B.C.), the sixth king of this First Dynasty of Babylon, built a sizable empire through treaties, vassalage, and conquest. From his time forward, Babylon was considered to be the political seat of southern Mesopotamia, the region called Babylonia. The Amorite dynasty of Babylon reached its apex under Hammurabi. Subsequent rulers, however, saw their realm diminished, and in 1595 B.C. the Hittites sacked Babylon. After their withdrawal members of the Kassite tribe seized the throne. The Kassite Dynasty ruled for over four centuries, a period of relative peace but also stagnation. Little is known up to about 1350 B.C. when

Babylonian kings corresponded with Egypt and struggled with the growing power of Assyria to the north. After a brief resurgence the Kassite dynasty was ended by the Elamite invasion in 1160 B.C.

When the Elamites withdrew to their Iranian homeland, princes native to the Babylonian city of Isin founded the Fourth Dynasty of Babylon. After a brief period of glory in which Nebuchadnezzar I (about 1124–1103 B.C.) invaded Elam, Babylon entered a dark age for most of the next two centuries. Floods, famine, widespread settlement of nomadic Aramean tribes, and the arrival of Chaldeans in the south plagued Babylon during this time of confusion.

During the period of the Assyrian Empire, Babylon was dominated by this warlike neighbor to the north. A dynastic dispute in Babylon in 851 B.C. brought the intervention of the Assyrian king Shalmaneser III. Babylon kings remained independent, but nominally subject to Assyrian "protection."

A series of coups in Babylon prompted the Assyrian Tiglath-pileser III to enter Babylon in 728 B.C. and proclaim himself king under the throne name Pulu (Pul of 2 Kings 15:19; 1 Chron. 5:26). He died the next year. By 721 B.C. the Chaldean Marduk-apal-iddina, Merodach-baladan of the OT, ruled Babylon. With Elamite support he resisted the advances of the Assyrian Sargon II in 720 B.C. Babylon gained momentary independence, but in 710 B.C. Sargon attacked again. Merodach-baladan was forced to flee to Elam. Sargon, like Tiglath-pileser before him, took the throne of Babylon. As soon as Sargon died in 705 B.C., Babylon and other nations, including Judah under King Hezekiah, rebelled from Assyrian domination. Merodach-baladan had returned from Elam to Babylon. It is probably in this context that he sent emissaries to Hezekiah (2 Kings 20:12-19; Isa. 39). In 703 B.C. the new Assyrian king, Sennacherib, attacked Babylon. He defeated Merodach-baladan, who again fled. He ultimately died in exile. After considerable intrigue in Babylon, another Elamite-sponsored revolt broke out against Assyria. In 689 B.C. Sennacherib destroyed the sacred city of Babylon in retaliation. His murder, by his own sons (2 Kings 19:37) in 681 B.C., was interpreted by Babylonians as divine judgment for this unthinkable act.

Esarhaddon, Sennacherib's son, immediately began the rebuilding of Babylon to win the allegiance of the populace. At his death the crown prince Ashurbanipal ruled over Assyria, while another son ascended the throne of Babylon. All was well until 651 B.C. when the Babylonian king rebelled against his brother. Ashurbanipal finally prevailed and was crowned king of a resentful Babylon.

Assyrian domination died with Ashurbanipal in 627 B.C. In 626 B.C. Babylon fell into the hands of a Chaldean chief, Nabopolassar, first king of the Neo-Babylonian Empire. In 612, with the help of the Medes, the Babylonians sacked the Assyrian capital Nineveh. The remnants of the Assyrian army rallied at Haran in north Syria, which was abandoned at the approach of the Babylonians in 610 B.C. Egypt, however, challenged Babylon for the right to inherit Assyria's empire. Pharaoh Necho II, with the last of the Assyrians (2 Kings 23:29-30), failed in 609 to retake Haran. In 605 B.C. Babylonian forces under the crown prince Nebuchadnezzar routed the Egyptians at the decisive Battle of Carchemish (Jer. 46:2-12). The Babylonian advance, however, was delayed by Nabopolassar's death that

Painted relief of a bull from the famous Ishtar Gate of Babylon.

B

Reconstruction of ancient Babylon.

obliged Nebuchadnezzar to return to Babylon and assume power.

In 604 and 603 B.C. Nebuchadnezzar II (605–562 B.C.), king of Babylon, campaigned along the Palestinian coast. At this time Jehoiakim, king of Judah, became an unwilling vassal of Babylon. A Babylonian defeat at the border of Egypt in 601 probably encouraged Jehoiakim to rebel. For two years Judah was harassed by Babylonian vassals (2 Kings 24:1-2). Then, in December of 598 B.C., Nebuchadnezzar marched on Jerusalem. Jehoiakim died that same month, and his son Jehoiachin surrendered the city to the Babylonians on March 16, 597 B.C. Many Judeans, including the royal family, were deported to Babylon (2 Kings 24:6-12). Ultimately released from prison, Jehoiachin was treated as a king in exile (2 Kings 25:27-30; Jer. 52:31-34). Texts excavated in Babylon show that rations were allotted to him and five sons.

Nebuchadnezzar appointed Zedekiah over Judah. Against the protests of Jeremiah, but with promises of Egyptian aid, Zedekiah revolted against Babylon in 589 B.C. In the resultant Babylonian campaign, Judah was ravaged and Jerusalem besieged. An abortive campaign by the Pharaoh Hophra gave Jerusalem a short respite, but the attack was renewed (Jer. 37:4-

10). The city fell in August of 587 B.C. Zedekiah was captured, Jerusalem burned, and the temple destroyed (Jer. 52:12-14). Many more Judeans were taken to their exile in Babylonia (2 Kings 25:1-21; Jer. 52:1-30).

Apart from his military conquests, Nebuchadnezzar is noteworthy for a massive rebuilding program in Babylon itself. The city spanned the Euphrates and was surrounded by an 11-mile long outer wall that enclosed suburbs and Nebuchadnezzar's summer palace. The inner wall was wide enough to accommodate two chariots abreast. It could be entered through eight gates, the most famous of which was the

The ruins of the Hanging Gardens of Babylon (modern Iraq), one of the Seven Wonders of the World.

northern Ishtar Gate, used in the annual New Year Festival and decorated with reliefs of dragons and bulls in enameled brick. The road to this gate was bordered by high walls decorated by lions in glazed brick behind which were defensive citadels. Inside the gate was the main palace built by Nebuchadnezzar with its huge throne room. A cellar with shafts in part of the palace may have served as the substructure to the famous "Hanging Gardens of Babylon," described by classical authors as one of the wonders of the ancient world. Babylon contained many temples, the most important of which was Esagila, the temple of the city's patron god, Marduk. Rebuilt by Nebuchadnezzar, the temple was lavishly decorated with gold. Just north of Esagila lay the huge stepped tower of Babylon, a ziggurat called Etemenanki and its sacred enclosure. Its seven stories perhaps towered some 300 feet above the city. No doubt Babylon greatly impressed the Jews taken there in captivity and provided them with substantial economic opportunities.

Nebuchadnezzar was the greatest king of the Neo-Babylonian Period and the last truly great ruler of Babylon. His successors were insignificant by comparison. He was followed by his son Awel-marduk (561–560 B.C.), the Evil-Mero-dach of the OT (2 Kings 25:27-30), Neriglissar (560–558 B.C.), and Labashi-Marduk (557 B.C.), murdered as a mere child. The last king of Babylon, Nabonidus (556–539 B.C.), was an enigmatic figure who seems to have favored the moon god, Sin, over the national god, Marduk. He moved his residence to Tema in the Syro-Arabian Desert for 10 years, leaving his son Belshazzar (Dan. 5:1) as regent in Babylon. Nabonidus returned to a divided capital amid a threat from the united Medes and Persians. In 539 B.C. the Persian Cyrus II (the Great) entered Babylon without a fight. Thus ended Babylon's dominant role in Near Eastern politics.

Babylon remained an important economic center and provincial capital during the period of Persian rule. The Greek historian Herodotus, who visited the city in 460 B.C., could still remark that "it surpasses in splendor any city of the known world." Alexander the Great, conqueror of the Persian Empire, embarked on a program of rebuilding in Babylon that was interrupted by his death in 323 B.C. After Alexander, the city declined economically but remained an important religious center until NT times. The site was deserted by A.D. 200.

In Judeo-Christian thought Babylon the metropolis, like the Tower of Babel, became

The site of the ancient city of Babylon in modern Iraq.

symbolic of man's decadence and God's judgment. "Babylon" in Rev. 14:8; 16:19; 17:5; 18:2; and probably in 1 Pet. 5:13 refers to Rome, the city which personified this idea for early Christians.

Religion Babylonian religion is the best known variant of a complex and highly polytheistic system of belief common throughout Mesopotamia. Of the thousands of recognized gods, only about 20 were important in actual practice. The most important are reviewed here.

Anu, Enlil, and Ea were patron deities of the oldest Sumerian cities and were each given a share of the universe as their dominion. Anu, god of the heavens and patron god of Uruk (biblical "Erech," Gen. 10:10) did not play a very active role. Enlil of Nippur was god of the earth. The god of Eridu, Ea, was lord of the subterranean waters and the god of craftsmen.

After the political rise of Babylon, Marduk was also considered one of the rulers of the cosmos. The son of Ea and patron god of Babylon, Marduk began to attain the position of prominence in Babylonian religion in the time of Hammurabi. In subsequent periods Marduk (Merodach in Jer. 50:2) was considered the leading god and was given the epithet Bel (equivalent to the Canaanite term Baal), meaning "lord" (Isa. 46:1; Jer. 50:2; 51:44). Marduk's son Nabu (the Nebo in Isa. 46:1), god of the nearby city of Borsippa, was considered the god of writing and scribes and became especially exalted in the Neo-Babylonian Period.

Astral deities—gods associated with heavenly bodies—included the sun god Shamash, the moon god Sin, and Ishtar, goddess of the morning and evening star (the Greek Aphrodite and Roman Venus). Sin was the patron god of Ur and Haran, both associated with Abraham's origins (Gen. 11:31). Ishtar, the Canaanite Astarte/Ashtaroth (Judg. 10:6; 1 Sam. 7:3-4; 1 Kings 11:5), had a major temple in Babylon and was very popular as the "Queen of Heaven" (Jer. 7:18; 44:17-19).

Other gods were associated with a newer city or none at all. Adad, the Canaanite Hadad, was the god of storms and thus both beneficial and destructive. Ninurta, god of war and hunting, was patron for the Assyrian capital Calah.

A number of myths concerning Babylonian gods are known, the most important of which is the Enuma elish, or Creation Epic. This myth originated in Babylon, where one of its goals was to show how Marduk became the leading god. It tells of a cosmic struggle in which, while other gods were powerless, Marduk slew Tiamat (the sea goddess, representative of chaos). From the blood of another slain god, Ea created mankind. Finally, Marduk was exalted and installed in his temple, Esagila, in Babylon.

The Enuma elish was recited and reenacted as part of the 12-day New Year Festival in Babylon. During the festival statues of other gods arrived from their cities to "visit" Marduk in Esagila. Also, the king did penance before Marduk and "took the hand of Bel" in a ceremonial procession out of the city through the Ishtar Gate.

The gods were thought of as residing in cosmic localities but also as present in their image, or idol, and living in the temple as a king in his palace. The gilded wooden images were in human form, clothed in a variety of ritual garments, and given three meals a day. On occasion the images were carried in ceremonial processions or to visit one another in different sanctuaries. It is very difficult to know what meaning the images and temples of the various gods had for the average person and even more difficult to ascertain what comfort or help he might expect through worship of them. It seems clear, however, that beyond the expectations of health and success in his earthly life, he was without eternal hope. See *Babel; Hammurabi.*

Daniel C. Browning, Jr.

BACA (Bā´ cá) Place-name meaning "Balsam tree" or "weeping." A valley in Ps. 84:6 which reflects a poetic play on words describing a person forced to go through a time of weeping who found God turned tears into a well, providing water.

BACHRITE (Băch´ rīt) KJV spelling of Becherites (NASB, NRSV) or Bekerite (NIV). See *Becher.*

BACKSLIDING Term used by the prophets to describe Israel's faithlessness to God (Isa. 57:17 RSV; Jer. 3:14,22; 8:5; 31:22; 49:4; Hos. 11:7; 14:4). In these passages it is clear that Israel had broken faith with God by serving other gods and by living immoral lives. See *Apostasy.*

BADGER Burrowing mammal; largest of the weasel family. It is a carnivore with claws on toed feet and considered unclean by the

Israelites. The KJV uses "badger skins" in Exod. 26:14; 36:19 and other passages, but other translations disagree. This animal has also been identified as the rock hyrax or coney. See *Badger Skins; Coney.*

BADGER SKINS KJV translation of the skin used to cover the tabernacle (Exod. 26:14; 36:19; 39:34), the ark, and other sacred objects (Num. 4:6-14). The leather was also used for shoes (Ezek. 16:10). Bible students do not agree on the kind of skin intended. The KJV translation of "badger skin" seems doubtful, as the word used is not the normal word for badger. The badger was considered an unclean animal making it very doubtful that the skin of the badger would have been used as a covering for sacred objects. Additionally, it is doubtful that the badger was plenteous enough to provide the necessary hides. The translation of "goatskin" (RSV) also fails on the grounds that the word used is not a normal word for goat. Thus NRSV reads "fine leather" with a note that the meaning of the Hebrew is uncertain. Some have proposed the simple translation "leather," noting the similarity of the Hebrew and Egyptian words for leather (TEV). Others have proposed dolphin or "porpoise skins," noting the similarities between the Hebrew and Arabic words for dolphin or porpoise (NASB). Still others have proposed "hides of sea cows" (that is, dugongs, REB)—sea creatures that have been found in the Red Sea (NIV). See *Sea Cow.*   *Phil Logan*

BAG Flexible container that may be closed for holding, storing, or carrying something. **1.** Large bags in which large amounts of money could be carried (2 Kings 5:23; Isa. 3:22; KJV, "crisping pins"). **2.** Small bag (purse) used to carry a merchant's weights (Deut. 25:13; Prov. 16:11; Mic. 6:11) or smaller sums of money (Prov. 1:14; Isa. 46:6). This may be the same as the purse mentioned in the NT (Luke 10:4; 12:33; 22:35-36). **3.** Cloth tied up in a bundle is translated as "bag" (Job 14:17; Prov. 7:20; Hag. 1:6) or "bundle" (Gen. 42:35; 1 Sam. 25:29; Song 1:13). The size of the bundle would depend on its use. This type of bag was used to hold money (Gen. 42:35; Prov. 7:20; Hag. 1:6; see 2 Kings 12:10 where the verb form, "to tie up in bags," is used) or "something loose" such as myrrh (Song 1:13). This term for bag is used figuratively to speak of one's sins being bundled up (and perhaps sealed,

"bag of transgressions," Job 14:17) and one's life being bundled up and protected by God ("bundle of the living," 1 Sam. 25:29). **4.** The shepherd's bag (KJV "scrip" or "vessel"). Used by shepherds and travelers to carry one or more days' supplies, it was made of animal skins and slung across the shoulder. Joseph's brothers carried grain in such a bag (Gen. 42:25). Saul's bag was empty of bread when he went to meet Samuel (1 Sam. 9:7), and David collected stones in his shepherd's bag when confronting Goliath (1 Sam. 17:40,49). An Israelite traveler whose bag of provisions was empty could eat from a fellow Israelite's vineyard but was not permitted to fill his bag for the rest of the journey (Deut. 23:24). Jesus commanded His disciples not to carry a bag when He sent them out to preach (Matt. 10:10; Mark 6:8; Luke 9:3; 10:4). They were to be totally dependent on God and the hospitality and support of God's people (cp. Num. 18:31; 1 Cor. 9:3-14). The disciples learned from this experience that they would be cared for, but because of the critical nature of what they were about to face, Jesus later instructed His disciples to begin carrying a purse, bag, and—very curiously—a sword (Luke 22:35-36). The Hebrew word for shepherd's bag is also translated as "carriage." See *Carriage.* **5.** Large sack used to carry grain (Gen. 42:25,27,35; Josh. 9:4; Lev. 11:32). The same Hebrew word is translated as sackcloth worn during times of mourning or humiliation. See *Sackcloth.* **6.** KJV translates *glossokomon* as "bag" in John 12:6; 13:29. The *glossokomon* was actually a money box.   *Phil Logan*

BAGGAGE See *Carriage.*

BAGPIPE Modern translation of a musical instrument translated as "dulcimer" by the KJV (Dan. 3:5,10,15). See *Music, Instruments, Dancing.*

BAHARUM (Bá·hā´ rŭm) NRSV reading of Baharumite (KJV, NASB, NIV). A person from Bahurim. See *Bahurim.*

BAHURIM (Bá·hū´ rĭm) Place-name meaning "young men." Village on road from Jerusalem to Jericho in tribal territory of Benjamin. David demanded Ishbosheth, Saul's son, to send back Michal, Saul's daughter and David's wife. Ishbosheth took her from her husband Phaltiel, who followed her weeping to Bahurim until

B

Abner, the general, forced him to return home (2 Sam. 3:16). When David fled from his son Absalom, a kinsman of Saul named Shimei met him at Bahurim, cursed him, and threw stones at his party. David prevented immediate punishment (2 Sam. 16:5; 19:16). Two messengers taking secret messages about Absalom from the priests hid from Absalom's servants at Bahurim (2 Sam. 17:18). Solomon followed David's orders and had Shimei of Bahurim killed (1 Kings 2:8-9,36-46). Azmaveth, one of David's valiant soldiers, was from Bahurim (1 Chron. 11:33). Second Samuel 23:31 lists the city as Barhum, due to a copyist's mistake. Bahurim was probably located at modern Ras et-Tmim, east of Mount Scopus near Jerusalem.

BAJITH (Bā´ jĭth) (KJV, Isa. 15:2) Modern translations read "temple." KJV interprets as name of Moabite worship place.

BAKBAKKAR (Băk·băk´ kär) Levite living in Judah after the exile (1 Chron. 9:15).

BAKBUK (Băk´ bŭk) Personal name meaning "bottle." Levite who was a temple servant after returning from Babylonian exile with Zerubbabel about 537 B.C. (Ezra 2:51; Neh. 7:53).

BAKBUKIAH (Băk·bū·kī´ äh) Personal name meaning "Yahweh's bottle." Leader among the Levites in Jerusalem after the exile (Neh. 11:17; 12:9,25).

BAKEMEATS Old English term for any food prepared by a baker.

BAKER'S STREET Jerusalem street known as "baker's street" where most, if not all, the bakeries of the city were located. It was common in ancient cities for trades and crafts to locate near others of the same kind. In all likelihood the baker's residence was part of the bakery. Zedekiah promised Jeremiah, whom he had imprisoned, that he would have food for as long as bread was available on baker's street (Jer. 37:21).

BAKING OT speaks most often of the baking of bread and cakes, which were the main part of the meal for Hebrews and Canaanites alike (Gen. 19:3; Exod. 12:39; Lev. 26:26; 1 Kings 17:12-13; Isa. 44:15). The bread of the presence (Lev. 24:5) and other offerings (Lev. 2:4-6) were also baked. See *Bread; Bread of the Presence; Cooking and Heating; Food; Kneading, Kneading Bowl.*

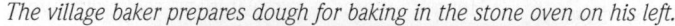

The village baker prepares dough for baking in the stone oven on his left.

BALAAM (Bā´ lăm) Non-Israelite prophet whom Balak, king of Moab, promised a fee if he would curse the invading Israelites.

Old Testament Balaam was one of many prophets of eastern religions who worshiped all the gods of the land. Many of these false teachers had great power and influence. When they pronounced a blessing or a curse, it was considered as true prophecy. When Moses led his people across the wilderness, God commanded him not to attack Edom or Moab (Deut. 2:4-9). He did not. When Edom attacked, "Israel turned away from him" (Num. 20:21). As the great nation journeyed north on the east side of Jordan, King Balak of Moab faced the invasion of Israel. Balak sought a strategy other than battle to stop Moses. He decided to use a prophet to curse Israel. Balaam was chosen; Balak sent his messengers with fees to secure Balaam's services. Balaam asked God's permission to curse Israel. Permission was refused, but Balaam journeyed to confer further with Balak. On this journey Balaam's donkey talked with him as he traveled a narrow trail (Num. 22:21-30; 2 Pet. 2:16). Here Balaam clearly understood that an angel's drawn sword enforced his obedience to speak only God's message to Balak. Later in four vivid messages Balaam insisted that God would bless Israel (Num. 23–24). God used Balaam to preach truth. He even spoke of a future star and scepter (Num. 24:17), a prophecy ultimately fulfilled in the coming of Jesus as the Messiah. Balak's actions brought God's anger upon Moab (Deut. 23:3-6). In a battle against the Midianites, Balaam died (Num. 31:8; Josh. 13:22). Balaam could not curse Israel, but he taught the Moabites to bring the men of Israel into Baal worship with its immorality. For this God would punish Israel. What Balaam could not accomplish with a curse he did through seductive means.

New Testament Peter warned against false teachers and described their destruction. He referred to the fallen angels, the watery destruction of the unbelievers in Noah's time, and the fiery judgment on lawless Sodom and Gomorrah in Lot's day. Peter described his generation of false leaders as those with eyes full of adultery, who never stop sinning by seducing the unstable. He further said that they bore a curse as experts in greed. Peter wrote that they left the straight way and followed the way of Balaam (2 Pet. 2:15). In Rev. 2:14 the church at Perga-

mum was complimented for faithfulness under persecution but also warned that some followed after Balaam in offering meat to idols and in immorality.   *Lawson G. Hatfield*

BALAC (Bā´ lăc) (KJV) See *Balak*.

BALADAN (Băl´ á-dăn) Akkadian personal name meaning "God gave a son." Father of Merodach-baladan, king of Babylon (722–711; 705–703 B.C.). See *Merodach-baladan*.

BALAH (Bā´ lăh) Place-name meaning "used, worn out." City in tribal territory of Simeon (Josh. 19:3), apparently the same as Baalah (Josh. 15:29) and Bilhah (1 Chron. 4:29). Location in southwest Judah is unknown.

BALAK (Bā´ lăk) In Num. 22:2 the king of Moab who sent for Balaam the prophet to pronounce a curse on the Israelites. Balaam, however, spoke no curse; and Balak was denied a military victory over Israel. See *Balaam; Moab*.

BALANCES Used to measure weights early in the development of civilization. Balances were well-known to the Hebrews and in common use in the OT (Lev. 19:36; Job 6:2; Hos. 12:7). They consisted of two pans hung on cords attached to a balancing beam. The beam was suspended by a cord in its center. Sometimes the beam was suspended by a ring or hook. Sometimes balances were held in the hand. The Hebrews probably used the common balances of Egypt, which are shown in Egyptian tomb reliefs and papyri writings.

Balances were the basis of economic life. Money came in weighted units of gold and silver. These had to be weighed in the balance for every business transaction or purchase (Jer. 32:9-10). Balances could be easily manipulated, especially by having weights that did not measure up to the proper amount or by having two sets of weights, one for buying and one for selling. God called on Israel for economic justice that began with proper weights and balances (Prov. 11:1; 16:11; 20:23; Ezek. 45:9-12; Hos. 12:7; Amos 8:5; Mic. 6:10-11). In a figurative sense the balance was employed to ask for a fair trial or judgment for the persecuted (Job 31:6; Ps. 62:9).

Balances help teach about God. Only He can weigh the mountains in a balance (Isa. 40:12-13). Just balances show a person belongs to Him (Prov. 16:11), while foolish people weigh out lavish amounts of gold to make idols to worship (Isa. 46:6).   *Jimmy Albright*

BALD LOCUST (KJV, Lev. 11:22) See *Insects; Locust.*

BALDNESS Natural baldness was apparently rare in Israel. It is mentioned only in the Levitical laws on leprosy (Lev. 13:40-43), where the bald man is declared "clean" unless the bald area has evidence of redness or swelling. Archaeology has uncovered no depictions of bald men from Israel. Elisha was ridiculed for being bald, but he may have shaved his head to mourn Elijah's departure (2 Kings 2:23). Shaving the head for appearance or in grieving for the dead was prohibited by law (Lev. 21:5; Deut. 14:1, and especially for priests (Ezek. 44:20). However, Isaiah told of God's calling the people to acknowledge their sin with baldness and the wearing of sackcloth (Isa. 22:12). A shorn head is frequently mentioned in conjunction with shaving the beard and wearing sackcloth to signify loss of loved ones or loss of hope (Isa. 3:24; 15:2-3; Jer. 48:37). Deuteronomy 21:11-13 may refer to a practice of making captives bald, possibly to baldness in mourning, or to a symbol of a change in lifestyle. Ezekiel described men made to work so hard "every head was made bald, and every shoulder was peeled" (Ezek. 29:18), but there is no evidence that slaves were forced to shave their heads. See *Grief and Mourning; Hair; Leprosy.*   *Tim Turnham*

BALLAD SINGERS Refers to the makers and repeaters of proverbs (Num. 21:27). KJV "they that speak in proverbs" gives that sense.

BALM Aromatic resin or gum widely used in the ancient Near East for cosmetic and medical purposes. Egyptians used them for embalming. Despite the widespread usage, balm is difficult to identify. Ancient writers refer to balm by a variety of names, which adds to the difficulty of identification. Most ancient references seem to be to the resin from *Balsamodendron opobalsamum* or balm of Gilead. At times the reference seems to be to *Balanites aegyptiaca* Delile—a small shrub that still grows in North Africa and exudes a sticky resin used for medicinal purposes (Gen. 37:25; Jer. 8:22; 46:11; 51:8). In another place the mastic tree (*Pistacia lentiscus*) seems to be referred to (Gen. 43:11). A yellow aromatic resin was extracted from the mastic tree by cutting the branches.

BALM OF GILEAD Substance known in the ancient world for its medical properties. Exported from Gilead to Egypt and Phoenicia (Gen. 37:25; Ezek. 27:17). See *Balm.*

BALSAM Translation of two Hebrew words. *Baka'* is translated as "balsam trees" in the modern versions (2 Sam. 5:23-24; 1 Chron. 14:14-15 NASB, NIV, NRSV, TEV). The KJV reads "mulberry trees," while REB has "aspens." Neither the balsam nor mulberry tree has been known to grow around Jerusalem, making the identification of the tree uncertain. Poplar and mastic tree have also been suggested as translations. *Balsam* is also a translation of *basam* in the NASB, where other versions have "spice" and "spices" (Song 5:1,13; 6:2).

BAMAH (Bā´ măh) Hebrew noun meaning "back, high place." Word is used frequently to describe places of worship, usually false worship of Yahweh containing Canaanite elements. In Ezek. 20:29 a particular place is named Bamah in a wordplay ridiculing high places. If a location was intended for Bamah, it can no longer be found. See *High Place.*

BAMOTH (Bā´ mŏth) Place-name and common noun meaning "high places." A place in Moab where Israel stayed during the wilderness wanderings (Num. 21:19-20). Some would equate it with Bamoth-baal.

BAMOTH-BAAL (Bă´ mŏth-bā´ ăl) Place-name meaning "high places of Baal." Mesha, king of Moab about 830 B.C., mentioned it in the Moabite stone. Numbers 22:41 speaks of Bamoth or high places of Baal near the Arnon River. There Balak and Balaam could see all Israel. Joshua 13:17 lists it as a city Moses gave the tribe of Reuben. It may be modern Gebel Atarus.

BAN See *Accursed; Anathema.*

BAND (KJV, Matt. 27:27; Mark 15:16) See *Battalion; Cohort.*

BAND, MAGIC See *Magic Bands.*

BANGLES See *Anklet.*

BANI (Bā´ nī) Personal name meaning "built." **1.** Man from tribe of Gad in David's special 30 warriors (2 Sam. 23:36). **2.** Levite descended from Merari (1 Chron. 6:46). **3.** Ancestor of Uthai of tribe of Judah who was among first Israelites to return to Palestine from Babylonian exile about 537 B.C. (1 Chron. 9:4). **4.** Original ancestor of clan of whom 642 returned from Babylonian exile with Zerubbabel about 537 B.C. (Ezra 2:10). Nehemiah 7:15 spells the name Binnui and says 648 returned. Same clan apparently had members who had married foreign wives and agreed to divorce them to avoid bringing religious temptation to the covenant community (Ezra 10:29,34,38). **5.** Father of Rehum, a Levite who helped Nehemiah repair the wall of Jerusalem (Neh. 3:17). May be same man who helped Ezra interpret the law to the people (Neh. 8:7), led the worship service of repentance leading to Nehemiah's covenant to obey God's law (Neh. 9:4-5; a second Bani was also involved here), sealed Nehemiah's covenant along with the second Bani (Neh. 10:13-14). His son Uzzi was leader (chief officer) of the Levites (Neh. 11:22).

BANKING Ancient Israel had no lending institutions or banks in the modern sense. Commercial transactions and the lending of credit were entirely in the hands of private individuals, landowners, and merchants. Contemporary cultures in Mesopotamia lent money or produced at interest (in some cases as much as 33 ⅓ percent per annum). The temptation among the Israelites to do this was suppressed by laws forbidding the charging of interest on loans (Exod. 22:25; Lev. 25:36-37; Ezek. 18:8). According to these statutes, only foreigners could be charged interest on a debt (Deut. 23:20).

Pledges were sometimes required to guarantee a loan (Gen. 38:17), but essential items, like a cloak, could not be kept past nightfall (Deut. 24:12; Amos 2:8). A strict protocol of debt collection was also to be followed with the lender forbidden to enter the home of the debtor to "fetch his pledge" (Deut. 24:10-11). In periods of famine or high taxation a man might mortgage his home and fields, pledging his labor as a debt-slave or the labor of his family to satisfy the loan (Neh. 5:1-5; Ps. 109:11). Abuse of this system occurred often enough that the prophets condemned it (Neh. 5:6-13; Ezek. 22:12). Proverbs called it folly (17:18; 22:26).

The widespread introduction of coined money after 500 B.C. and the expansion of travel and commerce in the Roman Empire aided the establishment of banking institutions in the NT period. Money lending (Gk., *trapezites*, from the table *trapeza* where business was conducted) was a common and acceptable activity in the cities. Jesus' parables of the talents (Matt. 25:14-30) and the pounds (Luke 19:11-27) lend credence to the practice of giving sums to the bankers to invest or to draw interest. The older custom of burying one's money for safekeeping (Josh. 7:21) Jesus condemned as "wicked and slothful" (Matt. 25:25-27 KJV).

Some who were involved in finance, however, took advantage of the large number of currencies in circulation in Palestine. Farmers and merchants came to them to weigh coinage and exchange it for the Tyrian drachma favored in the city. The regulations regarding the temple tax in Jerusalem also worked in the financiers' favor. The "money changers," known as *kollubistes*, charged a fee of 12 grains of silver (a *kollubos*) and set up their tables in the Court of the Gentiles. They exchanged foreign currency for the silver didrachma required by the law (Matt. 17:24). Jesus' cleansing of the temple may have been in part a response to the unfair practices of these money changers (Matt. 21:12-13; Mark 11:15-17; John 2:14-16).

With sums coming into the temple from Jews throughout the empire, the temple itself became a bank, lending money to finance business, construction, and other programs. Pilate raised a storm of protest when he tapped one of the temple funds (*Corban*), which was to be used exclusively for religious purposes, to build an aqueduct. After the destruction of the temple in A.D. 70, the Roman emperor Vespasian ordered the continued payment of the tax and its deposit in the temple of Jupiter.

Victor H. Matthews

BANKRUPTCY Declaring bankruptcy as a legal means of escaping debt was not an option during the biblical period. If a person could not repay his debts, his creditors could seize his property (Neh. 5:3-4; Ps. 109:11) or children (Exod. 21:7-11; 2 Kings 4:1-7; Neh. 5:5; Job 24:9) until sufficient payment was deemed to have been made, or the debtor himself could be sold into slavery (Lev. 25:39-43; cp. Prov. 22:7) or imprisoned (Luke 12:58-59).

The regular remission of debts in ancient Israel (Deut. 15:1-3) was never intended to encourage irresponsible borrowing. Rather, the writers of the Bible simply expected that God's people would repay their debts, even if by doing so they would incur great loss (Exod. 22:14; cp. Ps. 15:4). Those who did not repay their debts were considered to be wicked (Ps. 37:21) and foolish (cp. Luke 14:28-29).   *Paul H. Wright*

BANNER Sign carried to give a group a rallying point. Hebrew terms translated with the English word "banner" are *degel* and *nes*. A third term, *'ot* (sign), seems related to these, as *degel* and *'ot* appear in the same verse (Num. 2:2), "Every man of the children of Israel shall pitch by his own standard (*degel*), with the ensign (*'ot*) of their father's house." The terms may describe two different banners, or the terms may be in parallel, expressing the same thing in different words. A banner was usually a flag or a carved figure of an animal, bird, or reptile. It may have been molded from bronze, as was the serpent in Num. 21:8-9. Each tribe of Israel may have had some such animal figures as their standard, or banner. The banner was used as a rallying point for groups with a common interest, such as a call for an army to assemble, or as a signal that a battle was to begin. When the Israelites left Sinai for the land of Canaan, they marched under the banner of four major tribes: Judah, Reuben, Ephraim, and Dan (Num. 10). The prophet Isaiah used the term in reference to a signal God would raise against Babylon as a warning of impending destruction (Isa. 13:2). In Isa. 49:22 God's upraised hand is a signal (*nes*) for the nations to bring the sons of the exiles home to the land of Canaan. The practice of using banners, or standards, was widespread in ancient times in many cultures and lands. Israel probably borrowed the custom from her neighbors.
Bryce Sandlin

BANQUET Elaborate meal, sometimes called a "feast." In the OT and NT banquets and feasts are prominent in sealing friendships, celebrating victories, and for other joyous occasions (Dan. 5:1; Luke 15:22-24). The idea of hospitality ran deep in the thought of those in the Near East (Gen. 18:1-8; Luke 11:5-8).

Most banquets were held in the evening after the day's work. Usually only men were invited. The women served the food when no servant was present. Hosts sent invitations (Matt. 22:3-4) and sometimes made elaborate preparations for the guests. Those who dined reclined on bedlike seats and lay at right angles to the table. Even though our English translations usually speak of "sitting down" at a meal, the Greek actually means "recline" (Mark 6:39; Luke 12:37).

Typical foods served at banquets were fish, bread, olives, various kinds of vegetables, cheeses, honey, dates, and figs. Beef or lamb was used only by the rich or on special occasions (Mark 14:12; Luke 15:23). Wine was also an important part of the feasts, so that they were sometimes called "a house of drinking" in the Hebrew (KJV, "banqueting house," Song 2:4) or "drinkings" in the Greek (KJV, "banquetings," 1 Pet. 4:3).

Some "seats" at the banquet table were preferred over others (Mark 10:37; Luke 14:7-11; John 13:23). In Luke 14:8-10 Jesus referred to these "lowest" and "highest" places. He often used banquets and feasts to present His message to various people (Matt. 9:9-10; Mark 14:1-9; Luke 7:36-50; 19:1-6; John 2:1-11; 12:1-8). The image of the feast as an occasion of celebrating victory is seen in Jesus' reference to the messianic banquet (Matt. 8:11; Luke 13:29). Also, in Revelation, the final victory day is described in terms of a "marriage feast of the Lamb" of God (Rev. 19:9 HCSB).   *W. Thomas Sawyer*

BAPTISM The Christian rite of initiation practiced by almost all who profess to embrace the Christian faith. In the NT era persons professing Christ were immersed in water as a public confession of their faith in Jesus, the Savior. This was accomplished in direct obedience to the explicit mandate of the Lord (Matt. 28:16-20).

Jewish Background Among Palestinian Jews of the first century, a form of ritual cleansing was practiced, one which undoubtedly constituted the foreshadowing of Christian baptism. The unearthing of hundreds of *mikvaot* (ritual cleansing pools) in various locations from the Temple Mount to the fortress of Masada and the community of Qumran testify to the widespread practice of both proselyte baptism and ritual cleansings. The existence of deep pools accessed by stairs provides sufficient evidence that the Jewish practice employed a form of self-baptism or self-immersion. A typical use of the *mikveh* would find a Gentile who had embraced

Judaism and accepted circumcision walking into the *mikveh*, citing the *shema*, "Hear, O Israel; the Lord our God, the Lord is one" (Deut. 6:4), and then immersing himself in the pool.

John's Baptism Consequently, when John the Baptist began baptizing in the Jordan River, the practice of baptism *per se* was hardly shocking to the Jews. The introduction of an administrator who immersed others was John's novel addition. The church maintained this development in its post-resurrection worship and elevated it to prominence as the first public act of identification with Christ. John insisted that those who sought baptism at his hand give testimony to a radically changed life, evidenced by repentance. Those who thus acquiesced formed a purified community awaiting the advent of Messiah. That Jesus of Nazareth was among those who sought John's baptism puzzled the church through the ages and seems to have mystified John at the time (Matt. 3:14). John's protest sug-

gests that he observed no need for repentance in Jesus. He relented and immersed Jesus in response to the Lord's assurance that in so doing this act would "fulfill all righteousness" (Matt. 3:15). In addition to identifying with the ministry of John, the act declared the nature of the Messiah's mission. He would be a crucified, buried, and resurrected Messiah. Additionally, the event provided one of the most important declarations of the Trinitarian nature of God with the baptism of the Son, the voice of the Father, and the descent of the Spirit in the form of a dove (Matt. 3:16-17).

Baptism in the New Testament The word "baptism" has several uses in the NT. In addition to its usual sense of faith-witness initiation, the Bible speaks of a baptism of fire (Matt. 3:11-12), baptism by/in the Holy Spirit (1 Cor. 12:13), baptism for the dead (1 Cor. 15:29), and even the baptism of the Hebrew people into Moses and the Sea (1 Cor. 10:2). But overwhelmingly

B

Ancient Byzantine baptistry at Avdat, Israel, showing the importance given baptism by the early church.

the most prominent use of the word refers to the first response of obedience by a new follower of Jesus. The word "baptize" is itself a loanword borrowed from the Greek term *baptizo*. Few scholars contest that the meaning of the term is "immerse," and not "to pour" or "to sprinkle." In classical Greek, the word is used, for example, to describe the sinking of a ship that is, therefore, "immersed" or totally enveloped in water. Five important issues about baptism are: (1) the meaning of the ordinance, (2) the appropriate candidate for baptism, (3) the proper mode of baptism, (4) the right time for baptism, and (5) the correct authority for baptism.

Meaning In its simplest form baptism is a public identification with Jesus the Christ. As such it pictures the death of Jesus for the sins of the world, His subsequent burial, and His triumphant resurrection. There is also a reenactment of the believer's death to sin, the burial of the old man, and a resurrection to walk in newness of life with Christ (Rom. 6:4). There is also an eschatological hint, a prophetic look to the future in baptism. Though we die and are interred in the ground, we shall rise again at the coming of the Lord. There are those who see baptism as a sacrament, bestowing grace or even bringing salvation. In this view baptism effects the removal of original sin in infants and/or secures salvation for the one baptized. Advocates of such a position cite Acts 2:38 and a few other verses as supporting texts. The believers' church tradition understands baptism to be symbolic of salvation, a public profession of faith, and a witness to the work of salvation. The Bible clearly teaches that salvation is appropriated solely by faith based on the grace of God. Baptism, being an act of man, can never cleanse a person of sin or procure God's forgiveness (Rom. 4:3).

Proper Candidate for Baptism Accordingly, the only appropriate candidate for the witness of baptism is someone who has something about which he can bear witness (Acts 2:38; 8:12-13,36-38; Eph. 4:5). There is no precedent for infant baptism in the NT; in addition, only one who has experienced regeneration can give genuine witness to that experience. Only one sufficiently mature to have recognized, confessed and repented of his sin, and made a conscious commitment of faith in Christ should be baptized (Acts 2:41).

Correct Time for Baptism In certain areas of the world, baptism is delayed, sometimes as much as two years, during which time candidates "prove themselves" and/or are carefully taught, but the NT knows no such practice. Baptism is a public confession of faith, an initiatory ordinance of a new believer desiring to be obedient to Christ (Acts 8:35-38). The accompanying safeguard is a scriptural program of church discipline. Therefore, as soon as one is saved, he should be baptized.

The Proper Form of Baptism The correct form of baptism is determined by the meaning of the act. While it is true that *baptizo* means "immerse," and while it is further the case that Jewish and first-century Christian baptisms were all by immersion, it is the significance of death, burial, and resurrection that determines the form. The new believer is buried in a watery grave and raised up as a symbol of his trust in the death, burial, and resurrection of Christ for the atonement of sins. Only immersion adequately pictures a burial and a resurrection (Rom. 6:4-6). Immersionist baptistries dating from early Christian churches are common in Europe and the Middle East. Not a few contemporary Roman Catholic churches have even recognized the antiquity of the practice of immersion and have begun constructing immersionist pools. Eastern Orthodoxy has always practiced immersion.

The Correct Authority for Baptism Who has the authority to administer or perform baptism? Here the Scriptures are not explicit. However, in the NT, wherever people professed Christ and were baptized, they were assimilated into local assemblies of believers. The possible exception to this is the Ethiopian eunuch (Acts 8:35-38). Lacking more precise instruction, it seems safe to say that to identify with Christ as the head of the church without also identifying with the church, which is the body of Christ, would be unfathomable. The local church is the proper authority to administer baptism.

Finally, it should be noted that the two ordinances given to the church—baptism and the Lord's Supper—together tell the story of Christ's atoning work. In the Supper the death of Christ is acknowledged and proclaimed; whereas in baptism His burial and resurrection are depicted. These comprise the only rituals assigned to the church by Jesus. See *Baptism with/in the Holy Spirit; Infant Baptism; Ordinances.*

Paige Patterson

BAPTISM FOR THE DEAD The only biblical mention of this is 1 Cor. 15:29. Paul refers to something being practiced without commenting on it. He does not commend, condone, or condemn it. Baptism for the dead is not Paul's point but is used to bolster his argument for the reality of the resurrection that some are denying (1 Cor. 15:12). He argues on the basis of Christ's resurrection (vv. 13-16) and the Corinthians' salvation (vv. 17-19). The order of resurrection is that first Christ was raised (v. 20), then those who are Christ's at His coming (v. 23), and finally death itself is abolished (v. 26). Paul reinforces his logic by pointing to their practice; if there is no resurrection, then "what will they do who are being baptized for the dead?" (v. 29 HCSB).

No explanation of this practice is given. A straightforward reading of "baptism for the dead" is that people were being baptized vicariously on behalf of someone already dead. Some have suggested a symbolic understanding. If "baptism" is symbolic, it would parallel Jesus' use in Mark 10:38 ("Are you able ... to be baptized with the baptism I am baptized with?"), a metaphorical reference to His crucifixion and death. Paul's words could then refer to martyrdom. If "death" is symbolic, it could refer to the believer's death to his old nature, self, and sin as symbolized by baptism (Rom. 6:4).

Other suggestions understand the preposition to mean baptism "over" the graves of believers, baptism "with reference to" the converts' own future deaths, or baptism "with a view towards" being reunited with fellow believers already dead. Another possibility is "Why be baptized if there is no resurrection from the dead?"

These symbolic or syntactic suggestions have little to support them. The natural reading is preferable, that this is vicarious baptism on behalf of the dead. No information is provided concerning how this was done or what it was believed to accomplish. We simply cannot know. Nevertheless, any idea that a living person could be baptized and impact the salvation of one already dead contradicts the clear teaching of Scripture on both salvation and baptism. It could not be a practice of which Paul approved.

David R. Beck

BAPTISM OF FIRE Central to the message of John the Baptist was the teaching that the Messiah whose coming he announced would also baptize but in a manner that superceded John's baptism. The Messiah would baptize "with [or "in"; the Greek can be translated either way] the Holy Spirit (Mark 1:8; John 1:33; Acts 1:5; 11:16) and fire" (Matt. 3:11; Luke 3:16). The fact that there is only one Greek article governing the two nouns, "Spirit" and "fire" indicates that only one baptism is in view and the addition of "and fire" further defines the character of the Messiah's baptism. Whereas water temporarily cleanses the outside, fire permanently purifies the whole.   *E. Ray Clendenen*

BAPTISM WITH/IN THE HOLY SPIRIT Phrase used in one form or another by John the Baptist, Jesus, Simon Peter, and Paul. John the Baptist proclaimed, "I baptize you with [Gk., *en*] water for repentance. But the One who is coming after me is more powerful than I; I am not worthy to take off His sandals. He Himself will baptize you with [Gk., *en*] the Holy Spirit and fire" (Matt. 3:11 HCSB). All four Gospels carry this prediction, though John and Mark leave out the words "and fire" (Mark 1:8; Luke 3:16; John 1:33). Jesus referred to the words of John just before His ascension, affirming to the disciples that they would soon ("not many days from now") receive this baptism (Acts 1:5). The promise was then fulfilled on the Day of Pentecost, when the Holy Spirit came upon the 120 disciples in the upper room (Acts 2:4) and tongues of fire rested on each of them (Acts 2:3). To demonstrate publicly that He had given the Spirit, God miraculously enabled the 120 to speak in the foreign languages of the pilgrims present in Jerusalem that day (Acts 2:4-12).

In Acts 10 God sent Simon Peter to the house of the Gentile, Cornelius. There the Lord poured out the Spirit on the Gentiles, enabling them to speak in tongues, thus showing Peter that the Gentiles had received the same gift as the Jews. When he made his report to the Jerusalem church about this matter, Peter quoted the words of Jesus about Spirit-baptism from Acts 1:5, causing the disciples present to affirm, "So God has granted repentance resulting in life to even the Gentiles" (Acts 11:18 HCSB). These first six references to Spirit-baptism all point to the fulfillment of the promise of the gift of the Spirit (John 14:25-27; 15:26-27; 16:7-11), first to the Jews in Jerusalem, then to the Gentiles. Christian Jews and Gentiles are now one not only because they have a common Savior but because they have the same gift of the Spirit (Eph. 2:11-3:6; Gal. 3:28; Rom. 2:9-29; Col. 1:26-27).

Paul also speaks of being Spirit baptized (1 Cor. 12:13 HCSB). "For we were all baptized by one Spirit into one body—whether Jews or Greeks, whether slaves or free—and we were all made to drink of one Spirit." Similar to the earlier references, this text notes the unity of both Jews and Gentiles as having the Spirit, emphasizing that by referring to the Spirit as "one Spirit." There are, however, some unique features in Paul's statement. First, it refers to a past experience shared by Paul and the Corinthians, while the other references have a future orientation. Second, it is significant that none of these persons was present in the events found in the two texts in Acts, yet Paul asserts that they also have been baptized in the one Spirit. Third, Paul says that this Spirit baptism has the result of incorporating believers into the body of Christ (cp. 1 Cor. 12:14-27; Eph. 1:23; 4:12; Col. 1:24).

Over the last century Bible interpreters have differed over the interpretation of these texts in three specific ways. First, the question has been asked, is Spirit-baptism an experience subsequent to conversion, or does it happen at the same time as conversion? Second, should the Spirit-baptized person speak in tongues as "evidence" of the experience? Third, is Paul talking about the same essential experience in 1 Cor. 12:13 as John, Jesus, and Peter are talking about in the other texts? The questions do yield a fairly certain response.

Taking the last item first, it is clear that Paul is speaking about essentially the same kind of experience as did John, since he uses the same construction in the Greek, with the only difference being the addition of the word "one" [Spirit] and the past tense. He also uses the passive voice, but that is to be expected with the subject shifting from "He" [Jesus] to "we" [Christians]. If we conclude that Paul is speaking of the same experience as the other texts, then it should be clear that Spirit baptism could not be subsequent to conversion, since Paul says it is the means by which believers are incorporated into the body of Christ. It must happen at conversion, as was the case in Acts, as one of the constellations of Spirit blessings bestowed on believers at that moment—they are born of the Spirit (John 3:5), sealed in the Spirit (Eph. 1:13),

and receive the gift of the indwelling Spirit (Rom. 8:9-11). What of the matter of tongues as initial evidence of Spirit baptism? At Pentecost and at the house of Cornelius, the Spirit-baptized believers spoke in tongues, but this was to show that both Jews and Gentiles alike had received the promised gift of the Spirit. Nowhere in Scripture are believers told that tongues is the evidence of Spirit baptism outside of these initial moments in salvation history, and nowhere are believers commanded to be baptized in the Spirit or to speak in tongues.

The initial promise of John the Baptist about Spirit baptism is fulfilled in the Jew and Gentile "Pentecosts" (Acts 2; 10). Since Paul tells the Corinthians that they have been Spirit-baptized, the blessing of the pentecostal gift is applied to all disciples at the moment of conversion. The seven texts assembled together make clear that Jesus is the one who baptizes believers, the Spirit is the element into or with which they are baptized, and incorporation into the body of Christ is the result. See *Holy Spirit; Tongues, Gift of.*   *Chad Brand*

BAPTIST See *John.*

BAR Aramaic translation of the Hebrew word *ben.* Both words mean "son of." "Bar" is often used in the NT as a prefix for names of men telling whose son they were: Barabbas (Matt. 27:16-26), Bar-Jesus (Acts 13:6), Bar-jona (Matt. 16:17 KJV), Barnabas (Acts 4:36; 9:27; etc.), Barsabbas (Acts 1:23; 15:22), Bartholomew (Matt. 10:3; Acts 1:13), and Bartimaeus (Mark 10:46). See *Ben.*

BARABBAS Name means "Son of the Father." A murderer and insurrectionist held in Roman custody at the time of the trial of Jesus (Mark 15:15). All four Gospels record that when Pilate offered to release Jesus or Barabbas, the crowd demanded the release of Barabbas. Pilate gave in to the demand, ordered Jesus crucified, and set Barabbas free. Nothing is known of his subsequent history.

The current critical text of the Greek NT, following Origen, various ancient versions of the NT, and a number of Greek manuscripts, has Pilate calling him Jesus Barabbas (Matt. 27:16-17). The reading is not certain but is likely. If it is correct, Pilate offered the crowd a choice between "Jesus Messiah" (Jesus Christ) and

"Jesus, son of the father" (Jesus Barabbas). See *Christ; Christology; Cross; Crucifixion.*

Charles W. Draper

BARACHEL (Bär´ á·kĕl) Personal name meaning "God blessed." Father of Job's friend Elihu (Job 32:2).

BARACHIAH (Bär´ á·kī´ ăh) (NRSV, NT) See *Berechiah.*

BARACHIAS (Bär·á·kī´ ăs) (KJV, NT) See *Berechiah.*

BARAK (Bā´ răk) Son of Abinoam whom the Prophetess Deborah summoned to assume military leadership of the Israelites in a campaign against Canaanite forces under the command of Sisera (Judg. 4:6). Barak mustered Zebulunite and Naphtalite troops and set out to engage the Canaanites in battle near Mount Tabor. Though the Canaanites were routed, Sisera escaped. He was subsequently killed by Jael, the wife of Heber the Kenite. In 1 Sam. 12:11, where he is called Bedan, Barak is mentioned as one who delivered the Israelites from their enemies. See *Judges.*

BARAKEL (Bär´ á·kĕl) (NIV, TEV) See *Barachel.*

BARBARIAN Originally referred to stammering, stuttering, or any form of unintelligible sounds. Even the repeated syllable "bar-bar" mimics this. The term "barbarian" came to be synonymous with "foreigner," one who did not speak Greek, or one who was not a Greek. The Septuagint or earliest Greek translation translated Ps. 114:1 using "barbarian" for "a people of strange language." In the NT "barbarian" occurs six times. Paul uses the term twice in 1 Cor. 14:11 where he deals with the problem of unintelligible speech in the church. The more common use of "barbarian" seems related to those who spoke a foreign language, especially other than Greek. Paul's description of the islanders of Melita (Acts 28:2,4) as barbarians meant only that they did not speak Greek. With the rise of the Greek Empire, there was the tendency to include all who were not privy to this language and culture as barbarians. Thus, Paul makes the distinction between Greek and non-Greek in Rom. 1:14. Also, in Col. 3:11, "barbarians" are distinguished from the Greeks. As the

Romans came to power and absorbed the Greek culture, they removed themselves from barbarian classification. The term came to be a reproach during the Persian wars and in time was associated with those who were crude and contemptible. See *Gentile; Greeks; Hellenist.*

C. Kenny Cooper

BARHUMITE (Bär·hū´ mīt) Variant Hebrew spelling for Baharumite. See *Bahurim.*

BAR-JESUS (Bär·jē´ sŭs) Jewish magician and false prophet at Paphos (Acts 13:6). Paul the apostle denounced him, and he was struck blind. In Acts 13:8 he is called Elymas.

BAR-JONA (Bär·jō´ nà) Surname of Simon Peter (Matt. 16:17). The meaning is "son of John."

BAR-KOCHBA (Bär-Kōk´ bà) Means "son of the star" and was the title given by Jewish rebels to Simeon bar Kosevah, the leader of their revolt in A.D. 132–135. The title designated him as the Messiah (Num. 24:17). The revolt erupted because the Roman Emperor Hadrian had begun to rebuild Jerusalem as a pagan city with plans to replace the ruined Jewish temple with one dedicated to Jupiter. Circumcision was also forbidden. At first the Jews prepared for war secretly. When Hadrian left Syria, they openly revolted. By using guerrilla tactics they were able to overpower the Roman forces and liberate Jerusalem in A.D. 132. Bar-Kochba was the civil leader of the people, and Eleazar was the high priest. Their initial success led to such widespread rebellion that even some Gentiles and Samaritans joined them. Hadrian had to recall Severus from Britain to suppress them. It was a long and costly war for the Romans. Severus avoided direct confrontation, weakening the rebels instead by capturing them in small groups, cutting supply lines, besieging fortresses, and starving them. Bar-Kochba made his last stand at Betar, where most of the remaining insurgents died in 135. Some retreated to caves in the Judean desert and had to be starved to death. *(See map on page 182.)*   *Ricky L. Johnson*

BARKOS (Bär´ kŏs) Aramaic name possibly meaning "son of Kos" (a god). The original ancestor of a clan of Nethinim or temple employees who returned to Jerusalem from exile in Babylon with Zerubbabel about 537 B.C. (Ezra 2:53).

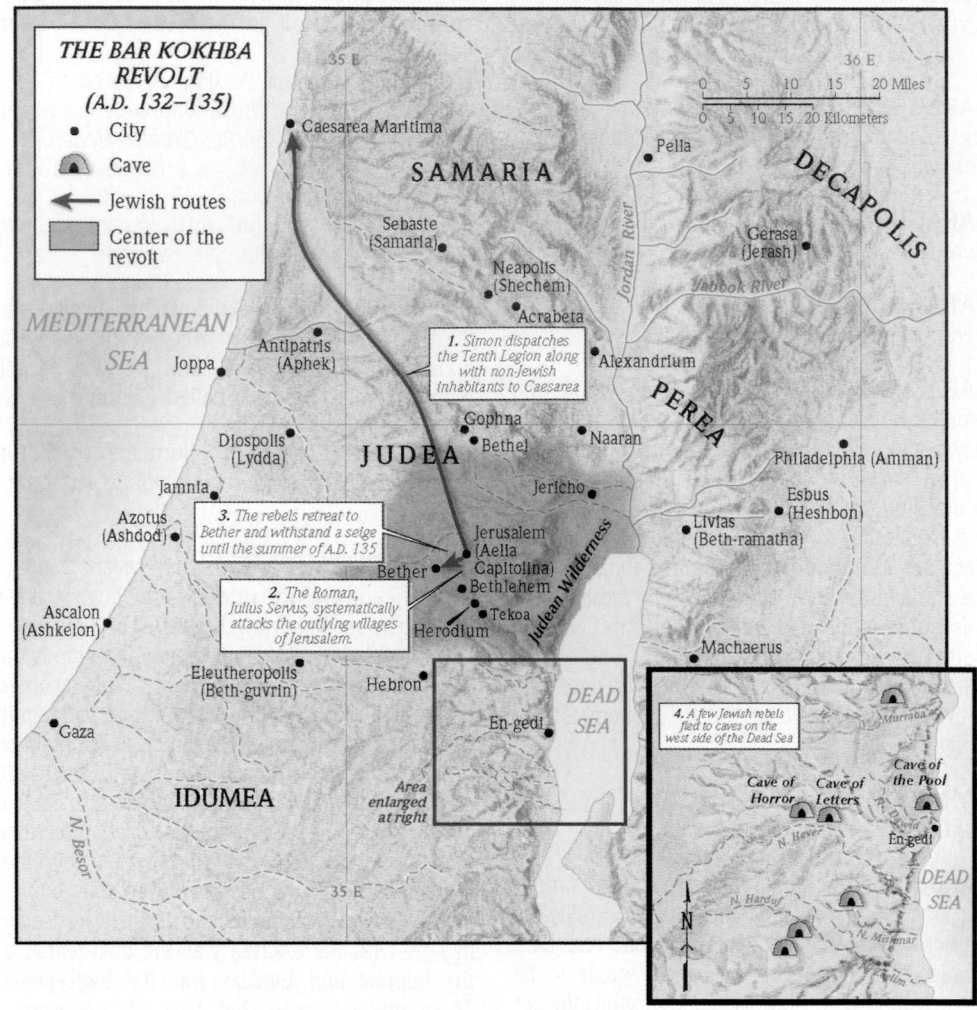

THE BAR KOKHBA
REVOLT
(A.D. 132–135)
• City
🏠 Cave
← Jewish routes
▨ Center of the revolt

BARLEY Grain for which Palestine was known (Deut. 8:8). Failure of the barley crop was a disaster (Joel 1:11). Barley was the food of the poor (Lev. 23:22; Ruth 3:15,17; 2 Sam. 17:28; 2 Kings 4:42; 7:1,16,18; 2 Chron. 2:10,15; 27:5; Jer. 41:8). Barley flour was used to make bread (Judg. 7:13; Ezek. 4:12) and was the kind of bread Jesus used to feed the multitude (John 6:9,13). Barley was also used as feed for horses, mules, and donkeys (1 Kings 4:28). There was a spring variety (*Hordeum vulgare*) and a winter variety (*Hordeum hexastichon*).

BARLEY HARVEST Began in late April or early May and preceded the wheat harvest by about two weeks (Exod. 9:31-32). At the beginning of the barley harvest (Ruth 2:23), the firstfruits were offered as a consecration of the harvest (Lev. 23:10).

BARN Storage place for seed (Hag. 2:19) or grain (Matt. 13:30). A full barn is a sign of prosperity (Deut. 28:8; Prov. 3:10; Luke 12:18) while an empty barn is a sign of calamity of some kind (drought, war, etc; Joel 1:17). Equivalent to modern granaries or silos.

BARNABAS (Bär´ nȧ·bȧs) Name appears 23 times in Acts and five times in Paul's letters and probably means "son of prophecy" or one who prophesies or preaches ("son of exhortation," Acts 4:36). Barnabas was a Levite and native of the island of Cyprus, named Joseph (Joses), before the disciples called him Barnabas.

He sold his property and gave the proceeds to the Jerusalem church (Acts 4:36-37). He introduced Saul of Tarsus to the Jerusalem church (9:26-27). The church chose Barnabas to go to Syrian Antioch to investigate the unrestricted preaching to the Gentiles there. He became the leader to the work and secured Saul as his assistant. They took famine relief to the Jerusalem church (11:19-30). On Paul's "first missionary journey," Barnabas at first seems to have been the leader (chaps. 13–14). Paul and Barnabas were sent to Jerusalem to try to settle the questions of how Gentiles could be saved and how Jewish Christians could have fellowship with them (15:1-21). They agreed to go on another missionary journey but separated over whether to take John Mark with them again (15:36-41). Barnabas (Gal. 2:1-10) went with Paul to Jerusalem and the apostles approved of their Gentile mission (probably the same event as Acts 15). In Gal. 2:13, however, Paul indicated that on one occasion Barnabas wavered on the issue of full acceptance of Gentile Christians. In 1 Cor. 9:6 Paul commended Barnabas for following his (Paul's) practice of supporting himself rather than depending upon the churches. Colossians 4:10 simply states that Mark was Barnabas's cousin. In the third century Barnabas was identified by Clement of Alexandria as one of the 70 of Luke 10:1; Tertullian referred to him as the author of Hebrews; and the *Clementine Recognitions* stated he was the Matthias of Acts 1:23,26. All of these are most unlikely. In the second century an epistle bearing Barnabas's name appeared, became quite popular, and even received some consideration for a place in the NT. Later an apocryphal Acts of Barnabas and perhaps even a Gospel of Barnabas were circulated.   *James A. Brooks*

BARREL KJV translation found in 1 Kings 17:12-16; 18:33. Modern versions translate the same word as "jar." Jars were used for carrying water and storing flour. See *Pottery.*

BARREN, BARRENNESS Term used to describe a woman who is unable to give birth to children: Sarai (Gen. 11:30), Rebekah (Gen. 25:21), Rachel (Gen. 29:31), Manoah's wife (Judg. 13:2), Hannah (1 Sam. 1:5), and Elizabeth (Luke 1:7,36). Also described as "solitary" (Job 3:7), "desolate" (2 Sam. 13:20; Isa. 49:21; 54:1), or "dead, deadness" (Rom. 4:19). Barren-

ness was considered a curse from God (Gen. 16:2; 20:18; 1 Sam. 1:5), which explains Elizabeth's statement that God had taken away her "disgrace among the people"—that she was a sinner and cursed by God as evidenced by her barrenness (Luke 1:25). The barrenness of Sarai, Rebekah, and Rachel (the mothers of the Israelite nation) is significant in that their ability finally to bear children is a sign of the grace and favor of God toward His elect people.

BARSABAS (Bär´ så·bås) (KJV) or **BARSABBAS** Personal name meaning "son of the Sabbath." **1.** Name given Joseph Justus, candidate not elected when church chose replacement for Judas, the traitor (Acts 1:23). **2.** Last name of Judas, whom the Jerusalem church chose to go with Paul and Silas to Antioch after the Jerusalem council (Acts 15:22). See *Apostle; Disciple; Judas; Joseph; Justus.*

BARTHOLOMEW (Bär·thŏl´ ō·mēw) One of the 12 apostles (Mark 3:18). The name Bartholomew means "son of Talmai" and may have been a patronymic, a name derived from that of the father or a paternal ancestor. It occurs in all four lists of the apostles in the NT (Matt. 10:2-4; Mark 3:16-19; Luke 6:14-16; Acts 1:13); in each of the Synoptic Gospels it immediately follows the name of Philip. The name does not occur at all in John's Gospel. In the first chapter of John, however, the account of Philip's call to discipleship is closely related to the call of a person named Nathanael (vv. 43-51). This circumstance has led to the traditional identification of Bartholomew with Nathanael. See *Apostle; Disciple; Nathanael.*

BARTIMAEUS (Bär·tĭ·mā´ ŭs) or **BARTIMEUS** (KJV) Blind beggar near Jericho who cried to Jesus for mercy despite efforts to silence him. Jesus said that his persistent faith had made him whole. Able to see, he followed Jesus (Mark 10:46-52). The name means "son of Timaeus." His blindness had reduced him to anonymity, the witnesses not even knowing his personal name. The story demonstrates the value Jesus placed on all persons, even the lowliest and seemingly least significant.   *Charles W. Draper*

BARUCH (Bä´ rūk) **1.** Son of Neriah who served as Jeremiah's scribe and friend. He helped Jeremiah purchase a field from the prophet's cousin Hanameel and used the purchase as a

B

symbol of hope (Jer. 32:12). Baruch, whose name means "blessed," served Jeremiah as an amanuensis or scribe. He appears, moreover, to have had a close personal association with the prophet and to have exercised a significant influence in the ministry of Jeremiah. He wrote down Jeremiah's preaching and read it to the king's counselors who took it to the king. Jehoiakim burned it, but Jeremiah dictated it again (Jer. 36). Jeremiah was even accused of being a mere instrument of Baruch's enmity (Jer. 43:3). The prophet counseled Baruch to place his confidence wholly in the Lord and not to seek great things for himself (Jer. 45). A wide range of later literature was attributed to Baruch in Jewish tradition. See *Jeremiah*. **2.** A priest, son of Zabbai, during the time of Nehemiah. He "diligently" repaired part of the eastern wall of Jerusalem (Neh. 3:20). It is usually assumed that he is the same Baruch who was a signer (Neh. 10:6) of the covenant described in Neh. 8–10 in which the postexilic community officially recommitted itself to the law of God as authoritative in their lives (see especially 10:28-29). **3.** Baruch mentioned in Neh. 11:5 is from the tribe of Judah. Nothing else is known of him but that his son Maaseiah volunteered to endure danger as a settler in postexilic Jerusalem.

BARZILLAI (Bär·zĭl´ lī) Personal name meaning "made of iron." **1.** Man from Gilead east of the Jordan who met David at Mahanaim as he fled from Absalom. Barzillai and others gave needed supplies for David's company (2 Sam. 17:27-29). When David returned to Jerusalem, the 80-year-old Barzillai accompanied him across the Jordan but refused to go to Jerusalem (2 Sam. 19:31-39). Barzillai may have served as David's host while he stayed east of the Jordan. His sons went to Jerusalem, and the dying David ensured their welfare (1 Kings 2:7). **2.** Father of Adriel whose sons David delivered to the Gibeonites for execution in payment for Saul's inhumane slaying of Gibeonites (2 Sam. 21:8). This Barzillai could be the same as 1. above. **3.** Priestly clan whose ancestor had married the daughter of 1. above and taken his name. Some of these priests returned from exile in Babylon with Zerubbabel about 537 B.C. (Ezra 2:61).

BASEMATH (Băs´ ĕ·măth) Personal name meaning "balsam." **1.** Hittite woman whom Esau married, grieving his parents, Isaac and Rebekah (Gen. 26: 34-35; 27:46). Some differences in her name and ancestors appear. In Gen. 28:9 Esau married Mahalath, daughter of Ishmael and sister of Nebajoth. In Gen. 36:3 Basemath is Ishmael's daughter and Nebajoth's sister. Apparently, all three passages refer to the same woman. How one explains the complexity of names, relationships, and backgrounds is not certain. Some talk of literary sources; others of new names given women at marriage; others of copyists' changes of the text. Reuel, Basemath's son, became father of four clans in Edom (Gen. 36:10,13,17). **2.** Daughter of Solomon who married Ahimaaz, district supervisor providing supplies for the royal court from Naphtali (1 Kings 4:15).

BASHAN (Bâ´ shăn) Northernmost region of Palestine east of the Jordan River. Though its precise extent cannot be determined with certainty, it was generally east of the Sea of Galilee. In the time of Moses, it was ruled over by a king named Og, whom the Israelite army defeated (Num. 21:33-35). It was assigned to the tribal area of Manasseh (Deut. 3:13; Josh. 13:29-31). Probably on account of its frontier location, it changed hands several times during the course of Israelite history. It was known as a particularly fertile area (Deut. 32:14; Ezek. 39:18). See *Palestine*.

BASHAN-HAVOTH-JAIR (Bá´ shăn-hā´ vŏth-jáīr) (KJV) See *Havoth-jair*.

BASHEMATH (Băsh´ ĕ·măth) (KJV) See *Basemath*.

BASIN (KJV, "bason") Used interchangeably with "bowl" to refer to various sizes of wide hollow bowls, cups, and dishes used for domestic or more formal purposes (John 13:5). The most common material used to make such instruments was pottery. However, basins were also made of brass (Exod. 27:3), silver (Num. 7:13), and gold (2 Chron. 4:8). The largest basins were usually banquet bowls or mixing bowls for wine, although one of the largest was used in the sacrificial ritual at the great altar of the temple (Zech. 9:15). Generally, the largest basins were also used as lids for other vessels. The basin used by Jesus to wash the disciples' feet (John 13:5) was of a special sort. The Greek word is found nowhere else in Scripture but from the context is understood to mean a vessel specifically suited for washing a particular part of the body, such as the hands or the feet, and is therefore used with a definite article, "the basin." See *Laver; Sacrifice and Offering.*   C. Dale Hill

BASKET Five kinds of baskets are mentioned in the OT. The precise distinctions of size and shape are not clear. Some had handles, others lids, some both, others neither. The most common term always refers to a container for carrying food (Gen. 40:16-18). Another term is used to signify a cage or "bird net" (Jer. 5:27). A third term for basket is the common household utensil used in harvesting grain (Deut. 26:2; 28:5). A fourth term refers to a larger basket used for heavy burdens such as clay for bricks or even the heads of the 70 sons of Ahab delivered to Jehu (2 Kings 10:7). The final term was used to describe both the basket (ark) in which Moses was placed as an infant (Exod. 2:3,5) and the ark which Noah built (Gen. 6:14-16). The NT uses two words for basket. The smaller basket is referred to in the story of the feeding of the 5,000 (Matt. 14:20). The larger basket is mentioned in the feeding of the 4,000 (Matt. 15:37). The Apostle Paul also used the larger basket as a means of escape over the wall of Damascus (Acts 9:25). It might logically be considered a hamper.
                                            C. Dale Hill

BASMATH (Băs´ măth) (KJV, 1 Kings 4:15) See *Basemath.*

BASON (KJV) See *Basin.*

BASTARD KJV translation of a word for the offspring of an illegitimate union. The term could refer to an incestuous union or of a marriage that was prohibited (Lev. 18:6-20; 20:11-20). Illegitimate children were not permitted to enter the assembly of the Lord (Deut. 23:2). According to Hebrews, those who do not have the discipline of the Lord are illegitimate children (12:8). Also translated as "a mongrel people" (Zech. 9:6 NRSV).

BAT Order (*Chiroptera*) of nocturnal placental flying mammals; quadruped with wings. The Hebrew word translated "bat" is the generic name for many species of this mammal found in Palestine (Isa. 2:20). Although the bat is listed among unclean birds in the Bible (Lev. 11:19; Deut. 14:18), it belongs to the mammals because it nurses its young. It is nocturnal and

lives in caves (Isa. 2:20). Modern zoologists have cited at least 20 different species in the area of Palestine.

BATH Liquid measure roughly equivalent to five and one-half gallons (U.S.). It was used to measure the molten sea in the temple (1 Kings 7:26,38) as well as oil and wine (2 Chron. 2:10; Ezra 7:22; Isa. 5:10; Ezek. 45:11,14). The bath was $\frac{1}{10}$th of a homer. See *Weights and Measures.*

Second-century Roman baths in the upper agora at Ephesus.

BATHING Biblical languages make no distinction between washing and bathing primarily because the dry climate of the Middle East prohibited bathing except on special occasions or where there was an available source of water (John 9:7). Therefore, where "bathe" occurs in the biblical text, partial bathing is usually intended. However, two notable exceptions are that of Pharaoh's daughter in the Nile River

Bathing room in the baths at Roman Herculaneum (modern Italy) showing mosaics and shelves.

(Exod. 2:5) and that of Bathsheba on her rooftop (2 Sam. 11:2). Public baths of the Greek culture were unknown in Palestine before the second century. The chief use of the word has to do with ritual acts of purification (Exod. 30:19-21). It is probably safe to say that the masses of people in both the OT and NT had neither the privacy nor the desire for bathing, as we know it today. Priests washed clothes, hands, feet, or bodies before approaching the altar for sacrifice. Ceremonial defilement was removed by bathing the body and washing the clothes (Lev. 14:8). During a time of mourning or fasting the face and clothes were left unwashed (2 Sam. 12:20), a practice forbidden by Jesus (Matt. 6:17). Lambs were washed at shearing time (Song 4:2), babies after birth (Ezek. 16:4), and bodies in preparation for burial (Acts 9:37). Sometimes other elements such as wine and milk were used to symbolize washing in a metaphorical sense. According to Josephus, the Essene community practiced daily bathing for ceremonial reasons, a practice which excavations at Qumran appear to confirm. See *Clean, Cleanness.*   *C. Dale Hill*

BATH-RABBIM (Băth-răb´ bĭm) Place-name meaning "daughter of many." A gate of Heshbon, which was near pools of fish. Song of Songs 7:4 uses its beauty as comparison for the beauty of the beloved lady's eyes. See *Heshbon.*

BATHSHEBA (Băth·shē´ bà) Daughter of Eliam and the wife of Uriah the Hittite (2 Sam. 11:3). She was a beautiful woman with whom David the king had an adulterous relationship (2 Sam. 11:4). When David learned that she had become pregnant as a result of the intrigue, he embarked on a course of duplicity that led finally to the violent death of Uriah. David then took Bathsheba as his wife. She was the mother of Solomon and played an important role in ensuring that he be made king (1 Kings 1:11–2:19). See *David.*

BATHSHUA (Băth´ shū·à) Personal name meaning "daughter of nobility." **1.** Canaanite wife of Judah and mother of Er, Onan, and Shelah (1 Chron. 2:3 NASB, TEV, NRSV). KJV, NIV read "daughter of Shua." Genesis 38:2 says her name was Shuah, while Gen. 38:12 calls her daughter of Shuah or Bath-shua. See *Shuah.* **2.** Name for Bathsheba in 1 Chron. 3:5. See *Bathsheba.*

BATTALION RSV translation of 1/10th of a Roman legion, about 600 men. KJV translates "band," HCSB uses "whole company." When Pilate handed Jesus over to be crucified, the whole battalion assembled together before Jesus (Matt. 27:27; Mark 15:16). This battalion would have been the Second Italian Cohort. See *Cohort.*

BATTERING RAM See *Arms and Armor.*

BATTLE See *Arms and Armor; Army.*

BATTLE-AX See *Arms and Armor.*

BAVAI (Bā´ vī) (KJV) or **BAVVAI** (NASB, TEV, RSV) Government official in Keilah who helped Nehemiah rebuild wall of Jerusalem (Neh. 3:18). NRSV, NIV read Binnui on basis of Neh. 3:24 and other textual evidence. See *Binnui; Keilah.*

BAY KJV translation of a term referring to horses in Zech. 6:3,7. KJV took the term as referring to the color of the horses. The earliest translators had trouble with the word, as do modern versions. Recent interpreters take the Hebrew word as referring to the strength of the horses (NIV, NASB), though NRSV reads "gray" in verse 3 and "steeds" in verse 7, while REB omits the word in verse 3 and emends the text in verse 7.

BAY TREE KJV translation in Ps. 37:35. The Hebrew word (*'ezrach*) means "native" or "indigenous." While the bay tree is native to Palestine, Ps. 37:35 gives no indication when referring to "that tree." NRSV and TEV hardly come closer to a correct translation with "cedar tree." NASB, NIV, and REB are closer to the meaning of the Hebrew text when they speak of a "tree in its native soil."

BAZAAR Section of a street given over to merchants. Ben-hadad of Damascus gave Ahab permission to set up bazaars in Damascus as Ben-hadad's father had done in Samaria (1 Kings 20:34).

BAZLITH (Băz´ lĭth) or **BAZLUTH** (Băz´ lŭth) Personal name meaning "in the shadow" or "onions." Original ancestor of clan of temple employees who returned from exile in Babylon with Zerubbabel in 537 B.C. (Neh. 7:54). Name is spelled Bazluth in Ezra 2:52, which NIV reads in Neh. 7:54.

BDELLIUM Translation of *bedolach*, a word of uncertain meaning. It has been identified as a gum or resin, pearl, or stone. Genesis 2:12 (KJV) mentions bdellium, gold, and onyx as products of Havilah. Numbers 11:7 likens manna to bdellium in appearance. Terms in other languages using words very similar to *bedolach* favor the identification with a resinous gum. In droplet form the gum may have the appearance of a pearl or stone.

BEADS RSV translation of a term for articles of gold jewelry (Num. 31:50). The exact identification of these objects is uncertain. They are variously identified as tablets (KJV), armlets, pendants (REB, NRSV), necklaces (TEV, NIV, NASB), and breastplates.

BEALIAH (Bē·à·lī´ ah) Personal name meaning "Yahweh is Lord." Literally, "Yahweh is baal." Soldier who joined David at Ziklag while he fled from Saul and served the Philistines (1 Chron. 12:5).

BEALOTH (Bē´ ā·lŏth) Place-name meaning "female Baals" or "ladies." **1.** Town on southern border of tribal territory of Judah (Josh. 15:24). This may be the same as Baalath-beer (19:8). **2.** Region with Asher making up a district to supply food for Solomon's court (1 Kings 4:16). KJV, NIV read "in Aloth." This could be a common noun meaning "in the heights." If a town is meant, its location is unknown.

BEANS Leguminous plant (*Faba vulgaris*) grown in the ancient world as food. Beans mentioned in 2 Sam. 17:28 and Ezek. 4:9 were the horse or broad bean. These beans were sown in the autumn and harvested sometime in mid-April just before the barley and wheat. They were cooked green in the pods or cooked after being dried. Dried beans were threshed and winnowed like other grains.

BEAR Large, heavy mammal with long, thick, shaggy hair. It eats insects, fruit, and flesh. The bear of the Bible has been identified with a high degree of certainty as the Syrian bear. They may grow as high as six feet and weigh as much as 500 pounds. In biblical times the bear was a threat to vineyards and to herds of sheep and goats (1 Sam. 17:34-35). The two largest and

Modern Middle Eastern market on the island of Crete reminiscent of an ancient bazaar.

strongest beasts of prey—the bear and the lion—are often listed together (1 Sam. 17:37). A narrative about Elisha pictures the ferocity of the bear (2 Kings 2:23-24). Within the last century the Syrian bear has disappeared from the Holy Land, with the last bear being killed in Galilee just before World War II. It still survives in Syria, Persia, and Turkey. For the constellation, see *Arcturus*.

BEARD Hair growing on a man's face often excluding the mustache. Ancient Hebrews are often depicted in ancient Near Eastern art with full, rounded beards. This is in contrast to Romans and Egyptians who preferred clean-shaven faces and to other desert nomads and others living in Palestine who often clipped or cut their beards (on the latter see Jer. 9:26; 25:23; 49:32). Israelites were forbidden to mar the edges of their beards by cutting them (Lev. 19:27), and priests were forbidden to cut the corners of their beards (Lev. 21:5). To have one's beard shaved was an insult (2 Sam. 10:4-5; Isa. 50:6) or used as a sign by the prophets of coming destruction (Isa. 7:20; 15:2; Jer. 41:5; 48:37; Ezek. 5:1). The regular Hebrew word for "beard" (*zaqan*) also means "old" and was applied to men (Judg. 19:16), slaves (Gen. 24:2), women (Zech. 8:4), and elders (Exod. 19:7). The word translated as "beard" in 2 Sam. 19:24 (*sapham*) probably means "mustache." The same word is also translated "lip" (Lev. 13:45; Ezek. 24:17,22; Mic. 3:7 KJV, NRSV), "[lower part of the] face" (NIV, TEV), "mouth" (Mic. 3:7 NASB, REB), "mustache" (Lev. 13:45; Ezek. 24:17,22 NASB), "upper lip" (Lev. 13:45 REB), and "beard" (Ezek. 24:17,22 REB).

BEAST Several Hebrew and Greek words and phrases are translated as "beast." "Beast" may refer to any animal in distinction from people (Eccles. 3:18-21), reptiles (Gen. 1:24), and sometimes cattle (Gen. 1:30). Beasts were divided into categories of clean and unclean (Lev. 11:1-8) and wild and domesticated (Gen. 1:24; 2:20; Exod.19:13; 22:10; Num. 3:13; etc.).

Apocalyptic literature such as Daniel and Revelation utilize beasts of various sorts in their symbolism. The OT used "beast" as a symbol for an enemy, and the writers of Daniel and Revelation may have built on that (Ps. 74:19; Jer. 12:9). Daniel saw four great beasts who repre-

sented four great kings arise out of the sea (Dan. 7:2-14). These four beasts would threaten God's kingdom, but God's people would prevail over them (Dan. 7:18). See *Apocalyptic*.

The book of Revelation speaks of two beasts. The first beast arises out of the sea (Rev. 13:1), is seven headed, and derives its authority from the dragon (Rev. 12:3; 13:4). This beast has several of the characteristics of the four beasts of Dan. 7. The second beast arises out of the earth (Rev. 13:11). It serves the first beast by seeking devotees for it and is referred to as the "false prophet" (Rev. 16:13; 19:20; 20:10). Both the beast and the false prophet persecute the church but are finally judged by Christ (Rev. 19:20; 2 Thess. 2:6-12). See *Behemoth; Leviathan*.

BEATEN GOLD Thin sheets of gold produced by hammering; used to overlay objects of lesser value. Several objects were overlaid with gold in this manner: the golden shields of Solomon (1 Kings 10:16-17), the lampstands of the tabernacle (Exod. 25:18,31,36; 37:7,22; Num. 8:4), and idols (Isa. 40:19).

BEATEN OIL Highest grade of olive oil produced by crushing ripe olives in a mortar. The second grade of oil was produced by pressing the olives. The third grade of oil was produced by further crushing and pressing the pulp. Beaten oil was used in the lamps of the sanctuary (Exod. 27:20; Lev. 24:2) and with the daily sacrifices (Exod. 29:40; Num. 28:5). Solomon also used beaten oil in his trade with Hiram (1 Kings 5:11).

BEATEN SILVER Thin sheets of silver produced by hammering and used to overlay objects of lesser value such as the wooden core of an idol (Jer. 10:6-10).

BEATING See *Scourge*.

BEATITUDES Beatitudes or "blessed sayings" are so designated because they begin with the expression "blessed is" or "happy is" (Hb. *ashre*; Gk. *makarios*; Lat. *beatus*). "Happy," however, may not be the best rendering since it has been spiritually devalued in modern usage. The idea is that of a fortunate, blissful state based not on worldly circumstances but on divine conditions. These conditional blessings are frequent in OT wisdom literature, especially the Psalms (Job

Church of the Beatitudes on the traditional site of the Sermon on the Mount by the Sea of Galilee.

5:17; Pss. 1:1; 32:1-2; 33:12; 41:1; 106:3; Prov. 8:34; 28:14).

The most widely known and extensive collection of such blessings introduces Jesus' Sermon on the Mount (Matt. 5:3-12; cp. Luke 6:20-26). The Beatitudes set the tone for the Sermon by emphasizing man's humility (5:3-5,7,9) and God's righteousness (5:6,8,10). Each of the eight Beatitudes (5:11-12 is an expansion on 5:10) portrays the ideal heart condition of a kingdom citizen—a condition that brings abundant spiritual blessing. "Poor in spirit" refers to an awareness of spiritual bankruptcy apart from Christ (5:3). To "mourn" is to be grieved and broken over sin (5:4; Isa. 61:1-3; 2 Cor. 7:10). The "meek," like Christ, exemplify gentleness and self-control (5:5; 11:29). "Hunger and thirst" is a vivid description of those who crave God's righteousness (5:6; Ps. 42:1-2). The "merciful" are both forgiving and compassionate (5:7; 6:12-15). To be "pure in heart" refers to that internal cleansing necessary for entering God's presence (5:8; Ps. 24:3-4). The "peacemakers" are those who invite men to be reconciled to God and to one another (5:9; Rom. 10:15; 12:18; 2 Cor. 5:20). Finally, there is a blessing for those who are "persecuted for righteousness." It is normal for the world to oppose kingdom citizens (5:10-12; 1 Pet. 3:14; 4:14). See *Sermon on the Mount.*   *Pete Schemm*

BEAUTIFUL GATE Scene of the healing of a lame man by Peter and John (Acts 3:2,10). Neither the OT nor other Jewish sources mention a "Beautiful Gate." Christian tradition has identified the gate with the Susa (or Shushan) or Golden Gate on the east side of the temple leading from outside into the Court of the Gentiles. Modern scholars, however, identify the gate as the one on the east side of the Court of Women leading from the Court of the Gentiles. Others

Mount of Beatitudes as viewed from the Sea of Galilee. Church of the Beatitudes is in center of photo.

place it east of the Court of the Men. Josephus, a Jewish historian in the first century, described a gate of "Corinthian bronze" outside the sanctuary. Jewish sources refer to this gate as Nicanor's Gate. See *Jerusalem; Temple.*

BEBAI (Bē´ bā-ī) Babylonian personal name meaning "child." **1.** Original ancestor of clan of whom 623 (628 in Neh. 7:16) returned with Zerubbabel from exile in Babylon about 537 B.C. (Ezra 2:11). His son, or at least a member of the clan, led 28 men from Babylon to Jerusalem with Ezra (Ezra 8:11). Members of the clan had married foreign wives (Ezra 10:28). **2.** Signer of Nehemiah's covenant to obey God's law (Neh. 10:15).

BECHER (Bē´ kĕr) or **BEKER** (NIV) **1.** Personal name meaning "firstborn" or "young male camel." Son of Benjamin and grandson of Jacob (Gen. 46:21). He had nine sons (1 Chron. 7:8). **2.** Original ancestor of clan in tribe of Ephraim (Num. 26:35). First Chronicles 7:20 spells the name "Bered."

BECHERITE (Bē´ kĕr-īt) Member of clan of Becher. See *Becher.*

BECHORATH (Bē-kō´ răth) (KJV) or **BECORATH** (Bē-cō´ răth) Personal name meaning "firstborn." Ancestor of King Saul (1 Sam. 9:1).

BED, BEDROOM Place to sleep or rest. A bed may be a simple straw mat or an elaborate frame of wood, metal, stone, or ivory. A bedroom is a designated room designed for sleep or rest.

A bed for the very poor was a mere thin straw mat or cloth pad rolled out on the ground with no more than a stone for a pillow (Gen. 28:10-11; John 5:9) and an outer garment for cover. For the more fortunate poor, a multipurpose, one-room, mud house served as protection from the elements, and as a kitchen, workspace, and sleeping quarters. For the very few affluent, households and palaces contained many rooms including kitchens, living rooms, libraries, and bedrooms with elaborately decorated beds (Esther 1:6; Prov. 7:16-17; Amos 6:4). A bed of iron attracted attention (Deut. 3:11). Sometimes the bed was a symbol of both the highest and the lowest moral codes of mankind. The bed is a symbol that there is no secret place secure from deception (2 Kings 6:12). In Isa. 28:20 the bed that is too short and the cover too narrow is a

Bedroom in Herculaneum showing the Roman-style bed and walls originally decorated with frescoes.

symbol that there is no escape from judgment. The Scripture teaches that marriage is honorable among all people, that the marriage bed should be kept undefiled, and that God will judge the adulterer and the sexually immoral (Heb. 13:4; Rev. 2:22).   *Lawson G. Hatfield*

BEDAD (Bē´ dăd) Personal name meaning "scatter" or "be alone." Father of Hadad, king of Edom (Gen. 36:35).

BEDAN (Bē´ dăn) Personal name of uncertain meaning. **1.** Listed as a judge in 1 Sam. 12:11. Usually seen as the work of a copyist, but the original reading is uncertain. The closest name of the judges would be Barak (Judg. 4–5). Bedan is a son of Gilead in 1 Chron. 7:17 and could be another name for Jephthah, a son of Gilead (Judg. 11:1). Early Jewish rabbis read *ben-Dan,* "son of Dan," and thought Samson was intended (Judg. 13:2,24). Others read "Abdon" (Judg. 12:13-15). NIV, TEV, NRSV read "Barak" for Bedan. **2.** Descendant of Machir and Manasseh (1 Chron. 7:17).

BEDEIAH (Bē-dē´ äh) Personal name meaning "Yahweh alone" or "branch of Yahweh." Man with foreign wife who divorced her under Ezra's leadership to prevent tempting Israel with foreign gods (Ezra 10:35).

BEE See *Insects.*

BEELIADA (Be-li´ ä-dà) Personal name meaning "Baal knows" or "the Lord knows." Son of David born in Jerusalem (1 Chron. 14:7). In 2 Sam. 5:16 the Baal part of the name is replaced with "El," a Hebrew word for God, becoming "Eliada."

BEELZEBUB (Bē·ĕl´ zē·bŭb) (KJV, NIV) or **BEELZEBUL** (NASB, TEV, NRSV, HCSB) Name for Satan in NT spelled differently in Greek manuscripts. The term is based on Hebrew Baal-zebub, "lord of the flies." See *Baal-zebub.*

BEER See *Strong Drink.*

BEER (Bē´ ĕr) Place-name meaning "well." It frequently occurs in compound constructions of place-names. For example, Beer-sheba means "well of seven." The generally arid climate of much of Palestine made wells particularly significant locations. **1.** One of the camps of the Israelites during the wilderness wandering (Num. 21:16). **2.** Jotham fled to Beer when he feared his brother Abimelech would kill him (Judg. 9:21). This may be modern Bireh.

BEERA (Bē·ē´ rà) Personal name meaning "a well." A descendant of the tribe of Asher (1 Chron. 7:37).

BEERAH (Bē·ē´ răh) Personal name meaning "a well." A leader of the tribe of Reuben taken captive by Tiglath-pileser, king of Assyria, about 732 B.C. (1 Chron. 5:6).

BEER-ELIM (Bē´ ĕr·ē´ lĭm) Place-name meaning "well of the rams, the heroes, the terebinths, or the mighty trees." Place involved in mourning according to Isaiah's lament over Moab (Isa. 15:8). It is probably the same as Beer (Num. 21:16), where Israel sang the song of the well. The location may be in the Wadi et-Temed, northeast of Dibon.

BEERI (Bē·ē´ rī) Personal name meaning "well." **1.** Hittite father of girl Esau married, grieving his parents Isaac and Rebekah (Gen. 26:34-35; 27:46). **2.** Father of Hosea, the prophet (Hos. 1:1).

BEER-LAHAIROI (Bē´ ĕr·là·haî´ roî) Place-name meaning "well of the Living One who sees me." Interpretation of the name and location of the place are difficult. After Sarai had Abraham put Hagar out of the house, an angel appeared to Hagar announcing the birth of a son. Hagar interpreted this as a vision of the living God and named the well where she was Beer-lahairoi (Gen. 16:14). Isaac passed there as he went to meet and wed Rebekah (Gen. 24:62). Isaac lived

there after his father Abraham died (Gen. 25:11).

BEEROTH (Bē·ē´ rŏth) Place-name meaning "wells." **1.** Wells of the sons of Jaakan, where Israel camped in the wilderness (Num. 33:31; Deut. 10:6). **2.** City of the Gibeonites to which Joshua and his army came to defend the Gibeonites after making a covenant with them (Josh. 9:17). The city was allotted the tribe of Benjamin (Josh. 18:25). Ishbosheth's army captains came from Beeroth (2 Sam. 4:2), whose citizens had fled to Gittaim when Israel, possibly under Saul, conquered Beeroth (2 Sam. 4:3). Compare 2 Sam. 21:1-9 for Saul's dealing with the Gibeonites. Joab's armor bearer, one of David's 30 heroes, came from Beeroth (2 Sam. 23:37). Citizens of Beeroth returned with Zerubbabel from exile in Babylon about 537 B.C. (Ezra 2:25). The city had to be close to Gibeon, but its exact location is debated. Among suggestions are: el-Bireh, Tell en-Nasbeh, Nebi Samwil, Khirbet el-Burj, Biddu, Khirbet Raddana, Ras et-Tahune.

BEEROTH-BENE-JAAKAN (Bē·ē´ rŏth-bē´ nē-jā´ à·kăn) (NASB, NRSV, Deut. 10:6) See *Beeroth.*

BEER-SHEBA (Bē´ ĕr-shē´ ba) Beer-sheba and its surrounding area factors significantly in the OT from the earliest sojourns of the patriarchs (Gen. 21; 22; 26) to the return of the Hebrew exiles with Nehemiah (Neh. 11:27,30). Since it was an important crossroad to Egypt in the geographic center of the dry, semidesert region known as the Negev, Beer-sheba also served as the administrative center of the region. Settlement of the Beer-sheba area began before 3000 B.C.

Abraham and a nearby king, Abimelech, swore to protect Abraham's right to the water of this region (Gen. 21:22-33). Abraham then named the place "Beer-sheba," meaning "well of the oath" or preferably "well of the seven," referring to seven lambs involved in the agreement. Here he called on the Lord (Gen. 21:33) and lived for some time (Gen. 22:19). The Lord confirmed His promises with Isaac at Beer-sheba (Gen. 26:23-25), where Isaac renamed his father's well "Shibah." A well is found today outside the ruins of biblical Beer-sheba (Tell es-Saba'); however, it cannot be the patriarchal well

B

since it is dated much later, around the twelfth century. Isaac also lived in the area of Beer-sheba, and his son Jacob left there for Haran to seek a wife (Gen. 28:10). A crossroad to Egypt, Beer-sheba was a stopping place for Jacob many years later when he was encouraged by the Lord to continue on to Egypt where Joseph was awaiting him (Gen. 46:1-5). Because of these patriarchal events at Beer-sheba, it is thought that the city eventually and unfortunately became a pilgrimage destination for idolatry later during the monarchy (Amos 5:5; 8:14).

Joshua gave Beer-sheba to the tribe of Judah (Josh. 15:28) and then to the tribe of Simeon whose territory lay within Judah's boundaries (Josh. 19:1-2,9). Samuel's sons Joel and Abiah were unfair judges in Beer-sheba right before the monarchy began with Saul (1 Sam. 8:1-3).

Beer-sheba is mentioned idiomatically 12 times to indicate the northern and southern extremes of Israel, "Dan to Beersheba" (2 Sam. 24:2, 1 Kings 4:25). This type of phrase served to speak of Israel in its entirety and its unity, for instance, in its resolve to punish the tribe of Benjamin (Judg. 20:1) and its recognition of Samuel as a true prophet (1 Sam. 3:20). This idiom also served to show the extent of the reforms of three southern kings: Jehoshaphat (2 Chron. 19:4 KJV, "Beer-sheba to mount Ephraim"), Hezekiah

Various millstones and stone mortars from the area around Beer-sheba.

(2 Chron. 30:5 KJV, "Beer-sheba even to Dan"), and Josiah (2 Kings 23:8 KJV, "from Geba to Beer-sheba").

Archaeology has shown Beer-sheba to be the administrative center of the Negev by uncovering its large commercial storerooms and fortifications that were superior to the lesser cities in the area. The fortifications were inadequate, however, against the Assyrians who sacked the

Tel Beer-sheba well.

city and left it in ruins until the Persian period. After the punitive exile of Judah, the people returned to Beer-sheba and its surrounding satellite towns with Nehemiah in the fifth century (Neh. 11:27,30).

As the "gateway to the desert," Beer-sheba was in a precarious place climatically, which is the backdrop of two persons' prayers concerning death. Hagar pleaded at a distance not to see her son die (Gen. 21:14-16), and Elijah prayed for death in the desert rather than at the order of Queen Jezebel (1 Kings 19:3-4).

Daniel C. Fredericks

A well found at Beer-sheba which may date as early as the 14th or 13th century B.C.

BEESHTERAH (Bē·ĕsh´ tə·răh) Place-name meaning "in Ashtaroth" or representing a contraction of "Beth Ashtaroth," which means "house of Ashtaroth." Place east of the Jordan from territory of tribe of Manasseh set aside for the Levites (Josh. 21:27). First Chronicles 6:71 spells name "Ashtaroth." See *Ashtaroth.*

BEGINNING AND END See *Alpha and Omega.*

BEHEADING See *Capital Punishment; Crimes and Punishments.*

BEHEMOTH (Bē´ hə·mŏth) Large beast known for its enormous strength and toughness. Described in detail in Job 40:15-24, this animal has been variously identified as an elephant, a hippopotamus, and a water buffalo, with the hippopotamus the most likely. Identification as a hippopotamus is based on the description in Job 40 of its size and strength, where it lived, and its manner of eating. The modern Hebrew word for the animal means "beast" or "cattle." In Lev. 11:2 the word translated "beasts" (KJV) is translated "animals" in the NIV. See *Hippopotamus; Leviathan.*

Excavated storerooms at the site of ancient Beer-sheba in the Negev.

BEKA or **BEKAH** One-half a shekel. The amount contributed by each Israelite male for the use of the temple (Exod. 38:26). See *Weights and Measures.*

BEKER (NIV) See *Becher.*

BEL (Bĕl) Name of Babylonian god, originally as city patron of Nippur but then as a second name for the high god Marduk of Babylon. Isaiah mocked Babylon by describing their gods burdening down donkeys in procession out of the city into captivity. People did not bow before them. The idols bowed down to get out of the city gates (Isa. 46:1). Similarly, Jeremiah prophesied shame coming on Bel (Jer. 50:2). Bel would have to spit out the nations he had swallowed up (Jer. 51:44). An apocryphal book is called Bel and the Dragon. See *Apocrypha; Babylon.*

BELA (Bē´ là) or **BELAH** Personal and place-name meaning "he swallowed." **1.** Name for Zoar. Its king joined coalition to fight off attacks from eastern kings (Gen. 14:2). See *Zoar.* **2.** King of Edom who ruled in city of Dinhabah before Israel had a king (Gen. 36:32). **3.** Son of Benjamin and grandson of Jacob (Gen. 46:21). He became original ancestor of clan of Belaites (Num. 26:38; 1 Chron. 7:7). **4.** Descendant of Reuben (1 Chron. 5:8).

BELAITES Descendants of Bela (Num. 26:38). See *Bela.*

BELIAL (Bē´ lĭ·àl) Transliteration of a Hebrew common noun meaning "useless" or "worthless." KJV interprets it as a proper name 16 times, but modern translations translate it as a common noun, "worthless" or "wicked." It is a term of derision (Deut. 13:13). In Nah. 1:15, where the KJV translates it as "the wicked," Belial appears to be the name of some specific malevolent power.

In the NT the word occurs one time (2 Cor. 6:15), where Paul the apostle declared the mutual irreconcilability of Christ and Belial, who thus appears to be equated with Satan. See *Antichrist; Satan.*

BELIEF, BELIEVE See *Faith.*

BELL Golden object fastened to the garments of the high priest that served as a signal or warning of the high priest's movements (Exod. 28:33-35; 39:25-26).

BELLOWS Instrument that blows air on a fire, making it burn hotter. The term is used only in Jer. 6:29. God appointed Jeremiah as the assayer of His people to test their purity. God's people remained like impure metal despite the fact that the bellows had blown fiercely on the fire, making it hot enough to consume lead. The refining process was in vain; the wicked remained; the people were like refuse silver. The idea of a bellows is alluded to elsewhere (Job 20:26; 41:21; Isa. 54:16; Ezek. 22:20-21). See *Assayer.*

BELOVED DISCIPLE Abbreviated expression used to refer to a disciple for whom Jesus had deep feelings. He has been variously identified as Lazarus, an anonymous source or author of the Gospel, an idealized disciple, or John's reference to himself without using his own name. Church tradition and interpretation of biblical evidence appear to point to John. Modestly he declined to put his name on his literary works. For this reason the one-time "son of thunder" referred to himself as the other disciple whom Jesus loved (John 20:2; 21:7 HCSB). See *John.*

Lawson G. Hatfield

BELSHAZZAR (Bĕl·shăz´ zàr) Name meaning "Bel's prince." Babylonian king whose drunken feast was interrupted by the mysterious appearance of the fingers of a human hand that wrote a cryptic message on the palace wall (Dan. 5:1). When the Babylonian seers were unable to interpret the writing, Daniel the Hebrew was called. He interpreted the message for the king, explaining that it meant the kingdom would be taken from Belshazzar and given to the Medes and Persians (Dan. 5:28). According to Dan. 5:30, Belshazzar was slain on the very night of this incident. See *Babylon.*

BELTESHAZZAR (Bĕl·tĕ·shăz´ zàr) Babylonian name meaning "protect the king's life." Name the prince of eunuchs under Nebuchadnezzar, king of Babylon, gave to Daniel (Dan. 1:7). See *Daniel.*

BEN (Bĕn) Hebrew noun meaning "son of." A Levite who became head of a clan of temple porters under David (1 Chron. 15:18 NASB, KJV). Other translations follow the Septuagint or earliest Greek translation and some Hebrew manuscripts that omit Ben. See *Bar.*

BEN-ABINADAB (Běn-à·bǐn´ à·dăb) Personal name meaning "son of Abinadab." The district supervisor over Dor in charge of provisions for Solomon's court one month a year. He married Solomon's daughter, Taphath (1 Kings 4:11). KJV reads "son of Abinadab."

BENAIAH (Bē·nī´ ah) Personal name meaning "Yahweh has built." **1.** Captain of David's professional soldiers (2 Sam. 8:18; 20:23), known for heroic feats such as disarming an Egyptian and killing him with his own sword as well as killing a lion in the snow (2 Sam. 23:20-23). Still he was not among the top three military advisors of David (2 Sam. 20:23). His unquestioned loyalty to David led Adonijah not to include him as he attempted to replace David as king instead of Solomon (1 Kings 1:8-26). He followed David's orders and helped anoint Solomon as king (1 Kings 1:32-47). He became Solomon's executioner (1 Kings 2:25-46) and army commander (1 Kings 4:4). **2.** A Pirathonite who is listed among the 30 elite warriors of David (2 Sam. 23:30). **3.** In 1 Chron. 4:36 a Simeonite prince who was involved in a defeat of the Amalekites. **4.** In 1 Chron. 15:18 a Levitical musician involved in the processional when the ark of the covenant was brought to Jerusalem. **5.** In 1 Chron. 15:24 a priest who sounded a trumpet when the ark was brought to Jerusalem. **6.** In 2 Chron. 20:14 an Asaphite, the grandfather of Jahaziel. **7.** In 2 Chron. 31:13 one of the overseers who assisted in the collection of contributions in the house of the Lord during the reign of Hezekiah. **8.** In Ezek. 11:1 the father of Pelatiah. **9.** In Ezra 10 the name of four Israelite men who put away their foreign wives.

BEN-AMMI (Běn-ăm´ mī) Personal name meaning "son of my people." Son of Lot and his younger daughter after his two daughters despaired of marriage and tricked their father after getting him drunk (Gen. 19:38). Ben-ammi was the original ancestor of the Ammonites. See *Ammon.*

BENCHES KJV translation for the planks of a ship's deck (Ezek. 27:6). Modern translations give the wood of the deck variously: boxwood (NASB), pine (NRSV, TEV), or cypress (NIV, REB). These translations understand the deck to be inlaid with ivory rather than made of ivory as the KJV suggests.

BEN-DEKER (Běn-dē´ kĕr) Personal name meaning "son of Deker" or "son of bored through." Solomon's district supervisor in charge of supplying the royal court for one month a year. His district bordered the Philistine territory on the west, reached to Aphek in the north, and to Beth-shemesh in the south (1 Kings 4:9).

BENE-BERAK (Běn·à-bà·räk´) Place-name meaning "sons of Barak" or "sons of lightning." City of tribe of Dan (Josh. 19:45). It is located at modern Ibn Ibraq, four miles southeast of Joppa. Sennacherib, king of Assyria, in 701 B.C. claims he conquered Bene-berak.

BENEDICTION Prayer for God's blessing or an affirmation that God's blessing is at hand. The most famous is the priestly benediction (or Aaronic blessing) in Num. 6:24-25. Most NT epistles close with benedictions as well (Rom. 15:13; 16:25-27; 1 Cor. 16:23; 2 Cor. 13:14; Gal. 6:18; Eph. 3:20-21; 6:23-24; Phil. 4:23; 1 Thess. 5:28; 2 Thess. 3:18; 1 Tim. 6:21b; 2 Tim. 4:22; Titus 3:15b; Philem. 25; Heb. 13:20-21,25; 1 Pet. 5:14b; 2 Pet. 3:18; 3 John 15a; Jude 24-25). See *Blessing and Cursing.*

BENEDICTUS Latin word meaning "blessed." The first word in Latin of Zacharias' psalm of praise in Luke 1:68-79 and thus the title of the psalm. See *Magnificat; Nunc Dimittis.*

BENEFACTORS Honorary title bestowed on kings or other prominent people for some meritorious achievement or public service. The title in Greek is *Euergetes* and was held by some of the Hellenistic kings of Egypt. One would not earn the title "benefactor" from service rendered in the kingdom of God. In contrast to the conspicuous work needed to earn the title "benefactor," the members of the kingdom are to devote themselves to humble, obscure, and perhaps menial service (Luke 22:24-27).

BENE-JAAKAN (Běn´ à-jā´ à·kan) Place-name meaning "sons of Jaakan." Same as Beeroth-bene-jaakan. See *Beeroth-bene-jaakan.*

BEN-GEBER (Běn-gē´ bĕr) Personal name meaning "son of Geber" or "son of a hero." Solomon's district supervisor in the towns northeast of the Jordan River around Ramoth-gilead (1 Kings 4:13). He provided supplies for the royal court one month a year. KJV reads "son of Geber."

BEN-HADAD (Bĕn-hā´ dăd) Personal name or royal title meaning "son of (the god) Hadad." References to Israel's interaction with Damascus and other city-states in Syria show the power of the kings of Damascus. The kings either bore a title, "ben-hadad," son of the God, much like Israel's kings seem to have been called "son of God" at their coronation (Ps. 2:7) and as emperors of Rome were called caesars, or Ben-hadad was the personal name of several kings. See *Damascus; Syria.*

BEN-HAIL (Bĕn-hā´ ĭl) Personal name meaning "son of strength." Official under King Jehoshaphat of Judah (873–848 B.C.), who sent him to help teach God's law in the cities of Judah (2 Chron. 17:7).

BEN-HANAN (Bĕn-hā´ năn) Personal name meaning "son of the gracious one." Son of Shimon in lineage of Judah (1 Chron. 4:20).

BEN-HESED (Bĕn-hē´ sĕd) Personal name meaning "son of mercy." Solomon's district supervisor over the Mediterranean coastal region between Aphek on the south and Hepher. He supplied the royal court one month a year (1 Kings 4:10).

BEN-HINNOM (Bĕn-hĭn´ nŏm) Place-name meaning "son of Hinnom." A valley south of Jerusalem serving as northern border of tribe of Judah (Josh. 15:8) and southern boundary of tribe of Benjamin (Josh. 18:16). Pagan child sacrifices occurred here, some kings of Judah included (Ahaz, 2 Chron. 28:3; Manasseh, 2 Chron. 33:6). Jeremiah announced God's judgment on the valley because of such practices (Jer. 19:1-15). The valley would be renamed "valley of slaughter" (Jer. 19:6). The sin of the valley gave God reason to bring the Babylonians to destroy Jerusalem (Jer. 32:35). King Josiah defiled and did away with the altars there (2 Kings 23:10). The valley served as the northern boundary of the Judean villages where the returning exiles settled (Neh. 11:30).

BEN-HUR (Bĕn-hûr) Personal name meaning "son of a camel" or "son of Horus." Solomon's

district supervisor over Mount Ephraim in charge of supplying the royal court one month a year (1 Kings 4:8).

BENINU (Bē·nī´ nū) Personal name meaning "our son." A Levite who sealed the covenant Nehemiah made to obey God's law (Neh. 10:13).

BENJAMIN (Bĕn´ jȧ mĭn) Personal name meaning "son of the right hand" or "son of the south." The second son Rachel bore to Jacob (Gen. 35:17-18). He became the forefather of the tribe of Benjamin. His birth was difficult, and his mother named him Ben-oni, which means "son of my sorrow." She died giving him birth. His father Jacob, however, did not let that name stand. He gave the child the name Benjamin.

The tribe of Benjamin occupied the smallest territory of all the tribes. Yet it played a significant role in Israelite history. Saul, Israel's first king, was a Benjamite. Furthermore, the city of Jerusalem was near the border between the territories of Benjamin and Judah and may have been in Benjamin originally (Josh. 18:16; Judg. 1:21). Benjamin's appetite for territory may be seen in Jacob's blessing (Gen. 49:27). Moses' blessing highlights Benjamin's special place in God's care (Deut. 33:12). Late in the period of the judges Benjamin almost disappeared from history when they mistreated a Levite and his concubine (Judg. 19–21).

In the NT the Apostle Paul proudly proclaimed his heritage in the tribe of Benjamin (Rom. 11:1; Phil. 3:5). See *Patriarchs; Tribes of Israel.*

BENJAMIN GATE Jerusalem gate (Jer. 37:13; 38:7). Identified by some with Nehemiah's Sheep Gate or with the Muster Gate, it could indicate a gate that led to tribal territory of Benjamin. See *Jerusalem.*

BENO (Bē´ nō) Proper name meaning "his son." A Levite under David (1 Chron. 24:26-27).

BEN-ONI (Bĕn ō´ nī) Personal name meaning "son of my sorrow." See *Benjamin.*

BEN-ZOHETH (Bĕn-zō´ hĕth) Personal name meaning "son of Zoheth." Son of Ishi in the tribe of Judah (1 Chron. 4:20).

BEON (Bē´ ŏn) Place-name of uncertain meaning. Probably a copyist's change from original Meon (Num. 32:3), a short form of Beth-meon or Beth-baal-meon. See *Beth-baal-meon.*

BEOR (Bē´ ôr) Proper name meaning "burning." **1.** Father of Bela, king of Edom centered in Dinhabah, before Israel had a king (Gen. 36:32). **2.** Father of prophet Balaam (Num. 22:5). See *Balaam.*

BERA (Bē´ rà) Personal name, perhaps meaning "with evil" or "victory." King of Sodom in days of Abraham and Lot (Gen. 14:2). He joined coalition of local kings against group of invading eastern kings.

BERACAH (Bĕr´ à·kăh) or **BERACHAH** (KJV) Personal name meaning "blessing." **1.** Skilled soldier able to use right or left hand with slingshot and with bow and arrows. He joined David's band in Ziklag, when David fled from Saul and joined the Philistines (1 Chron. 12:3). **2.** Valley where King Jehoshaphat of Judah (873–848 B.C.) and his people blessed God after He provided miraculous victory over Ammon, Moab, and Edom (2 Chron. 20:26). A valley near Tekoa and a modern village retain the name: Wadi Berekut and Khirbet Berekut.

BERACHIAH (Bĕr·à·kī´ ăh) (KJV, 1 Chron. 6:39) See *Berechiah.*

BERAIAH (Bà·raî´ ăh) Personal name meaning "Yahweh created." A descendant of the tribe of Benjamin (1 Chron. 8:21).

BERAKIAH (Bĕr·à·kī´ ah) (NIV, Matt. 23:35) See *Berechiah.*

BEREA (Bà·rē´ à) Place-name meaning "place of many waters." City in Macedonia to which Paul escaped after the Jews of Thessalonica rioted (Acts 17:10). See *Macedonia.*

BERECHIAH (Bĕr·ĕ·kī´ ăh) Personal name meaning "Yahweh blessed." **1.** Descendant of David in period after Jews returned from exile in Babylon (1 Chron. 3:20). **2.** Father of Asaph (1 Chron. 6:39). See *Asaph.* **3.** Leader of the Levites after the return from exile who lived around the city of Netophah (1 Chron. 9:16). **4.** Levite in charge of the ark when David moved it to Jerusalem (1 Chron. 15:23). He

could be identical with 2. above. **5.** Leader of the tribe of Ephraim who rescued prisoners of war that Pekah, king of Israel (752–732 B.C.), had taken from Ahaz, king of Judah (735–715) (2 Chron. 28:12). **6.** Father of Meshullam, who repaired the wall with Nehemiah (Neh. 3:4). His family was tied in marriage to Tobiah, Nehemiah's enemy (Neh. 6:17-19). **7.** Father of the prophet Zechariah (Zech. 1:1; Matt. 23:35).

BERED (Bē´ rĕd) Personal name meaning "cool." **1.** Place used to locate Beer-lahai-roi (Gen. 16:14) but a place that cannot be located today. **2.** Son of Ephraim (1 Chron. 7:20). Numbers 26:35 spells the name "Becher."

BERI (Bē´ rī) Personal name of unknown meaning. A descendant of Asher (1 Chron. 7:36). Many Bible students think a copyist has changed original text that may have read *bene* (sons of).

BERIAH (Bà·rī´ ăh) Personal name meaning "Yahweh created." **1.** Son of Asher and grandson of Jacob (Gen. 46:17). He thus became original ancestor of clan of Beriites (Num. 26:44). **2.** Son of Ephraim born after his sons Ezer and Elead died in battle against Gath. Beriah's name is explained here not as a compound of *bara'* + *Yah (Yahweh created)* but as a compound of *b* + *ra'ah (with evil)*. His daughters built the two cities named Beth-horon (1 Chron. 7:20 25). **3.** Clan leader of the tribe of Benjamin in the area of Aijalon. He helped drive out the inhabitants of Gath (1 Chron. 8:13). **4.** Levite under King David (1 Chron. 23:10).

BERIITE (Bà·rī´ īt) Member of clan descended from Beriah. See *Beriah.*

BERITE (Bē´ rīt) Word of unknown meaning (2 Sam. 20:14). Some Bible students think original text read Bichrites, referring to clan to which Sheba, son of Bichri belonged (2 Sam. 20:13; see TEV, NRSV). Some would identify the Berites as residents of a town called Biria in northern Palestine.

BERITH (Bē´ rīth) Hebrew word meaning "covenant." See *Baal-berith; Covenant.*

BERNICE (Bĕr nēs´) Name meaning "gift." Companion of Herod Agrippa II (Acts 25:13). She was the daughter of Herod Agrippa I, born probably about A.D. 28. Prior to her appearance in Acts, she had been married first to a person named Marcus, then to her own uncle, Herod. Two sons were born as a result of the latter union before Bernice was widowed in A.D. 48. In the following years an incestuous relationship is suggested between Agrippa II and her. Later she was married again, to Polemo, the king of Cilicia. According to the Roman historian Tacitus, she was also the mistress of the Roman emperor Titus. See *Herod*.

BERODACH-BALADAN (Bə·rō´ dăk-băl´ ȧ·dăn) King of Babylon who wrote Hezekiah, king of Judah (2 Kings 20:12). Parallel passage in Isa. 39:1 reads Merodoch-baladan, so most Bible students think Berodach resulted from a copyist's change in the text (cp. NIV, TEV, NRSV). See *Merodach-baladan*.

BEROEA (Bə·rē´ ȧ) (NRSV) See *Berea*.

BEROTHAH (Bə·rō´ thäh) Place-name meaning "wells." Northern border town in Ezekiel's vision of restored promised land (Ezek. 47:16). It may be located east of the Jordan River about seven miles south of Baalbeck at Bereiten. See *Berothai*.

BEROTHAI (Bē·rō´ thī) Place-name meaning "wells." City in Syria from which David took brass as tribute after he defeated King Hadadezer (2 Sam. 8:8). The parallel passage (1 Chron. 18:8) reads Chun or Cun and says Solomon used the brass for temple vessels. The exact relationship of Berothah, Berothai, and Cun cannot be determined. The three are usually identified as the same place, but some Bible students dispute this. At the date when Chronicles was written, Cun may have been better known than nearby Berothai. See *Cun*.

BEROTHITE (Bē´ rŏth-īt) Person from Beeroth (1 Chron. 11:39). See *Beeroth*.

BERYL Light-green precious stone closely related to emeralds and aquamarines. See *Jewels, Jewelry; Minerals and Metals*.

BESAI (Bē´ sī) Personal name of unknown meaning. A clan of temple employees who returned from exile in Babylon with Zerubbabel about 537 B.C. (Ezra 2:49).

BESODEIAH (Bĕs-ō-dī´ ah) Personal name meaning "in Yahweh's counsel." Father of Meshullam, who helped Nehemiah repair the gate of Jerusalem (Neh. 3:6).

BESOM Broom made of twigs (KJV, Isa. 14:23).

BESOR (Bē´ sôr) Place-name, perhaps meaning "wadi of the good news." Brook where David left 200 weary soldiers while he and the remaining 400 pursued the Amalekites after they had burned Ziklag and captured David's wives (1 Sam. 30:9-10). David rewarded those who stayed as well as those who fought (1 Sam. 30:21-24). The Besor is probably Wadi Ghazzeh about 15 miles south of Ziklag.

BESTIALITY Sexual intercourse between a human and an animal, punishable by death in OT legal codes (Exod. 22:19; Lev. 18:23; 20:15-16; Deut. 27:21). Israel's neighbors practiced bestiality in fertility worship and worship of animal gods.

BETAH (Bē´ täh) Place-name meaning "security." City from which King David took brass after defeating King Hadadezer (2 Sam. 8:8). First Chronicles 18:8 lists Betah as Tibhath. NIV reads Tebah in 2 Sam. 8:8. See *Berothai; Tibhath*.

BETEN (Bē´ tĕn) Place-name meaning "womb." Border town of tribe of Asher (Josh 19:25). It may be located at Khirbet Abtun, 11 miles south of Acco.

BETH-ABARA (Bĕth-ăb´ ȧ-rȧ) Place-name meaning "house of crossing." KJV reading for Bethany in John 1:28 following some Greek manuscripts. See *Bethany*.

BETH-ANATH (Bĕth-ā´ năth) Place-name meaning "house of Anath." A fortified city in the territory of the tribe of Naphtali (Josh. 19:38). The tribe could not drive out the Canaanites from the city (Judg. 1:33). Beth-anath was apparently a worship center for the Canaanite goddess Anath. It may have been located at modern Safed el-Battik, 15 miles east of Tyre.

BETH-ANOTH (Bĕth-ā´ nŏth) Place-name meaning "house of Anath" or "house of being heard." A city of Judah (Josh. 15:59), a temple to the Canaanite goddess Anath may have been here. The modern location may be Khirbet Beit Ainur, one and a half miles southeast of Halhul.

BETHANY (Bĕth´ ȧ nē) Known primarily in the Gospels as the home of Mary, Martha, and Lazarus. Ancient Bethany occupied an important place in the life of Jesus. Jesus often found Himself staying in Bethany at the home of his closest friends as He ministered in Jerusalem.

Located on the Mount of Olives' eastern slope, Bethany sat "about two miles" (John 11:18 HCSB) southeast of Jerusalem. Bethany became the final stop before Jerusalem just off the main east-west road coming from Jericho. Being at the foot of the mountain, the people could not see Jerusalem, thus giving Bethany a sense of seclusion and quietness. The road between Bethany and Jerusalem provided a ready avenue for travel across Olivet with the journey taking about 55 minutes to walk.

The primary event in the NT taking place in Bethany involved the raising of Lazarus from the dead (John 11-12). This magnificent miracle by Jesus demonstrated His authority, prepared for His resurrection, and was even magnified through the name of His friend, Lazarus (an abbreviation of Eleazar, "God has helped").

Another significant event in Jesus' life occurred in Bethany at the home of Simon the Leper (Matt. 26:6; Mark 14:3). Late on the Tuesday night of Jesus' last week, a woman (recognized as Mary in John 12:3) gave Jesus His "burial anointing." Coming to Jesus in the sight of all, she brought a costly alabaster vial of perfume and emptied its contents upon Jesus' head ("feet" in John 12:3).

Besides a number of smaller references to Bethany, one final event took place there.

View of the ancient city of Bethany, the hometown of Mary, Martha, and Lazarus.

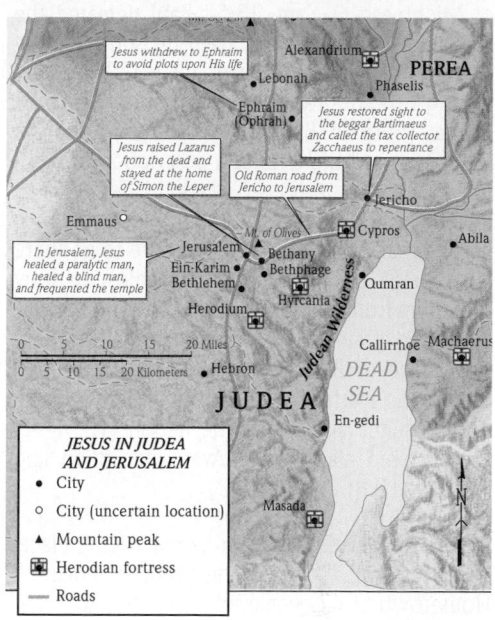

Bethany provided the location for Jesus' final blessing to His disciples and His subsequent parting. This encounter made up the final scene of ascension in Luke's Gospel (24:50-53).

Larry McGraw

BETH-ARABAH (Bĕth-är´ ȧ-băh) Place-name meaning "house of the desert." A border town of tribe of Judah (Josh. 15:6,61) also claimed as a city of Benjamin (Josh. 18:22). It may be modern Ain el-Gharbah southeast of Jericho.

BETH-ARAM (KJV) See *Beth-haram*.

BETH-ARBEL (Bĕth-är´ bĕl) Place-name meaning "house of Arbel." Site of infamous battle that Hosea could use as example of what would happen to Israel (Hos. 10:14). The battle is unknown to us. The site may be Irbid in Gilead, four miles northwest of Tiberias. See *Shalman*.

BETH-ASHBEA (Bĕth-ăsh´ bə-ȧ) Place of unknown location in Judah known for clans of linen workers, thus giving evidence of craft guilds in Israel (1 Chron. 4:21).

BETH-AVEN (Bĕth-ā´ vĕn) Place-name meaning "house of deception" or "of idolatry." **1.** City near Ai east of Bethel (Josh. 7:2). It formed a border of Benjamin (Josh. 18:12) and was west of Michmash (1 Sam. 13:5). Saul defeated the Philistines here after God used his son Jonathan to start the victory (1 Sam. 14:23). The exact location is not known. Suggestions include Burqa, south of Bethel; Tell Maryam; and Ai. **2.** Hosea used the term as a description of Bethel. Instead of a house of God, Beth-el had become a house of deception and idolatry. Thus he commanded worshipers to refuse to go there (Hos. 4:15), to prepare for battle against an army marching from the south against Benjamin (5:8), and to be afraid of the golden calves in the worship place of Beth-el, not because they represented the fearful presence of God but because they brought disaster on the nation (10:5). All the worship places were Aven, deception and idolatry (10:8).

BETH-AZMAVETH (Bĕth-az·mā´ vĕth) Place-name meaning "house of the strength of death." Hometown of 42 people who returned to Palestine with Zerubbabel from exile in Babylon about 537 B.C. (Neh. 7:28). Ezra 2:24 calls the town Azmaveth. It may be modern Hizmeh about two miles north of Anathoth.

BETH-BAAL-MEON (Bĕth-bā´ ál-mē´ ŏn) Place-name meaning "house of Baal's residence." City allotted tribe of Reuben (Josh. 13:17). Same as Baal-meon. See *Baal-meon.*

BETH-BARAH (Bĕth-bâr·ah) Place-name meaning "house of God." A ford over the Jordan River and/or the village there if text of Judg. 7:24 is correct. Many Bible scholars think copyists have changed the original text, introducing a place-name not in the text.

BETH-BIREI (Bĕth-bir´ ə·ī) (KJV) or **BETH-BIRI** (Bĕth-bir´ ī) Place-name meaning "house of my creation." Town allotted tribe of Simeon (1 Chron. 4:31). It is apparently the same as Lebaoth (Josh. 15:32) and Beth-lebaoth (Josh. 19:6). The location is uncertain.

BETH-CAR (Bĕth´ cär) Place-name meaning "house of sheep." Final site of battle where God thundered from heaven to defeat the Philistines for Samuel (1 Sam. 7:11). The location is not known unless copyists changed an original Beth-horon, as some Bible students think.

BETH-DAGON (Bĕth-da´ gŏn) Place-name meaning "house of Dagon." Apparently the

name indicates a worship place of Philistine god Dagon. **1.** Town in tribal territory of Judah (Josh. 15:41). It is probably modern Khirbet Dajun on the road connecting Ramalleh and Joppa. **2.** Town in Asher (Josh. 19:27) without certain present location.

BETH-DIBLATHAIM (Bĕth-dĭb·là·thā´ ĭm) Place-name meaning "house of the two fig cakes." Town in Moab on which Jeremiah prophesied judgment (Jer. 48:22). About 830 B.C., Mesha, king of Moab, bragged that he built the city, as recorded on the Moabite Stone. It may be present-day Khirbet et-Tem. See *Almon-diblathaim.*

BETH-EDEN (Bĕth-ē´ dĕn) Place-name meaning "house of bliss." Amos announced God's threat to take the royal house out of Beth-eden or the "house of Eden" (KJV) (Amos 1:5). He was obviously referring to a place in Syria. Assyrian records refer to Bit-adini, a city-state between the Euphrates and Balik rivers, somewhat north of Syria proper. Ashurbanipal II conquered it in 856 B.C. An Assyrian representative bragged about conquering Beth-eden, urging Hezekiah to surrender about 701 B.C. (2 Kings 19:12). Ezekiel included Eden as one of the states who had traded with Tyre (Ezek. 27:23).

BETH-EKED (Bĕth-ē´ kəd) Place-name meaning "house of shearing" (KJV, "shearing house"). Place where Jehu, after slaughtering all members of King Ahab's house in Jezreel, met representatives from King Ahaziah of Judah and killed them (2 Kings 10:12-14). It is traditionally located at Beit Qad, four miles northeast of Jenin, but recent studies question this location. Whatever its location, it must have been a meeting place and perhaps a marketplace for shepherds.

BETHEL (Bĕth´ ĕl) Name meaning "house of God." **1.** Bethel was important in the OT for both geographic and religious reasons. Because of its abundant springs, the area was fertile and attractive to settlements as early as 3200 B.C., and first supported a city around the time of Abraham. Today the village of Beitin rests on much of the ruins of Bethel. Located at the intersection of the main north-south road through the hill country and the main road from Jericho to the coastal plain, Bethel saw much domestic and international travel. Bethel became a prominent border town between tribes and the two kingdoms later. Religiously, Bethel served as a sanctuary during the times of the patriarchs, judges, and the divided kingdom, hence was second only to Jerusalem as a religious center.

Entering Canaan, Abraham built an altar at Bethel, calling on "the name of the Lord" (Gen. 12:8), and returned here after his time in Egypt (Gen. 13:3). His grandson, Jacob, spent the night here on his way to Syria to find a wife. In a dream the Lord confirmed the Abrahamic covenant, and Jacob responded by renaming this locale, which was previously called Luz, "Bethel" ("house of God"; Gen. 28:10-22). Probably the name "Bethel" is referred to but out of chronological sequence in the earlier Abraham passages. When he returned with his large family, Jacob came to Bethel again to hear the Lord's confirmation of the covenant and his name was changed to "Israel." Here again Jacob set up a stone monument (Gen. 35:1-16; Hos. 12:4-5). Extensive fortification of Bethel came after this patriarchal period.

At the time of the conquest, Bethel and Ai were taken together (Josh. 7:2; 8:3-17; 12:9,16), but the definitive defeat of Bethel is recounted later in Judg. 1:22-26. It was a Benjamite border town initially (Josh. 16:1-2; 18:13,22). Later it was a part of the Northern Kingdom (1 Chron. 7:28), only briefly annexed to Judah by Abijah (2 Chron. 13:19).

The ark of the covenant was kept in Bethel during a period of the judges (Judg. 20:27), so the tribes converged there upon Benjamin to avenge the moral atrocity at Gibeah (Judg. 20:18-28), offering sacrifices and seeking the Lord's direction (Judg. 21:1-4). Bethel also was a place where both Deborah (Judg. 4:5) and Samuel (1 Sam. 7:16) judged the civil and religious affairs of the Israelites in the area. Bethel was evidently vulnerable at the time of the judges, since archaeology shows it to have been destroyed several times in this period.

David considered the city significant enough to send it gifts during his flight as a fugitive from Saul, hoping to establish a friendship of diplomatic value in the future (1 Sam. 30:27). When he eventually named Jerusalem his capital, Bethel grew and prospered.

Whereas Bethel had been a place of orthodox worship from Abraham to the judges, Jeroboam I made it a religious center of his innovative, apostate religion of the Northern Kingdom. He erected a golden calf both here and in Dan with non-Levitic priests and an illegitimate feast to compete with the celebrations and religion of Jerusalem, 10.5 miles to the south in Judah (1 Kings 12:29-33). Bethel was the prominent site over Dan. There an anonymous prophet from Judah found and rebuked Jeroboam I and brought destruction to the king's altar (1 Kings 13:1-10). Another anonymous prophet from Bethel entrapped the first prophet into disobedience. Because of his disobedience, the Lord caused a lion to kill the first prophet (1 Kings 13:11-25).

Other true prophets seem to have been attached to Bethel even during the time of northern apostasy, since Elijah encountered a group of them there as he traveled (2 Kings 2:2-3). Amos was sent to Bethel to rebuke the kingdom of Jeroboam II in the eighth century (Amos 7:10-13) since it was the center of northern idolatry and a royal residence. He met the resistance of Amaziah, the priest, who vainly ordered him to leave the city. In addition to Amos's prophetic charges against those who sacrificed there (Amos 4:4), he predicted the destruction of Bethel and its false altars (Amos 3:14, 5:5-6), as did Hosea (Hos. 10:14-15). Hosea seems to have played with the name of Bethel ("city of God"), by referring to it as "Beth-aven" ("city of a false [god]," Hos. 5:8-9; 10:5).

The religious significance of Bethel is confirmed also by Assyria's appointment of a priest to this city to teach the new residents of the north who displaced the Israelites (2 Kings 17:28). Later, Josiah desecrated another false altar of Bethel during his reforms (2 Kings 23:4-19) and perhaps annexed the city to his Southern Kingdom. Bethel was destroyed in the sixth century during the exile; however, some returned there when released by the Persians (Ezra 2:28; Neh. 7:32; 11:31). Since it was a late first-century Roman garrison town, it was probably a city of importance at the time of Christ.

2. Another city variously spelled Bethul (Josh. 19:4), Bethuel (1 Chron. 4:30), and Bethel (1 Sam. 30:27). This may be modern Khirbet el Qaryatein north of Arad. **3.** Bethel was apparently the name of a West Semitic god. Many scholars find reference to this deity in Jer. 48:13. Others would find the mention of the deity in other passages (especially Gen. 31:13; Amos 5:5).   *Daniel C. Fredericks*

BETHEL-SHAREZER See *Sharezer*.

BETHELITE (Bĕth´ el·īt) Resident of Bethel (1 Kings 16:34). See *Bethel*.

BETH-EMEK (Bĕth-ē´ mĕk) Place-name meaning "house of the valley." A border town in the tribal territory of Asher (Josh. 19:27). Located at modern Tel Mimas, six and a half miles northeast of Acco.

BETHER (Bē´ thĕr) Place-name meaning "division." A mountain range used as an emotional image in Song 2:17. NIV reads "rugged hills."

BETHESDA (Bē thĕs´ dà) Name of a pool in Jerusalem where Jesus healed a man who had been sick for 38 years (John 5:2). The name, appropriately, means "house of mercy." Most ancient manuscripts identify Bethesda as the place of the pool. Some ancient manuscripts name it Bethzatha or Bethsaida. The third edition of the *United Bible Societies Greek New Testament* places Bethzatha in the text and the other readings in footnotes. The waters of the pool were popularly believed to possess curative powers. Truly, the man who was healed after 38 years experienced the outpouring of God's mercy on the Sabbath. The references to the pool being stirred by angels (John 5:3b-4) are not found in either the oldest or the majority of manuscripts. However, regardless of the disagreement among manuscripts on the name of the pool or the angel passage, the pool did exist. Today this pool is identified with the series of pools found near the church of St. Anne. See *Healing, Divine*.

BETH-EZEL (Bĕth-ē´ zĕl) Proper name meaning "house of the leader" or "house at the side." City Micah used in a wordplay to announce judgment on Judah about 701 B.C. All support would be taken away from the house of the leader or the house beside (Mic. 1:11). The location may be Deir el-Asal two miles east of Tell Beit Mirsim.

BETH-GADER (Bĕth-gā´ der) City founded by or controlled by descendants of Hareph, a descendant of Caleb (1 Chron. 2:51). It is probably the same as Geder (Josh. 12:13), if that is the proper reading. Some students of Joshua suggest the original text read Gezer or Gerar.

BETH-GAMUL (Bĕth-gā´ mŭl) Place-name meaning "house of retaliation." City in Moab on which Jeremiah announced judgment (Jer. 48:23). Its location was modern Khirbet el-Jemeil about seven miles east of Dibon.

BETH-GILGAL (Bĕth-gĭl´ gäl) Place-name meaning "house of the wheel or circle." A village of Levitical singers near Jerusalem whose occupants participated in the dedication of the newly built city wall under Nehemiah (Neh. 12:29). It is probably the same as Gilgal. See *Gilgal*.

BETH-HACCEREM (Bĕth-hăk´ ē·rĕm) or **BETH-HACCHEREM** Place-name meaning "house of the vineyard." City used to signal that enemies approached from the north (Jer. 6:1). Its leading official helped Nehemiah repair the Dung Gate (Neh. 3:14). It is probably modern Ramat Rahel halfway between Jerusalem and Bethlehem. Archaeological excavations show it was founded about 800 B.C. It sits high on a hill surveying the surrounding countryside. One of the later kings of Judah built a grand palace there. Apparently Jehoiakim (609–597) built the palace, which fits the description of Jer. 22:13-

The Pool of Bethesda at Jerusalem, a spring-fed pool near the Sheep Gate where the sick used to come to receive healing. Jesus healed a man there who had been stricken with an unidentified infirmity for 38 years.

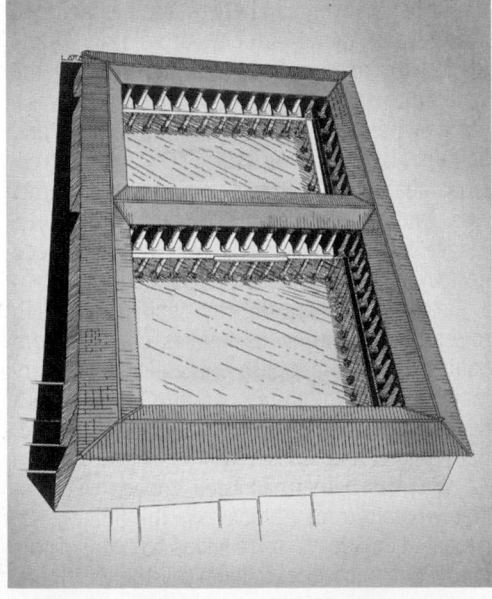

19. After the return from exile, it served as an administrative center.

BETH-HAGGAN (Bĕth-hăg´ găn) Place-name (NIV, TEV, NRSV) or common noun (KJV, NASB) meaning "house of the garden." King Ahaziah of Judah (841 B.C.) fled there from Jehu, but Jehu finally caught up and killed him (2 Kings 9:27). It is probably modern Jenin, southeast of Tanaach.

BETH-HANAN (Bĕth-hā´ năn) Place-name meaning "house of grace." A city in Solomon's second district (1 Kings 4:9 TEV). See *Elon.*

BETH-HARAM (Bĕth-hā´ răm) Place-name meaning "house of the exalted one" or "house of height" (KJV, Beth-aram). A city Moses allotted to the tribe of Gad (Josh. 13:27). It is probably Tell er-Rameh though others suggest Tell Iktanu. It is probably the same as Beth-haran. See *Beth-haran.*

BETH-HARAN (Bĕth-hā´ răn) Place-name meaning "house of height." Town east of the Jordan that the tribe of Gad strengthened after Moses gave it to them (Num. 32:36). It is probably the same as Beth-haram. See *Beth-haram.*

BETH-HOGLAH (Beth-hŏg´ lăh) Place-name meaning "house of the partridge." Border city between tribes of Judah and Benjamin (Josh. 15:6; 18:19,21). It is probably modern Ain Hajlah, four miles southeast of Jericho.

BETH-HORON (Bĕth-hō´ rŏn) Place-name of uncertain meaning. Suggestions include "house of caves," "house of anger," "house of the hollow," "house of (the god) Hauron." Twin cities, one higher than the other, were called Upper and Lower Beth-horon. An important road here dominates the path to the Shephelah, the plain between the Judean hills and the Mediterranean coast. Joshua used the road to chase the coalition of southern kings led by the king of Jerusalem (Josh. 10:10). Here God cast hailstones on the enemies. The border between the tribes of Ephraim and Benjamin was at Beth-horon (Josh. 16:3,5; 18:13-14). The city belonged to Ephraim but was set aside for the Levites (Josh. 21:22). The Philistines sent one unit of their army the way of Beth-horon to attack Saul and Jonathan (1 Sam. 13:18). Solomon rebuilt the lower city as a stone city

and as a defense outpost (1 Kings 9:17). The chronicler preserved an even earlier tradition of a descendant of Ephraim, a woman named Sheerah, building the two cities (1 Chron. 7:22-24). When King Amaziah of Judah (796–767 B.C.) followed a prophet's advice and sent home mercenary soldiers he had hired from Israel, those soldiers fought the cities of Judah, including Beth-horon (2 Chron. 25:13). Upper Beth-horon is modern Beit Ur el-Foqa, five miles northwest of Gibeon and 10 miles northwest of Jerusalem. It is 1,750 feet above sea level. Lower Beth-horon is two miles to the east and only 1,050 feet above sea level. It is modern Beit Ur et-Tahta.

BETH-JESHIMOTH (Bĕth-jĕsh´ ĭ-mŏth) or **BETH-JESIMOTH** (KJV) Place-name meaning "house of deserts." A town in Moab where Israel camped just before Moses died and Joshua led them across the Jordan (Num. 33:49). Joshua 12:3 lists it as land Israel took from Sihon, king of the Amorites. Moses gave it to the tribe of Reuben (Josh. 13:20). Ezekiel described it as one of three frontier cities of Moab, these being "the glory of the country" (Ezek. 25:9), but one facing God's judgment. It is usually located at modern Tell el-Azeme, 12 miles southeast of Jericho.

BETH-LE-APHRAH (Bĕth-lĕ-aph´ răh) Place-name meaning "place of dust." Town Micah used in a wordplay to announce judgment on Judah. The house of dust would roll in dust, a ritual expressing grief and mourning (Mic. 1:10). The location is uncertain, perhaps et-Taijibe between Beit Gibrin and Hebron. KJV reads "house of Aphrah"; NIV, "Beth Ophrah."

BETH-LEBAOTH (Bĕth-lĕb´ ā-ŏth) Place-name meaning "house of lionesses." City in territorial allotment of tribe of Simeon (Josh. 19:6). It is apparently the same as Lebaoth in Judah's inheritance (Josh. 15:32). This is called Beth-birei in the parallel passage (1 Chron. 4:31). Its location is not certain.

BETHLEHEM (Bĕth´ lə hĕm) Place-name meaning "house of bread," "fighting," or "Lahamu" [god]. **1.** Approximately five miles southwest of Jerusalem just off the major road from Jerusalem to the Negev lies the modern Arabic village Bethlehem. The popular understanding is that the name, *beth-lechem*, means "house of bread." Perhaps the first mention of

Traditional site of the manger of the infant Jesus, inside the Church of the Nativity in Bethlehem.

Small entrance to the Church of the Nativity in Bethlehem. Archway was filled to keep out horsemen.

the village occurred before 1300 B.C. in the Amarna letters (No. 290) where the ruler of Jerusalem complained to the Egyptian pharaoh that the people of *Bit-Lahmi* had gone over to the side of the "Apiru," apparently a people without local citizenship who caused disturbances in Canaanite society.

In the OT the parenthetical reference to Bethlehem in Gen. 35:19 is perhaps derived from a traditional burial site for Rachel near the village. Bethlehem appears in Judg. 17:7-13 as the home of the Levite who became priest to Micah. The concubine of the Levite of Ephraim

was from the village of Bethlehem (Judg. 19). The book of Ruth takes place in the region of Bethlehem (Ruth 1:1-2,19,22; 2:4; 4:11). This story leads to the events that gave major importance to the village as the home and place of anointing of David (1 Sam. 16:1-13; 17:12,15).

Other OT references to the village include the mention of a Philistine garrison being there during David's early kingship (2 Sam. 23:14), Elhanan's home (2 Sam. 23:24), the burial place of Asahel (2 Sam. 2:32), and a fort of Rehoboam (2 Chron. 11:6). Bethlehem is also mentioned

View of Bethlehem with Herodium in the background.

Stained glass window depicting the nativity scene at the Church of the Nativity in Bethlehem.

with reference to the Babylonian exile (Jer. 41:17; Ezra 2:21).

It is the relationship of Bethlehem to Christ that has ensured its place in Christian history. Micah 5:2 was understood to indicate that the Messiah, like David, would be born in Bethlehem not Jerusalem. Matthew (2:1-12), Luke (2:4-20), and John (7:42) report that Jesus was born in that humble village. It appears that early Christians believed that some caves east of the village were the holy site of the birth. A field southeast of town has been identified as the place where the shepherds had the vision of the angels. **2.** Town in the territory of Zebulun, about seven miles northwest of Nazareth (Josh. 19:15), which was the burial site of Ibzan (Judg. 12:10), in modern Beit Lahm. **3.** Personal name as in 1 Chron. 2:51,54.   *George W. Knight*

BETHLEHEM-EPHRATAH (KJV) or **BETHLE-HEM-EPHRATHAH** (NASB, NIV, NRSV) Place-name used by Mic. 5:2 to designate birthplace of new David who would come from Bethlehem, David's birthplace, and of the clan of Ephrathah, that of Jesse, David's father (1 Sam. 17:12). See *Bethlehem.*

BETHLEHEMITE Citizen of Bethlehem. See *Bethlehem.*

BETH-MAACAH (Bĕth-mā´ à·cäh) (NASB, NRSV) or **BETH-MAACHAH** (KJV) Place-name meaning "house of Maacah" or "house of pressure." Usually appears as Abel Beth-Maacah (always so in NIV). Beth-Maacah apparently appears as final stop on Sheba's trip through Israel to gain support against David (2 Sam. 20:14). See *Abel-Beth-Maacah.*

BETH-MARCABOTH (Bĕth-mär´ cà·bŏth) Place-name meaning "house of chariots." City allotted to tribe of Simeon (Josh. 19:5). Its location is uncertain.

BETH-MEON (Bĕth-mē´ ŏn) Place-name meaning "house of residence." City in Moab on which Jeremiah pronounced judgment (Jer. 48:23). Apparently the same as Beth-baal-meon and Baal-meon. See *Beth-baal-meon; Baal-meon.*

BETH-MILLO (Bĕth-mîl´ lō) Place-name meaning "house of fulness." **1.** Part of Shechem or a fortress guarding Shechem, where the citizens of Shechem proclaimed Abimelech king. Jotham, Jerubbaal's (or Gideon's) son asked citizens to overthrow Abimelech at Beth-millo (Judg. 9:6,20). **2.** Fortification in Jerusalem where two of his servants killed King Joash (835-796 B.C.; 2 Kings 12:19-20). It is also called "Millo." See *Jerusalem; Millo; Shechem.*

BETH-NIMRAH (Beth-nĭm´ räh) Place-name meaning "house of the panther." City east of the Jordan that tribe of Gad rebuilt after Moses allotted it to them (Num. 32:36). It provided good grazing land (Num. 32:3). It is located at either Tell Nimrin or nearby at Tell el-Bleibil, about 10 miles northeast of the mouth of the Jordan.

BETH-OPHRAH (Bĕth-ōph´ räh) (NIV) See *Beth-le-aphrah.*

BETH-PALET (Bĕth-pā´ lĕt) (KJV, Josh. 15:27) See *Beth-pelet.*

BETH-PAZZEZ (Bĕth-păz´ zĕz) Place-name meaning "house of scattering." Town in tribal allotment of Issachar (Josh. 19:22). It may be modern Kerm el-Hadetheh.

BETH-PELET (Bĕth-pē´ lĕt) Place-name meaning "house of deliverance." Southern town in tribal allotment of Judah (Josh. 15:27). After the return from exile in Babylon, the Jews lived there (Neh. 11:26). KJV spellings are Beth-palet and Beth-phelet. The location is not known.

BETH-PEOR (Bĕth-pē´ ôr) Place-name meaning "house of Peor." A temple for the god Peor or Baal Peor probably stood there. Town in whose valley Israel camped as Moses delivered the sermons of the book of Deuteronomy (Deut.

3:29). It had belonged to Sihon, king of the Amorites (Deut. 4:46). Moses died and was buried near there (Deut. 34:6). It belonged to tribe of Reuben (Josh. 13:20). It was located at modern Khirbet Uyun Musa, 20 miles east of the north end of the Dead Sea. Numbers does not use the place name, but evidently at least part of the shameful worship of Baal Peor (Num. 25:1-5) occurred at Beth-peor. Hosea described the actions of Peor as a turning point in Israel's blissful honeymoon with God (Hos. 9:10). See *Baal-peor; Peor.*

BETHPHAGE (Bĕth´ phȧ·ġē) Place-name meaning "house of unripe figs." A small village located on the Mount of Olives near Bethany on or near the road between Jerusalem and Jericho. Reference is made to the village in each of the Synoptic Gospels (Matt. 21:1; Mark 11:1; Luke 19:29). In each account Bethphage was where Jesus gave instruction to two disciples to find the colt on which he would ride into Jerusalem for His triumphal entry. This may also be the place where the fig tree was cursed (Matt. 21:18-22; Mark 11:12-14,20-26). Today one may still find rolling stone tombs in Bethphage, such as our Lord was buried in. See *Olives, Mount of; Triumphal Entry.* *William H. Vermillion*

BETH-PHELET (Bĕth-phē´ lĕt) See *Beth-pelet.*

BETH-RAPHA (Bĕth-rā´ phȧ) Place-name meaning "house of a giant." First Chronicles 4:12 says the otherwise unknown Eshton "became the father of Beth-rapha" (NASB). This apparently describes the beginning of a clan who lived at the town whose name is not known. The name could have distant relationships to the Rephaim (Deut. 3:11), though the Bible nowhere makes such relationships.

BETH-REHOB (Bĕth-rē´ hŏb) Place-name meaning "house of the market." Town near where tribe of Dan rebuilt Laish and renamed it Dan (Judg. 18:28). Rehob was the father of Hadadezer, the Syrian king of Zobah (2 Sam. 8:3). Beth-rehob may have been their hometown. When the Ammonites made David angry by humiliating his officials, Ammon sent to Beth-rehob for Syrian soldiers, evidently indicating that Syria controlled the city. The town lay at the southern foot of Mount Hermon. See *Rehob.*

BETHSAIDA (Bĕth sā´ ĭ dȧ) Place-name meaning "house of fish." The home of Andrew, Peter, and Philip (John 1:44; 12:21), located on the northeast side of the Sea of Galilee. This town was rebuilt under Philip the tetrarch, one of the sons of Herod the Great, who named it Julius in honor of the Emperor Augustus' daughter. Near here Jesus fed the 5,000 (Luke 9:10) and healed a blind man (Mark 8:22). Jesus pronounced judgment upon Bethsaida for its lack of response to His message and miracles (Matt. 11:21; Luke 10:13). The site of Bethsaida has yet to be identified archaeologically. Some scholars do propose two sites named Bethsaida: the one northeast of the Sea of Galilee, as already discussed; and another, west of the Sea of Galilee, close to Capernaum. This postulation is based on Mark 6:45, where following the feeding of the 5,000 outside Bethsaida, Jesus tells His disciples to sail to Bethsaida. However, there is no contemporary mention of two Bethsaidas, and the Mark 6 text can just as easily refer to a short trip to the known city of Bethsaida-Julias as to an unknown town. *William H. Vermillion*

BETH-SHAN, BETHSHAN (Bĕth-Shän), or **BETH-SHEAN** (Bĕth-shē´ ȧn) Place-name meaning "house of quiet." Beth-shean stood at the crossroad of the Jezreel and Jordan Valleys, commanding the routes north-south along the Jordan and east-west from Gilead to the Mediterranean Sea. Tell el-Husn, site of ancient Beth-shean, stands above the perennial stream of Harod, the city's primary water supply, giving the city a commanding view of the two valleys.

The University of Pennsylvania in several campaigns from 1921 to 1933 carried on excavation of Tell el-Husn and its surroundings. Settlements at Beth-shean were found to date back to the Neolithic and Chalcolithic periods. The city became an important Canaanite site in the early and middle Bronze Ages (3300–1500 B.C.) but came under the domination of Egypt's 18th dynasty in the late Bronze Age. The name Beth-shean (or -shan) is mentioned in the Egyptian texts of Thutmose III (1468 B.C.), the Amarna letters (1350 B.C.), Seti I (1300 B.C.), Rameses II (1280 B.C.), and Shishak (925 B.C.). Excavations have confirmed the Egyptian role in the life of Beth-shean in these periods (for example, through the discovery of scarabs and a cartouche bearing the name Thutmose III).

Biblical references to Beth-shean relate to the period from Joshua until the United Monarchy. The city is listed among the allocations of the tribe of Manasseh, though the city was within the territory of Issachar (Josh. 17:11). Yet Manasseh was unable to control Beth-shean until the Canaanites were subdued in the reign of David (Josh. 17:16; Judg. 1:27). After the defeat of Saul and the Israelite army by the Philistines (ca. 1006 B.C.), the bodies of Saul and his sons were hung on the walls of Beth-shean, where a temple to the Ashtaroth was located. Some valiant men from Jabesh-gilead rescued the bodies from this sacrilege and disposed of them in Jabesh (1 Sam. 31). Later David's men brought the bodies to the land of Benjamin to be buried (2 Sam. 21:12-14). The city is listed among those under the administration of Baana (fifth district) during Solomon's reign (1 Kings 4:12). Though the city is not specifically mentioned in the 1 Kings 14:25-28 account of the invasion of Shishak from Egypt, Beth-shean is listed among the cities plundered. Afterward, the city played little role in Israelite history, though the city was occupied by Israelites of the Northern Kingdom from 815–721 B.C.

The city remained abandoned for the most part until the Hellenistic period (third century B.C.), when it was rebuilt and renamed Scythopolis ("city of Scythians"). This city formed the foundation of a significant Hellenistic and Roman occupation that included temples, theater, amphitheater, colonnaded street, hippodrome, tombs, and many public buildings, which had spread to the northern, eastern, and southern quadrants around the earlier "tell." Scythopolis was the largest city of the Decapolis (Matt. 4:25; Mark 5:20), and the only city of the

The Greco-Roman theater at Beth-shean (Tel el-Husn) in Israel.

Beth-shean.

league west of the Jordan River. The city continued to flourish in the Byzantine period until Arabs destroyed it in A.D. 636. The modern village of Beisan preserves the ancient name of the city.   *R. Dennis Cole*

BETH-SHEMESH (Bĕth-shē´ mĕsh) Place-name meaning "house of the sun." Beth-shemesh is a name applied to four different cities in the OT. The name probably derives from a place where the Semitic god Shemesh (Shamash) was worshiped. **1.** Beth-shemesh of Issachar was situated on the tribal border with Naphtali between Mount Tabor and the Jordan River (Josh. 19:22). Present scholarship identifies the city with either el-Abeidiyeh, two miles south of Galilee, or Khirbet Shemsin, east of Tabor. **2.** Beth-shemesh of Naphtali was probably located in central upper Galilee because of its association with Beth-anath (Josh. 19:38; Judg. 1:33). This Canaanite town remained independent and unconquered until the time of David. The site Khirbet er-Ruweisi has been suggested as a possible location. **3.** Beth-shemesh of Egypt is to be identified with Heliopolis (five miles northeast of Cairo) according to the Septuagint or early Greek translation (Jer. 43:13). Jeremiah told of the Lord's judgment upon the gods of

Excavations at Beth-shemesh showing what appears to be a portion of the massive city walls.

Egypt by depicting the destruction of the worship centers. **4.** Beth-shemesh of Dan is located on the south tribal border with Judah (Josh. 15:10; 19:41) overlooking the Sorek Valley about 24 miles west of Jerusalem. The ancient name was preserved in the Arab village of Ain Shems, and the "tell" is identified with Tell er-Rumeilah. Beth-shemesh guarded the lush farmlands of the Sorek Valley at the point at which the Shephelah (foothills) borders the Judean hill country. It was also situated in the strategic "buffer zone" between the Philistines and the Israelites during the period of the judges.

The Danite tribe was unable to control the lands of its inheritance because of the Amorites (Judg. 1:34-35) and/or the Philistines. Some were forced into the hills near Zorah and Eshtaol (as was Samson's family, Judg. 13:1-2). Beth-shemesh was apparently controlled by Israel (ca. 1050 B.C.) when the ark of the covenant passed through the city upon returning from the Philistines (1 Sam. 6:13). Around 795 B.C. the city was the scene of a battle in which Jehoash of Israel was victorious over Amaziah of Judah, resulting in the pillaging of the temple (2 Kings 14:11-14; 2 Chron. 25:21-24). Beth-shemesh is last mentioned in Scripture during the decadent reign of Ahaz. The Philistines captured Beth-shemesh from Judah (ca. 734), seen as judgment from God (2 Chron. 28:18-19).

Beth-shemesh was excavated by D. Mackenzie in 1911–1912 and Haverford College in 1928–1931, 1933. The city was first settled about 2200 B.C. by a relatively small group. The city achieved importance after being conquered and rebuilt by the Hyksos about 1720 B.C. A huge city wall, three defensive towers, and several tombs were uncovered. The Hyksos city was captured by the Egyptians of the Eighteenth Dynasty about 1550 B.C. Beth-shemesh flourished in the late Bronze Age under Egyptian and Canaanite rule, evidenced by imported wares from Mycenae and Egypt, as well as quality Canaanite finds, including inscriptions. Iron Age I (Judges) finds show that Beth-shemesh was heavily influenced by the Philistines, but the city was in general decline. After David defeated the Philistines, the city was rebuilt. Excavations indicate the Israelite city had olive oil, wine, copper, fabric dyeing, and wheat production industries. After Beth-shemesh was destroyed by the Babylonians (588–587 B.C.) under Nebuchadnezzar, the city was largely unoccupied, except for remnants of the Roman/Byzantine city at Ain Shems (monastery on the corner of the tell).   *R. Dennis Cole*

BETH-SHEMITE (Běth-shē´ mit) Resident of Beth-shemesh. See *Beth-shemesh*.

BETH-SHITTAH (Běth-shǐt´ tăh) Place-name meaning "house of Acacia." Battle scene when Gideon and his 300 men defeated the Midianites (Judg. 7:22). It may be modern Tell es-Saidiya or Tell Umm Hamad. It may be east of the Jordan River.

BETH-TAPPUAH (Běth-tăp´ pū·ăh) Place-name meaning "house of apples." Town assigned tribe of Judah in Judean hills (Josh. 15:53). It is modern Taffah, about four miles west of Hebron.

BETH-TOGARMAH (Beth-tō·gär´ măh) Place-name meaning "house of Togarmah." Listed in the Table of Nations (Gen. 10:3) as son of Gomer and great grandson of Noah, Togarmah is a city mentioned in Assyrian and Hittite texts. It was north of Carchemish on an Assyrian trade route. It may be related to modern Gurun between the Halys and Euphrates Rivers. Ezekiel notes Togarmah's trading relations in horses and mules with Tyre (Ezek. 27:14) and warned it of judgment along with Gog (Ezek. 38:6).

BETHUEL (Bě·thū´ ěl) or **BETHUL** (Bē´ thŭl) Place-name and personal name meaning "house of God." **1.** Nephew of Abraham and son of Nahor (Gen. 22:22). His daughter Rebekah married Isaac (Gen. 24:15,67). He was an Aramean or Syrian from Paddan-aram (Gen. 25:20). His relationship to Rebekah's brother Laban (Gen. 24:29) is not clear, since Laban takes the chief role protecting Rebekah (Gen. 24:55; 27:43), and Nahor is Laban's father (Gen. 29:5). Genesis 28:5 says Laban was the son of Bethuel. Nahor was actually Bethuel's father (Gen. 22:22-23). **2.** Town where the children of Shimei lived (1 Chron. 4:30). Joshua 19:4 apparently reads the same town as Bethul. It may be modern Khirbet el-Qarjeten, three miles north of Tell Arad.

BETHZATHA (Běth·zā´ tha) TEV, NSRV reading of place-name in John 5:2 based on different Greek manuscripts than those followed by other translators. See *Bethesda*.

BETH-ZUR (Běth´ zûr) Place-name meaning "house of the rock." **1.** City allotted to tribe of Judah (Josh. 15:58). Rehoboam, Solomon's son and successor as king of Judah (931–913 B.C.), built it up as a defense city (2 Chron. 11:7) in view of the threat of Shishak of Egypt (2 Chron. 12:2). A city official of Beth-zur helped Nehemiah repair Jerusalem and its wall (Neh. 3:16). It played a significant role in the wars of the Maccabeans in the period between the Testaments. It is located at Khirbet et-Tubeiqeh, 18 miles southwest of Jerusalem and four miles north of Hebron on a major highway intersection. This is one of the highest sites above sea level in Palestine. **2.** Son of Maon in line of Caleb (1 Chron. 2:45), apparently indicating the clan that settled the city.

BETONIM (Bět´ ō·nǐm) Place-name meaning "pistachios." A border town in tribal allotment of Gad (Josh. 13:26). It is located at Khirbet el-Batne, two and a half miles southeast of es Salt on Mount Gilead.

BETROTHAL Act of engagement for marriage in Bible times and was as binding as marriage.
Old Testament The biblical terms, betrothal and espousal, are almost synonymous with marriage and as binding. Betrothal and marriage comprised a moral and spiritual principle for the home and society. The penalty under the law of Moses for disrupting this principle by adultery, rape, fornication, or incest was death by stoning (Deut. 22:23-30). Later under some circumstances the Jewish legal system allowed divorce. The forgiving love and grace of God for his adulterous people is demonstrated by Hosea's buying back his adulterous wife and restoring her to his home and protection (Hos. 2:19-20). This means that forgiveness takes precedence over stoning or divorce.
New Testament Mary and Joseph were betrothed but did not live together until their wedding. When Mary came to be with child during betrothal, Joseph decided to quietly divorce her. In a dream from God, the apparent unfaithfulness of Mary was explained to Joseph as a miracle of the Holy Spirit. This miracle gave emphasis to the unique human and divine nature of Jesus Christ. Paul used the betrothal concept to explain the ideal relationship that exists between the church as a chaste virgin

being presented to Christ (2 Cor. 11:2).

Lawson G. Hatfield

BEULAH (Bū´ lah) Symbolic name meaning "married," used in reference to Jerusalem (Isa. 62:4 KJV). The other name, Hephzibah, means "my delight is in her." Both names connote good fortune. The name symbolizes the closeness of Zion and her sons and that Zion is restored to her God. The name suggests fertility in the Messianic Age based on righteousness, with the Lord as husband (Isa. 62:1-2).

BEVELED WORK NRSV translation describing scrollwork on the bronze stands of the laver in Solomon's temple (1 Kings 7:29; KJV, "thin work"; NASB, "hanging work"; REB, NIV, "hammered work"). It was wreathlike in appearance and may have been gold plating.

BEWITCH KJV translation of two Greek words. In Gal. 3:1 Paul criticized the Galatians for being "captivated by the falsehood" (*baskaino*) of the Judaizers to the point of straying from the gospel. The Greek word used here has a history in magical evil and the casting of spells. "Bewitch" is also used as a translation of another word (*existemi*) that modern versions translate as "amazed," "astonish," or "astound" (Acts 8:9,11).

BEYOND THE JORDAN Often used to describe the territory on the east side of the Jordan River (also referred to as the Transjordan). Five times the phrase describes the territory on the west side of the Jordan (Gen. 50:10-11; Deut. 3:20,25; 11:30).

BEYOND THE RIVER Refers to the Euphrates River in Mesopotamia. From the perspective of those living in Palestine, "beyond the river" meant on the east side of the Euphrates River. The expression is often used when speaking of the ancestral home of the patriarchs (Josh. 24:3,14-15; KJV has "on the other side of the flood"). From the perspective of those living in Persia, "beyond the river" meant on the west side of the Euphrates River. Darius I, the great organizer of the Persian Empire, named his fifth satrapy "Beyond the River" (Ebir-nari). This satrapy included Syria and Palestine. The official Persian usage is reflected in the books of Ezra (4:10-20; 5:3,6; 6:6,8,13; 7:21,25; 8:36) and Nehemiah (2:7,9; 3:7).

BEZAI (Bē´ zā-ī) Contraction of Bezaleel. **1.** Clan of 323 (Ezra 2:17) who returned from Babylonian exile with Zerubbabel about 537 B.C. **2.** Man who signed Nehemiah's covenant to obey God's law (Neh. 10:18).

BEZALEEL (Bĕz´ à leêl) or **BEZALEL** (Bĕz´ à-lel) Personal name meaning "in the shadow of God." **1.** Son of Uri, a member of the tribe of Judah (Exod. 31:2) and great grandson of Caleb (1 Chron. 2:20). He and another man, the Danite Aholiab, were skilled craftsmen who were responsible for making the tabernacle, its furnishings, and trappings. His skill derived from his being filled with the Spirit of God. Most modern translations render the names of these men Bezalel and Oholiab. **2.** Man who followed Ezra's leadership and divorced his foreign wife (Ezra 10:30).

BEZEK (Bē´ zĕk) Place-name meaning "lightning." Place where Judah and Simeon defeated Canaanites who were led by Adoni-bezek (literally "lord of Bezek") (Judg. 1:4). In Bezek Saul numbered the Israelites to rally an army against Nahash the Ammonite and deliver Jabesh-gilead (1 Sam. 11:8). Bezek was located at Khirbet Ibziq, 12 miles northeast of Shechem and 13 miles from Jabesh-gilead, six miles north of Tirzah, though the Judges' site may be a distinctive city. If so, it would be at Tell Bezqah near Gezer.

BEZER (Bē´ zĕr) Place-name meaning "inaccessible." A city of refuge in tribal territory of Reuben (Deut. 4:43; Josh. 20:8), set aside as a city for the Levites (Josh. 21:36). It may be Umm el-Amad, eight miles northeast of Medeba. Mesha, king of Moab about 830 B.C., claimed to have rebuilt Bezer as a Moabite city.

BIBLE FORMATION AND CANON "Bible" derives from the Greek term for "books" and refers to the OT and NT. The 39 OT books and 27 NT books form the "canon" of Holy Scripture. "Canon" originally meant "reed" and came to signify a ruler or measuring stick. In this sense the Bible is the rule or standard of authority for Christians. The concept of "canon" and process of "canonization" refers to when the books gained the status of "Holy Scripture," authoritative standards for faith and practice.

Organization of the Bible The OT was written primarily in Hebrew, with some portions of Ezra–Nehemiah and Daniel in Aramaic. The Hebrew OT is divided into three sections: the Law or Torah, (Genesis, Exodus, Leviticus, Numbers, and Deuteronomy); the Prophets, divided into Former Prophets (Joshua, Judges, 1–2 Samuel, and 1–2 Kings) and Latter Prophets (Isaiah, Jeremiah, Ezekiel, and the book of the Twelve—Hosea through Malachi); and the Writings. The Writings fall into three groups: Poetic Books (Job, Psalms, Proverbs), the Festival Scrolls or Megilloth (Ruth, Esther, Ecclesiastes, Song of Solomon, and Lamentations), and the Historical Books (1–2 Chronicles, Ezra–Nehemiah, and Daniel). Our current order of OT books is based upon the Septuagint, the Greek translation of the OT.

The NT, written in Greek, is organized with the narrative books (the four Gospels and Acts) followed by the epistles (Pauline Epistles and General Epistles) and concluding with Revelation. In many Greek NT manuscripts, the General Epistles (James, 1–2 Peter, 1–3 John, and Jude) precede the Pauline Epistles (Romans through James, plus Hebrews), likely due to the more direct links between Jesus and James, Peter, John, and Jude.

Development of the Old Testament Canon The common critical view, which may be traced to Hebert E. Ryle (1892, rev. 1895), is that the three-fold designation of the OT books—Law (Torah), Prophets (Neviim), and Writings (Kethubim)—is based on the gradual acceptance of each of these three "collections" as canon. This view is based largely upon the premises that Moses could not have authored the Pentateuch and that the OT historical books would have been compiled after the reign of King Josiah (Judah, 640–609). Recognition of the Torah (Law) by the fifth century B.C. is based on the fact that the Samaritans, whose canon comprised only the Torah, split from the Jews just after the exile. The Prophets is thought to have been closed by 200 B.C., explaining why the Prophet Daniel was not included (his book is in the Writings in the Hebrew canon)— critical scholars date his book to the second century B.C. The Writings are usually said to have been set at a meeting of rabbis at Jamnia (Jabneh) sometime between A.D. 70 and 135.

Roger Beckwith (1985), benefiting from the work of Jack P. Lewis (1964), S. Z. Leiman

Oldest complete Coptic Psalter.

(1976), and others, addressed and refuted many issues raised by the liberal-critical school and concluded that the OT collection could have been settled as early as the fourth century B.C., although it was more probably settled by the second century B.C. For example, the Samaritans' acknowledgment of only the Torah may not be a clue to the canon's history but rather involved a rejection of the previously recognized prophets. Second, the rabbis at Jamnia were concerned not with canonization but with interpretation. Finally, although the designation of Law, Prophets, and Writings was known and important (as noted in the prologue to Ecclesiasticus; Luke 24:44; Josephus, *Against Apion* I:8; DSS mss.; and the writings of Philo), Beckwith proved this is not a credible guide to the process of canonization.

When God chose to reveal Himself to His people and to establish a permanent relationship with them, He used the principle of the covenant, a concept familiar from ancient Near Eastern culture. The formation of a covenant commonly involved the creation of a covenant document. Furthermore, the history of the covenant would naturally be reflected in updating that covenant document. Therefore with the Mosaic covenant came the Mosaic document, and as each book of the OT was written, its authority as the revealed word of God evoked the immediate embracing of it as sacred and binding upon the emerging Israelite community. Moses, as the covenant mediator, wrote the Torah under divine leadership. The remainder of Scripture, the early and latter prophets, the poetry and wisdom literature, and the postexilic books, were likewise accepted immediately as each one was delivered and received into the Israelite community. The closure of this process would have come as the last book was accepted as authoritative and binding (referred to as "defiling the hands"). This may have been Malachi (usually acknowledged as the last prophet) or Chronicles (the last book in the Hebrew canonical order). In any case, what Protestants attest as the 39 books of the OT canon (same as the 22 or 24 books in the Jewish community [e.g., minor prophets were counted as one book; Jeremiah and Lamentations as one; Ezra and Nehemiah as one, etc.]) was settled very close to the time of the last book's writing. See *Covenant*.

Development of the New Testament Canon

The canonization process for the NT is easier to trace, even though some questions cannot be fully answered. The Pauline Epistles were collected and considered authoritative at least during the first half of the second century, as evidenced by Marcion's canon (ca. A.D. 140) of 10 Pauline Epistles and Luke. The four Gospels became a canonical unit during the second half of the second century, with Irenaeus (A.D. 180) defending the fourfold Gospel canon. By the end of the second century, the core of the NT canon was fixed, with the four Gospels, Acts, 1 Peter, 1 John, and 13 Pauline Epistles all accepted as authoritative texts by the leading churches. Revelation enjoyed early acceptance as well but later, near the middle of the third century, began to be questioned both on content and authorship. Hebrews was debated likewise due to authorship doubts. James, 2 Peter, 2–3 John, and Jude came to be accepted by many churches during the late third century, but they were not fully canonical until the fourth century. The first mention of a 27-book NT canon was made by Athanasius, the bishop of Alexandria, who in his Easter letter of 367, instructed the churches about the NT, listing exactly the 27 books we have. Even at that point, however, some groups such as Syriac churches used a 22-book NT canon (lacking 2 Peter, 2–3 John, Jude, and Revelation) or a 26-book canon (lacking Revelation). However, over time, the 27-book NT canon prevailed in virtually all of the churches.

The early church's task of ascertaining God's will regarding the NT canon was not easy. Marcion promoted a very limited canon in Rome (see above) that represented an extreme reaction against Judaism. He rejected the OT as well as NT writings that were "too Jewish," keeping only Paul and Luke (the only Gentile NT writer).

In reaction the church defended the OT and began defining its own NT canon, much broader than Marcion's.

In the late second century Montanism promoted an ongoing "prophetic" voice in the church. This assertion of new revelation caused the church to become more restrictive in defining the canon, limiting the NT to books that could be traced to the apostolic authorship or influence.

As the task continued, the Spirit-led process was guided by certain standards. For a book to be considered Holy Scripture (canonical), it had to enjoy widespread acceptance among the churches. Regional acceptance was not adequate. Also, criteria were needed to separate later works from those of the first century. Books must date to the apostolic era and be connected to an apostle, whether by authorship or direct association (for example, Mark and Luke were associated with Peter and Paul, respectively). The books also had to prove beneficial to the churches that heard them read. This spiritual dimension was likely paramount. Our NT books were included in the canon because they spoke so strongly to people that they could not be kept out of the canon. Lastly, the books had to be deemed suitable for public reading in the church. Since illiteracy was widespread, the reading of the text in worship was the primary contact with the text for most of the people. Those texts read in worship were heard as the authoritative Word of God. Such texts were on the path of full canonization.

A further stage of canonization occurred during the Reformation. The reformers, echoing Jerome, held that the Jewish OT canon should be followed, and so they accepted only the 39 books of the Hebrew OT, instead of the expanded OT often found in the Septuagint. These additional books (the Apocrypha) were also in the Latin Vulgate, the primary Bible of the Western Church for over 1,000 years prior to the reformation. Bibles for both the Roman Catholic Church and the Orthodox Churches still generally include the Apocrypha, but since Vatican II they have a lesser level of canonicity, being called deuterocanonical. Protestants, while not denying these books are helpful, do not accept them as canonical Holy Scripture. See *Apocrypha, Old Testament; Apocrypha, New Testament*.

Bill Warren and Archie W. England

BIBLE HERMENEUTICS The theory of biblical interpretation—its goals, methods, principles, and evaluative criteria used in interpreting Scripture. This may sound esoteric and impractical, but, in fact, hermeneutical theory has far-reaching consequences for believers and the church.

Every person who approaches the Bible is operating with some hermeneutical theory. The results of a person's encounter with the Bible will be heavily influenced by the interpretative understandings that person brings to the text. Humans develop their interpretive skills as they learn their first language. Early in acquiring their first language, children learn what it is to misunderstand and to be misunderstood. They learn that interpretations can be right or wrong.

This early insight is the basis of a long-standing assumption in biblical hermeneutics: that a text has at least one meaning and that one's interpretation of that meaning will be right or wrong. That assumption has been challenged in recent years by postmodernists. Persons in small group Bible studies may not have read any of the postmodernists. But postmodernist assumptions can be seen in such Bible study groups where every interpretation is seen as being as good as another. In these kinds of subtle ways our hermeneutical theory is modified by the cultural milieu we imbibe without being aware of what has happened. For that reason, having an overview of biblical hermeneutics can help students of the Bible become aware of the hermeneutical principles and assumptions that they bring to the Bible every time they read it. See *Bible, Methods of Study.*

How we interpret the Bible shares much in common with how we interpret other texts. But the difference between biblical texts and texts from law, literature, and the sciences is that despite the 66 biblical books having been written by many people over a period of 1,500 years, the Bible claims God as its ultimate author. This raises the stakes on reading it and accurately understanding what it says. It is one thing to misinterpret Shakespeare but quite another to misread God. Nevertheless there has been and is much disagreement over what the Bible means at various points. This encourages us to look at the different interpretative approaches that give rise to a diversity of interpretations, many of which are incompatible with each other.

An assumption held in common by both Jesus and the religious leaders of His time was that the Hebrew Scriptures were the word of God. Also held in common was a number of methods of interpreting Scripture: literal, midrash, pesher, and typological. Yet, Jesus and the religious leaders interpreted Scripture very differently.

One of the first activities of the risen Christ was interpreting Scripture. As He walked with Cleopas and another disciple on the road to Emmaus, "beginning with Moses and all the Prophets, He interpreted for them in all the Scriptures the things concerning Himself" (Luke 24:27 HCSB). Jesus' interpretation of who He was and His mission in light of the Hebrew Scriptures is the foundation of the church and historically is the factor that created separation between the church and the synagogue.

This interpretative activity of Jesus forges a connection between the Hebrew Scriptures and what later came to be called the New Testament. Not only does Jesus' teaching bring the two Testaments together, but it provides the key for seeing how they fit together, how they are mutually dependent.

What seems so clear in Luke 24 was not seen clearly by some in the second century. Alongside the Hebrew Scriptures, a body of Christian writings were being collected (2 Pet. 3:16). By A.D. 140 the relationship between the Hebrew Scriptures and this body of Christian writing began to be questioned. Marcion, a wealthy shipbuilder from Pontus, came to Rome and sought to use his influence to remove the Hebrew Scriptures from the church. He believed the God revealed in the Hebrew Scriptures was incompatible with the God revealed in Jesus. Marcion proposed that only some of Paul's letters and an edited version of the Gospel of Luke should be viewed as Scripture.

Marcion forced the church to decide whether or not to keep the Hebrew Scriptures and how to interpret them in light of Jesus. While Marcion wanted to make the canon considerably smaller, there was another group, the Montanists who wanted to add to it Montanist writings.

Between these two extremes was a third group who wanted to keep the Hebrew Scriptures alongside Christian writings that had apostolic authority. It was not required that an apostle be an author of a canonical writing but that it be written under the authority of an apostle. Some documents that carried apostles' names were rejected because they were incompatible with apostolic teaching about Jesus Christ.

This apostolic understanding of Jesus Christ came to be an important element in biblical interpretation in the early church. Written documents are often subject to multiple interpretations. They are somewhat like a series of dots on a piece of paper. There are numerous pictures that can be made by connecting the dots in a variety of ways. A vital question for the early church was how are the dots to be connected.

The Gnostics were taking the Scriptures and reinterpreting them according to their own opinions. Irenaeus likened what they were doing to a person taking the beautiful image of a king created by an artist out of precious jewels and rearranging the gems into the image of a fox or a dog (Irenaeus, *Against Heresies,* I,8:1 [A.D. 180], in ANF, I:326).

In the face of these distortions of Scripture, Irenaeus formalized an interpretive framework that had been implicit in the church for a number of decades. This framework came to be called the rule of faith. The rule of faith was not something additional to Scripture. It was derived from Scripture and became a template against which to test interpretations.

The rule of faith has taken numerous forms in the history of the church. The Apostles' Creed approximates the rule of faith. Later creeds and confessions of faith have functioned historically in ways similar to the rule of faith. The rule of faith has served both a positive and negative function in the history of biblical interpretation. Positively it has kept interpretation from going far afield and becoming something that suited only the tastes of the interpreter. Negatively, at times, it has kept the church looking at the biblical text with fresh eyes.

While the rule of faith was recognized in Alexandria, it did not keep Clement and Origen from creativity in biblical interpretation. The allegorical method of interpretation flourished there long before the time of Clement and Origen. It was used in Alexandria to interpret both the Greek classics and the Hebrew Scriptures. Clement and Origen used allegory as a way to deal with difficult passages in the OT and to interpret both the life and teachings of Jesus. One of the most famous of Origen's allegories is his interpretation of the Good Samaritan. Every element in the parable symbolizes something other than itself. While this interpretation is creative, the question is whether this is what Jesus intended to convey when He told the parable. See *Allegory.*

Allegory as practiced in Alexandria came under criticism from biblical interpreters in Antioch. The Antiochenes were concerned that allegorical interpretation detracted from the literal truth expressed in Scripture. They believed the spiritual import of Scripture was derived from an accurate, literal reading of the text rather than from interpretations that mapped unrelated spiritual meanings on to the primary sense of Scripture.

Perhaps the most influential biblical interpreter for the next millennium was Augustine. His first encounter with the Bible was anything but promising. Compared to Cicero, Augustine found the Bible lacking in dignity. Some of Augustine's first reactions to the Bible may have stemmed from the primitive Latin translation he read.

Augustine's early training led him to believe that the goal of interpretation was fidelity to the intent of the author as expressed in the text. This being said, there is some irony in the fact that Augustine's conversion was made easier after he heard Ambrose apply the allegorical method in his preaching. As Augustine interpreted Scripture, he did not neglect the literal sense but went beyond it in passages that were ambiguous at the literal level.

Augustine set forth a number of principles that have become part of sound biblical interpretation to the present. He recognized that the interpreter must know the text, preferably in the original languages, and have a broad knowledge of numerous subjects that are a part of biblical content. Augustine recognized that the Bible contains obscure and difficult passages. He taught that the interpreter should begin with the clear passages and interpret obscure passages in light of the clear.

For Augustine the goal of biblical interpretation is spiritual—nothing less than the transformation of the persons who read and study the Bible. This goal cannot be achieved through a mechanical process. Knowing language and history well are necessary for understanding the Scriptures, but they are not sufficient. The spiritual dimension of the interpreter is integral to the process of understanding Scripture, but neither is it sufficient. Augustine recognized that biblical interpretation was a task that engaged both the intellect and the heart.

Augustine made a distinction between knowledge of language *(linguarum notitia)* and knowledge of things *(rerum notitia)*. In On the Teacher Augustine maintains that language (signs) does not provide knowledge but prompts the reader to remember what they already know. In spiritual matters Christ is the teacher and source of this knowledge. Augustine distinguished between literal signs and figurative signs. The language of Genesis that gives the account of Abraham taking Isaac to Mount Moriah uses literal signs. This same language can be read figuratively as pointing to the death of Christ.

Augustine's model of biblical interpretation influenced Gregory the Great, a pivotal figure in the medieval era. Gregory began with a literal reading of the text. With this reading as a foundation, Gregory derived the doctrinal (allegorical) and the moral (tropological) import of the passage. This threefold interpretation later added a fourth level, the anagogical that pointed to the future.

The fourfold approach to biblical interpretation was summarized in a rhyme:

> *Littera gesta docet,* (The letter teaches facts)
> *Quid credas allegoria,* (allegory what one
> should believe)
> *Moralia quid agas,* (tropology what one
> should do)
> *Quo tendas anagogia* (anagogy where one
> should aspire).

We see this fourfold method of interpretation at work in Thomas Aquinas' exegesis of Exod. 20:8-11. In his literal interpretation Thomas makes a distinction between the moral import and the ceremonial import of this commandment. Christians are to give time to the things of God. The ceremonial part of the command specifies that time as the seventh day. The allegorical interpretation signifies Christ's seventh-day rest in the grave. The tropological reading calls for Christians to desist from sin and rest in God. The anagogical reading points forward to the eternal rest and enjoyment of God in heaven.

A way of reading Scripture that originated in the medieval era resonated strongly with Augustine's emphasis on the spiritual dimension of Bible study. *Lectio divina* had these steps:

(1) Spiritual preparation denotes that Scripture should be approached in an attitude of prayer. The text should be read with a quiet receptivity, listening for the voice of the Holy Spirit speaking through the text. Listening is closely related to readiness to act on what was revealed in the passage.

(2) Reading scripture requires close attention to the many details that compose Scripture. The text is to be approached with the expectation that each detail has been put there for a reason and that it is for our spiritual good to attend to these details.

(3) Giving careful attention to biblical imagery is important in seeing beyond the words to the realities they convey.

Increased knowledge of the original languages of the Bible was a catalyst for a new era of biblical interpretation and knowledge. Desiderius Erasmus is a significant transitional figure. His careful work in developing a series of editions of the Greek New Testament gave him an attention to detail that shifted the emphasis in interpretation from many levels of meaning to a passion for discovering what the author intended in the text. What Erasmus saw in the approach to interpretation of the past troubled him. Creativity of interpretation had the effect of leading readers away from the author's intent. It was almost as if they were playing a game.

In this milieu and in the context of his own spiritual crisis, Martin Luther moved gradually from the largely allegorical interpretation of Scripture to an approach that sought the historical sense of a passage. Luther caricatured allegorical interpretation as a wax nose that could be shaped by the interpreter rather than having a definitive form of which the interpreter had to take account. Yet, even in criticizing allegory, Luther continued to practice it.

Luther's controversy and eventual break with Rome gave focus to another important question in biblical interpretation: in the midst of competing interpretations of Scripture, what is the source of authority? With the crisis occasioned by Gnosticism, the rule of faith was the touchstone for discerning the correct interpretation of Scripture. Now in the crisis with Rome, Luther answers, *"Sola Scriptura!"* Not reason. Not church tradition. Scripture alone.

B

This does not mean that Luther and other reformers did not value church tradition. They had been shaped by it and continued to be influenced by it. However, they became aware that church tradition had itself been shaped by influences other than Scripture. *Sola Scriptura* was a call to recognize and act on first things first.

John Calvin, the leading Bible interpreter of the 16th century, saw that the first purpose of the interpreter is to hear and understand what the author is saying rather than to say what the author should have said. Calvin interpreted Scripture in light of Scripture and stressed the importance of the Holy Spirit who inspired the text being an integral part of the interpretative process.

An assumption held in common by the majority of exegetes from the second century through the 18th century came to be increasingly abandoned in the 18th century and beyond. The assumption is that God is the ultimate author of Scripture. In the absence of this assumption, both the nature of Scripture and the goal of interpretation began to change.

A number of factors contributed to the change in how Scripture was seen and interpreted. Both the church fathers and medieval interpreters were guided by the authority of tradition. As noted earlier the Reformers did not eliminate tradition but were critical of it in order to emphasize that Scripture alone was the touchstone of what the church teaches and practices.

In other fields of learning, traditional authorities gradually came into question. Human reason and experience came to be viewed as the sources of knowledge. The explanatory power of Newtonian physics reinforced the belief that revelation was not needed to understand God and the world. The logical progression of this was Laplace saying that he no longer needed God as a hypothesis to explain anything in the world.

In the 19th century the writings of Charles Darwin strongly reinforced the naturalistic worldview that began to displace a theistic worldview that had been dominant in the West for a thousand years.

The Bible was now seen as just a human book, to be studied with the same methods as are used to study any other human document. The goal of interpretation now was to understand what the human authors were saying and to reconstruct the process by which they came to write the documents.

It is not that all of a sudden new discoveries were made about Scripture. The earliest interpreters of Scripture were aware of different accounts of the same events. Within their frame of reference, these differences were not that significant and in themselves did not call into question Scripture's self-attestation as the word of God. These same observations made from the perspective of naturalism, however, were seen as confirmation that the Scripture was just a human document.

From the late 19th century to the present, the academic study of Scripture has seen a proliferation of methods used to understand Scripture. Some sought to reconstruct the history of the document under study, including the history and motives of the community out of which the document was composed. Another broad approach was less concerned with the historical, cultural, and religious background of the document and gave attention to its literary form. For many scholars who took this approach, the history behind the document and the historicity of the events of the narrative were of minimal interest.

While historical-critical biblical interpreters differ from traditional interpreters on the issue of the nature of Scripture, they do hold in common the belief that the goal of interpretation is to understand what the author(s) intended to say. The fact that one can never establish this with certainty does not mean that the goal is not valid and important. In recent years this assumption has been called into question by postmodernists. It is interesting that philosophers as different as Jacques Derrida and W. V. Quine have come to this conclusion. Both Derrida and Quine acknowledge that meaning is a useful pragmatic concept. Yet they, for different reasons, hold that the meaning in semantics or hermeneutics lacks explanatory power. Our common-sense understanding of meaning leads us to give it the kind of reality that physical objects have, but meaning as a kind of entity does not exist.

The implication of this for biblical interpretation is that not only can we not be sure when we have the correct interpretation of a text, but there is no correct interpretation of the text. There is no authorial intent to be wrong or right about. As different as the starting points for Derrida and Quine are, what they share in common is an attempt to account for language within a naturalistic worldview. The conclusions they come to from very different directions may be an indicator of the bankruptcy of naturalism as a research program for understanding human language and developing hermeneutical theory that takes account of the complexity and richness of human language.   *Steve Bond*

BIBLE, METHODS OF STUDY Most people who read the Bible do so without a clearly defined goal. It is better to study the Bible with a more defined purpose in mind, for its subject matter and its intended meaning.

Study for Subject Matter One way to study the Bible is with specific questions in mind—for example, questions about doctrine, history, or moral and spiritual guidance.

Theological Doctrines and Teachings The Bible is above all a book that talks about God and His relationship to the world. What is God like? What is His relationship to His creation? What is His intended purpose for creation?

For Christians the Bible is the ultimate source for knowledge of theology (the person and nature of God), anthropology (the makeup of human beings), soteriology (the doctrine of salvation), Christology (the doctrine of the person of Christ), ecclesiology (the doctrine of the church), and eschatology (the doctrine of the last things). As the only infallible source for doctrine, Christians scrutinize the Bible. However, great harm has been done by using the Bible as a source of "proof-texts" to support theological doctrines. The Bible should be studied not to support our belief system but to determine it. True respect for the Bible involves subjecting what we believe to its teaching. For example, we should not study NT passages dealing with Christian baptism to support our particular understanding of baptism but rather to see if our understanding is in harmony with the teaching of these passages. To the degree that our understanding is correct, the biblical texts will support it. We must judge our interpretation in light of the authors' intended meaning.

In seeking to discover what the Bible teaches concerning a particular doctrine, two general principles can be mentioned. One is that important doctrines tend to be repeated. Things referred to only once or twice in the Bible are not as important as those teachings found repeatedly. For example, we read of baptism for the dead only once in the entire Bible (1 Cor.

15:29). Whatever Paul may have meant by this, it cannot be an important issue or doctrine. Building a theological system on it is foolish. Similarly, the vast importance some groups place on Peter as the rock upon which the church is built or on speaking in tongues, belies the fact that the former is referred to only once in the Bible (Matt. 16:17-19), and the latter occurs in only two NT books (Acts and 1 Corinthians). Because of relatively rare occurrences in the Bible their importance cannot be great. Far more important are the repeated teachings that love and service are to typify the Christian life, that salvation is by grace through faith, and that a day is coming when God will judge the world. Another principle is that the NT interprets the OT. Without denying that the OT throws light on the NT, it is clear that the more recent revelation reveals those aspects of the older revelation that are no longer operative (the ceremonial aspects of the law involving clean-unclean, regulations concerning circumcision, the Sabbath, and others) and those that have found their fulfillment (the promised successor of David is Jesus of Nazareth, the arrival of the Kingdom of God with the Spirit as its firstfruits, and so on).

Biblical History One of the most popular reasons people study the Bible is to learn about the historical events it records. The most important area involves the life and teachings of Jesus. Christians want to learn as much as they can about Jesus. The primary source for this is the four canonical Gospels. These are read to discover what we can learn about the birth of Jesus, the chronology of His life, His baptism and temptation, the calling of the disciples, His teaching and healing ministry, the confession of Peter and Jesus' teaching of His forthcoming death, the transfiguration, Palm Sunday, the cleansing of the temple, the Last Supper, Gethsemane, the arrest and trial, the crucifixion, burial, resurrection, resurrection appearances, ascension, and other historical events. Another popular area of historical investigation involves the life and ministry of the Apostle Paul. There are numerous other areas of biblical history: the lives of biblical characters (from well-known people like Abraham, Moses, and John the Baptist to lesser-known people like Hagar and Jehoshaphat); various events (the call of Abraham; the exodus; the fall of Jerusalem; the return from exile). So much of the Bible is devoted to history (cp. Genesis–Exodus, Joshua–Esther, Matthew–Acts, also various portions of Leviticus–Deuteronomy, the prophets, and Paul's letters) because biblical faith is largely founded on what God has done in history.

It must be remembered, however, that understanding what happened is not the same as understanding its full meaning. A clear example of this is the empty tomb on Easter morning. This event is not self-explanatory and is subject to more than one explanation. Jesus' enemies did not deny the fact of the empty tomb, but they gave a different explanation to it than did the writers of the NT. The enemies said that Jesus' body was stolen (Matt. 28:13-15; John 20:13-15). However, the fact of the empty tomb coupled with numerous appearances of the risen Christ over a period of 40 days provided a different interpretation: the tomb was empty because Jesus conquered death and rose triumphantly from the grave. In the study of biblical history the reader should seek to understand the meaning of historical facts. The biblical writers did not consider themselves mere reporters of facts but as authoritative interpreters of those facts. Thus, when reading a historical passage, we should seek to learn "why" the author recorded this historical event. We should not be content with understanding what happened but must seek to understand what the inspired authors sought to teach by the events they recorded.

Moral Teachings for Living Another reason people read the Bible is for moral and spiritual guidance. The Bible contains all one needs to know concerning what must be done to be saved and to live a life pleasing to God. Intuitively, following the plain and simple meaning of the biblical texts, people with normal intelligence read the Bible for themselves and are able to understand the Scriptures. Thus we speak of the perspicuity or clarity of Scripture: all that is necessary for salvation and Christian living is clearly set forth in Scripture. One does not need to be a scholar or pastor to understand what to do to be saved or to live a life pleasing to God. This is understandable to the educated and uneducated alike. This reality makes possible in the fullest sense the priesthood of all believers. There are helpful principles that provide insight for interpreting the ethical teachings of the Bible.

The most helpful principle is to remember how ethical commands relate to the reception of

God's grace and forgiveness. Just as the Ten Commandments (Exod. 20) followed the deliverance from bondage in Egypt (Exod. 1–19), so the ethical teachings and commands of the Bible are addressed to people who are the recipients of God's grace and salvation. The commands of Scripture are part of a covenant entered into purely on the basis of grace alone. We are saved by grace through faith for good works (Eph. 2:8-10). We love God because He first loved us (1 John 4:19). The ethical teachings of the Bible are guides to those who have already experienced God's gift of salvation. They are not a means to achieve that salvation. See *Covenant.*

Two additional, helpful principles are that we should pay most attention to those ethical teachings frequently repeated in the Bible, and that we should note those teachings that Jesus and the inspired writers of the Bible emphasized. So we find at the center of Scripture the command to love God with all one's heart, mind, and soul, and one's neighbor as oneself (Lev. 19:18; Deut. 6:5; Josh. 22:5; Mark 12:28-31; John 15:12; Rom. 13:8-10). The repetition of this command and the emphasis that it receives indicates that this is the essence of biblical morality and the heart of the Judeo-Christian ethic.

Additional Areas of Information There are too many other subjects to give each of them a subheading. The Bible can be studied with respect to its geography; languages (the characteristics of biblical Hebrew, Aramaic, and Greek; the grammar, style, and vocabulary of biblical writers); temples (tabernacle, Solomonic, second, and Herodian); the specific regulations associated with marriage, sacrifice, diseases, circumcision, Jewish festivals, clean and unclean foods; teachings concerning hospitality; the plants and animals of the Bible; figures of speech used in the Bible (puns, parables, hyperbole, poetry); dates of various biblical events; when the books of the Bible were written; military weapons and strategy; musical instruments referred to in the Psalms; and others.

The amount of information contained in the Bible is enormous. No one could study all the subjects and information found in it, even with several lifetimes to do so. Some of the subjects are more important than others. Thus it is wise to investigate those areas which are most important. We must be aware, however, that the study of the Bible for its information or facts is insufficient without the determination and appropriation of meaning.

Study of the Bible for its Meaning Where the meaning of the Bible is to be found has been a spirited debate over the past hundred years. Since all communication involves three fundamental components (the author/speaker; the text/speech; and the reader/hearer), it is not surprising that each of these components has been advocated as the determiner of biblical meaning.

Study of the Bible for the Inspired Author's Meaning During the first half of the 20th century, a movement arose called the "new criticism" which maintained that texts such as the Bible are autonomous works of art whose meaning is totally independent of the original author and of the present-day reader. Thus what Paul meant in Romans or the meaning that a later reader gives to Romans is irrelevant; the text gives meaning to itself. However, whereas texts can convey meaning, they cannot "mean" anything. Meaning is a construction of thinking. Authors can think. Readers can think. A text, however, is an inanimate object (ink and paper) and thus cannot think or will a meaning. Therefore the meaning of a biblical text cannot be found in the ink or paper that make up a text but in either the human who thought and penned the thoughts or the one who reads it.

In the latter part of the 20th century a reader response emphasis became the dominant approach to interpretation. Here the reader is the one who determines the meaning of a text. He determines it not in the sense that he discovers the meaning of the original author of the text. Rather he gives the text its meaning. Thus it is, theoretically, perfectly acceptable to have different and even contradictory meanings ascribed to the same texts. The result of such an approach is that the reader, rather than being submissive to the text and its author, becomes their master, and what the biblical authors meant by their texts is considered irrelevant.

The more traditional understanding is that the author is the determiner of meaning and that readers should seek the meaning that the original authors intended when they wrote the texts. This is the basic presupposition of all communication: the speakers/authors determine the meaning of what they say/write. The fact that we seek to understand the meaning of Galatians with the help of Romans (not Revelation), the meaning of Acts with the help of Luke (not Plato's *Republic*), the meaning of John with the help of 1 John (not Hemingway's *For Whom the Bell Tolls*) witnesses to the fact that we want to know what the authors of Galatians, Acts, and John meant. The authors of Romans, Luke, and 1 John reveal this better than anyone else because they are the same authors writing at about the same time and on the same subject.

Role of the Holy Spirit in Interpretation The Bible teaches that both in its inception and its interpretation the Holy Spirit plays a major role. In understanding the Spirit's role in the interpretation of the Bible, it is helpful to distinguish between obtaining a correct mental grasp of what the author meant by the text and becoming convinced of the significance or truthfulness of what he wrote. Whereas all people with reasonable intelligence can understand the meaning of Scripture (some non-Christians write excellent commentaries), apart from the conviction of the Holy Spirit the teachings of the Bible are essentially "foolishness" (1 Cor. 2:14). It is through the convicting work of the Spirit that the believer knows these teachings are in reality the word of God.

Through the centuries some readers of the Bible have sought to find a deeper meaning than the meaning the authors consciously intended. It is arrogant, however, to seek a supposedly deeper and more ultimate meaning than the divinely inspired author possessed. Any such "spiritual" interpretation must itself be tested (1 John 4:1) by Scripture. In practice these deeper meanings often prove false. We have no access to God's revelation except through the willed meaning of the biblical authors, who are God's authoritative spokesmen. Those who claim that God has given them a deeper meaning beyond that of the biblical authors indeed possess a different meaning than that of the authors, but that meaning is theirs, not God's. See *Inspiration of Scripture.*

Importance of Genre Within the Bible we encounter numerous literary genres such as poetry, narrative, prophecy, proverbs, parables, letters, idioms, hyperbole, and others. Because the goal in studying each genre is the same—to understand the meaning of the biblical author—we need to know how these genres function. One does not interpret a love poem in the same way one interprets a medical report. The biblical writers expected their readers to understand

B

how various genres function and the rules governing them. Some genres and the rules associated with them are:

Proverbs A proverb is a short, pithy saying usually in poetic form, expressing a wise observation concerning life. The book of Proverbs involves wise observations of life seen through the lens of the revelation of God. What makes biblical proverbs different from other proverbs is that they have been formulated and shaped through the filter of divine revelation. Writers of proverbs expect their readers to understand that proverbs teach general truths. They are not universal laws but allow for exceptions. Such exceptions do not, however, negate the general rule (cp. Prov. 1:33; 3:9-10; 10:3-4; 13:21; 22:6; Matt. 26:52; Luke 16:10).

Poetry The difference in poetic and narrative description can easily be seen by how they describe the same event. In Judg. 4 we have a narrative description of how Deborah and Barak led the people of Israel over the Canaanites led by Sisera. Chapter 5 is a poetic version of that victory. It is only in the poetic description of the battle that we find the portrayal of the earth shaking, the mountains quaking (5:4-5), and the stars fighting from heaven (5:20). As poetry (5:1 calls it a song) this imagery should not be taken literally, as their complete absence from chapter 4 indicates. A similar narrative and poetic portrayal of another such victory is found in Exod. 14 and 15.

Prophecy For many readers prophecy is understood as the precise prediction of future events. Aside from the fact that much of prophecy deals less with prediction than with proclamation, the prophetic writers did not expect their readers to interpret their prophecies as reports for modern-day historical journals. Rather, they make considerable use of poetic or figurative language. When they refer to the destruction of Jerusalem in 587 B.C. or A.D. 70, they are referring to an actual event, but frequently the language describing this is the language of poets, not of modern-day military historians.

This can be seen in the frequent use of cosmic terminology in prophecies of events subsequently fulfilled (e.g., Isa. 13:9-11 which refers to the destruction of Babylon; Jer. 4:23-26 which refers to the destruction of Jerusalem in 587 B.C.; Acts 2:17-21 which refers to the coming of the Spirit at Pentecost). The purpose of such cosmic language is to indicate that God is about to act in a mighty way in history, and since God resides in the "heavens," cosmic terminology is used to refer to his bringing predicted events to pass.

An additional rule involved in the interpretation of prophecy involves prophecies of judgment. Such prophecies always assume, even if not stated, that repentance may avert or delay the prophecy. This is clear from Jonah's prophecy of judgment to the people of Nineveh in Jon. 3:4, its lack of fulfillment in 3:10, and Jonah's reaction in 4:2. This principle is clearly stated in Jer. 18:7-8 (cp. also Ezek. 33:13-15). Other examples of such prophecies of judgment are found in Mic. 3:12 and Jer. 26:16-19. Thus such prophecies often function less as absolute, unchangeable predictions than as warnings and opportunities for repentance.

Parables Since parables are essentially brief or extended comparisons (similes or metaphors), a distinction must be made between the picture part of a parable and the meaning the parable is seeking to teach. Usually a parable seeks to convey a basic point of comparison, teaching one main point. Like any simile or metaphor, the details generally are not intended to be pressed. Details in a parable tend simply to add color to the story and create interest. On the other hand, if the original audience would have seen allegorical significance in such details, it is legitimate for the reader today to see them as well (cp. for example Mark 12:1-11 with Isa. 5:1-7).

In order to understand the main point of a parable, several questions serve as guides. (1) Who are the two main characters? This helps to focus attention on the main point of the parable. (2) What comes at the end of the parable? This rule (called "end stress") recognizes that authors tend to emphasize the point they are making by how they end a story. (3) Who or what gets the most space in the parable? One tends to spend more time on the most important characters in the story. (4) What is found in direct discourse? The use of direct discourse in a story focuses the readers' attention on what is being said. These questions indicate that the focus of attention in the parable of the workers in the vineyard (Matt. 20:1-16) is upon the owner and the first-hour workers and in the parable of the prodigal son (Luke 15:11-32) on the father and the older brother.

Miscellaneous Genres Some other genres found in the Bible include idioms (the use of words in combination possessing a different meaning than the normal meaning of the individual words); narrative (the retelling of past events with the purpose of teaching a point); letters (what the writers meant by the individual words, the clauses in which these words appear, and the arguments created by these clauses); covenants (generally consisting of a prologue in which the covenant maker describes himself [the preamble], a description of his past graciousness [the historical prologue], stipulations of what the second party must do to remain in this covenantal relationship, references to witnesses of the covenant, a mandate for the regular reading of the covenant, a list of blessings and cursing based on the stipulations, and the oath by the second party); hyperbole and overstatement in which statements are exaggerated for emphasis, and so on. Every genre has rules that the writer understood. Even as one cannot understand what is going on in football without understanding the rules, so the present-day reader cannot understand what the biblical author meant without understanding the rules governing the genres he used.

Author's Meaning and Present-day Application Since the biblical author is the determiner of the meaning of the biblical text, that meaning can never change because what the author meant is locked in history. However, what authors meant in the past often has implications they were unaware of. Thus what authors meant in the past includes not only their specific but also all the legitimate implications flowing from that meaning. Thus the command not to commit adultery (Exod. 20:14) includes such implications as not to lust (Matt. 5:28). Since these implications flow from the specific meaning intended by the author, what implications are legitimate is determined by the author when he wrote. A reader may discover these implications, but the author created them.

Robert H. Stein

BIBLE TEXTS AND VERSIONS The text of the Bible is the best attested of any ancient writings, and we may be confident we have the original words of Scripture. Ancient copies of the Bible number in tens of thousands; other ancient works are known in a single manuscript, or a few, or rarely, a few hundred. Although no original documents survive, the great volume of manuscripts confirm the accuracy of the text. About 5,700 Greek NT manuscripts (as early as the second century A.D.) are extant and thousands of the Hebrew OT (as early as the second-third B.C.), some copied within 200 years of the final editing. Manuscripts of other ancient works are separated from their originals by much longer periods of time.

Old Testament Texts No document before the printing press was more carefully copied than the OT. Manuscripts were written on various materials. Papyrus, made from a reed abundant in Egypt, was used from the earliest times. Parchment was made of sheep, goat, and other animal hides. Paper, a Chinese invention (A.D. 105), began to be used in Egypt around A.D. 700 and in Europe around A.D. 1000. Old Testament manuscripts were in scrolls until A.D. 600; the codex, a book form, became popular thereafter.

The most important witness to the OT text is called the Masoretic text. Scribes, called Masoretes, were active A.D. 500–1000. They were not innovators but careful preservers of the consonantal text, the vowels, and accents of the Hebrew text. The most famous family was the ben Asher, especially Moses and his son Aaron, the most important Masorete.

Leningrad Codex Dated A.D. 1008, the Leningrad Codex was a direct copy of the text of Aaron ben Asher and is the basis of the current Hebrew Bible and most modern OT translations.

Aleppo Codex The Aleppo Codex (A.D. 925) is perhaps the best OT manuscript, but it is missing most of the Pentateuch because of a fire during the late 1940s. Solomon ben Buya copied the text (consonants), and Aaron ben Asher supplied the vowels. This Codex is the basis for a new critical Hebrew OT being produced by the Hebrew University in Jerusalem.

Codex Cairensis Codex Cairensis (A.D. 896), copied by Moses ben Asher, contains the Former and Latter Prophets. Taken from the Karaite Jews of Jerusalem by the Crusaders, it was later returned to the Karaites in Cairo, Egypt.

Dead Sea Scrolls Discovered 1947–1961 in caves near the Dead Sea, the Dead Sea Scrolls (ca. 250 B.C.– A.D. 70) are about 40,000 fragments from 600-1,000 scrolls (200 are OT). They predate the next oldest extant manuscripts by 800–1,000 years. Most are close to the Masoretic text, but some follow the Septuagint or Samaritan Pentateuch. The Dead Sea Scrolls testify to the careful transmission of the OT text and the reliability of the Masoretic Text.

Samaritan Pentateuch The Samaritan Pentateuch originated about the fifth century B.C. and was transmitted independently of the Masoretic Text, differing in about 6,000 places. It provides some added details, harmonizations, and sectarian theology. The oldest extant manuscripts date to the 11th century.

New Testament Texts The over 6,000 manuscripts of all or part of the Greek NT are written on papyrus, parchment, and paper. The categories of manuscripts are the Papyri, the Uncials (script similar to capital letters), the minuscules (lowercase cursive script), and the lectionaries (cursive texts designed for readings in worship). The text was transmitted in several types. Most scholars believe that the Alexandrian is oldest and closest to the original, followed by the Western, Caesarean, and the latest form, the Byzantine or Koine.

Papyri Only four papyri (of 115) are from scrolls; the rest are from the Codexes. None cover the entire NT. The papyri preserve a very early and accurate text, as many date to the second and third centuries. Some important papyrus manuscripts include:

P52: The oldest fragment of the Greek NT (A.D. 110–125), P52 contains John 18: 31–33,37–38. As John wrote his Gospel A.D. 90–95, P52 may reflect the original text of John.

P45, P46, P47: The Chester Beatty Papyri (acquired 1930–1931). Having 30 leaves (early third century), P45 contains sections of the Gospels and Acts. P46, ca. A.D. 200, with 86 leaves, has the Paulines and Hebrews (placed after Romans). P47, (mid-third century) has 10 leaves, Rev. 9:10–17:2.

P66, P72, P74, P75: The M. Martin Bodmer Papyri, published 1956–1962. P66, ca. A.D. 200, contains most of John. P72, ca. A.D. 250, contains 1–2 Peter and Jude. P74, ca. A.D. 750, contains portions of Acts, James, 1–2 Peter, 1–3 John, and Jude. Dating around A.D. 200, P75 contains extensive portions of John 1–15 and Luke 3–24. This is the earliest copy of Luke and one of the earliest of John.

Uncials Only about a fifth of the 309 Uncials have extensive sections of the NT. The Uncials are second in importance only to the Papyri. Important Uncials include:

Sinaiticus (a, 01): Discovered in 1859 at St. Catherine's Monastery on Mount Sinai by Constantin von Tischendorf, Sinaiticus (fourth century) is the only Uncial containing the entire Greek NT. The text is early Alexandrian and in some places Western.

Vaticanus (B, 03): Vaticanus (fourth century) contains most of the NT, except 1–2 Timothy, Titus, Philemon, Heb. 9:14–13:25, and Revelation, and is one of the most important witnesses to the NT text, reflecting a text very close to P75.

Alexandrinus (A, 02): Alexandrinus (fifth century) contains most of the NT, except Matt. 1–24, portions of John 6–8, and 2 Cor. 4–12. Alexandrinus is an important Alexandrian witness outside the Gospels, is Byzantine in the Gospels, and is one of the best texts of Revelation.

Minuscules Written with lowercase letters in cursive script (9th–17th centuries), minuscules reflect the Byzantine text, but preserve some early readings. Over 2,800 minuscules have been catalogued.

Family 1: Consisting of four 12th–14th century manuscripts (1, 118, 131, 209), Family 1 represents a Caesarean text of the third-fourth centuries.

Family 13: Comprised of about 12 11th–15th century manuscripts, Family 13 has affinities with the Caesarean text-type.

Ms 33: MS 33 (ninth century) contains the entire NT except Revelation. Generally Alexandrian, it shows the influence of the Byzantine in Acts and the Paulines.

Ms 81: MS 81 (A.D. 1044) contains Acts and the epistles, and in Acts often agrees with the Alexandrian text.

Ms 1739: MS 1739 (10th century), containing Acts and the epistles, apparently followed a fourth-century manuscript, except in Acts, which the scribe attributed to Origen (ca. 250 B.C.). MS 1739 preserves a relatively pure Alexandrian text.

Lectionaries The lectionaries are minuscule manuscripts that arrange the text of the NT into readings for each Sunday of the liturgical year. Over 2,400 lectionaries have been cataloged. Though most are late, scholars are finding that lectionaries may preserve a form of the text from much earlier than the date the manuscript was copied.

Old Testament and New Testament Versions Because of their antiquity, some ancient versions (translations) are important for establishing the original text of the Bible. Important versions include:

Septuagint (LXX) The first translation, from Hebrew to Greek (ca. 280–100 B.C.), the LXX is the most important non-Hebrew witness to the OT. Some books such as Genesis and Psalms are literal translations; others such as Isaiah are freer. The Septuagint generally represents the Masoretic text, but there are differences, at times significant (in Jeremiah and Ezekiel). Some books preserve a more accurate text than the Masoretic, especially Samuel and Kings.

Targums Targums, Aramaic renderings of the OT, according to tradition began with Ezra (Neh. 8:8), and portions of Job and Leviticus are among the Dead Sea Scrolls. The Targums are important for providing traditional synagogue interpretation, as well as witnessing to the Hebrew text. Some are rather literal and others are periphrastic.

Peshitta Syriac (a dialect of Aramaic) translation of the OT and NT (fifth-sixth centuries A.D.), the Peshitta generally follows the Masoretic text in the OT. In the NT the Peshitta follows various text types. The NT contains only 22 books, excluding 2 Peter, 2–3 John, Jude, and Revelation.

Vulgate The Latin Vulgate (A.D. 383–405) was the work of Jerome, the premier linguist in the Church of his era. It was the Bible of the Western Church for over 1,000 years. Jerome translated the Masoretic OT text into Latin, and over 8,000 Latin manuscripts are extant. He used Latin and several Greek manuscripts. His Greek manuscripts seem to have been a mixture of text-types. See *Textual Criticism; Textus Receptus.*

Russell Fuller and Charles W. Draper

BIBLE TRANSLATIONS The OT was written in Hebrew and Aramaic and the NT in Greek, the languages of both the writers and those who were expected to read the books in the first instance. All or part of the Bible has been translated into over 2,000 languages and dialects. The process of translation is ongoing in the effort to make God's Word available to all in languages that everyone can understand.

Early Translations The Samaritan Pentateuch used by the Samaritan community is a form of Hebrew written in a different script (Samaritan characters) from that which the Jewish community later came to use. The Aramaic translations called Targums have their beginning in the pre-Christian period and are represented in the Qumran finds; but the major Targums came later.

The OT was translated into Greek about 250 B.C. for the royal library of Alexandria. Named from the 70 translators who are said to have made it, the Septuagint, though made by Jews, has come down to us through Christian channels. Later Greek translations were made in the early period by Aquila, Symmachus, and Theodotion.

The evangelistic thrust of the early church gave impetus for many translations to impart the gospel to peoples in diverse language areas of the Roman Empire. Before A.D. 400 the Bible had been made available in Latin, Syriac, Coptic, Ethiopic, Armenian, and Georgian. The succeeding centuries brought still other translations.

In the West the church primarily used Latin after the end of the second century, and unofficial translations were made. In the fourth century Pope Damasus I invited Jerome to revise current Latin translations based on Hebrew and Greek manuscripts. Jerome completed the new translation after 18 years of work at Bethlehem. Jerome's translation came to be the accepted Bible, and by A.D. 1200 was called the Vulgate, the official version for the Roman Catholic Church.

Reformation Translations The invention of printing in 1443 and the onset of the Protestant Reformation in 1517 stimulated great interest in Bible translation. Most of the modern languages of Europe had printed translations made at that time: German, 1466; Italian, 1471; Spanish, 1478; and French, 1487. Each of these areas has a long history of manuscript translation prior to printing.

English Translations Efforts to render Scripture into English began with Caedmon's paraphrases into Anglo-Saxon (A.D. 670). Bede (A.D. 735) is said to have translated the Gospel of John, completing it on the last day of his life. It was, however, John Wycliffe and his associates (A.D. 1382) who are given credit for having first given the English the complete Bible in their own language.

B

Erasmus printed the Greek NT for the first time in 1516. Luther made his German translation in 1522–1524; and William Tyndale in 1525 brought out his English NT—the first printed one to circulate in England. Making use of Tyndale's material where available, Miles Coverdale brought out his complete Bible in 1535.

From this point the history of the English Reformation and the history of the English Bible go hand in glove with each other. Coverdale's Bible was followed by Matthew's Bible in 1537. Then in 1539 Coverdale, with the king's approval, brought out the Great Bible, named for its large size.

With the coming of Mary Tudor to the throne in 1553, the printing of Bibles was temporarily interrupted; but the exiles in Geneva, led by William Whittingham, produced the Geneva Bible in 1560. This proved to be particularly popular, especially with the later Puritans. Matthew Parker, archbishop of Canterbury, then had the Bishops' Bible prepared, primarily by bishops of the Church of England, which went through 20 editions. Roman Catholics brought out their Rheims NT in 1582 and then the OT in 1610. The period of Elizabeth was the time of England's greatest literary figures.

With Elizabeth's death and the coming of King James I to the throne, at the Hampton Court Conference in January 1604, the king accepted the proposal that a new translation be made. The outcome was the King James Version of 1611. It is number nine in the sequence of printed English Bibles and is a revision of the Bishops' Bible. The KJV was heavily criticized in its early days; but in time, with official pressure, it won the field and became "the Bible" for English-reading people—a position it held for almost 400 years. The KJV has undergone numerous modifications so that the currently circulating book differs from that of 1611 in over 75,000 places.

By 1850 large numbers of people felt the time had come for a revision. A motion made by Bishop Wilberforce in the Convocation of Canterbury carried, setting in operation the making of the Revised Version whose NT appeared in 1881 and its complete Bible in 1885. The best British scholars of the day participated in the revision, and American scholars were also invited for a limited role. Though launched with great publicity, the revision eventually provoked harsh criticism. In time it became obvious that people still preferred the KJV. The revised edition was more accurate; however, the style was awkward.

The Americans waited out the 15 years that they had promised before they would bring out a rival revision. The American Standard Revised Version was issued in 1901 with the American preferences in the text and the British in an appendix. It was more accurate than the KJV, but the revisers made the mistake of using an English style not native to English at any time. Wishing a literal translation, they produced one that is really English in Greek and Hebrew grammar and word order.

English Bible Translations in the Twentieth Century At the turn of the century, Adolf Deissmann, using study of the papyri from Egypt, persuaded scholars that the NT was in the common language (the Koine) of the first century, giving impetus to an effort to present the Bible in the language of the twentieth century. Accompanying this development was the rise of archaeological discovery that gave new manuscripts of both the OT and NT. The Cairo Genizah collection of Hebrew manuscripts was found at the end of the last century, and the Dead Sea Scrolls in 1947. Perhaps 25 Greek manuscripts of the NT could have been used in 1611. Now over 5,400 are known. More of the Uncial manuscripts (309) were available to 20th century translators. The papyrus manuscripts (115), most found in 20th twentieth century, are the oldest extant sources for the NT text. Wider knowledge of the nature of the biblical and related languages has been gained, making for more accurate definitions. New scholarly grammars, dictionaries, and anthologies of texts grew out of these developments. Besides these matters is the simple fact that the English language continually changes so that what is understandable at one period becomes less so at a later one.

Translation theory became a factor in Bible translation in the last half of the 20th century. The extremes are paraphrase and a "wooden" word-for-word literalism. Between the extremes, one choice is "formal equivalence," where the objective is to find a formal equivalent for the words of the text being translated. Supporters of this method suggest that it is necessary in order for the reader to know what Scripture says, and some see theological implications that, if the words of Scripture are the words of God, they should not be modified in translation more than is unavoidable. All translations may involve some interpretation, but interpretation is not the work of the translator. Another choice is "dynamic equivalence," where the priority is to communicate effectively the thoughts of the text being translated. Supporters of this view suggest that translation should communicate with the reader as effectively as the original did with its readers, and that translating "meaning for meaning" is necessary to accomplish this. Most of the previous translations were formal equivalence, including the King James, American Standard, and Revised Standard. Several recent translations fall into each category. Notably, the New English Bible (NEB, 1961) and its revision, the Revised English Bible (REB, 1989), the New International Version (NIV, 1978), the Good News Bible (GNB, 1976), the Jerusalem Bible (JB, 1966), and its thorough revision, the New Jerusalem Bible (NJB, 1985), and the New Living Translation (NLT, 1996) are dynamic equivalence. The New American Standard Bible (NASB, 1971) and its significant revision, the New American Standard Bible, Updated Edition (NASU, 1995), the King James II (KJ II, 1971), the New King James Version (NKJV, 1982), and the New Revised Standard Version (NRSV, 1989) are formal equivalence.

The first half of the 20th century saw a spate of translations which abandoned the effort to revise the KJV and attempted to reflect new trends, each from its own viewpoint. They had a limited vogue in some circles while being criticized in others. Some were works of groups while others were prepared by one person; none seriously threatened the dominance of the KJV.

The Revised Standard Version, with its NT ready in 1946 and the complete Bible in 1952, bore the brunt of criticism of modern translations because it was the first serious challenge after 1901 to the long dominance of the KJV. It retained the Old English forms in liturgical and poetic passages, as well as using Old English pronouns when deity is addressed. Eventually an edition was issued with modifications to make it acceptable for use by Greek Orthodox and Roman Catholics which is called the "Common Bible."

The New Revised Standard Version appeared in 1989. Chaired by Bruce Metzger, the translators sought to preserve all that is best in the English Bible and to make the language as accurate and clear as possible. Significantly different from the RSV, the NRSV removed archaic pronouns and is both dignified and lucid. It is sanctioned for public and private reading by the National Council of Churches.

The British have prepared the New English Bible (1970) which represents certain trends in British biblical scholarship. The American reader will see differences between British English and American English. A revision, the Revised English Bible (1989), is strongly oriented to dynamic equivalence in translation and retains many British colloquialisms, as did its predecessor.

Roman Catholics issued the Jerusalem Bible, which with its notes is used both in and out of Catholic circles. In 1985, a thorough revision, the New Jerusalem Bible, was published. Even more fluid and readable than its predecessor, it is widely used. Of more widespread influence is the New American Bible (1970) which was used in preparing the English version of the liturgy of the Roman church. While making some concessions, its notes support Catholic doctrine.

The Jewish community has produced the New Jewish Publication Society translation Tanakh (1962–1982). This translation follows the Masoretic Text for the most part, is very readable, and is among the best translations of the Hebrew Bible.

The Living Bible (1971, LB), by Kenneth N. Taylor, is a paraphrase of the Bible, based on the American Standard Version (1901, ASV). Extremely popular in its early years, but of uneven quality, it has been much criticized. Dr. Taylor freely admits that it is not a substitute for Bible translations. Its successor is a dynamic equivalence translation from the original languages, The New Living Translation (1996, NLT), with a dual goal of reliability and readability. The NLT is the product of a large group of transdenominational scholars and leans toward inclusive language.

Those who prefer literal translation found their representatives in the New American Standard Bible (NASB) prepared by the Lockman Foundation (1971). An attempt to give the ASV new life, this effort removes many archaisms from the ASV; it reflects different judgments on textual questions from the ASV, and it places words not represented in the original text but added by the translators for clarity in italics, as did the King James Version. The NASB was significantly revised in the New American Standard

Bible, Updated Edition (1995, NASU). Archaic pronouns are removed and readability is greatly enhanced without sacrificing accuracy. The NASU removes many of the common objections to the NASB and is without competitors as the most accurate English translation of the Bible. An effort to preserve as much of the old as possible is the New King James Bible (1982). This is a "halfway house" for those who know that something needs to replace the KJV but who are not willing to have a translation which represents the current state of knowledge and uses current language.

An effort to meet the needs of those who have English as a second language or those who have a limited knowledge of English is Today's English Version (TEV), also known as the Good News Bible (1976). Recasting of language, consolidation of statements, and paraphrasing have all been employed in the effort to make the message simple enough to be grasped by the reader.

The New International Version was issued in 1978 by the International Bible Society from a cooperative project in which more than 110 scholars representing 34 religious groups participated. Abandoning any effort to revise the KJV line of Bibles, the NIV is a new translation aiming at accuracy, clarity, and dignity. It attempts to steer a middle course between literalness and paraphrase while attaining a contemporary style for the English reader but does not always succeed, leaning heavily toward dynamic equivalence and containing many colloquialisms.

The NT of a new translation, the Holman Christian Standard Bible, was published in 2000. The OT is due in 2004. This translation strives for "optimal equivalence," using formal equivalence except when a formal equivalent cannot be easily understood, in those cases leaning toward a dynamic equivalent. Translated from the critical texts of the OT and NT, it is lucid, dignified, faithful to God's word, and accurate. Wide distribution indicates it is quite popular. The HCSB answers many of the common objections to formal equivalence translations.

The ESV, English Standard Version, is essentially a literal translation published in 2001. It emphasizes "word-for-word correspondence" but also readability. It is designed for personal reading and in-depth study as well as Scripture memorization and public worship.

Eugene Peterson has completed his translation of The Message (2002). It is a contemporary language paraphrase designed to express a personal message to the reader. It is an outgrowth of his work as a pastor. It is not designed to replace the more literal translations but is for the new believer and those who need a more modern slant to enhance their understanding.

Jack P. Lewis and Charles W. Draper

BIBLICAL THEOLOGY See *Theology, Biblical.*

BICHRI (Bĭk´ rī) Personal name meaning "first-born" or clan name "of the clan of Becher." Father of Sheba, who led revolt against David after Absalom's revolt (2 Sam. 20:1).

BICHRITE (Bĭk´ rīt) (RSV) See *Berites.*

BICRI (Bĭk´ rī) (NIV) See *Bichri.*

BIDKAR (Bĭd´ kär) Officer of Jehu who took body of Joram, king of Israel (852–841 B.C.), and threw it on Naboth's land after Jehu murdered the king (2 Kings 9:25). Bidkar and Jehu had originally served as chariot officers for Ahab, Joram's father.

BIER Litter or bed upon which a body was placed before burial. They were portable (2 Sam. 3:31; Luke 7:14). Biers in biblical times have been compared to the wooden boards used in Muslim funerals to carry bodies today. Asa's bier was of a more elaborate type of burial couch that was probably placed in the tomb. The Hebrew word for bier (*mittah*) is the normal word for bed and is translated bier only when referring to burials.

BIGTHA (Bĭg´ thá) Persian personal name possibly meaning "gift of God." A eunuch who served King Ahasuerus of Persia and took command to Queen Vashti to come to party (Esther 1:10). Bigthan (Esther 2:21) may be the same person. See *Bigthan.*

BIGTHAN (Bĭg´ thăn) May be identical with Bigtha. He plotted with Teresh, another of the king's eunuchs, to assassinate King Ahasuerus of Persia (Esther 2:21). Mordecai foiled the plot, thus setting up the king's need to honor Mordecai at Haman's expense (Esther 6:1-12). See *Bigtha.*

BIGTHANA (Bĭg·thā´ nȧ) Alternate spelling in Hebrew of Bigthan (Esther 6:2). See *Bigthan*.

BIGVAI (Bĭg´ vȧ·ī) Persian name meaning "god" or "fortune." **1.** Leader with Zerubbabel of exiles who returned from Babylon about 537 B.C. (Ezra 2:2). Either he or another person of same name was original clan ancestor of 2,056 people who returned (Ezra 2:14). When Ezra returned about 458 B.C., 72 members of the clan returned (Ezra 8:14). **2.** One who sealed Nehemiah's covenant to obey God's law (Neh. 10:16).

BIKRI (Bĭk´ rĭ) (TEV) See *Bichri*.

BILDAD (Bĭl´ dăd) Proper name meaning "the Lord loved." One of the three friends of Job (Job 2:11). He is identified as a Shuhite, perhaps a member of a group of nomadic Arameans. His speeches reveal him as a defender of tradition-alist theological views. He argues that a just God does not punish the innocent (chap. 8). Job should admit he was suffering the just fate of the wicked (chap.18), and no person can be right-eous before the awesome God (chap. 25). See *Job*.

BILEAM (Bĭl´ ē·ȧm) City given to Levites from tribal territory of western Manasseh. It is often identified with Ibleam. Joshua 21:25, a parallel passage reads "Gath-rimmon." See *Ibleam*.

BILGAH (Bĭl´ gah) Personal name meaning "brightness." **1.** Original ancestor of one of divi-sions of priesthood (1 Chron. 24:14). **2.** Priest who returned from exile with Zerubbabel about 537 B.C. (Neh. 12:5).

BILGAI (Bĭl´ gī) Priest who sealed Nehemiah's covenant to obey God's law (Neh. 10:8).

BILHAH (Bĭl´ hä) Personal name meaning "unworried." The handmaid of Rachel (Gen. 29:29). When Rachel failed to bear children to her husband Jacob, Bilhah became his concu-bine at Rachel's instigation. Bilhah became the mother of Dan and Naphtali (Gen. 29:29; 30:4-8). See *Patriarchs; Tribes of Israel*.

BILHAN (Bĭl´ hän) Personal name, perhaps meaning "afraid" or "foolish." **1.** Descendant of Seir or Edom (Gen. 36:27). **2.** Descendant of Benjamin (1 Chron. 7:10).

BILL OF DIVORCEMENT See *Divorce*.

BILSHAN (Bĭl shän) Akkadian personal name meaning "their lord." Leader of returning exiles with Zerubbabel from Babylon about 537 B.C. (Ezra 2:2).

BIMHAL (Bĭm´ häl) Descendant of tribe of Asher (1 Chron. 7:33).

B

BINDING AND LOOSING Simon Peter made the great confession that Jesus was the Christ, the Son of God, in Matt. 16:16. Jesus immedi-ately responded by telling Simon that his name would be Peter and that Christ would build His church on this great confession. He went on, "I will give you the keys of the kingdom of heaven, and whatever you bind on earth will have been bound in heaven, and whatever you loose on earth will have been loosed in heaven" (16:19 HCSB). Jesus gave a similar statement in Matt. 18:18, this time to all of the disciples.

Some have taken the statement to imply that the institutional church or the ecclesiastical head has the power to make authoritative statements that may supersede Scripture and that heaven is obligated to comply. Others have taken it to mean that Christians have the authority to "bind" and "loose" spiritual powers by use of the spoken word of faith. Neither of these views is a satisfactory interpretation.

A correct understanding of the two passages is tied to the grammar of the phrases "will have been bound in heaven" and "will have been loosed in heaven." The grammatical construc-tions in both phrases and in both verses are per-iphrastic future perfect passives. A more accurate translation of Matt. 16:19 might be "and whatsoever you shall bind on earth shall have been bound in heaven: and whatsoever you shall loose on earth shall have been loosed in heaven." Similarly, Matt. 18:18 might well read "Whatsoever you shall bind on earth shall be bound in heaven: and whatsoever you shall loose on earth shall have been loosed in heaven." In other words, that which would be declared and bound on the earth will have already been declared and bound in heaven first; that which would be declared and loosed on earth will have already been declared and loosed in heaven first.

In Matt. 16:19 the context involves the keys to the kingdom of heaven. This is a clear reference to the gospel, upon the truths of which Jesus would build His church. Simon and the other apostles are given authority to offer the gospel freely to loose those in bondage. This same gospel alienates some, so we find Peter shutting up the kingdom as well (Acts 4:11-12; 8:20-23). Those who are loosed by the church have already been loosed by heaven, and those bound by the gospel's narrowness will have been bound by heaven, as long as the church confines itself to simple, direct gospel proclamation. Heaven and earth come together then as disciples proclaim the message of salvation, confirming some in their sin, loosing others to the freedom of forgiveness.

Matthew 18:18 addresses the matter of church discipline. Here Jesus uses virtually the same words as in 16:19 to speak of the importance of confrontation and restoration. The gathered body has an obligation to exercise church discipline toward erring or sinful members, knowing that as it does so, heaven has already ratified its action. Even more, when churches exercise godly and appropriate discipline, which is a vital mark of true churches, they can be sure of the presence of the Lord in their midst at the time, "For where two or three are gathered together in My name, I am there among them" (18:20 HCSB). The "two or three" here are the same two or three that established the truth of the need for correction in Matt. 18:16. This text is not, then, a general statement about the presence of the Lord among His people but an assurance of His providential guidance in matters of church discipline. The Lord is present even with individual Christians, but it is a great comfort to know that He stands in the midst of the church when it exercises the most difficult of all of its functions—discipline.

David G. Shackelford and Chad Brand

BINEA (Bĭn´ ē·à) Descendant of the tribe of Benjamin (1 Chron. 8:37) and of King Saul (1 Chron.9:43).

BINNUI (Bĭn´ nū·ī) Personal name meaning "built." **1.** Father of Noadiah, Levite who assured the temple treasures Ezra brought back from exile were correctly inventoried (Ezra 8:33). **2.** Two men who divorced foreign wives when Ezra sought to remove temptation to idolatry and purify the community (Ezra 10:30,38). **3.** Man who helped Nehemiah repair the wall of Jerusalem (Neh. 3:24). **4.** Clan leader of 648 members who returned with Zerubbabel from Babylon about 537 B.C. (Neh. 7:15; Ezra 2:10—spells it "Bani" with 642 people). **5.** Levite who sealed Nehemiah's covenant to obey God's law (Neh. 10:9). Could be same as any of the above. He came up with Zerubbabel from Babylonian exile (Neh. 12:8).

BIRDS The Bible contains approximately 300 references to birds, scattered from Genesis to Revelation. The Hebrew people's keen awareness of bird life is reflected in the different Hebrew and Greek names used for birds in general or for specific birds. Although bird names are difficult to translate, many birds of the Bible can be identified from the descriptions of them given in the Scriptures.

Several general terms for birds occur. In the OT the Hebrew term *'oph*, the most general term for birds, is used collectively to refer to flying creatures or fowl, as well as to winged insects. The term *'oph* occurs repeatedly in the creation narrative of Gen. 1 and 2 (Gen. 1:20-22,26,28,30; 2:19-20). Genesis 6:20 notes the division of birds into species. Leviticus 20:25 categorizes them as clean or unclean. Leviticus 11:13-19 and Deut. 14:12-18 list the specific birds which the Hebrews regarded as unclean and therefore not to be eaten. All birds of prey, including eagles, vultures, hawks, and falcons, were classified as unclean.

A second general term used for birds in the OT is *tsippor*. Like *'oph*, *tsippor* may refer to birds of every kind (Gen. 7:14; Deut. 4:17), but it usually denotes game birds (Ps. 124:7; Prov. 6:5) or the perching birds (passerines, Ps. 102:7; Dan. 4:12). From the term *tsippor* the name of Moses' wife (Zipporah) is derived.

In the NT the Greek term *peteinon* is used for birds in general (Matt. 6:26; 8:20; 13:4; Luke 9:58; 12:24; Acts 10:12; 11:6; Rom. 1:23). The term *orneon* is used in Revelation to describe the completeness of Babylon's destruction (18:2) and to refer to flesh-eating fowl (19:17, 21).

Some of the specific birds mentioned are: cock (rooster), dove (turtledove), eagle, ostrich, pigeon, quail, raven, sparrow, and vulture. See other individual bird names in the alphabetical dictionary listing.

Birds of abomination The birds of abomination are in the list of 20 birds not to be consumed by Israelites (Lev. 11:13-19). The reason for the exclusion of these birds is unclear. Some have suggested that the birds were prohibited because they were associated with the worship of idols. Others have suggested that they were excluded because they ate flesh which contained blood or because they had contact with corpses—both of which would make one ritually unclean (Lev. 7:26; 17:13-14; 21:1-4,11; 22:4; Num. 5:2-3; 6:6-11).

BIRSHA (Bĭr´ shä) Personal name with uncertain meaning, traditionally, "ugly." King of Gomorrah who joined coalition of Dead Sea area kings against eastern group of invading kings (Gen. 14:2).

BIRTH Bringing forth young from the womb. The biblical writers, like other ancient people, did not fully understand the process of conception. Having no knowledge of the woman's ovum, they thought that only the male's semen (his "seed") produced the child. The woman provided her womb as a receptacle for the protection and growth of the child.

Midwives were often used in the birthing process (Gen. 35:17; 38:28; Exod. 1:15). Birthstools were also used (Exod. 1:16). The infant's navel cord was cut immediately after birth; the child was cleaned, rubbed with salt, and wrapped in cloths (Ezek. 16:4). Often the child was named at birth (Gen. 21:3; 29:32,35; 30:6-8). The woman was considered ritually unclean for a period from 40 to 80 days following birth (Lev. 12:1-8; Luke 2:22). See *Birthstool.*

When a son was born, he was placed immediately on his father's knees (Gen. 50:23; Job 3:12). The psalmist's words, "Upon thee was I cast from my birth," (KJV) reflects the father's receiving of his new son and signifies God's care from the moment of birth (Pss. 22:10; 71:6). Rachel, by receiving Bilhah's child upon her knees at birth, was adopting him as her own (Gen. 30:3-8).

Birth could be premature because of the shock of bad news (1 Sam. 4:19). The untimely birth—here, stillborn—enters the dark, finds rest, and does not know the agony of life (Eccles. 6:4-5; Job 3:11-13). A miscarriage was caused by accident or violence (Exod. 21:22-25) or may have been considered as divine judgment (Ps. 58:8; Hos. 9:14).

The birth of a child was a time of rejoicing, especially the birth of a son (Ruth 4:13-14; Jer. 20:15; Luke 1:14,57-58; 2:13-14; John 16:21). One's birthday was an occasion for celebration (Gen. 40:20; Matt. 14:6). If life became unbearable, one might be moved to curse the day of birth (Job 3:3; Jer. 20:14).

The birthing process was used in a figurative way in describing the relationship of God to His people. In Deut. 32:18 God gave birth to Israel as a mother would give birth to a child. Therefore, when the Israelites said to the tree "You are my father," and to the stone, "You gave me birth," they turned away from their true parent (the tree and stone pillar were symbols in the worship of idols). According to Jesus, it is just as necessary to be born of the Spirit as it is to be born of a woman (John 3:1-7). The birthing process is also used as an image to describe God's creative activity (Job 38:29). God is even pictured as a midwife (Isa. 66:7-9).

Many biblical writers used the pain of childbirth in a metaphorical way. Kings before God tremble like a woman giving birth (Ps. 48:6). The coming of the Day of the Lord will cause anguish similar to childbirth. There will be pangs, agony, cries, gasping, and panting (Isa. 13:8; 42:14; Jer. 6:24; 13:21; 22:23; 30:6; 48:41; 49:24; 50:43; John 16:21; Rev. 12:2).

Phil Logan

BIRTH CONTROL In response to God's command in the garden of Eden to "be fruitful and multiply, and fill the earth" (Gen. 1:28; cp. Gen. 9:1,7), men and women in ancient Israel and Judea placed a high value on human reproductivity (1 Sam. 1:8; Ps. 127:3-5). Emotional and economic security in ancient Israel was expressed through large families (Ps. 113:9) and protected by legal structures and customs which ensured genealogical continuity (Deut. 25:5-10; Ruth 4:5; Mark 12:18-23). One's personal identity was largely based on kinship and lineage so that a woman who was barren was considered incomplete (Gen. 30:22-23; 1 Sam. 1:5-6). For these reasons Onan's attempt at birth control was displeasing to both God and his family (Gen. 38:8-10).

Eunuchs were fairly common in the ancient world (e.g., Matt. 19:12; Acts 8:27). Castration was aimed not at birth control but performed for a variety of reasons such as punishment, to mark religious devotion, or to qualify a male for certain jobs which required undistracted loyalty, such as supervising women of the royal household (Esther 1:10-12; 2:3). However, Mosaic law recognized that castration was contrary to the created order and banned castrated persons from religious service (Deut. 23:1). This ban was evidently relaxed by the time of Isaiah (Isa. 56:3-5). *Paul H. Wright*

BIRTH DEFECTS The Bible records four clear cases of birth defects: a man "blind from birth" (John 9:1), a man "crippled from birth" (Acts 3:2), a man "crippled in his feet, who was lame from birth" (Acts 14:8), and a eunuch (male sterility) "born that way" (Matt. 19:12).

A variety of diseases and physical handicaps are mentioned in the Bible with no note as to their origin or cause (e.g., Matt. 9:2; Mark 7:32). Leviticus 21:18-21 lists physical deformities which disqualified a male descendant of Aaron from serving in the sanctuary of the Lord; these include blindness, lameness, disfigurement, dwarfishness, eye defects, and damaged testicles. In many instances such deformities must have been congenital.

The Bible is clear that while the development of a fetus may not be understood by people (Eccles. 11:5), it is both known and guided by God (Job 10:11; 31:15; Ps. 119:73; 139:13-16; Isa. 44:2; 46:3; 49:5; Jer. 1:5; Rom. 8:28). For this reason, every person must be embraced as a whole person in the eyes of God. *Paul H. Wright*

BIRTHRIGHT Special privileges that belonged to the firstborn male child in a family. Prominent among those privileges was a double portion of the estate as an inheritance. If a man had two sons, his estate would be divided into three portions, and the older son would receive two. If there were three sons, the estate would be divided into four portions, and the oldest son would receive two. The oldest son also normally received the father's major blessing. Esau forfeited his birthright to his brother Jacob for the sake of a meal of lentil stew and bread (Gen. 25:29-34). Indeed, the Hebrew word for blessing (*berakah*) is virtually an anagram of the word that means both birthright and firstborn (*bekorah*). Legal continuation of the family line may also have been included among the privileges of the firstborn son. Deuteronomy 21:15-17 prohibited a father from playing favorites among his

sons by trying to give the birthright to other than the firstborn.

BIRTHSTOOL Object upon which a woman sat during labor (Exod. 1:16 NASB, NKJV). The birthstool may have been of Egyptian origin. The same Hebrew word ('*obnayim*) is also translated as "potter's wheel" (Jer. 18:3). See *Birth*.

BIRZAITH (Bĭr·zā´ ĭth) or **BIRZAVITH** (Bĭr·zā´ vĭth) (KJV) Descendant of Asher (1 Chron. 7:31).

BISHLAM (Bĭsh´ lăm) Personal name or common name meaning "in peace." Apparently representative of Persian government in Palestine who complained about building activities (Ezra 4:7) of the returned Jews to Artaxerxes, king of Persia (464–423 B.C.).

BISHOP Term that comes from the Greek noun *episkopos*, which occurs five times in the NT (Acts 20:28; Phil. 1:1; 1 Tim. 3:2; Titus 1:7; 1 Pet. 2:25). "Overseer" more accurately identifies the function of the officeholder than does the term "bishop."

In ancient Greek literature *episkopos* is used of the gods who watch over persons or objects committed to their patronage. When referring to people, this term can likewise refer to one's protective care over someone or something but can be used also as an official title. Most commonly, the term is applied to local officials of societies or clubs but is found also as a title for religious leaders.

Of the five uses of *episkopos* in the NT, one is used of Jesus where He is called the "Shepherd and Overseer" of our souls (1 Pet. 2:25). The other four uses refer to officeholders in predominately Gentile congregations. In Acts 20:28 Paul exhorts the Ephesian elders to guard the flock since the Holy Spirit has made them "overseers" to shepherd the church of God. In Phil. 1:1 Paul addresses the "bishops and deacons." The qualifications for the office of bishop are given in 1 Tim. 3:1-7 and Titus 1:5-9. Although little is said concerning the duty of the bishop, one of the requirements that distinguished a bishop from a deacon was the bishop's responsibility to teach (cp. 1 Tim. 3:2; Titus 1:9 with 1 Tim. 5:8-13).

Since *episkopos* is used interchangeably with "elder" (Gk., *presbuteros*), it is likely that these two terms denote the same office in the

NT (many also equate *episkopos* with the "pastor and teacher" of Eph. 4:11). For example, in Acts 20 Paul summoned the Ephesian elders (v. 17), then stated that God had made them "overseers" (v. 28) to shepherd the church of God. Similarly, Titus is instructed to "appoint elders in every town" (Titus 1:5 HCSB), but when Paul gave the needed qualifications, he said, "For a bishop ... must be" (Titus 1:7 NRSV; cp. 1 Pet. 5:1-2). Yet, the fact that *episkopos* and *presbuteros* are used interchangeably is not the only evidence that the two terms denote the same office. If *episkopos* and *presbuteros* are two separate offices, then Paul never delineates the qualifications for elders, a striking omission given the importance of this office. Also, both the *episkopos* and the *presbuteros* have the same functions, leading and teaching (cp. 1 Tim. 3:2,4-5; Titus 1:7,9 with Acts 20:28; 1 Tim. 5:17). Furthermore, nowhere are the three offices mentioned together (bishop, elder, and deacon), which suggests that a three-tiered ecclesiastical system is foreign to the NT. It is also likely that more than one bishop (or elder) led each local congregation (Acts 20:28; Phil 1:1; cp. Acts 14:23; 20:17; 1 Tim. 5:17; Titus 1:5; James 5:14; 1 Pet. 5:1).

The related noun *episkope* occurs four times in the NT. Twice it refers to God's judgment (Luke 19:44; 1 Pet. 2:12) and twice it refers to officeholders (Acts 1:20; 1 Tim. 3:1).

It is not until the second century A.D. (in the epistles of Ignatius) that a distinction is made between the bishop and the elders. At first the bishop was simply the leader of the elders but soon gained more power and became sole head of the church, distinct from elders. Later, the bishop ruled not only one congregation but all the churches in a particular city or region. Today the Roman Catholic Church, Eastern Orthodox churches, Anglicans, Methodists, and Lutherans use bishops who have oversight of multiple churches.   *Ben L. Merkle*

BIT Metal bar fastened to the muzzle end of the horse's bridle. The bit is inserted in the horse's mouth between the teeth and is used to control the horse. The bit had loops on either end for attaching the reins. Some bits from the biblical period have spikes which would have stuck in the side of the horse's mouth when the reins were applied; the pain made the horse more responsive to the rider's commands. The bit and bridle were used figuratively in the Bible to refer to different forms of control (James 1:26; 3:2; 2 Kings 19:28; Isa. 37:29).

BITHIA (Bǐ´ thǐ´ å) (NASB) or **BITHIAH** (Bǐth´ ǐ·äh) Personal name meaning "daughter of Yahweh" or Egyptian common noun meaning "queen." Daughter of an Egyptian pharaoh whom Mered, a descendant of tribe of Judah, married (1 Chron. 4:17 NASB, RSV; 4:18 KJV, NIV). The verse stands in verse 18 in Hebrew but relates to the content of verse 17. Bithiah was the mother of Miriam, Shammai, and Ishbah. Throughout its history Israel incorporated foreigners into its tribes.

BITHRON (Bǐth´ rŏn) Place-name meaning "ravine" or common noun meaning "morning." As David ruled Judah in Hebron and Ishbosheth ruled Israel in Mahanaim, their armies clashed under generals Joab and Abner. Abner retreated. Joab and his brothers pursued. Abner killed Asahel. Finally when Joab quit pursuing, Abner crossed the Jordan and marched through Bithron (2 Sam. 2:29), either a ravine or mountain pass (KJV, NIV, TEV) or the forenoon (RSV, NASB).

BITHYNIA (Bǐ·thǐn´ ǐ·å) District in northern Asia Minor that Paul's missionary company desired to enter with the gospel (Acts 16:7). The Holy Spirit prevented them from doing so and directed them instead to Macedonia. Though no record exists of how the Christian faith took root in Bithynia, believers lived there during the first century. Those to whom 1 Peter was addressed included persons in Bithynia (1 Pet. 1:1).

BITTER See *Gall.*

BITTER HERBS Eaten with the Passover meal (Exod. 12:8; Num. 9:11), the herbs were interpreted as symbolizing the bitter experiences of the Israelites' slavery in Egypt. Some have suggested that the bitter herbs comprised a salad including lettuce, endive, chicory, and dandelion. The word translated "bitterness" in Lam. 3:15 is the same word translated "bitter herbs."

BITTERN KJV translation for an animal of desolation mentioned three times (Isa. 14:23; 34:11; Zeph. 2:14). The name "bittern" is applied to any number of small or medium-sized herons (*Botaurus* and related genera) with a characteristic booming cry. Bittern and heron are marsh and water birds and do not seem to be the animal referred to by the biblical writers. A number of alternatives have been suggested: bustard (REB), (screech) owl (NIV, TEV), porcupine, hedgehog (NASB, NRSV), and lizard. Of these suggestions, hedgehog and porcupine have the widest support. The animal represents the wild and mysterious world that humans do not control. See *Hedgehog.*

BITTER WATER Women suspected of adultery were given bitter water to drink (Num. 5:11-31). If a man suspected his wife had been unfaithful to him but was not a witness to the act and could not produce witnesses to the act, the woman was taken to the priest who arranged an ordeal to determine the woman's innocence or guilt. When the man brought the woman to the priest, he brought an offering of jealousy or remembrance (a cereal offering of barley). The priest seated the woman before the sanctuary facing the altar. The woman's hair was unbound as a sign of her shame. The woman held the offering, and the priest held the vessel containing the bitter water. The bitter water was a combination of holy water and dust from the sanctuary floor. At this point the woman took an oath: if she was innocent, the water would not harm her; if she was guilty, then her "thigh would rot" and her "body swell." The woman affirmed the oath with a double "amen." The priest wrote the curse (Num. 5:21-23) on a parchment and washed the ink off the page into the water. The priest then took the offering and burned it upon the altar, after which the woman drank the bitter water. If she was innocent, she would not be harmed and would conceive children as a blessing. If she was guilty, the curse would take effect. The man bore no guilt if his suspicions proved false—that is, he had not willingly broken the ninth commandment against bearing false witness. The woman, on the other hand, bore the consequences of her guilt (Num. 5:31).

BITUMEN (NRSV, RSV, ESV) Mineral pitch or asphalt (KJV has "slime"; NASB, NIV, "tar pits") found in solid black lumps in the cretaceous limestone on the west bank of the Dead Sea (Gen. 14:10). Other forms are found in Asia Minor. Bitumen was used as a mortar in setting bricks in the buildings and ziggurats in Meso-

potamia (Gen. 11:3) and as a caulking for rafts and basket boats on the Euphrates (Exod. 2:3; cp. Gen. 6:14). See *Babel; Pitch.*

BIZIOTHIAH (Bĭz´ ĭ-ō-thī´ ăh) or **BIZJOTH-JAH** (Bĭz·jŏth´ jah) (KJV) Place-name meaning "scorns of Yahweh." Southern town in tribal allotment of Judah (Josh. 15:28). The parallel list in Neh. 11:27 reads *benoteyha* ("her villages"), which the Joshua text of the Septuagint or early Greek translation also read. If that is not the correct reading in Josh. 15:27, then the location of Biziothiah is not known.

BIZTHA (Biz´ thà) Persian personal name of uncertain meaning. One of seven eunuchs who served King Ahasuerus in matters relating to his wives (Esther 1:10).

BLACK Often used to denote the color of physical objects: hair (Lev. 13:31,37; Song 5:11); skin (Job 30:30; Song 1:5-6; Lam. 4:8); the sky as a sign of rain (1 Kings 18:45); and animals (Gen. 30:32-43; Zech. 6:2,6; Rev. 6:5). "Black" is also used figuratively to describe mourning (Job 30:28; Jer. 4:28; 8:21; 14:2); a visionless day (Mic. 3:6); the abode of the dead (Job 3:5; Jude 13); and the treachery of Job's friends (Job 6:16). See *Colors.*

BLAINS KJV word for "sores" in Exod. 9:9-10. See *Boil.*

BLASPHEMY Transliteration of a Greek word meaning literally "to speak harm." In the biblical context blasphemy is an attitude of disrespect that finds expression in an act directed against the character of God.
Old Testament Blasphemy draws its Christian definition through the background of the OT. It is significant that blasphemy reflects improper action with regard to the use of God's name. God revealed His character and invited personal relationship through the revelation of His name. Therefore, the use of God's name gave the Israelites the opportunity of personal participation with the very nature of God.

Leviticus 24:14-16 guides the Hebrew definition of blasphemy. The offense is designated as a capital crime, and the offender is to be stoned by the community. Blasphemy involves the actual pronunciation of the name of God along with an attitude of disrespect. Under the influence of this interpretation, the personal name of

God (Yahweh) was withdrawn from ordinary speech and the title of Adonai (Lord) was used in its place.

Israel, at various times, was guilty of blasphemy. Specifically mentioned were the instances of the golden calf (Neh. 9:18) and the harsh treatment of the prophets (Neh. 9:26). David was accused by Nathan of making a mockery of God's commands and giving an occasion for the enemies of Israel to blaspheme—to misunderstand the true nature of God (2 Sam. 12:14).

The enemies of Israel blasphemed God through acts against the people of God. The Assyrians claimed that God was powerless when compared to their mighty army (2 Kings 19:6,22; Isa. 37:6,23). A contempt of God was shown by the Babylonians during the exile, as they continually ridiculed God (Isa. 52:5). Edom was guilty of blasphemy when it rejoiced over the fall of Jerusalem (Ezek. 35:12). God responded with judgment (2 Kings 19:35-37) or promised judgment (Isa. 52:6; Ezek. 35:12-15) to defend the dignity of His name.

New Testament The NT broadens the concept of blasphemy to include actions against Christ and the church as the body of Christ. Jesus was regarded by the Jewish leaders as a blasphemer Himself (Mark 2:7). When tried by the Sanhedrin, Jesus not only claimed messianic dignity but further claimed the supreme exalted status (Luke 22:69). Such a claim, according to the Sanhedrin, fit the charge of blasphemy and, therefore, deserved death (Matt. 26:65; Mark 14:64). However, according to the NT perspective, the real blasphemers were those who denied the messianic claims of Jesus and rejected His unity with the Father (Mark 15:29; Luke 22:65; 23:39).

The unity of Christ and the church is recognized in the fact that persecutions against Christians are labeled as blasphemous acts (1 Tim. 1:13; 1 Pet. 4:4; Rev. 2:9). It is also important that Christians avoid conduct that might give an occasion for blasphemy, especially in the area of attitude and speech (Eph. 4:31; Col. 3:8; 1 Tim. 6:4; Titus 3:2).

The sin of blasphemy is a sin that can be forgiven. However, there is a sin of blasphemy against the Holy Spirit that cannot be forgiven (Matt. 12:32; Mark 3:29; Luke 12:10). This is a state of hardness in which one consciously and willfully resists God's saving power and grace. It is a desperate condition that is beyond the situation of forgiveness because one is not able to recognize and repent of sin. Thus one wanting to repent of blasphemy against the Spirit cannot have committed the sin.   *Jerry M. Henry*

BLASTING Reference to the hot east winds which blow across Palestine for days at a time (Deut. 28:22 KJV, RSV; other versions read "blight"). This blasting wind dries up vegetation and ruins crops (Isa. 37:27; Ps. 90:5-6; 102:3-4; Isa. 40:6-8). This wind represents one of the great natural calamities (1 Kings 8:37; 2 Chron. 6:28) and one of the judgments of God upon the disobedient (Deut. 28:22; Amos 4:9; Hag. 2:17).

BLASTUS (Blăs´ tŭs) Personal name meaning "sprout." Official under Herod Agrippa I (A.D. 37–44). Won over by citizens of Tyre and Sidon, he tried to help them make peace with Herod. Herod's ensuing speech let him assume the role of God over the people, resulting in God striking him dead (Acts 12:20-23).

BLEACH See *Fuller*.

BLEMISH Condition that disqualifies an animal as a sacrifice (Lev. 22:17-25) or a man from priestly service (Lev. 21:17-24). In the NT, Christ is the perfect sacrifice (without blemish, Heb. 9:14; 1 Pet. 1:19) intended to sanctify the church and remove all its blemishes (Eph. 5:27). The children of God are commanded to live lives without blemishes (Phil. 2:15; 2 Pet. 3:14).

BLESSING AND CURSING Key biblical emphases, as reflected by 544 uses of various forms of the word "bless" and 282 occurrences of various forms of the word "curse" in the ESV.

In the OT the word most often translated "bless" is *barak*. The relationship between the concepts of "bless" and "kneel" thought formerly to meet in this word is generally no longer considered valid. The words for these concepts only sounded alike, like "spelling *bee*" and "bumble *bee*." To "bless" meant to fill with benefits, either as an end in itself or to make the object blessed a source of further blessing for others. God is most often at least the understood agent of blessing in this sense, and blessing a person often amounted to calling on God to bless them. In another sense the word could mean to "praise," as if filling the object of blessing with honor and good words. Thus individuals might bless God (Exod. 18:10; Ruth 4:14; Pss. 68:19; 103:1), while God also could bless men and women (Gen. 12:23; Num. 23:20; 1 Chron. 4:10; Ps. 109:28; Isa. 61:9). Persons might also bless one another (Gen. 27:33; Deut. 7:14; 1 Sam. 25:33), or they might bless things (Deut. 28:4; 1 Sam. 25:33; Prov. 5:18).

Words of blessing could also be used as a salutation or greeting, similar to an invocation of "peace" (*shalom*, Gen. 48:20). As such it may be used in meeting (Gen. 47:7), departing (Gen. 24:60), by messengers (1 Sam. 25:14), in gratitude (Job 31:20), as a morning salutation (Prov. 27:14), congratulations for prosperity (Gen. 12:3), in homage (2 Sam. 14:22), and in friendliness (2 Sam. 21:3). To be blessed by God was considered the essential ingredient of a successful and satisfying life. A related word ʾ*asher*, often translated "blessed" (Ps. 1:1 in KJV, RSV, etc.) refers especially to the state of happiness (cp. HCSB) resulting from being blessed.

In the NT the word "blessed" often translates *makarios*, meaning "blessed, fortunate, happy." It occurs 50 times in the NT, most familiarly in the "beatitudes" in Jesus' Sermon on the Mount (Matt. 5:3-11). Thus the NT concept stresses the joy people experience as children of God and citizens of his kingdom of God (Rom. 4:7–8; Rev. 1:3; 14:13).

For the act of "blessing," the NT generally used the verb *eulogeo*, whose etymology reflects the meaning "to speak well of" or "praise" (Luke 1:64). The related adjective *eulogetos* was especially used with this sense (Luke 1:68; Eph. 1:3). More often the verb refers to bestowing benefits (Gal. 3:9) or asking God to do so (Heb. 7:1). The noun *eulogia*, "blessing," has a range of meaning similar to the verb (e.g., Rev. 5:12; James 3:10; Heb. 6:7).

Of the 282 biblical uses of various forms of the word "curse" in the ESV, all but 34 are in the OT. The concept was clearly more prevalent in the OT. Depending on who is speaking, one who "curses" is either predicting, wishing or praying for, or causing great trouble on someone, or he is calling for an object to be a source of such trouble. As belonging to God and His people meant blessing, being cursed often meant separation from God and the community of faith. It thus involved the experience of insecurity and disaster.

The two most common words for "curse" in the OT are ʾ*arar* and *qalal*. The former is the one

that specifies the results of the fall and the entrance of sin into God's creation (Gen. 3:14,17; 4:11:5:29; 9:25). It is found 39 times in the OT as a passive participle ("cursed is the one who …") in pronouncements of judgment or deterrence from future sin (esp. Deut. 27–28). The other word, *qalal,* particularly invokes the experience of being insignificant or contemptible (Gen. 27:12–13; Exod. 21:17; Lev. 19:14).

At one time many scholars believed that the OT reflected the ancient Near Eastern idea that the formally spoken word had both an independent existence and the power of its own fulfillment. This concept was sometimes derived, for example, from Isa. 55:10–11, "my word … shall not return to me empty, but it shall accomplish that which I purpose, and shall succeed in the thing for which I sent it" (ESV). Blessings and curses were likewise thought to have such independent power. But other passages as Prov. 26:2 ("Like a flitting sparrow or a fluttering swallow, an undeserved curse goes nowhere," HCSB) demonstrate that for a word of blessing or curse to be effective it had to be appropriate and divinely sanctioned (cp. Ps. 109:17–20). Although the pagan king Balak may have believed in the self-fulfilling power of formally spoken words (Num. 22:6), even the pagan diviner Balaam knew otherwise (Num. 22:18–19). Isaac's blessing of his son Jacob was not irrevocable because it had already been uttered (Gen. 27:30–40) but because it had clearly been ordained by God (Gen. 25:22–23), and Isaac's preference for his son Esau could not change that.

In the NT the act of "cursing" sometimes means to wish misfortune on someone (Luke 6:28; Rom. 12:14; James 3:9-10). The concept of the "curse" is also applied to those who are outside God's blessings which are by His grace (Matt. 25:41). They are therefore under divine condemnation, the "curse of the law" because of sin (John 7:49; Gal. 3:10,13; 1 Cor. 16:22). Especially serious is the situation of those who reject or actively oppose the work of God (Gal. 1:8-9; 2 Pet. 2:14; Rev. 16:9,11,21).

E. Ray Clendenen

BLIGHT See *Blasting.*

BLINDNESS Physical blindness in the biblical period was very common. The suffering of the blind person was made worse by the common belief that the affliction was due to sin (John 9:1-3). Because of their severe handicap, blind persons had little opportunity to earn a living. A blind man was even ineligible to become a priest (Lev. 21:18). Frequently, the blind became beggars (Mark 10:46). The possibility of a blind person being mistreated was recognized and forbidden by God. The law prohibited the giving of misleading directions (Deut. 27:18) or doing anything to cause the blind to stumble (Lev. 19:14).

Physical Cause Many things caused blindness in ancient times. One could be born blind (John 9:1) due to some developmental defect or as a result of infection prior to birth. Usually, however, blindness began later. The most common cause was infection. Trachoma, a painful infection of the eye, is a common cause of blindness today and was probably prevalent in ancient times. Leprosy can also cause blindness. In old age vision may be severely impaired in some persons (Gen. 27:1). Some develop cataracts. Some have a gradual atrophy of portions of the eye.

Ancient people used salves of various types to treat disorders of the eye. Simple surgical procedures such as the lancing of boils near the eye and the extraction of inverted eyelashes were also employed.

In reality almost no effective treatment was available to those who suffered from diseases of the eye and blindness. There were no antibiotics, no effective surgical procedures for most problems, and no eyeglasses. Miraculous healing was often sought (John 5:2-3).

Jesus frequently healed blind persons (Matt. 9:27-31; 12:22; 20:30-34; Mark 10:46-52; John 9:1-7). Perhaps there is no greater evidence of His compassion and power than that seen in His willingness and ability to heal those who lived in darkness and hopelessness.

Spiritual Blindness The Bible addresses spiritual blindness as the great human problem. Israel was supposed to be God's servant (Isa. 42:19) but was blind to the role God wanted them to fill. Called to be watchmen protecting the nation, they instead blindly preyed on the people (Isa. 56:10). As the Pharisees gained leadership, they became blind leaders of the blind (Matt. 15:14; 23:16-26). Jesus came to reverse the situation, making clear who had spiritual sight and who was spiritually blind (John 9:39-41). Peter listed the qualities a person must have

to have spiritual sight. Without these a person is blind (2 Pet. 1:5-9). The problem is that the spiritually blind do not know they are blind (Rev. 3:17). They are blinded by the "god of this world" (2 Cor. 4:4). They walk in darkness, eventually being blinded by the moral darkness of hatred (1 John 2:11).

BLOOD Term with meanings that involve profound aspects of human life and God's desire to transform human existence. Blood is intimately associated with physical life. Blood and "life," or "living being," are closely associated. The Hebrews of OT times were prohibited from eating blood. "Only be sure not to eat the blood, for the blood is the life, and you shall not eat the life with the flesh. You shall not eat it; you shall pour it out on the ground like water" (Deut. 12:23-24 NASB). For agricultural people this command stressed the value of life. Though death was ever present, life was sacred. Life was not to be regarded cheaply.

Even when the OT speaks of animal sacrifice and atonement, the sacredness of life is emphasized. "For the life of the flesh is in the blood, and I have given it to you on the altar to make atonement for your souls; for it is the blood by reason of the life that makes atonement" (Lev. 17:11 NASB). Perhaps because an animal life was given up (and animals were a vital part of a person's property), this action taken before God indicated how each person is estranged from God. In giving what was of great value, the person offering the sacrifice showed that reconciliation with God involved life—the basic element of human existence. How giving up an animal life brought about redemption and reconciliation is not clear. What is clear is that atonement was costly. Only the NT could show how costly it was.

Flesh and Blood This phrase designates a human being. When Peter confessed that Jesus was the Messiah, Jesus told Peter, "Flesh and blood did not reveal this to you, but My Father in heaven" (Matt. 16:17 HCSB). No human agent informed Peter; the Father Himself disclosed this truth. When "flesh and blood" is used of Jesus, it designates His whole person: "The one who eats My flesh and drinks My blood lives in Me, and I in him" (John 6:56 HCSB). The next verse shows that eating "blood and flesh" is powerful metaphorical language for sharing in the life that Jesus bestows— "so the one who feeds on Me will live because of Me" (John 6:57 HCSB).

When Paul used the phrase "flesh and blood" in 1 Cor. 15:50, he referred to sinful human existence: "flesh and blood cannot inherit the kingdom of God." The sinfulness of human beings disqualifies them as inheritors of God's kingdom. In Gal. 1:16 Paul used "flesh and blood" as a synonym for human beings with whom he did not consult after his conversion. Paul said his gospel came directly from God.

In Eph. 6:12 Paul portrayed Christians in conflict—their wrestling is "not against flesh and blood" but with higher, demonic powers, "against the rulers, against the authorities, against the world powers of this darkness, against the spiritual forces of evil in the heavens." Of course, Christians do meet opposition to Christ and the gospel from other human beings, but behind all human opposition is a demonic-Satanic opposition. Human beings choose to identify with moral evil. We wrestle with the demonic leaders of moral revolt.

Finally, the phrase "flesh and blood" sometimes designates human nature apart from moral evil. Jesus, like other children of His people, was a partaker of "flesh and blood" (Heb. 2:14). Because He did so, He could die a unique, atoning death. He was fully human yet more than human; He was both God and man.

After the flood God renewed the original command that Noah and his sons be fruitful and multiply (Gen. 9:1). They were not to eat the flesh with its life, which means the blood (Gen. 9:4). Then murder is forbidden (Gen. 9:5-6). The reason is explained thus: "Whoever sheds man's blood, by man his blood shall be shed, for in the image of God He made man" (Gen. 9:6). Since a murderer destroys one made in God's image, murder is an attack upon God.

In Deut. 21:1-9 we read of an elaborate ceremony by elders concerning a person murdered in the fields near their city. They were to pray for the Lord's forgiveness by atonement: "Forgive Thy people Israel whom Thou hast redeemed, O Lord, and do not place the guilt of innocent blood in the midst of Thy people Israel. And the bloodguiltiness shall be forgiven them" (Deut. 21:8 NASB; see v. 9). The victim is assumed to be innocent, and the community is held responsible. A person who killed another accidentally had six cities to which he could flee and there establish his innocence (Josh. 20:1-9). He had to flee because the avenger of blood (the nearest of kin to the person murdered) was obligated to kill the individual who had murdered his relative (Num. 35).

When Pilate saw that justice was being distorted at the trial of Jesus, he washed his hands symbolically and declared his own innocence: "I am innocent of this man's blood. See to it yourselves" [i.e., that's your affair] (Matt. 27:24 HCSB). The people replied naively, "His blood be on us and on our children" (Matt. 27:25).

Blood of Sacrifices, Blood of the Covenant The great historic event of the OT was the exodus from Egypt. Central to that event was the offering of a lamb from the sheep or from the goats (Exod. 12:5). The blood of that lamb was put on the top and the two sides of the door frame (Exod. 12:7,22-23). When the angel passed through, destroying the firstborn in Egypt, he would pass by the houses in Israel's part of Egypt that were marked in this fashion. In terms of its redemptive effects, none of the daily sacrifices made throughout the OT (see Leviticus) were as dramatic as the Passover sacrifice.

Almost as dramatic as the Passover was the ceremony at the dedication of the covenant treaty at Sinai between Yahweh and His covenant people, the Israelites (Exod. 24:1-8). Moses took the blood of oxen and placed it in two bowls. Half of it he dashed upon the altar and half he dashed upon the people (Exod. 24:6-8). Moses declared "Behold the blood of the covenant, which the LORD has made (literally, cut) with you in accordance with all these words" (NASB). The people solemnly promised to act in agreement with this covenant (Exod. 24:3,7).

When Jesus inaugurated the new covenant after His last Passover with the disciples, He declared: "This is My blood of the covenant, which is shed for many for the forgiveness of sins" (Matt. 26:28 HCSB). Luke reads: "This cup is the new covenant in My blood, which is shed for you" (Luke 22:20). Testament means covenant here. Jesus, the God-man, gave up His life and experienced the reality of death so that those who identify themselves with Jesus might experience His life and never taste death as He did. He died as a sin-bearer that we might live for righteousness and become healed (1 Pet. 2:24).

Blood of Christ—Meaning and Effects The term "blood of Christ" designates in the NT the atoning death of Christ. Atonement refers to the basis and process by which estranged people become at one with God (atonement=at-one-ment). When we identify with Jesus, we are no longer at odds with God. The meaning of Christ's death is a great mystery. The NT seeks to express this meaning in two ways: in the language of sacrifice, and in language pertaining to the sphere of law. This sacrificial language and legal language provide helpful analogies. However, the meaning of Christ's death is far more than an enlargement of animal sacrifices or a spiritualization of legal transactions. Sometimes both legal and sacrificial language are found together.

In the language of sacrifice, we have "propitiation" (removal of sins, Rom. 3:25 HCSB); "sprinkling with the blood of Jesus Christ" (1 Pet. 1:1-2); redeemed "with the precious blood of Christ, like that of a lamb without defect or blemish" (1 Pet. 1:19); "blood of Jesus His Son cleanses us from all sin" (1 John 1:7); blood that will "cleanse our consciences" (Heb. 9:14); and "blood of the everlasting covenant" (Heb. 13:20). In legal language we have "justification" (Rom. 5:16,18); "redemption" (Eph. 1:7); been redeemed to God by His blood (Rev. 5:9). Such metaphors show that only God could provide atonement; Jesus, the God-man was both priest and offering, both Redeemer and the One intimately involved with the redeemed.

A. Berkeley Mickelsen

BLOOD, AVENGER OF See *Avenger; Bloodguilt; Cities of Refuge.*

BLOOD, FIELD OF See *Aceldama.*

BLOODGUILT Guilt usually incurred through bloodshed. Bloodguilt made a person ritually unclean (Num. 35:33-34) and was incurred by killing a person who did not deserve to die (Deut. 19:10; Jer. 26:15; Jon. 1:14). Killing in self-defense and execution of criminals are exempted from bloodguilt (Exod. 22:2; Lev. 20:9). Bloodguilt was incurred (1) by intentional killing (Judg. 9:24; 1 Sam. 25:26,33; 2 Kings 9:26; Jer. 26:15); (2) by unintentional killing (See Num. 35:22-28 where one who accidentally kills another may be killed by the avenger of blood implying that the accidental murderer

had bloodguilt. See *Avenger.*); (3) by being an indirect cause of death (Gen. 42:22; Deut. 19:10b; 22:8; Josh. 2:19); (4) a person was under bloodguilt if those for whom he was responsible committed murder (1 Kings 2:5,31-33); and (5) the killing of a sacrifice at an unauthorized altar imputed bloodguilt (Lev. 17:4). The avenger of blood could take action in the first two instances but not in the latter three.

When the murderer was known in instance (1) above, the community shared the guilt of the murderer until the guilty party had paid the penalty of death. No other penalty or sacrifice could substitute for the death of the guilty party, nor was there any need for sacrifice once the murderer had been killed (Num. 35:33; Deut. 21:8-9). The one who unintentionally killed another [(2) above] might flee to a city of refuge and be safe. If, however, the accidental killer left the boundaries of the city of refuge, the avenger of blood could kill in revenge without incurring bloodguilt (Num. 35:31-32; Deut. 19:13). The community was held to be bloodguilty if it failed to provide asylum for the accidental killer (Deut. 19:10).

In cases where the blood of an innocent victim was not avenged, the blood of the innocent cried out to God (Gen. 4:10; Isa. 26:21; Ezek. 24:7-9; cp. Job 16:18), and God became the avenger for that person (Gen. 9:5; 2 Sam. 4:11; 2 Kings 9:7; Ps. 9:12; Hos. 1:4). Even the descendants of the bloodguilty person might suffer the consequences of God's judgment (2 Sam. 3:28-29; 21:1; 1 Kings 21:29). Manasseh's bloodguilt and Judah's failure to do anything about it was the cause of Judah's downfall over 50 years after Manasseh's reign (2 Kings 24:4).

Judas incurred bloodguilt by betraying Jesus ("innocent blood," Matt. 27:4). Those who called for the crucifixion accepted the burden of bloodguilt for themselves and their children (Matt. 27:25). Pilate accepted no responsibility for the shedding of innocent blood (Matt. 27:24).

Phil Logan

BLUE Hebrew word translated "blue" (*tekelet*), also translated as "purple" (Ezek. 23:6) and "violet" (Jer. 10:9). The color was obtained from Mediterranean mollusks (class of Gastrohypoda) and used for dyeing. Blue was considered inferior to royal purple but was still a very popular color. Blue was used in the tabernacle (Exod. 25:4; 26:1,4; Num. 4:6-7,9; 15:38), in the temple (2 Chron. 2:7,14; 3:14), and in the clothing of the priests (Exod. 28:5-6,8,15; 39:1). See *Colors.*

BOANERGES (Bō à nẽr´ ģēs) Name meaning "Sons of Thunder," given by Jesus to James and John, the sons of Zebedee (Mark 3:17). The Gospel writer giving the meaning of the name did not explain why it was appropriate. The name might be indicative of the thunderous temperament these brothers apparently possessed. See *Apostle; Disciple.*

BOAR Male swine (Ps. 80:13). See *Swine.*

BOAT See *Ships, Sailors, and Navigation.*

BOAZ (Bō´ ăz) Personal name, perhaps meaning "lively." **1.** Hero of the book of Ruth; a wealthy relative of Naomi's husband. Ruth gleaned grain in his field. He graciously invited her to remain there and enjoy the hospitality of his servants, pronouncing a blessing on her for her goodness to Naomi. As he spent the night on the threshing floor to protect his harvest from thieves, Ruth lay down at his feet. Boaz agreed to marry her, according to the custom of levirate marriage by which the nearest male relative married a man's widow. Boaz bargained with the nearest relative, who gave up his right to marry Ruth. Boaz married her and became Obed's father, David's grandfather, and an ancestor of Christ (Matt. 1:5; Luke 3:32). See *Ruth.* **2.** The left or north pillar Solomon set up in the temple (1 Kings 7:21). The function of the pillars is not known. See *Jachin.*

BOCHERU (Bō´ kə·rū) Personal name meaning "firstborn." Descendant of King Saul in the tribe of Benjamin (1 Chron. 8:38).

BOCHIM (Bō´ kĭm) Place-name meaning "weepers." Place where angel of God announced judgment on Israel at beginning of the period of the judges because they had not destroyed pagan altars but had made covenant treaties with the native inhabitants. Thus the people cried and named the place Bochim (Judg. 2:1-5). It may have been between Bethel and Gilgal. An oak of weeping near Bethel was the burial place of Deborah, Rebekah's nurse (Gen. 35:8). See *Allon-bachuth.*

BODY Compared to most religions and systems of thought, both the OT and the NT place great value on the human body. In the OT there is not a term that refers to the body as such. The closest and most frequently used word is *basar*, translated as "flesh." *Basar* and *nephesh*, translated as "soul," are used interchangeably.

Bible Teachings The Bible makes basic claims about physical human existence.

The body as God's creation. The body is created by God—mortal, with physical needs, weak and subject to temptation. The body is not, however, without significance. In the body the person lives out the "I" of human existence, relating to God and to fellow humans. The body is the place of proper worship (Rom. 12:1), the temple of the Holy Spirit (1 Cor. 6:19-20), and thus is to be disciplined (1 Cor. 9:27). In Corinth the people did not properly understand God's purpose for the body. Paul followed Jesus in teaching that the inner spiritual life is not to be played off against the outer, physical life (Matt. 6:22; 1 Cor. 6:12-20; 2 Cor. 4:7,10). That means the war in the name of the spirit is not against the body but against sin. The goal is not liberation of a "divine" soul from the body but the placing of the body in service for God. Every action must be accounted for before God one day (2 Cor. 5:10).

The body and sexuality. Physical love is a gift of the Creator (Gen. 2:23-24). An entire book of the Bible rejoices over this reality—the Song of Songs. Humans express love with their entire person, not only with their sexual organs. This means that sexuality differs from eating and drinking, which satisfy only the requirements of the stomach. Sexual sin rules the body, that is, the entire person. Because the body of the Christian belongs to the Creator, Redeemer, and Holy Spirit, sexual sin is forbidden for the Christian (1 Cor. 6:12-20).

The redemption and resurrection of the body. The earthly human stands under the power of sin and of death. No persons can distance themselves from this power, but all long for redemption (Rom. 7:24; 8:23). Redemption is not guaranteed by a bodiless soul that continues to live after death. Such redemption is guaranteed only by God, who continues to care for the body and soul of humans even after death (Matt. 10:28). Death is not the redeemer; God is. He makes the gift of eternal life (Rom. 6:23) in that Jesus Christ became an earthly human and offered Himself for us (John 1:14; Rom. 7:4). Those who follow Him in faith and baptism experience the reality that the body does not have to remain a slave of sin (Rom. 6:6,12). A person will not be redeemed from the body; rather the body will be redeemed through the resurrection of the dead (Rom. 6:5; 8:11). The existence of the resurrected is a bodily existence. The earthly body of lowliness will be renewed like the glorious body of the resurrected Jesus, becoming an unearthly body or building or house (1 Cor. 15:35-49; 2 Cor. 5:1-10; Phil. 3:21).

Resurrection of the body does not mean that the personality dissolves into an idea, into posterity, or into the society. It means, instead, the total transformation of "flesh and blood" into a "spiritual body," that is a personality created and formed anew by God's Spirit. The resurrection body is that communion with the Lord and with people that begins before death and finds an unimaginable completion through the resurrection.

The body of Christ. Jesus Christ had a physical, earthly body which was crucified outside the gates of Jerusalem (Mark 15:20-47; Col. 1:22; Heb. 13:11-12). The body of Christ also designates the body of the Crucified One "given for you," with which the church is united together in the celebration of the Lord's Supper (Mark 14:24; 1 Cor. 10:16; 11:24). The continuing power of the sacrifice of Golgotha leads humans to join together in a church community, which in a real sense is joined together with the exalted Lord. Bodily is not, however, physical. The joining with the body of Christ does not occur magically through bread, but historically through the realization of the presence of the suffering and death of Jesus.

The church as the body of Christ. The image of the body calls the differing individual members into a unity (1 Cor. 12:12-27); however, the church is not just similar; it is one body, and, indeed, one body in Christ (Rom. 12:5; 1 Cor. 10:17). In Christ the body of the church community is incorporated. The community of Christians does not produce the body; the body is a previously given fact (1 Cor. 12:13). In the body of Christ, the body of the church community lives because Christ is greater than the church. He is the Head of the entire creation (Eph. 1:22-23; Col. 2:10) and as Head does not only belong to the church community but rather also stands over against the church. While the world stands in a relationship of subjection to Christ (Eph. 1:20-23; Phil. 2:9-11), only the church is His body (Col. 1:18,24; Eph. 4:4,12; 5:23,30), which He loves (Eph. 5:25). The church is joined to Him in organic growth (Col. 2:19; Eph. 4:15-16). The church grows by serving a future, which through Christ has already begun to be incarnate (Col. 2:9). The growth of the body occurs as the church marches out in service to the world (Eph. 4:12), even to the demonic world (Eph. 3:10). The individual Christian is joined to Christ only as a member of the body. The Bible knows nothing of a direct, mythical union of the individual with the Lord. The Bible knows of a union with Christ only as faith embodied in the realm of the church community and with the church in the realm of the world.   *Christian Wolf*

BODYGUARD Person or group of persons whose duty it is to protect another from physical harm. In the OT soldiers were included among the king's bodyguard because of acts of bravery. Members of a king's bodyguard mentioned in the Bible include: David (1 Sam. 22:14; 28:2), Benaiah ben Jehoiada (2 Sam. 23:23), Potiphar (Gen. 37:36), Nebuzaradan (2 Kings 25:8; Jer. 39:9-13; 52:12-16), and Arioch (Dan. 2:14).

BOHAN (Bō´ hăn) Place-name and personal name meaning "thumb" or "big toe." A place on the northern border of the tribal allotment of Judah called the "stone of Bohan," "the son of Reuben" (Josh. 15:6). This was the southern border of the tribe of Benjamin (Josh. 18:17). Some Bible students see this as evidence that some part of the tribe of Reuben once lived west of the Jordan. Others see an otherwise unknown heroic deed of Bohan honored with a memorial boundary stone.

BOIL General term used in the Bible to describe inflamed swellings of the skin. Boils are mentioned in connection with blains (KJV, an inflammatory swelling or sore) in the sixth plague on Egypt (Exod. 9:9-10). Since this plague affected both animals and men, many have suggested the malignant pustule of cutaneous anthrax as the sore or boil mentioned. Hezekiah's boil (2 Kings 20:7; Isa. 38:21) is identified as a furuncle—a localized swelling and inflammation of the skin caused by the infection of a hair follicle that discharges pus and has a central core of dead tissue. The boils suffered by Job (Job 2:7) have been identified with smallpox or with treponematosis (a parasitic infection).

BOKERU (Bō´ kə·rü) (NIV) See *Bocheru*.

BOKIM (Bō´ kîm) (NIV) See *Bochim*.

BOLDNESS Translation of four Greek words in the NT. Boldness denotes two things in the NT. First, boldness describes the courageous manner of those who preach the gospel (Acts 2:29; 4:13,31; 9:27-29; 13:46; 14:3; 18:26; 19:8; 26:26; 28:31; 1 Thess. 2:2; Phil. 1:20). The word translated as "boldness" in these texts (*parresia*) was used of the free citizen of a city-state who could say anything in the public assembly. In the NT it denotes the moral freedom to speak the truth publicly. Second, boldness describes the confidence with which Christians can now approach God because of the redeeming work of Christ (2 Cor. 3:4-6,12; Heb. 10:19; 1 John 2:28; 4:17).

BOLLED KJV translation (Exod. 9:31) of a term that means "having bolls"—that is, having seedpods. Some see the flax in this verse as being either in bud or in blossom.

BOLSTER KJV translation that means "the place where the head is while sleeping" (1 Sam. 19:13,16; 26:7,11-12,16). REB, NRSV translate "at his head" (cp. NIV, NASB).

BOND Translation of several Hebrew and Greek words with the meanings of "obligation," "dependence," or "restraint." Used literally to speak of the bonds of prisoners or slaves (Judg. 15:14; 1 Kings 14:10; Pss. 107:14; 116:16; Luke 8:29; Philem. 13). Used figuratively to speak of the bonds of wickedness or sin (Isa. 58:6; Luke 13:16; Acts 8:23), of affliction and judgment (Isa. 28:22; 52:2; Jer. 30:8; Nah. 1:13), the authority of kings (Job 12:18; Ps. 2:3), the obligation to keep the covenant (Jer. 2:20; 5:5; Col. 2:14), the bonds of peace and love (Eph. 4:3; Col. 3:14), and the bonds of an evil woman (Eccles. 7:26).

BONDAGE, BONDMAN, BONDMAID, BONDSERVANT See *Slave, Servant*.

BONES While often referring to the skeletal remains of humans (Gen. 50:25; Exod. 13:19; 1 Sam. 31:13), "bones" were also referred to metaphorically. "Rottenness in his bones" signified one whose wife caused shame and confusion (Prov. 12:4; 14:30, "to the bones" HCSB) or could refer to dejectedness and anticipation of approaching evil (Hab. 3:16). The "shaking of bones" denoted fear (Job 4:14) or sadness (Jer. 23:9). The "burning of the bones" indicated grief and depression (Ps. 102:3; Lam. 1:13) and the feeling of Jeremiah when he tried to refrain from proclaiming God's message (Jer. 20:9). "Dryness of bones" meant poor health (Prov. 17:22). Various other expressions using "bones" referred to mental distress (Job 30:17; Pss. 6:2; 22:14; 31:10; 38:3; 51:8; Lam. 3:4). "Bone of my bones" may mean having the same nature or being the nearest relation (Gen. 2:23; 2 Sam. 5:1).

BONNET KJV translation of two words. A conical-shaped cap placed on the head of the priest at the time of investiture. Made of fine white linen (Exod. 28:40; 29:9; 39:28; Lev. 8:13). See *Cloth, Clothing*.

BOOK OF LIFE Heavenly record (Luke 10:20; Heb. 12:23) written by God before the foundation of the world (Rev. 13:8; 17:8) containing the names of those who are destined because of God's grace and their faithfulness to participate in God's heavenly kingdom. Those whose names are in the book have been born into God's family through Jesus Christ (Heb. 12:23; Rev. 13:8); remain faithful in worship of God (Rev. 13:8; 17:8); are untouched by the practice of abomination and falsehood (Rev. 21:27); are faithful through tribulation (Rev. 3:5); and are fellow workers in the work of Jesus Christ (Phil. 4:3). The book of life will be used along with the books of judgment at the final judgment to separate the righteous and the wicked for their respective eternal destinies (Rev. 20:12,15; 21:27).

Christ Himself determines whether the names that are recorded in the book of life remain in that record and are supported by His confession that they belong to Him at the day of judgment or are blotted out (Rev. 3:5).

The OT refers to a record kept by God of those who are a part of His people (Exod. 32:32; Isa. 4:3; Dan. 12:1; Mal. 3:16). As in Revelation,

God can blot out the names of those in the book (Exod. 32:32; Ps. 69:28). In the OT this may simply mean people not in the book die, leaving the list of the living. Those whose names are written in the book are destined for life in a restored Jerusalem (Isa. 4:3) and deliverance through future judgment (Dan. 12:1). See *Apocalyptic; Book(s); Eschatology.*   *Jeff Cranford*

BOOK(S) Term which often refers to a scroll. A document written on parchment or papyrus and then rolled up. The "book" may be a letter (1 Kings 21:8) or a longer literary effort (Dan. 9:2). See *Letter; Library; Writing.*

Several books are mentioned in the Bible:

The Book of the Covenant Moses read from this book during the making of the covenant between God and Israel on Mount Sinai (Exod. 24:7). *The Book of the Covenant* included at least the material now found in Exod. 20:23–23:33. *The Book of the Covenant* is referred to at a later time (2 Kings 23:2,21; 2 Chron. 34:30). It probably included the Exodus passage in addition to other material.

The Book of the Law During the reign of Josiah, Hilkiah, the high priest, found a copy of *The Book of the Law* in the temple (2 Kings 22:8). Josiah based his reforms of the religion of Israel on the laws in this book (2 Kings 23). The book was not explicitly identified in 2 Kings, but by comparing the measures undertaken by Josiah and the laws of Deuteronomy, it is very likely that *The Book of the Law* was a copy of Deuteronomy.

The Book of the Wars of the Lord This book is quoted in Num. 21:14-15 (21:17-18 and 27-30 may also represent quotations from this book). The part of the book quoted describes the territory conquered by God in behalf of the Israelites. The book was probably a collection of poems that relate the conquest of the land during the time of Moses and Joshua. As the title of the book suggests, the Lord (acting as commander-in-chief) was responsible for the success of the conquest.

The Books of Joshua Joshua wrote one book detailing the allotment of Canaan to the Israelite tribes (Josh. 18:9) and a book similar to *The Book of the Covenant* listed above (Josh. 24:25-26).

The Book of Jashar (or Upright) A book quoted twice in the OT: Joshua's poetic address to the sun and the moon (Josh. 10:12-13) and David's lament for Saul and Jonathan (2 Sam. 1:17-27). Others would include Solomon's words of dedication of the temple (1 Kings 8:12-13), which the earliest Greek translation attributes to the book of song (Hb. *shir*), a transposition of letters of Hebrew *jshr* or *ishr* for Jashar. Deborah's song (Judg. 5) and Miriam's song (Exod. 15:20-21) are sometimes seen as part of Jashar. *The Book of Jashar* probably consisted of poems on important events in Israel's history collected during the time of David or Solomon. *The Book of Jashar* is often compared to or identified with *The Book of the Wars of the Lord* discussed above.

The Book of the Acts of Solomon Probably a biographical document that included such stories as Solomon's judgment between the two harlots (1 Kings 3:16-28), Solomon's administrative arrangements (1 Kings 4:1-19), and the visit of the Queen of Sheba (1 Kings 10:1-13).

Book of the Chronicles of the Kings of Israel Perhaps a continuous journal compiled by scribes from various sources but not to be confused with 1 and 2 Chronicles in the Bible. The writer of 1 and 2 Kings mentions this book 18 times as containing more complete information on the reigns of the kings of Israel (1 Kings 14:19; 15:31; 16:5,14,20,27; 22:39; 2 Kings 1:18; 10:34; 13:8,12; 14:15,28; 15:11,15,21, 26,31).

Book of the Chronicles of the Kings of Judah Source similar to the *Book of the Chronicles of the Kings of Israel,* not to be confused with 1 and 2 Chronicles in the Bible. The writer of 1 and 2 Kings mentions this book 15 times as containing more complete information on the reigns of the kings of Judah (1 Kings 14:29; 15:7,23; 22:45; 2 Kings 8:23; 12:19; 14:18; 15:6,36; 16:19; 20:20; 21:17,25; 23:28; 24:5).

Books Mentioned in 1 and 2 Chronicles Included are the *Book of the Kings of Israel* (1 Chron. 9:1; 2 Chron. 20:34), the *Book of the Kings of Israel and Judah* (2 Chron. 27:7; 35:27; 36:8), the *Book of the Kings of Judah and Israel* (2 Chron. 16:11; 25:26; 28:26; 32:32), the *Acts of the Kings of Israel* (2 Chron. 33:18), and the *Commentary on the Book of the Kings* (2 Chron. 24:27). Many think these titles are references to the same work and refer to it as the *Midrash of the Kings.* This work may contain the books of the chronicles of the kings of Israel and Judah listed above or at least be very similar in content to them.

B

Also mentioned in 1 and 2 Chronicles are books of various prophets: the *Book of Samuel the Seer* (1 Chron. 29:29), the *Book of Nathan the Prophet* (1 Chron. 29:29; 2 Chron. 9:29), the *Book of Gad the Seer* (1 Chron. 29:29), the *Prophecy of Ahijah the Shilonite* (2 Chron. 9:29), the *Visions of Iddo the Seer against Jeroboam the Son of Nebat* (2 Chron. 9:29), the *Book of Shemaiah the Prophet and Iddo the Seer* (2 Chron. 12:15), the *Story of the Prophet Iddo* (2 Chron. 13:22), the *Book of Jehu the Son of Hanani* (2 Chron. 20:34), the *Acts of Uzziah* (2 Chron. 26:22; written by Isaiah), the *Vision of Isaiah the Prophet* (2 Chron. 32:32), and the *Saying of the Seers* (2 Chron. 33:19). All of these, except for the last, may have been part of the *Midrash of the Kings*.

Various other works are also mentioned in 1 and 2 Chronicles: genealogies of the tribe of Gad (1 Chron. 5:17), the *Chronicles of King David* (1 Chron. 27:24), an untitled work containing the plan for the temple (1 Chron. 28:19), works on the organization of the Levites written by David and Solomon (2 Chron. 35:4), and lamentations for the death of Josiah by Jeremiah and others (2 Chron. 35:25).

Book of the Chronicles This is a work that contained genealogies and possibly other historical material (Neh. 7:5; 12:23) but was distinct from 1 and 2 Chronicles.

Books by the Prophets Isaiah (Isa. 30:8; cp. 8:16) and Jeremiah (Jer. 25:13; 30:2; 36; 45:1; 51:60,63) are said to have written books. These may have represented the first stages of the collections of their prophecies we now have.

Book (of Records) of the Chronicles or **Book of Memorable Deeds** The royal archives of Persia contained, among other things, books recording the way in which Mordecai saved the life of King Ahasuerus (Esther 2:20-23; 6:1; 10:2; cp. Ezra 4:15).

Book of Remembrance This book is mentioned in Mal. 3:16. It is probably the same as the Book of Life. See *Book of Life*.

Scripture (Book) of Truth This book is mentioned in Dan. 10:21. It is probably the same as the Book of Life.   *Phil Logan*

BOOT Figure mentioned in Isa. 9:5 of the booted Assyrian warrior (KJV translates the rare Hebrew word for boot as "battle"). Assyrian reliefs from the period of Sennacherib depict soldiers wearing leather boots laced up to the knee,

which is in contrast to the sandals worn by the Israelite soldier of the period. God's Messiah promised full victory, even over the more impressively dressed army.

BOOTH Temporary shelter constructed for cattle (Gen. 33:17) and people (Jon. 4:5), especially for soldiers on the battlefield (2 Sam. 11:11; 1 Kings 20:12,16). Israel after an invasion is compared to a deserted booth in a vineyard (Isa. 1:8). The booth is also used as a symbol of that which is flimsy and impermanent (Job 27:18). The booths used at the Feast of Booths were made of twigs woven together (Lev. 23:40-43; Neh. 8:15).

BOOTHS, FEAST OF See *Festivals*.

BOOTY Spoils taken by individuals in battle. Includes anything that might be of value or use to the captor including persons (Num. 31:53; Jer. 15:13; Ezek. 25:7). Booty is distinguished from spoil in the sense that booty was that taken by individual soldiers whereas spoil was plunder taken by the victor nation as a right of conquest.

BOOZ (Bō´ ŏz) (KJV, NT) See *Boaz*.

BOR-ASHAN (Bôr-ā´ shăn) Place-name meaning "well of smoke" or "pit of smoke." Place in most manuscripts of 1 Sam. 30:30; others read Chor-ashan (KJV). A town of the tribe of Judah to whom David gave part of his spoils of victory. It is usually equated with Asham, the town of Judah in which Simeon lived (Josh. 15:42; 19:7).

BORN AGAIN See *Regeneration*.

BORROW In Hebrew culture borrowing indicated economic hardship, not a strategy for expanding business or household. (See Lev. 25:35-37, which assumes that borrowers are poor.) In Deuteronomy God's blessings of prosperity was understood to exclude the need to borrow (15:6; 26:12). Thus poverty was not considered to be a desirable situation for anyone in the covenant community. The dire straits requiring borrowing are illustrated in Neh. 5:1-5. With typical shifts in fortune, borrowing was common practice in Hebrew society, and rules were needed so that the poor were not victimized by creditors. Laws for restitution were also established for borrowed property that was damaged (Exod. 22:14-15).

In Matt. 5:42 Jesus cites generosity "from the one who wants to borrow from you" as one example of an unexpected, loving response (instead of the typical self-protective response) to others' demands and abuses. In each example (5:38-42) the disciple's primary concern is the other person, not protecting one's own vested interests. The second person singular in verse 42 makes clear the personal nature of this response to the would-be borrower. This passage is part of Jesus' consistent emphasis on absolute loyalty to the way of God's kingdom, which necessitates a carefree regard for one's possessions (Matt. 6:24-34) and personal security (Matt. 5:43-48) as one unselfishly loves the neighbor.

David Nelson Duke

BOSCATH (Bŏs´ căth) (KJV, 2 Kings 22:1). See *Bozkath.*

BOSOR (Bō´ sôr) (KJV, 2 Pet. 2:15). See *Beor.*

BOSSED, BOSSES Knobs on the flat surfaces of shields. When shields were made of leather and wood, the bosses served to strengthen the shield. When shields were made of metal, the bosses were ornamental. Job 15:26 says that the wicked oppose God with a thick-bossed shield—that is, a reinforced shield. Thus some modern translations express the meaning rather than using literal translation: "strong shield" (NIV); "massive shield" (NASB).

BOTCH Old English term used in the KJV that means "boil" (Deut. 28:27,35).

BOTTLE Word used often in the KJV to translate several Hebrew and Greek words. Modern versions often translate these words as "skin" or "wineskin." Although glass and glass bottles were known in ancient times, ancient "bottles" were almost always made of animal skins since they were easier to carry than earthenware vessels. In Ps. 33:7 many modern scholars and translators emend the Hebrew text by adding an unpronounced Hebrew letter (*aleph*) to read "bottle" or "jars" (NIV, NRSV), but the traditional reading "heap" following the Hebrew text finds support in the parallel statement of Exod. 15:8.

Tiny Roman glass bottle.

BOTTOMLESS PIT Literal translation of the Greek in Rev. 9:1-2,11; 11:7; 17:8; 20:1,3. It represented the home of evil, death, and destruction stored up until the sovereign God allowed them temporary power on earth. See *Abyss; Hades; Hell; Sheol.*

BOW AND ARROW See *Arms and Armor.*

BOWELS Translation used in modern versions to refer to intestines and other entrails (Acts 1:18). In the KJV "bowels" is also used to refer to the sexual reproductive system (2 Sam. 16:11; Ps. 71:6) and, figuratively, to strong emotions (Job 30:27), especially love (Song 5:4) and compassion (Col. 3:12). Both Hebrew and Greek picture the entrails as the center of human emotions and excitement.

BOWL See *Basin.*

BOX KJV translation for jar or flask, a container of oil used for anointing (2 Kings 9:1; Mark 14:3).

BOX TREE KJV, REB and NASB translation in Isa. 41:19; 60:13. The box tree grows in Asia Minor and Persia but does not occur in

B

Painted relief of Persian soldier with lance, bow, and quiver of arrows on his left shoulder.

Phrygian cut-glass bowl.

Palestine. The tree has been identified as the pine (NRSV) or cypress (TEV, NIV). "Box tree" is based on early Greek and Latin translations. The Hebrew word means "to be straight" and apparently refers to the tall, majestic cypress trees. Such wonders of nature reflect the greatness of the Creator (Isa. 41:20).

BOZEZ (Bō´ zĕz) Place-name, perhaps meaning "white." A sharp rock marking a passage in the Wadi Suwenit near Michmash through which Jonathan and his armor bearer went to fight the Philistines (1 Sam. 14:4).

BOZKATH (Bŏz´ kăth) Place-name meaning "swelling." Town near Lachish and Eglon in tribal allotment of Judah (Josh. 15:39). It was the hometown of Adaiah, King Josiah's maternal grandmother (2 Kings 22:1). Its precise location is not known.

BOZRAH (Bŏz´ răh) Place-name meaning "inaccessible." **1.** Ancestral home of Jobab, a king in Edom before Israel had a king (Gen. 36:33). Isaiah announced a great judgment on Bozrah in which God would sacrifice His enemies (Isa. 34:6). A center of shepherds, it was known for woolen garments. God is pictured as returning from Bozrah with dyed garments as His spoil of victory (Isa. 63:1). Thus He demonstrated His righteousness and power to save from enemies. Jeremiah proclaimed doom on Bozrah (Jer. 49:13,22), as did Amos (1:12). A major city, which at times served as capital of Edom, Bozrah lay about 25 miles southeast of the southern end of the Dead Sea at modern Buseirah. See *Edom.* **2.** City of Moab Jeremiah condemned (Jer. 48:24). It may be equated with Bezer. See *Bezer.*

BRACELET Ornamental band of metal or glass worn around the wrist (as distinct from an arm-

Serpentine bracelet.

let worn around the upper arm). Bracelets were common in the ancient Near East and were worn by both women and men. They were made mostly of bronze, though examples of iron, silver, glass, and, rarely, gold bracelets have been found. The bracelets mentioned were usually of gold (Gen. 24:22,30,47; Num. 31:50; Isa. 3:19; Ezek. 16:11; 23:42). KJV, TEV and NASB translation for armlet in 2 Sam. 1:10. See *Armlet.*

BRAIDED, BRAIDING Fixing the hair in knots or weaving a wreath into the hair. Christian women were instructed that good works and spiritual grace were more important than outward appearances (1 Tim. 2:9; 1 Pet. 3:3). See *Lace.*

BRAMBLE Shrub (*Lycium europaeum*) with sharp spines and runners usually forming a tangled mass of vegetation (Judg. 9:8-15; Luke 6:44). It had beautiful, attractive flowers, but its thorns gave flocks trouble. Today we know that it prevents erosion on mountain slopes.

BRANCH Translation of many Hebrew and Greek words. Often refers to the branches of trees or vines or to the branches of the lampstands of the tabernacle and temple. There are, however, many metaphorical usages of "branch." The palm branch may stand for nobility, while the reed is symbolic for the common people (Isa. 9:14; 19:15). One's "being a branch" denotes membership in the people of God (John 15:1-8; Rom. 11:16-21). Spreading branches can symbolize fruitfulness and prosperity (Gen. 49:22; Job 18:16; Ps. 80:11), while withered, burnt, or cut branches symbolize destruction (Job 8:16; Isa. 9:14; Jer. 11:16; Ezek. 15:2). "Branch" or "shoot" is often used as a symbol for a present or coming king of Israel (Isa. 11:1; Jer. 23:5; 33:15; Zech. 3:8; 6:12). See *Messiah.*

BRASEN SEA See *Molten Sea.*

BRASEN SERPENT See *Bronze Serpent.*

BRASS Any copper alloy was called "brass" by the KJV translators. Brass is the alloy of copper and zinc, a combination unknown in the ancient Near East. A common alloy was copper and tin—that is, bronze—and this is what is indicated by the Hebrew of the biblical text. Some modern translations retain brass where hardness or persistence in sin is in view (Lev. 26:19; Deut. 28:23; Isa. 48:4), but they use "bronze" as a translation elsewhere. See *Minerals and Metals.*

BRAZEN SEA See *Molten Sea.*

BRAZEN SERPENT See *Bronze Serpent.*

BRAZIER Portable firepot (NIV) or fire pan used for heating a room during cold weather (Jer. 36:22-23; KJV has "hearth").

BREAD Appears 239 times in the NASB OT and 79 times in the NASB NT; but the seven Hebrew words which refer to bread, not always so translated, appear 384 times in the OT and the three Greek words 108 times in the NT. Frequency of mention is just one indication that bread (not vegetables and certainly not meat) was the basic food of most people (except nomads and the

Bread for sale in old Jerusalem.

wealthy) in Bible times. Indeed, several of the words alluded to above are often translated food.

Ingredients A course meal was ground from wheat (Gen. 30:14) or barley (John 6:9,13). American corn was unknown. (Use of the word in the KJV is a "Briticism" meaning grain in general.) Barley bread was less appetizing but also less expensive and therefore common among the poor. Grinding was done by a mortar and pestle or with millstones turned by an animal or human being (Num. 11:8; Matt. 24:41). For special occasions and offerings a fine flour was ground (Gen. 18:6; Lev. 2:7). The meal or flour was mixed with water, salt, sometimes leaven or yeast, sometimes olive oil, and rarely with other cereals and vegetables (Ezek. 4:9) and then was kneaded (Exod. 12:34).

Baking Usually the work of wives (Gen. 18:6) or daughters (2 Sam. 13:8), although in wealthy households it was done by slaves. Large cities or the royal court had professional bakers (Gen. 40:2; Jer. 37:21). There were three means of baking: on heated rocks with the dough being covered with ashes (1 Kings 19:6); on a clay or iron griddle or pan (Lev. 2:5); and in a clay or iron oven (Lev. 2:4). Most bread that was so baked had the appearance of a disk (Judg. 7:13) about one-half inch thick and 12 inches in diameter. Some was perforated. Some had a hole in the middle for storing or carrying on a pole. Some was heart shaped (the word for cakes in 2 Sam. 13:6,8,10 literally means heart shaped). Some took the shape of a small modern loaf (suggested by the arrangement of the Bread of Presence). Bread was broken or torn, not cut.

Use In addition to being used as a staple food, bread was used as an offering to God (Lev. 2:4-10). It was used in the tabernacle and temple to symbolize the presence of God (Exod. 25:23-30; Lev. 24:5-9). Bread was also used in the OT to symbolize such things as an enemy to be consumed (Num. 14:9, KJV, RSV), the unity of a group (1 Kings 18:19), hospitality (Gen. 19:3), and wisdom (Prov. 9:5). It is prefixed to such things as idleness (Prov. 31:27), wickedness (Prov. 4:17), and adversity (Isa. 30:20). In the NT it symbolizes Jesus Christ Himself (John 6:35), His body (1 Cor. 11:23-24), His kingdom (Luke 14:15), and the unity of His church (1 Cor. 10:17).

BREAD OF THE PRESENCE Also "bread of the faces." In Exod. 25:30 the Lord's instruc-

tions concerning the paraphernalia of worship include a provision that bread be kept always on a table set before the Holy of Holies. This bread was called the "bread of the Presence" or "showbread (shewbread)." The literal meaning of the Hebrew expression is "bread of the face." It consisted of 12 loaves of presumably unleavened bread, and it was replaced each Sabbath. Jesus took the staple diet of festival worship—unleavened bread—and gave it to His followers to symbolize the presence of His body broken to bring salvation and the hope of His return (1 Cor. 11:17-32). See *Shewbread; Tabernacle; Temple.* *James A. Brooks*

BREAKFAST See *Food.*

BREASTPIECE OF THE HIGH PRIEST Piece of elaborate embroidery about nine inches square worn by the high priest upon his breast. It was set with 12 stones with the name of one of the 12 tribes of Israel engraved on each stone. The breastpiece was a special item worn by the high priest as he ministered in the tabernacle or temple. Made like a purse, the breastpiece was constructed of gold metal; blue, purple, and scarlet yarn; and fine linen. It was securely tied to the ephod. Inside the breastpiece was placed two unknown stones, the Urim and Thummim, worn over the heart (Lev. 8:8). The breastpiece was called the breastpiece of judgment (Exod. 28:15) because these stones were the means of making decisions (Exod. 28:28-29). The purpose of the breastpiece was to show the glory and beauty of the Lord (Exod. 28:2) and to be a means of making decisions (Exod. 28:30) as well as to be a continuing memorial before the Lord (Exod. 28:29). See *Breastplate; Ephod; Urim and Thummim.* *Lawson G. Hatfield*

BREASTPLATE Piece of defensive armor. Paul used the military breastplate as an illustration of Christian virtues. Ephesians 6:14 reflects Isa. 59:17, symbolizing the breastplate as righteousness. Faith and love are symbolized in 1 Thess. 5:8. Breastplates were also strong symbols of evil (Rev. 9:9,17). See *Arms and Armor.*

Lawson G. Hatfield

BREATH Air coming out of or into the body of a living being. Two Hebrew terms are translated "breath." Generally *neshamah* is used in a milder manner to refer to the fact that breath is in all forms of life. It is concerned with the physiological concept of breath with a primary emphasis on breath as a principle of life. By contrast, *ruach* refers more to the force of breath in the extreme experiences of life, judgment, and death. At times it is intensified by the idea of a blast of breath. It thus contains the expanded meanings, wind and spirit. *Ruach* refers more to the psychological idea of breath by relating it to one's own will or purpose.

The term *neshamah* is often used with reference to God's breath. It identifies God as the source of life (Gen. 2:7; Job 27:3; 33:4; Dan. 5:23).

God is also the sovereign of life. He gave breath to humans initially in creation (Gen. 2:7), but He also takes breath away eventually at death (Gen. 7:22; Job 34:14). God has the power to restore life to the dead if He wishes to do so (Ezek. 37:9). He controls nature and the weather by His breath (Job 37:9-10). More important is the impact of God's breath on national life, for He can breathe anger and judgment on threatening enemies bringing festive joy to God's people (Isa. 30:33; cp. Job 41:21).

Neshamah is used several times to refer to human breath. It identifies breath as fragile during the times of God's wrath and in natural calamities (Isa. 2:21-22). Breath can become weak (Dan. 10:17); it is limited (Gen. 7:22; 1 Kings 17:17). Breath may be taken from a person, thus the experience of death (Josh. 11:11).

Breath (*neshamah*) refers to all living creatures. Those who breathe are expected to be responsive to God by offering Him praise (Ps. 150:6). Ultimately, they are responsible to God because He has the right to demand that they be put to death (Deut. 20:16; Josh. 10:40).

The NT contains a few references to breath as the life principle which God gives (Acts 17:25) and as the mighty wind at Pentecost (Acts 2:2). Acts 9:1 uses breath to express Saul's anger as a breathing of threats against the early Christians. In John 20:22 Jesus breathed the Holy Spirit upon His disciples. While the word *pneuma* parallels *ruach* in the OT in its multiple meanings, it is translated primarily as spirit or Holy Spirit. In Rev. 13:15 it refers to the power to breathe life into the image of the beast. See *Life; Spirit.*   *Donald R. Potts*

BREATH OF LIFE Translation of several Hebrew words and phrases. The phrase denotes the capacity for life. In the Bible God is the source of the breath of life (Gen. 1:30; 2:7; 7:15; Isa. 57:16). Just as God gave the breath of life, so can He take it away (Gen. 6:17; 7:22; Isa. 57:16). See *Immortality; Life.*

BREECHES Priestly garments made of linen covering the thighs for reasons of modesty. They were worn by the high priest on the Day of Atonement and by other priests on other ceremonial occasions (Exod. 28:42; 39:28; Lev. 6:10; 16:4; Ezek. 44:18). The garment ensured that priests fulfilled the commandment in Exod. 20:26.

BRIBERY Giving anything of value with intention of influencing one in the discharge of his or her duties. The danger of bribery is the opportunity it presents for the perversion of justice (1 Sam. 8:3; Prov. 17:23; Isa. 1:23; Mic. 3:11; 7:3). The poor, because they had no bribe to offer, were either discriminated against when the judgment was handed down or had difficulty getting a trial at all (see Job 6:22 where a bribe is necessary to get justice done). Bribery, because it perverted justice, is prohibited in the Bible (Exod. 23:8; Deut. 16:19).

BRICK Building material of clay, molded into rectangular-shaped blocks while moist and hardened by the sun or fire, used to construct walls or pavement.

The task of brick making was hard labor. It involved digging and moving heavy clay. Clay required softening with water, which was done by treading clay pits. After molding the bricks of approximately two by four by eight inches, they were dried in the sun or in kilns (ovens) for fire-hardened bricks. The tower of Babel (Gen. 11:3), made of bricks, had mortar of slime, a tar-like substance. Later, because of famine, Joseph

Mud-clay bricks in the ruins of the city of Ur.

moved his family to Egypt (Gen. 46:6). The 12 families multiplied greatly in 430 years. A new Pharaoh who "knew not Joseph" (Exod. 1:6-8) enslaved the Jews. They built storehouse cities of brick in Pithom and Rameses. Egyptian bricks were sometimes mixed with straw. When Moses confronted Pharaoh for Israel's freedom, the angered Pharaoh increased his demands of the slaves. They were required to produce their same brick quotas and gather their own straw. Both straw-made bricks and bricks of pure clay have been found at Pithom and Rameses. When David conquered the Ammonites, he required they make bricks (2 Sam. 12:31). Isaiah (65:3) condemned Israel for their paganlike practice of offering incense on altars of brick.

Lawson G. Hatfield

BRICK KILN Oven, furnace, or heated enclosure used for processing bricks by burning, firing, or drying. Some Bible students believe that sun-dried bricks were used in Palestine; they would translate the word as "brick-mold" (Nah. 3:14 NRSV, NASB, TEV). Others give the neutral translation "brickwork" (NIV, REB). Just as the Egyptians used the Israelites to make bricks, so David put the Ammonites to making bricks (2 Sam. 12:31).

BRIDE Biblical writers have little to say about weddings or brides. They occasionally mention means by which brides were obtained (Gen. 24:4; 29:15-19). Ezekiel 16:8-14 describes the bride, her attire, and the wedding ceremony. The Song of Songs is a collection of love poems in which the bride describes her love for her bridegroom.

The imagery of the bride is used widely in the Bible as a description of the people of God. In the OT, the prophets presented Israel as a bride who had committed repeated adulteries (Jer. 3; Ezek. 16; Hos. 3). The prophets also proclaimed that God was faithful to His unfaithful bride and would restore her (Jer. 33:10-11; Isa. 61:10; 62:5). In the NT, the bride imagery is used often of the church and her relationship to Christ. The bride belongs to Christ, who is the Bridegroom (John 3:29). In Revelation, the church, as the bride of the Lamb, has prepared herself for marriage by performing righteous deeds (19:7-8). In Rev. 21, the great wedding is portrayed with the church prepared for her bridegroom (21:2,9). Finally, the bride and the

Spirit issue an invitation "to come" (22:17). Paul used the metaphor of the bride to indicate his feelings toward the churches he had founded. In 2 Cor. 11:2 Paul wrote that he had betrothed the Corinthian church to Christ. He wanted to present the church as a pure bride to Christ. The Corinthians were in danger of committing "adultery." The imagery of the bride is used by various biblical writers, but they appear to have a single purpose. The bridal imagery is used to indicate the great love that God has for His people. For these writers, no image could express better this love than the ideal love between a bridegroom and bride.

Terence B. Ellis

BRIDE OF CHRIST See *Bride*.

BRIDE PRICE See *Dowry*.

BRIDLE See *Bit*.

BRIER Translation of various Hebrew words referring to thorny plants. Used metaphorically of the enemies of Israel (Ezek. 28:24) and of land which is worthless (Isa. 5:6; 7:23-25; 55:13; cp. Mic. 7:4).

BRIGANDINE KJV translation at Jer. 46:4; 51:3. Rendered elsewhere as "coat of mail" or "armor." See *Arms and Armor*.

BRIMSTONE Combustible form of sulfur. Used as a means of divine retribution (Gen. 19:24; Deut. 29:23; Job 18:15; Ps. 11:6; Isa. 30:33; 34:9; Ezek. 38:22; Luke 17:29; Rev. 14:10; 19:20; 20:10; 21:8). It lies on the shore of the Dead Sea and can burst into flame when earthquakes release hot gases from the earth's interior.

BROAD PLACE To be set in a broad place (Job 36:16) is to be delivered from danger, anxiety, want, or distress. The phrase is also translated as "large place" (2 Sam. 22:20; Pss. 18:19; 118:5; Hos. 4:16) and "large room" (Ps. 31:8). Related is the phrase applied to Canaan, "large land," which would appear to denote Canaan—the promised land—as a place of deliverance (Judg. 18:10; but see Isa. 22:18).

BROAD WALL A stretch of the wall of Jerusalem on the northwest corner near the

Gate of Ephraim, restored by Nehemiah (Neh. 3:8; 12:38).

BROIDERED See *Needlework.*

BRONZE See *Minerals and Metals.*

BRONZE SEA See *Molten Sea.*

BRONZE SERPENT Moses made a bronze serpent and set it on a pole in the middle of the Israelite camp (Num. 21). God had told Moses to do this so the Israelites bitten by serpents could express their faith by looking at it and be healed. The need for the serpent came in one of the times that Israel murmured against God and Moses. The people were in the wilderness after their refusal to obey God by entering the land of Canaan. Although God had provided food and water for them after their disobedience, they complained because of the monotony of the manna provided. As punishment for the people, God sent serpents among them. The serpents' bites were deadly, but God relented and chose to provide a way for rescue if those bitten would accept it. Anyone who looked on the bronze serpent set in the middle of the camp would be healed.

Nothing more is known of the bronze serpent until it is mentioned again in 2 Kings 18:4. There, in the account of King Hezekiah's purging of the temple, the Bible tells of the destruction of this symbol. Hezekiah wanted to purify temple worship. Apparently, the bronze serpent had become an object of worship as the Israelites burned incense to it.

Archaeological evidence from Mesopotamian and, more importantly, Canaanite sites reveals that the crawling serpent was a symbol of the fertility of the soil. The serpent was often represented associated with the fertility goddesses, the bull, the dove (life of the heavens), and water.

Jesus made the final mention of this symbol in John 3:14. There, in His conversation with Nicodemus, Jesus compared His own purpose with that of the bronze serpent. The serpent, lifted up in the wilderness, had been God's chosen way to provide physical healing. Jesus, lifted up on the cross, is God's chosen means of providing spiritual healing for all afflicted by sin. Whoever believes in Jesus "will not perish but have eternal life" (John 3:16 HCSB). See *Atonement; Hezekiah; Moses; Wilderness.*

Albert F. Bean and Karen Joines

BROOCH Class of jewelry brought by both men and women as offerings (Exod. 35:22). The Hebrew term denotes a golden pin (KJV has "bracelets"; REB, "clasp"; TEV, "decorative pins"). At a later time brooches were bow shaped and made of bronze or iron. Some recent interpreters think "nose rings" were meant.

BROOK OF EGYPT The southwestern limit of Canaanite territory given to Israel as a possession (Num. 34:5 NASB). It is usually identified with the Wadi el-'Arish, which flows from the middle of the Sinai Peninsula to the Mediterranean Sea. It empties into the Mediterranean about midway between the sites of Gaza and Pelusium. See *Rivers and Waterways.*

BROOK OF THE ARABAH Literally "brook of the wilderness." A streambed that is dry most of the year and marked the southern border of Israel, the Northern Kingdom (2 Kings 14:25; Amos 6:14). It has sometimes been located at the Brook of Zered that joins the Dead Sea at its southeastern corner from the east. More likely, it is either the Wadi el-Qelt, flowing from Jericho to the west, or the Wadi el-Kefren from the northern end of the Dead Sea flowing to the east.

BROOK OF THE WILLOWS Name appearing only in Isa. 15:7 as one of the borders of Moab. The Hebrew name can be read as a plural form of the Brook of the Arabah, but two separate waterways are meant. Probably the same as the Brook of Zered, modern Wadi el-Hesa. See *Brook of Zered; Arabim.*

BROOK OF ZERED Also called "valley of Zered." The Israelites crossed this brook marking an end to their wilderness wandering and entrance into the promised land (Num. 21:12; Deut. 2:13-14). It is usually identified with modern Wadi el-Hesa that flows into the southeast end of the Dead Sea. The wadi is about 35 miles long and forms the boundary between Moab and Edom. The Brook of Zered is the same as the Brook of the Willows (Isa. 15:7 KJV), the dry streambed of 2 Kings 3:16 (see 3:22), and perhaps the same as the Brook of the Arabah (Amos 6:14). See *Brook of the Arabah; Arabim.*

BROOM TREE Bush that often grows large enough to provide shade (1 Kings 19:4-5). Its foliage and roots were often used as fuel (Job 30:4; Ps. 120:4). Its white flowers with maroon center beautify the Dead Sea area. Bees buzz among its blooms. The name Rithmah—a place along the route of the exodus (Num. 33:18-19)—was named for this shrub (*rotem*). Although KJV, NASB identify the bush as the juniper, modern scholars agree that the bush intended by the Hebrew writer was the broom tree—*Retama raetam* (NIV, REB, NRSV).

BROTHERLY LOVE Concept that appears throughout the Bible, but the specific word for this type of love appears only in the NT. The word which is usually rendered "brotherly love" in the NT is the Greek *philadelphia* and is used only five times (Rom. 12:10; 1 Thess. 4:9; Heb. 13:1; 1 Pet. 1:22; 2 Pet. 1:7). A similar word, *philadelphos*, appears in 1 Pet. 3:8, and means "loving one's brother." However, the idea of brotherly love is much more extensive than these few occurrences.

Old Testament Two words in the OT cover the full range of ideas associated with "love," the Hebrew *ahab* and *chesed*, though the latter is often associated with covenant love. Israelites were called upon to love other people in many relationships: as friend to friend (Ps. 38:11; Prov. 10:12); between slave and master (Exod. 21:5; Deut. 15:16); with the neighbor (Lev. 19:18); with the poor and unfortunate (Prov. 14:21,31); and especially significant is the command to love the stranger and foreigner (Lev. 19:34; Deut. 10:19). Often the love relationship between people is in the context of covenant, as with David and Jonathan (1 Sam. 18:1-3).

New Testament Brotherly love in the ancient Christian literature means to treat others as if they were a part of one's family. This kind of love means "to like" another person and to want what is best for that individual. The basic word used for the brotherly type of love, *phileo*, sometimes means "to kiss," which was to show close friendship (Mark 14:44). This kind of love is never used for the love of God nor for erotic love.

Jesus constantly taught His followers the principle of "brotherly love." He declared that the second great commandment is, "You shall love your neighbor as yourself" (Mark 12:31 HCSB), and in the parable of the Good Samari-tan He explained who that neighbor is (Luke 10:25-37). He also encouraged forgiveness of a brother (Matt. 18:23-35) and offered the Golden Rule as a guide in relating to one's brother (Matt. 7:12; Luke 6:31).

Paul spoke of "brotherly love" in the context of the community of believers, the church. Twice he used the term *philadelphia*: first in 1 Thess. 4:9, then in Rom. 12:10. In both cases he encouraged Christians to live peaceably with one another in the church. He underlined the idea of love for the brethren in Gal. 5:14, "For the entire law is fulfilled in one statement: 'you shall love your neighbor as yourself.'" Also in Rom. 13:8-10, he declared, "Do not owe anyone anything, except to love one another." In 1 Cor. 8:13, on causing a weaker brother to stumble, he wrote, "If food causes my brother to fall, I will never again eat meat, so that I won't cause my brother to fall" (HCSB).

In the Johannine writings, brotherly love is a dominant theme. Jesus gave a new commandment "that you love one another" (John 13:34). The idea is repeated in John 17:26, "that the love with which You have loved Me may be in them." A series of emphatic statements on brotherly love in 1 and 2 John are designed to show that this is truly the central command of Jesus (1 John 2:9; 3:10,18,23; 4:8,20; 2 John 6).

In the Epistles the specific word *philadelphia* (brotherly love) appears in Hebrews and in 1 and 2 Peter. Hebrews 13:1-2 connects it with "hospitality to strangers," 1 Pet. 1:22 with being pure, and 2 Pet. 1:7 has it in a checklist of virtues which Christians should possess. See *Ethics; Hospitality; Love.*

W. Thomas Sawyer

BROTHERS In the OT the word "brother" usually refers to the blood relationship of siblings (Exod. 4:14; Judg. 9:5). In fact, the book of Genesis addresses the difficulties of sibling rivalry, or the "brother problem": Cain and Abel (Gen. 4); Jacob and Esau (Gen. 25–28); Joseph and his brothers (Gen. 37–50). In each instance the younger brother is the one favored by God. (See also David among Jesse's sons, 1 Sam. 16:11-13.)

The NT also reflects the use of the word "brother" to designate a physical relationship. Luke mentions that Herod and Philip are brothers (Luke 3:1). Among the disciples, Simon and Andrew are siblings (Mark 1:16); so also are

James and John (Mark 1:19). The four brothers of Jesus are mentioned in Mark 3:31 and named in Mark 6:3. Other examples of physical brothers are found in the parable of the rich man and Lazarus (Luke 16:28), the story of the disputed inheritance (Luke 12:13), and the parable of the prodigal son (Luke 15:11-32).

The term "brother" is also used in the OT to signify kinsmen, allies, fellow countrymen. The word is used in Gen. 13:8 to describe the relationship of Abram and his nephew, Lot ("we are brothers"). Solomon and Hiram of Tyre are called brothers after they entered into political alliance with one another (1 Kings 9:13). Often the term "brothers" is found in apposition to the phrase "the sons of Israel" (Lev. 25:46; Deut. 3:18; 24:7; Judg. 20:13; cp. Num. 25:6). Basic to this idea is the notion that the tribes and nation of Israel descended from a common father.

This shift of focus from blood to spiritual kinship is found in the teachings of Jesus when He designated as brothers "those who hear and do the word of God" (Luke 8:21 HCSB). The fledgling Christian community continued this emphasis on brother as expressing a spiritual relationship. Paul regularly addressed the Christian community as brothers (1 Cor. 1:10; 1 Thess. 1:4). In fact, in most of the NT passages where "brothers" is used to designate the entire Christian community (male and female), the word may be better translated as "fellow Christians" (Phil. 4:1-9). The dual function of the term "brother" as describing both a physical and spiritual relationship bears eloquent testimony to the importance in the Christian community of both the family of flesh and the family of faith. See *Early Church; Paul; Sister.*

Mikeal C. Parsons

BROTHERS, JESUS' Jesus grew up in a normal family with parents and brothers. Jesus' Nazareth critics listed them in Mark 6:3 as James, Joses, Judas, and Simon. Their names appear again in the parallel passage of Matt. 13:55, except Joseph is used as the alternate spelling of Joses (see NASB). His brothers may have been among the friends in Mark 3:21 who thought Jesus was "out of His mind"; ten verses later in 3:31 "His mother and His brothers" tried to get His attention while He was teaching in a house. Furthermore, John 7:5 reports that "not even His brothers believed in Him." After the resurrection, however, they changed their minds and joined the disciples in times of prayer (Acts 1:14). The risen Christ appeared to one of them, James, and he became the leader of the church in Jerusalem (Acts 12:17; 1 Cor. 15:7). Nevertheless, some writings in the early centuries raised questions about the brothers to protect their developing doctrine of Mary's perpetual virginity. One of them, often called the Gospel of James, tells the life story of Mary, using much fanciful material. It claims that Jesus' brothers were the sons of Joseph by an earlier marriage. This is the view of the Greek Orthodox Church. Later a famous scholar, Jerome, argued that Jesus' brothers were really his cousins because their mother was Mary of Cleophas and the sister of Mary the mother of Jesus (John 19:25). This is the view of the Roman Catholic Church, but Protestant scholars prefer the traditional view of the Gospels. Jesus was born of the virgin Mary. Mary and Joseph then had four sons in the way all humans normally do.   *W. J. Fallis*

BROWN KJV translation of a Hebrew word rendered as "black" (NASB, NRSV, TEV, REB) or "dark-colored" (NIV) by modern translations (Gen. 30:32,33,35,40). See *Black; Colors.*

BUBASTIS (Bū băs´·tĭs) (TEV, NIV) See *Pibeseth.*

BUCKET Reference is to water skin held open at the top by a stick in the shape of a cross (Num. 24:7; Isa. 40:15). The main purpose was for drawing water from a well and is still used in Palestine today.

BUCKLER Small rounded shield that was carried in the hand or worn on the arm. Larger shields were also used which covered the entire body. See *Arms and Armor.*

BUGLE NRSV, NASB, TEV translation of a Greek word in 1 Cor. 14:8 which is elsewhere translated as "trumpet." See *Music, Instruments, Dancing.*

BUKKI (Bŭk´ kī) Personal name shortened from Bukkiah, meaning "Yahweh proved" or "Yahweh has emptied." **1.** Representative of tribe of Dan on commission to distribute the promised land among the tribes (Num. 34:22). **2.** High priestly descendant of Aaron (1 Chron. 6:5,51) and ancestor of Ezra (Ezra 7:4).

B

BUKKIAH (Bŭk·kī´ ăh) Son of Heman among temple musicians David appointed (1 Chron. 25:4). He or a person of the same name headed the sixth course of musicians (1 Chron. 25:13). See *Bukki.*

BUL (Bŭl) Name of eighth month or parts of October and November meaning "harvest month." Solomon finished building the temple in this month (1 Kings 6:38).

BULL The term is a translation of several Hebrew words: *abbir, par,* and *shor.* The difference between *abbir* and *par* is not obvious but may be of some consequence. *Abbir* is used as an adjective most frequently to mean might or valiant one, either man, angels, or animals. *Par* seems to be used in reference to the male of the bovine species.

The bull was the symbol of great productivity in the ancient world and was a sign of great strength. Moses portrayed the future strength of Joseph with the term *shor* (Deut. 33:17). The king of Assyria boasted of his great strength with the term *abbir* (Isa. 10:13). The most frequent

Relief of festooned bull's head from Roman Philippi.

use of the bull in the OT was as a sacrificial animal. Leviticus specifies that no castrated animal could be so used and that the animal must be at least eight days old (22:17-28). The bull is specified as the sacrificial animal for a peace offering (Exod. 24:5), a burnt offering (Judg. 6:26), and as a sin offering (Ezek. 43:19). On the other hand, the sacrificial animal is not so restricted in other passages (Lev. 22:23; Num. 23:14). The bull was used most frequently in connection with the inauguration of the sacrificial system or with sacrifices on special days. It was used in connection with the consecration of the priests

A colossal Persian column capital from Susa decorated with the neck and head of two stylized bulls.

(Exod. 29:1-37); at the dedication of the altar of the tabernacle (Num. 7); for the purification of the Levites (Num. 8:5-22); at the beginning of the month, New Moon (Num. 28:11-15); the Feast of Weeks (Num. 28:26-31). The Feast of Booths had the distinction of requiring the largest numbers of bulls (71, Num. 29:12-40). The bull may have been introduced into the cultic system of Israel from the practice of her neighbors. It was a widespread practice in the region in which Israel resided. In the Canaanite religion, the chief of the assembly was called

Bulrushes at the so-called "Moses' Well" in the Sinai Desert.

"father bull El." The bull was closely associated with Baal and may have influenced Jeroboam to set up the golden bulls at Bethel and Dan (1 Kings 12:28). The bronze sea in the courtyard of the temple in Jerusalem was resting on the back of 12 bronze bulls. *Bryce Sandlin*

BULRUSH In Exod. 2:3 the material that was used to make the ark (basket) in which the infant Moses was placed to protect him from the edict of Pharaoh requiring that every male Hebrew child be drowned. It was a kind of reed plant. See *Plants*.

BULWARK Solid wall-like structure raised for defense, possibly a system of two walls with space between. God's salvation is a bulwark for His people (Isa. 26:1; Ps. 8:2; 1 Tim. 3:15).

BUNAH (Bū´ năh) Personal name meaning "understanding." Member of clan of Jerahmeel in tribe of Judah (1 Chron. 2:25).

BUNDLE See *Bag*.

BUNNI (Bŭn´ nī) Personal name meaning "built." Levite leader of worship service confessing Israel's sin in days of Ezra (Neh. 9:4). A man of the same name, probably same man, signed Nehemiah's covenant to obey God's Law (Neh. 10:15). His son Hasabiah was one of the Levites living in Jerusalem in the time of Nehemiah (Neh. 11:15).

BURGLARY See *Crimes and Punishments*.

BURIAL Partly because of the warm climate of Palestine and partly because the corpse was considered ritually impure, the Hebrews buried their dead as soon as possible and usually within 24 hours of death (Deut. 21:23). To allow a body to decay or be desecrated above the ground was highly dishonorable (1 Kings 14:10-14; 2 Kings 9:34-37), and any corpse found by the wayside was required to be buried (2 Sam. 21:10-14).

Though the Bible nowhere systematically describes Hebrew mortuary practice, several features can be gleaned from individual passages. Joseph closed his father's eyelids soon after Jacob's death (Gen. 46:4). Jesus' body was prepared for burial by anointing with aromatic oils and spices and wrapping in a linen cloth (Mark 16:1; Luke 24:1; John 19:39). The arms and legs

Burial caves carved out of bedrock along the south slope of the Hinnom Valley in Jerusalem.

of Lazarus' body were bound with cloth, and the face covered by a napkin (John 11:44). The body of Tabitha was washed in preparation for burial (Acts 9:37).

The dead were buried in caves, rock-cut tombs, or in the ground. It was desirable to be buried in the family tomb, so Sarah (Gen. 23:19), Abraham (Gen. 25:9), Isaac, Rebekah, Leah (Gen. 49:31), and Jacob (Gen. 50:13) were all buried in the cave of Machpelah, east of Hebron. Burial sites were marked by trees (Gen. 35:8), pillars (Gen. 35:19-20), and piles of stones (Josh. 7:26). The burials of the wealthy or politically powerful were sometimes accompanied by lavish accessories, including robes, jewelry, furniture, weapons, and pottery (1 Sam. 28:14; Isa. 14:11; Ezek. 32:27).

In contrast to its wide usage among the Greeks and Romans, cremation is not described as normal practice in the Bible. Bodies were cremated only in exceptional cases such as decay following mutilation (1 Sam. 31:12) or the threat of plague. Even in these instances, cremation was partial so that the bones remained. Embalming is mentioned only in the burial accounts of Jacob and Joseph (Gen. 50:2-3,26) and there only because of the Egyptian setting and plans to move the bodies. Apparently, embalming was an Egyptian practice.

When preparations for burial were completed, the body was usually placed on a bier and carried to the burial site in a procession of relatives, friends, and servants (Amos 6:10). The procession carried out the mourning ritual, which could include baldness and cutting of beard; rending garments and wearing sackcloth; loud and agonized weeping; and putting dust on the head and sitting in ashes (2 Sam. 1:11-12; 13:31; 14:2; Isa. 3:24; 22:12; Jer. 7:29; Ezek.

7:18; Joel 1:8). The Canaanite practices of laceration and mutilation are forbidden in the Torah (Lev. 19:27-28; 21:5; Deut. 14:1).

The period of mourning varied in response to circumstances. Mourning for Jacob lasted 70 days (Gen. 50:3), while for Aaron and Moses it lasted 30 days (Num. 20:29; Deut. 34:5-8). Women captured in war were allowed to mourn the deaths of their parents one month before having to marry their captors (Deut. 21:11-13).

The deaths of the famous prompted poetic laments. David mourned for the deaths of Saul and Jonathan (2 Sam. 1:17-27), and Jeremiah lamented the death of Josiah (2 Chron. 35:25).

Professional mourners are referred to in Jer. 9:17-18 and Amos 5:16 and in Matt. 9:23 as "flute players." In the latter account Jesus seemed to dismiss them as He healed the ruler's daughter. It is interesting to note that Jesus' own response to Lazarus' death was comparatively simple; He wept at the tomb (John 11:35-36).

Israel's mourning rites reflect in part the belief that death is something evil. All contact with death—whether it happened by touching a corpse, the bones of a corpse, a grave, or a house which contained a dead body—made the Israelite unclean and in need of purification. In addition to personal sorrow, the mourning rites reflected at least to a degree the mourner's humiliation because of his necessarily close contact with the body of the deceased.   *Joe Haag*

BURNING BUSH In Exod. 3:2 Moses' attention was arrested by the sight of a bush that burned without being consumed by the fire. When he turned aside to investigate, the Lord spoke to him from the bush, instructing him to return to Egypt to deliver the Hebrew people from slavery. Some attempts have been made to explain the phenomenon by claiming that the bush had foliage of a brilliant fiery color or that its leaves reflected the sunlight in an unusual manner. It is best, however, to regard the burning of the bush as a unique act of God. It appears

to have had significance primarily, perhaps solely, as a means of attracting Moses' interest and so enabling him to hear the divine word. See *Exodus; Moses.*

BURNT OFFERINGS See *Sacrifice and Offering.*

BUSHEL See *Weights and Measures.*

BUTLER Translation of a Hebrew word that literally means "one who gives drink." The butler was an officer of the royal court who had charge of wines and other beverages. The butler was a trusted member of the royal court as this person helped prevent the poisoning of the king. The term that is translated "butler" (Gen. 40:1-23; 41:9) is also translated "cupbearer" (1 Kings 10:5; 2 Chron. 9:4; Neh. 1:11).

BUZ (Bŭz) Place and personal name meaning "scorn." **1.** Son of Nahor, brother of Abraham (Gen. 22:21). **2.** A member of tribe of Gad (1 Chron. 5:14). **3.** A land in eastern Arabia (Jer. 25:23) which Jeremiah condemned.

BUZI (Bū´ zi) Personal noun meaning "scorn." Priest and father of Ezekiel, the prophet and priest (Ezek. 1:3).

BUZITE (Bŭz´ īt) Citizen of Buz. See *Buz.*

BUZZARD Unclean bird, not suitable for food. Listed in the NASB and NLT in Lev. 11:13; Deut. 14:12 with the birds of abomination. Revelation 18:2 (NLT) has "filthy buzzards" nesting in the fallen Babylon.

BYBLOS See *Gebal.*

BYWORD Object of ridicule and scorn among other peoples. Used to speak of the fate of faithless Israel (Deut. 28:37; 1 Kings 9:7; 2 Chron. 7:20; Job 17:6; 30:9; Ps. 44:14).

C

The bema (tribunal) where Paul stood before Gallio in Corinth.

CAB See *Kab; Weights and Measures.*

CABBON (Căb´ bŏn) Place-name of uncertain meaning. Town in tribal allotment of Judah (Josh. 15:40). Its location is uncertain.

CABIN KJV translation of Hebrew word appearing only in Jer. 37:16 and meaning vault, cellar, or prison cell (cistern, NRSV).

CABUL (Cā´ bûl) Place-name meaning "fettered" or "braided." **1.** Town on northeast border of Asher (Josh. 19:27). May be located at modern Kabul, nine miles southeast of Acco. **2.** Region of cities in Galilee Solomon gave Hiram, king of Tyre, as payment for materials and services in building the temple and the palace. Hiram did not like them and called them "Cabul," a Hebrew wordplay meaning "as nothing." Apparently, the "gift" expected a gift in return, according to Near Eastern etiquette, for Hiram gave Solomon 120 talents of gold (1 Kings 9:10-14).

CAESAR (Cē´ sàr) Family name of Julius Caesar assumed by following emperors as a title. Some Pharisees and Herodians asked Jesus about the propriety of paying taxes to Caesar. In reply the Lord said that those things pertaining to Caesar should be rendered to Caesar and those things pertaining to God should be rendered to Him (Matt. 22:15-21). In this passage the name Caesar is virtually a symbol for civil authority. Originally, Caesar was the family name of the founder of the Roman Empire. Julius Caesar was assassinated on March 15, 44 B.C. His successors kept Caesar's memory alive, and eventually his name came to be used as a title. Caesars mentioned or referred to in the NT include Augustus, Tiberius,

The turbulent waters of the Mediterranean Sea as seen from Caesarea Maritima.

Claudius, and probably Nero. See *Rome and the Roman Empire.*

CAESAREA (Cĕs·à·rē´ à) Located on the Mediterranean Sea 23 miles south of Mount Carmel is the city of Caesarea, known also as Caesarea-on-the-Sea (Maritima), Caesarea Sebaste, Caesarea of Palestine, and Caesarea of Judea.

Because of the lack of natural harbor between Sidon and Egypt, a Sidonian king, Abdashtart, established an anchorage in the forth century B.C. It became known as Strato's Tower, using the king's Greek name. A fortified town developed on this site. The first literary record is from the archive of the Egyptian Zenon who put in there for supplies in 259 B.C. The Hasmonean ruler Alexander Jannaeus brought it under Jewish control in 96 B.C., but Pompey returned it to Gentile rule in 63 B.C. The Jewish community apparently continued to thrive. Mark Anthony gave it to Cleopatra, but Octavian or Augustus defeated Antony at Actuim and placed Caesarea under Herod in 30 B.C.

Performances are once again held at the restored Herodian theater at Caesarea Maritima.

Byzantine street at Caesarea Maritima with two colossal statues, one possibly of the Emperor Hadrian.

The Mediterranean Sea as seen through the arches of the Herodian aqueduct at Caesarea Maritima.

Water was provided for Caesarea Maritima by an extensive system based on this Herodian aqueduct.

Herod determined to build a fine port facility and support it by a new city. The harbor, which he named Sebastos (Latin, Augustus), was a magnificently engineered project. The southern breakwater was built of huge mortared stones placed in a semicircle about 2,000 feet long, and the northern one is of similar construction almost 900 feet long. Great statues of Augustus and Roma were erected at the entrance. An inner harbor appears to have been dug into the land where mooring berths and vaulted warehouses were constructed. Josephus described the construction of the harbor and accompanying city in grandiose detail. The city was Hellenistic in design and style and named Caesarea for Caesar. In addition to the many buildings, a platform was raised near the harbor upon which a temple was built for Caesar with a colossus of Caesar.

After Archelaus was removed in A.D. 6, Caesarea became the capital of the province of Judea and served as the official home of the procurators. Hostilities between the Jewish and Gentile population apparently had been a way of life in this city. One of the public outbreaks resulted in the desecration of the synagogue Knestha d'Meredtha in A.D. 66 that precipitated the Jewish-Roman War. Vespasian gave it the status of colony.

The city appears in the book of Acts as a place of witness, travel, and the seat of government. Philip, having witnessed to the Ethiopian eunuch, is mentioned as arriving at Caesarea after a preaching mission. Peter led Cornelius, a centurion who was stationed there, to Christianity (Acts 10). Paul had several reported contacts with the city as a port (Acts 9:30; 18:22; and perhaps 21:8) and a place of imprisonment and trial

(Acts 23:23; 25:1-7). Herod Agrippa I had a residence there and died there (Acts 12:19-23).

George W. Knight

CAESAREA PHILIPPI (Čěs·á·rē´ á Phĭl´ ĭp pī) About 1,150 feet above sea level, Caesarea Philippi is located on a triangular plain in the upper Jordan Valley along the southwestern slopes of Mount Hermon. Behind it rise bluffs and rugged mountain peaks. The area is one of the most lush and beautiful in Palestine, with groves of trees and grassy fields abounding. Water is in abundance, for the city is near the spot where the spring Nahr Baniyas, one of the sources of the Jordan, gushes from a cave in the bluffs. The city is also in a strategic location, guarding the plains in the area. The extent of its ruins indicate that it was a city of considerable size. The modern town, which has dwindled drastically, is known as Banyas.

History Caesarea Philippi seems to have been a religious center from its earliest days. The Canaanite god Baal-gad, the god of good fortune, was worshiped here in OT times. Later, in the Greek period, a shrine in the cave was dedicated to the god Pan. In addition, many niches in the cave held statues of the Nymphs. When Herod the Great was king of the Jews, he built a temple out of white marble near the same spot and dedicated it to Emperor Augustus.

The city also has an important place in the history of the area. Paneas, as it was called before its name was changed, was the site of a famous battle (198 B.C.) in which Antiochus the Great defeated the Egyptians and thereby took control of Palestine for the Seleucids. In 20 B.C. the Romans under Augustus, who then controlled the area, gave the territory to Herod the Great. After Herod's death, it passed to his son Philip

Banias waterfall near Caesarea Philippi.

who ruled there from 4 B.C. until his death in A.D. 34. Philip rebuilt the city into a beautiful place and renamed it Caesarea Philippi in honor of Tiberias Caesar and himself.

When Herod Agrippa II (grandson of Herod the Great) inherited the city, he renamed it Neronias in honor of the emperor Nero. But after Nero's death the name was dropped. During the Jewish-Roman War of A.D. 66–70, the Roman general Vespasian rested his army here. After the war, Titus, who succeeded his father as general of the Roman armies, held gladiatorial shows here during which a number of Jewish prisoners were put to death. After subduing the Jews, the Romans changed its name back to Paneas.

New Testament Near here Jesus asked His disciples the famous question about His identity. When He asked them who men said He was, they answered that people were identifying Him with Elijah, John the Baptist, or one of the prophets (Mark 8:27-33; Matt. 16:13-23). Jesus then asked them, "Who do you say that I am?" (Matt. 16:15 HCSB). Peter, acting as the group's spokesman, replied with his famous statement that Jesus is the Christ.

Stone niche at Caesarea Philippi (Banias) in which the statue of a pagan god was placed.

Ruins of a Christian chapel on Mount Hermon near Caesarea Philippi, the site of Peter's confession.

The transfiguration, which occurred about a week after the confession at Caesarea Philippi, was probably also in the area. Caesarea Philippi, which had been the center for pagan worship, thus became an important site for Christians because of Jesus' association with it. See *Augustus; Baal; Herod; Nero.*   W. T. Edwards, Jr.

CAESAR'S HOUSEHOLD In Phil. 4:22 Paul the apostle sent greetings to the Philippian Christians from certain believers who were of Caesar's household. The phrase was used to refer to all persons, both slave and free, who were in the service of the emperor. In Phil. 1:13 Paul had indicated the fact that he was imprisoned for the cause of Christ had become well-known throughout the Praetorian Guard. Quite possibly, some members of the Praetorian Guard were included among the believers of Caesar's household. See *Caesar; Rome and the Roman Empire.*

CAIAPHAS (Kī´ a·phàs) personal name meaning "rock" or "depression." High priest at the time of the trial and crucifixion of Jesus (Matt. 26:3). He was the son-in-law of Annas and a leader in the plot to arrest and execute Jesus. Relatively little is known of his life. He was apparently appointed high priest about A.D. 18 and served until A.D. 36 or 37. His remains have been found in an ossuary box in a burial cave in Jerusalem, which also contains the remains of many of his family members. See *Cross, Crucifixion; Levites; Priests.*   Charles W. Draper

CAIN (Cān) Personal name meaning "acquisition." The firstborn son of Adam and Eve (Gen. 4:1). Although the meaning of the name is disputed, Eve's rationale for giving it suggests a relationship with a Hebrew root that means "to acquire." Cain was a farmer, and his brother Abel was a shepherd. When the two men each brought an offering to the Lord, Abel's was accepted, but Cain's was not. Subsequently, Cain murdered Abel his brother. In punishment, God took from him the ability to till the ground productively and made him to be a wandering vagabond. God marked him to protect him from anyone seeking to avenge Abel's murder.

CAINAN (Cā´ nän) Personal name of unknown meaning. **1.** Ancestor of Noah (Gen. 5:10-14), sometimes seen as a variant spelling of Cain (Gen. 4:17). He is included in Christ's ancestry (Luke 3:37). In 1 Chron. 1:2 the name is spelled Kenan, a spelling used in other places by many modern translators. **2.** Descendant of Noah listed in the Septuagint of Gen. 11:12 but not of Hebrew. Luke used this early Greek translation of the OT and included Cainan in Christ's ancestors (Luke 3:36). See *Kenan*.

CAKE Term referring more to the shape of a loaf of bread (flat and round) than to the type of batter or dough used to make the loaf (Exod. 29:23; 1 Kings 17:13). See *Bread*.

CALAH (Cā´ läh) Assyrian place-name. City that Nimrod built along with Nineveh and Rehoboth (Gen. 10:8-12). It is modern Tell Nimrud on the east bank of Tigris River where it joins Upper Zab River 20 miles south of Nineveh. Ashurnasirpal II (883–859 B.C.) made it the capital of Assyria. Major Assyrian archaeological discoveries including the six-acre palace of Ashurnasirpal have been dug up. See *Assyria*.

CALAMUS (Căl´ à·mŭs) Ingredient of holy anointing oil (Ezek. 30:23). It was a good-smelling spice made from an imported reed. It is also translated "fragrant cane" (NIV, NASB) or "aromatic cane" (NRSV). See *Plants*.

CALCOL (Căl´ cŏl) Personal name of uncertain meaning. Wise man who served as comparison for Solomon's

unsurpassed wisdom (1 Kings 4:31). First Chronicles 2:6 makes him a grandson of Judah, the son of Jacob.

CALDRON Cooking pot made of various materials used by different English translations for various Hebrew words. Used both in the home and in the temple (1 Sam. 2:14; 2 Chron. 35:13; Job 41:20; Ezek. 11:3,7,11; Jer. 52:18-19; Micah 3:3). See *Pottery*.

CALEB (Cā´ lĕb), **CALEBITE** Personal and clan name meaning "dog." Caleb, the son of Jephunneh, was one of the 12 spies sent by Moses to

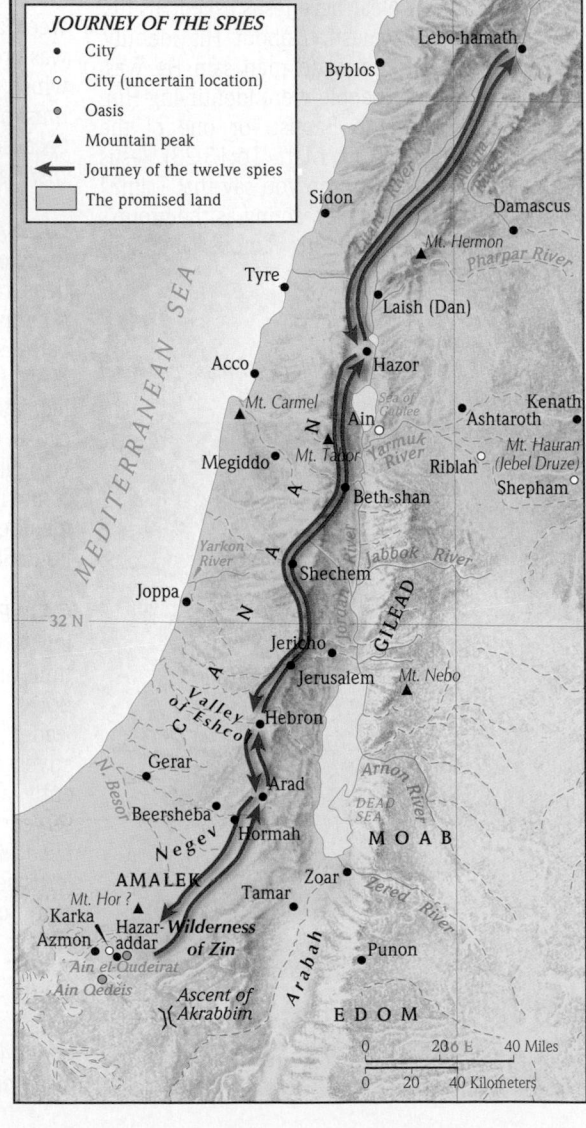

scout out the territory of Canaan (Num. 13:6). He was one of only two who brought back a positive report (Num. 13:30). Because of his steadfast loyalty to the Lord, God rewarded him by letting him survive the years of wilderness wandering and giving him the region of Hebron as his portion in the promised land. At the age of 85 Caleb conquered Hebron (Josh. 14).

The ethnological identity of the Calebites is uncertain. In Num. 13:6 Caleb is identified with the tribe of Judah. However, according to Num. 32:12, his father Jephunneh was a Kenezite. The Kenezites apparently were of Edomite origin (Gen. 36:9-11). Perhaps Caleb represented a Kenezite clan that had joined the Israelites and become incorporated into the tribe of Judah.

CALEB EPHRATAH (Cā´ leb Eph´ rà·tăh) (KJV), **CALEB-EPHRATHAH** (modern translations) Place where Hezron, Caleb's father, died (1 Chron. 2:24). The RSV (not NRSV) follows a slight change of Hebrew text to make Ephrathah the wife of Hezron whom Caleb took after his father's death. Ephrathah was another name for Bethlehem. Otherwise, Caleb-ephrathah is unknown. See *Bethlehem; Ephratah.*

CALENDAR OT mentions days, months, and years, the basic elements of a calendar, but it has no prescription for regulating one. It was in the rabbinical period that the written treatise on Jewish traditions, *Rosh Hashanah*, a part of the Mishna, organized the biblical data into the detailed calendrical system that the Jews observe today. We can assume that what the rabbis codified was in general practice among the Jews of the first century, the time of Christ and the apostles, but the NT offers little direct calendrical data. Periods into which certain important events are dated mention not the day and month but the name of one or another of the ancient Jewish festivals: the Passover (usually in the passion pericopae, Matt. 26, Mark 14, Luke 22, John 18–19; otherwise at Luke 2:41 and at seven passages in John preceding the passion); the day of Pentecost (the Jewish feast of Weeks, Acts 2:1; 20:16; 1 Cor. 16:8); and the feast of dedication (Jewish *Hanukkah*, John 10:22). The NT offers no evidence that the Jews inside or outside Palestine observed the Roman calendar commencing on January 1, but the apocryphal book 1 Maccabees and the Jewish historian Josephus do substitute Greek

(Macedonian) month names for Jewish month names. We may assume that in business dealings Greek-speaking Jews made free use of them. This was little more than a linguistic convention, however, since the Greek months corresponded with the Jewish months, making little difference in the basis of calendrical reckoning.

The Year Anthropological evidence from many regions shows that it was possible in the most ancient times to chart the course of the sun in its annual orbit, which occurs in approximately 365 days. The vernal and autumnal equinoxes (the day in the spring and fall, respectively, when days and nights are of equal lengths) were commonly designated as the beginning of a new year. From biblical data and from Near Eastern writings we know that all the peoples from the Mesopotamian area, as well as the Arabians, the Greeks, and the Romans, chose the first, unquestionably because spring is when new life sprouts forth. In Phoenicia, Canaan, and Israel, however, the fall date was chosen, probably for the reason that harvesting marked the end of one agricultural cycle and prepared for the next. In the exilic and postexilic periods, the Jews shifted to the spring new year, but since rabbinic times, the fall new year has been observed.

From biblical and archaeological evidence we are able to describe three different ways for reckoning the years and dividing up the months from one new year to the next. Each of them reflects a different social system and religious ideology.

First, a basically agricultural society is reflected in the "Gezer Calendar" discovered by R. A. S. Macalister. This is actually a schoolboy exercise in which primitive Hebrew letters are scratched on a clay tablet. It reads:

His two months are (olive) harvest,
   His two months are planting (grain),
      His two months are late planting;
His month is hoeing up of flax,
   His month is harvest of barley,
      His month is harvest and feasting;
His two months are vine-tending,
   His month is summer fruit.
(trans. by W. F. Albright, *Ancient Near Eastern Texts*)

Two things are important to observe: (1) the list commences in the fall and ends with the following summer; (2) because it alternates between two-month and one-month periods and does not name or number the months, we can see that the succession of agricultural activities determines the order of items and that the year is conceived on the succession of agricultural events rather than on astronomical observation.

Second, the entire OT moves on to a lunar-solar calendar that is based on observation of the heavenly bodies and regulates a more sophisticated order of economic and religious activity. This type of calendar had wide currency among the more advanced societies. It is called "lunar-solar" because it allowed the sun's orbit to mark the years' beginning but based the beginning of months on observation of the phases of the moon. The first appearance of the new moon would mark the new month. According to the Talmud, the priests would watch for this and proclaim it by sending messengers and blowing trumpets. The first problem is that the moon's circuit is about 29 ½ days, forcing a vacillation between a 30-day and a 29-day month; and second, that 12 of these moon/months equal 354 ¼ days, about 11 days short of the solar year. From the Babylonians the Hebrews learned to add an extra month every two or three years. In rabbinical times this "intercalary" month was inserted seven times in 19 years.

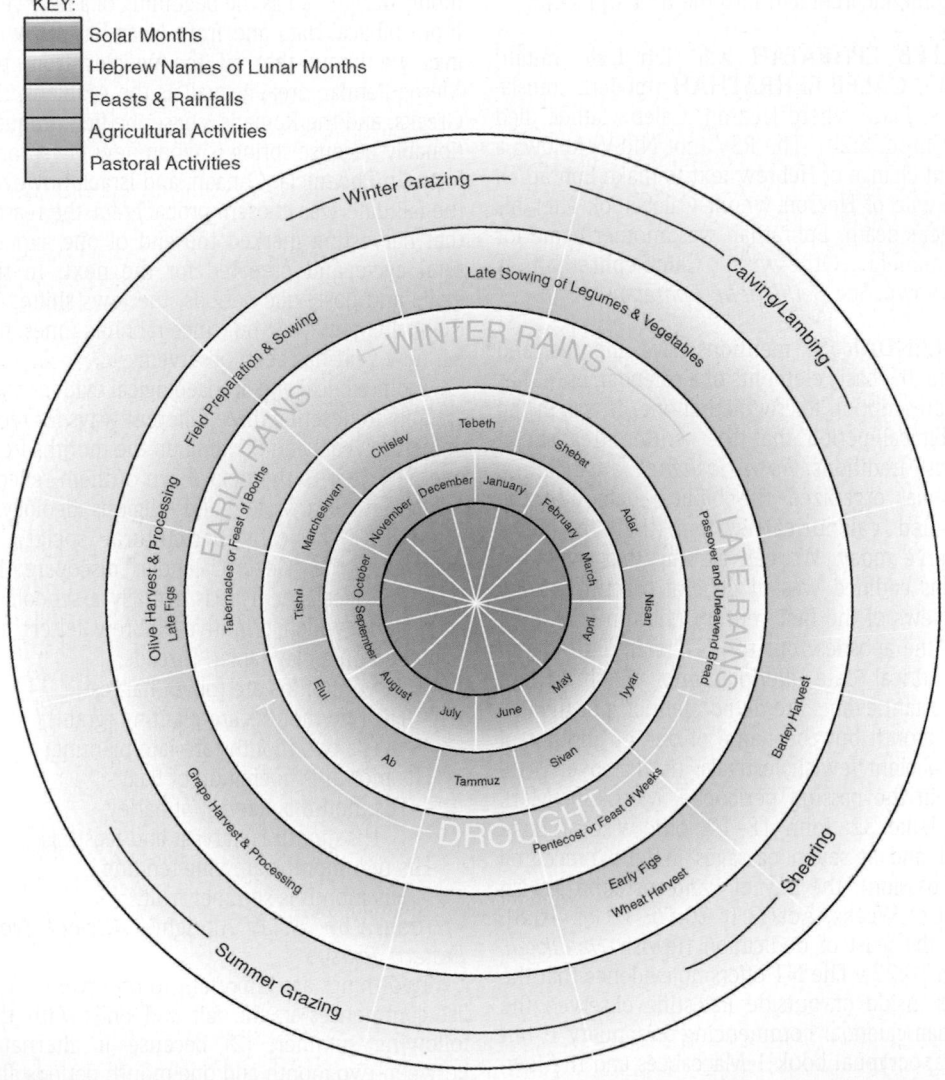

KEY:
- Solar Months
- Hebrew Names of Lunar Months
- Feasts & Rainfalls
- Agricultural Activities
- Pastoral Activities

Third, a sect known as the Essenes created a purely solar calendar that combined mathematical calculation with a special ideology. Discarding observation of the new moon, the Essenes gave each month 30 days but added a special day at the end of each three-month period, giving a year of 364 days. We have reason to believe that when this party tried to put this calendar into practice, the temple authorities drove them into exile. It would have disrupted the official religious festival cycle based on the lunar-solar year. We know about this erratic calendar only from sectarian books like the scrolls of Qumran.

The Month In addition to knowing that the length of months varied and that a new-year date in the spring or fall determined which of them was first, we are able to observe through Israel's history an interesting development in the naming of the months. These names reflected the presence of one or another dominating cultural influence: first that of the Canaanites, then that of Mesopotamia.

The earliest practice was to use the Canaanite month-names, of which four survive in the Bible: Abib (March-April); Ziv (April-May); Ethanim (September-October); and Bul (October-November) (Exod. 13:4; 23:15; 34:18; 1 Kings 6:1,37-38; 8:2). The other Canaanite months are known from Phoenician inscriptions. These are all agricultural names and reflect a seasonal pattern of reckoning, as in the Gezer calendar.

The usual practice in the OT is simply to number the months from first to 12th. Some of these numbered months are found in the passages mentioned above, hence the practice must be at least as early as the time of the Israelite monarchy. Because the first month is always in the spring, we must trace this practice back to the patriarchs, who would have learned it in Mesopotamia.

When the Jews returned from Babylonian exile, they brought with them the names of the Babylonian calendar, at the same time counting the new year from the spring. Although the rabbis returned to an autumnal new year, Judaism retains these Babylonian names as its own: Nisan (March-April); Iyyar (April-May); Sivan (May-June); Tammuz (June-July); Ab (July-August); Elul (August-September); Tishri (September-October); Marcheshvan (October-November); Chislev (November-December); Tebeth (December-January); Shebat (January-February); Adar

Bust of Caligula, the Roman Caesar from A.D. *37–41.*

(February-March). The inserted month is called *WeAdar*, "and-Adar."   *Simon J. DeVries*

CALF Young of the cow or other closely related animals. Calves were fattened in stalls to provide veal on special occasions (Gen. 18:7-8; 1 Sam. 28:24; Luke 15:23,27,30). Calves were also used in sacrificial settings (Lev. 9:2-3; Jer. 34:18; cp. Gen. 15:9-10, heifer). A calf symbolized the bullish Gentile armies (Ps. 68:30) and Egyptian mercenary soldiers (Jer. 46:21). The feet of one of the cherubim described by Ezekiel looked like those of a calf (Ezek. 1:7). One of the four creatures around the throne resembled a calf (Rev. 4:7 KJV, HCSB; other translations read "ox"). See *Golden Calf.*

CALIGULA Roman emperor, A.D. 37–41. See *Rome and the Roman Empire.*

CALKERS, CALKING Those who place some substance like bitumen into the seams of a ship's planking to make it watertight (Ezek. 27:9,27). See *Bitumen.*

CALL, CALLING Term often used of one being called by God to salvation and service.
Old Testament In the OT "call" carries several dominant connotations. These include to name,

to summon, to proclaim, to cry to God for help, and to choose.

In the OT the Hebrew word *qara'* is translated as "call" in the sense of naming items, animals, places, and persons (Gen. 1:5; 2:19; 16:14; 25:30). In other portions of the OT, the concept of "to summon" is more noticeable. Examples include the Hebrew midwives (Exod. 1:18), Moses and Aaron (Exod. 8:8), and the disastrous refusal of Dathan and Abiram to answer a divine summons (Num. 16:12,31-33). In Joel 2:15 the word is translated as "proclaim" in the NASB; it carries the idea of announcing an upcoming event in which the people are expected to participate. God's people are also instructed to "call" upon Him for salvation and deliverance in times of need (Isa. 55:6), and the false prophets of Baal called upon their god in the contest with Elijah on Mount Carmel (1 Kings 18:26), while Elijah called on the name of the Lord. In Isa. 45:3 the Lord is said to have "called" Cyrus by name, indicating that he was chosen to fulfill a specific role in the salvation history of God's people. See *Election; Predestination.*

New Testament The NT uses the concept of "call" in relation to one's station in life and a calling to Christian service. Jesus and the apostles appear to distinguish between two types of call—an external (gospel) call and an inner call.

In Acts 4:18 Peter and John are "called" back into the presence of the Sanhedrin after the body had completed its deliberations. In the parable of the unjust steward (Luke 16:2) the steward is "called" or summoned to give an accounting of his trust. The parable of the talents (Matt. 25:14-30) indicates again that a summons backed by divine authority is a most serious matter.

In the NT the concept of calling on the name of the Lord for deliverance is taken directly from key OT passages (Joel 2:32; cp. Acts 2:21; Rom. 10:13) and expanded into its fullest meaning of complete spiritual salvation from sin and judgment. In Acts 7:59 Stephen called on the Lord in prayer as he was about to die the martyr's death.

There is also a calling to Christian service. Paul refers to this directly when he says that he was called of God to be an apostle (Gal. 1:1; cp. Rom. 1:1).

In regard to the salvation of individuals, the word "call" is used in two distinct ways. In Matt. 22:14 Jesus said, "For many are called, but few are chosen" (NASB). Here the Lord indicates that the gospel call is intended to go out far and wide,

calling men and women everywhere to repent of sin and trust in Christ for salvation.

Not everyone will heed that "external" or "gospel" call. The Bible attributes the conversion of the sinner to an internal call effected by God. The Apostle Paul taught that this kind of call will be issued to all those whom God has predestined to salvation (Rom 8:28-30) and spoke of it in this passage with such certainty as to give the impression that such an internal call cannot fail to achieve its purpose (cp. Joel 2:32; Acts 2:39). Jesus spoke of the same thing under the concept of God's drawing power (John 6:44). This call is always ascribed to the loving and eternal purpose of the Father with the goal of redounding to the praise of his grace (Eph. 1:4-6).

God's gracious call does not lead to laziness. The Apostle Paul admonishes his readers to strive with all their God-given strength to live lives worthy of the calling they have received (Eph. 4:1) and press onward and upward "toward the goal for the prize of the upward call of God in Christ Jesus" (Phil. 3:14 NASB). In this context Paul's balance between responsibility and sovereignty comes into focus. In Rom. 10:9-15 Paul establishes the relationship between this internal call and the evangelistic imperative of the church: without the preaching of the gospel a person cannot hear, either of Christ, or from Christ, and so cannot call upon the name of the Lord and be saved. See *Election; Justification; Predestination; Salvation.*   A. J. Smith

CALNEH (Căl´ nĕh), **CALNO** (Căl´ nō) (Isa. 10:9) Place-name of uncertain meaning. **1.** A part of the kingdom of Nimrod in Babylonia (Gen. 10:10). Location or identity with any other recorded city is not known. **2.** City in Syria under Israel's control in the days of Amos and Isaiah (around 740 B.C.). Amos invited Israel to view Calneh's fate as a conquered city and see if Israel were really better in any way (Amos 6:2). Similarly, Isaiah warned Jerusalem that Calno (another spelling of Calneh) was as good as Jerusalem and yet had suffered conquest by Tiglath-pileser of Assyria in 738. This Calneh may be modern Kullan Koy in northern Syria, six miles from Arpad.

CALVARY English name for the place where Jesus was crucified (Luke 23:33), derived from the Latin *Calvaria*, which is the Vulgate's translation of the Greek *Kranion*, "skull." The other three Gospels (Matt. 27:33; Mark 15:22; John 19:17) refer also to the Semitic name "Golgotha," from the Aramaic *gûlgûltā',* "skull" or "head." This peculiar signification—"Place of a Skull" (*Kraniou Topos*)—has given rise to varied speculation about its origin. Common suggestions are that the site was a conventional and customary place of execution, or that it physically resembled a human skull, or even possibly that skulls were found there (or could be seen there). The biblical text sheds no light on the matter. What the NT does reveal is that the location was near Jerusalem (John 19:20), just outside the city walls (Heb. 13:12), apparently near a well-traveled road (Matt. 27:39), and seemingly stood conspicuously in its surroundings (Mark 15:40; Luke 23:49). Nearby was a garden (John 19:41; 20:15) in which was the tomb of Joseph of Arimathea, cut out of rock (Matt. 27:59-60; Luke 23:53), in which no one had ever been buried (Luke 23:53; John 19:41), and which, after Jesus' interment, was sealed with a large stone (Matt. 27:60; Mark 15:46).

Today, two locations in Jerusalem lay claim to being this ancient site: (1) the Church of the Holy Sepulchre, which is within the walls of the modern city and has the weight of tradition on its side (from about the 4th century), and (2) the much more recently noticed (19th century) Garden Tomb, which is just north and east of the Damascus Gate and conforms closely to the biblical details (also called Gordon's Calvary, after the British general Charles Gordon, who argued for its validity).   *B. Spencer Haygood*

CALVES, GOLDEN Representation of young bulls used to symbolize the god's presence in the worship place. The bull was used to represent many gods in the ancient Near East, particularly Amon-Re in Egypt and El and Baal in Canaan. As Moses was on Mount Sinai, Aaron formed a golden calf to use in a "feast to Yahweh" (Exod. 32:4-5). Similarly, Jeroboam placed calves in Dan and Bethel for the Northern Kingdom to use in its worship of Yahweh (1 Kings 12:28) so the people would not have to go to Jerusalem, the southern capital, to worship. In both instances the calves represent the gods who brought Israel up from Egypt. Thus the sin of the calves is not worshiping the wrong god but worshiping the true God in the wrong way through images (Ps. 106:19-20). Israel tried to make pedestals on which the invisible God could ride. The only such pedestal OT teaching allows was the ark of the covenant (1 Sam. 4:4). See *Bull; Golden Calf.*

Gordon's Calvary is one of two sites considered to be the possible location of Jesus' crucifixion.

CALVES OF THE LIPS KJV translation of a very difficult Hebrew phrase in Hos. 14:2. If this is the correct translation, the meaning is very obscure, possibly referring to vows to sacrifice cattle (REB). Modern translations supply different vowels to the consonants of the Hebrew text and read "fruit of the lips," which means giving praise to God.

CAMEL Large humpbacked mammal of Asia and Africa used for desert travel to bear burdens or passengers. Recent discoveries show it was domesticated before 2000 B.C.

Old Testament The camel, called the "ship of the desert," is adapted for desert travel with padded feet, a muscular body, and a hump of fat to sustain life on long journeys. A young camel can walk 100 miles in a day. Wealth was measured by many things, including camels (Gen. 24:35; Job 1:3). The Jews were forbidden to eat the ceremonially unclean camel, which chews the cud but does not have a split hoof (Lev. 11:4). An ill-tempered camel in an unhampered rampage could quickly trample down the tents of a family or clan. Jeremiah thus described the sins of Israel saying they were as a swift she-camel, running wild (Jer. 2:23). The wise men who worshiped Jesus (Matt. 2:1) are traditionally pictured as riding camels. This may be a prophecy of Isa. 60:6 that describes camel riders from Sheba coming to bring gold and incense and to proclaim praises of the Lord.

New Testament John the Baptist, a desert preacher, wore the rough and plain clothes of camel hair (Mark 1:6). His clothing and diet were revolutionary and consistent with his role as a forerunner of Jesus. A proverb picturing things impossible to accomplish was quoted by Jesus (Mark 10:25) when He said it is easier for a

Camels are still used by bedouins and others as a mode of travel in the Middle East.

camel to pass through the eye of a needle (Matt. 19:24) than for a rich man to enter heaven. A traditional but nonbiblical illustration describes an unburdened camel kneeling to creep under a low gate in a Jerusalem wall. This means that if a rich man will rid himself of pride and humble himself (kneel), he can get into heaven. Jesus describes hypocrites as persons who are very careful to strain out a gnat from a cup of drink but swallow a camel without notice (Matt. 23:24). They tithe the leaves of a small household herb but omit judgment, mercy, and faith.

Lawson G. Hatfield

CAMEL HAIR Very coarse material was woven from the hair of a camel's back and hump. A finer material was woven from the hair taken from underneath the animal. John the Baptist wore coarse camel hair (Mark 1:6). Jesus contrasted John's cloak to the "soft raiment" (KJV) of the members of the king's court (Matt. 11:8). Wearing a hairy mantle was the mark of a prophet (Zech. 13:4; cp. 2 Kings 1:8).

CAMON (Cā´ mŏn) (KJV) See *Kamon*.

CAMP, ENCAMPMENT Temporary settlement for nomadic and military people. In the OT, English translators usually use "camp" or "encampment" to translate Hebrew *machaneh*. A *machaneh* is a temporary settlement of travelers or warriors. Before the settlement in the promised land, Israel was a group of tribes on the move. Hence the frequent reference to "the camp" or "the camp of Israel" (Exod. 14:1,9; 16:13). Leviticus and Deuteronomy contain laws regulating life "in the camp."

Each tribe also had its own camp: Num. 2:3 speaks of "the camp of Judah"; Num. 2:25 of "the camp of Dan." After each tribe had secured a permanent place of residence in the promised land, the term "camp" designated a military settlement, whether of Israel (1 Sam. 4:3; 14:21) or of an enemy (2 Kings 7:10). The Hebrew word *machaneh* is often rendered "company" (Gen. 32:8,21), "host" (Exod. 14:24), and "army" (1 Sam. 17:1). The context in these instances calls for a word that designates the people of the camp rather than the settlement as such.

In the Greek translation of the OT, *machaneh* is rendered *parembole*, literally "a putting alongside." This word appears in Heb. 13:11,13 and in Rev. 20:9. In the last passage it is used figuratively of the church, "the camp of the saints," under attack by the forces of Satan. Its use in the two Hebrew citations is also figurative, drawing upon the time when the people of Israel lived as a camp and using that experience as a metaphor for the people of God at the time the author was writing. During Israel's years in the wilderness, sin offerings were burned outside the camp. When Jesus was put to death for the sins of mankind, He was led outside the Holy City and at a distance from the temple. The writer of Hebrews thus encouraged his fellow Christians to follow their Lord "outside the camp" of Israel's sacrificial system and of their Jewish religious heritage, even though that could mean bearing abuse. See *Castle*.

Thomas A. Jackson

CAMPHIRE KJV spelling of "camphor," Song 1:14; 4:13. Most modern versions read "henna." See *Henna*.

CANA (Cā´ nà) Place-name meaning "the nest." In John 2:1 the town that was the scene of a wedding during which Jesus changed water into wine. Its exact location is uncertain, though it was in Galilee. In Cana an unnamed nobleman sought out Jesus to ask Him to heal his son in Capernaum (John 4:46). Cana was also the home of Nathanael, one of the apostles (John 21:2).

CANAAN Territory between the Mediterranean Sea and the Jordan River reaching from the brook of Egypt to the area around Ugarit in Syria or to the Euphrates. This represents descriptions in Near Eastern documents and in the OT. Apparently Canaan meant different things at different times. Numbers 13:29 limits Canaanites to those who "live by the sea and along the Jordan" (HCSB; cp. Josh. 11:3). Israel was aware of the larger "promised land" of Canaan (Gen. 15:18; Exod. 23:20; Num. 13:17-21; Deut. 1:7; 1 Kings 4:21), but Israel's basic land reached only from "Dan to Beersheba" (2 Sam. 24:2-8,15; 2 Kings 4:25). At times Israel included land east of Jordan (2 Sam. 24:5-6). Other times the land of Gilead was contrasted to the land of Canaan (Josh. 22:9). After the conquest Israel knew "a great deal of the land remains to be possessed" (Josh. 13:1 HCSB). Canaan thus extended beyond the normal borders of Israel yet did not include land east of the Jordan. At times the land of Canaanites and the land of Amorites are identical. Whatever the land was called, it exercised extraordinary influence as the land bridge between Mesopotamia and Egypt and between the Mediterranean and the Red Sea.

History The word "Canaan" is not a Semitic name, although its appearance about 2300 B.C. in the Elba texts attests to its antiquity. Because of the final "n," it has been conjectured to be a Hurrian form. Quite probably the name was derived from a merchant designation; certainly Canaanite was ultimately equated in the biblical text with "trader" or "merchant" (Zech. 14:21). Isaiah 23:8 uses "Canaanites" as a common noun meaning "merchants" or "traders" as the aristocracy to Tyre in the prophet's day. Similar association may be found in passages such as Hos. 12:7-8; Ezek. 17:4; Zeph. 1:11. Canaan's identity as merchants probably goes back to a time when Canaan was limited to the area of Phoenicia, the rather small and narrow country along the seacoast of Canaan. Phoenicia was particularly known for a special purple dye produced from crushed mollusks. This product was shipped throughout the Mediterranean world. The word "Canaan" may be related to the special colored dye.

The biblical genealogical references are not particularly helpful in clarifying our understanding of Canaan. According to Gen. 9:18 and 10:6 Canaan was a son of Ham, one of the three sons of Noah. Genesis 10:15-20 clarifies the implications of this Hamitic descent in the sons of Canaan: Sidon, Heth, the Jebusites, the Amorites, the Girgasites, the Hivites, the Arkites, the Sinites, the Arvadites, the Zemarites, and the Hamathites. All of these people are characterized by being generally within the Egyptian sphere of influence.

Settlement within the land of Canaan is attested from Paleolithic times. Furthermore, a Semitic presence in the area is evidenced at least by 3000 B.C. Some of the best examples of cities indicating Semitic influences are Jericho, Megiddo, Byblos, and Ugarit.

The best attested period in Canaanite history is the Bronze Age (ca. 3200–1200 B.C.). During the Old Kingdom (ca. 2600–2200 B.C.), Egypt's power extended as far northward as Ugarit. From recoveries at several sites including Byblos and Ugarit, it is clear that Egypt controlled the area during the period of the 12th Dynasty (1990–1790 B.C.). From this general time period come the Egyptian Execration Texts that list peoples and princes of the area who owe their alle-

These twin basalt column bases are a part of one of four Canaanite altars excavated at Beth-shean.

giance to Egypt. Egyptian control over Canaan waned, being withdrawn about 1800.

Canaan had to contend with other aggressors besides Egypt. Approximately 2000 B.C. the Amorites invaded the area, having migrated via the Fertile Crescent from the southern Mesopotamian Valley. In addition, the Canaanites were beset by the Hyksos, who controlled Egypt from 1720 until 1570. Hurrians and Hittites also sought control of Canaan. The mingling of so many cultural influences still resulted in a rather unified culture.

When the Egyptians were able to expel the Hyksos in the 16th century, the Egyptians were able to extend their power over Canaan. Again, however, Egyptian power weakened. By 1400 B.C. a number of small, established nations in the area struggled with each other. From the 14th century the Amarna Letters are derived. These are approximately 350 letters written in cuneiform Akkadian. They represent correspondence between the Egyptian court at Tell el-Amarna and numerous Canaanite cities, including Jerusalem, Megiddo, and Shechem. These letters indicate the unrest characteristic of these Canaanite principalities socially and politically.

Prior to Israel's entrance into Canaan, the country seems to have been organized around major cities creating rather small principalities. There was apparently no attempt to organize centrally for defense, thus making possible the success the Israelites enjoyed in the 14th century and the parallel success of the Philistines in the 12th century. The biblical evidence is scant for any type of concerted Canaanite aggression against the Israelites. Stories in the book of Joshua (9:1-2; 10:1-5) indicate that in emergency situations the independent city-state kings formed defense coalitions, but no one had power to unite all Canaan against Israel. In the book of Judges only one judge, namely Deborah (Judg. 4–5), is depicted as having fought against the Canaanites. Rather than struggling with each other after the conquest, the Canaanites and Israelites gradually melded together, a phenomenon essentially completed by the end of David's rule.

The most significant finds have been the cuneiform tablets discovered in the royal library and/or temple of Ugarit. These tablets date from ca. 1400 B.C. to the final fall of Ugarit in ca. 1200 B.C. These tablets represent Canaanite culture in the second millennium B.C.

The Pantheon A pantheon of deities was worshiped at Ugarit. On the one hand, each deity had a clear duty assignment; while on the other hand, considerable fluidity flowed in deity perception. The role(s) of any given deity might be assumed by another.

El was acknowledged as the titular head of the pantheon. As king of the gods, he was both the creator god and a fertility god. He had earlier been more strongly associated with fertility than was true in the 14th century, although he was still depicted in the form of a bull. El lived at some distance from Ugarit upon a mountain (Mount Saphon) located to the north.

El was joined by *Athirat*, apparently his wife, who is represented in the OT as *Asherah*, with both feminine (*Asheroth*) and masculine (*Asherim*) plurals. Athirat was acknowledged as the mother of the deities, having given birth to some 70 gods and goddesses. Thus, she was predominately a fertility goddess and designated "creatress of the gods."

Baal was the chief god in the popular worship of the people. Baal means "master" or "lord" and could refer to any one of the numerous Baalim (Baals) who had authority in various locations. The Ugartic Baal, however, referred to the ultimate Baal.

Whereas El was located at some distance from the people, Baal was easily accessible. Baal statues have been recovered. These depict Baal wearing a conical hat with horns that convey the strength and fertility associated with bull imagery. In his right hand Baal holds a club that represents his military strength as well as thunder. In his left hand he grasps a stylized lightning bolt which symbolizes his role as a storm god. He is sometimes portrayed as seated on a throne, indicating his authority as king of gods.

Baal was joined in his task by *Anat*, represented in the Bible as *Anath*. She was portrayed as both sister and consort of Baal. In her role she was goddess of love, the perpetual virgin, and the goddess of warfare, whose exploits in Baal's behalf were sometimes remarkably cruel.

As Baal gradually supplanted El, many of the prerogatives earlier associated with El were naturally transferred to Baal. The biblical text derives from the period when this symbolic struggle between the deities had in essence been accomplished. Thus in the Bible Baal is often depicted with Asherah (i.e., Athirat) rather than Anath (i.e., Anat), as in Judg. 3:7.

Two additional gods fulfilled important roles in the popular mythology. *Mot* was the god of death and sterility. (In the Hebrew language the word for death is also *mot.*) Mot was associated with death, whether that refers to the seasonal cycle of vegetation, the sabbatical understanding of a seventh year of agricultural rest, or in some fashion to the individual's death. Mot was clearly understood as a power capable of rendering impotent Baal's regenerative powers.

Yam was called both "Prince River" and "Judge River." (Again, the Hebrew word for sea is *Yam.*) In the Ugaritic texts Yam was the chaotic god of the sea, capable of turning cosmos into chaos. The people of Ugarit, like their Mesopotamian counterparts (and unlike the Egyptians), apparently recognized both their dependency upon as well as the dangers associated with water. Cultically, the fear of chaos overcoming cosmos was represented in Baal's struggle with Yam.

This sampling of some of the more important members of the pantheon indicates that the Ugaritic schema, and thus that of the Canaanites in general, offered abundant options for worship. The mode of worship was tied especially to procreative sympathetic magic. The sexual union of god and goddess assured the fertility of mankind, the animals, and the larger world of nature. Crucial for this mode of worship was the worshiper's possibility to assist the process via sympathetic magic. In the temple a male priest or devotee fulfilled the goddess role. These two individuals became for the moment as god and goddess. In sympathetic magic humans ordain when and how the god and goddess act. This mode of human arrogance undergirded the tower of

A Canaanite altar located at Megiddo in Israel.

Babel story in Gen. 11. Practically all ancient worship structures operated from such a fertility-sympathetic magic orientation. The Israelites encountered this thought pattern when they entered Canaan. It took many centuries (note King Josiah's removal from the Jerusalem temple about 621 B.C. of the vessels made for Baal and Asherah as well as the houses of the male cult prostitutes—2 Kings 23) for Israel in daily practice of popular religion to resist Canaanite practices. The teachings of inspired leaders and the actual practice of religion often stood in stark contrast.

Canaanite Mythology The seven tablets upon which the Ugaritic mythological material was found are often mutilated, frequently making difficult an assured rendering of the material.

The mythology apparently centered on three primary exploits of Baal. Through these events he established himself as the god of supreme power within the pantheon, built the palace or temple which he merited by virtue of his victory over Yam, and in the third scenario struggled with, succumbed to, and ultimately escaped from the clutches of Mot.

El is portrayed as having been unashamedly afraid of Yam, this chaotic god of the sea. In fact, El was so frightened that he hid beneath his throne, fearful himself to encounter Yam but encouraging anyone to come forward who would confront this agent of chaos. Eventually, following some negotiations having to do with his role if successful against Yam, Baal stepped forward and proceeded to engage Yam. Baal was successful, bringing Yam under control by dividing him and thus making helpful an otherwise destructive, chaotic force. By this act Baal demonstrated himself worthy of exaltation.

The second mythological sequence emphasized that Baal was now worthy of his own palace or temple. Given the cyclic view of reality and the recurring danger posed by Yam, it is understandable that Baal did not want any windows in his palace. After all, the threat of chaotic flooding would surely occur again, for such recurrence is characteristic of mythological thought. Eventually Baal was convinced otherwise. Anat secured El's permission to build the palace, and the master craftsmen erected the structure. Baal opened the completed palace to all the pantheon for a type of sacred meal. During the meal Baal opened one of the windows and bellowed out the window, surely understood as an indication of thunder's origin, given Baal's association as god of the storm.

All should be well, but Baal had one more enemy to confront, Mot. According to the mythology, the two met in battle. Baal was defeated, being consigned thereby to the nether world. When Baal was separated from Anat, sterility reigned on earth. The wadis dried up, and Anat anxiously searched for Baal. While she could not find Baal, one day she chanced upon Mot. She had with her a blade with which she cut Mot into many pieces, which she then sifted, with the remains being scattered across the ground, probably an allusion to some type of grain festival. Regardless, this action by Anat enabled Baal to escape from his confinement. Rapidly thereafter, fertility returned! Thus the full cycle has been traversed, whether the intent be the annual cycle experienced in the world of nature, the seven-year sabbatical cycle, or perhaps the human birth-to-death cycle. What is transparent is the cyclic nature of the highly sensual, sympathetic magic worship. The Israelites were forced to contend with this mythology upon their entrance to Canaan. They faced a worship structure that had proved itself

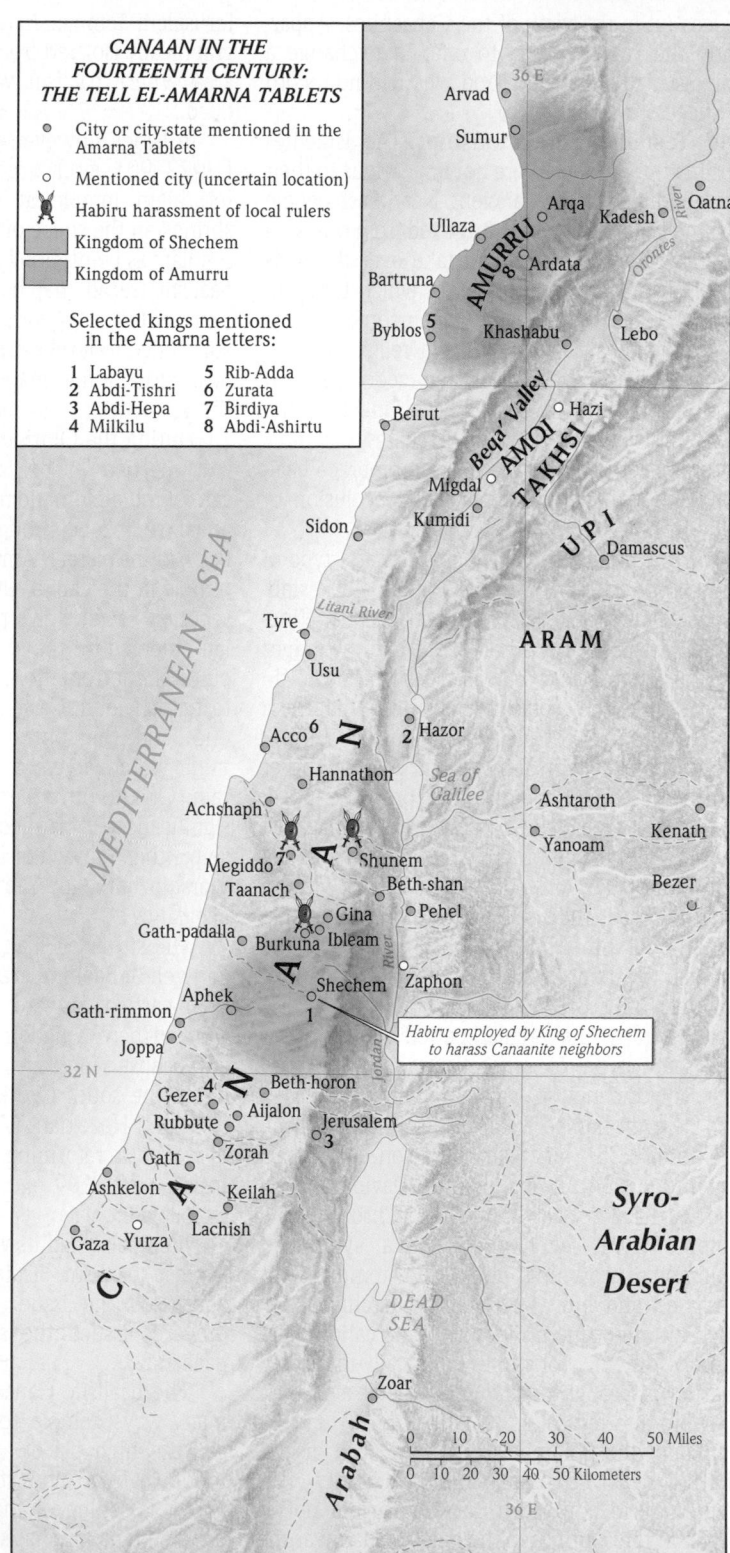

CANAAN IN THE FOURTEENTH CENTURY: THE TELL EL-AMARNA TABLETS

- ◉ City or city-state mentioned in the Amarna Tablets
- ○ Mentioned city (uncertain location)
- ⚔ Habiru harassment of local rulers
- Kingdom of Shechem
- Kingdom of Amurru

Selected kings mentioned in the Amarna letters:

1 Labayu	5 Rib-Adda
2 Abdi-Tishri	6 Zurata
3 Abdi-Hepa	7 Birdiya
4 Milkilu	8 Abdi-Ashirtu

Habiru employed by King of Shechem to harass Canaanite neighbors successful in the view of the Canaanites. Apparently the Israelites had to offer in exchange a non-agrarian wilderness God who had no record of success in agriculture!

Old Testament Relationships The Israelites settling into Canaan were not impervious to their surroundings. In the ancient Near East people assumed that as a people migrated from one area to another area they would take over the gods and religion of the new area in which they settled. At the least, they would incorporate the new religion into their own old religious structure. After all, these gods and goddesses had demonstrated their capability in meeting the inhabitants' needs. For the Israelites the most natural thing would have been to embrace baalism, although perhaps not to the exclusion of Yahwism.

Strong argument can be made that a type of Yahwism—baalism synthesis gradually established itself, particularly in the Northern Kingdom. During the period of Joshua and the judges a cultural struggle was waged which had to do more with the conflict between wilderness (Israelite) and agrarian (Canaanite) cultural motifs than between Yahweh and Baal. As earlier indicated, in the book of Judges only one judge, Deborah, is depicted as fighting directly against the Canaanites. Another judge could be called Jerub-baal (Judg. 6:32), having a father with an altar to Baal (Judg. 6:25). Without leadership Israel worshiped Baal-berith (Baal of the covenant) mixing baalism with the covenant of Yahweh (Judg. 8:33).

The early monarchial period demonstrates the same type of syncretistic behavior. Saul assuredly did not struggle to eliminate baalism, and he even named a son Eshbaal (man of Baal, 1 Chron. 8:33). Jonathan had a son, Merib-baal (1 Chron. 8:34). In like manner David named a son Beeliada ("Baal knows," 1 Chron. 14:7). Solomon was even more of a syncretist. Solomon's crowning glory, the temple, was designed and built by Canaanite architects. In such an atmosphere, lines of demarcation were loosely drawn. Solomon's politically-motivated marriages brought many other gods and their worship into Jerusalem (2 Kings 11:1-8).

Following Solomon's death and the disruption of the united monarchy, the identity crisis continued in both north and south, but not as much in the south as in the north. Judah was the base for worship of Yahweh and the site of the Jerusalem temple. In addition, Judah was geographically isolated from the northern Canaanite area where baalism was more regularly practiced.

In Israel, however, the initial king, Jeroboam I (922–901 B.C.), erected rival shrines to the Jerusalem temple at Dan and Bethel. These shrines, in the shape of bulls, are viewed by most scholars as being associated in some fashion with baalism (recall that both El and Baal could be represented in the form of a bull). Regardless, the adherence to Jeroboam's shrines was for the biblical writers the mark of apostasy for Israel's kings.

During the Omride dynasty, Ahab (869–850 B.C.) married Jezebel, a princess from Tyre, as a sign of the diplomatic relationship between Israel and Tyre. Jezebel brought the clearest infusion of baalism into Israel. Amidst the building of a Baal temple in the capital city of Samaria and the persecution of Yahweh's prophets, the Prophet Elijah emerged on the scene. In a classical story of cultural confrontation, Elijah encouraged a contest atop Mount Carmel (1 Kings 18–19). On the one hand, the contest was an attempt to determine which deity could provide the life-giving rain. On the other hand, it had a much greater significance. It clarified that a person must worship either Yahweh or Baal. It was not possible to worship both, for Yahweh demanded exclusive allegiance.

The struggle Elijah initiated with this either-Yahweh-or-Baal imperative, King Jehu (842–815 B.C.) carried forward politically. Religiously, in the Northern Kingdom, Hosea gave voice to the anti-baalistic message.

In the south two kings led the anti-baalistic struggle. Hezekiah (715–687 B.C.) is remembered as a reforming king (2 Chron. 29–31). Josiah (640–609 B.C.) was the reformer par excellence.

Judah also had its vocal prophetic spokesmen against baalism. Isaiah about 740–700 B.C. addressed the issue. Jeremiah from 615 B.C. onwards issued the strongest denunciation of baalism.

The baalistic Canaanites influenced Israel in many ways: temple construction, sacrificial rituals, the high places, a rejection of any sexual motif as a worship instrument (Deut. 23:17-18), and a lessening of the purely mythical with a concomitant emphasis upon the historical happening as with Yahweh's splitting of the sea (Yam

Suph) rather than a struggle with a mythological Yam (Exod. 14–15).

It is too easy for the biblical interpreter to focus on the numerous ways that Israel found the Canaanite religion to be offensive. In some cases, such as the use of sex in worship, the level of antipathy witnessed in the OT may not always have characterized Israel's actual practice, as prophetic denouncements like Hosea's show. The marked hostility (Deut. 20:16-18) which clamored for the wholesale destruction of the Canaanites came from inspired religious leaders who did not represent the majority of Israel's population. A priest could call a prophet to leave the king's place of worship (Amos 7:12-13). The prophet could command people not to go to traditional worship places (Amos 5:5).

In summary the Israelites did not settle into a cultural vacuum upon entering Canaan. They encountered a people with a proud history and a thriving religion. Historically speaking, that encounter could potentially have led to the elimination of Yahwism. It did not. Rather, a long historical process led to the eventual elimination of baalism and the other elements of Canaanite religion. Israel's battle with Canaanite religion gave new dimensions and depth to Israel's faith. The biblical record affirms that Yahweh, the Lord of history, has used the reality of historical encounter as a means to bring biblical religion to its mature development as revealed in the full canon of Scripture. See *Amorites; Anath; Asherah; Baal; El; Elijah; Gods, Pagan; Israel; Phoenicia; Ugarit.*

Frank E. Eakin, Jr.

CANALS Translation of a Hebrew word that refers to the branches of the Nile River (Exod. 7:19; 8:5; Isa. 19:6). The KJV uses "rivers."

CANANAEAN (Cā năn´ ē-ản) One of the 12 apostles is identified (Mark 3:18 RSV) as Simon the Cananaean (KJV renders "Simon the Canaanite"). In some other NT references this individual is called Simon the Zealot. Cananaean is probably the Aramaic equivalent of Greek zealot. See *Disciple; Apostle; Zealot.*

CANDACE (Căn´ dả-sē) In Acts 8:27 the queen of Ethiopia whose servant became a believer in Christ and was baptized by Philip. It is generally agreed that Candace was a title rather than a

proper name, though its meaning is uncertain. The title was used by several queens of Ethiopia.

CANDLE, CANDLESTICK (KJV) Candles as we know them were in use in biblical times. The reference is to "lamp" or "lampstand." See *Lamps, Lighting, Lampstand.*

CANE See *Calamus.*

CANKER KJV translation in 2 Tim. 2:17 and James 5:3. In general, canker may refer to any source of corruption or debasement. In 2 Tim. 2:17 the reference is to gangrene which is the local death of soft tissues due to loss of blood supply—a condition that can spread from infected to uninfected tissue. In James 5:3 the reference is to rust. See *Rust.*

CANKERWORM KJV translation in Joel 1:4; 2:25; Nahum 3:15-16. The Hebrew refers to a type of locust. See *Insects; Locust.*

CANNEH (Căn´ nĕh) Northern Syrian city that traded with Tyre and gained Ezekiel's mention in condemning Tyre (Ezek. 27:23). It may be variant spelling of Calneh or a city called Kannu in Assyrian documents.

CANON See *Bible Formation and Canon.*

CANTICLES See *Song of Songs.*

CAP See *Bonnet.*

CAPERBERRY Fruit—*Capparis spinosa*—thought to increase sexual powers and used in Ecclesiastes to symbolize the dying physical desire of the aging (Eccles. 12:5 NASB). Most modern translations omit the symbolism of the Hebrew and translate "desire."

CAPERNAUM (Cả pẽr´ nả um) Meaning "village of Nahum." On the northwest shore of the Sea of Galilee about 2½ miles west of the entrance of the Jordan is located the NT town of Capernaum.

Capernaum appears in the biblical record only in the Gospels where it is mentioned 16 times. As an economic center in Galilee, it was more significant than tradition has often allowed. The designation "city" distinguishes it from the "fishing village" category. Perhaps the proximity to a major east-west trade route explains the

Some of the intricately carved column pieces discovered in the excavations at Capernaum.

The foundational material of this third-century synagogue at Capernaum may date from the first century.

A house at Capernaum venerated by early local Chrisians as the home of the Apostle Peter.

An overview of the third-century synagogue at Capernaum.

need for a customs station there. The importance of the city is further demonstrated by the location of a military installation there under the command of a centurion. Fishing and farming were important to the economy, and archaeological evidence suggests that other light industries were contributing to the local prosperity.

In the NT, Capernaum was chosen as the base of operations by Jesus when He began His ministry. Teaching in the synagogue (Mark 1:21) and private homes (Mark 2:1) was basic to His work there, but the miracles performed there appear to have precipitated the controversy and opposition. The religious leadership challenged the direction of Jesus' ministry (Mark 2:24; 7:5), and the popular following attempted to take over and force Him into a political position (John 6:15). Mark (2:1) referred to Capernaum as Jesus' home, and Matthew (9:1) described it as "His own city." It appears that several of the disciples also lived in that town including Peter, Andrew, Matthew, and perhaps John and James. The populace apparently did not accept His messianic role because they fell under the same condemnation as Chorazin and Bethsaida for failing to repent (Matt. 11:20-24).   *George W. Knight*

CAPHTOR (Căph´ tôr) Original home of the Philistines (Amos 9:7). In Jer. 47:4 and in Deut. 2:23 its inhabitants are called Caphtorim (cp. Gen. 10:14). Though several places have at times been proposed for its location, current scholarship is generally agreed that Caphtor is the island of Crete. See *Crete; Philistines.*

CAPHTORIM (Căph´ tō·rĭm), **CAPHTORITES** (NIV) Citizens of Caphtor or Crete. See *Caphtor.*

CAPITAL PUNISHMENT Capital punishment, or the death penalty, refers to the execution by the state of those guilty of certain crimes. Though some have opposed capital punishment for ideological and practical reasons, it is important to note that God mandated its use. This divine mandate occurs first immediately after the Noahic flood. God instructed Noah and his sons, "Whoever sheds man's blood, by man his blood shall be shed" (Gen. 9:6 NASB). Human beings are created in the image of God (Gen. 9:6), and thus all human life is sacred, justifying a penalty as severe as death for murder.

Capital punishment is reserved for the state, not the individual. There is no place for personal revenge in administration of this punishment (Rom. 12:19). The state has responsibility, as God's civil servant on earth, to protect its citizens and to punish those who harm them (Rom. 13:4,6). Capital punishment provides the state the means to apply the appropriate punishment for murder (Deut. 19:21).

God instituted capital punishment as a legitimate punitive option for every state. Its institution predates Israel's birth as a nation and Moses' divinely inspired directions for its governance, eliminating the possibility that it was mandated solely for Israel. God issued guidance on capital punishment to earth's only surviving people (Gen. 7:20-24). God's instructions to them provided the foundation for all subsequent governments.

Capital punishment remains a valid instrument in the state's administration of justice. Paul affirms that the governing authorities do "not carry the sword (*machaira*) for no reason" (Rom. 13:4 HCSB). Paul is expressing the general principle that the state has the right to punish those who break its laws. More specifically, since the *machaira* (sword) typically describes an instrument of death in the NT, and certainly in Romans (cf. Rom. 8:35-36), it is evident that the state's authority to administer justice includes capital punishment.

The state possesses this power of death to punish evil (Rom. 13:4; 1 Pet. 2:13-14); however, only those acts identified by God as evil justify the use of capital punishment (Isa. 5:20). A state that uses capital punishment for other things abuses its power and violates God's standard for its use. An example of such an abuse of power is Nazi Germany's killing of millions of Jews.

The state does not violate the sixth commandment ("You shall not murder," Exod. 20:13 NASB) by its proper exercise of capital punishment. The Hebrew word *ratsach*, translated "kill" in some translations, refers to acts of murder or homicide. A different word, *harag*, often translated "kill," occurs more commonly in the OT. Rather than violating the sixth commandment by capital punishment, the state actually supports the commandment by executing those who murder.

In order to assure the fair administration of justice, God established some important guidelines for Israel, which any state would be wise to adopt, especially in a matter as serious as capital punishment:

1. The accused person must have committed a crime for which death is appropriate punishment. God states: "Life for life, eye for eye, tooth for tooth, hand for hand, foot for foot" (Deut. 19:21).

2. Clear evidence of guilt must be provided by two or more witnesses. One witness was not sufficient to warrant capital punishment (Num. 35:30; Deut. 17:6). Aware that unscrupulous people may use the death penalty for evil purposes, God requires multiple witnesses to the crime.

3. Those charged with crimes must be treated in a uniform and impartial manner, regardless of the status (Deut. 1:17) or class (Lev. 19:15) of the offender. Any society that favors some people and discriminates against others because of class or status, or deprives some of adequate defense, intentionally or through neglect, diminishes its integrity and creates serious doubts about its administration of justice (Lev. 24:22).

Some view the incident with the woman caught in adultery as evidence that Jesus opposed capital punishment (John 8:1-11). However, Jesus' reaction was not directed at the prescribed punishment but rather at those who sought to trap Him into participating in an illegitimate act (John 8:6). First, the scribes and Pharisees did not constitute an official governing body. Their efforts represented an illegitimate attempt to exercise the power of the state. Second, there is no indication there was any formal presentation of charges or official declaration of guilt. Third, there is no evidence that witnesses were present. At least two witnesses were necessary to prove capital cases, and in some instances, they had to throw the first stones (Deut. 17:6-7).

Jesus did not point out these failings. Instead, He used the incident to illuminate the hypocrisy of the scribes and Pharisees by calling for someone without sin to throw the first stone (John 8:7). Only a sinless person could claim the moral authority to execute this woman for a crime without due process. Knowing their situation was legally untenable and that they were not sinless, the scribes and Pharisees retreated (John 8:9). Obviously, Jesus' words were directed at the scribes and Pharisees, not the issue of capital punishment.

Though capital punishment remains a legitimate option for the state, it must be exercised under the strictest of conditions. The state that chooses to exercise the power of life and death over its citizenry must be certain all has been done to assure it is punishing the right person, that the punishment fits the crime, and that everyone, regardless of class or status, has had an adequate, vigorous defense.

Offenses requiring capital punishment in Israel: (1) intentional homicide (Exod. 21:12-13; Lev. 24:17; Num. 35:16-21,29-34); (2) false witnessing in capital cases (Deut. 19:16-21); (3) idolatry (Lev. 20:1-5; Deut. 13:6-11; 17:2-7), including human (Lev. 20:2) and animal sacrifices (Exod. 22:20); (4) blasphemy (Lev. 24:14-16, 23; 1 Kings 21:13; Matt. 26:65-66); (5) witchcraft and false claims to prophecy (Exod. 22:18; Lev. 20:27; Deut. 13:1-5; 18:20; 1 Sam. 28:3,9); (6) profaning the Sabbath (Exod. 31:14; 35:2; Num. 15:32-36); (7) rape (Deut. 22:23-27); (8) adultery (Lev. 20:10-12; Deut. 22:22); (9) sexual relations outside of marriage: (a) before marriage (Deut. 22:20-21), the woman alone to be executed; (b) consensual relations with another's betrothed (Deut. 22:23-24), both to be executed; (c) by a priest's daughter (Lev. 21:9); (10) acts of incest, homosexuality, and bestiality (Exod. 22:19; Lev. 20:11-17); (11) kidnapping (Exod. 21:16; Deut. 24:7); (12) cursing or striking one's parents (Exod. 21:15,17); (13) incorrigibility (Deut. 21:18-20; Ezek. 18:1-18); (14) refusing to obey the court (Deut. 17:12).

Because God held His covenant people to a high spiritual standard, He specified capital punishment for the above acts. Since no other nation has this same relationship with God, He has not specified that these acts are subject to the same penalty in other societies. However, because God mandated capital punishment prior to Israel's establishment, at the very least, it is a legitimate response to murder in other societies.

Forms of capital punishment stipulated or mentioned: stoning was the usual method (Exod. 19:13; Lev. 20:27; Deut. 22:24; Josh. 7:25); burning (Lev. 20:14; 21:9); sword (Exod. 32:27; Deut. 13:15); spear (Num. 25:7-8); shooting by arrow (Exod. 19:13); beheading (2 Sam. 16:9; 2 Kings 6:31-32); and crucifixion, only by Roman decree and Roman soldiers (Matt. 27:22-26,33-50; Mark 15:15-32; Luke 23:13-33; John 18:28–19:30). Jewish authorities under Roman rule were not normally permitted to execute anyone (John 18:31).   *Barrett Duke, Jr.*

CAPITALS See *Chapiter.*

CAPPADOCIA (Că̆p-pȧ-dō´ cĭ·ȧ) Roman province in Asia Minor mentioned twice in the NT: Acts 2:9; 1 Pet. 1:1. Although the extent of Cappadocia varied through the centuries depending on the currently dominant empire, it lay south of Pontus and stretched about 300 miles from Galatia eastward toward Armenia, with Cilicia and the Taurus Mountains to the south. Although mountainous country, its mostly rural population raised good crops, cattle, and

horses. While in NT times its mines were still producing some minerals, a large number of tablets written in cuneiform script discovered in 1907 at Tanish, now known as Kultepe, revealed that Assyrians were mining and exporting silver ore from Cappadocia about 1900 B.C.

From Acts 2:9 we know that Jews from Cappadocia were in Jerusalem when Peter preached at Pentecost. Those converted to Christianity that day must have given a good witness when they returned home because in 1 Pet. 1:1 believers there are mentioned along with others in Pontus.

Today the region of Cappadocia is in central Turkey, which is 98 percent Muslim.

CAPTAIN English translation of several Hebrew words usually referring to an officer or leader; often applied to Christ. See *Prince of Life.*

CAPTAIN OF THE TEMPLE Officer second in authority only to the high priest. Pashhur ("chief officer in the house of the Lord," Jer. 20:1 NASB) and Seraiah ("leader of the house of God," Neh. 11:11 NASB) held this office in the OT times. In Acts it appears that one of the main functions of this officer was to keep order in the temple (Acts 4:1; 5:24,26). The plural (Luke 22:4,52) may

Monastery of the Nuns at Cappadocia.

refer to officers under the command of the captain of the temple.

CAPTIVITY Term used for Israel's exile in Babylon between 597 B.C. and 538 B.C. See *Exile*.

CARAVAN Company of travelers (usually merchants) on a journey through desert or hostile regions with a train of pack animals (Gen. 37:25; Judg. 5:6; 1 Kings 10:2; Job 6:18-19; Isa. 21:13). Palestine lay along the main travel route between Egypt, Arabia, and Mesopotamia and had many caravans passing through it. See *Retinue*.

CARBUNCLE Precious stone used in the priest's breastpiece (Exod. 28:17 KJV) and part of the king of Tyre's apparel in the garden of Eden according to Ezekiel's ironic description (Ezek. 28:13). Equation with a stone used today is difficult if not impossible. NASB and NRSV read "emerald"; NIV, "beryl." KJV translates a different Hebrew term, "carbuncle," in Isa. 54:12. There NASB reads "crystal"; NRSV, "jewels"; and NIV, "sparkling jewels." In English, carbuncle is an obsolete term referring to various red jewels. See *Jewels, Jewelry; Minerals and Metals*.

CARCAS (Cär´ cȧs) Persian name meaning "hawk." One of the seven eunuchs under King Ahasuerus of Persia commanded to bring Queen Vashti to the king's party (Esther 1:10). See *Abagtha; Esther*.

CARCHEMISH (Cär´ kĕm ĭsh) Fort of Chemosh; modern Jerablus. An important city on the great bend of the Euphrates River. It was on the west bank of the river, at an important river crossing point on the international trade route. Carchemish lies mostly on the Turkish side of the modern Turkish-Syrian border.

Carchemish is mentioned about 1800 B.C. as the capital of a kingdom in alliance with the Assyrian king Shamshi-adad I against Yahdunlim, king of Mari.

After the Mari period, there is a short break in the known history of the city. When sources again become available, Carchemish was first under Hurrian influence, then was included within the Hittite sphere. Carchemish was a vassal and ally of the Hittite King Muwatallis against the Egyptian Pharaoh Rameses II at the important battle of Kadesh in 1286 B.C.

Following the destruction of the New Hittite Kingdom at the hands of the Sea Peoples shortly after 1200 B.C., Carchemish became the most important heir of the Hittite culture. The land of Hatti and the Hittites mentioned are probably these successors to the Anatolian Hittites centered on Carchemish. Carchemish again became the head of an independent kingdom and successfully resisted capture by the Assyrian Empire during the whole of its first period of expansion. Only under Sargon II were the Assyrians able to capture and destroy Carchemish in 717 B.C. Sargon helped to rebuild the city, and it became the capital of a western Assyrian province. Assyria's ultimate capture of the city was noteworthy enough that Isaiah used it as a rhetorical example in one of his oracles (Isa. 10:9).

The most important battle at Carchemish, however, was not fought over possession of the city. At the very end of the Assyrian period, when Nebuchadnezzar was incorporating all former Assyrian territory within the new Babylonian Empire, Pharaoh Neco II of Egypt came to Carchemish to try to save the remnants of the Assyrian army. He hoped to preserve a weak Assyria as a buffer between him and a strong and aggressive Babylon. He arrived too late to save the Assyrians, perhaps held up by Josiah's unsuccessful challenge at Megiddo (2 Chron. 35:20-24). Nebuchadnezzar defeated Neco at Carchemish. This victory gave Babylon authority over all of western Asia within the next few years; for this reason it ranks as one of the most decisive battles of all time. Jeremiah and the chronicler both took note of it; Jeremiah composed a poetic dirge commemorating the Egyptian defeat (Jer. 46:2-12). The city of Carchemish appears to have declined after the Babylonian period of power since references to it cease.

Carchemish and its ruins were visited by western travelers repeatedly during the 18th and 19th centuries. Excavations were carried out on the site from 1878 to 1881 and again from 1911 to 1914 and in 1920. A cuneiform inscription found during the excavations confirms the site as Carchemish. *Joseph Coleson*

CAREAH (Cȧ·rē´ ȧh) (2 Kings 25:23 KJV). See *Kareah*.

CAREER DECISIONS As a rule during the biblical period, sons entered the same line of work as their fathers. Occasionally, however, God chose careers for people, causing them to leave their family occupation in order to serve Him directly (e.g. Exod. 3:10; 1 Sam. 16:1-13; 1 Kings 19:19-21; Amos 7:14-15; Mark 1:16-20).

The Bible upholds any line of work that is honest and good (Titus 3:1; cp. Gen. 2:15; Neh. 2:18) and does not contradict the gospel (Acts 16:16-18; 19:23-27). All work should be done in the name of Jesus (Col. 3:17) and for the glory of God (1 Cor. 10:31) as if God Himself were the employer (Col. 3:23). This is true whether one works as a bishop, considered by Paul to be a "noble task" (1 Tim. 3:1), or at a job not highly regarded by the world (cp. the Egyptian attitude toward shepherding in Gen. 46:34). For this reason God is more concerned with one's attitude about work than the particular task performed (Eccles. 9:10; Col. 3:23).

God is concerned that each individual's full potential be met. For this reason He guides persons to choose careers (Ps. 73:24) that match their skills and areas of giftedness (cp. Exod. 39:43).

CARITES (Căr´ īts) Term of uncertain meaning in 2 Kings 11:4,19 and in Hebrew text of 2 Sam. 20:23, where "Cherethites" is usually read. The Carites were either mercenary soldiers recruited from Cilicia by Judah and other countries such as Egypt, or the meaning of the term can no longer be determined. They were military personnel who helped Jehoiada, the priest, install Joash as king and assassinate the queen mother Athaliah.

CARKAS (Căr´ kàs) NASB, NRSV, TEV spelling of Carcas (Esther 1:10). See *Carcas.*

CARMEL (Căr´ měl) Place-name meaning "park, fruitful field." **1.** Village in the tribal territory assigned to Judah (Josh. 15:55). King Saul set up a monument there after he defeated the Amalekites (1 Sam. 15:12). This is the place where Nabal treated David and his men with disrespect and disregard, an action eventually resulting in Nabal's death and David's marriage to his widow Abigail (1 Sam. 25:2-40). The village is modern Khirbet el-Kirmil, seven miles south of Hebron. **2.** The towering mountain (1 Kings 18:19) where Elijah confronted the prophets of Baal. The mountain is near the Mediterranean coast of Palestine between the Plain of Acco to the north and the Plain of

The western summit of Mount Carmel overlooking the modern Israeli port city of Haifa.

Sharon to the south. It reaches a maximum elevation of about 1,750 feet.

CARMEL, MOUNT (Cär´ mĕl) In 1 Kings 18:19 the scene of the confrontation between the prophet Elijah and the prophets of Baal. The mountain is near the Mediterranean coast of Palestine between the Plain of Acco to the north and the Plain of Sharon to the south. It is frequently mentioned in the Bible as a place of great beauty and fertility.

CARMELITE (Cär´ mĕl-īt) Citizen of Carmel. See *Carmel.*

CARMELITESS (Cär´ mĕl-ĭ-tĕs) Woman who resided in or was a citizen of the town of Carmel. See *Carmel.*

CARMI (Cär´ mī) Personal name meaning "my vineyard." **1.** Son of Reuben (Gen. 46:9) and thus original ancestor of a clan in the tribe of Reuben (Num. 26:6). **2.** Father of Achan (Josh. 7:1). **3.** Son of Judah (1 Chron. 4:1).

CARMITE (Cär´ mīt) Member of clan of Carmi (Num. 26:6). See *Carmi.*

CARNAL Anything related to the fleshly or worldly appetites and desires rather than to the godly and spiritual desires. Basic human nature is carnal, sold out to sin and thus living in the realm of death, unable to observe God's spiritual law (Rom. 7:14). People walk either in the flesh or in the Spirit, leading to death or to life. The carnal person is hostile to God, unable to please God (Rom. 8:1-11). Jesus Christ in human flesh overcame the condemnation of the fleshly way to offer the free life of the Spirit's way. Paul said that Gentiles had received the spiritual gospel through the Jews and should thus minister to the fleshly or material needs of the Jews (Rom. 15:27; cp. 1 Cor. 9:11).

Even church members can be carnal, being only babes in Christ, as Paul indicated in writing to the Corinthians (1 Cor. 3:1-4). Such Christians are jealous of one another and quarrel with one another. Christians should solve their problems with different "weapons" (2 Cor. 10:4). Such weapons serve God's purposes, destroy human arguments and human divisions, and bring glory to Christ.

Hebrews teaches that Christ had a distinct kind of priesthood from that of Jewish priests. Priests had always served on the basis of commandments written to meet fleshly needs. Christ served on the basis of His indestructible, eternal life (Heb. 7:16). In 9:10 the writer of Hebrews made clear the fleshly nature of the law. It consisted of commandments for the old order dealing with external matters until Christ came to deal with the spiritual matters of eternal redemption, sanctification, cleansing, and eternal life.

Using the same Greek word (*sarkikos*), Peter issued a battle cry against "fleshly lusts" so that glory would go to God and people would be attracted to His way of life (1 Pet. 2:11).

CARNELIAN Hard, red precious stone, a variety of chalcedony. It was used to decorate the king of Tyre (Ezek. 28:13 NRSV) and could be used to describe the one sitting on the heavenly throne (Rev. 4:3 NIV, NRSV, HCSB) and formed part of the wall of the New Jerusalem (Rev. 21:20 NIV, NRSV, HCSB). See *Minerals and Metals.*

CARPENTER Trade or skill lifted to a high position of honor by Jesus (Mark 6:3). See *Occupations and Professions.*

CARPUS (Cär´ pŭs) Personal name meaning "fruit." A Christian friend with whom Paul left his cloak in Troas. He asked Timothy to retrieve it for him (2 Tim. 4:13).

CARRIAGE KJV translation of several general Hebrew and Greek terms referring to utensils, baggage, supplies, or anything which can be carried. The term has nothing to do with transportation vehicles, as a more modern use of carriage would imply. Compare various translations of Judg. 18:21; 1 Sam. 17:22; Isa. 10:28; 46:1; Acts 21:15.

CARRION VULTURE NASB, NRSV translation of bird of prey (Lev. 11:18; Deut. 14:17). See *Vulture.*

CARSHENA (Cär shē´ nà) Wise counselor of King Ahasuerus of Persia to whom the king turned for advice on how to deal with his disobedient wife Vashti (Esther 1:14).

CASEMENT Window with latticework. The wisdom teacher looked through a latticed window to observe a foreign woman dealing with a naive youth (Prov. 7:6). Sisera's mother looked through a similar window as she impatiently waited for her son to return from the battle which he had lost to Deborah and Barak and after which he was killed by Jael (Judg. 5:28). Archaeologists have found such lattice windows in royal palaces. The queen or a goddess looking out the royal window seems to have been a popular motif in the ancient Near East.

CASIPHIA (Că sĭph´ ĭ á) Place-name meaning "silversmith." Place in Babylon where Levites settled in exile (Ezra 8:17) and from which Ezra summoned Levites to return with him to Jerusalem. The place is unknown outside this passage.

CASLUH (Căs´ lŭh), **CASLUHIM** (Căs´ lū hĭm), **CASLUHITES** (Căs´ lū hīts) Clan name of "sons of Mizraim (or Egypt)" and "father" of the Philistines in the Table of Nations (Gen. 10:14). Their origin is not known.

CASSIA Bark of an oriental tree (*Cinnamomum cassia Blume*) related to cinnamon. One of the ingredients used to make anointing oil (Exod. 30:24), it was acquired through trade with Tyre (Ezek. 27:19) and was desired for its aromatic qualities (Ps. 45:8). One of Job's daughters was named Keziah (Job 42:14), a name that means "cassia."

CASTANETS See *Music, Instruments, Dancing.*

CASTAWAY KJV translation of Greek *adokimos*, referring to battle-testing of soldiers, qualifications for office, or testing of metals to make sure they are genuine. Paul used his own example of personal discipline to ensure that his preaching proved true in life as a call to others to do the same (1 Cor. 9:27). He did not want to be cast away as impure metal or disqualified as an unworthy soldier or candidate. Paul played on the words *dokimos*, "qualified," and *adokimos*, "disqualified," in 2 Cor. 13:5-7. The Corinthians demanded a test or proof that Christ spoke through him (v. 3). Paul turned the argument on them, saying they needed to prove themselves that they had not failed the test of Christ and become reprobates. He hoped the Corinthians would recognize in Paul's life that he had not

failed the test and was thus not a reprobate. He prayed the Corinthians would not do wrong, not to prove himself qualified but so that the Corinthians would do what was right even if Paul proved to be unqualified.

Paul warned Timothy of evil persons in evil times with people resisting the truth, having corrupt minds, and being unqualified in the faith (2 Tim. 3:8). Similarly, he wrote Titus of persons professing to know God but unqualified in good works (Titus 1:16). With similar purpose, Hebrews compares people to ground which bears thorns and briers and is thus unqualified and fails to pass the test (Heb. 6:8).

CASTLE KJV translation for six Hebrew and one Greek word. NASB uses "castle" only for one Hebrew term in 2 Kings 15:25 and Prov. 18:19. RSV uses "castle" in Prov. 18:19 and also for a different Hebrew term in Neh. 7:2. NIV does not use "castle." See *Fortified Cities.*

Armon refers to the large, fortified home of the king, often translated palace or citadel (1 Kings 16:18). The term apparently referred to the massive masonry structures connected with the defense of the palace and possibly of the homes of other leading citizens (Amos 6:8; cp. 1:4). Apparently they served as storehouses for royal treasures and goods taken in battle (Amos 3:10). Israel prayed for peace in her fortress, but no fortress gave security from God's anger (Isa. 25:2; 34:13; Hos. 8:14). God promised to rebuild the fortified palaces of His people (Jer. 30:18). The palaces should witness to God's strength (Ps. 48:3,13-14). The wisdom teacher knew a more stubborn defense system than castles—that of humans (Prov. 18:19).

Birah is a late loanword from Accadian and refers to the fortified acropolis, usually built at the highest and most easily defensible part of a city (Neh. 1:1; Esther 1:2). It referred to the fortress near the temple in the rebuilt Jerusalem (Neh. 2:8). A military commander ruled the fortress (Neh. 7:2). The Chronicler used the term for Solomon's temple (1 Chron. 29:1,19) and used the term in the plural to describe Jehoshaphat's and Jotham's building (2 Chron. 17:12; 27:4).

Tirah refers to a stone wall used for protection around a camp of tents (Gen. 25:16; Num. 31:10; Ps. 69:25; Ezek. 25:4; cp. 1 Chron. 6:54; Ezek. 46:23b).

Migdal is a defense tower which may stand alone in the countryside as a watchtower (1 Chron. 27:25). They were also used to protect vineyards and other crops (Isa. 5:2). A famous *migdal* crowned one area of Shechem or served as a military outpost for Shechem (Judg. 9:46-49). Uzziah fortified the Jerusalem gates with such towers on top of which he placed modern weaponry (2 Chron. 26:9-10,15). Battle-axes were used to break down such towers (Ezek. 26:9). See *Shechem*.

Matsad and *metsudah* are closely connected to the Canaanite or Jebusite city of Jerusalem that David conquered (2 Sam. 5:7,9; 1 Chron. 11:5,7). The *metsudah* of Zion was probably a military citadel protecting the southeastern hill of Jerusalem, that part of Israel called "city of David." In general, the word described any place of hiding or refuge (Judg. 6:2; 1 Sam. 23:14). The basic biblical lesson is that Yahweh is our stronghold, refuge, and fortress (Pss. 18:2; 31:3). See *David, City of.*

Parembole is the Greek term for a fortified camp and designated the Roman army barracks or headquarters in Jerusalem (Acts 21:34; 22:24; 23:10). Hebrews refers to OT offerings burned outside the camp, comparing this to the place of Jesus' suffering and inviting Christians to be willing to suffer outside the camp, accepting disgrace as did Jesus (Heb. 13:11-13; cp. Rev. 20:9).

Trent C. Butler

CASTOR (Căs´ tôr) **AND POLLUX** (Pŏl´ lŭx) Greek deities, the twin sons of Zeus, represented by the astral sign of Gemini. They were supposed to watch particularly over sailors and innocent travelers. They were regarded as guardians of truth and punishers of those who committed perjury. In Acts 28:11, Castor and Pollux were the sign or figurehead of the ship that carried Paul from Malta toward Rome. See *Figurehead*.

CATERPILLAR Worm-like larvae of butterflies and moths. The term appears in different English versions to translate various Hebrew words, NIV not referring to caterpillars at all.

Chasil refers to a particular stage of the grasshopper or locust. Apparently in this stage wings have begun to develop but are not folded together. They could cause famine in a land, eating all the crops (1 Kings 8:37; Joel 1:4). They symbolized gathering booty or spoil of battle (Isa.

33:4). They made their mark on Israelite history in the plagues in Egypt (Ps. 78:46).

Yeleq is the first stage after emerging from the egg. The flying apparatus has begun to develop but is invisible. The word could be used to describe the plague on Egypt (Ps. 105:34). They were noted for covering or filling up an area (Jer. 51:14). They swarmed over a land as an army in formation marched into a country (Jer. 51:27; Joel 2:25). They multiplied quickly and ate up all in front of them before flying away to attack another land (Nah. 3:15-16). Obviously such language is not fully appropriate for the first stage of the animal, showing that the various terms became synonyms and could be used interchangeably to describe typical activities of the grasshopper or locust.

Gazam is traditionally defined as the just-matured grasshopper ready for flight. Other scholars would identify it as the true caterpillar. Its name comes from a Hebrew root word meaning "to cut off," thus describing the animal's destructive ability to bite through weeds, grain, fig leaves, grapes, olive trees, fruit, and even small twigs and branches (cp. Amos 4:9; Joel 1:4; 2:25). This stage is variously translated as "palmerworm" (KJV), "gnawing locust" or "caterpillar" (NASB), "locust" (NIV), "cutting locust" (NRSV).

Arbeh is the mature, swarming locust—schistocera gregaria—that grows to six centimeters in length. The exodus plague narrative features them (Exod. 10:14-19). They were classified as hopping animals (Job 39:20) with jointed legs and so were clean for Israel to eat (Lev. 11:20-23). Their devouring habits made them a part of God's threatened curses on a disobedient people (Deut. 28:38). Their wandering and swarming resembled that of an army (Judg. 6:5; 7:12; Prov. 30:27; Jer. 46:23; Nah. 3:17). They were harmless to the human body, since people could easily shake them off (Ps. 109:23). See *Insects*.

CATHOLIC EPISTLES NT letters not attributed to Paul and written to a more general or unidentifiable audience: James; 1 and 2 Peter; 1, 2, and 3 John; Jude. The title is from tradition and cannot be defined by modern standards.

CATTLE Domesticated quadrupeds used as livestock. In the Bible the term commonly refers to all domesticated animals. English translations use "cattle" for at least 13 different Hebrew words and six Greek words referring to animals.

Ox, bull, calf, and cow are among the names for cattle in the Bible. Sheep, goats, and other domesticated animals are also included under the designation of cattle (Gen. 1:24; John 4:12). The land of Goshen, where the Hebrews settled during the time of Joseph, was rich in cattle. From bones found at Megiddo, one archaeologist has identified cattle in ancient Israel as the present small Beiruti race, while another has identified five types of cattle of Gezer. Cattle were valued for sacrifices, for food, and as work animals (Deut. 25:4; Luke 14:19). They were divided into clean and unclean classifications (Lev. 5:2) and were covered by the law of firstlings and Sabbath rest (Exod. 13:12; 20:12). Bullocks and calves were used for sacrifices. Possession of considerable livestock was a sign of wealth (Gen. 13:2; 1 Sam. 25:2).

Shirley Stephens

CAUDA (Cou´ dä) or **CLAUDA** Small island whose name is variously spelled in the Greek manuscripts. Paul sailed by the island on his way to Malta and ultimately to Rome (Acts 27:16). The island is modern Gavdos, southwest of Crete.

CAUL Part of the liver which appears to be left over or forms an appendage to the liver, according to KJV. Other translations refer to the "lobe" (NASB), "covering" (NIV), or "appendage" (NRSV) of the liver (Exod. 29:13). Hosea 13:8 KJV speaks of the "caul of their hearts," which modern translations render more freely. The Hebrew apparently refers to the chest cavity in which the heart is located. KJV also uses "caul" to translate a rare Hebrew word in Isa. 3:18 taken by modern linguists to mean "headbands."

CAULKERS, CAULKING See *Calkers, Calking.*

CAVALRY Mounted soldiers of an army. Israel faced cavalry and chariots in the exodus (Exod. 14:9,18,28) and during the period of the judges (Judg. 4). God would not allow Israel to rely on the wealth and security represented by military horses (Deut. 17:16). David captured horses and chariots from Syria (2 Sam. 8:4). Solomon then developed a military force featuring horses (1 Kings 4:26; 9:19; 10:26). These references to horsemen may all refer to personnel connected with chariots rather than to individual riders or cavalry units. The Hebrew term *parash* refers to both with the context the only guide to

The east face of the Mount of Transfiguration showing caves used for shelter by the people of the area.

interpretation. Evidence outside Israel points to Assyria using cavalry troops shortly after 900 B.C. The cavalry provided a line of defense, served as scouts, and chased a defeated army. God warned Israel not to depend upon horses for security (Isa. 31:1).

CAVES Numerous caves pit the cliffs and mountains of Palestine. Such caves provided housing and burial sites for prehistoric people. Although occupation was not continuous, evidence for human habitation in some of the caves exists up until the Roman period. At this time they became places of refuge for Jews fleeing Roman persecution.

In the Bible caves were often used as burial places. Abraham bought the cave of Machpelah as a tomb for Sarah (Gen. 23:11-16,19). Lazarus was buried in a cave (John 11:38). David used the cave of Adullam for refuge (1 Sam. 22:1), as did five Canaanite kings at Makkedah (Josh. 10:16)   *Diane Cross*

CEDAR Tree grown especially in Lebanon and valued as building material (probably *Cedrus libani*). Cedar played a still-unknown role in the purification rites of Israel (Lev. 14:4; Num. 19:6). Kings used cedar for royal buildings (2 Sam. 5:11; 1 Kings 5:6; 6:9–7:12). Cedar signified royal power and wealth (1 Kings 10:27). Thus the cedar symbolized growth and strength (Ps. 92:12; cp. Ezek. 17). Still, the majestic cedars could not stand before God's powerful presence

One of the cedars of Lebanon.

(Ps. 29:5). The cedars owed their existence to God, who had planted them (Ps. 104:16). See *Plants.*

CEDRON (Cĕ′ drŏn) (KJV, John 18:1) See *Kidron.*

CELESTIAL BODIES Paul contrasted celestial bodies (sun, moon, and stars) with terrestrial bodies in explaining the difference between the present human body (physical) and the resurrection body (spiritual body, 1 Cor. 15:35-50). The two types of bodies are of an entirely different nature: one weak and perishing, the other glorious and eternal.

CELIBACY Abstention by vow from marriage. The practice of abstaining from marriage may be alluded to twice in the NT. Jesus said that some have made themselves eunuchs for the sake of the kingdom and that those who were able to do likewise should do so (Matt. 19:12). This statement has traditionally been understood as a reference to celibacy. Paul counseled the single to remain so (1 Cor. 7:8). Both Jesus (Mark 10:2-12) and Paul (1 Cor. 7:9,28,36-39; 9:5), however, affirmed the goodness of the married state. One NT passage goes so far as to characterize the prohibition of marriage as demonic (1 Tim. 4:1-3). See *Eunuch.*

CENCHREA (Cĕn′ chrə à) or **CENCHREAE** Eastern port city of Corinth. Phoebe served in the church there (Rom. 16:1), and Paul had his head shaved there when he took a vow (Acts 18:18).

CENSER Vessel used for offering incense before the Lord (Lev. 10:1). Nadab and Abihu used it improperly to bring God's destruction. It probably was also used for carrying live coals employed in connection with worship in the tabernacle or the temple, each priest having one (cp. Num. 16:17-18). Use of the censer in temple worship was restricted to members of the Aaronic priesthood, as King Uzziah discovered (2 Chron. 26:16-21). The heavenly worship also involved censers and incense, according to John's vision (Rev. 8:3-5). See *Tabernacle; Temple.*

CENSUS Enumeration of a population for the purpose of taxation or for the determination of manpower of war.

Moses took a census of Israel at Mount Sinai and assessed a half-shekel tax to each male over 20 to support the tabernacle (Exod. 30:13-16). Another census counted Israel's manpower available for war. This census excluded the Levites, separating them for service in the tabernacle (Num. 1). Another census was taken in Moab at the end of the wilderness wanderings, again excluding the Levites. The Hebrew may indicate that the units used in the count reflect tribal units and not thousands, thus accounting for the large totals. David also counted Israel's warriors. Second Samuel 24 says that the Lord incited David to carry out the census, and 1 Chron. 21 says that Satan moved David to do so. In both accounts a pestilence was sent upon Israel because of the census. Ezra 2 accounts for those who came out of exile with Zerubbabel and Nehemiah.

The first census referred to in the NT concerns the decree by Caesar Augustus "that the whole empire should be registered." This first census was taken by Quirinius, the governor of Syria (Luke 2:1-5). Luke used this benchmark both as a general time reference and, more importantly, to set the birth of Jesus in Bethlehem, the ancestral city of David. This passage has presented problems in that there is no specific record of such a census outside the Lukan account, and the date of Quirinius's governorship (A.D. 6–9) appears to be inconsistent with the previous statement that Jesus' birth was in the reign of Herod the Great (Luke 1:5), who died in A.D. 4. However, Luke's account is consistent with Roman practices, and such a census could well have been ordered by Quirinius functioning as a military governor alongside the political governor Sentius Saturnius around 6 B.C., when most scholars date the birth of Jesus. The other reference is that of Gamaliel's remark about Judas of Galilee, who rose up "in the days of the census" only to later perish (Acts 5:37).

Joel Parkman

CENTURION Officer in the Roman army, nominally in command of 100 soldiers. In Matt. 8:5 a centurion who lived at Capernaum approached Jesus on behalf of his ailing servant. In Mark 15:39 a centurion who witnessed the crucifixion identified Jesus as the Son of God. In Acts 10 the conversion of the centurion Cornelius marked the beginning of the church's outreach to the

The ruins of Cenchrea with the waters of its bay seen in the background.

Gentile world. In Acts 27:3 the centurion Julius treated the Apostle Paul with courtesy. These passages illustrate the generally favorable impression made by the centurions who appear in the NT. They were usually career soldiers, and they formed the real backbone of the Roman military force.

CEPHAS (Çē´ phȧs) See *Peter.*

CEREAL OFFERINGS See *Sacrifices and Offerings.*

CEREMONIAL LAW Laws which pertained to the festivals and cultic activities of the Israelites. See *Festivals; Laws; Priests and Levites; Sacrifices and Offerings; Worship.*

CERTIFICATE OF DIVORCE See *Divorce; Family.*

CHAFF Husk and other materials separated from the kernel of grain during the threshing or winnowing process. It blew away in the wind (Hos. 13:3) or was burned up as worthless (Isa. 5:24; Luke 3:17).

CHAINS English translation of at least eight different Hebrew terms for materials interlaced together into ornamental or restraining objects. **1.** Ornament worn around the neck either signifying investiture in office with political award (Gen. 41:42; Dan. 5:7) or for personal jewelry (Num. 31:50). Animals such as camels might also wear ornamental chains (Judg. 8:26). **2.** Decorations of gold worn on the high priest's breastplate (Exod. 28:14,22). **3.** Series of chains formed a partition in Solomon's temple (1 Kings 6:21). **4.** Architectural ornaments on the temple walls (2 Chron. 3:5,16). **5.** Restraining chains preventing prisoners from escaping (Jer. 39:7; Acts 28:20). God could loose His minister from chains (Acts 12:7).

CHALCEDONY Transliteration of Greek name of precious stone in Rev. 21:19. See *Jewels, Jewelry; Minerals and Metals.*

CHALCOL (Căl´ cŏl) (KJV, 1 Kings 4:31) See *Calcol.*

CHALDEA (Căl·dē´ ·ȧ) Refers either to a geographical locality (Chaldea) or to the people who lived there (Chaldeans). Chaldea was situated in central and southeastern Mesopotamia, i.e., the land between the lower stretches of the Tigris and Euphrates Rivers. Today Chaldea lies in the country of Iraq, very close to its border with Iran, and touching upon the head of the Persian Gulf.

The Chaldeans In OT times different peoples occupied southeastern Mesopotamia at various times. One such group was the Chaldeans, whose name derives from the ancient term *Kaldai,* which refers to several Aramean tribes who moved into lower Mesopotamia between 1000 and 900 B.C. Their new homeland was a flat, alluvial plain of few natural resources, many marshes, spring flooding, and very hot summers.

Relation to Babylonia At first the Chaldeans lived in tribal settlements, rejecting the urban society of the Babylonians to the northwest—so-called after the leading city-state of the region, Babylon, to which the OT refers over 300 times. Babylon was once the capital city of the great King Hammurabi (ca. 1763–1750 B.C.), remembered for the empire he created, and for the famous law code which bears his name.

As time passed, the Chaldeans gradually acquired domination in Babylonia. In the process they also took on the title "Babylonians," or more exactly, "Neo-Babylonians." As a result, the terms Chaldea(ns) and (Neo-)Babylonia(ns) may be used interchangeably (Ezek. 1:3 RSV, NIV; 12:13 NIV). See *Babylon.*

In the eighth century B.C. the Chaldeans emerged as the champions of resistance against Assyria, a dangerous, aggressive imperial force in upper Mesopotamia. At this time the Chaldeans begin to appear in the OT, first, as possible allies with Judah against Assyria, but later, as a direct threat to Judah and Jerusalem.   *Tony M. Martin*

CHALDEES (Căl´ dēēs) Another expression for Chaldeans. See *Chaldea.*

CHALKSTONE Soft stone easily crushed, used for comparison to destruction of altar (Isa. 27:9).

CHAMBER English translation of at least seven Hebrew words referring to a portion of a house or building. Included are sleeping quarters (2 Kings 6:12); bathroom (Judg. 3:24); private inner room reserved for a bride (Judg. 15:1; Joel 2:16); private, personal cubicle in the temple furnished with benches (1 Sam. 9:22; 2 Kings 23:11); storage rooms (Neh. 12:44); a cool upper room built on the roof (Judg. 3:20) or over the city gate (2 Sam. 18:33); and the ribs or beams forming side rooms in the temple (1 Kings 7:3). The NT speaks of inner rooms of a house (Matt. 6:6; 24:26; Luke 12:3) or of a storeroom (Luke 12:24). See *Architecture.*

CHAMBERING KJV translation of a Greek word in Rom. 13:13 rendered as "debauchery" or "sexual promiscuity" in modern versions.

CHAMBERLAIN High military or political official whose title is related to Hebrew term meaning "castrated" or "eunuch" but actually may be derived from Akkadian term for royal official. That all officials bearing the Hebrew title, sar, were actually eunuchs is doubtful. The Rab-saris of 2 Kings 18:17 is literally "chief of eunuchs" but more likely signifies the office held by a high military and administrative official (cp. Jer. 39:3; Dan. 1:3). Potiphar is described as Pharaoh's sar but had a wife (Gen. 37:36; 39:7). The Persian officials in Esther 1:10 may have been eunuchs, since they apparently protected the king's wives and harem (cp. 2 Kings 9:32). Hebrew officials also carried the title (1 Sam. 8:15; 1 Kings 22:9; 2 Kings 8:6; 23:11; 24:12,15; 25:19). See *Eunuch.*

CHAMBERS OF IMAGERY Phrase of uncertain meaning (Ezek. 8:12). It could refer to secret rooms containing idols or pictures on the walls (Ezek. 8:10; 23:14) probably related to pagan religions. Whatever "chambers of imagery" refers to, that which was taking place in the temple during the days of Ezekiel was displeasing to God.

CHAMBERS OF THE SOUTH Reference to some unknown phenomenon in the skies. Since "chambers of the south" is mentioned along with other stellar constellations (Job 9:9), the phenomenon is usually taken to mean some sort of constellation or group of constellations. Some have taken "chambers of the south" to be a reference to the bright portion of the sky from Argus to Centauri. Others have taken the term as a reference to the zodiac or perhaps to the southern portion of the zodiac (cp. Job 37:9; 38:22). See *Astrologer.*

CHAMELEON Unclean animal that moves on the ground (Lev. 11:30), usually identified as the *Chamaeleo calyptratus.* A Hebrew word with the same spelling but perhaps with different historical derivation occurs in Lev. 11:18 and Deut. 14:16, where it is apparently the barn owl, *Tyto alba.* See *Reptiles.*

CHAMOIS Small antelope (*rupicapra*) that stands about two feet high and is found in mountainous regions. Translated as "mountain-sheep" in modern versions (Deut. 14:5). See *Antelope; Sheep.*

CHAMPAIGN Open, unenclosed land or plain (Deut. 11:30 KJV). Hebrew has preposition meaning in front of or opposite Gilgal and Arabah. See *Arabah.*

CHAMPION Hebrew phrase in 1 Sam. 17:4,23 is literally "the man of the space between"—that is the man (like Goliath) who fights a single opponent in the space between two armies. The Hebrew word translated "champion" in 1 Sam. 17:51 is a different word meaning "mighty one, warrior."

CHANAAN (Cā´ nàan) KJV form of Canaan in Acts 7:11; 13:19.

CHANCELLOR Title of a royal official of the Persian government living in Samaria and helping administer the Persian province after Persia gained control of Palestine. English translations vary in the way they render the title, but it apparently refers to political administration rather than to military command and represents a high official but not the highest provincial office, that of governor (Ezra 4:8-9,17).

CHANT See *Music, Instruments, Dancing.*

CHAOS Transliteration of the Greek word. In the OT, several Hebrew words convey the idea meaning emptiness, waste, desolation, and void. Hebrew verbs denote sinking into obscurity, becoming nothingness, or falling prey to weakness. In Isa. 24:10 God announced judgment on the whole earth. This included breaking down the city of chaos so that no one could enter. Through God's power the line of desolation and the plumb line of emptiness are stretched over Edom (Isa. 34:11). In Jer. 4:23-26 the land is described as desolate, formless, void, and without light, a wilderness unfit for habitation. En route to Canaan, God cared for Israel in a howling wilderness waste (Deut. 32:10). God's power caused mighty leaders and princes to wander in the pathless wastes (Job 12:24; Ps. 107:40). Job compared his friends to waterless riverbeds that had lost themselves in nothingness (Job 6:18). Later Job longed for a place of deep shadow, of utter gloom without order (Job 10:21-22).

In Hebrew thought, however, the most prominent concept of chaos is that of the primeval disorder that preceded God's creative activity. When "darkness was over the surface of the deep" (Gen. 1:2 NASB), God through His word destroyed the forces of confusion.

Throughout the Scriptures chaos is personified as the principal opponent of God. In ancient Semitic legends, a terrible chaos-monster was called Rahab (the proud one), or Leviathan (the twisting dragon-creature), or Yam (the roaring sea). While vehemently denouncing idolatry and unmistakably proclaiming the matchless power of the One Almighty God, biblical writers did not hesitate to draw upon these prevalent pagan images to add vividness and color to their messages, trusting that their Israelite hearers would understand the truths presented.

God demonstrated His power in creation graphically in the crushing defeat of chaos. He quieted the sea, shattering Rahab, making the heavens fair, and piercing the fleeing serpent (Job 26:12-13). His victory over Leviathan is well-known (Job 41:1-8; Isa. 27:1); Leviathan and the sea are at His command (Ps. 104:26). In creation He curbed the unruly sea and locked it into its boundaries (Job 38:1-11). He stretched out the heavens and trampled the back of Yam, the sea (Job 9:8).

A second use of the chaos-monster figure involved God's victories at the time of the exodus, using the term Rahab as a nickname for Egypt. Through His power God divided the sea and crushed Leviathan (Ps. 74:13-14). He calmed the swelling sea and smashed Rahab like a carcass (Ps. 89:9-10). By slaying the monster Rahab, God allowed the people to pass through the barrier sea (Isa. 51:9-10). Mockingly, Isaiah called Egypt a helpless, vain Rahab whom God exterminated (Isa. 30:7). The psalmist anticipated the day when Rahab and Babylon would be forced to recognize God's rule (Ps. 87:4). In Ezek. 29:3; 32:2, the Pharaoh of Egypt is called the river monster that will be defeated at God's will.

Thirdly, the chaos theme is implied, if not used, in the NT depicting God's victory in Christ.

In the Gospels Christ confidently demonstrated mastery over the sea (Mark 4:35-41; 6:45-52; John 6:16-21). In Revelation, when the ancient serpent, personified as the satanic dragon, rises out of the sea challenging His kingdom, Christ utterly defeats the adversary forever.

So, beginning with Gen. 1:2, when God conquered the formless waste, and continuing through all the Scriptures, God's mighty power over chaos is shown repeatedly. Finally, the triumphal note is sounded in Rev. 21:1, "the sea existed no longer." A new heaven and new earth are proof once again that chaos is conquered!

Alvin O. Collins

CHAPITER KJV translation of Hebrew architectural term meaning a capital made to stand on top of a pillar (1 Kings 7:16) or the base on which the actual capital is placed. In Exod. 36:38; 38:17,19,28 KJV translates the Hebrew word for "head" as "*chapiter,*" while a different Hebrew term is so translated in 2 Chron. 3:15. See *Architecture.*

CHAPMAN Old English word for trader (2 Chron. 9:14 KJV). See *Commerce.*

CHARASHIM (Cär´ à shĭm) (KJV) See *Geharashim.*

CHARCHEMISH See *Carchemish.*

CHARGE See *Schoolmaster.*

CHARGER(S) 1. Large flat serving dish (Num. 7:13-85; Matt. 14:8,11 KJV). **2.** Horses used in battle to charge or attack (Nah. 2:3 NRSV; cp. TEV, REB based on early Greek translations; cp. Isa. 31:1,3; Jer. 8:6; Rev. 6:2).

CHARIOTS Two-wheeled land vehicles made of wood and strips of leather and usually drawn by horses. They were used widely in Mesopotamia before 3000 B.C. and were introduced into Canaan and Egypt by the Hyksos about 1800–1600 B.C. Their primary function was as mobile firing platforms in battles. They were also used for hunting, for transportation of dignitaries, and in state and religious ceremonies.
Old Testament Egyptian chariots were the first to be mentioned (Gen. 41:43; 46:29; 50:9). The iron chariots of the Philistines were fortified with plates of metal that made them militarily

stronger than those of the Israelites (Judg. 1:19; 4:3,13-17; 1 Sam. 13:5-7).

Chariots became an important part of Solomon's army and his commercial affairs (1 Kings 4:26; 9:15-19; 10:28-29). The military strength of Israel under Ahab was noteworthy because of the number of chariots available for use. According to Assyrian records, Ahab brought 2,000 chariots into the Battle of Qarqar in 853 B.C. Chariots were also seen in prophetic visions (Zech. 6:1-8) and applied figuratively to Elijah's and Elisha's power (2 Kings 2:12; 13:14). **New Testament** Chariots were used in prophetic imagery (Rev. 9:9; 18:13) and for transportation of the Ethiopian eunuch (Acts 8:26-38). See *Arms and Armor.*

Lai Ling Elizabeth Ngan

CHARIOTS OF THE SUN RSV translation in 2 Kings 23:11 for a sculpture that Josiah removed from the Jerusalem temple. Other translations speak of horses the kings of Judah had dedicated to the sun. The Assyrians called the sun god "chariot rider," so this could represent statuary introduced when Judah began to pay tribute to the Assyrian kings. Deuteronomy 17:3 records God's injunction to Israel not to worship the sun, but Ezekiel attested to persons in the temple worshiping the sun (Ezek. 8:16).

CHARITY KJV translation of Greek *agape.* Several translations use "charity" for *eleemosune,* "pity, alms" (Luke 11:41; Acts 9:36; 10:4,31). See *Alms; Love.*

CHARM Human grace and attractiveness; magic objects intended to ward off evil; and a method used to prevent poisonous snakes from biting. **1.** Human charm can be deceitful (Prov. 31:30), yet the Hebrew term used—*chen*—is a characteristic of God's gift of the Spirit (Zech. 12:10). God gave Joseph the ability to be charming or gain favor with the Egyptian jailer (Gen. 39:21). God also gives such grace to the afflicted (Prov. 3:34). Generally the term means to find favor or acceptance from another person (Gen. 6:8; 33:8), but English translations use "grace" or "favor" rather than "charm" as the translation at these points. "Charm" is used in cases like the harlot of Nah. 3:4. **2.** Magic charms sewn as wristbands (Ezek. 13:18 NIV) to ward off evil spirits and diseases receive prophetic condemnation (cp. Isa. 3:20). **3.** Snake charmers exercised

power in the community because they knew "magic words" or "magic acts" to prevent poisonous snakes from harming people. The psalmist compared the wicked to deaf snakes who were immune to such charmers (Ps. 58:4-5). The "enchanters" (NASB, NIV, NRSV) are listed among community leaders the prophet condemned (Isa. 3:3). Jeremiah warned God would send snakes whom no one could charm to punish His disobedient people (Jer. 8:17). The writer of Ecclesiastes reminded his audience that the price of unsuccessful charmers was great (Eccles. 10:11).

CHARRAN Greek and KJV spelling of Haran (Acts 7:2,4). See *Haran.*

CHASTE Holy purity demanded of God's people with special reference to the sexual purity of women. The Greek word *hagnos* originally referred to the holy purity of deities. Paul used the term to urge the Corinthians to remain pure so he could present them to Christ in the last days as a pure, virginal bride (2 Cor. 11:2-3). Titus was to teach young women to be pure in sincere worship, in general moral behavior, and in sexual matters (Titus 2:5; cp. 1 Pet. 3:2). Similarly, church leaders must be pure (1 Tim. 5:22). Purity is an essential element of Christian ethics (Phil. 4:8; James 3:17). Even preaching the gospel can be done from impure motives (Phil. 1:17). To be pure can also appear in a legal context, meaning to be declared innocent of a charge as Paul did in reference to the Corinthians (2 Cor. 7:11). Ultimately, Jesus is the pure One (1 John 3:3).

CHASTEN or **CHASTISEMENT** Refers to an act of punishment intended to instruct and change behavior. Two basic Hebrew words express the idea—*yakach*, "to settle a dispute, reprove"; *yasar*, "to instruct, a discipline." People fear the experience of God's angry chastisement (Pss. 6:1; 38:1). Still, the Father must correct His children (2 Sam. 7:14; cp. Deut. 8:5; 21:18; Prov. 13:24; 19:18). God's people should not despise God's chastening, for it leads to healing (Job 5:17-18; cp. Prov. 3:11; Heb. 12:5). Such chastisement is God's choice, not that of humans (Hos. 10:10; cp. 7:12). The purpose of chastising is to lead to repentance (Jer. 31:18-19) and bring blessing (Ps. 94:12), not to kill (Ps. 118:18). It shows God's greatness and power

(Deut. 11:2). The climactic OT word on chastisement is that the Suffering Servant has borne our chastisement, so that we do not have to suffer it (Isa. 53:5). Ultimately, chastisement shows God's love for the one chastised (Rev. 3:19). He seeks to lead us away from eternal chastisement (1 Cor. 11:32; cp. Heb. 12:10).

CHEBAR (Cē´ bär) River in Babylon where Ezekiel had visions (Ezek. 1:1; 3:15; 10:15; 43:3). This is probably to be identified with the nar Kabari, a channel of the Euphrates River southeast of Babylon. It may be the modern Satten-nil.

CHECKER WORK Part of the decoration of the pillars of the temple (1 Kings 7:17). The Hebrew word also denotes a lattice (2 Kings 1:2) or net (Job 18:8). With reference to the pillars of the temple, it thus denotes a crisscrossed design.

CHEDOR-LAOMER (Cĕd·ôr-lā·ō´ mēr) King of Elam who joined coalition of kings against kings of Sodom and Gomorrah, leading to Abraham's involvement and victory (Gen. 14:1). His Elamite name means "son of La'gamal," (a god). He apparently led the eastern coalition. He does not appear in the fragmentary Elamite records known today, so nothing else is known except what Gen. 14 records. See *Elam*.

CHEESE Dairy product forming a basic part of the diet. The three occurrences of cheese in English translations reflect three different Hebrew expressions. Job 10:10 refers to cheese; 1 Sam. 17:18 speaks literally of a "slice of milk"; and 2 Sam. 17:29 uses a phrase usually interpreted as meaning "curds of the herd."

CHELAL (Cē´ lăl) Personal name of a man with foreign wife in the postexilic community (Ezra 10:30).

CHELLUH (Cĕl´ lūl) Personal name of a man with a foreign wife in postexilic community (Ezra 10:35).

CHELUB (Cĕ´ lŭb) **1.** Descendant of the tribe of Judah (1 Chron. 4:11), probably to be identified with Caleb, the hero of the spy narrative of Num. 13–14. See *Caleb*. **2.** Father of Ezri, overseer of workers on David's farms (1 Chron. 27:26).

CHELUBAI (Cə·lu´ bī) Hebrew variant of Caleb, the hero of the spy narratives (Num. 13–14). See *Caleb*.

CHELUHI (Cĕl´ ūh·ī) (TEV, NRSV, NASB) See *Chelluh*.

CHEMARIM (Cĕm´ á·rĭm) KJV transliteration of Hebrew word meaning "priests of foreign or false gods" in Zeph. 1:4. The Hebrew term also appears in 2 Kings 23:5; Hos. 10:5.

CHEMOSH (Cē´ mŏsh) Divine name meaning "subdue." Deity the Moabites worshiped (Num. 21:29). He was expected to provide land for Moab (Judg. 11:24) though the meaning here is complicated by the fact that Ammonites are addressed. Solomon erected a sanctuary for Chemosh on a mountain east of Jerusalem (1 Kings 11:7). Josiah subsequently defiled the sanctuary (2 Kings 23:13). Jeremiah pronounced doom on Chemosh and his people (Jer. 48:7,13,46).

CHENAANAH (Cə·nā´ á·năh) **1.** Personal name meaning "tradeswoman." Father of the false prophet Zedekiah (1 Kings 22:11). See *Zedekiah*. **2.** Member of the tribe of Benjamin (1 Chron. 7:10).

CHENANI (Cə·nā´ nī) Personal name meaning "one born in month of Kanunu." A Levite who led Israel in a prayer of renewal and praise (Neh. 9:4).

CHENANIAH (Cĕn·á·nī´ ăh) Personal name meaning "Yahweh empowers." **1.** Chief of the Levites under David who instructed people in singing and played a leading role in bringing the ark back to Jerusalem (1 Chron. 15:22,27). **2.** Levite whose family had charge of business outside the temple, including work as officials and judges (1 Chron. 26:29).

CHEPHAR-AMMONI (Cē´ phär-ăm´ mō·nī) Place-name meaning "open village of the Ammonites." A village in the tribal territory of Benjamin (Josh. 18:24). Its location is not known.

CHEPHAR HA-AMMONAI KJV spelling, including the Hebrew definite article, *ha*, for Chephar-ammoni. See *Chephar-ammoni*.

CHEPHIRAH (Cə·phī´ răh) Place-name meaning "queen of the lions." It is located at Khirbet Kefire about four miles west of Gibeon. One of the four cities of the Gibeonites which Joshua delivered from the coalition led by the king of Jerusalem (Josh. 9:17). Joshua assigned it to the tribe of Benjamin (Josh. 18:26). Some of its exiled inhabitants returned to the post-exilic village with Zerubbabel (Ezra 2:25).

CHEPHIRIM (Cĕph´ ĭ·rĭm) Hebrew term for villages that NASB transliterates as place-name in Neh. 6:2.

CHERAN (Cē´ răn) Descendant of Seir (or Edom) listed in Gen. 36:26.

CHERETHITES, CHERETHIM People who lived south of or with the Philistines (1 Sam. 30:14). They were probably related to or paid soldiers for the Philistines. Crete may have been their original home. David used some of these soldiers as a personal bodyguard (2 Sam. 8:18). Ezekiel pronounced judgment on them (Ezek. 25:16), as did Zephaniah (Zeph. 2:5).

CHERITH (Cē´ rĭth) Place-name meaning "cutting" or "ditch." A wadi or brook east of the Jordan River, the modern Wadi Qilt south of Jericho. Elijah pronounced God's judgment to Ahab, king of Israel, in the form of a two-year drought and then found God's protection at the brook of Cherith, where he had water to drink (1 Kings 17:3). When Cherith finally went dry, he found refuge with the widow of Zarephath. See *Elijah*.

CHERUB (Cĕr´ ŭb) Man who left Tel-melah in Babylonian exile to go to Jerusalem with Zerubbabel about 537 B.C. He could not provide a family list to prove he was an Israelite (Ezra 2:59).

CHERUB or **CHERUBIM** (Chĕr´ ŭ·bĭm) Class of winged angels. The Hebrew *cherub* (plural, *cherubim*) is of uncertain derivation. In the OT it is the name of a class of winged angels who functioned primarily as guards (Gen. 3:24) or attendants (Ezek. 10:3-22). The only NT reference to cherubim is in a description of the furnishings of the holy of holies (Heb. 9:5).

Texts descriptive of the appearance and activities of cherubim reflect two contexts. One is in the visions of the presence of God attended by living creatures (cherubim and seraphim, Isa. 6:2-6; Ezek. 1:4-28; 10:3-22). The other is temple worship and the representations of cherubim which were a part of its furnishings (Exod. 25:18-22; 1 Kings 6:23-35; 2 Chron. 3:7-14).

The most impressive of the temple cherubim were the large sculptures (probably winged quadrupeds) in the holy of holies. If these were arranged as was common in the ancient Near East, the two cherubim would together form a throne. Their legs would be the legs of the throne, their backs the arm rests, and their wings the back of the throne. Consistent with the idea of a cherub throne are the texts which envision God dwelling between, enthroned upon, or riding upon the cherubim (1 Sam. 4:4; 2 Sam. 6:2; 22:11; 2 Kings 19:15; 1 Chron. 13:6; 28:18; Pss. 18:10; 80:1; 99:1; Isa. 37:16). Even Ezekiel's vision depicts the glory of God resting upon or between the cherubim as something of a living throne. See *Angels*.   *Michael Martin*

CHESALON (Cĕs´ à lŏn) Place-name meaning "on the hip." Village on eastern border of territory of tribe of Judah (Josh. 15:10). It is equated with Mount Jearim and is modern Kesla, about 10 miles west of Jerusalem. See *Jearim*.

CHESED (Cē´ sĕd) Personal name meaning "one of the Chaldeans." Son of Nahor, the brother of Abraham (Gen. 22:22). His name may indicate he was the original ancestor of the Chaldeans. See *Chaldea*.

CHESIL (Kə sēl´) Place-name meaning "foolish." A city of the tribe of Judah (Josh. 15:30). A similar list giving the boundary of Simeon in Josh. 19:4 spells the name Bethul, a reading supported for Josh. 15:30 by the Septuagint, the earliest Greek translation. First Chronicles 4:30 also reads Bethuel. Chesil is thus identical with Bethuel. See *Bethuel*.

CHESTNUT KJV translation for plane tree in Gen. 30:37. It apparently refers to the smooth-barked *Platanus orientalis*.

CHESULLOTH (Cə sŭl´ lŏth) Place-name meaning "on the hips." A border town of the tribe of Issachar (Josh. 19:18), probably the same as the border town of Zebulon called Chisloth-tabor in Josh. 19:12. It is the modern Iksal, four miles south of Nazareth.

CHEZIB (Kə zēb´) Place-name meaning "deceiving." Birthplace of Shelah, son of Judah and Shuah, a Canaanite (Gen. 38:5). Chezib is probably the same as Achzib. See *Achzib.*

CHICKEN Nesting, brooding bird. Both tame and wild chickens were known in Bible times. Jesus' compares His care for Jerusalem to the care of a mother hen for her nestlings. The Greek terms are general terms for birds and nestlings (Matt. 23:37; Luke 13:34).

CHIDON (Cī´ dŏn) Personal name meaning "crescent sword." First Chronicles 13:9 reads "Chidon" for "Nacon" in 2 Sam. 6:6. Chidon could be a place-name in the text. See *Nachon.*

CHIEF English translation of at least 13 different Hebrew words designating a leader in political, military, religious, or economic affairs. *'Abir* means the powerful one and is used of the chief of Saul's shepherds (1 Sam. 21:7). *'Ayil* is one who holds official power (Exod. 15:15; 2 Kings 24:15; Ezek. 17:13; 32:21). *'Aluph* is the leader of a clan or tribe (Gen. 36:15-43; Zech. 12:5-6). *Gibbor* is the manly one or hero (1 Chron. 9:26). *Gadol* is the great one or the big one (Lev. 21:10). *Ba'al* is the lord or master (Lev. 21:4). *Kohen* is literally a priest and then a leader (2 Sam. 8:18). *Nagid* is a leader (1 Chron. 29:22; 2 Chron. 11:11; Isa. 55:4; Jer. 20:1; Ezek. 28:2). *Nitsab* is the one in charge, the overseer or foreman (1 Kings 9:23). *Menatseach* is the eminent one or supervisor and is used in the titles of many psalms (Ps. 4:1), apparently referring to the choir director. *Nasi'* is a sheikh or tribal chief (Num. 25:18; Josh. 22:14). *Pinnah* is the corner or cornerstone (Judg. 20:2; 1 Sam. 14:38; Zech. 10:4). *'Attud* is a ram or he-goat and is used metaphorically for a chief or leader (Isa. 14:9; Zech. 10:3). *Qatsin* is the last one, the one who has to decide and thus the leader (Josh. 10:24; Judg. 11:6; Prov. 6:7; Isa. 1:10; Mic. 3:1). *Ro'sh* is the head (Num. 25:4; 2 Sam. 23:8,18; Job 29:25 and often in Chron., Ezra, Neh.). *Ri'shon* is number one, the first (Dan. 10:13). *Re'shith* is the first or beginning one (Dan. 11:41). *Sar* is one with dominion or rule, thus an official or ruler (Gen. 40:2; 1 Sam. 17:18; 1 Kings 4:2; 5:16; 1 Chron. 24:5; Dan. 10:20). *Rab* means numerous or great and is used in several compound words to represent the chief or greatest one (2 Kings 18:17; Jer. 39:13; Dan. 5:11).

In the NT the Greek word *arche* means "beginning" or "chief" and is used in several compound words to represent the chief priest or ruler (Matt. 2:4; 16:21; Luke 11:15; 19:2; John 12:42; Acts 18:8; 19:31; 1 Pet. 5:4). *Hegeomai* means to lead to command with official authority (Luke 22:26; Acts 14:12). *Protos* means first or foremost (Matt. 20:27; Luke 19:47; Acts 13:50; 16:12; 25:2; 28:7). *Chiliarchos* is the commander of a military unit supposed to have 1,000 members (Acts 21:31; 25:23; Rev. 6:15).

CHIEF PRIEST See *Aaron; Levites; Priests.*

CHILD See *Family.*

CHILD ABUSE Incidents of child abuse in the Bible usually involve the killing of infants or children. Reported instances of child abuse include the death of Israelite male babies in Egypt (Exod. 1:16-17,22), the male babies of Bethlehem (Matt. 2:16), the sons of Mesha (2 Kings 3:4,27), Ahab (2 Kings 16:3; cp. 2 Kings 23:10) and Manasseh (2 Chron. 33:6), and the daughters of Lot (Gen. 19:8) and Jephthah (Judg. 11:30-40). The Bible recognizes that some sinful activity is passed on from generation to generation (Exod. 34:7).

Ezekiel compared the origin of the people of Israel to an abandoned baby found and cared for by God (Ezek. 16:4-14). The psalmist likened God to a father who "has compassion on his children" (Ps. 103:13 HCSB), a teaching expanded by Jesus when He declared that God is more caring than even human fathers (Luke 11:11-13).

Jesus' actions in welcoming the little children (Mark 10:13-16) exemplify the care which parents and teachers should bestow on children who are under their protection. Parents are charged not to provoke their children (Eph. 6:4; Col. 3:21), a command that forbids all forms of abuse and neglect. Furthermore, Christians have a responsibility to expose and work to rectify acts which are harmful to others, especially persons who are innocent and helpless (Ps. 82:3-4; Jer. 22:3; Eph. 5:11).   *Paul H. Wright*

CHILDREN (SONS) OF GOD In the OT "sons of God" can refer to spirit beings (Job 1:6; 38:7; Ps. 89:6-7) but more often refers to persons who stand in covenant relationship with God. Thus, the people of Israel are called God's sons and daughters. At times this designation is due to

God's choice of Abraham and his descendants and often refers to the whole nation of Israel (Exod. 4:22; Deut. 14:1; Hos. 11:1). At other times the childhood of Israel is tied to obedience to and faith in God, and therefore, it refers only to a faithful remnant. Although children are disobedient (Is. 30:1), one's covenant status as a child of God can be forfeited (Deut. 32:5), because it applies only to individuals who can rightly be called by God's name (Isa. 43:6-7). This is the point of John the Baptist's criticism of some Jews' confidence in their Abrahamic descent (Luke 3:7-9).

The NT continues this dual emphasis on covenant relationship and faithfulness. The sonship of Israel through the covenant still stands (Rom. 9:4; Heb. 2:16), though not all Jews participate in the covenant blessings (Rom. 9:6). Only those who are "heirs according to the promise" to Abraham are truly God's children (Gal. 3:29). Jesus is the ultimate example and fulfillment of covenant relationship with the Father and, therefore, serves as the model of sonship. Our sonship is inextricably tied to the sonship of Christ (Heb. 1:5; Gal. 4:5). Adoption as God's children is received by union with Christ (Rom. 8:17), through the indwelling of the Holy Spirit (Rom. 8:14-16), and is available to both Jews and Gentiles. Adoption is based on faith in Christ Jesus (Gal. 3:26-27), though obedience is emphasized. The relationship between obedience and faith is mysterious but is one of reciprocity. The obedient are shown to be children of God (Phil. 2:15), and those who obey are God's children (1 John 3:9-10). Thus, divine childhood is based on faith in Christ (1 John 5:1), which flows out of love for God (1 John 5:2), and naturally leads to obedience (1 John 5:3-5).

Adoption as God's children is described as present with fulfillment at the end of the age. Paul says we are "eagerly waiting" (Rom. 8:23 HCSB) and tied to redemption of the body at the resurrection (Rom. 8:19). Jesus is the firstborn among many brethren (Rom. 8:29; 1 Cor. 15:20-23). John speaks of a childhood actualized by faith and revealed in future glory (1 John 3:2-3). See *Sons of God*.   *John Laing*

CHILDREN OF THE EAST See *Kadmonite*.

CHILEAB (Cĭl´ ə ăb) Personal name meaning "everything of the Father." David's second son (2 Sam. 3:3) born to Abigail. The name appears as Daniel in 1 Chron. 3:1. Whatever his exact name, David's second son disappeared from history here and did not figure in the later disputes over who would succeed David as king. His name could be associated with the clan of Caleb.

CHILION (Cĭl´ ĭ·ŏn) Personal name meaning "sickly." One of the two sons of Elimelech and Naomi (Ruth 1:2). With his parents he emigrated to Moab, where he married a Moabite woman named Orpah. Afterwards, he died in Moab. See *Ruth*.

CHILMAD (Cĭl´ măd) Place-name meaning "marketplace." A trading partner of Tyre according to Hebrew text of Ezek. 27:23, but many Bible students think copyists inadvertently changed the text from "all of Media" or a similar reading. Otherwise, Chilmad is identical with Kulmadara, a city in the Syrian Kingdom of Unqi. Its location may be modern Tell Jindaris.

CHIMHAM (Cĭm´ hăm) Personal name meaning "paleface." **1.** Apparently the son of Barzillai, the patron of David when he fled to Mahanaim east of the Jordan before Absalom (2 Sam. 19:37). Chimham returned with David to Jerusalem when Barzillai refused to leave his home. **2.** Village near Bethlehem. Johanan gathered his people there after the assassination of Gedaliah. From there they escaped to Egypt (Jer. 41:17).

CHINNERETH (Cĭn´ nə rĕth) Place-name meaning "harp shaped." **1.** Sea or lake otherwise called the Sea of Galilee, Lake of Gennesaret, or Sea of Tiberias. It formed the eastern border of Canaan, the promised land (Num. 34:11), marking the western boundary of the tribe of Gad (Josh. 13:27). **2.** City on the western edge of the Sea of Chinnereth, also called Chinneroth (Josh. 11:2), though this could be a reference to the Sea. The city belonged to the tribe of Naphtali (Josh. 19:35). The city apparently gave its name to the Sea and to the surrounding region with its several bays, thus explaining the plural form in 1 Kings 15:20, which tells of Ben-hadad of Syria defeating the area in answer to the request of King Asa of Judah. Thothmes III of Egypt also claimed to have conquered the city about 1475 B.C. The city is the modern Tell al-Oreimeh.

CHINNEROTH (Cĭn´ nə rōth) Hebrew plural form of Chinnereth. See *Chinnereth.*

CHIOS (Cī´ ŏs) Island with city of same name. Paul stopped here while returning from third missionary journey (Acts 20:15). The Greek poet Homer supposedly came from Chios. It lies in the Aegean Sea five miles off the coast of Asia Minor. It is now called Scio.

CHISEL English term NIV uses to translate several Hebrew expressions for working with wood and stone. The verb *pasal* means to hew out or dress stone (Exod. 34:1; Deut. 10:1; 1 Kings 5:18; Hab. 2:18). *Garzen* is an ax used in the stone quarries or forests (Deut. 19:5; 1 Kings 6:7). *Choqqi* is a verbal noun meaning cutting out or engraving (Isa. 22:16; 30:8). Isaiah employs a word used nowhere else and meaning a carpenter's tool for forming an idol. KJV, NASB, NRSV read "planes." *Ma'atsad* is apparently a small, curved cutting tool, perhaps an adze (Isa. 44:12; Jer. 10:3). KJV reads "tongs" in Isa. 44:12. See *Tools.*

CHISLEU (Cĭs´ lēū) or **CHISLEV** Name of the ninth month of the Jewish calendar after the exile, apparently borrowed from the Babylonian name Kisliwu (Neh.1:1; Zech. 7:1). See *Calendar.*

CHISLON (Cĭs´ lŏn) Personal name meaning "clumsy." Father of Elidad, who represented the tribe of Benjamin on the commission that divided the land for Israel (Num. 34:21).

CHISLOTH-TABOR (Cĭs´ lōth-tà´ bôr) See *Chesulloth.*

CHITLISH (Cĭt´ lĭsh) Place-name of foreign origin. It was a city of the tribe of Judah near Lachish (Josh. 15:40). KJV reads "Kithlish"; NIV, "Kitlish."

CHITTIM See *Kittim.*

CHIUN (Cī´ ŭn) KJV spelling of divine name meaning "the constant, unchanging one" (Amos 5:26). NRSV reads "Kaiwan;" NASB, "Kiyyun;" NIV, "pedestal." The Hebrew word *kiyun* appears to represent an intentional change by the Hebrew scribes, inserting the vowels of *shiqquts,* "abomination," for an original reading, *Kaiwan,* the name of a Babylonian god of the stars equiv-

alent to the Greek god, Saturn. Amos condemned the people of Israel for priding in their sophisticated worship of foreign gods. He called them back to the simple worship of the wilderness. See *Sikkuth.*

CHLOE (Clō´ ē) Personal name meaning "verdant." A woman whose household members informed Paul of dissension within the church at Corinth (1 Cor. 1:11). Where she lived and how her people learned of the situation in Corinth are not known.

CHOINIX Dry measure used to measure grain and was equivalent to about a quart, or a daily ration for one person (Rev. 6:6). See *Weights and Measures.*

CHORASHAN (Côr ăsh´ ăn) See *Bor-ashan.*

CHORAZIN (Cō´ rä zĭn) One of the cities Jesus censured because of the unbelief of its inhabitants (Matt. 11:21). It was located in Galilee. It has been identified with modern Khirbet Kerazeh, ruins located about two miles north of the site of Capernaum. Chorazin is mentioned in the Talmud as a place famous for its wheat. In the time of Jesus it must have been an important place, but by the second half of the third century A.D. it had ceased to be inhabited.

CHOSEN PEOPLE Israel as the elect of God. See *Election.*

CHOZEBA (Cō zē´ bà) (KJV) See *Cozeba.*

CHRIST, CHRISTOLOGY "Christ" is English for the Greek *Christos,* "anointed one." The Hebrew word is *Mashiach,* Messiah. Christology

Excavations at the site of Chorazin showing the synagogue area.

is a compound of the Greek words *Christos* and *logos* (word, speech). Christology is the study of the person (who He is) and work (what He did/does) of Jesus Christ, the Son of God.

Old Testament and Jewish Background See *Messiah.*

Jesus as the Christ in the Gospels The Gospels present distinctive yet complementary portraits of Jesus. The Synoptics' (Matthew, Mark, and Luke) presentations are similar, while John's is significantly different. The Synoptics give less prominence to the title "Christ" than we might expect. Jesus does not parade His messiahship nor overtly claim to be Messiah by announcing Himself as Israel's warrior king who would rid Palestine of Rome. He did claim to be the One in whom the kingdom of God was present (Mark 1:14-15; Luke 11:20). His parables enunciated both the arrival and character of the kingdom, showing how to be God's children (Matt. 13; Mark 4). His healing the sick, raising the dead, and casting out demons were demonstrations of His divine power and of God's presence in His ministry (Luke 5:17). His teaching on prayer demonstrated His awareness that God was uniquely and intimately His Father. He called God "Abba" ("my dear Father"), a word fondly used of a parent by Jewish children (Mark 14:36; Luke 10:21-22; 11:2). His mission was heralding the coming kingdom, which was bound to His sacrificial and substitutionary death on the cross (Mark 8:31-32; 9:31; 10:32-34; Luke 9:51; 13:32-35). Only through the cross could God's kingdom come and God's will be done by His anointed Servant and Son (Luke 4:16-19). See *Abba.*

Since God's redemption involved a suffering Messiah, Jesus took a reserved attitude to the title "Christ." When Peter confessed, "You are the Messiah" (Mark 8:29 HCSB), Jesus' response was guarded. He did not deny it, but He distanced Himself from common Jewish nationalistic expectations of a deliverer Messiah (Mark 10:35-45; Luke 24:19-21). Even the disciples entertained such a hope (Acts 1:6). At His trial before the Sanhedrin, Jesus affirmed He was "the Messiah, the Son of the Blessed One," then added the title "Son of Man" (Mark 14:61-62 HCSB). Before Pilate, however, He was more cautious (Matt. 26:63-64; Mark 15:2; Luke 22:67-68), not identifying with a political Messianic idea. Jesus was sentenced to death on a false charge of being a political messianic

claimant and rival to Rome (Mark 15:26,32). Jesus instead (Mark 10:45) viewed His mission as "Son of man," God's Representative who suffers, is loyal to truth, promoted to share God's throne (Dan. 7:13-14) and God's Suffering Servant (Isa. 42:14; 49:5-7; 52:13–53:12). At His baptism (Matt. 3:13-17; Mark 1:9-13; Luke 3:21-22), the voice of God revealed the kind of Messiah Jesus was. "This is My beloved Son" (cp. Ps. 2:7) is Messianic. "I take delight in Him!" (Matt. 3:17 HCSB; cp. Isa. 42:1) is from the first of the Suffering Servant songs. His Messiahship was realized through suffering and death as a sin-bearer. Understanding both His Messianic identity and mission, Jesus looked confidently beyond rejection by His own (John 1:11) and death on the cross to vindication by God in His bodily resurrection from the dead.

The Gospel of John makes unique contributions to Christology. Matthew and Luke narrate events related to the virgin conception and birth (Matt. 1–2; Luke 1–2) of Jesus. John, in contrast, focuses on the incarnation of the divine Son, the Word (*Logos*) of God (John 1:1-18). The Synoptics' Christology is "from below," beginning with the birth of Jesus; John's Christology is "from above," beginning with the preexistent Word (*Logos*) who was with God at creation and was God (1:1-2). John 1 and Col. 1 present the highest Christology in the NT. The background for John's use of Logos is the OT concepts of the "Word" and "Wisdom" (Prov. 8) of God. The Word is: the agent of creation (John 1:1-3; cp. Gen. 1:1; Ps. 33:6-9); the agent of revelation (John 1:4; cp. Gen. 12:1; 15:1; Isa. 9:8; Jer. 1:4; Ezek. 33:7; Amos 3:1); eternal (John 1:1-2; cp. Ps. 119:89) and the agent of redemption (John 1:12, 29; cp. Ps. 107:20). In Prov. 8 much of this is attributed to Wisdom. Wisdom was with God in the beginning and was present at creation (Prov. 8:22-31). Gen. 1–2 and Prov. 8 provide the OT context for John's prologue (1:1-18). Jesus spoke and taught as a wise man or sage. Much of His speech is wisdom speech, and He used many traditional wisdom forms (including parables and proverbs). Jesus is presented by Himself and others as a wise man (Matt. 12:42; 13:54; Mark 6:2; Luke 2:40,52; 11:31; 21:15; John 1:1-4; Rom. 11:33-36; Col. 2:2-3; Rev. 5:12; 7:10-12) and as the wisdom of God itself (1 Cor. 1:22-24,30; 2:6-8). This Wisdom Christology is an important feature of the NT portrait of Jesus. John also found *Logos* a valuable bridge word, speaking to multiple cultures at once, such as Jew and Greek. To the Greeks the Logos was the ordering principle of the universe. The Word (Jesus) in John's prologue became flesh (1:14) and has explicated the invisible God to man (1:18).

John also develops his Christology around seven signs and seven "I am" sayings, all of which point to the divine nature of the Son. The signs were miraculous, but their Johannine significance is in the fact that they proved who Jesus was.

THE SEVEN SIGNS IN JOHN

2:1-11	Jesus turns water into wine.
4:46-54	Jesus heals a nobleman's son.
5:1-16	Jesus cures a paralytic.
6:1-15	Jesus feeds the 5,000.
6:16-21	Jesus walks on water.
9:1-41	Jesus heals a blind man.
11:1-57	Jesus raises Lazarus from the dead.

THE SEVEN "I AM" STATEMENTS

"I AM the Bread of Life" (6:35,41,48,51).
"I AM the Light of the World" (8:12).
"I AM the Door of the Sheep" (10:7,9).
"I AM the Good Shepherd" (10:11,14).
"I AM the Resurrection and the Life" (11:25).
"I AM the Way, the Truth, the Life" (14:6).
"I AM the true Vine" (15:1,5).

In John 8:58 Jesus declares Himself to be the "I AM" of the OT. A more direct claim to deity cannot be found. John also develops a theology of glory through suffering for God's Messiah (12:27-28; 17:1-5). The self-awareness of Jesus as the Son of the Father is emphasized in John, though not absent in the Synoptics. The deity of Jesus receives a climactic confession at the end of John with Thomas' exclamation, "My Lord and my God!" (20:28).

This understanding was proclaimed in the apostolic church (Acts 2:22-36; 8:26-40), and in the hands of NT theologians such as Paul (Rom. 3:24-26) and the author of Hebrews (Heb. 8–10) is given further expression.

Christology: Methods Any study of Christology must consider methodology. Some start with creedal formulations confessing Jesus Christ as "true God" and "true man" (e.g., Nicea and Chalcedon), and then work backward to Christology of the early church and the NT. This method is Christology "from above." The alternative approach, Christology "from below," begins with the factual historical records and

theological data of the NT and traces the development of the church's understanding of the Lord before the creeds. In other words, is NT Christology ontological (concerned with Christ's transcendent role in relation to God, the world, and the church) or primarily functional (concerned mainly to relate the person of Jesus Christ to His achievements as Savior and Lord set in the context of earthly ministry)?

The two methods have different starting points. The first asks, "Who is Christ and how is He related to God?" The second raises questions, "What did the human Jesus do and how did the church come to see Him as God, according Him titles of divinity?" Or: "Is Jesus rightly called the Son of God because He saves me?" (functional Christology) or "Does He save me because He is God?" (ontological Christology). The two approaches reach the same goal and both are present in the NT.

John, especially the prologue (1:1-18), gives greater attention to ontological Christology as do other classic christological texts. Philippians 2:6-11 addresses the hypostatic union and the doctrine of kenosis; Col. 1:15-23, and 2:9-10 present the Son as the very image (*eikon*) of God and the Creator in whom all fullness (*pleroma*) dwells; and Heb. 1:1-3 affirms Christ as the radiance of God's glory and the exact representation of God's nature. The argument that the early church had little or no concerns about the ontological nature and status of Jesus as the Son of God are impossible. Christology "from above" was there from the beginning of the earliest church.

Approaching Christology from below, however, is also valuable and a way the apostles and early church knew Jesus and understood who He is and what He did. That a people wed to monotheism came to affirm His sinlessness (2 Cor. 5:21; Heb. 4:15), His deity, and His death on the cross as atonement for the sin of humanity is startling.

The Course of New Testament Christology
The earliest believers were Jews who accepted by faith Jesus as Messiah and risen Lord (Acts 2:32-36). Their appreciation of Jesus rose from the conviction that with His resurrection and exaltation, the new age of God's triumph, promised in the OT, indeed had dawned and the Scriptures (Ps. 110:1; Isa. 53:10-13) had been fulfilled. The cross required explanation, since Jesus' manner of death stood in direct contradic-

tion to current Jewish Messianic expectations. Deuteronomy 21:23 states anyone hanged on a tree died under God's curse (cp. Gal. 3:13). The early church responded in two ways: asserting that Jesus' rejection was foreseen in the OT (Ps. 118:22; Isa. 53) and that the resurrection vindicated God's Son and installed Him in the place of highest honor and power (Phil. 2:5-11). The first Christology had two thrusts: He was the Son of David in His human descent, and in the resurrection He is the Son of God with power (Rom. 1:3-4). The implicit messianic claims of His earthly life were overt in His resurrection and exaltation, and His true being was revealed in glory. Further, the new age He inaugurated was authenticated with the coming of the Holy Spirit at Pentecost (Acts 2:16-21, cp. Joel 2:28).

At a practical level this view of Jesus' life and resurrection gave believers a personal relationship with Jesus as a present reality. He was not a figure of the past, however recent. The first Christian prayer of record is "*Marana tha*" ("our Lord, come," 1 Cor. 16:22). Addressed to the risen Lord, it makes Him equal with Yahweh, Israel's covenant God (Rom. 10:9-13; cp. Acts 7:55-56,59) and as worthy of worship.

OT Scripture also illumines Jesus' true identity and explains His use of the title "Son of Man." Drawn from Dan. 7:13-18, Son of Man is a title of authority and dignity, two ideas the resurrection confirmed (Acts 7:56). Though seldom used by anyone other than Jesus, the church preserved this teaching for several reasons: (1) to show how Jesus was misunderstood and rejected as a false messiah, but as the "Son of Man" Jesus inaugurates God's kingdom and shares the divine throne; (2) to indicate how Jesus brought in a new age of revelation not tied to the law of Moses but universalized for all people. The "Son of Man" is head of a worldwide kingdom, far outstripping narrow Jewish hopes (Dan. 7:22,27); and (3) to find a missionary impulse to lead believers to evangelize non-Jews (Acts 7:59–8:1; 11:19-21; 13:1-3).

Such was the church's mission in the world of Greco-Roman culture and religion. The most relevant title was "Lord," used of gods and goddesses. More significantly, "Lord" designated the honor and divinity of emperor worship. Both areas proved fertile for application of Jesus' most common christological title, Lord. Already used for Yahweh in the Greek OT, it was now applied to the exalted Christ and became a useful point of contact between Christians and pagans familiar with their own deities (1 Cor. 8:5-6). Later "Lord" became the touchstone for Christian allegiance to Jesus when Roman authorities required homage to the emperor as divine, such as in Revelation, when the Emperor Domitian (A.D. 81–96) proclaimed himself "lord and god" (Rev. 17:14).

A further aspect of NT Christology is seen in Hebrews. The author of Hebrews proves the finality of Christ's revelation as Son of God and great "high priest" (5:5; 7:1–9:28), a theme unique to this book. Along with Paul (Rom 3:25) and John (1 John 2:2; 4:10), Hebrews sees the work of Christ as a propitiation (satisfaction) for sin (Heb. 2:17). Hebrews also affirms that in His death on the cross Jesus cleansed us of sins (1:3), puts away sins (8:12; 10:17), bore our sins (9:28), offered one sacrifice for sins for all time (10:12), made an offering for sin (10:18), and annulled sin by his sacrifice (9:26). From any perspective the Son has dealt with sin.

Even in these marvelous confessions (Rom. 9:5; Titus 2:13; 1 John 5:20), the church never compromised its belief in the unity and oneness of God (Deut. 6:4-6), a Christian inheritance from the Jews and an essential element of OT monotheism. Jesus and the Father are one (John 10:30). Jesus, the Logos, is with God and is God. There is a oneness in essence but a distinction in persons. Jesus is no new or rival deity in competition with the Father (John 14:28; 1 Cor. 11:3; Phil. 2:9-11). The worship of the Church is rightly directed to both, along with the Holy Spirit. The NT Church taught and practiced this without entering in-depth theological reflection on the relationships of the Godhead. How the two sides of Jesus' person (human and divine) relate is not explained. The writers bequeathed a rich legacy to the church which formed the substance of the Trinitarian and christological debates leading to the Councils of Nicea (A.D. 325) and Chalcedon (A.D. 451), where it was decreed and expressed that Jesus Christ is "God of God, Light of Light, very God of very God," and that Christ's two natures are united in one Person. This belief has remained the central position of the church ever since, a true confession of a Christology whose roots are in the soil of Holy Scripture. See *Messiah; Son of God; Lord.*

Daniel L. Akin, Ralph P. Martin,
and Charles W. Draper

CHRISTIAN The Greek suffix -*ianos* was originally applied to slaves. It came to denote the adherents of an individual or party. A Christian is a slave or adherent of Christ; one committed to Christ; a follower of Christ. The word is used three times in the NT. Believers "were first called Christians in Antioch" because their behavior, activity, and speech were like Christ (Acts 11:26 HCSB). Agrippa responded to Paul's witness, "Are you going to persuade me to become a Christian so easily?" (Acts 26:28 HCSB). He spoke of becoming an adherent of Christ. Peter stated that believers who suffer as a Christian are to do so for the glory of God (1 Pet. 4:16). A Christian is one who becomes an adherent of Christ, whose daily life and behavior facing adversity is like Christ.

Darrell W. Robinson

CHRISTIAN FESTIVALS See *Church Year.*

CHRISTMAS Of the major Christian festivals, Christmas is the most recent in origin. The name, a contraction of the term "Christ's mass," did not come into use until the Middle Ages. In the early centuries Christians were much more likely to celebrate the day of a person's death than the person's birthday. Very early in its history the church had an annual observance of the death of Christ and also honored many of the early martyrs on the day of their death. Before the fourth century, churches in the East—Egypt, Asia Minor, and Antioch—observed Epiphany, the manifestation of God to the world, celebrating Christ's baptism, His birth, and the visit of the magi.

In the early part of the fourth century, Christians in Rome began to celebrate the birth of Christ. The practice spread widely and rapidly, so that most parts of the Christian world observed the new festival by the end of the century. In the fourth century the controversy over the nature of Christ, whether He was truly God or a created being, led to an increased emphasis on the doctrine of the incarnation, the affirmation that "the Word became flesh" (John 1:14 HCSB). It is likely that the urgency to proclaim the incarnation was an important factor in the spread of the celebration of Christmas.

No evidence remains about the exact date of the birth of Christ. The December 25 date was chosen as much for practical reasons as for theological ones. Throughout the Roman Empire, various festivals were held in conjunction with the winter solstice. In Rome, the Feast of the Unconquerable Sun celebrated the beginning of the return of the sun. When Christianity became the religion of the Empire, the church either had to suppress the festivals or transform them. The winter solstice seemed an appropriate time to celebrate Christ's birth. Thus, the festival of the sun became a festival of the Son, the Light of the world. See *Church Year.*   *Fred A. Grissom*

CHRONICLES, BOOKS OF (Crŏ′ nĭ·kəls) First and Second Chronicles are the first and second books of a four-book series that includes Ezra and Nehemiah. These four books provide a scribal (priestly) history of Israel from the time of Adam (1 Chron. 1:1) to the rebuilding of the house of God and the walls of Jerusalem and the restoration of the people in the worship of God according to the law of Moses (Neh. 13:31). Special focus is on the fortunes of God's house in Jerusalem upon which God has set His name forever (2 Chron. 7:16). David found Israel to be like scattered sheep. As God's chosen shepherd and line through which God would build His house, David sought to order the life of Israel around the worship of God. Under God he made the city of Jerusalem his capital (1 Chron. 11:4-9), transferred the ark of God to the city (1 Chron. 16:1), and began to prepare for the building of the temple (1 Chron. 22:1-2). Solomon, his son, built the temple (2 Chron. 2:1), and Zerubbabel, his son of succeeding generations, rebuilt the temple (Ezra 3:8). The intervening sons of David, who served as kings of Judah, were judged by whether they were faithful to God and to His house. Compare, for example, the reign of wicked King Ahaz with that of good King Hezekiah (2 Chron. 28:1-4; 29:1-11). **Significance of the Title** The two books now called 1 and 2 Chronicles were originally one book. The division into two books was first made after 300 B.C. by the Jewish elders who translated the Hebrew OT into Greek, producing the Septuagint. The reason for making Chronicles into two books is quite simple. The Hebrew manuscript, which usually contained no vowels, could be written on one large roll. The Greek translation with its vowels, however, required nearly twice as much space. The division seems quite appropriate with 1 Chronicles concluding the reign of David and 2 Chronicles beginning the reign of Solomon.

The English title "Chronicles" is derived from the Latin *Chronicon*, which was applied to these writings by Jerome. He described these materials as "a chronicle of the whole of sacred history." The Septuagint (Greek) title is *Paraleipomena*, meaning "omitted things." That title reflects their understanding of Chronicles to be a supplement to the materials found in Samuel and Kings though this is not actually the case.

Closest to the heart is the Hebrew title. It means "the acts or deeds of the day or times." However, the books do more than recount the various acts of the people of that day. Chronicles focuses on the most important deeds of that time or indeed of any time—building the house of God. God's house was, of course, the temple in Jerusalem. But God's house transcends that building. David's dwelling "in the house of the Lord as long as I live" (Ps. 23:6 HCSB) means dwelling forever with God and His people in the abode of God. In the ultimate sense we would equate God's house with His kingdom. Accordingly, the writer(s) of Chronicles reminds us that the most important of all deeds are those by which God's kingdom is built in the hearts of people.

Significance of Chronicles' Place in the Canon Chronicles, Ezra, and Nehemiah stand among the *Hagiographa*, meaning "holy writings," which is the third division of the OT. The order of English versions with Chronicles, Ezra, and Nehemiah after Samuels and Kings goes back to the Septuagint.

The Hebrew Bible places Chronicles as the last book in the OT after even Ezra and Nehemiah. Chronicles doubtless occupied this position in the time of Christ, since He cited Zechariah as the last named prophet who suffered a violent death (2 Chron. 24:20-22; Matt. 23:35; Luke 11:51).

Three explanations are given as to why the Hebrews concluded the OT with Chronicles. One is the view that Chronicles was the last book to be accepted in the OT canon. The second is that the author(s) first wrote Ezra-Nehemiah and then Chronicles. The third and most likely is to have the OT conclude with God's providential control of history to build (rebuild) His house in Jerusalem. The final admonition of the Hebrew OT then is for God's people to go up to Jerusalem to build God's house (2 Chron. 36:23). Moreover, God's final promise is to bless with His presence those who indeed go up to build (2 Chron. 36:23).

Authorship, Date, and Sources We do not know for sure who wrote Chronicles. As has been noted, tradition names Ezra the "ready scribe," a priest descended from Zadok and Phinehas (Ezra 7:1-6), as author of Chronicles, Ezra, and Nehemiah. This tradition cannot be proved, but there is no valid objection to it. If he did not, we do not know who did. The position of these books in the *Hagiographa* indicates that the author was not a prophet. Moreover, the emphasis upon the priests and Levites suggests the author to be someone like Ezra who was one of them. Also, in the seventh year of his reign, Artaxerxes Longimanus, the Persian king from 465 to 425 B.C., sent Ezra to Jerusalem to order the civil and religious life of the Jews according to the law of Moses (Ezra 7:8,14). Accordingly, Ezra was the leader of the spiritual restoration effort these books were written to accomplish. An editor(s) could account for any material extending beyond the time of Ezra.

The use of sources by the author(s) is obvious. Much of the material came from the biblical books of Samuel and Kings. However, other sources are evident such as official chronicles (1 Chron. 27:24), the writings of the prophets (1 Chron. 29:29), and commentaries on the events of that day (2 Chron. 24:27). The genealogies reflect the carefully kept records of the Levites. Sources for the temple materials include "the works of Asaph and David" (2 Chron. 29:30) and the God-given "pattern" (1 Chron. 28:19).

Purposes and Enduring Value The principal purpose of 1 and 2 Chronicles is to show God's control of history to fulfill His desire to dwell among His people in a perfect relationship of holiness in which God is God and the redeemed are His people. God first shared His desire with Moses (Exod. 25:8). The tabernacle and the temple symbolize that desire. God is fulfilling His desire through the Lord Jesus Christ—the Son of David. When Christ shall have completed His redemptive work, "the tabernacle of God" will be "with men, and He will live with them. They will be His people, and God himself will be with them and be their God" (Rev. 21:3 HCSB). Chronicles shows how God worked from the time of Adam but particularly in the times of David through Ezra and Nehemiah to accomplish His desire to dwell in holiness with His people.

A second purpose is to show God's choice of a person and a people to build His house. The person is the Son of David—the Messiah. Solomon built the temple in Jerusalem, but the Son who is building and shall build to completion God's true house and the Son whose reign God will establish forever is the Lord Jesus Christ (1 Chron. 17:12; Luke 1:31-33; Acts 15:14-16). The people are those of faith whose lineage goes back to Adam through Seth to Shem to Abraham (1 Chron. 1:1,17,28) to whom God made the promise of the seed (the Christ) through whom He would bless all nations (Gen. 12:1-4; 15:4-6; 17:7; 22:16-18; Gal. 3:16). His people are those of Israel and indeed of all nations who will put their trust in Him.

A third purpose is to show that God who dwells in holiness must be approached according to the law that God gave to Moses. David, in seeking to unite his people around the presence of God, learned that God must be sought in the proper way (1 Chron. 15:13). Basic is the necessity to come to God by way of the altar of sacrifice as ministered by the Levitical priesthood. God in His merciful forgiveness of David revealed the place of the altar of sacrifice to be in Jerusalem at the threshing floor of Ornan (Araunah) (1 Chron. 21:18–22:1). There David erected the altar and built the temple according to God's directions. But most importantly, there the Son of God, our great High Priest, sacrificed Himself on the cross in our stead to bring His people into the glorious presence of God (Heb. 2:17; 5:1-10).

A fourth purpose of Chronicles is to encourage God's people to work together with God and with one another to build God's house. The author(s) shared with the people the challenge of God through King Cyrus to go up to Jerusalem to build God's house. Chronicles reminds the people of God's history of faithfulness to His people and to His house. God promised that He would bless their obedience to this challenge (2 Chron. 36:23), and He warned of judgment upon those who neglected, thwarted the building of, or desecrated the house of God.

Outline of 1 and 2 Chronicles:
Blessings for Building God's House

I. Israel's People of Faith
(1 Chron. 1:1–9:44)
  A. Godly line of Adam (1:1-4)
  B. Sons of Noah focusing on Shem
     (1:5-27)
  C. Sons of Abraham focusing on Isaac
     (1:28-34a)
  D. Sons of Isaac focusing on Israel
     (1:34b-54)
  E. Sons of Israel focusing on Judah and
     Levi (2:1–9:44)

II. David's Learning Obedience (10:1–22:1)
  A. God's replacing rebellious Saul with
     David (10:1-14)
  B. God's bringing David to power
     (11:1–12:40)
  C. David's bringing the ark back to
     Jerusalem and asking to build the
     temple (13:1–17:27)
  D. David's marring his victories by his
     sin (18:1–21:17)
  E. God's revelation in mercy of the site
     of the temple and the place of the
     altar of sacrifice (21:18–22:1)

III. David's Preparing to Build God's House
(22:2–29:30)
  A. Preparing workmen and materials
     (22:2-5)
  B. Preparing Solomon to build (22:6-16)
  C. Charging the princes to help Solomon
     (22:17-19)
  D. Making Solomon king (23:1)
  E. Ordering the priests and Levites and
     princes for service (23:2–27:34)
  F. Charging Solomon and the people
     (28:1-21)
  G. Inspiring gifts to build (29:1-9)
  H. Worshiping God and enthroning
     Solomon (29:10-25)
  I. Summarizing David's reign (29:26-30)

IV. Solomon's Building God's House
(2 Chron. 1:1–9:31)
  A. God's blessing of Solomon to build
     (1:1-17)
  B. Construction and consecration
     (2:1–7:22)
  C. Solomon's other achievements
     (8:1-18)
  D. Solomon's wisdom and wealth and
     fame (9:1-28)

E. Concluding Solomon's reign (9:29-31)

V. God's Judging Judah's Kings by Their Faithfulness to His House (10:1–36:21)

A. The wicked reign of Rehoboam (10:1–12:16)

B. The wicked reign of Abijah (13:1-22)

C. The sin-marred reign of good King Asa (14:1–16:14)

D. The godly reign of Jehoshaphat (17:1–21:1)

E. The wicked reign of Jehoram (21:2-20)

F. The wicked reign of Ahaziah (22:1-9)

G. The wicked reign of Athaliah (22:10–23:21)

H. The good reign of Joash (24:1-27)

I. Imperfect devotion of Amaziah (25:1-28)

J. Uzziah's violation of the priestly office (26:1-23)

K. Good but imperfect reign of Jotham (27:1-9)

L. Wicked reign of Ahaz (28:1-27)

M. Unqualified good reign of Hezekiah (29:1–32:33)

N. Conversion of wicked King Manasseh (33:1-20)

O. Wicked reign of Amon (33:21-25)

P. Unqualified good reign of Josiah (34:1–35:27)

Q. Wicked reigns of Jehoahaz and Jehoiakim: beginning of exile (36:1-8)

R. Wicked reigns of Jehoiachin and Zedekiah: final stage of exile (36:9-21)

VI. Providential Decree to Rebuild God's House (36:22-23)

A. Date and origin of decree (v. 22a)

B. Purpose of decree (v. 22b)

C. Motivating force of decree (v. 23)

D. Substance of decree (v. 23)

John H. Traylor, Jr.

CHRONICLES OF KINGS OF ISRAEL AND OF JUDAH Sources of information to which the writer of 1 and 2 Kings referred readers for more data concerning the various kings about whom he wrote (1 Kings 14:19). These are not the biblical books 1 and 2 Chronicles. They probably were official court records compiled for the use of each of the kings. Such records apparently were available to the author of Kings writing after the destruction of Jerusalem, but they are not available today. See *Kings*.

CHRONOLOGY OF THE BIBLICAL PERIOD When speaking of chronology, one must differentiate between relative and absolute chronology. Absolute chronology is tied to fixed dates—events that are known to have occurred on a specific date (i.e., John F. Kennedy was assassinated on November 22, 1963). Relative chronology places events in their chronological order but without a fixed date (i.e., Jesus was baptized, then tempted, then began His public ministry). Most of the biblical events are dated relatively rather than absolutely. For this reason many chronological charts have differences in specific dates, B.C. or A.D., but generally agree on the relative order of most events.

The Old Testament Period The primary tool by which absolute dates are provided for ancient Israel is Assyrian chronology, which is established through the use of lists of year names (eponyms) that can be tied to absolute chronology by reference to a solar eclipse known to have occurred in 763 B.C. Two Israelite kings, Jehu and Ahab, are referred to on Assyrian tablets. Thus we know that King Ahab (1 Kings 16–22) fought Shalmaneser III at the Battle of Qarqar and died in 853 B.C. Similarly, we know that King Jehu (2 Kings 9–10) in the first year of his reign paid tribute to the same Assyrian king in 841 B.C. Since the books of Kings give the names and length of reign of all the kings of Judah and Israel, the years of Solomon's reign are known with reasonable accuracy to have been 970 to 930 B.C., David's reign was 1010 to 970 B.C., and Saul's was 1050 to 1010 B.C.

Apparent numerical inconsistencies of dates between Kings and Chronicles can be resolved by recognizing (1) such common practices as coregencies (the overlapping reigns of a king and his successor) and rival kings and (2) differences between Israel and Judah in the manner of counting the years of a king's reign. The kings of Judah figured their reign from their first full year as king. A part of a year would be designated as the former king's last year of rule. In Israel a part year was designated as the previous king's last year and the new king's first year. Therefore, the length of reign for a king of Israel was counted as one year longer than a similar reign for a king of Judah. Uncertainty still remains at many points. Differences between ancient and modern calendars, for example, often necessitates the giving of alternate dates in the form 931/0 B.C. Furthermore, different methods of harmonizing

SIGNIFICANT DATES IN OLD TESTAMENT BIBLE HISTORY

	Traditional	Critical
Patriarchs	2100–1800	1800–1600
(Abraham, Isaac, Jacob)		
Exodus	1446	1290
Conquest	1400	1250
Judges	1350–1050	1200–1025

Kings of United Israel

	Traditional	Critical
Saul	1050–1010	1025–1005
David	1010–970	1005–965
Solomon	970–931/0	965–925

Kings of the Divided Kingdom

Judah		Israel	
Rehoboam	930–913	Jeroboam	930–909
Abijah (Abijam)	913–910		
Asa	910–869		
		Nadab	909–908
		Baasha	908–886
		Elah	886–885
		(Zimri	885)
		(Tibni	885–880)
		Omri	885–874
Jehoshaphat	872–848		
		Ahab	874–853
		Ahaziah	853–852
Jehoram (Joram)	853–841		
		Joram (Jehoram)	852–841
Ahaziah	841		
Athaliah	841–835		
		Jehu	841–814
Joash (Jehoash)	835–796		
		Jehoahaz	814–798
Amaziah	796–767		
		Jehoash (Joash)	798–782
Uzziah (Azariah)	792–740		
		Jeroboam II	793–753
Jotham	750–732		
		Zechariah	753
		Shallum	752
		Menahem	752–742
Jehoahaz (Ahaz)	735–715		
		Pekahiah	742–740
		Pekah	752–732
		Hoshea	732–722
Hezekiah	729–686		
		Fall of Samaria	722
Manasseh	697–642		
Amon	642–640		
Josiah	640–609		
Jehoahaz II	609		
Jehoiakim	608–598		
Jehoiachin	598–597		
Zedekiah	597–586		

Fall of Judah
Exile and Restoration

Babylonian conquest of Judah, Daniel and other nobles exiled	605
Jehoiachin and thousands exiled to Babylon, including Ezekiel	597
Jerusalem and temple destroyed, Zedekiah and others exiled	587/6
Governor Gedaliah assassinated, many fled to Egypt, taking Jeremiah	582(?)
Jehoiachin released from prison	562
Persian king Cyrus (559–530) captured Babylon	539
Jewish return to Judah led by Sheshbazzar and Zerubbabel	538
Persian king Cambyses	530–522
Persian king Darius	522–486
Preaching of Haggai and Zechariah, Temple building resumes	520
Temple completed	516/5
Persian King Xerxes/Ahasuerus	486–465
Persian King Artaxerxes	465–424
Ezra's arrival in Judah; wall rebuilding begins?	458
Nehemiah's arrival in Judah; wall completed	445
Nehemiah's temporary absence from Judah	433–431?

the dates of biblical kings yield slightly different results. The dates given for the divided kingdom in the chart "Significant Dates in the Old Testament Bible History" are according to the widely used system of Edwin A. Thiele.

Assuming a literal interpretation of 1 Kings 6:1, the exodus occurred in 1446 B.C., and the conquest period lasted about seven years around 1400 B.C. Continuing backwards, based on Exod. 12:40, Jacob's migration to Egypt would have been in 1876 B.C. Data regarding the ages of the patriarchs would place their births at 2006 B.C. for Jacob (Gen. 47:9), 2066 B.C. for Isaac (Gen. 25:26), and 2166 B.C. for Abraham (Gen. 21:5). Because the genealogical lists in Genesis are believed by most to be intentionally incomplete or "open," attempts are usually not made to establish historical dates prior to Abraham.

Many biblical scholars discount the Bible's chronological data. Even some who accept biblical authority nevertheless argue that many numbers in the Bible are figurative, especially "40" and its multiples. These scholars prefer to give priority to archaeological clues in establishing biblical chronology. Thus the Patriarchal period is often dated in the Middle Bronze Age between about 1800 and 1600 B.C. It is also supposed that the Hebrews migrated to Egypt during the Hyk-

sos period (about 1700 to 1500 B.C.) when Semitic people ruled Egypt. The exodus is then associated with the reign of Rameses II shortly after 1290 B.C. Following the wilderness-wandering period, the conquest of Canaan would have begun about 1250 B.C. Pharaoh Merneptah (1224–1214 B.C.) mounted a campaign against Canaan in the fifth year of his reign (about 1220). In his record of that campaign, he records that, among others, Israel was utterly destroyed. Thus by that date, the people Israel were a recognized group in Canaan.

The last days of the kingdom of Judah involve the kings of Babylon, thus giving an outside source to date Judah's history. These external synchronisms can be used to fix the date of the fall of Jerusalem at around 586 B.C.

The period of exile began with the capture of Jerusalem, the destruction of the temple, and the second deportation of leading citizens in 586 B.C. (An earlier deportation in 597 B.C. had taken King Jehoiachin and his family and many top officials to Babylon.) Ezekiel is a leading prophet among the exiles during this time. Exile ended in 538 B.C. after the capture of Babylon by the Persians under Cyrus in 539 B.C. and Cyrus' edict permitting displaced persons to return to their homelands. The rebuilding of the temple is dated between 520 and 515 B.C. according to dates from Hag. 1:1; Zech. 1:1; and Ezra 4:24; 6:15.

The Intertestamental Period During the Intertestamental Period, Palestine was first under the control of the Persians. Persian rule ended with the conquest of Palestine by Alexander the Great in 333–332 B.C. After the death of Alexander, Palestine fell first under Ptolemaic rule (323–198 B.C.) and then under Seleucid rule (198–164 B.C.). During the period of Ptolemaic rule the Septuagint (Greek translation of the OT) was made in Egypt. Seleucid rule brought a strong move to bring Hellenistic culture to Palestine, ending with the desecration of the temple in Jerusalem and the persecution of Jews by Antiochus IV (Epiphanes) in 167 B.C. The following Jewish revolt led by Judas Maccabeus resulted in the defeat of the Seleucids and the Second Jewish Commonwealth (164–63 B.C.). The temple was reconsecrated in 164 B.C. These events are recorded in the Apocrypha in 1 Maccabees 1–4. The successors to the Maccabees are usually called the Hasmonean rulers. Hasmonean rule ended in 63 B.C. when Pompey occupied Jerusalem and Judea was again under foreign domination.

The New Testament Period One might expect that the chronology of the NT would be much more certain than that of the OT. In some respects that is the case but not entirely so. Granted we have Greek and Roman histories and annals, but most of the biblical events still cannot be placed precisely in an absolute chronology. The complicating factors are at least twofold. In the first place, the events of the NT were not reported by the Greek and Roman historians, nor were many precise events from Greek and Roman history included in the NT. Secondly, the Romans and Jews used different calendars. The Romans had a solar calendar with the year beginning in January but reckoned most events from the accession date of the emperor. Thus they had internal differences in their own calendar. The Jewish calendar only confused the matter more. Basically, the Jews used a lunar calendar of 354 days. Periodically, they added an additional month to keep their calendar in line with the seasons. Because of several calendar changes, the Jews in their history had two New Year's days, one in the fall and the other in the spring. The spring New Year marked the beginning of the cultic calendar and the beginning of the next

year's reign of the Jewish king. The fall New Year marked the beginning of the civil year. The reign of foreign rulers was noted from this fall New Year. With such differences it is no wonder that absolute chronology for NT events is very difficult.

The Life and Ministry of Jesus The births of both Jesus (Matt. 2:1) and John the Baptist (Luke 1:5) are set in the reign of Herod the Great. From Josephus we learn that Herod died in the 37th year after the Roman Senate decree named him king (40 B.C.). This would place his death in 4 B.C. Herod's command to kill all the boys in Bethlehem two years old or less (Matt. 2:16) is another clue. The further evidence Luke gives of a census while Cyrenius was governor of Syria presents some difficulty (Luke 2:2). Cyrenius conducted a census while serving as governor in A.D. 6–7, but there is no corroborating historical reference to a census during Herod's reign nor to Cyrenius serving as governor at that time. This simply means that we cannot verify Luke's statement from presently available evidence. Luke may have referred to the census of A.D. 6–7 in Acts 5:37. With Herod's death placed in 4 B.C., Jesus' birth is usually dated between 7 and 5 B.C.

The beginning of John the Baptist's ministry is set in the 15th year of Tiberius (Luke 3:1-2), which was A.D. 28 or 29. Jesus' ministry would then have begun in A.D. 29 or 30 if John's ministry began one to two years before that of Jesus. On the other hand, if Tiberius' reign was considered to have begun when he co-ruled with Augustus, his fifteenth year would be A.D. 26 or 27. This latter date would fit better with Luke's statement that Jesus was about 30 when He began His ministry (Luke 3:23). Jesus' ministry would thus have begun about A.D. 27 or 28. The length of Jesus' ministry is also much debated. None of the four Gospels gives enough details to determine the precise length of the ministry. Lengths of one, two, and three years are most often proposed. John's Gospel mentions three Passover feasts (2:13; 6:4; 11:55). If these are distinct Passovers, they would indicate a ministry of at least a little more than two years.

The Roman historian Tacitus dated Jesus' crucifixion during the reign of Emperor Tiberius (A.D. 14–37) when Pilate was governor of Judea (A.D. 26–37). All the Gospel accounts agree that Jesus died on a Friday, the day before the Sabbath, at the beginning of Passover week. The chronological terms used by John and the Synoptic Gospels are not identical, resulting in disagreement over interpreting and reconciling the two. Nevertheless, it seems that after Jesus and the disciples celebrated the Last Supper on Thursday evening, Jesus was arrested and tried that night as well as the following morning. He was then crucified the next day, Nisan 14, which fell on a Friday in A.D. 30 and 33. If Jesus' ministry began in A.D. 29 or 30, His crucifixion must have been in A.D. 33. On the other hand, if His ministry began in A.D. 27 or 28, His crucifixion was in A.D. 30.

The Apostles Dating the events and activities of the apostles is as vexing as dating the events of Jesus' life. There are very few fixed dates. The death of Herod Agrippa I, mentioned in Acts 12:23, occurred in A.D. 44 according to Josephus. Likewise, the edict of Claudius expelling Jews from Rome (Acts 18:2) is usually dated to A.D. 49, and Gallio's term as deputy (Acts 18:12) belongs to A.D. 51–52.

Other events in Acts must be dated relatively, and problems remain. In particular, there is great difficulty in matching the chronology of Acts with the information in the Pauline epistles. However, in general, we can sketch with approximate dates the ministry of Paul as follows:

Conversion, A.D. 33/34
First visit to Jerusalem, A.D. 36
Second visit to Jerusalem, during famine, A.D. 46/47
First missionary journey, A.D. 47–48/49
Conference in Jerusalem, A.D. 49
Second missionary journey, A.D. 49/50–52
Third missionary journey A.D. 53–57
Final visit to Jerusalem, A.D. 57
Reaches Rome, A.D. 60
Further ministry in Asia A.D. 62–63
Return to Rome (execution under Nero) A.D. 64/65

The datable events in the NT all occurred before the fall of Jerusalem and destruction of the temple in A.D. 70.

Joel F. Drinkard, Jr. and E. Ray Clendenen

CHRYSOLITE Mineral from which the seventh stone of the foundation of the New Jerusalem is made (Rev. 21:20). The Greek *chrusolithos* means "golden stone," indicating a yellow-colored stone. It was thus a yellow topaz, beryl, or zircon. The modern chrysolite is green and is not identical with biblical chrysolite (cp. Ezek. 1:16). See *Jewels, Jewelry; Minerals and Metals.*

CHRYSOPRASE Mineral forming the tenth stone of the foundation of the New Jerusalem (Rev. 21:20). The Greek word literally means "green leek." The stone is apple-green, fine-grained hornstone or quartz colored with nickel oxide and is highly translucent. It may be closer to modern chalcedony than any other modern mineral. See *Jewels, Jewelry; Minerals and Metals.*

CHUB (Cŭb) KJV transliteration of Hebrew name of a people in Ezek. 30:5. Other translations follow an interpretation of the Septuagint, the earliest Greek translation, to find meaning in the text, reading "Lud" for "Chub," and translating "Libya." If "Libya" is not the original reading, "Chub" remains a people about whom nothing is known except that Ezekiel announced judgment on them as a partner of Egypt. See *Libya.*

CHUN (Cŭn) (KJV) See *Cun.*

CHURCH In the NT, the Greek word *ekklesia* refers to any assembly, local bodies of believers, or the universal body of all believers.

The Church as People of God Redemptive history demonstrates that God's purposes are not limited to redemption of individuals. Instead, God's intent was to form a people (Gen. 12:1-3).

The OT relates God's establishment of the Jewish nation, ruled by a king of His choosing, governed by divine revelation, and settled in the land of promise. The OT foresaw, however, a day when God would call Gentiles to Himself. After Pentecost, the apostles believed this prophecy was fulfilled as God created a new multinational, multiethnic church (Acts 2:14-42; 15:6-29). Jesus was the Son of David ushering in the eschatological ingathering of the nations (Acts 15:15-17).

The church's identity as the people of God is seen in terms of both Jewish and Gentile believers. Paul noted that the Gentiles have been "grafted on" to the people of God along with believing Israel (Rom. 11:11-25). Pagans once cut off from God and excluded from the commonwealth of Israel became "fellow citizens" with the Jews in God's planned redemption (Eph. 2:11-22 HCSB). Indeed, now there is "no Jew or Greek" in the church (Gal. 3:28 HCSB). Using language once reserved only for Israel, Peter wrote of the church as a "holy priesthood" and a house of "living stones" (1 Pet. 2:4-10 HCSB). Indeed, Peter, echoing Hosea (Hos. 1:9), reminds Gentile believers that "once you were not a people, but now you are God's people" (1 Pet. 2:10).

John's end-time vision is of a vast multitude from every "tribe, people, and language" redeemed before God's throne (Rev. 7:9-10). Jesus commissioned His disciples to carry the gospel even "to the ends of the earth" (Acts 1:8). The multinational, multiethnic character of the NT church testifies not only to the universality of the gospel message (Rom. 10:11-12) and to the personal reconciliation accomplished at the cross (Eph. 2:14-16), but also to the global extent of the coming reign of Christ (Ps. 2:8). Thus, obedience to the Great Commission (Matt. 28:16-20) is not simply a function of the church but is essential to her identity as the people of God.

Similarly, worship is not incidental. Because God has assembled a people "to the praise of His glorious grace" (Eph. 1:6), worship is necessary to the corporate life of the church. This is seen not only in Israelite practice but also in the practice of the earliest church (John 4:20-24; Eph. 5:18-20).

The Church as Body of Christ The church is not merely a sectarian religious society. Jesus speaks of personally building this new community on the confession of His lordship (Matt. 16:18-19). The apostles recognized the birth of the church at Pentecost as the work of Jesus Himself. At Pentecost (Acts 2:14-39), Peter tied the events there to the promises of a Davidic Messiah (2 Sam. 7; Pss. 16; 110).

Various terms are used in the NT to describe the church: body of Christ (Eph. 5:22-23,30), "new man" (Eph. 2:14-15), "His (God's) household" (Heb. 3:6; 1 Pet. 4:17), and others. Paul repeatedly calls the church the "body of Christ;" believers united to Christ in His death and resurrection. The persecution of the church, therefore, is the persecution of Christ Himself. The body metaphor shows the unity of believers in Christ and emphasizes differing roles and gifts of believers in the larger community (1 Cor. 12:12-31).

The description of the church as the body of Christ designates Jesus' rule over the community. As the exalted Son of David, He exercises sovereignty by His Spirit and by His Word. Through His resurrection He is named "head" of the church (Col. 1:18). Jesus' headship shows

that believers are subject to the One who loved them and purchased them with His blood (Eph. 5:23-27). Individual gifts are to be exercised according to the sovereign distribution of the Holy Spirit (Eph. 4:4-16).

The body of Christ does not only refer to the universal church but also applies to each local congregation of believers. In writing to the Corinthians, Paul teaches that God has gifted members of the congregation to edify one another for the glory of Christ (1 Cor. 12:1-31). As such, each local congregation is autonomous, governed by the risen Christ, through submission to the authority of biblical revelation (Eph. 5:24).

The fact that the church is the body of Christ necessarily entails that individual members belong to Christ. As such, each church must be composed of a regenerate membership, those giving evidence of faith in Jesus Christ. The NT inextricably ties personal regeneration to local church membership (Heb. 10:19-25). Because baptism is both an initiatory rite into the church and a testimony of conversion, it is to be administered only to those who confess Jesus as Savior and Lord (Acts 10:47-48). Baptism is reserved for those united to Christ in His death and resurrection (Rom. 6:3-4). Likewise, the Lord's Supper testifies to a regenerate church membership. Those who partake of the Lord's Supper remember the death of Christ on their behalf and testify to their union with Him (1 Cor. 11:23-34).

The Church as Covenant Community The NT refers to the church as "the pillar and foundation of the truth" (1 Tim. 3:15 HCSB). From the beginning, the church was to serve as a confessional body, holding to the truth of Christ as revealed by the prophets and apostles He had chosen (Eph. 2:20).

A local congregation is organized around a confession of faith. The church's leaders are to guard the doctrinal fidelity of the congregation by faithfully preaching the Scriptures (Acts 20:25-30; 1 Tim. 4:1-11; 2 Tim. 3:13-17). When doctrinal error comes, the church is to confront and uproot it, even if it means expulsion of unrepentant false teachers (1 Tim. 1:19-20; 6:3-5; 2 Tim. 3:1-9; James 5:19-20).

The covenant nature of the local congregation is also seen in the accountability of believers to one another. The members of a church are responsible to edify one another (Eph. 5:19) and are charged with restoring those who falter in the faith (Gal. 6:1-2). When personal attempts fail to restore, the church is to exercise discipline (Matt. 18:15-20). If a church member will not repent, the ultimate step is removal from membership (1 Cor. 5:1-13).

The Church and the World The Bible presents the church as sharply distinct from the world. The church is to be composed of regenerate believers called out of a world hostile to the gospel of Christ. As such, the church is called to confront the world with the reality of coming judgment and the gospel of redemption through Christ.

The Bible presents the church as an alternative society, called to countercultural life in the Spirit. The church is to be a colony of the kingdom, holding ultimate loyalty to Christ. As opposed to a world that slavishly worships raw political power, like Caesar's, the church proclaims, "Jesus is Lord." As opposed to a world of deadly power struggles, the church is self-sacrificial and serves others. This does not mean, however, that the church is to disengage from the world. The church is in the world but is not to conform to it (Rom. 12:2). The NT speaks repeatedly of the early church confronting synagogues, cultic paganism, and Greek philosophy. The church is not to abandon earthly relationships and responsibilities but to transform these by their regenerated lives.

The church, however, cannot coerce the world (John 18:11). The church's message is that God regenerates sinners and adds them to the body of Christ. If genuine conversion is prerequisite to membership in the church, then such transformation cannot be forced. The church testifies to the sovereignty of God through the persuasive power of the preached word. Sinners thus are cut to the heart, regenerated, and rescued "from the domain of darkness" (Col. 1:13).

Thus the church and the state are to be kept separate. The church has prerogatives over which the state has no jurisdiction (1 Cor. 5:1-13). The state has responsibilities that are not part of the church's mission (Rom. 13:1-4).

The Mission of the Church The church is nowhere equated in the NT with the kingdom of God. The body of Christ is related to the kingdom, but the use of kingdom language for the church (Matt. 16:18-19; Col. 1:11-18) suggests that the church is an initial manifestation of the coming kingdom.

Confessing Jesus as Lord, every local congregation is a visible reminder to worldly powers that judgment will come. The just and righteous King will one day crush the kingdoms of this world and the entire cosmos will tremble before the church's sovereign risen Head (Dan. 2:44; Phil. 2:5-11). As such, although believers submit to governing authorities, their ultimate loyalty is not to transient political entities but to the coming messianic kingdom.

The Government of the Church The fact that God has gifted each member of the church does not mean that the church is to be without leadership. To the contrary, the NT speaks of God's calling out leaders for His church for the building up of the body (Eph. 4:11-16). The officers of a NT church are pastors (called "overseers" or "bishops" or "elders") and deacons (1 Tim. 3:1-13). These men are gifted by God and called out from the congregation to serve the church.

The pastor is called to lead the congregation by teaching the truth of Scripture, by setting a godly example, and by shepherding the flock (Heb. 13:7). The ultimate decision-making of the church, however, is given to the congregation under the lordship of Christ. The NT writers confronted various issues of conflict within church life. They often addressed these issues of polity not to a supra-congregational "board," but to the congregations themselves (1 Cor. 5). As such, each member of the congregation is responsible before God for decisions of the local body. The called leadership of the church, however, bears an even greater responsibility before God (James 3:1) as those who will give account for the soul of each member of the congregation (Heb. 13:17).

Because each congregation is so gifted and responsible for internal polity, the local congregation does not submit to external control. Churches may cooperate together for the work of the kingdom of God. The early church, for example, called a council of church leaders to address pressing doctrinal questions vexing congregations (Acts 15:1-35). Similarly, Paul called on and organized local churches for the relief of impoverished fellow believers in other churches (2 Cor. 8–9; Phil. 1:15-18). See *Apostle; Bishop; Deacon; Elders; Missions.*   *Russell D. Moore*

CHURCH AND STATE SEPARATION There was very little separation between governmental and religious institutions in ancient Israel during

OT times. Before the Israelite monarchy, Israel operated under a theocracy; during the monarchy Israel's religious institutions fell under the direct influence of the king (e.g., 1 Kings 5–8; 2 Kings 16:10-18; 22:1–23:25). Some prophets, however, acted outside of royal control (e.g., 1 Kings 17:1; Amos 7:12-15).

In the NT period individual Christians were subject to the authority of Caesar and his officials, yet local churches, if they remained quiet, were able to function relatively independent of governmental control. As the Christian movement grew in power and influence, the Roman Empire's interests invariably came into contact—and conflict—with those of the church.

God bestows all power, civil (Jer. 27:5-6; Dan. 2:21; John 19:11; Rom. 13:1) and religious. Religious freedom is grounded in the reality of God and the freedom of human conscience to worship Him as is seen fitting. Ultimately, all governmental authorities—and individuals—are subject to God (Rom. 13:4,6), whether a particular state removes religion from civil control or not. It is the responsibility of Christian citizens to obey their governmental authorities (Rom. 13:1-5; 1 Tim. 2:1-2; 1 Pet. 2:13-17) yet promote biblical values in society through all possible spheres of influence.

CHURCH YEAR Although the dates of observance and specific practices of the Christian festivals developed over the centuries, the major festivals all center on the life of Christ. As the church grew and the need for ordered worship increased, the need for focusing on the central affirmations at the heart of the Christian message also increased. By the fifth century, the basic elements of the church calendar were firmly established, although modifications continued to be made throughout the Middle Ages and the Reformation. Even today, the symbols and rituals of the festivals vary according to denomination, culture, and personal preference.

The original Christian festival and the basic building block for all the church year is the Lord's day, Sunday. The earliest Christians set aside Sunday, the day of the resurrection, as a time of special remembrance of Christ. By the second century, most Christians were observing a special celebration of the resurrection at Easter. In most areas, the season before Easter, later called Lent, was a time of penitence and the training of new Christians. Similarly, the 50-day period after Easter was one of triumph during which fasting and kneeling to pray were forbidden. This period culminated in Pentecost, which means "50th day," the celebration of the descent of the Holy Spirit. By the next century, at least in the East, many churches held a special observance of Christ's birth and baptism at Epiphany. In the fourth century, most Christians began to celebrate Christ's birth at Christmas and to observe Advent as a period of preparation.

As the dates and practices for these celebrations became more standard throughout the Christian world, the dimensions of the church year were established. Advent came to be regarded as the beginning of the church year and the half-year between Advent and Pentecost, the period during which all the major festivals occurred, came to be regarded as a time for Christians to concentrate on the life and work of Christ. The rest of the year, from Pentecost to Advent, became a time for concentrating on the teachings of Jesus and the application of those teachings in the lives of Christians. The development of the church calendar helped to assure that Christian worship would deal with the entire breadth and depth of the Christian gospel. See *Advent; Christmas; Easter; Epiphany; Holy Week; Lent; Lord's Day.*   *Fred A. Grissom*

CHUSHAN-RISHATHAIM (Cū´ shăn-rĭsh-á-thä-ĭm) KJV spelling of Cushan-rishathaim, Mesopotamian king who oppressed Israel until he was defeated by Othniel the son of Kenaz (Judg. 3:8). The name of this Mesopotamian ruler means Chushan of double iniquity. It probably was a derogatory epithet rather than his actual name. See *Judges.*

CHUZA (Chū´ zà) Personal name meaning "seer." The steward of Herod Antipas (Luke 8:3). He was the husband of Joanna, one of the women who provided material support for Jesus. See *Joanna.*

CILICIA (Çĭ-lĭ´ shà) Geographical area and/or Roman province in southeastern Asia Minor. The region was home to some of the people who opposed Stephen (Acts 6:9). It was located on the coast of the Mediterranean Sea in the southeast part of Asia Minor. One of its important cities was Tarsus, the birthplace of Paul the apostle (Acts 21:39; 22:3). By the time of the Council of Jerusalem (Acts 15), Christianity had already

The famous Cilician Gates, a mountain pass through the Taurus Mountains, 30 miles north of Tarsus.

penetrated Cilicia. Paul passed through the region during the course of his missionary travels (Acts 15:41; 27:5; Gal. 1:21).

The western portion of the geographical area, about 130 miles long east to west and 50 to 60 miles wide, consisted almost entirely of the westernmost extension of the Taurus Mountains. It was called "mountainous" Cilicia and was sparsely populated, important primarily for timber. The eastern portion, about 100 miles long east to west and 30 to 50 miles wide, consisted of a fertile coastal plain and was called "level" Cilicia. Through the Cilician Gates (pass) in the Taurus Mountains to the north, through "level" Cilicia itself, and through the Syrian Gates in the Ammanus Mountains to the east, ran the great international highway between central Asia Minor and Syria, Mesopotamia, and Egypt.

The area was conquered by the Romans between 102 and 67 B.C. Until A.D. 72 the western portion had the status of a client kingdom or was part of another such kingdom. In 38 B.C. the eastern portion was joined to the Province of Syria, which then became Syria and Cilicia. In A.D. 72 the parts were united in a separate province.

In the OT the same region is called Kue (1 Kings 10:28; 2 Chron. 1:16 RSV, NASB, NIV). See *Helech; Kue; Paul; Tarsus.*

James A. Brooks

CINNAMON Spice used in making fragrant oils. Such oil was used to anoint the wilderness tent of meeting (Exod. 30:23). It was part of the lucrative international spice trade (Rev. 18:13; cp. Prov. 7:17; Song 4:14). Cinnamon comes from the bark of a large tree belonging to the laurel family. Both the English and Greek words are derived from the Hebrew *qinnamon.* See *Plants; Spices.*

CINNEROTH (Cĭn´ nē rōth) (KJV, 1 Kings 15:20) See *Chinnereth; Chinneroth.*

CIRCUIT Circular route that a person, a geographical feature, or a natural object follows. Underlying the English word are at least four Hebrew words indicating round, surround, around, or turning. Samuel went around a circuit of cities to judge Israel (1 Sam. 7:16). The human eye views heaven as a circular vault or dome, where God takes His daily walk (Job 22:14). Similarly, the sun passes along the circuit of the heavens (Ps. 19:6). The wind appears to run a meaningless circular course going nowhere (Eccles. 1:6). Jerusalem within its walls represented a circle or circuit, which David repaired (1 Chron. 11:8 NRSV). The villages around Jerusalem formed a circuit (Neh. 12:28 NRSV; cp. 2 Kings 3:9 NASB).

CIRCUMCISION Act of removing the foreskin of the male genital. In ancient Israel this act was ritually performed on the eighth day after birth upon children of natives, servants, and aliens (Gen. 17:12-14; Lev. 12:3). Circumcision was carried out by the father initially, utilizing a flint knife (cp. Josh. 5:3). Later specialists were employed among the Jewish people.

Origin Several theories seek to explain and describe the nature and origin of circumcision: (1) initiatory rite—before marriage (as the Shechemites in Gen. 34:14-24) or at puberty; (2) physical hygiene—to prevent the attraction or transmission of diseases; (3) tribal mark of distinction; (4) rite of entry into the community of faith. In the OT the origin of Israelite practice was founded upon the circumcision of Abraham as a sign of the covenant between God and the patriarch (Gen. 17:10).

Ancient Near Eastern Background Several Semitic and non-Semitic peoples practiced circumcision according to biblical and other sources. Jeremiah depicts Egyptians, Edomites, Ammonites, Moabites, and the desert-dwelling Arabians as circumcised peoples (Jer. 9:25-26; cp. Ezek. 32:17-32). On the other hand Philistines, Assyrians, and Babylonians are counted among the uncircumcised. That the Canaanites are not mentioned in either regard is noteworthy. Evidence of their perspective of circumcision is lacking.

Ethical implications of circumcision can be observed in the metaphorical usage of the term. The uncircumcised are those who are insensitive to God's leadership. Circumcision of the heart implies total devotion to God (Deut. 10:16; Jer. 4:4); however, the uncircumcised ear cannot hear so as to respond to the Lord (Jer. 6:10); and the uncircumcised of lips cannot speak (Exod. 6:12). Circumcision was therefore an external sign of an internal singularity of devotion of Yahweh.

Circumcision and Christianity Controversy arose in the early church (Acts 15:1-12) as to whether Gentile converts needed to be circumcised. First-century A.D. Jews disdained the uncircumcised. The leadership of the Apostle Paul in the Jerusalem Council was crucial in the settlement of the dispute: circumcision was not essential to Christian faith and fellowship. Circumcision of the heart via repentance and faith were the only requirements (Rom. 4:9-12; Gal. 2:15-21). *R. Dennis Cole*

CIS (Cĭs) (KJV, Acts 13:21) See *Kish*.

CISTERN Translation of a Hebrew term that means "hole," "pit," or more often "well." The difference between "cistern" and "well" often is not apparent. The innumerable cisterns, wells, and pools that exist in Palestine are evidence of the efforts of ancient people to supplement the natural water supply. The cistern of Palestine was usually a bottle or pear-shaped reservoir into which water could drain from a roof, tunnel, or courtyard. The porous limestone out of which the cisterns were dug allowed much of the water put into the cistern to escape. After 1300 B.C.

A cistern with a stone mortar in the foreground probably used for grinding grain at Beersheba.

Large, extensive water cistern at Masada, Herod's mountain fortress.

The circular opening to a cistern at the site of Lachish in Israel.

A water system at Gibeon was based on this large rock-cut pool connected by tunnel to another cistern.

cisterns began to be plastered, which resulted in a more efficient system of water storage. The mouth of a cistern was sometimes finished and covered with a stone. Some cisterns have been found with a crude filter to trap debris.

The biblical writers revealed that cisterns were used for purposes other than holding water. Joseph was placed in a "broken" cistern by his brothers (Gen. 37:20-29). The prophet Jeremiah was imprisoned in the cistern of Malchijah, King Zedekiah's son (Jer. 38:6 NASB). In Jer. 14 the pagan gods were symbolized as broken cisterns that could not hold water. Cisterns also served as convenient dumping places for corpses (Jer. 41:7,9). See *Waterworks; Wells.*

James Newell

CITADEL NRSV, NASB, NIV translation of Hebrew *'armon.* See *Castle.*

CITIES AND URBAN LIFE Cities form a major indicator of civilization. Indeed, the emergence of cities often marks the move to civilization. The oldest city excavated to date is found in Palestine; it is Tell es-Sultan, OT Jericho. This site was already a bustling city between 8000 and 7000 B.C. Even before its citizens used pottery, the city had a massive defense wall and a high circular watchtower inside the wall.

The terms "city" and "urban life" had quite a different meaning in the biblical period, especially in the earlier times. Modern usage has given us at least five terms to describe a range of population. In increasing size of population we speak of open country, village, town, city, metropolis. The OT uses two words for "city" (*'eer* and *qir*) and one for "village" (*chatser*). The OT differentiation seems to be based not on

size primarily, but on the presence or absence of a defense wall. Cities had walls, while villages were without walls.

Size of Cities Ancient cities tended to be much smaller in both size and population than our typical understanding of a city. The oldest walled city at Jericho mentioned above covered less than 10 acres. Even during the OT period, Jericho was no more than 10 acres in area. Some of the great cities of Mesopotamia were much more like the size we consider for a city. At the height of the Assyrian empire in the eighth century B.C., Nineveh covered approximately 1,720 acres or over two and a half square miles. The mound of Calah (ancient Nimrud) covered over 875 acres or one and a quarter square miles. None of the cities in Palestine from the OT period come close to the size of the great cities of Mesopotamia. Jerusalem at the time of Solomon covered only 33 acres; even at the time of Jesus it covered less than 200 acres. This is not to say that Palestine had no larger cities. Hazor, in northern Israel, was over 175 acres in area. However, most of the well-known biblical sites were smaller rather than larger.

Closely related to the area of a town is its population. Recent population projections based on the density of cities from cultures similar to those of biblical times along with a count of the number of house units found in excavations suggest that most cities could support 160–200 persons per acre. Thus Shechem might have had a population of 2,000 to 2,500 during the OT period; Jerusalem in Solomon's time could have supported 5,000 to 6,500. Even when Jerusalem expanded in Josiah's time, it would have had no more than 25,000 inhabitants. An inscription found at Ebla in northern Syria and dated to about 2400–2250 B.C. states that Ebla had a population of 250,000. However, it is unclear whether this figure referred to the city, or the entire kingdom controlled by Ebla, or was an exaggeration to impress others of the size of Ebla. By A.D. 300, the city of Rome may have had nearly a million inhabitants.

Cities and the Surrounding Region At least two types of phrases are used to describe the region surrounding a city. One phrase described the chief city of a region in relation to the smaller villages around it. Thus in a literal Hebrew translation the OT speaks of a city "with its villages" (Josh. 19:16; Neh. 11:30) or "with its daughters" (Num. 21:25; 2 Chron. 13:19). These two phrases indicate that the city was the most important center of activity for the region. Outlying villages were closely related to the central city for their existence. Most of the commercial activity for the region was carried out in the city. Usually, the city was located on the main highway or intersection of highways and trade route through the area. The major sanctuary or worship place would be most frequently located in the city, making it a center of religious pilgrimages and celebrations. Whenever war or invasion threatened, the people of the surrounding villages would flee to the walled city for protection.

Among the chief concerns a city would be built at a particular location was the presence of food and water nearby, along with the raw materials for shelter, tools, and industry. Furthermore, a site that was easy to defend would be most likely to be chosen. A number of common features may be found in a typical city of the ancient Near East. Each of these features will be discussed briefly.

Walls City walls in the ancient Near East were formed of courses of stone or mudbrick, at times quite thick. The rampart at Hazor in northern Israel about 1700 B.C. is almost 50 feet high at places and up to 290 feet thick. Furthermore, the perimeter of this enclosed area was over two miles.

Gate The most important and most vulnerable part of the wall structure was the gate. Massive guard towers usually flanked the gate. The entrance itself was narrow, usually 12 to 15 feet wide. Two heavy wooden doors could be shut and braced with metal bars at night or in case of attack. The gate complex itself had two or three separate sets of doors through which one had to pass to gain entry to the city.

Water supply Adequate water supply was another necessity for a city. During peaceful times, the water supply could be outside the wall and within a reasonable distance from the city. A protected water supply accessible from within the city was necessary to endure a siege during wartime. Most cities were located near springs, streams, or wells. Many homes had cisterns, especially in the more arid regions. The springs were usually at the foot of the tell outside the city wall. Hazor, Megiddo, and Gibeon provide examples of water systems the Israelites constructed during the monarchy. Extensive water

tunnel and pool systems were built by cutting through the bedrock of the tell to reach the level of the springs. At Hazor, the tunnel system had to cut through 70 feet of soil and rock to reach the water level. Hezekiah's tunnel in Jerusalem is another example of the water tunnel system. Second Kings 20:20 mentions the construction of this system about 700 B.C. The Romans often constructed great aqueducts to bring water from long distances to a city. Portions of two such aqueducts still remain at Caesarea-by-the-Sea, which brought the water from over five miles away. One of the Hellenistic-Roman aqueducts at Jerusalem covers nearly 25 miles.

Agricultural land Earliest towns were surely self-sufficient and must have had fertile farming land nearby. The OT speaks of the fields of a city or village (Lev. 25:34; Josh. 21:12; Neh. 11:25,30) and indicates that some of the land was held in common and some was owned by a family or clan. Large cities would not have had enough land surrounding to meet its food needs, so they would depend on the trade of the surplus produce from the smaller villages. The villages in turn would depend on the cities for the manufactured goods and items of trade from distant areas. Agricultural land was not supposed to be sold out of the family or clan (Lev. 25:25-28). Isaiah strongly denounced those wealthy who would add "field to field, until there is no more room" (Isa. 5:8 NASB).

Acropolis The highest elevation of many cities often formed an acropolis or inner citadel. In addition to serving as a stronghold, the acropolis also served as residence for the aristocracy or royalty. As one might expect, the houses located here would be the largest and best constructed of the city. Not only would the security be strongest in the acropolis, but the higher elevation would catch any breeze and cool the house in the summer. In addition, the major shrines or temples were often located on the acropolis.

Street plan Ancient Near Eastern cities usually had a regular street plan. In Babylon, major streets led from the gates into the city center. In the period of the monarchy, Israelite cities regularly had an open court just inside the gate. A circular street led from the court around the perimeter of the city. This circular street gave easy access to all sections of the city, and provided the military with quick access to any part of the city wall. Other streets branched off this circular street and led into the center of the city.

In the Roman cities, the major road was usually the *cardo*, a wide, flagstone paved highway which ran north-south. The major east-west road was the *decumanus*. A section of the *cardo* of Jerusalem has been excavated recently in the Jewish Quarter. Although the portion excavated belongs to the Byzantine period, it may well reflect what the Roman *cardo* there was like. The street was colonnaded and was 39 feet wide. It had covered sidewalks, each an additional 17 feet wide. The street even had a covered drainage system.

House plans Along with the street plan, one can note something of a development in house plans in Israel. The earliest houses had one main room and courtyard. By the period of the monarchy, the typical Israelite house was a four-room house.

Dramatic changes took place in the Hellenistic and Roman periods. The successors to Alexander the Great built many Greek cities in Palestine. Greek culture was the pattern in the Decapolis and other Hellenistic cities. See *Architecture.*   *Joel F. Drinkard, Jr.*

CITIES OF REFUGE Safe place to flee for a person who had accidentally killed another. The city provided asylum to the fugitive by sheltering and protecting him until a trial could be held to determine his guilt or innocence. If, in the judgment of the city elders, the death had occurred accidentally and without intent, the man was allowed to stay there without fear of harm or revenge by the dead man's relatives (Josh. 20:2-6).

Four major passages in the OT describe the right of asylum and the sanctuary provided by a city of refuge (Exod. 21:12-14; Num. 35:6-34; Deut. 19:1-13; Josh. 20:1-9). A literal translation of the Hebrew phrase means "a city of intaking." This right of asylum was offered before the settlement of the promised land but was available only to one charged with accidental manslaughter. Exodus 21:12 records that "He who strikes a man so that he dies shall surely be put to death" (NASB). The passage continues, however, to promise that "if he did not lie in wait for him," a place would be designated to which he could flee (v. 13). Prior to the establishment of these cities, temporary safety could be gained by fleeing to a sanctuary and grasping the horns of the altar there. First Kings 1:50 and 2:28 record two examples of men seeking safety by clinging to

the altar in Jerusalem. Neither Adonijah nor Joab were innocent, though, and later were executed.

Moses was commanded to establish six cities of refuge from the total of 48 given to the Levites (Num. 35:6-7). Three were located on each side of the Jordan. In the east were Bezer in the territory of the Reubenites, Ramoth in Gilead, and Golan in the area of Bashan (Deut. 4:43). On the west side of the Jordan were Kedesh in Galilee, Shechem in Ephraim, and Kirjath-arba or Hebron in the hill country of Judah (Josh. 20:7-8). Sanctuary was not limited to the people of Israel but was extended to the stranger and sojourner among them (Num. 35:15).

The OT reveals the importance and sacredness of human life by its laws regarding the taking of life. The reason for distributing the cities of refuge throughout Israel on both sides of the Jordan was so that a city was easily accessible to a person responsible for an accidental homicide. He needed to find asylum immediately because a member of the dead man's family would pursue him. The avenger of blood sought to kill the slayer of his kin for the harm done to the family or clan. In the early period of Israel's history before the development of the cities of refuge, this action could result in a blood feud that terminated only with the extinction of one family. The establishment of the cities of refuge served a humanitarian purpose by transforming a case of homicide from a private feud between two families to a judicial matter settled by a group of elders.

Numbers 35 lists several requirements to be met prior to seeking sanctuary in a city of refuge. The primary requisite was that the death must have occurred by accident without premeditation or intent. Case studies are presented in Num. 35:16-18,20-23 to provide examples of those incidents that prevented or allowed a slayer to seek refuge in such a place.

A second major requirement for asylum in a city of refuge was that the slayer, once being admitted to the city, could not leave until the death of the high priest (Num. 35:25; Josh. 20:6). If he chose to leave the city before that time, he could be killed by the avenger of blood (Num. 35:26-28). In contrast to the temporary sanctuary offered by grasping the horns of an altar, the city of refuge provided a permanent place of asylum for the manslayer. In a punitive way, the city also served as a place of detention. The manslayer was not guiltless. He could not leave under penalty of death by the avenger of blood nor could he buy his way out by offering a ransom to the relatives of the deceased. A similar example of this punishment may be found in Solomon's confinement of Shimei to Jerusalem under a death threat if he left the city (1 Kings 2:36-46).

The taking of a life imposed a guilt that could not be paid for by any means short of death. The death of the high priest, even as a result of natu-

ral causes, served to pay the price of the required penalty. One man died in place of another. During his life, one of the functions of a high priest was to bear the sins of the people (Exod. 28:38). In accordance with this regulation, all the cities of refuge were Levitical cities, given to that tribe during the division of the promised land among the Israelites. These locations probably contained local sanctuaries in which a priest served. After the death of the high priest, the one guilty of

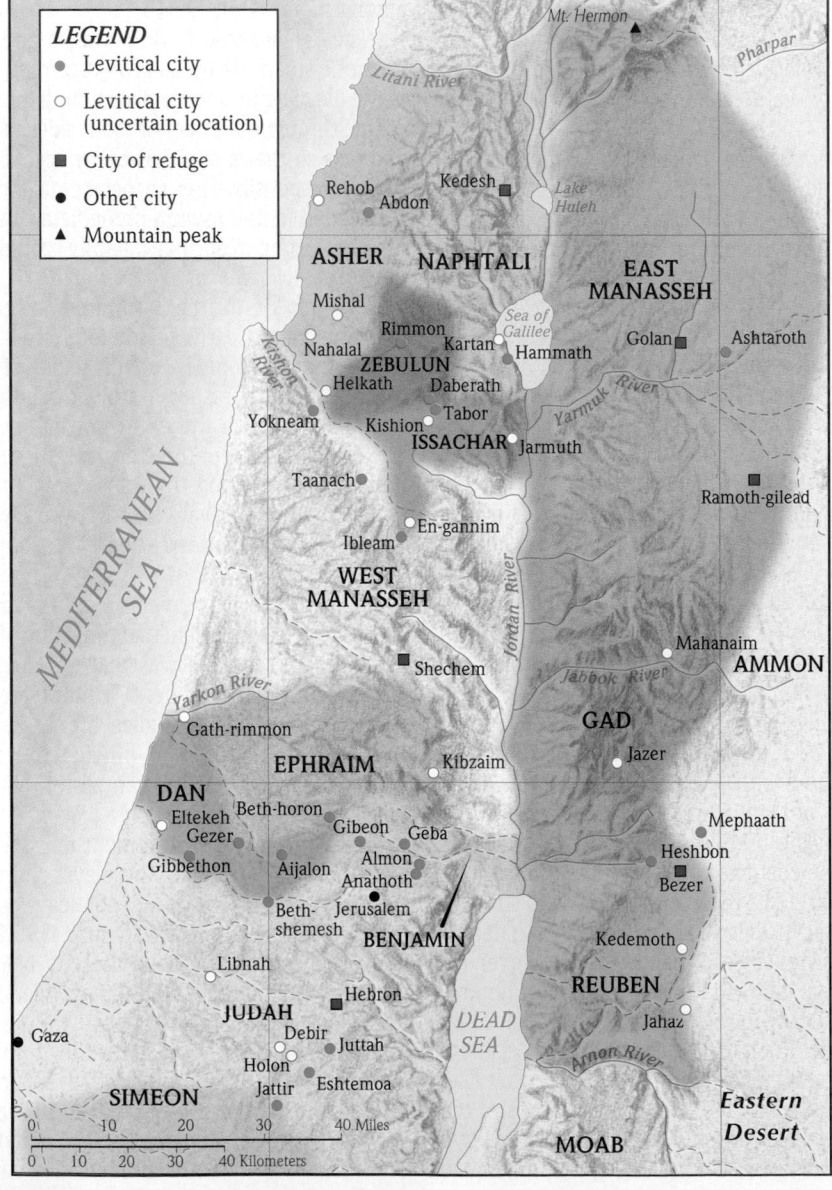

LEGEND

- ● Levitical city
- ○ Levitical city (uncertain location)
- ■ City of refuge
- ● Other city
- ▲ Mountain peak

manslaughter was free to leave the city and return to his home without fear of the avenger of blood. See *Avenger; Bloodguilt.*

Brenda R. Hockenhull

CITIES OF THE PLAIN Cities of the Plain (RSV, "cities of the valley") are the five cities—Sodom, Gomorrah, Admah, Zeboiim, and Zoar—thought to be located near the southern end of the Dead Sea. The narrative of Gen. 14 associates these five cities and locates them in the Valley of Siddim, the Dead Sea. All these cities except Zoar were destroyed for the wickedness of Sodom and Gomorrah (Gen. 19:24-29).

Most recent scholarship has located the five cities in the shallow water of the southern end of the Dead Sea, south of the Lisan, the tongue of land along the southeastern shore that protrudes into the sea. However, no conclusive evidence has been found to support this proposal. Excavations along the eastern shore of the Dead Sea in recent years have convinced some scholars that the cities of the Plain might be located in that region, especially at Bab-ed-Dhra and Numeira near the Lisan.

The particular phrase, "cities of the Plain," occurs in Gen. 13:12 as the place Lot chose to dwell, and in Gen. 19:29 concerning the destruction. The Hebrew word translated "plain" more nearly means "round." Thus it seems better to think of these cities as being ones "around" the Dead Sea or "around" the Jordan Valley. This interpretation may indicate simply that these cities were allies that lay in the Jordan Valley near the Dead Sea. As such, these cities may have been on a trade route and themselves involved in the trade of bitumen, salt, and sulphur.

Joel F. Drinkard, Jr.

CITIZEN, CITIZENSHIP Officially recognized status in a political state bringing certain rights and responsibilities as defined by the state. Paul raised the issue of citizenship by appealing to his right as a Roman citizen (Acts 16:37; 22:26-28). Roman citizenship rights were first formulated in the Valerian Law at the founding of the Roman Republic in 509 B.C., but citizenship rights changed as Roman governments changed. In NT times the definition came in the Julian Law passed near 23 B.C.

Becoming a Citizen Roman citizenship could be gained in several ways: birth to Roman par-

ents, including birth to a Roman woman without regards to identity of the father; retirement from the army; being freed from slavery by a Roman master; buying freedom from slavery; being given citizenship by a Roman general or emperor as an individual or as part of a political unit; purchase of citizenship. Paul was born a citizen, but how his family gained citizenship we do not know.

Citizenship Rights and Responsibilities A citizen became liable for Roman property taxes and municipal taxes. A citizen had the right to vote in Rome, though different social classes had different rights at this point. A citizen became a member of a Roman tribe. A citizen was promised a fair trial without certain forms of harsh punishment. A citizen could not be executed without a trial and would not be crucified except by order of the emperor. A citizen could appeal to Caesar and had to be taken to Rome for trial. Paul made use of these rights as he faced opposition and persecution (Acts 16:37; 25:11).

CITRON NASB, NIV translation of Greek *thuinos,* a scented wood that formed part of the rich international trade (Rev. 18:12). KJV translates "thyine," while NRSV has "scented."

CITY GATE Gates in the biblical period bring to mind two images: the massive defensive structures that protect the entrance way, and a place of various activities "in the gate." Gates and walls together mark the boundary between outside and inside, but gates are more frequently mentioned simply because they give access in and out.

Gates have existed since defensive walls first appeared in towns and villages. If walls are necessary to protect a town, an entrance through the wall is also necessary, and a gate to protect the entrance would likewise be required. The two developments probably coincided. In the ancient Near East, archaelogoists have uncovered town gate foundations dating back at least to the early Bronze Age (3300–2200 B.C.) and have a fully preserved four chamber mud-brick gate complex from the middle Bronze Age (ca. 1800 B.C.) at Tel Dan [see below]. Earlier during the Chalcolithic period (4500–3300 B.C.) at Ein Gedi remains of a temple and sacred area which has an enclosure wall with two entrances have been found. One of the entrances has the clear foundations of a two-chamber gate. Much earlier, at prepottery neolithic Jericho (ca. 8300 B.C.) evidence of a wall around the town and a circular tower, probably to serve as a watchtower. Although no evidence of a gate for that time has yet been excavated, there must have been a gate to provide entry into the town.

The gate is usually the most vulnerable part of a town's defenses, simply because it stands at an opening into the town. In addition, the gate was often located at a low point in the town's topography for several reasons: the low point would provide the easiest access to the town by travelers or merchants—they wouldn't have to maneuver their animals and wares to higher points in the town; the marketplace was often located just inside the gate for the same reason; and the low point would offer a good drainage channel for rainfall throughout the town to run outside the city walls through the gate. Because of its vulnerability, strong towers often flanked the gateway to help protect it. In addition, heavy wooden or metal doors would be closed to shut the gate at night or in times of imminent attack.

During the Iron Age, the period of Israelite monarchy, two-, four-, and six-chamber gates are found. Rather than a developmental scheme, the choice of gate type seems most likely related to local topography and defensive needs. Undoubtedly, the development of new weapons, including more effective battering rams, required new defensive strategies. Among such innovations were the introduction of inner and outer gate structures. Such double-gate structures may well have been intended to strengthen defenses. Assaulting an outer-gate structure would not give access into the city proper; it would only lead through a narrow passage (where an invading army would be under continual assault by defenders on the walls above) to an inner-gate structure, likewise well defended. Sites with inner- and outer-gate structures include Tel Dan, Megiddo, and Lachish. Typical gate openings during the Iron Age were from 3.5 to 4 meters, from 11 to 13 feet. Such openings would allow easy passage for animals laden with goods, for chariots, as well as for pedestrian traffic.

Just outside the city gate one would often find a well or spring. Since access to the water supply is quite important, the city gate was often located near the water. Recent excavations at the Jebusite and Davidic city of Jerusalem have found a gate with massive towers protecting access to the spring Gihon. Beersheba had a well just outside the city gate. John 4 has the story of Jesus meeting a woman of Sychar at the well just outside the city.

In the typical town plan, the marketplace, often an open plaza, was just inside the gate complex. Close by might be either administrative buildings, military buildings, or a shrine or temple. The biblical description of various activities within the gates of the city/town indicates the business of that area. When Abraham was negotiating for the purchase of a burial plot for Sarah, he met with the landowner and the elders of the town at the city gate (Gen. 23: 10,18), as did Boaz when he negotiated the purchase of Elimelech's property (Ruth 4:1-11). Elders gathered at the city gate to administer justice or judgment (Deut. 21:19; 22:15,24) as well as transact sales. The prophets have a number of references to proper justice at the city gate (Amos 5:10-15; Zech. 8:16). King David had a seat at the gate (2 Sam 19:8). At Tel Dan a platform has been discovered just inside the gate complex that may have been for a royal throne or may have been a shrine. Shrines have been excavated at several sites around the gate complex. In particular Bethsaida, probably ancient Geshur, had a cultic platform adjacent to the gate and several steles in the gate complex. Also at Mudayna on the Wadi eth-Thamid in Jordan, a shrine has been discovered adjacent to the gate complex.

Many have suggested the various activities described above took place literally in the city gate. "Benches" have been found within the chambers of some city gates. However, the benches are often of such height and size that it is unlikely they were used for sitting. It is more likely such benches were for depositing and storing items or for other purposes. It is probable that the activities took place "at" the city gate or "inside" the city gate [i.e., within the open plaza] rather than necessarily "in" the gate itself. The presence of the marketplace and of administrative buildings just inside the gate complex provided the rationale for the elders to gather there. And where the elders gathered would be the ideal place for transacting business or dispensing justice that fell to them.   *Joel F. Drinkard, Jr.*

CITY OF CONFUSION (CHAOS) Name applied to Jerusalem in Isa. 24:10.

CITY OF DAVID In the OT the phrase "the city of David" refers to Jerusalem. The name was given to the fortified city of the Jebusites after David captured it (2 Sam. 5:6-10). Its original reference may have been only to the southeastern hill and the Jebusites' military fortress there. In Luke 2:4,11 the reference is to Bethlehem, the birthplace of David (John 7:42). See *Jerusalem; Zion.*

CITY OF DESTRUCTION See *Heliopolis.*

CITY OF MOAB City where Balak went to meet Balaam (Num. 22:36). Some identify the city as Ar. See *Ar.*

CITY OF PALM TREES Probably to be identified with a site near Jericho where the Kenites lived (Judg. 1:16; see Deut. 34:3; Judg. 3:13; 2 Chron. 28:15). Jericho itself lay in ruins from the time of the conquest until the time of Ahab. Some identify the region with Zoar on the south side of the Dead Sea or with Tamar about 20 miles south of the Dead Sea. See *Jericho.*

CITY OF SALT City allotted to the tribe of Judah "in the desert" (Josh. 15:62). Its precise location is not known. Archaeological finds do not support identification with Qumran that some have tried to make.

CITY OF THE SUN (NRSV) Usually taken as a reference to Heliopolis (Isa. 19:18). Also translated "city of destruction." See *Heliopolis.*

CITY OF WATERS City in Ammon, probably to be identified with part or all of Rabbah, the capital. Joab captured it for David (2 Sam. 12:27).

CIVIL LIBERTIES Civil liberty is grounded in the biblical teaching that all persons have integrity and worth before God (Gen. 1:26-28; Ps. 8:5-8; Rom. 5:6-8) and that governments are established to maintain order in society (Rom. 13:4). The same Spirit of God who provides liberty from sin and from enslavement to the Mosaic law (2 Cor. 3:17; Gal. 5:1) also provides the power and wisdom by which Christians may live under civil authority (Rom. 13:1-5; 1 Tim. 2:1-2; 1 Pet. 2:13-17).

Christians are enjoined to lead quiet lives (1 Thess. 4:11; 2 Thess. 3:12; 1 Tim. 2:2) and be good citizens (Rom. 13:6-7; 1 Pet. 2:17). Both Jesus and Paul called for the voluntary subordination of personal liberty for the sake of others (Luke 22:26; 1 Cor. 8:9-13; 9:12,15; Eph. 5:21;

Phil. 2:4). By so doing, Christians are able to live freely yet responsibly in a pluralistic society (Gal. 5:13-15; 1 Pet. 2:16).

CIVIL RIGHTS Basis for civil rights is grounded in the impartiality of God (Deut. 10:17-18; Acts 10:34; cp. Luke 20:21), in the created order by which all persons are made in the image of God (Gen. 1:27-28; 9:6), and in the redemptive work of Christ (Gal. 3:28).

Mosaic law distinguished between sojourners (non-Israelite residents of the land of Israel) and foreigners (persons who were not resident in Israel). Sojourners were subject to the same laws as were Israelites (Exod. 12:49; Num. 15:15-16; cp. Deut. 10:18-19), but the rights of foreigners were somewhat restricted (Exod. 12:43; Deut. 15:3; 17:15).

Both the OT and NT acknowledged the practice of slavery in the ancient world and held that the rights of slaves were to be protected to a degree greater than was typically found among neighboring cultures (Exod. 12:44; Lev. 25:39-55).

The NT recognizes the fundamental equality of all who are in Christ (Gal. 3:28) and advocates the voluntary subordination of individual rights for the benefit of others (Luke 22:26; 1 Cor. 8:9-13; Phil. 2:4-8).

CLAN Term used to distinguish a kin group more extensive than a family. The boundaries of such a group are not always clearly delineated. Each clan was governed by the heads of the families (elders). Several clans formed a tribe, and 12 tribes formed Israel. The clan is sometimes referred to as "division," "kindred," "family," "thousand," or even "tribe."

CLAUDA (Clou´ dĭ á) KJV, NASB spelling of Cauda in Acts 27:16 for an island where Paul landed on his way to Rome. See *Cauda.*

CLAUDIA (Clau´ dĭ á) Woman who sent greetings to Timothy (2 Tim. 4:21).

CLAUDIUS (Clau´ dĭ ŭs) **1.** Roman emperor from A.D. 41 to 54. He made Judea a Roman province in A.D. 44. He expelled Jews from Rome in about A.D. 49 (Acts 18:2), probably due to conflict between Jews and Christians in Rome. Apparently his fourth wife Agrippina poisoned him in A.D. 54 and took charge of the empire for

Marble bust of Claudius from the island of Malta, dating from the first century.

her son Nero. The prophet Agabus announced a coming famine during Claudius' reign (Acts 11:28). See *Caesar.* **2.** Roman army captain who protected Paul from Jews who wanted to assassinate him (Acts 23:26-27). Referred to as Claudias Lysias.

CLAY Basic building and artistic material consisting of various types of earth combined with water to form a material that could be molded into bricks for building, sculptures, pottery, toys, or writing tablets. A piece of clay marked by a signet ring gave proof of ownership or approval. The type of soil—sand, quartz, flint, limestone, along with coloring patterns, gives archaeologists a key for dating deposits uncovered from ancient sites. See *Archaeology and Biblical Study; Pottery.*

CLEAN, CLEANNESS The idea of cleanness includes a surprisingly wide range of human behavior. On the purely physical side a person is considered clean when obvious indications of dirt or similar defilement have been removed. A clean person is also one who habitually maintains a pattern of personal cleanliness and

hygiene, while at the same time taking care to ensure that his or her environment is in a clean condition so as to forestall possible accidents, infection, and disease.

Because the mind is an integral aspect of the human personality, cleanness must also be applied to attitudes and motives that govern particular forms of behavior. Impure thoughts as the expression of the mind can result in shameful activities (Mark 7:15), unless they are checked firmly, and bring disgrace to the individual concerned as well as harm to others. A "clean-living" person is generally understood to be one who does not give evidence of being a criminal, a victim of such vices as alcoholism and drug addiction, or an individual who habitually flaunts God's moral code.

Cleanness, however, is a relative term when the human condition is being considered. Mankind's fall from divine grace as a result of defying God's commands and yielding to temptation has made sin a genetic issue (Gen. 3:1-19). This means that the tendency to sin is inborn, with the inevitable result that, as the ancient psalmist said, there is none righteous (Ps. 14:3; Rom. 3:10). Paul stated the situation with equal emphasis by proclaiming that all have sinned and come short of God's glory (Rom. 3:23). Human sin places a barrier between sinners and a just, holy God. Sinners are unclean in God's eyes.

The religious rituals of Leviticus had much to say about the way in which the sinner could be cleansed from iniquity and be reconciled to God. This was a matter of great importance to the Israelites because God required them to be a kingdom of priests and a holy nation (Exod. 19:6). In the ancient Near Eastern religions the idea of holiness was applied to a person in a state of consecration to the service of a deity, whose cultic worship could, and frequently did, involve acts of a gross sexual nature. For the Hebrews holiness demanded that they should reflect in their living and thinking the exalted moral and spiritual qualities of God as revealed in His laws.

Cleanness was thus fundamental to the establishing and preservation of holiness in the Israelite community. As distinct from all other nations, the Hebrews were provided with specific instructions concerning cleanness and how to recover it when it had been lost through carelessness or disobedience. The principles of cleanness touched upon all aspects of individual and community life. They were ultimately capable of a moral interpretation since in the holy nation, secular and spiritual matters were closely connected.

God established for the Israelites a special group of laws dealing with clean and unclean animals (Lev. 11:1-47; Deut. 14:1-21) to provide guidance for dietary and other circumstances. While the nations of the ancient Near East maintained a general distinction between clean and unclean species, the principles of differentiation were in no sense as explicit as those provided for the Hebrews. Clean animals were allowed to be eaten, but unclean ones were prohibited strictly. The terms "clean" and "unclean" were defined by illustration, and clear principles were enunciated to enable anyone to make the distinction correctly.

Very simply, whatever animal had a cleft hoof and chewed the cud was clean and therefore suitable for food. Any animal that did not meet these specifications was unclean and consequently was not to be eaten. If an animal such as a camel possessed only one of the two stated requirements, it was still regarded as unclean. Because birds formed part of the Israelites' diet, a list of those species suitable for food excluded the ones that might carry communicable diseases.

There has been much discussion about the purpose of these regulations. Some writers claimed that they were designed so as to avoid pagan idolatrous practices. Others have focused upon preserving the separated nature of the Israelites in matters of food as well as in ethical and religious considerations. Yet another view emphasized the hygienic aspects of the laws as a means of preventing the spread of infectious ailments. Most probably, all three concerns underlay the legislation, and therefore each should be given due weight. Animals associated with pagan cults were prohibited as were unfamiliar or repulsive creatures and those species that fed upon carrion. If the rules for food were followed, the Hebrews could expect to enjoy good physical health. Clearly the overall objective of the dietary laws was the prevention of uncleanness and the promoting of holiness in the community (Lev. 11:43-44).

Uncleanness also applied to certain objects and situations in life that conveyed impurity to those involved. Thus contact with a dead person (Lev. 5:2; 21:1), a creeping insect or animal (Lev. 22:4-5), or the carcass of an animal (Lev. 11:28;

Deut. 14:8) required ritual purification to remove it. Following childbirth, women were ritually unclean and had to go through a rite of purification (Lev. 12:4-5; Luke 2;22). Leprosy was particularly dangerous as a source of uncleanness and required special cleansing rituals (Lev. 14) when the sufferer was pronounced cured. Unclean persons transmitted their condition to whatever they touched so that others who handled such things became unclean also. Even God's sanctuary needed to be cleansed periodically (Lev. 4:6; 16:15-20).

As noted previously, cleanness had a specific moral dimension. Because God's priests were to be clothed with righteousness (Ps. 132:9), the entire nation was involved in manifesting the priesthood of all who believed sincerely in the covenant relationship with God that had been forged on Mount Sinai. Thus to be clean meant not merely the negative aspects of being free from disease or defilement but the positive demonstration in daily life of God's high moral and ethical qualities of absolute purity, mercy, justice, and grace.

Cleanness was a part of the moral stipulations of the Law. Thus murder was both a pollution of the land and a violation of the Decalogue's express commands. The killing of the innocent called for a response in justice from the entire Israelite community, based upon a principle of blood retribution (Num. 35:33; Deut. 19:10). Grave moral offenses that violated God's law and polluted the nation included adultery (Lev. 18:20)—a capital offense (Lev. 20:10)—and perverted sexual activity which included bestiality, with death as the prescribed punishment (Lev. 20:13).

Ceremonial holiness thus involved distinguishing between clean and unclean. Moral holiness required the Israelites to behave as a nation separated from the pollutions of contemporary society and to live upright and righteous lives in obedience to God's laws (Lev. 21:25-26). For the penitent transgressor a complex system of purificatory rites cleansed from both physical and moral defilement. These involved various kinds of washing by water as a natural cleansing process (Lev 6:28; 8:6; 14:8-9; Num. 8:7; 19:9); the use of ashes (Num. 19:17) and hyssop (Num. 19:18) for ritual and accidental contamination; and sacrificial blood, which made atonement for sin and reconciled the worshiper to God. The Law established the principle that blood made atonement for human life (Lev. 17:11), and thus a blood sacrifice involved the highest form of purification (Lev. 14:6,19-20) or dedication to God (Lev. 8:23-24). Yet even this form of sacrifice was powerless against sins deliberately committed against the spirituality of the covenant (Num. 15:30).

In the NT, cleansing was associated only with the ritual customs of contemporary Judaism. Thus the infant Jesus was presented in the temple for the traditional purification ritual (Lev. 12:2-8; Luke 2:22). Cleansing (*katharismos*) was a matter of contention between the Pharisees and the disciples of John the Baptist (John 3:25), but Christ obeyed the Law in sending healed lepers to the priest for cleansing (Lev. 14:2-32; Matt. 8:4). On other occasions He asserted His superiority to the ordinances that He would subsequently enrich and fulfill (Matt. 12:8; Mark 2:28; Luke 6:5).

In His teaching Christ made the OT cultic regulations concerning cleanness even more rigorous by stressing a person's motivation rather than the external or mechanical observance of rules and regulations. He taught that adultery had been committed just as fully by a man's lusting after a woman (Matt. 5:27-28) as if the physical act had occurred. In John 15:3 the word that Christ had proclaimed made them clean by regenerating their characters and instilling holiness of life.

Jesus was not only a moral Teacher. He came to earth to give His life as a ransom for humanity's sin (Mark 10:45). In this way He became the Lamb of God, taking away the sin of the world (John 1:29). His atoning death as our great High Priest transcended all that the Law's cleansing rituals could ever be expected to do in the single offering of Himself for us on Calvary (Heb. 7:27). There He instituted a new covenant of divine grace in His blood (Heb. 8:6), achieving human redemption and making possible eternal life for the penitent individual who has faith in His atoning work.

One of the most gracious assurances of His new covenant is that the blood of Jesus cleanses us from all sin (1 John 1:7). Sacrifices and offerings are now unnecessary, for what Jesus demands is a penitent spirit that confesses the merits of His atonement. For the Christian the cultic provisions of the OT are nullified. All meats have been declared clean (Mark 7:19; Acts 10:9-16), and the only sacrifices that God requires are those that emerge from a humble and contrite heart (Ps. 51:17).   *R. K. Harrison*

CLEMENT (Clĕm´ ĕnt) Fellow worker in the gospel with Paul (Phil. 4:3). He was apparently a member of the church at Philippi. Otherwise, no more information about him is available.

CLEOPAS (Clē´ ō·pȧs) Follower of Jesus, who with a companion was traveling toward the village of Emmaus on the day of Christ's resurrection (Luke 24:13-25). A person whom they did not recognize joined them. Later, they discovered that the stranger was Jesus Himself.

CLEOPHAS (Clē´ ō·phȧs) (KJV, John 19:25) See *Clopas.*

CLOAK Outer garment. See *Cloth, Clothing.*

CLOPAS (Clō´ pȧs) Relative of one of the Marys who were near the cross during the crucifixion (John 19:25). "Mary, who [was] of Clopas" is the literal Greek text and has been interpreted to mean that Clopas was the husband of Mary. See *Mary.*

CLOSET Private room in a dwelling where Jesus encouraged people to pray (Matt. 6:6). He also noted that not even words said in the inner room privacy could be kept secret (Luke 12:3), indicating the Pharisees' hypocrisy could not be hidden. A biblical closet is an actual room, not a storage place. See *Architecture; Chamber.*

CLOTH, CLOTHING Biblical and archaeological sources concur that the earliest clothing resources were the hides of wild animals (Gen. 3:21). The Bible contains little information, however, about the process of manufacturing clothes from vegetable fibers. Technological developments predate biblical history.

Natural Resources Cloth production in the ancient Near East dates to the Neolithic period when natural flax fibers were spun and woven into linen fabric. Nomadic cultures continued to prefer the hides of animals, some of which were left with small amounts of fur. The growing sedentary urban cultures preferred fabrics made from vegetable fibers such as flax and cotton and from animal fibers such as wool, goats' hair, silk, and the limited use of other wild animals.

Wild flax originated in the regions of Palestine and the Caucasus. Domesticated plants were brought to Egypt early where they grew abundantly and were used to produce fine linen (Gen. 41:42) for soft garments and sails (Ezek. 27:7). Linen from Syrian flax was deemed finer than Egyptian. The importance of flax production in Palestine is reflected in the Gezer calendar. Quality fabrics were made from plants grown in Galilee and the Jordan Valley. Flax stalks were also used in making sturdy baskets.

Cotton, which seems to have originated in the Indus Valley region, was grown on small trees. In the Iron Age the cotton tree was introduced into Assyria, but the climate of southern Mesopotamia was more suitable to crop cultivation. Cotton needs a warm humid climate for quality growth and processing and thus was produced less widely in Palestine. Still, it was highly prized by leaders from Egypt to Babylon for its bright color and its soft, yet durable, qualities. During the Hellenistic period, production and usage increased dramatically.

Wool was the most commonly used raw material among the Semitic peoples for felt and other fabrics. By patriarchal times wool spinning was advanced sufficiently to warrant no description in the Bible. Natural wool tones ranged from white to yellow to gray. These gave rise to a multitude of color possibilities in conjunction with natural dyes. The development of metallic shears in the Iron Age greatly facilitated removal of wool and hair. Wool was at first plucked by hand and later by a toothed comb. Wool fabrics were quite fashionable among the Sumerians, who spoke extensively of all aspects of wool production.

Other resources included silk, hemp, camel hair, and goat hair. Silk was imported from China and spread to Mesopotamia and eventually to the Mediterranean islands, where the moths were cultivated. Silk was generally reserved for royalty and the wealthy. Hemp and hair produced coarse garments when used alone but, when used with wool, produced rugged quality garments.

The fuller would take the newly shorn wool or flax, and sometimes woven linen, and prepare the products for use in garments. Oil, dirt, or other residues were removed by first washing the material in an alkaline-based liquid made from ashes, lime, etc. and then repeatedly rinsing with clean water. Sometimes it would be tread upon and beaten against rocks in the rinse stage. Finally, the material would be left in the sun to

dry, bleach, and shrink before final usage (Isa. 7:3). God's justice is compared to the fuller's wash soap (Mal. 3:2). In Jesus' transfiguration (Mark 9:3), His garments are said to have been whiter that the best fuller's work.

Weaving Biblical sources indicate that the raw materials were spun and woven into fabric sections about six feet in width and as long as necessary (Exod. 26:1-2,7-8). Egyptian murals indicate that their looms were large and technologically advanced. Three kinds of looms were employed during Bible times: the Egyptian vertical, the Greek vertical, and the horizontal. Models of the horizontal loom have been found in Egyptian tombs. The Greek vertical primarily was used in wool production. Primitive warp-weighted vertical looms, using hand-molded clay weights, were prominent even in the Iron II period in Israel. Examples of the baseball-sized loom weights have been excavated in numerous OT sites. These looms consisted of two uprights, a horizontal beam, and a warp stretched between the beam and a series of loom weights. Greek vase-paintings also show many excellent examples of this type.

In the construction of the tabernacle, skilled women spun wool with their hands and even interwove gold threads into the fabric (Exod. 35:25; 39:3). Spinning wheels were better developed in Egypt and Mesopotamia. The book of Proverbs depicts a woman who spends much time spinning and weaving fabric (Prov. 31:13-24).

Dyes and Colors Predynastic Egyptians (about 3000 B.C.) had begun to master the art of dyeing fabrics. Reds, purples, and blues (indigo) were the known natural dyes of the Mediterranean and African regions, having been derived from

Modern Arab man wearing typical head cloth (called kaffiyeh) worn by Middle Easterners for millennia.

marine life, plants, and insects. Natural tones from different breeds of animals gave some variety to fabric colors (brown and black goat hair; white, gray, and yellow wool). Available natural dyes and variable natural tones offered a wide spectrum of color possibilities. Mixing of dyes and fabrics could result in colors such as green, orange, brown, yellow, black, and pink, each with varied shades. Natural Tyrian purple was considered the most beautiful color of all throughout ancient history, according to Strabo.

Those who could afford them preferred more colorful garments. Biblical descriptions indicate that dyed textiles were generally reserved for special garments and occasions. In Exod. 26:1, indigo, purple, and scarlet are listed as hues of tabernacle raiments. Jealousy over favoritism in the gift of a brightly colored coat is reflected in the Joseph conflict with his brothers (Gen. 37:3-4).

Clothing Styles The Bible gives only general descriptions of the types of garments worn in biblical times. Egyptian, Assyrian, Roman, and Hittite monuments provide extensive pictorial evidence of dress in the ancient world. The need for clothing derives its origin from the shame of nakedness experienced by Adam and Eve in the garden (Gen. 3:7-8). God's provision for His people is reflected in the animal skin garments given in response to human need.

Men and women wore tunics made of linen or wool hanging from the neck to the knees or ankles. The Beni Hasan Tableau from the tomb of Khnum-hotep in Egypt depicts tunics worn by Semitic peoples as having diverse patterns and colors.

Loincloths or waistcloths of linen (Jer. 13:1) or leather (2 Kings 1:8) were worn by men and used to gird up the tunic for travel. For comfort it could be loosened at night or when resting. Priests were to have their hips and thighs covered (Exod. 28:42) so as not to be exposed when in service to Yahweh.

The cloak was an outer garment used for a night covering, and thus was not to be loaned (Deut. 24:13). This article is often referred to as a mantle, which was worn by sojourners (Deut. 10:18; Ruth 3:3). In John 19:2 Jesus' outer cloak was draped over Him during the beatings inflicted by the Roman soldiers. Jesus' tunic was probably the garment for which the Roman soldiers cast lots at His death (John 19:23). Long sleeveless external robes of blue or purple fabric were worn by royalty, prophets, and the wealthy (1 Sam. 18:4; Ezra 9:3; Luke 15:22). Mantles of various types were worn by kings, prophets, and other distinctive persons. In times of sorrow or distress, this garment might be torn (Job 1:20). Another kind of outer garment was the ephod, usually a special white robe (1 Sam. 2:18).

Women likewise wore inner and outer garments, but the differences in appearance must have been noticeable since wearing of clothes of the opposite sex was strictly forbidden (Deut. 22:5). The undergarments were loose-fitting or baggy apparel (Prov. 31:24), and the outer robes were more flowing. The woman also wore a head cloth of brightly colored or patterned material which could be used as a wrapped support for carrying loads (Isa. 3:22), a veil (Gen. 24:65; Song 5:7) or a hanging protective garment against the hot sun. A long train or veil adorned women of high social stature (Isa. 47:2).

Festive clothing for both men and women was generally made of costly white material, adorned with colorful outer wrappings and head cloths. Gold, silver, or jewels further decorated one's festive attire (2 Sam. 1:24). Priestly dress (Exod. 39:1-31) likewise consisted of only the best of fine linen, which was dyed scarlet, indigo, and purple, and of gold ornamentation. See *Linen; Silk; Wool.*   *R. Dennis Cole*

CLOUD, PILLAR OF Means by which God led Israel through the wilderness with His presence and still hid Himself so they could not see His face. By day Israel saw a pillar of cloud, while by night they saw a pillar of fire (Exod. 13:21-22). The night before the exodus, the cloud gave light to Israel but darkness to the Egyptians so they could not come near one another (Exod. 14:19-20). God came down to speak to Israel in the cloud during crisis times (Num. 11:25; 12:5). Coming to the tabernacle in the cloud, God spoke to Moses face-to-face (Exod. 33:11; Num. 14:14). Paul used the protection of the cloud theme to warn Christians that living under God's presence calls for holy living (1 Cor. 10:1-14).

CLOUDS OT uses eight different Hebrew words in 167 passages to refer to clouds of rain, dust, smoke, storm, and fog. Both meteorological (1 Kings 18:44-45) and metaphorical meanings appear. The latter can be both positive (beneficial to life, Prov. 16:15; Isa. 25:5) and negative (hindrance to life, Eccles. 12:1-2). Clouds symbolize fluidity and transitoriness (Job 30:15; Isa. 44:22; Hos. 6:4), massive expansion and height (Ps. 36:5; Ezek. 38:9,16). More important are the statements in contexts speaking of God.

Old Testament Clouds demonstrate the power of God as Creator. Particularly Job 36–38 witnesses to the sovereignty of the Creator, who directs and controls the clouds. The clouds accompany God's revelation. God dwells in the dark clouds (1 Kings 8:12; Ps. 18:11). When He comes forth from His unapproachable holy being for judgment or for salvation, rain, lightning, and thunder break out from the clouds (Judg. 5:4; Pss. 68:33-35; 77:14-18; 97:2). When Yahweh appears as a Warrior, the clouds are His battle chariots in which He travels (Pss. 68:33; 104:3; Isa. 19:1) and from which He shoots down the lightning as arrows (Pss. 18:14; 77:17; Zech. 9:14). Dark clouds overshadow the judgment day of Yahweh, which the prophets announced (Ezek. 30:3,18; Joel 2:2; Zeph. 1:15).

Clouds conceal and reveal the secrets of God at the same time. In the tent of revelation during the wilderness period (Exod. 40:34-38), in the Jerusalem temple (1 Kings 8:10-11), on Mount Sinai (Exod. 34:5), and in His direction and protection by means of the clouds and the pillar of fire, Israel experienced that God came to them (Exod. 33:7-11) but still remained wholly other (Lev. 16:2,13) even when he came as the Son of Man (Dan. 7:13).

New Testament Strictly meteorological meaning appears only in Luke 12:54. Metaphorical meaning occurs in Jude 12; 2 Pet. 2:17; Heb. 12:1 (using a distinct Greek word). Clouds are not used in the NT to point to the power of God as Creator except for indirect references (Matt. 5:45; Acts 14:17). All other references to clouds in the NT have a relationship to God.

Clouds accompany the revelation of God in Jesus Christ. As God on Sinai was glorified and concealed in the clouds, so was Jesus on the mountain of transfiguration and in His ascension to heaven (Mark 9:7; Acts 1:9). The clouds, into which Jesus entered with Moses and Elijah as Moses had once entered on Mount Sinai (Exod. 24:18), are "light" but at the same time concealing. The voice out of the clouds no longer referred to the Torah of Moses but to the teaching of the Son. No longer must a tent be set up to experience the presence of God, for the clouds have set God's presence free to appear in Jesus

alone. As the resurrected One was exalted to the Father, the clouds veiled Him.

Clouds mark the conclusive and final revelation of the lordship of Christ. Mark 13:26; 14:62; and Rev. 1:7 combined the motif of the Son of Man from Dan. 7 with the word of judgment from Zech. 12:10 and referred them to the *parousia* or coming of Christ. Clouds thus became only signs of the revealing of the lordship and majesty of the Lord; they no longer concealed anything. In Rev. 14:14-16 the returning Christ sits on "white" (light, shining, majestic) clouds. In this transparent purity, both the living and the deceased believers are joined with their Lord (1 Thess. 4:17).

In 1 Cor. 10:1-2 the clouds and the sea of the exodus of Israel form a type of the baptism of Christians that had been misunderstood by the Corinthians. Thus we see that the word "clouds" in the parabolic language of the Bible makes spiritual contexts clear.   *Christian Wolf*

CLOUT KJV translation in Jer. 38:11-12 for Hebrew word meaning "tattered clothes, rags."

CLUB Weapon of war used in close combat to strike an enemy. See *Arms and Armor.*

CNIDUS (Cnī´ dŭs) Place-name of city in southwest Turkey. Paul's ship passed by here on the way to Rome (Acts 27:7).

COAL Charred wood used for fuel. The altar of sacrifice burned coals (Lev. 16:12), as did the blacksmith's fire (Isa. 44:12) and the baker's (Isa. 44:19). Coals provided heat for refining metal (Ezek. 24:11). Burning coals became a symbol of divine judgment, apparently representing God's coming to earth and causing volcanoes to erupt and throw burning coals on His enemies (Ps. 18:13). See *Cooking and Heating.*

COAST Land bordering a major body of water and used by KJV in obsolete sense of territories, borders, frontiers.

COAT See *Cloth, Clothing.*

COAT OF MAIL Protective device worn from the neck to the girdle. Also called a brigandine (Jer. 46:4; 51:3 KJV) or habergeon (2 Chron. 26:14 KJV). Usually made of leather, though it may at times have been covered with metal scales of some kind. Part of the usual equipment of the soldier (1 Sam. 17:5; 2 Chron. 26:14; Neh. 4:16; Jer. 46:4; 51:3). David refused to wear Saul's coat of mail (1 Sam. 17:38). Leviathan's skin is described as a double coat of mail (Job 41:13 NRSV, NASB following early Greek translation). See *Arms and Armor.*

COBRA Poisonous snake. See *Reptiles.*

COCK Strutting, crowing bird (rooster), *Zarzir motnayim* (Prov. 30:31). The crowing of the cock is probably the most well-known bird sound in the Bible. All of the NT references to the cock (except the mention of "cockcrow" in Mark 13:35) relate to Peter's denial of Christ. Jesus warned Peter that before the cock crowed twice, Peter would deny Him three times (Mark 14:30). Roosters first crowed about midnight and a second time around three o'clock in the morning. Their crowing occurred so punctually that the Romans relied on this bird sound to signal the time to change the guard. See *Chicken.*

COCKATRICE KJV translation of legendary serpent and poisonous snakes (Isa. 11:8; 14:29; 59:5; Jer. 8:17). It is probably the *Vipera xanthina.* See *Reptiles.*

COCKCROWING The third watch of the night in the Roman system (Mark 13:35), thus midnight until 3 a.m. Jewish system had only three watches; Roman had four.

COCKLE Plant whose name derives from Hebrew word for "stink." It appears in Scripture only at Job 31:40 and is identified as *Lolium temulentum.* Modern translations refer to brier or thorns.

A cobra pictured in the famous Nile Mosaic.

CODEX A collection of manuscript pages, especially of the Bible or sections of it, bound together in book form.

The word comes directly from the Latin meaning "tree trunk," possibly describing a stack of wooden tablets, each coated with wax on one side for writing and held together by leather thongs inserted in holes bored along one side. For centuries papyrus and parchment made from animal skins were popular writing materials because they could be shaped into long strips and rolled into a scroll. Using the scroll required both hands, however, and someone decided to cut a scroll into equal-sized sheets, stack them in order, and stitch them together along one edge. So, the scroll became a codex.

Biblical manuscripts produced in the codex form were all hand copied in Greek capital letters on parchment from older manuscripts. Nearly 250 of these manuscripts in codex form are now preserved in various libraries and museums. They have been dated from the fourth to the eleventh centuries. The oldest and most complete is Codex Sinaiticus now in the British Museum. It contains about 350 sheets that measure 15 by 13 ½ inches with four columns of lettering per page. It was discovered accidentally in 1844 by a Russian scholar in a monastery at the foot of Mount Sinai. It contains all the NT and most of the OT. Another important codex from the fourth century is in the Vatican Library in Rome. A fifth-century manuscript of the four Gospels is known as Codex Washingtonianus and is housed in the Freer Gallery of Art in Washington, D.C. *William J. Fallis*

COFFER Old English word for box in 1 Sam. 6:8,11,15 (KJV).

COHORT Roman military unit with capacity of 1,000 men; ten cohorts formed a legion. Cornelius (Acts 10:1) apparently belonged to a cohort of archers named the Cohors II Miliaria Italica Civium Romanorum Voluntariorum that had 1,000 members, Cornelius commanding 100 of them. Originally, the unit had been formed in Rome of freed slaves who received citizenship. It was transferred to Syria at least by A.D. 69. Bible narrative places the cohort in Caesarea before A.D. 41. An infantry cohort was stationed in Jerusalem and protected Paul from zealous Jews (Acts 21:31). They were stationed in the citadel Antonia on the northwest corner of the temple. A centurion attached to the cohort Augusta had command of Paul and other prisoners, transporting them from Caesarea to Rome (Acts 27:1). KJV translates "cohort" as "band."

COINS are stamped metal disks issued by a government for trade and valuation.

Before money was invented, a man might trade or swap with a neighbor something he owned for something he wanted. Because of their intrinsic value and mobility, cattle were very popular in the barter system. Such trading took place also on a grand scale. When Hiram of Tyre agreed to furnish building materials for the temple, Solomon pledged large annual payments in wheat and olive oil (1 Kings 5:11). Eventually the discovery and use of metals for ornaments, implements, and weapons led to their dominating the primitive exchanges. Silver, gold, and copper in various forms, such as bars, bracelets, and the like represented wealth in addition to land, cattle, and slaves. The silver shekel, weighing about four-tenths of an ounce, became the standard measure. When Abraham bought the cave of Machpelah, he "weighed out... four hundred shekels of silver" (Gen. 23:16). At that time the shekel was a weight rather than a coin.

The talent was another weight frequently associated in the OT with gold and silver. The crown that David took from the king of the Ammonites weighed one talent (2 Sam. 12:30). After Judah's defeat at Megiddo, the victorious pharaoh appointed a puppet king and required the Jews to pay Egypt a heavy tribute in silver and gold (2 Kings 23:30). Although its weight varied slightly from one country to another, the talent was approximately 75 pounds.

Determining the weight and purity of any metal was a tedious business and sometimes subject to dishonesty. To establish some standards, the first coins were minted about the same time around 650 B.C. both in Greece and in Lydia of Asia Minor. Excavations in Shechem have uncovered a Greek silver coin dating after 600 B.C., about the time the Jews were returning from Babylon to Judah. First mention of money in the Bible appears in Ezra 2:69, describing funds collected for rebuilding the temple. KJV lists among other resources 61,000 "drams of gold," but the RSV has "darics of gold," (NASB, NIV, "drachmas") referring to a Persian gold coin. Years later, about 326 B.C., after Alexander overran the Persian Empire, Greek coinage was

A gold coin of Lysimachos from Thrace (323–281 B.C.).

circulated widely in Palestine, according to archaeological research.

The Maccabean Revolt began in 167 B.C. Twenty-four years later (123 B.C.), Judea became an independent state, and about 110 B.C. the reigning high priest minted in bronze the first real Jewish coins. Only dominant political entities could produce silver coins. In accord with the Second Commandment, Jewish coins did not bear the image of any ruler, but they used symbols such as a wreath, a cornucopia, or the seven-branched lampstand of the temple. Such symbols continued to be used by Herod and other appointed Jewish rulers after Palestine submitted to Roman domination. Many small copper coins from this early NT period have been discovered.

The coin most often mentioned in the Greek NT is the *denarion*, translated "penny" in the KJV and "denarius" in the RSV, NASB, NIV. It was a silver coin usually minted in Rome. It carried on one side the image of the emperor (Matt. 22:21), and on the reverse might be some propaganda symbol. Of course, the "penny" translation was an attempt to equate the value of an ancient coin with a familiar one of the King James era. Its value in NT times can be more accurately assessed by knowing the labor that the ancient coin could buy. The denarius was the daily pay for Roman soldiers and the wage of a day laborer in Palestine (Matt. 20:2).

Another reference to silver money occurs in Matt. 26:15 in the agreement between the high priest and Judas for betraying Jesus. Although the original text mentions only "silver" with no specific coin, scholars feel that the figure "30" recalls the compensation required by law for killing a slave by accident (Exod. 21:32). So, Judas' pay could have been 30 silver shekels. By this time the shekel had developed from only a measure of weight to a specific coin weighing a little less than half an ounce. It is possible also that the "large money" (KJV) paid to the soldiers guarding Jesus' tomb (Matt. 28:12) referred to large silver coins or shekels.

A third coin mentioned in the NT was the one the poor widow put into the temple treasury as Jesus watched (Mark 12:42). KJV translates the original words as "two mites, which make a farthing" while the RSV reads "two copper coins, which made a penny" (NIV: "two very small copper coins, worth only a fraction of a penny"). The first noun describes the smallest Greek copper coin (*lepta*) and the second noun translates the Greek (*Kodrantess*) for the smallest Roman copper coin. In either case they were the smallest coins available, but Jesus said they were greater in proportion than the other donations.

From two parables told by Jesus, we get the impression that the word "talent" had come in NT times to represent a large sum of money instead of just a measure of weight. In Matt. 18:24 He told of a man who owed a certain king "10,000 talents." A few chapters later He described a wealthy man assigning different responsibilities to three servants. At the reckoning time he rebuked the one who had merely hidden his talent by saying that at least he could have deposited the money to let it earn interest

A coin from Pamphylia (190–36 B.C.)

(Matt. 25:27). Such a talent had been estimated to have a current value of about a thousand dollars. *William J. Fallis*

COLHOZEH (Cŏl hō´ zĕh) Personal name meaning "he sees everything" or "everyone a seer." Father whose son Shallun was ruler of part of Mizpah and who helped Nehemiah repair Jerusalem's gates (Neh. 3:15). Apparently he had a grandson living in Jerusalem in Nehemiah's day (Neh. 11:5). The name Colhozeh may indicate a family of prophets.

COLLAR Word used to translate various Hebrew words and may describe the opening for the head in a garment (Exod. 28:32 NIV; Job 30:18; Ps. 133:2 NIV); a decorative ornament around the necks of the Midianite Kings (NRSV) or their camels (Judg. 8:26; Prov. 1:9; Song 4:9); stocks or a pillory used to restrain a person (Jer. 29:26 NRSV, NASB); and a shackle of iron placed around the neck of a prisoner (Ps. 105:18 NRSV, REB, TEV).

COLLECTION FOR THE POOR SAINTS Near the end of Paul's ministry, he took up a collection for the poor of the Jerusalem church. Why the Jerusalem church had so much poverty is not clear. Jews in Jerusalem may have isolated Christian Jews from the economic system. Paul and Barnabas promised to help (Gal. 2:1-10), so Paul collected this money from the Gentile churches which he administered. These included churches in Philippi, Thessalonica, Corinth, and Galatia. He mentioned this offering on three occasions in his letters. In 1 Cor. 16:1-4 Paul indicated that he wanted the church to put something aside on the first day of each week. In 2 Cor. 8–9 Paul wrote that the churches of Macedonia had given liberally and Titus would oversee the completion of the offering in Corinth. Finally, in Rom. 15:25 Paul stated that at the present time he was going to Jerusalem to deliver the gift. A sense of spiritual indebtedness to the founding church in Jerusalem prompted the offering. Luke never mentioned the offering specifically in Acts. There is a list of men in Acts 20:4 who accompanied Paul to Jerusalem. (This trip corresponds to the plans of Rom. 15:25.) The importance of this offering for Paul was twofold. First, the offering met an economic need in Jerusalem. Political instability and general economic depression were problems in Palestine. There were dependent widows (Acts 6:1), and the sharing of property offered only temporary relief (Acts 4:32-37). For this reason Paul was anxious to "remember the poor" (Gal. 2:10). Second, the offering had a theological importance for Paul. The fact that the Gentiles were willing to aid the Jews in this manner validated Paul's Gentile mission. The offering was evidence that in the Christian family there was neither "Jew nor Greek" (Gal. 3:28).

Terence B. Ellis and Lynn Jones

COLLEGE KJV translation (2 Kings 22:14) of Hebrew word meaning "repetition, copy, second," referring to the second district or division of Jerusalem (cp. Zeph. 1:10).

COLONY Only Philippi is described as a colony of Rome (Acts 16:12), though many cities mentioned in the NT were considered as such. Roman colonization as practiced under Julius Caesar provided land for veteran soldiers and healthy individuals on the relief rolls of Rome. The cities of Corinth and Philippi were Roman colonies during the time of Caesar. Augustus founded colonies in Antioch (Psidian), Lystra, Troas, and Syracuse (all mentioned in Acts). Other Roman colonies included Ptolemais (Acco) and Iconium. Colonies had autonomous local governments and in some cases were exempt from poll and land taxes. The functioning of the local governments of Roman colonies is seen in Acts 16:12-40.

COLORS Writers of biblical literature reflected little or nothing of an abstract sense of color. Nevertheless, they made frequent references to a select group of colors when their purposes in writing so demanded it.

References to Colors Moving beyond color in the abstract sense, one does find frequent references to certain objects that have color designations. When reference is made to a particular color or colors, it is likely made for one of two basic reasons. First, a writer may wish to use color in a descriptive sense to help identify an object or clarify some aspect about that object. Color usages in the descriptive sense may apply to such categories as the natural world, animate and inanimate objects, and aspects of personal appearance. For instance, earthly vegetation is depicted as green; clothes are often of varying shades of red or blue; horses are identified by col-

ors such as red, black, or white; and human features such as eyes, hair, skin, and teeth are described colorfully as well.

A second reason for color designations in the Bible involves a more specialized usage. At times a writer may use color in a symbolic sense to convey theological truth about the subject of his writing. Color designations have general symbolic significance. For instance, white may be symbolic of purity or joy; black may symbolize judgment or decay; red may symbolize sin or life-blood; and purple may be symbolic of luxury and elegance. Color symbolism became for the writers of apocalyptic literature (Daniel, Revelation) an appropriate tool for expressing various truths in hidden language. In their writings one may find white representative of conquest or victory, black representative of famine or pestilence, red representative of wartime bloodshed, paleness (literally "greenish-gray") representative of death, and purple representative of royalty.

Color Designations of Frequent Use Color designations that appear in the Bible offer relatively little in the way of variety. The matter is further complicated by the fact that of those colors which appear, a precise translation of the underlying Hebrew and Greek terms is difficult.

Colors mentioned most frequently are those that refer to the dyed products manufactured by the peoples of Israel and her neighbors. Particularly common are the varying shades in the red-purple range. Purple was the most valued of the ancient dyes and was used in the coloring of woven materials. The peoples of Crete, Phoenicia, and Canaan produced the dye from mollusks taken from the Mediterranean Sea. Purple is noted to be the color of some of the tabernacle furnishings and priests' garments in the OT (Exod. 26:1; 28:4-6). In the NT the robe put on Christ and Lydia's occupation are associated with the color purple as well (Mark 15:17; Acts 16:14). By varying the dye-making process, other shades of blue became possible and are noted in Scripture (Exod. 28:5-6; Ezek. 23:6; Rev. 9:17).

Shades of red dye were produced from the bodies of insects, vegetables, and reddish-colored minerals. These were, likewise, used to color garments. In addition, natural objects are sometimes designated red, scarlet, or crimson, including such items as pottage, wine, the sky, and horses (Gen. 25:30; Prov. 23:31; Matt. 16:2-3; Rev. 6:4). Isaiah used the color red as a symbol of the nature of sin (Isa. 1:18).

The neutrals, white and black, are mentioned on occasion in the Bible. Natural objects such as milk, leprous skin, and snow are designated white (Gen. 49:12; Lev. 13:3-4; Isa. 1:18). White is used in the NT of the garments of Jesus and angels to indicate the glory of the wearer (Matt. 17:2; 28:3; Acts 1:10). Natural objects designated black include such items as hair, skin, the sky, and even the sun itself (Lev. 13:31; Job 30:30; 1 Kings 18:45; Rev. 6:12).

Other color designations used less frequently but not any less significantly are green, yellow, vermillion, and gray.   *James Sexton*

COLOSSAE See *Asia Minor, Cities of; Colossians, Letter to the.*

COLOSSIANS, LETTER TO THE (Cŏ·lŏs´sĭans) Letter from Paul to the church at Colossae. It is one of the Prison Epistles (along with Ephesians, Philemon, and Philippians). Traditional date and place of writing is A.D. 61 or 62 from Rome. The letter itself does not name the place where Paul was imprisoned, and Caesarea and Ephesus have been suggested as alternatives to Rome. If written from Ephesus, the time of writing would be in the mid-50s; if from Caesarea, the late 50s. The primary purpose of Colossians was to correct false teachings that were troubling the church.

Authorship of Colossians The authenticity of Colossians has been debated, as has also the exact nature of the relationship between Ephesians and Colossians. In favor of Pauline authorship it may be noted that the early church accepted the letter as genuinely Pauline. While it is true that the style and vocabulary differ somewhat from Paul's other letters, this occurs primarily in the section which attacks the Colossian heresy (1:3–2:23). The unusual terminology in this section is at least partly the result of addressing an unusual problem.

Some would rule out Pauline authorship by identifying the heresy attacked in Colossians as second century Gnosticism. Such arguments are not convincing, however, because the heresy cannot be identified with certainty, and gnostic thought was already encroaching on the church by the middle of the first century.

One should note also the relationship between Philemon and Colossians. They mention many of the same people and were apparently carried by the same messenger (Col. 4:7-18; Philem. 1-2,10,23-24). The undoubted authenticity of Philemon argues in favor of the Pauline authorship of Colossians as well.

The City of Colossae Colossae was located in the southwest corner of Asia Minor in what was then the Roman province of Asia. Hierapolis and Laodicea were situated only a few miles away. All three were in the Lycus River Valley. A main road from Ephesus to the east ran through the region. See *Asia Minor, Cities of.*

Colossae was prominent during the Greek period. By Paul's day it had lost much of its importance, perhaps due to the growth of the neighboring cities. Extremely detrimental to all of the cities of the region were the earthquakes that occasionally did severe damage. Shortly after Paul wrote Colossians, the entire Lycus Valley was devastated by an earthquake (about A.D. 61) which probably ended occupation of the city.

The region included a mixture of people native to the area, Greeks, Romans, and transplanted Jews. The church probably reflected the same diversity. As far as we know, Paul never visited Colossae. His influence was felt, however, during his ministry in Ephesus. (Acts 19:10 records that all Asia heard the gospel.) The letters to Philemon and to the Colossians indicate that many of Paul's fellow workers (if not Paul himself) had worked among the churches of the Lycus Valley. As a result, the relationship between the apostle to the Gentiles and the Colossian church was close enough that when trouble arose some of the church turned to Paul for instruction.

Content Colossians may be divided into two main parts. The first (1:3–2:23) is a polemic against false teachings. The second (3:1–4:17) is made up of exhortations to proper Christian living. The introduction (1:1-2) is in the form of a Hellenistic, personal letter. The senders (Paul

A view of the tell of Colossae.

and Timothy) and the recipients (the Colossian church) are identified, and a greeting is expressed (the usual Pauline "grace and peace" replaced the usual secular "greeting").

Typical of Paul, a lengthy thanksgiving (1:3-8) and prayer (1:9-14) lead into the body of the letter. Paul thanked God for the faith, hope, and love (1:4-5) which the Colossians had by virtue of their positive response to the gospel. He prayed that they might have a full knowledge and understanding of God's will and lead a life worthy of redeemed saints, citizens of the kingdom of Christ (1:9-14).

The doctrinal section which follows begins with a description of the grandeur of the preeminent Christ (1:15-20). Though the precise meaning of some words and phrases is uncertain, there is no doubt as to Paul's intent. He meant to present Jesus as fully God incarnate (1:15,19), as supreme Lord over all creation (1:15-17), as supreme Lord of the church (1:18), and as the only Source of reconciliation (1:20).

The origin of this grand statement on the nature and work of Christ is debated. The structure, tone, and vocabulary of the passage have led many to speculate that 1:15-20 is a doctrinal statement (hymn) that was in use in the church of Paul's day. This passage and Phil. 2:6-11 are thought by the majority of scholars to be the most obvious examples of pre-Pauline tradition in the letters of Paul. However, difficulty in recreating a balanced hymnic structure has convinced most that Paul rewrote portions of the hymn, if indeed he was not the author of the entire confession. Author or not, the apostolic stamp of approval is on these words which Paul used to state unambiguously that Christ is Lord and Savior of all.

The purpose of the first two chapters was to correct the false teaching that had infiltrated the church. The heresy is not identified, but several characteristics of the heresy are discernible. (1) An inferior view of Christ is combated in 1:15-20. This christological passage implies that the heretics did not consider Jesus to be fully divine or perhaps did not accept Him as the sole Source of redemption. (2) The Colossians were warned to beware of plausible sounding "philosophies" which were antichrist (2:8). (3) The heresy apparently involved the legalistic observance of "traditions," circumcision, and various dietary and festival laws (2:8,11,16,21; 3:11). (4) The worship of angels and lesser spirits was encouraged by the false teachers (2:8,18). (5) Asceticism, the deprivation or harsh treatment of one's "evil" fleshly body, was promoted (2:20-23). Finally, (6) the false teachers claimed to possess special insight (perhaps special

The Lycus River Valley as seen from Colossae.

revelations) that made them (rather than the apostles or the Scriptures) the ultimate source of truth (2:18-19).

Scholars cannot agree on who these false teachers were. Some of the characteristics cited above seem to be Jewish; others sound like gnostic teachings. Some see the teachings of a mystery religion here. Dozens of alternatives have been proposed by very capable authors. It is even argued that Paul was not attacking one specific heresy (or if he was, he did not have a clear understanding of it himself) but rather was warning the Colossians about a variety of false teachings which had troubled the church or which might trouble it in the future. While the passage does not clearly identify the heretics, it does clearly state that Christ (not angels, philosophies, rituals, traditions, asceticism, or anything else) is the Source of redemption.

Colossians 3:1-4 provides the link connecting the theology of chapters 1 and 2 with the exhortations to live a Christian life in chapters 3 and 4. The command to "put to death" (3:5 NIV) and to "rid yourselves of all such things" which will reap the wrath of God (3:5-11) is balanced by the command to "clothe yourselves with" (3:12 NIV) those things characteristic of God's chosen people (3:12-17). The changes are far from superficial, however. They stem from the Christian's new nature and submission to the rule of Christ in every area of one's life (3:9,10,15-17).

Rules for the household appear in 3:18–4:1. The typical first-century household is assumed, thus the passage addresses wives and husbands, fathers and children, masters and slaves. Paul made no comment about the rightness or wrongness of the social structures; he accepted them as givens. Paul's concern was that the structures as they existed be governed by Christian principles. Submission to the Lord (3:18,20,22; 4:1), Christian love (3:19), and the prospect of divine judgment (3:24–4:1) must determine the way people treat one another regardless of their social station. It is this Christian motivation which distinguishes these house rules from those that can be found in Jewish and pagan sources.

A final group of exhortations (4:2-6) and an exchange of greetings (4:7-17) bring the letter to a close. Notable in this final section are the mention of Onesimus (4:9), which links this letter with Philemon; the mention of a letter at Laodicea (4:16), which may have been Ephesians; and Paul's concluding signature which indicates that the letter was prepared by an amanuensis (secretary) (4:18).

Outline

I. Warnings Against Heresy (1:1–2:23)
  A. Greeting, thanksgiving, and prayer (1:1-14)
  B. Christ and no other is supreme in the universe (1:15-17).
  C. Christ, having reconciled all creation to God and embodying the fullness of God, is supreme in the church (1:18-20).
  D. Believers experience Christ's supremacy in the saving power of the gospel (1:21-23).
  E. The supreme Christ fulfills God's eternal saving purpose (1:24-29).
  F. Christians should have full confidence in Christ's supremacy and forget heretical teachings (2:1-5).
  G. Elemental human traditions must not lead away from faith in Christ (2:6-10).
  H. Legal practices cannot supplement Christ's work of salvation on the cross (2:11-23).
II. The Supreme Rule of Christ Leads to Rules for Life with Christ (3:1–4:18).
  A. Believers seek the fullness of the new life in Christ (3:1-4).
  B. Life in Christ cleanses believers of old practices (3:5-11).
  C. The life in Christ gives power for unity, mutual love, and forgiveness (3:12-14).
  D. Church life includes mutual encouragement and worship (3:15-17).
  E. Life in Christ brings faithfulness and compassion in family relationships (3:18–4:1).
  F. Closing greetings and blessings for those in Christ (4:2-18)

Michael Martin

COLT Young of various riding animals. Modern understanding is that of a young male horse, but in the sixteenth century, the range of meaning was broader. **1.** Young camels (Gen. 32:15), noted by the Hebrew term for "sons." **2.** Young donkeys (Gen. 49:11), also "son" in Hebrew (cp. Judg. 10:4; 12:14, where Hebrew is "donkeys"). The NT uses the reference in Zech. 9:9 as a prediction of Jesus' triumphal entry into Jerusalem (Matt. 21; Mark 11; Luke 19; John 12:15). Zechariah apparently used parallelism, the basic structure of Hebrew poetry, to describe a rider on one young donkey. Mark, Luke, and John told the story of Jesus' entry with reference to one animal. Matthew mentioned two animals, including both the ass and the colt from Zechariah as separate animals.

COMFORTER Commonly used translation of the Greek word *paracletos*. The compound noun refers to "one called alongside." John's Gospel features five passages in which this word details the work and ministry of the Comforter for believers. Jesus told His disciples He was going away and that it was to their advantage because He would send another Comforter, the Holy Spirit, who would never be taken away from them. There are a number of ministries that the Comforter would carry out in the life of the believer. He will teach believers all things (John 14:26), bear witness to Christ (15:26), expose the world's error and bring conviction of sin (16:8), guide believers in the way of truth (16:13), and glorify Jesus (16:14).

The same word is rendered in 1 John 2:1 as "Advocate" and is a reference to Jesus' intercessory work for believers. The "two Comforters" can be seen as working simultaneously: the Spirit Paraclete working in and for us on earth, and Jesus the Paraclete, working for us in heaven, as One who "always lives to intercede" for us (Heb. 7:25 HCSB). See *Advocate; Holy Spirit; Paraclete.*   *W. Dan Parker*

COMMANDER See *Chancellor.*

COMMANDMENTS, TEN See *Ten Commandments.*

COMMERCE Commercial activity in the ancient Near East took many forms. The economy centered around agriculture, but some manufactured goods were produced and natural resources mined. Farm goods, products, and resources had to be transported to market centers and other countries. Barter and the buying and selling of goods and services held a prominent place in the life of villages and towns. This is demonstrated by the large number of economic texts uncovered in excavations and the importance placed on transactional dialogue and the use of commercial scenes to highlight major events in the biblical text.

Products The irrigated fields of Mesopotamia and Egypt and the terraced hillsides of Palestine produced a variety of agricultural products. Barley and wheat were crushed, winnowed, sieved, and distributed on the threshing floor (*goren*) for local consumption (Deut. 15:14; Ruth 3:15). Surpluses were transported to regional marketplaces and major cities. Whole grain, meal, flax, nuts, dates, olive oil, fish in the Galilee area, and a variety of animal by-products found their way into every home and paid the taxes imposed by the government. The kings like Uzziah (2 Chron. 26:10) also had large holdings of land and vast herds that contributed to the overall economy.

Village craftsmen produced pottery, metal and wooden implements, weapons, and cloth. Evidence of their commercial self-sufficiency is seen in the recovery of loom weights in excavations of private homes throughout Israel. These balls of clay provide evidence of how widespread the local weaving and cloth-making industries were in ancient times. Manufactured products were distributed among the inhabitants of the village. The finer items were traded to traveling merchants or transported overland to Jerusalem or some other commercial center.

Manufactured goods most commonly introduced into national or international commerce included fine pottery, weapons, glassware, jewelry, cosmetics, and dyed cloth. Distinctive styles or fine workmanship created markets for these products and thus made it worth the costs and hazards of sea and overland transport. Evidence of how widespread trade was in the ancient world can be traced by the different styles and decoration of pottery. Seal markings showing place of origin are also found on many jugs and storage jars used to transport wine, oil, grain, and spices.

Another indication of the diversity of trading products that circulated throughout the ancient Near East is found in Ezekiel's "lamentation over Tyre," one of the principal Phoenician seaports (Ezek. 27:12-24). Their ships and those of Tarshish carried iron, tin, and lead, exchanging them for slaves, horses, mules, ivory, and ebony at various ports of call. Aram or Edom (NIV with footnote) traded "emeralds, purple, embroidered work, fine linen, coral, and rubies" (27:16 NASB), and Judah sent honey, oil, and balm along with wheat as trade goods to Tyre (Ezek. 27:17). The Phoenicians also supplied their trading partners with wool and cloth dyed purple with a glandular secretion from the murex mollusk.

Merchant quarters were established in many trading centers like that at Ugarit, a seaport in northern Syria (1600–1200 B.C.). Phoenician seaports of Tyre and Sidon also had their resident alien communities, adding to the cosmopolitan nature of these cities and facilitating the transmission of culture and ideas. Economic and political importance of these trading communities is seen in Solomon's construction of storehouse cities in Hamath (2 Chron. 8:4 and in Ahab's negotiations with Ben-Hadad of Syria for the establishment of "market areas in Damascus" (1 Kings 20:34 NIV).

Places of Business Metropolitan centers, like Babylon and Thebes, had open areas or market squares where commerce took place. This was also the case in the Hellenistic cities of the Near East that had one or more *agoras*. The narrow confines of the villages and towns in Palestine, however, restricted commercial activity to shops or booths built into the side of private homes or to the open area around the city gate.

For most Palestinian villages and towns, the gate was a vital place where commercial, judicial, and social activities of all sorts took place. Lot sat in the gate, demonstrating his status as a privileged resident alien (Gen. 19:1). The gate of Samaria served as a market center where the people purchased measures of barley and fine meal (2 Kings 7:18). In Prov. 31:23 one sign of a prosperous man with a well-ordered house was his ability to sit with the elders in the gate.

Large urban centers, like Jerusalem, had several gates and commercial districts, thus allowing for diversification of commercial activity throughout the city. Jeremiah 18:2 speaks of the Potsherd Gate (author's translation; known as the Dung Gate in Neh. 2:13) where Jeremiah enacted a prophecy of doom by smashing a pot. He also mentions the bakers' street as the principal area of production and supply of bread in Jerusalem (Jer. 37:21). In the Roman period, Josephus lists several commercial activities in the city: wool shops, smithies, and the clothes market.

Weights and Measures Inscribed stone, clay, or metal weights were used throughout the Near East and have been found in large quantities by archaeologists. They range from the talent (2 Sam. 12:30; 2 Kings 18:14) to the mina (Ezra 2:69 NASB), the shekel (2 Sam. 14:26; Ezek. 4:10), and various smaller weights. Until the establishment of the monarchy, commercial transactions were governed in each Israelite town by a local standard of exchange. Evidence has been found (markings on the weights) of the use of both the Egyptian standard of weights as well as Babylonian measures. Even these standards were apparently negotiable, however, and sometimes subject to abuse. Thus, Abraham was forced before witnesses in the gate of Hebron to pay an exorbitant rate (400 shekels of silver) for the cave of Machpelah (Gen. 23:16), and Amos condemned those merchants who planned "to make the bushel smaller and the shekel bigger, and to cheat with dishonest scales" (Amos 8:5 NASB).

Until coinage was introduced after 600 B.C., foodstuffs and other goods were obtained through barter in the marketplace or purchased with weights of precious metals (Gen. 33:19; Job 42:11). When minted coinage came into general use during the Hellenistic period (after 200 B.C.), it created a revolution in commerce. Transactions in accepted coinage, known to bear a definite weight, added to the confidence of the public and eliminated some of the abuses of the marketplace. Coins also facilitated the payment of taxes (Mark 12:15-17) and wages (Matt. 20:2). See *Coins*.

Business Law Hammurabi's law code (about 1750 B.C.) contains a model of business law in the ancient Near East. Many facets or trade are governed by this code. They are sometimes echoed in the biblical codes as well. For instance, Hammurabi's law protected a man who consigned a portion of his grain to storage from losses due to natural events and the corrupt practices of the owner of the storage room (cp. Exod. 22:7-9). Lending at interest to fellow Israelites was forbidden in Exod. 22:25 and Deut. 23:19. This injunction, however, does not seem to apply to the practice of investment of surplus capital found in Matt. 25:14-30 and Luke 19:12-25.

The parables of the pounds and the talents suggest the existence of a sophisticated banking and investment community, which lent out sums for commercial enterprises and garnered profits for those who left their money with them. A portion of the vast sums that came into the temple treasury in Jerusalem as taxes each year (Matt.

17:24) were probably lent out as investment capital. Several of Hammurabi's laws speak of similar practices requiring that those who engage in commercial transactions obtain receipts to show proof of their investments and sales.

Trade and Trade Routes From earliest times caravans of traders carried goods throughout the Near East. Obsidian, brought by Neolithic traders from Anatolia, has been discovered at sites hundreds of miles from its place of origin. Palestine, situated on a land bridge between Mesopotamia and Africa, naturally became a center of commercial travel. Groups of Semitic traders, like the Ishmaelites and Midianites (Gen. 37:27-28), are recorded in Egyptian texts and on the walls of tombs, such as the Benihasen tomb paintings (about 1900 B.C.), which depict whole families with their donkeys transporting "ox-hide" ingots of metal. They used hilltop pathways as well as the Via Maris coastal highway and the King's Highway in Transjordan to move between Mesopotamia and Egypt. Eventually, the introduction of the camel and the establishment of caravansaries (inns where caravans can rest at night) as storage and rest centers, made it possible for merchants to take a more direct route across the deserts of northern Syria and Arabia. These lucrative trade routes were controlled in the Roman period by the city of Tadmor, the capital of the Palmyran kingdom, and by the Nabateans.

During the monarchy period, Israel's trade horizon expanded. Solomon imported vast quantities of luxury and exotic goods (ivory, apes, peacocks—1 Kings 10:22b) from all over the Near East. He also purchased horses and chariots for his fortress garrisons like those at Gezer, Hazor, and Megiddo (1 Kings 10:26). The nation had no deep-water ports on its coastline, so the Gulf of Aqaba became the prime point of entry for goods coming from Africa (spices, precious stones, gold from Ophir, algum wood). The Aqaba port of Elath (Ezion-geber) served the needs of the court of Solomon and subsequent kings as well. The shipping trade of Israel, as well as many other nations, joined with or was carried by Phoenician merchantmen (1 Kings 10:22). These more experienced sailors could avoid the storms and other hazards that sank many ships in the Mediterranean (2 Chron. 20:37 NIV).

Even in NT times, shipping was restricted to particular routes and seasons (Acts 27:12). Travel seems to have been more common in this period as seen by the movements of Paul, the other apostles, and those associated with the establishment of the early church, such as Aquila and Priscilla (Rom. 16:3). Passengers and cargo might be transported on one leg of a journey on one ship and then transferred to a number of others to complete their journey (Acts 27:1-8). Underwater excavations off Cyprus and the Herodian port of Caesarea Maritima demonstrate, however, that many of these ships never made it to port (Acts 27:39-44).

For those who chose to take the overland routes, the Romans constructed paved roads that facilitated the movement of their armies, as well as people and wagons loaded with goods for sale. Mile markers set up along these roads show how often they were repaired and which emperors took a special interest in the outlying districts of his domain. See *Agriculture; Banking; Economic Life; Marketplace; Transportation and Travel; Weights and Measures.*   *Victor H. Matthews*

COMMON In the OT that which was common (alternately profane) was contrasted with that which was holy. Thus common bread was contrasted with the bread of the Presence (1 Sam. 21:4); the common journey was contrasted with the military campaign for which David and his men would need to be consecrated (1 Sam. 21:5). The common people (*'am ha'arets*, "people of the land") were contrasted with rulers or people of standing in the community (Lev. 4:22,27) and were buried in cemeteries for the common people (2 Kings 23:6; Jer. 26:23). By NT times the concept of "common" also carried with it the connotation of "unclean." Thus Peter declares that he has never eaten anything "common or unclean." The response to Peter was: "What God has made clean, you must not call common" (Acts 10:14-15 HCSB).

COMMON LIFE See *Community of Goods.*

COMMONWEALTH Group of people united by common interests. Before the coming of Christ, the Gentiles were separated from the commonwealth of Israel (Eph. 2:12). Paul reminded the Philippians that more important than their citizenship in a Roman colony was their citizenship in heaven (Phil. 3:20). See *Citizen, Citizenship.*

COMMUNION Paul's term describing the nature of the Lord's Supper and thus the term used by many church groups to refer to their celebration of Jesus' final, memorial supper with His disciples. Paul used the Greek term *koinonia* to express the basic meaning of the Christian faith, a sharing in the life and death of Christ which radically creates a relationship of Christ and the believer and of the believers with one another in a partnership or unity. See *Fellowship; Lord's Supper.*

COMMUNITY OF GOODS Jerusalem church's practice of having "everything in common" (Acts 2:41-47; 4:32-37) had contemporary parallels: the Greek utopian ideal of common property among friends, the compulsory communalism of the Jewish sect at Qumran, and even the precedent of Jesus and the Twelve (Luke 8:3; John 13:29). The immediate context of both references in Acts (2:1-40; 4:31) indicates that the community of goods was not an ideal to which the church aspired but was itself evidence of the community's nature: that the entire range of their life together was shaped and directed by the Holy Spirit.

"Common" (*koina*) in 2:44 and 4:32 has the same root as *koinonia* ("fellowship" in 2:42); thus the issue was not economic theory but the common life together ("daily" in 2:46) with no separation between physical and spiritual needs. (See 6:1-6, which depicts the investment in care for the needy.) The parallel between Acts 4:34 and Deut. 15:4 indicates that the early church fulfilled God's intention for Israel to be generous.

The Jerusalem church chose to practice the selfless generosity in a form that closely resembled the lifestyle of Jesus and the Twelve. Other early churches practiced sacrificial generosity in different forms (Acts 11:27-30; 1 Cor. 16:1-4; Rom. 12:13; 1 John 3:17), for Jesus' call to set aside possessions took more than one form (cp. Matt. 19:16-22 with Luke 19:1-10. What these incidents have in common is an emphasis on sacrificial giving (Luke 21:1-4), requiring a complete change of heart so that God, not possessions, is served (Matt. 6:24) with a clear recognition of riches' dangers (Mark 10:23-31; Luke 6:24; 12:13-31).

This danger of riches manifested itself in the context of the community of goods (Acts 4:36–5:11). In contrast to Barnabas who sold some land and gave the proceeds to the apostles, Ananias and Sapphira held back some of the proceeds from their sale. Their subsequent deaths testified to the severity of abandoning the common life for selfish interest. Possessiveness led to lying to the Spirit (5:3,9) and therefore rejecting the bond ("one heart and of one soul" in 4:32) created by the Spirit. The voluntary nature of this community of goods was therefore not a matter of individuals independently choosing when and if to give, but the ongoing spontaneous generosity of a community unified and directed by the Spirit. See TEV translation of Acts 2:45 and 4:34b ("would sell") which identifies the ongoing nature of the generosity. See *Ananias; Borrow; Essenes; Fellowship; Gift, Giving; Holy Spirit; Mammon; Qumran; Teachings of Jesus.*

David Nelson Duke

COMPANY See *Cohort.*

COMPASSION Meaning "to feel passion with someone" or "to enter sympathetically into one's sorrow and pain." In various translations of the Bible, this English word is used to translate at least five Hebrew words in the OT and eight Greek words in the NT. The subtle variations in the original terms are emphasized below, with the inevitable overlapping of meanings being apparent.

Old Testament *Chamal* means "to regret," "to be sorry for (i.e., to pity)," "to grieve over," or "to spare someone." See 2 Sam. 12:4 for an example in which a rich man "spared" [KJV] his own sheep ("refrained" [NIV] from taking his own lamb) and took the lamb of a poor man to feed his guest. He obviously had more compassion for his sheep than he had for his poor neighbor. Pharaoh's daughter "had pity" on the baby Moses (Exod. 2:6); David "spared" Mephibosheth (2 Sam. 21:7); in anger, God often showed no "pity" on rebellious people (Zech. 11:6); but, in exercising grace, God more often showed "compassion for" or "grief over" His people (Joel 2:18; Mal. 3:17; Gen. 19:16; 2 Chron. 36:15; Isa. 63:9).

Chen represents "grace" and "charm." The term identifies what is "gracious." For example, God planned to demonstrate a spirit of "grace" or "compassion" (NRSV) on His people (Zech. 12:10). He would enable them to "mourn" the one they pierced (possibly a messianic reference). The term is used again in Job 8:5 where

Bildad instructed Job to implore the "compassion of the Almighty" (NASB).

Chus seems to be close in meaning to the English word "empathy," which suggests an identification with the person with whom one is "sympathizing" or for whom one is having "compassion." With the emotional content goes the intellectual intent to help. God forbade Israel to have such "pity" on the tribal peoples who were to be driven from the promised land (Deut. 7:16). God, Himself, refused to have such "pity" on a disobedient people, either Israel or its neighbors (Ezek. 5:11). An interesting contrast appears where Jonah had "compassion" on a plant (Jon. 4:10 NASB) while he did not want God to have "compassion" on the entire population of a city (Jon. 4:11).

Nichum or *nocham* are two forms of another Hebrew word for "compassion" which contains more than emotion. It means to "be sorry for," "regret," "comfort," or "console." This word includes the will to change the situation. God "was sorry" He made people (Gen. 6:6), but He still acted to preserve human life (Gen. 8:21). Though, in His basic nature, God does not "change His mind" (a translation of the Hebrew word *nicham* in 1 Sam. 15:29 NASB), there is a sense in which God (YAHWEH) does "repent" (which means normally to change one's mind and action). Examples are found in a number of OT texts (Exod. 32:14; 2 Sam. 24:16; and Jon. 3:10). Basically, what happened in each case was that the people or the circumstances changed enough for God to deal with them differently. Thus, Hos. 11:8 is translated, "My repentings are kindled together" (KJV) and "All my compassion is aroused" (NASB), suggesting a compassionate change in God which favored His people.

Racham is related to the Hebrew word for "womb" and expresses a mother's (Isa. 49:15) or a father's (Ps. 103:13) compassion for a helpless child. This deep emotion seeks expression in aggressive acts of selfless service (Gen. 43:14; Deut. 13:17). In Scripture, this compassion is protective, reflecting the feelings of the more powerful for the inferior. The majority of Bible uses of *racham* have God as the subject (the giver) and someone or something in the temporal world as the object (the recipient). Compare Hos. 2:4,23; Zech. 1:16; 10:6, and Ps. 145:9.

New Testament *Eleos* is one of the two principle NT words for compassion. The other is *splanchnizomai*. The first, *eleos*, is used in the

Greek OT, the Septuagint, to translate most of the Hebrew words listed above. In the NT *eleos* is the word Jesus chose to challenge the Pharisees to learn of God's desire for compassion (Matt. 9:13; 12:7). Jesus used the term again when He challenged Peter to understand that even slaves should practice compassion and forgiveness (Matt. 18:33). Paul reminded his readers that the demand for compassion is rooted in the very nature of God, who is full of compassion (Eph. 2:4; 1 Pet. 1:3).

Splanchnizomai is related to the Greek noun for "inward parts" or "bowels of mercies" [KJV]. The expression "pit of the stomach" suggests that the "inward parts" are the seat of human emotion. This and similar contemporary expressions like "go with your gut" show that this concept of compassion is still valid. The common first-century practice was to use the term to refer to courage rather than to mercy or compassion, even though some nonbiblical Jewish writings before Christ used the term to mean mercy.

Jesus took the term a step further and used it to define the attitude that should capture the life of every believer. In the parable of the unforgiving servant, the master had compassion and forgave the servant's debt (Matt. 18:27). The prodigal son's father had compassion on him (Luke 15:20). The good Samaritan had compassion on the injured traveler (Luke 10:33). Jesus had compassion on the crowd (Mark 6:34). People needing help asked Jesus for compassion (Mark 9:22; cp. Matt. 9:36; 20:34).

Oiktirmos is another of the eight Greek terms translated "compassion" in the NT. It is normally related to mourning the dead, expressing sympathetic participation in grief. In the Septuagint, the Greek OT, translated approximately 250 B.C., this Greek term is used to translate the Hebrew words *chen* and *racham*. Such compassion stands ready to help the one who is sorrowing. Paul taught that God is the source of the believer's capacity for showing genuine compassion (2 Cor. 1:3; cp. James 5:11).

Sumpathes is the fourth term translated "compassion." *Sun*, the Greek preposition meaning "with" is changed to *sum* when prefixed to the verb form *patheis*, from *pascho*, the basic verb meaning "to suffer." The word means "to suffer with" or "to suffer alongside." The English language borrowed this word directly from the Greek and spells it "sympathize." Peter listed *sumpathes* (compassion) among the basic Christian virtues (1 Pet. 3:8). *Don H. Stewart*

CONANIAH (Cŏn á nī´ ăh) Personal name meaning "Yahweh has established." **1.** Levite in charge of collecting temple offerings under King Hezekiah (2 Chron. 31:12). **2.** Perhaps the grandson of 1. He and other Levites contributed 5,000 sheep and goats and 500 bulls for Josiah's Passover offering (2 Chron. 35:9).

CONCISION Archaic English noun meaning "a cutting off." KJV uses "concision" in Phil. 3:2 to describe Paul's opponents who insisted on circumcision as necessary for right relationship with God (Phil. 3:2). See *Circumcision; Paul.*

CONCOURSE KJV translation of Hebrew "noisy places" in Prov. 1:21 referring to a place of community gathering and meeting.

CONCUBINE A wife of lower status (usually a slave) than a primary wife. Taking of concubines dates back at least to the patriarchal period. Both Abraham and Nahor had concubines (Gen. 22:24; 25:6; 1 Chron. 1:32). Tribal chiefs, kings, and other wealthy men generally took concubines. Gideon had a concubine (Judg. 8:31). Saul had at least one concubine named Rizpah (2 Sam. 3:7; 21:11). David had many (2 Sam. 5:13), but Solomon took the practice to its extreme, having 300 concubines, in addition to his 700 royal wives (1 Kings 11:3). Deuteronomy 17:17 forbids kings to take so many wives.

The concubines (and wives) of chiefs and kings were symbols of their virility and power. Having intercourse with the concubine of the ruler was an act of rebellion. When Absalom revolted against his father David, he "went in to his father's concubines in the sight of all Israel" (2 Sam. 16:22 NASB) on the palace roof. When David returned to the palace, the 10 concubines involved were sent away to live the rest of their lives in isolation (2 Sam. 20:3).

A concubine, whether purchased (Exod. 21:7-11; Lev. 25:44-46) or won in battle (Num. 31:18), was entitled to some legal protection (Exod. 21:7-12; Deut. 21:10-14) but was her husband's property. A barren woman might offer her maid to her husband hoping she would conceive (Gen. 16:1-3; 30:1-4).

Although the taking of concubines was not explicitly prohibited, monogamous marriage was set forth as the biblical pattern (Gen. 2:24; Mark 10:6-9). See *Family; Marriage; Polygamy; Slavery.* *Wilda W. Morris*

CONCUPISCENCE KJV translation of Greek *epithumia,* "desire, lust." The Greeks used the term to mean excitement about something in a neutral sense and then in an evil sense of wrongly valuing earthly things. The NT knows desire can be good (Matt. 13:17; Luke 22:15; Phil. 1:23; 1 Thess. 2:17). In fact, the NT uses the verb form more often in a good sense than in a bad one.

The bad sense of *epithumia* is desire controlled by sin and worldly instincts rather than by the Spirit (Gal. 5:16). Everyone has been controlled by such desires before their commitment to Christ (Eph. 2:3; Titus 3:3). Such desire is part of the old life without Christ and is deceitful (Eph. 4:22). Such desire can be for sex (Matt. 5:28), material goods (Mark 4:19), riches (1 Tim. 6:9), and drunkenness (1 Pet. 4:3). The Christian life then is a war between desires of the old life and desire to follow the Spirit (Gal. 5:15-24; 1 Pet. 2:11), the Spirit-led life crucifying worldly desires (Gal. 5:24). (Note the list of fleshly desires in Gal. 5:19-21.) As the new life comes through the Spirit, so old desires come through Satan (John 8:44) and the world of which he is prince (1 John 2:16). Such desires can make slaves of people (2 Pet. 2:18-20). Desire brings temptation, leading to sin, resulting in death (James 1:14-15). People cannot blame God, for He allows them freedom to choose and gives them over to what they choose (Rom. 1:24). God did give the law which defined wrong desires as concupiscence or sin. The power of sin then changed the good commandment into an instrument to arouse human desires to experience new arenas of life. Thus they sin and die rather than trust God's guidance through the law that such arenas are outside God's plan for life and thus should not be experienced (Rom. 7:7-8). Either sin brings death, or believers in Christ murder evil lusts (Col. 3:5).

In a very limited sphere of life, Paul called on believers to rise above the normal activities caused by lust in society. He called on faithfulness in marriage rather than on the immoral practices of the Greek and Roman world of his day (1 Thess. 4:4-5).

CONDEMN Act of pronouncing someone guilty after weighing the evidence.

Old Testament The word appears first in the context of a court of law (Exod. 22:9) where a judge hears a charge against a thief and condemns the culprit. Another juridical instance appears in Deut. 25:1 where judges are instructed to hear cases, decide on the issue, and "condemn the wicked." In Ps. 94:20-21 the writer accuses corrupt judges who "condemn the innocent," and in Ps. 109:31 he thanks God for saving the poor man "from those who condemn him to death" (TEV).

"Condemn" is also used in making everyday personal judgments as in the book of Job. Feeling helpless before God's power and righteousness, Job knew that no matter how he tried to defend himself, his own mouth would condemn him (9:20). He begged God not to condemn him but to explain why He was making him suffer (10:2). After Job's advisors had had their say, Elihu saw that all three "had condemned Job" (32:3). Other instances of the word being used in everyday judgments appear in Isa. 50:9; 54:17.

The more significant use of "condemn" is in connection with God's judgment. In dedicating the new temple, Solomon prayed that God would judge His people, "condemning the wicked ... and justifying the righteous" (1 Kings 8:32 NASB). The writer of Proverbs expected the Lord to condemn "those who plan evil" (12:2 TEV). The psalmist was sure God would not forsake a good man or allow him "to be condemned when he is on trial" (37:33 TEV). On the other hand, the Lord asked Job whether he wanted to condemn Him just to prove his own righteousness (40:8).

New Testament Several Greek words are translated "condemn" and "condemnation" with a progression of meaning from just making a distinction to making an unfavorable judgment. The three-way usage of the word in the OT continued into the NT. The law court context is seen in Jesus' prediction of His coming trial in Jerusalem (Matt. 20:18), in a remark of one of the men crucified with Jesus (Luke 23:40), and in the final vote of the Sanhedrin (Mark 14:64).

"Condemn" was also used in Jesus' day in making personal judgments of others. For instance, Jesus said the men of Nineveh would condemn His own unrepentant generation (Matt. 12:41); James warned the brethren that teachers were subject to greater criticism (James

3:1); and Paul urged Titus to use healthful speech in his teaching to avoid criticism (Titus 2:8). As in the OT, God is also the source of condemnation in the NT. He was responsible for the destruction of Sodom and Gomorrah (2 Pet. 2:6), and He condemned sin in human nature by sending His own Son (Rom. 8:3).

NT usage of "condemn" is unique in its reference to the final judgment, especially in John 3:17-19. A similar teaching appears in John 5:24. Paul felt that avoiding that final condemnation was a reason for accepting the Lord's chastening in this life (1 Cor. 11:32).   *William J. Fallis*

CONDUIT Water channel or aqueduct in or near Jerusalem channeling water into the city (2 Kings 18:17; 20:20; Isa. 7:3). The same Hebrew word refers to a trench built up to conduct water flow (1 Kings 18:32-38; Job 38:25; Ezek. 31:4). The location of the Jerusalem conduit is a matter of debate with different scholars favoring the Pool of Siloam, the Gihon Spring, or outside the wall to the northwest of the city beside the major north-south highway leading to Samaria. The latter location may be the most likely. Aqueducts had been built for Jerusalem before David conquered it with a tunnel providing water for the city (2 Sam. 5:8). Israel's kings evidently supplemented this. In a marvelous engineering feat, Hezekiah had workmen start at both ends and meet in the middle to construct a water tunnel connecting Gihon Spring and the Pool of Siloam (2 Kings 20:20; 2 Chron. 32:2-4,30). The tunnel was discovered in 1880.

CONEY Wild hare—*Procavia syriaca*, also called *Hyrax syriacus*.

Resembled a rabbit in size and color. The badger of Exod. 23:5; 26:14 has been identified by some scholars as the Syrian coney. It was unclean because it did not have divided hooves (Lev. 11:5; Deut. 14:7). It established its home in the rocky cliffs (Ps. 104:18; Prov. 30:26) from the Dead Sea Valley to Mount Hermon. The design of its feet helped the coney maintain footing on the slippery rocks.

CONFESSION Admission, declaration, or acknowledgment, that is a significant element in the worship of God in both OT and NT. The majority of the occurrences of the term can be divided into two primary responses to God: the confession of sin and the confession of faith.

Confession of Sin Numerous OT passages stress the importance of the confession of sin within the experience of worship. Leviticus speaks of ritual acts involving such admission of sin: the sin (or guilt) offering (5:5–6:7) and the scapegoat that represents the removal of sin (16:20-22). Furthermore, confession can be the act of an individual in behalf of the people as a whole (Neh. 1:6; Dan. 9:20) or the collective response of the worshiping congregation (Ezra 10:1; Neh. 9:2-3). Frequently, it is presented as the individual acknowledgment of sin by the penitent sinner (Ps. 32:5; Prov. 28:13; Pss. 40 and 51, which are individual confessions although the word "confession" is not used).

Likewise, in the NT confession of sin is an aspect of both individual and corporate worship. At the Jordan, John's followers were baptized, confessing their sins (Matt. 3:6; Mark 1:6). Similar confessions were made by Paul's converts in Ephesus (Acts 19:18). Christians are reminded that God faithfully forgives the sins of those who confess them (1 John 1:9). James admonished his readers not only to pray for one another but also to confess their sins to one another (5:16), probably within the context of congregational worship. By the end of the first century, routine worship included confession as the prelude to the observance of the Lord's Supper as seen in *Didache* 14:1. See *Apostolic Fathers.*

Confession of Faith Closely related to the confession of sin in the OT is the confession of faith, that is, the acknowledgment of and commitment to God. In 1 Kings 8:33,35 (as well as 2 Chron. 6:24,26) acknowledgment of the name of God results in forgiveness of sins. Such acknowledgment came to be standardized in the confessional formula known as the Shema (Deut. 6:4-5).

Such declaration of commitment to God, or particularly to Christ, is also found in the NT. One's public acknowledgment of Jesus is the basis for Jesus' own acknowledgment of that believer to God (Matt. 10:32; Luke 12:8; cp. Rev. 3:5). Furthermore, as Paul described the process by which one is saved, he explicitly drew a parallel between what one believes in the heart and what one confesses with the lips (Rom. 10:9-10)—belief and confession are two sides of the same coin. Probably the earliest confession of faith was the simple acknowledgment of the lordship of Christ (Rom. 10:9; 1 Cor. 12:3; Phil. 2:11), but the rise of heresy seems to have

caused the addition of specific data about Christ to the confession—for example, that He is Son of God (1 John 4:3,15) or that He has come in the flesh (1 John 4:2). A firmly set outline of Christian beliefs then appears to be what is meant by confession in later NT writings (Heb. 4:14). See *Faith; Scapegoat; Sin; Repentance.*

Naymond Keathley

CONFESSIONS AND CREDOS Theological statements of faith. Although individual Christians can produce such treatises, Christian groups or denominations normally produce confessions and credos. These proclamations are intended to declare the doctrinal perspective of the group on the matters addressed in the document.

The OT depicts the people of God confessing truths about Him and then offering their allegiance to him. Deuteronomy 6:4-25 calls for Israel to confess the truth about God (His oneness) and salvation (deliverance from Pharaoh's armies), and then to offer allegiance to Him in terms of personal devotion (love Him with all your heart, v. 5), passing on the heritage of God's message (teach [the commands] diligently to your children, v. 7), be always remembering God's Word (vv. 8-10), telling the story of their deliverance to the next generation (vv. 20-15). This passage has for centuries served a confession used regularly in Jewish homes. Psalm 78 demonstrates how Israel regularly called to mind God's work in its history. It speaks in narrative form of God's sovereignty (vv. 12,22-26), His wrath (vv. 21,27-29), His salvation (vv. 12-16,70-72), His mercy (vv. 38-39), His judgment (vv. 41-67), and His elective grace (vv. 67-72). Other confession texts can be found in Exod. 19–20, Josh. 24, Deut. 26.

The NT gives evidence of the early church's use of confessions and credos. The expression "Jesus is Lord" is an early confession intended to signify those who were genuinely born again and in whom the Holy Spirit dwelt (Rom. 10:9; 1 Cor. 12:3; Phil. 2:11). A baptismal candidate immediately prior to baptism may have used the confession to profess faith in Christ. Such public confessions often resulted in persecution and death. Credos may have been tools used to instruct new converts or to combat heresy. For example, the expression "Jesus Christ has come in the flesh" appears to be a credo designed to refute the false teaching that Jesus Christ only appeared to be a human being (1 John 4:2; 2 John 7). Other examples of succinct statements that encapsulate the faith of the early church in a confessional/creedal format are: Col. 1:15-20; 1 Tim. 3:16; 1 Pet. 3:18-22; Heb. 1:1-3; Phil. 2:5-11.

In the early church, confessions and credos were used to profess the faith of martyrs or those who withstood persecution. The concept eventually came to mean a resolved affirmation of religious convictions. These declarations may or may not be in conjunction with persecution.

Following the biblical precedent, confessions and credos ultimately developed into formal doctrinal statements. This concept has several forms. One form of confessionalism is the production of confessions of faith. Confessions of faith are theological documents intended to provide doctrinal identity and promote denominational unity. Confessions of faith often identify and articulate common areas of belief among different Christian denominations. Most denominations have used confessions of faith throughout their history. Exceptions would include Campbellites (followers of Alexander Campbell, now represented by these denominations: Church of Christ, Christian Church, Disciples of Christ) and Quakers. The former have held that the NT is sufficient, and thus there is no need for any confession of faith, while the latter have held to a radical individualism in which each person under the guidance of the Spirit's "inner light" is the arbiter of truth. Baptists and other Protestants have generally rejected such arguments.

Another understanding of confessionalism is the formal presentation of beliefs produced by Protestants. These presentations provide interpretative guides to Scripture, usually expounding the recognized creed of faith of a particular denomination. Confessionalism in this sense concerns formal theological treatises that are classified as "confessional theologies." These confessional theologies normally profess a Protestant understanding of the faith, often in contrast to Roman Catholicism, or even to other Protestant traditions.

Confessionalism can also be the endeavor of deriving doctrinal, core insights from within a particular Christian community of faith. This form of confessionalism finds its theological starting point from a perspective that is unique to a particular Christian religious community. This doctrinal interpretation may or may not be an interpretation of the formal creedal statements of a particular denomination.

Debate today surrounds the distinction between confessions of faith and creeds. Distinctions between the two are often difficult to clarify and define. Confessions of faith and creeds both provide denominational and doctrinal identity to particular Christian denominations. Further, both articulate explicit doctrinal statements that require a voluntary, conscientious adherence. One distinction, however, may be in the use of such documents. Creeds can be used to require conformity by all members of a particular tradition. In other words, creeds require a complete subscription by an individual in order to be a member of the denomination. Confessions of faith, while providing a consensus opinion of the majority of adherents, do not generally require such a subscription in order to belong to the specific body.   *Stan Norman and Chad Brand*

CONFIRM To establish an agreement and to show that a word is true and reliable. English translations use "confirm" for general Hebrew terms meaning "to prove reliable, trustworthy," "to be strong," "to fill, fulfill," "to stand," "to rise." The Greek terms mean "to be reliable" and "to set up." The terms are regularly used to speak of humans establishing God's words, covenant, or law by practicing them (Deut. 27:26) and more often of God confirming His message or His covenant by setting it up with His people and bringing to pass the promises He made (Lev. 26:9; 2 Sam. 7:25; 1 Chron. 16:17; Isa. 44:26; Rom. 15:8). At times human agreements or promises are confirmed (Ruth 4:7; 1 Kings 1:14; Esther 9:29; Jer. 44:25; Heb. 6:16). One could also establish oneself in a position or institution (2 Kings 15:19; 1 Chron. 17:14). Believers seek to confirm the gospel message through a Christian life (1 Cor. 1:6; Phil. 1:7). In so doing one also confirms the individual's calling and election (2 Pet. 1:10).

CONFISCATION Appropriation of private property for public or governmental use. Confiscation was not practiced in Israel until the rise of the monarchy and was not permitted by God. This practice was foretold by Samuel before Israel elected its first king (1 Sam. 8:14) as an inherent danger of kings following Near Eastern patterns. Ahab exercised this royal right when he confiscated the property of a person (Naboth) executed by the state (1 Kings 21:15-16), but he had to bear God's punishment for his act (1 Kings 21:18-19). Ezekiel reacted strongly against the abuses of this royal prerogative (Ezek. 45:7-8; 46:16-18).

CONFLICT, INTERPERSONAL

The Bible illustrates, explains, and offers solutions for interpersonal conflict. Among the more notable instances of interpersonal conflict recorded in the Bible are the hostilities between Cain and Abel (Gen. 4:1-16), Abram and Lot (Gen. 13:8-18), Jacob and Esau (Gen. 25–27; 32–33), Jacob and Laban (Gen. 29–31), Saul and David (1 Sam. 18–31), Mary and Martha (Luke 10:38-42), Jesus' disciples (Mark 9:33-37; Luke 22:24-27), Paul and Barnabas (Acts 15:36-41), and the Corinthian believers (1 Cor. 1:10-12; 3:2-4; 11:18).

The root cause of interpersonal conflict is sin (Gal. 5:19-20). James explains that fighting is the result of uncontrolled passions and desires (James 4:1-3). The book of Proverbs characterizes those who stir up conflict as persons given to anger (Prov. 15:18; 29:22), greed (Prov. 28:25), hate (Prov. 10:12), gossip (Prov. 16:28), and worthless perversions (Prov. 6:12-15). Such conflicts inevitably result in personal destruction (Prov. 6:15), discord (Prov. 6:14), and strife (Prov. 10:12; 16:28). It is no wonder that "the Lord hates … one who stirs up trouble among brothers" (Prov. 6:16,19 HCSB).

The Bible places great value on the ability to live at peace with one another (Ps. 34:14; Mark 9:50; Rom. 14:19; 1 Thess. 5:13; Heb. 12:14; 1 Pet. 3:11), in unity (Ps. 133:1), and harmony (Rom. 15:5-6). At the same time, the Bible declares unequivocally that such peace is given only by God (Num. 6:26; John 14:27; 16:33; 2 Cor. 13:11; 2 Thess. 3:16) and lived out only as believers pattern their lifestyles after that of Jesus (Phil. 2:3-8).

CONGREGATION

Assembled people of God. Congregation translates the Hebrew words *'edah* and *qahal* primarily. These terms may apply to any individual or class collectively such as "the wicked," "the hypocrites," and others. While *'edah* is once used to refer to a herd of bulls (Ps. 68:30) and once to a hive of bees (Judg. 14:8), both words primarily describe the Israelite people as a holy people, bound together by religious devotion to Yahweh rather than by political bonds. There is no apparent distinction in meaning between the two. Every circumcised Israelite was a member of the congregation. The congregation was subdivided into the tribe and then the most basic unit, the family. The congregation of Israel functioned in military, legal, and punishment matters.

In the Greek OT *'edah* was usually translated by *sunagoge*, *qahal* by *ekklesia*. In late Judaism *sunagoge* depicted the actual Israelite people and *ekklesia* the ideal elect of God called to salvation. Hence *ekklesia* became the term for the Christian congregation, the church. *Sunagoge* in the NT is almost entirely restricted to the Jewish place of worship. (An exception is James 2:2, which may refer to a Christian assembly.) The English word "synagogue" is merely a transliteration of *sunagoge*. *Ekklesia* means "called out," and in classical Greek referred to the body of free citizens called out by a herald. In the NT the "called out ones" are the church, the assembly of God's people. There is a direct spiritual continuity between the congregation of the OT and the NT church. Significantly the Christian community chose the OT term for the ideal people of God called to salvation (*ekklesia*), rather than the term which described all Israelites collectively (*sunagoge*). *Joe E. Lunceford*

CONGREGATION, MOUNT OF

Mountain considered by Israel's neighbors to stand in the far north and serve as a meeting place of the gods (Isa. 14:13).

CONIAH

(Cō·nī´ ăh) See *Jehoiachin*.

CONQUEST OF CANAAN

The book of Joshua and the first chapter of the book of Judges describe the conquest of Canaan, which resulted in Israel's settlement in the land of promise.

Historical Setting Israelite conquest came at a time when Egyptian control of Canaan was weakened. Historians disagree over when the conquest of Canaan occurred because they disagree over the date of the exodus. Archaeological evidence is largely ambiguous because of the close similarities between the Israelite and Canaanite cultures and because the Israelites refrained in general from destruction and burning of cities. The traditional date of the exodus based on a literal interpretation of 1 Kings 6:1 is about 1445 B.C., placing the conquest at about 1400–1350 B.C. Those who place more faith in archaeology than in the biblical data, and those who understand 1 Kings 6:1 and similar passages as figurative, commonly date the exodus around 1280 B.C. Such a date would place the conquest at about 1240–1190 B.C.

While it is not possible to be definitive about the date of the conquest, it is possible to draw some general conclusions regarding the situation of Canaan in the approximate time frame of the conquest. Shortly after 1500 B.C. Egypt subdued Canaan. Canaanite society operated according to a feudal system whereby the kings of city-states paid tribute to their Egyptian overlords. The city-states were numerous in the heavily populated Palestinian coastal plain; the mountainous regions were lightly populated. From about 1400 B.C. onward, Egyptian control of Canaan weakened, opening the land up for possible invasion by an outside force.

Joshua's Strategy Joshua led a three-campaign invasion of Canaan. At the close of the wilderness wanderings the Israelites arrived on the plains of Moab in the Transjordan ("beyond the Jordan"). There they subdued two local kings, Sihon and Og (Num. 21:21-35). Some of the Israelite tribes—Reuben, Gad, and half of the tribe of Manasseh—chose to settle in this newly conquered territory (Num. 32).

After Moses died, Joshua became the new leader of the Israelites. As God instructed him, Joshua led the people across the Jordan River into Canaan. The crossing was made possible by a supernatural separation of the water of the Jordan (Josh. 3–4). After crossing the river the Israelites camped at Gilgal. From there Joshua led the first military campaign against the Canaanites in the sparsely populated central highlands, northwest of the Dead Sea. The initial object of the attack was the ancient stronghold of Jericho. The Israelite force marched around the city once a day for six days. On the seventh day they marched around it seven times, then blasted trumpets and shouted. In response the walls of Jericho collapsed, allowing the invaders to destroy the city (Josh. 6).

The Israelites then attempted to conquer the nearby city of Ai, where they met with their first defeat. The reason for the failure was that Achan, one of the Israelite soldiers, had kept some booty from the invasion of Jericho—an action which violated God's orders to destroy everything in the city. After Achan was executed, the Israelites were able to destroy Ai (Josh. 7–8).

Not all of the Canaanites tried to resist Israel's invasion. One group, the Gibeonites, avoided destruction by deceiving the Israelites into making a covenant of peace with them

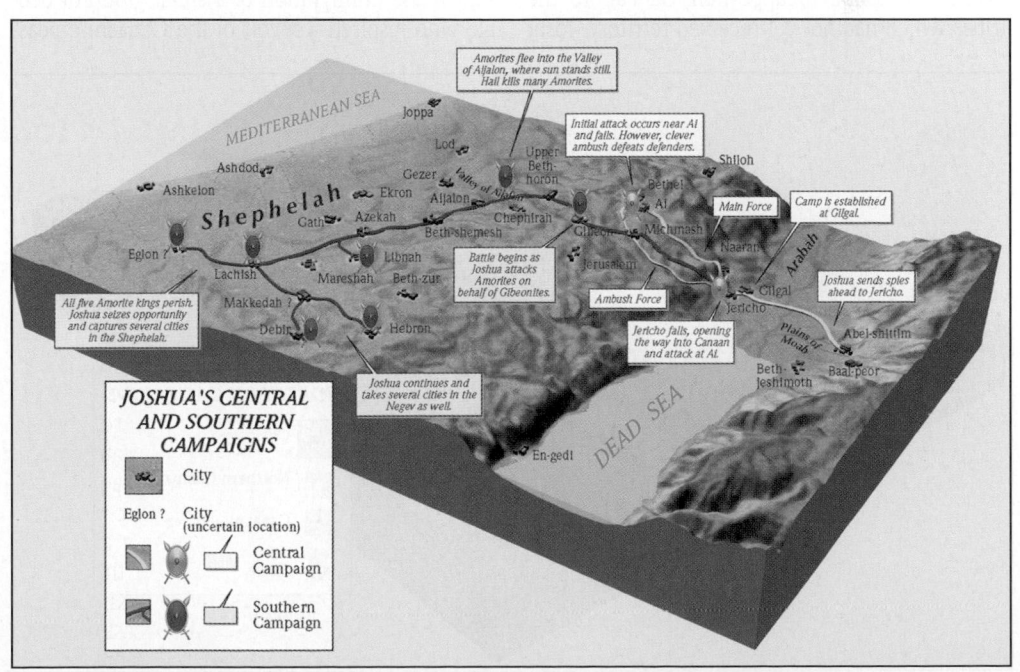

JOSHUA'S CENTRAL AND SOUTHERN CAMPAIGNS

(Josh. 9). Alarmed by the defection of the Gibeonites to Israel, a group of southern Canaanite kings, led by Adoni-zedek of Jerusalem, formed a coalition against the invading force. The kings threatened to attack the Gibeonites, causing Joshua to come to the defense of his new allies. Because of supernatural intervention, the Israelites were able to defeat the coalition. Joshua then launched a southern campaign that resulted in the capture of numerous Canaanite cities (Josh. 10).

Joshua's third and last military campaign was in northern Canaan. In that region King Jabin of Hazor formed a coalition of neighboring kings to battle with the Israelites. Joshua made a surprise attack upon them at the waters of Merom, utterly defeating his foe (Josh. 11:1-15).

The invasion of Canaan met with phenomenal success; large portions of the land fell to the Israelites (Josh. 11:16–12:24). However, some areas still remained outside their control, such as the heavily populated land along the coast and several major Canaanite cities like Jerusalem (Josh. 13:1-5; 15:63; Judg. 1). The Israelites struggled for centuries to control these areas.

Israelite Settlement The Israelite tribes slowly settled Canaan without completely removing the native population. Even though some sections of the land remained to be conquered, God instructed Joshua to apportion Canaan to the tribes which had not yet received territory (Josh.

13:7). Following the land allotments, Israel began to occupy its territory. Judges 1 describes the settlement as a slow process whereby individual tribes struggled to remove the Canaanites. In the final analysis the tribes had limited success in driving out the native population (Judg. 1). As a result, Israel was plagued for centuries by the infiltration of Canaanite elements into its religion (Judg. 2:1-5).

Conquest Reconstructions Scholars have proposed varying models for understanding the conquest of Canaan. The previous description of the nature of the conquest and settlement presents a traditional, harmonizing approach to the interpretation of the biblical material. Some scholars have proposed other interpretive models. One is the immigration model, which assumes that there was no real conquest of Canaan but that peoples of diverse origins gradually immigrated into the area after 1300 B.C. They eventually took control of the city-states and became the nation of Israel. The difficulty with this model is that it ignores the general biblical picture of God constituting the nation of Israel in the desert and leading them to invade the promised land.

Other scholars have put forth a revolt model for understanding the nature of the conquest. This approach suggests that there was no major invasion of Canaan from an outside force but simply the immigration of a small group of people who inspired a revolt of the Canaanite peas-

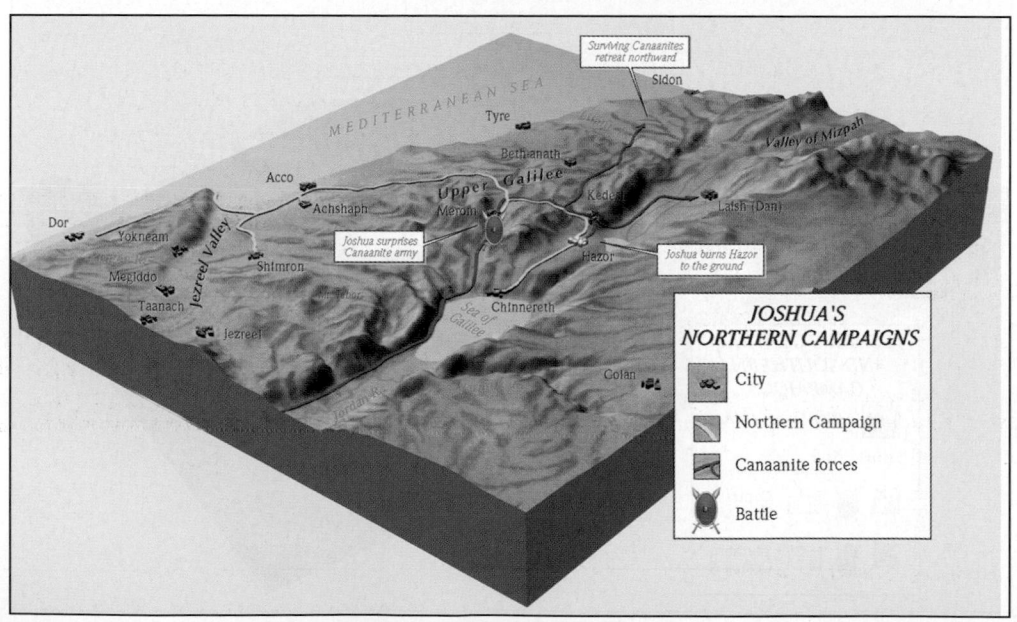

Surviving Canaanites retreat northward

Sidon

MEDITERRANEAN SEA

Tyre

Valley of Mizpah

Bethanath

Acco

Upper Galilee

Kedesh

Laish (Dan)

Dor

Achshaph

Meron

Yokneam

Jezreel Valley

Joshua surprises Canaanite army

Hazor

Joshua burns Hazor to the ground

Megiddo

Shimron

Taanach

Sea of Galilee

Chinnereth

Jezreel

Golan

JOSHUA'S NORTHERN CAMPAIGNS

City

Northern Campaign

Canaanite forces

Battle

Ruins of a temple at Hazor destroyed by Joshua in the conquest of Canaan.

ants. The result was the overthrow of the feudal city-state kings and the emergence of what became the Israelite nation. This interpretation of the conquest diverges from the biblical record in its claim that the bulk of the population of Israel was made up of former Canaanite peasants. It also reveals a tendency to read back into Israelite history modern Marxist theory about the struggle between classes. The best approach to understanding the conquest of Canaan is one that is rooted in the biblical materials. See *Achan; Ai; Exodus; Gilgal; Jericho; Joshua.*

Bob R. Ellis and E. Ray Clendenen

CONSCIENCE Human capacity to reflect upon the degree to which one's behavior has conformed to moral norms. For the believer these norms should be those established by God. The word does not occur in the OT, although clearly there are times when the concept is present (1 Sam. 25:31 NLT). The primary background for conscience, however, is Greek. While it originally referred simply to one's self-awareness, conscience gradually came to be associated with moral awareness. The Jewish writer Philo (ca. A.D. 40) is probably the first to state explicitly that the conscience is given by God to reprove unacceptable behavior.

In the NT two-thirds of the occurrences of the term are in Paul's writings. The majority of these are in his letters to the Corinthians, which hints to some that the Corinthians were the ones who had first used the term in a letter to Paul. Paul states that his "boasting" about his ministry is the witness of his conscience (2 Cor. 1:12; 5:11). He goes on to state that this witness is based on the fact that he has conducted himself in sincerity and purity in the grace of God, not in

"fleshly" wisdom, before both unbelievers ("the world") and the believing recipients of his letter (Acts 23:1; 24:16). Thus, the conscience examines both one's behavior, as well as one's motives. If one thinks and acts consistently with what one's conscience dictates, then a believer has reason to believe that others will ultimately respond positively to one's message (1 Pet. 3:16).

Weak Conscience In 1 Cor. 8:7 the phrase "weak conscience" does not refer to a conscience that is less sensitive than it should be. In context, Paul refers to persons who may know intellectually there is only one God, yet when they eat meat in an idol temple, they still feel as if they are worshiping an idol. Thus, a "weak conscience" refers to a conscience that may be overly sensitive or one that does not act in concert with what the person knows to be true. Nevertheless, other believers, then, must not influence the "weak" to engage in any practice that would go against or "defile" the conscience (1 Cor. 8:7-10).

The conscience should not limit the believer's freedom in Christ, however. In 1 Cor. 10:25 Paul addresses the practice of eating meat purchased in the market which probably had been slaughtered in an idol temple. Paul states believers may eat this meat and should not ask questions "because of conscience." He means that consumption of this meat is permissible, and the conscience must not dictate otherwise. In matters of indifference (*diaphoros*) the conscience should not limit Christian freedom. Those with "seared" consciences are those who deceive others by prohibiting actions that are entirely permissible (1 Tim. 4:2-3). The conscience, then, is not one's ultimate judge. Paul uses the verbal form of the word when he states in 1 Cor. 4:4 (HCSB), "I am not conscious (*sunoida*) of anything against myself, but I am not justified by this. The One who evaluates me is the Lord." As Martin Luther pointed out, the conscience must be obeyed, but the conscience must be "captive" to God's Word.

The Conscience of Unbelievers In Rom. 2:15 Paul states that the consciences and thoughts of Gentiles, who do not know the law of God, act as witnesses in both an accusatory and apologetic manner. While the focus is on past behavior, it appears that the conscience here could direct future conduct as well. Nevertheless, verse 16 makes clear that the ultimate verdict will be at the last judgment. While the conscience can be an important component in evaluation of thoughts and behavior, both believers and unbelievers stand ultimately under God's judgment.

C. Hal Freeman, Jr.

CONSCIENTIOUS OBJECTORS While the Bible does not speak directly to the issue of conscientious objectors, it does offer principles which can help an individual determine whether it is proper to invoke the status of conscientious objector in any given situation.

The Bible entreats Christians to be good citizens, and in principle this involves subjection to the governing authorities (Rom. 13:1-7; Titus 3:1; 1 Pet. 2:13-17). As much as it depends on the ability of each individual believer, Christians are commanded to live peaceably with others (Rom. 12:18).

At times Christians find it necessary to disobey the laws of men in order to follow higher standards set by God (Acts 4:19-20; 5:29). Each individual is given a conscience which, when purified by God, helps that person determine a proper course of action within a given set of circumstances (Rom. 14:4; 1 Tim. 1:5,19; Heb. 13:18; 1 Pet. 3:16). When Shadrach, Meshach, and Abednego (Dan. 3:16-18), Daniel (Dan. 6:10-16), the apostles (Acts 5:40-42), and Paul (Acts 25:11) chose to disobey the civil government, they willingly accepted the consequences of their actions.

The issue of a "just war" is complex. While at times God called His people to battle (Josh. 6:2-5; Judg. 1:1-2), the Bible records other instances when war was to be opposed (cp. Isa. 7:1-16; 22:8b-11). It is incumbent on every believer to trust God for guidance in each situation.

Paul H. Wright

CONSECRATION Persons or things being separated to or belonging to God. They are holy or sacred. They are set apart for the service of God. The Hebrew *qadesh* and Greek *hagiazo* are translated by several different English words: holy, consecrate, hallow, sanctify, dedicate.

Old Testament God is said to be *qadesh* or "holy." When persons or things were "consecrated," they were separated to or belonged to God. "You shall be holy, for I the Lord your God am holy" (Lev. 19:2 NASB). "You shall be to Me a kingdom of priests and a holy nation" (Exod. 19:6 NASB). When persons were "consecrated,"

they were set apart to live according to God's demands and in His service.

In the OT the ordination of persons to the service of God is indicated by the phrase "to fill the hand." This phrase is usually translated "consecrate" or "ordain."

Numbers 6:1-21 sets forth the vow of the Nazirite. *Nazir* from which Nazirite is derived, means "to separate" and is translated "consecrate" in Num. 6:7,9,12.

New Testament This ethical understanding of God's holiness is found throughout the NT. In Matt. 23:16-24 Jesus criticized the scribes and Pharisees on the basis of their neglect of justice, mercy, and faith. He said it is "the altar that sanctifies the gift" (Matt. 23:19 HCSB). The cause to which persons give themselves determines the nature of the sacrifice. When the cause is God's, the gift is consecrated. Jesus' mission was to sanctify persons. Paul said that Christians are called to be "saints," and their sanctification comes through Christ.

H. Page Lee

CONSERVATISM Disposition to appreciate, conserve, and foster in the present teachings and values that are rooted in the past. In the Bible, conservatism is most clearly seen in the attitude that Paul took toward faith and Scripture. Paul recognized that he was heir to a body of sacred writings and traditions which must be learned, believed, and carefully taught to others (1 Cor. 11:2; 2 Thess. 2:15; 2 Tim. 1:13-14; 3:14-15; Titus 1:9).

The Pharisees, who placed great stress on observing the traditions of their elders (Mark 7:3-4; cp. Deut. 6:6-7; Prov. 1:8; 4:1-4), criticized Jesus for His apparent lack of conservatism (Mark 7:5). Jesus' response was to distinguish between human traditions and the words of God (Mark 7:6-13), the latter which, by implication, were intended to enliven men's hearts in a way that mere tradition could not.

CONSOLATION Comfort which eases grief and pain. The Hebrew terms are closely related to the words for compassion—*nichum, nocham.* Job's integrity with God's instructions gave him consolation despite his grief and pain (Job 6:10). David sent servants to console Hanun, king of Ammon, after his father died (2 Sam. 10:1-2). People brought food and drink to console the grieving (Jer. 16:7; cp. John 11:19). God's response to prayer brings consolation to the worried soul (Ps. 94:19). Even as God destroyed Jerusalem, He provided consolation in the person of faithful survivors (Ezek. 14:22-23).

Israel's ultimate hope was the consolation that only the Messiah could bring. The faithful waited expectantly for this (Luke 2:25; cp. Isa. 40:1-2). Those who trust in riches rather than in the coming of the Son of Man have all the consolation they will receive (Luke 6:24). Believers receive consolation through the ministry of proclamation (1 Cor. 14:3). See *Compassion.*

CONSTELLATIONS See *Heaven; Stars.*

CONSUMMATION End of history and the fulfillment of God's kingdom promises. The term comes from Dan. 9:27 speaking of the complete destruction God had decreed on the prince who threatened His sanctuary. See *Eschatology.*

CONSUMPTION Wasting or emaciating disease that would be inflicted upon those who disobeyed the law (Lev. 26:16; Deut. 28:22). The disease has been identified as pulmonary tuberculosis (*phthisis*) or as the side effects of wasting and emaciation from prolonged bouts of malarial fever. Some have even suggested cancer. The KJV uses consumption in Isa. 10:22; 28:22 where modern versions translate "destruction."

CONTAINERS AND VESSELS See *Basin; Basket; Glass; Pottery; Vessels and Utensils.*

CONTENTMENT Internal satisfaction which does not demand changes in external circumstances. The NT expresses this with the Greek word *arkeo* and its derivatives. Hebrews 13:5 summarizes the teaching in advising believers to be free of the love of money and to depend on God's promise not to forsake His people. Food and lodging should be enough for the godly (1 Tim. 6:6-10; cp. Matt. 6:34; contrast Luke 12:19). The believer can be content no matter what the outward circumstances (Phil. 4:11-13). Believers are content to know the Father (John 14:8-9) and depend on His grace (2 Cor. 12:9-10; cp. 2 Cor. 9:8-11).

CONTRITE To be humble and repentant before God, crushed by the sense of guilt and sinfulness. This OT concept is expressed by the Hebrew word *daqaq* and its derivatives. The basic meaning is to be crushed or beaten to pieces. This

meaning appears in the crushing of the golden calf (Exod. 32:20) or the crushing of grain during threshing (Isa. 28:28). Crushing enemies is a frequent theme (Ps. 89:10). God taught Israel not to crush the poor (Prov. 22:22). Indeed, the king is to crush the oppressor who harms the poor (Ps. 72:4). In Ps. 9:9 the poor are referred to as the crushed (literal translation) and assured that God is their "refuge" (cp. Ps. 143:3). They can thus come to God in prayer, knowing what God wants is a broken spirit and a contrite heart (Ps. 51:17). God will revive the spirit of such a one (Isa. 57:15; cp. 66:2; Ps. 34:18).

God's plan of salvation rests on God being pleased to crush His Suffering Servant (Isa. 53:10 NASB). This One will finally be exalted (Isa. 52:13).

CONVERSATION Communication between two or more people (Jer. 38:27 in modern translations) or personal conduct or behavior in KJV's now obsolete use of the term (Ps. 37:14; Gal. 1:13; James 3:3).

CONVERSION Turning or returning of a person to God, a crucial biblical and theological concept. The word itself is relatively rare in Scripture. In the OT the word is *shub*, translated usually as "turn" or "return." In the NT the basic verb is *epistrepho*, and the noun is *epistrephe*. This word group is more similar to our common conception of conversion. *Metanoeo* (and the related noun) is usually translated "repent(ance)." Theologically, "conversion" is usually understood as the experiential aspect of salvation, founded on the logically prior divine work of regeneration (the "new birth"; John 3:3,5-8; Titus 3:5). It refers to a decisive turning from sin to faith in Jesus Christ as the only means of salvation (John 14:6; Acts 4:12; 1 Tim. 2:5). It is a once-for-all unrepeatable and decisive act. One is either converted or not. There is no middle or third way. Humanly speaking, conversion is the initiation of the overall process of salvation. In only one case is *epistrepho* used in the NT of a believer "returning" to obedience and faith—when Peter "turned back" after denying Christ (Luke 22:32).

In the OT the concept of conversion occurs in a number of ways. (1) One can speak of a group conversion such as that of a pagan city like Nineveh in the past (Jon. 3:7-10) or the nation of Egypt (Isa. 19:22) or all the nations in the future

(Ps. 22:27). More commonly the concept applies to a turning of Israel back to God. Israel's conversion is marked by the making of a covenant and a renewed commitment to loyalty and faithfulness to God, whom they had forsaken in the past (Josh. 24:25; 2 Kings 11:4; 2 Chron. 15:12; 29:10; 34:31). (2) There are accounts of individuals turning to God (Ps. 51:13; 2 Kings 5:15; 23:25; 2 Chron. 33:12-13). (3) There are even occasions when it is God who is said to be the one who turns or returns to His people (Isa. 63:17; Amos 9:14).

The psalmist affirms that the word of God is essential in conversion (19:7). Isaiah connects conversion with righteousness (1:27), healing (6:10), mercy and pardon (55:7). Jeremiah identifies conversion with the putting away of idols (4:1-2). Conversion is a genuine turning to God, which involves repentance, humility, a change of heart, and a sincere seeking after God (Deut. 4:29-30; 30:2,10; Isa. 6:9-10; Jer. 24:7). It results in a new knowledge of God and of His purposes (2 Chron. 33:13; Jer. 24:7).

In the NT a key text is Matt. 18:3, "unless you are converted and become like children, you will never enter the kingdom of heaven" (HCSB). Conversion is possible for anyone who comes to God with simple trust like a child before his parents.

In Acts we discover calls to be converted as well as the record of a number of conversion experiences. Peter connected conversion with repentance and having one's sins blotted out (3:19). Acts 11:20-21 affirms that believing in Jesus is involved in conversion. Paul affirms at Lystra that conversion involves turning from useless things to the living God (14:15, cp. 1 Thess. 1:9; 1 Pet. 2:25). The only occurrence of the noun form of the word "conversion" in the NT describes Gentiles coming to salvation and the great joy it caused (15:3; cp. Luke 15:7,10).

In recounting his own conversion, Paul said the Lord commissioned him to preach to the Gentiles in order "to open their eyes that they may turn from darkness to light and from the power of Satan to God, that they may receive forgiveness of sins and a share among those who are sanctified by faith in Me" (Acts 26:18 HCSB). There are conversions of various groups recorded in Acts: Jews at Pentecost (2:22-41), Samaritans (8:5-25), Gentiles (10:44-48), and disciples of John (19:1-7). There are also the conversion experiences of individuals. Some are quite dramatic with accompanying physical manifestations (e.g. Paul, 9:5-18; Cornelius, 10:44-48; also 15:7-35; note 15:19; the Philippian jailer, 16:29-34). Others are quiet and calm (the man from Ethiopia, 8:26-40; Lydia, 16:14). It is also interesting to note that Luke has three accounts of the conversion of Paul (9:5-18; 22:6-21; 26:12-23) as well as of the Gentile Cornelius (10:44-48; 11:15-18; 15:7-35). God makes no racial distinction concerning those who may turn to Him. James adds a word of encouragement to the faithful evangelist, informing us that "whoever turns a sinner from the error of his way will save his life from death and cover a multitude of sins" (James 5:20).

In a biblical theology, conversion has two sides, divine and human. It represents the infusion of divine grace into human life and a resurrection from spiritual death to eternal life. We can turn only through the power of God's grace and the calling of the Holy Spirit. Conversion is an event that initiates a process. It signifies the moment in time we are moved to respond to Jesus Christ in repentance and faith. It begins the sanctifying work of the Holy Spirit within us, purifying us and conforming us to the image of Christ. Conversion is the beginning of our journey to Christian maturity. We can and should make progress toward perfection, but we can never attain it in this life. Even the converted need to maintain a life of ongoing repentance, and even the sanctified need to turn again to Christ and be cleansed anew (cp. Ps. 51:10-12; Luke 17:3-4; 22:32; Rom. 13:14; Eph. 4:22-24; 1 John 1:6-2:2; Rev. 2:4-5, 16; 3:19). See *Regeneration; Repentance.*   *Daniel L. Akin*

CONVICTION Sense of guilt and shame leading to repentance. The words "convict" and "conviction" do not appear in the KJV. The word "convince" (KJV) comes closest to expressing the meaning of "conviction."

The Hebrew word *yakah* expresses the idea of conviction. It means "to argue with," "to prove," "to correct." God may be the subject and persons the object (Job 22:4), or a person may be the subject who convicts another person (Ezek. 3:26).

The Greek term meaning "convict" is *elencho.* It means "to convict" "to refute," "to confute," usually with the suggestion of shame of the person convicted. Young ministers like Timothy and Titus had the responsibility of "convicting" (rebuking, refuting) those under their charge (1 Tim. 5:20; 2 Tim. 4:2; Titus 1:13; 2:15). John the Baptist "convicted" Herod Antipas because of his illicit marriage to Herodias, his brother's wife (Luke 3:19). No one could convict Jesus of sin (John 8:46).

John 16:8-11 is a classic passage on conviction. The Holy Spirit is the One who convicts, and the (inhabited) world is the object of conviction. A study of this passage yields the following results. First, conviction for sin is the result of the Holy Spirit awakening humanity to a sense of guilt and condemnation because of sin and unbelief. Second, more than mental conviction is intended. The total person is involved. This can lead to action based on a sense of conviction. Third, the conviction results in hope, not despair. Once individuals are made aware of their estranged relationship with God, they are challenged and encouraged to mend that relationship. The conviction not only implies the exposure of sin (despair) but also a call to repentance (hope). See *Forgiveness; Repentance; Sin.*

Glenn McCoy

CONVOCATION, HOLY See *Festivals.*

COOKING AND HEATING Only in recent times have cooking and heating become separated, so that central heating, for example, works independently of the microwave. In Bible times the means of heating was the means of cooking. Heating was by open fire, and cooking was done at the same time. This is not to say that fire was always produced in the same way or that the methods of cooking were identical; it is the differences that provide the interest.

The basic focus for cooking and heating was the open fire. The Bedouin encampment could be recognized by the fires at night outside and in front of the tents. The fire was laid in a hollow scooped out of the ground or on flat stones. The fire was ignited by friction or by firing tinder with sparks (Isa. 50:11). Many of the stories of the Bible were preserved, originally as folk memories, remembered word-for-word around the campfires lit for warmth on cool evenings in the arid climate or in the high terrain. The people of the Bible were fortunate because the white broom plant was useful in making fires. Its embers stayed hot for a long time and could be fanned into a blaze even when they looked dead. Less useful but equally combustible materials were thorns (Isa. 10:17), dried grass (Matt. 6:30), charcoal (John 18:18 NRSV, HCSB), sticks, and dried animal dung (Ezek. 4:15).

When people of the Bible moved from tents and settled in houses, fires for cooking were still generally lit out-of-doors. If the house had a courtyard, the fire was made somewhere in the corner as the farthest place away from the smoke. Very few houses had a chimney; and even though the fire was put into an earthenware box or was contained in a metal brazier, there was no exit for the smoke. Life must have been quite miserable during the damp and cold winters of the Holy Land. A fire was necessary to keep warm, but the only window needed rough curtaining with a blanket. The smoke had little space to exit, so it blackened the rough ceiling and made the householders choke and splutter. Later better homes were provided with a chimney, and the houses of royalty actually had a form of central heating in which the heat of underfloor fires was ducted underneath paved rooms.

In patriarchal times food consisted basically of bread, milk products, meat, and honey. Wine was the most common drink. Cooking, therefore, consisted of the preparation of such foods. Grain (spelt, barley, or wheat—preferred in that order) had first to be cleaned and selected. It was necessary to remove any poisonous seeds such as darnel (tares, Matt. 13:25). Then it was ground either in a pestle and mortar or in a hand mill. The hand mill was made of two disks of stone about 12 inches in diameter. The lower stone had an upright wooden peg at its center, and the upper stone had a hole through the center that fitted over the peg. A handle fixed to the upper stone allowed it to be rotated about the peg.

Middle Eastern woman sifting grain with a type of sifting frame.

Grain was fed through the central hole. As the upper stone was rotated, the grain was crushed, coming out as flour between the two stones and falling onto a cloth placed below. Any woman could manage a hand mill, but it was much easier if two women shared in the task, sitting with the mill between them and alternately turning the handle (Matt. 24:41). It was a chore and was therefore given to the slaves when this was possible (Lam. 5:13), but it was a chore which made a sound always associated with home (Jer. 25:10). The flour was mixed with water and formed into dough cakes in a trough called a kneading trough. Salt was added, and most days of the year, leaven was added too. Leaven was fermented dough from the previous day's baking. It took longer to penetrate the dough than if fresh yeast was used, but that was reserved for the time following the festival of unleavened bread, and the normal method was just as certain. Some of the grain was finely ground and was given a special name. It was the finely ground flour which was used in sacrificial offerings (Exod. 29:40).

Cooking consisted of the application of (relatively) clean heat. In some cases large flat stones were put in the hot fire. When the flames had died down, the dough was placed on the hot stones. In other cases, where the fire was placed in a hole in the ground, the dough was actually placed on the hot sides of the depression. Another common method was to invert a shallow pottery bowl over the fire and place the dough cakes on the bowl's convex surface. It was many years before the pottery "oven" was invented. It consisted of a truncated cone that was placed over the fire. The cakes of bread were then placed on the inside of the cone at the top, away from the flames. Not until Roman times were pottery ovens in use where the firebox was separated from the cooking area by a clay dividing piece. This method was maintained for centuries. The cooking resulted in different shapes of bread. Some loaves were paper-thin and were most suitable for scooping food from a common pot (Matt. 26:23). Other loaves (John 6:9) were heavier, like biscuits, and a still heavier loaf is described in Judg. 7:13 where it knocked down a tent.

As communities grew larger, the baker developed his trade and provided facilities for the whole village. His oven was tunnel shaped. Shelves lined the sides for the dough, and fires were lit on the floor. It was possible for the housewife to take her own dough to be cooked in the communal oven and possible for the children to collect hot embers at the end of the day for kindling fires in their homes (Hos. 7:4-7).

Bread is being cooked in an outdoor truncated cone-shaped "pottery oven."

Jeremiah received a bread ration from the local bakery while he was in prison (Jer. 37:21).

Not all of the grain was ground. A metal baking sheet was sometimes placed over the hot fire and grain put on the metal surface. The grain "popped" and provided what the Bible calls parched corn (1 Sam. 25:18), which was used as an occasional snack.

The basic food to go with the bread was vegetable soup prepared from beans, green vegetables, and herbs. A large cooking pot was put directly on the fire and was used for this purpose. The pottage that Jacob gave to Esau was lentil soup (Gen. 25:30). It was eaten by forming a scoop with a piece of bread, and dipping it in the central pot. When soups were made, the cook had to remember that ritual law forbade the mixing of seeds for this purpose (based on Lev. 19:19). When a special occasion was called for, as at the arrival of a guest, meat would be added to the stock. Most meat was boiled or stewed in this way and was taken either from the herd or in the hunt. Boiling was the easiest way to deal with meat because ritual law required that the blood should be drained from the animal (Lev. 17:10-11). It was therefore easiest to cut up the carcass before putting it in a stew. Meat was normally roasted only at festivals and very special days such as Passover (Exod. 12:8-9). It was sometimes roasted on a spit that was speared through the animal and supported over the fire. Since the main altar at temple and tabernacle was a kind of barbecue in which the carcass was laid on a grill above a fire, it would be unusual if similar arrangements were not sometimes used domestically. Meat was always available from the sheep and goats of the flock, but hunting wild animals that came up from the jungle in the Jordan Valley was popular. Veal was served to Abraham's guests in Gen. 18:7, while Gideon's guests ate goat meat (Judg. 6:19). Milk, too, was used as a basic cookery material; but it was forbidden to stew a kid in its mother's milk (Exod. 23:19). The reason for this is not clear. Guesses have been made that the commandment was given for "humanitarian" reasons or that the practice was somehow associated with magic in contemporary religious life.

By the time the Jewish people had settled in the promised land, additions had been made to their diet. While they were in Egypt, they had gotten used to some of the food which was popular in that country—cucumber, garlic, leeks,

Arab woman using an ancient hand mill to grind grain.

onions, and melons (Num. 11:5). Some of these plants were uncooked and were used to eat with bread or as a salad. Others were cooked to give additional flavor to the cooking pot. The leek was a salad leek, and the cucumber was the "snake cucumber" which was common in Egypt. With the growth of trade under the Israelite monarchy, these items became fairly common in the diet. In addition to onions and garlic, herbs were used in cooking to add to the flavor. Salt was collected during the hot season from the shores of the Dead Sea after evaporation had left it behind. Salt was used for preservation as well as for seasoning. Liberal use was made of dill, cumin (Isa. 28:25-27) and coriander, and sugar. Spicy chutneys were also prepared to give added flavor to the food. The charoseth used at the Passover was chutney made of dates, figs, raisins, and vinegar.

The big difference when the settlement took place was that the Jews began to use fruit from the trees. They built plantations and orchards. Most significant in this respect was the olive. After the olives had been beaten from the trees and crushed in the olive press, the olive oil was used instead of water for binding the flour and for frying. A whole new era of cookery was opened. The woman from Zarephath who cared for Elijah needed only some flour (meal) and some olive oil to be able to survive through the time of famine (1 Kings 17:12). Other trees provided basic food which was eaten either raw or stewed—figs, sycamore figs, pomegranates, and nuts.

Milk has already been mentioned as a liquid for stewing meat and vegetables. It was also drunk for itself and used in the preparation of other foods. Some milk was fermented to produce yogurt. It is in fact still called "milk" in some versions of the Bible (Judg. 4:19). Milk was used to make cheese (1 Sam. 17:18), and when placed in a skin bag to be shaken and squeezed by turn, butter was produced. Buttermilk was presumably used as well, but there is no mention of this in the Bible.

By NT times fish was a common addition to the diet. Much of the fish was imported from the Phoenicians, who caught fish in the Mediterranean. Fishing industry also thrived on the Sea of Galilee. Fish was most commonly grilled over a fire (John 21:9) or was salted and eaten later. Magdala, the home of Mary Magdalene, was a well-known center for the salting of fish.

Wine was always available, even among the nomadic people. When entry to the promised land took place, it was possible for the people of the Bible to go into viticulture in a big way, and the preparation of the grapes was an important aspect of cooking. Some grapes were dried in the hot sun to become raisins—a substantial snack when they were needed. Most of the grapes however were crushed to obtain their juice. This was a long "cooking" operation. Picked between July and September, the grapes were placed in a winepress—a stone "tank" cut out of the ground with an exit hole in the bottom where the juice ran out and could be collected outside. The juice stood in the collecting vessels for about six weeks to allow natural fermentation to take place. It was then carefully poured off to leave any sludge undisturbed in the bottom and was placed in another jar, sealed except for a small hole to allow gases to escape until the fermentation process was complete. Wine was the most natural and safest drink because water supplies were often suspect. Not all of the wine was used for drinking. The housewife sometimes boiled up the juice to make a simple grape jelly or jam, which was spread on the bread. This was so plentiful that it may well be one of the senses of "honey" which is referred to in the phrase "land flowing with milk and honey" (Exod. 3:8,17).

Ralph Gower

COOS (Cō´ ŏs) (KJV) See *Cos.*

COPING Traditional translation of a Hebrew architectural term in 1 Kings 7:9. The meaning of the Hebrew word is unknown. NIV, TEV reads "eaves." Recent scholars see it as the "framework," meaning a row of stone or wood headers and stretchers above the various levels of the foundation on which bricks were laid.

Bread being cooked on an inverted shallow skillet over an open flame.

COPPER Reddish metal that can be shaped easily by hammering and can be polished to a shining finish.

While gold was probably the first metal humans used, the oldest tools and utensils recovered by archaeologists in Bible lands are of copper, usually combined with some alloy. The word "copper" appears in the KJV only in Ezra 8:27 and in the word "coppersmith" in 2 Tim. 4:14. On the other hand, the word "brass" appears about 100 times in the KJV. In most instances the same Hebrew word is translated as "bronze" in the RSV. Copper had limited use by itself in Bible times. Combining copper with from two to 16 percent tin produced bronze that was hard enough to be used for weapons, armor, utensils, and sculpture.

Cyprus was the chief source of copper in the Mediterranean world, but Egypt probably secured some from the Sinai Peninsula. Besides the usual promised bounty of Canaan, Deuteronomy said it would include "a land whose stones are iron, and out of whose hills you can dig copper" (8:9 RSV; cp. NASB, NIV). The Hebrews mined a limited supply in the Arabah, the region south of the Dead Sea. Palestinian remains of copper mines have been found only in that area, and archaeologists have discovered at the north end of the Gulf of Aqaba the remains of copper mines. The original excavator thought these were built by Solomon for processing both copper and iron, but subsequent research has shown them to be earlier than Solomon.

In the OT the Hebrew word for copper may refer to that basic metal or to bronze. If an object described as copper could be shaped by hammering, it was probably made of pure copper. However, if the metal for an object had to be melted and cast into a form, the word meant bronze. Thus, the fixtures and furnishings of the tabernacle were of bronze (Exod. 26:11–39:39). So also were the two huge pillars, the mammoth tank, and other major features for the temple designed by Hiram of Tyre for Solomon (1 Kings 7:14-47). Also before the days of iron, bronze was the best metal for weapons and armor, as shown in the equipment of Goliath (1 Sam. 17:5-6). While not considered a precious metal,

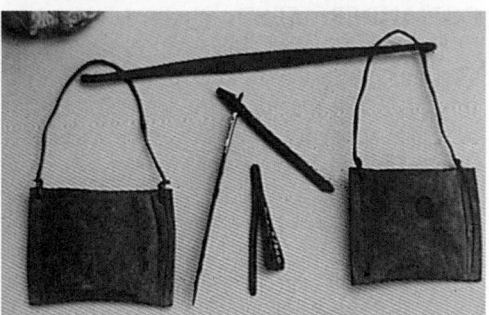

Miniature copper tools for shawabtis (small god symbols) from Egypt, New Kingdom.

bronze was a significant prize of conquest (2 Kings 25:13-15). See *Minerals and Metals.*

William J. Fallis

COPPERSMITH Term applied in ancient times to metalworkers or blacksmiths in general. The name Kenite means "smith." A certain Alexander was a coppersmith who caused trouble in the early church (2 Tim. 4:14). See *Kenites.*

COR Large liquid and dry measure of unknown quantity. See *Weights and Measures.*

CORAL Calcareous or horny skeletal deposit produced by anthozoan polyps. The red or precious coral found exclusively in the Mediterranean and Adriatic seas (*Corallium rubrum*) is the type known to the biblical writers. The value of wisdom surpasses the value of gold, silver, a variety of precious stones, crystal, or coral (Job 28:12-18). Coral was among the goods of trade between Israel and Edom (Ezek. 27:16).

CORBAN (Côr´ băn) Gift particularly designated for the Lord and so forbidden for any other use (Mark 7:11). Jesus referred to some persons who mistakenly and deliberately avoided giving needed care to their parents by declaring as "corban" any money or goods that could otherwise be used to provide such care. Thus what began as a religious act of offering eventually functioned as a curse, denying benefit to one's own parents. See *Sacrifice and Offering.*

Gene Henderson

CORD See *Lace.*

CORE (Cō´ rə) KJV transliteration of Greek spelling of Korah in Jude 11. See *Korah.*

CORIANDER SEED Herb (*Coriandrum sativum*) of the carrot family with aromatic fruits used much as poppy, caraway, or sesame seeds are today. The manna of the wilderness period was like coriander seed either in appearance (Exod. 16:31) or taste (Num. 11:7).

CORINTH One of four prominent centers in the NT account of the early church, the other three being Jerusalem, Antioch of Syria, and Ephesus. Paul's first extended ministry in one city was at Corinth. On his first visit to Corinth, he remained for at least 18 months (Acts 18:1-18). Paul's three longest letters are associated with Corinth. First and Second Corinthians were written to Corinth, and Romans, from Corinth. Prominent Christian leaders associated with Corinth include Aquila, Priscilla, Silas, Timothy, Apollos, and Titus.

History of Corinth Located on the southwest end of the isthmus that joined the southern part of the Greek peninsula with the mainland to the north, the city was on an elevated plain at the foot of Acrocorinth, a rugged hill reaching 1,886 feet above sea level. Corinth was a maritime city located between two important seaports: the port of Lechaion on the Gulf of Corinth about two miles to the north and the port of Cenchreae

on the Saronic Gulf about six miles east of Corinth.

Corinth was an important city long before becoming a Roman colony in 44 B.C. In addition to the extant works of early writers, modern archaeology has contributed to knowledge of ancient Corinth.

The discovery of stone implements and pottery indicates that the area was populated in the late Stone Age. Metal tools have been found that reveal occupation during the early Bronze Age (between 3000 B.C. and 2000 B.C.). The rising importance of Corinth during the classical period began with the Dorian invasion about 1000 B.C.

Located at the foot of Acrocorinth and at the southwest end of the isthmus, Corinth was relatively easy to defend. The Corinthians controlled the east-west trade across the isthmus as well as trade between Peloponnesus and the area of Greece to the north. The city experienced rapid growth and prosperity, even colonizing Siracuse on Sicily and the Island of Corcyra on the eastern shore of the Adriatic. Pottery and bronze were exported throughout the Mediterranean world.

For a century (about 350 to 250 B.C.) Corinth was the largest and most prosperous city of mainland Greece. Later, as a member of the Achaean League, Corinth clashed with Rome. Finally, the

The columns of the temple of Apollo at Corinth.

city was destroyed in 146 B.C. L. Mummius, the Roman consul, burned the city, killed the men, and sold the women and children into slavery. For a hundred years the city was desolate.

Julius Caesar rebuilt the city in 44 B.C., and it quickly became an important city in the Roman Empire. An overland ship road across the isthmus connected the ports of Lechaion and Cenchreae. Cargo from large ships was unloaded, transported across the isthmus, and reloaded on other ships. Small ships were moved across on a system of rollers. Ships were able, therefore, to avoid 200 miles of stormy travel around the southern part of the Greek peninsula.

Description of Corinth in Paul's Day When Paul visited Corinth, the rebuilt city was little more than a century old. It had become, however, an important metropolitan center. Except where the city was protected by Acrocorinth, a wall about six miles in circumference surrounded it. The Lechaion road entered the city from the north, connecting it with the port on the Gulf of Corinth. As the road entered the city, it widened to more than 20 feet with walks on either side. From the southern part of the city a road ran southeast to Cenchreae.

Approaching the city from the north, the Lechaion road passed through the Propylaea, the beautiful gate marking the entrance into the agora (market). The agora was rectangular and contained many shops. A line of shops divided the agora into a northern and a southern section. Near the center of this dividing line the Bema was located. The Bema consisted of a large elevated speaker's platform and benches on the back and sides. Here is probably the place Paul was brought before Gallio (Acts 18:12-17).

Religions of Corinth Although the restored city of Paul's day was a Roman city, the inhabitants continued to worship Greek gods. West of the Lechaion road and north of the agora stood the old temple of Apollo. Probably partially destroyed by Mummius in 146 B.C., seven of the original 38 columns still stand. On the east side of the road was the shrine to Apollo. In the city were shrines also to Hermes, Hercules, Athena, and Poseidon.

Corinth had a famous temple dedicated to Asclepius, the god of healing, and his daughter Hygieia. Several buildings were constructed around the temple for the sick who came for healing. The patients left at the temple terra cotta replicas of the parts of their bodies that had

been healed. Some of these replicas have been found in the ruins.

The most significant pagan cult in Corinth was the cult of Aphrodite. The worship of Aphrodite had flourished in old Corinth before its destruction in 146 B.C. and was revived in Roman Corinth. A temple for the worship of Aphrodite was located on the top of the Acropolis.

Summary The city of Corinth as Paul found it was a cosmopolitan city composed of people from varying cultural backgrounds. Being near the site of the Isthmian games held every two years, the Corinthians enjoyed both the pleasures of these games and the wealth that the visitors brought to the city. While their ships were being carried across the isthmus, sailors came to the city to spend their money on the pleasures of Corinth. Even in an age of sexual immorality, Corinth was known for its licentious lifestyle.

R. E. Glaze

CORINTHIANS, FIRST LETTER TO THE

First Corinthians is a practical letter where Paul dealt with problems concerning the church as a whole and also with personal problems.

Paul's First Ministry in Corinth A brief survey of Paul's contacts with Corinth will aid in understanding his correspondence with Corinth. In a vision at Troas on his second missionary journey, Paul heard the call, "Cross over to Macedonia and help us!" (Acts 16:9 HCSB). Paul and his party went to Philippi and established work there. Following their release from prison, Paul and Silas went to Thessalonica. Although a work was established there, persecution arose due to the jealousy of the Jews. Paul and Silas moved on Berea, where they were well received. However, Jews from Thessalonica came and stirred up the crowds.

The decision was made for Paul to minister alone in Athens. A comparison of Acts 17:13-15 with 1 Thess. 3:6 indicates that Timothy returned to Thessalonica. Silas probably remained at Berea. Paul's ministry was brief in Athens. Some converts were made, but a church was not established. Paul left Athens alone and probably discouraged.

Paul went from Athens to Corinth, where later Silas and Timothy joined him (Acts 18:5). Paul ministered in Corinth at least 18 months (Acts 18:1-18). He began working with Aquila

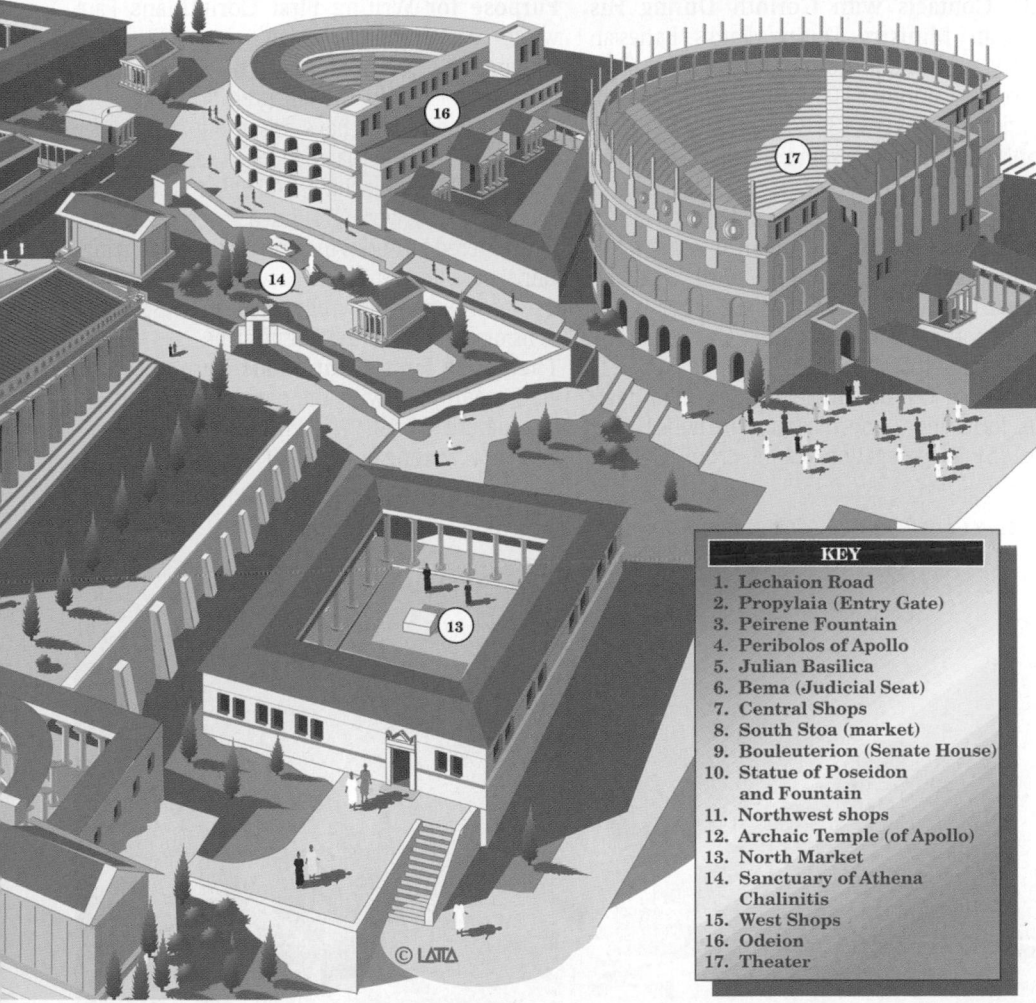

CORINTH
FIRST · CENTURY

KEY

1. Lechaion Road
2. Propylaia (Entry Gate)
3. Peirene Fountain
4. Peribolos of Apollo
5. Julian Basilica
6. Bema (Judicial Seat)
7. Central Shops
8. South Stoa (market)
9. Bouleuterion (Senate House)
10. Statue of Poseidon and Fountain
11. Northwest shops
12. Archaic Temple (of Apollo)
13. North Market
14. Sanctuary of Athena Chalinitis
15. West Shops
16. Odeion
17. Theater

© LATTA

and Priscilla in tent making. Probably, they were already Christians.

Paul left Corinth accompanied by Aquila and Priscilla (Acts 18:18). He left them at Ephesus and promised the Ephesians that he would return. In the meantime, Aquila and Priscilla instructed Apollos; and he left for Corinth, where he preached for some time (Acts 18:24-28). After visiting Jerusalem and Antioch of Syria, Paul returned to Ephesus for a ministry of more than two years (Acts 19:8-10).

Paul's Contacts with Corinth During His Ephesian Ministry During Paul's Ephesian ministry a series of disturbing events took place relative to Corinth: (1) A party spirit arose in Corinth (1 Cor. 1:12-13; 3:3-4). (2) A series of reports came to Paul, some by those of Chloe (1 Cor. 1:11). These reports included attacks upon Paul (1 Cor. 2:1-10) and problems of immorality (1 Cor. 5:1). (3) Paul wrote a letter warning against fellowship with sexually immoral people (1 Cor. 5:9). This letter is lost unless a portion of it remains in 2 Cor. 6:14–7:1. (4) The Corinthians wrote to Paul (1 Cor. 7:1) asking about certain problems concerning marriage, fornication, and disorders in public worship. (5) A delegation came from Corinth (Stephanas, Fortunatus, and Achaicus) with news from Corinth (1 Cor. 16:17). (6) Apollos quit his work in Corinth and returned to Ephesus. Even under Paul's urging, he refused to go back to Corinth (1 Cor. 16:12). (7) Paul sent Timothy to Corinth (1 Cor. 4:17) in an effort to heal the problems. Timothy probably went by way of Macedonia (Acts 19:22; 1 Cor. 16). (8) Paul wrote 1 Corinthians from Ephesus (1 Cor. 16:8), expecting them to receive the letter before the arrival of Timothy (1 Cor. 16:10).

Purpose for Writing First Corinthians Paul wrote 1 Corinthians to give instruction and admonition that would lead to the solving of the many problems in the congregation. Some of these problems may have arisen out of a "super spiritualist" group that had been influenced by incipient gnostic teachings. All of the problems in chapters 1–14 were grounded in egocentric or self-centered attitudes in contrast to self-denying, Christ-centered attitudes. Chapter 15 concerning the resurrection may reflect sincere misconceptions on the part of the Corinthians.

Theme of First Corinthians The egocentric life is contrasted with the christocentric life, or, the mature Christian is characterized by "giving," not "getting."

A street in Corinth from the first century A.D. with the Acrocorinth in the background.

Outline

The bema or judgment seat at Corinth.

R. E. Glaze

CORINTHIANS, SECOND LETTER TO THE

After writing the first letter to the Corinthians, Paul continued his ministry at Ephesus. This ministry was so successful that "the inhabitants of the province of Asia, both Jews and Greeks, heard the word of the Lord" (Acts 19:10 HCSB). Not so successful, however, was his attempt to solve the problems at Corinth. Even after the writing of 1 Corinthians, trouble continued to grow worse, especially the Corinthians' harsh attacks upon Paul. Divisions within the church and their attacks upon Paul denied the very essence of the gospel that "in Christ, God was reconciling the world to Himself ... and He has committed the message of reconciliation to us" (2 Cor. 5:19 HCSB).

Contacts between Paul and the Corinthians continued. Reports from Corinth indicated increasing hostility toward Paul. Timothy, whom Paul had sent with the hope that he could resolve the problems, returned to Ephesus and was with Paul when he wrote 2 Corinthians (2 Cor. 1:1).

Paul made a painful visit to Corinth that is not recorded in Acts. Second Corinthians contains three references to this visit. After making this visit, Paul wrote, "I made up my mind about this: not to come to you on another painful visit" (2 Cor. 2:1 HCSB). The first visit of Acts 18:1-18 was not a painful visit; therefore, the painful visit was a second visit. Also, 2 Cor. 12:14 and 13:1 indicate that Paul's forthcoming visit would be his third visit.

Paul also wrote a letter of strong rebuke that he regretted after sending it (2 Cor. 7:8). Later he rejoiced because the letter provoked them to repentance. Titus probably was the bearer of this letter (2 Cor. 8:7,16-17). This letter was not preserved unless it is chapters 10–13 of 2 Corinthians.

After Titus departed for Corinth, Paul left Ephesus. His heart was heavy because of Corinth. He expected Titus to meet him at Troas with news of reconciliation. Titus did not meet him. Even though Paul found an open door at Troas, his heart was so heavy that he could not minister (2 Cor. 2:12-13). He went on to Macedonia, where Titus finally met him (2 Cor. 7:6-7) and reported improved conditions at Corinth. In response Paul wrote 2 Corinthians, promising an early visit to them.

Questions have been raised concerning the unity of 2 Corinthians. These questions concern 6:14–7:1 and chapters 10–13. Some see 6:14–7:1 as a part of the previous letter mentioned in 1 Corinthians 5:9. Two arguments favor this view: (1) The verses interrupt the thematic connection between 6:13 and 7:2. (2) Their content fits the description of the letter in 1 Corinthians 5:9. Two arguments oppose this view: (1) There is no manuscript evidence for these verses ever existing outside of 2 Corinthians. (2) It was characteristic of Paul to insert other matters into his main argument.

The suggestion has been made that chapters 10–13 refer to the letter written "out of an extremely troubled and anguished heart" (2 Cor.

The excavations at Corinth showing the shops in the Agora.

2:4 HCSB). Two arguments favor this: (1) The tone changes between chapters 9 and 10. Chapters 1–9 reflect restored relations and the absence of hostility. Chapters 10–13 are filled with rebuke and Paul's defense of his apostleship and conduct. (2) Chapters 1–9 reflect Paul's joy and optimism. This is hard to account for if even a minority remained stubborn. Two arguments are given against chapters 10–13 being the harsh letter: (1) There is no manuscript evidence for such a division. (2) Chapters 1–9 could be addressed to the repenting majority and chapters 10–13 to an unrepentant minority.

We can be sure that all was written by Paul and is God's message given to Paul through divine inspiration. Paul wrote 2 Corinthians to deal with problems within the church and to defend apostolic ministry in general and his apostleship in particular. In so doing Paul revealed much about himself, his apostleship, and his apostolic ministry. This epistle is essential for anyone who would know as much as possible about Paul.

Second Corinthians is relevant for today in its teachings concerning ministers and their ministries. Among these teachings are the following: (1) God was in Christ reconciling the world to Himself and has given to us a ministry of reconciliation. (2) True ministry in Christ's name involves both suffering and victory. (3) Serving Christ means ministering in His name to the total needs of persons. (4) Leaders in ministry need support and trust from those to whom they minister.

Outline

I. Salutation (1:1-3)
II. The Nature of Apostolic Ministry (1:3–7:16)
    A. Defined in terms of Paul's relations with the Corinthians (1:3–2:17)
    B. Defined in light of its glory and shame (3:1–7:16)
III. The Expression of Apostolic Ministry through the Collection for Jerusalem (8:1–9:15)
    A. Examples of sacrificial giving (8:1-15)
    B. Care in handling the collection (8:16-24)
    C. An appeal for a generous response (9:1-15)
IV. Paul's Defense of His Apostolic Ministry (10:1–12:13)
    A. Defended by answering allegations (10:1-18)
    B. Defended by resorting to the foolishness of boasting (11:1–12:13)
V. Paul's Future Plans (12:14–13:10)
    A. Anticipation of a third visit to Corinth (12:14-21)
    B. Paul's warning that he will deal forthrightly when he comes (13:1-10)
VI. Farewell (13:11-14)   *R. E. Glaze*

CORMORANT Large seafowl (*Phalacrocorax carbo carbo*) listed among the unclean birds (Lev. 11:17; Deut. 14:17). Other translators call it a fisher owl (REB).

CORN General term used by the translators of the KJV for any grain.

CORNELIUS (Côr nē´ lĭ ŭs) Centurion in the Roman army who lived at Caesarea (Acts 10:1). Although he was a Gentile, he was a worshiper of the one true God. He also treated the Jewish people with kindness and generosity. After an angel appeared to this pious soldier, he sent to Joppa for Simon Peter, who came to him with the message of forgiveness of sins through faith in the crucified and risen Christ. Cornelius became a Christian as a result of this incident. His conversion marked the beginning of the church's missionary activity among Gentiles. It also helped to set the stage for an important early controversy in the church, for it raised the question of the possibility of salvation for those who were not Jews. See *Acts of the Apostles; Peter.*

CORNER BUTTRESS (NASB, 2 Chron. 26:9) See *Turning of the Wall.*

CORNER GATE Gate of Jerusalem in the northwest corner of the city not far from the Ephraim Gate (2 Kings 14:13; 2 Chron. 25:23). It is not mentioned in Nehemiah's restoration of Jerusalem. See *City Gate.*

CORNERSTONE Stone laid at the corner to bind two walls together and to strengthen them. Used symbolically as a symbol of strength and prominence in the Bible. The figure is often applied to rulers or leaders (Pss. 118:22; 144:12; Isa. 19:13 NIV, REB, NASB; Zech. 10:4). God promised through Isaiah that Zion would be restored, resting on the cornerstone of the renewed faith of Israel (Isa. 28:16). Jeremiah declared that Babylon would be so utterly devastated that nothing useful would remain, not even a stone for use in a foundation (Jer. 51:26).

In the NT Ps. 118:22 and Isa. 28:16 are quoted (or alluded to) and applied to Christ. The symbolism is clear: Jesus Christ is the only sure foundation of faith. The Synoptic Gospels quote Ps. 118:22 after the parable of the wicked tenants to show the rejection and ultimate triumph of Christ (Matt. 21:42; Mark 12:10; Luke 20:17; cp. Acts 4:11; Eph. 2:20-22).

In 1 Pet. 2:4-8 the two cornerstone passages are quoted in addition to Isa. 8:14. Here the appeal to the reader is to come to the living stone (Jesus) the people rejected but precious in God's sight. This is substantiated by a quote from Isa. 28:16. There then comes a warning: those who believe consider the stone to be something precious, but those who do not believe are warned that the stone which they have rejected has become the head of the corner (Ps. 118:22), and further, this stone will make them stumble and fall (Isa. 8:14; cp. Rom. 9:33). Believers are encouraged to themselves become living stones like *the* Living Stone and be built into a spiritual house (1 Pet. 2:5). See *Rock; Stone. Phil Logan*

CORNET KJV for several different kinds of musical instruments. See *Music, Instruments, Dancing.*

CORNFLOOR KJV for threshing floor in Hos. 9:1.

CORPORAL PUNISHMENT Punishment of, relating to, or affecting the body. The Bible teaches that corporal punishment can play an important role in correcting misbehavior (Prov. 20:30). Proverbs especially encourages parents to "use the rod" of discipline judiciously in child rearing (Prov. 13:24; 22:15; 23:13-14).

Other instances of corporal punishment are noted in the Bible. Gideon beat the men of Succoth with thorns and briars for refusing to help in pursuing the Midianite kings Zebah and Zalmunna (Judg. 8:16). God declared that David's son would be subject to punishment "with floggings inflicted by men" should he do wrong (2 Sam. 7:14), a figurative use of corporal punishment indicating subjection to his enemies. The Mosaic law regulated the severity of a beating as punishment for a crime (Deut. 25:1-3).

The Bible recognizes that corporal punishment, like other forms of discipline, is most effective if received with a willing and submissive spirit. A fool, however, will not be responsive to a large number of lashes (Prov. 17:10).

Paul H. Wright

CORRUPTION Used especially in the KJV to denote the transient nature of the material world—that is, the world's bent toward change and decay (Rom. 8:21; 1 Cor. 15:42-57; 1 Pet. 1:4). The world's corruption stands in contrast to the permanent, eternal nature of the resurrection hope.

CORRUPTION, MOUNT OF Hill east of Jerusalem near the Mount of Olives where Solomon built altars to the gods of his foreign wives (1 Kings 11:7). These places of worship were destroyed by Josiah (2 Kings 23:13). The name is probably a wordplay by the biblical writer on Mount of Oil, an early name of the Mount of Olives and a word spelled much like Mount of Corruption or Destruction.

COS (Cŏs) Island and its chief city between Miletus and Rhodes where Paul landed briefly on his return voyage after his third missionary journey (Acts 21:1). It was a center for education, trade, wine, purple dye, and ointment. Hippocrates founded a school of medicine there. It is modern Kos.

COSAM (Cō´ săm) Personal name meaning "diviner." Ancestor of Jesus (Luke 3:28).

COSMETICS Materials used for personal care and beautification. In the ancient Near East, both men and women used cosmetics. Men primarily made use of oil, rubbing it into the hair of the head and the beard (Ps. 133:2; Eccles. 9:8). Women used cosmetic preparations which included eye paint, powders, rouge, ointments for the body, and perfumes. There are only limited references made to cosmetics in the Bible.

Utensils, Colors, and Manufacture of Cosmetics Cosmetic utensils of glass, wood, and bone have been found in archeological excavations in Palestine, Egypt, and Mesopotamia. In Ur, utensils have been discovered dated as early as 2500 B.C. In Egypt a scene on a sarcophagus dated about 2000 B.C. depicts a woman holding a mirror. In Palestine most frequently uncovered are limestone bowls or palettes. These are ordinarily in the form of small bowls, about four inches in diameter, with flat bases and a small shallow hole in the center. The wide rim was usually decorated with incised geometric designs. They were used to prepare colors for making up the face. Mixing was done by means of bone spatulas or small pestles. Possibly imported from Syria, the palettes were common in the northern part of Palestine from about 1000 B.C. on.

Other paraphernalia uncovered include small glass vials and small pottery juglets used as perfume containers, alabaster jars used for ointments, ivory flasks, cosmetic burners, and perfume boxes such as that mentioned in Isa. 3:20. Ivory combs, bronze mirrors, hairpins, kohl sticks, unguent spoons, and tweezers also were used by women in biblical times. In the excavations at Lachish, an object was discovered which appears to be a curling iron and is dated about 1400 B.C. In the Cave of Letters, one of the hiding places of some rebels of the Bar Kochba War (A.D. 132–135), findings included a woman's mirror and cosmetic utensils of glass, wood, and bone.

The colors for cosmetic preparations came from various minerals. Red ocher was used for lip color. White was obtained from lead carbonate. Green eyelid coloring was derived from turquoise or malachite, and black was often made from lead sulfate. Kohl or manganese was used for outlining the eyes. Colors were also produced from ivories, bitumen, and burned woods.

Expert craftsmen made the cosmetics. They imported many of the raw ingredients from India and Arabia. Oils for skin creams were extracted from olives, almonds, gourds, other trees and plants, and animal and fish fats. Fragrances came from seeds, plant leaves, fruits, and flowers, especially roses, jasmines, mints, balsams, and cinnamon.

Eye Paint Women painted their eyelids to make their eyes appear larger (Jer. 4:30 NASB). There may also have been some medicinal value by preventing dryness of the eyelid or discouraging disease-carrying flies. However, biblical references often seem to associate the practice of painting the eyes with women of questionable reputation (2 Kings 9:30; Ezek. 23:40).

Dry powders for eye coloring were stored in pouches, reeds, reed like tubes of stone, or small jars. The reference to Job's daughter, "Keren-hap-puch" (horn of antimony or eye paint, Job 42:14), indicates the powders were also carried in horns. The powders were mixed with water or gum and applied to the eyelids with small rods made of ivory, wood, or metal. Egyptian women favored the colors of black and green, painting the upper eyelid black and the lower one green. Mesopotamian women preferred yellows and reds. Heavy black lines were traced around the eyes to make them appear more almond-shaped.

Ointments and Perfumes Creams, ointments, and perfumes were especially important in the hot Near Eastern climate. Creams protected the skin against the heat of the sun and counteracted body odors. Ointments were applied to the head (Matt. 6:17) or to the whole body (Ruth 3:3) as part of hygienic cleansing. They were considered part of the beautification process (Esther 2:12). Anointing one's head with oil was a sign of gladness (Ps. 45:7). In worship services anointing was a special part of consecration (Exod. 30:30-32). The formula was given by God and was a priestly secret (Exod. 30:22-38). Ointments were used by prophets in anointing new kings. Elijah anointed Jehu (2 Kings 9:3), and Jehoiada anointed Joash (2 Kings 11:12). In NT times a good host displayed hospitality by anointing guests with ointments (Luke 7:37-50). Ointment was sometimes used to anoint the sick (James 5:14). Perfumed ointments were part of the preparation for burial (Mark 14:8; Luke 23:56).

The use of perfume is an ancient practice. The first recorded mention is on the fifteenth century B.C. tomb of Queen Hatshepsut who had sent an expedition to the land of Punt to fetch frankincense. Herodotus (450 B.C.) mentioned Arabia's aromatics. To the magi who bore gifts to the Christ child, the offering of frankincense symbolized divinity.

Perfumes mentioned in the Bible include aloes (Num. 24:6); balm (Ezek. 27:17); cinnamon (Prov. 7:17); frankincense (Isa. 43:23; Matt. 2:11); myrrh (Song 5:5; Matt. 2:11); and spikenard (John 12:3). The perfumes were derived from the sap or gum of the tree (frankincense, myrrh), the root (spikenard), or the bark (cinnamon). They were often quite expensive and imported from Arabia (frankincense, myrrh) and India (aloes, spikenard, and Ceylon (cinnamon).

The perfumes could be produced as a dry powder and kept in perfume boxes (Isa. 3:20), or as an ointment and kept in alabaster jars, such as the spikenard with which Mary anointed Jesus

C

(John 12:3). They could also be obtained in the natural form as gum or pellets of resin. In this form they were placed in cosmetic burners and the resin burned. In close or confined quarters, the resulting incense smoke would act as a fumigation for both the body and the clothes, such as that which seems to be described in the beautification process noted in Esther 2:12. See *Anoint; Perfume, Perfumer.* *Darlene R. Gautsch*

COULTER KJV word for both mattock and plowshare.

COUNCIL, HEAVENLY A meeting of God and the heavenly hosts which points to God's role as King of the universe. Some scholars have proposed an analogy with Mesopotamian and Canaanite myths about meetings of the pantheon of gods to decide the fate of the cosmos. For example, angels are depicted as presenting themselves before God, perhaps to report their contributions to His plan (Job 1:6; 2:1) or to discuss how that plan will be effectuated (1 Kings 22:20b; possibly Gen. 1:26, though this is doubtful). However, important differences exist. The monotheism of the Hebrew people is *proclaimed*, rather than *called into question*, by the council texts. Yahweh (the LORD) sits enthroned amidst the adoration and worship of the angelic creaturely beings (Ps. 29:1), and in the assembly He is greatly feared as well as praised (Ps. 89:5-8). His presiding over the assembly is directly tied to His sole claim as Ruler and Judge (Ps. 82:1,8).

Humans are sometimes privy to the workings of God's council. A true prophet of Yahweh is someone who has stood in God's council. In his ordeal with the false prophets, Micaiah reports his observation of council deliberations (1 Kings 22:19-23). Likewise, Eliphaz asks Job if he stood in God's council, implying that his claims would thereby be substantiated (Job 15:8). Jeremiah condemns those prophets who have not stood in God's council, for if they had, they would know God's plan and would not lead His people astray (Jer. 23:18,22). Participation in the council by the prophet, then, leads to predictive success.

Demons sometimes appear before the council. In the story of Ahab's fall, an evil spirit is enlisted to deceive the false prophets. God questions the spirits regarding Ahab's enticement, but this does not mean that God is consulting the angels about His plan. His response to the lying spirit indicates that its success has been ordained (1 Kings 22:23). Satan appears before God's throne to accuse the saints (Job 1:9-11; 2:4-5; Zech. 3:1-2), yet he does not seem to be a regular attendee. The text states that Satan *came* with the angels (Job 1:6; 2:1) after *roaming the Earth* (Job 1:7; 2:2). This is to be contrasted with the angelic beings who perpetually stand around God's throne (Rev. 4:6b-8). It may be safely concluded that evil spirits participate in the council when they have a function to serve in God's plan. See *Sons of God.* *John Laing*

COUNCIL OF JERUSALEM Name given to the meeting described in Acts 15:6-22. The purpose of the council was to determine the terms on which Gentile converts to Christianity would be received into the church. The occasion of the meeting was a significant turning of Gentiles to Christ as a result of missionary activity by Barnabas and Paul. Some maintained that all Gentile converts must submit to circumcision and observe the whole of the Mosaic law. Paul and Barnabas, however, contended that imposing such requirements on Gentiles was unreasonable. The solution proposed by the Jerusalem Council was that Gentile believers would not be required first to become Jewish proselytes but that they would be asked to refrain from idolatry, from sexual misconduct, and from eating blood. See *Acts of the Apostles; Paul.*

COUNSELOR One who analyzes a situation and gives advice to one who has responsibility for making a decision. Israelite kings seem to have employed counselors on a regular basis (2 Sam. 16:23; 1 Kings 12:6-14; Isa. 1:26; 3:3; Mic. 4:9). God is often regarded as a counselor (Pss. 16:7; 73:24) as is His Messiah (Isa. 9:6; 11:2) and the Holy Spirit (John 14:16,26; 15:26; 16:7). See *Advocate; Comforter.*

COUNTENANCE One's face as an indication of mood, emotion, or character (Gen. 4:5-6; Prov. 15:13; Eccles. 7:3; Mark 10:22). Having God's countenance upon one is a way of speaking about being in God's presence (Ps. 21:6). Being in God's presence may bring peace (Num. 6:25-26), blessing (Pss. 4:6; 89:15), or victory (Ps. 44:3). It may also bring destruction (Ps. 80:16) or judgment for sin (Ps. 90:8).

COUNTERVAIL Old English word meaning "to equal," "be commensurate with," "compensate for" in Esther 7:4.

COURIERS Members of the royal guard who carried messages throughout the kingdom (2 Chron. 30:6,10; Esther 3:13,15; 8:10,14). Roman couriers were empowered to confiscate transportation or the help of citizens of the empire in the fulfillment of their duties (Matt. 5:41; Mark 15:21).

COURT OF THE GUARD or **COURT OF THE PRISON** Open court in the Jerusalem palace reserved for the detention of prisoners during the day of Jeremiah (Jer. 32:8,12; 33:1; 37:21; 38:6,13,28; 39:14-15 KJV). Translated in the modern versions as "court of the guard."

COURTS OF THE GENTILES, WOMEN, ISRAELITES, PRIESTS See *Temple.*

COURT SYSTEMS Court systems of ancient Israel are not fully described in the OT or in any extrabiblical source. Laws governing the conduct of judges and witnesses, reports about leaders who were consulted for legal decisions, and narratives of judicial proceedings supplement the accounts of Moses' appointment of assistant judges (Exod. 18) and Jehoshaphat's judicial reform (2 Chron. 19). Archaeological investigation has not yet discovered court documents from ancient Israel.

Legal disputes could be settled at the level of society in which they arose. The head of a family had authority to decide cases within his household without bringing the matter before a professional judge (Gen. 31; 38). The law codes limit his authority in some cases (Num. 5:11-31; Deut. 21:18-21; 22:13-21). When persons from more than one family were involved, the case was taken before the elders of the town, who were the heads of the extended families living together in that place and represented the community as a whole. The elders would serve as witnesses to a transaction (Deut. 25:5-10; Ruth 4:1-12), decide guilt or innocence (Deut. 19; 22:13-21; Josh. 20:1-6), or execute the punishment due the guilty party (Deut. 22:13-21; 25:1-3). The elders helped to preserve the community by seeing that disputes were settled in a manner that everyone would recognize as just.

Disputes between tribes were more difficult to resolve. When a Judahite woman who was the concubine of a Levite living in the territory of Ephraim was raped and murdered in Gibeah of Benjamin, several tribes were involved (Judg. 19–21). The Levite, therefore, appealed to all the tribes of Israel for justice. The initial attempts at negotiation were rebuffed when the men of Benjamin refused to hand over the guilty persons for punishment. Israel then went to war against the whole tribe of Benjamin, defeated them, and vowed not to let them intermarry with the rest of the tribes. The biblical historian comments regretfully that this sort of thing happened when there was no king to execute the law (Judg. 21:25).

During the period of Israelite history covered by the book of Judges, several individuals appointed by God possessed special judicial authority. The so-called "minor judges" (Judg. 10:1-5; 12:8-15) are not credited with delivering Israel from oppression by military means, so their function may have been purely judicial or political. Some scholars have identified their office as "judge of all Israel" in the tribal league, but others have argued that their jurisdiction was over a smaller area. Deborah, and later Samuel, also decided cases. Their judicial activities took place in a limited area (Judg. 4:4-5; 1 Sam. 7:15-17). We do not know whether they only heard cases on appeal. The Bible does not say how any of these individuals came to possess their authority as judges. Both Deborah and Samuel were prophets. The other deliverer judges were called by God and possessed by God's Spirit, so judicial authority was probably also a divine gift.

A hierarchical system of courts and judges could exist when political authority was centralized. In Exod. 18:13-26 Moses appointed assistant judges to decide the smaller cases so that his own energy could be preserved for the difficult ones. A system in which local courts referred complex cases to the supreme judges is described in Deut. 17:2-13; 19:16-19. This was not an appeals court to which dissatisfied parties could bring their cases for reconsideration; it was a court of experts who could pass judgment in cases too complicated for the local judges to decide themselves. The court system instituted by Jehoshaphat also followed this pattern (2 Chron. 19:4-11). Although appointed by the king, the judges were responsible directly to God (2 Chron. 19:6). It is not clear whether the residents of Jerusalem went directly to the central court. We only know that Jeremiah was tried in Jerusalem by "the princes of Judah" after being charged by the priests and prophets with a crime worthy of death. The system described in Deut. 17; 19 and 2 Chron. 19 has both priests and secular officials as judges in the central court in Jerusalem.

The king possessed limited judicial authority. Despite his supreme political power, he was not personally above the law. Saul's death sentences on Jonathan (1 Sam. 14:39) and the priests at Nob (1 Sam. 22:6-23) were not accepted by the people. Jonathan was not punished, and the priests were finally killed by a non-Israelite. David was led to convict himself of his crimes against Uriah and his mistreatment of Absalom (2 Sam. 12:1-6; 14:1-24). Unlike Saul, David and Solomon were able to exercise authority to execute or spare persons who represented a threat to their reigns (2 Sam. 1:1-16; 4:1-12; 19:16-23; 21:1-14; 1 Kings 2:19-46). Jezebel used the existing town court to dispose of Naboth and confiscate his vineyard. God, however, punished her and Ahab, for having Naboth executed on trumped-up charges even though Ahab was king (1 Kings 21–22). Deuteronomy 17:18-20 places the king at the same level as his subjects with respect to the requirements of God's law. In Israel the king did not have the authority to enact new laws or to make arbitrary legal rulings contrary to the prevailing understanding of justice.

The ideal of the just king who oversees the dispensing of justice for all his subjects was known in Israel. In this role the king himself was the leading example of a just and honest judge and was personally involved in hearing cases as well as appointing other judges. Absalom was able to take advantage of David's failure to live up to this ideal (2 Sam. 15:1-6). Solomon is the supreme example of the just king, having been granted discernment and wisdom by God (1 Kings 3).

The relationship of the king's court to the rest of the judicial system is uncertain. The wise woman from Tekoa appealed to David a decision that had been made within her extended family (2 Sam. 14). The Shunammite widow successfully appealed to the king of Israel for the restoration of her house and land, which she had abandoned during a time of famine (2 Kings 8:1-6). The famous case of the two prostitutes and their infant sons was brought directly to Solomon without any previous judgment (1 Kings 3:16-28). All of these cases seem to be exceptional. Powerful third parties were involved in the first two cases; Joab set up the audience with David, and the Shunammite had an advocate present in the person of Gehazi, Elisha's servant. The two prostitutes had no families to settle their dispute. We are not certain, therefore, what these accounts can tell us about how cases usually came to be heard by the king. There are no OT laws that define the process of judicial appeal to the king.

Priests also possessed judicial authority. The passages about the high court in Jerusalem mention priests alongside the secular judge (Deut. 17:9; 19:17; 2 Chron. 19:8,11). Some scholars believe that this division between religious and civil courts reflects the postexilic period, in which the secular authority was that of the Persian king and Jewish priests who administered the law of God (Ezra 7:25-26). Israelite priests, however, possessed a body of knowledge from which they ruled on matters pertaining to the worship of God and the purity of the community. The cult and the judicial system were both concerned with removing bloodguilt from the community (Deut. 21:1-9). We cannot determine how the priestly judges were related to the other court systems or how cases were assigned to the various judges.

Actual court procedures may be partially reconstructed as follows. There were no prosecutors or defense attorneys; accuser and accused argued their own cases. The burden of proof lay with the defendant. Physical evidence was presented when necessary (Deut. 22:13-21), but proving one's case depended primarily on testimony and persuasive argument. The word of at least two witnesses was required to convict (Deut. 19:15). The system depended on the honesty of witnesses and the integrity of judges (Exod. 18:21; 20:16; 23:1-3,6-9; Lev. 19:15-19; Deut. 16:19-20; 19:16-21; 2 Chron. 19:6-7). The prophets condemned corrupt judges (Isa. 1:21-26; Amos 5:12,15; Mic. 7:3) and those who supported them (Amos 5:10). Cases brought by a malicious witness giving false testimony were referred to the central court (Deut. 19:16-21). In some circumstances the accused could submit to an ordeal or an oath to prove his or her innocence (Exod. 22:6-10; Num. 5:11-31; Deut. 21:1-8). If guilty, he or she would be punished directly by God. Casting lots to discover the guilty party was another extraordinary procedure. In both cases reported in the Bible the person identified also confessed his guilt (Josh. 7; 1 Sam. 14:24-46). The judges were responsible to administer punishment, often with the whole community participating (Deut. 21:21). The court systems could only function well when the community agreed with their decisions and cooperated to enforce them. By judging justly, the courts taught God's law and the principles of divine justice. The courts worked together with the people to restore the community to peace and wholeness under God whenever they recognized the one in the right and imposed an appropriate penalty on the guilty one.

Pamela J. Scalise

COUSIN At times the KJV uses "cousin" when a distant relative is referred to (Mark 6:4; Luke 1:36,58; 2:44; 14:12). The same Greek word in all these passages means relatives, kin, or countryman.

COVENANT Oath-bound promise whereby one party solemnly pledges to bless or serve another party in some specified way. Sometimes the keeping of the promise depends upon the meeting of certain conditions by the party to whom the promise is made. On other occasions the promise is made unilaterally and unconditionally. The covenant concept is a central, unifying theme of Scripture, establishing and defining God's relationship to man in all ages.

In the OT, the Hebrew word translated "covenant" is *berit*. The term probably derives from the verb *bara*, "to bind." The noun *berit* originally denoted a binding relationship between two parties in which each pledged to perform some service for the other. The NT, following the Septuagint, uniformly uses the Greek word *diatheke* for the covenant idea, avoiding the similar term *suntheke*, which would wrongly portray a covenant as a mutual contract or alliance rather than an oath-bound promise. This does not mean that a covenant may not, in some cases, take on characteristics common to a mutual agreement or contract, but the essence of the covenant concept is clearly that of a binding pledge.

Covenant Rituals and Signs The technical language used when covenants were made was "to cut a covenant" (*karat berit*). This terminology

referred to ritual sacrifices that accompanied covenant making. Often animals sacrificed would be cut in two. In some covenant rituals part of the animal would be eaten by the covenanting parties and part burned in honor of their god. Sometimes the parties would walk symbolically between the pieces of the animal. In any case, the shedding of blood in such rituals signified the solemnity of the covenant, each party vowing not to break the covenant on pain of death.

The making of covenants often included signs as well. A sign served as a memorial, reminding the parties of their promises. Abraham gave Abimelech seven ewe lambs "as a witness" to their covenant (Gen. 21:30); Jacob and Laban used a heap of stones (Gen. 31:46-48); the sign of God's covenant with Noah was the rainbow (Gen. 9:12-15); circumcision was the sign of the Abrahamic and Mosaic covenants (Gen. 17:10-14; Exod. 12:47-48); and baptism is the sign of the new covenant (Col. 2:9-12; Rom. 6:3-4).

Covenants Between Humans The Bible records many covenants between human beings. Abraham and Abimelech made a covenant at Beersheba (Gen. 21:22-34), Abraham promising to deal kindly with Abimelech's family, and Abimelech promising to recognize Abraham's ownership of a well. Jacob and Laban made a covenant (Gen. 31:44-54), swearing to do each other no harm. Jonathan and David cut a covenant in which Jonathan acknowledged David's right to the throne of Israel (1 Sam. 18:3; 23:18).

The Gibeonites, who were under God's ban to be slaughtered, deceived Joshua into a covenant to live in peace and protect them (Josh. 9:15). Abner covenanted with David to lead the northern tribes of Israel to break with Ish-Bosheth and join David (2 Sam. 3:12-13). Solomon made a covenant of peace with Hiram, King of Tyre, committing their countries to mutual trade (1 Kings 5:12). King Asa led Judah to make a covenant to seek the Lord after many years of rebellion (2 Chron. 15:9-15).

There are many other human covenants in the Bible, some of which were ill advised. For example, Hosea warned Israel of God's judgement for her covenant with Assyria (Hos. 12:1), and God punished Asa for a covenant with Ben-Hadad of Aram (2 Chron. 16:2-13). The dire consequences of these covenants were brought about because Israel relied upon foreign military power rather than God (cp. 2 Chron. 16:7).

Of special interest among human covenants is marriage. Malachi 2:14 clearly indicates that marriage was understood as a covenant. In marriage one man and one woman vow to live together in a lifelong commitment (Gen. 2:24; Matt. 19:4-6), involving sexual union, sacrificial love, and mutual support.

The Divine Covenants Most significant in Scripture are several covenants God makes with man. These covenants provide a unifying principle for understanding the whole of Scripture and define the relationship between God and man. The heart of that relationship is found in the phrase, "I will be their God and they shall be My people" (cp. Gen. 17:7-8; Exod. 6:6-7; Lev. 26:12; Deut. 4:20; Jer. 11:4; Ezek. 11:20).

The first covenant that God made is the covenant of redemption. This was a covenant that God the Father established with God the Son to redeem fallen humanity. In 2 Tim. 1:9-10 (HCSB) we learn that God has saved us not by works but by grace "which was given to us in Christ Jesus before time began." And in Titus 1:2 (HCSB) Paul declares that God promised the elect eternal life "before time began." The term "covenant" is not here, but the concept of an oath-bound promise is evident. This promise was made to Christ who came to fulfill an eternal plan to save those the Father gave him (John 6:37-40; 17:1-5). God the Father bestowed (lit. "covenanted") upon Him a kingdom which He in turn bestows upon His disciples (Luke 22:28-30).

The biblical covenant that appears first is the Edenic covenant or covenant of works which God made with Adam in the garden of Eden (Gen. 2:15-17). Hosea 6:6-7 states plainly that this arrangement was a covenant. God promised man in his state of innocence that he would give him everlasting life on the condition of his perfect obedience. Obedience would be measured by whether he kept God's command to refrain from eating of the tree of the knowledge of good and evil. However, Adam and Eve ate the forbidden fruit, thus breaking this covenant and falling under its terrible curse: "in the day that you eat of it you shall surely die."

It is important to note that the covenant of works provided no method of restoration. Since it demanded perfection, this covenant, once broken, left Adam and his posterity without hope. It

is in this context that we find the inauguration of another covenant, the covenant of grace. After the fall, God cursed the serpent and promised the seed of the woman would crush the serpent's head, though his own heel would be bruised (Gen. 3:15). This promise was an unconditional guarantee that God would graciously rescue fallen man from the curse of the covenant of works. The NT makes clear that the "seed of the woman" who fulfills this promise is Christ (Gal. 3:19; Col. 2:13-15; 1 John 3:8). The covenant of Grace, then, is God's promise to save sinful humanity from the fall's curse by grace alone through the redemptive work of Christ. This redemptive work is foreshadowed even in Gen. 3 where God apparently slays an animal to provide coverings for Adam and Eve's nakedness (v. 21).

Genesis 4–6 describes the rapid moral decline of the human race after the fall that led God to destroy most of them with a flood. However, "Noah found grace in the eyes of the Lord" (Gen. 6:8), and God preserved the human race by instructing him to build an ark in which he and his family and the animal species could survive the floodwaters. After the flood, God established the Noahic covenant (Gen. 9:9-17), promising never again to flood the earth. This covenant called for no human response. God simply and graciously bound himself to preserve the human race and other living creatures.

The next biblical covenant is the Abrahamic covenant (cp. Gen. 12:1-3; 15:1-19; 17:1-14; 22:15-18). God called Abraham out of Ur to go to Canaan, promising to make him a great nation which in turn would bless all nations (Gen. 12:1-3). The utter graciousness of this covenant is seen clearly in the ratification ceremony in Gen. 15. God promised the aging Abraham that he would have a son and heir from his own body and that he would inherit the land of Canaan. Abraham believed God, which resulted in God's declaring him righteous (v. 6). Yet Abraham desired confirmation, asking, "How shall I know that I will inherit it?" In response God had Abraham cut several animals in two in accordance with the custom for cutting a covenant. However, unlike the custom, God alone passed between the animal pieces, signifying that His promise was unconditional and certified by His own vow to suffer violent death if He failed to keep His promise to Abraham. God repeats His oath in Gen. 22:18, adding further that it would be through Abraham's seed that all nations would someday be blessed. Paul applies the singular noun "seed" as a reference to Christ (Gal. 3:16). It is through Christ, Abraham's prophesied descendent, that the blessings of the Abrahamic Covenant would come to every nation. Paul understands that the blessing the nations receive is, like Abraham, to be justified by faith alone rather than works, and to receive the gift of the Holy Spirit (Gal. 3:8-14).

In the course of time, Abraham's descendants were enslaved in Egypt. They cried out to God for deliverance, and because God "remembered His covenant with Abraham, Isaac, and Jacob" (Exod. 2:24 NASB), He sent Moses to confront Pharaoh and lead the people out of bondage. Once free, the Israelites gathered at Mount Sinai. There God established with them the Sinai or Mosaic covenant (Exod. 19:5). This covenant bears the closest resemblance to the suzerainty treaties found in other ancient near-eastern nations. In such treaties, the suzerain (i.e., overlord or king) would pledge to provide benevolent rule and protection to conquered peoples in exchange for their loyalty. Suzerainty treaties had certain stylized features that are paralleled in the Mosaic covenant (Exod. 19–23). These features include:

1. a historical prologue reviewing the past relationship between the parties;

2. a statement of obligations the parties have to each other;

3. provisions for occasionally reading the treaty in public; and

4. lists of blessings and curses to follow from keeping or breaking the treaty.

Though the Mosaic covenant followed this familiar pattern, its purpose and content differed significantly. For one thing, the Mosaic covenant was brought about not by an act of conquest but by God's gracious deliverance of Israel from bondage. Further, God's covenant with Israel established not simply an agreement between a suzerain and his vassals, but an intimate relationship based on loyal love (Hb. *chesed*).

The unique feature of the Mosaic covenant was the Law, summarized in the Ten Commandments (Exod. 20:10-17). By promulgating the Law, God established Israel as a distinct people and nation, existing under His own theocratic rule. God promised Israel that they would be His special possession, His "holy nation," and the Lord promised to be their God (cp. Exod. 19:5-

6; 20:2). This promise was conditioned on Israel's obedience to the Law. God's grace singled out Israel as the recipient of this covenant (Deut. 7:7), but they were warned that the temporal blessings promised would be theirs only if they kept his commandments (Deut. 7:12-26; 28:1-14). Failure to keep God's commandments would result in calamitous curses including being "divorced" by God and no longer being His special people (Deut. 8:19-20; 28:15-68; cp. Jer. 3:6-8; Hos. 1:1-8). Under the Mosaic covenant, Israel repeatedly rebelled against God, incurring divine wrath on numerous occasions, but God mercifully limited the severity of judgment because of His promise to Abraham (cp. 2 Kings 13:22-23). However, God's patience finally wore out, and He imposed the curses first on Israel (722 B.C.) and then Judah (586 B.C.) by the Assyrian and Babylonian exiles. But, again, because of the unconditional promises to Abraham and David, God preserved a remnant of Judah and brought them back to Palestine (cp. 1 Kings 11:11-13; Neh. 9:7-8,32).

The NT adds insight into the meaning and significance of the Mosaic covenant. Hebrews indicates that the covenant's stipulations for animal sacrifices were "a shadow of the good things to come" and that they were not efficacious in atoning for sin (Heb. 10:1-4). Rather they were symbolic pointers to the substitutionary sacrifice of Christ that alone can wash away sins (Heb. 10:11-14). Paul explains that the Mosaic covenant was added to the Abrahamic covenant "until the Seed to whom the promise was made would come" (Gal. 3:18-19 HCSB). That is, God established the Mosaic covenant with national Israel as a temporary arrangement whose purpose would be completed at the first coming of Christ. Further, the purpose of this covenant was that the law would serve as "our guardian until Christ" (Gal. 3:24 HCSB). It does so by giving God's righteous demands, which sinners are incapable of keeping (cp. Rom. 5:13,20; 8:7-8), and the breaking of which earns them the wrath of God. Realizing their helplessness before law, penitent sinners may see their need of a Savior and be driven to Christ.

God made another unconditional covenant with David (2 Sam. 7:1-17; 23:1-5). In the Davidic covenant, God made a promise that He would establish for David a perpetual kingdom, one of his descendants sitting upon the throne of Israel forever. Moreover, God promised David's seed, "I will be a father to him and he will be a son to Me" (2 Sam. 7:14 NASB). The promise is unconditional, God being determined to keep it despite the wickedness of subsequent kings descended from David (1 Kings 11:11-13; 2 Kings 20:4-6). Of course, the eventual destruction of the Davidic dynasty seems to call into question the perpetuity of this covenant, but the prophets looked forward to eventual restoration of David's kingdom (Amos 9:11).

The NT also provides insight into the Davidic covenant. For example, several NT authors use the theme of the king's sonship to God to connect the Davidic King to Jesus Christ (cp. Ps. 2:6-7; Heb. 1:5-6; Acts 13:32-34; Rom. 1:3-4). As the actual Son of God, He is the ultimate fulfillment of the covenant with David. Further, Christ's resurrection and ascension mark His coronation as the Davidic King seated on David's throne (Acts 2:29-36). And the establishment of the church with the influx of Gentile converts is taken by James as marking the restoration of David's kingdom prophesied by Amos (Amos 9:11-12; Acts 15:13-18).

Finally, God established what both testaments call the new covenant. Jeremiah was the first to speak of it (Jer. 31:27-34). In the wake of Israel's covenant-breaking disobedience, God promised that He would someday establish a new covenant with Israel unlike the old covenant that they broke. In this new covenant God says, "I will put My law within them, and on their heart I will write it; and I will be their God, and they shall be My people...[and] they shall all know Me ... for I will forgive their iniquity, and their sin I will remember no more" (vv. 33-34 NASB). Ezekiel echoes this theme, saying that in the new covenant God will "give you a new heart and put a new spirit within you ... and cause you to walk in My statutes" (Ezek. 36:26-27 NASB). This new covenant is contrasted with the old Mosaic covenant and promises several blessings that the old covenant could not provide: regeneration or new birth, the full forgiveness of sins, an intimate knowledge of God, and the assurance that this new covenant is unbreakable. The promises of the new covenant signify the fulfillment of all of the redemptive purposes that God established in the covenant of grace, bringing to an end the curse of the Fall and providing full salvation for the human race.

Jesus announced the fulfillment of the new covenant in His institution of the Lord's Supper (Luke 22:20; 1 Cor. 11:23-25). Jesus' substitutionary death on the cross, which the Lord's Supper symbolizes, brought the new covenant into being and made the old covenant obsolete (cp. Heb. 8:6-13; 9:11-15). In the new covenant, Christ brings to fulfillment the promises and purposes of the previous covenants. As indicated above, Christ is the "seed of the woman" that God promised would crush the serpent's head; He is the seed of Abraham who would bless all the nations; He is the goal of the Mosaic law; He is the King who sits forever on David's throne. Moreover, as Christ is "Immanuel" or "God with us" (Matt. 1:23; John 1:14), He brings to its consummation the intercovenantal theme that God "will be their God, and they shall be [His] people." Also the new covenant fulfills all the OT promises to Israel in the life and ministry of the New Israel, the church (cp. Gal. 6:16; 1 Pet. 2:9-10; Acts 15:14-17; Heb. 11:8-16; Rev. 21:12-14). Of course, not all the blessings of the New Covenant have been fully realized. The ultimate consummation of the new covenant awaits the return of Christ.

The Unity of the Divine Covenants Despite their differences, the divine covenants exhibit a structural and thematic unity which unifies the whole of Scripture. Their structural unity is seen in the fact that each successive divine covenant grows out of and depends upon previous ones. Each covenant forms a new phase in one overarching divine plan. Both the covenant of works and the covenant of grace are the historical outworking of the more fundamental covenant of redemption. The covenant of grace, in which God unilaterally promises graciously to redeem fallen humanity, presupposes the failure of the covenant of works. But both of these covenants depend upon that eternal covenant made between God the Father and God the Son to redeem sinners from sin and misery. Before time began, God promised to give salvation to a sinful human race. That promise necessitated the establishment in history of the covenants of works and grace.

All of the subsequent divine covenants are stages of the covenant of grace in which God progressively unfolds the promise made in Gen. 3:15. The covenant with Noah preserves the human race from destruction so that the seed of the woman might be born. It demonstrates the grace of God in that God promises to forbear patiently with the human race until the coming of Christ (cp. Acts 17:30). The Abrahamic covenant follows from the covenant of grace as well, creating a historical lineage through which the promised seed would come. In all subsequent covenants, God graciously preserves this lineage despite the wickedness of Abraham's descendants. The Mosaic covenant, too, is part of the covenant of grace and an extension of the Abrahamic covenant. Indeed, the Scriptures explicitly state that the Mosaic covenant is established because God "remembered His covenant with Abraham, Isaac, and Jacob" (Exod. 2:24). By delivering Israel from Egypt and forming them into a nation through the promulgation of the Law, God established an arrangement in which all of mankind might see their inability to live up to the covenant of works and thus realize their need for a Savior. Within the context of national Israel, God also founded the Davidic covenant that provided the divine monarchy through which God will govern His redeemed people for all eternity. God also kept this covenant unconditionally, preserving the rebellious Hebrew nation and bringing them back from exile "for My own sake and for My servant David's sake" (2 Kings 20:4-6 NASB). Lastly, the new covenant brings the covenant of grace to its consummation with the life, death, resurrection, and ascension of Jesus Christ who is the promised seed of the covenant of grace. Thus, in the progressive revelation of these covenants, we can see the unfolding of one eternal plan.

The unity of the covenants is further seen in the single theme present in all of them: "I will be your God and you shall be My people" (cp. Gen. 17:7-8). The divine covenants are designed to bring fallen human beings into intimate personal relationship with God. This theme is developed in Scripture in close connection with the "Immanuel Principle" of God actually dwelling in the midst of his people. The OT tabernacle was the place where God met personally with Israel. When the tabernacle was consecrated, God Himself connected the Immanuel Principle with the covenant theme: "I will dwell among the sons of Israel and will be their God" (Exod. 29:45 NASB). Christ embodies the consummate form of this principle in the new covenant. He is called "Immanuel, which is translated 'God with us'" (Matt. 1:23), and John explicitly states that in Christ God "became flesh and took up residence [lit. 'tabernacled'] among us" (John 1:14 HCSB). The final mention of this covenant theme is found in Rev. 21:3. After the second coming of Christ, we find God's covenant promise fully and finally realized: "Look! God's dwelling is with men, and He will live with them. They will be His people, and God Himself will be with them and be their God" (HCSB).

Steven B. Cowan

COVENANT BOX (TEV) See *Ark of the Covenant.*

COVENANT OF SALT Often utilized in covenant making, probably as symbolic of that which preserves and prevents decay. The hope was that the covenant thus enacted would endure (Num. 18:19; 2 Chron. 13:5). Salt was an essential element of the cereal offerings made to God (Lev. 2:13).

COVERING OF THE LIVER See *Caul.*

COVERING THE HEAD In 1 Cor. 11:1-16 Paul dealt with the matter of covering the head in worship services. This extended treatment shows that this must have been a subject of considerable interest in Corinth.

The Jewish custom was for all women to cover their heads with a veil when they went outside their homes. To appear in public without a veil was a sign of immodesty and lack of virtue. To appear in a worship service without a veil was unthinkable.

Some of the Corinthian Christian women had evidently appeared in worship without a veil on their heads. Perhaps they had understood Paul's emphasis on Christian freedom to mean that they no longer had to observe any of the old Jewish customs—including that of wearing a veil.

The effects of such a change in dress style had been disruptive to the worship services and Christian witness in Corinth. This led Paul to state that a woman should cover her head during the worship service. At the same time, he encouraged the men to follow the Jewish custom of worshiping with uncovered heads.

Paul cited various reasons in 1 Cor. 11:1-16 for his position. He referred to: (1) the order in creation (v. 3), (2) social customs of the time (vv. 4-6), (3) the presence of angels (v. 10), (4) nature itself (vv. 13-15), and (5) the common practice in the churches (v. 16).

The principle here is that Christians must be sensitive to the cultures in which they live. They should not needlessly flout local customs unless there is some moral reason to do so. To be insensitive to the culture in which one lives causes one to offend many of the people whom the church is trying to win to Jesus Christ. It diverts attention away from the most important thing and focuses it on peripheral matters. See *Corinth; Woman; Worship.* *Lynn Jones*

COVET, COVETOUS Inordinate desire to possess what belongs to another, usually tangible things.

While the Hebrew word for "covet" can also be translated "to desire," in the tenth commandment it means an ungoverned and selfish desire that threatens the basic rights of others. Coveting was sinful because it focused greedily on the property of a neighbor that was his share in the land God had promised His people. After Israel's defeat at Ai, Achan confessed that his selfish desire for treasure was so great that he disobeyed God's specific commandment (Josh. 7:21). In defense of Judah's poor, Micah declared the Lord's judgment against the land-grabbers for coveting small farms and actually seizing them from their powerless owners (Mic. 2:2). Although the commandment against coveting seems concerned only with motivation, some passages indicate that coveting in the heart was expected to end with taking what was desired.

In the NT the same Greek word is translated "covet" in the KJV and "earnestly desire" in the RSV (1 Cor. 12:39). So covet could be used in a good sense. Another Greek word describes the ruthless self-assertion that the Tenth Commandment forbids (Luke 12:15; Eph. 5:5). In the Luke passage Jesus said that the covetous man will not be "rich toward God." In the Ephesian passage Paul classed the covetous man with the idolater. So the greedy person—one who covets—denies his faith in God and scorns His values.

William J. Fallis

COW Designates domestic bovine animals, especially the female. Cows are mentioned in relation to giving birth and nurturing calves (Lev. 22:27-28; 1 Sam. 6:7). They were among the cattle gift that Jacob offered to Esau (Gen. 32:15). Amos called the wealthy, selfish women of Samaria "cows of Bashan" (Amos 4:1), referring to the area that was wellknown for raising cows (Deut. 32:14). See *Cattle.*

COZ (Cŏz) (KJV, TEV) See *Koz.*

COZBI (Cŏz´ bī) Personal name meaning "my falsehood." A Midianite woman who was slain by Phinehas after being brought into the tent of an Israelite man named Zimri (Num. 25:15). When both she and Zimri were executed, a plague that was sweeping through the Israelite camp was stopped.

COZEBA (Cō zē´ bá) Place-name meaning "deceptive." Home of descendants of Judah (1 Chron. 4:22). Its location is uncertain.

CRACKNEL Old English word for a hard brittle biscuit (1 Kings 14:3 KJV).

CRAFT Occupation or trade requiring manual dexterity or artistic skill. Several crafts were practiced in biblical times: carpentry, boat building, carving (wood, ivory, ebony, and alabaster), metalworking (gold, silver, bronze, and iron), weaving and spinning, tanning, tent making, basket weavers, potter's trade, fuller's trade, dyeing, sculpting, jeweler's trade, glassmaking, perfumery, embroidering, masonry, plastering, etc. See *Occupations and Professions.*

CRANE KJV translation of the Hebrew word in Isa. 38:14; Jer. 8:7. Modern translations read "swift" (NIV, NASB, REB) or dove (REB). See *Birds.*

CRAWLING THINGS NRSV translation of Hebrew term in Mic. 7:17. The Hebrew word also appears in Deut. 32:24,33 where it refers to poisonous snakes. See *Creeping Things.*

CREATION The nature of the Bible's teaching on creation is at once theological, doxological, and factual. Theologically the Bible counters pagan cosmological theories both ancient and modern: this world is not ultimate reality. Doxologically not only the creation itself declares the glory of God, but even the teaching of creation in Scripture is presented as praise to God. For instance, scholars recognize the pleasing literary symmetry in the structure of the creation days in Genesis. Factually the biblical texts reveal something about God's creative and formative actions in this world. Therefore, though the doctrine of creation is more than science, it is not unscientific—otherwise biblical theology and doxology are groundless. Indeed these emphases are bound together in the doctrine of creation as a central theme throughout the Bible.

The Message of Creation God is eternal and transcendent; creation is not (Gen. 1:1; cp. Jesus' allusions to the "beginning of creation which God created" Mark 13:19 KJV; cp. Matt. 19:4; Mark 10:6). Everything owes its creaturely existence (Isa. 44:24; 45:12; Ps. 33:6; Rev. 4:11) to the work of the Father, Son, and Holy Spirit (cp. Gen. 1:1; John 1:1; Gen. 1:2), with Christ as the preeminent agent of creation (John 1:10; Col. 1:16). Biblical teaching implies that God created the world out of nothing (Heb. 11:3). Unlike God, any created thing can be shaken; only what He desires will continue to exist (Heb. 1:3; 12:27; Col. 1:17).

In spite of its present subjection to ethical and material corruption, God's creation still bears the original impress of its complete goodness (Gen. 1:31; 1 Tim. 4:4). The human race alone enjoys the privilege of bearing His image (Gen. 1:27—all subsequent people, though not directly created as were Adam and Eve, are regarded as God's special handiwork; Ps. 89:47; cp. Ps. 102:18). Divine purpose (Col. 1:16) and design (e.g., the marking of time by the movements of the heavenly bodies in Gen. 1:14) pervade creation. The creation speaks of the glory of God in bold contrast with man (Pss. 8; 19:1-4).

The defacement of creation, then, is not original. Due to Adam's sin, creation now bears evidence of its subjection to futility, slavery to corruption, groaning and suffering (Rom. 8:20-22). Nevertheless, God's handiwork faithfully continues to attest of His eternal power and divine nature, despite the rebellion and idolatry of a race which chooses to turn away from this revealed knowledge (Rom. 1:18-23). The good news is that though God's image in the human race is marred due to the fall, the image is being renewed (Col. 3:10; Eph. 4:24) in those who are new creatures in Christ (2 Cor. 5:17; Gal. 6:15). One day the entire creation will be released into the freedom of the coming glory of the children of God (Rom. 8:20-22). Therefore, as foreshadowed by Adam, Christ is the true prototype for the company of the redeemed (Rom. 5:14; 1 Cor. 15:45).

Care in Interpreting Scripture and Science Especially since the Enlightenment, the scriptural teaching of creation has become the object of dissection and doubt. Relevant biblical texts are commonly treated today as prescientific mistakes or mythology. In this milieu teachers and preachers of the doctrine of creation can expect inquiry as to the truthfulness of the Bible in relation to the physical and literary "sciences."

Historical critics typically view the creation narrative in Genesis as dependent on Mesopotamian or Egyptian parallel accounts. Yet none of the various scholarly reconstructions of dependence in Genesis has captured a scholarly consensus. Creation stories certainly do exist which are similar to Genesis in some aspects, but differences, even radical ones, are often ignored in the comparisons. For instance, the serene monotheism of Genesis stands in bold relief to the turbulent polytheism typically found in Babylonian tales. Some points of contact between Genesis and other creation accounts are, in fact, likely due to the biblical repudiation of the pagan ideas in those cosmogonies.

What has become a standard charge of modernist biblical critics is that Genesis not only contains mythology but is even comprised of two conflicting mythological accounts of creation in its opening chapters. Attempting to explain the first two chapters as a source and tradition compilation, the common conjecture is that a priestly source (P) underlying Gen. 1:1-2:4a is in conflict with the Yahwist (J) account in the rest of chapter 2. A growing scholarly tendency, however, is to reject the view that these chapters represent two competing creation accounts. Congruity in the literary structure of the two chapters indicates one hand rather than separate traditions. Rhetorical studies also imply that the two chapters present a unified narrative; and comparative studies indicate that origin stories in Sumeria and Babylon were told in doublet, with the general account followed by the more detailed. All of this lends support to the traditional view: chapter 2 presents a more detailed elaboration of the themes in chapter 1.

With the rise of modern science, another challenge to the biblical doctrine of creation has been mounted. An all too common perception is that the teachings of the Bible and science are either diametrically opposed or else completely irrelevant to each other. A healthier view, yet which requires more care and work, is that Scripture and science complement each other when each is correctly interpreted. Past interpretive mistakes and incomplete understandings of science and Bible are well known. For instance, Isaac Newton was mistaken in his corpuscular theory of light. Quantum phenomena continue to perplex our understanding. Biblical interpreters once believed the Bible taught a geocentric universe (also the scientific understanding of those times). Many interpretive biblical conundrums also remain such as the creation of light before the sun and stars in Gen. 1, or when and how to date creation. What is clear is that the church must not surrender to interpretive skepticism or doubts about biblical veracity and at the same time must resist interpretive fads.

The church must also stand firm in the face of speculative worldviews dressed up as scientific truth. The Bible does seem to recognize genetic variability within the various creaturely orders (e.g., since all humans have descended from Adam and Eve, there is only one human race—cp. Acts 17:26). But the almost infinite plasticity of species as postulated in Darwinism is rejected in the scriptural doctrine of creation (note that reproduction is "after their kind"; see Gen. 1:11-12). It is vital to recognize that the rejection of any possibility of design in macro-evolutionary theory flies in the face of the biblical creation account and cannot be harmonized with it.

Believers are grateful when science, intentionally or not, lends some confirmation of scriptural truth (e.g., recent cosmology has begun to debate again whether there is scientific evidence of a creation *ex nihilo*). Ultimately, however, faith in God's revealed word in Scripture is paramount for understanding the origin of all things (Heb. 11:3). Not dependent upon incomplete or faulty human understanding, the revealed truth of God's sovereign creative work is a settled matter (Ps. 119:89-91). *Ted Cabal*

CREATION AND SCIENCE The forward progress of science has been made possible by the scientific method, which includes observing a phenomena, formulating a hypothesis to explain the observation, and performing a designed experiment to gather data to assess the validity of the hypothesis. These steps illustrate two important fundamentals of science. First, science is limited to the present. No matter how sophisticated the scientific equipment, it will never allow a person to analyze data other than in his present time. The scientist can examine artifacts, catalogue them, and make guesses using the techniques of historiography, but he can never perform a controlled experiment to discern what happened in the past.

Second, the scientific method provides data independent of the scientist's worldview. A scientist who is a Christian (and there are many) will arrive at exactly the same data using the scientific method as an atheist. Science does not depend upon a particular belief system and is, therefore, not the sole domain of evolutionists. Thus, the attempt to cast the debate between evolutionists and creationists as one of science versus religion or fact versus faith is erroneous.

Today, evolution stands as a theory in crisis. Experiments demonstrating how life could arise from non-life in a primordial, pre-biotic soup have all failed leaving evolutionists with no explanation for the presence of life today. Stanley Miller's 1953 experiment in which he produced a few amino acids is no longer considered valid even though it is still in every college textbook as proof of evolution. Miller assumed the earth's primitive atmosphere was a reducing atmosphere that contained ammonia and methane gases but no oxygen. Being a chemist, he knew that a reducing atmosphere was absolutely necessary if any molecules were to form spontaneously. New understanding of the data (from an evolutionary perspective) suggests that a neutral atmosphere produced by volcanic gases was present in the early earth. These gases form no building blocks of life in Miller's apparatus. To complicate matters for evolutionists, certain artifacts (rocks and water) suggest that oxygen was indeed present very early. A. G. Cairns-Smith, an evolutionist, has demonstrated that the production of naturally occurring, pure, usable chemicals to build molecules would be impossible in the waters of the primitive earth (*Seven Clues to the Origin of Life,* Cambridge University Press, 1985, p. 43).

One must ask, "If it was possible for building blocks of life to form, could they spontaneously assemble into a living cell?" Sir Fred Hoyle calculated this probability (which is a very conservative number) and determined that there is only one chance in $10^{40,000}$ that a cell could be assembled from organic molecules (*The Universe: Past and Present Reflections,* University College, 1981). Most scientists consider probabilities greater than 10^{50} to be impossible. Francis Crick, the biologist who won the Nobel Prize for discovering the structure of DNA, determined that the four billion years evolutionists have determined was available for evolution was not enough time for life to arise out of a primordial soup (*Life Itself: Its Origin and Nature,* Simon and Schuster, 1981).

The shortcomings of the Darwinian theory continue to manifest themselves. Darwin wrote, "If it could be demonstrated that any complex organ existed which could not possibly have been formed by numerous, successive, slight modifications, then my theory would absolutely break down" (*The Origin of the Species,* New York University Press, 1988, p. 154). How does Darwin fare today? Two lines of scientific research provide evidence against Darwin.

The first line of evidence shows that mutations do not build new genes. Pierre-Paul Grassé, past president of the Académie des Sciences, stated that mutations are only trivial changes resulting from the alteration of genes already present, whereas creative evolution requires the synthesis of new genes (*Evolution of Living Organisms,* Academic Press, 1977, p. 217). His studies provided evidence that mutations do not take succeeding generations farther away from a starting point, but instead the succeeding generations stay within firmly fixed boundaries. Bacteria, despite their innumerable mutations, have not transgressed the structural framework within which they have always fluctuated and still do. Lee Spetner has not only confirmed these findings but has shown that mutations result in a loss of genetic information—exactly the opposite of what Darwinism predicted. Spetner concluded, "The failure to observe even one mutation that adds information is more than just a failure to find support for a theory. It is evidence against the theory" (*Not by Chance: Shattering the Modern Theory of Evolution,* Judaica Press, 1998, p. 160). Worse yet, a key piece of evidence long held as "proof" for evolution through mutation was the development of antibiotic resistance in bacteria. Antibiotic resistance is caused by switching on a gene already present in the bacteria. As it turns out, there was no mutation at all.

The other line of scientific proof that discredits evolution is irreducible complexity. Darwin's simple-to-complex scheme has not stood up under scientific scrutiny. Biochemist Michael Behe declared that irreducible complexity extends not only to the cell but to the parts that make up the cell (*Darwin's Black Box: The Biochemical Challenge to Evolution,* Free Press,

1996). This means that the cell could not have been built by a process of simple steps. In order for the cell to function, it had to have all its complexity from the start. Anything less would have been nonfunctional, organic rubbish. Behe's famous mousetrap example illustrates the fallacy that part of an eye (organ, limb, etc.) is better than no eye at all. Part of an eye works no better than having only half the parts of a mousetrap. One simply does not expect to catch fewer mice with half the parts of a mousetrap missing. Irreducible complexity down to the smallest parts demands an intelligent Creator who by His wisdom created an amazingly complex cell to confound the wisdom of the world.

The impossibility of life appearing spontaneously is an insurmountable problem for evolutionists but clearly fits within the truth claims of the Scripture that God, in the beginning, created life. The reason life looks as if an organizing "principle" worked itself out in a definite plan is because God, the Great Designer, formed life in intricate detail. God did not create the cell and set things in motion (theistic evolution), but God created every living thing as He said in the first two chapters of Genesis.

As the mainstays of evolution crumble, creation remains the only realistic explanation of life. It best explains the artifact evidences seen today, such as the absence of transitional forms of life witnessed by the fossil record. Missing links between fish and amphibians, amphibians and reptiles, etc., in the fossil record are missing because they did not exist. God created the kinds to bring forth after their own kind. Yet God designed genetic diversity within the cell which allows for the variation observed within the kinds.

If evolution is in such a state, then why do so many cling to it? As it turns out, the argument is not really between creation and science. The argument is on a philosophical level. Rationalistic thinking rules out the supernatural and looks for other explanations than the work of an all wise Creator, who left His imprint in a designed creation. Should the theory of rationalistic, fallible man mold our thinking, or ought we to acknowledge the God, who is our Sovereign Creator, and believe His word?   *David Mapes*

CREATURE Something having life, either animal or human. The phrase used in the Hebrew Bible *nephesh chayah* is translated by "creature," "living [thing, soul]," and "beast." In Gen. 2:7 it is used of mankind and translated "living soul." In all of the other references the phrase applies solely to animals. Because the same term is used of mankind and the other creatures, interpreters believe that it applies to the similar physical makeup (same matter) rather than the higher relationship with God that is special to humans.   *Mike Mitchell*

CREDIT, CREDITOR The biblical attitude toward borrowing is summarized in Prov. 22:7, which declares that to be a borrower is tantamount to being a lender's slave. Paul taught that it is better to owe no one anything (Rom. 13:8). Nevertheless, the Bible recognizes that some loans are necessary and so counsels against unjust interest rates (Ps. 15:5; Prov. 28:8; Ezek. 18:8,13). Those who borrow and do not repay are called "wicked" (Ps. 37:21) and will face a day of economic reckoning (Hab. 2:6-7).

The social and economic difficulties incumbent on heavy borrowing were anticipated by the Mosaic law, which commanded that fellow Israelites should not be charged interest on loans (Exod. 22:25; Deut. 23:19-20; cp. Neh. 5:7-12). This practice runs counter to the modern banking and credit card industries, as does Jesus' maxim to lend without expecting repayment (Luke 6:34). See *Loan.*   *Paul H. Wright*

CREEPING THINGS English translation sometimes used for a general Hebrew term designating small animals that appear to creep or crawl along the ground. English translators sometimes use "moving things" or other equivalents for the Hebrew word. The term was applied to all land animals in general (Gen. 1:24-26,28; 7:23; 9:3), fish (Pss. 69:34; 104:25; Hab. 1:14), forest animals (Ps. 104:20), and "creatures that swarm" (Lev. 11:29-30,44,46 NRSV, NASB, that is, weasels, mice, lizards, snails, moles, and perhaps even crocodiles). See *Reptiles.*

CREMATION Referred to in the OT by the phrase "burning the bones of" (1 Kings 13:2; 2 Kings 23:16, 20; Amos 2:1). In ancient Israel, death by burning was reserved as a punishment for the worst of criminals (Gen. 38:24; Josh. 7:15, 25; Lev. 20:14; 21:9). Both it and cremation, burning the body after death, were stigmatized as abhorrent by the Israelites. Because burning human bones was considered to be the ultimate desecration of the dead (1 Kings 13:2; 2 Kings 23:16, 20), it was subject to punishment by God (Amos 2:1).

The ancient Greeks cremated bodies after a plague or battle for sanitary reasons or to prevent their enemies from mutilating the dead. A similar attitude was found among the Israelites and perhaps explains why the dead bodies of Saul and his sons were burned (1 Sam. 31:12; cp. 2 Sam. 21:11-14). Saul's cremation also reflects God's rejection of his ignominious reign. When Amos (6:9-10 NIV) described the burning of bodies after battle, evidently for sanitary reasons, he intended to depict the horrors faced by victims of war.

Early Christians were hesitant to practice cremation because of their understanding that the body was the temple of the Holy Spirit (1 Cor. 6:19) yet recognized that cremation has no effect on the integrity of one's eternal state (Rev. 20:13).   *Paul H. Wright*

CRESCENS (Crĕs´ cĕns) Personal name meaning "growing." Christian worker with Paul who had gone to Galatia when 2 Timothy was written (2 Tim. 4:10).

CRESCENTS Translation used in some modern versions for the ornamental jewelry on necklaces in the shape of the crescent moon. It probably had magical connotations. Midianites (Judg. 8:21,26) and unfaithful Israelites (Isa. 3:18) wore them.

CRETANS (Crē´ tăns), **CRETES, CRETIANS** Citizens of Crete. See *Crete.*

CRETE (Crēt) Long, narrow, mountainous island south of mainland Greece, running 170 miles east-west but never more than about 35 miles wide. Crete was the center of the Minoan maritime empire named after the legendary King Minos and associated especially with the famous palaces of Cnossos and Phaestos, which flourished from 2000 to 1500 B.C. This artistically brilliant civilization fell suddenly, perhaps by earthquake followed by conquest, about 1400 B.C., leaving written tablets in the oldest known scripts of Europe, including the undeciphered "Linear A" and the apparently later proto-Greek "Linear B," found also on the mainland. The Minoans of Crete were known to the Egyptians as "Keftiu," which may be the same as biblical

"Caphtor," though the biblical term may include a wider reference to coastlands and islands of the Aegean area. The Philistines came to Palestine from Caphtor (Jer. 47:4; Amos 9:7) and may have been part of the widespread migrant "Sea Peoples" rather than Cretans proper.

In classical Greek times Crete had many city-states, but they played relatively little part in mainstream Greek history. It had become a center of piracy before the Roman occupation in 67 B.C. Under the Romans it became part of a double province, Crete with Cyrene, under a governor with the title "proconsul," who ruled the island and the opposite coast of North Africa from the Roman capital Gortyna. This had already been among the cities to whom the Romans had appealed a century before for fair treatment of their Jewish minorities (1 Macc. 15:23). Cretans were among those listed as present in Jerusalem on the day of Pentecost (Acts 2:11), and the gospel may first have reached the island through them.

Paul made his voyage to Rome as a prisoner on a Roman grain ship. The voyage followed the route south of Crete, which gave partial shelter from the northwest winds and avoided the peril of the lee shore on the north coast, while still involving the need to beat against largely adverse winds. The journey had already been very slow, and it was getting dangerously late in the summer sailing season. The ship doubled Salmone, the eastern cape of Crete, and with difficulty reached Fair Havens, a small anchorage near the city of Lasea (Acts 27:8). There the emergency council called by the centurion and shipmaster overruled Paul's advice, and a risky attempt was made to reach Phoenix, a regular port for servicing the grain ships, some 40 miles further west along the coast. The gentle south wind gave way to a violent northeaster (Euroclydon, Acts 27:14) when they came out of the shelter of Cape Matala (Loukinos) into an open bay, and the ship was driven helplessly, managing only some emergency action in the lee of the offshore island of Cauda, and thence to shipwreck on Malta.

The only other references to Crete in the NT are in the epistle to Titus. Paul had left Titus in Crete to exercise pastoral supervision over the churches there (Titus 1:5). The character of the people is described in a quotation from a prophet of their own: "Cretans are always liars, evil beasts, lazy gluttons" (Titus 1:12 HCSB), words attributed to the Cretan seer Epimenides, who was also credited with having advised the Athenians to set up altars to unknown gods (cp. Acts 17:23).

A harbor on Crete through which Paul likely passed on his journey from Caesarea Maritima to Rome.

It is a problem to know when Paul (or Titus) visited Crete, apart from Paul's voyage as a prisoner. It is difficult to fit the occasions of the Pastoral Epistles (to Timothy and Titus) into Paul's life as recorded in Acts. The most satisfactory answer to this difficulty still seems to be that which argues that Paul was released from his two years' imprisonment in Rome (Acts 28:30) and undertook further travels in the East which can only be traced in these epistles. At this last period of his life he may have focused his work on establishing and strengthening the churches throughout the Greek East.   *Colin J. Hemer*

CRIB Feeding trough for the ox (Prov. 14:4 KJV) or the ass (Isa. 1:3; cp. Job 39:9) and probably for any number of other domesticated animals.

CRICKET Hebrew term translated "cricket" (Lev. 11:22 NIV, NASB, NRSV, TEV) is difficult to identify, probably a locust or grasshopper. See *Insects*.

CRIMES AND PUNISHMENTS Israel, like most peoples in the ancient Near East, considered their law to be the direct revelation from God. Since the law came from God, any transgression of the law was a transgression of God's revealed will.

The responsibility for the fulfillment and enforcement of the law lay with the entire community. The transgression of the law by one person or group within Israel involved the whole community in the guilt of the act. This is especially true in cases of homicide, idolatry, and sexual offenses (Deut. 19:10; 21:1-9; 2 Kings 24:1-7). When Israel failed to purge the offender and rebellion against God's Law from their midst, God punished Israel (Lev. 18:26-28; 26:3-45; Deut. 28).

Israelite law with respect to crime and punishment was distinct from the laws of other cultures in several ways. First, Israel, in contrast to many of its neighbors, did not consider crimes against property to be capital crimes. Israel observed a system of corporal punishment and/or fines for lesser crimes. Second, Israel restricted the law of retaliation (eye for an eye; *lex talionis*) to the person of the offender. Other cultures permitted the family to be punished for the crimes of the offender. Third, Israel did not observe class differences in the enforcement of the Law to the extent that their neighbors did.

Nobility and commoner, priest and lay people were treated equally in theory. However, slaves and sojourners (foreigners) did not have an equal standing with free Israelites—though their treatment in Israel was often better than in surrounding nations; women did not have equal standing with the men in Israelite culture—especially in regard to marriage and divorce laws and laws pertaining to sexual offenses. Finally, Israelites (in contrast to the people of surrounding nations) could not substitute sacrifices for intentional breaches of the law; sin and guilt offerings were allowed only in the cases of unwitting sins (Lev. 4–5).

Crimes and Capital Punishment in the Old Testament Israelite law considered some crimes serious enough to warrant capital punishment. See *Capital Punishment.*

Being "Cut Off" from Israel Often in the OT the punishment for a particular crime is termed being "cut off" from Israel. The meaning of the phrase is somewhat ambiguous. Some interpret the phrase to mean excommunication or exile from Israel or the community of faith, while others interpret it as the pronouncement of the death penalty. The latter position is accepted in this article. Often the phrase "cut off" is used in parallel with words or phrases or in contexts which clearly indicate death (Exod. 31:14; 2 Sam. 7:9; 1 Kings 11:16; Jer. 7:28; 11:19; Zech. 13:8). See *Excommunication.*

The offenses that make one liable to being "cut off" are: the men of Israel who are uncircumcised (Gen. 17:14; cp. Exod. 4:24; Josh. 5:2-9), eating leavened bread during the feast of unleavened bread (Exod. 12:15,19), trying to copy or using the holy anointing oil on outsiders (30:33), profaning the Sabbath (Exod. 31:14), partaking of sacrifices in an unclean state (Lev. 7:20-21,25; 19:8; cp. 1 Sam. 2:33), eating blood (Lev. 7:27; 17:10,14), offering sacrifices in a place other than the tabernacle (Lev. 17:3-4,8-9), certain sexual offenses (18:29; 20:17-18), child sacrifices to Molech (Lev. 20:3,5), consulting wizards or mediums (Lev. 20:6; Mic. 5:12), approaching holy things in an unclean state (Lev. 22:3; Num. 19:13,20), improperly observing the Day of Atonement (Lev. 23:29), not observing the Passover (Num. 9:13), committing a high-handed sin (sinning intentionally or defiantly; Num. 15:30-31), idolatry (1 Kings 9:6-7; 14:9-10,14; 21:21; Ezek. 14:7-8; Mic. 5:13; Zeph. 1:4; Zech. 13:2), and those God curses (Ps.

37:22). The idea of being "cut off" is also mentioned in the NT (Rom. 9:3; 11:22; cp. 1 Cor. 16:22; Gal. 1:6: 5:12).

Crimes and Corporal Punishment in the Old Testament Crimes of a lesser nature (usually those involving premeditated bodily injury) were punished with some sort of corporal punishment. The law of retaliation (eye for an eye; *lex talionis*) was the operative principle in most cases involving corporal punishment (Exod. 21:23-25; Lev. 24:19-22; Deut. 19:21).

The law of retaliation may seem to some to be rather harsh and even crude. In our own modern world, we would sue a person responsible for putting out an eye before we would put that person's eye out. In the ancient world, however, the law of retaliation served to restrict the vengeance taken on one who inflicted bodily injury. For example, it prevented the killing of a person who had put out the eye of another. The law of retaliation helped make the punishment fit the crime.

Besides the law of retaliation, corporal punishments also included scourging (Deut. 25:1-3), blinding (Gen. 19:11; 2 Kings 6:18; cp. Judg. 16:21; 2 Kings 25:7), plucking out hair (Neh. 13:25; Is. 50:6), and the sale of a thief into slavery who could not pay the monetary penalties (Exod. 22:1-3; cp. Lev. 25:39; 2 Kings 4:1; Neh. 5:5). In one instance, mutilation is prescribed (Deut. 25:11-12).

Crimes and Fines in the Old Testament Fines were always paid to the injured party. Fines were prescribed for causing a miscarriage (Exod. 21:22), deflowering a virgin (Exod. 22:16-17; cp. Deut. 22:29), sexually violating a slave woman promised to another man in marriage (Lev. 19:20), and in some cases where an ox gored a person causing death (Exod. 21:28-32). A thief (one who steals by stealth) may be fined double, fourfold, or five-fold the value of the stolen goods, depending on what was stolen (Exod. 22:1-4,9). A robber (one who steals by force or intimidation) must return the stolen property plus one-fifth of its value plus make a guilt offering (Lev. 6:1-7). The difference between the penalties for thievery and robbery is difficult to explain. Should a man falsely accuse his bride of being unchaste, the man is fined double the marriage present (100 shekels of silver; Deut. 22:19). One who inflicted unpremeditated bodily injury must compensate the victim for the loss of income plus pay the costs of recovery

(Exod. 21:18-19). If a person should cause the loss of eye or tooth of his slave, the slave was freed (Exod. 21:26-27).

Crimes and Punishments in the New Testament There is no body of legal material in the NT comparable to that found in the OT. Jesus did comment in the Sermon on the Mount on some of the matters discussed above. He expanded the prohibition of killing to include anger (Matt. 5:21-26) and the prohibition against adultery to include lust (Matt. 5:27-30). In contrast to the OT, Jesus forbade divorce except on the grounds of unchastity (Matt. 5:31-32). With regard to the law of retaliation, Jesus desired that his disciples waive their rights to reparations (Matt. 5:38-42).

During the period of the NT, the Jews seem to have had relative autonomy in the matters of their religious law and customs. Even Jewish communities outside Palestine were under the authority of the high priest (Acts 9:1-2) and were allowed some measure of autonomy in religious matters (Acts. 18:12-17).

Whether the Jews had the authority under the Roman government to impose the death penalty is a debated question. When Jesus was brought to trial, the Jews' reason for bringing him to Pilate was that they did not have the power to execute criminals (John 18:31). One ancient rabbinic tradition in the Babylonian Talmud (Abodah Zarah 8b) holds that the Jews lost the power to execute criminals for about 40 years. However, incidents in the NT seem to indicate otherwise: statements made at Peter's trial (Acts 5:27-42), the stoning of Stephen (Acts 7:57-60), attempted lynchings (Acts 9:23-24; 14:19; 23:12-15), the authority to kill foreigners caught trespassing in certain areas of the temple (Acts 21:28-31, a practice reported by Josephus, an ancient Jewish historian), and a statement made by Paul (Acts 26:10). Other ancient Jewish records of stonings and burnings indicates that the Jews may have had the authority to impose the death penalty.

The Jews during the period of the NT had the power to impose corporal punishment. This consisted primarily of scourgings (Matt. 10:17; Acts 5:40; 22:19; 2 Cor. 11:24) and excommunication (Luke 6:22; John 9:22; 12:42; 16:2).

The procurator was Rome's legal representative in the provinces of the Roman Empire. He intervened in local affairs when the public peace and order were threatened—especially by sedition, riot, or brigandage (cp. Acts 5:36-37). The charge against Jesus was a claim to be "King of the Jews" (Matt 27:37). Roman punishments included crucifixion (usually reserved only for slaves and the lower classes), beheading (Matt. 14:10; Rev. 20:4), lifetime sentences to work in the mines (that is, kept in bonds; Acts 23:29; 26:31), scourging (Acts 16:22; 22:24), and imprisonment (Acts 16:23-24). See *Appeal to Caesar.* *Phil Logan*

CRIMSON Red color taken from the bodies of dead kermes (*Coccus ilicis,* which attached itself to the kermes oak—*Quercus coccifera*) or cochineal insects (*Coccus cacti*). The same Hebrew words translated as crimson are also translated "scarlet" ("red" comes from a root word from which the Hebrew word for "blood" comes and designates a different color). Crimson or scarlet thread (Gen. 38:28,30), cord (Josh. 2:18,21), and cloth (Lev. 14:4; Num. 4:8; 2 Sam. 1:24; 2 Chron. 2:7,14; 3:14; Prov. 31:21; Jer. 4:30; Nah. 2:3) are mentioned in the Bible. Crimson or scarlet along with purple were considered royal colors (Matt. 27:28; Rev. 17:3-4; 18:11-12,16). Isaiah used scarlet as the imagery to describe sins (Isa. 1:18). See *Colors.*

CRISPING PIN KJV translation in Isa. 3:22. A crisping pin was used for curling the hair. Modern versions translate the word "handbag," or "flounced skirt" (REB). See *Bag.*

CRISPUS (Crĭs´ pŭs) Personal name meaning "curly." Leader of synagogue in Corinth (Acts 18:8) and one of few whom Paul personally baptized (1 Cor. 1:14). Church tradition says he became bishop of Aegina.

CROCUS Plant with abundant blossoms. Several species of crocus grow in Palestine. The flower mentioned in Song 2:1 and Isa. 35:1 has been identified as either the narcissus (*N. tazetta*), the meadow saffron (genus *Calchicum*), or the asphodel (*asphodelos*). The Hebrew word is sometimes translated "rose" (cp. KJV, NRSV, REB, NASB, NIV Song 2:1 and Isa. 35:1). See *Flowers.*

CROSS, CRUCIFIXION Method the Romans used to execute Jesus Christ. The most painful and degrading form of capital punishment in the ancient world, the cross became also the means by which Jesus became the atoning sacrifice for the sins of all mankind. It also became a symbol for the sacrifice of self in discipleship (Rom. 12:1) and for the death of self to the world (Mark 8:34).

Historical Development Originally a cross was a wooden pointed stake used to build a wall or to erect fortifications around a town. Beginning with the Assyrians and Persians, it began to be used to display the heads of captured foes or of particularly heinous criminals on the palisades above the gateway into a city. Later crucifixion developed into a form of capital punishment, as enemies of the state were impaled on the stake itself. The Greeks and Romans at first reserved the punishment only for slaves, saying it was too barbaric for freeborn or citizens. By the first century, however, it was used for any enemy of the state, though citizens could only be crucified by direct edict of Caesar. As time went on, the Romans began to use crucifixion more and more as a deterrent to criminal activity, so that by Jesus' time it was a common sight.

The eastern form of crucifixion was practiced in the OT. Saul was decapitated and his body displayed on a wall by the Philistines (1 Sam. 31:9-10), and the "hanging" found in Esther 2:23; 5:14 may mean impalement (cp. Ezra 6:11). According to Jewish law (Deut. 21:22-23) the offenders were "hung on a tree," which meant they were "accursed of God" and outside the covenant people. Such criminals were to be removed from the cross before nightfall lest they "defile the land." During the intertestamental period the western form was borrowed when Alexander Janneus crucified 800 Pharisees (76 B.C.), but on the whole the Jews condemned and seldom used the method. Even Herod the Great refused to crucify his enemies. The practice was abolished after the "conversion" of the emperor of Constantine to Christianity.

A person crucified in Jesus' day was first of all scourged (beaten with a whip consisting of thongs with pieces of metal or bone attached to the end) or at least flogged until the blood flowed. This was not done just out of cruelty but was designed to hasten death and lessen the terrible ordeal. After the beating, the victim was forced to bear the crossbeam to the execution site in order to signify that life was already over and to break the will to live. A tablet detailing the crime(s) was often placed around the criminal's neck and then fastened to the cross. At the site the prisoner was often tied (the normal method) or nailed (if a quicker death was desired) to the crossbeam. The nail would be driven through the wrist rather than the palm, since the smaller bones of the hand could not support the weight of the body. The beam with the body was then lifted and tied to the already affixed upright pole. Pins or a small wooden block were placed halfway up to provide a seat for the body lest the nails tear open the wounds or the ropes force the arms from their sockets. Finally the feet were tied or nailed to the post. Death was caused by the loss of blood circulation and coronary failure. Especially if the victims were tied, it could take days of hideous pain as the extremities turned slowly gangrenous; so often the soldiers would break the victims legs with a club, causing massive shock and a quick death. Such deaths were usually done in public places, and the body was left to rot for days, with carrion birds allowed to degrade the corpse further.

Four types of crosses were used: (1) The Latin cross has the crossbeam about two-thirds of the way up the upright pole; (2) St. Anthony's cross (probably due to its similarity to his famous crutch) had the beam at the top of the upright pole like a T; (3) St. Andrew's cross (supposedly the form used to crucify Andrew) had the shape of the letter X; (4) the Greek cross has both beams equal in the shape of a plus sign.

The Crucifixion of Jesus Jesus predicted His coming crucifixion many times. The Synoptic Gospels list at least three (Mark 8:31; 9:31; 10:33-34 and parallels), while John records three others (3:14; 8:28; 12:32-33). Several aspects of Jesus' passion are predicted: (1) it occurred by divine necessity ("must" in Mark 8:31); (2) both Jews ("delivered") and Romans ("killed") were guilty (Mark 9:31); (3) Jesus would be vindicated by being raised from the dead; (4) the death itself entailed glory (seen in the "lifted up" sayings which imply exaltation in John 3:14; 8:28; 12:32-33).

The narration of Jesus' crucifixion in the Gospels emphasized Jewish guilt, but all four carefully separated the leaders from the common people, who supported Jesus all along and were led astray by the leaders at the last. Yet Roman guilt is also obvious. The Sanhedrin was no longer allowed to initiate capital punishment; only the Romans could do so. Furthermore, only Roman soldiers could carry it out. Roman customs were followed in the scourging, mock

enthronement, bearing the crossbeam, and the crucifixion itself. The site on a hill and the size of the cross (the use of the hyssop reed shows it was seven to nine feet high) showed their desire for a public display of a "criminal." The Jewish elements in the crucifixion of Jesus were the wine mixed with myrrh (Mark 15:23), the hyssop reed with vinegar (Mark 15:36), and the removal of Jesus' body from the cross before sunset (John 19:31).

The four Gospels look at Jesus' crucifixion from four different vantage points and highlight diverse aspects of the significance of His death. Mark and Matthew centered upon the horror of putting the Son of God Himself to death. Mark emphasized the messianic meaning, using the taunts of the crowds to "save yourself" (15:30-31) as an unconscious prophecy pointing to the resurrection. Matthew took Mark even further, pointing to Jesus as the royal Messiah who faced His destiny in complete control of the situation. Jesus' vindication was found not only in the rending of the veil and the centurion's testimony (Matt. 27:51,54 paralleling Mark) but in the remarkable raising of the OT saints (vv. 52-53) which links the cross and the open tomb. For Matthew the cross inaugurated the last days when the power of death is broken and salvation is poured out upon all people.

Luke has perhaps the most unique portrayal, with two emphases: Jesus as the archetypal righteous Martyr who forgave His enemies and the crucifixion as an awesome scene of reverence and worship. Luke omitted the negative aspects of the crucifixion (earthquakes, wine with myrrh, cry of dereliction) and overturned the taunts when the crowd "returned home beating their breasts" (23:48 RSV). Luke included three sayings of Jesus which relate to prayer (found only in Luke): "Father, forgive them" (v. 34, contrasted with the mockery); "today you will be with Me in paradise" (v. 43 HCSB, in response to the criminal's prayer); and "Father, into Your hands I entrust My spirit" (v. 46 HCSB). A wondrous sense of stillness and worship color Luke's portrayal.

John's narration is perhaps the most dramatic. Even more so than Luke, all the negative elements disappear (the darkness and taunts as well as those missing also in Luke), and an atmosphere of calm characterizes the scene. At the core is Jesus' sovereign control of the whole scene. The cross becomes His throne. John noted that the inscription on the cross ("JESUS THE NAZARENE, THE KING OF THE JEWS") was written in Aramaic, Latin, and Greek (19:19-20), thereby changing it into a universal proclamation of Jesus' royal status. Throughout the account to the final cry, "It is finished" (v. 30), Jesus was in complete control.

One cannot understand Jesus' crucifixion until all four Gospels are taken into account. All the emphases—the messianic thrust, Jesus as Son of God and as the righteous Martyr, the sacrificial nature of His death, the cross as His throne—are necessary emphases of the total picture of the significance of His crucifixion.

Theological Meaning While a theology of the cross is found primarily in Paul, it clearly predates him, as can be demonstrated in the "creeds" (statements of belief/teaching) Paul quoted. For instance, 1 Cor. 15:3-5 says Paul had "received" and then "passed on" to the Corinthians the truth that Jesus "died for our sins according to the Scriptures." Three major themes are interwoven in this and other creeds (Rom 4:25; 6:1-8; 8:32; Col. 2:11-12; 1 Tim. 3:16; Heb. 1:3-4; 1 Pet. 1:21; 3:18-22): Jesus death as our substitute (from Isa. 53:5; cp. Mark 10:45; 14:24); Jesus' death and resurrection as fulfilling Scripture; and Jesus' vindication and exaltation by God.

For Paul the "word of the cross" (1 Cor. 1:18 NASB) is the heart of the gospel, and the preaching of the cross is the soul of the church's mission. "Christ crucified" (1 Cor. 1:23; cp. 2:2; Gal. 3:1) is more than the basis of our salvation; the cross was the central event in history, the one moment which demonstrated God's control of and involvement in human history. In 1 Cor. 1:17–2:16 Paul contrasted the "foolishness" of the "message of the cross" with human "wisdom" (1:17-18), for only in the cross can salvation be found and only in the foolish "message of the cross" and "weakness" can the "power of God" be seen (1:21,25). Jesus as the lowly One achieved His glory by virtue of His suffering—only the crucified One could become the risen One (1:26-30). Such a message certainly was viewed as foolish in the first century; Roman historians like Tacitus and Suetonius looked upon the idea of a "crucified God" with contempt.

The cross is the basis of our salvation in Paul's epistles (Rom. 3:24-25; Eph. 2:16; Col. 1:20; 2:14), while the resurrection is stressed as the core in the book of the Acts (2:33-36; 3:19-21; 5:31). Romans 4:25 makes both emphases.

The reason for the distinct emphases is most likely seen in the fact that Acts chronicles the preaching of the early church (with the resurrection as the apologetic basis of our salvation) and the epistles the teaching of the early church (with the crucifixion the theological basis of our salvation). The three major terms are: "redemption," stressing the "ransom payment" made by Jesus' blood in delivering us from sin (Titus 2:14; 1 Pet. 1:18); "propitiation," which refers to Jesus' death as "satisfying" God's righteous wrath (Rom. 3:25; Heb. 2:17); and "justification," picturing the results of the cross, the "acquittal" ("declaring righteous") of our guilt (Rom. 3:24; 4:25; Gal. 2:16-21; 3:24).

The cross did even more than procure salvation. It forged a new unity between Jew and Gentile by breaking down "the dividing wall of hostility" and "made the two one" (Eph. 2:14-15 NIV), thereby producing "peace" by creating a new access to the Father (v. 18). In addition the cross "disarmed" the demonic "powers" and forged the final triumph over Satan and his hordes, forcing those spiritual forces to follow his train in a victory procession (Col. 2:15 NIV). The cross was Satan's great error. When Satan entered Judas in betraying Jesus, he undoubtedly did not realize that the cross would prove his greatest defeat. He could only respond with frustrated rage, knowing that "his time is short" (Rev. 12:12 NIV). Satan participated in his own undoing.

The Symbolic Meaning Jesus Himself established the primary figurative interpretation of the cross as a call to complete surrender to God. He used it five times as a symbol of true discipleship in terms of self-denial, taking up one's cross, and following Jesus (Mark 8:34; 10:38; Matt. 16:24; Luke 9:23; 14:27). Building upon the Roman practice of bearing the crossbeam to the place of execution, Jesus intended this in two directions: the death of self, involving the sacrifice of one's individuality for the purpose of following Jesus completely; and a willingness to imitate Jesus completely, even to the extent of martyrdom.

Closely connected to this is Paul's symbol of the crucified life. Conversion means the individual "no longer live(s)" but is replaced by Christ and faith in Him (Gal. 2:20). Self-centered desires are nailed to the cross (Gal. 5:24), and worldly interests are dead (Gal. 6:14). In Rom. 6:1-8 we are "buried with him" (using the imagery of baptism) with the result that we are raised to "a new way of life" (v. 4). This is taken further in 2 Cor. 5:14-17. The believer relives the death and resurrection by putting to death the old self and putting on the new. In one sense this is a past act, experienced at conversion. Yet according to Eph. 4:22,24 this is also a present act, experienced in the corporate life of the church. In other words, both at conversion and in spiritual growth, the believer must relive the cross before experiencing the resurrection life. The Christian paradox is that death is the path to life. See *Atonement; Christology; Justification; Passion; Propitiation; Redemption.*

Grant Osborne

CROWN Special headdress worn by royalty and other persons of high merit and honor. The crown probably evolved from the cloth headband or turban worn by a tribal leader; the headband eventually became a metal diadem, with or without ornamentation. Some years ago archaeologists discovered in a Jericho tomb a copper headband or crown dating from about 2000 B.C.

Both the king and the high priest of Israel wore crowns, but we have been told more about the latter than the former (Exod. 28:36-37; 29:6, Lev. 8:9). David's golden crown was a prize of battle (2 Sam. 12:30). As a symbol of his authority, the crown was worn when the king was on his throne and when leading his forces in combat (2 Sam. 1:10). The word "crown" was also used figuratively referring to the old man's gray head (Prov. 16:31), a man's virtuous wife (Prov. 12:4), and God's blessings on mankind (Ps. 8:5). Occasionally the word referred to a festive wreath (Song 3:11).

While most references to "crown" in the OT point to the actual headdress, in the NT it usually has a figurative significance. Paul envisioned "a crown of righteousness" for himself and others (2 Tim. 4:8), and James anticipated "the crown of life" (James 1:12). While the winning runner of that day received a garland of myrtle leaves, Paul looked forward to a crown that would not decay (1 Cor. 9:25). Not even the victorious athlete would receive his reward unless he obeyed the rules (2 Tim. 2:5). Conversely, the word evokes revulsion when we read of Roman soldiers weaving briers into a crown of Jesus' head (Matt. 27:29).

In the book of Revelation, crowns are both realistic and figurative. The 24 elders seated around God's throne were wearing "gold crowns" (4:4), and as they worshiped, they "cast their crowns before the throne" (4:10). Later, a seven-headed dragon appeared wearing a crown on each head (12:3), but opposing all the evil forces was the "Son of Man" wearing "a golden crown" (14:14). In each case the crown symbolized power, either good or evil. *William J. Fallis*

CROWN OF THORNS Crown made by the Roman soldiers to mock Jesus, the "King of the Jews" (Matt. 27:29; Mark 15:18; John 19:3; not mentioned in Luke). The identification of the plant used to plait this crown is unknown. Jesus used the imagery of "thorns" in his teaching in a negative sense (Matt. 7:16; Mark 4:7,18; Heb. 6:8). See *Plants.*

CRUCIBLE Melting pot or "fining pot" (KJV), probably made of pottery, used in the refining of silver. The crucible is used in the Bible as a figure for testing of people (Prov. 17:3; 27:21).

CRUSE Elongated pottery vessel about six inches tall used for holding liquids such as oil (1 Kings 17:12,14,16) or water (1 Kings 19:6). Modern readers would understand the vessels to serve the purpose of a modern canteen (1 Sam. 26:11-16). The bowl (2 Kings 2:20 NIV) reflects a different Hebrew term but a similar type vessel. See *Flask.*

CRYSTAL Nearly transparent quartz that may be colorless or slightly tinged. "Crystal" is the modern translation of several Hebrew and Greek words used to describe something valuable (Job 28:17), a clear sky (Ezek. 1:22), a calm sea or river (Rev. 4:6; 22:1), or the radiance of the new Jerusalem (Rev. 21:11). Translators differ in their usage in the various passages.

Fragment of a slate measuring rod divided into fractions of the cubit, from Egypt around the time of Akhenaton's reign.

CUB See *Chub.*

CUBIT Unit of measure. It was reckoned as the distance from a person's elbow to the tip of the middle finger, approximately 18 inches. See *Weights and Measures.*

CUCKOW KJV for an unclean bird (Lev. 11:16; Deut. 14:15); also spelled "cuckoo." Since the bird in question is grouped with carrion-eating or predatory birds, the cuckoo would seem to be eliminated since it only eats insects. Modern versions read "seagull."

CUCUMBER See *Plants.*

CUMIN, CUMMIN Herb of the carrot family (*Cuminum cyminum* L.) mentioned with dill. Used in Bible times to season foods. Isaiah portrayed the planting and threshing of cumin (Isa. 28:25,27). Jesus faulted the Pharisees for giving attention to small things like tithing mint, dill, and cumin while ignoring the weightier matters of the law (Matt. 23:23; Luke 11:42). See *Plants.*

CUN (Cūn) Place-name of city in Syria belonging to Hadadezer, king of Zobah. David took bronze from the city as tribute, and Solomon used the materials in furnishing the temple (1 Chron. 18:8). The parallel passage in 2 Sam. 8:8 reads "Berothai." The two are apparently separate cities, Cun being northeast of Byblos and Berothai southeast of Byblos. Evidently, Cun was more familiar to the Chronicler's readers than Berothai. See *Berothai.*

CUNEIFORM (Cū·nē´ ĭ·fōrm) Most widely used system of writing in the ancient Near East until it was supplanted by alphabetic scripts like Aramaic. The word "cuneiform" is derived from the Latin *cuneus,* "wedge," and is used to refer to characters composed of wedges. The system of writing was originated apparently by the Sumerians before 3000 B.C. The earliest documents are commercial tablets consisting of pictographs (of sheep, grain, etc.) and numbers. Because the documents were written on tablets of moist clay, the scribes soon found it more convenient to indicate objects with stylized pictures composed of wedges made by a stylus. The earliest cuneiform signs were ideographs (a sign standing for a word); but as literary needs increased, the signs were given phonetic values.

Cuneiform tablet and its envelope dealing with the sale of some land.

The cuneiform system of writing was adapted and developed to suit the requirements of several other languages, including Akkadian, Hurrian, Hittite, Elamite, and Eblaite. The people at Ugarit and the Persians used wedges to form their alphabetic scripts.

The decipherment of the cuneiform scripts of Mesopotamia was aided by the existence of trilingual inscriptions, such as the Behistun Rock inscriptions written in Persian, Babylonian, and Elamite cuneiform. The decipherment of the Persian written in an alphabetic cuneiform opened the way for the decipherment of the more difficult syllabic Babylonian and Elamite scripts. Due to the pioneering efforts of H. Rawlinson, E. Hincks, and J. Oppert and others, by the end of the 19th century it was possible to read with confidence the cuneiform inscriptions known up to that time.

The decipherment of the Ugaritic alphabetic cuneiform script was accomplished simultaneously but independently by H. Bauer, E. Dhorme, and Ch. Virolleaud in 1930–31. Unlike any other cuneiform writing, Ugaritic consists of 31 signs or characters used to record documents in a language similar to Phoenician and Hebrew. The Ugaritic inscriptions and documents date from the 14th century and are of crucial importance for the study of the Bible. See *Akkadian; Assyria; Babylon; Sumer; Writing.*

Thomas Smothers

CUP Drinking vessel made of pottery or various metals such as gold, silver, or bronze. During biblical times cups came in two different forms. Some resembled their modern counterparts. However, most ancient cups were shallow bowls that were produced in a multitude of sizes. They also could be used in divination (Gen. 44:5). In addition, the term "cup" was used to designate the receptacles for holding lamps on the lampstand of the tabernacle (Exod. 25:31-35 NASB).

In the Bible the word "cup" frequently is used in a figurative sense. The contents of the cup are accentuated, since symbolically God serves the drink. Thus the cup might represent blessings or prosperity for a righteous person (Pss. 16:5; 23:5; 116:13). Likewise, it portrayed the totality of divine judgment on the wicked (Pss. 11:6; 75:8; Isa. 51:17,22; Jer. 25:15; 49:12; 51:7; Ezek. 23:31-34; Rev. 14:10; 16:19; 17:4; 18:6). Jesus voluntarily drank the cup of suffering (Matt. 20:22; 26:39,42; Mark 10:38; 14:36; Luke 22:42; John 18:11). For Jesus that cup was His death and everything that it involved.

The cup had a prominent place in the liturgy of the Jewish Passover meal and so, subsequently, in the Lord's Supper. In the Christian ordinance the cup is a symbolic reminder of the atoning death of Jesus (Matt. 26:27-28; Mark 14:23-24; Luke 22:20; 1 Cor. 11:25-26). See *Divination and Magic; Lamps, Lighting, Lampstand; Lord's Supper; Passover; Pottery; Vessels and Utensils.*   *LeBron Matthews*

CUPBEARER High-ranking official in the courts of ancient Near Eastern kings. The cupbearer was responsible for serving wine at the king's table and protecting the king from poisoning. The cupbearer was often taken into the king's confidence and had no small amount of influence on the king's decisions. The "chief cup-

Gold cup decorated with gazelles, late second millennium B.C., from southwest Capian region.

bearer" of the Joseph story (Gen. 40:2) was one who was overseer of a staff of his own. Nehemiah was the highly esteemed cupbearer for Artaxerxes (Neh. 1:11; 1 Kings 10:5; 2 Chron. 9:4). The Rabshakeh may have been the title given to cupbearers in the Assyrian court (2 Kings 18:17-37; Isa. 36:2). See *Occupations and Professions.*

CURSE See *Blessing and Cursing.*

CURTAIN Piece of cloth or other material, sometimes arranged so that it can be drawn up or sideways, hung either for decoration or to cover, conceal, or shut off something. "Curtain" is often used synonymously with "tent" (Song 1:5; Isa. 54:2; Jer. 4:20; 10:20; 49:29; Hab. 3:7). The tabernacle which was constructed to house the ark of the covenant was made of 10 curtains (Exod. 26:2). At a later time in Israelite history, two curtains were used to close off the holy place and the holy of holies in the temple. The curtain separating the holy of holies and the holy place was torn from top to bottom at the time of Jesus' death signifying the access that all people had to God from that time forward (Matt. 27:51). The writer of Hebrews speaks of the curtain in the heavenly sanctuary (Heb. 6:19; 9:3). Jesus also opened this curtain to his followers by his death (Heb. 10:20).

CUSH (Cŭsh) **1.** Member of the tribe of Benjamin about whom the psalmist sang (Ps. 7:1). Nothing else is known of him. **2.** Son of Ham and grandson of Noah (Gen. 10:8). Thus in the Table of Nations he is seen as the original ancestor of inhabitants of the land of Cush. **3.** Nation situated south of Egypt with differing boundaries and perhaps including differing dark-skinned tribes (Jer. 13:23) at different periods of history. The Hebrew word *Cush* has been traditionally translated "Ethiopia," following the Septuagint, or earliest Greek translation, but Cush was not identical with Ethiopia as presently known. Moses' wife came from Cush (Num. 12:1), probably a woman distinct from Zipporah (Exod. 2:21). Cush was an enemy of Egypt for centuries, being controlled by strong pharaohs but gaining independence under weak pharaohs. Zerah, a general from Cush, fought against Asa, king of Judah (910–869 B.C.) (2 Chron. 14:9). Finally, Pi-ankhi of Cush conquered Egypt and established the Twenty-fifth Dynasty of Egyptian rulers (716–656) with their capital at Napata above the fourth cataract. Isaiah 18 may describe some of the political activity involved in Cush's establishing their power in Egypt. Tirhakah (2 Kings 19:9) was one of the last of the pharaohs from Cush. Isaiah promised that people who fled from Judah and were exiled in Cush would see God's deliverance (Isa. 11:11; cp. Zeph. 3:10). Isaiah acted out judgment against Cush, probably as the rulers of Egypt (Isa. 20:3-5; cp. 43:3; 45:14; Ps. 68:31; Jer. 46:9; Ezek. 30:4-5,9). In Ezekiel's day Cush represented the southern limit of Egyptian territory (Ezek. 29:10). Cush's strength could not help Thebes escape from Ashurbanipal, king of Assyria, in 663 B.C. Nahum used this historical example to pronounce doom on Nineveh, the capital of Assyria (Nah. 3:9). Ezekiel listed Cush as one of the allies of Gog and Magog in the great climatic battle (Ezek. 38:5). The psalmist proclaimed that God's reputation had reached even unto Cush (Ps. 87:4). Job saw Cush as a rich source of minerals, especially topaz (Job 28:19). By the time of Esther, Cush represented the southwestern limits of Persian power (Esther 1:1). Cambyses (530–522) conquered Cush for Persia.

Cush is mentioned in Gen. 2:13 as surrounded by the Gihon River. The Gihon is usually associated with Jerusalem as a spring (1 Kings 1:33). Some Bible students identify Cush here with the Kassites, the successors to the old Babylonian Empire, who controlled Babylon between about 1530 and 1151 B.C. Such students connect this with Gen. 10:8 where Cush is associated with Nimrod, whose kingdom centered in Babylon (Gen. 10:10). Other Bible students would see Gihon here as another name for the Nile River and Cush as referring to the land south of Egypt. A clear solution to this problem has not been found.

CUSHAN (Cū´ shăn) Tent-dwelling people that Habakkuk saw experiencing God's wrath (Hab. 3:7). The parallel with Midian makes people think of an Arabian tribe, possibly nomads. Some identify Cushan with Cush, either as a territory controlled by Cush or as an otherwise unknown kingdom of Cush on the northeast shore of the Gulf of Aqaba near Midian. This would account for Cushites near Arabs (2 Chron. 21:16).

CUSHAN-RISHATHAIM (Cū´ shăn rĭsh á thä´ ĭm) Personal name meaning "dark one of double evil." King of Aram Naharaim to whom Yahweh gave Israel in the early period of the Judges (Judg. 3:8). Othniel finally defeated him. We have no other information about him. Some have tried to see Aram as an unintentional copying error for an original Edom, but no evidence exists for this conjecture. *See Aram-Naharaim.*

CUSHI (Cū´ shĭ) Personal name meaning "Cushite." **1.** Father of the prophet Zephaniah (Zeph. 1:1). **2.** Ancestor of a royal official under King Jehoiakim (Jer. 36:14).

CUSHITE (Cū´ shīt) Citizen or inhabitant of Cush. The Hebrew word is the same as the proper name "Cushi." God has concern for and control over them just as He does for His own people (Amos 9:7). **1.** Unnamed Cushite served as Joab's messenger to bring the news of Absalom's death to David (2 Sam. 18:21-32). **2.** Eunuch under King Zedekiah who helped Jeremiah escape from a cistern into which the king had had him thrown (Jer. 38:6-12; 39:16). See *Cush; Ebed-melech.*

CUSTODIAN Wealthy Greek and Roman families often had a slave who attended boys under the age of about 16. The major responsibilities of the custodian were to escort the boys to and from school and to attend to their behavior. The pedagogue or custodian had responsibility to discipline or punish the boy. Once the boys reached manhood, they no longer needed the services of the custodian. Often the young man rewarded the custodian by granting him freedom. Paul spoke of the law as the custodian of God's people until Christ came (Gal. 3:23-26). The law could not save; but it could bring us to the point where we could have faith in Christ by showing us our unrighteousness (Gal. 3:19; cp. Rom. 7:7-12). Of course, the law was not nullified by Christ's death or by becoming Christians. We are still expected to live according to the moral principles found in the law (Rom. 7:12,16; cp. Matt. 5:17-48). See *Guardian; Schoolmaster.*

CUTH (Cŭth), **CUTHAH** Place-names with two spellings in Hebrew and English. Cuthah was the center of worship of Nergal, god of death in Mesopotamia. Residents of the city were exiled by the Assyrians to live in Israel (2 Kings 17:24). Once settled, they made an idol to worship Nergal (2 Kings 17:30), thus aggravating the tendency to worship Yahweh of Israel along with other gods. Cuth was located at Tell Ibrahim, about 18 miles northeast of Babylon. See *Nergal.*

CUZA (Cü´ zà) (NIV) See *Chuza.*

CYMBAL See *Music, Instruments, Dancing.*

CYPRIOT (Cÿ´ prĭ ot) Citizen or resident of Cyprus. See *Cyprus.*

CYPRUS (Cÿ´ prŭs) Large island in the eastern Mediterranean Sea mentioned most prominently in Acts. In the OT scattered references refer to the island as Kittim ("Chittim," Isa. 23:1; Jer. 2:10), although in some passages the term has a wider scope and includes lands other than Cyprus lying west of Palestine (Dan. 11:30). The island is 138 miles long east to west and 60 miles wide from north to south; it is eclipsed in size only by Sicily and Sardinia. Much of Cyprus is mountainous; the Troodos Mountains (5,900 feet) dominate the western and central sections, while the Kyrenia Mountains (3,100 feet) extend along the northern coast.

Historically Cyprus was important as a source for timber used in shipbuilding and copper, both vital commodities in the ancient world. The strategic position of Cyprus just off the coasts of Asia Minor and Syria coupled with the presence of favorable currents and reliable summer winds encouraged wide-ranging trade contacts. Evidence of trade with Cyprus between 2000 and 1000 B.C. has been found in Asia Minor, Egypt, Palestine, and Syria; contacts also were maintained with Crete, the Aegean Islands, and Greece. After 1500 B.C. Cyprus was influenced heavily by the Mycenean culture of mainland Greece which left an indelible stamp.

After 1000 B.C. several city-states, each ruled by a king, were the basis of the political structure on Cyprus. Among the most important cities were Salamis and Kition. The Phoenicians, a Semitic people who established a trading empire throughout the Mediterranean, colonized Kition about 850 B.C. Tyre and Sidon were the center of Phoenician trade, and the OT underscores the connection between these cities and Cyprus in several passages (Isa. 23:1-2,12; Ezek. 27:4-9).

From the time the kings of Cyprus submitted to Sargon II of Assyria in 707 B.C., the political fortunes of the island were determined by successive empires that dominated the Near East. Egyptian and Persian kings controlled Cyprus prior to the coming of Alexander the Great in 333 B.C. After his death, Cyprus became a part of

Limassol, a modern city on the southern coast of Cyprus.

the Ptolemaic Empire (294–258 B.C.). During this period many Jews settled on the island, forming an important part of the population. In 58 B.C. Rome annexed Cyprus; with the establishment of the Roman Empire under Augustus, the island became a Senatorial Province in 22 B.C. governed by a proconsul from Paphos.

Cyprus is first mentioned in the NT as the birthplace of Joseph surnamed Barnabas, a Hellenistic Jewish convert who later accompanied Paul (Acts 4:36-37). As a result of the persecution associated with the martyrdom of Stephen in Jerusalem, Jewish Christians journeyed to Cyprus and preached the gospel to the Jewish community on the island (Acts 11:19-20). In A.D. 46 or 47 Paul undertook his first missionary journey accompanied by Barnabas and John Mark (Acts 13). Arriving at Salamis on the eastern side of Cyprus, the group crossed the island to Paphos, preaching the new faith. The reference to Paphos is to Neapaphos, "New Paphos," founded in the fourth century B.C., and the center of Roman government on Cyprus. The conversion of the deputy, Sergius Paulus, was brought about in part by the blinding of the magician Bar-jesus. Whether Paul visited Paleapahos, "Old Paphos," is unclear; Paleapaphos was an ancient city associated with the worship of the

A portion of the agora area at the site of ancient Salamis on the island of Cyprus.

The excavations at Paphos on Cyprus showing the traditional site where Paul was beaten.

Greek goddess Aphrodite, who reputedly emerged from the foam of the sea nearby.

John Mark and Barnabas returned to Cyprus a second time after parting company with Paul (Acts 15:39). Later, Paul twice passed by the island on voyages, once on a return to Jerusalem (Acts 21:3) and finally while traveling to Rome (Acts 27:4). See *Elisha; Kittim; Phoenicians.*

Thomas V. Brisco

CYRENE (Cȳ rē´ nē) Home of a certain Simon who was compelled to carry Jesus' cross to the place of crucifixion (Matt. 27:32). Located in northern Africa, it was the capital city of the Roman district of Cyrenaica during the NT era. Cyrenaica and Crete formed one province. Simon of Cyrene may have belonged to the rather large population of Greek-speaking Jews who resided in the city during the first part of the first century A.D.

CYRENIAN (Cȳ rē´ nǐ ăn) Citizen and/or resident of Cyrene. See *Cyrene.*

CYRENIUS (Cȳ rē´ nǐ ǔs) Roman official mentioned in Luke 2:2 as the governor of Syria when the birth of Jesus took place. Some translations of the NT use the name Cyrenius, an Anglicized form of his Greek name, while others use the Latin form Quirinius. His full name is Publius Sulpicius Quirinius. Throughout his varied career Quirinius served as consul of Rome, military leader, tutor to Gaius Caesar, and legate (governor). He died in A.D. 21.

Luke's reference to Quirinius as governor during the nativity has caused some scholars to question Lukan historical accuracy. It is established that Quirinius was legate in Syria from A.D. 6 to 9, but this date is far too late for Jesus' birth, which occurred prior to the death of Herod the Great who died in 4 B.C. Luke's historical reference seems in direct conflict with nonbiblical sources establishing that either Saturninus (9–7 B.C.) or Varus (6–4 B.C.) was legate of Syria during Christ's birth.

The discovery of an ancient inscription has shown that a legate fitting the description of Quirinius served two different times in Syria. Apparently the nativity occurred during Quirinius' first tenure in Syria as legate with primary responsibilities for military affairs, while Varus was the legate handling civil matters. Quirinius served a second term in A.D. 6–9.

This solution affirms Lukan accuracy without overlooking other known historical sources.

Stephen Dollar

CYRUS (Cȳ´ rǔs) Third king of Anshan, Cyrus (the Great) assumed the throne about 559 B.C. According to the best histories, Cyrus was reared by a shepherd after his grandfather, Astyages, king of Media, ordered that he be killed. Apparently, Astyages had dreamed that Cyrus would one day succeed him as king before the reigning monarch's death. The officer charged with the execution instead carried the boy into the hills to the shepherds.

As an adult, Cyrus organized the Persians into an army and revolted against his grandfather and father (Cambyses I). He defeated them and claimed their throne.

One of his first acts as king of Medio-Persia was to launch an attack against Lydia, capital of Sardis and storehouse for the riches of its king, Croesus. Turning eastward, Cyrus continued his campaign until he had carved out a vast empire, stretching from the Aegean Sea to India.

The Babylonian Empire next stood in his path, an obstacle that appeared to be insurmountable. Engaging the Babylonian army at Opis, Cyrus' troops routed them and moved on Babylon. The people in the capital welcomed Cyrus with open arms, seeing him as a liberator rather than a conqueror. All that remained was Egypt, which he left for his son, Cambyses II. Cyrus truly was the ruler of the world.

Cyrus' military exploits have become legendary. However, he is best remembered for his policies of peace. His famous decree in 539 B.C. (2 Chron. 36:22-23; Ezra 1:1-4) set free the captives Babylon had taken during its harsh rule. Among these prisoners were the Jews taken from

The Cyrus Cylinder, inscribed with the famous Edict of Cyrus the Great in 538 B.C. (2 Chron. 36:23; Ezra 1:2-3).

Jerusalem in 586 B.C. They were allowed to return to rebuild the temple and city. Along with this freedom Cyrus restored the valuable treasures of the temple taken during the exile. Since the Jews had done well in Babylon financially, many of them did not want to return to the wastes of Judah. From these people Cyrus exacted a tax to help pay for the trip for those who did wish to rebuild Jerusalem.

An astute politician, Cyrus made it a practice publicly to worship the gods of each kingdom he conquered. In so doing he won the hearts of his subjects and kept down revolt. He is referred to as Yahweh's shepherd and anointed (Isa. 44:28–45:6) because of his kindness to the Jews and worship of Yahweh.

His last years are obscure. Cyrus was killed while fighting a frontier war with the nomadic Massagetae people. His tomb is in Pasargadae (modern Murghab).   *Mike Mitchell*

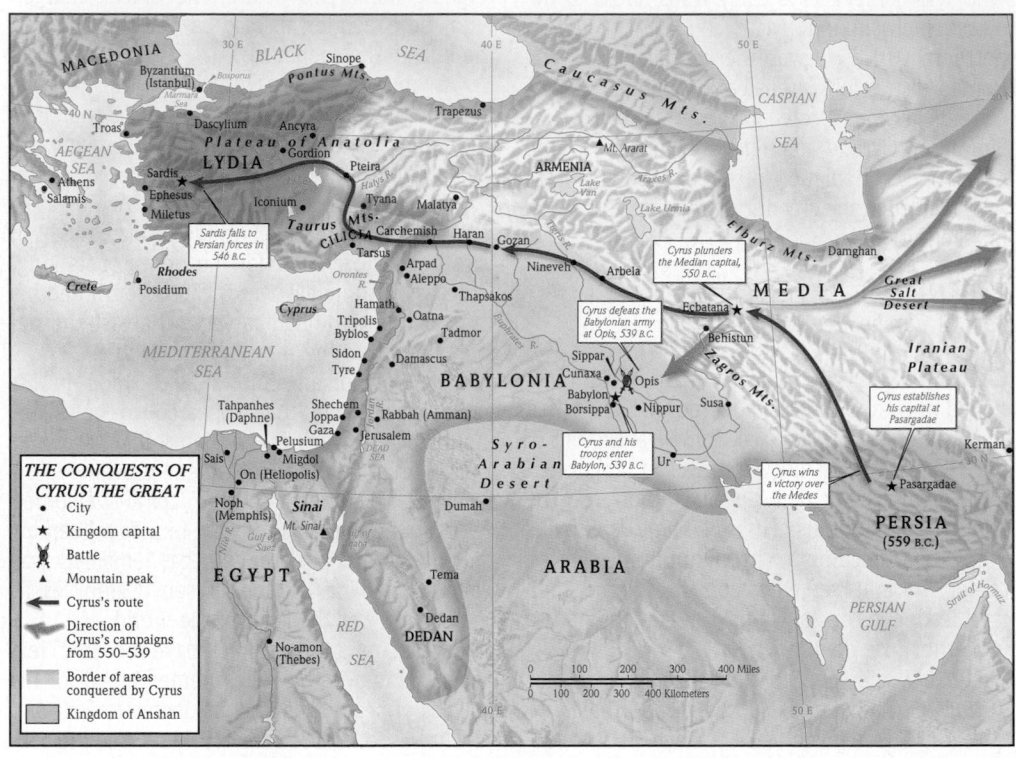

THE CONQUESTS OF CYRUS THE GREAT

- • City
- ★ Kingdom capital
- ⚔ Battle
- ▲ Mountain peak
- ← Cyrus's route
- ← Direction of Cyrus's campaigns from 550–539
- Border of areas conquered by Cyrus
- Kingdom of Anshan

D

The Dead Sea

DABAREH (Dăb´ á rĕh) (KJV, Josh. 21:28). See *Daberath*.

DABBASHETH (Dăb´ bá shĕth) or **DABBESHETH** Place-name meaning "hump." A border town of the tribe of Zebulun (Josh. 19:11). It is modern Tell esh-Shammam northwest of Jokneam.

DABERATH (Dăb´ ĕ răth) Place-name meaning "pasture." Border city of Zebulun near Mount Tabor (Josh. 19:12). In Josh. 21:28 it is a city given the Levites from the territory of Issachar. It is modern Daburiyeh at the northwest foot of Mount Tabor.

DAGGER KJV translation for the short, double-edged weapon of Ehud, the judge (Judg. 3:16-22). Other translations use "sword." Ehud's weapon was one cubit in length (18-22 inches), enabling him to conceal it under his cloak.

DAGON (Dā´ ğŏn) Name of a god meaning "little fish" or "dear." Dagon is a god associated with the Philistines. However, his origin was in Mesopotamia during the third millennium B.C. By 2000 B.C. a major temple was erected for him in the maritime city of Ugarit. Ugaritic commerce carried his cult into Canaan when Canaan was still a part of the Egyptian Empire. When the Philistines conquered the coastal region of Canaan, they adopted Dagon as their chief deity.

According to a popular etymology of Dagon, the name came from the Hebrew word for fish, and so it was postulated that he was a sea god. However, archaeological evidence does not support this view. The name probably was derived originally from the word for grain or possibly from a word for clouds. Thus Dagon was a grain god or a storm god, much like Baal. According to Ugaritic documents from the fourteenth century B.C., Dagon was the father of Baal. Little else is known about his mythology or cult.

After the Philistines subdued Samson, they credited the victory to Dagon (Judg. 16:23). However, when Samson collapsed Dagon's temple upon himself and the Philistines, he proved the superiority of Israel's God. Likewise, the overthrow of the idol of Dagon before the ark of the covenant demonstrated God's predominance (1 Sam. 5:1-7). Nevertheless the Philistines later

displayed the head of Saul as a trophy in the temple of Dagon (1 Chron. 10:10). See *Philistines*.

LeBron Matthews

DALAIAH (Dá laî´ ăh) (KJV) See *Delaiah*.

DALMANUTHA (Dăl má nū´ thá) Place to which Jesus and His disciples came following the feeding of the 4,000 (Mark 8:10). Its location is not known. The parallel reference in Matt. 15:39 suggests it was in the area of Magdala. See *Magdala*.

DALMATIA (Dăl mā´ shĭ á) Place-name referring to the southern part of Illyricum, north of Greece and across the Adriatic Sea from Italy. At the writing of 2 Timothy, Titus had left Paul to go to Dalmatia (2 Tim. 4:10). Paul had preached in Illyricum (Rom. 15:19). Illyricum included most of modern Yugoslavia and Albania.

DALPHON (Dăl´ phŏn) Personal name apparently derived from Persian word, perhaps meaning "sleepless." One of 10 sons of Haman, chief enemy of Mordecai and Esther. The sons were killed when the Jews protected themselves against the Persian attack (Esther 9:7).

DAMARIS (Dăm´ á rĭs) Personal name meaning "heifer." An Athenian woman who became a Christian following Paul's sermon at the Aeropagus, the highest court in Athens (Acts 17:34).

DAMASCENE (Dăm´ á sēn) Resident and/or citizen of Damascus. See *Damascus*.

DAMASCUS (Dá măs´ cŭs) Capital of important city-state in Syria with close historical ties to Israel. Apparently Damascus has been occupied continuously for a longer period of time than any

Wall of the New Testament period in Damascus from which Paul escaped to begin his ministry.

other city in the world and can claim to be the world's oldest city.

Setting Its geographical location enabled Damascus to become a dominant trading and transportation center. Standing 2,300 feet above sea level, it lay northeast of Mount Hermon and about 60 miles east of Sidon, the Mediterranean port city. Both major international highways ran through Damascus: the Via Maris from Mesopotamia in the east through Damascus and the Jezreel Valley to the Plain of Sharon and the Mediterranean coast, then south to Egypt; and the King's Highway from Damascus south through Ashtaroth, Rabbath-ammon, and Bozrah to Elath on the Red Sea and to Arabia. By the same token, Damascus saw armies march along the highways, often using Damascus as the staging area.

History Archaeology cannot contribute much to the study of Damascus since the continued existence of the city makes excavation difficult, if not impossible. Explorations do indicate settlement from before 3000 B.C. Tablets from the Syrian center of Ebla mention Damascus about 2300 B.C. Thutmose III of Egypt claimed to have conquered Damascus about 1475 B.C. The Hittites battled Egypt for control of Damascus until the Hittites were defeated by the Sea Peoples about 1200 B.C. At this time Arameans from the nearby desert came in and took control of an independent Damascus, gradually establishing a political power base.

In the Bible Abraham chased invading kings north of Damascus to recover Lot, who had been taken captive (Gen. 14:15). Abraham's servant Eliezer apparently came from Damascus (Gen. 15:2).

Soldiers of Damascus attempted to help Hadadezer, king of Zobah another Syrian city-state against David. David won and occupied Damascus (2 Sam. 8:5-6). The weakness of Zobah encouraged Rezon to organize a renegade band, much as David had in opposing Saul (1 Sam. 22:2). Rezon became the leader of Syria headquartered in Damascus (1 Kings 11:23-25). God used him to harass Solomon.

The new Syrian city-state faced a strong opponent from the east as Assyria rose to power. Ben-hadad strengthened Damascus to the point that Asa, king of Judah (910–869), paid him tribute to attack Baasha, king of Israel, and relieve pressure on Judah (1 Kings 15:16-23). This gave

The city wall of biblical Damascus.

Damascus reason to interfere repeatedly in politics in Palestine.

First Kings 20 also features Ben-hadad of Damascus, giving reason to believe that Ben-hadad (literally, "son of Hadad") was a royal title in Syria, identifying the king of Damascus as a worshiper of the god Hadad, another name for Baal. The Syrian king attacked Samaria under King Ahab (874–853). A prophet revealed the way to victory for Ahab over a drunken Ben-hadad. The Syrian king decided Israel's God controlled the hills but not the plains, so he attacked at Aphek (1 Kings 20:26). Again a prophet

The window in the city wall of Damascus which may be the site of Paul's escape in a basket from the city.

The traditional street called Straight in Damascus, Syria.

pointed the way to Israel's victory. Ahab agreed to a covenant treaty with the defeated Syrian king, for which he met a prophet's strong judgment (1 Kings 20:35-43).

Naaman, a Syrian officer, sought Elisha's help in curing his skin disease but decided Abana and Pharphar, the great rivers of Damascus, offered greater help than did the Jordan (2 Kings 5:12). These rivers made Damascus an oasis in the midst of the desert. Elisha helped deliver Samaria when Ben-hadad besieged it (2 Kings 6-7). Elisha also prophesied a change of dynasty in Damascus, naming Hazael its king (2 Kings 8:7-15). Shalmaneser III of Assyria (858–824) claimed to have defeated both Ben-hadad and Hazael. The first important battle came at Qarqar in 853 B.C. Ahaziah, king of Judah (841), joined Joram, king of Israel (852–841), in battle against Hazael with Joram being wounded. Jehu took advantage of the wounded king and killed him (2 Kings 8:25–9:24).

Having fought against Damascus in campaigns in 853, 849, 848, and 845, Shalmaneser III of Assyria severely weakened Damascus, besieging it in 841 and then receiving tribute again in 838. After this, Hazael of Damascus exercised strong influence, gaining influence in Israel, Judah, and Philistia (2 Kings 10:32-33). His son Ben-hadad maintained Damascus' strength (2 Kings 13:3-25). Finally, Jehoash, king of Israel (798–782), regained some cities from Damascus (2 Kings 13:25). Jeroboam II, king of Israel (793–753), expanded Israelite influence and gained control of Damascus (2 Kings 14:28). This was possible because Assyria threatened Syria again, as Adad-nirari III, king of Assyria (810–783), invaded Syria from 805 to 802 and again in 796. About 760 B.C. Amos the prophet

condemned Damascus and its kings Hazael and Ben-hadad (Amos 1:3-5).

Tiglath-pileser III, king of Assyria (744–727), threatened Damascus anew. King Rezin of Damascus joined with Pekah, king of Israel, about 734 B.C. in an effort to stop the Assyrians. They marched on Jerusalem, trying to force Ahaz of Judah to join them in fighting Assyria (2 Kings 16:5). The Prophet Isaiah warned Ahaz not to participate with Syria and Israel (Isa. 7). He also said that Assyria would destroy Damascus (Isa. 8:4; cp. chap. 17). Rezin of Damascus had some military success (2 Kings 16:6), but he could not get Ahaz of Judah to cooperate. Neither could Isaiah. Instead, Ahaz sent money to Tiglath-pileser, asking him to rescue Judah from Israel and Damascus. The Assyrians responded readily and captured Damascus in 732 B.C., exiling its leading people (2 Kings 16:7-9). Damascus had one last influence on Judah; for when Ahaz went to Damascus to pay tribute to Tiglath-pileser, he liked the altar he saw there and had a copy made for the Jerusalem temple (2 Kings 16:10-16). Damascus sought to gain independence from Assyria in 727 and 720 but without success. Thus Damascus became a captive state of first the Assyrians, then the Babylonians, Persians, Greeks, Ptolemies, and Seleuccids. Finally, Rome gained control under Pompey in 64 B.C. Jews began to migrate to Damascus and establish synagogues there. Thus Saul went to Damascus to determine if any Christian believers were attached to the synagogues there so that he might persecute them (Acts 9). Thus the Damascus road became the site of Saul's conversion experience and Damascus the site of his introduction to the church. He had to escape from Damascus in a basket to begin his ministry (2 Cor. 11:32-33). Damascus gained importance, eventually becoming a Roman colony. See *Baal; Ben-hadad; Hadad; Syria.*   *Trent C. Butler*

DAN (Dăn) Personal name meaning "judge." First son born to Jacob by Rachel's maid Bilhah (Gen. 30:6). He was the original ancestor of the tribe of Dan. When the Israelites entered Canaan, the tribe of Dan received land on the western coast. They could not fully gain control of the territory, especially after the Philistines settled in the area. The last chapters of Judges show Samson of the tribe of Dan fighting the Philistines. Eventually Dan migrated to the north and was able to take a city called Laish.

Excavations at Dan showing the stone steps leading to the mud-brick gate in the background.

They renamed the city Dan and settled in the area around it. Dan was always a small tribe, and it never exercised significant influence in Israel. The most prominent Danites mentioned in the Bible are Oholiab and Samson.

The biblical city of Dan is often mentioned in the description of the land of Israel, namely "from Dan even to Beersheba" (Judg. 20:1). It has been identified with modern Tell el-Qadi (or Tell Dan). The tell, which covers about 50 acres, is situated at the northern end of the richly fertile Huleh Plain at the base of Mount Hermon. The abundant springs of the site provide one of the three main sources of the Jordan River.

The city was formerly named Laish (Judg. 18:7, or Leshem in Josh. 19:47) when occupied by the Canaanites. This city is mentioned in the Egyptian execration texts and Mari tablets from the eighteenth century B.C. Later Thutmose III listed Laish among the cities conquered in his 1468 B.C. campaign.

Excavation of Tell Dan has been led by A. Biran of Hebrew University in Jerusalem since 1966. Laish was founded at the end of the early Bronze II Age (about 2700 B.C.) near the springs

View of the mud-brick arched gateway just after its discovery and before it was completely uncovered.

and flourished until about 2300 B.C. Significant pottery remains of this era were uncovered along with remains of floors and walls. The city probably remained unoccupied until the middle Bronze II period (about 2000 B.C.), when a large, well-fortified city was constructed. A massive earthen rampart similar to that of Hazor was built for defensive purposes, and set into the rampart (about 1750 B.C.) was a well-preserved, mud-brick "triple-arched gate." The 15-meter square gate system stood 12 meters above the surrounding plain and contained the earliest arched entryways known in the world.

The late Bronze Age is represented by a richly supplied tomb containing Mycenaean and Cypriote imported wares; ivory inlaid cosmetic boxes; gold, silver, and bronze objects; and 45 skeletons of men, women, and children.

Iron Age Laish was rebuilt by local inhabitants in the late thirteenth century B.C. but destroyed about 1100 B.C. by the migrating tribe of Dan. Scripture describes the conquest of the city as if the local people were unsuspecting of

Base for a canopy at Dan, possibly from Ahab's time.

the coming invasion. Danites utilized the earlier rampart for defense and built their homes on the ruins of the previous city. The first Danite city, which contained some Philistine pottery remnants, was destroyed a century after its founding. The city was soon rebuilt and became a prominent Israelite city of the Iron Age.

Following the establishment of the Israelite kingdom under David and Solomon, Jeroboam led the Northern tribes in revolt against Rehoboam (about 925 B.C.). As an alternative to worship in Jerusalem, Dan and Bethel were fortified as border fortress/sanctuaries (1 Kings 12:29) with temples containing golden calf representations of Yahweh. This may have represented a combination of Baal worship with worship of Yahweh. The extent to which the Baal cult influenced Northern Israel is seen in the reign of Jehu, who did not destroy the altars at Dan and Bethel, despite eradicating the Baal priests from the land (2 Kings 10:23-29). Excavations at Dan have uncovered the "high place" of Jeroboam along with a small horned altar, the city gate (with royal throne) and walls (12 feet thick), hundreds of pottery vessels, buildings, and inscribed objects. This city was soon taken by Ben-hadad of Aram and then recaptured by Jeroboam II in the eighth century B.C. (2 Kings 14:25). The Israelite city of Dan fell to the Assyrians under Tiglath-pileser III (Pul of OT) about 743 B.C. (2 Kings 15:29). He annexed the city into an Assyrian district. Many Danites were deported to Assyria, Babylon, and Media following the fall of Samaria in 722 or 721 B.C. (2 Kings 17:6) to Sargon II. Foreigners were brought in from Babylon, Aram, and other lands to settle Israel's territory. The writer of Kings ascribed the fall of the kingdom to the worship of gods other than Yahweh (2 Kings 17:7-20), and Dan was one of the key centers of this idolatry.

As Josiah came to the throne of Judah in 639 B.C., Assyria was on the decline. Josiah incorporated the former Northern Kingdom territories into a united country, restoring the classical borders of Israel to "from Dan to Beersheba." An upper gate to the city was built during this period, and the inscription found at this level, "belonging to Ba'alpelet," demonstrates that Baal worship continued to influence this area after the Assyrian destruction. The partially rebuilt city survived until the onslaught of the Babylonian army of Nebuchadnezzar (about 589 B.C.; cp. Jer. 4:14-18).

Base for a canopy at Dan, probably from the time of Ahab.

Dan again was occupied in the Hellenistic, Roman, and Byzantine periods. In the area of the high place, statues and figurines of Greco-Roman and Egyptian gods such as Osiris, Bes, and Aphrodite have been excavated. The Greek and Aramaic inscription, "To the god who is in Dan, Zoilos made a vow," further evidences the religious significance of the city. See *Patriarchs; Tribes of Israel.*   *R. Dennis Cole*

DANCING Essential part of Jewish life in Bible times. According to Eccles. 3:4, there is "a time to mourn, and a time to dance" (NASB). Dances were performed on both sacred and secular occasions, though the Hebrew mind would not likely have thought in these terms.

The OT employs 11 terms to describe the act of dance. This suggests something about the Hebrew interest in the subject. The basic Hebrew term translated "dance" means to twist or to whirl about in circular motions. Other terms for dance mean "to spring about," "to jump," "to leap," "to skip." One term seems to have been used of processional marches or dances at feasts and holidays.

The Greek terms for dance mean "row" or "ring." The two terms are used five times in the NT (Matt. 11:17; 14:6; Mark 6:22; Luke 7:32; 15:25). Dances were performed for different purposes. The mood behind the dance was one of celebration and praise.

Military victories were celebrated with dances. Women sang and danced, accompanied by musical instruments. Miriam and other Israelite women sang and danced in celebration of the victory at the Red Sea (Exod. 15:20-21). Jephthah's daughter danced before her victorious father (Judg. 11:34) as did the Israelite women when David returned from having defeated the Philistines (1 Sam. 18:6). Men also danced to celebrate military victory (1 Sam. 30:16).

Dances were customary at weddings. On some occasions young ladies, dressed in their best clothing, danced in a bride-choosing ceremony (Judg. 21). Dances were performed in honor of the bride (Song 6:13b NRSV, NIV).

Some dances were performed for the sheer entertainment of guests. Salome danced before the princes and politicians gathered to celebrate her father's birthday (Matt. 14:6; Mark 6:22). Children played games of "dance" (Job 21:11), often with the accompaniment of a musical

Jewish men dancing during a private ceremony in the Court of the Men at the Wailing Wall in Jerusalem.

instrument (Matt. 11:17; Luke 7:32). The return of a long lost son was cause for celebration and dancing (Luke 15:25).

Religious celebration was most often the occasion for dancing. David danced before the ark as it was brought into Jerusalem (2 Sam. 6:14,16; 1 Chron. 15:29). The psalmist exhorted others to praise God with music and dancing (Pss. 149:3; 150:4). Also pagans used the dance as a means of honoring their gods (1 Kings 18:26).

In summary, the dance of the Jewish people was similar to what we today call the folk dance. It was performed by both males and females, though apparently not in mixed groups. Both group and individual dances were performed. See *Music, Instruments, Dancing.*

Glenn McCoy

DANIEL (Dăn´ yĕl) Personal name meaning "God is judge" or "God's judge." **1.** Son of David and Abigail, the Carmelitess (1 Chron. 3:1), who is also called Chileab in 2 Sam. 3:3. **2.** Priest of the Ithamar lineage (Ezra 8:2; Neh. 10:6) who returned with Ezra from the Babylonian captivity. **3.** Daniel of Ezek. 14:14,20; 28:3 is spelled differently in Hebrew from all the other forms in the OT. This Daniel was a storied figure of antiquity mentioned with Noah and Job. He was famous for wisdom and righteousness. Due to the similarity in the spelling of the name and the common attributes of wisdom and righteousness, some interpreters identify this Daniel with the Daniel of the canonical book of Daniel. Most interpreters, however, take note of the differences in the spelling and also the fact of antiquity. Some identify the "Daniel" of Ezekiel with "Danel" of ancient Ugaritic literature.

4. The most common usage of "Daniel" refers to the hero of the book of Daniel. This young man of nobility was taken captive by Nebuchadnezzar, king of Babylon, and elevated to high rank in the Babylonian and Persian kingdoms. The Babylonians sought to remove all vestiges of Daniel's nationality and religion. For this reason they sought to change the name of Daniel to Belteshazzar (Dan. 1:7; 2:26; 4:8–9,18–19; 5:12; 10:1).

Daniel was transported from Judah to Babylon in his early youth at the battle of Carchemish, 605 B.C. The text does not indicate his precise age. Daniel was given the name Belteshazzar and his three Hebrew companions, Hananiah, Mishael, and Azariah, came to be called Shadrach, Meshach, and Abednego (Dan. 1:6-7). He was trained in the arts, letters, and wisdom in the Babylonian capital. Eventually, he rose to high rank among the Babylonian men of wisdom. He was active throughout the long reign of Nebuchadnezzar (604–562 B.C.). No mention is made in Daniel of the times of Evil-Merodach (561–560 B.C.), Neriglissar (559–555 B.C.), or Labashi-Marduk (555 B.C.). However, much information is provided concerning Daniel's involvement during the reign of Nabonidus (555–539 B.C.). While Nabonidus was absent from his country for extended periods of time, he put his son Belshazzar in charge of the affairs of government.

Daniel was in Babylon when the forces of Cyrus, the Persian, captured Babylon. Successively, Daniel was a high governmental official during the reigns of Cyrus (539–529 B.C.) and Cambyses (529–522 B.C.). He served also during his old age into the reign of Darius I, the son of Hystaspes (522–486 B.C.). Daniel would probably have celebrated his one hundredth birthday during the reign of Darius. He had outstanding physical attraction. He demonstrated at an early age propensities of knowledge, wisdom, and leadership. In addition to his wisdom, he was skilled in dream interpretation. Throughout his entire life he demonstrated an unshakable faith in his God. It took courage to resist the temptations and threats that confronted him repeatedly. He recognized that God was continuously judging him. He remained faithful.   *J. J. Owens*

DANIEL, BOOK OF The book of Daniel is one of the most intriguing works in the Bible. Its stories are beautifully told and its visions are awe inspiring. Timeless truths fill its pages. Yet it is also one of the most controversial books in Scripture with key differences centering on interpretation and authorship and date of composition.

Daniel and the Canon In the English versions, Daniel appears as the last of four major prophetic books, whereas in the Hebrew Bible it is grouped with the section of Scripture known as the *Hagiographa* or the *Writings*. Daniel is referred to in Scripture as a prophet in a general sense, like Abraham (Gen. 20:7) or Moses (Deut. 18:15) because he received messages from God and shared these with the people, but primarily Daniel was a statesman and an administrator. He never preached sermons to the nation of Israel in the manner of Isaiah or Jeremiah, and for this reason those responsible for finalizing the canon of the Hebrew Bible did not include the book with the prophets. Daniel's position in the prophetic section in the English versions follows the pattern of the majority of Greek translations.

Authorship and Date The traditional position is that Daniel wrote the book in the sixth century B.C., the prophecy is historically reliable, and its predictions are supernatural and accurate. In modern times some scholars have maintained the view (first proposed by the Neo-Platonist Porphyry in the third century A.D.) that the prophecy in its present form was produced by an anonymous Jew during the second century B.C. writing under the pseudonym (false name) Daniel. The book consists of non-historical accounts and pseudo-prophecies (*vaticinia ex eventu*). Its purpose was to encourage Jewish believers in their struggle against the Syrian-Greek tyrant, Antiochus IV Epiphanes (175–163 B.C.) during the Maccabean period. According to this Maccabean thesis, the book of Daniel would be the latest of the OT Scriptures. Generally, those who hold the Maccabean view consider chapters 7–12 essentially to be an original cre-

ation of the second-century author who introduced his material with the tales of chapters 1–6, a collection borrowed from a Danielic corpus dating to the previous century. Often the second century writer is identified as a member of the religious sect known as the Hasidim.

Those who espouse the Maccabean hypothesis contend that the book's language, theology, position in the Hebrew canon with the Writings rather than the prophets (discussed above), and inaccuracies concerning historical events before the second century suggest a late date of composition. However, the historical reliability of the book has been confirmed in many instances by archaeological discoveries (e.g., the historicity of Belshazzar and the invasion of Jerusalem by the Babylonian armies in 605 B.C.), and the alleged historical inaccuracies on close examination are found to have reasonable solutions. Neither does the language necessitate a late date. Daniel completed his book after the Persian conquest of Babylon and even served in the new administration, thus the presence of Persian loan words is not surprising. Actually, the Persian expressions seem to be rather strong evidence for an early time of composition, for they are old Persian words that ceased to be used by about 300 B.C. Neither would the three Greek loanwords in the book (3:5,7,10,15) demand a late date since archaeological evidence has demonstrated extensive contact between Greece and the nations surrounding the Mediterranean Sea well before the sixth century B.C. On the other hand, if the book was written between 170–164 B.C. during Greek control of Palestine, we would expect to find a plethora of Greek words in the text. The Aramaic of Daniel (and Ezra) exhibits striking parallels with early examples of the language found in documents (e.g., the Elephantine papyri) also written in Imperial Aramaic and dated to the fifth century B.C. and earlier. Furthermore, the Aramaic of the book does not conform to later samples of the language found at Qumran (e.g., Genesis Apocryphon). Finally, arguments for dating documents based on theology are precarious. If Daniel is dated to the sixth century by other objective criteria, the theology in the book is sixth-century theology.

Arguments for the traditional view are: (1) The NT writers and Jesus Himself seem to have accepted the traditional understanding of the prophecy (cp. Matt. 24:15 to Mark 13:14; Matt. 26:64 to Mark 14:62 to Luke 22:69; Heb.

11:32-34). (2) The book professes to have been written by Daniel (cp. 7:1; 12:4), to be an account of a historical individual who experienced the exile and lived in Babylon, and to be a prediction of future events (e.g., Dan. 7:2,4, 6-28; 8; 9:2-27; 10:2-21; 12:4-8). (3) One of the eight manuscripts of Daniel discovered at Qumran (4QDan^c) has been dated to ca. 125 B.C. and may have been written earlier. Some scholars have argued that there would have been insufficient time for the book of Daniel to have gained such universal acceptance if written only forty years earlier. (4) The Septuagint (LXX) is the name commonly designated for a Greek translation of the OT by Jewish scholars in Egypt (Alexandria) that came to be used widely by the Jews of the Diaspora. Scholars generally agree that at least the Pentateuch was translated in the middle of the third century B.C. It is probable that all of the Bible books were translated into Greek about the same time. Certainly by ca. 130 B.C. (when the grandson of Ben Sirach wrote the Prologue to Ecclesiasticus) Daniel had been translated into Greek. According to the Maccabean hypothesis, only 30 years after Daniel was written, the book had been received into the canon and carried to Alexandria, Egypt, approximately three hundred miles away, and there translated into Greek. Such a proposal seems unlikely. (5) Ezekiel, the sixth-century prophet, alluded to Daniel three times in his book (14:14,20; 28:3), and these references would appear to be decisive evidence for the traditional view. Since the discoveries at Ras Shamra, however, scholars who accept the late date have attempted to explain these passages by declaring that Ezekiel was referring to a mythological figure named, Danel, who appears in the Ugaritic epic, "The Tale of Aqhat." A devastating argument against the theory that Ezekiel's Daniel is this Ugaritic hero is that Danel was an idolater! Ezekiel must have been referring to the author of the book of Daniel. If so, the historicity of Daniel and his book would seem to be established.

Type of Literature The first division of the book (chaps. 1–6) consists of historical material and some prophecy (chap. 2); the second division (chaps. 7–12) contains both history and apocalyptic messages. Daniel is the classic example of the apocalyptic genre. The term "apocalyptic" is derived from a Greek word, *apokalupsis*, "revelation, disclosure." In this genre a divine revelation is given to a prophet

through a divine mediator concerning future events. Symbolism and numerology are often employed. The major theme of apocalyptic is the eschatological triumph of the kingdom of God over the kingdoms of the earth. Apocalyptic grants the world a glimpse of God and the future.

Language An unusual feature of the book is that it is written in two languages. Daniel 1:1–2:4a and 8:1–12:13 (157 ½ verses) are written in Hebrew, whereas 2:4b–7:28 (199 ½ verses) are in Aramaic. Various theories have been offered to explain this phenomenon, but the most satisfying proposal is that the employment of the two languages was a deliberate device on Daniel's part. Aramaic (the *lingua franca* of this period) was reserved for the parts of the book that had universal appeal or special relevance to the Gentile nations, and Hebrew was employed for those portions that most concerned the Jewish people.

Texts and Versions The Hebrew and Aramaic text of Daniel has been well preserved, and few of the textual variations are significant. Of the versions, the Greek translations designated Theodotion and the Septuagint (LXX) are by far the most important. Theodotion's translation more exactly corresponds to the Hebrew text and for this reason largely replaced the LXX for Christian usage. Three lengthy additions are inserted in the LXX that are not found in the Hebrew-Aramaic text of Daniel: the Prayer of Azariah and the Song of the Three Young Men, Susanna, and Bel and the Dragon. Although these expansions make for interesting reading, they were not accepted by the Jews in Palestine as Scripture and were not included in the Palestinian canon. Since none of the LXX additions is found in the Qumran texts, it is reasonable to assume that they originated outside of Palestine, possibly in Egypt. Today Protestants and Jews include these works in the Apocrypha, whereas in Roman Catholic editions the first is inserted in the book itself following 3:23, and the last two appear at the end as chapters 13 and 14.

Eight manuscripts of the text of Daniel have survived two millennia in the caves of Qumran. These documents were produced sometime between the second century B.C. and the first century A.D. The Qumran fragments demonstrate the faithfulness with which the biblical text was preserved over the centuries.

Theological Emphases Without doubt the principal theological theme of the book is the sovereignty of God. Every page reflects the author's conviction that his God is the Lord of individuals, nations, and all of history. Daniel also emphasizes the person and work of the Messiah (e.g., 7:13-14, 9:24-27). Eschatology is another prominent theme in Daniel's prophecies. Believers will experience tribulation in the last days (7:21,25; 9:27; 12:1), but the Messiah will appear and establish a glorious, eternal kingdom (2:44-45; 7:13-14,26-27; 9:24). In this wonderful new world, the saints will be rewarded and honored (12:2-3).

Structure That the book of Daniel should be divided according to the type of literature—the stories of Daniel (1:1–6:28) and the prophecies of Daniel (7:1–12:13)—is indicated by the chronological scheme set forth by the author of the book and by the fact that the author himself grouped homogeneous literary accounts together.

Interpretation Those who hold to the Maccabean thesis interpret virtually every aspect of the book of Daniel to address the persecutions of the Jews by Antiochus IV in the second century B.C. The author believed that the kingdom of God would be ushered in upon the death of the Syrian-Greek tyrant. Among those who follow the traditional view, key differences of interpretation concern whether the kingdom of God described in chapter 2 refers to Christ's first or second coming, the nature of the 70 weeks in chapter 9 (symbolic periods or weeks of years) and their culmination (first century A.D. or Christ's second coming), and whether certain prophetic passages refer to the nation of Israel or the church, as a spiritual Israel (e.g., 9:24).

Outline
I. The Ministry of Daniel in Babylon (1:1–6:28)
   A. Daniel's identity and godly character are described (1:1-21).
   B. Daniel interprets Nebuchadnezzar's dream of the four Gentile empires and the coming kingdom of God (2:1-49).
   C. Daniel's three friends refuse to bow before the king's idolatrous statue, are thrown into the fire, but are miraculously delivered (3:1-30).
   D. Nebuchadnezzar is humbled by the Lord of heaven for his pride (4:1-37).
   E. The handwriting on the wall warns Belshazzar of his doom for blasphem-

ing Israel's God at an immoral feast (5:1-31).
   F. Daniel is thrown into a den of lions for his faithfulness to God but is delivered (6:1-28).
II. The Visions of Daniel in Babylon (7:1–12:13)

In vision Daniel is shown four world empires (symbolized by beasts), the last of which will be overcome by the "son of man" who establishes an everlasting kingdom populated by the saints of the Most High (7:1-28).

The vision of the ram, the goat, and the little horn symbolizes the victories of Alexander the Great over Persia and the coming of Antiochus IV from a division of the Greek Empire (8:1-27).

In response to Daniel's prayer, God assures the prophet through the vision of the 70 weeks that Israel will be reestablished and preserved as a nation (9:1-27).

Daniel's final vision furnishes a preview of great world empires, a description of the deliverance of the saints in the end times, and final instructions to the prophet (10:1–12:13).

Stephen R. Miller

DANITE (Dăn´ īt) Resident and/or citizen of city of Dan or member of tribe of Dan. See *Dan*.

DAN-JAAN (Dăn-jā´ ăn) Place-name of uncertain meaning in 2 Sam. 24:6. Many Bible students think the scribes have not preserved the correct Hebrew text at this point and read only "Dan" (NRSV) or "Dan and Ijon" (NEB). If the present Hebrew text is correct, the location of the town is not known except that it is apparently in the territory of the tribe of Dan.

DANNAH (Dăn´ năh) Place-name meaning "fortress." Town assigned tribe of Judah in the hill country (Josh. 15:49). Its location is uncertain.

DAPPLED Variegated gray color of the horses in the vision in Zech. 6:3,6. KJV translates the rare Hebrew term as "bay." Modern translators follow the earliest Greek translation in reading "dappled." The Hebrew term also appears in Gen. 31:10,12 and in a few manuscripts of Neh. 5:18. KJV reads "grisled," while modern translations have "spotted," "speckled," or "mottled."

DARA (Dâr´ à) Hebrew reading in 1 Chron. 2:6 for Darda of 1 Kings 4:31. See *Darda*.

DARDA (Där´ dȧ) Personal name possibly meaning "pearl of knowledge." Famous wise man whose father is listed as Mahol in 1 Kings 4:31 but as Zerah in what appears to be a parallel list in 1 Chron. 2:6. Mahol may mean "dancer," "musician," or "chorister," representing an occupation or guild rather than the father's name.

DARIC Persian gold coin equivalent to four days' wages, probably introduced by Darius I (522–486 B.C.) and possibly the earliest coined money used by the Jews who became acquainted with it during the exile. Offerings for the reconstruction of the temple were made in darics (Ezra 2:69 ESV; Neh. 7:70,72). Some interpreters understand the 20 gold basins in Ezra 8:27 to be worth 1,000 darics each. Others take this as a weight of about 19 pounds or 8.5 kilograms. See *Coins*.

DARIUS (Dȧ·rī´ ŭs) Name of several Medo-Persian kings, three of whom are mentioned in the OT. **1.** Darius the Mede (Dan. 5:31), ruler who took Babylon from Belshazzar. Against his own will, he had Daniel thrown to the lions and later decreed that "in all … my kingdom men are to fear and tremble before the God of Daniel" (Dan. 6:26 NASB). He was an enigma to scholars because ancient sources indicate that the Persian Cyrus was the conqueror of Babylon. Furthermore, archaeological evidence for him is lacking. Some deny the existence of Darius the Mede and say the biblical text is a fictional attempt to fulfill prophecies of Median conquest over Babylon (Isa. 13:17-18; 21:2; Jer. 51:1,27-28). Others have suggested several possibilities, but evidence points to only one likely candidate. This person was Gubaru (or Gobyrus), governor of Gutium, who seized Babylon for Cyrus and

Remains of the throne of Darius the Great.

was viceroy over Mesopotamia, exercising royal powers. His age and ancestry are unknown, but Gutium was in Median territory, and an army he led would have been Median. Daniel 6:28 seems to indicate that Cyrus and Darius ruled simultaneously. **2.** Darius I (521–486 B.C.), also known as Darius Hystaspes or the Great, was both extremely cruel and generous. Darius seized power following the death of Cambyses II, son of Cyrus. Being only a cousin of Cambyses, Darius emphasized his royal ancestry, but his rule was not recognized in all provinces, and he endured numerous revolts. Once control was established, Darius demonstrated great military prowess. He extended his empire from northern India in the east to the Black Sea and parts of Greece in the west, making his the largest empire known to that time. He made two attempts to invade mainland Greece. The first was stopped by a storm in the Aegean, and the second came within 20 miles of Athens. The Athenians defeated him at Marathon (490 B.C.), stopping westward expansion. Darius unified the Persian Empire, establishing 20 satrapies or provinces and decreeing Aramaic the official language. He instituted a system of weights and measures, extended trade routes, and probably introduced gold coins (darics) as currency. Also, he undertook several impressive building projects. This is the Darius of Ezra (Ezra 4–6; Haggai; Zech. 1–8), under whom the temple in Jerusalem was reconstructed, completed in the sixth year of his reign. Darius continued Cyrus' policy of restoring disenfranchised peoples who were victims of Assyrian and Babylonian conquests. Darius reaffirmed Cyrus' authorization and also provided for maintenance of the temple. **3.** Darius the Persian (Neh. 12:22), although scholars differ as to his identity, is believed by many to be Darius III Codomannus

Relief of Darius I giving an audience.

(336–331 B.C.). He was defeated by Alexander the Great, which brought an end to Persian rule. But this is highly unlikely, as his rule postdates Nehemiah. This Darius coincides with the priesthoods of Jaddua and Johanan (Neh. 12:11,22-23), which identifies him as Darius II (423–404 B.C.), given name Ochus. He was son of Artaxerxes I by a Babylonian concubine and was the governor of Hycania on the Caspian Sea. His half brother, Sogdianus, killed Xerxes II and seized his throne in 423 B.C. Ochus soon executed Sogdianus and seized the throne for himself. Uprisings and corruption plagued his reign, but he won the Peloponnesian War, conquering Greek coastal cities on the Aegean.   *T. J. Betts*

DARKNESS Absence of light is used in both physical and figurative senses in both the OT and NT. The darkness that covered the deep before God's creation of light symbolizes chaos in opposition to God's orderly creation (Gen. 1:2-3). Elsewhere darkness, as well as light, is recognized as the creation of God (Isa. 45:7). Darkness is a place where "workers of iniquity may hide" (Job 34:22 NASB); however, darkness does not hide one from God (Ps. 139:11-12; Dan. 2:22).

Darkness was thought of as a curse. Thus the OT speaks of death as a land of darkness (Job 10:21-22; 17:13; Ps. 88:6). Darkness is frequently associated with supernatural events involving the judgment of God, such as the plagues of Egypt (Exod. 10:21), the coming of the Lord (Isa. 13:9-10; Joel 2:31; Matt. 24:29), and Christ's crucifixion (Matt. 27:45). The day of God's judgment is often described as a day of darkness (Joel 2:2; Amos 5:18-20). Elsewhere darkness forms part of God's punishment on the disobedient (Deut. 28:29; 1 Sam. 2:9; Job 5:14; 15:30; 20:26; Ps. 107:10; Isa. 47:5; Jer. 13:16; Ezek. 32:8).

In the NT the place of punishment for humans and sinful angels is designated "the outer darkness" (Matt. 8:12; 22:13; 25:30; cp. 2 Pet. 2:4; Jude 6,13). Darkness often has an ethical sense. Scripture speaks of ways of darkness (Prov. 2:13; 4:19), walking in darkness (John 8:12; 1 John 1:6; cp. 2 Cor. 6:14; Eph. 5:8), and works of darkness (Rom. 13:12; Eph. 5:11). In this ethical sense God has no darkness in Himself (1 John 1:5). Powers hostile to God can be termed darkness. People thus face a choice of whether to yield allegiance to God or to darkness (Luke 22:53; John 1:5; 3:19; Col. 1:13; 1 Thess. 5:5). Darkness also symbolizes ignorance, especially of God and of God's ways (Isa. 8:22; 9:2; John 12:46; Acts 26:18; 1 Thess. 5:4; 1 John 2:9). God's deliverance (either from ignorance or hostile powers) is described as lighting the darkness (Isa. 9:2; 29:18; 42:7-16; Mic. 7:8; 1 Pet. 2:9). See *Light.*   *Chris Church*

DARKON (Där´ kŏn) Personal name, perhaps meaning "hard." A servant of Solomon whose descendants returned from exile with Zerubbabel about 537 B.C. (Ezra 2:56).

DART Thrusting or throwing weapon used for medium range combat, either similar to a spear or javelin (2 Sam. 18:14) or else an arrow (Prov. 7:23; Eph. 6:16). The use of flaming arrows (Pss. 7:13; 120:4) becomes in Eph. 6:16 a picture of the assault of the evil one on believers. KJV uses "darts" to translate two different Hebrew words, the first meaning "stick" or "staff," and the second, "arrows."

DATES Fruit of the date palm (*Phoenix dactylifera*), highly valued by desert travelers who consume dates fresh, dry them, or form them into cakes for a portable and easily storable food. As part of the celebration of bringing the ark to Jerusalem, David gave gifts of food to each Israelite gathered in Jerusalem (2 Sam. 6:19; 1 Chron. 16:3). The meaning of the Hebrew term is uncertain. NASB and NIV use "cake of dates" at 2 Sam. 6:19 (also TEV margin). Other modern translations follow the KJV, understanding the food as a piece of meat. The NIV, but not the NASB, uses "cake of dates" in the parallel account in 1 Chronicles.

The NASB of Song 5:11 describes the hair of the king as "like a cluster of dates," perhaps a

Dates growing on a date palm tree.

An Arab date vendor.

reference to a full head of hair. The REB translates the same term as "like palm-fronds." Other translations speak of bushy hair (KJV), curly hair (KJV margin), or wavy hair (NIV, NRSV, TEV). See *Palms; Plants.*

DATHAN (Dā´ thăn) Personal name meaning "fountain" or "warring." The son of Eliab from the tribe of Reuben, Dathan and his brother Abiram were leaders of a revolt challenging Moses' authority over the Israelites. The attempted coup failed, and Dathan and Abiram, along with their families, were swallowed up by the earth (Num. 16). See *Abiram; Numbers, Book of.*

DAUGHTER-IN-LAW Wife of one's son. Famous daughters-in-law include Sarah, daughter-in-law of Terah (Gen. 11:31); Tamar, daughter-in-law of Judah (Gen. 38:11,16; 1 Chron. 2:4); and Ruth, daughter-in-law of Naomi (Ruth 2:20,22; 4:15). Daughters-in-law might be addressed simply as daughter (Ruth 2:2,8,22). Marriage made them an integral member of the family. Ruth was hailed as more to Naomi than seven sons (Ruth 4:15). The breakdown of the relationship between mothers-in-law and daughters-in-law illustrated the collapse of moral society (Mic. 7:6). In the NT differing responses to

the gospel created the same breakdown of relationship (Matt. 10:35; Luke 12:53). Jewish law prohibited incest between a man and his daughter-in-law (Lev. 18:15). This crime was punishable by death (Lev. 20:12). In Ezek. 22:11 this crime illustrates the moral decline of the nation. See *Family.*

DAVID Personal name probably meaning "favorite" or "beloved." The first king to unite Israel and Judah and the first to receive the promise of a royal messiah in his line. David was pictured as the ideal king of God's people. He ruled from about 1005 to 965 B.C.

Selection as King When Saul failed to meet God's standards for kingship (1 Sam. 15:23,35; 16:1), God sent Samuel to anoint a replacement from among the sons of Jesse, who lived in Bethlehem (1 Sam. 16:1). God showed Samuel He had chosen the youngest, who still tended sheep for his father (16:11-12). David's good looks were noteworthy.

In Saul's Court David's musical talent, combined with his reputation as a fighter, led one of Saul's servants to recommend David as the person to play the harp for Saul when the evil spirit from God troubled him (1 Sam. 16:18).

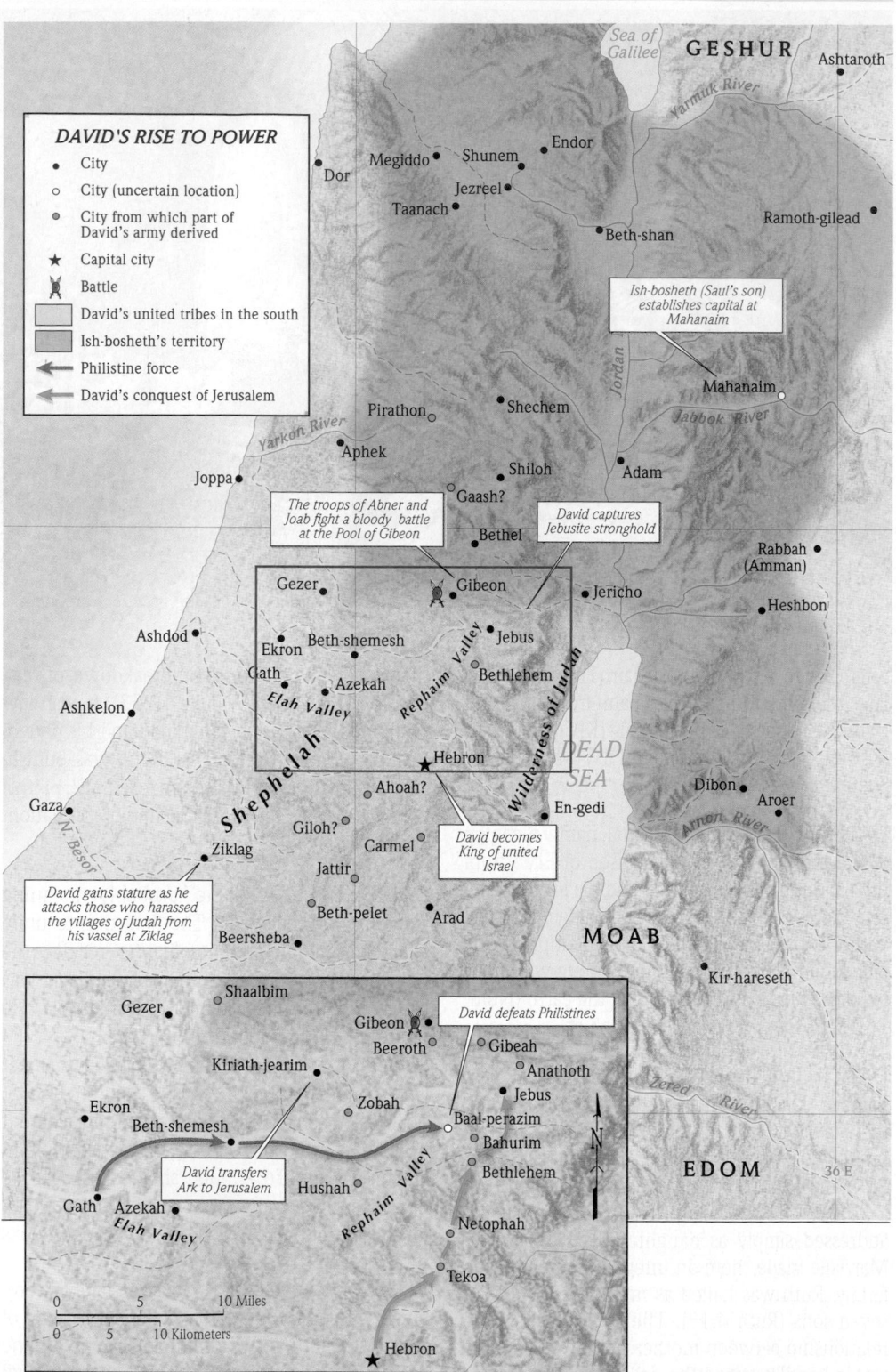

DAVID'S RISE TO POWER

- • City
- ○ City (uncertain location)
- ● City from which part of David's army derived
- ★ Capital city
- ⚔ Battle
- ▭ David's united tribes in the south
- ▭ Ish-bosheth's territory
- ← Philistine force
- ← David's conquest of Jerusalem

Sea of Galilee

GESHUR

Ashtaroth

Yarmuk River

Dor
Megiddo
Shunem
Endor

Jezreel

Taanach

Beth-shan

Ramoth-gilead

Ish-bosheth (Saul's son) establishes capital at Mahanaim

Jordan

Mahanaim

Jabbok River

Pirathon
Shechem

Yarkon River

Aphek

Shiloh
Adam

Joppa

Gaash?

The troops of Abner and Joab fight a bloody battle at the Pool of Gibeon

Bethel

David captures Jebusite stronghold

Rabbah (Amman)

Gezer
Gibeon
Jericho

Heshbon

Ashdod

Beth-shemesh

Rephaim Valley

Jebus

Ekron

Gath
Azekah

Bethlehem

Elah Valley

Wilderness of Judah

Ashkelon

Shephelah

Hebron

DEAD SEA

Ahoah?

En-gedi

Dibon
Aroer

Gaza

N. Besor

Giloh?
Carmel

David becomes King of united Israel

Arnon River

Ziklag

Jattir

David gains stature as he attacks those who harassed the villages of Judah from his vassal at Ziklag

Beth-pelet
Arad

Beersheba

MOAB

Kir-hareseth

Inset map:

Shaalbim

Gezer

Gibeon

David defeats Philistines

Beeroth
Gibeah

Anathoth

Kiriath-jearim

Zobah

Jebus

Ekron

Beth-shemesh

Baal-perazim

Bahurim

David transfers Ark to Jerusalem

Bethlehem

Hushah

Rephaim Valley

N

Zered River

Gath
Azekah

EDOM

Elah Valley

Netophah

36 E

Tekoa

0   5   10 Miles
0   5   10 Kilometers

Hebron

Saul grew to love David and made him armor bearer for the king (16:21-22).

At a later date the Philistines with the giant Goliath threatened Israel (1 Sam. 17). David returned home to tend his father's sheep (17:15). Jesse sent David to the battlefield with food for his warrior brothers. At least one brother did not think too highly of him (17:28). Saul tried to persuade David, the youth, from challenging Goliath; but David insisted God would bring victory, which He did.

Saul's son Jonathan became David's closest friend (1 Sam. 18:1). David became a permanent part of Saul's court, not returning home (18:2). Saul gave David a military commission, which he fulfilled beyond expectations, defeating the Philistines and winning the hearts of the people. This stirred Saul's jealousy (18:8). Moved by the evil spirit from God, Saul tried to kill David with his spear; but God's presence protected David (18:10-12). David eventually earned the right to marry Michal, Saul's daughter, without being killed by the Philistines as Saul had hoped (18:17-27). With the help of Michal and Jonathan, David escaped from Saul and made contact with Samuel, the prophet (19:18). Jonathan and David made a vow of eternal friendship, and Jonathan risked his own life to protect David (1 Sam. 20).

Independent Warrior David gathered a band of impoverished and discontented people around him. He established relationships with Moab and other groups and gained favor with the people by defeating the Philistines (1 Sam. 22–23), but all Saul's efforts to capture him failed. God protected David, and David refused to injure Saul, instead promising not to cut off Saul's family (24:21-22).

Abigail of Maon intervened with David to prevent him from punishing her foolish husband Nabal. God brought Nabal's death, and David married Abigail. He also married Ahinoam of Jezreel, but Saul gave Michal, David's first wife, to another man (1 Sam. 25).

After again refusing to kill Saul, the Lord's anointed, David attached himself to Achish, the Philistine king of Gath. Saul finally quit chasing him. Achish gave Ziklag to David, who established a headquarters there and began destroying Israel's southern neighbors (1 Sam. 27). Despite the wishes of Achish, the other Philistine leaders would not let David join them in battle against Saul (1 Sam. 29). Returning home, David found the Amalekites had destroyed Ziklag and captured his wives. David followed God's leading and defeated the celebrating Amalekites, recovering all the spoils of war. These he distributed among his followers and among the peoples of Judah (1 Sam. 30).

King of Judah Hearing of the deaths of Saul and Jonathan, David avenged the murderer of Saul and sang a lament over the fallen (2 Sam. 1). He moved to Hebron, where the citizens of Judah crowned him king (2 Sam. 2). This led to war with Israel under Saul's son Ish-bosheth. After much intrigue, Ish-bosheth's commanders assassinated him. David did the same to them (2 Sam. 4).

King of Israel The northern tribes then crowned David king at Hebron, uniting all Israel under him. He led the capture of Jerusalem and made it his capital. After defeating the Philistines, David sought to move the ark of the covenant to Jerusalem, succeeding on his second attempt (2 Sam. 6). He then began plans to build a temple but learned from Nathan, the prophet, that he would instead build a dynasty with eternal dimensions (2 Sam. 7). His son would build the temple.

David then organized his administration and subdued other nations who opposed him, finally gaining control of the land God had originally promised the forefathers. He also remembered his promise to Jonathan and cared for his lame son Mephibosheth (2 Sam. 9).

A Sinner David was a giant among godly leaders, but he remained human as his sin with Bathsheba and Uriah showed. He spied Bathsheba bathing, desired her, and engineered the death of her faithful warrior husband, after committing adultery with her (2 Sam. 11). Nathan, the prophet, confronted David with his sin, and David confessed his wrongdoing. The newborn child of David and Bathsheba died. David acknowledged his helplessness in the situation, confessing faith that he would go to be with the child one day. Bathsheba conceived again, bearing Solomon (2 Sam. 12:1-25).

Family Intrigue Able to rule the people but not his family, David saw intrigue, sexual sins, and murder rock his own household, resulting in his isolation from and eventual retreat before Absalom. Still, David grieved long and deep when his army killed Absalom (2 Sam. 18:19-33). David's kingdom was restored, but the hints of division between Judah and Israel remained (2 Sam.

D

View of Jerusalem from the southeast during the time of David (1000–962 B.C.), showing the Taberna-cle pitched atop the threshing floor of Araunah (or Ornan) the Jebusite (upper right). David's palace (center, right) overlooked the Tabernacle. The Citadel fortress (center), and City of David (left, center) can also be seen. The Tyropoeon Valley (top, center) and the Kidron Valley (lower right) flanked each side of the city perched high on the escarpment of Zion.

D

A view of the excavations led by Kathleen Kenyon of the City of David.

19:40-43). David had to put down a northern revolt (2 Sam. 20). The last act the books of Samuel report about David is his census of the people, bringing God's anger but also preparing a place for the temple to be built (2 Sam. 24). The last chapters of 1 Chronicles describe extensive preparations David made for the building and the worship services of the temple. David's final days involved renewed intrigue among his family, as Adonijah sought to inherit his father's throne, but Nathan and Bathsheba worked to ensure that Solomon became the next king (1 Kings 1:1–2:12).

Prophetic Hope David thus passed from the historical scene but left a legacy never to be forgotten. He was the role model for Israelite kings (1 Kings 3:14; 9:4; 11:4,6,33,38; 14:8; 15:3,11; 2 Kings 14:3; 16:2; 22:2). David was the "man of God" (2 Chron. 8:14), and God was "the God of your father David" (2 Kings 20:5 NASB). God's covenant with David was the deciding factor as God wrestled with David's disobedient successors on the throne (2 Chron. 21:7). Even as Israel rebuilt the temple, they followed "the directions of King David of Israel" (Ezra 3:10 NASB).

God's prophets pointed to a future David who would restore Israel's fortunes. "There will be no end to the increase of His government or of peace, on the throne of David and over his kingdom, to establish it and to uphold it with justice and righteousness from then on and forevermore" (Isa. 9:7 NASB). Jeremiah summed up the surety of the hope in David: "If you can break My covenant for the day, and My covenant for the night, so that day and night will not be at their appointed time, then My covenant may also be broken with David My

servant that he shall not have a son to reign on his throne .... As the host of heaven cannot be counted, and the sand of the sea cannot be measured, so I will multiply the descendants David My servant" (Jer. 33:20-22 NASB; cp. 33:15,17,25-26; Ezek. 34:23-24; 37:24-25; Hos. 3:5; Amos 9:11; Zech. 12:6-10).

New Testament The NT tells the story of Jesus as the story of the Son of God but also as the story of the Son of David from His birth (Matt. 1:1) until His final coming (Rev. 22:16). At least 12 times the Gospels refer to Him as "Son of David." David was cited as an example of similar behavior by Jesus (Matt. 12:3), and David called Him "Lord" (Luke 20:42-44). David thus took his place in the roll call of faith given in Heb. 11:32. This was "David the son of Jesse, a man after My heart, who will carry out all My will" (Acts 13:22 HCSB).

DAVID, CITY OF Most ancient part of Jerusalem on its southeast corner representing the city occupied by the Jebusites and conquered by David (2 Sam. 5:7). The Kidron Valley bordered it on the east, and the Tyropoeon Valley on the west. The entire area occupied no more than 10 acres. It is also called Zion. This part of Jerusalem dates back at least to about 2500 B.C., when it is mentioned in the Ebla documents. Its strong defense walls on which the Jebusites prided themselves originated about 1750 B.C.

DAWN First appearance of light in the morning as the sun rises. Job 3:9 indicates that the stars are still visible at dawn. Dawn is used in the literal sense of the beginning of the day (Josh. 6:15; Judg. 19:26; Matt. 28:1; Acts 27:33). Matthew 4:16 uses the picture of the dawn in Isa. 9:2-3 as a figure for the new age of hope and promise that Jesus brought.

DAY OF ATONEMENT Tenth day of the seventh month of the Jewish calendar (Sept.–Oct.) on which the high priest entered the inner sanctuary of the temple to make reconciling sacrifices for the sins of the entire nation (Lev. 16:16-28). The high priest was prohibited from entering this most holy place at any other time on pain of death (Lev. 16:2). Nor was any other priest permitted to perform duties within the temple proper during the ritual for the Day of Atonement (Lev. 16:17). The days' ritual required the high priest to bathe and be dressed in pure linen garments as a symbol of purity (Lev. 16:4). The ceremony began with the sacrifice of a young bull as a sin offering for the priest and his family (Lev. 16:3,6). After burning incense before the mercy seat in the inner sanctuary, the high priest sprinkled the blood from the bull on and in front of the mercy seat (16:14). The priest cast lots over two goats. One was offered as a sin offering. The other was presented alive as a scapegoat (16:5,7-10,20-22). The blood of the goat used as the sin offering was sprinkled like that of the bull to make atonement for the sanctuary (16:15). The mixed blood of the bull and goat were applied to the horns of the altar to make atonement for it (16:18). The high priest confessed all of the people's sins over the head of the live goat which was led away and then released in the wilderness (16:21-22). Following the ceremony, the priest again bathed and put on his usual garments (16:23-24). The priest then offered a burnt offering for the priest and the people (16:24). The bodies of the bull and goat used in the day's ritual were burnt outside the camp (16:27-28). The Day of Atonement was a solemn day, requiring the only fast designated by the Mosaic law. All work was also prohibited (16:29; 23:27-28).

The writer of Hebrews developed images from the Day of Atonement to stress the superiority of Christ's priesthood (8:6; 9:7,11-26). Hebrews 13:11-12 uses the picture of the bull and goat burned outside the camp as an illustration of Christ's suffering outside Jerusalem's city walls. According to one interpretation, Paul alluded to the day's ritual by speaking of Christ as a sin offering (2 Cor. 5:21). See *Atonement.*

Chris Church

DAY OF CHRIST See *Day of the Lord; Judgment Day.*

DAY OF THE LORD Time when God reveals His sovereignty over human powers and human existence. The Day of the Lord rests on the Hebrew term, *yom,* "day," the fifth most frequent noun used in the OT and one used with a variety of meanings: time of daylight from sunrise to sunset (Gen. 1:14; 3:8; 8:22; Amos 5:8); 24-hour period (Gen. 1:5); a general expression for "time" without specific limits (Gen. 2:4; Ps. 102:3; Isa. 7:17); the period of a specific event (Jer. 32:31; Ezek. 1:28). The "Day of the Lord"

then does not give a precise time period. It may mean the daylight hours, the 24-hour day, or a general time period, perhaps characterized by a special event. Zechariah 14:7 even points to a time when all time is daylight, night with its darkness having vanished.

"Day of the Lord" does not in itself designate the time perspective of the event, whether it is past, present, or future. Lamentations 2:1 can speak of the "day of the Lord's anger" in past tense, describing the fall of Jerusalem. Joel 1:15 could describe a present disaster as the "Day of the Lord."

The OT prophets used a term familiar to their audience, a term by which the audience expected light and salvation (Amos 5:18), but the prophets painted it as a day of darkness and judgment (Isa. 2:10-22; 13:6,9; Joel 1:15; 2:1-11,31; 3:14-15; Amos 5:20; Zeph. 1:7-8,14-18; Mal. 4:5). The OT language of the Day of the Lord is thus aimed at warning sinners among God's people of the danger of trusting in traditional religion without commitment to God and His way of life. It is language that could be aimed at judging Israel or that could be used to promise deliverance from evil enemies (Isa. 13:6,9; Ezek. 30:3; Obad. 15). The Day of the Lord is thus a point in time in which God displays His sovereign initiative to reveal His control of history, of time, of His people, and of all people.

New Testament writers took up the OT expression to point to Christ's final victory and the final judgment of sinners. In so doing, they used several different expressions (HCSB): "day of Christ Jesus" (Phil. 1:6), "day of our Lord Jesus Christ" (1 Cor. 1:8); "Day of the Lord" (1 Cor. 5:5; 1 Thess. 5:2); "day of Christ" (Phil. 1:10; 2:16); "day of judgment" (1 John 4:17); "this day" (1 Thess. 5:4); "that day" (2 Tim. 1:12); "day of wrath" (Rom. 2:5).

People who take a dispensational perspective on Scripture often seek to interpret each of the terms differently, so that the "day of Christ" is a day of blessing equated with the rapture, whereas the day of God is an inclusive term for all the events of end time (2 Pet. 3:12). In this view the Day of the Lord includes the great tribulation, the following judgment on the nations, and the time of worldwide blessing under the rule of the Messiah.

Many Bible students who do not take a dispensational viewpoint interpret the several expressions in the NT to refer to one major event: the end time when Christ returns for the final judgment and establishes His eternal kingdom. Whichever interpretation one makes of specific details, the Day of the Lord points to the promise that God's eternal sovereignty over all creation and all nations will one day become crystal clear to all creatures. See *Dispensation.*

DAY'S JOURNEY Customary, though inexact, measure of distance traveled in a day. The distance varied with the terrain and with the circumstances of the traveler. The typical day's journey of the Jews was between 20 and 30 miles, though groups generally traveled only 10 miles per day (Gen. 30:36; 31:23; Exod. 3:18; 8:27; Deut. 1:2; Luke 2:44).

DAYSMAN KJV term for a mediator, arbitrator, or umpire (Job 9:33). In the Near East such mediators placed their hands on the heads of the parties in a dispute. The mediator may have attempted to bring both parties together in reconciliation or may have had authority to impose a settlement on both parties. Job's point is that no human is capable of standing in judgment of God. The NT points to "the man Christ Jesus" as the "one mediator between God and men" (1 Tim. 2:5).

DAY STAR NRSV translation of Hebrew term called "Lucifer" by KJV and "morning star" or "star of the morning" by other translations. The planet Venus appears as a morning "star" at dawn. Isaiah 14:12 compares the splendor of the Babylonian king to the day star (NRSV). Second Peter 1:19 describes Christ as the morning star which outshines the light of the earlier prophetic witness. The Hebrew term appears only in Isa. 14:12. The translation "Lucifer" comes from the Latin translation called the Vulgate. See *Lucifer.*

DEACON Term "deacon" comes from the Greek noun *diakonos,* which occurs 29 times in the NT and is most commonly translated "servant" or "minister." This noun is derived from the verb "to serve" and is used to signify various types of service. Paul not only refers to himself as a *diakonos* (1 Cor. 3:5; 2 Cor. 3:6; 6:4; Eph. 3:7; Col. 1:23,25), but he also applies this term to his coworkers Phoebe (Rom. 16:1), Apollos (1 Cor 3:5), Tychicus (Eph. 6:21; Col. 4:7), Epaphras (Col. 1:7), and Timothy (1 Tim. 4:6). This term is also used with respect to governments

(Rom. 13:4) and Christ (Rom. 15:8; Gal. 2:17). Less frequently it is found as a designation for an officeholder in the local church (Phil. 1:1; 1 Tim. 3:8,12; possibly Rom. 16:1).

Although it is difficult to prove that the origin of the diaconate is found in the choosing of the seven in Acts 6:1-6, since the noun *diakonos* is not used, it is reasonable to believe that these seven leaders were at least the prototypes of the first deacons. For just as the apostles needed help taking care of logistics so that they might be freed up to devote themselves to prayer and teaching, what distinguishes the deacons from the bishops (or elders) is the bishops' ability to teach (1 Tim. 3:2; 5:17; Titus 1:9). The laying on of the apostles' hands in Acts 6:6 is often seen as the origin of ordaining deacons.

The first mention of deacons as officeholders in the local congregation appears in Phil. 1:1 where Paul addresses the church at Philippi "including the bishops and deacons." Although the qualifications for deacons are found in 1 Tim. 3:8-13, there is no explicit text that states their duties. Because deacons are mentioned after bishops in Phil. 1:1 and 1 Tim. 3, and because of the connotations of the term *diakonos,* most agree that they fulfilled a supporting role to the bishops. In later centuries the deacons were involved in administering goods to the poor, assisting in the ordinances of baptism and the Lord's Supper, and performing other ministerial and administrative tasks. Some have suggested that the qualification of not being double-tongued [hypocritical, HCSB] (1 Tim. 3:8) perhaps indicates close contact with church members in home visitations. Others maintain that the requirement of not being greedy (1 Tim. 3:8) indicates that deacons were responsible for collecting and distributing funds.

In Rom. 16:1 it is uncertain as to whether *diakonos* should be rendered "servant" or the more official "deacon." Since *diakonos* most commonly is not used in its technical meaning of deacon, many conclude that Phoebe was not an officeholder in her church. Yet, there are several factors that might indicate otherwise. First, Paul uses the masculine *diakonos* to refer to a woman instead of a feminine form. Second, Paul specifically states that Phoebe is a *diakonos* of the church at Cenchrea, which is the only place Paul speaks of someone being a *diakonos* of a local church (cp. Eph. 6:21; Col. 1:7; 1 Tim. 4:6). Third, Paul urges the Romans to aid

Phoebe since she is sent to perform an official task on behalf of the Apostle Paul and her church. It is argued that such an official task requires an official office.

Another text related to the question of women deacons (deaconesses) is 1 Tim. 3:11. The problem is that the text is ambiguous since Paul uses the Greek term *gunaikes* ("women" or "wives"), which could refer to the deaconesses or wives of deacons. The arguments for the latter position are the following: (1) First Timothy 3:11 begins with "likewise" as does v. 8 and therefore also introduces a new office. (2) Since there is no requirement for the bishops' wives, why should there be one for deacons' wives? (3) The word "their," although added in some translations, is not found in the Greek. The text simply reads "wives" or "women," not "their [i.e., deacons'] wives." (4) A serving ministry would not require women to be in authority over men and thus not violate 1 Tim. 2:1 That is why deacons do not have to be "able to teach" as do the overseers since that is an authoritative act.

Yet, there are good arguments countering the four previously mentioned: (1) First Timothy 2:9 also begins with "likewise" but is not a parallel idea (men are to pray ... likewise women are to dress appropriately). Also, it would seem awkward for Paul to address deacons in vv. 8-10, interrupt himself to introduce the office of deaconess, and then go back to speaking about deacons in vv. 12-13. (2) It is possible that the wives of deacons are mentioned but not the wives of bishops if the former participated in their husbands' ministry (such as ministering to widows). Furthermore, there are other requirements of deacons that are not made of overseers. (3) The possessive pronoun "their" is not required to make the passage refer to the wives of deacons in the present context. If Paul had meant to speak of an office of deaconess, he could have used the word "deaconess" rather than using the word often translated as "wives." (4) Even if deacons do not teach, they still exercise authority, which would be inappropriate for women. See *Bishop; Elder*.   *Ben L. Merkle*

DEAD SEA Inland lake at the end of the Jordan Valley on the southeastern border of Canaan with no outlets for water it receives; known as Salt Sea, Sea of the Plain, and Eastern Sea. Its current English name was applied to it through writings after A.D. 100. It is about 50 miles long and 10 miles wide at its widest point. The surface of the sea is 1,292 feet below the level of the Mediterranean Sea. At its deepest point the lake is 1,300 feet deep. At its most shallow, it is only 10 to 15 feet deep.

The main source of water for the sea is the Jordan River, but other smaller rivers empty into the sea also. The Jordan River empties an average of six million tons of water every 24 hours into the sea. Despite this and the fact that the sea has no outlet, the surface does not rise more than 10 to 15 feet. Since the Dead Sea lies below sea level, the heat and aridity of its location cause rapid evaporation of the water.

This, plus other geographical factors, gives it a salt content that is approximately five times the concentration of the ocean. This makes the body of water one of the world's saltiest. The salt content also causes a condition in which no form of marine life can live, although some fish have reportedly been found in adjacent less salty pools. The surrounding land area, however, can

Aerial photo of central Israel showing the topography of the Dead Sea region. Courtesy of NASA.

The Dead Sea's high salt content makes it virtually impossible for a person to sink in its waters.

support vegetation and life. These features of the Dead Sea as well as its location in a hot and arid area inspired the biblical writers to use it as an example of a life apart from the law of God.

Bob Sheffield

DEAD SEA SCROLLS A large collection of biblical and extra-biblical manuscripts and fragments discovered in caves and buildings in the vicinity of the western shorelines of the Dead Sea. The completion of the official publication of the scrolls (*Discoveries in the Judean Desert*) was celebrated in 2001.

Discovery and Excavation Discovery began in the winter of 1946–47 when two young bedouins, while herding their sheep and goats, discovered in a cave several large storage jars containing leather materials wrapped in linen. These collected materials were eventually sold to a cobbler/antiquities dealer in Bethlehem who then sought buyers for the scrolls. Two sets of scrolls were sold to the Archbishop of the Syrian Orthodox Church in Jerusalem and Eleazar Sukenik of the Hebrew University in Jerusalem.

Authentication was provided initially by Professor Sukenik, John Trever, the acting director of the American Schools of Oriental Research in Jerusalem, and the noted American scholar William F. Albright.

Two archaeologists were enlisted for a systematic exploration of the cave region, located about eight miles south of Jericho: Dr. G. L. Harding, Director of the Amman Dept. of Antiquities, and Fr. Roland de Vaux of the Ecole Biblique in East Jerusalem. In their exploration no additional caves were found, but they examined the surface remains of some ruins known to the Arabs as Khirbet Qumran, named after the nearby Wadi Qumran. Fr. De Vaux was appointed to carry out a systematic excavation of the Khirbet Qumran ruins, while the bedouins continued to search secretly for more scrolls in nearby caves.

Excavation began in the spring of 1952, two months after the bedouins had discovered Cave 2 near the first, and de Vaux soon realized the connection between the scrolls of Cave 1 and the ruins of Khirbet Qumran. During the first season of excavation, many caves were explored and among them were four additional caves containing scrolls, some found by the excavation team and some by the local bedouins. In Cave 4, immediately adjacent to the site, bedouins discovered the richest cache of written material, with 8,000+ fragments representing 200+ documents. In 1955–56 five more caves were found to contain manuscripts and fragments. On the Israeli side of the West Bank border, Yigael Yadin led a team of explorers in the deep precipitous wadis near En-gedi, including Mishmar, Muraba`at, Hever, and Zeelim. Many contained scrolls and papyri dated to the Second Jewish Revolt of Bar Kochba (A.D.132–135) along with coins dating variously from 40 B.C. to A.D. 135. In the excavation of the Herodian and Zealot fortress of Masada in 1964–65, the Yigael Yadin team uncovered several biblical and extrabiblical manuscript fragments.

The excavations of Qumran yielded remains dating back to the late Judahite kingdom, perhaps representing one of the towers in the wilderness built by Uzziah (2 Chron. 6:10). A large tower with storage rooms, two pottery kilns, and one two-story building on the interior of the site was interpreted as the Scriptorium. The excavated remains of the "scriptorium" included two inkwells and sections of long bench-like tables upon which the Qumran scribes are believed to have sown together pieces of sheepskin parchment and produced copies of the various documents. The site was dramatically destroyed by fire and earthquake between 40 and 31 B.C.

Scroll Contents The scrolls are divided among biblical and sectarian documents including a number of commentaries on biblical books. Apocryphal and pseudepigraphic texts abound in the collection that also contains numerous texts composed by the community that evidence their doctrines and practices. The original seven Cave 1 manuscripts included such a mixture of documents. The Syrian Archbishop purchased **1QIsª**, a complete scroll of Isaiah, **1QpHab**, a commentary on Habakkuk 1–2 (**p** = pesher, a kind of interpretation by divine illumination), **1QGenApoc**, an apocryphal version of Genesis, and **1QS**, the Seder (order) of the Community consisting of doctrines and rules governing the sectarian group. This latter document also contained a portion identified as **1QSa**, sometimes referred to as the "Messianic Rule." These four scrolls were eventually sold to the Israeli Yigael Yadin through an intermediary for approximately $250,000. Professor Sukenik purchased three scrolls, identified as **1QIsᵇ**, containing a major portion of Isaiah, **1QM** (**M**=Hb. mil'hamah, "war") known as the "War Scroll"

and **1QH** (**H**= Hb. hodayot, "thanksgivings") containing numerous psalms and songs composed by the sect leaders and members.

All the 39 books of the Hebrew Bible are represented at least in fragments except for Esther and possibly Nehemiah. Esther is represented in a somewhat paraphrastic Aramaic version (six fragments). If Nehemiah was combined with Ezra at this time, as many scholars believe, then one can say it is represented since a portion of Ezra is extant in the corpus. Some biblical books, such as the Chronicles, are found with only a few verses in one small fragment, whereas others such as Isaiah are represented completely in the collective multiple copies (21). The largest numbers of biblical manuscripts occur in the Pentateuch, Isaiah, and the Psalms (36). Some of the biblical texts are found in the Greek Septuagint form and language, and a number of primarily Pentateuchal texts are written in the Paleo-Hebrew script used by Israelites prior to the Babylonian captivity. By paleographic analysis of the formation of the Hebrew characters, a few biblical manuscripts have been dated to the third century B.C., suggesting the original founders of the Qumran sect brought with them copies of biblical books which were already nearly 100 years old.

The sectarian documents are categorized into five categories: (1) Rules and Halakah,

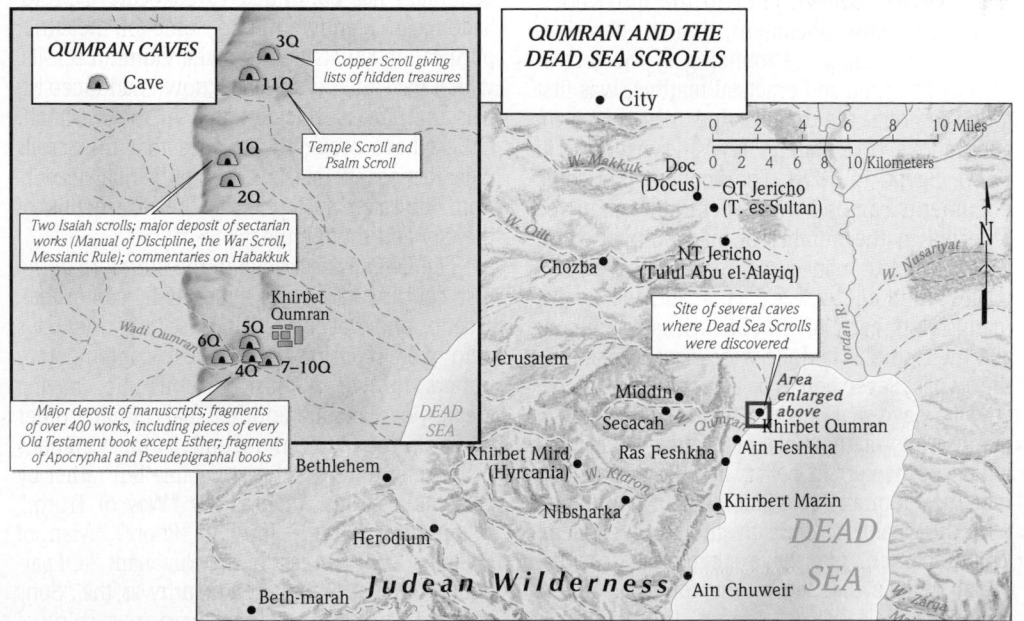

QUMRAN CAVES
🔺 Cave

3Q
11Q
Copper Scroll giving lists of hidden treasures

1Q
Temple Scroll and Psalm Scroll

2Q

Two Isaiah scrolls; major deposit of sectarian works (Manual of Discipline, the War Scroll, Messianic Rule); commentaries on Habakkuk

Khirbet Qumran
Wadi Qumran 6Q 5Q 4Q 7–10Q

Major deposit of manuscripts; fragments of over 400 works, including pieces of every Old Testament book except Esther; fragments of Apocryphal and Pseudepigraphal books

QUMRAN AND THE DEAD SEA SCROLLS
● City

0   2   4   6   8   10 Miles
0   2   4   6   8   10 Kilometers

W. Makkuk
Doc (Docus)
OT Jericho (T. es-Sultan)

W. Qilt

Chozba
NT Jericho (Tulul Abu el-Alayiq)

W. Nusariyat

Site of several caves where Dead Sea Scrolls were discovered

Jerusalem

Middin
Secacah
Ras Feshkha
Ain Feshkha

Area enlarged above
Khirbet Qumran

Bethlehem
Khirbet Mird (Hyrcania)
W. Kidron

Khirbert Mazin

Nibsharka

Herodium

DEAD SEA

Beth-marah
Judean Wilderness
Ain Ghuweir

DEAD SEA

D

Caves at Qumran in which the Dead Sea Scrolls were discovered.

Teacher. Nine copies were discerned of the War Scroll, which describes the preparation for and a sequence of conflicts in the 50 years of eschatological battles leading up to the establishment of the messianic kingdom.

The Qumran hermeneutic was governed by the principle of *pesher*, by which the Righteous Teacher was believed to be endowed by God with special illumination in order to discern the times and the Scriptures in understanding what God was doing in the present age of wrath. This perspective is evident in the Habakkuk *pesher* on 2:1-2, "and God told Habakkuk to write down that which would happen to the final generation, but He did not make known to him when the time would come to an end.... This concerns the Righteous Teacher to whom God made known all the mysteries of the prophets." Hence, the Qumran eschatology was governed by their view of themselves in God's plan as bringing the culmination of the ages to fruition in that day.

Sectarian Identity Since the early publication of the scrolls, the majority of scholars have noted the parallels between the content of the scrolls and the setting of the community with the Essenes who were known from the writings of Josephus, Philo of Alexandria, and Pliny the Elder. Other early suggestions included known groups such as the Pharisees, Sadducees, Zealots, and even the Medieval Karaites. L. Schiffman has continued to advocate a proto-Sadducean identity due to some of the strict purification rituals noted in the Qumran scrolls, which have affinity to later known Sadducee rituals that are specifically cited in the Mishnah. Others have proffered the idea that the scrolls were deposited in the caves by scribal leaders from Jerusalem just prior to the destruction of the city and the temple.

The Essenes described in the literature of the first century A.D. were a peaceful, communal, ascetic, and deeply religious sect of the Jews who were considered by most contemporary writers to live a most virtuous life, having greater love for one another than did any other group. In the Qumran documents the sectarians never refer to themselves by name but rather by descriptive terms, such as the "Way of Truth," "Community" (or "Unity"), "Poor," "Men of Holiness," or "Keepers of the Covenant." Of particular interest is their self-identity as the "Sons of Light" who in this age were in a spiritual

(2) Hymns, Liturgies, and Wisdom, (3) Bible Interpretation and Paraphrase, (4) Apocrypha and Pseudepigrapha, and (5) Astronomical and Calendrical Texts. Some of these were known from earlier Jewish and Christian sources, yet many were unknown prior to the discoveries. The Damascus Document, which describes issues surrounding the founding of the sect as well as doctrinal and practical matters, was first found among the manuscripts discovered in excavations of a Karaite Jewish synagogue in Cairo, Egypt, in 1890. The popularity of some documents among the sectarians may be reflected in the number of manuscripts found. For example, Jubilees is represented by 15 copies found in Caves 1, 2, 3, 4, and 11. Twelve manuscripts each of the Damascus Document and the Community Rule were discerned among the scrolls. Seven copies of 1 Enoch were uncovered in Cave 4. From the same cave came six manuscripts of the Halakhic Letter (4QMMT), which posits certain beliefs and ritual practices that the Qumran sectarians held in contention with the established priestly circle in Jerusalem. This document may have served as a foundational treatise that led to the founding of the group by a leader known as the Righteous

eschatological battle against the "Sons of Darkness" composed of the Gentile nations and the ungodly of the covenant (unfaithful Jews). Among the arguments against the Essene hypothesis are the differences between initiatory stages for entry into the communities, the practice of marriage at Qumran vs. celibacy suggested by the writers on the Essenes, and the non-occurrence of the term Essene in the Qumran texts. Still a majority of the evidence points to the Essenes or possibly a sub-group among the several thousand Essenes in existence in the latter half of the first century A.D.

Community Life and Theology In the beginning of the Damascus Document the writer describes the setting for the founding of the community in an "age of wrath" which had continued since the Babylonian captivity. In the second century B.C. a group of repentant "guilty men" who sought God's forgiveness and favor were blessed by God with a Righteous Teacher who guided the faithful "in the way of His heart." They were opposed by an unfaithful priest, called the "Scoffer," who abandoned the true teaching of the covenant and who eventually forced them to withdraw from Jerusalem to an isolated location overlooking the Dead Sea where they could prepare themselves for the coming of God's kingdom. Calling themselves "the Sons of Zadok the Priest," they took quite literally Isa. 40:3 and sought to "prepare the way for the Lord in the wilderness." The community was led by a council composed of priests and lay persons devoted to the study and discussion of the Torah and exemplary in their faithfulness to the teachings of the Scriptures as interpreted by the Righteous Teacher. Sect members were to spend one-third of their hours in the study of the Scriptures, often in the context of a group of at least 10 men with a learned priest present. Various other members contributed to the whole by carrying out agricultural and animal husbandry practices, pottery production, tanning of skins for sandals and text parchment, preparing meals, and other daily necessities.

Entry into the sect was a three-year process during which one was taught thoroughly and was expected to exemplify in lifestyle the doctrines of the sect. An annual examination reviewed the initiate's progress, and gradually one could participate in the "holy things" of the community, such as the ritual washings, community meals, and festive activities. By the end of the process one's worldly goods, which had been registered at the initial stage, would be incorporated into the community possessions.

One was taught from the beginning to discern the ways of humanity, to determine whether they were of the spirit of light and truth or the spirit of darkness and falsehood, the two categories into which God has apportioned all of humanity. The sectarian theology ascribed to God as being the Creator of both spirits but that "He loves the one everlastingly and delights in its works forever; but the counsel of the other He loathes and for ever hates its ways" (1QS IV.2-3). The sectarians held the belief in the immortality of the soul in common with the Pharisees and the description of the Essenes in Josephus (Jewish War II.154-55; Antiquities XVIII.i.2–6; 1QS IV; 1QH 3.19-23). Yet in the final stage of the eschaton (last days), the Community Rule (IV.10-11) suggests that the ultimate end of the wicked and spirit of falsehood is "shameful extinction in the fire of the dark regions. The times of all their generations shall be spent in sorrowful mourning and in bitter misery and in calamities of darkness until they are destroyed without remnant or survivor."

The Dead Sea Scrolls and the Old Testament Text Prior to the discovery of these scrolls, the oldest complete or almost complete manuscripts of the Hebrew Old Testament were

Dead Sea Scroll fragment.

The Shrine of the Book (Museum for the Dead Sea Scrolls) in Jerusalem, Israel.

the Leningrad Codex (A.D. 1009) and the Aleppo Codex (A.D. 930). The discovery of the Dead Sea Scrolls has extended our knowledge of the Hebrew text back 1,000 years. The most important lesson to be learned from this is how carefully the Jewish scribes preserved the integrity of the text during that time. Moreover, among the recovered manuscripts was the early textual tradition that later became the standard text, known as the Masoretic Text (MT). This discovery indicated that the Jewish Masoretes were not creating a text but were faithfully preserving an ancient form of the Hebrew Old Testament. The state of the Hebrew text at Qumran also witnesses that other forms of the Hebrew text existed at Qumran. Multiple scribal traditions can be discerned in some of the earliest texts in the areas of orthography (spelling; some more influenced by Aramaic than others), paleography (letter formation), and textual readings. Hebrew manuscript fragments of Jeremiah, 1 Samuel, Joshua, and others suggest that the Greek Septuagint, translated in Egypt in the third and second centuries B.C., was done from a Hebrew text that differed in some respects from the text later standardized and preserved by the Masoretes. Also, other Hebrew texts from Qumran agreed with different readings known in the Samaritan Pentateuch (ca. 150 B.C.). Scholars believe that the standard form of the Hebrew text was determined by ca. A.D. 100. Through the scholarly discipline of textual criticism (establishing the original words of the text), scholars are in a better position than ever before as a result of the discovery of the Dead Sea Scrolls to identify the best Hebrew readings. In summary, the field of OT textual criticism has advanced in its analysis and recovery of the Hebrew Scriptures.

The Dead Sea Scrolls and Christianity Soon after the discovery of the first of the scrolls, certain scholars posited the idea that some of the ideology of early Christianity may have had its origins in the theology of the Qumran sectarians. Self-identifying phrases such as the "Called-out Ones" (*ekklesia*), "the Way," "the Poor," "the Elect," and "the Saints" were common to both groups, as well as their general identities as messianic communities. Both held to a "new covenant" theology and saw their founders and leaders as the fulfillment of the prophetic promise of the OT. Both groups held that the religious leadership in Jerusalem had become corrupt and was in need of divine intervention to bring correction. Communal meals and property sharing in the early church were paralleled with those at Qumran, and both were seen as practicing forms of baptismal ritual. However these might appear as parallel upon a surface reading of the texts, there are notable differences. At the core of the distinctiveness is the personal identity, teaching, and work of Jesus of Nazareth. Qumran sectarians were looking for possibly two messiahs, one of the lineage of Aaron (priestly) and one of the branch of David (royal); whereas for Christianity the Messiah had come and fulfilled the Law and the Prophets and would return in the eschatological future for the saints.

In a number of cases the NT evidences that the biblical writers drew from a broad range of Jewish theological viewpoints, including those espoused at Qumran, in proclaiming the person and work of Jesus Christ. M. Abegg has suggested that Paul may have drawn upon concepts related in the 4QMMT (Halakic Letter) when he referred to the "works of the Law" in Gal. 2:16. The Hebrew equivalent of this phrase (*ma'asey haTorah*) is only found in this work of all extant Jewish literature. John the apostle's use of dualistic imagery in referring to the "children of light" and "spirit of falsehood" have their closest parallels in the pronounced dualism of the Dead Sea Scrolls.

Several scholars have examined the parallels between John the Baptist and the Qumran sectarian life. Parallels include the general ascetic lifestyle, the meager diet composed of locusts and wild honey (both listed in the dietary supplements at Qumran), priestly background and lineage and yet, at the same time, strong confrontations with the religious leadership in Jerusalem, the relative closeness of John's baptismal activity to the Qumran location, and finally the messianic role as fulfillment of Isa. 40:3. The evidence is largely circumstantial, and yet some points may have validity. If John the Baptist had some contact with the community, by the time of his public ministry he had differentiated himself from the community teaching and saw anew his God-given role in preparing for the advent of the Messiah Jesus.

R. Dennis Cole and E. Ray Clendenen

DEAFNESS Inability to hear. According to the OT God makes persons deaf or hearing (Exod. 4:11). The deaf were protected by the Mosaic law (Lev. 19:14). The inability to hear is used as an image for waiting on God rather than resisting attackers (Ps. 38:13-14). Deafness is also symbolic of inattentiveness to and rebellion against God (Isa. 42:18-20; 43:8). Part of the future hope of the prophets is that the deaf will hear (Isa. 29:18). The enemies of Israel would experience deafness in response to God's restoration of Israel (Mic. 7:16).

The NT interprets Jesus' healing of the deaf as evidence of Jesus' messiahship (Matt. 11:5; Luke 7:22). Strangely, only Mark narrated the healing of a deaf person (Mark 7:33-35; cp. 9:14-29). Mark 9:25 attributes deafness to an evil spirit. The parallel narratives (Matt. 17:14-19; Luke 9:37-42) emphasize epileptic-like fits rather than deafness.

DEATH The biblical portrait of death is not that of a normal outworking of natural processes. Instead, the Bible presents human death as a reaffirmation that something has gone awry in God's created order. The Scriptures do not, however, picture death as a hopeless termination of human consciousness but instead brim with the hope of resurrection. Biblical scholars group the Bible's teachings on death into three distinct but interrelated categories—physical, spiritual, and eternal.

Physical Death The opening chapters of the Pentateuch pinpoint the origin of human death in the Edenic rebellion (Gen. 3:19). This mortality eventually overtook Adam (Gen. 5:5) and is a certainty for all his descendants (1 Cor. 15:21-22). Apart from direct miraculous provision, as in the case of the prophet Elijah (2 Kings 2:11), God has fixed an hour of death for each human being (Heb. 9:27). In their fallen and finite state,

human beings are powerless to avert the reality of death (Ps. 89:48).

The reality of death pervades the Scriptures. Within the OT community, the touching of a corpse rendered an individual unclean (Num. 5:2). Even contact with the bones of the dead or with a grave necessitated seven days of ritual uncleanness (Num. 19:16). The people of God were forbidden to mourn their departed with the customs of the pagan nations around them such as ceremonial cutting of skin and head shaving (Deut. 14:1).

Because God is the giver of life (Acts 17:25), He has the sovereign prerogative to take human life at His own good pleasure. At times in the old covenant theocracy, God by direct revelation through His prophets appointed His people to exercise His judgment on the enemies of the people of God (Num. 31:1-11; Deut. 7:22-26; 20; 1 Sam. 15:1-8). The new covenant church, however, was not given such authority. The church's power does not extend to bodily life or death but only to the power to expel unrepentant sinners from the body (1 Cor. 5:9-13). Even so, the Bible does speak of death as a drastic manifestation of God's divine discipline over those within the believing community who remain unrepentant in their sinful activity (Acts 5:1-11; 1 Cor. 11:27-34).

Throughout the Bible, death is a reminder of the brevity of human life. The Bible calls for joyful living in light of one's certain destiny in the grave (Eccles. 9:9-10), compares the shortness of life to the fleeting existence of a flower (Job 14:2), and contrasts the shortness of human life with the eternal faithfulness of God (Pss. 90:2-12; 103:14-17). Jesus spoke of the suddenness of death as a warning to those who trust in their earthly possessions rather than in the gracious provision of God (Luke 12:16-20). James, describing human existence as a "vapor," argues that impending death exposes the tentativeness of all human plans (James 4:13-16).

The Bible nowhere presents physical death as a painless transition from material existence to the spiritual plane. Facing the death of His friend Lazarus, for instance, Jesus did not react with a detached resignation but was moved to tears of compassion by the pain death had left in its wake (John 11:35,38). The Apostle Paul seems ambivalent about his own foreseen death at the hands of the state. The goodness he finds in death is not an escape from life. Rather, Paul rejoices in the knowledge that in death he both would glorify and be in the presence of His Messiah, the Lord Jesus (Phil. 1:19-23).

Scripture closely associates death with the malevolent activity of Satan, whom Jesus labeled a "murderer from the beginning" (John 8:44 HCSB). The entrance of death into the creation came through the cunning temptation of the Serpent (Gen. 3:1-6). The writer of Hebrews ascribes to the evil one the "power of death," namely a paralyzing and universal fear of death, from which believers are liberated by the atonement of Christ (Heb. 2:14-15).

Although physical death is sometimes compared to sleep (Deut. 31:16; John 11:11; 1 Cor. 11:30; 1 Thess. 4:15), Scripture does not teach that one's consciousness lapses after death to reawaken at the day of resurrection and judgment. Jesus promised the repentant thief on the cross that He would see paradise the very day of his death (Luke 23:43). Paul teaches that, for believers, being absent from the body means being present with Christ (2 Cor. 5:8).

Spiritual Death The cataclysmic results of Adam's fall are not limited to bodily death. Scripture characterizes fallen humanity as "dead in trespasses and sins" (Eph. 2:1; Col. 2:13). Human beings are born with the sentence of death hanging over their heads, but they are also born with corrupted desires and inclinations that render them completely "dead" to the peril of their own accumulating guilt (Eph. 4:18-19).

As such, humans are alienated from their Creator. The mind suppresses what can be clearly seen of God in His creation, preferring to worship idols (Rom. 1:21-23). The will refuses to acknowledge the truth of God's self-disclosure (Rom. 3:10). The affections cling to sinful cravings, preferring them to the righteousness of God (John 3:19; Phil. 3:19). This spiritual deadness, if not counteracted by the gracious activity of God in the gospel, will lead to eternal judgment (James 1:14-15).

Eternal Death Bodily death does not end the accountability of rebellious humans before the holy tribunal of God. After the appointed hour of death comes judgment (Heb. 9:27). The Bible uses the word "death" at times to describe the wrath of God visited upon unbelievers in the afterlife (Rev. 20:14). Though this hellish reality is sometimes called "perishing" (John 3:16; 2 Pet. 2:12) and "destruction" (Matt. 10:28; 2 Thess. 1:9), it cannot be understood as the

annihilation of the person. In contrast with the momentary sting of physical death, the death that awaits the sinner at the last judgment is pictured as conscious (Matt. 8:12) and eternally unrelenting (Mark 9:43). The universality of sin means that each human being, with the exception of the sinless Jesus of Nazareth, stands deserving of this paramount expression of God's justice (Rom. 3:23).

Death and the Work of Christ The OT does not picture death as a permanent condition within the created order. Instead, the prophets point to the day when God will call the righteous from their graves and into everlasting life (Dan. 12:2). The prophets proclaim that death has no place in the consummation of the eschatological kingdom of God (Isa. 25:8). The resurrection from the dead at the last day is seen as a vindication of the glorious faithfulness of God to His covenant promises (Ezek. 37:12-14).

In Jesus of Nazareth, the promised destruction of death in the Kingdom of God has arrived. Jesus exercised His sovereignty over life and death by raising the dead (Matt. 9:18-26; Mark 5:35-43; Luke 7:11-17; 8:49-56), while claiming Himself as the source of bodily resurrection and eternal life (John 11:25). Jesus asserted that at the last day He personally would call His people from their graves (John 6:39), a promise reiterated in the apostolic preaching of the early church.

The decisive turning point in God's purposes to overturn the reign of death came in the sacrificial death and resurrection of Jesus. Jesus endured death for the world, bearing in His body the holy judgment of God against rebellious creation. His resurrection from the dead vindicated Him as the anointed Messiah and beneficiary of God's covenant promises (Rom. 1:3-4; Acts 2:22-36). The apostles preached Jesus' resurrection as His triumph over death. As the Second Adam, He is the firstfruits of the resurrection of the righteous (1 Cor. 15:20-23). Those who believe in Him will find themselves resurrected, not because of their righteousness, but because they are united to the resurrected Christ.

Paul, having established death as the consequence of a universal human depravity, heralds the resurrection of Jesus as pronouncing the death knell for death itself (2 Tim. 1:10). Proclaiming that the end times have come in Christ as the "last enemy" is destroyed in the resurrection of the Messiah (1 Cor. 15:26), Paul mocks the power of death in light of the victory of Jesus (1 Cor. 15:55). He assures believers on the basis of God's resurrection of Jesus that the same bodies buried in the graves will be raised to life in the new creation (1 Cor. 15:35-49). Believers, therefore, have no reason for despair in the face of death (1 Thess. 4:13-18).

The Bible posits the believer's hope in the face of death not only in Jesus' resurrection triumph over death but also in the present ministry of the Holy Spirit. The OT prophets linked the resurrection from the dead to the coming of the Spirit of God in the eschatological kingdom (Ezek. 37:13-14). The Spirit's regeneration of the people serves as a guarantee of the coming regeneration of the universe (2 Cor. 1:22; 5:1-5; Eph. 1:14).

The Bible compares Jesus' reversal of physical death in resurrection with His reversal of spiritual death in the regeneration of the human heart, an act that is likened to God's calling light into existence at the creation event (2 Cor. 4:6). Regeneration is said to be God "making alive" those who had been "dead" in their sins (Eph. 2:1) that they may walk in the newness of the new creation (Rom. 6:4). See *Resurrection*.

Russell D. Moore

DEATH OF CHRIST See *Cross, Crucifixion; Christ, Christology; Jesus Christ.*

DEBIR (Dě·bēr´) Personal and place-name meaning "back, behind." As a common noun, the Hebrew term refers to the back room of the temple, the holy of holies. **1.** King of Eglon who joined in Jerusalem-led coalition against Joshua and lost (Josh. 10:3). Nothing else about him is known. See *Eglon.* **2.** Important city in hill country of tribe of Judah whose exact location is debated by archaeologists and geographers. Joshua annihilated its residents (Josh. 10:38; cp. 11:21; 12:13). Joshua 15:15 describes Caleb's challenge to Othniel to capture Debir, formerly called Kiriath Sepher (cp. Judg. 1:11). Joshua 15:49 gives yet another name, Kiriath Sannah, to Debir. It became a levitical city for the priests (Josh. 21:15). Different scholars locate Debir at Tell Beit Mirsim, 13 miles southwest of Hebron; Khirbet Tarrameh, five miles southwest of Hebron; and Khirbet Rabud, seven and a half miles west of Hebron. It may have been the most important town south of Hebron. **3.** A town on the northern border of Judah (Josh. 15:7). This may be located at Thoghret ed Debr, the "pass of Debir," 10 miles east of Jerusalem. **4.** A town in Gad east of the Jordan given various spellings in the Hebrew Bible: *Lidebor*

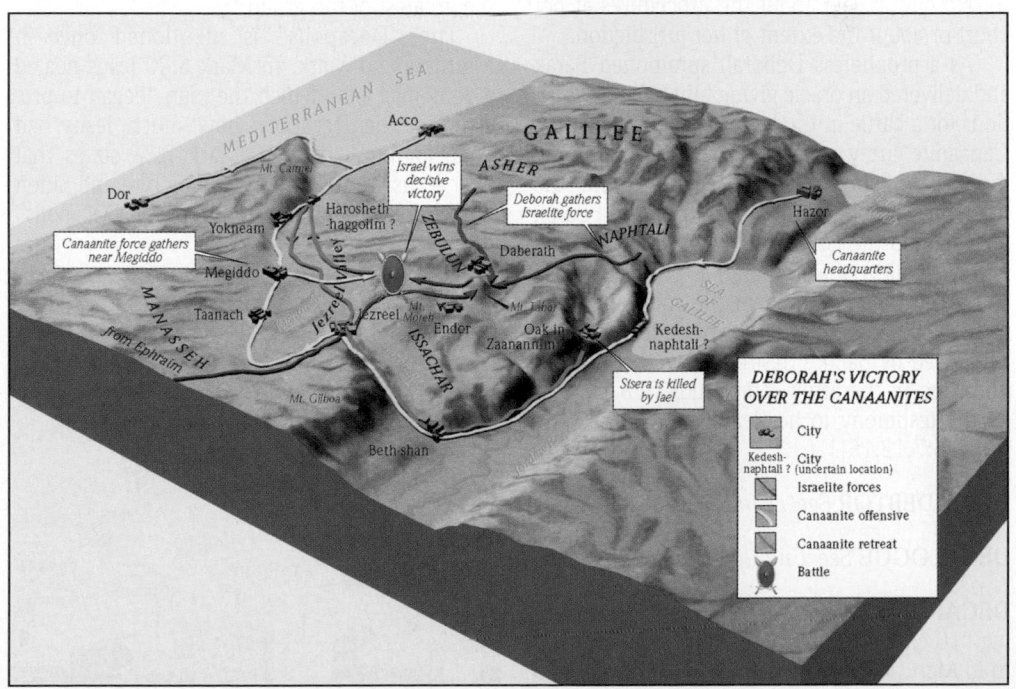

DEBORAH'S VICTORY OVER THE CANAANITES

City

Kedesh-naphtali ? City (uncertain location)

Israelite forces

Canaanite offensive

Canaanite retreat

Battle

(Josh. 13:26); *Lwo Debar* (2 Sam. 9:4-5); *Lo' Debar* (2 Sam. 17:27); *Lo' Dabar* (Amos 6:13). The city may be modern Umm el-Dabar, 12 miles north of Pella. It apparently was near Mahanaim, where first Ish-bosheth and then David, while fleeing Absalom, made their head-quarters. Some Bible students have suggested a location at Tell el-Chamme or Khirbet Chamid.

DEBORAH (Dĕb´ ô räh) Personal name meaning "bee." Deborah is the name of two women in the Bible, Rebekah's nurse (Gen. 35:8) and a leader of premonarchic Israel (Judg. 4–5).

Deborah, Rebekah's nurse, died and was buried near Bethel. She had been part of the household of Jacob, Rebekah's son.

Deborah, the leader of Israel, is identified as a prophetess, a judge, and the wife of Lapidoth (Judg. 4:4). She probably lived about 1200 B.C. or slightly later during a period of Canaanite oppression. Deborah is described in Judg. 5:7 as "a mother in Israel" because of her role in deliv-ering God's people. After Moses, only Samuel filled the same combination of offices: prophet, judge, and military leader.

Deborah served regularly as a judge, hearing and deciding cases brought to her by the people of Israel. She held court at "the palm tree of Deborah," in the southern part of the territory of Ephraim, between Ramah and Bethel (Judg. 4:4-5). Nothing is said about the procedures at her court or about the extent of her jurisdiction.

As a prophetess Deborah summoned Barak and delivered an oracle giving him God's instruc-tions for a battle in the Jezreel Valley against the Canaanite army commanded by Sisera (Judg. 4:6-9; cp. Samuel, 1 Sam. 15:2-3, and the unnamed prophet, 1 Kings 20:13-15). Barak obeyed, and the Israelites won the battle. Some scholars believe that Deborah as prophetess also composed the victory poem she and Barak sang in Judg. 5. Deborah's authority under God was evidenced by Barak's desire to have her present with him in the army camp (Judg. 4:8,14) and by the testimony to her leadership in the song (Judg. 5:7,12,15). *Pamela J. Scalise*

DEBT, **DEBTOR** See *Loan.*

DECALOGUE See *Law, Ten Commandments.*

DECAPOLIS (Də căp´ ō lĭs) Place-name mean-ing "10 cities." A group of Greek cities referred to in Matt. 4:25; Mark 5:20; 7:31, originally 10

Colonnade along the main road through the ruins of the ancient Decapolis city of Gerasa (modern Jerash).

in number but including more cities at a later time. The second century A.D. writer Pliny named the 10 cities as Damascus, Philadelphia (modern Amman), Canatha, Scythopolis, Pella, Hippos, Gadara, Dion, Raphana, and Gerasa (modern Jerash). Ptolemy, another second-cen-tury writer, names 18 cities in the Decapolis, omitting Raphana but adding nine others. A later source mentioned 14 cities in the group. Thus the number varied from time to time. They were established after the time of Alexander the Great and were predominantly Greek in culture and influence. These cities were scattered south and east of the Sea of Galilee. Only Scythopolis was west of the Jordan River. Josephus named it as the greatest of the group.

The "Decapolis" is mentioned only in Matthew and Mark. In Mark 5:20 Jesus healed a demoniac after which the man "began to pro-claim in the Decapolis how much Jesus had done for him" (HCSB). Mark 7:31 states that after Jesus went to the region of Tyre and Sidon He went "through the region of the Decapolis"

Greco-Roman theater in Amman, Jordan (the ancient Decapolis city of Philadelphia).

(HCSB). Matthew 4:25 adds no more to our knowledge of these cities.

Traditionally the Decapolis is assumed to be a league of cities that preserved the stronghold of Greek thought and life in Palestine and resisted the Semitic influences of the Jews. According to Pliny, however, it was not a very solid political alliance. A recent view is that it was not even a league but a geographical region. These cities do seem to have much in common; they were centers for the spread of Greco-Roman culture and had no great love for the Jews. They were associated with one another closely enough that in some ways they were considered as a group, if not as a league. See *Palestine*.

W. Thomas Sawyer

DECISION, VALLEY OF (Joel 3:14) See *Jehoshaphat, Valley of.*

DECREE Royal order or decision. Decrees were proclaimed publicly by criers (Jon. 3:5-7), designated as "heralds" (Dan. 3:4), often throughout the territory of the monarch (1 Sam. 11:7; Ezra 1:1). Decrees were written and stored in archives for later reference (Ezra 6:1-2). Scripture attributes just decrees to divine wisdom (Prov. 8:15). Scripture also recognizes unjust decrees (Isa. 10:1). Some important decrees include: Cyrus's decree on rebuilding the temple (Ezra 6:3-5); Esther's decree on the celebration of Purim (Esther 9:32); and the decree of Caesar Augustus which set the scene for the birth of Christ (Luke 2:1).

As King of the earth, God issues decrees regulating the world of nature (the sea, Prov. 8:29; rain, Job 28:26) and of humanity (Dan. 4:24). God also decrees the reign of the Messianic King (Ps. 2:7).

The KJV uses "decree" to describe the decision of the Apostolic Council (Acts 16:4) and of a human inward decision not to marry (1 Cor. 7:37). NIV refers to God's righteous decree of death for sinners (Rom. 1:32). NASB uses "decree" for God's law that led to disobedience and death (Col. 2:14,20). NRSV uses "decree" to speak of God's eternal wisdom and plan for creation. Any translator using "decree" is interpreting the meaning of a more general Hebrew or Greek term, resulting in each translation using "decree" for several different words of the original language.

DEDAN (Dē´ dăn) Personal and place-name of unknown meaning. **1.** The original ancestor of an Arabian tribe listed in the Table of Nations as a son of Cush (Gen. 10:7). See *Cush.* **2.** Grandson of Abraham (Gen. 25:3). Here, as in 10:7, Dedan's brother is Sheba. Three otherwise unknown Arabian tribes descended from Dedan, according to Gen. 25:3. **3.** Arabian tribe centered at al-Alula, 70 miles southwest of Tema and 400 miles from Jerusalem. It was a station on the caravan road between Tema and Medina. Jeremiah pronounced judgment against the Arabian tribes (Jer. 25:23), perhaps looking to Nebuchadnezzar's raid in Arabia in 599–598 B.C. Nabonidus, king of Babylon (556–539), left control of his kingdom to his son Belshazzar and worked in Arabia for a period, controlling Dedan among other cities. Dedan was a caravan center for incense trade (Isa. 21:13). Isaiah warned the traders from Dedan to avoid the regular caravan stations and spend the night in the wilderness. Neighbors from Tema would have to meet their food needs. Jeremiah warned merchants from Dedan working or staying in Edom to flee the country because God was bringing judgment on it (Jer. 49:8). Ezekiel warned Edom that their soldiers fleeing even to Dedan would be struck down (Ezek. 25:13). In judging Tyre, Ezekiel noted they, too, traded with Dedan (Ezek. 27:15,20; cp. 38:13).

DEDANIM (Dĕd´ à nĭm) or **DEDANITE** (Dĕd´ à nīt) Resident or citizen of the tribe of Dedan. See *Dedan.*

DEDICATE, DEDICATION General term used to describe an act of setting apart or consecrating persons or things to God (or gods), persons, sacred work, or ends. The act is usually accompanied by an announcement of what is being done or intended and by prayer asking for divine approval and blessing. In the OT the people who were set apart included all Israel (Exod. 19:5,6; Deut. 7:6; 14:2) and the priests (Exod. 29:1-37). The things that were set apart included the altar in the tabernacle (Num. 7:10-88), images of pagan deities (Dan. 3:2-3), silver and gold (2 Sam. 8:11), temple (1 Kings 8:63; Ezra 6:16-18), walls of Jerusalem (Neh. 12:27), and private dwellings (Deut. 20:5). The idea of dedication is embodied in the NT word "saints." The whole church is set apart to God (Eph. 5:26). The individual believer is one of a dedicated, sanctified, consecrated, priestly people; set apart "to offer spiritual sacrifices acceptable to God through Jesus Christ" (1 Pet. 2:5 HCSB).

Ray F. Robbins

DEDICATION, FEAST OF Term for Hanukkah in John 10:22. See *Festivals; Hanukkah*.

DEEP, THE English translation of the Hebrew term *tehom*. The deep constitutes the primeval waters of creation in Gen. 1:2. This concept is echoed dramatically in Ps. 104:5-7, where God is pictured as rebuking the waters of the deep, separating the waters from the mountains and valleys, and setting the boundaries for each. Creation includes the concept of bringing order by separating or dividing what is made, and keeping each in its proper place (Prov. 8:22-31). This thought is expressed in an interesting metaphor in Ps. 33:7, where God is said to have gathered the waters into a bottle (NRSV) and put the deeps into a storehouse.

In the account of the Exodus from Egypt, God's action in parting the waters for the Israelites to pass is expressed poetically as a dividing of the waters of the deep (Exod. 15:8). God held the waters in place as the Israelites crossed the sea and released the waters when they reached the other side, shielding them from the Egyptians (Ps. 77:16-20). This was, theologically speaking, an act of creation—creating a people for the Lord, by freeing them from slavery in Egypt.

The waters of the deep can be destructive or constructive, curse or blessing. When the waters of the deep burst their bounds, the result is a flood (Gen. 7:11). At the extreme described in Gen. 7, it is a reversal of creation which can only be checked when God again sends the wind or spirit (*ruach*) which began creation (Gen. 1:2) and closes the fountains of the deep (Gen. 8:1-3). Storms at sea are also associated with the deep (Ps. 107:23-26; cp. Jon. 2:5-6). In the poetry of the Psalms, the deep is a metaphor for the trials of life that seem overwhelming (Ps. 69:14-15). It could even represent the abode of the dead (Ps. 71:20).

On the other hand, the waters of the deep are a blessing, without which life could not continue. Deuteronomy 8:7 describes the promised land as a land of brooks, fountains, and deeps, which irrigate the land so that grain and fruit can be grown (Ezek. 31:4). When Jacob blessed his son Joseph with "blessings of the deep that lies beneath," he was attempting to bestow fertility on Joseph and his offspring and on their land (Gen. 49:25 NASB; cp. Deut. 33:13-17). As blessing and as curse, the deep reflects as power which only the Creator God can control (Ps. 95:4).

The Greek Bible or Septuagint translated *tehom* as "abyss," bringing it into relationship with the pit, the abode of the dead (Rom. 10:7) and place of evil spirits (Luke 8:31), including the beast of the apocalypse (Rev. 17:8).

Wilda W. Morris

DEER Antlered animal (all male and some female have antlers) with two large and two small hooves. It is believed that three species of deer lived in Palestine in Bible times: red, fallow, and roe. The red deer seems to be the one most easily identified and probably was the species in the list of daily provisions for Solomon's table (1 Kings 4:23). The hart is the male red deer (Ps. 42:1), and the hind, the female (Job 39:1). The fallow deer, a small specie with especially large horns, is native to the Middle East and still survives in northern parts of that area. The tribe of Naphtali is described as "a doe set free that bears beautiful fawns" (Gen. 49:21). Certain characteristics of deer are noted in the Bible in the form of similes (Prov. 5:19; Isa. 35:6; Hab. 3:19).

DEFILE To make ritually unclean. See *Clean, Cleanness*.

DEGREES, SONG OF KJV phrase used in the titles of 15 psalms (Pss. 120–134). Modern speech translations render the phrase "Song of Ascents." Though the origin of the phrase is obscure, the generally accepted view is that the Hebrew term *ma'alot* (goings up) is a reference to pilgrims going up to Jerusalem for the three required festivals (Pss. 42:4; 122:4). Jerusalem was surrounded by mountains (Pss. 121:1; 125:2; 133:3), thus such trips involved a literal going up. It is conjectured that these psalms were sung on such occasions (Isa. 30:29; Ps. 132:7). Others have suggested that "ascents" is a reference to the rising melody of the psalms, the steplike poetic form of some of the psalms, or to the steps upon which the Levites performed music in the temple. Jewish tradition relates the title to the 15 steps leading from the court of the women to the court of Israel in the temple.

DEHAVITE (Dǝ hā´ vīt) KJV transliteration of Aramaic text in Ezra 4:9. Modern translators read the text as two Aramaic words—*di-hu'*—meaning "that is."

DEKAR (Dē´ kär) KJV reads "son of Dekar" in 1 Kings 4:9, where modern translations transliterate the Hebrew text to read "Ben-deker." See *Ben-deker.*

DELAIAH (Dǝ lā´ yǎh) Personal name meaning "the Lord rescued." **1.** Head of one of the 24 divisions of the priestly order organized by David (1 Chron. 24:18). **2.** Son of Shemaiah and a courtier who counseled Jehoiakim not to burn Jeremiah's scroll (Jer. 36:12,25). **3.** One of the exiles who returned under Zerubbabel to Jerusalem (Ezra 2:60; Neh. 7:62). **4.** Descendant of David and son of Elioenai (1 Chron. 3:24). **5.** Contemporary of Nehemiah (Neh. 6:10).

DELILAH (Dě lī´ lǎh) Personal name meaning "with long hair hanging down." A woman from the valley of Sorek who was loved by Samson (Judg. 16:4). She was probably a Philistine. She enticed Samson into revealing to her that the secret of his great strength lay in his hair, which had never been cut. Then she betrayed him to the Philistines. While he slept, she had his head shaved, and he was captured, blinded, and bound by the Philistines. See *Judges, Book of; Samson.*

DELIVERANCE, DELIVERER Rescue from danger. In Scripture God gives deliverance (Pss. 18:50; 32:7; 44:4), often through a human agent. In the OT deliverance most often refers to victory in battle (Judg. 15:18; 2 Kings 5:1; 13:17; 1 Chron. 11:14; 2 Chron. 12:7). Joseph was God's agent to deliver His people from famine (Gen. 45:7). The OT consistently stresses God as the giver of deliverance rather than the human agent. Thus Mordecai warned Esther that if she failed to act out her role as deliverer, God would provide another way (Esther 4:14). KJV also uses "deliverance" to describe the remnant that survives a battle or exile (Ezra 9:13). In KJV both NT uses of deliverance refers to release of prisoners (Luke 4:18; Heb. 11:35).

Modern translations use "deliverance" to refer to rescue from danger in Acts 7:25; Phil. 1:19.

A deliverer is one who rescues from danger. Two of the judges, Othniel and Ehud (Judg. 3:9,15), are called deliverers in the sense of military heroes. More often God is spoken of as the Deliverer of His people (2 Sam. 22:2; Pss. 18:2; 40:17; 144:2). The picture of God as deliverer is paralleled with the images of a rock, fortress, helper, and strong tower. Acts 7:35 refers to Moses as a deliverer. Romans 11:26-27 refers to the Messianic King as the Deliverer who will take away Israel's sins.

The verb "deliver" is used in a wide range of contexts. According to Job 5:19-26, God delivers in seven ways: from famine, war, the scourge of the tongue, wild animals, to safety, abundant offspring, and long life. Scripture also speaks to deliverance from sin (Pss. 39:8; 79:9); the way of evil (Prov. 2:12); the power of evil (Matt. 6:13; Gal. 1:4; Col. 1:13); the law (Rom. 7:6); the body of death (Rom. 7:24); and the coming wrath of God (1 Thess. 1:10). God is the agent of deliverance in Col. 1:13 and Rom. 7:24-25. Christ is the agent in 1 Thess. 1:10 and Gal. 1:4, where He brings deliverance by giving Himself for sins.

DELUGE See *Flood.*

DEMAS (Dē´ mȧs) Companion and coworker of Paul the apostle (Col. 4:14). Though in Philem. 24 Paul identified Demas as a "coworker," 2 Tim. 4:10 indicates that this man later deserted Paul, having "loved this present world."

DEMETRIUS (Dǝ mē´ trĭ ŭs) Personal name meaning "belonging to Demeter, the Greek goddess of crops." **1.** Silversmith in Ephesus who incited a riot directed against Paul because he feared that the apostle's preaching would threaten the sale of silver shrines of Diana, the patron goddess of Ephesus (Acts 19:24-41). Demetrius may have been a guild master in charge of producing small silver copies of Diana's temple with a figure of the goddess inside. **2.** Apparently a convert from the worship of Demeter, the god worshiped in the mystery religion at Eleusis near Athens. John commended him, saying, he "has a good testimony from everyone, and from the truth itself" (3 John 12 HCSB). He may have carried 3 John from John to its original readers.

DEMONIC POSSESSION Demons are identified in Scripture as fallen angels who joined Satan in his rebellion. They follow Satan, doing evil and wreaking havoc. They have limited power and like Satan are already defeated (Col. 2:15).

Old Testament In the OT no individuals are said to have been possessed, but demonic beings were attested. Two of the more prominent demonic beings are the *Sedim* and the *Se'irim*. The *Sed* are mentioned twice (Deut. 32:17; Ps. 106:37), as are the *Se'irim* (Lev. 17:7; 2 Chron. 11:15). These beings are referred to as "demons" and are the recipients of forbidden sacrifices. The sacrifices consisted of adults, children, or an unclean animal. Lilith and Azazel are also considered to represent the demonic. Lilith is pictured as a female associated with unclean animals and desolate places (Isa. 34:14). Azazel is mentioned in connection with the scapegoat sent into the wilderness (Lev. 16:8,10,26). An evil spirit is mentioned three times (1 Sam. 16:15-16; 18:10). The evil spirit was sent to King Saul to torment him.

New Testament Various kinds of activity are attributed to demons. In demonic possession an individual is so affected that his actions are influenced by a demonic spirit. Terms such as "evil spirit," "deceitful spirits," and "unclean spirits" are used to identify demons in the NT. Demonic possession has various manifestations which include: muteness (Matt. 9:32; 12:22; Mark 9:17,25; Luke 11:14); deafness (Mark 9:25); blindness (Matt. 12:22; John 10:21); convulsions (Mark 1:26; 9:26); superhuman strength (Mark 5:4); and self-destructive behavior (Matt. 17:15). The NT does not separate the actions of the person from those of the demon. Physical changes such as masochism (Mark 5:5) and an unnatural voice (Mark 5:7) are understood as the demon's control of the individual. Paul understands demons as idols which men sacrifice to and worship (1 Cor. 10:20-22).

The NT distinguishes between demonic possession and physical disease. Matthew 4:24 states that Jesus healed "all those who were afflicted, those suffering from various diseases and intense pains, the demon-possessed, the epileptics, and the paralytics" (HCSB). Thus the theory that demonic possession should be equated with epilepsy or any other neurotic ailment is weak. Some of the demons made assertions of Christ's divinity when the disciples did not show such recognition. Mental or physical illness would not impart this type of knowledge (Mark 5:13; Luke 4:33-35; 8:29-33).

The cure for demonic possession was faith in the power of Christ. Never were magic or rituals used to deliver one from demonic possession. The exorcisms of Jesus show His power over Satan and his demons. The Beelzebul passages (Matt. 12:25-29; Mark 3:23-27; Luke 11:17-22) demonstrate the presence of the kingdom of God in the present world order (Luke 11:20). The exorcisms of Jesus were accomplished by the power of His speech. He issued simple commands, such as "be quiet, and come out of him!" (Mark 1:25), or "you mute and deaf spirit, I command you: come out of him and never enter him again!" (Mark 9:25 HCSB). The disciples were given Christ's authority and cast out demons (Luke 10:17-20; Acts 16:18). This success led Jewish exorcists to include the names of Jesus and Paul in their rituals (Acts 19:13). Despite Christ's authority over demons, the Gospels portray a continuing battle in the present age (Matt. 13:36-49). The final outcome of the battle is not in doubt. The fate of Satan and his demonic hoard is assured (Rev. 20:10).

Joe Cathey

DENARIUS (De nǎr´ ǐ ǔs) Coin representing a typical day's wage for an ordinary laborer (Matt. 20:2). KJV translates it "penny." This unit of Roman currency is the most frequently mentioned coin in the NT. See *Coins; Economic Life.*

DEN OF LIONS Place where lions live, at times a thicket (Jer. 50:44) or cave (Nah. 2:12). See *Lion.*

A Roman denarius.

DENY To disown or disassociate oneself from someone or to dispute that an assertion (Mark 14:70) or event (Acts 4:16) is true. The OT speaks of disassociating oneself from God (Josh. 24:27; Prov. 30:9). Peter's denial of Jesus (Matt. 26:34,69-75; Mark 14:30,66-72; Luke 22:34, 56-62) should be understood in this sense, since Peter three times disassociated himself from Jesus, claiming not to be one of His group. Fear of death or persecution leads some to deny, that is, disassociate themselves from Jesus (Matt. 10:33; Mark 8:38; Luke 12:9; 2 Tim. 2:12), resulting in Jesus' disassociation from them at the judgment. It is possible that 2 Pet. 2:1 and Jude 4 should be understood in this sense as well. To deny oneself is a special case in which a person disassociates oneself from self-interest to serve a higher cause. Here the idea of denial is paralleled by the picture of taking up Jesus' cross and following Him (Matt. 16:24; Mark 8:34; Luke 9:23).

John the Baptist denied or disputed the assertion that he was the Christ (John 1:19-20). The "antichrists" of 1 John 2:22 disputed the teaching that Jesus is the Christ. Possibly 2 Pet. 2:1 and Jude 4 are to be understood in this sense.

DEPOSIT Something given as a down payment; money invested with a banker for the purpose of drawing interest (Matt. 25:27); something given to another for safekeeping (Exod. 22:7). Exodus 22:7-13 gives guidelines for cases in which property left for safekeeping is stolen or a deposited animal is injured or dies. Lev. 6:2-7 gives guidelines for one wishing to confess mishandling a deposit. See *Pledge.*

DEPTHS Deep places of the sea (Exod. 15:5,8; Pss. 68:22; 77:16; 78:15); an underground spring (Deut. 8:7; Prov. 8:24); the earth's interior (Ps. 95:4; Isa. 44:23); and by extension Sheol, the subterranean abode of the dead (Pss. 63:9; 71:20). "The depths" is used figuratively for the unsearchable (Prov. 25:3), for the womb (Ps. 139:15), and perhaps for tragedy (Ps. 130:1). See *Deep, The.*

DEPUTY Official of secondary rank (1 Kings 22:47); KJV term for a Roman proconsul (Acts 13:7; 18:12; 19:38). See *Proconsul.*

DERBE (Dêr´ bə) Important city in region of Lycaonia in province of Galatia in Asia Minor. It is apparently near modern Kerti Huyuk. The res-idents of Derbe and Lystra spoke a different language from the people to the north in Iconium. Paul visited Derbe on his first missionary journey (Acts 14:6), fleeing from Iconium. Persecution in Lystra led to a successful preaching mission in Derbe (14:20-21). On the second journey Paul returned to Derbe (Acts 16:1). He apparently visited again on the third journey (18:23). Paul's fellow minister Gaius was from Derbe (20:4). See *Asia Minor, Cities of.*

DESCENT Path down a mountain (Luke 19:37); a genealogy, line of ancestors (Heb. 7:3,6).

DESCENT INTO HADES Phrase in the Apostles' Creed describing the work of Christ. Acts 2:27 says "You will not leave My soul in Hades, or allow Your Holy One to see decay" (HCSB). Acts 2:31 says, "He was not left in Hades, and His flesh did not experience decay" (HCSB). Ephesians 4:9 says that Christ "descended to the lower parts of the earth" (HCSB). First Peter 3:19 says Christ "went and made a proclamation to the spirits in prison" (HCSB). Many explanations have been offered for this. The time may be seen as the days of Noah (1 Pet. 3:20) and thus describe the activity of the preexistent Christ or the work of Christ's spirit through Noah. The time may have been immediately after the death of Christ on the cross or after the bodily resurrection of Christ. The content of His preaching may have been judgment; it may have been affirmation of His victory over "angels, authorities, and powers" (1 Pet. 3:22); it may have been release from Sheol or Hades for saints who preceded Him. The spirits may have been the "sons of God" of Gen. 6:2, the people of Noah's day, OT era sinners, OT people who were true to God, fallen angels (2 Pet. 2:4), or evil spirits (demonic powers) whom Jesus contested in His earthly ministry. The prison may have been Sheol or Hades, a special place of captivity for sinners, a place of punishment for fallen angels, a place of security for such angels where they thought they could escape Christ's power, or a place on the way to heaven where the faithful of old waited to hear the message of Christ's final atoning victory. Whatever the detailed explanations, the ultimate effect and purpose is to glorify Christ for His completed work of salvation through His death, burial, resurrection, and ascension, demonstrating His sovereign control of all places and powers.   *Charles W. Draper*

DESERT Areas with little rainfall to the east and south of Palestine and inhabited by nomads with flocks and herds. Three major deserts figure in biblical events: the plateau east of the mountains to the east of the Jordan River; the area south of Edom; and the triangle bordered by Gaza, the Dead Sea, and the Red Sea. The Bible pictures raiders from the desert—Amalekites, Midianites, Ishmaelites—threatening Palestine farmers. Saul relieved some of this pressure (1 Sam. 14:48).

Palestine's desert areas received brief hard rains in March and April. At times they blossomed briefly, but long dry spells returned its normal desert characteristics. The Hebrew language distinguishes with several words what English describes as desert or wilderness.

Midbar is the most prominent and inclusive term but is used in several different contexts with differing meaning. It can describe the southern boundary of the promised land (Exod. 23:31; Deut. 11:24). This southern wilderness can be divided into various parts: Shur (Exod. 15:22), Sin (Exod. 16:1), Paran (Num. 12:16), Zin (Num. 13:21). This entire southern desert

Wasteland of the northern Negev in southern Israel.

region can be called the wilderness of Sinai (Exod. 19:1) above which rises Mount Sinai. North of this is the wilderness of Judah (Judg. 1:16), lying east of the road connecting Jerusalem and Hebron. Here deep, narrow gorges lead down from the Judean hills to the Dead Sea. *Midbar* also describes the area surrounding a settlement where herds are pastured (1 Sam. 23:24; 24:1; 2 Chron. 20:20; cp. Josh. 8:24). Settlements in the desert arose particularly during times of political stability and served as military stations against Bedouin invasions and as protection for commerce on the desert trade routes.

Arabah often appears as a synonym for *midbar*. This is the basic term for the long rift reaching from the Sea of Galilee to the Dead Sea and on down to the Red Sea. It describes ground dominated by salt with little water or plants. *Arabah* is never used to describe pasturelands. It serves as the eastern boundary of the promised land and is often translated "plain," if it is not transliterated as "Arabah" (Deut. 3:17; Josh. 12:1).

Yeshimon designates the wasteland, which is unproductive. The word appears either in parallel with midbar or as part of a territorial designation such as in 1 Sam. 23:24. God holds out hope for restoration of the wild lands (Isa. 43:19-20). See *Jeshimon.*

Chorbah describes hot, dry land or land with destroyed settlements. It can designate dry land opposed to water-covered land (Gen. 7:22; Exod. 14:21). It describes the desert in Pss. 102:7; 106:9; Isa. 25:5; 50:2; 51:3; 64:10; Jer. 25:9.

Tsiyyah points to a dry region (Job 30:3; Pss. 78:17; 105:41; Isa. 35:1; Jer. 50:12; Zeph. 2:13).

Shamamah is a desolate and terrifying land and often indicates God's destruction of a place (Exod. 23:29; Lev. 26:33, Jer. 4:27; Ezek. 6:14; 23:33).

Negev (Negeb) refers to the dry land and is a technical name for the southern desert whose northern border lies north of Beersheba. Annual rainfall ranges from 100 to 300 millimeters a year. Rainfall varies drastically year to year. *Negev* came to mean "south" in Hebrew and could be translated the "south country" (Gen. 24:62).

For Israel the dry, mostly uninhabited desert engendered fear and awe. It could be described like the original chaos prior to creation (Deut. 32:10; Jer. 4:23-26). Israel was able to go through the desert because God led them (Deut. 1:19). Its animal inhabitants caused even more fear—snakes and scorpions (Deut. 8:15); wild donkeys (Jer. 2:24). The desert lay waste without humans or rain (Job 38:26; Jer. 2:6). The desert was a "terrifying land" (Isa. 21:1 NASB). The only expectation for a person in the wilderness was death by starvation (Exod. 16:3).

God's judgment could turn a city into desert (Jer. 4:26), but His grace could turn the wilderness into a garden (Isa. 41:17-20).

In the NT the desert was the place of John the Baptist's ministry (Luke 1:80; 3:4) and where demon-possession drove a man (Luke 8:29). The crowds forced Jesus into the unpopulated desert to preach (Mark 1:45). Jesus took His disciples there to rest (Mark 6:31). See *Wilderness.*   *Trent C. Butler*

DESIGN Modern translations' reading for an artistic pattern (Exod. 31:4; 39:3; 2 Chron. 2:14; KJV, "cunning works"); RSV translation for plans, generally in the negative sense of schemes or wiles (Job 10:3; 2 Cor. 2:11). KJV has "counsel" and "devices."

DESIRE See *Concupiscence; Lust.*

DESIRE OF ALL NATIONS Phrase that Haggai used in his prophecy of a renewed temple (Hag. 2:7). Some translations (KJV, NIV) interpret the underlying Hebrew as a prophecy of the coming Messiah. Other translations render the phrase "treasure" (TEV, NRSV, REB) or "wealth" (NASB) of all nations in parallel to the gold and silver of 2:8. The messianic interpretation first appears in the Latin Vulgate translation, while the treasures would show Yahweh's power to restore the glory of His house despite the people's poverty.

DESOLATION, ABOMINATION OF See *Abomination, Abomination of Desolation.*

DESTINY Word used in modern translations for God's act in electing or predestinating people and nations. See *Election; Fate; Predestination.*

DESTROYER Invading army (Isa. 49:17; Jer. 22:7) or a supernatural agent of God's judgment (Exod. 12:23; Heb. 11:28), often termed an angel (2 Sam. 24:15-16; 2 Kings 19:35; Ps.

78:49). All stand under God's sovereign control as he directs human affairs.

DESTROYING LOCUSTS See *Insects; Locust.*

DETAINED BEFORE THE LORD To remain in the presence of the Lord at the tabernacle or temple (1 Sam. 21:7). The reason for Doeg remaining at the tabernacle is not given. Perhaps he was there to fulfill a vow, receive an oracle, perform an act of penance, or to celebrate a holiday. First Samuel 21:6 suggests that it was the Sabbath (Mark 2:25-26).

DEUEL (Deū´ĕl) Personal name meaning "God knows." In Num. 1:14 the father of Eliasaph, the leader in the wilderness of the tribe of Gad. Numbers 2:14 identifies Eliasaph's father as Reuel. Deuel and Reuel may be alternative forms of the same name, probably representing a copyist's misreading of Hebrew "d" and "r," which are quite similar.

DEUTERONOMY, BOOK OF English name of fifth book of OT taken from Greek translation meaning "second law." Deuteronomy is the last of five books of Law and should not be read in isolation from the other four books (Genesis, Exodus, Leviticus, Numbers). Pentateuch (five books) is the familiar title associated with these five books of Law, the first and most important division of the Hebrew Bible. By longstanding tradition and for good reason, these books have been associated with Moses, the human instrument of God's deliverance of Israel from bondage in Egypt and the negotiator of the covenant between God and Israel. It is quoted or alluded to in the NT more than any other OT book except Psalms and Isaiah.

The probable origin of the title "Deuteronomy" is the translation in the Septuagint (Greek translation of the Hebrew OT) of Deut. 17:18-19. These two verses contain instructions to the king about making "a copy of this law" to be read regularly and obeyed faithfully. The Septuagint translators rendered the above phrase "this second law" instead of "a copy of this law." The Septuagint translation implies a body of legislation different from that contained in the previous books of Law. That does not seem to be the point of the instruction in Deut. 17:18-19. This apparent Greek mistranslation is the likely source of the title "Deuteronomy."

The title used in the Hebrew Bible, "these (are) the words" (two words in Hebrew), follows an ancient custom of using words from the first line of the text to designate a book. Sometimes the title in the Hebrew Bible was shortened to "words." This title more accurately defines the contents of the book than our familiar English title, Deuteronomy. In the main the book consists of the words by which Moses addressed Israel prior to their entry into the promised land. The style is sermonic, that of a preacher addressing his congregation with words designed to move them to obedience and commitment.

Background Deuteronomy is not primarily a law book or a book of history. It claims to be Moses' instruction to Israel on the eve of their entry into Canaan. Their wanderings in the wilderness were at an end. Their early efforts at conquest of the promised land east of the Jordan had met with success.

Israel's exodus from Egypt and the covenant at Sinai were the stages of Israel's birth as a nation. As yet they were a nation without a homeland. God's covenant with Israel at Sinai was in part a renewal of earlier covenants made with the patriarchs. Included in those covenants were the following promises: (1) that Israel would be God's special nation, (2) that Yahweh God would be their God, (3) that they would be obedient to God, and (4) that God would give them a homeland and innumerable descendants.

Now Israel was poised on the borders of Canaan ready to enter and to possess the land of promise. Moses, knowing that Israel's future hung on their obedience and commitment to God, led the people in a covenant renewal ceremony. Moses' approaching death and resulting transfer of human leadership to Joshua, plus Israel's approaching battles in conquest of the land, formed the basis for renewal of the covenant.

Contents Deuteronomy contains not one but three (or more) addresses from Moses to Israel. Most interpreters agree that the structure of the book is patterned after Near Eastern vassal treaties.

Deuteronomy 1:1-5 is an introduction, giving the time and place of the addresses. The time is "the fortieth year" (Deut. 1:3) of wilderness wandering, "in the eleventh month, on the first of the month" (HCSB). The place is "across the Jordan in the wilderness" (Deut. 1:1) and, more particularly, "in the land of Moab" (Deut. 1:5).

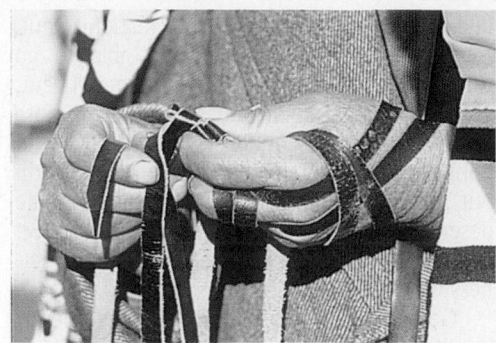

The hands of a Jewish man with the long strips of his phylactery intertwined with his fingers as he prays.

Deuteronomy 1:6–4:40 is Moses' first address in which he recounted Israel's journey from Horeb to Moab and urged Israel to be faithful to Yahweh. Moses used Israel's immediate past history to teach the present generation of Israelites the importance of trusting God. Israel's obedience was imperative if they were to expect to possess the land of Canaan. Moses set up cities of refuge on the east bank of the Jordan (Deut. 4:41-43).

Deuteronomy 4:44–28:68 contains Moses' second address to Israel. The address is introduced in Deut. 4:44-49. Then Moses proceeded to teach Israel lessons from the Law. These are not laws to be used in the courts to decide legal cases but instructions for life in the land of Canaan. Chapters 5–11 contain general laws, including the Ten Commandments (5:6-21) and the command to "Love the LORD your God with all your heart, with all your soul, and with all your strength" (6:5 HCSB). The specific laws are given in chapters 12–26, followed by a series of promised blessings or curses dependent on whether Israel would be loyal to God's covenant and keep His law.

Moses' third address is found in Deut. 29:1–30:20. The focus is upon covenant renewal. Repentance and commitment would assure life and the blessings of God. Rebellion would result in their death as a nation. The choice was theirs.

Deuteronomy 31:1-29 is Moses' farewell address. The song of Moses is given in Deut. 31:30–32:52. Moses' blessing is reported in chapter 33, and his death is recounted in chapter 34.

Date and Authorship The testimony of the text is that "These are the words Moses spoke to all Israel across the Jordan" (Deut. 1:1), "Across the Jordan in the land of Moab, Moses began to explain this law" (1:5), and "Moses wrote down this law and gave it to the priests"(31:9 HCSB). Jesus also identifies Deut. 24:1-4 as coming from Moses (Matt. 19:8), Paul identifies the law of the ox in Deut. 25:4 as coming from "the law of Moses" (1 Cor. 9:9), and the author of Hebrews regards the legal requirement of two or three witness in Deut. 17:2-6 as coming from "Moses' law" (Heb. 10:28). Nevertheless, scholars have hotly debated the extent of Moses' connection to the book of Deuteronomy. Did he write all, or part, or none of the book? Few would claim that the book came exactly as it is from the hand of Moses. The account of his death in chapter 34 suggests that some changes may have been made after his time. Evidence used to discount Mosaic authorship of much of the book, however, is inconclusive. Third person references to Moses, for example, would argue against the Mosaic authorship of most of the Pentateuch, which the Bible repeatedly refers to as "the book of Moses" (e.g., 2 Chron. 25:4, which quotes Deut. 24:16). Such references are apparently a matter of style. Reference to Moab as "across the Jordan" (Deut. 1:1) does not necessarily indicate the location of the writer west of the Jordan since the "Transjordan" tribes used the same expression in Gilead when describing their own inheritance in Num. 32:19.

The structural similarities between Deuteronomy and Near Eastern treaty texts from the second millennium B.C. have furnished strong evidence for the unity and antiquity of the book. Comparison to Hittite treaties suggests a date no later than about 1300 B.C. Scholars seeking to maintain an eighth or seventh century B.C. (or later) date for Deuteronomy have pointed to similarities to Neo-Assyrian treaties from the seventh century B.C. This later treaty form, however, is missing important elements found in Deuteronomy and the Hittite texts, such as the historical prologue (Deut. 1:6–4:43) and the list of blessings (Deut. 28:1-14). The conclusion is that Moses' authorship of Deuteronomy essentially as we have it is the most reasonable view for the person who accepts the testimony of Scripture.

The "book of the law" found during the repair of the temple in the 18th year of Josiah's reign (621 B.C.) has been identified as Deuteronomy since the early church fathers shortly after A.D. 300. That identity cannot be proved, but the nature of the reforms of Josiah and the contents of Deuteronomy show an interesting similarity. For example, the call for centralization of worship (Deut. 12) is matched by Josiah's destruction of all altars except the one in the temple in Jerusalem (2 Kings 23:4-20).

Purpose The theme of the land as a promised gift from God is the major theme of the book. References to the land as a gift occur at least 66 times. Israel is told 69 times they will "possess" and "inherit" the land. Moses' messages in Deuteronomy are necessary to prepare Israel to take possession of the land in view of the death of the first generation and Moses' impending death. It was time for Moses to turn around and remind Israel of who they were and what God expected them to do. They needed to bear in mind that the land was an undeserved gift and that they could not acquire it on their own. The land God promised was not just a location but represented the Lord's abundant provisions, His protection, and most important, His presence. Moses also warned Israel of threats to His gift: fear of the Canaanites, the corrupting influence of the Canaanites, and their own sinful tendency

Jewish man in prayer at the Wailing Wall wearing his phylactery containing Scripture from Deuteronomy.

to forget the Lord. Most of all, Moses tried to impress Israel with the importance of complete and loving loyalty to the Lord, expressed in reverential obedience and in joyful, thankful worship.

Teaching The truths in Deuteronomy have a perennial relevance. Jesus knew Deuteronomy well. When Satan tempted Him at the beginning of His ministry, He responded to each of the three temptations with a quotation from Deuteronomy. This book is either quoted or alluded to nearly 200 times in the NT.

Deuteronomy calls for a complete and undivided devotion to God. It sets forth the consequences of obedience and recognizes the inclination of God's people to forget who He is and what He has done for them. For that reason, Moses urges the people to continually be on guard against forgetting God and not to allow their children to be ignorant of Him and His expectations.

Billy K. Smith and E. Ray Clendenen

Outline

I. Moses' First Address (1:1–4:43)
   A. Narrative Preamble (1:1-5)
   B. The Address: The Historical Prologue (1:6–4:40)
      1. Moses' Survey of Israel's Recent History (1:6–3:29)
      2. Call for Response to the Torah of the Lord (4:1-40)
         a. The Grace of Torah (4:1-8)
         b. The Grace of Covenant (4:9-31)
         c. The Grace of Salvation (4:32-40)
   C. The Narrative Postscript (4:41-43)
II. Moses' Second Address (4:44–29:1)
   A. Narrative Preamble (4:44-49)
   B. The Stipulations of the Covenant (5:1–26:19)
      1. The General Stipulations of the Covenant (5:1–11:32)
         a. The Origins of God's Covenant with Israel (5:1-33)
         b. The Challenge of Covenant Relationship with the Lord (6:1–8:20)
         c. The Grace of Covenant Relationship with the Lord (9:1–11:25)
         d. The Call for Decision (11:26-32)

2. The Specific Stipulations of the Covenant (12:1–26:15)
   a. The Religious Life of the Holy People (12:1–16:17)
   b. The Government of the Holy People (16:18–21:9)
      (1) The Structures of Government (16:18–18:22)
      (2) The Conduct of Government (19:1–21:9)
   c. Family Matters (21:10–22:30)
   d. The Sanctity of the Holy Assembly (23:1-8)
   e. Miscellaneous Regulations of Israelite Life (23:9–25:15)
   f. Two Special Offerings (26:1-15)
3. The Concluding Covenantal Oath (26:16-19)
C. Interlude: The Provision for Future Covenant Renewal (27:1-26)
D. The Covenant Blessings and Curses (28:1–29:1)

A Jewish rabbi opening a Torah (Genesis through Deuteronomy) case for a ceremony at the Western, or Wailing, Wall in Jerusalem. Jewish people consider the wall sacred but were forbidden to worship at it during Turkish, British, and Jordanian rule.

1. A Summary Preamble (28:1)
2. The Covenant Blessings (28:2-14)
3. The Covenant Curses (28:15-68)
4. The Narrative Postscript (29:1)

III. Moses' Third Address: A Paradigm For Covenant Renewal (29:2–30:20)
A. Recapitulation of the Basic Principles of the Covenant (29:1–30:10)
1. A Summary Historical Prologue to Covenant Relationship (29:2-9)
2. The Privilege of Covenant Relationship (29:10-13)
3. The Responsibilities of Covenant Relationship (29:14–30:10)
a. The Scope of the Covenant (29:14-17)
b. The Way of Judgment (29:18-29)
c. The Sufficiency of the Torah for Israel (29:29)
d. The Way of Hope (30:1-10)
B. The Final Appeal (30:11-20)
1. The Accessibility of the Covenant (30:11-14)
2. The Promise of the Covenant (30:15-20)

IV. Moses' Arrangements for the Future (31:1–32:47)
A. The Designation of a Successor (31:1-8)
B. The Provision of a Written Torah (31:9-13)
C. The Provision of an Anthem (31:14–32:47)
1. The Context (31:14-29)
2. The Song (31:30–32:47)

V. The Death of Moses (32:48–34:12)
A. The Lord's Summons to Moses (32:48-52)
B. Moses' Blessing of the Tribes (33:1-29)
C. The Departure of Moses (34:1-12)

Daniel I. Block

DEVIL, SATAN, EVIL, DEMONIC Evil appears early in Genesis with the serpent figure (Gen. 3:1-5). While Genesis does not identify this figure as "Satan," Revelation alludes to him as such (Rev. 12:9). The Scriptures portray Satan as a personal being in direct opposition to God and His purposes. Satan is not equal to God, nor does he threaten God's power (Isa. 45:5-7).

Old Testament The word *satan* is used as a verb or noun in the OT and translated as "adversary." When used as a verb, it means to act as an adversary, accuser, or in a hostile manner (Gen. 27:41; 49:23; 50:15; Zech. 3:1). A person may act in such a manner toward others or God (1 Sam. 29:4; 1 Kings 5:4; 11:14,23,25; Pss. 71:13; 109:4,6,20).

Satan is chief of the fallen angels. From mankind's creation Satan and the fallen angels were active rebels against God. It appears that pride was the source of Satan's downfall (1 Tim. 3:6). The most extensive discussion of Satan is found in Job. In Job 1–2 Satan appears as an agent of God, whose purpose appears to be testing human beings (Job 1:8). When he appears before God, he comes with the "sons of God," members of the heavenly council (Job 1:6). Satan asks God, "Does Job fear God for nothing?" (Job 1:9). Thus he impugns the faith of the righteous Job. In order to disprove Satan's claim God grants him certain powers. He attacks Job but only with God's permission. In Zech. 3:1 Satan stands at the high priest's right hand in order to accuse him. In 1 Chron. 21:1 Satan tempts King David to take a census of Israel.

Apocrypha and Pseudepigrapha In the Intertestamental period the idea of Satan receives more detailed definition. In deutero-canonical books (Jubilees, The Assumption of Moses, and Tobit), Satan is portrayed as a much more malevolent force. These works identify Satan as the chief of the evil spirits. Many of these texts attribute some of God's questionable behavior (sacrifice of Isaac, the attacking of Moses on his way to Egypt) to Satan. During this period many of the demons were given names and personalities.

New Testament By the time of the NT, the doctrine of Satan was well developed. The origin of evil was placed in Satan, recognizing the reality of evil beyond the scope of human will. The NT mentions Satan over 35 times. The NT has many different names for Satan. The Gospels refer to Satan as "tempter" (Matt. 4:3), "ruler of demons" (Matt. 9:34; 12:24; Mark 3:22; Luke 11:15), "evil one" (Matt. 13:38), "enemy" (Matt. 13:39), "the father of lies" (John 8:44), "a murderer" (John 8:44), and "ruler of this world" (John 12:31; 14:30; 16:11). Paul referred to him as "the god of this world" (2 Cor. 4:4), "the prince of the powers of the air" (Eph. 2:2), "the ruler of the darkness of this age" (Eph. 6:12);

D

and "tempter" (1 Thess. 3:5). Paul warned the Corinthians that Satan may appear as an "angel of light" (2 Cor. 11:14). In the General Epistles he is referred to as "an adversary" (1 Pet. 5:8) and "the evil one" (1 John 5:19). Revelation refers to him as "one who deceives" (Rev. 12:9), "an accuser" (Rev. 12:10), "a serpent" (Rev. 12:9), and "a dragon" (Rev. 12:3-17; 13:2,11).

In the Synoptic Gospels Satan is responsible for the temptation of Christ in the wilderness (Matt. 4:1). He is the leader of demonic forces which are able to inflict disease (Matt. 17:14-18; Luke 13:16) and possess people (Luke 22:3). Paul portrayed Satan as the god of this age (2 Cor. 4:4). He is the chief power of the demonic forces often referred to as "powers of the air" (Eph. 2:2; 6:12). In the General Epistles Satan is graphically portrayed as a roaring lion that seeks to devour (1 Pet. 5:8). Second Peter 2:4 and Jude 6 refer to angels which did not keep their place and thus sinned.

Although the NT teaches that this world is under the power of Satan, it must be remembered that neither he nor the demons are coequal with God. Satan and the demonic beings are creatures who are subject to God's sovereign will. The evil host may tempt but not coerce a person to sin. The NT is clear that Satan and his demonic following have already been judged and decisively defeated by the death and resurrection of Jesus Christ (Col. 1:13; 2:15). Believers have the armor of Christ as spiritual security (Eph. 6:11-19).   *Joe Cathey*

DEVOTED, DEVOTED TO DESTRUCTION
See *Anathema*.

DEVOUT Careful in fulfilling religious duties; pious; used only in Luke and Acts. Simeon is described as a righteous and devout person who welcomed the coming of the Messiah and on whom the Holy Spirit rested (Luke 2:25). Cornelius is described as a devout person who reverenced God, gave alms, and prayed continuously (Acts. 10:2). Ananias is described as a devout person according to the standard of the Jewish law. He had a "good reputation with all the Jews" (Acts 22:12 HCSB).

DEW Moisture that forms into drops of water on the earth during a cool night. Moist air drawing from the sea is largely responsible for the dew in western Palestine. Downward dew occurs in the summer when the soil is loose, thus providing good cooling conditions. Upward dew results from the condensation of water vapor from damp soil and is, therefore, more frequent in the winter season.

Dew is used in the Bible as a symbol of refreshment (Deut. 32:2; Ps. 133:3); a symbol of the loving power of God that revives and invigorates (Prov. 19:12); a symbol of the sudden onset of an enemy (2 Sam. 17:12); a symbol of brotherly love and harmony (Ps. 133:3); a symbol of God's revelation (Judg. 6:36-40); and a symbol of God's blessing (Gen. 27:28).

Gary Bonner

DIADEM English translation of three Hebrew terms designating a head covering symbolizing authority and honor. *Mitsnephet* is the turban of the high priest (Exod. 28:4,39) or king (Ezek. 21:26). The priest's was made of fine linen (Exod. 28:39) with a golden plate (KJV, NASB, NIV) or a flower rosette of pure gold (NRSV) on its front. The plate or rosette is apparently called a *nezer* (literally, "sign of dedication") in Exod. 29:6 ("crown" NASB, KJV; "diadem" NIV, NRSV; cp. Exod. 39:30).

The turban was worn by both religious and royal persons. Aaron the High Priest wore one (Exod. 28:37; 29:6; Lev. 16:4; Zech. 3:5) as did Queens Vashti (Esther 1:11) and Esther (Esther 2:17).

Tsaniph or *tseniphah* is the turban worn by a man (Job 29:14) or woman (Isa. 3:23) or by the king (Isa. 62:3) or high priest (Zech. 3:5). *Tsephirah* is a braided crown, garland, or wreath signifying God's glorious power and authority to come (Isa. 28:5).

The word "diadem" was used in a metaphorical sense of the prudent person (Prov. 14:18), of justice (Job 29:14), of God (Isa. 28:5), of God's presence (Ezek. 21:26), and of Jerusalem (Isa. 62:3).

Just before the NT era, "diadem" was applied by Greeks to the symbol of royalty worn by the Persians. Since all levels of people wore the turban, the king's diadem was distinguished by its color and perhaps by jewels worn on it. To the Greeks and Romans the diadem was the distinctive badge of royalty and was usually white. Later a wreath was used as a crown for Greek kings.

The diadem should be distinguished from the wreath given for victory in athletic games

(1 Cor. 9:25), for civil accomplishments, for military bravery, and for weddings.

In Rev. 12:3; 13:1; 19:12 the diadem conveys the idea of power and authority.

Glenn McCoy

DIAL See *Sundial.*

DIAMOND Precious stone used in jewelry and engraving. It is the hardest mineral known, formed of pure carbon crystals. Two Hebrew words stand behind English "diamond." *Yahelom* is a stone on the high priest's breastplate (Exod. 28:18; NIV, "emerald"; NRSV, "moonstone") and among the jewels of the king of Tyre (Ezek. 28:13). *Shamir* is the stone used on the point of an engraving tool to cut into stone surfaces (Jer. 17:1; NIV, "flint"; others suggest "emery"). The term also appears in Ezek. 3:9 and Zech. 7:12 as the hardest stone known.

Apparently Alexander the Great around 330 B.C. first discovered diamonds for the western world in India. This would indicate "diamonds" are not meant in the OT references. Emery stones or adamant stones were widely used for engraving. Emery was a variety of corundum and was composed of aluminum oxide. See *Jewels, Jewelry; Minerals and Metals.*

DIANA (Dī ăn´ à) Roman goddess with similar characteristics to the Greek Artemis. KJV reads "Diana" in Acts, where Greek and most modern translations read "Artemis." See *Artemis.*

DIASPORA Scattering of the Jews from the land of Palestine into other parts of the world. The term "dispersion" is also often used to describe this process.

The Diaspora took place over several centuries. While its exact beginnings are difficult to date, two major events greatly contributed to it. In 722 B.C. the Assyrians captured the Northern Kingdom (Israel). Following this victory, the Assyrians resettled large numbers of the Israelites in Assyria (2 Kings 17:6). In 586 B.C. the Babylonians captured the Southern Kingdom (Judah) and followed the same policy of resettlement. Many of the residents of Judah were transported to Babylon (2 Kings 25:8-12). While some of these persons later returned to Judah, many of them remained permanently in Babylon. Later other wars fought by the Greeks and Romans in Palestine helped scatter more of the Jewish people.

The result of the Diaspora was that by NT times as many Jews lived outside of Palestine as lived within the land. In almost every city Paul visited on his missionary journeys, he found a Jewish synagogue (Acts 14:1; 17:1,10; 18:4). The Diaspora thus helped pave the way for the spread of the gospel. See *Assyria; Babylon; Exile; Synagogue.* *Lynn Jones*

DIBLAH (Dĭb´ lăh) or **DIBLATH** (Dĭb´ lăth) Place-name with variant manuscript spellings and English transliterations in Ezek. 6:14. The Hebrew term may mean "cake of figs." Ezekiel used the term to describe the northern border of Israel as joined with the southern wilderness to describe all the territory of Israel which faced judgment—"from the desert to Diblah" (NIV). With slight manuscript support from the Latin Vulgate, many Bible students read "Riblah" supposing that in the earliest history of the text tradition a copyist made the simple mistake of changing a Hebrew "r" to a Hebrew "d," the two letters being easily confused. See *Riblah.*

DIBLAIM (Dĭb lā´ ĭm) Personal or place-name meaning "two fig cakes." Hosea 1:3 lists Diblaim as a parent of Gomer, Hosea's harlot wife. Some Bible students see Hosea's father-in-law so named; others, his mother-in-law. The latter case is combined with an understanding that she was also a harlot whose price was two fig cakes. Others would equate Diblaim with the place-name Beth-diblathaim. The most direct explanation seems to be that Diblaim is Gomer's father, of whom nothing more is known. See *Beth-diblathaim.*

DIBON (Dī´ bŏn) or **DIBON-GAD** (Dī´ bŏn-găd) Place-name possibly meaning "pining away" or "fence of tubes." **1.** Capital city of Moab captured by Moses (Num. 21:21-31). Gad and Reuben asked for it as their tribal territory (Num. 32:3). Gad took control and fortified Dibon (Num. 32:34). It thus became known as Dibon-gad and was one of Israel's camping spots east of the Jordan (Num. 33:45-46). Joshua reported that Moses gave Dibon to the tribe of Reuben (Josh. 13:9,17). In pronouncing judgment on Moab, Isaiah described the religious mourning at the worship place in Dibon (Isa. 15:2), showing that Moab had gained control of Dibon by about 730 B.C. The Moabite stone of King Mesha, discovered in Dibon, shows that

Moab controlled Dibon about 850 B.C. About 700 B.C. Jeremiah again announced destruction for Moab and Dibon (Jer. 48:18-22). Dibon stood on the northern hill across the valley from modern Dhiban. It is about 40 miles south of Amman, Jordan, and three miles north of the Arnon River. Occupation of the site apparently goes back to about 2500 B.C., but the main occupation period began after 1200 B.C., climaxing about 850 with Mesha. Nebuchadnezzar destroyed the city in 582 B.C. Nabateans built a temple there during Jesus' childhood. It was apparently abandoned about A.D. 100. **2.** In Nehemiah's day (about 445 B.C.) Jews lived in a Dibon in Judah. This may be the same as Dimonah. See *Dimonah.*

DIBRI (Dĭb´ rī) Personal name meaning "talkative" or "gossip." Father of an Israelite woman who had a son with an Egyptian father. The son cursed God's name and was stoned to death (Lev. 24:10-23).

DIDACHE See *Apostolic Fathers.*

DIDRACHMA Greek coin worth two drachmas or a Jewish half shekel, the amount of the temple tax paid by every male Jew above age 19 (Matt. 17:24). After the temple's destruction in A.D. 70, the Roman government apparently continued to collect the temple tax, possibly to support a Roman temple. The first readers of Matthew's Gospel would have understood the temple tax in the Roman context.

DIDYMUS (Dĭd´ ĭ mŭs) Personal name meaning "twin." An alternative name for the Apostle Thomas (John 11:16). It appears only in John's Gospel. See *Thomas.*

DIETING For most people of the ancient world, and certainly for the common man, starvation was a constant and very real threat. For this reason, when the biblical writers wanted to describe someone who was blessed, they often said that such persons would eat rich, fat, and sweet foods, or eat in abundance (e.g., 2 Sam. 6:19; Neh. 8:10; 9:25; Prov. 24:13; Song 5:1; Isa. 7:22; 25:6; Ezek. 16:13; Joel 2:26). Weight loss was something to be avoided.

God created within humanity a wide variety of body shapes and sizes. God also created a wide variety of foods for the nourishment and pleasure of people (Gen. 1:29; 9:3). Yet biblical

teaching implies that not all foods are equally beneficial for human consumption and that for some people the desire for certain foods can lead to enslavement (1 Cor. 6:12).

The book of Proverbs cautions that excessive eating and drinking is the mark of a fool (Prov. 23:20-21; cp. Eccles. 5:18; 9:7; 1 Cor. 15:32) and urges bodily restraint (Prov. 23:2; 25:16). The writer of Ecclesiastes noted that one who is blessed "eats at a proper time—for strength and not for drunkenness" (Eccles. 10:17). Daniel and his friends refused the rich foods of Babylon in favor of vegetables and water (Dan. 1:5-16) and were healthier as a result.

New Testament teaching holds that a person's body is the temple of the Holy Spirit (1 Cor. 6:19) and that it must therefore be subdued (1 Cor. 9:27) and cared for in a way that honors God (1 Cor. 6:20). For this reason, excessive eating is contrary to Christian discipline (Phil. 3:19).   *Paul H. Wright*

DIGNITIES KJV translation of Greek *doxas* (literally, "glorious ones") in 2 Pet. 2:10. The people whom Peter condemned in his second letter willingly blasphemed the "dignities," who are either good angels or evil angels (cp. Jude 8).

DIKLAH (Dĭk´ läh) Personal name apparently meaning "date palm." Grandson of Eber (Gen. 10:27). He was apparently the original ancestor of a tribe in Arabia that settled in an oasis where dates were grown, but nothing more is known of him.

DILEAN (Dī´ lə ăn) Place-name meaning "protrusion" or "ledge." Village in tribal territory of Judah (Josh. 15:38). Tell en-Najileh southwest of Tell el-Hesi has been suggested as a possible modern site.

DILL Spice cultivated in Israel (Isa. 28:25-27). KJV translates "fitches"; NIV, "caraway." It was probably black cumin, *Nigella satina.* Jesus accused the scribes and Pharisees of tithing their dill but neglecting justice, mercy, and faith (Matt. 23:23). See *Plants.*

DIMNAH (Dĭm´ năh) Place-name meaning "manure." Town in tribal territory of Zebulun given to Levites (Josh. 21:35). First Chronicles 6:77 appears to refer to the same city as Rimmon (cp. Josh. 19:13). A scribe copying the text could easily confuse the two names. See *Rimmon.*

DIMON (Dī´ môn) Place-name, perhaps meaning "blood." City in Moab on which Isaiah announced judgment (Isa. 15:9). Dead Sea Scrolls text and Latin Vulgate read "Dibon" here. This may be the original reading, but that would go against the normal type of copying mistakes scribes make in that it would substitute an unknown place for a famous place. It may be that transcription of a Moabite name into the Hebrew language or the development of the language resulted in a change of pronunciation so that the two names represent one place. If Dimon is a separate town, it was probably located at modern Khirbet Dimme, about seven miles north of Kerak. Jeremiah 48:2 calls a Moabite town "Madmen." The Hebrew word, *madmen*, may involve a play on words referring to Dimon. See *Dibon*.

DIMONAH (Dī mō´ năh) Place-name related to Hebrew word for blood. A town on southeast border of tribal allotment of Judah (Josh. 15:22). Some have suggested its location at Tell ed-Dheib near Aroer. It may be the same as Dibon mentioned in Neh. 11:25.

DINAH (Dī´ năh) Personal name meaning "justice" or "artistically formed." The daughter of Jacob and Leah (Gen. 30:21). According to Gen. 34 she was sexually assaulted by a man named Shechem, who wished to marry her. Simeon and Levi, her brothers, took revenge by killing the male residents of the city of Shechem. See *Jacob; Leah; Patriarchs; Shechem.*

DINAITE (Dī´ nȧ īt) KJV transliteration of Aramaic word in Ezra 4:9. Modern translations translate the word as "judges."

DINHABAH (Dĭn´ hȧ băh) City name of unknown meaning. Residence of one of earliest kings of Edom in period prior to Saul in Israel (Gen. 36:32). Nothing else is known of the city.

DINOSAURS Some interpreters hold that many of the biblical references to Leviathan (Job 41:1-34; Pss. 74:14; 104:26; Isa. 27:1), dragons (Ps. 74:13; Isa. 27:1; 51:9), and the behemoth (Job 40:15-24) preserve early memories of dinosaurs. Most, however, prefer to explain these great monsters in terms of large and terrifying animals known to man today.

The word "Leviathan" (perhaps derived from a verb meaning "to twist") is the proper

name of a large sea creature that defies easy zoological classification. Suggestions as to the identity of Leviathan include the crocodile, the dolphin, the whale, or the sea serpent.

The Hebrew word for dragon (*tannin*), which often refers to serpents (e.g., Exod. 7:9; Deut. 32:33; Ps. 91:13), is used generically in Gen. 1:21 for large sea creatures. Other passages mentioning *tannin* indicate a specific kind of large sea creature (Job 7:12; Ps. 74:13; Isa. 27:1; 51:9) which cannot be identified with certainty.

Behemoth (the plural form of the common Hebrew noun for cattle) occurs as a great monster only in Job 40:15-24. The description in Job suggests a hippopotamus or elephant.

God created all life for His enjoyment and glory, including dinosaurs (cp. Ps. 148:7). However, difficulties in interpretation preclude us from knowing to what extent the biblical writers knew about dinosaurs.   *Paul H. Wright*

DIONYSIUS (Dī ō nўs´ ĭ ŭs) Athenian aristocrat who was converted to Christianity through the preaching of Paul the apostle (Acts 17:34). He was a member of the Areopagus, an elite and influential group of officials. See *Areopagus.*

DIOTREPHES (Dī ŏt´ rə phēs) Personal name meaning "nurtured by Jove." An individual whose self-serving ambition is cited unfavorably (3 John 9). John declared that Diotrephes rejected his authority. See *John, Letters from.*

DIPHATH (Dī´ phăth) NRSV, NASB reading of great grandson of Noah in 1 Chron. 1:6. KJV, NIV follow other Hebrew manuscripts and versions and Gen. 10:3 in reading Riphath. See *Riphath.*

DIRECTIONS In the Western world we take as our cardinal points for directions, the compass points, north, south, east, and west. We also take north as our primary reference point. At least since Roman times, this has been the pattern. But in the ancient Near Eastern world of Semitic speaking peoples, the primary reference was east, the direction of the rising sun. We know this from the vocabulary used for directions. Often the phrase "rising of the sun" or simply "rising" is used to express the direction east (Deut. 4:41,47; 4:49). The Hebrew word *qedem* and its related forms means both "in front of" and "east of." The clearest example demonstrating that *qedem* means "east of" is Josh. 19:12, where the border of Zebulun is being described. One portion of this border is said to go from Sarid eastward (*qedmah*) toward the rising of the sun. Thus the direction "in front of" one was east. Ai is said to lie *miqedem*, "east of," Bethel (Josh. 7:2). Other words describing what was before or in front of one could also mean "east of." The Cave of Machpelah where Abraham buried Sarah is located *al pene*, "east of," Mamre (Gen. 23:19; 25:9,18). Another reference locates the cave *liphne*, "east of" Mamre (Gen. 23:17). Both these word phrases use the literal words "to the face of" or "in front of" to indicate the direction east. Also, the biblical reference to the Tigris River as being "in front of" Assyria, means that the Tigris is east of Assyria (Gen. 2:14).

The OT expresses "west" in terms of the setting sun. The phrase "from the rising of the sun to its setting" expresses the concept "from east to west" (Isa. 45:6; Mal. 1:11; Pss. 50:1; 113:3). West was also often indicated by reference to the major geographical feature west of Israel-Canaan, the Mediterranean Sea. In Hebrew it was most often called simply "the sea" or "the great sea." Joshua 1:4 describes "the Great Sea toward the setting of the sun" as the western border of Israel. Other times the direction west could be indicated by "sea" or "seaward" (Gen. 12:8; 13:14; Josh. 11:2,3).

The Hebrews used both specific words for the cardinal directions and terms related to the body for those directions. Just as *qedem*, "in front of," could indicate "east, the Hebrew word *achor* and related forms can mean both "behind" and "west." Thus the Mediterranean Sea is described in Hebrew as the "Behind Sea" or "Western Sea" (Deut. 11:24; 34:2; Josh. 2:20).

The specific Hebrew word for north was *tsaphon*. The northern boundary of Israel is described as running from the Mediterranean Sea to Mount Hor to Lebo-hamath to Zedad to Ziphron and to Hazar-enan (Num. 34:7-9). "North" was also that which was on the left hand using body position for directions. Samaria and her daughter towns are located north (literally, "left") of Judah and Jerusalem (Ezek. 16:46). North is often specifically the direction from which God said He would bring judgment on Israel-Judah (Jer. 1:13-15), but it is also the

direction from which the restoration would come (Jer. 31:8).

The direction "south" in Hebrew is *negev*. The word *negev* can be used to refer to the arid region in the south of Judah, usually to the south of Hebron and Beersheba (Gen. 20:1). It also is used for the direction "south" in general: the tribe of Manasseh's southern border ended at Wadi Kenah; towns south of that wadi belonged to Ephraim (Josh. 17:9). South was also that which was on the right hand. Thus Manasseh's southern border was also described as that which was on the right (Josh 17:7). The name "Benjamin" literally means "son of the right hand" or "son of the south." Benjamin was the southernmost tribe of the 10 tribes of the Northern Kingdom, Israel.

The OT uses all the cardinal directions in several passages. God tells Abraham to look north and south, east and west (that is, in all directions), and all that land will be his and his descendants (Gen. 13:14). In the NT, ones from all directions, east and west, north and south, will sit at the table in God's kingdom (Luke 13:29).   *Joel F. Drinkard, Jr.*

DIRGE Modern translation term for lamentation. See *Music, Instruments, Dancing; Psalms, Book of.*

DISABILITIES AND DEFORMITIES See *Diseases.*

DISAPPOINTMENT The Bible recognizes the emotional and physical stress which can accompany disappointment and proclaims that hope is always found in God. Examples of disappointment recorded in the Bible include Samuel (1 Sam. 16:1), the men on the road to Emmaus (Luke 24:17-21), and Paul (1 Thess. 2:17-20). Many of the psalmist's cries reflect the depths of his disappointment in life and, at times, in God Himself (e.g., Pss. 39:12-13; 42:5a,9-11a).

Disappointment and discouragement break the spirit (Prov. 15:13), dry up the bones (Prov. 17:22), and can lead to death (Prov. 18:14).

In spite of his circumstances, the psalmist learned to trust in God who, in the end, overcame his disappointment (Pss. 22:5; 40:1; 42:5b). Isaiah saw a day when all who were feeble and fearful would become strengthened (Isa. 35:3-4). In the meantime, Jesus commands that those who are disappointed continue to wait on

God, pray, and not lose heart (Luke 18:1; cp. Matt. 5:4). Every believer is called to recognize that suffering produces endurance, endurance produces character, and character produces a hope in God that does not disappoint (Rom. 5:3-5).   *Paul H. Wright*

DISCERNING OF SPIRITS One of the gifts of the Spirit (1 Cor. 12:10). It apparently refers to the God-given ability to tell whether a prophetic speech came from God's Spirit or from another source opposed to God.

DISCHARGE Modern translation term for bodily excretion that rendered one ceremonially unclean (Lev. 15:2-33; Num. 5:2; KJV, "issue"). The nature of the discharge of males (Lev. 15:2-25) is unclear. Suggestions include hemorrhoids, spermatorrhea, that is, the involuntary release of sperm due to a weakening of the sexual organs, or a discharge related to an inflammation of the urinary tract. In the case of women, the discharge is the monthly period (15:19) or bleeding outside this period (15:25). A discharge rendered unclean the person and anything or anyone coming into contact with the source of uncleanness.

DISCIPLE Follower of Jesus Christ, especially the commissioned Twelve who followed Jesus during His earthly ministry. The term "disciple" comes to us in English from a Latin root. Its basic meaning is "learner" or "pupil." The term is virtually absent from the OT, though there are two related references (1 Chron. 25:8; Isa. 8:16).

In the Greek world the word "disciple" normally referred to an adherent of a particular teacher or religious/philosophical school. It was the task of the disciple to learn, study, and pass along the sayings and teachings of the master. In rabbinic Judaism the term "disciple" referred to one who was committed to the interpretations of Scripture and religious tradition given him by the master or rabbi. Through a process of learning which would include a set meeting time and such pedagogical methods as question and answer, instruction, repetition, and memorization, the disciple would become increasingly devoted to the master and the master's teachings. In time, the disciple would likewise pass on the traditions to others.

Jesus' Disciples In the NT 233 of the 261 instances of the word "disciple" occur in the Gospels, the other 28 being in Acts. Usually the word refers to disciples of Jesus, but there are also references to disciples of the Pharisees (Matt. 22:16; Mark 2:18), disciples of John the Baptist (Mark 2:18; Luke 11:1; John 1:35), and even disciples of Moses (John 9:28).

The Gospels often refer to Jesus as "Rabbi" (Matt. 26:25,49; Mark 9:5; 10:51; 11:21; John 1:38,49; 3:2,26; 6:25; 20:16 NIV). One can assume that Jesus used traditional rabbinic teaching techniques (question and answer, discussion, memorization) to instruct His disciples. In many respects Jesus differed from the rabbis. He called His disciples to "follow Me" (Luke 5:27). Disciples of the rabbis could select their teachers. Jesus oftentimes demanded extreme levels of personal renunciation (loss of family, property, etc.; Matt. 4:18-22; 10:24-42; Luke 5:27-28; 14:25-27; 18:28-30). He asked for lifelong allegiance (Luke 9:57-62) as the essential means of doing the will of God (Matt. 12:49-50; John 7:16-18). He taught more as a bearer of divine revelation than a link in the chain of Jewish tradition (Matt. 5:21-48; 7:28-29; Mark 4:10-11). In so doing Jesus announced the end of the age and the long-awaited reign of God (Matt. 4:17; Luke 4:14-21,42-44).

The Twelve As the messianic proclaimer of the reign of God, Jesus gathered about Himself a special circle of 12 disciples, clearly a symbolic representation of the 12 tribes (Matt. 19:28). He was reestablishing Jewish social identity based upon discipleship to Jesus. The Twelve represented a unique band, making the word "disciple" (as a reference to the Twelve) an exact equivalent to "apostle" in those contexts where the latter word was also restricted to the Twelve. The four lists of the Twelve in the NT (Matt. 10:1-4; Mark 3:16-19; Luke 6:12-16; Acts 1:13,26) also imply from their contexts the synonymous use of the terms "disciples"/"apostles" when used to refer to the Twelve.

A Larger Group of Followers The Gospels clearly show that the word "disciple" can refer to others besides the Twelve. The verb "follow" became something of a technical term Jesus used to call His disciples, who were then called "followers," (Mark 4:10). These "followers" included a larger company of people from whom He selected the Twelve (Mark 3:7-19; Luke 6:13-17). This larger group of disciples/followers included men and women (Luke 8:1-3; 23:49) from all walks of life. (Even the Twelve included a variety: fishermen, a tax collector, a Zealot.) Jesus was no doubt especially popular among the socially outcast and religiously despised, but people of wealth and of theological training also followed (Luke 8:1-3; 19:1-10; John 3:1-3; 12:42; 19:38-39).

The Twelve were sent out as representatives of Jesus, commissioned to preach the coming of the kingdom, to cast out demons, and to heal diseases (Matt. 10:1,5-15; Mark 6:7-13; Luke 9:1-6). Such tasks were not limited to the Twelve (Luke 10:1-24). Apparently Jesus' disciples first included "a great multitude of disciples" (Luke 6:17). He formed certain smaller and more specifically defined groups within that "great multitude." These smaller groups would include a group of "70" (Luke 10:1,17), the "Twelve" (Matt. 11:1; Mark 6:7; Luke 9:1), and perhaps an even smaller, inner group within the Twelve, consisting especially of Peter, James, and John—whose names (with Andrew) always figure first in the lists of the Twelve (Matt. 10:2; Mark 3:16-17; Luke 6:14; Acts 1:13), whose stories of calling are especially highlighted (Matt. 4:18-22; John 1:35-42 and the tradition that John is the "Other"/"Beloved Disciple" of the Gospel of John—13:23; 19:26; 20:2; 21:20), and who alone accompanied Jesus on certain significant occasions of healing and revelation (Matt. 17:1; Mark 13:3; Luke 8:51).

All Followers of Jesus The book of the Acts of the Apostles frequently uses the term "disciple" to refer generally to all those who believe in the risen Lord (6:1-2,7; 9:1,10,19,26,38; 11:26,29). In addition, the verb form "to disciple" as it appears in the final commissioning scene of Matthew's Gospel (28:19-20) also suggests a use in the early church of the term "disciple" as a more generalized name for all those who come to Jesus in faith, having heard and believed the gospel.

Conclusion We have seen that, as references to the Twelve, the words "apostle" and "disciple" could be synonymous. However, just as the term "disciple" could mean other followers of Jesus than the Twelve in the time of His ministry, so also after His resurrection the term "disciple" had a wider meaning as well, being clearly applied to all His followers. Whereas the term "apostle" retained a more specific meaning, being tied to certain historical eyewitnesses of the resurrected Lord, the word "disciple" tended to lose its narrower associations with the

Twelve, and/or those who followed the historical Jesus, or who saw the risen Lord, and became a virtual equivalent to "Christian" (Acts 11:26). In every case, however, the common bond of meaning for the various applications of the word "disciple" was allegiance to Jesus. See *Apostle.*   *Robert B. Sloan, Jr.*

DISCIPLINARIAN See *Schoolmaster.*

DISCIPLINE Usually refers in the Bible to moral training, which includes the positive aspect of instruction and the negative aspect of correction, sometimes punitive. The result of receiving discipline with humility is wisdom and a satisfying, successful life (Prov. 4:13; 5:23; 10:17; 13:18). These various aspects of discipline are intertwined in the spiritual life of the believer and of the church.

In the OT the word usually renders a form of the Hebrew *yasar,* "to instruct, rebuke, warn." "Discipline" in the NT usually renders a form of *paideuo,* "to instruct, correct."

Discipline in Proverbs The book of Proverbs speaks of moral training more than any other biblical book. Its very purpose is to develop wisdom through "instruction in righteousness, justice, and integrity" (1:3 HCSB). Only an ungodly fool would refuse such training (1:7), which includes instruction in God's Torah or Law (1:8; 6:23; Deut. 6:6-7; Ps. 94:12; Eph. 6:4). A son must diligently pay attention to his father's and mother's discipline (4:1; 6:20; 13:1; 15:5), and a faithful and loving parent must be willing to punish wrongdoing as part of a child's training (13:24; 15:10; 19:18; 22:15; 29:15).

One effect of such training should be the development of self-discipline or self-control, an essential characteristic of one who is wise (1 Cor. 9:27; 1 Pet. 4:7). The Bible teaches that one needs moral training and the discipline of self to defeat the natural tendencies to wantonness and sinful selfishness that result from moral depravity resulting from the fall (Gen. 4:7).

Divine Discipline Divine discipline is distinct from God's judgment or punishment. While God's judgment and punishment is meted out on the unrighteous, God's discipline is reserved only for His children. The writer to the Hebrews exhorted his readers to be encouraged by God's discipline in their lives because it serves as the ultimate proof that God is indeed their father (Heb. 12:5-11). Representing God's gracious intention toward His children, he explained that He [God] does it for our benefit, so that we can share His holiness (v. 10) and that it yields the fruit of peace and righteousness to those who have been trained by it (v. 11).

Church Discipline Perhaps the discipline most neglected by Christians of the 21st century is church discipline. If church members are commanded to be concerned about one another in order to promote love and good works (Heb. 10:24), then we are also commanded to confront one another lovingly whenever a member falls into sin. During His earthly ministry Jesus commanded the church to practice discipline and outlined the procedure by which it should be executed (Matt. 18:15-20). If one member sins against another, the aggrieved party should privately confront the member who is in sin in hopes of restoring the relationship. If the member who is in sin refuses to repent and be restored after the initial private meeting, then the offended party should take one or two others along for a second confrontation. If he or she still will not repent, then the church must be told and action taken against the unrepentant member.

While Matthew's Gospel does not spell out precisely which sins are serious enough for church discipline, Paul's epistles do. In three separate passages, the apostle explains that a member needs to be disciplined for gross immorality that is publicly known (1 Cor. 5:1-13), doctrinal heresy (Rom. 16:17-18), and intentionally creating division in the church (Titus 3:10-11). Though the purpose of church discipline is always restoration (Gal. 6:1), when the persons in question will not admit that they have been in sin, they should be put out of the fellowship of the church and denied any privileges of church membership, including but not limited to partaking of the Lord's Supper (1 Cor. 5:11). This action removes the spiritual protection of the church from them and allows satanic attack to reveal their true spiritual status "for the destruction of the flesh, so that his spirit may be saved in the Day of the Lord" (1 Cor. 5:5 HCSB). Paul holds out the hope that the satanic assault may drive them back to the church in repentance.

Related to church discipline is the discipline of church leaders, a special circumstance about which Paul teaches in 1 Tim. 5:19-20: "Don't accept an accusation against an elder unless it is supported by two or three witnesses. Publicly

rebuke those who sin, so that the rest will also be afraid" (HCSB).

Hershael W. York and E. Ray Clendenen

DISEASES Physical and/or mental malfunctions that limit human functions and lessen the quality of life. Successful treatment of disease depends primarily on prompt, correct diagnosis, and the use of effective therapeutic agents. Unfortunately, people living in biblical times had limited means to diagnose and treat illness. The best-educated people in biblical times had a meager understanding of human anatomy and physiology and even less knowledge about the nature of disease and its effect on the body. No one knew about bacteria and viruses. This fact hampered diagnosis. Illness was often attributed to sin or to a curse by an enemy. The main diagnostic tools were observation and superficial physical examination. The physician had few aids to use in his work.

Providers of Medical Care Ancient Near Eastern literature contains numerous references to physicians and medical practice. A Sumerian physician, Lulu, lived in Mesopotamia about 2700 B.C. A few decades later, a famous Egyptian named Imhotep established a reputation as a physician and priest. He also became noted as a great architect. He designed the Step Pyramid at Saqqara.

The Code of Hammurabi, from about 1750 B.C., contains several laws regulating the practice of medicine and surgery by physicians in the Old Babylonian Kingdom. Although the profession of medicine was in its infancy, the many practitioners slowly improved their skills.

The Egyptians made more rapid progress in medical knowledge and its application to patients than did the Babylonians. Their physicians tended to specialize. Each would limit his practice to one part of the body, such as the eye, the teeth, or the stomach. Egyptian doctors, like others, often used herbs in their medications. These were collected from many areas of the world and were often grown in gardens connected with the temples of Egypt. Egyptian physicians became respected throughout the ancient world. Their skill was even admired in a later period by the Greeks, who eventually became the foremost physicians.

The OT has only a few references to physicians. These persons most likely had been trained in Egypt. Physicians were called upon to embalm the body of Jacob (Gen. 50:2). King Asa sought medical care from physicians for his diseased feet (2 Chron. 16:12). Some nonmedical references are made to physicians (Jer. 8:22; Job 13:4). It is unlikely that many trained physicians lived among the ancient Hebrews.

The great Greek physician, Hippocrates, born about 460 B.C., is often referred to as the Father of Medicine. Hippocrates believed that disease had natural causes. He relied mainly on diet and various herbs to treat his patients. Around 300 B.C. the Greeks established an important medical school in Alexandria, Egypt, which flourished for several centuries and trained many physicians. The school was noted for its large library and laboratory facilities. Dissection of the human body was permitted, and some limited advances were made in the knowledge of anatomy.

By the time of Jesus, the city of Rome had become an important medical center. Many physicians practiced there. Originally they were in the slave class, but their profession gradually became esteemed. Julius Caesar granted Roman citizenship to Greek physicians practicing in Rome. The Romans made significant contributions in the area of public health, including the provision of a relatively pure water supply, an effective sewage disposal system, and the establishment of a food inspection program. The Romans also established a network of hospitals, initially founded to care for the needs of the army.

Outlying regions of the empire, such as Palestine, apparently had few well-trained doctors, although little information is available concerning professional medical care outside the large cities. The majority of people probably were born and died without ever being treated by a trained physician.

The NT mentions physicians only a few times. Jesus noted the purpose of a physician is to treat the ill (Matt. 9:12; Mark 2:17; Luke 5:31), and He referred to a common proverb, "Doctor, heal yourself" (Luke 4:23 HCSB). Mark and Luke related the story of a woman who had sought the help of physicians but had not been healed (Mark 5:25-34; Luke 8:43-48). Paul, in Col. 4:14, remarks that his colleague, Luke, was a physician. Luke was a Gentile, but his hometown is unknown. The source of his medical training is also unknown, but it is possible that he went to medical school in Tarsus, Paul's hometown.

In many lands priests were assigned medical duties. This was true among the ancient Hebrews, where priests were major providers of medical services. They were especially responsible for the diagnosis of diseases that might pose a threat to the community (Lev. 13). Priests in Israel apparently played little role in the actual treatment of ill persons.

During the time of the NT, the Roman god of healing, Aesculapius (known by the Greeks at an earlier time by the name of Asklepios), was popular. Many of his temples, staffed by his priests, were scattered throughout the Mediterranean world. Persons seeking healing thronged these temples. They often brought small replicas of the portion of the body that was afflicted by disease to these temples and left them with the priests. Other sites, for one reason or another, became renowned as places of healing. A good biblical example of this is the Pool of Bethesda (John 5:1-15). The pool of Siloam also is connected with Jesus' ministry of healing (John 9:7).

Most of the medicine practiced in ancient Palestine and in other outlying parts of the Roman Empire was probably unprofessional. This was certainly true in OT times. Women, trained by apprenticeship and experience, served as midwives. Some persons became adept at setting broken bones. Families were left to apply their own folk remedies in most cases of illness, perhaps in consultation with someone in the community who had become known for his or her success in the treatment of various ailments. Fortunately, the human body has considerable ability to heal itself. Despite obvious medical limitations, many of the patients recovered; and many of the remedies used were "successful."

Methods of Treating Disease The Bible contains little information about the treatment of disease, except through miraculous means. Much of the data concerning this subject has to be obtained from other ancient literature. Most of these records come from the ancient Babylonians, Egyptians, Greeks, and Romans. Some are even older. For example, a clay tablet containing 15 prescriptions from a Sumerian source has been found. This dates to about 2200 B.C.

An examination of these old records, often fragmentary and obscure, reveals that most medicines were derived from three sources. The majority came from various parts of many different plants. Early physicians also used substances obtained from animals, such as blood, urine, milk, hair, and ground-up shell and bone. In addition, certain mineral products were commonly used, including salt and bitumen. The use of these medicines was often accompanied by magical rites, incantations, and prayers. In the earliest periods, in particular, lines were not clearly drawn between religion, superstition, and science.

Modern doctors and Bible students have an almost impossible task as they try to diagnose accurately ailments mentioned in the Bible. Various infectious diseases undoubtedly accounted for a large number of the cases of serious illness and death. Nutritional deficiencies, birth defects, and injuries were common. The symptoms produced by these and other types of physical afflictions were treated by a variety of means.

Prevention is always the best form of treatment. Since the cause of most illness was unknown in the biblical period, relatively little could be done, however, to prevent disease. Ancient people did realize a contagious nature to some illnesses. In these cases, attempts were made to quarantine the afflicted person and prevent close contact with healthy individuals (Lev. 13).

The Hebrew word translated "leprosy" in Lev. 13 is a general term used to describe a number of different skin eruptions. Although true leprosy occurred in ancient times and often caused changes in the skin, many of the persons brought to the priests undoubtedly suffered from more common bacterial and fungal infections of the skin. The priests had the duty of determining, on the basis of repeated examination, which of these eruptions posed a threat to others. They had the authority to isolate persons with suspected dangerous diseases from the community.

Isaiah 38 relates the story of the very serious illness of King Hezekiah. The cause of his illness was a "boil" (v. 21). The Hebrew word translated "boil" is translated "sore boils" in Job 2:7. It is also the word used to describe the eruption occurring on men and beasts mentioned in Exod. 9:8-11 (cp. Lev. 13:18-20; Deut. 28:27).

The illness of Hezekiah was treated by applying a poultice of figs (Isa. 38:21). Hezekiah almost certainly had some type of acute bacterial infection of the skin. Prior to the discovery of antibiotics, these dangerous infections could cause death. Although it is unlikely that the figs

had any medicinal value, they were probably applied in the form of a hot compress. Heat is an effective treatment for infections of the skin.

The use of hot and cold compresses and baths was widely employed in the ancient world to treat illness, although the Bible itself has little to say about this.

Medical care in biblical times frequently employed the use of different kinds of salves and ointments. Olive oil was used widely, either alone or as an ingredient in ointments. The use of oil for the treatment of wounds is mentioned in Isa. 1:6 and Luke 10:34. Oil also became a symbol of medicine, and its use was coupled with prayer for the ill (Mark 6:13; James 5:14).

Herbs and various products obtained from many different plants were among the most popular of ancient medicines. These were applied to the body as a poultice, or, in many cases, taken by mouth. Frankincense and myrrh—gum resins obtained from trees—were commonly used to treat a variety of diseases, although their main use was in perfumes and incense.

Wine was commonly thought to have medicinal value. One of its uses was to alleviate pain and discomfort. Wine, mixed with gall and myrrh, was offered to Jesus prior to His crucifixion, but He refused to drink it (Matt. 27:34; Mark 15:23). Wine also was used to sooth stomach and intestinal disorders (1 Tim. 5:23) and to treat a variety of other physical problems. Beer was also widely used as an ingredient in several medicines, especially by the Babylonians.

Mental illness and epilepsy were not uncommon in the ancient world, and the victims suffered greatly. Their sickness was usually associated with demonic powers. The afflicted person was often isolated and even abused in some cases. King Saul became mentally unstable, and it is of interest that he gained some help from music (1 Sam. 16:23), a form of therapy that has proved to be beneficial in some cases of mental illness. Perhaps the most dramatic example of mental illness related in the Bible concerns the Babylonian king, Nebuchadnezzar (Dan. 4). No treatment is described, but the king's sanity was restored when he acknowledged the true God.

Sterility was a great burden in biblical times. A childless couple was pitied by all. When Leah suffered a temporary period of sterility, she sent her son, Reuben, to the field to obtain mandrakes. Her barren sister, Rachel, also asked for some of the mandrakes (Gen. 30:9-24). The root of the mandrake was widely used in the ancient world to promote conception, although there is no reason to believe it was truly effective. It was also used as a narcotic.

Most babies were born without the benefit of a physician. Midwives were frequently sought to give help, especially in the case of difficult deliveries (Gen. 35:16-21; 1 Sam. 4:19-22). Babies were often born with mothers seated on a special stool (Exod. 1:16). Many mothers and babies died during childbirth or in the first few days and weeks after delivery. The high death rate was due to infection, blood loss, poor nutrition, and the absence of good medical care before, during, and after childbirth. The custom of breast-feeding fortunately did help prevent some illness.

Several examples of sickness are mentioned in the Bible where no description of the treatment given is described. King Asa had a disease of the feet (2 Chron. 16:12). The nature of the treatment provided by his physicians is not given, but it was unsuccessful, and he died after two years. He may have been afflicted with gout, but this is uncertain.

King Jehoram died with a painful intestinal disorder (2 Chron. 21:18-20). King Uzziah died of leprosy (2 Chron. 26:19-23). King Herod Agrippa I died of some kind of parasitic disease (Acts 12:21-23). Several kings died of injuries received in battle. Ahaziah died following a fall from the upper portion of his home in Samaria (2 Kings 1:2-17). When illness or accident occurred in the ancient world, it mattered little whether one was a royal person or a commoner—in either case, only limited medical help was available.

Several illnesses accompanied by fever are mentioned in Matt. 8:14-15; John 4:46-52; Acts 28:8. In the last cited reference, the ill man also had dysentery. Dysentery has several causes, but a very common and serious type was caused by amoeba, an intestinal parasite. Most fevers were due to infectious diseases, including malaria. There was no effective treatment for any of these infections, and death was all too often the outcome. Infections of the eye often resulted in blindness.

Small children were particularly vulnerable to illness, and the death rate could be high. The Bible tells of many children who suffered illness and sometimes death (2 Sam. 12:15-18; 1 Kings 17:17-24; 2 Kings 4:18-37; Luke 7:11-15; 8:40-56; John 4:46-52).

Since there was relatively little good medical care available and since illness so often led to disastrous results, it is not unexpected that sick persons in biblical times frequently asked for divine help. The Hebrew people were no exception to this practice. They often sought the help of God directly through prayer or through some person who was believed to possess special God-granted power to heal. A large number of the miracles described in the Bible are miracles of healing.

Surgery The only surgical procedure mentioned in the Bible is circumcision. This was done for religious rather than medical reasons and was not ordinarily performed by a doctor. In many ways, however, advances in surgery occurred more rapidly than progress in other branches of medicine in many countries. Descriptions of operations have been found in ancient literature, and some old surgical tools have been found in the ruins of ancient cities. Skeletons and mummies sometimes bear the traces of ancient surgical procedures.

Boils were lanced; broken bones were set; arms and legs were amputated. Holes were drilled into skulls to relieve pressure, and stones were removed from the urinary bladder. Teeth were also extracted. Ancient mummies have been found with gold fillings in their teeth. In addition, false teeth, using human or animal teeth, were being prepared by at least 500 B.C. Other kinds of daring operations were performed. Surgery called for boldness on the part of both the doctor and the patient.

Jesus and the Treatment of Disease One of the major ministries of Jesus was the healing of ill persons. They flocked to Him in large numbers, often after having tried all the remedies available in their day. They were desperate for help.

Jesus did not believe that all illness was the direct result of sin (John 9:1-3). He had the power, however, both to forgive sin and to heal (Matt. 9:1-8; cp. Mark 2:1-12; Luke 5:17-26). Ordinarily, He did not use any kind of secondary means to treat the afflicted, although on several occasions He used spittle (Mark 7:32-35; 8:22-25; John 9:6-7). Some of the illnesses treated by Jesus probably had a psychosomatic basis; but many others undoubtedly had organic causes, including birth defects, accidental injuries, and infections.

Regardless of the cause of their distress, people found that Jesus could truly help. There can be no doubt that the ability of Jesus to perform miracles is seen most vividly in His healing ministry. The blind, the deaf, the lame, and sufferers of all varieties found in Him the help that was often not available through regular medical channels.   *Kenneth Eakins*

DISH Utensil for holding or serving food. The OT uses three terms for dish: a large, shallow metal dish (Judg. 5:25; 6:38), a platter (2 Kings 21:13), and a deep dish or bowl (Exod. 25:29; 37:16; Num. 4:7; 7:13). Dishes were generally made of earthenware. Those made of wood were more highly prized (Lev. 15:12). Dishes made of precious metal were used by the rich and in the temple. In the ancient Near East, those gathered at a meal usually ate out of one central dish (Matt. 26:23; Mark 14:20). To offer a person a choice piece of food from the common dish was a special sign of hospitality. See *Pottery; Vessels and Utensils.*

DISHAN (Dī´ shăn) Personal name meaning "bison" or "antelope." This may be a variant spelling/pronunciation of Dishon. A Horite chief and son of Seir (Gen. 36:21,28,30). Apparently these Horites controlled the land of Edom before the Edomites entered the land. See *Dishon; Edom; Horites; Seir.*

DISHON (Dī´ shŏn) Name of Horite chief of Edom (Gen. 36:21,25-26,30). The name may be the same as Dishan with the variant spelling used to identify the separate individuals. See *Dishan.*

DISHONOR See *Shame and Honor.*

DISPENSATION English term derived from the Latin *dispensatio* that is commonly used to translate the Greek *oikonomia.* Etymologically the Greek word refers to the law or management of a household. The verb form *oikonomeo* means to manage, administer, regulate, or plan. It had connotations of financial responsibility as seen in Rom. 16:23, which mentions Erastus the treasurer of the city of Corinth. The term is employed to describe the administration of Paul's apostolic ministry in 1 Cor. 9:17. So beyond the monetary responsibility and account-

ability it is broadened to include all kinds of stewardship.

In the teaching of Jesus, it appears in his famous parable of the shrewd steward (Luke 16:1-13). Here particularly the task and the officer are closely aligned. Jesus used the word *oikonomeo* with its cognates eight times. The remaining uses in the NT are from Paul's pen (except one by Peter, 1 Pet. 4:10), bringing the total to over 20 occurrences.

The biblical usage of *oikonomia* reveals a theological usage and meaning. In Eph. 3:2 and 3:9 the dispensation is linked to the mystery of Christ, which Paul says is a revelation from God. The dispensation is hence an arrangement or management in which a responsibility is placed on mankind by God. As it is related to Jesus Christ, who had not been revealed for a long time (3:5), it is new with regards to time. Paul indicated earlier in the epistle that there is coming a "dispensation of the fullness of the times" (1:10 KJV; cp. HCSB, NASB), which appears as a future phenomenon. Colossians 1:25-29 indicates that there existed a previous dispensational arrangement different from the present one. This suggests that in Paul's thought at least three dispensations of God's dealings with mankind are evident: past, present, and future.

When seen in light of the progress of revelation (e.g., John 1:17; Gal. 3–4), the dispensations can be interpreted as taking on added significance. There is progression of revelation as salvation history unfolds. The different ages incorporate different (sovereignly appointed) ways or dispensations of relating to God. These must not be seen as multiple ways of salvation. Salvation is always by grace through faith alone (Rom. 4). The church of the present age has a unique feature of including both Jews and Gentiles in a position of equality that had not been realized before (Eph. 2:11-22). The Mosaic economy as a whole is superseded (particularly important here is Galatians) as was predicted in the OT itself. In 2 Cor. 3:6, Paul mentions himself and his colaborers as ministers of the New Covenant (cp. Luke 22:20). An initial and partial fulfillment of the promises made to Israel in Jer. 31:31-34 and Ezek. 36:22-32 have come to pass in the ministry of the life, death, and resurrection of Jesus Christ. In the future ministry of Christ, at His return other remaining aspects of salvation history shall also come to pass. These dispensational arrangements are, therefore, to be seen as both a theology of progressive revelation in relation to time and as a hermeneutical tool for correctly interpreting God's relations to humanity.

Dispensationalism is a system of biblical interpretation that has been prominent in the church since the resurgence of biblical study in the mid 1800s, though its roots go back much further. John Nelson Darby, C. I. Scofield, and Lewis Sperry Chafer were among the most famous advocates of a system of theology and interpretation emphasizing the distinguishable elements within the dispensations. The most characteristic hermeneutical concern for Dispensationalism is the consistent distinction between National Israel and the Church. Some Classical Dispensationalists even held that Israel and the church had divergent final destinies, the one on renewed earth and the other in heaven. In the past seven or eight decades, this theology has witnessed remarkable numerical growth but also significant development. In the 1950s and '60s the extreme form of the dual nature of God's eternal plan was relaxed somewhat, especially in the writings of Charles Ryrie and John Walvoord. Instead of the previously taught permanent land or earthly fulfillment of God's promises to Israel as opposed to the spiritual heavenly promises held out to the Church, these theologians taught that one united future remained for both Jews and Gentiles in soteriological unity. More recently still, reconciliation has begun between some adherents of Dispensationalism and those of nondispensational theology. Particularly significant is the eschatological understanding of the NT with its already/not yet approach to fulfillment of promises made in the OT. Progressive Dispensationalism as advocated by evangelicals such as Craig Blaising, Darrell Bock, and Robert Saucy has emerged as a recent effort to fine-tune the hermeneutical system. This approach has been criticized by supporters of the earlier school but has gained a large hearing. This newer approach is closest to nondispensational thinking and could thereby serve as a bridge to unite evangelicals on biblical and theological matters. Dispensationalism remains a vibrant force within evangelical interpretations of the Bible. See *Millennium; Revelation, Book of.*

Doros Zachariades

DISPERSION See *Diaspora.*

DISSIPATION Deceptive desires leading to a lifestyle without discipline resulting in the dizzy hangovers of drunkenness. The Greek word *apate* means "deception" caused by riches (Matt. 13:22) and sin (Heb. 3:13). This is founded in the deceptive lusts of the unredeemed human heart (Eph. 4:22). People following such a way of life will suffer "the penalty for doing wrong" as they continue "reveling in their dissipation" (2 Pet. 2:13 NRSV). *Asotia* means to be hopelessly sick and refers to a lifestyle by which one destroys oneself. It is the prodigal son's "wild living" (Luke 15:13 NIV). It is the life of "dissipation" resulting from drinking wine (Eph. 5:18 NASB; cp. Titus 1:6; 1 Pet. 4:3-4). The Bible speaks against a disorderly life, whereas the Greeks used the term to mean a wasteful or luxurious life. The Bible teaches believers to avoid both lifestyles.

DISTAFF Part of the spindle used in spinning wool (Prov. 31:19). The obscure Hebrew word may refer to a small disk at the bottom of the spindle used to make the wheel spin faster. See *Cloth, Clothing; Spindle.*

DISTRICT Translates several different Hebrew and Greek words referring to a region, territory, or land. In the OT district often connotes a part of a larger whole, either the provinces of an empire (1 Kings 20:14-19), regions within a country (2 Chron. 11:23), or sections of a city (Neh. 3:9-18). In the NT "district" often refers to the area around a city (Matt. 15:21; 16:13; Mark 8:10). At Acts 16:12 the reference is to an administrative area (perhaps Matt. 2:22 also). At times district means no more than the general area (Matt. 9:26,31).

DIVERSITY Characteristic of human and animal populations (Gen. 10; Acts 17:26-27). Out of His richness God created an unfathomable number of creatures to fill the earth (Gen. 1:11-12,20-22,24-25) and respond to Him in praise (Ps. 148).

Although God chose the family of Abraham from among the nations to be His special possession, an ethnically diverse element has always been present in His people (Exod. 12:38; cp. Luke 4:25-27). At times Israel responded negatively to diverse populations within their midst, such as when Nehemiah criticized the Jews of Jerusalem for marrying foreign women (Neh.

13:23-30). The issue of diversity became critical during the initial spread of the church to the Gentile world (Acts 10:1-48; 15:1-21) and was resolved on the side of unity in Christ (Gal. 3:28). John saw that the population of heaven will contain persons "from every nation, tribe, people, and language" (Rev. 7:9 HCSB).

God provides a variety of spiritual gifts to equip and empower His church for service in a diverse world (1 Cor. 12:4-31; Eph. 4:11-13).

DIVES (Dī´ vēs) Name sometimes given to the rich man of whom Jesus spoke in Luke 16:19-31. *Dives* actually is the Latin word for "rich" used in Luke 16:19 in the Vulgate translation. The idea that this was the name of the man emerged in medieval times. See *Lazarus.*

DIVIDED KINGDOM Two political states of Judah and Israel that came into existence shortly after the death of Solomon (1 Kings 11:43) and survived together until the fall of Israel in 722 B.C. The Northern Kingdom, known as Israel, and the Southern Kingdom, known as Judah, were operated as separate countries from approximately 924 B.C. until 722 B.C. (1 Kings 12). At times, the two countries were at war with one another. At other times, they cooperated in a friendly alliance. The Northern Kingdom came to an end in 722 B.C. when the Assyrians destroyed the capital city, Samaria. The Southern Kingdom fell to the Babylonians in 587 B.C.   *James Newell*

DIVIDING ROCK See *Selah-Hammahlekoth.*

DIVINATION AND MAGIC Practice of making decisions or foretelling the future by means of reading signs and omens. Several types of divination are mentioned in the Bible. Ezekiel 21:21 mentions consulting idols, the use of arrows, and examining the liver of an animal. Arrows were shaken in a quiver and either poured out on the ground or one was drawn out to indicate where to attack. The position, size, color, etc., of a dead animal's liver was seen as indicating the best choice or one's fate. Divination by looking into a cup filled with liquid was also practiced (Gen. 44:5).

Divination and magic, or sorcery, was common among the nations surrounding ancient Israel. Egyptian court magicians could imitate some of Moses' miracles (Exod. 7:11,22; 8:7), though not all of them (Exod. 8:18; 9:11). Div-

ination was one reason the nations were driven out of Canaan (Deut.18:12). Divination was practiced by the Philistines (1 Sam. 6:2). Babylonian court magicians were advisers to the king (astrologers, charmers, diviners, and Chaldeans; Dan. 1:20; 2:2,10; 4:7; 5:7).

God condemned divination and magic in every form. The law of Moses repeatedly condemns the practice. In Exod. 22:18 and Lev. 20:27 it brings the death penalty. Leviticus 19:26 forbids the practice. Leviticus 20:6 commands the people to avoid those who engage in such practices, linking it to harlotry. To engage in divination is to be unfaithful to the Lord and to commit abomination (Deut. 18:9-22). People are exhorted to listen to God's prophets instead.

Condemnation of divination and magic is found in the historical writings. In 2 Kings 9:22 the sorceries of Jezebel are condemned. Manasseh, king of Judah, was considered evil for divination and idolatry (2 Kings 21:1-7; 2 Chron. 33:6). Divination and sorcery are listed among the sins that caused the fall of Israel to Assyria (2 Kings 17:17-18).

The prophetic writings also contain many references condemning divination. Isaiah mentions it repeatedly (Isa. 2:6; 3:1-3; 44:25; 47:9,12-15). Zechariah 10:1-2 admonishes to look to the Lord for rain, not to diviners. Jeremiah also said that diviners should not be listened to (Jer. 27:9; 29:8).

Consulting mediums, who contact the dead, is also forbidden, carrying the death sentence (Lev. 20:6,27; Isa. 8:19). Saul was guilty of consulting a medium to contact Samuel (1 Sam. 28), despite the fact that Saul had banished all mediums from the land.

In the NT magic and divination get less attention. Simon, a sorcerer in Samaria, was rebuked by Peter for attempting to buy the power of the Holy Spirit (Acts 8:9-24). Paul and Silas encountered a slave girl at Philippi who had a demonic power of foretelling the future (Acts 16:16-26). Paul commanded the demon to leave her, which led to their imprisonment. Witchcraft is among the things condemned as a work of the flesh in Gal. 5:20.

The Bible consistently condemns the practice of divination. Only rarely does it regard such practices as fraudulent. They are condemned, not because they are not supernatural, but because the source is often demonic and practitioners are trying to circumvent God to find guidance for the future. Christians should heed the biblical injunctions against astrology, fortune-telling, and mediums.   *Fred Smith*

DIVINE FREEDOM One of God's unique attributes is freedom. Scripture declares, "Our God is in heaven and does whatever He pleases" (Ps. 115:3 HCSB), and "The LORD does whatever He pleases in heaven and on earth, in the seas and all the depths" (Ps. 135:6 HCSB). God is of such a nature that He is self-determining. He acts according to His nature and choosing at all times. God's actions are always voluntary. God cannot be compelled to act by any other person or exterior force. Only His nature and will are determinative for His actions (Isa. 42:21; Eph. 1:11). Because He is absolutely true and faithful, His actions are always consistent with His nature, purposes, and promises.

God's greatness ensures that He thus accomplishes all that He intends. No task is beyond God's power or too difficult for Him to perform (Jer. 32:17). Nevertheless certain actions are contrary to His character. God's goodness renders him unable to perform certain actions. He cannot lie (Heb. 6:18). He can neither be tempted by evil nor tempt anyone to evil (James 1:13). Such restrictions need not be understood as limitations upon His freedom because they are self-caused, deriving from His free nature, and because such actions are not proper objects of power. The power to lie or to be the cause of evil does not contribute to greatness. In fact, just the opposite is the case; such abilities diminish greatness. Because God does not lie, His ultimate purposes are eternal and unchanging (Num. 23:19).

God's freedom is such that He is free *from* limitations upon either His goodness or His greatness. Additionally God is free from spatial or temporal limitations. As such He is supratemporal and supraspatial (eternal and omnipresent). God's greatness ensures that His decisions are perfectly wise and consistent. He is thus a God who never acts illogically or absurdly, or frustrates Himself. Nor does God act arbitrarily or capriciously. So despite the fact that He is thoroughly free, His freedom is *perfect freedom.* He always acts for good and not evil (James 1:17) and in ways that reveal His glory and greatness.   *Robert B. Stewart*

DIVINE RETRIBUTION Repayment without stipulation of good or evil. The application of the word in theology is, however, almost always viewed as the response of a just and holy God to evil. Like other prominent theological terms (i.e., Trinity, etc.), the word is not found in the Bible, but the idea of God's repayment for evil is prominent in at least three ways.

First, the law of sowing and reaping is part of God's economy (Gal. 6:7-8). In the OT this takes the form of blessings and cursings. When Israel entered Canaan, half stood on Mount Ebal and half on Mount Gerizim and acknowledged that certain kinds of behavior bring consequences either for good or evil (Deut. 27:1-26). In the NT the certainty of reaping what one sows is plain (Rom. 6:21-22).

Second, coming judgment at the end of history includes repayment from God for rebellion. In the Great White Throne Judgment (Rev. 20:11-15), two criteria of judgment seem to be involved. Unbelievers are said to be judged from both the books (plural) and the book (singular). Specifically, the "books" are examined to demonstrate that the deeds of the condemned have demonstrated God's justice in judgment. A search of the "book" confirms that those being turned into hell are not named in the Lamb's Book of Life, and hence divine retribution falls because they failed to respond to God's gracious offer of salvation.

Finally, the justice of God's condemnation of sinners gives rise to the necessity of the grace of God in salvation and the substitutionary death of Jesus on the cross. In the OT Isaiah noted this pointedly (Isa. 53:6), "All of us like sheep have gone astray ... but the Lord has caused the iniquity of us all to fall on Him" (NASB). In the NT Peter declares Christ suffered for us since He "bore our sins in His body on the tree" (1 Pet. 2:24 HCSB). An eternal principle of justice exists. God in His grace extends to sinners an offer of pardon rather than the retribution they deserve, because Jesus paid the price for human sin in His vicarious death, making it possible for the Father to be both "just" and still the "justifier" of the sinner who places his faith in Jesus (Rom. 3:26).

Retribution takes several forms in the Bible. Sometimes, the response of God is temporal and physical. Defeat by one's enemies, drought in the land (1 Kings 8:33-40), or even illness can be retributive acts of God (1 Cor. 11:30; 1 Chron.

21:12-13). More serious, the inevitability of physical death is a residual effect of God's retribution (Gen. 2:17; Rom. 6:23). More serious, indeed irremediable, is "spiritual death" and the estrangement of the soul from God forever. This retribution carries with it confinement of the sinner in hell (Rev. 21:8; Matt. 18:19). For this reason the beginning of wisdom is still the "fear" of God (Luke 12:5). See *Eschatology; Eternal Life; Everlasting Punishment; Future Hope.*

Paige Patterson

DIVINERS' OAK Place visible from the gate of Shechem (Judg. 9:35,37). Some translations understand the underlying Hebrew to refer to a plain (KJV, plain of Meonenim; NRSV, Elon-meonenim). Others translate as the "diviners' oak" (NASB), "Soothsayers' terebinth" (REB), "soothsayers' tree" (NIV) or "oak tree of the fortune tellers" (TEV). In this case the tree formed part of a sanctuary. The terebinth was designated the diviners' or soothsayers' tree since persons would go to the sanctuary seeking an oracle. The tree is perhaps that associated with Abraham (Gen. 12:6), Jacob (Gen. 35:4), and Joshua (Josh. 24:26) (cp. Deut. 11:30; Judg. 9:6). It may well have played an important role in Canaanite worship at Shechem before Israel took over the ancient worship place. It was apparently located near the east gate of the city.

DIVINITY OF CHRIST See *Christ, Christology; Incarnation; Jesus.*

DIVORCE Breaking of the marriage covenant. An action contrary to the pattern of "one man, one woman, one lifetime" revealed by God in Gen. 1:27; 2:21-25. The root idea implied a cutting of the marriage bond. While ancient cultures differed in details, most had a concept of marriage and a corresponding concept of divorce.

The OT has numerous references to divorce. The concept that divorce constituted sin appeared in Mal. 2:14-16. First, Malachi stated that marriage represented a covenant between a man and a woman. Further, marriage provided companionship, brought oneness, and promoted a godly seed. The dissolution of marriage represented treacherous behavior before the Lord. God hated divorce, and He issued a warning to those who had not divorced.

Under certain conditions, divorce could occur under OT law (Deut. 24:1-4). Though a wife might abandon her husband, only the husband could seek a divorce. If a husband found "some indecency in her" (NASB), he was allowed, but not required, to write a "certificate of divorce" against his wife. The rejected wife might marry again, but she could not remarry her original husband. Deuteronomy 24 has been interpreted to mean either that any displeasing thing allowed for divorce or that only sexual immorality allowed for divorce. The most scripturally consistent interpretation would seem to be that if upon marriage a husband found that his wife had been sexually active during the engagement period (or even before), then he could divorce her. This was an important safeguard since, under OT law, adultery (sexual immorality during marriage) was punishable by death (Lev. 20:10). After the Babylonian captivity of Israel, Ezra (Ezra 10) led the Israelites to "put away all the wives and their children," so as to remove idolatrous foreigners from Israel. Intermarriage with the idolatrous peoples around Israel had been forbidden in Deut. 7:3. Since other foreigners had been accepted into Israel (i.e., Ruth), this may have indicated a refusal to worship the Lord as God on the part of the foreign wives.

Divorce regulations appear in other parts of the OT. Priests were not allowed to marry divorced women (Lev. 21:14), indicating a higher standard for their actions. Also, the vow of a divorced woman was considered legally binding since she had no husband to affirm or to overrule her actions (Num. 30:9). Finally, the Lord used divorce as a symbol of his displeasure with Israel (Jer. 3:8), though He elsewhere indicated His future plans for Israel.

The NT also sheds light on the subject of divorce. The Lord Jesus stated that divorce, except in the case of sexual immorality, would cause complications for remarriage. An improper divorce would make the divorced wife and her future husband adulterers in their relationship (Matt. 5:31-32). In Matt. 19:3-12, Jesus stated that God did not intend for divorce to occur. Further, He stated that the Mosaic law allowed for divorce only because of the hardness of Israelite hearts. Jesus' disciples considered this a hard saying and said so; nevertheless, He affirmed His position on divorce (Matt. 19:7-12; Mark 10:4-12).

The Apostle Paul twice dealt with divorce. In his discussion of the law in Rom. 7:1-3, Paul used the illustration of marriage to show the authority of the law. He reaffirmed the principles of the sanctity of marriage, the wrongfulness of divorce, and the potential consequences of remarriage. In 1 Cor. 7:10-16 Paul reiterated the need to preserve the marriage commitment.

Based on Rom. 7:1-3 and 1 Cor. 7:39, Paul believed that divorce was no longer an issue once one spouse had died. The remaining spouse was free to marry as long as the new marriage was "in the Lord" (1 Cor. 7:39). Therefore, marriage in Scripture represented a sacred bond between one man and one woman for one lifetime. The concept of marriage was ordained by God and applied to believers and nonbelievers alike. This had ramifications for the leadership qualifications for God's other institution, the church (1 Tim. 3:1-13; Titus 1:5-9). A breaking of the marriage covenant opposed the plan of God and divided the God-ordained institution of the family. See *Marriage.*   *Michael R. Spradlin*

DIZAHAB (Dĭz´ à hăb) Place-name meaning "place of gold." Place east of Jordan River used in Deut. 1:1 to locate where Moses spoke to Israel. Nothing else is known of it. It may be located in Moab in modern ed-Dhebe.

DOCTOR See *Diseases.*

DOCTRINE Christian truth and teaching passed on from generation to generation as "the faith that was delivered to the saints" (Jude 3 HCSB).

Specifically, doctrine refers to Christian teaching and most specifically to Christian teaching about God, the gospel, and the comprehensive pattern of Christian truth. The word itself means "teaching" and generally refers to the accepted body of beliefs held by the Christian church universally and to those beliefs specific to individual denominations and congregations in particular.

The Christian church cannot avoid teaching and thus must formulate a framework for understanding and teaching the basic rudiments and principles of the faith and for developing those basic doctrines into more comprehensive and thorough understandings. Without such a framework, the church has no coherent system of beliefs and no means of discriminating between true and false beliefs.

Doctrine thus serves a vital and necessary role within the life of the church and the life of the believer. The biblical focus on doctrine is not based upon the notion of static and dead beliefs but upon living truths cherished and defended by all true Christians.

The foundation, sourcebook, and authority for developing doctrine is the Bible. The Bible is "profitable for teaching" (2 Tim. 3:16), and it forms the structure, content, and authority for the development of doctrine.

The structure of Christian doctrine is rooted in the character of the Bible as the inerrant and infallible Word of God. As God's revelation, the Bible establishes a structure for thought and conveys truth in doctrinal form. Doctrine is most clearly rooted in the propositional nature of biblical revelation. The Bible sets forth a unified and comprehensive structure of Christian truth, and the church bears the responsibility to correlate these truths into a unified system of truth.

The content of Christian doctrine is derived from a careful consideration of the totality of the Bible's teaching. Doctrines are developed as Christians seek to understand the contents of the Bible and to express those teachings in understandable form appropriate for instructing believers.

The authority for Christian doctrines is the Bible itself. In formulating doctrine, the church takes other authorities into consideration. Experience often reveals the need for doctrinal attention, and true Christian doctrine is to be lived out in faithful Christian experience, not just received as matters of intellectual interest. Reason is also important in doctrinal formulation, for the tools of reason are indispensable to the task of expressing biblical truths in doctrinal form. Tradition also plays a role, for every generation of Christians inherits patterns of belief and practice from previous generations. We do not begin with a blank slate unformed by received traditions.

Nevertheless, the Bible cannot function merely as one authority among others. The Bible is the controlling and ultimate authority for all matters of Christian belief and practice. Experience, reason, and tradition are to be judged by Scripture, and Scripture is not to be judged by other authorities. This principle has characterized the church in every period of doctrinal strength and purity. When compromised, false teachings and heresies inevitably follow.

This principle was expressed during the Reformation as *sola Scriptura*, for Scripture alone is the final and controlling authority for all true Christian teaching and doctrinal formulation.

Once formulated, doctrines are often expressed and taught through catechisms and adopted as creeds and confessions. Every Christian denomination expresses its beliefs in some doctrinal form, whether highly developed or rudimentary. Likewise, every Christian must have a basic understanding of Christian doctrine in order "to give a defense to anyone who asks you a reason for the hope that is in you" (1 Pet. 3:15 HCSB).

The church must give constant attention to doctrine, for aberrant teachings and heresies are constant threats to the biblical integrity of the people of God. Like the Christians of ancient Berea, the church must continually examine its beliefs by Scripture (Acts 17:11). Heresies are to be confronted and corrected on Scriptural authority. False teachers are to be revealed and removed from fellowship (1 Tim. 6:3-5 KJV; Titus 3:10). The church cannot be unconcerned about false teachings but must protect the purity of true Christian faith in mutual submission to the Bible as the Word of God.

Doctrines are to be formulated, taught, and passed down from one generation to the next in a succession established by the apostles (Acts 2:42; 2 Tim. 2:2). The faith "once for all delivered" (Jude 3) is to be cherished, believed, defended, and protected by true Christians. Parents are responsible for teaching their children, and church leaders are to teach the flock of God with faithfulness.

No human formulation can express Christian truth in total comprehensiveness. Our doctrinal formulations are never coextensive with the fullness of biblical truth. Nevertheless, the church is called to express the structure and content of biblical truth and to be continually about the task of correcting our doctrines by Scripture, seeking to teach the gospel and the pattern of biblical truth as it was first received by the apostles.   *R. Albert Mohler, Jr.*

DODAI (Dō´ dī) Personal name related to Hebrew word meaning "favorite" or "beloved." First Chronicles 27:1-15 describes David's army as being divided into 12 monthly divisions with an officer over each. Dodai was in charge for the second month. Second Samuel 23:9 and 1 Chron. 11:12 refer to Dodo the Ahohite, which is probably a variant spelling referring to the same person as Dodai. See *Ahohite; Dodo*.

DODANIM (Dō´ dä nĭm) Great grandson of Noah and son of Javan in the Table of Nations (Gen. 10:4). In 1 Chron. 1:7 the name is Rodanim. Early copyists made the easy confusion between Hebrew "r" and "d." If Rodanim is correct, the reference may be to inhabitants of Rhodes. If Dodanim is original, the identification of the people is not simple. It could refer to a land of Danuna known from the Amarna letters. This was apparently north of Tyre. A people with a similar name were among the Sea People who fought with Rameses III. Homer says Danaeans besieged Troy. Sargon II describes Yadanana who lived on Cyprus. Despite specific information, they were apparently from the Greek area and may have been Greek speaking.

DODAVAH (Dŏd´ å väh) or **DODAVAHU** (Dō dä va´ hū) Personal name meaning "beloved of Yahweh." Father of Eliezer the prophet (2 Chron. 20:37).

DODO (Dō´ dō) Personal name meaning "his beloved." **1.** Grandfather of Tola, the judge (Judg. 10:1). **2.** Father of Eleazar, one of David's three mighty men (2 Sam. 23:9). In 1 Chron. 27:4 he is called Dodai. **3.** Citizen of Bethlehem and father of Elhanan, one of David's warriors (2 Sam. 23:24).

DOE Modern translation where KJV has "hind" or "roe." The Hebrew has two words. *Ya 'aalah* refers to the female ibex or mountain goat (Prov. 5:19), the mate of the ibex, *Capra nubiana* or *Capra sinaitica* (Ps. 104:18). *Ayalah* is the female fallow deer (Gen. 49:21; 2 Sam. 22:34; Job 39:1; Pss. 18:33; 29:9; Jer. 14:5; Hab. 3:19; Song 2:7; 3:5). The male, *Cervus captrolus*, is the hart or deer of Deut. 12:15,22; 14:5; 15:22; 1 Kings 4:23; Isa. 35:6; Ps. 42:2; Song 2:9,17; Lam. 1:6. See *Deer*.

DOEG (Dō´ ĕg) Personal name meaning "full of fear." An Edomite in the service of King Saul (1 Sam. 21:7). He was present at Nob at the time David arrived there during the course of his flight from Saul. Doeg subsequently reported to Saul that the priest Ahimelech had given assistance to David. After confronting Ahimelech, Saul ordered his guards to slay the priests of

Nob. When the guards refused to obey, Saul told Doeg to kill the priests. In a grisly show of obedience, Doeg took the lives of 85 people. The title of Ps. 52 refers to this incident. See *Saul.*

DOG Considered an unclean animal; often wild, scavenger animal that ran in packs (Pss. 22:16-21; 59:6) but sometimes kept as domestic pet. Dogs served as watchdogs for herds (Isa. 56:10; Job 30:1) and for the dwelling (Exod. 11:7). Some were trained for hunting (Ps. 22:16), but some ran stray in the streets (Exod. 22:30; 1 Kings 14:11).

Metaphorically, "dog" was a term of contempt (1 Sam. 17:43) and self-abasement (1 Sam. 24:14). "Dog" may refer to a male cult prostitute (Deut. 23:18), though the exact meaning of "dog's wages" is disputed. The term "dog" was a designation for the wicked (Isa. 56:10-11). The prophet insulted the priests by saying their sacrifices were no better than breaking a dog's neck and sacrificing the dog (Isa. 66:3). This means that sacrifices are not needed in the new age and that the priests had neglected their first task, that of determining God's will.

Jesus used dogs to teach people to be discriminating in whom they chose to teach (Matt. 7:6). In Mark 7:27, Jesus probably was referring to the small dogs that people kept as pets. Jews contemptuously called Gentiles "dogs." Paul insulted his Judaizing opponents, calling them dogs (Phil. 3:2; cp. 2 Pet. 2:22; Rev. 22:15).

DOMINION Either political authority (Num. 24:19; Dan. 7:6,12,14) or the realm in which such authority is exercised (1 Kings 4:24; 9:19). Dominion may have a positive connotation as when humankind is given dominion over creation (Gen. 1:26,28; Ps. 8:6) or a negative connotation that approximates the idea of domination (Gen. 37:8; Judg. 14:4; Neh. 9:28). Though humans exercise dominion in the political sphere and over creation, ultimate dominion belongs to God (Ps. 72:8; Dan. 4:3,34). Dominion is used figuratively for the authority of the law (Rom. 7:1) and for the domination of sin (Ps. 19:13; Rom. 6:14) and death (Rom. 6:9). The dominions of Col. 1:16 are angelic powers that are subordinated to Christ.

DOMITIAN See *Rome and the Roman Empire.*

DONKEY See *Ass.*

DOOR Opening for entering or leaving a house, tent, or room. At least five Hebrew words and one Greek term are translated "door" in the English Bible. The two most common Hebrew words have distinct usages, though they may be interchanged. *Petach* refers to the doorway, to the actual opening itself. *Delet* alludes to the door proper, usually made of wood sheeted with metal, though a slab of stone could be used. The Greek term *thura* is used for both of these Hebrew words.

"Door" is often used in a figurative sense in the Bible. In the OT "sin is crouching at the door" (Gen. 4:7 NASB) means that sin is very near. The valley of Achor, a place of trouble (Josh. 7:26), is later promised as "a door of hope" (Hos. 2:15). It will become a reason for God's people to trust Him again.

In the NT Jesus calls Himself "the door" (John 10:7,9). Faith in Him is the only way to enter the kingdom of God. God gave to the Gentiles "the door of faith" or an opportunity to know Him as Lord (Acts 14:27). Paul constantly sought a "door of service," an occasion for ministry in the name of Christ (1 Cor. 16:9). Jesus stands at the door and knocks (Rev. 3:20). He calls all people to Himself but will not enter without permission.   *Bradley S. Butler*

DOORKEEPER Person guarding access to an important or restricted place. Temple doorkeeper was an important office in biblical times. The doorkeepers collected money from the people (2 Kings 22:4). Some Levites were designated doorkeepers (or "gatekeepers") for the ark (1 Chron. 15:23-24). The Persian kings used eunuchs for doorkeepers (Esther 2:21). Women also served this function (John 18:16-17; Acts 12:13).

The Hebrew word underlying the translation "doorkeeper" in Ps. 84:10 (KJV, RSV, NIV) appears only once in the OT. The root idea is threshold. Thus some translations (NASB, REB, TEV) render the word "at the threshold" or some similar expression. The reference is to those waiting outside the temple either to beg alms or to seek admission. The thought of the verse is that it is better to be standing outside the temple than to be inside the tents of the wicked.

DOPHKAH (Dŏph´ käh) Place-name, perhaps meaning "(animal) drive." Station in the wilderness between Wilderness of Sin and Rephidim where Israel camped (Num. 33:12). It has been located at modern Serabit el-Chadim, but this is uncertain.

DOR (Dôr) Place-name meaning "dwelling." Canaanite city located at modern Khirbet el-Burj, 12 miles south of Mount Carmel. Its early history shows connections with Egypt under Rameses II and with the Sea Peoples, who are closely related to the Philistines. Apparently the Tjeker, one of the Sea Peoples, destroyed the city shortly after 1300 B.C. Its king joined the northern coalition against Joshua (Josh. 11:2; 12:23) but met defeat. The Hebrew expression here, *naphoth dor*, or heights of Dor is unexpected since Dor lies on the seacoast. The reference must be to Mount Carmel. Dor lay in the territory assigned Asher, but the tribe of Manasseh claimed it (Josh. 17:11). The Canaanites maintained political control (Josh. 17:12; Judg. 1:27). Dor served as a district headquarters under Solomon, governed by Solomon's son-in-law Ben-abinadab (1 Kings 4:11).

DORCAS (Dôr´ cảs) Personal name meaning "gazelle." A Christian woman of Joppa who was known for her charitable works (Acts 9:36). She was also called Tabitha, an Aramaic name. When she became sick and died, friends sent for the Apostle Peter. He came to Joppa. Through him Dorcas was restored to life. This was the first such miracle performed through any of the apostles, and it resulted in many new believers.

DOT REB translation of Greek term "little horn" (Matt. 5:18; cp. Luke 16:17), rendered in various ways in English translations (e.g., tittle, KJV; stroke of a letter or pen, NASB, NRSV, NIV). The dot is generally held to be a mark distinguishing

View of the ancient harbor at Dor in Israel.

similarly shaped letters, either the raised dot distinguishing *sin* from *shin* or else the hooks used to distinguish others (e.g., *beth* and *kaph*). Others suggest the letter *waw* is intended. *Iota*, translated "jot" or "smallest letter" is the smallest Greek vowel and is generally taken to represent the smallest Hebrew letter, *yodh*. Jesus thus contended that it was easier for heaven and earth to pass away than for the smallest detail of the law to be set aside. Matthew's qualification "until all things are accomplished"(HCSB) is perhaps a reference to the saving work of Christ as the fulfillment of all Scripture.

DOTHAN (Dō´ thăn) Place-name of uncertain meaning, also known as Dothaim. A city of the tribe of Manasseh, west of the Jordan, northeast of Samaria, southeast of Megiddo, and now identified as Tell Dotha. It was located in an area less productive for agriculture and was traversed by

Excavations of the ruins at Dothan in Israel.

roads used for commerce. Dothan is the area to which Joseph traveled to find his brothers (Gen. 37:17). From there, Joseph was sold to a caravan of Ishmaelites and carried to Egypt, following an ancient trade route over the Plain of Dothan to Egypt. Dothan was the place Elisha stayed (2 Kings 6:13). The king of Syria sought to capture Elisha by laying siege to the city. Elisha then led the Syrian army away from Dothan to Samaria and defeat. Dothan is five miles southwest of Genin, 11 miles northeast of Samaria, and 13 miles north of Shechem.

David M. Fleming

DOUBLE-MINDED Words used only by James in the NT to express a lack of purity of heart or a lack of absolute trust in God. The term literally means "of two minds or souls" (Greek *dipsychos*). It describes one who is trusting in God while also trusting in something else, such as self or the world. James encouraged those who were lacking in wisdom to ask God. The one who asks God and doubts is described in James 1:8 as an "indecisive man" (HCSB). He is one who is wavering between asking God in faith and not believing God will or can answer. He may also be one who asks God yet resorts to his own wisdom instead of that which God provides. This person is described as one who was "unstable in all his ways" indicating that his entire life was lived without a complete trust in God.

Later in his letter James encouraged his readers to purify their hearts (James 4:8), because they were "double-minded people." James was calling for these Christians to make a commitment to trust in God and His ways while denying their own ways and trusting in themselves.

Thomas Strong

DOUBLE-TONGUED One of the qualifications of deacons is that they not be double-tongued, that is, inconsistent in speech (1 Tim. 3:8; HCSB, "hypocritical"). James 3:9-10 warns of the inconsistency of those who bless God while cursing those made in the image of God. First John 3:18 encourages consistency of loving words with loving actions. Inconsistency of speech might be taken as thinking one thing and saying another or as saying one thing to one, another thing to another.

DOUGH Flour or meal mixed with liquid, usually water but sometimes olive oil as well, which is baked as bread. Dough was normally leavened, given time to rise, and then kneaded before baking (Jer. 7:18; Hos. 7:4). The necessity for haste at the Hebrews' departure from Egypt caused them to carry their dough before it was leavened (Exod. 12:34). See *Bread.*

DOVE The term "dove" is applied rather loosely to many of the smaller species of pigeon. The first mention of the dove occurs in Gen. 8:8-12. Noah released a dove from the ark to determine if the floodwaters had subsided from the earth.

The moaning of the dove sometimes functions metaphorically (Isa. 38:14; 59:11; Ezek. 7:16). Psalm 55:6 notes the dove's powers of flight; Jer. 48:28 describes its nesting habits; Ps. 68:13 indicates its rich colors. Because of the

gentleness of the dove and because of its faithfulness to its mate, this bird is used as a descriptive title of one's beloved in the Song of Songs (2:14; 5:2; 6:9). In Matt. 10:16 the dove symbolizes innocence.

All four Gospels describe the Spirit of God descending like a dove upon Jesus after His baptism (Matt. 3:16; Mark 1:10; Luke 3:22; John 1:32).

The term "turtledove" also is applied to any of the smaller varieties of pigeon. The turtledove played a significant sacrificial role in the Bible (Gen. 15:9; Lev. 1:14; 5:7,11; 12:6; 14:22,30; 15:14; Luke 2:24). For those who could not afford a lamb, the law prescribed that two turtledoves or pigeons be offered for the sacrifice of purification after childbearing. Mary brought such an offering after the birth of Christ (Lev. 12:8; Luke 2:24). The turtledove also signified the arrival of spring (Song 2:12; Jer. 8:7).

Janice Meier

DOVE ON FAR-OFF TEREBINTHS Part of the superscription of Ps. 56 (NRSV; cp. REB, NIV); probably a reference to the secular tune to which the psalm was to be sung. "Hind of the Dawn" (Ps. 22 REB) and "Lilies" (Ps. 45 NIV) are possibly other hymn tunes. An alternative explanation relates to the association of doves with the ritual of atonement. In this case the title indicates an atonement psalm. KJV transliterates the Hebrew, Jonath-elem-rechokim. See *Terebinths.*

DOVE'S DUNG An item sold as food for an incredible price (2 Kings 6:25) during the siege of Samaria. Some interpret dove's dung as bird droppings since 2 Kings 18:27 indicates that in time of siege persons could be reduced to eating their own excrement and drinking their own urine. Others have suggested that the dung was to be used as fuel or as a salt substitute. Probably Dove's Dung refers to a bulbous plant similar to a wild onion that was edible after boiling or roasting. Still others emend the text to read some type of bean pods (REB, NIV).

DOWNSIZING The Bible's statements regarding God's providence in times of hardship are directly applicable to personal difficulties which result from corporate and financial downsizing. The biblical record is ample proof that no one is exempt from trouble (Job 5:7; Ps. 40:12). Job experienced a greater degree of downsizing than perhaps anyone before or since (Job 1:13-19). While Job apparently never understood the reasons for his misfortune (Job 42:1-6), God eventually restored both his wealth and position (Job 42:10-17).

The Apostle Paul learned "the secret of being content ... whether in abundance or in need" (Phil. 4:12 HCSB). Paul understood that while circumstances are often beyond the control of individuals, nothing is beyond the realm of God, who cares for even the smallest part of His creation (Ps. 24:1; Matt. 6:25-33). For this reason God answers those who wait for Him (Ps. 40:1).

Paul H. Wright

DOWRY Marriage present that ensured the new wife's financial security against the possibility her husband might forsake her or might die. The husband-to-be or his father paid the dowry or bride price to the bride's father to be kept for the bride. The bride could protest if her father used the dowry for other purposes (Gen. 31:15). In addition the bride received wedding gifts from her father and husband (Gen. 24:53; 34:12; Judg. 1:15). The amount of the dowry depended on customs of the specific tribes or clans and upon the economic and social class of the parties involved (1 Sam. 18:23-27, a passage also showing that service could be substituted for money; cp. Gen. 29:15-30; Josh. 15:16-17). Besides guaranteeing future financial security, the dowry also compensated the bride and her family for the economic loss represented to her family by her leaving to join her husband's family. Deuteronomy 22:29 apparently puts the price at 50 shekels of silver, a much larger price than paid for a slave—30 shekels (Exod. 21:32; cp. Lev. 27:1-8). Payment of the dowry made the marriage a legal fact even before the official wedding ceremonies or consummation of the marriage. Ancient Near Eastern texts from different cultures show similar practices. Often the bride receives the dowry directly or indirectly through her father. See *Family; Marriage*.

DOXOLOGY Brief formula for expressing praise or glory to God. Doxologies generally contain two elements, an ascription of praise to God (usually referred to in third person) and an expression of His infinite nature. The term "doxology" ("word of glory") itself is not found in the Bible, but both the OT and NT contain many doxological passages using this formula.

Biblical doxologies are found in many contexts, but one of their chief functions seems to have been as a conclusion to songs (Exod. 15:18), psalms (Ps. 146:10), and prayers (Matt. 6:13), where they possibly served as group responses to solo singing or recitation. Doxologies conclude four of the five divisions of the psalter (Ps. 41:13; 72:19; 89:52; 106:48), with Ps. 150 serving as a sort of doxology to the entire collection. Doxologies also occur at or near the end of several NT books (Rom. 16:27; Phil. 4:20; 1 Tim. 6:16; 2 Tim. 4:18; Heb. 13:21; 1 Pet. 5:11; 2 Pet. 3:18; Jude 25) and figure prominently in the Revelation (1:6; 4:8; 5:13; 7:12).

David W. Music

DRACHMA (Drăk´ mȧ) Greek term used to refer to silver coins (Luke 15:8-9). It was a Greek unit of silver coinage that, during the time of the NT, was considered equivalent to the Roman denarius. In 300 B.C. a sheep cost one drachma, but apparently by NT times the drachma was worth much less. See *Coins; Economic Life*.

DRAGNET Large fishing net equipped with a weighted bottom edge for touching ("dragging") the river or lake bottom and a top with wooden floats allowing the net to be spread across the water (Isa. 19:8). Such nets were normally let down from a boat and then drawn to shore by a crew positioned on the beach. In the case of a large catch, the net was hauled to shore by boat (John 21:6-8).

Habakkuk 1:14-17 pictures the residents of Judah as helpless fish before the Babylonian army, pictured as the fishermen. Here the fishing nets and hooks symbolize the Babylonian military machinery. The text is not evidence that ancient fishermen sacrificed to their nets or that the Babylonians sacrificed to their weapons of war. Rather the text points to the worship of military might.

Jesus compared the kingdom of God to a dragnet, containing both good and bad fish until the time of separation and judgment (Matt. 13:47).

DRAGON Term used by the KJV to translate two closely related Hebrew words (*tannim* and *tannin*). At times the terms appear to be interchangeable. Context indicates that the first term refers to a mammal inhabiting the desert (Isa. 13:22; 35:7; 43:20; Lam. 4:3). Most modern speech translations equate the animal with the jackal, though perhaps the wolf (REB) is intended. The second term has four possible uses: (1) "great sea monster" (KJV, "great whales") in the sense of a large sea creature (Gen. 1:21; Ps. 148:7), possibly a whale; this sense of *tannin* as created being may serve as a correction of sense 4; (2) a snake (Exod. 7:9-10,12; Deut. 32:33; Ps. 91:13); (3) a crocodile (Jer. 51:34; Ezek. 29:3; 32:3); here the beast is used as a symbol of Nebuchadnezzar of Babylon or the Egyptian Pharaoh; (4) a mythological sea monster symbolic of the forces of chaos and evil in opposition to God's creative and redemptive work (Ps. 74:12-14; Job 7:12; 26:12-13; Isa. 27:1; 51:9-10). Leviathan and Rehab are used as parallel terms.

In the NT Revelation develops sense 4, describing the dragon as a great, red monster with seven heads and ten horns. This dragon is clearly identified with Satan (the Devil) and is termed the deceiver and the accuser of the saints. As in the OT texts, the dragon is put under guard (Rev. 20:1-3; Job 7:12) and later released for final destruction (Rev. 20:7-10; Isa. 27:1).

DRAGON WELL Jerusalem landmark in the time of Nehemiah which can no longer be identified with certainty (Neh. 2:13). The water source is described as a well (KJV, NASB, NIV), a spring (REB, NRSV), or a fountain (TEV). The NIV takes the underlying Hebrew word as jackal rather than dragon. The Dragon Well has been identified with the Gihon spring, the main water source during the time of Hezekiah, the Siloam pool which was fed by the Gihon, the En-rogel spring located 210 meters south of the confluence of the Hinnom and Kidron valleys, or with a spring along the east side of the Tyropoeon Valley which has since dried up.

DRAWERS OF WATER Water carriers (Josh. 9:21,23,27). See *Occupations and Professions.*

DREAMS In the ancient Near East dreams were one of several ways people sought to see the future and to make decisions that would be beneficial to them. In some societies, people went to temples or holy places to sleep in order to have a dream that would show them the best decision to make.

The dreams of common people were important to them, but the dreams of kings and of holy men or women were important on a national or international scale. One of the results was that many of the nations surrounding Israel had religious figures skilled in the interpretation of dreams. These figures could be consulted at the highest level of government for important decisions. In such nations as Egypt and Assyria, these interpreters even developed "dream books" by which they could give interpretations according to the symbols of a dream.

Dreams were important in the OT, too. Israel was forbidden to use many of the divining practices of her neighbors, but over a dozen times God revealed something through a dream. When we recognize that night visions and dreams were not strictly distinguished, we can find many more times in the OT and NT that God used this method to communicate. In fact, prophecy and the dreaming of dreams were to be tested in the same way according to Deut. 13.

What Dreams Were Interpreted? Not every dream was thought to be from God. Not every dream was significant. Some could be wishful thinking (Ps. 126:1; Isa. 29:7-8). In times of need and especially when a person sought a word from God, dreams could be significant.

Not every dream needed to be interpreted. To note this we can distinguish three types of dreams. A simple "message dream" apparently did not need interpretation. For instance, Joseph, in Matt. 1 and 2, understood the dreams concerning Mary and Herod even though no mention is made of interpretation. A second type, the "simple symbolic dream," used symbols, but the symbolism was clear enough that the dreamer and others could understand it. The OT Joseph had this kind of dream in Gen. 37. Complex symbolic dreams, though, needed the interpretive skill of someone with experience or an unusual ability in interpretation. The dreams of Nebuchadnezzar described in Dan. 2 and 4 are good examples of this kind of dream. Even Daniel himself had dreams in which the symbolism was so complex that he had to seek divine interpretation (Dan. 8).

Were Dreams Ever Wrong or Wrongly Interpreted? Dreams were neither foolproof nor infallible. Both Jeremiah and Zechariah spoke against relying on dreams to express the revelation of

God. Dreams could come without being God's word (Jer. 23:28). Jeremiah lumped dreamers together with soothsayers, sorcerers, and false prophets (Jer. 27:9). He cautioned exiles in Babylon not to listen to dreamers and false prophets who told them that the exile would not be long (Jer. 29:8). Zechariah pointed people toward the Lord, apparently because they were relying on dreamers and others to give them the truth (Zech. 10:1-2). Thus, while God often used dreams to reveal His will, there is a warning, too, not to rely on this method to know the will of God. See *Inspiration of Scripture; Oracles; Prophecy, Prophets; Revelation of God.*

Albert F. Bean

DRESS See *Cloth, Clothing.*

DRESSER OF SYCAMORE TREES One of the occupations of the prophet Amos (Amos 7:14). The tending involved slitting the top of each piece of fruit to hasten its ripening and to produce a sweeter, more edible fruit. Fruit infested with insects might be discarded at this time as well. The significance of Amos' trade is twofold: (1) he was a prophet solely because of the call of God, not because of training in a prophetic school; and (2) contrary to the accusation of the priest Amaziah (7:12), Amos did not earn his living by prophesying.

DRIED GRAPES Raisins. Grapes were dried in clusters for a food that was easily stored and transported (1 Sam. 25:18; 30:12; 2 Sam. 16:1; 1 Chron. 12:40). Nazarites were prohibited from eating dried grapes (Num. 6:3).

DRINK Beverages. Water was the primary drink. It was drawn from cisterns (2 Sam. 17:18; Jer. 38:6) or from wells (Gen. 29:2; John 4:11). In times of drought it was necessary to buy water (Deut. 2:28; Lam. 5:4). Milk was also a common beverage though it was considered a food rather than a drink. Several types of wine were consumed. "New" or "sweet" wine was likely wine from the first drippings of juice before the grapes had been trodden. Some interpreters argue that new wine was unfermented. Some texts in which it is mentioned, however, allude to its intoxicating effects (Hos. 4:11; Acts 2:13). In a hot climate before the invention of refrigeration, it was not possible to keep wine many months past the harvest before fermentation began. Sour wine, perhaps vinegar mixed with oil, was a common drink of day laborers (Ruth 2:14; Luke 23:36). Wine was considered a luxury item which could both gladden the heart (Ps. 104:15) or cloud the mind (Isa. 28:7; Hos. 4:11). See *Milk; Water; Wine.*

DRINK OFFERING See *Sacrifice and Offering.*

DROMEDARY One-humped species of camel. See *Camel.*

DROPSY Edema, a disease with fluid retention and swelling. Dropsy is a symptom of disease of the heart, liver, kidneys, or brain. The condition involves the accumulation of water fluid in the body cavities or in the limbs. Thus the TEV speaks of a man whose arms and legs were swollen (Luke 14:2).

DROSS Either the refuse from impure metal which is separated by a process of smelting (Prov. 25:4; 26:23) or else the base (impure) metal before the smelting process. Litharge (lead monoxide) from which silver was to be extracted is perhaps meant at Isa. 1:22,25. The same sense is required if the reading dross is preferred over the emendation glaze (REB, NRSV, NIV) at Prov. 26:23. Dross is a symbol of impurity. The wicked are pictured as dross (Prov. 25:4; Ps. 119:119) that renders the whole of society impure. Both Isa. 1:22,25 and Ezek. 22:18-19 speak of silver turned to dross as a picture of Israel's lost righteousness.

DRUGS (Illegal Narcotics) Several biblical principles address the scourge which results from the use of illegal narcotics. The Bible's strong counsel against drunkenness (Prov. 20:1; 23:20-21,29-35; Isa. 28:1, 7-8; Hab. 2:15-16; Gal. 5:16, 21; Eph. 5:18) is clear indication that illegal narcotics, which adversely affect the mind and body to an even greater degree than does alcohol, should be stringently avoided. Like alcohol abuse, drug abuse destroys one's ability to live a reasonable life (Isa. 5:11-12).

The Bible recognizes the compelling reality of temptation to give in to peer pressure, abuse oneself, and shut out one's surroundings (Prov. 31:4-7; Isa. 56:12; 1 Cor. 10:13; 15:33). Peter speaks of the importance of maintaining an alert mind in the face of difficult circumstances (1 Pet. 1:13; 5:8; cp. 1 Thess. 5:6). Even on the cross Jesus refused the drugging effects of wine mixed with gall (Matt. 27:34).

Christians are commanded to honor God with their bodies, which the Apostle Paul aptly calls temples of the Holy Spirit (1 Cor. 6:19-20). The Bible teaches the value of self-control (Prov. 25:28; Gal. 5:23) as one means to withstand temptation (1 Cor. 10:13). Ultimately, it is the work of Christ which breaks the cycle of sin and death (Rom. 7:18–8:2). *Paul H. Wright*

DRUNKENNESS Result of consuming a quantity of alcohol; the outcome being the impairment of faculties. This impairment may be mild (deep sleep) to severe (dizziness, vomiting, hallucination, and death). The physical symptoms mentioned in Scripture are: staggering (Job 12:25; Ps. 107:27); wounds and beatings (Prov. 20:1; 23:29-35; Lam. 2:12); vomiting (Isa. 19:14; Jer. 25:27; 48:26); and hallucinations (Isa. 28:1-8; Prov. 23:33). The mental effects of alcohol mentioned in Scripture are a false sense of one's abilities and strengths (Isa. 28:11; Hos. 4:11). The spiritual effects of alcohol are the deadening of one's self to God and all religious thought (Isa. 5:11-12).

There are many cases of drunkenness in the OT. Among the better known cases of drunkenness are: Noah (Gen. 9:21), Lot (Gen. 19:33), Nabal (1 Sam. 25:36), Uriah the Hittite (2 Sam. 11:13), Elah king of Israel (1 Kings 16:9), and Ben-Hadad (1 Kings 20:16). Interestingly misfortune befalls each of these people either in their drunken stupor or shortly after they awake. Thus Scripture issues strong warnings against drunkenness (Lev. 10:9; Deut. 21:20; Prov. 24:29-35; 1 Cor. 5:11; Gal. 5:21; Eph. 5:18). The Scriptures often refer to drunkenness as a great social problem. Consequently in Proverbs the drunkard is depicted as one who spends his money to feed his habit, only to suffer ill health and misfortune at the hands of his fellowmen. In the Prophets the drunken rich often take advantage of the poor in society (Amos 4:1; 6:6; Isa. 5:11-12; 28:1-8; 56:11-12). The Prophets also point out the foolishness of drunkenness (Jer. 25:27; 48:26; 51:39,57; Hab. 2:15). Jeremiah uses the metaphor of spiritual drunkenness to indicate not a state of spiritual bliss or enthusiasm but of foolishness and idolatry (Jer. 25:27-33). In the NT the Lord explicitly warned against the use of alcohol (Luke 21:34). In Paul's letters there are numerous warnings against the indulgence of alcohol (1 Cor. 5:11; 6:10; Gal 5:21; Eph. 5:18). Likewise a person desiring the office of a bishop cannot be addicted to wine (1 Tim. 3:2-3; Tit. 1:7-8; 2:2-3). *Joe Cathey*

DRUSILLA (Drū sĭl´ là) Wife of Felix, the Roman governor of Judea who heard Paul's case. Drusilla was a Jew and listened to Paul's arguments with her husband (Acts 24:24). She was the youngest daughter of Herod Agrippa I. She had been engaged to Antiochus Ephiphanes of Commagene, but he refused to become a Jew. King Aziz of Emesa did agree to be circumcised, and they were married. Atomos, a magician from Cyprus, helped Felix win Drusilla away from her husband. Apparently, her son Agrippa died when Mount Vesuvius erupted in A.D. 79. She may have also died in this disaster. See *Herod*.

DUGONG See *Sea Cow*.

DUKE (KJV) See *Chief*.

DULCIMER Apparently a Greek word used to name a musical instrument in Dan. 3:10. Many think the bagpipes are meant here (NASB). NRSV translates "drum."

DUMAH (Dū´ măh) Place-name meaning "silence" or "permanent settlement." **1.** Son of Ishmael and the original ancestor of the Arabian tribe (Gen. 25:14) centered in the oases of Dumah, probably modern el-Gof, also called Dumat el-Gandel, meaning Dumah of the Rocks. Rulers in Dumah apparently led coalitions supported by Damascus and later by Babylon against Assyria between 740 and 700 B.C. Thus Assyria punished Dumah in 689 when they also defeated Babylon. Sennacherib conquered Dumah. The remainder of Assyrian history is filled with troubled relationships with Arabian vassals, particularly those around Dumah. Isaiah proclaimed an oracle against Dumah (Isa. 21:11). **2.** City of the tribe of Judah (Josh. 15:52). It is probably modern Khirbet ed-Dome about nine miles southwest of Hebron. It may be mentioned in the Amarna letters.

DUMBNESS See *Muteness*.

DUNG Excrement of man or beast. "Dung" translates several different Hebrew and Greek words. An ash heap or rubbish heap was used to convey the haunt of the destitute (1 Sam. 2:8; Luke 14:35).

The first mention of dung in the Bible is in connection with the sacrificial rites. The sacred law required that the dung, along with other parts of the animal, should not be burned on the altar but should be burned outside the camp (Exod. 29:14; Lev. 4:11-12).

A major disgrace for a Jew was to have one's carcass treated as dung (2 Kings 9:37). Dung has been used as fertilizer for centuries. It is recorded in Luke 13:8 and Isa. 25:10 that the people of Palestine used it for that purpose. Dry dung was and is often used as fuel (Ezek. 4:12-15). Animal dung was used as fuel when it was mixed with straw and dried to a suitable state for heating the simple bread ovens.

Paul used a powerful metaphor with the word "dung" when he made a comparison between his personal knowledge of Christ and those who did not know Christ (Phil. 3:8). The word is used also in Scripture to indicate symbolically the degradation to which a person or a nation might fall (2 Kings 9:37; Jer. 8:2).

Gary Bonner

DUNG GATE Jerusalem landmark; one of the 11 gates in the time of Nehemiah (Neh. 2:13; 3:13-14; 12:31). Located at the southwest corner of the wall, the gate was used for the disposal of garbage, rubbish, and dung that was dumped into the Hinnom Valley below the city. Referred to as the Refuse Gate by NASB, and Rubbish Gate by TEV.

DUNGEON See *Prison, Prisoners.*

DURA (Dū´ rä) Akkadian place-name meaning "circuit wall." Plain in Babylonia where King Nebuchadnezzar set up a mammoth golden image of a god or of himself (Dan. 3:1). The common place-name does not lend itself to an exact location.

DUST Loose earth, used both literally and figuratively. Dust is used in figures of speech for a multitude (Gen. 13:16; Num. 23:10; Isa. 29:5) or for an abundance (of flesh, Ps. 78:27; of silver, Job 27:16; of blood, Zeph. 1:17). Dust is used as a metaphor for death, the grave, or Sheol (Job 10:9; Eccles. 12:7; Dan. 12:2). Dust on a balance is a picture of something insignificant (Isa. 40:15). Human lowliness in relationship with God as well as humanity's close relationship with the rest of creation is expressed in the making of persons from dust (Gen. 2:7; Job 4:19; Ps.

104:29). To return to dust is to die (Gen. 3:19; Job 10:9; 17:16). To place dust on one's head was a sign of mourning (Lam. 2:10; Ezek. 27:30; Rev. 18:19). This act was sometimes accomplished by rolling in dust (Mic. 1:10). Dust on the head may have been a sign of defeat and shame as well as mourning in Josh. 7:6. To throw dust was a sign of contempt (2 Sam. 16:13), though to throw it in the air may have been a demand for justice (Acts 22:23).

To defile a crown in dust (Ps. 89:39) was to dishonor the office of king. To eat or lick dust (Gen. 3:14; Ps. 72:9; Isa. 65:25; Lam. 3:29; Mic. 7:17) was to suffer humiliation and powerlessness before an enemy. To lay one's horn (glory) in the dust was to experience humiliation and loss of standing (Job 16:15). To lay a soul in the dust (Pss. 7:5; 22:15) is to kill. To make something dust (Deut. 9:21; 2 Kings 13:7) is to destroy it completely. To raise from the dust (1 Sam. 2:8) is to rescue or exalt. To sit in the dust (Isa. 47:1) is to suffer humiliation.

For Jews to shake dust off their feet was a sign that Gentile territory was unclean. In the NT this action indicates that those who have rejected the gospel have made themselves as Gentiles and must face the judgment of God (Matt. 10:14-15; Acts 13:51).

Chris Church

The Dung Gate in old Jerusalem.

DWARF Person of abnormally small size, especially one with abnormal body proportions. The Hebrew word translated as dwarf by most English translations of Lev. 21:20 is used in Gen. 41:3,23 to describe the emaciated cows and shriveled heads of grain. Some thus understand the word to mean lean or emaciated. The early Greek and Latin versions understood the word to mean a type of eye disorder (cp. REB). Though denied the privilege of making the offering to God, priests with such a blemish were permitted to eat the holy food with other priests and Levites.

DWELLING Place where someone lives, in biblical times either a tent (Gen. 25:27), house (2 Sam. 7:2), or the territory in which one lives (Gen. 36:40,43). The OT repeatedly promises that those who keep the covenant will dwell in safety (Lev. 25:18-19; Zech. 2:10-11).

References to the dwelling place of God highlight both the immanence and transcendence of God. References which focus on God's drawing near to speak, listen, and fellowship include the following references to God's dwelling place: in the bush at Sinai (Deut. 33:16); in the tabernacle (Exod. 25:8; 29:45-46; 2 Sam. 7:2); at Shiloh (Ps. 78:60); in the land of Israel (Num. 35:34); in the temple (Pss. 26:8; 43:3; 135:2; Matt. 23:21); on Mount Zion (Pss. 9:11; 20:2; 132:14); and in Jerusalem (Pss. 76:2; 135:21; Ezra 7:15). The OT idea of God's dwelling with His people (Ezek. 37:27) is developed in a variety of ways in the NT.

The Word become flesh dwelt among humankind (John 1:14). The church is the dwelling place of God (Eph. 2:22). Christ dwells in believers' hearts (Eph. 3:17). Believers are the temple of God (1 Cor. 3:16) and their bodies the temple of His Holy Spirit (6:19). The NT closes with an echo of Ezekiel's hope of God's dwelling with His people in Rev. 21:3.

References focusing on the transcendency of God include those in which God is said to dwell in clouds and thick darkness (1 Kings 8:12), in a high and holy place (Isa. 57:15), or in light (1 Tim, 6:16). Though heaven is spoken of as God's dwelling (1 Kings 8:30,39,43,49), even heaven cannot contain God (1 Kings 8:27).

Dwelling is used figuratively for the body. To dwell in a house of clay (Job 4:19) is to possess a mortal body. The heavenly dwelling of 2 Cor. 5:2 is the resurrection body.   *Chris Church*

DYEING Process of coloring materials. The dying process is not mentioned in Scripture, though dyed material is. Blue, purple, and scarlet thread was used in the making of the tabernacle curtains (Exod. 25:4; 36:8,35,37). Dyed material was an important part of the spoils of war (Judg. 5:30). The work of the guild of linen workers (1 Chron. 4:21) may have included dyeing thread. Solomon requested the King Hiram of Tyre send him someone skilled in dyeing purple, blue, and crimson for the temple curtains (2 Chron. 2:7; 3:14). Job 38:14 as emended by some modern translators (NRSV) speaks of the dawn's "dyeing" the sky (most refer to "clay"). In the NT, Lydia was a seller of purple dyed goods (Acts 16:14).

The dyeing process involved soaking the material to be dyed in vats of dye then drying it. This process was repeated until the dyed material was the desired color. The process was concluded by soaking it in a fixing agent that rendered the cloth colorfast. Blue dye was made from the rind of pomegranates, crimson from grubs or worms that fed on oaks, and purple from the shell of the murex shellfish. Since this shellfish was found only in the vicinity of Acre on the Phoenician coast and since only a small amount of a dye material could be extracted from each shell, this dye was especially valued. Archeological evidence suggests that in Palestine of biblical times thread was dyed rather than whole cloth. See *Cloth, Clothing.*

DYSENTERY Disease characterized by diarrhea, painful bowel spasms, and ulceration and infection of the bowels resulting in blood and pus in the excreta. Modern speech translations of Acts 28:8 render the "bloody flux" of the KJV as dysentery. Many interpreters also understand the chronic bowel disease which afflicted King Jehoram (2 Chron. 21:15,18-19) as dysentery. The nontechnical language of the account does not permit a precise diagnosis excluding other diseases of the bowels such as chronic diarrhea or colitis. There is some disagreement on the nature of the symptoms given in 2 Chron. 21:15. The REB together with many commentators understand the phrase usually rendered his bowels came out as a reference to a prolapsed bowel, that is, his bowel slipped from its normal position. Others understand the text to refer to excretion of the bowel itself.

E

The Temple of Luxor, Egypt, at night.

EAGLE The term "eagle" refers to several large birds of prey active in the daytime rather than at night. The Hebrew term translated "eagle" (*nesher*) also sometimes is translated "vulture." The eagle, the largest flying bird of Palestine, may reach a wingspread of eight feet or more. The Palestinian eagle builds great nests of sticks on rocky crags in the mountains (Job 39:27-28; Jer. 49:16). As one of the most majestic birds, it occupies a prominent role in the Bible. The eagle appears in the lists of unclean birds (Lev. 11:13; Deut. 14:12). OT writers noted the eagle's swift movement (Deut. 28:49; 2 Sam. 1:23; Jer. 4:13), the sweep and power of its flight (Prov. 23:5; Isa. 40:31), and the eagle's concern for its young (Exod. 19:4; Deut. 32:11).

In the ancient world the eagle or vulture often was associated with deity. The prophets and apocalyptists chose this bird to play a figurative or symbolic role in their writings (Ezek. 1:10; 10:14; Dan. 7:4; Rev. 4:7; 8:13).

In Exod. 19:4 and Deut. 32:11 the eagle is used figuratively of God's protection and care. In these passages God is pictured as a loving parent who redeems and protects His people even as the parent eagle cares for its young.

Janice Meier

EAR Physical organ of hearing. In the OT "ears" are involved in several rites. The right ear of a priest was consecrated with blood (Exod. 29:20; Lev. 8:24). The right ear of a leper was also sprinkled with blood and oil as part of being cleansed (Lev. 14:14,17). If a slave volunteered to serve a master for life, the slave's ear was pierced with an awl into the master's doorpost (Exod. 21:6; Deut. 15:17).

The ears appear in a variety of expressions in both Testaments. To speak to someone's ears was to speak to them or to speak in their hearing (Gen. 44:18; 50:4). To incline the ear was to listen (2 Kings 19:16) or even to obey (Jer. 11:8). To give ear was to pay careful attention (Job 32:11). To turn the ears toward wisdom (Prov. 2:2) was to desire understanding. Dull, heavy, closed, or uncircumcised ears expressed inattentiveness and disobedience (Isa. 6:10; Jer. 6:10; Acts 7:51). To stop the ears was to refuse to listen (Acts 7:57). Open ears were obedient, hearing ears. Open ears are a gift of God (Ps. 40:6) who sometimes uses adversity to open deaf ears (Job 36:15). To awake the ears was to make someone teachable (Isa. 50:4). To uncover or open the ear was to reveal something (Isa. 50:5). To let words sink into one's ears was to understand thoroughly (Luke 9:44). Sometimes the functions of the mind were attributed to the ear. Thus the ear exercised judgment (Job 12:11) and understanding (13:1).

EARLY RAIN See *Rain*.

EARNEST Sincerity and intensity of purpose or a deposit paid to secure a purchase. "Earnest" does not relate directly to any Hebrew or Greek word, but represents the attempts of translators to relay the sense of several grammatical constructions and words. For instance, KJV uses "earnest" or "earnestly" 24 different times as the translation of 13 different words, phrases, or constructions in the original languages. Some expressions have important theological significance. The fallen creation waits earnestly for redemption (Rom. 8:19). The Corinthians' earnest desire for Paul's welfare comforted him (2 Cor. 7:7). Believers should give earnest heed to Christian teachings (Heb. 2:1). In the agony of the cross Christ prayed earnestly (Luke 22:44). Paul urged the Corinthians to "earnestly desire the greater (spiritual) gifts" (1 Cor. 12:31 NASB). Christians earnestly await the new resurrection body (2 Cor. 5:2). Meanwhile, they earnestly contend for the faith (Jude 3).

The Greek *arrabon* is a first payment on a purchase that obligates the purchaser to make further payments. A payment made in advance, it secures legal claim to an article or validates a sales contract before the full price is paid. The concept is a Semitic one with the word being adopted into Greek. The related Hebrew term appears in Gen. 38:17, where Judah promised to send Tamar a young goat and she asked for a pledge to hold until she received the promised animal. God has given believers the Holy Spirit in their hearts as an earnest or pledge of the salvation to come (2 Cor. 1:22; 5:5; Eph. 1:14). Daily relationship with the Spirit brings total confidence that God will complete His plan and the believer will share His gift of eternal life.

EARRINGS See *Jewels, Jewelry*.

EARS OF GRAIN Fruit-bearing spike of a cereal such as maize that included both seed and protective structures. American corn was unknown in the ancient Near East. It is more proper to speak of the common grains of that area, namely, wheat and barley, as having heads. The law permitted passersby to handpick heads of grain from a neighbor's field (Deut. 23:25).

EARTH, LAND Various terms are translated as "earth" or "land" in the OT. The primary term *erets* is often distinguished from the other major term *adamah* by denoting a geographical or political territory (Gen. 11:28, "the land of his birth"; Gen. 13:10, "the land of Egypt"; Gen. 36:43 "the land of their own possession"), while both terms may denote the ground's surface, the soil that supports vegetation and all life (Gen. 1:11-12, *erets*; Deut. 26:2, *adamah*; Gen. 2:5-6, both). When not clearly specified by a modifier, it is often difficult to decide whether *erets* refers to the whole earth or just a part of it. However, *adamah* usually does not refer to the whole earth (but see for example Gen. 12:3 and 28:14, "all the families of the earth [*adamah*]" NASB). Other related terms include *yabbashah* (Gen. 1:10: "God called the dry land [*yabbashah*] earth" [*erets*]), *sadeh* ("field," Gen. 2:5), and *migrash* ("pastureland," Lev. 25:34). In the Septuagint and NT, *ge* is the usual equivalent of *erets*, with *oikoumene* occasionally rendered "inhabited earth." Of the various senses associated with earth and land, the earth and the land of Israel stand out most prominently in biblical theology.

The earth is intimately linked with both God and humanity. The phrase "heaven and earth" refers to the totality of the created order (Gen. 1:1; 2:4). As Creator, Yahweh is the universal God, Sovereign, and Owner of heaven and earth (Gen. 14:19; 24:3; Exod. 9:14-16,29; 19:5; Deut. 4:39; Josh. 3:11; Ps. 24:1; Isa. 48:13). He is also Judge of the whole earth (Gen. 18:25; 1 Sam. 2:10; Isa. 24) and its Sustainer (Ps. 104:10-21, 27-30). At the same time, God transcends His creation (Isa. 40:12,22; 66:1-2; cp. 1 Kings 8:27; 2 Chron. 2:6).

The earth is humankind's God-given dwelling (Gen. 1:28-29; 9:1-3; Ps. 115:16). Man [*adam*] was formed out of the dust of the ground (*adamah*; Gen. 2:7) to serve (*'bd*) and keep (*shmr*) it (Gen. 2:15), and thus the destiny of humankind and the earth are bound together. The ground (*adamah*) was cursed on account of Adam and Eve's rebellion (Gen. 3:17-19). When the earth became corrupt in the sight of God because of the wickedness of humankind, God sent a flood to destroy the earth (Gen. 6; 9:11; cp. Isa. 24:5-6). At the revelation of the sons of

God (the redemption of our bodies at the final resurrection), creation will also be freed from the bondage of corruption (Rom. 8:19-23), and there will be a "new heavens and a new earth" (Isa. 65:17; 2 Pet. 3:13; Rev. 21:1).

With the Abrahamic covenant God narrowed the focal point of His redemptive mission (the Noahic covenant confirmed a virtual new creation—Gen. 8:17; 9:7—but did not stop human rebellion, epitomized at Babel). Nevertheless, the promise of a specific land, Canaan, to Abraham and his descendants (Gen. 12:7; 13:15,17; 15:7; 17:8; 26:3-4; 35:12; 48:4; 50:24) is accompanied by the promise of blessing to "all the families of the earth" (Gen. 12:3; 28:14; "all the nations of the earth" in 22:18 and 26:4). Israel was to obey Yahweh in its land the way humankind should on the earth but failed to do. The good land was given to Israel as a possession (Deut. 9:6), providing abundance ("land flowing with milk and honey," e.g., Exod. 3:8; Num. 13:27; cp. Deut. 8:7-9; 11:10-12) and rest from wandering (Josh. 1:13; cp. Deut. 12:9).

In the history of Israel, blessings and curses on the land reflected Israel's obedience to or rebellion against Yahweh in the land. The prophets employed imagery of the land mourning as a result of people's evil deeds (Hos. 4:1-3; Jer. 12:4; 23:10; Amos 1:2). Israel was warned that the land would vomit them out the way it had vomited out the Canaanites if they followed the Canaanites in their wickedness (Lev. 18:25-28). The covenant curses, which culminated in removal from the land and scattering among the nations for their disobedience (Lev. 26:32-39; Deut. 28:63-65), came first upon the Northern Kingdom (2 Kings 17:6-23; Amos 7:11) and then the Southern Kingdom of Judah (2 Kings 23:26-27; Jer. 7:15). Nevertheless, Yahweh promised a restoration to the land (e.g., Isa. 14:1; 27:12-13; Jer. 16:15; 23:8; Ezek. 28:25; Amos 9:15; Zeph. 3:10), which partially occurred under Zerubbabel, Ezra, and Nehemiah.

In the NT proclamation is focused on the kingdom of God and Jesus Christ as its embodiment (references to the promised land are rare: e.g., Acts 7:3-7; 13:17-19; Heb. 11:9). Some argue that land is not a NT concern. More likely, the symbol of land is universalized in light of Christ. Abraham and his descendants will inherit the world (Rom. 4:13; cp. Matt. 5:5 where "the earth" is apparently parallel with "the kingdom of heaven," Matt. 5:3,10 and 25:34,46 where

E

the inherited kingdom is the context for entrance into eternal life). Using the pattern of an exodus followed by possession of the land, the Father "who has enabled you to share in the saints' inheritance in the light. He has rescued us from the dominion of darkness and transferred us into the kingdom of the Son He loves" (Col. 1:12-13 HCSB; cp. 1 Pet. 1:3-5). Abraham and other OT believers were seeking after and longing for a better homeland, a heavenly one (Heb. 11:13-16). The redemption of God's people will include the redemption of all creation as their inheritance (Rom. 8:14-25). In the meantime, God's people are to respond with careful obedience to God's grace, so as to enter into God's rest (Heb. 4:1-11).

Will the Jews enjoy a restoration to their land, perhaps in a future millennium? One's answer depends in part on one's interpretation of OT prophecy and stance on eschatology (for example, whether Rev. 20 refers to a future literal millennium and whether the OT prophecies will be fulfilled in a more literal fashion for the Jews then). The NT's emphasis, however, is on the inauguration of the kingdom of God at Christ's first coming and its consummation when Christ returns. In the new heaven and new earth, where God dwells in harmony with His people, God's creation and redemption of humankind and the earth and His promise of land and His people's entrance into blessing, rest, and eternal life will reach their final goal (Rev. 21–22). *Randall K. J. Tan*

EARTHQUAKE Shaking or trembling of the earth due to volcanic activity or, more often, the shifting of the earth's crust. Severe earthquakes produce such side effects as loud rumblings (Ezek. 3:12-13 RSV), openings in the earth's crust (Num. 16:32) and fires (Rev. 8:5). Palestine has two to three major quakes per century and two to six minor shocks per year. The major quake centers in Palestine are Upper Galilee, near the biblical town of Shechem (Nablus) and near Lydda on the western edge of the Judean mountains. Secondary quake centers are located in the Jordan Valley at Jericho and Tiberias.

The Bible mentions an earthquake during the reign of Uzziah (Amos 1:1; Zech. 14:5). The oracles of Amos are dated two years before this earthquake. The precise year of this quake has not been settled to everyone's satisfaction. Most would view the period between 767 and 742 B.C. as the likely dates for the earthquake.

Many times God's judgment or visitation is described using the imagery of an earthquake (Ps. 18:7; Isa. 29:6; Nah. 1:5; Rev. 6:12; 8:5; 11:13; 16:18) and is often seen as a sign of the end of time (Matt. 24:7,29). Many times an earthquake is a sign of God's presence or of God's revelation of Himself (1 Kings 19:11-12; Ps. 29:8; Ezek. 38:19-20; Joel 2:10; 3:16; Acts 4:31; Rev. 11:19). At times the whole universe is described as being shaken by God (Isa. 13:13; 24:17-20; Joel 3:16; Hag. 2:6-7; Matt. 24:29; Heb. 12:26-27; Rev. 6:12; 8:5).

Even though earthquakes were usually seen as things to escape (Isa. 2:19,21), they could be used by God for good purposes (Acts 16:26). The earth quaked in revulsion at the death of Jesus (Matt. 27:51-54), and the earth quaked to move the stone from Jesus' tomb (Matt. 28:2). Those who love God and are faithful to Him have no need to fear the trembling of the earth (Ps. 46:2-3). *Phil Logan*

EAST See *Directions.*

EAST COUNTRY Designation for territories lying in the direction of the rising sun. At Gen. 25:6 the reference signifies desert lands more than direction. At 1 Kings 4:30 the wisdom of the East, either of Mesopotamia or of the desert dwelling Arabs, together with the wisdom of Egypt signifies all wisdom. The East Country of Ezek. 47:8 lies in the direction of the Dead Sea. The East Country and West Country of Zech. 8:7 refer to the whole world.

EAST GATE This designation refers to three different gates. **1.** KJV refers to the East Gate of Jerusalem as leading to the Hinnom Valley (Jer. 19:2). This valley lies to the south of the city rather than the east. Modern speech translations render this phrase "Potsherd Gate." This gate may be identified with the Valley Gate (2 Chron. 26:9; Neh. 2:13,15; 3:13) or perhaps to the Refuse or Dung Gate (Neh. 2:13; 3:13-14; 12:31) located 1,000 cubits away. **2.** The East Gate of the outer court of the temple. Since the temple faced east, this gate was the main entrance to the temple complex (Ezek. 47:1). Levites in charge of the East Gate of Solomon's temple had responsibility for the free-will offerings (2 Chron. 31:14). In a vision Ezekiel saw the glory of the Lord depart through the East Gate before the destruction of the city (Ezek. 10:19). His vision of the new temple included the return of God's glory through the same gate (Ezek. 43:1-2). God's use of this gate rendered it holy. It was to remain closed. Only the prince (messianic king) was allowed to enter it (Ezek. 44:1-3). **3.** The East Gate of the inner court of the temple. This gate was closed on the six working days but open on the Sabbath (Ezek. 46:1).

EAST SEA Ezekiel's expression for the Dead Sea (Ezek. 47:18). See *Dead Sea.*

EAST WIND See *Wind.*

EASTER The special celebration of the resurrection at Easter is the oldest Christian festival, except for the weekly Sunday celebration. Although the exact date was in dispute and the specific observances of the festival developed over the centuries, it is clear that Easter had special significance to the early generations of Christians. Since Christ's passion and resurrection occurred at the time of the Jewish Passover, the first Jewish Christians probably transformed their Passover observance into a celebration of the central events of their new faith. In the early centuries the annual observance was called the *pascha,* the Greek word for Passover, and focused on Christ as the paschal Lamb.

Although the NT does not give any account of a special observance of Easter and evidence from before A.D. 200 is scarce, the celebrations were probably well established in most churches by A.D. 100. The earliest observance probably consisted of a vigil beginning on Saturday evening and ending on Sunday morning and included remembrance of Christ's crucifixion as well as the resurrection. Evidence from shortly after A.D. 200 shows that the climax of the vigil was the baptism of new Christians and the celebration of the Lord's Supper. By about A.D. 300 most churches divided the original observance, devoting Good Friday to the crucifixion and Easter Sunday to the resurrection. See *Church Year.* *Fred A. Grissom*

EATING See *Cooking; Food.*

EBAL (Ē´ băl) Personal name and place-name possibly meaning "bare." **1.** Grandson of Seir and son of clan leader Shobal among the Horite descendants living in Edom (Gen. 36:23). **2.** Son

of Joktan in line of Shem (1 Chron. 1:22). He is called Obal in Gen. 10:28 through a scribal copying change. **3.** Mountain near Shechem on which Moses set up the curse for the covenant ceremony (Deut. 11:29; 27:13). An altar was also on Ebal (Deut. 27:4-5). Ebal rises 3,100 feet with its stark rock, bare of vegetation, giving the appearance of curse. On the north of Shechem, it stands opposed to the fruitful Mount Gerizim, the mount of blessing to the south. Joshua carried out the covenant ceremony on Ebal and Gerizim (Josh. 8:30-35), building an altar on Ebal. Later the Samaritans built their temple on Mount Ebal (cp. John 4:20). See *Gerizim and Ebal.*

EBED (Ē´ běd) Personal name meaning "servant." **1.** Father of Gaal, who led revolt in Shechem against Abimelech (Judg. 9:26-40). See *Abimelech; Gaal.* **2.** Clan leader who returned from exile under Ezra (Ezra 8:6).

EBED-MELECH (Ē bĕd-mē´ lĕk) Personal name meaning "servant of the king." An Ethiopian eunuch in the service of King Zedekiah of Judah (Jer. 38:7). When Jeremiah was imprisoned in a cistern used as a dungeon, Ebed-melech was responsible for the prophet's rescue. As a result of his faith in the Lord, he received the promise recorded in Jer. 39:15-18.

EBENEZER (Ĕb ĕn ē´ zĕr) Place-name meaning "stone of help." The name of a site near Aphek where the Israelites camped before they fought in battle against the Philistines (1 Sam. 4:1). During the second of two engagements in the area, the Philistines captured the ark of the covenant. Later, after the recovery of the ark and a decisive Israelite victory over the Philistines, Samuel erected a monument to which he gave the name Eben-ezer.

EBER (Ē´ bĕr) Personal name meaning "the opposite side." **1.** The ancestor of Abraham and the Hebrew people, and a descendant of Shem (Gen. 10:21-25; 11:14-17). Numbers 24:24 apparently refers to him as the original ancestor of a people associated with the Assyrians and threatened by Balaam with destruction by Kittim. Precisely who was meant at this point is not known. **2.** A member of the tribe of Gad, called Heber by KJV (1 Chron. 5:13). The name entered Israel's record about 750 B.C. (v. 17). **3.** Clan leader in tribe of Benjamin (1 Chron.

E

8:12). **4.** Another clan leader of Benjamin (1 Chron. 8:22). **5.** Head of priestly family of Amok (Neh. 12:20) in days of Jehoiakim (609–597 B.C.).

EBEZ (Ē′ bĕz) Spelling of Abez in modern translations. See *Abez.*

EBIASAPH (ə bī′ à săph) Personal name meaning "my father has collected or taken in." A Levite descended from Kohath (1 Chron. 6:23). The same person may be mentioned in verse 37, but the precise relationship of these family lists is uncertain with one or both possibly incomplete. He and his family kept the gate of the tabernacle (1 Chron. 9:19). The Abiasaph of Exod. 6:24 is apparently the same person. See *Abiasaph.*

EBLA (Ĕb′ là) Major ancient site located in Syria about 40 miles south of Aleppo. Covering about 140 acres, the mound is known today as Tell Mardikh. Excavations have been conducted since 1964 by an Italian team headed by P. Matthiae. The discovery of over 17,000 clay tablets in the mid-1970s revealed a major Syrian civilization in the mid-third millennium and brought the site worldwide prominence by the late 1970s.

Though few of these tablets are published yet, they appear to date from about 2500 B.C. Most were discovered in the two rooms of Palace G in fallen debris, but in a way that allowed for reconstructing the original shelving. They are written in a cuneiform script similar to that used in Mesopotamia. Sumerian was used on a limited scale as well as a new language that has come to be called Eblaite. The later language was correctly assumed to be Semitic so that decipherment was almost immediate. Nevertheless, the complexity of reading the cuneiform signs has created significantly different readings, with attending controversies. At least four categories of texts are known: (1) administrative texts relating to the palace make up the majority (about 80%), (2) lexical texts for the scribes, (3) literary and religious texts, including accounts of creation and a flood, and (4) letters and decrees.

Many early attempts to draw connections between Ebla and the Bible have not proven to be convincing. The term *Ebla* never occurs in the Bible, and no biblical personalities or events have yet been identified in the Ebla tablets. Some biblical personal names such as Ishmael have been attested at Ebla; but since they can be attested elsewhere in the ancient Near East, this has no special significance. Claims that the Ebla tablets mention biblical cities such as Sodom, Gomorrah, Jerusalem, and Hazor have not been substantiated. Efforts to identify the Israelite God Yahweh with the *-ya* elements of Eblaite personal names have not been compelling because these *-ya* elements can frequently occur in both Semitic and non-Semitic languages.

On the other hand, valuable general information can be gleaned from Ebla for the study of the Bible. Ebla was a major religious center, and over 500 gods are mentioned in the texts. The chief god was Dagon, a vegetation deity associated in the Bible with the Philistines (1 Sam. 5:2). Other gods include Baal, the Canaanite god of fertility, and Kamish (the biblical Chemosh), god of the Moabites (Judg. 11:24). In addition, there is reference to "the god of my father" (cp. Gen. 43:23). Some similarities between prophets at Ebla and Mari can be drawn with Israelite prophets, especially their call by the deity and their role as messengers of the deity to the people.

Actually, contacts between Ebla and the Bible are by necessity limited for three reasons: (1) The illumination of the Bible using other ancient Near Eastern civilizations is usually general cultural background rather than specific and direct connection. (2) A more specific limitation in this case is that the Elba tablets are generally too early to have specific bearing on the OT. (3) Finally, the study of Ebla is in its infancy with very few texts already published. As more texts are published, we can expect additional information to illuminate not only the Bible but the rest of the ancient Near East as well.

James C. Moyer

EBONY See *Plants.*

EBRON (Ē′ brŏn) City in territory of Asher (Josh. 19:28), spelled Hebron in KJV. Several manuscripts in Josh. 19:28 plus the lists in Josh. 21:30; 1 Chron. 6:74 have Abdon. See *Abdon.*

EBRONAH (ə brō′ năh) (KJV) See *Abronah.*

ECBATANA (Ĕc′ bă tà nà) Modern translation spelling of Achmetha. See *Achmetha.*

ECCLESIASTES, BOOK OF The English title, Ecclesiastes, was derived from the Greek Septuagint's translation of the Hebrew, *Qohelet* (1:1-2,12; 7:27; 12:8-10). Both Qohelet and Ecclesiastes denote one who presides over an assembly, that is, a preacher or teacher.

Authorship and Date Traditionally Solomon has been identified as the author of Ecclesiastes, but in modern times many, including a large number of conservative scholars, have followed Martin Luther's lead in assigning the book to the postexilic period (usually between ca. 300–200 B.C.). Scholars who espouse the latter view generally consider the book to be a unified composition of one author while recognizing some editorial work, particularly in the prologue and epilogue.

Those who accept the late date point out that the name of Solomon is nowhere expressly mentioned as the author. More serious is the charge that Aramaisms, two apparently Persian words, parallels to Mishnaic Hebrew, and other signs of late Hebrew demand a postexilic date. Sometimes it is also alleged that the author shows evidence of dependence on Greek thought and that the book reflects late theology.

In defense of the traditional view, the following evidence has been cited. (1) Both Christian and Jewish tradition (e.g., Talmud) named Solomon as the author. (2) While the text does not state specifically that Solomon wrote the book, in 1:1 the author identifies himself as the "son of David, king in Jerusalem," and in 1:12 he adds that he was "king over Israel in Jerusalem." Only one son of David, Solomon, ruled over the United Kingdom of Israel (excepting Rehoboam whose brief reign over the 12 tribes and weak character would hardly satisfy the requirements of the text). References in the book to the author's unrivaled wisdom (1:16), opportunities for pleasure (2:3), extensive building programs (2:4-6), and unequaled wealth (2:7-8) all point to Solomon. Like Solomon the writer also penned many proverbs (12:9). Those who deny Solomonic authorship generally respond that Solomon is merely the central character of the book or that the writer is putting his words into Solomon's mouth. (3) Many recent examinations of the language of Ecclesiastes have also supported a pre-exilic date of composition. The amount of Aramaic influence in the book has been greatly exaggerated. For example, a recent study concludes that there are only seven terms of Aramaic origin in the book, four of which are attested elsewhere in early biblical Hebrew. Con-

cerning the Persian words, one is questionable (*pardes*) and the other (*pitgam*) may have entered the Hebrew language early. Various other studies have indicated no grounds for asserting Mishnaic Hebrew influence and have suggested that supposed late linguistic forms are actually early Canaanite-Phoenician in nature. (4) Evidence for dependence on Greek thought is lacking as the vast majority of scholars recognize. Moreover, if Ecclesiastes was written in the third century B.C.—the heart of the Greek Empire—we would expect significant Greek influence on the language of the book. (5) Late theology is not demonstrable. (6) Numerous affinities exist between Proverbs and Ecclesiastes.

Whether the author was Solomon or another, based on the many admonitions in the book that reflect the experiences of the elderly, we may assume that he was an old man who felt death was imminent.

Canon Ecclesiastes was included in the Septuagint (third century B.C.), and Ben Sira (Ecclesiasticus) knew and used the book (ca. 190 to 180 B.C.). Qumran fragments of Ecclesiastes confirm its canonical status in the mid-second century B.C. While no quotations exist, passages in the NT seem to refer to Ecclesiastes (e.g., Rom. 8:20; James 4:14). Josephus and early Christian writers like Melito of Sardis, Epiphanium, Origen, and Jerome allude to the book.

In the English Bible, Ecclesiastes is placed with the books of poetry following the order in the Greek Septuagint. Yet in the Hebrew Bible it is included in the *Hagiographa* or *Writings*, specifically the section of the *Hagiographa* referred to as the *Megilloth*. Five scrolls are included there—Ruth, Song of Songs, Ecclesiastes, Lamentations, and Esther. These books are diverse in content but have one thing in common. They were each read publicly at one of the great annual Jewish festivals: the book of Ruth at the Feast of Weeks (Pentecost), the Song of Songs at the Passover festival, Ecclesiastes at the Feast of Tabernacles, Lamentations at the commemoration of the destruction of Jerusalem in 586 B.C. (the ninth of Ab), and the book of Esther at the Purim festival. Doubtless Ecclesiastes was read at the Feast of Tabernacles, probably Israel's most joyous feast, because of the book's many exhortations to enjoy the life that God has given (2:24-25; 3:13; 5:18-20; 8:15; 9:9).

E

Text The text of Ecclesiastes is well preserved, and disputed passages are rare. Three manuscripts of Ecclesiastes (dating to the second century B.C.) were recovered at Qumran. These contain part of 5:13-17, substantial portions of 6:3-8, and five words from 7:7-9. Besides orthographic (spelling) differences, variants from the Masoretic Text are few and insignificant.

Type of Literature Ecclesiastes, Job, and Proverbs are generally classified as the OT wisdom books. Proverbs deals with practical (didactic) wisdom, but Ecclesiastes and Job are more philosophical in nature. Job tackles the problem of why the righteous suffer, while Ecclesiastes examines the question of the meaning of life. Much of Ecclesiastes was written in poetical form as may be readily observed from a modern translation of the Bible. Hebrew poetry is characterized by parallelism—primarily synonymous or repetition, (1:9a,18; 3:1), synthetic or development of a thought (1:3; 2:13), and antithetic or contrast (1:4; 7:26b; 10:12).

Theme Probably no biblical book is so dominated by one leading theme as is Ecclesiastes. In 1:2 the author declares that "everything is meaningless" (NIV) or better, "vanity" (KJV, NRSV, NASB, NKJV, ASV). The Hebrew word translated "meaningless" or "vanity" is *hebel* (literally, "breath"), the key word in the book. Here it occurs 38 times, roughly half of its appearances in the OT. In Ecclesiastes *hebel* primarily seems to denote items (approximately two dozen) that are fleeting as breath (6:12; 7:15; 9:9; 11:10), senseless (4:7-8; 5:7, 10; 7:6), or like breath have no substance or lasting value (2:1,11). At first glance the declaration that "all is vanity" (1:2) seems negative, but the phrase in the following verse (1:3), "under the sun" (only in Ecclesiastes in the Bible, 29 times), clarifies the author's perspective. The meaning is that earthly existence is brief and mere worldly accomplishments are of no eternal worth. The author developed this theme using what may be labeled the "quest motif." His search covered all the main areas of human existence: the city, fields, gardens, the temple, a house, a bedroom, courts of justice, seats of power, and even warfare. He examined wealth, power, religion, relationships, work, and play.

Interpretation Of all the books in the Bible, Ecclesiastes is usually considered to be the most problematic. The work has been called pessimistic, shocking, unorthodox, and even heretical. For example, certain statements in the book have been interpreted to deny life after death (3:18-21; 9:5-6,10). Yet, when these passages are considered in light of the overall theme of the book, it becomes clear that the author is not denying the existence of the human spirit after death but is stating an obvious fact: at death earthly life (life "under the sun") with its joys, sorrows, and opportunities is over. In 12:7 the author explicitly declares that the body "returns to the ground it came from, and the spirit returns to God who gave it" (NIV).

The author of Ecclesiastes has been deemed a pessimist, or even an existentialist. Others have argued he was an apologist who defended faith in God by pointing to the grimness of life without God. However, it may be best to regard the author as a realist. He observed that all persons (both good and bad) experience injustice, grow old, die, and are forgotten. The lives of all human beings are brief. Earthly possessions and mere worldly endeavors are temporary and have no eternal value for believers or nonbelievers. Only what is done for God will endure. Therefore, human beings should live in light of eternity realizing that someday they will give an account to God (12:13-14).

Outline

I. The author identifies himself and announces the theme of the book (1:1-3).

II. The Teacher sets forth observations concerning life under the sun on various topics (1:4–12:7).

  A. The vanities of earthly life, earthly wisdom, pleasure, worldly success, earthly wisdom, and earthly work, as well as the first exhortation to enjoy life (1:4–2:26)

  B. A proper time for all of life's activities, observations concerning the worker, time and eternity, a second exhortation to enjoy life, God's works and actions, and a third exhortation to enjoy life (3:1-22)

  C. Various evils of life (4:1–6:6)

  D. Miscellaneous observations on various subjects with a fifth and sixth exhortation to enjoy life (6:7–11:6)

  E. Living in light of the reality of death (11:7–12:7)

III. The author restates the theme, emphasizes the truth and purpose of his instruction, and presents the grand conclusion of the book: "Fear God and keep his commandments" (12:8-14).

Stephen R. Miller

ECONOMIC LIFE In ancient Palestine economic life involved the simple desire to improve the condition of life and to expand contact with other people. The people's success in doing this was determined to a large extent by the environmental conditions in which they lived. Adequate rainfall or water sources, arable farm and grazing lands, and the availability of natural resources were the most important of these ecological factors. Once the nation was formed and the monarchy established, the demands of the local and international markets, government stability, and the effects of international politics also came into play. Throughout their history, however, the economic life of the people of Israel was at least in part governed by the laws of God that concerned the treatment of fellow Israelites in matters of business and charity.

Like most of the rest of the Near East, the economy of ancient Palestine was primarily agricultural. However, unlike the major civilizations of Mesopotamia and Egypt, Israel's economy was not as completely dominated by the concerns of palace or temple as they were in other nations. For instance, there was no state monopoly on the ownership of arable land. Private ownership of land and private enterprise were the rule during the early history of the tribes of Israel. This changed somewhat after the establishment of the monarchy when large estates were formed (2 Sam. 9:10) to support the kings and the nobility. Attempts were also made by the royal bureaucracy to control as much of the country's land and economic activity as possible (1 Kings 4:1-19).

Further changes took place after the conquest of the nation by Assyria and Babylon. From that point on, the economic efforts (farm production, industry, and trade) of the nation were largely controlled by the tribute demands of the dominant empires (2 Kings 18:14-16) and the maintenance of international trade routes. This pattern continued into the NT period when Roman roads speeded trade but also held the populace in submission. The economy, while relatively stable, was burdened with heavy taxes (Matt. 22:17-21) to support the occupation army and government.

Environmental Conditions Many aspects of the economic life of the people were determined by the environmental conditions in which they lived. Palestine has a remarkably varied geographic pattern and huge shifts in climate. Within its environs are steppe and desert to the south and east in the Negev and the corresponding areas of the Transjordan. In these areas only dry or irrigation farming is possible, and much of the land is given over to pastoralists guiding their flocks and herds. A desolate wilderness region lies near the Dead Sea, while well-watered farmlands are found in the Shephelah plateau (between the coastal plain and the hill country) and in the Galilee area of northern Palestine. Rolling hill country dominates the center of the country where agriculture must be practiced on terraced hillsides and where water conservation and irrigation are necessary to grow crops.

The semitropical climate of Palestine includes a hot, dry summer and autumn during which no rains fall for six months. The drought is broken in September or October with rains continuing throughout the winter and into March and April. Yearly amounts of rainfall, which may all come in torrents within a few days, average 40 inches a year in the north and in the western areas of the hill country and Shephelah. Under the influence of the desert winds and the barrier of the hill country, these amounts decrease to the south and east, with less than eight inches a year in the desert regions of the Judean wilderness and the Negev. Average temperatures also vary widely, again with the highlands and northern coastal strip remaining cooler while the desert regions and low-lying areas see temperatures well into the 90 degree range.

Uncertain climatic conditions often determined the economic activity of the local village, the region, and the nation. The fact that Abram's first experience in Palestine was a famine (Gen. 12:10) is not surprising. Drought, which destroyed crops (1 Kings 17:1; Jer. 14:1-6), had a ripple effect on the rest of the economy. Some people left the country for the more predictable climate of Egypt (Gen. 46:1-7) or went to areas in Transjordan unaffected by a famine (Ruth 1:1). Economic hardship brought on by climatic extremes also hurt the business of the local potter, tanner, blacksmith, and weaver.

Local Village Economy Agriculture in ancient Palestine took three basic forms: grain production (barley and wheat), cultivation of vines and fruit trees, and the care of oleaginous plants (olive, date, sesame) from which oil was extracted for cooking, lighting, and personal care uses. Most of the energies of the village population were taken up with plowing fields (1 Kings 19:19) and the construction and maintenance of the hillside terraces where vineyards (Isa. 5:1-6; Mark 12:1) and grain were planted. In the hill country water sources were usually in the valleys, and thus it would have been too much work to carry water up to the hillside terraces. As a result, irrigation channels were dug to ensure that the terraces were evenly watered by rain and dew. Roof catch basins and plastered cisterns were constructed to augment water supplies from the village's wells and springs during the dry summer months.

The ideal situation for every rural Israelite was to spend his days "under his vine and his fig tree" (1 Kings 4:25 NASB). To ensure this possibility for his sons, a man's ownership of land was considered part of a family trust from one generation to the next. Each plot of land was a grant to the household by Yahweh and as such had to be cared for so that it would remain productive. Its abundance was the result of hard work (Prov. 24:30-34) and was to be shared with the poor (Deut. 24:19-21). Yahweh's grant of the land was repaid (Num. 18:21-32) through the payment of tithes to the Levites and through sacrifices.

The family's holdings were duly marked off. It was strictly against the law to remove the boundary stones (Deut. 19:14; Prov. 22:28). Inheritance laws were well defined with every eventuality provided for in the statutes. Normally, the oldest son inherited the largest portion of the lands of his father (Deut. 21:17; Luke 15:31). Sometimes this was all a man had to pass on to his children. It thus became traditional that land not be permanently sold outside the family or clan (Lev. 25:8-17). The tradition was so strong that Naboth could refuse King Ahab's request to purchase his vineyard saying he could not give him "the inheritance of my fathers" (1 Kings 21:3). In later periods, however, the prophets spoke of rich men "who add house to house and join field to field" (Isa. 5:8 NASB), taking advantage of the poor farmer whose land has been devastated by invading armies (Mic. 2:2) or drought.

If a man died without a male heir, his daughters would receive charge of the land (Num.

27:7-8), but they were required to marry within the tribe to ensure it remained a part of the tribal legacy (Num. 36:6-9). A childless man's property passed to his nearest male relative (Num. 27:9-11). The tragedy of childlessness was sometimes resolved through the levirate obligation. In these cases the nearest male relative married the dead man's widow to provide an heir for the deceased (Gen. 38). The duty of the redeemer, or *go'el*, as the relative was called, also included the purchase of family lands that had been abandoned (Jer. 32:6-9).

Since life was uncertain and disease and war often took many of the village's inhabitants, laws were provided to ensure that the widow, the orphan, and the stranger would not go hungry. Each field owner was required to leave a portion of the grain unharvested and some grapes on the vine (Lev. 19:9-10). This belonged to the poor and the needy who had the right to glean in these fields (Ruth 2:2-9). The land was also protected from exhaustion by the law of the sabbatical year, which required that it be left fallow every seventh year (Lev. 25:3-7).

Despite the backbreaking work of harvesting fields with flint-edged sickles (Joel 3:13), the grain and the fruits meant the survival of the village and was cause for celebration (Judg. 21:19). Following the harvest, the threshing floor became the center of the economic activity of the village and countryside (Joel 2:24). The sheaves of grain from the harvested fields of the district were brought here (Amos 2:13) to be trampled by oxen (Deut. 25:4) and threshing sledges (2 Sam. 24:22; Isa. 41:15). The grain was further separated from the chaff with winnowing forks (Ruth 3:2; Isa. 41:16; Jer. 15:7) and finally with sieves (Amos 9:9; Luke 22:31). Once this process was complete, the grain was guarded (Ruth 3:2-7) until it could be distributed to the people. The village may have had a communal granary, but most kept their grain in home storage pits or private granaries (Matt. 3:12).

Because of the importance this distribution held for the wellbeing of the people, the threshing floor gradually became associated with the administration of justice for the community. This is seen in the Ugaritic epic of Aqhat (dated to about 1400 B.C.) where the hero's father Daniel is said to be judging the cases of widows and orphans at the threshing floor. Similarly, Ruth's coming to Boaz as he lay on the threshing floor after the winnowing (Ruth 3:8-14) may have been an attempt to obtain justice regarding the ownership of her dead husband's estate. In another instance from the monarchy period, it can be seen how the threshing floor evolved into a symbolic place of judgment used by kings to augment their authority. First Kings 22:10 (NASB, NIV) portrays Kings Ahab and Jehoshaphat sitting enthroned before the gates of Samaria on a threshing floor as they judge the statements of the Prophet Micaiah.

Village economies also included the maintenance of small herds of sheep and goats. Nomadic pastoralism, like that described in the patriarchal narratives, was not a part of village life. The flocks were moved to new pastures in the hill country with the coming of the dry summer season, but this would have required only a few herdsmen (1 Sam. 16:11). Only the shearing of the sheep would have involved large numbers of the community (2 Sam. 13:23-24).

What little industry existed in Israelite villages was designed to complement agricultural production and provide both necessities and some trade goods. This activity included the making of bricks and split timbers for house construction, and the weaving of material for clothing. Some households had the skill to shape cooking utensils and farm tools from clay, stone, and metal. Few, however, had the ability to shape their own weapons, relying in many cases on clubs and ox goads (Judg. 3:31) for protection.

In exceptional cases village craftsmen may have set up stalls or business where they provided some of the more specialized items, especially fine pottery, bronze weapons, and gold and silver jewelry. Anything additional could either be done without or obtained in trade with other villages or nations who might possess a particularly fine artisan (1 Sam. 13:20). It is also possible that during a yearly visit to the city (Luke 2:41) to attend a religious festival the villager could visit the stalls of traders from all over the Near East and buy their wares.

Urban Economic Life Local trade expanded beyond the sale of surplus commodities and handcrafted items as the villages and towns grew in size. Population growth, sparked by the establishment of the monarchy and social stability, also increased the needs and appetites for metals (gold, tin, copper, iron), luxury items, and manufactured goods. A network of roads gradually developed to accommodate this economic activity and to tie together the villages and towns throughout the nation. More sophisticated road construction, designed to allow heavy vehicular traffic, was introduced by the kings who marshaled large numbers of corvée workers (persons who worked in lieu of paying taxes) to construct public works projects (1 Kings 9:15-22). Eziongeber, a port on the Red Sea, was acquired from the Edomites and serviced a fleet of ships bringing gold from Ophir and rare woods and other luxury items to the royal court (1 Kings 9:26; 10:11-12). Another fleet joined that of Hiram of Tyre in the Mediterranean trade (1 Kings 10:22).

Within the walled cities and towns, most commercial activity occurred within the gate complex or its environs. This would have been the site of the heaviest traffic in any town and the most likely spot, other than private homes (Jer. 18:2-3), for stalls and shops to be set up for business. Since legal matters were also handled here (Deut. 21:18-19), business contracts could be witnessed (Gen. 23:15-16) and disputes settled (Ruth 4:1-6). Shops may have also been established within the walls of those cities that had hollow-wall (casemate) construction.

Since this was an economy without coined money until about 550 B.C., barter and specified weights (shekel, mina, talent) of precious metals were used as rates of exchange. Prices, as always, were determined by the law of supply and demand (2 Kings 6:25; Rev. 6:6), with an extra markup to cover the costs of transport, and, where applicable, manufacturing. For instance, luxury items such as spices and perfumes from Arabia and ivory and rare animals commanded high prices. They were portable enough to make the venture worthwhile.

Weights and measures also fitted into the sale of commodities in the town marketplace. These weights varied from one district and time period to the next (2 Sam. 14:26; Ezek. 45:10). However, the law required that Israelites provide a fair measure to their customers (Lev. 19:35-36). The fact that the law did not prevent fraud in every case is seen in the prophets' cries against deceitful weights (Mic. 6:11) and false balances (Amos 8:5). Archaeological evidence shows some attempt by the royal administration to standardize shekel weights. Hieratic symbols on these markers demonstrate a reliance on the Egyptian system of weights and measures.

Slave labor was also an outgrowth of the urbanization of Israel and the constant military

E

campaigns of the kings. The large number of military prisoners joined the levies of forced labor gangs (1 Kings 5:13; 9:20-22) building roads and repairing the walls of the fortresses which guarded the kingdom. Royal estates were managed by stewards (1 Chron. 27:25-31) and worked by large bands of state-owned slaves and a levy of free men (1 Sam. 8:12).

It is unlikely that private individuals held as many slaves as the monarchy or the social elite. Since the laws regarding slaves were quite stringent (Exod. 21:1-11,20,26; Lev. 25:39-46), it is more likely that day laborers were hired by most landowners (Matt. 20:1-5). The leasing of land to tenant farmers was another alternative to the labor problem, but this was not common in Israel until the NT period (Matt. 21:33-41; Mark 12:9).

Israelites could sell their families or themselves into slavery to resolve a debt (Exod. 21:7-11; Lev. 25:39; Matt. 18:25). This was regulated by the law so that the normal term of slavery or indenture was no more than six years. Then the slave was to be released and given a portion of the flock and the harvest with which to make a new start (Deut. 15:12-14). Perpetual slavery was only to occur if the Israelite himself chose to remain a slave. This choice might be made because he did not want to be separated from a wife and children acquired during his term of enslavement (Exod. 21:1-6) or because he did not feel he would have a better life on his own (Deut. 15:16).

Urbanization and the imposed demands of foreign conquerors brought greater complexity to the economic life of the people of Palestine. Travel and trade increased, and the variety of goods and services was magnified by the increased demands of consumers and the influx of new ideas and technologies from outside the country. Agriculture remained the staple of the economy, but it was augmented by the public works projects of the kings and foreign rulers. The increase in commercial and private traffic was facilitated by better highways and means of transport. Slave labor also became more common, but the majority of slaves came from a pool of military prisoners acquired in the wars that solidified and protected the nation's borders. See *Agriculture; Commerce; Slave, Servant; Transportation and Travel; Weights and Measures.*

Victor H. Matthews

ECZEMA See *Diseases; Scurvy.*

ED (Ĕd) Place-name meaning "witness." Altar that the tribes assigned territory east of the Jordan built as a witness that Yahweh is God of both the eastern and western tribes. The building resulted in a dispute between the two groups of tribes, but Phinehas, the priest, helped settle the dispute, ensuring the altar was a symbol and would not be used for burnt offering (Josh. 22:34). NASB, NIV, NRSV read "witness."

EDAR (Ē´ där) (KJV, Gen. 35:21) See *Eder.*

EDEN (Ē´ dĕn) Garden of God. "Eden" is probably derived from the Sumerian-Akkadian *edinu*, meaning "flatland" or "wilderness." The similarity to the Hebrew verb *eden*, meaning "delight" or "pleasure," resulted in the Septuagint's translation of the expression "garden of Eden" as "garden of delight," hence paradise.

"Eden" appears 20 times in the OT but never in the NT. Two usage's refer to men (2 Chron. 29:12; 31:15). Twice the name is used to designate a city or region in the Assyrian province of Thelassar (Isa. 37:12; 2 Kings 19:12). Ezekiel 27:23 mentions a region named Eden located on the Euphrates. Amos 1:5 refers to the ruler of Damascus as holding the scepter of the house of Eden.

The 14 remaining appearances relate to the idyllic place of creation. In Genesis (2:8,10,15; 3:23-24; 4:16) the reference is to the region in which a garden was placed. Though details seem precise, identification of the rivers that flow from the river issuing forth from Eden cannot be accomplished with certainty. The Euphrates and the Tigris can be identified, but there is no agreement on the location of the Pishon and the Gihon.

Joel 2:3 compares Judah's condition before its destruction with Eden. In Isa. 51:3 and Ezek. 36:35 Eden is used as an illustration of the great prosperity God would bestow on Judah. These exilic prophets promised that the nation God restored after the exile would be like Eden's garden. Ezekiel also refers to the trees of Eden (31:9,16,18) and calls Eden the garden of God (28:13). See *Paradise.*

Robert Anderson Street

EDER (Ē´ dĕr) Place and personal name meaning "water puddle" or "herd." **1.** Tower near Bethlehem (Gen. 35:21; cp. v. 19). The exact location is not known. Micah referred to Jerusalem as the "tower of the flock," the same Hebrew expression as in Genesis (Mic. 4:8). **2.** A town in the southern limits of the tribal territory of Judah near Edom (Josh. 15:21). Its location is not known. **3.** A Levite of the clan of Merari (1 Chron. 23:23; 24:30). **4.** A leader of the tribe of Benjamin (1 Chron. 8:15); KJV spelling is Ader.

EDICT See *Decree.*

EDIFICATION Literally "building up," it approximates encouragement and consolation (1 Cor. 14:3; 1 Thess. 5:11), though with edification focus falls on the goal, defined as being established in faith (Col. 2:7) or attaining unity of faith and knowledge, maturity, and the full measure of Christ (Eph. 4:13). Edification is the special responsibility of the various church leaders (Eph. 4:11-12) and is the legitimate context for the exercise of their authority (2 Cor. 10:8; 13:10). The work of building up is, however, the work of all Christians (1 Thess. 5:11). Spiritual gifts are given for the edification of the church. Of these gifts, those which involve speaking are especially important (1 Cor. 14; Eph. 4:29). All elements of Christian worship should contribute to edification (1 Cor. 14:26). Prophecy and instruction are especially important (1 Cor. 14:3,18-19). Edification is not all talk, however, but involves demonstrating love (1 Cor. 8:1) and consideration for those weak in faith (Rom. 15:1-2).

EDOM (Ē´ dŏm) Area southeast and southwest of the Dead Sea, on opposite sides of the Arabah, was known as Edom in biblical times and was the home of the Edomites. The name "Edom" derives from a Semitic root that means "red" or "ruddy" and characterizes the red sandstone terrain of much of the area in question. Moreover, the Edomite area was largely "wilderness"— semidesert, not very conducive to agriculture— and many of the inhabitants were semi-nomads. Thus, the boundaries of Edom would have been rather ill defined. Yet not all of Edom was wilderness; the vicinity of present-day Tafileh and Buseireh, east of the Arabah, is fairly well watered, cultivable land, and would have boasted numerous villages during OT times. This would have been the center of Edomite population. Buseireh is situated on the ruins of ancient Bozrah, the capital of Edom. Note that the mod-

The hills of Edom between Petra and Bozrah toward the Wadi Arabah.

ern name, "Buseireh," preserves memory of the ancient one, "Bozrah."

Most of the biblical passages pertaining to Edom refer to this Edomite center east of the Arabah. Isaiah 63:1, for example, speaks of one that "comes from Edom, with garments of glowing colors from Bozrah, this One who is majestic in His apparel, marching in the greatness of His strength" (NASB). (See also Jer. 49:22; Amos 1:11-12.) Yet there are other passages that presuppose that the territory west of the Arabah, south of the Judean hill country and separating Judah from the Gulf of Aqaba, was also part of Edom. See especially the description of Judah's boundary in Num. 34:3-4 and Josh. 15:1-3, where Judah's south side is described as extending to "the border of Edom, southward to the wilderness of Zin" (NASB). Certain of the tribal groups that ranged this wilderness area south of Judah are listed in the Edomite genealogy of Gen. 36. In NT times even the southern end of the Judean hill country (south of approximately Hebron) was known officially as Idumea (Edom).

The "land of Seir" seems to be synonymous with Edom in some passages (Gen. 32:3; 36:8; Judg. 5:4). Egyptian texts from about 1300 to 1100 B.C. know of Shasu (apparently seminomadic tribes) from Seir and Edom. "Teman" also is used in apposition to Edom in at least one biblical passage (Amos 1:12) but normally refers to a specific district of Edom and possibly to a town by that name. One of Job's visitors was Eliphaz the Temanite (Job 2:11; cp. Ezek. 25:13).

The Israelites regarded the Edomites as close relatives, even more closely related to them than the Ammonites or Moabites. Specifically, they identified the Ammonites and Moabites as descendants of Lot, Abraham's nephew, but the Edomites as descendants of Esau, Jacob's brother

(Gen. 19:30-36; 36). Thus Edom occasionally is referred to as a "brother" to Israel (Amos 1:11-12). Edomites seem not to have been barred from worship in the Jerusalem temple with the same strictness as the Ammonites and Moabites (Deut. 23:3-8). Yet, as is often the case with personal relations, the closest relative can be a bitter enemy. According to the biblical writers, enmity between Israel and Edom began with Jacob and Esau (when the former stole the latter's birthright) and was exacerbated at the time of the Israelite exodus from Egypt (when the Edomites refused the Israelites passage through their land). Be that as it may, much of the conflict also had to do with the fact that Edom was a constant threat to Judah's frontier and moreover blocked Judean access to the Gulf of Aqaba.

Both Saul and David conducted warfare with the Edomites—probably frontier wars fought in the "wilderness" area southwest of the Dead Sea (1 Sam. 14:47-48; 2 Sam. 8:13-14). David achieved a decisive victory in the valley of salt, probably just southwest of Beer-sheba where the ancient name still is preserved in modern Arabic Wadi el-Milk. Apparently this secured Davidic control of the Edomite area west of the Arabah as well as access to the Gulf of Aqaba. Thus we read that Solomon built a fleet of ships at Ezion-

geber and sent them to distant places for exotic goods. Later Hadad of the royal Edomite line returned from Egypt and became an active adversary to Solomon. This would have involved Edomite attacks on Solomon's caravans that passed through traditionally Edomite territory from Ezion-geber to Jerusalem (1 Kings 11:14-22).

Apparently Judah gained the upper hand against Edom again during the reign of Jehoshaphat. Once again we read of a Judean attempt (unsuccessful this time) to undertake a shipping venture from Ezion-geber (1 Kings 22:47-50). Edom regained independence from Judah under Joram, who succeeded Jehoshaphat to the throne (2 Kings 8:20-22). A later Judean king, Amaziah, is reported to have defeated the Edomites again in the valley of salt and then to have pursued 10,000 survivors to "the top of the cliff" from which they were thrown down and dashed to pieces (2 Chron. 25:11-12).

Conflict between Judah and Edom and efforts on the part of Judean kings to exploit the commercial possibilities of the Gulf of Aqaba continued (2 Kings 14:22; 16:6; 2 Chron. 26:1-2; 28:17) until eventually the Edomites, like the other peoples and petty kingdoms of Syria-Palestine, fell under the shadow of the major eastern

The mountainous landscape of the land of Edom.

empires—the Assyrians, then the Babylonians, finally the Persians and the Greeks. Some scholars hold that the Edomites aided the Babylonians in their attacks on Jerusalem in 597 and 586 B.C. and then took advantage of the Judeans in their helpless situation. This would explain, for example, the bitter verbal attacks on Edom in passages such as Jer. 49:7-22 and the book of Obadiah. Yet there is no clear evidence to support this view.

By NT times a people of Arabic origin known as the Nabateans had established a commercial empire with its center in the former Edomite territory east of the Arabah. Their chief city was Petra, and the whole region southeast of the Dead Sea had come to be known as Nabatea. Only the former Edomite territory west of the Arabah was still known as Idumea (Edom). Herod the Great was of Idumean ancestry. See *Bozrah; Esau; Nabateans; Petra; Sela; Transjordan.*

EDOMITES See *Edom.*

EDREI (Ĕd´ rə ī) Place-name of unknown meaning. **1.** Royal city of Og, king of Bashan (Josh. 12:4). Invading Israel defeated Og there (Num. 21:33-35). It is also known from Egyptian records. Its location is modern Dera, halfway between Damascus and Amman. The clan of Machir in the tribe of Manasseh laid claim to the city (Josh. 13:31). **2.** Fortified city in the tribal territory of Naphtali (Josh. 19:37).

EDUCATION IN BIBLE TIMES Most teaching and learning in the biblical periods consisted of informal training and concentrated on the goal of passing along an approach to life centered on guidance for a moral and religious lifestyle. Formal education was restricted to the elites of society (the rulers and their immediate workers) throughout most of the biblical period. Literacy in the sense of reading and writing was normally linked to the ruling classes and their helpers due to the requirement for a more formal setting for such training. On the other hand, the gradual acceptance of the OT as canon brought a greater need and reason for teaching, at least, an ability to read to a larger segment of the population, with the synagogues serving as settings for such training (likely during the time of the exile). In general, however, the lower classes did not need literacy to fulfill their everyday obligations or had no free time for the required training in what

would have been an unnecessary luxury among life's primary demands. Due to this, informal learning is the major form of education referenced in the biblical text, with home and community settings serving as the vehicles for such training.

Informal and Semiformal Learning Three major types of learning are mentioned in the Bible with different emphases in each setting. The first and most common setting was the home in which moral instruction, cultural patterns, historical events, and spiritual guidance were taught by parents to children on an informal level with extended family involved in the task many times as well. A prime example of this setting is found in Deut. 6 (which includes the "Shema") where parents are commanded to recite the commandments of God to their children and discuss them throughout the day. The normal discipleship of children by their parents is engaged as the vehicle of choice for passing along the religious heritage of the group. Of course virtually all aspects of daily life were taught in the home, but ideally even these should have had a religious tone in the instruction since all of life was religious in nature. What is specific in the OT is that a conscious effort is demanded in this endeavor with the content delineated in its broad contours from the religious standpoint. Other examples of household education include instruction in holiness codes (laws about what was clean and unclean, dietary laws, and Sabbath rules), teachings about the importance of such historical events as the Passover, and the passing along of work skills through apprenticeship in the father's trade.

A second type of learning related especially to the needs of the political elites for helpers such as scribes in keeping government records and promoting their image in the public domain. These needs are reflected in the tax lists and conquest records found in several archaeological finds from the region in the OT period. Sumerian remains on clay tablets attest to this type of record keeping among them as well as among the Babylonians and Assyrians, with increased use of scribal recording of materials during the first millennium before Christ, as seen in the literary advances of this time period in both the Hebrew culture and the surrounding cultures. The training requirement for such scribal work was quite complicated, and only a small segment of the society outside of the elites (upper class)

E

achieved a high level of literacy training. This semiformal structured educational training was directly related to literacy and did not necessarily involve learning in other areas of study (in fact, such instruction was not likely a part of the training of scribes) unless the retainers (helpers of the elites) were being trained to teach the children of the elites in a formal education setting.

In the OT context Ezra is the prime example of a religious emphasis on scribal training and activity. Ezra marks a turning point as a class of religious scribes emerges in order to copy the sacred texts and to read them to the people. Members of this scribal group often became interpreters of the text during the intertestamental and NT time periods.

The emergence of the synagogue gatherings provided further settings for offering training in at least minimal levels of reading literacy as required for reading the sacred text in the synagogue services. Also, spiritual instruction and moral guidance were taught to children through the synagogue organization during the week. For the NT period this is the likely source for any educational training outside of the home that Jesus and His disciples would have had.

Formal Learning A third setting for learning in the biblical time period involved the education of elites themselves, those in the upper stratum of society. In these settings a more formal education system existed that included training by others outside of the family unit who were hired for that purpose (or slaves were used). While records of this type of training in the OT time period are limited, a general picture includes royal courts and wealthy urban elites with at least some collections of important works. In Egypt and the Babylonian, Assyrian, and Persian empires, the levels of formality, breadth, and sophistication of such learning were quite high. By the fifth century Athens had achieved a remarkable level of literacy, training, and education, with a widespread scope of involvement that went beyond simply the elites of the city. The philosophical giants Socrates, Plato, and Aristotle are examples of the heights of learning that were being introduced to the urban public of this period. But by the time of the Greek conquests under Alexander the Great, the more traditional pattern of formal education as a privilege of the elites again prevailed, with the teaching responsibilities often placed in the hands of the retainers (slaves and employees) of these elites.

The pattern for formal education in the Greco-Roman culture of the NT period included beginning with grammar instruction during the early childhood years, followed by guidance in the art of rhetoric and speech. Sometimes the student received instruction from a tutor in the home and at other times by attending a school, with various combinations possible between these two options. Quintilian, one of Rome's greatest teachers in the first century, described the education system and its various components in detail. The young pupil started in the care of the *grammaticus* (grammar teacher) to learn grammar and then passed into the hands of the *rhetor* for instruction in rhetoric and speech. The grammar teaching included reading and writing, with a beginning process of copying the writings of others, then recasting those writings into one's own words, and finally composing original works. This last step of composition was then developed more fully in the next stage of training in rhetoric. Moral instruction was normally part of the entire process by means of readings, role models, and discussions. Quintilian also noted the importance of the father/family in the education process and goals, the need for a strong grasp of grammar, and the challenge to continue learning throughout one's lifetime.

Although none of the leaders of the early church or writers of the NT was likely a member of the ruling elites, Paul and Luke may have had some formal educational training. Paul is stated to have studied under Gamaliel in Jerusalem and may have had some formal training in Tarsus before going to Jerusalem, but even if this was so, his training would have been at a lower level than that afforded the ruling classes. He would not have been from the ruling elites of Tarsus since his trade was tent-making, which implied a status at most fitting for the retainers of the elites or possibly affiliated with the merchant stratum on a lower level. Taking at face value the tradition of Luke being a physician, Luke also belonged to a social stratum no higher than the retainer class. So Luke as well would not have been likely to have passed through all of the formal training afforded to the elites. However, Luke's reference to the "most excellent Theophilos" may reflect a relationship to one of the ruling elites befitting a member of the retainer stratum. At any rate, Luke's introduction to his Gospel indicates a level of training suitable to digesting and investigating both oral and written sources, thus implying at least some level of training in literacy for Luke.

Libraries In conjunction with the training of elites and the prestige of learning opportunities, libraries emerged in some of the leading cities of the Roman Empire. The most famous library in antiquity was the Alexandria library, which at its height of prestige had over 500,000 scrolls of writings between the main library and the smaller "daughter's library" beside it. The goal was for the library to have all of the known works of any type extant. The excellence of the Alexandria library is seen in the practice of comparing (and correcting) copies in other libraries to those in Alexandria due to the "old text" being preserved there. As a byproduct of this goal, the Torah from the OT was translated into Greek and added to the library in the mid-third century B.C., and then later over a period of time the Prophets and the Writings as well as other books were added to that translation. This Greek Old Testament became the version used predominantly in the early church.

While the library at Alexandria was the best known in the ancient world and reputed to be the largest in holdings, libraries also were located in other cities such as Antioch, Pergamum, Athens, Rhodes, Carthage, and Rome. By the time of Christianity, many of the larger cities had libraries, with at least some public access in the major centers. During the time of the Roman Empire, Alexandria remained the best center for studying Greek works, with Rome housing the best collection of works by Latin writers (as well as a substantial collection of Greek works).

The function of libraries was to provide access to the works of the classic Greek writers of antiquity, such as Homer, Plato, and Aristotle, as well as to those of others of less stature or contemporary authors. The copies of the works were stored in the library with duplicates made for those who wished to use the works outside of the library setting. Sometimes the author would pay to have copies made for friends, while at other times the buyer would underwrite the copying of the book. Borrowing books, while allowed in some locations, was limited at best and may often have been restricted to certain citizens of standing. See *Library.*   *Bill Warren*

EGLAH (Ĕg´ lăh) Personal name meaning "heifer, young cow." David's wife and mother of his son Ithream (2 Sam. 3:5).

EGLAIM (Ĕg´ lā ĭm) Place-name meaning "two cisterns." Place in Moab used by Isaiah to describe far limits of Moab's distress. It is modern Rugm el-Gilimeh, southeast of el-Kerak. It is distinct in location and Hebrew spelling from En-eglaim (Ezek. 47:10).

EGLATH-SHELISHIYAH (Ĕg´ ləth-shĕ lĭsh´ ĭ yäh) Place-name meaning "the third heifer." Place apparently in Moab where Moab fugitives fled in Isaiah's description of disaster (Isa. 15:5). The name has given translators and interpreters many problems. The location is not known. The words do not apparently fit the poetic structure and are unexpected in the syntax and context, there being no adverb or preposition between Zoar and Eglath-Shelishiyah in the Hebrew. KJV makes the phrase an identifying statement with Zoar—"an heifer of three years old." The same problems arise in the closely related Jer. 48:34.

J. Maxwell Miller

EGLON (Ĕg lŏn) **1.** Moabite king who oppressed the Israelites (Judg. 3:12). Aided by the Amalekites and Ammonites, Eglon dominated Israel for 18 years. He was finally slain by the Benjamite judge Ehud, who ran the obese monarch through with a short sword. **2.** Canaanite city whose king entered an alliance with four other Canaanite rulers against Gibeon (Josh. 10:3). The Gibeonites had made a treaty with Israel (Josh. 9). Subsequently, Eglon was captured by the Israelite army under Joshua. It became a part of the territory of the tribe of Judah. Most scholars long held that the modern site of Tell el-Hesi was the location of ancient Eglon. More recently, however, some have contended for Tell `Eton. Both places are to the southwest of Lachish. See *Ehud; Joshua; Judges.*

EGYPT Land in northeastern Africa, home to one of the earliest civilizations, and an important cultural and political influence on ancient Israel. **Geography** Egypt lies at the northeastern corner of Africa, separated from Palestine by the Sinai wilderness. In contrast to the modern nation, ancient Egypt was confined to the Nile River Valley, a long, narrow ribbon of fertile land (the "black land") surrounded by uninhabitable desert (the "red land"). Egypt proper, from the first cataract of the Nile to the Mediterranean, is some 750 miles long.

Classical historians remarked that Egypt was a gift of the Nile. The river's three tributaries converge in the Sudan. The White Nile, with its source in Lake Victoria, provides a fairly constant water flow. The seasonal flow of the Blue Nile and Atbara caused an annual inundation beginning in June and cresting in September. Not only did the inundation provide for irrigation, but also it replenished the soil with a new layer of fertile, black silt each year. The Nile also provided a vital communication link for the nation. While the river's flow carried boats northward, prevailing northerly winds allowed easy sailing upstream.

Despite the unifying nature of the Nile, the "Two Lands" of Egypt were quite distinct. Upper Egypt is the arable Nile Valley from the First Cataract to just south of Memphis in the north. Lower Egypt refers to the broad Delta of the Nile in the north, formed from alluvial deposits. Egypt was relatively isolated by a series of six Nile cataracts on the south and protected on the east and west by the desert. The Delta was the entryway to Egypt for travelers coming from the Fertile Crescent across the Sinai.

The temple of Luxor.

History The numerous Egyptian pharaohs were divided by the ancient historian Manetho into 30 dynasties. Despite certain difficulties, Manetho's scheme is still used and provides a framework for a review of Egyptian history.

The unification of originally separate kingdoms of Upper and Lower Egypt about 3100 B.C. began the Archaic Period (First and Second Dynasties). Egypt's first period of glory, the Third through Sixth Dynasties of the Old Kingdom (2700–2200 B.C.) produced the famous pyramids.

Low Nile inundations, the resultant bad harvests, and incursions of Asiatics in the Delta region brought the political chaos of the Seventh through Tenth Dynasties, called the First Intermediate Period (2200–2040 B.C.). Following a civil war, the 11th Dynasty reunited Egypt and began the Middle Kingdom (2040–1786 B.C.). Under the able pharaohs of the Twelfth Dynasty, Egypt prospered and conducted extensive trade. From the Middle Kingdom onward, Egyptian history is contemporary with biblical events. Abraham's brief sojourn in Egypt (Gen. 12:10-20) during this period may be understood in light of a tomb painting at Beni Hasan showing visiting Asiatics in Egypt about 1900 B.C.

Under the weak 13th Dynasty, Egypt entered another period of division. Asiatics, mostly Semi-tes like the Hebrews, migrated into the Delta region of Egypt and began to establish independent enclaves, eventually consolidating rule over Lower Egypt. These pharaohs, being Asiatics rather than native Egyptians, were remembered as Hyksos, or "rulers of foreign lands." This period, in which Egypt was divided between Hyksos (15th and 16th) and native Egyptian (13th and 17th) dynasties, is known as the Second Intermediate or Hyksos Period (1786–1550 B.C.). Some believe Joseph's rise to power (Gen. 41:39-45) may have taken place under a Hyksos pharaoh. See *Hyksos.*

Funerary statuettes from the tomb of King Tut (Pharaoh Tutankhamun).

The Hyksos were expelled and Egypt reunited about 1550 B.C. by Ahmose I, who established the 18th Dynasty inaugurated the Egyptian New Kingdom. Successive 18th Dynasty pharaohs made military campaigns into Canaan and against the Mitannian kingdom of Mesopotamia, creating an empire that reached the Euphrates River. Foremost among the pharaohs was Thutmose III (1479–1425 B.C.), who won a major victory at Megiddo in Palestine. Amenhotep III (1391–1353 B.C.) ruled over a magnificent empire in peace—thanks to a treaty with Mitanni—and devoted his energies to building projects in Egypt itself. The great successes of the Empire led to internal power struggles, especially between the powerful priesthood of Amen-Re and the throne.

Amenhotep III's son, Amenhotep IV (1353–1335 B.C.), changed his name to Akhenaton and embarked on a revolutionary reform which promoted worship of the sun disc Aton above all other gods. As Thebes was dominated by the powerful priesthood of Amen-Re, Akhenaton moved the capital over 200 miles north to Akhetaton, modern Tell el-Amarna. The Amarna Age, as this period is known, brought innovations in art and literature; but Akhenaton paid little attention to foreign affairs, and the Empire suffered. Documents from Akhetaton, the Amarna Letters, represent diplomatic correspondence between local rulers in Egypt's sphere of influence and pharaoh's court. They especially illuminate the turbulent situation in Canaan which, depending upon one's preference for a 15th or 13th century date for the exodus, could be a century after or prior to the Israelite invasion.

The reforms of Akhenaton failed. His second successor made clear his loyalties to Amen-Re by changing his name from Tutankhaten to Tutankhamen and abandoning the new capital in favor of Thebes. He died young, and his comparatively insignificant tomb was forgotten until its rediscovery in 1921. The 18th Dynasty would not recover. The General Horemheb seized the throne and worked vigorously to restore order and erase all trace of the Amarna heresy. Horemheb had no heir and left the throne to his vizier, Ramesses I, first king of the 19th Dynasty.

Seti I (1302–1290 B.C.) reestablished Egyptian control in Canaan and campaigned against the Hittites, who had taken Egyptian territory in North Syria during the Amarna Age. Construc-

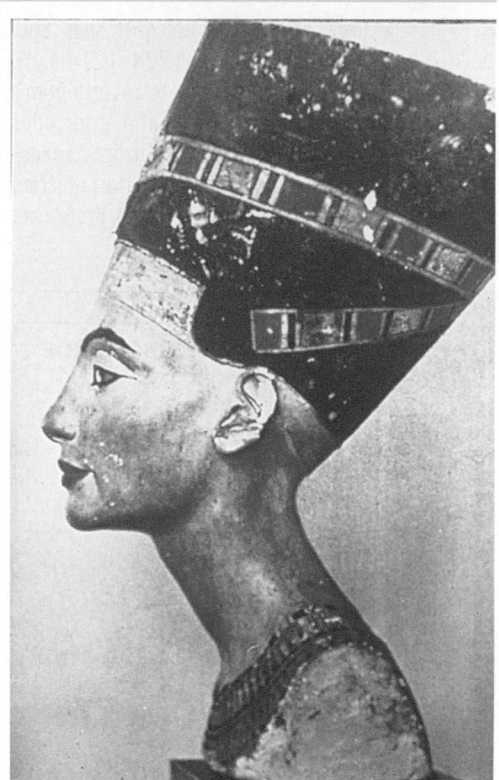

Bust of the Egyptian queen Nefertiti, wife of Pharaoh Akhenaton.

tion of a new capital was begun by Seti I in the eastern Delta near the biblical Land of Goshen. Thebes would remain the national religious and traditional capital. See *Hittites.*

Ramesses II (1290–1224 B.C.) was the most vigorous and successful of the 19th Dynasty pharaohs. In his fifth year he fought the Hittites at Kadesh-on-the-Orontes in north Syria. Although ambushed and nearly defeated, the pharaoh rallied and claimed a great victory. Nevertheless, the battle was inconclusive. In 1270 B.C. Ramesses II concluded a peace treaty with the Hittites recognizing the status quo. At home he embarked on the most massive building program of any Egyptian ruler. Impressive additions were made to sanctuaries in Thebes and Memphis, a gigantic temple of Ramesses II was built at Abu Simbel in Nubia, and his mortuary temple and tomb were prepared in Western Thebes. In the eastern Delta, the new capital was completed and called Pi-Ramesse ("domain of Ramesses"; cp. Gen. 47:11). Many scholars view this as the biblical Ramesses (Exod. 1:11), a storage city built for the unnamed pharaoh of the exodus.

After a long reign, Ramesses II was succeeded by Merneptah, his son (1224–1214 B.C.). A stele of 1220 B.C. commemorates Merneptah's victory over a Libyan invasion and concludes with a poetic account of a campaign in Canaan. It includes the first extrabiblical mention of Israel and the only one in known Egyptian literature.

After Merneptah the 19th Dynasty was a period of confusion.

Egypt had a brief period of renewed glory under Ramesses III (1195–1164 B.C.) of the 20th Dynasty. He defeated an invasion of the Sea Peoples, among whom were the Philistines. The remainder of 20th Dynasty rulers, all named

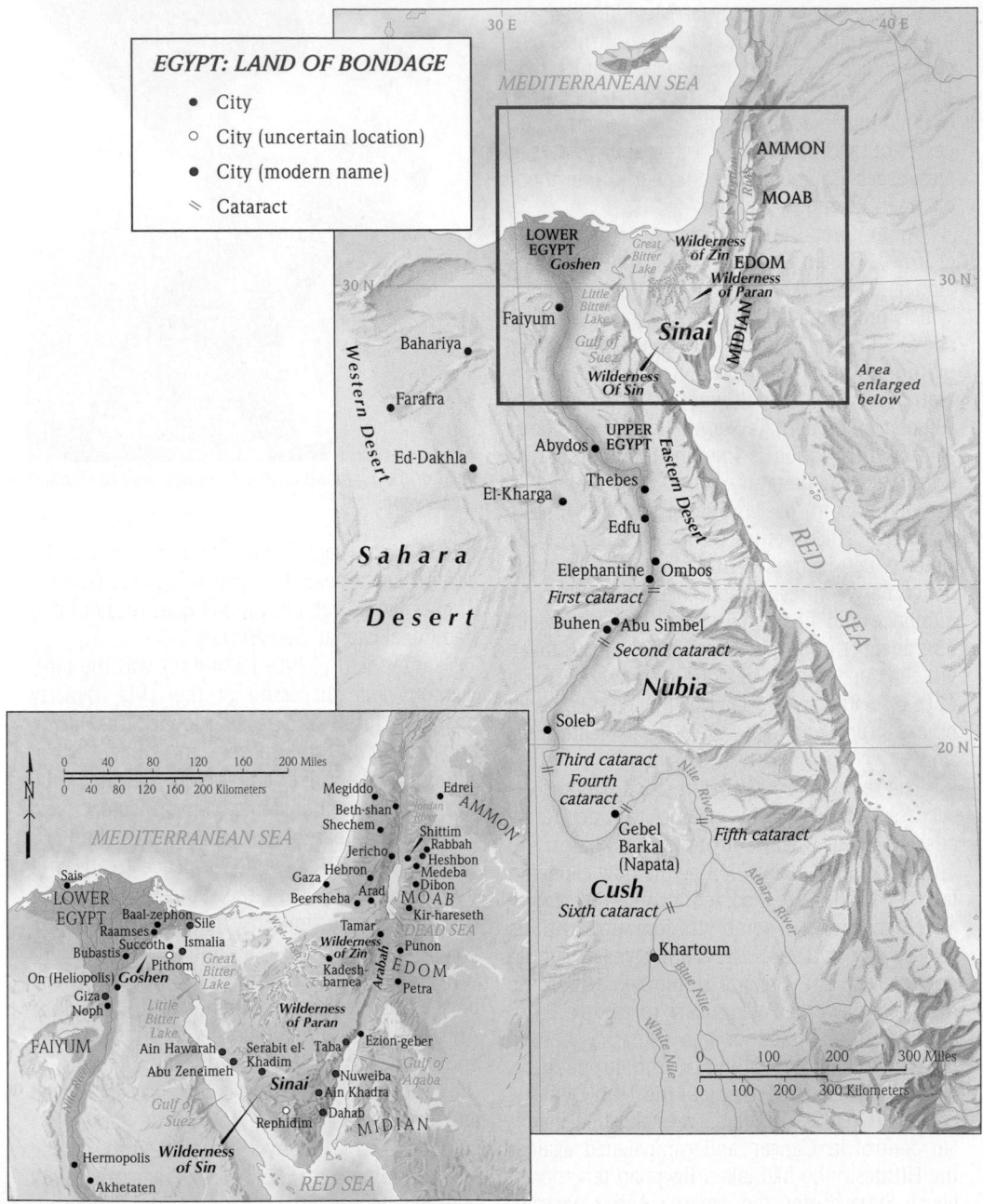

Ramesses, saw increasingly severe economic and civil difficulties. The New Kingdom and the Empire came to an end with the last of these rulers in 1070 B.C. The Iron Age had taken dominance of the Near East elsewhere.

The late period (1070–332 B.C.) saw Egypt divided and invaded but with occasional moments of greatness. While the high priesthood of Amen-Re controlled Thebes, the 21st Dynasty ruled from the east Delta city of Tanis, biblical Zoan (Num. 13:22; Ps. 78:12; Ezek. 30:14; Isa. 19:11; 30:4). It was likely a pharaoh of this dynasty, perhaps Siamun, who took Gezer in Palestine and gave it to Solomon as his daughter's dowry (1 Kings 3:1; 9:16). The 22nd Dynasty was founded by Shoshenq I (945–924 B.C.), the Shishak of the Bible, who briefly united Egypt and made a successful campaign against the newly divided nations Judah and Israel (1 Kings 14:25; 2 Chron. 12). Thereafter, Egypt was divided between the 22nd through 25th Dynasties. The "So king of Egypt" (2 Kings 17:4), who encouraged the treachery of Hoshea, certainly belongs to this confused period, but he cannot be identified with certainty. Egypt was reunited in 715 B.C., when the Ethiopian 25th Dynasty succeeded in establishing control over all of Egypt. The most important of these pharaohs was Taharqa, the biblical Tirhakah who rendered aid to Hezekiah (2 Kings 19:9; Isa. 37:9).

Assyria invaded Egypt in 671 B.C., driving the Ethiopians southward and eventually sacking Thebes (biblical No-Amon; Nah. 3:8) in 664 B.C. Under loose Assyrian sponsorship, the 26th Dynasty controlled all of Egypt from Sais in the western Delta. With Assyria's decline, Neco II (610–595 B.C.) opposed the advance of Babylon and exercised brief control over Judah (2 Kings 23:29-35). After a severe defeat at the Battle of Carchemish (605 B.C.), Neco II lost Judah as a vassal (2 Kings 24:1) and was forced to defend her border against Babylon. The Pharaoh Hophra (Greek Apries; 589–570 B.C.) supported Judah's rebellion against Babylon but was unable to provide the promised support (Jer. 37:5-10; 44:30). Despite these setbacks, the 26th Dynasty was a period of Egyptian renaissance until the Persian conquest in 525 B.C. Persian rule (27th Dynasty) was interrupted by a period of Egyptian independence under the 28th through 30th Dynasties (404–343 B.C.). With Persian reconquest in 343 B.C., pharaonic Egypt had come to an end.

Sailboat on the Nile River near Luxor.

Alexander the Great took Egypt from the Persians in 332 B.C. and founded the great city of Alexandria on the Mediterranean coast. After his death in 323 B.C., Egypt was home to the Hellenistic Ptolemaic Empire until the time of Cleopatra, when it fell to the Romans (30 B.C.). During the NT period, Egypt, under direct rule of the Roman emperors, was the breadbasket of Rome.

Religion Egyptian religion is extremely complex and not totally understood. Many of the great number of gods were personifications of the enduring natural forces in Egypt, such as the sun, Nile, air, earth, and so on. Other gods, like Maat ("truth," "justice"), personified abstract concepts. Still others ruled over states of mankind, like Osiris, god of the underworld. Some of the gods were worshiped in animal form, such as the Apis bull that represented the god Ptah of Memphis.

Many of the principal deities were associated with particular cities or regions, and their position was often a factor of the political situation.

This is reflected by the gods' names that dominate pharaohs' names in various dynasties. Thus the god Amen, later called Amen-Re, became the chief god of the Empire because of the position of Thebes. The confusion of local beliefs and political circumstances led to the assimilation of different gods to certain dominant figures. Theological systems developed around local gods at Hermopolis, Memphis, and Heliopolis. At Memphis, Ptah was seen as the supreme deity who created the other gods by his own word, but this notion was too intellectual to be popular. Dominance was achieved by the system of Heliopolis, home of the sun god Atum, later identified with Ra. Similar to the Hermopolis cycle, it involved a primordial chaos from which appeared Atum who gave birth to the other gods.

Popular with common people was the Osiris myth. Osiris, the good king, was murdered and dismembered by his brother Seth. Osiris' wife, Isis, gathered his body to be mummified by the jackal-headed embalming god Anubis. Magically restored, Osiris was buried by his son, Horus, and reigned as king of the underworld. Horus, meanwhile, overcame the evil Seth to rule on earth. This cycle became the principle of divine kingship. In death, the pharaoh was worshiped as Osiris. As the legitimate heir Horus buried the dead Osiris, the new pharaoh became the living Horus by burying his dead predecessor.

The consistent provision of the Nile gave Egyptians, in contrast to Mesopotamians, a generally optimistic outlook on life. This is reflected in their preoccupation with the afterlife, which was viewed as an ideal continuation of life on earth. In the Old Kingdom it was the prerogative only of the king, as a god, to enjoy immortality. The common appeal of the Osiris cult was great, however, and in later years any dead person was referred to as "the Osiris so and so."

To assist the dead in the afterlife, magical texts were included in the tomb. In the Old Kingdom they were for royalty only, but by the Middle Kingdom variations were written inside coffin lids of any who could afford them. In the New Kingdom and later, magical texts known as *The Book of the Dead* were written on papyrus and placed in the coffin. Pictorial vignettes show, among other things, the deceased at a sort of judgment in which his heart was weighted against truth. This indicates some concept of sin, but the afterlife for the Egyptian was not an offer from a gracious god but merely an optimistic hope based on observation of his surroundings.

The Bible mentions no Egyptian gods, and Egyptian religion did not significantly influence the Hebrews. There are some interesting parallels between biblical texts and Egyptian literature. An Amarna Age hymn to the Aton has similarities to Ps. 104, but direct borrowing seems unlikely. More striking parallels are found

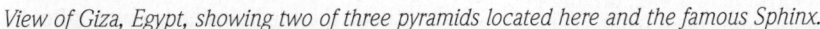

View of Giza, Egypt, showing two of three pyramids located here and the famous Sphinx.

in wisdom literature, as between Prov. 22 and the Egyptian *Instruction of Amen-em-ope.*

Daniel C. Browning, Jr. and Kirk Kilpatrick

EGYPTIAN, THE Leader of an unsuccessful attempt to capture Jerusalem in about A.D. 54. In Acts 21:38 the tribune commanding the Antonia fortress mistook Paul for this revolutionary who led 4,000 "assassins" into the wilderness. Josephus mentioned two incidents involving the same, or a similar, character. In the first, an Egyptian false prophet led a group into the desert. The procurator Felix dispersed this revolutionary band with cavalry and foot soldiers. Later the Egyptian gathered 30,000 in the wilderness, leading the multitude to the Mount of Olives from which, so he promised, they would see the walls of Jerusalem fall at his command. Felix again responded with force, killing 400 and taking 200 captive. The Egyptian ringleader escaped.

Such a sizable following suggests that either an Egyptian Jew or a proselyte to Judaism was the leader of the revolt rather than a pagan Egyptian. The tribune presumed that the Egyptian was a barbarian (unable to speak Greek). This presumption together with Paul's response that he was a Jew of Tarsus, an important city of Cilicia, suggests a rural origin for the Egyptian rebel.

EHI (Ē′ hī) Personal name meaning "my brother." A son of Benjamin (Gen. 46:21), but he does not appear in the lists of Benjamin's sons in Num. 26:38-40; 1 Chron. 8:1-2.

EHUD (Ē′ hŭd) Personal name meaning "unity, powerful." **1.** A left-handed Benjamite whom the Lord raised up to deliver the Israelites from Moabite oppression (Judg. 3:15). By a ruse he gained access to the Moabite King Eglon and assassinated him. **2.** Great grandson of Benjamin and clan leader in that tribe (1 Chron. 7:10). **3.** Clan leader in tribe of Benjamin who originally lived in Geba but were deported by someone unknown to Manahath (1 Chron. 8:6). The name Ehud appears unexpectedly in the text, so that scholars search for other names in the lists of Num. 26 and 1 Chron. 8:1-5 who might be the same person without sure results.

EKER (Ē′ kĕr) Personal name meaning "root" or "offspring." Son of Ram and grandson of Jerahmeel in the tribe of Judah (1 Chron. 2:27).

EKRON (Ĕk′ rŏn) Northernmost of the five major Philistine cities known as the Pentapolis. The site of ancient Ekron has been much debated but now is generally agreed to be modern Tell Miqne, about 14 miles inland from the Mediterranean Sea and 10 miles from Ashdod. The site is one of the largest in Palestine, cover-

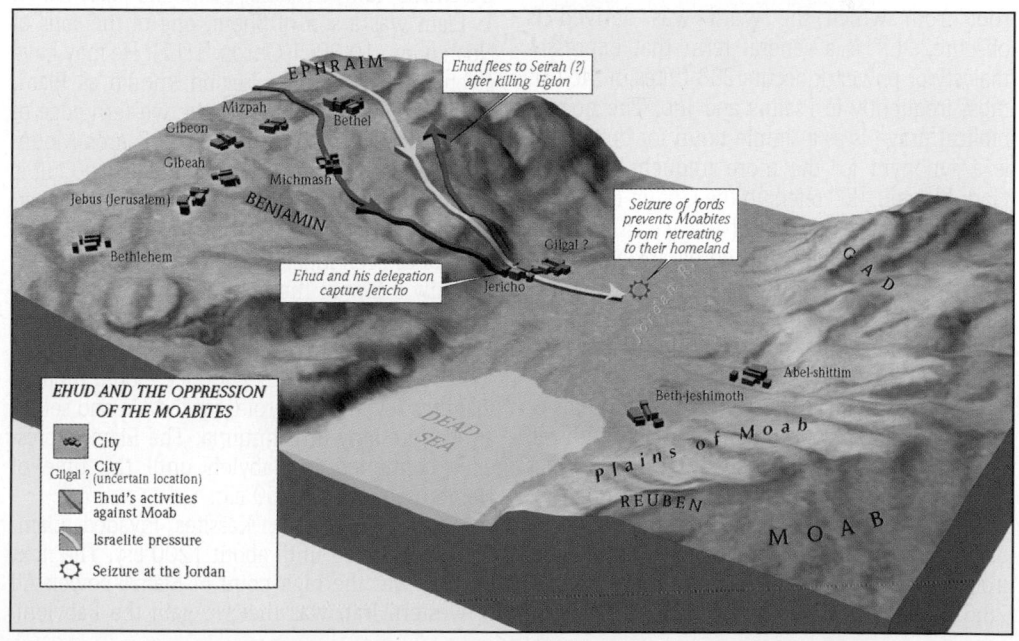

EHUD AND THE OPPRESSION OF THE MOABITES

City
Gilgal ? City (uncertain location)
Ehud's activities against Moab
Israelite pressure
Seizure at the Jordan

Ehud flees to Seirah (?) after killing Eglon

Seizure of fords prevents Moabites from retreating to their homeland

Ehud and his delegation capture Jericho

ing some 50 acres. Ekron lies on the road leading from Ashdod into the Judean hill country and up to Jerusalem through the Sorek Valley.

Ekron was assigned to both Judah (Josh. 15:11,45-46) and Dan (Josh. 19:43) in the tribal allotments. It probably lay on the border between the tribes. Judges 1:18 reports that Judah captured Ekron along with other parts of the Philistine coast, but Ekron was certainly in Philistine hands at the time the ark was captured (1 Sam. 5:10). It was also the place to which the Philistines retreated after David slew Goliath (1 Sam. 17:52). Ahaziah, the son of King Ahab of Israel, called on the god of Ekron, Baal-zebub, when he was sick (2 Kings 1:2-16).

Excavations at Tell Miqne have discovered much pottery that is typically Philistine. From the last period before Tell Miqne was destroyed by the Babylonians, the excavators found an important industrial complex near the city gate. A hoard of iron agricultural tools was found. Hundreds of whole pottery vessels were present. Perhaps most importantly, a well-preserved olive press was discovered. This press is the largest and best preserved known in Israel. A horned altar was also found during the excavations.

Joel F. Drinkard, Jr.

EL (Ĕl) One of several words for God found in biblical Hebrew and the name of the high god among the Canaanites. The word is common to Hebrew, Aramaic, and Arabic, yet the origin and root from which the word was derived is obscure. "El" is a general term that expresses majesty or power. It occurs 238 times in the OT, most frequently in Psalms and Job. The normal biblical usage is as a simple noun for deity. "El" is a synonym for the more frequent noun for God: Elohim. "El" refers to the God of Israel and in other passages to one of the pagan gods. In some instances qualifying words are associated with "El" in order to distinguish which god is being addressed. Exodus 34:14 is an example of the expression "other god"; Pss. 44:20 and 81:9 are translated "strange god."

"El" was frequently combined with nouns or adjectives to express the name for God with reference to particular attributes or characteristics of His being. El Shaddai, "God Almighty," appears in Gen. 17:1. El-elohe-Israel, in Gen. 33:20, was used to distinguish the God of Israel from all others. El Elyon, in Gen. 14:18 and Ps. 78:35, was written to suggest the exalted nature

of God. El Gibbor (Isa. 9:6; Jer. 32:18) has been interpreted as a portrayal of God as a mighty warrior. El Roi, the God who sees, is found only in Gen. 16:13. See *Canaan.*   *James Newell*

ELA (Ē´ là) Personal name of unknown meaning, perhaps related either to *el*, Hebrew word for God, or to Elah, a slightly different Hebrew spelling not noted in KJV. Father of one of Solomon's district superintendents (1 Kings 4:18). See *Elah.*

ELADAH (Ĕl´ ə däh) (KJV) See *Eleadah.*

ELAH (Ē´ lăh) Personal name and place-name meaning "oak," "mighty tree," or "terebinth." See *Terebinth.* **1.** Clan chief descended from Esau (Gen. 36:41) and thus an Edomite. See *Edom; Esau.* **2.** A valley where Saul and his army set up battle lines against the Philistines (1 Sam. 17:2). The valley runs east and west just north of Socoh. There David defeated Goliath (1 Sam. 21:9). **3.** King of Israel (732–723 B.C.), killed while he was drunk during rebellion that Zimri, his general, led successfully (1 Kings 16:6-14). **4.** Father of Hoshea, who led a revolt and became king of Israel (732–723 B.C.) (2 Kings 15:30). **5.** Son of Caleb and father of Kenaz among clans of Judah (1 Chron. 4:15). **6.** Head of a clan from Benjamin who settled in Jerusalem after the exile (1 Chron. 9:8).

ELAM (Ē´ lăm) Personal name and place-name. **1.** Elam was a son of Shem, one of the sons of Noah (Gen. 10:22; 1 Chron. 1:17). He may have given his name to the region known as Elam. **2.** The region of Elam is on the western edge of ancient Persia, modern Iran. The Zagros Mountains lie east and north while the Persian Gulf is to the south and the Tigris River is on the west. The ancient capital of the area is Susa. The region has been inhabited since before 3000 B.C., but only a few of the periods are of importance for biblical history.

Elam appeared in history when Sargon of Akkad subdued it about 2300 B.C. Soon, though, Elamites reversed the role, sacked Ur, and set up an Elamite king in Eshnunna. The Elamite presence continued in Babylon until the time of Hammurabi about 1700 B.C.

After Hammurabi, Kassites invaded Elam. Their rule lasted until about 1200 B.C. The next century was the high point of Elam's power. All of western Iran was theirs. Again the Babylonians brought Elamite power to an end. The Assyrian Ashurbanipal brought an end to the periods of strength and weakness. He swept through the region in a series of campaigns and captured Susa in 641 B.C. He may have moved some Elamites to Samaria at that time (Ezra 4:9). Earlier, Elam had incorporated Anshan, later home of Cyrus the Great, into the kingdom. As Assyria weakened, Elam and Anshan became part of the kingdom of the Medes. Thus, they participated with the Babylonians in the defeat of the Assyrian Empire. Elam had little subsequent independent history, but it continued to be part of the Medes' and the Persians' empires. In Scripture Elam's importance may have been due to its role as a vassal of the great empires, supplying troops for them.

Elam is mentioned in Scripture in narratives and oracles. Abraham fought Chedorlaomer, king of Elam, to secure the return of Lot and others (Gen. 14). Although this king cannot be identified from other records, the events may have occurred during Elam's time of strength prior to Hammurabi. Prophets mentioned Elam in oracles.

Other biblical references mention Elam as a personal name or homeland. Perhaps most interesting is the presence of men from Elam on the day of Pentecost. These may have been Jews from the region of Elam or converts to Judaism (Acts 2:9). God was still gathering His people from there. See *Persia; Cyrus; Assyria.* **3.** Clan head of tribe of Benjamin living in Jerusalem (1 Chron. 8:24). **4.** Priestly gatekeeper under David (1 Chron. 26:3). **5.** Two clan leaders among the exiles who returned to Jerusalem with Zerubbabel in 537 B.C. (Ezra 2:7,31; cp. 8:7; 10:2,26). **6.** Postexilic leader who signed Nehemiah's covenant to obey God (Neh. 10:14). **7.** Priest who helped Nehemiah lead the people in celebrating the completion of the Jerusalem wall (Neh. 12:42).   *Albert F. Bean*

ELASAH (Ĕl ā´ săh) Personal name meaning "God has made." **1.** Son of Shaphan, the royal scribe. He took Jeremiah's message to the exiled community in Babylon while on a mission for King Zedekiah (Jer. 29:3). **2.** Descendant of Jerahmeel in tribe of Judah (1 Chron. 2:39-40); spelled "Eleasah" in English translations. **3.** Descendant of Saul and Jonathan in tribe of Benjamin (1 Chron. 8:37; cp. 9:43); spelled "Eleasah" in English translations. **4.** Priest with a

foreign wife who agreed to divorce her to avoid temptation of foreign gods in the time of Ezra (Ezra 10:22).

ELATH (Ē´ lăth) or **ELOTH** (Ē´ lōth) Place-name meaning "ram," "mighty trees," or "terebinth." See *Terebinth.* Port city on northern end of Red Sea. Israel passed through it on way through Edom in wilderness (Deut. 2:8). It was significant enough to serve as a point of reference to identify Ezion-geber, where King Solomon made his naval vessels (1 Kings 9:26; cp. 2 Chron. 8:17-18). Later King Uzziah (792–740) rebuilt the seaport and controlled it for Judah (2 Kings 14:22). Archaeologists have usually identified Elath as another name for Ezion-geber and located it at Tell el-Kheleifeh. More recent archaeological work has attempted to show that Ezion-geber was the port city on the island of Jezirat Faraun. Elath would then be the mainland base to which goods were transferred for loading onto pack animals for the long caravan travels northward to Judah, Israel, Syria, or Phoenicia or for travels eastward to Assyria or Babylonia or westward to Egypt. See *Ezion-geber.*

Aqaba, Jordan, at the mouth of the Gulf of Aqaba with Elath in the distance.

EL-BERITH (El-bĭr´ ĭth) Name of a god meaning "god of the covenant." A god worshiped in a temple at Shechem. It had a stronghold or citadel guarding it. There the citizens of Shechem sought protection when Abimelech attacked them, but Abimelech set the citadel on fire (Judg. 9:46-49). KJV translates "god Berith." See *Baal-berith; Shechem.*

EL-BETHEL (Ĕl-bĕth´ ĕl) Place-name meaning "god of the house of El (god)." Either Bethel or place in or near Bethel, where Jacob built an altar to God as memorial to his previous visit to Bethel when he had seen a vision of God (Gen. 35:7; cp. 28:10-19). Apparently the name used for God was used as a place-name. See *God of the Fathers*.

ELDAAH (Ĕl dā´ ăh) Personal name meaning "God has called," "God has sought," or "God of wisdom." Son of Midian and grandson of Abraham thus original ancestor of clan of Midianites (Gen. 25:4).

ELDAD (Ĕl´ dăd) Personal name meaning "God loved." Along with Medad, he was one of 70 elders of Israel that God selected to help Moses, but the two did not meet at the tabernacle with the others. Still the Spirit came upon Eldad and Medad in the camp, and they prophesied. Joshua attempted to stop them, but Moses prayed that all God's people might have the Spirit (Num. 11:16-29). See *Medad; Prophet; Spirit*.

ELDER Prominent member of both Jewish and early Christian communities. In the OT, "elder" usually translates the Hebrew word *zaqen* from a root that means "beard" or "chin." In the NT, the Greek word is *presbuteros*, which is transliterated in English as "presbyter" and from which the word "priest" was derived.

Old Testament From the beginning of Israelite history, the elders were the leaders of the various clans and tribes. When the tribes came together to form the nation of Israel, the elders of the tribes naturally assumed important roles in governing the affairs of the nation. Moses was commanded to inform the "elders of Israel" of the Lord's intention to deliver Israel from Egypt and to take the elders with him to confront the pharaoh (Exod. 3:16,18). Similarly, 70 of the elders participated with Moses at the covenant meal at Sinai (Exod. 24:9-11). As the task of governing Israel grew in complexity, part of the burden was transferred from Moses to a council of 70 elders (Num. 11:16-17).

During the period of the judges and the monarchy, the elders were prominent in the political and judicial life of Israel. They demanded that Samuel appoint a king (1 Sam. 8:4-5); they played crucial roles in David's getting and retaining the throne (2 Sam. 3:17; 5:3; 17:15; 19:11-12); and they represented the people at the consecration of the temple of Solomon (1 Kings 8:1,3). In the legal codes of Deuteronomy, the elders are responsible for administering justice, sitting as judges in the city gate (Deut. 22:15), deciding cases affecting family life (Deut. 21:18-21; 22:13-21), and executing decisions (Deut. 19:11-13; 21:1-9).

Although elders were less prominent in the post-exilic period and the term was apparently not used much in Jewish communities outside Palestine, the "council of elders" was an integral part of the Sanhedrin at Jerusalem. In the NT, frequent reference is made to the elders of the Jews, usually in conjunction with the chief priests or scribes (Matt. 21:23; Mark 14:43). In this context the elders, apparently members of leading families, had some authority but were not the principal leaders in either religious or political affairs.

New Testament In the earliest Jewish Christian churches, at least the church in Jerusalem, the position of "elder" was almost certainly modeled after the synagogue pattern. Although there are few specific details about the function of elders in the Jerusalem church, they apparently served as a decision-making council. They are often mentioned in conjunction with the apostles, and some passages give the impression that the apostles and elders of Jerusalem considered themselves to be a decision-making council for the whole church (Acts 15; 21:17-26).

Other churches also had elders. Acts 14:23 reports that Paul and Barnabas appointed elders in churches on their missionary journey. These elders do not seem to fit the Jewish pattern, however. In the address to the Ephesian elders, Paul referred to them as overseeing the church and serving as shepherds of the church (Acts 20:28). Paul did not use the term "elders" often, usually referring to the functions of ministry rather than titles of offices. For example, in Rom. 12:6-9 Paul referred to those with gifts for prophecy, serving, teaching, and several other aspects of ministry (cp. 1 Cor. 12). Although those exercising such gifts in churches are not expressly called elders, it is likely that at least some of them were elders. Thus, elders in the Pauline churches were probably spiritual leaders and ministers, not simply a governing council.

One of the most debated questions concerning the pattern of early Christian ministry is the relationship between bishops and elders. Some scholars believe the two terms are interchangeable; others argue that they refer to distinct offices. Nowhere in the letters of Paul is there any explicit reference to the duties of either, nor is there any listing of the qualifications of elders. Titus 1:5-9 is the only passage that mentions both terms. The passage begins with a direction that elders be appointed in every town and continues with a description of the qualifications for a bishop. The context leads to the conclusion that the directions and the qualifications refer to the same persons, thus implying that the terms are interchangeable.

The qualifications in Titus 1:6-9 and in 1 Tim. 3:1-7 apparently apply to elders. It becomes apparent that the elders were the spiritual leaders of the churches. Taken as a whole, the qualifications describe one who is a mature Christian of good repute, with gifts for teaching, management, and pastoral ministry. The only specific reference to the ministry of elders is the description (James 5:14-15) of elders praying for and anointing a sick person. Although "bishop" usually occurs in the singular form, none of these passages indicate that there was only one elder in each congregation. The nature of the relationship between the various elders is nowhere described.   *Fred A. Grissom*

ELEAD (Ĕl´ ə ăd) Personal name meaning "God is a witness." Member of tribe of Ephraim killed by men of Gath for stealing their cattle (1 Chron. 7:21). See *Ezer*.

ELEADAH (Ĕl ə ā´ dăh) Personal name meaning "God adorned Himself." Modern translation spelling for KJV Eladah, a descendant of Ephraim (1 Chron. 7:20).

ELEALEH (Ĕl ə ā´ lĕh) Moabite place-name meaning "God went up" or "high ground." Town that tribe of Reuben requested from Moses and strengthened (Num. 32:3,37). Isaiah announced judgment on the town (Isa. 15:4; 16:9; cp. Jer. 48:34). It is modern el-'Al, a mile north of Heshbon in a fertile plain.

ELEASAH (Ĕl ə ā´ săh) Personal name meaning "God acted," or "God made," using same Hebrew spelling as Elasah. **1.** Member of clan of Jerahmeel in tribe of Judah (1 Chron. 2:39-40). See *Elasah*. **2.** Descendant of Saul and Jonathan in tribe of Benjamin (1 Chron. 8:37; 9:43).

ELEAZAR (Ĕl ə ā´ zăr) Personal name meaning "God helps." **1.** The third son of Aaron (Exod.

6:23) and high priest of Israel (Num. 20:28). After Aaron's death Eleazar took his place as Moses' helper. It was in the presence of Eleazar that Moses commissioned Joshua (Num. 27:22). According to Josh. 14:1 Eleazar and Joshua were the key figures in the distribution of Canaanite territories among the Israelite tribes. When he died, Eleazar was buried on a hill belonging to his son Phinehas (Josh. 24:33). He was an ancestor of Ezra the scribe (Ezra 7:5). See *Aaron; Priests and Levites*. **2.** Son of Abinadab who was sanctified by the men of Kirjath-jearim to have responsibility for the ark of the Lord (1 Sam. 7:1). **3.** One of David's renowned warriors, the son of Dodo (2 Sam. 23:9). **4.** Son of Mahli who died having had no sons, but only daughters (1 Chron. 23:21-22). **5.** Son of Phinehas who assisted in weighing out the silver and gold utensils in the house of God (Ezra 8:33). **6.** One of the sons of Parosh in a list of persons who had married foreign wives. He later put away his wife because of Ezra's reform banning foreign marriage (Ezra 10:25). **7.** Musician involved in the dedication of the wall of Jerusalem (Neh. 12:42). **8.** Son of Eliud and father of Matthan. He was an ancestor of Joseph the husband of Mary (Matt. 1:15).

ELECT LADY Recipient of John's second letter (2 John 1) sometimes understood to be an individual, but the phrase probably is a way of referring to a local church congregation. The members of the church would then be the "children" who are mentioned in the same verse. The "elect sister" of verse 13 would be another congregation whose members were sending greeting.

ELECTION God's plan to bring salvation to His people and His world. The doctrine of election is at once one of the most central and one of the most misunderstood teachings of the Bible. At its most basic level, election refers to the purpose or plan of God whereby He has determined to effect His will. Thus election encompasses the entire range of divine activity from creation, God's decision to bring the world into being out of nothing, to the end time, the making anew of heaven and earth. The word "election" itself is derived from the Greek word, *eklegomai*, which means, literally, "to choose something for oneself." This in turn corresponds to the Hebrew word, *bachar*. The objects of divine selection are the elect ones, a concept found with increasing frequency in the later writings of the OT and at many places in the NT (Matt. 22:14; Luke 18:7; Col. 3:12; Rev. 17:14). The Bible also uses other words such as "choose," "predestinate," "foreordain," "determine," and "call" to indicate that God has entered into a special relationship with certain individuals and groups through whom He has decided to fulfill His purpose within the history of salvation.

Israel as the Object of God's Election The doctrine of election is rooted in the particularity of the Judeo-Christian tradition, that is, the conviction that out of all the peoples on earth God has chosen to reveal Himself in a special, unique way to one particular people. This conviction resonates through every layer of OT literature from the early awareness of Israel as "the people of Yahweh" through the Psalms (147:19-20a, "He declares His word to Jacob, His statutes and judgments to Israel. He has not done this for any nation" [HCSB]; cp. Isa. 14:1; Ezek. 20:5). We can identify five major motifs in the OT portrayal of God's election of Israel.

(1) Election is the result of the sovereign initiative of God. At the very beginning of Israel's role in salvation history is the call of Abraham to leave his homeland for a new one that would be shown unto him (Gen. 12:1-7). This directive came to Abraham from God who also promised to bless his descendants and all peoples on earth through them. While Abraham responded to this call in obedience and faith, his election was not the result of his own efforts, but solely of God's decision. (2) The central word in Israel's vocabulary for describing their special relationship with God was "covenant." This covenant was not a contract between equal partners, but a bond established by God's unmerited favor and love. The gracious character of the covenant is a major theme in Deuteronomy. "For you are a holy people to the LORD your God; the LORD your God has chosen you to be a people for His own possession out of all the peoples who are on the face of the earth. The LORD did not set His love on you nor choose you because you were more in number than any of the peoples, for you were the fewest of all peoples" (Deut. 7:6-7 NASB). (3) Within the covenanted community God selected certain individuals to fulfill specific functions. The following persons are said to be elected in this sense: Abraham (Neh. 9:7), Moses (Ps. 106:23), Aaron (Num. 16:1–17:13), David (Ps. 78:70),

Solomon (1 Chron. 28:10), and Zerubbabel (Hag. 2:23). Kings, priests, and prophets are all chosen by God, though in different ways and for various purposes. Jeremiah believed that he had been elected and set apart as a prophet even before he was born (Jer. 1:4-5). (4) Israel's election was never intended to be a pretext for pride but rather an opportunity for service. "I am the LORD, I have called you in righteousness, ... as a light to the nations" (Isa. 42:6 NASB). From time to time the children of Israel were tempted to presume upon God's gracious favor, to assume, for example, that because the Lord had placed His temple at Jerusalem, they were exempt from judgment. Again and again the prophets tried to disabuse them of this false notion of security by pointing out the true meaning of the covenant and their mission among the nations (Jer. 7:1-14; Amos 3:2; Jonah). (5) In the later OT writings, and especially during the intertestamental period, there is a tendency to identify the "elect ones" with the true, faithful "remnant" among the people of God. The birth of the Messiah is seen to mark the dawn of the age of salvation for the remnant (Ezek. 34:12-13,23-31; Mic. 5:1-2). The community of Essenes at Qumran saw themselves as an elect remnant whose purity and faithfulness presaged the Messianic Age.

Election and the New Covenant Early Christians saw themselves as heirs of Israel's election, "a chosen race, a royal priesthood, a holy nation, a people for His possession" (1 Pet. 2:9 HCSB). Paul treats this theme most extensively, but we should not overlook its central importance for the entire NT. Again, certain individuals are singled out as chosen by God: the 12 apostles (Luke 6:13), Peter (Acts 15:7), Paul (Acts 9:15), and Jesus Himself (Luke 9:35; 23:35). In the Synoptic Gospels the term "elect ones" is always set in an eschatological context, that is, the days of tribulation will be shortened "because of the elect, whom He chose" (Mark 13:20 HCSB). Many of the parables of Jesus, such as that of the marriage feast (Matt. 22:1-14) and that of the laborers in the vineyard (Matt. 20:1-16), illustrate the sovereignty of God in salvation. In John, Jesus is the unmistakable Mediator of election: "You did not choose Me, but I chose you," He reminded the disciples (John 15:16a HCSB). Again, His followers are those who have been given to Him by the Father "before the world existed" and "not one of them is lost" (John 17:5,12 HCSB). Also in John the shadow side of election is posed in the person of Judas, "the son of destruction." Though his status as one of the elect is called into question by his betrayal of Christ, not even this act was able to thwart the fulfillment of God's plan of salvation.

There are three passages where Paul deals at length with different aspects of the doctrine of election. In the first (Rom. 8:28-39) divine election is presented as the ground and assurance of the Christian's hope. Since those whom God has predestinated are also called, justified, and glorified, nothing can separate them from the love of God in Christ Jesus. The second passage (Rom. 9–11) is preoccupied with the fact of Israel's rejection of Christ that, in the purpose of God, has become the occasion for the entrance of Gentile believers into the covenant. In the third passage (Eph. 1:1-12) Paul pointed to the Christocentric character of election: God has chosen us "in Christ" before the foundation of the world. We can refer to this statement as the evangelical center of the doctrine of election. Our election is strictly and solely in Christ. As the eternal Son, He is, along with the Father and the Holy Spirit, the electing God; as the incarnate Mediator between God and humankind, He is the elected One. We should never speak of predestination apart from this central truth.

Election and the Christian Life Paul admonished the Thessalonians to give thanks because of their election (2 Thess. 2:13), while Peter said that we should confirm our "calling and election" (2 Pet. 1:10 HCSB). However, in the history of Christian thought, few teachings have been more distorted or more misused. The following questions reveal common misperceptions. (1) Is not election the same thing as fatalism? Predestination does not negate the necessity for human repentance and faith; rather it establishes the possibility of both. God does not relate to human beings as sticks and stones but as free creatures made in His own image. (2) If salvation is based on election, then why preach the gospel? Because God has chosen preaching as the means to awaken faith in the elect (1 Cor. 1:21). We should proclaim the gospel to everyone without exception, knowing that it is only the Holy Spirit who can convict, regenerate, and justify. (3) Does the Bible teach "double predestination," that God has selected some for damnation as well as some for salvation? There are passages (Rom. 9:11-22; 2 Cor. 2:15-16) that portray God as a potter who has molded both

vessels of mercy and vessels of destruction. Yet the Bible also teaches that God does not wish any one to perish but for all to be saved (John 3:16; 2 Pet. 3:9). We are not able to understand how everything the Bible says about election fits into a neat logical system. Our business is not to pry into the secret counsel of God but to share the message of salvation with everyone and to be grateful that we have been delivered from darkness into light. (4) Does not belief in election result in moral laxity and pride? Paul says that God chose us "for salvation through sanctification by the Spirit" (2 Thess. 2:13 HCSB). We are to work out our salvation with fear and trembling, even though to be sure, it is God who is at work within us both to will and do His good pleasure (Phil. 2:12-13). The proper response to election is not pride but gratitude for God's amazing grace that saves eternally. Election, then, is neither a steeple from which we look in judgment on others, nor a pillow to sleep on. It is rather a stronghold in time of trial and a confession of praise to God's grace and to His glory.

Timothy George

EL-ELOHE-ISRAEL (Ĕl-əl ō´ hĕ-Ĭs´ rā ĕl) Divine name meaning "God, the God of Israel." Name that Jacob gave the altar he set up in the land he bought near Shechem (Gen. 33:20). See *Patriarchs.*

EL-ELYON See *El; God.*

ELEMENTS, ELEMENTARY SPIRITS Greek term (*ta stoicheia*) used in a number of ways in ancient sources and in the NT.

First, "elements" could refer to the primary or elementary points of learning, especially for a religion or philosophy. This seems to have been the earliest meaning of the phrase and appears to be the way in which the writer of Hebrews uses it (cp. Heb. 5:12). Second, the term could refer to the four basic elements out of which all other materials were thought to have emerged: fire, air, water, and earth. Peter refers to the destruction of the elements in 2 Pet. 3:10. The term is also associated with the stars or other heavenly bodies, which were thought to consist of fire, the purest of the elements. Finally, the term came to be used in association with "elementary spirit-beings" who were thought by some to exercise a certain amount of control over the heavenly bodies—for either good or evil.

There are a number of different interpretations concerning how Paul uses the term (Gal. 4:3,9; Col. 2:8,20). The immediate context in Galatians favors "elementary spirits," since Gal. 4:8-9 connects the *stoicheia* with "[beings] that by nature are not gods" (HCSB). One problem, however, is that no other evidence for this meaning of the term can be found prior to the second century. Further, the broader context equates returning to the Torah with returning to the *stoicheia*, which perhaps would favor equating the elements with philosophical principles or a nationalistic view of the Torah. On balance, Paul probably is using the term to refer to "elementary spirits," but certainty eludes us.

C. Hal Freeman, Jr.

ELEPH (ə´ lĕph) (KJV) See *Haeleph*.

ELEPHANTS While elephants are not specifically referred to in the Bible, ivory is mentioned in connection with King Solomon, that ivory was among the riches he imported (1 Kings 10:22). Ivory tusks were used in trading among nations in Ezek. 27:15, and in Rev. 18:12 ivory is again mentioned among products traded or bought. See *Ivory*.

ELHANAN (Ĕl hā´ năn) Personal name meaning "God is gracious." The Bethlehemite who slew the brother of Goliath (2 Sam. 21:19). The Hebrew text, however, does not contain the words "the brother of." It states that Elhanan killed Goliath. First Chronicles 20:5 does indicate that Elhanan killed Lahmi, the brother of Goliath. A further variation in the texts from 2 Samuel and 1 Chronicles lies in the name of Elhanan's father: in 2 Sam. 21:19 it is Jaare-oregim; in 1 Chron. 20:5, Jair. The proper reconciliation of these two passages, along with their relationship to 1 Sam. 17 (according to which Goliath was slain by David), constitutes one of the OT's more baffling puzzles. See *David*.

ELI (Ē´ lī) Personal name meaning "high." The priest at Shiloh who became the custodian of the child Samuel (1 Sam. 1:3). He was the father of Hophni and Phinehas. After Samuel's birth, his mother Hannah brought him to the sanctuary at Shiloh in fulfillment of a vow she had made to the Lord. Eli thereby became the human agent largely responsible for the religious and spiritual training of the boy. When Samuel mistook the voice of God for the voice of Eli, Eli instructed him to ask the Lord to speak the next time he heard the voice (1 Sam. 3). Eli's death was precipitated by the news of the death of his sons and the capture of the ark of God by the Philistines (1 Sam. 4:18).

ELI, ELI, LAMA SABACHTHANI This cry of Jesus on the cross, traditionally known as the "fourth word from the cross," means "My God, My God, why have You forsaken Me?" (Matt. 27:46; Mark 15:34 HCSB). It is a quotation from Ps. 22:1. The Markan form, *Eloi*, is closer to Aramaic than Matthew's more Hebraic *Eli*.

This saying of Jesus from the cross strikes a dissonant chord for some Christians, because it seems to indicate that Jesus felt forsaken by the Father. There are several ways to consider the meaning of this passage in reverent faith. It is possible to interpret these words as a beautiful testimony to Jesus' love of His Bible, the OT, and His quoting of it in this hour of darkest crisis. In this case, such verses in Ps. 22 (5,7,8,12,14,18) indicate that Jesus sees Himself and His fate in this psalm. However, since the Gospels record only the first verse of the psalm and we do not know whether Jesus quoted the entire Psalm, this view may run the risk of not taking the phrase at face value.

Another view sees this cry as indicating a genuine forsaking of Jesus by the Father, a forsaking that was necessary for our redemption. This view leads some to questions about the nature of the godhead and theories of atonement that we cannot address in this brief discussion. Perhaps the most serious difficulty of this view is that it raises the question of whether the idea of God the Father turning His back on the obedient Son is consistent with the general biblical teaching of the steadfastness and faithfulness of God. Would He desert a trusting child in such an hour?

A view that takes into consideration the full humanity—as well as full divinity—of Jesus seems most helpful. Obviously Jesus felt deserted as He bore the burden of human sin and suffered the agony of crucifixion. This feeling of His death as a "ransom for many" may, indeed, have obscured for a time His feeling of closeness with the Father, so that even in dying He was tempted as we are. Rather than forsaking the Father in that moment, He cried out to Him in prayer.

Earl Davis

ELIAB (ə lī´ăb) Personal name meaning "God is father." **1.** Leader of tribe of Zebulun under Moses (Num. 1:9). He brought the tribe's offering at the dedication of the altar (Num. 7:24). **2.** Member of tribe of Reuben and father of Dathan and Abiram. See *Abiram; Dathan*. **3.** First son of Jesse to pass by and be rejected when Samuel searched for king to replace Saul (1 Sam. 16:6). He fought in Saul's army (1 Sam. 17:13) and became angry at David's interest in fighting Goliath (1 Sam. 17:28). His daughter married King Rehoboam (2 Chron. 11:18). He is apparently called Elihu in 1 Chron. 27:18. **4.** Levite in the line of Kohath and ancestor of Samuel (1 Chron. 6:27). The same person is apparently called Elihu in 1 Sam. 1:1 and Eliel in 1 Chron. 6:34. **5.** Levite appointed as a temple musician under David (1 Chron. 15:18,20; 16:5). **6.** Military leader from the tribe of Gad under David (1 Chron. 12:9).

ELIADA (ə lī´ ə dà) Personal name meaning "God has known." **1.** Son born to David after he established his rule in Jerusalem (2 Sam. 5:16). In 1 Chron. 14:7 he is listed as Beeliada ("Baal has known" or "the lord has known"). **2.** Father of Rezon, who established himself as king of Damascus after David conquered Zobah (1 Kings 11:23). **3.** Military commander of the tribe of Benjamin (2 Chron. 17:17) under King Jehoshaphat (873–848 B.C.).

ELIADAH (ə lī´ ə dáh) (KJV, 1 Kings 11:23) See *Eliada.*

ELIAH (ə lī´ áh) (KJV, 1 Chron. 8:27; Ezra 10:26) See *Elijah.*

ELIAHBA (ə lī´ əh bà) Personal name meaning "God hides in safety" or "my god is Chiba." A leading soldier in David's army (2 Sam. 23:32).

ELIAKIM (Ē lī´ ə kǐm) Personal name meaning "God will raise up." **1.** Son of Hilkiah who was in charge of the household of King Hezekiah of Judah (2 Kings 18:18). That responsibility had previously belonged to Shebna; Isa. 22:15-25 deals with the displacing of Shebna by Eliakim. **2.** Son of Josiah who was placed on the throne of Judah by Pharaoh Neco of Egypt (2 Kings 23:34). The Pharaoh changed the name of Eliakim to Jehoiakim. The latter name is the one by which this individual is more widely known. See *Jehoiakim*. **3.** Priest who was involved in the

dedication of the wall of Jerusalem (Neh. 12:41). **4.** Ancestor of Joseph, the husband of Mary (Matt. 1:13). **5.** Son of Melea, mentioned in Luke's genealogy of Jesus (Luke 3:30).

ELIAM (ə lī´ ăm) Personal name meaning "God is an uncle or relative" or "God of the people." **1.** Father of Bathsheba (2 Sam. 11:3). The two parts of his name are reversed in 1 Chron. 3:5, becoming Ammiel. **2.** Leading warrior under David (2 Sam. 23:34). The related list in 1 Chron. 11 does not have Eliam but in a similar position has Ahijah ("my brother is Yahweh").

ELIAS (ə lī´ás) NT spelling of Elijah (KJV), transliterating the Greek spelling. See *Elijah.*

ELIASAPH (ə lī ə sǎph) Personal name meaning "God has added." **1.** Leader of the tribe of Gad under Moses (Num. 1:14). He presented the tribe's offerings at the dedication of the altar (Num. 7:42). **2.** Levite of the family of Gershon (Num. 3:24).

ELIASHIB (ə lī´ ə shǐb) Personal name meaning "God repays or leads back." **1.** Descendant of David in Judah after the return from exile in Babylon (1 Chron. 3:24). **2.** Leading priest under David (1 Chron. 24:12). **3.** High priest in time of Nehemiah who led in rebuilding the sheep gate in the Jerusalem wall, a gate through which sheep were led to the nearby temple for sacrifice (Neh. 3:1). His house was built into the city wall (Neh. 3:20). He was the son of Joiakim and the father of Joiada (Neh. 12:10). His grandson married the daughter of Sanballat, who strongly opposed Nehemiah's efforts (Neh. 13:28), possibly indicating some tension between Nehemiah and the priestly leaders. He may be the Eliashib whose son had a room in the temple (Ezra 10:6). **4.** Priest in the time of Nehemiah who administered the temple storerooms and provided a place for Tobiah, Nehemiah's strong opponent (Neh. 13:4-9). This may be the Eliashib of Ezra 10:6. **5.** Levite and temple singer in Ezra's day who agreed to divorce his foreign wife to avoid tempting Israel to worship other gods (Ezra 10:24). **6.** Two Israelites who agreed to divorce their foreign wives under Ezra's leadership (Ezra 10:27,36).

ELIATHAH (ə lī´ ə thǎh) Personal name meaning "my God has come." A temple musician appointed under David to play and prophesy

(1 Chron. 25:4). He headed a division of temple workers (1 Chron. 25:27, where the Hebrew spelling of the name varies slightly). Many scholars of the Hebrew language think the names of the last nine sons of Heman in verse 4b originally formed a verse of a Hebrew psalm in which Eliathah would have meant "my God are You."

ELIDAD (ə lī´ dăd) Personal name meaning "God loved" or "my God is uncle or friend." The name in Hebrew is a variant spelling of Eldad. Representative of tribe of Benjamin on committee that God chose to help Joshua and Eleazar divide the land of Canaan among the tribes (Num. 34:21). See *Eldad*.

ELIEHOENAI (Ĕl ĭ ē hō ē´ nī) Personal name meaning "to Yahweh are my eyes" (cp. Ps. 123:2). **1.** One of the temple porters or gatekeepers under David (1 Chron. 26:3). **2.** One of the 12 clan heads who returned to Jerusalem from Babylon with Ezra (Ezra 8:4).

ELIEL (ə lī´ ĕl) Personal name meaning "my God is God" or "my God is El." **1.** Clan leader in the tribe of Manasseh east of the Jordan River (1 Chron. 5:23-24). **2.** Levite and ancestor of the singer Heman (1 Chron. 6:34). **3.** Member of the tribe of Benjamin (1 Chron. 8:20). **4.** Another Benjaminite (1 Chron. 8:22). **5.** Military leader under David (1 Chron. 11:46), not listed in 1 Sam. 23. **6.** Another military leader under David not listed in 1 Sam. 23 (1 Chron. 11:47). **7.** Warrior from the tribe of Gad who served under David in the wilderness (1 Chron. 12:11). **8.** Chief Levite in the time of David (1 Chron. 15:9,11). **9.** Overseer of temple offerings among the Levites (2 Chron. 31:13) under King Hezekiah (715–686 B.C.).

ELIENAI (Ĕl ĭ ē´ nī) Abbreviated form of the Hebrew personal name Eliehoenai. The abbreviated form's literal meaning is "my God, my eyes." A member of the tribe of Benjamin (1 Chron. 8:20). See *Eliehoenai*.

ELIEZER (Ĕl ĭ ē´ zēr) Personal name meaning "God helps." **1.** Servant of Abram who would have been the patriarch's heir if Abram had remained childless (Gen. 15:2). **2.** Second son of Moses and Zipporah (Exod. 18:4). **3.** One of the sons of Becher the Benjamite (1 Chron. 7:8). **4.** One of the priests who blew the trumpets when the ark of the covenant was brought to

Jerusalem (1 Chron. 15:24). **5.** A ruler of the Reubenites (1 Chron. 27:16). **6.** Son of Dodavah, who prophesied against Jehoshaphat (2 Chron. 20:37). **7.** One of the leaders whom Ezra sent for (Ezra 8:16). **8.** Priest who put away his foreign wife (Ezra 10:18). **9.** Levite who put away his foreign wife (Ezra 10:23). **10.** Member of the clan of Harim who put away his foreign wife (Ezra 10:31). **11.** Son of Jorim mentioned in the genealogy of Jesus (Luke 3:29).

ELIHOENAI (Ĕl ĭ hō ē´ nī) (KJV, Ezra 8:4) See *Eliehoenai*.

ELIHOREPH (Ĕl ĭ hō´ rĕph) Personal name meaning "my God repays," or "my God is the giver of the autumn harvest," or borrowed from Egyptian, "Apis is my God." One of Solomon's two royal scribes with his brother Ahijah (1 Kings 4:3). Their father may have been Egyptian. The name could indicate that Solomon's father-in-law (1 Kings 3:1) had helped him organize and staff his administration. Shisha, the name of Elihoreph's father, is the Egyptian word for scribe. REB takes Elihoreph as a title: "adjutant general."

ELIHU (E lī´ ə hū) Personal name meaning "he is God." **1.** Son of Barachel the Buzite who addressed Job after the latter's first three friends had ended their speeches (Job 32:2). Elihu's words fill Job 32–37. Interpreters differ with regard to the significance of Elihu's speeches. His words seem to be somewhat more insightful than those of the other three friends, yet they still prove finally unsatisfactory as an explanation of Job's suffering. See *Job*. **2.** Samuel's great grandfather (1 Sam. 1:1). **3.** Member of tribe of Manasseh who defected to David (1 Chron. 12:20). **4.** Mighty military hero under David (1 Chron. 26:7). **5.** David's brother in charge of the tribe of Judah (1 Chron. 27:18).

ELIJAH (ə lī´ jăh) Personal name meaning "my God is Yah." The prophet from the ninth century B.C. from Tishbe of Gilead in the Northern Kingdom has been called the grandest and the most romantic character that Israel ever produced (1 Kings 17:1–2 Kings 2:18). He was a complex man of the desert who counseled kings. His life is best understood when considered from four historical perspectives that at times are interrelated: his miracles, his struggle against baalism, his prophetic role, and his eschatological relationship to Messiah.

Miracles His first miracle was associated with his prophecy before King Ahab (1 Kings 17:1) in which he said there would be no rain or dew apart from his declaration. Immediately after the prophecy, he retreated to the brook Cherith where he was fed by ravens. His next refuge was Zarephath where he performed the miracle of raising the widow's dead son (1 Kings 17:17-24). Here he was first called "a man of God."

On Mount Carmel his greatest public miracle involved his encounter with the 450 prophets of Baal and the 400 prophets of Asherah (1 Kings 18:19-40). The contest was to determine the true God. The false prophets called on their gods, and Elijah called on His God to see which would rain fire from heaven. After the false prophets failed to hear from their gods, Elijah wet the wood on his altar to the true God by pouring four jars of water over it three times. In response of Elijah's prayer, Yahweh rained fire from heaven to consume the wet wood. As a result of their deception, Elijah ordered the false prophets killed.

Elijah next prophesied that the drought was soon to end (1 Kings 18:41) after three rainless years. From Carmel, Elijah prayed. He sent his servant seven times to see if rain was coming. The seventh time a cloud the size of a hand appeared on the horizon. Ahab was told to flee before the storm. Elijah outran his chariot and the storm to arrive at Jezreel.

Baalism Interwoven in the life of Elijah is his struggle with Baalism. Jezebel, daughter of Ethbaal, king of Sidon and Tyre (1 Kings 16:31), was Ahab's wife and Israel's queen. She brought the worship of her god Baal into Ahab's kingdom. Even "Ahab served Baal a little" (2 Kings 10:18). The contest on Carmel showed a contrast between the contesting deities. Yahweh's power and Baal's impotence was further revealed through the drought. Jezebel planned revenge toward Elijah for ordering the false prophets slain, so Elijah retreated to Judah and finally Mount Horeb. There he observed the power of the wind, earthquake, and fire; but the Lord was not seen in these forces. In a small voice the Lord commanded him to go anoint Hazael king of Syria, Jehu king of Israel, and Elisha as his own successor (1 Kings 19:1-17).

Prophet His prophetic role constantly placed Elijah in opposition to the majority of the people of

Entrance to Elijah's cave near Tyre.

his nation. His prophetic confrontations involved King Ahab and later his son Ahaziah. Their toleration of polytheism was the ongoing reason for Elijah's prophetic denunciations.

When Ahaziah fell and injured himself, he sent messengers to ask Baal-zebub (lord of flies) about his fate. Elijah intercepted them and sent word back to Ahaziah that he was soon to die (2 Kings 1). Ahaziah sent three different detachments of 50 soldiers each to arrest Elijah. The first two units were destroyed by fire from heaven. The captain of the third group pleaded for his life. He safely escorted Elijah to the king where he delivered the prophecy of his pending death personally.

Relationship to Messiah Elijah and Elisha were involved in the schools of the prophets when Elijah struck the waters of the Jordan and they parted to allow their crossing (2 Kings 2:1-12).

Malachi promised God would send Elijah the prophet before the coming "day of the LORD" (Mal. 4:5). John the Baptist was spoken of as the

The Chapel of Elijah on Mount Sinai, commemorating the traditional site to which Elijah fled.

one who would go before Messiah "in the spirit and power" of Elijah (Luke 1:17 HCSB). John personally denied that he was literally Elijah reincarnate (John 1:21,25). Some considered Jesus to be Elijah (Matt. 16:14; Mark 6:15).

Elijah appeared along with Moses on the Mount of Transfiguration with Jesus to discuss His "departure." Here Peter suggested that three tabernacles be built for Jesus, Moses, and Elijah (Matt. 17:4; Mark 9:5; Luke 9:33).

The two witnesses referred to in Rev. 11:6 are not identified by name, but their capacity "to close the sky so that it does not rain" (HCSB) leads many to conclude they are Moses and Elijah.   *Nelson Price*

ELIKA (ə lī´ kà) Personal name meaning "my God has arisen" or "my God has vomited." One of David's military heroes from the village of Harod (2 Sam. 23:25). He does not appear in the parallel list in 1 Chron. 11.

ELIM (Ē´ lĭm) Place-name meaning "trees." One of the encampments of the Israelites after the exodus from Egypt (Exod. 15:27). It was the first place where they found water. It had 12 wells of water and 70 palm trees (Num. 33:9). Its exact location is unknown.

ELIMELECH (ə lĭm´ ə lĕk) Personal name meaning "my God is king." Husband of Naomi,

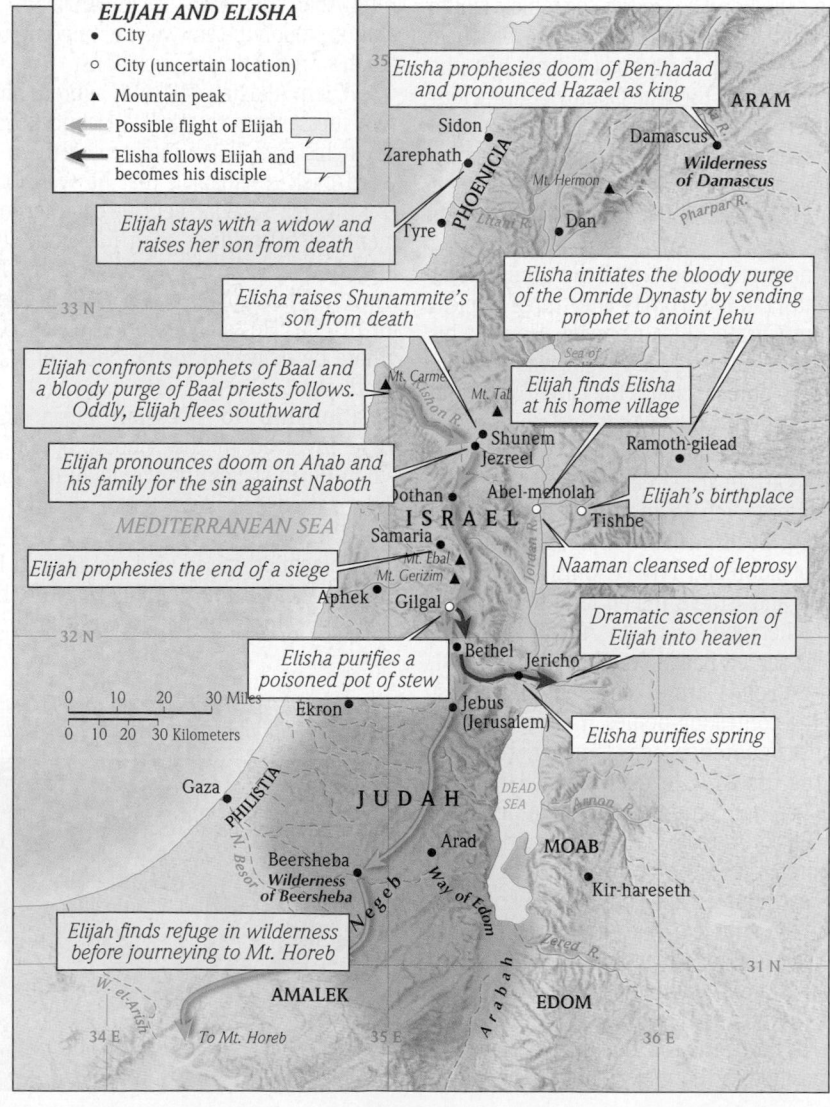

ELIJAH AND ELISHA
- City
- City (uncertain location)
- ▲ Mountain peak
- Possible flight of Elijah
- Elisha follows Elijah and becomes his disciple

Elisha prophesies doom of Ben-hadad and pronounced Hazael as king

Elijah stays with a widow and raises her son from death

Elisha raises Shunammite's son from death

Elisha initiates the bloody purge of the Omride Dynasty by sending prophet to anoint Jehu

Elijah confronts prophets of Baal and a bloody purge of Baal priests follows. Oddly, Elijah flees southward

Elijah finds Elisha at his home village

Elijah pronounces doom on Ahab and his family for the sin against Naboth

Elijah's birthplace

Naaman cleansed of leprosy

Elijah prophesies the end of a siege

Dramatic ascension of Elijah into heaven

Elisha purifies a poisoned pot of stew

Elisha purifies spring

Elijah finds refuge in wilderness before journeying to Mt. Horeb who led his family from Bethlehem to Moab to escape famine and then died in Moab. This prepared the scene for the book of Ruth (Ruth 1:2-3; cp. 4:3).

ELIOENAI (Ēl ĭ ō ē´ nī) Personal name meaning "to Yo [Yahweh] are my eyes," a Hebrew spelling variant of Eliehoenai. See *Eliehoenai.* **1.** Postexilic descendant of David, maintaining Israel's royal line (1 Chron. 3:23-24). **2.** Clan leader of the tribe of Simeon (1 Chron. 4:36). **3.** Grandson of Benjamin and thus great grandson of Jacob (1 Chron. 7:8). **4.** Priest who agreed under Ezra's leadership to divorce his foreign wife to protect the community from false worship (Ezra 10:22). **5.** Israelite who agreed to divorce his foreign wife (Ezra 10:27). **6.** Priest who led in the service of dedication and thanksgiving for the completion of repairs of the wall around Jerusalem (Neh. 12:41).

ELIPHAL (ə lī´ phăl) Personal name meaning "God has judged." Military hero under David (1 Chron. 11:35). In 2 Sam. 23:34 the name appears as Eliphelet. See *Eliphelet.*

ELIPHALET (ə lĭph´ ə lĕt) (KJV, 2 Sam. 5:16; 1 Chron. 14:7). See *Eliphelet.*

ELIPHAZ (Ēl´ ĭ phăz) Personal name meaning "my god is gold." **1.** Son of Esau by his wife Adah, the daughter of Elon the Hittite (Gen. 36:4). Eliphaz became the ancestor of the chieftains of several Edomite clans (Gen. 36:15-16). **2.** One of three men who visited Job and engaged the sufferer in dialogue (Job 2:11). He is identified as a Temanite, meaning he was from Teman in Edom. His recorded speeches to Job are marked by a simplistic theological traditionalism and a tone of moral superiority. He may have been a descendant of Eliphaz the son of Esau. See *Job.*

ELIPHELEH (ə lĭph´ ə lĕh) (KJV) or **ELIPHELEHU** (ə lĭph´ ə lē hū) Personal name meaning "God treated him with distinction." Levite and musician in temple under David (1 Chron. 15:18,21).

ELIPHELET (ə lĭph´ ə lĕt) Personal name meaning "God is deliverance." **1.** David's son born in Jerusalem (2 Sam. 5:16). He is apparently listed twice in both 1 Chron. 3:6,8 and 14:5,7, with an abbreviated Hebrew spelling in 14:5. **2.** Descen-

dant of Saul and Jonathan in the tribe of Benjamin (1 Chron. 8:39). **3.** Clan leader who accompanied Ezra on his return from exile in Babylon (Ezra 8:13). **4.** Man who divorced his foreign wife under Ezra's leadership to avoid false worship among God's people (Ezra 10:33). **5.** Famous warrior under David (2 Sam. 23:34).

ELISABETH (Ĕ´ lĭs ´ ə bĕth) Personal name meaning "my God is good fortune" or "my God has sworn an oath." A woman descended from Aaron who was the wife of Zacharias the priest (Luke 1:5). Both she and her husband are described in Luke 1:6 as being noteworthy examples of piety and devotion to the Lord. However, she was barren in her old age. God removed from her the stigma of childlessness, and she became the mother of John the Baptist, forerunner of Christ. She also was kin to Mary the mother of Jesus, but the Bible does not indicate the exact degree of relationship between the two women. See *Annunciation; John.*

ELISEUS (Ĕl ĭ sē´ ŭs) KJV spelling of Elisha, following the Greek transliteration of the Hebrew, in Luke 4:27. See *Elisha.*

ELISHA (ə lī´ shà) Personal name meaning "my God is salvation." A ninth century B.C. Israelite prophet, son of Shaphat of Abel-meholah (1 Kings 19:16).

His Name and Call Experience Elisha was plowing one day when "Elijah passed over to him and threw his mantle on him" (1 Kings 19:19 NASB). This action symbolically manifested God's plan to bestow the prophetic powers of Elijah upon Elisha. The chosen one understood the call of God for, "he left the oxen and ran after Elijah" (1 Kings 19:20). That Elisha felt the call of prophetic succession is again clear following Elijah's dramatic ascent into heaven. There Elisha "took up the mantle of Elijah that fell from him" (2 Kings 2:13).

The beginning of Elisha's ministry should be dated to the last years of King Ahab's rule (1 Kings 19) or approximately 850 B.C. The prophet then served faithfully during the reigns of Ahaziah (about 853 B.C.), Jehoram or Joram (852 B.C.), Jehu (ca. 841 B.C.), Jehoahaz (ca. 814 B.C.), and Jehoash or Joash (798 B.C.).

His Miracles After Elijah insisted to his chosen successor that he, "Ask what I shall do for you, before I am taken from you," Elisha answered,

E

"Let a double portion of spirit be upon me" (2 Kings 2:9). Taking up the mantle of the departed prophet, he parted the Jordan River. Following this miracle the prophetic order or "sons of the prophets" declared, "The spirit of Elijah rests on Elisha" (2 Kings 2:15).

Soon thereafter, Elisha made bad water wholesome (2 Kings 2:19-22). His reputation soon assumed so sacred an aura that harassment of the prophet merited severe punishment. For mocking the bald prophet, 42 boys were attacked by two she-bears (2 Kings 2:23-24).

The prophet used his power to provide a widow with an abundance of valuable oil to save her children from slavery (2 Kings 4:1-7). He made a poisonous pottage edible (2 Kings 4:38-41), fed a hundred men by multiplying limited resources (2 Kings 4:42-44), and miraculously provided water for thirsting armies (2 Kings 3:13-22). Once he made an iron ax head float (2 Kings 6:5-7).

Some of the miracles of Elisha are quite well known and loved. This barren woman and her

Elisha's spring at Jericho which is the source for Elisha's well (located in the covered area).

husband who had graciously opened their home to the prophet had in turn been given a son by the Lord. One day while the boy worked in the field with his father, he suffered an apparent heatstroke and died. The compassion and tenacious hope of the mother met its reward when she sought and found the man of God and pleaded for help. God's power through Elisha raised the boy from the dead (2 Kings 4:8-37).

Yet another well-known story is the healing of Naaman the leper and the subsequent affliction of Gehazi the dishonest servant of Elisha (2 Kings 5:1-27). The miraculous powers of the prophet were prominently displayed still further in the war between Syria and Israel. The Syrian soldiers were blinded, then made to see. Then, at last, divine intervention totally foiled the Syrian siege of Samaria (2 Kings 6:8-7:20).

Elisha's power did not end at death. For when a dead man was thrown into Elisha's grave and touched his bones, "he revived and stood up on his feet" (2 Kings 13:21).

In carrying out the second and third commands of the "still small voice" to Elijah (1 Kings 19:11-16), Elisha enhanced his legacy beyond the realm of miracle worker. He played a major role in Hazael becoming king of Syria (2 Kings 8:7-15) and also in the anointing of Jehu as king of Israel (2 Kings 9:1-13).

Powerful enough to perform miracles and appoint kings, yet sensitive enough to weep over the fate of Israel (2 Kings 8:11-12), Elisha, disciple and successor to Elijah, proved to be both prophet and statesman.   *J. Randall O'Brien*

ELISHAH (ə lī´ shăh) Place-name of unknown meaning. Elishah, or Alashiya as it appears in Hittite, Akkadian, and Ugaritic texts, is a name for all or part of the island of Cyprus, which exported copper and purple cloth. Others would locate it as the present Haghio Kyrko in Crete. Among the Amarna letters from Egypt are letters from the king of Elishah to the pharaoh mentioning copper exports. The Greeks established a colony on Cyprus by about 1500 B.C. This would explain the relationship of Elishah as a son of Javan or the Greeks in the Table of Nations (Gen. 10:4; cp. 1 Chron. 1:7). Ezekiel noted in his lament over Tyre that Tyre had imported from Elishah the purple fabric for which Tyre was famous (Ezek. 27:7).

ELISHAMA (ə lĭsh´ ə mȧ) Personal name meaning "God heard." **1.** Leader of the tribe of Ephraim under Moses in the wilderness (Num. 1:10). He presented the tribe's offerings at the dedication of the altar (Num. 7:48-53; cp. 1 Chron. 7:26). **2.** David's son born after he captured and moved to Jerusalem (2 Sam. 5:16). He is apparently listed twice in 1 Chron. 3:6,8, though 1 Chron. 14:5 reads the first Elishama as Elishua, as in 2 Sam. 5:15. **3.** Royal scribe under King Jehoiakim (609–597 B.C.). Baruch's scroll of Jeremiah's preaching was stored in Elishama's room before it was taken to be read to the king (Jer. 36:12-21). **4.** Ancestor with royal bloodlines of Ishmael, the person who murdered Gedaliah and took over political control of Judah immediately after Babylon had destroyed Jerusalem (2 Kings 25:25). **5.** Descendant of the clan of Jerahmeel in the tribe of Judah (1 Chron. 2:41). **6.** Priest under King Jehoshaphat (873–848 B.C.). He taught the book of the law to the people of Judah at the king's request (2 Chron. 17:7-9).

ELISHAPHAT (ə lĭsh´ ə phăt) Personal name meaning "God had judged." Military captain who helped Jehoiada, the priest, overthrow Queen Athaliah and establish Joash (835–796 B.C.) as king of Judah (2 Chron. 23:1).

ELISHEBA (ə lĭsh´ ə bȧ) Personal name meaning "God is good fortune." Wife of Aaron, the high priest (Exod. 6:23).

ELISHUA (Ĕl ĭ shū´ ȧ) Personal name meaning "God is salvation." David's son born after he captured and moved to Jerusalem (2 Sam. 5:15). See *Elishama 2.*

ELIUD (ə lī´ ŭd) Personal name meaning "God is high and mighty." Great, great grandfather of Joseph, the earthly father of Jesus (Matt. 1:14-15).

ELIZABETH (ə lĭz´ ȧ bĕth) Americanized spelling used in modern translations of KJV Elisabeth. See *Elisabeth.*

ELIZAPHAN (Ĕl ĭ zā´ phăn) Personal name meaning "God has hidden or treasured up." **1.** Clan leader among the sons of Kohath among the Levites in the wilderness with Moses (Num. 3:30; cp. 1 Chron. 15:8; 2 Chron. 29:13). **2.** Representative of tribe of Zebulun on the

council to help Joshua and Eleazar divide the land among the tribes (Num. 34:25).

ELIZUR (ə lī´ zûr) Personal name meaning "God is a rock." Leader of tribe of Reuben under Moses in the wilderness (Num. 1:5). He presented the tribe's offerings at the dedication of the altar (Num. 7:30-35).

ELKANAH (Ĕl kā´ nah) Personal name meaning "God created." **1.** One of the sons of Korah, the priest (Exod. 6:24). **2.** Son of Jeroham. He became the father of Samuel (1 Sam. 1:1). **3.** Person named in a list of Levites (1 Chron. 6:23-26). **4.** Father of Asa who is mentioned in a list of Levites (1 Chron. 9:16). **5.** Benjaminite warrior who deserted Saul and joined David (1 Chron. 12:6). **6.** One of two gatekeepers for the ark of the covenant (1 Chron. 15:23). **7.** An official in the service of King Ahaz of Judah who was assassinated by Zichri the Ephraimite (2 Chron. 28:7). See *Samuel.*

ELKOSH (Ĕl´ kŏsh) Place-name of unknown meaning. Home of Nahum the prophet (Nah. 1:1). Although several traditions exist that identify various places as the site of Elkosh, its location remains unknown. That it was in Judea is fairly likely.

ELLASAR (Ĕl lā´ sär) Babylonian place-name of unknown meaning. The capital city of King Arioch, who joined the eastern coalition against Sodom and Gomorrah, resulting in Abraham's involvement in war (Gen. 14:1). Identification with Larsa in Babylon was based on a false identification of Arioch. The Mari texts mention Ilanzura between Carchemish and Harran. Other scholars suggest Ellasar is an abbreviation for Til-Asurri on the Euphrates River. Others suggest it is located on the southern coast of the Black Sea near Pontus in Asia Minor. Thus the question of exact identification still remains open.

ELM See *Plants; Terebinth.*

ELMADAM (Ĕl mā´ dăm) or **ELMODAM** (Ĕl mō´ dăm) (KJV) Personal name of unknown meaning. An ancestor of Jesus Christ (Luke 3:28).

ELNAAM (Ĕl nā´ ăm) Personal name meaning "God is a delight." Father of military leaders under David (1 Chron. 11:46). He is not listed in 2 Sam. 23.

ELNATHAN (Ĕl nā´ thăn) Personal name meaning "God has given." **1.** Father of King Jehoiachin's mother (2 Kings 24:8). **2.** Possibly to be identified with 1. He was the member of King Jehoiakim's advisory staff who brought the prophet Uriah back to the king from Egypt for punishment (Jer. 26:22-23). He tried to prevent the king from burning Baruch's scroll of Jeremiah's preaching (Jer. 36:12-26). **3.** Three men of the same name plus a "Nathan" are listed in Ezra 8:16 as part of the delegation Ezra sent to search for Levites to return from Babylon to Jerusalem with him. Many Bible students feel that copying of the manuscripts has introduced extra names into the list.

ELOI (ə lō´ ī) Greek transliteration of Aramaic *'elohi*, "my God." See *Eli, Eli, Lama Sabachthani*.

ELON (Ē´ lŏn) Personal name and place-name meaning "great tree" or "tree of god" (cp. Gen. 12:6; Judg. 9:6,37). See *Terebinth*. **1.** The Hittite father of Esau's wife Bashemath (Gen. 26:34). **2.** Site where Deborah, Rebekah's nurse, was buried, called "Allon-bachuth" or "the oak of weeping" (Gen. 35:8). See *Allonbachuth*. The same point may be referred to as the "oak of Tabor" (1 Sam. 10:3) or the "palm tree of Deborah" (Judg. 4:5). See *Bochim*. **3.** The Hittite father of Adah, Esau's wife (Gen. 36:2), Bashemath being listed as Ishmael's daughter (36:3). See *Basemath*. **4.** Son of Zebulun and grandson of Jacob (Gen. 46:14). A clan in Zebulun was thus named for him (Num. 26:26) **5.** City in tribal territory of Naphtali (Josh. 19:33), often transliterated into English as Allon. See *Allon*. The reference may simply be to a large tree that served as a boundary marker. **6.** City in tribal territory of Dan (Josh. 19:43). It may be located at Khirbet Wadi Alin. It is probably the same place as Elon-beth-hanan (1 Kings 4:9), though some read Ajalon and Bethhanan or "Elon, and Beth-hanan" (REB). **7.** Judge from the tribe of Zebulun (Judg. 12:11-12). **8.** A leader in the tribe of Simeon (1 Chron. 4:37).

ELON-BETH-HANAN (Ē lŏn-bĕth-hā´ năn) See *Elon*.

ELON-MEONENIM (Ē lŏn-mē ŏn´ ə nĭm) See *Diviner's Oak*.

ELONITE (Ē´ lŏn īt) Citizen of Elon. See *Elon*.

ELOTH (Ē´ lŏth) Variant spelling of Elath. See *Elath*.

ELPAAL (Ĕl pā´ ăl) Personal name meaning "God has made." A clan name in the tribe of Benjamin, mentioned twice in 1 Chron. 8 (vv. 11-12,18). Bible students debate whether the references refer to the same clan ancestor or to two individuals. It is also uncertain whether he or his sons receive credit for building Ono and Lod (v. 12).

ELPALET (Ĕl pā´ lĕt) (KJV) See *Elpelet*.

ELPARAN (Ĕl pā´ răn) Place-name meaning "tree of Paran." The place where the eastern coalition of kings extended its victory over the Horites (Gen. 14:6). It is apparently a place in or near Elath. See *Elath; Paran*.

ELPELET (Ĕl pĕl´ ĕt) David's son born after he captured and moved to Jerusalem (1 Chron. 14:5). This is apparently an abbreviated spelling of Eliphelet. See *Eliphelet*.

EL-SHADDAI See *El; God*.

ELTEKE or **ELTEKEH** (Ĕl´ tĕ kĕ) Place-name meaning "place of meeting," "place of hearing," or "plea for rain." A city in Dan (Josh. 19:44) assigned to the Levites (Josh. 21:23). Egyptian pharaohs claim to have conquered an Altaku, which may be the same. Sennacherib of Assyria met an Egyptian army there about 701 B.C. It has been variously located at Khirbet el-Muqenna on the eastern edge of the coastal plain, at Tell esh-Shalaf, and at Tell el-Melat, northwest of Gezer.

ELTEKON (Ĕl´ tə kŏn) Place-name meaning "securing advice." Village in tribal territory of Judah in southern hill country (Josh. 15:59). Its location is unknown, though some have suggested Khirbet ed-Deir, west of Bethlehem.

ELTOLAD (Ĕl tō´ lăd) Place-name meaning "plea for a child." Village in tribal territory of Judah (Josh. 15:30), given to tribe of Simeon (Josh. 19:4). First Chronicles 4:29 apparently abbreviates it as Tolad. Its location is not known.

ELUL (ə´ lūl) Sixth month of Hebrew year, name taken over from Akkadian. It included parts of August and September. See Neh. 6:15.

ELUZAI (ə lū´ zī) Personal name meaning "God is my strength." A member of King Saul's tribe of Benjamin, who became a military leader for David, while he lived as a fugitive in Ziklag (1 Chron. 12:5).

ELYMAS (Ĕl´ y̆ măs) Personal name possibly meaning "wise." A magician and false prophet also known as Bar-jesus (Acts 13:6-11). At Paphos on the island of Cyprus, Elymas tried to dissuade the deputy Sergius Paulus from listening to the words of Barnabas and Paul. He was denounced by Paul and stricken temporarily blind. See *Sergius Paulus.*

ELYON See *El; God.*

ELZABAD (Ĕl zā´ băd) Personal name meaning "God made a gift." **1.** Soldier who fought for David while he was a fugitive in Ziklag (1 Chron. 12:12). **2.** Levite and grandson of Obed-edom, identified as a valiant man (1 Chron. 26:7). He was a porter or gatekeeper in the temple.

ELZAPHAN (Ĕl zā´ phăn) Personal name meaning "God has hidden or treasured up." An abbreviated form of Elizaphan. A son of Uzziel, Aaron's uncle (Exod. 6:22). He helped carry the dead bodies of Nadab and Abihu out of the wilderness camp after God punished them (Lev. 10:4-5).

EMBALMING Process of preserving bodies from decay. Embalming originated in Egypt and was seldom used by the Hebrews. The practice is rarely mentioned in the Bible, and the human remains unearthed in Palestinian tombs generally show no signs of having been embalmed. In Gen. 50:2-3 it is recorded that Joseph ordered the embalming of Jacob's body and that "physicians" required 40 days to perform the process. Verse 26 says Joseph was embalmed and laid to rest in Egypt. The embalming of these two patriarchs testifies both to their importance in the community and to plans to remove their bodies for burial in Canaan (Gen. 50:13; Exod. 13:19).

Related passages including 2 Chron. 16:14 describe the burial of Asa and the John 19:39-40 account of Jesus' burial. The use of spices mentioned in both of these passages did not constitute embalming but ceremonial purification.

The Egyptian art of mummification was an elaborate version of embalming that required 70 days for completion.   *Joe Haag*

EMEK-KEZIZ (Ē´ mĕk-kē´ zĭz) Place-name meaning "the cutoff valley" or "the valley of gravel." It is listed as one of the cities assigned to the tribe of Benjamin (Josh. 18:21). Its location is not known.

EMERALD See *Minerals and Metals.*

EMERODS Archaic form of the word "hemorrhoids" used by the KJV for the disease(s) in Deut. 28:27 and 1 Sam. 5–6. It is impossible to identify the disease with certainty. Whatever its precise nature, the disease was regarded as incurable and fatal. Modern speech translations are agreed that the malady is likely not hemorrhoids. The underlying Hebrew term is rendered tumors except for the passage in Deuteronomy where NRSV and TEV opt for ulcers or sores. The presence of tumors associated with an infestation of mice has suggested bubonic plague to some interpreters. On the basis of the earliest Greek OT reading, the NIV includes the margin reading "tumors of the groin."

EMIM (Ē´ mĭm) or **EMITES** (Ē´ mīts) (NIV) National name meaning "frightening ones." They lost a war to the eastern coalition of kings (Gen. 14:6) and are identified with a place in northern Moab, Shaveh Kiriathaim. They were ancient giants or Rephaim (Deut. 2:10-11). See *Rephaim.*

EMMANUEL (Em măn´ ū ĕl) See *Immanuel.*

EMMAUS (Ĕm mā´ ŭs) Place-name meaning "hot baths." A village that was the destination of two of Jesus' disciples on the day of His resurrection (Luke 24:13). As they traveled, they were joined by a person whom they later realized was the risen Christ. Emmaus was about 60 furlongs (approximately seven miles) from Jerusalem. That statement is the only clue to its location. As many as four sites have been proposed as the location of Emmaus, but certainty is not possible. See *Resurrection.*

EMMOR (Ĕm´ môr) (KJV, Acts 7:16) See *Hamor.*

EMPEROR WORSHIP Practice of assigning the status of deity to current or deceased rulers.

Old Testament Although the term "emperor worship" is usually applied to the Roman cult, there were similar beliefs and practices in OT times. In Egypt, for example, the current ruler was considered the incarnation of the god Horus, son of Re, and at death he became Osiris. The most obvious example of emperor worship in the OT is the well-known story of Shadrach, Meshach, and Abednego (Dan. 3). King Nebuchadnezzar made an image of gold, presumably of himself, and commanded everyone to fall down and worship the image or be killed (3:5-6). Shadrach, Meshach, and Abednego refused to commit idolatry by worshiping the image (3:16-18). They were thrown into a furnace but were not burned (3:27). Thereafter, Nebuchadnezzar permitted them to worship their God unhindered (3:29). See *Gods, Pagan.*

New Testament Although the Greeks believed the gods could appear as men, (cp. Acts 14:12-13), they usually rejected the deification of rulers. Yet, Alexander the Great began to refer to himself as "son of Zeus" after encountering the priest of Amun in Egypt. After his burial in Alexandria, a temple and cult were dedicated to him there, which spread to Asia Minor and even Athens. The Ptolemies and Seleucids, who considered themselves heirs of his empire, also considered themselves heirs of his divinity and built temples in their names. This ruler cult was also inherited by the Roman Empire. In Ephesus in 48 B.C., Julius Caesar was decreed "god on earth, descended from Ares and Aphrodite, and universal savior of human life." After his death the people of Rome echoed this declaration, and the Senate made it official in 42 B.C., building an altar to him. Again in the Eastern provinces, Julius Caesar's adopted son and heir of the empire, Octavian, who became known as Augustus, was likewise worshipped. His birthday was celebrated as "the beginning of good news [*euangelia*]" for the world, and temples were dedicated to "Rome and Augustus." Then like his predecessor, at Augustus's death in 14 B.C. he took his place in Rome among the gods.

The emperors Tiberius and Claudius likewise waited until their deaths for deification, but Tiberius's successor Caligula and Claudius's successor Nero were not so patient. Caligula represented himself as Helios the sun god, and Nero claimed the designation Apollo. Domitian (A.D.

Forum and temple of Augustus in Rome—the major center of emperor worship.

81–96) even issued his orders as coming from a god. He built a temple with a huge statue of himself in Ephesus.

Determined to return his empire to its traditional Roman religion, Domitian was especially vicious toward Christians. But they were also victims of the royal cult during the reigns of Nero and other Roman emperors. Persecution of Christians was severe, partly because of gross misconceptions regarding the practice of the Christian faith. Christians were considered undesirable and were vigorously rooted out. When on trial, if they worshiped the pagan gods, that is, the emperor and the imperial cult, they would be freed. If not, they would suffer all manner of punishments and death. All the suspected Christian had to do was sprinkle a few sacrificial grains of incense into the eternal flame burning in front of the statue of the emperor. Since the punishments were so horrible and the means of escape so easy, many Christians gave in. Many did not and were burned alive, killed by lions in the arena, or crucified.

A specific NT example of emperor worship is the worship of the beast in the book of Revelation. Revelation 13 speaks of a beast that is given ruling authority. An image is made of the beast, and all are commanded to worship it (13:4,12,14-15; see also Dan. 8:4,8-12). See *Rome and the Roman Empire.*

Donna R. Ridge and E. Ray Clendenen

ENAIM (ə nā´ ĭm) or **ENAM** (Ē´ năm) Place-name meaning "two eyes or springs." A village near Timnah, where Tamar seduced Judah (Gen. 38:14). It is probably the same as Enam in the tribal territory of Judah (Josh. 15:34). The exact location is not known. See *Timnah.*

ENAN (Ē´ năn) Personal name meaning "eyes or springs." Father of Ahira, the leader of the tribe of Naphtali under Moses (Num. 1:15). See *Ahira*.

ENCHANTER See *Divination and Magic*.

EN-DOR (Ĕn´ dôr) Place-name meaning "spring of Dor," that is, "spring of settlement." **1.** Home of witch who brought up Samuel from the grave (1 Sam. 28:7). Psalm 83:10 says Jabin died there (cp. Judg. 4–5). It is modern Khirbet Safsafe, three miles south of Mount Tabor. **2.** City tribe of Manasseh claimed but could not conquer (Josh. 17:11; cp. Judg. 1:27).

ENDURANCE See *Perseverence; Steadfastness*.

ENEAS (ə nē´ ås) Variant spelling of Aeneas. See *Aeneas*.

EN-EGLAIM (Ĕn-ĕg´ lā ĭm) Place-name meaning "spring of the two calves." A spring near the Dead Sea where Ezekiel predicted a miracle, the salt waters being made fresh and becoming a paradise for fishing (Ezek. 47:10). It is apparently Ain Feshcha on the western coast of the Dead Sea.

ENEMY Adversary or foe; one who dislikes or hates another and seeks to harm the person. Sometimes referring to an individual opponent or to a hostile force, either a nation or an army.

The natural inclination of all people is to hate their enemies. Some have even misconstrued God's law to teach hatred. Jesus taught rather to love one's enemies and to seek their good (Matt. 5:43-47). This is also the teaching of the OT (Prov. 24:17; 25:21).

In the Bible a person who disobeys divine commands is declared to be God's enemy. Paul referred to sinners as the enemies of God (Rom. 5:10). Job felt that God had become his enemy, too (Job 13:24). Because of this severed relationship, God has made provision for our forgiveness in the life, death, and resurrection of Jesus Christ.

Satan is also called "the adversary" (1 Tim. 5:14-15 HCSB). He has revealed himself as such throughout history by seeking to hurt men and women, leading them away from God.

The greatest and final enemy is death itself (1 Cor. 15:26). It is feared by all because of its finality and unknown nature. But the Bible teaches that Jesus has "abolished" death once for all (2 Tim. 1:10). Those who have trusted Christ for the salvation He freely gives need not fear death.   *Bradley S. Butler*

EN-GANNIM (Ĕn-găn´ nĭm) Place-name meaning "the spring of gardens." **1.** Town in the tribal territory of Judah located in the Shephalah (Josh. 15:34). It has been located at modern Beit Jemal, about two miles south of Beth-shemesh or at 'umm Giina one mile southwest of Beth-shemesh. **2.** Town in tribal territory of Issachar designated as city for Levites (Josh. 19:21; 21:29). Anem (1 Chron. 6:73) is apparently an alternate spelling. The same place may be meant in 2 Kings 9:27 by Beth Haggan (NIV, REB, NRSV) or the "garden house" (KJV, NASB). It is located at modern Jenin west of Beth-shean and about 65 miles north of Jerusalem.

EN-GEDI (Ĕn-gĕ´ dĭ) Place-name meaning "place of the young goat." A major oasis along the western side of the Dead Sea about 35 miles southeast of Jerusalem. The springs of En-gedi are full, and the vegetation is semitropical. Both biblical and extra-biblical sources describe En-gedi as a source of fine dates, aromatic plants used in perfumes, and medicinal plants (Song 1:14). It was a chief source of balsam, an important plant used for perfumes, and a major source of income for the area. En-gedi apparently lay on a caravan route that led from the east shore of the Dead Sea around to its south, then up the west side to En-gedi. From there the road went up to Tekoa and then to Jerusalem.

En-gedi, also called Hazazon-tamar (2 Chron. 20:2), was inhabited by Amorites in the time of Abraham and was subjugated by Chedorlaomer (Gen. 14:7). In the tribal allotments, it was given to Judah and was in the district of Judah known as the wilderness district (Josh. 15:62). When David was fleeing from Saul, he hid in the area of Engedi (1 Sam. 23:29). Saul was in a cave near En-gedi when David cut off a piece of his robe but spared his life (1 Sam. 24). During the reign of Jehoshaphat, Moabites, Ammonites, and others gathered at Engedi to attack Judah (2 Chron. 20:1-2).

Recent excavations at En-gedi have uncovered a fortress belonging to the period of the monarchy, a workshop used in producing

E

E

One of few natural waterfalls in Israel is located at En-gedi on the west side of the Dead Sea.

perfumes, and a sanctuary belonging to the Chalcolithic or early Bronze Age.

Joel F. Drinkard, Jr.

ENGINE Catapult or battering ram. See *Arms and Armor.*

ENGRAVE To impress deeply, to carve. Many materials were engraved including clay writing tablets (Isa. 8:1), metal, precious gems, stone (Zech. 3:9), and wood. Engraving was frequently done with an iron pen, a stylus, sometimes with a diamond point (Job 19:24; Jer. 17:1). Signet rings engraved with the sign or symbol of the owner were quite common throughout the ancient world (Gen. 38:18; Esther 3:12; Jer. 22:24). In fact, "like the engravings of a signet" ring or cylinder is a set phrase used to describe the various engraved gems of the high priest's vestments (Exod. 28:11,21,36; 39:6,14). The Hebrew words translated "engrave" are used both for carving wood and working with precious stones in the construction of the tabernacle and temple (Exod. 31:5; 35:33; 1 Kings 6:18,35; 2 Chron. 2:7). A graven image (Exod. 20:4) is a carved idol (as opposed to one cast in a mold).

EN-HADDAH (Ĕn-hăd´ dàh) City in tribal lot of Issachar (Josh. 19:21). It is apparently el-Hadetheh about six miles east of Mount Tabor.

EN-HAKKORE (Ĕn-hăk´ kōr rə) Place-name meaning "spring of the partridge" or "spring of the caller." Place where God gave Samson water after he threw down the jawbone he had used to kill a thousand Philistines (Judg. 15:18-19). It is near Lehi, or literally translated, "Jawbone," which is probably near Beth-shemesh.

EN-HAZOR (Ĕn-hā´ zôr) Place-name meaning "spring of the enclosed village." A fortified city in the tribal territory of Naphtali (Josh. 19:37). It may be located at Khirbet Hazireh, west of Kadesh. Others would locate it southwest of Kedesh on the border joining Naphtali and Asher.

EN-MISHPAT (Ĕn-mĭsh´ pàt) Place-name meaning "spring of judgment." Another name for Kadesh, where the eastern coalition of kings defeated the Amalekites and Amorites. The location is usually called Kadesh-barnea and identified with the oasis now called ain Hudeirat. See *Kadesh-barnea.*

ENOCH (Ē´ nŏk) Personal name meaning "dedicated." **1.** The son of Jared who was taken up to God without dying (Gen. 5:18). He became the father of Methuselah. Enoch lived in such close fellowship with God that he was translated into the presence of God without dying. Hebrews 11:5 attributes his translation to faith. According to Jude 14, he prophesied. The name of Enoch is associated with a large body of ancient extrabiblical literature. See *Genesis; Resurrection; Apocalyptic; Apocrypha; Pseudepigrapha.* **2.** Son of Cain for whom Cain built a city and named it (Gen. 4:17-18).

ENON CITY (Ē´ nŏn Cĭtĭ) TEV translation of Hazar-enan (Ezek. 47:17). See *Hazar-enan.*

ENOS (Ē´ nŏs) or **ENOSH** (Ē´ nŏsh) Personal name meaning "humanity" or "a man." Son of Seth and therefore the grandson of Adam (Gen. 4:26). The period following his birth is identified as the time when people began to worship Yahweh. See Gen. 5:6-11.

EN-RIMMON (Ĕn-rĭm´ mōn) Place-name meaning "spring of the pomegranate." A town in Judah (Neh. 11:29) where people lived in Nehemiah's day (about 445 B.C.). Ain and Rimmon or Remmon appear as separate cities in the tribal territory of Judah (Josh. 15:32), settled by the tribe of Simeon (Josh. 19:7). These two are sometimes read as one city (19:7 RSV but not NRSV), but this makes the numbers of the cities in the lists inaccurate. It is located at Khirbet er-Ramamin, about two miles south of Lahav.

EN-ROGEL (Ĕn-rō´ gĕl) Place-name meaning "spring of the fuller" or "spring of the foot." A border town between the tribal territory of Judah (Josh. 15:7) and that of Benjamin (Josh. 18:16). Jonathan and Ahimaaz, the priests' sons, stayed at En-rogel as messengers to relay to David what the priests might learn from Absalom when he took over Jerusalem from his father (2 Sam 17:17). Adonijah staged a party there to proclaim himself as David's successor as king of Judah (1 Kings 1:9). En-rogel lay near Jerusalem where the Kidron and Hinnom Valleys met at modern Bir Ayyub.

EN-SHEMESH (Ĕn-shē´ mĕsh) Place-name meaning "spring of the sun." Town on border between tribal territories of Judah (Josh. 15:7) and Benjamin (Josh. 18:17). It is located at Ain

E

En-rogel with the traditional site of Jacob's well located under the dome in the center of the photo.

el-Hod, "the spring of the apostles," about two miles east of Jerusalem on the eastern edge of Bethany.

EN-TAPPUAH (Ĕn-tăp pū´ ăh) Place-name meaning "spring of apple." A spring near the town of Tappuah which marked the border of the tribe of Manasseh and Ephraim (Josh. 17:7). See *Tappuah.*

ENTRANCE ROOM See *Arch.*

ENVIRONMENTAL PROTECTION The earth and its resources belong to God (Lev. 25:23; Job 41:11; Pss. 24:1; 89:11) yet have been entrusted to people (Gen. 1:28-30; 2:15; 9:1-4; cp. Deut. 8:7-10). For this reason, people have a sacred responsibility to care for the earth (cp. Luke 12:41-48) with the same diligence that God cares for it (Deut. 11:12; Pss. 65:5-13; 104:10-22). Adam's initial activity in the garden of Eden consisted of tilling the ground (Gen. 2:15) and naming the animals (Gen. 2:19-20), thus signaling his active stewardship of creation.

The Mosaic law included statutes which seem to have been aimed specifically at protecting the environment. Among these were injunc-

tions that the land was to lay fallow every seven years (Exod. 23:10-11; Lev. 25:3-7) and that fruit was not to be picked from trees under four years of age (Lev. 19:23-25).

The connection between God's covenant and the land, however, ran much deeper than individual statutes. The Israelites understood that their adherence to the stipulations of God's covenant as a whole had direct consequences for the land. Obedience to God's commands resulted in a land that was blessed, that is, productive and fertile (Deut. 28:1-6), while disobedience adversely affected the fertility of the land (Gen. 3:17-19; Deut. 11:13-17; 28:1-4,15-18), creating an ecological imbalance (Deut. 29:22-28; Jer. 4:23-28; Hos. 4:2-3).   *Paul H. Wright*

ENVY Painful or resentful awareness of another's advantage joined with the desire to possess the same advantage. The advantage may concern material goods (Gen. 26:14) or social status (30:1). Old Testament wisdom frequently warns against envying the arrogant (Ps. 73:3), the violent (Prov. 3:31), or the wicked (Ps. 37:1; Prov. 24:1,19). In the NT "envy" is a common member of vice lists as that which comes out of the person and defiles (Mark 7:22), as a characteristic of humanity in rebellion to God (Rom. 1:29), as a fruit of the flesh (Gal. 5:21), as a characteristic of unregenerate life (Titus 3:3), and as a trait of false teachers (1 Tim. 6:4). "Envy" (sometimes translated "jealousy" by modern translations) was the motive leading to the arrest of Jesus (Matt. 27:18; Mark 15:10) and to opposition to the gospel in Acts (Acts 5:17, 13:45; 17:5). Christians are called to avoid envy (Gal. 5:26; 1 Pet. 2:1).

Envy is sometimes a motive for doing good. The Preacher was disillusioned that hard work and skill were the result of envying another (Eccles. 4:4). Paul was, however, able to rejoice that the gospel was preached even if the motive was envy (Phil. 1:15).

The KJV rightly understood the difficult text in James 4:5, recognizing that it is a characteristic of the human spirit that it "lusteth to envy." Contrary to modern translations, the Greek word used for "envy" here (*phthonos*) is always used in a negative sense, never in the positive sense of God's jealousy (Greek *zelos*). God's response to the sinful longings of the human heart is to give more grace (4:6). See *Jealousy.*

EPAENETUS (ə pē′ nĕ tŭs) Personal name meaning "praise." The first Christian convert in Achaia and thus a friend with special meaning for Paul (Rom. 16:5). See *Achaia*.

EPAPHRAS (Ĕp′ à phrăs) Personal name meaning "lovely." A Christian preacher from whom Paul learned of the situation of the church in Colossae (Col. 1:7). He was a native of Colossae whose ministry especially involved Colossae, Laodicea, and Hierapolis. Later he was a companion of Paul during the latter's imprisonment. Though Epaphras is mentioned in the NT only in the letters to the Colossians and to Philemon, Paul evidently held this man in high regard.

EPAPHRODITUS (ə păph rō dī′ tŭs) Personal name meaning "favored by Aphrodite or Venus." A friend and fellow worker of Paul the apostle (Phil. 2:25). He had delivered to Paul a gift from the church at Philippi while the apostle was in prison. While he was with Paul, Epaphroditus became seriously ill. After his recovery, Paul sent him back to Philippi, urging the church there to receive him "with all gladness" (Phil. 2:29). The name Epaphroditus was common in the first-century Greek-speaking world.

EPENETUS (ə pē′ nə tŭs) Variant spelling of Epaenetus. See *Epaenetus*.

EPHAH (Ē′ phàh) Personal name meaning "darkness." **1.** Son of Midian and grandson of Abraham (Gen. 25:4). The line came through Abraham's wife Keturah rather than Sarah and did not inherit as did Isaac. Ephah was thus the original ancestor of a clan of Midianites, and the clan name could be used in poetry in parallel with Midian to talk about the Midianites (Isa. 60:6). **2.** Concubine of Caleb and mother of his children (1 Chron. 2:46). **3.** Son of Jahdai and apparently a descendant of Caleb (1 Chron. 2:47).

4. An entirely different Hebrew word with a different first letter lies behind the English "ephah" as a dry measure of grain. It is one-tenth of a homer and equal to one bath of liquid (Ezek. 45:11). It is also equal to 10 omers (Exod. 16:36). Thus it is about 40 liters, though we do not have enough information to make precise estimates. Estimates place it about half a bushel. The vision of Zech. 5:7 of a woman sitting in an ephah basket contains the imaginative images of visions, for any ephah would be far too small for a woman to sit in. Israel was constantly warned not to have two ephah measures, one for buying and the other for selling (Deut. 25:14; Prov. 20:10; cp. Lev. 19:36; Ezek. 45:10; Amos 8:5).

EPHAI (Ē′ phī) Personal name meaning "bird." Father of men who joined Ishmael in revolt against and murder of Gedaliah, the governor of Judah after Babylon captured and destroyed Jerusalem in 586 B.C. (Jer. 40:8). Ephai was from Netophah near Bethlehem.

EPHER (Ē′ phĕr) Personal name meaning "young deer." **1.** Son of Midian, grandson of Abraham through his wife Keturah, and clan father among the Midianites (Gen. 25:4). **2.** Descendant of Caleb in the tribe of Judah (1 Chron. 4:17). **3.** Original ancestor of clan in tribe of Manasseh (1 Chron. 5:24).

EPHES-DAMMIM (Ē′ phĕs-dăm′ mĭn) Place-name meaning "end of bloodshed." Town between Socoh and Azekah where Philistines gathered to fight Saul (1 Sam. 17:1) preceding David's killing of Goliath. It is apparently the same as Pas-dammim (1 Chron. 11:13). It is modern Damun, four miles northeast of Shocoh.

EPHESIANS, LETTER TO THE (Ē phē′ shĕnz) While it is not the longest of the Pauline Epistles, Ephesians is the one that best sets out the basic concepts of the Christian faith.

Paul and the Ephesians Precise information on the introduction of Christianity to Ephesus is not available. From Acts 13:1–14:28 we know Christianity was introduced to the Asian peninsula early. Paul and Barnabas, during the first missionary journey about A.D. 45–48, established Christianity in Cilicia, Pamphylia, and Phrygia. The newly established religion moved inevitably westward to the coast and to the flourishing city of Ephesus, a city of multiple religions, gods, and goddesses.

At the close of his second missionary journey about A.D. 49–52, Paul left Achaia (Greece) taking Aquila and Priscilla with him. They stopped at Ephesus and surveyed the situation in that city where religions flourished. The Ephesians urged Paul to stay there, but he declined. Leaving Aquila and Priscilla and perhaps Timothy there to carry on the Christian witness (Acts 18:18-21), Paul sailed to Antioch. He returned to Ephesus during a third missionary journey and

E

experienced the triumph over the challenge of Jewish religious leaders as well as that of the Greco-Roman religions represented in the worship of the Greek goddess Artemis (Roman name—Diana; Acts 19:24).

His ministry in Ephesus lasted three years (Acts 20:31). From there he journeyed to Jerusalem where he was arrested by the Jews and turned over to the Romans. He was imprisoned in Caesarea for two years (Acts 21:15–26:32). He was sent to Rome where he was imprisoned for another two years (Acts 27:1–28:31).

Interpreters are divided in opinion as to the time and place of the writing of Ephesians. These two imprisonments of Paul are the only ones which might bear on the question of where and when the Imprisonment Epistles were written. In all four of these epistles, Paul mentioned his imprisonment.

A related and much debated question is the year of Paul's writing each epistle and the place. To our knowledge only two places appear to be viable options—Caesarea and Rome. Majority opinion through Christian history has favored Rome. A much smaller minority of interpreters has argued for Caesarea.

A third opinion has grown out of Col. 4:16 in which Paul urged the church at Colossae to exchange letters with the church at neighboring Laodicea so both might get the benefit of both letters. This opinion, which was never widely held, took the position that Paul was writing from an imprisonment in Ephesus and that the "Laodicean" letter was what we have as "Ephesians."

Careful review of this very extensive and complex issue leaves the subjective opinion that all four Prison Epistles were written by Paul during his imprisonment in Rome about A.D. 61–62. Also subjective is the opinion that they were written in this order: Ephesians A.D. 61; Colossians A.D. 61; Philemon A.D. 61; Philippians A.D. 62.

Introduction to the Epistle Paul's motive for writing this letter was the challenge that Christianity faced in confrontation with other religions and philosophies of the day. Paul was convinced that the religion he proclaimed was the only way of redemption from sin and sonship to God.

The challenge was the struggle for human minds as they sought the "good life." Even in Judaism, the cradle in which it was born, Christianity faced that aggressive encounter.

Paul opposed a Judaism he considered to have become a religion of human attainment, doing the works of the law as a means of being right with God. He offered instead Christianity as a religion of divine provision, salvation by faith in God's providing what humans could never attain.

That distinction was also what brought Christianity into conflict with Greek philosophy and with the Greco-Roman nature religions. The Christian view is that the "good life" comes by faith, not by intellectual processes, speculations, and rules of conduct in the integration of personality.

Analysis of the Epistle: Theology and Ethics Following the pattern of all of his epistles, Paul introduced himself as an apostle of Christ Jesus by the will of God—not by human will, not even by his own will, but God's will. That was the driving force in his life.

The expression "at Ephesus" is not in the oldest manuscripts of Ephesians, but it is in many of the best ones. Its absence has led to speculation that in writing the epistle Paul left a blank space and that he meant the epistle to be a circular one to go to several churches. As the epistle was read in the churches, the public reader would insert the name of that church; such as, at Laodicea, at Hierapolis, at Colossae, and so forth. Indeed one manuscript of about the middle of the second century had "at Laodicea" in that place.

"Grace to you and peace from God our Father and the Lord Jesus Christ" (Eph. 1:2 HCSB) is in all of Paul's epistles. It is always in that order, grace and peace. Grace is the work of the Father by which salvation from sin comes. Peace is the condition of the believer's heart after grace has done its work. They are in that order because there can be no peace in the heart until grace has done its work.

Following a frequently used pattern in Paul's epistles, two basic themes are developed. First there is a major section on some theological theme. Second there follows a major section in ethics growing out of the theological theme. In the NT theology and ethics are bound together; they are never to be separated.

In his theological part (1:3–3:21) Paul centered attention on the plan and propagation of redemption. He began with a literary pattern of a poem or song to praise God for what He has done in providing salvation for sinful humanity. The provision of redemption is presented as the work of the Trinity: Father, Son, and Holy Spirit. A refrain "to the praise of His glorious grace" repeats itself after each section, each with a slight variation.

Paul turned to thanksgiving to show the blessings of redemption (1:15–2:10). He wanted his readers to know Christ better, the Christ who enables believers to have the incomparable power that resurrected Christ and that now rules in this age and the one to come. This power can come to persons who were dead in sin but are saved by grace, being raised up with Christ to participate in His rule but also to live out of grace in the good works God has planned for His people to do.

Paul turned to the language of imperative to explain the propagation of redemption (2:11–3:21). A people without hope, separated from the people of the covenant have been brought to salvation through the blood of Christ. Thus unity of all races is accomplished through Him. In the cross He brought peace and provided access to God through the one Holy Spirit. All are joined together in Christ's church built on the foundation of the apostles and serving as the residence of God the Spirit. This good news is a mystery, a mystery God calls people to share with other people through His grace and a mystery which allows all people to approach God in confidence and freedom.

Paul turned to prayer to conclude this section and reveal the goal of redemption (3:14-21). His prayer was that Christ may dwell in the believers who will be rooted in love and can grasp the marvelous greatness of that love.

In his ethical part (4:1–6:24) Paul looked at the application of redemption to the church, to personal life, and to domestic life. Ethical imperatives dominate the section. He sought unity in the Spirit—one body, one Spirit, one hope, one Lord, one faith, one baptism, one God and Father. Within the unity he celebrated the diversity of the individuals within the church, a diversity stemming from the differing gifts Christ gives. The use of the gifts within the church leads to maturity for the church and its members. Maturity involves growing in Christ, in His love, each doing the work Christ gives and not seeking to do the work assigned another.

This has consequences for personal life, calling for a complete transformation from the lifestyles of unbelievers. Without faith the individual is devoted to selfish lust and earthly dissipation. The believer becomes like God in holiness, purity, and righteousness. A central element of this is human speech, speaking the truth and saying that which helps build up others. Anger and malice must turn to love, compassion, and forgiveness. Walking in the light means pleasing God and showing the sinfulness of evil deeds. This is the wise path avoiding spirits that make one drunk but turning to the one Spirit who leads to praise and worship. This changes one's role at home. Submission to one another becomes the key, a submission motivated by loyalty to Christ and love to the marital partner. That love follows the example of Christ's love for His church. Parents expect honor from children while training children in the Lord's way of love. Similarly, masters and servants respect and help one another.

To complete his letter, Paul called his readers to put on God's armor to avoid Satan's temptations. This will lead to a life of prayer for self and for other servants of God. This will lead to concern for and encouragement from other Christians. As usual, Paul concluded his letter with a benediction, praying for peace, love, faith, and grace for his beloved readers.

Outline

I. Salutation: The apostle greets the church (1:1-2).

II. Theology: The plan of redemption leads to the propagation of redemption (1:3–3:21)

  A. The plan of redemption (1:3–14)

    1. The work of the Father: He has blessed and chosen us in Christ, predestining us for sonship in Him (1:3-6).

    2. The work of the Son: He brings redemption and forgiveness from sin through His blood (1:7-12).

    3. The work of the Spirit: He seals us as God's cherished possession (1:13-14).

  B. The blessings of redemption (1:15–2:10)

    1. A clear insight into the nature of redemption (1:15-19)

    2. A full insight into the nature of Christ (1:20-23)

    3. A transition from spiritual death to spiritual life (2:1-9)

4. A life of good works wrought out in Christ (2:10)

C. The propagation of redemption (2:11–3:21)
1. Redemption is for all without regard to race (2:11-13).
2. Redemption makes all people one in Christ (2:14-22).
3. Redemption is to be revealed to people through other people (3:1-13).
4. Redemption has a goal: revelation of the nature of God's love through Christ (3:14-21).

III. Ethics: Redemption is applied in church life, personal life, and domestic life (4:1–6:24).
A. The application of redemption in church life (4:1-16)
1. The Holy Spirit produces unity (4:1-6).
2. Christ provides a diversity of gifts (4:7-11).
3. The Spirit's unity and Christ's gifts result in maturity (4:12-16).
B. The application of redemption in personal life (4:17–5:21)
1. Desires and practices of old life are ended (4:17-32).
2. In the new way of life the redeemed learn to walk in love (5:1-5).
3. In the new way of life the redeemed learn to walk in light (5:6-14).
4. In the new way of life the redeemed learn to walk in wisdom (5:15-21).
C. The application of redemption in domestic life (5:22–6:9)
1. Mutual duties of husbands and wives to each other (5:22-33)
2. Mutual duties of parents and children to each other (6:1-4)
3. Mutual duties of masters and servants to each other (6:5-9)

IV. Conclusion: Prepare for the spiritual conflict of life (6:10-24).
A. Know God is your Ally and Satan your enemy (6:10-12).
B. Put on the armor God supplies (6:13-17).
C. Pray for boldness for Christian leaders (6:18-20).
D. Communicate with and encourage one another (6:21-22).

E. Live under God's benediction of peace, love, faith, and grace (6:23-24)

Ray Summers

EPHESUS (Ĕph´ ə sŭs) One of the largest and most impressive cities in the ancient world, a political, religious, and commercial center in Asia Minor. Associated with the ministries of Paul, Timothy, and the Apostle John, the city played a significant role in the spread of early Christianity. Ephesus and its inhabitants are mentioned more than 20 times in the NT.

Location The ancient city of Ephesus, located in western Asia Minor at the mouth of the Cayster River, was an important seaport. Situated between the Maeander River to the south and the Hermus River to the north, Ephesus had excellent access to both river valleys that allowed it to flourish as a commercial center. Due to the accumulation of silt deposited by the river, the present site of the city is approximately five to six miles inland.

Historical Background The earliest inhabitants of Ephesus were a group of peoples called Leleges and Carians who were driven out around 1000 B.C. by Ionian Greek settlers led by Androclus of Athens. The new inhabitants of Ephesus assimilated the native religion of the area, the worship of a goddess of fertility whom they identified with the Greek goddess Artemis, the virgin huntress. (Later the Romans identified Artemis with their goddess Diana.)

Around 560 B.C. Croesus of Lydia conquered Ephesus and most of western Asia Minor. Under Croesus' rule the city was moved farther south and a magnificent temple, the Artemision, was constructed for the worship of Artemis. In 547 B.C., following the defeat of Croesus by Cyrus of Persia, Ephesus came under Persian control. Disaster struck the city in 356 when fire destroyed the Artemision.

Alexander the Great, who was reportedly born on the same day as the Artemision fire, took over the area in 334 B.C. His offer to finance the ongoing reconstruction of the temple was diplomatically declined. The rebuilt temple, completed about 250 B.C., became known as one of the Seven Wonders of the World.

Lysimachus, one of Alexander's generals, ruled over Ephesus from about 301 to 281 B.C., when he was killed by Seleucus I. Under Lysimachus the city was moved again, this time to higher ground to escape the danger of flooding.

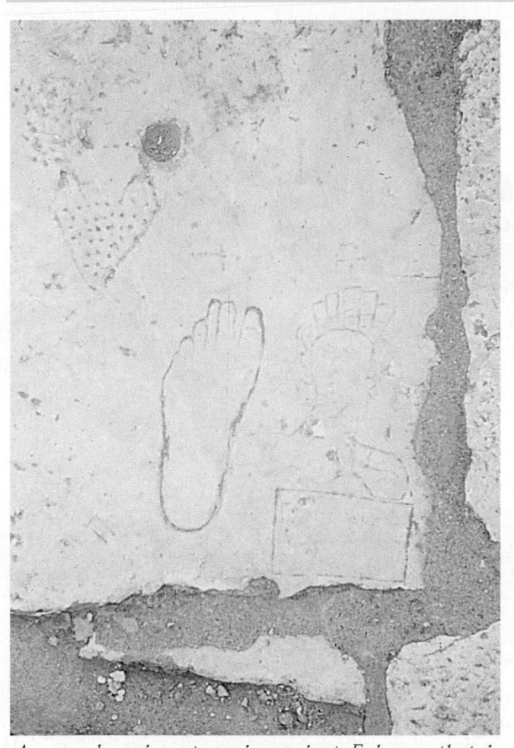

E

A carved paving stone in ancient Ephesus that is probably an advertisement for a brothel.

A part of the Roman Harbor baths and gymnasium complex excavated at ancient Ephesus.

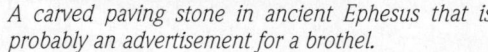

The Great Theater of ancient Ephesus as viewed from the Arcadian Way on the way to the harbor.

EPHESUS

A.D. 48 – A.D. 400

E

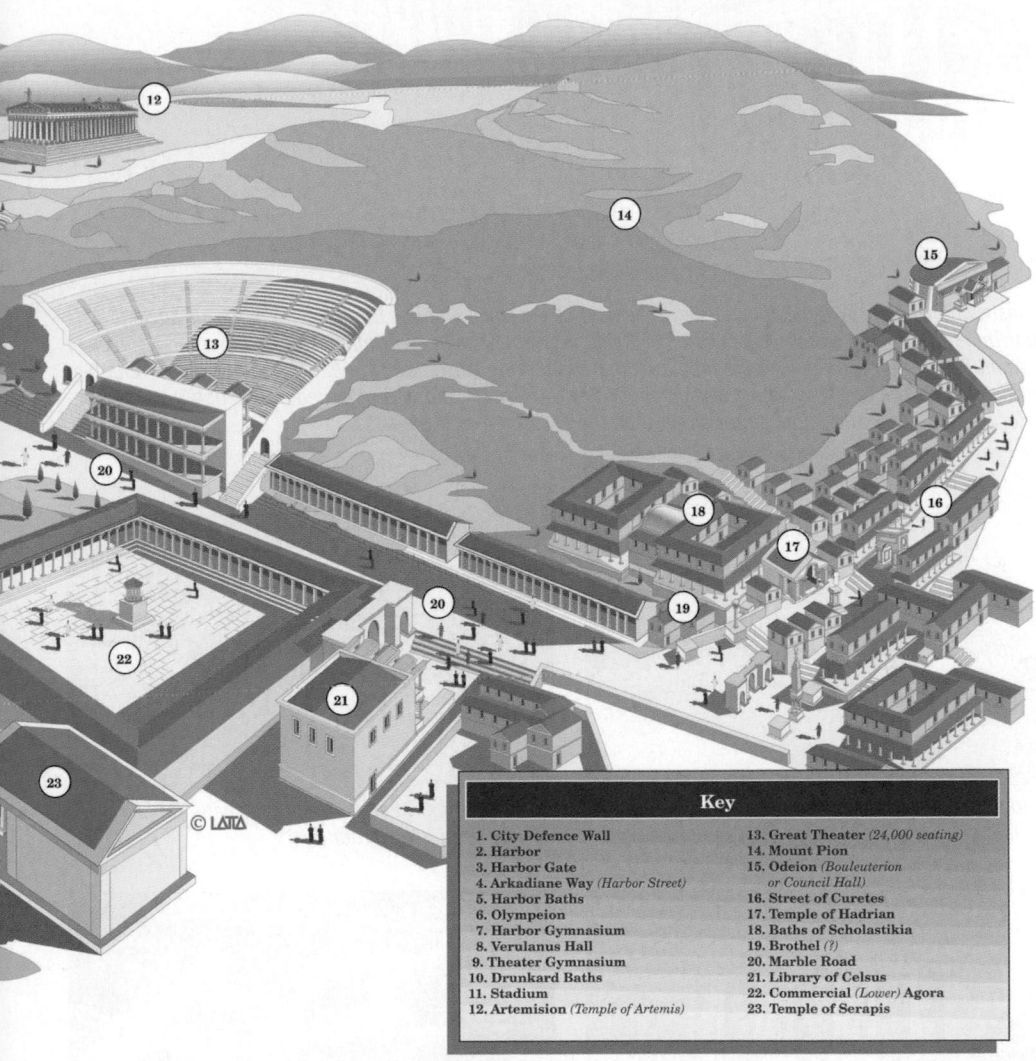

© LATA

Key

1. City Defence Wall
2. Harbor
3. Harbor Gate
4. Arkadiane Way *(Harbor Street)*
5. Harbor Baths
6. Olympeion
7. Harbor Gymnasium
8. Verulanus Hall
9. Theater Gymnasium
10. Drunkard Baths
11. Stadium
12. Artemision *(Temple of Artemis)*

13. Great Theater *(24,000 seating)*
14. Mount Pion
15. Odeion *(Bouleuterion or Council Hall)*
16. Street of Curetes
17. Temple of Hadrian
18. Baths of Scholastikia
19. Brothel *(?)*
20. Marble Road
21. Library of Celsus
22. Commercial *(Lower)* Agora
23. Temple of Serapis

E

Reconstruction of the Artemesion, the great temple of Artemis (Roman Diana) at Ephesus in ancient Asia Minor (modern Turkey) which was begun in 360 B.C. to honor the ancient many-breasted mother goddess of the Anatolian region. The cult was adopted by the conquering Alexander the Great of Greece and renamed Artemis (Roman Diana). The temple was completed by the Greeks and was recorded as one of the seven wonders of the ancient world—four times larger than the Parthenon at Athens.

A baptismal pool from the Roman period located in the Double Church of Mary at ancient Ephesus.

Curetes Street in ancient Ephesus with the Library of Celsus in the background.

The re-erected marble façade of the Library of Celsus at ancient Ephesus.

The Great Theater of Ephesus with the Arcadian Way in the background leading to the ancient harbor.

City walls were built; a new harbor was constructed; and new streets were laid out. After the death of Lysimachus, Ephesus fell under the control of the Seleucids until their defeat by the Romans in 189 B.C. Rome gave the city to the king of Pergamum as a reward for his military assistance. In 133 B.C., at the death of the last Pergamum ruler, the city came under direct Roman control.

Under the Romans, Ephesus thrived, reaching the pinnacle of its greatness during the first and second centuries of the Christian era. At the time of Paul, Ephesus was probably the fourth largest city in the world, with a population estimated at 250,000. During the reign of the emperor Hadrian, Ephesus was designated the capital of the Roman province of Asia. The grandeur of the ancient city is evident in the remains uncovered by archaeologists, including the ruins of the Artemision, the civic agora, the temple of Domitian, gymnasiums, public baths, a theater with seating for 24,000, a library, and the commercial agora, as well as several streets and private residences. Also discovered were the head and forearm of a colossal statue of the emperor Domitian. Today the Turkish town of Seljuk occupies the site of ancient Ephesus. See *Asia Minor, Cities of; Ephesians, Letter to the; Revelation of Jesus Christ; Timothy, First Letter to.*

Mitchell G. Reddish

EPHLAL (Ĕph´ lăl) Personal name meaning "notched" or "cracked." Descendant of Jerahmeel in tribe of Judah (1 Chron. 2:37).

EPHOD (Ē´ phŏd) Priestly garment connected with seeking a word from God and used in a wrong way as an idol. The exact meaning and derivation of the term "ephod" are not clear.

In early OT history there are references to the ephod as a rather simple, linen garment, possibly a short skirt, apron, or loincloth. It is identified as a priestly garment (1 Sam. 14:3; 22:18). It was worn by Samuel (1 Sam. 2:18) and by David when he danced before God on the occasion of the transfer of the ark of the covenant to David's capital city of Jerusalem (2 Sam. 6:14). From its earliest forms and uses, it appears that the ephod was associated with the presence of God or those who had a special relationship with God. It is portrayed as a source of divine guidance, as when David wanted to know if he should trust the people of Keilah (1 Sam. 23:9-12) or when

he wanted to know if he should pursue the Amalekites (1 Sam. 30:7-8).

There are references to a special ephod associated with the high priest. It appears to have been an apron-like garment worn over the priest's robe and under his breastplate. It is described in detail in Exod. 28–35. Woven of gold, blue, purple, and scarlet materials, it was very elaborate and ornate. On top of each of the shoulders the ephod was fastened by two onyx clasps on which were engraved the names of six of the 12 tribes. Twelve gemstones on the breastplate contained the names of the 12 tribes. Some scholars believe that this breastplate also contained a pouch where the sacred lots, Urim and Thummim, were kept (Exod. 28:30). The ephod was fastened around the waist by a beautiful and intricately woven girdle. The robe worn with the ephod was equally elaborate. It was blue in color, with a fringe at the bottom comprised of golden bells and blue, purple, and scarlet pomegranates (Exod. 28:31-34). Apparently, the ephod of the high priest was not only worn by the high priest, but also prominently displayed in the tabernacle. It may have been placed upon a divine image and used as an object of worship at some times in Israel's history. This usage, plus the importance of the ephod, may have led to idolatrous use in worship during the time of the judges (Judg. 8:27; 17:5-6).

The importance of the ephod in Hebrew worship is seen in the fact that, even after the division of the nation into the Northern and Southern Kingdoms, there is mention of the ephod in worship in the Northern Kingdom (Hos. 3:4). See *Ark of the Covenant; Priests; Tabernacle; Teraphim.* *Daniel B. McGee*

EPHPHATHA (Ĕph´ phá thá) Aramaic expression that Jesus spoke when He healed a person who was deaf and had a speech impediment. It is translated "be opened." When Jesus had said it, the individual was healed (Mark 7:34).

EPHRAIM (Ē´ phră ĭm) Personal and tribal name meaning "two fruit land" or "two pasture lands." The younger son of Joseph by the Egyptian Asenath, daughter of the priest of On (Gen. 41:52). He was adopted by his grandfather Jacob and given precedence over his brother Manasseh (Gen. 48:14). He was the progenitor of the tribe of Ephraim, which occupied a region slightly to the northwest of the Dead Sea (Josh. 16) and was the leading tribe of the Northern Kingdom, ever ready to assert its rights (Josh. 17:15; Judg. 3:27; 4:5; 7:24–8:3; 12:1).

Ephraim played an important role in Israelite history. Joshua was an Ephraimite (Josh. 19:50). Samuel was an Ephraimite (1 Sam. 1:1). Jeroboam I was an Ephraimite (1 Kings 12:25). The important sanctuary at Shiloh was located in the territory of Ephraim. From the eighth century B.C., Ephraim was often used as a designation for Israel (Isa. 11:13; Jer. 7:15; Hos. 5:13). See *Patriarchs; Tribes of Israel.*

EPHRAIM, CITY OF Another name for Ephron. See *Ephron.*

EPHRAIM, FOREST OF Densely wooded site of the battle between the forces of King David and the rebel army of Absalom (2 Sam. 18:6,8). The location of the forest presents difficulties. The account in 2 Samuel suggests a site on the east side of the Jordan near enough to the city of Mahanaim in the Jabbok Valley to allow David to send reinforcements. The difficulty arises since the tribal allotment for Ephraim was west of the Jordan. Joshua 17:14-18 predicts Ephraim's expansion north into the wooded Jezreel Valley and the vicinity of Beth-shan, both within Issachar's territory. It is possible that this dominant tribe also settled in the wooded hills to the east of the Jordan.

EPHRAIM GATE Entrance to Jerusalem located 400 cubits (about 200 yards) from the Corner Gate (2 Kings 14:13). The section of wall between these two gates was destroyed by King Jehoash of Israel in the eighth century. In Nehemiah's time the city square at the Ephraim Gate was one of the sites where booths for the celebration of the feast of tabernacles were set up (Neh. 8:16).

EPHRAIMITE (Ē′ phrǎ ĭm īt) Member of tribe of Ephraim. See *Ephraim.*

EPHRAIM, MOUNT KJV designation for the hill country belonging to Ephraim. Modern translations use the phrase "hill country of Ephraim" since an entire region is intended rather than a particular mount. Scripture specifies that the following cities were located in the hill country of Ephraim: Bethel (Judg. 4:5); Gibeah (Josh. 24:33); Ramah (Judg. 4:5); Shamir (10:1);

Shechem (Josh. 20:7); Timnath-heres or -serah (Josh. 19:50; Judg. 2:9).

EPHRAIN (Ē′ phrā în) KJV reading of city in 2 Chron. 13:19 following the earliest Hebrew scribal note. Hebrew text reads "Ephron," as do most modern translations. See *Ephron.*

EPHRATAH (Ěph′ rá tǎh) or **EPHRATH** (Ē′ phrǎth) or **EPHRATHAH** (Ěph′ rá thǎh) Place and personal name meaning "fruitful." **1.** Town near which Jacob buried his wife Rachel (Gen. 35:16-19; usually translated in English as Ephrath, NRSV). Genesis 35:16 seems to indicate that Ephrath(ah) must have been near Bethel. This is supported by 1 Sam. 10:2; Jer. 31:15, which place Rachel's tomb near Ramah on the border between the tribal territories of Ephraim and Benjamin. Genesis 35:19, however, identifies Ephrath(ah) with Bethlehem (cp. Gen. 48:7). It is part of Judah's tribal territory according to the earliest Greek translation of the OT, words omitted in current Hebrew manuscripts (Josh. 15:59 REB). Micah 5:2 also appears to equate Bethlehem and Ephrath(ah) as the home of the coming Messiah. This, in turn, was based on Bethlehem (1 Sam. 16:1) and Ephrath(ah) (1 Sam. 17:12) as the home of David's father Jesse and thus of David. In sending Messiah, God chose to start over at David's birthplace. Naomi's husband Elimelech was an Ephrathite from Bethlehem (Ruth 1:2). In Ruth 4:11 Bethlehem and Ephrathah are apparently identified in poetic parallelism. It may be that Ephrathah was a clan name of a family in Bethlehem whose importance made the clan name a synonym for the city. The parallelism in Ps. 132:6 seems to equate Ephrathah with "the field of Jaar" (NASB and most modern translations). This would be Kiriath-jearim, though two different resting points of the ark—Bethlehem and Kiriath-jearim—may be intended here. The identification with Kiriath-jearim could be supported by the genealogy in 1 Chron. 2 that lists both personal names and place-names. Shobal, the founder of Kiriath-jearim, was the son of Ephrathah, Caleb's wife (1 Chron. 2:19,50). In 1 Chron. 4:4 Ephrathah's son Hur was the father of Bethlehem. Ephrathah may have been a clan name associated with several different geographical localities, the most famous of which was Bethlehem. The textual and geographical connections are not always easy to figure out.

The entrance to the Church of the Nativity in Bethlehem (Ephratah).

2. Caleb's wife (1 Chron. 2:50; spelled Ephrath in 2:19; cp. 4:4).

EPHRATHITE (Ĕph´ rà thīt) Citizen or clan member of Ephratah. See *Ephratah*.

EPHRON (Ē´ phrŏn) Personal name and place-name meaning "dusty." **1.** Hittite who sold the cave of Machpelah to Abraham (Gen. 23:8-20). The narrative follows the normal manner of concluding a purchase agreement among Near Eastern people. Abraham was also buried in the cave with Sarah (Gen. 25:9-10). It became the patriarchs' burying place (Gen. 49:30-33; 50:13). **2.** Mountain marking the tribal border of Judah with Benjamin (Josh. 15:9). It is located northwest of Jerusalem near Mozah at el-Qastel. **3.** City that King Abijah of Judah (913–910 B.C.) took from King Jeroboam of Israel (926–909 B.C.), according to spelling of Hebrew text (2 Chron. 13:19). The earliest Hebrew scribes suggested that "Ephrain" was the correct spelling (KJV). It is apparently identical with Ophrah in Benjamin (Josh. 18:23; 1 Sam. 13:17), located at et-Taiyibeh about four miles north of Bethel. The city of Ephraim (2 Sam. 13:23; John 11:54) is probably the same city. If et-Taiyibeh is the correct location, it is a high city, 300 feet higher than Jerusalem and could be quite cold. Some would locate the city of Ephraim in the lower valley at ain Samieh, on the edge of the desert.

EPICUREANISM (Ĕp ĭ cū rē´ ăn ĭsm) School of philosophy which emerged in Athens about 300 B.C. The school of thought was founded by Epicurus who was born in 341 B.C. on the Greek island of Samos. Epicurus founded his school (The Garden) in Athens. Around him he gathered his students and refined his philosophy. Epicurean thought had a significant impact on the Hellenistic world and later on Rome. Paul met Epicureans as he preached about Jesus and the resurrection in Athens (Acts 17:18).

Epicurean philosophy centered on the search for happiness. Pleasure is the beginning and fulfillment of a happy life. Often today, Epicurus' ideas are distorted. Many think he proposed a life of sensual pleasure and gluttony. This concept is far from his philosophy and his own lifestyle. To Epicurus, happiness could only be achieved through tranquillity and a life of contemplation. The goal of Epicureanism was to acquire a trouble-free state of mind, to avoid the pains of the body, and especially mental anguish. Epicureans sought seclusion from worldly temptations. Epicurus taught that a man should not become involved in politics or affairs of the state. These activities simply served to distract one from the life of contemplation. He believed in gods, but he thought that they were totally unconcerned with the lives or troubles of mortals.   *Gary Poulton*

EPILEPSY Disorder marked by erratic electrical discharges of the central nervous system resulting in convulsions. In ancient times epilepsy was thought to be triggered by the moon. The term in Matt. 4:24, translated as "epileptics" by most modern translations, is literally "moonstruck." The KJV term "lunatick" from the Latin *luna* (moon) assumes the same cause for the disorder. Many interpreters understand the symptoms of the boy in Mark 9:17-29 (inability to speak, salivation, grinding teeth, rigid body, convulsions) as expressions of epilepsy.

EPIPHANY Term "epiphany" comes from a Greek word which means "appearance" or "manifestation." In Western Christianity the festival of Epiphany, observed on the sixth of January, celebrates the manifestation of Christ to the Gentiles, the coming of the Magi to see the child Jesus (Matt. 2:1-12). The 12 days between Christmas and Epiphany have often been called the "Twelve Days of Christmas."

In much of Eastern Christianity, Epiphany is a celebration of the baptism of Jesus, a recognition of His manifestation to humanity as the Son of God (Mark 1:9-11). In the early centuries before the observance of Christmas, Epiphany celebrated both the birth of Jesus and His baptism. See *Church Year.*   *Fred A. Grissom*

EPISTLE See *Letter.*

ER (Ĕr) Personal name meaning "protector" or "watchful." **1.** Oldest son of Judah and grandson of Jacob (Gen. 38:3). He married Tamar but was so wicked that God killed him (Gen. 38:6-7). **2.** Grandson of Judah (1 Chron. 4:21). **3.** Ancestor of Jesus (Luke 3:28).

ERAN (Ē´ răn) Personal name meaning "of the city" or "watchful." Some of the earliest translations and the Samaritan Pentateuch read "Eden" rather than Eran. Eran was grandson of Ephraim and a clan leader in the tribe of Ephraim (Num. 26:36).

ERANITE (Ē´ răn īt) Member of clan of Eran (Num. 26:36).

ERASTUS (ə răs´ tŭs) Personal name meaning "beloved." **1.** Disciple Paul sent with Timothy from Ephesus to Macedonia to strengthen the churches during his third missionary journey (Acts 19:22). **2.** City financial officer of Corinth who joined Paul in greeting the church at Rome (Rom. 16:23). He may have been a slave or a freed slave working for the city government; he may well have been a high-ranking and influential government leader—city treasurer. If so, he would have political power, prestige, and probably some wealth. **3.** Disciple who remained at Corinth and was not with Paul when he wrote Timothy (2 Tim. 4:20). He may have been identical with either of the other men named Erastus or may be a separate individual.

ERECH (Ē´ rĕch) Hebrew transliteration of Akkadian place-name: Uruk, one of the oldest Sumerian cities founded before 3100 B.C. Genesis' Table of Nations reports that Nimrod, the mighty hunter, included Erech in his kingdom (Gen. 10:10). Ashurbanipal, king of Assyria (668–629 B.C.), exiled "men of Erech" (NASB) to Samaria about 640 B.C. (Ezra 4:9). Sumerian literature lists Erech as one of the first cities after the flood. Gilgamesh, the hero of Akkadian flood stories, appears as king of Erech. Excavations at Erech provide early evidence of pictographic writing and numerical notation on clay tablets and reveal an astronomical observatory and a scribal school. It is modern Warka, about 120

miles southeast of Babylon and 40 miles northwest of Ur.

ERI (Ē´ rī) Personal name meaning "of the city of" or "watchful." A son of Gad and grandson of Jacob (Gen. 46:16). Original ancestor of clan of Erites (Num. 26:16).

ERITE (Ē´ rīte) Member of clan of Eri. See *Eri.*

ESAIAS (ə sī´ ŭs) KJV transliteration of Greek spelling of Isaiah in the NT. See *Isaiah.*

ESARHADDON (Ē sär hăd´ dŏn) Assyrian royal name meaning "Ashur (the god) has given a brother." King of Assyria (681–669 B.C.). He was the favorite son of Sennacherib, whom he succeeded as king (2 Kings 19:36-37; Ezra 4:2; Isa. 19:4; 37:37-38). In Isa. 19:4 he is probably the "cruel lord" and "fierce king" who conquered Egypt. In Ezra 4:2 he is recognized as the king who colonized Samaria. See *Assyria.*
                                                                    M. Stephen Davis

ESAU (Ē´ sau) Personal name whose meaning is not known. Son of Isaac and Rebekah; elder twin brother of Jacob (Gen. 25:24-26; 27:1,32,42; 1 Chron. 1:34); father of the Edomite nation (Gen. 26:34; 28:9; 32:3; Deut. 2:4-29; Mal. 1:2-3). At birth his body was hairy and red "and they named him Esau" (Gen. 25:25,30; 27:11,21-23). The second born twin, Jacob, father of the nation Israel, held Esau's heel at birth (Gen. 25:22-26); thus depicting the struggle between the descendants of the two which ended when David led Israel in the conquest of Edom (2 Sam. 8:12-14; 1 Chron. 18:13; cp. Num. 24:18).

From the first Jacob sought to gain advantage over Esau (Hos. 12:3). Esau, the extrovert, was a favorite of his father and as a hunter provided him with his favorite meats. Jacob was the favorite of his mother Rebekah.

As a famished returning hunter, Esau, lacking self-control, sold his birthright to Jacob for food (Gen. 25:30-34). Birthright involved the right as head of the family (Gen. 27:29) and a double share of the inheritance (Deut. 21:15-17). This stripped Esau of the headship of the people through which Messiah would come. Thus, the lineage became Abraham, Isaac, and Jacob.

Having lost his birthright, he was still eligible to receive from Isaac the blessing of the eldest son. Rebekah devised a deception whereby Jacob received this blessing (Gen. 27:1-30).

A well that marks the traditional site where Jacob met Esau.

Years later the two brothers were reconciled when Jacob returned from Mesopotamia. Esau had lived in the land of Seir. As Jacob neared Palestine, he made plans for confronting his wronged brother and allaying his anger. Esau, with an army of 400, surprised Jacob, his guilty brother, and received him without bitterness (Gen. 33:4-16).

The two reconciled brothers met again for the final time at the death of their father (Gen. 35:29). Though their hostility was personally resolved, their descendants continue to this day to struggle against each other.   *Nelson Price*

ESCHATOLOGY Derived from the combination of the Greek *eschatos*, meaning "last," and *logos*, meaning "word" or "significance." Refers to the biblical doctrine of last things. The doctrine of last things normally focuses on a discussion of the return of Christ at the end of the age, the coming judgments, various expressions of the kingdom of heaven and the kingdom of God, the nature of the glorified body, and the prospects for eternal destiny. Generally, eschatology sets itself apart as a theology of the future and in juxtaposition to both history and the present age.

This general consensus about the nature of eschatology was challenged by C. H. Dodd and others in the early part of the 20th century. In a 1935 publication entitled *The Parables of the Kingdom*, Dodd noted NT passages in which Jesus and others seemed to speak of the kingdom of heaven as if it were already present. John the Baptist spoke of the kingdom of God as being "at hand" (Matt. 3:2), and Jesus Himself seems to have employed that same terminology (Matt. 10:7). Even more specifically Jesus declared, "If I drive out demons by the Spirit of God, then the kingdom of God has come to you" (Matt. 12:28 HCSB). In Luke 17:20 and following, Jesus again seems to insist that the kingdom of God is in the midst of the disciples. Dodd concluded that Jesus believed He was bringing the kingdom in His own person. Dodd reinterpreted passages that had always been given a futuristic cast in light of his theory, which became known as realized eschatology, meaning that the fulfillment of all endtime anticipation was secured in Christ.

Dodd's critics, however, responded by pointing to his failure to deal adequately with texts such as Matt. 6:10 where Jesus Himself taught His disciples to pray, "Your kingdom come. Your will be done on earth as it is in heaven" (HCSB). Again Jesus said that the gospel of the kingdom will be preached to all the earth as a witness to all the nations "and then the end will come" (Matt. 24:14 HCSB). Jesus seemed also to allude to a future time when He spoke of people coming from the east and west and north and south to "recline at the table in the kingdom of God" (Luke 13:28-29 HCSB). Paul seems to be speaking of a future act when he says, "Then comes the end, when He hands over the kingdom to God the Father, when He abolishes all rule and all authority and power. For He must reign until He puts all His enemies under His feet" (1 Cor. 15:24-25 HCSB).

This debate, which at first seems to be merely another scholarly discussion, is important because it gave rise to a new emphasis on the eschatology of the NT as being an eschatology of "already—and not yet." In other words, Jesus does seem to indicate that in some meaningful sense the kingdom of God came with the advent of the Messiah. Still there are other respects in which the kingdom does not arrive in its ultimate expression until the end times. Consequently, one may conclude that the study of last things begins with the incarnation of Christ and does not end until the events associated with His return.

In this regard, to speak of the return or coming again of Christ is more technically accurate than to refer to the second coming. There are two reasons for this. First, in only one text does the Bible approximate the language of "second coming." The author of Hebrews says that "the Messiah ... will appear a second time, not to bear sin, but to bring salvation to those who are waiting for Him" (Heb. 9:28 HCSB). The other references in the NT simply speak of His coming

E

or His presence among us. The second reason for caution at this point is the fact that there do seem to be theophanies or more precisely Christophanies (appearances of Christ) in the OT. If this is the case, then to speak of His incarnation would be the proper terminology for the beginning of the *eschatos* and to speak of His return the best way to think of the final fulfillment of all prophecy.

Eschatological Material in the Old Testament The OT, not just the NT, is intensely eschatological in its nature. If eschatology does indeed begin with the coming of the Christ, then all messianic prophecies fall in the category of eschatological material. For example, Isa. 9:6-7, a passage about the birth of Christ, becomes eschatological because not only does it speak of a child (a son) being given but also that "the government will be upon His shoulders" and that "of the increase of His government and peace there will be no end." Other books of the OT have large segments of material that are clearly eschatological, having to do with the end time. For example, Dan. 9 records the famous seventieth week prophecy of Daniel. A portion of the prophecy seems to have been fulfilled at the time of the death of the one to whom the passage refers as "the Prince." Clearly, the "Prince" is used as a synonym for the Messiah (Dan. 9:25). But again the prophecy also speaks of the 70 weeks being apportioned not only "to make an atonement for iniquity" but also "to bring in everlasting righteousness" and "to seal up vision and prophecy" (Dan. 9:24 NASB). Once again, the events seem to indicate a continuum beginning at the incarnation and atonement of Christ and culminating in the fulfillment of all prophecy and the bringing of everlasting righteousness.

The Prophet Ezekiel boasts many eschatological passages but from chapters 36 to 48 there can be little question but that the end times are in view. These chapters include a magnificent view of an eschatological temple, salient information on God's plan for the restoration of the Jewish nation, and in chapter 36 an explanation of God's again dealing with the Jewish people after their recalcitrance (Ezek. 36:19-24). Meantime Zechariah sees a day coming when there will be a fountain open for the house of David and for the house of Jerusalem "for sin and for impurity" (Zech. 13:1). The marvelous prophecies of Isaiah contain significant and far-reaching prophecies of the end times. For example, the days will come, predicted Isaiah, "in the last days" when all nations will "hammer their swords into plowshares, and their spears into pruning hooks" and learn of war no more (Isa. 2:2,4 NASB). The same prophet sees a return to domesticity on the part of the animals—a day when "the wolf will dwell with the lamb, and the leopard will lie down with the kid" (Isa. 11:6). He further anticipates a day when the original fruitfulness of the earth will be restored and the desert "will rejoice and blossom" (Isa. 35:1).

Eschatological Material in the New Testament The NT takes up where the OT ended. Jesus Himself spoke frequently about the *eschatos*. His remarks are enshrined in what is known as the Olivet Discourse in Matt. 24–25, a discourse provided in succinct form in what is called the Little Apocalypse in Mark 13. In those passages Jesus spoke specifically of cataclysmic upheavals belonging to the end times and such devastation during the period known as the Great Tribulation that "unless those days were cut short, no one would survive" (Matt. 24:22 HCSB). Jesus announced that men would see Him coming in the clouds of heaven with power and great glory (Matt. 24:30) but that no one would know the day nor the hour of these events, only His Father in heaven (Matt. 24:36). He spoke of two who would be in the field—one of whom would be taken and another left (Matt. 24:40). He illustrated the whole theme of His return with the parable of the wise and foolish virgins (Matt. 25:1-13), which culminated in a warning concerning watchfulness. Jesus concluded this discourse with the gathering of all nations and God's final judgment for them (Matt. 25:31-46).

Paul frequently visited eschatological themes as in 1 Cor. 15, where he explicated carefully the nature of the glorified body that the saints will receive at the coming of the Lord. In Rom. 9–11, Paul picked up the question of God's program with the Jewish people, which he sees them as continuing and flourishing again in the last days. He speaks of an olive tree whose original branches (the Jews) were taken away and of the branches of a wild olive tree (the Gentiles), which were grafted in. However, he anticipates a time coming when the original branches will be grafted in again (Rom. 11:17-26). Finally, he speaks of "a partial hardening" that "has come to Israel until the full number of the Gentiles has come in" and then anticipates "all Israel will be saved" (Rom. 11:25-26 HCSB).

In addition to all of these passages, the Apocalypse of John (the book of Revelation) is a book that is eschatological almost from the outset. A vision of the glorified Christ in chapter one is followed by messages to seven historical churches in Asia Minor in chapters two and three. But beginning with the throne room scene of heaven in chapter four, the remainder of the book seems to be futurist in its orientation, dealing principally with the unfolding of the catastrophic events during the Great Tribulation and concluding with the anticipation of the final judgment (Rev. 20:11-15) and the unveiling of the new heavens and new earth in chapters 21 and 22.

Systems of Thought about the *Eschatos* At no point in biblical interpretation is a hermeneutical presupposition more compelling than in the study of the end times. In approaching eschatological materials that often make use of highly symbolic language, the questions arise: "To what degree are the subjects broached in the text to be taken literally?" and "To what degree should they be taken in a figurative fashion?" As an example of the problem, the passages in Isaiah that foretell a wolf lying down with a lamb might be interpreted to belong to an actual kingdom age in which all animals live at peace with other animals and with their human neighbors. On the other hand, some interpreters insist that this be understood figuratively. In this case, the passage would not anticipate a literal fulfillment but depicts the peace of God that exists in the heart of the believer and, for that matter, in the cosmos when Christ is honored as King. The discussion comes ultimately to a head in Rev. 20:1-10, a section in which a period of "a thousand years" is mentioned no less than six times in seven verses. This thousand years, which is spoken of in theological literature as the millennium (from Latin *mil* meaning one thousand and *annum* meaning years) is a period in which Satan is not allowed to deceive the nations for a thousand years and in which the saints of God live and reign with Christ for a thousand years. If one approaches these verses with a hermeneutical decision that they are to be understood in a straightforward way, then he would anticipate a thousand-year reign of Christ on the earth at the end of the age. If, on the other hand, the material is to be treated as merely "Jewish apocalyptic genre" that should be understood spiritually

instead of literally, then the passage becomes simply another way of speaking of the ultimate sovereignty of God and His reign over all things. The basic decision one makes about this will then determine in which of the following ways he understands the eschatology of the Bible.

Amillennialism The amillennialists (the alpha negative prefix has the sense of "no") is the position of those who believe that most of the eschatological materials in the Bible referring to the end of the age should not be understood in a strictly literal fashion. They anticipate no kingdom age on this earth and understand the kingdom solely in the terms of its eternal expression.

Postmillennialism On the other hand, postmillennialists (so called because the word post means "after") believe that there will be a kingdom age of sorts on the earth that will be consummated by the coming of Christ. Hence, the coming of Christ is "post" (after) the millennium. This view, which was more popular in church history prior to World War II, sees the church and its missionary movement as being wonderfully prolific and successful. Consequently, at some point the reign of Christ through the church is experienced on the earth, the culmination of which is the coming of Christ at the end of the millennium.

Premillennialism Another popular view that attempts to understand the Scriptures generally in a more literal fashion sees Christ returning to the earth before the millennium (hence, the prefix "pre"). According to this view, the kingdom age on earth cannot begin without the King in residence. Hence, Christ returns to the earth, subdues all of His enemies, and establishes a kingdom of righteousness for a thousand years.

The Tribulation As indicated earlier, Jesus spoke of a coming time of trouble on the earth such as has never been duplicated in all the history of the world. This message seems also to be the clear teaching of the seventieth week of Daniel, the book of Revelation, and other texts. One of the questions that theologians have debated, particularly in recent years, has been the relationship of the church to the tribulation. This debate is one in which neither amillennialists nor postmillennialists, but only premillennialists, have a stake. Among premillennial scholars there are three primary positions and a number of subsidiary positions. The three major positions are designated pretribulationism, midtribulationism, and posttribulationism.

Pretribulationists believe that Christ will be revealed at the outset of the tribulation period of seven years. The dead in Christ will rise, and every true believer will be caught up to be with the Lord in the air. A period of seven years of the outpouring of the wrath of God upon the earth, which will conclude with the return of Christ to establish His millennial kingdom, will follow. Hence, Christ comes for the church prior to the tribulation and prior to the millennium to establish His kingdom.

Midtribulationism, on the other hand, notes that the Apocalypse divides the tribulation into two periods of three and one-half years each. Midtribulationists suggest that Christ will return for the church after the first half of the tribulation. The church, therefore, will have to experience the first forty-two months of the tribulation period but will be rescued from the most debilitating portion of it.

Posttribulationism (referred to as historic premillennialism by its advocates), however, argues that the church endures the Great Tribulation but is not the object of God's wrath poured out on the wicked. They see only one return of Christ in Scripture, in opposition to the two posited by either pretribulationism or midtribulationism. Therefore, Christ comes at the end of the tribulation to receive the church to Himself and then returns immediately to the earth to establish the kingdom age.

Other views that have been advocated by a few include partial rapturism (the view arguing that only the watching church will be taken) and pre-wrath-rapturism (a view that simply moves the time of the rapture later in the tribulation than midtribulationists maintain). The view, however, is still essentially a midtribulationist view.

Other Eschatological Issues Other issues that are debated among those studying eschatology include (as indicated above) the coming of Christ. The issue here is whether or not one may discern the return of Christ to happen in two segments—one for the church and one to establish His kingdom—or whether there is but one return of Christ to establish the kingdom age.

Still another question revolves around the nature and number of the judgments. At least three passages of Scripture address the question of end-time judgments. First Corinthians 3:11-15 seems to envision a judgment of believers that is also mentioned in Rom. 14:10 and 2 Cor. 5:10,

referred to as the "judgment seat of Christ" in the latter reference. Matthew 25:31-46 recalls the words of Jesus regarding the "sheep and goat judgment." Revelation 20:11-15 has been called the "Great White Throne Judgment" and seems to focus on the judgment of the lost. Amillennialists and some premillennialists tend to believe that all these judgments are simply varying pictures of the final judgment of all men. On the other hand, other premillennialists argue that they are three separate judgments—the judgment seat of Christ representing a judgment that will take place immediately following the rapture of the church prior to the tribulation. It is a judgment for believers only and has to do with the bequeathal of rewards. The sheep and goat judgment in Matt. 25, on the other hand, is a determination of who enters the millennial era or the kingdom age by the Lord at the conclusion of the tribulation. Sheep enter; goats are excluded. The Great White Throne Judgment, however, is a judgment at the end of all time in which only unbelievers are judged.

A final question relates to eternal destiny. The Bible makes it reasonably clear that those who are not found written in the Book of Life are turned aside into the lake of fire or into hell. The righteous, on the other hand, are admitted into heaven. Few evangelical Christians question either the existence of heaven or the eternal longevity of it. However, the possibility of a place of punishment that provides suffering for eternity has proved an intolerable conception for some theologians in the present era. Theologians as prominent as John Stott and Clark Pinnock, therefore, have argued that the lost are turned aside into hell where after a period of suffering for their sins they are annihilated. Annihilationism is viewed by most evangelical scholars as radically inconsistent with the testimony of the biblical narrative. Those who agree point out that if the words used to describe hell are not to be taken literally, then it is difficult to imagine that the same words used to describe heaven should be taken in a different way.

Conclusion Eschatology has too often become a battlefield of contention rather than an oasis of hope in the desert of life. Attitudes toward the study of eschatology range from preoccupation with such matters alone to the desire to avoid the subject altogether as one that has caused too much contention and that is too difficult. Both approaches seem less than wholesome. The object of the information given in the Bible concerning eschatology seems to be not so much to provide every detail but rather to create hope and anticipation as the church looks for "the blessed hope and glorious appearing of our great God and Savior Jesus Christ" (Titus 2:13). See *Apocalyptic; Kingdom of God; Millennium; Rapture; Revelation, Book of; Tribulation.*

Paige Patterson

ESDRAELON (Ĕs drā´ lŏn) Greek translation of the word "Jezreel," indicating the low-lying area that separates the mountains of Galilee from the mountains of Samaria.

Old Testament Esdraelon, also called the Great Plain of Esdraelon or the Plain of Jezreel, is the area assigned to Zebulun and Issachar (Josh. 19:10-23). It extends from the Mediterranean Sea to the Jordan River at Beth-shean. Included are the Valley or Plain of Megiddo in the east and the Valley of Jezreel in the west.

Sources disagree on the actual naming of the area. Some scholars say that the Valley of Jezreel is the name for the entire region; Esdraelon being the western portion, comprised of the Plain of Accho and the Valley of Megiddo. Whatever the entire region is called, it is assumed that references to Jezreel indicate both the town of Jezreel and the valley in which it is located; and references to Megiddo indicate both the town and the plain on which it is located.

The historical and biblical significance of Esdraelon in the OT is its association with war and bloodshed. As a battleground, it was a strategically favored place. It was occupied by Canaanites who were less than willing to relocate when the tribes of Israel tried to settle there (Judg. 1:27). The Song of Deborah in Judg. 5 celebrates the battle "at Taanach, by the waters of Megiddo" (Judg. 5:19) where Barak finally routed the Canaanites.

Other important battles were fought in Esdraelon. Frequently the question of Israel's leadership was settled there. Josiah died in battle against Pharaoh Neco at Megiddo (2 Chron. 35:20-24). Saul and Jonathan died at the hands of the Philistines in the Valley of Jezreel (1 Sam. 29:1,11; 31:1-7). Jehu killed his rivals Joram and Ahaziah at Jezreel (2 Kings 9). He later slaughtered all the men of Ahab and Ahaziah and all the prophets of Baal there (2 Kings 10).

Brutal slaughter for other than political reasons took place in Esdraelon. Naboth owned a vineyard in Jezreel. Jezebel and Ahab wanted to buy the vineyard, but Naboth refused because it had been handed down to him from his ancestors (1 Kings 21:3). Jezebel arranged Naboth's murder so Ahab could take possession of the vineyard (1 Kings 21:5-16).

The tragedies at Esdraelon did not go unnoticed by God. For her part, Jezebel was later murdered at Jezreel as prophesied by Elijah (1 Kings 21:23; 2 Kings 9:36). Hosea prophesied vengeance on the house of Jehu for his role in the slaughter at Jezreel (Hos. 1:4-5).

New Testament Esdraelon is mentioned in the NT as Armageddon or har-Megiddon, meaning hill or city of Megiddo. Revelation 16:16 echoes the OT portrayal of Esdraelon as a place of war and tragedy. The final battle of the Lord will be waged there (Rev. 16:14-16; 19:19).

Donna R. Ridge

The Valley of Armageddon, or Plain of Esdraelon, as seen from the site of ancient Megiddo.

ESDRAS See *Apocrypha.*

ESEK (Ē´ sĕk) Place-name meaning "strife." A well that Isaac's servants dug in the valley near Gerar to find water for their herds. The shepherds of Gerar disputed Isaac's claim to the watering place. Isaac apparently gave in to the claim without warfare, thus receiving God's assurance of blessing (Gen. 26:18-24).

ESHAN (Ē´ shăn) or **ESHEAN** (KJV) Place-name meaning "I lean on." Town in the hill country of Judah assigned to tribe of Judah (Josh. 15:52). A text tradition in the earliest Greek translation reads "Soma" instead of Eshan, possibly pointing to a location at modern Khirbet Hallat Sama. Otherwise, the location is not known.

ESH-BAAL (Ĕsh-bā´ ăl) Personal name meaning "man of Baal." Son of Saul, the first king of Israel (1 Chron. 8:33; 9:39). In 2 Sam. 2:8 the name is Ish-bosheth, "man of shame," apparently an intentional corruption in the Hebrew tradition to avoid the name of the Canaanite god and to characterize the person with such a name. First Samuel 14:49 lists Ishui or Ishvi as Saul's son, possibly another way of respelling the name to avoid Baal. In Saul's day "baal" may have been a title applied to Yahweh indicating "He is Lord or Master." In this case Esh-baal would mean "the man of the Lord." Otherwise, Saul's name for his son would seem to indicate some devotion to the Canaanite god Baal at the period in his life when he named the son. Saul's son Jonathan named his son Merib-baal. See *Ish-bosheth; Ishvi; Jonathan; Merib-baal.*

ESHBAN (Ĕsh´ băn) Personal name of unknown meaning. An Edomite listed as a descendant of Seir the Horite (Gen. 36:26).

ESHCOL (Ĕsh´ cŏl) Place-name meaning "valley of grapes" or "cluster." **1.** A valley in Canaan that was explored by the 12 Israelites sent to spy out the land (Num. 13:23). From the valley of Eshcol they brought back an exceptionally large cluster of grapes. Apparently the valley was given the name on account of grape clusters such as the one found by the Israelite spies. **2.** Brother of Mamre and Aner (Gen. 14:13). He and his brothers were Amorites who were allies of Abram in the defeat of Chedorlaomer.

ESHEK (Ē´ shĕk) Personal name meaning "oppression" or "strong." A member of the tribe of Benjamin descended from King Saul (1 Chron. 8:39).

ESHKALONITE (Ĕsh´ kə lŏn īt) Citizen of Ashkelon. See *Ashkelon.*

ESHTAOL (Ĕsh´ tā ŏl) Place-name meaning "asking (for an oracle)." Town in lowlands of Shephelah of Judah allotted to the tribe of Judah (Josh. 15:33) but also to the tribe of Dan (Josh. 19:41). Near there, God's Spirit stirred Samson of the tribe of Dan (Judg. 13:25). Samson was buried near Eshtaol (Judg. 16:31). The tribe of Dan sent men from Eshtaol to seek a new homeland (Judg. 18:2-11). Its citizens were kin to the clan of Caleb and to residents of Kiriath-jearim (1 Chron. 2:53). It may be located at modern Irtuf, a mile south of Ishwa.

ESHTAOLITE (Ĕsh´ tā ə līt) or **ESHTAULITE** (Ĕsh´ tá ū līte) (KJV) Citizen of Eshtaol. See *Eshtaol.*

ESHTARAH (Ĕsh´ tə räh) (NIV; REB, Beashtaroth) See *Beeshterah.*

ESHTEMOA (Ĕsh tə mō´ á) Place and personal name meaning "being heard." The name may indicate an ancient tradition of going to Eshtemoa to obtain an oracle or word of God from a prophet or priest. **1.** City in tribal allotment of Judah (Josh. 15:50, with variant Hebrew spelling; see *Eshtemoh*). God set it aside for the Levites (Josh. 21:14). While living in exile in Ziklag, David sent some of the plunder from his victories to Eshtemoa (1 Sam. 30:28). **2.** Member of clan of Caleb in tribe of Judah (1 Chron. 4:17), probably listed as the clan father of those who settled in Eshtemoa. The relation between the two Eshtemoas in 1 Chron. 4:17,19 is not clear. The city is the modern es-Samu about eight and a half miles south-southwest of Hebron and 14 miles northeast of Beersheba.

ESHTEMOH (Ĕsh´ tə mōh) Variant Hebrew spelling of Eshtemoa (Josh. 15:50). See *Eshtemoa.*

ESHTON (Ĕsh´ tŏn) Personal name of uncertain meaning. Member of the tribe of Judah Chron. 4:11-12).

ESLI (Ĕs´ lī) Personal name of unknown meaning. Ancestor of Jesus (Luke 3:25), spelled Hesli in NASB. Some scholars equate him with Elioenai (1 Chron. 3:23). See *Elioenai.*

ESPOUSAL See *Betrothal.*

ESROM (Ĕs´ rŏm) (KJV, NT) See *Hezron.*

ESSENES Members of a Jewish sect that existed in Palestine during the time of Christ. They are not mentioned in the NT. They were ascetics who practiced community of goods, generally shunned marriage, refrained from attending worship in the temple, and attached great importance to the study of the Scriptures. Many scholars associate the Dead Sea Scrolls discovered in 1947 with an Essene community. See *Dead Sea Scrolls; Qumran.*

ESTHER (Ĕs´ tẽr)Persian personal name meaning "a star." Since this is not the biblical Esther's given name at birth (Esther 2:7), some have suggested that this name is linked to the planet Venus and the goddess Ishtar. Whether the name was given to her by her cousin Mordecai to hide her identity as a Jew or given to her when she was presented to the king, from the mind-set of the Persians a name linked to the goddess of fertility would be appropriate for the queen's role.

ESTHER, BOOK OF Placed by the Jews in the third section of the Hebrew Bible known as the Writings. While some debate over the book occurred due to the lack of inclusion of the name of God, the activity of the Lord was so obvious in the book that this objection was overruled.

According to the book of Esther, the woman more popularly known as Esther in the Bible was named Hadassah (meaning "myrtle") when she was born. Orphaned at some point in childhood, she was raised by her cousin Mordecai among the Jews living in Persia. Hadassah became queen when the King of Persia's wife Vashti refused to appear before him at a banquet for his nobles. She was chosen as the most beautiful of all of the eligible maids in the entire empire of the Persian monarch. Hadassah's remarkable beauty was not an accident. In accord with the emphasis on the providence of God in this book, her incredible beauty must be seen as from the hand of God. Her identity as a Jew was unknown to the king.

About the time that Esther was named the new queen, Mordecai discovered a plot against the king's life. He made the plot known to

The ruins of ancient Qumran probably inhabited by Essenes from 130 B.C. until A.D. 70.

Esther, who in turn passed on the information so that the plot was foiled.

Haman the Agagite (who seems to be identified as a descendant of Agag, king of the Amalekites) was made prime minister of Persia. Infuriated by Mordecai's refusal to bow to him, Haman began to plot against Mordecai and all of the Jews. After Haman had the Persian monarch sign a decree against the Jews for their destruction on an appointed day, Mordecai and all of the Jews lamented their potential approaching doom.

Mordecai then called on Esther to approach the king. He reminded her that as a Jew she would not escape and that it might be the case that "for such a time as this" God had allowed her to rise to the position of queen of Persia. Esther, after fasting and prayer, risked her life by entering the king's throne room unbidden. After the king extended the royal scepter to her, she requested the king's presence at a banquet prepared in his honor. Haman was also invited.

Meanwhile, Haman was busy plotting Mordecai's death and building a gallows on which he intended to hang him. Providentially the king happened to read about Mordecai's faithfulness in revealing the earlier plot against his life. The king then purposed to honor Mordecai and asked Haman what should be done for the man that the king would like to honor. Thinking that he was prescribing his own treatment, Haman found out to his chagrin that the high honors he prescribed would be performed by him for Mordecai.

At the banquet on the second day, Esther revealed Haman's plot to the king. Haman was then hanged upon the gallows that he had prepared for Mordecai. After another decree was sent out allowing the Jews to defend themselves, many of those of the provinces became Jews. On the appointed day the Jews were victorious. The celebration continues each year with the Feast of Purim (9:24-28).

The Historical Period of the Book The Hebrew "Ahasuerus" is usually identified with Xerxes I (486–465/64 B.C.). The Persian was *khshayarsha.* The Elephantine papyri spell the name *kshy'resh* which is close to the Greek Xerxes. Evident throughout the book is the intimate knowledge possessed by the writer of Persian customs, of the topography of Susa, and of the interior of the Persian royal palaces. Persian names and loanwords were used throughout the book.

It is suggested that Mordecai may have been linked to the household of Otanes, one of the seven noble families of Persia. When the Persians chose a king from the seven nobles, Otanes requested that his name not be put in with the other six nobles on the condition that his household would remain free in Persia only to obey the commands of the new king with which they were in agreement (Herodotus III, 83). This could explain why Mordecai was not obliged to bow to Haman.

The Traditional Use of the Book The book of Esther provides the historical background for the feast of Purim. In plotting against the Jews, Haman cast lots (*purim* from Assyrian *puru*) to determine their fate (9:24-28). The story of God's preservation of His people is a reminder of His covenant with Abraham that He will not only bless those who bless His people, but he will also curse those who curse them. The preservation of the Jews kept alive messianic expectations in the intertestamental period.

When this story is rehearsed to groups of Jewish children during the feast of Purim, it is customary for the children to hiss (like a snake) loudly and stomp their feet every time the name of Haman occurs in order to block out even the sound of his name. As such he is seen as a "satanic" figure.

Outline

I. Vashti Dismissed (1:1-22)
   A. The Feast and the King's Summons (1:1-11)
   B. The Queen's Refusal and Dismissal (1:12-22)
II. Esther Made Queen (2:1-23)

The traditional site of the tombs of Esther and Mordecai in the modern country of Iran.

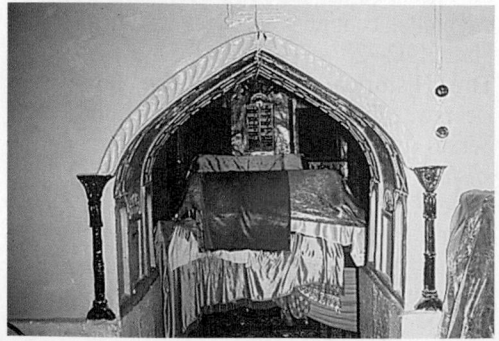

   A. A Replacement for Vashti Sought (2:1-4)
   B. Esther Taken into the King's Harem (2:5-16)
   C. Esther Crowned the New Queen (2:17-20)
   D. Mordecai Discovers a Plot against the King's Life (2:21-23)
III. Haman and the Decree of Death (3:1-15)
   A. Haman Made Prime Minister (3:1)
   B. Mordecai's Refusal to Bow (3:2-4)
   C. Haman's Wrath and Plot against the Jews (3:5-9)
   D. The Decree Is Sealed and Sent Out (3:10-15)
IV. Esther's Dilemma (4:1-17)
   A. Mordecai Mourns (4:1-2)
   B. The Jews Mourn (4:3)
   C. Mordecai Gives Esther Counsel (4:4-14)
   D. Esther Asks for the Jews to Fast (4:15-17)
V. Esther's Banquet: Day One (5:1-14)
   A. Esther Enters the King's Court (5:1-2)
   B. The King and Haman Invited to a Banquet (5:3-5)
   C. The King and Haman to Return (5:6-8)
   D. Haman's Gallows (5:9-14)
VI. Esther's Banquet: Night One (6:1-14)
   A. The Restless King (6:1-3)
   B. Mordecai Honored (6:4-14)
VII. Esther's Banquet: Day Two (7:1-10)
   A. The Request of the Queen (7:1-7)
   B. Haman Is Hanged (7:8-10)
VIII. Mordecai and the Counter-Decree (8:1-17)
   A. Mordecai Is Promoted (8:1-2)
   B. The Decree Written by Mordecai (8:3-17)
IX. Victory for the Jews: The Feast of Purim (9:1-32)
X. Mordecai Prospers (10:1-3)

Kirk Kilpatrick

ETAM (Ē´ tăm) Place-name meaning "place of birds of prey." **1.** Rocky crag where Samson camped during his battles with the Philistines (Judg. 15:8-13), conferring there with men of Judah who wanted to bind him and hand him over to the Philistines. The exact location is not known. It must be near Lehi. See *Lehi*. **2.** Town in territorial allotment of tribe of Judah according to earliest Greek translation of the OT but omitted from present Hebrew manuscripts (Josh. 15:59 REB). Rehoboam, king of Judah (931–913 B.C.), fortified the city (2 Chron. 11:5-6), which seems to indicate that Etam stood between Bethlehem and Tekoa. Rehoboam probably feared attack from Egypt, which had sheltered Jeroboam, king of Israel (2 Chron. 10:2). Pharaoh Shishak did, indeed, attack (2 Chron. 12:2-4). Some scholars think Rehoboam's fortification program came after Shishak's attack. A road ran along the ridge through or near Hebron, Bethzur, and Bethlehem to Jerusalem. Etam protected the approach to this road from the east. Etam is located at Khirbet el-Khokh, southwest of Bethlehem. **3.** Member of tribe of Judah and apparently clan father of town of same name associated with Jezreel (1 Chron. 4:3). **4.** Village assigned to Simeon (1 Chron. 4:32), though it is not listed in Simeon's tribal territory in Josh. 19:7. It may be modern Aitun, about 11 miles southwest of Hebron.

ETERNAL LIFE Life at its best, having infinite duration characterized by abiding fellowship with God. This important term in the NT is emphasized in the Gospel of John but also appears in the other Gospels and in Paul's writings. Eternal life in the NT eliminates the boundary line of death. Death is still a foe, but the one who has eternal life already experiences the kind of existence that will never end.

Yet, in this expression, the emphasis is on the quality of life rather than on the unending duration of life. Probably some aspects of both quality and duration appear in every context, but some refer primarily to quality of life, and others point to unending life or a life to be entered into in the future.

In terms of quality, life is (1) life imparted by God; (2) transformation and renewal of life; (3) life fully opened to God and centered in Him; (4) a constant overcoming of sin and moral evil; and (5) the complete removal of moral evil from the person and from the environment of that person.
Eternal Life as Experience in the Present This term in John has important implications. The one trusting in the Son has eternal life; the one disobeying the Son has the wrath of God abiding on him (John 3:36). Trusting and obeying go together; they leave no room for neutral-

ity. The one who hears Christ's message and believes or trusts in the Father who sent Him has eternal life. This person does not come into condemnation but has passed out of death into life (John 5:24). The perfect tense—one who has passed and remained in the state of having passed from death into life—emphasizes eternal life as a permanent, present reality. But no presumption is possible here. Eternal life is a present reality for the one hearing and trusting (John 5:24).

The bold metaphors of eating and drinking point to active involvement with Christ. "Anyone who eats My flesh and drinks My blood has eternal life" (John 6:54a HCSB). Verse 57 explains that "the one who feeds on Me will live because of Me." Since Christ is our life, we must make that life part of us by "sharing in Christ," by actively coming to Him and drawing life-giving strength from Him.

Eternal life is defined in Jesus' high priestly prayer: "This is eternal life: that they may know You, the only true God, and the One You have sent—Jesus Christ" (John 17:3 HCSB). The present tense of the verb "to know" indicates that this knowledge is by experience—not from intellectual facts. Genuine knowledge of God by experience brings eternal life. Such experience transforms life.
Eternal Life as Experienced in the Present and Future John compared the lifting up of the serpent in the wilderness to the lifting up of the Son of Man on the cross and His exaltation to heaven. People who respond to Christ by constant trust have eternal life (John 3:15). They have healing from something more deadly than snakebite—the destructive effects of sin. Here eternal life involves a present healing, a present reality. But John 3:16 refers both to the present and the future.

Christ defined His true sheep as those who hear or listen to His voice and follow Him (John 10:27). To such disciples, He gives eternal life, and they will not perish (John 10:28). Again, no presumption is possible. Those are secure who persistently listen, hearken, and follow. For such people eternal life is both a present and a future reality.
Eternal Life as a Future Experience "What must I do to inherit eternal life?" the rich young ruler asked. (Mark 10:17 HCSB; cp. Matt 19:16; Luke 18:18). He saw eternal life as a final inheritance. His earnestness moved Jesus, and Jesus

loved this young man (Mark 10:21). But he had to make a decision: Would he follow Jesus without his possessions? (Mark 10:22). His action said, "No." He could not part with his possessions first and then follow Jesus.

In Matt. 19:27 Peter asked Jesus, "What will there be for us?" The disciples had left their dear ones and their possessions to follow Jesus. Jesus promised them loved ones and lands (possessions) with persecutions. Then He added: "And eternal life in the age to come" (Mark 10:30 HCSB). Eternal life here refers to an unending future reality.

John 12:20-26 tells of some Greeks who wanted to see Jesus. We do not know how Jesus interacted with these Greeks. We do know He spoke about His death and what it meant to be a disciple: "The one who loves his life will lose it, and the one who hates his life in this world will keep it for eternal life" (John 12:25 HCSB). Jesus here contrasted eternal life with the present life. Believers are to guard their persons or souls by serving Christ and following Him (John 12:26). Such servants will be where Christ is, and the Father will honor them (John 12:26). To be where Christ is means to come into eternal life—a life freed from sin or moral evil.

Paul declared that "the one who sows to the Spirit will reap eternal life from the Spirit" (Gal. 6:8 HCSB). Eternal life is given by Jesus and the Holy Spirit. This future reality, already experienced to some limited degree in the present, involves the Father, Son, and Spirit. Fellowship in life eternal means fellowship with the triune God.   *A. Berkeley Mickelsen*

ETHAM (Ēʹ thăm) Place-name meaning "fort." The second station in Israel's wilderness wandering out of Egypt (Exod. 13:20; Num. 33:6-8). The nearby wilderness was called the wilderness of Etham (Num. 33:8). Its precise location is not certain.

ETHAN (Ēʹ thăn) Personal name meaning "long lived." **1.** Man so famous for his wisdom that Solomon's outstanding wisdom could be described as exceeding Ethan's (1 Kings 4:31). Ezrahite may indicate Ethan was at home in Canaan before Israel entered, though this is uncertain. A list similar to 1 Kings 4:31 appears among the descendants of Judah in 1 Chron. 2:6,8. See *Ezrahite*. **2.** Levite and temple singer (1 Chron. 6:42,44; 15:17) and instrumentalist

(1 Chron. 15:19). He is associated with Pss. 88 and 89 in their titles.

ETHANIM (Ĕthʹ á nĭm) Canaanite name of the seventh month taken over by Israel (1 Kings 8:2), who also called the month Tishri. This was the first month of the civil year. Ethanim means "always flowing with water" and refers to the flooding streams fed by heavy fall rains.

ETH-BAAL (Ĕth-bāʹ ál) Personal name meaning "with him is Baal." King of Sidon and father of Jezebel (1 Kings 16:31), who married Ahab, king of Israel (793-753 B.C.). Through her influence Baal worship pervaded the Northern Kingdom. See *Jezebel*.

ETHER (Ēʹ thĕr) Place-name meaning "smoke of incense." **1.** Town in tribal territory of Judah (Josh. 15:42). **2.** Town occupied by tribe of Simeon (Josh. 19:7). Some Bible students identify this with the town in Judah, since Simeon's territory was within Judah's boundaries. Other scholars warn us not to identify the two places. Ether in Judah is modern Khirbet Attir, south of Lahav and a mile northwest of Beth Gibrin.

ETHICS Study of good behavior, motivation, and attitude in light of Jesus Christ and biblical revelation. The discipline of ethics deals with such questions as: What ought I do? How should I act so as to do what is good and right? What is meant by good? Who is the good person?

Biblical ethics likewise addresses some of the identical questions. While neither Testament has an abstract, comprehensive term, or definition that parallels the modern term "ethics," both the OT and the NT are concerned about the manner of life that the Scripture prescribes and approves. The closest Hebrew term in the OT for "ethics," "virtue," or "ideals" is the word *musar*, "discipline" or "teaching" (Prov. 1:8) or even *derek*, "way or path" of the good and the right. The closest parallel Greek term in the NT is *anastrophe*, "way of life, lifestyle" (occurring nine times in a good sense with 2 Pet. 3:11 being the most significant usage). Of course the Greek term *ethos* appears 12 times in the NT (Luke 1:9; 2:42; 22:39; John 19:40; Acts 6:14; 15:1; 16:21; 21:21; 25:16; 26:3; 28:17; Heb. 10:25). The plural form appears once in 1 Cor. 15:33. It is usually translated "conduct," "custom," "manner of life," or "practice."

The Biblical Definition of Ethics Is Connected with Doctrine The problem with trying to speak about the ethics of the Bible is that ethical contents are not offered in isolation from the doctrine and teaching of the Bible. Therefore, what God is in His character, what He wills in His revelation, defines what is right, good, and ethical. In this sense then, the Bible had a decisive influence in molding ethics in western culture.

Some have seriously questioned whether there is a single ethic throughout the Bible. Their feeling is that there is too much diversity to be found in the wide variety of books and types of literature in the Bible to decide that there is harmony and a basic ethical stance and norm against which all ethical and moral decisions ought to be made. Nevertheless, when following the claims made by the books of the Bible, some conceive their message to be a contribution to the ongoing and continuous story about the character and will of God. This narrative about the character and will of God is the proper basis for answering the questions: What kind of a person ought I to be? How then shall we live so as to do what is right, just, and good?

As some have pointed out, the search for diversity and pluralism in ethical standards is as much the result of a prior methodological decision as is the search for unity and harmony of standards. One may not say the search for diversity is more scientific and objective than the search for harmony. This fact must be decided on the basis of an internal examination of the biblical materials, not as an external decision foisted over the text.

Three Basic Assumptions Can ethical or moral decisions rest on the Bible, or is this idea absurd and incoherent? Three assumptions illustrate how a contemporary ethicist or moral-living individual may be able to rest his or her decision on the ethical content of the biblical text from a past age. The three are: (1) the Bible's moral statements were meant to be applied to a universal class of peoples, times, and conditions; (2) Scripture's teaching has a consistency about it so that it presents a common front to the same questions in all its parts and to all cultures past and present; (3) the Bible purports to direct our action or behavior when it makes a claim or a demand. In short the Bible can be applied to all people. It is consistent and seeks to command certain moral behavior.

To take Scripture's universality first: every biblical command, whether it appeared in a biblical law code, narrative text, wisdom text, prophetic text, Gospel, or epistle, was originally addressed to someone, in some place, in some particular situation. Such particulars were not meant to prejudice their usage in other times, places, or persons. Lurking behind each of these specific injunctions can be found a universal principle. From the general principle, a person in a different setting can use the Bible to gain direction in a specific decision.

Are our problems, our culture, and our societal patterns so different that, even though we can universalize the specific injunctions from Scripture, they have no relevance to our day? Can we assume consistency between cultures and times for this ethic? All that is required here is that the same biblical writer supplied us elsewhere with a whole pattern of ethical thought that has led up to this contextualized and particular injunction. If we may assume that the writer would not change his mind from one moment to the next, we may assume that he would stand by his principle for all such similar situations regardless of times or culture.

Finally, the Bible claims to command mortals made in the image of God. Whether the ethical materials are in the imperative or indicative moods makes little difference. The writers of Scripture intended to do more than offer information; they purported to direct behavior.

Five Basic Characteristics of Biblical Ethics In contrast to philosophical ethics, which tends to be more abstract and human centered, biblical morality was directly connected with religious faith. Hence immoral men and women were by the same token irreligious men and women, and irreligious persons were also immoral persons (Ps. 14:1).

Biblical ethics are, first of all, personal. The ground of the ethical is the person, character, and declaration of an absolutely holy God. Consequently, individuals are urged, "You shall be holy, for I the LORD your God am holy" (Lev. 19:2 NASB).

In the second place, the ethics of the Bible are emphatically theistic. They focus on God. To know God was to know how to practice righteousness and justice.

Most significantly, biblical ethics are deeply concerned with the internal response to morality rather than mere outward acts. "The LORD looks at the heart" (1 Sam. 16:7 NASB) was the cry repeatedly announced by the prophets (Isa. 1:11-18; Jer. 7:21-23; Hos. 6:6; Mic. 6:6-8).

Scripture's ethical motivation was found in a future orientation. The belief in a future resurrection of the body (Job 19:26-27; Ps. 49:13-15; Isa. 26:19; Dan. 12:2-3) was reason enough to pause before concluding that each act was limited to the situation in which it occurred and bore no consequences for the future.

The fifth characteristic of biblical ethics is that they are universal. They embrace the same standard of righteousness for every nation and person on earth.

The Organizing Principle: God's Character That which gives wholeness, harmony, and consistency to the morality of the Bible is the character of God. Thus the ethical directions and morality of the Bible were grounded, first of all, in the character and nature of God. What God required was what He Himself was and is. The heart of every moral command was the theme that appeared in Lev. 18:5-6,30; 19:2-4,10,12,14,18,25,31-32,34,36-37, "I am the LORD" or "You shall be holy: for I the LORD your God am holy." Likewise, Phil. 2:5-8 (HCSB) agreed: "Make your own attitude that of Christ Jesus, who, existing in the form of God … He humbled Himself by becoming obedient to the point of death—even to death on a cross."

The character and nature of the holy God found ethical expression in the will and word of God. These words could be divided into moral law and positive law. Moral law expressed His character. The major example is the Ten Commandments (Exod. 20:1-17; Deut. 5:6-21). Another is the holiness code (Lev. 18–20). Positive law bound men and women for a limited time period because of the authority of the One who spoke them. Positive law claimed the peoples' allegiances only for as long and only in as many situations as God's authority determined when He originally gave that law. Thus the divine words in the garden of Eden, "from the tree of the knowledge of good and evil you shall not eat" (Gen. 2:17 NASB) or our Lord's, "Untie [the colt]" (Luke 19:30 HCSB) were intended only for the couple in the garden of Eden or the disciples. They were not intended to be permanent commandments. They do not apply to our times. A study of biblical ethics helps us distinguish between the always valid moral law and the temporary command of positive law.

The moral law is permanent, universal, and equally binding on all men and women in all times. This law is best found in the Decalogue of Moses. Its profundity can be easily grasped in its comprehensiveness of issues and simplicity of expression. A few observations may help in interpreting these Ten Commandments. They are:

(1) The law has a prologue. This established the grace of God, as seen in the exodus, as the basis for any requirement made of individuals. Ethics is a response to grace in love, not a response to demand in fear.

(2) All moral law is double sided, leading to a positive act and away from a negative one. It makes no difference whether a law is stated negatively or positively, for every moral act is at one and the same time a refraining from a contrary action when a positive act is adopted.

(3) Merely omitting or refraining from doing a forbidden thing is not a moral act. Otherwise, sheer inactivity could count as fulfilling a command, but in the moral realm this is just another name for death. Biblical ethics call for positive participation in life.

(4) When an evil is forbidden in a moral command, its opposite good must be practiced before one can be considered obedient. We must not just refuse to murder, but we must do all in our power to aid the life of our neighbor.

The essence of the Decalogue can be found in three areas: (1) right relations with God (first command, internal worship of God; second, external worship of God; third, verbal worship of God); (2) right relations with time (fourth command), and (3) right relations with society (fifth command, sanctity of the family; sixth, sanctity of life; seventh, sanctity of marriage and sex; eighth, sanctity of property; ninth, sanctity of truth; and tenth, sanctity of motives).

The Content of Biblical Ethics Biblical ethics is based on the complete revelation of the Bible. The Decalogue and its expansions in the three other basic law codes join the Sermon on the Mount in Matt. 5–7 and the Sermon on the Plain in Luke 6:17-49 as the foundational texts of the Bible's teaching in the ethical and moral realm. All other biblical texts—the narratives of wrongdoing, the collection of Proverbs, the personal requests of letters—all contribute to our knowledge of biblical ethics. The Bible does not offer a list from which we choose. It hammers home a life-style and calls us to follow.

Several examples of the content of biblical ethics may help to understand better how the character of God, especially of His holiness, sets the norm for all moral decision-making.

Honor or respect for one's parents was one of the first applications of what holiness entailed according to Lev. 19:1-3. This should come as no surprise, for one of the first ordinances God gave in Gen. 2:23-24 set forth the monogamous relationship as the foundation and cornerstone of the family.

Husband and wife were to be equals before God. The wife was not a mere possession, chattel, or solely a "childbearer." She was not only "from the LORD" (Prov. 19:14) and her husband's "crown" (Prov. 12:4), but she also was "a power equal to" him (the word "helper" Gen. 2:18 NASB is better translated "strength, power"). The admonition to honor parents was to be no excuse to claim no responsibility to help the poor, the orphan, and the widow (Lev. 25:35; Deut. 15:7-11; Job 29:12-16; 31:16-22; Isa. 58; Amos 4:1-2; 5:12). The oppressed were to find relief from the people of God and those in authority.

Similarly, human life was to be regarded as so sacred that premeditated murder carried with it the penalty of capital punishment in order to show respect for the smitten victim's being made in the image of God (Gen. 9:5-6). Thus the life of all persons, whether still unborn and in the womb (Exod. 21:22-25; Ps. 139:13-6) or those who were citizens of a conquered country (Isa. 10; Hab. 3), were of infinite value to God.

Human sexuality was a gift from God. It was not a curse, or an invention of the devil. It was made for the marriage relationship and meant for enjoyment (Prov. 5:15-21), not just procreation. Fornication was forbidden (1 Thess. 4:1-8). Sexual aberrations, such as homosexuality (Lev. 18:22; 20:13; Deut. 23:17) or bestiality (Exod. 22:19; Lev. 18:23-30; 20:15-16; Deut. 27:21) were repulsive to the holiness of God and thus condemned.

Finally, commands about property, wealth, possessions, and concern for the truth set new norms. These norms went against the universal human propensity for greed, for ranking things above persons, and for preferring the lie as an alternative to the truth. No matter how many new issues were faced in ethical discourse, the bottom line remained where the last commandment had laid it: the motives and intentions of the heart. This is why holiness in the ethical realm began with the "fear of the LORD" (Prov. 1:7; 9:10; 15:33).

The greatest summary of ethical instruction was given by our Lord in Matt. 22:37-39: to love God and to love one's neighbor. There also was the "Golden Rule" of Matt. 7:12. The best manifestation of this love was a willingness to forgive others (Matt. 6:12-15; 18:21-35; Luke 12:13-34).

The NT, like the OT, included social ethics and one's duty to the state as part of its teaching. Since God's kingdom was at work in the world, it was necessary that salt and light also be present as well in holy living.

While both Testaments shared the same stance on issues such as marriage and divorce, the NT often explicitly adopted different sanctions. Thus, church discipline was recommended in the case of incest in 1 Cor. 5 rather than stoning.

The main difference between the two Testaments is that the NT sets forth Jesus as the new example of uncompromising obedience to the will and law of God. He came not to abolish the OT but to fulfill it. The NT is replete with exhortations to live by the words and to walk in the way set forth by Jesus of Nazareth, the Messiah (1 Cor. 11:1; 1 Thess. 1:6; 1 Pet. 2:21-25).

Some of the motivators to live ethical and moral lives carry over from the previous Testament but to these are added: the nearness of God's kingdom (Mark 1:15); gratitude for God's grace in Christ (Rom. 5:8); and the accomplished redemption, atonement, and resurrection of Jesus Christ (1 Cor. 15:20-21). Like the OT love is a strong motivator; however, love does not take the place of law. Love is not itself the law; it is a "how" word, but it will never tell us "what" we are to do. Love is a fulfillment of the law (Rom. 13:9) because it constrains us to comply with what the law teaches. Thus, love creates an affinity with and affection for the object of its love. It gives willing and cheerful obedience rather than coerced and forced compliance.

Finally, the content of biblical ethics is not only personal, but it is wide-ranging. The letters of Paul and Peter list a wide range of ethical duties; toward one's neighbors, respect for the civil government, and its tasks, the spiritual

E

significance to work, the stewardship of possessions and wealth, and much else.

The ethic which Scripture demands and approves has the holiness of the Godhead as its standard and fountainhead, love to God as its impelling motivation, the law of God as found in the Decalogue and Sermon on the Mount as its directing principle, and the glory of God as its governing aim. *Walter C. Kaiser, Jr.*

ETHIOPIA (Ē thǐ ō´ pǐ á) Region of Nubia just south of Egypt, from the first cataract of the Nile into the Sudan. Confusion has arisen between the names Ethiopia and Cush. The OT Hebrew (and Egyptian) name for the region was Cush. The ancient Greek translation of the OT, the Septuagint, rendered Cush by the Greek word *Aithiopia*, except where it could be taken as a personal name. English translations have generally followed the Septuagint in designating the land as Ethiopia and its inhabitants as Ethiopians. In some passages such as Gen. 2:13 and Isa. 11:11, various English versions alternate between Cush and Ethiopia. See *Cush*.

The biblical Ethiopia should not be confused with the modern nation of the same name somewhat further to the southeast. In biblical times Ethiopia was equivalent to Nubia, the region beyond the first cataract of the Nile south, or upstream, of Egypt. This region, with an abundance of natural resources, was known to the Egyptians as Cush and was occupied by them during periods of Egyptian strength. During the New Kingdom (1550-1070 B.C.), Ethiopia was totally incorporated into the Egyptian Empire and ruled through an official called the "viceroy of Cush."

When Egyptian power waned, Nubia became independent under a line of rulers who imitated Egyptian culture. When Egypt fell into a period of chaos about 725 B.C., Nubian kings extended their influence northward. In 715 B.C. they succeeded in establishing control over all of Egypt and ruled as pharaohs of the 25th Dynasty. The most influential of these Ethiopian pharaohs was Taharqa (biblical Tirhakah), who rendered aid to Hezekiah of Judah during the Assyrian invasion of Sennacherib in 701 B.C. (2 Kings 19:9; Isa. 37:9).

The Assyrian Empire invaded Egypt in 671 B.C., driving the Ethiopian pharaohs southward and eventually sacking the Egyptian capital Thebes (biblical No-Amon; Nah. 3:8) in 664 B.C.

Thereafter, the realm of Ethiopian kings was confined to Nubia, which they ruled from Napata. Ethiopia continued to be an important political force and center of trade (Isa. 45:14). Some time after 300 B.C. Napata was abandoned and the capital moved further south to Meroe, where the kingdom continued for another 600 years. Excavations in Nubia have revealed numerous pyramid tombs at Napata and Meroe as well as several temples to the Egyptian god Amun.

In NT times several queens of the kingdom of Meroe bore the title Candace. The Ethiopian eunuch to whom Philip explained the gospel was a minister of "Candace, queen of the Ethiopians" (Acts 8:27 HCSB). Candace should be understood as a title rather than a personal name.

Daniel C. Browning, Jr.

ETHIOPIAN EUNUCH (Ē thǐ ō´ pǐ ǎn) Unnamed person who was returning to his homeland after having been to Jerusalem to worship (Acts 8:27). He was an official in the court of the queen of Ethiopia. As he traveled, he met Philip the evangelist. Philip had come to the desert area in response to God's call. Philip declared the gospel to the eunuch, and the eunuch received Christian baptism at Philip's hands (Acts 8:26-39). His conversion illustrates the Christian faith transcending national boundaries and embracing one whose physical mutilation would have excluded him from full participation in Judaism.

ETHKAZIN (Ěth kā´ zǐn) Place-name, perhaps meaning "time of the chieftain." Town in tribal territory of Zebulun (Josh. 19:13). Its location is not known.

ETHNAN (Ěth´ nǎn) Personal name meaning "gift." Member of tribe of Judah (1 Chron. 4:7).

ETHNI (Ěth´ nī) Personal name meaning "I will give." Levite, ancestor of Asaph (1 Chron. 6:41).

EUBULUS (yū byū´ lǔs) Personal name meaning "good counsel." Companion of Paul who sent greetings to Timothy (2 Tim. 4:21).

EUNICE (yū´ nǐs) Personal name meaning "victorious." The mother of Timothy (2 Tim. 1:5). Paul commended both her and her mother Lois for their faith. She was a Jewish woman whose husband was a Gentile. No details are known about her conversion to Christianity. See *Timothy.*

EUNUCH A male deprived of the testes or external genitals. Such men were excluded from serving as priests (Lev. 21:20) and from membership in the congregation of Israel (Deut. 23:1). Eunuchs were regarded as especially trustworthy in the ancient Near East and thus were frequently employed in royal service. By extension, the Hebrew word translated eunuch could be used of any court official (Gen. 37:36 and 39:1 refer to a married man). The Greek term translated eunuch is literally "one in charge of a bed," a reference to the practice of using eunuchs as keepers of harems (Esther 2:3,6,15). Part of Isaiah's vision of the messianic era was a picture of the eunuch no longer complaining of being "a dry tree," one without hope of descendants, because God would reward the faithful eunuch with a lasting monument and name in the temple which would be far better than sons or daughters (Isa. 56:45). Ethiopian eunuch of Acts 8:27 was reading from Isaiah's scroll.

A eunuch for the sake "of the kingdom of heaven" (Matt. 19:12 HCSB) is likely a metaphor for one choosing single life in order to be more useful in kingdom work (cp. 1 Cor. 7:32-34).

EUODIA or **EUODIAS** (yū ō′ dĭ às) Female leader in the church at Philippi whose disagreement with Syntyche concerned Paul (Phil. 4:2-3). The name Euodia means either prosperous journey or pleasant fragrance. Euodia and Syntyche were perhaps deacons or else hostesses of house churches that met in their respective homes. Paul commended these women as two who struggled by his side for the spread of the gospel in a way comparable to Clement and other church leaders. See *Philippians, Letter to the.*

EUPHRATES AND TIGRIS RIVERS (yū phrā′ tēs and Tī′ grĭs) Two of the greatest rivers of Western Asia. They originate in the mountains of Armenia and unite about 90 miles from the Persian Gulf to form what is now called the Shatt-al-Arab that flows into the gulf. In ancient times the Tigris flowed through its own mouth into the gulf. The Euphrates and Tigris were included among the four rivers of Paradise (Gen. 2:14).

Boats on the Euphrates River in modern Iraq (ancient Mesopotamia).

The Euphrates was known as "the great river" (Gen. 15:18; Josh. 1:4) or "the river" (Num. 22:5) to the Hebrews. It formed the northern boundary of the land promised by Yahweh to Israel (Gen. 15:18; Deut. 1:7). The Euphrates is mentioned in the book of Revelation as the place where angels were bound (9:14) and where the sixth vial was poured out (16:12).

The Euphrates is the longest, largest, and most important river in Western Asia. Many significant cities were located on the Euphrates, Babylon being the most important. Others located on its banks were Mari and Carchemish, the latter being the site of a famous battle between Babylon and Egypt in 605 B.C. (Jer. 46:2).

The Tigris is not as prominent in the Bible as is the Euphrates, but it is the site of the major vision of the Prophet Daniel (Dan. 10:4). Like the Euphrates, some significant cities were located on its banks. Nineveh, the ancient capital of the Assyrian Empire, was located on its east bank. Farther south was the site of Asshur, religious center and original capital of Assyria. See *Babylon; Nineveh.* *M. Stephen Davis*

A young Iraqi man gazing across the Euphrates River that flows through Iraq and into the Persian Gulf.

EURAQUILO (yu rǎ′ quǐ lō) NASB transliteration of Greek name for northeast wind in Acts 27:14. See *Euroclydon.*

EUROCLYDON (yū rŏc′ lǐ dŏn) Noun meaning "southeast wind raising mighty waves." KJV reading of traditional Greek text in Acts 27:14, but most modern translations follow other Greek texts that read *Eurakulon,* the northeast wind. Whichever reading is correct, the wind created a mighty storm that shipwrecked the ship taking Paul to Rome.

EUTYCHUS (yū tǐ kǔs) Personal name meaning "good fortune." A young man who listened to Paul the apostle preach in Troas (Acts 20:9-10). Overcome with sleep, Eutychus fell from a third-floor windowsill and was picked up dead. Paul, however, embraced the youth, and Eutychus was restored to life.

EVANGELISM Active calling of people to respond to the message of grace and commit oneself to God in Jesus Christ. While many think of evangelism as a NT phenomena, profound concern for all people is also obvious in the OT (1 Kings 8:41-45; Ps. 22:27-28; Isa. 2:2-4). God's care for the first couple after they had sinned, His

plan to "bless" all people through the Israelite nation, and His continuing attempts through the prophets and through discipline to forge His people into a usable nation all speak of His concern.

While Israel's influence was primarily national and magnetic in nature, there were instances of individual and external witness (Dan. 3–6; 2 Kings 5:15-18; Jon. 3:1-10). Though Israel was largely a failure in carrying out her mission, the large number of God fearers at the beginning of the Christian era show that her magnetic attraction and proselytizing efforts were not entirely unfruitful.

It is, however, the NT that manifests the dynamic thrust of evangelism. While the word "evangelism" does not occur in the Bible, it is woven into the very fabric of Scripture.

Despite its obvious importance, a wide range of opinion seeks to define what it means and what it should include. Definitions range from the extremely narrow to the exceedingly broad.

Evangelism is derived from the Greek word *euangelion,* meaning "gospel" or "good news." The verbal forms of *euangelizo,* meaning "to bring" or "to announce good news" occur some 55 times (Acts 8:4,25,35; 11:20) and are normally translated with the appropriate form of the word "preach." Evangelism has to do with the proclamation of the message of good news.

In the light of the wide range of definitions and the continuing debate, it is well to consider two kinds of definitions. First, many insist on defining evangelism only in the strictest sense of the above NT words. It is preaching the gospel, communicating God's message of mercy to sinners. Such a definition places strict limits to arrive at a precise definition of evangelism. It refuses to speak in terms of recipients, results, or methods, laying all its emphasis on the message.

This type of definition is certainly correct, as far as it goes. It would represent the view of many evangelicals concerning evangelism. Many others, however, believe that such definitions are inadequate for the present day and that they are partly responsible for a truncated sort of evangelism too often practiced in the past.

Many would, therefore, prefer what might be described as a "holistic" definition or one that takes into account the "good news of the kingdom." This might be stated: evangelism is the Spirit-led communication of the gospel of the kingdom in such a way or ways that the recipients have a valid opportunity to accept Jesus Christ as Lord and Savior and become responsible members of His church. Such a definition takes into account the essential work of the Holy Spirit, the various ways of conveying the good news, holistic concern for the persons involved, the need for actual communication and understanding of the message, and the necessity of productive church membership on the part of the convert.

Luke 8:2-56 shows how Jesus brought the good news. He not only preached; He demonstrated His power over the forces of nature in saving His fearful disciples. He exorcised a demon, healed a poor woman who had hemorrhaged for 12 years, and raised Jairus's daughter from the dead. Clearly He brought the good news by word and deed, and not by word only.

Paul, in similar fashion, described how he had been used to "make the Gentiles obedient by word and deed, by the power of miraculous signs and wonders, and by the power of God's Spirit. As a result, I have fully proclaimed the good news about the Messiah" (Rom. 15:18-19 HCSB).

Some warn that such definitions are dangerous, opening the door to an overemphasis on the social dimension of the gospel to the exclusion of the spoken message. Indeed they can be. A complete evangelism will include the verbalized gospel. Balance is a necessity, although different situations may sometimes call for more emphasis on one aspect or the other. The biblical mandate remains to "become all things to all people, so that I may by all means save some" (1 Cor. 9:22 HCSB).   *G. William Schweer*

EVE (Ēv) Personal name meaning "life." The first woman created and thus original ancestor of all people (Gen. 3:20; cp. 4:1-2,25). She also faced the serpent's temptation first (3:1; 2 Cor. 11:3; 1 Tim. 2:13-14). Her fall illustrates the ease with which all persons fall into sin (2 Cor. 11:3). See *Adam and Eve*.

EVERLASTING PUNISHMENT God's unending punishment of sinners beyond this life is known as eternal punishment. The Bible teaches that unrepentant, unforgiven sinners will be punished (Dan. 12:2; Matt. 10:15; John 5:28-29; Rom. 5:12-21). The unending nature of this punishment is emphasized in Scripture in several ways. Isaiah 66:24 asserts that the wicked will be consumed with an unquenchable fire: "Then they shall go forth and look on the corpses of the men who have transgressed against Me. For their worm shall not die, and their fire shall not be quenched; and they shall be an abhorrence to all mankind" (NASB). Jesus Himself alludes to the endlessness of the punishment of the wicked in Mark 9:47-48: "And if your eye causes your downfall, gouge it out. It is better for you to enter the kingdom of God with one eye than to have two eyes and be thrown into hell, where 'their worm does not die, and the fire is not quenched'" (HCSB). The emphasis of these and similar passages is that the fire in which the wicked are cast inflicts a torment upon them, but the fire does not consume them.

Further evidence for the endless duration of everlasting punishment is found in phrases describing the future abode of the unrepentant wicked. Concepts such as fire or burning (Isa. 33:14; Jer. 17:4; Matt. 18:8; 25:41; Jude 7), contempt (Dan. 12:2), destruction (2 Thess. 1:9), chains (Jude 6), torment (Rev. 14:11; 20:10), and punishment (Matt. 25:46) are linked with terms like "everlasting" or "eternal" to underscore that these states are unceasing. The wicked will experience and endure this horrific existence without reprieve or relief. The punishment never ends.

Several theological concepts have developed in the history of Christian thought that attempt to eliminate or limit the notion of everlasting punishment. One of the more notable of these is Annihilationism. This is the idea that human beings are not innately immortal. Immortality, or more properly eternal life, is the gift of God bestowed upon believers. Some forms of this belief (conditional immortality) teach that the wicked simply cease to exist after death. Other forms assert that the wicked may experience a time of punishment after death, but that the person will eventually "burn out" or cease to exist. They are "annihilated." In all its varied forms, this school of thought denies the unending duration of punishment.

Two common reasons are typically offered as grounds for denying everlasting punishment. One of these is that everlasting punishment denies God's eternal love. For God to allow His creatures to exist in eternal torment is a contradiction of His loving nature. Another argument against everlasting punishment is that endless torment contradicts God's sovereignty because He allows unbelievers to exist for eternity. As significant as these points are, they both seem to lack any support from the Bible.

One of the more significant passages of Scripture that supports the doctrine of everlasting punishment and refutes the denials of endless punishment is Matt. 25:46. In this verse, the states of the righteous and the unrighteous are juxtaposed, with the word "eternal" applied to the final state of both. Jesus said that the righteous will enter "eternal life," but the unrighteous will enter into "eternal punishment." Although the word "eternal" may mean "quality of life," the concept most certainly includes the notion of unlimited duration. Further, consistent rules of biblical interpretation necessitate that the duration of the life of the righteous, which is deemed eternal, be equally applied to the duration of the punishment of the wicked, also called eternal.

God is the Creator of all things. It may be that part of His plan was to make humanity in such a way that those persons who volitionally decide to live separate from God would experience eternal anguish as the consequence of their choice. God's intention for humanity is to live eternally in bliss and fellowship with God. Those who pervert this intention will and must experience the eternal consequences of that act. See *Gehenna; Hell; Judgment; Wrath of God.*   *Stan Norman*

EVI (Ē´ vī) Personal name of uncertain meaning, perhaps "desire." King of Midian killed in battle by Israelites during wilderness wanderings (Num. 31:8). He apparently ruled as a vassal of Sihon (Josh. 13:21).

EVIL Since pre-Christian times, philosophers have wrestled with the coexistence of a completely good sovereign God and evil and suffering. Christian theologians have struggled with how to relate God's providence and evil. Many believers have asked "Why me?" when personally faced with suffering. In contrast with other religions and philosophies, however, the Bible provides adequate answers.

Whereas many philosophers and theologians have discarded belief in divine omnipotence and goodness, or even the existence of God or evil, according to the Bible there is no true philosophical problem of evil. Instead, the Bible simply teaches that God has His reasons for allowing evil. Christian thinkers have traditionally classified God's reasons into two categories: (1) Creaturely volition (at least in the case of Satan and Adam) would not be free if there were no possibility to disobey God's will. Evil results, therefore, from the abuse of freedom. (2) Suffering can be providentially used to develop Christian character. Scripture, however, provides more than two reasons and in doing so never compromises the reality of either the living God or evil.

Biblical Reasons for Evil Isaiah 45:7 (KJV) reads: "I make peace, and create evil. I the LORD do all these things." This translation has misled some to surmise that the simple explanation for evil is that God is its source. Exegetes, though, have long noted that the verse is not about the source of evil but rather about divine providence "causing well-being and creating calamity" (NASB). Biblical teaching steers clear from attributing evil to the Holy One: "God is not tempted by evil, and He Himself doesn't tempt anyone" (James 1:13 HCSB). The following scriptural reasons for evil often overlap and correlate (cp. J. Newport's *Life's Ultimate Questions*).

Free will At the very least, God created Adam and Eve (and by implication, Satan) with freedom to choose for or against God (Gen. 1–3). Their free moral agency, exercised in rebellion and issuing in disastrous evils, would not have been truly free without ability to disobey. God's providence is not compromised thereby. He is still sovereign over history and His justice and goodness are not impugned by the fall.

Retribution God must punish evil as the righteous guarantor of the moral order. Thus, some present suffering as a result of His judgment upon sin (Deut. 30; Isa. 3:11; Rom. 1:18), not including judgment in the age to come (Rom. 14:10-12; 2 Cor. 5:10; Rev. 20:11-15).

Discipline God uses suffering to make His people more like Christ. Indeed, God's goodness ensures that He trains and matures His children through trials (Prov. 3:11-12; Jer.18:1-6; Rom. 5:3-5; Heb.12:5-11).

Probation The godly await the final overthrow of evil. In the interim their faith is tested by evil which seems to have the upper hand, thus obscuring God's present rule (Pss. 37; 73). But by enduring testing, true saving faith is finally revealed and confirmed (Heb.10:32-39; James 1:2-4; 1 Pet. 4:12-19; 5:8-10).

Revelation Suffering can issue in a fuller knowledge of God. Hosea's domestic troubles were used by God to reveal truth to Israel (Hos. 1–3). Though suffering may induce further blasphemy in the ungodly (Rev. 16:9-11,21), the righteous are victorious in the knowledge that God's love is at work for them in their tribulations (Rom. 8:28-38).

Redemption Suffering is sometimes borne redemptively for others. The supreme instance is Christ's vicarious atonement for sinners (Isa. 53:4-12; 1 Pet. 2:21-24; 3:18), but believers may suffer on behalf of others (Col. 1:24).

Mystery The book of Job teaches that reasons behind one's suffering may be hidden from the sufferer and misunderstood by observers. Job ultimately learns to rest in God, even without a full explanation (Job 42:1-6). Even the Lord Jesus cried out on the cross: "My God, My God, why have You forsaken Me?" (Matt. 27:46 HCSB; cp. Ps. 22:1).

Final victory The full solution to evil awaits the coming age. At history's darkest moment, Christ will return to conquer evil (2 Thess. 1:5-10; Rev. 19:1-21). God will vindicate His children and wipe away their tears (Isa. 25:8; Rev. 7:16-17; 21:4).   *Ted Cabal*

EVIL-MERODACH (Ē´ vĭl-mə rō´ dǎk) Babylonian royal name meaning "worshiper of Marduk." Babylonian king (562–560 B.C.) who treated Jehoiachin, king of Judah, with kindness (2 Kings 25:27). The Babylonian form of the name is Amel-Marduk. He was the son of Nebuchadnezzar. See *Babylon*.

EXACTOR KJV term for a taskmaster or a tax collector used only at Isa. 60:17 (ruler, HCSB). Most often the KJV translated the underlying Hebrew word as "oppressor" (Job 3:18; Isa. 3:12; 9:3; 14:2,4; Zech. 9:8; 10:4). Elsewhere

the term is translated "taskmaster," one who "exacts" labor (Exod. 3:7) or as "raiser of taxes" (Dan. 11:20). The image is of one who drives people like a mule driver drives his beast (Job 39:7). Isaiah's picture is striking. In the future God is preparing for the only "rule" known to be peace and the only "oppression" known to be righteousness (60:17).

EXCOMMUNICATION Practice of temporarily or permanently excluding someone from the church as punishment for sin or apostasy.

Old Testament In the OT excommunication came as a curse from God as punishment for sin (Deut. 27:26; 28:15; Ps. 119:21; Mal. 2:2-9; 4:6). The Jewish community assumed authority to curse on God's behalf (Num. 23:8; Isa. 66:5). Old Testament terms for excommunication include: *karat*, to be excluded or cut off (Exod. 12:15,19; Lev. 17:4,9); *cherem*, banish, devote, or put to destruction (Exod. 22:19; Lev. 27:28-29; Josh. 6:17); and *qelalah*, desolation or thing of horror (2 Kings 22:19; Jer. 25:18). The covenant community protected itself from curse and temptation by distancing covenant-breakers from the community even to the point of executing them.

New Testament Expulsion from the synagogue was one form of NT excommunication. Christians were frequently subject to expulsion, which was punishment for blasphemy or for straying from the tradition of Moses (Luke 6:22; John 9:22; 12:42; 16:2). Many early Christians thus endured excommunication from the worship place of their fathers to be Christians. The apostles practiced excommunication based on the binding and loosing authority Jesus gave to them (John 20:23; Matt. 18:18). They excommunicated church members for heresy (Gal. 1:8) for gross, deliberate sin (1 Cor. 5; 2 John 7) and perhaps for falling away from church belief and practice (Heb. 6:4-8). The purpose was to purify the church and to encourage offenders to repent (1 Cor. 5:5-6; 2 Cor. 2:6-10; 2 Thess. 3:15). Punishment ranged in scope from limited ostracism to permanent exclusion and may even have included some form of physical punishment if the church continued synagogue practice (Luke 4:28-30; John 8:2-11; Acts 5:1-5; 7:58). New Testament terms for excommunication include: being delivered to Satan (1 Cor. 5:5; 1 Tim. 1:20); anathema or cursed and cut off from God (Rom. 9:3; 1 Cor. 16:22; Gal. 1:8). The NT

E

churches apparently used excommunication as a means of redemptive discipline. See *Apostasy; Binding and Loosing.*

In Church History During the Middle Ages when church and state became intertwined, excommunication was often used as a political tool. In 1054 the Catholic Church was divided into east and west. Each claimed primacy as the true church. They "resolved" the issue by excommunicating each other.

Contemporary In its broadest sense, excommunication now means denial of sacraments, congregational worship, or social contact of any kind. Excommunication is practiced in this manner by both Protestant and Catholic churches. However, the term itself is used mainly in the Catholic Church and usually indicates the permanent ban. Lesser punishments are called censures. *Donna R. Ridge*

EXECRATION Act of cursing; an object of cursing. The term appears in the KJV twice (Jer. 42:18; 44:12), both times in reference to the fate of the remnant who disobeyed God's word and sought safety in Egypt. The text may be understood in at least two ways. First, their name would become an object of cursing (NIV), that is, others would curse the remnant. Alternately, their name might be used as a curse (TEV) in the form "May you be like the remnant whom God destroyed." See *Blessing and Cursing.*

EXECUTIONER One who puts another to death, especially as a legal penalty. KJV uses the term only once (Mark 6:27 for the one beheading John the Baptist). Some modern translations prefer a more generic term such as "soldier of the guard" (NRSV, REB) or simply "guard" (TEV). The OT law does not make provision for the role of the representative executioner who acts on behalf of society. Where "official" executioners are mentioned, they are portrayed as the agents of despotic rulers (Dan. 2:14,24; Mark 6:27). The execution of Jesus is the chief example of such abuse of power. See *Capital Punishment.*

EXERCISE The Bible speaks only briefly of physical exercise. First Timothy 4:8 recognizes the value of bodily training but subordinates it to the greater value of godliness. Because the human body was created by God, it is incumbent on people to care for their bodies. This is particularly true for Christians whose bodies are temples of the Holy Spirit (1 Cor. 6:19), which are to be presented to God as living sacrifices (Rom. 12:1). Using the imagery of a runner, the Apostle Paul speaks of the need to pommel and subdue his body in order to qualify it for life's race (1 Cor. 9:24-26). *Paul H. Wright*

EXHORTATION Argument (Acts 2:40) or advice intended to incite hearers to action. The ability to exhort or encourage to action is a spiritual gift (Rom. 12:8) sometimes associated with prophets/ preachers (Acts 15:32; 1 Cor. 14:3). Elsewhere mutual exhortation is the responsibility of all Christians (Rom. 1:12; 1 Thess. 5:11,14; Heb. 3:13, 10:24-25). Hebrew Scriptures provided NT preachers with a source of exhortation (Rom. 15:14; Heb. 12:5-6). The synagogue sermon was described as a "word of exhortation" (Acts 13:15 KJV; HCSB, message of encouragement). As such it called for applying the truths of the scriptural text to life. Indeed, exhortation is the goal of orderly worship (1 Cor. 14:31). Letters of exhortation were common in the ancient world. Messengers often supplied additional encouragement to supplement the written message (2 Sam. 11:25; Eph. 6:22; Col. 4:8). Two NT documents describe themselves as exhortations (1 Pet. 5:12; Heb. 13:22). The effect of the letter of the Apostolic Council was similarly described as exhortation (Acts 15:21). Though it does not designate itself as such, the letter from James is an exhortation.

EXILE Events in which the northern tribes of Israel were taken into captivity by the Assyrians and the southern tribes of Judah were taken into captivity by the Babylonians. Sometimes the terms "captivity" and "carried into captivity" refer to the exiles of Israel and Judah.

In OT times the Assyrians and Babylonians introduced the practice of deporting captives into foreign lands. Deportation was generally considered the harsher measure only when other means had failed. Rather than impose deportation, Assyria demanded tribute from nations it threatened to capture. As early as 842 B.C., Jehu, king of Israel, was paying tribute to Shalmaneser, king of Assyria. Not until the reign of Tiglath-pileser (745–727 B.C.) did the Assyrians begin deporting people from the various tribes of Israel.

In 734 B.C. Tiglath-pileser captured the cities of Naphtali (2 Kings 15:29) and carried away as captives the inhabitants of the tribes of Naphtali,

Reuben, Gad, and the half-tribe of Manasseh (1 Chron. 5:26). In 732 Tiglath-pileser took control of Damascus, the capital city of Syria. At that time he appointed Israel (the Northern Kingdom) her last king—Hoshea (732–723 B.C.). Hoshea rebelled about 724 B.C. and was taken captive by the Assyrians (2 Kings 17:1-6).

Samaria, the capital city of Israel, held out until early 721 B.C. Shalmaneser V (727–722 B.C.) laid siege to the city. The eventual fall of Samaria occurred at the hands of Sargon II (722–705 B.C.). These events marked the end of the 10 northern tribes (2 Kings 17:18).

The Assyrians exiled the Israelites into Halah, Gozan, and Media (2 Kings 17:6; 18:11; Obad. 20). The Assyrians brought into Samaria people from Babylon, Cuthah, Ava, Hamath, and Sepharvaim (2 Kings 17:24; Ezra 4:10). Sargon II recorded that 27,290 Israelites were deported.

The prophets Hosea and Amos had prophesied the fall of Israel. These two prophets proclaimed that Israel's fall was due to moral and spiritual degeneration rather than to the superior military might of the Assyrian nation. Assyria was only the "rod of mine anger"' (Isa. 10:5).

History of the Exile of Judah More than a hundred years before the Babylon exile, Isaiah, the prophet, had predicted Judah's fall (Isa. 6:11-12; 8:14; 10:11). In addition, the prophets Micah, Zephaniah, Jeremiah, Habakkuk, and Ezekiel agreed that Judah would fall.

There were three deportations of Jews to Babylon. The first occurred in 598 B.C. (2 Kings 24:12-16). The second deportation took place in 587 B.C. (2 Kings 25:8-21; Jer. 39:8-10; 40:7; 52:12-34). After the second deportation, Gedaliah was appointed governor of Judah by the Babylonians but was assassinated (2 Kings 25:22-25). A third deportation, a punishment for Gedaliah's assassination, occurred in 582 B.C. (Jer. 52:30).

Life in the Exile meant life in five different geographical areas: Israel, Judah, Assyria, Babylon, and Egypt. We possess little information about events in any of these areas between 587 and 538 B.C.

Israel Assyria took the educated, leading people from the Northern Kingdom and replaced them with populations from other countries they had conquered (2 Kings 17:24). They had to send some priests back to the area to teach the people the religious traditions of the God of the land (2 Kings 17:27-28). Such priests probably served a population that contained poor Jewish farmers dominated by foreign leaders. When Babylon took over the area, they established a provincial capital in Samaria. Leaders there joined with other provincial leaders to stop Zerubbabel and his people from rebuilding the temple (Ezra 4:1-24). Gradually, a mixed population emerged (Ezra 10). Still, a faithful remnant attempted to maintain worship of Yahweh near Shechem, producing eventually the Samaritan community. See *Samaritans.*

Assyria Exiles from the Northern Kingdom were scattered through the Assyrian holdings (2 Kings 17:6). Apparently, their small communities, isolated from other Jews, did not allow them to maintain much national identity. We do not know what happened to these people, thus the popular title: the lost tribes of Israel. Some may have eventually returned to their original homeland. Others may have established the basis of Jewish communities that appear in later historical records.

Judah The Babylonians did not completely demolish Judah. They left farmers, in particular, to care for the land (Jer. 52:16). Some citizens who had fled the country before the Babylonian invasion returned to the land after Jerusalem was destroyed (Jer. 40:12). The Babylonians set up a government that may or may not have been dependent on the provincial government in Samaria. Jews loyal to the Davidic tradition assassinated Gedaliah, the governor (2 Kings 25:25). Then many of the people fled to Egypt (2 Kings 25:26; Jer. 43). People remaining in the land continued to worship in the temple ruins and seek God's word of hope (Lamentations). Many were probably not overjoyed to see Jews return from Babylon claiming land and leadership.

Babylon The center of Jewish life shifted to Babylon under such leaders as Ezekiel. Babylon even recognized the royal family of Judah as seen in 2 Kings 25:27 and in recovered Babylonian records. Exiled Jews based their calendar on the exile of King Jehoiachin in 597 (Ezek. 1:2; 33:21; 40:1). Jehoiachin's grandson, Zerubbabel, led the first exiles back from Babylon in 538 (Ezra 2:2; Hag. 1:1). Most of the exiles in Babylon probably followed normal Near Eastern practice and became farmers on land owned by the government. Babylonian documents show that eventually some Jews became successful merchants in Babylon. Apparently religious leaders like Ezekiel were able to lead religious meetings

E

(Ezek. 8:1; cp. Ezra 8:15-23). Correspondence continued between those in Judah and those in exile (Jer. 29), and Jewish elders gave leadership to the exiles (Jer. 29:1; Ezek. 8:1; 14:1; 20:1). First Chronicles 1–9, Ezra, and Nehemiah show that genealogies and family records became very important points of identity for the exiles. People were economically self-sufficient, some even owning slaves (Ezra 2:65) and having resources to fund the return to Jerusalem (Ezra 1:6; 2:69). Still, many longed for Jerusalem and would not sing the Lord's song in Babylon (Ps. 137). They joined prophets like Ezekiel in looking for a rebuilt temple and a restored Jewish people. They laughed at Babylonian gods as sticks of wood left over from the fire (Isa. 44:9-17; 45:9-10; 46:1-2,6-7; Jer. 1:16; Ezek. 20:29-32). A Babylonian Jewish community was thus established and would exercise strong influence long after Cyrus of Persia permitted Jews to return to Judah. These Jews established their own worship, collected Scriptures, and began interpreting them in the Aramaic paraphrase and explanations which eventually became the Babylonian Talmud, but continued to support Jews in Jerusalem.

Egypt Jews fled Jerusalem for Egypt (2 Kings 25:26) despite God's directions not to (Jer. 42:13–44:30). Many Jews apparently became part of the Egyptian army stationed in northern border fortresses to protect against Babylonian invasion. As such, they may have joined Jews who had come to Egypt earlier. Archaeologists have discovered inscriptions at Elephantine in southern Egypt showing a large Jewish army contingent there also. They apparently built a temple there and worshiped Yahweh along with other gods. These military communities eventually disappeared, but Jewish influence in Egypt remained. Finally, a large community in Alexandria established itself and produced the Septuagint, the earliest translation of the Hebrew Bible into Greek.

The Edict of Cyrus in 538 B.C. (2 Chron. 36:22-23; Ezra 1:1-4) released the Jews in Babylon to return to their homeland. Though conditions in the homeland were dismal, many Jews did return. The preaching of Haggai and Zechariah (520–519 B.C.) urged these returning captives to rebuild their temple in Jerusalem. The temple was completed in 515 B.C., the date which traditionally marks the end of the Babylonian exile. *Gary Hardin*

EXODUS Israel's escape from slavery in Egypt and journey towards the promised land under Moses. Historically and theologically this is the most important event in the OT. More than a hundred times in all parts of the OT except the Wisdom Literature, Yahweh is proclaimed as "the one who brought you up from the land of Egypt, out of the house of bondage." Israel remembered the exodus as God's mighty redemptive act. She celebrated it in her creeds (Deut. 26:5-9; 1 Sam. 12:6-8). She sang of it in worship (Pss. 78; 105; 106; 114; 135; 136). The prophets constantly reminded Israel that election and covenant were closely related to the exodus (Isa. 11:16; Jer. 2:6; 7:22-25; Ezek. 20:6,10; Hos. 2:15; 11:1; Amos 2:10; 3:1; Mic. 6:4; Hag. 2:5). (The English word "exodus" does not occur in the KJV.) The exodus in the OT was to Israel what the death and resurrection of Christ was to Christians in the NT. Just as Israel commemorated her deliverance from Egyptian bondage in the feast of Passover, Christians celebrate their redemption from sin in the observance of the Lord's Supper (Luke 22:1-20; 1 Cor. 11:23-26).

Historicity The only explicit account of the exodus we have is the biblical account (Exod. 1–15). No extrabiblical witnesses directly speak of the sojourn of Israel's ancestors in the land of the Nile. However, Egyptian sources do confirm the general situation that we find in the end of Genesis and the beginning of the book of Exodus. There are many reports in Egyptian sources of nomadic people called Habiru coming into Egypt from the east fleeing from famine. Extrabiblical evidence from Egypt indicates that Egypt used slave labor in building projects (Exod. 1:11). At one time the land in Egypt was owned by many landholders; but after the reign of the Hyksos kings the Pharaoh owned most of the land, and the people were serfs of the king (Gen. 47:20). Old Testament scholars accept the essential historicity of the exodus.

The Nature of the Event Some scholars see the exodus as the miraculous deliverance of the people of God from the grip of Pharaoh's army at the Red Sea. Others see it as an escape across a sprawling wilderness and sweltering desert of a small mixed band of border slaves. Some argue that the military language in the account indicates that the event was a military skirmish. Such language may be the language of holy war.

The Bible stresses that the exodus was the work of God. God brought the plagues on Egypt

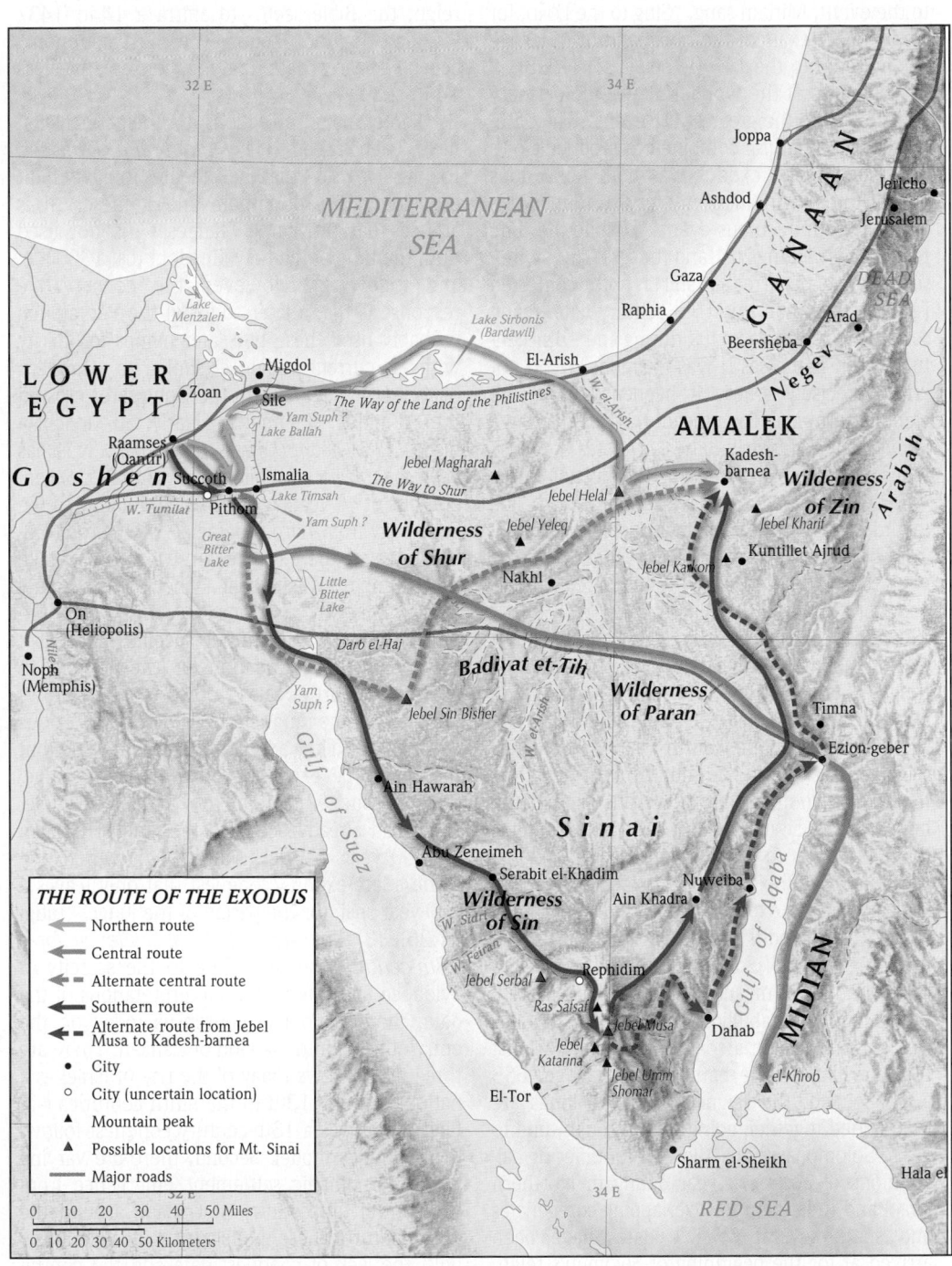

THE ROUTE OF THE EXODUS

→ Northern route
→ Central route
⇢ Alternate central route
→ Southern route
⇢ Alternate route from Jebel Musa to Kadesh-barnea
• City
○ City (uncertain location)
▲ Mountain peak
▲ Possible locations for Mt. Sinai
— Major roads

0 10 20 30 40 50 Miles
0 10 20 30 40 50 Kilometers

(Exod. 7:1-5). The miracle at the sea was never treated merely as a natural event or as Israel's victory alone. In the earliest recorded response to the event, Miriam sang, "Sing to the LORD, for He is highly exalted; the horse and his rider He has hurled into the sea" (Exod. 15:21 NASB).

Elements of the wonderful and the ordinary contributed to the greatest OT events. The natural and supernatural combined to produce God's deliverance. The exodus was both miraculous and historical. An air of mystery surrounds this event as all miraculous events. Despite the time reference in 1 Kings 6:1 and Judges 11:26, when the exodus occurred is still a hotly contested issue. Rather than this 15th century date, many scholars place the exodus during the 13th century when Ramesses II was Pharaoh. We do not know precisely where it happened since the Hebrew term may have meant the Red Sea as we know it, one of its tributaries, or a "sea of reeds" whose location is unknown. We do not know who or how many may have been involved. The record makes it clear that God delivered Israel from bondage because of His covenant with the patriarchs and because He desired to redeem His people (Exod. 6:2-8).

The Date of the Exodus The Bible does not give an incontrovertible date for the exodus. First Kings 6:1 says, "In the four hundred and eightieth year after the sons of Israel came out of the land of Egypt, in the fourth year of Solomon's reign over Israel, in the month of Ziv which is the second month, that he began to build the house of the LORD" (NASB). Though this verse refers primarily to the beginning of the building of Solomon's temple and only in a general way to the time of the exodus, it does indicate a 15th century B.C. exodus event. One problem is that the fourth year of Solomon's reign is calculated by a round-about means. First, King Ahab is mentioned in an extrabiblical inscription that states that Ahab fought in a coalition of armies against the Assyrians in the battle of Qarqar (ca. 853 B.C.). Second, the reigns of Israelite kings are then added together, going back through time to get to Solomon's reign. Allowing for differing calculations of accession year dating in Northern Israel and Judah and for overlapping coregencies and such, several possible dates have been arrived at for the beginning of Solomon's reign. However, the competing chronological systems for the beginning of Solomon's reign differ by no more than a decade (970; 967; 966; 961 B.C.).

The fourth year of Solomon's reign would then be dated anywhere from 966 to 957 B.C. So even without the precise date for the beginning of his reign, the Bible seems to affirm a 1446–1437 B.C. date for the exodus. The most commonly accepted early date (among conservatives) is 1446 B.C.

Three major objections to this conclusion have been raised. (1) *Pithom and Rameses.* Exodus 1:11 says that the Israelites in Egypt built the store cities of Pithom and Rameses. It is argued that the name "Rameses" is not used until the time of the new kingdom (ca. 1300 B.C. and following). However, the conservative response is that a later editor of the Pentateuch probably used these two later names for clarity with his current audience (similar to a modern historian saying, William the Conqueror crossed the "English Channel"—clearly an anachronism). (2) *The 480 years time span.* This has been taken as a symbolic length of time (12 generations of 40 years each; possibly relating to the genealogy from Aaron to Zadok in 1 Chron. 6:3-8). However, there is no definitive reason to take this number as symbolic. The phrasing only appears this way in 1 Kings 6:1, and the continuation of the verse further specifies the exact timing of the foundation of the temple in Solomon's fourth year. Another problem shows up when all the numbers are added from Exodus to 1 Samuel. They add up to over 550 years, but these may be explained by overlapping judgeships and such. According to Jephthah the judge, Israel had already occupied the land of Canaan for 300 years before his time. This would preclude a late exodus/conquest that only leaves a 200-year span for the period of the judges (Judg. 11:26). (3) *The archaeological evidence for a 13th-century conquest.* Due to the scarcity of evidence and the differing interpretations of the data, there is no real consensus today on the entry of Israel into the land of Canaan. There are three major views today of the rise of Israel as a nation from the 13th to the ninth centuries B.C. First, there was a 13th-century conquest following Albright's model. Second, there are varying views of nomadic settlement/emergence from the central hill country of Canaan around the 13th century. These models try to deal seriously with the lack of conquest data and the contradiction of mixed cultural evidence in the central hill country in the late Bronze Age (ca. 1200 B.C.). Third, there are those who use the scarcity of data to minimize the historicity of the Bible text and thus hold to a ninth-century date for the nation of Israel beginning with Omri/Ahab. As for data, the Merneptah Stele (ca. 1220 B.C.) indicates Israel was in Canaan by this date—but does not preclude an early date. The data from Lachish, Bethel, Hazor, Debir, and so forth could be interpreted to support a 13th-century conquest, but some of these destruction levels could be attributed to the time of Judges. Bryant Wood's analysis of the Jericho evidence has shown that John Garstang's original interpretation of an early (ca. 1400 B.C.) destruction level at Jericho was correct. Wood's latest pottery analysis of an Italian excavation at Jericho indicates that the retaining fortification wall around Jericho was both built and destroyed in the late Bronze I period. This is further evidence for an early date for the destruction of Jericho (and conquest) as well as an early date for the exodus. The identification of Ai with Et-Tell has shown to be inconclusive since the site did not exist as a town at either the early or the late date. However the site of Khirbet el-Maqatir, excavated by Bryant Woods and Garry Byers, did exist nearby in the late Bronze Period and may be the biblical Ai. Nelson Glueck's survey of the Transjordan, where he concluded there was no evidence of Edomites, Moabites, or nomadic tribes for the Israelites to run into in the early date, has been overturned. Maxwell Miller's survey of the Transjordan (specifically the Moabite plateau) has shown that there is evidence of nomadic tribes throughout the time periods in question for both dates of the exodus. See *Pithom and Rameses.*

The Pharaoh of the Exodus The pharaoh of the exodus is tied directly to the interpretation of the data for the dating of the exodus/conquest. If one takes the late exodus date (ca. 1270 B.C.), the pharoah of the oppression would have been Seti I, and the pharaoh of the exodus would have been Ramesses II (1304–1237 B.C.). However, taking the early exodus date (ca. 1446 B.C.), the pharaoh of the oppression was Thutmose III, and the pharaoh of the exodus was Amenhotep II (1450–1425 B.C.). Neither date has absolute conclusive chronological evidence, which leads many to conclude the exodus/conquest did not happen or at least happened in stages. While there is conflicting evidence, there is no concrete reason to contradict 1446 B.C. dating for the exodus as alluded to in the Bible. Amenhotep II is depicted in ancient texts as a strong warrior and military pharaoh who made several campaigns into Canaan and then abruptly stopped his military activity. Amenhotep II's father, Thutmose III,

Lake Timsah, possibly the place where the Hebrews crossed the Red Sea.

was one of the strongest and wealthiest pharaohs of the 18th dynasty. Egypt was at the zenith of its power and wealth when Amenhotep II rose to rule and became the pharaoh of the exodus. Though not conclusive, the Dream Stele of Thutmose IV, son and successor of Amenhotep II, indicates that Thutmose IV was not the firstborn son of Amenhotep II—a possible allusion to the tenth plague on the firstborn of Egypt.

The Number Involved in the Exodus In our English Bibles Exod. 12:37 says, "Now the sons of Israel journeyed from Rameses to Succoth, about six hundred thousand men on foot, aside from children" (NASB). For various reasons (water/food supply in Sinai; evidence of burials, etc.) current scholarship translates the Hebrew word for "thousand" as "clan or military unit." This view results in drastically reducing the numbers of Israelites in the exodus, as well as in the rest of OT. However, they must admit that this translation cannot be used consistently in this manner throughout the OT for some numbers are more specific. Numbers 1:46 states more specifically that God commanded Moses to take a census in the second year after the exodus from Egypt and the men of war numbered 603,550. It is not unusual for round numbers to be used at times both in the Bible and the Ancient Near

East, but this does not mean the rounded numbers lack historicity, or veracity. Just prior to entering the promised land, in Numbers 26, God commanded Moses to take a census after the plague caused by immorality with the Moabite women. The Israelites numbered 601,730 men of war (Num. 26:51) over the age of twenty (Num. 1:3). The differences in the numbers found in Exod. 12 and Num. 26 may be attributed to the death of the older exodus generation through both divine judgment and natural causes as well as the increase through new births in the first 20 of the 40 years of wandering in the wilderness of Sinai. Some scholars try to get around large numbers which are specific by breaking the number into two parts—the thousands being military units/clans and the hundreds standing for the actual number of men, but this method breaks down when we see in Num. 1:46 [603,550] 603 military units/clans but a total of only 550 men. If the statistics are correct that males over the age of twenty make up approximately 25 percent of the total population, then the Israelites numbered well over two million people at both the beginning and the end of the wilderness wanderings.

The exodus was the work of God. It was a historical event involving a superpower nation and

Interior chapel of Hatshepsut's festival hall. Hatshepsut was the wife of Thutmose II and the aunt and step-mother of Thutmose III, believed by some to be the pharaoh of the Exodus.

an oppressed people. God acted redemptively in power, freedom, and love. When the kingdom of God did not come, the later prophets began to look for a second exodus. That expectation was fulfilled spiritually in Christ's redemptive act.

Ralph L. Smith and Eric Mitchell

EXODUS, BOOK OF Central book of the OT, reporting God's basic saving act for Israel in the exodus from Egypt and His making of His covenant with the nation destined to be His kingdom of priests.

Literary Setting The book of Exodus is the second book of the OT and of the Pentateuch. (See *Pentateuch* for discussion of date and authorship.) Exodus builds on the Genesis narrative of creation, human sin, divine punishment and renewal, the call of Abraham to bless the world, and the struggles of Isaac and then Jacob to carry out God's call. This ends with Joseph taking his father's family into Egypt to avoid the harsh sufferings of famine. Exodus takes up the story of the children of Jacob in Egypt, now under a new pharaoh and seen as feared foreigners instead of welcomed deliverers from famine. Israel thus became slave laborers in Egypt (chap. 1). God delivered the baby Moses from danger, and he grew up in pharaoh's court as son of pharaoh's daughter. Still he cared for the Israelites. Trying to protect one of his own people, he killed an Egyptian. Thus, Moses had to flee to the wilderness of Midian, where he helped seven endangered shepherd girls. He settled among them and married one of the girls. There, God called him at the burning bush of Mount Horeb/Sinai and sent him back to rescue Israel from Egypt (chaps. 2–4). With his brother Aaron, he faced a stubborn pharaoh, who refused to release the Israelites. When pharaoh made life harder for Israel, the Israelites complained about Moses. God took this as opportunity to reveal Himself to Israel, to pharaoh, and to the Egyptians. God brought the plagues upon Egypt. Pharaoh stubbornly refused to let Israel go until his firstborn son and the eldest sons of all Egypt died in the final plague. This tenth plague became the setting for Israel's central religious celebration, that of Passover and Unleavened Bread in which Israel reenacted the exodus from Egypt and rejoiced at God's supreme act of salvation for His people (chaps. 5–13). As Israel fled Egypt, the pharaoh again resisted and led his army after them. The miracle of the Red Sea (or perhaps more literally, the Sea of Reeds) became the greatest moment in Israel's history, the moment God created a nation for Himself by delivering them from the strongest military power on earth as He led them through the divided waters of the sea and then flooded the sea again as the Egyptians tried to follow (chap. 14).

After celebrating the deliverance in song and dance (15:1-21), Israel followed God's leadership into the wilderness, but soon the difficult wilderness life proved too hard. The Israelites cried for the good old days of Egypt, even after God supplied their food and drink needs and after He defeated the Amalekites (15:22–17:15). Moses' father-in-law Jethro brought Moses' wife and children back to him in the wilderness and praised God for all that He had done for Moses and the people. Jethro also advised Moses how to organize a more efficient judicial system, relieving Moses of stress (chap. 18). Then Israel came to Sinai, where God called them to become His covenant people, a holy nation to carry out Abraham's mission of blessing the nations. God gave the Ten Commandments and other laws central to the covenant (chaps. 19–23), and then confirmed the covenant in a mysterious ceremony (chap. 24). Moses went to the top of the mountain to receive the remainder of God's instructions, especially instructions for building the sacred place of worship, the tabernacle (chaps. 24-31). Impatient Israel got Aaron to build an object of worship they could see, so he made the golden calf. The people began worshiping. This angered God, who sent Moses back down to the people. Moses prayed for the people despite their sin but then saw the people's sinful actions and threw the tablets with the law to the ground, breaking them. Moses again went up and prayed for the people. God punished them but did not destroy them as He had threatened. God showed His continued presence in the Tent of Meeting and in letting His glory pass by Moses (chaps. 32–33). God then gave Moses the law on two new tablets of stone and renewed the covenant with the people, providing further basic laws for them. Such intense communication with God brought radiance to Moses' face (chap. 34). Moses then led Israel to celebrate the Sabbath and to build the tabernacle (chaps. 35–39). Moses set up the tabernacle and established worship in it. God blessed the action with His holy glorious presence (chap. 40). This provided the sign for Israel's future journeys, following God's cloud and fire.

Theological Teaching In Exodus Israel learned the basic nature of God and His salvation. They also learned the nature of sin, the characteristics of God's leader, the components of worship, and the meaning of salvation. In Exodus Israel learned the identity of the people of God.

God is Ruler of the world, able to act for His people even on the home territory of the world's most powerful political and military force. God chooses to act for the people He elects. God knows the situation of His people even when another nation has forced them into slavery. God saved His people through calling out a leader to communicate God's will and to face their enemies. God empowered the leader at a time of the leader's personal weakness rather than at a time of strength. He worked in the forces of nature to show His unequaled power and to demonstrate His concern for His own people.

Salvation, power, and concern were not all that God revealed of Himself. He also showed a holy nature in that special preparations were made to enter His presence. He revealed His great glory, so majestic even the leader could not view it. Most of all, He revealed His will to be present among His people and lead them through their daily activities.

In so doing, He showed the way He expected His people to live, a way of holiness, a way of priesthood among the nations. This way centered on life guided by the Ten Commandments. Such a life reflected the nature of God Himself, who could be identified as "The LORD God, compassionate and gracious, slow to anger, and abounding in lovingkindness and truth; who keeps lovingkindness for thousands, who forgives iniquity, transgression and sin; yet He will by no means leave the guilty unpunished" (Exod. 34:6-7 NASB).

God expected His people to live the way of holiness, the way of the Ten Commandments. Failure to do so is sin. Sin centers particularly in giving another god credit for what God has done and in worshiping what human hands have made rather than the true God who allows no images of Himself. To avoid sin, God's people had to follow God's chosen leader, even when the path led through the wilderness and demanded a lifestyle lacking in some of the food and luxuries they had learned to take for granted. The leader followed God's will and not the people's. In so doing, the leader interceded with God for a sinful people, willing to give up his own place with God in exchange for the people's salvation. Only a leader who communed face-to-face with God could develop such an attitude. Thus Moses became the leader without parallel for Israel.

The leader's lasting role included the establishment of a worship place and worship practices. God's people gained their identity in worship. The leader showed them when, where, and how to worship.

The people offered worship because they had experienced God's salvation. For them salvation meant physical deliverance in military action against a powerful world enemy. It involved following God's instructions and waiting for God's miraculous help. Salvation set up a relationship between God and the people, a relationship based on God's initiative in delivering the people and on God's initiative in inviting the people into covenant relationship. This meant the people could trust God to lead them through their personal and national history. It also meant that God expected a trusting people to obey Him as He set out the way of life they should follow. Salvation was not just receiving God's salvation. It was following in faith the lifestyle God described for them. See *Covenant.*

Outline

I. God Saves His People (1:1–4:17).
 A. God's people face oppression in fear (1:1-22).
 B. God raises up a deliverer for His oppressed people (2:1–4:17).
II. God Sends His Leader on a Difficult Mission (4:18–7:2).
 A. God uses all means to accomplish His will against an ungodly ruler (4:18-26).
 B. God fulfills His angry promise to provide a helper for His leader (4:27-31).
 C. God's leader delivers God's message to pagan leaders (5:1-23).
 D. God promises deliverance to a deaf people (6:1-9).
 E. God reaffirms His insecure leaders (6:10–7:2).
III. God Reveals Himself in Punishing His Enemy (7:3–12:30).
 A. God is sovereign over enemy powers (7:3-13).
 B. Miracles do not bring belief (7:14-25).

C. Enemy powers seek compromise not conversion (8:1-15).

D. God's power convinces enemy religious leaders (8:16-19).

E. Political deceit cannot defeat God's purposes (8:20-32).

F. God's power is superior to pagan religious symbols (9:1-7).

G. God's power affects people as well as animals (9:8-12).

H. Terror and admission of sin are not adequate responses to the actions of the only God (9:13-35).

I. God's saving acts are to be taught to coming generations (10:1-20).

J. God's will must be followed completely (10:21-29).

K. God distinguishes between His people and His enemies when He punishes (11:1-10).

L. God judges other gods but preserves an obedient people (12:1-13).

M. God's people are to remember and celebrate His deliverance (12:14-28).

N. God punishes His proud, stubborn enemies (12:29-30).

IV. God Reveals Himself by Delivering His People from Bondage (12:31–15:21).

A. God delivers and blesses His people and those who join them (12:31-51).

B. God instructs His people to remember, celebrate, and teach His mighty salvation (13:1-16).

C. God leads and protects His obedient people (13:17-22).

D. God gains glory and evokes faith by saving His troubled people (14:1-31).

E. God's people praise Him for their deliverance (15:1-21).

V. God Provides for His Doubting, Complaining People (15:22–18:27).

A. God promises healing to an obedient people (15:22-27).

B. God reveals His glory and tests His people's faith while meeting their needs (16:1-36).

C. Doubting people test God's presence (17:1-7).

D. God delivers His people and permanently curses their enemy (17:8-16).

E. Foreign relatives testify to God's superiority over all gods (18:1-12).

F. God's people must have effective teaching and administrative leadership (18:13-27).

VI. God Covenants with His People (19:1–20:21).

A. God's covenant is based upon His act of deliverance and upon the people's obedience as a kingdom of priests (19:1-8).

B. God prepares His people for His coming down to make a covenant (19:9-15).

C. God's awesome presence confirms His covenant (19:16-25).

D. The Ten Commandments are God's covenant ground rules for life with Him (20:1-17).

E. Awestruck people need a human mediator with the holy God (20:18-21).

VII. God Gives Civil, Ceremonial, and Criminal Laws to Help His People (20:22–23:33).

A. Instructions for acceptable worship (20:22-26).

B. Treatment of Hebrew slaves (21:1-11).

C. Dealing with a person who injures or kills another person (21:12-32).

D. Justice for damage done to another's property (21:33–22:15).

E. Justice when a virgin is seduced (22:16-17).

F. Punishment for sorcery, bestiality, and idolatry (22:18-20).

G. Care for the stranger, widow, orphan, and poor (22:21-27).

H. Respect for God and human rulers, dedication of children, and being holy (22:28-31).

I. Practice honesty; do not hurt the righteous or innocent (23:1-9).

J. Keep the sabbatical year, the Sabbath day, sacred occasions (23:10-19).

K. God will provide spiritual guidance (23:20-33).

VIII. God and His People Must Ratify the Covenant (24:1-18).

A. The people commit themselves to do God's will (24:1-11).

B. God ratifies the covenant with His holy presence (24:12-18).

IX. God Plans to Be Present with His People (25:1–31:17).

E

A. As their hearts move them, people are to give for God's worship place (25:1-7).

B. God will dwell among His people in His place of holy worship (25:8–27:21).

C. God's minister mediates His holy presence for a holy people (28:1–29:37).

D. People respond to the holy Presence with sacrificial giving (29:38–30:38).

E. Craftsmen respond to the holy Presence by dedicating God-given skills (31:1-11).

F. People respond to the holy Presence with Sabbath worship (31:12-17).

X. God Restores a Sinful People (31:18– 34:35).

A. God provides guidelines for life in His presence (31:18).

B. An impatient people break the covenant by making and worshiping other gods (32:1-6).

C. God reacts against a disobedient people in wrath (32:7-10).

D. Intercessory prayer brings divine repentance (32:11-14).

E. Judgment comes to a disobedient people through God's chosen leaders (32:15-29).

F. A mediator's majestic intercession is not sufficient (32:30-35).

G. God withdraws His immediate presence from a sinful people (33:1-4).

H. Mourning and repentance, even by a disobedient people, catch God's attention (33:5-6).

I. Worship at God's chosen place is an essential element in restoring the covenant (33:7-11).

J. The unseeable presence of God reaffirms the covenant relationship (33:12-23).

K. God renews His covenant with His people (34:1-35).

XI. God Honors the Obedience of His People with His Holy Presence (35:1–40:38).

A. God gives His people specific requirements (35:1-19).

B. Obedient people provide resources and skills needed for God's work (35:20–36:7).

C. Obedient people use their resources to build God's dwelling place (36:8–39:43).

D. The leader of God's people prepares for worship (40:1-33).

E. God's presence fills the worship place continually for His obedient people (40:34-38).   *Trent C. Butler*

EXORCISM Practice of expelling demons by means of some ritual act. Although the Hebrew Bible does make reference to demonic beings (Lev. 17:7; Deut. 32:17; Isa. 13:21; 34:14; 2 Chron. 11:15; Ps. 106:37 NRSV), there is no account of demons being cast out of a person or a place. The office of the exorcist, long known in the religious practice of Mesopotamia, is totally absent from the Hebrew Bible. The demons that are mentioned there are usually dreadful earthly beings, sometimes resembling goats or satyrs who live in dry regions. Twice a loanword, *shedim* (Akkadian: *shedu*, "protecting spirit"), is used to describe the foreign gods (Deut. 32:17; Ps. 106:37) and is usually translated "demons" in English.

In the NT the demons were earthly powers or spirits allied with Satan. Jesus' power to exorcise is demonstrated in the Synoptic Gospels of His power over Satan (Matt. 15:21-28; Mark 1:23-38; 5:1-20; 7:24-30; 9:14-29). Exorcism is included in the list of wonders Jesus performed at Capernaum and in Galilee (Mark 1:34,39). Mark 3:11 reports that Jesus had to silence the unclean spirits because they recognized Him and proclaimed Him Son of God.

Jesus gave His disciples authority over unclean spirits (Mark 3:14-15; 6:7) which they generally exercised with success (Mark 6:13) but not always (Mark 9:18). Mark 9:38-41 makes reference to someone who did exorcisms in the name of Jesus even though he was not a follower of Jesus. Jesus told the disciples not to forbid him. In another vein, Acts 19:13-16 tells of wandering Jewish exorcists in Ephesus who attempted to exorcise demons in the name of the Jesus preached by Paul but without success.

John says nothing of Jesus exorcising demons, but the issue of demons is not lacking in that Gospel, for His opponents often accused Jesus of being possessed (John 7:20; 8:48-49,52; 10:20). Similarly, in the Synoptics, the scribes accused Him of casting out demons by the power of the prince of demons (Mark 3:22).

The usual technique of exorcism, as shown by contemporary magical papyri, was to adjure the demon (by name, if possible) through the power of one or more gods to depart the one possessed. This was often accompanied by preparations of herbs and the imposition of amulets. Magical words of extended, repeated syllables were also part of almost all exorcistic formulas. By contrast, the exorcisms of Jesus in the Synoptics involved His command without reference to other divine beings (Mark 1:25; 9:25) and with only a single reference to anything like technique in saying about the boy the disciples could not exorcise that the demon involved could only be cast out by prayer (Mark 9:29). Something close to the usual technique of exorcism was demonstrated by the Gerasene demoniac who tried unsuccessfully to exorcise Jesus, calling Him by title and adjuring Him in the name of the Most High God to leave him alone (Mark 5:7). Jesus relied on His own unique power to demonstrate demons had no place or power in His kingdom. See *Demonic Possession; Divination and Magic; Healing; Miracles.*   *Fred L. Horton, Jr.*

EXPIATION, PROPITIATION Terms used in Christian theology that directly correlate and define the nature and effect of the atonement in relation to God and believers. The two terms have somewhat different meanings and are sometimes placed in opposition to each other by theologians, though it is also possible to see them as complementary. Expiation speaks of the process by which sins are nullified or covered. Propitiation, taking a personal object, speaks of the appeasement of an offended party—specifically the Christian God—from wrath or anger. Expiation falls under the concept of propitiation. In Scripture it cannot exist without propitiation. Other terms used for propitiation are appeasement and placation.

Biblical Terminology In the OT, the Hebrew word *kaphar* normally translated into English as "to make an atonement" is used almost always in the context of quenching the wrath of God. For example, Num. 25:11-13 states that the Lord told Moses that Aaron "has turned away my wrath" because he "made atonement for the sons of Israel" (NASB). Other examples are Exod. 32:30-33; Num. 16:41-50; Isa. 47:11; and Mal. 1:9-10. In relation to man being the object of appeasement, Gen. 32:20, 2 Sam. 21:3-14;

and Prov. 16:14 are used. Other texts speak to gods or idols being the object of appeasement (Deut. 32:17; Jer. 32:35; and Ps. 106:37-38). Although the word *kaphar* is sometimes translated as "to cover" or "to wipe" (cp. Ps. 85:2-3), which would lean toward the idea of expiation, the word is almost always in context of propitiation. Therefore, the satisfaction of God's wrath is a theme addressed in context of OT sacrifice.

Although the controversy over expiation and propitiation is found in the OT, the tension builds upon the NT Greek word *hilasmos* (*hilaskomai* is the verb form, *hilasterion* is the cognate noun form) with four key passages: Rom. 3:25; Heb. 2:17; 1 John 2:2; and 4:10. The diverse renderings of this word in modern translations illustrate the great controversy surrounding the meaning and effect of the atonement. For example, the word *hilasterion* in Rom. 3:25 is translated as "propitiation" (NASB, KJV, HCSB), "expiation" (RSV), "means of expiation" (NEB) and "a sacrifice of atonement" (NIV, NRSV). The NIV, supporting the idea of placation of wrath, offers a marginal option as "the one who would turn aside his wrath, taking away sin." The NRSV's marginal option for Rom. 3:25—"place of atonement"—leaves the reader ambivalent about the function of the atonement but appeals to the locus (site) of the blood sprinkled on the Day of Atonement, the Mercy Seat. The Septuagint uses the word *hilasterion* 28 times, all of which refer to the Mercy Seat, except Amos 9:1. This rendering of *hilasterion* as "mercy seat" in the NT carries a certain ambiguity, however, since Christ was the personal incarnation of Deity and the means of atonement, not an impersonal place of atonement. It is best not to translate the word as "mercy seat."

Paul has articulated that God's wrath is fixed on all human beings due to their heinous sin (Rom. 1–3, especially 1:18-32). Paul, in Rom. 3:25, demonstrates God's initiation in satisfying his wrath in Christ as the *hilasterion* or propitiation. If Paul intended to discuss expiation alone in this verse, he would have forsaken his theme up to that point in his letter.

Hebrews 2:17 has *tas harmartias* (the sins) as the direct object of *hilaskomai*, which might cause one to think the best translation would be "expiation." However, this passage, while speaking of the atonement washing away our sins, does not negate the notion that God's wrath is under consideration and even mentions of a "merciful high priest," which indicates placation of righteous anger. The other passage is found in 1 John 2:2, which tells of an "Advocate" needed to avert the angered God. Although 2 Cor. 5:18-20 does not use the word *hilasmos*, it does speak of God who "reconciled us to Himself through Christ" (HCSB) denoting a previous enmity between God and believers. This imagery could not be explained by expiation alone but must build upon propitiation, thus the translations should reflect this proper meaning.

Theological Formulation The necessity of propitiation is found in God Himself in that sin provokes His wrath. However, some scholars, such as C. H. Dodd and A. T. Hanson, either believe that the wrath of God is nonexistent or it is an impersonal, cause-and-effect occurrence. Dodd believed that the word *hilasmos* in Greek (classical and Koine) means "to propitiate" and that pagan worship involved a similar appeasement of their deities through sacrifice. Nonetheless, he did not feel this applied to Hellenistic Judaism or the NT. He then interpreted the OT and NT texts solely in an expiation fashion, thereby denying propitiation. Dodd's theological concern to redefine God's nature without reference to His righteous wrath against sin seems to have determined his conclusions. Other scholars, such as Leon Morris and Roger Nicole, have adequately defended and supported the reality of God's wrath and the doctrine of a propitiatory atonement.

The doctrine of propitiation in Scripture is in stark opposition to the propitiation of pagan ritualistic sacrifice. First, the object of pagan sacrifice would be either personal deities who are not absolute in power or an impersonal, absolute deity, neither of which can produce atonement. The object of scriptural sacrifice is the personal, absolute Triune God. Second, deities of pagan worship display wrath in an irrational and capricious manner. The Deity of Scripture displays wrath due to His internal nature, not whimsical, external causes. Third, the subject of pagan propitiation is the worshipers who offer the sacrifice. The subject of averting the wrath of God the Father is God the Son who voluntarily brings effectual atonement, because humanity is unworthy to sacrifice to the God against whom they have rebelled. This manner of sacrifice is displayed in the OT in Lev. 17:11, where God has given Israel the atonement to propitiate His wrath.

The effect of the atonement is directly linked to God's wrath. If God has no wrath or anger towards sinners, there is no need for propitiation. Mere expiation will do. If there is expiation without propitiation, God is both indifferent to sin and therefore unjust. Propitiation is the only way God can offer mercy and forgiveness to sinners and, at the same time, be just. "He presented Him to demonstrate His righteousness at the present time, so that He would be righteous and declare righteous the one who has faith in Jesus" (Rom. 3:26 HCSB).

Another attribute of God which some scholars believe is incompatible with God's wrath is love, but the two attributes are shown to be compatible through the atonement, "in that while we were still sinners Christ died for us" (Rom. 5:8 HCSB; cp. Exod. 34:7). The tension must be reconciled because this theological flaw—namely, not reconciling the seeming paradox of God's love and wrath—is probably the reason for much of the controversy over whether expiation or propitiation is the correct understanding. Those who cannot reconcile the apparent paradox reject wrath and propitiation in exchange for love, a move that is unnecessary. In 1 John 4:9-10, the author states that "by this (atonement) the love of God was manifested" (NASB). The crucifixion is the very incarnation of love. While sinners hated their Creator, he sought a way for reconciliation for his people. Isaiah 53:10 further states that "the LORD was pleased to crush Him, putting Him to grief" (NASB). Jesus was not a victim. This act on His part was love without parallel, a complete giving of Himself for us, "a sacrificial and fragrant offering to God" (Eph. 5:2 HCSB).   *Jeremiah H. Russell*

EYE Organ of sight.
Literal Uses The eyes were especially valued organs. If a master stuck a slave, blinding him in an eye, the slave was to go free as compensation for the eye (Exod. 21:26). The OT law of retribution limited vengeance of personal loss to "an eye for an eye" (Lev. 24:20). Jesus replaced this concept of justice with His requirement of love for enemies (Matt. 5:38-48). An eye defect disqualified one for priestly service (Lev. 21:20). An exceptionally cruel punishment was to gouge out the eyes of an enemy (Judg. 16:21; 2 Kings 25:7). This act was interpreted as bringing disgrace on the land of the blinded ones (1 Sam. 11:2). The description of Leah's eyes (Gen.

29:17) is of uncertain meaning. The KJV rendering "tender" can be understood either positively (lovely, NRSV) or negatively (weak, NASB).

Extended Uses The OT often speaks of the eye where we would speak of the person, reflecting the Hebrew concept of bodily parts as semi-independent entities. The eye can thus approve actions (Job 29:11). The eyes can be full of adultery (2 Pet. 2:14) and can desire (Ps. 54:7) or lust (Num. 15:39; 1 John 2:16). The eyes despise (Esther 1:17), are dissatisfied (Prov. 27:20; Eccles. 4:8), and can dwell on past provocation (Job 17:2). Job even spoke of entering a covenant with his eyes as if they were a second party (31:1). Eyes can be evil, that is, greedy or stingy. Such an evil eye refuses to loan when the sabbatical year is near (Deut. 15:9) and begrudges a brother food (28:54). The evil eye of Matt. 6:23 is often interpreted as an unhealthy eye in contrast to the single (whole, healthy) eye of 6:22. The Matthean context of teaching on treasure in heaven (6:19) and serving mammon or riches (6:24) as well as the usage in Matt. 20:15 suggest that the familiar OT idea of the evil eye as the stingy eye is in mind here also. The eyes can be generous to the poor (Prov. 22:9 KJV). The eyes can scorn and mock (Prov. 30:17), spare an enemy (1 Sam. 24:10; Isa. 13:18), or wait for a time to sin (Job 24:15). The eyes can offend (Matt. 5:29), that is, cause someone to sin. Jesus' call to pluck out the offending eye is an exaggerated call to let nothing cause one to sin.

Expressions The "apple of the eye" is a description of the pupil. Proverbs 7:2 called for making God's law the apple of one's eye, that is, something of value to be guarded (kept) carefully. To "make any baldness between your eyes" (Deut. 14:1 KJV) means to shave one's forelocks (NRSV, REB). Bribes blind the eyes of judges causing them to ignore justice (Deut. 16:19; 1 Sam. 12:3). The difficult expression "covering the eyes" (Gen. 20:16 KJV) denotes either compensation for injury (REB), covering the offense (NIV), or else exoneration or some similar term (NRSV, NASB, TEV). In some way Sarah was vindicated; Abimelech and his company could see nothing to criticize in her behavior; and her marriage was saved.

The difficult expression, "daughter of the eye" (Lam. 2:18 NASB margin), rendered "apple of the eye" by the KJV, is generally understood as a poetic equivalent for the eye. To see "eye to

Sunrise ("eyelids of the morning" in Job 3:9) over the Mediterranean coast of Israel.

eye" (Isa. 52:8) is either to see in plain sight (NRSV) or to see with one's own eyes.

Eyes which have been enlightened or brightened (1 Sam. 14:27) are likely an image for being refreshed (REB, TEV) (cp. Ps. 13:3). Light of the eyes can parallel strength (Ps. 38:10; cp. Prov. 15:30). The Lord's commands could enlighten the eyes (Ps. 19:8) in this sense of giving strength or in the sense of giving understanding.

To fasten one's eyes (Acts 11:6) is to look closely. Heavy eyes (Mark 14:40) are drowsy eyes. To have one's eyes opened (Gen. 3:5; 21:19) is to be made aware or to recognize. The image of tearing out ones eyes (Gal. 4:15) pictures willingness to do anything. Winking one's eyes (Ps. 35:19; Prov. 6:13; 10:10; cp. 16:30) is associated with hate, treachery, and troublemaking.

God's Eye(s) God's eye or eyes is a frequent picture of God's providential care. God guides with His eye (Ps. 32:8), that is, gives counsel while offering His watch care. Deliverance from death and famine result from God's watchful eye (Ps. 33:18-19). The image of God's eye(s) roving throughout the earth (2 Chron. 16:9; Prov. 15:3; Jer. 16:17) symbolizes God's knowledge of all human activity and His control over it.

Apocalyptic pictures involving numerous eyes (Ezek. 1:18; 10:12; Rev. 4:6), likewise, reassure of God's awareness of His people's plight wherever they might be.

Other Uses The Hebrew term for eye is used in a variety of expressions not related to sight or seeing. The word can be translated "spring" (Gen. 16:7; Num. 33:9). The term can refer to the (sur)face of the land (Exod. 10:5,15; Num. 22:5,11) or to facets (faces) of a stone (Zech. 3:9). The term is used for the sparkling of wine (Prov. 23:31) perhaps in reference to bubbles that resemble eyes. The word sometimes translated "color" in Num. 11:7 is also a word for eye.   *Chris Church*

EYELIDS OF THE MORNING Phrase meaning "the glow of dawn" used to describe the eyes of Leviathan (Job 41:18). See *Leviathan.*

EYE OF A NEEDLE See *Needle.*

EYE PAINT See *Cosmetics.*

EZAR (Ē´ zər) (KJV, 1 Chron. 1:38) See *Ezer.*

EZBAI (Ĕz´ bī) Personal name of unknown meaning. Father of one of David's military leaders (1 Chron. 11:37). The parallel list (2 Sam. 23:35) contains a word of similar appearance: "the Arbite." The Samuel reading may be the original with the Chronicles reading the result of early copying, but no certain decision can be made.

EZBON (Ĕz´ bōn) Personal name, perhaps meaning "bare." Son of Gad and grandson of Jacob (Gen. 46:16). Numbers 26:16 has a similar sounding Hebrew name, "Ozni." The Samaritan Pentateuch has a longer Hebrew name of similar sound, so that the precise spelling and pronunciation of the name are not known. Whatever the name, he was one of the Hebrews who entered Egypt with Joseph.

EZEKIAS (Ĕz ə kī´ əs) KJV spelling of Ezekiel in the NT following the Greek spelling there. See *Ezekiel.*

EZEKIEL (ə zē´ kĭ əl) Personal name meaning "God will strengthen." Ezekiel was a sixth-century B.C. prophet who ministered to the Judean exiles in Babylon. All that is known of Ezekiel derives from his book. He was a son of Buzi

(1:3), taken captive to Babylon in 597 B.C., along with King Jehoiachin and 10,000 others, including political and military leaders and skilled craftsmen (2 Kings 24:14-16). Ezekiel lived in his own house near the river Chebar, an irrigation canal that channeled the Euphrates River into surrounding arid areas. He was married and ministered from his own home (3:24; 8:1; 33:30-33). His wife died suddenly (24:18), but he was not allowed to mourn the loss.

Ezekiel's Role We know Ezekiel primarily as a prophet who received oracles from God and passed them on to the people (cp. 2:5; 33:33). However, his pronounced priestly interests give good reason to interpret him primarily as a priest who also was a prophet. The Lord's call to him came in his 30th year (1:1), the age priests normally were inducted into office (Num. 4:30). In Jerusalem, he would have inherited the priestly office and prepared for it by traditional means. However, in exile the call came dramatically and directly from God. In a vision he was called into divine service and ushered into the presence of God. In autobiographical notes Ezekiel described his reactions to events with priestly sensitivities, especially to issues involving cleanness and uncleanness (4:14). Some of the actions God assigned to him were appropriate only for a priest: "bearing the iniquity" of the people (4:4-6) and not mourning the death of his wife (24:15-27; cp. Lev. 21:4-5). This is especially true of temple visions in which the Lord Himself took Ezekiel into the temple and guided him throughout the building (chaps. 8–11; 40–43). In both visions Ezekiel's legitimate presence in the temple is contrasted with the illegitimate presence of others (8:7-18; 44:1-14). In his preaching and teaching Ezekiel fulfilled the role of a priest charged with the responsibility of teaching the Torah in Israel (Lev. 10:11; Deut. 33:10a). Ezekiel delivered oracles received from God, permeated by Mosaic theology and forms.

Priestly ministry is associated with sacrifices and other tabernacle/temple rituals (cp. Deut. 33:10b). But removed from Jerusalem, Ezekiel could not carry out temple duties. The primary priestly function left was teaching. Ezekiel is a model of the priest as teacher of the Torah. This is not to deny him the prophetic. Normally priests engaged in prophetic ministry through the Urim and Thummim (Num. 27:21). However, denied official priestly vestments, Ezekiel could not use these objects. Instead he received messages directly and verbally from God.

Like his contemporary, Jeremiah, Ezekiel initially resisted God's call. This accounts for the nature of the opening vision, with intent to overwhelm him and break his resistance (1:1-28a); for the Lord's warning to him not to be rebellious (2:8); for Ezekiel's deep emotional disturbance at his call (3:15); for the harshness of the Lord's warning not to fail as a watchman (3:16-21); and for the severe restrictions of his call (3:22-27).

Once he accepted the call, he proclaimed God's messages fearlessly. Because he displayed many bizarre actions, some have characterized Ezekiel as neurotic, paranoid, psychotic, or schizophrenic. However, his unusual behavior derives from his utter obedience to God. Ezekiel was gripped by the Spirit of God, had a profoundly theological perspective on contemporary historical events, and an unflinching determination to deliver the messages just as God gave them.

Historical Background to Ezekiel's Ministry Ezekiel was the only Israelite prophet to carry out his ministry entirely outside Israel's homeland. He received his call five years after he was deported to Babylon by Nebuchadnezzar in 597 B.C. This tragedy, foreseen by the Prophet Isaiah more than 100 years earlier (2 Kings 20:16-18), represented the culmination of a series of historical events. After the horrendous apostasies of Manasseh, the godly king Josiah (640–609 B.C.) attempted sweeping religious reforms (2 Kings 23:1-25), but it was too little and too late. The doom of the nation had already been determined. All Josiah's successors were wicked. His son, Jehoahaz, ruled only three years before the Egyptians deposed him and replaced him with his brother Jehoiakim (609–598 B.C.).

Babylon replaced Egypt as the dominant political force in the ancient Near East after the battle of Carchemish in 605 B.C. Under Nebuchadnezzar the Babylonian army marched as far south as Jerusalem, claiming Judah as his vassal. At this time Daniel and his three friends were taken to Babylon as hostages in order that they might prepare the way for the arrival of masses of Judeans in 597. Because Jehoiakim rebelled against Babylon in that same year, Nebuchadnezzar removed him from the throne and replaced him with his son Jehoiachin, but he too resisted the Babylonians, and Nebuchadnezzar deported him and all the upper classes (including Ezekiel) to Babylon and put his uncle Zedekiah

on the throne. Remarkably, Zedekiah too resisted Nebuchadnezzar's authority. Finally, in 587 B.C. Nebuchadnezzar's armies besieged Jerusalem, which fell in 586.   *Daniel I. Block*

EZEKIEL, BOOK OF Classified with the major prophets and placed in the OT canon following Lamentations. Ezekiel is a series of oracles delivered in a number of identifiable literary forms such as woe oracle, judgment oracle, riddle, and other. Unlike Jeremiah, the order of Ezekiel is approximately chronological.

Because of the bizarre nature of Ezekiel's opening vision, well-intentioned people often give up reading the book before they even get through the call narratives. While many different theories concerning the significance of this vision have been proposed, the vision makes perfect sense if one interprets it within the context of ancient Near Eastern iconography. Virtually every feature of the heavenly throne chariot has been attested on images and reliefs from the ancient world. While the images may be confusing to us, in Ezekiel's day they made perfect sense. To a community that had lost its spiritual way and its confidence in the Lord, God broke through, declaring that He remained absolutely and gloriously sovereign over all things. Nebuchadnezzar's razing of Jerusalem was not a sign of Marduk's superiority over Yahweh; he came as the agent of Yahweh. God departed from the temple (chaps. 8–11) but appeared to Ezekiel far away in a defiled and pagan foreign land.

Since virtually all of Ezekiel's oracles are in the first person, readers seem to have access to the private memoirs of the prophet. Only once, in the editorial note in 1:2-3, is the I-form abandoned in favor of the third person. Elsewhere the prophet is named only in 24:24, in the context of a divine speech introduced by the first person. This contrasts with other prophets, who rarely use the first-person autobiographical form. Ironically, although the oracles are in autobiographical narrative style, occasions when the prophet actually admits the reader into his mind are rare. Only six times does he express his reaction to circumstances, venting revulsion or acknowledging the incomprehensibility of God's actions (4:14; 9:8; 11:13; 21:5 [20:49]; 24:20; 37:3). Elsewhere his responses are drafted as divine oracles. Although he must have heard the chatter of the people, the Lord repeatedly reminds him of what they are saying (11:15; 12:22,27; 33:30-33;

37:11), even of their reactions to his performed sign-acts (12:9; cp. 17:12; 24:19). In spite of the autobiographic form of the text, one wonders if the real Ezekiel is ever exposed. We see a man totally under the control of the spirit of the Lord; only what God says and does matters.

Ezekiel's Message Although many of Ezekiel's oracles are addressed to the population in Jerusalem or to foreign nations, his primary audience was fellow exiles in Babylon. Prior to 586 B.C. the elders of the community came to him at his house to hear a word from God (8:1; 14:1; 20:1), hoping for an announcement of their imminent return to Jerusalem. However, the exiles refused to acknowledge that they had been exiled because of their own rebellion against the Lord. Eventually they came to look on Ezekiel primarily as an actor performing theatre in his home. He could declare a word from God, but they did not care for the message; they wanted to be entertained (33:30-33).

Economically the exilic community fared relatively well. However, spiritually they were in shock and bitter over the Lord's "betrayal." While in Jerusalem they staked their security on God's four immutable promises: (1) He had entered into an eternal covenant with Israel from which there would be no divorce; (2) He had given them the land of Canaan as an eternal possession; (3) He had established the Davidic kingship, promising them eternal title to the throne of Israel; (4) He had chosen Zion as His eternal dwelling place. Based on these promises, even as the enemy camped around Jerusalem, Judeans perceived themselves absolutely secure; their covenant God had obligated Himself to them, the land, the king, and the temple irrevocably and unconditionally. They forgot that the blessings associated with these promises are contingent on active demonstration of fidelity through lives characterized by obedience to God, in response to the privilege of being His covenant people. But God had abandoned them; they thought He had proved unfaithful; He had let Nebuchadnezzar into the city, in effect conceding that Marduk, the Babylonian god was stronger. Disillusioned and depressed, they continued the idolatrous ways that caused their exile in the first place.

Ezekiel's rhetorical strategy in chapters 4–24 is to demolish illusions of security by exposing the peoples' crimes. He argued that far from being innocent in this "divorce," they were

guilty and had brought the calamity on themselves. Although the order in which these major themes are addressed appears to be somewhat random, all his oracles were deliberately aimed at demolishing the four pillars on which they had based their security. Systematically he undermined the validity of their reliance on God's eternal promises of an immutable and unconditional covenant (e.g., 15:1-8; 16:1-60), of eternal and unconditional title to the land (4:1-3; 6:1-14; 7:1-27; 11:1-23), of the Davidic kings as an irrevocable symbol of His commitment to them (12:1-16; 17:1-24; 19:1-14), and of Jerusalem as the eternal dwelling place of God (8:1–10:22; 24:16-27). Courageously he declared they could not sin with impunity. On the contrary, built into the covenant were warnings of judgment if they persisted in rebellion (Lev. 26; Deut. 28). This was the eternal word that God would certainly fulfill. Not only were the promises eternal, so was judgment for ingratitude and disobedience.

When Jerusalem fell in 586, Ezekiel's message changed. Judgment had fallen, and he was vindicated as a true prophet. With few exceptions, thereafter, his messages were proclamations of hope. But Ezekiel emphasized always that Israel's future restoration would be a work of divine grace. First, he declared that God will deal graciously with Israel by destroying the threat of all their enemies (chaps. 25–32), and ultimately the worldwide conspiracy under the leadership of Gog of Magog (chaps. 38–39). Second, he declared that God would restore Israel to full status and wellbeing as His own covenant people. Ironically, he based that hope on the very promises of God that he had so systematically shown to be false bases of security in chapters 1–24. His restoration oracles show those ancient promises to be indeed eternal. The deportations were not the last word: Israel must return to the land promised to their fathers, the Davidic kingship would be restored, and God would again dwell in their midst and never abandon them again (chaps. 40–48). Ezekiel 36:22-38 are the theological heart of the restoration oracles. Ezekiel summarized the process. After the Lord cleansed the land, He would again gather the people and bring them back to the promised land. Then He would replace their hearts of stone with hearts of flesh and put His Spirit within them, so that they might walk in His ways and experience His generous blessing.

Ezekiel's Method In the past Ezekiel was described as emotionally unstable, a victim of neurotic and psychotic abnormalities. Today scholars recognize that he was not a man on the verge of a breakdown but used deliberate rhetorical tactics to get his message across to a hardened and resistant audience. No prophet was as creative as Ezekiel in the strategies employed to communicate his message. Inspired by God, he crafted powerful word pictures (17:1-24; 19:1-14; 27:1-9), demolished populist slogans with impeccable logic (11:1-21; 18:1-32), played the role of prosecuting attorney (16:1-63; 23:1-49), and, like watchman on the wall, warned them of certain doom (3:16-21; 7:1-27; 33:1-9). Once the judgment had fallen, he assumed a sympathetic stance, like a pastor (34:1-31), a bearer of good news (6:8-10; 36:16-38; 37:1-14), and like a second Moses, heralding a new constitution (40–48). But he also performed symbolic acts to expose the condition of the nation and her kings (chaps. 4–5; 12:1-20). Later he used the same strategy to declare his message of hope (37:15-28), but this was more than "street theatre." In his own body Ezekiel bore his message of doom (2:8–3:3; 3:22-27; 24:15-27; 33:21-22).

The Significance of Ezekiel in History and Tradition Ezekiel offers little evidence of any positive fruits for his labors. On the contrary, the Lord tells him otherwise (3:4-11). The only encouragement he received was that however hardened his audience might be, God would make his forehead even harder. However, God did promise to vindicate him, declaring that when the disaster had struck, the people would recognize that a true prophet of God has been in their midst (2:5; 33:33).

To evaluate Ezekiel's effectiveness we must look to the events that followed his book. According to the internal evidence, Ezekiel delivered his last oracle in 571 B.C. (29:1), more than two decades after his call. Even then, there was no hint of positive response among the exiles. However, the following three decades witnessed a remarkable development: when Cyrus issued a decree in 538 B.C., permitting the Judeans to return home and rebuild the temple, more than 40,000 people returned, totally weaned off idolatry and eager to rebuild (Ezra 2:64). Most likely they came through the ministry of Ezekiel, having experienced a widespread spiritual revival. Whether he lived long enough to witness these developments, we do not know. The preserva-

tion of his prophecies testifies to his impact on the exiles.

Ezekiel's influence lasted long beyond his own century. Allusions to his book are common in the NT, beginning with Jesus' appropriation of the title "Son of Man." This was the form by which God consistently addressed Ezekiel in the book (93 times), presumably to remind him that, though he was called into divine service, he was of the same *genus* as his audience. Echoing Ezek. 34, in John 10 Jesus explicitly identified Himself as the Good Shepherd, in contrast to the wicked shepherds. The efforts to stone Him for claiming this title reflect recognition that this was a title of divinity (cp. John 10:31-33). Jesus' parable of the vine and the vinedresser in John 15 has its roots in Ezek. 15. The book of Revelation contains many allusions to Ezekiel, at times taking over and adapting entire oracles. The living creatures of Ezek. 1 and 10 reappear in Rev. 4:6-9, and the picture of the throne of God in Ezek. 1:26-28 is picked up in Rev. 4:2-3. Revelation 20 makes heavy use of Ezekiel's oracle against "Gog, the land of Magog" (Ezek. 38:2). The vision of the Holy City Jerusalem in Rev. 21–22 is dependent upon Ezekiel's temple vision (40–48). Especially striking is the reference to the river flowing from the throne of God.

The prophecies of Ezekiel now are generally ignored. However, enslaved African American Christians expressed their hope through spirituals, and some have their origin in Ezekiel: "Swing Low Sweet Chariot" and "Ezekiel Saw Dem Dry Bones." Scholars cannot agree on the significance of Ezekiel's prophecies of Israel's restoration. Covenant theologians tend to see these prophecies fulfilled in a spiritual sense in the church, while dispensationalists see Ezekiel's prophecies of Gog and Magog (chaps. 38–39) and the vision of the temple and the land (chaps. 40–48) are to be interpreted literally. The truth probably lies between the extremes.

Difficulties in Interpreting the Book of Ezekiel Although his language and themes are firmly rooted in the Sinai revelation and Deuteronomy, many of his oracles betray other influences, both in their language and in their motifs. His oracles against Tyre and Egypt (chaps. 27–32), for example, feature Canaanite and Egyptian mythological and environmental motifs. At other times, the language is simple Hebrew, but his choice of expressions is shocking, bordering on pornographic (chaps. 16 and

23). Apparently, the only way to penetrate his audience and wake them out of lethargy was using outrageous language and reconstructing Israel's history as God saw it in startling, if not repugnant, terms. Perhaps more than in other prophetic books, to understand Ezekiel one must ask not only "What does the text say?" (the text-critical question) or, "What does the text mean?" (the hermeneutical question), but also, "Why does he say it like that?" Having explored his world and his audience, the answers to all three questions become clearer.

Outline

Daniel I. Block

EZEL (Ē´ zĕl) Place-name of uncertain meaning, perhaps, "disappearance." Rock where David hid from Saul and watched for Jonathan's signal

(1 Sam. 20:19). He had hidden there previously, an apparent reference to David's escape in 1 Sam. 19:2. In 1 Sam. 20:41 the Hebrew text apparently refers to the same place as the "south side" (NASB), using a word for side which sounds much like Ezel. Early translations and modern translators have sought a different text to read at this point. Thus "the pile of stones there" (TEV; cp. NRSV) or "the mound there" (REB). The name and location of the site is uncertain. The point of the narrative is clear: David used a natural hiding place to escape Saul and to gain vital information from his friend, the king's son.

EZEM (Ē´ zĕm) Place-name meaning "mighty" or "bone." Town in Judah's tribal territory but settled by tribe of Simeon (Josh. 15:29; 19:3; 1 Chron. 4:29). KJV spells Azem in Joshua. Ezem is modern Umm el-Azam about 15 miles south of Beersheba and southwest of Aroer. Archaeologists at Tell esh-Sharia about 13 miles northwest of Beersheba have found a broken piece of pottery with the name Ezem on it.

EZER (Ē´ zēr) English spelling of two Hebrew names with different spellings and meanings. The first Hebrew meaning is "gathering" or "pile." Ezer was a leader in Edom and a descendant of Esau (Gen. 36:21,27,30). He was a Horite and lived in Seir or Edom.

The second Hebrew meaning is "help" or "hero." **1.** Descendant of Judah (1 Chron. 4:4) in the clan of Caleb. **2.** Son of Ephraim and grandson of Jacob. With his brother Elead, he was killed as he tried to take cattle from the inhabitants of Gath (1 Chron. 7:21). Ephraim was born and lived in Egypt with his family (Gen. 46:20). When any of his immediate family would have had opportunity to visit Gath and steal cattle is a difficult question. It may be history of clans of Ephraim and refer to a moment of mourning in the history of families descended from Ephraim. The place in the middle of the list of descendants of Ephraim and ancestors of Joshua points to a time after that of Ephraim himself. Otherwise, a different Ephraim from the son of Jacob is meant, or Ephraim, the son of Jacob, entered Palestine, but the Bible did not preserve a story of his travels. **3.** Member of tribe of Gad who joined David's wilderness army before he became king (1 Chron. 12:9). **4.** Person who helped Nehemiah repair the Jerusalem wall. His father had political authority over Mizpah (Neh. 3:19).

5. Temple musician who helped Nehemiah dedicate the completion of the Jerusalem wall (Neh. 12:42, with a slightly different Hebrew spelling). See *Ebenezer.*

EZION-GABER (KJV, Num. 33:35-36; Deut. 2:8; 2 Chron. 20:36) or **EZION-GEBER** (Ē zĭ ŏn-gē´ bēr) Port city of Edom located on the northern shore of the Gulf of Aqaba. It is first mentioned in the Bible among the cities on the route of the exodus (Num. 33:35-36; Deut. 2:8). Solomon utilized this city for shipbuilding purposes. During this time it was a port from which ships manned by Phoenician sailors sailed to Ophir for gold and other riches (1 Kings 9:26-28; 10:11,22; 2 Chron. 8:17).

Nelson Glueck led excavations of the site of the ancient city and discovered the remains of four towns, the first dating to the time of Solomon. Interestingly, this first city shows evidence of being a carefully laid-out complex, built at one time according to a plan rather than gradually. A notable feature of this first town was a series of structures with flues and air ducts in the floors and walls. Glueck concluded that this city was a refinery for the copper and iron that were mined in the area. However, in 1962 Rothenburg challenged this view and persuaded Glueck that the remains indicate that the city was a large storehouse for grain and supplies.

After the division of the kingdom, the city fell to the kingdom of Judah. It was destroyed probably during the invasion of Palestine by Shishak (925 B.C.). The city was rebuilt by Jehoshaphat, king of Judah, who attempted a similar enterprise as Solomon but with disastrous results (1 Kings 22:48; 2 Chron. 20:35-37). The city was again destroyed in the reign of Jehoram when the Edomites revolted (2 Kings 8:20-22). Azariah rebuilt the city, and according to many scholars it was renamed Elath (2 Kings 14:22; 2 Chron. 26:2), though recent study sees Elath as a separate city. During the reign of Uzziah, the Edomites regained possession of the city. From that time on the city remained under the control of the Edomites. It was abandoned sometime between the eighth and fourth centuries B.C. and was never rebuilt.

Recent archaeological study has questioned the identification of Ezion-geber with Tell el-Kheleifeh. Its lack of a good harbor and of the proper pottery finds has led to exploration of the island of Jezirat Faraun, where a natural harbor

E

exists. Also known as Pharaoh's Island and Coral Island, it is seven miles south of modern Eilat and 900 feet offshore from the Sinai Peninsula. The island is 1,000 feet from north to south and 200 feet from east to west. It may have served as the harbor and port while Tell el-Kheleifeh was Elath. See *Commerce; Elath.*

Paul E. Robertson

EZNITE Word of uncertain meaning describing the family or tribal relationship of Adino (2 Sam. 23:8), but most modern translations take a clue from the parallel text in 1 Chron. 11:11 and from the earliest Greek translation, omitting Adino the Eznite from the text. (Compare modern translations.) See *Adino.*

EZRA (Ĕz´ rȧ) Priest and scribe of the fifth century B.C. He descended from Aaron through Phinehas and later Zadok (Ezra 7:1-5; 1 Chron. 6:4-14). Ezra was sent with a large company of Israelites to Jerusalem by King Artaxerxes of Persia in 458 B.C. (Ezra 7:7). His mission was "to study the law of the LORD, and to practice it, and to teach His statutes and ordinances in Israel" (7:10 NASB).

He was supplied with silver and gold and the vessels of the former temple from the king's treasury and given the power to appoint public officials to enforce the law. After he divided up the supplies among the tribes of Israel, he made sacrifices unto the Lord and began to initiate reform. His first act of reform was to deal with the issue of mixed marriages. The Israelites had intermarried among the surrounding nations. Through prayer, intercession, and preaching he quickly achieved some measure of success (10:19). Nehemiah records that he read the law before all of the people in 444 B.C. at the reinstitution of the Feast of Tabernacles (Neh. 8). Ezra was of profound importance to Israel and biblical scholars today. He was the main instigator of reform just after Israel's return from exile and one of the most important preservers and teachers of law in Jewish history. (He was probably the author of the books of Chronicles and Ezra and the final editor of the OT.) Additionally, he is the main source of information about the first return from exile. *Kevin Burris*

EZRA, BOOK OF Name "Ezra" may be shortened form of a name meaning "God/Yahweh is my help." Several had the name: a family head in

Judah (1 Chron. 4:17), a priest in the return with Zerubbabel (Neh. 12:1,13), and a prince at the dedication of Jerusalem's walls built by Nehemiah (Neh. 12:32-33). The most famous is the chief character in the book of Ezra.

The book of Ezra is intimately connected with Chronicles and Nehemiah. The connection is so obvious that possibly one person wrote and compiled all three. This unknown person is referred to as the Chronicler.

Ezra and Nehemiah were actually one book in the ancient Hebrew and Greek OT. Each book contains materials found in the other (e.g., the list in Ezra 2 is also in Neh. 7). Each book completes the other; Ezra's story is continued in Nehemiah (chaps. 8–10). Both are necessary to the history of Israel. A whole century would be unknown (538–432 B.C.), historically, apart from Ezra and Nehemiah. They are the next chapter of the history recorded in Chronicles.

The book chronicles two major events, that of Zerubbabel and the group of returnees who rebuilt the temple (chaps. 1–6), and that of Ezra (chaps. 7–10, completed in Neh. 8–10). Peculiarities in the book include the naming of Sheshbazzar (chap. 1) as the leader of the first group to return and not Zerubbabel. Two approaches are possible. One is that Sheshbazzar was a real historical person who actually led a small group of anxious Jews to Jerusalem. The other is that Sheshbazzar might have been another name for Zerubbabel. But it seems unlikely that a Jew would have two Babylonian names.

Another peculiarity, found in both Ezra and Nehemiah, is the use of lists. The list in Ezra 2 of those who returned with Zerubbabel is in Neh. 7. Other lists include those who returned with Ezra (Ezra 8:1-14) and "the sons of the priests who had married foreign wives" (Ezra 10:18-43).

Another peculiarity is the Aramaic in Ezra. This was a widely used language of Ezra's era, related to Hebrew, used by Jews and Gentiles alike. Most of the book is written in Hebrew, but there are two large sections of Aramaic (Ezra 4:7–6:18; 7:12-26). The Aramaic generally deals with official correspondence between Palestine and Persia.

The lists and the Aramaic show that the author was determined to use official documents where possible. Establishing the legitimacy of the Jews was an important objective, and these helped do that.

Ezra begins with the story of Sheshbazzar and Zerubbabel and the first Jews to return to Jerusalem from captivity in 538 B.C. Their main objective was to rebuild the temple. Its foundation was laid in 536 B.C. Then there was a long delay. Haggai and Zechariah (Ezra 5:1) in 520 B.C. had encouraged the people to finish the project, which they did in 515 B.C. (6:14-15), and they "celebrated the dedication of this house of God with joy" (6:16 NASB).

Almost 60 years passed before Ezra went to Jerusalem (458 B.C.), six decades of silence. He left Persia with "the copy of the decree which King Artaxerxes gave to Ezra the priest, the scribe" (7:11 NASB), giving him unusual power and authority (7:12-26). As he "viewed the people, and the priests, and [he] found there none of the sons of Levi" (8:15). These were essential for his teaching program to implement the law of God in Jerusalem. During a three-day delay more than 200 ministers "for the house of our God"

(8:17) were enlisted. Four months later the group, probably less than 2,000, arrived in the Holy City.

Soon Ezra was informed of the most glaring sin of the Jews, intermarriage with non-Jews, those not in covenant relation with Yahweh (9:2). Ezra was greatly upset (9:3-4). He prayed (9:6-15). In assembly people reached what must have been a heartrending decision: "Let us make a covenant with our God to put away all the wives and their children" (10:3 NASB). The book concludes with the carrying out of this decision (chap. 10).

Ezra's story reaches its climax in Neh. 8–10. There he read from "the book of the law of Moses, which the LORD had commanded to Israel" (Neh. 8:1). A great revival resulted.

Ezra's greatest contribution was his teaching, establishing, and implementing "the book of the law of the LORD" (Neh. 9:3) among the Jews. Ezra evidenced strong theology; he believed in

E

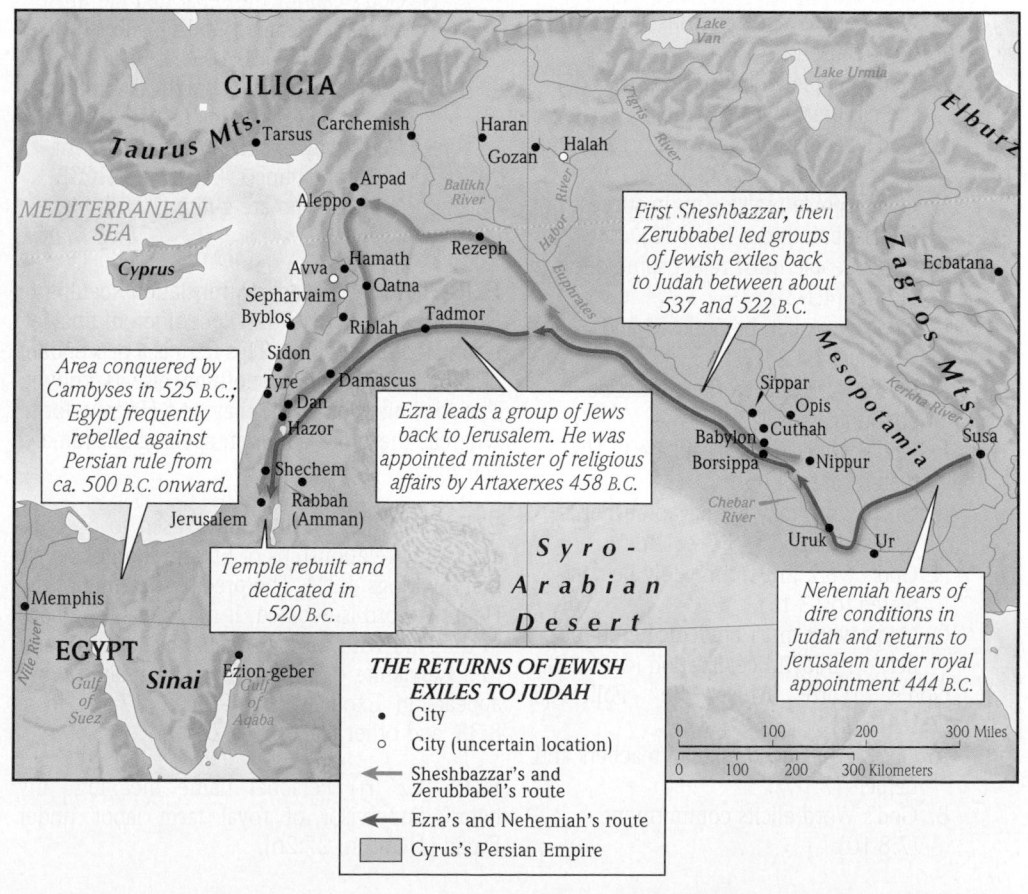

First Sheshbazzar, then Zerubbabel led groups of Jewish exiles back to Judah between about 537 and 522 B.C.

Area conquered by Cambyses in 525 B.C.; Egypt frequently rebelled against Persian rule from ca. 500 B.C. onward.

Ezra leads a group of Jews back to Jerusalem. He was appointed minister of religious affairs by Artaxerxes 458 B.C.

Temple rebuilt and dedicated in 520 B.C.

Nehemiah hears of dire conditions in Judah and returns to Jerusalem under royal appointment 444 B.C.

THE RETURNS OF JEWISH EXILES TO JUDAH
- • City
- ○ City (uncertain location)
- ← Sheshbazzar's and Zerubbabel's route
- ← Ezra's and Nehemiah's route
- ▨ Cyrus's Persian Empire

| 0 | 100 | 200 | 300 Miles |
| 0 | 100 | 200 | 300 Kilometers |

the sovereignty of God, who could use a Cyrus, an Artaxerxes, and a Darius to accomplish His purposes. He believed in the faithfulness of God, who brought home the exiles who wanted to return. He believed in the sacredness and practicality of the Scriptures; he read them to his people and insisted that their teachings be carried out. He was a person of prayer; note his long confessional prayers (Ezra 9:5-15; Neh. 9:6-37). He was a preacher: he used a pulpit (Neh. 8:4); he publicly read the Scriptures; and he helped to interpret them to his congregation (8:8).

Outline

I. God's Worship Must Be Restored (1:1–6:22).
   A. God can use a pagan "to fulfill the word of the LORD" (1:1-4).
   B. God's people respond to God's ways (1:5-6).
   C. God will recover and reclaim His possessions (1:7-11).
   D. God's people, by name and as individuals, are important (2:1-67).
   E. God's people are generous givers for a good cause (2:68-70).
   F. God's people worship, regardless of the circumstances (3:1-6).
   G. God's people will give and organize to get a job done (3:7-9).
   H. God's people praise Him in success or in disappointment (3:10-13).
   I. God's people must reject some offers of help (4:1-3).
   J. God's work can be opposed and stopped (4:4-24).
   K. God's work and workers must be encouraged (5:1-2).
   L. God's work and workers are in His watch care (5:3-5).
   M. God's work may get pagan authorization and support (5:6–6:12).
   N. God's work must ultimately be completed (6:13-15).
   O. God's work must be dedicated publicly with joyful celebration (6:16-22).
II. God's Word Must Be Followed (7:1–10:44).
   A. God's Word needs skilled teachers and helpers (7:1-7).
   B. God's Word elicits commitment (7:8-10).
   C. God's work accepts all the help it can get from many different sources (7:11-26).
   D. God blesses His workers and expects to be praised (7:27-28).
   E. God's work warrants good records (8:1-14).
   F. God's work must enlist trained workers (8:15-20).
   G. God's work calls for faith, prayer, and humility (8:21-23).
   H. God's work warrants division of responsibility (8:24-30).
   I. God's work necessitates good stewardship and generous sacrifice (8:31-36).
   J. Gross violations of God's Word must be acknowledged (9:1-5).
   K. Acknowledged sin leads to prayer and confession with deep theological insights (9:6-15).
   L. God's grace and human confession call for active commitment (10:1-4).
   M. God's people must unite (10:5-9).
   N. God's call for the separated life must be made clear by God's leaders to God's people (10:10-11).
   O. God's way utilizes practical solutions for difficult problems (10:12-17).
   P. God's way expects "fruit consistent with repentance" (Matt. 3:8 HCSB) from all who are guilty (10:18-44).

D. C. Martin

EZRAH (Ĕz´ rá) Modern translation spelling of Ezra in 1 Chron. 4:17 to reflect different final letter in Hebrew spelling. This Ezra is a descendant of Judah about whom nothing else is known. The spelling of his name may be a Hebrew form, whereas the more common spelling is Aramaic. See *Ezra*.

EZRAHITE (Ĕz´ rá hīt) Term used to describe the family relationships of Ethan, a famous wise man (1 Kings 4:31). The precise meaning of the Hebrew word is debated. It may mean one born in the land with full citizenship rights and point to a Canaanite origin for Ethan. A related word appears in Exod. 12:19,49; Lev. 17:15; Josh. 8:33, and other places. See *Ethan*.

EZRI (Ĕz´ rī) Personal name meaning "my help." Supervisor of royal farm labor under David (1 Chron. 27:26).

F

Floor mosaic from the church at Tabgha in Galilee, Israel, shows the bread and fish.

FABLE Short, fictitious story that uses animals or inanimate objects as characters to teach ethical or practical lessons. Typically, the characters are portrayed as having human personality traits that are good or evil. The practical or moral lesson is obvious in the story when these character traits lead to either failure or success. Fables are rarely found in the Bible, but there are two clear examples in the OT. The fable of the trees of the forest selecting a king (Judg. 9:8-15) is designed to warn Israel of the dangers in selecting a weak and ruthless king. In 2 Kings 14:8-10 (2 Chron. 25:17-19), there is a fable addressed to Amaziah, king of Judah, about the folly of arrogance. In this story a thistle thinks that it is equal to the giant cedars of Lebanon and gets trampled by a wild beast of the forest.

Daniel B. McGee

FACE The front of a person's head. In the Bible several words are translated as "face." In the OT *panim* is the most common and has the actual meaning of "face." *Aph* (nose) and *ayin* (eyes, aspect) are also at times translated as face. In the NT the words used are *opsis* and *prosopon*.

The word "face" has a variety of meanings. It is used literally to refer to the face of man or animals (Gen. 30:40), seraphim (Isa. 6:2), and the face of Christ (Matt. 17:2). Figuratively, it is used in reference to the face of the earth (Gen. 1:29), waters (Gen. 1:2), sky (Matt. 16:3), and moon (Job 26:9). Also, the word "face" is used theologically with regard to the "presence of God" (Gen. 32:30). Face may be the physical "face" or the surface seen. Being "face to face" (literally, "eye to eye") is being squared off with each other, front to front, and fully visible (Num. 14:14). The face (eye) of the earth is the visible surface of the earth (Exod. 10:5,15), and the face of the waters is that surface which is seen (Gen. 1:2).

The word "face" may stand for the entire countenance. It is in the face that the emotions are expressed. The face of the sky expresses the weather, stormy and red, or fair (Matt. 16:2-3). Bowing one's face (nose or face) expresses reverence or awe (Num. 22:31; Luke 5:12). Bowing one's face (nose) toward the ground also includes the involvement of the entire person (1 Sam. 20:41; Matt. 26:39), indicating complete submission. When angry or sad, one's countenance (face) will fall (Gen. 4:5). "A joyful heart makes a face cheerful" (Prov. 15:13 HCSB). To express displeasure or disgust, the face is averted or "hid" (Ezek. 39:23; Ps. 102:2); to "seek his face" is to desire an audience (Ps. 105:4). To "set my face against" is to express hostility (Jer. 21:10), while turning away the face shows rejection (Ps. 132:10). To "set their faces to" indicates determination (Jer. 42:17; Luke 9:51). The wicked man "puts on a bold face" (Prov. 21:29 HCSB), and "covered his face with his fat" (Job 15:27 NASB). When in mourning, the face is covered (2 Sam. 19:4).

Because the face reflects the personality and character of a person, the word is frequently translated as "person" (Deut. 28:50; 2 Sam. 17:11; 2 Cor. 2:10), or "presence" (Exod. 10:11). Sometimes it is translated merely as the indefinite pronoun "many" (2 Cor. 1:11). Frequently, the word "face" is translated with the phrase "respect persons" (KJV), or "being partial" (RSV), (Deut. 1:17; Prov. 24:23; Matt. 22:16; Gal. 2:6).

Many idioms and phrases also apply to "the face of God." His face "shines" (Ps. 4:6), indicating good will and blessing. He sets His face against sinners (Lev. 17:10), and hides His face (Ps. 13:1). Frequently, the word "face" is used in a theological sense with regard to the person or presence of God. Sometimes "face" is translated as "presence" (Gen. 4:16; Exod. 33:14; 2 Thess. 1:9). In the tabernacle, the "shewbread" (KJV) or "Bread of the Presence" (RSV), was a local manifestation of the presence of God. The literal Hebrew reads "bread of the faces." At other times, other words are substituted although the direct meaning is the "face of God." Moses asked to see God's "glory" (Exod. 33:18), but God answered that "you cannot see My face" (Exod. 33:20). The correlation indicates that in seeing God's face, one would experience His actual presence, and thereby be exposed to God's nature and character. Sinful and nonholy beings cannot survive being in God's holy presence without God's grace or merciful intervention (Exod. 33:17-23). Thus Moses (Exod. 3:6), Elijah (1 Kings 19:13), and the seraphim (Isa. 6:2) hide their faces in God's presence. See *Glory; Shewbread; Presence of God; Eye.* *Darlene R. Gautsch*

FACETS NRSV, TEV translation of the Hebrew *ayinim*, meaning small plane surfaces, especially those on a cut gem (Zech. 3:9). The basic idea of the Hebrew *ayin*, as reflected in most English versions, is eye. By extension the root can designate a face or surface, hence the translation "facet." Some commentators understand the Hebrew root to mean springs of water (cp. Gen. 16:7). The translation "eyes" points ahead to "the seven eyes of God which roam throughout the world" (Zech. 4:10), a symbol of the omniscience or omnipresence of God. The translation "springs" fits well with the idea of the removal of iniquity (3:9b). The eschatological spring or stream is well-known in visions of the temple (Joel 3:18; Ezek. 47; Zech. 13:1; 14:8). Zechariah 3:9, however, uses the masculine plural form rather than the feminine form used in other references to springs. Perhaps the masculine form is an Aramaism. Some scholars believe the stone was a stone slab occupying the place held by the ark of the covenant in the first temple. In this case the seven eyes represent the full presence of God in a way corresponding to the ark of the covenant.

FAIR HAVENS An open bay on the southern coast of Crete near the city of Lasea. Protected only by small islands, it did not appear to be a safe harbor for winter, so the sailors of the ship carrying Paul to Rome decided to try to reach Phoenix. They refused to listen to Paul's warnings and were caught in a ferocious storm (Acts 27:8-20).

FAIRNESS Prerequisite for wisdom (Prov. 2:9-10) and therefore an important value for life (Ps. 99:4; Prov. 1:2-3). The prophets linked fairness with righteousness (Isa. 11:4; cp. Ps. 98:9) and saw that when fairness was lacking, life became tenuous and uncertain (Isa. 59:9-11; Mic. 3:9-12). Biblical persons who exhibited fairness in their words or actions include Jacob (Gen. 31:38-41), Solomon (1 Kings 3:16-27), Jesus (John 7:53–8:11) and the thief on the cross (Luke 23:40-41).

Many injunctions in the Mosaic law are based on the principle of *lex talionis* ("an eye for an eye"). This principle holds that a person's misdeeds were to be punished by actions commensurate with their crime (Exod. 21:23-25; Lev. 24:17-21; Deut. 19:16-21). Later biblical writers understood that reciprocity also attained for behavior which was merely selfish or unwise but not criminal (Ps. 7:15-16; Prov. 26:27; Matt. 7:2; 2 Cor. 11:15; Gal. 6:7-10).

Biblical injunctions uphold fairness in matters of business (Lev. 19:36; Deut. 25:15; 1 Tim. 5:18), law (Exod. 23:3; Deut. 16:19), speech (Exod. 23:1), and family relationships (e.g., Deut. 21:15-17; Eph. 6:1-9).

God's fairness in His treatment of sin was understood by the biblical writers in different ways. During the early days of ancient Israel, God's fairness was viewed through the concept of corporate solidarity, so that the responsibility for a person's actions carried through to his family (Exod. 34:6-7). By the time of the exile and in the NT, responsibility for sin was seen to be an individual matter (Ezek. 18:10-32) and God's judgment of individuals as individuals was accepted as fair.

FAITH, FAITHFULNESS Contemporary English word "faith" derived from the Latin *fides*. Today faith denotes trust. Faith does not function as a verb in contemporary English; the verb "to believe" has replaced the verb "to faith." The English noun "faithfulness" denotes trustworthiness or dependability.

The Biblical Concept The concept of faith has been radically redefined in some philosophical and theological circles during the past century. Those definitions rarely address the complexities of the biblical concept, a concept in which the whole person, the physical world, God's Word, and God Himself play crucial roles. Those alternative definitions often do not grasp the objective and subjective characteristics of biblical faith.

Throughout the Scriptures faith is the trustful human response to God's self-revelation via His words and His actions. God initiates the relationship between Himself and human beings. He expects people to trust Him; failure to trust Him was in essence the first sin (Gen. 3:1-7). Since the fall of humanity God nurtures and inspires trust in Him through what He says and does for the benefit of people who need Him. He provides evidence of His trustworthiness by acting and speaking in the external world to make Himself knowable to people who need Him. Thus, biblical faith is a kind of limited personal knowledge of God.

Hebrew Terminology The most significant Hebrew word for faith is *aman*, a root word that denotes reliability, stability, and firmness. *Aman* concretely meant to support or to uphold, as for example the strong arms of a parent would uphold an infant. Those arms are sure, certain, and firm. Forms of this root were used metaphorically to describe faith (a human response to God) and faithfulness (a virtue of God and his servants). When employed to describe relationships between God and people, *aman* is used to express a complex concept. It describes both the subjective and objective nature of trust in God and an objective quality of God Himself. God, who exists objectively outside of human beings, receives trust generated from within individuals (Deut. 7:9). He and His words are objectively faithful, constant, and reliable (Ps. 119:86). God enables people to possess these objective virtues, faithfulness and reliability (Josh. 24:14; Isa. 7:9).

Another significant Hebrew word used to convey the idea of faith is *yare'*, usually translated "to fear." *Yare'* occurs more often in the OT than *aman*, although the two express very similar concepts. To fear God is to believe Him with a reverential awe, even to the point that emotional trepidation occurs. To fear Him is to maintain a firm conviction that the Lord's directives are reliable (Ps. 119:89-91), protective (Ps. 33:18-19), and beneficial to the believer (Ps. 31:19). Someone who fears God dreads disappointing Him, but the fear of the Lord produces joy and fulfillment in the life of the one who fears (Eccles. 12:13). "To fear the LORD" is used synonymously with "serve Him in sincerity and truth" in Josh. 24:14. An element of human responsibility resides in this fear; "choose for yourselves today whom you will serve" (24:15). God does not force faith upon unwilling people. He presents His expectations and promised benefits to people, but their freedom to choose and to receive the consequences of their choices remain (Deut. 30:19). Refusal to choose Him can be followed by God's hardening the unbeliever's resistance (Exod. 10:20).

Like *aman*, the Hebrew root *yare'* reveals much about the objective and subjective characteristics of genuine faith. Old Testament authors used "the fear of the LORD" to underscore the importance of submission to God through what He has revealed objectively; this submission should occur subjectively in the minds, wills, and emotions of people who trust God's word. This submission results in objective behavior that reflects God's character.

As the OT period progressed, God gave more information about how He planned to empower more people with genuine faith or "the fear of the LORD." Through Jeremiah, for example, God predicted that He would make an everlasting covenant through which he would enable people to fear him forever (Jer. 32:40). God describes a covenant in which He will write his law on the hearts of His people and allow them all to know Him personally (31:33-34). God's description reveals that to fear Him is to know Him personally. Such a relationship empowers people to please Him. OT prophets decried human inability to maintain this kind of fear toward the Lord.

Theme of Faith in the Old Testament The OT provides a clear definition of faith in the context of the unfolding purpose of God to redeem. God makes faith possible by providing for human beings verbal information about Himself and His plans; this information is connected to His redemptive actions in the world. These words and actions combine to offer an objective basis for the faith (Exod. 4:29-31). His words interpret and explain His saving acts so that people may receive from Him the blessings that the acts make available (Exod. 12:21-28; Deut. 11:1-11; and Isa. 55:1-3). Just as one may know another human by the words and actions of that human, so God has chosen to become knowable through His words and actions.

A consistent theme of salvation by faith can be traced through God's acts and deeds in the OT. People were saved by faith in God's self-revelation during that period, just as they would be saved through faith in His self-revelation during the NT period and beyond. God has always required faith as the proper response to His self-revelation.

Two pivotal OT passages reveal the theme of salvation by faith. Abram was proclaimed "righteous" by God when Abram believed God's promise (Gen. 15:6). In this verse a form of *aman* is used to describe Abram's response to what God said He planned to do for Abram. Abram linked himself to God through that promise, becoming convinced internally of the reliability of the promise-maker. Abram's confidence prompted God to label Abram "righteous," completely acceptable in relationship to God. Abraham would go on to prove God's label was accurate. After years of seeing God's faithfulness, Abraham would obey God's call to sacrifice Isaac, to which Yahweh said "now I know you fear God" (Gen.

22:12). Abraham's faith was the kind of faith that withstood a serious test, showing therefore that Abraham's faith was synonymous with the fear of the Lord.

A second thematic statement appears in Hab. 2:4, "the righteous will live by his faith." The nation of Judah was facing an enormous threat to its future existence, the Babylonian army, sent by God to judge Judah. But God offered a promise that the righteous will survive and thrive through the judgment. Because they believe the God who promises, they are "righteous." Habakkuk 2:4 would be interpreted as a scriptural thematic statement by the Apostle Paul in the NT and seen as a hermeneutical key to understanding how God consistently relates to people. He justifies them by faith.

Genesis 15:6 and Hab. 2:4 unveil a grand soteriological principle: God saves people (whenever or wherever they may live) who trust sincerely both Him and what He says about how they can properly relate to Him. Both verses reveal that saving faith in the OT is viewed as a response to a verbal revelation from God about Himself, about His plan for the future, and about the accessibility of God and His future to a human in need. This verbal revelation is propositional; it is communicated in statements made by God. Those statements contain claims about the present and the future. God's *modus operandi* during the OT and NT periods was to make Himself knowable through words about how people can relate properly to Him. Those words are not the object of the believer's faith; God is the object. But His words mediate faith in Him. His words guide people to Him. Without the words, no one would know how to respond properly to Him. Old Testament believers praised God for revealing His word of salvation (Ps. 56:4).

New Testament Amplification The dominant NT term for faith is the Koine Greek word *pistis*, usually translated "faith." It conveys the idea of trust, a firm internal conviction regarding the truthfulness of someone or some claim. The verb form, *pisteuo*, is usually translated, "I believe" or "I trust." *Pistis* and *pisteuo* in the NT correspond to the OT terms *aman* and *yare'*. *Pistis* also appears in the NT with the definite article to describe particular Christian beliefs, termed "the faith."

New Testament writers often show continuity with the OT's concept of faith. Paul argues that Abram's experience provides a model for how God continues to save by faith (Rom. 4). Paul's citation of "the righteous will live by faith" (HCSB) supports his arguments in his letter to the Romans (1:17) and the Galatians (3:11). Just as was true prior to the coming of Christ, it is impossible after the coming of Christ for someone without faith to please God (Heb. 11:6).

Faith in the NT continues to be a personal trustful response to God's self-revelation, although the content of that self-revelation has increased dramatically with the life, ministry, death, and resurrection of Christ. In the NT faith toward God responds to that which God has revealed verbally and actively in Jesus Christ. As the incarnate Son of God, Jesus is the perfect means by which one may know God (John 17:3).

In words and in actions God the Father made available in Christ His personal and propositional revelation. In the death and resurrection of the Son, the Father communicated His love, His justice, and His mercy (Rom. 5:8). These events, especially the resurrection of Christ, were interpreted by the NT writers as evidence that God had declared that Jesus is the unique Son of God (Rom. 1:4).

God communicated not only through His actions in Christ; He also communicated verbally. Jesus appointed apostles as His personal representatives (Matt. 10:2-4). In the power and under the leadership of God's Spirit, the apostles broadcast through their teachings and/or writings this propositional revelation. For example, John states plainly that his Gospel was written to help people believe (John 20:31). God provided actions and words to enable people to understand what He had done and can do for them in Christ.

Underscoring the objective nature of Christian faith, "the faith" was used by NT authors when referring to the essential Christian doctrines or propositions to which believers held (Acts 6:7; 14:22; Gal. 1:23; 3:25). Those doctrines help to mediate the object of the faith, God in Christ. Paul calls upon his readers to examine whether their beliefs are consistent with "the faith" (2 Cor. 13:5).

Role of Faith in Justification The *euangelion* or gospel, embodies the core beliefs by which saving faith in Christ can be mediated and whereby He can be known. According to 1 Cor. 15 the *euangelion*'s objective veracity was evidenced by Jesus' postresurrection appearances.

The Apostle Paul challenged readers to examine eyewitness evidence for the resurrection of Christ (15:1-6). God makes an enormous amount of evidence available from historical witnesses to the resurrection. Jesus did pronounce a blessing on those who believe without seeing His resurrected body, but eyewitnesses to that resurrected body were made available by Him (John 20:29; Acts 1:8). See *Justification.*

Paul was even willing to concede that, if Jesus did not rise from the dead, then Christian faith is meaningless and useless (1 Cor. 15:14-19). Christ's resurrection would be evidence that God wants people to believe that Jesus is the solution to human sinfulness, but without the resurrection people cannot rightly draw such a radical conclusion. Thus, the resurrection of Jesus serves at the primary historical basis for Christian faith.

Faith in Christ is based on the evidence of the testimony of eyewitnesses, but the evidence is not an end in itself. The gospel must be heard and understood before faith can happen; faith occurs when someone moves through the words and the evidence and "calls upon" or asks Christ to save (Rom. 10:9-13). To ask Christ to save is to trust what God says the death of Christ makes available, particularly regarding forgiveness and freedom from sin's power. When God saves, the believer internally identifies Christ's death as the death of his or her own sin (Rom. 6:1-14), making genuine and consistent obedience to God possible for the future. This is the kind of faith that will prove its genuineness by the transformed life God produces through it, as occurred with Abraham (James 2:14-26). Saving faith is never merely a superficial or verbal response. Nor is it merely an intellectual acceptance of the claims of the gospel. The kind of faith by which God justifies sinners moves through acceptance of those claims to Christ Himself.

An element of subjective personal choice is retained in the NT concept of faith (Luke 13:34). People still must choose, but this subjective choice should be understood in light of the objective elements that guide and empower the choice. Underscoring the subjective nature of the choice, saving faith occurs within the person's "heart," where the Holy Spirit illuminates the person's need of what Christ has done and can do for the person (Rom. 10:9-10; 1 Thess. 1:5). Recognition of need always precedes saving faith. God's Spirit enables someone to under-

stand how Christ's death and resurrection were for the hearer. God gives the unbeliever the capacity to choose to trust God through what He says through His human witnesses about Christ. God's Spirit also bears witness by personally applying the words of the gospel internally to the hearer. The Spirit activates, guides, and empowers the choice.

If God left humans totally untouched by the work of the Spirit, then humans would naturally choose against God (Rom. 1–3). The Spirit "gives" Christian faith, enabling people to trust what God says He has done and will do to save. Faith, therefore, is a spiritual gift (Rom. 12:3). No one will be able to boast of self-produced saving faith; God chooses to enable some people to believe (Eph. 2:8-9). He alone deserves praise for producing faith within people. A paradoxical tension between divine sovereignty and human responsibility is maintained in the NT's depiction of saving faith.

Role of Faith in Sanctification God allows the testing of faith in order to sanctify the believer, as occurred with Abraham (James 1:2-8; 2:14-26). God uses trials to test and to grow the quality of the faith of believers, to prove that His justification of them was an accurate appraisal. He desires that they grow in their relationship to Him that He might produce Christ's virtue of faithfulness within them (Matt. 25:21). As Christians learn to trust what God says they possess in Christ, they can discover freedom from sin and the power to glorify God as Christ produces his character in them (Eph. 1:15-23). God's Spirit enables sanctification in the same way that He enables justification, through faith in what God says He has done and will do in Christ (Gal. 3:1-5; 5:25).

Faith yields in the believer a confidence or sense of assurance as he or she continues to trust God through His promises (Heb. 11:1). This confidence becomes possible when a believer can identify with the help of the Spirit of God ways God has transformed him or her (Rom. 8:13-16; Phil. 3:10; 1 John 2:3; 3:14; 5:18-20). New Testament authors unashamedly refer to this confident faith as a knowledge of God, albeit a partial knowledge (1 Cor. 13:9). Only when Christ returns and consummates His kingdom will faith be unnecessary for the Christian. Then this knowledge of God will not be partial.

The Holy Spirit gives to some Christians a special *charisma* or grace-gift of faith whereby they discern God's will and trust God accordingly in particular situations where His will has not been objectively revealed (1 Cor. 12:9). For example, some Christians have been given the ability to discern God's will to heal a sick person and to pray successfully for the healing (James 5:15). All Christians have a gift of faith (Rom. 12:3) but not the gift (*charisma*) of faith, given to some for the purpose of ministry.

Conclusion The God of the Bible has consistently related to people via trust in what He says and does. Biblical faith is a complex idea; God, His word, His actions, the whole human being, and the physical world all play critical roles. When saving faith occurs, God has enabled someone to know Him through His revelation of Himself in words and actions in Christ. God Himself activates faith in the hearer of His word, enabling that hearer to become faithful in Christ, just as He is faithful (Rev. 19:11). *D. Mark Parks*

FALCON (NIV, NASB) (Deut. 14:13; Lev. 11:14; Job 28:7) See *Eagle; Vulture.*

FALL Traditional name for the first sin of Adam and Eve that brought judgment upon both nature and mankind.

In Genesis people are the dominion-havers created in the image of God (Gen. 1:26-28). Man and woman are placed on earth with a commandment to obey (Gen. 1:28). The biblical understanding of dominion suggests a serving stewardship rather than mere power (Matt. 20:25-28).

Sin in the Garden Genesis pictures humans as the special creation of God (2:7) placed in the special garden created by God (2:8-15). Three features are crucial for understanding the human role in the garden: (1) Adam was put in the garden to "cultivate it and keep it" (2:15 NASB). God provided this vocation for man's fulfillment. (2) The first people were granted great freedom and discretion in the garden. This freedom permitted them to take from the goodness of God's creation (2:16). (3) Yet their freedom and discretion were limited. God prohibited the taking of the fruit from the tree of knowledge of good and evil (2:17). Scholars have pointed out that these three features belong uniquely to humans. Each person faces vocation, freedom, and yet prohibition. Full humanity is experienced only when all three of these are maintained.

The "knowledge of good and evil" would make humans godlike in some way (Gen. 3:5,22). Some Bible students understand the tree to hold all knowledge—that is the complete range of experience. Others claim the tree provides knowledge of a moral nature. Some claim the acquired knowledge was simply sexual experience.

The tree's purpose within the narrative provides a clue toward a more satisfactory explanation. The tree was the object and symbol of God's authority. The tree reminded Adam and Eve that their freedom was not absolute but had to be exercised in dependence upon God. In prideful rebellion the couple grasped for the capacity to be completely self-legislating—establishing an absolute self-directing independence. Such absolute dominion belongs only to God. Their ambition affected every dimension of human experience. For example, they claimed the right to decide what is good and evil.

The Serpent The serpent made a sudden intrusion into the story. The serpent is identified in Genesis only as a creature. Theological reflection has identified him as an instrument of Satan and, thus, legitimately cursed and pictured as the enemy of woman's seed (Gen. 3:14-15). Later Scripture also declares that Satan is the ultimate tempter (1 John 3:8; Rev. 12:9). His presence, however, does not diminish mankind's responsibility. Scripture stipulates that man cannot blame his sin on demonic temptation (James 1:12-15).

The serpent began the conversation with a question that obviously distorted or at least extended God's order not to eat of the tree (Gen. 3:1). The questioner invited the woman to enter into a conversation about God and to treat Him and His word as objects to be considered and evaluated. Moreover, the serpent painted God as one who sadistically and arbitrarily placed a prohibition before the couple to stifle their enjoyment of the garden.

The woman apparently felt inclined to defend God's instruction. In her response to the serpent, she included a citation of God's command. The text does not tell us how she or the snake came to know God's command. Adam may have passed on this information that he initially received prior to woman's creation (Gen. 2:17-18). She may thus represent all who receive the word of God through "human" instrumentality but who are nevertheless called to believe (cp. John 20:29). She responded with a restatement of God's permission to eat freely of the garden provision (Gen. 3:2). She then told of God's prohibition of that one tree in the middle of the garden. Perhaps anxiety over doubting God's character moved her then to add to God's own words; she extended the instruction to include touching the tree, thereby making her own law. It is interesting that the first challenge to God's word did not involve deletion but addition by both the serpent and the woman. Mankind's first surrender to temptation began with doubting God's instruction and His loving character.

The woman's willingness to judge and her addition to God's instruction, though seemingly harmless, permitted the serpent boldly to continue with a direct attack on God's character. He declared that the couple would not really die. Instead, he argued that God's motive was to keep the couple from being like God. The serpent claimed that the phrases "your eyes will be opened, and you will be like God, knowing good and evil" (Gen. 3:5 NRSV, NIV) are God's reasons for giving the prohibitive command; in reality, these phrases express the human reasons for breaking the command. The couple was unhappy with their freedom as long as they thought more could be had. They sought unrestricted freedom—to be responsible to no one, not even God. The serpent seemed sure that eating would produce equality not death.

The woman stood before the tree. Crudely, she saw the fruit was good for food. In a more refined manner she judged it to be pleasant to the eye. More appealing to her vanity still was the newfound faith that it would bring knowledge (Gen. 3:6; cp. 1 John 2:16). She ate of the fruit and gave it to Adam who ate as well.

Results of Sin Sin had immediate results in the couple's relationship; the "self-first" and "self-only" attitude displayed toward God affected the way they looked at one another. The mutual trust and intimacy of the one-flesh bond (Gen. 2:24) was ravaged by distrust. This does not suggest that the knowledge of good and evil was sexual awareness. Intercourse was the command and blessing of God prior to the fall (Gen. 1:28). In the absence of mutual trust, complete intimacy implies complete vulnerability (Gen. 3:7).

The couple also felt compelled to hide from God when they heard Him walking in the garden. When loving trust characterized the couple's attitude, they were apparently comfortable in God's presence. After their sin, shame appro-

priately marked their relationships—both human and divine (Gen. 3:8). The sinners could not remain hidden. God pursued, asking, "Where are you?" (Gen. 3:9 NRSV). This may be a normal question, but some see it as God's sorrowful anticipation of what follows. Sinners finally must speak to God. Adam admitted that God's presence now provoked fear, and human shame provoked hiding (Gen. 3:10).

God's next question drew the man's attention away from his plight to his sin (Gen. 3:11). The couple had to face their Maker. The man admitted his sin but only after emphatically reminding God that the woman was instrumental in his partaking. Woman shared equally in the deed, but she quickly blamed the deceiving serpent (Gen. 3:12-13). Along with shame, blame comes quite naturally to humankind.

God moved immediately to punish. The serpent was not interviewed because he was not an image-bearer in whom God sought a representation and relationship. The snake's (literally) low status is symbolic of the humiliation God would bring on those who oppose Him. The ensuing strife would not merely occur on a natural level between the snake and other animals (v. 14) or between the snake and humans (v. 15). The "seed" of the woman is representative of the Messiah, and the "seed" of the serpent represents Satan and his followers. Thus, a fuller meaning of the verse promises Christ's ultimate victory over Satan (Gen. 3:14-15).

The woman's punishment was linked to her distinctive role in the fulfillment of God's command (Gen. 1:28). Her privilege to share in God's creative work was frustrated by intense pain. Despite this pain she would nevertheless desire intimacy with her husband, but her desire would be frustrated by sin. She would long to control her husband, though God had given him the role of "ruling" over her (Gen. 3:16).

Adam's punishment also involved the frustration of his service. He was guilty of following the woman's sinful advice and eating of the forbidden tree (Gen. 3:17). The fruitful efficiency known prior to the fall was lost. Now even his extreme toil would be frustrated by the cursed earth. The earth was apparently cursed because it was within Adam's domain. This corporate mentality is strange to us, but biblical writers recognize nature's need for redemption (Isa. 24; Rom. 8:19-23; Col. 1:15-20).

Results—Epilogue Man's prerogative to name woman (Gen. 3:20) was a sign of the fallen order, but hope persists. Mankind can carry on because the woman has the capacity to bear children. Hope ultimately emerged from divine determination to preserve His creation. Some may expect God to retreat and leave the sinful people alone to taste the misery that would follow, but grace-giving Yahweh provided clothing for fallen mankind (Gen. 3:20-21).

Yahweh acknowledged the partial truth of the serpent's claim: Adam's and Eve's autonomy had made them like the divine (Gen. 3:5,22). In these circumstances, access to the tree of life is inappropriate. Numerous questions regarding the conditional nature of the tree of life are left unanswered here (Ezek. 47:12; Rev. 2:7; 22:2,14,19). As a tragic judgment, the sinful pair was driven out of the garden, intended by God as His dwelling place. Guardian cherubim protected the garden and the tree (Gen. 3:22-24) and, thus, graciously protected people from entering into an infinite period of struggle. The serpent's lie concerning death (Gen. 3:4) became visible. Human sin brought death (Gen. 3:19,22). Some readers question why death did not come "on that day" as God had apparently promised (Gen. 2:17), but the Hebrew expression may mean simply "when" (NIV; cp. REB). One should also be reminded of God's grace to allow life to continue and the Hebrew understanding that death involves separation from God as much as physical death (Job 7:21; Ps. 88:5,10-12; Isa. 38:18-19).

New Testament The NT writers assumed the fallen state of both humans and nature. Both groan for redemption (Rom. 8:19-23). When comparing Adam and Christ, Paul declared that sin and death gained entrance into the world through Adam and that sin and death are now common to all people (Rom. 5:12; 6:23). Adam is pictured as a representative of mankind, all of whom share in his penalty (Rom. 5:19).

Randy Hatchett

FALLOW DEER (1 Kings 4:23 KJV) See *Deer*.

FALLOW GROUND Virgin soil or else soil that has not recently been planted (Jer. 4:3; Hos. 10:12). The central thrust of the prophetic message is clear: the nation Israel, "Jacob," is to return to Yahweh by "cultivating" the covenant values of righteousness and steadfast love. The precise significance of the fallow ground is unclear. Perhaps the unplowed earth represents Israel's failure to do what was needed to keep the covenant. Or perhaps the virgin soil represents a new relationship with God. Here the call is for Israel to abandon the worn-out fields of unrighteousness (symbolized by thorns) and to move on to the new, fertile (Prov. 13:23) ground of covenant living.

FALSE APOSTLES Designation for Paul's opponents in 2 Cor. 11:13; also designated deceitful workers (11:13) and servants of Satan (11:15). Such "apostles" were characterized as preaching a "rival Jesus" (likely a lordly, miracle-working "success story"), possessing a different spirit (a self-seeking motivation evidenced by a different lifestyle than Paul's), and a different gospel which disregarded the cross (and its corollary of suffering for those who follow Christ). The false apostles appear to have been Jewish Christians (11:22), well-trained in speech (11:6), who perhaps claimed "visions and revelations of the Lord" (12:1) as authenticating marks of apostleship (cp. the role of Paul's Damascus Road experience, Acts 9:15; 22:14-15; 26:16-19). Though they cut in on Paul's missionary territory, the "false apostles" are characterized as boasting (2 Cor. 10:13-16) according to human standards. Their leadership style was oppressive (11:20). In contrast to Paul, these false apostles relied on the Corinthian Christians for financial support (11:7-11,20; 12:14). They perhaps accused Paul of being "paid what he was worth." Paul countered that suffering for Christ was the mark of true apostleship (11:23). Weakness, not dominating power, reveals God's power (11:30; 12:5,9). If the "super-apostles" (11:5; 12:11 NRSV, REB, NIV) are identified with the leaders of the Jerusalem church, they should be distinguished from the false apostles at Corinth. The latter may have claimed the authority of the former.

The false apostles of Rev. 2:2 are characterized as evil men and liars. They should perhaps be identified with the Nicolaitans active at Ephesus (2:6) and Pergamos (2:15), and with the followers of the "false prophetess" at Thyatira (2:20).

FALSE CHRISTS Imposters claiming to be the Messiah (Christ in Greek). Jesus associated the appearance of messianic pretenders with the fall of Jerusalem (Matt. 24:23-26; Mark 13:21-22).

Jesus warned His followers to be skeptical of those who point to signs and omens to authenticate their false messianic claims. Jesus also urged disbelief of those claiming the Messiah was waiting in the wilderness or was in "the inner rooms" (perhaps a reference to the inner chambers of the temple complex). Josephus mentioned several historical figures who might be regarded as false christs: (1) Theudas, who appeared when Fadus was procurator (A.D. 44–46) and summoned the people to the Jordan River wilderness with the promise that he would divide the Jordan like Joshua and begin a new conquest of the land; (2) various "imposters" during the term of Felix (A.D. 52–59) who led crowds into the wilderness with promises of signs and wonders; (3) an "imposter" during the term of Festus (A.D. 60–62) who promised deliverance and freedom from the miseries of Roman rule for those who would follow him into the wilderness; (4) Manahem ben Judah (alias "the Galilean") during the term of Florus (A.D. 64–66) who came to Jerusalem "like a king" and laid siege to the city. These messianic imposters and the barely distinguishable false prophets repeatedly urged the Jewish people to take up armed resistance to Rome or to stay in Jerusalem to fight. In contrast, Jesus urged His disciples to attempt to save themselves by fleeing the city. The Christian inhabitants of Jerusalem remembered this advice when the war with Rome broke out (A.D. 66) and fled to safety in Pella in Transjordan. Some interpreters expect false christs to arise before the future coming of Christ.

FALSE PROPHET Person who spreads false messages and teachings, claiming to speak God's words.

Old Testament While the term "false prophet" does not occur in the OT, references to false prophets are clear. The pages of the OT are filled with men and women who fit the description of a false prophet given in Jer. 14:14 (NASB): "The prophets are prophesying falsehood in My name. I have neither sent them nor commanded them nor spoken to them; they are prophesying to you a false vision, divination, futility and the deception of their own minds." Other examples are in Jer. 23:21-33 and Zech. 10:2. Punishment for prophesying falsely was severe. False prophets were cast away from God's presence and permanently humiliated. They suffered the destruction of their cities (Jer. 7:14-16; 23:39).

A false prophet was also one who prophesied on behalf of another god. A familiar example is the story of Elijah and the prophets of Baal (1 Kings 18:20-39). In a test against Elijah and the true God, the prophets of Baal suffered humiliating defeat.

Israel could not always distinguish between the true and the false prophet as seen in 1 Kings 22; Jer. 28. The prophet could only say, wait and see whose prophecy proves true in history (Deut. 18:22; 1 Kings 22:28; Jer. 29:9; cp. 1 Kings 13).

New Testament Jesus and the apostles spoke many times about false prophets. In the Sermon on the Mount, Jesus taught about the marks of a false prophet and the consequences of being one (Matt. 7:15-23). He also cautioned His followers to beware of false prophets who would arise during times of tribulation and in the end times (Matt. 24:11,24; Mark 13:22). He said to be careful when the world loves a prophet's words because a prophet who is false is apt to be popular (Luke 6:26).

The apostles instructed believers to be diligent in faith and understanding of Christian teachings, in order to discern false prophets when they arise (2 Pet. 1:10; 1:19-2:1; 1 John 4:1). The tests of a prophet are: (1) Do their predictions come true (Jer. 28:9)? (2) Does the prophet have a divine commission (Jer. 29:9)? (3) Are the prophecies consistent with Scripture (2 Pet. 1:20-21; Rev. 22:18-19)? (4) Do the people benefit spiritually from the prophet's ministry (Jer. 23:13-14,32; 1 Pet. 4:11)?

Punishments for false prophets were just as severe in the NT as they were in the OT. Paul caused a false prophet to be stricken with blindness (Acts 13:6-12), but most other punishments were more permanent in nature. Jesus said the false prophets would be cut down and burned like a bad tree (Matt. 7:19). Second Peter 2:4 describes being cast into pits of darkness. The ultimate punishment appears in Rev. 19:20; 20:10—the false prophet, the beast, and the devil will be thrown into a lake of fire and brimstone and be tormented forever. See *Prophecy, Prophets.* *Donna R. Ridge*

FALSE WORSHIP Broad category of acts and attitudes that includes worship, reverence, or religious honoring of any object, person, or entity other than the one true God. It also includes impure, improper, or other inappropriate acts directed toward the worship of the true God.

Worship offered to a false object is the most obvious and easily recognized form of false worship. Worship of idols is but a part of false worship in the biblical world. Many times other gods were worshiped, not because of the appeal of the idols or images but out of a false sense of the power of the "god." The most consistent problem with false worship seen in the OT is with the nature or fertility deities—Baals and Ashtaroth, Anath, Astarte—the male and female representations of reproduction and growth. Understanding of the basic form and nature of this kind of false worship has been clarified by discoveries made at Ugarit and the subsequent interpretation and study of these. Baal was commonly believed to have control over growth of all crops and reproduction of all flocks. Many of the forms of this false worship involved sexual acts—activities abhorred in the OT laws. Yet the appeal and practice of these rituals continued, probably because of Baal's reputed power in those areas so entwined with life and livelihood of the ancient Hebrews. During the time of great Assyrian power in the ancient world, even the Hebrews seem to have thought that the Assyrian gods were more powerful than their Yahweh; so they began to worship them. The Prophet Zephaniah, who lived and prophesied in this time, condemned those who "bow down on the housetops to the host of heaven" (Zeph. 1:5 NASB). Associated with this type of worship was the fairly prevalent view in the OT world that a god had his own territory and that he was relatively powerless outside that place. Perhaps the most direct statement of this is in the story of Naaman (2 Kings 5, esp. v. 17). After the Syrian commander was cured of his leprosy, he requested a "two-mules' burden" of dirt from Israel to take with him to Syria so that he could worship the true God.

The many references to false gods with obviously false worship in the OT coupled with the almost total absence of such in the NT might suggest that there was little problem with other gods in the NT world. Such is far from true. The world of the first century was filled with religions other than Judaism and Christianity. The presence of falseness in worship because it was directed to false gods continued to be a religious problem. Native national gods and fertility deities similar to Baal and Ashtaroth of the OT period still abounded. A new force was present in the mystery religions—Hellenistic religions that focused on the hope for life beyond death. The Orphic and Eleusinian mysteries were perhaps the most common of these. Emperor worship was a serious challenge in the days of the early church. Probably most Romans saw the emperor cult as merely an expression of patriotism and loyalty to the state. However, the Christian standard was to "give back to Caesar the things that are Caesar's, and to God the things that are God's" (Luke 20:25 HCSB). Often the Christian was faced with imperial orders to participate in this kind of false worship. Refusal could bring serious penalties, often execution. In late NT times and the years following, Mithraism became the primary competitor with Christianity. This pagan worship of Mithra, represented by *sol invictus* (the invincible sun) was a powerful challenge to Christianity. Exclusively a male religion, emphasizing power and strength, Mithraism was especially popular in the Roman army.

False worship does not necessarily center in practice of pagan or idolatrous cults. It is often a problem for those who proclaim worship of the one true God. False worship of this sort usually centers in some form of deliberate or unintentional disobedience. Its presence in the Bible extends from the self-exalting disobedience in the Garden of Eden to compromising accommodation with the emperor cult and other pagan religions seen in the book of Revelation.

The primary forms of false worship are addressed in the Decalogue (Exod. 20): "You shall have no other gods before [in addition to] Me" (v. 3)—a command for exclusive loyalty to and worship of Yahweh; "You shall not make for yourself an idol" (v. 4a)—a clear requirement of worship without images; and "You shall not take the name of the LORD your God in vain" (v. 7a)—a command to honor in all of life the God whose name the Hebrews claimed and bore.

The Hebrews were guilty of syncretistic or artificially mixed religious practices. The temples built by Jeroboam, son of Nebat, the first king of Israel (the Northern Kingdom) after its break from the Jerusalem-centered Kingdom of Judah, were probably dedicated to such worship. When these temples were established in Bethel and Dan, Jeroboam the King "made two golden calves, and he said to them, 'It is too much for you to go up to Jerusalem; behold your gods,

O Israel, that brought you up from the land of Egypt'" (1 Kings 12:28 NASB). This mixing of the gold calf—a symbol of Baal—with the worship of the God who delivered the Hebrews from their Egyptian bondage was false worship.

A very similar practice was prevalent in the time of Elijah. In his confrontation with the Baal prophets on Mount Carmel in the time of Ahab and Jezebel (1 Kings 18:20-46), the prophet of the Lord addressed the assembled people. "How long will you hesitate between two opinions? If the LORD is God, follow Him; but if Baal, follow him" (1 Kings 18:21 NASB).

False worship includes trusting in military power (Isa. 31:1), trusting in the "works of your hands" (Jer. 25:7), serving God in order to receive physical and material blessings (as Job's friends), offering unacceptable, tainted or maimed sacrifices to God instead of the best (Mal. 1:6-8). False worship also occurs when one prays, fasts, or gives alms before men "to be seen by them" instead of in sincere devotion to God (Matt. 6:1-18 HCSB).

The subjects of false and true worship are best presented in Mic. 6:8, "What does the LORD require of you but to do justice, and to love kindness, and to walk humbly with your God" and in the words of Jesus to the Samaritan woman in John 4:23-24: "True worshippers will worship the Father in spirit and in truth. Yes, the Father wants such people to worship Him. God is Spirit, and those who worship him must worship in spirit and truth" (HCSB). See *Canaan; Worship.*

Bruce C. Cresson

FAMILIAR SPIRIT See *Medium.*

FAMILY A group of persons united by the ties of marriage, blood, or adoption, enabling interaction between members of the household in their respective social roles. God has ordained the family as the foundational institution of human society.

Terminology Within the ethnic "people" (*am*) of Israel descended from Jacob were three levels of family relationships. One was the tribe (*shevet* or *mateh*) comprising the descendants of one of Jacob's sons. Within the tribe were the "clans" (*mishpachah*), and within the clan were the family units, which were the basic units of Israel's social structure. They were typically referred to as "the father's house" (*bet-'av*; Josh. 7:16-18). This unit would be similar to what we mean by

"family," but it was usually larger than our "nuclear family," including three or four generations of sons and their wives and children, who lived on the same land under the leadership of the family patriarch or "head." The group of elders who judged at the gate of a town (e.g., Deut. 21:19) probably comprised all the local "heads." The perception and value of the two-generation "nuclear family" may be inferred from repeated references to the parent-child relationship.

The terms "father" and "mother" could refer to any male or female ancestor, whether one or more generations removed, and whether living or dead. Likewise, "son" or "daughter" could refer to any of one's male or female descendants. Similarly, the terms "brother" and "sister" could refer to any other relative in the same clan (cp. Gen. 12:5 with 14:16).

The term most frequently used in the NT is *oikos* and the equivalent, *oikia*, "house, household." Synonymous with the Hebrew expression, "father's house," it was used of the members of a household, even including servants and any other dependents.

Old Testament The importance of the family unit in Israel is suggested by the fact that about half of the capital crimes were family related, including adultery, homosexuality, incest, persistent disobedience to or violence against one's parents, and rape (Lev. 20; Deut. 21–22). The basis for the family unit was the married couple (Gen. 2:4–5:1). From the union of the husband and wife, the family expanded to include the children, and also various relatives such as grandparents, and others.

Along with paternal authority over the family came responsibility to provide for and protect the family. The father was responsible for the religious and moral training of his children (Deut. 6:7,20-25; Exod. 12:26-27; Josh. 4:6-7), and before the law he acted as the family priest (Gen. 12:7-8; Job 1:2-5). After establishment of the Levitical priesthood, the father led the family in worship at the sites designated by God with the priests performing the sacrifices (1 Sam. 1). Moral purity was stressed for men and women in Israel with severe penalties for either party when sin occurred (Lev. 18; Prov. 5). The father was to give his daughter in marriage (Deut. 22:16; 1 Sam. 17:25; Jer. 29:6) to only an Israelite man, usually one from his own tribe. A daughter found to have been promiscuous before she married was to be stoned on her father's doorstep (Deut. 22:21).

Contrary to the practices of the surrounding nations, wives were not considered property. Though most marriages in the OT were arranged, this does not mean that they were loveless. The Song of Songs extols the joys of physical love between a husband and wife. God is used as an example of the perfect husband who loves His "wife" Israel (Hos. 1–2) and delights to care for her and make her happy.

Mothers gave birth and reared the children, ran the home under her husband's authority, and generally served as her husband's helper (Gen. 2:18; Prov. 31:10-31).

The importance of children in ancient Israel may be inferred from the law of Levirate marriage, which provided for the continuance of the family line (Deut. 25:5-10; Ps. 127:3-5). They were also the instruments by which the ancient traditions were passed on (Exod. 13:8-9,14; Deut. 4:9; 6:7). God delights to be praised by children (Ps. 8:2). Children were taught to respect their mothers as well as their fathers (Exod. 20:12; Deut. 5:16; 21:13; 27:16; Prov. 15:20; 23:22,25; 30:17) and to heed their instruction (Prov. 1:8; 6:20). Discipline was one way of showing love to one's children (Prov. 3:11-12; 13:24).

Polygamy (more specifically "polygyny") was one of the abnormal developments of the family in the OT and was first practiced by Lamech, a descendant of Cain. It is never cast in a positive light in Scripture but is a source of rivalry and bickering, as is seen in the lives of Abraham and Jacob (Gen. 16; 29–30). The harems of the kings of Israel are presented as excess that is rebuked in the monarchy (Deut. 17:17). Because of polygamy the kings of Israel were persuaded to worship false gods (1 Kings 11:1-10). The normal family unit in Israel was never polygamous, nor was polygamy widely practiced outside of the monarchy.

Relatives identified as off-limits for marriage (that is, incestuous; see Lev. 18:6-18; 20:11-14,19-21) seem to have been those normally considered members of the "father's house." This included one's father or mother, son or daughter (of whatever generation), sister or brother, uncle or aunt, or a step-relation, half-relation, or in-law, that is, one's father, mother, son, daughter, sister, brother, uncle, or aunt by marriage. The exception was in the case of "Levi-rate marriage," that is, an unmarried male's marriage to the childless widow of his deceased brother.

New Testament As the family is the basic unit in society and in OT Israel, it was also essential to the life and growth of the early church. The apostolic missionaries sent by Jesus were to focus on households (Matt. 10:11-14), early worship consisted in part of "break[ing] bread from house to house" (Acts 2:36; see also 5:42; 12:12; 20:20), and later churches met regularly in homes (Rom. 16:23; 1 Cor. 16:19; Col. 4:15). Conversions even sometimes happened by household (Acts 10:24,33,44; 16:15,31-34; 18:8; 1 Cor. 1:16). The family also served as a proving ground for church leaders, who should exhibit marital faithfulness, hospitality, competent household management, including wise parenting skills, and having wives "worthy of respect" (1 Tim. 3:2-13; Titus 1:6-9).

In the NT family structure is not discussed as much as the roles and responsibilities of those in the household. The common family unit was a monogamous relationship that included the extended family. By the first century there was a greater measure of independence within the family based upon Roman culture and urban living. Close ties were common between members of the family in Israel.

Jesus reaffirmed the monogamous family and rebuked immorality and divorce during His ministry. He spoke about the indissolubility of the family and that even the civil courts could not break the family bonds (Mark 10:1-12). The responsibility to care for those in the family is seen at the cross where Jesus, though suffering, gave the Apostle John the responsibility to care for His mother (John 19:26-27).

Much of the NT teaching on the family is found in Paul's writings. Household ethics are described in Eph. 5–6 and Col. 3–4. In these texts husbands are responsible for the physical, emotional, religious, and psychological health of wives. A wife's submission is in the marriage context.

Wives are called to be household administrators. As household managers wives are responsible to give the family guidance and direction. Paul states that performing these tasks will inhibit gossiping and other unprofitable activities (1 Tim. 5:14). Thus any decision made within the family without the counsel and guidance of the wife is unwise.

Family roles in the NT also include children, who are commanded to obey their parents (Eph. 6:1-4). Each member of the family has responsibilities. Jesus affirms the importance of children and their importance to Him in Matt. 18:2-14; 19:13-14; Mark 10:14-16.

Family as Metaphor The OT often uses familial terms to describe God's relationship to the people of Israel. They are sometimes said to be His "son" or His "sons/children," and at other times they are His wife. (Ps. 103:13). Unfortunately Israel is often described as a wayward wife, or rebellious children, because of their rebellion against God (Jer. 2:32; 3:14).

The church of Jesus Christ could be described as "God's household" of which both Jewish and Gentile believers were family members (Eph. 2:19; see Mark 10:29-30; 1 Tim. 3:15). The result is that one's responsibility to his spiritual family is similar to his responsibility to his physical family (Gal. 6:10; 1 Pet. 3:8), though one should not depend on the church to meet the needs of his own family (1 Tim. 5:3–8). See *Education; Fatherless; Father's House; Incest; Levirate Law, Levirate Marriage; Marriage; Mother; Woman.*

Brent R. Kelly and E. Ray Clendenen

FAMINE AND DROUGHT Famine is an extreme shortage of food, and drought is an excessive dryness of land. The Bible reports or predicts the occurrence of several famines and droughts.

Causes of Famine Drought was the most common cause of famines mentioned in the Bible. Drought caused famines in the time of Abraham (Gen. 12:10), Isaac (Gen. 26:1), Joseph (Gen. 41:27), and the judges (Ruth 1:1). Drought and famine also plagued the Israelites in the days of David (2 Sam. 21:1), Elijah (1 Kings 18:2), Elisha (2 Kings 4:38), Haggai (Hag. 1:11), and Nehemiah (Neh. 5:3). At times the coming of droughts and famines was predicted by prophets (2 Kings 8:1; Isa. 3:1; Jer. 14:12; Acts 11:28). Other natural forces also caused famines: locusts, wind, hail, and mildew (Joel 1:4; Amos 4:9; Hag. 2:17). The Israelites also experienced famines caused by enemies. Occasionally oppressors destroyed or confiscated food (Deut. 28:33,51; Isa. 1:7). The siege of cities also resulted in famine, such as the siege of Samaria by Ben-hadad (2 Kings 6:24-25) and the siege of Jerusalem by Nebuchadnezzar (2 Kings 25:2-3).

The famines that Israel experienced were often severe, some lasting for years (Gen. 12:10; 41:27; Jer. 14:1-6). During famines, starving people resorted to eating such things as wild vines, heads of animals, garbage, dung, and even human flesh (2 Kings 4:39; 6:25,28; Lam. 4:4-10).

Famine and Drought as the Judgment of God God created the world as a good environment that would normally provide ample water and food for mankind (Gen. 1). However, the productiveness of the earth is related to people's obedience to God. For example, the sins of Adam, Eve, and Cain resulted in unfruitfulness of the earth (Gen. 3:17-18; 4:12). Israel's relationship with God also directly affected the fertility of the promised land. When the people obeyed God, the land was productive (Deut. 11:11-14). However, when they disobeyed, judgment came on the land by drought and famine (Lev. 26:23-26; Deut. 11:16-17; 1 Kings 8:35). Furthermore, the NT reports that famine will be a part of God's coming judgment of the earth in the last days (Matt. 24:7; Rev. 6:8).

While the Bible states that some famines and droughts are the judgment of God (2 Sam. 21:1; 1 Kings 17:1; 2 Kings 8:1; Jer 14:12; Ezek. 5:12; Amos 4:6), not all such disasters are connected to divine punishment (Gen. 12:10; 26:1; Ruth 1:1; Acts 11:28). When God did send drought and famine on His people, it was for the purpose of bringing them to repentance (1 Kings 8:35-36; Hos. 2:8-23; Amos 4:6-8). Moreover, the OT contains promises that God will protect His faithful ones in times of famine (Job 5:20,22; Pss. 33:18-19; 37:18-19; Prov. 10:3). See *Ben-hadad; Jerusalem; Nebuchadnezzar; Samaria; Water.*

Bob R. Ellis

FAN KJV term for a long wooden fork used to toss grain into the air so that the chaff is blown away. Shovels were also used for this purpose (Isa. 30:24). Modern translations render the underlying Hebrew and Greek terms "shovel," "winnowing fork," or "winnowing shovel."

FARM, FARMING See *Agriculture.*

FARMER See *Agriculture; Occupations and Professions.*

FARTHING See *Coins.*

A relief of a plowing scene from the Roman period.

Ox turning an ancient type of water pump used for irrigation in the region of Goshen of Egypt.

Young Israeli farmer plowing furrows behind his donkey-drawn wooden plow.

F

Arab farmer plowing his field with a simple double-yoked plow and team of two donkeys.

FASHION The practice of using clothing to make a statement regarding one's status or position in society was just as prevalent in the biblical world as it is today. However, clothing styles did not change as rapidly in antiquity and so the effort to remain stylish was less hectic.

The exact meanings of many technical terms in the Bible describing specific articles of clothing and accessories remain lost; other terms are clearer. The basic wardrobe in biblical times included a long shirt-like undergarment (the tunic—e.g., John 19:23), an outer garment that could be decorated according to one's status (the robe—e.g., 1 Sam. 18:4), various girdles (loincloths, belts and sashes—e.g., Matt. 3:4; Rev. 1:13), headgear (e.g., 2 Sam. 15:30; Zech. 3:5), footwear (e.g., Ezek. 24:17), and jewelry (e.g., Exod. 32:2; Judg. 8:24-26).

Fine clothing was worn by kings and priests (Exod. 28:1-43; 39:1-31; Matt. 11:8) or others worthy of status (Gen. 37:3; Luke 15:22). Such clothing was a valued commodity (cp. Josh. 7:21) and made a precious gift (Gen. 45:22; 2 Kings 5:5; Esther 6:8) but could lead to showiness (Isa. 3:18-26). Believers are instead instructed to clothe themselves modestly so that their true, inward beauty might prevail (1 Tim. 2:9; 1 Pet. 3:3-5).

The outward adornment of clothing was used by the biblical writers to signal the inner spiritual nature of God's people. Once elegantly adorned (Ezek. 16:10-14), Israel sinned and became dressed in filthy rags (Isa. 64:6; Zech. 3:3-4; cp. Rev. 3:4). Those who become righteous are clothed in fine white robes (Zech. 3:4-5; Rev. 3:4-5; 7:9,13). *Paul H. Wright*

FASTING Refraining from eating food. The Bible describes three main forms of fasting. The *normal fast* involves the total abstinence of food. Luke 4:2 reveals that Jesus "ate nothing"; afterwards "He was hungry." Jesus abstained from food but not from water.

In Acts 9:9 we read of an *absolute fast* where for three days Paul "did not eat or drink" (HCSB). The abstinence from both food and water seems to have lasted no more than three days (Ezra 10:6; Esther 4:16).

The *partial fast* in Dan. 10:3 emphasizes the restriction of diet rather than complete abstinence. The context implies that there were physical benefits resulting from this partial fast. However, this verse indicates that there was a revelation given to Daniel as a result of this time of fasting.

Fasting is the laying aside of food for a period of time when the believer is seeking to know God in a deeper experience. It is to be done as an act before God in the privacy of one's own pursuit of God (Exod. 34:28; 1 Sam. 7:6; 1 Kings 19:8; Matt. 6:17).

Fasting is to be done with the object of seeking to know God in a deeper experience (Isa. 58; Zech. 7:5). Fasting relates to a time of confession (Ps. 69:10). Fasting can be a time of seeking a deeper prayer experience and drawing near to God in prevailing prayer (Ezra 8:23; Joel 2:12). The early church often fasted in seeking God's will for leadership in the local church (Acts 13:2). When the early church wanted to know the mind of God, there was a time of prayer and fasting. *C. Robert Marsh*

FATE That which must necessarily happen. The OT speaks of death as the common fate of humankind (Pss. 49:12; 81:15; Eccles. 2:14; 3:19; 9:2-3). The OT similarly speaks of violent death as the destiny of the wicked (Job 15:22; Isa. 65:12; Hos. 9:13). See *Election; Predestination*.

FATHER See *Family; God*.

FATHERLESS Person without a male parent, often rendered orphan by modern translations. Orphans are often mentioned with widows as representatives of the most helpless members of society (Exod. 22:22; Deut. 10:18; Ps. 146:9). In societies where the basic social unit was the clan headed by a father (the eldest male relative, perhaps a grandfather or uncle), those without a father or husband were social misfits without one to provide for their material needs and represent their interests in the court (Job 31:21). Life for the fatherless was harsh. Orphans were often forced to beg for food (Ps. 109:9-10). They suffered loss of their homes (Ps. 109:10), land rights (Prov. 23:10), and livestock (Job 24:3). The fatherless were subject to acts of violence (Job 22:9), were treated as property to be gambled for (6:27 TEV, NRSV, NASB, NIV), and were even murdered (Ps. 94:6).

God, however, has a special concern for orphans and widows (Deut. 10:18; Pss. 10:14-18; 146:9; Hos. 14:3) evidenced in the title "a father of the fatherless" (Ps. 68:5). Old Testament law provided for the material needs of orphans and widows who were to be fed from the third year's tithe (Deut. 14:28-29; 26:12-13), from sheaves left forgotten in the fields (24:19), and from fruit God commanded to be left on the trees and vines (24:20-21). Orphans and widows were to be included in the celebrations of the worshiping community (Deut. 16:11,14). God's people were repeatedly warned not to take advantage of orphans and widows (Exod. 22:22; Deut. 24:17; 27:19; Ps. 82:3; Isa. 1:17). In the NT James defined worship acceptable to God as meeting the needs of orphans and widows (1:27).

God's exiled people were described as orphans without home or inheritance (Lam. 5:2-3). The OT image of the orphan without a helper at the court perhaps forms the background for Jesus' promise that His disciples would not be left orphans (John 14:18 NASB, NIV, NRSV; "comfortless," KJV; "bereft," REB). They would not be defenseless since the Holy Spirit would act as their advocate (14:16). Paul described his painful separation from the Thessalonian Christians as being orphaned (1 Thess. 2:17 NRSV). See *Poor, Orphan, Widow.*   *Chris Church*

FATHER'S HOUSE Name given to extended family units in the ancient Near East reflecting a social organization in which a dominant male headed the family. These units might be large (Jacob's house included 66 descendants when he entered Egypt, Gen. 46:26). A father's house could designate the clans within a tribe (Exod. 6:14-25) or even an entire tribe (Josh. 22:14). The common designations "house of Jacob" (Exod. 19:3; Amos 3:13), "house of Israel" (Exod. 40:38), and the unusual designation "house of Isaac" (Amos 7:16) all refer to the nation of Israel in terms of a father's house.

During patriarchal times a marriage was expected to be within the house of one's father (Gen. 11:29; 20:12; 24:4,15,38,40; 29:10; Exod. 6:20; Num. 36:8-10). Some of these marriages within the clan were later prohibited (Lev. 18:9,12; 20:17,19). In patriarchal times married women were regarded as remaining part of their father's house (Gen. 31:14; cp. 46:26 where the enumeration of Jacob's house does not include his sons' wives). In later times married women were regarded to have left their father's houses (Num. 30:3,16). Widows were expected to return to their fathers' houses (Gen. 38:11).

Genesis 31:14 suggests that in patriarchal times married women might normally expect to share in their father's inheritance. Later law limited this right to cases in which there were no sons to inherit (Num. 27:8).

In John 2:16 "My Father's house" is a designation for the temple which was then equated with Christ's body (2:21). The reference to "My Father's house" with its many dwelling places (14:2) can be explained in two ways. "House" can be understood as a place or as a set of relationships, a household. Already in the Psalms the temple is the house of God where the righteous hope to dwell (23:6; 27:4). It is a short step to the idea of heaven as God's dwelling where there is ample room for the disciples. If house is understood as household, the focus is on fellowship with God. In contrast to servants, a son abides in his father's house (John 8:35). As Son of God, Jesus enjoys unique fellowship with God. By believing in Christ, we are empowered to become children of God (1:12), members of God's household, and share in fellowship with the Father. The two meanings do not exclude each other. Both are included in Jesus' promise in John 14:2.   *Chris Church*

FATHOM Measure of depth equaling six feet (Acts 27:28). See *Weights and Measures.*

FATLINGS, FATTED Generally a young animal penned up to be fed for slaughter. Sometimes a general reference to the strongest or to the choice among a flock or herd is intended. In Pharaoh's dream fat cows (Gen. 41:2,18) symbolized years of prosperity. Saul was tempted to spare the choice animals of the Amalekites (1 Sam. 15:9). In Ezek. 34:3,16,20 the fat sheep symbolize the prosperous leaders of Israel. As choice specimens, fattened animals made an appropriate offering to God (2 Sam. 6:13; Ps. 66:15; Amos 5:22). Fattened animals are often associated with banquets.

Fattened cattle formed part of the menu for the wedding banquet of the king's son in the parable in Matt. 22:4. In the parable of the loving father, a son is welcomed home with a banquet of a fatted calf (Luke 15:23,27,30). Fattened animals were used as a symbol for slaughter. In the NT James pictured the oppressive rich as fattening their hearts for a day of slaughter, perhaps a reference to God's judgment on them (5:5).

F

FAWN Young deer; term used in modern translations for KJV's "hind" and "roe." See *Deer*.

FEAR Natural emotional response to a perceived threat to one's security or general welfare. It ranges in degree of intensity from a sense of anxiety or worry to one of utter terror. It can be a useful emotion when it leads to appropriate caution or measures that would guard one's welfare. On the other hand, fear can be a hindrance to the enjoyment of life if it is induced by delusion or if it lingers and overpowers other more positive emotions such as love and joy, perhaps leading to an inability to engage in the normal activities of life. In the Bible, however, fear is perhaps more often than in popular culture regarded not as pure emotion but as wise behavior.

Terminology The concept of fear is referred to in the Bible several hundred times, either explicitly or by implication through effects such as trembling, shaking, shuddering, or cringing. The word group most often associated with fear in the OT (occurring 435 times) is the verb *yara'*, "to fear, honor," the adjective *yare'*, "in fear of, fearful," and the related nouns, *mora'*, "fear, terror, awe," and *yir'ah,* "fear, worship." These are supplemented by other word groups such as one related to the root *chatat*, "be terrified, disheartened, dismayed," and *pacad*, "tremble, be in dread."

In the NT the concept of fear is most often associated with the root *phob-* (146 times), as in the verb *phobeo*, "to fear, reverence, or respect," related nouns, *phobos*, "fear, terror, reverence, respect" and *phobetron*, "terrifying sight," and the adjective *phoberos*, "fearful." Synonyms are also found, such as *tarasso*, "disturb, terrify," and the word group *deilia*, "cowardice," *deiliao*, "be cowardly, fearful," and *deilos*, "cowardly, timid."

Emotions of Terror and Anxiety The familiar concept of fear induced by a threatening situation is common in the Bible. The first emotion explicitly referred to is Adam and Eve's fear of divine retribution for eating the forbidden fruit (Gen. 3:10). In this case, their fear induced them to hide. Jacob's fear of Esau caused him to pray in Gen. 32:11. Sometimes fear causes silence or inhibits action, as when "Ish-bosheth did not dare to say another word to Abner, because he was afraid of him" (2 Sam. 3:11; cp. 2 Chron. 17:10).

A common biblical theme is fear of one's enemies, often found in passages of divine encouragement not to fear. For example, before engaging in battle Israel's priest was to exhort them not to be "fainthearted or afraid; do not be terrified or give way to panic before them" (Deut. 20:3). And the Lord commanded Joshua, "Be strong and courageous. Do not be terrified; do not be discouraged, for the LORD your God will be with you wherever you go" (Josh. 1:9; Deut. 31:6; Isa. 44:8; Luke 12:32; John 16:33). On the contrary, the Lord promised Israel that He would cause their enemies to panic and flee from them in terror (Exod. 15:14-16; 23:27; Deut. 2:25; 11:25). It may be said that a believer is one who fears nothing but God (Deut. 7:21; Prov. 29:25; Isa. 8:13; Matt. 10:28).

We should notice from these verses that the Bible does not portray fear of danger simply as an emotion over which the believer has no control. The biblical command not to fear is a command not to panic or be immobilized by fear or not to allow one's fear of perceived danger to hinder obedience to God. The antidote to such fear is the conviction that God is able to protect and to accomplish His will and that His promises can be trusted (2 Kings 6:15-17; 2 Chron. 15:7-8; Pss. 34:4; 56:3-4; Prov. 3:24-26; Isa. 41:10, 43:1; Matt. 10:26-31; Heb. 13:6; 1 Pet. 3:13-17; Rev. 2:10).

The same can be said of anxiety, which can be no less destructive to faithfulness than terror (Phil. 4:6). It was probably Abraham's anxiety over his childlessness that prompted the Lord's charge not to fear in Gen. 15:1, and it was failure to heed that charge that led to the birth of Ishmael in chapter 16. Anxious fear or worry becomes the sin of pride and unbelief when it diverts one's attention from following the Lord (Isa. 51:12-13; Mark 4:19; Luke 10:41) or causes someone to trust their own resources or abilities or those of someone else rather than God's (Matt. 6:19-34; Ps. 55:22).

Attitude of Respect and Submission Another indication that the biblical concept of fear was not necessarily an involuntary emotion is that the same words were also used of one's proper response to someone in authority: a child to parents (Lev. 19:3), citizens to their leaders (Josh 4:14; Rom. 13:7), a servant to his master (Mal. 1:6; Eph. 6:5), and a wife to her husband (Eph. 5:33). In these cases, "fear" carries with it the expectation of obedience. Respect or honor may be the sense in which Israel "feared" Solomon when they saw evidence that he possessed God's wisdom (1 Kings 3:28). Respect or reverence is also the proper attitude toward God's sanctuary (Lev. 19:30). Fear can be the opposite of treating someone or something as common, insignificant, irrelevant, or otherwise unworthy of attention (Esther 5:9).

Fear of God Any of these senses—terror, honor, submission—may be involved when God is the object of fear, with the additional sense of worship. For those who are enemies rather than followers of the Lord, terror is most appropriate (Jer. 5:22). Such terror is limited by the fact that God is not capricious but acts consistently according to His righteous character and revealed will. Nevertheless, those guilty of idolatry and injustice have every reason to fear His coming wrath in judgment (Ps. 90:11; Isa. 13:6-11; 30:30-33; Zeph. 1:18; Heb. 10:26-31). Terror is the only reasonable response when confronted by a Being whose knowledge and power have no limits, unless one's safety has been assured. The Bible contains many cases of a divine or angelic appearance to which fear is the natural response (Exod. 3:6; 20:18-20; Dan. 10:10-12; Luke 1:12-13,30). Following the resurrection of Christ, for example, an angelic appearance caused the guards at the tomb to faint with fear, but the believing women were told they had nothing to fear (Matt. 28:4-5).

The proper attitude of believers toward God is often said to be respect, reverence, or awe rather than fear. The biblical terminology, however, is the same, and God's character remains unchanged. The description of God often translated "awesome" is literally "feared" or "fearful" (Exod. 15:11; Neh. 1:5; Job 37:22; Ps. 89:7; Dan. 9:4). Confining the believer's attitude toward God to "reverence" or "awe" rather than "fear" may lose sight of those aspects of the divine character that compel obedience—His perfect holiness and righteousness and His unlimited knowledge and power. Knowing that God's wrath has been satisfied in Christ relieves the believer from the fear of condemnation but not from accountability to a holy God (2 Cor. 5:10-11; 7:1; 1 Tim. 5:20; 1 Pet. 1:17).

"Fear" and "love" are both terms found in ancient Near Eastern literature associated with covenant loyalty. To fear God is to have alle-giance to Him and consequently to His instructions, thus affecting one's values, convictions, and behavior (Gen. 20:11; Lev. 25:17,36,43; 1 Sam. 12:14,24; Ps. 128:1; Prov. 8:13). True believers are often referred to as those who fear God (Gen. 22:12; Job 1:9; Pss. 31:19; 33:18; 103:11,13,17; 115:11,13; 118:4; Mal. 3:16; 4:2; Luke 1:50). So the fear of God expressed in humble submission and worship is essential to true wisdom (Prov. 9:10; 15:33; Isa. 33:6). A true believer may be defined as one who trembles at God's word (Gen. 22:12; Exod. 1:17; Ps. 119:161; Isa. 66:2,5; Jer. 23:9). See *Awe, Awesome; Reverence.*   *E. Ray Clendenen*

FEAR OF ISAAC Name or title that Jacob used in referring to God (Gen. 31:42; cp. 31:53; 46:1). Evidently the patriarchs used various names to refer to God until He revealed His personal name to Moses (Exod. 6:3). Some scholars translate the Hebrew expression "Kinsman of Isaac" or "Refuge of Isaac." See *God of the Fathers; Patriarchs.*

FEASTS See *Festivals.*

FELIX (Fē´ lĭx) Procurator of Judea at the time Paul the apostle visited Jerusalem for the last time and was arrested there (Acts 23:24). Antonius Felix became procurator of Judea in A.D. 52, succeeding Cumanus. He remained in office until A.D. 60, when the emperor Nero recalled him. He is depicted in Acts as a man who listened with interest to Paul's defense but failed to make any decision with regard to the case or with regard to the personal implications of Paul's message. Rather, he hoped Paul would pay him a bribe (Acts 24:26). Contemporary historians Tacitus and Josephus paint Felix as a brutal, incompetent politician who was finally replaced (cp. Acts 24:27). See *Paul; Rome and the Roman Empire.*

FELLOES (KJV, REB) Rim of a wheel (1 Kings 7:33).

FELLOWSHIP Bond of common purpose and devotion that binds Christians to one another and to Christ. "Fellowship" is the English translation of words from the Hebrew stem *chabar* and the Greek stem *koin-*. The Hebrew *chabar* was used to express ideas such as common or shared house (Prov. 21:9), "binding" or "joining"

(Exod. 26:6; Eccles. 9:4), companion (Eccles. 4:10), and even a wife as a companion (Mal. 2:14). *Chaber* was used for a member of a Pharisaic society. Pharisees tended to form very close associations with one another in social, religious, and even business affairs. A most important dimension in the life of these *cheberim* was a sharing together in the study of Scripture and law and table fellowship.

The Gospels record no sayings of Jesus in which He used the *koin*-stem to describe "fellowship" among disciples, though certainly the close association shared by Jesus and His followers laid the foundation for the church's post-Easter understanding of fellowship.

Koinonia was Paul's favorite word to describe a believer's relationship with the risen Lord and the benefits of salvation which come through Him. On the basis of faith, believers have fellowship with the Son (1 Cor. 1:9). We share fellowship in the gospel (1 Cor. 9:23; Phil. 1:5). Paul probably meant that all believers participate together in the saving power and message of the good news. Believers also share together a fellowship with the Holy Spirit (2 Cor. 13:14), which the apostle understood as a most important bond for unity in the life of the church (Phil. 2:1-4).

The tendency of many Christians to refer to the Lord's Supper as "communion" is rooted in Paul's use of the term *koinonia* in the context of his descriptions of the Lord's Supper. He described the cup as "sharing in the blood of Christ," and the bread as "sharing" of the body of Christ (1 Cor. 10:16 HCSB). Paul did not explain precisely how such "sharing" takes place through the Supper. He emphatically believed the Supper tied participants closer to one another and to Christ. Such "sharing" could not be shared with Christ and with other gods or supernatural beings. Thus Paul forbad his readers from partaking in pagan religious meals, which would result in sharing "fellowship" with evil, supernatural forces or demons (1 Cor. 10:19-21).

Immediately after Paul spoke of "fellowship" with Christ through participation in the Lord's Supper (1 Cor. 10:16), he said, "Since there is one bread, we who are many are one body" (1 Cor. 10:17 HCSB). This illustrates clearly Paul's belief that fellowship with Christ was to issue into fellowship between believers. Once we grasp this, it is easy to understand why Paul was so angry over the mockery that the Corinthi-

ans were making of the Lord's Supper. While claiming to partake of this sacred meal, many Corinthian Christians ignored the needs of their brothers and sisters and actually created factions and divisions (1 Cor. 11:17-18), "For in eating, each of you takes his own supper ahead of others, and one person is hungry while another is drunk!" (1 Cor. 11:21 HCSB). Because the "fellowship" among the Corinthians themselves was so perverted, Paul could go so far as to say "when you come together in one place, it is not really to eat the Lord's Supper" (1 Cor. 11:20 HCSB).

Koinonia with the Lord results not only in sharing His benefits (the gospel and the Holy Spirit), but also sharing His sufferings (Phil. 3:10; Col. 1:24). These texts express clearly just how intimate was Paul's perception of the close relationship between the believer and the Lord. The pattern of self-sacrifice and humility, demonstrated most profoundly through Jesus' suffering on the cross (Phil. 2:5-8), is to mark the current life of the disciple. Just as Jesus gave so completely of Himself for the sake of His people, so, too, are believers to give completely of themselves for the sake of the people of God (2 Cor. 4:7-12; Col. 1:24). The pattern of following Christ in suffering continues for the believer, in that just as Christ entered into glory following His suffering (Phil. 2:9-11), so, too, will the believer in the future share in the glory of Christ if "we suffer with Him" (Rom. 8:17 HCSB; cp. Phil. 3:10-11).

Paul believed that Christians were to share with one another what they had to offer to assist fellow believers. Paul used the *koin*-stem to refer to such sharing. One who has received the word ought to "share" it with others (Gal. 6:6). Though it is not translated "fellowship" in English versions, Paul actually used the term *koinonia* to denote the financial contribution which he was collecting from Gentile believers to take to Jerusalem for the relief of the saints who lived there (Rom. 15:26; 2 Cor. 8:4; 9:13). The reason he could refer to a financial gift as *koinonia* is explained by Rom. 15:27: "For if the Gentiles have shared in their [the Jewish Christians'] spiritual benefits, then they are obligated to minister to Jews in material needs" (HCSB). In this case, each offered what they were able to offer to benefit others: Jewish Christians their spiritual blessings, Gentile Christians their material blessings. Such mutual sharing of one's blessings is a clear and profound expression of Christian fellowship.

Finally, for Paul, *koinonia* was a most appropriate term to describe the unity and bonding that exists between Christians by virtue of the fact that they share together in the grace of the gospel. When Paul wished to express the essential oneness of the apostolic leadership of the church he said concerning James, the Lord's brother, Peter, and John, that they "gave the right hand of fellowship to me" (Gal. 2:9 HCSB). When we realize that this expression of *koinonia* came on the heels of one of the most hotly debated issues in the early church, namely the status of Gentiles in the people of God (Gal. 2:1-10; Acts 15), we can see how powerful and all encompassing Paul's notion of Christian fellowship was.

Like Paul, John also affirmed that *koinonia* was an important aspect of the Christian pilgrimage. He affirmed emphatically that fellowship with God and the Son was to issue in fellowship with the other believers (1 John 1:3,6-7). See *Lord's Supper; Holy Spirit.*   *Bradley Chance*

FENCED CITY KJV term for a fortified or walled city. See *Cities and Urban Life; Fortified Cities.*

FERRET White European polecat mentioned by KJV in Lev. 11:30. Other translations read "gecko."

FERTILE CRESCENT Crescent-shaped arc of alluvial land in the Near East stretching from the tip of the Persian Gulf to the southeastern corner of the Mediterranean Sea. The term was coined by James Henry Breasted in 1916 and does not occur in the Bible.

Conditions in the Fertile Crescent in antiquity were favorable for settled life, and the rise of civilization occurred along its river valleys. This band of land between the desert and the mountains was suitable for farming and was somewhat isolated by geographical barriers on all sides. The northeast is bordered by the Zagros Mountains, the north by the Taurus and Amanus ranges. On the west lies the Mediterranean Sea, and the concave southern limit is determined by the vast Syro-Arabian Desert. The Fertile Crescent is composed of Mesopotamia in the east and the Levant, or Palestine and Syria in the west.

Egypt was separated from Palestine by the Sinai, and thus is not a part of the Fertile Crescent. The Nile River, however, provided an ideal situation for the rise of early civilization parallel

City walls and buildings outside Hazor, one of Israel's most heavily fortified cities.

to that of Mesopotamia. See *Mesopotamia, Palestine.* *Daniel C. Browning, Jr.*

FERTILITY CULT General term for religions marked by rites which reenact a myth accounting for the orderly change of the seasons and the earth's fruitfulness. Such myths often involve a great mother-goddess as a symbol of fertility and a male deity, usually her consort but sometimes a son, who like vegetation dies and returns to life again. In Mesopotamia the divine couple was Ishtar and Tammuz (who is mourned in Ezek. 8:14); in Egypt, Isis and her son Osiris; in Asia Minor, Cybele and Attis. In Syria the Ugaritic myths of the second millennium B.C. pictured Baal-Hadad, the storm god, as the dying and rising god. (A local manifestation of this god is mourned in Zech. 12:11; Syrian kings derived their names from this deity, 1 Kings 15:18; 2 Kings 6:24; 13:24). His wife was the goddess Anath. In the earliest Ugaritic myth Asherah, the great mother-goddess, was the consort of El, the chief god in the pantheon. As Baal replaced El as the major deity, he became associated with Asherah (Judg. 6:25-30; 1 Kings 18:19). Ashtoroth, the daughter of Asherah, is used as the Hebrew word for womb or the fruit of the womb (Deut. 7:13; 28:4,18,51).

Fertility cults attribute the fertility of the cropland and herds to the sexual relations of the divine couple. Sacral sexual intercourse by priests and priestesses or by cult prostitutes was an act of worship intended to emulate the gods and share in their powers of procreation or else an act of imitative magic by which the gods were compelled to preserve the earth's fertility (1 Kings 14:23-24; 15:12; Hos. 4:14). Transvestism (prohibited in Deut. 22:5) may have been part of a fertility rite like that practiced by the Hittites. Sacrifices of produce, livestock, and even children (2 Kings 17:31; 23:10) represented giving the god what was most precious in life in an attempt to restore order to the cosmos and ensure fertility.

Elijah's struggle with the priests of Baal and Asherah at Mount Carmel is the best known conflict between worship of Yahweh and a fertility cult (1 Kings 18:17-40). Under Ahab, Baalism had become the state religion (1 Kings 16:31). The account of the priests of Baal lacerating themselves (1 Kings 18:28) is illuminated by the Ugaritic myths where El gashes his arms, chest, and back at the news of Baal's death. The priests

of Baal customarily reenacted this scene from the myth at plowing time. Both skin and earth were cut as a sign of mourning (prohibited by Deut. 14:1). Baal's resurrection came with the return of the rains. The biblical narrative is clear that Yahweh, not Baal, is the Lord who withholds and gives rain (1 Kings 17:1; 18:20-45).

The Israelites' sacred calendar celebrated the same seasons as their neighbors (barley harvest, same as feast of unleavened bread; wheat harvest, same as Pentecost; fruit harvest, same as feast of booths). The Israelites interpreted these seasons in light of God's redemptive acts in their history. Israel recognized God as the one responsible for rain (1 Kings 18), grain, wine, oil, wool, and flax (Hos. 2:8-9). Israel conceived of the earth's fruitfulness in a way quite unlike that of her neighbors. Yahweh had no consort; thus fertility was not tied to Yahweh's return to life and sexual functioning. Rather, the ability of plants and animals to reproduce their own kind was rooted in creation (Gen. 1:11-12,22,28). The orderly progression of the seasons was not traced to a primordial battle but was rooted in God's promise to Noah (Gen. 8:22). The fertility of the land was ensured not by ritual reenactment of the sacred marriage but by obedience to the demands of the covenant (Deut. 28:1,3-4,11-12).

In the NT Diana or Artemis of the Ephesians (Acts 19:35) was a many-breasted fertility goddess. Aphrodite was also associated with fertility. Her temple at Corinth was the home of cult prostitutes responsible for the city's reputation for immorality (cp. 1 Cor. 6:15-20). Many of the mystery religions that competed with Christianity in the early centuries of the church developed the myths of the older fertility cults. See *Asherah; Ashtoroth; Baal; Canaan; Dagon; Diana; Gods, Pagan; High Place; Prostitution; Tammuz; Ugarit.* *Chris Church*

FESTAL GARMENTS, FESTAL ROBES Terms used by modern translations for two Hebrew expressions. The Hebrew expressions underlying "festal garments" mean a change of clothing (Gen. 45:22; Judg. 14:12-13,19; 2 King 5:5,22-23); the term underlying "festal robes" means clean, pure, or white clothing (Isa. 3:22; Zech. 3:4). Modern translations are not consistent in translating the terms, translation depending on the context. In the ancient Near East possession of sets of clothing was regarded as a sign of wealth. Common people would own few clothes. Thus a change of clothes might suggest clothes reserved for a special occasion as reflected in some translations (Judg. 14:12-13,19 NRSV, TEV; 2 King 5:5,22-23 TEV). The white garments of Isa. 3:22 are likely fine linen robes. The reference in Zech. 3:4 is either to the high priest's robes (perhaps the special robes reserved for the Day of Atonement, Zech. 3:9), which represent the restoration of the priesthood, or a simple reference to clean robes as a symbol of Joshua's innocence of any charges (symbolized by the filthy rags).

FESTERING SORES See *Diseases; Scurvy.*

FESTIVALS Regular religious celebrations remembering God's great acts of salvation in the history of His people. Traditionally called "feasts" in the English Bibles, these can conveniently be categorized according to frequency of celebration. Many of them were timed according to cycles of seven. The cycle of the week with its climax on the seventh day provided the cyclical basis for much of Israel's worship; as the seventh day was observed, so was the seventh month (which contained four of the national festivals), and the seventh year, and the fiftieth year (the year of Jubilee), which followed seven cycles each of seven years. Not only were the festivals as a whole arranged with reference to the cycle of the week (Sabbath), two of them (the feast of unleavened bread and the feast of tabernacles) lasted for seven days each. Each began on the 15th of the month—at the end of two cycles of weeks and when the moon was full. Pentecost also was celebrated on the 15th of the month and began 50 days after the presentation of the firstfruits—the day following seven times seven weeks.

Sabbath The seventh day of each week was listed among the festivals (Lev. 23:1-3). It functioned as a reminder of the Lord's rest at the end of the creation week (Gen. 2:3) and also of the deliverance from slavery in Egypt (Deut. 5:12-25). The Sabbath day was observed by strict rest from work from sunset until sunset (Exod. 20:8-11; Neh. 13:15-22). Each person was to remain in place and not engage in travel (Exod. 16:29; Lev. 23:3). Despite such restrictions even as kindling a fire (Exod. 35:3) or any work (Exod. 31:14; 35:2), the Sabbath was a joyful time (Isa. 58:13-14). See *Sabbath.*

New Moon This festival was a monthly celebration characterized by special offerings, great in quantity and quality (Num. 28:11-15), and blowing of trumpets (Num. 10:10; Ps. 81:3). According to Amos 8:5, business ceased. The festivals of the new moon and Sabbath are often mentioned together in the OT (Isa. 1:13; 66:23; Ezek. 45:17; 46:1,3). This festival provided the occasion for King Saul to stage a state banquet and for the family of David to offer a special annual sacrifice (1 Sam. 20:5,6,24,29). David's arrangements for the Levites included service on the new moon (1 Chron. 23:31), and the ministry of the prophets was sometimes connected with this occasion (2 Kings 4:23; Isa. 1:13; Ezek. 46:1; Hag. 1:1). Ezekiel mentioned four times receiving a vision on the first day of the month (Ezek. 26:1; 29:17; 31:1; 32:1). This day (along with others) is included in prophetic denunciations of abuses of religious observances (Isa. 1:13-14). The new moon of the seventh month apparently received special attention (Lev. 23:24; Num. 29:1-6; Ezra 3:6; Neh. 8:2). Although the exile brought a temporary cessation (Hos. 2:11), the festival was resumed later (Neh. 10:33; Ezra 3:1-6). It was on the first day of the seventh month that Ezra read the law before the public assembly (Neh. 7:73b—8:2). For Paul, new moon festivals were viewed as only a shadow of better things to come (Col. 2:16-17; cp. Isa. 66:23).

Annual festivals required the appearance of all males at the sanctuary (Exod. 34:23; Deut. 16:16). These occasions—called "feasts to the LORD" (Exod. 12:14; Lev. 23:39,41)—were times when freewill offerings were made (Deut. 16:16-17).

Passover The first of the three annual festivals was the Passover. It commemorated the final plague on Egypt when the firstborn of the Egyptians died and the Israelites were spared because of the blood smeared on their doorposts (Exod. 12:11,21,27,43,48). Passover took place on the 14th day (at evening) of the first month (Lev. 23:5). The animal (lamb or kid) to be slain was selected on the 10th day of the month (Exod. 12:3) and slaughtered on the 14th day and then eaten (Deut. 16:7). None of the animal was to be left over on the following morning (Exod. 34:25). The uncircumcised and the hired servant were not permitted to eat the sacrifice (Exod. 12:45-49).

The Passover was also called the feast of unleavened bread (Exod. 23:15; Deut. 16:16)

A young Jewish boy receives his first phylactery during his bar mitzvah.

because only unleavened bread was eaten during the seven days immediately following Passover (Exod. 12:15-20; 13:6-8; Deut. 16:3-8). Unleavened bread reflected the fact that the people had no time to put leaven in their bread before their hasty departure from Egypt. It was also apparently connected to the barley harvest (Lev. 23:4-14).

During NT times large crowds gathered in Jerusalem to observe this annual celebration. Jesus was crucified during the Passover event. He and His disciples ate a Passover meal together on the eve of His death. During this meal Jesus said, "This is My body," and "this cup is the new covenant in My blood" (Luke 22:17,19-20 HCSB). The NT identifies Christ with the Passover sacrifice: "For Christ our Passover has been sacrificed" (1 Cor. 5:7 HCSB).

Feast of Weeks The second of the three annual festivals was Pentecost, also called the feast of weeks (Exod. 34:22; Deut. 16:10,16; 2 Chron. 8:13), the feast of harvest (Exod. 23:16), and the day of firstfruits (Num. 28:26; cp. Exod. 23:16; 34:22; Lev. 23:17). It was celebrated seven complete weeks, or 50 days, after Passover (Lev. 23:15-16; Deut. 16:9); therefore, it was given the name Pentecost.

Essentially a harvest celebration, the term "weeks" was used of the period of grain harvest from the barley harvest to the wheat harvest, a period of about seven weeks. At this time the Lord was credited as the source of rain and fertility (Jer. 5:24). It was called "day of firstfruits" (Num. 28:26) because it marked the beginning of the time in which people were to bring offerings of firstfruits. It was celebrated as a sabbath with rest from ordinary labors and the calling of a holy convocation (Lev.23:21; Num. 28:26). It was a feast of joy and thanksgiving for the com-

pletion of the harvest season. The able-bodied men were to be present at the sanctuary, and a special sacrifice was offered (Lev. 23:15-22; Num. 28:26-31). According to Lev. 23:10-11,16-17, two large loaves were waved before the Lord by the anointed priests. These were made of fine flour from the new wheat and baked with leaven. They were a "wave offering" for the people. They could not be eaten until after this ceremony (Lev. 23:14; Josh. 5:10-11), and none of this bread was placed on the altar because of the leaven content. Also two lambs were offered. The feast was concluded by the eating of communal meals to which the poor, the stranger, and the Levites were invited.

Later tradition associated the feast of weeks with the giving of the law at Sinai. It had been concluded by some that Exod. 19:1 indicated the law was delivered on the fiftieth day after the exodus. Some thought that Deut. 16:12 may have connected the Sinai event and the festival, but Scripture does not indicate any definite link between Sinai and Pentecost. In the NT the Holy Spirit came upon the disciples at Pentecost (Acts 2:1-4), at the festive time when Jews from different countries were in Jerusalem to celebrate this annual feast. See *Firstfruits; Pentecost.*

The Day of Atonement The third annual festival came on the 10th day of the seventh month (Tishri-Sept./Oct.) and the fifth day before the feast of tabernacles (Lev. 16:1-34; Num. 29:7-11). According to Lev. 23:27-28, four main elements comprise this most significant feast. First, it was to be a "holy convocation," drawing the focus of the people to the altar of divine mercy. The holy One of Israel called the people of Israel to gather in His presence and give their undivided attention to Him. Second, they were to "humble their souls" ("afflict your souls," Lev. 23:27 KJV). This was explained by later tradition to indicate fasting and repentance. Israel understood that this was a day for mourning over their sins. The seriousness of this requirement is reiterated in Lev. 23:29, "If there is any person who will not humble himself on this same day, he shall be cut off from his people" (Lev. 23:29 NASB). Third, offerings are central to the Day of Atonement. The Bible devotes an entire chapter (Lev. 16) to them; they are also listed in Num. 29:7-11. In addition to these, when the day fell on a sabbath, the regular Sabbath offerings were offered. The fourth and final element of the day involved the prohibition of labor. The Day of

Atonement was a "sabbath of rest" (Lev. 23:32), and the Israelites were forbidden to do any work at all. If they disobeyed, they were liable to capital punishment (Lev. 23:30).

The center point of this feast involved the high priest entering the holy of holies. Before entering, the high priest first bathed his entire body, going beyond the mere washing of hands and feet as required for other occasions. This washing symbolized his desire for purification. Rather than donning his usual robe and colorful garments (described in Exod. 28 and Lev. 8), he was commanded to wear special garments of linen. Also, the high priest sacrificed a bullock as a sin offering for himself and for his house (Lev. 16:6). After filling his censer with live coals from the altar, he entered the holy of holies where he placed incense on the coals. Then he took some of the blood from the slain bullock and sprinkled it on the mercy seat ("atonement cover," Lev. 16:13 NIV) and also on the ground in front of the ark, providing atonement for the priesthood (Lev. 16:14-15). Next he sacrificed a male goat as a sin offering for the people. Some of this blood was then also taken into the holy of holies and sprinkled there on behalf of the people (Lev. 16:15). Then he took another goat, called the "scapegoat" (for "escape goat"), laid his hands on its head, confessed over it the sins of Israel, and then released it into the desert where it symbolically carried away the sins of the people (Lev. 16:8,10). The remains of the sacrificial bullock and male goat were taken outside the city and burned, and the day was concluded with additional sacrifices.

According to Heb. 9–10 this ritual is a symbol of the atoning work of Christ, our great high Priest, who did not need to make any sacrifice for Himself but shed His own blood for our sins. As the high priest of the OT entered the holy of holies with the blood of sacrificial animals, Jesus entered heaven itself to appear on our behalf in front of the Father (Heb. 9:11-12). Each year the high priest repeated his sin offerings for his own sin and the sins of the people, giving an annual reminder that perfect and permanent atonement had not yet been made; but Jesus, through His own blood, accomplished eternal redemption for His people (Heb. 9:12). Just as the sacrifice of the Day of Atonement was burned outside the camp of Israel, Jesus suffered outside the gate of Jerusalem so that He might redeem His people from sin (Heb. 13:11-12).

Feast of Tabernacles The fourth annual festival was the feast of tabernacles (2 Chron. 8:13; Ezra 3:4; Zech. 14:16), also called the feast of ingathering (Exod. 23:16; 34:22), the feast to the Lord (Lev. 23:39; Judg. 21:19). Sometimes it was simply called "the feast" (1 Kings 8:2; 2 Chron. 5:3; 7:8; Neh. 8:14; Isa. 30:29; Ezek. 45:23,25) because it was so well-known. Its observance combined the ingathering of the labor of the field (Exod. 23:16), the fruit of the earth (Lev. 23:39), the ingathering of the threshing floor and winepress (Deut. 16:13), and the dwelling in booths (or "tabernacles"), which were to be joyful reminders to Israel (Lev. 23:41; Deut. 16:14). The "booth" in Scripture is not an image of privation and misery but of protection, preservation, and shelter from heat and storm (Pss. 27:5; 31:20; Isa. 4:6). The rejoicing community included family, servants, widows, orphans, Levites, and sojourners (Deut. 16:13-15).

The feast began on the fifteenth day of Tishri (the seventh month), which was five days after the Day of Atonement. It lasted for seven days (Lev. 23:36; Deut. 16:13; Ezek. 45:25). On the first day, booths were constructed of fresh branches of trees. Each participant had to collect twigs of myrtle, willow, and palm in the area of

A Jewish mother and child celebrate the Jewish tradition of lighting of the candles at Hanukkah.

The Jewish Calendar

	Sacred	1	2	3	4	5	6
Year	Civil	7	8	9	10	11	12
Month		Nison/Abib 30 days	Iyyar/Ziv 29 days	Sivan 30 days	Tammuz 29 days	Ab 30 days	Elul 29 days
English Months (nearly)		April	May	June	July	August	September
Festivals		**1** New Moon **14** The Passover **15-21** Unleavened Bread	**1** New Moon **14** Second Passover (for those unable to keep first)	**1** New Moon **6** Pentecost	**1** New Moon **17** Fast. Taking of Jerusalem	**1** New Moon **9** Fast. Destruction of temple	**1** New Moon
Seasons and Productions		Spring rains (Deut. 11:14) Floods (Josh. 3:15) Barley ripe of Jericho	**Harvest** Barley Harvest (Ruth 1:22) Wheat Harvest Summer begins No rain from April to Sept. (1 Sam. 12:17)		**Hot Season** Heat increases	The streams dry up Heat intense Vintage (Lev. 26:5)	Heat intense (2 Kings 4:19) Grape Harvest (Num. 13:23)

Note 1

The Jewish year is strictly lunar, being 12 lunations with an average of 29-1/2 days making 354 days in the year.

The Jewish sacred year begins with that new moon of spring which comes between our Marc 22 and April 25 in cycles of 19 years.

We can understand it best if we imagine our New Year's Day, which now comes on Jan. 1, without regard to the moon, varying each year with Easter, the time of the Passover, the time of the full moon which , as a new moon, had introduced the New Year two weeks before.

7	8	9	10	11	12	13
1	2	3	4	5	6	Leap year
Tishri/ Ethanim 30 days	Marchesran/ Bul 29 days	Chislev 30 days	Tebeth 29 days	Shebat 30 days	Adar 29 days	Veadar/Adar Sheni
October	November	December	January	February	March	March/April
1 New Year. Day of Blowing of Trumpet. Day of Judgment and Memorial 10 Day of Atonement (Lev. 23:24) 15 Booths 21 (Lev. 23:24) 22 Solemn Assembly	1 New Moon	1 New Moon 25 Dedication (John 10:22,29)	1 New Moon 10 Fast. Siege of Jerusalem	1 New Moon	1 New Moon 13 Fast. of Esther 14–15 Purim	1 New Moon 13 Fast. of Esther 14–15 Purim
Seed Time		Winter				
Former or early rains begin (Joel 2:23) Plowing and sowing begin	Rain continues Wheat and barley sown	Winter begins Snow on mountains	Coldest month Hail and snow (Josh. 10:11)	Weather gradually warmer	Thunder and hail frequent Almond tree blossoms	Intercalary Month

Note 2	Hence the Jewish calendar contains a 13th month, Veadar or Adar Sheni, introduced 7 times every 19 years, to render the average length of the year nearly correct, and to keep the seasons in the proper months.
Note 3	The Jewish day begins at sunset of the previous day.

Jerusalem for construction of the booths (Neh. 8:13-18). Every Israelite was to live for seven days in these during the festival, in commemoration of when their fathers lived in such booths after their exodus from Egypt (Lev. 23:40; Neh. 8:15). The dedication of Solomon's temple took place at the feast (1 Kings 8:2).

After the return from exile, Ezra read the law and led the people in acts of penitence during this feast (Neh. 8:13–9:3). Later, Josephus referred to it as the holiest and greatest of the Hebrew feasts. Later additions to the ritual included a libation of water drawn from the pool of Siloam (the probable background for Jesus' comments on "living water," John 7:37-39) and the lighting of huge menorahs (candelabra) at the Court of the Women (the probable background for Jesus' statement, "I am the light of the world," John 8:12 HCSB). The water and the "pillar of light" provided during the wilderness wandering (when the people dwelt in tabernacles) was temporary and in contrast to the continuing water and light claimed by Jesus during this feast which commemorated that wandering period.

Feast of Trumpets Modern *Rosh Hashanah* is traced back to the so-called "Feast of Trumpets," the sounding of the trumpets on the first day of the seventh month (Tishri) of the religious calendar year (Lev. 23:24; Num. 29:1). The trumpet referred to here was the *shophar*, a ram's horn. It was distinctive from the silver trumpets blown on the other new moons.

This day evolved into the second most holy day on the modern Jewish religious calendar. It begins the "ten days of awe" before the Day of Atonement. According to Lev. 23:24-27 the celebration consisted of the blowing of trumpets, a time of rest, and "an offering by fire." The text itself says nothing specifically about a New Year's Day, and the term itself (*rosh hashanah*) is found only one time in Scripture (Ezek. 40:1) where it refers to the 10th day. The postexilic assembly on the first day of the seventh month, when Ezra read the law, was not referred to as a feast day (Neh. 8:2-3). The fact that the OT contains two calendars—a civil and a religious one—further complicates our understanding of the origins of this holiday. Until modern times this day did not appear to be a major feast day.

Two feasts of postexilic origin are noted in Scripture—Purim and Hanukkah.

Purim Purim, commemorating the deliverance of the Jews from genocide through the efforts of Esther (Esther 9:16-32), derives its name from the "lot" (*pur*) which Haman planned to cast in order to decide when he should carry into effect the decree issued by the king for the extermination of the Jews (Esther 9:24). In the apocryphal book of 2 Maccabees (15:36), it is called the Day of Mordecai. It was celebrated on the fourteenth day of Adar (March) by those in villages and unwalled towns and on the 15th day by those in fortified cities (Esther 9:18-19). No mention of any religious observance is connected with the day; in later periods, the book of Esther was read in the synagogue on this day. It became a time for rejoicing and distribution of food and presents.

Hanukkah The other postexilic holiday was Hanukkah, a festival that began on the 25th day of Kislev (Dec.) and lasted eight days. Josephus referred to it as the Feast of Lights because a candle was lighted each successive day until a total of eight was reached. The festival commemorates the victories of Judas Maccabeus in 167 B.C. At that time, when temple worship was reinstated, after an interruption of three years, a celebration of eight days took place. The modern celebration does not greatly affect the routine duties of everyday life. This feast is referred to in John 10:22, where it is called the Feast of Dedication.

Two festivals occurred less often than once a year: the Sabbatical year and the Year of Jubilee.

Sabbatical Year Each seventh year Israel celebrated a sabbath year for its fields. This involved a rest for the land from all cultivation (Exod. 23:10,11; Lev. 25:2-7; Deut. 15:1-11; 31:10-13). Other names for this festival were sabbath of rest (Lev. 25:4), year of rest (Lev. 25:5), year of release (Deut. 15:9), and the seventh year (Deut. 15:9). The Sabbatical year, like the Year of Jubilee, began on the first day of the month Tishri. This observance is attested by 1 Maccabees 6:49,53 and Josephus. Laws governing this year of rest included the following: (1) the soil, vineyards, and olive orchards were to enjoy complete rest (Exod. 23:10-11: Lev. 25:4-5); (2) the spontaneous growth of the fields or trees (Isa. 37:30) was for the free use of the hireling, stranger, servants, and cattle (Exod. 23:10-11; Lev. 25:6-7), fruitful harvest was promised for the sixth year (Lev. 25:20-22); (3) debts were released for all persons, with the exception of foreigners (Deut. 15:1-4) (probably this law did not forbid voluntary payment of debts, no one was to oppress a poor man); (4) finally, at the Feast of Tabernacles during this year, the law was to be read to the people in solemn assembly (Deut. 31:10-13).

Jewish tradition interpreted 2 Chron. 36:21 to mean that the 70 years' captivity was intended to make up for not observing sabbatical years. After the captivity this Sabbatical Year was carefully observed.

Year of Jubilee This was also called the year of liberty (Ezek. 46:17). Its relation to the Sabbatical Year and the general directions for its observance are found in Lev. 25:8-16,23-55. Its bearing on lands dedicated to the Lord is given in Lev. 27:16-25.

After the span of seven sabbaths of years, or seven times seven years (49 years), the trumpet was to sound throughout the land; and the Year of Jubilee was to be announced (Lev. 25:8-9).

The law states three respects in which the Jubilee Year was to be observed: rest for the soil—no sowing, reaping, or gathering from the vine (Lev. 25:11); reversion of landed property (Lev. 25:10-34; 27:16-24)—all property in fields and houses located in villages or unwalled towns, which the owner had been forced to sell through poverty and which had not been redeemed, was to revert without payment to its original owner or his lawful heirs (exceptions noted in Lev. 25:29-30; 27:17-21); and redemption of slaves—every Israelite, who through poverty had sold himself to another Israelite or to a foreigner settled in the land, if he had not been able to redeem himself or had not been redeemed by a kinsman, was to go free with his children (Lev. 25:39-41).

It appears that the Year of Jubilee was a time of such complete remission of all debts that it became a season of celebration of freedom and grace. In this year oppression was to cease, and every member of the covenant family was to find joy and satisfaction in the Lord of the covenant. God had redeemed His people from bondage in Egypt (Lev. 25:42), and none of them was again to be reduced to the status of a perennial slave. God's child was not to be oppressed (Lev. 25:43,46); and poverty could not, even at its worst, reduce an Israelite to a status less than that of a hired servant, a wage earner, and then only until the Year of Jubilee (Lev. 25:40).

After the institution of the Year of Jubilee laws (Lev. 25:8-34), the year is mentioned again in Num. 36:4. No reference to the celebration of this festival is found in Scripture apart from the idealistic anticipation of Ezek. 46:17, but the influence of such laws illuminate such passages as the conduct of Naboth and Ahab in 1 Kings 21:3-29; and the prophetic rebukes found in Isa. 5:8 and Mic. 2:2.   *Larry Walker*

FESTUS (Fĕs´ tŭs) Successor of Felix as procurator of Judea (Acts 24:27); assumed this office at Nero's appointment in A.D. 60. He held it until his death in A.D. 62. Paul the apostle appealed to Porcius Festus for the opportunity of being tried before Caesar, and Festus granted that request. See *Paul; Herod; Rome and the Roman Empire.*

FETTER Translation of several Hebrew and Greek terms referring to something that constrains, especially a shackle for the foot. Fetters were made of wood, bronze (Judg. 16:21; 2 Chron. 33:11), or iron (Ps. 149:8). Fetters worn on the feet were often joined by a rope or chain to hobble the prisoner (Mark 5:4). Fetters were painful to the feet (Ps. 105:18). Paul claimed that though he wore fetters, the word of God was not fettered (2 Tim. 2:9 REB, RSV).

FEVER Elevated body temperature or disease accompanied by such symptoms. The "burning ague" (Lev. 26:16) is an acute fever marked by regular periods of fever, sweating, and then chills. Fever accompanying "consumption" or "wasting disease" (Deut. 28:22 REB) could refer to any number of diseases: malaria, typhoid, typhus, dysentery, chronic diarrhea, or cholera. The "extreme burning" of Deut. 28:22 is understood by most modern translations as a reference to the weather ("fiery heat" RSV, NASB; "scorching wind" TEV) rather than to a fever. Jesus healed two persons afflicted with fevers—Peter's mother-in-law (Matt. 8:14-15; Mark 1:30-31; Luke 4:38-39) and an official's son (John 4:52). In Luke the healing was portrayed as an exorcism. In Acts 28:8 Paul healed Publius's father of a fever and dysentery ("bloody flux" KJV). See *Diseases.*

FIELD Unenclosed land. In the Hebrew definition of field, both the use of land (pasture, Gen. 29:2; 31:4; cropland, Gen. 37:7; 47:24; hunting ground, Gen. 27:3,5) and the terrain (land, Num. 21:20, literal translation, "field of Moab";

F

Judg. 9:32,36) were insignificant. The crucial distinction is between what is enclosed and what is open. A field may be contrasted with a tent (Num. 19:14,16), a camp (Lev. 14:3,7), vineyards which were customarily enclosed (Exod. 22:5; Lev. 25:3-4), or with a walled city (Lev. 14:53; Deut. 28:3,16). Villages without walls were regarded as fields (Lev. 25:31). Fields were likewise distinguished from barren wasteland (Ezek. 33:27). Fields were marked with landmarks (Deut. 19:14).

The NRSV translated the Hebrew term *shedemah*, one of the words generally translated "field," as "vineyard" at Deut. 32:32. The REB rendered the term differently each place it was used (terraces, Deut. 32:32; slope, 2 Kings 23:4; vineyard, Isa. 16:8; field, Jer. 31:40; orchards, Hab. 3:17).

FIELD OF BLOOD See *Akeldama*.

FIERY SERPENT God used snakes of fiery appearance or burning bite to teach His people. The Hebrew word for burning or fiery is the same as for seraphim in Isa. 6 but refers to different kinds of creatures. To punish the Israelites for complaining about their lot in the wilderness, God sent fiery serpents among them. As a result, many died. The serpents were natural residents of the wilderness (Deut. 8:15). Subsequently, God directed Moses to make a representation of a fiery serpent and place it on a pole. The brass serpent made by Moses became the means of healing for those that had been bitten by the fiery serpents but had not died. Jesus used this to point to His own fate of being lifted up on a cross (John 3:14; cp. 12:32). See *Moses; Numbers*.

Isaiah used the fear of snakes to warn complacent Philistines that God would raise up a more fearful enemy who could be compared only to a serpent (*saraph*) which flew or darted (Isa. 14:29 NIV; cp. 30:6).

FIG, FIG TREE Important fruit and tree of the Holy Land. Adam and Eve used leaves from the plant to make clothing (Gen. 3:7). Jesus cursed a fig tree because it was without fruit (Mark 11:13-14,20-21). See *Plants*.

FIGURED STONE Idol of carved stone (NIV) in contrast to one of molten metal, associated with Canaanite worship (Lev. 26:1; Num. 33:52), according to modern translations. KJV reads, "image of stone" and "pictures." The same

Hebrew term is used in Ezek. 8:12 for idolatrous shrines decorated with base reliefs of gods in the form of animals (8:10; prohibited in Deut. 4:16-18). Various identifications of the animals have been suggested, beasts similar to the lions and serpent-dragons of the "Ishtar Gate" in Babylon, animals similar to those serving as mounts for the gods in stone carvings at Maltaya, Egyptian mortuary deities, and totem animals.

FIGUREHEAD Emblem on the prow of a ship (Acts 28:11 NIV, NRSV, NASB). The figure ("sign" KJV) in Acts is the Twin Brothers Castor and Pollux, sons of Zeus and Leda, identified with the constellation Gemini. Sight of the constellation was a good omen in bad weather. Thus the figurehead was something of a good luck charm.

FILIGREE Modern translation of ornamental work, especially of fine metal wire. KJV reads, "ouches"; REB, "rosettes." Gold filigree was used in the settings of precious stones (Exod. 28:11,20; 39:6,13) and as clasps (Exod. 28:13,25; 39:16,18) for clothing or jewelry. The design in Exodus was likely a rosette or simple floral pattern.

FILLETS Either metal bands binding the tops of pillars used in construction of the tabernacle (Exod. 36:38; 38:10-12,17,19) or else rods connecting the pillars to one another (TEV). Jeremiah 52:21 uses a different Hebrew word to refer to a measuring line used to measure the circumference of a pillar.

FINANCIAL PLANNING The Bible provides examples of both effective and ineffective financial planning in the face of economic adversity. Examples of good financial planning include Joseph's preparation for famine in Egypt (Gen. 41:34-36), the servants who wisely invested their master's money (Luke 19:13-19) and the Corinthian believers who laid aside money to help others (1 Cor. 16:1-2; cp. 2 Cor. 9:1-5). Proverbs 27:23-27 counsels a shepherd to know well the condition of his flocks so that they will provide for him in the future. Diversification of investments is advised in Ecclesiastes 11:2.

Poor financial planning can be seen in the man who built bigger barns without thought of his impending death (Luke 12:16-21), the man who started to build a tower without the money to complete it (Luke 14:28-30) and the servant who refused to invest his master's money (Luke 19:20-21).

The Bible recognizes that having sound plans helps ensure a successful venture (Prov. 6:6-8; 21:5; 27:23-27; 30:25; Isa. 32:8; 2 Cor. 9:5). A key element in planning is the wise counsel of others (Prov. 13:18; 20:18), especially God, who causes plans to succeed or fail (Ps. 32:8; Prov. 3:6; 16:1-4, 9; Isa. 29:15).   *Paul H. Wright*

FINANCIAL RESPONSIBILITY Two maxims underlie the Bible's principles of financial responsibility: the earth and its resources belong to God (Lev. 25:23; Job 41:11; Pss. 24:1; 89:11; Hag. 2:8), and they have been entrusted to people to use wisely (Gen. 1:29-30; 9:1-4). The overall message of the Bible regarding finances is one of personal thrift combined with generosity toward others. The Bible places a high value on saving money to provide for oneself and others in times of need (Gen. 41:1-57; Prov. 6:6-8; 21:20; Eccles. 11:2; Luke 12:16-21; 1 Cor. 16:2). Because God blesses those who give to others (Deut. 15:10; Ps. 112:5; Prov. 11:25; 22:9; Mal. 3:10; 2 Cor. 9:6-12), the willingness to give generously (Matt. 25:31-46; 2 Cor. 8:3) and without thought of return (Deut. 15:11; 23:19; Ps. 15:5; Matt. 5:42; Luke 6:34; Rom. 11:35) is considered a mark of financial responsibility. Those who save to provide only for themselves, or are unable to save because of extravagant spending, are held to be foolish (Job 20:20-22; Prov. 21:20).

Other marks of financial responsibility include careful financial planning (Prov. 27:23-27), hard work (Prov. 28:19; Eph. 4:28; 2 Thess. 3:10; cp. Prov. 24:33-34), diversification of investments (Eccles. 11:2), paying debts when they become due (Prov. 3:27-28), providing for one's family (1 Tim. 5:8), and leaving an inheritance to one's children (Num. 27:7-11; Prov. 13:22; cp. Ruth 4:6; Eccles. 5:13-14).

Jesus' stewardship parables speak of financial responsibility as a precursor of greater areas of responsibility in the kingdom of God (Matt. 25:14-30; Luke 16:1-13; 19:11-27).
          Paul H. Wright

FINERY Modern translation of Hebrew term for the luxuriousness of the jewelry and clothing worn by the society women of Jerusalem (Isa. 3:18). KJV reads "bravery"; NASB, "beauty." The Hebrew word describes the beauty or glory of Aaron's priestly clothes (Exod. 28:2), the glory of God's house (Isa. 60:7), battlefield honor (Judg. 4:9), and the pompous (NASB) pride (NIV) of the Assyrian king (Isa. 10:12). Thus finery in itself is not bad, but prideful human attitudes concerning it soon became sinful. See *Fashion*.

FINGER OF GOD Picturesque expression of God at work. The finger of God writing the Ten Commandments illustrated God's giving the law without any mediation (Exod. 31:18; Deut. 9:10). Elsewhere the finger of God suggests God's power to bring plagues on Egypt (Exod. 8:19) and in making the heavens (Ps. 8:3). Jesus' statement, "If I drive out demons by the finger of God, then the kingdom of God has come to you" (Luke 11:20 HCSB) ,means that since Jesus cast out demons by the power of God, God's rule had become a reality among His hearers.

FINING POT KJV term for a crucible (NRSV, NIV) or smelting pot (REB), a vessel used to heat metal to a high temperature as part of the refining process (Prov. 17:3; 27:21). See *Crucible*.

FIR TREE KJV term for a tree most often identified with the pine (NIV, REB, TEV). Others have identified the tree with the juniper (NASB at Isa. 41:19 and 60:13 only) or cypress (NRSV, NASB elsewhere). See *Plants*.

FIRE The word "fire" in our English Bibles normally translates the Hebrew word *esh* in the OT and the Greek word *pur* (the root from which such English terms as "pyromaniac" and "pure" are derived) in the NT. Both terms signify the physical manifestations of burning: heat, light, and flame. Ancient peoples kindled fire either by rapidly rubbing dry pieces of wood together creating enough fiction to ignite dry vegetation or by striking flint rocks thus creating sparks (cp. 2 Macc.10:3). Normally, fires were maintained and perpetuated to avoid the need for kindling. Abraham, for example, apparently carried a torch with him on his way to sacrifice Isaac in order to prevent having to kindle one at the altar (Gen. 22:6-7).

Throughout both the OT and NT, fire functions as a significant theological symbol. It is frequently associated with such important concepts as God's presence, divine judgment, and purification. In fact, in the OT, fire served as the primary means by which God manifested His presence and exercised judgment. Because of the sacrificial system, fire was an important aspect of early Israelite worship; it was the means by which animal sacrifices were offered up to God as a "pleasing aroma" (Gen. 1:8; Exod. 29:18,25,41).

The first time God appeared to a human in Scripture, He assumed the form of a smoking firepot and a flaming torch (Gen. 15:17). Similarly, God appeared to Moses as a fiery bush when He first revealed His covenant name (Exod. 3:2), and He spoke from the midst of a fire on top of Mount Sinai when He gave the Ten Commandments to Israel (Exod. 19:8; 24:17; Deut. 4:11-15). God also led the Israelites through the desert by means of a pillar of cloud by day and a pillar of fire by night (Deut. 1:32-33).

God often communicates the protective nature of His presence by means of fire as well. The Prophet Elisha was surrounded by an angelic army of flaming horses and chariots when the king of Aram tried to attack him (2 Kings 6:17). Zechariah foresaw a future Jerusalem without the usual protective outer wall because God told the prophet "For I ... will be a wall of fire around her" (Zech. 2:5 NASB).

The NT continues to portray God's presence in the form of fire especially in the person of the Holy Spirit. The outpouring of the Spirit at Pentecost was signaled by the appearance of fire on each believer's head (Acts 2:3). In his first letter to the Thessalonians, Paul warns believers not to "quench the Holy Spirit" (1 Thess. 5:19 NASB). The word "quench" normally refers to extinguishing a fire. Since God so frequently indicated His presence by means of fire, fire became a metaphor for God emphasizing both His holiness and His retributive justice (Deut. 4:24; Heb. 12:29).

In addition to symbolizing God's presence among His people, fire serves as an instrument of divine judgment. The destruction of Sodom and Gomorrah is the first example of God's use of fire to judge and destroy wickedness (Gen. 19:24). Later in Scripture, the destruction of Sodom and Gomorrah became a type indicating the severity of future judgment (Deut. 29:22-23; Isa. 13:19; Lam. 4:6; Luke 17:29; 2 Pet. 2:6; Jude 7). A special fire called the "fire of the LORD" consumed the outer edges of Israel's camp in the wilderness when the Israelites complained, and the same supernatural fire fell from heaven and consumed the soldiers whom Ahaziah had sent to seize Elijah the prophet (2 Kings 1:12). On numerous occasions Jesus described the eternal punishment of the damned in terms of an unquenchable fire (Matt. 5:22; 13:40; 18:8; 25:41; Mark 9:48; John 15:6).

Even in contexts where divine judgment is not explicitly mentioned, fire was a preferred means of destruction, especially for things associated with extreme defilement or evil. For example, the city of Jericho, along with certain other Canaanite cities, was completely burned—all the inhabitants, animals, and goods—as an act of devotion to God and as a means of purging the land from the abominable practices of the Canaanites (Josh. 6:24). Idols were also frequently destroyed with fire (Deut. 7:5; 9:2; 12:3; 2 Kings 19:18).

Certainly, fire played an important role in day-to-day domestic activities such as cooking (Exod. 12:8), warming homes (Isa. 44:16), and purifying metals (Jer. 6:29). The preponderance of biblical references to fire, however, express its power as a symbol of divine presence, divine protection, and divine judgment. See *Baptism of Fire; Molech.*   *Kevin J. Youngblood*

FIREPAN Utensil made of bronze (Exod. 27:3) or gold (1 Kings 7:50, KJV, "censers") used to carry live coals from the altar of burnt offering (Exod. 27:3; 38:3), as censers for burning incense (Num. 16:6,17), and as trays for collecting the burnt wicks from the tabernacle lamps (Exod. 25:38; 37:23; the "snuffdishes" of the KJV).

FIRKIN Unit of liquid measure (John 2:6). Firkin is an archaic English word that was used to translate a Greek term referring to a measure of approximately 10 gallons. See *Weights and Measures.*

FIRMAMENT Great vault or expanse of sky that separates the upper and lower waters. God created the firmament on the second day to separate the "waters from the waters" (Gen. 1:6-7). One use of "heaven" in the Bible is to refer to the ceiling or canopy of the earth. Heaven in this sense is also referred to as the firmament or sky (Gen. 1:8). Into this expanse God set the sun, moon, and stars (Gen. 1:14-18).

In Gen. 1:6 the firmament separates the mass of waters and divides them into layers. The fir-

F

mament is mentioned 17 times (KJV) in Genesis, the Psalms, Ezekiel, and Daniel. It is described as bright, transparent like crystal, revealing the handiwork of God, and signifying His seat of power (Pss. 19:1; 150:1; Ezek. 1:22; Dan. 12:3).

Some scholars argue that the Hebrews had a primitive cosmology where the firmament was visualized as a rigid, solid dome—a celestial dam (Gen. 7:11; 2 Sam. 22:8; Job 26:8; 37:18; Prov. 8:28; Mal. 3:10). Above the firmament flowed the heavenly waters. The firmament was punctuated by grilles or sluices, "windows of heaven" through which rain was released. Others argue that such interpretations are unsound, in that they confuse poetic and figurative language with literal prose. Others say Israel's inspired writers used language of experience and appearance rather than language of precise scientific description. See *Heaven*.   *Paul Robertson*

FIRST AND LAST See *Alpha and Omega*.

FIRSTBORN First son born to a couple and required to be specially dedicated to God. The firstborn son of newly married people was believed to represent the prime of human vigor (Gen. 49:3; Ps. 78:51). In memory of the death of Egypt's firstborn and the preservation of the firstborn of Israel, all the firstborn of Israel, both of man and beast, belonged to Yahweh (Exod. 13:2,15; cp. 12:12-16). This meant that the people of Israel attached unusual value to the eldest son and assigned special privileges and responsibilities to him. He was presented to the Lord when he was a month old. Since he belonged to the Lord, it was necessary for the father to buy back the child from the priest at a redemption price not to exceed five shekels (Num. 18:16). The husband of several wives would have to redeem the firstborn of each.

The birthright of a firstborn included a double portion of the estate and leadership of the family. As head of the house after his father's death, the eldest son customarily cared for his mother until her death, and he also provided for his sisters until their marriage. The firstborn might sell his rights as Esau did (Gen. 25:29-34) or forfeit them for misconduct as Reuben did because of incest (Gen. 35:22; 49:3-4).

The firstborn of a clean animal was brought into the sanctuary on the eighth day after birth (Exod. 22:29-30). If it were without blemish, it was sacrificed (Deut. 15:19; Num. 18:17). If it

had a blemish, the priest to whom it was given could eat it as common food outside Jerusalem (Deut. 15:21-23), or it could be eaten at home by its owner. Apparently the firstborn of a clean animal was not to be used for any work since it belonged to the Lord (Deut. 15:19).

The firstborn of an unclean animal had to be redeemed by an estimation of the priest, with the addition of one-fifth (Lev. 27:27; Num. 18:15). According to Exod. 13:13; 34:20, the firstborn of an ass was either ransomed by a sheep or lamb, or its neck had to be broken.

Figuratively, Israel was God's "firstborn" (Exod. 4:22; Jer. 31:9) and enjoyed priority status. God compared His relationship to Israel with the relationship of a father and his firstborn son. Within Israel, the tribe of Levi represented the firstborn of the nation in its worship ceremony (Num. 3:40-41; 8:18).

Christ is the "firstborn" of the Father (Heb. 1:6 NIV) by having preeminent position over others in relation to Him. He is also described as "firstborn among many brothers" (Rom. 8:29 HCSB) and "firstborn over all creation" (Col. 1:15 HCSB). Paul (Col. 1:18) and John (Rev. 1:5) refer to Christ as "firstborn from the dead"—the first to rise bodily from the grave and not die again.

Hebrews 12:23 refers to the "assembly of the firstborn whose names have been written in heaven" (HCSB). Christian believers, united with and as joint heirs with Christ, enjoy the status of "firstborn" in God's household. See *Family*.   *Larry Walker*

FIRSTFRUITS Choice examples of a crop harvested first and dedicated to God. In accordance with Mosaic law, individual Israelites brought to the house of the Lord "the choice (that is, "the best") first fruits of your soil" (Exod. 23:19 NASB; 34:26), including grain, wine, and oil, which were used—except for the grain (Lev. 2:14-16)—for the support of the priests (Num. 18:12; Deut. 18:4). According to Deut. 26:1-11, the offering was brought in a basket to the sanctuary for presentation. The book of Proverbs promises prosperity to those who honor the Lord with the firstfruits (Prov. 3:9-10).

According to Lev. 23:9-14, the first sheaf of the new crop of barley was presented as a wave offering before the Lord. This took place on the day after the Passover Sabbath and was a public acknowledgment that all came from God and belonged to Him (Num. 28:26; cp. Exod. 23:16; 34:22). Not only were the Israelites to be mindful that the land of Canaan was the Lord's possession and that they had only the rights of tenants (Lev. 25:23), but they were also to be aware that the fertility of Canaan's soil was not due to one of the Baals but rather to the Lord's gift of grace.

Israel was described as God's "firstfruits" (Jer. 2:3). Christ in His resurrection is described as the "firstfruits" of them that slept (1 Cor. 15:20,23). The Holy Spirit is spoken of as a "firstfruits" (Rom. 8:23), and believers are also spoken of as "a kind of firstfruits" (James 1:18). The saved remnant within Israel is described as "firstfruits" (Rom. 11:16), as are the 144,000 of the tribulation period (Rev. 14:4). The first converts of an area were designated "firstfruits" (Rom. 16:5; 1 Cor. 16:15). In each case the emphasis was on special dedication and blessing. See *Festivals.*   *Larry Walker*

FIRST RAIN KJV term at Deut. 11:14 for the early rain. See *Rain.*

FISH, FISHING Animals living in water and breathing through gills; the profession and/or practice of catching fish to supply a family or society's need for food. Methods of catching fish included angling with a hook (Job 41:1), harpoons and spears (Job 41:7), use of dragnets (John 21:8), and thrown hand nets (Matt. 4:18). **Old Testament** Fish are mentioned often but not by the different kinds. Fish were a favorite food and a chief source of protein (Num. 11:5; Neh. 13:16). The law regarded all fish with fins and scales as clean. Water animals that did not have fins and scales were unclean (Lev. 11:9-12).

Fish abounded in the inland waters of Palestine as well as in the Mediterranean. Fish caught in the Mediterranean were brought to ports such as Tyre and Sidon. The Sea of Chinnereth or Galilee was also a fishing center. The fish were preserved in salt and brought to Jerusalem where they were sold at a specially named "Fish Gate" in the city. The strong currents of the Jordan River carried many fish to the Dead Sea where they died (Ezek. 47:7-11).

References to fishing as an occupation are rare in the OT because, for the most part, in OT times the Mediterranean coast was controlled by the Philistines and Phoenicians. The Israelites depended largely on foreign trade for their fish (Neh. 13:16). Two OT texts (Song 7:4 KJV; Isa. 19:10 KJV) speak of fishpools and fishponds, possibly an indication of commercially raised fish or of fish farming.

The most famous OT fish was the great fish of the book of Jonah (1:17), one that God prepared especially for the occasion and one whose species the OT does not indicate.

New Testament During NT times commercial fishing businesses were conducted on the Sea of Galilee by fishermen organized in guilds (Luke 5:7,11). Fishermen were hard workers, crude in manner, rough in speech and in their treatment of others (John 18:10). Fishermen owned their ships, took hirelings into their service, and sometimes joined to form companies (Mark 1:20; Luke 5:7).

Fish provided food for the common people (Matt. 14:17; 15:34). The risen Lord ate fish with the disciples in Jerusalem (Luke 24:42) and by the Sea of Galilee (John 21:13). The primary method of preparing fish was broiling (John 21:9). The most famous NT fish was the one used to pay the temple tax for Jesus and Peter (Matt. 17:27).

Theological The Bible contains numerous figurative uses of fish and fishing. Human helplessness is compared to fish taken in a net (Eccles. 9:12; Hab. 1:14). Fish caught in a net symbolized God's judgment (Ps. 66:11; Ezek. 32:3). Jesus mentioned fishing when He called disciples to be witnesses (Matt. 4:18-19). Jesus compared the kingdom of heaven to a net thrown into the sea and loaded with fish of many varieties (Matt. 13:47).

In early Christian churches the Greek word for fish (*ichthus*) came to be interpreted as a

A building stone from Ephesus carved with the figure of a fish.

cipher for Jesus. The first letter of each of the Greek words for "Jesus Christ, Son of God, Savior" spell *ichthus.* We do not know when this cipher was first used; but once the identification was made, the fish became a standard Christian symbol.   *Gary Hardin*

FISH GATE A north gate of the second quarter of Jerusalem (Zeph. 1:10) mentioned in connection with fortifications built by Manasseh (2 Chron. 33:14). The gate was rebuilt during the time of Nehemiah (Neh. 3:3; 12:39). The name is perhaps derived from the proximity of the gate to the fish market (cp. Neh. 13:16-22).

FISHHOOK Curved or bent device of bone or iron used in biblical times for catching or holding fish (Job 41:1-2; Isa. 19:8 KJV, "angle"; Matt. 17:27). Habakkuk described God's people as helpless fish who would be captured by hooks (1:15) and nets. Amos 4:2 refers to the practice of ancient conquerors of leading captives with hooks through their lips. Such was the fate of Manasseh according to one interpretation (2 Chron. 33:11 NASB, NIV, TEV).

FITCHES KJV term for two different plants. The first is black cummin (Isa. 28:25,27). Ezekiel 4:9 refers to either spelt, an inferior type of wheat (NASB, NIV, TEV), or else vetches (REB), a plant of the bean family. See *Plants.*

FLAG KJV term for a water plant generally translated as "reed" (Exod. 2:3,5; Job 8:11) or rush (Isa. 19:6) by modern translations. See *Plants.*

FLAGON Large, two-handled jar for storing wine (Isa. 22:24 KJV; Exod. 25:29; 37:16 REB, NRSV). The Hebrew term *ashishah* translated as "flagon" by the KJV (2 Sam. 6:19; 1 Chron. 16:3; Song 2:5; Hos. 3:1) refers to a cake of raisins, often used as offerings to idols.

FLAGSTAFF Pole on which a standard is displayed (Isa. 30:17). The same Hebrew term is translated "mast" elsewhere (Isa. 33:23; Ezek. 27:5). The REB used the translation "mast" at Isa. 30:17 as well. The NASB preferred the translation "flag" for this text though the margin note, pole, can account for all occurrences of the term.

FLASK General term translators use to describe vessels. It does not appear in KJV. The term refers to a small container of perfume oil in 2 Kings

Statue of an aged woman holding a flagon of wine in her lap.

9:1-3. The same Hebrew word appears in 1 Sam. 10:1. At Jer. 19:1 (RSV) refers to an earthenware water jar or jug. The vessel perhaps had a narrow neck making it impossible to mend (19:10). This Hebrew word recurs in 1 Kings 14:3. At Matt. 25:4 small containers for lamp oil are meant. The Greek term appears only here in the NT. Luke 7:37 refers to a small alabaster container such as had been used for expensive perfumes for thousands of years. See Cruse.

FLAX Plant *(Linum usitatissimumro)* used to make linen. The fibers of the flax stem are the most ancient of textile fibers. Flax was cultivated by the Egyptians before the exodus (Exod. 9:31) and by the Canaanites before the conquest (Josh. 2:6). The making of linen was a common household chore in biblical times. Proverbs 31:13 described the virtuous wife as one who sought wool and flax. The linen making process involved pulling and drying flax stalks (often on rooftops, Josh. 2:6). The stalks were deseeded, soaked until the fibers were loosened (retted), and redried. A hackle, a comb or board with long teeth, was used to separate the outer fibers from the inner core. Further combing (carding) cleansed and ordered the fibers so that they might be spun into thread for weaving (Isa. 19:9). The remaining short, tangled fibers (the

Fishing boats on the Nile River in Egypt.

tow) were used to weave a course fabric or make twine (Judg. 16:9; Isa. 1:31).

Flax fibers were also used to make torches and lamp wicks. Isaiah 43:17 pictures armies as a wick which the Lord would extinguish. In Isa. 42:3 the Servant of the Lord is one who will not quench a dimly burning wick. The picture suggests one who will help and comfort the powerless rather than bring harsh judgment. Matthew understood Jesus' ministry as the fulfillment of this Scripture (Matt. 12:20). See *Linen.*

FLEA See *Insects.*

FLEET Group of ships. Solomon built a fleet of ships at Ezion-geber with the help of Hiram of Tyre (1 Kings 9:26-27; 10:11,22). KJV translated "fleet" as "navy" or "navy of ships." Solomon's fleet was used for commercial rather than military purposes. See *Ezion-geber; Ships, Sailors, and Navigation.*

FLESH The term "flesh," while prevalent in older English translations of the Bible such as the KJV and ASV (1901), has largely been replaced by numerous other terms in most modern English translations. Undoubtedly this shift is due to the wide variety of nuances the word "flesh" can have in the biblical context that are better rendered by other words in a modern setting. Nonetheless, such seemingly unrelated terms as "skin," "food," "meat," "relatives," "humankind," and "sinful nature" in modern English translations often render the same single word in the original languages: *basar* in Hebrew and *sarx* in Greek. Due to the obvious flexibility of the word, each of its primary meanings is listed below followed by an explanation and biblical examples.

"Flesh" as a Designation for the Body or Parts of the Body "Flesh" frequently refers to the skin or the body—all the material that covers the skeleton of humans and animals. For example, "flesh" clearly refers to the body as a whole in Lev. 14:9 where cleansed lepers are commanded to bathe "their flesh" in water. The psalmist also uses "flesh" in reference to his whole body when he says "my flesh trembles in fear of you" (Ps. 119:120 NIV).

While the term predominately refers to the human body, it can also refer to the bodies of animals. For example, when Joseph explains Pharaoh's dream concerning the seven fat cows

and the seven lean cows, he consistently refers to the lean cows as "thin of flesh," a Hebrew idiom meaning "skinny" (Gen. 41:1-3). Paul distinguishes between various kinds of animal "flesh" or body types when he explains the physical resurrection to the Corinthian Christians (1 Cor. 15:39). Since "flesh" can be used of animal bodies, it can, by extension, refer to meat or food as well (Exod. 21:28; Isa. 22:13).

The term can also, however, refer to part of the body. For example, the Bible often uses "flesh" as a euphemism for the male genitals. This use of the term is most common in contexts related to the covenant sign of circumcision (Gen. 17:11,14; Rom. 2:28; Gal. 6:13).

Occasionally, "flesh" is used in contrast to the term "soul" (*nephesh* in Hebrew) thus distinguishing a person's physical existence from his spiritual existence (Isa. 10:18; Pss. 63:1; 84:3). Similarly, "flesh" is used in contrast to the word for heart/mind (*leb* in Hebrew) to distinguish the body from the mind, will, and emotions (Ps. 16:9; Prov. 14:30).

Flesh as a Designation for Mankind or Blood Relatives Scripture occasionally uses the term "flesh" as a general designation for all living things. In Gen. 6:17, God warned that the flood He was about to bring upon the earth would destroy "all flesh." This included animals and human beings alike. More narrowly, "flesh" can be used as a designation for all humanity. The famous prophecy in Joel 2:28-32 which is quoted and fulfilled in Acts 2:17-21 promised that God's Spirit would be poured out on "all flesh." Clearly, in this case, only humanity is in view.

In an even narrower sense, "flesh" can refer to one's relatives. Leviticus 18:6, for example, employs the terms in prohibitions against sexual intimacy with close family members.

The use of the term "flesh" as a designation for humanity suggests an important contrast between man and God. Man is "flesh," but God is "spirit"; man is finite and mortal, but God is infinite and immortal. Numerous passages stress this contrast by pairing the word "flesh" with the word "spirit" (Gen. 6:3; Isa. 31:3; Matt. 26:41). The word "flesh" by itself, however, can also stress the weakness and sinfulness of humanity in contrast to the power and holiness of God (Pss. 56:5; 78:39; 2 Chron. 32:8).

Flesh as a Designation for the Sinful Nature In the NT, especially in the Pauline epistles, the term "flesh" takes on a specialized theological meaning. Paul consistently uses the term "flesh" in reference to the fallen human nature that is incapable of conforming to God's holy expectations (Rom. 7:5,18; 8:3-9; Gal. 3:3). In this sense, "flesh" is unaided human effort—mere human strength without the power of the Holy Spirit. It is this "flesh" that offers sin a foothold in a believer's life (Rom. 8:3-4,9; Gal. 3:3; 5:16-17). Paul explains that the flesh and the Spirit are in conflict with each other within believers necessitating the believer's denial of sinful desires and cooperation with the Holy Spirit (Rom. 8:13; Gal. 2:19-21; Col. 3:5).

Unfortunately, many have misunderstood Paul's specialized use of the term "flesh" and have taken the passages mentioned above to mean that our bodies are inherently evil. Nothing, however, could have been further from Paul's mind. Paul taught that Christ Himself came in the flesh and yet lived a sinless life (Rom. 1:3; 1 Tim. 3:16). Furthermore, the body is God's creation and therefore is good when it is devoted to God in holy service (1 Tim 4:4). In fact, Paul referred to the believer's body as the temple of the Holy Spirit indicating its sacred nature and purpose (1 Cor. 6:19-20). The notion that the physical body is inherently evil and therefore an obstacle to spirituality came not from Paul but from Plato. See *Anthropology; Body.*   *Kevin J. Youngblood*

FLESH AND SPIRIT Terms noticeably used in tandem in the NT to contrast diametrically opposed lifestyles. The term "flesh" is often ascribed the connotation of an ungodly lifestyle of selfishness and sensual self-gratification. The term "spirit" signifies the opposite characteristics. One who walks by the Spirit lives with a conspicuous God consciousness that directs his or her dispositions, attitudes, and actions.

This use of these terms is evident especially in Paul's writing. In Rom. 7 Paul spoke frankly about his constant struggle between the continuing power of his flesh and the sincere intentions of his will to live obediently to God. "For I do not do the good that I want to do, but I practice the evil that I do not want to do" (Rom. 7:19 HCSB). This battle is because of the "flesh" the believer battles even after salvation. Paul poses the question then, "Who will rescue me from this body of death?" (Rom. 7:24 HCSB). He answers with confidence, "I thank God through Jesus Christ our Lord! So then, with my mind I myself am a slave to the law of God, but with my flesh, to the law of sin" (Rom. 7:25 HCSB). Even though believers wrestle with the flesh, those who are in Jesus Christ are no longer under compulsion to live in a fleshly manner. In Gal. 5 Paul provides the most extensive treatment of this subject. He encourages Christians who indeed "live by the Spirit" also to "walk by the Spirit" so that they may avoid carrying "out the desire of the flesh." The admonition here as well as in other Pauline passages is for Christians not to live carnally. A carnal Christian is a believer who, although regenerate, persists in living a life ruled by fleshly desires (Rom. 8:7; 1 Cor. 3:1).

Other texts in the NT use the terms "flesh" and "spirit" to underscore this same struggle. John instructed believers not to behave in such a way as to fulfill the "lust of the flesh" (1 John 2:16 HCSB).

This contrast should not be pushed to mean that human, physical existence is evil. Literal human flesh was created "good." Some early Christian Gnostic groups perverted this concept and taught that anything related to physical existence should be considered evil in and of itself. This false dichotomy led some sects to become ascetic, depriving their physical bodies of proper food, sleep, and care in an attempt to purify them. Other groups came to the conclusion that what one did with the body was of no consequence spiritually, even acts of moral license.

Through the power and freedom of Christ, one must determine to live godly and not turn this freedom into "an opportunity for the flesh" (Gal. 5:13 HCSB). The goal is to demonstrate a life ruled by the constant presence of the Holy Spirit characterized by the traits of "love, joy, peace, patience, kindness, goodness, faith, gentleness, and self control" (Gal. 5:22-23 HCSB).

D. Cornett

FLESH HOOK Large fork used for handling large pieces of meat, especially at the sacrificial altar. Those in the tabernacle were of brass (Exod. 27:3; 38:3), those in the temple of bronze (2 Chron. 4:16) or gold (1 Chron. 28:17).

FLESHPOT Kettle used for cooking meat. The murmuring of the Israelites against Moses (Exod. 16:3) included the exaggerated claim that they customarily relaxed by the fleshpots in Egypt and had more than enough bread. In the ancient

F

Near East meat was not part of the common people's regular diet.

FLINT Three Hebrew terms which are applied loosely to any hard, compact rock or specifically to nearly opaque, cryptocrystalline varieties of quartz. Flint may be flaked to give a very sharp, hard edge. Flint tools, including scrapers, ax heads, knives (Exod. 4:25; Josh. 5:2-3 REB, NIV, NASB, NRSV, TEV), arrowheads, sickle blades, and other tools were used from the earliest prehistoric times.

The hardness of flint is proverbial. God's miraculous provision for the Israelites in the wilderness is pictured as water (Deut. 8:15; Ps. 114:8) or oil (Deut. 32:13) flowing from flinty rock. God protected the Prophet Ezekiel by making his forehead harder than flint (Ezek. 3:9). A face set like flint pictured the determination of the Servant of the Lord (Isa. 50:7; cp. Luke 9:51). Zechariah 7:12 pictures the people's unwillingness to repent as hearts of flint.

FLOAT KJV translation of two Hebrew terms (1 Kings 5:9; 2 Chron. 2:16) rendered raft by

modern speech translations. The pine and cedar logs for construction of the temple were lashed together to form rafts which were floated down the coast.

FLOCK Sheep and goats under the care of a shepherd (Gen. 30:31-32). God' people are sometimes described as sheep without a shepherd (Num. 27:17; Ezek. 34:5,8; Matt. 9:36; Mark 6:34), that is, in need of leaders who would rule them justly and nurture them spiritually. God's people can be described as a flock shepherded by God (Ps. 100:3; Jer. 23:3; Ezek. 34:31) or by Christ, "the great Shepherd of the sheep" (Heb. 13:20; cp. John 10:11; 1 Pet. 5:4).

The unity of all Christians is pictured by the image of one flock composed of many folds (John 10:16). Flocks can refer to individual congregations under the care of a pastor (1 Pet. 5:2-3).

Judgment is sometimes pictured as the sorting of a flock. In Ezek. 34 the fat, strong sheep (the oppressive leaders of Israel) are separated from the weak sheep that they victimized (34:16-17,20-21). In Matt. 25:32-46 sheep are

Shepherd with a flock of sheep.

separated from goats on the basis of concrete acts of love shown to the needy.

FLOGGING Punishment by repeated lashes or blows of a whip or rod(s). The OT recognized flogging as a form of punishment (Deut. 25:1-3) though limiting it to 40 blows so that the neighbor who was punished would not be degraded. Children were disciplined with rods (Prov. 23:13-14). Floggings were sometimes inflicted unjustly (Prov. 17:26; Isa. 53:5).

Jesus warned His disciples that they would face flogging (Matt. 10:17; beatings, Mark 13:9) in the synagogue. Paul had believers flogged in his days as a persecutor of the church (Acts 22:19-20). The apostles were flogged by order of the Sanhedrin (Acts 5:40). Paul received the "forty lashes minus one" at the hands of the synagogue five times (2 Cor. 11:24 HCSB). Paul was also beaten with rods three times (11:25), perhaps at the hands of Gentile officials as at Philippi (Acts 16:22-23).

FLOOD Genesis 6-9 tells the story of the flood that covered the whole earth, and of Noah, the man used by God to save the world of men and beasts.

The Events The deluge was brought on by sin. The first six verses of Gen. 6 speak of the "sons of God" having relations with the "daughters of men." Some have seen the sons of God as angelic (or demonic) beings, and thus the evil as demons cohabiting with humans. More likely, the sons of God were the sons of the godly line of Seth, and the daughters of men were women from the profane line of Cain. The evil then was the righteous being unequally yoked with unbelievers, thus stamping out the remnant on the earth, so that "the earth was corrupt in the sight of God, and the earth was filled with violence" (Gen. 6:11 NASB). Noah was apparently the only remnant left. "But Noah found favor in the eyes of the LORD" (Gen. 6:8). He was a man of faith, whose trust in God "condemned the world" (Heb. 11:7).

The Lord commanded Noah to construct an ark of "gofer wood." Into this ark went 14 ("by sevens") of all clean animals and two each of the unclean animals (Gen. 7:1-5). There were more of the clean animals since they would be needed for food and for sacrifice once the flood was over (8:20-22; 9:2-4). God then sent judgment in the form of rain, which fell on the earth for 40 days

(7:17) and prevailed for 150 days (7:24). Finally the ark settled on the mountains of Ararat. Noah sent out doves three times until the last one did not return. He then opened the ark, praised God, offered a sacrifice, and received God's covenant promise not to judge the world by water again (8:21-22).

The Issues Few texts have inspired more interest than this one. It has become the source for discussion about ethics (capital punishment), theology (the Noahic Covenant), and apologetics (evidence for the flood). Of the latter, several issues have been most prominent. The first has to do with the ark's remains. Over the last 30 years much interest has been focused on photographs which seem to depict a large wooden structure buried atop Mount Ararat in Turkey. It remains to be seen whether this will ever be resolved and whether it actually is the ark. Second, there is much discussion over evidence for the flood. New data pours in seemingly by the week. Not long ago scientists discovered the remnants of a city a hundred feet or more beneath the surface of the Black Sea. It appears that this sea was not always there or not always so expansive. This would be clear evidence of a flood in ancient times. The third issue is whether the flood was local or worldwide. Proponents of a local flood only, some of whom are evangelicals, stand in sometimes vocal opposition to those who believe the flood to have been universal. Both OT and NT texts seem clearly to teach that the flood was universal (Gen. 7:19-24; 2 Pet. 3:6). But that does not mean that any one way of arguing for a universal flood, such as the catastrophist approach, for instance, is the last word on the matter. Much work remains to be done. What can be said is that the scientific evidence for a flood, even for a universal flood, is strong and growing daily.   *Chad Brand*

FLOUR Fine-crushed and sifted grain used in making bread (Exod. 29:2; 1 Sam. 28:24), often translated as fine or choice flour. Typically meal, which was ground course from the whole kernels of grain together with the bran, was used to make bread (Lev. 2:16; 1 Kings 17:12). The firstfruits cereal offering was of course grain since it represented the common table fare. Most often cereal offerings were of fine flour (Lev. 2:1-2,4-5,7), ground from the inner kernels of wheat only, the best part of the grain (Deut. 32:14). Fine flour was a luxury item (Ezek.

16:13; Rev. 18:13) such as might be baked as bread for an honored guest (Gen. 18:6; 1 Sam. 28:24).

FLOWERS Colorful blooms containing a plant's reproductive organs. Flowers grew abundantly during springtime in Palestine. Flowers grew mostly in open fields, since flower gardens as we now know them were not cultivated. Flowers grew in crop fields and in groves of trees around houses. Numerous kinds of wild flowers could be found in the plains and mountains of Palestine. The words "flower" or "flowers" refer to colorful blossoms, towering plants, open flowers, and flourishing flowers. In Palestine the warm spring temperatures joined with the winter rains to produce beautiful, blooming plants and flowers.

Almond blossoms (Gen. 43:11; Exod. 25:33-34; 37:19-20; Num. 17:8; Eccles. 12:5). This tree, a member of the rose family, had beautiful pink blossoms that the Israelites used as models for engravers to adorn the cups of the golden lampstand.

Bulrush (Exod. 2:3; Job 8:11; Isa. 18:2; 35:7). Sometimes referred to as "flag," "papyrus" (NIV), "reed" (NASB), or "rush" (NEB). This tall, slender reedlike plant grew along the banks of the Nile River and provided the earliest known material for making paper and covering the frames of boats (Isa. 18:2).

Calamus leaves (Exod. 30:23; Song 4:14; Isa. 43:24; Jer. 6:20; Ezek. 27:19). The leaves from

A type of flour mill from the Roman period. The flour falls into the wooden box.

this plant were a sweet-smelling cane or ginger grass. The leaves, when crushed, gave a much relished ginger smell. It was apparently imported from India for use in worship (Jer. 6:20). Several Hebrew expressions lie behind "calamus." The basic Hebrew term *qaneh* means "cane." It is modified in Exod. 30:23 by the word for balsam,

An ancient flour mill in Capernaum.

apparently referring to sweet cane or *Cymbo-pogon.* A similar plant may be meant by *qaneh tob* in Jer. 6:20, *tob* meaning either "good" or "perfumed." Elsewhere, *qaneh* occurs without modification and may refer to different types of cane. For example, in 1 Kings 14:15 the giant reed *Arundo donax* may be meant (cp. Job 40:21; Isa. 19:6; 35:7).

Camphire flowers (sometimes referred to as Henna) (Song 1:14; 4:13; 7:11; see REB). The camphire was a small plant or shrub that bore beautiful cream-colored flowers that hung in clusters like grapes and were highly scented. It was used for orange dye.

Caperberry flowers (Eccles. 12:5 NASB). The caperberry was a prickly shrub that produced lovely flowers and small, edible berries as it grew in rocks and walls. It was supposed to stimulate sexual desires and powers. KJV, NRSV, NIV, TEV translate the Hebrew term as "desire" in Eccles. 12:5, but REB and NASB follow recent Hebrew dictionaries in translating it "caperberry" or "caper-buds."

Cockle flowers (Job 31:40). Purplish red flowers of a noxious weed called the "cockle" or "darnel" (*Lolium temulentum*). This plant grew abundantly in Palestinian grain fields. Its Hebrew name is spelled like the Hebrew word for "stink" and thus is translated "stinkweed" by NASB.

Crocus (Song 2:1; Isa. 35:1). Spring flowering herb with a long yellow floral tube tinged with purple specks or stripes. It is sometimes translated as rose. Technically, it was probably the asphodel (Isa. 35:2 REB).

Fitch (Isa. 28:25-27). KJV calls this flower the "fitch," but the better designation is probably the nutmeg flower. This flower was a member of the buttercup family and grew wildly in most Mediterranean lands. The plant was about two feet high and had bright blue flowers. The pods of the plant were used like pepper. Technically the plant is probably dill (NRSV, NASB, REB) or more precisely black cummin (*Nigella sativaro*). NIV translates "caraway." See *Fitches.*

Leek (Num. 11:5). Member of the lily family, a bulbous biennial plant with broad leaves. The bases of the leaves were eaten as food. The bulbs of this plant were used as seasoning. Israel relished the memory of leeks (*Allium porrumro*) from Egypt.

Lily (1 Kings 7:19,22,26; 2 Chron. 4:5; Song 2:1-2,16; 5:13; 6:2-3; 7:2; Hos. 14:5). The term "lily" covered a wide range of flowers. The most

Cyclamen is one of the flowers found in Israel. The flowers appear between December and early May, but there is a single region near Jericho where the plants flower in the autumn.

common was *Lilius candidum.* The lily mentioned in Song 5:13 refers to a rare variety of lily that had a bloom similar to a glowing flame. The "lily of the valley" (Song 2:1-2,16) is known as the Easter lily. The lily mentioned in Hos. 14:5 is more akin to an iris. The beautiful water lily or lotus was a favorite flower in Egypt and was used to decorate Solomon's temple (1 Kings 7:19,22,26; 2 Chron. 4:5). The "lilies of the field" (Matt. 6:28; Luke 12:27; HCSB, wildflowers) were probably numerous kinds of colorful spring flowers such as the crown anemone.

Mandrake (Gen. 30:14-16; Song 7:13). The mandrake, an herb of the nightshade family, had a rosette of large leaves and mauve flowers during winter and fragrant and round yellow fruit during spring. The mandrake grew in fields and rough ground. It was considered to give sexual powers and probably can be identified as *Atropa Mandragora,* often used for medicine in ancient times.

Mint (Matt. 23:23; Luke 11:42). Aromatic plant with hairy leaves and dense white or pink flowers, probably *jucande olens.* Mint was used to flavor food. The Jews scattered it on the floors of houses and synagogues for its sweet smell.

Myrtle branches (Neh. 8:15; Isa. 41:19; 55:13; Zech. 1:8-11). Myrtle bushes (*Myrtus communisro*), which grew on Palestinian hillsides, had fragrant evergreen leaves and scented white flowers. The flowers on the myrtle branches were used as perfumes.

Pomegranate blossoms (Exod. 28:33, Num. 13:23; 1 Sam. 14:2; 1 Kings 7:18). Blossoms from the pomegranate tree (*Punica granatumro*) had dark green leaves with large orange-red blossoms. Decorators carved pomegranates on public buildings. The fruit symbolized fertility and was used to tan leather and for medicine.

Rose (Song 2:1; Isa. 35:1). Several varieties of roses could be found in Palestine. The rose was a member of the crocus family. Traditionally, what is considered a rose is not the flower mentioned in Scripture. The "rose" is more generally considered an asphodel. See *Crocus* above.

Saffron (Song 4:14) (*Curcuma longa* or *Crocus sativasro*). A species of crocus. In ancient times the petals of the saffron flower were used to perfume banquet halls. The type meant in Song 4:14 may be an exotic plant imported from India.

The blossoms and fruit of a pomegranate tree growing in Israel. The pomegranate is one of seven species with which the land of Israel is blessed (Deut. 8:8). It is a frequent theme in Jewish art and is found atop the columns on the façade to the temple.

Other Though not specifically mentioned by kind in the Bible, other varieties of flowers grew in Palestine. Appearing as early as January were the pink, white, and lilac blossoms of the cyclamen. Dominating many landscapes were the various shades of reds and pinks of the crown anemones, poppies, and mountain tulips. Some short-lived summer flowers were the yellow and white daisylike chrysanthemums.

Figurative Uses of "Flowers" The striking manner in which flowers burst into bloom for a few short weeks in spring and then faded into withered leaves was viewed as an illustration of the transient nature of human life (Job 14:2; Ps. 103:15; Isa. 40:6; 1 Pet. 1:24). The flowers of spring (Song 2:12) signify renewal. The "fading flower" of Isa. 28:1 represented the downfall of God's disobedient people. The "lilies of the field" (Matt. 6:28) grew unassumingly and without any outward signs of anxiety. If God takes care of the lilies, so God will take care of His children who need not worry uselessly. The phrase "flower of her age" (1 Cor. 7:36 KJV) described a girl reaching womanhood. The rich pass away just as quickly as the period of time for blooming flowers passes away (James 1:10-11). See *Garden; Plants.*   *Gary Hardin*

FLUTE See *Music, Instruments, Dancing.*

FLUX, BLOODY KJV term for dysentery (Acts 28:8). See *Dysentery.*

FODDER Feed for domestic animals. The Hebrew suggests a mixed feed, either of several

Israel's Star of Bethlehem flower.

grains (though barley was the common grain for livestock, Judg. 19:19; 1 Kings 4:28) or a mix of finely cut straw, barley, and beans formed into balls. Silage refers to fodder which has been moistened and allowed to ferment slightly (Isa. 30:24 NRSV). Fodder was salted to satisfy the animals' need for salt and to give a tastier feed.

FOOD When Jesus was a guest at a meal, He referred to the two main meals of the day: "When you give a lunch or a dinner, don't invite your friends, your brothers, your relatives, or your rich neighbors, because they might invite you back, and you would be repaid. On the contrary, when you host a banquet, invite those who are poor, maimed, lame, or blind" (Luke 14:12-13 HCSB). There were only two main meals for the Jewish family. Breakfast was taken informally soon after getting up and normally consisted of a flat bread cake and a piece of cheese, dried fruit, or olives. Sometimes the bread was wrapped around the appetizer, and sometimes the bread was split open to make a bag where the morsels might be placed. To eat bread for a meal in such a way was so natural and normal that "eating bread" came to have the same meaning as "having a meal." "Give us today our daily bread" is a request that God will meet our need for daily food (Matt. 6:11 HCSB). It was quite usual for the men and boys to leave the house for their work, eating their breakfast as they went, while mother, daughters, and the younger children were kept at home. There was no midday meal as such, although a rest may have been taken for a drink and a piece of fruit. When Ruth stopped with the reapers, she ate parched grain moistened with wine (Ruth 2:14 NRSV).

While the men in the family were at work, the women and children would, among their daily activities, prepare for the evening meal. Water for cooking was collected by the older girls who drew it from the well or spring at the beginning of the day before it began to get hot, and the goats were milked too. Water collection was quite a serious business as well water could be polluted by animal usage, and house runoff from mud roofs was not normally safe to drink. Water collected, the girls then went to the market to purchase food for the meal. Fresh vegetables were bought from traders who sat with their produce around them on the ground of the market place, and if needed, olive oil and seasoning. Some families collected bread from the village

baker, who owned a communal oven, returning the bread that each family had left as dough the night before (Hos. 7:4-6). Other families baked their own bread upon returning home. The house had in the meantime been cleaned (Luke 11:25) and the washing done. Grain had been crushed in the handmill, and the fire fanned so that it was hot enough for baking bread. After the midday rest, the evening meal was prepared on the fire; a vegetable or lentil stew was made in the large cooking pot, herbs and salt being used to add to the flavor. Only on special occasions such as a sacrifice or festival day was any meat added to the stew, and only on very rare occasions was the meat roasted or game or fish eaten. When the time came for the meal, the pot was placed on a rug on the floor as the whole family sat around it. A blessing or thanksgiving was made, and each member of the family used a piece of bread as a scoop to take up some of the contents of the pot because there was no cutlery. (Communal dipping into the pot made it essential that hands were washed before the meal.) Later in history a table and benches sometimes replaced the rug on the ground (1 Kings 13:20), but the communal pot was still at the center. At the close of the meal, fruit would be eaten and the wine would be drunk.

Formal meals were always preceded by an invitation. The host then insisted that people come until the invitations were accepted (Luke 14:16-24). When the guests arrived, their feet were washed by the most humble slaves, and their sandals were removed (John 13:3-11). This was to protect the carpeted floors from dirt as well as to make it more comfortable to sit on one's heels. Their heads were anointed with olive oil scented with spices. The oil was rubbed into the hair (Luke 7:36-50). Drinking water was then provided. In large houses the special guest moved to the "top table" in a room with a raised floor and would sit on the right-hand side of the host. The second guest would sit on the host's left-hand side (Luke 14:7-11; 20:46).

One did not so much "sit" at table as recline at table. Couches were drawn up to the tables, head towards the table, and cushions provided so that guests could rest on their left arm and use the right to serve themselves from the table. Using this arrangement it was possible for the servants to continue to wash the feet (Luke 7:46), but to make conversation persons had to turn almost on their backs and literally be "on the bosom" of the person to the left (John 13:23-25). In the time of Jesus, the triclinium or couch arranged around three sides of a table, was the height of fashion. Servants used the open side so that they had access to the tables to bring in or to take away dishes of food.

The meal started with a drink of wine diluted with honey. The main dinner that followed was of three courses, beautifully arranged on trays. There were no forks, so guests ate with their fingers except when soup, eggs, or shellfish were served. Then spoons were used. Finally there was a dessert of pastry and fruit. During the meal the host provided entertainment of music, dancing (individual, expressive dances), and readings from poetry and other literature. Such an occasion was an important local event, and people of humbler means were able to look in from the darkness outside (Luke 7:37). When the meal was completed, there was a long period devoted to talking. Stories were related, and gossip was shared. Such festivities were always the envy of poorer people who tried to copy them in their own way.

Whether such meals were formal or informal, abundant or scant, there were always food laws that had to be observed. Only animals which chewed the cud and had divided hoofs, fish which had fins and scales, and birds which did not eat carrion could be eaten (Lev. 11:1-22).

Ralph Gower

FOOD OFFERED TO IDOLS A cause of controversy in the early church centering on what Christians were permitted to eat.

"Food offered to idols" is a translation of a single Greek word which has also been rendered "things offered unto idols" (KJV) and "meat sacrificed to idols" (NIV). The identification of the object of the offering by the term "idol" suggests that it was a name that originated outside first-century paganism. It reflects the perspective and conclusion of someone who spoke as a Jew or Christian.

Pagan sacrifices could be thought of as typically consisting of three portions. One small part would be used in the sacrificial ritual. A larger portion would be reserved for the use of the priests or other temple personnel. The largest part would be retained by the worshiper to be used in one of two ways. The one who offered the sacrifice sometimes used the remaining portion as the main course in a meal that might be served at or near the pagan temple. It is this type of religio-social event that stands behind the question raised by the letter (1 Cor. 8:1) from the church at Corinth to Paul and consequently as the background for Paul's response in 1 Cor. 8. The second method of disposing of the worshiper's portion would be to offer it for sale at the local marketplace. Meat that was sold in this fashion would be bought and then served as a part of a regular family meal. This situation is reflected in Paul's comments in 1 Cor. 10:23–11:1.

Robert Byrd

FOOL, FOOLISHNESS, AND FOLLY Translations of several uncomplimentary words that appear approximately 360 times throughout the OT and NT to describe unwise and ungodly people. The words are especially predominant in the Wisdom Literature of the OT. Persons who do not possess wisdom are called "fools"; their behavior is described as "folly." The picture, which emerges from the biblical material, is quite simple: folly is the opposite of wisdom, and a fool is the opposite of a wise person. Both wisdom and folly are depicted as philosophies or perspectives on life. The religious person chooses wisdom, whereas the nonreligious person opts for folly. Wisdom leads to victory; folly to defeat. Wisdom belongs to those who fear God, and the "fear" of the Lord is the beginning of wisdom (Prov. 1:7). Wisdom is the essence of life. The foolish person is the one who is thoughtless, self-centered, and obviously indifferent to God.

Old Testament Usage Seven different Hebrew words are usually translated by the single English word "folly." Some of the shades of meaning suggested by these various words include: (a) deliberate sinfulness; (b) simple-mindedness; (c) malicious simple-mindedness; and (d) brutal or subhuman activity.

The fool may be the one who is aloof. "Fools fold their hands" (Eccles. 4:5a NRSV). This aloofness is also described in terms of the farmer who "chases fantasies" instead of tending to the farm (Prov. 12:11b HCSB).

In other passages the fool is described as the one who denies that God exists: "The fool says in his heart, 'God does not exist'" (Ps. 14:1 HCSB). Foolish behavior is also characterized by an inability to recognize the true character of God. Job chastised his wife for behaving as the foolish do when she denied the steadfast love of God (Job 2:10).

The simple-minded fool is encouraged to change in Prov. 9:4-6. But the fool may be the one who is intentionally perverse. Nabal and Saul represent this kind of intentional and malicious folly toward David (1 Sam. 25:25; 26:21). **New Testament Usage** The contrasting elements of wisdom and folly evident in the OT were clearly in the mind of Paul when he asked, "Hasn't God made the world's wisdom foolish?" (1 Cor. 1:20b HCSB). However, in the NT, this polarity between wisdom and folly is not always stressed. In fact, it is possible that a certain kind of wisdom can actually be folly. In Matt. 7:26; 25:2-3; Rom. 2:20 "folly" is used synonymously with "experiential wisdom." Wisdom based only on human intellect and experiences without considering God is folly.

In Matt. 23:17 folly is equated with blindness. The characteristics of folly include thoughtlessness, the pursuit of unbridled aspirations, and a lifestyle characterized by envy, greed, and pride.

Foolishness is also described in paradoxical terms in the NT. In 1 Cor. 1–3 the incarnation is portrayed as "foolishness," but it is precisely this kind of perceived "foolishness" which is better than worldly wisdom. Our understanding of this paradoxical relationship affects the manner in which Christ is proclaimed (1 Cor. 1:18–2:5). We must rely on God's gift and power of proclamation not on human powers and wisdom. The writer of Matthew records Jesus stating that "whoever says to his brother, 'Fool,' will be subject to the Sanhedrin. But whoever says, 'You moron!' will be subject to hellfire" (5:22b HCSB). See *Wisdom and Wise Men*.

Kenneth Craig

FOOT Part of the human and animal body used for walking. In Scripture "foot" refers mainly to the human foot (Exod. 12:11; Acts 14:8). It may also be used of the feet of animals (Ezek. 1:7) or, anthropomorphically, of God's feet (Isa. 60:13). The "foot" as a measure of length does not appear in Hebrew or Greek, but some English versions give the equivalent in feet (Gen. 6:15 NIV; KJV, NRSV, NASB, cubits).

In the ancient world with unpaved roads, feet easily became dirty and had to be washed often. From earliest times hosts offered to wash their guests' feet (Gen. 18:4), usually done by the lowest servant (John 13:3-14). High honor was paid by anointing another's feet (Deut. 33:24; Luke 7:46; John 12:3).

Because it was so easy to soil one's feet, to remove the shoes was a sign of getting rid of dirt and so indicated holiness in worship (Exod. 3:5). To shake the dust off one's feet meant total rejection of that place (Acts 13:51). For both the Israelites and the Romans, punishment might include binding the feet in stocks (Job 13:27; Acts 16:24). Often "feet" symbolize the whole person, since it is hard to act without using the feet ("refrained my feet from every evil way" [KJV] means "kept myself from evil," Ps. 119:101; cp. Luke 1:79; Acts 5:9; Rom. 3:15).

Several biblical expressions contain "feet." "Put your feet upon the necks of these" suggested total victory over someone (Josh. 10:24). This was also implied by the phrase to put someone "under your feet" (Rom. 16:20; 1 Cor. 15:25). "To fall at [someone's] feet" showed humble submission, often when one had a request (1 Sam. 25:24; Luke 17:16). "To cover [one's] feet" was a euphemism for relieving oneself (1 Sam. 24:3). For one's foot "to slip" or "to be taken in a snare" meant calamity (Pss. 9:15; 66:9). "The feet of him who brings good news" meant the person's coming (Isa. 52:7). To sit "at the feet" meant to be a listener or disciple of someone (Acts 22:3). "Laid them down" at someone's feet suggested that the thing was a gift (Acts 4:35).   *Kendell Easley*

A perfume bottle in the shape of a sandaled foot from around 550 B.C. in Sicily.

FOOTMAN KJV translation of two unrelated Hebrew terms. The first refers to foot soldiers as distinguished from cavalry (2 Sam. 8:4), to soldiers in general (1 Sam. 4:10; 15:4), or to men of military age (Exod. 12:37). The second term refers to a runner who served in the honor guard that ran ahead of the king's chariot (1 Sam. 8:11; 2 Sam. 15:1), to the king's guards in general (1 Kings 14:27-28; 2 Kings 10:25), or to royal couriers (Esther 3:13,15).

FOOTSTOOL Piece of furniture for resting the feet, especially for one seated on a throne (2 Chron. 9:18; James 2:3). The footstool of Tutankhamen of Egypt was carved with pictures of his enemies. Other Pharaohs were portrayed with their feet on their enemies' heads. The footstool thus became a symbol for dominion. God is pictured as a king enthroned in heaven with the earth as His footstool (Isa. 66:1; Matt. 5:35). In Ps. 99:5 and Lam. 2:1 it is difficult to determine with certainty whether God's footstool is the ark, the temple, or Zion (cp. Isa. 60:13; Ezek. 43:7). Only 1 Chron. 28:2 is an unambiguous reference to the ark as a resting place for God's feet.

In Ps. 110:1 God makes the messianic King triumph over His enemies, who are then made His footstool. This text is quoted six times in the NT. It served as the basis for Jesus' riddle about David's son who is also his Lord (Matt. 22:44; Mark 12:36; Luke 20:43). Elsewhere, the Scripture was applied to the ascension of Christ (Acts 2:34-35), the exaltation of Christ (Heb. 1:13), and the future victory of Christ (Heb. 10:13).

FOOTWASHING An act necessary for comfort and cleanliness for any who have traveled dusty Palestinian roads wearing sandals. Customarily, a host provided guests with water for washing

Bronze statuette from the Roman period of two soldiers carrying a wounded comrade.

their own feet (Judg. 19:21; Luke 7:44, where the complaint was that Simon had not provided water). Footwashing was regarded as so lowly a task that it could not be required of a Hebrew slave. In this context the statement of John the Baptist that he was unworthy to untie the sandal (to wash the feet) of the One coming after him (Mark 1:7) indicates great humility. As a sign of exceptional love, a disciple might wash a master's feet (contrast John 13:13-14). The initiative of the woman who was a "sinner" in washing Jesus' feet (Luke 7:37-50) was more than expected hospitality. Hers was an act of great love that evidenced the forgiveness of her sins (7:47).

Jesus' washing of the disciples' feet (John 13:4-5) has both an ethical and a symbolic sense. The ethical sense is emphasized in John 13:14-15 where Jesus presented Himself as the example of humble, loving service (cp. Luke 22:27). The command to do for one another what Christ had done for them ought not to be confined simply to washing feet. What Jesus did for the disciples was to lay down His life for them (John 15:13). Thus the ethical imperative calls for giving our lives in extravagant acts of selfless service. Footwashing is one expression of this. Like the Lord's Supper, the footwashing is an enacted sermon on the death of Christ. This symbolic sense is highlighted in the picture of Jesus' laying aside His garments and then taking them up (a picture of Christ's laying down and taking up His life, John 10:17-18), the note that the footwashing is necessary for the disciples to receive their inheritance ("part" 13:8), and the statement that it affects cleansing (13:10). Some interpreters see a connection with baptism (and the Eucharist) as sacraments of cleansing. Instead, the footwashing, like baptism and the Supper, bears witness to the same salvific event, the selfless giving of Christ in the humiliating death of the cross.

Washing the feet of other Christians was a qualification for service as a "widow" in the early church (1 Tim. 5:10). Footwashing is here representative of humble acts of service (TEV).

The ceremonial washing of feet was first attested by Augustine in connection with Easter baptism. The association of the rite with Maundy Thursday was fixed by the council of Toledo (694). The developed Catholic practice involves a priest washing the feet of 12 poor men. Martin Luther criticized ecclesiastical authorities who washed feet as an act of humility and then demanded greater humility in return. The Anabaptists practiced footwashing as a symbol of washing in the blood of Christ and to impress the example of Christ's deep humiliation. Footwashing was commonly practiced by Baptists in early America. Today the regular practice is confined to smaller Baptist bodies, Mennonites, and some others.   *Chris Church*

FORBEARANCE Specifically, a refraining from the enforcement of a punishment; generally, a synonym for patience. Forbearance makes it possible to influence a ruler (Prov. 25:15 NASB; patience, NIV, NRSV, HCSB; patient persuasion, TEV). Jeremiah prayed that God not take him away in His forbearance (15:15 NRSV), that is, that God not be so patient with Jeremiah's enemies as to allow them to destroy him. In Rom. 2:4; 3:25 forbearance refers to God's patience expressed in God's willingness to hold back judgment for a time. God's forbearance does not mean that God condones sin but that God gives opportunity for repentance. God is able to maintain His reputation as a righteous judge in spite of God's overlooking the past sins of Israel and the present sins of those who place faith in Christ (3:26) because the cross was an effective sacrifice of atonement. God's forbearance is an opportunity for salvation (2 Pet. 3:15).

FORD Shallow place in a stream or river that permits crossing by foot. The Romans were the first to build bridges in Palestine. Before their time river crossings were generally limited to fords. Fords are mentioned in connection with three rivers in Palestine: the Arnon (literally "rushing torrent," Isa. 16:2), the Jabbok (Gen. 32:22), the Jordan. All three rivers have swift currents and offer few fording places. Fords were thus strategic points. To secure the fords meant success in battle (Judg. 3:28; 12:5-6); their loss meant defeat (Jer. 51:32).

FOREHEAD Part of the face above the eyes. Because it is so prominent, the appearance of the forehead often determines our opinion of the person.

The Emblem of Holiness was placed on Aaron's forehead (Exod. 28:38). This symbolized acceptance before the Lord. A mark was put upon the foreheads of those in Jerusalem who mourned for the wickedness of Jerusalem. They were spared in a time of terrible judgment (Ezek. 9:4).

The Bible indicates that a person's character can be determined by observing the forehead. A set forehead indicates opposition, defiance, and rebellion (Jer. 3:3). Hardness of the forehead indicates determination to persevere (Isa. 48:4; Ezek. 3:8-9). It has been used as a representation of Satan (Rev. 13:16-17). The forehead is used as a very dishonorable word when read of the harlot's forehead (Jer. 3:3), indicating utter shamelessness. At the same time, it stands for courage as when God told Ezekiel that He had made the prophet's forehead harder than flint against the foreheads of the people (Ezek. 3:9).

In the apocalyptic literature of the NT the foreheads of the righteous were marked (Rev. 7:3; 9:4; 14:1; 22:4). The apocalyptic woman dressed in purple and scarlet had her name written on her forehead (Rev. 17:5). See *Face*.

Gary Bonner

FOREIGN AID Financial assistance provided by the government or citizens of one country to citizens of another country in times of economic hardship. The best known instance involved the sale of grain by the government of Egypt "to all the earth" during a prolonged famine in the days of Joseph (Gen. 41:57). Perhaps in response to this event, Moses noted that God's blessing to Israel included the conditional promise that Israel would one day be prosperous enough to lend to other nations rather than having to borrow from them (Deut. 15:6; 28:12).

The NT reports that Christians from Antioch, Macedonia, and Achaia provided financial assistance to believers in Judea and Jerusalem (Acts 11:27-30; Rom. 15:26; 2 Cor. 8:1-7; 9:1-5).

These examples suggest that Christians should be willing to aid persons who live in other countries in times of need, whether through the church or government.

FOREIGNER See *Alien*.

FOREKNOW, FOREKNOWLEDGE To know beforehand. The verb (Gk. *proginosko*) and the noun (Gk. *prognosis*) are composites formed from the prefix, *pro* (before) and the verb, *ginosko* (know, understand, perceive, be acquainted with). Scripture uses these terms to signify knowledge of events before they occur or knowledge of things before they exist. Of the seven occurrences of these terms in the NT, two refer to human knowledge: Acts 26:5 refers to previous knowledge that the Jews had of Paul, and 2 Pet. 3:17 refers to the believer's knowledge of future events based on divine revelation. All other references are to God's foreknowledge. Although the idea of foreknowledge is present in the OT, there is no Hebrew equivalent to the Greek terms.

Scripture reveals God as being omniscient, that is, having exhaustive knowledge of all things—past, present, and future. Both the OT and the NT testify to God's comprehensive knowledge. The Lord's eyes run to and fro throughout the whole earth (2 Chron. 16:9); God's eyes are everywhere (Prov. 15:3). His understanding has no limit (Ps. 147:5). God has comprehensive knowledge of the actions of men (Job 34:21), man's thoughts (1 Sam. 16:7; 1 Kings 8:39; Ps. 139:2; Prov. 5:21), and even his motives (1 Chron. 28:9). To underscore the range of God's knowledge, Jesus spoke of God's awareness of the birds in the air and the hairs on human heads (Matt. 10:29-30). Nothing is hidden from God's sight (Heb. 4:13). John captured the essence of the biblical teaching: "God ... knows all things" (1 John 3:20 HCSB).

God's foreknowledge is that aspect of God's omniscience that relates to the future. Scripture clearly indicates that God's knowledge is not limited to the past and present. He is the One who announces events before they occur, and He makes known the end from the beginning (Isa. 42:9; 46:10a). It is this knowledge of the future, among other things, that distinguishes God from the false gods (Isa. 44:6-8; 48:14). It was not the prophets' clairvoyance but God's foreknowledge that made possible their predictions. Nathan foretold the death of David's son (2 Sam. 12:14); Elijah foretold the deaths of Ahab and Jezebel (1 Kings 21:19, 23); Amos foretold Israel's captivity (Amos 5:27) and restoration (Amos 9:14). By God's foreknowledge the prophets foretold that Jesus would be born in Bethlehem (Mic. 5:2); that He would suffer vicariously (Isa. 53:4-6); that He would be raised from the dead (Ps. 16:10). Predictive prophecy was possible only because God revealed His foreknowledge to the prophets.

While it is clear that the Greek words *prognosis* and *proginosko* have the connotation of knowing something beforehand (prescience), many interpreters find that a richer meaning is intended in their NT usages. Some passages indicate that God's foreknowledge is closely related to His foreordination. In the OT, events of history are the unfolding of God's eternal plans (Gen. 45:4-8; Isa. 14:24-27; 42:9; Jer. 50:45). The NT writers perceived in the life, death, and resurrection of Jesus the outworking of God's eternal plan to save sinful humanity. The Gospels declare that those things which the prophets had said were now fulfilled in the life and death of Jesus (Matt. 1:22-23; 2:5-6,15; John 19:24). Using forms of the word prognosis, Scripture teaches that the crucifixion was not a chance happening in history. It was according to the foreknowledge of God, according to His eternal plan. Speaking of Jesus' death, Peter proclaimed, "This man was handed over to you by God's set purpose and foreknowledge" (Acts 2:23a NIV). In his first epistle, Peter wrote of Christ: "Who verily was foreordained before the foundation of the world" (1 Pet. 1:20a AV, KJV). This foreknowledge involves more than prior knowledge; it includes foreordination.

Other passages indicate that God's foreknowledge is of people. God's foreknowledge of people is not primarily a reference to His intellect but to His benevolent will by which He sets people apart to Himself. Here foreknowledge means to set one's affections upon beforehand.

This is apparent in Paul's two uses of this verb in Romans. "For those He foreknew He also predestined to be conformed to the image of His Son" (8:29 HCSB); "God has not rejected His people whom He foreknew" (11:2 HCSB). God is depicted, not as having awareness of events or circumstances (prescience), but of people. It is not *what* God foreknew but *whom* He foreknew. It often is argued that Paul is using the Hebrew meaning of knowledge (*yada*) as found in such passages as Amos 3:2 and Jer. 1:5. This knowledge involves a personal relationship with Israel, His people. He did not choose them based on something good that He foresaw in them but by His mercy. Thus, whereas God has prior knowledge (prescience) about the other nations, He is not said to foreknow them. Likewise, God has prior knowledge of all people, but He foreknows only those who are His redeemed (Rom. 8:29).

Attempts to reconcile divine foreknowledge with human freedom and responsibility have occupied theologians and philosophers throughout church history. Some have argued that God's foreknowledge, whether construed as prescience or foreordination, entails the denial of human freedom. On such grounds some have denied that God knows the future, either because He has chosen not to know it, or, as the "open theists" have more recently argued, that He is unable to know it. Others have tended to stress foreknowledge and foreordination to the near exclusion of human choice. A better approach is to accept the biblical teaching that God foreknows and foreordains all things while not violating human free agency and moral responsibility. The biblical writers were not ashamed to place these truths together. In Acts 2:23 Peter proclaimed that the crucifixion of Jesus was according to God's foreknowledge and foreordained plan. Yet Peter held Christ's tormenters accountable for their actions, seeing that they acted on their own malicious desires.

Walter Johnson

FORERUNNER Greek term *prodromos* (one who runs ahead) occurs only once in the NT (Heb. 6:20) where it serves as a designation for Christ. In secular Greek the term was frequent as a military term for advanced scouts or cavalry that prepared for a full assault. This sense is seen in the earliest Greek translation of the Apocryphal book, the Wisdom of Solomon (12:8), where wasps were the forerunners of the armies of Israel (cp. Exod. 23:28; Deut. 7:20; but also Josh. 24:12 where the hornets completed driving out the Amorite kings so that no Israelite assault was necessary). Elsewhere in the earliest Greek translation of the OT (Septuagint) *prodromos* is used metaphorically for the first ripe fruit (Num. 13:20; Isa. 28:4). This usage suggests that the Christian hope of entering God's presence is guaranteed by the forerunner's already reaching this goal (cp. the idea of Christ as firstfruits of the dead, 1 Cor. 15:20,23.) A similar idea is expressed in the image of Christ as the pioneer of salvation (Heb. 2:10), the first of many children that God brings to glory through suffering. Significantly, Christ is forerunner for us. Having run ahead on the road of suffering, Christ became the source of salvation that makes our following possible (Heb. 5:8-10).

In English, forerunner indicates one who precedes and indicates the approach of another. In this sense John the Baptist is termed the forerunner of Jesus, though the NT does not use this term of John. The OT used the common image of advance agents sent ahead of a king to make arrangements for his travel to picture the mission of a prophetic messenger preparing the way for God's coming (Isa. 40:3; Mal. 3:1). The application of these texts to John by the NT writers (Matt. 11:10; Mark 1:2; Luke 1:76; 7:27) affirms that the coming of Jesus is the coming of God.

FORESAIL Small sail used to steer a vessel in strong wind (Acts 27:40). KJV refers to the "mainsail." Paul's ship likely had a large central mast with a long yardarm supporting the large, square mainsail and a smaller foremast, sloping forward like a bowsprit, which carried the foresail.

FORESKIN Loose fold of skin covering the glans of the penis which is removed in circumcision. Removal of the foreskin was a bodily reminder of God's covenant with Abraham (Gen. 17:11,14,23-25). In Deut. 10:16 the "foreskin of the heart" (KJV, NRSV) is associated with stubbornness in disobedience. The difficult text in Hab. 2:16 is likely a scribal corruption of the word "stagger" involving the inversion of two letters. NRSV, TEV, and REB thus translate "stagger" together with the Dead Sea Scrolls and several ancient versions. The reading in the Masoretic text, "to show oneself to be uncircumcised," does not mean simple exposure (NIV, NASB) but to be recognized as one cut off from the covenant. See *Circumcision; Covenant.*

FOREST Large, naturally wooded areas, characteristic of the central hill country, the Galilee, and the Bashan.

Large expanses of forest covered the majority of the hills in Palestine during the OT period. After the exodus, the inability of the Israelite tribes to conquer much of their inheritance forced them to develop new settlements and camps in the wooded hill country. Unable to rescue their portion from the hands of the Canaanites, the clans of Ephraim and Manasseh cleared the forests among the hills in their territory to provide room for settlement (Josh. 17:15-18). Forests also provided excellent staging areas for warfare, such as the rebellion of Absalom against David that ended with a battle in the forests of Ephraim (2 Sam. 18:6-8). The valuable cedars of Lebanon were imported from Tyre by Solomon for his extensive building projects in Jerusalem (1 Kings 5:8-10). Solomon's palace, "the house of the forest of Lebanon," was so named for its

F

extensive use of these cedars (1 Kings 7:2). As the population expanded, forested areas were cut down, and terraced orchards took their place. Large portions of the forests around Jerusalem were destroyed during the Roman siege of the city in A.D. 70.   *David Maltsberger*

FOREST OF LEBANON, HOUSE OF See *House of the Forest of Lebanon.*

FORGE See *Furnace.*

FORGETFULNESS, LAND OF Name for Sheol, the abode of the dead, in Ps. 88:12 (land of oblivion, HCSB). See *Sheol.*

FORGIVENESS Term used to indicate pardon for a fault or offense; to excuse from payment for a debt owed.
Terminology The two main terms for forgiveness in Hebrew are *nasa'*, "to take away (sin)" and *salach*, "to pardon." God is always the subject of the latter. The LXX expands the OT's forgiveness vocabulary to 20 terms. The NT expresses forgiveness with a select group of words, especially *aphiemi.*
Old Testament God is characterized early in the life of Israel as a God who both forgives and holds the guilty accountable (Exod. 34:7; cp. Neh. 9:17). He is the source of forgiveness for Israel at Sinai (Exod. 32:32; 34:9). He provides forgiveness for sin through the sacrificial system (Lev. 4:20,26,28,31; 5:10,13,16, 18; 6:7; 19:22). Solomon trusts God to forgive the repentant in his prayer of dedication for the temple. He utilizes the formula "Then hear ... and forgive," establishing God's sovereignty and willingness to forgive. God's forgiveness is directed primarily to His covenant people to sustain His covenant through them. However, outsiders may also become the object of God's merciful forgiveness (1 Kings 8:41-43; cp. 2 Chron. 6:32-33). Forgiveness is tied to the cultic setting in both the 1 Kings narrative and the 2 Chronicles narrative. Thus, forgiveness is the vehicle in which God reappropriates the blessings of His gracious covenant.

The prophets hold this same covenant grace out to Israel if she would only repent from her presumption on God's grace and her election (Dan. 9:9; Isa. 33:74; Jer. 33:8; Mic. 7:8). Social injustices that arise are often the fruit of Israel's indifference towards God's covenant and become the target of God's wrath (Amos 2:6, etc.). Israel also must repent of land/covenant defiling sins such as idolatry, bloodshed, and sexual sins, before forgiveness is procured.

The Psalms reveal the God of Israel as the same God found in the Torah. He does not allow the guilty to go unpunished, yet He is a God of forgiveness. In particular, the psalmist finds God to be the only source of forgiveness (Pss. 19:12; 25:11; 32:5; 65:3; 78:38). This reliance on God results in hymns of praise to God (Ps. 136).
New Testament Forgiveness is a vital idea for NT theology. John's baptism was for repentance and the forgiveness of sins (Mark 1:4; Luke 1:76-77). The idea is found in the confession of the Christ child's destiny (Matt. 1:21; Luke 1:77). It is the blood of Jesus' atonement that yields eternal forgiveness of sins (Matt. 26:28; Heb. 10:11-12; Lev. 16; 17:11). Jesus places enormous emphasis on horizontal (human to human) forgiveness. Matt. 18:21-35 details the parable of the unforgiving slave, enclosed by the divine demand to forgive. In Jesus' model prayer, the forgiveness the individual receives is dependent upon the forgiveness the individual gives to those who offend him. Jesus distinguishes His own ministry as one by which forgiveness is mediated to sinners through His blood (Matt. 26:28).

Paul discusses forgiveness, using the terminology mentioned above, only scarcely. He prefers to discuss the concept under the idea of righteousness. However, he defines forgiveness as the fundamental condition for Christian fellowship (2 Cor. 2:7-10). He refers to the idea of redemption as the "forgiveness of sins," (Col. 1:14). Because Christians have been redeemed, they are obligated to forgive as they have been forgiven (Col. 3:13).
Guaranteed Forgiveness? The idea that God's business is to forgive and thus forgiveness is secured by any and all who ask, regardless of intent, has no biblical ground. God established the sacrificial system for the dissolution of ritual impurity and the forgiveness of moral impurities. Yet for the "person who does anything defiantly" there is no forgiveness of sin via sacrifice (Num. 15:30-36). The illustration used in Numbers is a young man who breaks the Sabbath. His judgment occurs on the spot. This defiant sin is treated differently in other cases (Josh. 7; 1 Sam. 12; cp. Ps. 51), so it would be inaccurate to say there is no forgiveness for it. However, there is a

grave risk of immediate and irrevocable judgment.

The NT also speaks of a sin that will not be forgiven (Mark 3:29; Luke 12:10). Presumably the sin of indignantly categorizing the spirit of Jesus, whom Jesus identifies as the Holy Spirit, as demonic reveals the desire to vilify God and to deny Him any place as sovereign.   *Jeff Mooney*

FORK Two types of forks (pronged implements) are mentioned in Scripture: an implement used in the sacrificial cult and a farm tool used to winnow grain. See *Fan; Flesh Hook; Winnowing.*

FORMER RAIN KJV term at Joel 2:23 for the early rain. See *Rain.*

FORNICATION Various acts of sexual immorality, especially being a harlot or whore.
Old Testament Normally women are the subject of the Hebrew verb *zanah*, but in Num. 25:1 "people began to play the harlot" (NASB). The clearest example is that of Tamar sitting on the roadway to entice Judah (Gen. 38:12-30). Such action was subject to criminal prosecution bringing the death penalty (Gen. 38:24; cp. Lev. 21:9; Deut. 22:21). Fornication meant being unfaithful to a marriage commitment (Judg. 19:2).

Israel's neighbors practiced a fertility religion in which prostitution was part of the worship. This led naturally to describing worship of other gods as prostitution (Exod. 34:15-16; Judg. 8:27,33; Hos. 4:13). This concept is central for Hosea's preaching based on his experience with his unfaithful wife Gomer. Ezekiel also used this concept (Ezek. 16; 23) and extended it to include political treaties with foreign enemies (Ezek. 16:26,28; 23:5).
New Testament The NT also condemns prostitution. Here again prostitution played a central role in worship in places like Corinth and Athens. Greek philosophers could even distinguish the roles of prostitutes for pleasure, slave mistresses to give daily care to the master's body, and wives to produce legitimate children. Some Stoic philosophers reacted against such practices and condemned sex outside marriage. Many women used the situation to take slave lovers for themselves or become lesbians.

Jesus went against Jewish tradition and forgave prostitutes and opened the way for them to enter God's kingdom through faith (Matt. 21:31-32; cp. Heb. 11:31; James 2:25), though He still regarded fornication as evil (Mark 7:21).

Paul extended the use of the Greek term for fornication to cover all sinful sexual activity. He dealt with the problem particularly in writing the Corinthians who faced a society permeated with sexual religion and the sexual sins of a seaport. A believer must decide to be part of Christ's body or a prostitute's body (1 Cor. 6:12-20). The believer must flee sexual immorality and cleave to Christ, honoring Him with the physical body. Fornication is thus a result of sinful human nature (Gal. 5:19) and unsuitable for God's holy people (Eph. 5:3; 1 Thess. 4:3).

The book of Revelation also says much about fornication, condemning those guilty to eternal punishment (Rev. 2:21-22). Revelation, as well as the prophets, extends the meaning of fornication to include political and religious unfaithfulness (Rev. 14:8; 17:2,4; 18:3; 19:2).

As a whole, the NT uses *porneia*, most often translated "fornication," in at least four ways: voluntary sexual intercourse of an unmarried person with someone of the opposite sex (1 Cor. 7:2; 1 Thess. 4:3); as a synonym for adultery (Matt. 5:32; 19:9); harlotry and prostitution (Rev. 2:14,20); various forms of unchastity (John 8:41; Acts 15:20; 1 Cor. 5:1). See *Adultery; Divorce.*   *Gary Hardin*

FORT, FORTIFICATION Walled structures built for defense against enemy armies. Cities of the ancient world were fortified for defensive purposes as far back as archaeological records exist. The oldest fortifications in Israel are at Jericho, where a Neolithic stone tower and part of a wall have been dated to 7000 B.C. No other examples exist until 3000 B.C., the Chalcolithic Period (about 4000–3000 B.C.) being one of open villages without fortification. Beginning in the Early Bronze Age, mudbrick walls, towers, and gates were built on stone foundations at Ai, Arad, Beth Yerah, Gezer, Jericho, Megiddo, and elsewhere. From this time until the Roman Period (the time of Christ), cities were almost always surrounded by walls. The stone foundations and those portions of wall above the ground that utilized stone construction were made of uncut fieldstone. In the time of Solomon, however, well-dressed ashlars (carefully trimmed limestone blocks) began to be used in the construction of unique fortification systems. These included casemate walls (that is,

F

two parallel stone walls with dividing partitions connecting them) and huge six-chambered gates allowing easy entrance and exit for his chariots (a gate plan introduced much earlier by the Hyksos invaders, around 1700 B.C., who also used chariots). Similar, but smaller four-chambered gates were used later in the time of Ahab and Jeroboam II, attached to offsets-insets solid walls. A glacis was sometimes built against the outside wall for added protection against the battering ram. A glacis was a sloping embankment of beaten earth, clay, gravel and stones, sometimes covered with plaster. Examples of huge, dressed stone walls and gate towers of the Hellenistic/Roman Periods may be seen today at Samaria, Caesarea Maritima, and Tiberias. Citadels were often built on the acropolis of the enclosed city. *John McRay*

FORTIFIED CITIES The term "fortified city" (often "fenced city" or "defenced city" in the KJV) refers to a town with strong defenses, usually a massive wall structure and inner citadels or strongholds. In general the fortified city was a major military or administrative center for a region. Size was not so much the factor, though many of the fortified cities were large cities. Location was much more critical.

The Bible contains two lists of fortified cities, one for Naphtali (Josh. 19:35-38), and a list of cities Rehoboam fortified for Judah (2 Chron. 11:5-12). These two lists seem to include most of the walled cities within the tribal area.

Fortified cities served a strategic function. They could guard a major highway (as did Lachish and Hazor). They could protect mountain passes (Megiddo and Taanach). They could serve as border fortresses (Arad and Hazor).

Masada, the site of a palace built by Herod the Great, provides its own natural fortification.

Surely troops would be garrisoned in a fortified city. At times of imminent danger, much of the populace from the surrounding area might find protection in a fortified city (Jer. 4:5; 8:14).

Other closely related terms used in the Bible include chariot cities and store cities (1 Kings 9:19). Chariot cities were major military centers where the chariot troops were garrisoned. Store cities probably served as central supply bases for the military. *Joel F. Drinkard, Jr.*

FORTRESS See *Castle*.

FORTUNATUS (Fŏr tū nā´ tŭs) Corinthian Christian who together with Stephanus and Achaicus ministered to Paul at Ephesus (1 Cor. 16:17). The three perhaps brought Paul a letter from Chloe's household in Corinth. In view of their anticipated return to Corinth, they perhaps delivered First Corinthians as indicated in the superscription of the Textus Receptus.

FORTUNE See *Destiny*.

FORTUNE TELLER See *Divination and Magic*.

FORUM The open place of a market town or the town itself. The Appii Forum (Acts 28:15) or market town of Appius was located 43 miles to the southeast of Rome on the Appian Way.

FOUNDATION That on which a building is built; the first layer of a structure that provides a stable base for the superstructure. Bedrock was the preferred foundation (Matt. 7:24). The best alternative was a solid platform of close-fitting cut stone (1 Kings 5:17). Modest homes had foundations of rough stone. Generally, building sites were leveled by filling in the foundation trenches with gravel or small stones. Often, the

A panoramic view of the ruins of the Forum.

foundation is all that remains of ancient structures. The prohibition of laying a foundation for Jericho (Josh. 6:26) was a prohibition of rebuilding the city as a fortified site rather than of inhabiting the place. The splendor of the new Jerusalem is pictured in its foundation of precious stones (Isa. 54:11; Rev. 21:19).

The OT pictured the earth (dry land) as resting on foundations (2 Sam. 22:16; Pss. 18:15; 82:5). God is pictured as a builder who marked out the foundations (Prov. 8:29) and set the stone (Ps. 104:5). The mountains (Deut. 32:22; Ps. 18:7) and the vault of the heavens (2 Sam. 22:8; Job 26:11) are also pictured as resting on foundations. God's great power is expressed in the images of the earth's foundations trembling (Isa. 24:18) or being exposed (2 Sam. 22:16) before the Almighty. "From the foundation of the world" (HCSB) means from the time of creation (Isa. 40:21; Matt. 13:35; John 17:24).

Christ's teaching is compared to a rock-solid foundation (Matt. 7:24; Luke 6:48). Foundation serves as a metaphor for the initial preaching of the gospel (Rom. 15:20; Heb. 6:1-2 which outlines the foundational topics), for the apostles and prophets as the first generation of preachers (Eph. 2:20; cp. Rev. 21:14,19); and for Christ as the content of preaching (1 Cor. 3:10-11).

The foundations of Ps. 11:3 are the foundations of life, security, community, justice, and religion. To lay a good foundation for the future (1 Tim. 6:19) is to be generous and ready to share. The foundation of 2 Tim. 2:19 is an enigma. The context suggests that God's foundation is the core of true believers known only to God. Other suggestions include Christ, God's work, the church, Christ's teaching, and God's eternal law.   *Chris Church*

FOUNTAIN Spring of water flowing from a hole in the earth. The limestone rock of Palestine is especially suited for the formation of springs. In semi-arid country springs are highly prized as water sources and often determine the location of settlements. Thus the frequency of the Hebrew root *En*, meaning spring, in place-names: En-dor (Josh. 17:11); En-eglaim (Ezek. 47:10); En-gannim (Josh. 15:34); En-gedi (15:62); En-haddah (19:21); En-hakkore (Judg. 15:19); En-hazor (Josh. 19:37); En-rimmon; (Neh 11:29); En-rogel and En-shemesh (Josh. 15:7); and En-tappuah (17:7). Enaim (Enam, Josh. 15:34) means "two springs." The goodness

During the Roman period man-made fountains such as this one at Pompeii (first century A.D.) supplemented natural spring-fed fountains.

of Canaan was seen in its abundant water supply, "a land of brooks of water, of fountains and springs, flowing forth in valleys and hills" (Deut. 8:7 NASB).

The OT portrays the earth's dry land resting on foundations over the fountains of the deep (Gen. 7:11). The unleashing of these waters amounted to a return to the chaos before the creation (Gen. 1:1,9).

Provisions of spring water is an expression of God's providential care (Ps. 104:10). God's special concern for the poor and needy is pictured in terms of providing fountains and springs (Isa. 41:17-18). The blessedness of the endtime

Fountain in the center of Cisterna, a possible site for The Three Taverns in Italy.

includes pictures of fountains flowing from the temple (Ezek. 47:1-12; Joel 3:18), Jerusalem (Zech. 14:8), or the throne of God (Rev. 22:1-2) with amazing life-giving powers.

The metaphorical use of fountain for source is common. The teaching of the wise is a fountain (source) of life (Prov. 13:14; contrast 25:26).

Chris Church

FOUNTAIN GATE A city gate at the southeast corner of the walls of ancient Jerusalem (Neh. 2:14; 3:15; 12:37), probably so named because people brought water from the En-rogel or Gihon springs into the city through this gate. The gate is possibly identical with the "gate between the two walls" (2 Kings 25:4; Jer. 39:4; 52:7). See *Gate.*

FOWL See *Birds.*

FOWLER One who traps birds. All biblical references are figurative. A variety of means are mentioned in Scripture: snares (Pss. 91:3; 124:7); traps (Ps. 141:9; Jer. 5:26-27); ropes (Job 18:10 KJV, "snare"); and nets (Hos. 7:12). God is praised as One who delivers from the fowler's snare (Pss. 91:3; 124:7), an image of the power of the wicked. Opposition to the Prophet Hosea is pictured as a fowler's snare set in the temple (Hos. 9:8). Hosea 7:12 pictures Israel as a dumb bird that God will catch with a net so the nation can be disciplined. Prov. 6:1-2,5 picture indebtedness as a snare to be avoided. Jesus warned that the day of God's coming judgment would be as unexpected as the closing of a trap (Luke 21:35).

FOX Doglike carnivorous mammal, smaller than the wolf with shorter legs (Neh. 4:3). It has large erect ears and a long bushy tail (Judg. 15:4). It is referenced as cunning and crafty (cp. Luke 13:32).

FRACTURE Breaking of a bone (Lev. 24:20, KJV "breach"). The law of retribution limited retaliation to "fracture for fracture."

FRAME Term used by modern translations to render a number of Hebrew terms. Frame refers to the "carrying frame" (NRSV) for the lamps and tabernacle utensils (Num. 4:10,12; KJV, NASB, bars; REB, poles); the rim that served as a brace for the legs of the table of the presence (Exod. 25:25,27; KJV, border); the frames for the side panels of the stands used to transport the temple lavers (1 Kings 7:28-36; 2 Kings 16:17; KJV, ledge); the skeletal structure over which the tabernacle curtains were spread (Exod. 26:15-29; 35:11; KJV, NASB, boards); and the casing of windows and doors (1 Kings 7:4-5). Frame is also used in reference to the human form (Job 41:12; Pss. 103:14; 139:15). Frame can be interpreted either as "how we are formed" (NIV) or "what we are made of" (TEV). Frame is also used as a verb, meaning "to join." The tongue's "framing words" is a picturesque expression for speech (Ps. 50:19). Most often frame means to plan or devise (Ps. 94:20) or to act on plans (Jer. 18:11).

FRANKINCENSE Ingredient used in making the perfume for the most holy place in the tabernacle (Exod. 30:34). It is a resinous substance derived from certain trees in the balsam family. Frankincense was one of the gifts presented to the child Jesus by the magi (Matt. 2:11).

FREEDMEN, SYNAGOGUE OF THE Greek-speaking synagogue in Jerusalem involved in instigating the dispute with Stephen (Acts 6:9; KJV "Synagogue of the Libertines"). The Greek syntax suggests two groups of disputants. The first consisted of the Synagogue of the Freedmen, composed of Cyrenians and Alexandrians (NASB, TEV). It is possible that this first group has three parties, the freedmen (freed slaves), the Cyrenians, and Alexandrians. Some early versions have Libyans in place of "libertines," giving three groups of North African Jews. The second party in the dispute was composed of Greek-speaking Jews of Asia and Cilicia. These may have belonged to the Synagogue of the Freedmen as well (REB). Some have identified the freedmen as the descendants of Pompey's prisoners of war (63 B.C.).

FREEWILL OFFERING Gift given at the impulse of the giver (Exod. 35:21-29; 36:3-7; Lev. 7:16). The distinctive mark of the freewill offering was the "stirred hearts" and "willing spirits" of the givers. The tabernacle was constructed using materials given as freewill offerings (Exod. 35:29). The people's desire to give was so great that Moses was compelled to ask that no more gifts be given (Exod. 36:3-7). Freewill offerings were traditionally given at Pentecost (Deut. 16:10). See *Sacrifice and Offering.*

FREEDOM A key biblical theme finding expression in both the spiritual and social ramifications of salvation in Christ. Scripture portrays freedom in a complex and multifaceted manner. It addresses issues related to political freedom, freedom from the institution of slavery, freedom from oaths and obligations, freedom from guilt and punishment, and freedom from sinful, destructive habits. Naturally, these categories are not airtight; there is considerable overlap, but these constitute the basic categories for understanding the Bible's conception of freedom.

Political Freedom The central redemptive event of the OT, the exodus, resulted in Israel's freedom from Egyptian domination. While it is true that the exodus involved freedom from slavery, the more significant result was the fulfillment of the divine promise ensuring the formation of Abraham's offspring into an independent political entity with its own land (Gen. 12:1-3; 15:18). Israel's political freedom, however, did not take the form of a democracy; God formed a covenant with Israel in which He ruled over the nation as king and the nation worshiped and served Him as devoted subjects—a form of government referred to as a "theocracy" (Exod. 19:5-6). Israel's freedom consisted of her independence from other human kingdoms, not of an independence from her divine king.

Freedom from Slavery In many biblical contexts, freedom is a social category standing in contrast to the social category of slavery. Though the institution of slavery did exist in the social structure of ancient Israel, it was regulated by strict laws ensuring the humane treatment of slaves. The Torah, for example prohibited any Hebrew from owning a Hebrew slave longer than six years unless the slave voluntarily agreed to remain in the service of the master (Exod. 21:2-5; Deut. 15:12-18). In fact, the Law commanded that any Hebrew who became poor and sold himself into slavery was not to be treated as a slave but as a hired worker. Furthermore, he was to be released on the year of Jubilee (Lev. 25:39-43). Any slave who suffered physical injury at the hands of his master was to be freed (Exod. 21:26). Thus, it was God's intention that His chosen people enjoy social freedom in the ancient Israelite economy. They were not to live in the promised land as they had lived in Egypt before their redemption.

In the NT, Paul advised slaves to gain their freedom if possible, but if not, to serve Christ faithfully as a slave. Their social position was irrelevant to their status in Christ's kingdom and their calling in ministry (1 Cor. 7:21-22). Though a believer may be a slave in society, he is free in Christ and can thus live in spiritual liberty while enduring social bondage. Paul's letter to Philemon appears to be singularly concerned with the release of Onesimus, a runaway slave who belonged to Philemon. In social terms, therefore, the Bible acknowledges that freedom is preferable to slavery but not essential to enjoying the spiritual freedom offered by the Gospel.

Freedom from Obligation and Guilt Scripture also relates the concept of freedom to the concepts of obligation, oath, and guilt. In the OT, people commonly are bound to and released from oaths (e.g., Gen. 24:8,41). The two-and-a-half tribes that lived on the east side of the Jordan were under obligation to help the rest of the Israelites conquer the land of Canaan. God said that once the land was subdued they would be free from this obligation (Num. 32:22). Similarly, Paul speaks of a spouse's freedom from marriage in the case of the mate's death or in the event that an unbelieving spouse forsakes the marriage (1 Cor. 7:15,39).

This concept is then broadened to include freedom from punishment brought on by guilt. For example, a woman suspected of marital infidelity was subjected to a bitter water ritual to determine her guilt or innocence. Before administering the test, the priest would say, "If you are innocent of uncleanness, may you be free from the curse of the bitter water" (cp. Num. 5:19-22). Paul uses the term freedom in a similar sense in Rom. 8:1-2 when he says, "Therefore no condemnation exists for those in Christ, because the Spirit's law of life in Christ Jesus has set you free from the law of sin and of death" (HCSB).

Freedom from Confinement and Distress Scripture frequently describes God as one who "sets prisoners free" (Pss. 102:20; 146:7; Isa. 45:13; 58:6; 61:1; Luke 4:18). In these contexts, God is freeing people from either literal or metaphorical confinement. The concept is frequently broadened to include distress or dire circumstances (Ps. 118:5; Zech. 9:11; 1 Cor. 7:32).

Freedom from Sin The work of Christ brought new depth and significance to the biblical concept of freedom. Paul in particular proclaims a new freedom available in Christ, freedom from sin. Beyond freedom from the penalty of sin, Paul also speaks of freedom from the power of

F

sin, the Spirit-empowered ability to resist habitual disobedience (Rom. 6:7-22; Gal. 4:1-7). Closely related to this is Paul's declaration of freedom from the law, not freedom from God's standard of righteousness but freedom from the frustration of our fallen nature's inability to keep God's law (Rom. 7:7-20). Not only did Christ fulfill the demands of the law in His own life and sacrificial death, He continues, through the Holy Spirit, to fulfill it in the lives of transformed believers.

Thus, contrary to popular opinion, freedom is not the ability to do whatever one desires. This inevitably leads to enslavement to one's own passions. Rather, the Bible defines freedom as the ability to deny one's self, to deny one's desires in the interest of pleasing and glorifying God. See *Election; Slave, Servant.*   *Kevin J. Youngblood*

FRIEND, FRIENDSHIP Close trusting relationship between two people. Nowhere does the Bible present a concise definition of "friend" or "friendship." Instead, both the OT and NT present friendship in its different facets.

Two Hebrew root words, *rʿh* and *ʾhb*, are used to describe friendship. *Rʿh* denotes an associate or companion, while *ʾhb* connotes the object of one's affection or devotion—a friend. Consequently, friendship may be simple association (Gen. 38:12; 2 Sam. 15:37) or loving companionship, the most recognizable example being that between David and Saul's son, Jonathan (1 Sam. 18:1,3; 20:17; 2 Sam. 1:26).

Friendship, however, was not limited to earthly associates. The OT also affirms friendship between God and human persons. The relationship between God and Moses (Exod. 33:11) is likened to friendship because they conversed face-to-face. Both 2 Chron. 20:7 and Isa. 41:8 characterize Abraham as the friend of God. Friendship between God and His people is alluded to in Isa. 5:1-7, the song of the vineyard. Proverbs features the most references to friendship, nearly all of them cautioning against dubious friendships or extolling the virtues of a true friend (14:20; 17:17-18; 18:24; 19:4,6; 22:11, 24; 27:6,10,14).

In the NT, the predominant word for friend is *philos.* A derivative, *philia,* is often used for friendship. Jesus is described as the "friend of ... sinners" (Matt. 11:19 HCSB). He called His disciples "friends" (Luke 12:4; John 15:13-15). The NT highlights the connection between friends

and joy (Luke 15:6,9,29), as well as warning of the possibility of friends proving false (Luke 21:16). Echoing the OT, James pointed to Abraham, the friend of God, as one whose example of active faith is to be followed (James 2:23). James also warned against friendship with the world (James 4:4).

Only in 3 John 14 is "friend" a self-designation for Christians. As a means of describing the relations between church members, friendship was overshadowed by the model of family relations, brotherhood and sisterhood (1 Tim. 5:1-3; 1 Pet. 1:22; 2:17). See *Body of Christ; David; Jonathan; Love; Neighbor.*

William J. Ireland, Jr.

FRIEND OF THE KING Title of a court official (1 Kings 4:5). The king's friend was counselor and companion to the monarch. He functioned somewhat as a secretary of state. Hushai evidently held this office in David's court; Zabud held it in Solomon's.

FRINGE Tassels of twisted cords fastened to the four corners of the outer garment, worn by observant Jews as a reminder of covenant obligations (Num. 15:38-39; Deut. 22:12; cp. Zech. 8:23). The woman suffering from chronic hemorrhage touched the tassel of Jesus' cloak (Matt. 9:20; Luke 8:44). The English translations (with the exception of the NRSV) obscure this point by using different terms to translate the Greek *kraspedon* when it refers to Jesus' outer cloak (hem, KJV; fringe, NASB; edge, NIV, TEV; simply garment, RSV) and to the outer garment of the Pharisees (borders, KJV; tassels, NASB, NIV, TEV; fringe, RSV). Though Jesus observed the OT requirement, He criticized those who wore excessively long tassels to call attention to their piety (Matt. 23:5).

FROG Amphibious animal specifically used by God as a plague against Pharaoh and his people. When the Lord sent Moses to free the Israelites, Pharaoh's heart was hard. Moses told Pharaoh that frogs would come into the palace and to the houses of his officials and his people. Aaron stretched out his hand over the waters, and frogs covered the land. The court magicians also did the same, and more frogs came on the land. Pharaoh called on Moses to pray to the Lord to take the frogs away and he would let the people go. Moses prayed, the frogs died, but Pharaoh still refused to let the Israelites go free (Exod. 8:2-15). See *Animals.*

FRONTLETS Objects containing Scripture passages worn on the forehand and between the eyes, primarily at prayer times. Jews followed scriptural commands, literally, writing Exod. 13:1-16; Deut. 6:4-9; 11:13-21 on small scrolls, placing these in leather containers and placing these on their forehead and left arm (Exod. 13:9,16; Deut. 6:8; 11:18).

By NT times, the frontlets were known as phylacteries (Matt. 23:5). Jewish men wore phylacteries during prayer times, except on the Sabbath and feast days.

Phylacteries were bound with thongs to the forehead, though some phylacteries were worn on the upper arm so that when a person crossed his arms the Scriptures contained in the phylactery would be close to the heart.

Jesus condemned individuals who called attention to themselves by wearing larger than usual phylacteries (Matt. 23:5).   *Gary Hardin*

FRUIT Edible pulp surrounding the seed(s) of many plants. Various types of fruit are mentioned; among the most common are grapes, figs, olives, pomegranates, and apples (perhaps to be identified with apricots or quince). Israel, in contrast to her neighbors, recognized the process by which trees reproduce by means of seeds carried in fruit to be a part of God's good plan at creation (Gen. 1:12,29). The continuing fruitfulness of Israel's trees was dependent on faithfulness to the covenant (Deut. 28:4,11,18). The first fruit to ripen was offered to God (Exod. 23:16; Neh. 10:35).

Figuratively, "the fruit of the womb" is a common expression for descendants (Gen. 30:2; Deut. 7:13; Ps. 127:3; Isa. 13:18). Fruit often indicates a thought close to our word "results." The fruit of the Spirit is the results of the Spirit's workings in the lives of believers (Gal. 5:22-23). Similar is the use of fruit where we would speak of manifestations or expressions. The fruits of righteousness (Phil. 1:11; James 3:18), of repentance (Matt. 3:8), of light (Eph. 5:9) are expressions of righteousness, repentance, and moral purity. Jesus cautioned that false prophets could be identified by the fruit they produced (Matt. 7:15-20), that is, by the qualities manifested in their lives. Jesus similarly warned of the necessity of bearing fruit that was compatible with cit-

A modern orthodox Jewish man praying at the Wailing Wall in Jerusalem wearing his frontlet.

izenship in the kingdom of God (Matt. 21:43). Fruit sometimes has the sense of reward (Isa. 3:10; John 4:36; Phil. 4:17). Fruit is also used as a picture for Christian converts (Rom. 1:13; 1 Cor. 16:15).

FRUSTRATION Hebrew verb "to frustrate" (from *parar*) means to make ineffective or void and is used primarily to describe God's response to the plans of people. The Bible declares that God frustrates the plans of those who trust in their own devices or who operate according to their own agendas (Job 5:12; Ps. 33:10; Isa. 44:25) and relates several instances of persons who became frustrated in opposing God. These include Pharaoh (Exod. 8–12), Ahithophel (2 Sam. 17:14,23), Ahab (1 Kings 18:17; 21:1-4), the men of Sanballat and Tobiah (Neh. 4:7,15), and Pilate (John 19:1-16).

Those who strive to follow God often experience frustration in its more general sense of a dissatisfaction arising over unmet expectations. The psalmist cried out in frustration over God's apparent inactivity on his behalf (Ps. 22:1-2; 38:1-22; 39:1-13), and Paul expressed frustration over the lack of faith evident in the Galatian believers (Gal. 3:1-5). Partly in response to such frustrations, Paul learned to be content in every situation (Phil. 4:11-13) and counseled that everything eventually works for good for those who love God and are called according to His purpose (Rom. 8:28). God's promises of comfort extend to those who are frustrated (Isa. 40:1; 1 Cor. 1:3-7), while the spiritual maturity, which enables believers to overcome frustration, arises from trust in God in the midst of trials (Ps. 22:5; Prov. 3:5-6; Phil. 1:6; James 1:2-4).

FRYING PAN KJV term for the vessel used for cooking the cereal offering (Lev. 2:7; 7:9), simply "pan" in modern translations. A kettle for deep fat frying is perhaps intended.

FUEL Materials used to start and maintain a fire. Numerous types of fuel are mentioned in Scripture: wood (Isa. 44:14-16); charcoal (Jer. 36:22; John 18:18); shrubs (Ps. 120:4); thornbushes (Eccles. 7:6; Nah. 1:10); grass (Matt. 6:30); weeds (Matt. 13:40); vines (Ezek. 15:4,6); branch trimmings (John 15:6); animal or even human dung (Ezek. 4:12); and the blood-stained clothing of fallen warriors (Isa. 9:5). Oil was used as a fuel for lamps (Matt. 25:3). Coal was not known to the Hebrews.

Fuel is frequently used figuratively as a symbol of total destruction. Disobedient Israel is portrayed as "fuel for the fire" (Isa. 9:19; Ezek. 15:6; 21:32). For Jesus, God's extravagant love evidenced in clothing grass destined to be burned as fuel with beautiful flowers illustrated even greater care for human beings (Matt. 6:30).

FULFILL Verb used in three senses that merit special attention: an ethical sense of observing or meeting requirements; a prophetic sense of corresponding to what was promised, predicted, or foreshadowed; and a temporal sense related to the arrival of times ordained by God. The ethical sense of "fulfill" appears in the OT only in connection with meeting the requirements of a vow (Lev. 22:21; Num. 15:3), never in connection with the law. In the NT Jesus submitted to John's baptism, identifying Himself with sinful people, in order "to fulfill all righteous" (Matt. 3:15 HCSB), that is, to meet God's expectation for His life. Jesus described His mission not as coming "to destroy the Law or the Prophets" but "to fulfill" (Matt. 5:17 HCSB). The NT repeatedly speaks of love as the fulfilling of the law (Rom. 13:8-10; Gal. 5:14; James 2:8).

"Fulfill" is most common in Scripture in the prophetic sense of corresponding to what was promised, predicted, or foreshadowed. The fulfillment of prophecy in the life of Jesus is a major theme in Matthew's Gospel. Isaiah's prophecy (7:14) found fulfillment not only in Christ's virgin birth but also in His nature as "God is with us" (Matt. 1:22-23 HCSB; cp. 28:20). Jesus' ministry in both word (Matt. 4:14-17) and deed (8:16-17) fulfilled Scripture (Isa. 9:1-2; 53:4). Jesus' command of secrecy (Matt. 12:16) and His habit of teaching in parables (13:35) likewise fulfilled Scripture (Isa. 42:1-3; Ps. 78:2), as did His humble entry into Jerusalem (Matt. 21:4-5; Zech. 9:9) and His arrest as a bandit (Matt. 26:55-56). At several points Jesus' life story gave new meaning to the history of Israel. Like Israel, Jesus was God's Son called out of Egypt (Matt. 2:15; Hos. 11:1). The suffering of Israel's mothers (Jer. 31:15) was echoed by the mothers of Bethlehem (Matt. 2:17-18). Both foreshadowed the fate of the Christ child who was spared only to die at a later time.

Luke and Acts are especially interested in Christ's suffering and later glorification as the fulfillment of the expectations of all the OT, the Law, Prophets, and Writings (Luke 24:25-26,44-47; Acts 3:18; 13:27-41) .Jesus interpreted His journey to Jerusalem as a second "exodus" (Luke 9:31), an event that would result in freedom for God's people.

In John the failure of the people to recognize God at work in Jesus' signs or to accept Jesus' testimony was explained as fulfillment of Scripture (12:37-41; cp. Mark 4:11-12). John also viewed details of the passion story as the fulfillment of Scripture (John 19:24,28; Pss. 22:18; 69:21). Typological fulfillment in which Jesus corresponded to OT institutions is more common than correspondence to predictive prophecy. Jesus was "the Lamb of God, who takes away the sin of the world" (John 1:29 HCSB), likely a reference to the Passover lamb (John 19:14). Like Bethel (Gen. 28:12) Jesus offered access between heaven and earth (John 1:51). At Cana Jesus' gift of wine corresponded to the blessings of God's future (John 2:1-11; Isa. 25:6; Joel 3:18; Amos 9:13; Zech. 9:17). Jesus' body which was to be destroyed and raised was identified with the temple (John 2:19,21). In His being lifted up on the cross (John 3:14), Christ corresponded to the serpent Moses raised in the wilderness (Num. 21:9). In the same way, Christ in giving His life corresponded to the life-giving manna from heaven (John 6:31-32; Exod. 16:15). Often, time references in the Gospel of John suggest that Jesus gave new meaning to the celebrations of Israel (Passover, 2:13; 6:4; 11:55; booths, 7:10; dedication, 10:22).

Paul spoke of Christ as the One in whom "every one of God's promises is 'yes'" (2 Cor. 1:20 HCSB). Like John, Paul made frequent use of typology. Christ was foreshadowed by Adam (Rom. 5:12-21; 1 Cor. 15:22,45-49), by the rock in the wilderness (1 Cor. 10:4), and by the Passover lamb (1 Cor. 5:7).

Temporal phrases such as "the time is fulfilled" point to times ordained by God, for example, the time of Christ's ministry (Mark 1:15; Gal. 4:4; Eph. 1:10), the time of Gentile domination of Israel (Luke 21:24), or the time of the appearance of the lawless one (2 Thess. 2:6).

Chris Church

FULLER One who thickens and shrinks newly shorn wool or newly woven cloth; also one who washes or bleaches clothing. The Hebrew term comes from the root "to tread" and refers to the common method of cleansing clothing by treading them by foot. Cleansing was also done by beating clothing with sticks. The ancient Hebrews were not acquainted with bar soap. Clothing was cleansed in a solution of alkali obtained by burning wood to ash. Putrid urine was sometimes used in the process. Due to the foul smell, fullers worked outside the city gates. All the biblical references are metaphorical (Ps. 51:7; Jer. 2:22; 4:14; Mal. 3:2) and refer to cleansing from sin.

FULLER'S FIELD Site outside Jerusalem's walls, located near the conduit between the Gihon Spring and the upper pool (2 Kings 18:17; Isa. 7:3; 36:2). The road to the Fuller's Field was the scene of an encounter between Rabshakeh, agent of the king of Assyria, who stopped within hearing distance of those on the city walls, and the leaders of Jerusalem. See *Rabshakeh.*

FULLNESS Completeness or totality. "The earth is the Lord's, and the fulness thereof" (Ps. 24:1 KJV). Scripture sees that nothing is really complete until it serves the purpose for which God has created it. Thus Eph. 1:23 (NRSV) speaks of God as "him who fills all in all." He is the one who gives everything its ultimate significance

and richness. This fullness is most clearly expressed in Jesus Christ (Col. 1:19; 2:9) from whom all true believers receive the divine life of fullness (John 1:16; 10:10). It is a life full of joy (John 15:11) and peace despite the fact of tribulations in this world (John 16:33). See *Eternal Life.*   *Joe Baskin*

FULLNESS OF TIME Traditional rendering of two similar Greek expressions in Gal. 4:4 and Eph. 1:10. The first refers to a past event, the sending of Christ to redeem those born under the law. While the sending of God's Son encompasses the whole of Christ's incarnate ministry, the NT specifically relates the sending to Christ's death as a saving event (John 3:17; Rom. 8:3; 1 John 4:9-10). The sending of Christ in the fullness of time refers not so much to world conditions in the sense that the prevalence of Greek as a common spoken language, Roman roads, and the Roman enforced peace made the rapid spread of the gospel possible. Rather the emphasis is on God whose sending of Christ is not a "last-ditch effort" but part of God's gracious plan from the beginning.

The reference to the fullness of time in Ephesians is more difficult. Some translations understand the time when all things are gathered together in Christ to lie in the future (NIV, TEV); others, in the past (REB). A major theme of Ephesians is that Christ has already broken down the dividing wall of hostility between Jew and Gentile (2:11-22, esp. 2:14,21). Therefore, it seems likely that the crucial shift in time between the past with its hopelessness and hostility and the present age of reconciliation has already occurred.   *Chris Church*

FURNACE Device, generally of brick or stone, used to heat materials to high temperatures. In biblical times furnaces were not used for central heating. Rather furnaces were used to smelt ore, melt metal for casting, heat metal for forging, fire pottery or bricks, and to make lime. The furnace of Dan. 3 was probably a large furnace used for smelting ore or for firing bricks. Biblical references to furnaces are mostly figurative for experiences of testing (of the Egyptian bondage, Deut. 4:20; 1 Kings 8:51; Jer. 11:4; of adversity, Isa. 48:10). God's stubbornly rebellious people are pictured as "rejected silver" (Jer. 6:30) and as dross, the waste product of the smelting process (Ezek. 22:17-22). Such pictures may form the

F

background of the furnace of fire which symbolizes divine punishment (Matt. 13:42,50).

FURNACES, TOWER OF KJV and NASB designation (Neh. 3:11) for a tower designated "Tower of the Ovens" in other modern translations. The tower was adjacent to the "corner gate" located at the northwest angle in the second or middle wall of Jerusalem. The "Baker's Street" (Jer. 37:21) may have passed by this tower.

FURNITURE Equipment in a home used for rest, beautification, storage, and workspace.

Sacred Furniture Biblical interest in furniture focuses on the sacred furnishings of the tabernacle and the temple. We have in Exod. 25–27; 30; 37–38 a full description of the tabernacle with all its objects of furniture. Lovingly detailed accounts of the ark of the covenant, the altar of incense, and other furnishings are so clear that we can easily visualize and reconstruct them in the form of models. Likewise, 1 Kings 6–7 provides similar data about the temple of Solomon. See *Tabernacle; Temple.*

Common Furniture But this is not the case regarding the furniture of the common people living out their daily lives in their tents and houses. The Bible occasionally refers to basic furniture items such as beds, chairs, etc., but we have virtually nothing about manufacturers, building materials, designs, or appearances.

Biblical terminology illustrates the problem. Old Testament Hebrew has no word equivalent to the English terms "furniture" and "furnishings." The Hebrew word *keli* is so translated in passages such as Exod. 31:7, but in this very same context the very same word (*keli*) is also rendered as "utensils," "articles," or "accessories." In fact, the word *keli* is so fluid that it may refer to any humanly manufactured material object.

Similarly, the NT carries us no further, for it uses no word that could be translated as "furniture" in the English versions.

Sources of Data The Bible remains a source of data, however, at least to the degree that it refers to such items as beds and chairs. Beyond the Bible itself we must resort to artifacts recovered by archaeology. Palestine, however, does not enjoy the climate that would have saved wooden furnishings for study today. Only a few such objects have survived, and even these have greatly disintegrated over time. This being the case, we must resort to secondary artifacts such as written records, seals, sculpture, ivories, and tombs.

Individual Objects of Furniture Domestically, Israelite furniture reflected the simplicity of the ordinary household dwelling. Some Israelites preferred to live in tents (Jer. 35), preserving the traditions of nomadic and wilderness days. The furnishings of such a living place would have to be readily portable and as light as possible. Chests of some sort would be used when the family or clan was settled, then double as carriage crates when on the move. A few simple rugs covered the ground floor. The tent itself and all its paraphernalia—pegs, ropes, interior curtains for separating the "rooms" inside, along with a few sleeping mats—might be all the "furniture" such a family owned. The same would apply to those living in small shelters.

A more permanent home would be furnished according to the family's relative wealth or poverty. Like the tent-dwellers mentioned above, a poorer family would own, at the minimum, simple bedding and kitchen equipment. Reed mats would be rolled out on the floor for resting and sleeping. In some cases these mats would have to serve as tables and chairs, as well, since real ones were probably beyond the means of poorer families. All homes needed interior lighting, of course, so even the poor would own, in all probability, several lamps, i.e., saucer-shaped bowls with a pinch in the rim for a wick fueled by a pool of olive oil; such a lamp often sat on a supporting stand. Widemouthed jars for food and water were essential, as were also some sort of stone and clay oven and a grinding mill for preparing grain. A few of these houses might also have stone or wooden benches, some covered with cloth or carpet material around the inner walls; but this was likely the exception among the poor rather than the rule. Since most homes of biblical days had few windows, they would also have had few, if any, curtains.

Even the homes of the comfortable and the wealthy would also seem all but bare in contrast to the homes of any socioeconomic class in a developed nation of the West today. Consider the home of the "wealthy woman" of Shunem (in lower northern Palestine about five miles east of Megiddo), found in 2 Kings 4:8-37. Because of her special concern for the prophet Elisha, she and her husband built "a small room on the roof"

(4:10 NIV) of their house for him to use when he was passing through their vicinity. They furnished it with "a bed and a table, a chair and a lamp" (4:10 NIV), for which he was sincerely grateful.

Only a century later Amos (760–750 B.C.) condemned the decadent prosperity of the wealthy class in his day. He spoke of the mansions of Samaria (Amos 3:15; 5:11; 6:11) and their opulent beds and couches encrusted with ivory (3:12,15; 6:4). By then the gap between the relatively poor and the relatively rich had grown to scandalous proportions, as evidenced by the quality of their furniture (cp. Esther 1:6). It seems most likely that apart from the highly ornamented furniture mentioned in Amos, the household furniture of the vast majority of Israelites was merely functional, rather than aesthetic.

Furniture and Artifacts Archaeology has shed some (but not much) light on ancient Palestinian furniture. The excavation of ancient Jericho in the 1950s discovered a series of tombs containing both the skeletal remains of the dead and practical provisions to serve their needs in the afterlife. The pertinent finds date to about 1600 B.C. Furniture styles were slow to change, and the artifacts found at Jericho were probably like those used by the Israelites long after.

One body had been laid on a wooden bed consisting of a rectangular frame enclosing wooden crosspieces tenoned to the rails. The crosspieces and rails enclosed five panels of woven rush. The bed probably supported a mattress about six inches above the floor.

Beside the bed was a table measuring about 58 inches by 16 inches, supported by only three legs about 10 inches above the floor. Each leg tenoned into a rounded corner extension below the underside of the table. Survivors left a wooden platter of mutton on the table.

Two cylinder seals from Tell es-Sa'idiyeh on the Jordan River and dated to about 750 B.C. show simple chairs in their impressions. One has a tall straight back and, apparently, a seat of woven rush. Further details are unclear. The other chair has a curved, ladder-back design with four cross-slats.   *Tony M. Martin*

FURROW Narrow trench cut in the earth by a plow (1 Sam. 14:14; Job 31:38; 39:10; Pss. 65:10; 129:3; Hos. 10:4; 12:11). The KJV rendered two Hebrew terms as "furrow" which are best translated otherwise. At Ezek. 17:7,10 modern translations opt for bed (NASB, RSV), plot (NIV), or garden (TEV). At Hos. 10:10 modern translations understand a reference to two sins (iniquity, NRSV; guilt, NASB; sin, NIV, TEV; shameful deed, REB).

FUTURE HOPE Expectation of individuals after their death and of the world when God brings present world affairs to an end.

Future hope focuses upon the expectancy of the consummation of the individual's salvation at the close of the age. With the ushering in of the eternal order at the return of Christ, the believer's hope becomes experienced reality rather than anticipation of future experience (Rom. 8:24-25). This eschatological orientation of NT future hope grows out of the OT prophetic anticipation of God's future deliverance (Isa. 25:9; see especially Paul's use of Isa. 11:10 in Rom. 15:12).

Old Testament Terms In the Hebrew OT several terms are used to convey the idea of hope: *qawah* (to be stretched out towards, to long after, wait for [with God as object 26 times]), *yachal* (to wait, long [for God, 27 times]), *chakah* (to wait [for God, 7 times]), *sabar* (to wait, hope [for God, 4 times]). The corresponding nouns are not commonly used; only nine times in reference to hope in God. Of the 146 uses of these verbs or nouns, only half have the thrust to spiritual reality rather than a nonreligious meaning. In these 73 religious uses the concept of hope is closely related to trust. God is the ground and frequent object of hope; "to hope in Yahweh," "to wait for Yahweh" are common expressions. Implicit to hoping in God is submission to His sovereign rule. Consequently, hope and fear of God are often expressed together (Pss. 33:18-20; 147:11; Prov. 23:17-18). To hope in God is to stand in awe of Him and His power with the confidence that God will faithfully perform His word. Thus hope becomes trust in the righteous character of Yahweh.

Between the Testaments In the interbiblical period the eschatological thrust of hope became prominent but also confusing with its differing expectations. This future hope was often directed toward the expectation of the Messiah and the restoration of the kingdom of Israel. With the emergence of numerous individuals making messianic claims, arousing the expectations of the people, but then collapsing into defeat and destruction, the future hope of Israel took on a pessimistic tone especially in rabbinical thought. Not before Israel achieved complete obedience to the law could God's kingdom be established.

This national uncertainty tended to create a personal uncertainty about what constitutes the required obedience for pleasing God, thus ensuring the resurrection of the body and inclusion in that coming messianic kingdom. In contrast to this pessimistic view, one finds in Qumran a confident eschatological hope. However, this hope was only possible for the select few who were the elect of God. In Hellenistic Judaism, future hope was submerged into the Greek concept of the immortality of the soul, as Philo's writings illustrate.

New Testament The writers in the NT express the concept of future hope primarily by the Greek word *elpis* and its cognates.

The use of hope in reference to the return of Christ is seen in Matt. 24:50 (also Luke 12:46) and in 2 Pet. 3:12-14. In Jesus' teaching on watchfulness, failure to be expecting the return of the Son of man can cause disaster. In 2 Peter this expectation of the day of the Lord stands as the incentive to holy living. In both passages the element of uncertainty often associated with the Greek word has disappeared and is replaced with the sense of confidence based upon the promise of the Lord to come again.

Content of Future Hope The objects of the various Greek words relating to future hope provide insight into what constitutes this hope. Most basic is the expectancy of the return of Christ, described as the revelation of our Lord Jesus Christ (1 Cor. 1:7) and as the coming of the day of God (*parousia*; 2 Pet. 3:12), or just simply as hope in our Lord Jesus Christ (1 Thess. 1:3; cp.

Luke 12:36; Phil. 3:20; Heb. 9:28). This expectancy constitutes a blessed hope and is defined as the manifestation of the glory of our great God and our Savior Jesus Christ (Titus 2:13; cp. Rom. 5:2; Col. 1:27). Accompanying this manifestation of Christ is the expectancy of a new heaven and a new earth (2 Pet. 3:13; Rev. 21:1); the resurrection of the righteous and the wicked (Acts 24:15); the revelation of the sons of God (Rom. 8:19); our adoption as sons which is defined as the redemption of our bodies (Rom. 8:23); the mercy of our Lord Jesus Christ for life eternal (Jude 21); God's grace (1 Pet. 1:13). As Abraham awaited the Holy City, so the believer looks forward to it (Heb. 11:10). The hope of Israel in the promise of God is realized in the Christian hope of resurrection (Acts 26:6-8). These constitute the hope of life eternal long promised beforehand (Titus 1:2; 3:7), of salvation (1 Thess. 5:8) and of righteousness (Gal. 5:5).

The basis of this hope lies in God. In Him who is the Savior of all mankind one puts hope (1 Tim. 4:10; 5:5; Rom. 15:12; 1 Pet. 1:21), rather than in uncertain riches (1 Tim. 6:17); in His name is hope placed (Matt. 12:21), or in Christ (1 Cor. 15:19). This hope is linked closely to the gospel (Col. 1:23), to our calling into God's grace (Eph. 1:18; 4:4) and to faith and the presence of the Holy Spirit (Gal. 5:5). It is a dynamically living hope (1 Pet. 1:3) which motivates one to holy and righteous living (2 Pet. 3:14). As such it stands as a member of the Christian triad of faith, hope, and love (1 Cor. 13:13; 1 Thess. 1:3; Col. 1:4-5). See *Day of the Lord; Eschatology; Eternal Life; Faith; Faithfulness; Hope; Resurrection; Return of Christ; Salvation.*   *Lorin L. Cranford*

Sunset on the Sea of Galilee at Tiberias.

GAAL (Gā´ ǎl) Personal name meaning "abhorrence," "neglect," or perhaps "dung beetle." Man who usurped Abimelech's leadership in Shechem but met sudden defeat from Abimelech and left the city (Judg. 9:26-41). The early translations spell his name and that of his father in several different ways, showing perhaps that Israelites intentionally distorted his name to shame his reputation.

GAASH (Gā´ ǎsh) Personal name meaning "rising and falling noisily." A height in the hill country of Ephraim that cannot be located any more precisely. Joshua was buried there (Josh. 24:30). Hiddai, one of David's 30 military heroes, came from the brooks of Gaash (2 Sam. 23:30).

GABA (Gā´ bà) (KJV) See *Geba*.

GABBAI (Găb´ bā ī) Personal name traditionally interpreted as meaning "tax collector." Member of tribe of Benjamin who settled in Jerusalem in time of Nehemiah (Neh. 11:8). Many modern commentators think copying errors have introduced the name into the text from an original Hebrew text meaning "heroic men," though no existing Hebrew text has this reading.

GABBATHA (Găb´ bà thà) English transliteration of Greek transliteration of Aramaic place-name meaning "elevation." A platform in front of the praetorian or governor's palace in Jerusalem, where Pilate sat in judgment over Jesus (John 19:13), pronouncing the sentence to crucify Jesus. Before announcing the decision, however, Pilate introduced Jesus as King of the Jews, giving the Jewish leaders one last chance to confess their Messiah. The Greek name for the place was *lithostrotos*, or "stone pavement." The location is either the fortress Antonia or Herod's palace. Tourists see the Antonia site at the present Convent of the Sisters of Zion, but archaeologists have dated the pavement there later than Jesus' time.

GABRIEL (Gā´ brǐ ĕl) Personal name meaning "strong man of God." The heavenly messenger who interpreted to Daniel the meaning of the vision of the ram and the goat. He appears four times in the Bible, each time bringing to human beings a message from the Lord. Twice he appeared to Daniel (8:15-27; 9:20-27). In the NT he appeared to announce the births of John the Baptist (Luke 1:8-20) and Jesus (Luke 1:26-38). See *Angels*.

GAD (Găd) Personal name meaning "good fortune." **1.** Seventh son of Jacob and the progenitor of the tribe of Gad (Gen. 30:9-11). His mother was Leah's maid Zilpah. At the conclusion of the period of wilderness wandering, when the Israelites were preparing to occupy Canaan, the tribe of Gad requested permission, along with the tribe of Reuben and half the tribe of Manasseh, to settle east of the Jordan. Their reason was that they owned large numbers of livestock and the territory east of the Jordan was particularly suitable for raising livestock (Num. 32). This territory became known as Gad (Jer. 49:1). Though the exact limits of Gad's tribal territory are difficult to determine, the Gadites generally occupied land to the northeast of the Dead Sea (Josh. 13:24-28). See Tribes of Israel. **2.** Syrian god known from inscriptions from Phoenicia and Palmyra and used in biblical names such as Baal-gad (Josh. 11:17) and Migdal-gad (Josh. 15:37). It also apparently is meant in Isa. 65:11 where the prophet condemned the people for setting "a table for Fortune" (NASB; Hb. *Gad*). **3.** Prophet who advised David as he fled from Saul (1 Sam. 22:5) and who brought God's

Entrance to the Church of St. Gabriel in Nazareth.

options for punishment after David took a census of Israel (2 Sam. 24:11-14). Gad also brought David God's orders to build an altar, apparently on the site of the future temple (2 Sam. 24:18-19). The Chronicler pointed his readers to records of David's reign by Gad (1 Chron. 29:29) and of Gad's assistance in showing David God's plan for temple worship (2 Chron. 29:25).

GADARA (Găd´ à rà) Place-name for home of Gadarenes used in TEV (Matt. 8:28). See *Gadarene.*

GADARENE (Găd´ à rēn) Resident of Gadara, one of the cities of Decapolis (Mark 5:1; Gerasenes, HCSB). In the NT it is mentioned only in the Gospel accounts of the healing of the Gadarene man who was afflicted by demons (Matt. 8:28-34; Mark 5:1-17; Luke 8:26-37). The textual tradition in the Greek manuscripts of each of these passages shows confusion among Gadarenes, Gerasenes, and Gergesenes. Textual evidence appears to favor Gadarenes in Matthew, Gerasenes in Mark and Luke. Origen, an early church father, apparently introduced Gergesenes into the tradition. Gadarene, in the context, would have to refer to the larger area, not just the city of Gadara. Gergasenes points to the modern city of Kersa on the lake's edge. Gerasene comes from the city of Gerasa about 30 miles southeast of the lake. Early tradition may have confused the Hebrew or Aramaic spelling of Gedara and Gerasa or may have seen Gerasa as the dominant town in the area. Whatever the original name, Gentiles and their pigs dominated the area. It has been identified with modern Um Keis, approximately five miles southeast of the Sea of Galilee. The designation "country of the Gadarenes" evidently applied to an area that extended as far as the shore of Galilee.

GADDI (Găd´ dī) Personal name meaning "my good fortune." Spy from the tribe of Manasseh sent by Moses to examine the land of Canaan prior to Israel's conquest (Num. 13:11).

GADDIEL (Găd´ dĭ ĕl) Personal name meaning "God is my good fortune." Spy from tribe of Zebulun that Moses sent to examine Canaan, the land to be conquered (Num. 13:10).

GADFLY (Jer. 46:20 NIV, NRSV) Stinging insect (stinging fly, TEV), either a horsefly (*Tabanidae*, NASB) or a botfly (*Oestridae*). See *Insects.*

GADI (Gā´ dī) Personal name meaning "my good fortune." A variant Hebrew spelling of Gaddi using same word as Gadite. Father of Menahem, king of Israel (752–742 B.C.) (2 Kings 15:14,17).

GADITE (Găd´ īte) Member of tribe of Gad. See *Gad; Gadi.*

GAHAM (Gā´ hăm) Personal name meaning "flame." Son of Nahor, Abraham's brother, by his concubine Reumah (Gen. 22:24).

GAHAR (Gā´ här) Personal name meaning "drought" or "small in spirit" or "red-faced." Clan head of family of temple servants who returned from Babylonian captivity with Zerubbabel about 537 B.C. (Ezra 2:47).

GAIUS (Gā´ ŭs) Greek form of Latin name *Caius* meaning "I am glad, rejoice." **1.** Macedonian Christian who was one of Paul's traveling companions (Acts 19:29). Along with Aristarchus, he was seized during the riot in Ephesus incited by Demetrius the silversmith. **2.** Christian from Derbe who accompanied Paul the apostle into Asia (Acts 20:4). **3.** Paul the apostle's host in Corinth (Rom. 16:23). According to 1 Cor. 1:14 he was one of the individuals in Corinth whom Paul personally had baptized. **4.** The Christian John loved and to whom he addressed 3 John (3 John 1).

GALAL (Gā´ lăl) Personal name meaning "roll" or "turtle." **1.** Levite among those who settled in Jerusalem after the exile (1 Chron. 9:15). **2.** Grandfather of Adda, a Levite who led in Nehemiah's thanksgiving (Neh. 11:17). He came up and settled in Jerusalem after the exile (1 Chron. 9:16).

GALATIA (Gà lā´ tià) Geographical name derived from Gaul because its inhabitants were Celts or Galli (Gauls). The original settlement was in central Asia Minor. King Nicomedes of Bithynia invited the Celtic warriors across the Bosporus River to help him fight his brother in 278 B.C. The invaders fought on their own, capturing cities until stopped by Antiochus I in 275 B.C. They then occupied the northern part of Asia Minor, bounded on the north by Pontus and Bithynia, on the east by Tavium and Pessinus in the west. For the most part, true Galatians lived in open areas, leaving city occupation to their

G

predecessors, the Phrygians. The true Galatians constantly switched sides in ongoing battles in the area. Finally, in 25 B.C. Rome made Galatia a province of the empire and extended its borders, adding Lycaonia, Isauria, and Pisidia with Ancyra serving as the governmental center. Various Roman rulers added and subtracted territory from the province, so its precise boundaries are difficult to draw. Paul visited Galatia (Acts 16:6; 18:23), though his precise route is not clear. It is not known whether he visited Phrygian-dominated cities or the true Galatians in the countryside or whether his letter was addressed to the original territory in the north or to the Roman province with its southern additions (cp. 1 Cor. 16:1; 2 Tim. 4:10, where some manuscripts have Gaul, and 1 Pet. 1:1). See *Asia Minor, Cities of; Galatians, Letter to the.*

GALATIAN (Gȧ lā´ shən) Specifically, a member of the Celtic or Galli tribes which invaded and settled Galatia, but more generally any resident of the territory or province of Galatia. See *Galatia.*

The image of a dying Gaul. The Gauls or Galli who inhabited the region of Galatia were a warlike people.

GALATIANS, LETTER TO THE Galatians is Paul's most intense letter. His anger at their situation is evidenced by the omission of his usual expression of praise after the salutation. The Galatian churches were founded by Paul (4:13-15), but others, probably from Jerusalem, visited the Galatians espousing views contrary to what Paul had taught. Their teachings centered around the need to supplement faith in Christ with obedience to the law of Moses. Circumcision was required, since it marked the "conversion" of a Gentile male to Judaism. The false teachers were referred to as "Judaizers."

Paul forcefully presented his position that justification comes by the grace of God, by faith alone in Christ alone. By justification Paul means both being declared guiltless before God and being granted status as a member of God's covenant community. One's salvation is in no way contingent on observing the law of Moses. Relying on observance of the law demonstrates that one lacks the necessary faith that Christ alone is sufficient for salvation.

Two problems make determining the origin and destination of Galatians difficult. The first is the exact identity of the Galatians. The word itself referred either to an ethnic group (also known as Gauls or Celts) in northern Galatia or to those living in the Roman province of Galatia. If Paul used the term in its provincial sense, then he probably wrote to believers in cities in the south such as Iconium, Lystra, Derbe, and Pisidian Antioch, in churches established on Paul's first missionary journey. If so, Paul could have written Galatians as early as A.D. 49, although others maintain he wrote from Corinth about A.D. 53. On the other hand, some scholars have held that Paul wrote to ethnic Galatians living in northern Galatia. They believe Acts 16:6 and 18:23 should be interpreted that Paul went north on his second journey. If so, Paul did not write Galatians until around A.D. 55. It is more likely Paul addressed those in the south for two reasons. First, Paul tends to use provincial titles (cp. 2 Cor. 9:2). Second, we have no evidence Paul ever visited northern Galatia.

The second problem is how visits to Jerusalem mentioned in Galatians correlate with those visits in Acts. Acts describes five visits by Paul to Jerusalem (Acts 9:26; 11:27-30; 12:25; 15:4; 18:21; 21:7,15), and Paul mentions two visits in Galatians. Galatians 1:18-19 describes

Paul's first postconversion visit to Jerusalem. Most agree this is the visit of Acts 9:26. Many traditionally held that the second visit mentioned in Galatians (2:1-2) is the third visit of Acts, the "Jerusalem Conference" visit. Yet it seems more likely the visit of Gal. 2:1 is the "famine relief" visit in Acts 11:27 and 12:25 for these reasons. First, Gal. 1–2 describes his visits to Jerusalem (1:20). It is unlikely he would neglect to mention a visit, since the issue had become highly charged. Second, Paul describes a private meeting in Galatians; the meeting in Acts 15 is public. Meeting with the apostles in private would explain why Luke does not mention details of the visit in Acts 11–12. Third, the agreement in Gal. 2 is for Paul to go to the Gentiles and Peter to the "circumcision." The agreement in Acts 15 was that Gentiles need not be circumcised to be saved but that they should observe certain restrictions. Nothing is mentioned about spheres of ministry in Acts 15. Fourth, reference to a request by the apostles "that we would remember the poor" (Gal. 2:10 HCSB) would be natural if the visit was for famine relief, as was the case in Acts 11:27 and 12:25.

The letter can be divided into three main sections. In the first (Gal. 1:10–2:21) Paul defends his apostleship as given directly by God through Christ, not dependent on Jerusalem or those who were apostles before him. He describes his relationship with Jerusalem as distant but largely positive. Paul fulfilled his commission without authority from Jerusalem. The only problem came in a confrontation with Peter over table-fellowship with Gentiles at Antioch. Paul concludes by stating the main argument of the epistle: Justification is by faith in Christ and the works of the law must not be added. Faith is living one's life in constant submission to Christ and in relationship to Christ. In fact, Paul says, "Christ lives in me."

In the second section (3:1–5:12) he supports his thesis by appeals to the Galatians' own experience, inheritance practices, and the experiences of Abraham. His first appeal to the Galatians' experience reminds them of their receiving the Spirit, which Paul equates with conversion (3:1-5). They received the Spirit by believing the message Paul preached. Now they thought they could add something to the Spirit by works of the flesh, that is, circumcision. Paul reminds them that Abraham was declared right-eous when he was uncircumcised. He, too, had simply believed God and this faith was credited to him as righteousness (3:6-9). Reliance on the law placed one under the curse of the law (3:10-14). The purpose of Christ's work was to free (redeem) from the curse.

Paul also appeals to their knowledge of inheritance and adoption practices. Once an adoptee was placed in a will, it could not be changed. A promise was made to Abraham concerning a blessing to be given to all nations. God would never alter a promise (3:17). That would be like changing a will after it was put into effect.

Paul continues the same reasoning in chapter 4 but changes the hypothetical to that of a "minor" treated as a slave until a time set by the father for the child's legal status to change. When that time comes, then things are completely different (4:1-7). So with the coming of Christ, in the fullness of time, the children of God are no longer slaves to the law.

After a reminder they once welcomed Paul despite physical infirmity, Paul concludes by appealing to the birth of Abraham's sons. Isaac was the son through whom the promise came. Ishmael's birth was natural or "of the flesh." Isaac, born to Sarah late in life, was born according to the promise of God. Believers too are children of the promise and should not depend on the flesh. To be circumcised was to depend on the flesh. They must trust the promise of God in Christ.

The third major section (5:13–6:10) contains Paul's appeal to live by the Spirit. They must not lose their spiritual freedom by giving in to sin. Life in the Spirit does not rule out moral absolutes. Paul's emphasis on justification by faith was an argument for the Galatians to live out their freedom. That freedom, however, must not be taken as meaning there is no moral accountability. The command that they not live by the law of Moses is not inconsistent with directions on how to live. The "works of the flesh" are obvious and must be avoided. They must nurture the fruit of the Spirit (5:22-23a) and act in love toward each other. In this way they will fulfill the law of Christ.

The closing section is written in Paul's own hand and again challenges them not to return to dependence upon the law (6:11-18).

Outline

   I. Introduction (1:1-10).

A. Paul greets the Galatians and reminds them his commission came from God (1:1-5).

B. Paul reprimands the Galatians (1:6-10).
1. They are turning to another gospel of a different kind (1:6).
2. There is no other (true) gospel than the one he preached to them (1:7).
3. People who preach another gospel are to be accursed, eternally condemned (1:8-9).
4. Paul seeks to please God and not other persons (1:10).

II. Paul Defends His Gospel (1:11–2:21).
A. He received his gospel directly from Jesus Christ (1:11-12).
B. He recounts his previous life in Judaism (1:13-14).
C. He reminds them of his calling to preach to the Gentiles (1:15-17).
D. He visited Jerusalem for 15 days (1:18-24).
E. After 14 years he made a second visit to Jerusalem (2:1-10).
F. He confronted Peter at Antioch for withdrawing from Gentile believers (2:11-14).
G. He summarizes his understanding of the true gospel—faith alone justifies (2:15-21).

III. Paul Explains His Gospel (3:1–5:12).
A. The Galatians received the Spirit without obeying the law (3:1-5).
B. Abraham was accounted as righteous without obeying the law (3:6-9).
C. All under the law are under the curse of the law (3:10-14).
D. The promises to Abraham could not be altered by the law (3:15-18).
E. The law had a temporary role (3:19-22).
F. Christ came to give to all who believe status as God's children (3:23-29).
G. Christ's coming means we can call out to God as "Abba" (4:1-7).
H. Knowing God makes observance of special days or celebrations unnecessary (4:8-11).
I. Paul recounts his visit with the Galatians (4:12-20).
1. They received him well despite his physical infirmity (4:12-13).
2. They welcomed him as if an angel, or as Jesus Christ Himself (4:14).
3. They would have done anything for him (4:15).
4. Paul appeals to them to return to their former belief and trust (4:16-20).

J. Paul appeals to the example of Sarah and Hagar (4:21-31).
1. Isaac was born of the promise to the free woman.
2. Ishmael was born to the slave girl by natural means.

K. Conclusion: They must not forfeit their freedom (5:1-12).

IV. Paul Explains Freedom in the Spirit (5:13–6:10).
A. Freedom is to be used to serve each other through love (5:13-15).
B. Freedom results in being led by the Spirit (5:16-26).
1. The "works of the flesh" are obvious and dangerous (5:16-21).
2. The "fruit of the Spirit" are borne by those who crucify the flesh (5:22-26).
C. Freedom is to be used to minister to others (6:1-10).
1. They must help the wayward, the burdened, and those who teach them (6:1-6).
2. They will reap what they sow in due time (6:7-10).

V. Conclusion (6:11-18).
A. The Judaizers have false motives (6:11-13).
B. Paul will boast only of Jesus Christ (6:14).
C. Being a new creation, not being circumcised, is the intent of the gospel (6:15-16).
D. Farewell (6:17-18).

C. Hal Freeman, Jr.

GALBANUM (Exod. 30:34) See *Plants*.

GALEED (Găl´ ə ĕd) Place-name meaning "pile for witness." Place where Jacob and his father-in-law Laban made a formal agreement or covenant determining the boundary line between their peoples and agreeing not to harm one another

(Gen. 31:43-52). The place was also called Sahadutah and Mizpah. The heap of stones marking Galeed was in Gilead, north of the Jabbok River. See *Mizpah*.

GALILEAN (Găl ĭ lē´ ȧn) Person who lived in Galilee. Dialect distinguished them from Jews in Jerusalem and Judah, particularly the difficulty in distinguishing the sounds of the gutturals that are important in Hebrew and Aramaic. Peter's Galilean style of speech set him apart from the courtyard crowd during Jesus' trial (Mark 14:70; cp. Acts 2:7). Jesus was identified as being from Galilee (Matt. 26:69). Pilate used this as an excuse to get Herod to hear Jesus' case (Luke 23:6-7). Galileans had a reputation for rebellion and disregard of Jewish law (Acts 5:37), so they could be regarded as sinners (Luke 13:2). Apparently, Pilate had killed some Galileans while they offered the Passover sacrifices in Jerusalem (Luke 13:1). On His return to Galilee from Judea and Samaria, Jesus received a warm welcome from the Galileans. This surprising statement is modified by the story that followed showing the welcome apparently depended on an expectation of miracles, not on appreciation for whom Jesus was or from faith in Him (John 4:43-54).

Sea of Galilee with a view of the boat landing at Capernaum.

GALILEE (Găl´ ĭ lē) Place-name meaning "circle" or "region." The northern part of Palestine above the hill country of Ephraim and the hill country of Judah (Josh. 20:7). The Septuagint or early Greek translation referred to a king of the nations of Galilee in Josh. 12:23, though the Hebrew reads, "Gilgal." Many scholars see the Greek as original (NRSV, REB). This would indicate a leader of a coalition of city-states whom Joshua defeated. Kedesh in Galilee was a city of refuge (Josh. 20:7) and a city for the Levites (Josh. 21:32). Solomon paid Hiram of Tyre 20

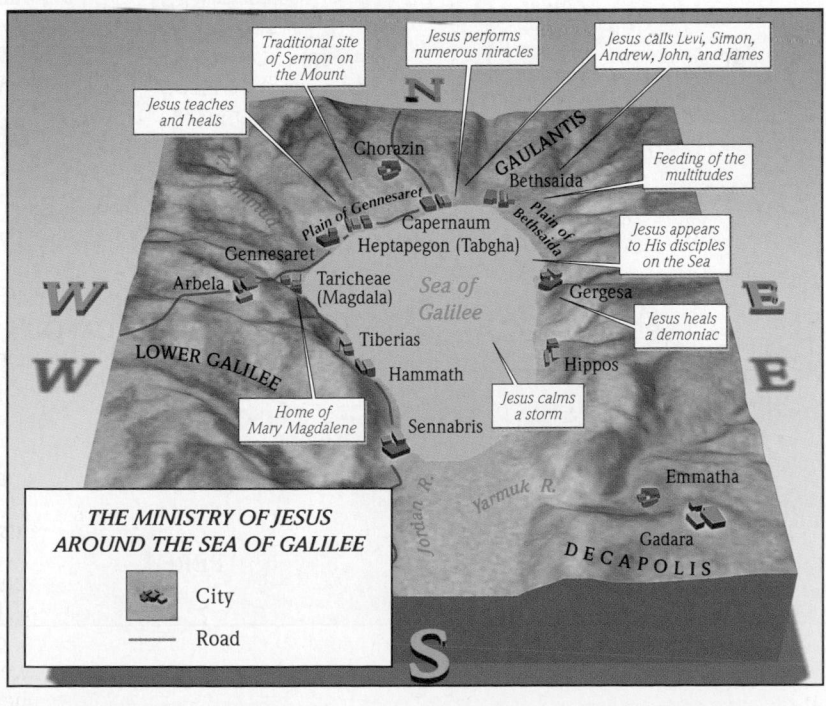

THE MINISTRY OF JESUS AROUND THE SEA OF GALILEE

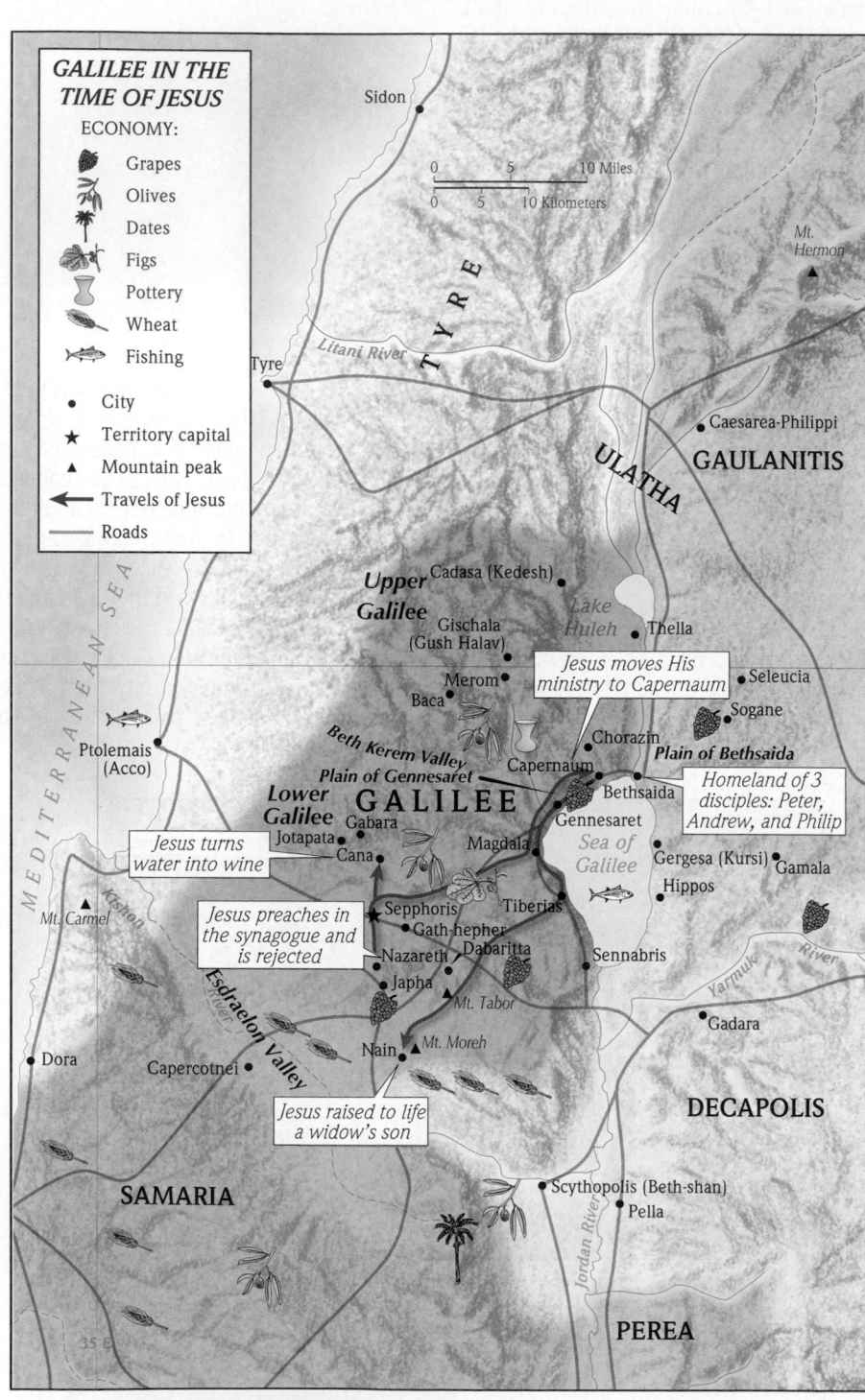

GALILEE IN THE TIME OF JESUS

ECONOMY:

- Grapes
- Olives
- Dates
- Figs
- Pottery
- Wheat
- Fishing

- • City
- ★ Territory capital
- ▲ Mountain peak
- ← Travels of Jesus
- — Roads

Sidon

TYRE

Mt. Hermon ▲

Caesarea-Philippi •

ULATHA

GAULANITIS

Litani River

Tyre

Upper Galilee

Cadasa (Kedesh)

Lake Huleh

Thella •

Gischala (Gush Halav)

Jesus moves His ministry to Capernaum

Seleucia •

Merom •

Baca •

Sogane

Chorazin •

Plain of Bethsaida

Beth Kerem Valley

Ptolemais (Acco) •

Plain of Gennesaret

Capernaum •

Bethsaida •

Homeland of 3 disciples: Peter, Andrew, and Philip

MEDITERRANEAN SEA

Lower Galilee

GALILEE

Gabara •

Gennesaret •

Jotapata •

Magdala •

Sea of Galilee

Gergesa (Kursi) •

Gamala

Jesus turns water into wine

Cana •

Hippos •

Mt. Carmel ▲

Kishon

Sepphoris •

Tiberias •

Jesus preaches in the synagogue and is rejected

Gath-hepher •

Nazareth •

Dabaritta •

Sennabris •

Japha •

Mt. Tabor ▲

Esdraelon Valley

Nain •

Mt. Moreh

Gadara •

Dora •

Capercotnei •

Yarmuk River

DECAPOLIS

Jesus raised to life a widow's son

SAMARIA

Scythopolis (Beth-shan) •

Pella •

Jordan River

PEREA

35 E

cities of Galilee for the building materials Hiram supplied for the temple and royal palace (1 Kings 9:11), but the cities did not please Hiram, who called them Cabul, meaning "like nothing" (1 Kings 9:12-13). Apparently, Galilee and Tyre bordered on each other. The cities may have been border villages whose ownership the two kings disputed. The Assyrians took the north under Tiglath-pileser in 733 (2 Kings 15:29) and divided it into three districts—the western coast or "the way of the sea" with capital at Dor, Galilee with capital at Megiddo and beyond Jordan or Gilead (Isa. 9:1).

The term "Galilee" apparently was used prior to Israel's conquest, being mentioned in Egyptian records. It was used in Israel but not as a political designation. The tribes of Naphtali, Asher, Issachar, Zebulun, and Dan occupied the territory which covered approximately the 45-mile stretch between the Litani River in Lebanon and the Valley of Jezreel in Israel north to south and from the Mediterranean Sea to the Jordan River west to east.

In the time of Jesus' Galilee, Herod Antipas governed Galilee and Perea. Jesus devoted most of His earthly ministry to Galilee, being known as the Galilean (Matt. 26:69). After the fall of Jerusalem in A.D. 70, Galilee became the major center of Judaism, the Mishnah and Talmud being collected and written there.

GALILEE, SEA OF Place-name meaning "circle." A freshwater lake nestled in the hills of northern Palestine. Its surface is nearly 700 feet below the level of the Mediterranean, some 30 miles to the west. The nearby hills of Galilee reach an altitude of 1,500 feet above sea level. To the east are the mountains of Gilead with peaks of more than 3,300 feet. To the north are the snow-covered Lebanon Mountains. Fed chiefly by the Jordan River, which originates in the foothills of the Lebanon Mountains, the Sea of Galilee is 13 miles long north and south and eight miles wide at its greatest east-west distance. Because of its location, it is subject to sudden and violent storms that are usually of short duration.

In the OT this sea is called Chinnereth. It is named only rarely, however, and all references but one relate to the Hebrew conquest of Palestine under Joshua. In NT times it was also called the "lake of Gennesaret." Luke referred to it by that name once (5:1); the Jewish historian Josephus always called it by that name, and so did

The Sea of Galilee as viewed from the northwest.

Looking eastward across the Sea of Galilee.

the author of First Maccabees. Once John called it the "Sea of Tiberias" (6:1).

In the first century the Sea of Galilee was of major commercial significance. Most Galilean roads passed by it, and much travel to and from the east crossed the Jordan rift there. Fish was a major food in the area, and the fishing industry flourished because there was no other significant freshwater lake in the region. Capernaum, which played a major role in the ministry of Jesus, was a center of that industry. The other lake towns of importance were Bethsaida, which means "the fishing place," and Tiberias, a Gentile city constructed by Herod Antipas when Jesus was a young man. See *Chinnereth.*   *Roger Crook*

GALL 1. Bitter, poisonous herb (perhaps *Citrullus colocynthis*), the juice of which is thought to be the "hemlock" poison that Socrates drank. Gall was frequently linked with wormwood (Deut. 29:18; Jer. 9:15; 23:15; Lam. 3:19; Amos 6:12) to denote bitterness and tragedy. Wormwood and gall were often associated with unfaithfulness to God, either as a picture of the unfaithful (Deut. 29:18) or as their punishment. Modern speech translations generally translate the Hebrew word for gall in light of the context of the passage (poisonous growth, Deut. 29:18 NRSV; poisonous water, Jer. 8:14; 9:15; 23:15 NRSV; poison, Amos 6:12 NRSV). Gall is still used at Lam. 3:19. On the cross, Jesus was offered sour wine drugged with gall, perhaps opium, which He refused (Matt. 27:34; cp. Ps. 69:21). Simon the magician was described as full of the gall of bitterness (Acts 8:23) because he wanted to prostitute the gift of the Holy Spirit. **2.** Expressed by two different Hebrew words, used in three senses in connection with the liver: (1) as an organ, either the liver or the gallbladder,

through which a sword might pass when one was run through (Job 20:25); (2) as bile, a sticky, yellow-greenish, alkaline fluid secreted by the liver, which might be poured out on the ground when one was disemboweled (Job 16:13); (3) in a figurative sense (Job 13:26) for bitterness (bitter things, NASB, NIV, NRSV; bitter charges, REB, TEV).

GALLERY Architectural feature of the temple annex (Ezek. 41:15-16) and two buildings near the temple (42:3,5). The English "gallery" is an ambiguous term referring to a number of features: a corridor (REB); a roofed walkway or colonnade; an outdoor balcony or terrace. The meaning of the underlying Hebrew word is contested. Some suggest the meaning was "passageway" on the basis of similarities with Akkadian. Others suggest the term means slope or embankment. In this case the temple measurements in 41:15-16 would refer to the base of the elevated inner court. English translators understand either a reference to interior corridors of the temple annex or columned porches (contrast 42:6). The two buildings in chapter 42 were apparently constructed "stair-step" style with each floor smaller than the one beneath it. Here the gallery is perhaps the terrace formed by the flat roof of the floor below. Others have suggested the Hebrew refers to underlying rock formations that protruded into the structure.

GALLEY Long, narrow ship propelled mainly by oars. The galleys were used as warships (Isa. 33:21). Such vessels were designed to sail near the shore or on rivers. The image in Isaiah is of a Jerusalem free from the threat of invasion.

GALLIM (Găl´ lĭm) Place-name meaning "heaps." Village near Anathoth in tribal territory of Benjamin. Saul gave his daughter Michal as wife to a citizen of Gallim after taking her away from David (1 Sam. 25:44; cp. 2 Sam. 3:14-15). Gallim lay on the road that conquerors took from Bethel down to Jerusalem (Isa. 10:30). It may be modern Khirbet Kakul, northwest of Anathoth or even further to the northwest just south of Ramah at Khirbet Ercha. See *Michal.*

GALLIO (Găl´ lĭ ō) Personal name of unknown meaning. The deputy or proconsul of Achaia headquartered in Corinth, where his judgment seat has been discovered. Certain Jews brought

Paul before Gallio seeking to get Roman punishment of him. They charged that Paul advocated an unlawful religion (Acts 18:12-17). Gallio refused to involve himself in Jewish religious affairs, even ignoring the crowd's beating of Sosthenes, the ruler of the synagogue.

Gallio was the son of Marcus Annaeus Seneca, a Spanish orator and financier, and the elder brother of Seneca, the philosopher and tutor of Nero. Lucius Junius Gallio, a rich Roman, adopted Gallio, naming him Lucius Junius Gallio Annaeus. Gallio's name appears on an inscription at Delphi that refers to the twenty-sixth acclamation of Claudius as emperor. This places Gallio in office in Corinth between A.D. 51 and 53. He was apparently proconsul from May 1, 51, to May 1, 52, though dates a year later are possible. The date gives evidence from outside the Bible for the time Paul was in Corinth and founded the church there.

Finding the climate at Corinth unhealthy, Gallio apparently welcomed the opportunity to return to Rome, where he counseled Nero until he and Seneca joined a conspiracy against the emperor. First Seneca died; then Nero forced Gallio to commit suicide about A.D. 65. See *Achaia; Corinth; Corinthians, First Letter to the; Corinthians, Second Letter to the; Paul; Rome and the Roman Empire.*

GALLON Word used by modern translations to transfer Greek *metretes* into modern terminology. A *metretes* contained about nine gallons (cp. John 2:6; KJV reads "firkins"). See *Weights and Measures.*

GALLOWS English translation referring to the platform on which a person was hanged. The Hebrew term translated "gallows" in Esther (2:23; 7:9-10; 9:25) is the word for "tree." It is frequently suggested that tree should be understood as "stake" and that those executed by the Persians were impaled rather than hung. The earliest Greek translation understood the passage in this sense.

GAMAD (Gā´măd) (NRSV, TEV) or **GAMMAD** (NIV, REB) Place-name of uncertain meaning in Ezek. 27:11. The early translations apparently read a Hebrew text with letters easily confused with those of Gamad and meaning "watchers." Others interpreted it as "dwarf" or "pygmies." Others have pointed to a people called Kumudi

The interior of the traditional site of the tomb of Gamaliel.

from northern Syria listed in early Egyptian sources. They were apparently allies of Tyre in its fight against Babylon.

GAMALIEL (Gȧ mā´ lĭ ĕl) Personal name meaning "God rewards with good." **1.** Son of Pedahzur; a leader of the tribe of Manasseh, who helped Moses take the census in the wilderness (Num. 1:10; cp. 7:54-59). **2.** Highly regarded Pharisee who was a member of the Sanhedrin (Acts 5:34). He squelched a plan by the Sanhedrin to kill the apostles by reminding the members that interference with what the apostles were doing might prove to be opposition to God. If the work of the apostles were a purely human work, Gamaliel said, it would come to nothing anyway. According to Acts 22:3, this Gamaliel had been Paul's teacher. He was the grandson of the great Rabbi Hillel. He died about A.D 52. **3.** A leading Jewish rabbi in the late first and early second centuries A.D. He was the grandson of the Gamaliel mentioned in the book of Acts. He is credited with many of the adaptations in Judaism necessitated by the destruction of the temple in A.D. 70.

GAMES Archaeological finds from the ancient Near East provide ample evidence for the existence in antiquity of numerous types of games, including early forms of checkers and chess. Likewise, various children's toys found in Palestine confirm that Hebrew children, like their counterparts in nearly every culture and era, played recreational games. There is, however, no specific mention of organized games of any kind in the OT. Skills frequently mentioned in the OT, such as running (1 Sam. 8:11), archery (1 Sam. 20:20), using a sling (1 Sam. 17:49), or wrestling

Mosaic of gladiators from the Roman period with the victor standing triumphantly over his opponent.

(Gen. 32:24), imply training and practice, but there are no specific references to competitive events. Israelites either avoided athletic competition or refrained from writing about it.

In contrast to Hebrew culture, Hellenistic culture prized games and competitive events as a central part of life. In order to become good citizens Greek youths received both intellectual and physical training. At the gymnasium a well-rounded education included skills such as boxing and running. The gymnasium, a central part of Hellenistic towns and cities, was also the site of a marketplace, as well as a training facility for mature athletes. Prevalent also in Hellenistic culture were organized competitive events such as chariot racing, wrestling, footraces, boxing, and archery. The Olympic games are a primary example of the important role of athletic games in Hellenistic culture. Competitive games continued, with some changes, in the Roman era but with an added emphasis on combative events such as gladiatorial contests and fighting wild animals. For both Greeks and Romans, these events were connected to the worship of the gods.

With Alexander the Great's conquest of Palestine in 332 B.C., Hellenistic culture swept into Israel, including Greek games and competitions. As a result, arenas and gymnasiums began to appear in Israel. A descendant of one of Alexander's generals, Antiochus IV Epiphanes, who reigned over Palestine (175–164 B.C.), even had a gymnasium built in Jerusalem. Apparently many Jews, including some priests, participated in the events held there (see 1 Macc. 1:14; 2 Macc. 4:9). For many Jews the spectacle of a gymnasium in Jerusalem was repulsive (not least because athletes competed in the nude). Although Hellenistic games became less prevalent in Israel after the Maccabean revolt (167 B.C.), the presence of Hellenistic culture and ath-

A training track for footracing at Olympia.

letic competition remained in Israel. Herod the Great (47–4 B.C.) built, among other things, a stadium and hippodrome in Caesarea, a theater in Jerusalem, and possibly a hippodrome in Jericho. By the first century, Jews in Palestine and in the Diaspora, and of course Gentiles throughout the Mediterranean world, were familiar with competitive games.

In the NT there are direct references to games and competitions, particularly in Paul's epistles. For those living in Corinth in the first century, illustrations from competitive games would be easily understood not only from everyday life but also because it was the site of the Isthmian games (A.D. 51), an event second only to the Olympics in prestige. Paul used the footrace as an illustration of Christian endurance, reminding them that even though all competitors run in the race, only the winner receives the prize (1 Cor. 9:24). He used the strict and severe training of the athletes competing in the games as an analogy to the discipline required for the Christian life, reminding his readers that athletes undergo training to win a "perishable wreath." The celery wreath given to the winners at the Isthmian games may have come to their minds. Paul's message was clear: if athletes do all this to win a perishable crown, how much more should Christians endure and undergo discipline to receive an "imperishable crown" (1 Cor. 9:25). Turning to his own life, Paul used himself as an example of one who does "not run aimlessly." The runners in the games ran toward a fixed mark, perhaps a stone (what we would call a "finish line"). They did not run carelessly but for one purpose: to finish the race (Paul used a similar analogy in Phil. 3:12-14). Furthermore he says, "I do not ... box like one who beats the air. Instead, I discipline my body and bring it under strict control" (1 Cor. 9:26-27 HCSB). Paul fought against his sinful desires with the pitiless intensity of competitors in a boxing match. Thus Paul utilized two of the most well-known events to make a clear illustration about the Christian life.

Paul also used athletic games as an analogy for his whole life. He concluded that he had "finished the race" and therefore would receive the "crown of righteousness" (2 Tim. 4:7).

The writer to the Hebrews also used competitive games as a metaphor for perseverance: "Therefore since we also have such a large cloud

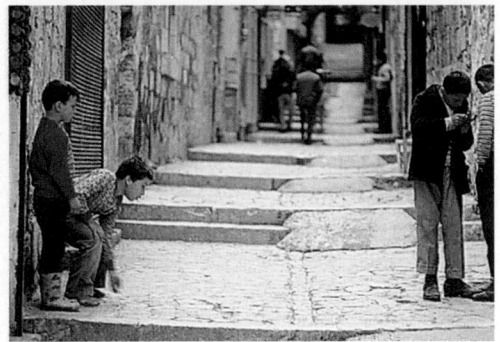

Children in present-day Jerusalem playing a game in the street on the Via Dolorosa.

of witnesses surrounding us," comparing the saints who have gone before to the crowds gathered in the athletic arenas, every effort should be made to "run with endurance the race that lies before us." Moreover, the focus, the finishing line, is Jesus "the source and perfecter of our faith" (Heb. 12:1-4). *Bryan J. Vickers*

GAMMADIM (Găm´ mȧ dĭm) Citizen of Gamad. See *Gamad.*

GAMUL (Gā´ mŭl) Personal name meaning "receiver of good deeds." Head of one of the priestly divisions in the temple under David and Solomon (1 Chron. 24:17).

GANGRENE Greek *gangraina* (2 Tim. 2:17) can refer either to gangrene, a death of soft tissue resulting from problems with blood flow (NASB, NRSV, REB) or to an ulcer (canker, KJV; open sore, TEV). In 2 Timothy *gangraina* is used figuratively for false teachings which destroy people who accept them.

GANGS It was not unusual in antiquity for persons who saw themselves as poor, oppressed, or disenfranchised to gather themselves together under a charismatic leader and live largely under their own authority, sometimes cooperating with existing authority structures and sometimes opposing them. Whether such groups should be called "gangs," "brigands," or simply "bands of adventurers" depends largely on the particular circumstances involved.

The tendency toward gang formation was greatest in times of weakened centralized authority. Hence Abimelech (Judg. 9:4), Jephthah (Judg. 11:3), men attached to Ish-bosheth son of Saul (2 Sam. 4:1-3), Jeroboam (2 Chron.

G

13:6-7), and even David (1 Sam. 22:2) became commanders of gangs of men who had withdrawn from mainstream society. While David's gang was composed of men who had been oppressed, it is implied, by the economic policies of King Saul (1 Sam. 22:2), that the gangs of Abimelech, Jephthah, and Jeroboam consisted of "worthless fellows."

The Bible mentions other instances of gang-like behavior in the rape of the Levite's concubine by the men of Gibeah (Judg. 19:22-26), the attempted rape of Lot's guests by the men of Sodom (Gen. 19:4-11), and the taunting of Elisha by boys (2 Kings 2:23-24).

Paul H. Wright

GARDEN In biblical times an enclosed plot of ground on which flowers, vegetables, herbs, and fruit and nut trees were cultivated (Gen. 2:8; 1 Kings 21:2; Esther 1:5; Isa. 51:3; John 18:1-2). **Characteristics** The primary OT words for "garden" (*gan* and *gannah*) derive from a root meaning "to surround." Gardens were plots of ground enclosed or surrounded by walls or hedges. Some were large (Esther 1:5), the most prominent gardens being royal ones (2 Kings 25:4; Neh. 3:15; Jer. 39:4). Most gardens were situated close to the owner's residence (1 Kings

21:2). Occasionally a house might be located in the garden (2 Kings 9:27). An abundant supply of water was especially important (Gen. 13:10; Num. 24:6; Isa. 1:30; 58:11; Jer. 31:12). Gardeners were employed to tend the more substantial gardens, sowing seed and watering (Deut. 11:10; John 20:15). Orchards or small vineyards were sometimes called gardens.

Uses Obviously a garden provided food for its owner (Jer. 29:5,28; Amos 9:14), but it also served other aesthetic and utilitarian purposes. It was a place of beauty where plants were pleasing to the sight (Gen. 2:9). As a guarded and protected place (Song 4:12), persons could retreat there for prayer (Matt. 26:36-46), for quiet or solitude (Esther 7:7), or even for bathing (Susanna 15). It provided a cool escape from the heat of the day (Gen. 3:8; Susanna 7). Friends could meet in gardens (John 18:1-2), or banquets could be served there (Esther 1:5). It thus was often associated with joy and gladness (Isa. 51:3). On the other hand, pagan sacrifices were sometimes offered in gardens (Isa. 65:3; 66:17); and gardens were used as burial sites (2 Kings 21:18,26; John 19:41-42).

Important Gardens The garden of Eden (Gen. 2:8; 3:23-24) was planted by God (2:8) and entrusted to Adam for cultivating and keeping

A Roman courtyard and garden in the Villa of Menander at Pompeii.

The Garden of Gethsemane looking west toward the city wall of old Jerusalem.

(2:15). Following their sin, Adam and Eve were banished from the garden; but "Eden, the garden of God" (Ezek. 28:13) continued as a symbol of blessing and bounty (Ezek. 36:35; Joel 2:3). The "king's garden" in Jerusalem was located near a gate to the city that provided unobserved exit or escape (2 Kings 25:4; Neh. 3:15; Jer. 39:4; 52:7). The "garden" (John 18:1) called Gethsemane (Matt. 26:36; Mark 14:32) was a place where Jesus often met with His disciples (John 18:2) and where He was betrayed and arrested.

Michael Fink

GAREB (Gā´ rĕb) Personal name and place-name meaning "scabby." **1.** Member of David's personal army (2 Sam. 23:38). **2.** Hill in Jerusalem marking point of city wall which Jeremiah promised would be rebuilt (Jer. 31:39).

GARLAND In modern translations two Hebrew and one Greek term, all referring to wreaths worn on the head. Garlands symbolized instruction or the benefit of wisdom (Prov. 1:8-9; 4:7-9). In Isa. 61:3,10 garlands form part of the bridegroom's wedding apparel (ASV, NEB). Israel's days of exile, pictured as mourning, would give way to the celebration of God's salvation, pictured as a wedding. At Acts 14:13 the priest of Zeus brought Paul and Barnabas garlands. In Greek mythology the gods were frequently portrayed wearing garlands. Mistaking the apostles for Zeus and Hermes, the priest deemed garlands a suitable gift.

GARLIC (Num. 11:5) See *Plants.*

GARMITE (Gär´ mīt) Title or designation meaning "my bone" used for Keilah in the line of the tribe of Judah (1 Chron. 4:19). The Hebrew text and the exact meaning of Garmite are obscure.

Relief from Philippi of bull's head draped with a garland.

GARNER KJV term for a barn, storehouse, or granary (Ps. 144:13; Joel 1:17; Matt. 3:12; Luke 3:17). To garner (Isa. 62:9 NASB, NRSV) means to gather (a crop) for storage. See *Granary*.

GARRISON Body of troops stationed for defense, often in the sense of occupying forces. In the tenth century B.C. the Philistines had garrisons deep in Jewish territory at Gibeath-elohim (1 Sam. 10:5), Geba (1 Sam. 13:3), and Bethlehem (2 Sam. 23:14). David, in turn, placed garrisons in Damascus (2 Sam. 8:6) and in Edom (2 Sam. 8:14) with the result that the natives became his servants, that is, they were subjugated and forced to pay tribute.

The KJV has garrisons at Ezek. 26:11 where modern translations have a reference to pillars in honor of the gods of Tyre. The KJV of 2 Cor. 11:32 mentions that the city of Damascus was guarded with a garrison. Modern versions simply note the city was guarded. The parallel in Acts 9:24 only mentions guards at the gate.

GASH In modern translations to cut the skin as a sign of mourning (NASB, Jer. 41:5; 47:5; 48:37) or in the worship of pagan deities (1 Kings 18:28). See *Fertility Cult*.

GASHMU (Găsh´ mū) Aramaic form of *Geshem* used in Neh. 6:6. See *Geshem*.

GATAM (Gā´ tăm) Personal name of uncertain meaning. Son of Eliphaz and grandson of Esau (Gen. 36:11). He headed a clan of Edomites (Gen. 36:16).

GATE A gate, like a door, a wall, or a threshold, sets a boundary between that which is inside and that which is outside. "Gate" is the more prominent term since it provided the most common access into towns and villages, temples, and even houses. In reality a gate serves both to allow access and to limit access. Open gates allowed entrance, though gatekeepers were often employed to ascertain that only authorized persons gained entry (1 Chron. 9:22). Shut gates offered protection and safety for those inside (Josh. 2:5). Because the gate was the primary means of entry, it was often the site where enemies assembled for attack or forced entry (Jer. 1:15).

Those who resided inside a household compound were members of that household: family members, workers attached to the family unit, servants, or guests. All within the gate were treated as part of the family—they were included under Sabbath rest commandment (Exod. 20:9-10) and as participants in major festivals (Deut. 16:11,14). Guests were to be offered the same protection as family members (see Gen. 19; Judg. 19). Likewise those within the gates of the city were to be afforded the same protection as citizens.

Biblical examples of those excluded by the gate include lepers who were kept outside the gates (2 Kings 7:3), the poor man Lazarus in the parable Jesus told (Luke 16:20), as well as the lame man outside the temple (Acts 3:2). All of these were "outsiders," outside the gate. They were not considered part of the community or family within.

Physically, a gate might be a simple opening in a wall, or it might be an elaborate entry complex with multiple chambers and doors, and several sharp turns designed to impede access. Gates typically had doors of wood or metal that were shut at night and in the event of threatened attack. Towers were often built adjacent to the gate to provide additional protection for the gate entry.

The Bible has several figurative or symbolic allusions to gates. Jacob, after his dream at Bethel, describes the place as "the house of God, … the gate of heaven" (Gen. 28:17 NASB). In effect for Jacob this spot marked a symbolic boundary between heaven and earth. Both Job and the psalmist speak of the gates of death (Job 38:17; Ps. 107:18). The gates of death mark the boundary between life and death. King Hezekiah in the book of Isaiah speaks of being consigned to the gates of Sheol the rest of his days, a clear reference to his death (Isa. 38:10). Jesus says of the church "the gates of Hades shall not overpower it" (Matt. 16:18 NASB). Hades, the realm of the underworld and the dead, has no power over Christ's church.

In summary, "gate" marks a boundary, either physical or figurative between inside and outside. It serves to permit or prevent movement from without to within. See *City Gate; Gates of Jerusalem and the Temple*.

Joel F. Drinkard, Jr.

GATE BETWEEN THE TWO WALLS City gate on the southeast side of Jerusalem, perhaps identical with the Fountain Gate. Zedekiah and his sons were captured by the Babylonians after escaping through this gate (2 Kings 25:4; Jer. 39:4; 52:7). See *City Gate; Fountain Gate; Gate.*

GATEKEEPER One who guards access to a place, either a city (2 Sam. 18:26; 2 Kings 7:10-11), a residence (John 18:17), the sacred precincts of the ark (1 Chron. 15:23-24), or the temple (1 Chron. 23:5). KJV uses "porter." Temple gatekeepers were charged with preventing anyone unclean from entering the temple (2 Chron. 23:19) and with guarding the temple treasuries and storehouses (1 Chron. 9:26; 26:20-22; Neh. 12:25).

GATES OF JERUSALEM AND THE TEMPLE Jerusalem's many gates have varied in number and location with the changing size and orientation of its walls throughout its long history. Persons could enter through an important city gate on the west from Jaffa (Tel Aviv) Road, as they do today. On the east, those coming from the Kidron Valley entered principally through the Sheep Gate (modern Stephen or Lion Gate) in NT times and by a recently found gate (spring 1986) south of the modern city walls in OT times. This latter gate may date to the reign of

The Joppa (modern Jaffa) Gate at Jerusalem.

Solomon, being similar to Solomonic gates found at Megiddo, Gezer, and Hazor. Entrance to the temple itself was on its eastern side through the Beautiful Gate (Acts 3:10), near the Golden Gate recently found beneath the city eastern wall. On the north, the principal gateway (Damascus

The Dung Gate at Jerusalem was the entry to Jerusalem from the Tyropoeon Valley.

The Damascus Gate at Jerusalem as seen from outside the old city walls.

G

Stephen's (or Lion's) Gate at Jerusalem.

Gate) opened onto the Damascus Road. Seven gates now allow entrance to the old city of Jerusalem. *John McRay*

GATH (Găth) One of the five cities that comprised the Philistine city-state system (1 Sam. 6:17). The inhabitants of Gath were referred to as the Gittites (1 Sam. 17:4; 2 Sam. 6:10-11). Because the Hebrew term *gat* meant "winepress" and since vineyards and winepresses were widespread in the land, a number of towns in Palestine were named Gath. Usually the name was used with another name that helped distinguish one site from another, such as, Gath-Hepher, Gath-Rimmon, and Moresheth-Gath.

By far the most frequently mentioned Gath in the OT is Gath of the Philistines. In addition to Gath, the other towns of the Philistine city-state system were Ekron, Ashdod, Ashkelon, and Gaza (1 Sam. 6:17). We may reasonably assume that Gath was the principal city among the five and served as the hub of the Pentapolis.

Gath was strategically located for Philistine purposes. While we do not know the exact location, we do know the general area in which Gath was located. Based on information from the bib-

lical accounts, Gath was located inland as opposed to the other Philistine towns that were on or near the coast. It was located in the Shephelah, that is, the band of foothills that lay between the coastal plain on the west and the central hill country on the east. Since the Israelites, at least during the period of the settlement, occupied the central hill country, Gath was in a position to protect Philistine territory from raids by the Israelites. At the same time it was convenient for the Philistines to initiate raids on Israelite communities from the city of Gath. Since a number of sites have been eliminated in recent years based on archaeological excavations, one of the most likely candidates for Philistine Gath is Tell es-Safi, 12 miles east of Ashdod.

A number of the highlights of Gath's history are reflected in the OT. Prior to the coming of the Israelites, Gath was a Canaanite city occupied by the Anakim, a group known for their large stature (Josh. 11:21-22). During the conquest of Canaan, Joshua and the Israelites apparently did not take the sites of Gaza, Gath, and Ashdod (Josh. 11:22). We may assume that the Philistines took these towns at this point. Gath was one of the locations to which the Philistines took the ark (1 Sam. 5:8-9) and was the hometown of Goliath (1 Sam. 17:4) and Obed-edom (1 Chron. 13:13). One of the most interesting bits of information is that at one point while Saul was in pursuit of David, David found sanctuary with Achish, the king of Gath, and perhaps became a vassal of the Philistines (1 Sam. 27:1-7). Eventually David defeated the Philistines and made Gath an Israelite town (1 Chron. 18:1). Apparently Achish continued to be the king of Gath, perhaps as a vassal king, even during the reign of Solomon (1 Kings 2:39). During the

Panoramic view of the tel of ancient Gath.

period of the divided monarchy, Gath's history went through a series of changes. Rehoboam, the king for Judah (931–913 B.C.) fortified Gath and made it a fortress city of Judah (2 Chron. 11:5-12). Hazael, king of Syria (about 843–797 B.C.), besieged the city and captured it (2 Kings 12:17). Shortly thereafter, the inhabitants of Gath apparently rebelled against Hazael and established to some degree their independence. Finally, Uzziah, king of Judah (792–740 B.C.), partially destroyed Gath and made it once again a part of the territory of Judah (2 Chron. 26:6). Around 711 B.C., Sargon II, the king of Assyria, conquered and perhaps destroyed the city. Apparently, at this point, Gath's history came to an end. This conclusion is reinforced by the fact that Gath is obviously omitted in the lists of Philistine sites mentioned by the prophets (Jer. 25:20; Amos 1:6-8; Zeph. 2:4; Zech. 9:5-6). See *Philistines.*   *LaMoine DeVries*

GATH-HEPHER (Găth-hē´ phĕr) Place-name meaning "winepress on the watering hole." A city on the eastern border of Zebulun's tribal allotment (Josh. 19:13). The prophet Jonah came from Gath-hepher (2 Kings 14:25). It is located at modern el-Meshed or nearby Khirbet ez-Zurra, three miles northeast of Nazareth.

GATH-RIMMON (Găth-rĭm´ mon) Place-name meaning "winepress on the pomegranate tree." Town in tribal territory of Dan (Josh. 19:45) and set aside for Levites (Josh. 21:24). It is usually located at Tell Jerisheh on the Yarkon River in modern Tel Aviv, but some scholars locate it two miles to the northeast at Tell Abu Zeitun. First Chronicles 6:69 lists Gath-rimmon in the tribe of Ephraim, but this is usually understood as a copyist's omission of a sentence at the beginning of verse 69. Gath-rimmon also appears in the Hebrew text of Josh. 21:25 though not in the earliest Greek translation or in the parallel in 1 Chron. 6:70. Most scholars recognize that a copyist repeated Gath-rimmon from verse 24, the original reading probably being Ibleam. See *Ibleam.*

GAUZE, GARMENTS OF One of the fine items associated with Jerusalem socialites (Isa. 3:23 NRSV). The meaning of the underlying Hebrew is debated. The sense is either a gauze garment (NRSV; interpreted as a revealing garment, TEV; scarves of gauze, REB) or a mirror

(hand mirror, NASB). The KJV has glasses in the sense of looking glasses. At this time a mirror would be a piece of polished metal. At Isa. 8:1 the Hebrew word translated as gauze garment (or mirror) is translated as (writing) tablet.

GAZA (Ga´ zȧ) Place-name meaning "strong." Philistine city on the coastal plain about three miles inland from the Mediterranean Sea. It was the southernmost town of the Philistine city-state system which also included Ashkelon, Ashdod, Ekron, and Gath (1 Sam. 6:17).

While the site is especially associated with the Philistines, many other groups have inhabited it throughout history. That history extends from a period prior to the arrival of the Philistines, a period when the Avvim occupied the village (Deut. 2:23), on down to the present. The inhabitants of Gaza at times were referred to as the Gazites or Gazathites (Judg. 16:2).

Gaza's important role in ancient history was due to its strategic location on the major coastal plain highway that connected Egypt with the rest of the ancient Near East. Because of its strategic location, Gaza witnessed the passage of

A mythical figure wearing a gauze-thin garment of Roman style.

G

numerous caravans and armies and often got caught in the middle of the political struggles of the ancient Near East. This is reflected in a brief review of the highlights of Gaza's history. According to the records of Thutmose III, Thutmose captured Gaza on his first campaign to Palestine and made it a major Egyptian center. The Amarna Letters identify Gaza as the district headquarters for Egyptian holdings in southern Palestine. For Solomon, Gaza was the major center on the southern border of his kingdom which ran "from Tiphsah even to Azzah (Gaza)" (1 Kings 4:24 KJV).

Gaza was often affected by the political struggles and turnovers that took place during the Assyrian and Babylonian periods. Tiglath-pileser III collected tribute from Gaza during his military campaign against Israel and Syria about 734 B.C. Hezekiah "smote the Philistines, even unto Gaza" (KJV) as he tried to re-establish Judah's independence (2 Kings 18:8) about 705-704 B.C. Sennacherib reinforced his control of Gaza as a vassal state as he invaded Judah in 701 B.C. Pharaoh Neco conquered Gaza about 609 B.C. and made it an Egyptian holding, but it remained in Egyptian hands for only a few years. Sometime after 605 B.C. the Babylonian King Nebuchad-nezzar conquered Gaza and made it a part of his empire. *LaMoine DeVries*

GAZATHITE (Gā´ zăth ĭt) (KJV, Josh. 13:3) See *Gaza.*

GAZELLE Fleet-footed animal noted for its attractive eyes. Native to the Middle East, this animal resembles an antelope but is smaller. They were considered clean by the Israelites and

Gold cup decorated with the raised figure of a gazelle from the Treasure of the Oxus.

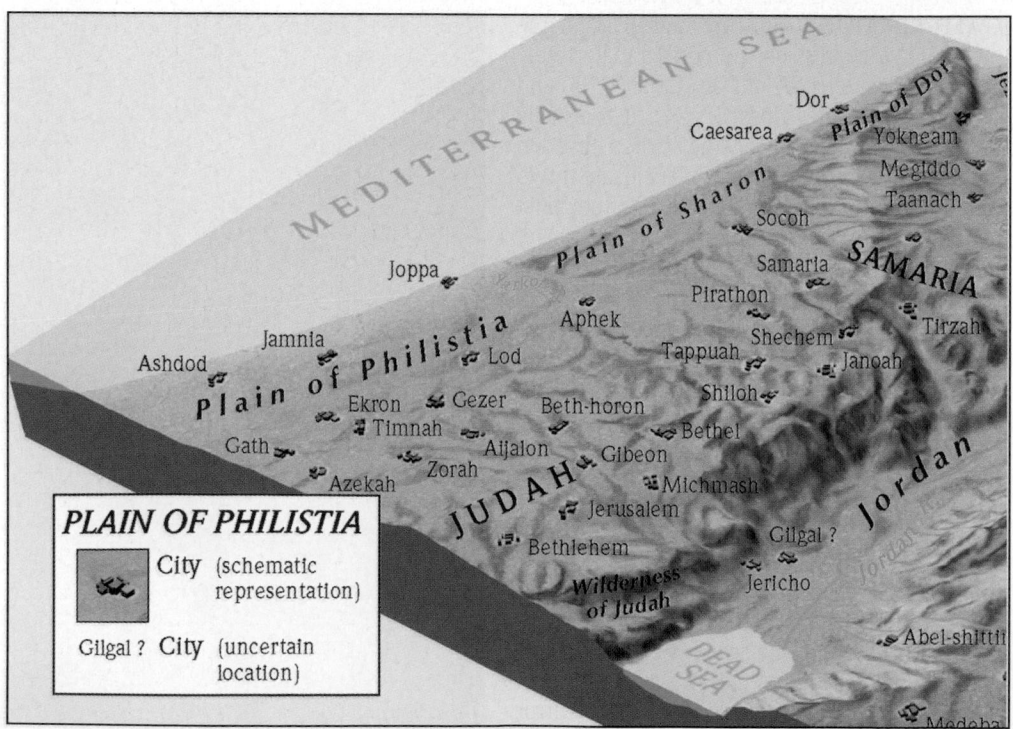

PLAIN OF PHILISTIA

thus were permitted as food (Deut. 12:15,22). See *Antelope*.

GAZER (Gā´ zēr) KJV spelling of Gezer based on Hebrew accented form (2 Sam. 5:25; 1 Chron. 14:16). See *Gezer*.

GAZEZ (Gā´ zĕz) Personal name meaning "sheepshearing." Name both of Caleb's son and grandson (1 Chron. 2:46). As other names in the list represent cities in southern Judah occupied by the clan of Caleb, Gazez may also be a city, though nothing else is known about it.

GAZITE (Gā´ zīt) Citizen of Gaza. See *Gaza*.

GAZZAM (Găz´ zam) Personal name meaning "caterpillar" or "bird of prey." Leader of a clan of temple servants who returned from Babylonian captivity with Zerubbabel (Ezra 2:48).

GEAR Context of Acts 27:17 indicates that the Greek term underlying "gear" (RSV) refers to some type of nautical equipment or apparatus. The two interpretations most often given are "lowered the sail" (KJV, TEV) and "let out the (sea) anchor" (NASB, NIV, NRSV, REB). Some commentators suggest that the passage means that all the ship's gear (ropes, sails, yards, pulleys) was secured or stored below deck.

GEBA (Gē´ bȧ) Place-name meaning "hill," and variant Hebrew spelling of Gibeah, with which it is sometimes confused, though the two represent different towns in the territory of Benjamin. Geba was given to Benjamin (Josh. 18:24) but set aside for the Levites (Josh. 21:17). This is evidently the base camp for Saul and Jonathan in their fight with the Philistines (1 Sam. 13:16–14:18), though the Hebrew texts and modern translations confuse Geba and Gibeah here. King Asa of Judah (910–869 B.C.) strengthened the city (1 Kings 15:22). In the days of King Josiah (640–609 B.C.) Geba apparently represented the northern border of Judah as opposed to the southern border in Beersheba (2 Kings 23:8). Isaiah described the ominous march of the Assyrian army coming through Geba on its way to Jerusalem (Isa. 10:29). For Zechariah (Zech. 14:10), Geba represented the northern border of a Judah to be flattened out into a plain dominated by God ruling on Mount Zion in Jerusalem. At some period Geba's inhabitants were forced to move to Manahath (1 Chron.

The southern site of Geba, modern Jeba, a few miles north of Jerusalem.

8:6), perhaps when the tribe of Benjamin first settled there or during the exile. Exiles returned to Geba under Zerubbabel (Ezra 2:26). Some citizens of Geba lived in Michmash and other cities in Nehemiah's day, unless the Hebrew text is read differently (REB) to mean they lived in Geba as well as the other towns (Neh. 11:31). Levite singers lived there (Neh. 12:29).

Geba is variously located, some scholars going so far as to locate a southern Geba of Benjamin at Jeba across the Wadi Suweinit from Michmash, about five-and-a-half miles north of Jerusalem, and a northern Geba (Josh. 18:24) at Khirbet et-Tell, seven miles north of Bethel. At neither of these places has archaeology yet shown evidence to correlate with the biblical materials.

GEBAL (Gē´ bȧl) Place-name meaning "mountain." **1.** Seaport known to Greeks as Byblos whose help for Tyre Ezekiel described (Ezek. 27:9). Mentioned in Egyptian texts before 2000 B.C. and in many Egyptian and Assyrian texts through the centuries, Gebal was located at modern Dschebel about 25 miles north of Beirut. It was the most famous of the Syrian ports. It belonged to land that remained for Joshua to conquer (Josh. 13:5). Stone masons from Gebal cut stones for Solomon's temple (1 Kings 5:18). Archaeologists have discovered settlements here as early as 8000 B.C. The fine sarcophagus of King Ahiram found there contained the earliest evidence we have of the Phoenician alphabet. About 900 B.C. Tyre replaced Gebal as the strongest city of Phoenicia. Still its fame for building ships and trading throughout the world continued. **2.** Member of a coalition against Israel which the psalmist lamented (Ps. 83:7). It is the

G

The ruins of the ancient seaport city of Byblos (Gebal), located in the modern country of Lebanon.

northern part of Arabia near Petra in the mountainous country south of the Dead Sea. The Genesis Apocryphon from the Dead Sea Scrolls also mentions it.

GEBALITE (Gē´ bȧ līt) Citizens of Gebal. See *Gebal*.

GEBER (Gē´ bēr) Personal name meaning "young man" or "hero." Solomon's district governor for Gilead beyond the Jordan (1 Kings 4:19) was the son of Uri. He collected provisions to supply the royal court. The district governor over Ramoth-gilead was Ben-geber or the son of Geber. See *Ben-geber*.

GEBIM (Gē´ bĭm) Place-name meaning "water ditch." It lay on the line of the march that conquerors took against Jerusalem (Isa. 10:31). The exact site is not known, but it lay between Tell el-Ful and Mount Scopus near Jerusalem.

GECKO See *Reptiles*.

GEDALIAH (Gĕd ȧ lī´ ah) Personal name meaning "Yahweh has done great things." **1.** Son of Ahikam who was appointed ruler of Judah by Nebuchadnezzar of Babylon in 587 B.C. (2 Kings 25:22). Jerusalem had fallen to the Babylonians, and many of the residents of Judah had been deported. Ahikam, the father of Gedaliah, was an ally of the Prophet Jeremiah (Jer. 26:24; 39:14), and Gedaliah may have been in sympathy with Jeremiah's political views. That could explain why Nebuchadnezzar selected Gedaliah to be governor. Gedaliah's time in office was brief. After only two months he was murdered by a group of fanatically zealous nationalists under the leadership of Ishmael (Jer. 40:1–41:18).

2. Royal official under King Zedekiah (597–586 B.C.) who was with the group that got the king's permission to imprison Jeremiah in a cistern (Jer. 38). **3.** Temple singer and prophet who played the harp with his father Jeduthun and five brothers (1 Chron. 25:3). He headed one of the 24 divisions of temple servants (1 Chron. 25:9).

An abbreviated form of the Hebrew name is given to a priest with a foreign wife under Ezra (Ezra 10:18) and the grandfather of the Prophet Zephaniah (Zeph. 1:1).

GEDEON (Gĕd´ ə on) KJV transliteration of Greek for Gideon in Heb. 11:32. See *Gideon*.

GEDER (Gē´ dēr) Place-name meaning "stone wall." City whose king Joshua killed (Josh. 12:13). The site is unknown and could be easily confused with several places called Beth-geder, Gederah, Gederoth, or Gederothaim. Some scholars believe a copyist confused this text with the preceding Gezer or miscopied a similarly appearing Gerar. First Chronicles 27:28 mentions an official from Geder, but the relationship of this Geder to that of Josh. 12 to the other cities mentioned above cannot be determined.

GEDERAH (Gə dē´ rah) Place-name meaning "sheepfold" or "stone wall." A village in the Shephalah or valley of Judah (Josh. 15:36). It is located at modern Tell el-Judeireh north of Maraeshah and 10 miles southeast of Lod. Villagers were noted for skill in making pottery, much of which was made for the king (1 Chron. 4:23). The home of one of David's soldiers (1 Chron. 12:4) apparently belongs in Benjamin (1 Chron. 12:2), but he may have been living in Judah before joining David at Ziklag. Otherwise, this is a different Gederah located at Jedireh near Gibeon. See *Geder*.

GEDERATHITE (Gə dē´ rȧ thīt) See *Gederah*.

GEDERITE (Gə´ dēr´ īt) Citizen of Geder. See *Geder*.

GEDEROTH (Gə dē´ rŏth) Place-name meaning "walls." City in tribal allotment of Judah in the Shephelah or valley (Josh. 15:41). It may be an alternate spelling of Gederah or Qatra near Lachish. When the Philistines took Gederoth with other cities, King Ahaz (735–715 B.C.) sent to Assyria for help (2 Chron. 28:18). See *Geder; Gederah*.

GEDEROTHAIM (Gĕd ə rō thā´ ĭm) Place-name meaning "two walls" or common noun referring to sheepfolds (cp. REB translation, namely both parts of Gederah). A town in the valley or Shephelah of Judah allotted to Judah (Josh. 15:36). The list contains 14 cities without Gederothaim, causing several commentators to identify Gederothaim as a part of Gederah or as a copyist's duplication. See *Gederah*.

GEDOR (Gē´ dôr) Place-name meaning "wall." **1.** Town in hill country of Judah allotted to tribe of Judah (Josh. 15:58). It is located at Khirbet Judur three miles north of Hebron and Beth-zur and west of Tekoa. **2.** In 1 Chron. 4:18 Jered is the father of Gedor. See *Socho*. **3.** The Gedor in 1 Chron. 4:39 probably represents an early copyist's change from Gerar, which is quite similar in appearance in Hebrew and appears in the earliest Greek translation. If Gedor is the original reading, its location in the tribal allotment of Simeon (1 Chron. 4:24) is not known. A Benjaminite from Gedor had two sons in David's wilderness army (1 Chron. 12:7). This could be a city in Benjamin of unknown location or one of other Gedors discussed above. A member of the tribe of Benjamin was named Gedor (1 Chron. 8:31). See *Geder; Gederoth*.

GEHARASHIM (Gē här´ ə shĭm) Place-name meaning "valley of the handcrafts workers." A member of the genealogy of Judah and Caleb in 1 Chron. 4:14, a list which often includes place-names. It is listed as a place where members of the tribe of Benjamin lived in the time of Nehemiah (Neh. 11:35). This might indicate that descendants of Judah and Caleb had once occupied territory in Benjamin. It is apparently near Lod in Benjamin's allotment about 30 miles northwest of Jerusalem.

GEHAZI (Gə hā´ zī) Personal name meaning "valley of vision" or "goggle-eyed." Servant of the Prophet Elisha (2 Kings 4:12). The Bible portrays him as a man of questionable character. On one occasion he tried to force a grieving woman away from the prophet (2 Kings 4:27). Despite the prophet's commission, he could not restore a child to life (2 Kings 4:31). Later he tried to secure for himself the reward Elisha had refused from Naaman the Syrian and then lied to Elisha (2 Kings 5:20-25). For his duplicity with regard to Naaman, Gehazi was stricken with the disease of which Naaman had been cured. Gehazi did testify to the king of Elisha's good deeds and helped the widow get her lands restored (2 Kings 8:1-6). See *Elisha*.

GEHENNA (Gə hĕn´ na) English equivalent of the Greek word (*geena*) derived from the Hebrew place-name (*gehinnom*) meaning "valley of Hinnom" and came to be used in NT times as a word for hell. The valley south of Jerusalem now called the Wadi er-Rababi (Josh. 15:8; 18:16; 2 Chron. 33:6; Jer. 32:35) became the place of child sacrifice to foreign gods. The Jews later used the valley for the dumping of refuse, the dead bodies of animals, and executed criminals. The continuing fires in the valley (to consume the refuse and dead bodies) apparently led the people to transfer the name to the place where the wicked dead suffer. In the period between the OT and NT, Jewish writing used the term to describe the hell of fire in the final judgment. In some writings, but not in the Bible, Gehenna was also seen as the place of temporary judgment for those waiting the final judgment.

The NT uses "Gehenna" to speak of the place of final punishment. Jesus warned that those who called another "You moron!" faced the danger of the fire of Gehenna (hellfire, Matt. 5:22 HCSB). He taught that it is better to destroy a part of one's body than to have one's whole body thrown into Gehenna (Matt. 5:29; 18:9; Mark 9:43,45,47). In Gehenna worms are constantly at work in a fiery environment that burns forever (Mark 9:48). Only God can commit people to Gehenna and so is the only One worthy of human fear (Matt. 10:28; Luke 12:5). Jesus condemned the Pharisees for making converts but then turning them into sons of Gehenna, that is, people destined for hell (Matt. 23:15). He scolded the Pharisees, warning they had no chance to escape Gehenna through their present practices (Matt. 23:33). James warned many that they could not control their tongues that Gehenna had set on fire (James 3:6). See *Hades; Hell; Hinnom*.

GELILOTH (Gĕ lī´ lŏth) Place-name meaning "circles" or "regions." Border point north of Jerusalem in tribal allotment of Benjamin (Josh. 18:17). It appears to correspond to Gilgal in the description of Judah (Josh. 15:7). See *Gilgal*.

G

GEM See *Jewels, Jewelry; Minerals and Metals.*

GEMALLI (Gə măl´ lī) Personal name meaning "my camel" or "camel driver." Spy who represented tribe of Dan in searching out the land of Canaan (Num. 13:12).

GEMARA Portion of the Talmud containing commentary on the Mishnah. The word "Gemara" (Aramaic, "to learn") refers specifically to the discussions on the Mishnah conducted in the rabbinic academies of ancient Palestine and Babylon. The Mishnah and Gemara combined comprise the Talmud. Most of the Gemara is written in Aramaic. Two Gemaras exist, the Palestinian and the Babylonian. See *Mishnah.*

GEMARIAH (Gĕm ə rī´ a) Personal name meaning "Yahweh has completed or carried out." **1.** Messenger King Zedekiah (597–586 B.C.) sent to Babylon. He carried a letter from Jeremiah to the exiles (Jer. 29:3). **2.** Son of Shaphan, the court scribe, who had a room in the temple, where Baruch read from Jeremiah's sermons to the congregation (Jer. 36:10). Later, Gemariah sought to keep the king from burning Jeremiah's scroll (v. 25). See *Shaphan.*

GENDER EQUALITY Adam and Eve were created in God's image to be equal in personhood but distinct in gender (Gen. 1:26-27; 5:1-2). The phrase "a helper who is like him" (Gen. 2:18), conveys equality and compatibility on the one hand but also indicates a functional distinction that was part of creation.

Adam and Eve were co-participants in the fall, but Adam as head of the race was the one held responsible by God (Gen. 2:16-17; Ps. 90:3; Rom. 3:18; 5:12,15; 1 Cor. 15:22). The fall introduced distortions into the male-female relationship resulting in martial conflict (Gen. 3:16b).

Redemption in Christ aims to reverse the effects of the fall.

Although gender differences remain, all persons—male and female—are one in Christ (Gal. 3:26-28) and participate in unique ways through the work of the Holy Spirit in the life of the church (Acts 2:17-18; 1 Cor. 12:7). The Apostle Paul appealed to the order of creation—man first, then woman—to argue for the submission of women to men in certain functions of the church, namely teaching and preaching (1 Tim. 2:11-12; cp. 1 Cor. 11:8-9). Husbands have been given headship over their wives in a way analogous to the headship of Christ over the church

View of the Valley of Genenna (Hinnom Valley) looking northeast toward the new city of Jerusalem.

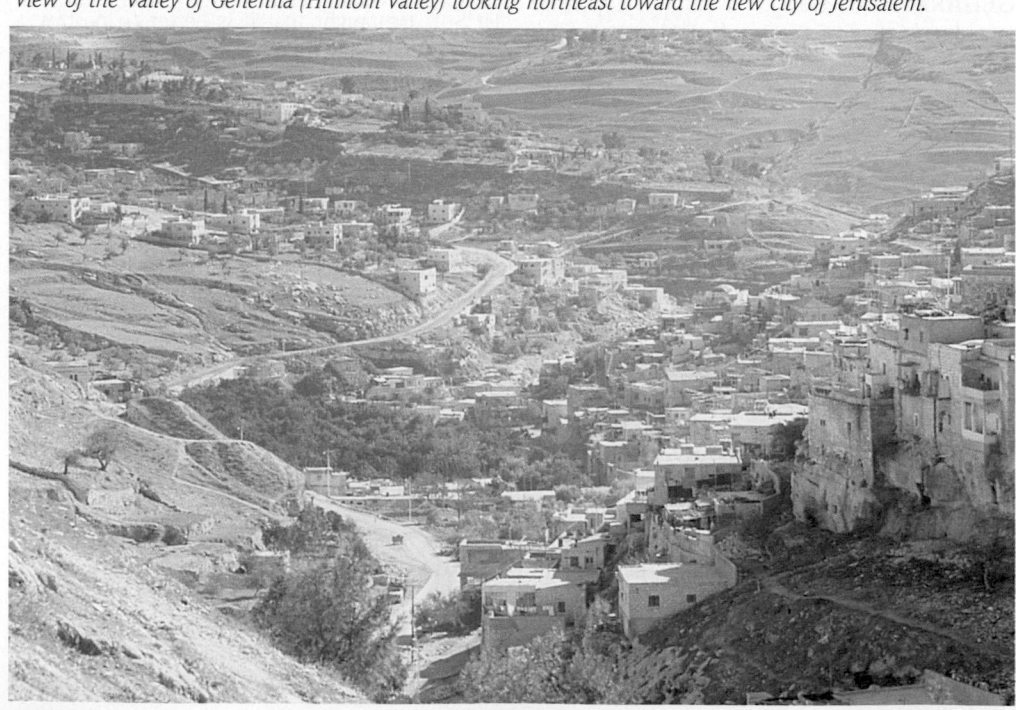

(Eph. 5:23) and must be motivated in their relationship by agape love (Eph. 5:25).

Women held important positions of authority in both the OT (Exod. 15:20; Judg. 4:4-14; 2 Chron. 34:22-28; Prov. 31:29) and NT (Acts 1:14; Rom. 16:1-3; 1 Cor. 1:11; 16:19; Phil. 4:2-3). Both men and women exercise leadership in raising and nurturing their children (Exod. 20:12; Prov. 1:8; Eph. 6:1-4).   *Paul H. Wright*

GENEALOGIES Written or oral expressions of the descent of a person or persons from an ancestor or ancestors.

Old Testament Genealogies are presented in two forms: in concise lists or within narratives that will contain additional information. Genealogies may be *broad* or display *breadth*, presenting only the first generation of descendants ("The sons of Leah … the sons of Rachel … the sons of Bilhah … the sons of Zilpah" Gen. 35:23-26). They may be *deep* or *linear*, listing several sequential descendants, usually from two to 10 ("the son of Solomon was Rehoboam, Abijah his son, Asa his son," 1 Chron. 3:10). Linear genealogies serve to legitimate the last-named person(s) in the list of names. Segmented genealogies display both depth and breadth ("These are the generations of the sons of Noah, Shem, Ham, and Japheth.... The sons of Japheth were Gomer … the sons of Gomer" Gen. 10:1-29). Descending genealogies progress from parent to child (1 Chron. 9:39-44; see also Matthew's genealogy of Jesus in Matt. 1:1-16), and ascending genealogies proceed from child to parent (1 Chron. 9:14-16; see also Luke's genealogy of Jesus in Luke 3:23-38). Biblical genealogies do not always name all the members of the family line. They serve a selective function, depending on the purpose(s) of the author. For example, Exod. 6:14-26 presents a five-generation list of ancestors of Moses and Aaron. The purpose of this genealogy is to legitimize Moses and Aaron in their new leadership roles. The genealogy of Ephraim (1 Chron. 7:23-27) demonstrates that there were at least 12 generations from Joseph to Joshua, suggesting that some of the ancestors of Moses and Aaron were not included in the Exodus genealogy.

M. D. Johnson identified nine functions/purposes of genealogies. (1) Demonstrate existing relationships between Israel and neighboring tribes by tracing them back to common ancestors, showing simultaneously the degree of kinship as well as the distinction between Israel and her neighbors. The genealogies of Lot (Gen. 19:36-38), Nahor (Gen. 22:20-24), Keturah (Gen. 25:1-6), Ishmael (Gen. 25:12-16), and Esau (Gen. 36) are examples of this function. (2) Create a coherent and inclusive genealogical system for Israel. An example is the Genesis *toledot* book. (3) Establish continuity through the periods not covered by the biblical narratives. Genesis 5 and 11 are examples of this purpose. Ruth 4:18-22 also serves this purpose. (4) Assign dates for the flood (Gen. 5), the birth of Abraham (Gen. 11), or dividing Israel's preexilic history into two equal parts (1 Chron. 6:1-15) by listing the high priests prior to and following Solomon's reign. Because some genealogies are selective, this function is not a measure of absolute chronological reckoning. (5) Perform the military function of numbering the warriors of Israel. Examples are Num. 1 and 26. (6) Demonstrate the legitimacy of an individual in his office, particularly with respect to the priesthood. Examples are Ezra 8 and Neh. 7, and Exod. 6:14-26. (7) Establish and preserve the homogeneity of the Jewish community. The genealogies of Ezra and Nehemiah and the rabbinic tradition serve this purpose. (8) Assert the continuity of the children of God through the period of national disruption (the exile). Thus the postexilic community is the same Israel of the monarchy. The genealogies of 1 Chron. 1–9 are examples. (9) Divide history into orderly periods and demonstrate that the course of history is governed and ordered according to the divine plan.

New Testament The genealogy of Jesus in Matt. 1:1-17 traces the family of Jesus in three lists of 14 ancestors: from Abraham to David, David to the exile, and from the exile to Joseph. Luke presents an ascending genealogy from Jesus to Adam, the son of God (Luke 3:23-38). Several proposals have been presented to harmonize the two genealogies. One widely accepted view is that Matthew focused on the messiahship of Jesus and the legal descent of the heir to the throne of David, by listing the line of kings from David to Jechoniah. Luke's purpose was to focus on the physical descent of Jesus through His mother, Mary. Luke was concerned to present Jesus' humanity while Matthew emphasized His kingship. Both emphasized Jesus' virgin birth and His divine nature. With regard to other figures of the NT, the writers demonstrated much

G

less concern with the ancestry of the men and women than does the OT. God has now revealed the One through whom He would reunite humanity, not by a common ancestor but by a common spiritual rebirth.   *Francis X. Kimmitt*

GENERAL With reference to Sisera (Judg. 4:7) and Joab (1 Chron. 27:34), a general (NRSV) is the highest-ranking officer in command of an army. General, commander, and (chief) captain are used interchangeably for such an officer in English translations. KJV consistently translates "captain" or "chief captain."

GENERATION Period of time and its significant events comprising the life span of a person but also used to talk of a more indefinite time span. Two Hebrew words are at times translated "generation." The more significant of these is *toledot*, derived from the Hebrew verb, "to bear children." *Toledot* gives structure to the book of Genesis (2:4; 5:1; 6:9; 10:1,32; 11:10,27; 25:12-13,19; 36:1,9; 37:2). Thus creation, Adam, Noah, Noah's sons, Shem, Terah, Ishmael, the sons of Ishmael, Isaac, Esau, and Jacob each provide a generation and a structural unit in the Genesis narrative. In writing a narrative this way, Israel followed a pattern long used by Near Eastern neighbors, that of describing creation as a series of births. Israel, as so often under divine inspiration, radically changed the pattern. Israel's neighbors spoke of the birth of gods, such births representing at the same time a part of the universe, since the sun, the moon, the stars were all looked upon as gods. Israel simply spoke of the birth of creation by God's words and actions. This started a process by which human generations would endure as long as the creation generation endured. Each human generation lasts from the death of the father through the death of the son. This was the time when the son functioned as head of the larger Hebrew extended family. Often the aged patriarch presided over the active leadership of his sons as seen particularly in the cases of Isaac and Jacob. Human history in its simplest form of family history is then the way God tells His story of working with human beings to bless them and to accomplish His purposes for them. He works not only in miraculous, unique events; He works also in the continuing series of human births and deaths. Elsewhere *toledot* appears in genealogical lists such as Exod. 6, Num. 1, 1 Chron. 1–9.

The Hebrew term *dor* is related to the word for circle and refers to the life circle of an individual, either from birth to death or from birth to the birth of the first child. It can have extended uses in metaphorical language. *Dor* occurs over 160 times in the OT. A generation was a general term for those persons living at a particular time. A generation did not necessarily have a specific number of years. Genesis 15:13-16 apparently equates 400 years with four generations, thus 100 years per generation. Numbers 32:11-13 may reckon a generation as 60 years; it included people 20 and above and giving them 40 more years to die. Or one may interpret this to mean a generation is the 40 years of adulthood between ages 20 and 60. God promised Jehu his sons would rule to the fourth generation, apparently meaning four sons (2 Kings 10:30; 15:12). Jehu began ruling about 841 B.C., his first son Jehoahaz about 814 B.C., and the fourth generation Zechariah died about 752 B.C. The five generations ruled less than 90 years, while the four sons' generations ruled about 60 years. In this instance a generation would be fewer than 20 years. After his tragedies Job lived 140 years and saw four generations (Job 42:16). This would make a generation about 35 years. Basically, generation is not a specific number of years but a more or less specific period of time (cp. Job 8:8; Isa. 51:9). The literal Hebrew expression "generation and generation" thus means through all generations or forever (Ps. 49:11). Similarly, "to your (his, their) generations" means forever (Num. 10:8).

The generations come and go (Eccles. 1:4). A generation also represents those who can gather for worship, so that the gathered worship community forms a generation (Pss. 14:5; 24:6; 73:15). The generations of people change, but God has given His name Yahweh to be remembered through all generations (Exod. 3:15). He is the refuge for all generations (Ps. 90:1). The danger is that a generation will arise that does not know Yahweh (Judg. 2:10; cp. Ps. 12). Thus one generation must tell God's acts and write them down for the next generation (Pss. 22:30-31; 102:18; cp. Ps. 79:13).

God's people must be taught faithfulness. God is faithful to a thousand generations by His very nature (Deut. 7:9). His salvation is available through the generations; that is forever (Isa. 51:8).

In the NT "generation" refers to a specific contemporary audience. Jesus often used the term to describe the evil nature of the people He addressed (Matt. 11:16; 12:39; Luke 17:25). The message of the NT can be summarized: "to Him be glory in the church and in Christ Jesus to all generations, forever and ever" (Eph. 3:21 HCSB).   *Trent C. Butler*

GENESIS, BOOK OF The first book of the Bible and the first of five written by Moses. Genesis describes the creation of all things by the mighty acts of the one true God, human rebellion, punishment, and restoration (Gen. 1–11:9). The remainder explains the origins of the people of God, Israel, and their place in God's plan of redemption (Gen. 11:10–50:26). See *Pentateuch*.

Contents Most understand that the structure of Genesis is related to the repeated phrase variously translated, "These are the generations of X," "These are the records of X," or "This is the account of X." The Hebrew word *toledot* occurring in this phrase normally means "descendants," but in Genesis it usually means "family history." It has a figurative sense in its first occurrence in 2:4 of the heavens and the earth. There it introduces a section that recounts what happened to God's creation, namely, the introduction of sin and death. Furthermore, the first 11 chapters of Genesis recount the earliest history of the earth, showing why God's plan of redemption through Abraham was needed so badly. The rest of the book concerns (1) the patriarchs—Abraham, Isaac, Jacob, and his sons, (2) God's oath to bless and redeem mankind through them, and (3) how Abraham's descendants came to be in Egypt.

Genesis 1:1–11:9 Genesis 1:1–2:3 describes the origin of the universe, "the heavens and the earth": six days of creation and the seventh day when God rested. Genesis 2:4–4:26 describes in more detail God's creation of mankind and how mankind corrupted itself through sin. Genesis 5:1–6:8 surveys what became of Adam's descendants down to the time of Noah. Genesis 6:9–9:29 recounts the story of the flood, God's covenant with Noah, and God's curse on Canaan and the Canaanites. Finally, Gen. 10:1–11:9 records the geographical distribution of Noah's sons (10:1-32) and explains the

reason for so many human languages and nations as God's curse on man's pride at the Tower of Babel (11:1-9).

Genesis 11:10–50:26 Genesis 11:10-26 surveys the descendants of Noah's son Shem down to the time of Terah and his sons Abram, Nahor, and Haran. Some consider this section as concluding the first main division of the book. Genesis 11:27–25:11 recounts the story of God's dealings with Abram (meaning "exalted father"), whose name God changed to Abraham (meaning "father of a multitude"). God promised to bless Abraham, to make his name great, to be an enemy to Abraham's enemies, and to give him a multitude of descendants who would become a great nation. Most important, God promised to bless all nations through him (Gen. 12:1-3). In Genesis 15 God reaffirmed His covenant with Abraham and guaranteed the covenant unconditionally. Abraham tried to fulfill God's promise of a son by taking his wife's servant Hagar as a slave-wife, who bore for him Ishmael (Gen. 16). However, God's promise was fulfilled by giving Abraham and Sarai (whose name God changed to Sarah) a son, Isaac (Gen. 21). The story of Abraham ends with the account of his death after providing a wife for Isaac. After listing the descendants of Ishmael, whom God blessed for Abraham's sake (Gen. 25:12-18), the story of Isaac's descendants is given in Genesis 25:19–35:29. This is primarily the story of God's dealings with Isaac's son, Jacob, whom God chose over Esau as the one through whom the promise of redemption would be fulfilled. After listing the descendants of Esau (36:1–37:1), the account of Jacob's descendants is given in Gen. 37:2–50:26. This is primarily the story of Joseph and how God brought Jacob and his sons to live in Egypt. Although the family was preserved by the godly character of Joseph, Jacob's fourth son Judah would be the one through whom God's redemptive promise would be fulfilled (49:8–12). Genesis 47–50 completes the story of the patriarchs, following both Jacob and Joseph to their deaths, and foreshadowing the return to Canaan in the book of Exodus. See *Abraham; Adam and Eve; Anthropology; Creation; Earth; Flood; God of the Fathers; Humanity; Image of God; Isaac; Jacob; Joseph; Names of God; Noah; Sin.*

Interpretive Issues Until the 19th century Moses' authorship of the first five books, the

G

Pentateuch, was commonly accepted by both Jews and Christians. Six passages in the Pentateuch explicitly cite Moses as the author of at least parts of the work (Exod. 17:14; 24:4-8; 34:27; Num. 33:1-2; Deut. 31:9,24-26; 31:22,30). Although Genesis contains no such citation, the book is an integral part of the Pentateuch; Exodus makes no sense without it. Exodus through Deuteronomy give abundant testimony that God's revelation to the people of Israel came first through Moses, and the rest of the OT refers to "the book of the law" as coming from Moses (e.g., Josh. 1:7-8; 2 Kings 14:6; 2 Chron. 34:14; Dan. 9:11-13). Jesus and the NT writers considered the Pentateuch, including Genesis, as coming from Moses (see Luke 16:29,31; 24:27,44; John 1:17; 5:45-47; 7:19,22-23; Acts 3:22; 13:39).

With the enlightenment, however, many biblical scholars began following a critical path that radically diverged from the traditional view. They were motivated in part by a desire to peel away the layers of religious tradition to discover what *really* happened in the past and to free religious faith from its dogmatism and bondage to biblical literalism. Signs believed to point down this path were such features of the biblical text as (1) variations in the names used for God (*Elohim/Yahweh*); (2) the appearance of supposed redundancies such as two creation accounts (Gen. 1–2) and two wife-sister narratives (Gen. 12 and 20); (3) variant names for persons and places such as Canaanites/Amorites, Ishmaelites/Midianites, and Sinai/Horeb; (4) supposedly differing ideas such as the remoteness or immanence of God; and (5) anachronisms such as references to kings of Israel (Gen. 36:31) or to the city of Dan (Gen. 14:14 versus Josh. 19:47). Consequently, a new understanding of how and when the Pentateuch was produced arose in Europe especially in the 19th century. It came to be called "the documentary hypothesis" because the theory proposed four main documentary sources, J, E, D, and P, which were written and spliced together between the ninth and fifth centuries B.C. Through his work first published in 1878, Julius Wellhausen was the scholar most responsible for propagating this revisionist theory, not only of Pentateuchal origins but also of Israel's history.

This classic critical view has undergone many revisions but has shown an amazing resilience in spite of being contrary to what the Bible says about itself. Several troubling implications have also aroused various responses. First, if we cannot trust how the Bible describes its own origins, why should we trust it in other areas? Second, if the Pentateuch did not originate from the time of Moses, its reliability as a source for Israel's early history is called into question. Third, if the Pentateuch is a composite of sources whose theology and perspective is at odds with each other, how may the voice of God be heard? We may suggest that the path that has led to this unfriendly territory can be retraced and avoided by a reading of the biblical texts that is (1) more sensitive to literary conventions in the ancient Near East in the Mosaic era, (2) more tolerant of practices of ancient writers that are different than our own, (3) more open to the principle of divine verbal revelation, and (4) open to scribal practices of updating biblical texts during the process of transmission. The signs that have led so many down this critical path can in this way be understood as not diverging significantly from the traditional position of Mosaic authorship for Genesis and the rest of the Pentateuch. Many outstanding scholarly commentaries have been written on these books from this perspective. On Genesis see especially commentaries by V. P. Hamilton, K. A. Mathews, G. J. Wenham and Bruce Walker. See *Pentateuch*.

The creation and flood accounts of Genesis bear similarities to stories from ancient Sumer, Babylon, and Assyria—another testimony to the antiquity of Genesis. Some even see this as evidence that Genesis borrowed from other cultures. The differences, however, are just as striking as the similarities. The Genesis accounts present a sovereign and gracious God of moral purity. The other accounts portray the gods (multiple) as worse than the worst of men, and creation as the result of sexual activity by the gods. A better explanation is that creation occurred as Genesis reveals. All people are descended from Noah, thus ancient cultures had "memory" of the beginnings and shaped the stories in their own way. See *Creation; Flood*.

The historicity of the flood has been rejected as mythological. Geological evidence shows a flood strata around the world. Fossils of fish are found on mountaintops. Yet scientists whose assumptions deny the possibility of a universal flood "conclude" one did not occur. The existence of Abraham and the patriarchs has been questioned. Assertions were made that he was a mythological or legendary figure, as was his city Ur. Yet Ur now has been discovered and excavated for many years, and the name Abram has been found carved in stone there.

Scholarship rightly practiced does not prove Genesis is not true in all that it teaches us about creation and the fall, the flood, the patriarchs, and the rest. There is every reason to conclude that Genesis is a reliable guide to what really happened.

Teachings God is the central character of Genesis. He is sovereign Lord and Creator of all things. Genesis assumes the fact of divine creation but does not try to prove it. Genesis does not specify when creation occurred or exactly how long it took. Genesis eloquently teaches that God created all things, including Adam and Eve, by special creation for fellowship with Himself. They were created innocent and with free wills. Freely they chose to disobey God, fell from innocence, and lost their freedom. Their fallen nature was passed to every other human being. The freedom of human wills is limited by fallen human nature. Humans are moral agents who make choices, but their wills are not free to obey God. Death came because of sin, and humanity was so corrupt that God wiped them out and started over with Noah. The second humanity also proved corrupt, and God confused their languages and scattered them. God's plan of redemption began to unfold by His calling of one man to found a family, one family chosen from among all the families of the earth. That family would be the source of blessing and salvation for all peoples. Through each generation in Genesis God demonstrated that the promise depended only on His sovereign power and that no circumstance, person, family, or nation could thwart His purposes. Human sin could not destroy God's plan, but rather provided Him opportunity to demonstrate His glory. Joseph may lie dead in a casket in Egypt, but his dying command was that his bones be carried home to Canaan when, not if, God brought His people again into the land He promised Abraham, Isaac, and Jacob.

Outline
I. Prepatriarchal History (1:1–11:9)
  A. Creation of All Things (1:1–2:3)
  B. Origin and Corruption of Mankind (2:4–4:26)
  C. From Adam to Noah (5:1–6:8)
  D. The Flood and Its Aftermath (6:9–9:29)
  E. The Table of Nations and Tower of Babel (10:1–11:9)
II. Patriarchal History (11:10–50:26)
  A. From Noah to Abram (11:10-26)
  B. The Abraham Cycle (11:27–25:11)
    1. Abram's Family (11:27-32)
    2. God's Call of Abram (12:1-9)
    3. God's Protection of Abram and His family (12:10–14:24)
    4. God's Covenant with Abram (15:1-21)
    5. Abram's Impatience (16:1-16)
    6. God's Renewed Promise (17:1–18:15)
    7. Abraham's Intercession for Sodom and Gomorrah (18:16–19:38)
    8. God's Fulfillment of the Promise of a Son (20:1–21:34)
    9. God's Ultimate Test of Abraham's Faith (22:1-24).
    10. Abraham's First Portion of Land (23:1-20)
    11. Isaac's Wife (24:1-67)
    12. Abraham's Death (25:1-11)
  C. Ishmael's Descendants (25:12-18)
  D. The Jacob Cycle (25:19–35:29)
    1. Esau's Birthright (25:19-34)
    2. God's Deliverance of Isaac (26:1-35)
    3. God's Protection and Blessing of Jacob (27:1–33:20)
    4. Jacob's Trouble with the Canaanites (34:1-31).
    5. Jacob's Return to Bethel (35:1-15)
    6. Rachel's and Isaac's Deaths (35:16-29)
    7. God Blesses Esau for the Sake of Abraham and Isaac (36:1-43)
  E. Esau's Descendants (36:1–37:1)
  F. The Joseph Cycle (37:2–50:26)
    1. Joseph's Slavery in Egypt (37:1-36)
    2. Judah's Unfaithfulness (38:1-30)
    3. Joseph's Success in Egypt (39:1–40:23)
    4. Joseph's Exaltation in Egypt (41:1-52)

G

5. Joseph's Test of his Brothers
   (41:53–44:34)
6. Joseph's Reunion with His
   Brothers (45:1-28)
7. Jacob's Family Moves to Egypt
   (46:1–47:31)
8. Jacob's Family Blessing and Death
   (48:1–49:33)
9. Joseph's Death (50:1-26)

Charles W. Draper and E. Ray Clendenen

GENNESARET (Gĕn nĕs´ à rĕt) Another name for the Sea of Galilee. Also used for the fertile valley northwest of this sea. See *Galilee, Sea of.*

GENTILES People who are not part of God's chosen family at birth and thus can be considered "pagans." Though not synonymous in English, "Gentiles," "nations," "pagans," "heathens" are variants chosen by translators to render *goyim* in Hebrew and *ethnoi* in Greek. "Gentile" and "nation" suggest race or territory, while "pagans" and "heathen" suggest religion.

The doctrine of election in which Israel became a holy nation (Exod. 19:6; Lev. 19:2) among the nations by the covenant at Sinai draws attention to the fact that no other nation has such a God or such laws. The writer of Deuteronomy forbade communion with the nations (Deut. 7:3,6,16). The OT noted the filthy ways (Ezra 6:21) and worship abominations (2 Kings 16:3) of the nations.

Affliction by other nations increased tension between Israel and the nations which gave rise to invoking curses on the nations in the Psalms (Pss. 9; 59; 137). The ultimate punishment of Israel for disobedience was being scattered among the nations.

According to the prophets, the nations were under God's control and were unconsciously being used (Isa. 10:5-7) but in turn would be punished (Isa. 10:12-16). Joel depicted the judgment of the nations who had abused Israel in the valley of Jehoshaphat (Joel 3:12-16).

Solomon's prayer of dedication made clear that the door was never closed to the foreigner who wished to serve the Lord (1 Kings 8:41-43), and prophetic words and some psalms depict the nations gathering to worship the God of Jacob (Pss. 86:9; 102:15-17; Isa. 2:2-4; Zeph. 3:9-10). The Lord is the sole God of all peoples (Isa. 45:22-24). Israel's mission was to bring justice (Isa. 42:1) and light to the nations (Isa. 49:6).

Jesus' ministry is interpreted in the Gospels in terms of OT expectations for the Gentiles. He was a light to the Gentiles (Matt. 4:16-17; Luke 2:32). Though Jesus directed His work to Jews (Matt. 15:24) and at first limited His disciples to them (Matt. 10:5), He threatened that the kingdom would be taken from the Jews and given to a nation bringing its fruits (Matt. 21:43). Though Jesus was crucified by Gentiles (Matt. 20:19), equal blame is placed on both Gentiles and Jews (Acts 4:27).

Following the resurrection of Jesus, the commission included "all nations" (Matt. 28:19). The judgment scene in Jesus' parable envisioned "all nations" gathered before the glorious throne (Matt. 25:31-32). The promises included all those afar off (Acts 2:39). At the house of Cornelius, the Spirit was poured out on the Gentiles (Acts 10:45; 11:1,18; 15:7). The apostolic gathering in Jerusalem, by the apostolic letter, freed Gentiles from obedience to the law (Acts 15:19; cp. 21:19,21,25).

In the apostolic preaching the promise to Abraham (Gen. 12:3; 18:18) found fulfillment (Gal. 3:8). Though in times past the Gentiles had been without God (Eph. 2:12-22), God in Christ broke through all boundaries. Paul, sent to preach among the Gentiles (Acts 9:15; 22:21; 26:17; Gal. 1:16; 2:9), endured many dangers (2 Cor. 11:26). When rejected in the synagogues, he turned to the Gentiles (Acts 13:46; 18:6; 28:28), understanding his work in the light of OT predictions (Acts 13:47-48; Rom. 15:9-12). As the apostle to the Gentiles (Gal. 2:8-9), claiming that in Christ racial distinctions were obliterated (Gal. 3:28), Paul proclaimed an equal opportunity of salvation (Rom. 1:16; 9:24; Col. 3:11; cp. Acts 26:20,23). Gentiles were the wild branches in the allegory grafted into the olive tree (Rom. 11:16-25).

Paul experienced great resentment among the Jews because of the opportunity he was offering the Gentiles (1 Thess. 2:14-16). Nevertheless, in NT thought, the church made up of Jews and Gentiles was the holy nation, God's own people (1 Pet. 2:9).

The apocalypse with its shifting views, depicts a redeemed multitude of all nations (Rev. 5:9; 7:9), and the One who overcomes has power over the nations (Rev. 2:26), Babylon (Rev. 14:8; 18:2,23), the beast (Rev. 13:4), and the harlot (Rev. 17:15) are the deceivers of the nations. The devil is bound to deceive them no more (Rev. 20:3). All nations come to worship (Rev. 15:4) One born to rule with a rod of iron (Rev. 12:5). In the closing scenes of the book the nations walk in the light of the lamp of the Lamb; the glory of the nations is brought into the city (Rev. 21:23-24,26); the leaves of the tree of life are for the healing of the nations (Rev. 22:2).

Jack P. Lewis

GENUBATH (Gə nū´ băth) Personal name meaning "theft" or "foreign guest." Son of Hadad, king of Edom, and the sister of Tahpenes, the wife of Egypt's pharaoh (1 Kings 11:19-20). The name of the Egyptian pharaoh is not known. See *Hadad.*

GERA (Gē´ rȧ) Personal name meaning "stranger," "alien," or "sojourner." **1.** Son of Benjamin and grandson of Jacob (Gen. 46:21). **2.** Grandson of Benjamin (1 Chron. 8:3,5). Son of Ehud and clan head in Geba who was exiled to Manahath (1 Chron. 8:6-7 [see 1, above]). **3.** Father of Ehud (Judg. 3:15). **4.** Father of Shimei, who cursed David (2 Sam. 16:5). See *Shimei.*

GERAH (Gē´ rah) Smallest biblical measure of weight equaling one-20th of a shekel. Archaeological discoveries show a gerah weighed about half a gram. See *Shekel; Weights and Measures.*

GERAR (Gə rär´) Place-name possibly meaning "drag away." City located between Gaza and Beersheba. Abraham and Isaac made treaties with the king of Gerar (Gen. 20; 26). Gerar was on the border of Canaanite territory (Gen. 10:19). TEV reads Gerar with the earliest Greek translation of 1 Chron. 4:39-40. Other translations follow the Hebrew reading "Gedor." Gerar was the limit of Asa's pursuit of the defeated Ethiopians (2 Chron. 14:13-14). The site is possibly that of Tell Abu Hureirah on the northwest side of Wadi Esh-Sheriah. Numerous potsherds from the middle Bronze period (1800–1600 B.C.) indicate that the city flourished during the time of the patriarchs.

GERASA (Gĕr´ ȧ sa) Two places bear this name. One of them is referred to in the Bible; the other is not.

According to some excellent ancient manuscript evidence, Mark 5:1 and Luke 8:26 located the healing of the demon-possessed man who lived among the tombs in "the country of the Gerasenes (Gadarenes)" ("Gerasenes" in NIV, NASB). This would point to a place named Gerasa. Such a place existed on the east side of the Sea of Galilee. Selecting among Gadara, Gergesa, and Gerasa as the scene of the healing of the demoniac is one of the more challenging tasks in NT studies. See *Gadarene.*

The other Gerasa was located some 26 miles north of present-day Amman in Jordan. Its ruins are among the most excellently preserved in the Middle East. See *Arabia.*

GERASENES (Gĕr´ ȧ sēns) Citizens of Gerasa. See *Gerasa.*

The ruins of ancient Gerasa located in the modern country of Jordan.

GERGESENES (Gĕr´ gĕ sēns) KJV reading in Matt. 8:28. Modern translations read "Gadarenes." See *Gadarenes.*

GERIZIM AND EBAL (Gĕr´ ĭ zĭm and Ē´ bàl) Closely related place-names meaning "cut-off ones" and "stripped one" or "baldy." Two mountains that form the sides of an important east-west pass in central Israel known as the valley of Shechem. Ancient Shechem lies at the east entrance of this valley, and modern Nablus stands in the narrow valley between the two mountains.

Gerizim (modern Jebel et-Tor) stands 2,849 feet above the Mediterranean and 700 feet above the valley. Ebal (modern Jebel Eslamiyeh) was located directly opposite Gerizim and is 2,950 feet above sea level. Both of the mountains are steep and rocky and perhaps gave reason to the probable meaning of Shechem: "shoulder(s)." The mountains, standing like two sentinels, could be fortified and assure control of this important valley.

When the Israelites conquered central Israel, Joshua carried out the directive given by Moses, and placed half of the tribes on Mount Gerizim to pronounce the blessing (Deut. 27:12) and the other half on Mount Ebal to pronounce the curses (Deut. 11:29; Josh. 8:30-35). Joshua built an altar on Ebal (Josh. 8:30).

Jotham proclaimed his famous kingship fable to the citizens of Shechem from Mount Gerizim (Judg. 9:7), thus using its sacred tradition to reinforce the authority of his message. After the Assyrians captured the Northern Kingdom, the mixed race of people began mixing pagan worship and worship of Yahweh (2 Kings 17:33).

Gerizim disappears from biblical history until after the Babylonian exile and the Persian restoration. The Jewish historian Josephus reported that Alexander the Great gave permission to the Samaritans to build a temple on Mount Gerizim. Archaeologists think they have found remains of this temple, 66 by 66 feet and 30 feet high, built of uncut rocks without cement. Josephus also reported that John Hyrcanus destroyed the temple in 128 B.C. Archaeologists have also found remains of the temple to Zeus Hypsistos which Hadrian, the Roman emperor, built after A.D. 100. Over 1,500 marble steps led to the pagan temple. The small Samaritan community continues to worship on Gerizim today, just as they did in Jesus' lifetime when He met the Samaritan woman drawing water from Jacob's well. She pointed to traditional worship on the mountain (John 4:20). See *Samaritans.*

Jimmy Albright

GERSHOM (Gĕr´ shŏm) Personal name meaning "sojourner there," "expelled one," or "protected of the god Shom." **1.** Firstborn son of Moses and Zipporah (Exod. 2:22). The inspired writer interpreted his name to mean "stranger" or "sojourner" from the Hebrew word *ger,* "sojourner." His birth became a further sign for Moses that he had done right in escaping Egypt, the birth occurring in Midian. Apparently Gershom was the son circumcised in the unusual ritual of Exod. 4:24-26 in which Zipporah delivered Moses when God sought to kill him. Thus Gershom represented protection for Moses. **2.** Son of Levi and head of a clan of Levitic priests (1 Chron. 6:16-20,43,62,71; 15:7). First Chronicles 23:14 shows that Moses' sons had been incorporated into the line of Levites (cp. 1 Chron. 26:24). **3.** Man who accompanied Ezra on the return from Babylon to Jerusalem (Ezra 8:2). See *Gershon; Levites; Moses.*

The forum and colonnaded road of Gerasa (modern Jerash) as seen from the temple of Zeus.

GERSHOMITES (Gĕr´ shō mīts) NRSV term for "sons of Gershom" (1 Chron. 6:62,71). See *Gershom.*

GERSHON (Gĕr´ shŏn) Personal name meaning "expelled" or "bell." Eldest son of Levi (Gen. 46:11). He was the progenitor of the Gershonites, who had specifically assigned responsibilities regarding the transporting of the tabernacle during the years of Israel's nomadic existence in the wilderness (cp. Exod. 6:16-17; Num. 3:17-25; 4:22-41; 7:7; 10:17; 26:57; Josh. 21:6,27). First Chronicles often spells the name "Gershom." See *Gershom; Levi; Priests and Levites.*

GERSHONITE (Gĕr´ shŏn īt) Descendant of Gershon. See *Gershon.*

GERUTH (Gĕ´ rüth) Part of a place-name meaning "hospitality" (Jer. 41:17) translated differently—KJV: "habitation of Chimham"; NASB, NRSV: "Geruth Chimham"; REB: "Kimham's holding." Fugitives stopped there near Bethlehem on their way to Egypt fleeing from Ishmael, who had killed Gedaliah, whom Babylon had appointed governor of Judah after the fall of Jerusalem in 586 B.C. It apparently designated an inn or lodging place near Bethlehem. It may have represented the first stop across the border from Judah into Egyptian-controlled territory.

GESHAM (Gĕsh´ ăm) Personal name with variant spellings, perhaps meaning "rain." Son of Jahdai (1 Chron. 2:47). Earliest translations give varying spellings, followed by modern translators. Thus NASB, NIV, NRSV, REB read "Geshan," which is the actual Hebrew spelling. The early Greek traditions read "Gershom" and "Sogar." Many of the names in the list are towns associated with Caleb, so that Gesham (Geshan) may also be a town.

GESHAN (Gĕsh´ ăn) Personal name of uncertain meaning. See Gesham.

GESHEM (Gĕsh´ ĕm) Personal name meaning "rain." Arabian ruler of Kedar who joined Sanballat and Tobiah in opposing Nehemiah's efforts to rebuild the wall of Jerusalem (Neh. 2:19; 6:1-19). His name appears on a silver vessel dedicated by his son Qainu to the goddess Han-Ilat at Tell el-Maskhuta in Lower Egypt. An inscription found in Dedan also appears to describe extensive territories Geshem controlled. He was in name a vassal of Persia but apparently wielded great personal power with tribes in the Syrian Desert, southern Palestine, the delta of Egypt, and northern Arabia. He may have hoped to gain further control in Palestine and certainly did not want a local power to threaten him there. In 6:6 a variant spelling of his name—Gashmu (KJV, NASB)—appears.

GESHUR (Gĕ´ shûr) Place-name, perhaps meaning "bridge." Small Aramean city-state between Bashan and Hermon. It served as a buffer between Israel and Aram. David married Maacah, daughter of the king of Geshur, who became mother of Absalom (2 Sam. 3:3), which caused the two lands to be on friendly terms. Absalom later retreated to his mother's homeland (2 Sam. 13:37-38). Nowhere do David's battle reports mention Geshur (2 Sam. 8; 10). Many scholars think Josh. 13:2 and 1 Sam. 27:8 refer to a group of southern Philistine cities about which nothing else is known.

GESHURI (Gə shū´ rī) KJV spelling for Geshurites. See *Geshur.*

GESHURITE (Gĕsh´ ū rīt) Citizen of Geshur. See *Geshur.*

GESTURES Movements of either a part or all of the body to communicate one's thoughts and feelings. Gestures often may involve external objects such as the tearing of one's clothing (Joel 2:13) or the casting down of one's crown before God (Rev. 4:10). A gesture does not have to accompany verbal speech. Just a piercing look (Luke 22:61) is sufficient to communicate persuasively. In a certain sense all gestures are visual symbols.

Cultural-Corporal Gestures These are the most common to the everyday life and customs of the ancient Near East.

Whole Body Gestures (1) Standing to pray indicates respect to God (1 Sam. 1:26; 1 Kings 8:22; Mark 11:25). (2) Sitting may communicate several things. David's sitting before the Lord indicated reverence, humility, and submission (2 Sam. 7:18), while the sitting down of Jesus at the right hand of God indicates finality and completion as well as power and authority (Heb. 10:12). (3) Kneeling and bowing express honor, devotion, and submission in worship (1 Kings 19:18; Isa. 45:23; Rev. 4:10; 5:8) and reverence in prayer (1 Kings 8:54; 18:42; Dan. 6:10; Luke 22:41). (4) Weeping is not only a sign of sorrow (Job 16:16; Jer. 9:10; Luke 22:62; John 11:35), but also of happiness (Gen. 46:29). (5) Dancing shows joy (Exod. 15:20; Judg. 11:34) and celebration in praise (2 Sam. 6:16; Ps. 149:3). (6) Tearing of one's clothes and heaping of ashes upon one's head signify deep grief (2 Sam. 1:11; 13:19), shocking horror (Num. 14:6; Josh. 7:6), and sudden alarm (Matt. 26:65; Acts 14:14).

Head Gestures (1) Shaking one's head communicates scorn and reproach (Ps. 22:7; Lam. 2:15; Matt. 27:39; Mark 15:29). (2) Lifting one's head can indicate exaltation (Ps. 27:6), contempt (Ps. 83:2), and freedom (2 Kings 25:27). (3) Bowing of one's head shows reverence in worship and prayer (Gen. 24:26; Neh. 8:6).

Face Gestures (1) Eye gestures are numerous and quite expressive. Winking the eye may show mischief and deceit (Prov. 6:13), which also can lead to sorrow (Prov. 10:10). Wanton eyes are sensual eyes that deserve condemnation (Isa. 3:16). Jesus' looking at Peter at the point of his denial is an example of eyes showing both hurt and condemnation (Luke 22:61). The lifting up of one's eyelids expresses haughtiness and pride (Prov. 30:13). One's eyes can show anger (Mark 3:5). The eyes, when uplifted in prayer, signify not only respectful acknowledgment of God but also devotion to Him (Mark 6:41; Luke 9:16). To fail to lift one's eyes up to God while praying indicates one's sense of unworthiness (Luke 18:13). Jesus' lifting up of His eyes upon the disciples shows His personal regard for them (Luke 6:20). (2) Mouth gestures also are plentiful in the Scriptures. To smile and laugh can mean more than just happiness and joy; it also can show goodwill (Job 29:24), scorn (Ps. 22:7; Mark 5:40; Luke 8:53) or even rebuke (Ps. 2:4). The shooting out of the lip communicates the idea of contempt (Ps. 22:7). Kissing is an act that expresses the warmth of a friendly greeting (Rom. 16:16; 1 Cor. 16:20), the affection of one for another (Song 8:1), the sorrow of one who dearly cares for another (Ruth 1:14; Acts 20:37), the deceit of one who hides true intentions (Prov. 27:6; Matt. 26:48), the submission of the weak to the strong (Ps. 2:12), and the seduction of a foolish man by a loose woman (Prov. 7:5-23). Spitting is an emphatic way of showing contempt in order to shame another (Deut. 25:9; Isa. 50:6; Matt. 26:67; 27:30). (3) To incline

one's ear is to give attention to another (Ps. 45:10; Jer. 7:26). (4) An obscure gesture is the putting of the branch to the nose. This pagan gesture is an offense to God and possibly has obscene connotations (Ezek. 8:17). (5) A hardened neck indicates stubbornness (Neh. 9:16; Prov. 29:1; Jer. 7:26), while an outstretched neck reveals haughtiness (Isa. 3:16).

Hand Gestures (1) The raising of hands in prayer is a gesture signifying one's request is unto God (Ps. 141:2; 1 Tim. 2:8). The raising of one's hands can also be a symbol of blessing (Lev. 9:22; Neh. 8:6; Luke 24:50), or it can be an act that gives emphasis to an oath (Deut. 32:40; Ezek. 20:5,15,23,28). (2) The covering of one's mouth with the hand signifies silence (Job 29:9). (3) The lifting up of one's hand or the shaking of one's fist means defiance (2 Sam. 18:28; Isa. 10:32; Zeph. 2:15). (4) The laying of a hand or hands on someone can mean violence (Gen. 37:22), or it can mean favor and blessing as on a son (Gen. 48:14) or in healing (Luke 4:40; Acts 28:8). The placing of hands on someone's head shows favor and blessing as in the acknowledgment of an office (Acts 6:6) or in the coming of the Holy Spirit (Acts 8:17). The striking or shaking of hands indicates a guarantee or confirmation (Prov. 6:1; 17:18; 22:26), while the giving of one's hand to another is a sign of fellowship (2 Kings 10:15; Prov. 11:21). (5) To clap one's hands can mean either contempt (Job 27:23; Lam. 2:15; Nah. 3:19) or joy and celebration (2 Kings 11:12; Pss. 47:1; 98:8; Isa. 55:12). (6) The waving of one's hand can mean to beckon (Luke 5:7; John 13:24), to call for silence in order to speak (Acts 12:17; 13:16; 19:33), or to call on God for healing (2 Kings 5:11). (7) The dropping of hands shows weakness and despair (Isa. 35:3; Heb. 12:12). (8) A hand on one's head communicates grief (2 Sam. 13:19; Esther 6:12; Jer. 2:37). (9) The washing of one's hands in public declares one's innocence (Deut. 21:6-7; Matt. 27:24). (10) The pointing of a finger can show ill favor (Prov. 6:13) or accusation (Isa. 58:9). (11) The hand or arm outstretched is a sign of power and authority (Exod. 6:6). (12) To hug or embrace is to show warmth in greeting another (Gen. 33:4).

Foot Gestures (1) The placing of a foot upon one's enemy is a twofold gesture: it shows victory and dominance for the one standing and defeat and submission for the one downfallen and vanquished (Josh. 10:24; Ps. 110:1; 1 Cor. 15:25). (2) To shake the dust off of one's feet is a sign of contempt and separation (Matt. 10:14; Acts 13:51). (3) To wash the feet of another is to humble oneself as a servant (John 13:5-12). (4) The lifting of one's heel against another shows opposition (Ps. 41:9; John 13:18). (5) To cover one's feet is to relieve oneself with some degree of privacy (Judg. 3:24; 1 Sam. 24:3). (6) To uncover one's feet or to walk barefooted indicates grief or repentance (2 Sam. 15:30; Isa. 20:2). (7) The act of uncovering one's feet as in the case of Ruth with Boaz (Ruth 3:4) was an established practice indicating not only one's willingness to marry but also the protection of the husband over his wife.

Religious-Ceremonial Gestures These are a more specialized category of gestures in which prescribed body movements take on a more clearly religious meaning than that found in the previous category.

Old Testament Sacrificial Gestures Two examples are sufficient to represent this limited category of gestures. (1) Within the instructions given by Moses concerning the Passover are the following words: "Now you shall eat it in this manner: with your loins girded, your sandals on your feet, and your staff in your hand; and you shall eat it in haste—it is the LORD's Passover" (Exod. 12:11 NASB). All of these actions symbolize urgency and readiness. This whole body gesture is one of the profound ways that God chose to emphasize the abruptness and costliness of their freedom from bondage. (2) Another whole body gesture with special emphasis upon the hands is the act of offering a burnt offering unto God. If the offering came from the herd it was to be a male without blemish, and it was to be offered at the door of the tabernacle of the congregation as a free will offering. "And he shall lay his hand on the head of the burnt offering, ... And he shall slay the young bull before the LORD" (Lev. 1:4-5). The offering of this sacrifice emphasized God's holiness (a male without blemish) and human sinfulness and separation (only as far as the altar could a sinful person enter into the court of the tabernacle). The act expressed the need for substitution and death (the killing of the animal) and mediation (the ministry of the priests). In an ideal sense the act of coming to the entrance of the tabernacle was a public testimony of confession and commitment. The offering of a sacrifice was the language of covenant acted out in prayerful imagery. The act of putting one's hand upon the head of the animal and killing it served as the focal point of the offering for the sinner.

New Testament Sacrificial Gestures The two ordinances of the church continue the sacrificial theme. Both ordinances testify to the sacrificial death of Jesus Christ. (1) The ordinance of baptism is a whole body gesture that expresses one's identification with Christ's atoning work: His death, burial, and resurrection. To be baptized (Matt. 28:19) is to testify publicly of one's total commitment to Jesus Christ as Savior and Lord. (2) The Lord's Supper (Matt. 26:26-30; 1 Cor. 11:23-29) also emphasizes one's identification with the sacrificial death of Christ. It is through the observance of the Lord's Supper that one testifies to a willingness to deny oneself and take up the cross (Matt. 16:24) to follow Christ.

Prophetic-Symbolical Gestures Prophets dramatized their message with symbolic gestures. Here examples are limited to the prophets Isaiah, Jeremiah, and Ezekiel. The use of symbolical gestures by the prophets could range from the simple and obvious, such as Ezekiel's mock attack against a clay model of Jerusalem to symbolize God's impending judgment on the city (Ezek. 4:1-3) to the complex and theological, such as Jeremiah's purchase of a field (Jer. 32:1-44) to symbolize God's future restoration of the Southern Kingdom as its Kinsman (*go' el*) Redeemer.

In Isa. 20:3 Isaiah had "gone naked and barefoot three years" (NASB) as a symbol of the humiliation that Egypt and Ethiopia were to know when Assyria conquered them. In Jer. 27:1-7 Jeremiah wore a yoke of wood around his neck as a symbol of the future domination of the Babylonians over Judah and her neighbors; therefore, Jeremiah's message was one of submission to Babylonian rule. Ezekiel more than any other was known for his use of prophetic-symbolic acts. His laying on his side for many days (Ezek. 4:4-8) indicated a year for each day of their iniquity and of their impending siege. His eating of scant rations (Ezek. 4:9-17), the cutting of his hair and its various consequences (Ezek. 5:1-17), and the setting of his face toward the mountains of Israel (Ezek. 6:1-7) were all symbolic gestures which showed the judgment of God that soon was to come upon his people (Ezek. 12:1-28).

See *Festivals; Ordinances; Prophecy, Prophets; Sacrifice and Offering; Symbol.*

Gary A. Galeotti

GETHER (Gē´ thĕr) Aramean tribal name of uncertain meaning. They are Semites, their original ancestor being the grandson of Shem and great grandson of Noah (Gen. 10:23). Nothing else is known of them.

GETHSEMANE (Gĕth sĕm´ ȧ nə) Place-name meaning "olive press." Place where Jesus went after the Last Supper, a garden outside the city, across the Kidron on the Mount of Olives (Matt. 26:36-56; Mark 14:32-52; Luke 22:39-53; John 18:1-14). Here Jesus charged the disciples to "watch" as He prayed. Judas led the enemies of Jesus to Gethsemane where Jesus was arrested and taken away for trial. Here Jesus, the Son, showed He had learned obedience to the Father even in suffering (Heb. 5:7-9).

Gethsemane was probably a remote walled garden (Jesus "entered" and "went out") where Jesus went often for prayer, rest, and fellowship with His disciples. See *Kidron Valley; Judas; Olives, Mount of.*

Wayne Dehoney

Inside the garden of Gethsemane, the olive trees and foliage provide a beautiful and tranquil scene.

GEUEL (Gə ū´ ĕl) Personal name meaning "pride of God." Spy from tribe of Gad that Moses sent to inspect the land before conquering it (Num. 13:15).

GEZER (Gĕz´ ĕr) An important city in the biblical period, located on a main juncture of the Via Maris, the Way of the Sea. It guarded the Aijalon Valley and the route from the coast up to Jerusalem and the Judean Hills. Gezer is located at Tell Jezer (Tell Jazari). It is a 33-acre mound situated in the foothills of Judah. It is known from biblical, Egyptian, and Assyrian sources.

Looking toward the garden of Gethsemane with the Church of All Nations in the center of the photo.

Gezer is mentioned in the annals of Thutmose III (ca. 1468 B.C.), Amarna Letters (14th century B.C.), and Merneptah's Victory Stela. Gezer is mentioned in an inscription and relief of Tiglath-Pileser III (eighth century B.C.). In addition to the historical sources, the site is well-known due to several archaeological expeditions. Two major excavations were carried out in 1902–1909 by R. A. S. Macalister and in 1964–1973 by William G. Dever and Joe D. Seger. Several smaller excavations were conducted by Alan Rowe (1934) and Dever (1984, 1990).

Gezer was a major Canaanite city-state throughout the second millennium B.C. The mound of Gezer was initially occupied around 3500 B.C. and the settlement continued to grow until it was a walled city during the middle Bronze Age (ca. 2000–1500 B.C.) when major fortifications (gate, tower, glacis) were built and the "High Place" was founded. The city was destroyed (ca. 1500 B.C.) and rebuilt during the late Bronze Age when it came under Egyptian hegemony as evidenced by several palaces and residencies. Joshua defeated the king of Gezer who was part of a Canaanite coalition (Josh. 10:33). Gezer remained in Canaanite hands throughout the period of the judges (Josh. 16:10; Judg. 1:29) even though it formed the boundary for Ephraim's tribal allotment (Josh. 16:3) and was assigned as a Levitical city (Josh. 21:21). David fought against the Philistines near Gezer (2 Sam. 5:25; 1 Chron. 20:4).

Gezer was conquered by Egypt and given to Solomon as a dowry for his marriage to Pharaoh's daughter. It finally came under Israelite control as Solomon fortified Gezer along with Jerusalem, Hazor, and Megiddo (1 Kings 9:15-17). This Solomonic rebuilding is evidenced by construction of a four-entryway monumental city gate, a palace, and a casemate wall. This city was destroyed by Shishak (ca. 950–925). The city was rebuilt and experienced another destruction at the hands of the Assyrians (Tiglath-Pileser III, 733 B.C.). Gezer became known as Gazara in the Hellenistic Period and became an important city for the Hasmonean rulers.   *Steve Ortiz*

GEZRITE (Gĕz´ rīt) KJV spelling of name of people in 1 Sam. 27:8, where the Hebrew text tradition shows both Girzites (NIV, NASB, NRSV, TEV) and Gezrite. REB reads Gizrite. Gezrite or Gizrite would refer to inhabitants of Gezer, but Gezer is too far north for the Samuel context. We

Tel Gezer.

know nothing else of the Girzites. First Samuel 27:8 says they had lived in the southwestern edge of Palestine from time immemorial and that David raided them from his base at Ziklag.

GHOST KJV uses "ghost" in two senses, for the human life force and for God's Holy Spirit. KJV never uses "ghost" for the disembodied spirits of the dead. All 11 OT references involve the phrase "give up the ghost" (for example, Gen. 25:8; 35:29), which means to cease breathing or simply to die. This phrase occurs eight times in the NT (Matt. 27:50; Acts 5:5; 12:23). The predominant NT use is for the Holy Spirit.

Modern translations use "ghost" (rather than "spirit" as the KJV) for the disembodied spirits of the dead. Jesus' disciples mistook Him for a ghost when He walked on water (Matt. 14:26; Mark 6:49) and when He appeared after the resurrection (Luke 24:37,39).

GIAH (Gī´ ah) Place-name meaning "bubbling." Place where David's general Joab confronted Abner, Saul's general, after Abner killed Joab's brother Asahel (2 Sam. 2:24). The earliest translations saw Giah as a common noun meaning "valley." Its location near Gibeon is not known.

GIANTS Persons of unusual stature who often are reputed to possess great strength and power. The earliest biblical reference to giants is to the nephilim born to the "daughters of men" and the "sons of God" (Gen. 6:1-4). Interpreters differ on the origin of these giants. Some understand the "sons of God" to be angelic beings who intermarried with human women (Jude 6). Others view them as descendants of Seth who intermarried with the ungodly. Later descendants of the *nephilim* were called "the sons of Anak" (Num. 13:33) or Anakim (Deut. 2:11; 9:2). They inhabited the land of Canaan prior to Israel's conquest. Egyptian records testify to their presence as early as 2000 B.C. Similar races of giants had also inhabited Moab (Deut. 2:9-10) and Ammon (Deut. 2:19-20).

A second class of giants who inhabited pre-Israelite Palestine was the *repha'im*. Their last survivor was Og, king of Bashan (Deut. 3:11,13). A valley near Jerusalem (Josh. 15:8; 18:16) and part of the wooded country in the tribal territory of Ephraim (Josh. 17:15) retained their name.

The OT also records cases of individual giants. The well-known Goliath (1 Sam. 17) was a Philistine champion. A family of giants from Gath were among the Philistine enemies slain by David and his followers (2 Sam. 21:16-22; 1 Chron. 20:4-8). *Michael Fink*

GIBBAR (Gĭb´ bär) Personal name meaning "young, powerful man." A man, 95 of whose descendants returned from Babylonian captivity with Zerubbabel in 537 B.C. (Ezra 2:20). The corresponding list in Neh. 7:25 has Gibeon. The correct reading cannot be determined.

GIBBETHON (Gĭb´ bə thŏn) Place-name meaning "arched," "hill," or "mound." City in the tribal territory of Dan (Josh. 19:44) but assigned to the Levites (Josh. 21:23). During the monarchy the Philistines controlled Gibbethon. Nadab of Israel (909-908 B.C.) besieged it. During the siege Baasha murdered Nadab and assumed the kingship (1 Kings 15:25-28). The Israelite army was encamped against Philistine Gibbethon when Zimri assumed rule by assassinating Elah, the son of Baasha (1 Kings 16:15-17). Gibbethon has been variously identified as Tell el-Melat north of Ekron, and with Agir, two and a half miles west of Tell el-Melat.

GIBEA (Gĭb´ ĭ ä) Personal name meaning "hill." Son of Caleb by his concubine Maacah (1 Chron. 2:49). See *Gibeah*.

GIBEAH (Gĭb´ ĭ äh) Place-name meaning "a hill," closely related to names of Geba and Gibeon. Gibeah or Gibeath was the name of four different places in the OT. **1.** City in hill country of Judah allotted to tribe of Judah (Josh. 15:57). This may be the home of King Abijah's wife Maacah (2 Chron. 13:2) and could be the same as the place-name presupposed in the list of Caleb's descendants (1 Chron. 2:49), a list

including city names rather than personal names, perhaps indicating the clans who originally inhabited the cities. This Gibeah has usually been located at el-Jeba, seven and a half miles southwest of Bethlehem, but this is too far north to be connected with clans of Caleb. Otherwise, the location is not known. **2.** City closely connected with Phinehas, the high priest and grandson of Aaron. Phinehas buried his father Eleazar there (Josh. 24:33). Some try to locate this on a hill near Shechem or Bethel. Others would identify it with the Levitical city of Geba in Joshua 21:17 in the territory of Benjamin. The Bible simply uses the general term "hill country of Ephraim." It could even be near Shiloh. **3.** The ark was lodged on a hill (Hb., Gibeah) during the period between its return by the Philistines and David's initial effort to move it to Jerusalem (2 Sam. 6:3-4). The Hebrew word is probably not a proper noun (Hebrew writing does not distinguish proper names with capital letters as does English). The best translation may be "hill" (NASB, NIV, NRSV, REB; cp. 1 Sam. 7:1-2). The hill here is apparently near Kiriath-jearim or Baalah (cp. Josh. 15:9-11). See *Baalah*. **4.** The most significant Gibeah was the city in the tribal territory of Benjamin (Josh. 18:28). A bloody civil war between Benjamin and the other Israelite tribes broke out when the men of Gibeah raped a traveling Levite's concubine (Judg. 19:1–21:25). Saul had close family connections to the city (1 Chron. 8:29-33 also connects them with the nearby and similarly sounding Gibeon) and made it his capital after he became king (1 Sam. 10:5,26; 15:34; 23:19). If the "hill of God" (1 Sam. 10:5 KJV, NASB, REB) or "Gibeath-elohim" (NRSV) should be translated "Gibeah of God" (NIV) and equated with Gibeah of Saul, then the Philistines controlled the city prior to Saul gaining control. Apparently the Philistines built a fortress there which Saul took over, or Saul constructed his own royal complex, since archaeologists have uncovered a fortress from this period. After Saul's death, the city declined. Hosea and Isaiah referred to it during the eighth century B.C. (Isa. 10:29; Hos. 5:8; 9:9; 10:9). Isaiah shows it was on the natural path for an enemy army such as the Assyrians attacking Jerusalem from the north. Archaeologists have shown the city flourished once more after the destruction of Jerusalem and again in the Maccabean age. Gibeah is located at Tell el-

Ful on a high ridge, three and a half miles north of Jerusalem. See *Benjamin; Geba; Gibeon; Saul.*

LeBron Matthews

GIBEATH (Gĭb´ ĭ ăth) Alternative Hebrew spelling for Gibeah (Josh. 18:28) preserved in KJV spelling. See *Gibeah.*

GIBEATH-ELOHIM (Gĭb´ ĭ ăth-ĕ lō´ hĭm) Place-name meaning "hill of God." See *Geba; Gibeah.*

GIBEATH-HAARALOTH (Gĭb´ ĭ ăth-hà är´ à lŏth) Place-name meaning "hill of foreskins." KJV translates the place-name in Josh. 5:3, while modern translations transliterate it. Joshua used traditional flint stone knives rather than more modern metal ones to circumcise the Israelite generation about to conquer Canaan.

GIBEATHITE (Gĭb ĭ à thīt) Citizen of Gibeah (1 Chron. 12:3). See *Gibeah.*

GIBEON (Gĭb´ ĭ ŏn) Place-name meaning "hill place." This "great city" (Josh. 10:2) played a significant role in OT history, especially during the conquest of Canaan. Archaeology has demonstrated that the city was a thriving industrial area that made it a primary community in Canaan.
Background of the City Little was known of Gibeon's exact location until the twentieth century. Originally the city was assigned to the tribe of Benjamin following Israel's victory in Canaan (Josh. 18:25) and made a city for Levites (Josh. 21:17). Beginning in 1956, excavations led by James B. Pritchard gave proof that the modern city of el-Jib was the site of ancient Gibeon. Lying eight miles northwest of Jerusalem, Gibeon was in an area of moderate climate, ample rainfall, with a wine-led economy. With an elevation of about 2,400 feet, Gibeon towered above most other cities, making it easily defended. Dating to about 3000 B.C., Gibeon served as the fortress city at the head of the valley of Aijalon that provided the principal access from the coastal plain into the hill country. Gibeon's power was strong as archaeology has found no sign of the city's destruction.
Role of the City Forty-five OT references are made to Gibeon. Its first major appearance in Israel's history involved the conquest of Canaan. The people of Gibeon concocted a deceptive strategy to protect themselves from the Israelites (Josh. 9). Pretending to be foreigners also, the

Gibeonites made a treaty with Joshua. When Joshua later discovered the truth, he forced the Gibeonites to become water carriers and woodcutters for the Israelites. Honoring this covenant, Joshua led Israel against the armies of five kings who had attacked Gibeon. During these victories the Lord caused the sun and moon to stand still (Josh. 10; cp. Isa. 28:21).

By the time of David, Gibeon had become part of Israel's United Monarchy. Saul's family seems to have had some connections to Gibeon (1 Chron. 8:29-33; 9:35-39). Following Saul's death a crucial meeting occurred in Gibeon involving Abner and Joab, the respective generals of Saul and David (2 Sam. 2:12-17). A "sporting" battle (v. 14) by the pool of Gibeon ensued in which the men of Joab proved to be victorious. Archaeologists have discovered a spiraling shaft and tunnel with circular stairway leading to water and providing the city a way to get water inside the city walls during enemy attacks.

Gibeon also played host to part of Sheba's rebellion against David (2 Sam. 20:8-13). Joab pursued Amasa, a leader of the revolt, to the great stone in Gibeon where Joab left him "wallowing in his blood in the middle of the highway" (v. 12 NASB). Discovering that Saul had broken the covenant by killing some of the Gibeonites, David gave seven of Saul's male descendants to the people of Gibeon who then put the seven to death (2 Sam. 21:1-9). During one of the sacrifices Solomon made in Gibeon, the Lord appeared and granted the new king's request for wisdom (1 Kings 3:3-14; cp. 9:2). Apparently Gibeon was Israel's major place of worship before Solomon built the temple.

The pool at ancient Gibeon with a spiral staircase leading down to the water level.

G

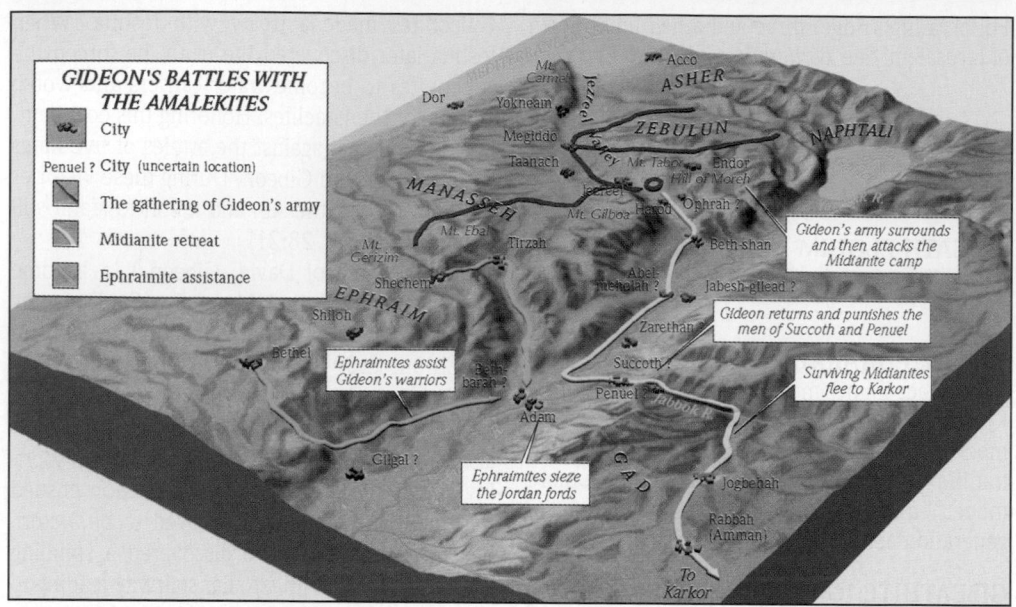

GIDEON'S BATTLES WITH
THE AMALEKITES

City

Penuel ? City (uncertain location)

The gathering of Gideon's army

Midianite retreat

Ephraimite assistance

Gideon's army surrounds
and then attacks the
Midianite camp

Gideon returns and punishes the
men of Succoth and Penuel

Surviving Midianites
flee to Karkor

Ephraimites assist
Gideon's warriors

Ephraimites sieze
the Jordan fords

To
Karkor

The next references to Gibeon took place about 600 B.C. Jeremiah spoke of the coming destruction of Jerusalem, contradicting Hananiah of Gibeon who predicted Nebuchadnezzar's doom (Jer. 28). Fleeing from justice, Ishmael, the murderer of the Babylonian-appointed "governor" Gedaliah, was overtaken at Gibeon (Jer. 41).

Final references to Gibeon highlighted the city's role in postexilic Israel. The Gibeonites assisted in rebuilding Jerusalem's walls (Neh. 3:7). Nehemiah's list of the returning exiles also included an entry concerning the number of "the children of Gibeon" (7:25). See *Canaan; David; Gibeah; Joshua.*   *Larry McGraw*

GIBEONITE (Gĭb´ ĭ on īt) Citizen of Gibeon. See *Gibeon.*

GIBLITE (Gĭb´ līt) (KJV) See *Gebal.*

GIDDALTI (Gĭd dăl´ tī) Personal name meaning "I brought from there" or "I made great, praised." Son of Heman to whom David gave the task of prophesying through playing musical instruments (1 Chron. 25:4). He became a leader of a clan of temple musicians (1 Chron. 25:29).

GIDDEL (Gĭd´ dĕl) Personal name meaning "he made great, praised." **1.** Clan leader of a group of temple servants who returned from the Babylonian captivity with Zerubbabel about 537 B.C.

(Ezra 2:47). **2.** Original clan father of a group of royal servants who returned from the Babylonian exile with Zerubbabel about 537 B.C. (Ezra 2:56).

GIDEON (Gĭd ĭ ŏn) Personal name meaning "one who cuts to pieces." The fifth major judge of 12th century Israel. He was also called Jerubbaal and was the son of Joash of the tribe of Manasseh. He judged for 40 years (Judg. 6:11–8:35).

Gideon was given the task of delivering the Israelites from the Midianites and Amalekites, desert nomads who repeatedly raided the country. Their use of the camel allowed them to ride in, destroy crops, take plunder, and then escape back into the desert with such speed the Israelites could not catch them. Gideon was not a willing volunteer. Although he knew the will of God, twice he laid out the fleece in what seems an effort to avoid the will of God by imposing impossible conditions. God met his conditions both times and then set out the strategy that would guarantee victory for Israel.

To reduce their number, two tests were given to the 32,000 men in Gideon's army. This was done that Israel could not claim victory by any other means than continued dependence upon God. Those who were afraid and those who knelt down to get a drink of water were sent home. The remaining 300 were given pitchers,

The springs of Harod where Gideon divided his men for battle against the Midianites.

G

torches, and trumpets, and placed around the Midianite encampment. The strategy was one of terror: at Gideon's signal the pitchers were broken, the torches then became visible, and the trumpets sounded, giving the enemy the impression they were surrounded. They took flight, their leaders were killed, and the Midianite oppression was brought to an end.

The hero of faith (Heb. 11:32) ended life on a sad note. He angrily punished Succoth and Penuel for not helping in his war against the Midianite kings (Judg. 8:1-17). He refused the people's offer to crown him king, testifying that only God was King (Judg. 8:22-23), but he ordered the people to give him their golden earrings, taken as war spoil from the Ishmaelites. He made a worship symbol, an ephod, out of it and led his people astray with it (Judg. 8:24-27). His family did not follow his God (Judg. 8:33). See *Camel; Jerubbaal; Judges, Book of; Midianites.*

Darlene R. Gautsch

GIDEONI (Gĭd ĭ ō´ nī) Personal name meaning "one who cuts down or cuts to pieces." Father of Abidan, a leader of the tribe of Benjamin during the encampment in the wilderness (Num. 1:11; 2:22; 7:60; 10:24).

GIDOM (Gī´ dŏm) Place-name meaning "cleared land." Place where tribes of Israel punished tribe of Benjamin by killing 2,000 of Benjamin's soldiers (Judg. 20:45) for grossly mistreating a traveling Levite and his concubine. REB follows some scholars in omitting Gidom. No one knows its exact location between Gibeah and Bethel.

GIFT, GIVING Favor or item bestowed on someone. Gifts were given on numerous occasions for a variety of purposes: as dowry for a wife (Gen. 34:12); as tribute to a military conqueror (2 Sam. 8:2); as bribes (Exod. 23:8; Prov. 17:8; Isa. 1:23); as rewards for faithful service and to ensure future loyalty (Dan. 2:48); and as relief for the poor (Esther 9:22). Since gifts might be required by custom, law, or force, modifiers are sometimes used to specify gifts given voluntarily: "willing" or freewill offerings or gifts (Exod. 35:29); free gift or gift of grace (Rom. 5:15-17; 6:23); bountiful gift not motivated by covetousness (2 Cor. 9:5).

Both OT and NT witness to God as the giver of every good gift (1 Chron. 29:14; James 1:17).

Human life is God's gift (Job 1:21), as are all things necessary for physical life: the sun for light (Jer. 31:35); plants (Gen. 1:29) and animals for food (Gen. 9:3); water (Num. 21:16); clothing (Gen. 28:20); grass for herds (Deut. 11:15); seasonal rains for crops (Lev. 26:4); companionship of male and female (Gen. 2:18-24; cp. 3:12); the ability to have children (Gen. 17:16); and sleep (Ps. 127:2). Various human abilities are likewise given by God: the ability to work (Deut. 8:18); artistic abilities (Exod. 31:6); the ability to acquire learning and master communication skills (Dan. 1:17). These gifts demonstrate God's general providence.

Scripture also witnesses to God's gifts as evidence of a special providence. In the OT such gifts include the promised land (Gen. 12:7), including its successful conquest (Deut. 2:36), possessing its cities (Deut. 6:10) and its spoils (Deut. 20:14); the Sabbath (Exod. 16:29); the promises (1 Kings 8:56); the covenants (2 Kings 17:15); the law (Exod. 24:12); and peace (Lev. 26:6). In the NT God's special providence is especially evident in the gift of God's Son (John 3:16) and of God's Holy Spirit (Luke 11:13).

God makes relationship with Himself possible by giving His people wisdom (1 Kings 4:29), understanding (1 Kings 3:9), a new heart (Ezek. 36:26), and a good Spirit to teach them (Neh. 9:20). The NT expresses these gifts as the power to become children of God (John 1:12), justification from sin (Rom. 3:24; 5:15-17), and eternal life (John 10:28; Rom. 6:23).

Both Testaments witness to God's gift of leadership to God's people as: priests (Num. 8:19; Zech. 3:7); Davidic kings (2 Chron. 13:5); deliverers (2 Kings 13:5); shepherds with godlike hearts (Jer. 3:15); apostles, prophets, evangelists, and pastor-teachers (Eph. 4:11-12). Paul spoke of God's giving the ministry of reconciliation (2 Cor. 5:18), authority for building up the church (2 Cor. 10:8), and grace for sharing the gospel with the Gentiles (Eph. 3:8). The NT also stresses God's gift of spiritual abilities to every believer (Rom. 12:6; 1 Cor. 12:4; 1 Pet. 4:10).

God's gifts should prompt the proper response from the recipients. This response includes not boasting (1 Cor. 4:7; Eph. 2:8); amazement at God's inexpressible goodness (2 Cor. 9:15); the using of gifts for the further-

G

ance of Christ's kingdom (1 Tim. 4:14; 2 Tim. 1:6-11); and a life of good works (Eph. 2:10).

Chris Church

GIFTS, SPIRITUAL See *Spiritual Gifts.*

GIHON (Gī´ hŏn) Place-name meaning "gushing fountain." The primary water supply for Jerusalem and one of the four rivers into which the river of Eden divided (Gen. 2:13). The river cannot be identified with any contemporary river.

During the OT period the spring of Gihon was the primary water supply for the city of Jerusalem. The name comes from a Hebrew word meaning "a bursting forth" and is descriptive of the spring that is located in the Kidron Valley. It does not produce a steady flow but gushes out at irregular intervals, twice a day in the dry season to four or five times in the rainy season. Water issues from a crack 16 feet long in the rock. At some point in the ancient past, a wall was built at the eastern end of the crack, diverting water into a cave at the other end. In the Jebusite period before David, a shaft went from the spring to a pool under the city. Water jugs were let down into the pool through another vertical shaft. This probably was the way Joab entered into the city and captured it for David (2 Sam. 5:8; 1 Chron. 11:6). During the early Israelite occupation, water was collected outside the city walls in an open basin called the "upper pool" (Isa. 7:3). An open aqueduct carried water from there to the "old pool" at the southern end of the city (Isa. 22:11; cp. Isa. 8:6). Along this conduit Isaiah confronted Ahaz (Isa. 7:3), and later Sennacherib's army demanded the city's surrender (2 Kings 18:17). Before Sennacherib's arrival, Hezekiah plugged the aqueduct and dug his famous water tunnel (2 Kings 20:20; 2 Chron. 32:30). See *Eden; Hezekiah; Jerusalem; Kidron Valley; Siloam; Water.*

LeBron Matthews

GILALAI (Gīl´ à lī) Personal name, perhaps meaning "rolled away." Temple musician who helped Nehemiah lead the thanksgiving service for the completion of the Jerusalem wall (Neh. 12:36).

GILBOA (Gīl bō´ à) Place-name of uncertain meaning, perhaps, "hill country" or "bubbling fountain." Location of an Israelite encampment (1 Sam. 28:4). The Israelites under Saul were preparing to do battle against the Philistines. At Mount Gilboa Saul and his three sons were slain (1 Sam. 31:8). David sang a lament over the Gilboa tragedy (2 Sam. 1:17-27). Mount Gilboa has been identified with modern Jebel Fuqus, on the eastern side of the Plain of Esdraelon. See *Palestine; Saul.*

GILEAD (Gīl´ ĭ àd) Place and personal name meaning "raw" or "rugged." **1.** The north-central section of the Transjordanian highlands. The name may originally have applied to a very small area. Usage of the name then grew and could be applied in different contexts depending on present political situations (cp. Judg. 10:17; Hos. 6:8). It occupies the mountain slopes and tableland east of the Jordan, northeast of the Dead Sea. Gilead is bisected by the Jabbok River; in OT times the kingdom of Ammon occupied its eastern fringe. It was often contested by other nations (Amos 1:3). Gilead extends about 50 miles from southern Heshbon not quite to the Yarmuk River in the north. Its east-west extent is about 20 miles.

Physically, Gilead is a rugged country; the Hebrew name *Gil'ad* may be translated "rugged." Some of its peaks reach over 3,500 feet. It also has plains with grassland suitable for cattle, and in antiquity the northern half of the region particularly was heavily forested. The King's Highway, an important international trade route, passed through Gilead. Gilead was an agriculturally significant region as well. It was famous especially for its flocks and herds and also for the balm of Gilead, an aromatic and medicinal preparation, probably derived from the resin of a small balsam tree.

Mount Gilboa.

G

Many famous persons and events are associated with Gilead. The judges Jair and Jephthah (Judg. 11:1), Israel's King Jehu, and the Prophet Elijah were all Gileadites. Jacob and Laban met at its northeastern border (Gen. 31:22-23). Jacob encountered the angel of God at Peniel in Gilead (Gen. 32:30). Saul's son Ish-bosheth (2 Sam. 2:8-9), David (2 Sam. 17:24-26), and Jesus all retreated to Gilead for a time. Old Testament cities of importance were Heshbon in the south, Rabboth-ammon on the eastern desert fringe, Jabesh-gilead, and Ramoth-gilead. Rabboth-ammon is the NT Philadelphia; Pella and Jerash (Gerasa) are other important NT cities.

2. Great grandson of Joseph and original clan leader in tribe of Manasseh (Num. 26:28-32; 36:1). The clan was so strong it could be listed with Israel's tribes in Deborah's song (Judg. 5:17). They fought for recognition among other tribes (Judg. 12:4-7).   *Joseph Coleson*

GILEADITE (Gĭl´ ĕ ȧd īt) Citizen of Gilead. See *Gilead.*

GILGAL (Gĭl´ găl) Place-name meaning "circle" and probably referring to a circle of stones or a circular altar. Such a circle of stones could be found almost anywhere in Palestine and led eas-

ily to naming towns "Gilgal." The many references to Gilgal in the OT cannot thus be definitely connected to the same town, since several different Gilgals may well have existed. **1.** Gilgal is most closely associated with Joshua, but the number of Gilgals involved continues an unsolved question. After crossing the Jordan, Joshua established the first camp at Gilgal (Josh. 4:19). There Joshua took 12 stones from the bed of the river to set up a memorial for the miraculous crossing. Gilgal, the first foothold on Palestinian soil, became Israel's first worship place, where they were circumcised and observed the Passover. There God appeared to Joshua and affirmed his mission (Josh. 5). This Gilgal apparently became Israel's military base of operations (Josh. 9:6; 10:6; 14:6), though some scholars would identify this with a Gilgal farther north near Shechem. Joshua set up Gilgal as the border between Judah and Benjamin (Josh. 15:7; cp. 18:17), though many Bible students think the border town must be south of the original camp. Ehud, the judge, passed Gilgal in his mission to slay the king of Moab (Judg. 3:19,26). David passed through Gilgal as he fled from Absalom (2 Sam. 19:15,40). This Gilgal is often located at modern Khirbet Mefjir, a little more than a mile

The rugged hill country of Gilead.

east of Jericho. Others would locate it at Khirbet en-Nitleh, two miles southeast of Jericho. Still others remain baffled at finding a location. The boundary town is often seen as Khan el-Ahmar or Araq ed-Deir. The military camp is at times located at Tell Jiljulieh east of Shechem but without archaeological support. This could be the same Gilgal of Deut. 11:30, if Joshua's original town is not meant. Gilgal was also one of the three places where Samuel annually held circuit court (1 Sam. 7:16). This could be near Tell Jiljulieh or at Joshua's first landing place near the Jordan. Saul was both crowned and rejected as king at Gilgal (1 Sam. 11:14-15; 13:14-15). Gilgal established itself as a major place of worship for Israel with ancient traditions. However, it also permitted worship associated with other gods and became the object of prophetic judgment (Hos. 4:15; Amos 4:4; 5:5). **2.** Elijah and Elisha were associated closely with Gilgal. At one time Elisha made his headquarters there (2 Kings 4:38), where Elijah was taken up into heaven (2 Kings 2:1). This was apparently Tell Jiljulieh about three miles southeast of Shiloh, though it could still be Joshua's original Gilgal. **3.** Gilgal of the nations is mentioned as a royal city near Dor (Josh. 12:23). The earliest Greek translation reads this as "kings of the nations in Galilee," which many scholars think is the original reading, a copyist of the Hebrew text using the word "Gilgal" since it had become familiar in the earlier chapters of Joshua. If the Hebrew Gilgal is original, its location is not known. See *Beth-gilgal; Elisha; Joshua; Samuel; Saul.*

Kenneth Craig

GILO (Gī´ lō) RSV, TEV spelling of Giloh to refer to Gilonite (2 Sam. 23:34). See *Giloh.*

GILOH (Gī´ lōh) Place-name meaning "uncovered" or "revealed." Town in tribal allotment of Judah in Judean hills (Josh. 15:51). David's counselor Ahithophel came from Giloh (2 Sam. 15:12). Some scholars locate it at Khirbet Jala in the suburbs of Jerusalem, but most think Giloh was actually further south.

GILONITE (Gī´ lō nīt) Citizen of Giloh. See *Giloh.*

GIMZO (Gĭm´ zō) Place-name of uncertain meaning. Town in the Shephelah or valley of Judah which the Philistines captured from King Ahaz of Judah (735–715 B.C.), leading him to ask Assyria for help and pay tribute to them (2 Chron. 28:18). It is located at Gimzu, about four miles east of Ramleh and three miles southeast of Lod.

GIN KJV term for a trap or snare. With the exception of Amos 3:5, all scriptural uses are figurative, either of the fate of the wicked (Job 18:9; Isa. 8:14) or of the schemes of the wicked (Pss. 140:5; 141:9). See *Fowler.*

GINATH (Gī´ năth) Place-name or personal name meaning "wall" or "enclosure." Father of Tibni, the favorite of half of Israel for kingship when Omri became king about 885 B.C. (1 Kings 16:21). See *Tibni.*

GINNETHO (Gĭn´ nə thō) KJV spelling in Neh. 12:4 of Levite who returned from Babylonian captivity with Zerubbabel about 537 B.C. Hebrew texts have various spellings followed by modern translations: Ginnethon (NIV; REB); Ginnethoi (NASB, TEV, NRSV). This is apparently the same person listed as head of a clan of priests in 12:16. Probably the person who signed Nehemiah's covenant (10:6) belonged to the same family.

GINNETHOI (Gĭn´ nə thŏī), **GINNETHON** (Gĭn´ nə thŏn) See *Ginnetho.*

GIRDLE Several items of clothing in KJV. **1.** An ornate sash worn by the officiating priests (Exod. 28:4,40) and by the wealthy of Jerusalem (Isa. 3:24). **2.** A decorated band (NRSV), woven belt (TEV, NASB), or waistband (NIV, REB) for the high priest's ephod (Exod. 28:8,27-28). **3.** A belt on which a sword or bow might be carried (1 Sam. 18:4; 2 Sam. 20:8; perhaps Isa. 5:27); a leather belt forming part of the proverbial garb of the prophets (2 Kings 1:8; Matt. 3:4). **4.** An undergarment (Job 12:18; Jer. 13:1-11), often rendered waistcloth or loincloth.

To gird up one's loins means literally to tuck the loose ends of one's outer garment into one's belt. Loins were girded in preparation for running (1 Kings 18:46), for battle (Isa. 5:27), or for service for a master (Luke 12:35). The call to "gird your minds" (1 Pet. 1:13 NASB) means to be spiritually alert and prepared. See *Cloth, Clothing.*

GIRGASHITE (Gĭr´ gȧ shīt) or **GIRGASITE** (Gĭr´ gȧ sīt) Tribal name possibly meaning "sojourner with a deity." One on the list of original tribal groups inhabiting Canaan, traced back to Canaan, son of Ham and grandson of Noah (Gen. 10:16). The Ugaritic texts from Ras Shamra also apparently mention them.

GIRZITE (Gĭr´ zīt) See *Gezrite*.

GISHPA (Gĭsh´ pȧ) or **GISPA** (Gĭs´ pȧ) (KJV) Personal name of uncertain meaning. Supervisor of temple servants in days of Nehemiah (Neh. 11:21). It does not appear in the lists in Chronicles and Ezra, so some Bible students think the name is a copyist's change from Hasupha, which the Jews would pronounce similarly (Ezra 2:43; Neh. 7:46).

GITTAH-HEPHER (Gĭt´ ta-hē´ phēr) KJV spelling for Gath-hepher (Josh. 19:13) based on a variant Hebrew spelling in the text. See *Gath-hepher*.

GITTAIM (Git´ tā ĭm) Place-name meaning "two winepresses." City to which people of Beeroth fled after Israel entered Canaan. The Bible does not tell the precise time (2 Sam. 4:3). After the exile, part of the tribe of Benjamin settled there (Neh. 11:33). This could be the same as the Gath of 1 Chron. 7:21; 8:13, but that is not certain. The location is not certain, probably near Lydda and thus in Philistine territory at Rash Abu Hamid.

GITTITE (Gĭt´ tīt) Citizen of Gath.

GITTITH (Gĭt´ tĭth) Word of uncertain meaning used in the titles of Pss. 8; 81; 84. It may represent a musical instrument resembling a Spanish guitar, a musical tune, or a rite or ceremony as part of a festival.

GIZONITE (Gī´ zō nīt) Citizen of Gizah or Gizon, a place not otherwise mentioned. It may be modern Beth-giz southwest of Latrun. David had military leaders from there (1 Chron. 11:34), though Gizonite does not appear in the parallel in 2 Sam. 23:34. Some Greek manuscript evidence points to Guni as the original reading. Some Bible students suggest the original reading was Gimzoni from Gimzo. See *Gimzo; Guni*.

GIZRITE (Gĭz´ rīt) Citizen of Gezer. REB reading in 1 Sam. 27:8 for Girzite. See *Gezrite*.

GLAD TIDINGS KJV phrase for good news (Luke 1:19). A synonym for gospel as the news Jesus brought of God's kingdom (Luke 8:1; Acts 13:32; Rom. 10:15). See *Gospel*.

GLASS Amorphous substance, usually transparent or translucent, formed by a fusion of silicates (sometimes oxides of boron or phosphorus) with a flux and a stabilizer into a mass that cools to a rigid condition without crystallization.

Glass has a long history in the Middle East. Obsidian (volcanic glass) was brought into Palestine from Anatolia as early as 5000 B.C. Manufactured glass began to appear after 2500 B.C., but vessels made of glass did not appear until about 1500 B.C. The glass industry reached its zenith in Egypt between 1400 and 1300 B.C. One of the few artifacts not from Egypt is a conical beaker from Mesopotamia, found at Megiddo.

In Egypt and Phoenicia glass was opaque and was used chiefly to make ornamental objects—especially beads, jewelry, and small bottles. Highly skilled artisans created pieces that imitated precious stones such as lapis lazuli and turquoise.

The value of glass in ancient times may be indicated in Job where the glass is equated with gold and is used in parallel with jewels (Job 28:17). The Egyptians and Phoenicians made small bottles for perfume by welding sticks of glass around a core of sand and clay built around a bar of metal. The core and bar were removed after the glass cooled.

Glass drinking bowls became popular in Palestine by 200 B.C. Most of that found in Palestine originated in Phoenicia. The method still used was molding the glass over an object. About 50 B.C. came the revolutionary invention of glass blowing. This method was quicker and less expensive than creating molds for each desired type of vessel. Discovered probably in Phoenicia, blown glass became the vessels of choice in Palestine during the Roman period. Palestinian artists became famous for their brown glass. Many even began signing their creations—the first known designer products in history.

Transparent glass was not made until NT times as a luxury item. During this period, Alexandria, Egypt, became world famous as a

Glass vase in the shape of a fish from Tel el-Amarna in Egypt.

center for the production of glassware. Such items as beakers, bowls, flasks, goblets, and bottles were made from the transparent glass. Corinth became known for the production of glass after the time of Paul.

John probably had the transparent variety of glass in mind when he wrote Revelation. He described the walls and streets of the new Jerusalem being made of pure gold. The gold of the walls and streets was so pure that it was as clear as glass (Rev. 21:18,21).

John also described the sea as being like glass (Rev. 4:6; 15:2). Here the reference is probably not so much to transparency as to calmness. It has often been stated that the Israelites had a fear of the sea that always seemed to be in a state of chaos and tumult. The sea that John saw around the throne of God was not in a constant uproar; this sea was as smooth as glass.

The KJV uses glass in five other passages where a polished metal mirror is probably being referred to (Job 37:18; Isa. 3:23; 1 Cor. 13:12; 2 Cor. 3:18; James 1:23). Glass was not used to make mirrors in biblical times.

Phil Logan and Mike Mitchell

GLAZE Oxide mixture (usually of silica and aluminum) applied to ceramic surfaces that renders them impervious to moisture and gives them a glossy appearance. Some modern translations (NIV, REB, NRSV, TEV) divide the consonants of the Hebrew text of Prov. 26:23 differently from the KJV and NASB and find a reference to a glaze rather than to silver dross. The TEV gives the sense of the passage: "Insincere talk that hides what you are really thinking is like a fine glaze on a cheap clay pot." See *Pottery.*

GLEANING Process of gathering grain or produce left in a field by reapers or on a vine or tree by pickers. Mosaic law required leaving this portion so that the poor and aliens might have a means of earning a living (Lev. 19:9-10; 23:22; Deut. 24:19-21; cp. Ruth 2). Isaiah compared the few grapes or olives left for gleaners to the small remnant of Israel God would leave when He judged them (Isa. 17:5-9). One day, however, God would again gather or glean His remnant one by one and return them to worship in Jerusalem (Isa. 27:12).

GLEDE KJV term for an unclean bird of prey (Deut. 14:13). The identity of the bird (Hb. *ra'ah*) is impossible to determine. The following suggestions have been offered: buzzard (NRSV); kite (REB); red kite (NIV, NASB). The Hebrew root suggests a bird with keen eyesight, for example a member of the hawk family. An easily confused Hebrew word (*da'ah*) occurs in Lev. 11:14 and in some manuscripts and early translations of Deut. 14:13. The bird in question may be the red kite *(Milvus milvus).* See *Kite.*

GLISTERING STONES See *Antimony.*

GLORY Weighty importance and shining majesty that accompany God's presence. The basic meaning of the Hebrew word *kavod* is heavy in weight (cp. 1 Sam. 4:18; Prov. 27:3). Thus it can refer to a heavy burden (Exod. 18:18; Ps. 38:4; cp. more idiomatic uses in Gen. 12:10; 47:4; Exod. 4:10; 7:14). On the other side, it can describe extreme good fortune or mass numbers, a use with many different English translations (cp. Gen. 13:2; Exod. 12:38; Num. 20:20; 1 Kings 10:2).

The verb thus often comes to mean "give weight to, honor" (Exod. 20:12; 1 Sam. 15:30; Ps. 15:4; Prov. 4:8; Isa. 3:5). Such honor that people give to one another is a recognition of the place of the honored person in the human community. A nation can have such honor or glory (Isa. 16:14; 17:3). This is not so much something someone bestows on another as a quality of importance that a person, group, or nation has and which another recognizes.

"To give glory" is to praise, to recognize the importance of another, the weight the other carries in the community. In the Psalms people give such glory to God; they recognize the essential nature of His "godness" that gives Him importance and weight in relationship to the human worshiping community (cp. Pss. 22:23; 86:12; Isa. 24:15). Human praise to God can be false, not truly recognizing His importance (Isa. 29:13; cp. 1 Sam. 2:30). At times God creates glory for Himself (Exod. 14:4,17; Ezek. 28:22). As one confesses guilt and accepts rightful punishment, one is called upon to recognize the righteousness and justice of God and give Him glory (Josh. 7:19; 1 Sam. 6:5). God thus reveals His glory in His just dealings with humans. He also reveals it in the storms and events of nature (Ps. 29; cp. Isa. 6). Glory is thus that side of God which humans recognize and to which humans respond in confession, worship, and praise (cp. Isa. 58:8; 60:1). Still, for the OT, the greatest revelation of divine glory came on Sinai (Deut. 5:24). Yet such experiences are awesome and fearful (Deut. 5:25). Such revelation does not, however, reveal all of God, for no person can see the entirety of the divine glory, not even Moses (Exod. 33:17-23).

The NT uses *doxa* to express glory and limits the meaning to God's glory. In classical Greek *doxa* means opinion, conjecture, expectation, and then praise. The NT carries forward the OT meaning of divine power and majesty (Acts 7:2; Eph. 1:17; 2 Pet. 1:17). The NT extends this to Christ as having divine glory (Luke 9:32; John 1:14; 1 Cor. 2:8; 2 Thess. 2:14).

Divine glory means that humans do not seek glory for themselves (Matt. 6:2; John 5:44; 1 Thess. 2:6). They only look to receive praise and honor from Christ (Rom. 2:7; 5:2; 1 Thess. 2:19; Phil. 2:16).

GLOSSOLALIA Technical term for speaking in tongues (Gk. *glossa*). See *Tongues, Gift of*.

GLUTTON One habitually given to greedy and voracious eating. Gluttony was associated with stubbornness, rebellion, disobedience, drunkenness, and wastefulness (Deut. 21:20). A more general meaning for the Hebrew term as a "good-for-nothing" (Prov. 28:7 TEV) is reflected in some translations: wastrel (Deut. 21:20 REB); profligate (Deut. 21:20 NIV; Prov. 28:7 REB); riotous (Prov. 28:7 KJV). When Jesus was accused of being "a glutton and a drunkard" (Matt. 11:19 HCSB; Luke 7:34), it was in this expanded sense of being one given to loose and excessive living. Gluttony makes one sleepy,

leads to laziness, and eventually to poverty (Prov. 23:21).

GNASHING OF TEETH Grating one's teeth together. In the OT gnashing of teeth was an expression of anger reserved for the wicked and for one's enemies (Job 16:9; Pss. 35:16; 37:12; Lam. 2:16). In the NT gnashing of teeth is associated with the place of future punishment (Matt. 8:12; 13:42,50). There the gnashing of teeth is perhaps an expression of the futility of the wicked before God's judgment or else a demonstration of their continuing refusal to repent and acknowledge the justness of God's judgment (cp. Rev. 16:9,11), See *Hell; Punishment, Everlasting.*

GNAT See *Insects.*

GNOSTICISM (nŏs´ tĭ sĭ zəm) Modern designation for certain dualistic religious and philosophical perspectives that existed prior to the establishment of Christianity and for the specific systems of belief characterized by these ideas, which emerged in the second century and later. The term "Gnosticism" is derived from the Greek word *gnosis* (knowledge) because secret knowledge was such a crucial doctrine in Gnosticism.

Importance of Gnosticism Gnosticism emerged in schools of thought within the church in the early second century and soon established itself as a way of understanding Christianity in all of the church's principal centers. The church was torn by heated debates over the issues, and by the end of the second century many of the gnostics belonged to separate, alternative churches or belief systems viewed by the church as heretical. Gnosticism was thus a major threat to the early church, many of whose leaders, such as Irenaeus (died about 200), Tertullian (died about 220), and Hippolytus (died about 236), wrote voluminously against it. Many of the features of Gnosticism were incorporated into the sect of the Manichees in the third century, and Manichaeism endured as a heretical threat to the church into the fourth century.

Gnosticism is also important for interpreting certain features of the NT. Irenaeus reported that one of the reasons John wrote his Gospel was to refute the views of Cerinthus, an early gnostic. Over against the gnostic assertion that the true

God would not enter our world, John stressed in his Gospel that Jesus was God's incarnate Son.

Heretical Gnostic Sects The gnostics who broke away or were expelled from the church claimed to be the true Christians, and the early Christian writers who set themselves to refute their claims are the major source for descriptions of the heretical gnostic sects. Although wide variations existed among the many gnostic sects in the details of systems, certain major features were common to most of them—the separation of the god of creation from the god of redemption, the division of Christians into categories with one group being superior, the stress on secret teachings which only divine persons could comprehend, and the exaltation of knowledge over faith. The church rejected such teachings as heretical, but many people have continued to find attraction in varieties of these ideas.

Gnostics generally distinguished between an inferior god or "demiurge" whom they felt was responsible for the creation and the superior god revealed in Jesus as the Redeemer. This was a logical belief for them because they opposed matter to thought in a radical way. Matter was seen as evil; thought or knowledge distinguished persons from matter and animals and was imperishable, capable of revealing God, and the only channel of redemption. The gnostic Marcion thus rejected the OT, pointing out that the lesser or subordinate god revealed in it dealt with matter, insisted on law rather than grace, and was responsible for our decaying, tragedy-filled world. The God who revealed Himself in Jesus and through the additional secret teachings was, on the other hand, the absolute transcendent God. He was not incarnate in human flesh because the absolute God would not enter evil matter—Christ only seemed or appeared to be a human person, but He was not.

Gnostics divided Christians into groups, usually the spiritual and the carnal. The spiritual Christians were in a special or higher class than the ordinary Christians because they had received, as the elect of the good deity, a divine spark or spiritual seed in their beings that allowed them to be redeemed. The spiritual Christians were the true Christians who belonged to the heavenly world that was the true one. This belief that the spiritual Christians did not really belong to this world resulted in some gnostics seeking to withdraw from the world in asceticism. Other gnostic systems took an opposite turn into antinomianism (belief that moral law is not valid for a person or group). They claimed that the spiritual Christians were not responsible for what they did and could not really sin because their fleshly existence was not part of God's plan. Thus they could act in any way they pleased without fear of discipline.

Gnostics placed great stress on secret teachings or traditions. This secret knowledge was not a product of intellectual effort but was given by Jesus, the Redeemer from the true deity, either in a special revelation or through His apostles. The followers of the gnostic Valentinus claimed, for example, that Theodus, a friend of Paul's, had been the means of transmission of the secret data. The secret knowledge was superior to the revelation recorded in the NT and was an essential supplement to it because only this secret knowledge could awaken or bring to life the divine spark or seed within the elect. When one received the *gnosis* or true knowledge, one became aware of one's true identity with a divine inner self, was set free (saved) from the dominion of the inferior creator god, and was enabled to live as a true child of the absolute and superior deity. To be able to attain to one's true destiny as God's child, one had to engage in specific, secret rituals and in some instances to memorize the secret data which enabled one to pass through the network of powers of the inferior deity who sought to keep persons imprisoned. Salvation was thus seen by the gnostics in a cosmic rather than a moral context—to be saved was to be enabled to return to the realm of pure spirit with the transcendent God.

The gnostics thought faith was inferior to knowledge. The true sons of the absolute deity were saved through knowledge rather than faith. This was the feature of the various systems that gave the movements its designation: they were the gnostics, the knowers. Yet what this precise knowledge was is quite vague. It was more a perception of one's own existence that solved life's mysteries for the gnostic than it was a body of doctrine. The knowledge through which salvation came could be enhanced by participation in rituals or through instruction, but ultimately it was a self-discovery each gnostic had to experience.

Origins of the Gnostic Concepts Gnosticism would not have been a threat to the early church if it had not been quite persuasive in the first centuries of the Christian era, and the question of where such ideas came from and what human needs they met must be addressed.

The classic answer to the question of why Gnosticism arose is that it represents the "radical hellenizing of Christianity." In this view, Gnosticism resulted from the attempt of early Christian thinkers to make Christianity understandable, acceptable, and respectable in a world almost totally permeated by Greek assumptions about the reality of the world.

This classic view of the heretical gnostic sects as distortions of Christianity by Hellenistic thought has much strength because it is easily demonstrated how the gnostics could use NT texts, bending them to their purposes. In 1 Cor. 3:1-4, for example, Paul chides the Corinthian Christians for being "people of the flesh" (HCSB, NRSV) or carnal when they should be spiritual. This text could with ease be used as the foundation for supporting the Hellenistic idea of the superiority of certain persons in the Christian community.

The classic explanation does leave some problems unsolved, however. Little doubt exists that there are ideas, attitudes, and practices incorporated into many of the gnostic heresies that are found outside of Hellenistic thought and much earlier than the second century of the Christian era. In particular, the ultimate goal of the gnostics—to return to the absolute deity beyond matter and to be in some sense absorbed into the deity—belongs to near eastern pre-Christian mystical thought and not primarily to the Hellenistic world.

Although the radical conclusions of some scholars regarding a highly developed pre-Christian Gnosticism have been discounted, it does seem clear that there were many ideas, assumptions, and perceptions about deity, reality, and the relationships of persons to gods and the world that were incorporated into the gnostic sects from outside Hellenistic sources. Two literary discoveries have both inspired and tended to support this line of research—the Dead Sea Scrolls and the Nag Hammadi library with many gnostic documents.

Harold S. Songer and E. Ray Clendenen

GOAD Rod, generally about eight feet long, with a pointed end used to control oxen. During the time of the judges, the Israelites hired Philis-

tine blacksmiths to "sharpen the goads" (1 Sam. 13:21 KJV), either by fashioning metal points for the pointed ends or making metal casings for the blunt end which might be used to knock dirt clods from the plow. Goads might be used as a weapon (Judg. 3:31). The sayings of the wise are "goads" that "prod" (1 Sam. 13:21, God's Word; The Bible in Basic English) thought (Eccles. 12:11). God warned Paul not to "kick against the goads" (HCSB; KJV, pricks) by refusing to submit to the heavenly vision (Acts 26:14).

GOAH (Gō´ a) Place-name meaning "low" (as a cow) or "bellow." A place, apparently on the west side of Jerusalem, where Jeremiah promised the walls would be restored after the Babylonian destruction (Jer. 31:39).

GOAT Hollow-horned, cud-chewing mammal with long, floppy ears, usually covered with long, black hair. Sometimes, they were speckled. One type of goat mentioned in the Bible has been identified as the Syrian or Mamber goat. Domesticated long before the biblical era, the goat in biblical times probably had long ears and backward-curving horns. Both male and female had horns. The most common color was black. It was a prominent source of food; the male also was used for sacrifices (Lev. 22:27). A goat (called a scapegoat) was selected at random once a year on the Day of Atonement to bear symbolically the sins of the nation of Israel (Lev. 16:10-22). The skin of the goat was used to make garments, musical instruments, and water bottles; goat hair was woven into fabrics (Exod. 26:7). Goats are extremely destructive to vegetation and thereby contribute to erosion, as they tear plants out of the soil. Some of the earliest drawings available depict goats eating on trees. Sheep and goats grazed in the same pasture, but it was necessary to separate the herds because the male goat was often hostile toward the sheep (Matt. 25:32). Today goats are found in colors of black, gray, brown, white, and a variety of patterns and mixtures. See *Ibex*.

GOATH (Gō´ ăth) KJV and REB transliteration of Hebrew in Jer. 31:39 for Goah. See *Goah*.

GOATSKIN Hide of goats that desert dwellers used for clothing (Heb. 11:37) and for containers for water (Gen. 21:14) and wine (Josh. 9:4). In Gen. 27:16 Rachel placed goatskin on Jacob's neck and arms as part of the plan to deceive Isaac into giving his blessing. See *Goat.*

GOB (Gŏb) Place-name meaning "back" or "mountain crest." Site where David and his men fought two battles with the Philistines, killing Philistine giants (2 Sam. 21:18-19). The parallel passage (1 Chron. 20:4) names Gezer as the place. Some Hebrew manuscripts read Benob or "in Nob" as in verse 16. The Greek manuscripts presuppose either in Gath or in Gezer. The location of Gob is not known, though it appears to be a Philistine city.

GOBLET KJV term for a bowl-shaped drinking vessel without handles (Song 7:2). In contemporary English a goblet is a drinking vessel with a foot and stem. Modern translations are divided over the reference in Song of Songs: bowl (RSV, TEV), goblet (NASB, NIV, REB). The underlying Hebrew term is translated "basin" (Exod. 24:6) and bowls (Isa. 22:24) elsewhere. See *Vessels and Utensils.*

GOD Personal Creator and Lord of the universe, the Redeemer of His people, the ultimate author and principal subject of Scripture, and the object of the church's confession, worship, and service.

Knowledge of God The opening verses of Scripture not only begin with the affirmation of God's existence but also of God's unique action in speaking the universe into being out of nothing (Gen. 1:1; cp. Pss. 33:6; 148:5; John 1:1-2; Heb. 11:3). At the heart of the biblical presentation of God is that God alone is the personal Creator and Lord, and that if He is to be known truly by His creatures, He must take the initiative in making Himself known to us (1 Cor. 2:10-11; Heb. 1:1-2). No doubt His existence and power are disclosed in the created order, even though that order has been deeply scarred by human rebellion and its consequences (Ps. 19:1-2; Rom. 1:19-20; Gen. 3:18; Rom. 8:19-22). It is also true that a dim image of God's moral nature is reflected in the human conscience, even after the fall (Rom. 2:14-16). But Scripture is also very clear that apart from God's own gracious self-disclosure, both in Word and action, we could not know Him in any true sense.

In truth, God is incomprehensible, one that we cannot totally fathom (Pss. 139:6; 145:3; Rom. 11:33-36). But this in no way implies that we cannot know God truly. For in creating us in His image and giving us a Word, revelation of Himself, even though we cannot know God fully, we may know Him truly (Deut. 29:29). That is why any discussion of the Christian doctrine of God must be firmly rooted and grounded in Scripture as God's Word written (Pss. 19:7-14; 119; Prov. 1:7; 2 Tim. 3:14-17). Human speculation about God is never sufficient to lead us to the knowledge of God.

Nature of God Scripture identifies and describes God in many ways across the entire canon of Scripture and our understanding of Him must be based in the total presentation of Himself in all the Scriptures. However, for our purposes, we will attempt to summarize the sweep of biblical data by the words: God, the covenant Lord. First, God is the "Lord" (*Yahweh; kurios*). Even though Yahweh is not the only name of God in Scripture, it is uniquely the name by which God identifies Himself (Exod. 3:13-15; 34:6-7). He does this both at the beginning of His covenant with Israel and also as the name that has been given to Jesus Christ as the head of the new covenant (Exod. 6:1-8; 20; John 8:58; Phil. 2:11). Secondly, God is the "covenant" Lord. He is the God who not only talks the universe into existence but who is also active in it. His action in the world is supremely seen in covenantal relations that find their climatic fulfillment in Jesus Christ the Lord. Hence the expression, "the covenant Lord," nicely captures much of the biblical data regarding the identity of the God who creates, sustains, rules, and by grace, redeems a people for Himself. See *Names of God.*

Three important summary statements can be highlighted from this overall presentation of the God of Scripture. First, as the covenant Lord, God is both transcendent over and immanent in His world. God is presented as the Lord who is exalted above and over His world, that is, transcendent (Pss. 7:17; 9:2; 21:7; 97:9; 1 Kings 8:27; Isa. 6:1; Rev. 4:3). Transcendence is not primarily a spatial concept; rather it speaks of God's distinction and separateness from His creation and thus His complete lordship over it. In biblical thought, God alone is the all-powerful Creator and Lord, and everything else is His creation. He alone is self-existent, self-sufficient, eternal, and in need of nothing outside of Himself (Pss. 50:12-14; 93:2; Acts 17:24-25). That is why the God of Scripture is utterly unique and

G

thus shares His glory with no other created thing (Isa. 42:8). Furthermore, this is why God alone is to be worshiped, trusted, and obeyed. This presentation of God distinguishes Christian theism from all forms of dualism, pantheism, or polytheism.

But we must be careful that we do not misunderstand the biblical understanding of God's transcendence. God's transcendence is not to be viewed in either deistic or "wholly other" terms as has been common in some contemporary thought. For as the "covenant" Lord, Scripture clearly stresses that God is also immanent, that is, involved and present in His world (Ps. 139:1-10; Acts 17:28; Eph. 4:6). This is true not only in God's sustaining the world but also in effectively shaping and governing it towards its eternally planned end (Eph. 1:11). It is at this point that this view stands in direct opposition to process or pantheistic theism, which not only surrenders the transcendence of God but also wrongly views God's immanence as a struggling, evolving, and mutually dependent involvement with the world. Even though God is deeply involved in His world, He is also Lord over it.

Second, as the covenant Lord, God is infinite, sovereign, and personal. By infinite, Scripture presents God as having every attribute or quality to the most perfect degree as well as not being bound by any of the limitations of space or time that apply to us, His creatures. God is eternal spirit (John 4:24; cp. Exod. 3:14; Deut. 33:27; Ps. 90:2-4; 1 Tim. 1:17) and as spirit, He is not limited to any particular place or time nor can He in any way be brought under creaturely control. He is the invisible, transcendent, living God from which all derive their existence. Thus to affirm that God is infinite is to say that God is always present everywhere (omnipresent, Ps. 139:7-10; Acts 17:28) though invisibly and imperceptibly, and is at every moment conscious of all that ever was, is, or shall be (omniscient). Scripture nowhere affirms, as does open theism, that God does not know future free actions of human beings so that the future is to Him uncertain. Rather, God's knowledge is presented as comprehensive, certain, and immediate including things past, present, and future, things possible as well as actual (Ps. 139:1-4,16; Isa. 40:13-14; 41:22-23; 42:8-9; 46:9-11; Acts 2:22-24; 4:27-28; Rom. 11:33-36).

By sovereign, Scripture means that God's power and governance is so extensive that there is nothing whatsoever that takes place apart from His plan and rule, even including the free actions of human beings (Eph. 1:11; Prov. 21:1; Acts 2:22-24). In all things, without violating the nature of things including human free agency, God acts in, with, and through His creatures so as to accomplish everything He desires to do in the way He desires to do it (Isa. 10:5-11; Dan. 4:34-35). God is truly the sovereign-personal Lord. By personal, Scripture identifies God as the one who interacts with other persons as a person. God is never presented as some mere abstract concept or impersonal force or power. Rather He is the all-glorious God who knows, wills, plans, speaks, loves, becomes angry, asks questions, gives commands, listens to praise and prayer, and interacts with His creatures.

Third, God is Triune. Distinctive to biblical theism is the conviction that the covenant Lord is as truly three as He is one. Although the word "trinity" is not found in Scripture, theologians have employed it to do justice to the biblical teaching that God is not only one in nature but also three in person. As one follows the self-revelation of God in redemptive history, we discover not only the oneness of God (Deut. 6:4-5; Isa. 44:6), but also the affirmation that the Father is God (John 20:17), the Son is God (John 1:1,14; Rom. 9:5; Col. 2:9), and the Holy Spirit is God (Gen. 1:2; Acts 5:3-4; 1 Cor. 3:16). This is most clearly seen in the NT in the relationship between the Father, the Son, and the Spirit, and in the pervasive triadic references whereby the NT consistently presents salvation as the joint work of the three persons together (1 Cor. 12:3-6; 2 Cor. 13:14; Eph. 1:3-14; 2 Thess. 2:13-14; Matt. 28:19). Thus, within the complex unity of God's being, three personal centers of consciousness eternally coinhere, interpenetrate, relate to one another, and cooperate in all divine actions. Each person is co-equal and co-eternal in power and glory though each one's role and function distinguishes Him—the Father sends the Son, the Son obeys the Father, and the Holy Spirit brings glory to both (John 5:16-30; 16:12-16; Acts 2:14-36). It is no doubt true that the Trinity is to us a mystery, that is, a matter of incomprehensible fact. But the importance of the doctrine cannot be overstated. What is ultimately at stake in the doctrine is the biblical presentation of God as transcendent and self-sufficient while simultaneously personal and active in human history and redemption as that which is accomplished by a fully divine Father, Son, and Holy Spirit.

Character of God Throughout Scripture, in God's dealings with human beings, we see God's character fully revealed and displayed. In fact, we uniquely see God's character in action in Jesus Christ, the Lord of Glory, the Word made flesh (John 1:1,14). There are at least two statements that must be affirmed concerning the character of God.

First, God's character is holy love. It is important never to separate the holiness of God from the love of God. God is holy (Lev. 11:44; Isa. 6:3; Rev. 4:8). In the first instance, the word "holy" conveys the meaning of separateness and transcendence. God is the supremely holy one because "He is exalted above all the peoples ... He is holy" (Ps. 99:2-3 HCSB). However, it is the secondary meaning of the word that speaks of God's moral purity in the sense of God's separateness from sin. In this latter sense, as the holy one, God is pure, righteous, and just. That is why Scripture repeatedly emphasizes that our sin and God's holiness are incompatible. His eyes are too pure to look on evil and He cannot tolerate wrong (Exod. 34:7; Rom. 1:32; 2:8-16). Thus, our sins effectively separate us from Him, so that His face is hidden from us (Isa. 59:1-2). Closely related to God's holiness is His wrath, that is, His holy reaction to evil (Rom. 1:18-32; John 3:36). The wrath of God, unlike the holiness of God, is not one of the intrinsic perfections of God; rather, it is a function of His holiness against sin. Where there is no sin, there is no wrath, but there will always be holiness. But where God in His holiness confronts His image-bearers in their rebellion, there must be wrath; otherwise God is not the jealous God He claims to be, and His holiness is impugned. Ultimately, the price of diluting God's wrath is to diminish His holiness and moral character.

Nevertheless, God is also love. Often divine holiness and love are set over against one another, but in Scripture this is never the case. This is best seen in the context of the affirmation, "God is love" (1 John 4:8). John, in this context, does not view the love of God as mere sentimentality or a blind overlooking of our sin; rather, He views divine love as that which loves the unlovely and undeserving. In fact, the

supreme display of God's love is found in the Father giving His own dear Son as our propitiatory sacrifice that turns back God's holy anger against us and satisfies the demands of justice on our behalf (1 John 4:8-10). Thus, in the cross of Christ we see the greatest demonstration of both the holiness and love of God fully expressed, where justice and grace come together, and God remains both just and the justifier of those who have faith in Christ Jesus (Rom. 3:21-26).

Second, God's character is that of moral perfection. In all of God's dealings with His creation and with His people, God displays the wonder, beauty, and perfection of His own character. In His relation to His people, He shows Himself to be the God of grace and truth, slow to anger, abounding in love and faithfulness, wisdom, and goodness (Exod. 34:6-7; John 1:14-16; Deut. 7:7-8; Pss. 34:8; 100:5; 103:8; Mal. 1:2-3; 2 Cor. 1:3; Eph. 1:3-14; Heb. 4:16). Even in His relation to His rebel world, He displays His generosity, kindness, and patience, as well as His righteous and holy judgment (Pss. 65:9-13; 104:10-30; 136:25; Matt. 5:44-45; Acts 14:16-17; Rom. 2:4). In all of His ways, He is majestically perfect, unchanging (Exod. 3:14; Mal. 3:6; James 1:17), and good. Ultimately the purpose of human existence, and especially of God's redeemed people, the church, is to live before this great and glorious God in adoration, love, and praise and to find in Him alone our all in all (Ps. 73:23-28; Rom. 11:33-36). See *Christ; Holy Spirit; Trinity.*   *Steve Wellum*

GOD FEARER The book of Acts is our primary source for understanding the term "God fearer." In Acts 10:2 Luke describes Cornelius as "a devout man" who "feared God" (HCSB; cp. 10:22). Paul's address to those gathered in the synagogue at Pisidian Antioch begins, "Men of Israel, and you who fear God" (Acts 13:16; cp. 10:26). Similarly, there are several examples in Acts of people described as "devout" or as "worshipers of God." A group of "religious women" in Pisidian Antioch are incited by the Jews against Paul and Barnabas (13:50). Lydia, one of first converts in Philippi, is described as one who "worshiped God" (16:14). Among Paul's converts in Thessalonica were many "God-fearing Greeks" (17:4). In Athens Paul debated Jews and "those who worshiped God" in the synagogue (17:17). During Paul's first visit

G

to Corinth he stayed with Titius Justus, "a worshiper of God" (18:7).

The term "God fearer" is used to describe the Gentiles mentioned in Acts who were drawn to the Jewish religion, perhaps for ethical and moral reasons or because they were attracted to Jewish monotheism and worship practices. "God fearers" took part in Jewish practices such as tithing and regular prayers (Acts 10:2-4) and were apparently welcome to take part in some synagogue services. It has been suggested plausibly that God fearers were given the same rights and held to the same requirements as "resident aliens" in the OT. Given that, it is assumed that God fearers followed such practices as keeping the Sabbath (Exod. 20:10) and participating in sacrificial offerings (Lev. 17:8-9) and were expected not to commit offenses such as blasphemy (Lev. 24:16) or idolatry (Lev. 20:2). Perhaps another indication of the standards kept by the God fearers mentioned in Acts is found in the Sibylline Oracles (4:24-34). A blessing is spoken upon Gentiles who do things such as worship the one God and reject idolatry and who do not murder, steal, or commit sexual sins.

While God fearers attached themselves to many aspects of Judaism and certain Jewish practices, they never became full converts to Judaism. For instance, Luke seems to make a distinction between Gentiles who "feared God," and "devout proselytes" (Acts 13:16,43). It is likely, at least for Gentile men, that the prospect of circumcision was one of the reasons some "God fearers" never became full coverts. Other reasons, such as social or ethnic concerns could also have been factors. "God fearers," whatever their connection and affection for Judaism, remained fully Gentile.

It must be stressed that "God fearer" is a descriptive, rather than a technical, term. That is, it was probably not the "official" definition for Gentiles who followed nearly every tenet of Judaism short of circumcision. Descriptions like "devout" and "worshiper of God" can be applied to anyone, Jew or Gentile, and should not be thought of as synonymous with "God fearer." Moreover, one should be careful about drawing too sharp a distinction between "God fearer" and the technical term "proselyte." As long as these cautions are kept in mind, "God fearer" is a valid way of referring to the people mentioned in the passages cited above.

In Acts the "God fearers" are key figures in the unfolding of God's plan of redemption. One of the first Gentile Christians was Cornelius, a man who "feared God." Furthermore, as the gospel spread to Pisidian Antioch, to Philippi, to Corinth, to Athens, and beyond, the "God fearers" were among those who formed the earliest Christian congregations as the gospel spread to the Gentiles. See *Proselytes*.   *Brian J. Vickers*

GODHEAD Word used with reference to God when one speaks of God's divine nature or essence or of the three persons of the Trinity. See *Trinity*.

GODLESSNESS Attitude and style of life that excludes God from thought and ignores or deliberately violates God's laws. Romans 1:20-32 is a classic characterization of godlessness: the godless refuse to acknowledge God in spite of the evidence of creation (1:20-21), engage in willful idolatry (1:25), and practice a lifestyle unconstrained by divine limits (1:26-31). The godless not only have no fear of God's judgment but also seek to involve others in their wickedness (1:32). "Godless myths and old wives' tales" (NIV) refers to speech that encourages an attitude and lifestyle of godlessness (1 Tim. 4:7; cp. 6:20; 2 Tim. 2:16).

GODLINESS Respect for God that affects the way a person lives. The term "godliness" appears most frequently in the writings of Paul, specifically the Pastoral Epistles. Paul encouraged Timothy to pursue "godliness" in an active manner (1 Tim. 6:11). By so doing, he challenged him to develop a true respect for God and then, in turn, to live his life based on that respect. He emphasized the value of godliness by contrasting it to physical training (1 Tim. 4:8). Whereas physical training has benefit for this life, Paul noted that godliness would benefit the believer in this life and in the life to come. This characteristic was also recognized as being of "great gain" in the life of a Christian (1 Tim. 6:6). Peter likewise encouraged his readers to add to their lives "godliness" as a way of living (2 Pet. 1:6-7).

In addition, Paul used the term to refer to God's actions through Jesus that provided the basis for the Christian's godliness. According to 1 Tim. 3:16, this "mystery of godliness is great" (HCSB). Paul also referred to some who had a "form of godliness" but denied its power. These were ones who appeared to be people of piety, but their understanding and worship of God had little, if any, effect upon their lives (1 Tim. 6:5)

Thomas Strong

GOD OF THE FATHERS Technical phrase used as a general designation of the God of the patriarchs. Some references to the formula within the biblical narratives speak of the "God of my [your, thy, his, their] father" (Gen. 31:5,29; 43:23; 49:25; 50:17), without mention of a particular father. Other references include the name of a particular patriarch, as "the God of Abraham" (Gen. 31:53; 26:24; 28:13; 32:9), "the God of Isaac" (Gen. 28:13; 32:9; 46:1), or "the God of Nahor" (Gen. 31:53). Given the polytheistic environment of the time, originally the formula could refer to tribal or clan gods (Josh. 24:2, 14-15). Each of the patriarchs apparently had a special name for God: "Fear of Isaac" (Gen. 31:42), "Mighty One of Jacob" (Gen. 49:24).

The "burning bush" story (Exod. 3) identified the "God of the Fathers" with Yahweh. Faced with the prospect of telling the people that "The God of your fathers has sent me to you," Moses was worried that they would ask him, "What is His name?" (3:13). God commanded him to answer: "Yahweh (the Lord), the God of your fathers, the God of Abraham, the God of Isaac, and the God of Jacob, has sent me to you" (3:15). Exodus 6:2-3 reveals that the "God of the fathers" was not known by the name of Yahweh, but as "El Shaddai" (God Almighty).

The biblical witness consistently uses the formula to emphasize continuity between the God who is revealed to Moses and the God who guided the patriarchs, even by a different name. Likewise, in the OT, "God of your fathers" or "God of our fathers" functions to link the author's generation to the God of earlier generations, especially with reference to the promises to the patriarchs (Deut. 1:11,21; 4:1; 6:3; 12:1; 26:7; 27:3). In contrast, abandonment of this historic connection is also emphasized (1 Chron. 12:17; 2 Chron. 20:33; 24:24; 29:5; 30:7; 36:15; Ezra 7:27). In the NT the formula is transformed to mark the continuity between historic Israel and Christianity. The God revealed in Jesus Christ is the same as the God revealed to the patriarchs (Matt. 22:32; Mark 12:26; Acts 3:13; 5:30; 7:32; 22:14). See *Names of God; Patriarchs; Yahweh.*　　　　*Dixon Sutherland*

GODS, PAGAN One of the great distinctives of Judeo-Christian religion is monotheism—the recognition and reverence of only one God. By contrast, pagan religions of the biblical world were polytheistic, worshiping many gods. Although some OT passages are ambiguous regarding whether pagan gods actually existed, other passages are clear. When the Bible speaks of pagan gods, it speaks of either manmade concepts and worthless idols ("[Among the nations] you will serve gods made by human hands, wood and stone, which cannot see, hear, eat or smell," Deut. 4:28) or demonic spirits ("They sacrificed to demons, not God, to gods they had not known, new gods, recent arrivals, about whom your fathers knew nothing.... They have stirred up My jealousy with non-gods, they have provoked Me with their empty idols," Deut. 32:17,21; see also 2 Kings 17:29; 19:17-18; 1 Chron. 16:26; 2 Chron. 13:9; 32:19; Isa. 41:23; 42:17; Jer. 2:11; 5:7; 14:22; 16:20; Acts 19:26; 1 Cor. 8:4-6; Gal. 4:8). Old Testament passages that seem to imply a polytheistic worldview (e.g., Pss. 82:1; 86:8; 95:3; 96:4-5) should be understood as mockery or intended to vividly demonstrate the impotence of pagan worship.

Old Testament Most pagan gods began as gods of certain places such as cities or regions. Such gods or a combination of gods became nationalistic symbols as their cities or regions achieved political dominance. A by-product of the connection between gods and certain locales was the belief that a god's power may be limited to certain regions. Thus, officials of the Syrian king advised a battle with Israel on the plains observing, "Their gods are gods of the hill country. That's why they were stronger than we. But let's fight with them on the plain; surely then we'll be stronger than they" (1 Kings 20:23). Israel, against the background of this common belief, struggled with the concept that God was the Lord over all aspects of creation.

Egyptian Gods The names of about 40 deities from ancient Egypt are known, many by more than one name. Each of the 40 or so districts of Egypt had its own cult for its favorite god or gods. Few of the gods are known to have had only one area of involvement or persona, and they often overlapped. For example, creation is credited in various myths to Atum, Aten, Khnum, Thoth, Amun, or Ptah. Many deities were pictured as animals or part animals, such as

Hathor as a cow and Horus as a falcon-headed man.

Many were personifications of the enduring natural forces in Egypt. Several gods could be considered sun gods, the most common being Re or Atum. The sky was conceived as Hathor or as Nut bending over the earth god, Geb. Nut reputedly gave birth to the sun every morning and swallowed him every night. The sun was also described as *Re* traversing the sky in a boat by day and making the journey back through the underworld by night, emerging again after battling the serpent god, Apopis.

Thoth, god of the moon and patron god of scribes, was worshiped at Hermopolis. He was also pictured as the pilot of the sun god's boat and sometimes as the one who slew Apopis. Other gods connected with the moon were Osiris, Min, Shu, and Khnum.

Several gods were associated with the Nile. The main one held responsible for the annual flooding was Hapy, depicted as an obese man. Others were Sobek the crocodile god and Khnum, god of the first cataract.

Ma'at and Seth represented the duality of balance, order, and stability (Ma'at), and chaos, disorder, and death (Seth). Seth, who had slain his brother Osiris, represented the desert, foreign nations, and evil in general, constantly threatening life in Egypt. The Egyptian king or pharaoh whose enthronement was a reenactment of Re's daily victory over Apopis, was the primary weapon against the forces of evil. At his death the king became identified with Osiris, judge and lord of the dead, slain by Seth. The new king became Horus, god of fertility and the afterlife, son of Re. See *Egypt.*

Politics often played a part in the ascendancy of one god over another or the syncretism or identification of one god with another. The several major religious centers, such as Thebes, Hermopolis, Heliopolis, Abydos, and Memphis, explained the gods and the universe in ways that conflicted at various points.

The gods' names that dominate pharaohs' names in a dynasty show both the dominant city and its dominant god. Thus the god Amun, later called Amun-Re, became the chief god of the empire because of the position of Thebes. Under Amenhotep III, the successes of the empire led to internal power struggles between the powerful priesthood of Amun-Re and the throne.

Amenhotep IV changed his name to Akhenaten and embarked on a revolutionary reform that promoted worship of the sun disc Aten above all other gods. The reforms of Akhenaten failed. His second successor made clear his loyalties to Amun-Re by changing his name from Tutankhaten to Tutankhamen and abandoning the new capital in favor of Thebes. The following dynasty, while promoting Amun-Re seems to have favored gods of the north. The names of the gods Seth of Avaris, Re of Heliopolis, and Ptah of Memphis are evident in the 19th Dynasty names Seti, Rameses, and Merneptah.

The daily rituals in the temples of caring for the deities' statues were the means by which the Egyptians contributed to holding the forces of chaos at bay. Personal offerings also accompanied appeals for aid or relief from affliction. Also symbolizing devotion and appeals for help was the wearing of amulets, often devoted to such household deities as Bes, god of love, and his consort Tauert, a hippopotamus goddess of fertility and childbirth.

No Egyptian gods are mentioned in the Bible, and the complex Egyptian religion did not significantly influence the Hebrews. Some have tried to posit a relationship between the reforms of Akhenaten and the monotheism of Moses, but the differences between Atenism and the Mosaic view of God are far greater than the similarities.

Mesopotamian Gods The earliest civilization in Mesopotamia (third millennium B.C.) was that of the Sumerians. Their advanced culture, including their religion, was assimilated by their Semitic successors (Akkadians, then Assyrians and Babylonians), who ruled Mesopotamia for almost 2,000 years until the Persians. Most of the Sumerian deities continued to be worshiped, though usually by different names. More than 3,000 gods could be named, though only about 20 were highly regarded. They varied in rank at different historical periods and in different locations. Military incursions within and outside Mesopotamia usually included plundering the temples of one's enemies and capturing the statues of their gods.

One of the most important gods was An, god of the heavens and patron of Uruk (biblical Erech; Gen. 10:10). Enlil of Nippur, son of An, was the most prominent Sumerian deity. He possessed the "tablets of destiny" and was considered lord of the air and ruler of the earth. He was said to have created the human race by striking the earth with his hoe, but according to one story he also decreed human destruction in a flood because their excessive noise disturbed his sleep.

The god of Eridu, Enki, or Ea, was lord of the underground waters and the cunning god of craftsmen. He was thought to have originated human civilization and assigned gods to govern the various elements of creation and of culture. In one story he created mankind from the blood of the rebellious god Kingu and assigned them the task of serving the gods. In the Mesopotamian flood story, he divulged the plan for the flood to a human hero, who then built a boat and saved humanity.

The feared Nergal of Kutha (also called Erra) was the god of war, plagues, sudden death, and the underworld (cp. Jer. 39:3,13). His consort and coruler was Ereshkigal. The underworld, also called "the Land of No Return" and "the dark house," was viewed as a city surrounded by seven walls and entered through seven gates. It was a dark, dusty place full of frightening creatures, where the inhabitants ate dust and wore feathers like birds. The walls and gates were to protect the world of the living from the departed spirits, who were also kept from evil by mortuary cults, incantations, and mediums.

With Assyria's rise to power also came the prominence of the god and namesake of the original Assyrian capital, Ashur. Likewise, the political rise of Babylon was celebrated as a victory of their god, Marduk, son of Ea and god of thunderstorms. Many of the old myths were recast with him as the hero, defeating Tiamat, goddess of the sea, representing chaos, then organizing the world and receiving the tablets of destiny. He was referred to as "Lord of the Lands" and as *Bel* (equivalent to the Canaanite term Baal), meaning "lord" (Isa. 46:1; Jer. 50:2; 51:44). Marduk's son Nabu (Nebo in Isa. 46:1), the god of nearby Borsippa and of scribes, became especially exalted in the neo-Babylonian period as seen in the name Nebuchadnezzar.

Several important gods were associated with heavenly bodies. Shamash was god of the sun and played a prominent role among the Semites. The moon god Nanna or Sin was revered in the cities of Ur and Haran, both associated with Abraham's origins (Gen. 11:31). Thought to be Enlil's firstborn son, he traveled the night sky in a boat. During the moon's monthly disappearance he was believed to be serving as judge in the underworld, and special rites were performed to ensure his reappearance.

Ishtar (the Canaanite Athtart/Ashtart/ Astarte/Ashtoret) was variously associated with the date harvest, spring thundershowers, fertility, war, the morning and evening star (the planet Venus), and harlotry. She was very popular and was often referred to as the "mistress/queen of heaven" (Jer. 7:18; 44:17-19,25). In one story she tries and fails to usurp power in the underworld from her sister, Ereshkigal, who imprisons her there, spelling barrenness for the earth. Temple prostitution was an important part of her cult and gave Uruk, the city of her older Sumerian equivalent, Inanna, a sordid reputation. The practice was thought to promote fertility in the land. In Babylon where she was worshiped as Marduk's mistress, one of the city's impressive nine gates was named for her. Closely connected with Ishtar was her consort, the spring vegetation god Tammuz, who was remembered with wailing during the hot summer month that bore his name (cp. Ezek. 8:14). The Assyrians and Babylonians celebrated a sacred marriage ritual in which a statue of the god was symbolically brought into Ishtar's temple.

In addition to their cosmic nature, the gods were thought of as present in their image or idol and living in the temple as a king in his palace. The gold-plated wooden images were usually in human form with jewels for eyes (cp. Isa. 44:9-20; Jer. 10:1-16). Each day they were cleaned, dressed, and provided with meals by the priests (similarly in Egypt). The Assyrian king ministered before the image of his patron deity daily, but the Babylonian king only appeared before Marduk once a year at the *akitu*, the New Year festival.

Canaanite Gods The gods of the Canaanites made the greatest impact on the Israelites. While many of these are related to Mesopotamian gods, Canaanite religion was not well understood until the discovery of religious texts in the 1920s at the Syrian city of Ras Shamra, ancient Ugarit. These texts date from the 14th through the 12th centuries B.C. See *Canaan*.

At the top of the Canaanite pantheon of gods were two pairs of deities: El and Athirat (or Elat), the high god and his chief wife, and Baal and Anat, king of the gods and his chief consort and sister. El was the generic Semitic word for "god."

Like the Mesopotamian An, however, El was viewed as a grandfatherly, retiring god who did not play an active role.

By far the most prominent Canaanite god was Baal, around whom the Ugaritic myths revolve. These myths represent Baal as the storm god with power over rain, wind, and clouds, and thus over the fertility of the land. The term *ba'al*, which meant "lord, husband," may have been at first a title for the god whose personal name was Hadad, known among eastern and western Semites as god of storm, war, fertility, and divination (searching the future in the entrails of sacrificial animals, etc.). He was the main deity of the Aramaeans (cp. 2 Kings 5:18; Zech. 12:11).

The cycle of the seasons among the Canaanites was represented in the myths by Baal's struggle with Mot (literally, "death"), who represented drought and famine. Baal's death at the hands of Mot caused the dry season (summer), but his recurring return brought forth the rainy season (winter) and restored fertility to the land. In another myth, Baal defeated Yam (literally "sea"), the god of chaos, in much the way that the Babylonian Marduk defeated Tiamat.

In the Ugaritic myths, Baal's consort was his sister Anat, the bloodthirsty warrior goddess who rescued Baal from the underworld by defeating and dismembering Mot. But, apparently among the Canaanites in Palestine, her place was taken by Athirat, known in Ugarit as El's consort and the mother of the gods. In the OT she appears by the name Asherah, the Hebrew equivalent of Athirat (1 Kings 18:19). Her symbol was an "Asherah pole" (known in plural as Asherot/Asherim; e.g., Exod. 34:13; 2 Kings 17:10), probably representing a tree. Her worship included sacred prostitution, which in Canaan involved male and female prostitutes (Gen. 38:15-22; Deut. 23:17-18; 2 Kings 23:4-7; Jer. 2:20; Ezek. 16:16,31; Hos. 4:13-14). It was often conducted at "high places" that involved Asherah poles representing the goddess and sacred pillars representing the male deity (Lev. 26:30; Num. 33:52; 1 Kings 14:23-24; 2 Kings 18:4; 21:3; Ps. 78:58).

Another of Baal's consort's was Athtart. Although less prominent in Ugarit, she appears frequently in the OT as Ashtoret (probably derogatory, combined with boshet, "shame") and in Phoenician inscriptions as Ashtart, the Greek equivalent of which was Astarte. She may have played the role in Canaan that Anat played in Ugarit (cp. Judg. 10:6; 1 Sam. 7:4; 12:10; 1 Kings 11:5,33; 2 Kings 23:13). See *Asherah.*

The fertility aspect of the Canaanite gods was an inviting snare to the Israelites. New to farming and having just settled in Canaan after a generation of nomadic life in the desert, the Israelites were particularly tempted to serve the gods said to control the fertility of that land. Many of the Israelites practiced a syncretistic religion, mixing elements of Baalism with worship of Yahweh. Jeroboam's golden calves at Dan and Bethel may have been an attempt to identify Yahweh with Baal. A jar inscribed with a prayer to "Yahweh of Samaria and his Asherah" suggests a syncretistic belief that Asherah was Yahweh's consort.

Various other deities of Palestine impacted the OT story. The god Dagon of the Philistines (Judg. 16:23) was apparently a Semitic grain god acquired from the Canaanites. At Ugarit he is called Dagan, the father of Baal (although El is also said to be his father).

The national god of the Ammonites was Milcom (Hb. *milkom* or *malkam*; 1 Kings 11:5,33; 2 Kings 23:13; Zeph. 1:5), perhaps associated with the Canaanite deity Molek (or Molech), connected to a cult of the dead involving divination and child sacrifice—making one's children "pass through the fire" (Lev. 18:21; 20:2-5; 2 Kings 23:10; Jer. 19:5). In Judah this practice was conducted at Tophet in the Valley of Hinnom on the southwest side of Jerusalem (2 Chron. 28:3; Jer. 7:31; 32:35). The names Milcom and Molek are both related to the Semitic root *mlk*, "king," as is also the name of a west Semitic god variously known as Malik, Milku, and Muluk. He also was connected to a cult of the dead and was identified in antiquity with Nergal, the Mesopotamian god of the underworld. Some see an association as well with Chemosh (Hb., kamosh), the national god of the Moabites (Num. 21:29; Jer. 48:7), whose worship also involved child sacrifice (2 Kings 3:26-27) and who may have been identified with Nergal.

Another god identified with Nergal was Resheph (Hb. for "flame" or "pestilence" Hab. 3:5), god of plague and perhaps the same as Rapiu, patron god of the deified dead (Hb. *repha'im*; Isa. 14:9; 26:14; Prov. 2:18; 9:18). The cult of the dead at Ugarit involved a drunken orgy (perhaps at a family tomb) called a marzih.

New Testament The pagan gods of the NT world were the deities of the Greco-Roman pantheon and certain eastern gods whose myths gave rise to the mystery religions. The conquests of Alexander the Great of Macedon took the Greek culture throughout the Near East.

A few of the Greco-Roman gods are mentioned in the NT. At the head of the Greek pantheon was Zeus, the Roman Jupiter, god of the sky, originally the weather or storm god. With the syncretism of the Hellenistic period following Alexander the Great's conquests, Zeus was equated with the Semitic storm god Hadad. As the supreme Greek deity, however, Zeus was readily identified with the chief god of any region. Thus, when Antiochus IV attempted to force Hellenism on the Jews in 167 B.C., he transformed the Jewish temple into a temple to Zeus. A huge altar to Zeus at Pergamum is probably the "Satan's throne" of Rev. 2:13.

The messenger of the Greek gods was Hermes (Roman, Mercury). When the people of Lystra assumed Barnabas and Paul to be gods (Acts 14:8-18), they called Paul Hermes because he was the spokesman; and they identified Barnabas with Zeus or Jupiter. The oxen and garlands they brought forward were appropriate offerings for Zeus. Hermes was also the god of merchants and travelers.

Artemis was the Greek goddess of the wildwood, of childbirth, and, consequently, of fertility. The great mother goddess of Asia Minor worshiped at Ephesus was identified with Artemis, the Roman Diana. Her temple at Ephesus was one of the seven wonders of the ancient world and an object of pilgrimages. Artemis of the Ephesians was depicted in statues at Ephesus with many breasts, perhaps inspired by a sacred stone (Acts 19:35) kept in the temple. Paul's work in Ephesus resulted in an uproar incited by the silversmiths who sold souvenirs to the pilgrims (Acts 19:23-41).

Other Greco-Roman gods are not mentioned in the NT but formed an important part of Hellenistic culture. The most popular of the gods was Apollo, pictured in Greek art as the epitome of youthful, manly beauty. He served as the god of medicine, law, and shepherds. Aphrodite was the Greek goddess of sexual love and beauty. She was identified with the Semitic goddess Ishtar/Astarte and with the Roman Venus. Although not mentioned in the NT, a temple to Aphrodite at Corinth was said to employ a thousand cultic prostitutes and contributed to the city's reputation for immorality. The Semitic goddess of Byblos, *Ba ʿalat,* was identified in Greek sources as Aphrodite, who is said to have rescued the fertility god, Adonis (Semitic *Adon,* "lord") from Hades each year.

Athena, namesake and patron of the city of Athens, was a virgin goddess connected with arts and crafts, fertility, and war. She was identified with the Roman Minerva. Hera, whose Roman equivalent was Juno, was the wife of Zeus and goddess of marriage, women, and motherhood. Also not mentioned is the important Poseidon, Neptune to the Romans, god of the sea, earthquakes, and—oddly—horses. The war god of Greece was Ares, equated with the Roman god Mars. Hephaistos, the Roman Vulcan, was god of fire and the patron of smiths. Hades, called by the Romans Pluto, was the Greek god of the underworld. His name became the Greek word used in the NT for the abode of the dead (Matt. 11:23; 16:18; Luke 10:15; 16:23; Acts 2:27,31; Rev. 1:18; 20:13-14).

Certain Greek gods became the centers of cults that were quite influential in NT times. Foremost among these is the cult of Demeter or the Eleusinian mysteries. Demeter was the Greek goddess of grain who, according to the myth, ceased to function when her daughter Persephone was abducted into the underworld by Hades. Persephone was eventually released to her mother but forced to spend a third of each year in the underworld, which reflected the annual growth cycle of grain. Secret rites of initiation into the cult took place annually at Eleusis. The Greek god of wine, intoxication, and fertility was Dionysus, the Roman Bacchus. See *Babylon; Fertility Cult; Mystery; Mystery Religions.*

Daniel C. Browning, Jr. and E. Ray Clendenen

GOG AND MAGOG (Gŏg and Mā´ gŏg) **1.** In Ezek. 38–39 Gog of the land of Magog is the leader of the forces of evil in an apocalyptic conflict against Yahweh. In Rev. 20:8 Gog and Magog appear together in parallel construction as forces fighting for Satan after his 1,000-year bondage. The identity of Gog and Magog has been the subject of an extraordinary amount of speculation. In general, however, attempts to relate these figures to modern individuals or states have been unconvincing. Ezekiel's prophecy is apparently built on Jeremiah's sermons against a foe from the north (Jer. 4–6). Ezekiel's historical reference may have been Gyges, king of Lydia, who asked Ashurbanipal, king of Assyria, for help in 676 B.C. but then joined an Egyptian-led rebellion against Assyria about 665 B.C. His name became a symbol for the powerful, feared king of the north. Magog is apparently a Hebrew construction meaning "place of Gog." **2.** Gog is a descendant of the tribe of Reuben (1 Chron. 5:4).

GOIIM (Gôi´ ĭm) Proper name meaning "nations," particularly "Gentiles, foreign nations." **1.** Land where King Tidal joined the eastern coalition against a coalition from Sodom and Gomorrah. This action led to a war in which Abraham became involved (Gen. 14:1). To which nation the general term "Goiim" applies here is uncertain. Some would suggest the Hittites, since several Hittite kings between 1750 and 1200 B.C. were named Tudhaliya or Tidal. Others point to the Manda people, barbarian invaders who entered Mesopotamia about 2000 B.C. and had some association with Elamites. Goiim may mean a coalition of Hittite, Luvian, and/or other peoples. One Greek manuscript tradition points to Pamphylia, which means "rich in peoples." **2.** Joshua 12:23 lists a king of Goiim in Gilgal as one Joshua conquered. The earliest Greek translation reads "king of Goiim of Galilee," a reading many Bible students adopt since the immediate context refers to areas near Galilee and the copyist would easily write Gilgal since it plays such an important role in the early narratives of Joshua. Whatever the correct reading, we do not know the precise location or peoples referred to. **3.** Isaiah 9:1 also refers to Galilee of the nations. This may represent the Hebrew way of referring to Assyria's governmental district that the Assyrians called Megiddo. Assyria controlled this region after its wars with Israel in 733 and in 722 B.C. **4.** In Judg. 4:2 Sisera's residence was in Harosheth of the Gentiles (KJV) or Harosheth-ha-goiim (NRSV). See *Harosheth*.

GOLAN (Gō´ lăn) Place-name meaning "circle" or "enclosure." It was a city of refuge for people who unintentionally killed someone and was located in Bashan for the part of the tribe of Manasseh living east of the Jordan River (Deut. 4:43). It was also a city for the Levites (Josh. 21:27). It was located at modern Sahem el-Jolan on the eastern bank of the River el-Allan. See *Cities of Refuge; Levitical Cities.*

GOLD See *Minerals and Metals.*

GOLDEN CALF An image of a young bull, probably constructed of wood and overlaid with gold, which the Hebrews worshiped in the wilderness and in the Northern Kingdom of Israel. Living bulls were important in the religion of some regions of ancient Egypt, and bull images appear in the art and religious texts of Mesopotamia, Asia Minor, Phoenicia, and Syria. The primary references to "golden calf" are Exod. 32:1-8 and 1 Kings 12:25-33. The former passage records that the people summoned Aaron to make an image to go before them. The image was apparently intended to represent Yahweh, the Lord of Israel. The latter reference states that Jeroboam I constructed at Bethel and Dan two golden bulls, which were probably meant to represent the pedestals of God's throne. Interestingly, these passages are closely related to each other because they use the same terminology in the dedication of these images (Exod. 32:4; 1 Kings 12:28), and they both explore the sin of idolatry at crucial junctures in Israel's history.

Theological Significance These accounts demonstrate Israel's strong conviction that God cannot be lowered to the level of pictorial representation. God, as sovereign Lord, allows no physical image of Himself, and any human effort to create such an image invites His judgment. See *Aaron; Bethel; Bull; Calves, Golden; Dan; Exodus; Jeroboam; Moses; Yahweh.*

Robert William Prince III

GOLDEN RULE Name usually given to the command of Jesus recorded in Matt. 7:12 (cp. Luke 6:31)—"whatever you want others to do for you, do also the same for them" (HCSB). The designation "Golden Rule" does not appear in the Bible, and its origin in English is difficult to trace. The principle of the Golden Rule can be found in many religions, but Jesus' wording of it was original and unique.

GOLDSMITH See *Occupations and Professions.*

GOLGOTHA (Gŏl´ gō tha) Place-name transliterated from Aramaic and/or Hebrew into Greek and then into English meaning "skull." In Mark

Hill of Golgotha or Place of the Skull.

15:22 the Hebrew name for the place where Jesus was crucified. The Latin equivalent is *calvaria*. Both words mean "skull." See *Calvary; Crucifixion.*

GOLIATH (Go lī´ áth) In 1 Sam. 17:4 the huge Philistine champion who baited the Israelite army under Saul in the valley of Elah for 40 days. He was slain by the youthful David. See *Elhanan.*

GOMER (Gō´ mēr) Personal name meaning "complete, enough," or "burning coal." **1.** Daughter of Diblaim and wife of Hosea the prophet (Hos. 1:3). She is described in Hos. 1:2 as "a wife of harlotry" (NASB). Various explanations have been offered for that designation. Some have maintained that she was a common prostitute. Others have maintained that she was a cultic prostitute in the service of Baal. Some have suggested she symbolized Israel's worship of many gods. Still others have believed she was an ordinary woman who became unfaithful after her marriage to Hosea. Her unfaithfulness to her husband became a sort of living parable of Israel's unfaithfulness to Yahweh. See *Hosea.* **2.** Son of Japheth and grandson of Noah in the Table of Nations (Gen. 10:2). He is apparently seen as representing the Cimmerians, an Indo-European people from southern Russia who settled in Cappadocia in Asia Minor. Assyrian sources show they threatened Assyria after 700 B.C. He was the father of Ashkenaz or the Scythians of Jer. 51:27 who displaced the Cimmerians from their home in Russia. Gomer was also the father of Riphath (or Diphath in 1 Chron. 1:6) and of Togarmah.

GOMORRAH (Go mŏr´ ra) See *Sodom and Gomorrah.*

GONG Loud percussion instrument, perhaps like a type of cymbal used in the temple worship (1 Cor. 13:1; KJV, brass). The Greek is literally "noisy brass," referring to the metal from which the instrument was made.

GOOD In contrast to the Greek view of "the good" as an ideal, the biblical concept focuses on concrete experiences of what God has done and is doing in the lives of God's people. Scripture affirms that God is and does good (1 Chron. 16:34; Ps. 119:68). The goodness of God is experienced in the goodness of God's creative work (Gen. 1:31) and in God's saving acts (liberation of Israel from Egypt, Exod. 18:9; return of a remnant from captivity, Ezra 7:9; personal deliverance, Ps. 34:8; salvation, Phil. 1:6). God's goodness is extended to God's name (Ps. 52:9), God's promises (Josh. 21:45), God's commands (Ps. 119:39; Rom. 7:12), God's gifts (James 1:17), and God's providential shaping of events (Gen. 50:20; Rom. 8:28). Though God alone is truly good (Ps. 14:1,3; Mark 10:18), Scripture

Azekah in the Valley of Elah where young David killed Goliath.

G

repeatedly speaks of good persons who seek to live their lives in accordance with God's will. Christians have been saved in order to do good (Eph. 2:10; Col. 1:10) with the Holy Spirit's help.

GOODMAN KJV term for a husband or for the head of a household. At Prov. 7:19 "goodman" renders the Hebrew *ish*, the usual word for man. KJV on occasion translates the Greek term *oikodespotes* (rendered "goodman" at Matt. 20:11; 24:43; Mark 14:14; Luke 22:11) as master of the house (Matt. 10:25) or householder (Matt. 13:27). Modern translations use equivalents such as landowner or owner of the house.

GOPHER WOOD In Gen. 6:14 the material out of which Noah was instructed to construct the ark. The etymology of the Hebrew word is unknown, and there is no certainty as to the type of wood to which it refers. Even the earliest translators were uncertain. See *Ark*.

GOSHEN (Gō´ shən) **1.** The phrase, "land of Goshen," appears in the general description of territory occupied by Joshua's forces (Josh. 10:41; 11:16). Apparently it refers to the hill country between Hebron and the Negev. Some believe the phrase refers to a country. **2.** The "land of Goshen" may have been named after the city of Goshen located in the district of Debir (Josh. 15:51). Goshen may have been the chief city of the region at one time. The ancient city was either located at Tell el Dhahiriyeh, 12 miles southwest of Hebron or at a location further east. **3.** Goshen is primarily recognized as an area in the northeast sector of the Nile Delta. It was occupied by the Hebrews from the time of Joseph until the exodus.

Goshen is significant for biblical studies for four reasons. (1) The pharaoh assigned Goshen to Joseph's family when they entered Egypt (Gen. 47:6,11). The "Hebrew Sojourn" occurred there. (2) The territory lay on a route from Palestine to Egypt. (3) It may be possible to date Joseph's entrance to Egypt with the Hyksos control of the Delta. (4) Both of the cities that the Hebrews built, Rameses and Pithom, and the Hyksos capital at Zoan are key issues for settling on a date for the exodus.   *Gary D. Baldwin*

GOSPEL The term "gospel" occurs frequently in the NT in both noun and verb forms, literally meaning "good news" or "proclaiming good

The fertile land of Goshen in the delta country of northern Egypt.

news." The noun form, *euangelion*, occurs 75 times, and the verb *euangelizomai* occurs 56 times.

Background There are two views about the background of NT use of *euangelion* and *euangelizomai*. One is that these terms are taken from the Jewish context from which the church was established, particularly as they are used in the Septuagint (LXX). The second is that the terms were taken from a Hellenistic (pagan) setting. These have been incorrectly pitted against each other, causing interpreters to miss much the Bible says when using the term "gospel."

The meaning of these terms might arise from the LXX, but the singular use of *euangelion* does not occur. Because of this some argue that the primary, perhaps sole, external influence on NT use of *euangelion* comes from the pagan world. The important role that *euangelizomai* plays in OT passages (LXX) cited by the NT, however, makes the claim against a Jewish background difficult to sustain. In Isa. 40:9; 52:7-10; 60:6; 61:1, the herald of good news announces that Yahweh, God of Israel, has defeated the pagan enemies, ended the exile of His people, and established His reign. This fits well with the NT contexts.

The noun *euangelion* originally signified announcement of victory after battle and later the content of that message. The term also came to describe the birth or the rise to power of a new king. An inscription from Priene in Asia Minor, probably written around 9 B.C. describes the enthronement of Augustus as the new Roman emperor. Augustus is lauded as the savior who will bring peace and hails his birthday as "the beginning of the glad tidings (*euangelion*) that have come to men through him." This illustrates the religious content of the term in emperor worship.

When one compares pagan use of *euangelion* and the LXX's use of *euangelizomai*, a striking parallel arises of a king worshiped by his people. The gospel and its confession that Jesus is Lord confront the claim that Caesar is Lord and declare that in the cross and resurrection Jesus is enthroned as the King of kings. Caesar or any other created thing claiming lordship will bow before the crucified and risen Jesus.

Paul's Use of Gospel The gospel was the center of Paul's preaching and the rule by which he conducted himself to the glory of God. Paul employs *euangelion* 60 of the 75 times it is used in the NT. The congregations he addressed knew the content of the gospel, seen by the fact that Paul used the term without qualification 28 times. He also qualifies the term: the "gospel of Christ" (9 times), "the gospel of God" (6 times), "the gospel of peace," "the gospel of our salvation," and so forth. When Paul uses *euangelizomai*, it carries the same meaning as *kerusso*, both describing the act of preaching the gospel. In 1 Cor. 15 and Rom. 1 Paul explains the content of the gospel he preached.

First Corinthians 15 Paul begins discussing the certainty of the resurrection by asserting that the gospel they received from him sustains them and is the means by which they are saved. Paul defines the content of that gospel as the message he received from Jesus Christ. The two central features are that Jesus the Messiah died on the cross and rose from the dead according to the Scriptures. Paul's scriptural basis for his gospel comes from a few selected texts in the OT but also springs from his belief that the death and resurrection of Jesus the Messiah are that to which all Scripture points. By the cross and resurrection God undid the sin of Adam and the curse brought on all creation. In His death, Jesus took our sin and defeated it. Through the resurrection the power of death is destroyed and death no longer possessed any sting. The grave would no longer have the victory.

In 15:3-8 Paul demonstrates that the message he proclaimed had the same content as the message of Peter and the other apostles. He emphasizes the unity of the message because he and the other apostles have the same risen Lord. The encounter Paul had with Christ places him on the same level with these others who have seen the Lord, despite the fact that he was once a persecutor of the church. This description of the gospel opens the following discussion of the resurrection, for if Jesus has been raised, then all who believe in him shall also be raised. If Jesus has not been raised, the gospel has no power, and Jesus can only be described as a failed messianic pretender.

Romans 1:1-17 In the salutation, Paul again sets forth the content of his gospel, which is authored by God the Father and about His Son, Jesus Christ. Paul reminds his readers the gospel was promised beforehand in Scripture. He fortifies this argument through recognition that Jesus

G

was born of the seed of David, as the prophets had declared the Messiah would be. Jesus was designated the Son of God by virtue of His resurrection from the dead. The heart of the gospel is the cross and resurrection. All of history hangs on this, and a disservice to the gospel is done if the centrality of Jesus' death on the cross is minimized. The conclusion is the confession that Jesus the Messiah is Lord. In His death and resurrection, Jesus of Nazareth is vindicated as Yahweh's Messiah and established as the Lord before whom every knee shall bow and every tongue shall swear allegiance to the glory of God the Father (Phil. 2:10-11). This summary in Rom. 1:4-5 is almost identical to what Paul calls "my gospel" in 2 Tim. 2:8. In 2 Cor. 4:3-5 Paul describes the gospel as focusing on the glory of Christ and the confession that Jesus Christ is Lord is equated with the gospel Paul preached. When concluding this section (Rom. 1:16-17), Paul asserts the gospel is not just a body of information but rather the power of God for salvation. Through the cross and resurrection, salvation from sin is made available to all who believe, both Jews and Greeks.

Other Pauline Passages In Rom. 10:8c-13 the faith Paul preaches and the message that must be believed for salvation is that Jesus is Lord and that God has raised Him from the dead. Paul continues in 10:15, the one heralding the victorious return of Yahweh to Zion is closely linked to the suffering servant of Yahweh (Isa. 52:13–53:11). In Rom. 10:8c-13 the messenger proclaiming this word about Jesus is equated with the one heralding the return of Yahweh to Zion. Paul understands the gospel as the proclamation that Yahweh has defeated all enemies and established his kingdom.

The gospel is that Jesus of Nazareth, the Messiah, was crucified for our sins and raised from the dead, and is also the Lord of all creation. This message is the power of God for salvation and brings about all things that are a part of salvation (i.e., faith, regeneration, justification, etc.). Paul's message is the gospel (1 Cor. 9:14-18; Phil. 1:5; 2:22) and the reason for his imprisonment and suffering (Phil. 1:7; 2 Tim. 1:8, 2:8-9). Paul was called to proclaim this good news, and this calling strengthens him to preach the message of salvation to the Gentiles (Rom. 15:16-20; 1 Cor. 9:19-23; 2 Cor. 10:12-18; Gal. 1:15-23; 1 Thess. 2:2,8-9; 2 Tim. 2:11-12). The gospel also makes an ethical claim (Phil. 1:27; 1 Thess. 2:12; 2 Thess. 1:8). Paul links the gospel to the final judgment in that all will be judged by their response to the Savior that the good news proclaims (Rom. 2:16; Col. 1:23; 2 Thess. 1:8; 2 Tim. 4:1).

Gospel in the Gospels and Acts *Mark* Mark uses *euangelion* more than the other Gospels (8 times, including 16:15). He begins with the programmatic statement that the book is "the beginning of the gospel of Jesus Christ, the Son of God." This striking use of *euangelion* echoes both pagan and OT uses of the term through the arrival of a new king and the OT promise that Yahweh would return to Zion and defeat the enemies of His people. Everything Mark describes about the life and ministry of Jesus shows that Jesus is the Messiah sent by God to bring deliverance. In His miracles, Jesus is shown to be the Messiah, Son of God, who has power over nature, demons, disease, and even death. In His parables, the reader is taught about the kingdom Jesus is establishing. The ultimate purpose of the life of the Messiah was to die as a ransom for many. Through the resurrection, Jesus' messianic claims are vindicated and His status as the Son of God is shown to be unshakable.

Mark also employs *euangelion* to describe the ministry Jesus began after John the Baptist was jailed (1:14-15). Jesus came preaching the gospel, the proclamation that the time is fulfilled and the kingdom of God is near. Through the ministry of Jesus, the God of Israel is acting to restore His people. The corollary to this proclamation is the call to repent and believe in the gospel. Jesus' preaching echoes that of John the Baptist and brings fulfillment to it in that Jesus was the Messiah, the Son of God, who would establish Yahweh's reign. For Mark, the gospel is essentially about the establishment of the kingdom of God. Mark also uses *euangelion* as the object of *kerusso* when Jesus announces that the woman who anointed Him for burial would be remembered wherever the gospel is preached (Mark 14:3-9).

The importance of the kingdom is seen also in Mark's use of *euangelion* in 8:35 and 10:29-30. In 8:35, after his passion prediction, Jesus describes the cost of following Him and explains that one who follows Him must be willing to lose his life for the sake of Jesus and the gospel.

Matthew Matthew uses *euangelion* four times (4:23; 9:35; 24:14; 26:13) and *euangelizomai* one time (11:5; cp. Luke 7:18-23). Three times Matthew qualifies *euangelion* as the *euangelion tou basileias*, the gospel of the kingdom. Matthew summarizes Jesus' Galilean ministry in 4:23, by saying that He was teaching in their synagogues, preaching the gospel of the kingdom, and healing everyone with disease and sickness. The gospel for Matthew is focused on the kingdom Jesus came to establish through His life and death. This good news of the kingdom fits well with Jewish expectation that Yahweh would restore His people through the work of His Messiah and supports Matthew's argument that Jesus came in fulfillment of the Scriptures.

Luke-Acts Luke does not use *euangelion* in his Gospel but uses the verb (10 times) of the act of proclaiming the good news. In Acts, Luke uses *euangelizomai* 15 times and *euangelion* only twice. In the birth narratives of Jesus and John the Baptist, Luke uses *euangelizomai* in the proclamation of Gabriel to Zacharias (1:19) and to the shepherds by an angel on the night of Jesus' birth (2:10). When Jesus speaks at the synagogue in Nazareth (4:16-21), He reads from Isaiah of the restoration of Yahweh's people from their sin and exile (Isa 61:1; 58:6). Messiah will proclaim good news to the poor, declare release to the captives, sight for the blind, liberty to the oppressed, and declare the acceptable year of the Lord. After reading this text, Jesus tells the crowd this is fulfilled in Him. This text outlines the central focus of Luke's account of the life and ministry of Jesus. Luke uses this again, describing the message to John the Baptist when he seeks confirmation that Jesus is the one coming after him (7:22). The proclamation of the good news is focused on the kingdom of God and its fulfillment of the law and the prophets (8:1; 16:16).

In Acts, Luke's use of *euangelizomai* emphasizes proclamation about the life and ministry of Jesus. Eight times this proclamation is about Jesus the Messiah, who is Lord of all (5:42; 8:4-6,12,35; 10:36-44; 11:20; 13:16-41; 17:18). This good news about Jesus forms the center of the preaching by the missionaries of the early church (8:12,25,40; 14:7,15,21; 15:35; 16:10). The good news they preached was intimately linked to the promises of the OT and focused on the life and ministry of Jesus, particularly the cross and resurrection (8:26-39; 10:36-44; 13:16-41).

John John does not employ the terms *euangelion* and *euangelizomai* in his Gospel and prefers terms meaning "witness" and "truth." He also emphasizes the act of believing that Jesus is the Messiah, Son of God, and the life imparted as a result of this belief (John 20:20-31).

Gospel Elsewhere in the New Testament In 1 Pet. 1:3-12 Peter defines the gospel as the message promised by the prophets and completed in the suffering and glory of Jesus Christ. The resurrection of Jesus has provided a living hope and an eternal inheritance. This gospel is such good news that even the angels long to glimpse it. In 1:23 the gospel is called the living and abiding word of God. In discussing the time of trial and final judgment to come (4:1-19), Peter explains that a terrible outcome awaits those who reject the gospel. The verb form, *evangelizomai*, is used in Heb. 4:2 and 6 and refers to the message about Jesus the Messiah, similar to that found in 1:1-4. Revelation 14:6 describes the eternal gospel that is used in judgment.

Conclusion The gospel in the NT can be summarized as the message about the kingdom of God established in the life, death, and resurrection of Jesus the Messiah, who is enthroned as Lord of all. This good news describes events to which all Scripture points and declares that all principalities and powers are defeated once and for all by Jesus the Messiah. Finally, all of humanity will be judged according to their reception or rejection of this good news.   *Donny Mathis*

GOSPEL OF THOMAS See *Apocrypha, New Testament; Gnosticism.*

GOSPELS, SYNOPTIC The collective name for the Gospels of Matthew, Mark, and Luke. The term "synoptic" means "with the same eye," thus "with the same viewpoint."

In telling the gospel story, Matthew, Mark, and Luke share a common organization of their materials, with Jesus' ministry being oriented geographically, starting with His Galilee ministry, then moving to a transition stage that includes travel outside of Galilee, as well as within and through Galilee, and ending with the events in Jerusalem that conclude with Jesus' death and resurrection. John, on the other hand, has organized his telling of the story of Jesus in a different manner, with Jesus traveling numerous times between Galilee and Judea, due to His attendance at various Jewish festivals. While one organizational pattern is not better than the other, the similarities between the patterns of Matthew, Mark, and Luke are easily noted in a comparison of these Gospels. This common approach to telling the story of Jesus is highlighted especially by the relationship between Matthew and Mark. Of Mark's 661 verses (1:1-16:8), Matthew provides 606 of these in either exact or similar form. In other words, Matthew includes virtually all of Mark within his Gospel. And Luke, who included 320 verses that parallel Mark, is likewise closely related. Between Matthew and Luke, another 250 verses are paralleled that are not found in Mark. In some of these instances, the exact same wording is found in different Gospels, and not simply in the words of Jesus but also in the manner in which the narratives are told. See *Luke, Gospel of; Mark, Gospel of; and Matthew, Gospel of.*

So many indications of a literary relationship exist that scholars usually assume one or more common written sources were shared among these three Gospels. Various attempts have been generated to explain the nature of this literary relationship. Some scholars posit that Mark used both Matthew and Luke for his composition. But the vast majority of scholars hold that Mark wrote his Gospel first, with Matthew and Luke using Mark as one of their sources. The grammar of Matthew and Luke is generally in the direction of improving on Mark's, not the other way around. This pattern would indicate that Mark was prior to Matthew and Luke, since it would be unlikely that Mark would fail to copy the more sophisticated and often less coarse language of the other two. Mark's lack of inclusion of marvelous teachings from Jesus in Matthew and Luke, such as the Sermon on the Mount/Plain and the parables of Luke 15 would be incomprehensible if Mark had, indeed, used a copy of the others when writing. Mark seems to have written first, without the benefit of the Greek editions of Matthew and Luke that we know as our Gospels. Then, sometime after Mark had written, Matthew and Luke used Mark as an aid in their own writing.

On the other hand, Matthew and Luke also had a common source, which may have been an early form of Matthew (perhaps written in Aramaic), or a separate document, or documents, containing many teachings and sayings of Jesus. This common source material for Matthew and Luke is often designated as Q (*Quelle*), which is the word for "source" in German. Of course, Luke indicates that he knew of others who had sought to tell the gospel story and that he himself investigated the sources when writing his Gospel (Luke 1:1-4). So the fact that Matthew may have done the same and used several sources is not at all surprising. Since Mark was not an eyewitness, he would also have used various sources, with the preaching of Peter being a primary one according to the early church. The telling of the gospel story was such an important undertaking that the writers likely used as many reliable sources as they could access.

While all three of these Gospels have much in common and approach the telling of the story of Jesus from the same general organizational scheme, each one presents a unique vision of Jesus and the implications of discipleship. Each writer wrote to different groups, located in differing historical places and settings. So the common traits of these three Gospels should not be taken as indicating that they have only one viewpoint to present rather than three. In viewing these three Gospels side-by-side, the differences among the three can highlight the richness of the distinct emphases that each is making. Matthew, Mark, and Luke complement each other in their communication of the gospel story by means of their commonalities, even while presenting the message with a depth seen only by looking at each of them separately. See *Apocrypha, New Testament.*   *Bill Warren*

GOUGING THE EYES Cruel and degrading punishment sometimes inflicted on conquered peoples in biblical times. The Philistines put out Samson's eyes (Judg. 16:21). Nahash offered to make peace with the people of Gilead on the condition that he put out the right eye of every man in the city and thus bring disgrace upon all Israel (1 Sam. 11:2). After executing King Zedekiah's sons in his sight, the Babylonians put out his eyes (2 Kings 25:7). Scripture records such events as cruelty, not as examples to follow.

GOURD Inedible fruit with a hard rind of the genera *Lagenaria* or *Cucurbita*. Gourd motifs were used in the ornamentation of the interior of the temple (1 Kings 6:18 NASB; KJV, knops) and of the rim of the bronze sea (1 Kings 7:24). The gourd of Jon. 4:6-10 cannot be identified precisely. The KJV followed the earliest Greek translation with its rendering of gourd. The Vulgate or early Latin translation understood the plant as ivy. Many modern translations simply refer to a plant (NASB, RSV, TEV) or bush (NRSV). The NIV renders the term "vine"; REB, "climbing gourd." Many interpreters think a castor oil plant (*Ricinus communis*) is meant.

GOVERNMENT Defined in two general ways, either in terms of the officials or the institutions. In reference to officials, government refers to the sovereign authority over a body of people. In reference to institutions, government refers to the customs, mores, laws, and organizations of a people.

Many standard definitions of civilization include the presence of a strong centralized government as a constitutive element. The rise of the first empires at the beginning of the early Bronze Age is related in part to the rise of centralized governments. Centralized government was necessary for the building and maintaining of canals used for irrigation in Mesopotamia. It was also necessary for the development of a standing army. Extensive international trade required more centralized governmental power over the economic institutions.

In understanding the biblical view of government, one must remember that biblical theology presents early Israel as a theocracy, having God as king and ruler (Judg. 8:22-23; 1 Sam. 8:7-9; Pss. 93–99; Rom. 13:1-4). Ultimate authority resides in God and God alone. Human government is, therefore, always limited and always intended to be within the framework of God's will. The best ruler will be the one who best carries out God's design for just rule.

Early Hebrew Patterns of Government An understanding of biblical patterns of government must begin with the patriarchal period. During this time the Hebrews had no centralized government. The major unit was the extended family or, on a larger basis, the tribe. The government was family based. The first unit of authority or government was the household or the father's house.

This unit of society corresponds best to our designation of the extended family and would often involve two or more generations living together. The oldest male was usually the head of the family, the patriarch. As such, he was the chief official of family and government. The next level of social organization was the clan, often designated by the OT as the family (Hb. *mishpahah*). The clan was composed of several related extended families. One individual might be designated as chief or head of each clan. The next larger social level was the tribe (Hb. *shevet*), composed of several clans. A tribe might have a chief or even a prince as its leader. Finally, a group of tribes could be known as a people (Hb. ʿ*am*). The tribe was the most frequent social unit mentioned apart from the household or extended family. We should not necessarily consider the tribe to be overly large but more as rather small and isolated groups, especially before Saul and David. See *Family.*

It has been argued recently that the tribal and clan structures were based not on kinship but on grouping for common defense. Thus, two or three villages banding together might form a clan, and a tribe would be formed by two or three of the clan units. This would be true for the period after the conquest of Canaan. Thus, many scholars would argue that in the Song of Deborah (Judg. 5) the warriors are related to their tribal territories more than their tribes as a kinship group.

It is usually assumed that the patriarchal society was nomadic or semi-nomadic. Following the pattern of modern nomadic tribes with a patriarchal organization, the Hebrew society was probably democratic. Tribal decisions would be made on the basis of discussion by all the adult men. Not all men had equal authority. The elders held a major source of authority during this period and later periods as well.

The elders for a clan were probably the heads of the households that made up the clan. For a tribe the elders would have been all the household heads or selected elders from each clan. Thus, the elders were the leaders of the local community. They had the responsibility to decide many of the everyday matters, religious and judicial. The elders were representatives of the community as a whole in religious and military matters. They often accompanied the leader. The elders could conclude a covenant (2 Sam. 5:3) or treaty on behalf of the people. The elders regularly dispensed justice at the city gate (Deut. 21:19). The elders continued to function well into the period of the monarchy as a governing body. See *Elder.*

G

Beginning with the exodus, the OT presents Israel as a people composed of numerous tribes but with one leader. Joshua, who was succeeded in turn by the judges, succeeded Moses as leader. Although the depiction indicates a central leader, there is no indication of a centralized government. Granted, the leader had great authority, but the leader was not surrounded by the structure of a centralized government. A confederation of tribes was in existence during this period. In addition to the elder, Israel also had, following the period of Moses and Joshua, the office of judge. The judge was not primarily a judicial official but rather a charismatic military leader. Typically, the judge would rally the forces of Israel and defeat an oppressing power. From the time of Moses, the office of judge had included the element of deciding cases (Deut. 1:16; 16:18-20; 17:8-9). Much more frequently the emphasis was upon the military prowess of the judge (Judg. 3:7-30). The book of 1 Samuel brings a change in the emphasis of the judge. The judge became a priestly official, as in the case of Eli and Samuel. Thus the term "judge" seems to have a broader meaning than just a judicial term. Certainly the judge seems to have been the chief official of the confederacy of tribes in that period prior to the monarchy. It may be that the term was not specific as to the type of leader—priestly, military, or judicial—but simply indicated the leader. Although there were some cases where one judge attempted to have his sons succeed him (as did both Eli and Samuel), the office was not regularly hereditary (cp. the problems of Abimelech; Judg. 8:22–9:56). In this respect particularly, the office of judge differed from that of king that came later.

Although the period of judges may have led to the development of the monarchy, the two are quite different. The judge still retained a tribal character. Although several tribes might join together to fight a common enemy under the leadership of a judge, judgeship carried no sense of the permanence, hereditary character, or royal court of the monarchy. The judge was just an extension of the tribal chief or leader carried to a somewhat larger realm of a leader for several combined tribes. In actual function, the judge seldom played a strong role in maintaining the people's religious traditions until Samuel (Judg. 2:10; 17:6; 21:25).

Government during the Monarchy With the rise of the monarchy, a totally new organizational pattern emerged. Not only did the king stand as a single ruler for all the people, as a sort of chief raised to a national level, but the king was also surrounded by a new structure. The king had his royal court to carry out his mandate. Alongside the older tribal and town leaders, the king had a new cadre of officials. His officials included military officers and a professional army alongside the old militia from the tribes. The nation was divided into administrative districts with administrators who stood alongside the old system of elders. A royal court and professional army required revenue, so a taxation system was developed with its attendant officials. Evidence for this taxation system is found in the Samaria ostraca, which record the receipt of taxes paid from various estates to the government. Similarly, the *lamelek* jar handles (which bear an inscription literally meaning "for the king") indicate either taxation or produce of royal farms. Building projects required massive labor, and so the corvée or forced-labor contingents were organized. The old system of local government based on the city and the elder still existed, but a burgeoning bureaucracy developed parallel to the old system. The government also entered the international arena at this time, conducting warfare against international as well as local nations. It would negotiate treaties and alliances, trade and commercial agreements, and even arrange royal marriages. Surrounding the royal court were such officials as "the one who is over the house," a sort of secretary of state or prime minister; the recorder who was a herald, press secretary, and chief of protocol combined; the chief scribe; counselors; priests; and prophets (1 Kings 4). In addition, many attendants would minister to the king. The king embodied the rule of the entire nation. As he and his officials were just and faithful in ruling, the nation prospered. As he and the officials were unjust, the nation suffered. Likewise, the unjust actions of lesser officials ultimately were the responsibility of the king. Thus the prophets accused the king of his actions and of the actions of those under him.

Government under the Foreign Empires If the shift to a monarchy was the most revolutionary change in Israel's government, the collapse of the monarchy then marked the second most significant change. Self-government and independence were lost. In all likelihood this change was felt more on the national level than on the local level. The elders continued to function as local leaders, but the royal officials were replaced by new imperial and military officials of the conquering power—first Assyria, then successively, Babylon, Persia, and Hellenistic and Roman states. Now the tax revenues went to the treasury of that foreign state, and a new legal system had to be obeyed alongside the Hebrew law. This is seen especially in the trial of Jesus that involved hearings before the religious court (at that time the highest Jewish court) and before the Roman authorities. The chief ruler became a local governor appointed by the foreign power, as was Nehemiah, or even a foreigner, as were the Roman procurators. When local kings were allowed to rule, it was only at the pleasure of the foreign power and under the watchful eye of foreign military.

Beginning with the postexilic period, Jewish government fell more and more into priestly hands. The monarchy had ceased. The restructuring of society prevented too much power in political hands. The priesthood was strengthened and gradually assumed more and more of the judicial authority. Even the elders came to have an especially religious role as judicial officers. "Law" became virtually synonymous with the religious covenant, so that obeying the law meant keeping God's covenant. This affected every area of life. Such an arrangement was not necessarily new; it relates to the idea of God as king. The manner in which power was concentrated entirely in the sacred realm, as opposed to the secular, was new to the post-exilic and later periods. Since political power was not possible for the most part, power was consolidated where it could still be exercised, in the religious area. Religion was simply expanded to cover all of life.

In the NT we find Judea governed by a Herodian king appointed by the Roman government. Later direct Roman rule replaced the king. Religious authority still existed. The high priest and the priesthood exercised considerable authority, though it remained in name "religious" authority. The elders belonged to a formal body, the Sanhedrin, as also did certain priests. Just as in the case of the monarchy, two structures of authority existed side by side. Civil government now belonged basically to the foreign overlord, but religious power rested in the hands of the priests and Sanhedrin.   *Joel F. Drinkard, Jr.*

GOVERNOR Generally an appointed civil official charged with the oversight of a designated territory.

The KJV uses "governor" to translate a variety of Hebrew, Aramaic, and Greek terms. These terms represent a wide range of meanings that encompass almost every form of leadership or oversight. For example "governor" is used of city and tribal leaders (Judg. 5:9; 1 Kings 22:26), rulers (Ps. 22:28), temple officials (Jer. 20:1), managers of households (John 2:8; Gal. 4:2), and even pilots of ships (James 3:4). Recent versions of the Bible have translated the words more specifically with terms like "ruler," "leader," "prince," "commander," "officer," "representative," "prefect," "chief servant," "steward," and "pilot" (HCSB). This has allowed "governor" to be used to describe those officials serving as regional administrators over assigned territories or projects. Generally the governor exercised both law enforcement and judicial functions as a representative of his superior.

Old Testament The most widely used term for governor in the OT is the Akkadian loan-word *pechah*. This word occurs in Ezra and Nehemiah as a title for Tattenai (KJV, Tatnai), the Persian administrator of the province Trans-Euphrates or "Beyond the River" (Ezra 5:3). Tattenai's response to Darius's decree (Ezra 6:13) is indicative of the governor's allegiance to the king.

The title also is used of Sheshbazzar (Ezra 5:14) to describe his appointment as "governor of the Jews" (Ezra 6:7). Cyrus had commissioned him to rebuild the temple in Jerusalem at the end of the Babylonian exile. Nehemiah described his appointment by Artaxerxes I as "governor in the land of Judah" (Neh. 5:14). The prophet Haggai addressed his message to Zerubbabel, identifying him as "governor of Judah" (Hag. 1:1). *Pechah* is used of other leaders in the OT as well (2 Kings 18:24; 20:24; Isa. 36:9).

New Testament The Greek word *hegemon* and its derivatives predominate in the NT occurrences of "governor." The term often is used to describe Roman officials who exercised the tax and military authority of the emperor. Quirinius (Luke 2:2), Pontius Pilate (Luke 3:1; Matt. 27:2), Felix (Acts 23:24), and Porcius Festus (Acts 24:27) are specifically named. Joseph's rule in

Egypt also is classified as that of a governor (Acts 7:10).

Because governors are sent by the king "to punish those who do evil and to praise those who do good" (1 Pet. 2:13-14 HCSB), believers are to submit to their authority. Sent out by Christ, however, Christians will be brought before governors and kings for judgment. Faithfulness in such situations will bear witness for His sake (Matt. 10:18). *Michael Fink*

GOZAN (Gō´ zăn) Place-name of uncertain meaning, possibly, "quarry." A Syrian city-state to which the Assyrians exiled many of the people from Israel after they defeated Israel in 732 (1 Chron. 5:26) and 722 (2 Kings 17:6; 18:11). Assyria had previously conquered Gozan (2 Kings 19:12). Gozan is probably located at modern Tel Halaf in northwestern Mesopotamia on the southern bank of the River Khabur. Archaeology shows the city was built after 1000 B.C., though some Stone Age habitation is evidenced. The city included 150 acres with temples and government buildings. Excavators found documents with apparently Hebrew names, perhaps people deported by Assyria.

GRACE Undeserved acceptance and love received from another. Although the biblical words for "grace" are used in a variety of ways, the most characteristic use is to refer to an undeserved favor granted by a superior to an inferior. When used of divine grace toward mankind, it refers to the undeserved favor of God in providing salvation for those deserving condemnation. In the more specific Christian sense it speaks of the saving activity of God which is manifested in the gift of His Son to die in the place of sinners.
Old Testament In the OT "grace" is the translation of the Hebrew noun *chen* and the verb *chanan*. The verb *chanan* occurs some 56 times and is translated in the KJV as "be favorable or merciful." It refers to the kind turning of either God or humans to persons in an act of assistance in time of need (Prov. 14:3; Ps. 4:1). The noun *chen* occurs 69 times throughout a wide range of OT literature and is usually translated with one of two English words, "grace" or "favor," without any apparent difference in the two. It appears most often in the idiom, "find grace or favor in someone's eyes or sight" (cp. Gen. 19:19; 32:5; 33:8; 34:11; 47:25). The person from whom grace is sought is almost without exception in a

position of superiority or authority over the person seeking the favor. There is no obligation of the superior to show this grace. It is totally dependent on his generosity. The most frequent use of the term in the OT is to refer to human persons seeking or obtaining favor from another human: Joseph from Potiphar (Gen. 39:4), Joseph's brothers from Joseph (Gen. 47:25), Joseph from Pharaoh (Gen. 52:4), Ruth from Boaz (Ruth 2:10), David from Saul (1 Sam. 20:12,28), Joab from David (2 Sam 14:22).

If not the most frequent, the most significant use of "grace" in the OT is to express a divine/human relationship. Because the Hebrew word expresses an undeserved favor at the hands of a superior, God is never said to seek or obtain "favor in the eyes" of any of His creatures. There are, on the other hand, examples of humans seeking or receiving favor in the eyes of the Lord: Noah (Gen. 6:8), Moses (Gen. 33:12), Gideon (Judg. 6:17), Samuel (1 Sam. 2:26), the exilic remnant (Ezra 9:8; Jer. 31:2). In these examples "grace" denotes mostly God's undeserved gift in election. It is an expression of His sovereign love (Exod. 33:19). Furthermore "grace" forms the basis of all of God's relationship with man and His activity in behalf of man. Grace delivered Noah and his family from the flood (Gen. 6:8) and Lot from the destruction of Sodom and Gomorrah (Gen. 19:19). Grace gave Moses a personal knowledge of God and His ways (Exod. 33:12-13), assured him of God's presence with Israel and forgiveness of their sin (Exod. 33:17; 34:9), and caused him to see the glory of God (Exod. 34:18-23). It was grace that chose Israel for God's inheritance (Exod. 33:16) and preserved the remnant from captivity (Ezra 9:8). It was grace that chose David for kingship (1 Sam. 16:22) and, after a successful rebellion against him, restored him to his throne (2 Sam. 15:25). It is grace that will cause Israel one day to recognize the Messiah (Zech. 12:10). Grace brings mercy (Num. 11:15; Isa. 60:10), and the withholding of it brings judgment (Josh. 11:20).
New Testament The NT word for "grace" is the Greek *charis*. It is used approximately 150 times in the NT. The word had a long history in secular Greek before NT times. Originally it referred to something delightful or beautiful in a person, thing, or act which brought pleasure to others. From this came the idea of a favor or gift that brought pleasure to another. From the recip-

ient's standpoint it came to mean "thanks" or "thankfulness." Finally, it came to be used in an ethical sense of a favor done freely without any claim or expectation of something in return. When the OT was translated into Greek, *charis* was used to translate the Hebrew *chen* and thus in biblical Greek came to be associated with an objective relation of undeserved favor given by a superior to an inferior. This objective relation of undeserved favor given by God to man forms the background of the distinctively Christian meaning of grace in the NT.

Charis rarely appears in the Gospels. It is totally absent in Matthew and Mark. Luke uses the term eight times, four of which are uses by Jesus, but only in the ordinary sense of "thanks" (Luke 6:32-34; 17:9). Three of the remaining four occurrences are in the OT sense of "favor" (Luke 1:30; 2:40,52). In one reference Luke describes Jesus' words as "words of grace," which may have the secular meaning of "beautiful" or "attractive," but may also refer to the content of His message, which would make it synonymous with the gospel. In John's Gospel it appears four times, all in the prologue (1:14,16-17). It is used to describe Christ in His incarnation (v. 14), and as something that those who believe on Him receive as contrasted with the law (vv. 16-17). John's unusual expression, "grace for grace," has the idea of the continuance and inexhaustible supply of God's grace to believers. It is never interrupted and knows no bounds.

In Acts *charis* is used in three senses. The most frequent use is to refer to a power that flows from God or the exalted Christ. It gave the apostles success in their mission (4:33; 11:23; 13:43; 14:26), power to unbelievers to believe (18:27), and power to build up believers (20:32). It is used in the sense of human favor, and as such it is usually translated as "favor" or "pleasure" (2:47; 7:10, 46; 24:27; 25:3,9). The rarest, but most theologically significant, use is to refer to God's method of salvation in opposition to the legalism of the Judaizers. It is by "the grace of the Lord Jesus Christ" that both Jews and Gentiles are saved (15:11). The specific reference to the grace of the Lord Jesus Christ rather than to the more general "grace of God" indicates that Peter and the Jewish Christians viewed the saving grace of God as being manifested in the redemptive work of Christ.

Of the approximately 150 occurrences of *charis* in the NT, the great majority appear in the Pauline letters with a wide range of meanings. There are times when Paul employed it with its more secular meaning of a gift or act that brings pleasure to the recipient. His visit to Corinth was a *charis* (2 Cor. 1:15; KJV, "benefit"). The collection for the Jerusalem saints is called *charis* and was motivated by *charis* (1 Cor. 16:3; 2 Cor. 8:1,4,6-7,19). Often he used *charis* simply to mean thanks (1 Cor. 10:30; Col. 3:16), frequently employing the set expression "thanks (*charis*) be to God" (Rom. 6:17; 7:25; 1 Cor. 15:57; 2 Cor. 2:14; 8:16; 9:15; 1 Tim. 1:12; 2 Tim. 1:3).

Paul's most frequent and theologically significant use of *charis* is to refer to the grace of God. Twenty-five times he uses the expressions "grace of God" or "grace of our Lord Jesus Christ." There is no intended difference in the expressions. On one occasion he combines the terms with the expression "the grace of our God and the Lord Jesus Christ" (2 Thess. 1:12 HCSB). Commonly he refers to "His grace" which has either God or Christ as its antecedent. For Paul the grace of God is not so much a timeless attribute as an activity of God. It is the redeeming activity of God that manifests itself in the redemptive work of Christ by which sinners are forgiven and accepted by God. In Paul's thought the grace of God is necessary because of man's total inability to do anything to save himself and because of man's unworthiness to be saved. Paul's use of grace to refer to the undeserved nature of God's salvation was particularly illustrated by his own experience. His former life as a persecutor of Christians caused him to have a profound sense of his own unworthiness. It was only because of the grace of God that Christ appeared to him, changed him, and appointed him to be an apostle (1 Cor. 15:9-10; 1 Tim. 1:12-14).

So pervasive was Paul's sense of grace that he refers to it at the beginning and end of every one of his letters. For him the Christian life is summed up in the grace of God. Salvation from beginning to the end is all of grace. There can be no mixture of grace and works, or else it would not be grace (Rom. 11:6-7). Grace is synonymous with the gospel of Christ and to depart from it is to turn to a false gospel (Gal. 1:6). It was the grace of God that planned salvation for sinners in eternity past before the foundation of the world (Eph. 1:4; 2 Tim. 1:9). It was grace that provided salvation in the historical death of Christ (Rom. 3:24). It is grace that enables one to appropriate salvation, for it calls one to salvation, reveals Christ, and even gives the faith which is the condition of salvation (Gal. 1:6,15; Eph. 2:8-9; Phil. 1:29). It is the grace of God that calls and equips one for service in the Christian life (Rom. 15:15-16; 1 Cor. 3:10). Very much like Luke in Acts, Paul speaks of the grace of God as a power, almost as a person. The grace of God was something that was with him, produced labor, humility, godliness, and sustained him in times of difficulty (1 Cor. 15:10; 2 Cor. 1:12; 12:7-10). Everything, therefore, from first to last is of grace.

In the General Epistles and Revelation *charis* appears 24 times, most of these being found in Hebrews and 1 Peter. It has all the range of meanings found in Paul, the Gospels, and Acts. In Hebrews, grace is related to the atoning death of Christ (2:9). It is grace that allows us to come to God boldly for "help in time of need" (4:16). It is grace that strengthens the heart of the believer by which he is equipped with everything good to do the will of God (13:5). It is used in the secular sense of "thanksgiving" or "gratitude" in Heb. 12:28. In James, grace is used to refer to a power given to the humble to resist the devil and avoid spiritual adultery (4:6-7). In the Petrine letters grace has its source in God (1 Pet. 5:10) and has a manifold nature (1 Pet. 4:10). Peter equates grace with salvation and, like Paul, sees salvation as grace from first to last. It was prophesied by the prophets, accomplished by the sufferings of Christ, applied to people by a sovereign calling (1 Pet. 1:10-11; 5:10), and equips believers to serve (1 Pet. 4:10-11). All believers stand in a grace relationship with God, both men and women (1 Pet. 5:12; 3:7). The way to avoid being led astray by Satan into unfaithfulness is to "grow in the grace and knowledge of our Lord and Savior Jesus Christ" (2 Pet. 3:18). *Charis* is absent in 1 and 2 John and is found only in the closing verses of Revelation. However, the NT very appropriately closes with a benediction of grace (Rev. 22:21). See *Justification; Love; Mercy.* *Jimmy A. Millikin*

GRAFT To unite a scion (the detached, living portion of a plant that provides the leafy portion of a graft) with a stock (the part of the graft pro-

viding the roots). Olives were frequently caused to multiply by removing shoots from the base of a cultivated tree (cp. Ps. 128:3) and grafting them onto the trunks of wild olive trees. Paul's illustration (Rom. 11:17-24) portrays the incomprehensible grace of God who does what no farmer would do—break off cultivated limbs (representing descendants of Israel) to graft in wild limbs (representing Gentile believers). The illustration also serves as a warning to believing Gentiles not to be proud and despise the contribution of Israelites who made their faith possible but to stand firm in faith.

GRAIN General term for the edible seed of cultivated grasses. Common grains in the biblical world included wheat (Gen. 30:14), spelt or emmer (REB vetches) (Exod. 9:32), barley (Exod. 9:31), and millet (Ezek. 4:9). The KJV normally renders grain as corn, which does not mean "maize" (as in American usage), but any grain. See *Plants.*

GRANARY Storage facility for threshed and winnowed grain. Archeological evidence indicates that granaries varied in size and format. Granary

Various types of grains for planting on sale at an Arab market in old Jerusalem.

might refer simply to jars or bags of grain (Gen. 42:25), to plastered or unplastered pits, to silos (perhaps Luke 12:18), or even to large structures with numerous rooms (Hezekiah's storehouse, 2 Chron. 32:28, or those used by Joseph to store large amounts of grain, Gen. 41:49). Empty granaries was a sign of God's displeasure (Jer. 50:26; Joel 1:17). Gathering of grain into granaries was a picture of God's gathering of the righteous (Matt. 3:12; Luke 3:17). See *Garner.*

GRAPES See *Plants.*

A large grain silo at ancient Megiddo with a spiral access staircase leading down into it.

Storage facilities at Knossos, Crete. Oil, wine, and grain were stored here.

An Arab vineyard worker examining grapes on the vines in his vineyard.

GRASS Herbage suitable for consumption by grazing animals (Job 6:5). English translations use "grass" to translate at least five Hebrew words. **1.** *Deshe'* appears to be a comprehensive term for things that sprout and turn green (Gen. 1:11), being translated grass (KJV), vegetation (NASB, NRSV, NIV), all kinds of plants (TEV), or growing things (REB). With rain it forms green pastures (Ps. 23:2; cp. Isa. 66:14; 2 Kings 19:26). **2.** *Dethe'*, the Aramaic equivalent of *deshe'*, depicts the vegetation to be grazed in the field (Dan. 4:15,23). **3.** *Yereq* refers to pale yellow, green, or gold plants: the green herbs animals eat (Gen. 1:30; 9:3; Num. 22:4); the green sprouts of trees (Exod. 10:15); God's judgment destroys the green things (Isa. 15:6). *Yereq* can modify *deshe'* to emphasize the green color (2 Kings 19:26; Ps. 37:2; Isa. 37:2). The related term *yaraq* describes garden vegetables (Deut. 11:10; 1 Kings 21:2; Prov. 15:17). **4.** *Eseb* are the annuals the early rains bring forth (Gen. 1:11,29) as contrasted with the perennials; thus they are the herbs of the field (Gen. 1:30; 2:5; 9:3). Humans depend on God to make grass grow (Ps. 104:14; Mic. 5:7; Zech. 10:1). Grass illustrates the brevity of human life (Ps. 102:4,11) but also the rich, flourishing growth (Pss. 72:16; 92:7) and the king's enriching favor (Prov. 19:12). **5.** *Chatsir* is a general term for wild grass growing on roofs (2 Kings 19:26), mountains (Ps. 147:8), and even hanging on by watering places during drought (1 Kings 18:5). Humans in their mortality can be compared to grass in contrast to God's word (Isa. 40:6-8; cp. 51:12; Pss. 90:5; 103:15). The lily (Matt. 6:28) is later referred to as grass (v. 30).

GRASSHOPPER See *Insects*.

GRATE, GRATING Framework of crisscrossed bars. The grating of the tabernacle altar was made of bronze and held rings through which carrying poles could be inserted (Exod. 27:4-7; 35:16; 38:4-5,30; 39:39).

GRATITUDE See *Thanksgiving*.

GRAVE Pit or cave in which a dead body is buried. The variety of grave sites used by the Hebrews was determined by several factors: the circumstances of death, the surrounding terrain, and the time available for preparation and burial. The most usual grave was the shaft or trench.

While the use of pits for collective burial sites is not mentioned in the Bible, several have been excavated in Palestine. Caves were often chosen as a convenient alternative to the cost and time involved in cutting a rock tomb. Because they offered both an abundance of caves and ideal locations for constructing rock hewn shafts, Palestinian hillsides were a common choice for grave sites.

The tomb cut out of rock was sometimes fashioned to serve as a multiple grave with separate chambers. Ledges were often constructed to hold individual family members; and when the tomb was full, the bones from previous burials were set aside to make more room. The bones were placed in jars or stone boxes called "ossuaries," which resembled vessels used by the Romans to store ashes after cremation. Ossuaries sometimes held the bones of more than one person and were frequently marked with decorative or identifying designs. The entrances to tombs were secured either by hinged doorways or large flat stones that could be moved by rolling.

The most desirable grave site was the family tomb to which ample reference is made in the patriarchal narratives of Genesis. The Hebrews

A Roman grave at Pompeii. These were tombs with niches for jars containing cremated remains.

apparently envisioned a "shade" existence in death and preferred proximity to ancestors over solitude for the placement of their loved ones' remains.

While most graves were left unmarked, some were marked with trees (Gen. 35:8) or stone pillars. Second Samuel 18:18 anticipates the use of pillars, but this practice was never widespread in biblical times. The graves of the infamous dead were often marked with a pile of stones (Achan, Josh. 7:26; Absalom, 2 Sam. 18:17; the king of Ai and the five Canaanite kings, Josh. 8:29; 10:27). In NT times graves were whitewashed each spring so people could see them easily and avoid touching them to prevent ritual defilement during the Passover and Pentecost pilgrimages (Matt. 23:27; cp. Luke 11:44).

Coffins were generally not used in ancient Palestine. The body was placed on a simple bier and transported to the grave site. While Canaanites often placed containers of food and water in their tombs, the Israelites largely avoided this custom.

In Hebrew thought, graves were not simply places to deposit human remains. They were in a sense extensions of Sheol, the place of the dead. Since the realm of Sheol was threatening and since each grave was an individual expression of Sheol, the Israelites avoided burial sites when possible and treated them with circumspection. They performed purification rites when contact was unavoidable. See *Death; Eternal Life; Sheol.*

Joe Haag

GRAVEL Loose, rounded fragments of rock. One image of the suffering of conquered Zion was teeth broken by gravel (Lam. 3:16), perhaps the same as licking dust before the feet of the conqueror.

GRAVEN IMAGE See *Idol.*

GRAVING TOOL Sharp implement used to finish shaping the rough form of a statue cast from a mold (Exod. 32:4) or used for engraving tablets with writing (Jer. 17:1).

GRAY Usually a reference to hair color (Prov. 16:31; 20:29). See *Colors.*

GREAT Title claimed by the Samaritan magician Simon (Acts 8:9-10). The title represents a claim to divine honors though the precise meaning of the title is unclear. Justin Martyr held that the

The Mediterranean Sea along the coastline near Caesarea Maritima.

Samaritans revered Simon as the highest god of the Canaanite pantheon. Others have argued that Simon claimed to be a lesser god who represented the power of the high god, such as Baal Zebul or Athena.

GREAT LIZARD See *Reptiles; Snail.*

GREAT OWL See *Owl.*

GREAT SEA (KJV, Num. 34:6-7; Josh. 15:12). See *Mediterranean Sea.*

GRECIA (Grē´ shǐ a) (KJV, Dan. 8:21; 10:20; 11:2) See *Greece.*

GRECIAN Proper adjective referring to things or to people with origins in Greece. In the NT this refers to Jews who had adopted the Greek culture and language. They formed a significant part of the early church and created problems because of prejudice within the church (Acts 6:1; 9:29).

GREECE Located between the Italian Peninsula and Asia Minor, Greece itself is a peninsula with the Adriatic and Ionian Seas on the west and the Aegean Sea on the east. These seas, in turn, are a part of the larger Mediterranean Sea. Greece owes its rough terrain to the fact that it is the southern end of the central European mountain range. Another geographical feature is the numerous islands that lie in close proximity to the Greek mainland. The southernmost area, the Peloponnesus, is itself virtually an island, connected to the mainland by only a narrow neck of land known as the Isthmus of Corinth.

Its mountainous nature has played an important role in the development of the country. First of all, it has an unusually long shoreline for such a small area, resulting from the fact that there are numerous bays and inlets, giving it many natural harbors. Since its mountains were heavily forested in earlier times, shipbuilding and the sea trade developed. Secondly, the rough terrain discouraged a sense of unity among its people since communication between them was not easy. Finally, the land for agriculture, while fertile, was limited so that what was produced could not sustain a large population. Small grains, grapes, and olives were the main agricultural products while the mountains provided pastures for sheep and goats.

Historical Developments About the time of the great prophets in Israel (after 800 B.C.), city-states began to develop in Greece. The limited food supplies had forced Greeks to leave the homeland. As a result, colonies were established on the Mediterranean islands, Asia Minor, Sicily, Italy, and in the Black Sea area. Colonies provided the basis for trade, and trade, in turn, encouraged the growth of cities since the economy was not tied to agriculture.

Terracotta of woman with Grecian dress and hairstyle, dating from the second to first century B.C.

The high-water mark for the city-states was 500–404 B.C. The dominant city-states of the period were Athens and Sparta. About 500–475 B.C. Athens beat off a threat from the Persians. There followed what is known as the Golden Age of Athens. Under its great leader Pericles, art, architecture, and drama flourished. Peloponnesian city-states feared the power of Athens, however, and united under the leadership of Sparta to war against Athens. The defeat of Athens in 404 B.C. began a period of decline for the city-states.

About 350 B.C. Philip II came to the throne of Macedonia, a territory in what is now largely northern Greece. In the years that followed, Philip brought the entire Greek peninsula under his control, only to be assassinated in 336 B.C. He was succeeded by his 20-year-old son, Alexander, whose schoolmaster had been the great philosopher, Aristotle.

Alexander was one of the most outstanding military and organizational geniuses of human history. By the time of his death in 323 B.C., he had conquered an empire that spanned the Middle East from Greece to the western reaches of India, as well as Syria-Palestine and Egypt. Wherever he went, he left colonies that became dispensers of Greek language and culture, known as Hellenism. When the Romans took over much of this territory two centuries later, they imposed their legal and military system. They, in turn, were conquered by Greek culture. Thus we speak of the Greco-Roman culture. When Christianity arose, it had Greek, which many linguists call the most flexible language ever devised, as a vehicle to spread its concepts. Christian theologians in later centuries would wed Christian concepts with Greek philosophical methods and ideas to develop Christian theology.

Greece and the Bible Very few references to Greece appear in the OT with most of them being found in the book of Daniel (Dan. 8:21; 10:20; 11:2; Zech. 9:13). This is not true of the NT, however, especially in regard to Paul's ministry. Some of his most fruitful work was done in Greek cities. Philippi, in Macedonia, was the first church founded by Paul on European soil (Acts 16). It would become Paul's special favorite among his churches and would be the recipient of his most intimate and loving letter, which was to the Philippians. In the district of Thessaly, Paul founded two churches, Thessalonica and Berea

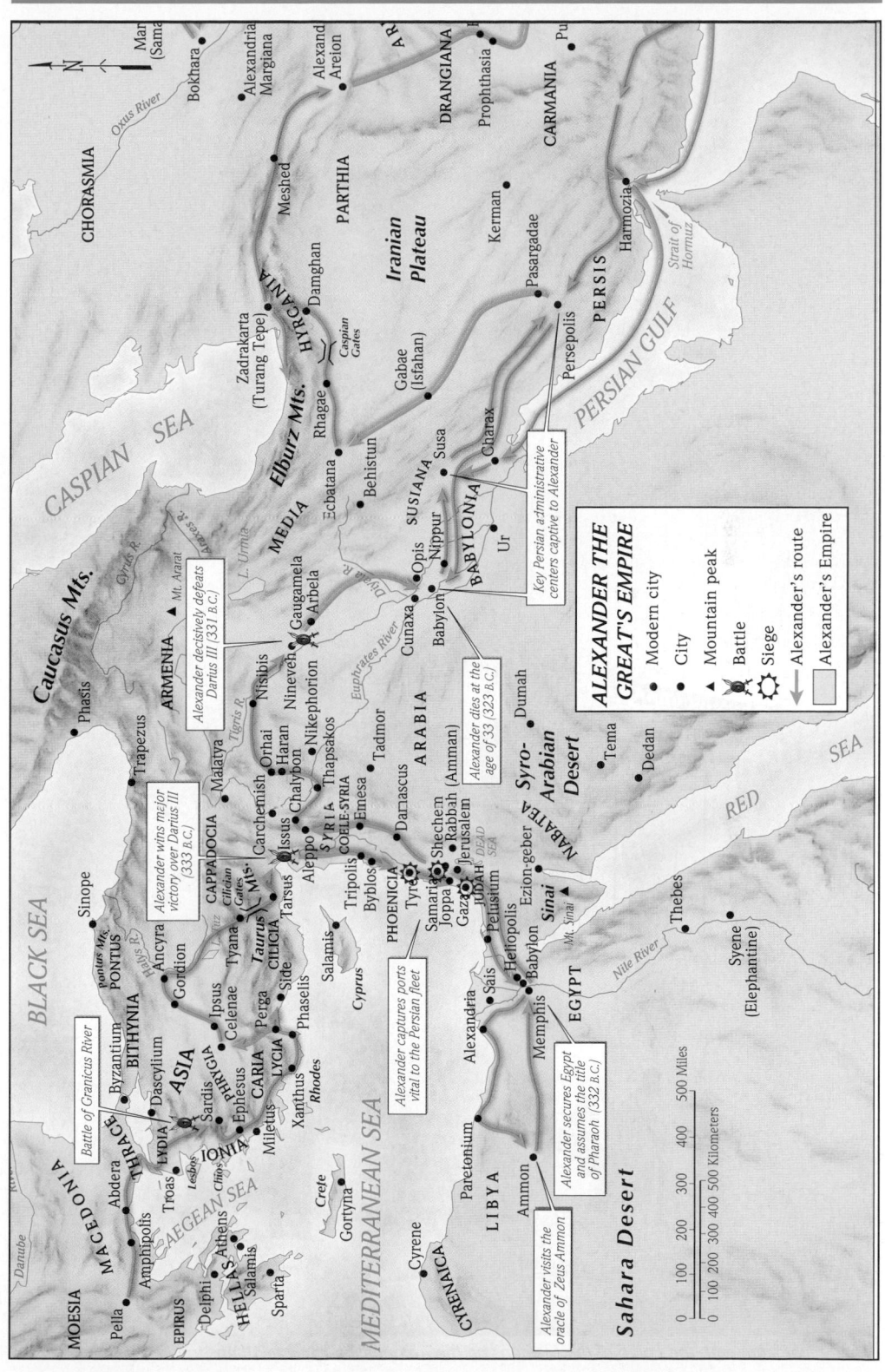

ALEXANDER THE
GREAT'S EMPIRE

- Modern city
- City
▲ Mountain peak
⚔ Battle
✺ Siege
→ Alexander's route
◻ Alexander's Empire

Alexander decisively defeats
Darius III (331 B.C.)

Key Persian administrative
centers captive to Alexander

Alexander wins major
victory over Darius III
(333 B.C.)

Alexander dies at the
age of 33 (323 B.C.)

Battle of Granicus River

Alexander captures ports
vital to the Persian fleet

Alexander secures Egypt
and assumes the title
of Pharaoh (332 B.C.)

Alexander visits the
oracle of Zeus Ammon

The Erechtheum with the Porch of the Maidens on the Acropolis of ancient Athens in Greece.

(Acts 17:1-14). The Thessalonians also would be the recipients of Pauline letters, two of which are in the NT (1 and 2 Thess.). Just as Paul had problems while at Thessalonica (Acts 17:1-9), so he had problems explaining to the church about the return of the Lord.

Bible students have long debated about Paul's success or lack of it at Athens (Acts 17:16-33). While the worship of the Greek gods had declined, Paul's experience in the marketplace at Athens shows that it was not entirely dead. It was, however, the sense of the failure of the older religions that led to the rapid acceptance of the Christian religion throughout the Roman Empire. Paul, however, did not win a large number of converts at Athens, but he did win some.

No city received more attention or provoked more correspondence from Paul than Corinth. Located on the narrow isthmus that connects the Peloponnesus to the rest of Greece, Corinth was a brawling, sinful seaport town, the crossroads of the Mediterranean (Acts 18:1-17). Here Paul met two people who would be among his most valuable helpers, Priscilla and Aquila. He would be brought to trial; he would establish one of his most troublesome and controversial churches, and later he would write at least four letters to

Relief of the myth of Telephus, son of Hercules, and his encounter with Achilles, who inflicted a wound that would not heal.

that church. Two survived to become a part of the NT.

The Greek influence on the NT and Christianity is immeasurable. Koine, the Greek of the streets, is the language of the NT. At least five NT books are written to churches in Greek cities (Phil., 1 and 2 Thess., 1 and 2 Cor.). All the other books in the NT are written in the Greek language. As the Christian gospel moved out into the Mediterranean world, it had to communicate its values to people who were steeped in Greek culture and religion. Both gained from the

The Acropolis at Athens, Greece.

G

relationship with people being transformed by the gospel and Christianity gaining a vehicle for its spread. *John H. Tullock*

GREED Excessive or reprehensible desire to acquire; covetousness. The greed of Eli's sons for the best part of the sacrifices disqualified them from the priesthood (1 Sam. 2:29). Hosea condemned priests who were greedy for the people's iniquity (4:8 NRSV), that is, greedy for the sin offerings.

Jesus warned against all types of greed (Luke 12:15; KJV, covetousness). The Pauline standard for Christian ministry gave no pretext for greed (1 Thess. 2:5; 1 Tim 3:3,8). Greed marked the Gentile or pagan way of life (Eph. 4:19).

GREEK LANGUAGE Greek was spoken broadly across the Roman Empire. Alexander the Great (336–323 B.C.) conquered the known world and stimulated the spread of Greek culture, including the Greek language. This Hellenization established many characteristics of the Western world. Early Greek independent city-states established individual dialects of Greek (Attic, Ionic, Doric). As a result of the conquests of Alexander, however, these dialects mixed together into a common tongue, a "Hellenistic Greek," that has come to be called "Koine." This was the common language understood almost anywhere. Historically this language stream flows into Byzantine Greek and then on into modern Greek.

Hellenistic Greek is a better term than Koine to describe the Greek of the first century. Hellenistic Greek represents a multilevel spectrum of Greek. The bottom level was Koine Greek. Koine was the Greek of the street, that is, colloquial daily speech.

A second level was less casual than Koine and more sophisticated. This was the Greek used to publish popular philosophy, such as the writings of Epictetus, and also standard business and legal materials.

A third level was even more formal. This level is an educated, literary Greek much less available to the general person, since only about 20 percent of the population was literate. Elite social classes used this level of Greek.

The fourth level, called Classical Greek, predated Alexander and was the Greek of ancient writers such as Homer. This style was not used in Jesus' day but was imitated. Some Greco-Roman writers of Jesus' day attempted to use Classical Greek. This imitating style is called Atticizing Greek. In normal speech few ever spoke that way.

All of the NT was written in Greek. This itself is an indication of how thoroughly hellenized was the world into which Jesus and his disciples preached. The Greek of the NT overall is like level two, the level of business and popular philosophy. New Testament Greek is generally better than simple Koine Greek but not as good as literary Greek. Some documents, of course, do show a literary flair, such as Hebrews, James, 1 Peter, and elements of Luke-Acts.

New Testament Greek is distinguished from Hellenistic Greek by several factors. One factor is its specialized religious subject matter, which involves a specialized vocabulary and ideas. Further, the distinctive nature of Jewish religion, which is the basic historical context for the Christian faith, is apparent against the broad sweep of other ancient religions. Fundamental monotheism, the Jewish way of life, and other religious elements set apart the Jews from the world around them.

Greek inscription on a sarcophagus at Thyatira containing the word "Thyatira" and verifying the site's identity.

Another factor distinguishing NT Greek in general is the broad use by NT writers of the Greek OT translation, the Septuagint. The Septuagint was necessary for Greek-speaking Jews to read the Scriptures. When many NT writers quoted Scripture, they used the Septuagint. The Septuagint established a Greek style of its own idiom in expressing Hebrew religious thought. This Septuagint language and style sometimes impacted how NT writers expressed themselves.

A third factor is the use of Aramaic, a variant of Hebrew, the mother tongue of Jews in Palestine in the first century. We have some evidence that Jews possibly were trilingual, speaking to lesser or greater degree some form of Greek, Hebrew (Aramaic), and Latin. The inscription recording the accusation against Jesus was in these three languages (John 19:20).

During foreign control, Syria and Palestine had been combined into one political unit, and the language adopted was Aramaic. Jesus probably taught in Aramaic. Mark especially gives hint of this by preserving sayings of Jesus in Aramaic and then translating for his Greek readers (Mark 5:41). The NT documents were written directly in Greek. But a few peculiarities of NT Greek might be explained as the influence of an underlying Hebrew or Aramaic stratum (whether oral or written). These effects on NT Greek are called "Semitisms."

Thus, while NT Greek in general is Hellenistic Greek of popular philosophy and commercial and legal writings, this Greek also has stylistic peculiarities traceable to the backgrounds of those writing. Unfortunately, the distinctions in Greek style among our NT documents is disguised or lost in translation.

Mark's Greek usually is described as the most Koine of our Gospels. Even so, Mark still has a vivid, direct style. An Aramaic stratum in Jesus' sayings comes more directly to the surface and more often in Mark.

Matthew's Greek is smoother and more cultivated than Mark. This Gospel is more like publication Greek of popular philosophy or commercial, legal documents. Semitisms, however, do show their effects in Matthew, as well as the influence of the Septuagint when Matthew quoted Scripture.

Of the Gospel writers, Luke uses the most cultured and educated Greek. Luke uses techniques of stylistic variety and more intelligent and sophisticated application of complex grammatical structures. Luke used sources (Luke 1:1-4) and was so careful with these sources that, in some cases, he even preserved or imitated the Greek style in them. For example, the prologue (1:1-4), which was Luke's own, is fine Greek of literary quality. On the other hand, the first two chapters about the early childhood of Jesus show a high level of Semitism, or even a Septuagintal style. This material probably represents some of the oldest data about Jesus directly from Palestine. One would expect such sources (whether oral or written) to be more Semitic. When Luke is on his own, such as the travel and narrative portions of Acts, he uses excellent Greek, tending to the literary level.

John's Greek is Koine and simple. The vocabulary is limited. The sentences are simple. John's style also is repetitive, so that translation is one of the easiest in the NT. At the same time, the thought-world of John is deeply theological and devotional. The Greek of the epistles of John is uniform and quite similar to the Gospel.

Paul's Greek is not characterized as educated, but he was a native Greek speaker, and his Greek is natural and forceful. Paul's emotional intensity is often obvious, and his letters were understood even by his opponents as a rhetorical tour de force (2 Cor. 10:10). He is capable of pun (Onesimus means "useful," and several words in Philemon are composed with this in mind) and poetry (1 Cor. 13 and many other lyric passages).

The General Epistles contain documents that preserve some of the best Greek in the NT. Hebrews probably ranks highest of all. While the author's subject required use of Septuagint material, the Greek style is literary and impressive, educated, and philosophical. The immense vocabulary is challenging and the sentence structure complex.

James and 1 Peter both have impressive Greek style, tending to the literary level. On occasion, though, a Semitic influence surfaces in James particularly.

Both Jude and 2 Peter show an Atticizing effect. The Greek is labored and somewhat forced, not as natural and flowingly beautiful as in Hebrews.

The Greek of Revelation is Koine. The sentence structure is simple, and the vocabulary descriptive, some terms recurring over and over. A Semitizing effect is notable, as well as

G

Septuagint influence. At the same time, the Greek of Revelation has various grammatical irregularities, unusual use and mixing of tenses, and other confusing elements. In some instances, rules of grammar are not followed. Various theories explaining the Greek of Revelation have not achieved any general consensus.

Gerald L. Stevens

GREEN Generally referring to grass, trees (wood), and plants. Revelation 6:8 in some translations (HCSB, NRSV) refers to a pale "green" horse for the horseman named Death. See *Colors.*

GREETING A salutation on meeting; an expression of good wishes at the opening (or in Hellenistic times, also the close) of a letter.

Among Semitic peoples the usual greeting was and is "peace": "Peace be to you, and peace be to your house, and peace be to all that you have" (1 Sam. 25:5-6 NASB; cp. Luke 10:5). The usual Greek greeting on meeting is *chairein,* translated "hail" or "greeting" (Luke 1:28; Matt. 28:9). A kiss was frequently part of such greeting (Gen. 29:13; Rom. 16:16; 1 Cor. 16:20; 2 Cor. 13:12; 1 Thess. 5:26; 1 Pet. 5:14). The command not to stop to exchange greetings (2 Kings 4:29; Luke 10:4) underlines the urgency of the commission given.

The opening greetings of ancient letters typically took the form: X (sender) to Y (addressee), greeting (Acts 15:23; 23:26; James 1:1). A letter addressed to a social superior took the form: To Y (addressee) from X (sender), greeting (Ezra 4:17). James is the only NT book to begin with the normal Greek greeting *chairein.*

Paul transformed the customary greeting *chairein* into an opportunity for sharing the faith, substituting "grace [*charis*] to you and peace from God our Father and the Lord Jesus Christ" (Rom. 1:7; 1 Cor. 1:3; 2 Cor. 1:2; Gal. 1:3; Eph. 1:2; Phil. 1:2; Titus 1:4). In Paul's opening greeting these terms always occur in this order, witnessing to the truth that peace cannot be experienced apart from the prior experience of God's grace.

The greetings of Hellenistic letters typically contained a prayer for the health of the recipients. Third John 2 provides the best NT example: "Dear friend, I pray that you may prosper in every way and be in good health, just as your soul prospers" (HCSB). Paul greatly expanded his opening prayers. Most of his letters begin with a prayer of thanksgiving, usually for the recipients. Ephesians begins with a benediction rather than a prayer of thanksgiving (1 Pet. 1:3-5; Rev. 1:4-6). In the Pauline corpus only Galatians lacks an opening prayer.

Hellenistic letters frequently included closing greetings. Most often these are "third person" greetings of the form X sends you greetings (by me) (1 Cor. 16:19-20; Col. 4:10-14) or send my greetings to Y (who is not directly addressed; Col. 4:15). Closing greetings often included a prayer or benediction. The simplest is "Grace be with you" (Col. 4:18; 1 Tim. 6:21; Titus 3:15; Heb. 13:25). Elsewhere the benediction is expanded (Rom. 16:25-27; 1 Cor. 16:23-24; Gal. 6:16; Eph. 6:23-24; Phil. 4:23). Some of the most familiar benedictions used in Christian worship come from such closing greetings: "The grace of the Lord Jesus Christ, and the love of God, and the fellowship of the Holy Spirit" (2 Cor. 13:13 HCSB); "Now may the God of peace, who brought up from the dead our Lord Jesus—the great Shepherd of the sheep—with the blood of the everlasting covenant, equip you with all that is good to do His will" (Heb. 13:20-21 HCSB); "Now to Him who is able to protect you from stumbling … to the only God our Savior" (Jude 24-25 HCSB).   *Chris Church*

GREYHOUND (KJV, Prov. 30:31). Modern translations read "strutting cock" or rooster.

GRIDDLE Flat surface on which food is cooked by dry heat (Lev. 2:5; 6:21; 7:9 modern translations; KJV, pan). In earlier days this would have been of stone. Later griddles were made of iron (Ezek. 4:3 where the same Hebrew word is often rendered "plate").

GRIEF AND MOURNING Practices and emotions associated with the experience of the death of a loved one or of another catastrophe or tragedy. When death is mentioned in the Bible, frequently it relates to the experience of the bereaved, who always respond immediately, outwardly, and without reserve. So we are told of the mourning of Abraham for Sarah (Gen. 23:2). Jacob mourned for Joseph, thinking he was dead: "Then Jacob tore his clothes, put sackcloth around his waist, and mourned for his son many days. All his sons and daughters tried to comfort him, but he refused to be comforted. 'No,' he said. 'I will go down to Sheol to my son, mourning.' And his father wept for him" (Gen. 37:34-35 HCSB). The Egyptians mourned for Jacob 70 days (Gen. 50:3). Leaders were mourned, often for 30 days: Aaron (Num. 20:29), Moses (Deut. 34:8), and Samuel (1 Sam. 25:1). David led the people as they mourned Abner (2 Sam. 3:31-32).

Mary and Martha wept over their brother Lazarus (John 11:31). After Jesus watched Mary and her friends weeping, we are told, "Jesus wept" (John 11:35). Weeping was then, as now, the primary indication of grief. Tears are repeatedly mentioned (Pss. 42:3; 56:8). The loud lamentation (wail) was also a feature of mourning, as the prophet who cried, "Alas! My brother!" (1 Kings 13:30; cp. Exod. 12:30; Jer. 22:18; Mark 5:38).

Sometimes they tore either their inner or outer garment (Gen. 37:29,34; Job 1:20; 2:12). They might refrain from washing and other normal activities (2 Sam. 14:2), and they often put on sackcloth: "David then instructed … 'Tear your clothes, put on sackcloth, and mourn over Abner.'" (2 Sam. 3:31 HCSB; Isa. 22:12; Matt. 11:21). Sackcloth was a dark material made from camel or goat hair (Rev. 6:12) and used for making grain bags (Gen. 42:25). It might be worn instead of or perhaps under other garments tied around the waist outside the tunic (Gen. 37:34; Jon. 3:6) or in some cases sat or lain upon (2 Sam. 21:10). The women wore black or somber material: "Pretend to be in mourning: dress in mourning clothes, and don't anoint yourself with oil. Act like a woman who has been mourning for the dead for many years" (2 Sam. 14:2 HCSB). Mourners also covered their heads, "[David's] head was covered, and he was walking barefoot. All the people with him, without exception, covered their heads and went up, weeping as they ascended" (2 Sam. 15:30 HCSB). Mourners would typically sit barefoot on the ground with their hands on their heads (Mic. 1:8; 2 Sam. 12:20; 13:19; Ezek. 24:17) and smear their heads or bodies with dust or ashes (Josh. 7:6; Jer. 6:26; Lam. 2:10; Ezek. 27:30; Esther 4:1). They might even cut their hair, beard, or skin (Jer. 16:6; 41:5; Mic. 1:16), though disfiguring the body in this way was forbidden since it was a pagan practice (Lev. 19:27-28; 21:5; Deut. 14:1). Fasting was sometimes involved, usually only during the day (2 Sam. 1:12; 3:35), typically for seven days (Gen. 50:10;

1 Sam. 31:13). Food, however, was brought by friends since it could not be prepared in a house rendered unclean by the presence of the dead (Jer. 16:7).

Not only did the actual relatives mourn, but they might hire professional mourners (Eccles. 12:5; Amos 5:16). Reference to "the mourning women" in Jer. 9:17 suggests that there were certain techniques that these women practiced. Jesus went to Jairus's house to heal his daughter and "saw the flute players and a crowd lamenting loudly" (Matt. 9:23 HCSB).

John W. Drakeford and E. Ray Clendenen

GRISLED KJV term for dappled (spotted) grey (Gen. 31:10,12).

GROVE In Gen. 21:33 a tree planted in Beersheba by Abraham. More than likely it was a tamarisk. The KJV also uses the word "grove" to translate the term *Asherah*. See *Asherah; Idol.*

GUARD Individual or body of troops assigned to protect a person or thing. "Guard" translates numerous Hebrew and Greek terms. *Tabbach* (literally "butcher" or "slaughterer") is a Hebrew term used only for officers of foreign kings (of Pharaoh, Gen. 37:36; 39:1; of Nebuchadnezzar, 2 Kings 25:8-20; Jer. 39:9-13). Two of the terms for guards are derived from the root *shamar* (to hedge about, guard, protect). The KJV often translated these terms by "watch" (Neh. 4:9; 7:3). The most common designation for the guards of the kings of Israel and Judah was "runners" (1 Sam. 22:17; 1 Kings 1:5; 14:27-28) from the use of such guards to escort the king's chariot. Modern translations frequently use the expression "court of the guard" where the KJV used "court of the prison" (Neh. 3:25; Jer. 32:2). Two terms for "guard" are used only one time. The first refers to the large guard gathered to defend the boy-king Joash (2 Chron. 23:10). The second refers to God as the guard of His people (Zech. 9:8).

Three Greek nouns are translated as "guard." *Huperetes* is used for those guarding the high priest's quarters (Matt. 26:58; Mark 14:54). *Koustodia* (Matt. 27:66; 28:11) is a Latin loanword, suggesting that this guard was indeed a Roman guard. *Phulake* is used for stations of guards in Acts 12:10.

GUARDIAN Adult responsible for the person and property of a minor (2 Kings 10:1,5). The Greek term *epitropos*, translated guardian at Gal. 4:2 (KJV, tutor), is a general word for a manager. Modern translations render the term as "steward," "foreman," or "manager" when it occurs elsewhere (Matt. 20:8; Luke 8:3). The basic thrust of Paul's message is clear: Before experiencing God's grace in Christ, the believers' lives were lives of slavery (Gal. 4:3,8). The guardian appears to be an image for the "elemental things of the world," that is, of celestial or demonic powers regarded as gods by pagan Gentiles. Paul earlier pictured the Jews as under the charge of the law (Gal. 3:22-25). See *Custodian; Schoolmaster.*

GUDGODAH (Gŭd gō´ da) Place-name of uncertain meaning. A stop on the Israelites' wilderness journey (Deut. 10:7). It is apparently the same place as Hor-hagidgad (Num. 33:32). The location is uncertain with some scholars looking at the area near the Wadi Chadachid.

GUEST One invited to a feast (1 Sam. 9:24; 2 Sam. 15:11). Jesus outraged those in Jericho by being a guest at the home of Zacchaeus, a well-known sinner (Luke 19:7). Peter crossed racial barriers by welcoming the Gentile messengers sent by Cornelius as guests in his home (Acts 10:23).

Figurative uses of guest include Zeph. 1:7 where consecrated guests are an image of invading armies the Lord invited to punish Judah. Jesus described His disciples as guests at a wedding feast who cannot mourn as long as He, the bridegroom, is with them (Matt. 9:15). God's salvation is pictured as a wedding hall full of guests who must have proper attire (Matt. 22:10-13).

GUEST ROOM or **CHAMBER** Single room where travelers could lodge. The guest room of Mark 14:14; Luke 22:11 was a room borrowed for the celebration of the Passover meal. The same Greek term is traditionally translated as "inn" at Luke 2:7.

GUILE Crafty or deceitful cunning; treachery; duplicity; deceit. Jacob dressed in his brother's clothes with the goatskins on his arms and neck is Scripture's best-known illustration of guile (Gen. 27:35; KJV, subtlety; modern translations, deceitfully). Jesus perhaps had this image of Jacob (Israel) in mind when pronouncing Nathanael "a true Israelite in whom is no deceit (guile)" (John 1:47 HCSB; cp. John 1:51 with Gen. 28:12). First Peter 2:22 describes Christ as one without guile in His mouth. Paul encouraged Christians to be "guileless as to what is evil" (Rom. 16:19 NRSV; cp. 1 Pet. 2:1), that is, innocent or naive when it comes to evil.

GUILT Responsibility of an individual or a group for an offense or wrongdoing. The most common Hebrew word for "guilt, be guilty" in the OT is *asham* and its derivatives (Gen. 26:10; Ezra 9:6,7,13,15; Ps. 69:5; used also of the guilt offering, also called the reparation, compensation, or trespass offering). Although the NT teaching on sin and its consequences is just as clear, explicit references to "guilt" are less frequent. The Greek words used for "guilt" in the NT are *enochos*, "liable, accountable" (Matt. 13:41; Mark 3:29; 1 Cor. 11:27; James 2:10), *opheilo*, "debt, obligation" (Matt. 6:12; 18:24,28,30; Luke 7:41; Rom. 4:4), and *aitia*, "grounds for punishment" (Luke 23:4,14,22; Acts 28:18).

The Bible teaches that the violation of God's moral law (that is, sin; 1 John 3:4), whether in act or attitude, results in an immediate state of culpability before God requiring either punishment or expiation. Sin results in guilt whether or not the sinner is a member of God's redemptive community (cp. Ezek. 25:12; Amos 1:3–2:16; Hab. 1:11).

Whereas this community is further accountable to obey God's written law, all men are accountable to God's moral law (Rom. 2:14-15). The basis for universal culpability is the covenant God made with the human race in Adam that obedience would bring blessing and disobedience would bring punishment (Gen. 2:16-17; 3:17-19,22-24; Hos. 6:7; Rom. 7:7-12; 10:5). Adam's choice of disobedience rendered the human race guilty before God and therefore under His wrath, deserving death (Rom. 5:12-21; Eph. 2:1-3). The principle that the sin of certain individuals can bring guilt on a group is also seen in such passages as Lev. 4:3, "If the anointed priest sins, bringing guilt on the people, he is to present to the LORD a young, unblemished bull as a sin offering for the sin he has committed" (HCSB; see also Gen. 26:10; Josh. 7:1; 1 Chron. 21:3).

Furthermore, everyone commits personal sins for which he is guilty (1 Kings 8:46; Pss.

51:5; 58:3; 143:2; Rom. 3:9-23; 1 John 1:8). Even one violation of God's law brings condemnation (Gal. 3:10; James 2:10-11), and the Bible teaches that no sin goes unnoticed or unrecorded by God (Eccles. 12:14; Matt. 12:36; Luke 12:2-3; Rom. 2:16).

God's righteousness demands that the guilt resulting from sin cannot just be overlooked (Prov. 11:21; Hab. 1:13). The "wages" for sin is death (Rom. 6:23), and God cannot leave the guilty unpunished and still be righteous (Exod. 34:7; Num. 14:18; Deut. 7:10; Nah. 1:3). The only way God can forgive sin in us is to impute that sin to Christ and punish it in Him: "He presented Him to demonstrate His righteousness at the present time, so that He would be righteous and declare righteous the one who has faith in Jesus" (Rom. 3:26; see also Isa. 53:6,12; John 1:29; 2 Cor. 5:21; Gal. 3:13; Heb. 9:26-28; 1 Pet. 2:24). The result is that one who is "in Christ" by faith has been freed of his guilt so that there is "no condemnation" (Rom. 8:1).

The presence or absence of the feeling or realization of one's guilt is not a reliable indication of true guilt because the heart is more deceitful than anything else (Jer. 17:9). Some who are "self righteous," that is, with no sense of guilt, may nevertheless be guilty (Matt. 5:20; 9:10-13), and those plagued by self-doubt may nevertheless be right with God (cp. 1 Cor. 8:7). On the other hand, the Bible gives several examples of the emotional anguish caused by sin (Pss. 32:1-5; 38; 51; Matt. 27:3-5; Luke 22:62). See *Atonement; Christ; Expiation, Propitiation; Forgiveness; Reconciliation; Sin.*

E. Ray Clendenen

GUILT OFFERING See *Sacrifice and Offering.*

GULF Term used by the KJV and REB for the gorge or pit (HCSB, chasm) separating the rich man's place of torment from Lazarus' place of comfort in the presence of Abraham (Luke 16:26).

GULL See *Birds.*

GUM Yellow to yellowish-brown product formed from the excretions of certain plants. Gum was an item of the Ishmaelites' caravan trade with Egypt (Gen. 37:25; KJV, spicery) and was regarded as one of the choice products of the land (Gen. 43:11). Some English translations focus on the nature of the substance (gum, NRSV; aromatic gum, NASB). Others focus on the use of the material (spices, KJV, NIV, TEV). Ladanum spice (Gen. 37:25 NASB margin) is the soft, dark resin of rock roses used in making perfume. Gum tragacanth (REB) is a resin used in the arts and in pharmacy.

GUN CONTROL Biblical analogy to gun control is recorded in 1 Sam. 13:19-22. The Philistines, who held a monopoly on the manufacture of iron implements, refused to allow the Israelites access to swords or spears. In spite of the Philistine attempt at armament control, the Israelites were able to defeat both the Philistines (1 Sam. 14) and Amalakites (1 Sam. 15) in battle.

More pointedly, David "prevailed over [Goliath] with a sling and with a stone … but there was no sword in David's hand" (1 Sam. 17:50 NASB; cp. vv. 31-40). The theological lesson of David's victory is that trust in God is more powerful than human attempts at armament, a lesson which Isaiah found necessary to repeat to Hezekiah in the face of the Assyrian invasion of 701 B.C. (Isa. 22:8b-11).   *Paul H. Wright*

GUNI (Gū´ nī) Personal name meaning "black-winged partridge." **1.** Son of Naphtali and grandson of Jacob (Gen. 46:24), thus head of the Gunite clan (Num. 26:48). **2.** Member of tribe of Gad (1 Chron. 5:15).

GUNITE (Gū´ nīt) Descendant of Guni and member of clan originated by Guni. See *Guni.*

GUR (Gûr) Place-name meaning "foreign sojourner" or "young animal." An unidentified mountain road near Ibleam where Jehu's men caught up with and mortally wounded Ahaziah, king of Judah (841 B.C.) (2 Kings 9:27).

GUR-BAAL (Gûr-bā´ ál) Place-name meaning "foreign sojourner of Baal" or "young animal of Baal." An Arabian or Bedouin city where God helped King Uzziah of Judah (792–740 B.C.) attack (2 Chron. 26:7). Greek manuscript evidence does not have Baal in the name. This would mean the city was Gur, also mentioned in the Amarna letters and situated east of Beer-sheba. Other scholars would identify the town with Jagur (Josh. 15:21).

The ruins of Ezion-Geber showing a water gutter or water shaft.

The open area (palaestra) of the gymnasium at Pompeii with gladiators' rooms to the left.

GUTTER KJV translation of two Hebrew terms. That is rendered in Gen. 30:38,41 (drinking) troughs (NIV, REB, NRSV TEV) or runnels, a small stream (RSV). The term used at 2 Sam. 5:8 is rendered water shaft (NIV, NRSV) or water tunnel (NASB, TEV).

GYMNASIUM Greek educational center. The word comes from a Greek word (*gumnos*) that means "naked." In ancient Greece the gymnasium was the center for physical and intellectual education for aristocratic adolescent boys. The gymnasium originated in Athens where the citizens sought the ideals espoused by Pericles that men should have wisdom without the loss of manly vigor. Physical education included wrestling, swimming, running, and use of the bow and sling, all in the nude. Intellectually, the boys were trained in reading, writing, mathematics, politics, philosophy, and music. As time passed, the gymnasiums became open to all citizens and were an integral part of all Greek cities.

During the second century B.C., when the Seleucids under Antiochus Epiphanes tried to convert the Jews to Greek culture, Jason, one of the Jewish high priests, built a gymnasium in Jerusalem (1 Macc. 1:14; 2 Macc. 4:7). Aristocratic Jewish young men began to frequent the gymnasium and to participate in Greek activities. The pious Jews were shocked at both their nudity, prohibited by Jews, and their practice of wearing the broad-brimmed Greek hats, associated with the worship of the Greek god Hermes. In addition some of the young men became ashamed of and tried to hide their circumcision. These practices were one of the causes for the Maccabean rebellion of 175 B.C.

There is no mention of the gymnasium in the NT, but there are references to the activities associated with it. In 1 Tim. 4:8, the expression "bodily exercise" is from the word for gymnasium. Paul also used metaphors from the gymnasium in 1 Cor. 9:24-27; Gal. 2:2; 5:7; Phil. 1:30; 2:16. No bad connotations are associated with the word in these passages.

W. T. Edwards, Jr.

A restored gymnasium at the ancient city of Sardis.

H

Herodium, one of Herod's most famous palace-fortresses located three miles southeast of Bethlehem. This is one of eleven fortresses Herod built or rebuilt. It stands on the site where Herod defeated Antigonus in 40 B.C.

HAAHASHTARI (Hā á hăsh´ tă rī) Personal and national name in Persian language meaning "kingdom." Member of tribe of Judah and clan of Caleb (1 Chron. 4:6), the form of the word indicating, as in many biblical genealogies, a political group as well as the ancestor. Nothing else is known of the person or nation.

HABAIAH (Há bā´ ya) Personal name meaning "Yahweh hides, keeps safe." Clan leader of exiled priests who returned from Babylon to Jerusalem with Zerubbabel about 537 B.C. (Ezra 2:61).

HABAKKUK (Há băk´ kŭk) Prophet of the late seventh century B.C., contemporary to Jeremiah. One explanation has his name based on a root meaning "to embrace." The Greek OT spelling "Hambakoum" suggests a root meaning "plant" or "vegetable."

The Times Judah had just experienced the exhilaration of the glorious days of Josiah, marked by freedom, prosperity, and a great religious revival. The Assyrians, once the scourge of the Middle East, were only a shadow of their former selves. In their place, however, stood the Babylonians. In the book of Habakkuk, they are called the Chaldeans, so named for the region from which their rulers came. The Babylonian armies were led by the energetic Nebuchadnezzar, who was soon to succeed his father Nabopolassar as king.

Nineveh, Assyria's capital, fell in 612 B.C. The powerful poetry of Nahum celebrates its fall. In 609 B.C. disaster struck. King Josiah, attempting to block the Egyptians as they moved north along the Palestinian coast to aid Assyria, was killed at Megiddo in northern Palestine. In his place the Egyptians set up Josiah's son, Jehoiakim. Unlike his father, Jehoiakim was a petty tyrant. Over the next 10 or 11 years, Jehoiakim tried to pit the Babylonians against the Egyptians until he finally exhausted the patience of Nebuchadnezzar. In 598 he laid siege to Jerusalem. That same year Jehoiakim died, leaving his son, Jehoiachin, to become Nebuchadnezzar's prisoner when Jerusalem fell in 597 B.C. People from the upper classes and skilled workmen were also among those taken to Babylon as captives.

The Man Other than his work as a prophet, nothing for certain of a personal nature is known about Habakkuk. Tradition makes him a priest of the tribe of Levi. The apocryphal work *Bel and the Dragon* (vv. 33-39) tells a story about Habakkuk being taken to Babylon by an angel to feed Daniel while he was in the lions' den.

HABAKKUK, BOOK OF One of the 12 Minor Prophets. After a brief statement identifying the prophet (1:1), the book falls into three distinct divisions: (1) Prophet's Questions and the Lord's Answers (1:2–2:5); (2) Five Woes against Tyrants (2:6-20); (3) Prayer of Habakkuk (3:1-19).

Of these three parts, only one, the woes (2:6-20) fits the traditional pattern of the prophets. The great prophets of the Lord saw themselves as spokesmen for the Lord to the people. In the first section (1:2–2:5), in what has been called "the beginning of speculation in Israel," Habakkuk spoke to the Lord for the people. He asked two questions, the responses to which give Habakkuk a unique niche in the prophetic canon. The first question, Why does violence rule where there should be justice? (1:2-5), expressed the prophet's sense of dismay, either about conditions within his own land caused by Jehoiakim or by the oppression of weak countries by stronger powers. In light of what follows, internal injustice seems to have been the object of his concern. In response, the Lord told the prophet that He was at work sending the Chaldeans as the instrument of His judgment (1:5-11).

The prophet shrank from such an idea and posed another question: Lord, how can you use someone more sinful than we are to punish us? (1:12-17). When the answer was not forthcoming immediately, he took his stand in the watchtower to wait for it. It was worth the wait: "Behold, as for the proud one, his soul is not right within him; but the righteous will live by his faith" (2:4 NASB). The term "faith" has more of the sense of faithfulness or conviction that results in action.

The woes (2:6-20), not unlike those of the other prophets, denounce various kinds of tyranny: plunder (2:6-8); becoming rich and famous by unjust means (2:9-11); building towns with blood (2:12-14); degrading one's neighbor (2:15-17); and idol worship (2:18-19). This section ends with a ringing affirmation of the sovereignty of the Lord.

The final section (3:1-19) is, in reality, a psalm, not unlike those found in the book of

Psalms. It is a magnificent hymn, extolling the Lord's triumph over His and His people's foes.

Habakkuk in History This book was a favorite of the people of the Dead Sea Scrolls. They interpreted the first two chapters as prophecy of their triumph over the Romans who were the overlords of Palestine at that time. Unfortunately, the Romans prevailed.

More important to us, however, is the influence this book had on the Apostle Paul. Habakkuk's declaration that "the righteous (just) will live by his faith" (2:4) was taken by Paul as a central element in his theology. As he did with many OT passages, he used it with a slightly different emphasis. Through Paul, this passage came alive for an Augustinian monk named Martin Luther, setting off the Protestant Reformation, one of history's greatest religious upheavals. Thus a so-called "Minor" prophet had a major influence on those who followed him.

Outline

                                    John H. Tullock

HABAZINIAH (Hăb á zĭ nī´ ah) or **HABAZZINIAH** Personal name meaning "Yahweh inflated or caused to make merry." Grandfather of Jaazaniah, the Rechabite leader Jeremiah tested with wine (Jer. 35:3). See *Jaazaniah*.

HABERGEON Short coat of mail covering the neck and shoulder worn as defensive armor. The KJV uses *harbergeon* to translate three Hebrew words. The first (2 Chron. 26:14; Neh. 4:16) is translated coats of mail or armor, body armor, or breastplate by modern translations. Modern translations agree that the second term (Job 41:26) refers to an offensive weapon, the javelin. There is much uncertainty regarding the meaning of the third term (Exod. 28:32; 39:23). NASB, NRSV follow the KJV in retaining "coat of mail." Other translations include: collar (NIV); garment (RSV); oversewn edge (REB following the earliest Greek translation). See *Arms and Armor*.

HABIRU (Hă bē´ rū) Appearing in texts from about 2300 through 1200 B.C. throughout the Near Eastern world, this word was used of a class of rootless mercenaries. Some scholars suggest that the Habiru were the Hebrews—ethnic Israel—citing the linguistic similarity of the terms. However, first, the Habiru were mentioned before the time of Abraham and therefore before the birth of the Hebrews as a nation. Second, the Habiru are referred to as nomadic mercenaries, whereas the Hebrews before their sojourn in Egypt were peaceful shepherds, and during the conquest they were not mercenaries

H

fighting on behalf of another nation but an army fighting on their own behalf. Finally, despite the apparent similarity, the terms Habiru and Hebrew do not in fact have a common etymology. The etymology of *Habiru/Hapiru/Apiru* is unknown, but Hebrew, from *Ibri*, goes back to Abraham's ancestor Eber; that is, Abraham and his descendants are Eberites (Gen. 10:21; 11:10-26).

Although the terms were technically separate, there may have been some confusion at times. The Amarna letters, written from Palestine shortly after the time of the conquest, probably mistakenly combine the Hebrews of Israel together with the Habiru, both of whom were causing turmoil in the region. The Habiru may have been directly or indirectly involved in the conquest, though much of the activity mentioned in the Amarna letters was outside the area of Joshua's campaigns. Of the cities within Canaan, the letters mostly refer to Shechem and Jerusalem. This agrees with the biblical account, which does not list those cities among the ones conquered in the first part of Joshua's campaigns.

After the conquest, some Habiru may have become proselytes of Israel while others moved on in order to engage in mercenary activity in other regions. One interpretation suggests that Saul employed Habiru mercenaries and referred to them as Hebrews, as opposed to his own ethnic "men of Israel" (1 Sam. 13:3). When hard pressed, the mercenaries deserted, leaving only the ethnic Israelites with Saul (13:6-7; 14:21).

It may be because of the poor reputation of the Habiru along with the occasional confusion of terms that the children of Abraham seldom referred to themselves as Hebrews, although foreigners sometimes used the term as if it were pejorative (Gen. 39:14,17; 1 Sam. 4:6,9).

David K. Stabnow

HABITATION Dwelling place; home; KJV translation of 10 different Hebrew words. Habitation is used for the dwellings of humans (Exod. 35:3; Isa. 27:10) and of birds (Ps. 104:12). Of special interest are references to the habitation of God. God's habitation is designated as heaven (Deut. 26:15; 2 Chron. 30:27), the temple (2 Chron. 29:6), or Jerusalem (Ps. 46:4). Jeremiah 50:7 pictures the Lord as the dwelling place of justice or "their true pasture" (NIV; cp. Pss. 71:3; 91:9). Ephesians 2:22 speaks of believers as "God's dwelling in the Spirit" (HCSB). Revelation 18:2

announces the fall of "Babylon," which "has become a dwelling for demons."

HABOR (Hā´ bôr) Akkadian river name. A major tributary of the Euphrates River. The Assyrians resettled many exiles from Israel there near Gozan when they captured the Northern Kingdom in 722 B.C. (2 Kings 17:6). See *Gozan*.

HACALIAH (Hăk á lī´ a) or **HACHALIAH** (KJV) Personal name meaning "wait confidently on Yahweh." Father of Nehemiah. See *Nehemiah*.

HACHILAH (Hā kī´ la) Hill where David and his men hid from Saul, south of Jeshimon in the Maon Desert. See *Jeshimon*.

HACHMON (Hăk´ mŏn) Clan name meaning "wisdom." Original ancestor of an Israelite clan called the Hachmonites. Most translations transliterate the Hebrew clan name as Hachmoni, including the Hebrew ending "i" that indicates membership in the clan or English "ite." TEV translates Hachmon (1 Chron. 11:11). Jashobeam, leader of David's army, was either a Hachmonite (1 Chron. 11:11) or a Tachmonite (2 Sam. 23:8), a copyist having either added or subtracted a "t" in transmitting the clan name. Jehiel, another of David's advisors, also belonged to the clan (1 Chron. 27:32). See *Jashobeam; Jehiel*.

HACHMONI (Hăk´ mō nī) or **HACHMONITE** (Hăk´ mō nīt) See *Hachmon*.

HACMONI (Hăk´ mō nī) NIV spelling of Hachmoni.

HACMONITE (Hăk´ mō nīt) NIV spelling of Hachmonite.

HADAD (Hā´ dăd) Personal name meaning "mighty." **1.** An Edomite king (Gen. 36:35). The name Hadad was borne by several members of the royal household of Edom. **2.** Hadad was also the name of the chief deity of the Ugaritic pantheon. This deity was identified as a storm-god. See *Canaan; Ugarit*.

HADAD-EZER (Hād ăd-ē´ zēr) Syrian royal name meaning "Hadad (god) helps." City-state king of Zobah in Syria whom David defeated to establish his control over Syria (2 Sam. 8:3-13).

Apparently, Hadar-ezer (2 Sam. 10:16) represents a copyist's change from Hadad-ezer in transmitting the text. Ammonites saw David was too strong for them and hired Syrian troops, including those of Hadad-ezer, to help them, but Joab, David's general, defeated them (2 Sam. 10:6-19). Hadad-ezer regrouped the Syrians but again met defeat. Some Bible students think the narrative in chapter 8 may be a summary looking forward to the fuller account in chapter 10 of the same event. Others think two separate battles are described.

First Kings 11:23 shows the troubled situation in Syria. Rezon revolted against Hadad-ezer (possibly the son of the one in 1 Sam. 8 or 1 Sam. 10 or even the same king). Rezon then established a kingdom for himself in the Syrian city of Damascus. Syria was thus a group of small city-states fighting among themselves for domination.

HADAD-RIMMON (Hā dăd-rĭm´ mŏn) Names of two Syrian gods combined into one word. Zechariah 12:11 describes the tragedy of the day of the Lord, including weeping and mourning in the Valley of Megiddo for Jerusalem. Such mourning could be compared only to the "mourning of Hadad-rimmon," apparently a reference to pagan worship ceremonies, perhaps for a dying and rising god. The exact interpretation of the passage is difficult, Hadad-rimmon being mentioned nowhere else.

HADAR (Hā´ där) Apparently a copyist's change of the name Hadad, a Syrian god, in Gen. 36:39 and in some manuscripts of Gen. 25:15. Translations differ on their readings, KJV reading Hadar in both cases. NIV, TEV read Hadad in both cases, while NASB, REB, NRSV retain Hadar in 36:39 but Hadad in 25:15. Parallel texts in 1 Chronicles read Hadad for both (1 Chron. 1:30,50-51). A reverent copyist may not have wanted to introduce the name of the pagan god into Genesis. See *Hadad.*

HADAR-EZER (Hā där-ē´ zĕr) Copying change in some manuscripts for Hadad-ezer. See *Hadad-ezer.*

HADASHAH (Hȧ dăsh´ a) Town name meaning "new." Town in tribal territory of Judah situated in vicinity of Lachish (Josh. 15:37).

HADASSAH (Hȧ dăs sa) Personal name meaning "myrtle." In Esther 2:7, another name for Esther. It was either her original Hebrew name or a title that was given to her. In the former case, it would mean "myrtle"; in the latter case, it would mean "bride." See *Esther.*

HADATTAH (Hȧ dăt´ ta) Place-name meaning "new." Part of name Hazor-hadattah (Josh. 15:25). The earliest Greek translations apparently read the Hebrew word for "their villages" that reappears in this section of Joshua instead of Hadattah. Some Bible students think Greek had the original reading. See *Hazor-Hadattah.*

HADES (Hā´ dēz) The Greek noun *hades* is used 61 times in the Greek OT (Septuagint) to translate the Hebrew term *she'ol,* which refers to the grave or the realm of the dead (Gen. 37:35; 1 Sam. 2:6; Prov. 15:24; cp. Ps 16:10 and Acts 2:27,31). Although the biblical writers were familiar with pagan concepts of a realm of departed spirits ruled by a deity (the meaning of *hades* in pagan Greek literature), and they occasionally alluded to such ideas, this concept is not taught in Scripture. The picture generally presented by Sheol is the tomb, where the bodies of the dead lie in silence.

Hades in the NT, on the other hand, can represent a place of torment for the wicked. Jesus uses the term in this way in His condemnation of Capernaum in Matt. 11:23 (parallel Luke 10:15) and in the parable of the rich man and Lazarus in Luke 16:23 where the rich man is said to be "in torment in Hades." When the term *hades* is used as the equivalent of the Hebrew *she'ol,* as it is in Acts 2:27,31 where Peter is quoting from Ps. 16:8-11, it refers simply to the grave. This is probably also the case in Rev. 20:13-14 whether the resurrection there includes only the wicked or also the righteous.

Old Testament teaching on the afterlife is less clear than in the NT (see Gen. 5:24; 1 Sam. 2:6; 2 Kings 2:11; Job 19:25-27; Pss. 16:8-11; 17:15; 49:15; 71:20; Eccles. 12:7; Dan. 12:2; Hos. 13:14). However, the NT is clear not only that there is a bodily resurrection (John 11:24-25; Rom. 6:5; 8:11; 1 Cor. 15:20-21) but that the believer who dies goes immediately to the Lord (Luke 23:43; 2 Cor. 5:1-8; Phil. 1:21-23). See *Gehenna; Hell; Sheol.*   E. Ray Clendenen

HADID (Hā´ dĭd) Place-name meaning "fast" or "sharpened." Home of people returning from exile with Zerubbabel (Ezra 2:33). Town is

H

modern el-Hadite about three miles east of Lydda (cp. Neh. 11:34).

HADLAI (Hăd´ lā ī) Personal name meaning "quit" or "fat sack." Leader in tribe of Ephraim and father of Amasa (2 Chron. 28:12). See *Amasa*.

HADORAM (Hà dō´ răm) Personal and tribal name ,perhaps meaning "Hadad (god) is exalted." **1.** Arabic tribe descended from Shem through Eber and thus distantly related to Hebrews according to the Table of Nations (Gen. 10:27). They lived in southern Arabia. **2.** Son of Tou, city-state ruler in Hamath of Syria. Hadoram brought tribute to David after David had defeated Hadad-ezer of Zobah (1 Chron. 18:10). See Hadad-ezer. **3.** "Taskmaster over the forced labor" (2 Chron. 10:18 NRSV) under Rehoboam, Solomon's son and successor as king of Judah. Rehoboam sent Hadoram to collect tribute from the Northern Kingdom immediately after they rebelled and refused to acknowledge Rehoboam as king. The children of Israel killed Hadoram. Thus they showed their contempt for Rehoboam's forced labor policies and made final the division between Israel and Judah, beginning the period of the divided monarchy.

HADRACH (Hā´ drăk) City-state name of uncertain meaning. Zechariah 9:1 claims this Syrian city-state will become a part of God's territory, though the precise meaning of the verse is difficult to interpret. Assyrian inscriptions frequently mention Hatarikka or *Hzrk* as an opponent that Tiglath-pileser III finally conquered and made part of his empire in 738 B.C. It was apparently the large mound Tell Afis, 28 miles southwest of Aleppo, and served as capital of Luhuti, which was an ally of Hamath from 854 to 773.

HAELEPH (Hă ē´ lĕph) Place-name meaning "the ox." KJV reads the initial "h" as the Hebrew definite article and thus has "Eleph." Some interpreters combine the preceding town name in Josh. 18:28 to read "Zelah Haeleph" as one town, following early Greek manuscript evidence. Town in tribal territory of Benjamin (Josh. 18:28). The location is not known. See *Zelah*.

HAFT KJV term for the hilt or handle of a dagger (Judg. 3:22).

HAGAB (Hā´ găb) Personal name meaning "grasshopper" or "chamberlain." Clan of temple servants who returned to Jerusalem from Babylonian exile with Zerubbabel (Ezra 2:46). The name also occurs on an ostracon from Lachish.

HAGABA (Hăg´ á bà) Clan of temple servants who returned home from Babylonian exile with Zerubbabel about 537 B.C. (Ezra 2:45).

HAGAR (Hā´ gär) Personal name meaning "stranger." The personal servant of Sarah, who was given as a concubine to Abraham and became the mother of Ishmael (Gen. 16:1-16; 21:8-21; 25:12; Gal. 4:24-25). Genesis 16:1-7 details the events of the initial conflict of Sarah with Hagar and the flight of Hagar. Verses 8-16 detail the visit of the messenger of Yahweh bringing the promise of a son to the mother in distress, encouraging Hagar to return to Sarah. These conflicts were related to the wife's and concubine's positions in the family and community (cp. similar conflicts in Gen. 29–30). Genesis 21:8-21 gives the story of the expulsion of Hagar and Ishmael and their miraculous deliverance. Pauline interpretation (Galatians) relates the superiority of a son born according to the Spirit over the son born according to the "flesh." In Gal. 4 Paul used the Hagar story to stand for slavery under the old covenant in contrast to freedom of the new covenant symbolized by Isaac.

David M. Fleming

HAGARENE (Hăg´ á rēn) (KJV, Ps. 83:6) See *Hagarite*.

HAGARITE (Hăg´ är īt) Name of nomadic tribe whom the tribe of Reuben defeated east of the Jordan River (1 Chron. 5:10,19-20). Reuben won because they called on and trusted in God. The tribal name is apparently taken from Hagar, Sarah's maid and mother of Ishmael (Gen. 16). David's chief shepherd was a Hagarite (1 Chron. 27:31). The psalmist asked God not to be silent when the Hagarites joined a coalition against God's people (Ps. 83:6). First Chronicles 11:38 names a Hagarite among David's military heroes, but some interpreters think that 2 Sam. 23:36 is evidence of an original Gadite, which would be written quite similar to Hagarite in Hebrew.

HAGERI (Hā´ gĕr ī) REB transliteration of Hebrew for Hagarite in 1 Chron. 11:38. See *Hagarite*.

HAGGADAH or **HALAKAH** In Judaism, rabbinic teaching is divided into two categories: halakah and haggadah (also spelled aggadah). Both of these terms refer to the oral teaching of the rabbis. Halakah refers to the legal teachings that are considered authoritative for religious life. Haggadah refers to the remaining nonlegal teachings.

Halakah, according to the early rabbis, goes back to oral law given to Moses at Sinai along with the written law (Torah) incorporated in the Bible primarily found in the Pentateuch. Therefore, the halakah is considered as binding as the written Torah. Modern scholars recognize that the halakah is the means by which the written Torah is interpreted to each new generation. Halakah extends the Torah of Moses into every aspect of Jewish life including personal, social, national, and international relations. It is essential for the preservation of Jewish life in new historical circumstances because it allows for a range of interpretive flexibility and development in the norms that govern the Jewish community.

Haggadah consists of a variety of amplifications of biblical texts primarily in the form of illustrative stories, parables or allegories, or, frequently, poetry. Many portions of the haggadah may go back to early Jewish synagogue preaching.

Much of early rabbinic halakah was eventually written down in the Mishnah (about A.D. 220) and Talmud (about A.D. 360) although it continues to be referred to as oral law even after these codifications. Likewise, haggadah was written down in various biblical commentaries as well as the Talmud.

These two types of rabbinic teaching are especially important as an aid in understanding Judaism at the time of Jesus and during the formation of the early church since some of these materials have their origin during the first century. Jesus probably referred to Pharisaic halakah (in part a precursor to rabbinic halakah) in Mark 7:1-23 and its parallel (Matt. 15:1-20). See *Mishnah; Pharisees; Talmud; Torah.*

Stephenson Humphries-Brooks

HAGGAI (Hăg´ gī) Personal name of one of the "postexilic" (sixth-century) prophets and of the book preserving his preaching. The name probably means that he was born on one of the Jewish feast days. He and the Prophet Zechariah roused the people of Judah to finish the Temple under Zerubbabel's leadership.

HAGGAI, BOOK OF One of the so-called Minor Prophets (also collectively known as "the Twelve"). It consists of four addresses the prophet delivered to the postexilic community of Judah and its leaders, Zerubbabel the governor and Joshua the high priest. The addresses are precisely dated according to the year of the Persian ruler and the month and day of the Jewish calendar.

Chronology of Haggai and Zechariah

August 29, 520 B.C.	Haggai's first message (Hag. 1:1-11)
September 21, 520	Temple building resumed (Hag. 1:12-15)
October 17, 520	Haggai's second message (Hag. 2:1-9)
October–November 520	Zechariah's ministry begun (Zech. 1:1-6)
December 18, 520	Haggai's third and fourth messages (Hag. 2:10-23)
February 15, 519	Zechariah's night visions (Zech. 1:7–6:8)
March 12, 515	Temple completed (Ezra 6:15-18)

Historical Background The Persian ruler Cyrus had freed the Jews to return from Babylonian exile shortly after he conquered Babylon in October 539 B.C. He had also promised to help them rebuild their temple in Jerusalem that the Babylonians had destroyed in 586 B.C. The first group of about 50,000 exiles to return were led by Sheshbazzar, who was appointed governor of the new province of Judah. Sanballot, governor of Samaria, was not pleased at Judah's new status and took every opportunity to oppose them. The returning Jews also clashed with Jews who had been left in Palestine who thought they were God's remnant and resented the newcomers taking over. Opposition continued and increased through the reigns of Cyrus (539–530 B.C.), Cambyses (530–522 B.C.), and Darius (522–486 B.C.; Ezra 4:4-5).

The temple foundation was laid fairly quickly under Zerubbabel's leadership, who eventually replaced Sheshbazzar as governor. This initial success was met not only with celebration but also with sadness when this temple was compared with Solomon's (Ezra 1–3; Hag. 2:3; Zech. 4:10). This is the first hint that perhaps this restoration would not satisfy entirely the prophetic announcements of Israel's glorious restoration. This discouragement together with the continuing opposition and concerns over personal affairs caused work on the temple to cease until the preaching of Haggai and Zechariah roused the people once more to work in faith (Ezra 4:24–5:2).

Message and Purpose The leaders and people of Judah had allowed external opposition, discouragement, and self-interest to keep them from completing the task of rebuilding the Lord's temple (1:2-4; 2:3). So they and their offerings to the Lord were defiled and displeasing to Him (2:14). The Lord's command through Haggai was to "build the house" for the pleasure and glory of God (1:8). Toward that end the Lord exhorted them not to fear but to "be strong ... and work" (2:4-5). Finally, by a parable Haggai instructed them of the need to dedicate themselves and their work to the Lord (2:11-16). The Lord called upon them to recognize His chastisement in the deprivation they had been experiencing (1:5-6,9-11; 2:16-17). He also informed the people that the completion of the temple would bring Him pleasure and glory (1:8). He further assured them of their success because of His presence (1:13-14; 2:4-5). He promised them that He would reward their renewed work and dedication to Him by glorifying the temple and granting them peace (2:6-9) and blessing (2:18-19). Finally, He promised to restore the Davidic throne on the earth through a descendant of Zerubbabel (2:20-23).

Structure Haggai's four sermons (1:1-15; 2:1-9; 2:10-19; 2:20-23) are marked by introductory date formulae. But repetition between messages one and three and between two and four shows that the book has a twofold structure. Both messages one and three refer to "this people" (1:2; 2:14) and include two commands to "think/consider carefully" (1:5,7; 2:15,18). Messages two and four both have the divine promise, "I am going to shake the heavens and the earth" (2:6,21) and have a threefold repetition of "the LORD solemnly declares" (2:4,23). Furthermore, the first and third messages are introduced by complete date formulae, giving year, month, and day, with the order in the third message reversed. The date formulae introducing the second and fourth messages have only the month and day, again with the fourth in reverse order.

Finally, at the end of the first and third messages, the date is repeated (1:15; 2:18).

The first two messages both deal with building the temple. The last two messages do not mention the temple explicitly but move beyond it to issues of defilement and restoration.

Contents *Message One: Instruction to Build the Temple (1:1-15)* The Lord's oracle is given in vv. 3-11 and the response to it in vv. 12-15.

In the context of the Mosaic covenant and Israel's restoration according to divine prophecy, they should have been able to discern God's displeasure with them by the trying circumstances they were experiencing.

The first message ends as it began with a date showing that 23 days after Haggai's message the rebuilding was underway again (the order in the Hebrew text of 1:15—day, month, year—is the mirror image of 1:1, showing the two dates to be part of the same section and stressing the comparison between the days). If God's earlier prophets had received such positive response the temple would never have been destroyed!

Message Two: Promises of God's Presence, Glory, and Peace (2:1-9) The time of the second message was during the Feast of Tabernacles (cf. Lev. 23:33-43), three weeks after the work began. The following day would be the concluding Sabbath on which Solomon had dedicated his newly built temple in 959 B.C. (2 Chron. 7:8-10).

Having motivated them to work by pointing to past events and present realities, the Lord also encouraged the remnant in vv. 6-9 with promises of the future. These verses describe the day of the Lord when the wicked will be removed and the nations shall be made subject to Him and will bring tribute to His temple (cp. Isa. 60:4-14). Thus its glory will exceed that of Solomon's temple, especially because the Lord Himself will be there. It is hard not to see a preliminary fulfillment of these verses in the appearance of Jesus at Herod's temple (cp. Matt. 2:11; 21:12-15; 27:51).

Message Three: Cleansing and Blessing (2:10-19) The Lord announces His determination to change Judah's deprivation to blessing because they have dedicated themselves to Him. The date is three months after the temple work began, just after the fall planting, which explains why there is no seed left in the barn (v. 19). After the introduction is a dialogue with the priests that functions like a parable (vv. 11b-13). The essence of the parable is that unlike holiness, defilement can be transmitted by touch. Then the parable is applied in vv. 14-19. Israel had been set apart for the Lord. Yet they had become defiled by sin and unbelief so that all they did was unacceptable to God, including offerings and temple building. Only God's grace in response to their humble dedication could cleanse them again, which He had done. Thus they are assured that God would turn their curse of deprivation into blessing, and they would have a plentiful harvest.

Message Four: Gentile Overthrow and Davidic Restoration (2:20–23) The Lord promises that He will destroy the kingdoms of this world and will establish a new kingdom ruled by a Davidic descendant, the Messiah (cp. Ezek. 39:19-23; Dan 2:44). The Messianic servant is named David in Ezek. 34:23-24 and 37:24 because He is the Davidic seed, the fulfillment of the Davidic covenant. Here He is named Zerubbabel as a divine promise that the Messiah will also be a descendant of Zerubbabel (cp. Matt. 1:12-13). The "signet ring" is appropriate as a Messianic metaphor because it was jealously guarded as a symbol of one's authority, used to sign official documents (cp. Esther 8:8). As God had cast off King Jehoiachin, so He had placed his grandson Zerubbabel on His finger (Jer. 22:24).

Theological Significance Several reasons can be given for the significance of the temple rebuilding. First, it was a sign of the people's priorities. Second, it showed that God was with the remnant and that His promises of restoration had begun to be fulfilled. Third, it declared God's glory and thus brought Him pleasure. Fourth, it served to vindicate the Lord since the temple's destruction had disgraced the Lord's name (Ezek. 11:23; 37:26-28.). Fifth, it served as a pledge of the new covenant and the Messianic age (Ezek. 37:26; Isa. 2:2-4; 44:28; 52:1-7; Mic. 4:1-4; Mal. 3:1). The restoration of the temple was a sign that God had not revoked His covenant with Levi or His covenant with David (cp. Jer. 33:17-22; Num. 25:11-13; Mal. 2:4). He will provide cleansing and restoration through a glorious temple and a messianic ruler.

Outline

I. Rebuilding the Temple (1:1–2:9).
   A. Message One: Instruction to Build the Temple (1:1-15).
   B. Message Two: Promises of God's Presence, Glory, and Peace (2:1-9).
II. Cleansing the People and Restoring the Kingdom (2:10-23).
   A. Message Three: Cleansing and Blessing (2:10-19).
   B. Message Four: Gentile Overthrow and Davidic Restoration (2:20-23).

E. Ray Clendenen

HAGGEDOLIM (Hăg gĕ dō´ lĭm) Personal name meaning "the great ones." Zabdiel, a leading priest, was the son of Haggedolim (Neh. 11:14; KJV, "the great men"; TEV, "a leading family"). Bible students have suggested that *haggedolim* is probably not a Hebrew proper name and have interpreted it as a copyist's change of an unfamiliar name for a more familiar word or title, an honorary title for a leading family, or a title for the high priest.

HAGGERI (Hăg gē´ rī) KJV transliteration of Hebrew for Hagarite in 1 Chron. 11:38. See *Hagarite.*

HAGGI (Hăg´ gī) Personal name meaning "my festival," indicating birth on a holy day. Son of Gad and grandson of Jacob and thus original ancestor of clan of Haggites (Gen. 46:16; Num. 26:15).

HAGGIAH (Hăg gĭ´ a) Personal name meaning "Yahweh is my festival." A Levite in the line of Merari (1 Chron. 6:30).

HAGGITE (Hăg´ gīt) Member of clan of Haggi. See *Haggi.*

HAGGITH (Hăg´ gĭth) Personal name meaning "festival." Wife of David and mother of Adonijah, who was born at Hebron (2 Sam. 3:4).

HAGIOGRAPHA Greek term meaning "holy writings," used as a designation for the third and final major division of the Hebrew Bible. In contrast to the first two divisions (the Law and the Prophets), "the Writings" (Hb. *Kethuvim*) are a miscellaneous collection. The Hagiographa in their Hebrew order include: Psalms, Proverbs, and Job; the "five scrolls" (*Megilloth*) read at major festivals, namely, Song of Songs, Ruth, Lamentations, Ecclesiastes, and Esther; Daniel; and Ezra-Nehemiah and Chronicles. These books were the last portion of the Hebrew Bible

H

to be recognized as canonical. Luke 24:44 uses "psalms" as a designation for these writings.

HAGRI (Hăg´ rī) Tribal or personal name probably referring to the Hagarites (1 Chron. 11:38) or a miscopying of "the Gaddite" from 2 Sam. 23:36. See *Hagarite*.

HAGRITE (Hăg´ rīt) Alternate spelling for Hagarite in modern translations. See *Hagarite*.

HAHIROTH (Hå hī´ rŏth) Reading of some manuscripts and translations for Pi-hahiroth in Num. 33:8. See *Pi-hahiroth*.

HAI (Hā´ ī) (KJV, Gen. 12:8; 13:3) See *Ai*.

HAIL (salutation) See *Greeting*.

HAIL (meteorological) Precipitation in the form of small balls consisting of layers of ice and compact snow, regarded as a plague by biblical writers. Hailstones generally have a diameter of half an inch to one inch. Large hailstones can destroy crops (Exod. 9:25,31; Ps. 78:47; Hag. 2:17; Rev. 8:7) and kill livestock and persons caught in the open (Exod. 9:19,25; Josh. 10:11; Ps. 78:48). The Bible speaks of hail to speak of divine presence, action, and punishment.

HAIR Covering of the human head and of animals. Ordinarily human hair is meant in biblical references (Num. 6:5), though animal hair

Jewish men of the orthodox tradition are prohibited from cutting off the hair above their ears.

Silver decorative bucket with scene of a servant combing the hair of her mistress.

(wool) may be in mind (Matt. 3:4). Beautiful hair has always been desirable for both women and men (Song 5:11). In OT times both men and women wore their hair long. Both Samson and Absalom were greatly admired for their long locks (Judg. 16:13; 2 Sam. 14:25-26). In the NT era, men wore their hair much shorter than women did (1 Cor. 11:14-15).

Gray hair and white hair were respected signs of age (Prov. 20:29). But baldness could be considered embarrassing or even humiliating (2 Kings 2:23; Ezek. 7:18). In Lev. 13, which gives extensive instruction on the diagnosis of leprosy (probably including other skin diseases), the color of the hairs in an infected area of skin indicated whether the disease was present or had been cured. A cured leper was required to shave his entire body (Lev. 14:8-9).

Hair among the Israelites required good care. Women usually wore their hair loose, but sometimes they braided it (2 Kings 9:30). New Testament writers cautioned against ostentation in women's hairstyles (1 Tim. 2:9; 1 Pet. 3:3). Hair that was anointed with oil symbolized blessing and joy (Ps. 23:5; Heb. 1:9). Some hosts provided oil to anoint honored guests (Luke 7:46). Mourning was indicated by disheveled, unkempt hair (Josh. 7:6; 2 Sam. 14:2). Jesus told His followers not to follow the custom of the Pharisees, who refused to care for their hair while they were fasting (Matt. 6:17).

Israelite men trimmed their hair, but the law prohibited them from cutting off the hair above their ears (Lev. 19:27). This restriction probably was a response to some pagan custom (Deut. 14:1-2), but orthodox Jews still wear long side curls. Those who took a Nazirite vow were forbidden from cutting their hair during the course of their vow, but afterward, their entire head was to be shaved (Num. 6:1-21; Acts 18:18; 21:24).

Because hairs are so many, they may symbolize the concept of being innumerable (Ps. 40:12). Because they seem so unimportant, they can stand for insignificant things (Luke 21:18).

Kendell Easley

HAKELDAMA (Hả kĕl´ dả mả) HCSB, NASB, NRSV spelling for Aceldama or Akeldama (Acts 1:19). See *Aceldama*.

HAKILAH (Hả kī´ la) (NIV) See *Hachilah*.

HAKKATAN (Hăk´ kả tăn) Personal name meaning "the small one, the lesser." Father of the clan leader who accompanied Ezra from Babylon to Jerusalem about 458 B.C. (Ezra 8:12).

HAKKORE (Hăk´ kō rə) TEV reading of En-hakkore (Judg. 15:19), translating *En* as spring. See *En-hakkore*.

HAKKOZ (Hăk´ kŏz) Personal and clan name meaning "the thorn." **1.** Clan leader in tribe of Judah (1 Chron. 4:8). See Koz. **2.** Clan of priests (1 Chron. 24:10; cp. Neh. 3:4,21). In the time of Ezra and Nehemiah, members of this clan could not prove their family roots, so they were not allowed to function as priests (Ezra 2:61). See *Koz*.

HAKUPHA (Hả kū´ phả) Personal name meaning "bent." Original ancestor of clan of temple servants (Ezra 2:51).

HALAH (Hā´ la) City-state or region in northern Mesopotamia to which Assyrians exiled some leaders of the Northern Kingdom after capturing Samaria in 722 B.C. (2 Kings 17:6). Some Bible students think the original text of Obad. 20 contained a promise for the captives in Halah. They read the Hebrew word for "host" as Halah. Halah may have been Hallahhu, northeast of Nineveh.

HALAK (Hā´ lăk) Place-name meaning "barren" or "naked." Mountain marking southern extent of Joshua's conquests (Josh. 11:17; 12:7). It is identified with Jebel Halak, about 40 miles southwest of the Dead Sea in Edom.

HALF TRIBE Used to designate a segment of the tribe of Manasseh that received territory on both sides of the Jordan River. The term usually refers to that part of Manasseh dwelling to the east of the Jordan along with Reuben and Gad (Num. 32:33; Deut. 3:13; Josh. 1:12; 4:12; 22:1). Those living west of the Jordan are sometimes called "the rest of the tribe of Manasseh" (Josh. 17:2 NRSV) or the "other half" (22:7). See *Tribes of Israel*.

HALF-SHEKEL TAX Temple tax required annually of every Israelite 20 years of age and upwards (Exod. 30:13,15; 38:26). Such payment brought atonement, but atonement price was equal for all (30:15). At Matt. 17:24 this tax is called the *didrachma* ("the two drachma") tax. The coin in the fish's mouth was a stater, a coin worth four drachmas or the temple tax for two (17:27). See *Atonement*.

HALHUL (Hăl´ hŭl) Place-name, perhaps meaning "circles." Town in hill country of Judah assigned to the tribe of Judah (Josh. 15:58). It is modern Halhul, four miles north of Hebron.

HALI (Hā´ lī) Place-name meaning "jewel." Border town assigned to tribe of Asher (Josh. 19:25). It may be Khirbet Ras Ali, north of Mount Carmel.

HALL Large, usually imposing, building, often used for governmental functions; the chief room in such a structure. NIV uses hall for the main room of the temple (1 Kings 6:3,5,17,33). Other translations have house (KJV), nave (NASB, NRSV), or sanctuary (REB). Modern translations designate several of Solomon's building projects as halls. The Hall of Pillars (KJV, porch of pillars) was part of the palace complex (1 Kings 7:6). It is unclear whether this hall was a separate building or the entrance to the House of the Forest of Lebanon or even the whole palace complex. The Hall of the Throne or Hall of Judgment (1 Kings 7:7; KJV, porch) was the throne room where legal decisions were rendered. The king's hall of Esther 5:1 was, likewise, the audience chamber of the Persian king. Archeological research indicates that Ahasuerus' Hall of Pillars was 193 feet square. The hall's name stemmed from the 36 massive pillars supporting the roof.

H

Banqueting halls are frequently mentioned. The hall of 1 Sam. 9:22 (KJV, parlour) was a chamber connected with the sanctuary where sacrificial meat was eaten. Belshazzar's banqueting hall (KJV, banquet house) was the scene of the famous handwriting on the wall (Dan. 5:10). This room was likely the large throne room (50 by 160 feet) which has been excavated.

KJV used the term "hall" to translate the Greek term *aule* (Luke 22:55). Elsewhere KJV translated the term "palace" (Matt. 26:58; Mark 14:54; John 18:15). Modern translations use "courtyard." KJV also used hall for the praetorian or Roman governor's headquarters (Pilate's, Matt. 27:27; Mark 15:16; John 18:28; Herod's, Acts 23:35). See *Architecture*.

HALLEL Song of praise. The name derives from the Hebrew "Praise Thou." The singing of psalms of praise was a special duty of the Levites (2 Chron. 7:6; Ezra 3:11). The "Egyptian" Hallel (Pss. 113–118) was recited in homes as part of the Passover celebration (cp. Ps. 114:1; Matt. 26:30). The "Great Hallel" was recited in the temple as the Passover lambs were being slain and at Pentecost, Tabernacles, and Dedication. Scholars disagree as to the original extent of the "Great Hallel" with some limiting the Hallel to Ps. 136, some including Ps. 135, and still others including the "Songs of Ascents" (Pss. 120–134).

HALLELUJAH (Hăl lə lū´ ya) Exclamation of praise that recurs frequently in the book of Psalms meaning "Praise Yahweh!" In particular, Pss. 146–150 sometimes are designated the Hallelujah Psalms. In the Psalms God is praised for His power, His wisdom, His blessings, and the liberation of His people. See *Psalms, Book of.*

HALLOHESH (Hăl lō´ hĕsh) Personal name meaning "the exorcist." Father of Shallum, who helped Nehemiah repair the Jerusalem wall. He is called "the official of half the district of Jerusalem" (Neh. 3:12 NASB), apparently meaning he administered one of the outlying districts near Jerusalem. The same man or a man of the same name sealed his name to Nehemiah's covenant (Neh. 10:24).

HALLOW To make holy; to set apart for holy use; to revere. See *Dedicate, Dedication; Holy; Sanctification.*

HALT Term that KJV sometimes uses as alternate translation for "lame" (Matt. 18:8; Mark 9:45; Luke 14:21; John 5:3).

HAM (Hăm) Personal name meaning "hot." Second of Noah's three sons (Gen. 5:32). Following the flood, he discovered Noah, his father, naked and drunken and reported it to Shem and Japheth (Gen. 9:20-29). When Noah learned of the incident, he pronounced a curse on Canaan the son of Ham. Ham became the original ancestor of the Cushites, the Egyptians, and the Canaanites (Gen. 10:6). See *Noah.*

HAMAN (Hā´ man) Personal name meaning "magnificent." The Agagite who became prime minister under the Persian king Ahasuerus (Esther 3:1). He was a fierce enemy of the Jews, and he devised a plot to exterminate them. In particular, he had a gallows erected on which he hoped to hang Mordecai because Mordecai would not bow to him. Through the intervention of Esther, however, his scheme was unmasked, and he was hanged on the gallows he had designed for Mordecai the Jew. See *Esther.*

HAMATH (Hā´ măth) Place-name meaning "fortress" or "citadel." City-state located in the valley of the Orontes River, roughly 120 miles north of Damascus. Excavation indicates this mound was occupied as early as Neolithic times. Hieroglyphic inscriptions first discovered by J. L. Burckhardt in 1810 attest early Hittite influence in Hamath. Throughout much of its existence, Hamath functioned as the capital of an independent kingdom.

The southern boundary of Hamath served as the northern boundary of Israel during the reigns of Solomon (1 Kings 8:65; 2 Chron. 8:4) and Jeroboam II (2 Kings 14:25,28). The "entrance of Hamath" was treated as the northern border of Israel (Num. 34:8; Josh. 13:5; Ezek. 47:15-17,20; 48:1) and served as an accepted geographical expression (Num. 13:21; Judg. 3:3).

Toi, king of Hamath, sent his son to congratulate David after David defeated King Hadadezer of Zobah. Toi had frequently fought with Hadad-ezer (2 Sam. 8:9-10; 1 Chron. 18:3,9-10). In 853 B.C. King Irhuleni of Hamath joined a coalition including Ben-hadad II of Damascus and Ahab of Israel which successfully thwarted the advance of Shalmaneser II of Assyria into northern Syria. In about 802 B.C. Adad-nirari III of Assyria crushed Damascus and levied a heavy tax upon it. During the following decades, the king of Hamath, probably named Zakir, waged a successful rivalry with Damascus. Hamath reached the zenith of its power between 800 and 750 B.C. See *Toi.*

In 738 B.C. Tiglath-pileser III of Assyria exacted tribute from Hamath together with other states including Israel. Following the fall of Samaria in 722–721 B.C., Hamath was devastated in 720 B.C. by Sargon II of Assyria (Amos 6:2). Refugees from Samaria may have been exiled to Hamath by the Assyrians, while refugees from Hamath were brought to Samaria along with their god, Ashima (2 Kings 17:24,30; Isa. 11:11). From this time, Hamath's history seems to merge with that of Damascus (Jer. 49:23).

In the Hellenistic period Antiochus IV changed its name to Epiphania. It was known by this name in the Greco-Roman period, though the natives continued to call it Hamath (modern Hamah). See *Lebo-Hamath.*   *Max Rogers*

HAMATH-ZOBAH (Hā măth-zō´ ba) Place-name meaning "fortress of Zobah." City that Solomon captured in Syria (2 Chron. 8:3). Both Hamath and Zobah are cities in Syria that David controlled (2 Sam. 8). Some interpreters see the combination here as the result of a damaged text available to the Chronicler. Others think the Chronicler reflects the Babylonian and Persian administrative system of his day including the two cities in one administrative district. Still others think this was simply another name for Zobah. The Chronicler in distinction from 2 Sam. 8 also combines the two cities into "Zobah-hamath" (1 Chron. 18:3 REB, reflecting the literal Hebrew text). See *Hamath; Zobah.*

HAMATHITE (Hā´ măth īt) Citizen of Hamath and originally descended from Canaan, son of Ham, son of Noah (Gen. 10:18). See *Hamath.*

HAMITES (Hăm´ īts) NIV designation for descendants of Ham (1 Chron. 4:40-41). See *Ham.*

HAMMATH (Hăm´ măth) Place-name meaning "hot spot," probably due to hot spring, and personal name meaning "hot one." **1.** Fortified city in the tribal territory of Naphtali (Josh. 19:35); probably the same as the Levitical town of Hammoth-dor (21:32). It may be located at Tell

Raqqat, just north of Tiberias. Others have tried to locate it at the famous hot springs of Hammam Tabiriyeh, south of Tiberias, but archaeologists have found no evidence of Iron Age occupation there. First Chronicles 6:76 reads "Hammon," apparently the same place, in the list of Levitical towns. **2.** Original ancestor of Kenites and Rechabites (1 Chron. 2:55; KJV reads "Hamath"; TEV, REB see a verbal construction meaning "intermarried" or "connected by marriage"). The context and grammatical construction of the verse makes certain understanding impossible. Hammath could be the founder of the city Hammath.

HAMMEDATHA (Hăm mə dā´ thà) Personal name meaning "given by the god." Father of Haman, the villain of the book of Esther (Esther 3:1).

HAMMELECH (Hăm´ mə lĕk) According to KJV, personal name translated "the king" (Jer. 36:26; 38:6). Modern translations read "son of the king."

HAMMER A striking tool. The earliest hammers were simply smooth or shaped stones. Beginning in the Bronze Age, stones were hollowed out to give a better grip or to receive a handle. Mallets of bone and wood were used (Judg. 5:26), though these have not normally been preserved. Hammers with metal heads were rare in Palestine, possibly because metal was reserved for tools needing a cutting edge.

Hammers were used in cutting stone (1 Kings 6:7), working common and precious metals (Isa. 41:7; 44:12), and for woodworking (Jer. 10:4). A hammer-like weapon was also used in battle (Jer. 51:20; "shatterer," NASB margin; Ezek. 9:2 "shattering weapon"). See *Arms and Armor.*

The hammer was a symbol of power. God's word is pictured as a hammer (Jer. 23:29). Babylon is mocked as a hammer whose strength has failed (Jer. 50:23). See *Tools.*

HAMMOLECHETH (Hăm mŏl´ ĕ kĕth) (TEV, NRSV, NASB) or **HAMMOLEKETH** (KJV, NIV, REB) Personal name meaning "queen." Sister of Gilead in genealogy of Manasseh in the unparalleled list of 1 Chron. 7:18.

HAMMON (Hăm´ mon) Place-name meaning "hot spot," probably from a hot spring. **1.** Town in tribal allotment of Asher (Josh. 19:28). It may be modern Umm el-awamid near the Mediterranean coast in Lebanon about five miles northeast of Rosh ha-niqra. **2.** See *Hammath*.

HAMMOTH-DOR (Hăm´ moth-dôr) See *Hammath*.

HAMMUEL (Hăm´ mū ĕl) Personal name meaning "El is my father-in-law" or "God is hot with anger." Member of tribe of Simeon (1 Chron. 4:26).

HAMMURABI (Hăm mŭ ra´ bĭ) (known also as Hammurapi) King of Babylon who reigned 43 years in the first half of the second millennium B.C. His absolute dates are uncertain; his reign began in 1848, 1792, or 1736 B.C. He was the son of Sin-muballit and the father of Samsu-iluna. He is most famous for issuing a famous law collection popularly known as "the code of Hammurabi."

Kingdom Hammurabi was the sixth in a line of Amorite kings of the First Dynasty of Babylon (about 2000–1600 B.C.). By forming coalitions against his enemies, and then later turning on his former allies, Hammurabi reunified Mesopotamia and founded the so-called Old Babylonian Empire.

Hammurabi spent the middle 20 years of his reign preoccupied with local affairs. Evidently he was consolidating and organizing his kingdom. He built religious shrines, civic buildings, defensive walls, and canals during this period, but there are virtually no remains of Hammurabi's capital. The archives at Mari reveal about 140 letters sent between Babylon and Mari during this era. The last 12 years of his rule were characterized by uninterrupted warfare. Whereas the early years witnessed military and political expansion, the latter years saw the kingdom shrink. Most of it was lost soon after his death, and the Hittites brought an end to the dynasty about 1600 B.C. See *Babylon*.

Religion With Babylon's rise to power came the rise of Babylon's patron god, Marduk. He was considered the son´ of Enki/Ea, god of fresh water and of wisdom. Marduk was god of thunderstorms and was worshiped at Babylon at the great temple called *Esagila*, apparently built during the first dynasty. The Babylonian creation epic *Enuma Elish*, dating to the second millennium, celebrated Marduk's defeat of evil Tiamat, goddess of the sea. For this feat the high god Enlil

rewards him with the "tablets of destiny" and the title "Lord of the Lands."

Lawgiver A French excavation of the ancient Persian city of Susa in A.D. 1901–02 uncovered a seven-foot high diorite stele inscribed with a collection of laws from Hammurabi's reign. The stele was probably set in the great Esagila temple with copies sent to other centers. It had been carried to Susa by the Elamites after a raid in 1160 B.C. At the top of the stele is a relief showing Hammurabi receiving the symbols of justice and order from the sun god Shamash, also god of justice and noted protector of the oppressed.

The stone contains 44 columns of ancient cuneiform writing. A poetic prologue and epilogue enclose 282 separate laws. (Compare the book of Job in which poetic dialogues are enclosed by prose prologue and epilogue.)

Hammurabi's law collection has much in common with the other cuneiform collections of Ur-Nammu (21st century B.C.), Lipit-Ishtar (19th century B.C.), the kingdom of Eshnunna (about 1800 B.C.), the Hittite laws (16th or 15th century B.C.), the Middle Assyrian laws (the 15th or 14th century B.C.), and the Neo-Babylonian laws (7th century B.C.), as well as with the law of Moses.

Much has been written about the purpose and function of these various law collections in the ancient Near East. That they did not function as binding and authoritative law codes in the modern sense is indicated by several factors. (1) In all the vast number of judicial records there is no example of a legal decision being based explicitly on one of these written laws. Legal decisions were based rather on precedent known through legal tradition. Legal decisions in the OT likewise do not cite written law, which has led some scholars to conclude that this shows ignorance of a written law of Moses. Comparison with how the legal systems of surrounding countries operated demonstrates the fallacy of this claim. (2) Another factor is that none of the law collections deal with every aspect of life, and they tend to deal primarily with exceptional cases. The Mosaic law is comparable here as well. Legal practices in the area of marriage, for example, often go beyond what is found explicitly in the law of Moses.

It is commonly held that Hammurabi's law collection contains the king's verdicts that were to serve as legal patterns to guide judges and so to produce political and social uniformity throughout his diverse kingdom. Their purpose, then, was either reform or education or both.

The collection was also intended to demonstrate to the people, to posterity, and especially to the gods that Hammurabi was a faithful and just shepherd of his people. The stele begins by describing the king's divine call to "make justice to shine forth in the land, to destroy the evil and the wicked, that the strong might not oppress the weak ... to give light to the land."

In his first year Hammurabi decreed the standard of law that would govern the economic and religious life of all Babylonians. This compares to the "reforms" of the Hebrew kings, who by restating allegiance to the Torah in their first year as king, "did right in the sight of the Lord" (2 Kings 18:3 NASB).

Hammurabi's law collection covers such general offenses as false accusations (cp. Deut. 5:20; 19:16-17), witchcraft (cp. Deut. 18:10; Exod. 22:18), evil judges (Exod. 23:6-9; Lev. 19:15; Deut. 16:18-21), and kidnapping (cp. Exod. 21:16). Many laws cover marital issues such as the rights of both parties, dowry settlements, bridal gifts, marriage offenses, and divorce. Legal marriage required a contract with the girl's parents. A man could divorce his wife if he returned the marriage gift and dowry and paid to educate the children (if any); a wife could divorce her husband if she had not been a "gadabout, thus neglecting her house and humiliating her husband" (cp. Deut. 24:1-4). Adultery with a married woman permitted the death penalty if the husband demanded it, but it was not required (cp. Deut. 22:22). Death was the punishment for rape as in Deut. 22:25. Incest is prohibited by each, but in Hammurabi the punishment is only exile.

Since property was such a great concern, many laws dealt with inheritance. As in Hebrew law (Exod. 13:2; Deut. 21:15-17), the firstborn had special rights. A father could disinherit a son who had done wrong or could adopt a son by oral pronouncement. Children of a slave wife would not inherit unless adopted.

Another category of laws concerned personal injury. The penalty for striking one's parent was loss of one's hand. In Hebrew law this was a capital offense (Exod. 21:15). Hurting pregnant women was severely punished as in Hebrew law but with no indication whether the injury was accidental, and in Hammurabi the woman is another man's daughter rather than wife (Exod.

21:22-25). The principle of "an eye for an eye" (*lex talionis*) was carried to the extreme that if someone caused the death of another's son or daughter, the penalty was the death of the offender's son or daughter.

Relationship to Biblical Law The law collections of Hammurabi, the Assyrians, Hittites, and others have much in common with Hebrew law. One area of similarity is form. As in other law collections, many of the Hebrew laws take the form of conditions: "When/if this happens, then this shall be the penalty" (e.g., Exod. 21:18–23:5). The first of Hammurabi's laws reads, "If a citizen accuses another citizen of murder but cannot prove it, the accuser shall be put to death." Similarities of content are of three types. Some laws are almost identical in content, some differ in penalties exacted or in other details, and some are similar only in that they deal with the same general situation. The latter type of similarity is the most common.

There are several critical differences between the Hammurabi law collection and Mosaic law. (1) Hammurabi's laws do not deal with religious affairs. (2) Penalties varied according to the class of the offender. Three classes were recognized: freedman, state dependent, and slave. (3) The immense value of property in Hammurabi's (and other) law collections is contrasted with the immense value placed on human life in the Mosaic laws. Only in biblical law was a clear distinction drawn between property and human life. Only biblical law, for example, required the death of an ox that had gored someone to death and also the owner's death if he had been negligent (Exod. 21:28-32). Conversely, in biblical law monetary compensation was never sufficient penalty for homicide. (4) Biblical law included laws of the absolute (apodictic) form, "Do not steal, etc." rather than just the more pragmatic emphasis on consequences. Israel was unique in having such laws that gave positive and negative commands directly to individuals, as in the Ten Commandments. (5) This in part may be the result of the divine authorship of Mosaic law, which also meant that not even the king had authority to change a law or even to reduce a penalty. The king also could not add to the laws God had given, a situation unique in the ancient Near East. (6) Finally, biblical law was unique in that it was understood in the context of the

H

covenant God had made with Israel. See *Law, Ten Commandments, Torah.*

Gary D. Baldwin and E. Ray Clendenen

HAMON-GOG (Hā´ mŏn-gŏg) Place-name meaning "horde of Gog." Place where Ezekiel predicted burial of defeated army of Gog (Ezek. 39:11,15). Its location is not known. See *Ezekiel; Gog and Magog; Hamonah.*

HAMONAH (Hȧ mō´ nah) Place-name meaning "horde." Town in valley of Hamon-gog where Israel would bury the defeated army of Gog (Ezek. 39:16). The exact meaning and location of the city are not clear except that Ezekiel was determined that Israel would keep the land ritually pure in all circumstances. TEV, REB translate Hamonah as "nearby" or "great horde" and thus do not mention the city. See *Ezekiel; Gog and Magog; Hamon-gog.*

HAMOR (Hā´ môr) Personal name meaning "donkey" or "ass." In Gen. 33:19, the father of Shechem. From the children of Hamor, Jacob purchased a parcel of land on which he erected an altar. Later the remains of Joseph, Jacob's son, were buried on this parcel of land (Josh. 24:32). Hamor and Shechem were killed by Simeon and Levi in an act of revenge for the outrage committed against Dinah (Gen. 34:25-26). Hamor was the original clan ancestor of the city of Shechem (Judg. 9:28).

HAMRAN (Hăm´ răn) Personal name of uncertain meaning, perhaps, "vineyard." Member of family of Esau (1 Chron. 1:35,41). KJV spells the name "Amram." The parallel list has Hemdan (Gen. 36:26); NIV picks up Hemdan in 1 Chronicles along with some Hebrew and Greek manuscripts. Apparently early copyists misread similar Hebrew letters. See *Hemdan.*

HAMSTRING To cripple by cutting the leg tendons. Horses captured in war were frequently hamstrung (KJV, hough) (Josh. 11:6,9; 2 Sam. 8:4; 1 Chron. 18:4). The hamstringing of oxen (Gen. 49:6 modern translations) is an example of rash anger.

HAMUEL (Hăm´ ū ĕl) (KJV) See *Hammuel.*

HAMUL (Hā´ mŭl) Personal name meaning "pitied, spared" or "El is father-in-law" or "El is hot, angry." Son of Pharez and grandson of Judah

(Gen. 46:12) and thus a clan leader in Judah (Num. 26:21).

HAMULITE (Hā´ mŭl īt) Member of clan of Hamul (Num. 26:21). See *Hamul.*

HAMUTAL (Hȧ mū´ tăl) Personal name meaning "father-in-law or kindred of the dew." Mother of King Jehoahaz (2 Kings 23:31) and King Zedekiah (2 Kings 24:18) of Judah. See *Jehoahaz; Zedekiah.*

HANAMEEL (Hȧ năm´ ə ĕl) Personal name meaning "God is gracious." Uncle of Jeremiah from whom the prophet bought the field in Anathoth (Jer. 32:7-12). Jeremiah's act symbolized God's long-range plans to restore the people to the land after exile.

HANAMEL (Hăn´ ȧ mĕl) Modern translation spelling of Hanameel. See *Hanameel.*

HANAN (Hā´ năn) Personal name meaning "gracious." Personal name probably originally connected to divine name such as El, Yahweh, or Baal. **1.** Clan or guild of prophets or priests living in the temple. Jeremiah used their temple chamber for his meeting with the Rechabites (Jer. 35:4). **2.** Clan of temple servants who returned to Jerusalem from Babylonian exile with Zerubbabel about 537 B.C. (Ezra 2:46). **3.** Man that Nehemiah appointed as assistant temple treasurer to receive and disperse tithes brought to care for the Levites (Neh. 13:13). **4.** One of David's military heroes (1 Chron. 11:43). **5.** Levite who instructed the people in the Lord's law while Ezra read it (Neh. 8:7). **6.** Levite who sealed Nehemiah's covenant to obey God's law (Neh. 10:10). **7.** Another signer of Nehemiah's covenant (Neh. 10:22). **8.** Another who signed Nehemiah's covenant (Neh. 10:26). **9.** Member of tribe of Benjamin (1 Chron. 8:23). **10.** Descendant of Saul in tribe of Benjamin (1 Chron. 8:38).

HANANEEL (Hȧ năn´ ə ĕl) (KJV) or **HANANEL** (Hăn´ ȧ nĕl) Place-name meaning "God is gracious." Tower marking northern wall of Jerusalem. Jeremiah predicted its rebuilding in the day of the Lord to come (Jer. 31:38; cp. Zech. 14:10). Nehemiah led the nation to rebuild the tower along with the rest of the Jerusalem wall (Neh. 3:1; 12:39). It may well have been part of the earliest fortress protecting the temple (Neh. 2:8; 7:2 NASB).

HANANI (Hå nā´ nī) Personal name meaning "my grace" or a shortened form of "Yahweh is gracious." **1.** Father of Prophet Jehu (1 Kings 16:1,7; 2 Chron. 19:2). **2.** Man who agreed under Ezra's leadership to divorce his foreign wife to protect the Jews from temptation to worship idols (Ezra 10:16-20,44). **3.** Nehemiah's brother who reported the poor conditions in Jerusalem to him while Nehemiah was still in Persia (Neh. 1:2). Nehemiah placed him in charge of the military protection of the restored Jerusalem (Neh. 7:2). Some have tried to identify him with the Hunani mentioned in the Elephantine Papyri, but this is far from certain. **4.** Priest musician at dedication of Jerusalem walls (Neh. 12:36). **5.** Temple musician and descendant of Heman (1 Chron. 25:4). Some would equate him with 4. above. **6.** Original leader of one course of temple musicians (1 Chron. 25:25). **7.** Prophetic seer who condemned King Asa of Judah (910–869 B.C.) for paying tribute to King Ben-hadad of Damascus rather than relying on God (2 Chron. 16:7). Asa imprisoned Hanani (2 Chron. 16:10).

HANANIAH (Hăn å nī´ a) Personal name with two Hebrew spellings meaning "Yah(weh) is gracious." **1.** Prophet from Gibeon who opposed Jeremiah by promising immediate deliverance from Babylon. Jeremiah could combat this false prophecy only by telling the people to wait until they saw it fulfilled in history (Jer. 28:8-9). Jeremiah could not even oppose Hananiah when he tried to embarrass Jeremiah by breaking the symbolic yoke that Jeremiah was wearing (vv. 10-11). Only later did Jeremiah receive a countering word from God to oppose Hananiah (vv. 12-17). **2.** Father of Zedekiah, a court official, in time of Jeremiah (Jer. 36:12). **3.** Grandfather of captain of guard who arrested Jeremiah as he left Jerusalem (Jer. 37:13). **4.** Jewish name of Daniel's friend Shadrach (Dan. 1:7). See *Shadrach.* **5.** Son of Zerubbabel in the royal line of David (1 Chron. 3:19). See *Zerubbabel.* **6.** Clan head in tribe of Benjamin living in Jerusalem (1 Chron. 8:24). **7.** Son of Heman among the priestly musicians in the temple (1 Chron. 25:4). He may be the same as the head of a course of priests (v. 23), though the latter's name has a slightly variant spelling in Hebrew.

8. Military leader under King Uzziah of Judah (792–740 B.C.) (2 Chron. 26:11). **9.** Man who followed Ezra's leadership and divorced his foreign wife to protect Judah from the temptation to worship foreign gods (Ezra 10:16-20,44). **10.** A member of the perfumers' guild who helped Nehemiah repair the Jerusalem wall (Neh. 3:8 NASB). **11.** Man who helped Nehemiah repair the Jerusalem wall (Neh. 3:30). **12.** Ruler of the temple fortress under Nehemiah (Neh. 7:2 NASB). Nehemiah set him up as one of two administrators of Jerusalem because he was trustworthy and reverenced God more than other men. **13.** Man who signed Nehemiah's covenant to obey God's law; perhaps the same as 12. above (Neh. 10:23). **14.** A priest immediately after the time of return from Babylonian exile (Neh. 12:12) when Joiakim was high priest. **15.** Priest musician who helped Nehemiah celebrate the completion of the Jerusalem wall (Neh. 12:41).

HAND Part of the human body, namely the terminal part of the arm that enables a person to make and use tools and perform functions. The Greek and Hebrew words that are translated by the English word "hand" appear approximately 1,800 times. Of these occurrences to which "hand" is referred, the literal sense is intended some 500 times, and the figurative sense some 1,300 times.

The references to "hand" often encompassed the idea of parts of a hand. Thus, in Gen. 41:42, when Pharaoh took his signet ring "from his hand" and placed it "on Joseph's hand," "hand" was used in the place of "finger." Likewise, in Ezek. 23:42, "hand" was used to mean wrists: "they put bracelets on the hands of the women." The context in which the word appears determines the meaning and usage of the word.

The largest number of figurative uses of "hand" relate to God. The "hand of God" or "in Thy hand" is an idiom referring to the supreme and almighty power and authority of God (1 Chron. 29:12). In Isa. 59:1 God's hand was described as mighty. Exodus 13:3-16 described God's deliverance of Israel from Egypt by His "strong hand." The creative work of God involved the use of His hands to make the heavens and the earth (Pss. 8:6; 95:5). God uses His hand to uphold and guide the righteous (Pss. 37:24; 139:10). Punishment and affliction come from the hand of God (Exod. 9:3; Deut. 2:15;

H

Judg. 2:15; 1 Sam. 7:13; 12:15; Ruth 1:13). The hand of God can be upon someone in either a good or bad sense. In a good sense, it meant to bring aid, while the negative connotation meant to hinder or distress (Amos 1:8).

The phrase "into someone's hand" was used figuratively to convey the idea of authority involving responsibility, care, or dominion over someone or something (Gen. 9:2). Examples of this concept include: Sarah's authority over Hagar (Gen. 16:6,9); Joseph's administration of Potiphar's house (Gen. 39:3-8); and the role of Moses and Aaron as leaders of Israel (Num. 33:1). Victory and deliverance were portrayed also by the use of this phrase. Victory over someone was conveyed by the phrase delivered "into your hand" (Josh. 6:2; cp. Gen. 49:8), while deliverance was understood as "out of the hand of" (Exod. 3:8 KJV).

Functions of the hand were often used by biblical writers to identify certain uses of the word. Since a person takes possession of objects with the hand, the biblical writers adapted "hand" to mean possession. A literal translation of Gen. 39:1 would include the statement that Potiphar bought Joseph "from the Ishmaelites." In 1 Kings 11:31 Jeroboam was told that the Lord was about to tear the kingdom "from the hand" of Solomon.

"To give the hand" meant that one had pledged or submitted to another, as in 2 Kings 10:15 and Ezra 10:19. Submission to the Lord is implied in 2 Chron. 30:8, where "yield to" is literally "give hand to."

"To stretch the hand" was used to convey two thoughts: attacking the enemy in battle (Josh. 8:19,26) and an intense desire for communion with God (Ps. 143:6).

Work or the action in which one is involved is expressed by the words "work of your hand" (Deut. 2:7; 30:9 NASB). In 1 Sam. 23:16 Jonathan's helping David is literally "he strengthened his hand in God," that is, increased his faith and hope in God's help.

The Hebrew phrase "high hand" indicated willful rebellion against God (Num. 15:30; Deut. 32:27) but also military power (Exod. 14:8; Mic. 5:9). A similar image is projected by the phrase "shaking the hand" (Isa. 10:32 KJV; 11:15). The movement of the hand was interpreted as a sign of contempt and displeasure, or lack of respect. When used in reference to God, it symbolized God's warning and punishment.

Hebrew "to fill the hand" expressed the consecration of a priest (Judg. 17:5) or a congregation's dedication (2 Chron. 29:31).

The word "hand" was used in a number of specialized ways. It came to mean "side," perhaps because of the location of the hands and arms on the body. A peculiar use was that of hand for "monument" (1 Sam. 15:12). The spreading of the hands denoted a large "space" (Gen. 34:21). See *Laying on of Hands; Work; Worship.* *James Newell*

HANDBAG See *Bag 1.*

HANDBREADTH Ancient measurement equal to the width of the hand at the base of the fingers (about three inches). Ezekiel's long cubit was six handbreadths, one more than the common cubit (Ezek. 40:5). In Ps. 39:5 "a few handbreadths" illustrates the shortness of life.

HANDKERCHIEF Greek term *soudarion* is borrowed from a Latin term used for a table napkin or a handkerchief. The term derives from the Latin root for sweat, suggesting that a *soudarion* was a cloth for wiping sweat or a sweatband. Such a cloth is likely intended at Acts 19:12. The same Greek term is used for a cloth in which money was buried (Luke 19:20) and for the cloth used to cover the face of the dead (John 11:44; 20:7).

HANDLES Literally "hands." The thumb pieces or knobs of the bolt or latch of a door (Song 5:5).

HANDMAIDEN See *Maid.*

HANDS, LAYING ON OF See *Laying on of Hands.*

HANDSTAVE Wooden staff used as a weapon by foot soldiers. KJV used "handstave" to translate a weapon at Ezek. 39:9. The nature of the weapon is unclear though the weapon was made of wood (39:10). The NRSV renders the term "handpike"; NASB and NIV, "war clubs"; REB, "throwing sticks." See *Arms and Armor.*

HANDWRITING See *Writing.*

HANES (Hā´ nēz) Egypt place-name. City to which Israel sent ambassadors in time of Isaiah to seek military and economic help (Isa. 30:4). Isaiah condemned the government policy of seeking Egyptian help rather than trusting Yahweh. Hanes has often been located at Heracleopolis Magna in southern Egypt just north of the Nile Delta, modern Ahnas. This would be a natural parallel to northern Zoan or Tanis. A more likely identification, however, is Heracleopolis Parva, modern Hanes, almost directly east of Tanis and much more likely to be the goal of Judah's ambassadors than the distant southern Heracleopolis. Ashurbanipal of Egypt also mentions Hanes in listing Egyptian cities. See *Zoan.*

HANGING A method of ridiculing, shaming, and desecrating an enemy. Hanging was not regarded as a means of capital punishment according to biblical law, although it was practiced by the Egyptians (Gen. 40:19,22) and the Persians (Esther 7:9). The Israelites, after putting an enemy or criminal to death, might hang them on a gibbet or tree for public scorn as added degradation and warning (Gen. 40:19; Deut. 21:22; Josh. 8:29; 2 Sam. 4:12), but biblical law demanded that the corpses be taken down and buried the same day (Deut. 21:22-23). Joshua 8:29; 10:26-27 record that the bodies of the kings of Ai and the kings of the Amorites were taken down and buried at sundown on the same day they were hanged. Contrast the undetermined length of exposure allowed by Pharaoh (Gen. 40:19), the Philistines (1 Sam. 31:10), and the Gibeonites (2 Sam. 21:8-10). A hanged man was considered an insult to God (Gal. 3:13) and therefore defiled the land.

According to the first-century Jewish historian, Josephus, all executed criminals were afterward hanged. The Mishnah prescribes hanging only for those put to death by stoning. Some Bible students think hanging was prescribed only for blasphemers and idolaters.

Hanging oneself is mentioned only once in the OT and once in the NT. Ahithophel, David's counselor, joined the conspiracy of Absalom, David's son (2 Sam. 15:31). Feeling his ploy for personal power evaporate, he set his house in order and hanged himself (2 Sam. 17:23). Judas, one of the 12 disciples of our Lord, in a desperate effort to resolve guilt and atone for the misdeed of betraying Jesus for 30 pieces of silver, went out into the night and hanged himself (Matt. 27:5). Acts 1:18 says he fell headlong and burst asunder, presumably as the rope broke.

C. Dale Hill

HANIEL (Hăn´ ĭ ĕl) (KJV, 1 Chron. 7:39) See *Hanniel.*

HANNAH (Hăn´ na) Personal name meaning "grace." One of the wives of Elkanah and mother of Samuel (1 Sam. 1:2). Because she had been barren for many years, she vowed to the Lord that if she should give birth to a son, she would dedicate the child to God (1 Sam. 1:11). Subsequently, she gave birth to the child Samuel. She fulfilled her vow by bringing her son to the sanctuary at Shiloh, where he served the Lord under the direction of Eli. Later on, Hannah had other sons and daughters. See *Samuel.*

HANNATHON (Hăn´ nȧ thŏn) Place-name meaning "grace." Town on northern border of tribal territory of Zebulun (Josh. 19:14). The El-Amarna tablets and the annals of Tiglath-pileser III of Assyria also mention it. It is probably present-day Tell el-Badawiye, about six miles north of Nazareth.

HANNIEL (Hăn´ nĭ ĕl) Personal name meaning "God is gracious." **1.** Representative of tribe of Manasseh on council that helped Joshua and Eleazar divide the land among the tribes (Num. 34:23). **2.** Member of tribe of Asher (1 Chron. 7:39).

HANOCH (Hā´ nŏk) Personal name with same Hebrew spelling as Enoch meaning "dedicated" or "vassal." See *Enoch.* **1.** Son of Reuben and grandson of Jacob (Gen. 46:9) and thus a clan leader in Israel (Exod. 6:14; Num. 26:5). **2.** Son of Midian and grandson of Abraham and thus one of the Midianites (Gen. 25:4). See *Midian.*

HANOCHITE (Hā´ nŏk īt) Member of clan of Hanoch. See *Hanoch.*

HANUKKAH An eight-day festival that commemorated the cleansing and rededication of the temple following the victories of Judas Maccabeus in 167/165 B.C. It is the only Jewish festival not specified in the Hebrew Bible. Hanukkah, also called the Feast of Dedication, begins on the 25th day of Kislev (December). One candle is lit each day until a total of eight are lit. Jesus was in Jerusalem once during this festival (John 10:22).

The word *hanukkah* means "consecration," "dedication." After Antiochus Epiphanes conducted pagan worship in the temple, Judas

Maccabeus cleansed the temple from the pollution of pagan worship. He made a new sacrificial altar and holy vessels, burned incense on the incense altar, lit the lampstands to give light to the temple, placed bread on the table, and hung new curtains. He dedicated the new altar with sacrifices, song, and joyous worship for eight days.

Hanukkah's ongoing significance lies in its commemoration of the victory of the few whose desire for freedom to practice their religion impelled them to battle against great odds. After the destruction of the temple in A.D. 70 the feast was observed by the lighting of lamps in private homes, thus, the description, Feast of Lights. See *Festivals*. *Gary Hardin*

HANUN (Hā´ nŭn) Personal name meaning "blessed" or "favored." **1.** King of Ammon whom David sought to honor and with whom he sought to renew the peace treaty. Hanun and his advisors misinterpreted David's act and treated David's messengers shamefully. David's military response brought victory over Ammon and Syria (2 Sam. 10). This set the stage for David's sinful relationship with Bathsheba. **2.** Man who repaired the Valley Gate of Jerusalem under Nehemiah (Neh. 3:13). See *Jerusalem*. **3.** Another man who worked under Nehemiah to repair the Jerusalem wall (Neh. 3:30).

HAPHRAIM (Hăph rā´ ĭm) (KJV) or **HAPHARAIM** (Hăph à rā´ ĭm) Place-name meaning "two holes" or "two wells." Town in tribal territory of Issachar (Josh. 19:17-19). It is modern et-Taiyibeh, about nine miles northwest of Beth-shean.

HAPIRU See *Habiru*.

HAPPIZZEZ (Hăp´ pĭ zĕz) Personal name meaning "the shattered one." Leader of one course of the priests (1 Chron. 24:6-7,15) and thus the original ancestor for that priestly clan. KJV, REB spell the name Aphses.

HAR-HERES (Här-hē´ rĕs) NRSV reading in Judg. 1:35 for Mount Heres, NRSV transliterating *har*, Hebrew word for "mountain." See *Heres*.

HAR MAGEDON (Här Mà gĕd´ ŏn) NASB, NRSV transliteration of Greek transliteration from Hebrew in Rev. 16:16 for place-name other

English translations transliterate as Armageddon. See *Armageddon*.

HARA (Hā´ rà) Place-name of uncertain meaning. City or region in northern Mesopotamia where, according to 1 Chron. 5:26, the Assyrians under Tiglath-pileser settled some of the exiles from east of the Jordan in the Northern Kingdom in 734 B.C. The name does not occur in the parallel passages (1 Kings 17:6; 18:11). The scribe copying Chronicles may have copied part of the Hebrew word for either Habor or for river a second time in a way that later generations made into the name Hara. The accounts in 1 Kings place the exile to these cities in 722 B.C.

HARADAH (Hà rā´ da) Place-name meaning "quaking" or "terror." Station in Israel's wilderness journey (Num. 33:24-25). It is probably modern el-Harada, over 50 miles south of Aqaba.

HARAN (Hā´ răn) Personal and place-name meaning "mountaineer" or "caravan route." Three men and an important city of northern Mesopotamia located on the Balik River. **1.** Terah's son and Lot's father (Gen. 11:26-29,31). **2.** Son of Caleb's concubine (1 Chron. 2:46). **3.** Son of Shimei and a Levite (1 Chron.

Vista of Haran from Crusader's castle.

23:9). **4.** The city became Abraham's home (Gen. 11:31-32; 12:4-5) and remained home for his relatives like Laban (Gen. 27:43). Jacob went there and married (Gen. 28:10; 29:4). In the eighth century Assyria conquered it (2 Kings 19:12; Isa. 37:12). It was a trade partner of Tyre (Ezek. 27:23). Through excavations begun in the 1950s, the city was determined to have been established by the middle of the third millennium and was occupied through the Assyro-Babylonian period until Islamic times. The city was also a major center of worship for the moon god Sin. Its name is spelled differently from that of the men in Hebrew.   *David M. Fleming*

HARAR (Hā´ rär) Geographical name perhaps related to Hebrew word for "mountain." The word appears in slightly difficult forms in its appearances in the Hebrew Bible. Three of David's military heroes are related to Harar (2 Sam. 23:11,33; 1 Chron. 11:34-35). Harar can either be a town, a region, a tribe, or a general reference to mountain country.

HARARITE (Ha´ rá rīt) Person from Harar. See *Harar.*

HARBEL (Här´ bĕl) TEV reading of place-name in Num. 34:11, usually translated Riblah but spelled in Hebrew with beginning "h," which can be the Hebrew definite article. See *Riblah.*

HARBONA (Här bō´ nä) Persian personal name, perhaps meaning "barren." A eunuch on the staff of King Ahasuerus of Persia (Esther 1:10; 7:9).

HARBONAH (Här bō´ na) Alternate spelling of Harbona, based on Hebrew text's alteration between Hebrew and Aramaic spelling. See *Harbona.*

HARD SAYING Teaching difficult to understand or accept (John 6:60).

HARDNESS OF HEART The action or state of resistance to and rejection of the Word and will of God. Hardness of heart can be a refusal to hear the Word of God, or it can be a refusal to submit and obey the will of God. This rejection can include both the message delivered and the messenger who delivers it.

"Hardening" is a process whereby a person ceases to have a conscience about an evil action

that is committed or a sinful attitude that is embodied, such as pride, godlessness, hatred, lust, etc. (Heb. 3:13; 1 Tim. 4:2). Sinful habits can produce or compound this hardened condition. Hardness of heart can eventually destroy one's sense of sin, ruling out the possibility of repentance.

One of the major issues in this topic concerns the agent of the hardening. The Bible pictures both God and individuals as agents of hardening. For example one passage in the book of Exodus states that Pharaoh hardened his own heart (Exod. 8:15). In other places, God is said to be the one who hardened Pharaoh's heart (Exod. 4:21; 10:1). Paul asserts that God will harden whomever He wants and will bestow mercy on whomever He chooses (Rom. 9:18). The Bible also gives strong warnings against hardening the heart, implying that persons are responsible for the condition of their hearts (Ps. 95:8; Heb. 3:8,15; 4:7). Hardening may therefore be considered both the work of God and the individual.

The significance of the passages that speak of hardness of heart is that God uses these destitute conditions as a means of accomplishing His purposes. Because of the hardness of Pharaoh's heart, God liberated the Israelites from Egyptian slavery and eventually led them to the promised land (Josh. 11:20). God used the hardness of Israel to bring salvation to the Gentiles (Rom. 11:7-25). In these passages God's sovereign purposes are manifested. The entrenched hardness of people's hearts may be the occasion through which God manifests His mercy and grace. The brightness of God's redemption is highlighted against the darkness of humanity's sin.

                                                                    Stan Norman

HARE Long-eared member of the rabbit family (*Leporhyidae*), especially those born with open eyes and fur. Hares were regarded as unclean (Lev. 11:6; Deut. 14:7) and were forbidden for Israelites to eat.

HAREPH (Hā´ rĕph) Personal name meaning "clever" or "reproach." Descendant of Caleb and thus member of tribe of Judah (1 Chron. 2:51).

HARETH (Hā´ rĕth) Place-name meaning "woodland." Forest where David went at advice of Gad, the prophet, as he hid from Saul (1 Sam.

22:5). It was in Judah, but the exact location is debated. Some students place it at Khirbet Khoreisa two miles south of Ziph and about six miles southeast of Hebron. Others think it is near the village of Kharas near Keilah. See *Hereth*.

HARHAIAH (Här hī´ a) Personal name of uncertain meaning. Member of goldsmiths' guild whose son helped Nehemiah repair the wall of Jerusalem (Neh. 3:8).

HARHAS (Här´ hăs) Foreign name of uncertain meaning. Grandfather of the husband of Huldah, the prophet (2 Kings 22:14). Second Chronicles 34:22 spells the name "Hasrah" with other manuscript evidence pointing to Hasdah or Harham. Many Bible students think Hasrah is original.

HARHUR (Här´ hŭr) Personal name meaning "glow, burn," possibly describing fever of mother at birth. A temple servant who returned from Babylonian exile with Zerubbabel about 537 B.C. (Ezra 2:51).

HARIM (Hā´ rĭm) Personal name meaning "dedicated." **1.** Clan leader from Bethlehem whose family returned from Babylonian exile with Zerubbabel about 537 B.C. (Ezra 2:32). **2.** Head of one course of priests appointed under David's leadership (1 Chron. 24:8; cp. Ezra 2:39; Neh. 12:15). Some members of this clan agreed under Ezra's leadership to divorce their foreign wives to protect the people from the temptation of false worship (Ezra 10:21). **3.** Another Israelite clan with members having to divorce foreign wives under Ezra (Ezra 10:31). The clan name may have come from an original ancestor but more likely from the town of residence— Charim, eight miles northeast of Joppa. One of these clan members helped Nehemiah build the Jerusalem wall (Neh. 3:11). **4.** Priest who signed Nehemiah's covenant to obey God's law (Neh. 10:5). **5.** Clan leader who signed Nehemiah's covenant (Neh. 10:27).

HARIPH (Här´ ĭph) Personal name meaning "sharp" or "fresh." **1.** Israelite clan whose members accompanied Zerubbabel in returning from Babylonian exile about 537 B.C. (Neh. 7:24). **2.** Leader of people who signed Nehemiah's covenant to obey God's law (Neh. 10:19).

HARLOT A prostitute. The most famous harlot in the Bible is Rahab of Jericho, who saved the Israelite spies sent by Joshua to scout out the promised land (Josh. 2). Israel spared her and her family when they conquered and destroyed Jericho. She continued to dwell with the Israelites (Josh. 6:23-25). She is listed in the genealogy of Jesus (Matt. 1:5). Her action on behalf of the Israelite spies won her a place in the roll call of the faithful (Heb. 11:31; cp. James 2:25).

The Bible gives few details of the ways in which harlots like Rahab practiced their trade. Evidently, harlots might solicit along the roadside (Gen. 38:14-15). Brothels, which often served as taverns and inns, were also known in the ancient Near East. Rahab's house may have been one (Josh. 2:1). It is possible that the prostitute had a distinctive mark on her forehead (Jer. 3:3) and breasts (Hos. 2:2). She might attract attention by her clothing, jewelry, and makeup (Jer. 4:30; Ezek. 23:40; Rev. 17:4). Flattering with words (Prov. 2:16) and making sweet music (Isa. 23:16) might be used to lure or soothe a client. Her payment might be in money, or it could be in jewelry (Ezek. 23:42) or other items of value (Gen. 38:15-18; cp. Luke 15:30).

Although harlots were considered socially inferior, they did have legal rights, as is evident from the incident recorded in 1 Kings 3:16-22. See *Fornication; Prostitution*.   *Wilda W. Morris*

HARMON (Här´ mon) Place-name of uncertain meaning in Amos 4:3 as translated by NRSV, NASB, NIV. KJV reads "palace," changing the first letter of the Hebrew word to a common Hebrew noun for royal fortresses. TEV does not translate the final Hebrew word, saying it is unclear. REB changes two Hebrew letters slightly to translate, "dunghill." The earliest Greek translation read "Mount Rimmon." Some Bible students change the first letter slightly to read "Mount Hermon." If Harmon, the unchanged Hebrew text, is read, we know nothing of the place meant. Whatever the precise reading of the original, Amos' intention was to describe the drastic fate waiting the sinful women of Samaria, a fate using terminology connected with slaughter of animals and exile.

HARMONY OF THE GOSPELS Arrangement of the Gospels in parallel columns for the purpose of studying their similarities and differences. Andreas Osiander (1498–1552), a German Bible scholar of the Protestant Reformation, was the first person to use the phrase "harmony of the

Gospels" for a parallel organization of Gospel texts which he designed. By choosing a musical term as a metaphor for his columnar arrangement, Osiander likened the total picture of Jesus supplied by all four Gospels to the sound of several musical notes being played together in one chord. A harmony of the Gospels may also be called a synopsis or a parallel of the Gospels.

History of Harmonies While the term "harmony of the Gospels" was not used until the sixteenth century, Bible scholars began efforts to compare and harmonize the four accounts of Jesus as early as the second century. At that time, Tatian, a Christian from Syria, compiled the four Gospels into a single paraphrased narrative called the *Diatessaron*. All we know about Tatian's work is from references to it by other writers.

The *Diatessaron* represents one approach to harmonizing the Gospels: the weaving together of material from the Gospels to present one continuous narrative of Jesus' life. Several biblical scholars in the past 200 years have attempted similar works.

Few contemporary scholars give credence to attempts to "harmonize" either the texts or the information contained in the Gospels into one, exhaustive record of Jesus. Rather, they recognize the differences and compare the variations between the Gospels and use their findings as an aid for interpretation. The first great work in this second approach to harmonizing the Gospels was done by Amonnius of Alexandria in the third century. Ammonius took the text of Matthew and wrote beside the text in parallel columns any passages from the other three Gospels that corresponded to them. Consequently, Ammonius' work only showed the relationship between Matthew and the other three Gospels. Any parallels that existed independently among the other three were ignored. In the fourth century the church historian Eusebius developed a cross-reference system which provided a way to locate and study a passage which had parallels in any of the other Gospels.

J. J. Griesbach, another German, made one of the most significant contributions to this field when he produced his *Synopse*, a parallel arrangement of the texts of the first three Gospels, in 1776. Griesbach derived his title from the Greek word that means "to view at the same time," and consequently gave Matthew, Mark, and Luke the designation "Synoptic Gospels" because of their similar perspective (in contrast to John) on the life of Jesus. Griesbach's work still serves as the basic model for scholars who make comparisons between the Gospels in order to aid their interpretation of a given text.

Need for Comparative Study Even the most casual reading of the NT reveals the need and helpfulness of a comparative study of Matthew, Mark, and Luke. Note the following: 1. Some of the material contained in one Gospel is repeated almost word for word in one or both of the other Gospels (the story of Jesus' disciples plucking grain on the Sabbath, Mark 2:23-27, Matt. 12:1-8; Luke 6:1-5). 2. Some material, part of which appears vital to the record of Jesus' teaching, is included in only one Gospel (the parable of the prodigal son, Luke 15:11-32).

The Synoptic Problem As noted above, scholars have long noted the particular similarities that abound between Matthew, Mark, and Luke. In all three Gospels: 1. The appearance of John the Baptist, Jesus' baptism and temptation, and the initiation of Jesus' public ministry are linked together. 2. Jesus' ministry is confined to Galilee until He attended the Passover celebration in Jerusalem where He was crucified. 3. The story ends with His crucifixion and resurrection.

In addition to the rough similarity in their plots and similar points of view, the three Gospels exhibit an undeniable interrelatedness with respect to actual content: Luke contains 50 percent of the substance of Mark's verses, while Matthew contains a full 90 percent of Mark. Yet, for all these similarities, the three Gospels also possess significant differences. Scholars have labeled the issues surrounding this question "the synoptic problem."

An Early Solution One of the earliest and most influential answers to the synoptic problem was offered by Augustine (A.D. 354–430). He decided that Matthew wrote first and that Mark produced his Gospel by abridging what Matthew had written. Luke was thought to be dependent on both of them. Augustine's position was the orthodox view for over 1,400 years.

Later Solutions During the 1800's advances were made in archaeology and the study of ancient languages. New methods were introduced to biblical studies. These changes produced several fresh solutions to the synoptic problem.

The first "modern" solution focused on the hypothesis of a single, original Gospel which is now lost to us. Some scholars believed it may have been an orally transmitted gospel that had become formalized through constant repetition, while others believed it was an actual document. In either case, those who believed this hypothesis assumed Matthew, Mark, and Luke individually selected material from this Gospel as they wrote their accounts.

Other solutions to the problem centered on the belief that the gospel writers used two documents. Reversing the established view that Matthew was written first, proponents of the two document theory concluded that Mark was actually the first Gospel and that the other two Synoptic Gospels were dependent upon Mark. Because of the similarities between teaching passages contained in both Matthew and Luke, these scholars also theorized that Matthew and Luke both had one other source, a collection of Jesus' teachings.

The Four-Document Hypothesis In the early part of the 20th century, B. H. Streeter, a British scholar, proposed the four-document theory as a solution to the synoptic problem. Streeter agreed with the two-document theory to a point but thought it failed to go far enough in explaining the existence of material that was exclusive to either Matthew or Luke. Therefore, Streeter offered the hypothesis that the writers of the Synoptic Gospels used a total of four documents as sources for their works.

a. The Priority of Mark Like the proponents of the two-document theory, Streeter believed Mark was written first and served as a source for both Matthew and Luke. Several facts led to this belief. First, all three Gospels usually agree on the order in which they arrange their material. However, when they do disagree, Matthew and Mark frequently agree compared to Luke, or Luke and Mark will agree compared to Matthew. Matthew and Luke hardly ever agree compared to Mark. The same is true in word usage and sentence structure. Mark often agrees with Matthew or Luke against the other, but Matthew and Luke rarely agree against Mark. These two facts would indicate that the other writers used Mark. A third piece of evidence indicating the priority of Mark is that statements in Mark which could offend or perplex readers are either omitted or presented in a less provocative form by the other two Synoptics (cp. Mark 4:38 with Matt. 8:25 and Luke 8:24). Streeter believed that when taken together, these three facts could

only lead to the conclusion that Mark was written first and used by Matthew and Luke.

b. The Existence of "Q" Streeter also agreed with the proponents of the two-document theory that Matthew and Luke used a common source other than Mark. German scholars gave this source the name "Q" from the German *Quelle*, which means "source." Its content can only be deduced by comparing passages common to Matthew and Luke but absent from Mark. Scholars agree that "Q" was primarily a collection of Jesus' teachings with little narrative and no mention of the crucifixion and resurrection. The most significant contribution of "Q" is the Sermon on the Mount (Matt. 5–7 and Luke 6:20-49).

c. The "M" Source Streeter believed Matthew had access to a body of material unknown to (or at least unused by) Mark and Luke. This source derives its name "M" from the initial for Matthew. Because Matthew's infancy story differs from Luke, it is considered part of the material contained in this source. "M" also contained many OT proof texts related to Jesus' role as Messiah.

d. The "L" Source The fourth and final source in the four-document hypothesis is believed to contain the material exclusive to Luke. This source contained at least an infancy story and many parables. The stories of the good Samaritan and the prodigal son are a part of this "L" source.

The Place of Inspiration Many people believe the discussion of "sources" used by the Gospel writers impinges on the inspiration of the Scriptures. If Matthew, Mark, and Luke used other documents to write their Gospels, does God still have a place in their authorship? Careful thought will reveal that "sources" and inspiration are not mutually exclusive. Old Testament writers clearly show they used written sources (Josh. 10:13; 2 Sam. 1:18; 1 Kings 11:41; 2 Chron. 9:29).

Luke says, "Since many have undertaken to compile a narrative about the events that have been fulfilled among us, just as the original eyewitnesses and servants of the word handed them down to us, it also seemed good to me, having carefully investigated everything from the first, to write to you in orderly sequence" (Luke 1:1-3 HCSB). Luke made an important admission in this statement: he indicated knowledge of other accounts of Jesus' life and message. No known theory of inspiration violates a person's humanity to the point of negating his or her memory. Therefore, the gospel authored by Luke would certainly have had something in common with the sources known to him. Additionally, no theory of inspiration states that the human authors of biblical material used information or words which, until the precise moment of writing, had been entirely unknown to the writer. To assume that inspiration cannot involve the process of helping a human being to recognize divine truth and to shape that truth into the specific message God wants communicated is to limit the abilities of God's Spirit. Inspiration of both Testaments included God's leading writers to proper sources and directing in the use of the sources.

Summary While most contemporary scholars hold to the four-document theory (or a theory very similar to it), one must recognize any solution to the synoptic problem is a theory and not a proven fact. Many Bible students today are returning to the view that Matthew was written first. It must be admitted that many of the answers we desire about the origins of the Gospels are not available to us. Therefore, some modern questioners will find themselves extremely frustrated when they expect scientifically precise answers about documents, the original purpose of which was to be religiously reliable about the exciting good news from God through Jesus Christ. We can trust and obey the gospels without having the answer to every question about their origins and relationships.

P. Joel Snider

HARNEPHER (Här´ nə phēr) Egyptian personal name meaning "Horus (god) is good." Member of tribe of Asher (1 Chron. 7:36).

HARNESS KJV translation of a term meaning breastplate (1 Kings 22:34; 2 Chron. 18:33) or weapons (2 Chron. 9:24), where RSV translation "myrrh" and REB "perfumes" reflect a different Hebrew text, changed to "weaponry" in NRSV. See *Arms and Armor.*

HAROD (Hā´ rŏd) Place-name meaning "quake," "terror," or "intermittent spring." Place where God led Gideon to test his troops to reduce their numbers before fighting Midian (Judg. 7:1). It is modern Ain Jalud near Gilboa, halfway between Affulah and Beth-shean. It is about two miles east-southeast of Jezreel. It was home for two of David's heroes (2 Sam. 23:25), though the parallel text in 1 Chron. 11:27 reads "Harorite," representing a copyist's confusion of two letters similar in appearance. The "fountain" of 1 Sam. 29:1 was probably Harod. Some Bible students see a reference to Judg. 7:1 in Ps. 83:10 and make a slight change in the Hebrew text to read "Harod" instead of "En-dor" (cp. REB).

HARODITE (Hā´ rŏd īt) Citizen of Harod. See *Harod.*

HAROEH (Hȧ rō´ ĕh) Personal name meaning "the seer." Descendant of Caleb in tribe of Judah (1 Chron. 2:52). The same person is apparently called Reaiah in 1 Chron. 4:2, an easy change to make in copying Hebrew and probably the original name. As other names in the list, this may represent a place-name as well as a personal name.

HARORITE (Hā´ rō rīt) Copyist's spelling of Harodite (1 Chron. 11:27). See *Harod.*

HAROSHETH (Hȧ rō´ shĕth) Place-name meaning "forest land." First part of compound Hebrew place-name Harosheth-hagoiim, meaning Harosheth of the Gentiles (KJV, REB, TEV) or nations. Home of Sisera, captain of the army of Jabin of Hazor (Judg. 4:2). He mustered his troops there and marched them to the river Kishon to face Barak and Deborah (v. 13). Barak chased the army back to Harosheth and killed them there (v. 16). It may be the same as Muhrashti of the Amarna letters. Its location is debated, some favoring Tell el-Ama at the foot of Mount Carmel about nine miles south of Haifa near the Arab village of Haritiyeh. Others would see Haroseth as a common noun meaning "woods" and locate it in the woods or forests of Galilee, using some evidence from the earliest Greek translation. This view would read Josh. 12:23 as "king of Goiim in Galilee" (TEV, NRSV), and equate the king with the ruler of the Galilean forests.

HAROSHETH HAGGOYIM (Hȧ rō´ shĕth Hȧg gôi´ ĭm) (NIV) See *Harosheth.*

HAROSHETH-HAGOIIM (Hȧ rō´ shĕth-hȧ gôi´ ĭm) Full Hebrew name of Harosheth. See *Harosheth.*

HAROSHETH-HAGOYIM (Hä rō´ shĕth-hä gôi´ ĭm) (NASB) See *Harosheth*.

HARP See *Music, Instruments, Dancing*.

HARPOON Barbed (KJV) spear or javelin used in hunting large fish or whales, mentioned as an inadequate weapon for catching the sea monster Leviathan (Job. 41:7) and thus showing God's sovereignty over human inadequacy.

HARROW To pulverize and smooth the soil by means of a harrow, a cultivating implement with spikes, spring teeth, or disks. The modern harrow was unknown in ancient Egypt. The biblical references to harrowing or breaking clods (Job 39:10; Isa. 28:24; Hos. 10:11) distinguish this process from plowing. Perhaps the dragging of branches to smooth the soil over seed is what is intended. The NIV replaced harrow with "till" (Job 39:10) and with "break up the ground" (Hos. 10:11). Modern translations replace the harrow of the KJV with iron picks (NIV, NRSV); iron hoes (TEV), or sharp iron instruments (NASB) at 2 Sam. 12:31; 1 Chron. 20:3. See *Agriculture; Tools*.

HARSHA (Här´ shä) Personal name meaning "unable to talk, silent" or "magician, sorcerer." Clan of temple servants who returned with Zerubbabel from Babylonian exile about 537 B.C. (Ezra 2:52). Tel-Harsha (Ezra 2:59 NASB) was one of the places where Jewish exiles lived in Babylon, so that the clan could have taken its name from the Babylonian home or given its name to the Babylonian home.

HART Adult male deer (Ps. 42:1; Isa. 35:6). See *Deer*.

HARUM (Hä´ rŭm) Personal name meaning "the exalted." A member of the tribe of Judah (1 Chron. 4:8).

HARUMAPH (Hä rū´ măph) Personal name meaning "split nose." Father of worker who helped Nehemiah rebuild the wall of Jerusalem (Neh. 3:10).

HARUPHITE (Hä rū´ phīt) Clan or place-name meaning "early" or "reproach." Reading of early Hebrew scribes in 1 Chron. 12:5. Written Hebrew text has Hariphites. Haruph is otherwise unknown. It could be a clan or a town from which Shephatiah came. Hariphite would refer to citizen or descendent of Hariph. See *Hariph*.

HARUZ (Hä´ rŭz) Personal name meaning "gold" or "industrious." Maternal grandfather of Amon, king of Judah (642-640 B.C.). He was from Jotbah (2 Kings 21:19). The home may not be in Judah and thus represent foreign influence on the king. See *Jotbah*.

HARVEST Festive occasion for gathering the crops, usually marked by important religious festivals. Among the more important crops grown were wheat, grapes, and olives. Other crops included barley, flax, and various vegetables and fruits. Crops that had been planted were harvested at various times. Olives were harvested between mid-September to mid-November by beating the trees with long sticks (Deut. 24:20; Isa. 17:6). Flax was gathered in the spring by cutting it off near the ground and then laying the stalks out to dry (Josh. 2:6). Barley was harvested from April to May; wheat from May to June; and summer fruits from August to September. The average harvesting period was set at a period of seven weeks (Lev. 23:15; Deut. 16:9). All members of the family were expected to work during harvest (Prov. 10:5; 20:4). Significant events were connected with harvest times (Exod. 34:18-20; Deut. 16:13-16; Josh. 3:15; 1 Sam. 16:13). Harvest time became the occasion for joyful festivals (Exod. 34:22; Isa. 9:3).

Several laws governed the harvest. Part of the crop was not harvested (Lev. 19:9) out of concern for the poor. The firstfruits of the harvest were presented as an offering to God (Lev. 23:10).

The OT provides several figurative uses of harvest. A destroyed harvest represented affliction (Job 5:5; Isa. 16:9). The "time of harvest" sometimes represented the day of destruction (Jer. 51:33; Joel 3:13). "Harvest is past" meant the appointed time was gone (Jer. 8:20).

Jesus spoke often of the harvest in connection with the harvesting of souls (Matt. 9:37; Mark 4:29; John 4:35). In the parable of the tares, Jesus related harvest to the end of the world (Matt. 13:30-39). The rhythm of harvest time (sowing and reaping) provided an illustration of a spiritual truth (Gal. 6:7-8). See *Agriculture; Festivals*.   *Gary Hardin*

H

HARVEST, FEAST OF Alternate name for Pentecost or the Feast of Weeks (Exod. 23:16; 34:22). See *Festivals; Pentecost.*

HARVESTER See *Occupations and Professions.*

HASADIAH (Hăs á dī´ a) Personal name meaning "Yahweh is gracious." Son of Zerubbabel and descendant of David (1 Chron. 3:20). See *Zerubbabel.*

HASENUAH (Hăs ə nū´ a) (KJV, 1 Chron. 9:7) See *Hassenuah.*

HASHABIAH (Hăsh á bī´ a) Personal name meaning "Yahweh has reckoned or imputed," appearing in longer and shorter Hebrew spellings. **1.** Ancestor of Merari among the Levite leaders (1 Chron. 6:45). **2.** Another member of the Merari priesthood (1 Chron. 9:14; Neh. 11:15). **3.** Temple musician and Levite under David (1 Chron. 25:1,3,6,19). **4.** Family of Levites from Hebron given authority to carry out God's business in the service of the king west of the Jordan (1 Chron. 26:30). This shows the close connection between temple and palace, religious and political activity in Israel. **5.** Leader of the tribe of Levi possibly connected with taking the ill-fated census under David (1 Chron. 27:17). He may be identical with 4. above. **6.** Levite leader under Josiah who provided animals for the Levites to celebrate Passover (2 Chron. 35:9). **7.** Levite leader Ezra conscripted to return to Jerusalem with him from Babylonian exile about 458 B.C. (Ezra 8:19). He shared responsibility for transporting temple treasures on the journey (vv. 24-30; cp. Neh. 12:24). **8.** Israelite called to divorce his foreign wife to protect the people from temptation to false worship according to Greek manuscripts of Ezra 10:25 (NRSV). **9.** Levite with administrative duties over city of Keilah who joined Nehemiah in repairing wall of Jerusalem (Neh. 3:17). He is probably the same one as the signer of Nehemiah's covenant to obey God's law (Neh. 10:11) and could be the same as both 7. and 8. above. **10.** Ancestor of chief Levite in Jerusalem in Nehemiah's day (Neh. 11:22). **11.** Priest one generation after the return from exile (Neh. 12:21).

HASHABNAH (Hă shăb´ nah) Personal name, perhaps meaning "reckoning." Signer of Nehemiah's covenant to obey God's law (Neh. 10:25).

HASHABNEIAH (Hăsh áb nē´ a) or **HASHAB-NIAH** (Hăsh áb nī´ a) (KJV) Personal name meaning "Yahweh has imputed to me." **1.** Father of man who helped Nehemiah repair the Jerusalem wall (Neh. 3:10). **2.** Levite who led worship in Nehemiah's covenant ceremony in which people reaffirmed their commitment to obey God (Neh. 9:5).

HASHBADANA (Hăsh bá dā´ na) (KJV) or **HASHBADDANAH** (Hašh băd´ dá na) Personal name of uncertain meaning. A member of the community leaders who stood with Ezra as he read the law to the people (Neh. 8:4). Some early translations provide evidence for a copyist having joined two names—Hashub and Baddanah into one. The precise function of these leaders is not stated.

HASHEM (Hā´ shĕm) Personal name meaning "the name." Father of some of David's heroes (1 Chron. 11:34) and said to be a Gizonite. The parallel passage in 2 Sam. 23:32 may preserve the original spelling: Jashen. See *Gizonite; Jashen.*

HASHMONAH (Hăsh mō´ na) Place-name of uncertain meaning. A station in Israel's wilderness journey (Num. 33:29-30). Some Bible students identify it with Azmon (Num. 34:4). See *Azmon.*

HASHUB (Hā´ shŭb) (KJV, Neh. 3:11,23; 10:23; 11:15) See *Hasshub.*

HASHUBAH (Hă shū´ ba) Personal name meaning "highly treasured." Son of Zerubbabel in the royal line of David (1 Chron. 3:20).

HASHUM (Hā´ shŭm) **1.** Personal name meaning "flat-nosed." Clan leader of group returning from Babylonian exile with Zerubbabel about 537 B.C. Some clan members divorced their foreign wives under Ezra's leadership to rid the community of religious temptations (Ezra 10:33). **2.** Community leader who stood with Ezra while he read the law to the people (Neh. 8:4). He also signed Nehemiah's covenant to obey God (Neh. 10:18).

HASHUPHA (KJV) See *Hasupha.*

H

HASIDEANS (Hăs ə dē´ ănz) Militant, religious community active in the Maccabean revolt (begun 168 B.C.). The group's name derived from the OT concept of the Hasidim, the "saints" or "faithful." The Pharisees and the Essenes likely derived from different streams of the Hasidean movement. See *Intertestamental History and Literature; Jewish Parties in the New Testament.*

HASMONEAN (Hăz mō nē´ an) Name given to the dynasty that ruled ancient Judea for almost a century, from the Maccabean wars (that ended in approximately 145 B.C.) until Roman occupation of ancient Palestine in 63 B.C. See *Intertestamental History and Literature.*

HASRAH (Hăz´ rah) Personal name, perhaps meaning "lack." See *Harhas.*

HASSENAAH (Hăs sə nā´ a) Personal or place-name, perhaps meaning "the hated one." Apparently the same name without "h," the Hebrew definite article, appears as Senaah, a clan who returned with Zerubbabel from Babylonian exile about 537 B.C. (Ezra 2:35). Members of the clan

helped Nehemiah rebuild the Fish Gate of the Jerusalem wall (Neh. 3:3).

HASSENUAH (Hăs sə nū´ a) Personal name meaning "the hated one." Leader in tribe of Benjamin (1 Chron. 9:7). The name without the Hebrew article "h" appears in Neh. 11:9 as father of a leader in postexilic Jerusalem from the tribe of Benjamin.

HASSHUB (Hăs´ shŭb) Personal name meaning "one to whom He has imputed or reckoned." **1.** Man who helped Nehemiah repair the Jerusalem wall (Neh. 3:23). He was apparently a Levite at the temple (1 Chron. 9:14; Neh. 11:15). **2.** Man who helped repair the bakers' ovens and apparently two parts of the wall, Neh. 3:23 describing the "other piece" or a "second section" (REB). He may be the one who signed Nehemiah's covenant to obey God (Neh. 10:23).

HASSOPHERETH (Hăs sō´ phə rĕth) Personal name meaning "the scribe" or "scribal office." Ezra 2:55 indicates it was either a family name of persons returning from Babylonian exile with

THE HASMONEAN DYNASTY

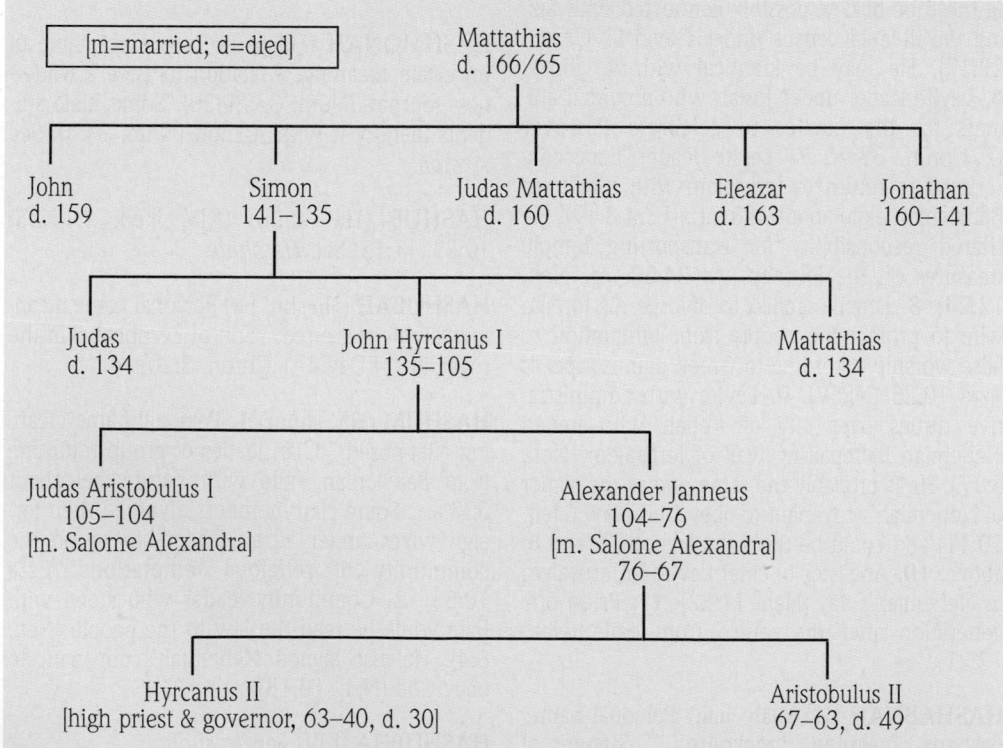

Zerubbabel about 537 B.C. or a guild of scribes who returned. The parallel passage (Neh. 7:57) omits "h," the Hebrew article, from the name, possibly indicating it was a guild.

HASUPHA (Hả sū´ phả) Personal name meaning "quick." A clan returning with Zerubbabel from Babylonian exile about 537 B.C. (Ezra 2:43).

HAT Article of clothing for the head (Dan. 3:21). The root word is similar to the Akkadian term for a helmet or cap. The NASB rendered the term "cap"; NIV, "turban." See *Cloth, Clothing.*

HATACH (Hả´ tăk) Personal name perhaps of Persian origin meaning "runner." A eunuch serving King Ahasuerus in the Persian court that the king assigned as Esther's servant (Esther 4:5-6). Esther assigned him to find why Mordecai was troubled, thus initiating Esther's appearances before the king to save her people.

HATE, HATRED Strong negative reaction; a feeling toward someone considered an enemy, possibly indicating volatile hostility.
Hatred of Other People Hatred of other people is a common response in human relations. Conflict, jealousy, and envy often result in animosity, separation, revenge, and even murder (Gen. 26:27; 27:41; Judg. 11:7; 2 Sam. 13:15,22). Some Hebrew laws explicitly deal with hatred or favoritism (Deut. 19:11-13; 21:15-17; 22:13-21).

Hatred of other people is frequently condemned, and love toward enemies is encouraged (Lev. 19:17; Matt. 5:43-44). Hatred characterizes the old age and the sinful life (Gal. 5:19-21; Titus 3:3; 1 John 2:9,11). Although Jesus cited the attitude of hating enemies (Matt. 5:43), the OT does not give an explicit command like this. The Dead Sea Scrolls, however, indicate that the Essenes at Qumran cultivated hatred for enemies, but they discouraged retaliation. Jesus stressed loving our enemies and doing good to those who hate us (Luke 6:27).

Believers can experience or practice hatred in certain contexts. For example, they are to hate whatever opposes God. Not a malicious attitude, this hate reflects agreement with God's opposition to evil (Pss. 97:10; 139:19-22; Prov. 8:13; 13:5; Amos 5:15). Although some of the psalms may sound vindictive, they leave punishment of the wicked to God's prerogative.

Jesus' disciples would have to hate their families to follow him (Luke 14:26). Hate here refers not to emotional hostility but to the conscious establishment of priorities. Hate means to love family less than one loves Jesus (Matt. 10:37). Similarly, one should hate one's personal life to gain eternal life (John 12:26).

Disciples can expect to be hated, just as Jesus was hated by the world (John 15:18-24; 17:14; 1 John 3:13). Hatred and persecution will also occur near the end of time (Matt. 24:9). Jesus encouraged His disciples to rejoice at this opposition (Luke 6:22-23).
Hatred of God People sometimes hate God (Pss. 68:1; 81:15) and His people. They are enemies of God who stubbornly rebel at His will and will be punished.
Divine Hatred Although God is love (1 John 4:8), some texts point to divine hatred. A holy, jealous God is displeased with human sin. For example, God hates pagan idolatry (Deut. 12:31) as well as hypocritical Hebrew worship (Isa. 1:14; Amos 5:21). God hates sin (Prov. 6:16-19; 8:13; Mal. 2:16), but He desires the sinner's repentance (Ezek. 18:32). Some texts imply God's hate is directed primarily to sinful actions rather than to sinful persons (Heb. 1:9; Rev. 2:6).

God's hate is not the vindictive, emotional hate often felt by human beings but is a strong moral reaction against sin. (God's attitude toward Edom in Mal. 1:3-4). In some cases the term "love" when contrasted with "hate" can mean "prefer" (e.g. Gen. 25:28; 29:30-33; Deut. 21:15-16), and "hate" can mean to "slight" or "think less of" (Gen. 39:30-31; Deut. 22:13; 24:3; Luke 14:26; 16:13). The terms "love" and "hate" can also express divine freedom in election (Mal. 1:2-5; Rom. 9:13). See *Enemy; Love; Retaliation; Revenge; Wrath.*

Warren McWilliams

HATHACH (Hả´ thăk) Modern translations' spelling of Hatach. See *Hatach.*

HATHATH (Hả´ thăth) Personal name meaning "weakling." Son of Othniel in the family line of Caleb and the tribe of Judah (1 Chron. 4:13).

HATIPHA (Hả tī´ phả) Aramaic personal name meaning "robbed." Clan who returned from Babylonian exile with Zerubbabel about 537 B.C. (Ezra 2:54).

HATITA (Hă tī′ tà) Aramaic personal name meaning "bored a hole" or "soft" or "festival." Clan of temple gatekeepers who returned from Babylonian exile with Zerubbabel about 537 B.C. (Ezra 2:42).

HATTIL (Hăt′ tĭl) Personal name meaning "talkative, babbling" or "long eared." Clan of temple servants who returned from Babylonian exile with Zerubbabel about 537 B.C. (Ezra 2:57).

HATTUSH (Hăt′ tŭsh) Personal name of uncertain meaning. **1.** Man in David's royal line after the return from exile (1 Chron. 3:22). He returned from Babylonian exile with Ezra about 458 B.C. (Ezra 8:2). His high place in the list may indicate that Ezra and his followers still placed hope in a Davidic monarch. **2.** Priest who signed Nehemiah's covenant to obey God (Neh. 10:4). It is not impossible that this was the same as 1. above. **3.** Priest who returned from Babylonian exile with Zerubbabel about 537 B.C. (Neh. 12:2). **4.** Man who helped Nehemiah repair the Jerusalem walls (Neh. 3:10).

HAURAN (Haw′ răn) Geographical name of uncertain meaning. One of four or five provinces through which the Assyrians and their successors administered Syria. Its northern boundary was Damascus; eastern, the Jebel Druze; western, the Golan Heights; and Southern, the Yarmuk River. It was a battleground among Assyria, Syria, Israel, Judah, and Egypt, appearing in Egyptian and Assyrian records. Ezekiel promised it would be in the restored promised land (Ezek. 47:16,18). The Maccabeans did control it for a time. The region was noted for its black basalt rocks, volcanoes, and rich harvests of grain.

HAVEN Place that offers safe anchorage for ships (Gen. 49:13; Ps. 107:30; Isa. 23:10 NRSV, NIV). See *Fair Havens*.

HAVILAH (Hăv′ ĭ la) Place-name meaning "sandy stretch." Biblical name for the sand-dominated region to the south covering what we call Arabia without necessarily designating a particular geographical or political area. The river from Eden is described as flowing "around the whole land of Havilah" (Gen. 2:11 NASB), a land noted for gold and other precious stones. The Table of Nations lists Havilah as a son of Cush or Ethiopia, showing Havilah's political ties (Gen. 10:7). Some Bible students think the name is preserved in modern Haulan in southwest Arabia. Havilah is also mentioned in the Table of Nations as a son of Joktan, the grandson of Shem (Gen. 10:29). The descendants of Ishmael, Abraham's son, lived in Havilah (Gen. 25:18). Saul defeated the Amalekites from "Havilah as you go to Shur, which is east of Egypt" (1 Sam. 15:7 NASB), a description whose meaning Bible students continue to debate. Some seek to change the Hebrew text slightly. Others look for a Havilah farther north and west than Havilah is usually located. Others talk of the fluid boundaries of the area. Thus Havilah refers to an area or areas in Arabia, but the precise location is not known.

HAVOTH-JAIR (Hā vŏth-Jā′ ĭr) or **HAVVOTH-JAIR** Place-name meaning "tents of Jair." Villages in Gilead east of the Jordan that Jair, son of Manasseh, captured (Num. 32:41). Deuteronomy 3:14 says Jair took the region of Argob and named Bashan after himself—Havvoth-jair. This passage equates land of Rephaim, Argod, Bashan, and Havvoth-jair (cp. Josh. 13:30; 1 Kings 4:13). Judges 10:3-4 concern Jair the Gileadite, a judge in Israel for 22 years. He "had thirty sons that rode on thirty donkeys; and they had thirty cities; which are in the land of Gilead, and are called Havvoth-jair to this day." First Chronicles 2:18-23 describes the genealogy of Caleb and his father Hezron. In late life Hezron married the daughter of Machir, the father of Gilead. She bore Segub, the father of Jair, who had 23 towns in Gilead. "But Geshur and Aram took from them Havvoth-jair, Kenath and its villages, sixty towns. All these were descendants of Machir, father of Gilead" (1 Chron. 2:23 NRSV). Apparently a group of villages east of the Jordan, perhaps varying in number at different times, were called Havvoth-jair. Israel laid claim to them and connected the name to that of different Israelite heroes at various time periods.

HAWK Bird of prey considered unclean (Lev. 11:16; Deut. 14:15) and not to be eaten. God reminded Job that He created the hawk to soar (Job 39:26). See *Birds*.

HAZAEL (Hăz′ ā ĕl) Personal name meaning "El (a god) is seeing." A powerful and ruthless king of the Syrian city-state of Damascus during the last half of the eighth century B.C. While an officer of Ben-hadad, king of Syria, Hazael was sent to Elisha the prophet to inquire about the king's health (2 Kings 8:7-15). Elisha prophesied Hazael's future kingship and his cruel treatment of Israel. Hazael returned to his master, murdered him, and became king of Syria in 841 B.C. These events had also been forecast by the Prophet Elijah (1 Kings 19:15-17). Soon after becoming king of Syria, Hazael joined in combat against both Ahaziah, king of Judah, and Joram, king of Israel (2 Kings 8:28-29; 9:14-15). He eventually extended his rule into both the Northern Kingdom of Israel (2 Kings 10:32-33; 13:1-9,22) and the Southern Kingdom of Judah (2 Kings 12:17-18; 2 Chron. 24:23-24). He was prevented from capturing the holy city of Jerusalem only by being allowed to carry off everything that was portable and of value in the city and the temple. The memory of Syria's ruthless power under Hazael was etched in Israel's memory. Half a century later, Amos used his name as a symbol of Syria's oppression that would be judged by God (Amos 1:4). See *Damascus; Syria.*   *Daniel B. McGee*

HAZAIAH (Há zī´ a) Personal name meaning "Yahweh sees." Member of tribe of Judah and ancestor of Jerusalem descendants in Nehemiah's day (Neh. 11:5).

HAZAR (Hā´ zär) Hebrew term meaning a court or enclosed space. *Hazar* is a common element in place-names: Hazar-enan (Ezek. 47:17); Hazar-gaddah (Josh. 15:27); Hazar-shual (Josh. 15:28); Hazar-susah (Josh. 19:5). The place-names perhaps recall the pitching of tents or building of homes in a circle for protection, resulting in an enclosed space. Alternately, settlements bearing the name Hazar were enclosed with walls or other defenses (cp. Num. 13:28; Deut. 1:28). See *Cities and Urban Life.*

HAZAR-ADDAR (Hā zär-ăd´ där) Place-name meaning "threshing floor." Station on Israel's wilderness journey (Num. 34:4) near Kadesh, possibly Ain Qedesh. See *Addar; Kadesh.*

HAZAR-ENAN (Hā zär-ē´ nan) Place-name meaning "encampment of springs." Site marking northeastern border of promised land (Num. 34:9-10; Ezek. 47:17). Its exact location is not known, but some locate it at Qaryatein about 70 miles east-northeast of Damascus.

HAZAR-ENON (Hā zär-ē´ nŏn) Variant Hebrew spelling of Hazar-enan in Ezek. 47:17 and reflected in NRSV. TEV calls the place Enon City. See *Hazar-enan.*

HAZAR-GADDAH (Hā zär-găd´ da) Place-name meaning "village of good luck." Town in tribal territory of Judah of unknown location near Beersheba (Josh. 15:27).

HAZAR-HATTICON (Hā zär-hăt´ tĭ cŏn) Place-name meaning "middle village." Ezekiel named it as the border of the future Israel (47:16). Some Bible students think the original text read Hazorenan (Ezek. 47:17; 48:1 REB). The location is not known.

HAZAR-MAVETH (Hā zär-mā´ věth) Place-name meaning "encampment of death." Name in the Table of Nations for son of Joktan in the line of Eber and Shem (Gen. 10:26). It is the region of Hadramaut east of Yemen.

HAZAR-SHUAL (Hā zär shū´ ăl) Place-name meaning "encampment of the foxes." Town near Beersheba in tribal territory of Judah (Josh. 15:28) but allotted to tribe of Simeon (Josh. 19:3; 1 Chron. 4:28). Jews returning from exile in Babylon lived there (Neh. 11:27). It may be modern Khirbet el-Watan.

HAZAR-SUSAH (Hā zär-sū´ sa) or **HAZAR-SUSIM** (Hā zär-sū´ sĭm) Place-name meaning "encampment of a horse." Town in tribal allotment of Simeon (Josh. 19:5). As most towns of Simeon also appear in Judah's allotment (cp. 19:1), many Bible students think this is another name for Sansannah in Josh. 15:31. Instead of the feminine form Susah, 1 Chron. 4:31 has the plural form Susim. It may be located at Sabalat Abu Susein.

HAZAZON-TAMAR (Hăz á zŏn-tā´ már) Place-name meaning "grave dump with palms." Home of Amorites who fought eastern coalition led by Chedorlaomer (Gen. 14:7). Edom (NIV; TEV; NRSV; REB following one Hebrew manuscript; most manuscripts and early translations read "Aram," meaning Syria, as read by NASB; KSV) captured the city and then attacked Jehoshaphat of Judah (873-848 B.C.), the text noting that Hazazon-tamar was another name for Engedi (2 Chron. 20:2). Some Bible students think Hazazon-tamar was actually located six miles north of Engedi at Wadi Hasasa, while others point to Tamar in southern Judah, Kasr Ejuniyeh or Ain Kusb, 20 miles southwest of the Dead Sea. See *Engedi.*

HAZEL KJV translation of a term meaning "almond" rather than "hazelnut" (Gen. 30:37).

HAZELELPONI (Hăz ə lĕl pō´ nī) Personal name meaning "Overshadow my face." Daughter of Etam in the tribe of Judah (1 Chron. 4:3 NASB; NIV, TEV, REB, NRSV). KJV follows Hebrew text, which reads "these the father of Etam." Many Bible students think a copyist omitted something in Hebrew. They would restore the text to read "these were the sons of Hareph: the father of Etam" Since many of the other names in the list are names of towns (e.g., Penuel, Bethlehem), Hazeleponi may also represent a town name. If so, its location is not known.

HAZER-HATTICON (Hā zər-hăt´ tĭ cŏn) NASB, NIV, NRSV spelling of Hazar-hatticon.

HAZERIM (Hȧ zē´ rĭm) KJV interpretation and transliteration of Hebrew word meaning "villages" or "hamlets" in Deut. 2:23. Modern translations interpret as common noun meaning villages near Gaza. See *Gaza.*

HAZEROTH (Hȧ zē´ rŏth) Place-name meaning "villages" or "encampments." Wilderness station on Israel's journey from Egypt (Num. 11:35). There Aaron and Miriam challenged Moses' sole authority, using his Cushite wife as an excuse (Num. 12). God punished Miriam with a hated skin disease. Deuteronomy 1:1 uses Hazeroth as one focal point to locate Moses' speech to Israel. Some geographers would locate it at modern Ain Khadra, south of Ezion-geber. Some Bible students try to locate all the sites in Deut. 1:1 near Moab. If they are right, the Hazeroth mentioned there is different from the wilderness station.

HAZEZON-TAMAR (Hăz ə zŏn-tā´ mȧr) (KJV) See *Hazazon-tamar.*

HAZIEL (Hā´ zĭ ĕl) Personal name meaning "God saw." A leading Levite in the time of David (1 Chron. 23:9).

HAZO (Hā´ zō) Abbreviated form of personal name Haziel meaning "God saw." Son of Abra-

ham's brother Nahor (Gen. 22:22). The 12 sons of Nahor apparently represented a closely associated group of tribes. Some Bible students think Hazo represents the city of Hazu known from an Assyrian source and located at al-Hasa near the Arabian coast by Bahrein.

HAZOR (Hā´ zôr)   Place-name meaning "enclosed settlement." **1.** Hazor was located in upper Galilee on the site now known as Tell el-Qedah, ten miles north of the Sea of Galilee and five miles southwest of Lake Huleh. The site of Hazor is composed of a 30-acre upper tell or mound rising 40 meters above the surrounding plain and a 175-acre lower enclosure which was well fortified. These dimensions make Hazor the largest city in ancient Canaan. Estimates set the population at its height at over 40,000. The upper tell had 21 separate levels of occupation beginning between 2750 and 2500 B.C. and continuing down to the second century B.C. Canaanites occupied Hazor until Joshua destroyed it. The Israelites controlled it until 732 B.C. when the Assyrians captured the city. Hazor then served as a fortress for the various occupying powers until the time of the Maccabees. The lower enclosure had five levels of occupation beginning about 1750 B.C. and continuing until Joshua destroyed it. It was never rebuilt.

Hazor's location was strategic both economically and militarily. It overlooked the Via Maris, the major overland trade route from Egypt to the north and east, and thus became a major trading center. It is mentioned extensively in both Egyptian and Mesopotamian records in conjunction with the other major trading cities of the day. Hazor also overlooked the Huleh Valley, a critical defense point against armies invading from the north. Joshua 11:1-15; 12:19 relate how Jabin, king of Hazor, rallied the forces of the northern

Storehouses dating from the ninth century B.C. at ancient Hazor in Israel.

H

cities of Canaan against Joshua. Hazor was "the head of all these kingdoms" (Josh. 11:10 NASB), that is, it was the dominant city-state of the Canaanite kingdoms. Joshua defeated the Canaanite forces, slew the leaders, including Jabin, and burned the city of Hazor. Modern archaeology lends support to this biblical account. The size and location of the city of Hazor, as well as references to it in other ancient literature, would indicate that Hazor probably controlled a vast portion of Canaan. In his initial interpretation of the archaeological evidence, Yadin dated the destruction to ca. 1400 B.C. He later adjusted this date to the mid-13th century B.C., but Bimson has argued that there was no good reason for this adjustment, and the original interpretation is the correct one.

Hazor is next mentioned in Judg. 4, where another Jabin is king of Canaan ruling from Hazor (Jabin was a dynastic name, much like Pharaoh and Ben-Hadad were used for a succession of rulers). The biblical narrative indicates that Joshua destroyed the city, but it does not say that he rebuilt it and occupied it. It was allotted to Naphtali (Josh. 19:36). The Canaanite dynasty maintained or regained control with one or more kings called Jabin. In the account of Judg. 4,

Jabin's troops led by Sisera of Harosheth-hagoyim were routed by Deborah and Barak. First Kings 9:15 mentions that Solomon rebuilt the walls of Hazor, Megiddo, and Gezer. Excavations have discovered conclusive evidence to support this short portion of Scripture. Two layers of Israelite occupation of Hazor between the destruction of the Canaanite city by Joshua and the rebuilding of the city by Solomon show merely semi-nomadic Israelite encampments, evidenced by tent or hut foundation rings, cooking pits, and storage pits. Apparently, no formal city or fortifications existed during the time of the judges. The city was clearly rebuilt at the time of Solomon, evidenced by the characteristically Solomonic gate structures, that is, casemate walls and a six-chamber gatehouse (three on each side) with two square towers. Comparing the gates at Hazor with those at Gezer and Megiddo, Yadin found them to be identical in both design and dimension. The Solomonic city was much smaller than the Canaanite city. It only covered half of the upper tell.

Second Kings 15:29 records that Tiglath-pileser III, king of Assyria, captured Hazor and carried its people captive to Assyria. The evidence of this destruction is very great. No less

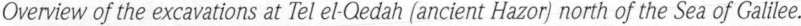

Overview of the excavations at Tel el-Qedah (ancient Hazor) north of the Sea of Galilee.

H

than three feet of ashes and rubble cover the ruins left by this destruction. Prior to the Assyrian invasion, Hazor had been greatly enlarged and strengthened by King Ahab of Israel in anticipation of the attack. The city had grown to fill the entire upper tell. Its fortifications had been strengthened and enlarged, and a special water shaft and tunnel 40 meters deep was dug down to the water table to bring the water supply inside the city. See *Conquest of Canaan.*

2. Town in tribal inheritance of Judah (Josh. 15:23), probably to be read with earliest Greek translation as Hazor-Ithnan. This may be modern el-Jebariyeh. **3.** Town in southern part of tribal inheritance of Judah, probably to be read as Hazor-Hadattah (Josh. 15:25) with most modern translations. This may be modern el-Hudeira near the Dead Sea's southern end. **4.** Town identified with Kerioth-hezron (Josh. 15:25). **5.** Town where part of tribe of Benjamin lived in time of Nehemiah (Neh. 11:33). This may be modern Khirbet Hazzur four miles north-northwest of Jerusalem. **6.** Name of "kingdoms" that Nebuchadnezzar of Babylon threatened (Jer. 49:28-33). Apparently, small nomadic settlements of Arab tribes are meant. Such settlements would still have rich treasures the Babylonian king coveted.   *John H. Brangenberg III*
and David K. Stabnow

HAZOR-HADDATTAH (Hā zôr-ha dăt´ ta) Place-name meaning "new Hazor." Town in tribal territory of Judah (Josh. 15:25). Its location is not known.

HAZZEBAIM (Hăz zē bā´ ĭm) See *Pochereth-hazzebaim.*

HAZZELELPONI (Hăz zə lel pō´ nī) Modern translations' spelling of Hazelelponi.

HAZZOBEBAH (Hă zō bē´ băh) NIV rendering of the name of the son of Coz (or Kos) and grandson of Helah (1 Chron. 4:8). Other English translations use the feminine name Zobebah.

HE Fifth letter of the Hebrew alphabet; it carries the numerical value five. In Judaism *he* is used as an abbreviation for the divine name Yahweh (Tetragrammaton). In some English versions he appears as a superscript to verses 33-40 of Ps. 119, each of which begins with this letter. See *Hebrew Language; Writing.*

HE ASS Male donkey. See *Ass.*

HEAD Literally, the uppermost part of the body, considered to be the seat of life but not of the intellect; and figuratively for first, top, or chief. The Jewish notion was that the heart was the center or seat of the intellect. "Head" meant the physical head of a person (Gen. 48:18; Mark 6:24) or of animals, such as a bull's head (Lev. 1:4). It was often used to represent the whole person (Acts 18:6). Achish made David "keeper of mine head" (KJV), that is, his bodyguard (1 Sam. 28:2).

"Head" was used frequently to refer to inanimate objects such as the summit of a mountain (Exod. 17:9) or the top of a building (Gen. 11:4). The word "head" often has the meaning of "source" or "beginning," that of rivers (Gen. 2:10), streets (Ezek. 16:25), or of periods of time (Judg. 7:19, translated here as "beginning").

In Ps. 118:22 "head of the corner"(KJV; HCSB, cornerstone) refers metaphorically to a king delivered by God when others had given him up (cp. Matt. 21:42; Acts 4:11; 1 Pet. 2:7, where it is used in reference to the rejection of Christ). "Head" designated one in authority in the sense of the foremost person. It can mean leader, chief, or prince (Isa. 9:15), and it can have the idea of first in a series (1 Chron. 12:9). Israel was the "head" (translated "chief") nation, God's firstborn (Jer. 31:7). Damascus was the "head" (capital) of Syria (Isa. 7:8). A husband is the "head of the wife" (Eph. 5:23).

A distinctive theological use of the word "head" was seen in the NT concept of the "headship" of Christ. Christ is the "head" (*kephale*) of His body the church; the church is His "bride" (Eph. 5:23-33, wife). In His role as "head," Christ enables the church to grow, knits her into a unity, nourishes her by caring for each member, and gives her strength to build herself up in love (Eph. 4:15-16). Not only is Christ "head" of the church, but also He is "head" of the universe as a whole (Eph. 1:22) and of every might and power (Col. 2:10). The divine influences on the world result in a series: God is the "head" of Christ; Christ is the "head" of man; man is the "head" of the woman, and as such he is to love and care for his wife as Christ does His church (Eph. 5:25-30). This theological use of the word may be an extension of the OT use of the word "head" for the leader of the tribe or community

H

or may be a reaction to early Gnostic tendencies. See *Gnosticism.*

Because the head was the seat of life, value was placed on it. Injury to it was a chief form of defeating an enemy (Ps. 68:21). As part of contemptuous insult, the soldiers struck Jesus' head with a reed and crowned Him with a crown of thorns (Mark 15:16-19). Decapitation was a further insult after the defeat. Herodias, through treachery and out of spite, had John the Baptist beheaded (Matt. 14:1-11). David cut off Goliath's head and brought it before Saul (1 Sam. 17:51). The Philistines cut off Saul's head (1 Sam. 31:9), and the sons of Rimmon cut off that of Ish-bosheth (2 Sam. 4:7). Attested to in many inscriptions and portrayed on several monuments, it was common for the Babylonians, Assyrians, and the Egyptians to cut off the heads of their dead enemies slain in battle.

Conversely, blessing comes upon the head (Gen. 49:26); and, therefore, hands are laid on it (Gen. 48:17). Anointing the head with oil symbolized prosperity and joy (Ps. 23:5; Heb. 1:9). In the service for ordination of priests and dedication to priestly service, the head of the high priest was anointed with oil (Exod. 29:7; Lev. 16:32). Human sins were transferred to the ani-

Unidentified sculpture of a head from the Roman period in Israel.

mal of the sin offering by laying on of hands upon the head of the animal (Exod. 29:10,15,19).

The head is involved in several colloquial expressions. The Jew swore by his head (Matt. 5:36). Sadness or grief was shown by putting the hand on the head or putting ashes on it (2 Sam. 13:19). In other instances, grief was shown by shaving the head (Job 1:20). To "heap coals of fire upon his head" was to make one's enemy feel ashamed by returning his evil with good (Prov. 25:21-22; Rom. 12:20). Wagging the head expressed derision (Mark 15:29), but bowing the head was a sign of humility (Isa. 58:5). Finally, "A gray head is a crown of glory; it is found in the way of righteousness" (Prov. 16:31 NASB).

Darlene R. Gautsch

HEAD OF THE CHURCH Title for Christ (Eph. 4:15; Col. 1:18). In Ephesians, the metaphor of Christ as head of His body, the church, is carefully developed. Headship includes the idea of Christ's authority (1:22; 5:23) and of the submission required of the church (5:24). More is in view than a statement of Christ's authority. The focus is on the character of Christ's relationship with the church. Unlike self-seeking human lords (Luke 22:25), Christ exercises His authority for the church (Eph. 1:22 NRSV, NIV), nourishing and caring for the church as one cares for one's own body (5:29). Christ's headship also points to the interrelationship of Christ and the church. The mystery of husband and wife becoming "one flesh" is applied to Christ and the church (5:31), which is "the fullness of the One fills all things in every way" (1:23 HCSB). In Col. 1:18 the idea of Christ as "head" is again complex, including not only the idea of head as authority but of head as source (1:15-20). The church is called to follow its head and to rest secure in its relationship with Him.

HEADBAND, HEADDRESS Headband refers to a head ornament, headdress to an ornamental head covering. Modern translations use "headband" to render an item of finery in Isa. 3:18. KJV rendered the same term as "caul," a loose-fitting, netted cap. KJV used "headband" to translate a different Hebrew term at Isa. 3:20. Modern translations render this term "sash." The same term is rendered "attire" (NASB, NRSV), "wedding ribbons" (REB), or "wedding ornaments" (NIV) at Jer. 2:32. Modern translations use "headdress" for a third Hebrew term

Headdresses and head coverings are still worn by the men and women of the Middle East.

(Isa. 3:20; KJV, bonnet). Such a headdress was wound around the head like a turban (Ezek. 24:17). The same Hebrew term is used for the bridegroom's "garland" (Isa. 61:10) and for the linen turbans of the priests (Ezek. 44:18). See *Cloth, Clothing.*

HEADSTONE KJV term for a top stone (NASB) or capstone (NIV) at Zech. 4:7. Zerubbabel's vision of a capstone quarried from the mountaintop was interpreted as an assurance that he would see the temple completed (4:8-9). New Testament writers spoke of Christ as a stone rejected by the builders which has become the head of the corner (Acts 4:11; 1 Pet. 2:7). Here, head of the corner refers either to a capstone (coping), a keystone of an arch, or to a cornerstone. See *Cornerstone.*

HEALING, DIVINE God's work through instruments and ways He chooses to bring health to persons sick physically, emotionally, and spiritually. The Bible not only tells of people's spiritual status but is also concerned about their physical condition. This concern appears in the emphasis on healing, particularly in the ministry of Jesus and in the early church. Nearly one-fifth of the Gospels report Jesus' miracles and the discussions they occasioned. The Gospels record 14 distinct instances of physical and mental healing. Jesus commissioned His disciples to continue His basic ministry, including healing (Matt. 10:5-10; Mark 6:7-13; Luke 9:1-6). In the book of Acts the healing ministry continued.

"Psychosomatic" is a word which literally means "soul and body," referring to the close relationship of body and spirit. The soul affects the body, and the health of the soul may be an indication of the health of the body. In the Bible John wished for his friend Gaius to "prosper in every way and be in good health, just as your soul prospers" (3 John 2 HCSB). This was an anticipation of the emphasis of psychosomatic medicine: a person is a unity; body and soul cannot be separated. Christianity and health are inextricably intertwined.

Most Christians believe in healing through faith, but trying to decide what techniques are scriptural, decorous, and psychologically helpful confuses the believer. Jesus used different methods in His healing ministry. They included calling upon the faith of the person or bystanders to be healed, touching the sick person, praying, assuring forgiveness of sin, uttering commands, and using physical media. On several occasions the faith of the individual was an important factor in the healing. Speaking to the woman who was hemorrhaging, Jesus said, "Your faith has made you well" (Mark 5:34 HCSB; cp. Matt. 9:29).

The faith of other people became a factor. Jesus stated to the father of the sick boy that healing was possible if people had faith, and the man responded, "I do believe! Help my unbelief" (Mark 9:23-24 HCSB). When the centurion sought Jesus to ask for healing his servant, the Savior responded, "I have not found anyone in Israel with so great a faith! ... And his servant was cured that very moment" (Matt. 8:10,13 HCSB; cp. Mark 2:5).

Christians are often confused about the ministry of healing, but these biblical teachings clearly appear:

(1) The Bible clearly states that Jesus believed in healing of the body.

(2) Jesus spoke of doctors in a positive way as He compared those in good health who have no need of a physician with those who do (Matt. 9:12; Mark 2:17; Luke 5:31). God has often healed by the way He has led dedicated scientists into the discovery of body functions.

(3) The methods of healing Jesus used included prayer, laying on of hands, anointing with oil, and assurance of forgiveness of sins. The church continued to use these methods (James 5:14-16).

(4) Jesus did not use healing as a means of gaining attention but tried to keep the experience private. "Praise the LORD ... He heals all your diseases" (Ps. 103:2-3 HCSB).

John W. Drakeford

HEALING, GIFT OF See *Spiritual Gifts; Healing, Divine.*

HEALTH Condition of being sound in body, mind, or spirit; used especially for physical health. Neither Hebrew nor Greek has a direct equivalent for our concept of health. Since a variety of terms is employed, English translations vary considerably in their use of the term "health." The KJV has the most numerous references to health (17 times). Modern translations frequently replace health with other terms. The substitutions of the NRSV are typical. The most common substitution is healing for health (Prov. 3:8; 4:22; 12:18; 13:17; Isa. 58:8). Elsewhere the NRSV substituted "well" as a broader statement of well-being (Gen. 43:28; 2 Sam. 20:9) or help (Pss. 42:11; 43:5) and saving power (Ps. 67:2) as more specific instances of God's assistance. The NRSV substituted "recovery" for health at Jer. 33:6, though rendering the underlying Hebrew as health elsewhere (Jer. 8:22; 30:17) as in KJV. At Acts 27:34 the NRSV has "help you survive" in place of "for your health."

The health wish of 3 John 2 is typical of Hellenistic letters (cp. 2 Macc. 1:10; 3 Macc. 3:12; 7:1). The basic Greek concept of health is what is balanced. Thus the Greeks frequently used the adjective "healthy" (*hugies*) to mean rational or intelligible. The adjective is frequently translated "sound" in the NT (1 Tim. 1:10; 6:3; 2 Tim. 1:13; 4:3; Titus 1:9; 2:1,8). See *Diseases; Healing, Divine.*

HEART Center of the physical, mental, and spiritual life of humans. The word "heart" refers to the physical organ and is considered to be the center of the physical life. Eating and drinking are spoken of as strengthening the heart (Gen. 18:5; Judg. 19:5; Acts 14:17). As the center of physical life, the heart came to stand for the person as a whole. It became the focus for all the vital functions of the body, including both intellectual and spiritual life. The heart and the intellect are closely connected, the heart being the seat of intelligence: "For this people's heart has grown callous ... otherwise they might ... understand with their hearts and turn back" (Matt. 13:15 HCSB). The heart is connected with thinking: As a person "thinketh in his heart, so is he" (Prov. 23:7 KJV). To ponder something in one's heart means to consider it carefully (Luke 1:66; 2:19). "To set one's heart on" is the literal Hebrew that means to give attention to something, to worry about it (1 Sam. 9:20). To call to heart (mind) something means to remember something (Isa. 46:8). All of these are functions of the mind but are connected with heart in biblical language.

Closely related to the mind are acts of the will, acts resulting from a conscious or even a deliberate decision. Thus, 2 Cor. 9:7 (HCSB), "Each person should do as he has decided in his heart" what he should give. Ananias contrived his deed of lying to the Holy Spirit in his heart (Acts 5:4). The conscious decision is made in the heart (Rom. 6:17). Connected to the will are human wishes and desires. Romans 1:24 describes how "God delivered them over in the cravings of their hearts to sexual impurity, so that their bodies were degraded among themselves" (HCSB).

Not only is the heart associated with the activities of the mind and the will, but it is also closely connected to the feelings and affections of a person. Emotions such as joy originate in the heart (Ps. 4:7; Isa. 65:14). Other emotions are ascribed to the heart, especially in the OT. Nabal's fear is described by the phrase: "his heart died within him" (1 Sam. 25:37; cp. Ps. 143:4). Discouragement or despair is described by the phrase "heaviness in the heart" which makes it stoop (Prov. 12:25 KJV). Again, Eccles. 2:20 (KJV) says, "Therefore I went about to cause my heart to despair of all the labor which I took under the sun." Another emotion connected with the heart is sorrow. John 16:6 says, "Because I have spoken these things to you, sorrow has filled your heart" (HCSB). Proverbs 25:20 describes sorrow as having "a troubled heart" (HCSB). The heart is also the seat of the affection of love and its opposite, hate. In the OT, for example, Israel is commanded: "You shall not hate your brother in your heart, but you shall reason with your neighbor, lest you bear sin because of him" (Lev. 19:17 RSV). A similar attitude, bitter jealousy, is described in James 3:14 as coming from the heart. On the other hand, love is based in the heart. The believer is commanded to love God "with all your heart" (Mark 12:30; cp. Deut. 6:5). Paul taught that the purpose of God's command is love that comes from a "pure heart" (1 Tim. 1:5 HCSB).

The heart is spoken of in Scripture as the center of the moral and spiritual life. The conscience, for instance, is associated with the heart. In fact, the Hebrew language had no word for conscience, so the word "heart" was often used to express this concept: "my heart does not reproach any of my days" (Job 27:6 NASB). The RSV translates the word for "heart" as "conscience" in 1 Sam. 25:31. In the NT the heart is spoken of also as that which condemns us (1 John 3:19-21). All moral conditions from the highest to the lowest are said to center in the heart. Sometimes the heart is used to represent a person's true nature or character. Samson told Delilah "all that was in his heart" (Judg. 16:17 NASB). This true nature is contrasted with the outward appearance: "man looks on the outward appearance, but the Lord looks on the heart" (1 Sam. 16:7 RSV).

On the negative side, depravity is said to issue from the heart: "The heart is more deceitful than all else and is desperately sick; who can understand it?" (Jer. 17:9 NASB). Jesus said that out of the heart comes evil thoughts, murder, adultery, fornication, theft, false witness, slander (Matt. 15:19). In other words, defilement comes from within rather than from without.

Because the heart is at the root of the problem, this is the place where God does His work in the individual. For instance, the work of the law is "written on their hearts," and conscience is the proof of this (Rom. 2:15 HCSB). The heart is the field where seed (the Word of God) is sown (Matt. 13:19; Luke 8:15). In addition to being the place where the natural laws of God are written, the heart is the place of renewal. Before Saul became king, God gave him a new heart (1 Sam. 10:9). God promised Israel that He would give them a new spirit within, take away their "heart of stone" and give them a "heart of flesh" (Ezek. 11:19 NASB). Paul said that a person must believe in the heart to be saved, "with the heart one believes, resulting in righteousness" (Rom. 10:10 HCSB; cp. Mark 11:23; Heb. 3:12.)

The heart is the dwelling place of God. Two persons of the Trinity are said to reside in the heart of the believer. God has given us the "down payment [of the Spirit] in our hearts" (2 Cor. 1:22 HCSB). Ephesians 3:17 expresses the desire that "the Messiah may dwell in your hearts through faith". The love of God "has been poured out in our hearts through the Holy Spirit who was given to us" (Rom. 5:5).

Gerald P. Cowen

HEARTH A depression in a floor, sometimes bricked to retain heat (Jer. 36:23), used for cooking food (Isa. 30:14). KJV used "hearth" to translate four Hebrew terms. Modern translations retain "hearth" at Isa. 30:14. Elsewhere modern translations substituted other terms: "furnace" (NRSV), "oven" (REB), or "glowing embers" (NIV) at Ps. 102:3; "brazier" (REB, NASB, NRSV) or "firepot" (NIV) at Jer. 36:22-23; "blazing pot" (NRSV), "brazier" (REB), or "firepot" (NASB, NIV) at Zech. 12:6. The altar hearth of Ezek. 43:15-16 refers to the upper part of the altar upon which the sacrifice was burnt (cp. Lev. 6:9). See *Cooking and Heating.*

HEATH Shrubby, evergreen plant of the heather family, used by the KJV (Jer. 17:6; 48:6). Various translations have been offered: juniper (NASB); bush (NIV); shrub (NRSV, 17:6). At Jer. 48:6 the RSV and TEV follow Aquila's Greek translation in substituting "wild ass" for the plant name. The REB takes the Hebrew figuratively for "one destitute." Arabic evidence points to the juniper *(Juniperus oxycedrus* and *Juniperus phoenicea).*

HEATHEN See *Gentiles.*

HEAVE OFFERING See *Sacrifice and Offering.*

HEAVEN Part of God's creation above the earth and the waters including "air" and "space" and serving as home for God and His heavenly creatures.

Old Testament The Hebrew word *shamayim* is plural in form and was easily related by the common people to the word *mayim,* "waters." Biblical writers joined their contemporaries in describing the universe as it appeared to the human eye: heavens above, earth beneath, and waters around and beneath the earth. Heaven could be described as a partition God made to separate the rain-producing heavenly waters from the rivers, seas, and oceans below (Gen. 1:6-8). The heavenly lights—sun, moon, and stars—were installed into this partition (Gen. 1:14-18). This partition has windows or sluice gates with which God sends rain to irrigate or water the earth (Gen. 7:11). This heavenly partition God "stretched out" (Isa. 42:5; 44:24; Ps. 136:6; cp. Ezek. 1:22-26; 10:1). The clouds serve a similar rain-producing function, so that KJV often translates the Hebrew word for "clouds" as "sky" (Deut. 33:26; Ps. 57:10; Isa. 45:8; Jer. 51:9; cp. Pss. 36:6; 108:4).

Only God has the wisdom to "stretch out the heaven" (Jer. 51:15). "Heaven" thus becomes the curtain of God's tent, separating His dwelling place from that of humanity on earth (Ps. 104:2; Isa. 40:22). Like a human dwelling, heaven can be described as resting on supporting pillars (Job 26:11) or on building foundations (2 Sam. 22:8; though the parallel in Ps. 18:7 applies the foundations to mountains). Just as He built the partition, so God can "rend" it or tear it apart (Isa. 64:1). Thus it does not seal God off from His creation and His people. English translations use "firmament" (KJV), "expanse" (NASB, NIV), "dome" (TEV, NRSV), or "vault" (REB) to translate the special Hebrew word describing what God created and named "Heaven" (Gen. 1:8).

Hebrew does not employ a term for "air" or "space" between heaven and earth. This is all part of heaven. Thus the Bible speaks of "birds of the heavens," though English translations often use "air" or "sky" (Deut. 4:17; Jer. 8:7; Lam. 4:19). Even Absalom, hanging by his hair from a tree limb, was "between heaven and earth" (2 Sam. 18:9; cp. 1 Chron. 21:16; Ezek. 8:3). The heaven is the source for rain (Deut. 11:11; Ps. 148:4), dew (Gen. 27:28), frost (Job 38:29), snow (Isa. 55:10), fiery lightning (Gen. 19:24), dust (Deut. 28:24), and hail (Josh. 10:11). This is the language of human observation and description, but it is more. It is the language of faith describing God in action, in and for His world (Jer. 14:22). Heaven is God's treasure chest, storing treasures such as the rain (Deut. 28:12), wind and lightning (Jer. 10:13), and snow and hail (Job 38:22). The miraculous manna came from God's heavenly storehouses for Israel in the wilderness (Exod. 16:11-15).

Heaven and earth thus comprehend the entire universe and all its constituents (Jer. 23:24), but God fills all these and more so that no one can hide from Him (cp. 1 Kings 8:27-30;

Isa. 66:1). Yet this One also lives in the humble, contrite heart (Isa. 57:15).

As God's dwelling place, heaven is not a divine haven where God can isolate Himself from earth. It is the divine workplace, where He sends blessings to His people (Deut. 26:15; Isa. 63:15) and punishment on His enemies (Pss. 2:4; 11:4-7). Heaven is a channel of communication between God and humans (Gen. 28:12; 2 Sam. 22:10; Neh. 9:13; Ps. 144:5).

As God's creation, the heavens praise Him and display His glory and His creativity (Pss. 19:1; 69:34) and righteousness (Ps. 50:6). Still, heaven remains a part of the created order. Unlike neighboring nations, Israel knew that heaven and the heavenly bodies were not gods and did not deserve worship (Exod. 20:4). It belonged to God (Deut. 10:14). Heaven stands as a symbol of power and unchanging, enduring existence (Ps. 89:29), but heaven is not eternal. The days come when heaven is no more (Job 14:12; Isa. 51:6). As God once spread out the heavenly tent, so He will wrap up the heavens like a scroll (Isa. 34:4). A new heaven and new earth will appear (Isa. 65:17; 66:22).

The OT speaks of heaven to show the sovereignty of the Creator God and yet of the divine desire to communicate with and provide for the human creature. It holds out the tantalizing examples of men who left earth and were taken up to heaven (Gen. 5:24; 2 Kings 2:11).

New Testament In the NT the primary Greek word translated "heaven" describes heaven as being above the earth, although no NT passage gives complete instructions regarding the location or geography of heaven. Other than Paul's reference to the three heavens (2 Cor. 12:2-4), the NT writers spoke of only one heaven.

The NT affirms that God created heaven (Acts 4:24), that heaven and earth stand under God's lordship (Matt. 11:25), and that heaven is the dwelling place of God (Matt. 6:9).

Jesus preached that the kingdom of heaven (God) had dawned through His presence and ministry (Mark 1:15). By using the image of a messianic banquet, Jesus spoke of heavenly life as a time of joy, celebration, and fellowship with God (Matt. 26:29). Jesus taught that there would be no marrying or giving in marriage in heaven (Luke 20:34-36).

Christians should rejoice because their names are written in heaven (Luke 10:20). Jesus

H

promised a heavenly home for His followers (John 14:2-3).

According to Paul, Christ is seated in heaven at the right hand of God (Eph. 1:20). Paul believed heaven is the future home of believers (2 Cor. 5:1-2). Paul referred to the hope of heaven as the hope of glory (Col. 1:27). The Holy Spirit is the pledge of the believer's participation in heaven (2 Cor. 5:5). Peter affirmed that heaven is the place where the believer's inheritance is kept with care until the revelation of the Messiah (1 Pet. 1:4).

The word "heaven" occurs more frequently in Revelation than in any other NT book. The Revelation addresses heaven from the standpoints of the struggle between good and evil and of God's rule from heaven. The most popular passage dealing with heaven is Rev. 21:1–22:5. In this passage, heaven is portrayed in three different images: (1) the tabernacle (21:1-8), (2) the city (21:9-27), and (3) the garden (22:1-5). The image of the tabernacle portrays heavenly life as perfect fellowship with God. The symbolism of the city portrays heavenly life as perfect protection. The image of the garden shows heavenly life as perfect provision.

Trent C. Butler and Gary Hardin

HEAVEN OF HEAVENS KJV designation rendered "highest heaven" by most modern translations (1 Kings 8:27; 2 Chron. 2:6; 6:18). According to an ancient understanding of the universe, above the canopy of the sky was a further canopy above which God dwelt. TEV understands "heavens of heavens" as "all (the vastness) of heaven."

HEAVENLY CITY The fulfillment of the hopes of God's people for final salvation. To the ancient world, cities represented ordered life, security from enemies, and material prosperity. Hebrews says the city "has foundations;" its "architect and builder is God" (11:10 NASB); God has prepared it (11:16); and it is "the city of the living God, the heavenly Jerusalem" (12:22). This city is the home to "an innumerable company of angels" (12:22), to the assembly of the firstborn (12:23; an image of believers redeemed by the death of Christ; cp. Exod. 13:13-15), and to the righteous made perfect by God (12:23; perhaps the OT saints). Some interpreters take these descriptions literally. The Christian goal is, however, not something that can be touched and sensed like Israel's Sinai experience (12:18). Indeed, believers have already come (12:22) to the heavenly Jerusalem, at least in part. Some interpreters thus take the Heavenly City as an image of the redeemed people of God whose "foundation" is the apostles and prophets (Eph. 2:20). The experience of the patriarchs whose hope lay beyond their earthly lives (Heb. 11:13-16) points to a final fulfillment of salvation in heaven.

The Heavenly City of Rev. 21:9–22:7 has also been interpreted both literally and figuratively. One interpretation sees the Heavenly City suspended above the earth like a space platform. Others see an earthly city. Still others see a city suspended in the air that later descends to earth. Others, pointing to the equation of the city as the bride of Christ (21:2,9), take the city as a symbol of the church. Whether understood as a literal city or as representing God's redeemed people experiencing their final salvation, the city is a place of fellowship with God (21:3,22), of God-ensured safety (21:4,25), and of God-given provision (22:1-2,5). See *Cities and Urban Life.*

Chris Church

HEAVENS, NEW Technical, eschatological term referring to the final perfected state of the created universe. It often is connected with the concept of a new earth.

The promise of a re-creation of the heavens and earth arose because of human sin and God's subsequent curse (Gen. 3:17). The biblical hope for mankind is tied to the conviction that persons cannot be completely set free from the power of sin apart from the redemption of the created order—earth as well as the heavens. The idea of a renewed universe is found in many passages of the Bible (Isa. 51:16; Matt. 19:28; 24:29-31; 26:29; Mark 13:24-27,31; Acts 3:20-21; Rom. 8:19-23; 2 Cor. 5:17; Heb. 12:26-28; 2 Pet. 3:10-13). However, the phrase "new heavens" is found in only four passages (Isa. 65:17; 66:22; 2 Pet. 3:13; Rev. 21:1).

The nature of the "new heavens and earth" is variously described in the Bible. First, God is the cause of this new creation (Isa. 65:17; 66:22; Rev. 21:22). In Heb. 12:28 the new heaven and earth are described as a "kingdom that cannot be shaken" (HCSB). This new heaven and earth will last forever (Isa. 66:22). In 2 Peter 3:13 the new world is described as one "where righteousness will dwell."

In Revelation, the nature of the new heaven and earth stands in marked contrast to the old heaven and earth. The Greek word translated "new" designates something that already exists but now appears in a new way: the new world is the old world gloriously transformed. Purity (Rev. 21:27) and freedom from the wrath of God (Rev. 22:3) are marks of the new heaven and earth. Further, the new world is marked by perfect fellowship of the saints with one another and with God. God and His people dwell together in the new age (21:1,3).

Clearly, God will bring the new order into existence at the end of history. But scholars disagree as to when this will occur within the events associated with the end times. Two main views are held. First, the new heavens and earth are created immediately after the second coming of Christ. Even among those within this camp there is disagreement. Some believe that the creation of the new heavens and earth will occur immediately after the "great white throne" judgment. Amillennialists generally hold to this theory. Some premillennialists associate the creation of the new heavens and earth with the beginning of the thousand year millennial reign of Christ. A second viewpoint commonly held by many premillennialists is that the new heaven and new earth are created at the end of the millennial reign of Christ. See *Angel; Creation; Eschatology; Heaven; Hell; Jerusalem; Kingdom.*

Paul E. Robertson

HEBER (Hē´ bĕr) Personal name meaning "companion." **1.** Grandson of Asher and great grandson of Jacob (Gen. 46:17). He was the original clan ancestor of the Heberites (Num. 26:45). **2.** Kenite related to family of Moses' wife (Judg. 4:11). His wife Jael killed Sisera, the Canaanite general, breaking a political alliance between Heber's clan and Jabin, Sisera's king (Judg. 4:17). This completed the great victory of Deborah and Barak over the Canaanites. **3.** A member of the tribe of Judah in a Hebrew text (1 Chron. 4:18), which apparently lists two mothers of Heber, one an Egyptian. Commentators generally change the text or consider that some words have fallen out of the text as it was copied. Heber was the father of Socho and thus apparently recognized as founding ancestor of town of Socho. See Socho. **4.** A member of the tribe of Benjamin (1 Chron. 8:17). **5.** A different Hebrew word lies behind Eber (1 Chron. 5:13; 8:22), which KJV

spells Heber. The Heber in Luke 3:35 (KJV) is the Eber of Gen. 11:15. See *Eber*.

HEBERITE (Hĕb´ ĕr īt) See *Heber*.

HEBREW (Hē´ brū) A descendant of Eber. It differentiates early Israelites from foreigners. After David founded the monarchy the term "Hebrew" seems to disappear from the Hebrew language. The designation apparently begins with Abraham (Gen. 14:13), showing that he belonged to an ethnic group distinct from the Amorites. It distinguished Joseph from the Egyptians and slaves of other ethnic identity (Gen. 39:14,17; 41:12; 43:32). Abraham's land has become the land of the Hebrews (Gen. 40:15), and his God, the God of the Hebrews (Exod. 5:3). Given the ethnic identity, special laws protected Hebrew slaves (Exod. 21:2; Deut. 15:12; cp. Lev. 25:40-41; Jer. 34:8-22). After the death of Saul (1 Sam. 29), the term "Hebrew" does not appear in the historical books, pointing possibly to a distinction between Hebrew as an ethnic term and Israel and/or Judah as a religious and political term for the people of the covenant and of God's nation. See *Eber; Habiru.*

HEBREW LANGUAGE The language in which the canonical books of the OT were written, except for the Aramaic sections in Ezra 4:8–6:18; 7:12-26; Dan. 2:4b–7:28; Jer. 10:11, and a few other words and phrases from Aramaic and other languages. The language is not called "Hebrew" in the OT. Rather, it is known as "the language (literally, 'lip') of Canaan" (Isa. 19:18) or as "Judean" (NASB), that is, the language of

Pottery handle from Lachish stamped with a Hebrew pottery seal containing a Hebrew inscription.

Judah (Neh. 13:24; Isa. 36:11). The word "Hebrew" for the language is first attested in the prologue to Ecclesiasticus in the Apocrypha. In the NT the references to the "Hebrew dialect" seem to be references to Aramaic. See *Apocrypha*.

Biblical or classical Hebrew belongs to the northwest Semitic branch of Semitic languages, which includes Ugaritic, Phoenician, Moabite, Edomite, and Ammonite. This linguistic group is referred to commonly as Canaanite, although some prefer not to call Ugaritic a Canaanite dialect.

Hebrew has an alphabet of 22 consonants. The texts were written right to left. The script was based on that of the Phoenicians, a circumstance that did not make it possible to represent or to distinguish clearly among all the consonantal sounds in current use in classical Hebrew.

The distinguishing characteristics of Hebrew are for the most part those shared by one or more of the other Semitic languages. Each root for verbs and nouns characteristically had three consonants, even in later periods when the use of four consonant roots was increased. Nouns are either masculine or feminine. They have singular, plural, or even dual forms, the dual being used for items normally found in pairs, such as eyes, ears, lips. While most nouns were derived from a verbal root, some were original nouns that gave rise to verbs (denominatives). The genitive relationship (usually expressed in English by "of") is expressed by the construct formation in which the word standing before the genitive is altered in form and pronunciation (if possible).

The Hebrew verb forms indicate person, number, and gender. Seven verbal stems serve to indicate types of action: simple action, active or passive; intensive action, active, passive, or reflexive; and causative action, active or passive. In classical Hebrew the isolated verb form did not indicate a tense, but rather complete or incomplete action. Thus verbs are often referred to as perfect or imperfect, there being no past, present, future, past perfect, present perfect, or future perfect. The tense can be determined only in context, and sometimes even that procedure produces uncertain results. Classical Hebrew is a verb-oriented language rather than a noun-oriented or abstract language. The usual word order of a sentence is verb, subject, modifiers, direct object. The language is quite concrete in expression. However, the relatively simple structure

and syntax of classical Hebrew did not keep biblical writers from producing countless passages of unparalleled beauty and power.

While historical development took place in classical Hebrew from the eleventh century to the emergence of Mishnaic Hebrew, it does not seem possible to write the history of that development. It is generally agreed that the most archaic texts are poetic, such as Gen. 4:23-24; Exod. 15; Judg. 5, although often it is difficult to decide what is archaic and what may be the result of an archaizing style. Books written toward the close of the OT period, such as Ezra, Nehemiah, Chronicles, and Ecclesiastes, show the Hebrew language undergoing a number of significant changes due primarily to Aramaic influence. Most of the Hebrew Bible now shows a homogeneous style which was most likely due to scribes in the late preexilic period copying the older texts in the dialect of Jerusalem. Thus, to be able to date an extant text does not necessarily mean that one can date the material contained in the text. There is some evidence of dialectical variations in the Hebrew spoken in biblical times. For example there is the Shibboleth-Sibboleth incident in Judg. 12:5-6. Some Bible students think many of the difficulties of the text of Hosea may be clarified by considering the Hebrew of that book as an example of northern or Israelite idiom.

The growing number of Hebrew inscriptions dating from the preexilic age provides an important supplement to the study of classical Hebrew. These inscriptions were chiseled into stone, written on ostraca (broken pieces of pottery), or cut into seals or inscribed on jar handles and weights. Some of the most important inscriptional evidence includes the Gezer calendar (tenth century), the Hazor ostraca (ninth century), the Samaria ostraca (early eighth century), the Siloam inscription (late eighth century), Yavneh-yam ostracon (late seventh century), jar handles from Gibeon (late seventh century), the Lachish ostracon (early sixth century), and the Arad ostraca (late seventh and early sixth centuries). To these may be added the Moabite Stone (Stele of Mesha, ninth century) and the Ammonite stele (ninth century) which contain inscriptions in languages very similar to classical Hebrew. Several benefits may be gained from these and other inscriptions for the study of classical Hebrew. First, we now have available an adequate view of the development of Hebrew

The Gezer Calendar is believed to be the oldest Hebrew inscription found to date. The inscription is on a limestone tablet and dates from 925 B.C.

script and orthography from the tenth century to NT times. Second, it now appears that literacy was earlier and more widespread in Israel than was thought previously. Third, the addition of new words and personal names and the like have enriched our knowledge of classical Hebrew. And fourth, details of the texts add new data on matters of history, material culture, and religion.

Thomas Smothers

HEBREWS, LETTER TO THE Language and imagery of the letter to the Hebrews seem distant from our world, but its message needs to be heard today.

Historical Context Both the author of Hebrews and the historical situation that prompted its writing are matters of speculation. Although Paul's name is included in the title in some manuscripts, the author never mentions his name. Nor does the author identify his recipients or their location. A monumental decision faced the audience, but the author never explicitly identified the situation forcing the decision.

We must reconstruct what we can about the historical context from clues in the text and from discussions by ancient church leaders. Authorship has been debated since the second century.

Clement of Alexandria and Origen, church leaders in Alexandria, Egypt, at the end of the second century, both recognized that the content of the letter was linked to Paul or someone associated with him. But the vocabulary and style were very different from Paul. Origen said the thoughts were Pauline but that they were written by someone else. His famous statement on authorship was, "God only knows." In addition to Paul, ancient nominations for the author included Luke, Barnabas, and Clement of Rome. More recently suggestions have included Apollos, Silvanus, Philip the deacon, Jude, and Priscilla, and others (at least 15).

More important than the name of the author is his character. The author had extraordinary knowledge of the OT. The letter contains 31 to 35 direct quotations from the OT plus numerous allusions and indirect references. The author used events, persons, and passages from the OT that he molded into a sustained argument for the superiority of Jesus.

The author was well educated, skillful in the use of language, and methods of argumentation. The Greek of Hebrews ranks with the best in the NT. From vocabulary to sentence construction, the author demonstrates creativity and finesse. One artistically crafted argument runs from beginning to end, using rhetorical techniques and imagery.

The author had a passion for people. Interwoven with biblical exposition is a plea to believers to stand fast in their faith. Poor decisions lead to disastrous spiritual consequences. The author would not rest until his readers realized the necessity of living out faith commitments in turbulent times.

Recipients The only geographical clue to the location of the church is found in Heb. 13:24b. However, the ambiguous phrase is open to two interpretations: Was the author in Italy writing to a church somewhere else ("Those here in Italy with me greet you") or was the author writing to Italy, especially Rome, from another location ("Those from Italy are here with me and greet you")?

At least two factors favor the second interpretation. The earliest quotations from and references to the book of Hebrews are found in the Letter of 1 Clement, which was written from Rome near the end of the first century. Also, some of the issues dealt with in The Shepherd of Hermas, written from Rome at about the same

H

time, appear to be responsive to issues raised in Hebrews. This early knowledge of Hebrews in Rome makes sense if that were the original destination of the letter.

The eastern church centered in Alexandria, Egypt, despite the questions of Origen, grouped Hebrews with the Paulines long before the western church centered in Rome did so. If the letter was originally sent to Rome, then the knowledge of the identity of the author may have prompted that hesitancy.

The date of the letter is also uncertain. The author labeled himself and his audience as "second generation" Christians, who heard the word from those who had known Jesus (Heb. 2:3b). This church also had its own history. Members who should have been leaders still needed someone to teach them (5:12). The church's history also included a period of persecution in earlier days when they gladly accepted various hardships (10:32-34; hinted at in 6:10). That persecution does not seem to have involved loss of life (12:4).

Establishing a time frame is difficult. The description in 2:3b could apply to most of the church after Pentecost. The latest possible date for composition is set by quotations found in 1 Clement, giving a date range from about A.D. 35 to 100. The history of the church in Rome during this period is not complete, and conclusions drawn must be tentative. However, if circumstances can be found that fit the evidence in the letter, then we can have a sense of historical concreteness.

Around A.D. 49 the emperor Claudius expelled Jewish leaders from Rome over a religious conflict creating a disturbance within the city. The expulsion included Jewish Christians (Priscilla and Aquilla, Acts 18:2). Such an expulsion would fit the humiliation, imprisonment, and loss of property without loss of life described in the letter (10:32-34).

A good candidate for the coming persecution is Nero's persecution of Christians in Rome during the mid 60s. Extremely intense, this persecution involved painful death for many Christians. If this scenario is accurate, then the author was writing to a house church/churches in Rome between the beginning of Nero's persecution after the great fire of the summer of A.D. 64 and Nero's suicide in A.D. 68.

The expulsion under Claudius was directed at Jews who accepted Jesus as Messiah and some

who did not. The purpose of the expulsion appears to have been to restore civil order. Jewish believers in the house churches in Rome potentially would have been affected by the order simply because they were Jews.

The persecution under Nero was an attempt to shift public criticism of Nero's involvement in the fire to a scapegoat, the followers of Jesus. Persecution was based on supposed crimes committed as believers. In the first situation, Jewish Christians could not escape expulsion either in the church or the synagogue for the order was based on their being Jewish. However, in the second situation, leaving the church and retreating to the synagogue would provide Jewish Christians with physical safety since the persecution was limited to Christians, not Jews in general.

Echoes of this concern run throughout the letter. The call to regular attendance in public meetings (10:24-25) may reflect the hesitancy of some to be associated with the church. The constant call throughout the letter was a reminder that everything in Judaism was fulfilled in Jesus. To turn from Jesus, no matter in which direction, was a move away from God. The only proper response to what God did in Jesus was to go outside the place of security (the synagogue) and bear Jesus' abuse with him (13:13).

To summarize, the letter was written by an unnamed author to a group of Christians, probably living in or near Rome, who were well versed in the OT Scriptures and familiar with Jewish history and the sacrificial system. They had faithfully endured hard times in the past but in the near future faced new and potentially more severe suffering. The author used a variety of means to encourage the Christians to stand firm and hold fast to their confession. The conjecture that links this group to Claudius' expulsion in the past and Nero's persecution in the near future must remain tentative, but if these two events do not provide the historical context for the letter, then it must have been events similar in nature.

Literary Context The literary context is just as problematic as the historical context. Hebrews is listed with NT letters. However, the book lacks the normal opening of a letter. The first four verses of Hebrews have been compared with the introduction to the Gospel of John, which serves as a prologue for the gospel. In this regard Hebrews is similar also to 1 John, which also lacks the normal letter opening. Unlike 1 John, which does not end like a letter either, Hebrews exhortations (13:1-18), followed by a benediction (13:20-21), concluding with personal references and greetings (13:22-24).

The incomplete epistolary form of Hebrews highlights its dual nature: it is a sermon or homily intended to be read orally but transmitted in written or letter form. The oral nature of the work is seen in the use of rhetorical devices that are crafted to arouse the emotions aurally as well as move the mind logically. The book begins with one such technique, alliteration: five words in the Greek text of 1:1 begin with the Greek letter *pi*. Even those NT letters containing all the formal elements of a letter were probably meant to be read orally. The original recipients of NT letters listened to them in public rather than reading them in private

The structure of the letter is also problematic. Hebrews is highly developed and well organized. However, there is little consensus as to how to outline the book. Two basic approaches to outlining have been followed, content based outlines and form based outlines. A limitation of content-based outlines is that they tend to force Hebrews into the Pauline pattern of doctrinal exposition followed by practical exhortation. However, although Hebrews contains both exposition and exhortation, the two elements are interwoven throughout the book rather than being sequential.

Form based outlines attempt to find keys in the text that can be used to determine the units of the text. Some of these keys are repeated themes, repeated words, and shifts in genre. For example, the theme of Jesus' superiority over the angels in 1:5-14 is indicated, in part, by the frequent repetition of the word "angels" in those verses. Beginning in 2:1 the author shifts from third person (he/they) to first person (we/us) and the word "angels" does not occur, indicating a shift in genre and content, from exposition to exhortation. Then in 2:5 the word "angels" is used again. This technique separates 2:1-4 as a warning or exhortation passage and links the material in 2:5-18 with the exposition of Jesus' superiority begun in chapter one. The most extensive study of the structure of Hebrews using this technique was by G. H. Guthrie in *The Structure of Hebrews: A Text-Linguistic Analysis*.

The most outstanding feature of the structure of Hebrews is this blending of expositional and exhortative material. The result is that the ser-mon does not develop in a logical, point-by-point fashion. Instead, the author constantly flashed warnings in the face of his audience. The doctrine expounded had practical implications. The readers were reminded repeatedly that sound decisions needed solid, theological foundations.

Theological Context The main theological theme is found early in chapter one. The God who spoke to the Israelites is the same God who spoke through Jesus (1:1-2). And when God speaks, His people ought to listen, a message reiterated in the climactic warning passage of the letter: "See that you do not reject the One who speaks" (12:25 HCSB). In what may be the climax of the whole letter (13:10-16), the author reintroduced the themes of high priest, altar, and Day of Atonement sacrifice, all of which were central images in chapters 8–10. In this passage these images were used to call the hearers outside their security zone. The synagogue might represent physical security for the audience, but Jesus was outside, suffering for the people. His people needed to be outside with Him.

Other theological themes give support to the call to obedience. One such theme is christological: Jesus is God's ultimate, superior revelation of Himself. He is superior to angels, Moses, the earthly priests, and His sacrifice is superior to anything offered in the temple. Through careful exposition of OT passages the author points out the temporal nature of the priesthood, the temple sacrificial system, and the initial covenant between God and His people. Jesus as the perfect high priest offered a once-for-all sacrifice that initiated the new covenant foretold by Jeremiah.

Another burning theological theme is the issue of apostasy. This issue is present in all the warning passages, but the focal point of discussion usually is 6:4-8. The passage leaves no doubt that those who fall away will be punished for their disobedience. What is often overlooked, however, is that the text is far from explicit about what they are falling away from and what the punishment will be.

The most common assumption is that they have fallen away from salvation and the burning (6:8) refers to eternal destruction. However, Herschel Hobbs' contention that these believers were in danger of falling away from God's world mission, and the punishment will be loss of opportunity is credible [see Herschel Hobbs, *Hebrews: Challenges to Bold Discipleship*]. The theme of God's mission can be seen in other

H

passages, such as the failed attempt at Kadesh-barnea to enter the promised land to fulfill their calling (chaps. 3 and 4). Another often suggested solution looks at those who fall away as phenomenological believers; in other words, they appeared to be believers but were not. A difficulty with this position is the strong language the author used in 6:4-5 to describe these people.

Outline

I. Prologue: Course and Climax of Divine Revelation (1:1-3)

II. The Pre-eminence of Christ (1:4–4:13)
  A. Superiority of Christ to angels (1:4-14)
  B. Warning against neglect (2:1-4)
  C. The reason Christ became human (2:5-18)
  D. Superiority of Christ to Moses (3:1-6)
  E. Warning against unbelief (3:7-3:19)
  F. Entering the promised rest (4:1-13)

III. The Priesthood of Jesus Christ (4:14–10:18)
  A. Importance of His priesthood for personal conduct (4:14-16)
  B. Qualifications of a high priest (5:1-10)
  C. The problem of immaturity (5:11-14)
  D. Warning against regression (6:1-12)
  E. Inheriting the promise (6:13-20)
  F. The greatness of Melchizedek (7:1-10)
  G. A superior priesthood (7:11-28)
  H. A heavenly priesthood (8:1-6)
  I. A superior covenant (8:7-13)
  J. Old covenant ministry (9:1-10)
  K. New covenant ministry (9:11-28)
  L. The perfect sacrifice (10:1-18)

IV. The Perseverance of Christians (10:19—13:25)
  A. Exhortations to godliness (10:19-25)
  B. Warning against willful sin (10:26-39)
  C. Heroes of Faith (11:1-40)
  D. The call to endurance (12:1-2)
  E. Fatherly discipline (12:3-13)
  F. Warning against rejecting God's grace (12:14-29)
  G. Final Exhortations (13:1-19)
  H. Benediction and Farewell (13:20-25)

                              Charles A. Ray

HEBRON (Hē´ brŏn) Place-name and personal name meaning "association" or "league." A major city in the hill country of Judah about 19 miles south of Jerusalem and 15 miles west of the Dead Sea. The region is over 3,000 feet above sea level. The surrounding area has an abundant water supply, and its rich soil is excellent for agriculture. According to archaeological

The mosque of the patriarchs at Hebron built over the traditional site of the Cave of Machpelah.

H

research the site has been occupied almost continuously since about 3300 B.C.

After his separation from Lot, Abraham moved to Hebron. At that time the area was known as Mamre and was associated with the Amorites (Gen. 13:18; 14:13; 23:19). Abraham apparently remained at Mamre until after the destruction of Sodom and Gomorrah. When Sarah died, the place was called Kirjath-arba; and the population was predominantly Hittite (Gen. 23:2; Josh. 14:15; 15:54; Judg. 1:10). From them Abraham purchased a field with a burial plot inside a nearby cave. Abraham and Sarah, Isaac and Rebekah, and Jacob and Leah were buried there (Gen. 23:19; 25:9; 35:29; 49:31; 50:13).

Four centuries later, when Moses sent the 12 spies into Canaan, the tribe of Anak lived in Hebron. According to Num. 13:22, Hebron was "built" seven years prior to Zoan, the Egyptian city of Tanis. Archaeological evidence suggests that the reference was to Tanis' establishment as the Hyksos capital around 1725 B.C. and not its beginning. Indeed both cities already were inhabited long before 2000 B.C. Therefore, the date may indicate that it was rebuilt by the Hyksos at that time, or it may specify when Hebron became a Canaanite city. After the Israelite conquest of Canaan, Hebron was given to Caleb (Josh. 14:9-13). It also became a city of refuge (Josh. 20:7). Later, Samson put the gates of Gaza on a hill outside of Hebron (Judg. 16:3).

After the death of Saul, David settled in the city (2 Sam. 2:3) and made it his capital during the seven years he ruled only Judah (1 Kings 2:11). His son, Absalom, launched an abortive revolt against David from Hebron (2 Sam. 15:10). Between 922 and 915 B.C. Rehoboam fortified the city as a part of Judah's defense network (2 Chron. 11:5-10). According to inscriptions found on pottery fragments, royal pottery was made in the city between 800 and 700 B.C.

When the Babylonians destroyed Jerusalem in 587 B.C., the Edomites captured Hebron. It was not recaptured until Judas Maccabeus sacked the city in 164 B.C. Although Herod the Great erected pretentious structures there, no mention of the city is made in the NT. The city was raided by both Jewish revolutionaries and Roman legions in A.D. 68 during the Jewish Revolt.

Two individuals in the OT also were named Hebron. The first was a Levite (Exod. 6:18; Num. 3:19; 1 Chron. 6:2,18; 23:12). The second is listed in the Calebite genealogy (1 Chron. 2:42-43). See *City of Refuge; Machpelah; Mamre.*   *LeBron Matthews*

HEBRONITE (Hē´ brŏn īt) Citizen of Hebron. See *Hebron.*

HEDGE Boundary formed by a dense row of usually thorny shrubs. In ancient Palestine hedges served to protect vineyards from damage by animals or intruders (Ps. 80:12-13; Isa. 5:5). To put a hedge around someone means to pro-

Stone fences on the island of Patmos with portions covered by thorny briars for added protection.

tect (Job 1:10). "To hedge in" means to hem in or obstruct (Job 3:23; Lam. 3:7; Hos. 2:6).

HEDGEHOG NASB, NRSV translation of the Hebrew *qippod*, a term of uncertain meaning (Isa. 14:23; 34:11; Zeph. 2:14). The term either refers to the hedgehog (or porcupine) or else to a type of bird. The decision of the NASB and RSV translators was based on the supposed Hebrew root *qaphad* (meaning to roll up, which is what hedgehogs do when frightened) and on cognate Arabic and Syriac words referring to hedgehogs and porcupines. Other English versions follow the KJV in seeing a reference to a type of bird. Context favors a reference to a bird. Various identities of the bird have been proposed: bittern, a nocturnal heron (KJV); owl, screech owl (NIV); owl (TEV); bustard, a game bird (REB). See *Bittern; Porcupine.*

HEEL, LIFTED HIS To lift one's heel against someone is to turn one's back and join rank with the enemies. Jesus applied the expression to

H

Judas, who accepted Jesus' hospitality but then plotted His arrest (John 13:18).

HEGAI (Hē´ gī) Persian name of unknown meaning. Eunuch in charge of King Ahasuerus' harem who befriended Esther (Esther 2:8-9,15).

HEGE (Hē´ gē) KJV spelling of Hegai in Esther 2:3 based on variant spelling in Hebrew text.

HEGLAM (Hĕg´ lam) NRSV interpretation of Hebrew text in 1 Chron. 8:7, taking as a proper name giving a second name to Gera what other translations translate as "who deported them."

HEIFER Young cow, especially one that has not yet calved. Heifers were used for plowing (Deut. 21:3; Judg. 14:18) and for threshing grain (Hos. 10:11). Heifers were used as sacrificial animals (1 Sam. 16:2). Heifers (or cows) were used in three different rites: to ratify a covenant (Gen. 15:9); to remove the guilt associated with a murder by an unknown person (Deut. 21:1-9); and to remove the uncleanness associated with contact with a corpse (Num. 19:1-10). The Hebrew term for the red "heifer" of Num. 19 is the common term for cow.

Samson characterized scheming with his wife as plowing "with my heifer" (Judg. 14:18). One of David's wives (2 Sam. 3:5) was named Eglah (heifer). The heifer was used as a symbol for the splendor of Egypt (Jer. 46:20) and of Babylon (50:11). Hosea 10:11 pictures obedient Ephraim as a trained heifer. In contrast, disobedient Israel is a stubborn cow.

HELAH (Hē´ la) Personal name meaning "jewelry for the neck." Wife of Ashur in the tribe of Judah (1 Chron. 4:5,7).

HELAM (Hē´ lam) Place-name meaning "their army." The earliest Greek translation of Ezek. 47:16 apparently locates it between Damascus and Hamath in Syria. First Maccabees 5:26 seems to indicate a place in the northern part of the territory east of the Jordan. Helam is the region, rather than a city, where David defeated the army of Hadadezer and thus gained control of Syria (2 Sam. 10:15-19).

HELBAH (Hĕl´ ba) Place-name meaning "forest." City in tribal territory of Asher which Asher could not drive out (Judg. 1:31). Some have seen this as an inadvertent copying of Ahlab. Most identify Helbah with Mahalib, mentioned in Assyrian monuments. It is four miles northeast of Tyre. See *Mahalab.*

HELBON (Hĕl´ bŏn) Place-name meaning "forest." City known for its trade in wine mentioned in Ezekiel's lament over Tyre (Ezek. 27:18). It is modern Halbun about 11 miles north of Damascus.

HELDAI (Hĕl´ dā ī) Personal name meaning "mole." **1.** Officer in charge of David's army for the twelfth month of the year (1 Chron. 27:15). He is apparently the same as Heled, David's military hero (1 Chron. 11:30), called Heleb in 2 Sam. 23:29. **2.** Man who returned from exile in Babylon, apparently with a gift of silver and gold, which God told Zechariah to take and have made into a crown for Joshua, the high priest (Zech. 6:10). Verse 14 calls him Helem, which probably represents a copying change. Some students think Heldai was a nickname and Helem the official name. The earliest Greek translation took the names in this verse as common nouns rather than as proper names, translating Heldai as "the rulers."

HELEB (Hē´ lĕb) Personal name meaning "fat" or "the best." One of David's military heroes (2 Sam. 23:29), probably a copyist's change from Heled in the parallel passage (1 Chron. 11:30), Heled also appearing in many manuscripts of 2 Samuel. See *Heldai.*

HELECH (Hē´ lĕk) Transliteration of Hebrew noun in NRSV, NIV which KJV, TEV, NASB interpret as meaning "your army." REB interprets Helech with many modern Bible students and reference books to refer to Cilicia. The precise meaning in the context is not known. Ezekiel described the good days of Tyre as having its massive city walls protected by foreign soldiers, but the precise home of these soldiers is not certain (Ezek. 27:11). See *Cilicia.*

HELED (Hē´ lĕd) Personal name meaning "life." See *Heldai; Heleb; Helem.*

HELEK (Hē´ lĕk) Personal name meaning "portion." Son of Gilead from the tribe of Manasseh and original clan ancestor of the Helekites (Num. 26:30). The clan received an allotment in the tribe's share of the promised land (Josh. 17:2).

HELEKITE (Hē´ lĕk īt) Member of clan of Helek. See *Helek.*

HELEM (Hē´ lĕm) Personal name meaning "beat, strike." Member of tribe of Asher (1 Chron. 7:35), probably the same name with a copying change as Hotham (v. 32). The same English spelling is derived from a different Hebrew word meaning "power." The name appears in Zech. 6:14 as a variant to Heldai in 6:10. See *Heldai.*

HELEPH (Hē´ lĕph) Place-name meaning "replacement settlement" or "settlement of reeds." Border city of the tribal allotment of Naphtali (Josh. 19:33). It is often identified with Khirbet Arbathah just northeast of Mount Tabor, but some Bible students think this location is too far south. Others think Heleph represents the southern border of Naphtali.

HELEZ (Hē´ lĕz) Personal name, perhaps meaning "ready for battle." **1.** David's military hero (2 Sam. 23:26) in charge of the army for the seventh month (1 Chron. 27:10). **2.** Member of the family of Caleb and Jerahmeel in the tribe of Judah (1 Chron. 2:39).

HELI (Hē´ lī) Hebrew personal name meaning "high." The son of Matthat and father of Joseph, Jesus' earthly father (Luke 3:23-24). His relationship to Jesus is variously explained by Bible students in light of Matt. 1:16, which makes Joseph's father to be Jacob. He has been seen as the father of Joseph, a more remote ancestor of Joseph, or an ancestor of Mary. Either Jacob and Heli are variant names of the same person ("son of" means "descendant of" as in other genealogies), or Luke preserved the genealogy of Mary rather than of Joseph. A totally satisfactory answer to the question has not been found. The name probably represents a Greek form of the Hebrew Eli (NASB).

HELIOPOLIS (Hē lǐ ŏp´ o lǐs) **1.** Greek name for Egyptian city that meant "city of the sun." Its name in Egyptian means "pillar town" and was rendered in Akkadian as *Ana* and in Hebrew as *On* or *Aven* (Gen. 41:45; 46:20; Ezek. 30:17). The city was sacred to the sun god Re or Atum and is designated *bet-shemesh*, "house/temple of the sun" in Jer. 43:13. Kings were crowned there during the new kingdom era. To the two cities of Pithom and Rameses, built in Egypt by

the Israelite slaves, the Septuagint adds "and On, which is the city of the sun." It has been identified as Tell Hisn in Matariyeh, just north of Cairo. See *On.* **2.** Ancient city of Baalbek ("Lord of the Valley") located in the Beqaa Valley of Lebanon about 50 miles east of Beirut. Although it was a very ancient city, it was renamed Heliopolis in the third or second century B.C. Baalbek was an important city in early times but declined through both the Hellenistic period and the early part of the Roman era. During the days of the later Roman Empire, its influence grew as a center for the cult worship of Juniper, Mercury, and Venus (which was based upon an older cult worship of the Semitic gods Hadad, Atargatis, and Baal). Impressive ruins have been excavated at Baalbek including a temple to Jupiter, a temple to Baachus, and one to Venus.

HELKAI (Hĕl´ kā ī) Personal name meaning "my portion." Priest when Joiakim was high priest one generation after the return from the exile under Zerubbabel (Neh. 12:15).

HELKATH (Hĕl´ kăth) Place-name meaning "flat place." Border town in the tribal allotment of Asher (Josh. 19:25) given to the Levites (Josh. 21:31). It is called Hukok in the parallel passage (1 Chron. 6:75). It is either modern Tell Qassis on the west bank of the Kishon River or Tell tel-Harbaj just south of Acco.

HELKATH-HAZZURIM (Hĕl kăth-hăz zū´ rĭm) Place-name meaning "field of flint stones" or "field of battle." Site of "play" (2 Sam. 2:14) battle between young warriors of Saul and those of David leading to defeat of Ish-bosheth's army (2 Sam. 2:12-17). The somewhat obscure Hebrew play on words to name the field near

View of magnificent architectural ruins at ancient Baalbek (Heliopolis).

H

Columns of the temple of Jupiter at Baalbek in Lebanon.

Gibeon has led to numerous translation attempts. REB reads "Field of Blades."

HELL Usually understood as the final abode of the unrighteous dead wherein the ungodly suffer eternal punishment; the term translates one OT word and several NT words.

Old Testament Usage The only Hebrew word translated "hell" in the KJV (though not in modern translatons) is Sheol. Sheol itself is a broad term that, depending on the context, may signify the abode of both the righteous dead and the ungodly dead. See *Sheol.*

New Testament Usage In the NT three words are translated "hell": *Gehenna* (Matt. 5:22,29-30; 10:28; 18:19; Mark 9:43,45,47; Luke 12:5; James 3:6), *Hades* (Matt.11:23; 16:18; Luke 10:15; 16:23; Acts 2:27,31; Rev. 1:18; 20:13-14), and *Tartarus* (2 Pet. 2:4). It is significant that, contrary to Sheol, none of the NT terms for hell or Gehenna are used simply for the grave. See *Gehenna; Hades.*

In paganism Hades originally referred to the god of the netherworld but later came to refer to the place of the dead. In Luke 16:23 Hades is definitely depicted as a place of torment (Luke 10:15). Revelation 20:13 depicts Hades as an interim place of habitation for the lost until the final judgment. Gehenna was the name of a valley on the southeast of Jerusalem into which little children were thrown as sacrifices to a god named Moloch.

There is a fundamental difference between Hades and Gehenna that is vital to the understanding of God's punitive justice. From its use in the NT, Hades is viewed as the place that receives the ungodly for the intervening period between death and resurrection. Gehenna may be equated with the everlasting fire that was originally prepared for the devil and his angels (Matt. 25:41), and the lake of fire in Rev. 20:14 into which are cast death and hell. Following the resurrection and the judgment of the lost, Gehenna becomes the final place of punishment by eternal fire.

Tartarus was regarded by the ancient Greeks as that abiding place where rebellious gods and other wicked ones were punished. Its only NT use is in 2 Pet. 2:4 which says that the angels that sinned "were confined in Tartarus" and "kept unto judgment."

Additional Descriptions of Suffering After final judgment, the lost experience continual and unimaginable suffering and torment. Such phrases as "weeping and gnashing of teeth" and "outer darkness" (Matt. 8:12; 22:13; 24:51; 25:30; 13:28) and "their worm does not die, and the fire is not quenched" (Mark 9:44,46,48 HCSB) indicate emotional and physical, as well as spiritual, suffering. Degrees of judgment and suffering are also indicated by such texts as Matt. 10:15; 11:22,24; 18:6; Mark 6:11; Luke 10:12,14.

Interpretations There are two broad questions to be answered which are vital to a proper understanding of the biblical teaching concerning hell. First, is the punishment of hell eternal or temporary? Second, does the Bible teach a literal or figurative hell?

Eternal or temporal? The Word of God teaches that the suffering of the lost in hell is eternal (Isa. 66:24; Matt. 25:46; Mark 9:44,46,48; Rev. 14:11). The assertion that God would be unfair to punish eternally a temporal sin underestimates the seriousness of sin, the spiritual nature of sin, and the supreme holiness of God.

Figurative or literal? That the Scriptures teach a literal hell is clear. The story of the rich man and Lazarus is most likely a true historical narrative revealed by Christ rather than a parable (Luke 16). Jesus teaches in Matt. 10:28 that both the soul and body can be cast into hell. This requires that hell be a literal place, for a physical body (the only kind of body there is) cannot be cast into anything metaphorical.

Among evangelicals, the most common difference of opinion is whether hell as a place of suffering is described with figurative language, literal language, or a combination of the two. Some believe the Bible teaches that hell is real, but the language used to describe it is figurative. This is an approach consistent with one taken by many concerning John's descriptions of heaven in Revelation. As heaven is more magnificent than the description in Revelation, also hell is so terrible that human language falls short.

However, there is strong evidence to indicate that literal language is used and that the Bible does in fact teach literal fire and other sufferings. The parable of the tares in Matt. 13, which discusses eternal judgment, is helpful here. The Son of man, the world, children of the kingdom, the children of the wicked one, the devil, the end of the world, the angels, the gatherings—all are literal figures in the parable. It is then natural to

H

conclude that the burning of the tares should also be taken literally.

Few would question that the Bible reveals hell as a place of spiritual and emotional torment for the finally impenitent. Since man is a physical being (body) as well as emotional and spiritual (soul and spirit), it is most consistent with Scripture to conclude that physical suffering is also a part of the destiny of the lost. It is no wonder why "it is a terrifying thing to fall into the hands of the living God" (Heb. 10:31 HCSB), and why the emphasis on evangelism is what makes the Great Commission great. See *Everlasting Punishment; Judgment Day; Wrath, Wrath of God.*

David G. Shackelford and E. Ray Clendenen

HELLENISM Used to describe any influence of classical Greek thought on Western heritage. It is derived from *hellas,* Greek for the nation Greece. Hellenism is often associated with the philosophy of Socrates, Plato, and Aristotle but is seen also in Greek philosophies such as Pythagoreanism, Stoicism, and Epicureanism. Hellenism was not merely academic. The various Greek philosophies were essentially religious, providing explanations of the universe and offering salvation through human reason.

While Greek philosophies differed on a number of issues, many shared a dualistic view of reality that drew a sharp distinction between physical and mental reality. Plato's "Allegory of the Cave" illustrates this bifurcation, describing an imaginary cave where prisoners were permanently chained. These prisoners heard people talking and saw their shadows on the wall but never saw the outside world. They believed the shadows were real, not knowing the real world lay beyond the cave. Plato's point is that we are like prisoners, trapped in this physical world of the five senses, believing only what we can see. Plato believed the natural world was really a shadow; the real world was the supernatural world of the soul. For many Greek thinkers, the physical world represented the temporal, transitory, and evil, while the world of the soul was eternal, real, and good. This principle shaped Greek thought that formed the intellectual context in which Christianity was born. This strain of Greek thought saw the human body as being evil but the mind or soul as being immortal and good. The soul was trapped in the body like a person in prison.

History Hellenism dates from early Greek culture but became dominant during the reign of Alexander the Great (336–323 B.C.). Alexander, tutored by Aristotle, believed that Greek philosophy offered the key to enlightenment for the barbarians. As Alexander conquered, his image was planted around the world, evidenced by the numerous cities named after him. He pursued an intentional process of indoctrinating conquered nations in Hellenistic philosophy. When the empire was divided after Alexander's death, the Ptolemaic dynasty (based in Egypt) reigned over the Holy Land (301–198 B.C.). The Ptolemies instituted a gentle policy of Hellenization, primarily through education and language. The Hellenistic culture of Alexandria strongly impacted Jewish and Christian communities. The Koine Greek language became the *lingua franca,* an influence seen in the Greek terms used to name the Jewish "synagogue" (*sunagoge*) and the NT "church" (*ekklesia*). In about 275 B.C. Jewish scholars produced the first translation of the Hebrew Scriptures, the Greek Septuagint (LXX). Philo the Jew (ca. 30 B.C.–A.D. 40) reinterpreted Judaism consistent with Greek philosophy. As the Church emerged from Alexandrian Judaism, early Christian thinkers such as Justin Martyr, Origen, and Clement of Alexandria viewed Christianity as the fulfillment of Greek philosophy, rather than being its rival.

While Jews thrived in Alexandria under the Ptolemies, the Palestinian Jews faced harsher Hellenization by the Seleucid dynasty, Syrian Greeks who dominated Palestine 198–167 B.C., having wrested control of Palestine from the Ptolemies. This forced Hellenization peaked during the reign of Antiochus IV (Antiochus Epiphanes), who sought to destroy Judaism, attacking on the Sabbath day and desecrating the

The temple of Apollo at the international Hellenistic shrine of Delphi.

Colossal statue of the Roman god Mars (Greek: Ares). Dual Greco-Roman gods was a mark of Hellenism.

book of Hebrews draws a sharp distinction between the earthly temple and the heavenly temple, utilizing the language of Plato. The earthly tabernacle was a shadow (*skia*) and type (*tupos*) of the heavenly tabernacle (Heb. 8:2-6; 9:21-24). Paul uses similar language in describing our citizenship in heaven (Phil. 3:20). These similarities do not suggest uncritical application of Greek philosophy to Christian theology, but that the church used existing Greek concepts to explain the unsearchable riches of Christ to a Hellenistic culture.

The Greeks found Christian doctrine scandalous, particularly the incarnation and resurrection, but the NT authors did not compromise the gospel (1 Cor. 1:18-25; 15:12). So while John utilized the philosophical term *logos*, he also claimed that "the Word became flesh and took up residence among us" (John 1:14 HCSB; 1 John 1:1-2; 2:22; 4:1-3; 5:1). That the immortal *logos* would take on evil human flesh was inconceivable to Greek thinkers. The resurrection caused a similar problem. The Greeks taught immortality of the soul for centuries, but Paul's

Bust of Demosthenes (384–322 B.C.), the greatest of Greek orators.

temple in Jerusalem. The account of the Jews' resistance, led by the Maccabee family, is recorded in the extracanonical books of 1–4 Maccabees. The Maccabees gained religious and political freedom for Palestine (167–63 B.C.), until Roman domination began.

Influence The early church experienced tension between hellenized Jewish believers and traditional Palestinian Jews, a dispute which led to the naming of the earliest deacons (Acts 6:1-6). Further, Jewish believers wanted to require Gentile believers to become Jews as a prerequisite to becoming Christian. Gentile believers challenged some Jewish traditions, leading to a conflict resulting in the Jerusalem Council (Acts 14:4-7; 15:1-3), which ruled that the Gentiles did not have to become Jewish to be saved.

The Greek language was crucial in the spread of the gospel. NT authors used and quoted from the Septuagint and the NT was written in Koine Greek. Some passages in the NT seem to reflect Greek thought as well as Greek terminology. Greek influence shows in the use of *logos* in John 1:1-14, a term Stoic philosophers used to describe the creative order of the universe. The

H

proclamation on Mars Hill of bodily resurrection to eternal life was scandalous (Acts 17:30-34).

Unfortunately, some Hellenistic Gnostic Christians did compromise the gospel to conform to Greek philosophy. Cerinthian Gnostics taught a docetic Christology that denied the full humanity of Christ, accepting Greek philosophical dualism. For God (spiritual, good) to come into flesh (evil) was incomprehensible. These docetic Gnostics taught that Jesus was wholly divine and was either a spirit adopting a human body or a ghostly apparition who had no real physical body. John directly confronted this heresy, affirming in graphic terms the full corporeal humanity of Christ (John 1:1-14; 1 John 1:1-2; 2:22; 4:1-3; 5:1). The pattern of the early church is a good example to the church in every age, making the gospel relevant to culture without compromising doctrine.

Later scholars proposed that the church borrowed from Greek philosophy and mystery religions. In particular, they asserted a similarity between the resurrection of Jesus and the sun worship in Greek mystery religions, in which the sun is reborn and dies repeatedly. This speculation is wrong. The Gospel writers carefully documented their historical narratives to ensure dramatic differences from mythology about dying and rising gods. These gods were mythological and imaginary; Jesus was historical and His miracles tangible and undeniable. So while the NT was produced in a Hellenistic culture, the Church consistently refused to compromise the Gospel in order to placate Hellenistic cultural expectations. *Steve W. Lemke*

HELLENISTS Group of early Christians whose language and culture was Greek rather than Hebrew. One of the first conflicts among believers in the early church was between those with a Greek background and those who had grown up in the Hebrew tradition (Acts 6:1; 9:29). See *Hellenism.*

HELMET See *Arms and Armor.*

HELON (Hē´ lŏn) Personal name meaning "powerful." Father of the leader of the tribe of Zebulun under Moses (Num. 1:9).

HELP, HELPS In addition to the usual sense of assistance, the KJV used "helps" in two technical senses: for equipment used to secure a ship in storm (Acts 27:17) and for a gift of ministry

Hellenistic tombs outside the west gate at Hierapolis.

(1 Cor. 12:28). Modern translations understand the "helps" of Acts 27 in various senses: ropes (NIV, TEV); supporting cables (NASB); tackle (REB); or generally as measures to undergird the ship (NRSV). The helps of 1 Corinthians refer to the ability to offer help or assistance. In the Septuagint, God is known as the help of those who lack strength and live in poverty (Sirach 11:12). It has been suggested that Paul refers to the ministry of the deacons who care for the poor and the sick. A general reference to all those who demonstrate love in their dealings with others is possible.

HELPER NASB translation of *parakletos*, a distinctive title for the Holy Spirit in the Gospel of John (14:16,26; 15:26; 16:7). Other versions translate the term "Comforter" (KJV), "Advocate" (NEB), or "Counselor" (HCSB, RSV, NIV). Because *parakletos* is difficult to translate with any single word, some interpreters opt for making "Paraclete" an English word and allowing the relevant Johannine passages to provide its meaning.

The Helper, who could not come until Jesus departed (John 16:7), functions as the abiding presence of Jesus among His disciples (John 14:16-18). Nearly everything said of the Helper is also said of Jesus in the Gospel, and the Helper actually comes as "another Counselor (*parakletos*)" (John 14:16), implying that Jesus had been the first (1 John 2:1).

Jesus described the role of the Helper primarily with verbs of speaking. The Helper would be sent by the Father to "teach" the disciples and to bring to remembrance all Jesus "said" to them (John 14:26; 16:14-15). Like Jesus, the Helper was "sent" to "bear witness" (John 15:26-27). The Helper's function in relation to the world involves "reproving" it concerning sin, righteousness, and judgment (John 16:8). The Helper would also "guide" Jesus' disciples into all truth by "speaking" what He hears and "showing" what is to come (John 16:13). By so doing He would "glorify" Jesus (John 16:14). See *Advocate; Comforter; Counselor; Holy Spirit; Paraclete.*   *R. Robert Creech*

HELP MEET KJV term for woman as a helper precisely adapted to man (Gen. 2:18). Modern translations supply various equivalents: helper suitable for him (NASB, NIV); helper as his partner (NRSV); a suitable companion to help him (TEV). The noun translated "helper" or "partner" does not suggest subordination. Elsewhere the term is used of God as Help (1 Chron. 12:18; Pss. 30:10; 54:4; 121:1) or of military allies (Jer. 47:4; Nah. 3:9). The adjective "meet" (translated "suitable," "comparable," or "corresponding") stresses that woman, unlike the animals (Gen. 2:20), can be truly one with man (2:24), that is, enjoy full fellowship and partnership in humanity's God-given task (Gen. 1:27-28) of rule and dominion.

HELVE KJV term used for the handle of an ax (Deut. 19:5).

HEM Border of a cloth article doubled back and stitched down to prevent the cloth from unraveling. Biblical references to the "hem" of a garment refer more generally to its edge or border. The border of Aaron's high priestly robe was decorated with blue, purple, and scarlet pomegranates and gold bells (Exod. 28:31-35; 39:22-26). Sometimes the woof (the vertical filling threads in woven cloth) were left long to prevent unraveling. The result of these long threads was a fringed border. The fringe on the corners of their garments was to remind the Israelites of the law of God (Num. 15:38-39). The fringed "hem" of Jesus' garment conveyed healing power to those who in faith touched it (Matt. 9:20; 14:36; Mark 6:56; Luke 8:44).

HEMAM (Hē´ măm) Personal name of uncertain meaning. Descendant of Seir (Gen. 36:22). The parallel passage spells the name Homam (1 Chron. 1:39).

HEMAN (Hē´ măn) Personal name meaning "faithful." **1.** In Gen. 36:22, one of the sons of Lotan mentioned among the descendants of Esau. KJV renders the name *Hemam.* **2.** In

1 Kings 4:31, a notable sage to whose wisdom that of Solomon is compared. **3.** In 1 Chron. 6:33, the son of Joel, a Kohathite. He was one of the temple singers under David and Solomon. In 1 Chron. 25:5, he is called a seer. Elsewhere in that chapter he is said to have prophesied using musical instruments. He may be the same as the Heman mentioned in 1 Kings 4:31. The psalm title attributes Ps. 88 to Heman.

HEMATH (Hē´ măth) (KJV) See *Hamath; Hammath.*

HEMDAN (Hĕm´ dăn) Personal name meaning "beauty, charm." Descendant of Seir and thus an Edomite (Gen. 36:26). The parallel passage spells the name Hamran (1 Chron. 1:41 NASB).

HEMLOCK KJV translation of two Hebrew terms. Modern translations agree in translating that in Hos. 10:4 as poisonous weed(s). The term at Amos 6:12 is translated as "bitterness" (NASB margins, NIV), "poison" (REB), and "wormwood" (NRSV, NASB). See *Gall.*

HEMORRHAGE Heavy or uncontrollable bleeding. The KJV translates the underlying Hebrew and Greek terms as "issue of blood" (Lev. 12:7; Matt. 9:20) or "fountain of blood" (Mark 5:29). Modern translations render these terms as hemorrhage, flow, or discharge of blood. Mosaic law said any discharge of blood, whether associated with the birthing process (Lev. 12:7), with menstruation (Lev. 15:19), or continued bleeding (Lev. 15:25; Matt. 9:20) rendered a woman unclean. Those ritually unclean were separated from God (represented by the tabernacle, Lev. 15:31) and from the congregation of Israel (Num. 5:2). The woman suffering from a hemorrhage (Matt. 9:20; Mark 5:29; Luke 8:43-44) was thus a religious and social outcast who only dared approach Jesus from behind. Contrary to expectations, the woman did not give her uncleanness to Jesus. Rather, Jesus' healing power made the woman clean.

HEMORRHOIDS Mass of dilated veins and swollen tissue in the vicinity of the anus. The KJV translators understood the affliction of Deut. 28:27; 1 Sam. 5:6,9,12 as hemorrhoids (or emerods). Modern versions are divided in their understanding of the term in Deuteronomy. Some take a reference to tumors (NASB, NIV, REB). Others find a reference to sores (TEV) or

H

ulcers (NRSV). Modern versions agree that the affliction of 1 Samuel was tumors, probably associated with bubonic plague.

HEN (*fowl*) Greek word translated "hen" can refer to the female of any bird, not just the domesticated fowl. Only two references to the hen occur in the Scriptures (Matt. 23:37; Luke 13:34). In both instances the term is used figuratively of God's care for His people. The hen stands as a figure of the self-sacrifice and tender motherliness of God revealed in Christ.

Janice Meier

HEN (*person*) Hebrew word for "grace, favor" used as either a proper name or a title (meaning "favored one") of Josiah son of Zephaniah (Zech. 6:14; cp. 6:10) if the present Hebrew text is original. The Syriac version (followed by the NRSV, REB, TEV) has the name Josiah in place of "hen" in 6:14. The earliest Greek version understood the name as a title.

HENA (Hē´ nȧ) Place-name of uncertain meaning. City Sennacherib, king of Assyria, captured prior to threatening Hezekiah and Jerusalem in 701 B.C. (2 Kings 18:34). Sennacherib used the historical example to brag and to persuade Hezekiah not to rely on God for protection against Sennacherib. Hena may be the same as Ana or Anat at the middle of the course of the Euphrates River.

HENADAD (Hĕn´ ȧ dăd) Personal name meaning "grace of Hadad (the god)." Clan of Levites who supervised the rebuilding of the temple under Zerubbabel after 537 B.C. (Ezra 3:9). Clan members also helped Nehemiah rebuild Jerusalem's walls (Neh. 3:18,24) and signed Nehemiah's covenant of obedience (Neh. 10:10).

HENNA See *Plants*.

HENOCH (Hē´ nŏk) (KJV, 1 Chron. 1:3,33) See *Enoch*.

HEPHER (Hĕ´ phĕr) Personal name meaning "well" or "shame." **1.** Original family ancestor in clan of Gilead and father of Zelophehad (Num. 26:28-37). He belonged to the tribe of Manasseh (Josh. 17:1-2). **2.** A hero in David's wilderness army (1 Chron. 11:36). 3. Member of the tribe of Judah (1 Chron. 4:6).

HEPHERITE (Hē´ phĕr īt) Descendant of family of Hepher. See *Hepher*.

HEPHZIBAH (Hĕph´ zĭ bȧ) Personal name meaning "my delight is in her." **1.** In 2 Kings 21:1 the mother of Manasseh, king of Judah. **2.** In Isa. 62:4 it is used as a symbolic name for Jerusalem. When Jerusalem is restored, she will no longer be forsaken and desolate; she will be called Hephzibah, for God's delight will be in her.

HERALD Official messenger. The herald of Dan. 3:4 was responsible for publicizing the king's law and the penalty of disobedience. Noah is described as a herald of righteousness (2 Pet. 2:5), that is, one who announced God's requirements. Paul was appointed as a herald or preacher of the gospel. First Timothy 2:5-7 outlines Paul's message as the uniqueness of God, Christ's unique role as mediator between God and humanity, and Christ's death as ransom. Second Timothy 1:9-11 outlines Paul's gospel as the good news that God has given grace by sending Christ who abolished death and brought life.

HERBS See *Plants*.

HERBS, BITTER Salad of bitter herbs was eaten as part of the Passover observance (Exod. 12:8; Num. 9:11). Such a meal could be quickly prepared and was appropriate to commemorate Israel's hasty retreat from Egypt (Exod. 12:11). Later the bitter herbs were associated with the bitterness of Egyptian slavery (cp. Exod. 1:14). Bitter herbs possibly included lettuce, chicory, eryngo, horseradish, and sow thistle. See *Plants*.

HERD Number of animals kept together under human control. In biblical usage "herd" generally refers to cattle in contrast to "flock" which refers to sheep or goats. Herds were a source of meat and dairy products, of agricultural labor (1 Chron. 12:40; Isa. 46:1), and of sacrifices (Num. 7:3; Ps. 69:31; Isa. 66:3). Herds were regarded as a sign of wealth (Gen. 13:5; 32:7; 45:10). Cattle were generally kept in open pasture. Pen-fed beef was a luxury item (Amos 6:4; Hab. 3:17). See *Cattle*.

HERDSMAN One who cares for cattle in contrast to a shepherd who cares for sheep. Amos served as a herdsman before receiving his prophetic call (Amos 7:14). Herdsmen were

H

sometimes included among high-ranking officials of ancient kings (1 Chron. 27:29; 28:1; cp. Gen. 46:34). Herdsmen were sometimes paid from the products of the herd (1 Cor. 9:7).

HERES (Hē′ rĕs) Place-name meaning "sun." A mountain pass over which Gideon traveled in returning from his battle with the Midianites (Judg. 8:13). It is distinct from the more western Mount Heres in Judg. 1:35, often identified with Beth-shemesh ("house of the sun"). KJV translates 8:13 as "before the sun was up" as compared to NASB, "by the ascent of Heres." Location of Gideon's pass is not known, though some scholars now locate it as the Ascent of Horus that leads to Tell Deir Alla east of the Jordan. Strong manuscript evidence reads "city of Heres" or Heliopolis in Isa. 19:18 (cp. REB, TEV, NRSV). See *Heliopolis.*

HERESH (Hē′ rĕsh) Personal name meaning "unable to speak." Levite who lived near Jerusalem after the return from exile about 537 B.C. (1 Chron. 9:15).

HERESY Opinion or doctrine not in line with the accepted teaching of a church; the opposite of orthodoxy. Our English word is derived from a Greek word that has the basic idea of "choice." In ancient classical Greek it was used predominantly to refer to the philosophical school to which one chose to belong. Later, it came to be associated with the teaching of philosophical schools.

The word had a similar usage in Jewish writings. Josephus, a Jewish historian of the first century from whom we learn much of what we know about the Judaism of NT times, used the word to refer to the various Jewish parties (or schools of thought) such as the Pharisees, Sadducees, and Essenes. Jewish rabbis employed the term in a bad sense applying it to groups who had separated from the main stream of Jewish teaching.

The word has several usages in the NT but never has the technical sense of "heresy" as we understand it today. It may be classified as follows:

(1) Most frequently, especially in Acts, it has the same meaning as Josephus. In Acts 5:17; 15:5; and 26:5, where it refers to the Pharisees and Sadducees, it simply means party or sect.

(2) In Acts 24:14 and 28:22 it is used in a slightly derogatory sense, referring to Christians as they were viewed to be separatists or sectarians by the Jews. This usage conforms to that of the rabbis.

(3) Paul used the term to refer to groups that threatened the harmonious relations of the church. In 1 Cor. 11:19, where he was writing about the disgraceful way in which the Corinthians were observing the Lord's Supper, the word has to do with the outward manifestations of the factions he mentioned in verse 18. In Gal. 5:20 it is one of the works of the flesh and is in a grouping including strife, seditions, and envyings. It apparently has to do with people who choose to place their own desires above the fellowship of the church. Titus 3:10 speaks of a man who is a heretic. Since the context of the verse has to do with quarreling and dissension, the idea in this passage seems to be that of a fractious person.

(4) In 2 Pet. 2:1 it comes closest to our meaning of the term. It clearly refers to false prophets who have denied the true teaching about Christ. Since the remainder of 2 Pet. 2 refers to the immoral living of the false prophets, the word also refers to their decadent living. The reference to the heretic in Titus 3:10 may belong to this category since the verse mentions disputes about genealogies, a doctrinal matter.

It is clear that in the NT, the concept of heresy had more to do with fellowship within the church than with doctrinal teachings. While the writers of the NT were certainly concerned about false teachings, they apparently were just as disturbed by improper attitudes.

In the writings of Ignatius, a leader of the church in the early second century, the word takes on the technical meaning of a heresy. Most frequently in the writings of the early church fathers, the heresy about which they were concerned was Gnosticism, a teaching which denied that Jesus was fully human. See *Christ, Christology; Gnosticism.*   *W. T. Edwards, Jr.*

HERETH (Hē′ rĕth) Modern translation spelling of Hareth; place-name meaning "cut in to." Forest in which David hid from Saul after settling his parents with the king of Moab (1 Sam. 22:4-5). Some identify it with Horesh (1 Sam. 23:15) located at Khirbet Khoreisa two miles south of Ziph. Others place it at the village of Kharas near

H

Keilah. From Hereth, David attacked the Philistines at Keilah (1 Sam. 23:1-5).

HERITAGE Legacy, inheritance, birthright. The OT frequently refers to the promised land as Israel's heritage from God (Exod. 6:8; Pss. 16:6; 135:12). Children are regarded as a heritage from God (Ps. 127:3). The law and God's protective care are likewise called a heritage (Ps. 119:111; Isa. 54:17). Israel is called God's heritage (Ps. 94:5; Jer. 12:7; Joel 3:2). This image is applied to the church in 1 Pet. 5:3 (cp. NASB margin, "allotment"). Revelation 21:7 speaks of the water of life as the heritage of those martyrs who conquered through their faithfulness. See *Inheritance*.

HERMAS (Hĕr´ màs) Christian to whom Paul sent greetings (Rom. 16:14). His name, the variant spelling of the Greek god Hermes, may indicate he was a slave, since many slaves were named for gods. See *Apostolic Fathers*.

HERMENEUTICS See *Bible Hermeneutics*.

HERMES (Hĕr´ mĕz) In Acts 14:12 the Greek deity for whom the superstitious people at Lystra took Paul. KJV uses the god's Latin name, Mer-

Marble head of Hermes dating from the first century B.C. to the first century A.D. from Dalmatia.

curius. Hermes was known as a messenger of the gods and was associated with eloquence. Paul's role as chief speaker made the Lystrans think of Hermes.

HERMETIC LITERATURE Greek writings composed in Egypt between A.D. 100 and 300 associated with the name "Hermes Trimegistos" (Thrice-great Hermes). The Hermetic literature is a diverse collection. Some of the texts are primarily astrological, magical, or alchemical. Others are primarily religious and philosophical texts. Some of the texts are monistic (viewing all reality as a unity) and pantheistic (seeing God present in everything). Others are dualistic (seeing God and the creation as separate).

The best-known Hermetic writing is the tractate titled *Poimandres* (perhaps from the Coptic for "knowledge of the sungod"). Poimandres offers to reveal to Hermes the secret nature of creation and God. According to the myth, God created the *nous* (mind, intelligence) which in turn created (physical) nature. God then created the *anthropos*, the original man. In the fall this man united with nature to produce the seven androgynous persons who were the source of the human race. Thus each person consists of a body (from nature) which imprisons the soul (from God). Salvation from the body and deliverance from the oppressive fate of the stars was achieved by receiving knowledge of the nature of things. Reception of such knowledge is described as rebirth. By repressing the bodily senses, the faithful Hermetic hoped to ascend past the seven astral spheres and to reunite with God.

The Hermetic doctrine has similarities with gnostic teaching. The Hermetic writings unlike Gnosticism did not regard nature itself as evil or the direct agent of creation (*demiurge*) as the enemy of God. Some scholars have seen the influence of Hermetic doctrine in the Gospel of John (creation by the *logos*, rebirth). More likely, both John and the later Hermetics developed earlier Jewish and Greek ideas independently. See *Gnosticism; John*.

HERMOGENES (Hĕr mŏg̀ ə nēz) Personal name meaning "born of Hermes." Follower who deserted Paul, apparently while he was in prison in Ephesus (2 Tim. 1:15). Paul's statement indicates acute disappointment in Hermogenes but does not say he became an apostate. Nothing else is known of him.

HERMON, MOUNT (Hĕr´ mon) Place-name meaning "devoted mountain." Site of sanctuary of Baal and northern boundary of Israel. The name Hermon was called Sarion (Sirion) by the Sidonians (Phoenicians) (Deut. 3:9; Ps. 29:6) and Sanir (Senir) by the Amorites (Deut. 3:9). Both appellations signify "breastplate," evidently because of the mountain's rounded snow-covered tip that gleaned and shone in the sunlight. The latter name appears twice in the OT, seemingly as the name of a peak adjacent to Hermon (1 Chron. 5:23; Song 4:8). It is also called Sion (Deut. 4:48), probably on account of its height. Once it is called "Hermons." KJV mistakenly renders this as "the Hermonites" (Ps. 42:6). This is probably a reference to the triple summits of the mountain.

The Hermon range is the southern spur of the Anti-Lebanon chain of mountains which runs parallel to the Lebanon range being separated from it by the valley of Beqaa. Hermon, being 9,100 feet above sea level, is the highest mountain in Syria. It can be seen from as far away as the Dead Sea—120 miles. The range is approximately 28 miles in length and reaches a width of 15 miles. Its peak is covered with snow two-thirds of the year. Water from its melting snow flows into the rivers of the Hauran and provides the principal source for the Jordan River. Although Hermon receives about 60 inches of precipitation (dew, snow, rain) per year, practically no vegetation grows above the snow line, where there is an almost complete absence of soil. Below it, the mountain slopes are covered with trees and vineyards. Wolves, leopards, and Syrian bears live in its forests. The biblical record praises the dew of Hermon (Ps. 133:3), its lions (Song 4:8), and its cypresses (Ezek. 27:5).

The mount is significant for four reasons. (1) It was the northern border of the Amorite kingdom (Deut. 3:8; 4:48). (2) It marked the northern limits of Joshua's victorious campaigns (Josh. 11:17; 12:1; 13:5). (3) It has always been regarded as a sacred mountain. (4) Some scholars believe the transfiguration of Jesus occurred on Hermon.   *Gary Baldwin*

HERMONITES KJV translators understood the Hebrew plural "Hermans" (Ps. 42:6) to refer to the inhabitants of the slopes of Mount Hermon. Modern translations take the plural to refer to the three "peaks of Hermon" (NASB).

HEROD (Hĕr´ od) Name given to the family ruling Palestine immediately before and to some

View of Mount Hermon from the ancient city-mound of Hazor in northern Galilee.

H

degree during the first half of the first Christian century. Their family history was complex, and what information has come down has been frequently meager, conflicting, and difficult to harmonize. The chief sources are the references in the NT, the Jewish historian Flavius Josephus, and a few obscure references by Roman historians, such as Dio Cassius, Plutarch, and Strabo.

The most prominent family member and ruler was Herod, son of Antipater who had been appointed governor of Idumea by Alexandra Salome, the Maccabean queen who ruled Palestine 78–69 B.C. With the permission of the Romans, Antipater left his son Phasael as Prefect of Jerusalem and his second son, Herod, governor of Galilee. See *Intertestamental History and Literature.*

Other Herods named in the NT include the following:

Agrippa I, the son of Aristobulus and grandson of Herod. He ruled with the title of king from A.D. 41–44. Agrippa I ordered James the son of Zebedee killed with the sword and imprisoned Peter (Acts 12:1-23).

Agrippa II, the son of Agrippa I, heard Paul's defense (Acts 25:13-27; cp. Acts 26:32). With his death the Herodian dynasty came to an end, in title as well as in fact.

Drusilla (Acts 24:24) was the third and youngest daughter of Agrippa I. She had been married briefly at age 14 to Azizus, king of Emessa, probably in the year 52. In 53 or 54 she was married to Felix, the Roman procurator.

Bernice was the sister of Drusilla and Agrippa II and also his wife. Paul appeared before them in Acts 25.

Herod Philip was the son of Herod the Great and Cleopatra of Jerusalem (Luke 3:1). He built Caesarea Philippi and was governor of the northeastern districts of Iturea, Gaulinitis, Trachonitis, and Decapolis. He was married to Salome, the daughter of Herodias.

A Herod Philip is mentioned in Mark 6:17 as the first husband of Herodias. In some places he is mentioned simply as Herod or Herod II. Most scholars do not believe that he was the same person as the governor of the northeastern districts.

Herodias (Matt. 14:3) was the daughter of Aristobulus (son of Herod and Mariamne I)

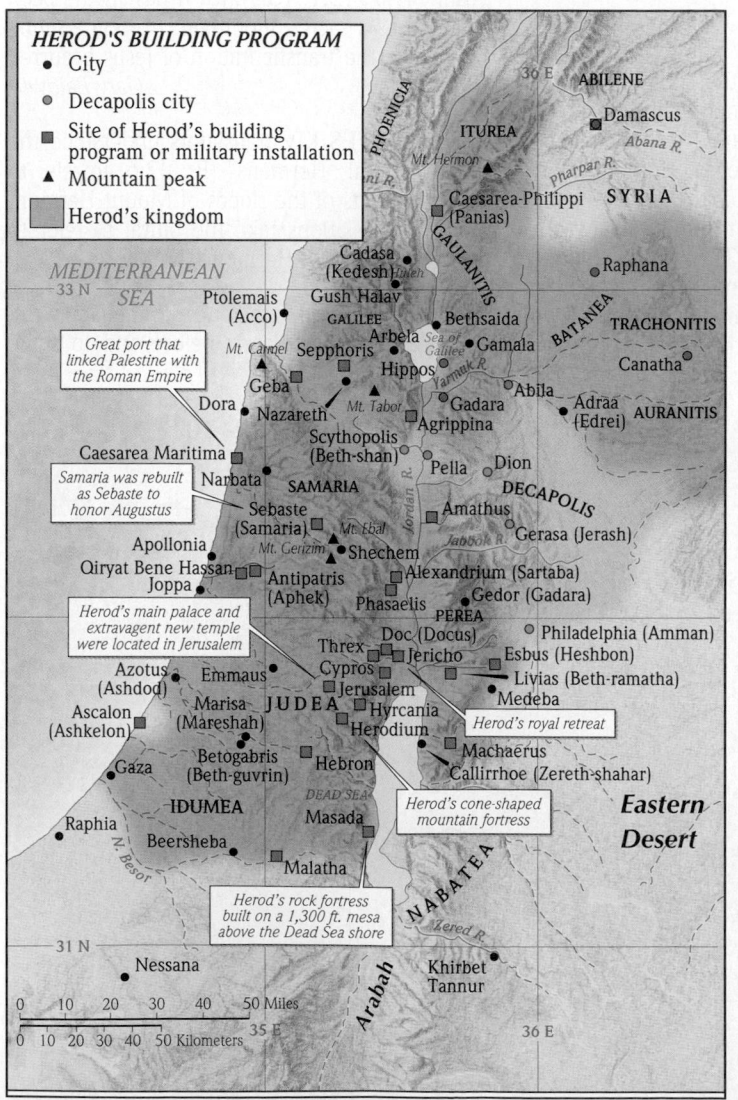

and Bernice, the daughter of Herod's sister, Salome. She was the second wife of Herod Antipas and called for the head of John the Baptist (Matt. 14:3-12; Mark 6:17-29; cp. Luke 3:19-20).

Salome was the daughter of Herodias. She was married to Philip. After his death in 34, she married a relative Aristobulus, prince of Chalcis and had three children (Matt. 14:6-12; Mark 6:22-29).

Herod was a paradox. He was one of the cruelest rulers of all history. His reputation has been largely one of infamy. He seemed fiercely loyal to that which he did believe in. He did not hesitate to murder members of his own family when he deemed that they posed a threat to him. Yet marital unfaithfulness and drunkenness did not seem to be among his vices. Because of his effective administration, he virtually made Palestine what it was in the first Christian century. He has gone down in history as "the Great," yet that epithet can only be applied to him as his personality and accomplishments are compared to others of his family.   *Robert Stagg*

Overview of the excavations of Herod's palace at Jerusalem as viewed from the Tower of David.

This aqueduct built by Herod the Great brought fresh water to Caesarea Maritima.

HEROD'S PALACE The probable scene of Herod's interrogation and mockery of Jesus (Luke 23:6-12). The palace was located along the western wall of the upper city to the west of the people's assembly hall. The palace was surrounded by a 45-foot wall surmounted by ornamental towers at fixed intervals. The palace was renowned for its circular porticoes, fine gardens, and a banquet hall seating over 100 guests. The palace was destroyed in September of A.D. 70.

HERODIAN (Hə rō´ dĭ ȧn) Member of an aristocratic Jewish group who favored the policies of Herod Antipas and thus supported the Roman government. Apparently they lived in Galilee, where Antipas ruled, and joined the Jerusalem religious authorities in opposing Jesus. They tried to trap Jesus into denying responsibility for Roman taxes (Matt. 22:15-22; Mark 12:13-17). Their plots began the road to Jesus' crucifixion (Mark 3:6). See Herod.

HERODIAS (Hə rō´ dĭ ȧs) Wife of Herod Antipas (Mark 6:17). She was the daughter of Aristobulus and Bernice. She was first married to the half brother of her father, identified in Mark 6:17 as Philip. By Philip she bore a daughter named Salome. Antipas, however, who was Philip's brother, divorced his own wife and wooed Herodias away from Philip. It was this gross marital misconduct that was denounced by John the Baptist. See *Herod; John the Baptist.*

HERODION (Hə rō´ dĭ on) Christian man to whom Paul the apostle sent a greeting (Rom. 16:11). Paul referred to him as a kinsman. This probably means that he was of Jewish birth. His name suggests that he might have been a member of the family of Herod. This possibility is

H

The Herodium against the Israeli sky.

strengthened by the fact that the name immediately preceding his is Aristobulus (Rom. 16:10). Herodion could have been one of those in the household of Aristobulus.

HERODIUM A fortress-palace built by Herod the Great about four miles southeast of Bethlehem. Herod was buried there. The fortress, captured in A.D. 72, was one of the last strongholds of Jewish resistance in the war with Rome. The Herodium served as a supply depot in the unsuccessful revolt of A.D. 132–135.

HERON Any of a family of wading birds with long necks and legs (*Areidae*), which were regarded as unclean (Lev. 11:19; Deut. 14:18).

HESED (Hē´ sĕd) Personal name meaning "grace" or "covenant love." Father of one of Solomon's district governors (1 Kings 4:10 KJV). Modern translations transliterate ben (Hb., son of). He brought provisions for the royal court one month of the year from his district of Arubboth. See *Arubboth*.

HESHBON (Hĕsh´ bŏn) Place-name meaning "reckoning." City in Moab ruled by Sihon and captured by Moses (Num. 21:21-30). Ancient Heshbon, to be identified with present-day Tell Hesban, was one of several ancient cities situated on the rolling and fertile plateau east of the Dead Sea and north of the Arnon River (present-day Wadi Mojib). Two of the other cities nearby, often mentioned by the biblical writers in connection with Heshbon, were Elealeh and Medeba. The agriculturally productive region in which these cities were located was much disputed territory during OT times. Generally it was regarded as part of Moab, as is assumed in Isa.

15–16 and Jer. 48. Yet the Israelite tribes of Reuben and Gad ranged with their sheep in this region (Num. 32:3,37). The Israelites laid claim to it on the grounds that Moses had taken all of the territory as far south as the Arnon from Sihon, an Amorite king who ruled from Heshbon (Num. 21:21-31). Certain of the stronger Israelite kings (David, Omri, and Ahab) were able to control all of that area. Apparently the Ammonites claimed the region as well, as implied by the exchange of messages between Jephthah and the Ammonite king related in Judg. 11:12-28.

Heshbon was assigned to the tribe of Gad and designated as a Levitical city according to Josh. 13:27-28; 21:38-39. Song of Songs 7:4, describing a maiden's beauty, proclaims "your eyes like pools in Heshbon" (HCSB). Herod the Great fortified the site, and it became a flourishing city (called Esbus) during late Roman times.

Excavations at Tell Hesban, conducted between 1968 and 1978, produced occupational remains ranging from the beginning of the Iron Age (about 1200 B.C.) through medieval times. No evidence of pre-Iron Age occupation was discovered at the site. That is the period when King Sihon was supposed to have ruled from the city. It is possible that Sihon reigned from another city called Heshbon; there are several near by sites that have evidence of occupation at that time. See *Gad; Moab; Reuben; Sihon*.

J. Maxwell Miller

HESHMON (Hĕsh´ mŏn) Place-name meaning "flat field." Town in tribal territory of Judah (Josh. 15:27). Its location is not known.

HESLI (Hĕs´ lī) (NASB) See *Esli*.

A view inside the Herodium, the magnificent fortress-palace built by Herod the Great.

HETH (Hĕth) Personal name of unknown meaning. Son of Canaan, great grandson of Noah, and original ancestor of the Hittites, some of the original inhabitants of Palestine (Gen. 10:15). Abraham bought his family burial ground from "sons of" or descendants of Heth (Gen. 23). See *Hittites.*

HETHLON (Hĕth´ lŏn) Place-name of unknown meaning on the northern border of Israel's promised land, according to Ezekiel's vision (Ezek. 47:15). Some see the word as a scribe's Hebrew abbreviation for mountain of Lebanon. Others see it as another name or a scribal change for Lebo-hamath (Num. 34:8). Others would identify it as modern Heitela, northeast of Tripoli, two and a half miles south of Nahr el-Kebir. Ezekiel pointed to a road near this place, perhaps the important transportation road otherwise known as Eleutheros.

HEW To cut with blows from a heavy cutting instrument. The references to "hewers of wood" together with "drawers of water" (Josh. 9:21,23,27; Deut. 29:11) probably refer to those who gathered firewood. Such work was a despised task relegated to foreigners and slaves. The "hewers that cut timber" (2 Chron. 2:10 KJV; NASB, woodsmen; cp. Jer. 46:22) were skilled lumberjacks. The "hewers of stone" (1 Kings 5:15 NASB) or "stonecutters" were royal servants mining rock from the mountains for royal building projects. Houses of "hewn stone" rather than rough stone were regarded as an extravagance (Amos 5:11).

HEXATEUCH Modern designation for the first six books of the OT viewed as a literary unity. The term was coined by source critics impressed with the supposed similarity of sources behind Joshua and the Pentateuch as well as the need for fulfillment of the promise of land to Abraham in the conquest of Canaan. More recent scholarship has evidenced a renewed appreciation of the canonical arrangement in which Joshua begins the "former prophets" or history of Israel from its entrance into the promised land until its departure with the exile. Joshua forms something of a bridge linking the promises to the patriarchs and the story of Moses with the later history of Israel.

HEZEKI (Hĕz´ ə kī) (KJV, 1 Chron. 8:17) See *Hizki.*

HEZEKIAH Son and successor of Ahaz as king of Judah (716/15–687/86 B.C.). Hezekiah

King Hezekiah's tunnel that brought water from the Gihon Spring to the pool of Siloam.

H

began his reign when he was 25 years old. At this time in history, the nation of Assyria had risen to power.

Hezekiah began his reign by bringing religious reform to Judah. Hezekiah was not willing to court the favor of the Assyrian kings. The temple in Jerusalem was reopened. The idols were removed from the temple. Temple vessels that had been desecrated during Ahaz's reign were sanctified for use in the temple. The sacrifices were initiated with singing and the sounds of musical instruments. The tribes in the Northern Kingdom (Israel) had been subjected to Assyrian dominance. Hezekiah invited the Israelites to join in the celebration of the Passover in Jerusalem. Places of idol worship were destroyed. Hezekiah even destroyed the bronze serpent Moses had erected in the wilderness (Num. 21:4-9) so the people would not view the bronze serpent as an object of worship. Hezekiah organized the priests and Levites for the conducting of religious services. The tithe was reinstituted. Plans were made to observe the religious feasts called for in the Law.

In 711 B.C., just a few years after Hezekiah had become king, Sargon II of Assyria captured Ashdod. Hezekiah anticipated the time when he would have to confront Assyrian armies.

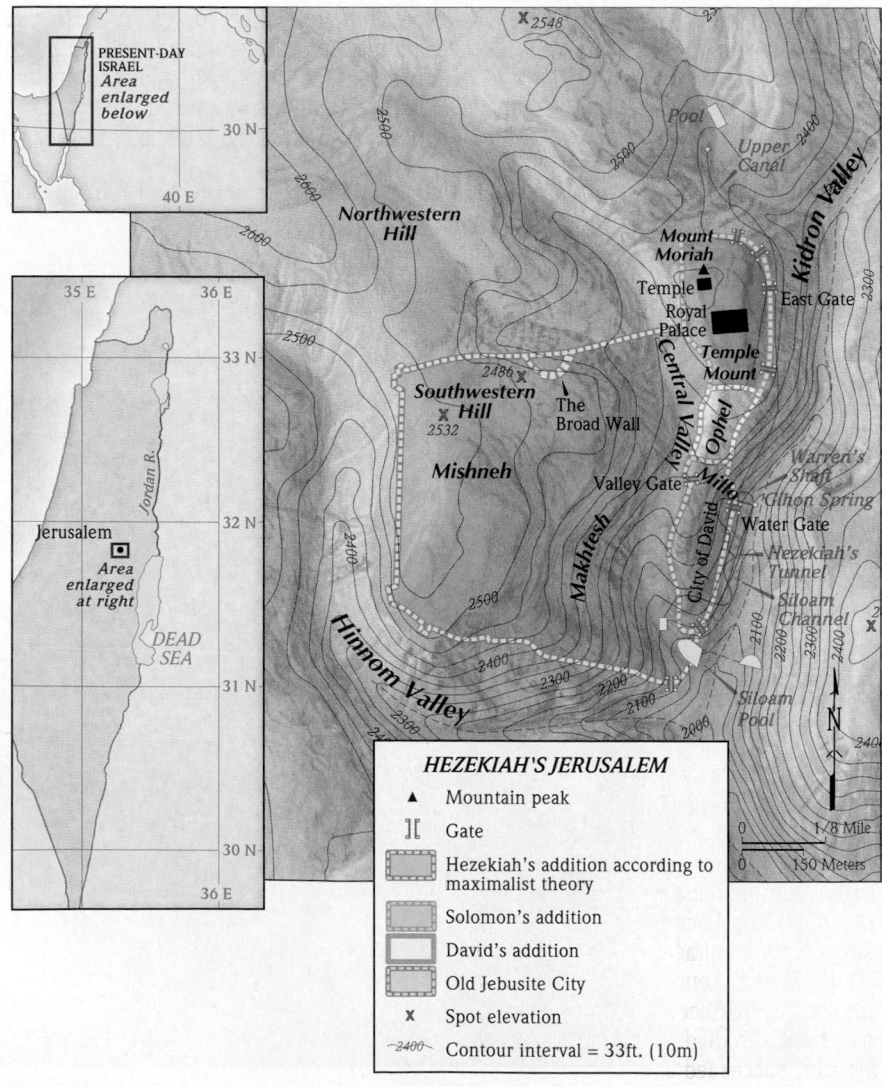

HEZEKIAH'S JERUSALEM

▲ Mountain peak

⫯ Gate

Hezekiah's addition according to maximalist theory

Solomon's addition

David's addition

Old Jebusite City

× Spot elevation

~2400~ Contour interval = 33ft. (10m)

Hezekiah fortified the city of Jerusalem and organized an army. Knowing that a source of water was crucial, Hezekiah constructed a tunnel through solid rock from the spring of Gihon to the Siloam pool. The city wall was extended to enclose this important source of water.

Isaiah warned Hezekiah not to become involved with Assyria (Isa. 20:1-6). The critical time for Hezekiah came in 705 B.C. when Sennacherib became king of Assyria. From Hezekiah, Sennacherib obtained a heavy tribute of silver and gold.

In 701 B.C. Hezekiah became seriously ill (Isa. 38:1-21). Isaiah warned the king to prepare for his approaching death, but Hezekiah prayed that God would intervene. God answered by promising Hezekiah 15 more years of life and deliverance of Jerusalem from Assyria (Isa. 38:4-6).

In the meantime, Sennacherib had besieged Lachish. Aware that Hezekiah had trusted God for deliverance, Sennacherib sent messengers to the Jerusalem wall to urge the people to surrender. Sennacherib boasted of having conquered 46 walled cities and having taken 200,000 captives. Sennacherib's messengers taunted that God would not come to Judah's defense. Hezekiah, dressed in sackcloth and ashes, went to the temple to pray. He also called for Isaiah, the prophet. Isaiah announced that Sennacherib would "hear a rumor" and return to his own land where he would die by the sword (2 Kings 19:7).

Hezekiah's faith and physical recovery brought him recognition from the surrounding nations (2 Chron. 32:33). The Babylonian leader, Merodach-baladan, even congratulated Hezekiah on his recovery. Hezekiah hosted this Babylonian leader at a reception, but Isaiah met this event with a warning that succeeding generations would be subjected to Babylonian captivity (Isa. 39:1-8).

Sennacherib destroyed the city of Babylon in 689 B.C. He then marched toward Egypt. Hoping to ward off any interference from Judah, Sennacherib sent letters to Hezekiah ordering him to surrender (Isa. 37:9-38). Hezekiah took the letters to the temple and prayed for God's help. From Isaiah came the message that Sennacherib would not prevail. In fact, Sennacherib's army was destroyed in a miraculous way (2 Kings 19:35-37). In 681 B.C. Sennacherib was killed by two of his sons as had been predicted by Isaiah in 701 B.C. Hezekiah died in 687/86 B.C. Manasseh, his son, succeeded him, although Manasseh had become co-regent with Hezekiah about 69 B.C.

The Gospel of Matthew lists Hezekiah in the genealogy of Jesus (Matt. 1:9-10).

Gary Hardin

HEZION (Hē´ zĭ ŏn) Personal name meaning "vision." Grandfather of King Ben-hadad of Damascus (1 Kings 15:18). His relationship to Rezon, founder of the Damascus dynasty, is not certain. Some think Hezion is a scribal change from Rezon in Hebrew. Others think both names have been changed from an original Hezron or Hazael. A more probable opinion is that Hezion is a personal name, while Rezon is a Syrian royal title or throne name. See *Rezon*.

HEZIR (Hē´ zĭr) Personal name meaning "wild pig." Ugaritic texts apparently show that the name came from the profession of herding swine. **1.** Leader of one of the 24 courses of priests (1 Chron. 24:15). **2.** Levite who signed Nehemiah's covenant to obey God's law (Neh. 10:20).

HEZRAI (Hĕz´ rā ī) or **HEZRO** (Hĕz´ rō) Personal name meaning "his stalk" or "stem." KJV reading of name of David's military hero (2 Sam. 23:35) following an early scribal note on the Hebrew text. The written text and modern translations read Hezro with 1 Chron. 11:37, where many early translations read Hezrai.

HEZRON (Hĕz´ rŏn) Personal and place-name meaning "camping place" or "reeds." **1.** Son of Reuben, grandson of Jacob (Gen. 46:9), and original clan ancestor of Hezronites (Num. 26:6). **2.** Grandson of Judah, great grandson of Jacob (Gen. 46:12), original clan ancestor of Hezronites (Num. 26:21) through whom David was born (Ruth 4:19). He was father of Caleb (1 Chron. 2:18) and of Segub (1 Chron. 2:21). The Hebrew text of 1 Chron. 2:24 can be interpreted and translated in different ways. KJV makes Hezron the father of Ashur (cp. NASB, NRSV, NIV). Some Bible students follow the lead of the earliest translations, changing the Hebrew text somewhat so that Caleb is the father of Ashur, Ephratah being Caleb's wife (cp. REB, TEV, RSV). Hezron's first son was Jerahmeel, original ancestor of the Jerahmeelites (1 Chron. 2:25).

H

HEZRONITE (Hĕz´ rŏn īt) Clan descended from Hezron both in tribe of Reuben and of Judah. See *Hezron*.

HIDDAI (Hĭd´ dā ī) Personal name, perhaps a short form for Hodai, meaning "my majesty." One of David's military heroes (2 Sam. 23:30). The parallel passage in 1 Chron. 11:32 spells the name Hurai. He was from Gaash. See *Gaash*.

HIDDEKEL (Hĭd´ də kĕl) Hebrew name for the third river flowing from the garden of Eden (Gen. 2:14). Most modern translations translate it as Tigris. This shows that the dependence of the important areas of subsequent world history owed their fertility to God's original garden of creation. KJV also retains the transliteration for Tigris in Dan. 10:4. See *Tigris*.

HIEL (Hī´ ĕl) Personal name meaning "God lives" or, following the Greek translation, a short form of Ahiel, "brother of God." Man from Bethel who rebuilt Jericho at the price of the life of two of his sons (1 Kings 16:34), fulfilling the divine curse Joshua issued when he destroyed Jericho (Josh. 6:26).

HIERAPOLIS (Hī ĕr ap´ ō lĭs) Place-name meaning "sacred city." Site of early church where Epaphras worked (Col. 4:13). Nothing else is known of the church. The city was 12 miles northwest of Colossae and six miles north of Laodicea on the Lycus River a short way above its junction with the Meander River. It is now called Pambuck Kulasi. Its fame rested on textile and cloth-dyeing industries. It began as a center for worship of the Phrygian mother goddess. A large Jewish community is evidenced by grave inscriptions and other literary remains.

Mineral deposits from the hot springs of Hierapolis used as a health spa during the Roman period.

The Roman west gate of Hierapolis with triple arches set between two defense towers (first century A.D.).

HIEROGLYPHICS Greek term meaning "sacred carvings," referring to the pictographic symbols used in ancient Egyptian writing. Normally hieroglyphs were carved in stone, though sometimes they were written with pen on papyrus. These picture-symbols consisted in both ideograms (representing an entire word or phrase) and phonograms (representing a consonant). A simplified cursive script (hieratic) was developed early. This was in turn simplified into the demotic script about 700 B.C.

HIGGAION (Hĭg gā´ yŏn) Transliteration of Hebrew word meaning "whispering" (Lam. 3:62 NASB) or "meditation" (Ps. 19:14) or musical sound a stringed instrument produces (Ps. 92:3). It appears as a worship notation with uncertain meaning in Ps. 9:16. It may mean to play quietly or to pause for meditation.

HIGHEST KJV designation for God (Luke 1:32,35,76; 6:35). Modern translations prefer "Most High" (NASB, NIV, NRSV) or "Most High God" (TEV). In the OT, "Most High" often occurs as a designation for the God of Israel when Gentiles are in view (Gen. 14:18-22; Num. 24:16; and frequently in Daniel). In the

Hieroglyphics on the wall of a partially restored temple at Saqqara, Egypt.

intertestamental period, the Highest or Most High became the most common designation for the Jewish God, occurring about 120 times in the Apocrypha.

HIGHEST HEAVEN See *Heaven of Heavens.*

HIGH GATE, HIGHER GATE KJV designations for a gate of the Jerusalem temple (2 Kings 15:35; 2 Chron. 23:20; 27:3). Most modern translations prefer the designation "Upper Gate." TEV reads "North Gate" or "Main Gate." Its location is not clear, possibly being the same as the Benjamin Gate. Parallel to 2 Chron. 23:20, 2 Kings 11:19 uses "guard" or "herald" as the gate's name, probably reflecting a change of names through history. See *Gates of Jerusalem and the Temple.*

HIGH HEAPS KJV translation of a Hebrew term for "marker" at Jer. 31:21. Modern translations render the term as "guideposts" (NASB, NIV, NRSV) or "signposts" (HCSB, REB).

HIGH PLACE Elevated site, usually found on the top of a mountain or hill; most high places were Canaanite places of pagan worship.
Heathen Worship at the High Place The average high place would have an altar (2 Kings 21:3; 2 Chron. 14:3), a carved wooden pole that depicted the female goddess of fertility (Asherah), a stone pillar symbolizing the male deity (2 Kings 3:2), other idols (2 Kings 17:29; 2 Chron. 33:19), and some type of building (1 Kings 12:31; 13:32; 16:32-33). At these places of worship the people sacrificed animals (at some high places children were sacrificed according to Jer. 7:31), burned incense to their gods, prayed, ate sacrificial meals, and were involved with male or female cultic prostitutes (2 Kings 17:8-12; 21:3-7; Hos. 4:11-14). Although most high places were part of the worship of Baal, the Ammonite god Molech and the Moabite god Chemosh were also worshiped at similar high places (1 Kings 11:5-8; 2 Kings 23:10). Scripture speaks negatively about these heathen places of worship; still they played a central role in the lives of most of the people who lived in Palestine before the land was defeated by Joshua. Archaeologists have discovered the remains of high places at Megiddo, Gezer, and numerous other sites.
God's Hatred of the High Places When the Israelites came into the land of Canaan, they were ordered to destroy the high places of the people who lived in the land (Exod. 23:24; 34:13; Num. 33:52; Deut. 7:5; 12:3) lest the Israelites be tempted to worship the Canaanite false gods and accept their immoral behavior. The Israelites were to worship God at the tabernacle at Shiloh (Josh. 18:1; 1 Sam. 1:3).

An exception to this practice existed in the years between the destruction of Shiloh by the Philistines and the construction of the temple in Jerusalem by Solomon. During this short period Samuel worshiped inside a city (possibly Ramah) at a high place dedicated to the worship of the God of Israel (1 Sam. 9:12-25), and a group of prophets of God worshiped at the "hill of God" (1 Sam. 10:5, probably Gibeah or Gibeon). David and Solomon worshiped the God of Israel at the high place at Gibeon where the tabernacle and the altar of burnt offering were located (1 Chron. 16:1-4,37-40; 21:29; 2 Chron. 1:3-4,13).

Stone fragments of what is probably an altar base at the high place in Lachish.

H

False Worship at High Places in Judah After the temple was constructed, the people were to worship God at this place which He had chosen (Deut. 12:1-14), but Solomon built high places for the gods of his foreign wives and even worshiped there himself (1 Kings 11:1-8). Because of the seriousness of this sin, God divided the nation by removing 10 tribes from the kingdom of his son Rehoboam (1 Kings 11:9-13,29-38). Following this, each new king that ruled in the Southern Kingdom of Judah and in the Northern Kingdom of Israel was evaluated in the books of Kings and Chronicles according to what they did with the high places where false gods were worshiped.

False Worship at High Places in Israel When Jeroboam created the new kingdom of Israel after the death of Solomon, he put two golden calves at high places at Dan and Bethel (1 Kings 12:28-32). An unnamed man of God came to Bethel and pronounced God's curse on this high place (1 Kings 13:1-3), but the following kings of the Northern Kingdom of Israel followed in the ways of Jeroboam and did not remove the high places where the false gods were worshiped.

The Israelite prophets also condemned the high places of Moab (Isa. 15:2; 16:12), Judah (Jer. 7:30-31; 17:1-3; 19:3-5; 32:35), and Israel (Ezek. 6:3,6; 20:29-31; Hos. 10:8, Amos 7:9) because they were places of sin where false gods were worshiped. See *Asherah; False Gods; Golden Calves; Prostitution.* *Gary V. Smith*

HIGH PRIEST One in charge of the temple (or tabernacle) worship. A number of terms are used to refer to the high priest: the priest (Exod. 31:10); the anointed priest (Lev. 4:3); the priest who is chief among his brethren (Lev. 21:10); chief priest (2 Chron. 26:20); and high priest (2 Kings 12:10).

Responsibilities and Privileges The high priesthood was a hereditary office based on descent from Aaron (Exod. 29:29-30; Lev. 16:32). Normally, the high priest served for life (Num. 18:7; 25:11-13; 35:25,28; Neh. 12:10-11), though as early as Solomon's reign a high priest was dismissed for political reasons (1 Kings 2:27).

A special degree of holiness was required of the high priest (Lev. 10:6,9; 21:10-15). This meant he had to avoid defilement by contact with the dead, even in the case of his own parents, and was forbidden to show any outward

The rock-cut altars of the high place at Petra in southern Jordan.

sign of mourning. He could not leave the sanctuary precincts. Such legislation identified the high priest as one totally dedicated to the Lord, always ritually pure and ready to serve the Lord.

If the high priest sinned, he brought guilt upon the whole people (Lev. 4:3). The sin offering for the high priest (Lev. 4:3-12) was identical to that required "if the whole congregation of Israel commits error" (4:13-21 NASB).

The consecration of the high priest was an elaborate seven-day ritual involving special baths, putting on special garments, and anointing with oil and with blood (Exod. 29:1-37; Lev. 6:19-22; 8:5-35). The special garments of the high priest included a blue robe with an ornate hem decorated with gold bells and embroidered pomegranates, an ephod of fine linen with colorful embroidered work and shoulder straps bearing stones engraved with the names of the twelve tribes, a breastplate with twelve precious stones engraved with the names of the 12 tribes, and a linen turban with a gold plate inscribed "Holy to Yahweh" (Exod. 28:4-39; 39:1-31; Lev. 8:7-9). The engraved plate and the stones engraved with the tribal names highlight the role of the high priest as the holy representative of all Israel before the Lord (Exod. 28:12,29). In his "breastpiece of judgment," the high priest kept the sacred lots, the Urim and Thummim, which were used to inquire of the Lord (Exod. 28:29-30; Num. 27:21). See *Breastpiece of the High Priest; Ephod; Lots; Urim and Thummim.*

The high priest shared in general priestly duties. Only the high priest, however, was allowed to enter the holy of holies and then only on the Day of Atonement (Lev. 16:1-25). See *Day of Atonement.*

The death of the high priest marked the end of an epoch. One guilty of involuntary manslaughter was required to remain in a city of refuge until the death of the high priest (Num. 35:25,28,32; Josh. 20:6). The expiatory death of the high priest removed bloodguilt that would pollute the land (cp. Num. 35:33).

History of the Office Some argue that the developed priesthood characterized by three divisions (high priest, priests, and Levites) was a late, possibly postexilic, development in the history of Israel's worship. Others take the biblical texts at face value and accept Mosaic institution of the fully developed priesthood.

The term "high priest" occurs in only one brief passage in the Pentateuch (Num. 35:25,28,32), once in Joshua (Josh. 20:6 where the legislation of Num. 35 is enacted), and never in the book of Judges. Aaron, Eleazar, and Phinehas are typically called the priest. Neither Eli, Ahimelech, Abiathar, nor Zadok are called high or chief priest, though all four headed priestly families and are mentioned in connection with items usually associated with the high priest (the ark, the ephod, the Urim and Thummim: 1 Sam. 3:3; 4:4-11; 21:6,9; 2 Sam. 15:24-29).

Eleazar was charged with supervision of the Levites (Num. 3:32; cp. 1 Chron. 9:20) and of the sanctuary apparatus (Num. 4:16). He figures in the narrative of Num. 16 where the offering of incense is affirmed as the exclusive prerogative of the priests and in the red heifer ceremony (Num. 19). The account of Eleazar's donning Aaron's priestly robe (Num. 20:25-28; cp. Deut. 10:6) provides Scripture's best report of high priestly succession. As chief priest Eleazar assisted Moses with the census (Num. 26). Eleazar served as an advisor to Moses (Num. 27:1) and to Joshua, consulting the Lord by means of the sacred lots. Such counsel formed the basis for the apportionment of the promised land among the tribes (Num. 34:17; Josh. 14:1; 17:4; 19:51; 21:1). One indication of the significance of Eleazar is that the book of Joshua concludes with the death of this chief priest (24:33).

Phinehas, son of Eleazar, is best known for his zealous opposition to intermarriage with the Moabites and the concomitant idolatry (Num. 25:6-13). For his zeal Phinehas was granted a covenant of perpetual priesthood (Num. 25:13) and was reckoned as righteous (Ps. 106:30). Phinehas accompanied the sanctuary vessels in holy war (Num. 31:6). Part of his ministry before the ark involved consulting the Lord for battle counsel (Judg. 20:27-28). Phinehas served as the major figure in the resolution of the conflict over the "commemorative" altar the tribes east of the Jordan built (Josh. 22:13,31-32).

Aaron, Eleazar, and Phinehas appear in biblical history as distinct personalities. Until Eli's appearance at the end of the period of the judges, a puzzling silence surrounds the high priesthood. First Chronicles 6:1-15 offers a list of seven high priests between Phinehas and Zadok, a contemporary of David and Solomon. Of these nothing is known except their names. Nor is Eli included among this list, though he functioned as the chief priest of the Shiloh sanctuary.

Eli is best known for his rearing of Samuel (1 Sam. 1:25-28; 3) and for his inability to control his own sons (1 Sam. 2:12-17,22-25; 3:13), which, in time, resulted in the forfeiture of the high priesthood by his line (1 Sam. 2:27-35). Following the death of Eli, the Shiloh priesthood apparently relocated to Nob. Saul suspected the priesthood of conspiracy with David and exterminated the priestly family of Ahimelech (1 Sam. 22:9-19). Only Abiathar escaped (22:20). When David moved the ark to Jerusalem, Abiathar and Zadok apparently officiated jointly as chief priests (2 Sam. 8:17; 15:24-29,35; 19:11), though Zadok already appears as the dominant figure in 2 Samuel. Solomon suspected Abiathar of conspiracy with his brother Adonijah and exiled him to his ancestral home (1 Kings 2:26-27). The high priesthood remained in the family of Zadok from the beginning of Solomon's reign (about 964 B.C.) until Menelaus bought the high priesthood (171 B.C.) in the days of Antiochus Epiphanes.

Azariah, the son of Zadok, was the first individual to be explicitly identified as the "high priest" (1 Kings 4:2). At times during the monarchy, individual high priests exercised major roles in the life of Judah. Jehoshabeath, wife of the high priest Jehoiada (2 Chron. 22:11), saved the infant Joash from the murderous Athaliah. Six years later Jehoiada was the mastermind of the *coup d'etat* in which Joash was crowned king (2 Kings 11:4-17). A second Azariah was known for opposing King Uzziah's attempt to usurp the priests' right to offer incense (2 Chron. 26:17-18). The high priest Hilkiah discovered the "Book of the Law," perhaps the book of Deuteronomy, which provided the incentive for King Josiah's reforms (2 Kings 22:8). Hilkiah removed all traces of Baal worship from the Jerusalem temple (2 Kings 23:4).

H

In the early postexilic period, the high priest Joshua is presented as the equal of the Davidic governor Zerubbabel (Hag. 1:1,12,14; 2:2,4). Both high priest and governor shared in the rebuilding of the temple (Ezra 3; 6:9-15; Hag. 1–2). Both are recognized as anointed leaders (Zech. 4:14; 6:9-15). A further indication of the heightened importance of the high priesthood in the postexilic period is the interest in succession lists of high priests (1 Chron. 6:1-15,50-53; 9:11; Ezra 7:1-5; Neh. 12:10-11), a new development in biblical literature.

In the period before the Maccabean revolt the high priesthood became increasingly political. Jason, a Hellenistic sympathizer, ousted his more conservative brother Onias III (2 Macc. 4:7-10,18-20). Jason was, in turn, ousted by the more radically Hellenistic Menelaus who offered the Seleucid rulers an even larger bribe to secure the office (2 Macc. 4:23-26). With Menelaus the high priesthood passed out of the legitimate Zadokite line.

The Maccabees combined the office of high priest with that of military commander or political leader. Alexander Balas, a contender for the Seleucid throne, appointed Jonathan Maccabee "high priest" and "king's friend" (1 Macc. 10:20). Simon Maccabee was, likewise, confirmed in his high priesthood and made a "friend" of the Seleucid King Demetrius II (1 Macc. 14:38). Temple and state were combined in the person of Simon who was both high priest and ethnarch (1 Macc. 15:1-2).

The Romans continued the practice of rewarding the high priesthood to political favorites. During the Roman period, Annas (high priest A.D. 6–15) was clearly the most powerful priestly figure. Even when deposed by the Romans, Annas succeeded in having five of his sons and a son-in-law, Joseph Caiaphas (high priest A.D. 18–36/37) appointed high priests. Some confusion has resulted from NT references to the joint high priesthood of Annas and Caiaphas (Luke 3:2). The passage is perhaps best understood as an acknowledgment of Annas as the power behind his immediate successors. Another possibility is that Annas retained the title of respect on the grounds that the high priesthood was for life. Ananias, one of Annas' sons, was the high priest to whom Paul was brought in Acts 23:2; 24:1.

High Priest and Chief Priests The ordination rite for the high priest included the consecration of his sons as well (Exod. 29:8-9,20-21). A number of terms refer to leading priests other than the high priest: anointed priests (2 Macc. 1:10); chief priests (Ezra 8:29; 10:5; Neh. 12:7); senior priests (2 Kings 19:2; Isa. 37:2; Jer. 19:1). More specific titles are also found. Zephaniah was described as the "second priest" (2 Kings 25:18; Jer. 52:24). Pashur was the "chief officer in the house of the Lord" (Jer. 20:1).

Table of High Priests
Aaron (Exod. 28-29)
Eleazar (Num. 3:4; Deut. 10:6)
Phinehas (Josh. 22:13-32; Judg. 20:28)
Eli (1 Sam. 1:9; 2:11)
Ahimelech (1 Sam. 21:1-2; 22:11)
Abiathar (2 Sam. 20:25; 1 Kings 2:26-27)
Zadok (1 Kings 2:35; 1 Chron. 29:22)
Azariah (1 Kings 4:2)
Amariah (2 Chron. 19:11)
Jehoiada (2 Kings 11:9-10,15; 12:7,9-10)
Azariah (2 Chron. 26:20)
Uriah (2 Kings 16:10-16)
Hilkiah (2 Kings 22:10,12,14; 22:4,8; 23:4)
Seraiah (2 Kings 25:18)
Joshua (Hag. 1:1,12,14; 2:2,4; Ezra 3; Zech. 3:6-7; 4:14; 6:9-15)
Eliashib (Neh. 3:1,20)
Simon the Just (Sirach 50:1-21)
Onias III (1 Macc. 12:7; 2 Macc. 3:1)
Jason (2 Macc. 4:7-10,18-20; 4 Macc. 4:16)
Menelaus (2 Macc. 4:23-26)
Alcimus (1 Macc. 7:9)
Jonathan Maccabee (1 Macc. 10:20; 14:30)
Simon Maccabee (1 Macc. 14:20,23)
John Hyrcanus (1 Macc. 16:23-24)
Annas (Luke 3:2; John 18:13,24; Acts 4:6)
(Joseph) Caiaphas (Matt. 26:57; John 18:13)
Ananias (Acts 23:2; 24:1)   *Chris Church*

HIGHWAY A road, especially an elevated road (Isa. 62:10). In addition to literal uses, there are figurative uses, especially in Isaiah. In Prov. 15:19 the highway of the righteous is an image for their way of conduct. The highway of Isa. 11:16 and 35:10 is an assurance that the exiles will have safe and speedy passage home. Isaiah 40:3 speaks of preparing a highway for the Lord. See *Palestine; Transportation and Travel.*

HILEN (Hī´ lĕn) Place-name, perhaps meaning "power." City in tribal territory of Judah given to Levites (1 Chron. 6:58). The parallel passage (Josh. 21:15; cp. 15:51) reads "Holon." The

Hebrew text in Chronicles actually reads "Hilez." Copying changes affected the various manuscript readings of this little-known town. See *Holon; Levitical Cities.*

HILKIAH (Hĭl kī´ ăh) Personal name meaning "Yah's portion." **1.** Father of Amaziah (1 Chron. 6:45). He was a Levite who lived before the time of David the king. **2.** Levite and temple servant who lived during the time of David (1 Chron. 26:11). **3.** Father of Eliakim, who was in charge of the household of King Hezekiah (2 Kings 18:18). **4.** Father of Jeremiah the prophet (Jer. 1:1). **5.** Father of Gemariah, who was an emissary from Zedekiah to Nebuchadnezzar, king of Babylon (Jer. 29:3). **6.** High priest who aided in Josiah's reform movement (2 Kings 22:4). **7.** Person who stood with Ezra the scribe at the reading of the law (Neh. 8:4). **8.** Priest who was among the exiles that returned (Neh. 12:7).

HILL, HILL COUNTRY Elevated land, usually distinguished as lower than a mountain or with a less distinct peak. Hills separating the Mediterranean coastal plain from the Jordan Valley run the length of Palestine. The area to the east of the Jordan and the Dead Sea is likewise hill country. The common Hebrew terms for hill and hill country (*gibe ʻah* and *har*) lack precise English equivalents, so a detailed knowledge of geography is required for proper translation. The RSV translated *gibe ʻah* as "hill" or "hills" 65 times. The RSV translated *har*, the usual term for mountain, as "hill" 40 times and as "hill country" 92 times. The KJV and REB understood the Hebrew Ophel as a fortress or citadel (2 Kings 5:24; Isa. 32:14; Mic. 4:8). Many English translations such as NASB translated the term as "hill." KJV uses tower, fort, and stronghold in the three passages.

HILLEL (Hĭl´ lĕl) Personal name meaning "praise." **1.** Father of the judge Abdon (Judg. 12:13). **2.** Influential rabbi and Talmudic scholar who flourished just prior to the time of the ministry of Jesus. He and his colleague Shammai presided over the two most important rabbinic schools of their time. Hillel was the more liberal of the two, and his emphases have largely determined the direction taken by Judaism since his era.

HILL OF GOD (Hb. *Gibe ʻat-elohim*) Site of a Philistine garrison and of a place of worship.

Here Saul met a band of ecstatic prophets and joined them in their frenzy (1 Sam. 10:5).

HILL OF THE FORESKINS (Hb. *Gibe ʻat-ha ʻaraloth*) Place near Gilgal where Joshua circumcised the Israelites born during the wilderness wandering (Josh. 5:3).

HILT Handle of a sword or dagger (Judg. 3:22 NRSV, REB). Other translations prefer "haft" (KJV) or "handle" (NASB, NIV, TEV).

HIN (hĭn) Unit of liquid measure reckoned as one sixth of a bath (Exod. 29:40). It would have been approximately equivalent to a gallon. See *Weights and Measures.*

HIND Female deer; doe (Prov. 5:19). "To make my feet like hinds' feet" (KJV, NASB) is a common expression (2 Sam. 22:34; Ps. 18:33; Hab. 3:19) of God's care in dangerous situations. See *Deer.*

HINGE Flexible device on which a door turns. Proverbs 26:14 compares a lazy person turning in bed to a door, turning on its hinges. The meaning of the term translated hinges at 1 Kings 7:50 (KJV, NASB, TEV) is disputed. NIV, NRSV prefer the translation sockets on the grounds that ancient doors swung on doorpins set in sockets rather than on jointed hinges. REB translates "panels."

HINNOM, VALLEY OF (Hĭn´ nŏm) Placename of uncertain meaning; also called the valley of the son(s) of Hinnom. The valley lies in close proximity to Jerusalem (2 Kings 23:10), just south of the ancient city (Josh. 15:8). The valley had a somewhat unglamorous history during the OT period. The worshipers of the pagan deities, Baal and Molech, practiced child sacrifice in the valley of Hinnom (2 Kings 23:10). The first specific mention of human sacrifice in Israel is in 2 Kings 16:3 and in Judah is in 2 Kings 17:17. The parallel passage in 2 Chron. 28:3 indicates that the scene of the abomination was the valley of Hinnom. See *Baal; Gehenna; Hell; Jerusalem; Molech.*   *Hugh Tobias*

HIP Part of the body where the thigh and torso connect. Jacob's hip came out of socket when he wrestled with God at the Jabbok (Gen. 32:25). The Israelites commemorated this encounter by not eating the thigh muscle on the hip socket (Gen. 32:32). To strike an enemy "hip and thigh" (Judg. 15:8) is to attack him fiercely (TEV)

H

The Hinnom (or Gehenna) Valley in Jerusalem, just south of the ancient city.

or viciously (NIV). Belshazzar's fear at the handwriting on the wall (Dan. 5:6 NASB) was evidenced by his hip joint going slack.

HIPPOPOTAMUS Large, thick-skinned, amphibious, cud-chewing mammal of the family *Hippopotamidae*. The Hebrew *behemoth* (Job 40:15-24) is sometimes understood as the hippopotamus (NASB, TEV margins). Others prefer to identify *behemoth* with the crocodile (REB), elephant (KJV margin), or with a mythical creature (TEV margin). Hippopotamus remains dating between 1200 and 300 B.C. have been found along the coastal plain near Tel Aviv. It is possible that the hippopotamus was also found in the Jordan River at this time, though archeological confirmation is lacking. See *Behemoth.*

HIRAH (Hī´ răi) Personal name of unknown meaning. A friend of Judah, the son of Jacob, whom Judah was visiting when he met Shuah, who bore three of his sons (Gen. 38:1-12). Hirah was from the Canaanite city of Adullam, about nine miles northwest of Hebron.

HIRAM (Hī´ răm) Personal name apparently meaning "brother of the lofty one." **1.** King of Tyre, associated with David and Solomon in building the temple. He is called Hiram (Samuel and Kings) and Huram (Chronicles), but both names refer to the same individual. Other information about him comes from the ancient Jewish historian, Josephus. Hiram was the son of Abibaal ("my father is Baal") and was 19 years old when he succeeded his father as king of Tyre on the Phoenician coast, just north of Israel. He reigned some 34 years and is said to have died at age 54, although the biblical references to him seem to necessitate a longer reign.

When he became king, he began to improve and to expand his kingdom. He raised banks at the eastern part of Tyre that enlarged the city, and he built a causeway to connect the city with the island temple of Jupiter Olympius in the harbor, after which he modernized the temple. When David became king of Israel, Hiram sent congratulatory gifts to him, including men and materials to build a palace (2 Sam. 5:11). The friendship between the men grew and was evidenced by the commerce that developed between their two nations. The close relationship continued into Solomon's reign, and the two men made an agreement that resulted in the construction of the temple in Jerusalem (1 Kings 5:1-12).

This relationship between Israel and Tyre was mutually beneficial. Jerusalem was inland and had the advantages of the overland trade routes. Tyre, as a major seaport, offered the advantages of sea trade. Hiram controlled the maritime trade during this time and was himself a respected world trader. His friendship with David and Solomon undoubtedly explains, at least in part, the prosperity and success of their reigns. See *David; Phoenicia; Solomon; Tyre.*

2. Craftsman who did artistic metal work for Solomon's temple (1 Kings 7:13-45). He lived in Tyre, his father's hometown but had a widowed Jewish mother from the tribe of Naphtali.

Hugh Tobias

HIRELING Worker who is paid wages; a laborer; a hired hand. The work of hired laborers was generally difficult (Job 7:1-2). Mosaic law required paying workers at the close of the day so that they might provide for their families (Deut. 24:14-15). Workers were frequently exploited (Mal. 3:5; James 5:4). John 10:12-13 contrasts the cowardice of a hired shepherd with an owner's self-sacrificing concern for his sheep.

HISS Sound made by forcing breath between the tongue and teeth in mockery or to ward off demons. In the OT an army or nation hissed at their enemy's city or land that suffered defeat or disaster (Jer. 19:8). Most often the reference is to astonishment at the fate of Israel, Jerusalem, or the temple lying in ruins (1 Kings 9:8; Jer. 18:16, 19:8; Lam. 2:15-16). Other nations and cities were also the objects of hissing: Edom (Jer. 49:17); Babylon (Jer. 50:13); Tyre (Ezek. 27:36); and Nineveh (Zeph. 2:15). Hissing was sometimes accompanied by wagging the head, clapping hands, gnashing teeth (Lam. 2:15-16), and shaking the fist (Zeph. 2:15).

HISTORY Biblical history is the written register of time—past, present, and future—which reveals that God created humanity and the environment, and that He is leading them through a linear progression of events to a meaningful conclusion. There are four primary aspects to the biblical understanding of history, especially when compared to other outlooks on history: providence, linear chronology, meaningfulness, and hope.

Providence: During the biblical period, most pagans viewed history as an unstable realm of conflict between competing deities. In opposition to the pagan view, and because of their encounter with Yahweh, the Hebrews embraced one all-powerful God as the Creator and Lord of history and of all its particular manifestations.

Linear chronology: The Hebrew understanding of time as a linear progression or non-repetitive chronology moving toward a definite goal differed with the pagan understanding of time as a circular repetition of events.

Meaningfulness: Although the Bible contains history understood in a chronological sense, its primary purpose is to convey the meaning of history. This comes out clearly in the lexical distinction between the Greek words *chronos*, "a span of time," and *kairos*, "a fateful and decisive point in time." The persistent use of *kairos* in the NT points to the Bible's intent to convey meaningful history.

Hope: The ancient Near East was generally pessimistic about the material world and wanted only to escape from history into a timeless, immaterial reality. The Bible, in stark contrast, pictures God as leading history to a beneficial conclusion for those who are in faithful covenant with Him.

Alternative Views of History Humans have often tried, to assign some meaning to the events they experience, and to discover the direction of history. These human efforts have generated alternative views which conflict with the divine revelation of history recorded in the Bible. The six alternatives are the cyclical, inevitable progress and mechanistic views, as well as the historicist, futurology, and chaos views.

(1) The cyclical view is one of the oldest documented views of history and was held in various forms in the ancient religions and philosophies of Europe, Asia, and Africa. In modern times, the cyclical view has been held by Friedrich Nietzsche who employed it in his attacks on Christianity. According to this view, time is a circle that inevitably and periodically repeats itself. Because history is not moving toward a specific goal, this view is accompanied by a profound sense of pessimism and resignation. Proponents of the cyclical view seek to escape from the historical cycle into an immaterial, impersonal reality. From the Christian perspective, the deficiency of the cyclical view is its lack of linear progression and of hope.

(2) The inevitable progress view has its origins in the 17th century Enlightenment. The inevitable progress view emphasizes the competency of human reason and is eager to discard traditional religious insights. Auguste Comte saw humanity as unavoidably passing through three stages, away from theology and toward scientific positivism. Charles Darwin's theory of biological evolution reinforced this view by stressing the principle of natural selection. Georg Hegel believed that the "Spirit," an absolute idea in which humans participate by knowing, leads history in a dialectical pattern from one advance to the next. History as dialectic means that a particular event, the thesis, encounters its opposite, the antithesis, and merges into a synthesis that becomes a new thesis set to encounter a new antithesis. History ultimately ends in the triumph of science (Comte), the survival of the fittest (Darwin), or the historical realization of the absolute idea (Hegel). From the Christian perspective, the inevitable progress view impinges upon the transcendent providence of God and mistakenly places its hope in something other

H

than the biblical hope of redemption from sin and death.

(3) The mechanistic view is related to the inevitable progress view. Ludwig Feuerbach believed that man makes his own history; moreover, he believed God is a false projection created by man to explain the universe, and that man will find salvation in realizing that he is the only true God. Karl Marx built his mechanistic view on the foundation set by Hegel and Feuerbach. According to Feuerbarch and Marx, the only reality is material. Marx believed history is trapped in a dialectical progression of economics. People are essentially economic beings who have developed through various stages that will end with the elimination of economic classes and the common sharing of all material resources. Religions and metaphysical philosophies are merely created by the upper classes to maintain their oppression of the other classes. From the Christian perspective, the mechanistic view has replaced the providence of God with the providence of fallible theories of economics or scientific materialism.

(4) The historicist view is not mechanistic or materialist in focus, but it is no less dismissive of the providence of God. According to historicism, cultural beliefs and customs are the products of a group's historical experience. Unlike the previous two views, historicism does not see history as progressing in a linear fashion toward some goal; moreover, intuition rather than reason allows the historian to make sense of events. Christians will be uncomfortable with the lack of divinely given human freedom which historicism teaches. Moreover, historicism does not believe that God is leading history through a linear progression of events to a definite goal.

(5) The futurology view is relatively recent in origin but is a secular parallel to the efforts of ancient false seers and false prophets. Futurologists like Alvin Toffler seek to discover future outcomes by utilizing sociological and anthropological analyses. The future outcomes can then be manipulated by humans to reach the desired result. Christians should be wary of this attempt to replace divine providence with human providence.

(6) The chaos view finds no purpose or pattern in human existence. According to the chaos view, God does not provide for humanity in history and history is going nowhere in particular. Therefore, history is not meaningful.

An individual's or society's view of history will shape the quality of that person's or society's life. Vestiges of the biblical view of history can be found in some of the alternative views of history. However, where the biblical view of history is lost in it's fullness, first there will be a spiritual decline, later followed by a decline in the individual morality, social cohesiveness, and economic vigor.

The Christian's hope of heaven has significant consequences in time, both for individuals and for the societies of which they are a part. John described the impact of this hope: "We know that when He appears, we will be like Him, because we will see Him as He is. And everyone who has this hope in Him purifies himself just as He is pure" (1 John 3:2-3 HCSB). C. S. Lewis said, "Aim at heaven and you will get earth thrown in. Aim at earth and you get neither."

Malcolm B. Yarnell III and Steve Bond

HITTITES (Hīt´ tīts) Non-Semitic minority within the population of Canaan who frequently became involved in the affairs of the Israelites. Hittites, along with the Hivites, were people of Indo-European origin, identified within the population of Canaan (as "sons" of Canaan) in the Table of Nations (Gen. 10:15,17), seemingly infiltrated from their cultural and political centers in the north and settled throughout Palestine. Although the history and culture of the Hittites is being clarified, a problem exists with the so-called "Hivites," a name of unknown origin without any extrabiblical references. That they were uncircumcised (Gen. 34:2,14) would suggest an Indo-European rather than Semitic origin. The more acceptable identification therefore would be with the biblical Horites (Hurrians) whose history and character are well known from extrabiblical sources and consistent with role attributed to them in the biblical text. The Septuagint reading "Choraios" (Horite) for the Masoretic "Hivite" in Gen. 34:2 and Josh. 9:7 suggests this identification. See Hivites; Horim or Horites.

Hittites appear among the ethnic groups living in urban enclaves or as individuals in Canaan interacting with the Israelites from patriarchal times to the end of the monarchy (Gen. 15:20; Deut. 7:1; Judg. 3:5). As a significant segment of the Canaan's population, these "children of Heth" permanently became identified as "sons"

Hittite relief showing the king Tudhaliya IV being protected by the god Sharruma (in the king's hand).

of Canaan (Gen. 10:15). In patriarchal times, the reference to King Tidal (in Hittite Tudhaliya II) in Gen. 14:1 is a possible link to early imperial Hatti. In Canaan, the Hittites established a claim on the southern hill country, especially the Hebron area. As a result, Abraham lived among this native population as "a stranger and a sojourner" (Gen. 23:4 NASB). He was forced to purchase the Cave of Machpelah from Ephron the Hittite as a family tomb, specifically for the immediate burial of Sarah (Gen. 23). Esau's marriage to two Hittite women ("daughters of Heth … daughters of the land") greatly grieved and displeased his parents (Gen. 26:34-35; 27:46).

The geographical reference to "all the land of the Hittites" (Josh. 1:4 NASB) on the northern frontier of the promised land may indicate a recognition of the Hittite/Egyptian border treaty established by Rameses II and the Hittites under King Hattusilis III of about 1270 B.C. Moses' listing of the inhabitants of the promised land included the Canaanites, Hittites, Amorites, Hivites, and Jebusites (Exod. 13:5), a situation that was confirmed by the 12 spies sent to explore the land. They reported that Amalekites occupied the Negev; the Hittites, the Jebusites, and Amorites lived in the hill country; and the Canaanites were concentrated along the

Ruins of the great temple at Boghaskoy, Turkey, the site of the ancient Hittite capital.

H

The King's Gate at the Hittite city of Hattusas in Asia Minor (modern Turkey).

Mediterranean coast and the Jordan Valley (Num. 13:29; Josh. 11:3). Thus the Hittites were doomed to displacement by the infiltrating and invading Hebrews (Exod. 3:8,17; 23:23; 33:2).

Devastation and pressures from the west by the Phrygians and the Sea Peoples brought

Hittite ornament portraying two stags encircled by a wreath standing on what may be an altar.

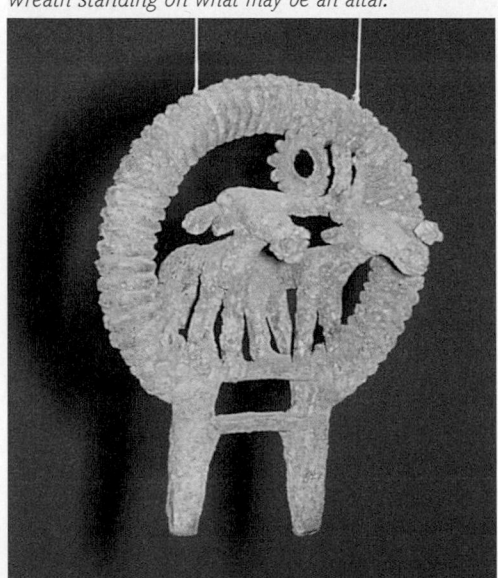

another Hittite population to Canaan about 1200 B.C. Ezekiel recalled that Jerusalem had Amorite and Hittite origins (Ezek. 16:3,45). David purchased a threshing floor from Araunah the Jebusite (2 Sam. 24:16-25) whose name may suggest a Hittite noble status (*arawanis* in Hittite, meaning "freeman, noble"). Later, the account of David's illicit love affair with Bathsheba indicates that Uriah and possibly other Hittites were serving as mercenaries in David's army (2 Sam. 11:3,6; 23:39). The Hittite woman among Solomon's foreign wives was probably the result of a foreign alliance with a neo-Hittite king of north Syria (1 Kings 10:29–11:2; 2 Chron. 1:17). Hittites together with other foreign elements appear to have been conscripted to forced labor during Solomon's reign (1 Kings 9:20-21).

George L. Kelm

HIVITES (Hī´ vīts) A name that occurs 25 times in the Bible though not in texts outside the Bible. Hivites are found in Gibeon (Josh 9:7; 11:19), Shechem (Gen. 34:2), below Hermon in the land of Mizpah (Josh. 11:3), and in the Lebanon mountains (Judg. 3:3). Most frequently the name appears in the list of nations God would drive out of the land during the Israelite conquest (e.g., Deut. 7:1).

Zibeon is identified as a Hivite (Gen. 36:2) but is listed among the Horites in Gen. 36:20,29. In addition, the Septuagint or earliest Greek translation reads "Horite" for "Hivite" in some texts (Gen. 34:2; Josh. 9:7). This may indicate an early linguistic confusion of "Horite" and "Hivite." It is unlikely that the two are identical, although the exact relationship is unclear. See *Horim or Horites.*   *James C. Moyer*

HIZKI (Hĭz´ kī) Personal name meaning "my strength" or a shortened form of "Yah is my strength." Modern translation spelling of Hezeki, a Benjaminite (1 Chron. 8:17).

HIZKIAH (Hĭz kī´ a) Personal name meaning "Yah is my strength." **1.** Abbreviated form in Hebrew for Hezekiah and used as alternate spelling of the king's name (2 Kings 18; Prov. 25:1). The ancestor of Zephaniah, the prophet, may have been the same king (Zeph. 1:1). See *Hezekiah; Zephaniah.* **2.** Apparently the Hebrew name of a clan that returned from Babylonian exile with Zerubbabel about 537 B.C., the Babylonian name being Ater (Neh. 7:21; parallel passage Ezra 2:16 in Hebrew has another variant spelling—Jehizkiah). Both Ater and Hizkijah appear, however, in the list of those who signed Nehemiah's covenant to obey God's law (Neh. 10:17). This would apparently represent men of the next generation. **3.** A descendant of David living after the return from exile (1 Chron. 3:23).

HIZKIJAH (Hĭz kī´ ja) KJV spelling of Hizkiah in Neh. 10:17. Modern translations usually use "Hezekiah." See *Hizkiah.*

HOARFROST or **HOAR FROST** KJV terms for frost from "hoar" (white) and "frost" (Exod. 16:14; Job 38:29; Ps. 147:16).

HOBAB (Hō´ băb) Personal name meaning "beloved" or "cunning." Father-in-law of Moses (Num. 10:29; Judg. 4:11). Some uncertainty exists concerning the identity of Moses' father-in-law. Jethro (Exod. 3:1; 18:2) and Reuel (Exod. 2:18) are also given as names for the father-in-law of the great lawgiver. Several explanations have been offered. Some say different groups within Israel handed down the story of Moses in oral tradition with different names for his father-in-law. Others say Reuel and Jethro were different names for the same person, while Hobab was the son of Reuel or Raguel (Num. 10:29) and

thus the brother-in-law of Moses. Others say that the Hebrew term for father-in-law really has the more general meaning of "related by marriage." Moses urged Hobab to accompany the Israelites through the wilderness as a guide. See *Moses; Jethro; Reuel.*

HOBAH (Hō´ ba) Place-name probably meaning "guilt" in Hebrew but "land of reeds" in Akkadian. Town in Syria to which Abraham pursued the coalition of eastern kings, who kidnapped Lot (Gen. 14:15). Attempts to identify Hobah with Apum or Upe in the Amarna letters from Egypt have recently been questioned. The town or region must lie somewhere north of Damascus, but its precise location is not known. It symbolizes Abraham's ability to drive his enemies completely out of the land of promise.

HOBAIAH (Hō bā´ ya) Personal name meaning "Yah hides." Clan of priests in time of Zerubbabel who did not have family records to prove their descent from pure priestly lines and were excluded from the priesthood (Ezra 2:61; Neh. 7:63). Some translations use "Habaiah" in one or both texts.

HOD (Hŏd) Personal name meaning "majesty." Member of tribe of Asher (1 Chron. 7:37).

HODAIAH (Hō dā´ ya) KJV, REB spelling of Hodaviah (1 Chron. 3:24) based on Hebrew text in which copyist has obviously transposed two letters and early scribes have noted proper reading in margin of text. See *Hodaviah.*

HODAVIAH (Hō dȧ vī´ ȧ) Personal name meaning "praise Yah." The longer form *Hodaviahu* appears in the scribal marginal note correcting the Hebrew text of 1 Chron. 3:24. See *Hodaiah.* **1.** The final generation of the sons of David that the Chronicler listed (1 Chron. 3:24). He appears to have been born about 420 B.C. The listing of seven brothers may be a cryptic note of hope in the Davidic dynasty for the Jewish community after the exile. **2.** Original ancestor of clan in half tribe of Manasseh living east of the Jordan (1 Chron. 5:24). The list leads to an explanation of Israel's loss of land east of the Jordan because of sin and idolatry. **3.** A member of the tribe of Benjamin (1 Chron. 9:7). **4.** A clan of Levites who returned to Judah under Zerubbabel about 537 B.C. (Ezra 2:40). He was kin to the leading priest Joshua or to a Levite with the same name (cp. Ezra 2:2,36). Ezra 3:9 reads Judah instead of Hodaviah, probably a copyists' change from the less familiar to the more familiar word. Similarly, in Hebrew Neh. 7:43 has "Hodevah," a copyist omitting one letter.

HODESH (Hō´ dĕsh) Personal name meaning "new moon." Wife of Shaharaim of the tribe of Benjamin who bore children in Moab (1 Chron. 8:9).

HODEVAH (Hō´ də va) Transliteration of Hebrew text in Neh. 7:43 for original "Hodaviah." See *Hodaviah*.

HODIAH (Hō dī´ a) Personal name meaning "Yah is majestic." **1.** Member of tribe of Judah (1 Chron. 4:19), though Hebrew text has led translators to interpret Hodiah as a wife (REB, KJV), the husband of Naham's sister (TEV), or the father (NASB, NIV, NRSV). Other scholars would assume copyists have changed the text from an original "sons of his wife the Jewess." **2.** A Levite who helped Ezra explain the meaning of the Law to the people (Neh. 8:7; note KJV spelling, Hodijah) and had a leading part in Israel's confession of sin and worship (Neh. 9:5). He signed Nehemiah's covenant to obey God's law (Neh. 10:10). Another Levite and a leader of the people with the same name also signed the covenant (Neh. 10:13,18).

HODIJAH (Hō dī´ ja) (KJV) See *Hodiah*.

HOE Tool for loosening the soil and cutting out weeds around cultivated plants (Isa. 7:25; KJV, "mattock"). See *Tools*.

HOGLAH (Hŏg´ lah) Personal name meaning "partridge." Daughter of Zelophehad in tribe of Manasseh (Num. 26:33). Her marriage to a son of her father's brothers helped ensure the family land inheritance remained within the tribe (Num. 36:11). See *Beth-hoglah; Zelophehad*.

HOHAM (Hō´ hăm) Personal name of uncertain meaning, perhaps related to "unlucky." King of Hebron who joined forces with the king of Jerusalem to punish Gibeon for making an alliance with Joshua (Josh. 10:3). He was one of five kings shut in a cave, used to show Israel's superiority over the kings by the symbol of Israel's captains putting their feet on the kings' necks, and then killed and hung on a tree (Josh.

10:15-26). Thus Joshua gained control of the south, destroying Hebron (10:36-37).

HOLD KJV term for a (fortified) place of refuge. Modern translations generally render the underlying Hebrew as "stronghold" (Judg. 9:46,49; 1 Sam. 22:4; 2 Sam. 5:7). Occasionally other terms are used in place of hold: "fortress" (2 Sam. 24:7 NIV, NRSV); "hill" (Mic. 4:8 NRSV, perhaps in the sense of "citadel"); "fortified cities" (Hab. 1:10 NIV); "refuge" (Nah. 1:7 NIV). In Acts 4:3 to be put in the hold means to be put in custody (NRSV) or in jail (NIV). See *Fort, Fortification*.

HOLM TREE Small, hollylike, evergreen oak (*Quercus ilex*). The identity of the tree of Isa. 44:14 is disputed: cypress (NASB, NIV); ilex (REB); holm oak or tree (NASB margin, NRSV); oak (TEV).

HOLON (Hō´ lŏn) Place-name meaning "sandy spot." **1.** Town in the hill country of Judah allotted to tribe of Judah and given as city for Levites (Josh. 15:51; 21:15). It may be modern Khirbet Illin near Beth-zur. The parallel passage (1 Chron. 6:58) has Hilez or Hilen in different manuscripts. **2.** City of Moab that Jeremiah condemned (Jer. 48:21). Its location is not known.

HOLY Biblical use of the term "holy" has to do primarily with God's separating from the world that which He chooses to devote to Himself. As God's redemptive plan unfolded through the OT, the "holy" became associated with the character of God's separated people conforming to His revealed law. When the time became ripe for the saving work of Jesus Christ, His redeemed people came to be known as saints (literally, "holy ones"). The cross made this possible by inaugurating the fulfillment of the preparatory OT teachings on the holy, opening the way for God's Holy Spirit to indwell His people.

God's Unique Holiness as Separation God alone is "majestic in holiness" (Exod. 15:11; cp. 1 Sam. 2:2; Rev. 15:4). The uniqueness of His holiness is stressed in the repetition of the seraphic cry: "Holy, holy, holy" (Isa. 6:3; cp. Rev. 4:8). Indeed, the frequent title of choice for God in Isaiah is "the Holy One of Israel" (e.g., 12:6; 17:7; 29:19,23; 41:14,16; 47:4; 60:9). But God's perfect holiness—the complete perfection of His attributes such as power and goodness—is a humbling and even terrifying thing when revealed to weak and sinful men (e.g., Isa. 6:5; Luke 5:8; Rev. 1:17).

Those things that God separates to Himself become holy, too. These objects of the Lord's choosing are set apart from the world. For instance, the holy place in the tabernacle and the temple is hidden from the eyes of the people, and the most holy place ("holy of holies") is only entered yearly by the high priest with the blood of atonement and a cloud of incense lest he die (Lev. 16). The privilege of being "a holy people to the Lord your God" (Deut. 7:6; 14:2,21; 28:9) is thus seen to carry weighty responsibility. Interestingly, not only can that which is holy be profaned (e.g., Lev. 21:6,12,15) but also contact with the holy transfers holiness to the profane (e.g., Ezek. 44:19; 46:20; cp. Exod. 29:37; 30:29; 1 Cor. 7:14).

The Ethical Mandate of God's Holiness God's chosen people, in separation from the world, are called to an ethical life in conformity to His revealed word. The command to His people is to "be holy; for I am holy" (Lev. 11:44-45; cp. 19:2; 20:26). This demand is not abrogated with the coming of Christ but is to find its fulfillment in the Christian community (1 Cor. 7:34; Eph. 1:4; Col. 1:22; 1 Pet. 1:16). Christians are to perfect "holiness in the fear of God" (2 Cor. 7:1 NASB). If necessary, God will discipline the followers of Christ for their own good so they "can share His holiness" (Heb. 12:10 HCSB).

The Ultimate Fulfillment of God's Holiness David, fearing that his sin would separate him from God, prays, "Do not ... take Your Holy Spirit from me" (Ps. 51:11 HCSB). John the Baptist, however, predicts that Jesus would inaugurate a new era for God's people by baptizing them with the Holy Spirit (Matt. 3:11). The atoning death of Jesus, by meeting the just demands of God's righteousness (Rom. 3:21-26), makes possible this intimate relationship of God and His people. Jesus, as the true Holy One, does not see decay in His death as the prophetic Scriptures foretold (Ps. 16:10; Acts 13:35). Thus His resurrection signifies the accomplishment of salvation and the inauguration of the age of the Holy Spirit (Rom. 1:4) in which the followers of Jesus are baptized with the Holy Spirit (Acts 2:4). This enduring promise for believers in every generation (Acts 2:38-39) is the empowerment to make them holy: the Holy Spirit makes them so (Rom. 15:16).   *Ted Cabal*

HOLY CITY Designation for Jerusalem (Neh. 11:1,18; Isa. 48:2; 52:1; Dan. 9:24; Matt. 4:5; 27:53; Rev. 11:2) and for the new, heavenly Jerusalem (Rev. 21:2,10; 22:19) because the holy God lived there. See *Holy.*

HOLY GHOST (KJV) See *Holy Spirit.*

HOLY OF HOLIES Innermost sanctuary of the temple. Separated from the other parts of the temple by a thick curtain, the holy of holies was specially associated with the presence of Yahweh. In the early years of the existence of the temple the holy of holies contained the ark of the covenant. See *Temple.*

HOLY ONE OF ISRAEL In Isa. 1:4, a designation for Yahweh. The title stresses God's nature as holy and His unique relationship to Israel. In the OT this designation is used especially in the book of Isaiah. In the NT Jesus is referred to as the Holy One. See *God; Holy.*

HOLY PLACE Courts, inner room, and outer room of the tabernacle (Exod. 26:33). Later the expression was used in reference to the temple and its environs. It was a holy place in the sense of being a place set apart for Yahweh. See *Temple.*

HOLY SPIRIT Third person of the Trinity through whom God acts, reveals His will, empowers individuals, and discloses His personal presence in the OT and NT.

Old Testament The term "Holy Spirit" in the OT is found only in Ps. 51:11; Isa. 63:10-11. References to the Spirit of God, however, are abundant. In one sense the Spirit of God is depicted as a mighty wind, Hebrew using the same word *ruach* for wind, breath, and spirit. During the time of the exodus, God deployed this wind to part the sea thus enabling the Israelites to pass through safely and elude Pharaoh and his army (Exod. 14:21). God used this agent in two ways: as a destructive force that dries up the waters (Hos. 13:15) and as the power of God in gathering clouds to bring the refreshing rain (1 Kings 18:45). The spirit exercised control over the chaotic waters at the beginning of creation (Gen. 1:2; 8:1; cp. Ps. 33:6; Job 26:13). Of the 87 times that the Spirit is described as wind, 37 describe the wind as the agent of God, mostly baneful and ever strong and intense. This property of the Spirit clearly reflects the power of

H

God. An additional quality of the Spirit is that of mysteriousness. Psalm 104:3 demonstrates that the Spirit as wind is able to transport God on its wings to the outer limits of the earth. No one can tell where He has been or where He is going. Power and mystery state the nature of God.

God's Spirit can be expressed as an impersonal force, or it can manifest itself in individuals. The OT has numerous examples when God inspired the prophets indirectly by the Spirit. The prime revelation of the Spirit in the OT, in the personal sense, is by means of prophecy. Joseph's dreams are perceived to be divinely inspired (Gen. 41:38); King David, as a mouthpiece for God, proclaimed that "the Spirit of the LORD spoke by me" (2 Sam. 23:2 NASB); and Zechariah announced the word of the Lord to Zerubbabel, "'Not by might nor by power, but by My Spirit,' says the LORD of hosts" (Zech. 4:6 NASB). Much like the power of the wind, the Spirit equipped the heroes of Israel with extraordinary strength (Judg. 14:6). The judges are described as being Spirit-possessed individuals as in the case of Othniel (Judg. 3:10). Sometimes, the Spirit came upon individuals mightily and altered their normal behavior (1 Sam. 10:16; 19:23-24).

The Spirit is also the ultimate origin of all mental and spiritual gifts, as it is in the underlying inspiration of the men of wisdom (Exod. 31:1-6; Isa. 11:2; Job 4:15; 32:8). Not only did the prophets benefit from the influence of the Spirit, but also the Spirit will be shed upon the people of God (Isa. 44:3) and upon all the people (Joel 2:28). Ezekiel and Isaiah express the idea of the Spirit more than any other OT source. Many of Ezekiel's allusions to the Spirit are in regard to Israel's restoration in the future. The reception of the new Spirit, prophesied in Ezekiel and Jeremiah, is dependent upon repentance (Ezek. 18:31) and is associated with the creation of a new heart (Jer. 31:31-34). This prophetic foreshadowing, in light of the individual, sporadic, and temporary manifestation of the Spirit in the OT, looked forward to a time when the Spirit of God would revitalize His chosen people, empower the Messiah, and be lavishly poured out on all humankind.

New Testament When John the Baptist burst on the scene proclaiming the advent of the kingdom of God, the Spirit-inspired prophetic voice returned after a 400-year absence. Zechariah and Elizabeth, John's parents, were informed that

their son would "be filled with the Holy Spirit while still in his mother's womb" (Luke 1:15 HCSB). Similarly, the angel Gabriel visited Mary with the news that "the Holy Spirit will come upon you, and the power of the Most High will overshadow you. Therefore the holy child to be born will be called the Son of God" (1:35).

A watershed in biblical history occurred at the event of Jesus' baptism when He was anointed by the Spirit of God (3:22). The Holy Spirit was then responsible for thrusting Jesus out into the wilderness to undergo temptation (4:1-13). Luke has many more references to the Holy Spirit than do the other synoptic accounts. This can be accounted for by Luke's theological interests that are extended in the Acts of the Apostles, which has been rightly named "The Acts of the Holy Spirit" because of the prominence given to the Spirit.

All apostolic writers witnessed to the reality of the Spirit in the church; however, the Apostle Paul, who wrote more than any other author, offers the most theological reflection on the subject. The main chapters to consult are Rom. 8; 1 Cor. 2; 12–14; 2 Cor. 3; and Gal. 5.

Johannine theology is rich in its doctrine of the Spirit. In the Gospel of John, the Spirit possesses Christ (1:32-33); is indicative of the new birth (3:1-16); will come upon Jesus' departure (16:7-11); and will endow the believer after the resurrection (20:22). The Christian community is anointed by the Spirit (1 John 2:20), and the Spirit assures the believer of the indwelling presence of Jesus (1 John 3:24). In the prophetic book of Revelation, John, in OT fashion, depicted himself as a prophet inspired by the Spirit. See *God; Spirit.*   *Paul Jackson*

HOLY SPIRIT, SIN AGAINST THE Attributing the work of the Holy Spirit to the devil (Matt. 12:32; Mark 3:29; Luke 12:10). See *Unpardonable Sin.*

HOLY WAR The Hebrew word for "war" occurs more than 300 times in the OT. The strategic position of Palestine between Mesopotamia and Egypt made war a harsh reality for most of its inhabitants during biblical times. Israel gained a foothold in this land by means of a war of conquest, and thereafter, by frequently defensive actions against intruders and invaders. Unfortunately, the history of war in Israel also included several civil conflicts.

For most of the ancient Near East, war was considered a sacred undertaking in which the honor and power of the national God was at stake. For Israel, however, war intimately involved the transcendent power of the God who created the heavens and the earth. The biblical writers refer to the conflicts Israel faced as the "Wars of the LORD" (Num. 21:14; 1 Sam. 18:17; 25:28). God is described as a "man of war" (Exod. 15:3; Isa. 42:13) and "mighty in battle" (Ps. 24:8). He is "the LORD of hosts, the God of the armies of Israel" (1 Sam. 17:45 NASB). It is God who leads them out and fights for them (Deut. 20:4; Josh. 10:14, 42; Judg. 4:14). God set the code of conduct in war (Deut. 20:10-18), and the spoils belong to Him (Josh. 6:19).

Before the armies of Israel went out to war, they offered a sacrifice to God (1 Sam. 7:9) and sought His guidance (2 Sam. 5:23-24). The warriors who marched into battle had to be pure and consecrated to God (Josh. 3:5). The presence of God in the arena of battle was symbolized by the ark of the covenant (1 Sam. 4:5-7). After the victory, praises were offered to God in a victory celebration (Exod. 15:1-3).

As the final act of battle, Israel was sometimes required to dedicate everything in a "ban" (*herem*), which meant that the people and possessions of an entire city would be set apart for God and destroyed (Deut. 7:2; 20:17; Josh. 8:2; 1 Sam. 15:3). Only the metal objects were saved (Josh. 6:18-24). Those who transgressed the ban faced dire consequences (Josh. 7).

Why would a loving God order the wholesale extermination of the nations living in the promised land? There is no simple answer to this difficult question. Three points, however, need to be remembered. First, the concept of the ban is also found among the nations surrounding Israel. In war, every living being and every piece of property was to be dedicated to the deity. Second, the rules for placing the spoils of war under the ban appear to apply only to the cities of the nations within the promised land that God had designated as inheritance for Israel (Deut. 20:16-18). In this context, it should be noted that the OT reports the use of the ban primarily at Arad (Num. 21:2-3), the cities of Sihon and Og (Deut. 2:24; 3:6), Jericho (Josh. 6:21), Ai (Josh. 8:26), the cities of southern Canaan (Josh. 10:28-43) and Hazor (Josh. 11:11). Finally, it must be remembered that Israel was only allowed to drive out the nations living in the promised land because of their sinful abominations (Deut. 9:4-5; 18:9-14; 20:16-18). In this sense, Israel served as the instrument of God's judgment against these sinful nations. In like manner, God would later allow another nation to march against Judah in judgment (Hab. 1:6-11).

Stephen J. Andrews

HOLY WEEK The week prior to Easter Sunday in which the church remembers the death and resurrection of Christ. As the observance of the Easter festival developed over the first few centuries, the week prior to Easter Sunday began to take on special significance for the early church. In the early centuries Easter Sunday celebrations included remembrance of both the crucifixion and the resurrection. By about 500, Good Friday came to be the focus of the remembrance of the crucifixion. *(See map on next page.)*

In a similar development Christians began to regard Thursday of Holy Week as a special time for participating in the Lord's Supper. The day came to be called "Maundy Thursday," a reference to Christ's giving a "new commandment" (John 13:34) to His disciples. The word "Maundy" comes from the Latin word for "commandment." Usually the early Maundy Thursday observances included a ceremonial foot washing, in imitation of Christ's washing the feet of the disciples (John 13:5-11). See *Church Year.*

Fred A. Grissom

HOMAGE Special honor, respect, or allegiance, such as that shown to a king; obeisance; reverence. Homage is most often paid to the king (1 Chron. 29:20 NASB, 2 Chron. 24:17 NIV) or to a high-ranking official (Gen. 43:28; Esther 3:2,5 NASB). Homage is sometimes paid to holy men (Samuel, 1 Sam. 28:14 NASB; Daniel, Dan. 2:46 NASB, NRSV). Homage is paid to God as the King of Israel (1 Chron. 29:20; Isa. 18:7 NASB). The Roman soldiers paid Christ mock homage before the crucifixion (Mark 15:19).

HOMAM (Hō´ măm) Personal name, perhaps meaning "confusion." Hebrew text name for grandson of Seir (1 Chron. 1:39). The parallel passage reads "Hemam" (Gen. 36:22).

HOMELESSNESS In a sense, all Christians, like Abraham, are "homeless" in that they are but sojourners in this world (Heb. 11:13). This reality, however, must not lessen the impact of the

H

THE PASSION WEEK IN JERUSALEM

Gate

Tower

Wall

Possible locations of the Chamber of Hewn Stone

MOVEMENTS OF JESUS

Sunday

Monday

Thursday/Friday

Jesus before the Sanhedrin

Begun by Herod Agrippa I (A.D. 41–44) and completed later

Josephus' Third North Wall

Kidron

Sunday
Jesus descends from Bethany and enters the temple precincts

Sunday night
Jesus returns to Bethany to lodge with His friends

Tuesday
Jesus teaches and disputes with authorities

Golgotha (Gordon's Calvary)

Tower of Psephinus

Josephus' Second North Wall

Sheep's Pool (Pool of Bethsaida)

Bezetha

Fish Gate

Via Dolorosa

Antonia Fortress

Israel's Pool

Tyropoeon Valley

Mt. of Olives

To Bethany (see inset below)

Gethsemane

Tuesday
Jesus teaches His disciples about end times on the Mount of Olives

Monday
Cleansing of the temple

Sheep Gate

Temple Mount

Solomon's Portico

Shushan Gate

Beautiful Gate

Thursday night
3. Jesus is arrested

Friday morning
9. Jesus is crucified

Golgotha (traditional location)

Wilson's Arch (bridge)

Altar

Temple

Friday daybreak
5. Jesus before the Sanhedrin

Tower's Pool

Tower of Hippicus

Gennath Gate

Josephus

First N. Wall

Xystus

Warren's Gate

Barclay's Gate

Royal Portico

Friday morning
8. Jesus again before Pilate

Tower of Phasael

Tower of Mariamne

Herod Antipas' Palace

Huldah Gates

Pinnacle of Temple (traditional location)

Friday daybreak
6. Jesus before Pilate

Praetorium

Herod's Palace

Thursday evening
2. Jesus retires to Gethsemane with His disciples

Herod's Family Tomb(s)

Thursday/Friday
4. Jesus is taken to the house of Caiaphas for a preliminary hearing

Upper City

Robinson's Arch (stairs)

Valley Gate

Ophel

Theater

House of Caiaphas, the High Priest

Escarpment

Friday morning
7. Jesus before Herod Antipas

Citadel

Gihon Spring

Hezekiah's Tunnel

Serpent's Pool

Essene Quarter

Lower City

City of David

Water Gate

Thursday
1. Jesus shares the Passover meal with His disciples

Upper Room (traditional location)

Siloam Pool

Essene Gate

Hinnom Valley

0 1/8 1/4 Mile
0 150 300 Meters

N

MEDITERRANEAN SEA

PRESENT-DAY ISRAEL

Area enlarged below

30 E 40 E 40 N

30 N 30 N

30 E 40 E

34 E 35 E 36 E

33 N 33 N

MEDITERRANEAN SEA

Jordan R.

Emmaus Jerusalem

Area enlarged at left

Bethany

32 N 32 N

31 N 31 N

DEAD SEA

30 N 30 N

34 E 35 E 36 E

responsibility of Christians who are able to own a house or pay rent on an apartment toward persons who, for a variety of reasons, are unable to do either.

The biblical term "sojourner" includes a variety of persons, native and nonnative, who did not have permanent homes of their own in the land in which they were living. While some sojourners were attached to a household (1 Kings 17:20; Job 19:15), others were transient (e.g., 2 Sam. 4:3; 2 Chron. 15:9), "like a bird wandering from its nest" (Prov. 27:8 HCSB). The rights of all were vulnerable. For this reason, sojourners, like the poor, orphans, and widows, fell under the special protection of God (Deut. 10:17-18; Ps. 146:9; cp. Rom. 8:38-39) and were to be treated as equals under the Mosaic law (Lev. 24:22; Deut. 24:17). Both the OT and NT declare that God's people are to provide for the homeless (Lev. 19:10; Deut. 10:18-19; Job 31:32; Isa. 58:7; Zech. 7:9-10; Matt. 25:31-46).

Other biblical examples of homelessness include Absalom, who fled his home as a fugitive (2 Sam. 14:13-14), various OT saints (Heb. 11:37-38), Jesus (Matt. 8:20), the prodigal son (Luke 15:13-16), and Paul (1 Cor. 4:11). The people of Israel considered themselves homeless when they were uprooted from their land in exile (Jer. 12:7; Lam. 4:14-15; 5:2; Hos. 9:17; Amos 7:17).

HOMER (Hō´ měr) Unit of dry measure (Lev. 27:16). According to Ezek. 45:11, it was equal to 10 ephahs. In liquid measure this was 10 baths. The actual volume represented by the term has been variously estimated between 3.8 and 6.6 bushels. It was the same volume as the cor (Ezek. 45:14). See *Weights and Measures.*

HOMOSEXUALITY Sexual relations between people of the same sex. When discussing homosexuality, the biblical emphasis is on behavior, and the verdict is always that it is sinful.
Homosexuality is a consequence of rejecting the created order. The *prima facie* case against homosexuality in the Scripture is found in God's creative plan for human sexuality. God created mankind as male and female, to procreate within the context of marriage (Gen. 1:27-28; 2:18-24). This creation order for human sexuality received the endorsement of both the Lord Jesus Christ (Mark 10:6-9; Matt. 19:4-6) and the Apostle Paul (Eph. 5:31). On the surface,

homosexual behavior should be recognized as sinful because it violates God's original plan for heterosexual monogamy.

Against this background of God's creation scheme for human sexual expression, Paul makes a theological argument in Rom. 1:18-32 that homosexuality is one consequence of rejecting God as Creator and His created order. Paul indicates that both male homosexuality and female lesbianism result from a denial of God. He begins by showing that through rejection of the "creation" (1:20) and "the Creator" (1:25) women "exchanged natural sexual intercourse for what is unnatural" (1:26 HCSB). He adds also that the men "left natural sexual intercourse with females and were inflamed in their lust for one another. Males committed shameless acts with males" (1:27 HCSB). Paul's argument: Because these people reject God, He gives them over to the desires of their own sinful hearts. In the course of this text, Paul uses several other negative terms to describe homosexuality, such as "uncleanness," "dishonor," "vile passions," "error," "debased mind," and "not fitting." In addition, homosexuality is included here in a serious list of vices that are deserving of death, not only for those who practice but also for those who approve (1:32).

As to modern notions of "homosexual orientation," a scriptural perspective will view any same sex inclinations at least as harmful as proclivities toward any other sin, as negative consequences of fallen human nature that is inclined towards sin. In light of Rom. 1, homosexual predisposition may also be an indication and outworking of earlier and other sin(s).
Homosexuality is a sin that results in judgment. The first mention of homosexuality in the Bible depicts God's judgment upon it as sin. It was the outstanding transgression of Sodom and Gomorrah. The severity of the judgment, which came because of homosexuality, indicates the seriousness of this sin (Gen. 19:1-11). Both cities were destroyed as "the LORD rained on Sodom and Gomorrah brimstone and fire" (19:24 NASB). The NT commentary on this event is that these two cities were turned to ashes as a matter of God's holy wrath, specifically because their inhabitants had given themselves to "sexual immorality and practiced perversions" (2 Pet. 2:6-7; Jude 7).

Some pro-homosexual interpreters have claimed that the sin of Sodom and Gomorrah

H

was not homosexuality per se, but homosexual gang rape. While it is accurate to say that the men of Sodom sought to rape Lot's guests, the text does not indicate that the sex would have been acceptable if only the angelic visitors had consented. Also, the fact that God's judgment came upon two entire cities argues that it was not just the one instance of gang rape in Sodom that was an offense to God. Instead, God's announced plan to destroy Sodom and Gomorrah before the rape incident occurred indicates that the practice of homosexual behavior in both cities was an affront to the holiness of God. When the homosexuals demanded carnally "to know" Lot's guests, they were merely attempting again what they had been doing for some time. Lot protested, "Do not act wickedly" (Gen. 19:7 NASB). But long before this, when Lot initially pitched his tent toward the city, we read "the men of Sodom were wicked exceedingly and sinners against the LORD" (13:13 NASB). Again, before the attempted gang rape, God said, "Their sin is exceedingly grave" (18:20 NASB), and Abraham also said they were "wicked" (18:23,25).

Another pro-homosexual interpretation is that the sin of Sodom and Gomorrah was inhospitality, not homosexuality or homosexual rape. An appeal is made from Ezek. 16:49 that Sodom was judged for violating the hospitality code. From this passage, the claim is made of Gen. 19 that the men of Sodom wanted "to know" (*yada‘*) Lot's guests only in the sense of "getting acquainted with them." However, *yada‘* is used in a sexual way in the OT at least 10 times, and half of these uses occur in Genesis. Added to this, the context of Gen. 19 argues for the sexual meaning of "to know." It makes no sense to say that *yada‘* means "acquainted with" in verse 8 where Lot says his daughters had not "known" any men. Certainly they were acquainted with men of the city. But they had not sexually "known" any men.

The "inhospitality" interpreters also point to the absence of any mention of homosexuality in other passages that hold up Sodom and Gomorrah as examples of judgment, such as Isa. 1:10; Jer. 23:14; Matt. 10:14-15; and Luke 10:10-12. There are also several problems with this approach. First, these texts do not exclude homosexuality. In the case of Ezek. 16:49, sexual sins should be viewed as a form of selfishness. Besides, the next verse (16:50) shows that

the sin was sexual by calling it an "abomination." In Lev. 18:22 this same word is used to describe homosexual sins. Most of all, the problem with this view is that the 2 Peter and Jude passages do link the judgment of the cities to the sexual sin of homosexuality, and this does not contradict in any way the other judgment passages. For this reason, those who take the authority of Scripture seriously will reject the pro-homosexual/inhospitality view (Judg. 19:16-24).

Violation of Old Testament law The Holiness Code, which conveyed God's demands for ordering the life of His covenant people, contained two clear prohibitions against homosexual activity. In a large section on sexual morality which should be viewed as an extension of the seventh commandment, "The LORD spoke to Moses saying ... 'You shall not lie with a male as one lies with a female'" (Lev. 18:1,22 NASB). Then later, repeating with 18:22 that homosexuality is an "abomination," Lev. 20:13 adds, "If there is a man who lies with a male as those who lie with a woman, both of them ... shall surely be put to death."

Violation of New Testament ethic In 1 Tim. 1:8-10 Paul discusses the value of the OT law in the present era, if used wisely. It is to be used to judge "sinners." Then he includes "homosexuals" (*arsenokoitai*) in his vice list, which delineates those who are "the ungodly." Also in 1 Cor. 6:9-11 "homosexuals" appears in a similar vice list, and Paul comments that anyone who continues in these sins will not inherit the kingdom of God. *Arsenokoites* refers to the active partner in the homosexual act. However, in addition to "homosexuals" in 1 Cor. 6:9, Paul adds a second word, "effeminate" (*malakoi*). *Malakoi* refers to the passive member in the homosexual relationship. The point is that both passive and active kinds of "homosexual" behavior are sinful, ungodly, and disqualify one from entrance into the kingdom of God.

Forgivable and changeable through Jesus Christ However ungodly and undeserving of heaven any homosexual might be, there is the opportunity to be forgiven, changed, and declared righteous through Jesus Christ. Paul continues in 1 Cor. 6:11 (HCSB) to say, "Some of you were like this." The Corinthian church evidently contained some former homosexuals who had been converted. Furthermore, Paul adds of them, "But you were washed, you were sanctified, you were justified in the name of the Lord Jesus Christ and by the Spirit of our God." The homosexual who repents and believes receives the same cleansing, sanctification, and justification as every other believer who turns from sin to Christ. *Jerry A. Johnson*

HONESTY Fairness and straightforwardness of conduct. KJV frequently used "honesty" or cognates where modern translations use other words: "honorable/honorably" (Rom. 13:13; Phil. 4:8; Heb. 13:18; 1 Pet. 2:12); "noble" (Luke 8:15; Rom. 12:17); "dignity" (1 Tim. 2:2); "properly" (1 Thess. 4:12). Men of "honest report" (Acts 6:3) are men of good standing (NRSV).

Someone in the right in a law case may be described as honest (Exod. 23:7 NIV). Isaiah lamented that "no one goes to law honestly" (59:4 NRSV). Honest or just balances, weights, and measures give fair and accurate measure (Lev. 19:36; Deut. 25:15; Prov. 16:11). Job (31:6) prays God's judgment to be weighed in an honest balance so God can know the person's integrity. Scripture often refers to honest or right speech (Job 6:25; Prov. 12:17; 16:13; 24:26). Those working on the temple construction were known for their honest business dealings (2 Kings 12:15; 22:7).

Jacob claimed honesty (Gen. 30:33) but manipulated the breeding of Laban's flocks (30:37-43). Jacob's sons repeatedly assured Joseph of their honesty (Gen. 42:11,19,31,33-34), never guessing that their brother knew their deceptive natures all too well (37:31-33).

HONEY Produced by bees providing a sweet foodstuff for people to eat.
Old Testament During Bible times, honey appeared in three forms: honey deposited from wild bees (Deut. 32:13); honey from domesticated bees (one of the products "of the field" 2 Chron. 31:5); and a syrup made from dates and grape juice (2 Kings 18:32). Honey served as a foodstuff (Gen. 43:11) and as an item of trade (Ezek. 27:17).

Almost all references to honey in the OT are to wild honey. Bees made their honeycombs and deposited their honey in holes in the ground (1 Sam. 14:25), under rocks or in crevices between rocks (Deut. 32:13), or in the carcasses of animals (Judg. 14:8).

Honey was prohibited from being used in burnt offerings because it fermented easily (Lev. 2:11). Honey was rare enough to be considered a luxury item (Gen. 43:11; 1 Kings 14:3). Honey was so ample in Canaan that the land there was described as a land "flowing with milk and honey" (Exod. 3:8).

Beekeeping is not mentioned specifically in the OT. In later times beekeeping was practiced by the Jews. The hives were of straw and wicker. Before removing the combs, the beekeeper stupefied the bees with fumes of charcoal and cow dung burnt in front of the hives.

The Lord's ordinances are "sweeter than honey" (Ps. 19:10). God's goodness to Jerusalem was expressed by the phrase "you ate honey" (Ezek. 16:13).
New Testament Honey is mentioned in three NT passages (Matt. 3:4; Mark 1:6; Rev. 10:9-10). In NT times, honey was viewed as a food eaten by those who lived in the wilderness (Matt. 3:4; Mark 1:6). *Gary Hardin*

HONOR See *Shame and Honor.*

HOOD KJV term for one of the items of finery worn by the elite women of Jerusalem (Isa. 3:23). Modern translations render the underlying Hebrew as "scarf" (TEV), "tiara" (NIV), or "turban" (NASB, NRSV, REB). It represented a fine Oriental head covering.

HOOF Curved covering of horn protecting the front of or enclosing the digits of some mammals. According to Mosaic law, ritually clean animals are those that both chew the cud and have cloven (divided) hooves (Deut. 14:6-7).

HOOK Curved or bent device for catching, holding, or pulling. Some biblical uses, for example, hanging curtains (Exod. 26:32; 27:10) or fishing (Isa. 19:8; Job 40:24; Hab. 1:15; Matt. 17:27), are familiar today. (KJV often uses "angle.") Less familiar is the practice of ancient conquerors who led their captives by means of hooks or thongs put through their noses or jaws (2 Chron. 33:11; Ezek. 38:4; Amos 4:2).

HOOPOE Any of the Old World birds of the family *Upupidae*, having a plumed head crest and a long, slender, curved bill. The identity of the unclean bird of Lev. 11:19 (Deut. 14:18) is disputed: lapwing (KJV); hoopoe (modern

English translations); waterhen (earliest Greek); woodcock (Targum).

HOPE Trustful expectation, particularly with reference to the fulfillment of God's promises. Biblical hope is the anticipation of a favorable outcome under God's guidance. More specifically, hope is the confidence that what God has done for us in the past guarantees our participation in what God will do in the future. This contrasts to the world's definition of hope as "a feeling that what is wanted will happen."

The Ground and Object of Hope In the OT God alone is the ultimate ground and object of hope. Hope in God was generated by His mighty deeds in history. In fulfilling His promise to Abraham (Gen. 12:1-3), He redeemed the Israelites from bondage in Egypt. He provided for their needs in the wilderness, formed them into a covenant community at Sinai, and led them into the successful occupation of Canaan. These acts provided a firm base for their confidence in God's continuing purpose for them. Even when Israel was unfaithful, hope was not lost. Because of God's faithfulness and mercy, those who returned to Him could count on His help (Mal. 3:6-7). This help included forgiveness (2 Chron. 7:14; Ps. 86:5) as well as deliverance from enemies. Thus, Jeremiah addressed God as the "Hope of Israel, its Savior in time of distress" (Jer. 14:8 NASB; cp. 14:22; 17:13).

A corollary of putting one's hope in God is refusing to place one's final confidence in the created order. All created things are weak, transient, and apt to fail. For this reason it is futile to vest ultimate hope in wealth (Pss. 49:6-12; 52:7; Prov. 11:28), houses (Isa. 32:17-18), princes (Ps. 146:3), empires and armies (Isa. 31:1-3; 2 Kings 18:19-24), or even the Jerusalem temple (Jer. 7:1-7). God, and God only, is a rock that cannot be moved (Deut. 32:4,15,18; Pss. 18:2; 62:2; Isa. 26:4) and a refuge and fortress who provides ultimate security (Pss. 14:6, 61:3; 73:28; 91:9). An accurate summary of the OT emphasis is found in Ps. 119:49-50.

A significant aspect of OT hope was Israel's expectation of a messiah, that is, an anointed ruler from David's line. This expectation grew out of the promise that God would establish the throne of David forever (2 Sam. 7:14). The anointed ruler (messiah) would be God's agent to restore Israel's glory and rule the nations in peace and righteousness. For the most part, however,

David's successors were disappointments. The direction of the nation was away from the ideal. Thus, people looked to the future for a son of David who would fulfill the divine promise.

The NT continues to speak of God as the source and object of hope. Paul wrote that it was "God who raises the dead" in whom "we have placed our hope" (2 Cor. 1:9-10 HCSB). Furthermore, "we have put our hope in the living God, who is the Savior of everyone" (1 Tim. 4:10 HCSB). Peter reminded his readers that "your faith and hope are in God" (1 Peter 1:21 HCSB). In the NT, as in the OT, God is the "God of hope" (Rom. 15:13).

For the early Christians, hope is also focused in Christ. He is called "our hope" (1 Tim. 1:1), and the hope of glory is identified with "Christ in you" (Col. 1:27). Images applied to God in the OT are transferred to Christ in the NT. He is the Savior (Luke 2:11; Acts 13:23; Titus 1:4; 3:6), the source of life (John 6:35), the rock on which hope is built (1 Pet. 2:4-7). He is the first and last (Rev. 1:17), the day-spring dispelling darkness and leading His people into eternal day (Rev. 22:5).

New Testament writers spoke of Christ as the object and ground of hope for two reasons: (1) He is the Messiah who has brought salvation by His life, death, and resurrection (Luke 24:46). God's promises are fulfilled in Him. "For every one of God's promises is 'Yes' in Him" (2 Cor. 1:20 HCSB). (2) They are aware of the unity between Father and Son. This is a unity of nature (John 1:1; Col. 1:19) as well as a unity in the work of redemption. Because "in Christ, God was reconciling the world to Himself" (2 Cor. 5:19 HCSB), hope in the Son is one with hope in the Father.

The Future of Hope While the NT affirms the sufficiency of Christ's redemptive work in the past, it also looks forward to His return in the future to complete God's purpose. Indeed, the major emphasis on hope in the NT centers on the second coming of Christ. The "blessed hope" of the church is nothing less than "the appearing of the glory of our great God and Savior, Jesus Christ" (Titus 2:13 HCSB). See *Future Hope.*

The Assurance of Hope Christians live in hope for two basic reasons. The first reason is because of what God has done in Christ. Especially important is the emphasis the NT places on the resurrection by which Christ has defeated the power of sin and death. "According to His great mercy, He has given us a new birth into a living hope through the resurrection of Jesus Christ from the dead" (1 Pet. 1:3 HCSB).

The second reason is the indwelling of the Holy Spirit. "The Spirit Himself testifies together with our spirit that we are God's children" (Rom. 8:16 HCSB).

Given the assurance of hope, Christians live in the present with confidence and face the future with courage. They can also meet trials triumphantly because they know "that affliction produces endurance, endurance produces proven character, and proven character produces hope" (Rom. 5:3-4 HCSB). Such perseverance is not passive resignation; it is the confident endurance in the face of opposition. There is, therefore, certitude in Christian hope that amounts to a qualitative difference from ordinary hope. Christian hope is the gift of God. "We have this hope—like a sure and firm anchor of the soul" (Heb. 6:19 HCSB). See *Eschatology*.

Bert Dominy

HOPHNI AND PHINEHAS (Hŏph´ nī and Phĭn´ ə hàs) Personal names meaning "tadpole" and "dark-skinned one" in Egyptian. In 1 Sam. 1:3, sons of Eli and priests at Shiloh. They were disreputable men who were contemptuous of sacred matters. They were slain in battle against the Philistines (1 Sam. 4:4). The news of their deaths precipitated the death of their father Eli (1 Sam. 4:18). See *Eli; Samuel.*

HOPHRA (Hŏph´ rà) Egyptian divine name meaning "the heart of Re endures." Egyptian pharaoh (589–569 B.C.). At the beginning of his reign he tried to drive the Babylonian army away from its siege of Jerusalem (Jer. 37:5). Apparently at that time Jeremiah mocked the pharaoh, making a pun on his name, calling him a loud-voiced boaster ("King Bombast, the man who missed his opportunity" Jer. 46:17 REB). Jeremiah warned that the pharaoh would be handed over to his enemies, at the same time warning Jews living in Egypt that salvation history was reversed and they would be destroyed (Jer. 44:26-30). Hophra's death would be a sign to the Jews that Jeremiah's words were true. Hophra eventually lost his power in a revolt by his general Amasis in 569 B.C. Condemnation of Hophra showed Jeremiah's consistency in opposing any opposition to Babylon, whom God had chosen to punish His disobedient people. See *Egypt.*

HOR, MOUNT (Hōr) Place-name, perhaps an ancient variant of Hebrew common noun, har, "mountain." **1.** Place where Aaron, the high priest, died, fulfilling God's word that he would be punished for rebelling at the water of Meribah (Num. 20:22-29; 33:38-39). Moses installed Aaron's son Eleazar as high priest on the mountain. It was apparently a brief journey from Kadesh and lay near the coast of Edom (Num. 20:22-23). The traditional location at Jebel Harun above Petra is too far inside Edom and too far from Kadesh, though high (4,800 feet) and impressive. Recently Bible students have pointed to Jebel Madurah, northeast of Kadesh on Edom's border. Deuteronomy 10:6 places Aaron's death at Mosera, an unknown site which may be under Mount Hor. Israel journeyed from Mount Hor to go around Edom (Num. 21:4; 33:41). **2.** Mountain marking northern boundary of promised land (Num. 34:7-8). The location is unknown, though some would see Hor as a variant name for Mount Hermon.

HORAM (Hō´ răm) Personal name perhaps meaning "high, exalted." King of Gezer, whose attempt to deliver Lachish from Joshua resulted in his death and the annihilation of his army (Josh. 10:33), though his city remained a Canaanite stronghold (Josh. 16:10; cp. 1 Kings 9:16).

HOREB (Hō´ rĕb) Alternative name for Mount Sinai (Exod. 3:1-12; 17:6-7; Deut. 1:19; 5:2; 1 Kings 19:8). See *Sinai, Mount.*

HOREM (Hō´ rĕm) Place-name meaning "split rock" but sounding like the word for "war booty under the ban." City in tribal allotment of Naphtali (Josh. 19:38). Location is unknown.

HORESH (Hō´ rĕsh) Place-name meaning "forest," KJV interpreting the term as a common noun. As David hid there from Saul, Jonathan, Saul's son, came out to help him and made a covenant of mutual help (1 Sam. 23:15-18). The people of Ziph revealed David's hideout, but David still escaped. If a proper name, Horesh may be modern Khirbet Khoreisa, two miles south of Ziph and six miles south of Hebron.

HOR-HAGGIDGAD (Hôr-hà gĭd´ găd) or **HOR-HAGIDGAD** (KJV) Place-name, perhaps meaning "hill of crickets." Station on Israel's wilderness journey (Num. 33:32-33). It may be in the Wadi Geraphi, though no certain location is known. It appears to be a variant spelling of Gudgodah (Deut. 10:7).

HORI (Hō´ rī) Personal name meaning "bleached," "lesser," or "Horite." **1.** Edomite descended from Seir (Gen. 36:22). **2.** Father of the leader of tribe of Simeon under Moses in the wilderness (Num. 13:5).

HORIM (Hō´ rĭm) (KJV) or **HORITES** (Hō rits) Pre-Edomite inhabitants of Mount Seir in the southern Transjordan. Hebrew word for Horites corresponds to the extrabiblical Hurrians, a non-Semitic people who migrated into the Fertile Crescent about 2000 B.C. The Hurrians created the Mitannian Empire in Mesopotamia about 1500 B.C. and later became an important element in the Canaanite population of Palestine. In locations where there is extrabiblical evidence for Hurrians, the Hebrew term *Hivites* appears (Gen. 34:2; Josh. 9:7; 11:3,19) as a designation for certain elements of the Canaanite population. The Septuagint (Gr. translation of the OT), however, substitutes Horites for Hivites in Gen. 34:2 and Josh. 9:7. Also, Zibeon, son of Seir the Horite (Gen. 36:20), is identified as a Hivite in Gen. 36:2. For these reasons, many scholars equate both Horites and Hivites (the names are quite similar in Hebrew) with the extrabiblical Hurrians.

Nevertheless, the Hebrew text only mentions Horites in Mount Seir where there is no record of Hurrians. Therefore, another suggestion holds that the biblical Horites were not Hurrians but simply the original cave-dwelling (Hb. *hor* means "cave") population of Edom (Mount Seir). The Hivites, according to this theory, should be identified with the extrabiblical Hurrians. See *Seir, Mount.*   *Daniel C. Browning, Jr.*

HORMAH (Hôr´ mah) Place-name meaning "split rock" or "cursed for destruction." City marking the limit of the Canaanite route of the Israelites after the failed Israelite attempt to invade Canaan that followed the report of the 12 spies (Num. 14:45). Though the exact location of Hormah is not known, it was in the territory assigned to the tribe of Simeon (Josh. 19:4). Some identify it with Tell Masos about seven miles east of Beersheba. Excavations have shown settlement in about 1800 B.C. and again just before 1200 B.C. The latter settlement

apparently lasted until the time of David (cp. 1 Sam. 30:30). A small fortress was built some time after 700 B.C. and destroyed shortly after 600 B.C.

The site controlled the east-west road in the Beersheba Valley and the north-south road to Hebron. Israel gained brief victory there (Num. 21:3) after their earlier defeat (Num. 14:45; cp. Deut. 1:44). The list of kings Joshua defeated includes Hormah (Josh. 12:14); the battle description says Judah and Simeon combined to take Hormah after Joshua's death (Judg. 1:1,17), the city earlier being called Zephath. See *Zephath.*

HORN Curved bonelike structures growing from the heads of animals such as deer or goats and vessels or instruments made from or shaped like such horns. In Scripture "horn" refers to trumpets, vessels, topographical features, and figurative symbols.

Old Testament The basic meaning of "horns" relate to animal horns (Gen. 22:13; Deut. 33:17; Dan. 8:5). Elephant tusks were also called horns (Ezek. 27:15). Horns are mentioned as being used as trumpets (Josh. 6:5). Such instruments were perforated horns of the ram or the wild ox used to sound ceremonial or military signals. Priests sounded trumpets to call to worship. Trumpets later were made of silver. Horns also were used as vessels. Being hollow and easy to polish, horns were used to hold liquids for drinking or storage, including ceremonial anointing oil (1 Sam. 16:1). Hornlike projections were built onto the corners of the altar of burnt offerings in the temple and in tabernacles (Exod. 27:2). The horns were smeared with the blood of the sacrifice, served as binding posts for the sacrifice, and were clung to for safety from punishment (1 Kings 2:28). See *Music, Instruments, Dancing.*

As a topographical feature, the peaks or summits of Palestinian hills were called horns (Isa. 51:1). Metaphorically, horn signified the strength and honor of people and brightness and rays. Such references are used in Scripture as emblems of the power of God (Heb. 3:4) and other physical or spiritual entities. There is an apocalyptic use of the word in Dan. 7:7. Horns budding or sprouting is a figurative language indicating a sign of revival of a nation or power.

New Testament Christ is called "a horn of salvation" (Luke 1:69 HCSB), which is a metaphorical use of the word signifying strength. Other figurative uses include the Lamb with seven horns mentioned in the book of Revelation (Rev. 5:6); the beast with 10 horns rising up out of the sea (Rev. 13:1); and the scarlet beast of the great prostitute also having 10 horns (Rev. 17:3,7). Those references represent anti-Christian powers. *J. William Thompson*

HORNED OWL Species of owl having conspicuous tufts of feathers on the head. NIV reckons the horned owl an unclean bird (Lev. 11:16; Deut. 14:15). The precise identity of the bird is unclear. Other possibilities include: desert owl (REB), owl (KJV), and ostrich (NASB, NRSV). See *Owl.*

HORNED SNAKE Venomous viper (*Cerastes cornutus*) of the Near East having a horny protrusion above each eye. Dan is compared to a horned snake (Gen. 49:17 NASB, REB). See *Reptiles.*

HORNETS See *Insects.*

HORONAIM (Hôr´ ō nā´ ĭm) Place-name meaning "twin caves." Prominent town in Moab upon which Isaiah (15:5) and Jeremiah (48:3,5,34) pronounced laments, warning of coming destruction. It apparently lay in the southwestern part of Moab, but students of biblical geography debate its exact location. Suggestions include Khirbet ad-Dubababout, three miles west northwest of Majra; Khirbet al-Maydan, west of modern Katrabba; and ed-Dayr, about two miles northwest of Rakin.

HORONITE (Hôr´ ō nīt) Citizen of Beth-horon or of Horonaim. A description of Sanballat, who led opposition to Nehemiah (Neh. 2:10). To which of the two possible places Sanballat belonged, we do not know.

HORSE Four-legged, solid-hoofed animal used for transportation and in war. The horse was probably first domesticated by nomads of Central Asia as long ago as 4,000 years. Babylonians used horses in battle, and military victories such as those of Genghis Khan and Alexander the Great would have been impossible without horses. The Hyksos warriors who invaded Egypt evidently brought these animals to the area from Persia. When the exodus occurred, Pharaoh's army was outfitted with horses and chariots (Exod.

A first century A.D. *relief of horses harnessed to and turning a mill.*

14–15). Herodotus reported the use of horses by the Persians in their postal system 3,000 years ago.

The horse is mentioned more than 150 times in the Bible, with the earliest reference being found in Gen. 47:17. However, there is no indication that the horse was in common use in Israel until the time of David and Solomon. David captured chariots from the Syrians and destroyed most of them but reserved 100 (2 Sam. 8:3-4). In so doing, he disobeyed God and introduced their use to Israel. David's son, Solomon, multiplied their numbers to strengthen the defense of his country, building chariot cities (1 Kings 9:19). The number of horses owned by Solomon was as many as 12,000. They were used to draw chariots (1 Kings 4:26; 10:26). Since the Mosaic law forbade the breeding of horses, Solomon imported horses from Egypt (Deut. 17:16; 2 Chron. 1:16). Likely, because of the superiority of the horse for warfare, this law was later ignored. The ruins of Solomon's well-known horse stables at ancient Megiddo are today marked as a historical and archeological site.

In Megiddo what appears to be stalls and feeding troughs from King Ahab's time have been discovered. These were sufficient for about 450 horses.

The horse was used for war by the Syrians (1 Kings 20:20), the Philistines (2 Sam. 1:6), the Medes and Persians (Jer. 50:42), and the Romans (Acts 23:23,32). By contrast, and as a sign of the peacefulness of the Messiah's kingdom, Jesus rode into Jerusalem upon an ass, not a horse (John 12:12-15).

Considerable opposition to the horse arose in Israel, seeing horses as symbols of pagan luxury and dependence on physical power for defense. Prophets condemned trusting in horses rather than the Lord for victory (Isa. 31:1; Ezek. 17:15). Yet horses became so common in Jerusalem that a royal palace near the city had a special horse gate (2 Chron. 23:15) and a gate of the city was also called the Horse Gate (Jer. 31:40; Neh. 3:28).

Horses are often used as symbols of swiftness (Jer. 4:13), strength (Job 39:19), and surefootedness (Isa. 63:13). The most detailed description of a horse is found in Job 39:19-25. In prophecy horses also play an important role as in Joel 2:4-5 and Rev. 6:1-8 where four horses of different colors are associated with different tragedies. See *Megiddo.*   *C. Dale Hill and Shirley Stephens*

HORSE GATE Gate on east side of city wall of Jerusalem near the temple. Jeremiah promised its rebuilding (Jer. 31:40), and the priests under Nehemiah rebuilt it (Neh. 3:28).

HORSELEACH (KJV) See *Leech.*

HORSEMAN Rider on a horse. The plural frequently refers to a cavalry (Exod. 14:9-28; Josh. 24:6; 1 Sam. 8:11). This association of horsemen with armed forces perhaps sparked the use of the four riders of Rev. 6:2-8 as symbols of military conquest, war, economic injustice, and death and Hades.

HOSAH (Hō´ sa) Personal name, and place-name perhaps meaning "seeker of refuge." **1.** Coastal city in tribal territory of Asher (Josh. 19:29), probably modern Tell Rashidiyeh near Tyre and known in ancient Egyptian and Assyrian texts as Usu. Other biblical geographers would see the fortified city of Tyre as Tell Rashidiyeh (Usu) and locate Hosah further from Tyre and the coast. **2.** Gatekeeper of the sanctuary under David (1 Chron. 16:38). He belonged to the priestly clan of Merari (1 Chron. 26:10).

He was in charge of the west gate (1 Chron. 26:16).

HOSANNA (Hō zăn´ nà) Cry with which Jesus was greeted on the occasion of His triumphal entrance into Jerusalem (Mark 11:9). The words with which the Savior was welcomed by the multitude are drawn from Ps. 118:25-26. "Hosanna" is a Hebrew or Aramaic word that is best translated as a prayer: "Save now," or "Save, we beseech Thee." When the residents of Jerusalem, carrying palm branches, met Jesus and hailed Him as the One who comes in the name of the Lord, they included in their acclamation a plea for salvation. See *Psalms, Book of; Triumphal Entry.*

HOSEA (Hō zā´ à) Personal name meaning "salvation." In Hebrew the name is the same as that of Joshua's original name (Num. 13:16; Deut. 32:44) and of the last king of Israel (2 Kings 17:1), who lived at the same time as the prophet. One of David's officers bore the name (1 Chron. 27:20) as did a clan chief in the time of Nehemiah (Neh. 10:23). English translators have often chosen to spell the prophet's name Hosea to distinguish him from the others whose names they spell "Hoshea."

Hosea's prophetic ministry included the period of Near Eastern history when Assyria emerged as a new world empire under the capable leadership of Tiglath-pileser III (745–727 B.C.). Assyria's rise to power posed a constant threat to Israel's national existence. Hosea's name symbolized the pressing need for national deliverance. His message pointed the nation to the deliverer (Hos. 13:4).

Hosea rebuked efforts at alliance with Assyria and Egypt as the means to national security. He witnessed the political chaos in Israel following the death of Jeroboam II. Four of the last six kings to sit on Israel's throne were assassinated. Hosea had the unenviable task of presiding over the death of his beloved nation, but he held out hope of national revival based on radical repentance (Hos. 14).

Placement of Hosea's ministry in the days of Uzziah, Jotham, Ahaz, and Hezekiah indicates that he was a contemporary of Isaiah. The title verse of Isaiah contains the same list of Judean kings. Jeroboam II is the only Israelite king named in the title to Hosea's book, in spite of the fact that internal evidence suggests that Hosea's ministry continued from the last days of Jeroboam II to near the end of the Northern Kingdom (approximately 750–725 B.C.).

Billy K. Smith

HOSEA, BOOK OF Title of the first book in the section of the Hebrew Bible called the Book of the Twelve, named after its prophetic hero. The small prophetic books that make up this section frequently are designated Minor Prophets. This title is not an assessment of worth but a description of size as compared to Isaiah, Jeremiah, and Ezekiel.

The two broad divisions of the book of Hosea are Hosea's Marriage (Hos. 1–3) and Hosea's Messages (Hos. 4–14). A pattern of judgment followed by hope recurs in each of the first three chapters. A similar pattern is discernible in the oracles of Hosea (Hos. 4–14) though the pattern is not balanced as neatly or revealed as clearly. Certainly the book ends on a hopeful note (Hos. 14), but most of the oracles in chapters 4–13 are judgmental in nature. The dominant theme of the book is love (covenant fidelity), God's unrelenting love for His wayward people and Israel's unreliable love for God.

Hosea is identified in the title verse (1:1) as a genuine prophet to whom "the word of the Lord" came. That phrase designates the source of his authority and describes his credentials. Not only are Hosea's oracles (Hos. 4–14) the word of the Lord to Israel but so also are the materials dealing with his domestic problems (Hos. 1–3). Based on information gleaned from his book, Hosea was from the Northern Kingdom of Israel. His familiarity with place-names, religious practices, and political conditions in Israel suggest that he was a native. In contrast, Amos, who ministered as a prophet in Israel shortly before Hosea's ministry there, was from Tekoa in Judah. Both prophets preached judgment, Amos with a lion's roar and Hosea with a broken heart.

Hosea's marriage and family life dominate chapters 1–3 and surface from time to time in the remainder of the book. References to Hosea's family serve as prophetic symbolism of God and His family Israel. God ordered Hosea to take a wife of harlotry and have children of harlotry "for the land commits flagrant harlotry, forsaking the Lord" (Hos. 1:2 NASB). Primary interest is not in Hosea and his family but in God and His family. How to interpret the prophet's marriage is not a settled issue. A few take the marriage to be an allegory. Some accept it as a literal marriage to a woman who became promiscuous after marriage. Most handle it as an actual marriage to a cult prostitute. Every interpreter must keep in mind the obvious intent of the material to serve as prophetic symbolism of God's relationship to Israel.

At the heart of Hosea's theology was the relationship between God and Israel. Yahweh alone was Israel's God. Israel was Yahweh's elect people. Hosea presented Yahweh as a faithful husband and Israel as an unfaithful wife. Hosea's stress is not upon righteousness and justice, as was the case with Amos, but the knowledge of God and loyal love. God's love for Israel would not permit Him to give up on them in spite of their lack of knowledge and infidelity. Hope for Israel's future lay in their repentance and God's forgiveness and love that made Him willing to restore their relationship.

Outline

I. God Loves His Unfaithful People (1:1–3:5).
  A. God's forgiveness has its limits (1:1-9).
  B. God promises a future reversal of His judgment upon His people (1:10–2:1).
  C. God works with His people to bring about reconciliation (2:2-15).
    1. God's legal actions call for His people's reform (2:2-5).
    2. God places obstacles in the path of His people to turn them back to God (2:6-8).
    3. God removes the bounty of His people to remind them that God is the Giver (2:9-13).
    4. God lures His people into the wilderness to open a door of hope (2:14-15).
  D. God initiates a new covenant with His people (2:16-23).
  E. God's love is the basis of future hope for His people (3:1-5).
II. Unfaithfulness Is the Basis of God's Controversy with His People (4:1–9:9).
  A. Unfaithful people break covenant commitments (4:1-3).
  B. Unfaithful ministers bring judgment on the people and on themselves (4:4-12a).
  C. An alien spirit dominates unfaithful people (4:12b-19).

H

D. God chastises His unfaithful people (5:1-15).
1. God disciplines unfaithful leaders (5:1-2).
2. God disciplines because He knows His people fully (5:3).
3. Pride prevents repentance and promotes stumbling (5:4-5).
4. Extravagant giving is no substitute for lapses in living (5:6-7).
5. God is the agent of punishment for His people (5:8-14).
6. God seeks the return of His people through discipline (5:15).
E. Surface repentance does not satisfy the sovereign God (6:1-3).
F. Sharp judgment comes upon fleeting loyalty (6:4-5).
G. Loyal love and personal knowledge of God meet His requirements (6:6).
H. Covenant breaking hinders restoration of God's people (6:7–7:2).
I. Making leaders by power politics shuts God out of the process (7:3-7).
J. Compromise leads to loss of strength and alienation from God (7:8-10).
K. Diplomatic duplicity interferes with God's redemptive activity (7:11-13).
L. Religious perversion ends in apostasy and bondage (7:14-16).
M. God's unfaithful people reap more than they sow (8:1–9:9).
1. The unfaithful disregard divine law (8:1-2).
2. The unfaithful reject God's goodness (8:3).
3. The unfaithful practice idolatry (8:4-6).
4. The unfaithful will reap foreign domination (8:7-10).
5. The unfaithful will reap religious and moral corruption (8:11-13a).
6. The unfaithful will reap national destruction (8:13b-14).
7. The unfaithful will reap exile in a foreign land (9:1-4).
8. The unfaithful will reap punishment for their sins (9:5-9).
III. God's Loyal Love Is the Only Basis for a Lasting Relationship with His People (9:10–14:9).
A. Without God's love His people perish (9:10-17).

B. Without reverence for God, His people have no future (10:1-8).
1. Ornate altars cannot hide deceitful hearts (10:1-2).
2. Bad leaders produce bad times (10:3-8).
C. Without righteousness God's people cannot experience God's unfailing love (10:9-15).
D. God's love for His people will not allow Him to give them up (11:1-11).
E. Covenant-making with alien powers is infidelity to God (11:12–12:1).
F. Judgment according to deeds is a universal principle (12:2-6).
G. Deception is repaid by destruction (12:7-14).
H. Rebellion against God leads to death (13:1-16).
I. Repentance results in restoration and life for God's people (14:1-9).

Billy K. Smith

HOSEN KJV term for hose or leggings (Dan. 3:21). The meaning of the underlying Aramaic term is disputed: leggings (NASB margin); robes (TEV); shirts (REB); trousers (NASB, NIV, NRSV); tunics (RSV).

HOSHAIAH (Hō shī´ ya) Personal name meaning "Yah saved." **1.** Father of Jewish leader who led delegation requesting Jeremiah's prayer support (Jer. 42:1) and then rejected Jeremiah's word from God (Jer. 43:2). **2.** Leader of Jewish group in celebration upon the completion of the Jerusalem wall under Nehemiah (Neh. 12:32).

HOSHAMA (Hŏsh´ á mà) Personal name, an abbreviated form of Jehoshama, "Yahweh heard." Descendant of David during the exile (1 Chron. 3:18).

HOSHEA (Hō shā´ á) See Hosea.

HOSPITALITY To entertain or receive a stranger (sojourner) into one's home as an honored guest and to provide the guest with food, shelter, and protection. This was not merely an oriental custom or good manners but a sacred duty that everyone was expected to observe. Only the depraved would violate this obligation.

Hospitality probably grew out of the needs of nomadic life. Since public inns were rare, a traveler had to depend on the kindness of others and had a right to expect it. This practice was extended to every sojourner, even a runaway slave (Deut. 23:15-16) or one's archenemy.

The Pentateuch contains specific commands for the Israelites to love the strangers as themselves (Lev. 19:33-34; Deut. 10:18-19) and to look after their welfare (Deut. 24:17-22). The reason for practicing hospitality was that the Israelites themselves were once strangers in the land of Egypt.

Some acts of hospitality were rewarded, the most notable of which was Rahab's (Josh. 6:22-25; Heb. 11:31; James 2:25). Breaches of hospitality were condemned and punished, such as those of Sodom (Gen. 19:1-11) and Gibeah (Judg. 19:10-25). The only exception was Jael who was praised for killing Sisera (Judg. 4:18-24).

Hospitality seemed to form the background of many details in the life of Jesus and the early church (Matt. 8:20; Luke 7:36; 9:2-5; 10:4-11). It was to be a characteristic of bishops and widows (1 Tim. 3:2; 5:10; Titus 1:8) and a duty of Christians (Rom. 12:13; 1 Pet. 4:9). It was a natural expression of brotherly love (Heb. 13:1-2; 1 Pet. 4:8-9) and a necessary tool of evangelism. Furthermore, one might even entertain angels or the Lord unaware (Heb. 13:2; Matt. 25:31-46).

Lai Ling Elizabeth Ngan

HOST OF HEAVEN Army at God's command, composed of either heavenly bodies (such as sun, moon, and stars) or angels.

"Host" is basically a military term connected with fighting or waging a war. The most frequent use of the word is to designate a group of men organized for war. In this sense, the Hebrew word often refers to a human army (Gen. 21:22,32; Judg. 4:2,7; 9:29; 1 Sam. 12:9; 2 Sam. 3:23; Isa. 34:2; Jer. 51:3). The term can refer to an act of war, as in Num. 1:3,20; Deut. 24:5; and Josh. 22:12. An extended meaning of "hosts" is that it designates a length of time of hard service (Job 7:1; Isa. 40:2, Dan. 10:1). The term is used in the book of Numbers to refer to the service of the Levites in the sanctuary.

The phrase "Host of Heaven" came into use because of the close connection between the realms of earth and heaven in ancient thought. The celestial bodies were thought to be organized in the same way as earthly military bodies. The sun, moon, and stars were regarded as the "host of heaven" (Gen. 2:1). The author of Ps. 33:6 stated that God created this host by His breath. God preserved the existence of the host of heaven (Isa. 40:26).

Old Testament writers warned Israel about the danger of worshiping the heavenly bodies (Deut. 4:19) and prescribed the death penalty for the crime of worshiping the sun, or the moon, or any of the "host of heaven" (Deut. 17:2-7). Unfortunately, Israel and Judah yielded to the temptation to worship the heavenly bodies from time to time, especially during the period of Assyrian and Babylonian influence (2 Kings 17:16-23; 21:3,5).

Manasseh, king of Judah (697–642 B.C.), built altars in Jerusalem for all the "host of heaven" (2 Kings 21:5). He attempted to merge the worship of other gods with the worship of Yahweh. Manasseh's efforts were reversed when Josiah came to the throne (2 Kings 23:7).

Another concept of the "host of heaven" is presented in passages similar to 1 Kings 22:19, in which the prophet Micaiah stated that he saw the Lord sitting on His throne "and all the host of heaven standing by Him" (NASB). The people of Israel drew comparisons between their God and the gods of Canaan and Babylonia. Yahweh came to be understood as a king who presided over a heavenly council, composed of angelic servants, sometimes called "sons of God." This concept is reflected in the first two chapters of Job. See *Angels; Council, Heavenly; Heaven; Sons of God.*   *James Newell*

HOSTAGE Person held as security against rebellion or aggression. When King Joash of Israel defeated King Amaziah of Judah, he took hostages (2 Kings 14:14; 2 Chron. 25:24).

HOSTS See *Sabaoth.*

HOSTS, LORD OF See *Names of God.*

HOTHAM (Hō´ thăm) Personal name meaning "seal" or "lock." **1.** Member of tribe of Asher (1 Chron. 7:32). **2.** Father of two warriors in David's army (1 Chron. 11:44; KJV, Hothan). Their home was Aroer.

HOTHIR (Hō´ thīr) Personal name meaning "he caused to be a remnant." Priestly musician in the clan of Heman under David (1 Chron. 25:4). He led the twenty-first course of Levites (1 Chron. 25:28).

HOUGH KJV term meaning "hamstring" (Josh. 11:6,9; 2 Sam. 8:4; 1 Chron. 18:4). See *Hamstring.*

HOUR Appointed time for meeting or for religious festival, a brief moment of time, one twelfth of the day or of the night, and in the Gospel of John the significant period of Jesus' saving mission on earth from His triumphal entry until His death and resurrection.

Biblical Hebrew has no word for "hour," only an expression for an appointed meeting time (1 Sam. 9:24 RSV). The NT term *hora* can refer to a general time of day, a "late hour" (Matt. 14:15 NRSV), to a brief moment of time (Rev. 18:17; cp. John 5:35), or to the time of an expected momentous event (Matt. 8:13; Mark 13:11). It also designates a period of time, somewhat flexible in duration, one twelfth of the daylight hours and one-twelfth of the night, a day being divided into the two periods (or watches) of light and darkness beginning at sunrise, making the sixth hour (Matt. 27:45) noon.

Jesus' hour is a central theme in John's Gospel, creating an emotional uncertainty and expectancy and a theological understanding of the central importance of Jesus' death and resurrection. In John's Gospel, "hour" usually refers to the period from the triumphant entry (12:23) until the climactic death and resurrection.

The Johannine theme of Jesus' "hour" makes a significant theological contribution to the Gospel. As the reader encounters this motif repeatedly, a perspective on Jesus' death develops that is quite different from that gained in the other Gospels. Without trivializing the reality of Jesus' suffering and death, the Gospel of John presents that event as the "hour" of Jesus' "glory," the time of His "exaltation (lifting up)." Jesus' death is the means by which eternal life is provided for the world (3:14-15; 6:51-53). From that hour on, human distinctions no longer apply (4:21-24; 11:51-53; 12:20-23). The glory of Jesus' death is found both in what it enabled him to offer the world (6:51-53; 7:37-39) and in its being the means by which He returned to the Father (13:1). The accounts of the empty tomb and the appearances of the risen Jesus in 20:1–21:23 serve to underscore the glory of His "hour." See *Glory; John, Gospel of; Time.*

R. Robert Creech

HOUSE Place where people live, usually in extended family units that can then be called a house. Abraham left Mesopotamia where he lived in houses made of mud brick (cp. Gen.

Cutaway of a first-century A.D. house in Israel.

11:3) and became a tent dweller (Heb. 11:9). Tents were made of goat hair and were suitable to nomadic life. His descendants apparently lived in tents until the time of Joshua, when they captured Canaan and began to build houses like the Canaanites. In the lowlands of the Jordan Valley, the houses were built of mud brick because stone was not readily available. This type of construction may still be seen in the refugee camps of modern Jericho. In the hill country fieldstones were used. Although slight differences existed in house construction over centuries of time, those that have been excavated manifest a similar style. The homes of the poor were small and modest, consisting of one to four rooms, usually, and almost always including a courtyard on the east of the house so that the prevailing westerly winds would blow the smoke away from the house. In this courtyard the family carried on most of its activity. Food was prepared here in an oven built of clay. Storage jars were kept here, and animals were often housed here. However, the house only met the essential needs of family life such as shelter, a place to prepare food, make clothing and pottery, care for animals, and such.

Social life was normally conducted at the community well or spring, the city gate, the marketplace, or in the fields at work. Because of the heat in summer and the cold in the winter, houses were built with few, if any, windows. This also provided more protection from intruders, but it meant that the houses were dark and uninviting. The only escape from the dim, cramped interior of the house was the courtyard and especially the flat roof. Here, the women of the house could do many of their daily chores— the washing, weaving, drying of figs and dates, and even the cooking. It was a wonderful place to enjoy the cool breezes in the heat of the day and to sleep in the summer (Acts 10:9; cp. 2 Kings 4:10). The roof was supported by beams laid across the tops of narrow rooms, which were then covered by brush and mud packed to a firm and smooth surface. The paralytic at Capernaum was let down to Jesus through a hole "dug out" of such a roof (Mark 2:4; it was covered with clay tiles—Luke 5:19). In the time of Moses, the Israelites were required to build a banister around the roof to prevent one from falling off (Deut. 22:8).

Reconstruction of an eighth-century B.C. Israelite house showing rooms for sleeping on straw mats and for storage. The outer courtyard was used for food preparation, cooking, and to house small animals. Construction of houses did not change much over the centuries until the NT period. So, this was a typical pattern for the average home of the OT period.

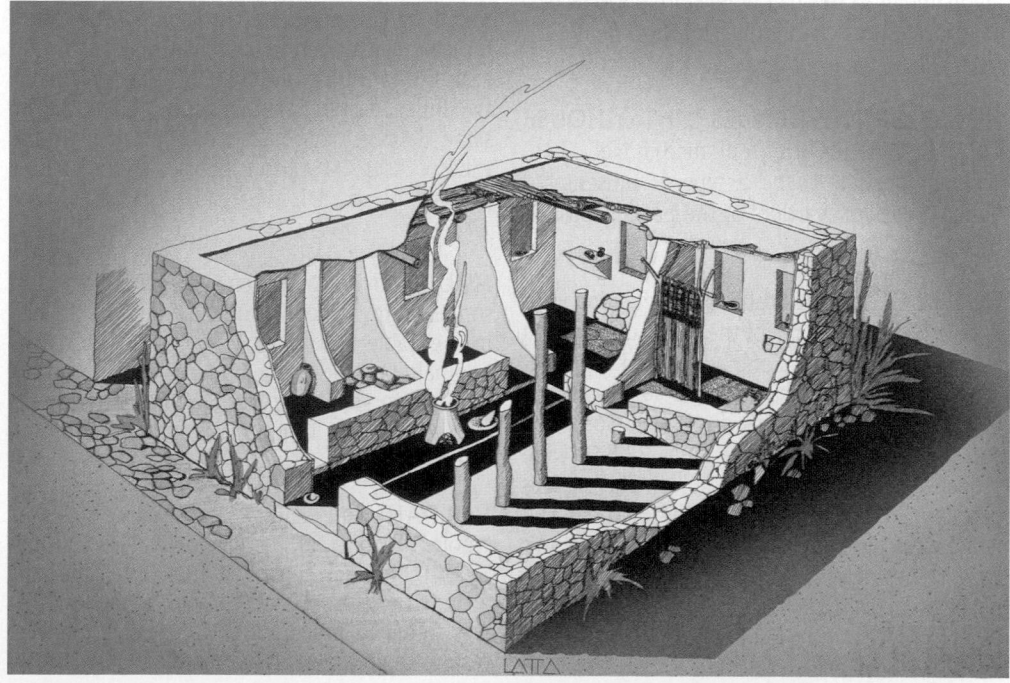

H

Unlike the poor, wealthy families built larger houses that sometimes utilized cut stone. They furnished them with chairs, tables, and couches that could double as beds. The poor had neither the space or the money for furniture. They ate and slept on floor mats that could be rolled out for that purpose. Most floors consisted of beaten earth, although some were made of mud and lime plaster and occasionally even limestone slabs. The wealthy in the time of the NT were able to cover their floors with beautiful mosaics and adorn their plastered walls with lovely frescoes. By this time, many of the better homes, under Roman influence, included atria, which added to the concept of outdoor living already experienced in the courtyards and on the roofs. There is evidence that two-story houses were built throughout biblical times, the upper floor being reached by outside stairs or ladders. See *Architecture.* *John McRay*

HOUSE OF THE ARCHIVES See *House of the Rolls.*

HOUSE OF THE FOREST OF LEBANON A designation for a great hall Solomon constructed as part of his palace complex in Jerusalem (1 Kings 7:2-5), so called because of the extensive use of cedar for the pillars, beams, and roofing material. In this hall were stored 300 shields of gold and vessels of gold (1 Kings 10:17-21). See *Hall.*

HOUSE OF THE HEROES (NIV) or **HOUSE OF THE WARRIORS** Mentioned in Neh. 3:16. Thought possibly to be a type of museum to honor heroes or warriors of the past. "House of the mighty" in KJV.

HOUSE OF THE ROLLS Place mentioned in Ezra 6:1 where records of the king's decrees and actions were kept. The archives were kept sometimes in the royal treasury (Ezra 5:17) or perhaps in the temple. Jeremiah's scroll (Jer. 36:20-26) and the scroll of the law (2 Kings 22:8-9) were probably kept in such an archive. The records pertaining to the reigns of the kings of Judah and Israel were probably also kept in archives of this kind. Genealogical records may have been stored in the archives (Ezra 4:15).

HOUSEHOLD See *Family.*

HOWLING CREATURES Identity of the "howling creature" (NRSV) of Isa. 13:21 is disputed. Suggestions include: the jackal (NIV); owl (NASB, KJV, TEV), porcupine (REB), and the laughing hyena. The precise identity of the creature is not so important as the complete desolation that its presence indicates, the awareness of the desolation of Babylon as a result of its sin.

HOZAI (Hō´ zā ī) Personal name meaning "seer." NASB literal transliteration of Hebrew text of 2 Chron. 33:19 making Hozai a prophet who recorded the reign of King Manasseh. Most translations follow Greek and one Hebrew manuscript in seeing one letter omitted from Hebrew, thus reading, "records of the seers" (NIV).

HUB Central portion of a wheel to which spokes are attached (1 Kings 7:33).

HUBBAH (Hŭb´ bah) NIV, NRSV reading of Jehubbah (1 Chron. 7:34) transliterating literally the Hebrew text. Most translations follow the early scribes' marginal note and the early translations in a slight change of the first Hebrew letter. See *Jehubbah.*

HUKKOK (Hŭk´ kŏk) or **HUKOK** (Hū´ kŏk) Place-name meaning "hewn out." **1.** Town on border of tribal allotment of Naphtali between Mount Tabor and the border of Zebulun. It has traditionally been located at Yaquq northwest of the sea of Chinnereth, but that may be too far east. Recent proposals look at Khirbet el-Jemeija, two miles west of Sakhmin (Josh. 19:34). **2.** The same Hebrew word names a Levitical city in the tribe of Asher (1 Chron. 6:75), but the parallel passage (Josh. 21:31) reads "Helkath." See *Helkath.*

HUL (Hŭl) Personal name meaning "ring." A son of Aram, son of Shem, and grandson of Noah in the Table of Nations (Gen. 10:23), thus the original ancestor of an Aramean or Syrian tribe. As often in genealogy lists, 1 Chron. 1:17 omits the father Shem to emphasize the kinship with Aram.

HULDAH (Hŭl´ dah) Personal name meaning "mole." Prophetess, the wife of Shallum (2 Kings 22:14). She was consulted after Josiah the king of Judah saw a copy of the book of the law that was found as preparations were being made to restore the temple. She prophesied judgment for the nation but a peaceful death for Josiah the king. See *Josiah*.

HUMAN SACRIFICE Ritual slaying of one or more human beings to please a god. This was widely practiced by many cultures in antiquity. Although the frequency of the practice is difficult to determine, the fact is that such rituals were performed for various reasons. For example, both Egyptians and Sumerians before 2000 B.C. killed servants and possibly family members to bury them with deceased kings to allow those who had served or been near the official in life to accompany him to the realm of the dead. In Mesopotamia, and perhaps elsewhere, the remains of animals and humans offered as sacrifice were deposited within foundations to protect the building from evil powers, a practice possibly reflected in 1 Kings 16:34.

In the OT, Jephthah sacrificed his daughter as a fulfillment of a vow, although the incident is clearly not normative (Judg. 11:30-40). In the ninth century Mesha, king of Moab, offered his own son as a burnt offering presumably to Chemosh, national god of Moab, upon the walls of his capital while under siege by Israel and Judah (2 Kings 3:27). The event was so shocking that the siege was terminated. However, although Israelite law specifically forbade human sacrifice (Lev. 18:21; 20:2-5), persistent references to the practice occur, especially between 800 and 500 B.C. Both Ahaz and Manasseh burned their sons as an offering in times of national peril (2 Kings 16:3; 21:6). The sacrifices were made in the valley of Hinnom that protected Jerusalem from the west and south. A portion of the valley bore the name Topheth, a name derived from the word for fireplace or hearth. Apparently Topheth was an open-air cultic area where Molech sacrifices were offered. The term Molech occurs frequently in connection with human sacrifice. In the Bible and elsewhere Molech apparently was used in two ways: as the name or title of a god to whom sacrifice was made (1 Kings 11:7) and as a specific type of sacrifice which involved the total consummation of a person, usually a child, by fire. Both usages of the term may be reflected in the OT. Both Jeremiah and Ezekiel condemn such offerings as an abomination to God (Jer. 7:31-32; 19:5-6; Ezek. 16:20-21; 20:31). Josiah defiled Topheth as a part of his reformation so that "no one might burn his son or his daughter as an offering to Molech" (2 Kings 23:10 RSV).

These practices, foreign to the worship of Yahweh, must have been adopted by Israel from the surrounding peoples. Direct evidence for human sacrifice during the first millennium B.C. comes from two cultures with which Israel had contact: the Phoenician colony of Carthage and the Arameans. The Carthaginians sacrificed children to Kronos during periods of calamity caused by war, famine, or disease. Pits filled with bones of animals and children have been excavated at Carthage with inscribed stones indicating these were Molech sacrifices. The Arameans of Gozan in northwest Mesopotamia sacrificed humans to the god Hadad. Interestingly, the Sepharvites, a people from an area dominated by Arameans deported to Palestine in 721 B.C. by Sargon II, burned their children as offerings to Adrammelech and Anammelech (2 Kings 17:31). Yet the abomination of human sacrifice, stated Jeremiah, never entered the mind of Yahweh (Jer. 19:5). See *Molech*.   *Thomas V. Brisco*

HUMAN SOUL See *Soul*.

HUMANITY Collective designation for all creatures who are made in the image of God, by which they are distinguished from all other creatures and from God Himself.

Humanity as Created by God Genesis 1–2 is foundational for understanding humanity as created by God. Humankind was created directly by God (Gen. 1:26) and did not evolve from lower forms of life. Empirical evidence favors the sudden appearance of full humanity, which is consistent with Scripture.

Man was also created in the image of God. The meaning of the image has been debated throughout Christian history. Some have equated it with reason and others with relationships, but neither of these is adequate. The biblical references fall into two groups. First, there are direct references to man's creation in God's image (Gen. 1:26-31; 9:6; James 3:9). God created humanity in His image for man to be God's representative, and He gave man dominion over creation (Ps. 8:3-8). The image of God is the foundation of the sanctity of human life (Gen. 9:6). Because man is God's representative, murder is an attack upon God. The image also means ownership (Mark 12:13-17). Humanity, being "stamped" with God's image, is God's special

H

possession. Second, biblical references to the image relate it to the transformation of character which accompanies salvation (Rom. 8:29; 1 Cor. 15:49; 2 Cor. 3:18; Eph. 4:24; Col. 3:10). These stress the believer's increasing conformity to the character of Jesus Christ, especially in holiness and righteousness.

God also created humanity male and female. Both bear the image of God (Gen. 1:27) and have equal standing before God. God's creation of humanity as male and female is the foundation of the biblical teaching concerning marriage, divorce, the family, and homosexuality (Gen. 2:18-25; Matt. 19:3-6; Rom. 1:26-27).

Man was also created by God as body and soul (Gen. 2:7). Man has a material part suited to life in this world and an eternal, immaterial part that survives physical death (2 Cor. 5:1-8). Some suggest that man's immaterial part may be further divided into soul and spirit. The Bible emphasizes man as a whole person more than as a composition of individual parts. The terms for "soul" and "spirit" are often used interchangeably in Scripture, and it is difficult to construct a biblical argument for a strong distinction between soul and spirit.

Humanity under Sin The sin of the first couple caused a profound change in humanity and humanity's relationship with God (Rom. 5:12). The image of God remained, but it is marred and distorted. Humanity continued to procreate as male and female, though relationships with others were deeply and immediately affected by sin (Gen. 4). Man remained body and soul, but his inmost being was particularly impacted by sin. Man's heart, the core of his being, is sinful (Gen. 6:5; Jer. 17:9; Mark 7:20-23), and his mind is darkened (Eph. 4:17-19). Man's will is in bondage to sin (Rom. 3:10-11; 2 Tim. 2:25-26), his conscience is defiled (Titus 1:15), and his desires are twisted (Eph. 2:3; Titus 3:3). Simply put, humanity is universally dead in sin (Eph. 2:1), in a state of hostility toward God (Rom. 5:10), and subject to physical death followed by eternal judgment (Rom. 5:12-21; 8:10; Heb. 9:27; Rom. 14:12).

Redeemed Humanity God in His grace did not leave humanity to perish eternally but provided for redemption. Humanity's participation in salvation begins at the individual level, when one places conscious faith in Jesus Christ. Saving faith includes a recognition of who Jesus is (fully divine and human Son of God), trust in the mer-

its of His atoning death, and submission of the will to Him. This is all made possible by God who, according to His eternal and gracious purpose, enables sinful humanity to believe (Eph. 2:4-9; 1 Tim. 1:14; Titus 3:5).

Differences of opinion exist regarding the nature of saved humanity. Some see two natures of totally opposite moral orientation, one utterly sinful, the other perfect (identified by some with the Holy Spirit), at work in the believer. Some who adhere to a strong distinction between soul and spirit identify the sinful nature with the soul and the perfect nature with the spirit. Paul described the believer as a new, though imperfect, creature (2 Cor. 5:17) indwelled by the Spirit of God (Rom. 8:9-17), involved in a gradual process of transformation (Rom. 8:12-13; 2 Cor. 3:18; Col. 3:10), and in conflict with his flesh (sinful nature) and the law of sin (Rom. 7:14–8:8).

Humanity's participation in salvation will be consummated at the end of the age with resurrection and entry into the eternal state (1 Cor. 15:50-57). Scripture emphasizes the perfect conformity of the believer to Christ (1 John 3:2), his eternal fellowship with God (John 14:2-3), and the joyful, worshipful assembly of all the redeemed (Rev. 7:9). This, of course, does not include all of humanity. Those who do not believe in Jesus Christ will spend an eternity suffering the just wrath of God (John 3:36; 2 Thess. 1:9). See *Anthropology; Image of God; Body; Soul; Spirit; Creation; Sin; Freedom; Church; Body of Christ.* *T. Preston Pearce*

HUMANITY OF CHRIST See *Christ, Christology; Incarnation; Jesus, Life and Ministry.*

HUMILIATION OF CHRIST See *Jesus, Death and Resurrection; Kenosis.*

HUMILITY The personal quality of being free from arrogance and pride and having an accurate estimate of one's worth.
Old Testament The OT connects the quality of humility with Israel's lowly experience as slaves in Egypt—a poor, afflicted, and suffering people (Deut. 26:6). The Hebrew word translated as humility is similar to another Hebrew word meaning "to be afflicted." In OT thought, humility was closely associated with individuals who were poor and afflicted (2 Sam. 22:28).

H

What God desires most is not outward sacrifices but a humble spirit (Ps. 51:17; Mic. 6:8). Such a humble spirit shows itself in several ways: a recognition of one's sinfulness before a holy God (Isa. 6:5), obedience to God (Deut. 8:2), and submission to God (2 Kings 22:19; 2 Chron. 34:37).

The OT promised blessings to those who were humble: wisdom (Prov. 11:2), good tidings (Isa. 61:1), and honor (Prov. 15:33).

The experience of many kings indicated that those who humble themselves before God will be exalted (1 Kings 21:29; 2 Kings 22:19; 2 Chron. 32:26; 33:12-19). Those who do not humble themselves before God will be afflicted (2 Chron. 33:23; 36:12). The pathway to revival is the way of humility (2 Chron. 7:14).

New Testament Jesus Christ's life provides the best example of what it means to have humility (Matt. 11:29; 1 Cor. 4:21; Phil. 2:1-11). Jesus preached and taught often about the need for humility (Matt. 23:12; Mark 9:35; Luke 14:11; 18:14). He urged those who desired to live by kingdom standards to practice humility (Matt. 18:1; 23:12).

The person with humility does not look down on others (Matt. 18:4; Luke 14:11). Humility in the NT is closely connected with the quality of gentleness (Matt. 5:5). While God resists those who are proud, He provides grace for the humble (James 4:6). Primary in the NT is the conviction that one who has humility will not be overly concerned about his or her prestige (Matt. 18:4; 23:12; Rom. 12:16; 2 Cor. 11:7).

Paul believed that quality relationships with other people, especially those who had erred spiritually, hinged on the presence of gentleness or humility (1 Cor. 4:21; Gal. 6:1; 2 Tim. 2:25). The NT affirms, as does the OT, that God will exalt those who are humble and bring low those who are proud (Luke 1:52; James 4:10; 1 Pet. 5:6). The Greek world abhorred the quality of gentleness or humility, but the Christian community believed these qualities were worthy (2 Cor. 10:18; Col. 3:12; Eph. 4:2).

Gary Hardin

HUMP Fleshy mound on the back of a camel where food is stored in the form of fat. Isaiah 30:6 refers to burdens carried on camels' humps (KJV, bunches). See *Camel.*

HUMTAH (Hŭm´ tah) Place-name meaning "lizards." Town in hill country of Judah in tribal territory of Judah (Josh. 15:54). Its exact location is not known.

HUNCHBACK One with a humped (curved or crooked) back. According to the Holiness Code, a hunchback was excluded from priestly service though allowed to eat the priests' holy food (Lev. 21:20). REB translates the unique Hebrew term, "misshapen brows."

HUNDRED, TOWER OF THE (KJV "Tower of Meah") Tower located on the north wall of Jerusalem that was restored by Nehemiah (Neh. 3:1; 12:39). The name perhaps refers to the height of the tower (100 cubits), the number of its steps, or the number of troops in its garrison. It may have been part of the temple fortress (Neh. 2:8).

HUNDREDWEIGHT Unit of weight equal to 100 pounds (Rev. 16:21 REB, RSV). The underlying Greek means "about the weight of a talent" (KJV). Most modern translations equate the talent with 100 pounds (NASB, NIV, NRSV, TEV).

HUNGER Strong need or desire for food. Scripture contains haunting pictures of hunger. Isaiah 29:8 uses the image of a hungry person dreaming of eating only to awake hungry again. In Lam. 4:9 those who fell by the sword are reckoned better off than those pierced by hunger. Hunger frequently takes on a theological significance. Exodus 16:3 recounts Israel's complaint that Moses led them from Egypt to kill them with hunger in the desert. God used this experience of hunger to humble the rebellious people and to teach them to hunger for His word (Deut. 8:3). Hunger was one penalty of disobedience of covenant obligations (Deut. 28:48; 32:24).

The cessation of hunger is frequently associated with God's salvation. Hannah anticipated God's reversing the fortunes of the hungry (1 Sam. 2:5; cp. Luke 6:21,25). Isaiah promised that those returning from exile would not be plagued by hunger (49:10). Ezekiel pictured God as providing for the needs of God's sheep so there would be no hunger (34:29). Part of the blessedness of the redeemed of Rev. 7:16 is the end of their hunger.

In Matt. 5:6 Jesus spoke of those who hunger and thirst for righteousness, that is, those who

H

earnestly desire to see God's will become a reality. In John 6:35 Jesus promised that anyone who came to Him would not hunger but would be satisfied.

HUNT, HUNTER To pursue game for food or pleasure. Hunting was an important supplementary food source, especially in the seminomadic stage of civilization. Genesis mentions several hunters by name, none of whom are Israelite ancestors (Nimrod, 10:9; Ishmael, 21:20; Esau, 25:27), perhaps suggesting that hunting was more characteristic of Israel's neighbors than of Israel. Hunting was, however, regulated by Mosaic law. The blood of captured game was to be poured out on the ground (Lev. 17:13). Deuteronomy 14:3-5 outlines what game was permitted as ritually clean food.

The tools of the hunter include bows and arrows (Gen. 21:20; 27:3), nets (Job 18:8; Ezek. 12:13), snares or pitfalls (Job 18:8), if the term does not refer to part of the net (NASB, NIV, REB); traps, snares, ropes (Job 18:9-10). Terror, the pit, and the trap of Isa. 24:17-18 (Jer. 48:43-44) perhaps allude to the Battue method of hunting whereby a group forms a cordon and beats over the earth, driving game into a confined area, pit, or net. Ancient Egyptian carvings depict such methods of hunting.

Hunting for pleasure was a popular pastime of ancient kings. The hunt is a popular motif in the art of the Assyrians, Egyptians, and Phoenicians. The Assyrian reliefs depicting Ashurbanipal's lion hunt are particularly well-known. The OT does not mention hunting as a pastime of the kings of Israel or Judah. Josephus did note Herod's love of the hunt.

Most often the hunt is used figuratively. A rare positive image is Jeremiah's picture of God's hunting the scattered exiles to return them to Israel (Jer. 16:16). Saul hunted David (1 Sam. 24:11). Matthew described the Pharisees' plotting "to entrap" Jesus (22:15), Luke their "lying in wait" for Him (11:54). The Pastorals speak of the devil's snare (1 Tim. 3:7; 2 Tim. 2:26). Ezekiel 13:17-23 pictures women practicing magical arts as fowlers ensnaring the people. In Mic. 7:2 the unfaithful are portrayed as hunting each other with nets. The warning of Prov. 6:5 is to save oneself (from evil) like the gazelle or roe flees the hunter. *Chris Church*

HUPHAM (Hū´ phăm) Original ancestor of clan of Benjamin in the wilderness (Num. 26:39). Hupham may be the original reading behind Huppim in Gen. 46:21 and 1 Chron. 7:12,15. Comparison of Gen. 46:21; Num. 26:38; 1 Chron. 7:6; 8:1-2 shows the difficulty in restoring precisely the names of Benjamin's sons. Similarly, the sons of Bela, Benjamin's son, are difficult to restore (Num. 26:39-40; 1 Chron. 7:7; 8:3-4). Part of the explanation may lie in the use of genealogies to claim membership in an important clan rather than to precisely reproduce family structures.

HUPHAMITE (Hū´ phăm īt) Member of clan of Hupham in tribe of Benjamin.

HUPPAH (Hŭp´ pah) Personal name meaning "shelter" or "roof" or "bridal chamber." Leader of thirteenth course of priests under David (1 Chron. 24:13).

HUPPIM (Hŭp´ pĭm) Personal name of unknown meaning. Son of Benjamin and grandson of Jacob (Gen. 46:21). See *Hupham*.

HUR (Hûr) Personal name of uncertain meaning, perhaps "white one" or "Horite" or perhaps derived from the name of the Egyptian god "Horus." **1.** Israelite leader who accompanied Moses and Aaron to the top of the mountain in the fight against the Amalekites. Hur helped Aaron hold Moses' hands up so Israel could prevail. In some way not explicitly stated, Moses' hands were the symbol of and instrument for God's power with Israel's army (Exod. 17:10-12). Hur and Aaron also represented Moses and settled any problems among the people while Moses ascended the mountain to receive God's instructions (Exod. 24:14). This same Hur was probably the grandfather of Bezaleel of the tribe of Judah, who was the artisan in charge of making the metal works for the tabernacle in the wilderness (Exod. 31:2). He was Caleb's son (1 Chron. 2:19). A genealogy of Hur appears both in 1 Chron. 2:50 and 4:1. The text is difficult to decipher at times. Apparently, like the Table of Nations in Gen. 10, these texts show geographical and political relationships of the descendants of Caleb. **2.** King of Midian whom Israel slew as they moved toward the promised land (Num. 31:8). Joshua 13:21 identifies the kings of Midian as vassals of Sihon (Num. 31).

3. District governor under Solomon over Mount Ephraim in charge of providing the royal table with provisions one month a year (1 Kings 4:8). His name may also be translated Ben-hur. **4.** Administrator over half the district of Jerusalem under Nehemiah or father of the administrator (Neh. 3:9).

HURAI (Hū´ rā ī) Variant reading in 1 Chron. 11:32 for David's warrior Hiddai in the parallel passage (2 Sam. 23:30).

HURAM (Hū´ răm) Personal name probably shortened from Ahuram meaning "exalted brother." **1.** Chronicler's spelling of Hiram, king of Tyre (2 Chron. 2). Also the Chronicler's form for Hiram, the artisan King Hiram sent to help with the metal work on the temple (2 Chron. 2:13). See *Hiram.* **2.** Descendant of Benjamin, often identified with Hupham of Num. 26:39. See *Hupham.*

HURAMABI (Hū răm a´ bĭ) Personal name, perhaps meaning "my father is an exalted brother." NASB, NIV, NRSV name for Huram/Hiram, the skilled artisan that Hiram, king of Tyre, sent to Solomon to help build the temple (2 Chron. 2:13). See *Huram.*

HURI (Hū´ rī) Personal name of uncertain meaning, perhaps "white one," "linen maker," "Horite," or "my Horus" (Egyptian god). A member of tribe of Gad (1 Chron. 5:14).

HURRIANS See *Horim* or *Horites.*

HUSBAND Male partner in a marriage. See *Family; Marriage.*

HUSBANDMAN KJV term for one who tills the soil; a farmer. Husbandry refers to farming. Modern translations replace husbandman and husbandry with other terms. The substitutions of the RSV are typical: plowman (Isa. 61:5); farmer (2 Chron. 26:10; Jer. 14:4; 31:24; 51:23; Amos 5:16); tiller of the soil (Gen. 9:20; Joel 1:11). The KJV's "ye are God's husbandry" was rendered with "you are God's field." See *Agriculture; Occupations and Professions.*

HUSHAH (Hū´ sha) Personal name and place-name meaning "hurry." Member of tribe of Judah (1 Chron. 4:4) listed along with Bethlehem and thus probably original ancestor of clan

who lived in town of Hushah, perhaps modern Husan near Bethlehem. Some Bible students think that in the copying process the name was changed from an original Shuah (1 Chron. 4:11) through transposition of Hebrew letters. Two of David's soldiers came from Hushah: Sibbechai (2 Sam. 21:18) and Mebunnai (2 Sam. 23:27).

HUSHAI (Hū´ shī) Personal name meaning "quick," "from Hushah," or "gift of brotherhood." The name could represent copying transposition from an original Shuah. This would designate his family as from Shuhu, the Syrian state in the central Euphrates region or a state in Edom or Arabia. The clan became a part of Israel as a clan of the tribe of Benjamin living in Archi southwest of Bethel (Josh. 16:2). Hushai was "David's friend" (2 Sam. 15:37), probably referring to an official government post as in Egypt, a close personal adviser somewhat like the secretary of state. As David escaped, leaving Jerusalem to his son Absalom, Hushai joined him, mourning (2 Sam. 15:32). David sent him back to deceive Absalom (2 Sam. 15:34; 16:16-19). His counsel to Absalom bought time for David to establish new headquarters and gather forces for new strategy (2 Sam. 17).

Solomon's commissioner in charge of collecting royal provisions in Asher was the son of Hushai, perhaps the same as "David's friend" (1 Kings 4:16). See *Hushah.*

HUSHAM (Hū´ shăm) Personal name, perhaps meaning "large-nosed" or "with haste." One of the early kings of Edom (Gen. 36:34) from Teman.

HUSHATHITE (Hū´ shăth īt) Citizen of Hushah. See *Hushah.*

HUSHIM (Hū´ shĭm) Personal name meaning "hurried ones." **1.** Son of Dan and grandson of Jacob (Gen. 46:23). **2.** Member of tribe of Benjamin (1 Chron. 7:12), though many Bible students think copying has caused omission of tribe of Dan in the list, Hushim here being the same as in Gen. 46:23. Dan's son is named Shuham in Num. 26:42, perhaps resulting from a copying transposition of Hebrew letters. **3.** Wife of Shaharaim of tribe of Benjamin (1 Chron. 8:8) and mother of Abitub and Elpaal (1 Chron. 8:11). Apparently, her husband sent her away either for safety or as part of family problems before he went to Moab.

H

HUSHITES (Hū´ shīts) NIV translation of Hushim (1 Chron. 7:12), interpreting it as the name of a population group rather than as an individual.

HUSK Outer covering of a seed or fruit, usually either dry (as the carob) or membranous (as the grape) (Num. 6:4; 2 Kings 4:42; Luke 15:16). Modern translations replace husk with skins when referring to grapes (Num. 6:4). The term translated "husk" at 2 Kings 4:42 is a *hapax legomena*, a term used only once in Scripture. NASB, RSV follow the Latin Vulgate in rendering the term "sack." Other modern translations follow other ancient versions in omitting the term. Modern translations give "pods" or "bean pods" for husks at Luke 15:16. The pods of the Carob tree (*Ceratonia siliqua*) are probably intended (NASB margin). The ripe pods are full of dark, honeylike syrup. These are ground and used as an animal feed.

HUT Modern translations' rendering for a lean-to or temporary shelter; shack (Isa. 1:8; 24:20). The image of Isa. 1:8 stresses the isolation of Jerusalem, the sole survivor of the cities of Judah (1:7-9). Isaiah 24:20 illustrates God's power in judgment in the picture of the earth's swaying like an unstable hut before the Lord.

HUZ (Hŭz) (KJV, Gen. 22:21). See *Uz*.

HUZZAB (Hŭz´ zăb) KJV transliteration of the Hebrew word in the context of Nah. 2:7 is not clear. KJV takes it as a city-state. Other translators take the word as a Hebrew verb meaning "fixed" (NASB) or "decreed" (NRSV, NIV). Others see a feminine noun: "train" of captives (REB), "queen" (TEV), "its mistress" (RSV). The verbal translation is probably correct, pointing to God's established plan announced through the prophet to defeat Assyria and its capital Nineveh. Otherwise, the term is describing Nineveh in figurative language, perhaps referring to deportation of dressed-up idols defeated in war.

HYACINTH Stone regarded as precious in ancient times. The hyacinth is sometimes identified with the sapphire (Rev. 9:17 NRSV, TEV) or turquoise (Exod. 28:19; Rev. 9:17; 21:20 REB; Exod. 28:19; Rev. 21:20 TEV). Others identify the hyacinth with zircon, a brown to grayish gem, or essonite, a yellow to brown garnet.

HYENA Any of a group of stocky built, carnivorous mammals of the genus *Hyaena*, located zoologically between the felines and canines. It is a striped scavenger looking much like a fox.

Hyenas feed on carrion and are known for their cowardice, cruelty, and disagreeable cry. They appear mainly at night. Because of its scavenger activity of digging up graves, the hyena was a repulsive animal in the ancient world. They were easily tamed, and the Egyptians kept them as pets. All the scriptural references concern judgment on foreign nations (Babylon or Edom) which are left desolate (Isa. 13:22; 34:14; Jer. 50:39). KJV translated the term for hyena as "wild beasts of the islands." The REB and NASB identify this animal with the jackal (Jer. 50:39). NASB uses wolves in Isa. 34:14.

The Hebrew term for hyena is used as a man's name (Zibeon, Gen. 36:20) and as the name for a town (Zeboim, Neh. 11:34) and valley (1 Sam. 13:18) in the territory of Benjamin.

HYKSOS (Hĭk´ sŏs) Racial name from the Greek form of an Egyptian word meaning "rulers of foreign lands" given to kings of the 15th and 16th Dynasties of Egypt. The word, which does not appear in the Bible, was later misinterpreted by Josephus as meaning "shepherd kings."

With the decline of the Middle Kingdom of Egypt (about 2000-1786 B.C.) large numbers of Asiatics, mostly Semites like the Hebrew patriarchs, migrated into the Nile Delta of northern Egypt from Canaan. These probably came initially for reasons of economic distress, such as famine, as did Abraham (Gen. 12:10). Unlike Abraham, many groups stayed in Egypt as permanent settlers. Under the weak 13th Dynasty, some Asiatics established local independent chiefdoms in the eastern Delta region. Eventually, one of these local rulers managed to consolidate the rule of northern Egypt as pharaoh, thus beginning the 15th Dynasty. The 16th Dynasty, perhaps contemporary with the 15th, consisted of minor Asiatic kings. As these dynasties of pharaohs were not ethnic Egyptians, they were remembered by the native population as "Hyksos."

While the Hyksos pharaohs ruled northern Egypt from Avaris in the eastern Delta, the native Egyptian 17th Dynasty ruled southern Egypt from Thebes. This period is known as the Second Intermediate or Hyksos Period (about 1786-1540 B.C.). The status quo was maintained

Hypostyle Hall in the Temple of Amun-Re at Thebes.

H

until war erupted between the Hyksos and the last two pharaohs of the 17th Dynasty. About 1540 B.C. Ahmose I sacked Avaris and expelled the Hyksos. As the first pharaoh of a reunited Egypt, Ahmose I established the 18th Dynasty and inaugurated the Egyptian New Kingdom or Empire.

Some have noted that Joseph's rise to power as pharaoh's second-in-command (Gen. 41:39-45) would have been far more likely under a Hyksos king. Like Joseph's family, the Hyksos were Semitic, whereas the native Egyptians regarded Semites with contempt. The biblical account of Joseph's rise to power, however, shows that it was anything but likely. There are also indications of great cultural differences between Joseph's family and that of the Egyptian rulers at the time (cp. Gen. 41:14; 42:23; 43:32; 46:34). The new pharaoh "who had not known Joseph" (Exod. 1:8 HCSB) and began oppressing the Israelites may have been Ahmose I, who drove out the Hyksos. But it would more likely have been one of the new Hyksos rulers, whom Manetho the Egyptian priest later described as "burning towns, razing the temples, and treating the inhabitants with terrible cruelty, cutting men's throats and leading the women and children into captivity."

Daniel C. Browning, Jr.
and E. Ray Clendenen

HYMENAEUS (Hī´ mĕ nē´ ŭs) or **HYMENEUS** (KJV) Personal name of the Greek god of marriage. Name of a fellow worker of Paul whose faith weakened and whose lifestyle changed, leading Paul to deliver him to Satan (1 Tim. 1:20). That probably means Paul led the church to dismiss Hymenaeus from the membership to purify the church, remove further temptation from the church, and to lead Hymenaeus to restored faith, repentance, and renewed church membership. Along with Philetus, Hymenaeus taught that the resurrection had already occurred (2 Tim. 2:17-18; cp. 1 Cor. 5). See *Gnosticism.*

HYMN A song of praise to God.
Old Testament Ceremonial religious singing is mentioned in the OT in connection with important events, such as the songs in celebration of the Hebrews' passage through the Red Sea (Exod. 15:1-21), Deborah and Barak's triumphal song after the defeat of the forces of Jabin, king of Hazor (Judg. 5:1-31), and the women's song at

David's victorious return from battle with the Philistines (1 Sam. 18:6-7). Moses also gave the Israelites some of his last warnings in a great song (Deut. 32:1-43). The book of Psalms is a hymnbook. The hymns in it were written by different authors over a long period of time and used by the people of Israel in their worship. The collection of 150 psalms eventually was included in Hebrew Scripture. Hymn singing in the Jerusalem temple was led by trained choirs, sometimes using instrumental accompaniment (2 Chron. 29:25-28). The people joined the choir in singing hymns in unison, responsively, and antiphonally.

Hymn is also the technical term for a specific literary type of material in Psalms. In this sense a hymn expresses the congregation's praise of God's greatness and majesty, usually addressing members of the congregation and inviting them to praise God. A hymn usually includes a call to the congregation to join in praise (Ps. 33:1-3), a list of reasons to praise God (Ps. 33:4-19), and a concluding call to praise or statement of trust (Ps. 33:20-22).

New Testament Singing of spiritual songs was a part of the early Christian church. Among the songs in the NT are several outstanding songs that have become a part of liturgical Christian worship: Luke 1:46-55, Mary's song—the *Magnificat*; Luke 1:68-79, Zacharias's prophetic song—the *Benedictus*; and Luke 2:29-32, Simeon's blessing of the infant Jesus and farewell—the *Nunc Dimittis.* Numerous doxologies (e.g., Luke 2:14; 1 Tim. 1:17; 6:15-16; Rev. 4:8) doubtless were used in corporate worship. Other passages in the NT give evidence of being quotations of hymns or fragments of hymns (Rom. 8:31-39; 1 Cor. 13; Eph. 1:3-14; Eph. 5:14; Phil. 2:5-11; 1 Tim. 3:16; 2 Tim. 2:11-13; Tit. 3:4-7). As for references to the word itself, the NT states that Jesus and His disciples sang a hymn at the end of the Last Supper (Matt. 26:30; Mark 14:26). Most Bible students think they sang part of Pss. 115–118, hymns known as the "Hallel," which traditionally were sung after supper on the night of Passover. The division of Christian song into psalms, hymns, and spiritual songs (Eph. 5:19; Col. 3:16) should not be taken to mean that there were three distinct types or styles of vocal music in use in those days. The reference indicates that Christian song was used in worship, to instruct in the faith, and to express joy. In another NT refer-

H

ence, Acts 16:25, the mention of singing "praises" to God obviously means that Paul and Silas sang hymns in prison. The author of the book of Hebrews stressed in 2:12 (a quotation of the messianic Ps. 22:22) that Jesus will declare His name to the church, that He will "sing praise," or hymns.

J. William Thompson

HYPOCRISY Pretense to being what one really is not, especially the pretense of being a better person than one really is. The word is based on the Greek *hupokrisis*, originally meaning to give an answer. A hypocrite in classical Greek could be an interpreter of dreams, an orator, a reciter of poetry, or an actor. Originally a neutral term, "hypocrite" gained the negative connotation of pretense, duplicity, or insincerity.

In the Bible the negative meaning prevails. Often hypocrisy refers to evil or sin in general, not pretense in particular. In the OT, "hypocrite" was used by the KJV whereas later translations (e.g., RSV, NIV) often use "godless" or "ungodly" (Job 8:13; 15:34-35; 17:8; Isa. 9:17; 33:14, etc.). This "godless" person was totally opposed to God or forgetful of God. The Hebrew word often translated "hypocrite" referred to pollution or corruption. Although the Hebrews were concerned about pretense or insincerity (Isa. 29:13; Jer. 12:2), there is no one Hebrew word exactly equivalent to "hypocrisy."

Hypocrisy in the narrower sense of playing a role is highlighted in the NT, especially in the teaching of Jesus in the Synoptic Gospels. Jesus criticized hypocrites for being pious in public (Matt. 6:2,5,16). They were more interested in human praise when they gave alms, prayed, and fasted than in God's reward. Hypocrites were also guilty of being judgmental of others' faults and ignoring their own (Matt. 7:1-5). Jesus often called the Pharisees hypocrites because of the conflict between their external actions and internal attitudes (Matt. 15:1-9). Their true attitudes would be revealed (Luke 12:1-3). The hypocrites could interpret the weather but not the signs of the times (Luke 12:56). They were more concerned about the rules for the Sabbath than a woman's physical health (Luke 13:15). Luke noted that the religious leaders pretended to be sincere when they asked Jesus about paying tribute to Caesar (Luke 20:20). Probably the most famous discussion of hypocrisy is Matt. 23. The religious leaders did not practice what they preached (Matt. 23:3). Jesus compared them to dishes that were clean on the outside and dirty on the inside and to whitewashed tombs (Matt. 23:25-28).

Hypocrisy is a concern throughout the NT. Although the term does not occur, it was part of the sin of Ananias and Sapphira (Acts 5:1-11). Paul accused Peter of hypocrisy for refusing to eat with Gentile Christians in Antioch (Gal. 2:12-13). Paul warned Timothy about hypocritical false teachers (1 Tim. 4:2). Peter included hypocrisy as one of the attitudes Christians should avoid (1 Pet. 2:1).

Six times NT writers stress that sincerity (without hypocrisy, *anupokritos*) should characterize the Christian. Christian love (Rom. 12:9; 2 Cor. 6:6; 1 Pet. 1:22), faith (1 Tim. 1:5; 2 Tim. 1:5), and wisdom (James 3:17) should be sincere. See *Lie; Pharisees; Sin; Truth.*

Warren McWilliams

HYRAX Small mammal making its home in the rock cliffs (Ps. 104:18; Prov. 30:26 NIV, HCSB). See *Coney; Rock Badger.*

HYSSOP Small (about 27 inches), bushy plant, probably *Origanum maru*, the Syrian marjoram. Stalks of hyssop bear numerous, small, white flowers in bunches. Hyssop was thus well suited for use as a "brush" to dab the lintels of Israelite homes with the blood of the Passover lambs (Exod. 12:22). The associations of hyssop with the events of the exodus perhaps led to its use in other rites, the cleansing of lepers (Lev. 14:4,6,49,51-52) and the cleansing of those unclean from contact with a corpse (Num. 19:6,18; see *Heifer*). Psalm 51:7 applies the well-known image of hyssop to spiritual cleansing from sin.

A branch of hyssop bore the sponge used to offer vinegar to Christ at His crucifixion (John 19:29; Matt. 27:48; Mark 15:36 mention a reed). Various attempts to resolve this tension have been offered. Most exegetes have attempted to harmonize the parallel accounts: (1) by suggesting that Christ was offered vinegar twice, once using a reed and once hyssop; (2) by suggesting both a reed and hyssop were simultaneously used to support the sponge; (3) by emending John's text to read "spike" which is more easily harmonized with reed; (4) by taking hyssop to refer to a plant other than marjoram which could be described as a reed, such as

H

Sorghum vulgare. An alternative approach is concerned primarily with the question of why (theological significance) rather than the details of what. These interpreters stress that John intends to link Jesus' death with the exodus event that marked liberation from Egyptian slavery and/or with the OT cleansing rituals involving hyssop. Hebrews 9:19 says the people were sprinkled with hyssop at the reading of the covenant. The account of Exod. 24:6-8 lacks this detail. See *Plants.*

Joseph E. Glaze, Mitchell G. Reddish,
and Charles R. Wade

I

Ancient bridge over the Tiber River in Rome.

I AM Shortened form of God's response to Moses' request for the name of the God of the patriarchs (Exod. 3:13-14). The fuller form of the name may be rendered "I am who I am," "I will be who I will be," or even "I cause to be what is." God's response is not a "name" that makes God an object of definition or limitation. Rather, it is an affirmation that God is always subject, always free to be and act as God wills. The earliest Greek rendering "I am the one who is" or "I am Being" has been especially significant in the development of theology.

Jesus' "I am" response in several NT passages suggests more than the simple identifying "I am he." The "I am" of Mark 6:50 means "I am Jesus and not a ghost," but suggests the divine "I am" who alone "tramples down the waves of the sea" (Job 9:8; Mark 6:48-49) and made the waves hush (Ps. 107:28-29; cp. Mark 4:39). John 8:24 makes recognition that Jesus is the "I am" a matter of eternal life and death: "If you do not believe that I am He, you will die in your sins" (HCSB). The Jews misunderstood, thinking it was a matter of identity ("Who are You?" 8:25). That the Jews rightly understood Jesus' claim "Before Abraham was, I am" (8:58) as a divine claim is evident from their picking up stones to throw at Him. The "I am" of John 18:5 again suggests more than "I am the man you are looking for." Rather, Jesus is the "I am" whose awesome presence forced the guard back and into a posture of reverence. Here Jesus was not the object of betrayal but the subject who won the release of His disciples (18:8). Though differing in form from the "I am" sayings, the references to the one "who is, who was, and who is coming" (Rev. 1:4,8 HCSB; 4:8; cp. 11:17; 16:5) are similar in thought. In a context of intense hardship that called into question God's sovereignty, the writer of Revelation reaffirmed Israel's faith in the "I am" who is the subject of history and not its victim. See *YHWH*.   *Chris Church*

IBEX Species of wild goat with large curved horns, native to high mountain areas. The ibex has been identified as the wild goat of the Bible (1 Sam. 24:2; Ps. 104:18). The Nubian ibex is found today in the area of En-gedi, an oasis near the Dead Sea. The ibex is included among clean game (Deut. 14:5). KJV's "pygarg" is a white-rumped antelope (cp. "white-rumped deer" REB). The precise identity of the animal

A vase handle in the shape of a beautiful winged ibex.

(whether goat or antelope) is uncertain. See *Goat*.

IBHAR (Ĭb´ här) Personal name meaning "he elected." Son born to David after he moved to Jerusalem (2 Sam. 5:15).

IBLEAM (Ĭ b´ lə ăm) Place-name meaning "he swallowed the people." City in tribal territory of Issachar but given to tribe of Manasseh (Josh. 17:11). Many Bible students think Ibleam was the original reading for the Levite city in Josh. 21:25, where the Hebrew text now reads "Gath-rimmon," also read in verse 24. A copyist may have copied the name from verse 24 into verse 25. Some Greek manuscripts read Iebatha, perhaps a corruption of Ibleam. First Chronicles 6:70 reads Bileam, pointing to Ibleam as original. Other Greek manuscripts read "Beth-shean." Manasseh could not conquer Ibleam (Judg. 1:27). Jehu, in his coup against Jehoram, king of Israel, also mortally wounded Ahaziah, king of Judah, near Ibleam (2 Kings 9:27). Many Bible students also read "Ibleam" as the place of attack in 2 Kings 15:10 (REB, TEV, RSV, but not NRSV).

The Hebrew text either uses an Aramaic pronoun otherwise unknown in Hebrew meaning "before," or it refers to a place Kabal-am otherwise unknown. Some Greek manuscripts read "Ibleam." Normal text procedure would see Ibleam as the easier reading adopted in view of 2 Kings 9:27 by a copyist or translator who did not understand the Hebrew text. Ibleam is modern bir Belalmeh about a mile southwest of Jenin.

IBNEIAH (Ĭb nī´ a) Personal name meaning "Yah builds." Benjaminite who returned from exile and settled in Jerusalem (1 Chron. 9:8).

IBNIJAH (Ĭb nī´ ja) Personal name meaning "Yah builds," a variant spelling of Ibneiah. Ancestor in tribe of Benjamin of one of persons returning from exile and living in Jerusalem (1 Chron. 9:8).

IBRI (Ĭb´ rī) Personal name meaning "Hebrew." A Levite under King David (1 Chron. 24:27). See Habiru.

IBSAM (Ĭb´ săm) Personal name akin to balsam, meaning "sweet smelling" in modern translations. KJV spelling is Jibsam. Member of tribe of Issachar (1 Chron. 7:2).

IBZAN (Ĭb´ zăn) Personal name, perhaps meaning "quick, agile." Judge of Israel from Bethlehem who participated in royal practice of marrying children to foreigners (Judg. 12:8-10).

ICE Frozen water. Job's poetry has several references to ice. Ice is described as hard as stone (Job 38:30). In picturesque language, ice is frozen by the "breath of God" (37:10). In an even bolder image, the Lord demanded to know "from whose womb has come the ice? And the frost of heaven, who has given it birth?" (38:29 NASB). Though lacking the knowledge of a meteorologist, the biblical writer saw clearly with wondering eyes that God was the ultimate source of weather phenomena. The Hebrew term translated "ice" is sometimes rendered "cold" or "frost" (Gen. 31:40; Jer. 36:30).

ICHABOD (Ĭk´ à bŏd) Personal name meaning "where is the glory?" The son of Phinehas, Eli's son (1 Sam. 4:21). His birth seems to have been precipitated by the news of the death of his father and the capture of the ark of the covenant

in battle against the Philistines. The mother of Ichabod died immediately after the child's birth. See Eli.

ICONIUM (Ī cō´ nĭ ŭm) City of Asia Minor visited by Barnabas and Paul during the first missionary journey (Acts 13:51). Paul endured sufferings and persecution at Iconium (2 Tim. 3:11). Its location is that of the modern Turkish provincial capital Konya. Iconium was mentioned for the first time in the fourth century B.C. by the historian Xenophon. In NT times it was considered to be a part of the Roman province of Galatia. Evidently it has had a continuous existence since its founding. See Asia Minor, Cities of.

IDALAH (Ĭd´ à la) Place-name of uncertain meaning, perhaps "jackal" or "memorial." Town in tribal territory of Zebulun (Josh. 19:15), probably modern Khirbet el-Hawarah south of Bethlehem in Zebulun, not to be confused with the more famous Bethlehem in Judah.

IDBASH (Ĭd´ băsh) Personal name meaning "sweet as honey." Son of Etam in the tribe of Judah (1 Chron. 4:3), according to modern translations and earliest Greek translation. KJV follows Hebrew text in reading father rather than son of Etam.

IDDO (Ĭd´ dō) English spelling of four different Hebrew personal names. **1.** Name of uncertain meaning. Person with authority in the exilic community during the Persian period to whom Ezra sent messengers to secure Levites to join him in the return to Jerusalem (Ezra 8:17). He apparently sent the needed Levites (vv. 19–20). **2.** Personal name, perhaps meaning "his praise." Leader of the eastern half of the tribe of Manasseh under David (1 Chron. 27:21). The written Hebrew text uses this name in Ezra 10:43 for a man with a foreign wife, but an early scribal note followed by English translations read Jadau. **3.** Name, perhaps meaning "Yahweh adorns Himself." A prophet whose records the chronicler refers to for more information about Solomon and Jeroboam (2 Chron. 9:29), Rehoboam (2 Chron. 12:15), and Abijah (2 Chron. 13:22). The latter indicates he wrote a *midrash*, which may indicate a Jewish exposition of Scripture. As early as Josephus, Iddo had been identified with the nameless prophet who spoke

I

against the altar of Bethel in 1 Kings 13. The Hebrew texts spell his name in different ways in the different occurrences. **4.** Grandfather of Zechariah, the prophet (Zech. 1:1,7 with different Hebrew spellings). Ezra 5:1; 6:14 put Zechariah as Iddo's son, using "son" to mean descendant, as often in Hebrew. He is included among the priestly families in the early postexilic community (Neh. 12:4,16). **5.** Father of Solomon's district supervisor who supplied the royal court provisions for one month a year in the area of Mahanaim (1 Kings 4:14). **6.** A Levite (1 Chron. 6:21).

IDLE Not engaged in earning a living; depending on the labor and generosity of others for support. Scripture distinguishes between those unwilling to work who should not eat (2 Thess. 3:10) and those unable to earn a living (e.g., "true" widows, 1 Tim. 5:9) for whom the community of faith is responsible. Hebrew wisdom literature frequently condemned idleness as the cause of hunger (Prov. 19:15), poverty (Prov. 10:4; 14:23), and inadequate housing (Eccles. 10:18). According to Hebrew wisdom, the ideal woman "is never idle" (Prov. 31:27 HCSB) but is an industrious, working woman who helps provide for the financial needs of her family (Prov. 31:16,24). In the NT, Paul called attention to his own example as a bivocational minister to encourage the Thessalonian Christians to be hard workers (2 Thess. 3:7-8). Though Scripture consistently condemns "willful" idleness, it is also aware of economic realities in which some who are willing workers stand idle because no one has hired them (Matt. 20:6-7). The biblical witness likewise does not trace all poverty to idleness. Some poverty results from the rich refusing to pay their poor day laborers (Lev. 19:13; Jer. 22:13; James 5:4).

IDOL Physical or material image or form representing a reality or being considered divine and thus an object of worship. In the Bible various terms are used to refer to idols or idolatry: "image," either graven (carved) or cast, "statue," "abomination." Both Testaments condemn idols, but with idols the OT expresses more concern than the NT, probably reflecting the fact that the threat of idolatry was more pronounced for the people of the OT.

The ancient Hebrews lived in a world filled with idols. Egyptians represented their deities in

Allat, the moon goddess of Syria and later of northern Arabia.

various human-animal forms. Similarly, the various Mesopotamian cultures used idol representations of their deities, as did the Hittites in ancient Asia Minor. More of a threat to Hebrew worship were the Canaanite Baal and Asherah fertility images, some of which are commonly found in excavations. Use of idols in worship continued to be commonplace in Greek and Roman religion.

One of the prominent distinguishing features of biblical religion is its ideal of "imageless" worship. Clearly expressed in the Decalogue is the command: "You shall not make for yourself an idol ... you shall not worship them or serve them" (Exod. 20:4-5 NASB). This is usually interpreted to be a negative statement concerning idols but with positive implications toward the spiritual worship desired by God.

Idols were a problem of long standing. One of the first acts of rebellion of the Hebrews centered around the golden calf made under Aaron's leadership in the wilderness (Exod. 32). The bronze serpent illustrates the Hebrews' propensity for idol worship. Moses set it up in the wilderness to allay a plague of serpents (Num. 21), but Israel retained it and made it an object of worship (2 Kings 18:4). Joshua called on the people to put away the gods their fathers had served in Mesopotamia and in Egypt (Josh. 24:14). Perhaps a misguided King Jeroboam intended to represent Yahweh by the gold calves set up in his temples at Bethel and Dan when he led the northern tribes to secede from the kingdom inherited by Rehoboam (1 Kings 12:28-33).

Biblical writers often denounced idolatry. None is more graphic and devastating than that in Isa. 44:9-20. The idol is made by a workman but is powerless to sustain the workman to complete his task. Further, the idol begins as a leftover piece of a tree from which a person makes a god. He then worships no more than a block of wood.

Many scholars believe that the threat of idolatry was much less in the Jewish community after the Babylonian exile and that it continued to be diminished though still present throughout NT times. The most noted problem in the NT concerns the propriety of eating meat that has previously been offered to an idol (1 Cor. 8–10). Paul seemingly broadened the scope of idolatry for Christianity when he identified covetousness with idolatry (Col. 3:5). See *Food Offered to Idols; Gods, Pagan.*   Bruce C. Cresson

IDOLATRY See *Idol.*

IDUMEA (Ĭd u mē´ à) In Isa. 34:5 a nation destined for judgment. "Idumea" is the term used in the Greek version of the OT and in the writings of the Jewish historian Josephus for Edom. The region was southeast of the Dead Sea. The Herods came originally from Idumea. Crowds from Idumea followed Jesus early in His ministry (Mark 3:8). See *Edom.*

IEZER (Ī ē´ zĕr) Personal name meaning "where is help" or a short form of "my father is help." (Hb. Aviezer, Josh. 17:2). Son of Gilead in tribe of Manasseh and original clan ancestor of Iezerites (Num. 26:30). KJV, REB spelling is Jeezer.

IEZERITES (Ī ē´ zĕr īts) See *Iezer.*

IGAL (Ī´ găl) Personal name meaning "he redeems." **1.** Spy representing tribe of Issachar whom Moses sent to investigate the land of Canaan (Num. 13:7). He voted with the major-

ity that the land was too difficult for Israel to conquer. **2.** One of David's heroic warriors, apparently a foreigner from Zobah (2 Sam. 23:36), though his name is spelled Joel, and he is the brother, not son, of Nathan in 1 Chron. 11:38. **3.** Descendant of David in the postexilic community (about 470 B.C.) and thus bearer of the messianic line and hope (1 Chron. 3:22), though the chronicler does not describe him in messianic terms here.

IGDALIAH (Ĭg dà lī´ a) Personal name meaning "Yahweh is great." Ancestor of the prophets whose chamber in the temple Jeremiah used to test the Rechabites loyalty to their oath not to drink wine (Jer. 35:4). This is apparently evidence for professional prophets on the temple staff. See *Jeremiah; Rechabites.*

IGEAL (Ī´ gĭ àl) (KJV, 1 Chron. 3:22) See *Igal.*

IGNORANCE Old Testament law distinguished between sins of ignorance, or sin unintentionally (Lev. 4:2,13-14; Num. 15:24-29), and premeditated sins ("sin presumptuously" or with a high hand, Num. 15:30-31). Sins committed in ignorance incur guilt (Lev. 4:13,22,27); however, the sacrificial system provided atonement for such sin (Lev. 4; 5:5-6). In contrast, "high-handed" or "presumptuous" sin is an affront to the Lord punishable by exclusion from the people of God. The Law provided no ritual cleansing for such sin (Num. 15:30-31). Common images for sins of ignorance include error (Lev. 5:18), straying (Ps. 119:10), and stumbling (Job 4:4). By extension these images can be applied to any sin. Thus Prov. 19:27 warns against willful "erring" from words of divine counsel.

The NT speaks of past ignorance that God excuses. Such was the ignorance of those Jews who participated in crucifying Jesus (Acts 3:17; 13:27), of Paul who persecuted Christians (1 Tim. 1:13), and of Gentiles who did not recognize the true God (Acts 17:30). Though God overlooks such past ignorance, He requires repentance (Acts 3:19; 17:30). Obedience characterizes lives of the converted just as ignorant desires characterize those without Christ (1 Pet. 1:14). The NT speaks of deliberate ignorance as well as "excusable" ignorance. Most often deliberate ignorance involves the stubborn refusal to acknowledge nature's witness to the powerful

I

existence of God (Rom. 1:18-21; Eph. 4:18; 2 Pet. 3:5).

IIM (Ī´ ĭm) Place-name meaning "ruins." **1.** Town on southern border of tribal territory of Judah (Josh. 15:29). Its location is not known, and it does not appear in parallel lists in Josh. 19:3; 1 Chron. 4:29. Many Bible students think a copyist copied parts of the following Ezem twice. **2.** Used in Num. 33:45 (KJV) as abbreviation for Iye-abarim. See *Iye-abarim.*

IJEABARIM (Ī jə ăb´ ȧ rĭm) (KJV) See *Iye-abarim.*

IJON (Ī´ jŏn) Place-name meaning "ruin." Place in northern Israel captured by King Ben-hadad of Damascus as a result of his agreement with King Asa of Judah (910–869 B.C.) to break the treaty between Damascus and Baasha, king of Israel (1 Kings 15:20). This forced Baasha to defend himself on the northern border and quit intruding on Judah's territory, giving Asa opportunity to strengthen his defenses (1 Kings 15:21-22). Tiglath-pileser conquered the city and carried many Israelites into captivity about 734 B.C. (2 Kings 15:29). Ijon is located near modern Marj Uyun between the rivers Litani and Hesbani at Tell Dibbin.

IKKESH (Ĭk´ kĕsh) Personal name meaning "perverted, false." Father of one of David's 30 heroes from Tekoa (2 Sam. 23:26).

ILAI (Ī´ lā ī) Personal name of uncertain meaning. One of David's military heroes (1 Chron. 11:29), apparently the same as Zalmon (2 Sam. 23:28), the different spelling resulting from a copyist's change.

ILLUSTRATION See *Imagery; Parables; Proverb; Wise Saying.*

ILLYRICUM (Ĭl lĭr´ ĭ cŭm) Place-name of uncertain meaning. A district in the Roman Empire between the Danube River and the Adriatic Sea. The Romans divided it into Dalmatia and Pannonia. It includes modern Yugoslavia and Albania. Illyricum represented the northeastern limits of Paul's missionary work as he wrote the Romans (Rom. 15:19), though the Bible nowhere mentions his work there. His work in Macedonia was only a few miles away, so he could easily have preached in or sent his associates to Illyricum. This does not mean he had covered all of Illyricum, only that he had introduced the gospel there in the dangerous limits of the empire. Paul had thus completed his missionary ministry of preaching the gospel and planting churches in the eastern end of the empire. Paul was now ready to preach in Rome and the western parts of the Roman Empire (Rom. 15:20-24).

IMAGE OF GOD Biblical designation for the unique nature, status, and worth of all human beings as created by God.

Christian thinkers have tried to locate the image of God (*imago Dei*) in various dimensions of man's being, including man's spirit, soul, rationality, will, mind, personhood, immortality, and even his physical body. But Scripture is not specific as to exactly what it is about man that constitutes the *image of God.* The image of God cannot be reduced to one attribute or any combination of attributes of man. The biblical portrait is more holistic. The entire man, as a human being, images God.

Creation The biblical depiction of the image of God begins "in the beginning" when "God said, 'Let Us make man in Our image, according to Our likeness,'" (Gen. 1:26a NASB). The Hebrew word "image" (*selem*) refers to a representation, image, or likeness; it often refers to the way that an idol represented a god. "Likeness" (*demut*) means "similar in appearance," usually visual appearance, but it can also refer to audible similarity. Taken together, "likeness" complements "image" to mean that man is more than a mere image; he is a likeness of God. Yet, regardless of whether one argues from definition or word order, attempts to distinguish sharply "image" from "likeness" are misguided. For centuries theologians have tried to contrast the "image" (as the physical, natural or rational part of man) over and against the "likeness" (as the spiritual, moral, and volitional part of man). While the terms *selem* and *demut* complement one another, three subsequent references to 1:26 all confirm that these two terms are essentially interchangeable ideas in the common Hebrew literary style of parallelism. On the one hand, in 1:27 "image" is used without "likeness." On the other hand, in 5:1 "likeness" is used without "image." In 5:3, both terms are used again in tandem but are in transposed order compared to 1:26. In any case, all three passages point back to

1:26 and communicate the big idea of God's image.

In understanding the image of God, it is more important that the immediate scriptural context of the original divine pronouncement in 1:26 is the creation of the animal kingdom. In contrast to the animal creation, humankind is made in the image of God in a separate act of creation. Man originates apart from any connection with the animal creation and certainly not from evolution. Also, for the first time in the creation narrative, the divine "let Us" is used in conjunction with the creation act. Added to this, the immediate scriptural context after this introduction of the "image of God" is the additional charge that man "subdue" the earth and "rule over" all of its other creatures (1:26,28). On the surface, man's earthly authority here sets him apart from the rest of creation. Below the surface, this dominion *imago Dei* motif stands in contrast to ancient pagan religious belief that only ruling kings enjoyed royal standing before the gods and men, as evidenced by their dominion which they presumed to exercise on behalf of their deities. In contrast the biblical picture of *imago Dei* means that all human beings, not just kings, possess special royal status as God's appointed stewards over the earth. By virtue of mankind's ruling over the rest of God's creatures and earth, every member of the human race somehow represents and reflects the sovereign Lord of creation.

Procreation Both sexes reflect the image of God as "male and female" (1:27) and were commanded to "be fruitful and multiply" (1:28). This population mandate was inaugurated in Gen. 5:1-3 with the clear implication that the *imago Dei* was passed from Adam and Eve to their son Seth. This text frames the image of God around the theme of sonship. When Luke references Gen. 5:1-3, he calls Adam the "son of God" (Luke 3:38 HCSB). These two passages together communicate a common idea: from God, Adam received the *imago Dei*; from Adam, Seth received the *imago Dei.* Adam's sin and its negative consequences for the entire human race without doubt marred the image of God, as no aspect of man's being was unaffected by the fall. Yet it is presumptive to assume that the image of God was completely lost through sin. To the contrary, Seth and his progeny received and passed down the image.

This multifaceted image of God in man, as represented in the creation-procreation themes of stewardship and sonship, is also present in Ps. 8. Here "man" and "son of man" are made "little less than God" and given glory, honor, and dominion (Ps. 8:3-8). So much does sinful man still bear that image that Paul states that fallen man "is God's image and glory" (1 Cor. 11:7 HCSB). While sin distorted and disfigured the image or God in man, it did not diminish its worth. In fact, post-fall human life is still sacred precisely because of the *imago Dei*, so sacred that it should not be taken (Gen. 9:6-7) or cursed (James 3:9).

Incarnation However, much of mankind images God by virtue of stewardship and sonship, only one man is the true image of God, with the full authority of the Father, as the only begotten Son of God. Jesus Christ "is the image of God" (2 Cor. 4:4 HCSB); "He is the image of the invisible God" (Col. 1:15 HCSB). This is the great fact of the incarnation (John 1:14,18; Phil. 2:5-8). As the only God-Man, among men Jesus Christ alone mirrors God as "the exact expression of His nature" (Heb. 1:3 HCSB). As such, Jesus Christ is God's ultimate steward and God's true Son (Heb. 2:6-8).

Redemption While the image of God in man was injured as a result of sin, that damage is more than countered by the redemptive work of Jesus Christ, for those who believe. The Christian is to "put on the new man, who is being renewed in knowledge according to the image of his Creator" (Col. 3:10 HCSB; cp. Eph. 4:24). "Reflecting the glory of the Lord," the believer is progressively sanctified, "being transformed into the same image from glory to glory" (2 Cor. 3:18 HCSB; cp. Rom. 8:28-29).

Glorification Because of the incarnation, life, death, and resurrection of Jesus Christ, believers are promised a final transformation into the likeness of Christ at His return. "As we have borne the image of the man made of dust, we will also bear the image of the heavenly man" (1 Cor. 15:49 HCSB; cp. 42,45-48). While there may be much about the image of God that Christians cannot understand or know in their current state, the revelation of Jesus Christ will change believers for eternity. "We know that when He appears, we will be like Him, because we will see Him as He is" (1 John 3:2 HCSB; cp. Phil. 3:21).   *Jerry A. Johnson*

IMAGE WORSHIP See *Idol.*

IMAGE, NEBUCHADNEZZAR'S Colossal figure in Nebuchadnezzar's dream (Dan. 2:31-45) that was erected on the plains of Dura (Dan. 3:1-18).

The interpretation of the statue in Nebuchadnezzar's dream is debated. Nebuchadnezzar is clearly the head of gold (2:38). The identification of the other materials (silver, bronze, iron mixed with clay) with historical references is less clear. For convenience, interpreters may be classed broadly as historicists and dispensationalists.

Historicists have proposed various solutions to the enigmatic historical references. According to one interpretation, the various materials refer to the line of Neo-Babylonian kings which came to an end with the conquest of Cyrus who is identified as the divinely ordained rock (Dan. 2:45; cp. Isa. 44:28; 45:1). Others see a succession of kingdoms rather than kings, for example, (1) Babylon, Media, Persia, and Greece, or (2) Babylon, Medo-Persia, Alexander the Great, and Alexander's Hellenistic successors. Interpreters divide over whether to identify the kingdom that rules the world (2:39) with that of Cyrus who made this claim or with Alexander who in fact conquered much of the known world. The fourth "divided" kingdom (2:41) is frequently identified with the division of Alexander's empire by his generals. The mixing of iron and clay is possibly a reference to failed attempts to unite these kingdoms by marriage treaties (2:43). For these interpreters, the God-ordained stone is the Maccabees who secured Jewish independence and reinstated temple worship. Many historicists recognize that the Maccabees only partially fulfilled the hopes of the writer of Daniel and thus find the ultimate fulfillment in the kingdom established by Christ.

Dispensationalist interpreters identify the succession of kingdoms as Babylon, Medo-Persia, Greece, and Rome. Rome is the empire divided into eastern and western halves and finally represented by a 10-nation federation. The Roman period extends until the time of Christ who is the God-ordained Rock that ends the power of the Gentiles (Dan. 7; Luke 21:24; Rev. 16:19).

The charge of not worshiping the gods of Nebuchadnezzar leveled against the Jews (Dan. 3:12,14) suggests a statue of Bel-merodach, the patron deity of Babylon, though the statue was possibly of Nebuchadnezzar himself. Here religion is a political tool to unite various peoples into one empire. Readers in Maccabean and Roman times no doubt understood the statue against contemporary use of the divine ruler cult.

Chris Church

IMAGERY Figurative language. Scripture prefers to convey truths by pictorial representations rather than through abstract language. Scripture abounds in word-pictures for God, God's people, and their experience of salvation.

The challenge of theology ("talk about God") is to express truths about God in human language. Scripture itself witnesses the difficulty of this task, "To whom would you liken Me, and make Me equal and compare Me, that we would be alike?" (Isa. 46:5 NASB). The living God is not to be equated with any one manageable image. Idolatry is essentially the attempt to reduce God to an image or label. The multiplicity of OT literary images for God serves as a corrective of human attempts to constrict one's view of God. Some images for God are inanimate: stone (Gen. 49:24); fortress (2 Sam. 22:2); fountain of living waters (Jer. 2:13). There is little danger of confusing God with such images. Other images of God are personal: father (Mal. 1:6); husband (Hos. 2:16); shepherd (Ps. 23:1); judge, lawgiver, and king (Isa. 33:22); teacher (Isa. 28:26); healer (Jer. 30:17); warrior (Exod. 15:1,3); farmer (Isa. 5:2-7). With such personal images, the danger of confusing "God is like" with "God is" is real. A challenging corrective is offered by the less familiar feminine images for God, for example, that of a mother bird sheltering her young (Ruth 2:12; Ps. 17:8). Also suggestive of a mother's tenderness are the images of carrying a child from birth (Isa. 46:3), teaching a child to walk (Hos. 11:3), child feeding (Hos. 11:4), and child rearing (Isa. 1:2).

In His parables, Jesus continued the OT practice of using vivid images for God: a shepherd seeking one lost sheep (Luke 15:4-7); a woman seeking one lost coin (Luke 15:8-10); a father waiting patiently for the return of one son and taking the initiative to reconcile the other (Luke 15:11-32). Images are also used to teach who Jesus the Christ is: word (John 1:1); light (John 8:12); bread and wine (Matt. 26:26-29); vine (John 15:1); the way (John 14:6).

Imagery is also used to depict the people of God and their experience of salvation. The OT pictures God's people as: a faithless wife (Jer. 3:20); a wild vine (Jer. 2:21); a wild donkey in heat (Jer. 2:24); God's beloved (Jer. 11:15); God's bride (Jer. 2:2); God's servant (Jer. 30:10); and God's son (Hos. 11:1). New Testament images include: light (Matt. 5:14); salt (Matt. 5:13); vine branches (John 15:5); a new creation (2 Cor. 5:17); God's temple (1 Cor. 3:16); and a royal priesthood (1 Pet. 2:9; cp. Exod. 19:6). Images for salvation are drawn from all walks of life: the law courts (Rom. 7:3; Heb. 9:16-17); slave market (Titus 2:14); marketplace (1 Cor. 6:20; 7:23); and the family (Rom. 8:17,23). The multiplicity of images again witnesses the rich experience of God's people. See *Anthropomorphism; Parables.*

Chris Church

IMAGERY, CHAMBER OF KJV phrase (Ezek. 8:12) understood as "room of his carved images" (NASB) or "shrine of his own idol" (NIV). The picture of the representatives of Israel worshiping idols within the Jerusalem temple in Ezekiel's vision (8:3,12) symbolizes the people's unfaithfulness to God.

IMAGES See Idol.

IMAGINATION KJV term for thought as the prelude to action, frequently in the sense of plotting or devising evil; can also refer to stubbornness from the Hebrew words meaning "formed" or "twisted." Imagination means evil plans (Prov. 6:18; Lam. 3:60-61). At Deut. 31:21, and possibly Rom. 1:21, "imagination" refers to the inclination to do evil. God opposes the imaginations of the proud (Luke 1:51; 2 Cor. 10:5). Imagination is also used in a neutral sense (1 Chron. 28:9). Most often, imagination means stubbornness (Deut. 29:19; Jer. 3:17; 7:24; 9:14; 11:8; 13:10; 16:12; 18:12; 23:17). Modern translations use imagination less frequently. For example, the RSV used imagination only four times: for the inclination to do evil (Gen. 6:5; 8:21; NRSV, "inclination"); for the plans of the proud (Luke 1:51; NSRV, "thoughts"); and in connection with the making of idols (Acts 17:29) where imagination may mean creativity or more likely a depraved mind. The NIV also used imagination four times: in reference to fabricating prophecy (Ezek. 13:2,17); and for evil plans (Isa. 65:2; 66:18).

IMITATE To mimic; to do what is seen to be done by another; sometimes it approximates "be obedient." Paul's uses can be divided into three groups: (1) To call attention to a comparison even when no conscious mimicking is in mind. The Thessalonians shared suffering at the hands of their compatriots comparable to that experienced by the earliest Judean Christians (1 Thess. 2:14). First Thessalonians 1:6 perhaps belongs here. (2) To follow an example (Phil. 3:17; 2 Thess. 3:7,9 where Paul's example of self-support is in view). Obedience may also be in mind as references to tradition (2 Thess. 3:6) and command (3:10) demonstrate. (3) An equivalent to "be obedient." Paul exhorted the Corinthians to follow him not primarily by following his personal example but by following his "ways in Christ" which he taught "everywhere in every church" (1 Cor. 4:16-17). The Corinthians were to follow Paul's example by heeding his counsel to do all for the glory of God without causing offense (1 Cor. 11:1; cp. 10:23-33). In Eph. 5:1 the command to be imitators is again linked with the previous series of commands, especially that of forgiveness (4:25-32). The image of children obedient to parents is common where the thought of imitation as obedience is primary (1 Cor. 4:14-16; Eph. 5:1).

Hebrews urges imitation of the faithfulness and patient endurance of those who inherited the promises (6:12) and the faithfulness of church leaders (13:7). The command of 3 John 11 is general, though specific examples of good (Demetrius) and bad (Diotrephes) are in view.

IMLA or **IMLAH** (Ĭm´ la) Personal name meaning "he fills," appearing in different spelling in Kings and Chronicles. Father of the prophet Micaiah (1 Kings 22:8). See *Micaiah.*

IMMANUEL (Ĭ m măn´ ū ĕl) Personal name meaning "God with us." Name of son to be born in Isaiah's prophecy to King Ahaz (Isa. 7:14) and fulfilled in birth of Jesus (Matt. 1:22-23).

When King Ahaz refused to show his faith by asking God for a sign (Isa. 7:10-12), Isaiah gave him a sign of the birth of Immanuel, using the traditional form of a birth announcement (7:14; cp. Gen. 16:11; Judg. 13:3,5). The Hebrew language apparently indicates that the prophet and king expected an immediate fulfillment. Recent study has pointed to Ahaz's wife as the woman expected to bear the child and show that God was still with the Davidic royal dynasty even in the midst of severe threat from Assyria. Such a sign would give hope to a king who trusted God

I

but would be a constant threat to one who followed his own strategy. The double meaning of the Immanuel sign appears again in Isa. 8:8. The Assyrian army would flood the land until Judah was up to its neck in trouble and could only cry out, "O Immanuel"; a cry confessing that God is with us in His destructive rage but at the same time a prayer, hoping for divine intervention. Isaiah followed this with a call to the nations to lose in battle because of Immanuel, God with us (8:10).

The Bible says nothing else about the effects of the Immanuel prophecy in the days of Isaiah and Ahaz. It does announce the great fulfillment in Jesus Christ (Matt. 1:22-23). Jesus' birth showed all humanity that God is faithful to fulfill His promises in ways far beyond human expectations, for Jesus was not just a sign of God with us. Jesus was God become flesh, God incarnate, God with us in Person.

IMMATERIALITY Not composed of matter. Acts 17:29 argues that "we shouldn't think that the divine nature is like gold or silver or stone" (HCSB). Rather "God is Spirit: and those who worship Him must worship in spirit and truth" (John 4:24 HCSB).

IMMER (Ĭm´ mĕr) Personal name probably meaning "lamb." **1.** Father of Pashhur, the priest and temple administrator (Jer. 20:1). **2.** Priest whose son Zadok helped Nehemiah repair Jerusalem's walls (Neh. 3:29). Ancestor of priests who dwelt in Jerusalem after the return from exile (1 Chron. 9:12). **3.** Leader of priestly division under David (1 Chron. 24:14). Son of Immer in other instances could mean, "descendant of Immer" and refer to this original priestly ancestor (cp. Ezra 2:37-38; 10:20; Neh. 7:40; 11:13).

IMMORALITY Any illicit sexual activity outside of marriage. Both in the OT and in the NT the word has a figurative meaning as well, referring to idolatry or unfaithfulness to God.

In the OT *zanah* regularly refers to wrongful heterosexual intercourse, primarily in regard to women (Judg. 19:2; Jer. 3:1; Hos. 4:13). The noun "harlot" or "whore" is derived from the same stem (Gen. 34:31; Josh. 2:1-3; Prov. 23:27; Hos. 4:13-14). In a figurative sense, *zanah* refers to Israel's unfaithfulness to God (2 Chron. 21:11; Isa. 1:21; Jer. 3:1-5; Ezek. 16:26-28). In addi-

tion, the sinfulness of Tyre (Isa. 23:17) and Nineveh (Nah. 3:4) are portrayed in this manner.

In Paul's letters, *porneia* and/or related words refer to an incestuous relationship (1 Cor. 5:1), sexual relations with a prostitute (1 Cor. 6:12-20), and various forms of unchastity both heterosexual and homosexual (Rom. 1:29; 1 Cor. 5:9-11; 6:9-11; 7:2; 2 Cor. 12:21; Eph. 5:3; 1 Thess. 4:3). Immorality is a sin against God (1 Cor. 3:16-17; 6:15-20; 1 Thess. 4:3-8). In the Gospels, the term, on occasion, is related to adultery (Matt. 5:32; 19:9) and in Revelation may refer to harlotry or prostitution (Rev. 2:14,20). The word "harlot" or "whore" is derived from the same root (Rev. 19:2). In Acts, the Apostolic Council requires that Gentiles avoid *porneia* (Acts 15:20,29). *Porneia* and related words also have a figurative meaning of unfaithfulness to God (Matt. 12:39; John 8:41; Rev. 2:21; 9:21; 14:8; 19:2). See *Adultery; Sex, Biblical Teaching on.* *Donald E. Cook*

IMMORTALITY Quality or state of being exempt from death. In the true sense of the word, only God is immortal (1 Tim. 6:16; 1:17; 2 Tim. 1:10), for only God is living in the true sense of the word. Humans may be considered immortal only insofar as immortality is the gift of God. Paul points us in this direction. In Rom. 2:7 Paul says, "To those who by patiently doing good seek for glory and honor and immortality, he will give eternal life" (NRSV). Paul also explained that the perishable nature of human life will put on the imperishable and that the mortal nature of human life will put on immortality. When that happens, the saying concerning victory over death will have been fulfilled (1 Cor. 15:53-55; Isa. 25:8; Hos. 13:14). As it is, humans in their earthly life are mortal; they are subject to death.

Thus, eternal life is not ours because we have the inherent power to live forever; eternal life and immortality are ours only because God chooses to give them to us. Those who escaped death—Enoch (Gen. 5:24) and Elijah (2 Kings 2:10-11)—did so only by the power of God and not by some inherent power they had to live forever. See *Eternal Life; Life.* *Phil Logan*

IMMUTABILITY OF GOD The unchangeability of God. In biblical theology God is described as unchanging in His nature and in His character. This includes God's being (essence), purposes, and promises.

Psalm 102:25-27 contrasts God's unchanging nature with that of the created order. Numbers 23:19 and 1 Sam. 15:29 indicate that God changes neither His plans nor His actions, for these rest on His unchanging nature. James finds assurance of God's future blessings in that there is in God "no variation or shadow cast by turning" (James 1:17 HCSB). After referring to His constant patience, long-suffering, and mercy, God concludes with a general statement of His immutability: "For I, the LORD, do not change" (Mal. 3:6 NASB).

Failure to allow the Bible to define precisely in what sense God changes, results in a distorted view of God. Being influenced more by Greek philosophy than by the Bible, some classical theologians have understood God's immutability to mean that God is unable to act and that He is uncaring and unresponsive to the created order. Overreaction to this error of viewing God as static results in an equally distorted view of God. Some recent thinkers have rejected the biblical teaching concerning God's immutability altogether. Being influenced more by process or existential thought, they understand God to be like the created order—experiencing change, maturing in knowledge and personal development, and having no certain knowledge of the future. Neither a static view of God nor a God in constant flux captures the biblical picture of God. Biblical theology portrays God as immutable, yet as acting, feeling emotions, and responding differently to various situations. In all such actions, feelings, and responses, God is constant and consistent.

On the surface it appears that some biblical passages represent God as changing. For example, He repents (Gen. 6:6; 1 Sam. 15:11; Joel 2:13; Amos 7:3,6; Jon. 3:9; 4:2); changes His purpose (Exod. 32:9-14; Jon. 3:10); becomes angry (Num. 11:1,10; Ps. 106:40; Zech. 10:3); and turns from His anger (Deut. 13:17; 2 Chron. 12:12; Jer. 18:8; 26:3). The apparent problem disappears upon close inspection of each text. These verses portray God changing in His relations and who sometimes appears to mere humans to alter His purposes but who never wavers or changes in His nature, purposes, or promises.

God's immutability is a great source of comfort to the believer. Whereas God is constant in His wrath against sin, He is equally constant in His forgiveness in response to faith and repentance.

God's immutability grants the assurance that "He who started a good work in you will carry it on to completion" (Phil. 1:6 HCSB). In a world that is in constant change, the believer finds peace in a God who does not change, knowing that truth and values are grounded in the nature and character of an unchanging God.

Walter Johnson

IMNA (Ĭm´ nă) Personal name meaning "he defends." A member of the tribe of Asher (1 Chron. 7:35). See *Imnah*.

IMNAH (Ĭm´ nă) Personal name meaning "he allots for" or "on the right hand, good fortune." **1.** Son of Asher and original ancestor of the Imnites (Num. 26:44; KJV, Jimna). **2.** Levite in the time of King Hezekiah (2 Chron. 31:14).

IMNITE (Ĭm´ nīt) See *Imnah*.

IMPEDIMENT IN SPEECH Disturbance of the vocal organs resulting in the inability to produce intelligible sounds (Mark 7:32). In Jesus' healing of a man who "had a speech difficulty" (HCSB; NIV, "hardly talk"), the crowds recognized a fulfillment of Isa. 35:5-6.

IMPERISHABLE Not subject to decay; ever enduring. Imperishable (KJV, incorruption) describes the spiritual resurrection body that, unlike the physical body, is not subject to the decay associated with death (1 Cor. 15:42-54). Imperishable describes the everlasting reward of the saints (1 Cor. 9:25; 1 Pet. 1:23). One of the Greek terms translated "imperishable" is also rendered "immortality" (Rom. 2:7; 2 Tim. 1:10). The same term is used in reference to "undying" love in Eph. 6:24 (KJV, "in sincerity").

IMPORTUNITY Troublesome urgency; excessive persistence. In Luke 11:8 importunity results in a favorable response to a midnight request for bread (KJV, RSV). Many modern translations read persistence (HCSB, NASB, NRSV, REB). The literal meaning of the term is shamelessness (NEB; cp. TEV: "not ashamed to keep on asking").

IMPOSITION OF HANDS See *Laying on of Hands*.

I

IMPOTENT Lacking power, strength, or vigor; helpless. Impotence in the KJV never refers to sexual inability. Modern translations replace "impotent" with other terms: "cripple" (Acts 4:9 NIV); "disabled" (John 5:3 NIV); "invalid" (John 5:3 NRSV); "sick" (John 5:3,7; Acts 4:9 NASB). Modern translations describe the man "impotent in his feet" (Acts 14:8) as one who could not use his feet (NRSV), without strength in his feet (HCSB, NASB), or crippled (NIV). See *Diseases*.

IMPRECATION, IMPRECATORY PSALMS Act of invoking a curse. In the Imprecatory Psalms the author calls for God to bring misfortune and disaster upon the enemies (Pss. 5; 11; 17; 35; 55; 59; 69; 109; 137; 140). These psalms are an embarrassment to many Christians who see them in tension with Jesus' teaching on love of enemies (Matt. 5:43-48). It is important to recall the theological principles that underlie such psalms. These include: (1) the principle that vengeance belongs to God (Deut. 32:35; Ps. 94:1) that excludes personal retaliation and necessitates appeal to God to punish the wicked (cp. Rom. 12:19); (2) the principle that God's righteousness demands judgment on the wicked (Pss. 5:6; 11:5-6); (3) the principle that God's covenant love for the people of God necessitates intervention on their part (Pss. 5:7; 59:10,16-17); and (4) the principle of prayer that believers trust God with all their thoughts and desires. See *Blessing and Cursing*.

IMPURITY See *Clean, Cleanness; Common*.

IMPUTE, IMPUTATION Setting to someone's account or reckoning something to another person. God reckoned righteousness to believing Abraham (Gen. 15:6). This means that God credited to Abraham that which he did not have in himself (Rom. 4:3-5). This does not mean that God accepted Abraham's faith instead of righteousness as an accomplishment meriting justification. Rather, it means that God accepted Abraham because he trusted in God rather than trusting in something that he could do.

Similarly, drawing from Ps. 32:1-3, Paul stated that only God can forgive sin. Those who are forgiven are not regarded as wicked since the Lord does not impute to them their iniquity. Instead these are considered or reckoned as children of God (Rom. 4:7-8,11,23-24).

The imputation of righteousness lies at the heart of the biblical doctrine of salvation. This righteousness is seen in Christ who purchased redemption. God grants righteousness to those who have faith in Christ (Rom. 1:17; 3:21-26; 10:3; 2 Cor. 5:21; Phil. 3:9). This righteousness imputed or reckoned to believers is, strictly speaking, an alien righteousness. It is not the believer's own righteousness but God's righteousness imputed to the believer. So, as Luther said, believers are simultaneously righteous and sinful.

Not only is the imputation of God's righteousness to the believer taught in Scripture, but the Bible in some sense implies that Adam's sin was imputed to humankind (Rom. 5:12-21; 1 Cor. 15:21-22). Likewise, it is taught that the sins of humanity were imputed to Jesus Christ (2 Cor. 5:21), although the exact nature of this divine imputation remains a mystery. The matter has been intensely debated in church history since the time of Augustine (A.D. 354–440). Nevertheless, for a consistent biblical witness, it must be maintained that in Adam God judged the whole human race guilty. Yet humankind has not merely been declared guilty; each human has acted out his or her guilt. More importantly, it is impossible for sinners to be righteous in God's sight apart from the gift of righteousness graciously granted to them in Christ through faith.

David S. Dockery

IMRAH (Ĭm´ ra) Personal name meaning "he is obstinate." Member of tribe of Asher (1 Chron. 7:36).

IMRI (Ĭm´ rī) Short form of personal name "Amariah" meaning "Yah has spoken." **1.** Ancestor of clan from tribe of Judah living in Jerusalem after the return from exile (1 Chron. 9:4). **2.** Father of Zaccur, who helped Nehemiah rebuild Jerusalem's wall (Neh. 3:2).

INCANTATIONS Chants used by magicians to control evil spirits and thus heal the sick or afflict enemies. No Palestinian incantations survive from the biblical period. Babylonian incantations had three parts: (1) an invocation of the names of the great gods, (2) identification of the spirit causing the illness, and (3) the call for the demon to leave. Compare Acts 19:13 where Jewish exorcists invoked the superior name of Jesus. Mosaic law prohibited the casting of spells (Deut.

18:10-11). The complaint that the wicked are like a snake, immune to the cunning enchanter perhaps refers to the futility of incantations (Ps. 58:3-5). The Babylonians hoped to gain success and terrorize their enemies by means of incantations (Isa. 47:12). Isaiah warned their incantations would be of no avail (47:9). The tongue muttering wickedness perhaps refers to incantations (Isa. 59:3). The books of magic of Acts 19:19 were likely collections of incantations. See *Blessing and Cursing; Imprecation; Divination and Magic.*

INCARNATION God's becoming human; the union of divinity and humanity in Jesus of Nazareth.

Definition of Doctrine Incarnation (Lat. *incarnatio*, being or taking flesh), while a biblical idea, is not a biblical term. Its Christian use derives from the Latin version of John 1:14 and appears repeatedly in Latin Christian authors from about A.D. 300 onward.

As a biblical teaching, incarnation refers to the affirmation that God, in one of the modes of His existence as Trinity and without in any way ceasing to be the one God, has revealed Himself to humanity for its salvation by becoming human. Jesus, the Man from Nazareth, is the incarnate Word or Son of God, the focus of the God-human encounter. As the God-Man, He mediates God to humans; as the Man-God, He represents humans to God. By faith-union with Him, men and women, as adopted children of God, participate in His filial relation to God as Father.

The Humanity of Jesus The angel of the Lord, in a prophecy of Jesus' birth, plainly stated the purpose of the incarnation: "[Mary] will give birth to a son, and you are to name Him Jesus, because He will save His people from their sins" (Matt. 1:21 HCSB; cp. Luke 19:10; John 3:17; 1 Tim. 1:15). The liberation of humanity from everything that would prevent relationship with God as Father requires incarnation. The biblical materials related to incarnation, though not systematically arranged, portray Jesus as the One who accomplished the mission of salvation because He was the One in whom both full divinity and full humanity were present.

Jesus referred to Himself as a man (John 8:40), and the witnesses in the NT recognized Him as fully human. (For example, Peter, in his sermon at Pentecost, declared that Jesus is "a man pointed out to you by God," Acts 2:22 HCSB). That the Word was made flesh is the crux of the central passage on incarnation in the NT (John 1:14). The respective genealogies of Jesus serve as testimonies to His natural human descent (Matt. 1:1-17; Luke 3:23-37). In addition, Jesus attributed to Himself such normal human elements as body and soul (Matt. 26:26,28,38). He grew and developed along the lines of normal human development (Luke 2:40). During His earthly ministry, Jesus displayed common physiological needs: He experienced fatigue (John 4:6); His body required sleep (Matt. 8:24), food (Matt. 4:2; 21:18), and water (John 19:28). Human emotional characteristics accompanied the physical ones: Jesus expressed joy (John 15:11) and sorrow (Matt. 26:37); He showed compassion (Matt. 9:36) and love (John 11:5); and He was moved to righteous indignation (Mark 3:5).

A proper understanding of the events preceding and including His death requires an affirmation of His full humanity. In the garden, He prayed for emotional and physical strength to face the critical hours that lay ahead. He perspired as one under great physical strain (Luke 22:43-44). He died a real death (Mark 15:37; John 19:30). When a spear was thrust into His side, both blood and water poured from His body (John 19:34). Jesus thought of Himself as human, and those who witnessed His birth, maturation, ministry, and death experienced Him as fully human.

Although Jesus was fully human in every sense of the word, His was a perfect humanity—distinct and unique. His miraculous conception highlights distinctiveness and originality of His humanity. Jesus was supernaturally conceived, being born of a virgin (Luke 1:26-35). To be sure, the Bible records other miraculous births such as those of Isaac (Gen. 21:1-2) and John the Baptist (Luke 1:57), but none attained to the miraculous heights of a human being supernaturally conceived and born of a virgin.

The NT also attests to the sinless character of Jesus. He, Himself, asked the question, "Who among you can convict Me of sin?" (John 8:46 HCSB). Paul declared, God "made the One who did not know sin to be sin for us" (2 Cor. 5:21 HCSB). The writer of Hebrews held that Christ was "without sin" (4:15). The NT presents Jesus as a man, fully human, and as a unique man, the ideal human.

The Deity of Jesus Paul, in a statement on the supremacy of Christ, asserted, "Because all the fullness was pleased to dwell in Him" (Col. 1:19 HCSB; cp. John 20:28; Titus 2:13). Jesus was aware of His divine status (John 10:30; 12:44-45; 14:9). With the "I am" sayings, He equated Himself with the God who appeared to Moses in the burning bush (Exod. 3:14). The assertion of the NT is that Jesus was God (John 6:51; 8:58; 10:7,11; 11:25; 14:6; 15:1).

The Bible affirms the preexistence of Jesus: "In the beginning was the Word; and the Word was with God, and the Word was God. He was with God in the beginning" (John 1:1-2 HCSB; 1:15; 8:58; 17:5; Phil. 2:5-11). Jesus realized accomplishments and claimed authority ascribed only to divinity. He forgave sins (Matt. 9:6) and sent others to do His bidding, claiming all authority "in heaven and on earth" (Matt. 28:18-20 HCSB). The central proclamation of the gospel is that He is the only way to eternal life, a status held by deity alone (John 3:36; 14:6; cp. Acts 4:12; Rom. 10:9). The NT pictures Him as worthy of honor and worship due only to deity (John 5:23; Heb. 1:6; Phil. 2:10-11; Rev. 5:12). He is the Agent of creation (John 1:3) and the Mediator of providence (Col. 1:17; Heb. 1:3). He raised the dead (John 11:43-44), healed the sick (John 9:6-7), and vanquished demons (Mark 5:13). He will effect the final resurrection of humanity either to judgment or to life (Matt. 25:31-32; John 5:27-29).

The titles ascribed to Jesus provide conclusive evidence for the NT's estimate of His person as God. Jesus is "Lord" (Phil 2:11), "Lord of lords" (1 Tim. 6:15), "the Lord of glory" (1 Cor. 2:8), "the mediator" (Heb. 12:24), and "who is God over all, blessed forever" (Rom. 9:5 HCSB). In addition, the NT repeatedly couples the name "God" with Jesus (John 1:18; 20:28; Acts 20:28; Rom. 9:5; 2 Thess. 1:12; Titus 2:13; Heb. 1:8; 2 Pet. 1:1; 1 John 5:20).

Formulation of the Doctrine The problem of the incarnation begins with John's assertion, "the Word became flesh" (1:14). Clear expression of the relation of the Word to the flesh, of divinity to humanity within the person of Jesus became a matter of major concern during the first five centuries of the Christian era. The unsystematized affirmations of the NT were refined through controversy, a process which culminated in the ecumenical councils of Nicaea (A.D. 325),

Constantinople (A.D. 381), Ephesus (A.D. 431), and Chalcedon (A.D. 451).

The Council of Nicaea marked the meeting of church representatives from throughout the Christian world. Its purpose was to settle the dispute over the teachings of Arius, a presbyter in the church of Alexandria. He taught a creature Christology—that is, he denied the Son's eternal divinity. Against Arius, the council asserted that the Son was of one substance with the Father. Jesus was fully divine.

The Council of Constantinople met to clarify and refute the Christology of Apollinarius, Bishop of Laodicea. Apollinarius insisted that Jesus was a heavenly man dissimilar to earthly men. If a human is body, soul, and spirit, the bishop asserted that Jesus was a body, soul, and Logos [lit. "Word"], a man not having a human spirit, or mind. Against this doctrine, the council affirmed the full humanity of Christ.

The Council of Ephesus considered the marriage Christology of Nestorius, Bishop of Constantinople. He held that the union of the human and divine in Jesus was like the marriage of a husband and wife. As a result, the Council accused him of teaching that there were two separate persons in Christ.

The Council of Chalcedon was perhaps the most significant church council for Christianity. It met in debate over the teaching of Eutyches, a monk from Constantinople. He denied that Jesus had two natures. This reaction against the Christology of Nestorius prompted the council to express the incarnation of Jesus in terms of one person with two natures—human and divine.

The mystery of the incarnation continues, and the statements of the first four councils of the Christian church preserve that mystery. Jesus, God incarnate, was one Person in two natures—fully divine and fully human. See *Christ.*   *Walter D. Draughon III*

INCENSE Mixture of aromatic spices prepared to be burned in connection with the offering of sacrifices (Exod. 25:6). The word is also used to refer to the smoke produced by the burning. In the KJV two Hebrew words are translated "incense"; however, the two words are practically synonymous. The incense used in worship was to be prepared according to exacting specifications and was to be offered only by the high priest. According to Luke 1:8-20, Zacharias was burning incense in the temple when he was visited by the angel Gabriel. See *Sacrifice and Offering.*

INCENSE ALTAR See *Tabernacle; Temple.*

INCEST Sexual intercourse between persons too closely related for normal marriage. The twofold theological rationale for the prohibition of incestuous unions is the divine claim "I am the Lord your God" (Lev. 18:2,4,6) and the note that such behavior characterized the Egyptians and Canaanites whom God judged (Lev. 18:3,24-25). Leviticus 18:6-16 prohibited unions between a man and his mother, stepmother, sister, half sister, daughter-in-law, granddaughter, aunt (by blood or marriage), or sister-in-law. Leviticus 18:17 prohibited a man's involvement with a woman and her daughter or granddaughter. Leviticus 18:18 prohibited taking sisters as rival wives. Penalties for various forms of incest included childlessness (Lev. 20:20-21), exclusion from the covenant people (Lev. 18:29; 20:17-18; cp. 1 Cor. 5:2,5), and death (Lev. 20:11-12,14). In patriarchal times marriage to a half sister (Gen. 20:12) and marriage to rival sisters (Gen. 29:21-30) were permissible, though such marriages proved troublesome to both Abraham and Jacob. Scriptural accounts of incest include Gen. 19:31-35; 35:22; and 2 Sam. 13.

INCH A unit of measure equal to a twelfth of a foot. Eighteen inches (Gen. 6:16 NIV, TEV) is the equivalent of a cubit. See *Weights and Measures.*

INCLUSIVENESS God chose Abraham from among the families of the earth to be the father of a great nation, which would then convey God's blessing to others (Gen. 12:3; Gal. 3:6-9).

Incense altar from the site of ancient Hazor.

Incense bowl from the island of Malta.

God's special relationship with Israel (Exod. 19:5-6) was never intended to be exclusive, however. Numerous non-Israelites (during the OT period) and non-Jews (during the intertestamental and NT periods) participated in the covenantal blessings of Abraham. These include the mixed multitude who left Egypt with Moses (Exod. 12:38), Rahab (Josh. 6:25; Matt. 1:5), Ruth (Ruth 1:4; Matt. 1:5), various Syrophoenician women (1 Kings 17:8-24; Luke 4:25-26), Naaman (2 Kings 5:1-19; Luke 4:27), the Ninevites (Jon. 3:5-10; 4:11), a Roman centurion (Matt. 8:5-13), the Samaritan woman (John 4:1-42), Simon of Cyrene (Mark 15:21), Cornelius (Acts 10:9-48), Timothy (Acts 16:1), and a host of Gentile converts throughout the history of the church. The population of heaven will include persons "from every nation, tribe, people, and language" (Rev. 7:9 HCSB).

With one exception, God shows no partiality in matters of judgment or salvation (Acts 10:34; Rom. 2:9-11; Eph. 2:11-14). The exception is that salvation is found in the work of Jesus Christ alone (John 14:6; Acts 4:12). The language which God used of Israel at Mount Sinai ("you shall be to Me a kingdom of priests and a holy nation," Exod. 19:6 NASB) was adopted by Peter to refer to Gentiles (1 Pet. 2:9) who, because of Christ, became fellow heirs with the believing descendants of Abraham (Gal. 3:29; 4:7). All barriers between people based on gender, ethnicity, or socioeconomic status are removed in Christ (Gal. 3:28-29).

INCONTINENCY, INCONTINENT KJV term for the lack of self-control (1 Cor. 7:5). Incontinent (2 Tim. 3:3) means lacking self-control (NASB), profligate (NRSV), or even violent (TEV).

I

INCORRUPTIBLE, INCORRUPTION KJV terms meaning imperishable and an imperishable state. See *Imperishable.*

INCREASE Multiplication or growth. In the OT increase often refers to the reproduction of livestock and to the harvest (Lev. 26:3-4; Deut. 7:12-13). The promise of increase is contingent on Israel's fulfilling its covenant commitments. Increase is used figuratively for Israel as the firstfruits of God's increase (KJV) or harvest. Isaiah 9:7 promises the increase of the government and peace of the coming Messiah. Isaiah 29:19 promises an increase in joy (KJV; "fresh joy," NRSV; cp. 9:3). Isaiah 40:29 promises increased strength to the powerless.

The increase of the word of God (Acts 6:7) refers to the spread of the gospel message. Increase is used both for the numerical growth of the church (Acts 16:5) and for maturation (Eph. 4:16; Col. 2:19). Christian maturity is evidenced by an increase in love (1 Thess. 3:12; 4:10) and knowledge of God (Col. 1:10). Boasting in the results of one's work for God is without a basis since God gives the increase (1 Cor. 3:6, Col. 2:19).

INDEPENDENCE OF GOD Doctrine that God does not depend on another for His existence or for the free exercise of His divine prerogatives. See *Divine Freedom; I Am; Sovereignty of God.*

INDIA Eastern boundary of the Persian Empire of Ahasuerus (Xerxes) (Esther 1:1; 8:9). Biblical references to India refer to the Punjab, the area of Pakistan and northwest India drained by the Indus River and its tributaries. India was possibly a port of call for Solomon's fleet (1 Kings 10:22). Trade between India and the biblical lands began before 2000 B.C.

INFANT BAPTISM Rite of initiation performed on infants born into Christian families, also called "paedobaptism." While there is no explicit record of infant baptism in the NT, it was an established practice in the church by the third century.

The significance of infant baptism is varied among the several Christian traditions in which the rite is observed. In some traditions, such as Roman Catholicism and Eastern Orthodoxy, it is held that baptism provides cleansing from sin. Many Protestant Reformers maintained the practice of infant baptism but developed a baptismal theology centered more on the covenantal significance of the rite.

There are a few arguments offered by paedobaptists in defense of the practice. First, household baptisms (Acts 16:15,33; 18:8; 1 Cor. 1:16) may have included the infant children of believing parents. Second, during His ministry Jesus welcomed children to Himself (Matt. 19:13-15; 21:16; Mark 10:14; Luke 10:21). Third, just as circumcision was a sign of the covenant promise of God in the OT, so baptism is seen as a sign of the covenant in the NT (Col. 2:11-12). Since infants (male) underwent circumcision in Judaism, so infants should undergo baptism in Christianity. Peter's statement in his Pentecost sermon that "the promise is for you and your children" (Acts 2:39 HCSB) is also seen by some as support for infant baptism. Further, the idea that God extends salvation to families or larger communities is evidenced in OT examples where Noah's family is delivered through the flood (cp. 1 Pet. 3:20-21) and the entire nation of Israel is delivered through the waters of the Red Sea (cp. 1 Cor. 10:1-2).

Adherents of believer's baptism argue against paedobaptism on the basis that: (1) the clear pattern in the NT is that baptism is preceded by repentance and faith (e.g., Acts 2:38; 8:12; 18:8); (2) it is not clear that household baptisms included infants; and (3) the NT parallel to circumcision is not baptism but circumcision of the heart (Rom. 2:29; Col. 2:11), which points to an inward spiritual reality based upon a confession of faith that is impossible for infants.

David P. Nelson

INFANT SALVATION See *Accountability, Age of; Salvation.*

INFINITE Unlimited in extent of space, duration, and quantity. Though Scripture does not use the term "infinite" to describe God, theologians have found the term a suitable summary of several attributes of God. God is not limited by space (Ps. 139:7-8); God is not limited by time; God existed before the creation (Gen. 1:1); the ordering of time is part of God's creative activity (Gen. 1:5). Because God is spirit (John 4:24), God cannot be quantified like a material object. God is regarded as infinite in many other qualities: God's steadfast love endures forever (Ps. 100:5); God's knowledge extends to the fall of a single sparrow and the number of hairs on our heads (Matt. 10:29-30; cp. Ps. 139:1-6); God is "the Almighty" (Gen. 17:1; Exod. 6:3).

INFIRMITY Disease, suffering, or sorrow. The KJV often used "infirmity" where modern translations have another term (e.g., weakness, diseases, sickness, menstruation, grief). Matthew saw in Jesus' healings the fulfillment of the servant of the Lord who took our diseases (Matt. 8:17; Isa. 53:4). Romans 15:1 calls upon the strong (in conscience) to bear with the weaknesses (KJV, infirmity) of those without strength. See *Diseases*.

INFLAMMATION Response to cellular injury characterized by redness, infiltration of white blood cells, heat, and frequently pain. Inflammation was one of the curses upon those disobedient to the covenant (Deut. 28:22; cp. Lev. 13:28).

INGATHERING, FEAST OF Alternate name for the Feast of Tabernacles (Booths) (Exod. 23:16; 34:22). See *Festivals*.

INHERITANCE Legal transmission of property after death. The Hebrew Bible has no exclusive term for "inheritance." The words often translated "inherit" mean more generally "take possession." Only in context can they be taken to mean "inheritance." The Greek word in the NT does refer to the disposition of property after death, but its use in the NT often reflects the OT background more than normal Greek usage.

In ancient Israel possessions were passed on to the living sons of a father, but the eldest son received a double portion (Deut. 21:17). Reuben lost preeminence because of incest with Bilhah (Gen. 35:22; 49:4; 1 Chron. 5:1), and Esau surrendered his birthright to Jacob (Gen. 25:29-34). These examples show that possession of this double portion was not absolute. Sons of concubines did not inherit unless adopted. Jacob's sons by the maidservants Bilhah and Zilpah (Gen. 30:3-13) inherited (Gen. 49) because those offspring were adopted by Rachel and Leah. Sarai promised to adopt the offspring of her maid Hagar when she gave Hagar to Abram (Gen. 16:2) but went back on that promise after Isaac's birth (Gen. 21:10).

Women were not to inherit from their fathers except in the absence of a son (Num. 27:1-11).

Before this ruling from the Lord, if a man had no offspring, the inheritance went to his brothers, to his father's brothers, or to his next kinsman.

Because the Hebrew words did not necessarily presuppose a death, they could be used in reference to God's granting of the land to Israel (Josh. 1:15; Num. 36:2-4). Levites had no share of the land, and the Lord Himself was their "inheritance" (Num. 18:20-24; Deut. 10:9; 18:2; Josh. 13:33). Jeremiah used the concept of "inheritance" to refer to the restoration of Israel to the land from "the north" after the time of punishment (Jer. 3:18-19).

Israel is the "inheritance" of the Lord (Jer. 10:16). Psalm 79:1 speaks of Jerusalem and the temple as God's "inheritance." In a broader sense, however, God can be said to "inherit" all nations (Ps. 82:8).

Anything given by God can be called an "inheritance." In Ps. 16:5 the pleasant conditions of the psalmist's life were his "inheritance" because he had chosen the Lord as his lot. In Ps. 119:111 God's testimonies are an "inheritance." In Job 27:13 "heritage" refers to God's punishment of the wicked. Proverbs 3:35 compares the honor the wise "inherit" with the disgrace of the fool.

In the NT "inheritance" can refer to property (Luke 12:13), but it most often refers to the rewards of discipleship: eternal life (Matt. 5:5; 19:29; Mark 10:29-30 and parallels; Titus 3:7), the kingdom (Matt. 25:34; James 2:5; negatively 1 Cor. 6:9-10; 15:50), generally (Acts 20:32; Eph. 1:14,18; Rev. 21:7). Christ is the Heir *par excellence* (Matt. 21:38 and parallels; Heb. 1:2). Through Christ Christians can be heirs of God and "co-heirs with Christ" (Rom. 8:17 HCSB; cp. Eph. 3:6). Only the book of Hebrews makes explicit use of the idea of "inheritance" as requiring the death of the testator, Christ. A "will" requires a death to come into effect, so the death of Christ brings the new "covenant" or "will" into effect (Heb. 9:16-17). See *Covenant; Land; Promise.*   *Fred L. Horton, Jr.*

INIQUITY See *Sin*.

INJURY Act that hurts, damages, or causes loss; the result of such an act. Old Testament law provided two responses to injuries; retaliation in kind ("eye for eye, tooth for tooth," Exod. 21:24) and compensation. For example, if the victim of an assault was confined to bed, the assailant was to pay the injured party for time lost from work as well as "health care" expenses to ensure recovery (Exod. 21:22). If an owner caused a slave to loose an eye or a tooth, the slave was to be freed as compensation for the loss (Exod. 21:26). Physical injuries excluded priests from service at the altar (Lev. 21:16-23). As part of the Hasmonean intrigue, Aristobulus had the ears of his uncle Hyrcanus II mutilated to disqualify him from priestly service (40 B.C.).

The extended use of the term is evidenced by Prov. 8:36 where those who miss wisdom injure themselves and Rom. 14:15 where Paul warned the Roman Christians not to injure other Christians for the sake of food (cp. Gal. 4:12).

INK Writing fluid. Ink for writing on papyrus (a plant product) was made of soot or lampblack mixed with gum arabic (Jer. 36:18; 2 Cor. 3:3; 2 John 12; 3 John 13). Red ink was made by replacing lampblack with red iron oxide. Because such ink did not stick well to parchment (a leather product), another ink was made from nutgalls mixed with iron sulfate.

Pen cases from ancient Egypt with containers in the tops for ink.

INKHORN KJV term for a case in which ingredients for making ink were kept (Ezek. 9:2-3,11). A scribe customarily carried his inkhorn in his belt.

INLET Bay or recess in the shore of a sea or lake. When Deborah and Barak went to battle against Sisera, the tribe of Asher stayed at home "by his inlets" ("landings," NRSV, Judg. 5:17).

INN Different kinds of shelters or dwellings. In the OT the Hebrew word translated "inn" or "lodging place" might refer to a camping place for an individual (Jer. 9:2), a family on a journey (Exod. 4:24), an entire caravan (Gen. 42:27; 43:21), or an army (Josh. 4:3,8). In these passages (with the possible exception of the reference in Jeremiah) the presence of a building is not implied. Often the reference is only to a convenient piece of ground near a spring. It is doubtful that inns in the sense of public inns with a building existed in OT times.

By the time of Christ, the situation is quite different. Public inns existed in Greek times and throughout the Roman period. The Greek word for "inn" in the NT implies some type of stopping place for travelers. At times it refers to a public inn. Such an inn of the first century consisted primarily of a walled-in area with a well. A larger inn might have small rooms surrounding the court. People and animals stayed together.

Inns generally had a bad reputation. Travelers were subjected to discomfort and at times robbery or even death. The primary services that could be depended upon were water for the family and animals and a place to spread a pallet.

In addition to referring to a public inn, the same Greek word for "inn" at times refers simply to a guest room in a private home (Mark 14:14; Luke 22:11).

In Bethlehem, Joseph and Mary could find no room at the inn (Luke 2:7). This may have been a guestroom in a home or some kind of public inn. The reference in Luke 10:34 is clearly to a public place where the wounded could be fed and cared for by the innkeeper. See *Hospitality; House.*   *Paul E. Robertson*

INNER MAN, INWARD MAN Component of human personality responsive to the requirements of the law. According to Paul's understanding (Rom. 7:22-23), human personality has three components: (1) the inmost self where the law dwells; Paul equated this with reason (*nous*, vs. 23); the inmost self approximates the rabbinic *yetser hatov* (inclination to good); (2) the members or the flesh that is responsive to desire; the flesh approximates the rabbinic *yetser hara'* (inclination to evil); and (3) the conscious "I" which is aware of both reason and desire. In rabbinic thought, the law served to tip the balance in favor of the good inclination. Paul, however, rejected this optimistic view of the law. Only the Spirit dwelling in the inner self can free the individual from the power of sin (Rom. 8:2; Eph. 3:16). The Pauline division of personality is reflected in Freud's threefold division—superego, id, and ego.

INNKEEPER One who serves as the host or hostess at an inn. The innkeeper of Luke 10:35 was responsible for providing food and medical care. A Targum (early Aramaic Free translation) on Josh. 2:1 identifies Rahab as an innkeeper.

INNOCENCE, INNOCENCY Condition of not offending God; freedom from sin and guilt. In the OT the adjective "innocence" is more common than the noun. Two roots are commonly translated "innocent." The basic idea of the first is clean or free from (Exod. 23:7; 2 Kings 24:4) and that of the second is righteousness (Gen. 20:4; Deut. 25:1; Job 9:15). Though the innocent are frequently mentioned, the biblical writers were well aware that only God can create a right heart and remove sin (Ps. 51:10; Jer. 24:7; 31:33-34).

In the NT four terms are used for innocent. The first means unmixed or pure (Matt. 10:16; Phil. 2:15); the second, free from (Matt. 27:4,24); the third, just, righteous, or upright (Matt. 23:35; Luke 23:47); and the fourth, clean or pure (Acts 18:6; 20:26). Innocence is always relative to some standard. Paul declared his innocence with respect to the demands of the law (Phil. 3:6). Only Christ, however, is absolutely pure (Rom. 3:9-18; 2 Cor. 5:21). Christ presents believers as holy and blameless before God (Col. 1:22; Eph. 5:27; 1 Cor. 1:8; 1 Thess. 5:23).

INNOCENTS, SLAUGHTER OF THE Herod's murder of all boys under two years of age as he attempted to destroy the baby Jesus (Matt. 2:16-18). The magi or wise men searched for the One born king of the Jews. Herod the Great saw a claimant to his throne. When the magi failed to report back their finding of the Christ child,

Herod ordered the slaughter of all male children in Bethlehem two years of age or less. The Gospel writer cites this as fulfillment of the prophecy of Jer. 31:15. This incident is not mentioned elsewhere in the NT. However, it can be found in ancient nonbiblical documents, such as the *Protoevangelium of James, Infancy Gospel of Thomas,* and *Gospel of Pseudo-Matthew.* These sources no doubt relied on the biblical Gospel for the record.

Flavius Josephus, our chief ancient source on Herod, is surprisingly silent on this episode. Nonetheless, an act of such ruthlessness on Herod's part is entirely in keeping with his character as reported by Josephus. For example, when lying near death Herod ordered that all the Jewish leaders be captured and slaughtered upon his death, thus assuring grief at his passing. Fortunately, that order was not carried out. See *Apocrypha, New Testament; Herod; Josephus; Magi.*   *Larry McKinney*

INQUIRE OF GOD Seek divine guidance, most often before battle (1 Sam. 23:2,4; 2 Sam. 5:19,23; 2 Kings 3:11; 2 Chron. 18:4,6-7), but in other situations as well. A variety of methods were employed to seek God's counsel: dreams (1 Sam. 28:6); priests with the ephod (1 Sam. 22:10; 23:9-13); prophets (2 Kings 3:11); and direct consultation. In the early history of Israel, priests were consulted for divine counsel (Judg. 18:14,17; 1 Sam. 22:10). The priests discerned God's will by the sacred lots, the Urim and Thummim (Num. 27:21; 1 Sam. 14:36-42). Since these lots apparently were kept in a pouch in the priest's ephod (Exod. 28:30), references to inquiring of the ephod likely refer to the lots (1 Sam. 23:9-13; 30:8). Prophets sometimes used music as an aid to achieve an ecstatic state in which God's will could be discerned (2 Kings 3:15; 1 Sam. 10:5-6). Prophets frequently took the initiative to announce God's will when no consultation was requested. With the rise of the synagogue, direct inquiring by prayer became the primary means of ascertaining the divine will.

Not all methods of inquiring of God were looked upon with favor. The Danites consulted a Levite in charge of Micah's sanctuary (Judg. 18:5-6,14). The method used by the Levite to ascertain the divine will is not clear. The sanctuary contained an ephod, a cast idol, and teraphim (household gods), any of which might have been consulted. Such shrines were regarded as one

I

example of the evil that resulted when there was no king and "every man did what was right in his own eyes" (Judg. 17:6 NASB). Other methods of discerning God's will rejected by the biblical writers include: consulting mediums (Deut. 18:10-11; 1 Sam. 28:3,7; Isa. 8:19), consulting teraphim (Judg. 17:5; 18:13-20; Hos. 3:4; Zech. 10:2), and consulting pagan deities (Baal-zebub, 2 Kings 1:2-3,16; Malcham or Milcom, Zeph. 1:5). See *Ephod; Lots; Milcom; Necromancy; Prophets, Prophecy; Teraphim; Urim and Thummim.*   *Chris Church*

INSANITY Mental illness. See *Diseases*.

INSCRIPTION Words or letters carved, engraved, or printed on a surface (Mark 15:26; Luke 23:38; superscription, KJV). Pilate likely intended the inscription above the cross in a derogatory sense: "See the defeated King of the Jews." According to John 19:21, the Jewish leadership found the inscription offensive. The Gospel writers saw in Pilate's mockery the truth about Jesus who in His suffering and death fulfilled His messianic role.

INSECTS Air-breathing arthropods which make up the class *Hexapoda*. Representatives are found on land and in water. They have three distinct body parts (head, thorax, and abdomen) as well as three pair of legs, one pair of antennae, and usually one or two pairs of wings. Fossil studies have shown that insects are among the most ancient of the animals. Their persistence demonstrates their ability to survive under the most difficult conditions. Today insects are the most widely distributed of all the animals. Though their numbers are limited in the Polar Regions, insects abound in the tropics and temperate regions. Their primary food is green plants, and they are found almost everywhere that a food source is available.

Insects are characterized by their ability to move about. Stimuli such as food, temperature, humidity, and change of season may initiate movement. Not only are insects mobile, but they are also migratory. Migration is usually a seasonal phenomenon. Many insects, such as the monarch butterfly, have an annual migration similar to some birds.

Insects comprise the largest number of species in the animal kingdom, numbering in the millions. They are abundant in population, as well as in species. This is due, in part, to the fact that insects lay enormous numbers of eggs. The average number of eggs laid by an insect is from 100 to 150, though the queen termite can lay 60 eggs per second until several million are produced. The short life cycle of insects also contributes to their great numbers. Most mature within a year. Others such as the red mite may have several generations in one season.

Some insects are characterized by specialized methods of reproducing. Polyembryony is a process by which hundreds of offspring can be produced from a single egg. Some species are able to reproduce with no mate, a function known as parthenogenesis.

Insects are among the most injurious of the classes of the animal kingdom. Most everything that man grows or manufactures is susceptible to the ravages of insects. Most insects feed on plants, causing much damage to agricultural products. Many attack man and other animals, as well as woodwork, wool, and clothing. Insects also transmit diseases such as malaria, the plague, and typhoid. However, some insects are beneficial, producing honey, wax, silk, pigments, and tannins. They are also a substantial food source for other animals, including man. Other insects are scavengers, helping to dispose of decaying flesh. The pollination of plants is another benefit provided by insects.

Insects occupy a prominent place among the animals named in the Bible. At least six orders are mentioned.

Hymenoptera These creatures generally have four wings. The female usually has a stinger as well as an ovipositor, or egg-laying organ, at the tip of the abdomen. Many of the species are social creatures.

Ants live in communities, sometimes as large as one-half million individuals. The nest is a maze of tunnels, showing much less planning than the nests of the wasps and bees. Young ants do not develop inside individual cells but are carried about in the nest. The workers are female, having neither wings nor the ability to reproduce. The queen and males have wings. Females are produced from fertilized eggs while males are born of unfertilized eggs. Ants are known to domesticate and enslave other insects, such as aphids and other ants. They also practice agriculture and conduct war on other ants.

The ant (Hb. *nemalah*) appears only in the book of Proverbs. Prov. 6:6-8 praises her as the supreme example of industry. The ant's wisdom and ability to provide food though "not a strong people" (HCSB) is noted in Prov. 30:25.

Bees have been domesticated for centuries. Herodotus, a Greek historian, wrote of how Egyptian beekeepers moved their hives according to the change of seasons. A beehive may contain 50,000 or more bees. Bees eat pollen and produce a wax that is used to build their combs and nests. A peculiar characteristic of bees and many of their relatives is their ability to determine the sex of their offspring. To do this, the queen bee stores in her body sperm received soon after she hatched. When she lays eggs, she releases one sperm cell for each egg she lays if females are needed. Males develop from eggs that have not been fertilized.

Bees (*devorah*) are mentioned several times in the OT. They were noted for their antagonism, and armies were compared to swarms of bees (Deut. 1:44). The bee gained fame in the story of Samson, for he ate honey from the carcass of a lion and later tested the Philistines with a riddle concerning the incident (Judg. 14:5-18). The bee also is referred to in Ps. 118:12 and Isa. 7:18.

Wasps and hornets (*tsir'ah*) are generally social creatures but to a lesser extent than bees

and ants. They construct nests by scraping dead wood and making a pulp that is used to form paper. The nest, like that of the bee, is made up of individual cells in the shape of a hexagon. Hornets are found in the OT. The Hebrew word may refer also to wasps and yellow jackets, but the precise Hebrew meaning is not known. "Hornet" comes from the earliest Greek translation. Some think the Hebrew word is a more general term for "terror" or "destruction." These insects are encountered in Exod. 23:28; Deut. 7:20; and Josh. 24:12. They were recognized for their venomous stings and were God's instruments for driving Israel's enemies out of Canaan. The reference could be to the hornet as traditional symbol of Egypt or as a symbol of God's terrifying Israel's enemies. The emphasis is on God's powerful action to give Israel the land.

Lepidoptera: *Butterflies and Moths* This order is divided into two groups: moths that generally fly at night and butterflies that are day fliers. Moths usually have feathery antennae while butterflies have hairlike or "clubbed" ones. The adults feed primarily on nectar. Larvae are called caterpillars and are plant feeders. Both butterflies and moths are characterized by wings that are covered with powderlike, overlapping

Hieroglyphic inscriptions on a temple wall at Karnak in Egypt.

scales. They have a proboscis or tongue, which may be more than twice the length of the rest of the body. Some moths have mouth parts specialized for piercing fruit and even other animals. While butterfly pupae have no covering, moths spin cocoons.

Moths and their larvae (Hb. *ash, ses*; Gk., *ses*) were known for their destructive ability (Job 4:19; 13:28; 27:18; Ps. 39:11; Isa. 50:9; 51:8; Hos. 5:12; Matt. 6:19-20; Luke 12:33; James 5:2). For people who had few possessions and no safe places for storage, moth infestation could be devastating.

Diptera The majority of these insects have one pair of wings. The adults feed upon plant and animal juices. Many species are considered injurious, to both animals and plants. Some of these creatures suck blood, transmitting diseases in the process. However, many species of this order are beneficial.

Flies are household pests, but they are primarily associated with livestock stables. Breeding in manure, the female may lay 75–150 eggs in the course of a single laying. This process is repeated several times during her 20-day productive period. A fly may lay a total of 2,000 eggs. The eggs hatch in 24 hours, producing larvae known as maggots. The maggots are active for two to three weeks, feeding on decaying matter. Then follows a resting stage in which the transformation into an adult occurs. The life cycle of the fly is relatively short. An egg becomes an adult within 12 to 14 days. Adults may live one or two months during the summer and longer in the winter.

The Hebrew word for fly, *zebub*, includes the common housefly as well as other species. As in modern times, flies were great pests for ancient peoples. When combined with poor sanitation and inadequate medical knowledge, flies could be a serious threat to health. The only clear references to this nuisance are found in Eccles. 10:1 and Isa. 7:18. The "swarms" of Exod. 8:21-31 may have been flies. The text is not clear, since a different word is used. The KJV translators added "of flies" for clarification, indicated by italics. The same is true in Pss. 78:45; 105:31. Second Kings 1 names the god of Ekron Baalzebub. Some interpret this name to mean "lord of the flies." If this interpretation is correct, flies may have been feared to the extent that the people worshiped a "fly-god," hoping to prevent infestation by the insects.

A cattle-biting fly, perhaps the gadfly (RSV, NIV) is found in Jer. 46:20. Due to the uncertain translation of the word, it also has been called a mosquito, as well as "destruction."

Gnats are another airborne nuisance. These insects are scarcely visible to the naked eye and leave bites that sting and burn. Some species fly at night, while others fly in the day, mainly in shaded woods. Others attack in bright sunlight. Some gnats do not bite but swarm in dense clouds numbering perhaps a million. The larvae of some species live in water and provide a source of food for aquatic life. The OT writers knew the gnat as *kinnam* or *kinnim*. As well as being pests, they also were known to be fragile creatures, as appears to be reflected in Isa. 51:6 (RSV). Jesus used the figure of the gnat (*konops*) to teach the scribes and Pharisees a lesson (Matt. 23:24). The use here simply highlights the small size of the gnat. Ancient people would strain liquids in order to remove gnats that had fallen into the open container. Jesus charged the "hypocrites" with giving attention to such details as tithing their herb gardens while neglecting more important matters.

The Egyptian plague of Exod. 8:16-18 perhaps should be understood as a plague of gnats or mosquitoes rather than lice. The Hebrew word used to describe the plague is identified by many scholars as pointing to the gnat. The same is true of the usage of the word in Ps. 105:31. Despite the uncertainty of the exact identification of the insect, the worth of the verses in question remains unaffected.

Siphonaptera *Fleas* are parasites that are particularly fond of birds and mammals as hosts. These insects are quite small and wingless, having a body that is tall and thin. This body shape allows the flea to pass easily between hairs and feathers. The adult female lays eggs on the host or in its nest or bed. Adults suck blood, while the larvae live on decaying animal and vegetable material. Adults usually feed at least once per day if a source of food is nearby, though they have been known to live more than four months without food.

The flea (*par'osh*) was a plague for people and animals during the time of the early history of Israel. Fleas were recognized both for their bite and for their size. Their small and insignificant nature even led to the formulation of proverbs of jest. Two such comparisons are found in 1 Sam. 24:14 and 26:20. In both instances

David stressed the difference in stature between Saul and himself, avoiding a confrontation with the king. Some scholars interpret the plague that fell upon the Assyrians as one caused by fleas, similar to the Bubonic plague (Isa. 37:36-37).

Anoplura *Lice* are found in at least two varieties: chewing and sucking lice. The lice of the Bible are almost certainly sucking lice. Small, wingless insects, they are noted for short legs and antennae, laterally flattened body, and specialized mouthparts. They have claws and are parasitic upon mammals. Both adults and larvae feed upon blood. They attach themselves to clothing, body hair, and bedding. Thus, they are passed easily from one person to another. Lice are also acknowledged as carriers of some serious diseases, such as typhus and trench fever.

Lice (*kinnim*) are mentioned in the KJV in two places. The Egyptian plague of Exod. 8:16-18 is one of dust becoming lice. Psalm 105:31 reminds the reader of the plagues upon Egypt. As stated above, both these occurrences of lice also could be understood as gnats or another biting insect.

Orthoptera *Grasshoppers and Locusts* The flying members of this order normally have two pairs of wings. This group contains grasshoppers, locusts, katydids, crickets, roaches, and mantids. Grasshoppers are powerful fliers with narrow wings and slender bodies. They are known to fly 15 miles per hour and have been found some 1,200 miles at sea. Locusts and grasshoppers are perhaps the best-known insects of the Bible. This group was so prolific that the Bible contains approximately a dozen words that describe them. The numerous words may indicate different species or even different stages of development. Disagreement exists as to the translation of many instances of the words. Thus, the different species cannot be identified positively from the Hebrew words.

One form of the locust (Hb. *arbeh*) has been called the migratory locust, or desert locust. It is remembered as the locust of the plague (Exod. 10:4-5). This type of locust invaded agricultural areas in immense numbers, so that they were said to "cover the surface of the land, so that no one will be able to see the land" (Exod. 10:5 NASB). The Egyptians had already suffered a hailstorm, only to have an infestation of insects that would "eat the rest of what has escaped— what is left to you from the hail" (Exod. 10:5 NASB). The destructive nature of this locust is highlighted again in Deut. 28:38; 1 Kings 8:37; 2 Chron. 6:28; Pss. 78:46; 105:34; Joel 1:4; 2:25. Many references point to the great numbers in which the swarms would come (Judg. 6:5; 7:12; Jer. 46:23; Nah. 3:15). Though the locust was a formidable enemy, it was not mighty in strength. This truth is reflected in Job 39:20; Ps. 109:23; Nah. 3:17. The locust is praised in Prov. 30:27 for its ability to work in orderly fashion while having no leader. Not only was the *arbeh* destructive, it was also edible. Permission is given for its consumption in Lev. 11:22.

The *gazam* is known as the palmerworm, certainly the caterpillar stage of one of the locust species (Joel 1:4; 2:25; Amos 4:9). Each of these citations recalls the destructive nature of the insect.

The *chagab* generally is translated "grasshopper" but is called a locust in 2 Chron. 7:13. This locust also was edible as can be seen in Lev. 11:22. It is mentioned in Eccles. 12:5 as being a "burden." Two OT verses recall the animal's small stature (Num. 13:33; Isa. 40:22).

The *chasil* is called a caterpillar and generally is mentioned in conjunction with "the locust." It has been suggested that the *chasil* was the second stage after the hatching of the locust egg. Others propose that it is the cockroach. Its voracious appetite is the subject of its biblical occurrences (1 Kings 8:37; 2 Chron. 6:28; Ps. 78:46; Isa. 33:4; Joel 1:4; 2:25).

The *chargol* is mentioned only in Lev. 11:22 and is called a beetle in the KJV. It also was one of the edible varieties. Most scholars propose that it be understood as some species of locust, perhaps a katydid.

The *sol'am* is called "the bald locust" in Lev. 11:22 and was also allowed for food.

The *tselatsal* has been called a katydid, cricket, mole cricket, and even a cicada. The KJV translates it "locust" in Deut. 28:42, where it is one of the curses for disobedience. The great numbers of an infestation of this insect may be reflected in Isa. 18:1. In that verse the land "shadowing with wings" reflects a group of Ethiopian ambassadors arriving in Jerusalem to enlist Judah's support in an anti-Assyrian alliance.

The *yeleq* is called the "cankerworm" in Joel 1:4; 2:25; Nah. 3:15-16. It is called the caterpillar (Ps. 105:34; Jer. 51:14) and the rough caterpillar (Jer. 51:27). It evidently was some form of locust larvae and was known to plague crops.

Akris is the NT word for locust. This insect was food for John the Baptist (Matt. 3:4; Mark 1:6). The locust also is used in Rev. 9:3,7 as an instrument of judgment. See *Locust.*

Miscellaneous Insects *Worms* Three Hebrew words and one Greek word are used to describe worms familiar to the biblical writers. The terms are rather vague and do not offer much help in identifying positively the insect in question. *Tola'im* is used to describe maggotlike worms (Exod. 16:20; Isa. 14:11). However, the same word is used to describe worms which probably were moth larvae (Deut. 28:39; Jon. 4:7). A scarlet dye was obtained from the insect, or perhaps its eggs (Exod. 25:4; Lev. 14:4). Other occurrences of this word include Job 25:6; Ps. 22:6; Isa. 41:14; 66:24. *Rimmah* describes maggots in Exod. 16:24; Job 7:5; 17:14; 21:26; 24:20; Isa. 14:11. It is also used in a more general sense in Job 25:6. These two Hebrew words are used together in Exod. 16; Job 25:6; Isa. 14:11. Such usage demonstrates that the meanings of the words overlapped. This is understandable, for the exact identification of species was not the intent of the writers of the biblical materials. *Zochel* was viewed as a worm by the KJV translators in Mic. 7:17, but in Deut. 32:24 is translated "serpent," a translation that modern translators use in both passages. In the NT only *skolex* is used to describe a worm. In Mark 9:44,46,48 reference is made to Isa. 66:24. A derivative of *skolex* vividly describes the fate of Herod (Acts 12:23).

Scale Insects appear only in connection with the crimson dye extracted from them or from their eggs. In addition to the scarlet dye made from the worm named above, a coloring material was manufactured from a member of the order *Rhynchota* known for its red scales. These insects, of the genus *Kermes*, are pea sized and of various colors. They generally are found on oak trees. At death, eggs are gathered from the females for the extraction of dye. The biblical references to these insects include 2 Chron. 2:7,14; 3:14. Some scholars identify the manna of Exod. 16; Num. 11 as an excretion of scale insects miraculously provided by God.

Insects are found often in the story of God's dealings with His people. These occurrences help the reader to understand the life of an ancient people. Insects are a part of the Bible because they were a part of life. Yet the references to these small creatures do more than give information. From them the reader can learn much about God.

God's sovereignty is reflected in His use of hornets to accomplish His divine purpose of driving Israel's enemies out of Canaan. He also could chasten the chosen people with a locust if they should disobey. The absence of advanced methods of insect control reminds us of Israel's utter dependence upon God. The Lord would inspire His servants to use the lowly ant and locust as examples for mankind to follow. The wisdom writers would use even the disgusting fly larva to remind humanity of its mortal nature.

Ronald E. Bishop

INSPECTION GATE Jerusalem city gate (Neh. 3:31 NASB, NIV). The KJV refers to the gate as the Miphkad Gate. The Hebrew word is related to that of Jer. 52:11, so some interpreters read, "prison tower" here. Others translate it as Muster Gate (NRSV, REB) and see it as a place where people drafted or conscripted into military service gathered. Some identify it with the Benjamin Gate. See *Benjamin Gate.*

INSPIRATION OF SCRIPTURE "All Scripture is inspired by God" (2 Tim. 3:16 HCSB). B. B. Warfield argued that the compound word (*theopneustos*), translated "inspired by God," misleadingly borrows from the Vulgate (Lat., *divinitus inspirata*). Instead of an inspiration (i.e., a breathing into by God), Paul's Greek suggests that Scripture is a divine "spiration" (that which God has breathed out, the product of His creative breath). Paul's point, then, is not that Scripture is inspiring to read (it is that), or that the authors were inspired (they were), but that Scripture's origin means it is the very Word of God.

Moreover, the verse is sometimes incorrectly translated as "every Scripture which is inspired," perhaps implying that Paul did not believe all Scripture is inspired. But in the preceding verse, he alludes not to just a portion but to the entire OT as the "sacred Scriptures."

For Paul and the writers of the Bible, the Scriptures are "the spoken words of God" (Rom. 3:2 HCSB). When Scripture speaks, God speaks (1 Cor. 6:16; Heb. 3:7; 10:15).

Theories of Inspiration Historically, biblical inspiration has been reckoned in four ways. (1) The Bible is only inspired like other good books with human authors. This is neither what

Scripture says nor what the church has believed. (2) The Bible is only partially inspired by God. Proponents hold that only the theological (not the scientific or historical) portions of Scripture are inspired, or that Scripture is just a record of God's saving historical acts, or that the Bible contains the word of God rather than being that word. But inspiration ensures that Scripture itself is the revealed word of God, not only testifying of God's redemptive work but also interpreting it. (3) The Bible is divinely inspired without use of human authors. Mechanical dictation theory renders Scripture analogous to myths regarding the origins of the Koran or Book of Mormon, and runs contrary to what the Bible says of its origins. (4) The Bible is divinely inspired because God concurrently worked with human authors to produce the very written message He desired. This classical view teaches the Holy Spirit superintended more than 40 authors from widely divergent backgrounds (shepherds, kings, prophets, fishermen, etc.), spanning a period of approximately a millennium and a half, to produce with supernatural congruity not just the thoughts but the very words of God to mankind.

Mode of Inspiration The Chicago Statement on Biblical Inerrancy (1978) confesses that the "mode of divine inspiration remains largely a mystery to us." But certain inferences can be drawn. For instance, the authors were divinely prepared to write God's word in much the same way as the prophets were made ready to speak His word. "Now the word of the LORD came to me saying, 'Before I formed you in the womb I knew you, and before you were born I consecrated you...all that I command you, you shall speak. ... Behold, I have put My words in your mouth" (Jer. 1:4-9 NASB; cp. Exod. 4:11-16; 1 Sam. 3; Isa. 6:1-9; Ezek. 2:3-3:11; Amos 7:14-15; Gal. 1:15; Rev. 1:10-11,19). New Testament apostles were received as authoritative by the early church in the same way as OT prophets under inspiration (1 Cor. 2:9-13; 14:37; Col. 4:16; 1 Thess. 2:13; 5:27; 2 Thess. 3:6; 2 Pet. 3:2). Peter referred to the writings of Paul as Scripture (2 Pet. 3:15-16; inferred also in Jude 17-18).

God Himself wrote the Decalogue (Exod. 24:12; 31:18; 32:16), and the writers of Scripture occasionally wrote what God dictated (Exod. 34:27-28; Rev. 1:10-11). But normally God used His chosen writers' personalities, theological meditations, and literary styles. Inspira-

tion was not always continuous in the writers' minds (Jer. 1:2; 14:1; 25:1; 26:1). The divine inscripturated message often surpassed the author's understanding (Dan. 12:8-9; Luke 10:23-24; 1 Pet. 1:10-12). Biblical authors were not always aware that divine inspiration was at work in them (Luke 1:3, Luke's historical research). The apostles could write divinely inspired letters in responding to questions and by stating their opinions (1 Cor. 7:1,25). The Holy Spirit saw to it that each biblical book actually has two authors, one human and one divine. Thus the divine superintendence of Scripture guarantees its inerrancy.

Inerrancy P. D. Feinberg defined inerrancy as "the view that when all the facts become known, they will demonstrate that the Bible in its original manuscripts and correctly interpreted is entirely true and never false in all it affirms, whether that relates to doctrine or ethics or to the social, physical, or life sciences" (*Evangelical Dictionary of Theology*).

Inerrancy extends only to the original biblical writings, the *autographa* (Chicago Statement: "Copies and translations of Scripture are the Word of God to the extent that they faithfully represent the original"). Though this stress by conservatives upon the *autographa* is often ridiculed, the emphasis is critical and sensible. Compared to a later copyist or translator, the author of the original text had a supernatural task for which the total superintendence of the Holy Spirit was needed. Only once for all time the text was written. Should the autograph be corrupted by errors, the following copies and translations of it would never be able to arrive at God's revealed truth. Therefore, the evangelical who emphasizes the inerrancy of the original manuscript does not undermine copies or translations, rather the undermining is done by those who deny the inerrancy of the *autographa*. The obvious order of transmission is from the original to copy to translation. Biblical faith, then, must not admit of error in the *autographa* but must be diligently aware of the possibility for error in copy or translation. This awareness has led to careful study of the textual transmission process and the original languages.

Thankfully, divine providence has overseen the transmission of scriptural copies for 3,000 years. The remarkable conserving work of the OT accomplished by Masoretic scribes is well documented, and NT copies abound more than any other work of antiquity, lending great confidence that we have what the apostles wrote. (It is simply not true that use of modern critical texts as opposed to the *Textus Receptus* will obscure or corrupt biblical doctrine. The widespread consensus among conservative textual scholars is that variants in the copies are insignificant regarding doctrine.) English readers are especially well served by an abundance of translations that faithfully make available the Word of God in the vernacular.

Inerrancy is a matter of faith and is not demonstrable by scholarship. But many attacks upon the veracity of Scripture are wrongheaded from the outset by those who insist upon arbitrary criteria for inerrancy. As the Chicago Statement notes, inerrancy is not undermined "by Biblical phenomena such as a lack of modern technical precision, irregularities of grammar or spelling, observational descriptions of nature, the reporting of falsehoods, the use of hyperbole and round numbers, the topical arrangement of material, variant selections of material in parallel accounts, or the use of free citations." Claims regarding other types of alleged errors are often greatly exaggerated. Indeed most Bible difficulties have yielded to the patient work of scholars that can be accessed in quality conservative commentaries.

So attempted harmonization of apparently discrepant texts is the appropriate first response, not the assumption of error. Some difficulties may not yield to investigation unless more archaeological or historical facts come to light. And if problems regarding some texts are not solved, evangelical confidence assumes that were all the pertinent facts known, no error would be found in the Bible. In the final analysis, the follower of Jesus exercises this kind of trust in the Word of God because it is mandated by the example of the Lord Himself.

Jesus' Attitude Toward Scripture Some today attempt to pit Christ as God's supreme revelation against scriptural revelation. Jesus reproved those in His day who searched the Scriptures but did not recognize that they bear witness to Him (John 5:39). But He did not reprove them for searching the Scriptures; after all, the Scriptures alone testify of Christ. There is no other way to know Him. Christ is the center of the Christian faith, and the way to Him is by that which the Spirit of God employs for this purpose, the God-breathed Bible.

The disciple's attitude should not be other than his Master's toward Scripture: Scripture is final and authoritative (Matt. 4:4,7,10; John 10:35) because it is the inspired Word of God. His reverence for and confidence in the OT was stunning (Matt. 5:17-19; 26:54; Luke 16:17; 18:31). See *Revelation of God.*   *Ted Cabal*

INSTANT Brief moment of time (Isa. 29:5; 30:13; Jer. 18:7-9); KJV uses it in the sense of insistent, pressing, or urgent. For example, "they were instant" (Luke 23:23, KJV) means "they kept urgently demanding" (NRSV); "continuing instant in prayer" (Rom. 12:12, KJV) means "persevere in prayer" (NRSV) or "faithful in prayer" (NIV); "be instant" (2 Tim. 4:2, KJV) means "be persistent" (NRSV) or "be prepared" (NIV).

INSTRUCTION Teaching or exhortation on aspects of Christian life and thought directed to persons who have already made a faith commitment. Instruction (*didache*) is frequently distinguished from missionary preaching (*kerugma*). Matthew's Gospel says of Jesus, "He was teaching them like one who had authority" (Matt. 7:29 HCSB). The Sermon on the Mount (Matt. 5–7) in particular is the rock-solid foundational teaching for Christian life (Matt. 7:24-27). Jesus Himself admonished His disciples to make disciples, baptizing them in the name of the Father, the Son, and the Holy Spirit, "teaching them to observe everything I have commanded you" (Matt. 28:20).

Teaching Ministry The church of Jesus Christ, therefore, is a teacher, instructing men and women in Christian faith and discipleship. The faith that the church proclaims must be strengthened by the teaching of the gospel. Paul reminded the early Christians that one of the offices of the church was the pastor/teacher who worked "to equip God's people for work in his service, for the building up of the body of Christ" (Eph. 4:12 REB). The church's teaching ministry has numerous dimensions.

The church teaches about Jesus. The church presents the basic details of Jesus' life and ministry: His death, burial, and resurrection. It helps members understand the meaning of these events for all times. In the early church, the catechumens or learners were those given instruction in Christian faith prior to receiving baptism and full membership in the community of faith. Later church leaders such as Martin Luther and

John Calvin wrote catechisms, books for instructing persons in faith and doctrine. The church is called to retell the story of Jesus in every generation. See *Gospel; Kerygma; Jesus, Life and Ministry of.*

The church teaches Christian spirituality. New Christians are not to remain "babies in Christ" but to "grow in the grace and knowledge of our Lord and Savior Jesus Christ" (1 Cor. 3:1-3; Heb. 5:13; 2 Pet. 3:18). Christian spirituality is the process of growing in faith. In its teaching ministry, the church guides Christians in the life of faith through prayer, Bible study, meditation, and spiritual reflection.

The church teaches Christian ethics. Those who follow Christ must be conformed to His image. The church instructs its members in faithfulness, morality, honesty, and integrity. Ethical instruction is not a new law but a way of life according to Christ's new commandment to love one another (John 13:34-35). Jesus is the ultimate moral teacher and example for the people of God. See *Ethics.*

The church instructs in Christian doctrine. The church teaches the basic truths of the Christian faith. It guides Christians in understanding significant beliefs. It opens the Scriptures to determine those doctrinal ideals upon which the church is founded. It guides faithful Christians to maturity so that its members may not be "tossed by the waves and blown around by every wind of teaching, by human cunning with cleverness in the techniques of deceit" (Eph. 4:14 HCSB). All doctrinal instruction leads to Christ who is the final source of the Christian's faith. See *Doctrine; Theology, Biblical.*

A Teaching Evangel As the church teaches, it also evangelizes. The teaching ministry of the church is another way in which the people of God declare their faith that others may know Christ and grow up in him. See *Evangelism.*

Bill J. Leonard

INSTRUMENT KJV term for a tool, utensil (1 Chron. 28:14), weapon (Gen. 49:5; 1 Chron. 12:33,37), or musical instrument (1 Chron. 15:16; 16:42; 23:5). Modern translations generally reserve the term "instrument" for musical instrument. See *Music, Instruments, Dancing.*

INSULT To treat with insolence, indignity, or contempt. The term does not appear in the KJV but becomes increasingly frequent in more recent translations, such as the NIV, where it replaces such terms as abuse, mock, revile, reproach, or ridicule. According to Hebrew wisdom, the wise person ignores insults (Prov. 12:16). Proverbs 14:31 warns that oppression of the poor is an insult to God. God's prophets were sometimes the objects of insults (Jer. 20:7-8; 2 Kings 2:23). As God's ultimate representative, Jesus anticipated insults as part of His passion (Luke 18:32). The Synoptic Gospels relate these insults (Matt. 26:68; 27:29,40-44; Mark 14:65; 15:16-20,29-32; Luke 22:63-65; 23:11,35-39). By suffering insult, Christ became the model for Christians who experience insult (Rom. 15:3, quoting Ps. 69:9; 1 Pet. 3:9). Jesus blessed those who suffered insult for His sake (Matt. 5:11). Paul was content with insults which are a natural consequence of mission involvement (2 Cor. 12:10). Jesus warned that one insulting a brother was in danger of standing before the Sanhedrin, the Jewish supreme court (Matt. 5:22).

INSURRECTION Rebellion against an established government. By the time of Artaxerxes (464–423 B.C.), Jerusalem had a well-established reputation for insurrection (Ezra 4:19). Barabbas was charged with insurrection (Mark 15:7; Luke 23:19,25). The tribune in charge of temple security confused Paul with an Egyptian insurrectionist (Acts 21:38). The insurrection of Acts 18:12 (KJV) is better rendered "united attack" (NRSV).

INTEGRITY Faithful support of a standard of values. Terms which occur in parallel with integrity (Hb. *tom, tomim*) suggest its shades of meaning: righteousness (Ps. 7:8); uprightness (Ps. 25:21); without wavering (Ps. 26:1 NRSV, NASB, NIV); blameless (Ps. 101:2 NRSV, Hebrew uses *tom* twice in this verse, otherwise translated "integrity"). Several OT characters are designated persons of integrity: Noah (Gen. 6:9); Abraham (Gen. 17:1); Jacob (Gen. 25:27); Job (Job 1:1,8; 2:3); and David (1 Kings 9:4). English translations frequently render the underlying Hebrew as perfect or blameless. Inclusion of Jacob is surprising since he is better known for his deceit (Gen. 27:5-27; 30:37-43; 33:13-17). English translators describe Jacob as a plain (KJV), peaceful (NASB), or quiet man (NRSV, NIV, REB).

In the NT integrity occurs only at Titus 2:7 (NRSV, NIV, REB) in reference to teaching. The idea of singleness of heart or mind is frequent (Matt. 5:8; 6:22; James 1:7-8; 4:8).

INTERCESSION Act of intervening or mediating between differing parties, particularly the act of praying to God on behalf of another person. In the OT the Hebrew verb *paga* is used of such pleading or interceding (Gen. 23:8; Isa. 53:12; 59:16; Jer. 7:16; 15:11; 27:18; 36:25). More general terms such as *palal*, "pray," or *chalah*, "appease," are also sometimes translated "intercede" (1 Sam. 7:5; 1 Kings 13:6). In the NT the Greek term is *entungkano* and its derivatives (Rom. 8:26-27,34; 1 Tim. 2:1; Heb. 7:25).

Old Testament Many OT characters noted for their faith are also noted for their intercessory prayer. Abraham asked God not to destroy Sodom in order to save his nephew Lot. He called on the righteous character of God, asking if God would "kill the righteous with the wicked" (Gen. 18:25). In so doing, Abraham acknowledged that he was not worthy to lay such claims before the holy God (v. 27). Abraham also interceded for Abimelech, fulfilling a prophetic function and bringing healing (Gen. 20:7,17).

Moses intervened between God and Pharaoh as he tried to get permission for the people to leave Egypt (for example, Exod. 8:8). At Sinai the people asked Moses to represent them before God since they feared to approach the awesome God (Exod. 20:19). After the people built the golden calf, Moses prayed for God's mercy, calling on God to remember His reputation among the nations and His promises to the patriarchs. As a result, God relented (Exod. 32:11-14). Through intercessory prayer Moses sought to make an atonement for sin, identifying himself so completely with the people that he asked to be blotted out of God's book if God would not forgive the people's sin (Exod. 32:30-34; cp. Deut. 9:25).

The priests had intercession as part of their job description (Joel 2:17; cp. 1 Sam. 2:25). The high priest's task was to make atonement for the people (Lev. 16). In face of the people's idolatry, Samuel asked God to forgive them (1 Sam. 7:5). Even when he did not agree with the people, Samuel took their plea for a king to God (1 Sam. 8; cp. chap. 12). When God rejected Saul, Samuel prayed in grief (1 Sam. 15:11). David interceded all night on behalf of his newborn baby, even knowing God had decreed the child's death because of David's sin (2 Sam. 12:14-18). After taking a census without God's direction, David asked God to punish him and not the innocent people (2 Sam. 24:17).

In dedicating the temple, Solomon asked God to hear the prayers of the sinful people and forgive them (1 Kings 8; cp. 3:3-14). Elijah accused God of bringing "tragedy upon the widow with whom I am staying by killing her son" (1 Kings 17:20) and prayed successfully that the child would live again (cp. 2 Kings 4:32-34). Hezekiah took Sennacherib's letter to the temple and opened it before God, praying for deliverance from the Assyrians (Isa. 37:14-20).

Intercession formed an important part of the prophet's task. Amos prayed that God's Word would not come to pass (Amos 7:5-6). Jeremiah responded to God's Word of judgment on the nation with a plea for God not to be a stranger among those who could not save themselves (Jer. 14:7-9). Lamentations is filled with prayers for the nation.

The Prophet Isaiah looked to a day when people from all nations could come to the temple and make intercession (Isa. 56:7). The prophetic hope centered in the Suffering Servant who would bear the sin of all people, making intercession for transgressors (Isa. 53:6,12).

Intercession was not always effective. God told Jeremiah to forsake the prophetic duty of intercession: "Do not pray for these people. Do not lift up a cry or a prayer on their behalf, and do not beg Me, for I will not listen to you" (Jer. 7:16). Even the great heroes of intercession would not succeed in such situations (Jer. 15:1; cp. Ezek. 14:14). In the final analysis, even the most righteous of people need an intercessor with God (Job 9:32-35; 19:25; 23:1-17).

New Testament The NT teaches that intercession is expected of all believers (1 Tim. 2:1-3). Intercession for the sick is particularly important (James 5:14). Paul in his letters constantly referred to his prayers for the readers, and Jesus set forth the supreme example of intercession (Luke 22:32; 23:34; John 17).

The Bible reveals that the Holy Spirit, Christ, and Christians intercede for mankind. Romans 8:26-27 shows that the Holy Spirit works to sustain the burdened believer, to intercede, to carry even inexpressible prayers to God. Romans 8:34 offers the truth that the risen Christ will maintain His intercession for the believer, being the Mediator between God and man. God accepts a believer's prayers and praises through Christ's intercession. His death secured removal of sin; His resurrection bestowed life on those who believe in Him; His ascension brought exaltation to power in heaven and on earth. Now He intercedes for us at God's throne of grace. Hebrews 7:25 proclaims the complete deliverance that comes through salvation accomplished through Christ and notes that He is ever present in heaven to intercede for those who come to Him. See *Prayer.*

J. William Thompson and Trent C. Butler

INTEREST Sum of money a borrower pays for use of loaned capital. Mosaic law prohibited the charging of interest to fellow Israelites (Exod. 22:25; Lev. 25:36-37; Deut. 23:19). Interest could be charged to foreigners (Deut. 23:20). The motive in loaning without interest to fellow Israelites was to prevent the formation of a permanent underclass in Israel. Ezekiel regarded the charging of interest as a watershed act separating the righteous from those practicing abominations (Ezek. 18:8,13,17; 22:12). Nehemiah challenged neglect of the Mosaic prohibition that had resulted in dire poverty for some of the returned exiles (Neh. 5:6-13).

The "harsh" master who expects interest and reaps what he did not sow (Matt. 25:24,26-27; Luke 19:21-23) is hardly to be taken as a model for Christian business practice. Luke's parable in particular contains reminiscences of the hated Archelaus (Luke 19:12,14; cp. Matt. 2:22). Jesus stood firmly in the OT tradition when He commanded His disciples to give freely to the needy who asked (Matt. 5:42; 10:8).

Many commentators feel compelled to defend the common, contemporary practice of charging interest. Any moral decision on the matter must carefully weigh rival claims: that capital loaned at interest provides an opportunity for persons to escape poverty and that the inability of both individuals and nations to pay interest on borrowed capital contributes to continued poverty. See *Archelaus; Banking; Loan.*

INTERPRETATION See *Bible Hermeneutics.*

INTERTESTAMENTAL HISTORY AND LITERATURE Events and writings originating after the final prophet mentioned in the OT (Malachi, about 450 B.C.) and before the birth of Christ (about 4 B.C.).

Shortly after 600 B.C. the Babylonians captured Jerusalem, destroyed the temple and took away many of the people as captives. After Cyrus overcame the Babylonian Empire, the Jews who desired were allowed to return. The temple was rebuilt. Under the leadership of Nehemiah and Ezra, the Jewish religious community established itself, and the worship and life of the people continued. Here OT history ends, and the Intertestamental Period begins.

The history of the Intertestamental Period can be divided into three sections: The Greek Period, 323 B.C. to 167 B.C.; the Period of Independence, 167 to 63 B.C.; and the Roman Period, 63 B.C. through the time of the NT.

The Greek Period, 323 to 167 B.C. Philip of Macedon sought to consolidate Greece so as to resist attack by the Persian Empire. When he was murdered in 336 B.C., his young son Alexander took up the task. He was only 19 years of age, but he was highly gifted and educated. Within two years he set out to destroy Persia. In a series of battles over the next two years he gained control of the territory from Asia Minor to Egypt. This included Palestine and the Jews. Josephus, a Jewish historian who lived about A.D. 37–100, tells of Alexander going to Jerusalem and offering sacrifice in the temple. Many elements of this story are undoubtedly false, but Alexander did treat the Jews well. When he founded the new city of Alexandria in Egypt, he moved many Jews from Palestine to populate one part of that city. In 331 B.C. Alexander gained full control over the Persian Empire.

Alexander's conquest had three major results. First, he sought to introduce Greek ideas and culture into the conquered territory. This is called Hellenization. He believed that the way to consolidate his empire was for the people to have a common way of life. However, he did not seek to change the religious practices of the Jews. Second, he founded Greek cities and colonies throughout the conquered territory. Third, he spread the Greek language into that entire region so that it became a universal language during the following centuries.

When Alexander died in 323 B.C., chaos resulted in his empire. Five of his prominent generals established themselves over different parts of his empire. Ptolemy chose the land of Egypt. Seleucus took control of Babylonia. Antigonus became ruler of Asia Minor and northern Syria.

The other two ruled in Europe and did not have direct influence over events in Palestine.

From the beginning, Ptolemy and Antigonus struggled over the control of Palestine. The battle of Ipsus in 301 B.C. settled the matter for a century. In this battle the other four generals fought against and killed Antigonus. Seleucus was given the territory of Antigonus, including Palestine. However, Ptolemy did not take part in the battle. Instead he took over control of Palestine. The result was that Palestine continued to be a point of contention between the Ptolemies and the Seleucids.

The Jews fared well under the Ptolemies. They had much self-rule. Their religious practices were not hampered. Greek customs gradually became more common among the people. During this period the translation of the OT into Greek began during the reign of Ptolemy Philadelphus, 285–246 B.C. This translation is known as the Septuagint, often abbreviated LXX. The early Christians used the Septuagint and NT writers often quoted it.

Antiochus III (the Great), 223–187 B.C., attempted to take Palestine from the Ptolemies in 217 B.C. without success. At the battle of Panium, 198 B.C., however, he defeated Ptolemy IV, and he and his successors ruled Palestine until 167 B.C. The situation of the Jews changed after Antiochus was defeated by the Romans in the battle of Magnesia, 190 B.C. Antiochus had supported Hannibal of North Africa, Rome's hated enemy. As a result, Antiochus had to give up all of his territory except the province of Cilicia. He had to pay a large sum of money to the Romans for a period of years, and he had to surrender his navy and elephants. To guarantee his compliance, one of his sons was kept as hostage in Rome. So the tax burden of the Jews increased, as did pressure to Hellenize, that is, to adopt Greek practices.

Antiochus was succeeded by his son Seleucus IV, 187–175 B.C. When he was murdered, his younger brother became ruler. Antiochus IV, 175–163 B.C., was called Epiphanes ("manifest" or "splendid"), although some called him Epimenes ("mad"). He was the son who had been a hostage in Rome. During the early years of his reign, the situation of the Jews became worse. Part of it was due to their being divided. Some of their leaders, especially the priests, encouraged Hellenism.

Up to the time of Antiochus IV, the office of high priest had been hereditary and held for life. However, Jason, the brother of the high priest, offered the king a large sum of money to be appointed high priest. Antiochus needed the money and made the appointment. Jason also offered an additional sum to receive permission to build a gymnasium near the temple. This shows the pressure toward Hellenism. Within a few years, Menelaus, a priest but not of the high priestly line, offered the king more money to be named high priest in place of Jason. He stole vessels from the temple to pay what he had promised.

Antiochus sought to add Egypt to his territory. He was proclaimed king of Egypt, but when he returned the following year to take control of the land, the Romans confronted him and told him to leave Egypt. Knowing the power of Rome, he returned home. When he reached Jerusalem, he found that Jason had driven Menelaus out of the city. He saw this as full revolt. He allowed his troops to kill many of the Jews and determined to put an end to the Jewish religion. He sacrificed a pig on the altar of the temple. Parents were forbidden to circumcise their children, the Sabbath was not to be observed, and all copies of the law were to be burned. It was a capital offense to be found with a copy of the law. The zeal of Antiochus to destroy Judaism was a major factor in its salvation.

Jewish Independence, 167 to 63 B.C. Resistance was passive at first; but when the Seleucids sent officers throughout the land to compel leading citizens to offer sacrifice to Zeus, open conflict flared. It broke out first at the village of Modein, about halfway between Jerusalem and Joppa. An aged priest named Mattathias was chosen to offer the sacrifice. He refused, but a young Jew volunteered to do it. This angered Mattathias, and he killed both the Jew and the officer. Then he fled to the hills with his five sons and others who supported his action. The revolt had begun.

Leadership fell to Judas, the third son of Mattathias. He was nicknamed Maccabeus, the hammerer. He probably received this title because of his success in battle. He was the ideal guerrilla leader. He fought successful battles against much larger forces. A group called the Hasidim made up the major part of his army. These men were devoutly committed to religious freedom. They

I

were dedicated to obedience to the law and to the worship of God.

Antiochus IV was more concerned with affairs in the eastern part of his empire than with what was taking place in Palestine. Therefore, he did not commit many troops to the revolt at first. Judas was able to gain control of Jerusalem within three years. The temple was cleansed and rededicated exactly three years after it had been polluted by the king, 164 B.C. (Dates through this period are uncertain and may be a year earlier than indicated.) This is still commemorated by the Jewish feast of Hanukkah. The Hasidim had gained what they were seeking and left the army. Judas had larger goals in mind. He wanted political freedom. He rescued mistreated Jews from Galilee and Gilead and made a treaty of friendship and mutual support with Rome. In

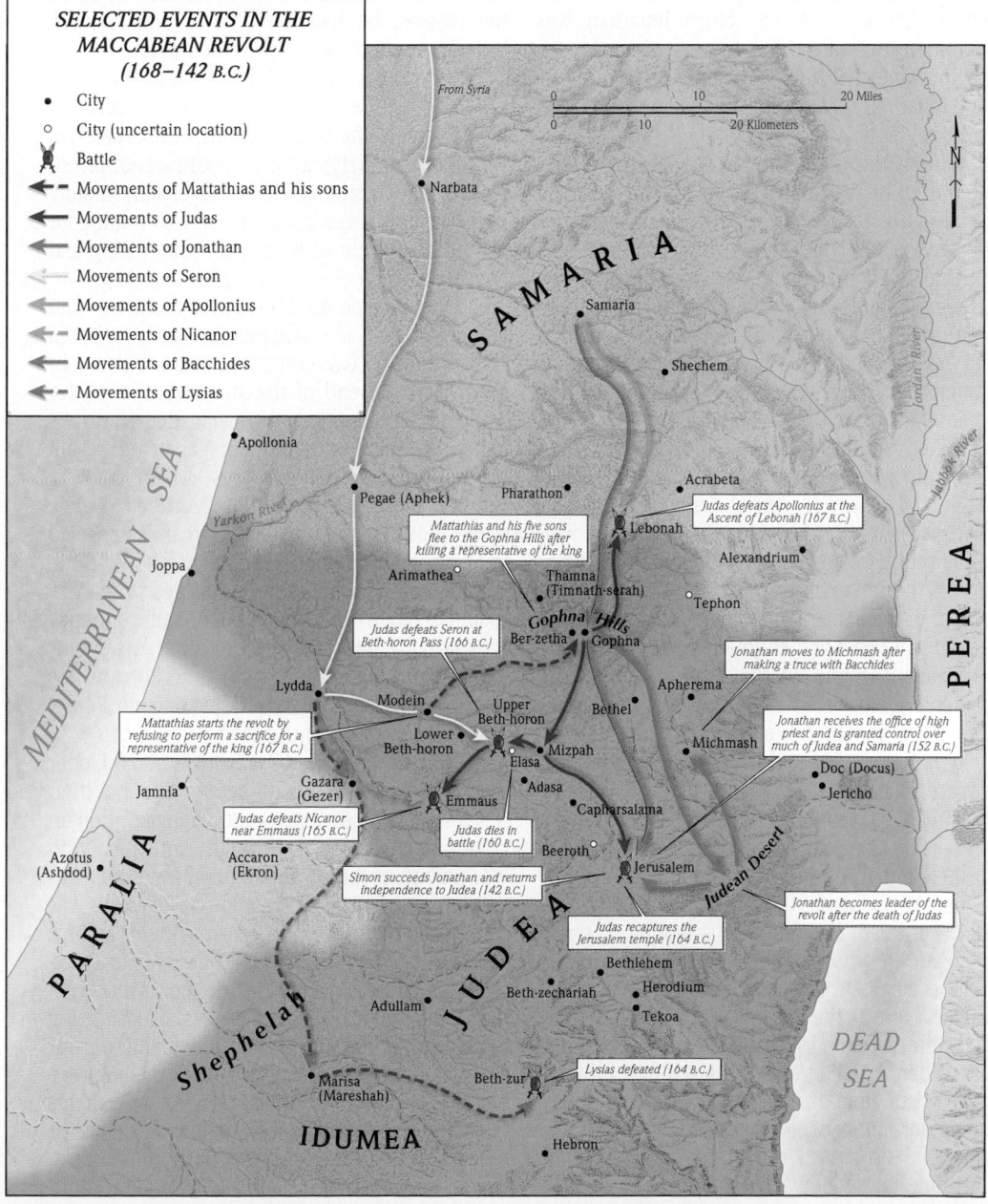

SELECTED EVENTS IN THE MACCABEAN REVOLT (168–142 B.C.)

- • City
- ○ City (uncertain location)
- Battle
- Movements of Mattathias and his sons
- Movements of Judas
- Movements of Jonathan
- Movements of Seron
- Movements of Apollonius
- Movements of Nicanor
- Movements of Bacchides
- Movements of Lysias

From Syria

0   10   20 Miles
0   10   20 Kilometers

N

Narbata

SAMARIA

Samaria

Shechem

Jordan River

Jabbok River

Apollonia

Pegae (Aphek)   Pharathon

Acrabeta

Judas defeats Apollonius at the Ascent of Lebonah (167 B.C.)

Lebonah

Alexandrium

PEREA

Yarkon River

MEDITERRANEAN SEA

Joppa

Arimathea

Mattathias and his five sons flee to the Gophna Hills after killing a representative of the king

Thamna (Timnath-serah)

Tephon

Judas defeats Seron at Beth-horon Pass (166 B.C.)

Ber-zetha   Gophna Hills   Gophna

Jonathan moves to Michmash after making a truce with Bacchides

Lydda   Modein   Upper Beth-horon   Bethel

Apherema

Jonathan receives the office of high priest and is granted control over much of Judea and Samaria (152 B.C.)

Mattathias starts the revolt by refusing to perform a sacrifice for a representative of the king (167 B.C.)

Lower Beth-horon   Mizpah   Michmash

Elasa   Doc (Docus)

Jamnia   Gazara (Gezer)   Adasa   Jericho

Judas defeats Nicanor near Emmaus (165 B.C.)   Emmaus

Caphar salama

Azotus (Ashdod)   Accaron (Ekron)   Judas dies in battle (160 B.C.)

Beeroth   Jerusalem   Judean Desert   Jonathan becomes leader of the revolt after the death of Judas

Simon succeeds Jonathan and returns independence to Judea (142 B.C.)

PARALIA

Judas recaptures the Jerusalem temple (164 B.C.)

Bethlehem

JUDEA   Herodium

Adullam   Beth-zechariah   Tekoa

Shephelah

DEAD SEA

Marisa (Mareshah)   Beth-zur   Lysias defeated (164 B.C.)

IDUMEA   Hebron

I

160 B.C. at Elasa, with a force of 800 men, he fought a vastly superior Seleucid army and was killed.

Jonathan, another son of Mattathias, took the lead in the quest for independence. He was weak militarily. He was driven out of the cities and only gradually established himself in the countryside. Constant struggle engaged those seeking the Seleucid throne. The rivals offered him gifts to gain his support. In 152 B.C. he gave his support to Alexander Balas, who claimed to be the son of Antiochus IV. In return Jonathan was appointed high priest. For the first time, Jewish religious and civil rule were centered in one person. Jonathan was taken prisoner and killed in 143 B.C.

Simon, the last surviving son of Mattathias, ruled until he was murdered by his son-in-law in 134 B.C. He secured freedom from taxation for the Jews by 141 B.C. At last they had achieved political freedom. Simon was acclaimed by the people as their leader and high priest forever. The high priesthood was made hereditary with him and his descendants. The Hasmonean dynasty, named after an ancestor of Mattathias, had its beginning.

When Simon was murdered, his son John Hyrcanus became the high priest and civil ruler (134–104 B.C.). For a brief time the Seleucids exercised some power over the Jews, but Hyrcanus broke free and began to expand the territory of the Jews. In the north he destroyed the temple of the Samaritans on Mount Gerizim. He moved southeast and conquered the land of the Idumeans, the ancient kingdom of Edom. The residents were forced to emigrate or convert to Judaism. This had great significance for the Jews, for it was from this people that Herod the Great was to come.

The oldest son of Hyrcanus, Aristobulus I (104–103 B.C.), succeeded him. He had his mother and three brothers put in prison. One brother was allowed to remain free, but he was later murdered. He allowed his mother to starve to death in prison. He extended his rule to include part of the territory of Iturea, north of Galilee. He was the first to take the title of king.

Salome Alexandra was the wife of Aristobulus. When he died, she released his brothers from prison and married the oldest of them, Alexander Jannaeus. He became high priest and king (103–76 B.C.). He made many enemies by marrying the widow of his brother. The OT stated that a high priest must marry a virgin (Lev. 21:14). He was an ambitious warrior and conducted campaigns by which he enlarged his kingdom to about the size of the kingdom of David. He used foreign soldiers because he could not trust Jews in his army. As high priest, he did not always follow prescribed ritual. On one occasion, the people reacted to his improper actions by throwing citrons at him. He allowed his soldiers to kill 6,000 of them. At another time he had 800 of his enemies crucified. As they hung on the crosses, he had their wives and children brought out and slain before their eyes.

Alexandra succeeded her husband as ruler (76–67 B.C.). Of course, she could not serve as high priest, so the two functions were separated. Her oldest son, Hyrcanus II, became high priest. He was not ambitious. Her younger son, Aristobulus II, was just the opposite. He was waiting for his mother to die so he could become king and high priest.

When Salome died, civil war broke out and lasted until 63 B.C. Aristobulus easily defeated Hyrcanus, who was content to retire. This might have been the end of the story were it not for Antipater, an Idumean. He persuaded Hyrcanus to seek the help of the king of Nabatea to regain his position. Aristobulus was driven back to Jerusalem. At this point Rome arrived on the scene. Both Aristobulus and Hyrcanus appealed to Scaurus, the Roman general charged with the administration of Palestine. He sided with Aristobulus. When the Roman commander Pompey arrived later, both appealed to him. Aristobulus ended up trying to fight against the Romans. He was defeated and taken as a prisoner to Rome. The Romans took control over Palestine.

The Roman Period, 63 B.C. to A.D. 70 Under the Romans, the Jews paid heavy taxes, but their religious practices were not changed. Roman power was exercised through Antipater, who was named governor of Palestine. Hyrcanus was made high priest. The situation in Palestine was confused due to the efforts of Aristobulus and his sons to lead revolts against Rome. While Palestine was successively under the control of various Roman officials, Antipater was the stabilizing force. He had one son, Phasael, named governor of Judea, and a second son, Herod, made governor of Galilee. Herod sought to bring order to his area. He arrested Hezekiah, a Jewish robber or rebel, and had him executed. The Sanhedrin in Jerusalem summoned Herod to give an account

I

of his action. He went, dressed in royal purple and with a bodyguard. The Sanhedrin could do nothing.

Antipater was murdered in 43 B.C. Antony became the Roman commander in the East in 42 B.C. In 40 B.C. the Parthians invaded Palestine and made Antigonus, the last surviving son of Aristobulus, king of Palestine. Hyrcanus was mutilated by having his ears cut or bitten off so he could not serve as high priest again. Phasael was captured and committed suicide in prison. Herod barely escaped with his family. He went to Rome to have his future brother-in-law, Aristobulus, made king, hoping to rule through him as his father had ruled through Antipater. However, the Roman Senate, at the urging of Antony and Octavian (Augustus), made Herod king (40 B.C.). It took him three years to drive the Parthians out of the country and establish his rule. He was king until his death in 4 B.C.

The years of Herod's rule were a time of turmoil for the Jewish people. He was an Idumean. Of course, his ancestors had been forced to convert to Judaism, but the people never accepted him. He was the representative of a foreign power. No matter how well he served Rome, he could never satisfy the Jews. Even his marriage to Mariamne, the granddaughter of Aristobulus II, gave no legitimacy to his rule in their sight. The most spectacular of his building achievements, the rebuilding of the Jerusalem temple, did not win the loyalty of the Jews.

Herod had many problems that grew out of his jealousy and fears. He had Aristobulus, his brother-in-law, executed. Later Mariamne, her mother, and her two sons were killed. Just five days before his own death, Herod had his oldest son Antipater put to death. His relations with Rome were sometimes troubled due to the unsettled conditions in the empire. Herod was a strong supporter of Antony even though he could not tolerate Cleopatra with whom Antony had become enamored. When Antony was defeated by Octavian in 31 B.C., Herod went to Octavian and pledged his full support. This support was accepted. Herod proved himself an efficient administrator on behalf of Rome. He kept the peace among a people who were hard to rule. To be sure, he was a cruel and merciless man. Yet he was generous, using his own funds to feed the people during a time of famine. He never got over the execution of Mariamne, the wife he loved above all others. His grief led to mental and emotional problems.

During the reign of Herod, Jesus was born (Matt. 2:1-18; Luke 1:5). Herod was the king who ordered the execution of the male babies in Bethlehem (Matt. 2:16-18).

At his death Herod left a will leaving his kingdom to three of his sons. Antipas was to be tetrarch ("ruler of a fourth") of Galilee and Perea (4 B.C.–A.D. 39). Philip was to be tetrarch of Gentile regions to the northeast of the Sea of Galilee (4 B.C.–A.D. 34). Archelaus was to be king of Judea and Samaria. Rome honored the will except that Archelaus was not given the title of king. He was ethnarch ("ruler of the people") of these two territories. He proved to be a poor ruler and was deposed in A.D. 6. His territories were placed under the direct rule of Roman procurators who were under the control of the governor of Syria.

Literature The Jews produced many writings during the Intertestamental Period. These writings can be divided into three groups. The Apocrypha are writings that were included, for the most part, in the Greek translation of the OT, the Septuagint. They were translated into Latin and became a part of the Latin Vulgate, the authoritative Latin Bible. Some are historical books. First Maccabees is our chief source for the history of the period from Antiochus Epiphanes to John Hyrcanus. Other books are Wisdom Literature. Others can be classified as historical romances. One is apocalyptic, giving attention to the end of time and God's intervention in history. One writing is devotional in nature. A second group of writings is the Pseudepigrapha. It is a larger collection than the Apocrypha, but there is no final agreement as to which writings should be included in it. Fifty-two writings are included in the two volumes, *The Old Testament Pseudepigrapha*, edited by James H. Charlesworth. These cover the range of Jewish thought from apocalyptic to wisdom to devotional. Their title indicates that they are attributed to noted people of ancient times, such as Adam, Abraham, Enoch, Ezra, and Baruch. For the most part they were written in the last centuries before the birth of Jesus, although some of them are from the first century A.D.

The final group of writings from this period is the Qumran scrolls, popularly known as the Dead Sea Scrolls. The first knowledge of these came with the discovery of manuscripts in a cave

I

above the Dead Sea in 1947. During subsequent years, fragments of manuscripts have been found in at least 11 caves in the area. These writings include OT manuscripts, writings of the Qumran sect, and writings copied and used by the sect that came from other sources. These writings show us something of the life and beliefs of one group of Jews in the last two centuries before Jesus. See *Apocrypha; Archelaus; Dead Sea Scrolls; Hasmoneans; Herod; Pseudepigrapha; Ptolemies; Septuagint; Seleucids; Temple.*

Clayton Harrop

IOB (Ī´ōb) Personal name of uncertain meaning but of different Hebrew spelling than the biblical sufferer Job, a difference not made in KJV. Son of Issachar, according to Gen. 46:13; but a copyist apparently omitted one Hebrew letter, the name appearing as Jashub in Samaritan Pentateuch and some Greek manuscripts of Genesis (followed by NRSV, NIV, TEV) and in Num. 26:24; 1 Chron. 7:1. See *Jashub.*

IOTA See *Dot.*

IPHDEIAH or **IPHEDEIAH** (Ĭph (ə) dē´ ya) Personal name meaning "Yah redeems." Member of tribe of Benjamin who lived in Jerusalem (1 Chron. 8:25).

IPHTAH (Ĭph´ ta) Place-name meaning "he opened." Town in tribal territory of Judah in the Shephelah (Josh. 15:43). It may be located at modern Terqumiyeh, halfway between Hebron and Beit Jibrin.

IPHTAHEL (Ĭph´ ta ĕl) Place-name meaning "God opens." Valley separating tribal territories of Zebulun and Asher (Josh. 19:14,27). It is modern Wadi el-Melek.

IR (Ĭr) Personal name meaning "city" or "donkey's calf." Member of tribe of Benjamin (1 Chron. 7:12). Some Bible students refer to Gen. 46:23 and think a copyist misread the name, writing Ir rather than an original Dan, which looks much like Ir in Hebrew (REB).

IRA (Ī´ rå) Personal name meaning "city" or "donkey's colt." **1.** Priest under David (2 Sam. 20:26). KJV and a few Bible students see "priest" here as a civil office rather than a religious one. Ira was apparently from Havoth-jair in Gilead (Num. 32:41), though some Bible students think

he was from Kiriath-jearim (1 Sam. 7:1). Ira is not identified as a Levite, and his function is not related to those of Abiathar and Zadok, the official priests. Thus some have concluded that he served on David's private staff as a personal priest to the king. Similarly, David's sons served as priests (2 Sam. 8:18 NRSV, REB, TEV). **2.** Two of David's military heroes were named Ira (2 Sam. 23:26,38). Ira from Tekoa was also an officer in charge of the sixth month's "national guard" army (1 Chron. 27:9).

IRAD (Ī´ răd) Personal name of uncertain meaning. Son of Enoch (Gen. 4:18).

IRAM (Ī´ răm) Personal name of uncertain meaning. Tribal leader in Edom (Gen. 36:43).

IRI (Ī´ rī) Personal name meaning "my city" or "my donkey's colt." Leader in tribe of Benjamin (1 Chron. 7:7).

IRIJAH (Ī rī´ ja) Personal name meaning "Yah sees." Army captain who accused Jeremiah of treason and turned him over to the authorities for punishment (Jer. 37:13) about 586 B.C. Apparently Jeremiah was going to inspect the field he had bought in Anathoth (Jer. 32:9). Since he had been preaching about ultimate victory for Babylon over Jerusalem, Irijah thought Jeremiah was trying to escape Jerusalem and join the Babylonian army, then retreat from Jerusalem. The prophet's mission included suffering. Loyalty to God did not always mean loyalty to the government or protection from the government. Both Irijah and Jeremiah thought they were serving God. History proved Jeremiah correct.

IRNAHASH (Ĭr nā´ hăsh) Place-name meaning "city of the snake" or "city of bronze." Modern Deir Nahhas about five and one half miles north of Lydda or Khirbet Nahash on the northern end of the Arabah. First Chronicles 4:12 lists it as a personal name in the descendants of Judah, using the Table of Nations (Gen. 10) and other passages of listing cities by original ancestors in the form of a genealogy.

IRON Metal that was a basic material for weapons and tools in the biblical period. The Iron Age began in Israel about 1200 B.C., though introduction of this metal into daily life occurred slowly. The Bible mentions iron in conjunction with Moses and with the Canaanite conquest, but at this time iron was rare and used mainly for jewelry. The availability of iron was a sign of the richness of the promised land (Deut. 8:9), and articles of iron were indications of wealth (Deut. 3:11; Josh. 6:19). Excavations of Israelite sites dating from the eleventh and twelfth centuries have uncovered rings, bracelets, and decorative daggers made of iron.

In early forging techniques iron was not much harder than other known metals and, unlike bronze and copper, it had to be worked while hot. As improved metalworking techniques became known, however, iron gradually became the preferred metal for tools such as plows, axes, and picks as well as for weapons such as spears and daggers. Iron chariots were a sign of great power in warfare (Josh. 17:18; Judg. 1:19; 4:3).

Older scholars taught that the Philistines held an iron monopoly over Israel. Increased availability of iron corresponds to the period of Philistia's collapse, and 1 Samuel records that the Philistines prevented smiths from working in Israel (1 Sam. 13:19-21). However, excavations in Philistia have uncovered no more iron implements than in Israelite cities. This suggests that the prohibition of smiths in Israel may refer to workers in bronze rather than iron or that for a period of history the Philistines had an economic and perhaps technological advantage, being able to control the iron industry.

Most likely, iron became common throughout the region due to disruption of sources of other metals and to increased trading to the north and over the sea. After 1000 B.C. iron became widely used. David emphasized the importance of taking metals as spoils of war, and he later used stockpiles of iron and bronze in preparation for building the temple (1 Chron. 22:3).

Iron is frequently used symbolically in the Bible. Related to the hardness of iron, it is used as a threat of judgment (Ps. 2:9; Rev. 2:27) or as a sign of strength (Isa. 48:4; Dan. 2:40). The imagery includes other aspects of ironworking: the furnace was a symbol of oppression (1 Kings 8:51), and the cauterizing effect of hot iron was used by Paul to describe those with no conscience (1 Tim. 4:2). See *Arms and Armor; Minerals and Metals; Mining; Philistines.*

Tim Turnham

IRON (Ī´ rŏn) Place-name meaning "fearful." Town in tribal territory of Naphtali (Josh. 19:38), sometimes spelled Yiron (RSV, TEV, NASB). It is modern Yarun in modern Lebanon a mile and a half north-northwest of Baram, nine miles southwest of Lake Huleh, on the modern border between Israel and Lebanon.

IRONSMITH One who works with iron, either one who smelts ore or one who works cast pieces. Barzillai (2 Sam. 17:27-29; 19:31-39), whose name means "man of iron," perhaps served as David's ironsmith. Solomon appealed to Hiram, the king of Tyre, for a skilled ironsmith (2 Chron. 2:7). Ironsmiths were among those assisting with Jehoiada's temple renovation (2 Chron. 24:12). The importance of smiths is highlighted by their inclusion in the classes singled out for deportation at the destruction of Jerusalem (2 Kings 24:14). Isaiah 44:12; 54:16 provide concise accounts of the ironsmith's work. See *Iron; Occupations and Professions.*

IRONY There are two basic meanings to the word "irony." First, irony is a use of words to communicate something different from, and often opposite to, the literal meaning of the words. A famous instance of irony in this sense is when Job told his conceited know-it-all companions, "Truly then you are the people, and with you wisdom will die!" (Job 12:2 NASB). Of course, Job meant the exact opposite of what he said, and this is made plain by the context. The above reference to Job's companions as "know-it-all" is an example of irony. In speech, irony is usually discerned through the speaker's expressions and tone of voice. In writing, however, irony is discerned only through context. For example, in John 5:31 Jesus says, "If I testify about Myself, My testimony is not valid" (HCSB). Later, in John 8:14, he says the exact opposite: "Even if I testify about Myself,… My testimony is valid" (HCSB). How may these two seemingly contradictory statements be reconciled? It is likely that in the first instance, John 5:31, Jesus is using irony, and His meaning is, "Although I am Truth, and can speak nothing but truth, your minds are so prejudiced against Me that you will not believe Me if I testify about Myself." The ironic meaning of His words would easily have been conveyed to His hearers with His tone of voice and gestures. Another example of ironic language is Paul's rebuking the

I

Corinthians for their arrogance and complacence by saying, "Already you are full! Already you are rich! You have begun to reign as kings without us" (1 Cor. 4:8 HCSB).

Second, irony refers to a turn of events that is different from, and often opposite to, what was expected. For example, when Joseph's brothers sold him into Egypt, they thought they were getting rid of their boastful brother. Joseph had told them about his dreams of one day ruling over them, and they hated him for it. It is "ironic" that they one day willingly bowed down to Joseph when he had been made ruler of Egypt. Again, the book of Esther records how wicked Haman built a gallows intending to hang the godly Mordecai on it. It is "ironic" that Haman himself was hanged on his own gallows. It is "ironic" that when Saul of Tarsus was on his way to Damascus to persecute the Christians, he became a Christian himself. In each of these examples there is an incongruity between what was expected to happen and what actually happened, and that is "irony" in the second sense of the word. *Jim Scott Orrick*

IRPEEL (Ĭr´ pə ĕl) Place-name meaning "God heals." Town in tribal territory of Benjamin (Josh. 18:27). Location is not known.

IRRIGATION Transportation of water by manmade means such as canals, dams, aqueducts, and cisterns.

Old Testament The dry climate of the ancient Near East made the transportation of water, often across long distances, a necessity. Large canal systems crossed the lands of Egypt and Mesopotamia, providing the vast amounts of water necessary to support crops during the dry months of March to October. In Egypt, the second highest official, the vizier, oversaw the maintenance of canals and the allocation of water to the provinces. Joseph may have fulfilled this role during his service for Pharaoh. Water was drawn from the Nile River and offshoot irrigation canals by means of a hinged pole with a hanging bucket on the end. Egypt's canal system allowed agricultural use of the highly fertile desert lands that the annual flooding of the Nile did not cover. During the exile of Judah in Babylon, canals as large as 25 yards wide and several miles long carried the waters of the Tigris and Euphrates to field and city. Commercial ships used these

At the second cataract of the Nile River a scene of primitive irrigation with the use of manpower.

waterways to transport produce between outlying farms and major cities.

The irrigation of fields was not widely practiced in ancient Israel. Instead, farmers relied upon the winter rains to provide all the water necessary for crops during the coming year. Fields and gardens close to water sources may have used small irrigation channels, and some fields may have been watered by hand in particularly dry years. Runoff from the rains was collected and diverted through conduits to both communal and private cisterns for drinking water. In larger cities such as Gezer, Megiddo, Hazor, and Jerusalem, engineers and workmen produced huge underground tunnel systems to provide the citizens with ample supplies of water. These tunnels maintained the cities needs in times of siege.

New Testament During Intertestamental and NT times massive Roman aqueducts were built to provide fresh water for the growing cities. A two-channeled canal ran 15 miles from its source to the coastal city of Caesarea. Water for Jerusalem was carried northward through an elaborate series of canals and pools from the Bethlehem area. Along the Dead Sea, where rain seldom fell, communities with elaborate canals and catch ponds thrived by capturing the runoff of rains that fell in the hill country and drained towards the Jordan Valley. Cities in the Negev developed an extensive network of dams to collect infrequent rains, allowing them to turn the desert into thriving orchards and wheat fields.

David Maltsberger

IRSHEMESH (Ĭr shē´ mĕsh) Place-name meaning "city of the sun." Town in tribal territory of Dan (Josh. 19:41) on the border of the tribe of

Judah (Josh. 15:10, called Beth-shemesh or house of the sun). See *Beth-shemesh*.

IRU (Ī´ rū) Personal name meaning "donkey's colt" or "they protect." Son of Caleb (1 Chron. 4:15). Many Bible students think the original text read Ir, a copyist joining the final *u* to the name when it should have been the first letter of the following word, meaning, "and."

ISAAC (Ī´ zək) Personal name meaning "laughter." Only son of Abraham by Sarah and a patriarch of the nation of Israel.

Old Testament Isaac was the child of a promise from God, born when Abraham was 100 years old and Sarah was 90 (Gen. 17:17; 21:5). Isaac means "he laughs" and reflects his parents' unbelieving laughter regarding the promise (Gen. 17:17-19; 18:11-15) as well as their joy in its fulfillment (Gen. 21:1-7). Sarah wanted Hagar and Ishmael banished. God directed Abraham to comply, saying that it would be through Isaac that his descendants would be reckoned (Gen. 21:8-13; cp. Rom. 9:7). Abraham's test of faith was God's command to sacrifice Isaac (Gen. 22:1-19).

Isaac married Rebekah (Gen. 24), who bore him twin sons, Esau and Jacob (Gen. 25:21-28). Isaac passed her off as a sister at Gerar (as Abraham had done). He became quite prosperous, later moving to Beersheba (Gen. 26). Isaac was deceived into giving Jacob his blessing and priority over Esau (Gen. 27). Isaac died at Mamre near Hebron at the age of 180 and was buried by his sons (Gen. 35:27-29).

Though less significant than Abraham and Jacob, Isaac was revered as one of the Israelite patriarchs (Exod. 3:6; 1 Kings 18:36; Jer. 33:26). Amos used the name Isaac as a poetic expression for the nation of Israel (Amos 7:9,16).

New Testament In the NT Isaac appears in the genealogies of Jesus (Matt. 1:2; Luke 3:34), as one of the three great patriarchs (Matt. 8:11; Luke 13:28; Acts 3:13), and an example of faith (Heb. 11:20). Isaac's sacrifice by Abraham (Heb. 11:17-18; James 2:21), in which he was obedient to the point of death, serves as a type looking forward to Christ and as an example for Christians. Paul reminded believers that "you, brothers, like Isaac, are children of promise" (Gal. 4:28 HCSB).   *Daniel C. Browning, Jr.*

ISAIAH (Ī zā´ a) Personal name meaning "Yahweh saves." Isaiah ministered primarily to the Southern Kingdom of Judah, although he was interested in the affairs of the Northern Kingdom of Israel during its time of demise and ultimate fall in 722/21 B.C. According to Isa. 1:1, the prophet ministered under the Judahite kings of Uzziah, Jotham, Ahaz, and Hezekiah. Neither the beginning nor closing dates of Isaiah's prophesying can be discerned with certainty.

Isaiah 6 dates the temple vision of Isaiah to the year of Uzziah's death in 740 B.C. Often the temple vision is assumed to be Isaiah's "call," but the experience is never stated specifically in those terms. Isaiah's temple vision took place in the year that Uzziah died. The assertion of 1:1 that the prophet served during the days of Uzziah is a strong indication he prophesied prior to Uzziah's death. Possibly, the prophet ministered earlier during Uzziah's reign with chapter 6 recounting a particularly momentous event in the life of the prophet but not the call experience itself. Similarly, the close of Isaiah's ministry cannot be dated with certainty. The last datable prophecy records the Sennacherib crisis of 701 B.C. (chaps. 36–37), although the prophet may have continued to minister beyond this point. The Assumption of Isaiah, an apocryphal book, preserves the tradition that the prophet was sawn in half at the command of Manasseh, who began to reign around 689 B.C.

Relatively little is known about the prophet in spite of the large book associated with him. He was the son of Amoz (1:1). Jewish tradition mentions Amoz as the brother of King Amaziah of Judah. If this assumption is correct, Isaiah and Uzziah were cousins, thus making Isaiah a member of the nobility. This family connection would explain the impact of Uzziah's death (chap. 6) on the prophet as well as the apparent ready access Isaiah had to the kings to whom he ministered.

Isaiah was married to "the prophetess" (8:3) and had at least two sons, Shear-jashub, "A Remnant will Return" (7:3) and Maher-shalal-hash-baz, "Speed the Spoil; Hasten the Prey" (8:3). The sons' names were symbolic and served as warnings to Isaiah's generation of God's coming judgment against Judah's rebellion.   *Harold Mosley*

ISAIAH, BOOK OF The book of Isaiah stands at the head of the classical prophetic books both in the order of the English canon as well as the Hebrew canon. The English division of Scripture into the "Major Prophets" and the "Minor Prophets" places Isaiah first among the Major Prophets. In the Hebrew canon Isaiah appears first among the "Latter Prophets," the section including also the books of Jeremiah, Ezekiel, and "The Twelve" (that is, the "Minor Prophets").

Division of the Book Of particular scholarly interest is the question of the division of the book and the related issues of authorship. In the late 18th century, different theories regarding the authorship of Isaiah began to emerge. The issue of authorship is directly related to the division of the book into sections. Different sections of Isaiah do contain different emphases, issues, vocabulary, style, and even historical perspectives. However, whether these differences demand different authors for the book is debated.

Isaiah 1–39 The issues and events found in Isa. 1–39 clearly relate to the times of Isaiah as an eighth-century prophet. In fact, in some of the oracles, Isaiah relates the story in first person (chaps. 6 and 8). Other oracles, although told in third person, refer to incidents in Isaiah's lifetime (chaps. 20; 36–39). The historical background of Isa. 1–39 involves Assyrian aggression and attempts on the part of Assyria to expand control into the areas of Israel and Judah. Isaiah 7 and 8 clearly have Assyrian interference in the region as their historical basis. Assyria is mentioned specifically in chapter 10, as well as chapters 20 and 36–37. Assyria is the major international power in the region in chapters 1–39.

Another indication that Isa. 1–39 comes from the time of the Prophet Isaiah is the frequent occurrence of the prophet's name (occurs 16 times in 1–39). Isaiah interacts with various people on several occasions in these chapters. The clear intent of the text is to show Isaiah acting and prophesying during the first 39 chapters.

A major emphasis in this section of the book is the prediction of exile because of the nation's rebellion against God. The clearest statement of this is Isa. 39:5-7. In the early chapters of Isaiah, judgment has not yet come upon the people, but it is predicted.

Isaiah 40–66 The situation changes in Isa. 40–66. The prophet's name does not appear at all nor is any indication given that the prophet is acting or speaking. Of greater importance is the change in the major world power. Assyria is no longer the emphasis; Babylon is now the power. Babylon and Babylon's gods receive attention

(Isa. 46–48). The mention of Cyrus (45:1), the Persian king who conquered Babylon, presumes a Babylonian background.

The judgment upon God's people for their sin that was prophesied in Isa. 1–39 is depicted as having already happened in Isa. 40–66. Jerusalem had received God's judgment (40:2) and was in ruins (44:26,28). God had given Judah into Babylon's hand (47:5-6). Jerusalem had drunk the cup of God's wrath (51:17). The temple had been destroyed (63:18; 64:10-11). The historical perspective of chapters 40–66 seems clearly different from the perspective found in 1–39. The explanation for this, some argue, is that Isaiah prophesied extensively about these future events; others, that someone(s) later appended what befell Judah as the consummation of what the prophet had earlier predicted. Clearly, the latter chapters need to be interpreted in the light of the events of the sixth-century exile to Babylon and return while the earlier chapters need to be interpreted based on events in the eighth century.

Authorship Issues *Multiple Authorship View* Scholars disagree on whether the difference in historical perspectives in the two sections of Isaiah demand different authors for those sections. Many modern scholars hold to multiple authorship. That is, Isaiah was responsible for the first 39 chapters, while "Deutero-Isaiah" (Second Isaiah), a prophet living during the exile, was responsible for the later chapters. Still other scholars would divide further the later chapters into "Deutero-Isaiah" (chaps. 40–55) and "Trito-Isaiah," or "Third Isaiah" (chaps. 56–66). The perspective of 56–66 focuses more on worship issues, thus some hold to a different author and setting for those chapters. Still further divisions are advocated by some scholars based upon the various genre and/or repetition in the text, e.g., apocalyptic material (24–27), history (36–39), "woe" statements (28–33), servant passages, and so on.

Discussion of the authorship of Isaiah emerged in the late 18th century with J. C. Döderlein (1775), who separated 40–66 from 1–39. In the 19th century, Bernard Duhm (1892) separated the book further by attributing 56–66 to "Trito-Isaiah." Among the reasons for the division of the book were internal evidence, stylistic concerns, and different theological emphases, though recent studies have shown that none of these actually require multiple settings or authors. Still a lingering, major concern for many scholars is the issue of the basic prophetic function, that is, the prophet primarily addressing his contemporary audience. However, in the latter portion of Isaiah, the focus is not on Isaiah's eighth-century setting but on the situation of the exile, an event that occurred over 100 years later. Not infrequently the prophets did address issues beyond their time frame, but for a prophet to devote such a large portion of material to a generation not yet born is indeed unusual though not beyond the scope of God's sovereignty. Likewise, numerous scholars have a problem with the specific mention of Cyrus since he would have been unknown to Isaiah (apart from divine revelation). So, this too causes some scholars to attribute the later chapters of Isaiah to a later prophet who knew of the rise of the Persian king.

Single Authorship View Although many scholars would divide the book of Isaiah among two or more authors, other scholars hold to single authorship of the book. The designation as "single author" may be misleading. Few would argue that Isaiah personally penned every word. Rather, this view holds that the messages themselves derive from the Prophet Isaiah, leaving open the possibility that Isaiah's disciples later organized or put the prophet's oracles in writing. Several reasons exist for the single author view.

One of the arguments for division of the book has to do with stylistic issues. Proponents for division argue that the style and vocabulary are different between the sections. These stylistic differences do exist; however, the importance of these differences has been overstated. Considering the differences in historical perspective, subject matter, and themes between the sections, one would expect stylistic alterations, especially if the sections were from different periods in Isaiah's life. Over the prophet's 40-plus years of ministry, events and perceptions could easily create changes in literary style.

Although differences are present, many similarities also exist between the sections of the book. Several images are used consistently throughout the book: light and dark (5:20,30; 9:2; 42:16; 50:10; 59:9; 60:1-3); blindness and deafness (6:10; 29:10,18; 32:3; 42:7,16-19; 43:8; 44:18; 56:10); human beings as fading flowers (1:30; 40:6-7; 64:6); God as potter and mankind as a vessel (29:16; 45:9; 64:8). Also, the distinctive name for God in Isaiah is "the

Holy One of Israel." This epithet occurs 31 times in Scripture, with 25 of them appearing in the book of Isaiah. (The occurrence in 1 Kings 19:22 was also spoken by Isaiah.) In Isaiah, the name occurs 12 times in chapters 1–39 and 13 times in 40–66, thus indicating a continuity of thought across the entire book.

The NT includes quotations and allusions from Isaiah on several occasions. In each instance, no indication is given that the book should be divided. For example, John 12:38-40 alludes to both Isa. 53:1 and Isa. 6:10, indicating both were spoken by Isaiah. Likewise, the Dead Sea Scrolls sheds light on the unity of the book. Among the discoveries at Qumran was a complete copy of Isaiah. The particular placement of Isa. 40 is interesting. Chapter 39 ends on the next to the last line on the page. Chapter 40 begins on the last line. If a break ever existed between chapters 39 and 40, the copyists at Qumran did not indicate it. However, a break of three blank lines does exist after chapter 33, with chapter 34 beginning on the following page. The Dead Sea Scrolls thus do not solve the problem of the division of Isaiah. Rather, they complicate the issue.

Theology of Isaiah *Holiness of God* In the temple vision Isaiah saw God as holy. The cry of the seraphim depicted God as "Holy, Holy, Holy." The holiness of God indicates the separateness of God from all other entities. God is transcendent, morally pure, and separated from sin. This attribute of God brings into contrast the attitude of the nation of Judah in Isaiah's day. The name, "the Holy One of Israel," contrasts the holiness of God with the sinfulness of God's people. The holy God seeks a relationship with human beings, and in that relationship, God demands holiness from His people.

Sin and Resulting Judgment God demands obedience and holiness from His people. The nations of Israel and Judah, however, constantly rebelled. Isa.1:2-4 depicts the people as rebellious children who refused to listen and obey. These actions prompted God's judgment in 1:24-25. God neither overlooks nor excuses sin. Instead, God seeks repentance on the part of human beings (1:16-20). If the offer for repentance is refused, judgment for sin is administered. Even judgment, however, has a redeeming purpose, with God seeking to restore people through the discipline of judgment (1:24-25). The themes of sin and judgment are echoed

I

throughout the book. The judgment of exile presupposed by chapters 40–66 is the exile prophesied because of sin in chapters 1–39. The judgment in the exile, however, was not designed to destroy the people but rather to purify them.

The recurring theme of "remnant" is associated with the theology of sin and judgment. The idea of remnant occurs often, even appearing in the name of Isaiah's son, Shearjashub, "A Remnant will Return." After the promised judgment in the form of exile fell upon God's people, a remnant would return to possess the land again. The remnant was both a positive and negative reminder to the nation. Although God would preserve and cause a remnant to return after the exile, many who entered the judgment would not return. The severe consequences of sin brought judgment, but God's grace promised a remnant.

God as the Sovereign Lord of History Although Assyria, and later Babylon and Persia, were the international powers who seemed to work at will among the nations, Isaiah pictured Israel's God as the controlling hand behind all powers. In Isa. 10:5-19, Assyria was nothing more than a rod in God's hand used to discipline Israel and Judah. Similarly, God controlled and used Babylon in Isa. 47. Babylon's boasting and arrogance was brought low by the hand of God. Assyria and Babylon thought of themselves as powerful. In reality, God controlled history, using sometimes Assyria, sometimes Babylon, sometimes Persia to accomplish His plan for history.

Faith in God Is True Security Judah and Israel tended to depend on themselves for security. Isaiah's words called for something much more secure. Isaiah 7 illustrates the need for trust in God. Ahaz, the newly installed king of Judah, was threatened by the combined armies of Syria and Israel. God through Isaiah counseled faith. Ahaz, however, refused to trust God, choosing instead to trust the power of Assyria. As a result of Ahaz's lack of faith, Assyrian influence entered Jerusalem. Rather than enjoying the blessings of obedience to God, the nation suffered the consequences of refusing to trust God. The opposing choices of trusting God or trusting other nations occur throughout the book of Isaiah. True security and safety does not lie in military armaments nor alliances with other nations.

Faith in the Sovereign Lord of history provides the only true security (7:9; 28:16; 30:15).

Messiah and Suffering Servant The word "messiah" simply means "anointed." Cyrus is the "messiah" or "anointed" in 45:1. The anointing of an individual indicated the empowering of God for a particular task. Thus, even the pagan king Cyrus could be "messiah" because God was empowering him for service to return the exiles to the land. The messiah concept later developed into a designation for the promised king from David's line.

The messiah of Isaiah is an enigmatic figure. Sometimes this image is a branch (11:1), other times a kingly figure (9:6-7), and other times a suffering servant (50:6; 53:3-6). Isaiah, however, never made a distinct connection between the messianic passages dealing with kingship and those having the suffering servant motif. The messiah and the suffering servant themes seem contradictory, at least initially. The messiah would rule while the servant suffered and died for the nation. From the NT perspective, one can easily see how Jesus fulfilled both images in His ministry. The church, knowing how Jesus suffered, yet believing He would also return to rule, combined the concepts into the ministry of the ultimate Messiah, the Christ.

Outline

I. Prophecies against Judah (1:1–12:6)
   A. Restoration through Repentance (1:1-31)
   B. Payday on the Way (2:1–4:6)
   C. Judgment against the Vineyard (5:1-30)
   D. Called, Cleansed, and Commissioned (6:1-13)
   E. The Assyrian Threat (7:1–10:4)
   F. God's Judgment of Assyria (10:5–12:6)

II. Prophecies against the Nations (13:1–23:18)
   A. Babylon (13:1–14:23)
   B. Assyria (14:24-27)
   C. Philistia (14:28-32)
   D. Moab (15:1–16:14)
   E. Damascus and Syria (17:1-14)
   F. Ethiopia (18:1-7)
   G. Egypt (19:1–20:6)
   H. Babylon (21:1-10)
   I. Edom (21:11-12)
   J. Arabia (21:13-17)

I

Harold Mosley and Steve Bond

ISAIAH, MARTYRDOM OF Jewish narrative elaborating the sins of Manasseh (2 Kings 21:16). The original was probably written in Hebrew or Aramaic and then translated into Greek in the pre-Christian era or perhaps in the first or early second century A.D. The narrative concerns Isaiah who makes predictions concerning the evil deeds of Manasseh. An evil priest offers Isaiah freedom if he will retract his prophecies of judgment. Empowered by God's Spirit, Isaiah resists and suffers martyrdom by being sawn in two. Hebrews 11:37 is a likely allusion to such a tradition of the faithfulness and martyrdom of Isaiah. Justin Martyr, Tertullian, and the Talmud are similarly aware of such a tradition. The familiarity of Origen (about A.D. 225) and IV Baruch (about A.D. 200) with details of the tradition suggests their dependence on the Martyrdom of Isaiah. See *Pseudepigrapha.*

ISCAH (Ĭs´ cǎ) Personal name, perhaps meaning "they look." Daughter of Haran and sister of Milcah (Nahor's wife) and Lot. Thus she was an intimate part of the ancestral family of Abraham (Gen. 11:29). Tradition has tried to make Iscah another name for Sarah or to say she was Lot's wife. No biblical information gives foundation for such late interpretations.

ISCARIOT (Ĭs câr´ ĭ ot) Personal name transliterated from Hebrew into Greek and meaning "man of Kerioth," or perhaps a name derived from Latin and meaning "assassin" or "bandit." Surname of both the disciple Judas who betrayed Jesus (Mark 3:19) and of his father Simon (John 6:71). If "bandit" is the meaning of the name, Judas and his father may have been members of a patriotic party, the Zealots. "Man of Kerioth" is probably the meaning of the surname, referring to town of Kerioth. See *Judas; Kerioth.*

I

ISHBAH (Ĭsh´ bà) Personal name meaning "he soothes." Member of tribe of Judah known as father of town of Eshtemoa (1 Chron. 4:17).

ISHBAK (Ĭsh´ băk) Personal name meaning "come before, excel." Son of Abraham and Keturah (Gen. 25:2). May be the same as Yasbuq in Assyrian sources and refers to a tribal ancestor of a tribe in northern Syria.

ISHBIBENOB (Ĭsh bī bē´ nŏb) Personal name meaning "inhabitant of Nob." Philistine who tried to kill David in battle (2 Sam. 21:16-17). He is described literally as "who (was) among the children of the Raphah." Traditionally, this has been connected with the Rephaim and translated "giant" (KJV, TEV, NASB, NRSV). NIV translates literally, "the descendants of Rapha." Some Bible students interpret this as being an elite group of warriors under a vow to the god Rapha, or it may mean "the men of the scimitar" or sword. Other Bible students use Greek manuscript evidence to replace the unusual name Ishbibenob with another—Dodo son of Joash—but this is a drastic solution. Another solution changes the text to read the name as a verb meaning "they camped in Nob," leaving the soldier unnamed. The soldier Ishbibenob was killed by David's faithful soldier Abishai. See *Nob.*

ISH-BOSHETH (Ĭsh-bō´ shĕth) Personal name meaning "man of shame." Son of Saul and his successor as king of Israel (2 Sam. 2:8). After Saul's death, Abner the commander of Saul's army proclaimed Ish-bosheth king. He reigned for two years. His own captains finally murdered him (2 Sam. 4:1-7). The name Ish-bosheth means "man of shame." Originally his name was Ish-baal (1 Chron. 8:33), which means "man of Baal." The repugnance with which Baal worship was regarded by the faithful in Israel frequently led to the substitution of the word for shame in the place of the name of the Canaanite deity. See *Saul.*

ISHHOD (Ĭsh´ hŏd) Personal name meaning "man of vigor and vitality." Member of tribe of Manasseh, east of the Jordan (1 Chron. 7:18).

ISHI (Ĭsh´ ī) Personal name meaning "my deliverer or salvation." **1.** Descendant of Jerahmeel in tribe of Judah (1 Chron. 2:31). **2.** Member of tribe of Judah (1 Chron. 4:20). **3.** Father of military leaders of tribe of Simeon who successfully fought the Amalekites (1 Chron. 4:42). **4.** Clan leader in tribe of Manasseh, east of the Jordan (1 Chron. 5:24). **5.** Transliteration of Hosea's wordplay between "my man" or "my husband" (Hb. ishi) and "my master" or "my lord" (Hb. *ba ´ali*) (Hos. 2:16 KJV, NASB). Hosea looked to the day when Israel would quit worshiping or even pronouncing the name of Baal and would be totally faithful to Yahweh as "her man" and "her master."

ISHIAH (Ĭsh ī a) (1 Chron. 7:3 KJV) See *Isshiah.*

ISHIJAH (Ĭsh ī´ ja) (KJV, NIV) See *Isshijah.*

ISHMA (Ĭsh´ mà) Short form of Ishmael meaning "God hears." Member of tribe of Judah (1 Chron. 4:3).

ISHMAEL (Ĭsh´ mā el) Personal name meaning "God hears." Son of Abraham by the Egyptian concubine Hagar (Gen. 16:11). He became the progenitor of the Ishmaelite peoples. The description in Gen. 16:12 points to an unruly and misanthropic disposition. Ishmael and his mother were expelled from the camp of Abraham at the insistence of Sarah following the birth of Sarah's son Isaac. The boy was near death in the wilderness when the angel of God directed Hagar to a well. Genesis 21:20 explains that God was with Ishmael and that he became an archer. See *Abraham; Midian, Midianites; Patriarchs.*

ISHMAELITE (Ĭsh´ mā ĕl īt) Tribal name for descendants of Ishmael. According to Gen. 25:12-16, Ishmael was the father of 12 sons. The Ishmaelites were regarded as an ethnic group, generally referring to the nomadic tribes of northern Arabia. The Ishmaelites were not, however, exclusively associated with any geographic area. References to them in the OT are relatively few. The people to whom Joseph was sold by his brothers are called Ishmaelites in Gen. 37:25. See *Abraham; Ishmael.*

ISHMAIAH (Ĭsh mī´ a) Long and short form of personal name meaning "Yah(weh) hears." **1.** Military hero from Gibeon in charge of David's select "30" warriors (1 Chron. 12:4), though he is not listed among the "30" in 2 Sam. 23 or 1 Chron. 11. He does illustrate early support for David from Saul's tribe of Benjamin. **2.** Head of tribe of Zebulun under David (1 Chron. 27:19).

ISHMERAI (Ĭsh´ mə rī) Short form of personal name meaning "Yah protects." Member of tribe of Benjamin (1 Chron. 8:18).

ISHOD (Ī´ shŏd) (KJV) See *Ishhod.*

ISHPAH (Ĭsh´ pa) Personal name, perhaps meaning "baldhead." Member of tribe of Benjamin (1 Chron. 8:16).

ISHPAN (Ĭsh´ păn) Personal name of uncertain meaning. Member of tribe of Benjamin (1 Chron. 8:22).

ISHTAR (Ĭsh´ tär) Mesopotamian goddess of fertility and war. In her role as goddess of fertility, Ishtar was associated with Tammuz, the god of vegetation. Ishtar was sometimes identified with the planet Venus and was designated "Mistress of Heaven" in the Amarna tablets. The goddess is perhaps the "Queen of heaven" of Jer. 7:18; 44:17-19,25; Ezek. 8:14. See *Ashtaroth; Babylon; Fertility Cult; Tammuz.*

ISHTOB (Ĭsh´ tŏb) Personal name meaning "man of good" or "man of Tob." KJV follows early translations in interpreting this as a proper name (2 Sam. 10:6,8). The standard Hebrew manuscript apparently has two words, indicating a common noun phrase. Thus most modern translations read "men of Tob." A manuscript from the Dead Sea Scrolls has Ishtob as one word and thus as a proper name, but modern Bible students still generally follow the standard manuscript rather than the older Dead Sea Scroll. "Man of Tob" could also refer to the ruler of Tob. See *Tob.*

ISHUAH (Ĭsh´ ū a) (Gen. 46:17 KJV) See *Ishvah.*

ISHUAI (Ĭsh´ ū ī) (1 Chron. 7:30 KJV) See *Ishvi.*

ISHUI (Ĭsh´ ū ī) (1 Sam. 14:49 KJV) See *Ishvi.*

ISHVAH (Ĭsh´ va) Personal name meaning "he is equal" or "he satisfies." Son of Asher (Gen. 46:17). He is not named in Num. 26:44, leading some scholars to think that a copyist duplicated the following name Ishvi with a minor variation.

KJV read the text with different vowel points than the standard Hebrew manuscript, spelling the name Ishuah.

ISHVI (Ĭsh´ vī) Personal name meaning "he is equal," "he satisfies," or "he rules." **1.** Son of Asher (Gen. 46:17) and original clan ancestor of Ishvites (Num. 26:44). **2.** Son of Saul (1 Sam. 14:49).

ISHVITE (Ĭsh´ vīt) See *Ishvi.*

ISHYO (1 Sam. 14:49 REB) See *Ishvi.*

ISLAND Tract of land surrounded by water. Modern translations sometimes replace the island or isle of the KJV with the terms coast, coastline, or coastland (cp. Gen. 10:5; Esther 10:1; Ps. 97:1; Isa. 11:11; Jer. 2:10). "Islands" frequently appears in parallel to people or nations (Isa. 41:1; 51:5; 66:19; Jer. 31:10) and to the earth (Isa. 42:4). Often the idea of distant people and places is stressed by the parallelism (Isa. 41:5; 49:1). The Hebrews were not a seafaring people and so easily equated the Mediterranean islands with the ends of the earth.

Scripture mentions many islands by name. Arvad (Ezek. 27:8,11) is an island two miles offshore from northern Phoenicia. Clauda or Cauda (NRSV) is a small island off Crete (Acts 27:16). Chios (Acts 20:15) is an island off the coast of Ionia. Coos or Cos (Acts 21:1 NIV) is an island 50 miles northwest of Rhodes. Crete (the OT Caphtor, Jer. 47:4; Amos 9:7) is an island 152 miles long located to the southeast of Greece (Titus 1:5,12). Cyprus (home of the OT Chittim, Jer. 2:10; Ezek. 27:6) is an island 75 miles long located toward the eastern end of the Mediterranean (Acts 4:36; 11:19-20 among others). Melita or Malta (NASB) is an island located 50 miles southwest of Sicily (Acts 27:39–28:10). Patmos is an island off the coast of Ionia west of Samos (Rev. 1:9). Rhodes is an island southwest of Asia Minor (Acts 21:1). Samos is an island located off the Ionian coast 12 miles southwest of Ephesus (Acts 20:15). Sardinia is a western Mediterranean island south of Corsica. Tyre (Ezek. 26:2) was a famous Phoenician island city.

ISMACHIAH (Ĭs mȧ kī´ a) Personal name meaning "Yahweh supports." Priest and administrator in the temple under Conaniah and Shimei when Hezekiah was king of Judah (2 Chron. 31:13).

I

ISMAIAH (Ĭs mā´ ya) (KJV) See *Ishmaiah*.

ISMAKIAH (Ĭs má kī´ a) (NIV) See *Ismachiah*.

ISPAH (Ĭs´ pa) (KJV) See *Ishpah*.

ISRAEL (Ĭz´ rā ĕl) **1.** Name of Northern Kingdom after Jeroboam led the northern tribes to separate from the southern tribes and form a separate kingdom (1 Kings 12). **2.** Personal name meaning "God strives," "God rules," "God heals," or "he strives against God." Name that God gave Jacob after he wrestled with the divine messenger (Gen. 32:28). Afterwards Jacob was a changed person, limping on a damaged thigh, with new food regulations and a new experience with God that influenced the way he lived. His 12 sons became known as the "sons of Israel," and the resulting nation became the nation of Israel. Thus Jacob's experience at the Jabbok became the foundation for the nation of God's chosen people. See *Jacob*.

ISRAEL, LAND OF The most common name in the OT for the land where the history of Israel takes place is Canaan. It occupies about 9,500 square miles, an area about the size of the state of Vermont, the upstate of South Carolina, or the country of Belgium. Canaan, or Palestine, reaches from the Mediterranean Sea on the west, to the Great Arabian Desert on the east, to the Lebanon and Anti-Lebanon Mountains on the north, and the Sinai Desert on the south. It is about 150 miles from north to south and 75 miles from east to west. The very location of Israel profoundly affected what was to happen to her over the centuries, for she sat uncomfortably in the middle of the "Fertile Crescent" (including Egypt, Palestine, Mesopotamia, Anatolia, and Armenia, or to use modern names: Egypt, Lebanon, Syria, Turkey, Jordan, Iraq, and Iran). This area was the very matrix of humankind, a veritable cradle for civilization.

Due to its strategic location, it served as a land bridge between Asia and Africa, a meeting place, and a contested battlefield for many ancient powers, including Egypt, Assyria, Babylonia, Medo-Persia, Greece, and Rome. To this day it remains one of the most geopolitically sensitive and important areas of the world.

From west to east the topographical features are the coastal plain, Galilee and the central hill country, flowing in a southerly direction from the Lebanon range; the Jordan Rift Valley, continuous with the Bekaa Valley, continuing south to the Dead Sea in the Arabah; and the Transjordanian highlands as the southern continuation of the Anti-Lebanon Mountains in Phoenicia/Lebanon on into the Moab-Edom plateau. It is an arid and exotic land of great variety. Mountains in the north are in stark contrast to the Arabah and the lowest point on the earth, the Dead Sea, some 1,300 feet below sea level.

The Preexilic Period *The Patriarchal Period* Biblical interest in Canaan begins with the call of Abram (Gen. 12). His journey to Canaan occurred about 2092 B.C. He left his home of Ur of the Chaldeans in Mesopotamia earlier with his family but lingered in Haran where his father Terah died. With Sarai, his wife, and Lot, his nephew, he came at last to Canaan. Abram was not a nomadic shepherd tending sheep and goats but rather a merchant prince who traded with monarchs and commanded a security force of 318 men to guard his family and his assets. The names of people and places and events described have a ring of authenticity, and we may be confident that the Abraham cycle is a reliable historical record. Abraham received a promise from God that the land of Canaan would be given to his descendants forever, but the only land he ever owned in the land of promise was a burial plot for Sarah and himself. Initiating a pattern, the younger of Abram's son, Isaac, was the child of the promise. Isaac had twin sons, Jacob and Esau. Continuing the pattern, the younger of the twins, Jacob, became the child of the promise. His 12 sons became the namesakes for the 12 tribes of Israel, but the child of the promise, Judah, was not the hero of his generation, rather Joseph became the savior of his family.

There is no reason to doubt that Joseph really existed. His story (Gen. 37–50) accurately reflects the history of Egypt in the 19th century B.C. Joseph's story falls into three parts: Joseph and his brothers in Canaan, Joseph alone in Egypt, and Joseph in Egypt with his father Jacob (by this time renamed Israel), his brothers, and their families.

One of the younger sons but favored by his father, Joseph was resented deeply by his brothers who sold him into slavery and told his father he was dead. In Egypt he repeatedly overcame great obstacles until he rose to the right hand of Pharaoh. Famine sent his brothers to Egypt for food where they came before Joseph who, after testing them, brought his father's family to live in safety in Egypt about 1875 B.C. The Joseph stories exhibit an overwhelmingly Egyptian context that fits well what is known of this period. Joseph's story provides the explanation for why Jacob's family and the tribes of Israel found themselves in Egypt for the next 430 years.

The Egyptian Period Several hundred years of relative silence separate the end of the story of Joseph (Gen. 37–50) from the beginning of the story told in the Book of Exodus. Joseph's story indicates that Israel probably entered Egypt in the middle of the illustrious Twelfth Dynasty (ca. 1875–1850 B.C.). The Hyksos (Egyptian for "rulers of foreign lands") were an Asiatic people who seized control of Egypt during a time of political instability, overthrowing native Egyptian dynasties around 1730–1710 B.C. The Hyksos established their capital in the Nile River Delta at Avaris and controlled northern Egypt for about 250–260 years. The Hyksos were the people of the king who "knew not Joseph." The Hyksos did not control all Egypt for much of their sojourn but were leaders of a federation of rulers over various parts of Egypt. With their accession the lot of the Israelites worsened. No longer favored by the pharaohs, they instead were reduced to servitude. The Hyksos were expelled from Egypt about 1570 B.C.

Moses appeared early in the new kingdom era, born about 1526 B.C. His parents Amram and Jochebed sought to save his life from Pharaoh's decree, that all male Hebrew infants be killed, by setting him adrift on the Nile in a basket. His basket came to rest at the place where a daughter of Pharaoh bathed. She took the child in and raised him as the grandson of Pharaoh. Educated in the palace of Egypt, Moses received one of the finest educations in the world. Learning a spectrum of languages and a wide variety of subject matter that prepared him well to lead and govern the Israelites after they left Egypt. Likely the Pharaoh of Moses' infancy was Amenhotep I, and the successor who especially oppressed the Israelites was Thutmose I who reigned 1526–1512 B.C. Thutmose II reigned 1512–1504 B.C. and Thutmose III 1504–1450 B.C. Moses' foster mother likely was a powerful woman named Hatshepsut, who effectively controlled Egypt while Thutmose III was still a minor after his accession to the throne. Thutmose III fits best the pharaoh who sought Moses' life when he had killed a prominent

Egyptian (at about age 40), and his successor Amenhotep II (reigned 1450–1425 B.C.) was probably the pharaoh of the exodus, which most likely occurred in 1447 or 1446 B.C.

The Exodus from Egypt—ca. 1447 B.C. The exodus from Egypt was to Israel what the Odyssey was to the Greeks and what the pilgrim fathers are to Americans. Israel's national identity was intimately tied to their deliverance from Egypt in the great exodus. This is graphically confirmed by the fact that some variation of the formula that Yahweh "brought you (Israel) up out of Egypt and the house of bondage" occurs 125 times in the OT.

Israel arrived at Mount Sinai around 1447 B.C. Though various locations have been suggested, the best option for the location of Mount Sinai is the traditional site Jebel Musa in the southern end of the Sinai Peninsula. At Sinai Israel entered into covenant with Yahweh, received the Ten Commandments, and began her first experience in self-governance.

The Wilderness Period—ca. 1447–1407 B.C. About a year later they started for the land of promise but were deterred from entry, first by disobedience and then by God, and did not arrive in Canaan for another 40 years. A remarkable sense of identity and mission emerged during the years in the Sinai wilderness. Also during these years Israel received all the legislation necessary for an orderly society. Good times and bad characterized Israel's wilderness experience. God supernaturally protected and preserved Israel, but the generation that refused to enter the land at God's command died out except for the two faithful spies, Joshua and Caleb.

Conquest of Canaan—ca. 1407–1400 B.C. One of the most dramatic stories ever told about the origin of a nation unfolded as Israel moved into the land of promise. A journey that could be made in eleven days stretched out for a total of 40 years. Near the end of this period Moses died and was buried by the Lord Himself and Joshua, an Ephraimite, assumed leadership of the nation. Joshua occupies comparatively little space in the record. He is introduced as Moses' successor and as the conqueror of Canaan (Deut. 1:38; 3:21,28; Josh. 1). Outside the book bearing his name, he is mentioned only in Exod. 17:8-16; Judg. 1:1, 2:6-9; 1 Kings 16:34; 1 Chron. 7:27; and Neh. 8:17.

Joshua did a remarkable job of organizing and executing the plan for the conquest of the land.

I

Miraculously Israel crossed Jordan on dry ground during flood season. Israel renewed the covenant at Gilgal where all those males were circumcised who had not been in the wilderness. The conquests were impressive, beginning with the miraculous collapse of the walls of Jericho, yet some of the existing people in the land were not completely driven out and remained a source of difficulty for Israel throughout her existence.

Joshua apportioned the land to the 12 tribes according to the instructions God gave Moses, and the occupation of Canaan began. Things went well during the lifetime of those who served with Joshua, but then a dark period of serious spiritual decline began.

Period of the Judges—ca. 1360–1084 B.C. Judges 1:1-29 forms a literary transition from the life of Joshua to the period of the judges. The downward spiral lasted about 280 years. The judges, *shophetim,* were more like leaders or rulers than legal functionaries. The period was characterized by a recurring cycle of decline, oppression, repentance, and deliverance. The reforms never lasted, and oppression came again repeatedly. The reports of the work of the various judges are not strictly chronological and overlapped frequently, explaining how the elapsed time of 280 years is so much shorter than the aggregate total of 410 years for the 15 judges mentioned. Progressive spiritual decline is seen in progressively declining character of the successive judges, until they and their people are much more like the surrounding peoples than they are like a people belonging to the one true and living God.

Toward the end of this period, hope emerged in the heroic saga of Naomi, Ruth, and Boaz, who demonstrate that faithful Israelites remained loyal to their covenant Lord. From this family would come the great King David.

The last of the judges was the greatest: Samuel, a Benjaminite whose mother dedicated him to the service of the Lord. Raised by the priest Eli, Samuel became priest and judge when God excised the family of Eli for its unfaithfulness. Samuel administered the nation wisely and fairly, and stability prevailed during the time of his stewardship. However, the people longed to be like the other nations and asked for a king.

The United Monarchy—ca. 1051–931 B.C. Samuel was provoked, but God commanded him to give the people what they asked for, a king of their desire, Saul, son of Kish, a wealthy Benjaminite. A tall, handsome, and humble man, Saul did not seek power and accepted it reluctantly. But, once in command, Saul demonstrated poor judgment and an ultimately fatal lack of spiritual discernment.

Saul made a good beginning by defeating the Philistines with the intervention of young David who killed the Philistine champion Goliath foreshadowing things to come. Almost immediately Saul became suspicious and resentful of David and kept him close by giving David his daughter Michal in marriage and by making David a commander of troops who reported to Saul (1 Sam. 18). Saul was determined to pass the throne to his son Jonathan and neglected the kingdom to pursue David for years, his reign lasting about 40 years.

David was the youngest son of Jesse of Bethlehem. He served his father as a shepherd. Samuel anointed David years before his accession to the throne, and David consistently honored the king and repeatedly passed up opportunities to kill Saul. Rather than attack Saul, David ran from him for years. As Saul's kingdom disintegrated, David grew stronger and gained a significant following.

Ultimately Saul and Jonathan were slain in battle, and David reigned over his tribe of Judah for seven years in Hebron, while the remaining tribes were led by Saul's son, Ish-Bosheth. After Ish-Bosheth's brutal assassination, David acceded to the throne of all Israel for an additional 33 years, establishing his capital in Jerusalem. He defeated Israel's enemies and established peace for his people. David was Israel's greatest king, described by God as "a man after My heart" (Acts 13:22 HCSB; 1 Sam. 13:14), but failed morally and spent years in personal and family turmoil as a result. David not only had an affair with the wife of one of his most loyal subordinates, but when threatened with exposure, he engineered Uriah's death. His household never knew peace again, ultimately costing the lives of some of his children. David developed the plans for the temple and gathered the resources, but because of his own sins God did not allow him to complete the project.

At the end of David's life, the accession of his son Solomon to the throne was a bloody interfamily struggle. Solomon made a marvelous beginning, building and dedicating a magnificent temple. Genuinely humble, God prospered him beyond his fondest hopes. Solomon was revered

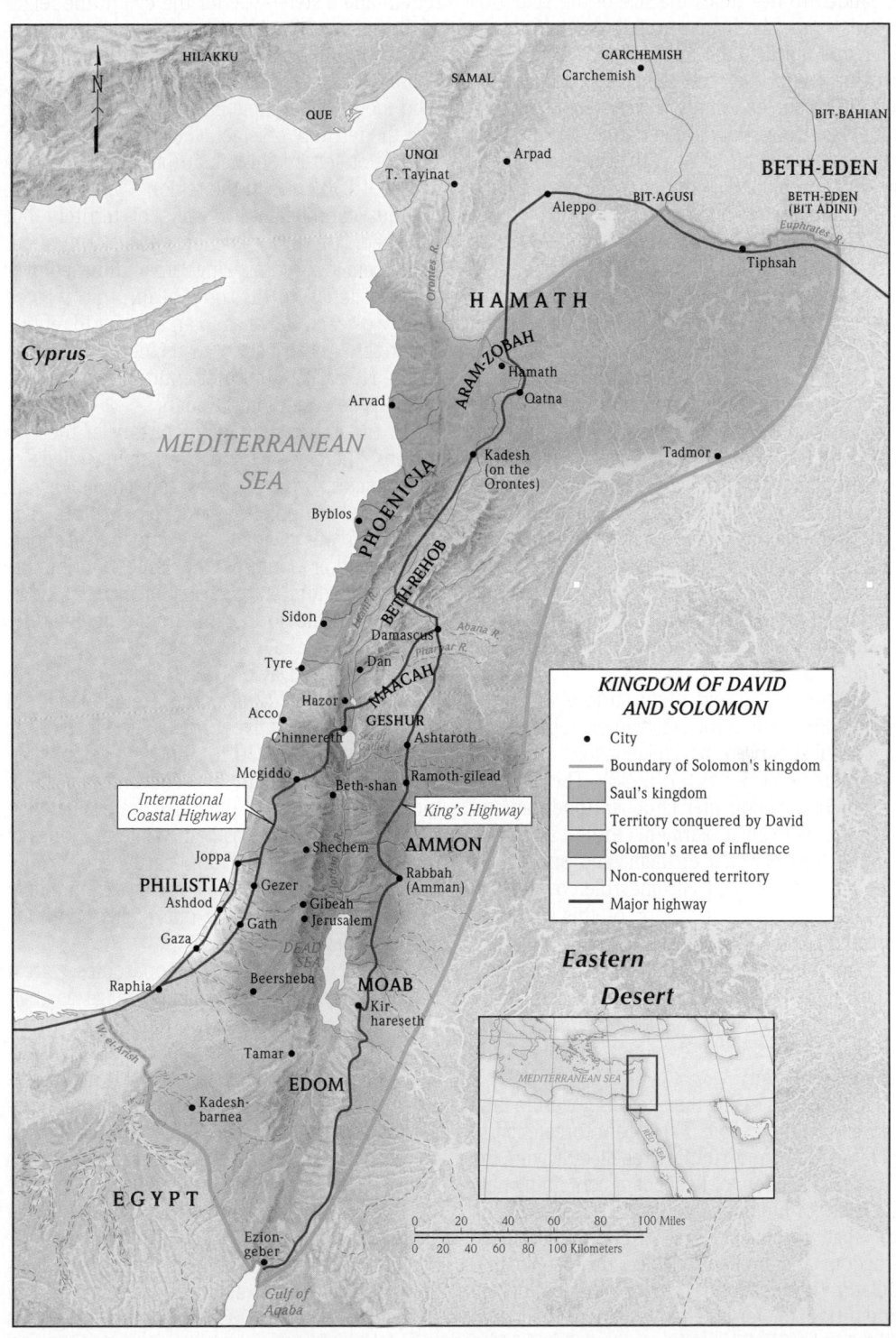

HILAKKU

QUE

CARCHEMISH
Carchemish •

SAMAL

BIT-BAHIAN

UNQI
T. Tayinat

Arpad •

BIT-AGUSI

BETH-EDEN

Aleppo •

BETH-EDEN
(BIT ADINI)

Euphrates R.

Tiphsah •

Orontes R.

HAMATH

Cyprus

ARAM-ZOBAH

Hamath •
Qatna •

Arvad •

*MEDITERRANEAN
SEA*

Kadesh
(on the
Orontes) •

Tadmor •

PHOENICIA

Byblos •

BETH-REHOB

Sidon •

Damascus •

Abana R.

Pharpar R.

Tyre •

Dan •

MAACAH

Hazor •

Acco •

GESHUR

Chinnereth •

Ashtaroth •

Megiddo •

Beth-shan •

Ramoth-gilead •

*International
Coastal Highway*

King's Highway

Shechem •

AMMON

Joppa •

Rabbah
(Amman) •

PHILISTIA

Gezer •

Ashdod •

Gibeah •
Jerusalem •

Gath •

Gaza •

*DEAD
SEA*

Raphia •

Beersheba •

MOAB

Kir-
hareseth •

*Eastern
Desert*

Tamar •

EDOM

Kadesh-
barnea •

W. el-Arish

EGYPT

Ezion-
geber •

*Gulf of
Aqaba*

**KINGDOM OF DAVID
AND SOLOMON**

•   City

—   Boundary of Solomon's kingdom

    Saul's kingdom

    Territory conquered by David

    Solomon's area of influence

    Non-conquered territory

—   Major highway

MEDITERRANEAN SEA

| 0 | 20 | 40 | 60 | 80 | 100 Miles |

| 0 | 20 | 40 | 60 | 80 | 100 Kilometers |

I

for his wisdom and maintained a kingdom expanded to five times the size of the land God promised to Abraham, extending south to the Sinai and north to the Euphrates River. Solomon became one of the most significant monarchs of his era. By the end of his 40-year reign, his kingdom was strong, but his commitment to the Lord had waned, and his latter years were troubled by internal problems. Soon after his death, the united monarchy ended.

The Divided Monarchy—ca. 931–586 B.C. The united kingdom of the 12 tribes suddenly divided in 931/930 B.C. The 10 tribes in the north would henceforth be known as Israel or Ephraim (its most influential tribe). The two southern tribes, Judah and Benjamin, remained loyal to the house of David and were known as Judah. Even before the united kingdom was founded, the unity of Israel was fragile. Petty rivalries and jealousies were common during the period of the judges. The division between Judah and Israel was apparent even during Samuel's lifetime, but David achieved a high degree of national unity. The heavy taxes of Solomon and the forced periods of labor imposed on the people under Solomon and Rehoboam brought the matter to a head.

Sedition boiled toward the surface late in the reign of Solomon. Jeroboam, son of Nebat, was a successful supervisor of civilian labor in Ephraim for Solomon (1 Kings 11:27-28). The Prophet Ahijah from Shiloh met Jeroboam one day and tore his (Ahijah's) garment into 12 pieces, handed Jeroboam 10 of them, and announced that Jeroboam would become ruler over Israel (1 Kings 11:31). The rumor of this prophecy spread quickly and Jeroboam fled to Egypt where he found refuge with Pharaoh Shishak, a political opportunist. Peace was preserved until the death of Solomon, but then trouble arose quickly and Rehoboam was not wise enough to salvage the tenuous situation.

Rather than easing the onerous governmental burdens on the people, Rehoboam threatened to increase them, and 10 tribes rebelled, leaving the Southern Kingdom of Rehoboam containing only the tribes of Judah and Benjamin. Jeroboam, son of Nebat, became the first king of the Northern Kingdom and immediately led the people into idolatry. In order to make up for the loss of religious ties to Jerusalem, Jeroboam had two golden calves fashioned for the two sites of Dan and Bethel. Because of his apostasy Jeroboam's family forfeited the kingship. His name became a refrain and a stereotype for the evil in the reigns of the rulers of the Northern Kingdom.

Rehoboam was attacked by Jeroboam's ally, Pharaoh Shishak (Shosenq I, ca. 945–924 B.C.), who looted the temple and then moved further into the territory of Israel, Gilead, and Edom. An inscription left by Shishak at Karnak claimed the defeat of 150 cities in the region. Oddly Shishak did not consolidate his gains of territory but returned to Egypt where he soon died. Rehoboam secured his kingdom and turned over a stable nation to his son Abijah, who reigned only two years. He failed in an attempt to reunite the tribes. Abijah's son Asa reigned 41 years in Judah. He partially, but not entirely, reversed the religious deterioration of Judah.

In the entire subsequent history of the two nations, there were nine overlapping reigns or co-regencies, which makes the chronology in Kings and Chronicles hard to establish. The north also was divided once into two factions, which further confuses the issue. During the divided kingdom era each nation had 19 kings. The kings of the north came from nine dynasties (families) while all the kings of Judah were descended from David. The 19 kings of the north ruled from 930–722 B.C.; the average length of each reign was relatively brief. The kings of the south served from 930 to 586 B.C., demonstrating the greater stability and continuity of life in Judah. All the kings of the north are evaluated in Kings and Chronicles as bad, while the kings of Judah were partly bad and partly good kings. Ironically, the worst of the kings was from Judah: Manasseh, who sacrificed one of his own children as a pagan sacrifice.

During the Israelite monarchies, great nations came across the biblical stage as their affairs intersected those of Judah and Israel. Because the focus of the biblical record is on God's people, only vignettes and brief glimpses are provided of the larger history of the era. The details provided in the Bible are confirmed repeatedly by the archives and artifacts of various kinds left by other ancient kingdoms.

The relationship between Israel and Judah fluctuated from hostile to civil to fraternal over the life of the Northern Kingdom. Sometimes they were allied and at other times involved in competing alliances. Overall both kingdoms enjoyed periods of peace and prosperity. An ominous development was the emergence of Syria as

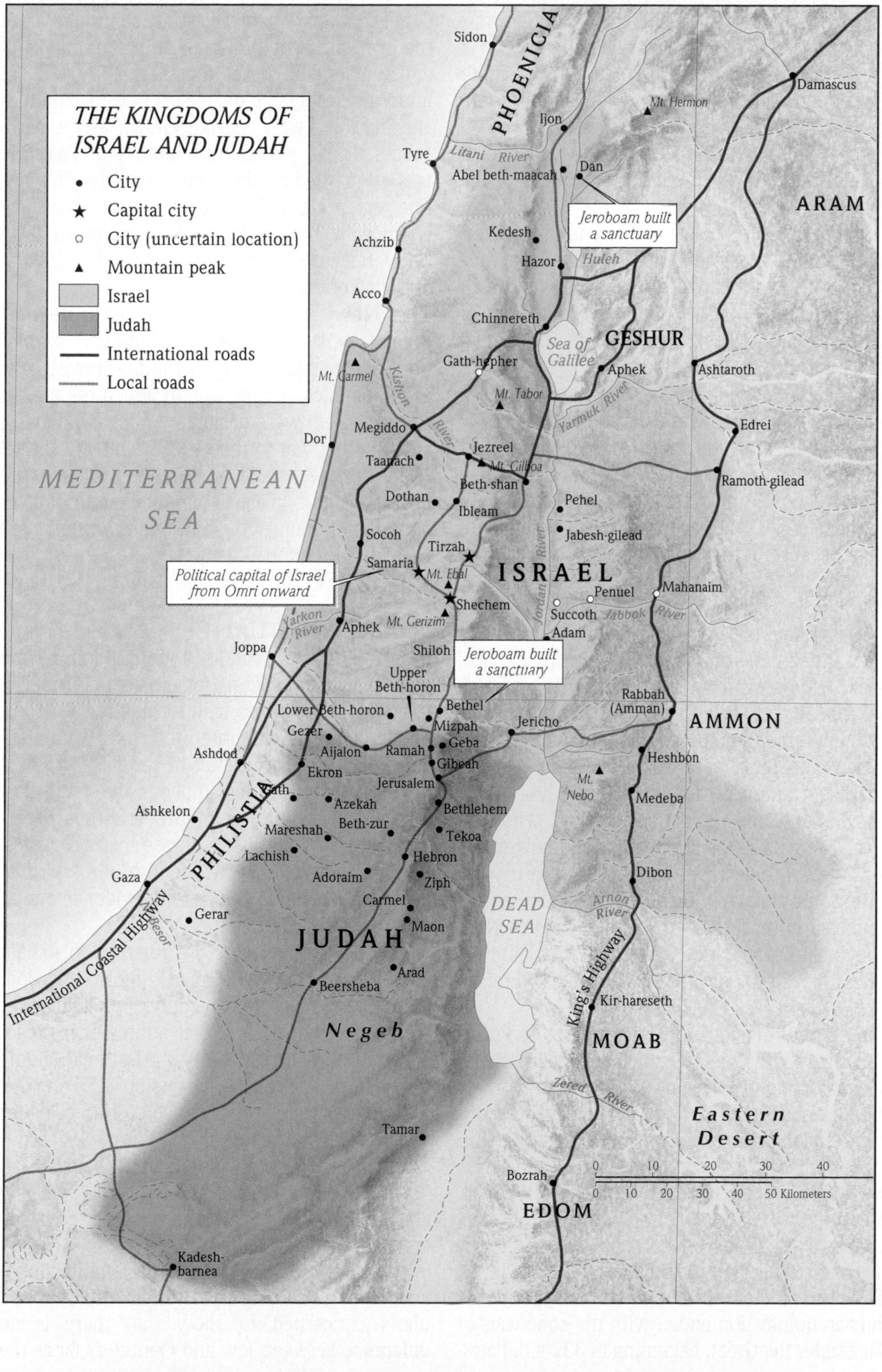

THE KINGDOMS OF ISRAEL AND JUDAH

- • City
- ★ Capital city
- ○ City (uncertain location)
- ▲ Mountain peak
- ▨ Israel
- ▨ Judah
- — International roads
- — Local roads

PHOENICIA

Sidon

Damascus

Ijon

Mt. Hermon

ARAM

Tyre

Litani River

Abel beth-maacah

Dan

Jeroboam built a sanctuary

Achzib

Kedesh

Hazor

Huleh

Acco

Chinnereth

Sea of Galilee

GESHUR

Mt. Carmel

Gath-hepher

Aphek

Ashtaroth

Kishon River

Mt. Tabor

Yarmuk River

Edrei

Dor

Megiddo

Jezreel

Mt. Gilboa

Taanach

Beth-shan

Ramoth-gilead

Dothan

Ibleam

Pehel

MEDITERRANEAN SEA

Socoh

Tirzah

Jabesh-gilead

Samaria

Mt. Ebal

ISRAEL

Political capital of Israel from Omri onward

Shechem

Penuel

Mahanaim

Yarkon River

Aphek

Mt. Gerizim

Succoth

Jabbok River

Joppa

Shiloh

Adam

Upper Beth-horon

Bethel

Jeroboam built a sanctuary

Rabbah (Amman)

Lower Beth-horon

Mizpah

Jericho

AMMON

Gezer

Geba

Ramah

Gibeah

Heshbon

Ashdod

Aijalon

Ekron

Jerusalem

Mt. Nebo

Medeba

Gath

Azekah

Bethlehem

Ashkelon

Mareshah

Beth-zur

Tekoa

Lachish

Hebron

Dibon

Gaza

Adoraim

Ziph

PHILISTIA

Carmel

DEAD SEA

Arnon River

Gerar

Maon

JUDAH

King's Highway

International Coastal Highway

Besor

Arad

Beersheba

Kir-hareseth

Negeb

MOAB

Tamar

Zered River

Eastern Desert

Bozrah

EDOM

Kadesh-barnea

0   10   20   30   40
0   10   20   30   40   50 Kilometers

a major power about the time of the division of the Israelite kingdom (ca. 930 B.C.). By about 850 B.C. Damascus was the capital of the most powerful state in the region. Assyria was in a time of domestic turmoil, which allowed more autonomy for other nations. After about a century of weakness, however, an Assyrian resurgence (ca. 745 B.C.) changed the geopolitical balance and foreshadowed future trouble for the Israelite kingdoms.

Syria became isolated and surrounded by territory under Assyrian control. With Syria thus preoccupied with problems of her own, Judah prospered most notably under the long reign of the good king Hezekiah. However, the end of Israel was just around the corner.

The last century of the Northern Kingdom (eighth century B.C.) was marked by the ministry of four great prophets: Amos, Hosea, Micah, and Isaiah, as well as Jonah. With perfect clarity they saw the demise of Israel and eventually Judah. Yet both nations believed themselves to be invincible because of their relationship with Yahweh. Most of the people ignored the prophets and clung to delusions of grandeur and safety.

Tragically the Assyrians swept Israel away after the fall of Samaria in 722 B.C. Twice, perhaps, Assyria came against Judah (701 and 688 B.C.) but was unable to conquer her because of divine intervention. Judah continued for another 135 years, often as a vassal state of Assyria. Jerusalem ultimately fell in 587–586 B.C. to the Babylonians under Nebuchadnezzar, who displaced Assyria as the dominant world power late in the seventh century B.C. (ca. 612–609).

The Babylonian Exile The Babylonians deported most of the people of Judah. The Neo-Babylonian ascendancy was short lived. Babylon fell to her former ally, the Medo-Persian Empire in 539 B.C.

The Postexilic Period Shortly after the fall of Babylon, Cyrus the Great, the Persian king, allowed conquered peoples to relocate to their native lands (Ezra 1:2-4). The Jews began returning to Judah about 537 B.C. Under the leadership of Zerubbabel, Ezra, and Nehemiah, Jerusalem was resettled and a second temple was built. A measure of autonomy existed throughout this period. The OT era ended about 400 B.C. with the ministry of the Prophet Malachi.

The Intertestamental Period The period of Persian domination ended with the conquests of Alexander the Great, beginning in 332 B.C. Pales-

tine changed hands several times between the Seleucid and Ptolemaic successors of Alexander. Greek domination of Palestine continued until the Jews succeeded in establishing an independent kingdom in a war that began in 167 B.C. under the leadership of an aged priest Mattathias and his sons, who became known as the Maccabees. In 63 B.C. Roman control of Palestine was established by the Roman General Pompey. The region was subdivided for purposes of governance by the Romans who sanctioned local rulers but also maintained control through the presence of the Roman military.

The New Testament Period and Beyond Roman control of Palestine continued beyond the NT era, culminating in the first Jewish War with Rome, ca. A.D. 66–72, in which the temple and Jerusalem were decimated (A.D. 70). Finally, after another war in the second century A.D. (ca. 135), the Jews were scattered throughout the Roman Empire. Palestine remained in Roman hands until about A.D. 400. See *Chronology of the Biblical Period.*

Walter C. Kaiser, Jr. and Charles W. Draper

ISRAEL, SPIRITUAL The phrase "spiritual Israel" is often used as a description of the church in contrast to national or ethnic Israel. It refers to all believers in all times regardless of ethnic identity. Some interpreters see Paul's language of "Israel according to the flesh" (1 Cor. 10:18) as necessarily implying its antithesis, "Israel according to the Spirit," and thus, "spiritual Israel." While Paul's phrase may be suggestive, it is not conclusive. The idea of a "spiritual Israel" must rest on the basis of evidence drawn from texts viewed together.

In the NT believers are referred to in language that is drawn from OT quotes and concepts that in their original context explicitly refer to Israel. For instance, Peter addresses his readers as "a chosen race, a royal priesthood, a holy nation, a people for His possession" (1 Peter 2:9 HCSB), a clear reference to Exod. 19:5-6. Other terms, such as "chosen" (1 Thess. 1:4 NIV), "sons of God" (Rom. 8:14), and "heirs" (Gal. 3:29), are all descriptions of believers, both Jew and Gentile, in terms the OT writers used in reference to Israel.

Other texts make it clear that ethnic boundaries have no bearing on salvation. Paul is particularly concerned to show that there is no difference between Jew and Gentile as far as the

PALESTINE IN THE TIME OF JESUS

- City
- City (uncertain location)
- Decapolis city
- Decapolis city (uncertain location)
- ★ Administrative capital
- ▲ Mountain peak
- — Major roads
- — Other roads
- First procuratorship
- Territory of Antipas
- Territory of Philip
- Syrian territory

Coponius was named the first prefect and established the administrative capital at Caesarea Maritima

ABILENE

Sidon

ITUREA

Damascus

Mt. Hermon ▲

Caesarea-Philippi (Panias)

Pharpar R.

Tyre

PHOENICIA (TYRE)

GAULANITIS

King's Highway

Raphana

TRACHONITIS

Cadasa (Kedesh)

Gischala (Gush Halav)

L. Huleh

BATANEA

Capernaum

Bethsaida

GALILEE

Jotapata

Sea of Galilee

Gergesa (Kursi)

Gamala

Sepphoris

Geba

Nazareth

Tiberias

Hippos

Mt. Carmel ▲

Xaloth (Chesulloth)

Mt. Tabor ▲

Gadara

Abila

Adraa (Edrei)

AURANITIS

Dora

Legio (Megiddo)

Esdraelon Valley

Bostra

Caesarea Maritima (Strato's Tower) ★

Scythopolis (Beth-shan)

Ginae (Jenin)

Pella

Dion

DECAPOLIS

SAMARIA

Aenon

Salim

Gerasa (Jerash)

Sebaste (Samaria)

Mt. Ebal ▲

Neapolis (Shechem)

Mt. Gerizim ▲

Amathus

Apollonia

Coreae

Antipatris (Aphek)

Yarkon R.

Alexandrium

Gedor (Gadara)

Joppa

Ephraim (Ophrah)

PEREA

Philadelphia (Amman)

Lydda

Archelais

JUDEA

Jericho

Jamnia

Emmaus (Nicopolis)

Cypros

Esbus (Heshbon)

Azotus (Ashdod)

Jerusalem

Bethany

Mt. Nebo ▲

Medeba

Eastern Desert

Ascalon (Ashkelon)

Hyrcania

Mesad Hasidim (Qumran)

Machaerus

Betogabris (Beth-guvrin)

Hebron

Callirrhoe (Zereth-shahar)

Gaza

En-gedi

DEAD SEA

Arnon R.

IDUMEA

Masada

King's Highway

N A B A T E A

Beersheba

Malatha

Arad

MEDITERRANEAN SEA

N. Besor

0 10 20 30 40 50 Miles

0 10 20 30 40 50 Kilometers

I

saving grace of God in Christ is concerned (Rom. 1:16; 3:29-30; 10:12; Gal. 3:28). In Ephesians Paul asserts that Gentiles, once "without the Messiah, excluded from the citizenship of Israel, and foreigners to the covenants of the promise" (Eph. 2:12 HCSB), are now "fellow citizens with the saints, and members of God's household" (Eph. 2:19).

Perhaps the most important text, and certainly the most debated, is Galatians 6:16. In this text Paul uses the phrase "the Israel of God." On one hand, Paul could be addressing Jewish Christians who are friendly to his ministry, as opposed to his Judaizing opponents. Thus the blessing, "May peace be on all those who follow this standard and mercy also be on the Israel of God" (HCSB) is extended to all believers, but Paul made the distinction in order to recognize ethnic Jews who are faithful to the gospel. On the other hand, in Galatians, Paul went to great lengths to de-emphasize the importance of ethnic boundaries since his opponents were adding Jewish customs and legal observances as requirements for Gentile believers. Therefore, to end his letter by making a distinction between believers along ethnic lines seems to work against the argument of the entire epistle. In Gal. 3:26 Paul stated that "you are all sons of God through faith in Christ Jesus," and then went on to add that "There is no Jew or Greek ... for you are all one in Christ Jesus. And if you are Christ's, then you are Abraham's seed, heirs according to the promise." Paul again refers to his readers as God's "sons" and "heirs" (Gal. 4:5-7), emphasizing the unity Jews and Gentiles have in Christ. Later Paul contrasts Hagar and Sarah as metaphors for two covenants (Gal. 4:21-31). The first, Hagar, stands for the covenant given from Mount Sinai which "corresponds to the present Jerusalem, for she is in slavery with her children" (Gal. 4:25). The second, Sarah, "the free woman" (Gal. 4:23) represents the covenant of promise and corresponds not to earthly but heavenly Jerusalem which is "free, and she is our mother" (Gal. 4:26). Paul's readers are "like Isaac ... children of promise." The references to readers as "heirs" and "Abraham's offspring," and "children of promise," strongly favor the view that Paul does have a "spiritual Israel" in view. Paul's summary statement could hardly be clearer: "For both circumcision and uncircumcision mean nothing; what matters instead is a new creation" (Gal. 6:15; cp. 5:6). Given the context of Galatians, Paul uses the term "Israel of God" in 6:16 to refer to all believers, all God's people apart from ethnic distinctions. This does not deny that elsewhere Paul speaks of Israel and the Jews in explicitly ethnic terms, the clearest example being Rom. 9–11. However, a word need not mean the same thing every time it is used. "Spiritual Israel" is a fair interpretation of Paul's meaning in Gal. 6:16, especially as a synthesis including the other NT texts cited above.

As a final note, the term "spiritual Israel" need not be equated with a term such as "new Israel" or as an assertion in favor of "replacement theology," which holds (since Tertullian and Justin Martyr) that the church has taken the place of ethnic Israel to the extent that every promise to Israel is now directed solely to the church. Nor does it mean that language about ethnic Israel must be "spiritualized" so as always to refer to the church.   *Bryan J. Vickers*

ISRAELITE (Ĭz´ rā ĕl īt) Citizen of nation of Israel.

ISSACHAR (Ĭs´ sà kär) Personal name meaning "man for hire" or "hireling." Ninth son of Jacob, the fifth borne by Leah (Gen. 30:18). He became the progenitor of the tribe of Issachar. Almost nothing is known about his personal history. The tribe of Issachar occupied territory in the northern part of Palestine, just southwest of the Sea of Galilee (Josh. 19:17-23). The tribe was not prominent in Israel's history. Tola, one of the so-called "minor" judges, was of the tribe of Issachar (Judg. 10:1-2). So was Baasha, the successor of Nadab as king of Israel (1 Kings 15:27). The city of Jezreel, which was an Israelite royal residence, was located in the territory of Issachar. See *Chronology of the Biblical Period; Tribes of Israel.*

ISSARON Transliteration of Hebrew word meaning "a tenth." A dry measure equal to one tenth of an ephah (Exod. 29:40; Lev. 14:10,21; 23:13,17; 24:5; Num. 15:4) or about two quarts. KJV translates a tenth deal. See *Ephah; Weights and Measures.*

ISSHIAH (Ĭs shī´ à) Personal name meaning "let Yahweh forget." In Hebrew the name appears in a longer form in 1 Chron. 12:6. **1.** Leader in the tribe of Issachar (1 Chron. 7:3). **2.** Soldier from Saul's tribe of Benjamin who joined David at Ziklag while he hid from Saul (1 Chron. 12:6). **3.** Member of the Kohath branch of Levites (1 Chron. 23:20; 24:24-25). **4.** Descendant of Moses among the Levites (1 Chron. 24:21; cp. 23:13-17).

ISSHIJAH (Ĭs shī´ jà) Personal name meaning "let Yahweh forget." Same Hebrew name as Isshiah. Israelite who had married a foreign wife, threatening Israel's total allegiance to Yahweh in the time of Ezra (Ezra 10:31).

ISSUE KJV term referring to offspring (Gen. 48:6; Isa. 22:24; Matt. 22:25; cp. 2 Kings 20:18; Isa. 39:7) or to a bodily discharge. The KJV applied "issue" to male pathological discharges such as that associated with gonorrhea (Lev. 15:2-15), to normal menstruation (Lev. 15:19-24), and to female pathological discharges (Lev. 15:25-30; Matt. 9:20). Normal discharges resulted in ritual uncleanness for one day that was removed by simple washing. Pathological discharges resulted in uncleanness until seven days after the return to full health and required an atoning sacrifice. In Ezek. 23:20 the seminal emission of stallions is one element in a graphic depiction of Judah's idolatry. See *Discharge*.

ISSUE OF BLOOD (Matt. 9:20 KJV) See *Hemorrhage*.

ISUAH (Ĭs´ ū à) (1 Chron. 7:30 KJV) See *Ishvah*.

ISUI (Ĭs´ ū ī) (Gen. 46:17 KJV) See *Ishvi*.

ITALIAN COHORT Name of the archery unit of the Roman army to which the Gentile centurion Cornelius belonged (Acts. 10:1). KJV calls it the Italian band. Probably 1,000 men who had been mustered in Italy composed the unit. Little is known about this Italian Cohort. Extrabiblical evidence exists for the presence in Caesarea of a unit called *Cohors II* Italica after A.D. 69. That date, however, is too late for the events recorded in Acts 10. Perhaps the *Cohors II* actually was in Caesarea prior to A.D. 69, or perhaps the Italian Cohort to which Cornelius belonged was a different unit. See *Cornelius*.

ITALY Boot-shaped peninsula between Greece and Spain which extends from the Alps on the north to the Mediterranean Sea on the south. Its long narrow shape contributed to its ethnic diversity, with so many Greeks occupying the

Temple of Serapis at the ancient port of Puteoli where Paul disembarked on his journey to Rome.

southern part that the citizens of Rome called it "Great Greece." Through the Punic Wars with Carthage (264–146 B.C.), the city of Rome extended its control over the whole country and eventually conquered the entire Mediterranean. The Roman Empire was created when Octavian became Augustus Caesar (27 B.C.) after the murder of Julius Caesar and of the demise of the Republic (44 B.C.). Italy is named in the NT in Acts 18:2; 27:1,6 and Hebrews 13:24.

John McRay

ITCH Skin disorder characterized by an irritating sensation in the upper surface of the skin. The itch included among the curses on those unfaithful to the covenant (Deut. 28:27) was possibly eczema or prurigo. NIV, NRSV use "itch" to distinguish a minor skin disorder from leprosy (Lev. 13:30-37). The KJV termed this disorder "scall," a malady characterized by dry scales or scabs. Other translations rendered this disorder "infection" (NASB), "scale" (REB), or "sore" (TEV). It has been suggested that *alopecia areata*, which produces patches of baldness (cp. Lev. 13:40-41) or ringworm is the cause of this disorder. Animals suffering from a skin disorder were unsuitable for sacrifice (Lev. 22:22). English translators divide over the nature of this disorder: eczema (NASB), itch (NRSV), scab (REB), scurvy (KJV), skin eruption (TEV). See *Diseases*.

ITHAI (Ī´ thā ī) Personal name, perhaps meaning "with me." A member of David's elite "30" military heroes (2 Sam. 23:29 NIV; NASB, Ittai).

ITHAMAR (Ĭth´ à mär) Personal name of uncertain meaning, perhaps "island of palms," or "where is Tamar," or shortened form of "father of

I

Tamar (palms)." Fourth son of Aaron the priest (Exod. 6:23). After the death of Nadab and Abihu, Ithamar and his surviving brother Eleazar rose to prominence. During the wilderness years Ithamar apparently was in charge of all the Levites (Exod. 38:21). Moses became angry when Ithamar and his brother did not eat part of an offering as commanded (Lev. 10:16). In addition, the house of Eli evidently was descended from Ithamar. See *Aaron; Priests and Levites.*

ITHIEL (Ĭth´ ĭ ĕl) Personal name meaning "with me is God." **1.** Member of the tribe of Benjamin in the time of Nehemiah after the return from exile (Neh. 11:7). **2.** Person to whom Prov. 30 is addressed, following standard Hebrew text (KJV, NASB, NIV. HCSB). Many Bible students put spaces between different letters of the Hebrew text assuming an early copying change. Then the text would read, "God is not with me, God is not with me, and I am helpless" (TEV), or "I am weary, O God, I am weary, O God. How can I prevail?" (NRSV; cp. REB, HCSB).

ITHLAH (Ĭth´ lȧ) Place-name, perhaps meaning "he hangs." Town in tribal territory of Dan (Josh. 19:42). Its location is not known, but some students of Bible lands geography follow some Greek manuscripts identifying Ithlah with Shithlah or Shilta, about four miles northwest of Bethhoron.

ITHMAH (Ĭth´ mȧ) Personal name meaning "orphan." Moabite soldier in David's army (1 Chron. 11:46).

ITHNAN (Ĭth´ năn) Place-name meaning "flowing constantly." Town on southern border of tribal territory of Judah (Josh. 15:23). Its location is not known unless some Bible lands geographers are correct in combining Hazor-ithnan into one town, which may have been located at modern el-Jebariyeh on the Wadi Umm Ethnan.

ITHRA (Ĭth´ rȧ) Personal name meaning "remnant" or "abundance." He was the father of Amasa, and the general that Absalom appointed to replace David's general Joab when he revolted against his father (2 Sam. 17:25). Ithra's wife, Abigail, was Joab's aunt. Ithra is called Jether in some Greek and old Latin manuscripts as well as

in 1 Kings 2:5,32; 1 Chron. 2:17. Some modern translations thus read Jether in 2 Sam. 17:25 (TEV, NIV). One early Greek manuscript and 1 Chron. 2:17 identify Ithra as an Ishmaelite rather than an Israelite, as the standard Hebrew text of 2 Sam. 17:25 reads. Many Bible students think Ishmaelite was the original reading in 2 Samuel, since it would be unusual and unnecessary to identify an Israelite (REB, TEV, NRSV).

ITHRAN (Ĭth´ răn) Personal name meaning "remnant" or "abundance." **1.** A Horite leader who lived in Edom (Gen. 36:26). **2.** Leader in the tribe of Asher (1 Chron. 7:37). He may be the same as the similarly spelled Jether (1 Chron. 7:38).

ITHREAM (Ĭth´ rȧ ăm) Personal name meaning "remnant of the people." David's son born in Hebron to Eglah, David's wife (2 Sam. 3:5).

ITHRITE (Ĭth´ rīt) Clan name meaning "of Jether." Descendants of Jether or Jethro (Exod. 4:18) or a clan whose home was Kiriath-jearim (1 Chron. 2:53). The latter may have been Hivites (cp. Josh. 9:7,17). Two of David's valiant "30" warriors were Ithrites (2 Sam. 23:38).

ITTAH-KAZIN (Ĭt tȧh-kā´ zĭn) (KJV) See *Ethkazin.*

ITTAI (Ĭt´ tā ī) Personal name meaning "with God." **1.** Gittite (from Gath) soldier who demonstrated loyalty to David by accompanying the latter in flight from Jerusalem after the outbreak of a rebellion led by David's son Absalom (2 Sam. 15:19-22). Gittite means a resident of Gath. Thus, this man was a Philistine who had cast his lot with the Israelite David. Later, Ittai shared command of David's army with Joab and Abishai (2 Sam. 18:2). See David. **2.** One of the "30" of David's army (2 Sam. 23:29) and son of Ribai of Gibeah from the tribe of Benjamin. The Hebrew text of 1 Chron. 11:31 spells the name Ithai.

ITURAEA (Ĭt ū rē´ ȧ) or **ITUREA** Place-name meaning "related to Jetur." Region over which Herod Philip was governor when John the Baptist began his public ministry (Luke 3:1). It was located northeast of Galilee between the Lebanon and Anti-Lebanon mountains, though its precise boundaries are almost impossible to

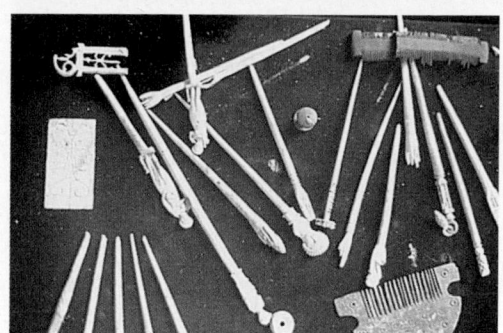

Ivory toilet articles and hair ornaments.

determine. Racially, the Ituraeans were of Ishmaelite stock; their origin probably should be traced to Jetur the son of Ishmael (Gen. 25:15). The earliest extant reference to the Ituraeans as a people dates from the second century B.C. Pompey conquered the territory for Rome about 50 B.C. Ituraea was eventually absorbed into other political districts, losing its distinct identity by the end of the first century A.D. See *Herod.*

IVAH (Ī´ vȧ) (KJV) See *Avva.*

IVORY English translation of the Hebrew word that means "tooth." Ivory was used for decoration on thrones, beds, houses, and the decks of ships (1 Kings 10:18; 22:39; 2 Chron. 9:17; Ps. 45:8; Ezek. 27:6,15; Amos 3:15; 6:4). Archaeologists in Palestine have unearthed numerous articles made of ivory: boxes, gaming boards, figurines, spoons, and combs.

First Kings 10:22 is cited by scholars as a possible explanation for the source of ivory in Palestine. Apparently, Solomon's ships returned with ivory as a part of their cargo. Sources outside the OT indicate that elephants existed in northern Syria during the second millennium B.C. Elephants were hunted into extinction in northern Syria by 800 B.C.

The Prophet Amos mentioned ivory as a token of luxury and wealth (Amos 3:15; 6:4). Lists of booty taken by victorious armies included ivory objects. Hezekiah was credited with giving Sennacherib tribute in 701 B.C. Sennacherib's account of the tribute included couches and chairs inlaid with ivory. Ivories have been found at Samaria that are thought to be from the time of Ahab, who reigned in Israel from about 869 to 850 B.C.   *James Newell*

IVVAH (Īv´ vȧ) Alternate spelling for Avva. See *Avva.*

IYE-ABARIM (Ī yȧ-ăb´ ȧ rĭm) Place-name meaning "ruins of the crossings." Station in the wilderness wanderings (Num. 21:11) near Moab. It is apparently near Mount Abarim. It is apparently abbreviated as Iim in Num. 33:45 (KJV). Some Bible geographers locate it at Khirbet Aii, southwest of Kerak or modern Mahay, but this is far from certain. See *Abarim.*

IYIM (Ī´ yĭm) Modern translations spelling of Iim (Num. 33:45), a shortened form of Iye-abarim. See *Iye-abarim.*

IZEHAR (Ī´ zȧ här) (Num. 3:19 KJV) See *Izhar.*

IZEHARITE (Ĭz´ ȧ här īt) (KJV) See *Izharite.*

IZHAR (Ĭz´ här) Personal name meaning "olive oil" or "he sparkles." **1.** Son of Kohath and grandson of Levi, thus original ancestor of a priestly clan (Exod. 6:18). He was father of Korah (Num. 16:1; cp. 1 Chron. 23:18). See *Korah.* **2.** Written Hebrew text of 1 Chron. 4:7 names Izhar as a member of the tribe of Judah but uses a different letter for "h," sometimes rendered "ch" in English. The resulting name is of uncertain meaning. An early Hebrew scribal note followed by the early Syriac and Latin translations makes the name Jezoar (KJV, REB) or Zohar (NIV).

IZHARITE (Ĭz´ här īt) Clan of Levites descended from Izhar. See *Izhar.*

IZLIAH (Ĭz lī´ ah) Personal name meaning "long-lived" or "Yahweh delivers." Leader in tribe of Benjamin living in Jerusalem after the return from exile (1 Chron. 8:18).

IZRAHIAH (Ĭz rȧ hī´ ȧ) Personal name meaning "Yahweh shines forth." Member of tribe of Issachar (1 Chron. 7:3). The same Hebrew name appears in Neh. 12:42 but is usually transliterated into English as Jezrahiah. See *Jezrahiah.*

IZRAHITE (Ĭz´ rȧ hīt) Clan name in 1 Chron. 27:8 for which the text tradition gives several variants: Harorite (1 Chron. 11:27 KJV); Harodite (2 Sam. 23:25 KJV). Other Hebrew manuscripts read "Zerahites." See *Harodite.*

I

IZRI (Ĭz´ rī) Clan leader of fourth course of temple musicians (1 Chron. 25:11). He is probably the same as Zeri (25:3), the name change occurring in copying the text.

IZZIAH (Ĭz zī´ á) Personal name meaning "Yah sprinkled." Priest who repented of marrying a foreign woman and thus tempting Israel with foreign gods in the time of Ezra (Ezra 10:25).

J

Courtyard of Church of the Holy Sepulchre in Jerusalem.

J Sign for one of the principal sources that critical scholars propose for the Pentateuch. The name derives from the personal name for God, Yahweh (German, *Jahweh*), that characterizes this source. The source is thought to have originated in Judah earlier than the E source (about 900 B.C.). Recent research has raised radical questions about this source and theory even among critical scholars. See *Bible Hermeneutics; Pentateuch.*

JAAKAN (Jā´ à·kăn) Personal name meaning "to be fast." Descendant of Esau and thus tribal ancestor of Edomites (1 Chron. 1:42; cp. Gen. 36:27; Num. 33:31-32; Deut. 10:6). Different translations transliterate the name differently— Akan, Jakan. The Hebrew text of Gen. 36:27 omits the first letter of the name. See *Bene-jaakan.*

JAAKANITES (Jā´ à·kà·nīts) (Deut. 10:6 NIV) See *Bene-jaakan.*

JAAKOBAH (Jā à·kō´ bah) Personal name meaning "may He protect." Leader in the tribe of Simeon (1 Chron. 4:36).

JAALA (Jā´ à·là) or **JAALAH** Personal name meaning "female ibex." A member of Solomon's staff whose descendants joined Zerubbabel in returning from Babylonian exile about 537 B.C. (Ezra 2:56; Neh. 7:58, which has an Aramaic ending rather than the Hebrew ending of the Ezra passage).

JAALAM (Jā´ à·lăm) (KJV, REB) See *Jalam.*

JAANAI (Jā´ à·nī) (KJV, REB) See *Janai.*

JAAR (Jā´ är) Place-name meaning "forest." Modern versions' transliteration of Hebrew in Ps. 132:6 (TEV, "Jearim," a plural form; KJV, "wood"). "Jaar" is probably a poetic abbreviation for Kiriath-jearim. The psalm celebrates David's returning the ark to Jerusalem from its Philistine captivity (cp. 1 Sam. 7:2; 2 Sam. 6; 1 Chron. 13:5). See *Kiriath-jearim.*

JAARE-OREGIM (Jā à·rə-ôr´ ə gĭm) Personal name meaning "forests of the weavers." Father of El-hanan from Bethlehem, who killed the brother of Goliath. Many modern Bible scholars follow early Greek translations and 1 Chron. 20:5 and omit Oregim (REB). Others interpret Oregim as a common noun, identifying Jair as a weaver (NIV translation note). This is partly based on 2 Sam. 23:24, where an El-hanan of Bethlehem is identified as the son of Dodo. Jaare may be an abbreviated form of Kiriath-jearim. See *El-hanan; Kiriath-jearim.*

JAARESHIAH (Jā´ à·rə·shī´ ah) Personal name meaning "Yahweh plants." Member of tribe of Benjamin (1 Chron. 8:27).

JAASAU (Jā´ à·sa) (KJV, REB) or **JAASU** (Jā´ à·sū) Personal name meaning "His product," a variant spelling of Jaasiel, which the earliest Hebrew copyists noted should be pronounced differently from the printed Hebrew text. An Israelite who agreed under Ezra's leadership to divorce his foreign wife to ensure the religious purity of the nation (Ezra 10:37).

JAASIEL (Jā ăs´ ĭ·ĕl) Personal name meaning "God makes or acts." **1.** Leader of tribe of Benjamin under David, apparently in charge of census in his tribe when David numbered the people (1 Chron. 27:21). His father Abner may be Saul's general who became David's general. **2.** Army hero under David whose hometown was Zobah (1 Chron. 11:47). KJV transliterates his name Jasiel. See *Mesobaite.*

JAAZANIAH (Jā·ăz à·nī´ ah) Personal name meaning "Yahweh hears." **1.** Member of party led by Ishmael who opposed Gedaliah after the Babylonians made him governor over Judah following their destruction of Jerusalem in 587 B.C. Jaazaniah may also have been in Ishmael's party that assassinated Gedaliah (2 Kings 25:23-25). A signet seal found at Tell en-Nasbeh dates from the same period and contains a depiction of a fighting cock. The seal inscription shows the seal belonged to Jaazaniah, the servant of the king. This is probably the same person and indicates he was on the king's staff, probably as an army captain. His name has a slightly different spelling in Jer. 40:8. See *Jezaniah.* **2.** One of the elders of Israel that Ezekiel found worshiping idols in the temple (Ezek. 8:11). His father Shaphan may have been the counselor of Josiah (2 Kings 22). If so, the son did not imitate the faithful father. **3.** A government official whom Ezekiel accused with his associates of giving wicked advice. His name in Hebrew is an abbreviated form of Jaaza-niah. **4.** The same abbreviated Hebrew name belonged to a Rechabite whom Jeremiah used as an example of faithful obedience to God (Jer. 35:3). See *Rechabite.*

JAAZER (Jā´ à·zēr) (KJV) See *Jazer.*

JAAZIAH (Jā-à-zī´ ah) Levitical priest in the time of David (1 Chron. 24:26). His name means "Yahweh nourishes."

JAAZIEL (Jā-à´ zǐ-ĕl) Variant form of Jaaziah meaning "God nourishes." Levite and temple musician (1 Chron. 15:18), apparently appearing in a variant Hebrew spelling in 15:20 as one who played the psaltery (1 Chron. 15:20), harp (NRSV, NASB, TEV), lute (REB), or lyre (NIV). See *Aziel.*

JABAL (Jā´ băl) Personal name meaning "stream." Son of Lamech by Adah (Gen. 4:20). A descendant of Cain, he was the first nomad, the progenitor of tent dwellers and herdsmen.

JABBOK (Jăb´ bŏk) Place-name meaning "flow-ing." River near which Jacob wrestled through the night with God (Gen. 32:22). Its modern name is Nahr ez-Zerqa. It is a tributary of the Jor-dan, joining the larger river from the east about 15 miles north of the Dead Sea. In biblical times various sections of its approximately 50-mile course served as the western boundary of Ammon, the boundary between the kingdoms of Sihon and Og, and a division in the territory of Gilead. The existence of numerous tells points to a dense population in the Jabbok Valley in ancient times. See *Jacob.*

JABESH or **JABESH-GILEAD** (Jā´ běsh-gĭl´ ə àd) Place-name meaning "dry, rugged" or "dry place of Gilead." City whose residents, with the exception of 400 virgins, were put to death by an army of Israelites (Judg. 21:8-12). The 400 women who were spared became wives for the Benjaminites. While certainty is elusive, the area in which Jabesh-gilead probably was located is east of the Jordan River about 20 miles south of the Sea of Galilee. The story illustrates the dras-tic steps taken to preserve the unity of the 12 tribes of Israel.

Jabesh-gilead figured prominently in the his-tory of Saul. His rescue of the people of Jabesh-gilead from Nahash the Ammonite marked the effective beginning of the Israelite monarchy (1 Sam. 11:1-11). Later, the men of Jabesh-gilead demonstrated the high regard in which they held Saul by retrieving the bodies of the slain king and his sons from the walls of Beth-shean (1 Sam. 31:11-13). David expressed thanks for the brave deed (2 Sam. 2:4-7) and eventually removed Saul's bones from Jabesh-gilead (2 Sam. 21:12).

JABEZ (Jā´ běz) Personal and place-name with a connotation of pain, hurt, and sorrow. **1.** Home of scribes whose location is not known (1 Chron. 2:55). **2.** Israelite who asked God for blessing and received it (1 Chron. 4:9-10). He illustrates the power of prayer.

JABIN (Jā´ bǐn) Personal name meaning "he understands." **1.** Leader of northern coalition of kings who attacked Joshua at the water of Merom and met their death (Josh. 11:1-11). The king of Hazor who controlled the Israelites when they turned away from God at Ehud's death (Judg. 4:1-2). The biblical writer referred to him as "King of Canaan," a title representing his

Panoramic view of the Jabbok River.

J

strong power in the northern part of the country, but a title that kings of the other Canaanite city-states probably would have strongly contested, since Canaan lacked political unity in that period. Jabin does not act in the story of Judg. 4; Sisera, his general, represents him and is killed, leading to Jabin's loss of power. **2.** Many scholars believe that a dynasty of kings in Hazor carried the name Jabin. Some have gone so far as to identify him with Ibni-Adad, who appears in Near Eastern documents from Mari.

JABNEEL (Jăb´ nə ĕl) or **JABNEH** (Jăb´ nĕh) Place-name meaning "God builds." **1.** Town marking northwestern boundary of tribal territory of Judah in land of Philistines (Josh. 15:11); modern Yibna. Uzziah took the town, called by the shortened form Jabneh, from the Philistines (2 Chron. 26:6). Later the city was called Jamnia and became a center of scribal activity for the Jews. See *Bible Formation and Canon*. **2.** Town in Naphtali's tribal territory (Josh. 19:33); modern Tell en-Naam or Khirbet Yemma, west-southwest of the Sea of Galilee and northeast of Mount Tabor.

JACAN (Jā´ kăn) or **JACHAN** (KJV) Personal name of unknown meaning. A member of tribe of Gad (1 Chron. 5:13).

JACHIN (Jā´ kĭn) Personal name meaning "Yah established." Son of Simeon and original ancestor of a clan in the tribe (Gen. 46:10; spelled "Jarib" in 1 Chron. 4:24). A priest who lived in Jerusalem in Nehemiah's day (Neh. 11:10; cp. 1 Chron. 9:10). This represented a priestly family connected to David's organization of the priesthood (1 Chron. 24:17).

JACHIN AND BOAZ (Jā´ kĭn and Bō´ ăz) Proper names meaning "he establishes" and "agile." In 1 Kings 7:21 the names of two bronze pillars that stood on either side of the entrance to Solomon's temple. They may have been 27 feet high and 6 feet in diameter with a 10-foot capital on top. Perhaps each word was the beginning of an inscription that was engraved on the respective pillars. Analogous pillars have been found in front of temples at Khorsabad, Tyre, Paphos, and other places. Their function appears to have been primarily ornamental, though some have suggested they may have been giant incense stands. It is possible that they took on

some symbolic religious significance with the passage of time. See *Temple*.

JACHINITE (Jā´ kĭn-īt) Family in tribe of Simeon descended from Jachin (Num. 26:12). See *Jachin*.

JACINTH Semiprecious stone more nearly orange in color than the hyacinth. Some English translations give "jacinth" as a gem in the high priest's breastplate (Exod. 28:19 NASB, NIV, NRSV), the color of one of the riders' breastplates (Rev. 9:17 KJV), and the eleventh foundation stone of the new Jerusalem (Rev. 21:20 HCSB, KJV, NASB, NIV, NRSV). See *Hyacinth; Minerals and Metals*.

JACKAL Golden jackal (*Canis aureus*), a yellow-coated, carnivorous mammal resembling the wolf but considerably smaller (34–37 inches, including tail of about one foot) with a shorter tail and ears. The same Hebrew word is translated both "jackal" and "fox" (Judg. 15:4, REB has "jackals"; NIV has "foxes"). KJV translated the term for "jackal" as either "dragon" (Isa. 13:22; Neh. 2:13) or "sea monster" (Lam. 4:3). Jackals are nocturnal. They hunt either alone, in pairs, or in packs. By hunting in packs, jackals have taken down large antelopes. This reputation accounts for the horror of one abandoned to jackals (Ps. 44:19). Jackals eat small mammals, birds, fruits, vegetables, and carrion (Ps. 63:10). They are scavengers, infamous for their distinctive nighttime wailing (Job 30:28-31; Mic. 1:8). Most biblical references associate jackals with desert ruins. For a city or nation to be made the haunt or lair of jackals is for it to be utterly destroyed (Isa. 13:22; 34:13; Jer. 9:11; 10:22; 49:33; 50:39; 51:37; Lam. 5:18; Mal. 1:3). See *Dragon*.

JACKAL'S WELL Water source outside Jerusalem, accessible from the Valley Gate (Neh. 2:13 NIV, RSV). Other English translations designate this water source as the Dragon('s) fountain (TEV), spring (NRSV, REB), or well (KJV, NASB). The spring is possibly En-rogel or more likely a water source in the upper part of the Hinnom Valley. See *Jackal; Jerusalem*.

JACOB (Jā´ cŏb) Personal name built on the Hebrew noun for "heel" meaning "he grasps the heel" or "he cheats, supplants" (Gen. 25:26;

27:36). Original ancestor of the nation of Israel and father of the 12 ancestors of the 12 tribes of Israel (Gen. 25:1–Exod. 1:5). He was the son of Isaac and Rebekah, younger twin brother of Esau, and husband of Leah and Rachel (Gen. 25:21-26; 29:21-30). God changed his name to "Israel" (Gen. 32:28; 49:2).

Texts from Ugarit and Assyria have persons named Jacob, but these are not Israelites. Their name is often connected with one of their gods, becoming Jacob-el or Jacob-baal. In such a form, it probably means "may El protect." The OT knows only one Jacob. No one else received the patriarch's name.

Between the Testaments other Jews received the name Jacob; the one NT example is the father of Joseph and thus the earthly grandfather of Jesus (Matt. 1:16). Jacob stands as a strong witness that the God who made all the people of the earth also worked in Israel's history, calling the patriarchs to a destiny He would fulfill even when they least deserved it.

Jacob in Genesis Jacob's story occupies half the book of Genesis. Living up to his name, Jacob bargained for Esau's birthright. Parental partiality fostered continuing hostility between Esau, the hunter loved by his father, and Jacob, the quiet, settled, integrated person favored by his mother. The tensions between brothers seemed to threaten the fulfillment of the divine promise.

Esau's thoughtlessness lost him his birthright and allowed Jacob to have material superiority. Nevertheless, Isaac intended to bestow the blessing of the firstborn upon Esau. The oracle Rebekah received (Gen. 25:23) probably encouraged her to counter Isaac's will and to gain the blessing for her favorite son by fraud. The blessing apparently conveyed the status of head of family apart from the status of heir. To his crass lies and deception, Jacob even approached blasphemy, using God's name to bolster his cause: "Because the LORD your God worked it out for me" (27:20 HCSB). The father's blindness deepened the pathos. The blind father pronounced the blessing he could never recall. Jacob became the bearer of God's promises and the inheritor of Canaan. Esau, too, received a blessing but a lesser one. He must serve Jacob and live in the less fertile land of Edom, but his day would come (27:40). The split between brothers became permanent. Rebekah had to arrange for Jacob to flee

to her home in Paddan-aram to escape Esau's wrath (27:41–28:5). See *Birthright.*

At age 40 Jacob fled his home to begin his life as an individual. Suddenly, a lonely night in Bethel, interrupted by a vision from God, brought reality home. Life had to include wrestling with God and assuming responsibility as the heir of God's promises to Abraham (28:10-22). Jacob made an oath, binding himself to God. Here is the center of Jacob's story; all else must be read in light of the Bethel experience.

In Aram with his mother's family, the deceiver Jacob met deception. Laban tricked him into marrying poor Leah, the elder daughter, before he got his beloved Rachel, the younger. Fourteen years he labored for his wives (29:1-30). Six more years of labor let Jacob return the deception and gain wealth at the expense of his father-in-law, who continued his deception, changing Jacob's wages 10 times (31:7,41). Amid the family infighting, both men prospered financially, and Jacob's family grew. Eventually he had 12 children from four women (29:31–30:24).

Intense bargaining ensued when Jacob told Laban he wanted to follow God's call and return to the land of his birth. Supported by his wives, who claimed their father had cheated them of their dowry (31:15), Jacob departed while Laban and his sons were away in the hills shearing sheep. Starting two days later, Laban and his sons could not overtake Jacob until they reached Gilead, 400 miles from Haran.

Laban complained that he had not had an opportunity to bid farewell to his daughters with the accustomed feast. More importantly, he wanted to recover his stolen gods (31:30,32). These gods were small metal or terra-cotta figures of deities (see *Teraphim*). Without the images, his family lost the magical protection that he thought the gods provided from demons and disasters. Since no fault could be found in Jacob's conduct in Haran, all Laban could do was to suggest a covenant of friendship. Laban proposed the terms as (1) never ill-treating his daughters, (2) never marrying any other women, and (3) establishing the site of the covenant as a boundary neither would cross with evil intent. Jacob was now head of his own household. He was ready to climb to a higher plane of spiritual experience.

J

As Jacob approached the promised land, a band of angels met him at Mahanaim (32:1-2). They probably symbolized God's protection and encouragement as he headed southward to meet Esau for the first time in 20 years. Esau's seemingly hostile advance prompted a call for clear evidence of God's guarding. Shrewdly, Jacob sent an enormous gift to his brother and divided his retinue into two groups. Each group was large enough to defend itself or to escape if the other was attacked. To his scheme Jacob added prayer. He realized that it was ultimately God with whom he must deal. When all had crossed the Jabbok River, Jacob met One who wrestled with him until daybreak (chap. 32). The two struggled without one gaining advantage, until the Opponent dislocated Jacob's hip. Jacob refused to release his Antagonist. Clinging to Him, he demanded a blessing. This would not be given until Jacob said his name. By telling it, Jacob acknowledged his defeat and admitted his character. The Opponent emphasized His superiority by renaming the patriarch. He became Israel, the one on whose behalf God strives. He named the place Peniel (face of God) because he had seen God face to face and his life had been spared (32:30).

Jacob's fear of meeting Esau proved groundless. Seemingly, Esau was content to forget the wrongs of the past and to share his life. As two contrary natures are unlikely to live long in harmony, Jacob chose the better course turning westward to the promised land. Esau headed to Seir to become the father of the Edomites. The twins did not meet again until their father's death (35:27-29).

From Succoth Jacob traveled to Shechem, where he built an altar to God. The son of the city ruler raped Jacob's daughter, Dinah. Jacob's sons demanded that the Shechemites be circumcised before any intermarriages were permitted. The leading citizens followed the king in the request. They hoped to absorb the Hebrews' wealth and property into their own. While the men of Shechem were recovering from surgery and unable to defend themselves, Simeon and Levi killed them to avenge their sister. Jacob condemned their actions but had to leave Shechem.

From Shechem he returned to Bethel. Once again he received the patriarchal promises. Losses and grief characterized this period. The death of his mother's nurse (35:8; 24:59) was followed by the death of his beloved wife Rachel while giving birth to Benjamin at Ephrath

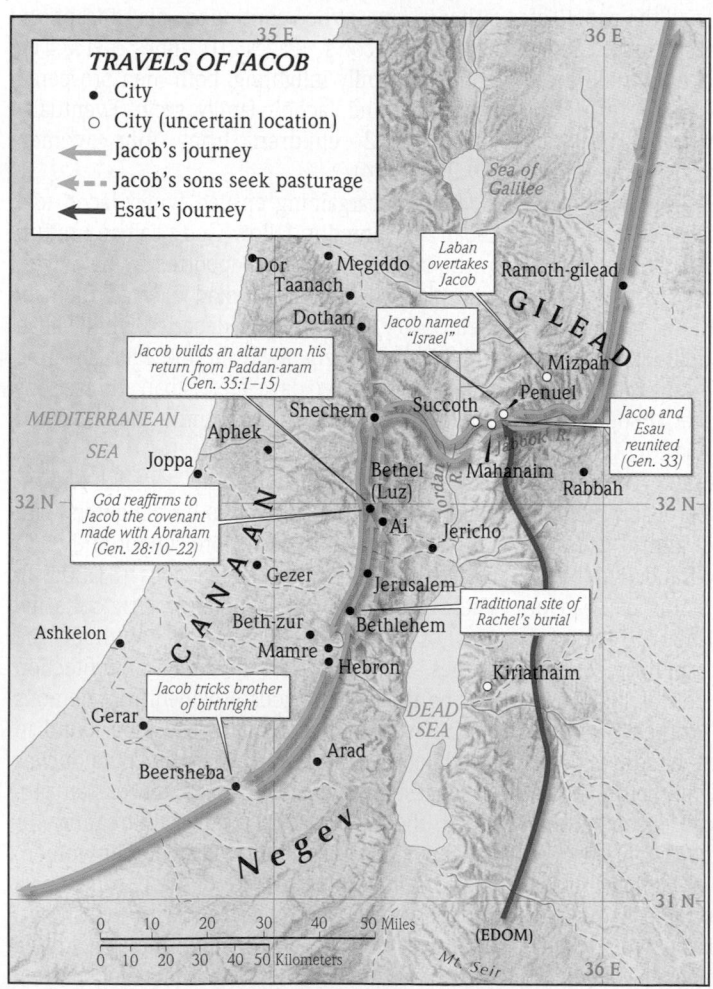

TRAVELS OF JACOB
- City
- ○ City (uncertain location)
- ← Jacob's journey
- ◄- - Jacob's sons seek pasturage
- ← Esau's journey

35 E · 36 E

Sea of Galilee

Dor · Megiddo · Laban overtakes Jacob · Ramoth-gilead
Taanach
Dothan · Jacob named "Israel" · GILEAD
Jacob builds an altar upon his return from Paddan-aram (Gen. 35:1–15)
Mizpah
Shechem · Succoth · Penuel
MEDITERRANEAN SEA · Aphek
Joppa · Jacob and Esau reunited (Gen. 33)
Bethel (Luz) · Mahanaim · Rabbah
32 N · God reaffirms to Jacob the covenant made with Abraham (Gen. 28:10–22) · 32 N
Ai · Jericho
Gezer
Jerusalem
Beth-zur · Bethlehem · Traditional site of Rachel's burial
Ashkelon · Mamre
Hebron · Kiriathaim
Jacob tricks brother of birthright · DEAD SEA
Gerar
Arad
Beersheba

Negev

0 10 20 30 40 50 Miles
0 10 20 30 40 50 Kilometers
(EDOM)
Mt. Seir
31 N
36 E

(35:19; 48:7). About the same time Reuben forfeited the honor of being the eldest son by sexual misconduct (35:22). Finally, the death of Jacob's father, who had been robbed of companionship with both sons, brought Jacob and Esau together again at the family burial site in Hebron.

Although chapters 37–50 revolve around Joseph, Jacob is still the central figure. The self-willed older sons come and go at his bidding.

Descent to Egypt When severe famine gripped Canaan, Jacob and his sons set out for Egypt. At Beer-sheba Jacob received further assurance of God's favor (46:1-4). Jacob dwelt in the land of Goshen until his death. Jacob bestowed the blessing not only upon his favorite son Joseph, but also upon Joseph's two oldest sons, Ephraim and Manasseh. He was finally laid to rest at Hebron in the cave Abraham had purchased (50:12-14).

Four NT passages recall events in his life. The woman at the well in Sychar declared to Jesus that Jacob provided the well (John 4:12). Stephen mentioned the famine and Jacob's journey to Egypt in the course of his defense before the Sanhedrin (Acts 7:8-16). Paul presented Jacob as an example of the sovereign choice of God and of the predestination of the elect (Rom.

9:10-13). The writer of Hebrews held up Jacob as one of the examples of active faith (Heb. 11:9,20-22).

Jacob's Character Throughout the narrative a persistent faith in the God of the fathers shines through. Jacob's life was a story of conflict. He always seemed to be running from someone or something—from Esau, from Laban, or from famine in Canaan. His life, like that of all Israelites, was a checkered history of rebellion and flight.

Jacob is no ideal. Jacob's better nature struggled with his sinful self. What raised Jacob above himself was his reverent, indestructible longing for the salvation of his God.

Jacob's Religion As the religion of Israel and thus the roots of Christianity claim to derive from the patriarchs, it is necessary to attempt to understand Jacob's spiritual life. See *God of the Fathers.*

Jacob's religion was consistent with the beliefs and practices of his fathers. He received instruction from Isaac concerning the history of Abraham, covenant, and the great promises. Jacob encountered God at Bethel at the moment of greatest need in his life. He was fleeing from home to distant unknown relatives. A secondhand

The traditional site of Jacob's Well in the city of Sychar.

J

religion would not do. Jacob's dream was his first-hand encounter with God. The threefold promise of land, descendants, and a blessing to all nations was personalized for him. Jacob saw in the vision the majesty and glory of God. At Bethel Jacob worshiped God and vowed to take Yahweh as his God.

At Peniel, Jacob wrestled face to face with God. He saw how weak he was before God. It taught him the value of continued prayer from one who is helpless. Jacob emerged from Peniel willing to let his life fall into God's control. He was wounded but victorious. God gave him a crippled body but a strengthened faith. It was a new Jacob—Israel—who hobbled off to meet Esau. He had learned obedience through suffering.

Theological Significance God did not choose Jacob because of what he was but because of what he could become. His life is a long history of discipline, chastisement, and purification by affliction. Not one of his misdeeds went unpunished. He sowed deception and reaped the same, first from Laban and then from his own sons.

Jacob's story is a story of conflict. The note of conflict is even heard before his birth (Gen. 25:22-23). However, in the midst of the all-too-human quarrels over family and fortune, God was at work protecting and prospering His blessed.

With the other patriarchs God acted directly, but with Jacob God seemed to be withdrawn at times. Yet, God was no less at work. He worked through unsavory situations and unworthy persons. Even in Jacob's web of conflict and tragedy, God's hand guided, though half hidden.

Gary D. Baldwin

JACOB'S WELL Place in Samaria where Jesus stopped to rest as He traveled from Judea to Galilee (John 4:6). There He met and conversed with a Samaritan woman on the subject of living water. The OT contains no reference to it. It was located near the Samaritan city of Sychar. The well currently shown as the scene of the encounter of Jesus with the Samaritan woman certainly is an ancient well and is generally accepted to be the place referred to in the Gospel. See *Jacob; Sychar.*

JADA (Jā´ dà) Personal name meaning "he knew." Grandson of Jerahmeel (1 Chron. 2:28,32).

JADAH (Jā´ dah) Abbreviated form of personal name Jehoaddah meaning "Yah adorned." NIV translation based on early Greek and Hebrew manuscripts for Jarah. See *Jarah.*

JADAU (Jǎ´ daw) KJV form of the name of a returned exile with a foreign wife (Ezra 10:43). Modern translations render the name Jaddai.

JADDAI (Jǎd´ dī) Modern translations' spelling of Jadau based on textual notes by earliest Hebrew scribes. See *Jadau.*

JADDUA (Jǎd´ dū à) Personal name meaning "well-known." **1.** Levite who placed his seal on Nehemiah's covenant (Neh. 10:21). **2.** A high priest, probably at the end of the Persian period when Alexander the Great approached Jerusalem about 333 B.C. (Neh. 12:11,22).

JADE See *Jewels, Jewelry; Minerals and Metals.*

JADON (Jā´ dŏn) Short form of personal name meaning "Yah rules" or "to be frail." Man from Meronoth near Gibeon who helped Nehemiah repair the wall of Jerusalem (Neh. 3:7).

JAEL (Jā´ əl) Personal name meaning "mountain goat." Wife of Heber the Kenite (Judg. 4:17). She received the Canaanite leader Sisera as he fled following his defeat by the Israelites under Deborah and Barak. Jael assassinated Sisera. Her action is celebrated in the Song of Deborah (Judg. 5:24-27). See *Deborah.*

JAGUR (Jā´ gûr) Place-name meaning "pile of stones." Village on southeastern border of tribal territory of Judah (Josh. 15:21). Its precise location is not known.

JAH (Jäh) Short form of divine name Yahweh in Ps. 68:4 (KJV) and in many proper names. See *God; YHWH.*

JAHATH (Jā´ hǎth) Personal name of uncertain meaning, perhaps "God will grab up." **1.** Member of clan of Zorathites in tribe of Judah (1 Chron. 4:2). **2.** Great grandson of Levi (1 Chron. 6:20; cp. v. 43). **3.** Leader of the Levites in time of David (1 Chron. 23:10-11). **4.** Levite in the line of Eliezer in clan of Izhar

(1 Chron. 24:22). **5.** Levite overseer of temple repair under King Josiah (2 Chron. 34:12).

JAHAZ (Jā´ hăz)**, JAHAZA** (Jȧ hā´ zȧ), or **JAHAZAH** (KJV, Josh. 21:36; Jer. 48:21) Moabite place-name, perhaps meaning "land-site." As they journeyed from the wilderness to the promised land, Israel defeated King Sihon there (Num. 21:23-24; Deut. 2:32-33; Judg. 11:20-21). Isaiah's oracle against Moab described the isolated city of Jahaz as hearing the mourning of Heshbon and Elealeh (Isa. 15:4). Jeremiah issued a similar warning (48:34; cp. v. 21). The name also appears with the Hebrew locative *ah* ending, thus being spelled Jahaza or Jahazah. Jahzah is also a variant spelling. It became part of the tribal territory of Reuben (Josh. 13:18) and a city of the Levites (Josh. 21:36; cp. 1 Chron. 6:78). On the Moabite stone King Mesha of Moab claims an Israelite king (perhaps Jehu) built Jahaz and used it as a base in his unsuccessful fight against Mesha, Chemosh, the Moabite god driving the Israelites out. Mesha then annexed the city to Dibon. It has been variously located at Libb, six miles north of Dibon; Aleiyan; Khirbet el-Mcdeiyineh; and Khirbet Iskander, four miles north of Dibon, being the most popular suggestions.

JAHAZIAH (Jā hȧ zī´ ah) (KJV) Personal name meaning "Yahweh looked." Person who opposed Ezra's plan to call for divorce in the mixed marriages (Ezra 10:15; cp. alternative interpretation of a difficult Hebrew text by KJV).

JAHAZIEL (Jȧ·hā´ zĭ·ĕl) Personal name meaning "Yah looks." **1.** Benjaminite military hero who supported David against Saul, also of the tribe of Benjamin (1 Chron. 12:4). **2.** Priest whom David appointed to blow the trumpet before the ark (1 Chron. 16:6). **3.** Levite of the clan of Hebron (1 Chron. 23:19; 24:23). **4.** Levite and a son of Asaph who received the Spirit of the Lord and prophesied, promising victory for Jehoshaphat and his people (2 Chron. 20:14-19). **5.** Clan leader who led 300 men among the exiles returning to Jerusalem with Ezra (Ezra 8:5).

JAHDAI (Jah´ dā ī) Personal name meaning "Yah leads." A descendant of Caleb (1 Chron. 2:47).

JAHDIEL (Jah´ dī ĕl) Personal name meaning "God rejoices." Military hero and leader in the East Manasseh tribe (1 Chron. 5:24).

JAHDO (Jah´ dō) Personal name meaning "his rejoicing." A member of tribe of Gad (1 Chron. 5:14).

JAHLEEL (Jah´ lȧ ĕl) Personal name meaning "God shows Himself to be friendly" or "he waits for God." A son of Zebulun and grandson of Jacob (Gen. 46:14) who became a clan leader in tribe of Zebulun (Num. 26:26).

JAHLEELITE (Jah´ lȧ ĕl īt) Clan in tribe of Zebulun (Num. 26:26).

JAHMAI (Jah´ mā ī) Personal name meaning "He protects me." Grandson of Issachar, great grandson of Jacob, and clan leader in tribe of Issachar (1 Chron. 7:2).

JAHWEH See *YHWH.*

JAHZAH (Jah´ zah) See *Jahaz.*

JAHZEEL (Jah´ zȧ ĕl) Personal name meaning "God apportions." Son of Naphtali, grandson of Jacob, and clan leader in tribe of Naphtali (Gen. 46:24; Num. 26:48). Jahziel (1 Chron. 7:13) represents a variant spelling.

JAHZEELITE (Jah´ zȧ ĕl īt) Clan in tribe of Naphtali. See *Jahzeel.*

JAHZEIAH (Jah zē´ yȧ) Modern translation spelling of Jahaziah (Ezra 10:15). See *Jahaziah.*

JAHZERAH (Jah´ zĕ rah) Personal name of uncertain meaning, possibly "careful"; "crafty"; or "let him turn back." A priest (1 Chron. 9:12). A similar list in Neh. 11:13 (KJV) lists Ahasai instead of Jahzerah.

JAHZIEL (Ja´ zĭ ĕl) (NIV, Gen. 46:24; 1 Chron. 7:13) See *Jahzeel.*

JAILER Keeper of a prison (Acts 16:23). See *Prison, Prisoners.*

JAIR (Jā´ īr) Abbreviated place-name meaning "Jah shines forth." **1.** Son of Manasseh who took possession of a number of villages in Gilead (Num. 32:41). See *Manasseh.* **2.** A Gileadite

J

who judged Israel for 22 years (Judg. 10:3-5). He was one of the so-called minor judges. His function probably was primarily judicial rather than military. He is described as having had 30 sons and 30 cities. At his death, he was buried in Camon. See *Judges.* **3.** Father of El-hanan (1 Chron. 20:5), whose name comes from a different Hebrew word, possibly meaning "Jah protects." His name is Jaare-oregim in 2 Sam. 21:19, though some translators would read the text "Jair of Bethlehem" (REB). **4.** Benjaminite who was the ancestor of Mordecai, Esther's guardian (Esther 2:5).

JAIRITE (Jā´ ĭr ĭt) Member of clan of Jair probably from Havvoth-jair, though possibly from Kiriath-jearim (2 Sam. 20:26). See *Jair.*

JAIRUS (Jī´ rŭs) Greek form of Hebrew personal name "Jair" meaning "Jah will enlighten." Synagogue official who came to Jesus seeking healing for his 12-year-old daughter (Mark 5:22). Before Jesus arrived at Jairus' house, however, the little girl died. Jesus reassured Jairus and entered the house with Peter, James, and John. Taking the girl by the hand, Jesus restored her to life, showing His power over death.

JAKAN (Jā´ kan) Personal name, perhaps meaning "he was fast." Descendant of or clan inhabiting territory of Seir (1 Chron. 1:42 according to KJV and Hebrew spelling). The Chronicles list repeats that of Gen. 36:27. Modern translations spell the name Akan or Jaakan here (cp. Deut. 10:6; Num. 33:31-32). See *Akan; Jaakan.*

JAKEH (Jā´ kĕ) Personal name meaning "prudent." Jakeh was the father or ancestor of Agur (Prov. 30:1).

JAKIM (Jā´ kĭm) Personal name meaning "He caused to stand." **1.** Member of tribe of Benjamin living in Ajalon (1 Chron. 8:19). **2.** Head of the 12th division of priests (1 Chron. 24:12).

JAKIN (Jā´ kĭn) (NIV) See *Jachin.*

JAKINITES (Jā´ kĭ nīts) (NIV) See *Jachinite.*

JALAM (Jā´ lam) Personal name meaning "their ibex or mountain goat" or "he is hidden or dark." Son of Esau and grandson of Isaac (Gen. 36:5), a clan leader among the Edomites (Gen. 36:18). KJV, REB spell the name Jaalam.

JALON (Jā´ lŏn) Personal name of uncertain meaning. Member of tribe of Judah and son of otherwise unknown Ezra (1 Chron. 4:17).

JAMBRES (Jăm´ brēs) See *Jannes.*

JAMES English form of Jacob, and the name of three men of the NT. See *Jacob.* **1.** James, the son of Zebedee and brother of John (Matt. 4:21; 10:2; Mark 1:19; 3:17; Luke 5:10). As one of the 12 disciples (Acts 1:13), he, with Peter and John, formed Jesus' innermost circle of associates. These three were present when Jesus raised Jairus' daughter (Mark 5:37; Luke 8:51), witnessed the transfiguration (Matt. 17:1; Mark 9:2; Luke 9:28), and were summoned by Christ for support during His agony in Gethsemane (Matt. 26:36-37; Mark 14:32-34).

Perhaps because of James' and John's fiery fanaticism, evidenced as they sought to call down fire from heaven on the Samaritan village refusing to receive Jesus and the disciples (Luke 9:52-54), Jesus called the brothers "Boanerges" or "sons of thunder" (Mark 3:17). James' zeal was revealed in a more selfish manner as he and John (their mother, on their behalf, in Matt. 20:20-21) sought special positions of honor for the time of Christ's glory (Mark 10:35-40). They were promised, however, only a share in His suffering. James was the first of the 12 to be martyred (Acts 12:2). His execution (about A.D. 44), by order of King Herod Agrippa I of Judea, was part of a larger persecution in which Peter was arrested (Acts 12:1-3).

2. James, the son of Alphaeus, one of the 12 disciples (Matt. 10:3; Mark 3:18; Luke 6:15; Acts 1:13). He is not distinguished by name in any occasion reported in the Gospels or Acts. He may be "James the younger," whose mother, Mary, was among the women at Jesus' crucifixion and tomb (Matt. 27:56; Mark 15:40; 16:1; Luke 24:10). In John 19:25, this Mary is called the wife of Cleophas, perhaps to be identified with Alphaeus. See *Cleophas; Mary.*

3. James, the brother of Jesus. Bible students debate the precise meaning of "the Lord's brother" (Gal. 1:19). Possibilities are the literal brother or stepbrother, a cousin, or intimate friend and associate. The literal meaning is to be preferred.

During the Lord's ministry, the brothers of Jesus (Matt. 13:55; Mark 6:3; 1 Cor. 9:5) were not believers (John 7:3-5; cp. Matt. 12:46-50; Mark 3:31-35; Luke 8:19-21). Paul specifically mentioned a resurrection appearance by Jesus to James (1 Cor. 15:7). After the resurrection and ascension, the brothers are said to have been with the Twelve and the other believers in Jerusalem (Acts 1:14).

Paul, seeking out Peter in Jerusalem after his conversion, reported, "I didn't see any of the other apostles except James, the Lord's brother" (Gal. 1:19 HCSB). In time, James assumed the leadership of the Jerusalem church, originally held by Peter. Evidently, such was achieved not through a power struggle but by James' constancy with the church while Peter and other apostles traveled. In a Jerusalem conference called regarding Paul's Gentile mission, James presided as spokesman for the Jerusalem church (Acts 15). See *Apostolic Council.*

James perceived that his calling was to the "circumcised," that is, the Jews (Gal. 2:9), and he is portrayed as loyal to Jewish tradition. He was, however, unwilling to make the law normative for all responding to God's new action in Christ. The death of James reportedly was at the order of the high priest Ananus and was either by stoning (according to Flavius Josephus, first-century historian of the Jews) or by being cast down from the temple tower (after Hegesippus, early Christian writer, quoted by the third-century Christian historian Eusebius). These accounts of James's death (about A.D. 66), are not confirmed in the NT.   *Joseph E. Glaze*

JAMES, LETTER FROM Letter from James belongs to the section of the NT usually described as the "General Epistles." The letter is one of exhortation for practical Christianity. The author stated principles of conduct and then frequently provided poignant illustrations. The author's concerns were clearly more practical and less abstract than those of any other NT writer. No other NT book has received criticism to the extent encountered by this epistle.

Author Verse one of the letter identifies James as the "servant of God" (NIV, NRSV, KJV) and the author of the letter. Several possibilities for proper identification of this "James" include

James the brother of John and the son of Zebedee, James the son of Alphaeus, one of the 12 apostles, or James the half brother of Jesus, a younger son of Mary and of Joseph. Of the three, James the brother of the Lord is the most likely choice. Tradition of the early church fathers universally ascribes the letter to James, the pastor of the church in Jerusalem. See *James 3.*

The general content of the letter is a call to holiness of life. This accords well with what is known of the life of James. Church tradition noted his exceptional piety, reporting that the knees of the saintly James were like those of a camel due to the unusual amounts of time spent on his knees before God. The author of the epistle was also steeped in the OT outlook in general and in Judaism in particular.

On the other hand, James the brother of John, the son of Zebedee, cannot be the author since he became an early martyr (Acts 12:1-2), his death almost certainly predating the writing of this letter from James. Little is known of James the son of Alphaeus—too little to conjecture that he was involved in the writing of the epistle.

Recipients Although some passages appear to address unbelievers (James 5:1-6), the letter is addressed to "the 12 tribes in the Dispersion" (1:1 HCSB). Reference to the "12 tribes" suggests that the recipients were Jews. Specifically, reference is made to the Jews of the Dispersion. This phrase recalled the scattering of the Jewish nation first in 722 B.C. when the Northern Kingdom of Israel fell to the Assyrian Empire and finally in 586 B.C. when the Southern Kingdom of Judah fell to the marauding Babylonians under Nebuchadnezzar.

However, James clearly had a still more narrow focus. Apparently, James had in mind the "Christian" Jews of dispersion. This may be conjectured from James' identification of himself (1:1) as a servant of Jesus Christ as well as from references like having "faith in our glorious Lord Jesus Christ" (2:1 HCSB).

Date Supposing an early date of writing may account for the peculiarity of the address. James' martyrdom by A.D. 66 provides us with the latest possible date of writing. Evidences of a very early date, such as the mention of those coming into the "assembly" (Gr. *sunagoge*), point to a time very early in Christian history, perhaps prior to the Jerusalem Conference in A.D. 49–50.

J

Though some Bible students date James after A.D. 60, many scholars are convinced that James is the first book of the NT to be written, some dating it as early as A.D. 48. As such, it provides the reader with a rather remarkable insight into the developing concerns of the church in its earliest era.

Occasion The letter was evidently the product of concerns on the part of early pastoral leadership about the ethical standards of early Christians. Therefore, the subject matter includes an analysis in chapter 1 of how to respond to temptation and trial (1:1-18). The necessity of "doing" the word as well as "hearing" the word is the focus of James 1:19-27. Treatment of the poor and the appropriate management of wealth are topics of concern in James 2:1-13 and 5:1-6. The waywardness of the tongue and the necessity of its taming are discussed in chapter 3. Conflicts and attitudes to other Christians are the subjects of chapter 4. Appropriate responses to life's demands and pressures are suggested in chapter 5.

James' Contributions Some scholars have compared James to the OT book of Proverbs. In many respects the two are quite different. However, the comparison is valid from the perspective of ethical instruction. The theme of the book is that practical religion must manifest itself in works that are superior to those of the world. The essence of such works covers the areas of personal holiness and service to others, such as visiting "orphans and widows," and keeping oneself "unstained by the world" (1:27 HCSB). These "works" further demand active resistance to the devil (4:7), submission to God (4:7), and even brokenhearted repentance for sins (4:9).

Patience in the wake of trials and temptations is the subject both of the introduction and of the conclusion of the epistle. Readers are to "consider it a great joy" when trials come (1:2 HCSB) and expect reward for endurance of those trials (1:12). In James 5:7-11 James returns to the subject, citing both Job and the prophets as appropriate examples of patience in the midst of tribulation.

Questions and Challenges of James Two difficult and widely debated passages in James challenge Bible students. In 2:14-26, James argued that "faith, if it doesn't have works, is dead by itself" (2:17 HCSB). This apparent contradiction to the teaching of the Apostle Paul has caused

much consternation among some theologians. For example, Martin Luther referred to the book as "an epistle of straw" when compared with Paul's writings.

More careful exegesis has shown that the contradiction is apparent rather than real. James argued that a faith that is only a "confessing faith," such as that of the demons (2:19), is not a saving faith at all. The demons believed in God in the sense of "intellectual assent," but they were void of belief in the sense of "commitment." Orthodoxy of doctrine that does not produce a sanctified lifestyle is, in the final analysis, worthless.

In 5:13-16 James spoke of healing and its means. Actually, this passage only treats the subject of healing incidentally. The actual purpose of the discussion is to stress the effectiveness of the earnest prayer of a righteous man (5:15-16). This is illustrated by a reference to Elijah, whose prayers were sufficient alternately to shut up the heavens and then to open them (5:17-18).

Whatever else may be intended, clearly the prayer of faith "will save the sick person" (HCSB). The anointing oil, whether medicinal, as some have argued, or symbolic, as others have held, is not the healing agent. God heals when He chooses to heal (5:14), as a response to the fervent prayers of righteous men.

The letter from James remains of lasting value and consequence to the Christian confronted by an increasingly secular world. Christ ought to make a difference in one's life. That is the theme and mandate of James.

Outline

I. Salutation (1:1)
II. True Religion Is Developed by Trials and Testing (1:2-15).
   A. Joy is the correct response to times of testing (1:2).
   B. Testing of faith can result in steadfastness that, when mature, enables us to be perfect, complete, and lacking in nothing (1:3-4).
   C. True wisdom comes from God and is available to those who ask in faith, not doubting (1:5-8).
   D. Wealth may be a test of faith, not a proof of faith (1:9-11).
   E. Perseverance under trial leads to blessing (1:12).

F. Temptation comes from within, not from God, and is to be resisted (1:13-15).

III. True Religion Is Initiated by Faith (1:16–2:27).
A. Salvation by faith is a gift from God, as are all good gifts (1:16-17).
B. Salvation as an expression of God's will is related to God's Word (1:18-27).
1. We are to receive God's Word (1:18-21).
2. We are to do God's Word, not just hear it (1:22-25).
3. We must control our speech and practice true religion (1:26-27).
C. Saving faith does not show favoritism but shows love to all (2:1-13).
D. Saving faith issues in godly attitudes and actions (2:14-26).

IV. True Religion Is Guided by Wisdom (3:1-18).
A. The wise person controls the tongue (3:1-12).
B. Earthly wisdom is characterized by evil attitudes and actions (3:13-16).
C. The wise person's life is characterized by moral behavior (3:17-18).

V. True Religion Is Demonstrated by Works (4:1–5:12).
A. Avoid acting selfishly instead of asking God (4:1-3).
B. Avoid being friendly with the world (4:4-5).
C. Possess the proper attitude toward self—being humble, not proud or presumptuous (4:6-10).
D. Avoid speaking against or judging other Christians (4:11-12).
E. Avoid presuming on God's time (4:13-16).
F. Do not fail to do what you know is right (4:17).
G. Avoid depending on wealth (5:1-3).
H. Avoid treating persons unjustly (5:4-6).
I. Do not be impatient, for the Lord is coming (5:7-11).
J. Do not take oaths (5:12).

VI. True Religion Is Expressed in Prayer (5:13-20).

A. Prayer, including intercession, is a significant part of true religion (5:13-16a).
1. Prayer is a proper response to suffering and illness (5:13-14).
2. Prayers are to be offered in faith, with right motives (5:15).
3. Prayer includes confession of sins (5:16a).
B. The righteousness of the person praying is related to the effectiveness of the prayer (5:16b).
C. All humans can pray and be heard (5:17-18).
D. Intercession for sinners is an important Christian responsibility (5:19-20).

Paige Patterson

JAMIN (Jā´ mĭn) Personal name meaning "on the right" or "good luck." **1.** Son of Simeon and grandson of Jacob, a clan leader in tribe of Simeon (Exod. 6:15; Num. 26:12). **2.** Grandson of Jerahmeel (1 Chron. 2:27). **3.** Levite who interpreted the law for the people as Ezra read it (Neh. 8:7). **4.** Component of name "Benjamin" meaning "right hand."

JAMINITE (Jā´ mĭn īt) Member of clan headed by Jamin. See *Jamin*.

JAMLECH (Jăm´ lĕk) Personal name meaning "May He cause to be king." Member of tribe of Simeon (1 Chron. 4:34).

JANAI (Jā´ nā ī) Personal name meaning "may He answer me." Member of tribe of Gad (1 Chron. 5:12).

JANGLING, VAIN KJV expression for idle talk (1 Tim. 1:6). Translation alternatives include foolish (TEV), fruitless (HCSB, NASB) or vain (RSV) discussion, meaningless talk (NIV, NRSV), and a wilderness of words (REB).

JANIM (Jā´ nĭm) Modern translation spelling of Janum following written Hebrew text (Josh. 15:53). See *Janum*.

JANNA (Jăn´ nȧ) or **JANNAI** (Jăn´ nī) Personal name of uncertain meaning. Ancestor of Jesus and head of final list of seven names before Jesus (Luke 3:24). Modern translations spell Jannai.

JANNES AND JAMBRES (Jăn´ nēs and Jăm´ brēs) Two opposers of Moses and Aaron (2 Tim. 3:8). Though the names do not appear in the OT, rabbinic tradition identified Jannes and Jambres as being among those Egyptian magicians who sought to duplicate for Pharaoh the miracles performed by Moses (Exod. 7:11). The Damascus Document from the Qumran Sect describes the two as brothers raised up by Belial, the evil one. Eusebius of Caesarea described them as sacred scribes of Egypt. The Jewish tradition makes several mentions of them, but in the end they could not match God's power displayed through Moses.

JANOAH (Jà nō´ ah) or **JANOHAH** (Jà nō´ hah) Place-name meaning "he rests." **1.** Town in tribal territory of Ephraim (Josh. 16:6-7). It is probably modern Khirbet Janun about seven miles south of Nablus. KJV transliterates the Hebrew *ah* meaning "towards" and so spells Janohah here. **2.** City in northern Israel that Tiglath-pileser, king of Assyria (744–727 B.C.), captured from Pekah, king of Israel (752–732 B.C.), about 733 B.C. Its location is uncertain, suggestions including Khirbet Janun; Janua, six miles south of Megiddo, and Janoah, nine miles east of Acco. Recently, interpreters have sought to establish a military pattern in the report and locate Janoah at Khirbet Niha just south of Kefar Giladi on the road south from Abel-beth-maacah.

JANUM (Jā´ nŭm) Place-name of uncertain meaning, perhaps "slumbering." Town in tribal territory of Judah (Josh. 15:53) near Hebron. The location is not known. KJV, NASB spelling follows vocalization by early Hebrew scribes. See *Janim.*

JAPHETH (Jā´ phĕth) Personal name meaning "may he have space." One of Noah's three sons, either the youngest or next to youngest (Gen. 5:32). Genesis 10:2 identifies Japheth's sons as Gomer, Magog, Madai, Javan, Tubal, Meshech, and Tiras. One of the titans of Greek mythology had a similar name. These names point to Japheth as having been the progenitor of the Indo-European peoples who lived to the north and west of Israel, farthest from Israel. Genesis 9:27 pronounces God's blessing on Japheth and his descendants, including living with Shem, thus getting to dwell in the land of promise, and being served by the Canaanites, thus sharing the

position as God's people. Here is an early indication of non-Israelites having a share with God's people. See *Noah; Table of Nations.*

JAPHIA (Jà·phī´ à) Place and personal name meaning "place situated high above" or "may He bring shining light." **1.** Border town of tribal territory of Zebulun (Josh. 19:12). In the Amarna Letters, the Egyptian pharaoh required the town to supply forced laborers after Labayu of Shechem destroyed Shunem. It is modern Yafa, southwest of Nazareth. **2.** King of Lachish who joined southern coalition against Joshua and met death by cave of Makkedah (Josh. 10:1-27,31-32). **3.** Son born to David in Jerusalem by unnamed wife (2 Sam. 5:15).

JAPHLET (Jăph´ lĕt) Personal name meaning "He rescues." Member of tribe of Asher (1 Chron. 7:32-33).

JAPHLETI (Jăph´ lĕt ī) or **JAPHLETITE** (Jăph´ lē tīt) Place-name according to KJV but name of tribal group—Japhletites—according to modern translations (Josh. 16:3). The clan's territory lay on border between Ephraim and Benjamin, though the clan apparently belonged to Asher. See *Japhlet.*

JAPHO (Jā´ phō) (KJV) See *Joppa.*

JAR See *Pottery; Vessels and Utensils.*

JARAH (Jā´ rah) Personal name meaning "goat." Descendant of King Saul (1 Chron. 9:42), apparently the same as Jehoadah in 8:36, the words being spelled the same except for one similarly written letter in Hebrew (cp. 1 Chron. 10:6).

JAREB (Jā´ rĕb) Personal name meaning "the great one" or "he contends" (in court). Modern translations see the term as part of a Near Eastern expression, "the great king," often applied to the king of Assyria, as in the Aramaic treaty inscriptions from Sefire and in the Assyrian equivalent in 2 Kings 18:19. Hosea accused Israel and Judah of turning to the "great king" of Assyria, probably Tiglath-pileser III (at least for Judah), to cure their ills rather than going to Yahweh, the great King of the universe and the Great Physician (Hos. 5:13). Hosea pronounced just punishment for Israel, their "calf-god" (REB) would be carried to Babylon as tribute to "the Great King" (10:5-6).

JARED (Jăr´ ĕd) Personal name meaning "slave." **1.** Father of Enoch (Gen. 5:15-20). **2.** Member of tribe of Judah (1 Chron. 4:18; English translations usually spell the same Hebrew word "Jered" here rather than Jared).

JARESIAH (Jâr·ə·sī´ ah) (KJV) See *Jaareshiah*.

JARHA (Jär´ hȧ) Personal name of uncertain meaning. Egyptian slave used by his master She-shan to maintain the family line in clan of Jerah-meel and tribe of Judah (1 Chron. 2:34-35).

JARIB (Jā´ rĭb) Personal name meaning "He contends against" or "He is legal opponent of" (Ps. 35:1; Isa. 49:25). **1.** Member of tribe of Simeon (1 Chron. 4:24) but called Jachin in Num. 26:12. See *Jachin*. **2.** Levite who served as messenger for Ezra in his search for Levites to accompany him back to Jerusalem (Ezra 8:16). **3.** Priest who pledged under Ezra's leadership to divorce his foreign wife to remove the temptation to worship the foreigners' gods (Ezra 10:18).

JARMUTH (Jär´ mŭth) Place-name meaning "height" or "swelling in the ground." **1.** City whose king joined southern coalition against Joshua and Gibeon (Josh. 10). Joshua "stored" the king in the cave of Makkedah before shaming him and slaying him (cp. 12:11). It lay in the western "lowlands" (NASB, NRSV), the "foothills" (NIV), or Shephelah (REB) of the tribe of Judah (Josh. 15:33,35). It is identified with modern Tell Jarmuth three miles southwest of Beth-shemesh and 15 miles southwest of Jerusalem. An Amarna letter from Tell el-Hesi mentions it. Brief excavations have shown early Bronze and Stone Age remains but as yet nothing from the late Bronze or early Iron Ages. In Nehemiah's time Jewish settlers lived there (Neh. 11:29). **2.** City of the Levites in the tribal territory of Issachar (Josh. 21:29; cp. 19:21; 1 Chron. 6:73, both spelled differently and differing from 1. above; thus spelling of Remeth, Ramoth). This city may be located at modern Kaukab el-Hawa.

JAROAH (Jȧ rō´ ah) Personal name meaning "smooth, gentle" or "shown mercy." Member of tribe of Gad (1 Chron. 5:14).

JASHAR, BOOK OF (Jăsh´ ȧr) An ancient written collection of poetry quoted by Bible authors. See *Books*.

JASHEN (Jā´ shĕn) Personal name meaning "sleepy." Member of David's elite military corps, the "30" or groups of threes perhaps (2 Sam. 23:32). First Chronicles 11:34 apparently spells the same name Hashem and calls him the Gizonite. See *Gizonite*.

JASHER (Jā´ shẽr) (KJV) See *Jashar*.

JASHOBEAM (Jȧ shō´ bə ăm) Personal name meaning "the uncle (or people) will return." Warrior of Saul's tribe of Benjamin who supported David at Ziklag as he fled from Saul (1 Chron. 12:6). He is listed first as "the chief of the thirty" (1 Chron. 11:11 NASB). Some interpreters would say the text listed him as a Hachmonite, while others would see "Hachmonite" as reference to a different individual. Second Samuel 23:8 spells the name Josheb-basshebeth (see modern translations), the last part of which represents the Hebrew word for "shame," at times used by scribes instead of an original name containing the Canaanite god's name Baal, leading some interpreters to see the original name here as Yishbaal. Some Greek manuscripts actually read Ishbaal. In 2 Sam. 23:8 REB reads Ishbosheth. KJV simply translates there: "that sat in the seat." Jashobeam commanded David's first course or division administering the kingdom for the first month of each year (1 Chron. 27:2). Here Jashobeam is the son of Zabdiel, a descendant of Perez who belonged to the tribe of Judah. Elsewhere Jashobeam is a member of the clan of Hachmon. See *Hachmonites*.

JASHUB (Jā´ shŭb) Personal name meaning "He turns to" or "He returns." The name is found in several Near Eastern cultures. **1.** Clan leader in tribe of Issachar (Num. 26:24). Genesis 46:13 (KJV) names him Job. **2.** Man with foreign wife condemned by Ezra as bringing temptation to foreign worship into the community (Ezra 10:29). **3.** Part of name of Isaiah's son (Isa. 7:3). See *Shear-jashub*. **4.** Some interpreters see a town named Jashub in Josh. 17:7, a border town

J

of the tribe of Manasseh (REB). This would be modern Jasuf, eight miles south of Shechem.

JASHUBI-LEHEM (Já shū bī-lē´ hĕm) Personal name meaning "Jashubites of bread" or "she returns for bread." Member of tribe of Judah (1 Chron. 4:22 NASB, KJV, NIV). Hebrew text has two words which modern interpreters read in different ways: but returned to Lehem (NRSV); then settled in Bethlehem (TEV).

JASHUBITE (Jā shŭb ī t) Member of clan founded by Jashub. See *Jashub.*

JASIEL (Jăs´ ĭ ĕl) (KJV) See *Jaasiel.*

JASON (Jā´ son) Personal name often used by Jews as a substitute for Hebrew Joshua or Joseph and also used by Gentiles. **1.** In Acts 17:5 Paul's host in Thessalonica. He was brought up on charges before the city officials when the angry Jewish mob was unable to find Paul (Acts 17:6-7). The Jason mentioned in Rom. 16:21 may have been the same person. He is identified as a Jew who joined Paul and others in greeting the Romans. **2.** Jewish high priest during the final years of Seleucid control of Palestine. His Greek name reflects the Hellenistic influence that increasingly permeated Jewish life during the period before the Maccabean revolt. See *Intertestamental History and Literature.*

JASPER Green chalcedony. Jasper commonly translates two Hebrew terms and one Greek term. The first term is used for the sixth stone in the headdress of the king of Tyre (Ezek. 28:13). The second term is used for a stone in the high priest's breastplate (Exod. 28:20; 39:13). This second term is rendered onyx at Ezek. 28:13. The third term describes the face of the One seated on the throne (Rev. 4:3) and the glory of the new Jerusalem (Rev. 21:11,18-19). The NIV used "jasper" to translate an obscure Hebrew term at Job 28:18. Other translation options include alabaster (REB), crystal (NASB, NRSV, TEV), and pearls (KJV). See *Minerals and Metals.*

JATHNIEL (Jăth´ nĭ ĕl) Personal name meaning "God gives." A Levite gatekeeper (1 Chron. 26:2).

JATTIR (Jăt´ tĩr) Place-name meaning "the remainder." Town in the hills of the tribal territory of Judah (Josh. 15:48). David gave some of war booty from victory over Amalekites to Jattir (1 Sam. 30:27). Joshua reserved it for the Levites (Josh. 21:14). It was located near modern Khirbet Attir about 13 miles south-southwest of Hebron and 14 miles northeast of Beersheba.

JAVAN (Jā´ văn) Personal name meaning "Greece." Son of Japheth (Gen. 10:2) and father of Elishah, Tarshish, Kittim, and Dodanim (Gen. 10:4), thus the original ancestor of Greek peoples. Elsewhere in the OT, the name Javan is used to denote Greece. See *Greece; Table of Nations.*

JAVELIN Light spear thrown as a weapon. See *Arms and Armor; Weapons.*

JAW Either of two bony structures that border the mouth and bear the teeth. The taking of captives in war is sometimes pictured using the

Statuette of Near Eastern warrior holding a spear or javelin from around 1500 B.C.

images of animals led with bridles in their jaws (Isa. 30:28) or fish carried away with hooks in theirs (Ezek. 29:4; 38:4). According to one understanding of Hos. 11:4, God, pictured as a farmer, "lifts the yoke from their jaws" (NASB), that is, looses the yoke so that the oxen might feed better.

JAZER (Jā´ zēr) Place-name meaning "May He help." Amorite city-state that Israel conquered while marching across the land east of the Jordan towards the promised land (Num. 21:32). The tribe of Gad rebuilt and settled Jazer (Num. 32:35; cp. Josh. 13:25). Joshua assigned it to the Levites (Josh. 21:39). Isaiah pronounced judgment on Jazer while preaching against Moab (Isa. 16:8-9). Jeremiah echoed him (Jer. 48:32). David found outstanding leaders there (1 Chron. 26:31-32). It was also an important city in the period between the Testaments (1 Macc. 5:8). Interpreters debate Jazer's exact location. German archaeologists appear to favor Tell el-Areme, while Israelis point to Khirbet es-Sar about eight miles west of Amman. Others point to Khirbet Jazzir about two miles south of es-Salt.

JAZIZ (Jā´ zĭz) Personal name meaning "he goads." Chief shepherd under David. He was probably a foreigner. See *Hagrite.*

JEALOUSY Used in three senses in Scripture: (1) as intolerance of rivalry or unfaithfulness; (2) as a disposition suspicious of rivalry or unfaithfulness; and (3) as hostility towards a rival or one believed to enjoy an advantage, a sense of envy. God is jealous for His people Israel in sense (1), that is, God is intolerant of rival gods (Exod. 20:5; 34:14; Deut. 4:24; 5:9) One expression of God's jealousy for Israel is God's protection of His people from enemies. Thus God's jealousy includes avenging Israel (Ezek. 36:6; 39:25; Nah. 1:2; Zech. 1:14; 8:2). Phinehas is described as jealous with God's jealousy (Num. 25:11,13, sometimes translated zealous for God). Elijah is similarly characterized as jealous (or zealous) for God (1 Kings 19:10,14). In the NT Paul speaks of his divine jealousy for the Christians at Corinth (2 Cor. 11:2).

Numbers 5:11-30 concerns the process by which a husband suspicious of his wife's unfaithfulness might test her. Most often human jealousy involves hostility towards a rival. Joseph's brothers were jealous (Gen. 37:11) and thus sold their brother into slavery (Acts 7:9). In Acts 17:5 a jealous group among the Jews incited the crowd against Paul. Jealousy, like envy, is common in vice lists (Rom. 13:13; 2 Cor. 12:20; Gal. 5:20-21). Jealousy is regarded as worse than wrath or anger (Prov. 27:4). James regarded jealousy (or bitter envy) as characteristic of earthy, demonic wisdom (3:14) and as the source of all disorder and wickedness (3:16). See *Envy.*

JEALOUSY, CEREAL OFFERING OF See *Jealousy, Ordeal of.*

JEALOUSY, IMAGE OF Term for an idol in Ezek. 8:3,5 (NRSV, KJV). The meaning is either that the idol evokes God's jealousy or that the idol is identified with Asherah, the goddess of passionate love (cp. 2 Kings 21:7; 2 Chron. 33:7). See *Jealousy.*

JEALOUSY, ORDEAL OF Test to determine guilt or innocence of a wife suspected of adultery but who had not been caught in the act (Num. 5:11-31). The ordeal consisted of two parts: "a grain offering of memorial, a reminder of iniquity" (5:15 NASB) and "the water of bitterness that brings a curse" (5:18). See *Bitter Water.*

JEALOUSY, WATER OF See *Bitter Water.*

JEARIM (Jē´ å·rĭm) Place-name meaning "forests" or "parks." Component of several OT place-names including Kiriath-jearim, Mount Jearim, Fields of Jearim, and the wood of 1 Sam. 14:26. See *Chesalon; Kiriath-jearim.*

JEATERAI (Jə ăt´ ə rī) or **JEATHERAI** (Jə ăth´ ə rī) Personal name of uncertain meaning. Levite (1 Chron. 6:21) perhaps to be identified with Ethni (1 Chron. 6:41).

JEBERECHIAH (Jə bĕr ə·kī´ ah) or **JEBEREKIAH** (NIV) Personal name meaning "Yahweh blesses." Father of Zechariah who served as witness for Isaiah (Isa. 8:2; cp. 2 Kings 18:2).

JEBUS (Jē´ bŭs) Place-name meaning "trodden under foot." Name of tribe originally occupying Jerusalem and then of city (Judg. 19:10; cp. Josh. 18:28; 1 Chron. 11:4). The name "Jebus" does not occur outside the Bible. See *Jebusi or Jebusites; Jerusalem.*

J

JEBUSI (Jĕb´ ū sī) (KJV, Josh. 18:16,28) or **JEBUSITES** (Jĕb´ ū sīts) Clan who originally controlled Jerusalem before David conquered the city. In the list of the descendants of Noah (Gen. 10) the Jebusites are traced through the line of Ham and Canaan and are listed alongside other clans such as the Amorites and Girgashites. In Josh. 10 the king of Jerusalem, Adonizedek, is considered one of the five Amorite kings who fought against Joshua. In the time of the judges, Jerusalem was attacked and burned by the men of Judah (Judg. 1:8), but the Jebusites were not expelled. Centuries later David captured the city and made it his capital. David purchased a stone threshing floor from a Jebusite named Araunah (2 Sam. 24:16-24), and this later became the site of Solomon's temple. The remnants of the Jebusites became bondservants during Solomon's reign (1 Kings 9:20-21). Jebusite names appear to be Hurrian rather than Semitic. See *Jerusalem.*

M. Stephen Davis

JECAMIAH (Jĕc á mī´ ah) (KJV) Personal name meaning "Yah causes to stand." **1.** Member of clan of Jerahmeel in tribe of Judah (1 Chron. 2:41). **2.** Son of King Jeconiah (Jehoiachin), the Judean king exiled by Babylon (1 Chron. 3:18). English translations sometimes spell these two names differently though they are the same Hebrew name.

JECHILIAH (Jĕk ĭ lī´ ah) NASB spelling (2 Chron. 26:3) following written Hebrew text. Other English translations follow early scribal note, versions, and 2 Kings 15:2, reading Jecoliah.

JECHOLIAH (Jĕk ō lī´ ah) (KJV, 2 Kings 15:2) See *Jechiliah.*

JECHONIAH (Jĕk ō nī´ ah) Personal name meaning "Jah establishes." Shortened form of Jehoiachin. Alternative spellings are Jeconiah and Jechonias. See *Jehoiachin.*

JECOLIAH (Jĕc ō lī´ ah) Mother of Uzziah, king of Judah (2 Kings 15:2; 2 Chron. 26:3). See *Jechiliah; Jecholiah.*

JEDAIAH (Jə dī´ ah) **1.** Personal name meaning "praise Yah" or "Yah has performed a merciful deed." Man who helped Nehemiah repair the wall of Jerusalem (Neh. 3:10) and a descendant

of the tribe of Simeon (1 Chron. 4:37). **2.** Personal name meaning "Yah knows." A priest or priests heading the second course or division of priests (1 Chron. 24:7), returned from Babylonian exile (1 Chron. 9:10; cp. Ezra 2:36; Neh. 7:39; 11:10; 12:6-7,19,21). The returning exile may be same as one from whom the prophet Zechariah received gold and silver (Zech. 6:10,14). English translations usually spell the names the same though they represent two distinct Hebrew names.

JEDIAEL (Jə dī´ ā ĕl) Personal name meaning "the one whom God knows." **1.** Member of tribe of Benjamin (1 Chron. 7:6,10-11). **2.** Military leader under David (1 Chron. 11:45). The same or a different warrior from the tribe of Manasseh joined David when he moved to Ziklag (1 Chron. 12:20). **3.** Levite and gatekeeper (1 Chron. 26:2).

JEDIDAH (Jə dī´ dah) Personal name meaning "darling" or "beloved." Mother of Josiah king of Judah (2 Kings 22:1).

JEDIDIAH (Jĕ dī dī´ ah) Personal name or nickname meaning "Yah's darling." A similar name meaning "El's darling" appears in the Ugaritic materials. A name God told David to give to his son Solomon (2 Sam. 12:25). Despite David's sin with Bathsheba and the death of the child of their sinful relationship, God showed His love to their child Solomon, thus underlining God's forgiving nature and His continued commitment to David and his royal house.

JEDUTHUN (Jə dū´ thŭn) Personal name meaning "praise." Prophetic musician and Levite in the service of King David (1 Chron. 25:1). The names Asaph and Heman appear along with that of Jeduthun as original ancestors of temple musicians. In 1 Chron. 15:17, however, Asaph and Heman are associated with Ethan, suggesting that Ethan and Jeduthun may be different names for the same person. If that is the case, Jeduthun would have been the son of Kushaiah and a member of the clan of Merari. Otherwise, nothing is known about Jeduthun's ancestry. In 1 Chron. 25:1,3 he is said to have prophesied using musical instruments; and in 2 Chron. 35:15 he is referred to as the king's seer, apparently working with Zadok at Gibeon (1 Chron. 16:37-42). Three psalms (39; 62; 77) include his name in their titles. The exact nature of Jeduthun's relationship to these psalms is uncertain. See *Music, Instruments, Dancing; Priests and Levites; Psalms, Book of.*

JEEZER (Jə ē´ zēr) Personal name meaning "where is help?" or a shortened form of "my brother helps" or "my father helps." Original head of a clan in tribe of Gilead (Num. 26:30 KJV). Apparently, the same name is intended in Josh. 17:2 where Abiezer occurs, quite probably the original name. Modern translations often use spelling Iezer. See *Abiezer.*

JEEZERITE (Jə ē´ zēr-īt) Member of clan of Jeezer. See *Jeezer.*

JEGAR-SAHADUTHA (Jē ğär-sä hȧ dū´ thȧ) Aramaic place-name meaning "stone marker." Aramaic equivalent of Galeed. See *Galeed.*

JEHALELEEL (Jə hȧ lē´ lə ĕl) or **JEHALELEL** or **JEHALLELEL** Personal name meaning "he praises God" or "God shines forth." **1.** Member of tribe of Judah (1 Chron. 4:16). **2.** Levite whose son helped King Hezekiah purify the temple (2 Chron. 29:12). English translations are not always consistent in transliterating this Hebrew name in its two occurrences.

JEHATH (Je´ hăth) (NIV, 1 Chron. 6:20) See *Jahath.*

JEHAZIEL (Jə hăz´ ĭ ĕl) See *Jahaziel.*

JEHDEIAH (Jĕh dē´ yȧ) Personal name meaning "Yahweh rejoices." **1.** Levite listed outside the 24 courses of Levites (1 Chron. 24:20). **2.** Keeper of the royal donkeys under David (1 Chron. 27:30). His home was Meronoth.

JEHEZEKEL (Jə hĕ´ zə kĕl) or **JEHEZKEL** (Jə hĕz´ kĕl) (NASB, NIV, TEV, REB, NRSV) Personal name meaning "God strengthens." Same Hebrew spelling as Prophet Ezekiel. Head of 20th course of priests (1 Chron. 24:16).

JEHIAH (Jə hī´ ah) Personal name meaning "may he live, O Yah." Guard of the ark when David brought it up from Philistine territory (1 Chron. 15:24).

JEHIEL (Jə hī´ ĕl) Personal name meaning "Let him live, O God." **1.** Apparently a variant name

for Jehiah (1 Chron. 15:18; cp. v. 24). See *Jehiah.* **2.** Levite musician who played the lute before the ark (1 Chron. 15:20; 16:5). **3.** Leading Levite (1 Chron. 23:8). **4.** Levite in charge of treasury for God's house under David (1 Chron. 29:8; cp. 26:20-22). **5.** Guardian of the royal sons under David (1 Chron. 27:32). **6.** Son of King Jehoshaphat slain by his brother King Jehoram when the latter ascended to the throne (2 Chron. 21:1-4). **7.** Levite who helped purify the temple under King Hezekiah (2 Chron. 29:14) according to ancient Bible translations and scribal note; the written Hebrew text has "Jehuel." Later, under Hezekiah possibly the same Jehiel served as an overseer in the temple (2 Chron. 31:13). **8.** Leading priest under Josiah who distributed large offerings to the priests for their Passover offerings (2 Chron. 35:8). **9.** Father of man who returned with Ezra to Jerusalem from Babylon (Ezra 8:9). **10.** Father of man who proposed that men with foreign wives divorce them in order not to tempt others to worship foreign gods under Ezra (Ezra 10:1-4). **11.** Priest who agreed to divorce his foreign wife under Ezra (Ezra 10:21). **12.** Layman who agreed to divorce his foreign wife under Ezra (Ezra 10:26).

JEHIELI (Jə hī´ ĕ lī) or **JEHIELITE** (Jə hī´ ĕ´ līt) (NASB) Member of clan founded by Jehiel (1 Chron. 26:21-22). See *Jehiel.*

JEHIZKIAH (Jē hĭz kī´ ah) Personal name meaning "Yahweh strengthens." **1.** Variant Hebrew spelling of Hezekiah (2 Kings 20:10; Isa. 1:1; 1 Chron. 4:41; 2 Chron. 28:27–33:3). **2.** Man of tribe of Ephraim who prevented people of Israel from bringing war prisoners from Judah into the city after Pekah of Israel defeated Ahaz of Judah about 733 B.C. (2 Chron. 28:12).

JEHOADAH (Jə hō´ ȧ dah) or **JEHOADDAH** (Jə hō´ ăd dah) Personal name, perhaps meaning "Yahweh is ornamentation." Descendant of Saul in tribe of Benjamin (1 Chron. 8:36), the list showing a continued interest in lineage of Saul long after his death.

JEHOADDAN (Jē hō ăd´ dȧn) Personal name meaning "Yahweh is bliss." Mother of King Amaziah of Judah (2 Kings 14:2).

JEHOADDIN (Jē hō ăd´ dĭn) Variant spelling of Jehoaddan in written Hebrew text of 2 Kings 14:2, where early Hebrew scribal note has Jehoaddan in agreement with 2 Chron. 25:1. See *Jehoaddan.*

JEHOAHAZ (Jə hō á hăz) Personal name meaning "Yahweh grasps hold." Two kings of Judah and one king of Israel bore this name. **1.** In 2 Chron. 21:17 the son and successor of Jehoram as king of Judah (841 B.C.). He is more frequently referred to as Ahaziah. **2.** In 2 Kings 10:35 the son and successor of Jehu as king of Israel (814–798 B.C.). His reign is summarized in 2 Kings 13. Although 2 Kings 13:1 states that he reigned for 17 years, a comparison of verse 1 with verse 10 seems to point to a reign of 14 years or a co-regency with his son for about three years. **3.** In 2 Kings 23:30 the son and successor of Josiah as king of Judah (609 B.C.). He is also known as Shallum. See *Chronology of the Biblical Period; Israel, Land of.*

JEHOASH (Jə hō´ ăsh) Personal name meaning "Yahweh gave." Variant spelling of Joash. See *Joash.*

JEHOHANAN (Jē hō´ hā năn) Personal name meaning "Yahweh is gracious." **1.** Priest in whose temple quarters Ezra refreshed himself and mourned for the sin of the people in taking foreign wives (Ezra 10:6). This Jehohanan is sometimes equated with the high priest of Neh. 12:22-23 who is considered then to be a grandson of the high priest Eliashib and also to be the high priest mentioned in the Elephantine Papyri as serving about 411 B.C. Such evidence is then used to date the ministry of Ezra to about 398 B.C. rather than being in the time of Nehemiah. The relationships between the priestly Eliashibs and Jehohanans of Scripture are too unclear to make dating decisions on them. This Jehohanan may have been related to the Eliashib of Neh. 13:4 who was not a high priest but was closely connected to temple chambers. See *Ezra.* **2.** Layman with a foreign wife under Ezra (Ezra 10:28). **3.** Son of Tobiah, who opposed Nehemiah's work in Jerusalem (Neh. 6:18). Jehohanan's marriage to a prominent Jerusalem family gave Tobiah an information system concerning Jerusalem happenings. See *Meshullam; Tobiah.* **4.** Head of a priestly family about 450 B.C. (Neh. 12:13). **5.** Priest who helped

Nehemiah celebrate completion of Jerusalem wall (Neh. 12:42). **6.** Levite and gatekeeper (1 Chron. 26:3). **7.** Military commander under King Jehoshaphat of Judah (2 Chron. 17:15). **8.** Father of a military commander under Jehoiada, the high priest, in the assassination of Queen Athaliah and the installation of Joash as king of Judah about 835 B.C. **9.** Father of military captain under King Pekah of Israel (2 Chron. 28:12).

JEHOIACHIN (Jə hoî´ á kin) Personal name meaning "Yahweh establishes." In 2 Kings 24:6 the son and successor of Jehoiakim as king of Judah. He was 18 years old when he came to the throne late in 598 B.C., and he reigned for three months in Jerusalem before being taken into captivity by Nebuchadnezzar of Babylon. The prominence in the account of his reign of his mother Nehushta suggests that she may have wielded considerable influence during the time that her son was in office. Jehoiachin evidently was a throne name taken at the time of accession to the kingship. Jehoiachin's original name seems to have been Jeconiah or Coniah. He retained the title "king of Judah" even in exile, but he never returned to Judah to exercise rule there. Nevertheless, he was ultimately released from prison by Evil-merodach of Babylon and accorded some honor in the land of his captivity (2 Kings 25:27-30). See *Chronology of the Biblical Period; Israel, Land of.*

JEHOIADA (Jə hoî´ á dà) Personal name meaning "Yahweh knows" or "Yahweh concerns Himself for." **1.** Priest who led the coup in which Queen Athaliah, who had usurped the throne of Judah, was slain and Joash (Jehoash), the legitimate heir to the monarchy, was enthroned (2 Kings 11:4). At the time, Joash was a child of seven, and Jehoiada evidently acted as regent for a number of years. Jehoiada's role was positive and beneficial; he influenced the young king to restore the temple. The death of Jehoiada marked a precipitous decline in the king's goodness and faithfulness to the Lord (2 Chron. 22–24). See *Athaliah; Joash; Priests and Levites.* **2.** Father of Benaiah, David's military leader (2 Sam. 8:18) apparently from Kabzeel (2 Sam. 23:20). This Jehoiada was apparently a Levite and military leader for David at Hebron (1 Chron. 12:27). **3.** Leading priest in the time of Jeremiah preceding Zephaniah (Jer. 29:25-26).

JEHOIAKIM (Jə hoî´ à kĭm) Personal name meaning "Yahweh has caused to stand." Son of Josiah who succeeded Jehoahaz as king of Judah (609–597). Jehoiakim was a throne name given to him by Pharaoh Neco of Egypt, who deposed his brother Jehoahaz. His original name had been Eliakim (2 Kings 23:34). He and his predecessor on the throne were brothers, sons of Josiah. He reigned for 11 years. At the beginning of his reign, Judah was subject to Egypt. Probably in 605 B.C., however, Babylon defeated Egypt. Jehoiakim, who apparently had been content to be a vassal of Egypt, transferred his allegiance to Babylon, but rebelled after three years. At his death he was succeeded by his son Jehoiachin. See *Chronology of the Biblical Period; Israel, land of.*

JEHOIARIB (Jə hoî´ à rĭb) Personal name meaning "Yahweh creates justice." **1.** Priest who was one of first settlers to return to Jerusalem from Babylonian exile about 538 B.C. (1 Chron. 9:10; cp. Neh. 12:6). **2.** Head of first course or division of priests (1 Chron. 24:7; cp. Neh. 12:19). This listing follows Hebrew text. English translations are not always consistent in transliterating this name and its shortened form Joiarib. See *Joiarib.*

JEHONADAB (Jə hŏn´ à dăb) Personal name meaning "Yahweh incites" or "Yahweh offers Himself freely." Son of Rechab who supported Jehu in the latter's bloody purge of the house of Ahab (2 Kings 10:15). He was representative of a group of austere ultraconservatives known as the Rechabites. Jeremiah 35 relates a meeting between the prophet and Rechabites, who cited the teaching of their ancestor Jehonadab (who in Jeremiah is called Jonadab). In the context of that meeting, some of the precepts of the Rechabites are articulated. They are reminiscent of the regulations that governed the Nazirites. The Hebrew word *rechav* means "chariot," so some scholars think Jehonadab belonged to Israel's chariot forces. See *Jehu; Rechabites.*

JEHONATHAN (Jə hŏn´ à thàn) Personal name meaning "Yahweh gave." **1.** Longer form of Jonathan often used in Hebrew text for Jonathan as in 1 Sam. 14:6,8. **2.** Son of Abiathar, the priest (2 Sam. 15:27,36; 17:17,20). He helped King David learn Absalom's plans when Absalom drove his father from Jerusalem. **3.** King David's

nephew who slew a giant from Gath (2 Sam. 21:21-22). **4.** Uncle of King David who served as royal counselor and scribe (1 Chron. 27:32). **5.** Military leader under David (2 Sam. 23:32). **6.** Supervisor of royal storehouses under David (1 Chron. 27:25). **7.** Scribe whose house King Zedekiah transformed into prison where he jailed Jeremiah (Jer. 37:15), a place Jeremiah did not like (37:20; 38:26). **8.** Levite King Jehoshaphat sent to teach God's law in the cities of Judah (2 Chron. 17:8). **9.** Head of a priestly family about 450 B.C. (Neh. 12:18). **10.** Founder of priesthood at worship place in Dan (Judg. 18:30). Earliest Hebrew scribes noted that Jonathan was a descendant of Moses, but the present Hebrew text says "Manasseh." The Hebrew text is at times inconsistent in using the longer or shorter form of the name, and modern translators are as equally inconsistent. This article follows the Hebrew text. See *Jonathan.*

JEHORAM (Jə hō´ ràm) Personal name meaning "Yahweh is exalted." Alternate form of Joram. See *Joram.*

JEHOSHABEATH (Jē hō shă´ bə ăth) Variant form of Jehosheba. See *Jehosheba.*

JEHOSHAPHAT (Jə hŏsh´ à phăt) Personal name meaning "Yahweh judged" or "Yahweh established the right." **1.** Son and successor of Asa as king of Judah (1 Kings 15:24). He occupied the throne for 25 years (873–848 B.C.). The biblical record of his reign is contained in the final chapters of 1 Kings and in 2 Chron. 17–20. He was an able ruler and a faithful worshiper of Yahweh (1 Kings 22:42-43). Nevertheless, he did one thing that ultimately proved to be disastrous: he made an alliance with Ahab, king of Israel. The immediate result was beneficial to both kingdoms. Years of conflict between them came to an end, and both kingdoms were strengthened. However, the alliance involved a marriage between Jehoshaphat's son Jehoram and Ahab's daughter Athaliah. Athaliah's influence in Judah finally proved to be horrific. See *Athaliah; Chronology of the Biblical Period; Israel, Land of; Micaiah.* **2.** Father of Jehu (2 Kings 9:2,14). **3.** Official at David's court (2 Sam. 8:16), called the "recorder" or "secretary of state" (REB). The Hebrew term's root meaning is "remember." Some Bible students compare the office to the Egyptian court herald who reported events to the king and made public announcements. Others think the office maintained public records, while others speak of a foreign minister. As with many Hebrew offices, certainty is not possible. Jehoshaphat retained the office under Solomon (1 Kings 4:3). **4.** Solomon's official in tribal territory of Issachar in charge of providing provisions for the royal court one month a year (1 Kings 4:17).

JEHOSHAPHAT, VALLEY OF Place-name meaning "valley where Yahweh judged." Place to which the Lord summons the nations for judgment (Joel 3:2). No evidence exists that any valley actually bore this name in Joel's time. Since the fourth century A.D. the Kidron Valley has been known as the Valley of Jehoshaphat; but there is no reason for believing Joel was referring to the Kidron Valley. The reference in Joel probably is meant to be symbolic. Through Joel, God promised all nations would ultimately be called to God's place of judgment. See *Joel.*

JEHOSHEBA (Jə hŏsh′ ə bà) Personal name meaning "Yahweh is fullness or fortune." Sister of King Ahaziah who, after his death, took young Joash and protected him from Queen Athaliah so Athaliah could not have him killed as she did the other royal children (2 Kings 11:2). Her name is spelled Jehoshabeath in 2 Chron. 22:11.

JEHOSHUA (Jə hŏsh′ ū à) (KJV, Num. 13:16) See *Joshua.*

JEHOVAH (Jĕ hō′ vah) English transliteration of Hebrew text's current reading of divine name Yahweh. Hebrew text, however, represents scribe's efforts to prevent people from pronouncing the divine name by combining consonants of Yahweh and vowels of Hebrew word *'adonai* ("Lord") so readers would pronounce *'adonai* rather than risk blasphemy by improperly pronouncing the divine name. See *God; Lord; Names of God; YHWH.*

JEHOVAH-JIREH (Jĕ hō vah-jī′ rĕh) Place-name meaning "Yahweh will provide" (Gen. 22:14). The name Abraham gave to the place where the Lord provided a sacrifice in place of Isaac. Modern translations translate the place-name whereas KJV transliterates it. See *Jehovah.*

JEHOVAH-NISSI (Jĕ hō vah-nĭs′ sī) Transliteration of place-name meaning "Yahweh is my banner." Name Moses gave to the altar he built after defeating the Amalekites (Exod. 17:15). Modern

Valley of Jehoshaphat (Kidron Valley) in Jerusalem showing the Church of All Nations.

versions translate the name instead of following KJV in transliterating it. See *Jehovah*.

JEHOVAH-SHALOM (Jĕ hō vah-shä lōm´) Place-name meaning "Yahweh is peace." Name Gideon gave to the altar he built at Ophrah (Judg. 6:24). Modern versions translate the name while KJV transliterated it. See *Jehovah*.

JEHOVAH-SHAMMA (Jĕ hō vah-shăm´ mà) Transliteration of a Hebrew name (Ezek. 48:35, margin) meaning "The LORD is there" which is better transliterated YHWH-shammah (NASB margin). The Jerusalem of Ezekiel's vision was known by this name (cp. Isa. 60:19-20; Rev. 21:3). See *YHWH*.

JEHOVAH-TSIDKENU (Jĕ hō vah-tsĭd kĕn´ ū) Hebrew name meaning "The LORD [is] our righteousness" (Jer. 23:6; 33:16, margin). The name is applied to a future Davidic king who would lead his people to do what is right and thus bring peace (23:6) and to the restored city of Jerusalem (33:16). The name is possibly a play on the name of Zedekiah ("Righteous [is] the Lord") who reigned from 597 to 587 B.C. See *YHWH*.

JEHOZABAD (Jə hŏz´ à băd) Personal name meaning "Yahweh bestowed." **1.** One of conspirators who killed King Joash of Judah (2 Kings 12:21). **2.** Porter or doorkeeper under King David (1 Chron. 26:4). **3.** Military commander under King Jehoshaphat of Judah about 860 B.C. (2 Chron. 17:18). See *Jozabad*.

JEHOZADAK (Jə hŏz´ à dăk) Personal name meaning "Yahweh deals righteously." High priest at the time Nebuchadnezzar carried Judah into Babylonian exile about 587 B.C. (1 Chron. 6:14-15). He was the father of Joshua, the high priest who returned from exile with Zerubbabel about 537 B.C. (Hag. 1:1; Zech. 6:11). An abbreviated Hebrew form Jozadak also appears, and English translations are inconsistent in spelling the name. See *Josedech; Jozadak*.

JEHU (Jā hū) Personal name meaning "Yah is He." **1.** Son of Jehoshaphat and king of Israel (841–814 B.C.). He was a commander of the army when Elisha the prophet sent one of the sons of the prophets to Ramoth-gilead to anoint him as king (2 Kings 9:1-10). Jehu embarked on a violent and bloody course that finally led him

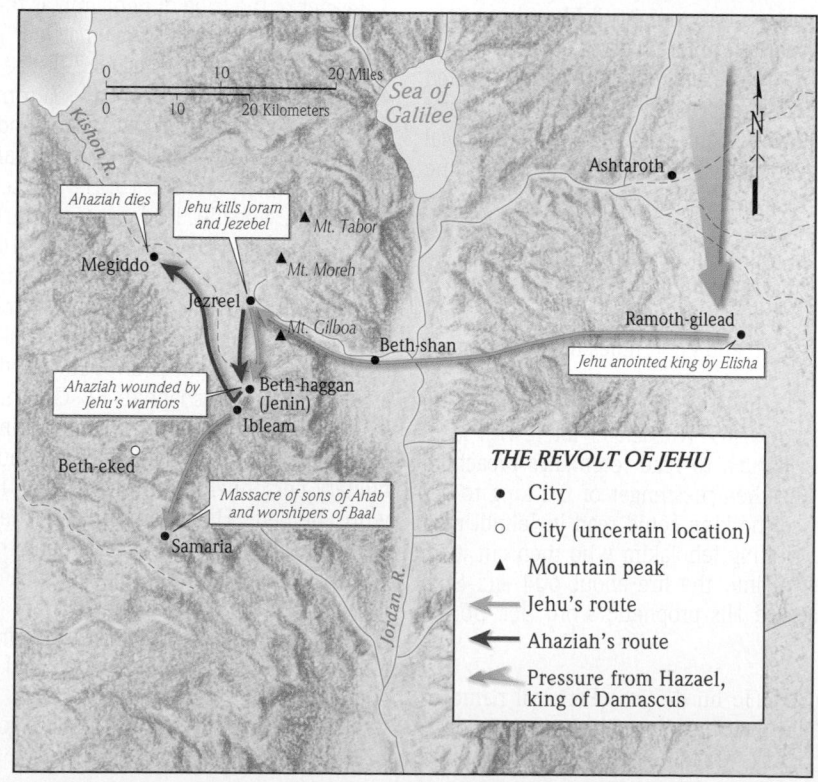

THE REVOLT OF JEHU
- • City
- ○ City (uncertain location)
- ▲ Mountain peak
- ← Jehu's route
- ← Ahaziah's route
- ← Pressure from Hazael, king of Damascus

to the throne. Along the way he was responsible for the deaths of Joram, king of Israel; Ahaziah, king of Judah; Jezebel, still powerful former queen of Israel, and some 70 surviving members of the household of Israel's late King Ahab. He used trickery to gather and destroy worshipers of Baal, so that Jehu destroyed Baal out of Israel (2 Kings 10:28). Jehu established a strong dynasty in Israel. He and his descendants held the throne for approximately a century. See *Chronology of the Biblical Period; Elijah; Israel, Land of.* **2.** Prophet who proclaimed God's judgment on King Baasha of Israel (1 Kings 16:1-12). He warned King Jehoshaphat of Judah (2 Chron. 19:2) and recorded the acts of Jehoshaphat in a record to which the chronicler referred his readers (2 Chron. 20:34). **3.** Member of David's army at Ziklag (1 Chron. 12:3). His home was Anathoth, in the tribal territory of David's opponent Saul. **4.** Leader of tribe of Simeon (1 Chron. 4:35).

JEHUBBAH (Jə hŭb´ bah) Personal name, perhaps meaning "He has hidden." Member of tribe of Asher (1 Chron. 7:34).

JEHUCAL (Jə hū´ căl) Personal name meaning "Yahweh proves to be mighty." Messenger King Zedekiah sent to ask Jeremiah to pray for him as he began to rule. Apparently, Zedekiah wanted blessing on his efforts to cooperate with Egypt against Babylon about 587 B.C. (Jer. 37:3). Jucal in 38:1 is probably a shortened form of the same name.

JEHUD (Jē´ hŭd) Place-name meaning "praise." Town in tribal territory of Dan (Josh. 19:45). It is located at modern Yehud about three miles south of Petah Tikvah and eight miles north of Joppa.

JEHUDI (Jə hū´ dī) Personal name meaning "Judean or Jewish." Messenger for Jewish leaders calling Baruch to read Jeremiah's preaching to them and then messenger of the king to get the scroll so the king could read it. Jehudi read the scroll to King Jehoiakim who then cut it up and threw it into the fire about 604 B.C. Still, God preserved His prophetic word (Jer. 36:11-32).

JEHUDIJAH (Jē hū dī´ jah) Personal name or proper adjective meaning "Jewess or Judean woman." KJV transliteration from Hebrew which modern translations read as adjective, "Judean" or "Jewish." TEV reads "from the tribe of Judah" (1 Chron. 4:18).

JEHUEL (Jə hū´ ĕl) Personal name meaning "God proves Himself active and alive." Written Hebrew text of 2 Chron. 29:14 followed by NRSV, TEV. Other translations read "Jehiel," following early Hebrew scribes. Levite who helped cleanse the temple under Hezekiah.

JEHUSH (Jē´ hŭsh) Variant spelling of Jeush. See *Jeush.*

JEIEL (Jə ī´ ĕl) Personal name, possibly meaning "God is strong" or "God heals." The early Hebrew scribes often used Hebrew vowel points in the text to indicate the name should be read as Jeiel where the written text indicated Jeuel (1 Chron. 9:35; 11:44; 2 Chron. 26:11; 29:13). The early translations point to similar early confusion at 1 Chron. 9:6. This article will deal with both Jeiel and Jeuel, since all occurrences of Jeuel show early textual evidence of being read Jeiel. **1.** Leader in the tribe of Reuben (1 Chron. 5:7). **2.** One of early members of tribe of Judah to return from Babylonian exile (1 Chron. 9:6). **3.** Leader of the tribe of Benjamin as they settled in Gibeon. He may have married a foreign woman (1 Chron. 9:35; cp. 8:29). See *Maacah.* **4.** Leader in David's army (1 Chron. 11:44). **5.** Levite and porter or gatekeeper under David (1 Chron. 15:18). **6.** Levite and harp player under David (1 Chron. 15:21). **7.** Levite who served as worship leader at the ark of the covenant under David (1 Chron. 16:5). The Hebrew text includes two Jeiels in this verse, and interpreters since the earliest translations have changed one or the other to a slightly different spelling. **8.** Ancestor of Levite who prophesied under Jehoshaphat (2 Chron. 20:14). **9.** Royal scribe or secretary under King Uzziah (792–740 B.C.). He maintained the numbers of military personnel (2 Chron. 26:11). **10.** Levite who helped Hezekiah purify the temple (2 Chron. 29:13). **11.** Officer among the Levites who provided them offerings to sacrifice at the Passover under Josiah about 622 B.C. (2 Chron. 35:9). **12.** Man who went with Ezra from Babylon to Judah about 458 B.C. (Ezra 8:13). **13.** Man condemned for having foreign wife and thus tempting Israel to worship foreign gods under Ezra (Ezra 10:43).

J

JEKABZEEL (Jə kăb´ zē ĕl) Place-name meaning "God assembled." A city in southern Judah settled by members of the tribe of Judah after the exile (Neh. 11:25). Jekabzeel was apparently south of the boundary of the Persian province of Judah, possibly at modern Khirbet Gharreh or Tell Ira. It is probably the same as Kabzeel, originally assigned to the tribe of Judah (Josh. 15:21) about halfway between Tell Beersheba and Tell Arad. See *Kabzeel.*

JEKAMEAM (Jĕk á mē´ ăm) Personal name meaning "the people deliver" or "the Kinsman saves." A priest set aside to work in God's house (1 Chron. 23:19; 24:23).

JEKAMIAH (Jĕk á mī´ ah) Personal name meaning "Yah delivers." **1.** Member of clan of Jerahmeel in tribe of Judah (1 Chron. 2:41). **2.** Son of King Jeconiah, also called Jehoiachin, of Judah about 597 B.C. (1 Chron. 3:18).

JEKUTHIEL (Jə kū´ thĭ ĕl) Personal name meaning "God nourishes." Member of tribe of Judah (1 Chron. 4:18).

JEMIMA (Jĕ mī´ mà) or **JEMIMAH** Personal name meaning "turtledove." Job's first daughter after God restored his fortunes (Job 42:14).

JEMUEL (Jə mū´ ĕl) Personal name meaning "day of God" or "sea of God." Son of Simeon, grandson of Jacob, and head of clan in Israel (Gen. 46:10; Exod. 6:15). Also called Nemuel (Num. 26:12; 1 Chron. 4:24).

JEPHTHAE (Jĕph´ thē) KJV transliteration of Greek for Jephthah (Heb. 11:32). See *Jephthah.*

JEPHTHAH (Jĕph´ thah) Personal name meaning "he will open." One of Israel's judges about 1100 B.C. (Judg. 11:1–12:7). A Gileadite, he was driven from his home because he was "the son of a harlot" (Judg. 11:1). He lived and raided in the land of Tob with a band of outlaws, becoming known as a "mighty warrior." When the Ammonites moved against Israel, Jephthah's people asked him to return and lead them. His victory over the Ammonites came about after a vow he made to offer as a burnt offering the first living thing he saw upon his return from the battle. Although it was his daughter who greeted him, Jephthah did fulfill his vow. Considered as one of

Yahweh's "chief" deliverers of His people (1 Sam. 12:11), Jephthah is hailed by the author of Hebrews as a hero of faith (Heb. 11:32). See *Ammon, Ammonites; Human Sacrifices; Judges, Book of.* Darlene R. Gautsch

JEPHUNNEH (Jə phŭn´ nĕh) Personal name meaning "he will be turned" or "appeased." **1.** Father of Caleb (Num. 13:6). See *Caleb.* **2.** In 1 Chron. 7:38, one of the sons of Jether in tribe of Asher.

JERAH (Jē´ rah) Personal name meaning "moon" or "month." A descendant of Shem, son of Noah, in the Table of Nations (Gen. 10:26). The moon was the chief god in South Arabia. Since the surrounding names in the list represent Arabian tribes, this probably indicates the relationship of Semitic tribes in Arabia to the Hebrews.

JERAHMEEL (Jə rah´ mē ĕl) Personal name meaning "God shows compassion." **1.** Son of Hezron (1 Chron. 2:9), brother of Caleb (1 Chron. 2:42), and original clan ancestor of Jerahmeelites (1 Sam. 27:10). See *Jerahmeelite.* **2.** Son of Hammelech (Hebrew, "the king" and so translated by modern versions), who was one of a group whom King Jehoiakim sent to arrest Baruch and Jeremiah (Jer. 36:26). Yet, the Lord showed He has more power than human rulers by hiding His faithful servants from the king. **3.** Levite in time of David (1 Chron. 24:29).

JERAHMEELITE (Jə rah´ mē ĕl īt) Member of clan of Jerahmeel which apparently lived south of Beersheba in the Negev. While dwelling with the Philistines, David told them he was fighting in the territory of the Jerahmeelites (1 Sam. 27:10), making Achish, the Philistine king, think he was fighting against parts of Judah, while he actually fought the other groups in the south who opposed Judah—Geshurites, Gezrites, Amalekites (1 Sam. 27:8). He divided the spoils of war with the Jerahmeelites (1 Sam. 30:29).

JERASH (Jĕr´ ăsh) Modern Arabic name of Gerasa. See *Gerasa.*

JERBOA (Jĕr´ bō à) Any of several species of leaping rodents having long hind legs and long tails of the family *Dipodidae.* The REB includes

J

Sunset at Jerash (ancient Gerasa).

the jerboa among the unclean animals of Lev. 11:29.

JERED (Jĕr´ ĕd) Alternate spelling used by English translations for Jared. See *Jared.*

JEREMAI (Jĕr´ ə mī) Personal name, abbreviated form of Jeremoth or Jeremiah. Israelite condemned for foreign wife which Ezra said would lead Israel to worship foreign gods (Ezra 10:33).

JEREMIAH (Jĕr ə mī´ ah) Personal name that may mean "may Yahweh lift up," "throw," or "establish." **1.** Head of a clan of the tribe of Manasseh in East Jordan (1 Chron. 5:24). **2.** Three soldiers of David's army at Ziklag (1 Chron. 12:4,10,13). **3.** Father-in-law of King Josiah of Judah (640–609 B.C.) and grandfather of the Kings Jehoahaz (609 B.C.) (2 Kings 23:31) and Zedekiah (597–586 B.C.) (2 Kings 24:18; Jer. 52:1). **4.** Representative of the sect of the Rechabites (Jer. 35:3). **5.** Three priests or heads of priestly families in the times of Zerubbabel about 537 B.C. (Neh. 12:1,12) and Nehemiah about 455 B.C. (Neh. 10:2; 12:34).

Other persons by the name of Jeremiah are referred to in Hebrew inscriptions from Lachish and Arad about 700 B.C. and in a number of ancient Jewish seals. The Bible has a short form of the name 17 times and a long form 121 times. Both forms are applied to the prophet. Inscriptions use the longer form.

JEREMIAH, THE PROPHET The Bible tells us more about personal experiences of Jeremiah than of any other prophet. We read that his father's name was Hilkiah, a priest from Anathoth (Jer. 1:1). He was called to be a prophet in the 13th year of King Josiah (627/6 B.C.) (Jer. 1:2). He was active under the Kings Jehoahaz/Shallum (609 B.C.) (22:11), Jehoiakim (609–597 B.C.) (Jer. 1:3; 22:18; 26:1; 35:1; 36:1,9), Jehoiachin/Jeconiah/Coniah (597 B.C.) (22:24; 24:1; 27:20; 28:4; 29:2; 37:1), and Zedekiah (597–586 B.C.) (1:3; 21:1; 27:1-12; 28:1; 32:1; 34:2; 37–38; 39:4; 52:8). When Jerusalem was destroyed by the Babylonians in 587 B.C., Jeremiah moved to Mizpah, the capital of Gedaliah, the newly appointed Jewish governor of the Babylonian province of Judah (40:5). When Gedaliah was assassinated (41:1-2), Jeremiah was deported to Egypt against his will by Jewish officers who had survived the catastrophes (42:1–43:7). In Egypt he continued to preach oracles against the Egyptians (43:8-13) and against his compatriots (44:1-30).

Jeremiah is depicted as living in constant friction with the authorities of his people, religious (priests, 20:1-6; prophets, 28:1; or both 26:8), political (kings, chaps. 21–22; 36–38), or all of them together (1:18-19; 2:26; 8:1), including Jewish leaders after the Babylonian invasion (42:1–43:13). Still his preaching emphasized a high respect for prophets whose warning words could have saved the people if they had listened (7:25; 26:4; 29:17-19; 35:13). He trusted in the promise of ideal future kings (23:5; 33:14-17). He recommended national surrender to the rule of the Babylonian Empire and called Nebuchadnezzar, Babylon's emperor and Judah's most hated enemy, the "servant of the Lord" (25:9; 27:6). He even incited his compatriots to desert to the enemy (21:8-9). He was accused of treason and convicted (37:12-13; 38:1-6), and yet the most aggressive oracles against Babylon are attributed to him (50–51). Enemies challenged his prophetic honesty and the inspiration of his message (43:1-3; 29:24), and yet kings and nobles sought his advice (21:1-2; 37:3; 38:14; 42:1-2).

J

He constantly proclaimed God's judgment upon Judah and Jerusalem, and yet he was also a prophet of hope, proclaiming oracles of salvation, conditioned (3:22–4:2) or unconditioned (30–31; 32:36-38; 33:6; 34:4). God forbade him to intercede for his people (7:16; 11:14; 14:11; cp. 15:1); yet he interceded (14:7-9,19-22). God ordered him to live without marriage and family (16:2). He had to stay away from the company of merrymakers (15:17) and from houses of feasting (16:8). He complained to and argued with God (12:1-17), complaining about the misery of his office (20:7-18). At the same time he sang hymns of praise to his God (20:13).

Although Jeremiah's call came in the 13th year of King Josiah, Josiah remains the only Jewish king contemporary with Jeremiah to and about whom no word is spoken in the whole book (but cp. 25:3). No concrete reference appears to any of the dramatic changes of national liberation and religious reformation within the last 18 years of Josiah's reign (2 Kings 22:1–23:30). The words of the call narrative: "Before I formed you in the womb I knew you, ... I have appointed you a prophet to the nations" (Jer. 1:5 NASB), have caused some to think that the date of Jeremiah's call and birth is one and the same. However, this is not likely the case.

JEREMIAH, BOOK OF The second longest book of the Bible, next to the Psalms, is the only one of the OT that tells us some details of its origin. According to Jer. 36:1-26, Baruch had written a first version at the dictation of Jeremiah. The scroll was read first in public and then again for the state officials and for the king. King Jehoiakim burnt it piece by piece. Jeremiah therefore dictated a second and enlarged edition of the first book to Baruch (Jer. 36:32). Additional references to Jeremiah's own writing activity (Jer. 30:2; 51:60; cp. 25:13) suggest that the scroll of Jer. 36:32 is not identical to the present form of the biblical book. Third person references to Jeremiah after chap. 25 suggest that perhaps the scroll of 36:32 may be confined to chaps. 1–25.

Structure and Content Biblical scholars have struggled to explain the arrangement of Jeremiah's prophecies. The complex nature of the structure is complicated by evidence from the earliest Greek translation. There the oracles against foreign nations are in a different order and appear immediately after 25:13 rather than at 46:1. This and other evidence suggest a complicated process of collection of the Jeremiah materials into a book. Traditional scholarly theories have tried to attribute poetic oracles to Jeremiah, stories about the prophet to Baruch, and prose sermons to a later editor who used the book of Jeremiah to exemplify and teach the theology of the book of Deuteronomy. Such theories are much too imaginative and must be discarded. Aside from the stories of the scroll's destruction, expansion, and recopying (chap. 36), we do not know the process through which the book of Jeremiah was produced, but the view that the overall product came from the Prophet Jeremiah's mature reflection makes the most sense of the text.

The book is not arranged chronologically as a whole, although some chronological arrangement is apparent. No theory has achieved a consensus, but various devices (such as theme, style, audience, and rhetoric) are summoned to explain certain connections. The book is often considered an anthology of prophetic units that were collected and combined at various times with little intentionality.

A useful proposal recently made by Richard Patterson is that the prophecies were arranged according to the prophet's divine call to be a prophet to the nations (1:4-19) and to Judah in particular (1:13-19). He identifies a twofold structure to the book that reverses those emphases: chaps. 2–24 focus on Jeremiah and his people, and chaps. 25–51 focus on Jeremiah and the nations. On either end are the description of the prophetic call and commission in chap. 1 and the historical appendix in chap. 52. The two main sections each begin with a subsection that sets forth the theme (2:1–3:5 and 25:1-38), followed by a subsection that develops the theme (3:6–23:40 and 26:1–51:58), and concluding with a sign (24:1-10 and 51:59-64).

The so-called confessions of Jeremiah (11:18-23; 12:1-4; 15:10-21; 17:14-18; 18:19-23; 20:7–18) are scattered through chapters 11–20. Oracles of hope (chaps. 30–31) interrupt the stories about Jeremiah (chaps. 26–45). Words against kings (21:11–22:30) and against prophets (23:9-40) appear to be independent collections.

Text of the Book The earliest Greek version of Jeremiah, dating back to pre-Christian centuries, is more than 12.5 percent shorter than the Hebrew text (although it adds about a hundred verses not found in the Hebrew). Only a few longer sections are missing (33:14-26; 39:4-13). The Greek text rather uses less titles and epithets, and single words and verses are missing throughout the book. More than 2,700 words of the Hebrew text do not have Greek equivalents. Fragments of Hebrew manuscripts from Qumran show that a longer and a shorter Hebrew text existed side by side in the time of Jesus.

The Message Theologically, the book of Jeremiah stimulates the search for the will of God in moments when all the institutions and religious representatives normally in charge of administrating His will are discredited. Neither the Davidic monarchy (Jer. 21:1–22:30), nor prophets and priests (Jer. 23:9-40), nor the cultic institutions of the temple (Jer. 7:1-34; 26:1-9) could help the people to prevent impending calamities. Neither could they detect that inconspicuous apostasy that mixes up the little aims of personal egoism (Jer. 2:29-37; 7:21-26; 28:1-17) with God's commission (Jer. 4:3). God's justice and righteousness cannot be usurped by His people. He can be a stumbling block even for His prophet (Jer. 12:1-6; 20:7-12). Execution of judgment and destruction is not God's delight. God Himself suffers pain because of the alienation between Himself and His people (2:1-37). Better than the prophet was able to admit, the apostate members of God's people remembered a correct notion of the nature of God. He continued to be their Father, and His anger would not last forever (3:4,12-13). Conversion is possible (3:14,22; 4:1-2), but this is no consolation for the apostate generation. Contrary to the expectations of the religious and political authorities, Judah and Jerusalem would meet the cruel catastrophe. This was not God's last word. His faithfulness prevails and creates new hope where all hope is lost (chaps. 30–33).

Outline

I. Prophetic Call (1:1-19).
II. Jeremiah and His People (2:1–24:10).
   A. Theme: Divine Punishment on Israel (2:1–3:5).
   B. Preliminary Plea to Repent (3:6–4:4).
   C. Development: Coming and Causes of Judgment (4:5–23:40).

      1. Coming Invasion of Jerusalem (4:5–6:30).
      2. Sins of the People (7:1–10:25).
      3. Judgment Declared and Plot Revealed (11:1–12:17).
      4. Ruined Wastecloth and Ruined People (13:1-27).
      5. Indelible Sin and Inescapable Catastrophes (14:1–17:18).
      6. Sabbath Warnings (17:19-27).
      7. Lesson from the Potter (18:1-23).
      8. Smashed Jug and Beaten Prophet (19:1–20:18).
      9. Zedekiah's Request (21:1-14).
     10. Unrighteous Kings and the Righteous King (22:1–23:8).
     11. False Prophets Condemned (23:9-40).
   D. Concluding Sign: Figs (24:1-10).
III. Jeremiah and the Nations (25:1-51:64).
   A. Theme: Pronouncement against Judah and the Nations (25:1-38).
   B. Preliminary Plea to Repent (26:1-6).
   C. Development: (26:7–51:58).
      1. Jeremiah and the Babylonian Crisis (26:7–36:32).
        a. Temple Sermon and Its Results (26:7-24).
        b. The Yoke of Babylon (27:1-22).
        c. Hananiah's False Prophecy (28:1-17).
        d. Jeremiah's Letter to the Exiles (29:1-32).
        e. Promise of a New Covenant (30:1–31:40).
        f. Jeremiah's Land Purchase (32:1-44).
        g. Reminder of God's Covenants with David and Levi (33:1-26).
        h. Word to King Zedekiah (34:1-7).
        i. The People and Their Slaves (34:8-22).
        j. Analogy of the Rechabites (35:1-13).
        k. Burning the Scroll (36:1-32).
      2. Jeremiah and the Fall of Jerusalem (37:1–45:5).
        a. Jeremiah's Imprisonment and Jerusalem's Fall (37:1–39:18).
        b. Jeremiah's Release and the Flight to Egypt (40:1–43:13).

c. Prophecy of Punishment
in Egypt (44:1-30).
d. God's Message to Baruch (45:1-
5).
3. God's Program for the Nations
(46:1–51:58).
a. Egypt in the South (46:1-28).
b. Philistia in the West (47:1-7).
c. Moab, Ammon, and Edom in
the East (48:1–49:22).
d. Damascus in the North (49:23-
27).
e. Babylon's Neighbors (49:28-39).
f. Babylon (50:1–51:58).
D. Concluding Sign: Sunken Scroll
(51:59-64).
IV. Historical Appendix (52:1-34).
Hans Mallau and E. Ray Clendenen

JEREMIAS (Jĕr ə mī´ ăs) KJV transliteration of Greek for Jeremiah (Matt. 16:14). See *Jeremiah, the Prophet.*

JEREMOTH (Jĕr´ ə mŏth) Personal name meaning "swellings." **1.** Member of tribe of Benjamin (1 Chron. 8:14), perhaps to be identified with Jeroham (8:27). **2.** Two Israelites with foreign wives condemned by Ezra (Ezra 10:26-27). **3.** Name written in Hebrew text of Israelite with foreign wife under Ezra (Ezra 10:29). Early Hebrew scribes and earliest translators read "and Ramoth." **4.** Descendant of Benjamin and leader in that tribe (1 Chron. 7:8). **5.** Priest in days of David and Solomon (1 Chron. 23:23; spelled Jerimoth in 24:30). **6.** Temple musician (1 Chron. 25:4, Jerimoth), possibly the same person as head of fifteenth division of priests (25:22). See *Jerimoth.*

JEREMY (Jĕr´ ĕ mĭ) KJV transliteration for Greek spelling of Jeremiah, the prophet (Matt. 2:17; 27:9). See *Jeremiah, the Prophet.*

JERIAH (Jə rī´ ah) Personal name meaning "Yahweh saw." Priest under David and Solomon (1 Chron. 23:19; 24:23).

JERIBAI (Jĕr´ ĭ bā ī) Personal name meaning "he defended my case." Military leader under David (1 Chron. 11:46).

JERICHO (Jĕr´ ĭ´ kō) Place-name meaning "moon." Apparently the oldest city in the world

and the first city Israel conquered under Joshua. Jericho is situated in the lower Jordan Valley, which, according to Gen. 13:10, "was well-watered everywhere … like the LORD's garden" (HCSB). The OT town lies beneath Tell es-Sultan near one of Palestine's strongest springs.

New Testament Jericho, founded by Herod the Great, was about one and one-half miles southward in the magnificent Wadi Qelt. The spring, Ain es-Sultan, issues some 30,000 cubic feet of water daily which falls about 160 feet in the first mile of its course down many channels to the Jordan River six miles away, irrigating about 2,500 acres.

The combination of rich alluvial soil, the perennial spring, and constant sunshine made Jericho an attractive place for settlement. Jericho could be called "city of palms" (Deut. 34:3; Judg. 1:16; 3:13; 2 Chron. 28:15) and has plenty of palm trees today. Only about 6.4 inches of rain fall there per year (mostly between November and February), and the average temperature in January is 59°F, while it is 88°F in August. Jericho is about 740 feet below sea level (accounting for its warm climate) but well above the Dead Sea, eight miles southward, which at 1,300 feet below sea level marks the earth's lowest point.

Jericho was an oasis situated in a hot plain, living in its own world with no major settlement in sight and lying between the two focal points of Jerusalem and Amman in the mountains to the west and east. It is mentioned in the Bible usually in association with some movement from one side of the Jordan to another—the Israelite invasion when Ehud takes tribute to the Moabite king, when David sends envoys to the king of Ammon, when Elijah and Elisha cross the

In the foreground the tel of NT Jericho with the tel of OT Jericho behind.

J

Step-trench cut into the tel of OT Jericho to uncover the many levels of destruction.

Gospels tell us (Matt. 20:29-34; Mark 10:46-52; Luke 18:35-43).

The archaeology of Jericho is closely associated with the names of John Garstang (1876–1956), who excavated there from 1930 to 1936, and especially Kathleen Kenyon, an Oxford University scholar who excavated there between 1952 and 1959. The earliest recognizable building on the site dates apparently (based on radiocarbon dating) from about 9250 B.C., a time marking the change from the Paleolithic to the Mesolithic period in Palestine. By 8000 B.C. a walled town (the world's earliest) of about 10 acres had been built. About 6000 B.C. pottery appeared in Jericho. About 4000 B.C. a period of abandonment began, but by 3300 B.C. Jericho was coming into her own again into what Kenyon calls the "Proto-Urban" age. Jericho came to have solid defense ramparts and walls. From about 2200 to 2000 B.C. the mound of Jericho was a campsite rather than a town, when some 346 excavated tombs show its occupants to be from various tribal units.

Jordan, or when Zedekiah attempts to escape the Babylonians.

In NT times Jericho was famous for its balm (an aromatic gum known for its medicinal qualities). This, along with its being the winter capital, made it a wealthy city. When Jesus was hosted by Zacchaeus (Luke 19:1-10), it was probably in one of Jericho's finest houses. Its sycamore trees were quite valuable. Such a city could expect to have its share of beggars, as the

Modern Arab citrus and vegetable vendors in the city of Jericho.

Inverted Corinthian column capital as found in situ in NT Jericho.

John Garstang's original excavation determined that Jericho was destroyed by fire around 1400 B.C. (corresponding to the biblical dating of the conquest). However, Kenyon's findings disagreed with Garstang, and she dated the destruction and city wall to a much earlier time. More recently archaeologist Bryant Wood's survey of both Garstang and Kenyon's work revealed that Kenyon was mistaken and Garstang's analysis of the lower city had been correct. While denying that the evidence affirms the biblical account, Lorenzo Nigro and Nicolo Marchetti's recent

Round Neolithic (New Stone Age) defense tower at OT Jericho.

J

Reconstruction of Herod the Great's winter palace at Jericho. Situated at the mouth of the Wadi Kelt along the lower slope of the western ridge of the Jordan Valley, the palace had a commanding view of NT Jericho and the arid, fertile Jordan River.

excavations at Jericho have found the stone revetment wall at the base of the tell, with part of the mud-brick wall built on top of it, still intact as well as evidence of collapsed walls. Again, this evidence affirms the biblical account. However, even today, Kenyon's view has held sway. While critical scholars underline the conflict between archaeological data and the biblical conquest nar-

View from atop the tel of NT Jericho showing the lush greenery of the oasis.

rative, in reality there is no conflict here. See *Archaeology; Conquest of Canaan; Joshua.*

Karen Joines and Eric Mitchell

JERIEL (Jĕr´ĭ ĕl) Personal name meaning "God sees." Member of tribe of Issachar (1 Chron. 7:2).

JERIJAH (Jə rī´ jah) Personal name meaning "Yah sees," a short form of Jeriah. Military hero of the Hebronite clan (1 Chron. 26:31), possibly identical with Jeriah. See *Jeriah.*

JERIMOTH (Jĕr´ĭ mŏth) Personal name, possibly meaning "fat belly." The name closely resembles Jeremoth, so that English translations are not consistent in following the Hebrew in spelling. The following represent spellings of the Hebrew text. See *Jeremoth.* **1.** Member of tribe of Benjamin (1 Chron. 7:7). **2.** Warrior of Saul's tribe Benjamin who joined David as he fled from Saul at Ziklag (1 Chron. 12:5). **3.** Levite of the house of Mushi (1 Chron. 24:30; cp. 23:23). **4.** Temple musician under David and Solomon

(1 Chron. 25:4; cp. v. 22). **5.** Leader of tribe of Naphtali under David (1 Chron. 27:19). **6.** Son of David, whose daughter married King Rehoboam (931–913 B.C.), according to 2 Chron. 11:18. Jerimoth does not appear in any other list of David's sons. **7.** An overseer of temple treasury under Hezekiah (2 Chron. 31:13).

JERIOTH (Jĕr´ ĭ ŏth) Personal name meaning "fearsome." Person related to Caleb, but the grammatical construction of Hebrew makes understanding of exact relationship difficult (1 Chron. 2:18): a second wife (KJV, NIV, NASB, NRSV); daughter (REB, TEV with many commentators).

JEROBOAM (Jĕr o bō´ ăm) Personal name possibly meaning "he who contends for justice for the people" or "may the people multiply." **1.** First king of the Northern Kingdom Israel about 926–909 B.C. Jeroboam had an interesting rise to power. He managed the laborers Solomon had conscripted for his huge building projects (1 Kings 11:28). During Solomon's reign Ahijah, a prophet from Shiloh, confronted Jeroboam, tore his own coat into 12 pieces, and gave 10 of them to Jeroboam (1 Kings 11:29-39). Ahijah interpreted this as God's pledge that Jeroboam would become king over 10 of the 12 tribes. Upon Solomon's death Jeroboam learned that the tribes would assemble at Shechem to make Solomon's son Rehoboam their king. Seizing upon the people's resentment toward Solomon's high-handed policies, Jeroboam led the 10 tribes to revolt against the house of David. They then crowned Jeroboam king.

The inspired biblical writers did not consider Jeroboam a good king. Rather he became the example of evil kings in Israel because he built temples in Dan and Bethel with golden calves representing God's presence. What appeared to be good politics diverted people from worshiping at Jerusalem, God's chosen place. All the following northern kings suffered the biblical writers' condemnation because they walked in the ways of Jeroboam, encouraging worship at Dan and Bethel (1 Kings 15:25-26,33-34; 16:18-19,30-31). Jeroboam also instituted new worship practices at his temples (1 Kings 12:25-33), intentionally making Israelite worship different from that in Jerusalem, though claiming to worship the same God with the same worship tradi-

tions. Prophetic warnings failed to move Jeroboam (1 Kings 13:1–14:20).

2. Powerful king of Israel in the dynasty of Jehu about 793–753 B.C. (2 Kings 14:23-29). He managed to restore prosperity and territory to a weak nation but continued the religious practices of Jeroboam I and thus met condemnation from the biblical writers. Jonah, Amos, and Hosea prophesied during his reign. Jeroboam basically restored the boundaries of David's empire, reaching even into Syria.

M. Stephen Davis

JEROHAM (Jə rō´ hăm) Personal name meaning "he found mercy." **1.** Father of Elkanah and grandfather of Samuel (1 Sam. 1:1; cp. 1 Chron. 6:27,34). **2.** Priest after the exile (Neh. 11:12). **3.** Member of tribe of Benjamin (1 Chron. 8:27, if proper reading is not Jeremoth as in v. 14; see *Jeremoth*). **4.** Father of one of first men to return to Jerusalem after Babylonian exile (1 Chron. 9:8). **5.** Priest whose son was one of first to return to Jerusalem from Babylonian exile (1 Chron. 9:12). **6.** Father of two of David's military leaders from Saul's tribe of Benjamin (1 Chron. 12:7). **7.** Father of leader of tribe of Dan under David (1 Chron. 27:22). **8.** Father of captain who helped Jehoiada, the high priest, overthrow Queen Athaliah and install Joash as king about 835 B.C. (2 Chron. 23:1).

JERUBBAAL (Jĕr ŭb bā´ ăl) Personal name meaning "Baal judges." Another name for Gideon (Judg. 6:32). See *Gideon*.

JERUBBESHETH (Jə rŭb´ bə shĕth) Personal name meaning "may shame judge" or "shame increases." A deliberate scribal corruption of the name Jerubbaal (2 Sam. 11:21), replacing the name of the Canaanite deity Baal with a form of the Hebrew word for "shame."

JERUEL (Jə rū´ ĕl) Place-name meaning "foundation of God." Place where Jahaziel, the prophet, predicted King Jehoshaphat and his army would find the Ammonite and Moabite army. The exact location is not known. It was on the rugged descent southeast of Tekoa going to En-Gedi.

JERUSALEM (Jə rū´ sá ləm) Jerusalem is a city set high on a plateau in the hills of Judah, considered sacred by Judaism, Christianity, and

J

Islam. Its biblical-theological significance lies in its status as Yahweh's chosen center of His divine kingship and of the human kingship of David and his sons, Yahweh's vice-regents. Besides the name "Jerusalem," the city is also called "the City of David" and "Zion" (originally referring to a part of the city, the "stronghold of Zion" that David captured from the Jebusites; see 2 Sam. 5:6-10).

In the Pentateuch, the city of Jerusalem is not directly mentioned. Moriah (Gen. 22:2; associated with the site of Solomon's temple in 2 Chron. 3:1) and Salem (Gen. 14:18; associated with Zion in Ps. 76:2) apparently refer to the same site and establish a link between the city and the patriarch Abraham. The city (known earlier as Jebus; see Judg. 19:10-11) was captured in Joshua's time (Judg. 1:8), but the Jebusites were not driven out (Josh. 15:63; Judg. 1:21). After

David captured it and made it Israel's capital (2 Sam. 5:6-10, 1 Chron. 11:4-9), David brought the ark of the covenant into Jerusalem (2 Sam. 6:17) and made it the seat not only of his own but also of God's monarchy (cp. 1 Kings 11:36; 14:21; and Ps. 132; which emphasize that it is Yahweh's own chosen/desired habitation). Jerusalem came to be "the city of our God," "the city of the great King," "the city of Yahweh of hosts" (Ps. 48). Under Solomon, the temple was constructed (2 Chron. 3–7) and the nation reached its political and economic zenith with Jerusalem at the center (2 Chron. 9).

In the Prophets, besides literal references to the city, "Jerusalem" appears as a corporate representative of the entire community in speeches of judgment and of future salvation. The theological centrality of Jerusalem and events such as God's historical deliverance of the city from the

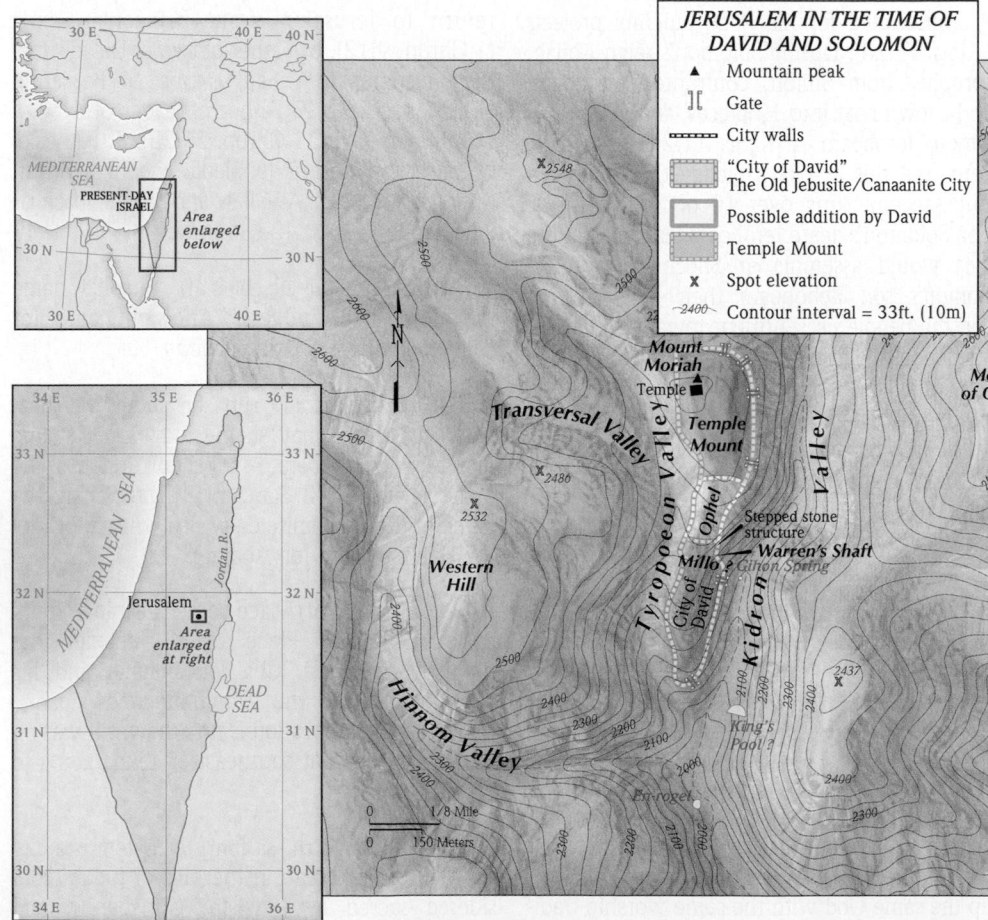

JERUSALEM IN THE TIME OF
DAVID AND SOLOMON

▲   Mountain peak

)(Gate

▭▭▭   City walls

   "City of David"
   The Old Jebusite/Canaanite City

   Possible addition by David

   Temple Mount

x   Spot elevation

-2400-   Contour interval = 33ft. (10m)

Model of first-century Jerusalem shows the three towers built by Herod to protect his palace.

hands of Sennacherib (2 Kings 19) led the people to a mistaken belief in the city's invincibility. This view is denounced by prophets such as Jeremiah (Jer. 7:1-15) and Micah (Mic. 3:11-12) as it abetted the people's apostasy from Yahweh. Since the people had abandoned Yahweh, Yahweh eventually abandoned His chosen city to the Babylonians in 586 B.C. (2 Kings 23:26-27).

Yet judgment was not Yahweh's final word. The Persian king Cyrus (decree in 538 B.C.) was Yahweh's servant in facilitating the return of many exiles and the rebuilding of the city and the temple (Isa. 44:26-28; 45:13; Ezra 6; Neh.

A tomb, possibly dating from as early as the first century A.D., in the city of Jerusalem.

1–6). Moreover, the future salvation of Jerusalem would exceed the temporal restoration of the postexilic community. All peoples would come to it (Isa. 2:2-4; Jer. 3:17). God's new work for Jerusalem would usher in nothing less than a new age (Isa. 65:18-25; Zech. 14:8-21).

The NT portrays the various Jerusalem-related prophecies as fulfilled in and through

David and his men may have captured Jerusalem through Warren's Shaft that runs from the Gihon Spring up to the old city of Jerusalem.

J

Jerusalem in the Time of Jesus

1. The temple (Herod's temple)
2. Women's court
3. The Soreg
4. The Court of the Gentiles
5. Royal Porch
6. Eastern Gate (the present-day Golden Gate)
7. Antonia Fortress
8. The Double Gate (the Western Huldah Gate)
9. The Triple Gate (the Eastern Huldah Gate)
10. Monumental Herodian Staircase (sections still remain today)
11. The City of David (established by David, the oldest part of the city)
12. Earliest defense wall (destroyed and constructed many times)
13. Heroidan outer defense wall around the expanded city
14. Herodian wall separating the Upper City (or affluent district) from the Lower City (or lower economic district)
15. The Second North Wall (possible location)
16. Garden of Gethsemane (the west side of the Mount of Olives)
17. Mount of Olives
18. Kidron Valley
19. Gihon Spring
20. Pool of Siloam
21. Tyropoeon Valley (Lower City)
22. Herodian aqueduct (possible location)
23. Shops and marketplace of Jesus' day
24. Additional shops and marketplace (probably added at a later time)
25. Staircase (Robinson's Arch) leading up from the Lower City

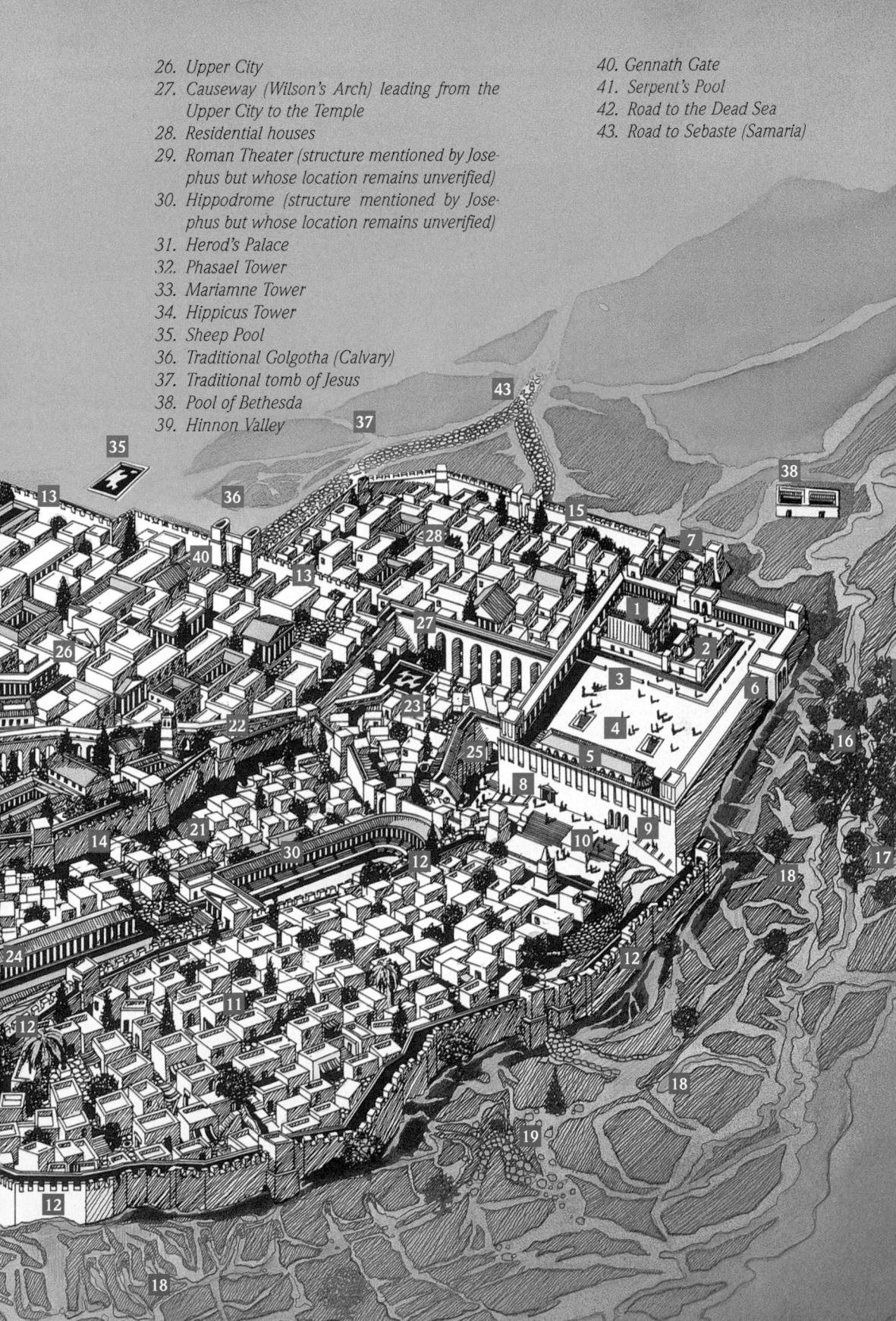

The Wailing Wall, revered by Jews for centuries as the only remaining wall of the ancient temple area.

J

Jesus, Israel's Messiah. In the Gospels, Jerusalem takes on ironic, contrasting roles. On one hand, it is "the city of the great King" (Matt. 5:35) and "the holy city" (Matt. 4:5; 27:53). On the other hand, it is the city "who kills the prophets and stones those who are sent to her" (Luke 13:34 HCSB). While there were those who longed for "the redemption of Jerusalem" (Luke 2:38), the city and its inhabitants will face awful judgment because they did not recognize the time of divine visitation by Jesus (Luke 19:41-44). Indeed Jesus' mission ended in His rejection by Jerusalem's rulers and His death outside the city walls (Mark 8:31; 10:32-34; chaps. 14–15).

While repentance for the forgiveness of sins is to be preached to all the nations "beginning at Jerusalem" (Luke 24:47), in the aftermath of Jesus' death and resurrection, biblical hope is centered on "the heavenly Jerusalem" (Heb. 12:22; cp. 11:10,16; 13:13-14). The true worshipers need not "worship the Father in Jerusalem ... but ... worship the Father in spirit and truth" (John 4:21,23 HCSB). The "Jerusalem above" (the mother of the free, who are children of the promise) stands in contrast to "the present Jerusalem," which is the mother of unbelieving slaves (Gal. 4:25-26). The city where the Lord Jesus was crucified was called "prophetically, Sodom and Egypt" (Rev. 11:8), but the "new Jerusalem" will come down from heaven with the coming of the new heaven and new earth (Rev. 3:12; 21:1-2).

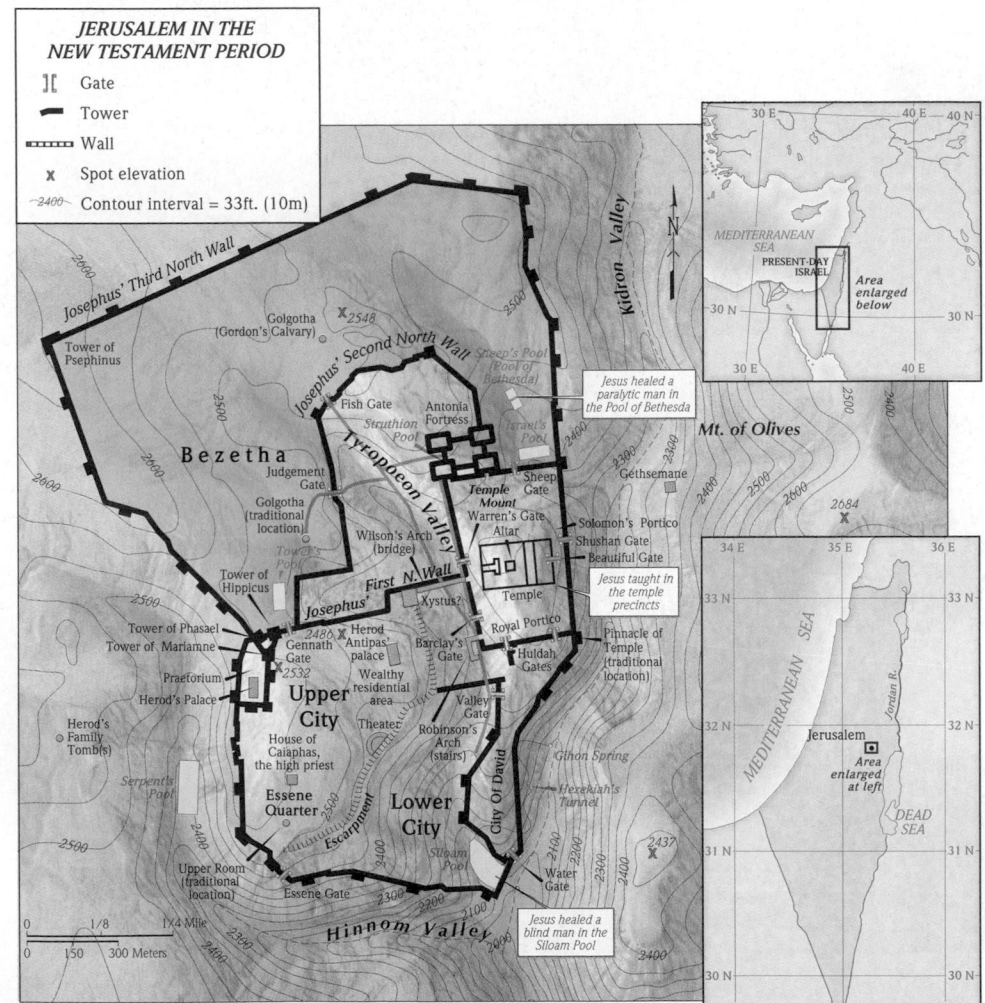

The modern city of Jerusalem looking south through the Kidron Valley from Mount Scopus.

The Muslim Dome of the Rock mosque built on the site of Solomon's temple.

J

The promises of Yahweh's reign ("the kingdom of God") and of the salvation of His people, both Jews and Gentiles, find their fulfillment in Jesus' death and resurrection and in the dawning of the new heaven and new earth. Biblical hope is now focused on "the city of the living God, the heavenly Jerusalem" (Heb. 12:22).

Randall K. J. Tan

JERUSALEM COUNCIL See *Apostolic Council.*

JERUSHA (Jə rū´ shà) Personal name meaning "one taken in possession." Mother of Jotham, king of Judah (2 Kings 15:33). She was the daughter of Zadok, possibly of the priestly line. In 2 Chron. 27:1 her name appears in the form Jerushah. The name of her father suggests that she may have been from a Levitical family.

JERUSHAH (Jə rū´ shà) Form of Jerusha in 2 Chron. 27:1, a variant spelling with different final "silent" consonant in Hebrew. See *Jerusha.*

JESAIAH (Jə sī´ ah) Variant form of Isaiah meaning "Yah has saved." Descendant of David in postexilic period (1 Chron. 3:21) and thus part of keeping messianic hope alive in Israel.

JESARELAH (Jĕs à rē´ lah) NIV, NRSV spelling of Jesharelah (1 Chron. 25:14), a variant spelling of Asharelah (25:2). See *Asharelah; Jesharelah.*

JESHAIAH (Jə shī´ ah) Variant English transliteration of Hebrew name Isaiah meaning "Yahweh delivered." **1.** Priest who used music to prophesy under David (1 Chron. 25:3). Apparently, they proclaimed God's will to the worshiping congregation. Leader of eighth course or division of priests (25:15). **2.** Member of family of Levites with responsibility for treasury of God's house under David (1 Chron. 26:25).

JESHANAH (Jə shā´ nah) Place-name meaning "old city." City that King Abijah of Judah captured from Jeroboam of Israel about 910 B.C. (2 Chron. 13:19). It was located at modern Burj el-Isane four miles south of Shiloh and eight miles northeast of Mizpah. Some interpreters follow early translations and read Jeshanah in 1 Sam. 7:12.

JESHARELAH (Jĕsh à rē´ lah) KJV, NASB, RSV transliteration of Hebrew name of leader of seventh division of Levites (1 Chron. 25:14). The Hebrew is more precisely transliterated Jesarelah and represents a variant Hebrew spelling or textual change from Asarelah (1 Chron. 25:2). Jesarelah in Hebrew is spelled like Israel with an additional final letter. See *Asarelah; Jesarelah.*

JESHEBEAB (Jə shĕ´ bə ăb) Personal name meaning "the father remains alive" or "He brings the father back." Head of 14th division of priests (1 Chron. 24:13).

JESHER (Jē´ shĕr) Personal name meaning "he sets right, establishes justice." Son of Caleb (1 Chron. 2:18).

JESHIMON (Jə shī´ mŏn) Place-name meaning "desert" or "wilderness." **1.** Wilderness site near where David hid from Saul. It apparently belonged to the Ziphites, who reported David's location to Saul (1 Sam. 23:19; 26:1). It lay somewhere between Hebron and the Dead Sea. **2.** Wilderness site east of the Jordan near Pisgah and Peor used to mark the places Israel passed under Moses on the way to conquer the promised land (Num. 21:20; 23:28). It may be another way to refer to the lower Jordan Valley. **3.** The Hebrew word also appears as a common noun meaning "desert" (Deut. 32:10; Pss. 68:7; 78:40; 106:14; 107:4; Isa. 43:19-20). Some interpreters take all occurrences of the word as the common noun. See *Beth-jeshimoth.*

JESHISHAI (Jə shĭsh´ ī) Personal name meaning "advanced in years." Member of tribe of Gad (1 Chron. 5:14).

JESHOHAIAH (Jĕ shō hī´ ah) Personal name of unknown meaning. Member of tribe of Simeon (1 Chron. 4:36).

JESHUA (Jĕ shū´ à) or **JESHUAH** Personal name spelled in Hebrew the same as Joshua and meaning "Yahweh is salvation." **1.** Leader of the ninth course of priests under David (1 Chron. 24:11, sometimes transliterated as Jeshuah). **2.** Priest under Hezekiah (715–686 B.C.) who helped distribute food collected in tithes and offerings to the priests living in the Levitical cities outside Jerusalem (2 Chron. 31:15). **3.** High priest taken into the exile by King Nebuchadnezzar of Babylon in 586 B.C. He returned to Jerusalem with Zerubbabel about 537 B.C. (Ezra

2:2). Descendants of his family or of 1. (above) also returned (Ezra 2:36; cp. 2:40). He led in rebuilding the altar and restoring sacrifice in Jerusalem (Ezra 3:2-6). They also began building the temple but quit when strong opposition arose and appealed to King Artaxerxes (Ezra 3:8–4:24). Later correspondence led King Darius to recover Cyrus' proclamation authorizing the rebuilding of the temple. This came after Jeshua followed the prophetic preaching of Zechariah and Haggai and renewed efforts to rebuild the temple (Ezra 5:2–6:15; Hag. 1:1,12-14; 2:4), finally finishing in 515 B.C. Still, some of his sons married foreign women and had to follow Ezra's teaching and divorce them (Ezra 10:18-19). Zechariah had a vision featuring Jeshua in which God announced the full cleansing of the high priest, preparing him to lead in the atonement rites for the people and pointing to the day when Messiah would come and provide complete and eternal atonement for God's people (Zech. 3). Jeshua was apparently one of the two anointed ones of Zechariah's vision (4:14; cp. 6:11-13). **4.** Clan related to the Pahath-moab or governor of Moab, some of whose members returned from exile with Zerubbabel (Ezra 2:6). **5.** Father of Exer, the Jewish governor of the district of Mizpah under Persian rule (Neh. 3:19). **6.** Levite who signed Nehemiah's covenant to obey God's law (Neh. 10:9). **7.** Clan of Levites in the postexilic community, probably having some connection with the clan of 1. **8.** Name for conquest hero Joshua, son of Nun (Neh. 8:17). See *Joshua.* **9.** Village in Judah where some Jews lived after returning from exile (Neh. 11:26). It may be modern Tell es-Sawi, northeast of Beersheba.

JESHURUN (Jə shū′ rŭn) Proper name meaning "upright" or "straight." Poetic name for Israel (Deut. 32:15; 33:5,26; Isa. 44:2). It may represent a play on Jacob, the original Israel, known for deception. Jeshurun would show Israel had quit deceiving and become upright or straight in actions.

JESIAH (Jə sī′ ah) Personal name meaning "Yahweh forgets." Member of Saul's tribe of Benjamin who joined David at Ziklag as David fled before Saul (1 Chron. 12:6). Modern translations read "Isshiah." A shortened form in Hebrew appears at 1 Chron. 23:20, a Levite; 7:3, leader in tribe of Issachar; 24:21, a Levite; 24:25,

another Levite; Ezra 10:31, a man with a foreign wife. See *Ishiah; Isshiah; Ishijah.*

JESIMIEL (Jə sĭm′ ĭ ĕl) Personal name meaning "Yahweh places." Member of tribe of Simeon (1 Chron. 4:36).

JESSE (Jĕs′ sē) Personal name meaning "man" or "manly." Father of David the king (1 Sam. 16:1). He was a Judahite who lived in Bethlehem, the son of Obed and the grandson of Boaz and Ruth (1 Sam. 16:1; Ruth 4:17). He had eight sons, of whom David was the youngest, and two daughters. He is mentioned in the genealogies of Jesus in the Gospels of Matthew and Luke. See *David.*

JEST Act intended to provoke laughter; an utterance intended as mockery or humor. Thinking Lot was jesting about Sodom's imminent destruction, his sons-in-law remained in the city (Gen. 19:14). The jesters of Ps. 35:16 (NASB) are mockers. Isaiah 57:4 describes idolatry as making God the object of a jest (KJV "sport"). Ephesians 5:4 characterizes jesting or mocking speech as part of a pagan life-style.

JESUI (Jĕs′ ū ī) KJV spelling of descendant of Asher (Num. 26:44), the same as Isui in Gen. 46:17. Modern translations spell both Ishvi. A son of Saul bears the same Hebrew name (1 Sam. 14:49), transliterated into English as Ishui (KJV), Ishvi (NASB, NRSV, NIV), or Ishyo (REB). See *Ishvi.*

JESUITE (Jĕs′ ū īt) Member of clan founded by Jesui (Num. 26:44 KJV). See *Jesui.*

JESURUN (Jə sū′ rŭn) (KJV, Isa. 44:2) See *Jeshurun.*

JESUS CHRIST The absolute fundamental to the Christian faith. The person Buddha is not essential to the teaching of Buddhism nor is the person Mohammed essential to the Islamic faith. Yet everything about Christianity rises or falls in the person of Jesus Christ. Liberal theologians have thought it possible to separate Christ from Christianity by suggesting that Jesus' teachings form the basis of the Christian faith. They want to assert that one may accept Christ's teachings without coming to a decision about Christ Himself.

J

To the contrary, biblical teaching affirms that a Christ-less Christianity is a contradiction of terms. This article, along with the one titled *"Jesus, Life and Ministry,"* seeks to summarize the biblical information on the uniqueness of Jesus. The names and titles applied to Him, His humanity, His deity, and His teaching and mighty works provide the framework for this discussion.

Names and Titles Jesus' proper name derives from the Hebrew "Joshua," meaning "Yahweh saves" or "salvation is from Yahweh" (Matt. 1:21). *Christ* is the Greek term for "anointed," equivalent to the Hebrew *Messiah*. This anointed Savior is also Immanuel, "God is with us" (Matt. 1:23; Isa. 7:14). Paul's favorite term for Jesus was *kurios*, "Lord," and the earliest Christian confession was that "Jesus is Lord." The sublime introduction of Jesus in the prologue to John's Gospel presents Him as the *logos*, the "Word" who created all things (1:3) and who became flesh and dwelt among us (1:14). He is the Life (1:4) and the Light of mankind (1:4); the Glory of God (1:14); the only begotten God who makes the Father known (1:18). The Gospels record Jesus' own self designation as Son of Man, the title He frequently used to speak of His humiliation, His identification with sinful mankind, His death on behalf of sinners, and His glorious return. While Jesus was the Son of Man in respect to His ministry and passion, He is also Son of God, the uniquely begotten one sent from God Himself (Mark 1:1; John 3:16). The book of Hebrews shows Jesus as God's great high priest (3:1; 4:14) who both makes sacrifice for His people and who is Himself the sacrifice (10:10-14). Hebrews also presents Jesus as the creator of all things (1:2), the perfect representation of God (1:3), and the apostle of our confession (3:1). The metaphors used of Jesus, particularly in John's Gospel, speak poignantly to the indispensable need for a person to know Jesus. He is the water of life (John 4:14), the bread of life (6:41), the light (8:12), the door (10:7), the way, the truth, and the life (14:6).

Humanity Jesus was fully human. He was not partially human nor did He function at times as a human and at times as God nor did He merely appear to be human. He was at once both man and God. *The Baptist Faith and Message* emphasizes this truth when it says, "Christ took upon Himself the demands and necessities of human nature, identifying Himself completely with mankind" (Art. II, B). The evidence for Jesus' humanity in Scripture is abundant. He displayed physical symptoms that all humans experience: fatigue (John 4:6), sleep (Matt. 8:24), hunger (Matt. 21:18), and suffering (Luke 22:43-44). Jesus also experienced the emotional reactions of mankind: compassion (Luke 7:13), weeping (Luke 19:41), anger and indignation (Mark 3:5), grief (Matt. 26:37), and joy (John 15:11). These physical and emotional traits, along with others mentioned in the Gospels, demonstrate that the NT everywhere assumes Jesus' real and full humanity. Yet Jesus was not just a real man; He was also a unique person. Though really human, Jesus differed from all other people in two ways. First, He was born to a virgin; He had no human father. He was conceived by the Holy Spirit in Mary's womb (Matt. 1:18-25). Second, unlike any other person, Jesus was without sin. He claimed to be sinless (John 8:46) and there is never a record of His confessing sin, though He told us to confess ours (Matt. 6:12). Other biblical writers ascribe sinlessness to Jesus. Paul said that Jesus became sin for us but that He personally knew no sin (2 Cor. 5:21). The writer of Hebrews says that Jesus never sinned (Heb. 4:15) and Peter affirmed that Jesus the righteous died for the unrighteous (1 Pet. 3:18).

Deity Throughout the centuries few people have denied the existence of the man Jesus. A fierce battle has always raged, however, concerning the supernatural nature of Jesus. If Jesus was virgin born and sinless, as noted above, then a supernatural element is already introduced into His nature that sets Him apart from all other people. Further, His resurrection denotes that this is a person who transcends time and space. The Gospel accounts record many eyewitnesses to the resurrected Christ (Matt. 28:1-10; Luke 24:13-35; John 20:19-31), and all attempts to refute such accounts fall short of credibility. However, the NT goes beyond these implicit references to deity and clearly states that Christ is divine. The demands of unabashed loyalty from His followers (Luke 9:57-62) and the claims that He will judge the world (John 5:27) sound strange if they come from a mere man. He also claimed that He could forgive sins (Mark 2:5), and He averred that in the judgment people will be condemned or approved according to their attitude toward the people who represent Him

(Matt. 25:31-46). Scripture says that Jesus created (John 1:3) and now sustains all things (Col. 1:17). He even has the power to raise the dead (John 5:25). Angels and people worship Him (Heb. 1:6; Matt. 2:2). He possesses equality with the persons of the Trinity (John 14:23; 2 Cor. 13:14). Beyond these assertions, the NT provides even clearer evidence regarding the deity of Christ. He is called God in Heb. 1:8. John's prologue (1:1-18) affirms that Jesus is from the beginning, that He is "with" (literally "face to face") God, and that He is God. John's intricate Greek declares Jesus to be equal in nature with God the Father but distinct in person! Another important passage is John 5:16-29. During a controversy with the Jews about healing a man on the Sabbath the Jews sought to kill Him because He blasphemed in making Himself equal with God. Rather than correcting them for mistaking His identity, Jesus went on to make even further claims regarding His deity: He has power to give life to people (v. 21), all judgment is handed over to Him (v. 22), and all should honor the Son with the same honor they bestow upon the Father (v. 23). Jesus' preexistence as God is demonstrated in John 8:58 where He affirmed that He transcends time. Romans 9:5 reveals that Paul called Jesus God, and there is no doubt that in Phil. 2:5-11 Paul understood Jesus to be the One who existed eternally in the form of God and on an equal nature with God. The outstanding christological passage in Col. 1:15-23 says that Christ is the image of the invisible God; that is, He is such a reproduction or likeness of the God who is invisible to mortal man that to look at Christ was to see God. Clearly, the Christ of the NT is not a man who was deified by His disciples (the view of classic liberalism), but He is the eternal Son of God who voluntarily became a man to redeem lost humanity.

Teaching and Mighty Works Jesus was a master teacher. Crowds that claimed no loyalty to Him were forced to admit, "No man ever spoke like this" (John 7:46 HCSB). At the close of His compelling Sermon on the Mount, the multitudes were amazed at how He taught (Matt. 7:29). He taught mainly about His Father and the kingdom that He had ushered in. He explained what that kingdom is like and the absolute obedience and love His followers are to have as citizens of the kingdom. His teaching often enraged the religious leaders of His day because they did not understand that He was the promised Messiah who appeared to usher in the kingdom through His death, resurrection, and second coming. He stressed that the kingdom, though inaugurated at His first appearing, will find its consummation in His second coming (Matt. 24–25). Until then, His disciples were to conduct themselves as salt and light in a dark, sinful world (Matt. 5–7). Often He spoke in parables, helping people to understand by using common things to illustrate spiritual truths.

Jesus' mighty works validated His unique and divine nature. He backed up His claims to deity by demonstrating His power over sickness and disease, over nature, and over life and death itself. One great miracle that demonstrates conclusively His claim to deity is His resurrection from the dead. Death could not hold Him. He rose from the dead and showed Himself alive by many "convincing proofs" (Acts 1:3). Despite rigorous attempts by liberalism to expunge the miracles from the Gospels, it is impossible to eliminate these supernatural elements from Jesus' life without consequently damaging the credibility of the Gospel records about Him.

Christianity affirms that Jesus is the only way to God (John 14:6; Acts 4:12). This view seems intolerant in light of our pluralistic, relativistic age. Yet, given the evidence presented above, one must deal with Jesus Christ either as the Lord God whom He claimed to be or as an imposter who somehow was deceived as to His own identity.   *Dale Ellenburg*

JESUS, LIFE AND MINISTRY The story of Jesus begins abruptly in the Gospel of Mark when He presented Himself at the Jordan River to the desert Prophet John the Baptist as a candidate for baptism. All that is said about His origin is that He came to the river "from Nazareth" (Mark 1:9). "Jesus of Nazareth" was a designation that followed Him to the day of His death (John 19:19).

His Origins Matthew's Gospel demonstrates that although Nazareth was Jesus' home when He came to John for baptism, He was not born there. Rather, He was born (as the Jewish messiah must be) in Bethlehem, the "city of David," as a descendant of David's royal line (Matt. 1:1-17; 2:1-6). This child born in Bethlehem ended up as an adult in Nazareth, described sarcastically by His enemies as a "Nazarene" (literally,

"Nazarite" 2:23). The play on words seems intended to poke fun simultaneously at Jesus' obscure origins and at the stark contrast (in the eyes of many) between His supposed holiness (like the Nazirites of the OT) and His practice of keeping company with sinners, prostitutes, and tax collectors (Mark 2:17). The Gospel of Luke supplies background information on John the Baptist, showing how the families of John and Jesus were related both by kinship and by circumstances (Luke 1:5-80). Luke added that Nazareth was the family home of Jesus' parents all along (Luke 1:26-27). Yet he confirmed Matthew's testimony that the family was of the line of David. Luke introduced the Roman census as the reason for their return to the ancestral city of Bethlehem just before Jesus' birth (Luke 2:1-7). More of a biographer than either Mark or Matthew, Luke provided glimpses of Jesus as an eight-day-old infant (2:21-39), a boy of 12 years (2:40-52), and a man of 30 beginning His ministry (3:21-23). Only when this brief biographical sketch was complete did Luke append His genealogy (Luke 3:23-38), which confirms in passing Jesus' Davidic ancestry (Luke 3:31; cp. 1:32-33), while emphasizing above all His solidarity with the entire human race in its descent from "Adam, son of God" (Luke 3:38 HCSB). The reflection on Jesus' baptism in the Gospel of John centers on John the Baptist's acknowledgement that Jesus "surpassed me, because He existed before me" (John 1:30; cp. v. 15). This pronouncement allowed the Gospel writer to turn the story of Jesus' origins into a theological confession by tracing Jesus' existence back to the creation of the world and before (John 1:1-5). Despite His royal ancestry and despite His heavenly preexistence as the eternal Word and Son of God, Jesus was of humble origins humanly speaking and was viewed as such by the people of His day. When He taught in Nazareth, the townspeople asked, "Isn't this the carpenter, the son of Mary, and the brother of James, Joses, Judas, and Simon? And aren't His sisters here with us?" (Mark 6:3; cp. Luke 4:22). When He taught in Capernaum, they asked, "Isn't this Jesus the son of Joseph, whose father and mother we know? How can He now say, 'I have come

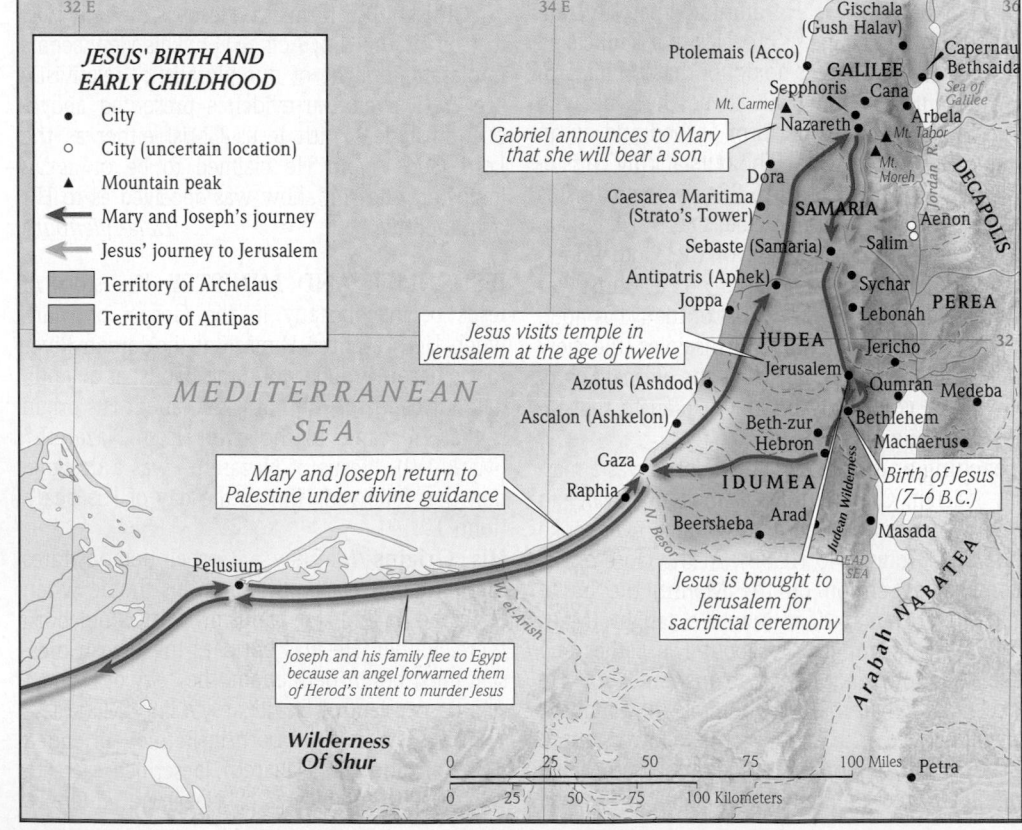

JESUS' BIRTH AND EARLY CHILDHOOD

- City
- City (uncertain location)
- Mountain peak
- Mary and Joseph's journey
- Jesus' journey to Jerusalem
- Territory of Archelaus
- Territory of Antipas

Gabriel announces to Mary that she will bear a son

Jesus visits temple in Jerusalem at the age of twelve

Mary and Joseph return to Palestine under divine guidance

Joseph and his family flee to Egypt because an angel forewarned them of Herod's intent to murder Jesus

Birth of Jesus (7–6 B.C.)

Jesus is brought to Jerusalem for sacrificial ceremony

MEDITERRANEAN SEA

Wilderness Of Shur

down from heaven'?" (John 6:42). Though two Gospels, Matthew and Luke, tell of His mother Mary's miraculous conception and of Jesus' virgin birth, these matters were not public knowledge during His time on earth, for "Mary was treasuring up all these things in her heart and meditating on them" (Luke 2:19; cp. v. 51). **Jesus and the God of Israel** Even after the momentous events associated with Jesus' baptism in the Jordan River—the descent of God's Spirit on Him like a dove and the voice from heaven announcing "You are My beloved Son; in You I take delight!" (Mark 1:10-11 HCSB)—His identity as Son of God remained hidden from those around Him. We have no evidence that anyone except Jesus, and possibly John the Baptist, either heard the voice or saw the dove. Ironically, the first intimation after the baptism that He was more than simply "Jesus of Nazareth" came not from His family or friends or from the religious leaders of Israel, but from the devil!

Twice the devil challenged Him: "If You are the Son of God, tell this stone to become bread" (Luke 4:3), and (on the pinnacle of the temple in Jerusalem), "If You are the Son of God, throw Yourself down from here" (Luke 4:9). Jesus made no attempt to defend or make use of His divine sonship but appealed instead to an authority to which any devout Jew of His day might have appealed—the holy Scriptures—and through them to the God of Israel. Citing three passages from Deuteronomy, Jesus called attention not to Himself, but to "the Lord your God" (Luke 4:8; cp. Mark 10:18; 12:29-30). Jesus apparently used this story out of His personal experience to teach His disciples that they, too, must "live ... on every word that comes from the mouth of God," (Matt. 4:4), must "not tempt the Lord your God" (Luke 4:12), and must "worship the Lord your God, and Him alone you shall serve" (Luke 4:8).

Two things about this temptation story have a special bearing on the ministry of Jesus as a whole. First, the God-centered character of His message continued in the proclamation He began in Galilee when He returned home from the desert: "The time is fulfilled, and the kingdom of God has come near. Repent and believe in the good news!" (Mark 1:15 HCSB; cp. Matt. 4:17). Mark called this proclamation "the good news of God" (Mark 1:14). John's Gospel presented Jesus as reminding His hearers again and

again that He had come not to glorify or proclaim Himself, but solely to make known "the Father," or "Him who sent me" (John 4:34; 5:19,30; 6:38; 7:16-18,28; 8:28,42,50; 14:10,28). Second, the issue of Jesus' own identity continued to be raised first by the powers of evil. Just as the devil challenged Jesus in the desert as "Son of God," so in the course of His ministry the demons (or the demon-possessed) confronted Him with such words as "What do You have to do with us, Jesus—Nazarene? ... I know who You are—the Holy One of God" (Mark 1:24), or "What do You have to do with me, Jesus, Son of the Most High God?" (Mark 5:7).

The mystery of Jesus' person emerged in pronouncements of this kind, but Jesus seemed not to want the question of His identity raised prematurely. He silenced the demons (Mark 1:25,34; 3:12); and when He healed the sick, He frequently told the people who were cured not to speak of it to anyone (Mark 1:43-44; 7:36a). The more He urged silence, however, the faster the word of His healing power spread (Mark 1:45; 7:36b). The crowds appear to have concluded that He must be the Messiah, the anointed King of David's line expected to come and deliver the Jews from Roman rule. If Jesus was playing out the role of Messiah, the Gospels present Him as a strangely reluctant Messiah. At one point, when the crowds tried to "take Him by force to make Him king, He withdrew again to the mountain by Himself" (John 6:15 HCSB). Seldom, if ever, did He apply to Himself the customary terms "Messiah" or "Son of God." He had instead a way of using the emphatic "I" when it was not grammatically necessary and a habit sometimes of referring to Himself indirectly and mysteriously as "Son of Man." In the Aramaic language Jesus spoke, "Son of man" meant simply "a certain man," or "someone." Though He made no explicit messianic claims and avoided the ready-made titles of honor that the Jews customarily applied to the Messiah, Jesus spoke and acted with the authority of God Himself. He gave sight to the blind and hearing to the deaf; He enabled the lame to walk. When He touched the unclean, He made them clean. He even raised the dead to life. In teaching the crowds that gathered around Him, He did not hesitate to say boldly, "You have heard that it was said ... but I tell you" (Matt. 5:21-22,27-28,31-34,38-39,43-44). So radical was He

J

Parables of Jesus

PARABLE	OCCASION	LESSON TAUGHT	REFERENCES
1. The speck and the log	When reproving the Pharisees	Do not presume to judge others	Matt 7:1-6; Luke 6:37-43
2. The two houses	Sermon on the Mount, at the close	The strength confered by duty	Matt 7:24-27; Luke 6:47-49
3. Children in the marketplace	Rejection by the Phaisee's of John's baptism	Evil of a fault-finding disposition	Matt 11:16-19; Luke 7:32
4. The two debtors	Pharisee's self-righteous reflections	Love to Christ proportioned to grace received	Luke 7:41
5. The unclean spirit	The Scribes demand a miracle in the heavens	Hardening power of unbelief	Matt 12:43-45; Luke 11:24-26
6. The rich man's meditation	Dispute of two brothers	Folly of reliance upon wealth	Luke 12:16-21
7. The barren fig tree	Tidings of the execution of certain Galileans	Danger in the unbelief of the Jewish people	Luke 13:6-9
8. The sower	Sermon on the seashore	The effects of preaching religious truth	Matt 13:3-8; Mark 4:3-8; Luke 8:5-8
9. The tares	The same	The severance of good and evil	Matt 13:24-30
10. The seed	The same	Power of truth	Mark 4:20
11. The grain of mustard seed	The same	Small beginnings and growth of Christ's kingdom	Matt 13:31-32; Mark 4:31-32; Luke 13:19
12. The leaven	The same	Dissemination of the knowledge of Christ	Matt 13:33; Luke 13:21
13. The lamp	To the disciples alone	Effect of good example	Matt 5:15; Mark 4:21; Luke 8:16; 11:33
14. The dragnet	The same	Mixed character of the church	Matt 13:47-48
15. The hidden treasure	The same	Value of religion	Matt 13:44
16. The pearl of great value	The same	The same	Matt 13:45-46
17. The householder	The same	Varied methods of teaching truth	Matt 13:52
18. The marriage	To the Pharisees who censured the disciples	Joy in Christ's companionship	Matt 9:15; Mark 2:19-20; Luke 5:34-35
19. The patched garment	The same	The propriety of adapting actions to circumstances	Matt 9:16; Mark 2:21; Luke 5:36
20. The wine bottles	The same	The same	Matt 9:17; Mark 2:22; Luke 5:37
21. The harvest	Spiritual wants of the Jewish people	Need of labor and prayer	Matt 9:37; Luke 10:2
22. The opponent	Slowness of the people to believe	Need of prompt repentance	Matt 5:25; Luke 12:58
23. Two insolvent debtors	Peter's question	Duty of forgiveness	Matt 18:23-35

Parables of Jesus

PARABLE	OCCASION	LESSON TAUGHT	REFERENCES
24. The good Samaritan	The lawyer's question	The golden rule for all	Luke 10:30-37
25. The three loaves	Disciples ask lesson in prayer	Effect of importunity in prayer	Luke 11:5-8
26. The good shepherd	Pharisees reject testimony of miracle	Christ the only way to God	John 10:1-16
27. The narrow gate	The question, Are there few who can be saved?	Difficulty of repentance	Matt 7:14; Luke 13:24
28. The guests	Eagerness to take high places	Chief places not to be usurped	Luke 14:7-11
29. The marriage supper	Self-righteous remark of a guest	Rejection of unbelievers	Matt 22:2-9; Luke 14:16-23
30. The wedding clothes	Continuation of the same discourse	Necessity of purity	Matt 22:10-14
31. The tower	Multitudes surrounding Christ	Need of deliberation	Luke 14:28-30
32. The king going to war	The same	The same	Luke 14:31
33. The lost sheep	Pharisees objected to his receiving the wicked	Christ's love for sinners	Matt 18:12-13; Luke 15:4-7
34. The lost coin	The same	The same	Luke 15:8-9
35. The prodigal son	The same	The same	Luke 15:11-32
36. The unjust steward	To the disciples	Prudence in using property	Luke 16:1-9
37. The rich man and Lazarus	Derision of the Pharisees	Salvation not connected with wealth	Luke 16:19-31
38. The slave's duty	Teaching the disciples	Humble obedience	Luke 17:7-10
39. Laborers in the vineyard	The same	The same further illustrated	Matt 20:1-16
40. The talents	At the house of Zaccheus	Doom of unfaithful followers	Matt 25:14-30; Luke 19:11-27
41. The importunate widow	Teaching the disciples	Perseverance in prayer	Luke 18:2-5
42. The Pharisee and tax-gatherer	Teaching the self-righteous	Humility in prayer	Luke 18:10-14
43. The two sons	The chief priests demand His authcrity	Obedience better than words	Matt 21:28
44. The wicked vine-growers	The same	Rejection of the Jewish people	Matt 21:33-43; Mark 12:1-9; Luke 20:9-15
45. The fig tree	In prophesying the destruction of Jerusalem	Duty of watching for Christ's appearance	Matt 24:32; Mark 13:28; Luke 21:29-30
46. The watching slave	The same	The same	Matt 24:43; Luke 12:39
47. The man on a journey	In prophesying the destruction of Jerusalem	The same	Mark 13:34
48. Character of two slaves	The same	Danger of unfaithfulness	Matt 24:45-51; Luke 12:42-46
49. The ten virgins	The same	Necessity of watchfulness	Matt 25:1-12
50. The watching slaves	The same	The same	Luke 12:36-38
51. The vine and branches	At the Last Supper	Loss and gain	John 15:1-6

Miracles of Jesus

MIRACLE	BIBLE PASSAGE			
Water Turned to Wine				John 2:1
Many Healings	Matt 4:23	Mark 1:32		
Healing of a Leper	Matt 8:1	Mark 1:40	Luke 5:12	
Healing of a Roman Centurion's Servant	Matt 8:5		Luke 7:1	
Healing of Peter's Mother-in-law	Matt 8:14	Mark 1:29	Luke 4:38	
Calming of the Storm at Sea	Matt 8:23	Mark 4:35	Luke 8:22	
Healing of the Wild Men of Gadara	Matt 8:28	Mark 5:1	Luke 8:26	
Healing of the Lame Man	Matt 9:1	Mark 2:1	Luke 5:18	
Healing of a Woman with a Hemorrhage	Matt 9:20	Mark 5:25	Luke 8:43	
Raising of Jairus's Daughter	Matt 9:23	Mark 5:22	Luke 8:41	
Healing of Two Blind Men	Matt 9:27			
Healing of a Demon-Possessed Man	Matt 9:32			
Healing of Man with a Withered Hand	Matt 12:10	Mark 3:1	Luke 6:6	
Feeding of 5,000 People	Matt 14:15	Mark 6:35	Luke 9:12	John 6:1
Walking on the Sea	Matt 14:22	Mark 6:47		John 6:16
Healing of the Syrophoenician's Daughter	Matt 15:21	Mark 7:24		
Feeding of 4,000 People	Matt 15:32	Mark 8:1		
Healing of an Epileptic Boy	Matt 17:14	Mark 9:14	Luke 9:37	
Healing of Two Blind Men at Jericho	Matt 20:30			
Healing of a Man with an Unclean Spirit		Mark 1:23	Luke 4:33	
Healing of a Deaf, Speechless Man		Mark 7:31		
Healing of a Blind Man at Bethesda		Mark 8:22		
Healing of Blind Bartimaeus		Mark 10:46	Luke 18:35	
A Miraculous Catch of Fish			Luke 5:4	John 21:1
Raising of a Widow's Son			Luke 7:11	
Healing of a Stooped Woman			Luke 13:11	
Healing of a Man with the Dropsy			Luke 14:1	
Healing of Ten Lepers			Luke 17:11	
Healing of Malchus's Ear			Luke 22:50	
Healing of a Royal Official's Son				John 4:46
Healing of a Lame Man at Bethesda				John 5:1
Healing of a Blind Man				John 9:1
Raising of Lazarus				John 11:38

Discourses of Jesus

WHERE DELIVERED	NATURE OR STYLE	TO WHOM ADDRESSED	THE LESSONS TO BE LEARNED	REFERENCES
1. Jerusalem	Conversation	Nicodemus	We must be "born of water and the Spirit" to enter the kingdom	John 3:1-21
2. At Jacob's Well	Conversation	Samaritan Woman	"God is spirit" to be worshiped in spirit and truth	John 4:1-30
3. At Jacob's Well	Conversation	The Disciples	Our food is to do His will	John 4:31-38
4. Nazareth	Sermon	Worshipers	No prophet is welcomed in his own hometown	Luke 4:16-31
5. Mountain in Galilee	Sermon	The Disciples and the People	The Beatitudes; to let our light shine before men; Christians the light of the world; how to pray; benevolence and humility; heavenly and earthly treasures contrasted; golden rule	Matt. 5-7; Luke 6:17-49
6. Bethesda-A pool	Conversation	The Jews	To hear Him and believe on Him, is to have everlasting life	John 5:1-47
7. Near Jerusalem	Conversation	The Pharisees	Works of necessity not wrong on the Sabbath	Matt. 12:1-14; Luke 6:1-11
8. Nain	Eulogy and Denunciation	The People	Greatness of the least in heaven; judged according to the light we have	Matt. 11:2-29; Luke 7:18-35
9. Capernaum	Conversation	The Pharisees	The unforgivable sin is to sin against the Holy Spirit	Mark 3:19-30; Matt. 12:22-45
10. Capernaum	Conversation	The Disciples	The providence of God; nearness of Christ to those who serve Him	Mark 6:6-13; Matt. 10:1-42
11. Capernaum	Conversation	A Messenger	Relationship of those doing His will	Matt. 12:46-50; Mark 3:31-35
12. Capernaum	Sermon	The Multitude	Christ as the bread of life	John 6:22-71
13. Capernaum	Criticism and Reproof	The Scribes and Pharisees	Not outward conditions, but that which proceeds from the heart defiles	Matt. 15:1-20; Mark 7:1-23
14. Capernaum	Example	The Disciples	Humility the mark of greatness; be not a stumbling block	Matt. 18:1-14; Mark 9:33-50
15. Temple–Jerusalem	Instruction	The Jews	Judge not according to outward appearance	John 7:11-40
16. Temple–Jerusalem	Instruction	The Jews	To follow Christ, is to walk into the light	John 8:12-59
17. Temple–Jerusalem	Instruction	The Pharisees	Christ the door; He knows His sheep; gives His life for them	John 10:1-21
18. Capernaum	Charge	The Seventy	Need for Christian service; not to despise Christ's ministers	Luke 10:1-24
19. Bethany	Instruction	The Disciples	The efficacy of earnest prayer	Luke 11:1-13
20. Bethany	Conversation	The People	Hear and keep God's will; the state of the backslider	Luke 11:14-36
21. House of Pharisee	Reproof	The Pharisees	The meaning of inward purity	Luke 11:37-54
22. Beyond Jordan	Exhortation	The Multitude	Beware of hypocrisy; covetousness; blasphemy; be watchful	Luke 12:1-21
23. Perea	Object Lesson	The Disciples	Watchfulness; the kingdom of God is of first importance	Luke 12:22-34
24. Jerusalem	Exhortation	The People	Death for life; way of eternal life	John 12:20-50
25. Jerusalem	Denunciation	The Pharisees	Avoid hypocrisy and pretense	Matt. 23:1-39
26. Mt. of Olives	Prophecy	The Disciples	Signs of the coming of the Son of man; beware of false prophets	Matt. 24:1-51; Mark 13:1-37; Luke 21:5-36
27. Jerusalem	Exhortation	The Disciples	The lesson of humility and service	John 13:1-20
28. Jerusalem	Exhortation	The Disciples	The proof of discipleship; that He will come again	John 14–16

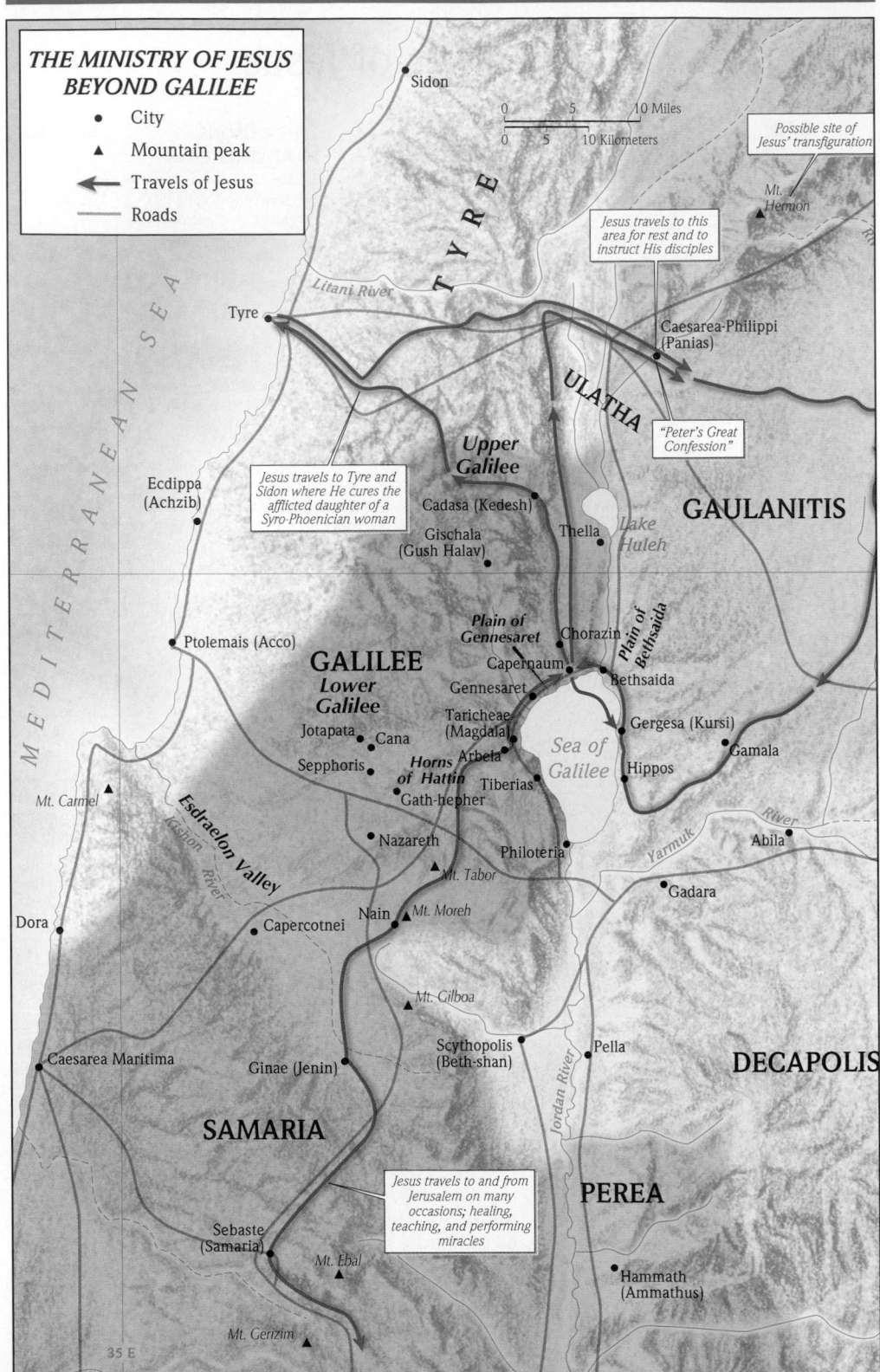

THE MINISTRY OF JESUS BEYOND GALILEE

- • City
- ▲ Mountain peak
- ← Travels of Jesus
- — Roads

Sidon

0   5   10 Miles
0   5   10 Kilometers

Possible site of Jesus' transfiguration

Mt. Hermon ▲

Jesus travels to this area for rest and to instruct His disciples

T Y R E

Litani River

Tyre

Caesarea-Philippi (Panias)

ULATHA

"Peter's Great Confession"

Ecdippa (Achzib)

Jesus travels to Tyre and Sidon where He cures the afflicted daughter of a Syro-Phoenician woman

Upper Galilee

Cadasa (Kedesh)

Gischala (Gush Halav)

Thella

Lake Huleh

GAULANITIS

MEDITERRANEAN SEA

Ptolemais (Acco)

GALILEE

Lower Galilee

Plain of Gennesaret

Chorazin

Plain of Bethsaida

Capernaum

Gennesaret

Bethsaida

Taricheae (Magdala)

Jotapata

Cana

Gergesa (Kursi)

Sepphoris

Horns of Hattin

Arbela

Gamala

Mt. Carmel ▲

Tiberias

Sea of Galilee

Hippos

Gath-hepher

Kishon River

Esdraelon Valley

Nazareth

Philoteria

Yarmuk River

Abila

▲ Mt. Tabor

Gadara

Dora

Nain ▲ Mt. Moreh

Capercotnei

Jordan River

▲ Mt. Gilboa

Scythopolis (Beth-shan)

Pella

DECAPOLIS

Caesarea Maritima

Ginae (Jenin)

SAMARIA

PEREA

Jesus travels to and from Jerusalem on many occasions; healing, teaching, and performing miracles

Sebaste (Samaria)

Mt. Ebal ▲

Hammath (Ammathus)

Mt. Gerizim ▲

35 E

J

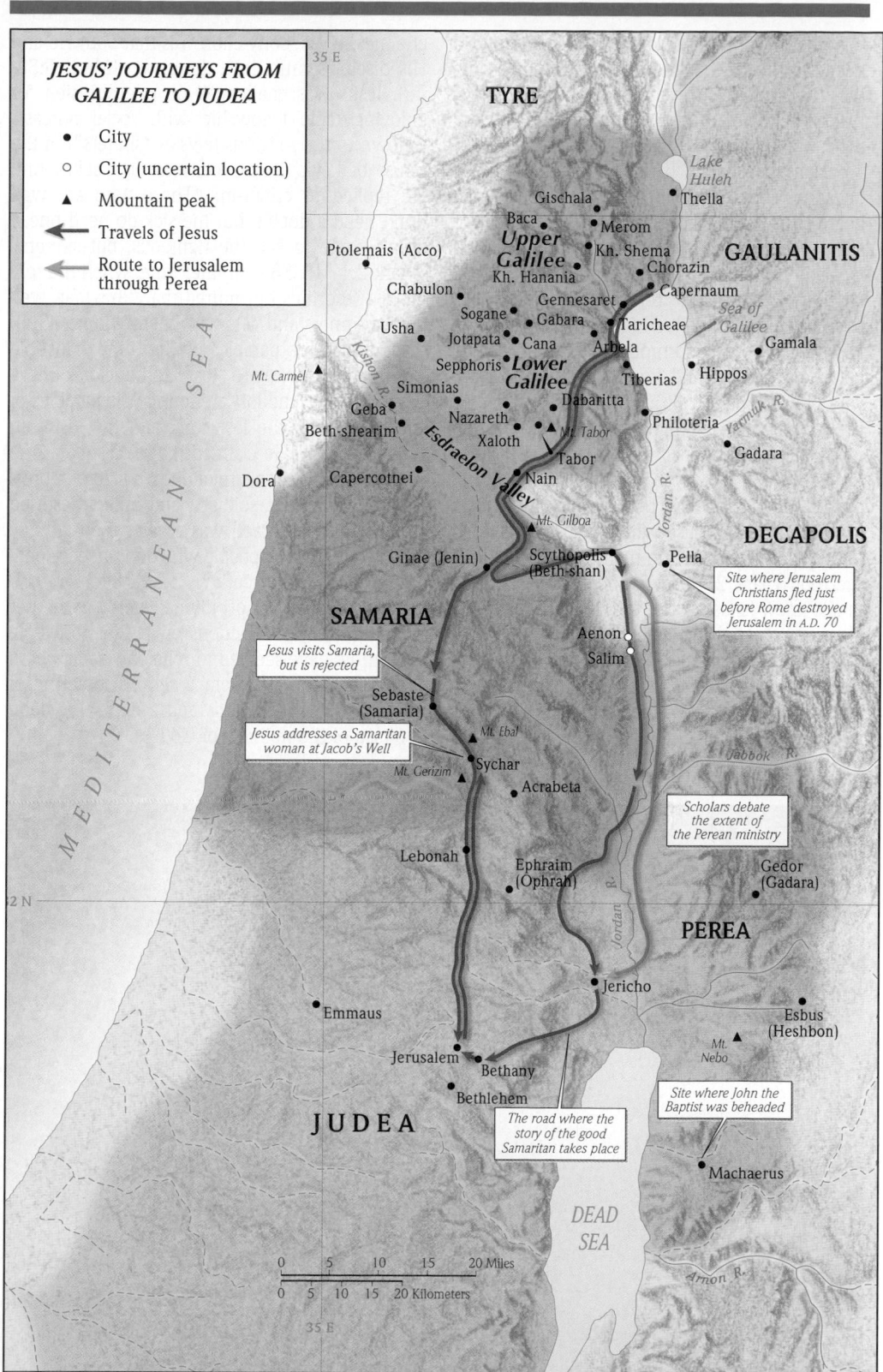

JESUS' JOURNEYS FROM
GALILEE TO JUDEA

- • City
- ○ City (uncertain location)
- ▲ Mountain peak
- → Travels of Jesus
- → Route to Jerusalem through Perea

TYRE

Lake Huleh

Gischala
Baca   Merom
Upper Galilee
Kh. Shema
Thella

GAULANITIS

Ptolemais (Acco)
Kh. Hanania   Chorazin
Chabulon   Capernaum
Sogane   Gennesaret
Usha   Gabara   Taricheae   *Sea of Galilee*
Jotapata   Cana   Gamala
Sepphoris   Arbela
Simonias   *Lower Galilee*   Tiberias   Hippos
Geba   Dabaritta
Beth-shearim   Nazareth   Philoteria
Xaloth   Mt. Tabor
Dora   Capercotnei   *Esdraelon Valley*   Tabor   Gadara
Nain

Mt. Carmel   ▲   *Kishon R.*

Yarmuk R.

DECAPOLIS

▲ Mt. Gilboa

Ginae (Jenin)   Scythopolis   Pella
(Beth-shan)

SAMARIA

Site where Jerusalem
Christians fled just
before Rome destroyed
Jerusalem in A.D. 70

Aenon
Salim

Jesus visits Samaria,
but is rejected

Sebaste
(Samaria)
▲ Mt. Ebal

Jesus addresses a Samaritan
woman at Jacob's Well   Sychar
Mt. Gerizim ▲   Acrabeta

Jordan R.

Scholars debate
the extent of
the Perean ministry

Lebonah
Ephraim
(Ophrah)   Gedor
(Gadara)

PEREA

Jabbok R.

M E D I T E R R A N E A N   S E A

Jericho   Esbus
(Heshbon)
Emmaus
Mt.
Nebo ▲

Jerusalem
Bethany
Bethlehem

JUDEA   The road where the
story of the good
Samaritan takes place

Site where John the
Baptist was beheaded

Machaerus

DEAD
SEA

0   5   10   15   20 Miles
0   5   10   15   20 Kilometers

Arnon R.

35 E

J

toward the accepted traditions that He found it necessary to state at the outset: "Don't assume that I came to destroy the Law or the Prophets. I did not come to destroy but to fulfill" (Matt. 5:17).

Such speech and behavior inevitably raised questions about Jesus' identity. The crowds who heard Him "were astonished at His teaching. For He was teaching them like one who had authority, and not like their scribes" (Matt. 7:28-29 HCSB). Despite His reluctance (or perhaps because of it), His following in the early days of His ministry was enormous. He had to get up before daylight to find time and a place for private prayer (Mark 1:35). So pressed was He by the crowds that He taught them on one occasion while sitting in a boat offshore on the lake of Galilee (Mark 4:1). Once when a group of people desired healing for a paralyzed man, the huge mob around the house where Jesus was staying forced them to lower the man through a hole in the roof (Mark 2:4). Everyone needed what he or she knew Jesus had to give. There was no way He could meet all their needs at once.

Jesus' Mission Jesus' primary mission was to reach the lost sheep of Israel. Through their carelessness about the law, the religious leaders had become the enemies of God; but God loved His enemies. Jesus' conviction was that both He and His disciples must love them, too (Matt. 5:38-48). Jesus was challenged on one occasion for enjoying table fellowship with social outcasts (known to the religious Jews as "sinners") in the house of Levi, the tax collector in Capernaum. He replied to criticism: "Those who are well don't need a doctor, but the sick do need one. I didn't come to call the righteous, but sinners" (Mark 2:17 HCSB). Another time, when the religious authorities murmured that "this man welcomes sinners and eats with them" (Luke 15:2), Jesus told three parables of God's inexhaustible love for those who are "lost" and of God's unbridled joy when the lost are found (the parables of the lost sheep, the lost coin, and the lost son; Luke 15:3-32). He claimed that God's joy at the recovery of all such sinners (tax collectors, prostitutes, shepherds, soldiers, and others despised by the pious in Israel) was greater than any joy "over 99 righteous people who don't need repentance" (Luke 15:7; cp. vv. 25-32). Such an exuberant celebration of divine mercy, whether expressed in Jesus' actions or in the stories He told, must have seemed to religious leaders both in Galilee and Jerusalem a serious lowering of ancient ethical standards and a damaging compromise of the holiness of God.

The traditional site on the Jordan River where Jesus was baptized.

We have little evidence that Jesus included non-Jews among the "sinners" to whom He was sent. Despite the reference in Luke 4:25-27 to Elijah and Elisha and their ministry to foreigners, Jesus explicitly denied that He was sent to Gentiles or Samaritans (Matt. 15:24; 10:5-6). Yet the principle, "not to the righteous, but to sinners," made the extension of the good news of the kingdom of God to the Gentiles after Jesus' resurrection a natural one. Even during Jesus' lifetime, He responded to the initiatives of Gentiles seeking His help (Matt. 8:5-13; Luke 7:1-10; Mark 7:24-30; Matt. 15:21-28), sometimes in such a way as to put Israel to shame (Matt. 8:10). Twice He traveled through Samaria (Luke 9:51-56; John 4:4): once He stayed in a Samaritan village for two days, calling a Samaritan woman and a number of other townspeople to faith (John 4:5-42); and once He made a Samaritan the hero of one of His parables (Luke 10:29-37).

None of this was calculated to win Him friends among the priests in Jerusalem or the Pharisees throughout Israel. He described visions that many would "come from east and west, and recline at the table with Abraham, and Isaac, and Jacob in the kingdom of heaven. But the sons of the kingdom will be thrown into the outer darkness" (Matt. 8:11-12 HCSB). He predicted that 12 uneducated Galileans would one day "sit on 12 thrones, judging the 12 tribes of Israel" (Matt. 19:28; cp. Luke 22:28-29). He warned the religious leaders sternly that they were in danger of "blasphemy against the Spirit" by attributing the Spirit's ministry through Him to the power of the devil (Matt. 12:31). The whole affair was complicated by the concern of Jesus' relatives over his safety and sanity (Mark 3:21) and by His consequent affirmation of His disciples as a new family based on obedience to the will of God (Mark 3:31-35).

The so-called "Beel-zebub controversy," triggered by his healing and saving activity, set a grim precedent for Jesus' relationship with the Jerusalem authorities and made His eventual arrest, trial, and execution almost inevitable (Mark 3:20-30). From that time Jesus began to speak in parables to make the truth about God's kingdom clear to His followers while hiding it from those blind to its beauty and deaf to its call (Mark 4:10-12; notice that Jesus is first said to have spoken in parables in Mark 3:23, in imme-

diate response to the charge of demon possession). He also began to intimate, sometimes in analogy or parable (Mark 10:38; Luke 12:49-50; John 3:14; 12:24,32) and sometimes in explicit language (Mark 8:31; 9:31; 10:33-34), that He would be arrested and tried by the religious leadership in Jerusalem, die on the cross, and rise from the dead after three days. From the start He had defined His mission, at least in part, as that of the "Servant of the Lord" (see, for example the citation of Isa. 61:1-2 in Luke 4:18-19). As His ministry moved toward its completion, the vicarious suffering of the Servant (Isa. 52:13–53:12) came into sharper and sharper focus for Jesus (Mark 10:45; 12:1-11). He also saw Himself as the stricken Shepherd of Zech. 13:7 (Mark 14:27) and, at the very end, in the role of the righteous Sufferer of the biblical psalms (e.g., Mark 15:34; Luke 23:46; John 19:28). Before His arrest He dramatized for the disciples His impending death by sharing with them in the bread and the cup of the Passover with the explanation that the bread was His body to be broken for them and that the cup of wine was His blood to be shed for their salvation. Only His death could guarantee the coming of the kingdom He had proclaimed (Matt. 26:26-29; Mark 14:22-25; Luke 22:14-20; cp. 1 Cor. 11:23-26).

His Death and Resurrection The Gospel accounts of Jesus' last days in Jerusalem correspond in broad outline to the predictions attributed to Him earlier. He seems to have come to Jerusalem for the last time in the knowledge that He would die there. Though He received a royal welcome from crowds who looked to Him as the long-expected Messiah (Matt. 21:9-11; Mark 11:9-10; John 12:13), no evidence points to this as the reason for His arrest. Rather His action in driving the money changers out of the Jerusalem temple (Matt. 21:12-16; Mark 11:15-17; cp. John 2:13-22), as well as certain of His pronouncements about the temple aroused the authorities to act decisively against Him.

During His last week in Jerusalem, Jesus had predicted the temple's destruction (Matt. 24:1-2; Mark 13:1-2; Luke 21:5-6) and claimed that "I will demolish this sanctuary made by hands, and in three days I will build another not made by hands" (Mark 14:58 HCSB; cp. Matt. 26:61). Jesus' intention to establish a new community as a "temple," or dwelling place of God (see Matt. 16:18; John 2:19; 1 Cor. 3:16-17), was

J

perceived as a very real threat to the old community of Judaism and to the temple that stood as its embodiment. On this basis He was arrested and charged as a deceiver of the people.

During a hearing before the Sanhedrin, or Jewish ruling council, Jesus spoke of Himself as "Son of Man seated at the right hand of the Power and coming with the clouds of heaven" (Mark 14:62 HCSB; cp. Matt. 26:64, Luke 22:69). Though the high priest called this blasphemy and the Sanhedrin agreed that such behavior deserved death, the results of the hearing seem to have been inconclusive. If Jesus had been formally tried and convicted by the Sanhedrin, He would have been stoned to death like Stephen in Acts 7, or like the attempted stoning of the woman caught in adultery in a story reported in some manuscripts of John 8:1-11. For whatever reason, the high priest and his cohorts apparently found no formal charges they could make stick. If Jesus were stoned to death without a formal conviction, it would be murder, a sin the Ten Commandments forbid. (John 18:31 refers to what was forbidden to the Jews by their own law, not to what was forbidden by the Romans.) The Sanhedrin decided, therefore, to send Jesus to Pontius Pilate, the Roman governor, with charges against Him that the Romans would take seriously: "We found this man subverting our nation, opposing payment of taxes to Caesar, and saying that He Himself is the Messiah, a King" (Luke 23:2 HCSB). Jesus' execution is therefore attributable neither to the Jewish people as a whole, nor to the Sanhedrin, but rather to a small group of priests who manipulated the Romans into doing what they were not able to accomplish within the framework of their law. Though Pilate pronounced Jesus innocent three times (Luke 23:4,14,22; cp. John 18:38; 19:4,6), he was maneuvered into sentencing Jesus with the thinly veiled threat, "If you release this man, you are not Caesar's friend. Anyone who makes himself a king opposes Caesar!" (John 19:12 HCSB). Consequently, Jesus was crucified between two thieves, fulfilling His own prediction that "as Moses lifted up the serpent in the wilderness, so the Son of Man must be lifted up" (John 3:14). Most of His disciples fled at His arrest; only a group of women and one disciple, called the disciple whom He loved, were present at the cross when He died (John 19:25-27; cp. Matt. 27:55-56; Mark 15:40; Luke 23:49).

The story did not end with the death of Jesus. His body was placed in a new tomb that

Painting from the 15th or 16th century showing the burial of Jesus, seen at the Church of the Holy Sepulchre in Jerusalem.

belonged to a secret disciple named Joseph of Arimathea (Luke 23:50-56; John 19:38-42). The Gospels agree that two days later, the morning after the Sabbath, some of the women who had remained faithful to Jesus came to the tomb. They discovered the stone over the entrance to the tomb rolled away and the body of Jesus gone. According to Mark, a young man was there (16:5; tradition calls him an angel) who told the women to send word to the rest of the disciples to go and meet Jesus in Galilee, just as He had promised them (Mark 16:7; 14:28). The most reliable manuscripts of Mark's Gospel end the story there, leaving the rest to the reader's imagination. According to Matthew, the young man's word was confirmed to the women by the risen Jesus Himself. When they brought word to the 11 disciples (the Twelve minus Judas, the betrayer), the disciples went to a mountain in Galilee, where the risen Jesus appeared to them as a group. He commanded them to make more disciples, teaching and baptizing among the Gentiles (Matt. 28:16-20). According to Luke, the risen Jesus appeared to the gathered disciples already in Jerusalem on the same day He was raised and before that to two disciples walking to the neighboring town of Emmaus. According to John, there was an appearance in Jerusalem on Easter day to one of the women, Mary Magdalene, another on the same day to the gathered disciples, another a week later (still in Jerusalem) to the same group plus Thomas, and a fourth appearance, at an unstated time, by the lake of Galilee, in which Jesus reenacted the initial call of the disciples by providing them miraculously with an enormous catch of fish. Luke adds in the book of Acts that the appearances of the risen Jesus went on over a period of 40 days in which He continued to instruct them about the kingdom of God. Whatever the precise order of the facts, the disciples' experience of the living Jesus transformed them from a scattered and cowardly band of disillusioned visionaries into the nucleus of a coherent movement able to challenge and change forever the Roman Empire within a few short decades.

Though the physical resurrection of Jesus cannot be proven, alternate "naturalistic" explanations of the disciples' experience and of the empty tomb require without exception more credulity than the traditional confession of the Christian church that on the third day He rose

from the dead. The unanimous witness of the Gospels is that the story goes on. Mark does it with the promise that Jesus will bring together His scattered flock and lead them into Galilee (Mark 16:7). Matthew does it more explicitly with Jesus' concluding words, "And remember, I am with you always, to the end of the age" (Matt. 28:20 HCSB). Luke does it with the entire book of Acts, which traces the spread of the message of the kingdom of God and the risen Jesus from Jerusalem all the way to Rome. John does it with his vivid picture of the Holy Spirit being given to the disciples directly from the mouth of Jesus Himself (John 20:21-22). Each Gospel makes the point differently, but the point is always the same. The story of Jesus is not over; He continues to fulfill His mission wherever His name is confessed and His teaching is obeyed, and the faith of Christians is that He will do so until He comes again.   *J. Ramsey Michaels*

JETHER (Jē´ thēr) Personal name meaning "remnant." **1.** Son of the judge Gideon who refused his father's command to kill enemy military leaders (Judg. 8:20). **2.** Father of Amasa, army leader under Judah (1 Kings 2:5,32), and descended from Ishmael (1 Chron. 2:17; cp. 2 Sam. 17:25). See *Ithra*. **3.** Member of clan of Jerahmeel in tribe of Judah (1 Chron. 2:32). **4.** Member of tribe of Judah (1 Chron. 4:17). **5.** Member of tribe of Asher (1 Chron. 7:38, called Ithran in 7:37). See *Ithran*.

JETHETH (Jē´ thĕth) Clan name in Edom of unknown meaning (Gen. 36:40).

JETHLAH (Jĕth´ lah) Place-name meaning "he or it hangs." Border town of tribe of Dan (Josh. 19:42). See *Ithlah*.

JETHRO (Jĕth´ rō) Personal name meaning "excess" or "superiority." In Exod. 3:1 a priest of Midian and the father-in-law of Moses. Some variation exists regarding the name of Moses' father-in-law. In Exod. 2:18 his name is Reuel; in Num. 10:29 it is Hobab. The nature of the relationship of these names to one another is uncertain. Of particular interest is that Jethro was a Midianite priest. The deity whom he served is not explicitly identified; in Exod. 18:11, however, he declared Yahweh to be greater than all gods. One school of thought has discovered the origin of Israel's Yahwism in the ancient

J

Midianite religion represented by Jethro. Such an origin is unlikely. Yahwistic faith probably is traceable at least as far back as Abraham. See *Moses; YHWH.*

JETUR (Jē´ tŭr) Personal name, perhaps meaning "he set in courses or layers." A son of Ishmael and thus original ancestor of Arabian tribe or clan (Gen. 25:15). The clan was a part of the Hagerites, probably descendants of Hagar (1 Chron. 5:19), who fought the East Jordan tribes. Israel's victory illustrated the conviction that trust in God brought victory in war. See *Hagarite; Ituraea.*

JEUEL (Jū´ ĕl) Personal name meaning "God is strong" or "God heals." See *Jeiel.*

JEUSH (Jē´ ŭsh) Personal name meaning "He helps." Hebrew is sometimes transliterated into English in different ways. **1.** Son of Esau and thus head of tribe in Edom (Gen. 36:5,18). **2.** Member of tribe of Benjamin (1 Chron. 7:10; cp. 8:39). **3.** Levite under David (1 Chron. 23:10-11). **4.** Son of King Rehoboam and grandson of Solomon (2 Chron. 11:19).

JEUZ (Jē´ ŭz) Personal name meaning "He brought to safety." Member of tribe of Benjamin (1 Chron. 8:10).

JEWELS, JEWELRY Jewels are stones valued for their beauty or scarcity. Most often they are cut and polished to enhance their appearance. Jewels have been more rare in archaeological finds in Palestine than in Egyptian, Greek, or Phoenician archaeological remains. There are two reasons for this. First, the land of Israel had no natural deposits of precious stones. Jewels (sometimes in the form of jewelry) were taken as booty during war (Num. 31:50), brought as gifts to the king (2 Chron. 9:1,9), or purchased from merchants (1 Kings 10:11; cp. Rev. 18:11-12). Secondly, Israel and Judah were pawns in power struggles between its neighbors. The wealth accumulated by the king and temple was carried off by conquerors (1 Kings 14:25-28). Jewels functioned as a medium of exchange in the ancient Near East before the invention of money. In Israel jewels were used primarily in relation to worship and the monarchy.

Worship First, jewels were a fitting contribution for a special offering (Exod. 35:22). Second, the

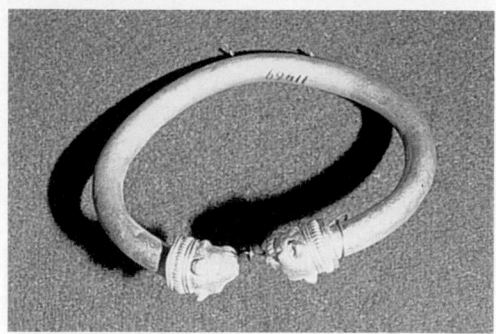

An example of Phrygian jewelry—an armlet with facing lioness heads (1200–650 B.C.).

high priest was garbed in fine clothing decorated with jewels (Exod. 28; 39). The ephod worn by the high priest had an onyx stone set in gold filigree and engraved with the names of the tribes of Israel on each shoulder. The breastpiece of the high priest (also called the "breastpiece of judgment," Exod. 28:15,29) was made of the finest cloth interwoven with gold, into which were set 12 precious stones in four rows of three each. On each stone was engraved the name of one of the 12 tribes. Thus the 12 tribes were symbolically present whenever the high priest ministered before the Lord. The Hebrew words for some of these jewels can be translated with some degree of assurance; in other cases translators must guess what stone is intended. Since the ancients had no way to cut diamonds, they were not yet precious stones. The word translated "diamond" in Exod. 28:18; 39:11 probably does refer to a very hard stone since it is based on a root word meaning "hammer, smite." Thus it is probably not what we call a diamond (NIV, "emerald"; REB, "jade"; NRSV, "moonstone"). The high priest would have looked quite elegant when presiding in worship.

The Monarchy Jewels were considered a fitting gift for kings. The Queen of Sheba brought them to Solomon (1 Kings 10:2,10). Jewels were used in royal crowns (2 Sam. 12:30) and probably royal garments (Ezek. 28:13). Jewels were a form of wealth that could be accumulated and easily kept in the royal treasury. The writer of Ecclesiastes considered such accumulation of royal wealth a matter of great vanity (Eccles. 2:4-11).

Unlike precious jewels, jewelry was widely used by ordinary people in the ancient Near East. Archaeologists have demonstrated that men and women have adorned themselves with various kinds of jewelry almost from the earliest known times. Jewelry was known in the patriarchal period. Abraham's servant, when sent to find a bride for Isaac, put a nose ring and bracelets on Rebekah (Gen. 24:47) and gave her other gold and silver jewelry. The Israelites are said to have "despoiled" the Egyptians by begging gold and silver jewelry of their neighbors in preparation for the exodus from Egypt (Exod. 3:22; 11:2-3). More Egyptian jewelry undoubtedly came into Israel through trade as well as with the daughter of Pharaoh who married Solomon (1 Kings 3:1). At least 15 precious stones were mined in ancient Egypt. Egyptian metalworkers were especially skilled in the art of making gold jewelry. The opulence of royal Egyptian jewelry has been demonstrated from archaeological finds, especially the tomb of Tutankhamen.

During the period of the monarchy, an ordinary man or woman might have had a few pieces of jewelry, something made of bronze or, if they could afford it, gold. Gold, which was used as a medium of exchange, was relatively plentiful and could be made into a necklace, bracelet, or ring by a local craftsman. Royalty, of course, could wear more expensive jewelry set with precious stones.

Many kinds of jewelry are mentioned in the OT. Not only women wore bracelets (Gen. 24:47); King Saul was wearing one when he died in battle (2 Sam. 1:10). Ankle bracelets might be worn (Isa. 3:16,18). Such bracelets have been found on the leg bones of women buried in ancient Israel. See *Anklet.*

Necklaces and pendants were popular (Song 1:10). A certain kind of gold necklace probably functioned as a symbol of authority. When Pharaoh appointed Joseph to high office, he put a gold chain around his neck (Gen. 41:42). Likewise, in the book of Daniel, King Belshazzar proclaimed that whoever could interpret the mysterious writing on the wall should have a gold chain put around his neck and be made "the third ruler in the kingdom" (Dan. 5:7,29). The crescents mentioned in Isa. 3:18, like those of Judg. 8:21,26, which were worn by the kings of Midian, were probably moon-shaped pendants worn on chains. Gold crescent jewelry has been discovered by archaeologists. The crescent may have functioned as a royal insignia. The items referred to as chains, collars, or pendants (Isa.

Gold Roman jewelry from the first century A.D.

3:19 NRSV; Judg. 8:26) were probably also worn around the neck, perhaps on cords.

Earrings were known in the patriarchal period. They may have had some religious significance (Gen. 35:4). Nose rings are mentioned in Gen. 24:22,30,47 (NIV) and Isa. 3:21 (NIV). The same term, *nezem,* is used for both, so the references are often ambiguous (Num. 31:50; Prov. 25:12).

Good-luck charms called "amulets" are not mentioned often in the Bible but have been widely found throughout Palestine in archaeological sites from all periods. Some represented gods and goddesses. Isaiah 3:20 may include a reference to amulets (see NRSV, NASB), though the translation is not sure. The earrings buried by Jacob under the oak near Shechem may have been amulets (Gen. 35:4). Such amulets were violations of the commandment not to make graven images (Exod. 20:4).

The most important item of jewelry mentioned in the OT is the signet ring. The signet was used to make an impression on clay or wax

Gold ring inlaid with precious stone from the first century A.D.

J

and thus to seal and authenticate documents. Generally the signet was a finely engraved semiprecious stone. A hole could be bored through the signet and it could be hung from a cord around the neck (Gen. 38:18), or it could be used as a setting for a ring or more elaborate necklace. Pharaoh gave Joseph his signet ring as a symbol of authority (Gen. 41:42). King Ahasuerus gave his signet ring first to Haman (Esther 3:10) and then to Mordecai (Esther 8:2).

Jewelry was also used to decorate animals, at least by the wealthy. The camels of the Midianite kings slain by Gideon wore crescents and decorated collars around their necks (Judg. 8:21,26). The reference in Prov. 11:22 to a ring in a swine's snout is metaphoric; one cannot draw conclusions from it concerning the use of decorative nose rings for animals. Amulets were sometimes worn by animals to ensure good fortune on a trip.

Isaiah 3:18-23 is sometimes interpreted as an attack on women's fashions and a denunciation of the uses of jewelry. The Hebrew terms used in the passage appear to refer rather to official insignia. Thus the passage is a condemnation of

Golden Phrygian necklace dating from 1200–650 B.C. from Gordium.

the misuse of wealth and power at the expense of the poor. In Ezek. 16:8-13 the Lord is portrayed as a bridegroom adorning his bride, Jerusalem, with fine clothing and jewelry including a nose ring, earrings, and a crown.

The NT does not often mention jewels and jewelry. Pearls were highly valued in NT time and thus a fitting metaphor for the kingdom of God (Matt. 13:45-46). James warned his readers not to discriminate on the basis of wealth as indicated by the wearing of gold rings and fine clothing (James 2:1-7). In 1 Tim. 2:9-10 women are reminded that the best adornment is not braids, gold, or pearls but good deeds.

In Rev. 21:2, which echoes the imagery of Ezek. 16:8-13, God is pictured as a bridegroom whose bride, the new Jerusalem, is adorned with jewels. The walls of the new Jerusalem are pictured as built of jasper, adorned with 12 kinds of jewels. Each of the 12 gates is made of a single pearl. The gems of the holy city, like those in so much jewelry, are to be put in a setting of gold. The idea of rebuilding Jerusalem with jewels as building material reflects Isa. 54:11-12. Unlike the old Jerusalem, the new Jerusalem—associated with the completion of the kingdom of God—will not be unfaithful. See *Minerals and Metals.*   *Wilda W. Morris*

JEWESS (Jū´ ĕs) Female Jew (KJV, NASB, NIV, RSV). Timothy's mother was Jewish, but his father was not (Acts 16:1). Drusilla, the wife of Felix the Roman governor, was a Jewess (Acts 24:24).

JEWISH PARTIES IN THE NEW TESTAMENT Judaism in NT times was diverse. We read of Pharisees, Sadducees, and Herodians. One man is called a Zealot. From other sources we learn of Essenes and the Sicarii.

Pharisees The Pharisees constituted the largest and most important group, Josephus stating that they numbered about 6,000. They appear in the Gospels as opponents of Jesus. Paul was a Pharisee (Phil. 3:5). They controlled the synagogues and exercised great control over much of the population.

No surviving writing gives us information about the origin of the Pharisees. The earliest reference to them is in the time of Jonathan (160–143 B.C.) when Josephus refers to Pharisees, Sadducees, and Essenes. Their good relations with the rulers ended in the time of John

Hyrcanus (134–104 B.C.). They came to power again when Salome Alexandra became Queen (76 B.C.).

The term "Pharisee" means "separated ones." Perhaps it means that they separated themselves from the masses or that they separated themselves to the study and interpretation of the law. A common assumption is that they developed from the Hasidim, the ultra-orthodox loyal freedom fighters in the time of Judas Maccabeus. They apparently were responsible for the transformation of Judaism from a religion of sacrifice to one of law. They were the developers of the oral tradition, the teachers of the two-fold law: written and oral. They saw the way to God as being through obedience to the law. They were the progressives of the day, willing to adopt new ideas and adapt the law to new situations.

The Pharisees were strongly monotheistic. They accepted all the OT as authoritative. They affirmed the reality of angels and demons. They had a firm belief in life beyond the grave and a resurrection of the body. They were missionary, seeking the conversion of Gentiles (Matt. 23:15). They saw God as concerned with the life of a person without denying that the individual was responsible for how he or she lived. They had little interest in politics. The Pharisees opposed Jesus because He refused to accept their interpretations of the oral law.

Sadducees The Sadducees were aristocrats. They were the party of the wealthy and of the high priestly families. They were in charge of the temple, its services, and concessions. They claimed to be descendants of Zadok, high priest of Solomon. True derivation of the term is unknown. In all our literature they stand in opposition to the Pharisees. They were social conservatives, seeking to preserve the practices of the past. They opposed the oral law, accepting the Pentateuch as the ultimate authority. The Sadducees were materialistic in their outlook. They did not believe in life after death or rewards or punishment beyond this life. They denied the existence of angels and demons. They did not believe that God was concerned with what people did. Rather, people were totally free. They were politically oriented, supporters of ruling powers, whether Seleucids or Romans. They tolerated no threats to their position and wealth, so they strongly opposed Jesus.

Herodians The Herodians are mentioned only three times in the NT (Matt. 22:16; Mark 3:6; 12:13). In Mark they joined the Pharisees in a plot to kill Jesus. The other references are to Pharisees and Herodians together asking Jesus about paying taxes to Caesar. They were Jews who supported Herod Antipas or sought to have a descendant of Herod the Great given authority over Palestine. At this time Judea and Samaria were under Roman governors.

Zealots The Zealots are mentioned rarely in the NT. Simon, one of the disciples, is called Zealot (Luke 6:15). John 18:40 uses a word for Barabbas that Josephus used for Zealot. Josephus said the Zealots began with Judas the Galilean seeking to lead a revolt over a taxation census (A.D. 6). He did not use the name Zealot until referring to events in A.D. 66, the first Jewish revolt against Rome. The Zealots were the extreme wing of the Pharisees. In contrast with other Pharisees they believed only God had the right to rule over the Jews. They were willing to fight and die for that belief. For them nationalistic patriotism and religion were inseparable.

Sicarii Literally meaning "dagger men," the Sicarii were the most extreme revolutionaries among the Jews of the first century. Committed to the overthrow of Roman power over Palestine, they used small concealed daggers to assassinate their enemies, principally Roman officials. They were willing to die in killing their targets and did whatever they could to disrupt Roman political and military policy.

Essenes We know of the Essenes through the writings of Josephus and Philo, a Jewish philosopher in Alexandria, Egypt. They are not mentioned in the NT. More information about the Essenes is known since the 1947 discovery of manuscripts from caves above the Dead Sea called the Dead Sea Scrolls. The common assumption is that the people of the Scrolls were either Essenes or associated with them. They may have begun at about the same time as the Pharisees and Sadducees. The Essenes were an ascetic group, many of whom lived in the desert region of Qumran near the Dead Sea. We now know that an active Essene community was located in Jerusalem as well. They took vows of celibacy and perpetuated their community by adopting male children. However, some Essenes did marry. When one joined the Essenes, he gave all his possessions to the community. A three-

J

PHARISEES

Dates of Existence	Name	Origin	Segments of Society	Beliefs	Selected Biblical References	Activities
Existed under Jonathan (160–143 B.C.) Declined in power under John Hyrcanus (134–104 B.C.) Began resurgence under Salome Alexandra (76 B.C.)	Pharisees = "the Separated Ones" with three possible meanings: (1) to their separating themselves from people (2) to their separating themselves to the study of the law ("dividing" or "separating" the truth) (3) to their separating themselves from pagan practices	Probably spiritual descendants of the Hasidim (religious freedom fighters of the time of Judas Maccabeus)	Most numerous of the Jewish parties (or sects) Probably descendants of the Hasidim—scribes and lawyers Members of the middle class—mostly businessmen (merchants and tradesmen)	Monotheistic Viewed entirety of the Old Testament (Torah, Prophets, and Writings) as authoritative Believed that the study of the law was true worship Accepted both the written and oral law More liberal in interpreting the law than were the Sadducees Quite concerned with the proper keeping of the Sabbath, tithing, and purification rituals Believed in life after death and the resurrection of the body (with divine retribution and reward) Revered humanity and human equality Missionary-minded regarding the conversion of Gentiles. Believed that individuals were responsible for how they lived	Matthew 3:7-10; 5:20; 9:14; 16:1,6-12; 22:15-22,34-46; 23:2-36 Mark 3:6, 7:3-5, 8:15; 12:13-17 Luke 6:7; 7:36-39; 11:37-44; 18:9-14 John 3:1; 9:13-16; 11:46-47; 12:19 Acts 23:6-10 Philippians 3:4b-6	Developers of oral tradition Taught that the way to God was through obedience to the law Changed Judaism from a religion of sacrifice to a religion of law Progressive thinkers regarding the adaptation of the law to a new situations Opposed Jesus because He would not accept the teachings of the oral law as binding Established and controlled synagogues Exercised great control over general population Served as religious authorities for most Jews Took several ceremonies from the Temple to the home Emphasized ethical as opposed to theological action Legalistic and socially exclusive shunned non-Pharisee as unclean Tended to have a self-sufficient and haughty attitude

SADDUCEES

Dates of Existence	Name	Origin	Segments of Society	Beliefs	Selected Biblical References	Activities
Probably began about 200 B.C. Demise occurred in A.D. 70 (with the destruction of the Temple)	Sadducees = Three possible translations: (1) "the Righteous Ones"—based on the Hebrew consonants for the word *righteous* (2) "ones who sympathize with Zadok," or "Zadokites"—based on their possible link to Zadok the high priest (3) "syndics," "judges," or "fiscal controllers"—based on the Greek word *syndikoi*	Unknown origin Claimed to be descendants of Zadok—high priest under David (see 2 Samuel 8:17; 15:24) and Solomon (see 1 Kings 1:34–35; 1 Chronicles 12:28) Had a possible link to Aaron Were probably formed into a group about 200 B.C. as the high priest's party	Aristocracy—the rich descendants of the high-priestly line (However, not all priests were Sadducees) Possibly descendants of the Hasmonean priesthood Probably not as refined as their economic position in life would suggest	Accepted only the Torah (Genesis through Deuteronomy—the written law of Moses) as authoritative Practiced literal interpretation of the law Rigidly conservative towards the law Stressed strict observance of the law Observed past beliefs and tradition Opposed oral law as obligatory or binding Believed in the absolute freedom of human will—that people could do as they wished without attention to the God Denied divine providence Denied the concept of life after death and the resurrection of the body Denied the concept of reward and punishment after death Denied the existence of angels and demons Materialistic	2 Samuel 8:17; 15:24 1 Kings 1:34 1 Chronicles 12:26-28 Ezekiel 40:45-46; 43:19; 44:15-16 Matthew 3:7-10; 16:1,6-12; 22:23-34 Mark 12:18-27 Luke 20:27-40 John 11:47 Acts 4:1-2; 5:17-18; 23:6-10	In charge of the Temple and its services Politically active Exercised great political control through the Sanhedrin of which many were members Supported the ruling power and the status quo Leaned toward Hellenism (the spreading of Greek influence)—and were thus despised by the Jewish populace Opposed both the Pharisees and Jesus because these lived by a larger canon considered more than only Genesis through Deuteronomy as authoritative.) Opposed Jesus specifically for fear their wealth/position would be threatened if they supported him.

ZEALOTS	Three possibilities for their beginning: (1) during the reign of Herod the Great (about 37 B.C.) (2) during the revolt against Rome (A.D. 6) (3) traced back to the Hassidim or the Maccabees (about 168 B.C.) Their certain demise occurred around A.D. 70–73 with Rome's conquering of Jerusalem.	Refers to their religious zeal Josephus used the term in referring to those involved in the Jewish revolt against Rome in A.D. 6—led by Judas of Galilee	(According to Josephus) The Zealots began with Judas (the Galilean), son of Ezekias, who led a revolt in A.D. 6 because of a census done for tax purposes.	The extreme wing of the Pharisees	Similar to the Pharisees with this exception: believed strongly that only God had the right to rule of the Jews, Patriotism and religion became inseparable. Believed that total obedience (supported by drastic physical measures) must be apparent before God would bring in the Messianic Age Were fanatical in their Jewish faith and in their devotion to the law—to the point of martyrdom	Matthew 10:4 Mark 3:18 Luke 6:15 Acts 1:13	Extremely opposed to Roman rule over Palestine Extremely opposed to peace with Rome Refused to pay taxes Demonstrated against the use of the Greek language in Palestine Engaged in terrorism against Rome and others with whom they disagreed politically [Sicarii (or Assassins) were an extremist Zealot group who carried out acts of terrorism against Rome.]
HERODIANS	Existed during the time of the Herodian dynasty (which began with Herod the Great in 37 B.C.)	Based on their support of the Herodian rulers (Herod the Great or his dynasty)	Exact origin uncertain	Wealthy, politically influential Jews who supported Herod Antipas (or any descendant of Herod the Great) as ruler over Palestine (Judea and Samaria were under Roman governors at this time)	Not a religious group—but a political one Membership was probably comprised of representatives of varied theological perspectives	Matthew 22:5-22 Mark 3:6; 8:15; 12:13-17	Supported Herod and the Herodian dynasty Accepted Hellenization Accepted foreign rule
ESSENES	Probably began during Maccabean times (about 168 B.C.)—around the same time as the Pharisees and the Sadducees began to form Uncertain demise—probably in A.D. 68–70 with the collapse of Jerusalem	Unknown origin	Possibly developed as a reaction to the corrupt Sadducean priesthood Have been identified with various groups: Hassidim, Zealots, Greek influence, or Iranian influence	Scattered throughout the villages of Judea (possibly including the community of Qumran) (According to Philo and Josephus) About 4,000 in Palestinian Syria	Very strict ascetics Monastic: most took vow of celibacy (adopting male children in order to perpetuate the group), but some did marry (for the purpose of procreation) Rigidly adherent to the law (including a strict rendering of the ethical teachings) Considered other literature as authoritative (in addition to the Hebrew Scripture) Believed and lived as pacifists Rejected Temple worship and temple offerings as corrupted Believed in the immortality of the soul with no bodily resurrection Apocalyptically oriented	None	Devoted to the copying and studying of the law Lived in a community sense with communal property Required a long probationary period and ritual baptisms of those wishing to join Were highly virtuous and righteous Were extremely self-disciplined Were diligent manual laborers Gave great importance to daily worship Upheld rigid Sabbath laws Maintained a non-Levitical priesthood Rejected worldly pleasures as evil Rejected matrimony—but did not forbid others to marry

year period of probation was required before full membership was granted. The Essenes devoted themselves to the study of the law. They went beyond the Pharisees in their rigid understanding of it. There is no hard evidence that either Jesus or John the Baptist had any relation to Qumran. Jesus would have strongly opposed their understanding of the law.

The vast majority of the people were not members of any of these parties, although they probably were most influenced by the Pharisees. See *Dead Sea Scrolls; Intertestamental History and Literature; Synagogue; Temple.*

Clayton Harrop and Charles W. Draper

JEWS IN THE NEW TESTAMENT The word "Jew" is derived ultimately from the tribe of Judah through Middle English *Iewe*, Old French *Ieu*, Latin *Iudaeus*, and Greek *Ioudaios* (cp. the woman's name Judith that originally meant "Jewess").

Old Testament Background Originally the Hebrew *yehudim* meant descendants of the tribe of Judah and then those who inhabited the territories claimed by them (2 Kings 16:6; 25:25; Jer. 32:12). With the deportation and subsequent assimilation of the "Ten Lost Tribes" of the Northern Kingdom by the Assyrians after 722 B.C., the only Israelites to survive into the exilic period (with a few from the tribe of Benjamin, such as Mordecai, who is called a "Jew" in Esther 2:5) were those from Judah, hence the name Jews (Neh. 1:2). The corresponding Aramaic word is used in Dan. 3:8,12.

The Intertestamental Period The Greek name *Ioudaios* (plural *Ioudaioi*) was used for the Israelites in the Greek and Roman world. This is the name used in the treaty between Judas Maccabeus and the Romans, described in 1 Macc. 8:23-32: "May all go well with the Romans and with the nation of the Jews" (v. 23).

Matthew, Mark, Luke The term *Ioudaios* occurs relatively rarely in the Synoptic Gospels, the first three Gospels which are closely parallel to each other. The word occurs only five times in Matthew, seven times in Mark, and five times in Luke, usually in the expression "King of the Jews" (12 of the total of 17). Of the remaining occurrences only Matt. 28:15 designates Jews as contrasted to Christian believers.

John By contrast, the word *Ioudaios* occurs 70 times in the Gospel of John. Some of these refer-

ences are quite positive, especially in the dialogue between Jesus and the woman of Samaria (chap. 4). In verse 9 the woman says to Jesus, "You, a Jew" (HCSB), and in verse 22 Jesus says, "Salvation is from the Jews." Many of the Jews believed in Jesus (8:31; 11:45; 12:11). Other references are neutral as in John 3:1 where Nicodemus is described as a ruler of the Jews.

The description of Jesus' opponents reveals a striking difference between the Synoptic Gospels and John. Whereas the former names Jesus' enemies as scribes and Pharisees, high priests, and Sadducees, the Gospel of John simply uses the general term "Jews." The term often implies Jewish authorities as in 7:13; 9:22; 19:38; 20:19.

The Jews impugned Jesus' birth and His sanity (8:48) and even alleged that He was demon possessed (8:52). The Jews questioned His statements about the temple (2:20) and were scandalized at His claim to be the bread from heaven (6:41). They regarded His affirmations of equality with the Father as blasphemous and picked up stones to kill Him (5:18; 7:1; 10:31,33; 11:8).

The heightened use of the term "Jews" in John to serve as a general designation for those who denied that Jesus was the Christ may be explained by the fact that John's Gospel was composed at a later date than the Synoptics—after such events as the destruction of Jerusalem in A.D. 70 and the insertion of a curse upon the minim ("heretics," especially Christians) into the daily synagogue prayer in A.D. 80 had increased mutual hostilities between Jews and Christians.

Acts Paul was a Jew from Tarsus (Acts 21:39; 22:3). After his dramatic conversion on the road to Damascus, his fellow Jews sought to kill him

From OT times faithful Jews have worn phylacteries on both forehead and arm as they pray.

(9:23). King Herod Agrippa I arrested Peter and killed the Apostle James, believing this would please the Jews (12:1-3).

Following his conviction that the gospel should be preached first to the Jews (Rom. 1:16), Paul on his missionary journeys began his preaching in the Jewish synagogues—at Salamis on Cyprus (Acts 13:5), at Iconium (14:1), at Thessalonica (17:1), at Athens (17:15-17), and at Corinth (18:1). Though he made some converts among the Jews, even converting the synagogue ruler at Corinth (18:8), and no doubt had success among the "God fearers" or proselytes who were interested in converting to Judaism (13:43; 17:4), the majority of the Jews reacted violently against Paul's message (13:50; 14:2; 17:5; 18:12). Paul therefore turned his efforts increasingly toward the Gentiles, the non-Jews.

Pauline Letters As the "apostle to the Gentiles," Paul argued against "Judaizers" that Gentile converts did not have to be circumcised, that is, become Jews first before they became Christians (Acts 15:1-5). His arguments were accepted by James and the church council at Jerusalem held about A.D. 49. Paul, who had been "a Hebrew born of Hebrews; as to the law, a Pharisee" (Phil. 3:5 HCSB) and had been more zealous in his pursuit of Judaism than his peers (Gal. 1:13-14), came to the radical conclusion that a true Jew is not one who was physically descended from Abraham (cp. John 8:31-41), adhered to the Torah or law of Moses (Rom. 2:17,28), and was circumcised. For Paul a true Jew is one who believes that Jesus is the Messiah or Christ (Gal. 3:26-29), relies on God's grace and not works of the law (Eph. 2:8-9), and has been circumcised in his heart by the Holy Spirit (Gal. 2:2-9; 5:6). In spite of his grief that most of his fellow Jews did not accept his message, Paul did not teach that God had abandoned the Jews but believed that God still has a plan for them (Rom. 9–11). (Note: the word *Ioudaios* is not found in any of the non-Pauline letters of the NT.)

Revelation The two references in the book of Revelation are to the church at Smyrna (2:9) and the church at Philadelphia (3:9), where there were those who claimed to be Jews but who were denounced as the "synagogue of Satan" because they opposed Christians. See *Hebrews; Israel, Land of; Pharisees; Sadducees.*

Edwin Yamauchi

JEZANIAH (Jĕ zà nī´ ah) Personal name meaning "Yahweh gave ear." Army captain loyal to Gedaliah, the governor that Babylon appointed over Judah immediately after Babylon destroyed Jerusalem and took the Jewish leaders into exile about 586 B.C. (Jer. 40:8). Jezaniah was one of the captains who refused to believe Jeremiah's prophecy calling the people to remain in Judah. Rather, he helped carry Jeremiah into Egypt (Jer. 42–43). In 43:2 the name is Azariah, which may be the correct reading in 42:1 rather than Jezaniah. See *Azariah.*

JEZEBEL (Jĕz´ ə bĕl) Personal name meaning "Where is the prince?" perhaps derived from Phoenician name meaning "Baal is the prince." Wife of King Ahab of Israel (874–853 B.C.), who brought the worship of Baal from Sidon where her father Ethbaal was king (1 Kings 16:31). Jezebel tried to destroy all God's prophets in Israel (1 Kings 18:4) while installing prophets of Baal and Asherah (1 Kings 18:19, modern translations) as part of the royal household. Elijah proved these prophets to be false on Mount Carmel (1 Kings 18), bringing Jezebel's threat to kill Elijah (1 Kings 19:2). Elijah ran for his life to Beer-sheba.

When Ahab wanted Naboth's vineyard, Jezebel connived with the leaders of the city who falsely accused and convicted Naboth, stoning him to death. Elijah then prophesied Jezebel's death, she being the one who had "stirred up" Ahab to wickedness (1 Kings 21). She continued her evil influence as her son Joram ruled (2 Kings 9:22). Elisha anointed Jehu to replace Joram. Jehu assassinated Joram and then went to Jezreel after Jezebel. She tried to adorn herself and entice him, but her servants obeyed Jehu's call to throw her from the window to the street where horses trod her in the ground (2 Kings 9:30-37).

Jezebel's name became so associated with wickedness that the false prophetess in the church at Thyatira was labeled "Jezebel" (Rev. 2:20).

JEZER (Jē´ zĕr) Personal name meaning "He formed." Son of Naphtali (Gen. 46:24) and founding ancestor of clan in that tribe (Num. 26:49). The name "Izri" (1 Chron. 25:11) means member of clan of Jezer, and Zeri (1 Chron. 25:3) is probably an abbreviated form of Izri.

J

JEZERITE (Jē´ zĕr īt) Member of clan of Jezer. See *Jezer*.

JEZIAH (Jĕ zī´ ah) Personal name meaning "Yah sprinkled." Israelite with foreign wife condemned by Ezra (Ezra 10:25). Modern translations transliterate the Hebrew as Izziah.

JEZIEL (Jē´ zĭ ĕl) Personal name meaning "God sprinkled." Military leader from tribe of Benjamin, Saul's tribe, who joined David at Ziklag as he fled from Saul (1 Chron. 12:3). The written Hebrew text has the name Jezuel, while the early Hebrew scribes noted the reading Jeziel.

JEZLIAH (Jĕz lī´ ah) Personal name meaning "long-lived." Member of tribe of Benjamin (1 Chron. 8:18). Modern translations transliterate the name Izliah.

JEZOAR (Jə zō´ är) Personal name, perhaps meaning "he was light-colored." Member of tribe of Judah (1 Chron. 4:7). The name in the Hebrew text is Jizhar or Izhar as read by modern translations. Early Hebrew scribes read it as "and Zohar" (NIV).

JEZRAHIAH (Jĕz rå hī´ ah) Personal name meaning "Yah shines forth." **1.** Leader in tribe of Issachar (1 Chron. 7:3; English transliteration is usually Izrahiah). **2.** Leader of Levite singers at Nehemiah's celebration of finishing the rebuilding of Jerusalem's wall (Neh. 12:42). REB transliterates Izrahiah.

JEZREEL (Jĕz´ rēl) Name, meaning "God sows," refers to a major valley, a northern city, a southern city, and the son of Hosea. **1.** Old Testament uses the name to refer to the entire Valley of Jezreel that separates Galilee from Samaria, including the valley of Esdraelon. The valley was important militarily as a battle site for Deborah (Judg. 4–5), Gideon (Judg. 6–7), Saul (2 Sam. 4), Jehu (2 Kings 9–10), and Josiah (2 Kings 22). The geography of Palestine made Jezreel a major route for travel from north to south and from east to west. See *Esdraelon*. **2.** Northern city of Jezreel, which guarded the corridor to Bethshan, was the site of the royal residence of Omri and Ahab where the incident of Naboth's vineyard occurred (1 Kings 21). **3.** David's wife Ahinoam was from the southern city of Jezreel that is located in the vicinity of Ziph (1 Sam. 25:43). **4.** Prophet Hosea named his son Jezreel as a

The Valley of Jezreel (Esdraelon or Megiddo) as viewed from the top of the Megiddo tel.

J

symbol to indicate the evil nature of the dynasty of Jehu, which began with much bloodshed in Jezreel. The name also symbolized that God will sow seeds of prosperity after the destruction (Hos. 1:4-5; 1:10–2:1).

Robert Anderson Street, Jr.

JEZREELITE (Jĕz´ rēl īt) A citizen of or from the hometown of Jezreel. See *Jezreel.*

JIBSAM (Jĭb´ săm) Personal name meaning "he smells sweet." Early leader in tribe of Issachar (1 Chron. 7:2). Modern translations often read Ibsam.

JIDLAPH (Jĭd´ lăph) Personal name meaning "he cries or is sleepless." Son of Nahor, Abraham's brother (Gen. 22:22).

JIMNA (Jĭm´ nȧ) or **JIMNAH** Proper name meaning "he allotted." **1.** Son of Asher, grandson of Jacob, and original ancestor of clan in tribe of Asher (Gen. 46:17; Num. 26:44). KJV spells the name "Imnah" in 1 Chron. 7:30, as do modern translations in all occurrences. **2.** Levite under Hezekiah (2 Chron. 31:14, spelled "Imnah" by English translations).

JIMNITE (Jĭm´ nīt) Member of clan of Jimnah. See *Jimna or Jimnah.*

JIPHTAH (Jĭph´ tah) Place-name meaning "he opened or broke up." City in tribal territory of Judah (Josh. 15:43). It may have been located at modern Terqumiyeh, halfway between Hebron and Beit Jibrin. Most modern translations transliterate as "Iphtah." The personal name Jephthah has the same Hebrew spelling. See *Jephthah.*

JIPHTHAH-EL (Jĭph´ thȧ-ĕl) Place-name meaning "God opened." A valley marking the border of the tribal territories of Asher and Zebulun (Josh. 19:14,27). The modern name is Wadi el-Melek. Modern translations transliterate Iphtah-el.

JOAB (Jō´ ăb) Personal name meaning "Yahweh is father." Military commander during most of David's reign. He was the oldest son of Zeruiah, the sister of David (2 Sam. 2:13; 1 Chron. 2:16). He was loyal to David and ruthless in achieving his objectives. After Saul's death David was negotiating with Abner, Saul's military commander.

Joab, whose brother had been slain in battle by Abner, deceived Abner and murdered him. David publicly lamented this assassination (2 Sam. 2–3).

Joab's exploits in the capture of Jerusalem led David to name him commander (1 Chron. 11:4-8). Joab successfully led David's armies against the Ammonites (2 Sam. 10). During this campaign David sent his infamous order to have Uriah, the husband of Bathsheba, killed (2 Sam. 11).

Joab was instrumental in the reconciliation of David and Absalom (2 Sam. 14). When Absalom led a rebellion, Joab remained loyal to David. Joab killed Absalom against the clear orders of David (2 Sam. 18:14). He also convinced David to end his obsessive grieving for Absalom (2 Sam. 19:4-8). Joab murdered Amasa, whom David had named commander (2 Sam. 20:10). He opposed David's plan for a census but carried it out when ordered to do so (2 Sam. 24:1-9).

When David was dying, Joab supported Adonijah's claim to the throne (1 Kings 1). David named Solomon king and told him to avenge Abner and Amasa by killing Joab. Although Joab fled to the tabernacle for sanctuary, Solomon ordered Benaiah to kill Joab (1 Kings 2).

Robert J. Dean

JOAH (Jō´ ăh) Personal name meaning "Jah is brother." **1.** Scribe under King Hezekiah about 715–686 B.C. (2 Kings 18:18). He was one of the king's messengers to listen to the Assyrian Rabshakeh and bring the message to the king. They did so in mourning (2 Kings 18:37). **2.** Son of royal scribe under King Josiah (640–609 B.C.). He helped repair the temple (2 Chron. 34:8). **3.** Levite (1 Chron. 6:21). **4.** Member of family of Levites who were porters or gatekeepers (1 Chron. 26:4). **5.** Levite who helped cleanse the temple under King Hezekiah about 715 B.C. (2 Chron. 29:12).

JOAHAZ (Jō´ ȧ hăz) Father of Joah (2 Chron. 34:8). See *Joah 2.*

JOANAN (Jō ā´ nan) Greek transliteration of Hebrew name "Johanan." Ancestor of Jesus (Luke 3:27). KJV reads Joanna. Some interpreters think his father Rhesa does not represent a personal name but is a transliteration of the Aramaic word for prince, a title for Zerubbabel. Joanan would then be the Hananiah of 1 Chron. 3:19. See *Johanan.*

JOANNA (Jō ăn´ nà) Personal name meaning "Yahweh's gift." **1.** In Luke 8:3 one of the women whom Jesus had healed and who ministered to Him out of their own private means. She was the wife of Herod's steward Chuza. Luke's Gospel, that gives particular prominence to women, also mentions her in 24:10. She was one of the women who came to Jesus' tomb on the Sunday following the crucifixion and reported to the eleven the message that He had risen. **2.** In Luke 3:27 (KJV) the son of Rhesa mentioned in the genealogy of Jesus. See *Joanan.*

JOASH (Jō´ ăsh) Personal name meaning "Yahweh gives." **1.** In Judg. 6:11 the father of Gideon. He was a member of the tribe of Manasseh who lived at Ophrah. **2.** In 1 Chron. 4:21-22 one of the sons of Shelah. **3.** In 1 Chron. 7:8 one of the sons of Becher. **4.** In 1 Chron. 12:3 one of David's warriors. He was a son of Shemaah the Gibeathite. **5.** In 1 Chron. 27:28 one of David's officers who was in charge of the stores of oil. **6.** In 1 Kings 22:26 a son of Ahab, the king of Israel, and one of those to whom Micaiah the prophet was handed over. **7.** In 2 Kings 11:2 the infant son of King Ahaziah of Judah who survived the bloodbath carried out by Athaliah, the queen mother, following the murder of Ahaziah. Joash was hidden by Jehosheba his aunt for six years, at the end of which time he was popularly proclaimed as the legitimate ruler of Judah in a move instigated by Jehoiada. Athaliah was executed, and Joash took the throne at the age of seven. During the king's minority, Jehoiada, the priest, exercised a strong positive influence in both the civil and religious life of the nation. The death of Jehoiada, however, marked a notable decline in the quality of the rule of Joash. Finally the king was assassinated as the result of a palace conspiracy. See *Athaliah; Chronology of Biblical Period; Israel, Land of; Jehoiada.* **8.** In 2 Kings 13:10 the son and successor of Jehoahaz as king of Israel. He ruled for 16 years during the early part of the eighth century B.C. His visit to the dying prophet Elisha is described in 2 Kings 13:14-19. During the course of that visit, the prophet promised the king three victories over Syria. Subsequently, Joash enjoyed military success not only against Syria but also against neighboring Judah. He

defeated Amaziah of Judah in battle at Beth-shemesh and actually entered Jerusalem and plundered the temple. At his death his son Jeroboam II succeeded him on the throne. See *Chronology of Biblical Period; Israel, Land of.*
Gene Henderson

JOATHAM (Jō´ à thăm) KJV transliteration of Greek for Jotham (Matt. 1:9). See *Jotham.*

JOB, BOOK OF (Jōb) Job apparently lived in the patriarchal or prepatriarchal days, for not only does he not mention the Law or the exodus, but he is pictured as a wealthy nomad (Job 1:3; 42:12) who is still offering sacrifices himself (Job 1:5; 42:8). Undoubtedly Job was a most respected man, for not only did the Prophet Ezekiel refer to him as one of the greatest of Israel's ancestors (Ezek. 14:14), but even James used him as an excellent example of patient and persistent faith (James 5:11).

The book of Job presents many problems concerning the person, time, and nature of its composition. First, the text does not indicate in any way its author. The text never speaks of Job as its author, just its subject. Thus, many have concluded that Job was written by Elihu, one of the three friends, or simply some anonymous writer of that or some other age. Second, though most will agree that the character Job lived in patriarchal times, many believe that the book was written many years later. The dates of such a composition will vary from the time of Abraham to that of the Greek Empire. Third, to further complicate the issue, many believe that Job is a compilation of several different stories coming from several different ages. As one can readily see, the question of date and authorship is a very complex issue that cannot yet be settled with certainty. However, the fact that one cannot identify the human agent in no way means that the book is not inspired, for it is God's Word and is a unit as it now stands.

Job Is a Perfect Illustration of True Faith Through the years, many purposes have been suggested for the book. Perhaps the one that has been mentioned more often than any other is that of answering the question of why the righteous suffer. Certainly this question was prominent in Job's day, for ancient society believed that human suffering was the result of one's sin or at least a god's displeasure. Even the meaning of the name Job (the persecuted one) seems to support this suggestion, but that may not be all that is involved in the book. Another popular suggestion is that the book has been preserved to illustrate for us the nature of true faith both from the point of view of people and of God. For humans, it is trusting in God as the Creator and Sustainer of life even when all is not going well and when He is not visibly present to help us. From God's point of view the story proves His faithfulness to His creatures despite their weaknesses and inability to understand what is happening. Another, and much less frequently suggested purpose, is that of a parable concerning the nation of Israel. In this case, Job becomes the nation Israel. Though this approach is possible, it seems unlikely since most parables have some type of interpretation close by which helps to explain them. Thus, perhaps it is best just to take the book as an illustration of the nature of God and His justice in dealing with humankind, a justice people often cannot recognize and never fully understand.

Job Is Unique in World Literature Though Job shows many similarities with other ancient Near Eastern texts, none come near to Job's beauty and message. Because the three friends have Edomite backgrounds, some have speculated that Job may have been an Edomite and that the setting for the book may have been Edom. However, there is not enough Edomite material available at this point to make any conclusions. Others have seen similarities between Job and the Egyptian poems concerning "The Protest of the Eloquent Peasant" and "A Dispute Over Suicide" or the Babylonian poems of "The Babylonian Theodicy" and "I Will Praise the Lord of Wisdom." In each of these cases, what similarities exist seem minor, indeed, and deal more with the topic than its content or form. Still others have suggested that Job is written in the form of a courtroom trial. No doubt many legal terms appear in the book, yet we still know too little about ancient legal procedure to make any such conclusions. Thus, it is best to simply take the book as a unique work depicting the life of one man and his efforts to understand his God and his own situation in life.

Job's Encounter with Life Brought Him Face to Face with God The book of Job is most frequently pictured as a drama with a prologue (chaps. 1–2) and an epilogue (42:7-17) enclosing three cycles of poetic speeches between Job and

his three friends (3–27), a beautiful wisdom poem from Job (28), Job's concluding remarks (29–31), the mysterious Elihu speeches (32–37), and God's whirlwind speeches (38:1–41:34), and Job's response (42:1-6).

The prologue describes the setting for the ensuing drama. Job was a very wealthy and religious man who seemed to have life under control (1:1-5). However, unknown to him, Satan challenged his righteousness. God allowed the challenge but limited Satan's power to Job's possessions (1:6-12). In quick succession Satan destroyed all of Job's possessions including even his children. However, Job did not blame God or question His integrity (1:13-22). Satan then challenged God to let him attack Job's personal health. God agreed but warned him not to kill Job (2:1-6). Without warning, a loathsome disease fell upon Job, yet he still refused to blame God (2:7-10). Job's friends were shocked and dismayed but nevertheless came to encourage him and offer their help (2:11-13). To this point Job displayed a traditional faith accepting suffering as inevitable and patiently enduring it.

After the traditional time of mourning had passed, Job cried out wondering why he was ever born or allowed to reach maturity (3:1-26). Job's faith turned to a challenging, seeking faith, confronting God, demanding escape and explanation. In all the bitter questioning, faith lived, for Job turned only and always to God for answers. At this point Job's friends could remain silent no longer and thus began to speak. The first to speak was Eliphaz who told Job that he must have sinned for God was surely punishing him. However, there was still hope if he would confess his sin and turn to God (4:1–5:27). Suffering did not have to endure always. Job was stunned and assured his friends that he was ready to meet God and work out any problem that he might have (6:1–7:21). Bildad added that if Job had not sinned it must have been his children, for obviously God was punishing him for some wrong. However, he too held out hope if Job would just confess (8:1-22). Job was deeply hurt and wondered aloud whether or not he could get a hearing before God (9:1–10:22). Zophar, the most brash of the friends, called upon God to meet with Job, for he was sure that when the two met, Job would see the error of his ways and repent (11:1-20). Job held to his integrity but continued to seek an audience with

J

God so that he could come to understand what was happening and why (12:1–14:22).

Job's friends were not satisfied, so Eliphaz spoke again and reminded him that all people (including Job) had sinned and needed to repent. Thus, if he would just repent, God would forgive him (15:1-35). Job realized that he was getting nowhere with his friends, so he called upon the rest of creation to witness to his integrity (16:1–17:16). Bildad reminded Job of the many proverbs that spoke of the fate of the wicked. In so doing, he was implying that what had happened to Job was the result of his sin (18:1-21). Job was becoming increasingly frustrated, for his friends and family seemed to have abandoned him. Yet he was unwilling to give up on God. Thus, in a most beautiful way he affirmed that he would be vindicated, if not in this world, then in the world to come (19:1-29). Zophar was hurt, for he and his friends were being ignored, if not totally disagreed with. Thus he declared that the wicked would suffer great pain and anguish and that all the forces of nature would turn against them. No doubt Zophar included Job in this group (20:1-29). Job turned to Zophar and harshly said, "No"; for as he observed, sometimes the wicked did prosper. However that did not mean that God was not in control or that He would not one day bring about real justice (21:1-34).

Though they listened to him patiently, Job's friends were also becoming increasingly frustrated. Thus Eliphaz intensified his charge that Job's suffering was the result of his own sinfulness by listing the various sins of which he thought Job was guilty. Then he called upon Job to repent (22:1-30). By this time Job was in such pain that he all but ignored Elipaz's comments and cried out for relief (23:1–24:25). Bildad, not to be outdone, reminded Job again to consider the nature and character of God, for since He was not unjust, Job surely must have sinned (25:1-6). Job, in sarcastic tones, asked the friends where they got their wisdom and then pleaded with them to look to God for real understanding and faith (26:1–27:23). Apparently, at this point, the three friends, having exhausted their arguments, once again became silent.

Job then turned and reflected both upon the true nature of wisdom and his own place in existence. In one of the most beautiful descriptions of wisdom found in the entire Bible, Job concluded that real wisdom (or meaning to life) can only be found in a proper faith relationship with God ("the fear of the Lord") (28:1-28). Though Job knew this was true and though he sought to live a righteous life, he was still hurting and did not understand why. Thus, in a beautiful soliloquy he cried out to God, reminding God of how he had lived faithfully in the past and had been respected for it (29:1-25), but now when he was suffering everyone had turned against him, and death seemed very near (30:1-31). Thus Job issued a final plea for God to vindicate him (31:1-40). With this, Job's case was made. He paused to await an answer from God.

At this point a young man named Elihu rose to speak. Though most of what he had to say had already been said, he gave four speeches, each of which sought to justify God's actions. First, Elihu contended that God speaks to all people, and thus, even though he was a young man, he had every right to speak and even had the understanding to do so (32:1–33:33). Second, he reiterated the view that God was just and thus what had happened to Job was well deserved (34:1-37). Third, he sought to show that God honored the righteous and condemned the prideful, just like He had Job (35:1-16). Fourth, he then pleaded with Job to accept what had happened to him as an expression of God's discipline and to humbly repent and seek His forgiveness (36:1–37:24). Finally, Elihu realized that Job really was not listening, so he stopped speaking.

Suddenly, out of the midst of a whirlwind, God began to speak. Basically, God said two things. First, He described the marvels of creation and then asked Job if he could have done any better (38:1–40:2). Job quickly responded that he could not for he, too, was just a creature (40:3-5). Second, God described how He controlled the world and everything in it and then asked Job if he could do a better job (40:6–41:34). Job admitted that he could not and that he did not need to for now he had seen God and clearly realized that God had everything well under control (42:1-6).

God was apparently very pleased with Job and his responses. However, He rebuked the three friends and commanded that they ask Job to seek intercession for them (42:7-9). Then God restored all Job's fortunes and even gave him more children (42:10-17). In the end Job found meaningful life, not in intellectual pursuits or even in himself, but in experiencing God and his faith relationship to Him.

Job's Message Is Still Relevant for Us Today

The book of Job thus wrestles with issues that all people eventually face. Such issues are not easily addressed. The different speakers in Job confront the issues from different perspectives, forcing us to admit the complexity of the issue before we accept simple answers. Two important issues are the cause and effect of suffering and the justice and care of God. Job begins by accepting suffering as a part of human life to be endured through trust in God in good and bad times. He begins to question, facing the theological issues head on. He illustrates human frustration with problems for which we cannot find answers. Yet he refuses to accept his wife's perspective of giving up on God and life. Rather, he constantly confronts God with cries for help and for answers. He shows faith can be more than simple acceptance. Faith can be struggling in the dark for answers but struggling with God, not with other people. Eliphaz notes that suffering will not last forever, especially for the innocent. Bildad notes that Job's punishment is not as bad as it could have been; after all, his children died. Being alive means Job's sin is not unforgivable and his suffering can be endured.

Zophar emphasizes Job's sin but notes that he could suffer even more. He should give God credit for mercy in not making him endure all the pain his sin deserves. Elihu pleaded for Job to listen to God's word in the experience, for his suffering should become a means of seeing God's will and God's way in the situation. This should lead Job to confess his sin and praise God. Job's complaint is that he cannot find God. He wants to present his case to God but cannot do so, for he is unequal to God. He cannot present his claims of innocence and get his name cleared and his body healed.

God's appearance shows that God cares, that He still controls the world, even a world with unexplainable suffering, and that His creative acts and the mysterious creatures He has created only prove that humans must live under God's control. The human mind cannot control all knowledge or understand all situations. People must be content with a God who speaks to them. They cannot demand that God give all the answers we might want. God can be trusted in the worst of circumstances as well as in the best. See *Faith; Suffering; Wisdom.*

Outline

I. Prologue: A Righteous Man Can Endure Injustice without Sinning (1:1–2:10).

II. First Round: Will a Just God Answer a Righteous Sufferer's Questions? (2:11–14:22).

   A. Job: Why must a person be born to a life of suffering? (2:11–3:26).

   B. Eliphaz: Do not claim to be just but seek the disciplining God, who is just (4:1–5:27).

   C. Job: Death is the only respite for a just person persecuted by God (6:1–7:21).

   D. Bildad: A just God does not punish the innocent (8:1-22).

   E. Job: Humans cannot win an argument in court against the Creator (9:1–10:22).

   F. Zophar: Feeble, ignorant humans must confess sins (11:1-20).

   G. Job: An intelligent person demands an answer from the all-powerful, all-knowing God, not from other humans (12:1–14:22).

III. Second Round: Does the Fate of the Wicked Prove the Mercy and Justice of God? (15:1–21:34).

   A. Eliphaz: Be quiet, admit your guilt, and accept your punishment (15:1-35).

   B. Job: Oh that an innocent person might plead my case with the merciless God (16:1–17:16).

   C. Bildad: Wise up and admit you are suffering the just fate of the wicked (18:1-21).

   D. Job: In a world without justice or friends, a just person must wait for a Redeemer to win his case (19:1-29).

   E. Zophar: Your short-lived prosperity shows you are a wicked oppressor (20:1-29).

   F. Job: Lying comforters do not help my struggle against the injustice of God (21:1-34).

IV. Third Round: Can the Innocent Sufferer Ever Know God's Ways and Will? (22:1–28:28).

A. Eliphaz: You wicked sinner, return to Almighty God and be restored (22:1-30).

B. Job: I cannot find God, but evidence shows He pays undue attention to me but gives no attention to the wicked (23:1–24:25).

C. Bildad: No person can be righteous before the awesome God (25:1-6).

D. Job: Neither your meaningless counsel nor God's faint word helps the innocent sufferer (26:1–27:23).

E. Job: Humans cannot know wisdom; only God reveals its content: Fear the Lord (28:1-28).

V. Job's Summary: Let God Restore the Good Old Days or Answer My Complaint (29:1–31:40).

A. In the good old days I had respect and integrity (29:1-25).

B. Now men and God are cruel to me (30:1-31).

C. In my innocence, I cry out for a hearing before God (31:1-40).

　1. I have not looked with lust on a maiden (31:1-4).

　2. I am not guilty of lying or deceit (31:5-8).

　3. I have not committed adultery (31:9-12).

　4. I have treated my servants fairly (31:13-15).

　5. I have been generous and kind to the poor and the disadvantaged (31:16-23).

　6. I have neither worshiped gold nor celestial bodies (31:24-28).

　7. I have not rejoiced in others' ruin (31:29-30).

　8. I have not refused hospitality to anyone (31:31-32).

　9. I have nothing to hide, but I wish God would give me a written statement of charges (31:33-37).

　10. I have not withheld payment for the laborers on my land (31:38-40).

VI. Elihu: An Angry Young Man Defends God (32:1–37:24).

A. Elihu is angry with Job and with the friends (32:1-22).

B. Elihu speaks to Job as a man; God speaks through dreams, visions, pain, and deliverance (33:1-33).

C. God is just; Job speaks without knowledge (34:1-37).

D. Is there any advantage in serving God? Human sin is no threat to God; human righteousness is no gift to Him (35:1-16).

E. God is just, all wise, mysterious, and sovereign over humans and nature (36:1–37:24).

VII. Dialogue: Prove Your Wisdom Is Sufficient to Contend with the Eternal Creator (38:1–42:6).

A. God: Can you control the inanimate and animate creation? (38:1–39:30).

B. Job: I am overwhelmed and powerless to answer (40:1-5).

C. God: Will you condemn God to justify yourself? (40:6-9).

D. God: Take charge of the universe. (40:10-14).

E. Two inexplicable creatures illustrate God's unfathomable ways (40:15–41:34).

F. Job: Seeing God, I confess His power and repent of sin (42:1-6).

VIII. Epilogue: Prayer Brings Reconciliation, Forgiveness, and Restoration (42:7-17).

Harry Hunt

JOBAB (Jō´ băb) Personal name, perhaps meaning "wilderness" or "arm oneself for battle." **1.** Son of Joktan in Table of Nations lineage of Noah's son Shem (Gen. 10:29). He was thus the original ancestor of a Semite tribe, probably in southern Arabia. **2.** Early king of Edom centered in Bozrah (Gen. 36:33). **3.** King of city-state of Madon who joined Jabin of Hazor in northern coalition against Joshua (Josh. 11:1). **4.** Two members of tribe of Benjamin (1 Chron. 8:9,18).

JOCHEBED (Jŏk´ ə bĕd) Personal name meaning "Yahweh's glory." In Exod. 6:20 the wife of Amram and the mother of Miriam, Aaron, and Moses. She was a member of the tribe of Levi. Her name includes the divine name Yahweh, evidence that the name Yahweh was known before the time of Moses. See *Moses*.

JODA (Jō´ dà) Greek transliteration of either Jehuda (KJV "Juda") or Joyada. An ancestor of Jesus (Luke 3:26).

JOED (Jo´ ĕd) Personal name meaning "Yah is witness." Member of tribe of Benjamin (Neh. 11:7).

JOEL (Jō´ ĕl) Personal name meaning "Yah is God." **1.** Son of Samuel who became an evil judge, leading Israel's leaders to ask Samuel to give them a king, thus introducing kingship as a form of government for Israel. Samuel argued strongly against this but to no avail (1 Sam. 8; cp. 1 Chron. 6:33). **2.** Levite (1 Chron. 6:36). **3.** Member(s) of tribe of Reuben (1 Chron. 5:4,8). **4.** Leader among the Levites under David (1 Chron. 15:7,11,17), who brought the ark of the covenant up to Jerusalem (cp. 1 Chron. 23:8; 26:22 for Levites named Joel). **5.** Member of tribe of Simeon (1 Chron. 4:35). **6.** Leader of tribe of Gad (1 Chron. 5:12). **7.** Leader of tribe of Issachar (1 Chron. 7:3). **8.** Military hero under David (1 Chron. 11:38; cp. Igal in 2 Sam. 23:36). **9.** Leader of the western half of the tribe of Manasseh under David (1 Chron. 27:20). **10.** Levite who helped King Hezekiah cleanse the temple about 715 B.C. (2 Chron. 29:12). **11.** Israelite Ezra condemned for having a foreign wife who might lead the nation to worship other gods (Ezra 10:43). **12.** Leader of the people from tribe of Benjamin living in Jerusalem in time of Nehemiah (Neh. 11:9). **13.** Prophet whose preaching ministry produced the book of Joel. Personal information concerning the prophet is minimal, only that he was the son of Pethuel, about whom we know nothing. That the prophet lived in Jerusalem is probable because of his avid interest in the city, his repeated references to Zion, his call to the people to assemble for worship, and his interest in the temple rituals and sacrifices.

His use of the popular formula, "The word of the Lord came," demonstrates his devotion as God's prophet. Distinguishing himself from the priests, he respectfully urged them to lead the people in repentance. As many as 20 references to and quotations from other prophets attest to his position in the prophetic ministry.

JOEL, BOOK OF Containing only 73 verses, the book of Joel is one of the shortest in the OT, comprising only three chapters in our English translations. The first of two natural divisions, the earlier section (1:1–2:17) describes a terrible locust plague concluding with a plea for confession of sins. The second section (2:18–3:21), written in the form of a first-person response from God, proclaims hope for the repentant people coupled with judgment upon their enemies.

An unprecedented locust plague was symbolic of the coming Day of the Lord. The insects, depicted in their four stages of development, moved through the land in successive swarms, utterly destroying everything in their path. Farmers were denied a harvest. Animals desperately roamed the wasteland groaning and perishing for lack of food. Drunkards cried out for a little taste of wine. Because priests could not find enough offerings for sacrifice, altars were empty. Drought and famine followed the locust infiltration. Vegetation was stripped; the weather was hot; water was scarce. All God's creation suffered because of the sinfulness of His people.

Priests were urged to call for fasting and prayer (2:15-17). Only God's grace could avert annihilation. Then, on the basis of their repentance, God answered that He would show pity and remove their plague (2:18-27).

As a result of their return to God, His people were promised the presence of God's Spirit among them. Locusts were used to tell about a greater Day of the Lord in the future. Judgment was pronounced against Phoenicia and Philistia (3:4) and eventually upon all nations as they were judged by God in the Valley of Jehoshaphat, which literally means "The Lord judges" (3:2,12). Judah faced unparalleled prosperity, but Egypt and Edom (traditional enemies) could look for terrible punishment (3:18-19). The Lord triumphed over his enemies in order that all shall "know that I am the LORD your God" (3:17 NASB; cp. 2:27).

Opinions differ regarding the date of the book. Internal evidence makes it clear that the priests were in a position of strong authority; the temple was standing; sacrifices were considered important; and certain foreign nations stood condemned. No mention was made of the world empires of Assyria or Babylonia. No reference was made to the Northern Kingdom of Israel; neither is the name of a king mentioned.

Two approximate dates generally are given as the possible times of the authorship of the book, either before the exile around the time of the

J

boy-king Joash (about 836–796 B.C.) or after the return from exile (about 500–400 B.C.). The position of the book among the early prophets in the Hebrew canon is considered evidence for an early date. Also the omission of a king's name would be appropriate if a young boy such as Joash had not achieved maturity.

In favor of the late date, strong arguments are given. The returning exiles, comprising a small group in Jerusalem, centered their worship in the temple. Sacrifices were important. Emphasis on ethical living, so characteristic of preexilic prophets such as Amos and Micah, was lacking. Idolatry and the high places were not mentioned, suggesting that they were no longer a serious problem. After the exile there would be no need for announcing the coming destruction of Assyria and Babylon. There would be no need to mention a king. Citation of the Grecian slave traffic (3:4-6) fits a late period. References to the scattering of the Israelites (3:2-6) would apply to an exilic period, and the use of the term "Israel" to refer to Judah (2:27; 3:2) would have been appropriate in postexilic times. In addition, the style and language reflects the period after the exile when the prophetic emphasis was beginning to give way to the apocalyptic.

Some early theologians viewed the entire book as an allegory with the locusts representing four heathen nations that opposed God's people. Few scholars hold to such an interpretation today. Other biblical students have seen in the book primarily a prediction of future events and have related it to certain apocalyptic literature of the NT (Rev. 9:3-11). Most scholars, however, accept the description of the locust plague as a literal invasion which the prophet used as a point of reference to speak to the people of his own day about the coming Day of the Lord, at the same time incorporating predictive elements concerning the messianic age.

Primary teachings of the book of Joel are numerous. (1) The Creator and Redeemer God of all the universe is in complete control of nature and can use calamities to bring His people to repentance. (2) All of God's creation is interdependent. People, animals, and vegetation all suffer when people sin. (3) Whereas the Jews considered the Day of the Lord as a time of punishment upon their enemies, Joel made it clear that although God controls the destinies of other nations, His people, with a responsibility to live in accordance with their relationship with Him, are not exempt from His vengeance. (4) The God of judgment also is a God of mercy who stands ready to redeem and restore when His people come before Him in repentance. (5) Of special significance is the forward look to a time when the Spirit of God would be present upon all people. All could become prophets, with no exclusions, no go-betweens, and all could know His salvation. On the day of Pentecost, Peter proclaimed that the new day of Spirit-filled people had arrived as it had been announced earlier by the Prophet Joel (Acts 2:17-21).

Outline

I. The Day of the Lord Calls for God's People to Respond (1:1–2:17).
   A. Witness to future generations (1:1-4).
   B. Mourn and grieve over the destruction (1:5-20).
   C. Sound the alarm because the Day of the Lord is dreadful (2:1-11).
   D. Repent inwardly because your gracious, patient God may have pity (2:12-14).
   E. Assemble the congregation for mourning and repentance (2:15-17).

II. God Will Respond to His People's Mourning and Repentance (2:18-27).
   A. God will have pity (2:18).
   B. God will provide food needs and remove shame from His people (2:19).
   C. God will defeat the enemy (2:20).
   D. God will replace fear and shame with joy and praise (2:21-26).
   E. God will cause His people to know and worship Him and Him alone (2:27).

III. God Is Preparing a Great Day of Salvation (2:28–3:21).
   A. God will pour out His Spirit to bring salvation to the remnant (2:28-32).
   B. God will judge all nations (3:1-17).
   C. God will bless His people (3:18-21).

Alvin O. Collins

JOELAH (Jō ē´ lah) Personal name meaning "female mountain goat." Warrior from Saul's tribe of Benjamin who joined David at Ziklag as he fled from Saul (1 Chron. 12:7). Early manuscripts and translations give various forms of the name such as Jaalah and Azriel.

JOEZER (Jō ē´ zẽr) Personal name meaning "Yah is help." Warrior from Saul's tribe of Benjamin who joined David at Ziklag as he fled from Saul (1 Chron. 12:6).

JOGBEHAH (Jŏg´ bə hăh) Place-name meaning "height, little hill." City east of the Jordan where Gideon defeated Zeba and Zalmunna, kings of Midian (Judg. 8:11). Its location is modern Khirbet el-Jubeihat 20 miles southeast of the Jordan and seven miles northwest of Amman. The tribe of Gad rebuilt it and settled it (Num. 32:35).

JOGLI (Jŏg´ lī) Personal name meaning "He reveals." Father of Bukki, who represented tribe of Dan in distributing the promised land (Num. 34:22).

JOHA (Jō´ hȧ) Apparently a short form of the personal name Johanan meaning "Yahweh is merciful." **1.** Member of tribe of Benjamin (1 Chron. 8:16). **2.** Military hero in David's army (1 Chron. 11:45).

JOHANAN (Jō hā´ nȧn) Short form of personal name Jehohanan meaning "Yahweh is merciful." **1.** Military leader among Jews who remained in Judah immediately after the exile began in 586 B.C. (2 Kings 25:23). He led the effort against Ishmael, who had assassinated Gedaliah, the governor Babylon appointed over Judah. Johanan led the people into Egypt to escape Babylonian retaliation. He forced Jeremiah to go with them, refusing to follow Jeremiah's word from God (Jer. 40–43). **2.** High priest about 411 B.C. known in the Elephantine papyri as Jehohanan but in Neh. 12:22-23 as Johanan. He was high priest at the time that Nehemiah's list of priests was compiled. Some interpreters would say that Jonathan (Neh. 12:11) is a copyist's error for Johanan, but this is not likely. Others would equate this Johanan with Jehohanan of Ezra 10:6 (note the KJV equation of names despite difference in Hebrew spelling), but Ezra does not indicate Jehohanan was high priest. See *Jehohanan.* **3.** High priest whom Josephus, the early Jewish historian, says murdered his brother named Jesus, perhaps under Artaxerxes III Ochus (358–338 B.C.). **4.** Eldest son of Josiah (1 Chron. 3:15). We know nothing else of this royal son who for some reason did not become king. **5.** Descendant of David in the postexilic period about 445 B.C. (1 Chron. 3:24). **6.** High priest in

the early period of Israel's monarchy (1 Chron. 6:9-10). His son Azariah was high priest under Solomon (cp. 1 Kings 4:2). **7.** Member of Saul's tribe of Benjamin who joined David at Ziklag when he fled from Saul (1 Chron. 12:4). **8.** Member of tribe of Gad who joined David at Ziklag, demonstrating that the people east of the Jordan supported him (1 Chron. 12:12). **9.** Man who led a group going with Ezra from Babylon to Jerusalem about 458 B.C. (Ezra 8:12).

JOHN Greek form of Hebrew name Yohanan.
John the apostle Son of Zebedee, the brother of James. Harmonizing Matt. 27:56 with Mark 15:40 suggests that John's mother was Salome. If she was also the sister of Jesus' mother (John 19:25), then John was Jesus' first cousin. This string of associations is so conjectural, though, that we cannot be sure of it. Because James is usually mentioned first when the two brothers are identified, some have also conjectured that John was the younger of the two.

The sons of Zebedee were among the first disciples called (Matt. 4:21-22; Mark 1:19-20). They were fishermen on the Sea of Galilee and probably lived in Capernaum. Their father was sufficiently prosperous to have "hired men" (Mark 1:20), and Luke 5:10 states that James and John were "Simon's partners."

John is always mentioned in the first four in the lists of the Twelve (Matt. 10:2; Mark 3:17; Luke 6:14; Acts 1:13). John is also among the "inner three" who were with Jesus on special occasions in the Synoptic Gospels: the raising of Jairus's daughter (Mark 5:37), the transfiguration (Mark 9:2), and the garden of Gethsemane (Mark 14:32-33). Andrew joined these three when they asked Jesus about the signs of the coming destruction of Jerusalem (Mark 13:3).

The sons of Zebedee were given the surname *Boanerges*, "sons of thunder" (Mark 3:17). When a Samaritan village refused to receive Jesus, they asked, "Lord, do You want us to call down fire from heaven to consume them?" (Luke 9:54 HCSB). The only words in the Synoptic Gospels attributed specifically to John are: "Teacher, we saw someone driving out demons in Your name and we tried to stop him because he wasn't following us" (Mark 9:38 HCSB; Luke 9:49). On another occasion the two brothers asked to sit in places of honor, on Jesus' left and right in His glory (Mark 10:35-41; cp. Matt.

J

20:20-24). On each of these occasions Jesus challenged or rebuked John. Luke 22:8 identifies Peter and John as the two disciples who were sent to prepare the Passover meal for Jesus and the disciples.

The Apostle John appears four times in the book of Acts, and each time he is with Peter (1:13; 3:1-11; 4:13-20; 8:14). After Peter healed the man, they were arrested, imprisoned, and then released. They were "uneducated and untrained men" (Acts 4:13 HCSB), but they answered their accusers boldly: "we are unable to stop speaking about what we have seen and heard" (Acts 4:20). Later, John and Peter were sent to Samaria to confirm the conversion of Samaritans (8:14).

Paul mentioned John only once: "James, Cephas [Simon Peter], and John, recognized as pillars" of the church agreed that Paul and Barnabas would go to the Gentiles, while they would work among the Jews (Gal. 2:9).

The Gospel of John does not mention James or John by name, and it contains only one reference to the sons of Zebedee (21:2). An unnamed disciple who with Andrew had been one of John the Baptist's disciples is mentioned in John 1:35, and an unnamed disciple helped Peter gain access to the house of the high priest in John 18:15-16. The disciple in these verses may have been the beloved disciple, who reclined with Jesus during the Last Supper (13:23-26), stood at the cross with Jesus' mother (19:25-27), ran with Peter to the empty tomb (20:2-10), and recognized the risen Lord after the great catch of fish (21:7). The need to clarify what Jesus had said about the death of the beloved disciple (21:20-23) probably indicates that the beloved disciple had died by the time the Gospel of John was put in final form by the editor who speaks in John 21:24-25 and attributes the Gospel to this beloved disciple.

Five books of the NT have been attributed to John the apostle: the Gospel, three letters, and Revelation. In each case, the traditional view that the apostle was the author of these books can be traced to writers in the second century. Neither the Gospel nor the letters identify their author by name. The author of Revelation identifies himself as "John" (1:1,4,9; 22:8) but does not further identify himself. Much of the weight of the traditional view of the authorship of the Gospel rests on the testimony of Irenaeus, bishop

of Lugdunum in Gaul (A.D. 130–200). This tradition fits the details of the Gospel, however. It also has historical credibility in that Irenaeus was from Asia Minor when he is said to have encountered Polycarp of Smyrna, who claimed to have been taught by the Apostle John.

Legends about the apostle continued to develop long after his death. According to tradition, John lived to an old age in Ephesus, where he preached love and fought heresy, especially the teachings of Cerinthus. The tomb of John was the site of a fourth-century church over which Justinian built the splendid basilica of St. John. The ruins of this basilica are still visible in Ephesus today.

The Apocryphon of John is an early gnostic work that purports to contain a vision of the Apostle John. Copies were found among the codices at Nag Hammadi. The work itself must go back at least to the second century because Irenaeus quoted from it.

The Acts of John is a third-century apocryphal writing which records miraculous events, John's journey to Rome, his exile on Patmos, accounts of several journeys, and a detailed account of John's death. In theology this work is Docetic, and it was eventually condemned by the Second Nicene Council in 787.

The Apostle John also has a place in the martyrologies of the medieval church. A fifth-century writer, Philip of Side, and George the Sinner, of the ninth century, report that Papias (second century) wrote that James and John were killed by the Jews (Acts 12:2), but these reports are generally dismissed as fabrications based on interpretations of Mark 10:39. See *John, Gospel of; John, Letters from; Revelation, Book of.*

John the Baptist Prophet from a priestly family, who preached a message of repentance, announced the coming of the Messiah, baptized Jesus, and was beheaded by Herod Antipas.

Luke 1:5-80 records the birth of John the Baptist in terms similar to the birth of Isaac. Zechariah, John's father, was a priest from the division of Abijah. Elizabeth, his mother, was a descendant of Aaron. The angel Gabriel announced John's birth, while Zechariah was burning incense in the temple. John would not drink wine or strong drink. He would be filled with the Holy Spirit, and as a prophet he would have the spirit and power of Elijah. His role would be to prepare the Lord's people for the coming of the Messiah.

Mark 1:3-4 records that John was in the wilderness until the time of his public ministry. There he ate locusts and wild honey. He wore the dress of a prophet, camel's hair and a leather girdle (Matt. 3:4; Mark 1:6; cp. 2 Kings 1:8). Because of his life in the wilderness, his priestly background, his preaching of repentance to Israel, and his practice of baptism, it is often suggested that John grew up among the Essenes at Qumran. This theory is attractive, but it cannot be confirmed. Neither can the origin of John's practice of baptizing be traced with certainty. Washings had long been part of Jewish piety, and by the time of John, Gentile converts to Judaism washed themselves as a form of ceremonial cleansing. The Essenes at Qumran practiced ritual washings and had an elaborate procedure for admission to the community. John's baptism may owe something to the Essene practices, but we cannot determine the extent of this influence.

According to Luke, John began his ministry around the Jordan River in the 15th year of the reign of Tiberius Caesar (Luke 3:1-3), which must have been A.D. 26 or 27 (according to the most common NT chronology). John's preaching emphasized the coming judgment, the need for repentance, and the coming of the Messiah. Luke also emphasizes the ethical teachings of John: he called the multitudes a "brood of vipers" (Luke 3:7); one who had two coats should give one to a person who had none; tax collectors were warned to collect no more than their due; and soldiers were instructed to rob no one and "be satisfied with your wages" (Luke 3:10-14 HCSB).

Jesus was baptized by John, a fact that all the evangelists except Mark attempted to explain. Matthew 3:15 explains that it was "to fulfill all righteousness." Luke recorded that John was thrown in prison before recording that Jesus also was baptized (3:20-21), and John told of the baptism of Jesus but only through the testimony of John the Baptist himself. Thus, the witness of John the Baptist to Jesus is featured, deflecting any possibility that later followers of the Baptist might argue that John was superior to Jesus (Matt. 3:11-12; Mark 1:7-8; Luke 3:15-17; John 1:15,19-36).

Various sayings give us glimpses of John's ministry. His disciples practiced fasting (Mark 2:18), and he taught them to pray (Luke 11:1).

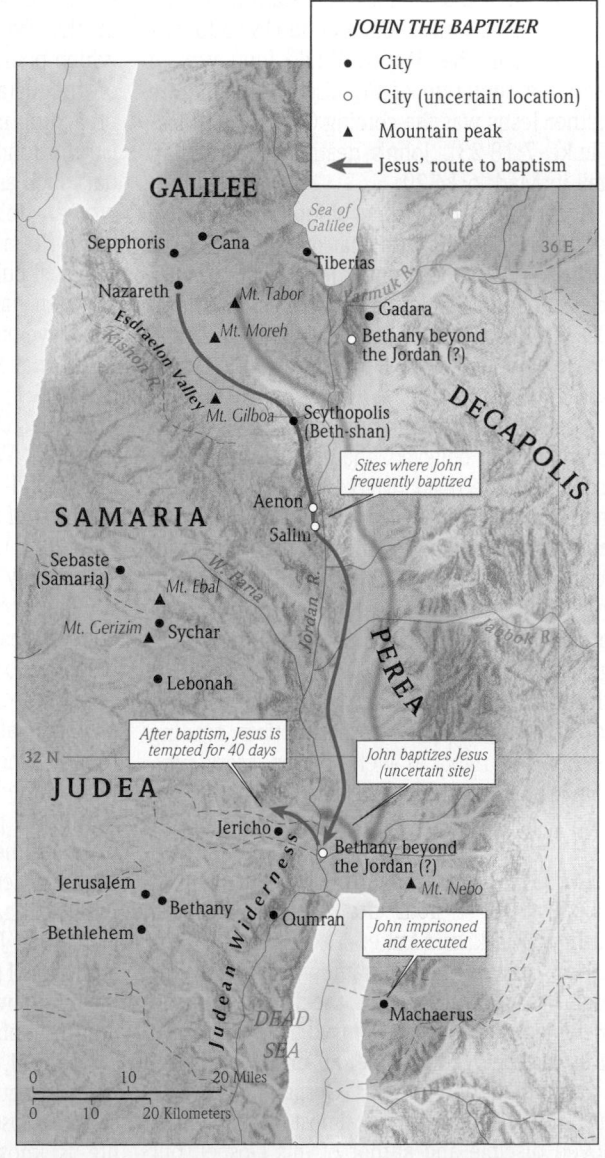

JOHN THE BAPTIZER

• City
○ City (uncertain location)
▲ Mountain peak
← Jesus' route to baptism

GALILEE

Sea of Galilee

Sepphoris • Cana • Tiberias

Nazareth • Mt. Tabor ▲

Esdraelon Valley
Kishon R.

▲ Mt. Moreh

Gadara

Bethany beyond the Jordan (?)

DECAPOLIS

▲ Mt. Gilboa — Scythopolis (Beth-shan)

Sites where John frequently baptized

SAMARIA

Aenon
Salim

Sebaste (Samaria) •

▲ Mt. Ebal

W. Faria

Jordan R.

PEREA

Jabbok R.

Mt. Gerizim ▲ • Sychar

• Lebonah

After baptism, Jesus is tempted for 40 days

John baptizes Jesus (uncertain site)

32 N

JUDEA

Jericho •

Judean Wilderness

Bethany beyond the Jordan (?)

▲ Mt. Nebo

Jerusalem • • Bethany • Qumran

Bethlehem •

John imprisoned and executed

DEAD SEA

• Machaerus

0   10   20 Miles
0   10   20 Kilometers

John was vigorous in his attacks on Herod. In contrast to Herod's household he lived an austere existence (Matt. 11:7-9). Some criticized John for his ascetic lifestyle (Matt. 11:16-19), but Jesus praised John as the greatest of the prophets (Matt. 11:11). John's popularity with the people is reflected in Matt. 21:31-32; Mark 11:27-32; Luke 7:29-30; John 10:41.

In an account that parallels the NT closely, Josephus stated that Herod Antipas arrested John and subsequently executed him at Machaerus because he feared that John's extensive influence over the people might lead to an uprising. Many believed that the defeat of Herod's armies by the Nabateans was God's judgment on Herod for the death of John the Baptist. While John was in prison, he sent two of his disciples to inquire whether Jesus was the coming One (Matt. 11:2-3; Luke 7:18-23). John's death is recorded in detail in Mark 6:14-29.

According to the Gospel of John, the ministry of Jesus overlapped with that of John (3:22-24; cp. Mark 1:14), and some of Jesus' first disciples had also been disciples of John the Baptist (John 1:35-37). Jesus even identified John with the eschatological role of Elijah (Matt. 17:12-13; Mark 9:12-13).

John's movement did not stop with his death. Indeed, some believed that Jesus was John, raised from the dead (Mark 6:14-16; 8:27-28). Years later a group of John's followers were found around Ephesus, among them the eloquent Apollos (Acts 18:24–19:7), and for centuries John's influence survived among the Mandeans who claimed to perpetuate his teachings. See *Baptism.*

Others A relative of Annas, the high priest, was also called John (unless manuscripts reading Jonathan are right) as well as John Mark who wrote the second Gospel. See *Annas; Mark, John.* R. Alan Culpepper

JOHN, GOSPEL OF Fourth Gospel account of the NT, distinct from the Synoptic Gospels, Matthew, Mark, and Luke.

Author Early Christian tradition indicates this Gospel was written by John, the disciple and son of Zebedee. The Gospel claims to have been written by the beloved disciple, an unnamed figure so designated only in this Gospel (21:20-24). John, son of Zebedee, is almost certainly the beloved disciple and author of this Gospel, but some doubts remain since John is not mentioned by name.

Distinct from Synoptics The Gospel of John is different from the three Synoptic Gospels. First, John omits events and references that are extremely important in the others. John does not describe the baptism of Jesus or the breaking of the bread and giving of the cup at the Last Supper. Jesus refers to the kingdom of God only in one conversation in John (3:3-6), whereas the kingdom was a central topic of Jesus' preaching in the Synoptics. Jesus performs no exorcisms in John or healing of lepers. Whereas Jesus performs many miracles, usually in front of crowds in the Synoptics, John records seven "signs" which point to Jesus' identity. John records none of the parables that are a mainstay of Jesus' preaching in the Synoptics. Second, Jesus' ministry in John features conversations with individuals such as Nicodemus (John 3), the Samaritan woman (John 4), and the disciples in the upper room (John 13–17). John does not record much of Jesus' public preaching.

John has much information that the Synoptics leave out. Over 90 percent of John is unique. Jesus makes at least four visits to Jerusalem (2:13; 5:1; 7:10; 12:12). The Synoptics record only one. The raising of Lazarus is recorded only in John. While John omits references to the bread and cup at the supper, he records washing of the disciples' feet. Jesus is called the "Lamb of God" only in John, a reference that recurs only in Revelation.

The most significant additions John makes concern Jesus' identity and the nature of proper response to him. First, John emphasizes the deity of Jesus from the beginning of his Gospel. The prologue affirms that He is the eternal Word (*logos*) who was both with God and was God. Jesus is the Word incarnate (1:14). Jesus uses the significant phrase "I am" seven times in John, claiming the personal name of God as His own. In John, Jesus is always in charge and knows what will happen in advance. For example, John states that Jesus knew what Judas would do all along (6:71). Jesus informed Pilate that he would have no power over Him "if it hadn't been given you from above" (19:11 HCSB).

Second, Jesus' teaching focuses on life, eternal and abundant, which is the present possession of those who believe (3:16; 10:10). Eternal life is knowing God and Jesus Christ (17:3).

Further knowledge of God comes from believing and knowing Jesus. Knowing and believing are key terms for John. Both occur over 90 times in this Gospel and are always used as verbs. Jesus' teaching in John reminds us that knowing God and believing in Jesus are expressed in action. Furthermore, while belief in Jesus may be based on the signs, Jesus' followers are to move to a deeper kind of faith. He wants them to believe in His Word (8:31; cp. 2:23-25).

Context Many scholars think a community following the teachings of the beloved disciple experienced two significant movements by the time John was written. First was a significant interest in persons expelled from synagogues for belief in Jesus while He ministered on earth (9:22; cp. 12:42; 16:2). Most scholars believe this interest indicates these later believers had similar experiences, perhaps while living in Judea or adjacent areas. These Jewish believers found comfort in knowing they were not the first to be expelled for their trust in Jesus. Second, the philosophical overtones of portions of John indicate that some recent challenges to the community came from those who, for philosophical reasons, either rejected the incarnation or the significance of the incarnation. This threat, sometimes referred to as "Docetism," seems to have become a problem by the time 1 John was written. John affirms that Jesus was both the eternal Word, which existed from the beginning, and that He really was flesh. The Gospel of John provides support for the doctrine that Jesus was both fully God and fully human.

Content John is divided into two main parts. In the first section (2–11) the focus is on both Jesus' ministry to "the world" and the signs He performed. Jesus performs seven signs that meet with varying responses. The disciples see the signs and believe (2:11). Some see the signs and still reject Jesus, as is illustrated by those who knew of the raising of Lazarus and yet did not believe (11:47). Moreover, there are some like Nicodemus who seem to be "secret believers" (3:1-2; 7:50-51).

The second major section (12–21) reveals Jesus' teaching to His disciples and the triumphant "hour" of His passion. Jesus instructs His followers that they will experience the presence of another Comforter (or "Paraclete"), the Holy Spirit. The disciples must live out their love for Him in obedience to Him. They must live as

He lived. He is the good shepherd, and they are His flock. His flock will hear His voice and follow Him. True believers are those who obey Jesus. He is the vine and they are the branches. Their life and unity is found in Him. Further, they must be known for their love for one another, sacrificial love, and even laying down of one's life for others.

John's record of the passion focuses on Jesus' control of the events. He has to instruct His adversaries on how to arrest Him (18:4-8). Pilate struggles with his decision, but Jesus knows what will happen. Jesus dies as the Lamb and is sacrificed at the very time lambs were being sacrificed for Passover (19:14).

John originally may have ended with 20:30-31. In the "epilogue" (21) we are told of the restoration of Peter and the prediction of his death. The rumor that John was not to die before the second coming is also refuted.

Purpose John wrote to assure fearful believers that they must believe Jesus and the words that He spoke. Further, he calls on others who sense a spiritual thirst to come to the One who gives the life-giving water. In Him one finds light, life, and love. See *John, Letters from; John the Apostle; Logos.*

Outline

   I. Introduction (1:1-51)
      A. The Prologue (1:1-18)
      B. The Calling of the Twelve (1:19-51)
   II. Jesus' Ministry to the World (2:1–11:57)
      A. Jesus' Ministry in the "Cana Cycle" (2:1–4:54)
         1. Jesus' first sign at the wedding in Cana (2:1-12)
         2. The cleansing of the temple (2:13-25)
         3. Jesus talks with Nicodemus (3:1-21)
         4. John witnesses to Jesus (3:22-36)
         5. Jesus talks with the Samaritan woman and the nobleman (4:1-45)
         6. Jesus returns to Cana (4:46-54)
      B. Jesus' Ministry in Jerusalem (5:1–11:57)
         1. The lame man healed at an unnamed festival (5:1-47)
         2. The Passover (6:1-71)
            a. Feeding of the multitude (6:1-15)
            b. Walking on the water (6:16-24)

J

JOHN, LETTERS FROM Three letters in the "General Epistles" section that, though technically anonymous, are attributed to John, the apostle.

Authorship Tradition has ascribed authorship of these three letters to the Apostle John, son of Zebedee and the brother of James (cp. Mark 1:19-20). He is credited by many to have penned five books of the NT (also the Gospel of John and Revelation), though some doubts were raised in the early church concerning John's authorship of 2 and 3 John and Revelation. Strong similarities between the first letter from John and the Gospel of John argue for common authorship of these books. This same conclusion is reached when a comparison is made between 1 John and the latter two letters. It should be noted that no other person than John the apostle was ever suggested by the early church as the author of the first epistle. This is not so with 2 and 3 John, though he was still the overwhelming choice.

Internal Evidence The author of 1 John claims to be an eyewitness of Christ (1 John 1:1-3). Throughout the book, he writes with an authoritative tone that is virtually apostolic. In 2 and 3 John the author identifies himself as "the elder," a title that would also convey a note of authority.

A comparison of 1 John and the Fourth Gospel reveals numerous similarities in theology, vocabulary, and syntax. There are contrasts such as: life and death; truth and falsehood; light and darkness; children of God and children of the devil; love and hate.

The term *parakletos* occurs only five times in Scripture and all are in the Johannine material (John 14:16,26; 15:26; 16:7; 1 John 2:1). The word *monogenes* as an expression of the Son's unique relationship to the Father occurs in John 1:14,18; 3:16,18; and 1 John 4:9.

External Evidence The early church was consistent in ascribing the authorship of the Fourth Gospel and 1 John to the Apostle John. Papias, who knew John (and was born ca. A.D. 60), is the first person to make a specific reference to a Johannine letter as the work of the Apostle John. Irenaeus (ca. A.D. 180) specifically makes reference to 1 and 2 John, and he clearly attributes both, as well as the Fourth Gospel, to the Apostle John. Indeed, the early Christian tradition is unanimous in ascribing 1 John to John, the disciple and apostle of the Lord.

External evidence for 2 and 3 John is not as early or strong as 1 John. This is probably because of their brevity and resulting limited circulation. A statement by Papias seems to imply the possibility of two Johns at Ephesus, the Apostle John and the elder John. However, the statement by Papias need not be interpreted as implying two Johns, and it seems that the better understanding is to see them as one and the same person. The Apostle John is the elder John. Both were appropriate designations for the last surviving member of Jesus' disciples.

Aside from the "elder John hypothesis," however, no one ever attributed 2 and 3 John to anyone other than the Apostle John. In spite of the questions occasionally raised in the early church, the obvious similarities in vocabulary, theme, and language argue for common authorship of all three letters.

Evidence both internal and external favors the view that the Apostle John is the author of the three letters that Christian tradition has attributed to him.

Date and Place of Writing Tradition is strong that John spent his latter years in the city of Ephesus ministering to the churches of Asia Minor. It would seem reasonable to see the place of writing for the three letters also as Ephesus. Internal evidence would indicate that John was an aged man when he wrote the letters. Church tradition says John was at Ephesus, "remaining among them permanently until the time of Trajan." Trajan reigned as Roman emperor from A.D. 98–117. This would indicate that John died toward the end of the first century, setting a terminus for his writings. A date of ca. A.D. 85–100 is reasonable.

The Occasion of 1 John First John was written to a church or group of churches in crisis—churches which were being attacked by false teaching (cp. 2:18-28; 4:1-6; 5:6-7). Some individuals who had once been associated with the Christian community had adopted heretical doctrine, particularly as it related to Christology, and had left the church (2:19). After their departure they continued to spread their teachings to those who remained within the Johannine churches. They went so far as to organize and send out itinerant teachers/missionaries who worked among the churches with the goal of converting those in the churches to their beliefs (cp. 2:26; 4:1-3; 2 John 7). This theological assault created confusion and crisis within the believing community. In response to this situation, the author penned 1 John, which has two primary objectives:

To combat the propaganda of the false teachers and to reassure the believers. To achieve the first objective John argues that these individuals are not genuine believers; they lack the marks of authentic Christianity in at least three areas.

(1) Doctrinally, they have compromised the person and work of Jesus Christ. They did not confess Jesus of Nazareth as the Christ (2:22) and denied that Jesus had come in the flesh (4:2-3). Most likely, these false teachers were influenced by early gnostic ideas, a heresy that emphasized the essential goodness of spirit and the inherent evil or inferiority of all matter. These false teachers may have viewed Christ as some type of spirit, perhaps a spirit who had come upon the man Jesus during part of His ministry (from His baptism until His crucifixion, cp. 5:6-8). However, they refused to directly associate "the Christ" with the human Jesus; this refusal led to a rejection of Jesus of Nazareth as the

Christ, the unique God-man. Combined with this faulty view of the person of Christ was a deficient view of His death. First John contains specific statements that emphasize the atoning results of Christ's death (2:2; 4:10). John highlights the importance of the incarnation, and he also stresses the distinctive nature of Christ's work of atonement.

(2) Morally, the false teachers minimized the seriousness of sin (1:6-10). They claimed that it was possible to have fellowship with God regardless of one's behavior (1:6). In contrast John insists that one's relationship to God has serious ethical implications (cp. 2:3-4). A genuine knowledge of and love for God demands obedience (2:3-6; 5:3).

(3) Socially, these heretics failed because their spiritual pride resulted in a lack of brotherly love (2:9,11). John will argue that love for other believers is a manifestation of genuine Christianity (3:14; 4:7-21).

John's second objective was to fortify believers in the assurance of their salvation. With the attacks of these false teachings, doubt and confusion developed among believers. What (who) were they to believe—"the traditional teachings of the apostle" or the doctrines of these false leaders? John reminds his churches of the truthfulness of Christianity that they had received in the beginning. He wants them to understand the reality of their faith so that they might know that they have eternal life (5:13). John provides his readers with tests or criteria by which they can evaluate the claims of those who have left the fellowship and with which they could reassure themselves that they were in the truth (1 John 1:5–2:2; 2:3-11; 3:7-10,14-15; 4:4-6,7-8,13-15; 5:13,18-20).

Though 1 John deals with specific problems caused by the secessionists who now evangelize for their cause, it does not indicate a specific destination (unlike 2 and 3 John). It is very probable that it was intended as a circular letter for the churches in the vicinity of Ephesus, the province of Asia Minor.

The Purpose of 1 John First John provides several keys that allow us to unlock the specific purpose(s) of this epistle. Four times in the letter John tells us why he writes:

(1) "We are writing these things so that our joy may be complete" (1:4 HCSB). (To promote in the child of God true joy.)

(2) "I am writing you these things so that you may not sin" (2:1 HCSB). (To prevent the child of God from committing sin.)

(3) "I have written these things to you about those who are trying to deceive you" (2:26 HCSB). (To protect the child of God from false teachers.)

(4) "I have written these things to you who believe in the name of the Son of God, so that you may know that you have eternal life" (5:13 HCSB). (To provide assurance of salvation for the child of God).

Theology of the Epistles *The Doctrine of God* John highlights two important characteristics of God. First, God is light (1 John 1:5). Second, God is love (1 John 4:8). Both of these qualities are essential attributes of God. To walk in the light is to walk in the life of God. To practice love is to demonstrate the character of God.

The Doctrine of Sin First John 3:8 states that the devil is the source of sin, for he "sinned from the beginning." Sin in the individual is the result of the devil's hold upon a person, and victory over sin is in reality victory over the devil himself. John describes sin as darkness (1 John 1:5-7), lawlessness or rebellion (1 John 3:4), and unrighteousness (1 John 5:17). Sin is universal and comprehensive. Therefore every person is a sinner and commits sins (1 John 1:8,10).

The Doctrine of Christology Jesus is presented as the Son of God, and the reality of the incarnation of the preexistent Word is stressed. Twenty-one times Jesus is called the Son in 1 John and twice in 2 John. John states that the Son "was with the Father" and is Himself the "life" of God (1 John 1:1-3, cp. John 1:1-5). Jesus is the "true God and eternal life" (1 John 5:20), a direct affirmation of the Son's deity. He was sinless (1 John 3:5), and He made atonement for the sins of the whole world (1 John 2:2, 4:10). He destroyed the devil's work (1 John 3:8), accomplishing all of this by His death (1 John 5:6). His death was a demonstration of the Father's love (1 John 4:9-11) for sinful humanity. He could do all of this because He took on tangible, real human flesh (1 John 1:1-3). The incarnation was a true and genuine wedding of perfect deity and sinless humanity.

The Doctrine of the Holy Spirit The Spirit witnesses to the believer concerning the true teaching about Jesus the Christ (1 John 2:27; 5:7-8). The Spirit Himself is a gift of anointing.

He has been given to the believer (3:24) and enables him to overcome the world (4:4). As the Spirit of truth (4:6), He helps the believer to recognize the false prophets who speak and teach wrongly concerning Jesus.

The Doctrine of Salvation The redemptive work of Jesus Christ has made possible our salvation (1 John 2:2; 3:16; 4:10). By believing and receiving the Son (1 John 5:10-13) one is born again (1 John 5:1), becomes a child of God (1 John 3:1-2), and receives the gift of eternal life. Through the new birth we are enabled to do "what is right" (2:29). We may commit individual acts of sin (1:8,10; 2:1), but we will not habitually live in sin (3:6-9). In salvation God has come to live (abide) in us and we in God (4:15-16).

The Doctrine of Eschatology John lived in the expectancy that the *parousia* was imminent. He said, "It is the last hour" (2:18 HCSB). The evidence included the presence of "many antichrists." John also looked to the eschatological coming of Antichrist as well (2:18; 4:3). John sees the world as already passing away (2:17), indicating that the victory of Christ won at the cross is already underway, yet it awaits a final and climactic consummation. The day of judgment is coming (4:17). Those who live in God and He in them will have confidence in that day and no fear (4:18). When He comes, our transformation will be made complete for "we know that when He appears, we will be like Him, because we will see Him as He is" (3:2 HCSB). Assured of a right standing before God through faith in His Son who provided atonement for sin, we love God and others, and with this hope in us, we purify ourselves, just as He is pure (3:3).

Canonicity The canonicity of 1 John was never questioned. Second and Third John were viewed as *antilegomena* or disputed. It is likely the books were not widely circulated due to their private nature and brevity, and as a result, they were not well-known among the churches. Athanasius included them in his 39th Paschal Letter (A.D. 367), and the Council of Carthage (A.D. 397) accepted them as canonical.

Structure and Form of 1 John The genre of 1 John is something of an enigma. It is the least letterlike in the absence of the identification of the sender or an address to any recipients except the non-specific "little children." It is more like a tract or treatise intended to address a particular situation. Its dominant themes are reoccurring, and no definitive analysis of its structure and form has been offered. The twin themes of "light" and "love" are central. The book itself is exhortative as John challenges his readers to follow his instruction.

Outline of 1 John

I. Prologue: The Word of Life (1:1-4)
II. God Is Light (1:5–3:10)
   A. Walk in the Light (1:5–2:2)
     1. God is Light (1:5-7)
     2. Resist sin (1:8–2:2)
   B. Obey the command to love (2:3-11)
     1. Know God and keep His commands (2:3-6)
     2. Learn the new command and love others (2:7-11)
   C. Know your spiritual status (2:12-14)
   D. Be warned of enemies of the faith (2:15-27)
     1. Beware of the world (2:15-17)
     2. Beware of the antichrists (2:18-27)
   E. Live like children of God (2:28–3:10)
     1. Be confident and ready for His coming (2:28–3:3)
     2. Be righteous and do not sin (3:4-10)
III. God Is Love (3:11–5:12)
   A. Love one another: part one (3:11-24)
     1. Love in action (3:11-18)
     2. Live in confidence (3:19-24)
   B. Test the spirits (4:1-6)
   C. Love one another: part two (4:7-21)
     1. Love others because God loves you (4:7-10)
     2. Love others because God lives in you (4:11-21)
   D. Obey God and experience the victory of faith (5:1-5)
   E. Believe in the Son and enjoy eternal life (5:6-12)
IV. Conclusion: The Confidence and Characteristics of the Child of God (5:13-21)
   A. Know you have eternal life (5:13)
   B. Be confident in prayer (5:14-17)
   C. Do not continue in sin (5:18-20)
   D. Keep yourself from idols (5:21)

Second John Second John is the second shortest book in the NT. It is only 245 words in the Greek text, and it would easily fit on a single piece of papyrus. Today we might call it (and 3 John) a "postcard epistle." It is an excellent example of hortatory (or exhortation) discourse. The elect lady, most likely a reference to a local church, must continue to walk in the truth, love one another, and be on guard against false teachers (the deceiver and the antichrist of v. 7). They must not extend hospitality to those who deny "the coming of Jesus Christ in the flesh" (v. 7 HCSB).

The letter follows the normal epistolary pattern of the NT period with opening (salutation), body, and closing. There are only two imperatives in the epistle: "watch yourselves" (*blepete*) in verse 8 and "do not receive" (*lambanete*) in verse 10. However, "love one another" in verse 5 virtually bears an imperatival force.

John builds this epistle around key words that tie the letter together. In this short letter of 13 verses, John repeatedly uses "truth" (five times), "love" (four times), "commandment" (four times), "walk" (three times), "teaching" (three times), and "children" (three times). He also utilizes a very rare word, "antichrist," which appears in Scripture only in 1 and 2 John (1 John 2:18,22; 4:3; 2 John 7), as a term describing false teachers.

John tells his children to (1) walk in the truth, (2) obey the commandments, (3) love one another, and (4) guard the teachings of Christ and they will not be deceived by the antichrist (v. 7). The spiritual safety of the believing community is confidently affirmed, as John begins and ends his letter with a reference to their chosen position (vv. 1,13).

Outline of 2 John

I. Love the Truth (1-3)
   A. Embrace the truth (1-2)
   B. Enjoy the truth (3)
II. Live the Truth (4-6)
   A. Be concerned with what you believe (creed) (4)
   B. Be concerned with how you behave (conduct) (5-6)
III. Look for the Truth (7-11)
   A. Recognize the deceptive (7)
   B. Resist the destructive (8)
   C. Reprove the destitute (9)
   D. Reject the dangerous (10-11)
IV. Long for the Truth (12-13)
   A. Experience the fullness of joy (12)
   B. Experience the fellowship of the family (13)

Third John Third John is the shortest book in both the NT and the Bible. It is only 219 words in the Greek text. It and 2 John are rightly described as "twin epistles," though they are rightly viewed as fraternal and not identical. There are some significant similarities worth noting:

(1) The author describes himself as "the elder" (2 John 1; 3 John 1).

(2) The recipients are those whom he loves "in truth" (2 John 1; 3 John 1).

(3) The recipients are the occasion of great rejoicing "I was very glad" (2 John 4; 3 John 3).

(4) The recipients are "walking in the truth" (2 John 4; 3 John 3).

(5) The elder has received good reports about both (2 John 4; 3 John 3,5).

(6) Both letters contain a warning (2 John 8; 3 John 9-11).

(7) The elder desires to see both face to face (2 John 12; 3 John 14).

(8) Others sent their greetings (2 John 13; 3 John 14).

Third John is a personal letter that revolves around three individuals: Gaius (the recipient), Diotrephes (the troubler), and Demetrius (probably the bearer of the letter). Like 2 John it follows closely the ancient epistolary form. It contains a word of exhortation to Gaius encouraging him not to imitate the bad example of Diotrephes but to continue the good work he is doing of receiving and supporting the traveling teachers/missionaries. The letter follows the basic epistolary pattern with an introduction (vv. 1-4), body (vv. 5-12), and a conclusion (vv. 13-14).

Though verses 1-4 clearly function as the salutation, it is possible to outline the letter for teaching purposes around the four (counting the elder) personalities of the book. Verses 1-8 contain a multifold commendation of Gaius. Verses 9-10 condemn the highhanded and malicious autocracy of Diotrephes. Verses 11-12, taken as a unit, praise the godly Demetrius. Verses 13-14 close with a glimpse into the heart of the elder. Four men and their reputations (growing out of their behavior) is the sum and substance of 3 John. John again constructs this letter with the building blocks of key word repetition: "beloved" (4; vv. 1,2,5,11; "dear" HCSB); "truth" or "true" (7; vv. 1,3 [twice]; 4,8,12 [twice]). The elder is understandably concerned that his authority is being challenged. He fears the power play of Diotrephes may succeed and that others might be influenced by him. He will

come if necessary for a face-to-face meeting where he will personally deal with the situation. In the meantime John seeks to enlist the support of Gaius. He praises him for his past performance and encourages him to keep it up. Demetrius comes to Gaius both as the bearer of the letter and a reinforcement in the crisis. Third John provides insight into a personality conflict that arose at the end of the first century and the strategy adopted by the elder to resolve it.

Outline of 3 John

I. Gaius Is a Commendable Christian (1-8)
   A. Live spiritually (1-2)
   B. Walk truthfully (3-4)
   C. Serve faithfully (5-6)
   D. Minster generously (7-8)

II. Diotrephes Is a Conceited Christian (9-10)
   A. Do not be driven by prideful ambition (9a)
   B. Do not display pompous arrogance (9b)
   C. Do not deliver perverse accusations (10a)
   D. Do not dominate with profane activity (10b)

III. Demetrius Is a Consistent Christian (11-12)
   A. Pursue a godly example (11)
   B. Possess a good testimony (12)

IV. John Is a Caring Christian (13-14)
   A. Desire the presence of fellow believers (13)
   B. Desires peace for fellow believers (14)

Daniel Akin

JOIADA (Jôi á da) Short form of personal name Jehoiada meaning "Yah knows." **1.** Man who helped repair the old gate of Jerusalem under Nehemiah (Neh. 3:6; KJV, Jehoiada). **2.** High priest about 425 B.C. (Neh. 12:10-11,22). Ezra suspected one of his sons, who married Sanballat's daughter, of being a traitor (Neh. 13:28). Such marriage of a high priest's family with a foreigner violated Jewish law (Lev. 21:14). See *Sanballat*.

JOIAKIM (Jôi´ á kĭm) Short form of Jehoiakim meaning "Yah has established, set up, delivered." Son of Jeshua and high priest of Israel about 510 B.C. (Neh. 12:10,12,26).

JOIARIB (Jôi á rĭb) Short form of Jehoiarib meaning "Yah establishes justice." See *Jehoiarib*.

1. Member of group that Ezra sent to get Levites to accompany him on return from Babylon to Jerusalem (Ezra 8:16). Many interpreters think Joiarib is a copyist's duplication of Jarib earlier in the verse. See *Jarib.* **2.** Ancestor of member of tribe of Judah who lived in Jerusalem after the exile (Neh. 11:5). **3.** Father of priest who lived in Jerusalem after the exile (Neh. 11:10). **4.** Priest who returned to Jerusalem from Babylonian exile about 537 B.C. with Zerubbabel (Neh. 12:6). **5.** Leading priestly family after return from exile (Neh. 12:19).

JOKDEAM (Jŏk´ də ăm) Place-name meaning "the people burned." City in tribal territory of Judah, possibly modern Khirbet Raqqa near Ziph (Josh. 15:56).

JOKIM (Jō´ kĭm) Short form of personal name Jehoiakim meaning "Yah has established or delivered." An early member of the tribe of Judah (1 Chron. 4:22).

JOKMEAM (Jŏk´ mə ăm) or **JOKNEAM** (Jŏk´ nə ăm) Place-name meaning "He establishes the people" or "the Kinsman establishes or delivers." **1.** Border city of fifth district of Solomon's kingdom (1 Kings 4:12; KJV, Jokneam). Its location was probably Tell Qaimun about 18 miles south of Haifa on the northwestern corner of the Jezreel Valley. A fortress city, it protected the pass into the Plain of Sharon. It lay on the border, perhaps outside of the tribal territory of Zebulun (Josh. 19:11) and was assigned the Levites (Josh. 21:34). Joshua defeated its king whose kingdom was near Mount Carmel (Josh. 12:22). Egyptian records of Thutmose III, Egyptian Pharaoh about 1504–1450 B.C., mentioned Jokmeam. **2.** City of the Levites from tribe of Ephraim (1 Chron. 6:68), either omitted in list in Josh. 21:22 or to be equated with Kibzaim there. It may be located at Tell es-Simadi or Qusen west of Shechem. See *Kibzaim.*

JOKSHAN (Jŏk´ shăn) Personal name meaning "trap, snare." Son of Abraham by Keturah and ancestor of Arabian tribes in wilderness east of Jordan (Gen. 25:2-3). He links the Jews and Arabs together as belonging to a common ancestor—Abraham.

JOKTAN (Jŏk´ tăn) Personal name meaning "watchful" or "he is small." Son of Eber in line from Shem in the Table of Nations (Gen. 10:25-26). He was original ancestor of several tribes in the Arabian Desert, particularly in Jemin. See *Mesha; Sephar.*

JOKTHEEL (Jŏk´ thə ĕl) Place-name meaning "God nourishes" or "destroys." **1.** Town in Shephelah or valley of tribal allotment of Judah (Josh. 15:38). **2.** King Amaziah captured Selah from Edom and renamed it Joktheel (2 Kings 14:7). It may be modern es-Sela northwest of Bozrah. See *Selah.*

JONA (Jō´ nà) Greek transliteration of Hebrew personal name "Jonah" meaning "dove." Father of Simon Peter (John 1:42; cp. 21:15-17).

JONADAB (Jŏn´ à dăb) Short form of personal name Jehonadab meaning "Yah proves himself to be generous." **1.** David's nephew who counseled Ammon how to take advantage of Tamar (2 Sam. 13). Jonadab also advised the sorrowing David that of his sons only Ammon was dead (vv. 32-33). **2.** Form used at times for Jehonadab in Jer. 35. See *Jehonadab.*

JONAH (Jō´ nah) Personal name meaning "dove." Jonah ben Amittai was a prophet of Israel from Gath Hepher, a village near Nazareth. He prophesied during the time of Jeroboam II (793–753 B.C.). God had earlier given Jonah the privilege of delivering the good news that Israel would experience a time of safety and prosperity (2 Kings 14:25). According to the book of Jonah God also used him against his will to deliver a warning to the pagans in Nineveh.

E. Ray Clendenen

JONAH, BOOK OF The book of Jonah is unique among the prophets in that it is almost entirely narrative. It recounts how Jonah learned that God was much bigger than he had thought, especially in the extent of His power and His compassion.

The major power in the Middle East during Jonah's time in the early eighth century B.C. was Assyria, of which Nineveh was a major city. Since the ninth century the Assyrians had been sending savage military expeditions west into Syria-Palestine. When Jonah prophesied, however, Assyria was in a weakened state, making possible the expansion of Jeroboam II in Samaria and Uzziah in Judah. Jonah and all Israel would have been glad if Assyria had continued to disintegrate. However, Assyria regained power in the later eighth century, conquered Syria-Palestine again, and in 722 B.C. destroyed Samaria and deported its citizens.

Jonah was not pleased when God commanded him to go to Nineveh and preach repentance. The Assyrians worshipped the vicious god Ashur and a multitude of other gods and goddesses. Assyrian brutality and cruelty were legendary. The Assyrians were known to impale their enemies on stakes in front of their towns and hang their heads from trees in the king's gardens. They also tortured their captives—men, women, or children—by hacking off noses, ears, or fingers, gouging out their eyes, or tearing off their lips and hands. They reportedly covered the city wall with the skins of their victims. Rebellious subjects would be massacred by the hundreds, sometimes burned at the stake. Then their skulls would be placed in great piles by the roadside as a warning to others. Jonah decided that he would rather quit the prophetic ministry than preach to such people. Nineveh was about 500 miles to the east, so he headed for Tarshish, probably what is now Spain, the farthest western location he knew, about 2,000 miles.

Many since the 19th century A.D. have regarded Jonah as a parable or didactic fiction, as if factual history were ruled out by literary artistry or the recounting of miraculous events. If this narrative, however, whose form bears at every point the mark of a historical account, was judged unhistorical on either of these bases, then most of the Bible would follow easily along. It is pointless to ask whether Jonah really could have been swallowed by a great fish without also asking whether God really could communicate with a prophet. Every aspect of man's encounter with God is miraculous. Jonah is clearly didactic, but it is not presented as fiction or interpreted as such by Jesus (cp. Matt 12:40–41). Also, as F. Page has pointed out (New American Commentary), "If one of the lessons of Jonah, as most would admit, is that God is sovereign over and responsive to human actions, how can we employ a method in its explication that denies that message by ruling out the possibility of miracles?" We might also question the likelihood of ancient Israel's having produced and accepted as Scripture a fictional account in which the two main characters were a historical prophet and Yahweh Himself.

The book has been called "a masterpiece of rhetoric" and a "model of literary artistry, marked by symmetry and balance." Its four chapters divide into two halves, as indicated by commands from the Lord in 1:1–2 and 3:1–2 to go preach in Nineveh. The first time Jonah fled (1:3), and the second time he obeyed (3:3). Each half begins with an introduction (1:1–3; 3:1–4) and has two episodes. In the first episode of each half, Jonah encounters a group of pagans, the sailors (1:4–16) and the Ninevites (3:5–10). Each group surpasses Jonah in sensitivity to the Lord's will. The second and climactic episode of each half finds Jonah talking with God (2:1–11; 4:1–11).

No indication of the book's author is given, only that it gives an account of an incident in the life of a prophet of Yahweh. On the other hand, there is no indication that Jonah was not or could not have been the book's author. Many scholars believe Jonah was written no earlier than the sixth century, which would rule out authorship by the prophet. Evidence of such a late date for the book's origin, however, is considered unpersuasive by many. Some have pointed to alleged historical inaccuracies in the book as evidence of a late date of origin and lack of factual concern. One example is that 3:3 describes Nineveh as larger than we know it to have been. It is described literally as "a great city to God, a walk of three days." Although this is often said to mean that a three-day journey would be required to circumscribe it, however, the point is probably that a three-day visit was required for Jonah to spread his God-given message. This would especially be the case if "the great city of Nineveh" referred to "greater Nineveh," that is, Nineveh and the surrounding towns. A second example is that the designation "king of Nineveh" (3:6) was not the normal way the Assyrians would refer to their king. This is true but irrelevant, since we have no reason to suppose that the book of Jonah was written by the Assyrians but by the Jews, who did sometimes refer to their kings in this way (1 Kings 21:1; 2 Kings 1:3). Besides, Assyria was at this time such a weakened state that it comprised little besides Nineveh.

Jonah is the story of how God teaches a lesson to a narrow-minded, sinful prophet, who represents all God's people who think we have a monopoly on God's grace. When Jonah refuses to go preach in Nineveh and God retrieves him and mercifully delivers him, Jonah is thankful. Yet when Jonah preaches in Nineveh and the people repent and are mercifully spared, Jonah is angry. The book of Jonah ends with an unanswered divine question regarding compassion, suggesting to the reader that Jonah repented, and inviting the reader to do the same. This must be regarded as the key to Jonah's overall purpose, to stir up compassion in God's people. The message of the book is that whether God's people like it or not, God desires all nations to worship Him. God has shown mercy to His people, who did not deserve it; they should desire that mercy be extended to all who repent, and they should rejoice when God shows His grace (cp. Acts 10:34–35). God is concerned for all human beings (John 1:7; 1 Tim. 2:1–6; 2 Pet. 3:9) and has the right to show mercy to whomever He wills (Exod. 33:19; Rom. 9:15).

Outline

I. Jonah Rejects God's Call (1:1–2:10)
   A. Introduction: Yahweh's Command and Jonah's Disobedience (1:1-3)
   B. Episode One: Jonah and the Sailors (1:4–16)
   C. Episode Two: Jonah and Yahweh in the Great Fish (2:1-11)
II. Jonah Fulfills God's Call (3:1–4:11)
   A. Introduction: Yahweh's Command and Jonah's Obedience (3:1-4)
   B. Episode One: Jonah and the Ninevites (3:5-10)
   C. Episode Two: Jonah and Yahweh in Nineveh (4:1-11)   *E. Ray Clendenen*

JONAM (Jō′ năm) or **JONAN** (Jō′ năn) Greek spelling of Hebrew personal name Jehohanan, meaning "Yahweh is gracious" (cp. 1 Chron. 26:3). Ancestor of Jesus (Luke 3:30). Greek uses the "m" ending, while Hebrew has the "n."

JONAS (Jō′ năs) (KJV, NT) See *Jonah; Jona.*

JONATH-ELEM-RECHOKIM (Jō năth-ē lĕm-rə kō′ kĭm) Transliteration of word in title of Ps. 56 (NASB, KJV). NIV reads "to the tune of 'A Dove on Distant Oaks'" (cp. REB, NRSV with Terebinths for oaks). HCSB reads "For the choir director: according to 'A Silent Dove Far Away.'" This was probably the name of a tune to which

the psalm was sung. See *Dove on Far-Off Terebinths.*

JONATHAN (Jŏn′ ả thản) Personal name meaning "Yahweh gave." **1.** Levite who served as priest of Micah in Ephraim and later with tribe of Dan (Judg. 17–18). **2.** Eldest son of King Saul; mother: Ahinroam; brothers: Abinadab, Malchishua and Ish-baal; sisters: Merab and Michal; son: Mephibosheth (Meribbaal).

Jonathan possessed courage, fidelity, and friendship. He led 1,000 soldiers to defeat the Philistines at Geba (Gibeah) (1 Sam. 13:2-3). Then Jonathan took only his armor-bearer to the rocky crags at Michmash and brought panic to the Philistines by killing 20 of them (1 Sam. 14:1-16). Saul discovered that Jonathan was missing, called for the ark of God, went to battle, and defeated the Philistines. Jonathan ate honey, unaware that Saul had forbidden the people to eat that day. Saul would have had Jonathan put to death, but the people spoke in praise of Jonathan and ransomed him from death (1 Sam. 14:27-46).

The next four accounts about Jonathan focus on his friendship with David. First, Jonathan formed a close friendship with David by giving him his robe, armor, sword, bow, and girdle (18:1-4). Second, Jonathan pleaded successfully with Saul to reinstate David (19:1-7). Third, Jonathan left Saul's table angrily to inform David that the king would never receive David again (20:1-42). Fourth, Jonathan held a final meeting with David at Horesh. They made covenant with one another as Jonathan acknowledged David as the next king (23:16-18).

The end of 1 Samuel reports the end of Saul and three of his sons, Jonathan, Abinadab, and Malchishua, at Mount Gilboa (1 Sam. 31:1-13). Their bodies were first hung on the wall of Beth-shan and later brought to Jabesh. Eventually David had the bones buried in the land of Benjamin, in Zela in the tomb of Kish, Jonathan's grandfather (2 Sam. 21:12-14). See *David; Mephibosheth; Saul.*

3. Son of Abiathar the priest in service to David (2 Sam. 15:24; 17:17,20; 1 Kings 1:42-43). **4.** An uncle of David who functioned as counselor and scribe in the royal court (1 Chron. 27:32). **5.** Son of Shimei or Shimeah, David's brother; slew a Philistine giant (2 Sam. 21:21; 1 Chron. 20:7). **6.** Son of Shammah; one of

David's 30 mighty men (2 Sam. 23:32-33; 1 Chron. 11:34). **7.** Son of Uzziah, a royal treasurer in reign of David; called Jehonathan (KJV) in 1 Chron. 27:25. **8.** House of a scribe or secretary where Jeremiah was imprisoned (Jer. 37:15,20; 38:26). **9.** Son of Kareah, "Johanan"; possibly same as 8. (Jer. 40:8). **10.** Father of Ebed, a returned exile (Ezra 8:6; 1 Esdras 8:32). **11.** Priest during high priesthood of Joiakim (Neh. 12:14). **12.** Priest, son of Joiada (Neh. 12:11). **13.** Priest, son of Shemaiah and father of Zechariah, in a group who played musical instruments (Neh. 12:35). **14.** Son of Asahel who supported foreign marriages in time of Ezra (Ezra 10:15; 1 Esdras 9:14). **15.** Descendant of Jerahmeel (1 Chron. 2:32-33). *Omer J. Hancock, Jr.*

JOPPA (Jŏp´ pà) Place-name meaning "beautiful." Situated on the Mediterranean coast, Joppa is located some 35 miles northwest of Jerusalem. Excavations have revealed that the city dates back at least to 1650 B.C. Originally Joppa was situated on a rocky hill just over 100 feet high, a hill that was just slightly beyond the coastline, forming a small cape. To the north stretches the Plain of Sharon, to the south the Plain of Philistia.

The ancient seaport of Joppa (Jaffa).

The OT name for Joppa was Japho (or Jaffe or Yafo), the name the Israeli nation has chosen as the modern designation for the city. The Phoenician form of the term comes from the name Jafe, the daughter of Aeolus, god of the winds.

Joppa is the only natural harbor on the Mediterranean between ancient Ptolemais and Egypt, and its facilities in biblical days were far less than outstanding. Reefs forming a roughly semicircular breakwater approximately 300 feet offshore made entrance from the south impossible. Entrance from the north was shallow and treacherous, but small vessels could navigate it.

The earliest historical reference to Joppa is found in inscriptions on the walls of the temple of Karnak at Thebes (Luxor). Thutmose III, who

Modern produce vendors at a busy market in Tel Aviv (adjacent to ancient Joppa).

ruled Egypt from 1490 to 1436 B.C., boasted of his conquest of the cities of Palestine; Joppa is one of those named. The Amarna Letters mention Joppa twice with observations about the beauty of her gardens and the skill of her workmen in leather, wood, and metal.

When Canaan was conquered, the tribe of Dan received Joppa, but it never came firmly into Hebrew hands. The Philistines took the city, but David recaptured it. Solomon developed it into the major port serving Jerusalem. To Joppa rafts of cedar logs were floated to be transported to Jerusalem for Solomon's splendid temple (2 Chron. 2:16).

Phoenicia gained control of Joppa by the time of Jonah. As the prophet fled from God's call, he caught a ship at Joppa for his well-remembered voyage toward Tarshish (Jon. 1:3). In 701 B.C. Sennacherib occupied the city, then, in turn, the Babylonians and the Persians. As it had been in Solomon's day, Joppa became the port that received cedar logs from Lebanon, now for the rebuilding of the temple under the leadership of Zerubbabel.

In 164 B.C. more than 200 Jewish citizens of Joppa were treacherously drowned by angry non-Jews. In retaliation Judas Maccabeus raided the city, burned the harbor installations, torching the anchored ships as well (2 Macc. 12:3-9). Joppa's history is linked with several notable names during the years of Roman control. Pompey conquered it in 63 B.C., joining it to the province of Syria. Antony later gave the city to Cleopatra of Egypt. Augustus Caesar added it to the kingdom of Herod the Great.

The NT records that Joppa was the home of Dorcas, a Christian woman known for her gracious and generous deeds. At her death the Christians of Joppa called for Simon Peter, who with the command "Tabitha, get up" (HCSB), restored her to life (Acts 9:36-41).

Simon Peter remained in Joppa at the home of Simon the Tanner. At noon, while Simon Peter waited for a meal to be prepared, he prayed on the flat roof of the tanner's house. In a trance Peter saw what seemed to be "a large sheet being lowered to the earth by its four corners" (HCSB) and learned that the Gentile world was a fit audience for the gospel (Acts 10:9-16).

Joppa is now annexed to the modern city of Tel Aviv, forming a part of the southern section of the largest city of Israel. Industrial, shipping, and

Traditional house of Simon the Tanner in Joppa where Peter received a vision from God.

residential complexes have been developed on this ancient site.   *Timothy Trammell*

JORAH (Jō´ rah) Personal name meaning "early or autumn rain." Group leader of Babylonian exiles returning to Jerusalem with Zerubbabel about 537 B.C. (Ezra 2:18). The parallel list (Neh. 7:24) has "Hariph" instead of Jorah (cp. Neh. 10:19). Many interpreters believe Hariph to be the original reading, though it is difficult to explain the change. See *Hariph*.

JORAI (Jō´ rā ī) Personal name, perhaps meaning "Yah has seen" or a short form of Joiarim, "Yah has exalted." Member of tribe of Gad (1 Chron. 5:13).

JORAM (Jō´ răm) Personal name meaning "Yahweh is exalted." Name of a king of Israel (849–843 B.C.) and a king of Judah (850–843 B.C.). The possibility of confusion between them is aggravated by several factors. For one thing, both are also called Jehoram. For another, they were contemporary with one another. Finally, each reigned in proximity to a person named

Ahaziah: Joram of Judah was succeeded on the throne by his son, whose name was Ahaziah; Joram of Israel came to the throne at the death of his brother, who was also named Ahaziah. The account of the reign of Joram (Jehoram) of Israel is found in 2 Kings 3. He led a coalition with Judah and Edom, advised by Elisha, to defeat Moab. The reign of Joram of Judah is treated in 2 Kings 8. He married the daughter of Ahab of Israel and brought Baal worship to Judah. Edom and Libnah gained independence from Judah in his reign. See *Chronology of Biblical Period; Israel, Land of.*

JORDAN RIVER (Jôr´ dȧn) Place-name meaning "the descender." River forming geographical division separating eastern and western tribes of Israel. It is the longest and most important river of Palestine. It rises from the foot of Mount Hermon and flows into the Dead Sea. The Jordan Valley proper is a strip approximately 70 miles long between the Sea of Galilee and the Dead Sea. The valley is divided by various rivers and wadis (small streams) into a number of geographically distinguishable sections. Due to the twists and turns of its course, the full length of the river is more than 200 miles. Its headwaters lie more than 1,000 feet above sea level, and its mouth nearly 1,300 feet below sea level. Along its descending course the river passes through a variety of climatic zones, as well as different types of terrain.

Four sources come together to form the Jordan River: Banias, el-Leddan, Hasbani, and Bareighit Rivers. They all arise at the foothills of Mount Hermon. The Jordan then flows south through what can be described as three stages: *(1) From the sources to Lake Huleh.* The Jordan flows almost seven miles before it enters Lake Huleh. Within this distance, the river makes its way through areas of marsh consisting of reeds, bulrushes, and papyrus—the chief writing material for centuries. In this area lions were seen in biblical times (Jer. 49:19). *(2) Between Lake Huleh and the Sea of Galilee.* On leaving Lake Huleh, the Jordan flows for about 10 miles to the Sea of Galilee. In this short stretch, it descends to 696 feet below sea level. The river has carved a deep and winding course for itself through the center of the valley. Much of its course is characterized by rocky gorges. *(3) From the Sea of Galilee to the Dead Sea.* After leaving the Sea of Galilee the river passes through an especially fertile region. The length of this stretch is around 65 miles, but the river curves and twists for three times this distance. The breadth of the valley is

The Jordan River flows south from Mount Hermon through Israel, finally emptying into the Dead Sea.

J

The green waters of the Jordan River as it meanders through Israel.

from three to 14 miles. The river drops 590 feet during this stretch.

Several major tributaries (e.g., Yarmuk, Jabbok) flow into the Jordan, emptying almost as great an amount of water as the Jordan itself. The deltas of these streams are always fertile areas that widen the extent of land that can be cultivated in the valley. Many cities of antiquity were built close to the point of juncture of the tributaries and the main river.

The Jordan River and Jordan Valley played an important role in a number of memorable events from both the OT and the NT. The first mention of the Jordan in the Bible occurs in the story of Abram and Lot. Lot, upon his separation from Abram, chose for himself "all the valley of the Jordan" (Gen. 13:11 NASB). Jacob wrestled with his adversary at the ford of the Jabbok (Gen. 32:22-26). Under the leadership of Joshua, Israel crossed the Jordan "on dry ground" (Josh. 3:15-17). During the period of the judges and the early monarchy, the possession of the fords of the Jordan more than once meant the difference between defeat and victory. The Jordan was a strong line of defense, not to be easily forded. The Jordan River is also featured in the miracles of Elijah and Elisha.

The essential story of the Gospels begins at the Jordan River. It was there that John the Baptist came preaching the coming kingdom of heaven. The most important NT event relating to the Jordan is the baptism of Jesus, which was performed by John the Baptizer (Mark 1:9). The first part of Jesus' ministry was centered in and around the Sea of Galilee. The second part of His ministry followed as he pursued His course down the east side of the Jordan Valley. There He performed new miracles and spoke to the multitudes in parables, especially those of the collection in Luke 12–18. See *Dead Sea; Hermon, Mount; Sea of Galilee.*   *Philip Lee*

JORIM (Jō´ rĭm) Personal name of unknown meaning. Ancestor of Jesus (Luke 3:29).

JORKEAM (Jôr´ kə ăm) Personal name meaning "the people is golden." Descendant of Caleb (1 Chron. 2:44). This, like other names in the list, may represent a city as well as a person. Many interpreters read Jokdeam here, equating the city with the tribal city of Judah. The location of the city is not known. See *Jokdeam.*

JORKOAM (Jôr´ kō ăm) (KJV) See *Jorkeam.*

JOSABAD (Jŏs´ à băd) (KJV, 1 Chron. 12:4) See *Jozabad.*

JOSAPHAT (Jŏs´ à phăt) (KJV, Matt. 1:8) See *Jehoshaphat.*

JOSE (Jō´ sə) KJV spelling of otherwise unknown ancestor of Jesus, representing Joshua in Hebrew and Jesus in Greek. Modern translations read Joshua (Luke 3:29).

JOSECH (Jō´ sĕk) Personal name of uncertain meaning. Ancestor of Jesus (Luke 3:26). KJV reads Joseph.

JOSEDECH (Jŏs´ ĕ dĕk) Personal name meaning, "Yahweh acts in righteousness." KJV spelling of short form of Jehozadak. See *Jehozadak.*

JOSEPH (Jō´ səph) Personal name meaning "adding." Name of several men in the Bible, most importantly a patriarch of the nation Israel and the foster father of Jesus.

Old Testament Joseph in the OT primarily refers to the patriarch, one of the sons of Israel. Joseph was the 11th of 12 sons, the first by Jacob's favorite wife, Rachel. His name, "may he [the Lord] add," was a part of Rachel's prayer at his birth (Gen. 30:24).

As the child of Jacob's old age and Rachel's son, Joseph became the favorite and was given the famous "coat of many colours" (Gen. 37:3 KJV; "long robe with sleeves," NRSV, REB; "richly ornamented robe" NIV) by his father. This and dreams which showed his rule over his family inspired the envy of his brothers, who sold Joseph to a caravan of Ishmaelites (Gen. 37).

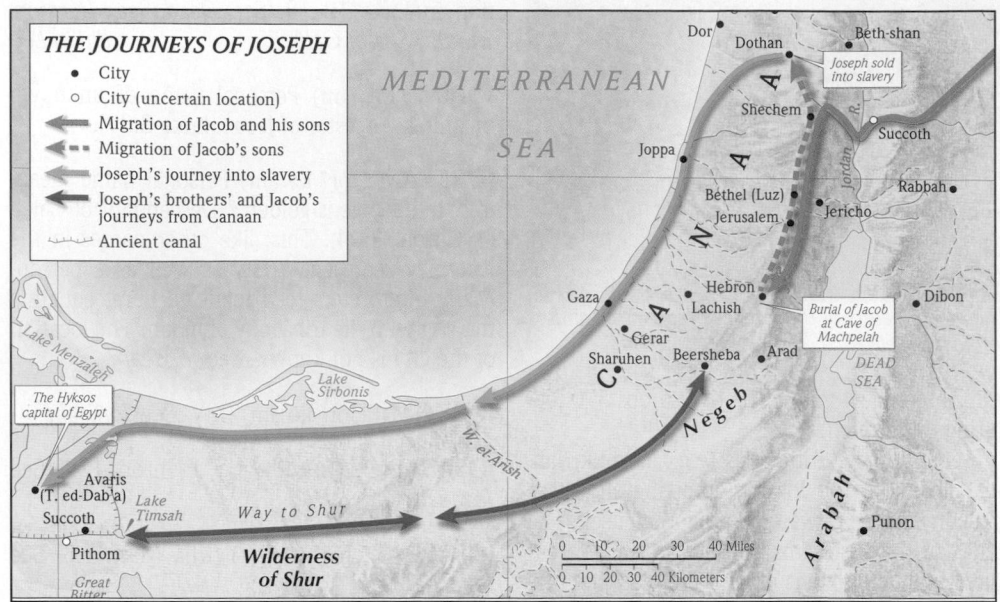

THE JOURNEYS OF JOSEPH
- City
- City (uncertain location)
- Migration of Jacob and his sons
- Migration of Jacob's sons
- Joseph's journey into slavery
- Joseph's brothers' and Jacob's journeys from Canaan
- Ancient canal

Joseph was taken to Egypt where he became a trusted slave in the house of Potiphar, an official of the pharaoh. On false accusations of Potiphar's wife, Joseph was thrown in the royal prison, where he interpreted the dreams of two officials who had offended the pharaoh (Gen. 39–40). Eventually Joseph was brought to interpret some worrisome dreams for the pharaoh. Joseph predicted seven years of plenty followed by seven years of famine and recommended a program of preparation by storing grain. Pharaoh responded by making Joseph his second in command (Gen. 41:39-45).

With the famine persons from other countries came to Egypt to buy food, including Joseph's brothers. They did not recognize him, but Joseph saw the fulfillment of his earlier dreams in which his brothers bowed down to him. After testing their character in various ways, Joseph revealed himself to them on their second visit (Gen. 42–45). Under Joseph's patronage Jacob moved into Egypt (Gen. 46:1–47:12). Joseph died in Egypt but was embalmed and later buried in Shechem (Gen. 50:26; Exod. 13:19; Josh. 24:32).

While in Egypt, Joseph became the father of two sons, Manasseh and Ephraim (Gen. 41:50-52), who were counted as sons of Jacob (48:5-6)

and whose tribes dominated the northern nation of Israel. The name Joseph is used later in the OT as a reference to the tribes of Ephraim and Manasseh (Num. 1:32; 36:1,5; 1 Kings 11:28) or as a designation for the whole Northern Kingdom (Ps. 78:67; Ezek. 37:16,19; Amos 5:6,15; 6:6; Obad. 18; Zech. 10:6). See *Hyksos*.

Four other men named Joseph are mentioned in the OT: the spy of the tribe of Issachar (Num. 13:7); a Levite of the sons of Asaph (1 Chron. 25:2); a contemporary of Ezra with a foreign wife (Ezra 10:42); and a priest in the days of high priest Joiakim (Neh. 12:14).

New Testament Several Josephs are mentioned in the NT. The most important is the husband of Mary, mother of Jesus. He was a descendant of David, a carpenter by trade (Matt. 13:55), and regarded as the legal or foster father of Jesus (Matt. 1:16,20; Luke 2:4; 3:23; 4:22; John 1:45; 6:42). Upon learning of Mary's pregnancy, Joseph, being a righteous man, sought to put her away without public disgrace. His response to God's assurances in a dream further demonstrated his piety and character (Matt. 1:18-25). Joseph took Mary to his ancestral home, Bethlehem, was with her at Jesus' birth, and shared in the naming, circumcision, and dedication of the child (Luke 2:8-33). Directed through dreams,

Joseph took his family to Egypt until it was safe to return to Nazareth (Matt. 2:13-23). As a dedicated father, he was anxious with Mary at the disappearance of Jesus (Luke 2:41-48). Joseph does not appear later in the Gospels, and it is likely that he died prior to Jesus' public ministry.

Also important in the NT is Joseph of Arimathea, a rich member of the Sanhedrin and a righteous man who sought the kingdom of God (Matt. 27:57; Mark 15:43; Luke 23:50). After the crucifixion, Joseph, a secret disciple of Jesus, requested the body from Pilate and laid it in his own unused tomb (Matt. 27:57-60; Mark 15:43-46; Luke 23:50-53; John 19:38-42). Arimathea is probably the same as Ramathaim-zophim (1 Sam. 1:1) northwest of Jerusalem.

Two Josephs are mentioned in the genealogy of Jesus (Luke 3:24,30). Another was a brother of Jesus, apparently named after his father (Matt. 13:55; KJV "Joses" as in Mark 6:3). It is likely but uncertain that the brother of James (Matt. 27:56; Joses in Mark 15:40,47) is a different person. Joseph was also another name of both Barsabbas (Acts 1:23) and Barnabas (Acts 4:36).

Daniel C. Browning, Jr.

JOSEPHUS, FLAVIUS (Jō sē´ phŭs, Flā´ vē ŭs) Early historian of Jewish life and our most important source for the history of the Jews in the Roman period. His four surviving works are *The Jewish War* (composed about A.D. 73), *The Antiquities of the Jews* (about A.D. 93), *Life* (an autobiographical appendix to *The Antiquities*), and *Against Apion*, penned shortly after *The Antiquities*. The date of Josephus' death is unknown but was probably after A.D. 100.

Following the conflict between Rome and the Jews of Palestine (A.D. 66–73), Flavius Josephus gave an account of the struggle in his seven books of *The Jewish War*, which include a prehistory reaching back to the second century B.C. Josephus came to Rome in 73 and lived in a house provided by Vespasian, who also gave him a yearly pension. *The Antiquities*, *Life*, and *Against Apion* were all written in Rome. In *The Antiquities* Josephus paraphrased the Septuagint (earliest Greek translation of the Bible) to tell the story of the Hebrews through the time of Cyrus and then employed other sources to complete the account through the first century. The account of the revolt against Rome is in many respects quite different in *The Antiquities* than it

is in the earlier *War. Against Apion* defends the Jews against charges of the grammarian Apion as well as against other common assaults on the antiquity and moral virtue of the Jews. Josephus' *Life* focuses primarily upon the six-month period in which he was commander of Jewish forces in the Galilee and refutes the charge made by Justus of Tiberias that Josephus had organized the revolt in the Galilee.   *Fred L. Horton, Jr.*

JOSES (Jō´ sēz) Personal name in Mark 6:3, one of the brothers of Jesus. In Matt. 13:55 KJV follows some Greek manuscripts in reading Joses for a brother of Jesus, but modern translations follow the earliest manuscripts in reading Joseph. Some Bible students see Joses as a dialectical pronunciation or a Greek substitute for the Hebrew Joseph (cp. Matt. 27:56). Mark 15:40 mentions another Joses, the brother of James the Less, whose mother's name was Mary. This latter Joses is mentioned as if he were a disciple of Jesus. Barnabas' original name was Joseph in the Greek of Acts 4:36. KJV reads this as Joses.

JOSHAH (Jō´ shah) Personal name of uncertain meaning. Member of tribe of Simeon (1 Chron. 4:34).

JOSHAPHAT (Jŏsh´ à phăt) Short form of personal name Jehoshaphat meaning "Yah judges." **1.** Military hero under David (1 Chron. 11:43). **2.** Priest who sounded the trumpet before the ark of the covenant as David brought it to Jerusalem (1 Chron. 15:24; KJV, Jehoshaphat).

JOSHAVIAH (Jŏ shà vī´ ah) Personal name meaning "Yah lets inhabit," probably a short form of Joshibiah. Military hero under David (1 Chron. 11:46). See *Joshibiah*.

JOSHBEKASHAH (Jŏsh bə kā´ shah) Personal name meaning "to live in misfortune." A Levite musician from clan of Heman, the seer, under David (1 Chron. 25:4). He headed the seventeenth course or division of temple musicians (1 Chron. 25:24).

JOSHEB-BASSHEBETH (Jō shĕb-băs shē´ bĕth) Personal name meaning "dweller of shame" (2 Sam. 23:8). See *Jashobeam*.

J

JOSHIBIAH (Jŏ shə bī´ ah) Personal name meaning "Yah lets inhabit." Member of tribe of Simeon (1 Chron. 4:35).

JOSHUA (Jŏsh´ ū à) Personal name meaning "Yahweh delivered." **1.** Leader of Israelites who first took control of promised land of Canaan. Joshua is one of the unsung heroes of the OT. He, not Moses, led the people into the promised land. He was a person of such stature that he could succeed the incomparable Moses and compile a record of notable success (Josh. 24:31). The Hebrew variations of Joshua are Oshea (Num. 13:16); Hosea (Hos. 1:1). English versions differ in their transliteration of the Hebrew names. Its NT equivalent is Jesus.

Joshua was born in Egypt during the period of slavery. He was a member of Ephraim, the important tribe that later formed the heart of the Northern Kingdom of Israel. He first appeared during the battle with the Amalekites during the desert travels. He was Moses' general, who led the troops in the actual fighting while Aaron and Hur held up Moses' hands (Exod. 17:8-13).

Joshua was Moses' servant (Exod. 24:13). He was on the mountain when Moses received the Law (Exod. 32:17). He was also one of the 12 spies Moses sent to investigate Canaan (Num. 13:8). He and Caleb returned with a positive, minority report. Of all the adults alive at that time, only the two of them were allowed to live to enter the land of Canaan (Num. 14:28-30,38).

The Lord selected Joshua to be Moses' successor long before Moses' death (Num. 27:15-23; Deut. 31:14-15,23; 34:9). Joshua was a military leader, a political leader, and a spiritual leader. He was quiet and unassuming, but he was not intimidated by his responsibilities or the task that lay before him. He was a battlefield genius, particularly in the areas of careful planning, strategy, and execution. He was a capable administrator for the nation, effective in maintaining harmony among people and groups. He was a spokesman to the people for the Lord. Though he did not receive the Law as Moses had, he communicated the Lord's will and the Lord's message much like Moses.

Joshua was at the helm of the nation during the conquest and the distribution and settlement of Canaan. He led in the covenant renewal at Mount Ebal and Shechem (Josh. 8:30-35; 24:1-28). He was able to challenge his people by both

word and example. His pattern is a hard one to better. See *Joshua, Book of; Moses*.

2. High priest of community who returned from Babylonian exile in 538 B.C. See *Jeshua 3*.
Dan Gentry Kent

JOSHUA, BOOK OF As the sixth book of the OT, the book of Joshua occupies a pivotal position between the Pentateuch and the Historical Books. It points backward to the exodus as well as forward to the time of the judges and the monarchy. The book is named after the successor to Moses and one of the greatest military leaders of the OT, Joshua the son of Nun.

However, the central character of the book is not Joshua but God. God fights for Israel and drives out the enemy before them. He is a faithful God who desires a true covenant relationship with His chosen people. God promised that He would give Israel the land that He had pledged to their fathers (Exod. 3:8; Gen. 12:1-3; 15:18-21). The book of Joshua documents how God fulfilled this promise.

The book of Joshua is also about Israel's response to God's covenant promise. Israel's lack of faith and rebellion prevented them from truly receiving God's promised rest (Heb. 3:11). Joshua challenges us to consider what a faithful promise-keeping God can do, and will do, in and through a people who are completely yielded to him.

Authorship and Date Jewish tradition in the Talmud states that Joshua wrote his own book. The book of Joshua itself notes that Joshua did some limited writing (8:32; 24:26), but Joshua is not credited with writing the entire text. Someone other than Joshua probably penned the account of Joshua's death (24:29-31). In addition, other material appears to be dated after his death (15:13-19,63; 19:47).

The author of Joshua may have been among the circle of officers mentioned in Josh. 1:10; 3:2; 8:33; 23:2; and 24:1. The Hebrew word for "officer" is related to an Akkadian verb that means to "write" or "record." These "officers" were contemporaries of Joshua, and eyewitnesses to many of the events recorded in the book. One of them may have been responsible for taking down the official record of Joshua's ministry. In any case, the author of the book was led by the Holy Spirit to render a faithful and trustworthy account of the conquest and settle-

TYRE

ARAM

THE TRIBAL ALLOTMENTS OF ISRAEL

- ● City
- ○ City (uncertain location)
- ▲ Mountain peak

Mt. Hermon ▲

Pharpar River

Ijon

Litani River

Tyre ●

Dan ●

Beth-anath ●

Kedesh ●

Lake Huleh

Yiron ●

Hazor ●

Merom ○

ASHER

NAPHTALI

EAST MANASSEH

Acco ●

Capernaum ●

Cabul ●

Aphek ●   ○Mishal

Nahalal ●

Golan ●

Ashtaroth ●

Achshaph ●   ○Hannathon

Rakkath ●

Sea of Galilee

Mt. Carmel ▲   *Kishon River*

Rimmon ●

Hammath ●

ZEBULUN

Chesulloth

Helkath ●   Daberath ●

Jabneel ●

Yokneam ●   Sarid ●   ▲   En-haddah ●

Tabor ● *Mt. Tabor*

Yarmuk River

Dor ●   Megiddo ●   Shunem ●   Endor ●

Lo-debar ○

Edrei ●

Jezreel ●

ISSACHAR   Jarmuth ●

Taanach ●

Beth-shan ●

Ramoth-gilead ●

En-gannim ○

Dothan ●   Ibleam ●

WEST MANASSEH

Jabesh-gilead ●

Jordan River

Socoh ●

Tirzah ●

Gerasa ●

Zaphon ●

Mt. Ebal ▲

Penuel ○

Mahanaim ○

Pirathon ●   Shechem ●

Mt. Gerizim   Succoth ●

Jabbok River

Janoah ●

AMMON

Aphek ●   Tappuah ●

Shiloh ●

GAD

Gath-rimmon ●

Joppa ●

Ophrah ●

Jazer ●

Jehud ●

EPHRAIM

Bethel ●

Amman ●

Lod ●   Upper Beth-horon ●

Mizpah ●   Naaran ●   Gilgal

Beth-nimrah ●

Gittaim ●

Shaalbim ●   Gibeon ●

Ramah ●

Abel-shittim ●

DAN

Chephirah ●

Jabneel ●   Gezer ●

Kiriath-jearim ●

Jericho ●

Heshbon ●

Baalath ○   ○Gibbethon

Aijalon ●   Chesalon ●

Adummim ●

Bezer ●

Ashdod ●

Ekron ●   Zorah ●   Eshtaol ●

Jerusalem ●   Beth-hoglah ●

Mt. Nebo ▲

Timnah ●

Beth-shemesh ●

BENJAMIN

Medeba ●

Gath ●

Bethlehem ●

Ashkelon ●

Beth-zur ●

Tekoa ●

Kedemoth ○

Lachish ●   Mareshah ●

REUBEN

Hebron ●

DEAD SEA

Jahaz ●

○Eglon

Dibon ●   Aroer ●

Gaza ●

JUDAH

Juttah ●

En-gedi ●

N. Besor

Gerar ●   Ziklag ●

Eshtemoa ●

Arnon River

Bethul ○   Jattir ●

MOAB

Ashan ●   Kabzeel ○

Arad ●

Sharuhen ●

Beersheba ●   Hormah ○

Kir-hareseth ●

Hazar-shual ●   Baalah ○

SIMEON

Eltolad ○

Ezem ○

0   10   20   30   40 Miles

0   10   20   30   40 Kilometers

Zered River

EDOM

MEDITERRANEAN SEA

ment of Canaan.

The book of Joshua appears to have been completed after the death of Joshua (24:29) and Eleazar the son of Aaron (24:33). The repeated phrase "to this day" (4:9; 5:9; 6:25; 7:26; 8:28-29; 9:27; 10:27; 13:13; 15:63; 16:10; 23:29; cp. 22:3,17) also suggests a time of composition later than the recorded events. However, this elapsed time span may not have been very long. Joshua 6:25 states that Rahab "lived in the midst of Israel to this day" (NASB). This may mean that Rahab herself was still living at the time of the writing of the book.

The date of the events recorded in the book of Joshua depends on the date of the exodus. Many evangelical scholars favor dating the exodus in 1446 B.C. This date would place Joshua and the Israelites in Canaan around 1400 B.C. Other scholars favor a later dating for the exodus, between 1250 and 1200 B.C.

Contents The book of Joshua documents the conquest and settlement of the land of Canaan. The book naturally divides itself into four main divisions with each section built around a particular Hebrew concept: "Going over" (1:1–5:15); "Taking" (6:1–12:24); "Dividing" (13:1–21:45); "Worshiping" (22:1–24:33). The first five chapters focus on the preparations made by Joshua and Israel to cross over the Jordan and invade the land. Highlights include God's charge to Joshua (chap. 1), the encounter of the spies with Rahab (chap. 2), the miraculous crossing of the Jordan River at flood stage (chaps. 3–4), and the celebration of the Passover (chap. 5).

Chapters 6–12 record the three-part campaign of Joshua and the Israelites to claim the promised land as their inheritance. The military strategy of the conquest is rather simple, and it reflects the political circumstances of the region during the Amarna period at the end of the late Bronze Age (1400 B.C.). Canaan at the time contained a mixture of powerful fortified city-states and coalitions of smaller city-states. Egypt held nominal control, but no one unified political power existed.

First, the victories at Jericho, Ai, and Bethel secured the central corridor of Canaan (chaps. 6–8). Next, a southern coalition of Amorites led by Adoni-zedek of Jerusalem was defeated at Gibeon and pursued through Beth-horon and the Valley of Aijalon (chaps. 9-10). Finally a powerful northern coalition led by Jabin the king of Hazor encamped together at the waters of Merom to fight against Israel (chap. 11). A list of conquered kings rounds out the record of the conquest (chap. 12).

When Joshua and the Israelites defeated this northern coalition, there was no power left in Canaan strong enough to pose a large-scale threat to Israel. The book of Joshua indicates that only Jericho, Ai, and Hazor were destroyed by fire. Many of the fortified cities were left standing, and the task of completing the conquest fell to the individual tribes who would inherit select portions of the land. As can be seen in the book of Judges, many of the tribes were not able to secure their own territory.

Chapters 13–21 document the inheritance and distribution of the promised land to Israel. God is the great "land giver." The detailed boundary descriptions and lists emphasize the fact that God is the owner of this land and has the authority to distribute it as He chooses. Emphasis is placed on the inheritance of Judah (chaps. 14–15) and of Joseph (chaps. 16–17). Provision is also made for the Cities of Refuge (chap. 20) and the Levitical Cities (chap. 21).

The final section of the book focuses on the farewell speeches of Joshua and the consecration of the land through the great covenant renewal ceremony at Shechem (chap. 24). Joshua blesses the people, calls on them to follow the Lord, warns them of the consequences of disobedience, and challenges them to reaffirm their covenant with God. Here Joshua expresses his personal commitment to the covenant Lord (24:15). After Joshua dies, he is given the title "the servant of the LORD" just like Moses (24:29).

Theological Themes Six major theological themes run throughout the book of Joshua.

The Divine Warrior In the book of Joshua God engages in combat as a divine warrior on behalf of Israel. Just as God fought against the Egyptians at the Red Sea (Exod. 14:14), He now fights for them in Canaan (Josh. 10:14).

Holy War In battle, every living being and every piece of property is to be dedicated to the deity. Why would a loving God order the wholesale extermination of the nations living in the promised land? There is no simple answer to this difficult question. But it must be remembered that Israel was allowed to drive out the nations living in the promised land because of their sin-

LIMITS OF ISRAELITE SETTLEMENT AND THE LAND YET TO BE CONQUERED

- ● City
- ○ City (uncertain location)
- ● City specified by Judges 1 as not taken by Israel
- ▲ Mountain peak
- Limit of Israelite control
- Areas yet to be conquered

PHOENICIA

Valley of Lebanon

Damascus

Sidon

Mt. Hermon

ARAM

Pharpar River

Ahlab

Litani River

Laish (Dan)

MAACAH

Tyre

Beth-anath

Kitron

Kedesh

Rehob

Achzib

Beth-shemesh

Hazor

Lake Huleh

GALILEE

Merom

Acco

Bashan

GESHUR

Aphek

Nahalal

Sea of Galilee

Golan

Ashtaroth

Mt. Carmel

Kishon River

Shimron

Mt. Tabor

Yarmuk River

Yokneam

Jezreel Valley

Endor

Dor

Megiddo

Taanach

Beth-shan

Ramoth-gilead

Ibleam

GILEAD

Socoh

Jabesh-gilead

Jordan River

Mt. Ebal

Mt. Gerizim

Shechem

Succoth

Mahanaim

MEDITERRANEAN SEA

Aphek

Tappuah

Jabbok River

AMMON

Joppa

Shiloh

Jazer

Jogbehah

Yarkon River

HILL COUNTRY OF EPHRAIM

Ai

Rabbah (Amman)

Gezer

Shaalbim

Gibeon

Jericho

Heshbon

Aijalon

Beth-shemesh

Jerusalem (Jebus)

Mt. Nebo

Bezer

Ashdod

Ekron

Bethlehem

Medeba

Ashkelon

Gath

Amorites pressure tribe of Dan near Aijalon (Judg. 1:34–36)

Eastern Desert

Lachish

Gaza

KENIZZITES

DEAD SEA

Dibon

Aroer

Gerar

Ziklag

En-gedi

Arnon River

JUDAH

KENITES

Beersheba

Arad

MOAB

Kir-hareseth

AMALEKITES

| 0 | 10 | 20 | 30 | 40 | 50 Miles |

| 0 | 10 | 20 | 30 | 40 | 50 Kilometers |

Zered River

J

ful abominations (Deut. 9:4-5; 18:9-14; 20:16-18).

The Promised Land God had promised to give Israel "a land flowing with milk and honey" (Exod. 3:8; Deut. 8:7-9; 11:8-12). The promise of land was conditional. God gave the land to Israel in its entirety, but Israel had to trust God and follow Him to occupy the gift. Israel's tenure on the land was also based on faithful worship of God (Deut. 7:12-15). The penalty for worshiping other gods was to be driven from the land (Deut. 6:14-15; 8:19-20; 11:8-9,17; 28:63).

The Covenant The covenant renewal ceremony of Josh. 24 has many similarities with the vassal-treaties formulated by the ancient Hittites. Both types of documents contain an introduction, a historical prologue, a set of stipulations, provisions for keeping the documents and for their public reading, a list of divine witnesses, and finally, curses for disobedience and blessings for obedience. Israel was to be faithful in keeping the covenant. Disobedience eventually brought about the exile.

The Holy and Redeeming God In the book of Joshua, a holy and redeeming God is graciously at work on behalf of Joshua and Israel. God's mercy is offered to non-Israelites as well. Both Rahab (6:17-25) and the Gibeonites (9:1-27) are brought within the covenant community.

A Rest for the People of God Joshua was to lead Israel into their inheritance, into their "rest" (1:13,15; 11:23; 14:15; 21:44; 22:4; 23:1). A faithful covenant relationship with God would secure a peaceful tenure on the land. Nevertheless, the rest provided by Joshua was temporary (Heb. 3:7–4:11). Soon after the death of Joshua, Israel would begin to serve the Canaanite gods and break the covenant relationship. See *Conquest; Joshua; Holy War.*

Outline

I. Claiming the Land (1:1–5:15)
    A. After the Death of Moses (1:1a)
    B. The Call of Joshua (1:1b-18)
    C. Rahab and the Spies (2:1-24)
    D. Crossing Over the Jordan (3:1–4:24)
    E. Covenant Consecration at Gilgal (5:1-15)

II. Conquering the Land (6:1–12:24)
    A. The Capture of Jericho (6:1-27)
    B. The Campaign at Ai (7:1–8:35)
    C. Victory Over the Southern Coalition (9:1–10:43)

    D. Victory Over the Northern Coalition (11:1–12:24)

III. Colonizing the Land (13:1–21:45)
    A. East of the Jordan (13:1-33)
    B. West of the Jordan, Part 1 (14:1–17:18)
    C. West of the Jordan, Part 2 (18:1–19:51)
    D. Cities of Refuge (20:1-9)
    E. Levitical Cities (21:1-45)

IV. Consecrating the Land (22:1–24:33)
    A. The Disputed Altar (22:1-34)
    B. Covenant Exhortations (23:1-16)
    C. Covenant Renewal at Shechem (24:1-33) *Stephen J. Andrews*

JOSIAH (Jō sī´ ah) Personal name meaning "Yahweh heals." Judah's king from about 640–609 B.C. He succeeded his father Amon, an idolatrous king, who ruled for only two years before being murdered by his servants (2 Kings 21:19-23; 2 Chron. 33:21-24). Josiah became king at the age of eight due to wishes of "the people of the land" who put his father's assassins to death (2 Kings 21:24). Josiah's reign lasted for 31 years (2 Kings 22:1; 2 Chron. 34:1).

The book of 2 Chronicles reveals much about the early years of Josiah. In his eighth year as king he began to seek the God of David (34:3). Josiah initiated a religious purge of Jerusalem, Judah, and surrounding areas during his 12th year on the throne (34:3-7). This purge included tearing down the high places, the Asherah, and the altars to Baal. The high places were essentially Canaanite worship centers that had been taken over by Israel. The Asherah were cult objects associated with the worship of Baal, the fertility god of Canaan. See *Asherah.*

In his 18th year as king, an unexpected event turned his energies in new directions. A "book of the Law" was discovered while repairs were being made on the temple. Hilkiah, the high priest, found the book and gave it to Shaphan, the scribe, who in turn read it to King Josiah. Upon hearing the message of the book, Josiah tore his clothes, a sign of repentance, and humbled himself before God. Josiah was assured that the promised destruction would not come in his time (2 Kings 22:8-20; 2 Chron. 34:15-28). The reading of this book prompted Josiah to instigate the most far-reaching religious reforms in Israel's history.

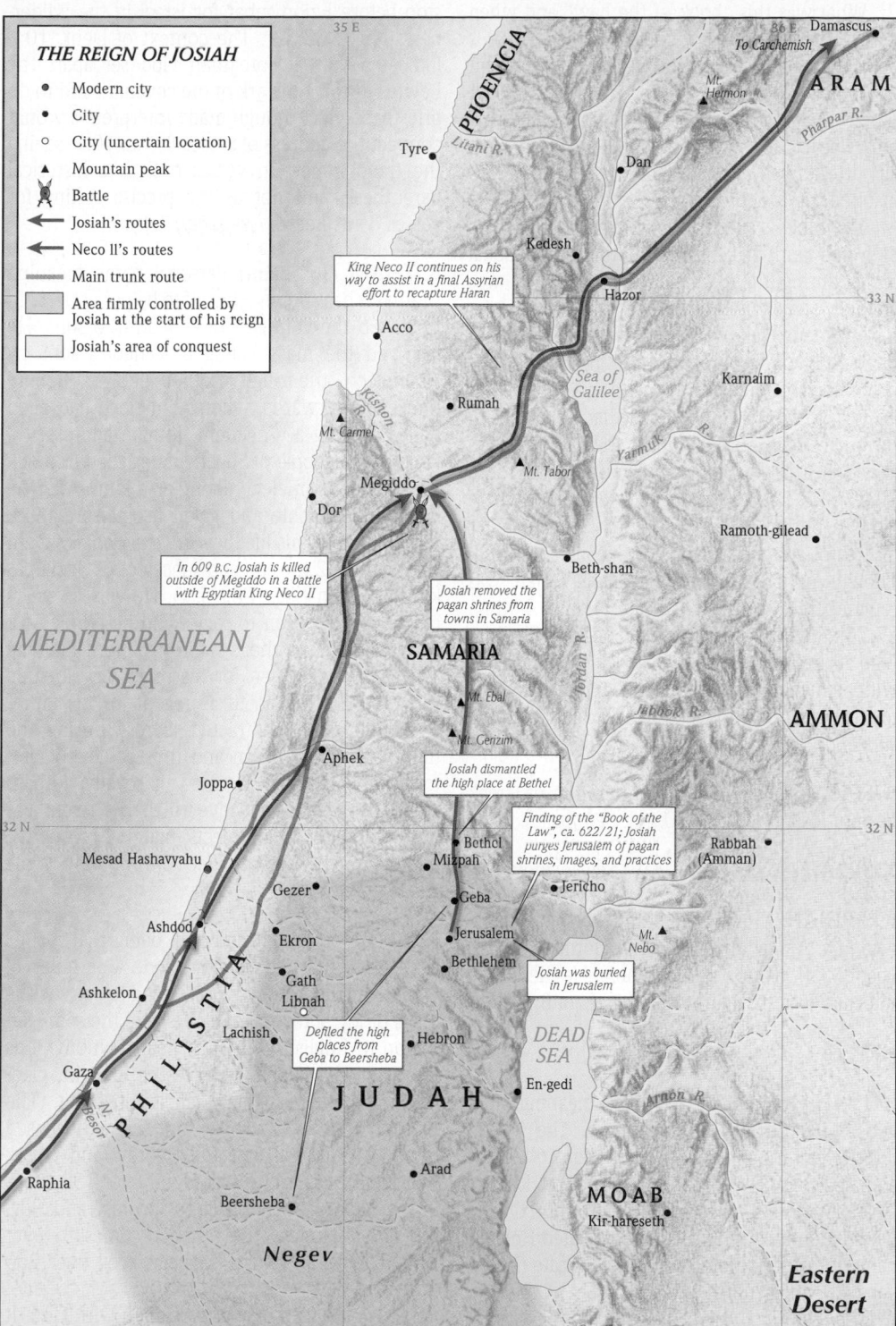

THE REIGN OF JOSIAH

- ● Modern city
- ● City
- ○ City (uncertain location)
- ▲ Mountain peak
- ⚔ Battle
- ← Josiah's routes
- ← Neco ll's routes
- ═ Main trunk route
- ▬ Area firmly controlled by Josiah at the start of his reign
- ▭ Josiah's area of conquest

King Neco II continues on his way to assist in a final Assyrian effort to recapture Haran

In 609 B.C. Josiah is killed outside of Megiddo in a battle with Egyptian King Neco II

Josiah removed the pagan shrines from towns in Samaria

Josiah dismantled the high place at Bethel

Finding of the "Book of the Law", ca. 622/21; Josiah purges Jerusalem of pagan shrines, images, and practices

Josiah was buried in Jerusalem

Defiled the high places from Geba to Beersheba

PHOENICIA

ARAM

Damascus
To Carchemish
Mt. Hermon
Pharpar R.
Tyre
Litani R.
Dan
Kedesh
Hazor
33 N
Acco
Sea of Galilee
Karnaim
Rumah
Mt. Carmel
Kishon R.
Mt. Tabor
Yarmuk R.
Megiddo
Dor
Beth-shan
Ramoth-gilead

MEDITERRANEAN SEA

SAMARIA

Mt. Ebal
Mt. Genzim
Jordan R.
Jabbok R.
AMMON

Aphek
Joppa
Bethel
Mizpah
Geba
Jericho
Rabbah (Amman)
32 N
Jerusalem
Mt. Nebo
Bethlehem
DEAD SEA

Mesad Hashavyahu
Gezer
Ekron
Gath
Libnah
Ashdod
Lachish
Hebron
En-gedi
Ashkelon
Gaza
Arnon R.
PHILISTIA
N. Besor
JUDAH
Arad
MOAB
Kir-hareseth
Raphia
Beersheba

Negev

Eastern Desert

35 E   36 E

J

What was this "book of the Law" and when was it written? Most scholars believe that this book included at least the core of our present book of Deuteronomy, either chapters 5–26 or 12–26. A major thrust of the book of Deuteronomy was to call the nation Israel to exclusive loyalty to Yahweh. Perhaps a thrust such as this inspired the Josianic revival.

The Bible is silent about the remaining years of Josiah until his death. On the international scene during those years Assyria's power was waning, and Babylon's was on the rise. Assyria had aligned itself with Egypt against Babylon. Pharaoh Neco's troops were passing through territory north of Judah en route to join forces with Assyria. Josiah's army blocked the movement of Egyptian troops at Megiddo. In the battle that followed Josiah was mortally wounded (2 Kings 23:29). His body was taken to Jerusalem where he was buried. There was great mourning for him throughout the land (2 Chron. 35:24-25). Though only 39 when he died, Josiah was remembered as Judah's greatest king (2 Kings 23:25): "Before him there was no king like him who turned to the LORD with all his heart and with all his soul and with all his might, according to all the law of Moses" (NASB). See *Deuteronomy, Book of; Jeremiah.*   *M. Stephen Davis*

JOSIAS (Jō sī´ ăs) KJV transliteration of Greek form of Josiah (Matt. 1:10-11). See *Josiah.*

JOSIBIAH (Jŏ sĭ bī´ ah) (KJV) See *Joshibiah.*

JOSIPHIAH (Jŏ sĭ phī´ ah) Personal name meaning "Yah adds to." A longer form of Joseph. Leader of group of Babylonian exiles who returned to Jerusalem with Ezra (Ezra 8:10).

JOT See *Dot.*

JOTBAH (Jŏt´ bah) Place-name meaning "it is good." Home of Meshullemeth, the queen mother of King Amon of Judah about 642–640 B.C. (2 Kings 21:19). It was located at Khirbet Gefat about nine miles north of Nazareth. Others would identify it with the closely related Hebrew name Jotbathah (Num. 33:34) and locate it at et-Taba 20 miles north of Akaba. See *Jotbathah; Meshullemeth.*

JOTBATHAH (Jŏt´ bà tha) Place-name meaning "good." Wilderness camping station, the second

stop before Ezion-geber for Israel in the wilderness (Num. 33:33). The context of Deut. 10:7 indicates that at Jotbathah God set apart the Levites to carry the ark of the covenant and to do priestly service, though many interpreters would connect the address of verses 8–9 to 10:1, seeing the travel report in verses 6–7 as a historical parenthesis and not as the precise setting for verses 8-11. See *Ezion-geber; Jotbah.*

JOTHAM (Jō´ thăm) Personal name meaning "Yahweh has shown Himself to be perfect." **1.** In Judg. 9:5 the youngest of Gideon's 70 sons. He survived the mass killing of Gideon's sons by Abimelech, their half brother, because he hid himself. Afterwards, when Abimelech had been hailed as king at Shechem, Jotham addressed a fable to the people of Shechem designed to mock the idea of Abimelech acting as a king. After he had told the fable and given its interpretation, Jotham fled for his life. See *Judges, Book of.* **2.** In 2 Kings 15:32 the son and successor of Uzziah as king of Judah (750–732 B.C.). He was 25 years old when he began to reign, and he reigned for 16 years. His mother's name was Jerusha. The 16-year period given for his reign may include the time that he acted as regent for his father Uzziah. Uzziah contracted leprosy during the final years of his reign and thus could not perform the functions required of royalty. Jotham evidently was an effective ruler. His reign was marked by building projects, material prosperity, and military successes. See *Chronology of the Biblical Period.*

JOY State of delight and well being that results from knowing and serving God. A number of Greek and Hebrew words are used to convey the ideas of joy and rejoicing. We have the same situation in English with such nearly synonymous words as joy, happiness, pleasure, delight, gladness, merriment, felicity, and enjoyment. The words "joy" and "rejoice" are the words used most often to translate the Hebrew and Greek words into English. Joy is found over 150 times in the Bible. If such words as "joyous" and "joyful" are included, the number comes to over 200. The verb "rejoice" appears well over 200 times.

Joy is the fruit of a right relation with God. It is not something people can create by their own efforts. The Bible distinguishes joy from pleasure. The Greek word for pleasure is the word from which we get our word "hedonism," the philosophy of self-centered pleasure seeking. Paul referred to false teachers as "lovers of pleasure rather than lovers of God" (2 Tim. 3:4 HCSB).

The Bible warns that self-indulgent pleasure seeking does not lead to happiness and fulfillment. Ecclesiastes 2:1-11 records the sad testimony of one who sought to build his life on pleasure seeking. The search left him empty and disillusioned. Proverbs 14:13 offers insight into this way of life, "Even in laughter a heart may be sad" (HCSB). Cares, riches, and pleasures rob people of the possibility of fruitful living (Luke 8:14). Pleasure seeking often enslaves people in a vicious cycle of addiction (Titus 3:3). The self-indulgent person, according to 1 Tim. 5:6, is dead while seeming still to be alive.

Many people think that God is the great killjoy. Nothing could be a bigger lie. God Himself knows joy, and He wants His people to know joy. Psalm 104:31 speaks of God Himself rejoicing in His creative works. Isaiah 65:18 speaks of God rejoicing over His redeemed people who will be to Him "a joy."

Luke 15 is the most famous biblical reference to God's joy. The Pharisees and scribes had criticized Jesus for receiving sinners and eating with them. Then Jesus told three parables—the lost sheep, the lost coin, and the lost son. The explicit theme of each parable is joy over one sinner who repents.

The joy of God came to focus in human history in Jesus Christ. The note of joy and exultation runs through the entire biblical account of the coming of Christ (Luke 1:14,44; Matt. 2:10). The most familiar passage is the angel's announcement of "good tidings of great joy, which shall be to all people" (Luke 2:10 KJV). Jesus spoke of His own joy and of the full joy He had come to bring to others (John 15:11; 17:13). He illustrated the kingdom of heaven by telling of the joy of a man who found treasure (Matt. 13:44). Zacchaeus was in a tree when Jesus called him, but he quickly climbed down and received Jesus joyfully (Luke 19:6). He had found life's ultimate treasure in Christ.

As Jesus' death approached, He told His followers that soon they would be like a woman in labor, whose sorrow would be turned into joy (John 16:20-22). Later they understood when the dark sorrow of the cross gave way to the joy of the resurrection (Luke 24:41). Viewed from this perspective, eventually they came to see that the cross itself was necessary for the joy to become real (Heb. 12:2). Because of His victory and the promise of His abiding presence, the disciples could rejoice even after the Lord's ascension (Luke 24:52).

The book of Acts tells how joy continued to characterize those who followed Jesus. After Philip preached in Samaria, the people believed and "there was great joy in that city" (Acts 8:8). After the work of Paul and Barnabas in Antioch of Pisidia, "the disciples were filled with joy and the Holy Spirit" (Acts 13:52 HCSB). Paul and Barnabas reported such conversions to other believers, "and they created great joy among all the brothers" (Acts 15:3). After the conversion of the Philippian jailer, he "rejoiced because he had believed God with his entire household" (Acts 16:34).

Joy in the Christian life is in direct proportion as believers walk with the Lord. They can rejoice because they are in the Lord (Phil. 4:4). Joy is a fruit of a Spirit-led life (Gal. 5:22). Sin in a believer's life robs the person of joy (Ps. 51:7-8,12).

When a person walks with the Lord, the person can continue to rejoice even when troubles come. Jesus spoke of those who could rejoice even when persecuted and killed (Matt. 5:12). Paul wrote of rejoicing in suffering because of the final fruit that would result (Rom. 5:3-5). Both Peter and James also echoed the Lord's teachings about rejoicing in troubles (1 Pet. 1:6-8; James 1:2).

Joy in the Lord enables people to enjoy all that God has given. They rejoice in family (Prov. 5:18), food (1 Tim. 4:3-5), celebrations (Deut. 16:13-15), fellowship (Phil. 4:1). They share with other believers the joys and sorrows of life: "Rejoice with those who rejoice; weep with those who weep" (Rom. 12:15 HCSB).

Robert J. Dean

JOZABAD (Jŏz´ å băd) Short form of personal name Jehozabad meaning "Yah gave." **1.** Person involved in assassination of King Joash about 782 B.C. (2 Kings 12:21, where Hebrew text says Jozabad, son of Shimeath and Jehozabad, son of Amaziah, but many Hebrew manuscripts read the first name of Jozachar). Second Chronicles 24:26 reads "Zabad son of Shimeath" and "Jehozabad son of Shimrith." Copying changes have made it impossible to determine precisely the original names. Chronicles shows that because Joash killed the sons of Jehoiada the priest, his own servants paid him back. They even refused to give him royal burial in the kings' tombs. See *Jehozabad; Joash.* **2.** Man from Gederah in tribe of Benjamin who joined David as he fled from King Saul (1 Chron. 12:4). **3.** Two men of tribe of Manasseh who joined David at Ziklag as he fled from Saul (1 Chron. 12:20). **4.** Priest who promised Ezra he would divorce his foreign wife to prevent temptation of foreign worship from invading Israel (Ezra 10:22). **5.** Priest who witnessed transfer of gold that Ezra's party brought from Babylon to the temple in Jerusalem (Ezra 8:33), though a Hebrew manuscript reads Jonadab here. **6.** Levite with foreign wife Ezra condemned (Ezra 10:23). **7.** Levite who helped the people understand God's law as Ezra read it (Neh. 8:7). **8.** Levite in charge of external affairs of the temple (Neh. 11:16). **9.** Supervisor of temple treasures under Hezekiah about 715 B.C. (2 Chron. 31:13). He helped give the Levites animals to sacrifice at Passover (2 Chron. 35:9).

JOZACAR (Jō´ zä cär) (NASB, NRSV, TEV) or **JOZACHAR** Personal name meaning "Yah thought of." KJV, REB reading of conspirator who helped kill King Joash about 782 B.C. (2 Kings 12:21) based on Hebrew manuscripts differing from the base manuscript normally used for the Hebrew text. See *Jehozabad; Jozabad.*

JOZADAK (Jŏz´ ä däk) Short form of personal name Jehozadak meaning "Yah acts in righteousness." Father of high priest Joshua (Ezra 3:2,8; 5:2; 10:18; Neh. 12:26). See *Jehozadak.*

JUBAL (Jū´ bäl) Personal name meaning "a ram," as a "ram's horn" used as a musical instrument. In Gen. 4:19-21 the son of Lamech and full brother of Jabal. He is associated with the invention of musical instruments.

JUBILEE See *Year of Jubilee.*

JUCAL (Jū´ cäl) Short form of Jehucal. See *Jehucal.*

JUDA (Jū´ dä) (KJV, NT) See *Judah.*

JUDAEA Alternate form of Judea used by the KJV (except in Ezra 5:8). See *Judea.*

JUDAH (Jū´ dah) Personal, tribal, and territorial name meaning "Praise Yahweh" but may have originally been related to the mountain of Jehud. **1.** In Gen. 29:35, the fourth son of Jacob and the progenitor of the tribe of Judah. His mother was Leah. Though Judah is prominent in the Genesis narratives, he seldom occupies center stage. Genesis 38 is an exception. It relates the seduction of Judah by his daughter-in-law Tamar. Their union resulted in the birth of Pharez and Zarah. Genesis 49:8-12 preserves the blessing of Judah by Jacob. Through Judah ran the genealogical line that led to Jesus. **2.** The tribe of Judah occupied the strategically important territory just to the west of the Dead Sea. The city of Jerusalem was on the border between Judah and Benjamin. David was from the tribe of Judah. **3.** When the kingdom was divided following the death of Solomon, the Southern Kingdom took the name Judah. See *Geography; Israel; Judas; Patriarchs; Israel, Land of; Tribes of Israel.* **4.** The province set up by the Persian government to rule a conquered Judean kingdom (Neh. 5:14; Hag. 1:1). Judah formed one small province alongside Samaria, Galilee, and Idumea. All these reported to the satrap of the Persian satrapy of Abarnaharah that encompassed the land west of the Euphrates River with its center in Damascus (Ezra 5:3,6; 6:6,13). The satrap reported to a higher official over Babylon and Abarnaharah with headquarters in Babylon. When Judah's exiles returned from Babylon, Zerubbabel was governor of Judah; Tattenai, satrap of Abarnaharah or Beyond the River; and Ushtannu, satrap of Babylon and Abarnaharah. **5.** Priest whose sons helped Zerubbabel and Joshua begin work on restoring the temple after 537 B.C. (Ezra 3:9; cp. Neh. 12:8). **6.** Levite whom Ezra condemned for having foreign wife who might tempt Israel to worship other gods (Ezra 10:23). **7.** Member of tribe of Benjamin who lived in Jerusalem after the return from exile and was second in command over the city (Neh. 11:9). He may be the official who joined Nehemiah in leading the celebration of the completion of the Jerusalem wall (Neh. 12:34). **8.** Priestly musician who helped in Nehemiah's celebration (Neh. 12:36). **9.** An obscure geographical reference in the description of the tribal borders of

Naphtali (Josh. 19:34). The earliest Greek translators could not understand the reference and so did not translate it (cp. TEV, NIV). Naphtali's territory does not touch that of the tribe of Judah. Some try to define Judah here as the 60 towns of Jair east of the Jordan (Josh. 13:30). Others translate Judah as "low-lying land" (REB). Some scholars try to make another place-name such as Jehuda out of the reference. It may be that a copyist confused Jordan and Judah, which resemble one another in appearance in Hebrew writing, and miscopied Jordan as Judah and then copied Jordan. No sure solution exists to explain Judah in this text. **10.** City of Judah (2 Chron. 25:28) is Jerusalem.

JUDAISM (Jūˊ dā ĭzm) Religion and way of life of the people of Judah, the Jews. Paul contrasted his Christian calling from his previous life in Judaism (Gal. 1:13-14). Foreigners could convert to Judaism. See *Jewish Parties in the New Testament; Proselytes.*

JUDAS (Jūˊ dăs) Greek transliteration of Hebrew personal name Judah meaning "Praise Yahweh." The proper name Judas was very common in the time of Christ because it was not only the Greek form of one of the 12 patriarchs, but it was also made popular by the Jewish hero Judas Maccabeus who led the nation in their fight for independence from Syria in 166 B.C. The NT mentions six men named Judas. Most of them are only mentioned in passing. **1.** Brother of the Lord (Matt. 13:55; Mark 6:3). **2.** Judas of Galilee was one of those who led a revolt against the Romans and died as a result. The exact year of this revolt is uncertain, perhaps A.D. 6 (Acts 5:37). **3.** After his experience on the road to Damascus Paul went to the house of a man named Judas who lived on Straight Street. Ananias found him there three days later (Acts 9:7-12). **4.** Judas, surnamed Barsabbas, was one of those chosen by the church of Jerusalem to go with Paul and Barnabas to deliver the letter from James to the church at Antioch concerning important matter of Gentile salvation (Acts 15:22). **5.** Jesus' 12 disciples include two named Judas. The first is always listed after James the son of Alphaeus and is called the son of James (Luke 6:16; Acts 1:13). He appears to have been known also by the name Lebbaeus Thaddaeus (Matt. 10:3; Mark 3:18). His only recorded words are found in John 14:22. **6.** The last of

these was Judas Iscariot. All of the Gospels place him at the end of the list of disciples because of his role as betrayer. *Iscariot* is an Aramaic word which means "man of Kerioth," a town near Hebron. He was the only disciple from Judea. He acted as treasurer for the disciples but was known as a miser and a thief (John 12:4-6). He was present at the Last Supper, during which Jesus predicted his betrayal (Luke 22:21; Matt. 26:20-21). The price of the betrayal was 30 pieces of silver, which Judas returned to Jewish leaders, then he went out and hanged himself. He died in sorrow but without repentance. The money, which could not be returned to the treasury because it was blood money, was used to buy a potter's field in Judas' name (Matt. 27:3-10; cp. Acts 1:18-19).   *Gerald Cowen*

JUDAS ISCARIOT (Jūˊ dăs Ĭs cărˊ ĭ ŏt) Personal name meaning "Judah from Kerioth." Betrayer of Jesus. See *Judas 6.*

JUDE, LETTER FROM The letter of Jude is often overlooked because of its brevity. Some are also troubled because Jude quoted 1 Enoch and alludes to the *Assumption of Moses*, but the latter is not a problem for citations from a source do not necessarily indicate that the document quoted is canonical. The message of Jude is alien to many in today's world, for Jude emphasized that the Lord will certainly judge evil intruders who are attempting to corrupt the churches addressed. The message of judgment strikes many in our world as intolerant, unloving, and contrary to the message of love proclaimed elsewhere in the NT. Nevertheless, this short letter should not be ignored. Some of the most beautiful statements about God's sustaining grace are found in Jude (vv. 1,24-25), and they shine with a greater brilliance when contrasted with the false teachers who have departed from the true Christian faith.

We can also say that the message of judgment is especially relevant to people today, for our churches are prone to sentimentality, suffer from moral breakdown, and too often fail to pronounce a definitive word of judgment because of an inadequate definition of love. Jude's letter reminds us that errant teaching and dissolute living have dire consequences. Hence, we should not relegate his words to a crabby temperament that threatens with judgment those he dislikes, but as a warning to beloved believers (vv. 3,17)

J

to escape a deadly peril. Jude was written so that believers would contend for the faith that was transmitted to them (v. 3) and so that they would not abandon God's love at a crucial time in the life of their church. Such a message must still be proclaimed today, for moral degradation is the pathway to destruction.

Author The author is identified in the first verse as "Jude, a slave of Jesus Christ, and a brother of James" (HCSB). The James mentioned is almost certainly James, the brother of the Lord Jesus Christ and the author of the letter from James (cp. also Acts 15:13-21; 1 Cor. 15:7; Gal. 2:9). We can conclude from this that Jude was well-known by his association with his famous brother who played a significant role in the apostolic church. Hence, Jude was also the half-brother of Jesus Christ (Matt. 13:55; Mark 6:3). External evidence from the early church also supports the view that Jude, the brother of Jesus, wrote the letter.

Some scholars have argued that another Jude wrote the letter. Calvin identified the author as the Apostle "Judas of James" (Luke 6:16; Acts 1:13). But if this were correct, the author would call himself an apostle. Others have speculated that the writer is "Judas Barsabbas" (Acts 15:22,27,32), but there is no evidence that the latter was James's brother. Even more unlikely is the theory that the author was the Apostle Thomas. Still others maintain that the letter is pseudonymous, but support for psuedonymity in canonical writings is lacking. To sum up, there are good reasons to accept the view that Jude, the brother of Jesus, is the author of the letter.

Recipients and Date It is extremely difficult to identify the recipients or narrow down the date of the letter. Most scholars today argue that 2 Peter borrows from Jude, and if this is the case, then Jude preceded 2 Peter, and the latter was written in the 60s. Presumably Jude was written in the same general time frame, but it is impossible to be certain. Suggestions for a destination include Palestine, Syria, Asia Minor, and Egypt. We must admit that we have no way of knowing with any certainty the recipients of the letter. Many think the readers were Jewish since Jude cites 1 Enoch and alludes to *The Assumption of Moses.*

Opponents The opponents of Jude have often been identified as gnostics, but this theory is less common today since NT scholars are recognizing

that the second century phenomenon of Gnosticism cannot be read back into the first century. Nor do the opponents betray many of the common features of Gnosticism. A precise label for the opponents eludes us. Verse 4 suggests that the opponents came from outside the church. It is clear from the letter that the opponents were libertines, perhaps abusing the Pauline doctrine of grace. They may have also appealed to personal revelation to support their libertinism (v. 8).

Structure The letter is vigorous, pointed, and well structured. Jude is particularly fond of triads in his writing.

Outline

I. Greeting: 1-2
II. The Purpose for Writing: 3-4
III. Judgment of the Intruders: 5-16
　A. God's Judgment: 5-10
　　1. Three Historical Examples of God's Judgment: 5-7
　　2. Application to Adversaries: Three Sins Warranting Judgment: 8-10
　B. Woe Oracle: 11-13
　　1. Three Types: 11
　　2. Application to Adversaries: 12-13
　C. Enoch's Prophecy: 14-16
　　1. The Prophecy: Judgment on the Ungodly: 14-15
　　2. Application to Adversaries: 16
IV. Exhortations to Believers: 17-23
　A. Remember the Apostolic Predictions: 17-19
　　1. The Apostolic Word: 17-18
　　2. Application to Adversaries: 19
　B. Keep Yourselves in God's Love: 20-21
　C. Show Mercy to Those Affected by Opponents: 22-23
V. Doxology: 24-25　　*Thomas R. Schreiner*

JUDEA (Jū dē´ à) Place-name meaning "Jewish." In Ezra 5:8 the Aramaic designation of a province that varied in size with changing political circumstances, but always included the city of Jerusalem and the territory immediately surrounding it. The area, formerly called Judah, was first given the name Judea following the Babylonian exile. During the Persian period, Judea occupied a very small area. Under the Maccabees, however, the territory was expanded in size and enjoyed a period of political independence. Herod the Great, appointed over roughly the same territory by Rome, had the title king of Judea. Judea, Samaria, and Galilee were generally considered, in Roman times, to be the three main geographical divisions of Palestine. See *Geography; Rome and the Roman Empire.*

JUDEAN (Jū dē´ ån) Resident or citizen of Judah in one of its several national and geographical meanings. See *Judah.*

JUDGE (OFFICE) 1. An official with authority to administer justice by trying cases. **2.** One who usurps the prerogative of a judge. **3.** A military deliverer in the period between Joshua and David (for this sense, see *Judges, Book of).*

Moses served as the judge of Israel, both deciding between persons and teaching Israel God's statutes (Exod. 18:15-16). At Jethro's suggestion Moses himself served as the people's advocate before God and their instructor in the law (18:19-20) and appointed subordinate judges to decide minor cases (18:21-23; Num. 11:16-17; Deut. 1:12-17; 16:18-20). Elders of a community frequently served as judges at the city gate (Deut. 22:15; 25:7; Ruth 4:1-9; Job 29:7-8). Difficult cases were referred to the priests or to the supreme judge (Deut. 17:8-13; cp. Num. 5:12-31, a case involving no wit-nesses). During the monarchy the king served as the supreme judge (2 Sam. 15:2-3) and appointed local judges (1 Chron. 23:4; 2 Chron. 19:5), along with an appeals process (2 Chron. 19:8-11). Following the exile Artaxerxes gave the priest Ezra the authority to appoint judges in Judea (Ezra 7:25).

Complaints against judges are frequent in the OT literature. Absalom took advantage of discontent with the legal system to instigate revolt (2 Sam. 15:4). Judges are accused of showing partiality (Prov. 24:23), of taking bribes (Isa. 61:8; Mic. 7:3; cp. Exod. 23:2-9), and of failing to defend the interest of the powerless (Isa. 10:2; Jer. 5:28). Zephaniah described the judges of Jerusalem as wolves on the prowl (3:3).

God is the ultimate Judge of all the earth (Gen. 18:25; Isa. 33:22; James 4:12). As God's representative Christ functions as Judge as well (John 8:16; James 5:9; 1 Pet. 4:5). See *Judging.*

Chris Church

JUDGES, BOOK OF In English Bibles the book of Judges is the second of the historical books of the OT (Joshua–Esther). Some scholars refer to Joshua–2 Kings as the Deuteronomistic History, so-called because the theology and style of these writings are heavily influenced by Deuteronomy.

Sunset over the Judean hills.

J

However, it is better to follow the Hebrew Bible and interpret these books as the Former Prophets. In all of them theological and spiritual concerns, common to Moses and the prophets, take precedence over the recording of historical facts and political agendas.

The book derives its name from the designation of the principal characters, *shophetim* (2:18), "governors." But they functioned as Israel's deliverers (*moshi'im*) from outside enemies. In most cases in the OT the term *shophet* denotes an official who decides legal cases in a court of law. However, the root bears a broader meaning, "to govern," which can involve internal issues such as disputes among citizens but may also involve external problems; settling national and tribal disputes with outsiders. This sense is reflected in both the name of the book and in the roles played by the major human characters.

Scholars and lay readers tend to read Judges differently. Many scholars interpret the book as a political document, demonstrating the need for a king to resolve the problems of Israel during the transitional period between the conquest of Canaan under Joshua and the establishment of the monarchy, and specifically to support the cause of David in opposition to the household of Saul. Taking their cue from Heb. 11:32, most lay people read Judges as a book of heroes who demonstrate strength of character in achieving great feats for God.

However, a close reading of Judges suggests that both interpretations miss the author's point. If we read Judges as a prophetic book, we discover that the focus is not on the judges but on God, on whose behalf they served as the nation's deliverers. Specifically, the book describes the Lord's response to the Canaanization of Israelite society during the period of settlement. As 2:6-10 declares, within a generation after the death of Joshua and those who had participated in the conquest, Israel's spiritual problems surfaced. This nation entered the land of promise triumphantly as the redeemed people of the Lord but became more and more like the people they were charged to displace.

More than most of the historical books, Judges has a tightly knit plot. The author shows awareness of other judges (Shamgar [3:31], Tola and Jair [10:1-5], Ibzan, Elon and Abdon [12:8-15]), but the events described in detail were carefully selected and deliberately crafted according to an intentional literary scheme. By doing so, the author presented a convincing case of the fundamental degeneration of Israel during the period of the judges. Each part of the book makes a vital contribution to the development of this theme.

The author sets the stage by summarizing the fortunes of the respective tribes as they claimed the land that the Lord had allotted them (1:1-36). He reported the results in a deliberate order, beginning with the successes of Judah and ending with the utter failure of Dan. This pattern anticipated the structure of the narratives that followed, as the portrait of the nation begins rather positively with Othniel (3:7-11), but with each cycle the picture became ever bleaker.

This historical introduction is followed by a heavily theological preamble (2:1–3:6). The fundamental problem is Israel's loss of the memory of the Lord's redemptive work on their behalf (2:1-10). This resulted in the sorry truth expressed in a refrain that is repeated seven times in the book: The Israelites did evil (literally "the evil") in the sight of the Lord; they served the Baals and abandoned the Lord their Redeemer (2:11-12; cp. 3:7,12; 4:1; 6:1; 10:6; 13:1). The following narratives of the individual judges, which take up the bulk of the book (3:7–16:31), describe the consequences of this apostasy. This preamble (2:1–3:6) invites the reader to interpret these accounts not merely as cyclical recurrences of the same problem but as illustrative of an intensification of the evil in Israel (2:17-19), offering the reader the key to understanding both the people of Israel and the judges who led them.

Because of the theological nature of the narrative and the author's selective use of data, it is difficult to reconstruct the history of Israel during the period of the judges from the accounts in the heart of the book (3:7–16:31). The events are deliberately arranged so that each judge is presented in a worse light than the previous, beginning with Othniel, an exemplary character (3:7-11), and ending with Samson, who embodies all that is wrong with Israel. Each cycle is structured after a literary pattern signaled by a series of recurring formulas:

(1) "The Israelites did evil in the eyes of the Lord" (2:11 NIV; 3:7,12; 4:1; 6:1; 10:6; 13:1).

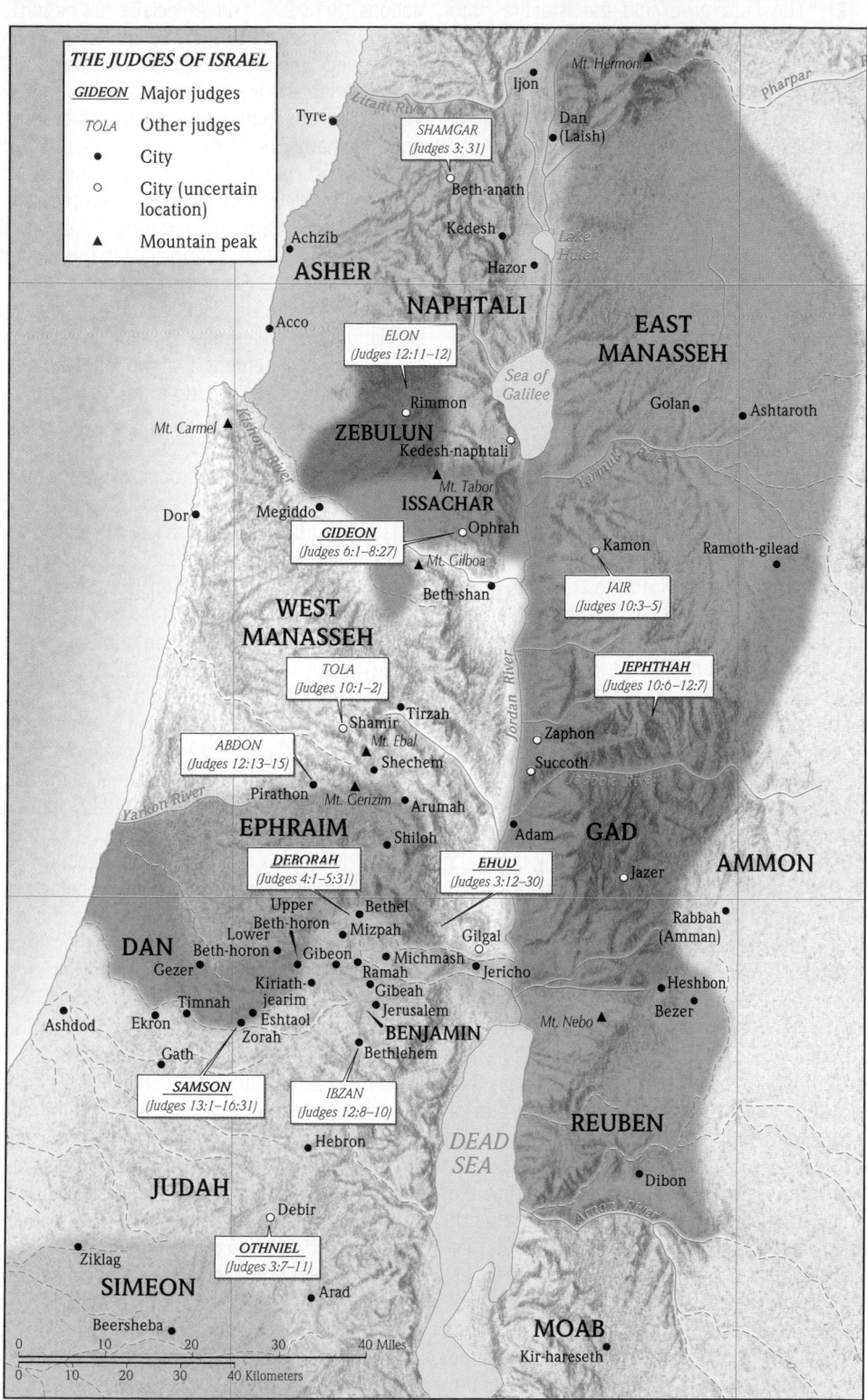

THE JUDGES OF ISRAEL

GIDEON Major judges
TOLA Other judges
• City
○ City (uncertain location)
▲ Mountain peak

Mt. Hermon ▲
Ijon
Pharpar R.
Litani River
Tyre
Dan (Laish)
SHAMGAR (Judges 3: 31)
Beth-anath
Kedesh
Lake Huleh
Achzib
ASHER
Hazor
NAPHTALI
Acco
ELON (Judges 12:11–12)
EAST MANASSEH
Kishon River
Mt. Carmel ▲
Rimmon
Sea of Galilee
Golan
Ashtaroth
ZEBULUN
Kedesh-naphtali
▲ Mt. Tabor
Yarmuk River
Dor
Megiddo
ISSACHAR
Ophrah
Kamon
Ramoth-gilead
GIDEON (Judges 6:1–8:27)
▲ Mt. Gilboa
Beth-shan
JAIR (Judges 10:3–5)
WEST MANASSEH
Jordan River
TOLA (Judges 10:1–2)
Tirzah
Zaphon
Jabbok River
Shamir
Mt. Ebal ▲
Succoth
ABDON (Judges 12:13–15)
Shechem
Pirathon
▲ Mt. Gerizim
Arumah
GAD
Yarkon River
EPHRAIM
Shiloh
Adam
AMMON
DEBORAH (Judges 4:1–5:31)
EHUD (Judges 3:12–30)
Jazer
Bethel
Rabbah (Amman)
Upper Beth-horon
Mizpah
Gilgal
Lower Beth-horon
DAN
Gibeon
Michmash
Heshbon
Gezer
Ramah
Jericho
Bezer
Kiriath-jearim
Gibeah
Timnah
Jerusalem
Mt. Nebo ▲
Ashdod
Ekron
Eshtaol
BENJAMIN
Gath
Zorah
Bethlehem
SAMSON (Judges 13:1–16:31)
IBZAN (Judges 12:8–10)
REUBEN
Hebron
DEAD SEA
Dibon
JUDAH
Arnon River
Debir
OTHNIEL (Judges 3:7–11)
Ziklag
Arad
SIMEON
Beersheba
MOAB
0 10 20 30 40 Miles
Kir-hareseth
0 10 20 30 40 Kilometers

J

(2) "The Lord gave/sold the Israelites into the hands of the enemy" (2:14; 6:1; 13:1).

(3) "The Israelites cried out to the Lord" (3:9,15; 4:3; 6:6; 10:10).

(4) "The Lord raised up a deliverer for Israel to save them" (2:16,18; 3:9,15).

(5) "And X [the oppressing nation] was made subject to Israel" (8:28; cp. 3:30; 4:23).

(6) "Then the land was undisturbed for X years" (3:11,30; 5:31; 8:28).

(7) "Then X [the judge] died" (2:19; 3:11; 4:1b; 8:28; 12:7).

From these formulas it is evident that the Lord is the most important character in the book, and the author's attention is fixed on His response to the Canaanization of His people. In judgment He sends in foreign enemies (as Lev. 26 and Deut. 28 predicted); then in mercy He hears their cry, raises up a deliverer, and provides victory over the enemy. But the Israelites do not learn the lesson; on the contrary the spiritual rot goes deeper and deeper into the very soul of the nation so that in the end Gideon acts like an oriental despot (8:18-32). Like the pagans around him, Jephthah tried to win the good will of God by sacrificing his daughter (11:30-40), and Samson's life and death looked more like that of a Philistine than one of the people of the Lord (chaps. 14–16).

Many interpret Judges 17–21 as more or less independent appendices. However, once we realize that the overall concern of the book is Israel's spiritual degeneration and God's response to it, we discover that, far from being an awkward add-on, these chapters represent the climax of the composition. The tone is set by variations of the four-fold refrain, "In those days there was no king in Israel; every man did what was right in his own eyes" (17:6; 18:1; 19:1; 21:25). This has traditionally been interpreted as a sign that the author looked forward to the institution of the monarchy as the solution to Israel's problems in this dark period. But this interpretation fails on four counts. First, it wrongly assumes that the primary problem in the book is politica when it is spiritual. Second, it overlooks the fact that far from solving the problem of apostasy in Israel, the monarchy actually sponsored the kinds of evils described in the book. Third, it discounts the negative view of kingship presented in the book of Judges itself. Gideon verbally rejects the office of hereditary king (8:22-23), but his actions (8:18-27), and especially his naming of his son Abimelech (which means "my father is king") belie his pious response. Abimelech, the only one labeled a king, epitomized the evils of Canaanite monarchy (see Jotham's fable, 9:7-15) and may hardly be looked to as an ideal. Fourth, if the author is looking forward to kingship as modeled by David as the solution to the crises in Israel at this time, it is curious that, unlike Hezekiah and Josiah centuries later, the accounts of David (1 and 2 Samuel) never portray him as abolishing idolatrous practices and cult centers in the land. It is preferable, therefore to see these refrains as a statement that no one, not even God, is king in this nation. All conduct their affairs as they see fit.

Chapters 17–21 illustrate this, dealing first with the religious symptoms of the problem (chaps. 17–18) and then the social consequences of Israel's Canaanization (chaps. 19–21). Micah, an Ephraimite, set up a pagan cult shrine in his home and instituted his own priesthood (17:1-13). Then the Danites, who cannot drive the Canaanites from the land God allotted to them, come along. On their migration northward to claim unallotted land north of the Sea of Galilee, they seize Micah's priest and his idolatrous images, and when they reach their destination they set up an official cult shrine at Dan. In the meantime, the conduct of the initially nameless Levite (18:30 identifies him as a grandson of Moses) illustrates the corruption infecting even those charged with the spiritual well-being of the nation. Chapters 19–21 illustrate the social rot that comes with the spiritual degeneration of Israel. In fact, in the account of the outrage at Gibeah (19:16-26) are deliberate echoes of the wickedness of Sodom (Gen. 19:1-14). Far from being an ethical community of faith, the Israelites became like the worst of the Canaanites. And instead of exposing the immoral criminals in their midst, the Benjaminites defend them. The book closes with Israel in total disarray politically, spiritually, and morally, with one tribe all but eliminated, leaving the reader to wonder what will become of this people of God.

What then is the enduring significance of this book? First, Israel as a nation survived the dark days of the judges entirely by the grace of God. In mercy He sent oppressors as reminders of their rebellion. In mercy He responded to their cries and raised up deliverers. Second, the book illustrates the fundamental problem of the human heart, depravity. When God's people forget His saving acts, they go after other gods. Third, the book illustrates the inevitable link between spiritual commitments and ethical conduct. There are few human heroes in the book. At the beginning the author presents Othniel as a good judge, but his successors are presented as progressively worse. Deborah is the exception. But then, contrary to popular perceptions, her primary role is not that of a military leader; she is the prophet through whom the Lord raises up Barak. Finally, as Hebrews 11:32-36 declares, despite the questionable morality of the judges, when they cry out to God in faith He enables them to achieve great victories. This is far more to God's credit than theirs. The statement in Hebrews should not be taken as a blanket endorsement of their characters. In the end the book of Judges illustrates the eternal truth: the Lord will build His kingdom/church, and the gates of hell shall not prevail against it. Because God's plan of salvation depended on the survival of Israel, He did not let them disappear. On the contrary, by His grace they survived, and later under the leadership of His anointed king David, His glory was proclaimed far and wide.

Theme: The Lord's Response to the Canaanization of Israel during the dark days following the death of Joshua.

Outline

JUDGING The interpretation of Matt. 7:1 that Christians should not make value judgments of the behavior of others is shown to be erroneous by multiple commands in Scripture to do exactly that (e.g., Matt. 7:15-20; John 7:24; 1 Cor. 5:12; 1 Tim. 3:10). As is frequently the case with biblical truths, the Christian's role in exercising judgment on others is found in a tension between warnings to avoid judging others and admonitions concerning how best to judge others. Christians are to judge others constructively with humility and gentleness (Gal. 6:1). We are forbidden to judge hypocritically, that is, when such judgment entails intolerance of another's sin coupled with blindness of one's own (Matt. 7:1-5; Luke 6:37; John 8:7; Rom. 2:1-4) or when human judgment impinges on God's prerogative as judge (Rom. 14:4; 1 Cor. 4:5; James 4:11-12). Instructions on proper exercise of judgment include (1) the call to judge reputed prophets by their fruits (Matt. 7:15-17), (2) encouragement

J

for Christians to arbitrate between fellow believers who have a dispute rather than going to pagan law courts (1 Cor. 6:1-6), and (3) instructions regarding church cases (Matt. 18:15-20). First Corinthians 5:3-5 illustrates the function of a church court.   *E. Ray Clendenen*

JUDGMENT DAY Appointed time in the future when God will intervene in history for the purpose of judging the wicked and upholding the righteous. In OT texts nations are pictured as being judged during this time. Yet in the NT the judgment seems to be more for individuals. In both Testaments the use of "day," "that day," or "great day," are often used in conjunction with or in place of the day of judgment. In the OT Yahweh is pictured as the Judge, whereas in the NT the Judge is Christ.

Old Testament Teaching "The Day of the Lord" (day of Yahweh) is the phrase indicative of judgment in the OT. This phrase "Day of the Lord" is used 16 times in the Prophets. However, other phrases connote the Day of the Lord. The Day of the Lord is called: "great" (Zeph. 1:14; Joel 2:11,31; Mal. 4:5); "day of trouble" (Zeph. 1:15); "a day of destruction" (Isa. 13:6; Joel 1:15); "a day of desolation and waste" (Zeph. 1:15); "darkness and not light" (Amos 5:18); "a day of fire" (Joel 2:30); "earthquake" (Isa. 2:12-22); "day of Yahweh's wrath" (Zeph. 1:15,18; Ezek. 7:19; Isa. 13:9); "a day of battle" (Zech. 14:3); and "a day of vengeance" (Jer. 46:10; Isa. 63:4).

On the day of judgment God will judge nations and peoples. He will judge Judah and Israel (Amos 2:5-16; 3:1-15; Hos. 13:9-11; 1 Chron. 27:24; 2 Chron. 24:18). Also other nations such as Babylon (Isa. 13; Jer. 51:9,52); Egypt (Isa. 7:18; 11:11,16; Ezek. 30:9-19; Mic. 7:12); Ammon (Ezek. 21:28-30); Edom (Isa. 34:5; Ezek. 35:11); and Moab (Jer. 48:21-47) will be judged. Joel 3 refers to Yahweh's judgment against all nations. The day of judgment will also be a personal day of recompense. Jeremiah, Ezekiel, and Isaiah are among the first to advance the idea of personal accountability during the day of judgment (Jer. 17:5-11; 31:29-30; Ezek. 18:1-32; 33:17-20; Isa. 1:28; 3:10-11; 10:1-4).

His wrath on that day will be like a consuming fire (Isa. 10:16; Ezek. 15:6; 22:31; 36:5-7) and yet a refining fire (Mal. 3:2-3). The day of

judgment will be carried out by Yahweh (Pss. 58:11; 96:10), the Son of Man (Ezek. 20:4; 22:2), or the new Davidic messiah (Isa. 11:1-4). The day of judgment is temporal in nature as seen by use of phrases such as "in that day," "in the coming day," "behold the days are coming," and "the end of days." The day of judgment has both future and past implications. Prophets such as Amos and Isaiah point to a future time of judgment upon all who shun God's divine law. Yet writers such as Jeremiah and Ezekiel point to a time past when Yahweh executed a day of judgment. The fall of Jerusalem was understood as a day of judgment to those who were taken captive (Lam. 1:12; 2:1,20-22; Ezek. 20:36; 23:11; 36:19).

New Testament Teaching New Testament teaching builds on both OT and intertestamental writings. Generally the NT understands the day of judgment as being closely associated with the *Parousia*, resurrection of the dead, and the coming kingdom of God. The day of judgment is often referred to as the "day of Christ" (Phil. 1:10; 2:16) or "Day of the Lord" (1 Cor. 5:5; 1 Thess. 5:2; 2 Thess. 2:2; 2 Pet. 3:10). The Gospels point to Christ as the agent who will judge mankind (Matt. 16:27; 19:28; 25:31; Luke 9:26; 17:24; 22:69). However, in the judging sayings of the Gospels often Jesus addressed Jews as recipients of the coming judgment. At the time Christ warned individuals (Matt. 5:22) and towns (Matt. 10:15; Luke 10:14) of the coming judgment. When Christianity broke from Judaism, Christians were warned of the coming judgment (2 Tim. 4:8; Heb. 4:1-13; James 5:7-11; 1 Pet. 1:13-17). Certain apocalyptic texts warn that all persons will be judged at the last day (Rom. 2:1-16; Heb. 4:13; Jude 14-15; Rev. 20:10-15). The day of judgment will be a time for even the angelic beings to be judged as well (1 Cor. 6:3; Jude 6).

The day of judgment will be a time in which all of mankind throughout eternity will be judged. Thus the living and dead of all humanity shall stand and make an account to God (Acts 10:42; 2 Tim. 4:1; 1 Pet. 4:5). While the basis for salvation is in Christ alone (John 3:36), one who is committed to Christ will have deeds of service (Matt. 25:31-46; James 2:14-26; 1 John 2:3-6). These deeds of service will be shown for what they are on the day of judgment (1 Cor. 3:11-15). See *Day of the Lord; Escatology;*

J

Place at the gate of Dan (during the Iron Age) where it is thought a judge sat to hear cases.

Future Hope; Heaven; Hell; Resurrection; Second Coming.   *Joe Cathey*

JUDGMENT SEAT In Matt. 27:19 the raised platform or bench occupied by Pontius Pilate while he was deliberating the accusations made against Jesus and the sentence he would pronounce in connection with Jesus' case. According to Acts 18:12, Paul the apostle was brought before the judgment seat in Corinth. In these two instances the judgment seat is to be understood in its ordinary literal sense. In Rom. 14:10 and 2 Cor. 5:10 the judgment seat of Christ is a theological concept. Those verses stress that individuals are accountable to the Lord for their lives and must one day face Him in judgment. See *Cross, Crucifixion; Jerusalem; Jesus; Judgment Day.*

JUDGMENT, HALL OF 1. One of Solomon's buildings (1 Kings 7:7). See *Hall.* **2.** KJV expression for the *praetorium* (John 18:28). See *Praetorium.*

JUDGMENT, LAST See *Judgment Day.*

JUDGMENTS OF GOD See *Eschatology; Judgment Day; Retribution, Divine.*

JUDITH (Jū´ dĭth) Personal name meaning "Jewess." **1.** One of Esau's Hittite wives who caused grief for his parents because they feared the women would lead Esau away from his culture and his God (Gen. 26:34-35). **2.** Heroine of the book of Judith in the Apocrypha. A pious widow, she beguiled Holfernes, Nebuchadnezzar's general, and delivered her people from him by cutting off his head. See *Apocrypha.*

JUG Large, deep, earthenware or glass container with a narrow mouth and handle. Neither KJV nor RSV use the term. NIV uses "jug" in three passages: a water jug (1 Sam. 26:11-12,16; KJV, cruse; NRSV, jar); an oil jug (1 Kings 17:12,14,16; KJV, RSV, cruse; NRSV, jug); and an unspecified container (Jer. 48:12; KJV, bottle; RSV, jar). The NASB uses jug in six passages. At 1 Sam. 1:24; 10:3; 16:20; 25:18; 2 Sam. 16:1 the translation "skins" is preferable (NIV, NRSV). At Jer. 13:12 the RSV translation "jar" is preferred (NIV, skin). The KJV generally rendered the underlying Hebrew terms as bottle. See *Cruse; Flask; Pottery; Vessels and Utensils.*

JULIA (Jū´ lĭ á) Common Roman name. In Rom. 16:15 a Christian woman to whom Paul the apostle extended a greeting. Her name suggests she may have had some association with the imperial household. She may have been sister or wife to Philologus and a slave of the emperor.

JULIUS (Jū´ lĭ ŭs) Common Roman personal name. In Acts 27:1 a centurion of the Augustan cohort assigned the responsibility of escorting Paul to Rome. Though Paul was his prisoner, Julius treated the apostle with kindness. He allowed Paul to go ashore at Sidon to visit with friends. Later he saved the apostle's life by restraining the soldiers who wanted to kill Paul to keep him from escaping. See *Centurion; Paul.*

JULIUS CAESAR See *Rome and the Roman Empire.*

JUNIA (Jū´ nĭ á) or **JUNIAS** (Jū´ nĭ ás) Roman personal name, possibly a shortened form of Junianus. In Rom. 16:7 Paul extended greeting to a certain Junia, whom he referred to as his kinsman, his fellow prisoner, and an apostle. The form of the name is feminine. Nothing is known of this individual beyond what may be inferred from this verse. Some recent commentators see the person as a woman and possibly as the wife of Andronicus. See *Andronicus; Disciple.*

JUNIPER In 1 Kings 19:4 a tree under which Elijah the prophet rested as he fled the wrath of Jezebel. The same plant is mentioned in Job 30:4 and Ps. 120:4. The Hebrew word thus translated probably refers to a kind of shrub that grows in

J

the Arabian deserts. Modern translations read "broom." See *Broom Tree.*

JUPITER (Jū´ pĭ tēr) Latin name of Zeus, king of Greek gods. KJV translates Zeus as Jupiter (Acts 14:12-13). God worked through Paul to heal a crippled man at Lystra. The people responded by claiming the gods had come to earth. They named Barnabas, Zeus, or Jupiter. The priest of Jupiter tried to offer sacrifices to them. Paul used the opportunity for evangelistic preaching. KJV also inserts Jupiter in Acts 19:35, referring to the image of Artemis or Diana, the goddess for whose worship Ephesus was famous. The Greek says the image fell from heaven (HCSB, NRSV, NASB, REB, NIV, TEV). See *Greece.*

JUSHAB-HESED (Jū shăb-hē´ sĕd) Personal name meaning "mercy is brought back." Royal son of Zerubbabel and descendant of David, thus

The temple of Jupiter at Baalbek (Heliopolis).

a part of keeping messianic hope alive (1 Chron. 3:20). See *Zerubbabel.*

JUSTICE Order that God seeks to reestablish in His creation where all people receive the benefits of life with Him. As love is for the NT, so justice is the central ethical idea of the OT. The prevalence of the concept is sometimes missed by the reader due to a failure to realize the wide range of meaning in the Hebrew word *mishpat,* particularly in passages that deal with the material and social necessities of life.

Nature of Justice Justice has two major aspects. First, it is the standard by which penalties are assigned for breaking the obligations of the society. Second, justice is the standard by which the advantages of social life are handed out, including material goods, rights of participation, opportunities, and liberties. It is the standard for both punishment and benefits and thus can be spoken of as a plumb line. "I shall use justice as a plumbline and righteousness as a plummet" (Isa. 28:17, REB).

Often people think of justice in the Bible only in the first sense as God's wrath on evil. This aspect of justice indeed is present, such as the judgment mentioned in John 3:19. Often more vivid words like "wrath" are used to describe punitive justice (Rom. 1:18).

Justice in the Bible very frequently also deals with benefits. Cultures differ widely in determining the basis by which the benefits are to be justly distributed. For some it is by birth and nobility. For others the basis is might or ability or merit. On the other hand, it might simply be whatever is the law or whatever has been established by contracts. The Bible takes another possibility. Benefits are distributed according to need. Justice then is very close to love and grace. God "executes justice for the orphan and the widow, and shows His love for the alien by giving him food and clothing" (Deut. 10:18, NASB; cp. Hos. 10:12; Isa. 30:18).

Various needy groups are the recipients of justice. These groups include widows, fatherless, resident aliens (also called "sojourners" or "strangers"), wage earners, the poor, and prisoners, slaves, and the sick (Job 29:12-17; Ps. 146:7-9; Mal. 3:5). Each of these groups has specific needs that keep its members from being able to participate in aspects of the life of their commu-

J

nity. Even life itself might be threatened. Justice involves meeting those needs. The forces which deprive people of what is basic for community life are condemned as oppression (Mic. 2:2; Eccles. 4:1). To oppress is to use power for one's own advantage in depriving others of their basic rights in the community (Mark 12:40). To do justice is to correct that abuse and to meet those needs (Isa. 1:17). Injustice is depriving others of their basic needs or failing to correct matters when those rights are not met (Jer. 5:28; Job 29:12-17). Injustice is either a sin of commission or of omission.

The content of justice, the benefits which are to be distributed as basic rights in the community, can be identified by observing what is at stake in the passages in which "justice," "righteousness," and "judgment" occur. The needs which are met include land (Ezek. 45:6-9; cp. Mic. 2:2; 4:4) and the means to produce from the land, such as draft animals and millstones (Deut. 22:1-4; 24:6). These productive concerns are basic to securing other essential needs and thus avoiding dependency; thus the millstone is called the "life" of the person (Deut. 24:6). Other needs are those essential for mere physical existence and well being: food (Deut. 10:18; Ps. 146:7), clothing (Deut. 24:13), and shelter (Ps. 68:6; Job 8:6). Job 22:5-9,23; 24:1-12 decries the injustice of depriving people of each one of these needs, which are material and economic. The equal protection of each person in civil and judicial procedures is represented in the demand for due process (Deut. 16:18-20). Freedom from bondage is comparable to not being "in hunger, in thirst, in nakedness, and in the lack of all things" (Deut. 28:48 NASB).

Justice presupposes God's intention for people to be in community. When people had become poor and weak with respect to the rest of the community, they were to be strengthened so that they could continue to be effective members of the community—living with them and beside them (Lev. 25:35-36). Thus biblical justice restores people to community. By justice those who lacked the power and resources to participate in significant aspects of the community were to be strengthened so that they could. This concern in Lev. 25 is illustrated by the provision of the Year of Jubilee, in which at the end of the 50-year period land is restored to those who had lost it through sale or foreclosure of debts (v. 28).

Thus they regained economic power and were brought back into the economic community. Similarly, interest on loans was prohibited (v. 36) as a process that pulled people down, endangering their position in the community.

These legal provisions express a further characteristic of justice. Justice delivers; it does not merely relieve the immediate needs of those in dire straits (Ps. 76:9; Isa. 45:8; 58:11; 62:1-2). Helping the needy means setting them back on their feet, giving a home, leading to prosperity, restoration, ending the oppression (Pss. 68:5-10; 10:15-16; cp. 107; 113:7-9). Such thorough justice can be socially disruptive. In the Jubilee year as some receive back lands, others lose recently acquired additional land. The advantage to some is a disadvantage to others. In some cases the two aspects of justice come together. In the act of restoration, those who were victims of justice receive benefits while their exploiters are punished (1 Sam 2:7-10; cp. Luke 1:51-53; 6:20-26).

The Source of Justice As the sovereign Creator of the universe, God is just (Ps. 99:1-4; Gen. 18:25; Deut. 32:4; Jer. 9:24), particularly as the defender of all the oppressed of the earth (Pss. 76:9; 103:6; Jer. 49:11). Justice thus is universal (Ps. 9:7-9) and applies to each covenant or dispensation. Jesus affirmed for His day the centrality of the OT demand for justice (Matt. 23:23). Justice is the work of the NT people of God (James 1:27).

God's justice is not a distant external standard. It is the source of all human justice (Prov. 29:26; 2 Chron. 19:6,9). Justice is grace received and grace shared (2 Cor. 9:8-10).

The most prominent human agent of justice is the ruler. The king receives God's justice and is a channel for it (Ps. 72:1; cp. Rom. 13:1-2,4). There is not a distinction between a personal, voluntary justice and a legal, public justice. The same caring for the needy groups of the society is demanded of the ruler (Ps. 72:4; Ezek. 34:4; Jer. 22:15-16). Such justice was also required of pagan rulers (Dan. 4:27; Prov. 31:8-9).

Justice is also a central demand on all people who bear the name of God. Its claim is so basic that without it other central demands and provisions of God are not acceptable to God. Justice is required to be present with the sacrificial system (Amos 5:21-24; Mic. 6:6-8; Isa. 1:11-17; Matt. 5:23-24), fasting (Isa. 58:1-10), tithing (Matt. 23:23), obedience to the other commandments

(Matt. 19:16-21), or the presence of the temple of God (Jer. 7:1-7).

Justice in Salvation Apart from describing God's condemnation of sin, Paul used the language and meaning of justice to speak of personal salvation. "The righteousness of God" represents God in grace bringing into the community of God through faith in Christ those who had been outside of the people of God (particularly in Romans but cp. also Eph. 2:12-13). See *Government; Law; Poverty; Righteousness; Welfare.*

Stephen Charles Mott

JUSTIFICATION Divine, forensic act of God, based on the work of Christ upon the cross, whereby a sinner is pronounced righteous by the imputation of the righteousness of Christ. The doctrine of justification is developed most fully by the Apostle Paul as the central truth explaining how both Jew and Gentile can be made right before God on the exact same basis, that being faith in Jesus Christ. Without this divine truth, there can be no unity in the body of Christ, hence its centrality to Paul's theology of the Church and salvation.

Old Testament The OT functioned as the Scriptures of the primitive NT Church, so that one must identify the sources in the OT that gave rise to the understanding of the term "justification" (and the related terms "just" and "to justify"). Clearly a wide range of uses of "just" or "righteous" (both fully valid translations of the Hebrew *tsadiq* and the Greek *dikaios*) can be seen in the OT, including the description of men as "just" or "righteous" in God's sight (Job 1:1). However, a specific set of passages provides the clearest background of the apostolic understanding. These include Exod. 23:7, "Stay far away from a false accusation. Do not kill the innocent and the just, because I will not justify the guilty" (HCSB), where the legal standing of the person described as "righteous" is in view. To "acquit" here is to "justify." This is clearly a forensic or legal context, the giving of a judgment. Deuteronomy 25:1 also uses the same language: "If there is a dispute between men, they are to go to court, and the judges will hear their case. They will clear the innocent and condemn the guilty," where the law court is again the context and "to justify" is clearly to render a verdict. Likewise Prov. 17:15 and Isa. 5:23 use these same terms in a forensic or judicial context. These uses show

that the apostolic use in the NT is not foreign to the OT Scriptural background.

The apostles were convinced the truth of justification by faith as a free and divine act of God based solely upon the exercise of faith and nothing more was not only consistent with the divine revelation of the OT, but they specifically drew from those Scriptures a positive witness to their teaching. Paul focused especially upon the key passage regarding Abraham, "Abram believed the LORD, and He credited it to him as righteousness" (Gen. 15:6 HCSB). This passage forms the central core of Paul's defense of his doctrine of justification in Rom. 4.

New Testament The centrality of the doctrine of justification comes out naturally in the writings of Paul, as it fell to him to explicate the ground of the believer's relationship to God in light of the relationship of Jew and Gentile in the one body of Christ. The conflict brought about by the Judaizers' insistence upon law keeping and circumcision forced the apostle to define with precision the basis of forgiveness and just how it is that any person, Jew or Gentile, can have peace with God. This explains the appearance of the doctrine primarily in those works directly related to the definition and defense of the gospel (Romans and Galatians).

The meaning of the family of Greek terms translated variously as "to justify" or "to declare righteous" is established clearly by its usage in the key passages in the NT. The term does not mean "to subjectively change into a righteous person" but instead means "to declare righteous," specifically, to declare righteous upon the act of faith based upon the work of another, the divine substitute, Jesus Christ. Justification then involves both the forensic, legal declaration of the righteousness of the believer as well as the imputation of the righteousness of Christ as the grounds and basis of their acceptance. The fact that it is the righteousness of Christ which is imputed to the believer accounts for the resulting perfection of the relationship between the believer and God: "Therefore, since we have been declared righteous by faith, we have peace with God through our Lord Jesus Christ" (Rom. 5:1 HCSB).

Paul's epistle to the churches of Galatia presents justification by faith as the focal point of attack by those he describes as "false brothers" (Gal. 2:4). The proclamation of a curse at the beginning of the epistle (1:6-8) places the entire discussion at the highest level of importance, and Paul's insistence that he is speaking of that which is the "truth of the gospel" (2:5) in contrast to a false gospel likewise focuses attention upon the argument he presents. The essence of his argument is placed in the context of his encounter with Peter and the Judaizers in Antioch. When Peter and even Barnabas withdrew from having table fellowship with the Gentiles in the fellowship, Paul recognized this action reflected an idea that one could be "more" Christian than someone else due to something one did, in this case, because one was circumcised. This would introduce a tiered fellowship of lesser and greater Christians. It is in this context that Paul insists upon justification by faith in opposition to justification by any work of righteousness, for faith, by nature, places all men on the same level and allows for no gradation. Hence, justification by "works of the law" is specifically denied and is instead contrasted to justification by faith (2:16). The very grace of God is nullified if there is any means of righteousness outside of faith in Christ, and specifically, through works of law (2:21). Instead, by citing the all encompassing scope of the law, the apostle proves that righteousness was never intended to come by law keeping (3:10,12). Instead, Paul derives from the testimony of Hab. 2:4, "the righteous man will live by faith," the conclusion that no one is justified before God by law keeping (3:11). Christ redeems from the curse of the law by His death and that blessing is passed on, not through the avenue of law but that of faith (3:13-17). So strong is Paul's condemnation of the opposite position that he describes it as "bondage" (5:1) and being cut off from grace and from Christ (5:4). The strongest language used in all the NT is employed by the apostle against those who added a single requirement of "good works" and "law keeping" to the gospel of grace.

The letter to the Romans comprises the single longest, thought-out presentation of the gospel in all of sacred Scripture. Justification takes up the focus of chapters 3–5. While the discussion in Galatians is marked by the passion of debate, Romans presents a relentless and logical argument, drawn from scriptural foundations. After establishing the universal sinfulness of man in Rom. 1:18–3:19, Paul provides an over arching summary of the truth of justification in 3:20-31,

followed by his scriptural defense, drawn primarily from the life of Abraham, in chapter four. He insists that no one will ever be justified by works of law before God (3:19-20). Instead, God's righteousness comes through "faith in Jesus Christ ... given to all who believe" (3:22), whether they are Jew or Gentile. God does not justify as a result of man's actions but instead justifies "freely" as a gift by His grace" (3:24). The Father can justify believers because of the redemption that flows from the work of Christ (3:25-26), so that Paul can conclude that justification is wholly the work of God, obtained solely by faith alone (3:28).

These broad assertions are proven through the example of Abraham, who was justified by faith without works of law in Gen. 15:6. The contrast is drawn between the "working" one who receives a wage (4:4) and the "not-working one" who instead believes in the God who justifies (4:5). Paul quotes from Ps. 32 and interprets these words to mean that God credits righteousness apart from works and then proves this by rhetorically asking if this mercy was shown to Abraham before, or after, he received circumcision. Since he was justified before he was circumcised, Paul concludes that the promise of Gen. 15 cannot be undone by the giving of law that comes afterward. In the same way, we are justified by faith and not by the observance of law.

Upon completion of his biblical defense, Paul can conclude that the relationship described by the word "justified" is one that brings true and lasting peace between God and man (Rom. 5:1). This is the essence of biblical justification: right relationship between God and man. But the beauty of justification by faith is seen in the fact that it is God who establishes this relationship through Christ, so that it is not merely a temporary state that can be destroyed by man's actions but is instead a state that results in eternal peace between the redeemed and the Redeemer.

James White

JUSTUS (Jŭs´ tŭs) Common Jewish personal name. **1.** In Acts 1:23 the surname of Joseph Barsabbas, one of two men put forward to replace Judas Iscariot among the Twelve. **2.** A pious man, probably a Roman citizen, whose home joined the synagogue in Corinth (Acts 18:7). Paul left the synagogue and moved into the home of Titius Justus (KJV omits Titius following some Greek manuscripts). Some scholars equate him with Titus (following some Greek manuscripts), while more identify him with Gaius of Rom. 16:23. Neither identification is more than a scholarly guess based on similarity of name. **3.** Surname of a fellow minister with Paul (Col. 4:11).

JUTTAH (Jŭt´ tah) Place-name meaning "spread out." Town in hill country of tribal territory of Judah (Josh. 15:55) given to the Levites (Josh. 21:16). It may be located at modern Yatta, six miles southwest of Hebron.

JUVENILE DELINQUENCY Juvenile delinquency was treated very seriously by the writers of the Bible because rebellion among children, in disrupting the authority structure of the family, tore at the very fabric of society. A well-ordered family prevented trouble outside the home which in turn ensured a stable society (cp. Eph. 6:2-3).

God expects parents to control their children and children to obey their parents (Exod. 20:12; Eph. 6:1-4; 1 Tim. 3:4) yet realizes that this is not always the case (Isa. 3:5; Ezek. 22:7). The sons of Eli (1 Sam. 2:22-25; cp. 8:3), the boys who jeered at Elisha (2 Kings 2:23-24), and the prodigal son (Luke 15:12-13) are all examples of juvenile delinquency. The Mosaic law categorized striking (Exod. 21:15), cursing, (Exod. 21:17) and dishonoring (Deut. 27:16) one's parents as acts of familial rebellion and mandated that a son who refused correction should be stoned in public (Deut. 21:18-21).

In spite of the responsibility placed on parents for child rearing (Deut. 6:7; Prov. 13:24; 19:18; 22:6; Eph. 6:1-4), the Bible recognizes that, ultimately, children are responsible for their own actions (Ezek. 18:10-13). Jesus used the example of the prodigal son to teach that everyone stands delinquent before God and must come to Him for forgiveness (Luke 15:11-32).

Paul H. Wright

J

K

The Gihon Spring in the Kidron Valley.

KAB (Kăb) A measure of volume mentioned only in 2 Kings 6:25. Descriptions in ancient sources indicate a kab would be slightly larger than a quart. See *Weights and Measures.*

KABZEEL (Kăb´ zə ĕl) Place-name meaning "may God gather"; same as Jekabzeel in Neh. 11:25. Located in the southeast part of Judah near the border of Edom (Josh. 15:21). The home of Benaiah, an officer under David and Solomon (2 Sam. 23:20; 1 Chron. 11:22). One of the towns reoccupied by the Jews after the return from the exile (Neh. 11:25).

KADESH (Kā´ dĕsh) or **KADESH-BARNEA** (Kā´ dĕsh-bär nē´ à) Place-name meaning "consecrated." The site where the Hebrews stayed for most of the 38 years after leaving Mount Sinai and before entering the promised land. The OT locates it between the Wilderness of Paran and the Wilderness of Zin (Num. 13:3-21,26). Moses sent out the 12 spies into Canaan from Kadesh-barnea (Num. 13:3-21,26). The Hebrews also attempted their abortive southern penetration into Canaan from there (Num. 13:26; 14:40-45). Kadesh-barnea is mentioned as a site where Abraham fought the Amalekites (Gen. 14:7) and as the southern border of the tribe of Judah (Josh. 15:3).

The actual site of Kadesh-barnea has been much debated, but the two most frequently mentioned sites are Ein-Qedeis and Ein el-Qudeirat. Both of these sites are in the northern part of the Sinai Peninsula, and both have a spring. Most scholars today accept Ein el-Qudeirat because of its abundance of water (the largest springs and oasis in northern Sinai). Ein el-Qudeirat is located on the crossroads of two major roads of antiquity—the road from Edom to Egypt and the road from the Red Sea to the Negev and southern Canaan, later southern Judah. The location on the road from Egypt to Edom would fit well the biblical context of Kadesh-barnea as the oasis home for the Hebrews during the wilderness-wandering period. Likewise, the location of Kadesh-barnea along the north-south road may explain the rationale for attempting the invasion of Canaan at Arad, since Arad lay north of Kadesh-barnea on that road.

Excavations of Ein el-Qudeirat have shown major fortresses dating from the period of Solomon to the fall of the monarchy (10th century B.C. to sixth century B.C.), but no remains from the period of the wilderness wandering

Iron Age fortress in the area of ancient Kadesh-barnea.

K

have been found to date. This raises the question about the identity of the site of Kadesh-barnea. The site has not been fully excavated, however, and as yet no better alternative site has come to light.   *Joel F. Drinkard, Jr.*

KADESH-MERIBAH (Kā´ dĕsh-mĕr´ ĭ bäh) TEV transliteration of a phrase from the Hebrew text of Ezek. 47:19. The name is translated in the KJV as "the waters of strife in Kadesh" (Num. 20:2-13; Deut. 32:51; cp. Exod. 17:1-7). RSV has "Meribath-kadesh," and NIV has "Meribah Kadesh" at Deut. 32:51; Ezek. 47:19. NASB has "Meribah-kadesh" at Deut. 32:51 and "Meri-

bath-kadesh" at Ezek. 47:19. TEV has "When you were at the waters of Meribah, near the town of Kadesh" at Deut. 32:51. The same town as Kadesh-barnea. See *Kadesh-barnea.*

KADMIEL (Kăd´ mĭ ĕl) Personal name meaning "God is of old" or "God goes before." **1.** Levite who returned from the Babylonian exile with Zerubbabel. A representative of the line of Hodaviah (Ezra 2:40; Neh. 7:43, Hodevah), also known as the line of Judah (Ezra 3:9). Helped rebuild the temple. **2.** Levite who helped Ezra in the reaffirmation of the covenant after the return from the exile (Neh. 9:4-5). **3.** Levite

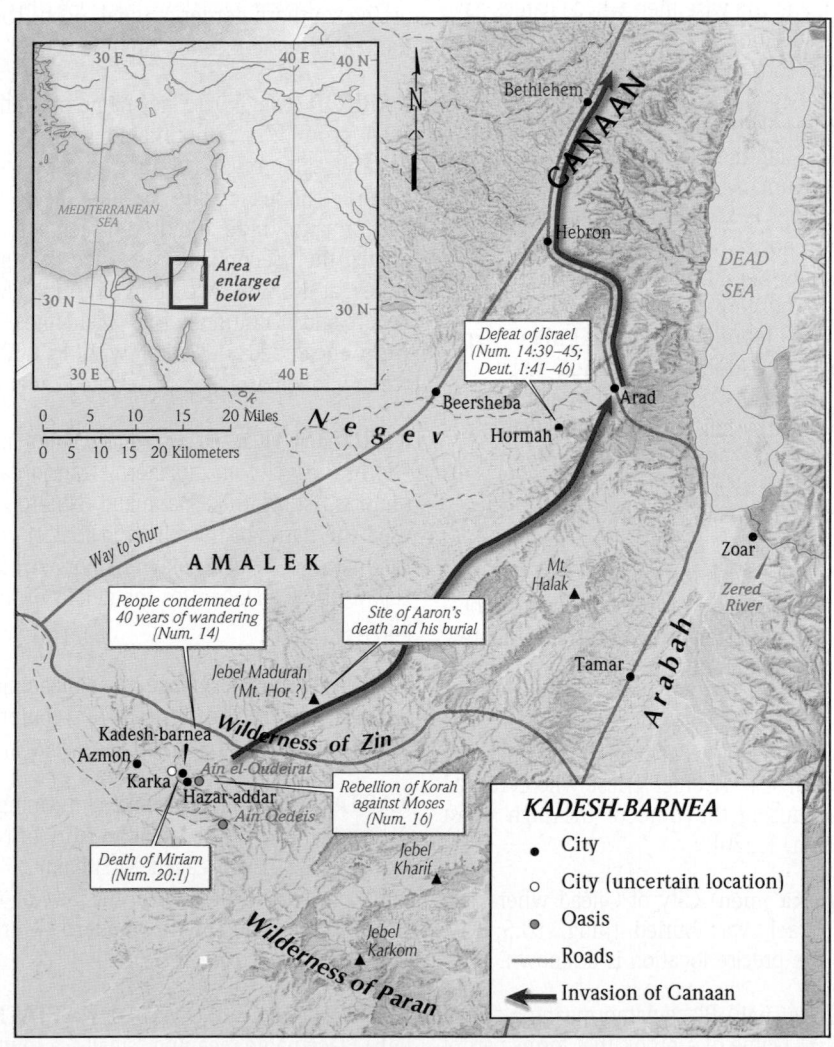

who signed the covenant after the exile (Neh. 10:9). The relationship between these persons is unclear. They may all represent the same person or be father and son.

KADMONITE (Kăd´ mon īt) Name of a people meaning "easterners." Tribe God promised (Gen. 15:19) Israel would dispossess. They probably inhabited the Syro-Arabian desert between Palestine-Syria and the Euphrates—which is to say areas to the east of Canaan. Their names often have Arabian associations. They may be related to the "children of the east" mentioned in Judg. 6:33. The sons of the concubines of Abraham were sent to live in the "east country" (Kedem) away from Isaac (Gen. 25:6). Job (Job 1:3), the camel-riding Midianite kings (Judg. 8:10-12,21,26), and the wise men whose names have Arabian associations (1 Kings 4:30-31) are all described as sons of the east.

KAIN (Kăn) Tribe and place-name meaning "smith." **1.** Clan mentioned in the fourth oracle of Balaam (Num. 24:22; KJV, Kenite). Adam and Eve's son Cain is spelled the same in Hebrew, and many scholars regard Cain as the ancestors of the Kenites. See *Kenites*. **2.** City southeast of Hebron in southern Judah (Josh. 15:57; KJV, NEB, Cain). Identified with Khirbet Yaqin. According to Arabian tradition Abraham watched the destruction of Sodom and Gomorrah from a nearby hill. Kain was a settlement of the Kenites.

KAIWAN (Kī´ wän) Babylonian god (Amos 5:26). KJV transliterates the name as Chiun. As is often the case when foreign gods were referred to, the original vowels of the name were probably replaced with the vowels of the Hebrew word for "abomination." See *Chiun; Gods, Pagan; Sakkuth*.

KALLAI (Kăl´ lā ī) Personal name meaning "swift" or "light." A chief priest who returned from exile during the time of the high priest Joiakim (Neh. 12:20).

KAMON (Kā´ mŏn) City of Gilead where Jair, judge of Israel, was buried (Judg. 10:5; KJV, Camon). The precise location is unknown.

KANAH (Kā´ nah) Place-name meaning "place of reeds." **1.** Name of a brook that forms part of the boundary between Ephraim and Manasseh (Josh. 16:8; 17:9). Some of the cities of Manasseh, however, were south of the brook Kanah (Josh. 16:9). Identified by some with the modern Wadi Qanah. **2.** City on the northern border of Asher (Josh. 19:28). Identified with modern Qana, about six miles southeast of Tyre. Not to be confused with Cana of the NT.

KAREAH (Ká rē´ ah) Personal name meaning "bald." Father of Johanan and Jonathan during the time of Jeremiah (Jer. 40:8,13,15-16; 41:11,13-14,16; 42:1,8; 43:2,4-5; 2 Kings 25:23 KJV, Careah).

KARKA (Kär´ ká) or **KARKAA** (Kär kā´ á) Place-name meaning "ground" or "floor." A city on the southern border of Judah (Josh. 15:3; KJV, Karkaa). Precise location unknown.

KARKOR (Kär´ kôr) Place-name meaning "soft, level ground." A mountainous village in the eastern region of Gilead during the period of the judges. The exact site has not been located. Gideon and three hundred Israelite men conducted their second surprise attack on the Midianites at Karkor. According to Judg. 8:10-11, Zebah and Zalmunna, two Midianites leaders, were encamped at Karkor with 15,000 troops when Gideon attacked and routed them.

KARNAIM (Kär nā ĭm) Place-name meaning "horns." A city in northern Transjordan. The same as Ashteroth-karnaim and Ashtaroth. Amos used the name of this city and that of Lo-Debar to make a word play (Amos 6:13). See *Ashtaroth; Lo-Debar* (for the details of the word play).

KARTAH (Kär´ tah) Place-name meaning "city." Levitical city in the territory of Zebulun (Josh. 21:34). Location unknown. See *Levitical Cities*.

KARTAN (Kär´ tăn) Place-name meaning "city." A Levitical city in the tribal territory of Naphtali (Josh. 21:32). Also called Kiriathaim (1 Chron. 6:76). It was located near the Sea of Galilee. Usually identified with modern Khirbet el-Qureiyeh. See *Levitical Cities*.

KATTAH (Kăt´ tah) (NASB) or **KATTATH** (Kăt´ tăth) Place-name meaning "small." A town in the tribal territory of Zebulun (Josh. 19:15). Probably the same as Kitron (Judg. 1:30). See *Kitron.*

KATYDID (Lev. 11:22 NIV) See *Insects.*

KEBAR (Kē´ bär) (NIV) See *Chebar.*

KEDAR (Kē´ dár) Personal name meaning "mighty" or "swarthy" or "black." The second son of Ishmael and a grandson of Abraham (Gen. 25:13; 1 Chron. 1:29). The name occurs later in the Bible presumably as a reference to a tribe that took its name from Kedar. Little concrete information is known about the group, however. Apparently the descendants of Kedar occupied the area south of Palestine and east of Egypt (Gen. 25:18). They may best be described as nomadic, living in tents (Ps. 120:5; Song 1:5) and raising sheep and goats (Isa. 60:7; Jer. 49:28-29,32), as well as camels, which they sold as far away as Tyre (Ezek. 27:21).

The Kedarites were led by princes (Ezek. 27:21) and were famous for their warriors, particularly their archers (Isa. 21:17). They evidently were of some importance during the time of Isaiah (Isa. 21:16). See *Abraham; Ishmael.*

Hugh Tobias

KEDEMAH (Kĕd´ ə mah) Personal and tribal name meaning "eastward." The last son of Ishmael (Gen. 25:15; 1 Chron. 1:31). Probably head of an Arabian tribe of the same name. Probably considered among the Kadmonites. See *Kadmonites.*

KEDEMOTH (Kĕd´ ə mŏth) Place-name meaning "ancient places" or "eastern places." One of the Levitical cities in the tribal territory of Reuben assigned to the family of Merari (Josh. 13:18; 21:37; 1 Chron. 6:79). From the wilderness nearby, Moses sent a delegation to Sihon, king of the Amorites, requesting passage through his country (Deut. 2:26). The city is associated with either Kasr ez-Za'feran or Khirbet er Remeil. Both of these cities are in the same vicinity and were in existence in Abraham's day. See *Levitical Cities.*

KEDESH (Kē´ dĕsh) Place-name meaning "sacred place" or "sanctuary." **1.** A city in the southern part of Judah (Josh. 15:23). Probably the same as Kadesh-barnea. See *Kadesh-barnea.* **2.** Canaanite town in eastern Galilee defeated by

Joshua (Josh. 12:22). The town was allotted to Naphtali (Josh. 19:32,37) and was called Kedesh in Naphtali (Judg. 4:6). It was also called Kedesh in Galilee and given to the Gershonite Levites as one of their cities (Josh. 20:7; 21:32). Kedesh in Naphtali was the home of Barak (Judg. 4:6) and the place where Deborah and Barak gathered their forces for battle (Judg. 4:1-10). Heber the Kenite pitched his tent in the vicinity where Sisera met his death at the hands of Jael, Heber's wife (Judg. 4:21; 5:24-27). Kedesh in Naphtali was captured by Tiglath-pileser III during the reign of Pekah of Israel. The inhabitants were exiled to Assyria (2 Kings 15:29). Usually identified with modern Khirbet Qedish, about two miles south of Tiberias. See *Levitical Cities.* **3.** City in Issachar allotted to the Gershomite Levites (1 Chron. 6:72). The town is also called Kishon (Josh. 21:28 KJV; Kishion in other versions). It has been suggested that "Kedesh in Issachar" may have arisen from a misreading of "Kishon" for "Kedesh." The site is uncertain, perhaps modern Tell Abu Qudeis, about two miles southeast of Megiddo.   *Phil Logan*

KEDESH IN NAPHTALI or **KEDESH-NAPH-TALI** See *Kedesh 2; Naphtali.*

KEDORLAOMER (Kĕd ôr lā´ ō mēr) (NIV) See *Chedorlaomer.*

KEHELATHAH (Kē hə lā´ thah) Place-name meaning "assembly." One of the desert camps of the Israelites during the wilderness wandering (Num. 33:22-23). Location unknown.

KEILAH (Kə ī´ lah) Personal and place-name, perhaps meaning "fortress." **1.** Descendant of Caleb (1 Chron. 4:19). **2.** Fortified city in the lowland plain (Shephelah) of the territory of Judah identified with modern Khirbet Qila, about eight miles northwest of Hebron and 18 miles southwest of Jerusalem. David rescued the city from a Philistine attack but later withdrew fearing the populace would hand him over to Saul (1 Sam. 23:1-13). The city was rebuilt by the returning exiles (Neh. 3:17-18). One of the traditional sites of the burial place of Habakkuk.

KELAIAH (Kə lī´ ah) Personal name, perhaps meaning "Yahweh has dishonored." One of the Levites who divorced his foreign wife during the

K

time of Ezra. Also identified as Kelita (Ezra 10:23). See *Kelita.*

KELAL (Kē′ lăl) (NIV) See *Chelal.*

KELITA (Kə lī′ tá) Personal name probably meaning "crippled, dwarfed one," but perhaps also meaning "adopted one." A Levite who assisted in interpreting the Law when it was read to the assembly of the people during the time of Ezra (Neh. 8:7) and who participated in the sealing of the covenant (Neh. 10:10). Kelita is perhaps a nickname for Kelaiah mentioned in Ezra 10:23. There Kelaiah (that is, the dwarf) gave up his foreign wife in accordance with the instructions of Ezra.

KELUB (Kē′ lŭb) (NIV) See *Chelub.*

KELUHI (Kĕl′ ū hī) (NIV, REB) See *Chelluh.*

KEMUEL (Kĕm′ ū) Personal name of uncertain meaning; perhaps meaning "helper of God" or "assembly of God." **1.** Father of Aram, and the son of Abraham's brother Nahor (Gen. 22:21). **2.** Son of Shiphtan and representative of Ephraim in the division of Canaan among the tribes of Israel (Num. 34:24). **3.** Father of Hashabiah, a Levite during the time of David (1 Chron. 27:17).

KENAANAH (Kĕ nā′ á nah) (NIV, REB) See *Chenaanah.*

KENAN (Kē′ nán) Personal name of uncertain meaning. Grandson of Adam, son of Enosh, and father of Mahalaleel (Gen. 5:9-14; KJV, Cainan; 1 Chron. 1:2). Listed as Cainan among the ancestors of Jesus (Luke 3:37). See *Cainan; Enosh.*

KENANI (Kə nā′ nī) (NIV, REB) See *Chenani.*

KENANIAH (Kĕ ná nī′ ah) (NIV, REB) See *Chenaniah.*

KENATH (Kē′ năth) Place-name of uncertain meaning. City in eastern Gilead taken by Nobah and given his name (Num. 32:42). The city was known as Kenath at a later time when it fell into the hands of Aram and Geshur (1 Chron. 2:23). The city is usually identified with the modern Qanawat in el-Hauran. Kenath was the easternmost city of the Decapolis. See *Decapolis.*

KENAZ (Kē′ năz) Personal name of unknown meaning. **1.** Son of Eliphaz and grandson of Esau, he was a clan chieftain of the Edomites (Gen. 36:11,15). **2.** Father of Othniel, Israel's first-mentioned judge (Josh. 15:17; Judg. 1:13) and a brother to Caleb; also was the father of Seriah (1 Chron. 4:13). **3.** Grandson of Caleb and son of Elah (1 Chron. 4:15). The Kenizzites are thought to be the people of Kenaz. Their land was promised to Abraham's offspring (Gen. 15:19). They were a nomadic people from the southeast who inhabited Hebron, Debir, and parts of the Negev. They are variously associated with Judah, Edom, and the Kenites. See *Kenizzite.*

KENEZITE (Kē′ nĕz īt) (KJV) See *Kenizzite.*

KENITES (Kĕn′ īts) Name of a tribe meaning "smith." Nomadic tribe, probably of blacksmiths, whose land, along with that of the Kadmonites and Kenizzites, God promised to Abraham (Gen. 15:19). Their home was the southeastern hill country of Judah. Balaam pronounced doom and captivity for them (Num. 24:21-22). Moses' father-in-law Jethro is called a "priest of Midian" (Exod. 3:1) and is described as a Kenite (Judg. 1:16). This association suggests a close relationship between the Kenites and Midianites. Some scholars have suggested that Moses learned about the worship of Yahweh through Kenite influence, but this theory contradicts the biblical witness.

The Kenites lived among the Amalekites during the time of Saul. The Kenites "showed kindness" to Israel during the time of the exodus (1 Sam. 15:6). The Chronicler includes the Kenite, Hemath, the father of the Rechabites, as one of the ancestors of the tribe of Judah (1 Chron. 2:55). No mention is made of the Kenites in the late history of Israel suggesting to many scholars that they disappeared or lost their identity shortly after 1000 B.C.

The word "Kenite" is probably related to an Aramaic word that means "smith." Some scholars think the traveling blacksmiths of the Middle Ages resembled the Kenites. This would account for their relations with different peoples. In addition to their nomadic character, the biblical evidence also indicates that the Kenites were never completely absorbed by another people but maintained a separate existence throughout their history. See *Amalekite; Cain; Jethro; Midian, Midianites; Moses.*

KENIZZITE (Kĕn´ ĭz zīt) Clan name of uncertain meaning. Clan that God promised Abraham the Israelites would dispossess (Gen. 15:19). The Kenizzites lived in the Negev, the southern desert region of Judah, before the conquest of the land by Joshua. The tribe of Judah absorbed some of the Kenizzites while Edom absorbed others. The Kenizzites were probably related to the Kenites from whom they would have learned the craft of metalworking (1 Chron. 4:13-14). They probably derived their name from Kenaz— a descendant of Esau (Gen. 36:11,15)—who is listed among the Edomite chieftains (Gen. 36:42). Jephunneh the Kenizzite may have married a woman of the tribe of Judah. Their son was Caleb (Num. 32:12; Josh. 14:6,14; 15:13). See *Kenaz; Kenites.*

KENOSIS View asserting that the eternal Son of God by virtue of the incarnation gave up some or all of the divine attributes which were incommensurate with a fully human existence. This view is primarily based on Phil. 2:5-11, especially verse 7, which states that Christ "emptied Himself." The idea of self-emptying is taken from the Greek verb *kenoo* which means "make empty."

Other Scriptures cited in support of this thesis are Mark 13:32 that shows Christ's ignorance of the time of the end and John 11:34 seeming to show Jesus' lack of omniscience, as He did not know where Lazarus lay.

Although, as originally construed, the kenosis view of Christ sought to do full justice to the real humanity of Jesus, in reality it is a serious assault on the true deity of Jesus Christ. Most evangelicals have resisted the kenotic view and have replaced it with what may be termed a subkenotic view stating that what Christ laid aside in the incarnation was not some or all of the divine attributes such as omniscience, omnipotence, and omnipresence. Instead, what Christ "emptied Himself" of was the independent use of these attributes in order to live a normal human life. His dependence on the Father for strength and wisdom is found in such passages as John 5:19,30 and 6:57. Also, in Matt. 12:22-30 Jesus is seen casting out demons by the Holy Spirit (Matt. 4:1; Mark 1:12; Luke 4:1). No doubt this is a valiant attempt to safeguard the full humanity of Jesus Christ, while also maintaining His full deity which Scripture clearly affirms (John 1:1-14; 8:58; 1 John 5:20; Rom. 9:5). The problem remains, however, whether it is truly successful. In light of Paul's clear affirmation that in Christ all the fullness of the deity dwells bodily (Col. 2:9), one must try to reconcile this very high and early Christology with the subkenotic theological understanding of Phil. 2:5-11. This appears impossible.

An alternative reading of the Phil. 2:5-11 passage affords a solution which discounts all types of kenotic doctrine concerning Christ. The real concern of Paul in Phil. 2 is not a preincarnate Christ who "empties Himself" in the incarnation, thereby equating the kenosis with his incarnation. Rather, the already incarnate Christ (see Phil. 2:5) is referred to as doing something with the expression "emptied Himself" (*heauton ekenosen*). Paul is thinking in scriptural categories, having Isaiah's prophecies concerning the servant of Yahweh in (Phil. 2:10-11 with Isa. 45:23). The words "emptied Himself" suggest that the incarnate Christ is to pour out His life, having taken a position of a servant and (already) the likeness of humanity, as a fulfillment of Isaiah's conceptual parallel in Isa. 53:12: "poured out Himself to death" (NASB). To this Paul adds "even to death on a cross" (Phil. 2: 8 HCSB).

In this passage the incarnation is the presupposition of the kenosis. A further comparison of Phil. 2:9 with Isa. 52:13 shows this "servant" section to be Paul's source material throughout this wonderful christological passage. A high Christology can therefore be maintained in this passage. For Paul the incarnation was an addition not a subtraction. Human nature was added to the person of the Son of God. Jesus Christ was not less than God; He was (and is) more. As the God-Man, Christ Jesus gave His life in obedience to the Father as a ransom for many (Mark 10:45). See *Christ, Christology; Incarnation.*

Doros Zachariades

KEPHAR-AMMONI (Kē phär-Ăm´ mō nī) (NIV, REB) See *Chephar-Ammoni.*

KEPHIRAH (Kə phī´ rah) (NIV, REB) See *Chephirah.*

KERAN (Kē´ răn) (NIV) See *Cheran.*

K

KERCHIEFS KJV translation of the Hebrew word translated as "veils" in modern translations of Ezek. 13:18,21. Ezekiel compares the kerchiefs or veils used by women who prophesied "from their own inspiration" (v. 17 NASB) to nets used to catch birds. According to this comparison, the kerchiefs were like nets used to catch the souls of persons. God declared through Ezekiel that he would free His people from the snares these women set for them.

KERE-KETHIB (Kĕ rā-kĕ thēv´) Transliteration of Hebrew terms meaning "read" and "written." The terms represent notations made in the margin of the Hebrew text by early scribes called Masoretes. In such cases the text has the written consonants of the traditional text, but the scribes had placed vowel points in the text indicating how the word should be read. In the margin of the text stand the consonants of the word to be read. An example is the perpetual *kere* involving God's personal name, where the Hebrew text contains the consonants *yhwh* with the vowels *a, o, a* from *adonai*, the Hebrew word for Lord in which *i* is actually a Hebrew consonant. The textual margin would read *'dni*, the consonants of *adonai*. How such readings developed in the history of the text is not known. They may have been early attempts to correct a text known to be incorrectly copied. They may have sought to make the text read in worship by the community conform to a standard written text. It may have been an attempt to record known differences between Hebrew texts at the time of the copyist. Some examples may have been theologically motivated, as the change in the divine name warned the reader not to pronounce the sacred name but to replace it with *adonai* or Lord.

KEREN-HAPPUCH (Kĕr ĕn-hăp´ pŭk) Personal name meaning "paint-horn," that is, "cosmetic box." The youngest daughter born to Job after his restoration to prosperity (Job 42:14).

KERETHITES (Kĕr´ ə thīts) (NIV, REB) See *Cherethites*.

KERIOTH (Kē´ rĭ·ŏth) Place-name meaning "cities." A fortified city of Moab (Jer. 48:24,41; Amos 2:2 [KJV, Kirioth]). Kerioth may be identical to Ar, the ancient capital of Moab, since Kerioth was treated as the capital of Moab by

Amos (2:2). Judas, the disciple of Jesus, may have been from Kerioth. Many scholars take the designation "Iscariot" to be derived from the Hebrew meaning "man of Kerioth." See *Iscariot*.

KERIOTH-HEZRON (Kē rĭ·ŏth-hĕz´ rŏn) Place-name representing one or perhaps two cities. KJV uses the Hebrew to refer to two cities in Josh. 15:25—thus, Kerioth and Hezron. Some scholars still follow this. If this is a reference to two cities, Kerioth would be identified with the Kerioth of Jer. 48:24; Amos 2:2. Hezron would be identified with the city of Hazor mentioned in Josh. 15:23, a city in the south of Judah near Kadesh-barnea (Josh. 15:3). Many scholars, however, take Kerioth-hezron to refer to a village of Judah in the Negev district of Beersheba and identify it with modern Khirbet el-Qaryatein, about four miles south of Maon. See *Hazor; Kerioth*.

KERITH (Kē´ rĭth) (NIV, REB) See *Cherith*.

KEROS (Kē´ rŏs) Personal name meaning "bent." One of the temple servants whose descendants returned from the exile with Zerubbabel (Ezra 2:44; Neh. 7:47).

KERUB (Kē´ rŭb) (NIV, REB) See *Cherub*.

KERYGMA (Kə·rĭg´ mȧ) Transliteration of the Greek *kerugma*, "the content of what is preached"; "the message"; closely connected with the act of preaching. The word occurs eight times in the NT (Matt. 12:41; Luke 11:32; Rom. 16:25; 1 Cor. 1:21; 2:4; 15:14; 2 Tim. 4:17; Titus 1:3). The verb form is *kerusso*. The one proclaiming, announcing, preaching is a *kerux*, a herald or preacher (1 Tim. 2:7; 2 Tim. 1:11).

Repentance comes, God saves those who believe (1 Cor. 1:21), believers are strengthened and confirmed (Rom. 16:25) through the message preached (Matt. 12:41; Luke 11:32). Foundational to preaching in the NT is utter dependence on the Spirit of God to accomplish its ends (1 Cor. 2:4-5).

The message God uses is about Jesus. Preaching in Acts is clear. In Him prophecy and promise find fulfillment (2:25-28,30-31,34-35; 13:32-33), the Messianic age has dawned, and the kingdom of God has come (2:16). Though attested by God (2:22), He was unjustly condemned (2:23,26; 13:28); though "the Holy and

Righteous One" (3:14), and "the Prince of Life" (3:15), and altogether undeserving of such treatment, He was hung on a cross (5:30) and put to death by crucifixion (10:39). God has raised Him from the dead (3:15; 4:10; 5:30; 10:40; 17:18,31). The execution has been reversed. God has exalted Jesus to His right hand, the place of honor and authority (2:33). Though despised by men, He is now Prince and Savior (5:31) and has sent the Holy Spirit (2:33; 5:32). Faith in His name saves (3:16; 4:10). Salvation is in no one else (4:12); He alone can grant repentance and forgiveness of sins (5:31; 10:43; 13:38-39). All who hear "all about this life" (5:20), "the message of this salvation" (13:26), are called on to "pay attention" (2:14), to "listen" (2:22) and "know with certainty" (2:36) their truth. The only option is to "repent" (2:38; 3:19), "be baptized" (2:38), "and turn back" (3:19). The call of the kerygma is "listen" (13:16) and "beware" (13:40), for to reject Jesus is to perish (13:41).

The kerygma is not limitable to a few common elements from passages where the word appears. Not a bare outline followed as an evangelistic method, it is rather the rich, powerful and comprehensive proclamation of what God has done in Christ. See *Gospel.*

Spencer Haygood

KESALON (Kĕs´ à·lŏn) (NIV, REB) See *Chesalon.*

KESED (Kē´ sĕd) (NIV, REB) See *Chesed; Kindness.*

KESIL (Kē´ sĭl) (NIV, REB) See *Chesil.*

KESITAH (Kə sē´ tà) (RSV) Transliteration of Hebrew meaning "part, measure, piece of money." Jacob paid 100 kesitahs for land near Shechem (Gen. 33:19; cp. Josh. 24:32). The earliest Greek translation translated kesitah as "lamb" (cp. REB). After God restored his fortunes, Job received a kesitah from each of his friends (Job 42:11).

KESULLOTH (Kə·sŭl´ lŏth) (NIV, REB) See *Chesulloth.*

KETHIB (Kĕ thēv´) See *Kere-Kethib.*

During the Roman period food was cooked in a kettle (pot) over hot coals.

KETTLE Translation of a Hebrew word for a vessel in which meat was prepared by the worshipers before being offered as a peace offering to God (1 Sam. 2:14). Hophni and Phinehas were not content with the priest's portion (1 Sam. 2:12-17; Lev. 7:14). They also reached into the worshipers' kettle with a fork to add to what was rightfully theirs. See *Hophni and Phinehas; Sacrifice and Offering.*

KETURAH (Kĕ·tū´ rah) Personal name meaning "incense" or "the perfumed one." In Gen. 25:1 Keturah is called Abraham's wife, while 1 Chron. 1:32 calls her a concubine. She was Abraham's second wife, apparently taken after Sarah's death.

Keturah bore six sons (daughters rarely are listed) to Abraham, the most notable being Midian. The list of Keturah's children substantiates the link between the Hebrews and the tribes that inhabited the areas east and southeast of Palestine. As children of a second wife, they were viewed as inferior to Isaac, Sarah's son.

K

KEYS An instrument for gaining access (Judg. 3:25).

Old Testament The holder of the keys had the power to admit or deny entrance to the house of God (1 Chron. 9:22-27; Isa. 22:22). In late Judaism this key imagery was extended to angelic beings and to God as keepers of the keys of heaven and hell.

New Testament In the NT keys are used only figuratively as a symbol of access (Luke 11:52) or of authority, particularly the authority of Christ over the final destiny of persons. The risen Christ holds the key of David and controls access to the New Jerusalem (Rev. 3:7). By overcoming death, He has the keys to the world of the dead (Rev. 1:18). See *Keys of the Kingdom.*

Barbara J. Bruce

KEYS OF THE KINGDOM What Jesus entrusted to Peter in Matt. 16:19, whose interpretation has been the subject of much debate between Catholics and non-Catholics. Any solution must consider: (1) the role of Peter as a leading apostle, (2) Peter's confession of Jesus as the Christ, (3) Jesus' wordplay regarding the "rock" (*petra*) upon which He would build His church, (4) the meaning of "binding" and "loosing," and (5) parallel references to both "keys" and the other above-mentioned terms in biblical literature (cp. Matt. 18:18; John 20:23; Rom. 9:32,33; Eph. 2:19-22; 1 Pet. 2:4-10; Rev. 1:18; 3:7-13).

The phrase "keys of the kingdom" relates to the authority given to Peter to "bind" and "loose." This authority was delegated to Simon Peter but should not be understood as an arbitrary or even individual authority of Peter to save or condemn. Peter is a representative of the apostles, a fact observed from his frequent role as leader and spokesman. In Eph. 2:20 it is not Peter but simply "the apostles and prophets" who are the foundation stone, with Christ Jesus the cornerstone. Moreover, in 1 Pet. 2:4-5 (which possibly reflects Peter's own interpretation of Christ's words to him) Christians themselves are "stones" built upon Christ the "living stone."

Furthermore, the authority given to Peter and the apostles cannot be separated from the heavenly insight and confession that Jesus is the Christ, the Son of God. It is the revelation given to (and confessed by) Peter that called forth our Lord's blessing. Thus, we cannot overlook the confessional/theological component of Peter's apostolic authority. Peter's authority as an apostle was based upon his divinely given confession. Paul (like Jesus, Matt. 16:23) certainly felt free to criticize Peter when Simon's theology/behavior warranted correction (Gal. 2:6-14). Moreover, the authority to "bind" and "loose," the result of receiving "the keys of the kingdom," is a stewardship, a delegated authority from Christ (cp. Matt. 16:19; John 20:21-23; Rev. 1:18; 3:7-8).

Finally, the related "key" passages in Scripture suggest that it is the preaching of the gospel that has been entrusted/delegated to the apostles. Though the gospel itself is certainly to be handed on (1 Tim. 6:20; 2 Tim. 2:2; 2 Pet. 1:12-16), Scripture nowhere suggests that the "power of the keys" was either a personal privilege or an ecclesiastical office that could be handed on by Peter or anyone else. Rather, it refers to the stewardship of the gospel (1 Cor. 3:10–4:1) entrusted to those historically unique eyewitnesses who as Christ's apostles could give authoritative testimony to the salvation that is found only in Him, a hope which could be confidently offered and promised ("on earth") as an already present gift ("in heaven") to those who confess Him. See *Binding and Loosing; Disciple; Keys.*

Robert B. Sloan

KEZIA (Kə zī´ à) (KJV) or **KEZIAH** Personal name meaning "cassia" or "cinnamon." The second daughter born to Job after his property had been restored (Job 42:14).

KEZIB (Kē´ zĭb) (NIV, REB) See *Chezib.*

KEZIZ, VALLEY OF (Kē´ zĭz) (KJV) See *Emek-Keziz.*

KIBROTH-HATTAAVAH (Kĭb rŏth-hăt-tā´ à vah) Place-name meaning "graves of craving, lust, gluttony." The first stopping place of the Israelites after they left Sinai (Num. 33:16). The Israelites craved meat, which the Lord gave them (Num. 11:31), but, because they overindulged, an epidemic broke out and many Israelites died. The dead were buried there, giving the place its name (Num. 11:34; Deut. 9:22; Ps. 78:30-31).

KIBZAIM (Kĭb´ zā-ĭm) Place-name meaning "double gathering" or "double heap." One of the

K

Levitical cities in the tribal territory of Ephraim also designated as a city of refuge (Josh. 21:22). In a parallel list of cities in Chronicles, the name Jokmeam appears (1 Chron. 6:68). This is not to be confused with Jokmeam (or Jokneam) of 1 Kings 4:12. The reason for the appearance of Jokmean in 1 Chronicles is unexplained. See *Cities of Refuge; Jokmeam; Jokneam; Levitical Cities.*

KID Translation of one of several Hebrew words referring to a young goat. See *Goat; Sacrifice and Offering.*

KIDNAPPING Act of capturing and holding a person using unlawful force and fraud. In modern times a person is usually kidnapped for the purpose of extorting ransom. In biblical times the usual purpose for kidnapping was to use or sell the person into slavery (Gen. 37:28; 40:15). NIV, NRSV translate the corresponding Greek term as "slave traders" (1 Tim. 1:10). Kidnapping free-born Israelites either to treat them as slaves or to sell them into slavery was punishable by death (Exod. 21:16; Deut. 24:7).

KIDNEY One of a pair of vertebrate organs lying in a mass of fatty tissue that excrete the waste products of metabolism.

In the Bible "kidney" is used both literally and figuratively. When the word is used figuratively of humans, KJV usually translates the term as "reins" (Jer. 12:2; Rev. 2:23, NRSV uses "mind"), "heart" (Job 19:27; Pss. 7:9; 16:7; 73:21; Jer. 12:2), "vitals" (Lam. 3:13), "soul" (Prov. 23:16), or "inward parts" (Ps. 139:13; cp. Job 16:13).

The kidneys are often associated with the heart as constituting the center of human personality (Pss. 7:9; 26:2; Jer. 11:20; 17:10; 20:12; Rev. 2:23). Because the areas around the kidneys are sensitive, the Hebrews believed the kidneys were the seat of the emotions (Job 19:27; Ps. 73:21; Prov. 23:16). The kidneys were also used figuratively as the source of the knowledge and understanding of the moral life (Ps. 16:7; Jer. 12:2).

When used literally of animals (except Isa. 34:6), the kidneys are mentioned in relation to sacrifice. The kidney, along with the fat surrounding it, were reserved for God as among the choicest parts of the animal (Exod. 29:13,22). Deuteronomy 32:14 (KJV) speaks of the best wheat as the "fat of kidneys" (NRSV, choicest wheat).

KIDON (Kī´ dŏn) (NIV, REB) See *Chidon.*

KIDRON VALLEY (Kĭd´ ron) Place-name meaning "turbid, dusky, gloomy." Deep ravine beside Jerusalem separating the temple mount and the city of David on the west from the Mount of Olives on the east. The spring of Gihon lies on the western slope. The garden of Gethsemane would have been above the valley on the eastern side. Cemeteries have been located in this area since the middle Bronze Age (before 1500 B.C.). David crossed the brook when he fled Jerusalem to escape from Absalom (2 Sam. 15:23). Solomon warned Shimei not to cross it or he would die (1 Kings 2:37). Here certain kings of Judah destroyed idols and other pagan objects removed from the temple area (1 Kings 15:13; 2 Kings 23:4,6,12; 2 Chron. 29:16; 30:14). After the Last Supper Jesus went through the Kidron Valley on His way to the Mount of Olives (John 18:1). See *City of David; Gihon; Jerusalem; Olives, Mount of; Valley of Hinnom.*

Ricky L. Johnson

KILEAB (Kīl´ ə·ab) (NIV) See *Chileab.*

KILION (Kīl´ ĭ·ŏn) (NIV) See *Chilion.*

KILMAD (Kĭl´ măd) NIV spelling of Chilmad. See *Chilmad.*

KILN Oven, furnace, or heated enclosure used for processing a substance by burning, firing, or drying. The Hebrew word *tannur* is used to refer to both the oven used in the home for baking bread and the large pottery kiln. The "pavement of sapphire" (NASB) in Exod. 24:10 probably refers to a glazed tile out of a potter's kiln. It is possible that the part of the wall around Jerusalem known as the "Tower of the Ovens" (Neh. 3:11 REB) got its name from a potter's kiln. The term "brickkiln" is used in Nah. 3:14, but this should probably read "brick mold" (NRSV, NASB) or "brick work" (NIV, REB), as the bricks in Palestine were usually sun dried. See *Pottery.*

KIMHAM (Kĭm´ hăm) (NIV, REB) See *Chimham.*

K

KINAH (Kī´ năh) Place-name meaning "lamentation." City in the southeast of Judah near the boundary of Edom (Josh. 15:22). Perhaps a settlement of the Kenites. Usually identified with modern Wadi el-Qeini, south of Hebron.

KINDNESS OT translation of the Hebrew term *chesed*. Throughout the OT the idea of *chesed* is that of compassion and faithfulness to one's obligations as well as to relatives, friends, and even to slaves (Gen. 21:23; 39:21; 1 Sam. 15:6). Kindness is seen in the marriage relationship of Abraham and Sarah (Gen. 20:13). It is also seen in the marriage story of Ruth and Boaz (Ruth 2:20). Kindness is shown to relatives and neighbors or even the stranger who comes into one's house (Gen. 19:1-3). The king as well as the common man was subjected to kindness in Israel. In 2 Chron. 24:22 the text shows that Joash did not remember the kindness that his father Jehoiada had shown him. Kindness can be in the form of kind deeds done for another person. In Gen. 40:14 Joseph asks the king's butler to remember the kindness that he has shown him. In the prophets the people of Israel are charged with ethical behavior. This behavior consists of "observing kindness and justice" (Hos. 12:6). Micah 6:8 declares what the Lord requires of man, that he do justice, love kindness, and to walk humbly before God. In Zech. 7:9 one is told to dispense true justice, practice kindness and compassion each to his brother. The praiseworthy woman and kind man both show kindness (Prov. 31:26; Ps. 141:5 [HCSB uses "faithful love"]).

In the NT kindness is translated from the Greek word *chrestotes*. This word can describe gentleness, goodness, uprightness, generosity, and graciousness. The NT describes kindness as an attribute of God (Titus 3:4; HCSB, love). Kindness is a characteristic of true love (1 Cor. 13:4). The Lord's people should possess kindness and not refuse to dispense it to others (Matt. 5:7; Acts 20:35; Rom. 15:2-5; Eph. 4:32; 1 Pet. 3:8; 4:8; 1 John 3:17). At the time of judgment Christ will reward those who have shown kindness to others (Matt. 25:34-36). Kindness can be seen in the deeds of people such as Joseph (Matt. 1:19), the centurion (Luke 7:2-6), John (John 19:27), Julius (Acts 27:3,43), and Onesiphorus (2 Tim. 1:16-18).   *Joe Cathey*

KINE KJV plural of cow. See *Cow*.

KING, CHRIST AS Biblical teaching that Jesus of Nazareth fulfilled the OT promises of a perfect King and reigns over His people and the universe. The OT hope for the future included a vision of a new king like David, called "the anointed one," or "the Messiah" in Hebrew (2 Sam. 7:16; 22:51). The Prophet Isaiah intensified the promises and pointed to the Messiah yet to come (Isa. 7:13-14; cp. Pss. 45; 110). The book of Daniel contains a vision of One to whom was given dominion, glory, and a kingdom, One that all peoples, nations, and languages would serve. His dominion is everlasting and shall never pass away. His kingdom shall never be destroyed (Dan. 7:13-14).

When Jesus Christ was born, His birth was announced in these categories. His earthly ministry then amplified these themes (Matt. 4:17; Luke 1:32-33). Similarly, John the Baptist proclaimed the presence of God's kingdom in the coming of Jesus (Matt. 3). The theme of Jesus as King, Ruler, or Lord dominates the NT from beginning to end. We find the culmination of this theme with the Lord seated on a throne, His enemies being made subject to Him and a new name given: "On His robe and on His thigh He has a name written, KING OF KINGS AND LORD OF LORDS" (Rev. 19:16 HCSB).

The question arises naturally, in what sense is Christ's kingship really operating in today's world? If He is king, how is it that the world is so little changed and His kingship so little acknowledged? Some would answer that Jesus' kingship is completely future. That fails to handle Christ's own statement that the kingdom of God is "in your midst" (Luke 17:21 NASB), "among you" (HCSB, NRSV), or "within you" (KJV, NIV). Christ's kingship is thus present yet still future, already here and still yet to come, spiritual and universal.

The present kingship of Christ is His royal rule over His people (Col. 1:13,18). It is a spiritual realm established in the hearts and lives of believers. He administers His kingdom by spiritual means—the word and the Spirit. Whenever believers follow the lordship of Christ, the Savior is exercising His ruling or kingly function. From this we understand that His kingship is more concerned with Jesus' reign than with the realm over which this takes place. When we pray

K

"Your kingdom come" as we do in the Lord's prayer (Matt. 6:10), we have in mind this present rule of Christ the King.

Christ's kingship is also present today in the natural world. Christ is the one through whom all things came into being (John 1:3) and through whom all things are held together (Col. 1:17). He is in control of the natural universe as He demonstrated during His earthly ministry (Mark 4:35-41).

The Bible recognizes Jesus' present kingship and presents the kingship as a spiritual one (John 18:36). The crowd proclaimed Jesus King during His triumphal entry on Palm Sunday (John 12:12-19). We might say the door of heaven opened a bit so that for a brief moment His true kingship appeared to people on earth. He claimed that if the people had kept silent on that historic occasion, the stones would have cried out to proclaim Him King.

In addition to Christ's present rule, His kingship will become fully evident in the future. We will see and understand this clearly when Jesus returns (Matt. 19:28). The future kingdom will be essentially the same as the present rule in the sense that men and women will acknowledge Christ's rule in their hearts. It will differ, however, in that His rule will be perfect and visible (1 Cor. 15:24-28). Once manifest, the future kingdom will endure forever. Christ will rule over all things in heaven and on earth. At this time God the Father will exalt Jesus, His Son, to the highest place of authority and honor. At the name of Jesus, every knee will bow, in heaven and on earth and under the earth, and every tongue will confess that Jesus is Lord to the glory of God the Father (Phil. 2:9-11).

Jesus established His kingship through His sacrificial death as each of the Gospels shows clearly. Pilate recognized more than he knew when he created the sign, King of the Jews, for the charge against Jesus. Jesus' kingship finds its highest exercise as He gives the blessings He secured for His people through His atoning work (Rom. 8:32; Eph. 1:3-11,20-22). Jesus will continue to reign as the second Person of the Trinity. His God/man personhood will not cease. Jesus Christ, the King, will reign as the God-man and will forever exercise His power for the benefit of the redeemed and for the glory of His kingdom.

David S. Dockery

KING, KINGSHIP Male monarch of a major territorial unit; especially one whose position is hereditary and who rules for life. Kingship includes the position, office, and dignity of a king. Though not so designated, the earliest known king in the Bible is Nimrod (Gen. 10:8-10), a Mesopotamia city builder who developed a mighty empire (perhaps early Babylonia). During the early Abrahamic period 10 more kings are named (Gen. 14:2-9), one being Melchizedek, the king of Salem. In Gen. 17:6 God promised Abraham that nations and kings would come from him. The Bible makes clear the flourishing of kings among the various people groups of the Canaanites, the Egyptians, and the Mesopotamians.

Kings were of three basic kinds in the ancient Near East: (1) kings of great nations often identified with a god (e.g., in Assyria, Babylon, and Egypt); (2) kings from a military elite who had taken control of a local population by force (e.g., Canaanite city kings); and (3) kings who arose from tribal or clan-oriented groups whose election to or inheritance of the kingship was determined in part by the people's will (e.g., Israel, Edom, Moab, and Ammon).

Transition from Judges to Kings From the time of Joshua to the time of Saul, the judges led Israel. Their leadership was temporary and local in nature, their main function being to lead those parts of Israel threatened by some outside force until the threat was gone. Israel during this period was bound together more by their covenant with God than by government.

As Israel became more settled in Canaan, they began to assimilate various aspects of Canaanite culture, and their complete trust in Yahweh alone for their welfare and security began to decline. This decline coupled with the threat of the Philistines to all tribes of Israel threatened the existence of Israel itself. Many in Israel began to feel a need for a hereditary and totalitarian leadership as a way of dealing with the threat (1 Sam. 8:20; 10:1; cp. Judg. 22-23).

The first national leader was Saul. Saul was anointed as the *nagid* over Israel (1 Sam. 11:15; 13:1; 15:1,11,35; 17:55; 18:6,22,25,27; 19:4; 24:8; 26:17; 29:3; 2 Sam. 5:25; 1 Chron. 11:2) Saul was a charismatic leader much in the mold of the judges. Israel remained a tribal league. Saul established no central government or

K

bureaucracy, had no court or standing army, and his seat at Gibeah was a fortress and not a palace.

The significant thing about Saul's leadership is that for the first time after settlement in Canaan, Israel had a permanent national military leader. This was a very important step in the transition from the system of judges to the establishment of the monarchy.

David was also a figure much in the likeness of the judges with a charismatic personality. A prophet designated him leader just as the judges and Saul had been designated before him.

David's leadership, however, represents the second stage in the transition. Unlike Saul, David was able to fuse the tribes of Israel together into a nation who owed allegiance to the crown, to establish and maintain a court, and to establish a standing army. What had been a loose union of 12 tribes became a complex empire centered on the person of David. Because of his charismatic personality and divine enabling, David was able to effect the union of the northern and southern tribes (something Saul was apparently unable to do). David captured Jerusalem and made it the religious and political center of Israel. The Canaanite population of Palestine was subject to the king. Subjugated lands paid tribute to David and not to the individual tribes.

When David passed the power of the kingship along to his son Solomon, the transition from the system of judges to that of monarchy was complete. The usual understanding of king is one whose position is hereditary and who rules for life. These conditions were met for the first time when Solomon inherited the throne from David.

Functions and Powers of the King The king functioned as military leader (1 Kings 22:29-36) and supreme judge (1 Kings 3:16-28). Israel, unlike some nations surrounding it, placed limitations on the power of its kings (1 Sam. 8:10-18). It was normal for the elders of the nation to make a covenant with the king (2 Sam. 5:3; 2 Kings 11:17) in which the rights and duties of the king were recorded and deposited in the sanctuary—possibly at the time of the anointment ceremony (1 Sam. 10:25). It was clearly understood that the king was not exempt from observing civil laws (1 Kings 21:4), nor was the king the absolute lord of life and death, a power David assumed in his murder of Uriah (2 Sam. 11; cp. Ahab's murder of Naboth 1 Kings 21:14-

18; also 2 Kings 5:7; 6:26-33). The prophetic denunciation of certain kings demonstrates that they were subject to the law (2 Sam. 12:1-15; 1 Kings 21:17-24; cp. Deut. 17:14-20).

The King's Court The officials at the king's court included the bodyguard (2 Kings 11:4), captain of the host or general of the army (1 Sam. 14:50; 2 Sam. 8:16), recorder (2 Sam. 8:16), secretary or scribe (2 Sam. 8:17; 2 Kings 18:18), chief administrator over the 12 district officers (1 Kings 4:5; cp. vv. 7-19), steward of the palace household (1 Kings 4:6; 18:3; 2 Kings 18:18; Isa. 22:15), overseer of forced labor (2 Sam. 20:24; 1 Kings 4:6; 5:13-17; 11:28; cp. modern translations for KJV tribute), friend of the king (2 Sam. 15:37; 1 Kings 4:5; 1 Chron. 27:33), counselor (2 Sam. 15:12), keeper of the wardrobe (2 Kings 22:14), officials in charge of the royal farms (1 Chron. 27:25-31), priests (2 Sam. 8:17; 20:25; 1 Kings 4:4), and prophets (1 Sam. 22:5; 2 Sam. 7:2; 12:25; 24:10-25).

To raise the necessary revenue to support a court of this size, Solomon introduced a system of taxation. Saul's court was simple and did not require extensive financial support while David depended on spoils of war (2 Sam. 8:1-14). Solomon divided the nation into 12 districts each of which would be responsible to support the court for one month out of the year (1 Kings 4:7-19,27-28).

Other revenue for the king's court included royal property (1 Chron. 27:25-31; 2 Chron. 26:10; 32:27-29) and forced labor (2 Sam. 20:24; 1 Kings 4:6; 11:28). Solomon also received revenue from a road toll on trade routes through Israel (1 Kings 10:15), trade in horses and chariots (1 Kings 10:28-29), a merchant fleet (1 Kings 9:26-28), and, according to archaeological evidence, possibly from copper mines.

God as King Israel's faith included the confession that God was its ultimate King. Some modern scholars see the covenant between God and Israel recorded in Josh. 24 as a royal covenant made between King and people (Exod. 19:6; Num. 23:21; Deut. 33:5; Judg. 8:23; 1 Sam. 8:7; 12:12). The fact that kingship is prophesied for Israel as early as Gen. 17:6; 35:11; 49:10; and Num. 24:17-19 indicates that God did not regard human kingship as inherently wrong or contrary to His will for Israel. What displeased God was the manner, timing, and motivation for Israel's demand for a king (cp. 1 Sam. 8:5-8; 12:12;

Judg. 8:22-23). The earthly king derived his authority from God as the Lord's anointed (1 Sam. 16:6; 2 Sam. 1:14) or the Lord's captain or prince (1 Sam. 9:16; 10:1; 13:14). Many of the Psalms speak of God as King (Pss. 24; 93; 95–98). See *Kingdom of God.*

Phil Logan and E. Ray Clendenen

KINGDOM OF GOD Concept of God's kingly or sovereign rule, encompassing both the realm over which rule is exerted (Matt. 4:8; 24:7; Mark 6:23; Luke 4:5; Rev. 16:10) and the exercise of authority to reign (Luke 19:12; Rev. 17:12,17-18). The kingdom of God is significant in the nation of Israel, the proclamation of the gospel, and presence of the church. The idea is a point of integration for both Testaments.

Old Testament God rules sovereignly over all His works as King. He desires His rule to be acknowledged in a bond or relationship of love, loyalty, spirit, and trust. Not surprisingly, then, one of the central themes of the OT is kingdom through covenant.

This theme is revealed on the first page of Scripture when God creates man in His own image. According to the grammar of the original text, ruling over the creatures in verse 26b is a result of creating man in the divine image. The fact that mankind is male and female prepares us for the command to be fruitful, and the fact that mankind is the divine image prepares us for the command to rule over the creatures.

The fact that mankind is male and female in itself has nothing to do with the divine image. Instead we should understand the divine image according to the background of the ancient Near East where the setting up of the king's statue was the equivalent to the proclamation of his domination over the area in which the statue was erected. Accordingly man is set in the midst of creation as God's statue. He is evidence that God is the Lord of creation. Man exerts his rule not in arbitrary despotism but as a responsible agent, as God's steward. His rule and his duty to rule are not autonomous; they are copies. Hence the concept of the kingdom of God is found on the first page of the Bible. Adam begins to rule the world under God by naming everything created on the earth just as God ruled by naming everything created in the heavens.

Careful attention must be paid to the language of the promises given to Abraham in Gen. 12 that are later incorporated into the covenant made in Gen. 15. The first promise that God gives to Abram is that He will make him a great nation (12:2). The last promise is that in Abram all the clans or families of the earth will be blessed (12:3). God speaks of Abram as becoming a great nation through three considerations. (1) The term "nation" emphasizes a people as a political entity defined by cultural, ethnic, geographical, or social factors. (2) In 12:3 the nations of the world are not called "nations" but rather "clans" or "families." The term family emphasizes a people with no real political structure and in which no system of final governmental headship or rule operates. (3) The background to Gen. 12 is chapter 11. There we have the history of Babel, where we see a complete confidence and naive optimism about human achievement and effort. Man is at the center of his world and he can achieve anything. This philosophy comes under divine judgment. By contrast Gen. 12 presents us with a political structure brought into being by God, with God at the center, and God as the governmental head and rule of that system. In other words, we have the kingdom of God brought into being by the promises to and covenant with Abraham (cp. Heb. 11:8-10).

When Abram's family does become a nation, God initiates with them the Sinai covenant or law of Moses as a means for the people being rightly related to God, to each other as God's true humanity, and to the creation as His stewards. Therefore, the covenant is the means for establishing His kingdom. The book of Judges proves that although each person did what was right in his own eyes (17:6), nonetheless, the Lord ruled over His people as King. Later God raised up a king after His own heart and made a special covenant with David. The Davidic covenant was God's king seeking to bring the people of God, and indeed all the nations, under this rule made explicit in the covenant (2 Sam. 7:19). Thus the king was the mediator of the covenant and the means of extending God's rule.

When the people failed to abide by the covenant, the prophets and the wise men were sent by God to call the people back to the covenant, the terms of God's rule. Zephaniah, for example, based his warnings on the covenant as found in Deuteronomy (cp. Zeph. 1:2 and Deut. 32:22; Zeph. 1:3 and Deut. 28:21; Zeph. 1:4-6

K

and Deut. 28:45; Zeph. 1:8-13 and Deut. 28:45; Zeph. 1:13 and Deut. 28:30,39; Zeph. 1:15 and Deut. 28:53,55,57). Moreover, the literary structure of Zephaniah is chiastic with 2:11 as the center of the book: "The nations on every shore will worship him, every one in its own land" (NIV). Zephaniah's theology, then, can be summed up by the theme, kingdom through covenant.

Although the prophets sought to bring the people back to the covenant, the Sinai covenant (law of Moses) failed to achieve the goal of establishing God's kingdom because it did not and, in fact, could not guarantee the obedience of the people of God. Hence the prophets begin to speak of a new covenant (Jer. 31) in which God's rule is guaranteed by an obedient people. As the failure of the Davidic line of kings became evident in history, the hope for a future king came more and more to the fore along with the promise of a new covenant through which God's kingship would be acknowledged in the hearts of His people in a new creation—new humanity in a new heavens and a new earth.

The OT ends (in the Hebrew Canon) with Chronicles, a book which focuses on good kings as the ideal of the future Messiah in whom Yahweh will be truly Lord over His people and over all His creation. So the last words of the OT call for a temple-builder from among the people to make this hope a reality—likely the Messiah Himself (2 Chron. 36:23).

New Testament In the NT the fullest revelation of God's divine rule is in the person of Jesus Christ. His birth was heralded as the birth of a king (Luke 1:32-33). The ministry of John the Baptist prepared for the coming of God's kingdom (Matt. 3:2). The crucifixion was perceived as the death of a king (Mark 15:26-32).

Jesus preached that God's kingdom was at hand (Matt. 11:12). His miracles, preaching, forgiving sins, and resurrection are an in-breaking of God's sovereign rule in this dark, evil age.

God's kingdom was manifested in the church. Jesus commissioned the making of disciples on the basis of His kingly authority (Matt. 28:18-20). Peter's sermon at Pentecost underscored that a descendent of David would occupy David's throne forever, a promise fulfilled in the resurrection of Christ (Acts 2:30-32). Believers are transferred from the dominion of darkness into the kingdom of the Son of God (Col. 1:13).

God's kingdom may be understood in terms of "reign" or "realm." Reign conveys the fact that God exerts His divine authority over His subjects/kingdom. Realm suggests location, and God's realm is universal. God's reign extends over all things. He is universally sovereign over the nations, humankind, the angels, the dominion of darkness and its inhabitants, and even the cosmos, individual believers, and the church.

In the OT the kingdom of God encompasses the past, present, and future. The kingdom of God had implications in the theocratic state. The kingdom of God is "already" present but "not yet" fully completed, both a present and future reality. The kingdom was inaugurated in the incarnation, life, ministry, death, and resurrection of Jesus. God's kingdom blessings are in some measure possessed now. People presently find and enter God's kingdom. God is now manifesting His authoritative rule in the lives of His people. God's kingdom, however, awaits its complete realization. His people still endure sufferings and tribulations. When fully consummated, hardships will cease. Kingdom citizens currently dwell alongside inhabitants of the kingdom of darkness. God will eventually dispel all darkness. The final inheritance of the citizens of God's kingdom is yet to be fully realized. The resurrection body for life in the eschatological kingdom is a blessing awaiting culmination.

God's kingdom is soteriological in nature, expressed in the redemption of fallen persons. The reign of Christ instituted the destruction of all evil powers hostile to the will of God. Satan, the "god of this age," along with his demonic horde, seeks to hold the hearts of individuals captive in darkness. Christ has defeated Satan and the powers of darkness and delivers believers. Although Satan still is active in this present darkness, his ultimate conquest and destruction are assured through Christ's sacrificial death and resurrection. Sinners enter Christ's kingdom through regeneration.

Many of Jesus' parables emphasize the mysterious nature of God's kingdom. For example, an insignificant mustard seed will grow a tree, as God's kingdom will grow far beyond its inception (Matt. 13:31-32). The kingdom of God is like seed scattered on the ground. Some seed will fall on good soil, take root, and grow. Other seed, however, will fall on hard, rocky ground and will not grow. Likewise, the kingdom will take root

K

in the hearts of some but will be rejected and unfruitful in others (Matt. 13:3-8). As wheat and tares grow side by side, indistinguishable from each other, so also the sons of the kingdom of God and the sons of the kingdom of darkness grow together in the world until ultimately separated by God (Matt. 13:24-30,36-43).

Although closely related, the kingdom and the church are distinct. George Eldon Ladd identified four elements in the relationship of the kingdom of God to the church. The kingdom of God creates the church. God's redemptive rule is manifested over and through the church. The church is a "custodian" of the kingdom. The church also witnesses to God's divine rule.

The kingdom of God is the work of God, not produced by human ingenuity. God brought it into the world through Christ, and it presently works through the church. The church preaches the kingdom of God and anticipates the eventual consummation. See *Jesus Christ; Salvation.*

Peter Gentry and Stan Norman

KINGS, BOOKS OF Covering the time frame between the final days of King David and the end of the Judean state, the books of 1 and 2 Kings are a vital part of the history of Israel. The title of these books is indicative of their contents: the kings and the kingdoms of Israel and Judah. First and Second Kings are part of a larger body of the OT known as the 12 Historical Books (Joshua–Esther). In the English Bible 1 and 2 Kings are the 11th and 12th books of the OT; however, until the 14th or 15th century A.D., Hebrew manuscripts placed 1 and 2 Kings together as a unified work. In the Greek translation of the OT, the Septuagint (third century B.C.), 1 and 2 Kings was coupled with 1 and 2 Samuel to form the four books of "kingdoms" or "reigns." Therefore, 1 and 2 Kings were known as 3 and 4 "kingdoms." In Jerome's Latin translation of the Bible, the Vulgate (ca. A.D. 400), 1 and 2 Kings are equivalent to 3 and 4 Kings, thus preserving the ancient tradition of viewing the books of Samuel and Kings as interrelated regarding the history of Israel and demonstrating a degree of superficiality in separating the two books.

Time Frame The historical beginning point for the narrative of 1 Kings is approximately 970 B.C. The final event in 2 Kings 25, Evil-Merodach's release of King Jehoiachin from prison, occurs in approximately 560 B.C. Thus, the narrative of 1 and 2 Kings spans 410 years of history. These 410 years witness monumental changes within the nation of Israel including the division of the kingdom in 930 B.C. (Israel as the 10 northern tribes and Judah as the two southern tribes), the height of the monarchy under Solomon (970–930 B.C.), and the exiles of both Israel and Judah (722 B.C. and 587/586 B.C.).

Author First and Second Kings are anonymous works. Since the texts themselves provide no direct internal evidence of authorship, two basic ideas dominate the theories concerning authorship. The first basic idea comes from the Jewish Talmud, which designates Jeremiah as the author. Jeremiah certainly fits the time frame for having composed these books with one exception: 1 Kings 25:27-30. Attributing Jeremianic authorship to these four verses is tenuous; however, one can assert the plausibility of prophetic authorship due to the strong prophetic outlook contained throughout the books.

German scholar Martin Noth advanced the second basic idea of authorship which is the hypothesis that a single "Deuteronomic Historian" wrote the entirety of Joshua–2 Kings (excluding Ruth) after 560 B.C. during the Babylonian exile (587–539 B.C.). This idea has garnered the largest following among critical biblical scholars since Noth first postulated the idea in the late 1940s. Noth based his idea on the assumption that the book of Deuteronomy was a type of foundational document upon which the Deuteronomistic Historian based his selection of events to include in his history of Israel. In the Hebrew Bible, the books Joshua—2 Kings are known as the Former Prophets.

Theology of 1 and 2 Kings Regardless of whether a single author called the Deuteronomistic Historian composed the books of 1 and 2 Kings, the books are nonetheless very "Deuteronomic" in theology. The book of Deuteronomy propounds this truth: obedience to God's laws brings blessings, while disobedience to God's laws brings curses. This theology provides an axis along which the historical narrative of the former prophets runs; however, a majority of the OT outside of the Former Prophets also has philosophical similarities to this theological idea (i.e., the Prophets and the Wisdom Literature).

K

When interpreting the Deuteronomic theology of the OT, an interpreter must exercise caution in understanding the promises of Deuteronomy in respect to the covenant relationship between Israel and Yahweh. Without understanding that Deuteronomy is the word of God to His chosen people (those who are already in a covenant relationship with Yahweh), an interpreter could broadly misapply the truth of the text by asserting that any person can receive the blessings of Yahweh by behaving in a manner commensurate with Deuteronomic theology. This misapplication fails to recognize the covenant relationship that was already present between the chosen seed of Abraham and Yahweh. In other words, Deuteronomic theology is a truth only for those who are already in a covenant relationship with Yahweh. Attempted obedience to the laws of God without a covenant relationship is nothing more than either a "salvation by works theology" or a "prosperity theology."

The other major Deuteronomic ideas that permeate 1 and 2 Kings are the ideas of centralized worship in Jerusalem (Deut. 12:1-28) and each particular king's faithfulness to promote complete devotion to Yahweh by ridding the land of idols (Deut. 12:29-32; 13:12-18). With the completion of the temple during Solomon's reign, worship became centralized in Jerusalem, thus bringing fulfillment to Deut. 12:5: "But you shall seek the LORD at the place which the LORD your God shall choose from all your tribes, to establish His name there for His dwelling, and there you shall come" (NASB). The kings that follow Solomon are judged on the basis of their faithfulness to promote complete obedience to Yahweh by ridding the land of idols, male cult prostitutes, Asherah poles, and so forth. In other words, the author of 1 and 2 Kings judged the kings of Judah and Israel based on their actions of devotion, or lack thereof, to the first and second commandments: (1) "You shall have no other gods before Me," and (2) You shall not make for yourself an idol, or any likeness of what is in heaven above or on the earth beneath or in the water under the earth. You shall not worship them or serve them; for I, the LORD your God, am a jealous God" (Exod. 20:4-6a NASB).

The author of 1 and 2 Kings gave a culminating statement of qualitative judgment regarding how well each king followed God's covenant.

These statements use David as the basis of judgment for each subsequent king of Judah. Second Kings 18:3 gives an example of such a statement regarding King Hezekiah: "And he did right in the sight of the LORD, according to all that his father David had done" (NASB). Twenty kings followed King Solomon in Judah. From these 20 kings, only eight remained faithful, to some degree, to God's covenant: Asa, Jehoshaphat, Joash/ Jehoash, Amaziah, Uzziah (Azariah in 2 Kings 15:1-7), Jotham, Hezekiah, and Josiah. Of these eight kings of Judah, only Hezekiah and Josiah received unmitigated praise for faithfulness to the covenant. The other six kings allowed at least some forms of idolatry to continue.

On a less positive note, all of the kings of the northern nation of Israel were wicked kings. The kings of the northern nation are judged on the basis that they did evil in the sight of the Lord and that they walked in the way of Jeroboam (the first king of the northern nation) and his sin (1 Kings 15:34). These evaluative formulas also seem to function as organizational markers.

Theological/Sacred History With verses like "now the rest of the acts of Solomon and whatever he did, and his wisdom, are they not written in the book of the acts of Solomon?" (1 Kings 11:41 NASB), a reader understands that the author of 1 and 2 Kings did not record every action that occurred in the history of Israel. This process of selectivity has been the impetus for the terms "Theological History" or "Sacred History." The author chose certain events to include in the account of Israel's history. These chosen events are Deuteronomic in theology, and the seeming intent of the author is to give an accurate account of these selected events.

Critical scholarship in the 1900s repeatedly questioned the historical reliability of the accounts found in the Pentateuch and the historical books of the OT by asserting that extrabiblical evidence to verify the biblical accounts was either sparse or nonexistent. While space prohibits the exploration of the entirety of these skeptical questions, an interpreter should note that both the Merneptah Stela (ca. 1224 B.C.) and the Tell-Dan inscription found in 1993 are two examples of extrabiblical support for the presence of Israel in the land of Canaan and for the historicity of David's kingship. Also, the Moabite Stone provides extrabiblical support for

K

the Omride dynasty of Israel found in 1 Kings 16:21-28. Furthermore, the Lachish letters and the Annals of Sennacherib offer additional extrabiblical material that accords with certain accounts in 1 and 2 Kings (albeit differences between the biblical texts and the extrabiblical texts do exist). With respect to the historicity of the events contained in the Bible, a reader would do well to heed the words of Walter Kaiser (*A History of Israel*, Broadman & Holman, 2000) by letting the Bible be "innocent until proven guilty." Also, one must remember that lack of extrabiblical evidence is not consummate proof that a biblical event did not occur.

Survey of Events The books of 1 and 2 Kings have three major sections. Using these three major sections, a survey of the events recorded in the books follows.

Solomon and His Reign (1 Kings 1–11) The narrative of 1 Kings begins with David at the end of his life. David's son Adonijah attempted to make himself king by acquiring a following and declaring himself to be the king, but Nathan the prophet and Bathsheba interceded, and David named Solomon as his successor. Once Solomon was declared king, he exercised "wisdom" and exterminated those who might oppose his kingship: Adonijah, Joab, and Shimei. Also, Abiathar the priest, who joined Adonijah's insurrection, was banished from the priesthood in fulfillment of the prophecy against the house of Eli in Shiloh (1 Sam. 2:27-36; 3:10-14). First Kings 3 relates the story of Solomon's request for wisdom, God's granting of wisdom to Solomon, and Solomon's classic display of wisdom in his arbitration between the two prostitutes disputing over a child.

With control of the kingdom firmly established, Solomon turned his attention to taking foreign wives and to building projects. The temple in Jerusalem is Solomon's most significant building project. The completion of the temple fulfilled the words of Deut. 12:1-28 regarding the place where Yahweh would establish His name. The biblical text reveals the magnificence of the temple, the conscription of laborers to build the temple, and the dedication of the temple. When the people brought the ark of the covenant into the temple, the glory of God returned as a cloud—hearkening back to the time of the tabernacle. As Solomon offered his dedicatory remarks, the reader sees the fulfill-ment of God's promise to David that his son would build the temple (2 Sam. 7:12-13). While the temple was of monumental importance to the Hebrews, Solomon also pronounced the importance of the temple for the foreigners who would come and pray to Yahweh (1 Kings 8:41-43). A visit from the Queen of Sheba and economic activity with the King of Tyre followed the dedication of the temple. Although Solomon's wealth exceeded that of any king of Israel either before or after him, he still had an "Achilles heel"—foreign gods. The foreign wives that Solomon had married brought other gods into Solomon's presence. These wives turned Solomon's heart away from total devotion to Yahweh, and Solomon both worshiped these foreign gods and built shrines to them. This sinful action is a blight on the magnanimous reign of Solomon, but true to Deuteronomic form, the author of 1 Kings recorded God's pronouncement of judgment—the tearing away of the kingdom from Solomon. God brought this judgment to pass after Solomon had died. Interestingly no spiritual evaluation of Solomon is present in the text as is so common in 1 and 2 Kings for all the kings that follow after Solomon.

The Divided Kingdom (1 Kings 12– 2 Kings 17) The once-united nation of Israel then entered a downward spiral. Solomon's son, Rehoboam, acted unwisely in pontificating his intention to place an even heavier burden of labor and taxation on the people than did his father. This action elicited Jeroboam, a former enemy of Solomon, to "break away" from the Jerusalem monarchy. The 10 northern tribes then became the nation of Israel, and the two southern tribes (Judah and Benjamin) became the nation of Judah (ca. 930 B.C.). Jeroboam became the first king of the northern nation, and he erected idolatrous shrines at Dan and Bethel thus attempting to keep the people from traveling to Jerusalem to worship. These idolatrous shrines contained golden calves, which hearken back to the rebellion of the Israelites at Mount Sinai. At this point in the narrative, the utter sinfulness of Rehoboam is emphasized; thus, he becomes the standard for the negative spiritual evaluation of all the northern kings that follow him. None of the 20 kings of Israel were faithful to the covenant with Yahweh, precipitating the destruction of the northern nation in 723/22 B.C. Second Kings 17 records that the Assyrians

K

destroyed Samaria, the capital city of the northern nation. This destruction was followed by the importation of other conquered peoples. The intermarriage of these imported people with the nondeported Israelites was the inception of the Samaritans.

Although the northern nation presents a "gloomy picture," the southern nation does have a few "bright spots" in her history. Eight of the 20 kings of Judah walked in some degree of faithfulness to the covenant with Yahweh. Through this chosen line of kings, God kept intact His promise to Abraham and the line through which He would bring His Son into the world.

The king formula comes to the fore in this section of the narrative. This introductory formula for the kings of Judah consists of four basic elements: (1) the regnal year of the king in the nation of Israel, (2) the age of the king when he began to reign, (3) the name of the queen mother, and (4) the spiritual evaluation of the king. This formula is an obvious organizing feature for the narrative; yet even with this formula, the similar names between the kings of the two nations and the plot movement from one nation to the other nation can be difficult to follow at times. The formula for the kings of Israel consists of the regnal year for the concomitant king of Judah and the length of the king's reign.

Though most of the kings of Israel have a scant amount of information concerning their exploits, the kings who reigned during the prophetic ministries of Elijah and Elisha do receive additional attention, such as Ahab and Jehu. Elijah enters the narrative in 1 Kings 17. With his confrontation of King Ahab (ca. 874/73–853), Queen Jezebel, and the prophets of Baal, Elijah appears as a champion for faithfulness to the covenant with Yahweh. Elijah was a miracle-working prophet who remained faithful to Yahweh in spite of persecution. After fleeing from Jezebel to the Negev/Sinai region, Elijah received the word of God regarding the concept of a remnant (1 Kings 19:18). Yahweh told Elijah that 7,000 people had not bowed their knees to Baal; therefore, God would spare their lives. After this word from God, Elijah then placed the prophetic mantle upon Elisha, who ministered during the ninth century B.C. The narrative records Elisha's interaction with Benhadad I, King of Assyria (ca. 880–842) and his interaction with Jehu, king of Israel (ca. 841–814/13).

Many miracles that Elisha performed are recorded in 2 Kings 4–8. This grouping of miracles is known as "miracle clustering."

This major section of 1 and 2 Kings ends with the destruction of the northern nation. What Shalmaneser V began by besieging Samaria, Sargon II finished by destroying Samaria. Occurring in 723/22 B.C., this cataclysmic event marked the end of the northern nation.

Judah Alone (2 Kings 18–25) This final section of the Kings narrative focuses on the nation of Judah. With Israel destroyed, Judah stood alone between the years of 722 and 587/86 B.C. During this time frame the two best kings of Judah came to the throne: Hezekiah and Josiah. In spite of the Deuteronomic reforms of these two kings, however, the nation of Judah continued to rebel against Yahweh. Therefore, God used the Babylonians as His instrument for punishing His people by destroying the city of Jerusalem and the temple in 587/86 B.C.

Hope for the Future Even though the history of God's people in 1 and 2 Kings is fraught with failure, God remained faithful to His chosen people. Even though both nations went into exile, God remembered His promise to Abraham, and He preserved His people while in exile. The last event in the book of 2 Kings is Evil-Merodach's goodness toward one of Judah's wicked kings, Jehoiachin (Jeconiah). Through Jehoiachin, God would bring His ultimate redemption to pass in the person of His Son, Jesus Christ. Thus, the Deuteronomic history of Israel ends on a "forward-looking" note to the inauguration of the new covenant (Jer. 31:31-34).   *Pete Wilbanks*

Outline
1 Kings
I.   God Works His Purposes Even through Human Revenge and Treachery (1:1–2:46).

II. God Works through the Wisdom He Gives His Humble Leader (3:1–7:51).
   A. God honors His humble leader's request and equips him with divine wisdom (3:1-28).
   B. God's leader administers his people wisely (4:1-34).
   C. God's leader wisely follows divine directives to build a house of worship (5:1–7:51).

K

III. God Responds to the Worship and Sin of His People (8:1–11:43).
  A. God fulfills His promise to His people and their leaders (8:1-21).
  B. The incomparable God of heaven hears the prayers of His repentant people anywhere (8:22-53).
  C. The faithful God leads His people to faithfulness and calls the nations to recognize His uniqueness (8:54-61).
  D. God's people worship joyfully in His house (8:62-66).
  E. God's favor is related to His people's obedience (9:1-9).
  F. God blesses the efforts of His faithful leader (9:10–10:29).
  G. A leader's unfaithfulness brings divine discipline on His people (11:1-43).
IV. Disobedience Brings Results (12:1– 16:34).
  A. Leaders who refuse to be servants lose their subjects (12:1-24).
  B. False worship leads to doom for God's people and their leader (12:25–13:10).
  C. God's prophets must obey God's voice (13:11-25).
  D. Disobedience leads a nation to eternal ruin (13:26–14:20).
  E. God is faithful to His promises even when a people disobey (14:21–15:8).
  F. In the midst of disobedience God honors a faithful leader (15:9-24).
  G. God fulfills His threats against evil leaders (15:25–16:34).
V. God Works in History through His Prophetic Messengers (17:1–22:53).
  A. God blesses and brings recognition to His faithful prophet (17:1-24).
  B. Yahweh proves His claim to be the only God of Israel through His prophet (18:1-46).
  C. God revives His depressed prophet and provides for His purposes to be worked out (19:1-21).
  D. God uses a prophet to prove His lordship over history (20:1-30a).
  E. God sends prophets to condemn His disobedient leaders (20:30b-43).
  F. God uses His prophets to bring guilty leaders to repentance (21:1-29).
  G. God speaks through His chosen prophet, not through those depending on human appointment and provisions (22:1-40).
  H. God blesses the faithful but is angry at the disobedient (22:41-53).

2 Kings
I. Through His Prophets God Guides History and Reveals His Will (1:1–8:29).
  A. God alone controls the fortunes of His people (1:1-18).
  B. God provides spiritual leadership for His people (2:1-25).
  C. The prophetic word from God controls history (3:1-27).
  D. God's minister helps God's faithful people in their time of need (4:1-44).
  E. God's mercy reaches across international lines (5:1-19a).
  F. Greedy ministers cannot deceive God (5:19b-27).
  G. God defeats the enemies of His people (6:1–7:20).
  H. God does not forget His faithful people (8:1-6).
  I. God controls the destiny of all nations (8:7-29).
II. God's Mercy Has Limits (9:1–17:41).
  A. God keeps His threats against false worship but honors those who carry out His will (9:1–10:36).
  B. God protects His chosen leader (11:1-21).
  C. God's people support His house of worship (12:1-16).
  D. God's offerings are not to be used for political purposes (12:17-21).
  E. God's mercy and faithfulness protect even His disobedient people (13:1–14:29).
  F. God works to punish a people who remain disobedient (15:1–16:20).
  G. God brings an end to the nation that refuses to follow the prophetic word (17:1-41).
III. God Honors Righteous Rulers but Punishes a Sinful People (18:1–25:30).
  A. God rewards those who trust in Him but punishes those who mock Him (18:1–19:37; cp. to Isa. 36:1–37:38)
  B. God hears the prayers of His faithful servant (20:1-11; cp. to Isa. 38:1-22).

K

C. God knows the future of His people (20:12-21; cp. to Isa. 39:1-8).
D. Rebellion against God brings divine rejection (21:1-26).
E. A righteous ruler can delay divine judgment (22:1-20).
F. A righteous ruler cannot avert judgment forever (23:1-30).
G. Deserved punishment comes to God's disobedient people (23:31–25:26).
H. God preserves hope for His people (25:27-30). *Phil Logan*

KING'S DALE See *Shaveh.*

KING'S GARDEN Place in Jerusalem adjacent to and probably irrigated by the overflow of the pool of Shelah (Siloam) (Neh. 3:15). See *King's Pool.*

KING'S HIGHWAY Major transportation route east of the Jordan River. Literally "the way of the king," this highway has been in continuous use for over 3,000 years. It runs from Damascus to the Gulf of Aqabah and is the main caravan route for the Transjordan. It is mentioned in Num. 20:17 and 21:22 as the route Moses and the Israelites would take through Edom and the land of Sihon. The Romans upgraded it during the reign of Trajan and renamed it Trajan's Road. The Arabic name is Tariq es-Sultani, which also means the way of the sultan or king. See *Transportation and Travel.*

KING'S POOL Probably the same as the Pool of Shelah, a reservoir in the king's garden in Jerusalem (Neh. 2:14), rebuilt by Shallum, ruler of the district of Mizpah (Neh. 3:15). See *King's Garden.*

KING'S TREASURE HOUSE See *House of the Rolls.*

KING'S VALE or **KING'S VALLEY** See *Shaveh.*

KINNERETH (Kĭn´ nə·rĕth) (NIV, REB) See *Chinnereth.*

KINSMAN Usually refers to a blood relative based on Israel's tribal nature. The most important relationship was that of the father to the oldest son.

Certain obligations were laid on the kinsman. In the case of an untimely death of a husband without a son, the law of levirate marriage becomes operative—that is, the husband's brother was obligated to raise up a male descendant for his deceased brother and thus perpetuate the deceased's name and inheritance. The living brother was the dead brother's *go'el*—his redeemer (Gen. 38:8; Deut. 25:5-10; Ruth 3:9-12).

The kinsman was also the blood avenger. A wrong done to a single member of the family was considered a crime against the entire tribe or clan. The clan had an obligation, therefore, to punish the wrongdoer. In the case of a murder committed, the kinsman should seek vengeance. According to the imagery of ancient people, the blood of the murdered man cried up from the ground for vengeance, and the cry was heard loudest by that member of the clan who stood nearest to the dead in kinship. Therefore the closest of kin followed through with the blood avenger responsibility (cp. Gen. 4:1-16, esp. v. 10).

The kinsman was also responsible to redeem the estate which his nearest relative might have sold because of poverty (Lev. 25:25; Ruth 4:4). It was the kinsman's responsibility also to ransom a kinsman who may have sold himself (Lev. 25:47-48).

The OT book of Ruth is the most striking example of a kinsman who used his power and Jewish law to redeem. Boaz demonstrated one of the duties of the kinsman—that of marrying the widow of a deceased kinsman. A correlation is sometimes made between the redemption of Ruth by Boaz and the redemption of sinners by Christ. See *Avenger; Cities of Refuge; Levirate Law; Redeem, Redemption, Redeemer; Vengeance.* *Gary Bonner*

KIOS (Kī´ ŏs) (NIV) See *Chios.*

KIR (Kĭr) Place-name meaning "wall." **1.** Moabite city mentioned in connection with Ar in Isaiah's prophecy against Moab (15:1). Many believe that Kir is the same as Kir-haraseth, an ancient capital of Moab along with Ar. Located at Kerak about 17 miles south of the Arnon River and 11 miles east of the Dead Sea. See *Kir-haraseth.* **2.** Kir is the Hebrew translation of the city name Der (a word from Akkadian that also means "wall"). Kir was a Mesopotamian city east of the lower Tigris River (which is now identified with the modern Badrah) on the main road from Elam (Persia) to Babylon. During the Neo-Babylonian period (605–539 B.C.), Kir was the capital of the province of Gutium. The governor of this province joined Cyrus the Persian in the overthrow of the Babylonian Empire in 539 B.C. See *Babylon.*

Kir was the city from which Arameans migrated to Syria (Isa. 22:6). Their migration—like the migration of the Philistines from Caphtor—is spoken of in terms similar to that of the exodus of Israel from Egypt (Amos 9:7; cp. Amos 1:5). When Tiglath-pileser III conquered the area during the reign of Ahaz (2 Kings 16:9), the descendants of the original immigrants to Syria were sent back to Kir (cp. the aversion of the ancient Hebrews to being sent back to Egypt in Deut. 17:16; 28:68). *Phil Logan*

KIR-HARESETH (Kĭr-hâr´ ĕ·sĕth) Place-name meaning "city of pottery." Known by various names in various texts and various versions of the OT: Kir-hareseth (2 Kings 3:25; Isa. 16:7), Kir-haraseth (2 Kings 3:25 KJV), Kir-heres (Isa. 16:11; Jer. 48:31,36), and Kir-haresh (Isa. 16:11 KJV). Perhaps also the same as Kir of Moab in Isaiah 15:1. See *Kir 1.*

During the reign of Jehoram of Israel, Mesha, king of Moab, rebelled against Israel (2 Kings 3:4-27). The kings of Judah (Jehoshaphat) and Edom joined Israel in the resulting war. The forces allied against Mesha crushed the rebellion, but they were unsuccessful in capturing Mesha. He took refuge in Kir-hareseth—a well-fortified and impregnable city. After Mesha tried unsuccessfully to break through the besiegers, he offered his son as a sacrifice upon the city walls. As a result, "there came great wrath against Israel" (2 Kings 3:27 NASB), and the allied forces withdrew, leaving Mesha alive in Kir-hareseth (2 Kings 3:4-27). Apparently the forces of Israel and Judah feared the power of the Moabite god Chemosh and gave up the victory that lay within their grasp. Jehoram and Jehoshaphat did not have faith that Yahweh would give them victory over the people of Chemosh.

The prophets would later correct this view. Isaiah (15:1; 16:7,11) and Jeremiah (48:31,36) prophesied that Kir-hareseth was no match for the power of God. All human kingdoms are ultimately subject to God. Kir-hareseth was destroyed by the Babylonians whom the prophets described as God's instrument of punishment (Jer. 4:5-31; 6:1-8,22-26; 25:1-14).

Kir-hareseth is identified with modern Khirbet Karnak, about 50 miles southeast of Jerusalem and 11 miles east of the Dead Sea. *Phil Logan*

KIR-HARESH (Kĭr-hā´ rĕsh) (KJV, Isa. 16:11) See *Kir-hareseth.*

KIR-HERES (Kĭr-hē´ rĕs) Believed to be an alternate spelling of Kir-hareseth found in Isa. 16:11; Jer. 48:31,36. The Greek translation of the name in Isa. 16:11 suggests that the translators of the Septuagint had a Hebrew text that read Kir-hadesheth, a name meaning "New City," which was mistaken for Kir-hareseth or Kir-heres. In the context Kir-hares (for Kir-hareseth) is likely the best reading (Isa. 16:7). The confusion between Kir-hadesheth and Kir-hareseth may be due to the similarity of the Hebrew "r" and "d." The name Kir-hares may be explained by the loss of the final Hebrew letter "th" from Kir-hareseth. See *Kir-hareseth.*

KIR OF MOAB See *Kir 1.*

KIRIATH (Kĭr´ ĭ ath) Place-name meaning "city" in tribal territory of Benjamin (Josh. 18:28 NASB, NIV; KJV, Kirjath). The same as Kiriath-jearim (Josh. 18:28 NRSV, REB, TEV). See *Kiriath-jearim.*

KIRIATHAIM (Kĭr ĭ á thā´ ĭm) Place-name meaning "double city" or "two cities." **1.** Levitical city and city of refuge in the tribal territory of Naphtali (1 Chron. 6:76; KJV, Kirjathaim). In the parallel list in Josh. 21:32 Kartan stands in the place of Kiriathaim and is probably another name for the same city. See *Cities of Refuge; Levitical Cities; Kartan.* **2.** City taken from the Emim by Chedorlaomer (Gen. 14:5, Shaveh-kiriathaim means "the plain of Kiriathaim"). Later the Israelites took it from the Amorites and assigned it to the tribe of Reuben (Num. 32:37: Josh. 13:19). The Moabites controlled the city during the exile (Jer. 48:1,23; Ezek. 25:9). Perhaps to be identified with el-Qereiyat, about five miles northwest of Dibon; however, no remains from before about 100 B.C. have been found on this site.

K

KIRIATH-ARBA (Kĭr ĭ ăth-är´ bà) Place-name meaning "city of Arba" or "city of four." The ancient name for the city of Hebron, the chief city in the hill country of Judah (Josh. 15:54). It was both a Levitical city (Josh. 21:11) and a city of refuge (Josh. 20:7). Caleb captured the city for Israel (Josh. 15:13-14). Bible students dispute the origin of the name. According to some, Kiriath-arba was originally named after Arba the Anakite hero (Josh. 14:15; 15:13). Others point to the nearby cave of Machpelah where, according to Jewish tradition, Adam, Abraham, Isaac, and Jacob were buried—thus, "city of four." See *Cities of Refuge; Hebron; Levitical Cities.*

KIRIATH-ARIM (Kĭr ĭ ăth-ā´ rĭm) Alternate spelling of Kiriath-jearim in Ezra 2:25. See *Kiriath-jearim.*

KIRIATH-BAAL (Kĭr ĭ ăth-bā´ àl) Place-name meaning "city of Baal." Another name for Kiriath-jearim in Josh. 15:60; 18:14. See *Kiriath-jearim.*

KIRIATH-HUZOTH (Kĭr ĭ ăth-hū´ zŏth) Place-name meaning "city of streets." City of Moab to which Balak took Balaam to offer a sacrifice (Num. 22:39). Some suggest a location near the Arnon River (Num. 22:36) not far from Bamoth-baal (Num. 22:41 NIV). The precise location is unknown.

KIRIATH-JEARIM (Kĭr ĭ ăth-jē´ à-rĭm) Place-name meaning "city of forests." Kiriath-jearim was located at modern Abu Gosh nine miles north of Jerusalem. It was on the border where Dan, Benjamin, and Judah joined before Dan began their migration northward (Josh. 15:9,60; 18:14-15). Dan's army camped there in their search for new territory (Judg. 18:12). After the Philistines returned the ark of the covenant, it was kept at Kiriath-jearim for a time (1 Sam. 6:21-7:2). David attempted to move the ark to Jerusalem from there, but because he did so improperly, God struck down Uzzah (2 Sam. 6:1-8). Among Kiriath-jearim's sons was Uriah, a faithful prophet and contemporary of Jeremiah. He was executed for prophesying against the king (Jer. 26:20-24).

The Romans built a fort over the ancient ruins to guard the main route from Jerusalem to the Mediterranean Sea. A garrison from the Tenth Legion was stationed there.

Kiriath-jearim is identified with Deir al-Azhar near the modern village of Qaryet el-Inab or Abu Gosh.

KIRIATH-SANNAH (Kĭr ĭ-ath-săn´ nah) Place-name, perhaps meaning "city of bronze." Another name for the city of Debir, also known as Kiriath-sepher (Josh. 15:15-16,49). See *Debir 2.*

KIRIATH-SEPHER (Kĭr ĭ-ăth-sē´ phĕr) Place-name meaning "city of book." Used in Josh. 15:15-16 as another name for Debir. Kiriath-sannah is the same city (Josh. 15:49). See *Debir 2.*

KIRIOTH (Kĭr´ ĭ-ŏth) (KJV, Amos 2:2) See *Kerioth.*

KIRIOTH-HEZRON See *Hazor 4.*

KIRJATH (Kĭr´ jăth) (KJV) See *Kiriath-jearim.*

KIRJATHAIM (Kĭr·jà·thā´ ĭm) (KJV) See *Kiriathaim.*

KIRJATH-ARBA (Kĭr jăth-är´ bà) (KJV) See *Kiriath-arba.*

KIRJATH-ARIM (Kĭr jăth-ā´ rĭm) (KJV) See *Kiriath-arim.*

KIRJATH-BAAL (Kĭr jăth-bā´ àl) (KJV) See *Kiriath-baal.*

KIRJATH-HUZOTH (Kĭr jăth-hū´ zŏth) (KJV) See *Kiriath-huzoth.*

KIRJATH-JEARIM (Kĭr jăth-jē´ à rĭm) (KJV) See *Kiriath-jearim.*

KIRJATH-SANNAH (Kĭr jăth-săn´ nah) KJV for Kiriath-sannah, another name for the city of Debir (Josh. 15:49). See *Debir 2.*

KIRJATH-SEPHER (Kĭr jăth-sē´ phĕr) KJV for Kiriath-sepher, another name for the city of Debir (Josh. 15:15-16). See *Debir 2.*

KISH (Kĭsh) Personal name of unknown meaning, perhaps "gift." **1.** Father of Saul (1 Sam. 9:1-2). A man of the tribe of Benjamin who lived in Gibeah. He is said to have been the son of Abiel (1 Sam. 9:1) and the son of Ner (1 Chron. 8:33). Some think he was the grandson of Abiel and son of Ner. He was apparently a man of wealth, owning both asses and servants (1 Sam. 9:3). The

K

description of Saul as being from the humblest family of the tribe of Benjamin is probably a good example of oriental modesty (1 Sam. 9:21). He was buried in Zela of Benjamin, where Saul and Jonathan were buried (2 Sam. 21:14). **2.** A Benjaminite, the third son of Jeiel of Gibeon and Maacah (1 Chron. 8:29-30; 9:35-36). **3.** Second son of Mahli who belonged to the Merari family of Levites. Kish's sons married his brother's daughters (1 Chron. 23:21-22). Kish's son, Jerahmeel, became the head of the family of Kish (1 Chron. 24:29). **4.** Son of Abdi, also of the Merari family of Levites. He assisted in cleansing the temple during the time of Hezekiah (2 Chron. 29:12). **5.** The Benjaminite ancestor of Mordecai (Esther 2:5).

KISHI (Kĭsh´ī) Personal name possibly meaning "gift." Levite of the Merari family (1 Chron. 6:44) also called Kushaiah (1 Chron. 15:17). See *Kushaiah.*

KISHION (Kĭsh´ĭ·ŏn) Place-name meaning "hard ground." A town in Issachar allotted to the Gershonite Levites (Josh. 21:28). A parallel list calls the town Kedesh (1 Chron. 6:72). It has been suggested that "Kedesh in Issachar" may have arisen from a misreading of "Kishon" for "Kedesh." The site is uncertain, perhaps modern Tell Abu Qudeis, about two miles southeast of Megiddo. See *Kedesh; Levitical Cities.*

KISHON (Kī´ shŏn) Place-name meaning "curving, winding." A small river which flows from east to west through the Valley of Jezreel. In the spring it achieves a width of about 65 feet and a length of 23 miles. It was at the Kishon that Deborah and Barak defeated the Canaanite Sisera when his chariots became mired in the marshes (Judg. 4:7,13; 5:21). Later the river was the place where Elijah brought the prophets of Baal to be executed following God's display and victory on Mount Carmel (1 Kings 18:40).

KISLEV (Kĭs´ lĕv) (NIV, REB, TEV) See *Chislev.*

KISLON (Kĭs´ lŏn) (NIV, REB) See *Chislon.*

KISLOTH-TABOR (Kĭs´ lŏth-tā´ bôr) (NIV, REB) See *Chisloth-tabor.*

KISON (Kī´ sŏn) (KJV, Ps. 83:9) See *Kishon.*

KISS Most often used of the touching of the lips to another person's lips, cheeks, shoulders, hands, or feet as a gesture of friendship, acceptance, respect, and reverence. The location of the kiss carried different meanings as Jesus made clear in the episode of the woman kissing his feet (Luke 7:36-50). With the exception of three occurrences (Prov. 7:13; Song 1:2; 8:1), the term is used without any erotic overtones. Kiss translates two Hebrew words and three Greek words; the basic Hebrew term is found 32 times, and the basic Greek term is found 7 times.

In the OT close relatives kissed at greeting and departing with the connotation of acceptance most often in the foreground (Gen. 27:26-27; 29:11; 50:1; Exod. 18:7; 1 Sam. 10:1; Ruth 1:9). The term was further used of the gesture of reverence to idols (1 Kings 19:18; Hos. 13:2) as well as to the Lord (Ps. 2:12). A kiss of betrayal is also found (2 Sam. 20:9). The term "kiss" in the NT is used of Judas (Mark 14:44-45), of the father to the prodigal as a sign of acceptance and reconciliation (Luke 15:20), of the Ephesian elders to Paul as a sign of gratitude (Acts 20:37), of the woman who kissed the feet of Jesus (Luke 7:38), and of the "holy kiss" (1 Thess. 5:26; 1 Cor. 16:20; 2 Cor. 13:12; Rom. 16:16).

The holy kiss was widely practiced among the early Christians as a manner of greeting, a sign of acceptance, and an impartation of blessing. This custom could well have been used to express the unity of the Christian fellowship. The substitute kiss involved kissing the hand and waving it in the direction of the object to be kissed (Job 31:27). The kiss of betrayal from Judas does not belong to the category of the kiss of Joab to Amasa (2 Sam. 20:9) but was the sign of respect from pupil to master. Either the action of Judas did not accord with his inner feeling, or his action had other motivation than betrayal.

The kiss still survives in the Near Eastern culture as a sign of love, respect, and reverence.

G. Al Wright, Jr.

KITCHENS Place of meal preparation, particularly involving cooking. Ezekiel's vision of the temple included four small courts at the corners of the Court of the Gentiles where the sacrifices that the common people were permitted to eat were boiled (Ezek. 46:24). The KJV has "the place of them that boil." The sin, guilt, and cereal offerings were cooked in the kitchens

K

within the priests' chambers to protect them from contact with persons who had not been consecrated (Ezek. 46:19-20). There is no mention in the Bible of separate rooms in homes where meals were prepared. See *Cooking and Heating.*

KITE Bird of prey, best described as a scavenger of the *Accipitridae* family (hawk), the subfamily of *Milvinae* of the genus *Milvus.* Medium sized with red coloring (Lev. 11:14; Deut. 14:13; Isa. 34:15). This bird was considered unclean and not for human consumption.

KITHLISH (Kĭth´ lĭsh) (KJV, REB) See *Chitlish.*

KITLISH (Kĭt´ lĭsh) (NIV) See *Chitlish.*

KITRON (Kĭt´ rŏn) Place-name of uncertain meaning. A city in the tribal territory of Zebulun from which the Israelites could not expel the Canaanites (Judg. 1:30). This city is probably the same as Kattath. See *Kattath.*

KITTIM (Kĭt´ tĭm) Tribal name for the island of Cyprus, sometimes spelled Chittim. This name was derived from Kition, a city-state on the southeastern side of the island. Long associated with maritime lore, the island was ruled first by Greece, then the Assyrians, and finally Rome. Genesis 10:4 traces the people's roots to Noah's son Japheth. Jeremiah and Ezekiel both mention it in their prophecies (Jer. 2:10; Ezek. 27:6; cp. Isa. 23:1,12).

Kittim is used in intertestamental writings as denoting all of the land west of Cyprus. First Maccabees credits it as being the land of Alexander the Great (1:1; 8:5). The writer of Daniel understood it to be a part of the Roman Empire (11:30) used to threaten Antiochus Epiphanes. The Dead Sea Scrolls contain several references to Kittim, the most notable being the defeat of her people (Romans) at the hands of God's people. See *Cyprus.*

KIYYUN (Kīy´ yŭn) NASB spelling of the word spelled Chiun in Amos 5:26 KJV. Other versions translate the word as "Kaiwan." See *Chiun; Kaiwan.*

KNEAD, KNEADING BOWL Process of making bread dough by mixing flour, water, and oil along with a piece of the previous day's dough with the hands in a kneading bowl or trough. The mixture was allowed to stand in the bowl to rise and ferment (Exod. 12:34). Kneading the dough was usually the work of the woman (Gen. 18:6; 1 Sam. 28:24) but was performed on occasion by men (Hos. 7:4). The bowls could be made of wood, earthenware, or bronze and were the objects of either God's blessing or curse (Deut. 28:5,17; Exod. 8:3).

KNEEL A common posture in worship (1 Kings 19:18; Ps. 95:6; Isa. 45:23) and prayer (1 Kings 8:54; 2 Chron. 6:13; Ezra 9:5; Dan. 6:10; Acts 7:60; 9:40; 20:36; Eph. 3:14), although other postures are also found in the Bible. In the OT prayers are most often offered while standing (e.g., 1 Sam. 1:26; 2 Chron. 20:9; Neh. 9:4; Mark 11:25; Acts 6:6). Kneeling is also considered a sign of reverence, obedience, or respect (2 Kings 1:13; Matt. 17:14; 27:29; Mark 1:40; 10:17; Luke 5:8). "Kneel" and "bless" were once thought to come from the same Heb. root, but this etymology is no longer widely accepted. Blessing a child often involved placing the child on one's knees (Gen. 30:3; 48:9–12; 50:23–24). References to God as "blessed" (e.g., Gen. 9:26; 14:20 NIV) probably refer to kneeling before Him, that is, worshiping or praising Him.

E. Ray Clendenen

KNIFE Small instrument made of flint, copper, bronze, or iron used mainly for domestic purposes. Joshua was ordered to make flint knives for the circumcision of Israelite males (Josh. 5:2-3). Since flint was not the common material used to make knives in the days of Joshua, the command to make the knives of flint probably reflects a very ancient practice of circumcision (Gen. 17:11). Knives were used most commonly for killing and skinning animals and for killing

Large, wide-bladed knife from the Roman era.

sacrificial animals (Lev. 7:2; 8:15,20,25; 9:8-15; 1 Sam. 9:24). Some Bible students think the pruning hooks of Isa. 18:5 were curved knives. Others believe that the lances of the priests of Baal were pointed knives with which they cut themselves to gain Baal's attention (1 Kings 18:28). According to Ezra 1:9 the furnishings for the temple included 29 knives (KJV, NRSV), but the meaning of the Hebrew term is uncertain as seen in modern translations: NIV, "silver pans"; REB, "vessels of various kinds"; RSV, "censers"; NASB, "duplicates." See *Circumcision.*

KNOB Ornamental detail on the seven-branched lampstand in the tabernacle (Exod. 25:31-36; KJV, knop; RSV, capital; NRSV, calyx; NIV, buds). Some suggest that the knob was an imitation of the almond. The word may also refer to the capital of a column (Zeph. 2:14).

KNOP An element of the candles that were part of the lampstand in the tabernacle (Exod. 25: 31-36). It may have resembled the fruit of the almond. An ornament in the shape of a gourd carved into the cedar wainscot in the temple (1 Kings 6:18). See *Knob.*

KNOWLEDGE Translation of several Hebrew and Greek words covering a wide range of meanings: intellectual understanding, personal experience, emotion, and personal relationship (including sexual intercourse, Gen. 4:1, etc.). Knowledge is attributed both to God and to human beings.

God's knowledge is said to be omniscient. He knows all things (Job 21:22; Ps. 139:1-18); His understanding is beyond measure (Ps. 147:5). He knows the thoughts of our minds and the secrets of our hearts (Pss. 44:21; 94:11). He knows past events (Gen. 30:22), present happenings (Job 31:4), and future events (Zech. 13:1; Luke 1:33).

The knowledge which God has of nations and human beings indicates that He has a personal interest—not merely an awareness—of people (Ps. 144:3). To be known by God may mean that a nation or individual is chosen by God to play a part in God's purposes in the world (Jer. 1:5; Amos 3:2; Gal. 4:9).

The Bible speaks often about human knowledge. Knowledge of God is the greatest knowledge (Prov. 9:10) and is the chief duty of mankind (Hos. 6:6). In the OT the Israelites

know God through what He does for His people (Exod. 9:29; Lev. 23:43; Deut. 4:32-39; Pss. 9:10; 59:13; 78:16; Hos. 2:19-20). This knowledge of God is not simply theoretical or factual knowledge; it includes experiencing the reality of God in one's life (cp. Phil. 3:10) and living one's life in a manner that shows a respect for the power and majesty of God (cp. Jer. 22:15-16).

In the NT one knows God through knowledge of Jesus Christ (John 8:19; Col. 2:2-3). The Apostle Paul closely connected knowledge to faith. Knowledge gives direction, conviction, and assurance to faith (2 Cor. 4:14). Knowledge is a spiritual gift (1 Cor. 12:8) which can grow, increase, be filled, and abound (Phil. 1:9; Col. 1:9-10; 2 Cor. 8:7). It consists in having a better understanding of God's will in the ethical sense (Col. 1:9-10; Phil. 1:9), of knowing that God desires to save people (Eph. 1:8-9), and of having a deeper insight into God's will given in Christ (Eph. 1:17; 3:18-19).

Though Paul recognized the importance of knowledge, he also knew that it could be a divisive factor in churches such as at Rome and Corinth where some Christians claimed to be more spiritual because of their knowledge of spiritual matters (Rom. 14:1–15:6; 1 Cor. 8:1-13). Paul argued that knowledge puffs up but love builds up, and the knowledge exercised by the "strong" in faith could cause the "weak" in faith to go against their Christian conscience and lead to their spiritual ruin. Knowledge can be misused (1 Cor. 8). Love is more important than knowledge (1 Cor. 13), yet knowledge is still a gift, necessary for Christian teaching (1 Cor. 14:6) and for Christian growth toward a mature faith (1 Cor. 8:7; 2 Pet. 1:5-6; 3:18).

In the Gospel of John knowledge is a key concept, although the noun "knowledge" itself never occurs in John's Gospel. John instead frequently uses the verbs "to know." Jesus and the Father have a mutual knowledge (John 10:14-15), and Jesus' knowledge of God is perfect (e.g., John 3:11; 4:22; 7:28-29).

Knowledge of God is closely related to faith, expressing the perception and understanding of faith. Full knowledge is possible only after Jesus' glorification, since the disciples sometimes failed to understand Jesus (John 4:32; 10:6; 12:16). In the Gospel of John knowledge is expressed in Christian witness which may evoke belief in

K

Jesus (John 1:7; 4:39; 12:17-18) and in love (John 17:26). Whereas Jesus' knowledge of the Father is direct, the disciples' knowledge of Jesus is indirect, qualified by believing. The Christian's knowledge of Jesus is the perception of Jesus as the revelation of God that leads to obedience to His word. So the Christian is caught up into God's mission of love to the world in order that the world may come to know and believe in Jesus as the revelation of the Father's love for the world.   *Roger L. Omanson*

KOA (Kō´ à) National name of unknown meaning. Ezekiel 23:23 lists the names of several nations God will bring against Israel. Koa, like Shoa, has not been identified to everyone's satisfaction. Some identify Koa with the Guti people of Babylon, but this is disputed.

KOHATH (Kō´ hăth) Personal name of unknown meaning. The second son of Levi (Gen. 46:11) and father of Amram, Izhar, Hebron, and Uzziel (Exod. 6:18) who became the heads of the Kohathite branch of the Levitical priesthood. Kohath went to Egypt with Levi (his father) and Jacob (his grandfather) (Gen. 46:11), had a sister named Jochebed (Exod. 6:20), and died at the age of 133 (Exod. 6:18). See *Kohathites.*

KOHATHITES (Kō´ hăth-īts) Descendants of Kohath, the son of Levi (Exod. 6:16). Since Kohath was the grandfather of Aaron, Moses, and Miriam (Exod. 6:20; Num. 26:59), the Kohathites were considered the most important of the three major Levitical families (that is, Kohathites, Gershonites, and Merarites). The Kohathites were further divided into four branches according to the four sons of Kohath: Amram, Izhar, Hebron, and Uzziel (Exod. 6:18; Num. 3:19; 1 Chron. 6:1-3,16,18,33,38; 23:6,12-13,18-20; 26:23).

The Kohathites were active throughout Israel's history. The Kohathites, along with the Gershonites and Merarites, were placed around the tabernacle and were charged with caring for and moving it. The Kohathites were to camp on the south side of the tabernacle and were responsible to care for and move the ark, table, lampstand, altars, vessels of the sanctuary, and the screen (Num. 3:29-31). The Kohathites could not touch these objects and could move them only after they had been properly prepared by Aaron and his sons. The result of attempting to move these objects without their first being fit with poles for carrying was death (Num. 4:15,17-20; 7:9; cp. 1 Sam. 5–6; 2 Sam. 6:6-11).

After the conquest, Kohathites descended from Aaron received 13 cities from the tribes of Judah, Simeon, and Benjamin (Josh. 21:4,9-19; 1 Chron. 6:54-60). The remaining Kohathites received 10 cities from the tribes of Dan, Ephraim, and Manasseh (Josh. 21:5,20-26; 1 Chron. 6:61,66-70). One of the latter 10 was Shechem, a city of refuge.

David appointed 120 Kohathites under the leadership of Uriel to bring the ark to Jerusalem (1 Chron. 15:5). When Jehoshaphat sought deliverance from the Moabites and Ammonites, the Kohathites led the people in prayer and praise (2 Chron. 20:19). Mahath and Joel of the Kohathites helped in the purification of Israel's worship during the time of Hezekiah (2 Chron. 29:12). During Josiah's religious reforms, two Kohathite priests (Zechariah and Meshullam) helped supervise the work (2 Chron. 34:12).

When the Israelites returned from the exile, some of the Kohathites were placed in charge of preparing the showbread every Sabbath (1 Chron. 9:32). See *Amram; Cities of Refuge; Gershonites; Kohath; Levites; Levitical Cities; Merarites.*   *Phil Logan*

KOHELETH (Kō-hěl´ ěth) English transliteration of the Hebrew title of Ecclesiastes (also spelled Qoheleth). Koheleth is a Hebrew word that is translated as preacher (KJV, RSV, NASB), teacher (NIV, NRSV), speaker (REB), or philosopher (TEV) in Eccles. 1:1.

KOLAIAH (Kō-lī´ ah) Personal name meaning "voice of Yah." **1.** Son of Maaseiah whose descendants lived in Jerusalem after the exile (Neh. 11:7). **2.** Father of the false prophet, Ahab (Jer. 29:21-23).

KOPH (Kōph) Nineteenth letter of Hebrew alphabet. Used as a heading for Ps. 119:145-152 and each verse in this section begins with the letter Koph (KJV), Qoph (NASB, NIV), or Qof (HCSB).

KOR (kōr) Some versions use *cor.* It is thought to be a dry measure equal to a homer or to about 6.3 imperial bushels, though estimates vary greatly. Those using the metric system have estimated a kor between 220 and 450 liters. It apparently represented the load a donkey could carry on its back. The measure in Luke 16:7 possibly represents a Greek transliteration of the Hebrew *kor*. See *Weights and Measures*.

KORAH (Kō´ rah) Personal name meaning "bald." **1.** Son of Esau (Gen. 36:5,14; 1 Chron. 1:35) who became chief of a clan of Edom (Gen. 36:18). **2.** Grandson of Esau, son of Eliphaz, and chief of a clan of Edom (Gen. 36:16). **3.** Leader of rebellion against Moses and Aaron while Israel was camped in the wilderness of Paran (Num. 16). Korah, Dathan, and Abiram led a confederacy of 250 princes of the people against Aaron's claim to the priesthood and Moses' claim to authority in general. The rebels contended that the entire congregation was sanctified and therefore qualified to perform priestly functions. As punishment for their insubordination, God caused the earth to open and swallow the leaders and their property. A fire from the Lord consumed the 250 followers. **4.** Levite descended from Izhar, of the family of Kohath (Exod. 6:21; 1 Chron. 6:22,37), probably to be identified with 3. above. The sons of Korah and Asaph were the two most prominent groups of temple singers (cp. 2 Chron. 20:19). Many of the psalms with the heading "A Psalm of the Sons of Korah" may have been taken from their hymnbook (Pss. 42; 44–49; 84–85; 87–88). In a later list of temple singers the group of Heman replaced Korah and was joined by Asaph and Ethan as the three groups of temple singers (1 Chron. 6:33-48). The members of the group of Korah were also gatekeepers (1 Chron. 9:19; 26:1,19) and bakers of sacrificial cakes (9:31). **5.** Son of Hebron in the lineage of Caleb (1 Chron. 2:43). **6.** Possibly a town in Judah near Hebron. The five Korahites who joined David at Ziklag may have been persons from this town (1 Chron. 12:6). However, since these five men are also identified as Benjamites (1 Chron. 12:2), they may have been from a town of this same name whose location has yet to be determined.

Mike Mitchell and Phil Logan

KORAHITES (Kôr´ á·hīts) Descendants of Korah who belonged to the Kohathite Levites. The name is also spelled Korathites (Num. 26:58) and Korhites (KJV). See *Kohathites; Korah*.

KORATHITE (Kō´ răth·īt) Alternate spelling of Korahites. See *Korahites*.

KORAZIN (Kō´·rā zĭn) (NIV) See *Chorazin*.

KORHITES (Kôr´ hīts) Alternate spelling of Korahites. See *Korahites*.

KORE (Kō´ rə) Personal name meaning "one who proclaims." **1.** Son of Ebiasaph, a Levite of the family of Korah and father of Shallum and Meshelemiah, gatekeepers at the tabernacle (1 Chron. 9:19; 26:1). **2.** Son of Imnah, the Levite, keeper of the eastern gate, and appointed by Hezekiah to receive the freewill offerings and distribute them among the priests (2 Chron. 31:14). **3.** Mistaken transliteration in 1 Chron. 26:19 (KJV). The name should be Korah (see modern versions).

KOUM (Kūm) NIV and TEV spelling of cumi. NASB has kum. All three represent the Aramaic word which means "arise" in Mark 5:41.

KOZ (Kŏz) Personal name meaning "thorn." **1.** Member of the tribe of Judah (1 Chron. 4:8). He may have belonged to the priestly family of Hakkoz. **2.** KJV transliterates the name Hakkoz in Ezra 2:61; Neh. 3:4,21; 7:63 with "Koz," apparently taking Hak to be the Hebrew article "the." The person in these passages is probably the same as the person in 1 Chron. 24:10. See *Hakkoz*.

KUB (Kŭb) (TEV) See *Chub; Libya*.

KUE (Kū´ ĕ) Believed by many to be an ancient name for Cilicia. The name occurs in 1 Kings 10:28 and 2 Chron. 1:16. The Masoretes (the Hebrew scholars who added the vowels to the Hebrew text which had been written only with consonants) did not seem to understand the reference and added vowels to the consonants which gave the reading now found in the KJV, "linen yarn." By adding different vowels to the consonants of the Hebrew text, modern Bible students read "from Kue." If the Masoretes and the KJV are correct, then Solomon imported horses and linen yarn from Egypt. If the NRSV, NASB, NIV, REB, and TEV are correct (which in all likelihood they are), then Solomon imported horses from Egypt and Kue—that is, Cilicia in southeast Asia Minor (NEB, Coa). Many think,

K

further, that the Hebrew word translated as "Egypt" (*Mizraim*) should be translated as "Musri," a country in Asia Minor near Cilicia. From Egypt, Solomon acquired chariots (1 Kings 10:29). Thus Solomon acted as the middleman, putting horses with chariots and exporting them to other kingdoms. This proved to be a very lucrative arrangement for Solomon. See *Cilicia; Mizraim; Musri; Solomon.*   *Phil Logan*

KUN (Kūn) TEV for Cun or Chun. See *Cun.*

KUSHAIAH (Kū·shī´ ah) Personal name of unknown meaning. Levite of the Merarite family listed as one of the sanctuary singers during the reign of David. His son Ethan was appointed as a chief assistant of Heman (1 Chron. 15:17). This same person is also listed under the name Kishi (1 Chron. 6:44).

K

L

The Lion of Amphipolis guards the old bridge over the Strymon River. Paul passed through Amphipolis on his way from Philippi to Thessalonica.

LAADAH (Lā´ à dah) Personal name meaning "throat" or "double chin." Member of tribe of Judah (1 Chron. 4:21).

LAADAN (Lā´ à dan) Personal name meaning "throat" or "double chin." **1.** Member of tribe of Ephraim (1 Chron. 7:26) and ancestor of Joshua. **2.** Original ancestor of clan of Levites and son of Gershon (1 Chron. 23:7-9; 26:21), though elsewhere Gershon's son is named Libni. Some suggest that Laadan originally belonged to family of Libni, but his clan became more prominent and overshadowed that of Libni in later times. See *Libni.*

LABAN (Lā´ bàn) Personal name meaning "white." **1.** Rebekah's brother (Gen. 24:29) and father of Leah and Rachel (Gen. 29:16). Laban lived in the city of Nahor that was probably close to the metropolis of Haran. Laban is known primarily from the two stories in Gen. 24 and 29–31. Laban was directly responsible for the betrothal of Rebekah to Isaac. After Abraham's steward relates that he has come to find a wife for Isaac, Laban and his father give their permission for the marriage (Gen. 24:50-51). Later Jacob fled to his uncle Laban's house after stealing the birthright from Esau. Laban agreed to give his daughter, Rachel, as payment for Jacob's seven years of labor. However, Laban deceived Jacob, making him marry the older daughter, Leah. After Jacob worked an additional seven years, Laban allowed him to marry Rachel (Gen. 29:15-30). See *Jacob; Leah; Rachel; Rebekah.* **2.** Town used to locate Moses' speeches in Deuteronomy (1:1). It is sometimes identified with Libnah (Num. 33:20). Assyrian and Egyptian texts mention its location on Canaan's southern border perhaps near the brook of Egypt at Sheikh ez-Zuweid or the nearby Tell Abu Seleimeh. See *Libnah.*   *Kenneth Craig*

LABOR See *Work, Theology of.*

LACE Ornamental braid used as a trim. Blue or purple cords were used to fasten the high priest's breastpiece to the ephod (Exod. 28:28; 39:21) and the golden plate to his turban (Exod. 28:37; 39:31). The translation "lace" (KJV, RSV) is frequently replaced with cord (NASB, NIV, NRSV, TEV) or braid (REB). The underlying Hebrew term is used elsewhere for a belt or signet cord (Gen. 38:18), for the cords or tassels on the cor-

ners of garments (Num. 15:38) or for strands of fiber (Judg. 16:9).

LACHISH (Lā´ kǐsh) An important OT city located in the Shephelah ("lowlands") southwest of Jerusalem. It has usually been identified in modern times with the archaeological site called Tell ed-Duweir. The same site has more recently come to be called Tel Lachish. Lachish is also mentioned in ancient Egyptian, Assyrian, and Babylonian records.

The earliest reference to Lachish is in the Amarna letters (about 1400 B.C.). It was evidently one of the important Canaanite cities of the time. The Hebrew army under Joshua's command defeated the king of Lachish, killed him, and conquered his city (Josh. 10:5,23,32-33). Later, Lachish was apportioned to the tribe of Judah (Josh. 15:39). The next biblical reference to Lachish comes in 2 Chron. 11:9, from the reign of Rehoboam who "fortified" or "built up" the city (11:5-6). Lachish was also the city of refuge for Amaziah, who fled there from Jerusalem to escape a conspiracy against him (2 Kings 14:19; 2 Chron. 25:27).

Lachish is perhaps most well-known for the story of its siege and conquest in 701 B.C. at the hands of the Assyrian King Sennacherib (2 Kings 18; 2 Chron. 32; Isa. 36). Two later brief references appear (Jer. 34:7; Neh. 11:30).

The archaeological excavations at Lachish have been extensive and rewarding. They have shown occupation at Lachish from about 4000 B.C. to the time of its conquest by the Persian Empire (539–333 B.C.). The rich and varied finds represent almost all of the periods, but the chief interest for the student of the Bible centers on the periods beginning with the time of the Hebrew invasion of Canaan. According to excavations by David Ussishkin, the archaeological evidence shows that the site contained two different Canaanite occupation levels both destroyed by fire, one in the late 1200s B.C. and one around 1150 B.C. (this latter date based upon, among other things, a cartouche of Rameses III of Egypt). The renowned OT scholar W. F. Albright had attributed the earlier destruction level to the Israelites, but Ussishkin prefers to attribute the later destruction to the Israelites (though he recognizes the possibility that the Philistines could have been the culprits). As shown here, the archaeological evidence is often assumed to correlate with a later dating of the

The definitive line of a wall at Lachish running from the south going northeast up to the high place.

Israelite conquest. However, according to Josh. 10, Joshua did not burn Lachish. In Joshua 11:13 it was reported as exceptional that the Israelites burned Hazor alone among a group of conquered cities. The conquest accounts in Joshua only mention the burning of three cities, Jericho, Ai, and Hazor (Josh. 6:25; 8:8,19; 11:11). According to the accounts in Joshua, the Israelites conquered Lachish and only killed its inhabitants; thus, perhaps the desire to correlate a fire level with the conquest is ill-advised. It is possible that Israel wiped out the inhabitants in a time frame correlating to the biblical dating of the conquest (1406 B.C.) leaving the site itself intact as a possible site of Israelite settlement (Deut.6:10-11) resulting in a later return of Canaanites to the site.

The biblical account of Sennacherib's conquest of Lachish in 701 B.C. is supported and amplified by Assyrian records of King Sennacherib's campaign (2 Kings 18; 2 Chron. 32; Isa. 36). This was graphically recorded in a large and elaborate bas-relief on the walls of the royal palace in Nineveh. Presently housed in the British museum in London, these carvings show Assyrian soldiers attacking the walled city, the city inhabitants defending their city, soldiers killing some of the defenders, families with possessions being led away captive, and the king on his throne reviewing the spoils taken from the city. A replica of this relief may be found in the library of The Southern Baptist Theological Seminary in Louisville, Kentucky.

The "Lachish Letters"—a group of messages in ancient Hebrew inscribed with ink on pottery shards dating to around 590 B.C.—are among the most significant finds from Lachish. They provide important linguistic and historical information about this period.

Bruce C. Cresson and Eric Mitchell

LADAN (Lā´ dăn) Modern translations' spelling of Laadan. See *Laadan*.

LADDER Series of steps used for ascent or descent. The Hebrew term may refer to steps carved out of rock or to steps constructed from wood, metal, stone, or even rope. The angels ascending and descending in Jacob's vision point to God's presence with Jacob (Gen. 28:12). Jesus' promise to Nathaniel points to Jesus as the one who incarnates God's presence (John 1:49-51).

LAEL (Lā´ ĕl) Personal name meaning "belonging to God." Levite leader in clan of Gershon (Num. 3:24).

LAHAD (Lā´ hăd) Personal name meaning "slow, lazybones." Member of tribe of Judah (1 Chron. 4:2).

LAHAIROI (Là hī rôı) See *Beer-Lahairoi*.

LAHMAM (Lăh´ măm) Place-name meaning "food" or "bread." Reading in many Hebrew manuscripts and early translations for Lahmas (Josh. 15:40). KJV, NRSV, TEV read Lahmam. Town in tribal territory of Judah near Lachish, possibly modern Khirbet el-Lahm, about two and a half miles south of Beth-gibrin.

LAHMAS (Lah´ măs) Place-name, perhaps meaning "violence." Reading of basic Hebrew manuscript (Josh. 15:40) adopted by REB, NIV, NASB. Possibly, early scribes confused final letter with similar appearing final "m" in Hebrew. See *Lahmam*.

LAHMI (Lah´ mī) Personal name meaning "my bread" or perhaps an abbreviated form of Bethlehemite. Brother of the giant Goliath. Elhanan the son of Jair killed him (1 Chron. 20:5). The parallel passage (2 Sam. 21:19) says Elhanan the Bethlehemite killed Goliath the Gittite (cp. 1 Sam. 17). The Chronicler may have been using a text of Samuel which copyists had made difficult to read and have interpreted it to the best of his ability. Some interpreters think the present text of Samuel represents copyists' confusion with the Chronicler's text accuracy. See *Elhanan; Goliath*.

LAISH (Lā´ ĭsh) Personal and place name meaning "strong" or "lion." The KJV form of Laishah. **1.** Laish was from Gallim in Benjamin. He was the father of Paltiel (Phalti in KJV) and father-in-law of Michal, King Saul's daughter (1 Sam. 19:11-12; 25:44) See *Michal*. **2.** Originally a Canaanite city in northern Palestine known for its quiet, secure, and isolated lifestyle (Judg. 18:7). It was spied out by the Danites as a place for their dwelling after the Philistines forced them from the coastal region. After finding it suitable, the Danites invaded Laish and renamed the city and area Dan. See *Dan*. **3.** Town apparently in tribal territory of Benjamin whose troubles from Assyrian invasion Isaiah mentioned

(Isa. 10:30). Its location is not known. Modern translations read Laishah.

LAISHAH (Lā´ ĭsh ah) Place-name meaning "lioness" or "towards Laish." City on military route from Bethel to Jerusalem which Isaiah warned of Assyrian army's approach (Isa. 10:30). It may be modern el-Esawijeh southwest of Anathoth or Ras et-Tawil south of Geba. See *Laish.*

LAKE OF FIRE See *Eschatology; Fire; Hell.*

LAKE OF GENNESARET See *Galilee, Sea of.*

LAKKUM (Lăk´ kŭm) or **LAKUM** (Lā´ kŭm) Place-name, perhaps meaning "rising" or "fortification." Border town in tribal allotment of Naphtali (Josh. 19:33). It may be modern Khirbet el-Mansurah near the southern end of the Sea of Galilee.

LAMA See *Eli, Eli, Lama Sabachthani.*

LAMB Young sheep. See *Lamb of God; Sheep.*

LAMB OF GOD Title specifically bestowed upon the Lord Jesus by John the Baptist (John 1:29), "Here is the Lamb of God, who takes away the sin of the world!" (HCSB). The title is found earlier than the NT but not with the specific meaning found there. For example, the phrase is used in a second century apocryphal book to refer to the Messiah ("honor Judah and Levi, for from them shall arise for you the Lamb of God, saving all nations by grace"). Also, Jer. 11:19 and Isa. 53:7 point to a prophetic significance of the Lamb. It is in the NT, however, that the term finds its distinctly Christian significance to refer to Christ as the Lamb who atoned for our sins.

The source of the expression is to be found in the important place that the "lamb" occupies in the sacrifices of the Jewish people. A lamb was used for sacrifice during the annual Passover (Exod. 12:1-36) as well as in the daily sacrifices of Israel (Lev. 14:12-21; Heb. 10:5-7). On the Sabbath the number of the offerings was doubled, and at some of the great festivals a still larger number were laid upon the altar (Exod. 29:38; Num. 28:3,9,13). All this would be familiar to John the Baptist, being a member of a priestly family.

The lamb of the Passover occupied a prominent place in the mind of a devout Israelite, and when John spoke the words of John 1:29, the Passover was not far off. The sacrificial significance of the term is much more important than the mere comparison of the character of our Lord with meekness and gentleness, as some have suggested. The sacrificial use is clearly in view in the words of the Apostles Paul (1 Cor. 5:7) and Peter (1 Pet. 1:18).

While uses of the word "lamb" are fairly sparse in the rest of the NT, in the book of Revelation the references to the Lamb take center stage. The term occurs 27 times, but the word used by the Apostle John differs from the one spoken by the Baptist. The *amnos* of John 1:29 becomes the *arnion* in Revelation, a diminutive form suggestive of affection. *Arnion* is also the word used by the Lord in His rebuke and forgiveness of Peter (John 21:15). While the *arnion* in Revelation is the Lamb of sacrifice (5:6-10; 12:11), He also is the one who will come in wrath and judgment (6:16-17).

The relation between John 1:29 and Isa. 53 has been the subject of significant discussion. In verse 10 Isaiah's "suffering one" "would render Himself as a guilt offering," and in verse 4 "our griefs He Himself bore" (NASB). The prophet's word for "bearing" (in the Septuagint [LXX], *pherein*) involves the conception of a sin offering possessing justifying power, and the idea of "taking away" is in view. John, however, did not use the LXX word *pherein* but *airein* when he said Christ will "take away" the sin of the world. Some scholars have maintained that John's term simply means "put away," or "support," or "endure." But this surely misses the meaning of the associated term "lamb," which John could not have employed without some reference to its sacrificial and therefore substitutionary force.

Between the two references, we find in Christ the fulfillment of the promise that God would provide a sacrifice who would both bear the curse of sin and provide salvation for the world. While Isaiah may not have had a complete dogmatic conception of the full relation of the death of Christ to the salvation of the world at large, at the very least the idea of bearing the curse of sin was in Isaiah's mind. See *Atonement; Christ, Christology; Passover; Redeem, Redemption, Redeemer; Sacrifice and Offering; Servant of the Lord.*   *Dale Ellenburg*

LAME, LAMENESS Physical condition in which walking is difficult or impossible. In the OT lame animals were not acceptable sacrifices (Deut. 15:21; Mal. 1:8,13). The lame were prohibited from serving as priests though they were allowed to eat from the priests' provisions (Lev. 21:18). The Jebusites boasted that their stronghold of Jerusalem was so impregnable that even the blind and lame would be able to turn back David's troops (2 Sam. 5:6 NRVS, NIV). A proverb excluding the blind and lame from "the house" (that is, the temple) is traced to the assault on Jerusalem (2 Sam. 5:8). In the NT the healing of the lame forms an important part of Jesus' messianic work (Matt. 11:2-6; 15:29-31). By healing the lame in the temple, Jesus restored these excluded ones to full participation in the worshiping community (Matt. 21:14). Acts tells of the early church continuing Jesus' healing ministry to the lame: Peter and John (Acts 3:2); Philip (8:7); Paul (14:8-10).

LAMECH (Lā´ mĕk) Personal name meaning "powerful." The son of Methuselah and father of Noah (Gen. 4:18; 5:25,29). He had two wives, Adah and Zillah, whose sons are credited with the rise of the nomadic way of life, music, and metalworking. Lamech is blamed with beginning polygamy (or bigamy) and the increase of sinful pride in the earth. The Song of Lamech (Gen. 4:23-24) is an ancient poem supporting unlimited revenge. Jesus may have had this in mind in teaching about unlimited forgiveness (Matt. 18:22).   *Mike Mitchell*

LAMED (La´ mĕd) Twelfth letter of the Hebrew alphabet used as a heading for Ps. 119:89-96. Each verse in this section of the psalm begins with the letter *lamed.*

LAMENT See *Grief and Mourning; Lamentations; Psalms, Book of.*

LAMENTATIONS, BOOK OF Composed of five poetic laments over the destruction of Jerusalem and the temple in 587 B.C. (Lam. 2:7) and over the pitiable condition of the people of Judah that resulted (2:11). The misery after the destruction is all the more deplorable compared to the glory beforehand (1:1). The author calls on the people to recognize that because of their sin God is just in what He has done (1:5), so the people should turn to Him, repent, and appeal for mercy (2:18; 3:25-26,40-41). See *Exile; Israel, Land of.*

The somber tone of Lamentations is suited to solemn services. The Jews read the book annually on the ninth of Ab to commemorate, among other things, the destruction of the first and second temples. Christians traditionally read it in services during the last three days of Holy Week.

The book does not state who its author was, but from ancient times it has traditionally been ascribed to Jeremiah. While some scholars find reason to doubt this, others defend it.

The following factors favor authorship by Jeremiah: (1) There are similarities between Lamentations and Jeremiah in tenor, theology, themes, language, and imagery (cp. Lam. 1:15 and Jer. 8:21; Lam. 1:2 and Jer. 30:14). (2) Like the book of Jeremiah, Lamentations affirms that Judah should submit to the exile because it is deserved (Lam. 1:5; 3:27-28; Jer. 29:4-10), yet there is hope for restoration (Lam. 3:21-33; 4:22; 5:19-22; Jer. 29:11-14). (3) Both books suggest that the prophets and priests share with the people the blame for the nation's sin (Lam. 2:14; 4:13; Jer. 14:14; 23:16).

An eyewitness to the destruction of Jerusalem seemingly wrote Lamentations, and the Prophet Jeremiah was an eyewitness (Lam. 2:6-12; Jer. 39:1-14). We know that Jeremiah wrote a lament over Josiah (2 Chron. 35:25); therefore it is entirely possible he also wrote these laments.

The canonicity of Lamentations has never been seriously challenged. The English Bible, like the Greek and Latin, places Lamentations after Jeremiah, probably for reasons of authorship and historical content. In the Hebrew Bible Lamentations is included with the "Writings," specifically among the five *Megilloth,* or "Scrolls," which are read during holy days.

Lamentations takes the form of a lament, a dirge. It shares literary attributes with laments in the Psalms (e.g., 44; 60; 74; 79; 80; 83; 89). Some scholars propose that there is a metrical pattern in the Hebrew poetry of chapters 1–4 that is found in other dirges in the Bible.

Chapters 1–4 are alphabetic acrostics. Because there are 22 letters in the Hebrew alphabet, chapters 1, 2, and 4 have 22 verses: each verse begins with a succeeding letter of the alphabet. Chapter 3 has 66 verses because three successive verses are allotted to each letter of the alphabet. (Chapter 5 also has 22 verses, but it is not composed as an acrostic.) The reason the author used the alphabetic acrostic may have been either to control and restrain the grief that would otherwise run rampant or to express his sorrow completely—from A to Z, as we would say. See *Acrostic.*

The facts of the fall of Jerusalem are given in 2 Kings 25 and Jer. 52; Lamentations expresses the emotion. Like Job, Lamentations wrestles with the problem of evil. Like Ezekiel, it expresses what results when God leaves His temple, His city, and His people. Throughout, it is acknowledged that Judah deserved its punishment; it is consistent with the curse in Deut. 28:15-68. But along with this admission of guilt is a call for the punishment to end, as in the psalms of lament, and a call for the enemies who carried it out to be punished in return (Lam. 4:22), as in the imprecatory psalms and Hab. 1:12-17.

Outline

I. Anguish of Jerusalem (1:1-22).
   A. Description of the desolation (1:1-11).
   B. Jerusalem pleads for mercy and vengeance (1:12-22).
II. God's Wrath on Jerusalem (2:1-22).
   A. God's wrath (2:1-10).
   B. Description of the ruin (2:11-19).
   C. Jerusalem's plea (2:20-22).
III. Suffering and Hope (3:1-66).
   A. Description of the suffering (3:1-18).
   B. Confidence in the Lord (3:19-39).
   C. Prayer for relief and vengeance (3:40-66).
IV. Sorrow and Horror (4:1-22).
   A. Jerusalem's glory replaced by horror (4:1-10).
   B. Causes and climax of the horror (4:11-20).
   C. Punishment for Edom (4:21-22).
V. Prayer (5:1-22).
   A. Prayer for remembrance (5:1-18).
   B. Prayer for restoration (5:19-22).

David K. Stabnow

LAMPS, LIGHTING, LAMPSTAND System and articles used to illuminate homes in biblical times. Lamps are mentioned often in the Bible but seldom described. Archaeological excavations have provided numerous examples of these lighting implements used in ancient times, dating from before Abraham to after Christ. Lamps of the OT period were made exclusively of pot-

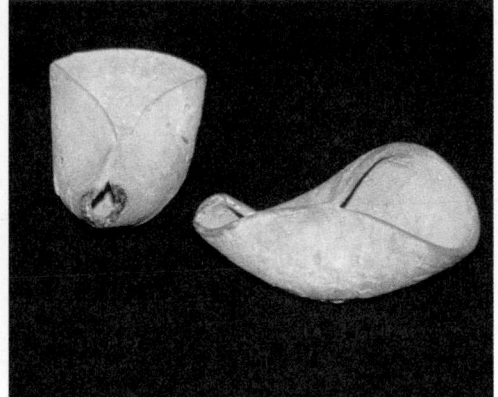

Hellenistic slipper lamps from Israel. These lamps are from the Maccabean era.

tery. These lamps were of the open-bowl design with a pinched spout to support the wick. Wicks were made generally of twisted flax (Isa. 42:3). Lamps burned olive oil almost exclusively (Exod. 25:6), though in later times oil from nuts, fish, and other sources were used. Lamps from the Bronze Age to the Hellenistic times were made on the pottery wheel, after which molds were made for the enclosed forms of the Greek and Roman periods (from about 500 B.C. onward). For outdoor lighting the torch (KJV, lantern) was used (Judg. 7:16; John 18:3).

A golden lampstand with three branches extending from either side of the central tier was placed in the tabernacle (Exod. 25:31-40). Each branch may have had a seven-spouted lamp

A multi-spout Roman oil lamp with ring-shaped oil chamber, made in Italy, first century A.D.

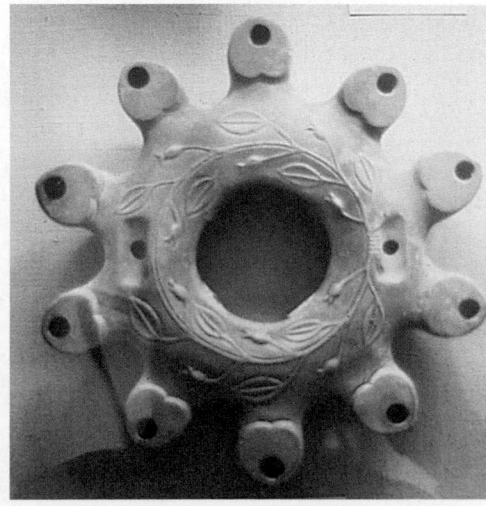

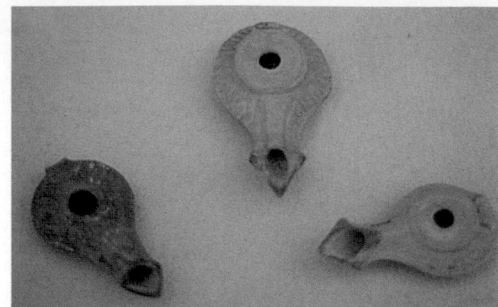

First-century B.C. pottery oil lamps.

(Zech. 4:2), as do some individual lamps found in Palestine. This seven-branched candelabrum (menorah), supporting seven lamps, continued in prominence through the first and second temple periods and later became symbolic of the nation of Israel. Surrounding nations also employed multitiered and multilegged lamps and lampstands.

Lamps (lights) were used symbolically in the OT and NT. Light depicted life in abundance, divine presence, or life's direction versus death in darkness (cp. Ps. 119:105; 1 John 1:5 with Job 18:5; Prov. 13:9). Jesus is depicted often in John as the light of the world (John 1:4-5,7-9; 3:19; 8:12; 9:5; 11:9-10; 12:35-36,46). Jesus' disciples are also described as the light of the world (Matt. 5:14-16). See *Light, Light of the World.*

R. Dennis Cole

LANCE, LANCET Weapon consisting of a long shaft with a metal head; javelin; spear (Judg. 5:8 NASB; 1 Kings 18:28 RSV; Jer. 50:42 KJV). In modern English a lancet is a two-edged surgical instrument. The KJV used "lancet" for a small lance (1 Kings 18:28). See *Arms and Armor; Weapons.*

LAND OF FORGETFULNESS Description of Sheol (Ps. 88:12; "land of oblivion" HCSB). See *Sheol.*

LANDMARK Pillar or heap of stones serving as a boundary marker (Gen. 31:51-52). Some Babylonian and Egyptian examples are elaborately carved. Many ancient law codes (Babylonian, Egyptian, Greek, Roman) prohibited the removal of a landmark (Deut. 19:14; cp. 27:17; Prov. 22:28). In Job 24:2 removal of a marker parallels theft. Proverbs 23:10 warns against removing markers to rob orphans. Hosea 5:10 condemns the ruthless rulers of Judah as like those who remove landmarks, that is, those who have no regard for justice or for the traditional law. Moving the landmark meant changing the traditional land allotments (cp. Josh. 13–19) and cheating a poor landowner of what little land he owned.

LANE Narrow, constricted passageway. In English "lane" evokes the image of a rural path between hedges or fences. The Greek term is used for a city alley (Luke 14:21 KJV, NASB,

This array of lamps shows the progression from the middle Bronze Age to the Persian and Hellenistic periods.

NRSV; alley, NIV, REB, TEV; "streets and alleys" HCSB). Compare Acts 9:11; 12:10 where the same Greek term is used.

LANGUAGE, CONFUSION OF See *Babel; Pentecost.*

LANGUAGES OF THE BIBLE
The OT was first written in Hebrew with the exceptions of much of Ezra 4–7 and Daniel 2:4b–7:28, which appear in Aramaic. The NT was written in Greek though Jesus and the early believers may have spoken Aramaic.

Characteristics of Hebrew Hebrew is a Semitic language related to Phoenician and the dialects of ancient Canaan. Semitic languages have the ability to convey abundant meaning through few words. Importance rests on the verb, which generally comes first in the sentence because action is the most significant element. Similarly, modifiers (such as adjectives) follow nouns, lending greater weight to the nouns. Typical word order for a sentence is: verb—subject—subject modifiers—object—object modifiers. Deviation from this order gives emphasis to the word that comes first.

Characteristics of Aramaic Aramaic is similar to Hebrew and shares a considerable vocabulary with it. It began as the language of Syria and was gradually adopted as the language of international communication. After about 600 B.C. it replaced Hebrew as the spoken language of Palestine. Hebrew then continued as the religious language of the Jews, but the Aramaic alphabet was borrowed for writing it.

Characteristics of Greek Greek belongs to the Indo-European language group. It spread throughout the Mediterranean world after about 335 B.C. with Alexander's conquests. The NT is written in a dialect called *koine* (meaning "common"), which was the dialect of the common person. New Testament Greek is heavily infused with Semitic thought modes, and many Aramaic words are found rendered with Greek letters (e.g., *talitha koum*, Mark 5:41; *ephphatha*, Mark 7:34; *Eloi, Eloi, lema sabachthani*, Mark 15:34; *maranatha*, 1 Cor. 16:22). So also are such Latin words as *kenturion* (centurion) and *denarion* (denarius). Greek's accurateness of expression and widespread usage made it the ideal tongue for the early communication of the gospel. Paul no doubt knew all three biblical languages and Latin as well. See *Aramaic;*

Daniel, Book of; Ezra, Book of; Greek Language; Hebrew Language.   *Larry McKinney*

LANTERN
Portable container with transparent openings used to display and protect a light. The Greek term used at John 18:3 is of uncertain meaning, though some type of light is clearly intended. In John's ironic scene, the mob comes with "artificial" lights to arrest Jesus, "the light of the world" (John 8:12; 9:5; 11:9; 12:35-36,40).

LAODICEA
(Lā ŏd ĭ sē´ á) City in southwest Asia Minor on an ancient highway running from Ephesus to Syria 10 miles west of Colossae and six miles south of Hierapolis. Christian communities existed in all three cities (Col. 2:1; 4:13-16), though the one in Colossae is the best known. Paul wrote a letter to the Laodiceans (Col. 4:16) which has not survived, though some scholars have attempted to identify this missing letter with either the letter to the Ephesians or to Philemon.

Laodicea was well-known in the ancient world for its wealth. The extent of its wealth is illustrated by the fact that Laodicea was rebuilt without the financial help of Rome after the disastrous earthquake of A.D. 60. Laodicea earned its wealth in the textile industry in the production of black wool and in the banking industry. Laodicea was also known for its medical school that concocted a spice nard for the treatment of ears and an eye salve. The major weakness of Laodicea was its lack of a water supply. This need was met by bringing water six miles north from Denizli through a system of stone pipes (another sign of Laodicea's wealth).

Laodicea is best known today to readers of Revelation where Jesus criticized Laodicea,

Exterior view of the archways in the top tier of one of the great theaters at ancient Laodicea.

An unexcavated Roman theater, smaller of the two theaters at ancient Laodicea.

using imagery drawn from its daily life (Rev. 3:14-22). First, Jesus said Laodicea is neither cold (like the cold, pure waters of Colossae) nor hot (like the therapeutic hot springs of Hierapolis). Laodicea is lukewarm and provides neither refreshment for the spiritually weary nor healing for the spiritually sick (Rev. 3:15-16). Despite their apparent spiritual uselessness, the Laodiceans were claiming a spiritual wealth equal to their material wealth; and further, they were claiming to have acquired both by their own efforts. In reality, however, the Laodiceans, while they may have had material wealth, were spiritually poor, blind, and naked (Rev. 3:17)— an obvious reference to the textile and banking industry and medical school of Laodicea. According to Jesus, what the Laodiceans needed more than anything else was the true gold, white (not black) garments, and ointment that only Christ could give (Rev. 3:18). A true spiritual foundation is laid only in Christ, not human effort.

The letter of the risen Christ to the church at Laodicea (Rev. 3:14-22) contains numerous allusions to conditions in the city. A five-mile-long aqueduct supplied the city with tepid water that served as an image for "lukewarm" Christianity

Archaeological remains of an early church located at Laodicea in Turkey.

(3:15-16). The Laodicean claim to be rich and prosperous reflects the self-reliant refusal of this city to accept Roman aid for rebuilding after an earthquake of about A.D. 60 (3:17). The charge that the Laodicean Christians were naked, blind, and in need of clothing and ointment (3:17-18) reflects the city's well-known school of ophthalmology and its fine garments of raven-black wool of local sheep.   *Phil Logan*

LAODICEAN (Lā ŏd ĭ sē´ an) Citizen of Laodicea. See *Laodicea*.

LAODICEANS, EPISTLE TO THE Short letter claiming Paul as its author. The letter was doubtless composed to fill in the gap suggested by Col. 4:16. The date of writing is unknown. Jerome (340?–420) warned against this spurious work. Despite Jerome's protests the letter was accepted as a genuine Pauline epistle by Pope Gregory the Great (590–604). About one half of the Latin manuscripts of the Pauline Epistles produced between 500 and 1600 contain the Epistle to the Laodiceans. With the Reformation the epistle quickly fell into disuse. The epistle was perhaps composed in Greek, though it survives only in Latin. Its 247 words are a patchwork of passages drawn from the authentic Pauline letters, chiefly Philippians but also Galatians, 1 and 2 Corinthians, and 1 and 2 Timothy. There are also echoes of Matthew and 2 Peter.

LAPIDOTH (Lăp´ ĭ dŏth) or **LAPPIDOTH** Personal name meaning "lightnings." Deborah's husband (Judg. 4:4).

LAPIS LAZULI See *Minerals and Metals*.

LAPWING (*Vanellus vanellus*) Shorebird with a short bill and a crest of feathers on its head. The lapwing is known for its irregular flapping flight and shrill cry. KJV included the lapwing among the unclean birds (Lev. 11:19; Deut. 14:18). Modern translations generally identify the Hebrew term with the hoopoe.

LASCIVIOUSNESS KJV term for an unbridled expression of sexual urges (Mark 7:22; 2 Cor. 12:21; Gal. 5:19; Eph. 4:19; 1 Pet. 4:3; Jude 4). RSV translated the underlying Greek as lenciousness; NASB, sensuality. Other translations used a variety of terms: debauchery, indecency, lewdness, sexual sin.

LASEA (Là sē´ à) Place-name of uncertain meaning. City on south coast of Crete (Acts 27:8).

LASHA (Lā´ shà) Place-name of uncertain meaning. A point on the original border of Canaan (Gen. 10:19). The traditional location is at Kallirhoe, east of the Dead Sea. Others identify it with Nuhashe or Laash in northern Syria near Hamath. The exact meaning of the prepositions and the direction of the borders are not clear.

LASHARON (Là shâr´ ŏn) Place-name meaning "belonging to Sharon." Listed as one of the towns whose king Joshua killed in conquering Canaan (Josh. 12:18). The early Greek translators had great difficulty with the text, some Greek manuscripts omitting the verse altogether. "L" represents the Hebrew preposition "of, to, belonging to." Sharon is the name of the plain in which the preceding town Aphek in the list is located. The original Hebrew text may have

A gold staff terminal decorated with lapis lazuli lion heads.

indicated Aphek in Sharon to distinguish it from other Apheks. See *Aphek.*

LAST DAY, LAST TIME See *Eschatology; Judgment Day.*

LAST SUPPER The last meal Jesus shared with His disciples before the crucifixion. The high point of the Bible and central event of the ages is the passion (betrayal, crucifixion, death, burial, resurrection, and ascension) of Jesus Christ. All that goes before it in the Bible anticipates His coming. All that comes after presents the full meaning of the person and work of Christ.

The Last Supper is reported in the four Gospels (Matt. 26:20-35; Mark 14:12-31; Luke 22:14-38; and John 13:1–17:26), but the oldest and most detailed description is in 1 Cor. 11:17-34, probably written before the Gospels were published. Even earlier is Isa. 52:13–53:12, which reads like eye-witness testimony. These two passages are used more than the Gospels to explain the significance of the passion.

As His last week unfolded, Jesus established a new celebration. The new communal meal forms the heart of Christian worship and will be celebrated until the second coming of Christ, when the symbolism will give way to the full reality the supper anticipates. The breaking and sharing of bread and the drinking of the cup were invested with new meaning, demonstrating continuity of the old and new covenants. The body and blood of Christ were given as a sacrifice to secure eternal salvation for all who trust Him as Lord and Savior. That night Jesus also demonstrated the principle of servant leadership. Judas Iscariot, one of the Twelve, though publicly honored that night, betrayed Christ into the hands of those who crucified Him.

Commentators love to explore apparent contradictions in timing and details of the Last Supper in relationship to the observance of Passover. The Synoptics relate it directly to the Passover meal, and John (if talking about the same event) places it on the day before. The assumption of conflict may not be correct. Often in his Gospel John related events not recorded in the other Gospels. Just as his narratives are different in other aspects, John may be describing another intimate meal with the disciples earlier in the final week of Jesus' life. See *Ordinances.*

Charles W. Draper

A stone slab found at Philippi, inscribed in Latin.

LATCHET KJV term for a leather thong or strap used to fasten sandals (Gen. 14:23; Isa. 5:27; Mark 1:7; Luke 3:16; John 1:27). According to the rabbis, untying sandals was a slave's task that could not be required of a disciple. John the Baptist thus claimed for himself a position lower than that of a slave before Jesus.

LATIN Language of ancient Italy and the Roman Empire and thus one of the languages in which the inscription over Christ's cross was written (John 19:20). See *Bible Texts and Versions.*

LATRINE Receptacle, generally a pit, used as a toilet (2 Kings 10:27; KJV, draught house). Jehu demonstrated his utter contempt for Baal by ordering that his temple be destroyed and converted into a latrine.

LATTER DAYS See *Eschatology; Judgment Day.*

LATTICE Structure of crisscrossed strips. Lattices were used as window covering to allow some light to penetrate while keeping heat and rain to a minimum (Judg. 5:28; 2 Kings 1:2; Prov. 7:6, KJV, casement; Song 2:9). According to one interpretation, in Ezekiel's temple vision

The public latrine of ancient Ephesus.

the windows were latticed (Ezek. 41:16,26 NASB). Other translations describe the windows as covered. The NASB also spoke of the lattices of the doves (Isa. 60:8). Other translations use home (TEV), nests (NIV), dovecots (REB), or windows (KJV, NRSV).

LAUGH To express joy or scorn with a chuckle or explosive sound. Laughter is central to the account of the birth of Isaac. Both Abraham (Gen. 17:17) and Sarah (18:12) laughed in contempt and disbelief at God's promise that Sarah would bear a son. The name Isaac (from the Hebrew word for laughter) served as a joyful reminder that the last laugh was on those slow to believe (Gen. 21:3,6). Laughter can serve as a sign of contempt (Gen. 38:23; 2 Chron. 30:10; Job. 22:19) or of confidence (Job 5:22; 39:18,22 NASB). References to God's laughing at the wicked demonstrate God's confident contempt (Pss. 2:4; 37:13; 59:8). Laughter is frequently contrasted with signs of mourning (Job 8:21; Ps. 126:2; Luke 6:21,25). Though Hebrew wisdom recognized a time to laugh as part of God's ordering of time (Eccles. 3:4), wisdom downplayed the value of laughter, associating it with fools (Prov. 29:9; Eccles. 7:4,6), calling it madness (Eccles. 2:2), and finding sorrow preferable (Eccles. 7:3).

LAUNDERER See *Fuller; Occupations and Professions.*

LAUREL Garlands of leaves from the laurel or bay tree (*Laurus nobilis*) were used by the Greeks to honor the winners of the Pythian games. The leaves of the tree were also used for medicine and seasoning. In Ps. 37:35 the wicked are compared to a "green bay tree" (KJV). HCSB, NASB, and NIV refer to a tree in its native soil.

An iron lattice over a window in ancient Pompeii dating from the first century A.D.

NRSV and TEV find a reference to the towering cedars of Lebanon.

LAVER Large basin or bowl used in purification rites. The OT describes the lavers used in the tabernacle and in Solomon's temple. The bronze laver of the tabernacle was constructed from metal mirrors provided by the women who ministered at the tabernacle entrance (Exod. 38:8). The priests used the laver for washing their hands and feet before priestly service (Exod. 30:18; 40:30-31). Levites also used water from this laver to purify themselves (Num. 8:7). Solomon's temple employed a large laver, the molten sea (1 Kings 7:23-26; 2 Chron. 4:2-5), and 10 smaller lavers (1 Kings 7:38-39; 2 Chron. 4:6). The priests washed in the molten sea. The 10 lavers were used for washing sacrifices (2 Chron. 4:6). See *Molten Sea; Temple.*

LAW, ADMINISTRATION OF See *Court System; Judges; Sanhedrin.*

LAW, ROMAN See *Roman Law.*

LAW, TEN COMMANDMENTS, TORAH Few expressions in the Bible are simultaneously more significant and more misunderstood than "law." Biblical interpreters apply the word to specific commandments, customs, legal judgments, collections of regulations/ordinances, the book of Deuteronomy (which means "second law"), the entire complex of regulations revealed at Sinai, the Pentateuch (in contrast to the Prophets), and the OT as a whole as opposed to the NT. The NT recognizes other laws as well, including natural laws (Rom. 1:26; 2:14) and "the law of sin" that results in inevitable death (Rom. 7:23,25; 8:2).

The conviction of a contrast between the OT, in which God's people were under the law, as opposed to the NT, where God's people are under grace, is determinative for many peoples' understanding of Scripture. Appeal is sometimes made to John 1:17, "For the law was given through Moses; grace and truth came through Jesus Christ" (HCSB). For this perception of a radical disjunction between the testaments two factors have been determinative. First, the Septuagint is virtually consistent in translating *torah* as *nomos,* "law" (202/220 occurrences). Second, Paul makes some strong assertions that whereas the law keeps us in custody and the letter [of the law] kills, through faith in Christ we

are delivered from the law and made alive by the Spirit (2 Cor. 3:6-7; Gal. 3:19-29; cp. Rom. 4:14). Accordingly many see a radical contrast between the old covenant, under which people were governed by the rule of law, and the new covenant, under which we are governed by the Spirit.

However, a closer look at the biblical evidence raises questions about the validity of both the Septuagint's rendering of *torah* and Luther's perception of the old covenant as a works oriented system. We begin with a survey of the OT perspective on "law" under the old covenant.

Old Testament Terms for "Law" The OT has a rich and varied legal vocabulary: *mitswot,* "commandments"; *huqqim/huqqot,* "ordinances, statutes, decrees"; *mishpatim,* "judgments, legal regulations"; *edot,* "covenant obligations, stipulations" (English "testimony" derives from the Greek Septuagint, *marturion*); *piqqudim,* "obligations, regulations"; *debarim,* "words, verbal utterances"; *torot,* "authoritative instructions, teachings."

The first five words usually refer to the specific laws and regulations prescribed by the Lord at Sinai and elsewhere. The most notable occurrence of the sixth, *debarim,* occurs in the expression, *aseret haddebarim,* "Ten Words," usually rendered "Ten Commandments" or "Decalogue." On occasion *torah* may be legitimately translated as "law." However, its everyday meaning is illustrated by the book of Proverbs, which applies the term to the "instruction" that the wise provide for the community (13:14), parents provide for children (1:8; 4:1-11), and the woman of the household to those under her influence (31:26). Its theological meaning is presented most clearly by the book of Deuteronomy, which, contrary to the Greek (and English) name of the book ("second law"), does not present itself as "law" but as a series of pastoral addresses (Deut. 1:1-5; 4:40). Even the so-called "Deuteronomic Code" (chaps. 16–26) has a pronounced pastoral and didactic (rather than legal) flavor.

This conclusion regarding the meaning of *torah* is confirmed when we observe how easily its scope was extended to the rest of the Pentateuch despite the fact that at least two-thirds of Genesis–Numbers is narrative, that is, the story of Yahweh's grace in election, salvation, and providential care for Israel, and His establishment of His covenant first with Abraham and then with the patriarch's descendants at Sinai.

These observations do not obscure the fact that the Pentateuch contains a great deal of prescriptive material with which the Lord sought to govern every aspect of the Israelites' lives. Scholars have identified several specific documents that might qualify as law: the "Passover Ordinance" (Exod. 12–13), the Decalogue (Exod. 20:2-17; Deut. 5:6-21), the "Covenant Document" (*seper habberit,* Exod. 21–23, cp. 24:7), the "Tabernacle Ordinance" (Exod. 25–31), the "Instructions Concerning Sacrifice" (Lev. 1–7), the "Holiness Code" (Lev. 17–25), and the "Deuteronomic Code" (Deut. 12–26). Maimonides, a Jewish rabbi, established that 613 commandments were scattered throughout the Pentateuch.

Old Testament Large portions of the Pentateuch, specifically the ordinances and covenant obligations, represent theological developments based on the Ten Commandments; there are seven.

First, God and Moses perceived obedience to the laws, not as a way of or precondition to salvation, but as the grateful response of those who had already been saved. God did not reveal the law to the Israelites in Egypt and then tell them that as soon as they had measured up to this standard He would rescue them. On the contrary, by grace alone, through faith they crossed the Red Sea to freedom. All that was required was belief in God's promise that He would hold up the walls of water on either side and see them safely through to the other shore.

The Decalogue begins, not with the first commandment, but with a preamble: "I am the LORD your God, who brought you out of the land of Egypt, out of the house of slavery" (Exod. 20:2; Deut. 5:6). Obedience to the Decalogue or any other law has never been intended as the way of salvation but as the appropriate response to salvation already received.

Second, obedience to the law was an expression of covenant relationship. Israel's primary commitment was not to a code of laws but to the God who graciously called Israel to Himself; they were to obey "His voice." In fact, He did not reveal His will to the people until He heard their declaration of complete and unconditional servitude to Him as covenant lord (Exod. 19:8).

Third, obedience to the law was the precondition to Israel's fulfillment of the mission to which she had been called and the precondition to her own blessing. The first point is highlighted in Exod. 19:5-6: if Israel will keep the Lord's covenant and obey His voice, she will be God's special treasure, His kingdom of priests, His holy nation (cp. Deut. 26:16-19). The second is spelled out in detail in Lev. 26:1-13 and Deut. 28:1-4.

Fourth, God's revelation of the law to Israel was a supreme act of grace and a unique sign of privilege (Deut. 4:6-8). In contrast to the nations who worshiped gods of wood and stone who never spoke (4:28; Ps. 115:4-8), Israel's God has spoken, clearly revealing to His people what He deemed an acceptable response to Him. Accordingly, for the genuinely faithful in Israel, obedience to the law was not a burden but a delight because of their deep gratitude for God's saving grace and covenant relationship and also because they knew God would respond to their obedience with favor (Deut. 6:20-25; Ps. 24:3-6).

Fifth, true obedience to the law was to be the external expression of an inward disposition of fear and faith in God and covenant love toward him. True biblical religion has always been a matter of the heart. This internal transformation is referred to metaphorically as a circumcised heart (Lev. 26:41; Deut. 10:16; 30:6-10; Jer. 4:4), a heart transplant (Jer. 24:7; 32:39; Ezek. 11:19; 36:26), the placement of God's Spirit within a person (Ezek. 11:19; 36:26), and the writing of God's *Torah* on the heart (Jer. 31:32).

Sixth, the laws viewed all of life holistically as under the authority of the divine suzerain. This is illustrated most impressively in Lev. 19, which, with its more than four dozen commandments, refuses to classify, let alone arrange in order of importance, civil, ceremonial and moral laws.

Seventh, the laws were perceived as comprehensible and achievable (Deut. 30:11-20) by those whose hearts were right with God. God did not impose upon His people an impossibly high standard but revealed to them in great detail a system of behavior that was uniquely righteous and also gracious (Deut. 4:6-8). At the same time there is a recognition of human depravity and the need for divine enablement for covenant faithfulness. Jeremiah anticipated a future new covenant when all Israel will love God and demonstrate with their lives that His *torah* has been written on their hearts (Jer. 31:31-34). God had a realistic view of His people. Recognizing their propensity to sin, within the law He graciously provided a way of forgiveness and communion through the sacrificial and ceremonial ritual.

Of course these seven facts did not prevent the Israelites from perverting obedience to the law into a condition for blessing and a condition for salvation. The prophets constantly railed against their people for substituting external rituals prescribed by the law for true piety, which is demonstrated first in moral obedience (Isa. 1:10-17; Hos. 6:6; Amos 5:21-24; Mic. 6:6-8). In every age Israelites misused the law, thinking that performance of rituals obligated God to receive them favorably. This did not prevent the Israelites from perverting the privilege of possessing the law into a divine right and unconditional guarantee of God's protection (Jer. 7:1-10,21-26; 8:8-12). Israel persistently perverted the law by placing great stock in rituals while disregarding God's ethical and communal demands. They imagined that God looked upon their hearts through the lenses of their sacrifices. They persisted in violating the moral laws even while they continued to observe the ceremonial regulations (Isa. 1; Jer. 7). In the end, Moses' predictions of disaster in Deut. 4 and 29–30 proved true in the exile of Judah in 586 B.C. The story of Israel as a nation was largely one of failure—not by God but by those whom He had called to be His people.

New Testament The legal vocabulary of the NT is more limited than that found in the OT. The most common term, *nomos,* "law," bears a range of meanings from a specific duty that God requires of a person, to the Mosaic law, the Pentateuch as a whole, and indeed the OT as a whole (John 10:34; 12:34; 15:25; 1 Cor. 14:21). In addition, the NT uses *entole,* "commandment" (e.g. Luke 23:56), and *dikaioma,* "regulation" (Luke 1:6; Rom. 2:26).

Like Moses and the psalmists, the NT views God's original revelation of the law to Israel as a climactic moment of grace. The basic disposition toward the law is expressed most eloquently in John 1:16-17: "From his fullness we have all received one demonstration of grace after another; for the *nomos* (= *torah*) was given through (*edothe dia*) Moses; grace and truth happened through (*egeneto dia*) Jesus Christ." The contrast here is not between law and grace as abstractions but between mediated grace in the form of *torah* and embodied grace in Jesus Christ.

Accordingly, when Jesus and Paul appear to be critical of the law, we should always ask whether their struggle was with the law itself or with misuse of the law. From the beginning Israelites had perverted the law by treating the law as a precondition of entrance into the kingdom of God rather than as a response to His grace; by adhering to the law's legal requirements as a matter of duty rather than a grateful expression of heartfelt covenant love for God and one's neighbor; and by treating physical descent from Abraham and membership in the Jewish nation as a guarantee of divine favor, rather than spiritual descent by faith as the precondition to blessing. It is to these abuses that many of the critical words concerning the law are addressed in the NT.

Jesus and the Law Jesus' own attitude toward the law is expressed fundamentally in two texts, Matt. 5:17-20 and 22:34-40 (cp. Mark 10:17-27; 12:28-31; Luke 10:25-37). In the first He declares that He came not to abolish (*kataluein*) the law or the prophets but to fulfill (*plerosai*) [them]." Here "law" refers not only to covenant obligations revealed at Sinai but to the entire Pentateuch. Here "fulfill" means to bring the OT revelation to its intended goal. Jesus goes on to declare the enduring validity and authority of every detail of the law until it is fulfilled. With Christ's first coming many aspects of the law are brought to complete fruition. As the eschatological fulfillment of the old covenant, in His person Jesus brings to an end the ceremonial shadows (sacrifices and festivals) and transforms old covenant customs into new covenant realities (baptism, the sign of the covenant made with the church, appears to replace circumcision, the sign of the covenant made with physical Israel); the Lord's Supper both replaces the Passover meal (Matt. 26:17-29; Mark 14:12-26; Luke 22:13-20) and anticipates the eschatological covenant meal (Rev. 19:6-10), of which the meal eaten on Sinai (Exod. 24:9-11; cp. Luke 22:20; 1 Cor. 11:25) was but a foretaste. However, other aspects of the law were to remain in force until Christ's return. When we read the OT law, we should always be open to both continuities and discontinuities with NT demands.

What Jesus means by a righteousness superior to that of the scribes and Pharisees He clarifies in Matt. 5:21–6:18. As God's Son who Himself fulfills the law and as the Lord of the covenant originally made with Israel at Sinai,

Jesus has the perfect perspective on the law and the full authority to declare its intention. He declared that God's demands cannot be reduced to a list of rules, but involve the commitment of one's whole being to Him and a genuine concern for the well-being of others. Jesus reiterated this perspective in Matt. 22:34-40 (cp. Mark 12:28-31; Luke 10:25-37) when He distilled all the covenant obligations laid on the human partner to love for God and love for one's neighbor, a point He illustrated dramatically with the story of the good Samaritan (Luke 10:25-37). Jesus' shift of focus from commitment to a set of rules and from external observation of the law to inward motivation and intent was new to His immediate audience. However, it is the same perspective Moses developed fully in Deuteronomy.

Paul and the Law The writings of Paul are the source of most of the confusion on the NT's view of the law. He spoke of the law as a way of death, in contrast to the Spirit that gives life (Rom. 7:10) and the law as a curse from which Christ has redeemed us (Gal. 3:13). He contrasted the letter (of the old covenant), which kills, with the Spirit (of the new covenant), that delivers life (2 Cor. 3:6). Such statements are difficult to reconcile with Moses' and the psalmists' celebration of the law as the supreme gift of grace and the way of life for God's people.

In resolving this apparent discrepancy we should recognize, first of all, that the unity of divine revelation precludes later inspired utterances contradicting earlier revelation. When we understand Paul correctly, we will discover his perspective to be in line with that of Moses.

Second, we recognize that Paul agrees with Moses in affirming the law, declaring that without it we would not know what sin was (Rom. 7:7; cp. Deut. 4:6-8), evaluating it as holy, just, and good (Rom. 7:12-14; 1 Tim. 1:8; cp. Ps. 119), and rooting his understanding of the ethical implications of the gospel firmly in the Torah (Rom. 13:8-10; 2 Cor. 6:14-18; cp. Exod. 20:1-17). Furthermore, Paul, like Jesus, captures the spirit of the OT law by reducing its demands to love God and one's neighbor (Rom. 13:8-10; Gal. 5:13).

Third, we recognize that many of Paul's negative statements concerning the law occur in contexts where he is debating with Judaizers the way of salvation for Gentiles. His frustrations are less with the law of Moses itself than with himself (Rom. 7:7-25) and with those who argue that

in order for Gentiles to become Christians they must first submit to the ritual of circumcision. If one looks to the law as a way of salvation, this also leads to death, for salvation comes only by grace through faith, which is precisely the way the Torah presents Israel's experience. Furthermore, his comment that apart from the Spirit it is impossible to satisfy the demands of the law is not contrary to Moses but a clarification of what Moses had meant by the circumcision of the heart.

In short, the problem is not with the law but with me because the law of sin inside me constantly wages war against the law of God. The glorious news of the Gospel is that in Christ God lifts the curse of sin, which the law proves we deserve. But this does not mean that the law has been suspended as a fundamental statement of God's moral will. The law served as a reflection of God's very nature. Since His nature does not change, neither does His moral will. Accordingly, those who fulfill the "Law of Christ," and those who love God with all their hearts and their neighbors as themselves will fulfill the essence of the law.

Since Paul's contrast of Sinai and Jerusalem in Gal. 4:21-31 is allegorical (*allegoroumena*, v. 24), we should not interpret him as categorically rejecting the Israelite covenant or as affirming a fundamental rift between the Davidic covenant (Jerusalem) and the Israelite covenant. Ishmael, the son of Hagar the maidservant of Sarah, was rejected as the son of promise. Ishmael provided Paul a convenient link to the covenant made with Israel at Sinai. But in associating Sinai with slavery, Paul adapts the material to his rhetorical needs. The consistent witness of the OT declares that the covenant God established with Israel at Sinai was a symbol of freedom, made with a privileged people whom he had rescued from the bondage of Egypt (see Exod. 19:4-6; Deut. 4:1-40). In Galatians Paul argued that his detractors have put the cart before the horse and in so doing reversed the true course of history. By demanding that Gentile Christians adhere to the Jewish law, specifically circumcision, they are putting Sinai before the exodus.

The Law in the General Epistles With its emphasis on works as a requisite evidence of faith, no document in the NT follows as obviously in the direct train of the Torah as James (cp. 2:14-26). First Peter is not far behind, being laced with echoes from the Pentateuch from beginning to end. Especially striking are Peter's call for holiness in 1:15-16, which is derived directly from Leviticus (Lev. 11:44-45; 19:2; 20:7,26), and his application of Exod. 19:5-6 to the church in 1 Pet. 2:9-12. The book of Hebrews applies the new covenant of Jer. 31:27-37 to Christians (Heb. 8:7-12) and declares explicitly that the old covenant is rendered obsolete in Christ. From the context it is evident that the author has in mind primarily the sacrificial system as the means of maintaining covenant relationship. Now in Christ the Aaronic priesthood, the sacrifices, and the Tabernacle/Temple itself are all superceded, and through Christ we have direct access to God. However this does not mean that nothing of the old covenant remains. If anything, from Heb. 10:26 to the end of the book the author draws on a series of OT texts to emphasize that his readers must respond to the grace of God with faith, perseverance, discipline, reverence, and high moral conduct.

Conclusion In Deut. 10:21 Moses declared that the God who redeemed Israel from Egypt and revealed to them his will is Israel's praise (*tehilla*). Yahweh, their God, is not a cruel taskmaster, who replaced the burdens of Egypt with the burdens of the law. Throughout Deuteronomy Moses presents the law as a glorious gift, and for one who observes it within the context of the covenant, it is the way to life and blessing. Into the dark world of human sin and alienation the Torah of Moses shone like a beacon of glory and grace. In the Torah Israel's God revealed Himself, declared the boundaries of acceptable and unacceptable conduct, and provided a way of forgiveness. No wonder the psalmists could celebrate the life to be found in the Torah with such enthusiasm (Ps. 119).

In the NT this Torah is fulfilled in Jesus Christ, and the apostles continue this tradition. There is no wedge between the law of the OT and the grace of the NT. The old covenant and its laws were grace. Having redeemed His people and having called them into covenant relationship, God could have left them to devise ceremonial and ethical responses to please Him, as did the nations whose gods neither hear, see, nor speak. At the same time the glorious grace proclaimed by the NT calls for response. Jesus, the divine Lord of both old and new covenants, declared that obedience to His commandments would be the inevitable and requisite proof of love for Him (John 14:15,21,23-24).

Obviously not all the laws associated with the old covenant continue under the new. With the shift from ethnic Israel to the transnational covenant community as the agent of divine blessing, the external demands intended to identify the nation of Israel as the covenant people are suspended. But what about the remainder? Theologians who divide the laws under the old covenant into civil, ceremonial, and moral requirements answer the question by declaring that the moral laws, especially as embodied in the Decalogue, continue in force. However, the OT refuses to draw such distinctions either between the three kinds of laws (all of life is equally holy) or between the Decalogue and the rest of the laws involved in God's covenant with Israel. Therefore a more careful approach is required, considering all aspects of the old covenant in the light of their fulfillment in Christ. Whatever else we may say about the relationship between the law of the old covenant and the law of the new, as grafted-in heirs of the covenant God made with Abraham and Israel, Christians are to give evidence of their faith and their privileged position through holy living. The Scriptures speak with a single voice in calling on all the redeemed to respond to God's grace with unreserved love for Him and self-sacrificing love for others. See *Pentateuch; Ten Commandments; Torah.*   *Daniel I. Block*

LAWGIVER One who gives a code of law to a people (Isa. 33:22; James 4:12). The KJV used "lawgiver" seven times. Modern translations replace "lawgiver" with "scepter" four times (Gen. 49:10; Num. 21:18; Pss. 60:7; 108:8). At Deut. 33:21 modern translations replace lawgiver with commander (NRSV), leader (NIV), ruler (NASB, REB), or an equivalent. The remaining two cases (Isa. 33:22; James 4:12) identify God as lawgiver. Contrary to popular opinion, Scripture never expressly identifies Moses as "lawgiver." The earliest Greek translation twice identified God as lawgiver (Ps. 9:21; 2 Esdras 7:89) and used the verb *nomotheteo* (to give law) with God as its subject several times (Exod. 24:12; Pss. 24:8,12; 26:11; 118:33,102). Once the Levitical priests are the subject (Deut. 17:10; cp. Heb. 7:11). The closest Scripture comes to identifying Moses as lawgiver is the question of John 7:19 ("Did not Moses give you the law?"). The NT more often identifies Moses as the intermediary through whom

L

the law was given (John 1:17; Gal. 3:19). The Epistle of Aristeas is unique among Hellenistic Jewish literature in expressly identifying Moses as the lawgiver (131,148,312).

Christ is sometimes regarded as the "second Moses" or "second lawgiver," though the NT does not expressly identify Him as such. Rather the NT designates Christ as the One who fulfills the law (Matt. 5:17) or is the end of the law (Rom. 10:4; cp. 7:4-6; 8:3-4). Christ does however set a new standard for judgment (Matt. 5:21) and gives a new commandment (John 13:34; 14:15,21; 15:10,12; 1 John 2:3-4,7-8).

LAWLESS, LAWLESSNESS Terms used by modern translations to describe people not restrained or controlled by law, especially God's law. As rebellion against God, sin is lawlessness (1 John 3:4; cp. 2 Thess. 3:4). Those responsible for Christ's death are characterized as lawless (Acts 2:23) as are Gentiles in their idolatry (1 Pet. 4:3). The leader of the eschatological (end-time) rebellion is called the man of lawlessness (2 Thess. 2:3; cp. 2:8). The lawless one is already at work but is presently restrained (2:6-7). The lawless one will be revealed before the return of Christ, who will destroy him with His breath (2:8).

LAWYER Authoritative interpreter of the Mosaic law. Characterization of the lawyers is especially harsh in Luke's Gospel: they rejected God's purpose for themselves by refusing John's baptism (7:30); they burdened others without offering any relief (11:45-46); they not only refused God's offer of salvation but hindered others from accepting it (11:52-53); they refused to answer Jesus' question concerning the legality of Sabbath healing (14:3). Lawyer is used in the general sense of a jurist at Titus 3:13.

LAYING ON OF HANDS Symbolic ceremonial act used to invoke a divine blessing or establish a connection for the purpose of sacrifice, ordination, or to impart spiritual gifts.
Old Testament A primary use of laying on of hands in the OT was sacrifices. In Lev. 16 the Lord instructed Moses and Aaron concerning the Day of Atonement. At a particular point Aaron was told that to place his hands upon a live goat and "confess over it all the wickedness and rebellion of the Israelites—all their sins—and put

them on the goat's head" (Lev. 16:21), transferring the sins of Israel to the goat.

The identification of the worshiper with a sacrifice is seen in discussions concerning the burnt, fellowship, sin, and ordination offerings (Lev. 1:4; 3:2; 4:4; Num. 8:12).

Laying on of hands was used to set one apart for a special office. Moses laid his hands on Joshua to identify him as Moses' successor and of Moses imparting his authority to Joshua (Num. 27:18-23).

Laying on of hands was used in blessings. Jacob blessed his grandsons, the children of Joseph, by placing his hands upon their heads. The laying on of hands in this instance signified future blessings of Joseph's sons, Ephraim and Manasseh (Gen. 48:12-19).

The laying on of hands also meant to chastise, arrest, capture, or do violence to someone (Exod. 22:11; 2 Chron. 23:15).
New Testament There is little difference between the OT and NT usages except that in the NT the sacrificial use is dropped and spiritual gifts are added. As in the OT this expression is used for the arrest or capture of a person (Matt. 26:50; Acts 4:3).

Jesus blessed children by laying His hands on them (Mark 10:16). He also laid hands upon the sick to heal them (Mark 6:5; Luke 5:13) as did the apostles (Acts 28:8).

Laying on of hands is used in the ordination of the "seven" in Acts 6:6. It is used in the commissioning of Barnabas and Saul for their mission (Acts 13:3). The act of laying on of hands as a method of ordaining or acknowledging a person's call to a ministry position is a sober task. Paul warned Timothy not to lay hands upon someone too quickly (1 Tim. 5:22). By the laying on of hands, the church acknowledges God's commission of an individual and identifies itself with the Spirit's enabling the person for the task of ministry.

In Acts are instances when the laying on of hands was associated with receiving the Holy Spirit (Acts 8:17-20; 19:6). In these cases the act confirmed the authenticity of the gospel. First Timothy 4:14 speaks of Timothy receiving a spiritual gift from elders who laid their hands on him. In 2 Tim. 1:6 Paul mentions the spiritual gift that Timothy received, "through the laying on of my hands." These references show that Timothy received authority, the spirit of power, love, and self-discipline (2 Tim. 1:7).

Brent R. Kelly

LAZARUS (Lăz´ á rŭs) Personal name meaning "one whom God helps." **1.** One of the principal characters in a parable Jesus told to warn the selfish rich that justice eventually will be done. Poor Lazarus sat outside the mansion of the nameless rich man to receive whatever food might fall from the banquet table (Luke 16:19-31). Because of his poverty, he lived in poor health, also. In death the roles of the two were reversed, with Lazarus residing comfortably in heaven and the rich man being tormented in hell. The rich man asked that Lazarus be allowed to relieve his thirst. This is refused because of the gulf fixed between heaven and hell. A second appeal came for Lazarus to go and warn the rich man's family so that they might not join him in hell. This was refused because they have had adequate warning already. **2.** Lazarus (a shortened form of Eleazer) of Bethany was a personal friend of Jesus and the brother of Mary and Martha (John 11:1-3). Jesus raised Lazarus from the dead after he had been in the tomb for four days to show the glory of God. Lazarus was at the Passover celebration in Bethany six days later. He became a target for murder by the chief priests because of his celebrity. Some believe Lazarus to be the "disciple whom Jesus loved" based on John 11:3 and

The traditional site of the tomb of Lazarus in Bethany.

21:20-22. He is not mentioned in the other Gospels, although Luke 10:38-42 names the sisters Mary and Martha. See *Beloved Disciple.*

Mike Mitchell

LEAD See *Minerals and Metals.*

LEADER See *Prince of Life.*

LEAF, LEAVES Foliage of plants or trees. Adam and Eve made their first clothes from leaves (Gen. 3:7). Leaves are frequently used to symbolize blessedness or cursedness. God's renewal of the earth following the flood was epitomized by an olive leaf (Gen. 8:11). God's providential care for the righteous is pictured by the image of a well-watered tree whose leaves do not wither (Ps. 1:3; cp. Jer. 17:8). Ezekiel's vision of the new Jerusalem included trees whose leaves never wither and whose leaves have healing power (Ezek. 47:12; cp. Rev. 22:2). Withered (Isa. 1:30), shaken (Isa. 33:9), fallen (Isa. 33:4), and faded (Isa. 64:4) leaves serve as images of judgment. A tree lacking fruit with withered leaves (Jer. 8:13) symbolizes a people found lacking when God judges (cp. Matt. 21:19; Mark 11:13). Jesus used the appearance of fig leaves which herald the arrival of summer to illustrate the need to heed the signs of the end (Matt. 24:32; Mark 13:28).

LEAGUE KJV used "league" at Dan. 11:23 in the sense of an agreement (NIV), alliance (NASB, NEB, NRSV), or treaty (TEV).

LEAH (Lē´ ah) Personal name meaning "wild cow" or "gazelle." Older daughter of Laban (Gen. 29:16) and Jacob's first wife. Jacob had asked for the younger Rachel's hand but was tricked into marrying Leah. Thus was preserved the ancient Near Eastern tradition of the elder marrying first. Leah bore six sons to Jacob (Reuben, Simeon, Levi, Judah, Issachar, Zebulun) and a daughter (Dinah). Her handmaid, Zilpah, bore two sons to Jacob (Gad, Asher), which by the law of that day were officially Leah's. When Jacob returned to Palestine from Padanaram, Leah and her children were placed in front of Rachel and Joseph, evidently to absorb any violence from Esau, Jacob's brother. This is indicative of the less-favored status of Leah to Rachel. Leah died in Palestine and was buried in the cave at Machpelah, where lay the remains of Abraham, Isaac, and their wives.

LEANNOTH (Lə ăn´ nōth) Transliteration of Hebrew word in title of Ps. 88 possibly meaning "to sing" or "for the poor," "for the sick." It may be part of the title of a tune to which the psalm was sung. The meaning remains obscure and uncertain.

LEATHER Animal skins tanned and prepared for human use. Elijah the prophet was recognized by his hairy garment and leather belt or girdle (2 Kings 1:8). The similar dress of John the Baptist marked him as a prophet (Matt. 3:4; Mark 1:6). Leather shoes are one of the gifts that symbolize God's lavish care for His beloved bride Jerusalem (Ezek. 16:10). See *Goatskin; Skin.*

LEAVEN Small portion of fermented dough used to ferment other dough and often symbolizing a corruptive influence. The common bread of OT times was made with leaven. Such bread was acceptable as wave offerings for the priests and as loaves to accompany the peace offerings (Lev. 7:11-13; 23:17). However, bread made with leaven or honey, both associated with the process of fermentation and thus a source of corruption, was never to be used as offerings to be burned on the altar (Lev. 2:11-12). Unleavened bread was also prepared in times of haste (1 Sam. 28:24) and was required for the Feast of Unleavened Bread that was celebrated in conjunction with the Passover festival (Lev. 23:4-8). This unleavened bread, or bread of affliction, reminded the Israelites of their hasty departure from Egypt and warned them against corruptive influences (Exod. 12:14-20).

In the NT "leaven" is a symbol of any evil influence that, if allowed to remain, can corrupt the body of believers. Jesus warned His disciples against the leaven of the Pharisees, their teaching and hypocrisy (Matt. 16:5-12; Luke 12:1). Paul urged the Corinthians to remove wickedness from their midst and become fresh dough, unleavened loaves of sincerity and truth (1 Cor. 5:6-13). Jesus also used leaven to illustrate the pervasive growth of the kingdom of God (Matt. 13:33). *Barbara J. Bruce*

LEBANA (Lə bā´ nà) Personal name meaning "white" or "full moon." Original ancestor of clan of temple servants (Ezra 2:45; Neh. 7:48). See *Nethinim.*

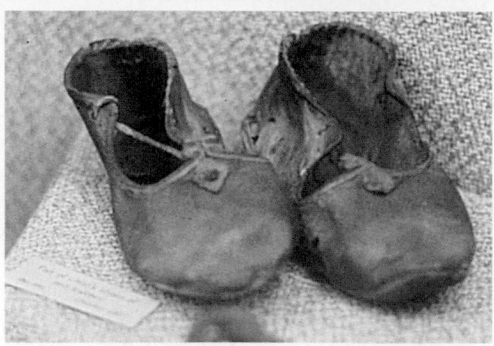

A child's leather shoes from Egypt (Roman era).

LEBANAH (Lə bā´ nah) Alternate spelling of Lebana (Neh. 7:48) in most English translations despite the same names in the Hebrew text (cp. REB). See *Lebana.*

LEBANON (Lĕb´ à nŏn) Place-name meaning "white" or perhaps "white mountain." A small country at the eastern end of the Mediterranean Sea and the western end of Asia. It has long been a world center of transportation and trade. The proper noun literally means the "White" (mountain), probably derived from the snow-capped Mount Hermon, also known as Sirion (Ps. 29:6). Hermon is often covered with snow, and its white crown offers a majestic and impressive view. The constant snow-coverage is contrasted with the fickleness and apostasy of Israel (Jer. 18).

Sandy beaches lie along its Mediterranean coast. Rugged mountains rise in the interior. The country itself is dominated by two mountain ridges, the Lebanon and Anti-Lebanon Mountains. Both ranges run parallel to the coast. The Lebanon range extends for about 105 miles along the coast, from modern-day Tripoli in the north to Tyre in the south.

The mountain ranges are about 6,230 feet high. Some summits reach a height of more than 11,000 feet: the highest peak is el-Qurnat el-Sawda (11,024 ft.). Between the higher parts of the range lie valleys and ravines.

The Holy Valley, which collects the water from the Mountain of the Cedars, is one of the most important valleys. It was in this region that the Maronites found refuge in the beginning of their history. This Holy Valley has retained its significance throughout the ages. Ain Qadisha (Spring of the Holy Valley) is highly revered. It gushes forth in the heart of a cedar forest and mountainside near Bsherrih. Another famous valley is the Valley of Adonis, through which the River of Adonis flows, and to where the pilgrimage of Adonis took place in the spring of the year. See *Gods, Pagan.*

In the Bible Lebanon is celebrated in various capacities. It is frequently featured in the OT, in a general way, as the northern boundary of Palestine (Josh. 1:4), dividing it from Phoenicia and Syria. Its imposing rage was emblematic of natural strength and solidarity, therefore a perfect poetic foil to the majesty of God revealed in a thunderstorm so powerful that it "makes Lebanon skip like a calf" (Ps 29:6 HCSB). It was a proverbially lush land, noted for its magnificent forests (Isa. 60:13), especially the "cedars of Lebanon" (Judg. 9:15; Isa. 2:13). For the tree-poor Palestinians, Lebanon's cedars symbolized the ultimate in natural wealth and beauty. The psalmist calls these ancient and beautiful cedars the "trees of the LORD ... that He planted" (Ps. 104:16 HCSB). It is said that some of the cedars remaining in Lebanon are at least 2,500 years old. They share with the famous redwoods of California the distinction of being the oldest living things on earth.

Cedars, as well as other woods of Lebanon, were used in great abundance in the construction of David's palace and Solomon's temple and palace buildings (1 Kings 5:10-18; 7:2). Cedar was obtained also for the building of the second temple or the temple of Zerubbabel (Ezra 3:7).

The forests of Lebanon have been victims of human greed and irresponsibility. They were exploited by Egypt and Mesopotamia long before biblical times, and they continued to supply precious timber well into the Roman Era. Under the Ottoman Empire (A.D. 1516), the forest almost entirely disappeared. Today there is not much left of the cedar woods; almost all of them are gone. The olive tree also played an important part in ancient times and is still cultivated.

Tyre, to which Ezek. 27–28 is devoted, was one of the most famous cities of the ancient world. Along with the older port of Sidon, it was one of the centers of Phoenician civilization. See *Phoenicia.*

Many foreign powers have controlled the Phoenician city-states. They include, in order of rule, the Egyptians, Hittites, Assyrians, Babylonians, and Persians. In 332 B.C. Alexander the Great conquered Lebanon. The region came under the control of the Roman Empire in 64 B.C.   *Philip Lee*

LEBAOTH (Lə bā´ ŏth) See *Beth-Lebaoth.*

LEBBEUS (Lĕb bē´ ŭs) Reading of some ancient Greek manuscripts for Thaddeus in Matt. 10:3 (KJV). Modern translations and interpreters follow earlier Greek manuscripts that read simply "Thaddeus." See *Thaddeus; Disciple.*

LEB-KAMAI, LEB-QAMAI (Lĕb-kā´ mī) Transliteration of Hebrew text. A code name for Babylon (Jer. 51:1, NASB, NIV, NRSV, REB, RSV margin; Kambul, NEB). The code employed is *athbash*, a code which replaces each letter of a word with a letter that stands as far from the end of the alphabet as the coded letter stands from the beginning (z=a; y=b). NASB marginal reading "the heart of those who are against me" arose when the Masoretes added vowels to the code.

LEBO-HAMATH (Lē bō-hā´ măth) Place-name meaning "entrance to or to come to Hamath." KJV, RSV translate, while other modern translations transliterate, the Hebrew name. Many modern interpreters think Lebo-hamath was an independent city in the city-state dominated by Hamath in Syria. It could be Lebwe north of Baalbek or Labau east of the Jordan. If a definite city is not meant, Lebo-hamath would represent the territory bordering the northwestern part of the Orontes River. Lebwe is close to the Litani River, about 43 miles north of Damascus. Whatever its precise location, Lebo-hamath represented the northern boundary of Canaan promised to Israel (Num. 13:21; cp. Ezek. 48:1), not conquered by Joshua (Josh. 13:5; Judg. 3:3), controlled by David (1 Chron. 13:5) and Solomon (1 Kings 8:65), and restored to Israel by Jeroboam II about 793–753 B.C. (2 Kings 14:25; cp. 13:25). Amos predicted complete defeat for Israel starting at Lebo-hamath (6:14). See *Hamath.*

LEBONAH (Lə bō´ nah) Place-name meaning "the white one." Town used to locate annual feast site by Israel's elders as they sought wives for decimated tribe of Benjamin (Judg. 21:19). It is probably modern el-Lubban, three miles northwest of Shiloh, and was known for its fine grapes.

LECAH (Lē´ cah) Personal name meaning "go!" Apparently the original ancestor for whom a town in Judah was named (1 Chron. 4:21). Its location is not known.

LEECH Wormlike, blood-sucking parasite of the class *Hirudinae,* which serves as a symbol of an insatiable appetite (Prov. 30:15; KJV, horseleach).

LEEKS Either *Allium porrum,* a bulbous vegetable, or *Tragonella foenumgraecum,* a grasslike herb. An Egyptian food eaten by the Hebrews during their captivity. After a steady diet of manna in the wilderness, they were ready to return to slavery and the foods of servitude (Num. 11:5). See *Plants.*

LEES Solid matter that settles out of wine during the fermentation process. In ancient Palestine wine was allowed to remain on the lees to increase its strength and flavor. Such wine "on the lees" was much preferred to the newly fermented product. At Isa. 25:6 a banquet of wine on the well-refined lees symbolizes God's people enjoying the best God can offer. Zephaniah 1:12 pictures the inhabitants of Jerusalem who did not believe God would act as wine resting on the lees (cp. Jer. 48:11). Since wine was normally strained before being drunk, the prophetic images point to a temporary respite. To drink dregs or lees is to endure the bitterness of judgment or punishment (Ps. 75:8).

LEG The upper leg or thigh was regarded as the one of the choicest parts of a sacrifice and was reserved for the priests (Lev. 7:32-34). The first term translated "leg" in Isa. 47:2 (KJV) is also translated robe (NRSV) or shirt(s) (NASB, NIV, REB).

LEGION In the NT a collection of demons (Mark 5:9,15; Luke 8:30) and the host of angels (Matt. 26:53). Behind this usage was the Roman military designation. The legions were the best soldiers in the army. At different times in Rome's history, the legion numbered between 4,500 and 6,000 soldiers. It was composed of differently skilled men: spearmen, commandos, skirmish specialists, calvary, and reserves. Originally, one had to be a property owner and Roman citizen to belong, but these requirements were waived depending on the need for troops.

Mike Mitchell

LEHAB (Lē´ hăb) National name meaning "flame." Singular of Lehabim. See *Lehabim.*

LEHABIM (Lē´ hā bĭm) "Sons" of Egypt in the Table of Nations (Gen. 10:13). Lehabim probably represents an alternative spelling of Lubim, the people of Libya. See *Lehab; Lubim; Libya.*

LEHABITES (Lē´ hà bīts) (NIV) See *Lehabim.*

LEHEM (Lĕ´ hĕm) Place-name meaning "bread" or "food." NRSV reading (1 Chron. 4:22) based on evidence from early Latin and Greek translations. The name appears in a list of members of tribe of Judah. Hebrew reads Jashubi-lehem (KJV, NASB, NIV). REB, TEV emend the text to read "came back to" or "settled in Bethlehem." See *Jashubi-lehem.*

LEHI (Lē´ hī) Place-name meaning "chin" or "jawbone." City where Samson killed 1,000 Philistines with the jawbone of a donkey and where God provided water from the jawbone (Judg. 15). Many interpreters read 2 Sam. 23:11 as occurring at Lehi (TEV, NRSV, REB). The site was apparently in Judah near Beth-shemesh.

LEISURE TIME The Bible usually speaks of "rest" in terms of cessation from toil, trouble, and sin (e.g., Exod. 33:14; Isa. 32:18; Heb. 4:1-11). While at rest, persons occupy themselves by enjoying God and one another's company, a foretaste of the activity of heaven.

The Bible recognizes the need for regularly scheduled breaks from work. The weekly Sabbath (Exod. 20:8-11) and several yearly festivals (Lev. 23:1-44; Deut. 16:1-17) were intended to focus on Israel's spiritual needs but also provided breaks from physical labor. The Mosaic law mandated a yearlong honeymoon for newlyweds (Deut. 24:5; cp. Luke 14:20). Jesus tried to find time to be by himself in order to rest and pray, but the press of the crowds often prevented Him from doing so (Matt. 14:13; Mark 3:20; 6:31; John 11:54).

The Bible cautions against the misuse of leisure time which leads either to idleness (Prov. 19:15; 24:33-34; Eccles. 10:18; Amos 6:4-6; 1 Tim. 5:13), excessive partying (Isa. 5:11-12), or troublemaking (2 Chron. 13:7; Prov. 6:10-15). See *Sabbath.*   *Paul H. Wright*

LEMUEL (Lĕm´ ū ĕl) Personal name meaning "devoted to God." A king who received words of wisdom from his mother concerning wine, women, and the legal rights of the weak and poor (Prov. 31:1-9). Exactly where his kingdom of Massa was is not known, although certain linguistic features in the text have led scholars to place it in north Arabia, possibly near Edom. This section of Proverbs apparently comes from a non-Israelite woman. See *Proverbs*.

LEND See *Banking; Interest; Loan*.

LENGTH, MEASURE OF See *Weights and Measures*.

LENT English word (stemming from an Anglo-Saxon word for "spring" and related to the English word "lengthen") that refers to the penitential period preceding Easter. Early Christians felt that the magnitude of the Easter celebration called for special preparation. As early as the second century, many Christians observed several days of fasting as part of that preparation. Over the next few centuries, perhaps in remembrance of Jesus' fasting for 40 days in the wilderness (Matt. 4:1-2), 40 days became the accepted length of the Lenten season. Since, from the earliest years of Christianity, it had been considered inappropriate to fast on the day of the resurrection, Sundays were not counted in the 40 days. Thus, the Wednesday 46 days before Easter came to be regarded as the beginning of Lent.

In the early centuries the season before Easter was also the usual period of intense training for new Christians. During this period, the catechumens (those learning what it meant to be Christians) went through the final stages of preparation for baptism, which usually occurred at dawn on Easter Sunday. As the practice of infant baptism increased, the emphasis on Lent as a training period decreased. See *Church Year*.

Fred A. Grissom

LENTILS See *Plants*.

LEOPARD Large cat with yellow fur, with black spots that form patterns. This animal was one of the most dangerous both to animals and human beings. Known for its gracefulness and speed, it was common in Palestine in OT times, especially in the forests of Lebanon but is seldom found there now. Five were killed around Jerusalem just before World War II, and one was killed in Southern Palestine near Beer-sheba soon after the war. The leopard still survives in Israel and is

protected by the government. Two locations suggest habitats of leopards—Beth-nimrah ("leopards' house," Num. 32:36) and "waters of Nimrim" ("waters of leopards," Isa. 15:6; Jer. 48:34). In Hos. 13:7, the lurking, noiseless movement of the leopard symbolizes God's wrath. Isaiah illustrated the serene peace of God's kingdom as creating the seemingly impossible occurrence of a leopard lying down with the goat (Isa. 11:6). Some translate Hab. 1:8 as "cheetah."

LEPROSY Generic term applied to a variety of skin disorders from psoriasis to true leprosy. Its symptoms ranged from white patches on the skin to running sores to the loss of digits on the fingers and toes.

For the Hebrews it was a dreaded malady which rendered its victims ceremonially unclean—that is, unfit to worship God (Lev. 13:3). Anyone who came in contact with a leper was also considered unclean. Therefore, lepers were isolated from the rest of the community so that the members of the community could maintain their status as worshipers. Other physical disorders or the flow of certain bodily fluids also rendered one unclean (Lev. 12:1—14:32; 15:1-33). Even houses and garments could have "leprosy" and, thus, be unclean (Lev. 14:33-57).

Jesus did not consider this distinction between clean and unclean valid. A person's outward condition did not make one unclean; rather that which proceeds from the heart determines one's standing before God (Mark 7:1-23; cp. Acts 10:9-16). Therefore, Jesus did not hesitate about touching lepers (Mark 1:40-45) and even commanded His disciples to cleanse lepers (Matt. 10:8). Jesus even made a leper the hero of one of His parables (Luke 16:19-31). See *Diseases*.

LESHEM (Lē´ shĕm) Place-name meaning "lion." City tribe of Dan occupied (Josh. 19:47). An alternate Hebrew spelling of Laish. See *Laish*.

LETTER FORM AND FUNCTION History and Form Letters in the ancient world were an important means of communication between people who were in different locations. They were, in fact, the only means available other than verbal messages. Letter writing is almost as ancient as writing itself, beginning in the second millennium B.C. Aids to composition were published in the ancient period, and two have

L

survived. *Tupoi Epsistolikoi* (*Epistlolary Types*), also referred to as *Pseudo-Demetrius* (written before A.D. 100) identified and explained 21 types of letters. The other, *Epistolimaioi Characteres*, (*Epistolary Styles*) also called Pseudo-Libanius, was written after A.D. 300 and presented 41 types of letters. In Demetrius each type of letter was defined, its logic presented, then illustrated by a sample letter. Libanius did not give actual sample letters but rather instructions and hints giving the gist of each type. In practice, types of letters were often mixed, so that any description of the contents of the "typical" ancient letter is artificial and misleading. Thousands of letters have survived from antiquity, demonstrating the influence of manuals like Demetrius and Libanius.

The method of classification of letters was related to rhetorical theory. Rhetoric is the art of persuasion and was the cornerstone of classical education. The various letter types employ the three principle types of rhetoric: judicial, deliberative, and epideictic. The setting for judicial rhetoric was the persuasion of judge and jury. Deliberative rhetoric was arguing for or against a course of action in the public arena or government assembly, the giving of advice. Epideictic rhetoric was the speech of praise or blame on occasions of celebration or commemoration, among them weddings and funerals. Epistolary theory developed from these categories, but most letter types were related to epideictic, expressing either praise or blame. Rhetorical training assisted letter writers in taking bare outlines and forms from manuals and adapting them, combining types for a particular situation.

As letter writing developed historically, many letters did not fit into any of the established categories of rhetoric, instead falling into another broad category, exhortation, which was only marginally related to rhetorical theory. The Greek term is *paraenesis*, which has carried over into English, as has the corresponding Latin term *praeceptio*, precept. Such letters are sometimes referred to as hortatory or paraenetic.

Letter writers often employed the services of an amanuensis. The closest modern equivalent is a secretary. The amanuensis might be trained in rhetoric and letter writing and could participate in the writing at several levels. He might simply take dictation and prepare the letter for the writer's signature. Often, however, he might edit what was written. Sometimes the amanuensis was a full participant, or collaborator, with the named writer in the content of the letter. He might even compose the letter according to guidelines given by the person sending the letter.

Dictation could be painfully slow, and interfere with the speaker's train of thought. The great Roman Cicero (106–43 B.C.) once complained of having to dictate slowly, syllable by syllable. The historian Plutarch credits Cicero with the development of shorthand (Gk., *tachugraphy*) and its introduction to Rome. Shorthand was in wide use by the time the letters of the NT were written. Seneca, writing in A.D. 63–64, described this shorthand as employing signs in place of whole words, allowing the transcriber to match the speed of the speaker.

Letters in the Bible *Old Testament* The first mention of a letter is in 1 Sam. 11:14-15, when David's treachery lead to the death of the letter bearer himself, Uriah, the husband of Bathsheba. The wicked Queen, Jezebel, wrote letters (1 Kings 21:8-9) when engineering the murder of Naboth. The king of Aram (Syria) sent a letter to the king of Israel concerning his general Naaman in 2 Kings 5:5-7. Jehu, king of Israel wrote letters that secured the deaths of the remaining sons of Ahab (2 Kings 10:1-7). Hezekiah, a righteous king of Judah, received letters from Kings of Assyria and Babylon (2 Kings 19:14; 20:12; Isa. 37:14; 39:1; 2 Chron. 32:17). Hezekiah also sent letters throughout the 12 tribes of Judah and Israel, inviting all the people to come and observe Passover (2 Chron. 30:1-12). Solomon exchanged letters with Huram, king of Tyre (2 Chron. 2:1-12). In 2 Chron. 21:12 the Prophet Elijah sent a letter pronouncing judgment and a painful death on Jehoram, king of Judah. When Ezra was rebuilding the temple, letters were exchanged between enemies of the Jews and the royal court of Persia (Ezra 4–5). Nehemiah received letters from the king of Persia, Artaxerxes, authorizing him to return to Jerusalem and complete the temple (Neh. 2:1-9). Numerous hostile letters were exchanged between the elders of Judah and Tobiah, their enemy (Neh. 6:17-19). The king of Persia, Ahasuerus, sent a number of letters in the book of Esther (1:22, 3:13; 8:5,10). Mordecai, uncle of Esther, sent letters to Jews in many locations (Esther 9:20-30). Jeremiah sent a letter to the exiles in Babylon (Jer. 29:1). Shemaiah wrote a letter to the exiles claiming the high priesthood for himself (Jer. 29:24-32).

New Testament Letters are even more common in the NT, and 21 out of 27 books are in the form of letters. Revelation contains seven brief letters. Thirteen books are letters written by the Apostle Paul, and eight, called the general letters, were written by others. The writer of Hebrews is unknown. James and Jude, brothers of Jesus, wrote letters. The Apostle Peter wrote two letters, and the Apostle John wrote three.

The first specific mention of letters is when Saul of Tarsus requested letters from the high priest to authorize the arrest of believers in Damascus, Syria (Acts 9:2; 22:5). The Jerusalem church sent a letter to the Gentile believers in Antioch, Syria, exempting them from the law of Moses (Acts 15:23-30). The Roman commander, Claudius Lysias, wrote to the Roman governor Felix about Paul (Acts 23:25-33).

The NT letters, for the most part, fall into the category of exhortation. Most are a mixture of letter types. In a number of them, significant elements of deliberative rhetoric are mixed in as well. The ancient rhetorical theorist Posidonius suggested three major kinds of paraenesis: advice related to actions, exhortation related to habits and character, and consolation related to emotions or passions. All of these are present in NT letters.

Scholars sometimes challenge the authenticity of several letters ascribed to Paul, but compelling evidence to overthrow the ancient testimony of Pauline authorship is lacking. We may have confidence that Paul indeed wrote all 13 letters bearing his name.

Like all correspondence, Paul's letters were "occasional" documents, written at a particular time for a reason. Most NT letters were written in order to be read aloud to the congregations who received them, serving as a substitute for the writer speaking to the church in person. Paul's surviving correspondence was with churches he started, at least one church he had not visited (Colossae), and with individuals (Timothy and Titus) working under his authority. Only God knows how many letters Paul wrote during 30 years of missionary activity, but we are blessed by the presence of his surviving letters in the NT canon.

As the major corpus of letters in the Bible, the Pauline letters have been studied more than the other letter collection (generals). Paul's letters indicate the use of an amanuensis in seven letters (Rom.; 1 Cor.; Gal.; Col.; 1–2 Thess.; and Philem.). The use of an amanuensis may be inferred in 2 Corinthians from grammatical features. That he used an amanuensis for all his letters is a reasonable assumption. One amanuensis names himself, Tertius (Rom. 16:23). In five letters Paul wrote a portion with his own hand (1 Cor.; Gal.; Col.; 2 Thess.; Philem.). The use of different amanuenses offers a reasonable explanation for some of the differences of style, vocabulary, and grammar among the letters of Paul. In eight letters Paul mentions associates as collaborators (1–2 Cor.; Gal.; Phil.; Col.; 1–2 Thess.; and Philem.). The collaborative efforts likely influenced style and vocabulary to some extent. Paul's letters demonstrate that he and his amanuenses knew and employed the conventional forms of letter writing in the first century A.D.

New Testament letters generally may be divided into three parts, the address, the body, and the conclusion. Within this framework the following features might be found, though few of the letters contain them all.

(1) The address, consisting of the identification of the writer and recipients, the opening greeting, the thanksgiving, and a prayer.

(2) The body of the letter, consisting of differing elements that vary widely from letter to letter. The closest thing to common features are a formal opening, paraenesis on the areas of primary concern, and application.

(3) Conclusion, including final blessings, greetings (sometimes to specific people), the "peace" wish, and postscripts.

The letters of the NT had to be carried from the writers to the recipients.

The Roman Empire had an efficient postal system, but it was restricted only to government use. The Latin word *positus*, associated with this system, is the origin of the English word postal and related terms. Mail was carried by horseback, and stations were maintained at intervals on the postal routes. Changes of horses, along with food and other supplies were kept at these stations in order to speed the mail carriers on their way. In the private sector letters and other documents were carried by a variety of means. Professional couriers were used, but for most people this was not an option. Friends, acquaintances, or other travelers carried letters for others. In Paul's case the couriers seem to have come from the circle of his coworkers and members of churches he was associated with. See *Greeting.*   *Charles W. Draper*

LETUSHIM (Lə tū´ shĭm) or **LETUSHITES** (Lĕ tū´ shīts) (NIV) Tribal name meaning "smiths." Descendants of Abraham and Keturah (Gen. 25:3). Nothing else is known of this tribe. They do not appear in the parallel passage (1 Chron. 1:32). See *Keturah.*

LEUMMIM (Lə ŭm´ mĭm) or **LEUMONITES** (Lə ŭm´ ŏ nīts) (NIV) Tribal name meaning "peoples." Descendants of Abraham and Keturah. Probably an Arabian tribe of which we know nothing. They do not appear in the parallel passage (1 Chron. 1:32). See *Keturah.*

LEVI (Lē´ vī) Personal name meaning "a joining." **1.** Third son of Jacob and Leah (Gen. 29:34) and original ancestor of Israel's priests. He is characterized in Scripture as savage and merciless, avenging the rape of his sister, Dinah, by annihilating the male population of an entire city (Gen. 34:25-31). Later Jacob spoke harshly of Levi rather than blessing him (Gen. 49:5-7). The tribe that bears his name is also characterized as an instrument of wrath. After the people of Israel sinned in the wilderness by making the molten calf, Moses commanded the people of Levi to slaughter those who had participated in the debacle (Exod. 32:28). Levi's descendants became a tribe of priests. See *Levites.* **2.** Name of two of Jesus' ancestors (Luke 3:24,29). **3.** A tax collector in Capernaum who became a follower of Jesus (Mark 2:14). In the parallel account in the Gospel of Matthew, the man's name is given as "Matthew" instead of "Levi" (9:9). The name of Levi appears in none of the lists of apostles.

LEVIATHAN (Lə vī´ á thán) Name of an ancient sea creature, meaning "coiled one," subdued by God. Leviathan appears in biblical and extrabiblical literature. A serpentine form is indicated in Isa. 27:1 ("Leviathan the fleeing serpent … the twisting serpent," NRSV). The sea creature is used interchangeably with other mysterious creations of the divine. Again, Isa. 27:1 refers to leviathan as "the dragon that is in the sea." The psalmist in 74:14 presents a many-headed leviathan among the supernatural enemies of God dwelling in the sea. Job 3:8; 41:1-9 present the sea creature as too formidable a foe for a person to consider arousing. Yet leviathan

was created by God and subject to Him (Ps. 104:24-30).

Apocalyptic literature depicts leviathan as throwing off his fetters at the end of the present age, only to be defeated in a final conflict with the divine. Ugaritic literature of Ras Shamra during the 1300s B.C. depicts the mythical Baal defeating the sea creature called *Lotan* (another linguistic form for Leviathan). The Hittites wrote of a struggle between the dragon *Illuyankas* and the mortal *Hupasiyos.* A cylinder seal found at Tel Asmar dated about 2350 B.C. shows two men fighting a seven-headed serpent.

Leviathan was seen in ancient legend as a sea monster engaged in primordial warfare with the gods. This creature represented chaos in a personified manner that any creator deity had to overcome in order to create. Leviathan was also seen as a threat to the orderliness of the universe and ultimately to be subdued at the end of time.

The ancient pagan myths concerning Leviathan were familiar to the Hebrews of the OT. To what degree these myths of Leviathan influenced the Hebrews, if any, may never be known. Scripture used the name known to so many people and removed fear connected with it, showing that God easily controlled Leviathan, which thus offered no threat to God's people. See *Apocalyptic; Creation; Rahab.*

Steve Wyrick

LEVIRATE LAW, LEVIRATE MARRIAGE Legal provision requiring a dead man's brother (levirate) to marry his childless widow and father a son who would assume the dead man's name and inherit his portion of the promised land (Deut. 25:5-10). The practice is an important element in the story of Ruth (Ruth 2:20; 3:2,9-13; 4:1-11). The Sadducees appealed to levirate law in asking Jesus a question about the resurrection (Matt. 22:23-33).

LEVITES (Lē´ vīts) Lowest of the three orders in Israel's priesthood. In the earliest biblical records, sacrifices were offered by the chief of a tribe, the head of a family (Gen. 12:7-8; 31:54) or possibly by a priest at a temple (Gen. 14:18). Originally, Israel's priests and temple personnel were to be drawn from the firstborn of every family in Israel (Exod. 13:11-15). Later God chose the tribe of Levi to carry out this responsibility for Israel (Num. 3:11-13). The tribe of Levi was appointed because it was the only tribe that stood with Moses against the people who worshiped the golden calf (Exod. 32:25-29; Deut. 10:6-9). The Levites were not given a tribal inheritance in the promised land (God was their inheritance) but were placed in 48 Levitical cities throughout the land (Num. 18:20; 35:1-8; Josh. 13:14,33). The tithe of the rest of the nation was used to provide for the needs of the Levites (Num. 18:24-32). Since the Levites were dependent on the generosity of others, families were encouraged to invite the Levites (as well as widows, strangers, and orphans) to join them in their eating and their celebration of the joyous national feast (Deut. 12:12,18; 16:11,14). These factors point to the total dedication of the Levites to the work of the Lord rather than the earthly concerns of making a good living.

The tribe of Levi included at least three separate families: Gershon, Kohath, and Merari (with the families of Moses and Aaron being treated somewhat separately from the rest of the tribe of Gershon). During the wilderness journey they were in charge of taking the tabernacle down, transporting it, setting it up, and conducting worship at the tent where God dwelt (Num. 1:47-54; 3:14-39). In some passages (Deut. 17:9,18; 18:1; 24:8) the terms "priest" and "Levite" (or Levitical priests) seem identical, but in Exod. 28 and Lev. 8–10 it is clear that only the family of Aaron fulfilled the priestly duties of offering sacrifices in the tabernacle. Because there appears to be a different way of handling the relationship between the priests and the Levites in these texts, interpreters differ in the way they understand the Levites. Although it is possible that the role of the Levites changed or that the distinction between the priests and Levites was not maintained in each period with equal strictness, the interpretation which maintains a general distinction between the priests and Levites seem to fit most texts.

The Levites were consecrated to God and given by God as a gift to Israel in order that they might perform the duties at the tabernacle (Exod. 29; Lev. 8). Their work made it possible for the people to come to the tabernacle and offer sacrifices for the atonement of sins. The Levites assisted the priests in their responsibilities (Num. 3:5-9; 16:9) by preparing grain offerings and the showbread, by purifying all the holy instruments used in the temple, by singing praises to the Lord at morning and evening offerings, by assisting the priests with burnt offerings

on Sabbaths and feast days, and by being in charge of the temple precinct and the chambers of the priests (1 Chron. 6:31-48; 23:1-13,24-32; 25:1-6; 2 Chron. 29:12-19). Because of their work, the holiness of the temple was maintained; and the glory of the Lord dwelt among Israel. During David's reign the Levites were integrated into the administration of the government, including the keeping of the gates, judges, craftsmen, musicians, and overseers of the royal treasury (1 Chron. 9:22-28; 23–26) In Jehoshaphat's time the Levites were involved with teaching the people the word of God (2 Chron. 17:7-9). This responsibility probably continued into the postexilic period of Ezra (Neh. 8:9-12). See *Levitical Cities.*   *Gary Smith*

LEVITICAL CITIES (Lĕ vĭt´ ĭ căl) Residence and pasturelands provided the priestly tribe of Levi in lieu of a tribal inheritance. Because of their priestly duties, the tribe of Levi did not receive any part of the land of Canaan as an inheritance (Num. 18:20-24; 26:62; Deut. 10:9; 18:1-2; Josh. 18:7). To compensate them for this, they received the tithes of Israelites for their support (Num. 18:21), and 48 cities were allotted to them from the inheritance of the other tribes. On the average four cities from each tribe were Levitical cities. The practice of setting cities aside in this manner was a common ancient Near Eastern practice.

The Levites were not the sole possessors or occupiers of these cities. They were simply allowed to live in them and have fields to pasture their herds. These cities did not cease to belong to the tribes within which they were located. Although 6 of the 48 were asylums for those guilty of manslaughter (Kedesh, Shechem, Hebron in Canaan, Bezer, Ramoth-gilead, and Golan), Levitical cities and cities of refuge are not synonymous. The privilege of asylum was not extended to all 48 Levitical cities. The aim of having cities of refuge was to control blood revenge by making it possible for public justice to intervene between the slayer and the victim's avenger of blood. The cities of refuge were probably priestly cities containing important shrines. Cities of refuge also served as punitive detention centers. The slayer was not permitted to leave until the death of the high priest. This was possibly interpreted as a vicarious expiation of life by life.

Levitical cities were a series of walled cities, apart from the lands surrounding them. Unwalled suburbs and fields outside the cities remained tribal property. The Levites could not sell any open plots of land. The legal status of Levitical houses within these cities differed from ordinary property. To prevent the dispossession of Levites, it was ordained that they might at any time redeem houses in their own cities which they had been forced to sell. Moreover, such a house, if not redeemed, reverted to its original Levitical owner during the year of Jubilee. Pastureland belonging to Levites could not be sold (Lev. 25:32-34).

Theological, political, and economic reasons led to establishing the cities. The cities formed bases of operation so that the Levites could better infiltrate each of the tribes to instruct them in God's covenant. Such bases would be most needed precisely where one finds them: in those areas least accessible to the central sanctuary. Obviously, there was also a political dimension. Certainly, the Levitical desire to secure Israel's loyalty to the Lord of the covenant would also imply a commitment to secure loyalty to the Lord's anointed, the king. There was a blending of covenant teaching and political involvement. The economic factor may have been the most significant. The list of cities describes the dispersion of the Levites who were not employed at the large sanctuaries, had no steady income, and who belonged, therefore, in the category of widows and orphans. The cities were established for men needing economic relief. See *Cities of Refuge; Year of Jubilee.*   *Gary D. Baldwin*

LEVITICUS, BOOK OF (Lĕ vĭt´ ĭ cŭs) Third book of the OT containing instructions for priests and worship. The Hebrew name of Leviticus comes from the first word in the book, *wayyiqra'*, "and he called." In the later rabbinic works and similarly in the Syuriac translation, the Peshitta, the book was called *torat hohanim,* "book of the priests." The English title comes from the Latin Vulgate translation of the Greek term *Leuitikon.* This is an adjectival form, "Levitical," which thus means "that which concerns the priests." Since Hellenistic Jews called the priests "Levites" (an equation already evident in Deut. 17:9,18; 18:1), the meaning of the Greek title is actually no different from the traditional title of the Jews, the "book of priests."

Authorship Christian and Jewish interpreters prior to the 18th and 19th centuries assumed the Mosaic authorship of Leviticus as well as the rest of the Pentateuch. By the end of the 19th century, however, it was commonly accepted that the Pentateuch was composed of four basic but different sources: J, E, D, and P. This reconstruction came to be known as "the documentary hypothesis." See *Pentateuch.*

The P source referred to the Priestly Code and contained most of the material in the Pentateuch that pertains to priesthood and sacrifice, including Leviticus (although some have proposed an additional source for Lev. 17–26, the H[oliness] source, composed about the time of Ezekiel). This source was regarded as the latest of the four and reflected a transcendent deity who can only be approached through the meticulous processes outlined in the Israelite sacrificial system. It was thought to have been composed in the postexilic period in the fifth century B.C. To give the contents of Leviticus an authoritative ring, the text is said to fictitiously portray the material as though it was revealed by God to Moses. Thus, the ancient sacrificial system, the Aaronic priesthood, and the tabernacle are nothing but a fabrication depicting practices of the postexilic period as though they occurred the second millennium B.C., during the time of Moses.

On the negative side one recent area of investigation that has demonstrated the falsehood of this reconstruction is the history of the Hebrew language. Based on sound and testable methodology, it has been demonstrated that the main premise that Ezekiel preceded Leviticus has been demolished because Ezekiel's language is of a later linguistic stratum than the language of Leviticus.

On the positive side Mosaic authorship of Leviticus and virtually all the Pentateuch is clearly affirmed by a straightforward reading of the biblical text. Leviticus is repeatedly said to comprise what God wanted Moses to tell the people of Israel. No other book claims divine inspiration more than the third book of the Pentateuch. No less than 38 times is the expression found, "The LORD said to Moses [or Aaron]" (1:1; 4:1; 6:1). Moses' authorship of the Pentateuch was assumed by later Jews in the postexilic community (1 Chron. 15:15; 2 Chron. 23:18; Ezra 3:2; Neh. 1:7) and by the NT writers (Matt. 8:4; Mark 12:26; Luke 16:31; John 1:17; 1:45; Acts

3:22). In Rom. 10:5 Paul claims that the statement from Lev. 18:5, "The one who does these things will live by them" (HCSB), was written by Moses. And speaking to the leper He had just healed, Jesus, citing Lev. 14, said, "See that you don't tell anyone; but go, show yourself to the priest, and offer the gift that Moses prescribed, as a testimony to them" (Matt. 8:4). Speaking in more general terms, Jesus said "If you believed Moses, you would believe Me, because he wrote about Me" (John 5:46-47) and "Didn't Moses give you the law?" (John 7:19). Thus, on the basis of the claims of Scripture, the testimony of Jesus, the virtual unbroken unilateral tradition among both Jews and Christians, and the scholarly evidence, we may assume with confidence that Moses is the author of Leviticus.

Mark F. Rooker

Contents The first section of Leviticus relates to the latter part of the book of Exodus. Exodus 26–27 gives the Lord's instruction for the building of the tabernacle, the place of worship during ancient Israel's sojourn in the wilderness. These instructions are carried out and the tabernacle accepted as an appropriate place of worship (Exod. 35–40). Exodus 28–29 recounts the Lord's instructions for ordaining Aaron and his sons as priests. This ordination takes place in Lev. 8–9. One of the primary tasks of the priests was to offer sacrifice at the tabernacle. Before beginning this practice, ancient Israel needed instruction on the offering of sacrifice. The book of Leviticus begins at that point. Before listing the major types of sacrifice, we should consider its basic significance. A sacrifice is in part a gift to God, not as a way to earn God's favor but as a way to give thanks for God's gift of life. Sacrifice is also a means of facilitating communion between God and worshipers. Another important purpose of sacrifice is atonement, restoring the relationship between God and worshiper. In the offering of sacrifice, worshipers give of themselves to God. In the shedding of the blood of the sacrificial victim, the vital power of life is released (Lev. 17:11). God honors this act and gives life back to the worshiper. Thus sacrifice was important in the relationship between the ancient Israelite and God.

Leviticus lists five main types of sacrifice: (1) The whole burnt offering: a means of atonement that symbolizes the dedication of the whole life to God. The entire animal was burned on the altar (Lev. 1:3-17). (2) The cereal or grain offering: indication that everyday life is a gift from God, since grain constituted the everyday diet in ancient Israel (Lev. 2:1-16). (3) The peace, or shared, offering: the sacrifice of part of the animal and a communal meal from the remainder of the meat (Lev. 3:1-17). (4) The sin, or purification, offering: a sacrifice of repentance for sin which has broken human relations to God and has endangered the welfare of the community (Lev. 4:1–5:13). This sacrifice is for unwitting sin (Lev. 4:2,13,22,27). (5) The guilt offering: might also be called a compensation or reparation offering; it calls for sacrifice and compensation to one who has been wronged. The guilty one repays that which has been taken plus 20 percent (Lev. 5:14–6:7).

Leviticus 6–7 provides further instruction on sacrifice for the priests, and Lev. 8–10 describes the beginning of sacrifice at the tabernacle.

Leviticus 11–15 provides instruction on that which is clean and unclean. A person who comes into contact with an unclean object becomes unclean and is not allowed to participate in worship. Thus it is important to avoid contact with that which is unclean because worship was such a central life-giving event in the life of the community of God's people. These chapters describe various causes of uncleanness, including improper diet, childbirth, and various skin diseases. Leviticus 11 presents the famous dietary regulations, and Lev. 12 describes uncleanness related to childbirth. Leviticus 13 gives instruction in determining uncleanness related to leprosy, and Lev. 14 describes the way to cleanse leprosy. Leviticus 15 lists bodily discharges that cause one to be unclean.

Leviticus 16 describes the ritual of the Day of Atonement, a way of removing the impact of sin and uncleanness. First, the priest made sacrifice for himself so that he was prepared to do the same for the community. Then two goats were brought, and one chosen for sacrifice. It was offered as a purification offering, and the blood was used to cleanse the sanctuary of any sin and uncleanness. The priest then took the other goat, the scapegoat, and confessed the sin of the people with his hands over the goat, symbolically passing the sin of the people to the goat. Then the goat was taken into the wilderness, a significant symbol of the removal of the sin of the people. This central ritual assumed that ancient Israel would encounter sin and uncleanness. Since God is perfectly holy, the Lord could

L

not dwell among sin and that which is unclean. This ritual then provided a means of removing sin and uncleanness so that God could continue to dwell among the people and be present in the sanctuary to give them life.

Leviticus 17–27 is the Holiness Code. This section gets its name from the frequent use of the phrase, "You shall be holy; for I the Lord Your God am holy." In the OT holiness means to be set apart; however, it does not indicate being set apart from the world in a separatist way. The term is used of ancient Israel's being set apart to God. As God is holy—set apart, unique, different, distinct, "There is no other like God"—so ancient Israel as people of God was to be holy, different from other people because they were people of God. These chapters then give instruction in how ancient Israel was to live a holy life. Leviticus 18 illustrates this. The chapter begins with a plea to live not as the Egyptians, whom ancient Israel had just left, nor as the Canaanites, whom ancient Israel would soon encounter, but as people of the Lord God. Then the chapter gives instruction in sexual conduct, particularly on forbidden sexual relations. Living according to such instruction would distinguish ancient Israel from other people in the land as people of the holy God. The conclusion of chapter 18 emphasizes this again in urging the people to be loyal to God. Holiness is not a means of removing the people from the world but of giving them a way to relate to the world as the people of God.

A number of the instructions in the Holiness Code relate to ethics and faithfulness to the Lord. Note the famous verse in Lev. 19:18, "You shall love your neighbor as yourself." There is also instruction on keeping the Sabbath as a day of rest and worship. Each seventh year was to be a Sabbath year for the land, to give it renewal and also as a sign that the land is not owned by ancient Israel but a gift from God. Each 50th year (7 x 7 + 1) was a Jubilee Year in which all slaves were to be freed and property revert to its original owner. This again shows that people do not own other persons or property; they are rather stewards of such gifts from God. This practice shows that life is to be structured for the good of the community rather than isolated individuals.

These chapters also contain instructions on worship. Regular worship in the tabernacle was to include the constant burning of the lamp. This symbolized both the Lord's presence with the people and light as the first of God's creations. Also of importance in the tabernacle was the bread that symbolized the relationship between God and ancient Israel and reminded the people that God gives the gift of food. The Holiness Code also gives instruction on the special feasts. In the spring came Passover and unleavened bread, reminders of the exodus from Egypt. The summer feast (Weeks and Pentecost) related to the harvest and celebrated the giving of the law. The fall festival included the Day of Atonement and the beginning of the new year. Also here was the Feast of Tabernacles, a harvest festival remembering the time in the wilderness.

The message of Leviticus begins with the fact that God is present with the people and continues with the notion that God is perfectly holy. This is why the book gives so much instruction on holiness and includes sacrifice as a means of removing the effects of sin and uncleanness so that this perfectly holy God can continue to dwell among and give life to the people. All of this instruction is a gift from God and helps the people understand how to live as God's covenant people. The book thus provides an important part of the story of God with the people, for it gives instruction on how to maintain and, when necessary, restore that relationship. The book seeks to explore further the instruction in Exod. 19:6, "You shall be to Me a kingdom of priests and a holy nation."

The NT uses Leviticus to speak of the atoning sacrifice of Christ. See *Atonement; Covenant; Holy; Purity, Purification; Sacrifice and Offering.*

Outline

I. Offer Yourself in Praise and Adoration to God (1:1–7:38).
   A. Offer pleasing sacrifices (1:1–6:7).
      1. Burnt offerings (1:1-17).
      2. Cereal offerings (2:1-16).
      3. Peace offerings (3:1-17).
      4. Sin offerings (4:1-35).
      5. Guilt offerings (5:1–6:7).
   B. Give instructions to the priests who offer pleasing sacrifices (6:8–7:38).
      1. Burnt offerings (6:8-13).
      2. Cereal offerings (6:14-23).
      3. Sin offerings (6:24-30).
      4. Guilt offerings (7:1-10).
      5. Peace offerings (7:11-38).
II. Consecrate Priests to Mediate between God and People (8:1–10:20).

A. Set apart priests who mediate (8:1-36).
B. Sacrifice for the priests who mediate (9:1-24).
C. Warn the priests who mediate (10:1-20).

III. Purify Yourself before God (11:1–16:34).
A. Eat clean animals; reject unclean animals (11:1-47).
B. Purify mother and child after childbirth (12:1-8).
C. Test for an infectious skin disease and remove the infected one from the camp (13:1-59).
D. Restore the cleansed inhabitant to the community (14:1-32).
E. Remove the threat of infection (mildew) from the house (14:33-57).
F. Cleanse unhealthiness within the community (15:1-33).
G. Make atonement for the community (16:1-34).

IV. Present Yourself in Holiness before God (17:1–26:46).
A. Give attention to acceptable slaughter of beasts (17:1-16).
1. Make proper sacrifices before the Lord (17:1-9).
2. Sanctify life by refusing to eat blood (17:10-16).
B. Follow the commandments of the Lord (18:1–20:27).
1. Reject abominable sexual practices (18:1-23; 20:10-21).
2. Warn concerning the danger of abominable practices (18:24-30).
3. Reverence God in worship (19:1-8).
4. Show love for your neighbor by righteous living (19:9-18).
5. Observe proper practices in agriculture, slavery, sacrifices, and the body (19:19-29).
6. Honor God through worship (19:30-31).
7. Honor God through life (19:32-37).
8. Worship only God; forsake other gods (20:1-8).
9. Honor father and mother (20:9).
10. Give diligence to obeying God (20:22-27).

C. Charge mediators to follow regulations which allow presence before God (21:1–24:23)
1. Present themselves holy before God (21:1-24).
2. Present holy gifts to God (22:1-33).
3. Lead worship at holy times (23:1-44).
4. Prepare the holy place (24:1-9).
5. Keep the congregation holy before God (24:10-23).
D. Present both land and people holy before God (25:1-55).
1. Observe the Sabbath Year (25:1-7).
2. Observe the Jubilee Year (25:8-22).
3. Care for the poor brother and his land (25:23-55).
E. Remember the blessings and curses concerning the covenant people (26:1-46).

V. Offer Proper Vows before God (27:1-34).
A. Vows related to people (27:1-13).
B. Vows related to a house (27:14-15).
C. Vows related to fields (27:16-25).
D. Vows related to firstborn animals (27:26-27).
E. Keep your vows (27:28-34).

W. H. Bellinger, Jr.

LEVY To impose or collect by authority (Num. 31:28). The priests and Levites were supported in part by a levy of war gains.

LEWDNESS Lust; sexual unchastity; licentiousness. Lewdness sometimes refers to an especially heinous crime: brutal gang rape resulting in murder (Judg. 19:25-27); murder by priests (Hos. 6:9); any vicious crime (Acts 18:14). Most often lewdness is used figuratively for idolatry (Jer. 11:15; 13:27; Ezek. 16:43,58; 22:9; 23:21,27,29,35,48-49; 24:13; Hos. 2:10). Since the cults of many of Israel's neighboring peoples were fertility cults that employed sexual acts as part of worship, the application of lewdness to idolatry or unfaithfulness is easily understood. See *Fertility Cults.*

LIBATION Act of pouring liquid as a sacrifice to a god. See *Sacrifice and Offering.*

LIBERALITY NASB term for generosity or openhandedness (Rom. 12:8; 2 Cor. 8:2). The KJV used "simplicity" for the text of Rom. 12:8 and "liberality" for 2 Cor. 8:2. The precise meaning of the underlying Greek is a matter of interpretation. "Simplicity" can mean wholeheartedly, generously (NIV, NRSV), or openhanded (REB). "Simplicity" can also mean purely, without mixed motives or desire for selfish gain. See *Stewardship*.

LIBERTINE KJV transliteration of Greek for "freedmen" (Acts 6:9). See *Freedmen, Synagogue of the*.

LIBERTY, LIBERATION Freedom from physical, political, and spiritual oppression. Throughout the Bible one of God's primary purposes for His people is to free them from physical oppression and hardship and to liberate them from spiritual bondage. One of the dominant themes of the OT is that Yahweh is the God who liberated the Israelites from their bondage in Egypt. In the NT God is the one who liberates people from bondage to sin through Jesus Christ. Jesus showed in Luke 4:18-19 that these purposes extend to all those who are oppressed, not just those who call on His name. This liberation always comes from God, but He desires to use His people to accomplish these purposes. If they refuse, He will use other means. See *Freedom*.

Steve Arnold

LIBNAH (Lĭb´ nah) Place-name meaning "white" or "storax tree." **1.** Wilderness station east of the Jordan (Num. 33:20). Its location is not known; Umm Leben 66 miles south of Haradah has been suggested. See *Haradah*. **2.** Town in the Shephelah of Judah that Joshua defeated (Josh. 10:29-30). Joshua allotted it to the tribe of Judah (Josh. 15:42) and separated it as a city for the Levites (Josh. 21:13). It illustrated western border rebellion against King Joram of Judah (853–841 B.C.) just as Edom represented rebellion in the east (2 Kings 8:22). It lay on the invasion route to Jerusalem followed by Sennacherib about 701 B.C. (2 Kings 19:8). The mother of Kings Jehoahaz (609 B.C.) and Zedekiah (597–586 B.C.) came from Libnah (2 Kings 23:31; 24:18). Debate continues concerning Libnah's location: Tell es-Safi at the head of the Elah Valley appears too far north; Tell Bornat just west of Lachish; Tell el-Judeideh, usually identified as Moresheth-gath. Tell Bornat is the most popular candidate but far from certain.

LIBNI (Lĭb´ nī) Personal name meaning "white." **1.** Original ancestor of clan of Levites

(Exod. 6:17; Num. 3:21; 26:58). See *Laadan*. **2.** A Levite in clan of Merari (1 Chron. 6:29).

LIBNITE (Lĭb´ nīt) Member of clan of Libni. See *Libni*.

LIBRARY Systematically arranged collection of writings. A private library is one owned by an individual; a public library is one owned corporately and is open to use by many. A special library of official records is an archive. Many of the earliest libraries were archives housed in palaces or temples.

Though the Bible does not use the word "library," it makes indirect allusions to collections of books. The Bible itself is a "library" and was called such in Latin: *bibliotheca*. It was probably not until about A.D. 300 that all 66 books were published in a single volume.

The Material and Form of Ancient Books The earliest writings, which were from Mesopotamia, were inscribed in cuneiform on clay tablets, which ranged in size from six-by-six inches up to seven-by-thirteen inches. Longer historical texts would be placed on clay barrels or prisms. One omen series required 71 tablets for 8,000 lines. Each tablet when translated would be the equivalent of a few pages in English rather than a complete book.

Egypt provided the ancient world with its famous papyrus, made from the stalks of a reed plant. As this was imported into Greece through the Phoenician harbor of Byblos, the Greeks called a book *biblos*. The word "Bible" is derived from its plural *ta biblia*, "the books," and the Greek word for library *bibliotheke* meant a container for such a book. Papyri sheets were normally written only on one side. They could be attached together to form long scrolls (an Egyptian royal papyrus could be over 100 feet long). Greek papyri rolls were generally shorter. The longer books of the NT, such as Matthew or Acts, would take a 30-foot scroll.

The Dead Sea Scrolls from Palestine were written on leather. The famous Isaiah Scroll is 23.5 feet long; the newly published Temple Scroll was originally 28.5 feet long. Late in 200s B.C. the city of Pergamum was supposedly forced by a shortage of papyrus to invent "parchment" (also called "vellum"), a specially treated animal skin that was stretched thin until it became translucent.

The Jews and pagan Greeks and Romans used both papyri and parchments in scroll form. Christians, perhaps as early as the first century, began to use the codex form, that is, the folding of several sheets of papyrus or parchment in a "book" form. This had several advantages. Both sides of the pages could be used; it was more compact; and above all one could more readily find Scripture references. Almost all of the early Christian Scriptures preserved in Egypt's dry climate are papyri codices.

When Paul was in prison in Rome, he requested "the scrolls, especially the parchments" (2 Tim. 4:13 HCSB). The books were probably scrolls of the OT. On the other hand, the parchments were probably parchment codices, possibly of his notes and letters.

Archives and Libraries in the Old Testament Era Abraham came from Mesopotamia, which had a well-developed tradition of palace and temple archives/libraries. Since 1974 over 20,000 tablets have been found in the archives of Ebla in northern Syria from pre-Abrahamic times. Many of the 25,000 tablets from Mari (1700s B.C.) and the 4,000 tablets from Nuzi (1400s B.C.) have helped to illuminate the backgrounds of the Hebrew patriarchs. Sumerian texts from among the 20,000 tablets at Nippur (before 1500 B.C.), and Akkadian texts from among the 20,000 tablets of Ashurbanipal's (about 668–629 B.C.) famous library at Nineveh have provided literary parallels to biblical stories such as the Gilgamesh Epic. Texts written in five scripts and seven languages from the libraries of Ugarit shed important light on the literary and religious background of the Canaanites. See *Archaeology; Ashurbanipal; Ebla; Mari; Nuzi; Sumer; Ugarit.*

Joseph and Moses (Acts 7:22) had access to the royal libraries of Egypt. The excavations of Amarna have uncovered a building with shelves for storing rolls and an inscription, "Place of the Records of the Palace of the King." Rameses II (1292–1224 B.C.) had some 20,000 rolls, which no doubt included medical works like the Ebers Papyrus, literary works like *The Shipwrecked Sailor*, and magical texts like *The Book of the Dead.*

Solomon, who was famed as a prolific author (1 Kings 4:32), must have had an extensive library. It was probably at the palace archives that such documents as Historical Record of Israel's Kings (1 Kings 14:19 HCSB) and of Judah's Kings (1 Kings 14:29) were housed. Sacred texts were kept in the temple (2 Kings 23:2)

We know from the Bible that Persian kings kept careful archives (Ezra 4:15; 5:17; 6:1). Ahasuerus (Xerxes) had a servant read from his chronicle one night as a cure for his insomnia (Esther 6:1).

In 1947 the Dead Sea Scrolls were discovered in jars in caves near Qumran. These were originally from the library of the Essene monastery. They included manuscripts of all of the OT books except for Esther, works from the OT Apocrypha and Pseudepigrapha, and sectarian compositions such as the *Manual of Discipline,* the War Scroll, and the Temple Scroll. The excavators also recovered a table, a bench, and inkwells from the scriptorium, where the manuscripts were copied. See *Dead Sea Scrolls.*

Greek and Roman Libraries The tyrants of the 500s B.C., Peisistratus of Athens and Polycrates of Samos, were the first Greeks to gather libraries. Individuals such as Euripides, Plato, and Aristotle also had their own libraries. Alexander the Great took with him copies of Homer, of the Greek tragedians, and of various poets.

The first corporate Hellenistic library was conceived by Ptolemy I at Alexandria in Egypt and then established by Demetrius of Phalerum (Athens) under Ptolemy II (285–247 B.C.). This became the greatest library in the ancient world, amassing up to 700,000 scrolls. The main building was in the palace area with a secondary collection near the Serapeum. Many of the first librarians were outstanding scholars and literary critics such as Zenodotus of Ephesus, Apollonius of Rhodes, Callimachus the poet, and Eratosthenes the geographer. Callimachus compiled an

The re-erected marble façade of the second-century A.D. Library of Celsus at Ephesus.

annotated catalogue, the *Pinakes,* in 120 scrolls. It is possible that the learned Apollos (Acts 18:24) may have made use of this famous library.

The second largest Hellenistic library was established at Pergamum (Rev. 1:11) by Eumenes II (197–158 B.C.) The excavators have identified a building next to the temple of Athena as the library. Rows of holes evidently held shelves for the scrolls; stone inscriptions identified the busts of authors. Antony gave Cleopatra its 200,000 scrolls in 41 B.C.

By the first century B.C. wealthy Romans, such as Cicero and Lucullus, had well-stocked libraries in their villas. Satirists mocked those like Trimalchio, who acquired books but never read them. Some 1,800 badly scorched papyri have been recovered from a wealthy man's library at Herculaneum, which was buried by volcanic mud from Vesuvius' eruption in A.D. 79.

Caesar was killed in 44 B.C. before he could erect Rome's first public library. This was built some time after 39 B.C. by Asinius Pollio. Augustus built three public libraries; Tiberius built another in the temple of Augustus. Most Roman libraries, such as Trajan's famous Biblioteca Ulpia, had both Greek and Latin collections.

The Use of Libraries The use of archives and libraries would be restricted, first of all, by literacy; and, secondly, in the case of temple or palace archives, to priests and scribes. At Alalakh (1700 B.C.) we have a record of only seven scribes out of a population of 3,000.

Though powerful individuals like the emperors could borrow books, most libraries did not permit books to circulate. An inscription from Athens reads: "No book shall be taken out, since we have sworn thus. [The library will be] open from the first hour (of daylight) until the sixth." See *Education in Bible Times; Paper, Papyrus; Writing.*   *Edwin Yamauchi*

LIBYA (Lĭb´ ў ȧ) Large land area between Egypt and Tunisia. Libya's northern border is the Mediterranean Sea. The people who inhabited the territory in biblical days are referred to variously as Chub (Ezek. 30:5), Put (1 Chron. 1:8; Nah. 3:9), Phut (Gen. 10:6; Ezek. 27:10), and Libyans (Ezek. 30:5; 38:5; Acts 2:10). Most of our knowledge of Libya comes from Egyptian records that mention border wars and invasions. Pharaoh Shishak I (about 950 B.C.) is thought to have been a Libyan. He began a dynasty in Egypt that reigned for over 200 years. He supported

Jeroboam I in establishing the kingdom of Israel in 922 B.C. (1 Kings 11:40; 14:25-28; 2 Chron. 12:1-12).   *Mike Mitchell*

LIBYAN (Lĭb´ ĭ ȧn) Person who comes from Libya. See *Libya.*

LICE See *Insects.*

LIEUTENANT KJV term for Persian officials of the rank of satrap (Ezra 8:36; Esther 3:12; 8:9; 9:3). See *Judea; Satrap.*

LIFE Principle or force considered to underlie the distinctive quality of animate beings. What is living has movement; in death movement ceases. "Life" is used in the Bible to describe the animating force in both animals and humans (e.g., Gen. 1:20). Living organisms grow and reproduce according to their kinds. Human life as bodily existence, the value of human life, and its transient nature is described (e.g., Pss. 17:14; James 4:14). This physical, bodily existence is subject to suffering, illness, toil, death, temptations, and sin (e.g., Pss. 89:47; 103:14-16; 104:23; Rom. 5:12-21; 6:21-23; 8:18). "Life," as used in the Bible, however, has a much wider application than only to physical, bodily existence.

God's Unique Life Only God has life in the absolute sense. He is the living God (Josh. 3:10; Matt. 16:16). All other life depends on God for its creation and maintenance (Acts 17:25; Rom. 4:17). God is spoken of as the God of life or as life giving (Deut. 32:40; Jer. 5:2). In stark contrast to God, the idols are dead (Isa. 44:9-20; Jer. 10:8-10,14) as are those who depend on them for life (Pss. 115:8; 135:18).

In the same way that God is Creator by giving His breath or spirit to living creatures, so no possibility of life exists when God withholds His breath or spirit (Job 34:14-15). Thus, God is Lord of both life and death (2 Cor. 1:9; James 4:15). Life is something which only God can give (Ps. 139:13-14) and which only God can sustain (Ps. 119:116).

This being the case, every life is solely the possession of God. No one has a right to end a life (Exod. 20:13; Deut. 5:17; cp. Gen. 4:10,19-24). Since life belongs to God, one must abstain from the consumption of blood, the vehicle of life (Gen. 9:4; Lev. 3:17; 17:10-14; Deut. 12:23-25). Thus, even animal life is valued by God as is evidenced by the fact that animals' blood was sacred to God.

Earthly Existence, Physical Life The Bible summarizes the lives of many people. Often the biblical account includes a statement about their life span, such as, "These are all the years of Abraham's life that he lived, one hundred and seventy-five years" (Gen. 25:7 NASB). The OT emphasizes quality of life. The person who finds wisdom is fortunate: "She [wisdom] is a tree of life to those who embrace her" (Prov. 3:18 HCSB). Wisdom affects how people live. Psalm 143 testifies to the dark moments of life. Then the psalmist prays for God to intervene: "For Your name's sake, LORD, let me live. In Your righteousness deliver me from trouble" (143:11 HCSB).

Jesus at His temptation quoted Deut. 8:3: "Man must not live on bread alone" (Matt. 4:4; Luke 4:4 HCSB). Rather each person must live "on every word that comes from the mouth of God" (Matt. 4:4). Earthly life involves God.

Jesus warned that "one's life is not in the abundance of his possessions" (Luke 12:15 HCSB). Yet many people see one's belongings as the criterion of success. Jesus healed people and raised some from the dead to relieve the harshness of life (cp. Mark 5:23-45). Jesus brought wholeness into human, physical life.

Life as Fellowship with God The OT uses bold metaphors for fellowship with God: "For with You is life's fountain. In Your light we will see light" (Ps. 36:9 HCSB). We come to God to receive life. We walk in fellowship with God, and in His light we see life. Otherwise, we are devoid of life and cannot see. Even when we do come to God, we may depart from Him. Another psalmist pleaded for God's hand to be upon him: "Then we will not turn away from You; revive us, and we will call on Your name" (Ps. 80:18 HCSB).

The proper response to life as the gift of God is to live life in service to God (Isa. 38:10-20) by obeying the Law (Lev. 18:5), doing God's will (Matt. 6:10; 7:21), and feeding on God's Word (Deut. 6:1-9; 8:3; 32:46-47; Matt. 4:4). Only that life which lives in obedience to God deserves to be called life in the true sense of the word (Deut. 30:15-20; Ezek. 3:16-21; 18:1-32).

The NT deepens this emphasis. Paul points out that Christians differ in terms of food they eat and days they celebrate (Rom. 14:1-6); these things are part of custom and tradition. All Chris-

tians are to make the Lord Jesus central and live so as to show that He is their purpose for living. "For none of us lives to himself, and no one dies to himself. If we live, we live to the Lord; and if we die, we die to the Lord. Therefore, whether we live or die, we belong to the Lord. Christ died and came to life for this: that He might rule over both the dead and the living" (Rom. 14:7-9 HCSB). Such living demands fellowship with the Savior who is the purpose for living.

Paul wrote that we died with Christ and were raised together with Him (Col. 3:1-3) and that the lives of Christians (individually) have been hidden with Christ in God. When Christ (the Christians' life) comes a second time, we will be manifested with Him in glory (Col. 3:4). Our fellowship with Him now is dependent on our constantly seeking and thinking on what is above (Col. 3:1-2). This is the new and transformed life.

Paul describes God's servants as an aroma for God among the people to whom they witness (2 Cor. 2:15). To those who are perishing, believers are a fragrance from death to death. To those who are being saved, they are a fragrance from life to life (2 Cor. 2:16). Those who reject the message continue on in death. Those who accept the message move from one level of life to another. The life that Christ initiates grows. Paul exclaimed: "Who is competent for this?" (2 Cor. 2:16 HCSB).

Paul set forth his picture of life: the process of living for me, Christ; the act of death, gain (Phil. 1:21). When Christ is central, life has no boundaries.

Christ as the Life, the One Who Imparts Life Old Testament believers identified life with God (Pss. 42:8; 27:1; 66:9). The "I am" sayings in the Gospel of John identify life with Jesus. "I am the bread of life" (John 6:35,48). "I have come that they may have life (John 10:10 HCSB). "I am the resurrection and the life" (John 11:25). "I am the way, the truth, and the life" (John 14:6). John states the purpose for his Gospel: "But these are written so that you may believe Jesus is the Messiah, the Son of God, and by believing you may have life in His name" (John 20:31). Since Jesus was God incarnate, He made genuine life a reality—not a distant prospect.

Life to Come, Life beyond This Life The genuine life that comes from Jesus to those who obey God is true or eternal life. Just as physical life is the gift of God, so is eternal life (John 6:63; Rom. 6:23; 1 Cor. 15:45; Eph. 2:8-10). Eternal life, or true life, refers as much to the quality of life one has as to the quantity of life. According to the Bible, all people will have an endless duration of life either in the blessing of God's presence or in the damnation of God's absence (e.g., Dan. 12:2; Matt. 25:31-46; John 5:28-29). The thing that distinguishes the life of these two groups of people is not its duration but its quality. Eternal life is of a quality like God's life. This kind of life is a true blessing (Luke 18:29-30; 1 John 5:12). The quality of this life is marked by freedom from the power of sin to destroy, by holiness, and by a positive relation with God (Rom. 6:20-23). True life is not only something to be hoped for in the future, it is a present reality. Believers share in the life of God in this life (Luke 11:20; Rom. 6:4,11; 8:6; 1 John 3:14), but the believer does not fully experience true life until the resurrection when believers obtain the crown of life (James 1:12; Rev. 2:10).

True life is offered to all, but it is received only by those who realize that the source of true life is what God has done in Jesus Christ and does not come from within the individual (Eph. 2:8-10). Those who have true life as a gift are to conform themselves to the manner of life Jesus exhibited (John 5:39-40). Christians are to lose themselves (2 Cor. 5:15) and serve God in love (Matt. 25:31-46; Gal. 2:19). Just as food maintains physical life, service to God maintains true life (John 6:27,32-58; Acts 7:38).

Eternal life is indestructible (1 Cor. 15:42-57; 1 Pet. 1:23), though threatened by the devil, the law, and death. The devil attempts to destroy this life (Luke 12:4-5; 1 Pet. 5:8), but he is not able to harm it for God protects the believer (Rom. 8:7-39; Eph. 6:10-18). The law threatens this life by tempting people to believe that they can attain this life by their own efforts (Rom. 7:10,13; 2 Cor. 3:4-6). Death is also an enemy of true life, but it is powerless to destroy the life that God gives (Rom. 5:12-21; 6:9-10; 7:24–8:11, 35-39).

Life beyond this life is not that of a "spirit" but that of a bodily resurrection. Paul highlighted both earthly existence and the life to come: "Godliness is beneficial in every way, since it holds promise for the present life and also for the life to come" (1 Tim. 4:8 HCSB). This "present" life is one of testing. James says those who pass this test "will receive the crown of life that He

has promised to those who love Him" (James 1:12 HCSB). This future life is one of open fellowship with God (Col. 3:4). See *Eschatology; Eternal Life; Resurrection.*

A. Berkley Mikelson and Phil Logan

LIFE, BOOK OF Heavenly document mentioned in Ps. 139:16 and further defined in the NT (Luke 10:20; Rev. 13:8). In it are recorded by God the names and deeds of righteous people.

LIFE, ORIGIN OF The Bible teaches that all matter (John 1:3), including living matter, was created by God ex nihilo (out of nothing—Heb. 11:3) through a series of special, decisive acts, each introduced in Gen. 1 by the phrase "and God said" (Gen. 1:3,6,9,14,20,24,26; cp. Ps. 148:5; Rev. 4:11). Plants and animals were created in self-reproducing "kinds" (Gen. 1:11-12,21,24). All of creation was God-directed and purposeful (Isa. 43:7; 45:18; Col. 1:16).

The Bible teaches the special creation of people (Gen. 1:26-28; 2:7; Matt. 19:4). God created people to bring glory to Himself (Isa. 43:7; cp. Col. 1:16) and made the earth to be their specially prepared home (Isa. 45:18). The psalmist stood in wonder at the intricate design of the human body and saw it as testimony of God's creative power (Ps. 139:13-15).

Each of the Bible's statements about creation is incompatible with the various theories of evolution. See *Creation and Science.*

LIFE SPAN The life expectancy in industrialized western countries closely approximates the natural life span of mankind according to Ps. 90:10: "Our lives last seventy years or, if we are strong, eighty years" (cp. 2 Sam. 19:32-35; Luke 2:36-37). While modern medicine, improved health care, and a healthy diet can increase this natural limit somewhat, it is unreasonable to assume that people will, or should, live as long as the patriarchs of old.

With the exception of Enoch, who "walked with God, and he was not, for God took him" (Gen. 5:24), each of the antediluvian fathers lived in excess of 595 years (Gen. 5:3-31). The recorded life span of the descendants of Noah gradually decreased after the flood so that the patriarchs each lived only twice today's normal span (Gen. 25:7-8; 35:28-29; 47:28; 50:26). While many scholars accept these year totals as accurate, others calculate them downward based on known or suggested genealogical or mathematical formulae.

The Bible records many tragic instances of human life cut off prematurely (e.g., Gen. 4:8; 1 Sam. 31:2; 2 Chron. 35:23-25; Job 21:21; Ps. 39:5,11; Luke 12:20). No one knows the day of their death (cp. Gen. 27:2). Because the years pass so quickly, the psalmist pleaded, "Teach us to number our days, that we may apply our hearts unto wisdom" (Ps. 90:12).

Paul H. Wright

LIFE SUPPORT (ARTIFICIAL) While the Bible does not speak directly to the issue of life support by artificial means, it does provide principles relevant to the time of one's death. These principles suggest that extreme measures to prolong life artificially encroach upon the prerogative of God to control life and death. For the same reason, any and all forms of euthanasia are contrary to the teaching of Scripture.

The Bible teaches that only God gives life and that only God should take life away (Exod. 20:13; Job 1:21; cp. Rom. 14:7-8). Human life is a sacred and precious gift because each person is created in the image of God (Gen. 1:26-27; Ps. 8:5). The writers of the OT voiced a strong preference for life over death (Deut. 30:19), even in the face of crushing pain and defeat (Job 2:9-10).

Yet there comes a God-appointed time for everyone to die (Eccles. 3:2; Heb. 9:27). Although Christians value life highly, they need not fear death (1 Cor. 15:54-55; Heb. 2:14-15; cp. 2 Cor. 5:8). The Apostle Paul, who was torn between life on earth and eternal life in heaven, was willing to follow either path that God desired for him (Phil. 1:19-26). *Paul H. Wright*

LIGHT, LIGHT OF THE WORLD Light is one of the Bible's most complex symbols. The primary term for light is *'or* in the OT and *phōs* in the NT. Light may denote daylight in contrast to darkness (Gen. 1:5,18; Isa. 5:30). It may refer to luminaries (sun, moon, or stars, Isa. 60:19; Ps. 136:7-9) or the light given by luminaries (Isa. 13:10; Jer. 31:35) or by other sources (lamp, Jer. 25:10; fire, Ps. 78:14). The expression *'or hab-boqer*, "light of the morning," means "dawn" (Judg. 16:2; 1 Sam. 14:36). In many of its figurative uses, the exact significance of light is uncertain, though some link to the notion of physical light as the basis for life on earth is often present. Light is linked with instruction (Isa. 2:5;

Ps. 119:105,130), truth (Ps. 43:3), good (Isa. 5:20), salvation (Ps. 27:1; Isa. 49:6), life (Ps. 36:9; Job 33:28,30), peace (Isa. 45:7), rejoicing (Ps. 97:11), covenant (Isa. 42:6), justice and righteousness (Isa. 59:9), God's presence and favor (Ps. 44:3; 89:15), or the glory of Yahweh (Isa. 60:1-3). Apocalyptic visions of the end are associated with the extinguishing of light (Isa. 13:10; Jer. 4:23; Matt. 24:29). In the new age, the new Jerusalem "does not need the sun or the moon to shine on it, because God's glory illumines it, and its lamp is the Lamb" (Rev. 21:23 HCSB; cp. Isa. 60:19; Zech. 14:6-7; Rev. 22:5).

On the first day God created light (Gen. 1:3), which implies that light existed before the sun and other luminaries (Gen. 1:14-18). God Himself is the source of that light (cp. Ps. 104:2; perhaps James 1:17). If so, this light likely signified the divine presence just as the luminous cloud of the Shekinah glory (cp. Exod. 24:15-18; 40:38; 2 Chron. 5:13-14; 7:2).

The identification of light with the divine presence of the Shekinah glory above sheds light on the meaning of light in the Gospel of John and 1 John. In the person of Jesus, "the true light, who gives light to everyone, was coming into the world" (John 1:9 HCSB). The only begotten God, who is in the bosom of the Father, has made the Father known (1:18) because he "became flesh and took up residence among us. We observed His glory, the glory as the One and Only Son from the Father, full of grace and truth" (1:14; cp. Exod. 34:6). In other words, in Jesus God was made manifest because in Him the Shekinah glory had returned to reside among us and this glory consisted of fullness of grace and truth (cp. John 1:16-17). Light thus signifies Jesus' glory, which is fullness of grace and truth. Jesus is "the light of the world" and His followers will have "the light of life" (i.e., the truth that brings life; John 8:12). Jesus, who is the light, the embodiment of grace and truth, also brings salvation (John 12:35-36,46-47) and the doing of God's works (John 9:4-5). This salvation and doing of God's works comes from guidance and instruction from the light (John 12:35,47). Notions of illumination, both positive manifestation of God's prior work of grace (John 1:13; 3:21) and negative reproof of human evil (John 3:20), are present as well. Human beings who reject the light are thus rejecting Jesus, the embodiment of grace and truth (John 3:14-21; cp. John 18:37-38, where Pilate apparently exemplifies one who rejects Jesus as the embodiment of truth).

The attribution of God (rather than the Word) as light in 1 John 1:5 falls into place in this line of interpretation. Not only is the only begotten God characterized by fullness of grace and truth, His Father, whom He makes known as characterized by fullness of grace and truth, is as well (John 1:17-18). John can thus deny that those who do not do the truth have fellowship with God, who is light (1 John 1:6). 1 John 2:8-10 is entailment of the truth—hating one's brother is incompatible with the character of both the Father and the Son (note "the true light is already shining" in v. 8). In addition, 1 John 1:7-10 indicates that walking in the light (i.e., the truth) includes the confession of our sins, which keeps us in fellowship with one another and effects cleansing from all sin through the blood of Jesus.

Paul's use of light in 2 Cor. 4:4-6 runs along parallel lines with John's usage (cp. Luke 2:32). "Light" (here *photismos*) is defined as "the gospel of the glory of Christ, who is the image of God" (2 Cor. 4:4 HCSB). "For God, who said, 'Light shall shine out of darkness,'" is the One who has "shone in our hearts to give the light (*photismos*) of the knowledge of God's glory in the face of Jesus Christ" (2 Cor. 4:6). Indeed, the beholding of the glory of the Lord results in our "being transformed into the same image from glory to glory; this is from the Lord who is the Spirit" (2 Cor. 3:18). Since they are being conformed to the glorious image of Jesus, who is the embodiment of grace and truth, it is fitting that Christ's disciples too are called "the light of the world" (Matt. 5:14,16). They have come to Christ to receive life (cp. Eph. 5:13-14) and thus are possessors and givers of light (1 Thess. 5:5; Rom. 13:12; Eph. 5:8; Phil. 2:15; cp. John 5:35). Like Paul (a prototypical disciple), they too are called "to open their [the Jewish people's and the rest of the nations'] eyes that they may turn from darkness to light and from the power of Satan to God, that they may receive forgiveness of sins and a share among those who are sanctified by faith in Me [Jesus]" (Acts 26:18 HCSB). As sons of light, they bear fruit in all goodness, righteousness, and truth (Eph. 5:9) and bring glory to the Father (Matt. 5:16).   *Randall K. J. Tan*

LIGHTNING Flash of light resulting from a discharge of static electricity in the atmosphere. In the OT lightning is always associated with God. God is the Maker of lightning and thunder (Job 28:26; Jer. 10:13) which reveal God's power and majesty (Pss. 77:18; 97:4). Lightning and thunder frequently accompany a revelation of God (the giving of the law, Exod. 19:16; 20:18; Ezekiel's first vision, Ezek. 1:13-14). In poetic language God's voice is identified with the thunder (Job 37:3-5). Lightning also appears as God's weapon in those passages in which God is portrayed as a warrior (arrows: 2 Sam. 22:15; Pss. 18:14; 77:17; 144:6; fire: Ps. 97:3; Job 36:32). Both the OT and the NT continue the association with power and majesty (4:5; 11:19) and with weapons/judgment (8:5; 16:18). Lightning serves as an illustration for Christ's clearly visible coming (Matt. 24:26-27) and of Satan's (sudden, catastrophic, visible) fall (Luke 10:18).

LIGHTS, FEAST OF Also known as Hanukkah. See *Festivals*.

LIGN ALOES KJV transliteration of the Vulgate (official Latin translation) reading at Num. 24:6 (*lignum aloes* means "wood of aloes"). NASB, NIV, NRSV simply read "aloes." The REB reflects the KJV tradition with the reading "aloe trees." See *Aloe*.

LIGURE KJV term for a gem usually identified with the jacinth, which was regarded as precious in ancient times (Exod. 28:19). See *Minerals and Metals*.

LIKENESS Quality or state of being like; resemblance. Old Testament passages center around two truths: (1) that God is wholly other and cannot be properly compared to any likeness (Isa. 40:18) and (2) that humanity is created in the image and likeness of God (Gen. 1:26). The first truth forms the basis for the prohibition of making any graven images (Exod. 20:4; Deut. 4:16-18) and perhaps explains Ezekiel's reluctance to speak of elements in his vision in concrete terms (Ezek. 1:5,10,16,22,26,28). The likeness of God in humanity (Gen. 1:26) has been interpreted variously. Likeness has sometimes been distinguished from image, though the terms are best regarded as synonyms. Interpreters have identified the divine likeness with the ability to think rationally, to form relationships with other humans and with God or with the exercise of dominion over creation (cp. Ps. 8:5-8). The divine likeness is sometimes thought to have been lost in the fall, but its passing to Seth (Gen. 5:3) argues against the popular form of this argument. Though the likeness of God was not lost with Adam's sin, neither Adam nor subsequent humanity fulfilled God's purpose. God's purpose for humanity was fulfilled in Jesus Christ who is in a unique sense the likeness of God (2 Cor. 4:4; cp. John 1:14,18; 14:9; Heb. 1:3). Paul's statement that Christ came "in flesh like ours under sin's domain" (Rom. 8:3 HCSB) parallels "taking on the likeness of men" (Phil. 2:7), testifying that the incarnate Christ was truly human. The Christian life is characterized as a new creation in the likeness of God (Eph. 4:24; cp. 2 Cor. 4:4). See *Idols; Image of God.*

LIKHI (Lĭk´ hī) Personal name meaning "taken." Member of tribe of Manasseh (1 Chron. 7:19).

LILY In biblical usage any of a number of distinctive flowers ranging from the lotus of the Nile (1 Kings 7:19) to wild field flowers in Palestine (Matt. 6:28). The lily was the inspiration for the rim of the molten sea in the temple in Jerusalem (1 Kings 7:26; cp. 1 Kings 7:19,22). The Song of Songs uses it to beautify the writer's description of love (2:1; 4:5). See *Flowers.*

LILY BLOSSOM See *Lily Work.*

LILY OF THE COVENANT, LILY OF THE TESTIMONY Translation of the Hebrew *shushan edut* in the title of Ps. 60, taken as a reference to the hymn tune (NASB margin, NIV, HCSB, REB). KJV, RSV simply transliterate the Hebrew.

LILY WORK Decorative work capping the two freestanding columns flanking the entrance to Solomon's temple (1 Kings 7:19,22). These columns were likely inspired by Egyptian columns with a lotus motif. The brim of the molten sea was perhaps also inspired by the shape of the lotus blossom (1 Kings 7:26). See *Temple.*

LIME White, caustic solid consisting primarily of calcium oxide obtained by heating limestone or shells to a high temperature. Mixed with water, lime was used as a plaster (Deut. 27:2,4). Burning someone's bones to lime amounts to complete annihilation (Isa. 33:12) and was

regarded as an especially heinous crime (Amos 2:1).

LINE Tool used for measuring length or distance; a plumb line; a cord; a row. Sometimes the distance to be measured is relatively short (1 Kings 7:23). Elsewhere the line serves as a surveying tool for measuring a larger distance (Ps. 16:6; Isa. 34:17; Jer. 31:39; Zech. 1:16; 2:1-2). The surveying image is applied both to contexts where judgment (Amos 7:17) and restoration (Jer. 31:39; Zech. 1:16; 2:1) are in view. In contrast, references to a plumb line refer to judgment (2 Kings 21:13; Isa. 34:11; Lam. 2:8) upon those who failed to meet God's high standards (Isa. 28:17). Line is used in the sense of a cord in the story of Rahab and the spies (Josh. 2:18,21). Line can also refer to a row (of men, 2 Sam. 8:2; of writing, Isa. 28:10,13).

LINEAGE KJV and RSV term (Luke 2:4) meaning descent (cp. NRSV) or family (NASB). HCSB has "family line." See *Genealogies.*

LINEAR MEASURES See *Weights and Measures.*

LINEN Most common fabric used in the ancient Near East. It was spun from the flax plant and bleached before being woven into clothing, bedding, curtains, and burial shrouds. The tabernacle curtains (Exod. 26:1) and the high priest's garments (Exod. 28:6) were of "fine linen," cloth woven so finely that it cannot be distinguished from silk without the aid of magnification. See *Flax.*

LINTEL Wooden crossbeam over a doorway. The lintel is most prominent in the celebration of the Passover. The people of Israel were to sprinkle the blood of the sacrificial lamb on the lintel and the doorposts as a sign to the death angel. Every household that had blood on the lintel would be spared the death of the firstborn (Exod. 12:22-23).

LINUS (Lī´ nŭs) Personal name possibly meaning "linen." Paul's companion who sent greetings to Timothy (2 Tim. 4:21). Early church tradition identified him as the first bishop of the church at Rome, but it is doubtful Rome had only one bishop or pastor that early in its history.

Statue of a lion standing over a bull's head.

LION Large, swift-moving cat. The male has a heavy mane. Mentioned approximately 135 times in the OT, the lion is the proverbial symbol for strength (Judg. 14:18). In Palestine lions seemed to prefer the vegetation of the Jordan Valley (Jer. 49:19). The Bible describes the lion as powerful and daring (Prov. 30:30) and distinguished by a terrifying roar (Isa. 5:29). It was a sign of the tribe of Judah (Gen. 49:9; Rev. 5:5). David defended his father's flock against lions and bears (1 Sam. 17:34-35). One of the most well-known stories in the Bible is about a young man being cast into a den of lions (Dan. 6:16-23). Since untamed lions were put in pits, it is possible that Daniel was cast into such a pit. Lions were kept as pets by pharaohs. The Hebrews seemed to make closer distinctions than does English in the lion family, since five unrelated Hebrew words are translated "lion." They have disappeared from Palestine, with the last one killed near Megiddo in the 13th century.

LIPS Fleshy, muscular folds surrounding the mouth. In the OT lips frequently take the character of the whole person. There are flattering and lying lips (Pss. 12:2; 31:18); joyful lips (Ps. 63:5); righteous lips (Prov. 16:13); fearful lips (Hab. 3:16). Uncircumcised lips (Exod. 6:12

KJV) most likely refer to stammering lips or lack of fluency in speech (Exod. 4:10). Mourning is expressed in part by covering the upper lip with one's hand (Lev. 13:45).

LITTER Covered and curtained couch with shafts so that it can be carried by porters (Song 3:7 NRSV, REB; Isa. 66:20 KJV, NASB, NRSV). The term used at Isa. 66:20 perhaps refers to covered wagons (NIV, REB). The NIV takes the term at Song 3:7 in this sense as well (carriage).

LITTLE OWL Any species of owl other than the great owl; included in the unclean birds of Lev. 11:17. See *Owl.*

LIVER Large organ that secretes bile. According to the NASB, the lobe of the liver was offered to God with the other choice parts of the burnt offering (Lev. 3:4,10,15). Only the covering of the liver was offered according to the NIV (also KJV). NRSV understood the offering to consist of the appendage to the liver, likely the pancreas. The ancients examined livers to discern the future. The only scriptural mention of the practice concerns the king of Babylon (Ezek. 21:21). In Lam. 2:11 the liver is likely regarded as the seat of emotions (liver, KJV, NASB margin; heart, NASB, NIV, RSV; bile, NRSV).

LIVING BEINGS, LIVING CREATURES Characters in Ezekiel's first vision (Ezek. 1:5,13-15,19-20,22; 3:13; 10:15,17,20). The creatures are later identified as cherubim (10:20). There were four creatures, each having a human form but with four faces. Perhaps the best interpretation views the creatures as a pictorial representation of the total sovereignty of God. Four creatures represent the four corners of the earth. The four faces represent four classes of creation: man, humanity; lion, king of wild beasts; ox, king of domestic beasts; and eagle, king of the birds. Central to this interpretation is the One seated on the throne above all the creatures (1:26-28). The book of Revelation develops a similar image to portray God's total sovereignty (Rev. 4:1-8).

LIZARD See *Reptiles; Bittern.*

LOAF (LOAVES) OF BREAD See *Bread.*

LO-AMMI (Lō-ăm′ mī) Symbolic personal name meaning "not my people." Son of Hosea the prophet whose name God gave to symbolize Israel's lost relationship with Him due to their sin and broken covenant (Hos. 1:9).

LOAN Grant temporary use. Because of Israel's experience of deliverance from slavery, her moral code gave special care to marginal folk (Exod. 22:21-24; Deut. 10:19; Ps. 82:3-4; Prov. 31:8-9). Thus loans were to be acts of generosity, not acts for profit at the expense of the poor (Lev. 25:35-37). Furthermore, because the earth was God's (Lev. 25:23; Deut. 10:14) and human possessions were gifts from God (Deut. 8:1-10), lending was sharing God's gifts.

Therefore the OT forbade charging interest to fellow Israelites (Exod. 22:25; Lev. 25:35-38; Deut. 23:19), for requesting loans indicated economic hardship. One might charge interest to sojourners (Deut. 23:20), though this arrangement was not meant to be exploitative (Exod. 22:21; Lev. 19:33-34; Deut. 10:19; Ezek. 22:7). Laws for collateral focused on protecting the debtor. The pledge must not threaten the debtor's dignity (Deut. 24:10-11), livelihood (Deut. 24:6), family (Job 24:1-3,9), or physical necessities (Exod. 22:26-27; Deut. 24:12-13). Compassionate lending was one measure of a righteous person (Ps. 15; Ezek. 18:5-9).

Years of release and the Jubilee Year (Exod. 23:10-11; Deut. 15:1-15; Lev. 25) provided a systematic means for addressing long-term economic hardship by returning family property, freeing slaves, and canceling debts. Deuteronomy 15:7-11 warns against scheming creditors who would refuse loans because a year of release was near; lending was to be an act of generosity (v. 10). As in most human communities, greed prevailed, and the prophets railed

Mosaic of loaves and fishes at the Tabgha church commemorating Jesus' feeding the five thousand.

against the exploitation of the poor (e.g., Amos 2:6-8; 8:4), including violations of charging interest and abusing pledges (Ezek. 18:12-13; 22:12; Hab. 2:6-9; Neh. 5:6-11). See *Borrow; Coins; Ethics; Justice; Levites; Poor, Orphan, Widow; Sabbatical Year; Slavery; Stranger; Year of Jubilee.*   *David Nelson Duke*

LOBE OF THE LIVER See *Caul.*

LOCK 1. A tuft, tress, or ringlet of hair. As a sign of their dedication to God, Nazirites were not permitted to cut their locks (Num. 6:5; Judg. 16:19). Priests were likewise prohibited from shaving their heads, though they could trim their hair (Ezek. 44:20). The Hebrew term that the KJV translated "locks" at Song 4:1,3; 6:7 and Isa. 47:2 is rendered "veil" by modern translations. **2.** A bolt used to secure a door. In the OT period door locks were bolts with holes into which small iron or wooden pins would drop to secure the bolt (Neh. 3:3,6,13,15; Song 5:5; cp. Judg. 3:23-24). The bolt was generally seven to nine inches long for an interior door, 14 inches to two feet for an outside door. The key had iron pegs corresponding to the position of the pins in the bolt and worked by forcing these pins up (Judg. 3:25).

LOCUST Insect species of the order *Orthoptera*, family *Acrididae*. In the Middle East the locust periodically multiplies to astronomical numbers. As the swarm moves across the land, it devours all vegetation, high and low. The Hebrew OT uses different words to describe the insect at its various stages of life, from egg to larvae to adult insect. Eaten in several ways (raw, boiled, roasted), the locust is an excellent source of protein (Lev. 11:21-22; Mark 1:6).

The locust plague is used as a symbol for what God's judgment will be like (Joel 2:1,11,25; Rev. 9:3,7; cp. Exod. 10:3-20; Deut. 28:38). The image of the locust plague was also used to symbolize being overwhelmed by a large and powerful army (Judg. 6:5; Isa. 33:4; Jer. 46:23; 51:27; Joel 2:20; Nah. 3:15). Similar imagery is used in other ancient Near Eastern literature. See *Insects.*

LOD (Lōd) Place-name of unknown meaning, later called Lydda, 11 miles southeast of Joppa. Shemed or perhaps Elpaal of the tribe of Benjamin is credited with building it (1 Chron. 8:12). Returning exiles settled there about 537

B.C. (Ezra 2:33; Neh. 7:37; 11:35) at what appears as the westernmost postexilic settlement though probably outside the governing authority of Sanballat of Samaria and of Judah (Neh. 6:2). See *Lydda.*

LO-DEBAR (Lō-Dē´ bàr) Place-name variously spelled in Hebrew to mean "no word" or "to him a word" or "to speak." After Saul and Jonathan had been defeated on Mount Gilboa (1 Sam. 31:1-13), Mephibosheth, Jonathan's lame son (2 Sam. 4:4) took refuge with Machir in the city of Lo-Debar (2 Sam. 9:3-4)—a city of Gad located in the eastern part of Gilead just south of the Sea of Chinnereth (Galilee). After David became king, he called for Mephibosheth so he could show kindness to the lone descendant of Jonathan (2 Sam. 9:1-5). David later needed the assistance of Machir of Lo-Debar during the rebellion of Absalom (2 Sam. 17:27-29).

The Hebrew text of Josh. 13:26 mentions the name of the city *Lidebir* near Mahanaim. This is usually translated "of Debir," but many see this as an alternate spelling of Lo-Debar. See *Debir.*

Lo-Debar is cryptically referred to in Amos 6:13. Prior to the delivery of this oracle, Lo-Debar and Karnaim had been recaptured by Jeroboam II from the Arameans in a campaign blessed by God (2 Kings 14:25-28). Israel had taken the victory as an indication of its own strength and greatness, forgetting that God had brought them the victory. Amos took the consonants of the name Lo-Debar and added new vowels to make the name read "a thing of nought." Amos was reminding Israel that its true strength and greatness lie not in their military achievements but in God who had blessed their efforts. Amos was calling the Israelites back to faith in this God.   *Phil Logan*

LODGE Temporary resting place, for example, in a private home (Josh. 2:1; Acts 10:18) or a campground (Josh. 4:3,8; Isa. 10:29). The temporary stay might be prolonged as was the case of Paul in Rome (Acts 28:23,30). Jeremiah longed to escape to a wayfarer's desert lodge to avoid his people's sinfulness (Jer. 9:2). See *Hut.*

LOFT KJV term for the upper room (NASB, NIV) or chamber (NRSV, cp. REB) of a house (1 Kings 17:19). See *Architecture; House; Upper Room.*

LOG 1. A liquid measure. See *Weights and Measures.* **2.** Section of a tree trunk. The Bible refers to splitting logs (Eccles. 10:9), to burning logs for cooking (Ezek. 24:10), and to felling logs to use in house construction (2 Kings 6:2,5). The timber that King Hiram of Tyre sent to Solomon was likely logs lashed together to form rafts (1 Kings 5:8-9). The "log" of Jesus' hyperbolic expression (Matt. 7:3-5; Luke 6:41-42) was a long, shaped piece of lumber (KJV, beam).

LOGIA (Lō gē´ à) Greek term applied to a collection of sayings. It comes from the same root as *logos,* a Greek word usually translated "word" (John 1:1,14). The Church Fathers used "logia" to denote a collection of the sayings of Jesus. In his *History of the Church,* Eusebius (ca. A.D. 260 to ca. 340) quoted Papias (A.D. 100s) who said that Matthew compiled the logia in Hebrew. Apparently this is not the same as the Gospel of Matthew itself. Rather the Hebrew logia were likely the sayings of Jesus contained in Matthew and Luke but not in Mark.

Exactly when the logia might have achieved written form is a subject of debate. In addition to NT evidence, two modern discoveries show that logia existed in early Christian communities. Around 1900 remnants of an actual logia were unearthed near Oxyrncus, Egypt. Three papyrus fragments were found containing sayings ascribed to Jesus. They have been dated to the A.D. 200s but are probably copies of an older collection. Each saying begins with "Jesus says." Some of them can be found in the Gospels, while others are known from the Church Fathers. In addition, two logia of a community with Gnostic tendencies were found in 1946 near Nag Hammadi, Egypt. Dating from between A.D. 300 and 400, they contain over 200 sayings attributed to Jesus.

The Gospels, as well as those NT sayings of Jesus found outside the Gospels (such as Acts 20:35), and the modern discoveries all demonstrate the early church's concern for preserving Jesus' sayings. The same concern can be seen today in our red-letter edition Bibles. See *Gnosticism; Logos; Luke; Mark; Matthew; Nag Hammadi.*   *Larry McKinney*

LOGOS John deliberately used *logos* (translated "Word") to describe Jesus (John 1:1). *Logos* had rich cultural meaning in the background of early Christians, both Jews and Greeks.

The Greek word *logos* ("word") ordinarily refers to an explanation or reason for something otherwise meaningless. *Logos* has a variety of uses depending on context. With regard to language or grammar, *logos* can mean "sentence" or "statement," while regarding logic or knowledge it can mean "reason," "explanation," "science," or "formula." A form of *logos* is utilized in English words to describe a particular discipline or science, such as theology, anthropology, and so forth.

Logos was given great significance by Greek philosophers, beginning with Heraclitus. The Stoics strongly emphasized the *logos spermatikos* ("seminal word"), the rational principle which pervades all reality, providing meaning and order to persons and the universe. The *logos* creates coherence and unity, provides an orderly pattern for existence, and holds everything together.

Foundational for biblical use of *logos*, however, is the OT concept of the "word" (*dabar*) of God. The Hebrews saw the word of God not as merely words but as a powerful and effectual means of accomplishing God's purposes (Isa. 40:8; 55:11; Jer. 23:29). By His word God spoke the world into existence (Gen. 1:3-31; Ps. 33:6; 2 Pet. 3:5). God communicated His word directly to persons, especially in the Law (Exod. 20:1-17; 34:28; Deut. 5:4-5) and the Prophets (1 Sam. 15:10; 2 Sam. 7:4; 23:2; 2 Kings 7:1; Isa. 38:4; Jer. 1:4,11; Ezek. 7:1; 11:14; Hos. 1:1; Joel 1:1; Jon. 1:1; Mic. 1:1; Hag. 1:1; Mal. 1:1). The wise person is the one who lives in accordance with the word of God (Gen. 15:1; Exod. 9:20-25; Num. 3:16; 1 Kings 6:11-12; Pss. 106:24; 119).

As Greek and Hebrew cultures overlapped, these concepts of "word" interacted. When Jewish scholars in Alexandria, Egypt, translated the Hebrew OT into Greek (the Septuagint, 275 B.C.), they utilized *logos* to translate *dabar*. An Alexandrian Jew, Philo (30 B.C.–A.D. 40), expressed Judaism in neo-Platonic terms, believing that Greek thinkers borrowed from Moses. Philo believed that Greek concepts such as *logos* were not contradictory to the OT view of the word and wisdom of God as personified in Prov. 8 and in the apocryphal books Wisdom of Solomon and Sirach. Just as the Stoic logos provided the rational order for creation, Philo reinterpreted the creation in Genesis to be through the *Logos*, the firstborn of creation.

In this cultural situation John described Jesus as the *Logos* (John 1:1-14). But John did not merely copy common cultural concepts. Writing under the inspiration of the Holy Spirit, he poured new meaning into the concept of *Logos*. In relation to God, Jesus as the *Logos* was not merely an angel or created being who was the agent of creation, nor another word from God or wisdom from God, but He was God Himself (John 1:1-4). In relation to humanity, Jesus the *Logos* was not the impersonal principle of Stoicism, but He was a personal Savior who took on human flesh in the incarnation (John 1:4-14). The Word's becoming flesh and living among us (John 1:14) was in sharp contrast to the Greek ideas. By depicting Jesus as the *Logos*, John portrays Him as the preexistent Creator of the universe, with God, and identical to God. From this perspective of Jesus' divinity and eternity, any view of Jesus as a mere prophet or teacher is impossible (Phil. 2:5-11; Col. 1:13-20; 2:9-10; Heb. 1:1-4; 1 John 1:1-3; Rev. 19:13).

In other NT texts *logos* is used to refer to Scripture, particularly as proclaimed in gospel preaching (Luke 5:1; 8:11-15; Acts 4:31; 8:14; 12:24; Rom. 10:8; 1 Thess. 2:13; 1 Pet. 1:23-25; Heb. 4:12). The preaching of the gospel brings order and meaning to lives shattered by sin. Those who put faith in Jesus, the *Logos*, will be welcomed into the family of God (John 1:11-12).   *Steve W. Lemke*

LOINS Hebrew and Greek terms refer to the hips and lower back. Loins are used in the literal sense of the body's midsection (Exod. 28:42; 2 Kings 1:8; Isa. 11:5; Jer. 13:1; Matt. 3:4). Tying up one's long, lower garments about one's waist or loins indicated readiness for travel (Exod. 12:11; 1 Kings 18:46; 2 Kings 9:1). In the NT to gird up one's loins is used in the figurative sense of preparedness (Luke 12:35; Eph. 6:14; 1 Pet. 1:13). The OT sometimes uses loins as the seat of physical strength (Nah. 2:1). Thus to make someone's loins shake or loosed is to render the person helpless (Ps. 69:23; Isa. 45:1). Scripture also uses the loins as a symbol of procreative powers (Gen. 35:11; 1 Kings 8:19; Acts 2:30; Heb. 7:5,10). Modern translations frequently hide the Hebrew expression "from his loins" behind the translation "descendant."

LOIS (Lō´ĭs) Personal name, perhaps meaning "more desirable" or "better." The mother of Eunice and grandmother of Timothy (2 Tim. 1:5). Paul exalted Lois as a model of Christian faith and saw her as instrumental in nurturing her grandson in the faith.

LONG LOBE OF THE LIVER See *Caul.*

LONG-SUFFERING See *Patience.*

LOOKING GLASS KJV term for a (hand)mirror (Exod. 38:8). In biblical times mirrors were made of polished metal (molten mirror, Job 37:18) which yielded a somewhat distorted image (1 Cor. 13:12). The women who ministered at the gate of the tabernacle donated their mirrors to be melted down for the bronze laver (Exod. 38:8). The KJV often refers to a mirror as a looking glass (Job 37:18; Isa. 3:23; 1 Cor. 13:12; James 1:23). See *Glass.*

LOOM Frame used for interlacing sets of threads at right angles to form cloth. The weaving of cloth was an important industry in the ancient world. Thus it is surprising that there are so few references to the process in Scripture. In a humorous scene, Samson convinced Delilah that his strength would be sapped should someone weave his hair into a piece of cloth on a loom. While he slept, Delilah did just that but was surprised when he easily freed himself from the loom (Judg. 16:14). Here "web" refers to cloth on a loom. Isaiah compared his finished life with cloth which is cut off from the loom (Isa. 38:12). Job 7:6 compares the brevity of life to the speed of the weaver's shuttle, the devise used to pass quickly the woof thread between the threads of the warp. Frequent references to a spear like a weaver's beam (1 Sam. 17:7; 2 Sam. 21:19; 1 Chron. 11:23; 20:5) perhaps suggest a javelin with a cord attached so that it might be easily retrieved. In this case, the heddle rod, a rod attached to cords or wires and used to guide warp threads, is possibly in mind. Other interpreters prefer to see a reference to the great size of the spear. See *Cloth, Clothing.*

LOOPS The inner and outer coverings of the tabernacle were each made of two large curtains held together by 50 clasps which passed through curved sections of blue cord for the inner tent or of leather for the outer tent (Exod. 26:4-5,10-11; 36:11-12,17).

LORD English rendering of several Hebrew and Greek words. Generally, the term refers to one who has power or authority.

God as Lord *Jehovah* (or *Yahweh;* Hebrew *YHWH,* "self-existent") is the name of God most frequently used in the Hebrew Scriptures. LORD commonly represents it in the English translations. The Jews meticulously avoided every mention of it and substituted in its stead another word, *Adonai.* They substituted the vowels in *Adonai* for those of *Yahweh* that produced the term *Jehovah.*

The importance of the name cannot be overstated. Exodus 3:14 furnishes a clue to the meaning of the word. When Moses received his commission to be the deliverer of Israel, God, who appeared in the burning bush, communicated to him the name to give as the credentials of his mission: "God said to Moses, 'I AM WHO I AM' [Heb. *ehyeh asher ehyeh*]; and He said, 'Thus you shall say to the sons of Israel, "I AM has sent me to you"'" (NASB). In both names, *ehyeh* and *YHWH,* the root idea is that of uncreated existence. When it is said that God's name is I am, simple being is not all that is affirmed. He *is* in a sense in which no other being is. He is, and the cause of His being is in Himself. He is because He is. The notice in Exod. 6:3, "By My name, LORD, I did not make Myself known to them" (NASB), does not imply that the patriarchs were completely ignorant of the existence or the use of the name. It simply means that previous to their deliverance from Egyptian bondage they had no experiential knowledge of such redemption. Under Moses they were to experience deliverance and have the redemptive power of God made real to them and the redemptive name of God entrusted to them. Previously, as shepherds in Palestine, Abraham, Isaac, and Jacob had known God as El Shaddai ("the Almighty," Gen. 17:1), proving His power, but not in this kind of redemptive relationship. This name affirms God's lordship over His people (Exod. 34:23), as well as His power over the whole creation (Josh. 3:13). By this name God avows His superiority over all other gods (Deut. 10:17).

Adonai is another important designation for God as Lord in the OT. It derives from the Hebrew word *Adon,* an early word denoting ownership, hence, absolute control. *Adon* is not properly a divine title as it is used of humans in some places. It is applied to God as the owner and governor of the whole earth (Ps. 114:7). It is sometimes used as a term of respect (like our "sir") but with a pronoun attached ("my lord").

It often occurs in the plural. *Adonai* is, in the emphatic form, "the Lord." Many regard this title as the plural of *Adon.*

"Lord" or "Master" (Gk. *kurios,* "supreme") signifies the one to whom a person or thing belongs, the master, the one having disposition of men or property, such as the "owner of the vineyard" (Matt. 20:8 HCSB; 21:40; Mark 12:9; Luke 20:15); the "Lord of the harvest" (Matt. 9:38 HCSB; Luke 10:2); the "master of the house" (Mark 13:35 HCSB); "Lord of the Sabbath" (Matt. 12:8 HCSB; Mark 2:28; Luke 6:5), who has the power to determine what is suitable to the Sabbath, and to release Himself and others from its obligation. This title is given to God, the ruler of the universe, both with the definite article *ho kurios* (Matt. 1:22; 5:33; Mark 5:19; Acts 7:33; 2 Tim. 1:16,18) and without the article (Matt. 21:9; 27:10; Mark 13:20; Luke 2:9,23,26; Heb. 7:21).

Jesus as Lord *Kurios* is the word normally employed in the NT to speak of Jesus as Lord. The word, however, has a wide range of reference, being used of God (Acts 2:34), of Jesus (Luke 10:1), of humans (Acts 16:19), and of angels (Acts 10:4). When characters in the Gospels speak of Jesus as Lord, they often mean no more than "sir." At other times the designation *kurios* expresses a full confession of faith, as in Thomas's declaration, "My Lord and my God!" (John 20:28 HCSB). "The Lord" came to be used as a simple yet profound designation of Christ in Luke and Acts. "The Lord Jesus" was used frequently in Acts as well (4:33) to speak of faith in Christ as Lord (16:31) and to identify baptism as being in the name of the Lord Jesus (8:16; 19:5). The phrase "Jesus is Lord" evidently was the earliest Christian confession of faith. In Acts 2:36 Peter declared that God had made Jesus both Lord and Christ.

Paul often used a fuller phrase to speak of Jesus' lordship, "the Lord Jesus Christ." It is significant that he used this in conjunction with the mention of God the Father and the Holy Spirit (1 Thess. 1:1; 2 Cor. 13:14). At other times Paul used the simpler formulas "the Lord Jesus" (2 Thess. 1:7) or "our Lord Jesus" (1 Thess. 3:13). In contrast to the many false gods and lords of pagans, there is for Christians one God, the Father, and one Lord, Jesus Christ (1 Cor. 8:5-6). Paul was certainly familiar with the early confession "Jesus is Lord" because he averred in 1 Cor. 12:3 that "no one can say, 'Jesus is Lord,'

except by the Holy Spirit" (HCSB). The word is used often in connection with the hope of Christ's second coming (Phil. 3:20; 4:5; 1 Cor. 16:22; Rev. 22:20).

In Revelation the title "Lord" has another connotation. The emperors demanded to be called "lord," and one emperor, Domitian, even issued a decree that began: "Our lord and god commands." John declared that such titles were blasphemous, and that Christ, the King of kings and Lord of lords, is the only emperor whom Christians can recognize (Rev. 19:16).

Second Peter 2:1 and Jude 4 speak of Jesus as *despotes,* "Master" (HCSB). It carries a more emphatic stress on the sovereignty of Jesus as Lord. Interestingly the same word is used to address God in Luke 2:29 and Acts 4:24. Revelation 6:10 also uses this term to address Jesus as the one who will avenge the blood of the martyrs.

To an early Christian accustomed to reading the OT, the word "Lord," when used of Jesus, would suggest His identification with the God of the OT. Contrary to some scholars who believe that the title was borrowed from pagan cults, the evidence of Acts, Corinthians, and Revelation shows that it belongs to the very earliest stratum of Christian confession. The crucified, resurrected Jesus is the Lord who will give back to the Father the judged and redeemed world (1 Cor. 15:28), and He is the eternal Lord over all humanity (Rom. 14:9).

Humans as Lord The Hebrew word *adon* is used more than 300 times in the OT to refer to human masters or as a term of respect for someone of equal rank and status. *Adon* is used of the owner of slaves (Gen. 24:14,27; 39:2,7, rendered "master"), of kings as the lords of their subjects (Isa. 26:13, "master"), and of a husband as lord of the wife (Gen. 18:12).

In the NT the Greek *kurios* is used to designate one who exercises authority over another person. It also serves as a term of respectful address (Matt. 21:29-30; Acts 25:26). The term *kurios* (Lord) is also a title of honor sometimes rendered "sir" and is expressive of the respect and reverence with which servants salute their masters (Matt. 13:27; Luke 13:8; 14:22). It is employed by a son in addressing his father (Matt. 21:30); by citizens toward magistrates (27:63); by anyone wishing to honor a man of distinction (8:2,6,8; 15:27; Mark 7:28; Luke 5:12); by the disciples in saluting Jesus, their teacher and master (Matt. 8:25; 16:22; Luke 9:54; John 11:12). See *Christ; God; Holy Spirit; Messiah; Jesus; Rabbi; Resurrection.*

Dale Ellenburg

LORD IS MY BANNER, THE See *Jehovah-nissi.*

LORD IS PEACE, THE See *Jehovah-shalom.*

LORD IS SHALOM, THE See *Jehovah-shalom.*

LORD IS THERE, THE See *Jehovah-shamma.*

LORD OF HOSTS See *Names of God.*

LORD WILL PROVIDE, THE See *Jehovah-jireh.*

LORD'S DAY Designation for Sunday, the first day of the week, used only once in the NT (Rev. 1:10). The Greek word for "Lord's," however, is precisely the same as that used in the term for "Lord's Supper" (1 Cor. 11:20). In fact, the *Didache,* an early Christian manual for worship and instruction, links the two terms together, indicating that the Lord's Supper was observed each Lord's Day (14:1). Herein may lie the origin of the term. Because the first day of the week was the day on which the early Christians celebrated the Lord's Supper, it became known as the Lord's Day, the distinctively Christian day of worship.

The earliest account of a first-day worship experience is found in Acts 20:7-12. Here Paul joined the Christians of Troas on the evening of the first day of the week for the breaking of bread (probably a reference to the Lord's Supper). The actual day is somewhat uncertain. Evening of the first day could refer to Saturday evening (by Jewish reckoning) or to Sunday evening (by Roman reckoning). Since the incident involved Gentiles on Gentile soil, however, the probable reference is to Sunday night.

The importance of Sunday to first-century Christians is also intimated in 1 Cor. 16:1-2. Giving instructions about a special relief offering he wanted to take to the Christians in Jerusalem, Paul suggested that the Corinthians should set aside their weekly contributions on the first day of the week. Paul probably mentioned this day because he knew that his readers routinely assembled on that day for worship and that

would be the logical time for them to set aside their offering.

Two other second-century documents also shed light on the significance of Lord's Day for the early church. First, Ignatius in his *Epistle to the Magnesians* (about A.D. 110–117) stressed the importance of Lord's Day by contrasting the worship done on that day with that formerly observed on the Sabbath (9:1). Second, Justin Martyr (ca. A.D. 150) wrote the first extant Christian description of a worship service. He noted that the early Sunday morning service began with baptism, included Scripture readings, expository preaching, and prayer, and then concluded with the observance of the Lord's Supper (*Apology* 65–67).

First- and second-century Christian documents indicate that Sunday quickly became the standard day for Christian worship, but they do not explain how or why this change from Sabbath to Lord's Day came about. The most obvious reason, of course, was the Resurrection of Jesus that took place on that first Lord's Day. Since the earliest collective experiences of the disciples with the risen Lord took place on Easter Sunday evening (Luke 24:36-49; John 20:19-23), one might naturally expect the disciples to gather at that same hour on subsequent Sundays to remember Him in the observance of the Supper. This pattern, perhaps, is reflected in the service at Troas in Acts 20.

The change in the time of worship from evening to morning, though, probably came about because of practical necessity. Writing to the emperor Trajan at the beginning of the second century, Pliny the Younger, governor of Bithynia, reported that in compliance with Trajan's edict against seditious assemblies, he had ordered that no group, including the Christians, could meet at night. Pliny then described an early morning service of the Christians. Forbidden to meet at night, they met for the observance of the Supper at the only other hour available to them on the first day of the week: early in the morning before they went to work. It is likely that the practice then spread throughout the empire wherever similar regulations against evening worship were in force.

Although some Jewish Christians probably also observed the Sabbath, the early Christians saw Sunday as a day of joy and celebration, not a substitute for the Sabbath. The use of the term "sabbath" to refer to Sunday did not become common until the English Puritans began to do so after A.D. 1500. Evidence from the early centuries clearly shows that Christians regarded Sunday as a day to rejoice in the new life brought by the resurrection. On other days Christians might fast and kneel when praying, but the joyous character of the Lord's Day made those actions inappropriate on Sundays. Soon after Christianity became the religion of the Roman Empire, Sunday was officially declared a day of rest. See *Didache; Lord's Supper; Sabbath; Worship.*

Fred A. Grissom and Naymond Keathley

LORD'S PRAYER Words Jesus used to teach His followers to pray. Three forms of the Lord's Prayer exist in early Christian literature—two in the NT (Matt. 6:9-13; Luke 11:2-4) and the other in the Didache 8:2, a noncanonical Christian writing of the early second-century from northern Syria. Their similarities and differences may be seen if the three forms are set side by side. (See next page)

Three conclusions derive from such comparison. First, it is the same prayer in all three cases. Second, the Didache likely uses the form of the prayer found in Matthew. Third, Matthew's version is longer than that of Luke at three points: at the end of the address to God, at the end of the petitions related to God, and at the end of the petitions related to humans. Also, study of the Greek manuscripts shows that the doxology that appears at the end of the Matthean form in some translations is not original; the earliest form of the prayer with a doxology is in Didache 8:2. It is likely that each evangelist gave the prayer as it was generally used in his own church at the time.

Matthew and Luke used the Lord's Prayer in different ways in their Gospels. In Matthew the prayer appears in the Sermon on the Mount where Jesus spoke about a righteousness that exceeds that of the scribes and Pharisees (5:20). It is located in a section that warns against practicing one's piety before men in order to be seen by them (6:1-18). Almsgiving, praying, and fasting are for God's eyes and ears. When praying one should not make a public display (6:5-6) or heap up empty phrases, thinking that one will be heard for many words (6:7).

In Luke the prayer comes in the midst of Jesus' journey to Jerusalem (9:51–19:46). In His behavior Jesus is an example of one who prays.

His prayer life caused one of His disciples to ask for instruction in prayer, as John the Baptist had given his disciples. What follows (11:2-13) is a teaching on prayer in which the disciples are told what to pray for (11:2-4) and why to pray (11:5-13). Here the Lord's Prayer is a model of what to pray for. To pray in this way is a distinguishing mark of Jesus' disciples.

Matthew	**Luke**	**Didache**
Our Father in heaven,	Father,	Our Father in heaven,
Your name be honored as holy.	Your name be honored as holy.	Your name be honored as holy.
Your kingdom come.	Your kingdom come.	Your kingdom come.
Your will done, be done on earth as it is in heaven.		Your will be as in heaven, so also on earth.
Give us today our daily bread.	Give us each day our daily bread.	Give us today our daily bread.
And forgive us our debts, as we also have forgiven our debtors.	And forgive us our sins, for we ourselves also forgive everyone in debt to us.	And forgive us our debt, as we also forgive our debtors;
And do not bring us into temptation, but deliver us from the evil one. [For Yours is the kingdom and the power and glory forever. Amen.]	And do not bring us into temptation.	And do not bring us into temptation but deliver us from evil, For yours is the power and glory, forever.

Although all three versions of the prayer exist only in Greek, the thought pattern and expressions are Jewish. In the address God is designated "Father" or "Our Father in heaven." One Jewish prayer begins: "Forgive us, Our Father" (Eighteen Benedictions, 6). Rabbi Akiba (ca. A.D. 130) said: "Happy are you Israelites! Before whom are

Tiles showing the Lord's Prayer in three of the many languages displayed at the Church of the Lord's Prayer, Jerusalem.

you purified, and who purifies you? Your Father in heaven" (Mishnah, *Yoma*, 8:9). The *Ahaba Rabba* (Great Love) prayer, which formed part or the morning worship in the Jerusalem temple, began: "With great love hast thou loved us, O Lord, our God, with great and exceedingly great forbearance hast thou ruled over us. Our Father, our King, be gracious to us."

The "You-petitions" are likewise Jewish in their thought and expression. The first two, "[Your name be honored as holy. Your] kingdom come," echo the language of the Jewish prayer, the Kaddish. It begins: "Magnified and hallowed [honored as holy] be his great name in the world.... And may he establish his kingdom in your lifetime and in your days ... quickly and soon." The third, "Your will be done," is similar to a prayer of Rabbi Eliezer (ca. A.D. 100): "Do thy will in heaven above and give peace to those who fear thee below" (Babylonian Talmud, *Berakot*, 29b).

The "Us-petitions" are also Jewish in their idiom. The first, "Give us our bread," is akin to the first benediction of grace at mealtime. "Blessed art thou, O Lord our God, king of the universe, who feedest the whole world with thy goodness ...; thou givest food to all flesh.... Through thy goodness food hath never failed us: O may it not fail us for ever and ever." The second, "Forgive us," echoes the Eighteen Benedictions, 6: "Forgive us, our Father, for we have sinned against thee; blot out our transgressions from before thine eyes. Blessed art thou, O Lord, who forgivest much." The accompanying phrase, "as we also have forgiven," reflects the Jewish teaching found in Sirach 28:2: "Forgive the

wrong of your neighbor, and then your sins will be forgiven when you pray." The third petition, "Do not bring us into temptation," is similar to a petition in the Jewish morning and evening prayers. "Cause me to go not into the hands of sin, and not into the hands of transgression, and not into the hands of temptation, and not into the hand of dishonor."

Just as it was a practice of Jewish teachers to reduce the many commandments to one or two (cp. Mark 12:28-34), so it was often the case that Jewish teachers would give synopses of the Eighteen Benedictions (Babylonian Talmud, *Berakot*, 29a). The Lord's Prayer seems to be Jesus' synopsis of various Jewish prayers of the time.

If the language of the Lord's Prayer and that of various Jewish prayers is similar, the meaning must be determined from Jesus' overall message. Jesus and the early Christians believed in two ages, the "Present Evil Age" and the "Coming Good Age." The "Age to Come" would be brought by a decisive intervention of God at the end of history. This shift of the ages would be accompanied by the resurrection from the dead and the last judgment. Before either of these events, there would be a time of great suffering or tribulation. One name given to the "Age to Come" was the "Kingdom of God." It was an ideal state of affairs when Satan would be defeated, sin would be conquered, and death would be no more. Jesus believed that in His ministry the activity of God that was to bring about the shift of the ages was already taking place. Within this world of thought, the Lord's Prayer must be understood.

The "You-petitions" are synonymous parallelism. They all mean roughly the same thing. "Your name be honored as holy," "Your kingdom come," and "Your will be done on earth as it is in heaven," are all petitions for the shift of the ages to take place and for the ideal state of affairs to come about. They constitute a prayer for the final victory of God over the devil, sin, and death. It is possible that they were also understood by the early Christians to be a petition for God's rule in their lives in the here and now.

The "Us-petitions" participate in the same tension between the ultimate future and the disciples' present. "Give us our bread for the morrow" (RSV note to Matt. 6:11) may refer to the gift of manna to be renewed at the shift of the ages. As the Jewish rabbi Joshua (ca. A.D. 90) said: "He who serves God up to the last day of his death, will satisfy himself with bread, namely the bread of the world to come" (*Genesis Rabbah* 82). It also refers to the bread necessary for daily life in this world as Luke 11:3 indicates: "Give us day by day." "Forgive us our debts or sins" may very well refer to the ultimate forgiveness of sins on the last day, but it also refers to the continuing forgiveness of the disciples by their heavenly Father as they, living in this age, continually forgive those indebted to them. "And do not bring us into temptation" may refer to protection of the disciples in the final tribulation (as in Rev. 3:10), but it also speaks about being helped to avoid something evil within history where we now live. In all of the petitions, therefore, there is a tension between the present and the future. All of the petitions can be understood to refer both to the shift of the ages and to the present in which we now find ourselves. This is not surprising, considering the tension between the two in both Jesus' message and the early church's theology. The concern about the shift of the ages in the prayer sets it apart from the Jewish prayers whose language was so similar.

The Lord's Prayer in the NT is a community's prayer: …"Our Father," "Give us … our … bread," Forgive us our debts," "as we … have forgiven our debtors," "Cause us," "Deliver us." It is the prayer of the community of Jesus' disciples.

The Lord's Prayer is a prayer of petition. It is significant that the model prayer for Christians is not praise, thanksgiving, meditation, or contemplation, but petition. It is asking God for something.

This prayer of petition seeks two objects. First, one who prays in this way implores God to act so as to achieve His purpose in the world. Second, one who prays in this manner requests God to meet the physical and spiritual needs of the disciples. It is significant that the petitions come in the order they do: first, God's vindication; then, disciples' satisfaction.

Such a prayer of petition assumes a certain view of God. A God to whom one prays in this way is assumed to be in control; He is able to answer. He is also assumed to be good; He wants to answer. The Father to whom Jesus taught His disciples to pray is One who is both in control and good. See *Eschatology; Kingdom of God; Midrash; Mishnah; Rabbi; Talmud; Targum.*

Charles Talbert

Stone relief of the Lord's Supper.

LORD'S SUPPER Church ordinance where unleavened bread and the fruit of the vine memorialize the death of the Lord Jesus and anticipate His second coming. Jesus established the Lord's Supper before His crucifixion while observing the Passover with His disciples (Matt. 26:26-29). Though other names occur, Paul used the phrase "Lord's Supper" in 1 Cor. 11:20.

In observing the Lord's Supper, church members eat unleavened bread and drink the "fruit of the vine" to symbolize the body and blood of Christ. This memorial meal is to be observed until Christ comes again. The frequency among churches for observing the Lord's Supper varies, but the Scripture does require that it be done regularly (Acts 2:42). See *Ordinances*.

Michael R. Spradlin

LO-RUHAMAH (Lō-rū hă´ mah) Symbolic personal name meaning "without love." Name that God gave Hosea for his daughter to symbolize that Israel, by rebelling against God and serving foreign gods, had forfeited God's love (Hos. 1:6).

LOSS See *Restitution*.

LOT (Lŏt) Personal name meaning "concealed." Lot was the son of Haran and nephew of Abraham (Gen. 11:27). Lot, whose father died in Ur (Gen. 11:28), traveled with his grandfather to Haran (Gen. 11:31). Terah had intended to travel to Canaan but stayed in Haran instead (Gen. 11:31). When Abraham left Haran for Canaan, he was accompanied by Lot and Lot's household (Gen. 12:5).

After traveling throughout Canaan and into Egypt, Abraham and Lot finally settled between Bethel and Ai, about 10 miles north of Jerusalem (Gen. 13:3). Abraham and Lot acquired herds and flocks so large that the land was unable to support both (Gen. 13:2,5-6). In addition, the herdsmen of Abraham and Lot did not get along (Gen. 13:7). Thus, to secure ample pasturelands for their flocks and to avoid any further trouble, Abraham suggested they separate. Abraham allowed Lot to take his choice of the land. Lot took advantage of Abraham's generosity and chose the well-watered Jordan Valley where the city of Sodom was located (13:8-12).

Some interesting details of the split between Abraham and Lot remind the reader of earlier events in Genesis. For example, the Jordan Valley is described as being well watered "like the LORD's garden" (Gen. 13:10), reminding one of the story of Adam and Eve in the garden of Eden. One wonders if Lot would be more successful in this garden spot than Adam and Eve had been. The prospect of success was thrown in doubt by the way Lot's journey is described—he journeyed east, a description that recalls Adam's and Eve's journey after their expulsion from the garden (Gen. 3:24).

The Jordan Valley is also described as being fertile like Egypt (Gen. 13:10). This detail not only recalls Abraham's nearly disastrous journey to Egypt to avoid the famine in Canaan (Gen. 12:10-20) but also foreshadows the journey that Jacob and his family would later make (Gen. 42–50)—a journey that did have disastrous consequences (Exod. 1:8-14).

The mention of the cities of the Jordan Valley also carries negative connotations. One is reminded of the story of the tower of Babel where the people had gathered in one place (they had migrated from the east) to build themselves a city and make a name for themselves, so that they would not be scattered over the face of the earth and live like sojourners (Gen. 11:1-4). One is also reminded that Terah gave up his pilgrimage to Canaan to settle in the city of Haran (Gen. 11:31). To add to the negative connotations that cities have in the stories of Genesis, we are told that the people of Sodom were great sinners against the Lord (Gen. 13:13).

All in all, things did not look as good for Lot as they might at first glance appear when he chose to live in the well-watered Jordan Valley. We begin to see this unfold in Gen. 14. Not only was the Jordan Valley attractive to herdsmen like Lot, but the riches of this valley were also attractive to foreign kings. Prominent among them was Chedorlaomer who, along with three other kings, captured and sacked Sodom, taking Lot as prisoner (Gen. 14:1-12). Abraham, upon hearing of Lot's fate, gathered an army and rescued his nephew (Gen. 14:13-16).

Lot is not mentioned again until Gen. 19 when two angels visited him. God had already told Abraham that He intended to destroy Sodom and Gomorrah (Gen. 18:20). Abraham interceded on behalf of Sodom, that if 10 righteous men were found in Sodom, then God would not destroy the city (Gen. 18:32-33). The two angels were apparently going to Sodom to inspect it. When the angels arrived, Lot received them with hospitality. When the townsmen heard that two strangers were staying with Lot, they wanted to have sexual relations with them. Lot protected his guests and offered them his daughters instead. The townsmen refused this offer and tried unsuccessfully to get the two strangers. For Lot's help the angels revealed God's desire to destroy Sodom and urged Lot to take his family to the hills to safety. They warned Lot and his family not to look on Sodom. Lot, instead of going to the hills for safety, decided to live in another city (Zohar). In their flight from Sodom, Lot's nameless wife looked at the destruction and turned to a pillar of salt (Gen. 19:1-29). Abraham "had rescued" Lot, again (Gen. 19:29; cp. 12:4).

As it turned out, Lot feared to live in the city of Zohar and decided to live in the surrounding caves instead. His daughters, fearing that they would never have offspring, decided to deceive their father into having intercourse with them. They got their father drunk; both conceived a son by him. The son of the elder daughter was called Moab and became the father of the Moabites. The son of the younger daughter was named Ben-ammi and became the father of the Ammonites (Gen. 19:30-38). Later in Israel's history, God desired to ensure the place of the Moabites and Ammonites in Palestine (Deut. 2:9). The Moabites and Ammonites betrayed their relationship, however, by joining with Assyria at a later period (Ps. 83:5-8).

In the NT the day of the Son of man is compared to the destruction of Sodom and Gomorrah (Luke 17:28-29). The followers of Jesus are warned not to desire their former lives, like Lot's wife, but to be willing instead to lose their lives. Losing one's life is the only way to gain life (Luke 17:32). The story of Lot is also used to show the faithfulness of God to rescue His people (2 Pet. 2:7-9).   *Phil Logan*

LOTAN (Lō´ tăn) Personal and tribal name of uncertain meaning. Son of Seir the Horite and apparently the original ancestor of clan in Edom (Gen. 36:20-29). See *Edom; Seir*.

LOTS (Lŏts) Objects of unknown shape and material used to determine the divine will. Often in the ancient Near East people, especially priests, made difficult and significant decisions by casting lots on the ground or drawing them from a receptacle. Several times Scripture mentions the practice. We do not know exactly what

the lots looked like. Nor do we know how they were interpreted. We do know that people of the OT and NT believed God (or gods in the case of non-Israelites or non-Christians) influenced the fall or outcome of the lots (Prov. 16:33). Thus, casting lots was a way of determining God's will.

One of the best examples of this use of lots is in Acts. Matthias was chosen to be Judas's successor by lot (Acts 1:26). The apostles' prayer immediately before shows the belief that God would express His will through this method. In the OT Saul was chosen as Israel's first king through the use of lots (1 Sam. 10:20-24).

In a similar fashion God communicated knowledge unknown to human beings through lots. Saul called for the casting of lots to determine who sinned during his daylong battle with the Philistines. Specifically, he called for the use of the Urim and Thummim (1 Sam. 14:41-42). When Joshua brought people near to the Lord to find the guilty party after the defeat at Ai, he may have used lots although the word is not found in the text (Josh. 7:10-15).

Lots helped God's people make a fair decision in complicated situations. God commanded that the promised land be divided by lots (Num. 26:52-56). Later, lots established the temple priests' order of service (1 Chron. 24:5-19). This practice continued into Jesus' day. Zechariah, father of John the Baptist, was burning incense in the holy place when the angel spoke to him. Zechariah was there because the lot fell to him (Luke 1:8-9). The awful picture of soldiers casting lots for Jesus' garments was this kind of "fair play" use of lots (Matt. 27:35). Proverbs teaches that the use of lots is one way to put an end to a dispute when decisions are difficult (Prov. 18:18).

Lots are memorialized in the Jewish Feast of Purim. *Purim*, the Akkadian word for "lots," celebrates the frustration of Haman's plan to destroy the Jews in Persia. Haman had used lots to find the best day for the destruction (Esther 3:7).

Finally, the word "lot" came to refer to one's portion or circumstance of life. The righteous could confess that God was their lot (Ps. 16:5). The lot of those who violated the people of God was terror and annihilation (Isa. 17:14). See *Oracles; Urim and Thummim.*   *Albert F. Bean*

LOTUS Thorny shrub (*Zizyphus lotus*), which serves as the habitat for behemoth (Job 40:21-

22) and flourishes in hot, damp areas of North Africa and Syria. The plant is especially abundant around the Sea of Galilee. This plant should be distinguished from the Egyptian lotus (*Nymphae lotus*) which is a water lily. The translation thorn bushes (TEV) or thorny lotus (REB) is preferable to the simple lotus (NASB, NIV, NRSV) which leaves the reader wondering what plant is in view.

LOVE Unselfish, loyal, and benevolent intention and commitment toward another. The concept of the love of God is deeply rooted in the Bible. The Hebrew term *chesed* refers to covenant love. Jehovah is the God who remembers and keeps His covenants in spite of the treachery of people. His faithfulness in keeping His promises proves His love for Israel and all humanity.

Another word, *ahavah*, can be used of human love towards oneself, another person of the opposite sex, or another person in general. It is used of God's love towards Jeremiah in Jer. 31:3, "I have loved you with an everlasting love [*ahavah*]; therefore, I have drawn you with lovingkindness [*chesed*]" (NASB).

In NT times three words for love were used by the Greek-speaking world. The first is *eros*, referring to erotic or sexual love. This word is not used in the NT or in the Septuagint. It was commonly used in Greek literature of the time.

The word *phileo* (and its cognates) refers to tender affection, such as toward a friend or family member. It is very common in the NT and extrabiblical literature. It is used to express God the Father's love for Jesus (John 5:20), God's love for an individual believer (John 16:27), and of Jesus' love for a disciple (John 20:2). The word *phileo* is never used for a person's love toward God. In fact, the context of John 21:15-17 seems to suggest that Jesus desired a stronger love from Peter.

The word *agapao* (and its cognate *agape*) is rarely used in extrabiblical Greek. It was used by believers to denote the special unconditional love of God and is used interchangeably with *phileo* to designate God the Father's love for Jesus (John 3:35), God the Father's love for an individual believer (John 14:21), and of Christ's love for a disciple (John 13:23).

Biblical love has God as its object, true motivator, and source. Love is a fruit of the Holy Spirit (Gal. 5:22) and is not directed toward the world or the things of the world (the lust of the eyes, the lust of the flesh, or the pride of life—1 John 2:15-16). The ultimate example of God's love is the Lord Jesus Christ, who said, " I give you a new commandment: that you love one another. Just as I have loved you, you should also love one another" (John 13:34 HCSB; cp. 15:12).

The definitive statement on love in Paul occurs in 1 Cor. 13. Rhetorical ability, preaching, knowledge, mountain-moving faith, charity towards the poor, or even martyrdom are nothing without *agape*.

First Corinthians 13:4-8a lists several characteristics of this love. First, it is long-suffering [*makrothumia*] (v. 4). This is a fruit of the Spirit (Gal. 5:22). It refers to a quality that does not seek revenge but suffers wrong in order to act redemptively.

Second, love is kind (translated gracious, virtuous, useful, manageable, mild, pleasant, benevolent—the opposite of harsh, hard, sharp, or bitter). Third, love is not envious (covetous), does not jealously desire what it does not possess.

Fourth, love does not promote itself; it is not puffed up (1 Cor. 8:1). Paul says in Phil. 2:3, "In humility consider others as more important than yourselves" (HCSB).

Fifth, love does not behave itself in an unbecoming fashion. Believers are to avoid even the appearance of evil (1 Thess. 5:22).

Sixth, love does not seek its own things. Paul once sent Timothy because "I have no one else like-minded who will genuinely care about your interests; all seek their own interests, not those of Jesus Christ" (Phil. 2:20-21 HCSB).

Seventh, love is not easily provoked (irritated, exasperated, or made angry). When Jesus was hit, He did not retaliate but said, "If I have spoken wrongly, ... give evidence about the wrong; but if rightly, why do you hit Me?" (John 18:23 HCSB).

Eighth, love believes the best about people; it "thinketh no evil" (KJV), "does not keep a record of wrongs" (HCSB). In other words, love overlooks insult or wrong (Prov. 17:9; 19:11; cp. Eph. 5:11).

Next, love finds no joy in unrighteousness (wrongdoing, injustice) but rejoices in the truth (1 Cor. 13:6). Paul concludes that love bears all, believes all, hopes all, and endures all things. Love never fails. Solomon said, "Many waters cannot quench love, neither can the floods drown it" (Song 8:7 KJV).

Paul uses the phrase "the bond of unity" in Col. 3:12-16. He admonishes the Colossians to put on hearts of compassion, kindness, humility, gentleness, patience, forbearance, and forgiveness. Above all these they are to put on love, which is the bond of maturity. The image is that of rods bound together, resulting in more strength.

To John, love is the test of authentic discipleship. The Jews centered their faith around the confession of the Shema: "Listen, Israel: The LORD our God, the LORD is One. Love the LORD your God with all your heart, with all your soul, and with all your strength" (Deut. 6:4-5 HCSB) and "You shall love your neighbor as yourself" (Lev. 19:18b; cp. Matt. 19:19; 22:39; Rom. 13:9; James 2:8). According to John, this was "an old command that you have had from the beginning" (1 John 2:7 HCSB). On the other hand, John was writing a new commandment to them (1 John 2:8-9). For John, love is not just a requirement for fellowship, but a test of salvation. "This is how God's children—and the Devil's children—are made evident. Whoever does not do what is right is not of God, especially the one who does not love his brother" (1 John 3:10 HCSB).

If we have a genuine relationship with God, that relationship should be made manifest by walking in the truth. "We know that we have passed from death to life because we love our brothers. The one who does not love remains in death. Everyone who hates his brother is a murderer, and you know that no murderer has eternal life residing in him. This is how we have come to know love: He laid down His life for us. We should also lay down our lives for our brothers ... we must not love in word or speech, but in deed and truth" (1 John 3:14-19 HCSB).

On the negative side, John admonishes the believer not to "love the world or the things that belong to the world. If anyone loves the world, love for the Father is not in him" (1 John 2:15 HCSB).

Jesus taught that believers are to love even their enemies (Matt. 5:44; Luke 6:27,35). Although believers are permitted, even commanded, to hate evil (Ps. 97:10; Prov. 8:13), we are not to hate the sinner. To insist that in order to accept a person the Christian must accept sin is unscriptural. Rather we are to reprove the sinner.   *David Lanier*

LOVE, BROTHERLY See *Brotherly Love*.

LOVE FEAST Fellowship meal that the Christian community celebrated with joy in conjunction with its celebration of the Lord's Supper. As a concrete manifestation of obedience to the Lord's command to love one another, it served as a practical expression of the *koinonia* or communion that characterized the church's life. While the only explicit NT reference to the agape meal is found in Jude 12, allusions to the practice may be seen in other NT texts. Thus, while the mention of "the breaking of bread" in Acts 2:42 is most likely a reference to a special remembrance of Jesus' last supper with His disciples, the allusion in Acts 2:46 to their taking of food "with gladness and simplicity of heart" implies that a social meal was connected in some way with this celebration. Paul's discussion of the Lord's Supper in 1 Cor. 11:17-34 also suggests a combining of the ceremonial act with a common meal. Such a practice is also suggested in Acts 20:7-12. By the second century the word *agapai* had become a technical term for such a common meal which seems to have been separated from the ceremonial observance of the Lord's Supper sometime after the NT period.

The origin of the love feast is probably to be found in the religious fellowship meals, a common practice among first-century Jews. While the Passover meal is the most familiar of these, such meals were also celebrated to inaugurate the Sabbath and festival days. On these occasions a family or a group of friends who had banded together for purposes of special devotion (known as *chaburoth* from the Hebrew word for "friends") would gather weekly before sundown for a meal in the home or another suitable place. After hors d'oeuvres were served, the company would move to the table for the meal proper. The host would pronounce a blessing (a thanksgiving to God), break the bread, and distribute it among the participants. The mealtime would be characterized by festive, joyous religious discussion. At nightfall lamps were lit and a benediction recited acknowledging God as the Creator of light. When the meal was over, hands were washed and a final benediction pronounced over "the cup of blessing" (1 Cor. 10:16) praising God for His provision and praying for the fulfillment of His purposes in the coming of His kingdom. The meal was concluded by the singing of a psalm. It was not uncommon for small groups of friends to gather weekly for such means.

Jesus and His disciples possibly formed just such a fellowship group. The fellowship meals of the early church appear to be a continuation of the table of fellowship that characterized the life of Jesus and His disciples. Such joyous fellowship served as a concrete manifestation of the grace of the kingdom of God that Jesus proclaimed. Jesus' last meal with His disciples may represent one specific example of such a fellowship meal causing some to trace the origins of the love feast directly to this event. See *Ordinances; Worship.*

Hulitt Gloer

LOVING-KINDNESS Occasional translation of the Hebrew, *chesed.* The OT's highest expression for love. It is variously called God's election, covenant-keeping, or steadfast love. It is a love that remains constant regardless of the circumstances. Although used mostly with God, it sometimes is used of love between people. See *Kindness; Love.*

LOWLAND See *Shephelah.*

LUBIM (Lū´ bĭm) Racial name of uncertain meaning apparently applied to all white North Africans, especially the inhabitants of Libya (2 Chron. 12:3; 16:8; Dan. 11:43; Nah. 3:9). Many English translations read Libyans. See *Libya.*

LUCAS (Lū´ căs) KJV transliteration of Greek for Luke (Philem. 24). See *Luke.*

LUCIFER (Lū´ sĭ fēr) Latin translation (followed by the KJV) of the Hebrew word for "day star" in Isa. 14:12, where the word is used as a title for the king of Babylon, who had exalted himself as a god. The prophet taunted the king by calling him "son of the dawn" (NIV, NASB), a play on a Hebrew term which could refer to a pagan god but normally indicated the light that appeared briefly before dawn. A later tradition associated the word with evil, although the Bible does not use it as such. See *Day Star.*

LUCIUS (Lū´ shŭs) Personal name of uncertain meaning. **1.** Christian prophet and/or teacher from Cyrene who helped lead church at Antioch to set apart Saul and Barnabas for missionary service (Acts 13:1). Early church tradition tried, probably incorrectly, to identify him with either Luke or with 2. below. Thus an African was one of the first Christian evangelists and had an important part in the early days of the church of Antioch and in beginning the Christian world missions movement. **2.** Relative of Paul who sent greetings to the church at Rome (Rom. 16:21). He was apparently one of many Jews who adopted Greek names.

LUD (Lŭd) Racial name for person from Lydia. Plural is Ludim. **1.** Son of Egypt in the Table of Nations (Gen. 10:13) and thus, apparently, a people living near Egypt or under the political influence of Egypt. **2.** Son of Shem and grandson of Noah in Table of Nations (Gen. 10:22). Attempts to identify them with peoples mentioned in other Near Eastern sources have produced varying results: Lydians of Asia Minor called the Luddu by Assyrian records or the Lubdu living on the upper Tigris River. They were known for skill with the bow (Jer. 46:9; Ezek. 30:5 which place them under Egyptian influence and may refer to 1. above if a distinction is to be made at all; otherwise, the reference is to mercenary soldiers from Lydia in Asia Minor serving in the Egyptian army, a practice apparently testified under Pharaoh Psammetichus before 600 B.C.). Lydian soldiers apparently served in Tyre's army (Ezek. 27:10). God promised that even the isolated people like Lydia who had never heard of His glory would be invited to share in that glory (Isa. 66:19). See *Lydia.*

LUDIM (Lū´ dĭm) Hebrew plural of Lud. See *Lud.*

LUDITES (Lū´ dĭts) NIV for Ludim. See *Lud.*

LUHITH (Lū´ hĭth) Place-name meaning "plateaus." It apparently identified a settlement in Moab on the road between Areopolis and Zoar, perhaps at present Khirbet Medinet er-rash. Isaiah mourned for Moabite refugees who would have to climb the heights of Luhith to escape the enemy taking over their country (Isa. 15:5; cp. Jer. 48:5).

LUKE Author of the Third Gospel and the book of Acts in the NT, as well as a close friend and traveling companion of Paul. The apostle called him "loved" (Col. 4:14). Luke referred to his journeys with Paul and his company in Acts 16:10-17; 20:5-15; 21:1-18; 27:1–28:16. Many scholars believe Luke wrote his Gospel and the book of Acts while in Rome with Paul during the apostle's first Roman imprisonment. Apparently Luke remained nearby or with Paul also during the apostle's second Roman imprisonment. Shortly before his martyrdom, Paul wrote that "only Luke is with me" (2 Tim. 4:11).

Early church fathers Jerome (ca. A.D. 400) and Eusebius (ca. A.D. 300) identified Luke as being from Antioch. His interest in Antioch is clearly seen in his many references to that city (Acts 11:19-27; 13:1-3; 14:26; 15:22,35; 18:22). Luke adopted Philippi as his home, remaining behind there to superintend the young church while Paul went on to Corinth during the second missionary journey (Acts 16:40).

Paul identified Luke as a physician (Col. 4:14) and distinguished Luke from those "of the circumcision" (Col. 4:11). Early sources indicate that Luke was a Gentile. Tradition holds that he was Greek. The circumstances of Luke's conversion are not revealed. An early source supplied a fitting epitaph: "He served the Lord without distraction, having neither wife nor children, and at the age of 84 he fell asleep in Boeatia, full of the Holy Spirit." See *Luke, Gospel of.*

T. R. McNeal

LUKE, GOSPEL OF Third and longest book in the NT. Luke is the first of a two-part work dedicated to the "most honorable Theophilus" (Luke 1:3 HCSB; Acts 1:1). The book of Acts forms the sequel to Luke, with the author explaining in Acts that Luke dealt with "all that Jesus began to do and teach until the day He was taken up" (Acts 1:1-2 HCSB).

Authorship Though the author of Luke-Acts never mentioned himself by name, he was obviously a close friend and traveling companion of Paul. In the "we" sections of Acts (16:10-17; 20:5-15; 21:1-18; 27:1–28:16), the author of the narrative apparently joined Paul on his journeys. Through a process of elimination, the most likely choice for this person is "Luke, the loved physician" (Col. 4:14 HCSB).

Tradition for Lukan authorship is very strong, dating back to the early church. Early lists and descriptions of NT books dating from between A.D. 160 and 190 agree that Luke, the physician and companion of Paul, wrote the Gospel of Luke. Many of the early Church Fathers from as early as A.D. 185 readily accepted Luke as the author of the Third Gospel.

With the early church tradition unanimously ascribing the Third Gospel to Luke, the burden of proof is on those who argue against Lukan authorship. See *Acts, Book of; Luke.*

Date and Place of Writing The book of Acts ends abruptly with Paul in his second year of house imprisonment in Rome. Scholars generally agree that Paul reached Rome around A.D. 60. This makes the book of Acts written at the earliest around A.D. 61 or 62 with the Gospel written shortly before. Luke 19:41-44 and 21:20-24 records Jesus' prophecy of the destruction of Jerusalem. This cataclysmic event in ancient Judaism occurred in A.D. 70 at the hands of the Romans. It hardly seems likely that Luke would have failed to record this significant event. Assigning a date to the Gospel later than A.D. 70 would ignore this consideration. Many scholars, however, continue to favor a date about A.D. 80.

A second historical consideration pushes the dating even earlier. Many scholars feel Paul was released from the Roman imprisonment he was experiencing as Acts concludes. The apostle was later imprisoned again and martyred under the Neronian persecution that broke out in A.D. 64. Paul was enjoying considerable personal liberty and opportunities to preach the gospel (Acts 28:30-31) even though a prisoner. The optimism of the end of the book of Acts suggests the Neronian persecution is a future event. One can hardly imagine that Paul's release would find no mention in the Acts narrative had it already occurred.

It seems best, then, to date the writing of Luke somewhere between A.D. 61 and 63. Those who argue that this does not allow Luke time to review Mark's Gospel (assuming it was written first) fail to take into account the tight web of association between those involved in Paul's ministry. See *Mark.*

As to where the Gospel was written, the most probable place is Rome. Luke reached Rome in Paul's company and was in Rome when Paul wrote Colossians (4:14) and Philemon (23-24) during this first Roman imprisonment. The circumstance would have allowed time for the composition of Luke-Acts. One ancient source suggested Achaia, a Greek province, as the place of writing. It seems reasonable to conclude that the Gospel, written in Rome, perhaps made its first appearance in Achaia or was finished there.

Purpose and Readership Luke himself identified the purpose of his writing the Gospel (Luke 1:1-4). He wanted to confirm for Theophilus the certainty of the things Theophilus had been taught. Luke also wanted this information available for a wider readership. Most scholars conclude that Luke's target audience was Gentile inquirers and Christians who needed strengthening in the faith.

Luke's purpose was to present a historical work "in order" (1:3). Most of his stories fall in chronological sequence. He often gave time indications (1:5,26,36,56,59; 2:42; 3:23; 9:28). More than any other Gospel writer, Luke connected his story with the larger Jewish and Roman world (2:1; 3:1-2).

A strong argument can be presented for a second, though clearly subordinate, purpose. Some see Luke-Acts as an apology for the Christian faith, a defense of it designed to show Roman authorities that Christianity posed no political threat. Pilate declared Jesus innocent three times (Luke 23:4,14,22). Acts does not present Roman officials as unfriendly (Acts 13:4-12; 16:35-40; 18:12-17; 19:31). Agrippa remarked to Festus that Paul could have been freed if he had not appealed to Caesar (Acts 26:32). Paul is pictured as being proud of his Roman citizenship (Acts 22:28). The apostle is seen preaching and teaching in Rome openly without hindrance as Acts draws to a close. It is possible to see in all this an attempt by Luke to calm Roman authorities' fears about any supposed subversive character of Christianity.

Beyond the immediate purposes of the author, the Holy Spirit has chosen Luke's Gospel to reach all nations with the beautiful story of God's love in Christ. Many claim the Lukan birth narrative (2:1-20) as their favorite. The canticles or songs in Luke (1:46-55,67-79; 2:13-14,29-32) have inspired countless melodies. Luke's Gospel has been a source for many artists, including Van Eyck, Van der Weyden, Rossetti, Plockhorst, Rubens, and Rembrandt.

Luke's Sources Though Luke was not an eyewitness to the earthly life and ministry of Christ, he was in intimate contact with many who were. Luke was with Paul in Palestine in the late 50s, especially in Caesarea and Jerusalem (Acts 21:1–27:2). Members of the Jerusalem church (including James, the brother of Jesus) would have provided much oral testimony to the physician intent on writing an account of Jesus' life. Luke's association with Paul brought him into contact with leading apostolic witnesses, including James and Peter.

Most scholars believe Luke (as well as Matthew) relied on Mark's written Gospel. Mark probably was an eyewitness to some events in Jesus' life. His Gospel is generally recognized to reflect Peter's preaching about Christ. Mark was in Rome with Luke and Paul during Paul's captivity (Col. 4:10,14; Philem. 24). It would be natural to assume Luke had access to Mark's writings. Scholars have identified a source, "Q" (an abbreviation for the German word *Quelle* meaning "source"), referring to passages and sections of written material apparently available to Matthew and Luke but either unavailable or unused by Mark (e.g., Matt. 3:7-10/Luke 3:7-9; Matt. 24:45-51/Luke 12:42-46). This source may have been a collection of Jesus' sayings written down by His followers.

John's Gospel certainly was not available for Luke (most scholars date John late in the first century). Any similarities between Luke's Gospel and John's can probably be accounted for by recognizing that a rich tradition, especially oral, provided a common source for all the Gospel writers.

Some scholars have posited an "L" source (an abbreviation for Luke) identifying some 500 verses exclusive to Luke, including the 132 verses of Luke 1 and 2. The argument that a separate document existed that only Luke had access to is not convincing. The new material introduced by Luke should be seen as the result of his own research and literary genius. One obvious example is the birth narratives of John the Baptist and Christ. The material that Luke uniquely presents gives the Third Gospel much of its character. See *Logia*.

Special Emphases and Characteristics As already noted, Luke took great pains to relate his narrative to contemporaneous historical events. Beginning with the birth narratives of John the Baptist and Jesus, he wrote with the eye for detail of a historian (1:5,36,56,59; 2:1-2,7,42; 3:23; 9:20,37,57; 22:1,7,66; 23:44,54; 24:1,13,29,33).

Luke stressed the universal redemption available to all through Christ. Samaritans enter the kingdom (9:51-6; 10:30-37; 17:11-19) as well as Gentiles (2:32; 3:6,38; 4:25-27; 7:9; 10:1; 23:47). Publicans, sinners, and outcasts (3:12; 5:27-32; 7:37-50; 19:2-10; 23:43) are welcome along with Jews (1:33; 2:10) and respectable people (7:36; 11:37; 14:1). Both the poor (1:53; 2:7; 6:20; 7:22) and rich (19:2; 23:50) can have redemption.

Luke especially notes Christ's high regard for women. Mary and Elizabeth are central figures in chapters 1 and 2. Anna the prophetess and Joanna the disciple are mentioned only in Luke (2:36-38; 8:3; 24:10). Luke included the story of Christ's kind dealings with the widow of Nain (7:11-18) and the sinful woman who anointed Him (7:36-50). He also related Jesus' parable of the widow who persevered (18:1-8).

Outline

I. Luke's Purpose: Certainty in Christian Teaching (1:1-4).

II. Jesus Fulfilled Judaism's Expectations (1:5–2:52).

III. Jesus Accepted Messianic Mission and Faced Rejection (3:1–4:44).

IV. Jesus Fulfilled His Mission in God's Way of Faith, Love, and Forgiveness (5:1–7:50).

V. God's Kingdom Involves Power but Demands Faithfulness to the Point of Death (8:1–9:50).

VI. The Kingdom Is Characterized by Faithful Ministry and Witness (9:51–13:21).

VII. Entrance Requirements for the Kingdom (13:22–19:27)

VIII. Jesus' Kingdom Power Aroused Opposition (19:28–22:6).

IX. Jesus Died as the True Passover Lamb (22:7–23:56).

X. Jesus' Resurrection Is the Doorway to Faith and Mission (24:1-53).

T. R. McNeal

LUKEWARM Tepid; neither hot nor cold (Rev. 3:16). The city of Laodicea received its water from an aqueduct several miles long. The lukewarm water that arrived at the city served as an appropriate illustration for a tasteless, good-for-nothing Christianity.

LUNATIC Term for epilepsy or insanity (Matt. 4:24; 17:15). The term "lunacy" derives from the Latin *luna* (moon) and reflects the popular notion that the mental state of the "lunatic" fluctuated with the changing phases of the moon. The Greek terms underlying Matt. 4:24 and 17:15 are likewise related to the Greek term for moon. Lunacy was not clearly distinguished from demon possession (Matt. 17:18; cp. Mark 9:17; Luke 9:39).

LUST In contemporary usage, a strong craving or desire, especially sexual desire. KJV and earlier English versions frequently used lust in the neutral sense of desire. This older English usage corresponded to the use of the underlying Hebrew and Greek terms which could be used in a positive sense: of the desire of the righteous (Prov. 10:24), of Christ's desire to eat the Passover with His disciples (Luke 22:15), or of Paul's desire to be with Christ (Phil. 1:23). Since lust has taken on the primary meaning of sexual desire, modern translations often replace the KJV's lust with a term with a different nuance. NRSV, for example, used crave/craving (Num. 11:34; Ps. 78:18); covet (Rom. 7:7); desire (Exod. 15:9; Prov. 6:25; 1 Cor. 10:6); long for (Rev. 18:14).

The unregenerate (preconversion) life is governed by deceitful lusts or desires (Eph. 4:22; 2:3; Col. 3:5; Titus 2:12). Following conversion, such fleshly desires compete for control of the individual with spiritual desires (Gal. 5:16-17; 2 Tim. 2:22). First John 2:16-17 warns that desires of the flesh and eyes are not from God and will pass away with the sinful world. Here lust or desire includes not only sexual desire but also other vices such as materialism. James 1:14-15 warns that desire is the beginning of all sin and results in death. Jesus warned that one who lusts has already sinned (Matt. 5:28). Part of God's judgment on sin is to give persons over to their own desires (Rom. 1:24). Only the presence of the Holy Spirit in the life of the believer makes victory over sinful desires possible (Rom. 8:1-2). See *Concupiscence*.

LUTE Stringed instrument with a large, pear-shaped body and a neck. NRSV used "lute" to translate two Hebrew terms (Pss. 92:3; 150:3). NASB translated the first term as "10-stringed lute" and the second as harp. The KJV translated both terms as psaltery. See *Music, Instruments, Dancing*.

LUZ (Lŭz) Place-name meaning "almond tree." **1.** Original name of Bethel (Gen. 28:19). Joshua 16:2 seems to distinguish the two places, Bethel perhaps being the worship place and Luz the city. Bethel would then be Burj Beitin and Luz, Beitin. See *Bethel*. **2.** City in the land of the Hittites that a man founded after showing the tribe of Joseph how to conquer Bethel (Judg. 1:26). Its location is not known. See *Hittites*.

LXX Roman numeral 70 which serves as the symbol for the Septuagint, the earliest Greek translation of the OT. According to one tradition, the Septuagint was the work of 70 scholars. See *Bible Texts and Versions; Septuagint.*

LYCAONIA (Lĭc ā ō´ nĭ à) Roman province in the interior of Asia Minor including cities of Lystra, Iconium, and Derbe (Acts 14:1-23).

LYCAONIAN (Lĭc ā ō´ nĭ ăn) Citizen of or language of Lycaonia. See *Lycaonia.*

LYCIA (Lĭs´ ĭ à) Geographical name indicating the projection on the southern coast of Asia Minor between Caria and Pamphylia (Acts 27:5).

LYDDA (Lĭd´ dà) Place-name of uncertain meaning. The OT Lod (1 Chron. 8:12), Lydda was a Benjaminite town near the Plain of Sharon. It was located at the intersection of the caravan routes from Egypt to Babylon and the road from Joppa to Jerusalem. According to Ezra 2:33 it was resettled after the exile (Neh. 7:37; 11:35). Later, it became a district capital of Samaria. The church spread to Lydda early (Acts 9:32) as the result of Peter's ministry. Christianity became a strong influence in Lydda by the second century.

LYDIA (Lĭd´ ĭ à; *from King Lydus*). Both a place and personal name of uncertain meaning. **1.** Country in Asia Minor whose capital was Sardis. Habitation of the area dates from prehistory. The Hittites left their mark on the land through monuments. Lydia's most famous ruler was Croessus (560–546 B.C.), a name synonymous with wealth. His kingdom was captured by Cyrus, who seven years later captured Babylon and freed the exiles. Lydians were named by Ezekiel as "men of war" or mercenaries who fought to defend Tyre (27:10) and who made an alliance with Egypt (30:5) **2.** Lydia was the first European converted to Christ under the preaching of Paul at Philippi (Acts 16:14). Her name originally might have been the designation of her home, "a woman of Lydia," since Thyatira was in the province of Lydia. Being a worshiper of God, Lydia could have been a convert to Judaism, although this cannot be stated with certainty. She did know enough about Judaism to converse with Paul about the religion. Lydia hosted Paul and his entourage in Philippi after her conversion. Her profession as a "seller of purple" meant that she probably was quite wealthy (Acts 16:12-15,40). *Mike Mitchell*

LYDIAN (Lĭd´ ĭ an) Person from Lydia. See *Lydia 1.*

LYE Substance used for cleansing purposes from the earliest times. Two Hebrew words are used in the OT for lye. *Neter* probably refers to sodium bicarbonate. This material occurs naturally and is referred to by ancient writers as appearing in Egypt and Armenia.

Bor likely refers to potassium carbonate and is sometimes called vegetable lye. It is a strongly alkaline solution made by burning certain plants like soapwort and leaching the lye from the ashes. This was the type of lye normally used in Palestine, for there are no known deposits of sodium bicarbonate there. The same Hebrew spelling also means "purity" (Ps. 18:20,24), leading to confusion in English translations.

LYSANIAS (Lī sā´ nĭ às) Personal name of unknown meaning. Roman tetrarch of Abilene about A.D. 25–30 and thus at the beginning of John the Baptist's ministry (Luke 3:1). See *Abilene.*

LYSIAS (Lĭs´ ĭ às) Second name or birth name of Roman tribune or army captain who helped Paul escape the Jews and appear before Felix, the governor (Acts 23:26). His name also appears in some Greek manuscripts at Acts 24:7 but not in the manuscripts followed by many modern translations as the earliest (cp. 24:22). See *Claudius.*

LYSTRA (Lĭs´ trà) City in south central Asia Minor and an important Lycaonian center. According to Acts 16:1, it probably was the home of young Timothy, one of Paul's companions in the ministry. Paul's healing of a crippled man at Lystra (Acts 14:8-10) caused the inhabitants to revere him as a god. Many believed his preaching but were turned against the missionary by Judaizers from Antioch and Iconium. Paul was dragged out of Lystra, stoned, and left for dead. He revived and later went back to the city to lend strength to the new Christians.

M

Megiddo overlooking the valley of Jezreel.

M Symbol designating one of the alleged sources of Matthew's Gospel according to the four-document hypothesis. The source purportedly consists of that part of Matthew not paralleled by Mark or Luke.

MAACAH (Mā´ à cah) Personal name of uncertain meaning, possibly "dull" or "stupid." **1.** Son of Nahor, Abraham's brother (Gen. 22:24); this Maacah perhaps gave his name to the Aramean kingdom west of Basham and southwest of Mount Hermon; the residents of this kingdom, the Maachathites (Mā´ ăch à thītes), were not driven out during the Israelite conquest of Canaan (Josh. 13:13). Later this people sided with the Ammonites against David (2 Sam. 10:6-8). This nation is perhaps personified as the wife (ally) of Machir at 1 Chron. 7:16. **2.** Concubine of Caleb (1 Chron. 2:48). **3.** Wife of Jeiel of Gibeon (1 Chron. 8:29; 9:35). **4.** Wife of David and the mother of Absalom (2 Sam. 3:3; 1 Chron. 3:2). **5.** Father/ancestor of one of David's warriors (1 Chron. 11:43). **6.** Father/ancestor of Shephatiah, who led the tribe of Simeon in David's reign (1 Chron. 27:16). **7.** Father/ancestor of Achish, king of Gath (1 Kings 2:39). **8.** Mother of King Abijam (1 Kings 15:2) and ancestress of King Asa (1 Kings 15:10,13).

MAACATH (Mā´ à căth) (NRSV, NASB, Josh. 13:13) or **MAACHAH** (Mā à kah) (KJV) See *Maacah.*

MAACHATHITES See *Maacah 1.*

MAADAI (Mā´ à dī) An Israelite forced to give up his foreign wife as part of Ezra's reforms (Ezra 10:34).

MAADIAH (Mā à dī´ ah) Personal name of uncertain meaning, perhaps "Yah assembles," "Yahu promises," or "Yah adorns." Priest who returned from exile with Zerubbabel (Neh. 12:5). He is perhaps the same as Moadiah (Neh. 12:17) or Maaziah (Neh. 10:8).

MAAI (Mā ī) Personal name of uncertain meaning. Musician participating in Nehemiah's dedication of the rebuilt Jerusalem walls (Neh. 12:36).

MAALEH-ACRABBIM (Mā à lĕh-à crăb´ bĭm) KJV transliteration of a phrase meaning ascent (NASB, NRSV, REB) or pass (NIV) of Akrabbim (Josh. 15:3). See *Akrabbim.*

MAARATH (Mā´ à răth) Place-name meaning "barren field." Name of a village in Judah's hill country (Josh. 15:59), possibly identical with Maroth (Mic. 1:12). The site is possibly modern Khirbet Qufin, two miles north of Beth-zur.

MAAREH-GEBA (Mā à rĕh-gē´ bà) Place-name meaning "clearing of Geba." Israel's army readied an ambush there for tribe of Benjamin (Judg. 20:33 NASB). Other translations translated the first part of the name or follow a Greek text in reading "west of Gibeah," a change of the final Hebrew letter. See *Gibeah.*

MAASAI (Mā´ à sī) Possibly a shortened form of Maaseiah meaning "work of Yah." One of the priests returning from exile (1 Chron. 9:12), Maasai is likely identical with Amashai (Neh. 11:13). KJV transliterated Amashai.

MAASEIAH (Mā à sā yà) Personal name meaning "work of Yahweh," appearing in a longer and shorter Hebrew form. Several of the many scattered references perhaps refer to the same person, though it is no longer possible to press identifications. **1.** Levite musician during David's reign (1 Chron. 15:18,20). **2.** Participant in high priest Jehoida's revolt which put Joash on the throne (2 Chron. 23:1). **3.** One of Uzziah's military officers (2 Chron. 26:11). **4.** Son of King Ahaz of Judah (2 Chron. 28:7). **5.** Governor of Jerusalem during the reign of Josiah (2 Chron. 34:8). **6.** Father of false prophet Zedekiah (Jer. 29:21). **7.** Father of the priest Zephaniah (Jer. 21:1; 29:25; 37:3). **8.** Temple doorkeeper (Jer. 35:4). **9.** Postexilic resident of Jerusalem from tribe of Judah (Neh. 11:5), likely identical with Asaiah (1 Chron. 9:5). **10.** Benjaminite ancestor of some returned exiles (Neh. 11:7). **11.–14.** Names of three priests and one layman in Ezra's time who had taken foreign wives (Ezra 10:18,21-22,30). **15.** Father/ancestor of the Azariah participating in Nehemiah's rebuilding of the wall (Neh. 3:23). **16.** Chief of the people who signed Ezra's covenant (Neh. 10:25), possibly identical with 14. and/or 18. **17.** One of those standing beside Ezra at the reading of the law (Neh. 8:4), possibly 14. and/or 16. **18.** One of the Levites interpreting the law which Ezra read (Neh. 8:7), possibly identical with 17. **19.-20.** Names of two priests participating in the dedication of the rebuilt walls of Jerusalem (Neh. 12:41-42), perhaps identical with 11. **21.** KJV form for Mahseiah. See *Mahseiah.*

MAASIAI (Mā á sī´ aī) (KJV) See *Maasai.*

MAATH (Mā´ ăth) Ancestor of Jesus (Luke 3:26).

MAAZ (Mā´ až) Personal name of uncertain meaning (possibly "angry"). See 1 Chron. 2:27.

MAAZIAH (Mā á zī´ ah) Personal name meaning "Yahweh is a refuge." **1.** Ancestor of a division of priests serving in David's time (1 Chron. 24:18). **2.** Priest who signed Ezra's covenant (Neh. 10:8).

MACBANNAI (Măc´ bán nī) (NIV) See *Machbanai.*

MACBENAH (Măc bē´ nah) (NIV) See *Machbenah.*

MACCABEES, BOOK OF See *Apocrypha.*

MACCABEES (Măk´ á bēz) Name given to the family of Mattathias, a faithful priest, who led in a revolt (Maccabean War) against the Hellenizing influences of the Seleucid King Antiochus Epiphanes in about 168 B.C. See *Apocrypha; Intertestamental History and Literature.*

MACE See *Weapons.*

MACEDONIA (Măs ə dō´ nĭ á) Now the northernmost province of Greece; in antiquity, the fertile plain north and west of the Thermaic Gulf from the Haliacmon River in the southwest to the Axios in the east ("Lower Macedonia") and the mountainous areas to the west and north ("Upper Macedonia," today divided between central northern Greece, southeastern Albania, and the Yugoslav province of Macedonia). Mace-

donia is the link between the Balkan Peninsula to the north and the Greek mainland and the Mediterranean Sea to the south. The important land route from Byzantium (Istanbul) in the east to the Adriatic Sea in the west (in Roman times the "Via Egnatia") crosses it as does the north to south road from the central Balkan (the area of the Danube and Save Rivers) which reached the Aegean Sea at the Thermaic Gulf and continued past Mount Olympus through the narrow valley of Tempe into Thessaly and central Greece.

History Philip II (359–336 B.C.) established firm control over the entire Macedonian area and extended it to the east beyond the Strymon into Thrace. There he founded the city of Philippi in place of the Thracian colony Crenides. It became the chief mining center for the gold and silver mines in the Pangaeon mountain. Philip II also subjected Thessaly to his rule and incorporated the Chalcidice peninsula into his realm. When he was assassinated in 336 B.C., Macedonia was the strongest military power in Greece. Its military strength and the wealth established by Philip II enabled his son Alexander to defeat the Persian Empire and to conquer the entire realm from the eastern Mediterranean to the Indus River (including today's Turkey, Egypt, Syria, Palestine, Iraq, Iran, and parts of Afghanistan and Pakistan).

The famous Greek tragedian Euripides spent some time at the court of the Macedonian kings, and Aristotle, before he founded his philosophical school in Athens, served as the teacher of the Macedonian prince Alexander.

In the Hellenistic period the capital was moved to Thessalonica, founded in 315 B.C. at the head of the Thermaic Gulf by Cassander and named for his wife Thessalia. During the Hellenistic period Macedonia was ruled by the Antigonids, descendants of Alexander's general Antigonus Monophthalmus. In 168 B.C. Perseus, the last Macedonian king, was defeated by the Romans. Rome first divided Macedonia into four independent "free" districts, then established it as a Roman province (148 B.C.) with Thessalonica as the capital and Beroea as the seat of the provincial assembly. During the time of Augustus, some of the Macedonian cities were refounded as Roman colonies: Dion, at the foot of Mount Olympus, became Colonia Julia

Augusta Diensis; Philippi, where Marc Antony had defeated the assassins of Caesar—Brutus and Cassius—was settled with Roman veterans and renamed Colonia Augusta Julia Philippensium. While the general language of Macedonia remained Greek, the official language of the Roman colonies was Latin (until after A.D. 300 almost all inscriptions found in these cities are in Latin). At the time of the Great Persecution of the Christians (303–311), Thessalonica was one of the four capitals of the Roman Empire and served as residence of the emperor Galerius, one of the most fanatic persecutors of Christianity.

Christianity in Macedonia The evidence for ancient Judaism in Macedonia is meager. An inscription (still unpublished) recently found in Philippi mentions a synagogue. The only evidence for Israelites in Thessalonica comes from a Samaritan inscription dating after A.D. 400. A Jewish synagogue has been excavated recently in the Macedonian city of Stobi in the valley of the Axios (Vardar) River (in Yugoslav Macedonia).

The Christian message came to Macedonia through the preaching of the Apostle Paul. Acts 16:9-10 describes the vision that came to Paul in Troas: a Macedonian appeared to him and invited him to Macedonia. Paul and his associates, sailing from Troas via Samothrace, arrived in Neapolis (today Kavalla), the most important port of eastern Macedonia, and went inland to Philippi where, according to the account of Acts 16:14-15, they were received by Lydia, a God fearer from Thyatira, and founded the first Christian community in Europe, probably in the year A.D. 50. The correspondence of Paul with this church, now preserved in the letter to the Philippians, gives testimony to the early development, organization, and generosity of this church. Forced to leave Philippi after an apparently brief stay (Acts 16:16-40 reports the incident of the healing of a possessed slave girl and Paul's subsequent imprisonment), Paul went to the capital Thessalonica via Amphipolis on the Via Egnatia (Acts 17:1). The church that he founded in Thessalonica (cp. Acts 17:2-12) was the recipient of the oldest Christian writing, the first letter to the Thessalonians, which Paul wrote from Corinth after he had preached in Beroea and in Athens (Acts 17:13-15).

Apart from this Pauline correspondence, our information about the Macedonian churches in the first three Christian centuries is extremely slim. Shortly after A.D. 100 Bishop Polycarp of Smyrna wrote to the Philippians who had asked him to forward copies of the letters of the famous martyr Ignatius of Antioch. Polycarp also wrote

Machaerus, Herod's fortress-palace where John the Baptist was imprisoned and executed.

to advise the Philippians with respect to the case of a presbyter who had embezzled funds. Otherwise, almost no detailed information is available for the time before Constantine.

Helmut Koester

MACEDONIANS Natives or residents of Macedonia (Acts 19:29; 27:2; 2 Cor. 9:2). See *Macedonia.*

MACHAERUS (Mȧ kēr´ ŭs) Palace-fortress located about 15 miles southeast of the mouth of the Jordan on a site rising 3,600 feet above the sea. Herod the Great rebuilt the fortress. Josephus gives the Machaerus as the site of the imprisonment and execution of John the Baptist. Mark's reference to Galilean nobles among Herod's guests has prompted some interpreters to suggest a site further north. The Gospels, however, associate John's ministry with the Judean wilderness (Mark 1:5; Matt. 3:1; John 3:22-23). That John's disciples claimed his body (Mark 6:29) suggests a site, such as the Machaerus, near the center of John's ministry.

MACHBANAI (Măk´ bȧ nī) (KJV) or **MACHBANNAI** (TEV) Military captain of tribe of Gad who served David (1 Chron. 12:13).

MACHBENA (Măk bē´ nȧ) (NASB) or **MACHBENAH** Descendant of Caleb or a village in Judah, possibly identical with Meconah, inhabited by descendants of Caleb (1 Chron. 2:49).

MACHI (Mā´ kī) Personal name, possibly meaning "reduced" or "bought" (Num. 13:15). Spy of tribe of Gad who explored the promised land.

MACHIR (Mā´ kĭr) Personal name meaning "sold." **1.** Oldest son of Manasseh and grandson of Joseph (Josh. 17:1). He was the father of Gilead (Josh. 17:1), Peresh, and Sheresh (1 Chron. 7:16), and a daughter whose name is not given (1 Chron. 2:21). He had a brother named Asriel (1 Chron. 7:14) and a wife named Maacah (1 Chron. 7:16). Machir was the head of the family called the Machirites (Num. 26:29). Apparently Machir along with his family had a reputation for being expert warriors. "Because he was a man of war,"

Machir was allotted the territory of Bashan and Gilead, east of the Jordan (Josh. 17:1). Apparently the territory of the Machirites started at the site of Mahanaim, on the Jabbok River, extended northward, and included the region around the Yarmuk River (Josh. 13:29-31). **2.** Son of Ammiel and member of the tribe of Manasseh. He came from the site of Lo-debar, perhaps a village near Mahanaim. He is recognized in the OT for the assistance he provided Mephibosheth, the son of Jonathan (2 Sam. 9, esp. vv. 4-5) and David during the period of Absalom's rebellion (2 Sam. 17:27-29). See *Manasseh.*

LaMoine DeVries

MACHIRITES (Mā´ kĭ rīts) See *Machir 1.*

MACHNADEBAI (Măk năd´ ĭ bī) Name, possibly meaning "possession of Nebo," of one of the laymen forced to give up their foreign wives in Ezra's reform (Ezra 10:40).

MACHPELAH (Măk pē´ lah) Place-name meaning "the double cave." Burial place located near Hebron for Sarah (Gen. 23:19), Abraham (25:9), Isaac, Rebekah, Jacob, Leah, and probably other members of the family. After Sarah's death Abraham purchased the field of Machpelah and its cave as a sepulcher. The owner, Ephron the Hittite, offered it to Abraham for free, but the patriarch refused the gift and paid the fair price of 400 shekels of silver. Such conversation was typical of negotiations to purchase land in that day. Both Ephron and Abraham expected a purchase to be made. The cave became the burial place for each of the succeeding generations. Jacob requested burial there before he died in Egypt and was returned there by his sons (Gen. 49:29-30; 50:13).

MACNADEBAI (NIV) See *Machnadebai.*

MADAI (Mā´ dī) Name of a son of Japheth (Gen. 10:2; 1 Chron. 1:5). The name means "Middle land," suggesting that Madai is to be understood as the ancestor of the Medians.

MADIAN (Mā´ dī ȧn) (KJV, Acts 7:29) See *Midian.*

M

M

MADMANNAH (Măd măn´ nah) Place-name meaning "dung heap." City in the Negev assigned to Judah (Josh. 15:31), possibly identical with Beth-marcaboth (Josh. 19:5). Suggested sites include the modern Khirbet umm Demneh and Khirbet Tatrit, both in the vicinity of Dharhiriyah. The reference to Shaaph as the father of Madmannah (1 Chron. 2:49) is open to various interpretations: (1) Shaaph (re)founded the city; (2) Shaaph's descendents settled in the city; or (3) Shaaph had a son named Madmannah.

MADMEN (Măd´ mĕn) Name meaning "dung pit," applied to a city of Moab (Jer. 48:2). Dimon (Dibon), the capital city, is perhaps the intended reference. Jeremiah's dirge perhaps refers to Ashurbanipal's suppression of a Moabite revolt in 650 B.C. See *Dimon*.

MADMENAH (Măd mē´ nah) Place-name meaning "dung hill." One of the points on the northern invasion route to Jerusalem (Isa. 10:31). The site is possibly Shu'fat. Isaiah perhaps refers to the invasion of Sennacherib in 701 B.C.

MADON (Mā´ dŏn) Place-name meaning "site of justice." Town in Galilee whose king joined in an unsuccessful alliance against Israel (Josh. 11:1; 12:19). The site has been identified as the summit of Qarn Hattim, northwest of Tiberias.

MAGADAN (Măg´ à dăn) Site on the Sea of Galilee (Matt. 15:39). At Mark 8:10 most translations follow other Greek manuscripts reading Dalmanutha. KJV follows the received text of its day in reading Magdala. The location of Magadan, if it is a correct reading, is not known.

MAGBISH (Măg´ bĭsh) Place-name meaning "pile." Town in Judah's territory, possibly identified with the modern Khirbet el-Mahbiyeh, three miles southwest of Adullam, to which exiles returned to reclaim their inheritance (Ezra 2:30).

MAGDALA (Măg´ dà là) Place-name, perhaps meaning "tower." City on the western shore of the Sea of Galilee and center of a prosperous fishing operation. The town was located on a main highway coming from Tiberias. A certain Mary, who had been healed of demon possession by Jesus, was from Magdala. See *Magadan; Mary*.

MAGDALENE See *Magdala; Mary*.

MAGDIEL (Măg´ dĭ´ ĕl) Personal (and tribal) name meaning "choice gift of God." Edomite chieftain or the area occupied by his descendants (Gen. 36:43; 1 Chron. 1:54).

MAGGOT Soft-bodied, legless grub that is the intermediate stage of some insects (Job 25:6; Isa. 14:11). The term always occurs in parallel with worm and serves to highlight human mortality. See *Insects*.

MAGI (Mă´ ġī) Eastern wise men, priests, and astrologers expert in interpreting dreams and other "magic arts." **1.** Men whose interpretation of the stars led them to Palestine to find and honor Jesus, the newborn King (Matt. 2). The term has a Persian background. The earliest Greek translation of Dan. 2:2,10 uses "magi" to translate the Hebrew term for astrologer (cp. 4:7; 5:7). The magi who greeted Jesus' birth may have been from Babylon, Persia, or the Arabian Desert. Matthew gives no number, names, or royal positions to the magi. Before A.D. 225 Tertullian called them kings. From the three gifts the deduction was made that they were three in number. Shortly before A.D. 600 the Armenian Infancy Gospel named them: Melkon (later Melchior), Balthasar, and Gaspar. The visit of the magi affirms international recognition by leaders of other religions of Jesus' place as the expected King. **2.** In Acts 8:9 the related verb describes

The village of Magdala on the western shore of the Sea of Galilee.

Simon as practicing sorcery, with a bad connotation. Such negative feelings had long been associated with some uses of the term. **3.** In Acts 13:6,8 Bar-Jesus or Elymas is designated a sorcerer or one of the magi as well as a false prophet. At Paul's word the Lord blinded Simon, showing God's power over the magic arts.

MAGIC See *Divination and Magic.*

MAGIC BANDS Bands or cushions placed on the wrist in magical practices (Ezek. 13:18,20). The KJV translates "pillows." Their precise nature is unknown. Apparently they represented part of a diviner's paraphernalia used to ascertain the destinies the gods had determined. See *Kerchiefs.*

MAGISTRATE Government official with administrative and judicial responsibilities. At Ezra 7:25 magistrate is perhaps a parallel title to judge. Possibly judges and magistrates handled different cases, for example, cases involving traditional law and royal cases in which the state had special interest. The term for magistrate at Dan. 3:2-3 is an Old Persian term of uncertain meaning. Since magistrates follows judges, officials with judicial responsibilities may again be in view. The term for magistrate at Luke 12:11 (KJV) and 12:58 (NRSV) is *archon,* a general term for ruler. The term rendered magistrates at Acts 16:20,22,35-36,38, *strategoi,* is a term used both for military commanders and for civil officials of a Greek city who were charged with administering the community finances, enforcing enactments of the council or citizen body and, in some cases, passing sentence in legal cases. In the case of Philippi, *strategoi* serves as the Greek equivalent of the Latin *duumviri,* the two magistrates who served as the chief judicial officials of a Roman city or colony.

MAGNIFICAT (Măg nǐ´ fǐ căt) Latin word meaning "magnify." The first word in Latin of Mary's psalm of praise (Luke 1:46-55) and thus the title of the psalm. Very similar to the psalm of Hannah (1 Sam. 2:1-10). See *Benedictus; Nunc Dimittis.*

MAGOG (Mā´ gŏg) See *Gog and Magog.*

MAGOR-MISSABIB (Mā gŏr-mǐs sā´ bǐb) Name meaning "terror on every side" that Jeremiah gave to Pashhur the priest after the latter had the prophet beaten and put in stocks (Jer. 20:3). The earliest Greek translation lacks the words "on every side," prompting some interpreters to conclude the words were added in imitation of the full phrase at Jer. 6:25; 20:10.

MAGPIASH (Măg´ pǐ ăsh) Personal name, perhaps meaning "moth exterminator." Magpiash was among the chiefs of the people who signed Ezra's covenant (Neh. 10:20).

MAHALAB (Mȧ hā´ lȧb) Town in Asher's tribal territory (Josh. 19:29 NRSV, TEV) according to the earliest Greek translation. The existing Hebrew text lacks Mahalab as do other English translations.

MAHALAH (Mȧ hā´ lah) (KJV, 1 Chron. 7:18). See *Mahlah.*

MAHALALEEL (Mȧ hā´ lȧ lē ĕl) (KJV) or **MAHALALEL** (Mȧ hă´ lȧ ləl) Personal name meaning "God shines forth" or "praise God." **1.** Son of Kenan, father of Jared, and ancestor of Christ (Gen. 5:12-17; 1 Chron. 1:2; Luke 3:37, Greek form Malaleleel [Mȧ´ lē lĕ ĕl´] appears). **2.** Ancestor of a postexilic member of the tribes of Judah (Neh. 11:4).

MAHALATH (Mā´ hȧ lăth) Personal name meaning "dance" or "sickness" and a term used in the superscriptions of Pss. 53; 88. **1.** Granddaughter of Abraham and daughter of Ishmael who married Esau (Gen. 28:9). **2.** Granddaughter of David and wife of King Rehoboam (2 Chron. 11:18). **3.** In Psalms perhaps a choreographic instruction; the second element in the composite term *mahalat-le'annot* (mā hȧ lăth-lē ăn´ nŏth) perhaps refers to an antiphonal performance by two groups answering and responding to each other (Ps. 88).

MAHALATH-LEANNOTH See *Mahalath 3.*

MAHALI (Mā´ hȧ lī) (KJV) See *Mahli.*

MAHANAIM (Mā hȧ nā´ ĭm) Place-name meaning "two camps." City somewhere in the hill country of Gilead on the tribal borders of Gad and eastern Manasseh (Josh. 13:26,30). It was a Levitical city (Josh. 21:38). It served as a refuge twice: for Ishbosheth after Saul's death (2 Sam. 2:8-9) and for David when Absalom usurped the throne (2 Sam. 17:24-27). During Solomon's administration the city served as a district capital (1 Kings 4:14). German archaeologists locate it at Tell Heggog, half a mile south of Penuel, while Israelis point to Tell edh-Dhabab el Gharbi.

MAHANEH-DAN (Mā há nĕh-dăn´) Hebrew term meaning "camp of Dan." During the period of the judges, the tribe of Dan lacked a permanent inheritance in the promised land (Judg. 18:1) and continued to live according to the earlier semi-nomadic pattern. Thus it is not surprising that two places are designated "camp of Dan." **1.** A site between Zorah and Eshtaol where the Lord's Spirit first stirred Samson (Judg. 13:25). **2.** A site west of Kiriath-jearim where the Danites camped on the way to the hill country of Ephraim (Judg. 18:12).

MAHARAI (Má hâr´ ā) Personal name meaning "hurried one." One of David's 30 elite warriors who came from the clan of the Zerahites and the town of Netophah in Judah and commanded the troops in the 10th month (2 Sam. 23:28; 1 Chron. 11:30, 27:13).

MAHATH (Mā´ hăth) Personal name meaning "tough." **1.** Levite of the Kohathite clan (1 Chron. 6:35). **2.** Levite assisting in Hezekiah's reforms (2 Chron. 29:12; 31:13). Both Mahaths are perhaps the same individual. The second may be the Ahimoth of 1 Chron. 6:25.

MAHAVITE (Mā´ há vīt) Family name of Eliel, one of David's 30 elite warriors (1 Chron. 11:46). See *Eliel 5.*

MAHAZIOTH (Má hā´ zĭ ŏth) Personal name meaning "visions." Son of Heman who served as a temple musician (1 Chron. 25:4,6-7,30).

MAHER-SHALAL-HASH-BAZ (Mā hĕr-shăl ăl-hash´-băz) Personal name meaning "quick to the plunder, swift to the spoil" (Isa. 8:1). Symbolic name Isaiah gave his son to warn of

the impending destruction of Syria and Israel as they threatened Judah and Ahaz, its king. The name appeared to show that God would deliver Judah from her enemies. The sign also called on Ahaz for faith. Without faith Judah could become part of the spoil. The prophecy was that the two enemies of Judah would be destroyed before they could attack the Southern Kingdom. Assyria defeated Syria in 732 B.C. and Israel in 722 B.C. Judah survived until 586 B.C.

MAHLAH (Mā´ lah) Personal name, perhaps meaning "weak one." **1.** Daughter of Zelophehad who with her sisters petitioned Moses to receive their father's inheritance in the promised land since he had no sons (Num. 26:33; 27:1-11). God granted their request (Num. 27:6-7). The tribe of Manasseh later petitioned that daughters who inherit be required to marry within their father's tribe (Num. 36:1-12). The daughters' persistence in pressing their claim is evidenced by Josh. 17:3. **2.** Descendant of Manasseh (1 Chron. 7:18).

MAHLI (Mă´ lī) Personal name, perhaps meaning "shrewd" or "cunning." **1.** Son of Merari, a Levite who gave his name to a priestly clan (Exod. 6:19; Num. 3:20; 1 Chron. 6:19,29; 23:21; 24:26,28; Ezra 8:18). **2.** Son of Mushi, the nephew of the above (1 Chron. 6:47; 23:23; 24:30).

MAHLITES (Mă´ līts) Descendants of Mahli. These Levites had charge of the set up and maintenance of the tabernacle (Num. 3:33-36; 26:58).

MAHLON (Mā´ lŏn) Personal name meaning "sickly." One of the two sons of Elimelech and Naomi (Ruth 1:2,5) and the husband of Ruth the Moabitess (4:9-10). Mahlon died while the family was sojourning in Moab because of a famine in their homeland of Israel. The reason for Mahlon's death is not given. Boaz, a distant relative to Mahlon, married the dead man's widow, Ruth.

MAHOL (Mā´ hŏl) Personal name meaning "place of dancing." The name belongs to the father of three renowned wise men (1 Kings 4:31). An alternate interpretation takes the phrase "sons of the place of dancing" as a title for those who danced as part of the temple ritual (cp. Pss. 149:3; 150:4). The wisdom of the temple dancers may be akin to the prophetic wisdom associated with musicians (1 Sam. 10:5; 2 Kings 3:15; esp. 1 Chron. 25:3).

MAHSEIAH (Mȧ sā´ yȧ) Personal name meaning "Yah is a refuge." Grandfather of the scribe Baruch (Jer. 32:12; 51:59).

MAID, MAIDEN Unmarried woman, especially of the servant class. In the KJV "maid" translated five Hebrew and four Greek terms. In the OT *amah* and *shiphchah* refer to female slaves. Alternate translations for these terms include: bondmaid; bondwoman; female slave; handmaid; and maidservant. Both terms are used as expressions of deep humility (Ruth 3:9; 1 Sam. 25:24-31; 28:21; 2 Sam. 14:6; 1 Kings 1:13,17). A special case involves the use of these terms for the "handmaid of the LORD" (1 Sam. 1:11; Pss. 86:16; 116:16), always with reference to prayer for the handmaid's son. KJV sometimes rendered *betulah* as maid (Exod. 22:16; Deut. 22:17). Modern translations generally render the term "virgin." KJV sometimes renders *almah* "maid." At Exod. 2:8 *almah* means simply "girl." At Prov. 30:19 a young man of marriageable age is intended. KJV translated the term as "virgin" at Isa. 7:14. The term *na'arah* is used both for young women (2 Kings 5:2) and specifically for servants (Ruth 2:8; Esther 2:4). In the NT *korasion* refers to a child or young girl (Matt. 9:24-25). *Paidiske* refers to a (young) female servant (Matt. 26:69; Mark 14:66; John 18:16). At Luke 8:51,54 *pais* means "child." Elsewhere, the term can mean "servant." Mary's reference to herself as the "Lord's slave [*doule*]" (Luke 1:38,48 HCSB) reflects the OT use. See *Servant of the Lord; Slave, Servant*.

MAIL, COAT OF See *Arms and Armor; Weapons*.

MAIMED Mutilated, disfigured, or seriously injured, especially by loss of a limb (Matt. 18:8; Mark 9:43). In the ancient world the maimed had difficulty finding work and relied on the generosity of others (Luke 14:13). A worthless shepherd (leader) does not care for the maimed (Zech. 11:16 NRSV). Christ, the Good Shepherd, cared for the maimed in His healing ministry (Matt. 15:30-31). He expected disciples to invite the maimed who could never repay (Luke 14:13). Cautioning His disciples to avoid what causes sin, Jesus taught it is preferable to enter (eternal) life maimed (or lame) than to go into eternal fire with whatever causes one to sin (Matt. 18:8).

MAINSAIL Principal sail of a vessel (Acts 27:40). Modern translations render the Greek term "foresail," understanding the sail to be a smaller, auxiliary sail used in strong winds when the full force provided by the mainsail would be unnecessary or dangerous.

MAKAZ (Mā´ kăz) Place-name meaning "cutting off" or "end." Center of Solomon's second administrative district (1 Kings 4:9). The site is possibly that of Khirbet-el-Muskheizin south of Ekron.

MAKHELOTH (Măk hē´ lŏth) Stopping place during the wilderness wandering. Makheloth (Num. 33:25-26), like Kehelathah (Num. 33:22-23), means "to assemble."

MAKI (Mā´ kī) (NIV) See *Machi*.

MAKIR (Mā´ kīr) (NIV) See *Machir*.

MAKIRITES (Mā´ kĭ rīts) (NIV) See *Machirites*.

MAKKEDAH (Măk kē´ dah) Name meaning "place of shepherds," of a Canaanite city, the site of Joshua's rout of the combined forces of five Canaanite kings (Josh. 10:10). The kings sought refuge in nearby caves but were trapped there (10:16). Joshua captured the city, killing all its population (10:28). Later Makkedah was assigned to the Shephelah (lowland) district of Judah (Josh. 15:41). Suggested locations include: Eusebius's suggestion of a site eight and a half miles from Eleutheropolis (Beit Jibrin); Tell es-Safi south of Hulda (Libnah); el-Muqhar ("the Caves") southwest of Ekron; and a site between Lachish and Hebron.

MAKTESH (Măk´ tĕsh) KJV transliteration of the Hebrew place-name meaning "mortar" (NASB, NRSV). District in or near Jerusalem

(Zeph. 1:11). Early commentators located the site in the Kidron Valley. Recently the site has been linked with an area of the Tyropoean Valley within the city walls (thus "lower town," REB; "market district," NIV).

MALACHI, BOOK OF (Măl´ á kī) Personal name meaning "my messenger." Author of the last prophetic book of the OT about which nothing more is known. The one prophesied in Mal. 3:1 to "prepare" the way for the Lord's coming to His temple is also identified as *mal'aki*, "My messenger." Some believe the book is actually anonymous, its name having been taken from 3:1. The emphasis of the book is clearly on the message rather than the messenger since 47 of the book's 55 verses are personal addresses from the Lord.

Historical Background Although the book is not dated by a reference to a ruler or a specific event, internal evidence, as well as its position in the canon, favors a postexilic date. Reference to a governor in 1:8 favors the Persian period when Judah was a province or subprovince of the Persian satrapy Abar Nahara, which included Palestine, Syria, Phoenicia, Cyprus, and, until 485 B.C., Babylon. The temple had been rebuilt (515 B.C.) and worship established (1:6-11; 2:1-3; 3:1,10). However, the excitement and enthusiasm for which the prophets Haggai and Zechariah were the catalysts had waned. The social and religious problems Malachi addressed reflect the situation portrayed in Ezra 9 and 10 and Neh. 5 and 13, suggesting dates either just before Ezra's return (ca. 460 B.C.) or just before Nehemiah's second term as governor (Neh. 13:6-7; ca. 435 B.C.).

Message and Purpose *Indictment* Malachi presents Judah's sins largely on their own lips, quoting their words, thoughts, and attitudes (1:2,6-7,12-13; 2:14,17; 3:7-8,13-15). Malachi was faced with the failure of the priests of Judah to fear the Lord and to serve the people conscientiously during difficult times. This had contributed to Judah's indifference toward the will of God. Blaming their economic and social troubles on the Lord's supposed unfaithfulness to them, the people were treating one another faithlessly (especially their wives) and were profaning the temple by marrying pagan women. They were also withholding their tithes from the temple.

Instruction Malachi calls the people to turn from their spiritual apathy and correct their wrong attitudes of worship by trusting God with genuine faith as living Lord. This includes honoring the Lord's name with pure offerings, being faithful to covenants made with fellow believers, especially marriage covenants, and signifying their repentance with tithes.

Judgment If the priests would not alter their behavior, the Lord would curse them and remove them disgracefully from service. Malachi also announces a coming day when the Lord of justice will come to purge and refine His people. At that time He will make evident the distinction between the obedient and the wicked and will judge the wicked.

Hope Malachi also bases his instruction on (1) the Lord's demonstration of love for Israel (1:2), (2) their spiritual and covenant unity with God and with one another (2:10), and (3) that coming day when the Lord will also abundantly bless those who fear Him (3:1-6; 3:16–4:3).

Messenger of the Covenant In 3:1-6 God promises a "messenger of the covenant," who would purge and purify God's people, including the priests (3:1-6). The divine-human nature of this messenger is indicated by his being both distinct from God who is speaking and also identified with Him (3:1; Zech. 12:10–13:9). "My messenger" is not the same but one who would announce the coming of the "messenger of the covenant" (cp. Heb. 9:15). The NT identifies "My messenger," as well as "Elijah" in 4:5 and the "voice" of Isa. 40:3, with John the Baptist (Matt. 3:3; 11:10; Mark 1:2-3; Luke 3:3-6; John 1:23).

Elijah's role as preparatory proclaimer of the time of divine intervention derives from his being viewed as quintessential prophet of repentance. As he appears with Moses in these final verses of the OT, so he appeared with Moses representing the prophets to testify to Jesus as the Messiah on the mountain of Jesus' transfiguration (Matt. 17:3; Luke 9:29-31). The prophecy in 4:5 was also fulfilled in part by John the Baptist (Matt. 11:14; 17:10-13; Luke 1:15-17). But Jesus indicated that an additional fulfillment awaits the time of His return (Matt. 11:14; 17:11), perhaps as reflected in the prophecy of the two witnesses in Rev. 11:3 (Deut. 19:15).

Style and Structure Although English versions of the prophecy of Malachi divide the book into four chapters, the Hebrew text divides it into only three (4:1-6 counted as 3:19-24). Malachi has a style that is unique among the OT prophetic books. In general it may be described as sermonic or oracular, but its frequent use of the rhetorical device of quotations from the audience, which constitutes a form of interaction that can be called pseudo-dialogue, give it a distinctive character. It is often said to comprise a series of "disputation speeches" or oracles where charges are raised and evidence presented in a confrontational mood. The six oracles are identified as 1:2-5; 1:6–2:9; 2:10-16; 2:17–3:5; 3:6-12; and 3:13–4:3 (in Heb. 3:21), followed by two appendices, 4:4 (in Heb. 3:22) and 4:5-6 (in Heb. 3:23-24) often considered to be later additions.

An alternative structure is to see the book as organized into three interrelated addresses, each comprising five sections that follow a pattern of alternation between indictment, instruction, judgment, and hope.

Outline

I. Priests Exhorted to Honor Yahweh (1:2–2:9).
   A. Hope: The Lord's love for Judah (1:2-5).
   B. Indictment: Failure to honor the Lord (1:6-9).
   C. Instruction: Stop worship that dishonors the Lord (1:10).
   D. Indictment: Profaning the Lord's name (1:11-14).
   E. Judgment: Priesthood cursed by the Lord (2:1-9).
II. Judah Exhorted to Faithfulness (2:10–3:6).
   A. Hope: Spiritual kinship (2:10a).
   B. Indictment: Marital unfaithfulness (2:10b-15a).
   C. Instruction: Guard against unfaithfulness (2:15b-16).
   D. Indictment: Judah's complaints of injustice (2:17).
   E. Judgment: Justice coming from the Lord (3:1-6).
III. Judah Exhorted to Return to the Lord and Remember the Law (3:7–4:6).
   A. Instruction: Bring tithes as evidence of repentance (3:7-10a).
   B. Hope: Promised blessing (3:10b-12).

C. Indictment: Complacency toward serving the Lord (3:13-15).
D. Hope and Judgment: Coming day of the Lord (3:16–4:3).
E. Instruction: Remember the Law (4:4-6).

E. Ray Clendenen

MALACHITE Green basic carbonate of copper used as an ore and for ornamental objects. According to the NEB and REB, a component of the mosaic pavement decorating the palace of the Persian king Ahasuerus at Susa (Esther 1:6). The Hebrew root means "glistening." Suggested meanings include: porphyry (NASB, NIV, NRSV), red marble (KJV), and white marble (TEV), in addition to malachite.

MALCAM (Măl´ căm) or **MALCHAM** (KJV for Malcam, 1 Chron. 8:9; Milcom, Zeph. 1:5) Name meaning "their King" is applied to: **1.** A Benjaminite (1 Chron. 8:9). **2.** Chief god of the Ammonites (Zeph. 1:5, KJV; Malcam, RSV and NASB margins). The Hebrew *malcam* is sometimes seen as a deliberate scribal misspelling of Milcom (cp. Jer. 49:1,3; Zeph. 1:5), the common name for the Ammonites' god (1 Kings 11:5,33; Zeph. 1:5). One text (1 Kings 11:7) links Milcom with Molech. At Amos 1:15 the Hebrew *malcam* is translated simply "their king," though the word choice suggests that the Ammonites' god will go with them into exile. See *Ammon; Milcom; Molech.*

MALCHIAH (Măl kī ah) Alternate form of Malchijah.

MALCHIEL (Măl´ kī ĕl) Name meaning "My God is king," given to a descendant of Asher (Gen. 46:17; Num. 26:45; 1 Chron. 7:31).

MALCHIELITES (Măl´ kī ĕl īts) Descendants of Malchiel (Num. 26:45).

MALCHIJAH (Măl kī´ jah) Personal name with long and short spelling meaning "My King is Yahweh." **1.** Ancestor of the musician Asaph (1 Chron. 6:40). **2.** Priest in David's time (1 Chron. 24:9; cp. 9:12; Neh. 11:12). **3.** Prince of Judah in Jeremiah's time, probably the father of Pashhur (Jer. 21:1; 38:1,6); **4.–6.** Three of Ezra's contemporaries with foreign wives (Ezra 10:25,31); some modern translations replace the second Malchijah in the Hebrew text of 10:25 with Hashabiah, the early Greek reading. **7.** One standing with Ezra at the reading of the Law (Neh. 8:4). **8.** Priest signing Ezra's covenant (Neh. 10:3); **9.–12.** Four contemporaries of Nehemiah involved in the rebuilding (Neh. 3:11,14,31) or dedication of the walls (Neh. 12:42). Several of the references in Ezra and Nehemiah may refer to the same person(s).

MALCHIRAM (Măl kī´ răm) Personal name meaning "My king is exalted." Son of King Jeconiah of Judah (1 Chron. 3:18).

MALCHISHUA (Măl kĭ shu´ à) Personal name meaning "My king is salvation." Son of King Saul and Ahinoam (1 Chron. 8:33; 9:39) killed in battle with the Philistines at Mount Gilboa (1 Sam. 14:49; 31:2; 1 Chron. 10:2).

MALCHUS (Măl´ kŭs) Personal name meaning "king," common among the Idumaeans and Palmyrenes, especially for their kings or tribal chiefs. High priest's servant whose ear Peter cut off (John 18:10). The name is unusual for slaves who commonly had names such as Onesimus ("Useful," Philem. 10-11). Perhaps the slave was chief of the temple guard. Only Luke recorded the healing of the ear (Luke 22:51). Possibly Luke desired to stress Jesus' compassion in the midst of His passion (cp. Luke 23:28,34,43) or respect shown to the high priest and his representative (cp. Acts 23:4).

MALEFACTORS Used in KJV to denote the two criminals who were crucified beside Jesus (Luke 23:32-33,39). The word is the Latin translation of the Greek *kakourgos*, meaning "robber" or "criminal." The Latin means "evildoer."

MALELEEL (Mà lē´ lə ĕl) Greek form of Mahalaleel used by KJV (Luke 3:37).

MALICE Vicious intention; desire to hurt someone. Malice is characteristic of preconversion life in opposition to God (Rom. 1:29; Titus 3:3). Christians are frequently called upon to rid their lives of malice (Eph. 4:31-32; Col. 3:8; 1 Pet. 2:1).

MALKIEL (Măl´ kĭ ĕl) (NIV) See *Malchiel.*

MALKIELITES (Măl´ kĭ ĕl īts) (NIV) See *Malchielites.*

MALKIJAH (Măl kī´ jah) (NIV) See *Malchijah.*

MALKIRAM (Măl´ kī răm) (NIV) See *Malchiram.*

MALLOTHI (Măl´ lō thī) Personal name meaning "I spoke." One of David's tabernacle musicians (1 Chron. 25:4,26). Like his father Heman (25:5), he may have exercised a prophetic role (king's seer). The sons' names may have formed a prayer (see REB note).

MALLOW In Scripture "mallow" refers to two plants. **1.** *Atriplex halimus L.,* the shrubby orache, is a salt marsh plant and unpleasant food (Job 30:4; "plant of the salt marshes," NASB margin). The saltwort (REB) is another possibility for this plant associated with the marshy areas around the Dead Sea. **2.** The true mallow (genus *Malva*) is a flowering plant prominent around Jerusalem. Its fading flowers provide an image for the unrighteous according to one interpretation of Job 24:24 (NRSV, REB). Here "mallow" is supplied from the earliest Greek translation. Other translations follow the Hebrew text in reading "all."

MALLUCH (Măl´ lŭk) Personal name meaning "being king." **1.** Ancestor of a Levitical singer in Solomon's temple (1 Chron. 6:44); **2.** Priest who returned from exile with Zerubbabel (Neh. 12:2, perhaps identical with the Malluchi of v. 14); **3.–6.** Four contemporaries of Ezra, two men with foreign wives (Ezra 10:29,32) and a priest (Neh. 10:4) and layperson (Neh. 10:27) who witnessed the covenant renewal. Some of the above may refer to the same person.

MALLUCHI (Măl´ lū kī) Family of priests in the time of Joiakim (Neh. 12:14). Some suggest Malluchi is a transcriptional error for Malluch (cp. 12:2).

MALTA (Mal´ tà) See *Island.*

MAMMON Greek form of a Syriac or Aramaic word for "money," "riches," "property," "worldly goods," or "profit." In general use it was a personification of riches as an evil spirit or deity. From about 1500 it has been current in English as indicating the evil influence of wealth. The word is not used in the OT. In the NT (KJV) it is used only by Jesus (Matt. 6:24; Luke 16:9,11,13). In the Sermon on the Mount, Jesus said, "Ye cannot serve God and mammon" (KJV). He meant that no one can be a slave of God and worldly wealth at the same time. The undivided concentration of mind to money-getting is incompatible with wholehearted devotion to God and to His service (Col. 3:5). In the parable of the unjust steward (Luke 15:1-13), Jesus commended the steward's foresight, not his method. His object was to point out how one may best use wealth, tainted or otherwise, with a view to the future. See *Stewardship*.
Ray Robbins

MAMRE (Măm´ rə) Place-name meaning "grazing land." Main area of habitation for Abraham and his family. It apparently was named after an Amorite (Mamre) who helped Abraham defeat the evil king, Chedorlaomer (Gen. 14:1-24). Mamre was famous for its oak trees. It was just east of Mamre that Abraham purchased a cave (Machpelah) for a family burial plot. Its location was at Ramet et-Chalil, two miles north of Hebron. See *Abraham; Machpelah*.

MAN See *Humanity*.

MAN OF LAWLESSNESS or **MAN OF SIN** (KJV) Ultimate opponent of Christ (2 Thess. 2:3). Modern translations follow other manuscripts in reading "man of lawlessness." See *Antichrist; Lawless, Lawlessness*.

MANAEN (Măn´ á ĕn) Greek form of Menahem ("Comforter"); the name of a prophet and teacher in the early church at Antioch (Acts 13:1). Manaen is described as the *suntrophos* of Herod the tetrarch (Herod Antipas, reigned 4 B.C. to A.D. 37). The term literally means "one who eats with." In the OT those who shared the king's table were persons recognized as valued members of the court (2 Sam. 9:10-13; 19:28; 1 Kings 2:7; 2 Kings 25:29; Neh. 5:17). The earliest Greek translation uses *suntrophoi* to refer to those generals who were reared with Alexander (1 Macc. 1:6) as well as for members of court (2 Macc. 9:29). The meanings "member of court" and "childhood companion" are both possible for Acts 13:1. A less likely alternative is the early Greek translation's use of *suntrophoi* for fellow Israelites to mean "kin" (1 Kings 12:24).

MANAHATH (Măn´ á hăth) Place or personal name meaning "resting place" or "settlement." **1.** Ancestor of the Horite subclan of Edomites (Gen. 36:23; 1 Chron. 1:40). **2.** Site, probably outside of Palestine, to which some Benjaminites from Geba were exiled (1 Chron. 8:6). **3.** City of tribal territory of Judah according to earliest Greek text of Josh. 15:59, there called Manocho, probably el-Malcha in the hill country of Judah three miles southwest of Jerusalem. The site is perhaps the same as Nohah ("resting place") associated with Benjaminites in Judg. 20:43 (1 Chron. 2:54).

MANAHATHITES (Măn á hăth´ īts) (NASB, NIV, NRSV) or **MANAHETHITES** (Má nā´ hĕth īts) (KJV, REB) Residents of Manahath (1 Chron. 2:54).

MANASSEH (Má năs´ sĕh) Personal name meaning "God has caused me to forget" (trouble). **1.** One of at least two sons born to Joseph by Asenath (Gen. 41:50-51). Manasseh was adopted by Jacob as one to receive his blessing. Along with Ephraim, Manasseh became one of the 12 tribes of Israel and received a portion of the land. In almost typical OT fashion, Manasseh, the elder brother, did not receive the blessing of the firstborn (Gen. 48:13-20). Jacob crossed his hands and gave that blessing to Ephraim. When the promised land was apportioned, half of the tribe of Manasseh settled on the east bank of the Jordan and half on the west. See *Tribes of Israel*. **2.** King of Judah (696–642 B.C.) who was a son of Hezekiah (2 Kings 20:21). His was the longest reign of any Judean king. Manasseh's reign was known as one of unfaithfulness to Yahweh. Second Kings blames him for Judah's ultimate destruction and exile (2 Kings 21:10-16).

MANASSEH, PRAYER OF See *Apocrypha*.

MANASSITES (Mả năs´ sīts) Members of tribe of Manasseh.

MANDRAKE Small, perennial plant (*Mandragora officinarum*) native to the Middle East. Although not grown for food, its root and berries are edible. The ancient Near East viewed it as an aphrodisiac and fertility drug. It is often called love apple or devil's apple. According to Gen. 30:14-16 a barren Rachel bargained with Reuben (Leah's oldest son) for some mandrakes which he had found. Leah, however, produced the children (Gen. 30:17-21). Only when God "remembered Rachel" did she bear Joseph (30:24).

MANEH KJV for mina at Ezek. 45:12. See *Weights and Measures*.

MANGER Feeding trough used for cattle, sheep, donkeys, or horses. Archaeologists have discovered stone mangers in the horse stables of Ahab at Megiddo. They were cut out of limestone and were approximately three feet long, 18 inches wide, and two feet deep. Other ancient mangers were made of masonry. Many Palestinian homes consisted of one large room that contained an elevated section and a lower section. The elevated section was the family's living quarters, while the lower section housed the family's animals. Usually a manger, in the form of a masonry box or a stone niche, was located in the lower section. Mangers were also put in cave stables or other stalls. The manger referred to in Luke 2:16 may have been in a cave stable or other shelter. There Jesus was laid to sleep after His birth. *Floyd Lewis*

MANNA (Măn´ nả) Grainlike substance, considered to be food from heaven, which sustained the Israelites in the wilderness and foreshadowed Christ, the true Bread from heaven.

Old Testament The small round grains or flakes, which appeared around the Israelites' camp each morning with the dew, were ground and baked into cakes or boiled (Exod. 16:13-36). Their name may have come from the question the Israelites asked when they first saw them: "What is it (*man hu*)?" Today a type of manna

A stone manger still in place in the archaeological excavations at ancient Megiddo.

has been identified with the secretions left on tamarisk bushes by insects feeding on the sap. The Bible emphasizes that God caused manna to appear at the right time and place to meet His people's needs.

New Testament Jesus assured the Jews that He, and not the wilderness food, was the true Bread from heaven which conferred eternal life on those who partook of it (John 6:30-58).

Barbara J. Bruce

MANOAH (Mả nō´ ah) Personal name meaning "rest." A member of the tribe of Dan and the father of Samson (Judg. 13). Manoah petitioned God for a son when his wife could not produce an heir. God promised a son on the condition that he be reared a Nazirite. Manaoh hosted the man of God that brought the news at a meal but was told to offer the food as a burnt offering. The man ascended in the smoke of the fire, revealing his identity as God's angel. Manaoh is buried between Zorah and Eshtaol.

MANSERVANT KJV, RSV for a male servant or slave. See *Slave, Servant*.

MANSION KJV translation of the Greek word *mone* [mō nā´] in John 14:2, meaning "dwelling place" or "room." Before going away Jesus promised to make provision of a dwelling place for His disciples. The Latin Vulgate had translated the word as *mansio*, which referred to a dwelling or home. KJV translated it as "mansions," which likewise meant a dwelling place but has come to represent an elaborate, expensive house in modern English. Thus modern translations read "dwelling places" or "rooms." Christian theology holds that Christ's followers will abide with Him eternally in heavenly dwelling places.

MANSLAYER One guilty of involuntary manslaughter; one who accidentally causes another's death (Num. 35:9-15,22-28; Deut. 19:1-10). English translations distinguish manslayer from murderer though the underlying Hebrew term (*ratsach*) is the same (cp. Exod. 20:13).

MANTLE Robe, cape, veil, or loose-fitting tunic worn as an outer garment. Many of the prophets wore them (1 Sam. 15:27; 1 Kings 19:13), as did women in Jerusalem (Isa. 3:22) and Job (Job 1:20). The transference of the mantle from Elijah to Elisha signified the passing of prophetic responsibility and God's accompanying power. These garments have been worn from at least the time of the exodus until the present. See *Cloth, Clothing; Veil.*

MANUSCRIPT Handwritten copy of a text. Before the invention of the printing press in the 1400s, all books were handwritten. Large numbers of NT and some OT manuscripts survive from the first few centuries B.C. until the 1500s. See *Bible Text and Versions; Paper, Papyrus; Writing.*

MAOCH (Mā´ ŏk) Personal name meaning "dumb, foolish." Father of King Achish of Gath (1 Sam. 27:2). Moach is perhaps identical with Maacah (1 Kings 2:39), perhaps his ancestor.

MAON (Mā´ ŏn) Name meaning "dwelling." **1.** Descendant of Caleb who founded Beth-zur (1 Chron. 2:45). **2.** Village in the hill country of Judah (Josh. 15:55). The site of Maon has been identified with Tell Ma'in about eight miles south of Hebron in the vicinity of Carmel of Judah (cp. 1 Sam. 25:2) and with Khirbet el-Ma'in 25 miles northwest of Beersheba. Pottery finds at Tell Ma'in demonstrate occupation from the time of David. David took refuge from Saul in the wilderness to the east of Maon (1 Sam. 23:24-25). Nabal, who foolishly refused hospitality to David, was a resident of Maon (1 Sam. 25:2).

MAONITES (Mā´ ŏn īts) One of the people groups who oppressed Israel during the period of the judges (Judg. 10:12). These Maonites are perhaps the Meunites, attacked by Hezekiah (1 Chron. 4:41) and Uzziah (2 Chron. 26:7), a band of marauding Arabs from south of the Dead Sea in the vicinity of Ma'an. The earliest Greek translation reads "Midianites" (REB).

MARA (Ma´ rà) Personal name meaning "bitter," chosen by Naomi to reflect God's bitter dealings with her in the death of her husband and sons (Ruth 1:20-21).

MARAH (Ma´ rà) Place-name meaning "bitter." Place in the Wilderness of Shur, so named because of the bitter water found there by the wandering Israelites (Exod. 15:23). The site is typical of pools in the Sinai Peninsula, having undrinkable water. The people complained against Moses because of their discomfort. God answered the leader's prayer by telling him to cast a tree into the water so that it became sweet and drinkable. Marah cannot be located definitely.

MARALAH (Mär´ à lah) Place-name meaning "site on mountain ledge." Border town in Zebulun (Josh. 19:11). The site is perhaps Tell Ghalta in the Jezreel Valley north of Megiddo or Tell Thorah.

MARANATHA (Mär à nă´ thà) Aramaic expression Paul used (1 Cor. 16:22) in closing a letter to the church at Corinth. Having prayed that those who do not love Christ (cp. 1 Cor. 13) would be *anathema*, Paul used a formula probably used in celebration of the Lord's Supper to pray that Christ would come. This highlighted the urgency of showing love to Christ. One way to show such love would be to obey Paul's instructions in 1 Corinthians. Maranatha is actually two Aramaic words. Dividing it as *Marana tha* means "Our Lord, come." *Maran atha* means "Our Lord has come." It reveals the expectant hope in which early Christians lived, watching for the imminent return of Christ. The division of the phrase is disputed by scholars. Whichever division is correct, the Aramaic formula shows that very early the church applied to Jesus the word Lord which otherwise belonged only to God. See *Anathema*.

MARBLE See *Minerals and Metals*.

MARCUS (Mär´ cŭs) Latin form of Mark ("large hammer") used by the KJV at Col. 4:10; Philem. 24; and 1 Peter 5:13. See *Mark*.

MARDUK (Mär´ dūk) Chief god of Babylon, sometimes called Merodach or Bel, the Babylonian equivalent of Baal meaning "lord." He was credited with creation, a feat reenacted each new year and celebrated with a festival. In typical ancient Near Eastern fashion, Marduk was proclaimed king. The reigning monarch was seen as the son of the god. As the kingdom grew, Marduk was attributed with more powers until he was acknowledged as lord of the heavens. The prophets mocked Marduk and his worshipers as products of human craftsmen who would lead Babylon to defeat and exile (Isa. 46:1; Jer. 50:2,38; 51:47). See *Babylon; Bel; Gods, Pagan*.

MARE Female horse. See *Horse*.

MAREAL (Mär ə ál) (RSV, TEV) See *Maralah*.

MARESHAH (Mà rē´ shà) Place and personal name meaning "place at the top" with two Hebrew spellings. **1.** Son of Caleb and founder of Hebron (1 Chron. 2:42). The Hebrew text apparently refers to this son as first Mesha, then Meresha. **2.** Member of the tribe of Judah (1 Chron. 4:21). **3.** A Canaanite city incorporated into the Shephelah district of Judah (Josh. 15:44). The city was fortified by Rehoboam (2 Chron. 11:8). Mereshah was near the site of the battle between the forces of King Asa and the Ethiopian commander Zerah (2 Chron. 14:9-14). Mareshah was

home to the Prophet Eliezar (2 Chron. 20:37). Micah foretold the destruction of the city (Mic. 1:15). The site has been identified with Tell Sandahannah one mile southeast of Beit Jibrin.

MARI (Ma´ rē) Ancient city accidentally discovered by Arab clansmen and later excavated by French archaeologists under the supervision of Andre Parrot. Today known as Tell el-Hariri, the site is comprised of about 135 acres (after erosion on its northeast sector), located adjacent to the right (west) bank of the Euphrates river, roughly 15 miles north of the modern Syrian-Iraqi border. Some 30 archaeological campaigns have unearthed city walls and various temples and palaces that date from about 3100 to 1760 B.C. when the city was demolished by Hammurabi of Babylon, never again to rise to a stature of prominence.

Located about midway between the great powers of Sumeria (Kish, Ur, Akkad) and Syro-Mesopotamia (Ebla, Aleppo), Mari played a significant role in the flow of trade as early as the third millennium, though, to judge from the documents which have already been published from this era, the city experienced a dependent status to these more powerful neighbors. By about 1800 no fewer than four trading routes converged on the city; the city's geographical and commercial horizons stretched from Iran in the east to the Mediterranean and Aegean in the west, including Turkey, Lebanon, Syria, Israel, and the Arabian Desert. From such an enviable position the kingdom of Mari played a crucial role in the international trade of timber, stone, wool, resin, garments, furniture, royal horses, wine, olive and sesame oils, myrtle, copper, lapis-lazuli and, perhaps most importantly, tin—an essential component in the forging or casting of bronze.

For about 25 years immediately prior to its destruction by Hammurabi, Mari experienced a "golden age" under its King Zimri-Lim. This era in Mesopotamian history has been compared by one noted historian to the age of Pericles in Greek history or of Caesar Augustus in Rome. For Mari it became a period of unsurpassed greatness in material prosperity, and its cultural remains have been matched by few sites in the neighboring areas of the ancient Near East.

The opulent prosperity in which Mari indulged is unmistakably etched into the remains of the magnificent palace of Zimri-Lim. Encompassing a nine-acre rectangular plot and containing more than 300 rooms, this palatial estate is one of the largest and best preserved buildings in all of Mesopotamian history. The excavators uncovered interior walls as thick as 13 feet and standing as high as 16 feet; lintels in some doorways were still intact. Apparently a two-story edifice, the palace was constructed to include many large open courts surrounded by a constellation of rooms that were interconnected by high doorways, thereby permitting ventilation and light to penetrate throughout a ground floor in which there were no windows. Floors were usually plastered or tiled; walls were plastered and frequently adorned with ornate sculpture or painting, and wood was used decoratively to add aesthetic luster.

Exhumed from this palace was Mari's greatest legacy of all: the royal archives. Embodying more than 25,000 texts and fragments, this documentation addresses almost every aspect within a culture: internal politics, international affairs, diplomacy and treaties, domestic policy, commerce and trade, agriculture, irrigation, law and jurisprudence, political intrigue, and religion. In point of fact, Zimri-Lim's reign is presently the most heavily documented of any king in antiquity, even including personal correspondence between himself and his wife, his daughters, his local administrators, and his territorial functionaries. His archive contains hundreds of bureaucratic registers that detail in a most graphic way certain aspects of daily life in a Mesopotamian court: where and how the king worshiped and his temples were serviced; where, what, and how often the king ate or was luxuriated; how courtiers were selected for the court or enticing female dancers were selected for the royal harem; what were various forms of entertainment for the court and/or visiting dignitaries; where, how far, and how frequently did the king journey; how was royalty attired.

Mari's bearing on biblical studies is significant, if indirect. Documentation from Mari has opened the historical, geographical, and social dimension of Northern Mesopotamia, the homeland of the biblical patriarchs. Certain patriarchal behavior attested in the writings of Moses may be seen to be reflected in the literature of Mari. This includes the prominence of the firstborn within family structure, the legal procedures entailed in adoption or formalizing inheritance, the centrality and interdependence of the clan as a model for social structuring, the notion of tribal or ethnic movement of people and the relocation and resettlement in a new area, the importance of genealogical registers similar to those of Gen. 5 and 11 as a means of establishing personal or clan authority, the prominent role and the forms of ritual in religious practices, the procedures for census taking, and the nature of prophets and prophecy. Mari's literary sources contribute to a richly textured reconstruction of Mesopotamian history during the early patriarchal period, just as they often provide linguistic elucidation of certain biblical concepts (compass points, tribal terms and leadership, flora and fauna, military terms). See *Hammurabi*.

Barry J. Beitzel

MARINER See *Ships, Sailors, and Navigation.*

MARJORAM See *Hyssop; Plants.*

MARK, GOSPEL OF Second book of the NT and shortest account of the ministry of Jesus.
Author The title "according to Mark" was added to this Gospel by scribes who produced the earliest copies of the Gospel. According to early church tradition Mark recorded and arranged the "memories" of Peter, thereby producing a Gospel based on apostolic witness. Although Mark was a common Roman name, the Gospel writer is probably John Mark. Mark became an important assistant for both Paul and Peter, preaching the good news to Gentiles and preserving the gospel message for later Christians. See *Mark, John.*
Readers Mark wrote his Gospel for Gentile Christians. He explains Jewish customs in detail for the benefit of readers unfamiliar with Judaism (7:3-4; 12:18). Mark translated several Aramaic expressions for a Greek-speaking audience (5:41; 7:11,34; 15:22). Gentiles would have especially appreciated Mark's interpretation of the saying of Jesus that declared all foods clean (7:19; cp. Matt. 15:17-20). Mark's Gentile audience may explain his omission of the genealogy of Jesus. Perhaps these Gentile readers were Roman Christians. Mark's Gospel contains many terms borrowed from Latin and written in Greek; consider "taking counsel" (3:6),

M

M

"Legion" (5:9), "tribute" (12:14), "scourged" (15:15).

Early Christian tradition placed Mark in Rome preserving the words of Peter for Roman Christians shortly before the apostle's death (1 Pet. 5:13). According to tradition Peter was martyred in Rome during the Neronian persecution, which would place the date of Mark's Gospel about A.D. 64 to 68. Such a hostile environment motivated Mark to couch his account of the life of Jesus in terms that would comfort Christians suffering for their faith. The theme of persecution dominates the Gospel of Mark (Mark 10:30; cp. Matt. 19:29; Luke 18:29). Jesus' messianic suffering is emphasized to inspire Christians to follow the same path of servanthood (10:42-45). Roman Christians would be encouraged knowing that Jesus anticipated that "everyone will be salted with fire" (9:49 HCSB; 13:9-13). Dying for the gospel would be equivalent to dying for Jesus (8:35; Matt. 16:25; Luke 9:24).

Style Mark has been called the "Gospel of action." One of his favorite words in telling the story of Jesus is "immediately." Jesus is constantly on the move. In one day, according to Mark, Jesus instructed the multitudes by the sea, traveled across the sea of Galilee and calmed the storm, healed the Gerasene demoniac, crossed the sea again, healed the woman with a hemorrhage, and raised a little girl from the dead (4:1–6:1). Mark apparently had more interest in the work of Jesus than in the words of Jesus. Thus he omitted the Sermon on the Mount. Jesus taught as He moved from region to region, using the circumstances of His travel as valuable lessons for His disciples (8:14-21). Geographical references serve only to trace the expansive parameters of His ministry. According to Mark's "motion" picture, Jesus moved quickly—as if He were a man whose days were numbered.

Good storytellers captivate audiences by using everyday language that provokes strong imagery. Mark's language is simple, direct, and common. His sometimes rough and unrefined Greek grammar facilitates his ability to communicate the gospel message by using familiar patterns of speech. When Mark told a story, he possessed a flair for the dramatic and an eye for detail. His description of events was replete with vivid images which evoke a variety of emotions in just one story (5:1-20; cp. Matt. 8:28-34). In the graphic account of Jesus' encounter with the demoniac boy, only Mark recorded the child's convulsion which caused him to fall on the

A colonnaded street by the agora in Perga, a city significant in the life of the Gospel writer Mark.

ground and roll "around, foaming at the mouth" (9:20,26 HCSB). Furthermore, Mark preserved Jesus' interrogation of the father as to the severity of the boy's condition and the depth of his own faith (9:21-24). Finally, only Mark recorded the actual words of Jesus' rebuke as well as the reaction of the crowd to the boy's lifeless body: "He's dead!" (9:25-26 HCSB).

Mark's concern for detail, sometimes to the point of redundancy (Mark 6:49-50 HCSB, "when they saw Him ... because they all saw Him ... He spoke to them and said"), demonstrates his reliance upon eyewitness testimony. Mark was careful to relate not only the words of Jesus but also His gestures, attitudes, and emotions (3:5; 6:34; 7:34; 8:12; 11:16). In the same fashion Mark recorded the reaction of the crowds, facial expressions of conversationalists, conclusions drawn by the disciples, and private remarks made by opponents (5:40; 10:22,32,41; 11:31; 14:40). Only an observant insider would relate stories with such pertinent information. Furthermore, the prominent role of Peter in the narrative (Peter remembered, 11:21; also 1:36; 14:37; 16:7) confirms early Christian tradition that Mark relied upon the recollections of the apostle when he produced "the gospel of Jesus Christ" (1:1).

Form Upon first reading the Gospel of Mark appears to be an arbitrary collection of stories about Jesus. After John the Baptist fulfilled his role as the forerunner to the Messiah (in a very brief appearance), Jesus began His public ministry in Galilee by preaching the "gospel of God" and collecting a few disciples (1:14-20). With these necessary introductions completed, Mark presented the life of Jesus by following a simple geographical scheme: from Galilee to Judea. The popular Galilean ministry of Jesus is recorded in chapters 1–9. The brief Judean ministry (10:1-31) serves primarily as a prelude to the approaching passion of Jesus. Over one-third of Mark's Gospel is devoted to describing the events of the last week in the life of Jesus (10:32–15:47). The story ends as abruptly as it began; Mark finished his Gospel account with the angelic announcement of the resurrection of Jesus the Nazarene (the earliest Greek manuscripts of the NT end Mark's Gospel at 16:8). Mark's chronology of Jesus leaves the reader with the impression that his only purpose in writing a Gospel was to preserve the oral tradition in written form. However,

upon closer inspection, it becomes apparent to the observant reader that Mark arranged the material in a more sophisticated fashion to convey truth on a higher level.

The stories of the cleansing of the temple and the cursing of the fig tree appear as isolated incidents in Matthew's Gospel, connected by chronological sequence (Matt. 21:12-22). In the Gospel of Mark, on the other hand, these two stories are interwoven to aid the reader in interpreting the parabolic activity of Jesus. Along the way to Jerusalem, Jesus indicated to His disciples that He was hungry and approached a fig tree to harvest its fruit. The tree was full of leaves, giving every indication of life, but it possessed no fruit. Mark recorded that Jesus "answered" the tree and announced, "May no one ever eat fruit from you again!" (11:14 HCSB). The disciples, who "heard it," must have been puzzled by Jesus' actions, for Mark recorded that "it was not the season for figs" (11:13 HCSB). Without explanation Jesus led His disciples into Jerusalem where He cleansed the temple. From a distance the daily activity of the temple gave every indication of spiritual life, but upon closer inspection Jesus found no spiritual fruit. Israel, the fig tree, was supposed to provide "a house of prayer for all nations" (11:17 HCSB). Instead, the religious leaders turned the devotion of worshipers into financial profit (11:15,17). In essence, when Jesus "answered" the fig tree, he pronounced a curse on the Jewish religious leadership and demonstrated His divine displeasure by cleansing the temple. It should have come as no surprise, then, for Peter and the disciples, during their return trip, to find the cursed fig tree dead (11:21).

Mark's Gospel is not just a collection of stories about Jesus; his book tells the story of Jesus as a whole. Mark developed the unifying "plot" of the Gospel story by unveiling the hidden identity of Jesus. The messianic secret is part of the mystery of the kingdom of God, understood only by insiders—"to those outside, everything comes in parables" (4:11,33-34 HCSB). Throughout Mark's Gospel Jesus sought to conceal His true identity. Jesus silenced demonic profession because they knew Him (1:34). He ordered those who witnessed miracles not to tell anyone what they saw, although silence was only a remote possibility (7:36). Even after the climactic profession of faith, when the disciples revealed that they had learned the secret ("You are the Messiah!"), Jesus warned them not to tell anyone about Him (8:30). Mark used the messianic secret to organize his story around the progressive revelation of Christ and the faith pilgrimage of His disciples. Even Gentiles demonstrated that they belonged to the community of faith when they understood Jesus' parables and recognized Him as the Christ.

The literary form of Mark's Gospel is no accident. The arrangement of the gospel material gives every indication that a skilled literary craftsman has been at work. For example, Mark found irony in pairing the story of the disciples questioning the identity of Jesus after the stilling of the storm, "Who then is this?" (4:41 HCSB) with the account of the demons who are quick to shout, "Jesus, Son of the Most High God" (5:7). When the disciples finally offered their superlative confession of faith at Caesarea Philippi (8:27-30), they failed to understand the full implications of Jesus' messiahship (8:31-38). Mark depicted their partial spiritual vision by recording the unique miracle of Jesus healing the blind man in two stages (8:22-25). Although the disciples saw the messianic secret, their vision would not be focused until the resurrection. Beyond doubt, Mark's portrait of Jesus is a "painting" which can be appreciated both up close (style) and from a distance (form).

Message Jesus' favorite self-designation, especially in Mark, was "Son of Man." In Mark's Gospel Jesus is identified with humanity in title and in kind. Mark portrayed Jesus as a Man possessing every human emotion. Moved by compassion, anger, frustration, mercy, and sorrow (1:41; 3:5; 8:17; 14:6,33), Jesus ministered among His own kind. Mark offered the full humanity of Jesus without reservation (3:21; 4:38; 6:3-6; 13:32); from the beginning of His earthly ministry (2:20) Jesus lived in the ominous shadow of the cross until the agony of Gethsemane almost overwhelmed Him (14:34). However, Mark penned a Gospel which was also designed to evoke faith in the deity of Jesus: the divine voice announced it from heaven, demons screamed it in agony, Peter professed it boldly, even a Roman soldier acknowledged, "This man really was God's Son!" (15:39 HCSB).

Outline

I. God Has Acted for His People by Sending His Son as His Agent (1:1-13).

II. The Appearance of God's Son as His Agent Signaled the Presence of the Kingdom (1:14-45).

III. The Old Order Failed to Recognize God's Agent or the Presence of the Kingdom (2:1–3:6).

IV. The Presence of God's Agent Provoked a Reaction from Others (3:7–6:6).

V. God's Agent Extended the Blessings of the Kingdom despite Opposition (6:7–8:30).

VI. God's Agent Exhibited the Kingdom Paradox: Suffering Precedes Vindication (8:31–10:52).

VII. The Presence of God's Agent in Jerusalem Intensified the Conflict between the Old Order and the Kingdom (11:1–12:44).

VIII. God's Agent Foresaw Impending Distress for Jerusalem and the Old Order (13:1-37).

IX. The Old Order Was Unified in Its Action against God's Agent (14:1–15:47).

X. The Resurrection of God's Agent Validated the Presence of the Kingdom (16:1-8).

XI. A Later Appendix: Proof of the Vindication of God's Agent (16:9-20).

Rodney Reeves

MARK, JOHN Author of the Second Gospel and an early missionary leader. John Mark, as Luke calls him in Acts, was the son of Mary, in whose house the church was meeting when Peter was miraculously freed from prison in Acts 12. Commonly called by his Greek name, Mark, in the NT, John was probably his Jewish name. Mark was a Jew, Barnabas' cousin (Col. 4:10), and a companion of Barnabas and Paul on their first missionary journey. On the first missionary journey Mark ministered with the group on Cyprus, the home territory of Barnabas, and also a place with family connections for Mark. However, when they left for Pamphylia, Mark returned to Jerusalem.

Mark was the cause of the split between Paul and Barnabas when Mark's participation in the second missionary journey was debated (Acts 15:39). Barnabas sided with his cousin, while Paul refused to take Mark since he had left them on the first journey. Later, however, Paul indicated that Mark was with him (in Rome likely) as Paul sent letters to the Colossians (Col. 4:10)

The south city gate (possibly Hellenistic) at Perga of Pamphylia, the port from which Mark returned home.

The area where the shops and agora of ancient Corinth were located.

and Philemon (Philem. 24). Mark was also summoned to be with Paul in 2 Tim. 4:11. Whatever rift existed earlier was healed sometime and their friendship renewed.

Mark is closely related to Peter. In 1 Pet. 5:13 Peter refers to Mark, his "son," as being with him in Rome (Babylon). Early church tradition supports the strong association between Peter and Mark. In the early second century, Papias mentioned that Mark was Peter's interpreter. Other early church figures associate Mark with Peter and note that the Gospel of Mark was based upon Peter's preaching.   *Bill Warren*

MARKETPLACE Narrow streets and clustered buildings of most towns and villages in ancient Palestine left little room for a public marketplace. Shops were built into private residences or clustered in the gate area to form bazaars (1 Kings 20:34). Merchants operated booths just inside the city gate or hawked their merchandise outside the gate area in an open space or square. This area also served as a marshaling place for troops (2 Chron. 32:6) and the site for public meetings (Neh. 8:1), victory celebrations (Deut. 13:16), and the display of captives (2 Sam. 21:12).

Herod rebuilt many of the cities of Palestine following the Greek pattern that included open areas for public gathering (Gr. *agora*). Amidst the shops children played (Matt. 11:16), day laborers gathered to be hired (Matt. 20:2-3), and Pharisees and other leading citizens wandered, exchanging greetings (Matt. 23:7; Luke 11:43). Paul went to the marketplace (Gr. *agora*) on his visits to Greek cities to speak to the crowd always gathered there (Acts 17:17). He and Silas were also tried by magistrates in the marketplace

at Philippi after angering the local merchants (Acts 16:19).   *Victor H. Matthews*

MAROTH (Mā´ rŏth) Place-name meaning "bitter" or "bitter fountain." Town in lowlands of Judah which would be attacked as invading armies approached Jerusalem (Mic. 1:12). The town is perhaps identical with Maarath (Josh. 15:59).

MARRIAGE The sacred, covenantal union of one man and one woman formed when the two swear before God an oath of lifelong loyalty and love to one another, the sign and seal of which is sexual intercourse.

Nature of Marriage God instituted the first marriage in the garden of Eden when He gave Eve to Adam as a wife (Gen. 2:18-25). That later marriages were to follow the pattern of the first is indicated by the concluding divine instruction (see Matt. 19:4-6): "This is why a man leaves his father and mother and bonds with his wife, and they become one flesh" (Gen. 2:24). A unique unity between Adam and Eve was seen in that the two became "one flesh." The oneness of marriage separated the couple from others as a distinct family unit.

Because God instituted it, marriage is more than just a ceremony. Biblical passages showing that the marriage relationship is based on a covenant or oath sworn before God are Prov. 2:17; Ezek. 16:8,59-62; Hos. 2:16-20; Mal. 2:14; Matt. 19:6. Any violation of that covenant invites God's judgment.

Purposes of Marriage *God's Glory* If man's chief purpose as the image of God is to glorify God and enjoy our relationship with Him forever (Ps. 73:28; 1 Cor. 10:31), clearly this is the chief purpose of marriage. Paul explains in Eph. 5:21-33 that the marriage relationship is to be patterned after that of Christ and the church. An inference to be drawn from that is that a husband and wife are to display in their relationship the nature of our relationship with Christ, our divine Husband, as His bride, the church. This same principle may also be inferred from the OT, where the marriage relationship was one of the key analogies used to describe Yahweh's relationship with Israel (e.g., Jer. 2:1; 3:6; 31:32; Hos. 1–3).

Marriage is also God's unique gift to provide the framework for intimate companionship, as a means for procreation of the human race and as the channel of sexual expression according to biblical standards.

Companionship Whereas the creation of male and female mankind was "very good" (Gen. 1:31), the creation of the male alone had not yet fulfilled God's purpose for man as the image of God (Gen. 2:18). This expresses no failure on God's part; instead, it instructs us that a male creature alone is not the perfect creation that God had in mind. Adam needed a wife to be all that God intended him to be, as is normally the case with all men unless God grants otherwise (see Matt. 19:10-12; 1 Cor. 7:6-7). The same, of course, would be true of the woman whom God made for the man (see 1 Cor. 11:9).

Adam needed "a helper who is like him," that is, someone to complement or complete him, whose nature corresponded to his own (Gen. 2:21-23). He needed more than a vessel for the production of children; he needed a "help," not a demeaning term since it is also used of God (Gen. 49:25; Exod. 18:4; Deut. 33:7,26; 1 Sam. 7:12; Isa. 41:10; Pss. 10:14; 33:20). Together, under God's direction and the husband's leadership, they could find satisfaction in fulfilling the purpose for which God had created them. The companionship that is shared between husband and wife in marriage enables physical, psychological, mental, emotional, and spiritual health.

Companionship within marriage is expressed in acts of love. The pattern of love that ought to define a marriage is found in 1 Cor. 13:1-7. Thus, marriage should be a place of patience, humility, joy, truth, peace, affirmation, and hope. Conversely, marriage is not a place for abuse. Nowhere in Scripture is a husband or wife given authority to strike or demean his/her spouse.

Procreation Marriage is also for the purpose of producing and rearing godly children (Gen. 1:28; Ps. 127). From the moment of conception children are a blessing and a heritage from the Lord. They are a source of joy in a marriage (Prov. 27:6). Parents are responsible for the moral and spiritual education of their children (Eph. 6:4). They are to lead their children by a consistent godly lifestyle and loving discipline so that children can learn to make choices based upon biblical truths. Children also have a responsibility to care for their parents in their old age. Though the OT places a high value on the firstborn son, all children are considered valu-

able to God from conception to maturity (Ps. 139:14-16; Prov. 17:6).

Sexual Intimacy Marriage is also for sexual intimacy. God's intention is for sexual acts to occur exclusively within the unique monogamous relationship of marriage as a reminder that they are "one flesh," bound together by covenant. Sexual intimacy was part of God's good creation (Gen. 1:27-28; 2:24-25). Intercourse is part of the natural expression of love within a marriage and provides emotional intimacy, deepens the couple's friendship, and helps to develop a servant attitude within the oneness of marriage (Gen. 2:24; Prov. 5:15-19; 1 Cor. 7:2-5). Sexual intimacy is to be a time of joy and mutual satisfaction for both the husband and wife (Song of Songs 6–7). God has given to both members of the marriage conjugal rights (1 Cor. 7:2-5).

Problems in Marriage ***Sexual Sins*** Adultery is a violation of the oath sworn before God that constituted the marriage. The Bible's condemnation of adultery includes such things as communal marriage, mate swapping, "open marriages," homosexuality, incest, and voyeurism such as pornography (Exod. 20:14; Lev. 18:22; Rom. 1:26-27; 1 Thess. 4:3; Heb. 13:4).

Sexual sins are serious because they undermine the foundation of family life, the oneness of the marriage relationship, and one's covenant commitment made before God. Moral purity was stressed for the husband and wife in Israel with severe penalties for either party when sin occurred (Lev. 18; Prov. 5). God likens idolatry to adultery because of the similarity of the divine-human and husband-wife relationships.

Unequally Yoked Biblical marriage is between Christians. The expectation for a Christian to marry a Christian is reflected in Paul's instruction to marry "only in the Lord" (1 Cor. 7:39). His expectation is also seen in his comments concerning not being "unequally yoked together with unbelievers" (2 Cor. 6:14). Those who choose to marry an unbeliever violate the commands of Scripture.

A Christian who is already married to an unbeliever is not given permission to leave him or her but should maintain the relationship in order to rear the children as believers and to win over the unbelieving spouse (1 Cor. 7:12-16; 1 Pet. 3:1). An example of the impact that a believing spouse can have on the children is seen in the life of Timothy. There is evidence that Timothy's father was not a believer (Acts 16:1), but his mother passed her faith along to her son (2 Tim. 1:5; 3:14-15).

Divorce There is some disagreement among Christians over the Bible's teaching on divorce. Almost all agree, however, that divorce is contrary to the biblical teaching that marriage, being based on a covenant by which a man and woman become "one flesh," is intended to last a lifetime. In Matt. 19:6 Jesus declared, "So they are no longer two, but one flesh. Therefore what God has joined together, man must not separate" (HCSB). In response to the Pharisees' question about Deut. 24:1-4 where divorce was allowed, Jesus further declared, "Moses permitted you to divorce your wives because of the hardness of your hearts. But it was not like that from the beginning" (Matt. 19:8). Nevertheless, under certain circumstances God appears to permit divorce and then, by implication, remarriage. In the same passage Jesus further declares that "whoever divorces his wife, except for sexual immorality, and marries another, commits adultery" (Matt. 19:9; see also 5:32). An inference is that to divorce one's spouse because he/she has committed sexual immorality (that is, adultery) and then to marry another person is not adultery but is acceptable to God. (Some question this inference, in part, because the parallels in Mark 10:11-12 and Luke 16:18 do not have the exception.) Some argue from 1 Cor. 7:10-11 that the legitimacy of divorce does not imply the legitimacy of remarriage. But Paul appears to be dealing in the Corinthian passage with a situation (such as abuse, perhaps) that does not involve adultery. It also seems that a Christian is permitted to divorce an unbelieving spouse who has deserted him/her (1 Cor. 7:15-16), although this interpretation is less clear.

Divorce, whether it is justified or not, is a tragedy that fractures the lives of men, women, children, and the Christian's witness for Christ to the lost world. Nevertheless, the Gospels are filled with examples of how Jesus dealt with persons who were struggling with guilt and failure, including one woman who had been married five times and who was living with a man who was not her husband (John 4:1-42). Where guilt and sin were involved, Jesus did not minimize it, but in every case He acted with redemption. His goal was to help them to begin anew through God's grace and strength.

Biblical Submission A Christian marriage is to be a place of refuge for a husband and wife, where they can be cheered and refreshed in a safe, healthy environment. Within Scripture there are clear roles for the husband and wife. These roles in no way lessen the value of either party. The husband and wife are each created in the image of God and are of equal worth in the sight of God (Gen. 1:27). The marriage relationship models the way God relates to His people.

The Bible describes the marriage that pleases God in terms of mutual submission empowered by the Holy Spirit (Eph. 5:18-21; see also Phil. 2:1-4). Such a marriage also provides the marital fulfillment and companionship God intends. However, mutual submission is to be expressed differently by the husband and the wife. The husband is to practice self-denying, nurturing love patterned after that of Christ (Eph. 5:25-33). He is the initiator and is responsible for leading his wife with wisdom and understanding. He is also to protect, provide for, and honor her (1 Pet. 3:7; Col. 3:19). A wife, on the other hand, is to express her submission by following her husband's leadership with respect (Eph. 5:22-24,33; Col. 3:18), maintaining a pure and reverent life with "a gentle and quiet spirit" (1 Pet. 3:1-6). See *Adultery; Divorce; Family.*

Brent R. Kelly and E. Ray Clendenen

MARROW Soft tissue within bone cavities. In OT times marrow was regarded as among the choicest of foods (Ps. 63:5; Isa. 25:6). Good health was characterized by bones with moist marrow (Job 21:24). To fear the Lord and shun evil is marrow (KJV) or refreshment (NASB, RSV) or nourishment (NIV) to the bones (Prov. 3:8). The image of the dividing of joints and marrow pictures the power of Scripture to penetrate a person's thoughts and motives (Heb. 4:12).

MARS HILL Prominent rise overlooking the city of Athens where the philosophers of the city gathered to discuss their ideas, some of which revolutionized modern thought. Paul discussed religion with the leading minds of Athens on Mars Hill. He used the altar to an "unknown god" to present Jesus to them (Acts 17:22). See *Areopagus; Greece.*

MARSENA (Mär´ sē nà) Aramaic or Persian personal name of uncertain meaning. One of the seven wise men or princes with access to the Persian King Ahasuerus (Esther 1:13-14; cp. Ezra 7:14).

MARSH Tract of soft, wet land (Job 8:11; 40:21). Ezekiel 47:11 refers to the salt marshes surrounding the Dead Sea.

MARSHAL Akkadian loanword for commander of troops (Jer. 51:27 NASB, NRSV; captain, KJV; commander, NIV, REB).

MARTHA Personal name meaning "lady [of the house]" or "mistress." Sister of Mary and Lazarus of Bethany and one of Jesus' best-loved disciples. True to her name, Martha is portrayed as a person in charge: she welcomed Jesus as a guest in her home (Luke 10:38); she was concerned with meeting the obligations of a hostess, whether preparing food (Luke 10:40; John 12:2) or greeting guests (John 11:20). Together with Mary, she sent for Jesus when Lazarus was ill (John 11:3). Luke 10:38-42 contrasts Martha's activist discipleship with Mary's contemplative discipleship. The church cannot minister without "Marthas" who are willing to serve alone. Jesus' gentle rebuke serves as a perpetual reminder not to major on minor matters. Jesus must not be neglected in the name of service. In John 11:21-27 Jesus led Martha from an inadequate to a lofty confession. Faced with the realities of death, Martha, however, later doubted (John 11:39).

MARTYR Transliteration of the Greek word *martus*, meaning "witness." In the Septuagint this term rarely denotes one killed for his or her testimony, although a case may perhaps be made thematically in reference to prophetic proclamation. The messages and oracles of God were often rejected, resulting in the messenger's maltreatment or death (Suffering Servant of Isa. 42; 49; 50; 52–53; other examples of suffering in persecution in Jer. 20:2; 1 Kings 19:2; 2 Chron. 18:7-27; 1 Kings 19:10; Jer. 20:1-6).

Witnesses also bear testimony about moral, religious, or spiritual truths and views of which they are convinced by faith. Those truths may be external facts or internal convictions, and it is understood that ultimately one would give one's life for those truths. The NT refers only three times to a martyr in this last sense (Acts 22:20;

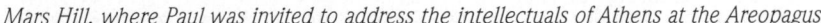

Mars Hill, where Paul was invited to address the intellectuals of Athens at the Areopagus.

"Mary's House" in Ephesus where tradition says that Mary the mother of Jesus lived out her last days.

Rev. 2:13; 17:6), but the early church greatly expanded this meaning and developed a theology of martyrdom during its centuries of persecution. See *Persecution; Testimony; Witness, Martyr.*   *Stefana Dan Laing*

MARY Greek personal name equivalent to Hebrew, Miriam. **1.** Mary, the mother of Jesus. Mary was a young woman, a virgin, living in Nazareth, and a relative of Elizabeth, mother of John the Baptist (Luke 1:5; 2:26). Pledged to marry a carpenter named Joseph, the angel Gabriel appeared to her, announcing she would give birth to "the Son of the Most High" who would sit on "the throne of His father David" (Luke 1:32 HCSB). When Mary raised the issue of her virginity, the angel indicated the conception would be supernatural (Luke 1:34-35). Matthew said this virginal conception was a fulfillment of Isa. 7:14. Subsequently, Mary visited Elizabeth (Luke 1:39-45). Later, after journeying to Bethlehem and giving birth to Jesus (Luke 2:1-20), Mary and Joseph presented the baby to the Lord at the temple (Luke 2:22-38). Matthew indicates that Mary, Joseph, and Jesus lived in Bethlehem until the visit of the magi, when the threat posed by Herod forced them to take refuge in Egypt (Matt. 2:1-18). The family then lived in Nazareth in Galilee (Matt. 2:19-23; Luke 2:39).

In later tradition a natural tendency to appreciate Mary took on added and unwarranted dimensions. She was venerated and claims about her uniqueness began to be made, including her "immaculate conception," "perpetual virginity," "bodily assumption," and continuing role as "co-mediatrix" of salvation. The Scriptures give no

support for these ideas. All appearances of Mary in the Gospels support a view of her as a normal human woman. Matthew 1:25 indicates that after the birth of Jesus, Joseph and Mary began normal marital relations, producing several other children (Matt. 13:54-56; Mark 6:3). When Jesus was 12, He gently rebuked His mother for failing to recognize His deep interest in the things of God. At a wedding in Cana, Jesus performed Mary's requested miracle but reproved her (John 2:1-11).

Mary was present at the cross when Jesus committed her care to John who took her into his home (John 19:26-27). After the ascension Mary and her sons were with the disciples in Jerusalem as they waited for the promised coming of the Holy Spirit (Acts 1:14).

2. Mary Magdalene, one of the women who followed and supported Jesus (Mark 15:41). She was from Magdala in Galilee. She experienced dramatic healing when seven demons came out of her (Mark 16:9; Luke 8:2). She was a key witness to Jesus' death (Matt. 27:56, Mark 15:40), burial (Matt. 27:61; Mark 15:47), the empty tomb (Matt. 28:1; Mark 16:1; Luke 24:1-10), and was the first to encounter the risen Christ (John 20:1-18). Her name being listed first may indicate a leadership role among the women. She has been identified as a sinful woman, perhaps a prostitute, perhaps even the "sinful woman" of Luke 7:36-50. However, there is no such evidence in any of the references to her.

3. Mary of Bethany, sister of Martha and Lazarus. Jesus stayed in this home more than once. Jesus commended Mary for her interest in His teaching (Luke 10:38-42). Mary and Martha sent for Jesus when Lazarus fell ill and died (John 11:1-45). Mary later anointed the feet of Jesus

Mosaic floors decorate the Western Palace area of Masada.

with perfume (John 12:1-8; Mark 14:3-9). A deep relationship existed between Jesus and this family. **4.** Mary, mother of James the Younger and Joses. Along with Mary Magdalene, this Mary is identified as an eyewitness to the death, burial, and resurrection of Jesus (Matt. 27:56–28:1; Mark 15:40–16:1; Luke 24:10). She was Galilean and a follower and supporter of the ministry of Jesus (Mark 15:40-41). **5.** Mary, the wife of Clopas. This Mary also was a witness to the death of Jesus and may be the same Mary, mother of James and Joses (John 19:25), but this view is problematic. **6.** Mary, mother of John Mark. When Peter was freed from prison in Acts

12, he went to the house of Mary, mother of John Mark, where the disciples were meeting. This home was apparently a gathering place for believers. John Mark was later associated with the missionary work of Paul, Barnabas, and Peter. **7.** Mary, from Rome. A believer in Rome greeted by Paul (Rom. 16:6), who noted her hard work on behalf of believers.

Clark Palmer

MASADA (Mă sa´ dă) A mesa on the western shore of the Dead Sea. It rises about 820 feet above the surrounding valleys and was used as a stronghold between 142 B.C. and A.D. 73. Jonathan Maccabeus first fortified the rock.

M

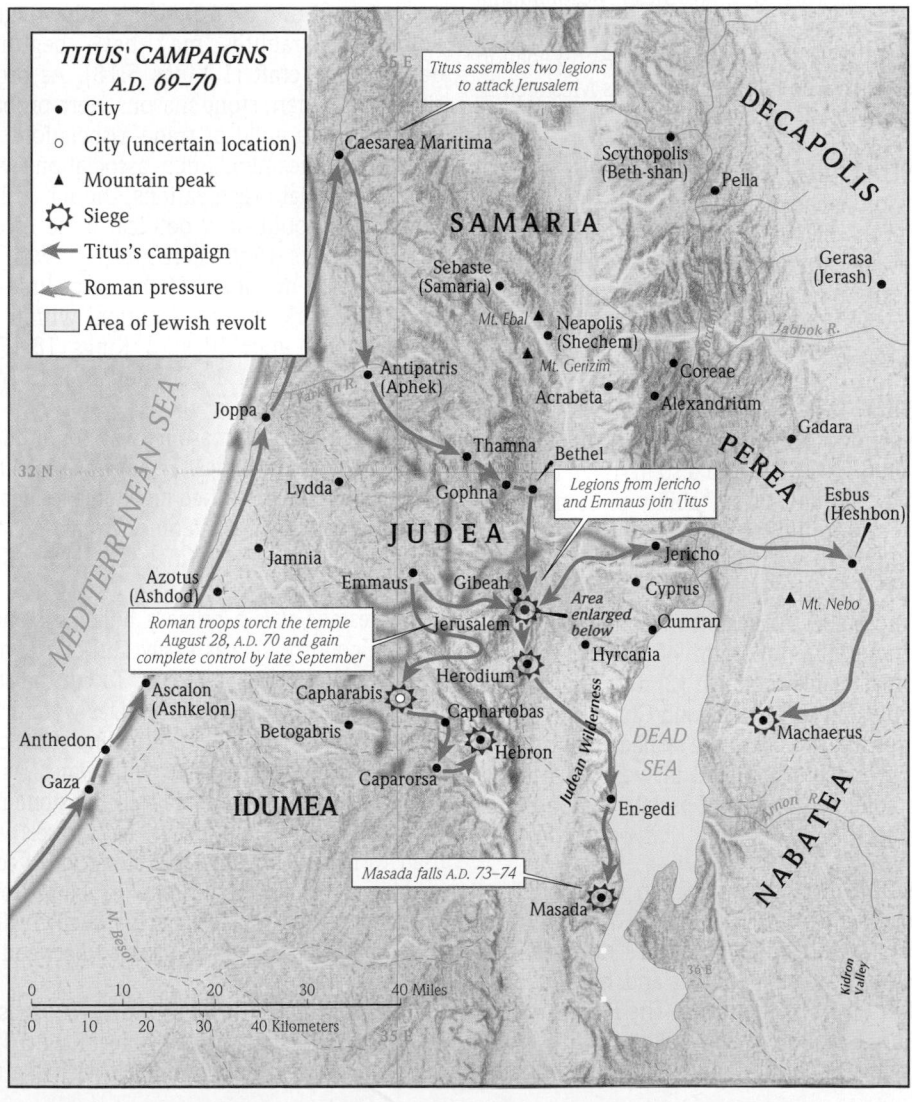

Herod the Great made it a monument to his building activity. A band of rebellious Jews held it briefly during the first revolt against Rome (A.D. 66–73). After a long struggle to recapture the fortress, the Tenth Legion raised an enormous siege ramp and broke through the walls. They found the bodies of over 900 men, women, and children, victims of a suicide pact to keep the Romans from taking them as prisoners.

MASCHIL (Mas´ kēl) See *Maskil.*

MASH (Măsh) Son of Aram (Gen. 10:23) in Table of Nations and thus original ancestor of Syrian tribal group, possibly from Mount Masius (Tur Abdin) in Northern Mesopotamia or the Mashu mountains of the Gilgamesh epic, probably the Lebanon and Anti-Lebanon Mountains. The name is copied as Meshech in 1 Chron. 1:17.

MASHAL (Mā´ shăl) **1.** City in the tribal territory of Asher later assigned to the Levites (1 Chron. 6:74). At Josh. 19:26; 21:30 the name appears as Misheal (KJV) or Mishal (modern translations). **2.** Technical Hebrew term for proverb, parable, simile. See *Proverbs, Book of; Wisdom and Wise Men.*

MASKIL (Mas´ kēl) Term *maskil* is in the superscription of Pss. 32; 42; 44; 45; 52–55; 74; 78; 88; 89; 142 and also in 47:7. The Septuagint translates it as "ability of comprehension," "intelligence," and the Vulgate translates it as "understanding," "intelligence." The origin and meaning of the term are uncertain. Suggested meanings are: (1) a didactic psalm (a psalm of wisdom, understanding, or instruction); (2) a skillful, artistic composition or song. Second Chronicles 30:22 mentions Levites who are skilled (*maskilim*) in singing and praising God in worship. Maskils were collected groups of psalms composed for worship. *Kyoungwon Choi*

MASONS Building craftsmen using brick or stone. The professional mason in Israel first appears in the Bible in David's time, though the craft was very ancient and highly developed in Egypt by that time. The Bible suggests that no Israelites were skilled in the art of quarrying, squaring, and setting fine building

Examples of Herodian masonry are visible around the Temple Mount in Jerusalem.

stones in David's time. David relied upon the king of Tyre for craftsmen (2 Sam. 5:11-12; 1 Chron. 22:2-4,14-18). Under the reign of Solomon, Israelites may have begun to develop this craft (1 Kings 5:18). As professional craftsmen, stone masons were probably members of a guild or trade association such as other tradesmen. Such associations were primarily social organizations, though in later times they could be a political force of concern to rulers (Acts 19:23-41). It was also common for members of the same trade to live and work in one location within the larger towns and cities (2 Kings 18:17; 1 Chron. 4:14; Neh. 11:35; Jer. 37:21; Matt. 27:7; Acts 18:3).

Dressed or ashlar masonry was not ordinarily used in private dwellings. The average man built his own home of sun-dried brick on a foundation of fieldstones. Biblical references to masons thus involve public works (2 Kings 12:11-15; 2 Kings 22:3-8; Ezra 3:7).

Limestone was a primary building stone in the hill country. It was easily cut, and it hardened when exposed to the air. To cut the stone loose from its bed, wooden wedges were driven into triangular slots cut along the line of the split. These wedges were soaked with water. As the wedges expanded, the force split the stone from the bed. Hammers, punches, and chisels were used to batter and dress the stone followed by rubbing with fine sandstone rubbing stones. Blocks could be squared and polished so finely that a blade could not be inserted between the joints.

Masons, under Herod's employ, cut massive limestone blocks as much as 46 feet long, 10 feet thick, and 10 feet high from quarries half a mile from where they were placed in the pediment of the temple mount. Some of these stones are estimated to weigh as much as 415 tons. They can be seen today in the southwest corner of the Wailing Wall. See *Architecture; Occupations and Professions.*   *Larry Bruce*

MASORA (Mả so´ rả) Hebrew term meaning "tradition," used for note added to the margins of manuscripts of the Masoretic text of the OT as a safeguard to transmission of the text. See *Bible Texts and Versions.*

MASREKAH (Măs´ rə kah) Place-name, perhaps meaning "vineyard." City in Edom whose king ruled the Edomites in the period before Israel had kings (Gen. 36:36; 1 Chron. 1:47). The site is perhaps Jebel el-Mushraq about 20 miles south-southwest of Ma'an. Eusebius (around A.D. 300) located Masrekah in Gabalene in northern Edom.

MASSA (Măs´ sả) Hebrew term with several meanings. **1.** Seventh son of Ishmael (Gen. 25:14; 1 Chron. 1:30). **2.** Arab tribe perhaps descended from 1. The Massa are listed among the people who paid tribute to King Tiglath-pileser III (745–727 B.C.) of Assyria. Some interpret the use of Massa in the titles of collections of proverbs (Prov. 30:1; 31:1) as referring to the nationality of the person mentioned (cp. RSV, JPS, NASB). **3.** Hebrew term for a load or burden (Exod. 23:5; Num. 4:24,32). **4.** Hebrew term found at the beginning of an OT book (Nahum, Habakkuk, Malachi) or a smaller unit identifying the nature of the following literary unit. Once thought to be the same as 3., it is now understood as a distinct word and is usually translated "oracle," "utterance," or "pronouncement." It often introduces a judgment oracle against a foreign nation (Isa. 13:1; 14:28; 15:1; 17:1; 19:1; 21:1,11,13; 23:1; Nah. 1:1; Zech. 9:1), against Israel (Isa. 22:1; 30:6; Ezek. 12:10; Hab. 1:1; Mal. 1:1), or against an individual (2 Kings 9:25). But it could also refer to a message of blessing or of blessing and judgment (cp. Jer. 23:33-34,36,38; Zech. 12:1; Mal. 1:1).
                    E. Ray Clendenen

MASSAH (Măs´ sah) Place-name meaning "to test, try." Stopping place during the wilderness wandering near the base of Mount Horeb (Sinai). Moses gave the name in response to the people's desire to put God to the test by demanding water (Exod. 17:7). Massah became a reminder of Israel's disobedience or hardness of heart (Deut. 6:16; 9:22; Ps. 95:8). Massah often appears together with Meribah (meaning "to strive with, contend, find fault with"; Exod. 17:7; Deut. 33:8; Ps. 95:8). Deuteronomy 33:8 gives a poetic account of the origin of the Levitical priesthood at Massah.

MAST Long pole rising from a ship's keel which supports a sail (Prov. 23:34; Isa. 33:23; Ezek. 27:5). See *Ships, Sailors, and Navigation.*

MASTER Scripture uses master in two basic senses: in authority and teacher. **1.** As one in authority, master applies to slaveholders and to heads of households (which in biblical times frequently included slaves or servants). Greek terms translated master (of servants or a household) include *despotes, kurios, oikodespotes* (Mark 13:35; Luke 13:25; 14:21; 16:13; Eph. 6:9). **2.** KJV regularly translated the Greek *didaskalos* (teacher) as master in the Gospels (Matt. 8:19; 9:11). KJV twice rendered *kathegetes* (guide, teacher) as master (Matt. 23:8,10). KJV sometimes also translated *rabbi* (rabbi, teacher) and *rabboni* (my rabbi, my teacher) as master (Matt. 26:25; Mark 9:5; John 4:31). Modern translations render the above terms as teacher or rabbi. Luke often uses *epistates* (manager, chief) where Matthew and Mark have teacher (*didaskalos*), rabbi, or Lord (e.g., Luke 5:5; 8:24,45; 9:33,49; 17:13).

MATHUSALA (Mả thū´ sả là) (KJV, NT) Ancestor of Christ (Luke 3:37). See *Methuselah.*

MATRED (Mả´ trĕd) Personal name possibly meaning "spear." The Hebrew text understands Matred to be the mother of Mehetabel (Gen. 36:39; 1 Chron. 1:50). The earliest Greek and standard Latin translations take Matred to be Mehetabel's father.

MATRI, MATRITES (Mā´ trī) The family within the tribe of Benjamin from which Saul came (1 Sam. 10:21).

MATRIX KJV term meaning "womb" (Exod. 13:12,15; 34:19; Num. 3:12; 18:15).

MATTAN (Măt´ tăn) Personal name meaning "gift of God." **1.** Queen Athaliah's priest of Baal in Jerusalem killed in Jehoiada's purge (2 Kings 11:18). **2.** Father of Shephatiah, a contemporary of Jeremiah (Jer. 38:1).

MATTANAH (Măt´ tă nah) Place-name meaning "gift." Stopping place in the wilderness (Num. 21:18-19). The site is perhaps identical with Khirbet el-Medeiyineh, about 12 miles southeast of Madeba. Pottery shards at that site indicate occupation from before 1200 to about 800 B.C.

MATTANIAH (Măt tă nī´ ah) Personal name meaning "gift of Yah." **1.** Tabernacle musician-prophet in David's time (1 Chron. 25:4). **2.** Ancestor of Jahaziel (2 Chron. 20:14). **3.** Member of the Asaphite subclan of Levites who participated in Hezekiah's reforms (2 Chron. 29:13). **4.** Original name of King Zedekiah of Judah (2 Kings 24:17). **5.** Asaphite among the first to return from exile (1 Chron. 9:15). **6.** Levitic leader of the temple choir in Zerubbabel's time (Neh. 11:17,22). **7.** Levitic temple gatekeeper (Neh. 12:25). **8.** Father of the Levite Shemaiah (Neh. 12:35). **9.** Grandfather of Hanan (Neh. 13:13). **10.–13.** Four of those who returned from exile with foreign wives (Ezra 10:26-27,30,37). Some of 5.–13. may be identical.

MATTATHA (Măt´ tă thă) Grandson of King David and ancestor of Christ (Luke 3:31).

MATTATHIAS (Măt tă thī´ ăs) **1.** Two ancestors of Christ (Luke 3:25-26). **2.** Priest whose refusal to obey Antiochus' decree to offer sacrifice initiated the Maccabean revolt (1 Macc. 2). **3.** Four high priests from 5 B.C. to A.D. 65. See *Intertestamental History and Literature; High Priest.*

MATTATTAH (Măt´ tăt tah) Personal name meaning "gift." Layman with foreign wife (Ezra 10:33).

MATTENAI (Măt´ tə nī) Personal name meaning "my gift." **1.** Priestly contemporary of the high priest Joiakim (Neh. 12:19). **2. and 3.** Two laymen with foreign wives (Ezra 10:33,37).

MATTHAN (Măt´ thăn) An ancestor of Christ (Matt. 1:15).

MATTHAT (Măt´ thăt) Two ancestors of Christ (Luke 3:24,29).

MATTHEW (Măth´ yū) Personal name meaning "the gift of Yahweh." A tax collector Jesus called to be an apostle (Matt. 9:9; 10:3). Matthew's office was located on the main highway that ran from Damascus, down the Jordan Valley to Capernaum then westward to Acre to join the coastal road to Egypt or southward to Jerusalem. His duty was to collect "toll" or "transport" taxes from both local merchants and farmers carrying their goods to market as well as distant caravans passing through Galilee. He was an employee of Herod Antipas. Matthew knew the value of goods of all description: wool, flax, linen, pottery, brass, silver, gold, barley, olives, figs, wheat. He knew the value of local and foreign monetary systems. He spoke the local Aramaic language as well as Greek. Because Matthew had leased his "toll" collecting privileges by paying the annual fee in advance, he was subjected to the criticism of collecting more than enough, growing wealthy on his "profit." Thus he was hated by his fellow Jews.

Matthew is the same person as Levi, a tax collector (Mark 2:14; Luke 5:27), and thus the son of Alphaeus. James the son of Alphaeus is also listed among the apostles (Mark 3:18; Matt. 10:3; Luke 6:15; Acts 1:13). This indicates that both Matthew and his (half) brother were in close association with Jesus. Mary, the mother of James, keeps the vigil at the foot of the cross with Mary, the mother of Jesus (Matt. 27:55-56; Mark 15:40). If the James mentioned here is the same as the son of Alphaeus, then we have a larger family closely associated with the family of Jesus.

Later legendary accounts tell of Matthew's travel to Ethiopia where he became associated with Candace, identified with the eunuch of Acts 8:27. The legends tell us of Matthew's martyrdom in that country.

Matthew had the gifts to be trained as a disciple, could keep meticulous records, and was a potential recorder/author of the Gospel. From earliest times Christians affirmed that Matthew wrote the Gospel that bears his name. See *Disciple; Matthew, Gospel of; Publican.*

Oscar S. Brooks

MATTHEW'S BIBLE The Thomas Matthew Bible was a revision of Tyndale's and Coverdale's versions likely prepared by John Rogers in 1537 in Antwerp. See *Bible Translations.*

MATTHEW, GOSPEL OF Opening book of the NT which appropriately begins with the declaration, "the historical record of Jesus Christ" (HCSB). When we begin reading this book today, we should, however, have in mind its ending (28:18-20). Matthew's purpose was to show that Jesus had the power to command His disciples to spread His gospel throughout all the world.

Matthew 28:16-20 is the scene of the resurrected Jesus meeting His disciples on a hill in Galilee. Jesus immediately declared His absolute authority: "All authority has been given to Me in heaven and on earth" (HCSB). The disciples would be reminded of many experiences during Jesus' ministry that proved His authority. Now with this knowledge of the resurrection, it was evident to them that He had received His authority from God. Jesus then gave the disciples a Commission to "make disciples of all nations" (HCSB). A disciple is (1) one who willingly becomes a learner of the Master's teaching and seeks to follow His example by implementing His teaching, and (2) who passes on to others what one has learned. Hearing Jesus' command, the disciples recalled His teaching and fellowship. Now they were called on to carry forward His mission. Jesus said they would make disciples as they went away from their meeting with Him. Their activities would include baptizing new disciples into the lordship of Jesus. This is the original commitment. The disciples would pass on to others all that Jesus taught them. In telling this story Matthew emphasized that Jesus has total authority, His teachings must be transmitted, and His message is for all people. If we, the modern readers, will keep these three themes in mind as we read the Gospel from the beginning, we will discover that the author

shows us how Jesus demonstrated His authority, the teachings He employed, and His concern for all nations.

The Gospel is easily divided into seven sections: a beginning and an end with five teaching sections between. Because of this, Matthew has been recognized for its emphasis on the teachings of Jesus.

Matthew 1:1–4:25 opens the Gospel with the royal genealogy and builds to the proclamation of God in 3:17: "This is My beloved Son." The genealogies confirm Jesus' authoritative, kingly lineage and remind the reader of His relation to all nations by mentioning Tamar, Rahab, Ruth, and the wife of a Hittite. The wise men (Gentiles) came seeking the King of the Jews (2:2). The angel affirmed Jesus' divine nature to Joseph. The child received a messianic name (1:18-23). Joseph took the holy family to Gentile territory (Egypt) to escape the threats of Herod. When Jesus came to John for baptism, the voice from heaven proclaimed Him as God's Son. As God's Son, Jesus had the authority and power to confront Satan and overcome. Jesus then went to Galilee of the Gentiles (4:15) to begin His public ministry. This opening section makes it obvious that Jesus is designated by God to be the Messiah with authority—for all nations.

Matthew 5:1–7:29 is commonly called the Sermon on the Mount. It should be called the Teaching from the Mount since that is what the text calls it (5:2). While teaching and preaching overlap, teaching emphasizes the essential principles that must be passed on to maintain the discipline or movement at hand. Jesus gave His essential doctrine in this teaching. He stressed the importance of His commandments in 5:19; emphasized the authoritative nature of His teachings by declaring, "But I tell you" (5:22,28,32,39,44) and was recognized by the crowds as a Teacher with authority (7:28-29). Matthew presented Jesus as an authoritative Teacher. When the disciples went out to teach, they knew what to teach.

Matthew 8:1–10:42 opens with a series of 10 miracles demonstrating Jesus' authority over disease, natural catastrophes, demons, and death. What He had demonstrated verbally in the teachings on the Mount, Jesus acted out through displays of power. His disciples were amazed, "even the winds and the sea obey Him!" (8:27 HCSB), and the crowds stood

M

amazed that He had the authority to forgive sins (9:8). His ministry to a Gentile centurion is in this section also. After demonstrating His power, Jesus gave authority to His disciples to go out and heal and teach as He had done (10:1), thus preparing them for their final Commission in 28:18-20. By continuing the emphasis on authority, teaching, and Gentiles, Jesus prepared His immediate disciples for their task after His death. Matthew continues to teach later generations of believers about Jesus' power and concern for all mankind.

Matthew 11:1–13:52 shows various people reacting to Jesus' authority. Various responses are noted in chapter 11, including Jesus' thanksgiving that the "infants" understand (vv. 25-30). When the leaders rejected Jesus' authority in chapter 12, Matthew implied that Jesus would go to the Gentiles by quoting Isaiah the prophet (12:18-21). Jesus continued His teaching in parables to those who were willing to listen (13:10-13). Therefore, when Jesus commissioned His disciples to go into all the world and teach, they were aware that He had already begun the movement by His example in His earthly ministry.

Matthew 13:53–18:35 opens with the story of Jesus' teaching in the synagogue in Nazareth. The people had the same response to Jesus' teaching as the crowds did at the end of the Sermon on the Mount. They were astonished (cp. 13:54; 7:28). Although Jesus presented His authoritative teaching, His hometown people rejected it (13:57). His disciples accepted Him (14:33) and so did the Gentile woman (15:22). Again Jesus taught authoritatively and related to Gentiles.

Matthew 19:1–25:46 makes the transition from Galilee to Jerusalem. Jesus dramatically presented His kingly authority by His triumphal entry into Jerusalem (21:1-9) and by cleansing the temple (21:10-17). Then, while He was teaching, the chief priests and elders challenged Him saying, "By what authority are You doing these things?" (21:23 HCSB). Jesus answered with parables and other teachings (21:28–22:46). Jesus warned the people about the examples of the Pharisees and Sadducees (23:1-38). He then concentrated His teaching only on His disciples (24:1–25:46). They could recall this when He commanded them to teach

what He taught. The modern believer must also hear what Jesus taught and teach it to others.

Matthew 26:1–28:20 has no teaching situations, but it tells of the conspiracy ending in Jesus' execution. In the midst of the trial scene, Jesus was asked if He was the Messiah. Jesus responded by affirming His authority: "You have said it" (26:64 HCSB). Pilate, a Gentile, recognized Jesus' kingly authority, placarding over the cross: "THIS IS JESUS THE KING OF THE JEWS" (27:37). The Gentile centurion proclaimed, "This man really was God's Son" (27:54). As in the birth story, so in the end, the author stressed Jesus' divine, kingly authority and emphasized the inclusion of the Gentiles.

When the resurrected Lord declared His authority to His disciples in 28:18, they understood because they had seen His authority displayed as they lived with Jesus. When modern readers come to 28:18, they understand because Matthew has shown us Jesus' authority from the beginning.

Matthew presented Jesus as the "Son of God," a term that appears 23 times in this Gospel. While the virgin birth story affirms Jesus' Sonship, the quotation from Hos. 11:1 (Matt. 2:15) confirms it. Twice God proclaimed Jesus' Sonship: at His baptism (3:17) and at the transfiguration (17:5). Peter confessed it (16:16). Jesus attested to His Sonship in the Lord's prayer (6:9), His thanksgiving to God (11:25-26), and the garden of Gethsemane (26:39). The author wanted the reader to be aware that Jesus, the Son of God, is the One crucified on the cross; so Jesus called out to "my God" from the cross (27:46), and a Gentile centurion confessed that the dying One "really was God's Son" (27:54).

Matthew wanted the reader to be aware that forgiveness of sins comes through the death of the divine Son of God. The angel had told Joseph that Jesus would "save His people from their sins" (1:21). Jesus Himself had assured His disciples that His destiny was "to give His life—a ransom for many" (20:28). Jesus left behind a continuing reminder of His role in the forgiveness of sins when He instituted the Lord's Supper, "For this is My blood of the covenant, which is shed for many for the forgiveness of sins" (26:28).

It is impossible to know the exact date when the Gospel of Matthew was written. Some contemporary writers date it as early as A.D. 60, some as late as A.D. 95. The place of writing was probably some place along the coast of Phoenicia or Syria such as Antioch. This is because of Matthew's several references to Gentiles, a reference to Phoenicia and Syria, and the terms (in the Greek text) used for coins (17:24,27). Although the Gospel nowhere identifies the author and many modern Bible students point to a complex history of editing and collecting sources, Matthew, the tax collector, the son of Alphaeus has been identified as the author since the second century. See *Matthew.*

Outline

I. Jesus' Birth Fulfilled Prophecy (1:1–2:23).

II. The Obedient Jesus Invites People to Kingdom Service (3:1–4:25).

III. Jesus Taught God's Way to Live (5:1–7:29).

IV. Jesus' Power and Call Reveal His Authority (8:1–10:42).

V. Jesus' Work Led to Controversy (11:1–12:50).

VI. Jesus Taught about the Kingdom (13:1-52).

VII. Jesus Confronts Conflict and Critical Events (13:53–17:27).

VIII. Jesus Gives Insight into Life in His Kingdom (18:1–20:34).

IX. Religious Authorities Reject Jesus as Messiah (21:1–23:36).

X. Jesus Has the Authoritative Word about the Future (23:37–25:46).

XI. Jesus Prepared for Death, Obeying God and Fulfilling Scripture (26:1-56).

XII. Jesus Conquered Death (26:57–28:20).

Oscar Brooks

MATTHIAS (Măt thī´ ås) Shortened form of Mattathias ("gift of Yah"). Disciple who followed Jesus from the time of John's ministry of baptism until Jesus' ascension, who was chosen by lot and prayer to succeed Judas as an apostle and official witness to the resurrection (Acts 1:20-26). This selection was regarded as necessary to fulfill Scripture concerning the band of apostles (Ps. 69:25; Acts 1:20). Scripture mentions nothing further about Matthias. See *Disciple; Acts, Book of.*

MATTITHIAH (Măt tĭ thī´ ah) Personal name meaning "gift of Yah." **1.** Levite whom David appointed as a tabernacle musician with special responsibility for leading lyre music

(1 Chron. 15:18,21; 25:3,21). Mattithiah also ministered before the ark (1 Chron. 16:5). **2.** Levite baker (1 Chron. 9:31). **3.** Layman with a foreign wife (Ezra 10:43). **4.** Man standing beside Ezra at the public reading of the Law (Neh. 8:4).

MATTOCK Tool used for digging. See *Tools, Agricultural Tools.*

MAUL KJV term for a club (HCSB, NASB, NIV, REB) or war club (RSV) at Prov. 25:18. See *Arms and Armor.*

MAUNDY THURSDAY See *Holy Week; Church Year.*

MAW KJV term for the fourth stomach of a cud-chewing animal. The "maw" was among the choice cuts of meat reserved for the priests' portion (Deut. 18:3). Modern translations use stomach (HCSB, NASB, REB, NRSV) or inner parts (NIV).

MAZZAROTH (Măz´ zå rŏth) Puzzling term in Job 38:32. Either a proper name for a particular constellation (KJV, NRSV), a collective term for the 12 signs of the Zodiac (KJV margin, REB), or a general term meaning constellation or stars (NASB, NIV, TEV; cp. 2 Kings 23:5).

MEADOW Tract of grassland, especially moist, low-lying pasture. The KJV used meadow at two passages. At Gen. 41:2,18 the reference is clearly to stretches of reed grass or papyrus thickets common along the Nile. The term rendered meadow in the phrase "meadows of Geba" (Judg. 20:33 KJV) is obscure. The NASB simply transliterates the phrase (Maareh-geba). In modern translations "meadows" illustrate God's blessing (Ps. 65:13 NASB, NIV, NRSV [pastures, HCSB]; Isa. 30:23; 44:4 NIV). Meadows are also used in pictures of God's judgment (Jer. 25:37; Hos. 4:16 NIV; Hos. 9:13 NASB; Zeph. 2:6 NRSV).

MEAH, TOWER OF (Mē´ ah) KJV transliteration of a Hebrew phrase meaning "Tower of the Hundred" (Neh. 3:1; 12:39). See *Hundred, Tower of.*

MEAL OFFERING See *Sacrifice and Offering, Grain Offering.*

MEALS See *Banquet; Food.*

MEARAH (Mə ā´ rah) Place-name meaning "cave." Part of the territory left unconquered following Joshua's conquest. The site is perhaps the caves called Mughar Jezzin located east of Sidon (Josh. 13:4).

MEASURING LINE Cord used to measure length (cp. 1 Kings 7:15,23; 2 Chron. 4:3). References to a measuring line point to the restoration of Jerusalem (Jer. 31:39; Zech. 2:1; cp. Ezek. 47:3).

MEASURING REED Ezekiel's measuring reed was a cane about 10 feet long used as a measuring tool (Ezek. 40:3,5-8; cp. Rev. 21:15-16). See *Weights and Measures.*

MEAT In modern English meat refers to animal tissue used as food, frequently in contrast to plant products. Modern translations use meat in this sense, where KJV used the term "flesh" (e.g., Num. 11:4-33; Judg. 6:19-21; 1 Sam. 2:13,15). KJV used "meat" in two senses: for food, especially solid food in contrast to drink (for example, 1 Cor. 3:2; Heb. 5:12,14); and for a meal, especially the evening meal (e.g., 1 Sam. 20:5; Matt. 26:7). The KJV used "meat" in the general sense of food about 250 times. The context frequently indicates that flesh is not in view (Gen. 1:29-30; Ezek. 47:12; Hab. 3:17). A special case of the use of "meat" to mean food is the frequent use of the term "meat offering" (about 130 times in the OT). Here "meat offering" means food offering in contrast to a libation (drink offering). Modern translations render the expression as cereal or grain offering. Modern translations, for example NRSV, frequently replace the KJV's "meat" with a more specific term in light of the context: provisions (Gen. 45:23); scraps [of food] (Judg. 1:7); present (2 Sam. 11:8); meager fare (2 Sam. 12:3); solid food (1 Cor. 3:2; Heb. 5:12). KJV also used "meat" in the sense of a meal. Modern translations generally replace the KJV's "sit at meat" with "sit at table" which means to take a meal (1 Sam. 20:5; Matt. 9:10; 26:7; Mark 2:15). "To come to meat" (1 Sam. 20:27) is to come to supper. A "morsel of meat" (Heb. 12:16) is "a single meal" (NRSV).

Dining area in a villa in Pompeii with spaces for several persons to be seated while eating a meal.

MEAT OFFERING KJV term used about 130 times in the OT for a food offering in contrast to a drink offering (libation). Modern translations render the term "grain offering." See *Sacrifice and Offering.*

MEAT TO IDOLS Offerings of animal flesh sacrificed to a god. Most religions of the ancient Near East had laws regarding offering sacrifices to the god(s). Israel's laws are in Lev. 1–8 and 16–17. Part of the ritual was for the people to eat some of the sacrifice. They believed that God and the people became closer by partaking of the same animal. Since most early Christians had Jewish backgrounds, a problem arose in the church when Gentile converts ate meat that had been offered to idols. The Jerusalem council decided that Christians should abstain from eating meat offered to idols so as not to cause weak believers to stumble. Paul echoed this sentiment in 1 Cor. 8:13.

MEAT, UNCLEAN See *Clean, Cleanness.*

MEBUNNAI (Mə bŭn´ nī) Personal name meaning "building of Yah." One of David's 30 elite warriors (2 Sam. 23:27). The name possibly resulted from scribal confusion of the first and third letters in the Hebrew name Sibbecai which replaces Mebunnai in the parallel lists (1 Chron. 11:29; 27:11).

MECHERATHITE (Mə kâr´ à thīt) The title of Hepher, one of David's warriors (1 Chron. 11:36). Mecherathite means inhabitant of Mecherah. The site is unknown unless it is to be identified with Maacah (2 Sam. 23:34).

MECONAH (Mə cō´ nah) Form of Mekonah preferred by modern translations.

MEDAD (Mē´ dăd) Personal name meaning "beloved." Israelite layman who prophesied in the wilderness camp (Num. 11:26-27). See *Eldad.*

MEDAN (Mē´ dăn) Personal name meaning "judgment." Third son of Abraham and Keturah (Gen. 25:2; 1 Chron. 1:32) and ancestor of a little-known Arab tribe. The Medan should perhaps be identified with the Badan, a people conquered by Tiglath-pileser III of Assyria (732 B.C.). Others argue for textual corruption of the term Media.

MEDEBA (Měd´ ə bȧ) Place-name meaning "water of quiet." City in Transjordan on the main north-south road (the King's Highway) about 25 miles south of Amman. The strategic importance of Medeba is indicated by frequent references to its changing hands. Sihon King of the Amorites took Medeba from Moab only to have the area pass into Israel's control (Num. 21:24,26,30). Medeba was included in Reuben's tribal allotment (Josh. 13:9,16). According to the Moabite stone, Omri King of Israel (885–874 B.C.) recaptured Medeba. Mesha King of Moab retook the city during the reign of Omri's son. An alliance of Israel, Judah, and Edom recaptured the city but quickly withdrew (2 Kings 3:25,27). Jeroboam II again secured control of the city of Israel (2 Kings 14:25). Isaiah 15:2 reflects the city's return to Moab. The site of Medeba is that of the modern city of Madeba.

MEDES, MEDIA (Mēdz, Mē´ dĭ ȧ) The region south and southwest of the Caspian Sea in the Zagros Mountains inhabited by the Medes, an Aryan people from north and west of the Caspian Sea. It is north of Elam and west of Assyria. The traditional capital of the region was Ecbatana.

Before 1500 B.C. the region was part of the Mitanni kingdom. Later the Elamites controlled the region and its nomadic inhabitants. The people known as the Medes entered the area over a long period between 1400 and 1000 B.C.

The Medes were first reported in history by the Assyrian Shalmaneser III about 850 B.C. They were a group of nomadic tribes rather than a state or kingdom. The Assyrians controlled them or sought to for more than 200 years, though the Medes enjoyed some periods of freedom before the Scythians conquered them in 653 B.C. Sometime before this, Deioces were united and organized the Medes. Despite the Scythians' invasion, the Medes continued to develop as a kingdom.

The greatest Median king was Cyaxares (625–585 B.C.). He was the third ruler of the united Medes and was able to defeat the Scythians. Afterwards Cyaxares turned his attention to the Assyrians, attacking Nineveh, the Assyrian capital. Before Nineveh fell in 612 B.C., Cyaxares conquered Asshur, the ancient center of the Assyrian Empire. Then, with the aid of the Scythians and Babylonians and others, Nineveh was taken. The end of the Assyrian Empire was near.

Babylon and Media divided the Assyrian Empire with Media taking the land east and north of the Tigris River. Nebuchadnezzar II and Cyaxares' granddaughter wed to seal the pact. The Medes turned their attention to the north and toward Asia Minor. After a five-year war with Lydia, Cyaxares concluded a peace in 584 B.C., again sealing it with a marriage. His son Astyages married the daughter of the Lydian king. Astyages became king of the Medes when Cyaxares died.

The end of the Median kingdom came with the rise of Cyrus II, founder of the Persian Empire. Cyrus was king of Anshan and a vassal to Astyages. Indeed, Cyrus' mother was Astyages' daughter. About 550 B.C., encouraged by Babylon, Cyrus rebelled against the Medes. His rebellion led to the defeat of Astyages. The kingdom of the Medes was replaced by the kingdom of the Persians.

Though conquered by the Persians, the Medes continued to hold a place of honor in the Persian Empire. Media was the second-most important portion of the Empire after Persia itself. Biblical references frequently combine "the Medes and the Persians" (Dan. 5:28; cp. Esther 1:19; 10:2). The kings of the Persian Empire are called "the kings of Media and Persia" (Dan. 8:20). The most famous Mede in Scripture is Darius the Mede (Dan. 5:31; 9:1). Media is sometimes referred to as the instrument of God, especially against Babylon (Isa. 13:17; 21:2; Jer. 51:11,28), but the Medes also

M

M

had to drink the cup of God's judgment (Jer. 25:25). Their final appearance in Scripture is the presence of Jews or Jewish converts from there at Pentecost (Acts. 2:9). See *Assyria; Babylonia; Cyrus; Darius; Elam; Persia.*   *Albert F. Bean*

MEDIATOR The term "mediator" occurs frequently in the Bible, though more frequently in the NT than in the OT. The idea of mediation, though, permeates Scripture, with human mediation being common in the OT, while the mediation of Christ is one of the key themes of the new covenant.

Old Testament In the Hebrew Scriptures priests and prophets are mediators, and, to a lesser degree, kings are as well. In older texts before the initiation of the sacrificial system, fathers stood the mediatorial role for their families (Gen. 8:20; 12:7-8; 15:9-11). The prophet stands between God and man and communicates God's will and word. Moses was the one through whom God revealed his plan for the covenant nation (Deut. 18:18-22). God raised up the prophet Samuel, to whom he spoke directly (1 Sam. 3:1-21). The later prophets were regularly the instruments of God's redemptive and corrective revelation (Isa. 1:2-20; Amos 1–2), and they were considered the "watchmen" of impending destruction who interceded for Israel (Ezek. 33:1-9; cp. Num. 14:11-19).

Priests were mediators also of the Word of God and interpreted his will by teaching Scripture (Neh. 8:1-8), and by appeal to the Urim and Thummim (Exod. 28:30; Lev. 8:8), but more than that, they stood between God and the sinfulness of Israel. The Levites were sanctified to do the work of ministry in the tabernacle/temple and had direct access to God in the services of the sanctuary. Between God and His people is fixed a sin-stained gulf that can only be breached by the sacrifice of an unblemished member of the herd or flock. These sacrifices can only be offered by an authorized person, a priest ordained by birthright and anointed for the task (Exod. 28–29). The priest derived his authority from the system, inaugurated by God's command to Moses; the system did not derive its authority from the priest. These duties were carried out by the priests daily in the various sacrifices (Lev. 1–7), though there were special sacrifices at appointed times, especially the Day of Atonement sacrifice performed only by the high priest once a year (Lev. 16).

In a lesser sense the king stood as mediator, since he was "Yahweh's anointed" (1 Sam. 16:6). As such, he was the type of the true mediatorial Messiah from the line of David who would be prophet, priest, and king (Isa. 61:1-3).

New Testament God the Son became incarnate as a man and fulfilled (and continues to fulfill) the role as the perfect mediator between God and man. Paul declared that man is unable to commune with God unless he comes to Him through Jesus, because there is only one mediator "between God and man, a man, Christ Jesus" (1 Tim. 2:5 HCSB). Christ, who is superior to Moses (Heb. 3:1-6), mediates a new covenant (8:6; 9:15; 12:24) based upon his "once for all" substitutionary death on the cross (7:27) that guarantees that it will be a better covenant (7:22). Jesus takes on the three-fold office as prophet, priest, and king in order to serve as the mediator of His people. As High Priest of the people of God, Jesus has offered up Himself as the propitiation for our sins, turning God's wrath from us (Rom. 3:25, 1 John 2:2) and bringing peace by reconciling us to God (Eph. 2:12-17; Rom. 5:1). Christ's ministry as mediator continues on as He sits enthroned in heaven. Because Jesus was raised and continues to live forever, so does His priesthood, which assures Christians that He will always save and intercede for them (Heb. 7:24-25; Rom. 8:34). Through the mediatorial work on the cross believers can boldly enter the sanctuary (holy of holies) and approach the throne of grace to find aid (Heb. 4:14; 9:12; 10:19-23). Christ, being both fully God and fully man, is a mediator and high priest who can sympathize with our weaknesses and therefore assures us that we will receive grace and mercy (Heb. 4:15-16).   *Chad Brand*

MEDICINE See *Diseases.*

MEDITATION Act of calling to mind some supposition, pondering upon it, and correlating it to one's own life. A wicked individual meditates upon violence (Prov. 24: 2). The meditation of a righteous person contemplates God or His great spiritual truths (Pss. 63:6; 77:12; 119:15,23,27,48,78,97,148; 143:5). He hopes to please God by meditation (Ps. 19:14). Thus meditation by God's people is a reverent act of worship. Through it they commune with God and are thereby renewed spiritually.

Most references to meditation occur in the OT, especially in the Psalms. The Hebrew words for meditation primarily were derived from two separate roots. The first (*hagah*) literally means "to utter in a low sound." The word is used to denote the growling of a lion (Isa. 31:4) or the cooing of a dove (Isa. 38:14). Therefore it has been suggested that in ancient Hebrew meditation Scripture frequently was recited in a low murmur. The second root word (*siach*) has the basic meaning of "to be occupied with," or "concerned about." Thus meditation is the repetitious going over of a matter in one's mind because it is the chief concern of life. The constant recollection of God's past deeds by the hearing of Scripture and repetition of thought produce confidence in God (Pss. 63:6-8; 104:34; 119:15,23,48,78,97,99,148; 143:5).

Meditation is only mentioned twice in the NT. Jesus instructed Christians to meditate beforehand on their attitude toward persecution (Luke 21:14). Paul advised Timothy to meditate on the matters about which Paul had written him (1 Tim. 4:15). Meditation is an important part of the Christian's relationship with Christ. See *Prayer.*   *LeBron Matthews*

MEDITERRANEAN SEA (Mĕd ĭ tẽr rā´ nə ăn) Designated in the OT and the NT simply as "the sea" (Josh. 16:8; Acts 10:6); also referred to as the "Western Sea" (Deut. 11:24 RSV, NIV); and as the "Sea of the Philistines" (Exod. 23:31). The Mediterranean Sea is an inland ocean extending about 2,200 miles from Gibraltar to the Lebanon coast and varies in width 100–600 miles. Most of the important nations of ancient times were either on the Mediterranean's shores or operated in its 2,200 miles of water: Israel, Syria, Greece, Rome, Egypt, Philistia, and Phoenicia. Strangely, nature has provided few natural harbors for Israel (Dor, Joppa, and Acco). The shoreline is almost straight. In many places a high ridge rises up sharply from behind a narrow strip of beach.

The Hebrews were not a seafaring people. A more apt description might be that they were a "sea-fearing" people. The Hebrew's fear of the sea was partially due to their desert origin; therefore, their culture developed chiefly around agriculture. The story of Jonah demonstrates the Hebrew's fear of the sea.

God exercises leadership over all creation. As part of God's creation, the sea is subservient to

M

Sunset over the Mediterranean Sea.

Him. He rules over the raging sea (Ps. 89:9) and causes a storm on it (Jon. 1:4).

For the Hebrews the Great Sea served as the western border for the land of Canaan (Num. 34:6) and the territory of Judah (Josh. 15:12). Only with the aid of the Phoenicians was Solomon able to assemble and operate a fleet of ships at Ezion Geber on the Red Sea. Timber was brought on rafts from Lebanon to Joppa (2 Chron. 2:16). Jehoshaphat's attempt at a navy ended in disaster (1 Kings 22:47-50). His ships were wrecked in the same harbor. Maritime commerce remained limited during most periods in Israel's history. Phoenicians were famous in the ancient world for their capacity as sailors and pilots.

Tyre eventually became the principal sea power in the Mediterranean. The extensive use of the Mediterranean by the Phoenicians was continued by the Romans who called it "Our Sea." Following the conquest of Palestine by Pompey in 63 B.C., traffic on the Mediterranean increased. This development helped to make possible the missionary activity of Paul, Silas, Barnabas, and others. Paul made three missionary journeys across the Mediterranean. Under Roman arrest, Paul made his final voyage across the Mediterranean Sea and shipwrecked (Acts 27). Paul's work involved such Mediterranean cities as Caesarea, Antioch, Troas, Corinth, Tyre, Sidon, Syracuse, Rome, and Ephesus. See *Phoenicia; Transportation and Travel; Tyre.*

Philip Lee

MEDIUM One possessed by (Lev. 20:6) or consulting (Deut. 18:11) a ghost or spirit of the dead, especially for information about the future. Acting as a medium was punishable by stoning (Lev. 20:27); consulting a medium, by exclusion from the congregation of Israel (Lev. 20:6). The transformation of Saul from one who expelled mediums (1 Sam. 28:3) to one who consulted a medium at En-dor (28:8-19) graphically illustrates his fall.

The Hebrew word translated medium (*'ov*) may refer to the spirit of a dead person, to the medium possessed by the spirit, or to images used to conjure up spirits. Manasseh made such images (2 Kings 21:6; 2 Chron. 33:6). Josiah destroyed them as part of his reforms (2 Kings 23:24). Saul's success in quickly locating a medium (1 Sam. 28:8) points both to the popu-

larity of the practice of consulting the dead and the difficulty of eradicating it.

Isaiah 8:19 suggests a possible connection between the consulting of mediums and ancestor worship. Those to be consulted are termed "fathers" and "gods" (cp. 1 Sam. 28:13 where Samuel is described as Elohim or "god"). The chirping and muttering of the spirits perhaps refers to the inarticulate sounds that must be interpreted by the medium. Consulting of mediums defiled the land and was described as prostitution. God's people were to trust God in times of distress and not resort to other "gods" in an attempt to learn the future.

MEEKNESS Moral quality of humility and gentleness, usually exhibited during suffering or difficulty and accompanied by faith in God. The word "meek" or "meekness" is often used in older versions of the Bible to translate the Hebrew word *anav*, the Greek word *praus*, and their related forms. The opposite of meekness is a harsh and proud wickedness that insists on immediate self-vindication (Prov. 3:33-34; 16:19; Isa. 32:7).

While the KJV employs "meek" or "meekness" 31 times, most modern English translations of the Bible favor "gentle" or "humble." Biblical meekness is usually not simply gentleness and humility but those qualities displayed with integrity during times of trial.

While God can be described as "meek" or "gentle" in His dealings with humanity (2 Sam. 22:36; Ps. 18:35), meekness is primarily a character trait associated with the human condition (Ps. 9:12; Prov. 15:33; 22:4; Zeph. 2:3). In the OT God often promises deliverance or salvation to the "meek," who are righteous persons suffering injustice, poverty, or oppression (Pss. 9:18; 10:12,17; 22:26; 25:9; 34:2; 37:11; 69:32; 76:9; 147:6; 149:4; Isa. 11:4; 29:19; 61:1). In the NT Jesus is presented as the preeminent example of meekness (Matt. 11:29; 21:5; 2 Cor. 10:1). Likewise, patient, humble, and faithful ("meek") disciples, although presently suffering the same rejection as their Messiah, will one day be vindicated by God (Matt. 5:5,11-12).

Paul and other NT writers teach that meekness should typify family, church, and societal relationships (Gal. 6:1; Eph. 4:2; Col. 3:12; 1 Tim. 6:11; 2 Tim. 2:25; Titus 3:2; James 1:21; 3:13; 1 Pet. 3:4,15). Such meekness is part of the "fruit of the Spirit," which is produced in believers by the indwelling Holy Spirit (Gal. 5:23). See *Humility; Patience; Poor in Spirit.*

Robert L. Plummer

MEGIDDO (Mə gĭd´ dō) Place-name, perhaps meaning "place of troops." One of the most strategic cities of Canaan since it guarded the main pass through the Carmel mountain range. This range was an obstacle along the International Coastal Highway that connected Egypt with Mesopotamia and even further destinations. Identified with current Tell el-Mutesellim, Megiddo had approximately 25 different eras of occupation during its life from the fourth millennium to the time of the Persian Empire. The city was very active while under Egyptian authority from the time of the patriarchs through to the judges (2000–1100 B.C.), but this golden age came to an end about 1125 B.C. when it was destroyed.

The city was allotted to Manasseh (Josh. 17:11; 1 Chron. 17:29) after the partial conquest of Joshua (Josh. 12:21), but neither it nor its surrounding villages were secured by the tribe. Due to its obvious strength, it was among many cities whose overthrow was delayed until later (Judg. 1:27). Deborah and Barak fought the

Manger and "hitching post" stones likely from a ninth-century B.C. storage area at Megiddo.

Canaanites and their leaders King Jabin and Sisera near the "waters of Megiddo," possibly the Wadi Qina running through the surrounding hills (Judg. 5:19).

When Megiddo was finally annexed to the nation Israel is not known. Probably by the time of David the city was serving Israel's defensive and security purposes. Certainly by the time of Solomon the city was firmly Israelite, since he

A view from Megiddo of the Valley of Jezreel with the town of Nazareth in the distance.

Model of ancient Megiddo.

M

fortified the city (1 Kings 9:15), including his mighty six-chambered gate which followed the pattern of his other two key fortress cities of Hazor and Gezer.

Megiddo was under the jurisdiction of Solomon's deputy, Baana (1 Kings 4:12). Buildings of current controversy have been excavated and explained variously as Solomon's or Ahab's stables, or storehouses where animals were loaded and unloaded.

During the divided monarchy, Megiddo's authority changed from Egyptian to Israelite to Assyrian. Five years into Jeroboam I's reign (ca. 920 B.C.), Pharaoh Shishak burst into both Israel and Judah, taking control of the coastal highway including Megiddo. However the Egyptian grip was not long lasting. Later the city was the place of death for the Judean king, Ahaziah, who was killed at the command of Jehu while fleeing from the scene of Jehoram's assassination (843 B.C., 2 Kings 9:27). Over a century later, the conquering Tiglath-pileser III chose Megiddo to be the seat of the Magidu administrative district in the Assyrian Empire (733 B.C.).

A Solomonic gateway area at ancient Megiddo.

After about 650 B.C. the city was no longer strongly fortified; however it was still strategically important. Josiah attempted to head off Pharaoh Neco II as he advanced along the coastal plain on his way to Carchemish (609 B.C.), but Josiah's attack ended when Neco II's archers fatally wounded him (2 Kings 23:29-30; 2 Chron. 35:22-24).

After returning from exile, Zechariah prophesied that the mourning for the false deities of Hadad and Rimmon (Hadad-rimmon) that took place in the plain below Megiddon (Megiddo) would be matched by Israel's mourning for its smitten Lord (Zech. 12:11).

Finally, in the NT, the Mount of Megiddo (har-Megiddon thus "Armageddon") will be where the kings of the world are gathered for that final battle in the last day of the Lord. Where Israel was initially frustrated during their conquest of Canaan is exactly where they will be victorious with Christ in the end (Rev 16:16).

Daniel C. Fredericks

MEGIDDON, VALLEY OF (Mə gĭd´ dŏn) KJV term for plain of Megiddo, the broad portion of the Jezreel Valley in the vicinity of Megiddo (Zech. 12:11). The passage perhaps alludes to the death of Josiah on this plain (2 Chron. 35:22). See *Megiddo*.

MEHETABEEL (Mə hĕt´ á bēl) Personal name meaning "God does good." Ancestor of Shemiah, a contemporary of Nehemiah (Neh. 6:10). Modern translations use the form Mehetabel.

MEHETABEL (Mə hĕt´ á bĕl) Personal name meaning "God does good." Wife of King Hadar of Edom (Gen. 36:39; 1 Chron. 1:50). Modern translations follow the Hebrew and also use Mehetabel for the KJV's Mehetabeel (Neh. 6:10).

MEHIDA (Mə hī´ dà) Personal name meaning "bought." Family of temple servants (KJV "Nethinim") at Ezra 2:52; Neh. 7:54.

MEHIR (Mē´ hĭr) Personal name meaning "purchased." Descendant of Judah (1 Chron. 4:11).

MEHOLAH (Mə hō´ lah) (TEV) or **MEHO-LATHITE** (Mə hō là thīt) Title meaning inhabitant of Abel-Meholah, given to Adriel, Saul's son-in-law (1 Sam. 18:19; 2 Sam. 21:8). Abel-Meholah is located in Gilead about 14 miles southeast of Beth-shean.

MEHUJAEL (Mə hū´ jā ĕl) Personal name meaning "struck by God" or "priest of God." Son of Irad (Gen. 4:18). Some interpreters see the name as a variant form of Mahalelel (Gen. 5:12-17).

MEHUMAN (Mə hū´ măn) Personal name meaning "trusty." Eunuch serving the Persian king Ahasuerus (Esther 1:10).

MEHUNIM (Mə hū´ nĭm) KJV form of Meunim or Meunites, an Arab tribe whose name likely derives from the city of Ma'an about 12 miles southeast of Petra. The Meunites raided Judah during the reign of Jehoshaphat (873–849 B.C.) according to 2 Chron. 20:1 (NASB, NIV, REB, NRSV following the Greek translation; the Hebrew text reads "Ammonites"). Uzziah (783–742 B.C.) subdued the Mehunites (2 Chron. 26:7). During the reign of Hezekiah (727–698 B.C.), Israelites dislocated the Meunites from the vicinity of Gedor in Transjordan about 18 miles north-northwest of Heshbon (1 Chron. 4:41; KJV, "habitations"). The Meunites are listed as temple servants in the postexilic period (Ezra 2:50; Neh. 7:52). They were perhaps the descendants of prisoners of war.

MEJARKON (Mĕ jär´ kŏn) Name meaning "waters of Jarkon" or "pale-green waters." Stream in the territory of Dan (Josh. 19:46), probably the Nahr el-'Auja ("winding river"), which, fed by springs at Ras el-'Ain about 10 miles from the coast, flows year-round to the Mediterranean about four miles north of Joppa.

MEKERATHITE (Mĕ kē´ rȧ thīt) (NIV) See *Mecherathite.*

MEKONAH (Mə kō´ nah) Place-name meaning "standing." KJV form of Meconah, town in southern Judah between Ziklag and Ain-rimmon (Neh. 11:28). The site is perhaps identical with Madmannah or Machbena (1 Chron. 2:49).

MELATIAH (Mĕ lȧ tī´ ah) Personal name meaning "Yah has set free." Man who assisted Nehemiah in building the wall (Neh. 3:7).

MELCHI (Mĕl´ kī) Personal name meaning "my king." Two ancestors of Christ (Luke 3:24,28).

MELCHIAH (Mĕl kī´ ah) (KJV, Jer. 21:1) See *Malchijah.*

MELCHISEDEC (Mĕl kĭz´ ə dĕk) (KJV, NT) See *Melchizedek.*

MELCHISHUA (Mĕl kī shū´ ȧ) (KJV, 1 Sam. 14:49; 31:2) See *Malchishua.*

MELCHIZEDEK (Mĕl kĭz´ ə dĕk) Personal name meaning "Zedek is my king" or "My king is righteousness." Priest and king of Salem, a city identified with Jerusalem.
Old Testament When Abraham returned from the Valley of Siddim where he defeated Chedorlaomer, king of Elam, and the kings aligned with Chedorlaomer, Melchizedek greeted Abraham with bread and wine. He blessed Abraham in the name of "God Most High." In return, Abraham gave Melchizedek a tenth of everything (Gen. 14:20).

Melchizedek and Abraham both worshiped the one true God. Abraham also appeared to recognize the role of Melchizedek as a priest. Psalm 110:4 refers to one who would be forever a priest in the "order of Melchizedek." This messianic psalm teaches that the leader or ruler of the Hebrew nation would be able to reflect in his person the role of priest as well as the role of king.
New Testament The writer of Hebrews made several references in chapters 5–7 to Jesus' priesthood being of the "order of Melchizedek" as opposed to Levitical in nature. The author of Hebrews cited Ps. 110:4. For the writer of Hebrews, only Jesus, whose life could not be destroyed by death, fit the psalmist's description of a priest of "the order of Melchizedek."

Judith Wooldridge

MELEA (Mē´ lē ȧ) Ancestor of Jesus (Luke 3:31).

MELECH (Mē' lĕk) Personal name meaning "king." Descendant of King Saul (1 Chron. 8:35; 9:41).

MELICU (Mĕl' ĭ kū) (KJV, Neh. 12:14) See *Malluchi.*

MELITA (Mĕ lēt' à) KJV form of Malta (Acts 28:1). See *Island.*

MELONS See *Plants.*

MELZAR (Mĕl' zär) KJV transliteration of what is likely an Assyrian loanword meaning "guard" (NIV), "overseer" (NASB), or "steward" (RSV) at Dan. 1:11,16. The KJV follows some early versions (Theodotian, Lucian, the Syriac, the Vulgate) in taking Melzar as a proper name. Modern translators point to the use of the article as evidence of a title.

MEM (Mĕm) Thirteenth letter of the Hebrew alphabet which serves as the heading for Ps. 119:97-104. Each of these verses begins with this letter.

MEMBERS Term used to describe body parts or individuals composing a group. Jesus warned of body parts which cause one to sin (Matt. 5:29). As a Christian Paul struggled with the reality of body parts which continue to give in to sin (Rom. 6:13). The bodily members are the sphere where the law of sin (Rom. 7:23) and passions (James 4:1) are at work. The image of various body parts cooperating in the life of one organism frequently serves to illustrate the unity of the church which is composed of different individuals exercising various, necessary functions (Rom. 12:4-5; 1 Cor. 12:12,27; cp. Eph. 4:25; 5:30). See *Body; Body of Christ; Church.*

MEMORIAL Something which serves as a reminder. Scripture witnesses to God's participation in human history for the salvation of God's people. Memorials to such events reinforced faith and provided opportunities for teaching. God's covenant name (Yahweh) was to be a "memorial name" (Exod. 3:15 NASB), a reminder of God's liberation of God's people. The Passover served as a similar reminder (Exod. 12:14; 13:9). The 12 stones taken from the Jordan's bed served as a reminder of God's provision of passage across the Jordan (Josh. 4:7). In the NT the Lord's Supper serves as a reminder of Christ's sacrificial death and an encouragement of His future coming (Matt. 26:13; Mark 14:9; 1 Cor. 11:25-26). All these memorials serve to "proclaim" the good news of what God has done.

MEMPHIS (Mĕm' phĭs) Place-name meaning "the abode of the good one." An ancient capital of Egypt located just south of modern Cairo on the west bank of the Nile River. It was founded by Menes, a pharaoh of the First Dynasty (about 2800 B.C.) and became the capital of Egypt as the Third Dynasty came to power (about 2686 B.C.). For over 300 years Memphis was the principal city of Egypt. Gradually, other cities grew in importance, and Memphis was eclipsed as the seat of power. During later dynasties Thebes and Avaris-Tanis served as the capital. Memphis regained its status as capital during the Hyksos reign (1750–1570) but was replaced when the alien occupation ended.

There remains little, architecturally, to attest to the glory and grandeur once enjoyed by the city. As the Moslems began to build Cairo, they raided the buildings of Memphis for material, even dismantling the temple of Ptah, which probably was the largest and most opulent structure in the city.

MEMUCAN (Mə mū' căn) One of the seven princes who served as advisors to King Ahasuerus of Persia (Esther 1:14,16,21). See *Marsena.*

One of several small sphinxes located at Memphis on the Nile River in Egypt.

MEN-PLEASERS Those who serve (only) to gain approval or win favor (Eph. 6:6; Col. 3:22).

MENAHEM (Mĕn´ à hĕm) Personal name meaning "consoler." King of Israel 752–742 B.C. Menahem became king by assassinating Shallum, who had killed King Zechariah only a month earlier (2 Kings 15:10-14). The period following the death of Jeroboam II in 753 B.C. was filled with turmoil. Several political factions fought for control. Shallum and Menahem each led an extremist party that sought the throne. They ruled by force. After becoming king Menahem attacked and destroyed one of Israel's cities because it resisted his rule (2 Kings 15:16). He ruled at least 10 years in Samaria. A significant event recorded about his reign is that he paid tribute to Tiglath-pileser III, the king of Assyria. This is the first mention of the Assyrian monarch in the biblical record. It is possible that Menahem obtained the throne of Israel with Tiglath-pileser's help. In any event, Menahem was little more than a puppet of the Assyrians during his reign. He was succeeded by his son, Pekahiah. See *Tiglath-pileser.*

MENAN (Mē´ năn) (KJV) See *Menna.*

MENE, MENE, TEKEL, UPHARSIN (Mē´ nə, mē´ nə, tĕk´ əl, Ū phär´ sĭn) Inscription that King Belshazzar of Babylon saw the fingers of a man's hand write on his palace wall as the king and his guests drank from the gold vessels taken from the temple in Jerusalem (Dan. 5:1-29). After the wise men of the kingdom could not decipher the writing, Daniel was brought in to give an interpretation.

Scholars have proposed a number of translations, the best of which probably is "mina, shekel, and halves." Daniel interpreted the inscription with a wordplay using Hebrew words which sound similar to each word of the inscription, taking it to mean "numbered, weighed, and divided."

Daniel's interpretation was that Belshazzar and his kingdom had been weighed in the balance and found wanting. The kingdom would be divided and given to his enemies, the Medes and Persians. Daniel 5:30 records that the overthrow occurred that very night. Thus God worked through Daniel to show His wisdom was greater than that of Persia's wise counselors and magicians, and only the God of Israel controlled history and human destiny.

MENI (Mə nē´) Personal name meaning "to count" or "to apportion." God of good luck worshiped together with the god Gad by Jewish apostates, probably in the postexilic period (Isa. 65:11 NASB margin). The god is possibly identical with Manat, a deity worshiped by the Arabs before the rise of Islam. The KJV translated the god's name as "that number." Modern translations prefer the translation "Destiny."

MENNA (Mĕn´ nà) Name of an ancestor of Christ (Luke 3:31). Form of Menan preferred by modern translations.

MENORAH (Mĕ´ nō rah) Candelabrum used in Jewish worship, specifically the branched lampstand used in the tabernacle (Exod. 25:31-35; 37:17-20; cp. Zech. 4:2,11). See *Lamps, Lighting, Lampstand.*

MENUHOTH (Mĕ nū´ hŏth) Name meaning "resting places." Family descended from Judah (1 Chron. 2:52 NRSV) or their town (TEV). Other English translations take this family as the other half of the Manahethites (KJV, REB; Manahathites, NASB, NIV) mentioned in 1 Chron. 2:54. Menuhoth was possibly located to the northwest of Jerusalem towards Kiriath-jearim.

MEONENIM, PLAIN OF (Mə ŏn´ ə nĭm) Meonenim is the Hebrew term for diviners or soothsayers (Deut. 18:10,14; Mic. 5:12). The KJV understood Meonenim as a proper name at Judg. 9:37. See *Diviner's Oak.*

MEONOTHAI (Mə ŏn´ ō thī) Personal name meaning "habitations of the Lord." A descendant of Judah (1 Chron. 4:14).

MEPHAATH (Mĕph ā´ ăth) Place-name meaning "height." Town in Reuben's tribal allotment (Josh. 13:18), assigned to the Levites (Josh. 21:37; 1 Chron. 6:79). In Jeremiah's time the town was in Moabite hands (Jer. 48:21). The site is perhaps that of modern Jawah about six miles south of Amman.

M

MEPHIBOSHETH (Mĕ phĭb´ ō shĕth) Personal name meaning "shame destroyer" or "image breaker." **1.** Son of Jonathan who was granted special position and privilege in David's court (2 Sam. 9). Jonathan was killed in battle when Mephibosheth was five years old. Fearing that the Philistines would seek the life of the young boy, a nurse fled with him, but in her haste she dropped him and crippled him in both feet (2 Sam. 4:4). Mephibosheth may be an intentional change by copyists to avoid writing the pagan god's name "baal." The original name would be Meribaal (1 Chron. 8:34). When David invited Mephibosheth to be a part of his court, he entrusted the family property to a steward, Ziba. During the Absalom rebellion Ziba tried unsuccessfully to turn David against Mephibosheth. Upon the king's return to Jerusalem, Mephibosheth vindicated himself and was allowed to remain in the king's house (2 Sam. 16; 19). See *Meribaal.* **2.** Son of Saul, who with six other members of Saul's household, was delivered by David to the Gibeonites to be hanged. This was in retaliation for Saul's earlier slaughter of a band of Gibeonites (2 Sam. 21:1-9). Mephibosheth's mother guarded the bodies until the time of burial.

MERAB (Mē´ răb) Personal name from the root "to become many." Eldest daughter of King Saul (1 Sam. 14:49), who was twice promised to David in exchange for killing Goliath (1 Sam. 17:25) and for fighting the Lord's battles against the Philistines (1 Sam. 18:17-19). Saul reneged on his promise and gave Merab to Adriel. Modern translators based on context and a few ancient texts often read "Merab" instead of the Hebrew text's "Michal" in 2 Sam. 21:8.

MERAIAH (Mə rī´ ah) Personal name meaning "Yah has promised" or "stubborn." Head of a priestly family in the time of the high priest Joiakim (Neh. 12:12).

MERAIOTH (Mə rā´ ŏth) Personal name meaning "obstinate" or "rebellious." **1.** Ancestor of the Zadokite high priests (1 Chron. 6:6-7,52). **2.** Ancestor of Ezra the scribe, perhaps identical with 1. (Ezra 7:3; 1 Chron. 9:11; Neh. 11:11). **3.** Priestly family in the postexilic period (Neh. 12:15), perhaps a scribal corruption of Meremoth (Neh. 12:3).

MERARI (Mə rär´ ē) Personal name meaning "bitterness" or "gall." Third son of Levi (Gen.

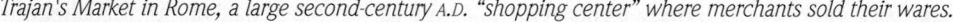

Trajan's Market in Rome, a large second-century A.D. "shopping center" where merchants sold their wares.

46:11; Exod. 6:16; Num. 3:17; 1 Chron. 6:1,16; 23:6). Merari was the ancestor of a division of priests, the Merarites.

MERARITES (Mə rär´ īts) Major division of priests descended from Merari, the third son of Levi. The Merarites and Gershonites were responsible for the setup, breakdown, and transport of the tabernacle (Num. 10:17; cp. 3:36-37; 4:29-33; 7:8). The Merarites received an allotment of 12 cities from the tribes of Reuben, Gad, and Zebulun, including Ramoth-gilead, a city of refuge (Josh. 21:7,34-40; 1 Chron. 6:63,77-81). Representatives of the Merarites participated in David's move of the ark to Jerusalem (1 Chron. 15:6), served as tabernacle musicians (1 Chron. 15:17,19) and gatekeepers (1 Chron. 26:10,19), shared in Hezekiah's (2 Chron. 29:12) and Josiah's (2 Chron. 34:12) reforms, and returned from exile to assist in the new temple (Ezra 8:19).

MERATHAIM (Měr á thā´ ĭm) Place-name meaning "double bitterness," or "double rebellion," possibly a play on the Akkadian phrase *mat marrati* ("Land of the Bitter River") or on *nar marratu*, a designation for the area touching the Persian Gulf known from Babylonian inscriptions. Jeremiah (50:21) announced God's judgment on the land.

MERCHANT Buyer and seller of goods for profit. With the exception of the period of Solomon (1 Kings 9:26-28; 10:15,22), Israel was not known in biblical times as a nation of merchants. References to Israelites involved in trade are surprisingly few. Israelites were prohibited from selling food to fellow Israelites for profit (Lev. 25:37) but could sell even carrion to a foreigner (Deut. 14:21). Merchants purchased cloth from housewives (Prov. 31:24); olive oil was sold (2 Kings 4:7). Abuses by merchants were often condemned: holding back grain to force up prices (Prov. 11:26); impatience for Sabbath or holy days to conclude so that commerce might resume; dishonest scales (Amos 8:5); forcing fellow Israelites into slavery to buy food (Neh. 5:1-8); violation of the Sabbath (Neh. 13:15-21). Jerusalem merchants assisted in Nehemiah's reconstruction of the walls, perhaps by providing finances (Neh. 3:32).

The majority of OT references to merchants concern nations other than Israel. The term translated as merchant or trader at Prov. 31:24 and Hos. 12:7 is, in fact, the word for Canaanite. Men of Tyre sold fish and all kinds of merchandise in postexilic Jerusalem (Neh. 13:16). Ezekiel 27:12-25 recounts the activities of the merchants of Tyre in full. They traded in common and precious metals, slaves, livestock, precious stones, ivory, wool, cloth, clothing, agricultural produce, wine, spices, and carpets (cp. Rev. 18:11-13). Tyre's trading partners included 22 nations or peoples encompassing Asia Minor, Palestine, Syria, Arabia, and Mesopotamia. Merchants generated great wealth. The prophets railed against the pride that accompanied merchants' material successes (Isa. 23; Ezek. 27).

In the NT Jesus used a merchant to illustrate the need to risk all to gain the kingdom of heaven (Matt. 13:45-46). Other references continue the prophetic attack on arrogant merchants. James 4:13 warns big businessmen who engaged in long-term foreign ventures not to dismiss God when making plans. Revelation condemns Roman merchants who grew rich on the sins of Rome (Rev. 18:3). See *Commerce; Economic Life.*   *Chris Church*

MERCURIUS (Měr cū´ rǐ ŭs) KJV translation of the Greek *Hermes* (Acts 14:12). The Roman god Mercury was identified with the Greek Hermes. See *Gods, Pagan; Hermes.*

MERCURY See *Gods, Pagan; Hermes.*

MERCY Characteristic and action that comes from the very nature of God. On the human level it is best described as one's consideration of the condition and needs of his fellowman. It is an essential disposition of a covenant people, especially Israel and the church. In the OT God's mercy was not primarily given to people outside His covenant community but was expressed mainly towards His people Israel. It also became the expected attitude and action of the people of Israel towards one another. This expectation was passed on to the church and became a chief tenet in the lifestyle of believers. Jesus made it an essential part of His Christian manifesto in the Sermon on the Mount (Matt. 5:7). In both OT and NT mercy is an action taken by the strong towards the weak, the rich towards the poor, the insider towards the outsider, those who have towards those who have not.

Mercy as given by God is the foundation of forgiveness. It is His faithfulness and steadfast love. God is not seen as displaying an emotion called mercy but as taking merciful action. This action was taken as Israel was in need: provisions such as manna in the wilderness (Exod. 13:31-35), protection such as the Shepherd who keeps Israel and does not sleep (Ps. 121), and deliverance (Pss. 56:12-23; 107) as Yahweh who delivered His people from Egypt (1 Sam. 10:18). Mercy has never been the benefit of God's people because of their merit but is always the gift of God. "The LORD, the LORD God, compassionate and gracious, slow to anger, and abounding in loving kindness and truth; who keeps loving kindness for thousands, who forgives iniquity, transgression and sin; yet He will by no means leave [the guilty] unpunished, visiting the iniquity of fathers on the children and on the grandchildren to the third and fourth generations" (Exod. 34:6-7 NASB).

God's justice and righteousness cannot be overlooked in this matter of mercy. Exodus 34:7 makes it clear that God's judgment will override His mercy where man's sinful rebellion turns away from His righteousness and love. Here God's mercy is manifested in His slow action and deferred punishment, not in ignoring sin and refusing to act in wrath. "The Lord does not delay His promise, as some understand delay, but is patient with you, not wanting any to perish, but all to come to repentance. But the Day of the Lord will come like a thief; on that day the heavens will pass away with a loud noise, the elements will burn and be dissolved, and the earth and the works on it will be disclosed" (2 Pet. 3:9-10 HCSB). God's wrath is the resulting action against man's rebellion after His mercy has been exhausted. In the OT God's wrath is exercised on the heathen nations as a result of their wickedness (Gen.18–19) and hostility to His people. God also expressed His wrath and withdrew His mercy from His beloved Israel and Judah.

Mercy in the NT is generally described by several root words: *splanchnon*, usually translated "compassion" or "bowels of mercy;" *eleos*, meaning "mercy;" *oiktirmos*, rendered "pity," "mercy," and "compassion." The word *hileos* is rarely used and translates "merciful" and "propitious." It is always used of God's mercy and is by some translated "forgive" (NIV). The HCSB translates Heb. 8:12, "For I will be merciful to their wrongdoing, and I will never again remember their sins." A form of the word is used in 1 John 2:2, "He Himself [Jesus] is the propitiation (*hilasmos*) for our sins, and not only for ours, but also for those of the whole world" (HCSB). This is the word in the Septuagint, *hilasterion*, which is used to translate the Hebrew *kapporet*, "mercy seat" where the blood of the atonement was sprinkled. In the greatest sense Jesus was the full expression of the mercy of God. No one embodies and personally illustrates the meaning of mercy as does Jesus. Like the Father, Jesus moved well beyond feeling compassion on the suffering. He always was "moved with compassion" and "showed mercy" when He encountered those hurting or down and out. His greatest illustration of the meaning of mercy is perhaps the story of the good Samaritan, which was used to answer the scribe's question, "Who is my neighbor?" In the story two of the words mentioned above are used. Jesus said that when the Samaritan saw the man, he had compassion (*splanchnizomai*). His resultant action described a mercy that does more than feel, a mercy that takes action. At the end of the story, Jesus asked the scribe which man proved to be the neighbor. The scribe's answer was, "The one who showed mercy (*eleos*)."

The many ways that Jesus expressed His mercy are woven throughout the Gospels. He is seen stopping in a crowded procession to invite Himself to be the social guest at the house of a despised little tax collector (Luke 19:1-10). He cleansed lepers (Mark 1:41), taught the ignorant multitudes, was moved with compassion and healed the sick, and relieved their hunger with a boy's small lunch (Matt. 14:14-21). Jesus gave sight to the blind (Matt. 20:34), made the lame to walk (John 5:2-9), and raised the dead (Luke 7:2-15). His words sent back to John the Baptist about His identity and ministry summarize the scope of His mercy. "Go and report to John the things you have seen and heard: The blind receive sight, the lame walk, lepers are cleansed, the deaf hear, the dead are raised, and the poor have the good news preached to them" (Luke 7:22 HCSB).

In both OT and NT mercy is always extended by the larger to the smaller, the rich to the poor, the strong to the weak, and the Righteous One to the sinner. God's chief disposition towards sinful man is mercy, spawned by His love, which exerts His power to bring sinful man back to Himself. Mercy from God is never deserved and is always generated by His character and not man's. The word *hilaskomai*, "to be merciful," "to be propitious," expresses God's mercy that makes atonement for undeserving man's sin. Salvation is God's merciful act of withholding His wrath and eternal punishment as well as His grace in granting forgiveness and eternal life. Paul points out that God has said to Moses, "'I will show mercy to whom I show mercy, and I will have compassion on whom I have compassion.' So then it does not depend on human will or effort, but on God who shows mercy" (Rom. 9:15-16 HCSB). He goes on to say that Jews and Gentiles, who are both vessels of wrath, have become vessels of mercy. "So then," continues Paul, "He shows mercy to whom He wills, and He hardens whom He wills" (9:18).

Mercy is not only a central focus of the ministry of Jesus and the Father; it is also to be the practice of all believers. Jesus made it an essential ingredient of the life and manner of the believer when He spoke the Beatitudes in the Sermon on the Mount; "Blessed are the merciful, because they will be shown mercy" (Matt 5:7 HCSB). As noted earlier in this article, the mercy of the good Samaritan is lifted up as an example for all believers. Paul introduced the idea that showing mercy is a spiritual gift. "According to the grace given to us, we have different gifts: ... if exhorting, in exhortation; giving, with generosity; leading, with diligence; showing mercy, with cheerfulness" (Rom. 12:6,8 HCSB). The church of Jerusalem in Acts 2 exhibited the essence of the heart and spirit required of every believer as they brought all their goods together in their time of hardship so they might survive (Acts 2:44-47). This was a spirit of mercy that came out of the heart of the faith demonstrated by Jesus. James taught what heavenly wisdom and true religion is: "The wisdom from above is first pure then peace-loving, gentle, compliant, full of mercy and good fruits, without favoritism and hypocrisy" (James 3:17 HCSB). He described "pure and undefiled religion before God our Father is this: to look after orphans and widows in their distress and to keep oneself unstained by the world" (James 1:27 HCSB). This is mercy in action that moves beyond mere emotion and brings about healing, restoration, or whatever need that sparks the act of mercy.

If mercy is action of the stronger based on response to plight or need of the weaker, it could be asked if mercy can be expressed in the opposite situation. The NT shows that it can be. The ethic that Jesus calls for is "turning the other cheek," "walking the second mile," and "blessing those who curse you." Jesus Himself embodied this very teaching. Mercy can be expressed by the person on the bottom towards the person on top. This is the very genius of the Christian faith. See for example the words of Jesus uttered in dying agony from the cross, "Father, forgive them, because they do not know what they are doing" (Luke 23:34 HCSB). Then there are the similar words of Stephen as the stones pounded upon his head and body: "Then he knelt down and cried out with a loud voice, 'Lord, do not charge them with this sin!' And saying this, he fell asleep" (Acts 7:60 HCSB). Thus, mercy is a feeling calling for action even by the oppressed towards the oppressor, the weak towards the strong, the victim towards the victor. "But I say to you who listen: Love your enemies, do good to those who hate you, bless those who curse you, pray for those who mistreat you" (Luke 6:27-28 HCSB).　　　　　*Dan Parker*

MERCY SEAT Slab of pure gold measuring about 45 inches by 27 inches that sat atop the ark of the covenant which was the same size. It was the base for the golden cherubim (Exod. 25:17-19,21) and symbolized the throne from which God ruled Israel (Lev. 16:2; Num. 7:89). On the Day of Atonement, the high priest sprinkled the blood of a sacrificial lamb on the mercy seat as a plea for forgiveness for the sins of the nation (Lev. 16:15). The Hebrew word means literally "to wipe out" or "cover over." This has led modern translators to render the term "cover" (REB, NRSV note), "lid" (TEV), or "atonement cover" (NIV). "Mercy seat" is based on the earliest Greek and Latin translations. The mercy seat has been replaced as the symbol and place of God's presence and atonement. Christ's cross and resurrection showed the perfect presence and accomplished atonement once for all (Heb. 9).

MERED (Mē´ rĕd) Personal name meaning "rebel." Descendant of King David who married Bithiah, a daughter of Pharaoh (1 Chron. 4:17-18), perhaps as part of a political alliance.

MEREMOTH (Mĕr´ ə mŏth) Personal name meaning "heights." **1.** Priest who returned from exile with Zerubbabel (Neh. 12:3). **2.** Priest in the time of Ezra and Nehemiah who assisted with the temple treasury (Ezra 8:33), with the repair of the walls (Neh. 3:4,21), and witnessed the renewal of the covenant (Neh. 10:5). **3.** Layman with a foreign wife (Ezra 10:36).

MERES (Mē´ rĕs) One of seven princes who served as counselors to King Ahasuerus of Persia (Esther 1:14). See *Marsena.*

MERIBAH (Mĕr´ ĭ bäh) See *Massah.*

MERIBAH-KADESH (Mĕr ĭ bah-kā´ dĕsh) See *Kadesh-meribah.*

MERIBATH-KADESH (Mĕr ĭ bäth-kā´ dĕsh) See *Kadesh-meribah.*

MERIBBAAL (Mĕr ĭb bā´ ál) Personal name of disputed meaning: "opponent of Baal," "obstinacy of Baal," "beloved or hero of Baal," or "Baal defends." Original name of Mephibosheth. Apparently later copyists of text changed name with Baal to avoid use of pagan god's name (1 Chron. 8:34; 9:40, the latter with the Hebrew spelling "hero" compared to the former's spelling "opponent"). See *Mephibosheth.*

MERNEPTAH (Mĕr´ nĕ pta) Personal name meaning "beloved of Ptah" (god honored in Memphis, Egypt). Ruler in the 19th Dynasty of Egypt 1236–1223 B.C. or 1224-1216 B.C. A stele produced during his rule is the earliest known nonbiblical reference to the Israelites. The stele praises Merneptah's conquest of Canaan, Ashkelon, Gezer, Yanoam, and Israel, Israel being marked as a people rather than a geographical place. Merneptah claimed to have "laid waste" to Israel. The stele shows that a people Israel existed in Canaan no later than 1220 B.C. and had sufficient strength to

fight Merneptah even though they lost, if his account is accurate. They may have been an ally of three city-states opposing Merneptah.

MERODACH (Mər ō´ dăk) Hebrew form of Marduk, the chief god of Babylon, also called Bel, corresponding to the Semitic Baal or "Lord" (Jer. 50:2). Merodach is an element in the names of the Babylonian kings Merodach-baladan (2 Kings 20:12; Isa. 39:1) and Evil-merodach (2 Kings 25:27; Jer. 52:31). With a different vocalization Merodach yields the name Mordecai (Esther 2:5). See *Gods, Pagan.*

MERODACH-BALADAN (Mə rō´ dăk-băl´ ȧ dan) Personal name meaning "god Marduk gave an heir." A ruler of the Bit-Yakin tribe in southern Babylonia and king of Babylon 721–711 B.C. and for a short time in 704 B.C. He was little more than a puppet of Assyria, answering to Sargon. Merodach-baladan sent envoys to King Hezekiah of Judah (Isa. 39:1; 2 Kings 20:12-13) who flaunted the palace treasure house and treasuries. Two years later Sennacherib laid his ill-fated siege to the Holy City. Merodach-baladan continued to rebel against the Assyrians, coming out of exile more than once to oppose the kings of Nineveh. He eventually was beaten back to his seashore tribal lands. See *Babylon; Hezekiah; Sargon; Sennacherib.*

MEROM (Mē´ rŏm) Place-name meaning "high place." Place in Galilee where Joshua led Israel to defeat a coalition of Canaanite tribes under King Jabin of Hazor in a surprise attack (Josh. 11:1-7). The location of the site has been debated but now appears to be the modern Merion. The town is near a wadi that is fed annually by a spring during the wet season. Thutmose III and Rameses II of Egypt claimed to have captured the area during their respective reigns.

MERONOTH (Mə rŏn´ oth) or **MERON-O-THITE** (Mə rŏn´-ō-thīt) Resident of Meronoth (1 Chron. 27:30; Neh. 3:7). The site is perhaps Beituniyeh, northwest of Gibeon.

MEROZ (Mē´ rŏz) Place-name of uncertain meaning. Town condemned in the Song of Deborah for failure to join in the Lord's battle against the oppressive forces of Sisera (Judg. 5:23). The site is unknown. Suggestions have included: Khirbet Marus three miles northwest of Hazor; Madon (Josh. 12:19); and (Shimron-)Merom (Josh. 11:5; 12:20), identified with Semuniyeh north of Megiddo on the edge of the Jezreel Valley. Marus is too far removed from the battle site to have been expected to participate. Madon is closer but still separated from the Jezreel by mountain terrain.

MESECH (Mē´ sĕk) (KJV, Ps. 120:5) See *Meshech*.

MESHA (Mē´ shȧ) English translation of three Hebrew names. **1.** Personal name meaning "Safety." Ruler of Moab who led a rebellion against Israel (2 Kings 3:4-27). The designation of Mesha as a sheep breeder (2 Kings 3:4 NRSV) is perhaps an honorary title for chief. The date of his revolt is uncertain. Second Kings 1:1 suggests the revolt followed immediately on Ahab's death (850 B.C.). Second Kings 3:4 sets the revolt in the reign of Jehoram (849–842 B.C.). The Moabite stone erected by Mesha to celebrate his exploits contains two apparently irreconcilable time notes: in the middle of the reign of Omri's son and 40 years after the beginning of Omri's oppressive taxation of Moab. If Omri's son is taken literally, the Moabite stone places the revolt in the reign of Ahab (869–850 B.C.). "Son of Omri" was, however, used as a title for any of the kings who succeeded Omri as king in Samaria, even of Jehu who overthrew Omri's dynasty. Jehoram, Omri's grandson, might thus be the "son" of Omri of the Moabite stone. Jehoram's reign, however, ended five years before the 40th anniversary of the earliest date of Omri's oppression of Moab. At the beginning of the revolt, Mesha succeeded in seizing Israelite border towns and in fortifying towns on his frontier. An alliance of Israel, Judah, and Edom, however, outflanked his defenses and attacked Mesha from the rear. Mesha retreated to Kir-hareseth from which he attempted, unsuccessfully, to escape to his Aramean allies. With no escape possible, Mesha sacrificed his firstborn son to his god Chemosh on the city walls. In response the Israelites lifted their siege and returned home. The Moabite stone describes

Mesha as a builder of cities and highways. Archaeological evidence, however, suggests a decline in Moabite civilization following the revolt. See *Moab and the Moabite Stone*. **2.** Descendant of Benjamin living in Moab (1 Chron. 8:9). **3.** Descendant of Caleb (1 Chron. 2:42; RSV follows early Greek translation in reading Mareshah). **4.** Place-name meaning "debt." City in the territory of the Joktanites (Gen. 10:30), most likely to be identified with Massa (Gen. 25:14; 1 Chron. 1:30), located between the head of the Gulf of Aqaba and the Persian Gulf. This Massa is identified with the Assyrian *Mash* and the Persian *Maciya*.   *Chris Church*

MESHACH (Mē´ shăk) Personal name of unknown meaning, apparently corrupted in transmission from Babylonian to Hebrew, perhaps to avoid pronouncing or acknowledging name of Babylonian god. One of Daniel's friends exiled to Babylon after the fall of Jehoiakim in 597 B.C. (Dan. 1:6-7). His Hebrew name was Mishael ("who is what God is") but was changed to Meshach (perhaps, "who is what Aku is") to mock Israel's God. Declining the rich food of the king's table, he and his friends proved that the simple fare of vegetables and water was to be desired to make one wise and strong. After refusing to bow to the king's golden image, he, Shadrach, and Abednego were thrown into a furnace but were delivered by God (Dan. 3). Thereafter, they were promoted in the king's court. See *Abednego; Daniel; Shadrach*.

MESHECH (Mē´ shĕk) Personal name meaning either "sowing" or "possession." **1.** A people of Asia Minor (Gen. 10:2; 1 Chron. 1:5), known for trading in copper vessels (Ezek. 27:13), frequently associated with Tubal (Ezek. 32:26; 38:2-3; 39:1). This Meschech is identical to the Assyrian *Mushki* and the Greek *Moschoi*. At Ps. 120:5 the name appears in the form Mesech (KJV). **2.** An otherwise unknown Aramean tribe (1 Chron. 1:17), perhaps identical with Mash (Gen. 10:23).

MESHEK (Mē´ shĕk) TEV for Meshech (1 Chron. 1:17).

MESHELEMIAH (Mə shĕl ĕ mī´ ah) Personal name meaning "Yahweh is recompense." Tabernacle gatekeeper in the time of David (1 Chron. 9:21; 26:1-2,9). Shelemiah is an abbreviated form of this name (1 Chron. 26:14). Other shortened forms include Shallum (1 Chron. 9:17, 19,31; Ezra 2:42) and Meshullam (Neh. 12:25). All may refer to the same Levite or various persons may be intended.

MESHEZABEEL (Mə shĕz´ á bēl) (KJV) or MESHEZABEL (Mə shĕz á bĕl) Personal name meaning "God delivers." 1. Ancestor of one of those working on the wall (Neh. 3:4). 2. One of the chiefs of the people witnessing Ezra's covenant renewal (Neh. 10:21). 3. Member of the tribe of Judah (Neh. 11:24). All three are perhaps the same individual.

MESHILLEMITH (Mə shĭl´ lĕ mĭth) or MESHILLEMOTH (Mə shĭl´ lĕ mŏth) Personal name meaning "reconciliation." 1. A priest (1 Chron. 9:12; Neh. 11:13). 2. Member of the tribe of Ephraim (2 Chron. 28:12).

MESHOBAB (Mə shō´ băb) Personal name from a root meaning "return." Leader of the tribe of Simeon (1 Chron. 4:34).

MESHULLAM (Mĕ shūl´ lăm) Personal name meaning "allied" or "given as a replacement." 1. Grandfather of Shaphan, King Josiah's secretary (2 Kings 22:3). See Josiah. 2. Son of Zerubbabel (1 Chron. 3:19). See Zerubbabel. 3. Member of the tribe of Gad who lived in Bashan (1 Chron. 5:13). 4. Son of Elpaal (1 Chron. 8:17). 5. Son of Hodaviah, father of Sallu (1 Chron. 9:7). 6. Son of Shephatiah (1 Chron. 9:8). 7. Member of the priestly family, a son of Zadok, and the father of Hilkiah (1 Chron. 9:11). See Zadok. 8. Son of Meshillemith of the priestly Zadokite family (1 Chron. 9:12). See Zadok. 9. Descendant of Kohath, one of the foremen during the repairs made in the temple following the finding of the book of Deuteronomy during Josiah's reign (2 Chron. 34:12). 10. One sent by Ezra to secure the services of a Levite for a group of returning exiles (Ezra (8:15-18). He later opposed Ezra's plan to end foreign marriages because he had a foreign wife himself (10:29). 11. Son of Berechiah, he helped Nehemiah repair the walls around Jerusalem following the return from Babylon (Neh. 3:4). 12. Son of Besodiah who helped repair the old gate (the Jeshanah Gate, NIV) when Nehemiah repaired the walls of Jerusalem (Neh. 3:6). See Nehemiah. 13. He stood beside Ezra as the scribe read the Law to the people of Jerusalem (Neh. 8:2-4). 14. One of the priests who joined Nehemiah and others setting his seal to the covenant between the people and God (Neh. 10:7). 15. One of the leaders of the people who set his seal to the covenant between the people and God (Neh. 10:20). 16. Son of Ezra, head of a priestly house during the time Jehoiakim was high priest (Neh. 12:13). 17. Another head of a priestly house when Jehoiakim was high priest; son of Ginnethon (Neh. 12:16). 18. Guard of the storerooms at the gates (Neh. 12:25 NIV). 19. Prince of Judah who participated in the procession to dedicate the rebuilt walls of Jerusalem (Neh. 12:33).

MESHULLEMETH (Mə shŭl´ lĕ mĕth) Personal name meaning "restitution." Wife of King Mannaseh and mother of Amon (2 Kings 21:19).

MESOBAITE (Mə sō´ bā īt) (KJV) or MEZOBAITE (Mə zō bā īt) (NASB, NIV, NRSV) Title of one of David's 30 elite warriors (1 Chron. 11:47). The REB and TEV amended the text to give the reading "resident of Zobah."

MESOPOTAMIA (Mĕs´ o po tā´ mĭ á) Strictly speaking, Mesopotamia (from the Greek "between the rivers") is the designation of the area between the Tigris and Euphrates rivers. Mesopotamia applies more generally to the entire Tigris-Euphrates valley. At times in antiquity the culture of Mesopotamia dominated an even larger area, spreading east into Elam and Media, north into Asia Minor, and following the Fertile Crescent into Canaan and Egypt.

The Scriptures witness to a long history of contacts between the Hebrew people and the people of Mesopotamia. Mesopotamia was the homeland of the patriarchs (Gen. 11:31–12:4; 24:10; 28:6). A Mesopotamian king subdued Israel for a time during the period of the judges (Judg. 3:8). Mesopotamia supplied mercenary chariots and cavalry for the Ammonites' war with David (1 Chron. 19:6; superscription of Ps. 60). Both the Northern Kingdom of Israel (2 Kings 15:29; 1 Chron. 5:26) and the Southern Kingdom of Judah (2 Kings 24:14-16; 2 Chron. 36:20; Ezra 2:1) went into exile in Mesopotamia.

MESSENGER One sent with a message. Messenger is often used in the literal sense (Gen. 32:3,6; Num. 20:14; 24:12; Deut. 2:26). In an extended sense, the prophets (2 Chron. 36:15-16; Isa. 44:26; Hag. 1:13) and priests (Mal. 2:7) are termed messengers in their role as bearers of God's message for humanity. The Hebrew and Greek terms for "messenger" are frequently rendered "angel," the heavenly messengers of God. Sometimes messengers made advance travel arrangements for their master (Luke 9:52). In this sense the prophetic messenger of Mal. 3:1 prepares for the Lord's coming. The Gospel writers applied this preparatory function to John the Baptist (Matt. 11:10; Mark 1:2; Luke 7:27). See *Angels; Herald.*

MESSIAH (Mĕs sī´ ah) Transliteration of Hebrew word meaning "anointed one" that was translated into Greek as *Christos*. "Christ" or Messiah is therefore a name admirably suited to express both the church's link with Israel through the OT and the faith that sees in Jesus Christ the worldwide scope of the salvation in Him.

The Old Testament and Early Jewish Background "Anointed" carries several senses in the OT. All have to do with installing a person in an office in a way that the person will be regarded as accredited by Yahweh, Israel's God. Even a pagan king such as Cyrus was qualified as the Lord's anointed (Isa. 45:1) to execute a divinely appointed task. The usual application of the term "anointed" was to God's representatives within the covenant people. Prophets such as Elisha were set apart in this way (1 Kings 19:16). Israel probably saw a close link between the anointed persons and God's spirit though the link is specifically mentioned only occasionally (2 Kings 2:9). Israelite kings were particularly hailed as Yahweh's anointed (cp. Judg. 9:8), beginning with Saul (1 Sam. 9–10 NIV) and especially referring to David (1 Sam. 16:6,13; 2 Sam. 2:4; 5:3) and Solomon (1 Kings 1:39).

The royal family of David as being the line of Israelite kings are mentioned by the title of the "anointed ones" (2 Sam. 22:51; cp. 2 Kings 11:12; 23:30; Pss. 2:2; 20:6; 28:8; 84:9). The king in Israel thus became a sacred person to whom loyalty and respect were to be accorded (1 Sam. 24:6,10; 26:9,11,16,23; 2 Sam. 1:14,16). The oracle spoken by Nathan (2 Sam. 7:12-16) is important since it centers the hope of Israel on the dynasty of David for succeeding generations.

The king, especially in the Psalms, became idealized as a divine son (Ps. 2:2,7; cp. 2 Sam. 7:14) and enjoyed God's protecting favor (Pss. 18:50; 20:6; 28:8). His dynasty would not fail (Ps. 132:17), and the people were encouraged to pray to God on his behalf (Pss. 72:11-15; 84:9). The fall of Jerusalem in 586 B.C. led to great confusion especially when Yahweh's anointed was taken into exile as a prisoner (Lam. 4:20) and his authority as king rejected by the nations (Ps. 89:38,51). This humiliation of the Davidic dynasty posed a set of problems to Israel's faith, even when the people were permitted to return to the land. No revival came for the Davidic kingship, yet that restoration became the pious longing of the Jews both in Babylonian exile (Jer. 33:14-18) and in the later centuries. One of the clearest expressions of the continuing hope was in the *Psalms of Solomon* (17–18) (70–40 B.C.), a Jewish writing of the Messiah as the son of David. There Messiah was a warrior-prince who would expel the hated Romans from Israel and bring in a kingdom in which the Jews would be promoted to world dominion.

After the exile the Israelite priesthood came into prominence. In the absence of a king, the high priest took on a central role in the community. The rite of anointing was the outward sign of his authority to function as God's representative. This authority was traced back to Aaron and his sons (Exod. 29:7-9; 30:22-33; cp. Ps. 133:2). The high priest was the anointed-priest (Lev. 4:3,5,16) and even, in one place, a "messiah" (Zech. 4:14; cp. 6:13; Dan. 9:25).

In the exilic and postexilic ages, the expectation of a coming Messiah came into sharper focus, commencing with Jeremiah's and Ezekiel's vision of a Messiah who would combine the traits of royalty and priestly dignity (Jer. 33:14-18; Ezek. 46:1-8; Zech. 4:1-14; 6:13).

Messianic Prophecies of the Old Testament

PROPHECY	O.T. REFERENCES	N.T. FULFILLMENT
Seed of the woman	Gen. 3:15	Gal. 4:4; Heb. 2:14
Through Noah's sons	Gen. 9:27	Luke 6:36
Seed of Abraham	Gen. 12:3	Matt. 1:1; Gal. 3:8,16
Seed of Isaac	Gen. 17:19	Rom. 9:7; Heb. 11:18
Blessing to nations	Gen. 18:18	Gal. 3:8
Seed of Isaac	Gen. 21:12	Rom. 9:7; Heb. 11:18
Blessing to Gentiles	Gen. 22:18	Gal. 3:8,16; Heb. 6:14
Blessing to Gentiles	Gen. 26:4	Gal. 3:8,16; Heb. 6:14
Blessing through Abraham	Gen. 28:14	Gal. 3:8,16; Heb. 6:14
Of the tribe of Judah	Gen. 49:10	Rev. 5:5
No bone broken	Ex. 12:46	John 19:36
Blessing to firstborn son	Ex. 13:2	Luke 2:23
No bone broken	Num. 9:12	John 19:36
Serpent in wilderness	Num. 21:8-9	John 3:14-15
A star out of Jacob	Num. 24:17-19	Matt. 2:2; Luke 1:33,78; Rev. 22:16
As a prophet	Deut. 18:15,18-19	John 6:14; 7:40; Acts 3:22-23
Cursed on the tree	Deut. 21:23	Gal. 3:13
The throne of David established forever	2 Sam. 7:12-13,16,25-26	Matt. 19:28; 21:4; 25:31; Mark 12:37;
	1 Chron. 17:11-14,23-27	Luke 1:32; John 7:4; Acts 2:30; 13:23;
	2 Chron. 21:7	Rom. 1:3; 2 Tim. 2:8;
		Heb. 1:5,8; 8:1; 12:2; Rev. 22:1
A promised Redeemer	Job 19:25-27	John 5:28-29; Gal. 4:4; Eph. 1:7,11,14
Declared to be the Son of God	Ps. 2:1-12	Matt. 3:17; Mark 1:11; Acts 4:25-26;
		13:33; Heb. 1:5; 5:5; Rev. 2:26-27;
		19:15-16
His resurrection	Ps. 16:8-10	Acts 2:27; 13:35; 26:23
Hands and feet pierced	Ps. 22:1-31	Matt. 27:31,35-36
Mocked and insulted	Ps. 22:7-8	Matt. 27:39-43,45-49
Soldiers cast lots for coat	Ps. 22:18	Mark 15:20,24-25,34; Luke 19:24;
		23:35; John 19:15-18,23-24,34; Acts
		2:23-24
Accused by false witnesses	Ps. 27:12	Matt. 26:60-61
He commits his spirit	Ps. 31:5	Luke 23:46
No bone broken	Ps. 34:20	John 19:36
Accused by false witnesses	Ps. 35:11	Matt. 26:59-61; Mark 14:57-58
Hated without reason	Ps. 35:19	John 15:24-25
Friends stand afar off	Ps. 38:11	Matt. 27:55; Mark 15:40; Luke 23:49
"I come to do Thy will"	Ps. 40:6-8	Heb. 10:5-9
Betrayed by a friend	Ps. 41:9	Matt. 26:14-16,47,50; Mark 14:17-21;
		Luke 22:19-23; John 13:18-19
Known for righteousness	Ps. 45:2,6-7	Heb. 1:8-9
His resurrection	Ps. 49:15	Mark 16:6
Betrayed by a friend	Ps. 55:12-14	John 13:18
His ascension	Ps. 68:18	Eph. 4:8
Hated without reason	Ps. 69:4	John 15:25
Stung by reproaches	Ps. 69:9	John 2:17; Rom. 15:3
Given gall and vinegar	Ps. 69:21	Matt. 27:34,48; Mark 15:23; Luke
		23:36; John 19:29
Exalted by God	Ps. 72:1-19	Matt. 2:2; Phil. 2:9-11; Heb. 1-8
He speaks in parables	Ps. 78:2	Matt. 13:34-35:34

Messianic Prophecies of the Old Testament

PROPHECY	O.T. REFERENCES	N.T. FULFILLMENT
Seed of David exalted	Ps. 89:3-4,19,27-29,35-37	Luke 1:32; Acts 2:30; 13:23; Rom. 1:3; 2 Tim. 2:8
Son of Man comes in glory	Ps. 102:16	Luke 21:24,27; Rev. 12:5-10
"Thou remainest"	Ps. 102:24-27	Heb. 1:10-12
Prays for his enemies	Ps. 109:4	Luke 23:34
Another to succeed Judas	Ps. 109:7-8	Acts 1:16-20
A priest like Melchizedek	Ps. 110:1-7	Matt. 22:41-45; 26:64; Mark 12:35-37; 16:19; Acts 7:56; Eph. 1:20; Col. 1:20; Heb. 1:13; 2:8; 5:6; 6:20; 7:21; 8:1; 10:11-13; 12:2
The chief corner stone	Ps. 118:22-23	Matt. 21:42; Mark 12:10,11; Luke 20:17; John 1:11; Acts 4:11; Eph. 2:20; 1 Pet. 2:4
The King comes in the name of the Lord	Ps. 118:26	Matt. 21:9; 23:39; Mark 11:9; Luke 13:35; 19:38; John 12:13
David's seed to reign	Ps. 132:11 cf. 2 Sam.7:12-13,16,25-26,29	Matt. 1:1
Declared to be the Son of God	Prov. 30:4	Matt. 3:17; Mark 14:61-62; Luke 1:35; John 3:13; 9:35-38; 11:21; Rom. 1:2-4; 10:6-9; 2 Pet. 1:17
Repentance for the nations	Isa. 2:2-4	Luke 24:47
Hearts are hardened	Isa. 6:9-10	Matt. 13:14,15; John 12:39,40; Acts 28:25-27
Born of a virgin	Isa. 7:14	Matt. 1:22,23
A rock of offense	Isa. 8:14,15	Rom. 9:33; 1 Pet. 2:8
Light out of darkness	Isa. 9:1,2	Matt. 4:14-16; Luke 2:32
God with us	Isa. 9:6,7	Matt. 1:21,23; Luke 1:32,33; John 8:58; 10:30; 14:19; 2 Cor. 5:19; Col. 2:9
Full of wisdom and power	Isa. 11:1-10	Matt. 3:16; John 3:34; Rom. 15:12; Heb. 1:9
Reigning in mercy	Isa. 16:4-5	Luke 1:31-33
Peg in a sure place	Isa. 22:21-25	Rev. 3:7
Death swallowed up in victory	Isa. 25:6-12	1 Cor. 15:54
A stone in Zion	Isa. 28:16	Rom. 9:33; 1 Pet. 2:6
The deaf hear, the blind see	Isa. 29:18-19	Matt. 5:3; 11:5; John 9:39
King of kings, Lord of lords	Isa. 32:1-4	Rev. 19:16; 20:6
Son of the Highest	Isa. 33:22	Luke 1:32; 1 Tim. 1:17; 6:15
Healing for the needy	Isa. 35:4-10	Matt. 9:30; 11:5; 12:22; 20:34; 21:14; Mark 7:30; John 5:9
Make ready the way of the Lord	Isa. 40:3-5	Matt. 3:3; Mark 1:3; Luke 3:4-5; John 1:23
The Shepherd dies for his sheep	Isa. 40:10-11	John 10:11; Heb. 13:20; 1 Pet. 2:24-25
The meek Servant	Isa. 42:1-16	Matt. 12:17-21; Luke 2:32
A light to the Gentiles	Isa. 49:6-12	Acts 13:47; 2 Cor. 6:2
Scourged and spat upon	Isa. 50:6	Matt. 26:67; 27:26,30; Mark 14:65; 15:15,19; Luke 22:63-65; John 19:1
Rejected by his people	Isa. 52:13–53:12	Matt. 8:17; 27:1-2,12-14,38
Suffered vicariously	Isa. 53:4-5	Mark 15:3-4,27-28; Luke 23:1-25,32-34
Silent when accused	Isa. 53:7	John 1:29; 11:49-52
Crucified with transgressors	Isa. 53:12	John 12:37-38; Acts 8:28-35
Buried with the rich	Isa. 53:9	Acts 10:43; 13:38-39; 1 Cor. 15:3; Eph. 7; 1 Pet. 2:21-25; 1 John 1:7,9
Calling of those not a people	Isa. 55:4,5	John 18:37; Rom. 9:25-26; Rev. 1:5
Deliver out of Zion	Isa. 59:16-20	Rom. 11:26-2

Messianic Prophecies of the Old Testament

PROPHECY	O.T. REFERENCES	N.T. FULFILLMENT
Nations walk in the light	Isa. 60:1-3	Luke 2:32
Anointed to preach liberty	Isa. 60:1-2	Luke 4:17-19; Acts 10:38
Called by a new name	Isa. 62:11	Luke 2:32; Rev. 3:12
The King cometh	Isa. 62:11	Matt. 21:5
A vesture dipped in blood	Isa. 63:1-3	Rev. 19:13
Afflicted with the afflicted.	Isa. 63:8-9	Matt. 25:34-40
The elect shall inherit	Isa. 65:9	Rom. 11:5,7; Heb. 7:14; Rev. 5:5
New heavens and a new earth	Isa. 65:17-25	2 Pet. 3:13; Rev. 21:1
The Lord our righteousness	Jer. 23:5,6	John 2:19-21; Rom. 1:3-4; Eph. 2:20-21; 1 Pet. 2:5
Born a King	Jer. 30:9	John 18:37; Rev. 1:5
Massacre of infants	Jer. 31:15	Matt. 2:17-18
Conceived by the Holy Spirit	Jer. 31:22	Matt. 1:20; Luke 1:35
A New Covenant	Jer. 31:31-34	Matt. 26:27-29; Mark 14:22-24; Luke 22:15-20; 1 Cor. 11:25; Heb. 8:8-12; 10:15-17; 12:24; 13:20
A spiritual house	Jer. 33:15-17	John 2:19-21; Eph. 2:20-21; 1 Pet. 2:5
A tree planted by God	Ezek. 17:22-24	Matt. 13:31-32
The humble exalted	Ezek. 21:26-27	Luke 1:52
The good Shepherd	Ezek. 34:23-24	John 10:11
Stone cut without hands	Dan. 2:34-35	Acts 4:10-12
His kingdom triumphant	Dan. 2:44-45	Luke 1:33; 1 Cor. 15-24; Rev. 11:15
An everlasting dominion	Dan. 7:13-14	Matt. 24:30; 25:31; 26:64; Mark 14:61,62; Acts 1:9-11; Rev. 1:7
Kingdom for the saints	Dan. 7:27	Luke 1:33; 1 Cor. 15:24; Rev. 11:15
Time of His birth	Dan. 9:24-27	Matt. 24:15-21; Luke 3:1
Israel restored	Hos. 3:5	John 18:37; Rom. 11:25-27
Flight into Egypt	Hos. 11:1	Matt. 2:15
Promise of the Spirit	Joel 2:28-32	Acts 2:17-21; Rom. 15:13
The sun darkened	Amos 8:9	Matt. 24:29; Acts 2:20; Rev. 6:12
Restoration of tabernacle	Amos 9:11-12	Acts 15:16-18
Israel regathered	Mic. 2:12-13	John 10:14,26
The Kingdom established	Mic. 4:1-8	Luke 1:33
Born in Bethlehem	Mic. 5:1-5	Matt. 2:1; Luke 2:4,10-11
Earth filled with knowledge of the glory of the Lord	Hab. 2:14	Rom. 11:26; Rev. 21:23-26
The Lamb on the throne	Zech. 2:10-13	Rev. 5:13; 6:9; 21:24; 22:1-5
A holy priesthood	Zech. 3:8	John 2:19-21; Eph. 2:20-21; 1 Pet. 2:5
A heavenly High Priest	Zech. 6:12-13	Heb. 4:4; 8:1-2
Triumphal entry	Zech. 9:9-10	Matt. 21:4-5; Mark 11:9-10; Luke 20:38; John 12:13-15
Sold for pieces of silver	Zech. 11:12-13	Matt. 26:14-15
Money buys potter's field	Zech. 11:12-13	Matt. 27:9
Piercing of his body	Zech. 12:10	John 19:34,37
Shepherd smitten—sheep scattered	Zech. 13:1,6-7	Matt. 26:31; John 16:32
Preceded by Forerunner	Mal. 3:1	Matt. 11:10; Mark 1:2; Luke 7:27
Our sins purged	Mal. 3:3	Heb. 1:3
The light of the world	Mal. 4:2-3	Luke 1:78; John 1:9; 12:46; 2 Pet. 1:19; Rev. 2:28; 19:11-16; 22:16
The coming of Elijah	Mal. 4:5-6	Matt. 11:14; 17:10-12

The people in the Dead Sea scrolls were evidently able to combine a dual hope of two Messiahs, one priestly and the second a royal figure. The alternation between a kingly Messiah and a priestly figure is characteristic of the two centuries of early Judaism prior to the coming of Jesus.

Messiahship in Jesus' Ministry A question posed in John 4:29 (cp. 7:40-43) is: "Could this be the Messiah?" (HCSB). It is evident that the issue of the Messiah's identity and role was one much debated among the Jews in the first century. In the Synoptic Gospels the way Jesus acted and spoke led naturally to the dialogue at Caesarea Philippi. Jesus asked His disciples, "Who do you say that I am?" a question to which Peter gave the reply, "You are the Messiah" (Mark 8:29 HCSB). Mark made clear that Jesus took an attitude of distinct reserve and caution to this title since it carried overtones of political power, especially in one strand of Jewish hope represented by the *Psalms of Solomon*. Jesus, therefore, accepted Peter's confession with great reluctance since with it went the disciple's objection that the Messiah could not suffer (Mark 9:32). For Peter, Messiah was a title of a glorious personage both nationalistic and victorious in battle. Jesus, on the other hand, saw His destiny in terms of a suffering Son of man and Servant of God (Mark 8:31-38; 9:31; 10:33-34). Hence He did not permit the demons to greet Him as Messiah (Luke 4:41) and downplayed all claims to privilege and overt majesty linked with the Jewish title.

The course of Jesus' ministry is one in which He sought to wean the disciples away from the traditional notion of a warrior Messiah. Instead, Jesus tried to instill in their minds the prospect that the road to His future glory was bound to run by way of the cross, with its experience of rejection, suffering, and humiliation. At the trial before His Jewish judges (Matt. 26:63-66), He once more reinterpreted the title Messiah (KJV, Christ) and gave it a content in terms of the Son of Man figure, based on Dan. 7:13-14. This confession secured His condemnation, and He went to the cross as a crucified Messiah because the Jewish leaders failed to perceive the nature of messiahship as Jesus understood it. Pilate sentenced Him as a messianic pretender who claimed (according to the false charges brought against Him) to be a rival to Caesar (Mark 15:9;

Luke 23:2; John 19:14-15). It was only after the resurrection that the disciples were in a position to see how Jesus was truly a king Messiah and how Jesus then opened their minds to what true messiahship meant (Luke 24:45-46). The national title "Messiah" then took on a broader connotation, involving a kingly role that was to embrace all peoples (Luke 24:46-47).

Messiah as a Title in the Early Church From the resurrection onward the first preachers announced that Jesus was the Messiah by divine appointment (Acts 2:36; Rom. 1:3-4). Part of the reason for this forthright declaration is to be traced to apologetic reasons. In the mission to Israel, the church had to show how Jesus fulfilled the OT prophecies and came into the world as the "Son of David," a title closely linked with the Messiah as a royal person. Matthew's Gospel is especially concerned to establish the identity (Matt. 1:1), but it is equally a theme common to Luke (Luke 1:32,69; 2:4,11; Acts 2:29-36; 13:22-23). Paul also saw in Jesus the fulfillment of the messianic hopes of the old covenant (1 Cor. 5:7-8). Peter, too, sought to show how the sufferings of the Messiah were foretold (1 Pet. 1:11,20; 2:21; 3:18; 4:1,13; 5:1). Luke stressed the link between Jesus as the One anointed by the Holy Spirit (Luke 4:16-22) in a way that looks back to Isa. 61:1, and he recorded Peter's statement (Acts 10:38 HCSB) that "God anointed Jesus of Nazareth with the Holy Spirit and with power" as a fulfillment of OT prophecy. The letter to the Hebrews is rich in this theme (Heb. 1:9; 2:2-4; 9:14-15).

The final stage of development in regard to the title "Messiah" came in the way that Paul used the word more as a personal name than as an official designation (Rom. 9:5, "Christ"). The reason for this shift lies in the intensely personal nature of Paul's faith which centered in Jesus Christ as the divine Lord (Phil. 1:21; Col. 3:4). Also Paul taught his converts, who were mainly converted to Christ from paganism, that Jesus was the universal Lord whose mission was wider than any Jewish hope could embrace. In Pauline thought, "Christ" is a richer term than "Messiah" could ever be, and one pointer in this direction is the fact that the early followers of the Messiah called themselves not converted Jews but "Christians," Christ's people (Acts 11:26; 1 Pet. 4:16) as a sign of their universal

M

faith in a sovereign Lord. See *Christ, Christology; Jesus Christ.*   *Ralph P. Martin*

MESSIANIC SECRET Term that Bible students use to describe Jesus' commands to His audience and His disciples not to reveal who He was after His performance of messianic wonders. Throughout the Gospel of Mark, Jesus made every attempt to conceal His true identity as the Christ. Although the messianic secret can be found in the Gospels of Matthew (8:3-4; 9:29-31; 12:15-16; 17:9) and Luke (4:41; 8:56; 9:21), Mark used the unveiling of the messiahship of Jesus as the unifying theme of his Gospel. Typically Matthew understood the messianic secret as the fulfillment of prophecy (Matt. 12:17-21); Luke provided no explanation. Mark, however, used the messianic secret to organize his story around the progressive revelation of the person of Christ and the messianic consciousness of the disciples. Demons demonstrated that they recognized Jesus immediately: "I know who You are—the Holy One of God!" (1:24-25,34; 3:11-12; 5:6-8; 9:20 HCSB); nevertheless, Jesus suppressed their confession. He prohibited public profession by those who experienced miraculous healing (1:43-44; 5:43; 7:36; 8:26). The parables of Jesus were offered in order to keep "outsiders" from learning the secret (4:11-12). Even the disciples, once they related that they understood the "secret of the kingdom of God" (4:11), were sworn to silence (8:30; 9:9).

Biblical interpreters have suggested a number of reasons why Jesus chose to conceal His identity for a time. Perhaps He avoided the title in light of the popular messianic expectations of the people—they were looking for a political deliverer. Some believe that Jesus prohibited messianic proclamation so that He could continue to move about freely in public. The only parable of Jesus that Mark recorded exclusively may provide a clue to the purpose of the messianic secret. Jesus introduced the parable of the secret growing seed (4:26-29) with the proverb: "For nothing is concealed except to be revealed, and nothing hidden except to come to light" (4:22 HCSB). Jesus intended for people of faith to learn the secret of His messiahship (4:11,34). He compared the mystery of the kingdom of God to a man who sows seed and discovers, to his amazement, that seeded ground produces plants which secretly grow at night—"he doesn't know how" (4:27). Like the seed that is covered by ground, the secret of Jesus' identity would be concealed for a season: discovering the messianic secret would take time. Jesus did not force people to accept Him as Messiah; "those who had ears to hear" must learn the secret on their own. The disciples not only needed time to recognize Jesus as Messiah (4:41; 6:52; 8:17-21), they also needed time to come to terms with His messianic agenda: messianic suffering precedes messianic glory (9:31-32). Complete human understanding of the messianic secret would only be possible after the resurrection (9:9-10). Therefore, no immediate messianic profession would possess any depth of understanding (especially demonic confession). Jesus wanted the disciples to think about the secret until they could articulate the secret. See *Christ, Christology; Jesus Christ; Messiah.*   *Rodney Reeves*

MESSIAS (Mĕs sī´ ås) Greek for Messiah (John 1:41; 4:25 KJV).

METALS, METALSMITH, METALWORKER See *Minerals and Metals; Mines and Mining; Occupations and Professions.*

METHEG-AMMAH (Mĕth ĕḡ-ăm´ mah) Phrase of uncertain meaning used at 2 Sam. 8:1. KJV, NIV, NRSV take it as a place-name. NASB translated the phrase as "the chief city." The parallel in 1 Chron. 18:1 has "Gath and its villages." Other suggestions for translation include: "bridle of the water channel," "reins of the forearm," "control of the mother city," "take the common land," or "wrest supremacy from."

METHUSAEL (Mə thū´ sā ĕl) (KJV) or **METHUSHAEL** (Mə thū´ shā ĕl) Personal name of uncertain meaning. "Man of God" is possible. Canaanite patriarch (Gen. 4:18). Some scholars regard the name as a variant of Methuselah (Gen. 5:21).

METHUSELAH (Mə thūz´ ə lah) Personal name meaning either "man of the javelin" or "worshiper of Selah." A son of Enoch (who walked with God) and grandfather of Noah (Gen. 5:21,26-29). According to the biblical record Methuselah is the oldest human ever, dying at age 969 (Gen. 5:27).

MEUNIM, MEUNITES (Mǝ´ ū nǐm; Mǝ ū´ nǐts) See *Mehunim.*

MEZAHAB (Měz´ á hăb) Either a personal name or a place-name meaning "waters of gold" (Gen. 36:39; 1 Chron. 1:50). If a person, Mezahab was the grandfather of Mehetabel, the wife of King Hadar of Edom. If a place-name, Mezahab was the home of Matred which should perhaps be identified with Dizahab (Deut. 1:1).

MEZUZAH (Mě zū´ zà) Hebrew term for "doorpost." Ancient doors pivoted on posts set in sockets. The blood of the Passover lamb was to be applied to doorposts (Exod. 12:7,22-23). At the beginning of the new year, blood was to be applied to the doorposts of the temple to make atonement for it (Ezek. 45:19). The command to write the words of the Shema (Deut. 6:4-9; 11:13-21) on the doorposts of one's home, like the command to write them on one's heart (Deut. 6:6), is a challenge to remember always that love of God is central to faith. At a later time these commands were understood literally. Today mezuzah refers to small scrolls inscribed with Deut. 6:4-9; 11:13-21 placed in a container attached to the doorjambs of some Jewish homes.

MIAMIN (Mī´ á mǐn) (KJV, Ezra 10:25; Neh. 12:5) See *Mijamin.*

MIBHAR (Mǐb´ här) Personal name meaning "best" or "chosen." One of David's 30 elite warriors (1 Chron. 11:38). The parallel at 2 Sam. 23:36, reflecting a copying error in transmission of the text, reads "of Zobah, Bani the Gadite."

MIBSAM (Mǐb´ săm) Personal name meaning "fragrant." **1.** Arab tribe descended from a son of Ishmael (Gen. 25:13; 1 Chron. 1:29). **2.** Descendant of Simeon (1 Chron. 4:25).

MIBZAR (Mǐb´ zär) Personal name meaning "fortification." Edomite clan chief and his tribe (Gen. 36:42; 1 Chron. 1:53). Mibzar is possibly Mabsara in northern Edom or Bozrah (Gen. 36:33; Amos 1:12).

MICA (Mī´ cà) Variant spelling that modern translations used for "Micah," reflecting Aramaic spelling in text of 2 Sam. 9:12; Neh. 10:11; 11:17,22; 1 Chron. 9:15. All passages reflect Levites. See *Micha 2.*

MICAH (Mī´ cah) Abbreviated form of the personal name Micaiah, meaning "Who is like Yahweh?" **1.** Ephraimite whose home shrine was the source of Dan's idolatrous worship (Judg. 17–18). **2.** Descendant of Reuben (1 Chron. 5:5). **3.** Descendant of King Saul (1 Chron. 8:34-35; 9:40-44; 2 Sam. 9:12 KJV, Micha). **4.** Leader of a family of Levites in David's time (1 Chron. 23:20; 24:24-25). **5.** Father of Abdon, a contemporary of Josiah (2 Chron. 34:20; 2 Kings 22:12, Micaiah). **6.** Eighth century B.C. prophet who came from Moresheth (NRSV, HCSB) which probably should be identified with Moresheth-gath. This village was located about 25 miles southwest of Jerusalem in the tribe of Judah. Micah, however, may have lived in Jerusalem during his ministry. He worked in the reigns of Jotham (750–732 B.C.), Ahaz (735–715 B.C.), and Hezekiah (715–686 B.C.) who were kings of Judah. The identification of these kings does not mean that he was active from 750 to 686 but that his ministry spanned parts of each reign. Jeremiah 26:17-18 refers to Micah as prophesying during the time of Hezekiah. Determining exact dates, however, for each of the prophecies contained in the book is difficult. Micah was a contemporary of Isaiah, Hosea, and possibly Amos. His prophecies addressed Samaria and Jerusalem. Samaria was the capital of the Northern Kingdom (Israel) and Jerusalem of the Southern Kingdom (Judah). Even though Micah ministered in Judah, some of his messages were directed toward Israel. See *Micaiah; Micha; Michaiah.*

MICAH, BOOK OF (Mī´ cah) Book named after the eighth century B.C. prophet, containing some of his messages. See *Micah.*
Historical Background In Micah's time many political and national crises occurred. Micah addressed those issues. The Assyrian Empire began to dominate the ancient Near East about 740 B.C. Judah and Israel became tribute-paying vassals of this new political power, and in 722 B.C. Israel felt the might of the Assyrian army. Shalmaneser V and Sargon II destroyed the Northern Kingdom and its capital Samaria

M

M

(2 Kings 16–17) because of an attempted rebellion. The records of Sargon II state that he "besieged and conquered Samaria, (and) led away as booty 27,290 inhabitants of it." While Judah survived, they still were vassals. Micah 1:2-7 associates the imminent destruction of Samaria as God's judgment for the people's idolatry. Hezekiah, king of Judah, instituted many reforms that caused the Assyrian king, Sennacherib, to respond with force. Many cities of Judah were destroyed, and Jerusalem was unsuccessfully besieged (2 Kings 18–19). The annals of Sennacherib boast that he laid siege to 46 cities and countless small villages. He took 200,150 people as booty along with the livestock. As for Hezekiah, Sennacherib says, "Himself I made a prisoner in Jerusalem, his royal residence, like a bird in a cage." Despite the failure to take Jerusalem, the citizens of the Southern Kingdom suffered greatly from the invasion.

Prophet's Message The subjects of Micah's messages reveal much about the society of his day. He constantly renounced the oppression of the poor by the rich. He characterized the rich as devising ways in which to cheat the poor out of their land (2:1-5). People were evicted from their homes and had their possessions stolen. Those who committed such crimes were fellow Israelites (2:6-11). The marketplace was full of deception and injustice (6:9-16). The rulers of the country, who had the responsibility of upholding justice, did the opposite (3:1-4).

Micah also denounced the religious practices of the nation. He predicted the destruction of Judah as an act of God's judgment. Other prophets, however, led the people to believe that this could never happen because God was residing in the nation and would protect them. Micah contended that the other prophets' message was not from God. Instead, the message from God was the imminent devastation of Judah (3:5-12).

Although the people worshiped other gods, they did not quit believing in and worshiping the God of Judah but combined this worship with devotion to the other deities (5:10-15). The people believed all that religion required of them was to bring their sacrifices and offerings to the temple. No relationship was acknowledged between their activity in the temple and their activity in daily life. Micah attempted to correct this misconception by arguing that God is not just interested in the physical act of making a sac-

rifice but is supremely concerned with obedience that extends into daily life (6:6-8).

Micah warned of impending judgment on God's people for their disobedience. At the same time he proclaimed messages of hope. Judgment would come, but afterwards God would restore a remnant of the people devoted to Him (4:1-13; 7:14-20). Unlike the unjust kings that the people were accustomed to, God would bring a ruler who would allow the people to live in peace (5:1-5). Ultimately Judah was destroyed in 586 B.C. by the Babylonians, but a remnant returned. Matthew saw in Micah's hope for a new ruler a description of Christ (Matt. 2:6). See *Ahaz; Assyria; Hezekiah; Israel; Jerusalem; Prophet; Samaria.*

Outline

I. God's Word Witnesses against All People (1:1-2).

II. God Judges His People for Their Sins (1:3–3:12).
   A. God judges religious infidelity (1:3-16).
   B. God judges economic injustice (2:1-5).
   C. God judges false preaching (2:6-11).
   D. God's judgment looks to the remnant's restoration (2:12-13).
   E. God judges unjust leaders (3:1-4).
   F. God judges those who preach peace and prosperity for sinners (3:5-7).
   G. God judges through His Spirit-filled messenger (3:8).
   H. God judges corrupt, greedy officials (3:9-12).

III. God Promises a Day of International Peace and Worship (4:1–5:15).
   A. God plans for His people to teach His way to the nations (4:1-5).
   B. God plans to redeem and rule His weakened remnant (4:6-11).
   C. God plans to show the world His universal rule (4:12-13).
   D. God plans to raise up a Shepherd from Bethlehem to bring peace and victory to His beleaguered flock (5:1-9).
   E. God plans to destroy weapons and idolatry from His people (5:10-15).

IV. God Has a Case against His People (6:1–7:6).
   A. God has done His part, redeeming His people (6:1-5).

B. God's expectations are clear: justice, mercy, piety (6:6-8).

C. God's people have not met His expectations (6:9-12).

D. God's punishment is sure for a corrupt people (6:13–7:6).

V. God in Righteousness, Love, and Faithfulness Will Forgive and Renew His People (7:7-20).

A. God's people can trust Him for salvation (7:7).

B. God's repentant people can expect better days ahead (7:8-14).

C. God's enemies face shameful judgment (7:15-17).

D. The incomparable God of patience, mercy, compassion, and faithfulness will forgive and renew His people (7:18-20).   *Scott Langston*

MICAIAH (Mī kā´ yả) Personal name meaning "Who is like Yahweh?" **1.** Son of Imlah and prophet of Yahweh who predicted the death of Ahab and the scattering of Israel's forces at Ramoth-gilead (1 Kings 22:7-28). Having witnessed Yahweh's heavenly council, Micaiah was certain Ahab's 400 prophets were possessed by a lying spirit. When accused and imprisoned on a charge of false prophesy, Micaiah replied, "If you indeed return safely the LORD has not spoken by me" (22:28 NASB). **2.** Form of Michaiah that modern translations prefer.

MICE See *Mouse.*

MICHA (Mī kả) KJV for Micah and Mica. **1.** Descendant of King Saul (2 Sam. 9:12). See *Micah* 3. **2.** One in a family line of temple musicians (Neh. 11:17,22). Nehemiah 12:35 uses the longer form Micaiah.

MICHAEL (Mī´ kәl) Personal name meaning "Who is like God?" **1.** Father of one of the 12 Israelite spies (Num. 13:13). **2–3.** Two Gadites (1 Chron. 5:13-14). **4.** Ancestor of Asaph (1 Chron. 6:40). **5.** Leader of the tribe of Issachar (1 Chron. 7:3) perhaps identical to the father of Omri (1 Chron. 27:18). **6.** Leader of the tribe of Benjamin (1 Chron. 8:16). **7.** Manassite who defected to David's army (1 Chron. 12:20). **8.** Son of King Jehoshaphat (2 Chron. 21:2). **9.** Ancestor of one of those who returned from exile with Ezra (Ezra 8:8). **10.** Archangel who served as the guardian of the nation of Israel (Dan. 10:13,21; 12:1). Together with Gabriel, Michael fought for Israel against the prince (angelic patron) of Persia. This angelic Michael figures in much extrabiblical literature in the intertestamental period. In Rev. 12:7 Michael commands the forces of God against the forces of the dragon in a war in heaven. Jude 9 refers to a dispute between the devil and Michael over Moses' body. According to Origen (A.D. 185 to 254), this account formed part of the extrabiblical work, *The Assumption of Moses.* The incident is not mentioned in the surviving fragments of this work. See *Angel.*

MICHAH (Mī´ kả) Abbreviated form of the personal name Micaiah that KJV used for the leader of a family of Levites in David's time (1 Chron. 23:20; 24:24-25). Modern translations prefer the form Micah.

MICHAIAH (Mī kā´ yả) KJV form of Micaiah, a personal name meaning "Who is like Yah?" **1.** Father of an officer of King Josiah (2 Kings 22:12). **2.** Wife of King Rehoboam and mother of Abijah (2 Chron. 13:1-2). **3.** Participant in Jehoshaphat's reforms (2 Chron. 17:7). **4.** Member of a leading family in Jeremiah's time (Jer. 36:11,13). **5.** Priest participating in Nehemiah's dedication of the walls (Neh. 12:41) and ancestor of a participating priest (Neh. 12:35).

MICHAL (Mī´ kảl) Personal name meaning "Who is like El (God)?" a variant form of Micah, "Who is like Yah?" and an abbreviated form of Michael. King Saul's younger daughter (1 Sam. 14:49), given to David in marriage for the price of 100 dead Philistines (1 Sam. 18:20-29). Saul may have thought David would be killed in the attempt. The king continued to set traps for David, but on one occasion Michal helped her husband escape (1 Sam 19:11-17). For revenge Saul gave her to Phaltiel (1 Sam. 25:44). Following Saul's death at Gilboa, David made a treaty with Abner, Saul's general. One of the points of the pact was that Michal would be returned to David, much to Phaltiel's regret (2 Sam. 3:14-16). David's dancing before the ark of the covenant as he brought the sacred box to Jerusalem enraged Michal, who criticized the king to his face. As punishment Michal was never allowed to bear children (2 Sam. 6:16-23; cp. 2 Sam. 21:8).

MICMASH, (Mĭk´ măsh) (NIV, NLT) **MICHMASH** Place-name meaning "hidden place." City in Benjamin about seven miles northeast of Jerusalem, four and a half miles northeast of Gibeah, rising 1,980 feet above sea level overlooking a pass going from the Jordan River to Ephraim. It is four and a half miles southeast of Bethel, which rises 2,890 feet above sea level. It is modern Mukhmas. Michmash served as a staging area, first for Saul (1 Sam. 13:2) and then for the Philistine army as they prepared to fight. It lay on the standard invasion route from the north (Isa. 10:28). The Philistines mustered 30,000 chariots and 6,000 horsemen there (1 Sam. 13:5-6). Before the battle could begin, Jonathan and his armor bearer sneaked into the Philistine camp, killed 20 sentries, and set off great confusion, resulting in the Philistines fighting each other (14:20). Exiles returning from Babylon rehabited the city (Neh. 11:31; cp. 7:31). It served as Jonathan Maccabeus' residence and seat of government (1 Macc. 9:73). See *Intertestamental History and Literature; Jonathan.*

MICHMETHAH (Mĭk´ mə thah) or **MICHMETHATH** (Mĭk mə thăth) (NASB, NIV, NRSV, REB) Place-name meaning "hiding place" or "concealment." Site near Shechem (Josh. 16:6; 17:7). Michmethath has been identified with Khirbet Makhneh el-Foqa about five miles southeast of Shechem and with Khirbet Juleijil east of Shechem.

MICHRI (Mĭk´ rī) Personal name meaning "purchase price." Member of the tribe of Benjamin (1 Chron. 9:8).

MICHTAM (Mĭk´ tăm) KJV form of Miktam. Heading for Pss. 16; 56–60. The meaning of the term is disputed. Suggestions include a musical notation or a title for psalms connected with expiation of sin. At Isa. 38:9 Hezekiah's "writing" (Hb. *miktav*) should perhaps be Miktam.

MICRI (Mĭc´ rī) (NIV) See *Michri.*

MIDDAY Noon or thereabouts (Neh. 8:3; Acts 26:13).

View of the gorge at Michmash.

MIDDIN (Mĭd´ dĭn) Place-name meaning "judgment." Village in the wilderness district of Judah (Josh. 15:61). The Septuagint identified Middin with Madon. Khirbet Abu Tabaq in the Achor Valley has been suggested as a possible site.

MIDDLE GATE City gate of Jerusalem (Jer. 39:3). Archeologists have found evidence of battle (arrowheads, charred wood) located outside the remains of a gate in the middle of the north wall of the preexilic city. It seems probable that the Babylonians attacked the city from the north and that these are, in fact, the remains of the Middle Gate. The gate is possibly identical to the Fish Gate (2 Chron. 33:14; Neh. 3:3; Zeph. 1:10). See *Gate.*

MIDDLE WALL Term is found in Eph. 2:14 and variously translated: "middle wall of partition" (KJV); "dividing wall of hostility" (HCSB, NRSV, NIV); "barrier of the dividing wall" (NASB); "barrier of enmity which separated them" (REB). Investigation of the term has yielded several possible interpretations. **1.** The wall that separated the inner and outer courts of the temple and prevented Jews and Gentiles from worshiping together. Inscriptions in Greek and Latin warned that Gentiles who disregarded the barrier would suffer the pain of death. **2.** The curtain that separated the holy of holies from the rest of the temple. This curtain was rent at the death of Jesus (Mark 15:38) and is representative of the separation of all humanity from God. **3.** The "fence" consisting of detailed commandments and oral interpretations erected around the law by its interpreters to ensure its faithful observation. In reality, the fenced-in law generated hostility between Jews and Gentiles and further divided them, as well as furthering the enmity between God and humanity. Destruction of the Law's mediators opens a new and living way to God through Christ Jesus (Eph. 2:18; 3:12; Heb. 10:20). **4.** The cosmic barrier that separates God and persons, persons themselves, and other powers in the universe (Eph. 1:20-21)—angels, dominions, principalities. **5.** Echoing Isa. 59:2, the term refers to the separation of humanity from God as a result of sin.

No one interpretation is sufficient by itself. The writer of Ephesians stressed that every conceivable barrier that exists between persons and between God and humanity has been destroyed by God's definitive work in Jesus Christ. See *Ephesians; Gentiles; Law; Salvation; Sin; Temple.*   *William J. Ireland, Jr.*

MIDIAN, MIDIANITES (Mĭd´ ĭ ăn, Mĭd´ ĭ ăn īts). Personal and clan name meaning "strife." Midian was the son of Abraham by his concubine Keturah (Gen. 25:2). Abraham sent him and his brothers away to the east, leading to the association of the Midianites with the "children of the east" (Judg. 6:3). Midianites took Joseph to Egypt (Gen. 37:28,36). Since the caravan in the passage is also described as Ishmaelite (37:25; 39:1), it is possible that these two groups descended from Abraham had become interrelated. Alternately, the term Ishmaelite in these verses may be a generic term for nomadic travelers. The OT mentions the Midianites in widely scattered geographical locations, but their main homeland seems to be east of the Jordan and south of Edom. Later historians located the land of Midian in northwestern Arabia east of the Gulf of Aqaba. The people of Israel had both good and bad relationships with the Midianites. When Moses fled from Pharaoh, he went east to Midian (Exod. 2:15). Here he met Jethro (also called Reuel), the priest of Midian, and married his daughter. During the wandering in the wilderness, Reuel's father-in-law Hobab served as a guide for the Israelites (Num. 10:29-32). The Midianites are associated with the Moabites in seducing Israel into immorality and pagan worship at Baal-peor (Num. 25:1-18). For this reason God commanded Moses to execute a war of vengeance against them (Num. 31:3; cp. Josh. 13:21). In the time of the judges the Midianites along with the Amalekites began to raid Israel using camels to strike swiftly over great distances. Gideon drove them out and killed their leaders (Judg. 6–8). They never again threatened Israel; but Midian did harbor Solomon's enemy Hadad (1 Kings 11:18). See *Amalekite; Baal-peor; Gideon; Ishmaelite; Jethro; Kenites.*   *Ricky L. Johnson*

MIDRASH Jewish interpretations of the OT included a form called Midrash. The Hebrew noun *midrash* is related to the verb *darash,* which means "to search" and thus refers to an "inquiry" or "examination." The word was commonly used to denote the process of biblical interpretation or the written expression of that interpretation.

The term "midrash" appears twice in the Bible. In both contexts the word describes a "study," "exposition," "interpretation," or "discussion." In 2 Chron. 13:22 the word refers to a literary work written by the Prophet Iddo that recounted the acts of Abijah. In 2 Chron. 24:27 the term seems to refer to a commentary on the *Book of the Kings.* In the Dead Sea Scrolls, the term refers to biblical interpretation and functions as a synonym of *pesher* ("interpretation"). In the Qumran community "midrash" referred to biblical interpretation that quoted or alluded to a biblical text and then sought to show how the text was meaningful to contemporary readers.

According to early rabbinic tradition, Hillel the Elder formulated seven rules which guided Jewish biblical interpretation. These rules were sensible guidelines for understanding the Bible and examples of the application of each rule appear in the NT. Later rabbis formulated many other rules that resulted in wild, fanciful interpretations that lost all connection with the literary and historical context of the passage under discussion.

Rabbinic Midrash may be divided into two basic categories: Halakah and Haggadah. "Halakah" (derived from the Hebrew verb meaning "to walk," which was often used to speak of one's legal or ethical conduct) investigated the legal parts of the OT with the aim of establishing rules of conduct. "Haggadah" was an interpretation of nonlegal portions of the OT that sought to inform, challenge, or inspire without establishing or supporting legal standards.

Ancient midrash appeared in several basic forms. The "Targums" were Aramaic paraphrases of the Hebrew OT. Another form of midrash completely rewrote OT narratives by editing, expanding, and paraphrasing rather freely. Another form of midrash quoted words from a biblical text and then interpreted them. Often the literary form resembled a modern commentary, although the rules that guided interpretation were sometimes very different from those used by modern commentators. Sometimes the interpreter gave a verse-by-verse explanation of a text, but at other times comments on the Scriptures were arranged according to topic.

The NT contains midrash and is midrashic in the sense that many portions of the NT offer interpretations of specific OT texts that follow the normal patterns of exegesis suggested by ancient rabbis. However, some recent critics who claim that the Gospels are midrash or contain midrash mean that the Gospel writers used narrative motifs from the OT to invent stories about the life of Christ that have no real basis in history. The search for these narrative motifs and the way in which they were used to create Gospel narratives is known as Midrash Criticism. Midrash critics claim that ancient Christians had no qualms about nonhistorical stories about Jesus as long as these stories expressed some spiritual truth. These claims however are unconvincing. The term "midrash," as it is used by the midrash critics, refers to a "theological tale" or Jewish myth. However 1 Tim. 1:4; 4:6-7; and Titus 1:14 show that Paul, no doubt expressing the prevailing conviction of the early church, disparaged "Jewish myths" and called for believers to reject them. Second Peter 1:16 adamantly denies that the apostolic accounts concerning the "power and coming of our Lord Jesus Christ" (HCSB) were "cleverly contrived myths." The NT may be described as midrashic since it contains quotations and interpretations of OT texts. But the NT is not midrash, if by this one means that the NT writers present their own imaginative creations as if they were history.

The study of midrash may offer the modern interpreter of Scripture a greater insight into the methods of interpretation used throughout Jewish history. As the student examines the strengths and weaknesses of these approaches to interpretation, he may learn how one's culture and worldview impact his understanding of the Bible and how he may more "accurately interpret the word of truth."   *Charles L. Quarles*

MIDWIFE Woman who assists in the delivery of a baby (Exod. 1:15-21). The duties of the midwife likely included cutting the umbilical cord, washing and salting the infant, and wrapping the child in cloths (Ezek. 16:4). The civil disobedience of the Hebrew midwives Siphrah and Puah confounded Pharaoh's plan to exterminate male Hebrews for a time (Exod. 1:15-21). Their faithfulness was rewarded with families of their own (Exod. 1:21), suggesting that childless women frequently served as midwives. The women of

Ruth 4:14-17 and 1 Sam. 4:20 were likely serving as midwives.

MIGDAL EDER NIV transliteration of tower of Eder (Gen. 35:21). See *Eder*.

MIGDAL-EL (Mĭg´ dăl-ĕl) Place-name meaning "fortress of God." Fortified town in Naphtali (Josh. 19:38). Migdal-el was located in northern Galilee in the vicinity of Iron (Yiron).

MIGDAL-GAD (Mĭg´ dăl-găd) Place-name meaning "Tower of Gad." Village near Lachish in the Shephelah district of Judah (Josh. 15:37). The site is perhaps that of Khirbet el-Mejdeleh five miles south of Beit Jibrin.

MIGDOL (Mĭg´ dŏl) Transliteration of Hebrew word meaning "tower, watchtower, fortress." A town or a border fortress located in the northeast corner of Egypt. The site is mentioned in reference to two events in biblical history—the exodus and the exile. One of the sites on or near the route of the exodus, Migdol was located near the sites of Pi-hahiroth and Baal-zephron, all of which were near the sea (Exod. 14:2). Jewish refugees fled to Migdol during the exile (Jer. 44:1). The coming doom of Egypt at the hand of Nebuchadnezzar was to be proclaimed there (Jer. 46:13-14). Ezekiel prophesied that the land of Egypt would be laid waste, "from Migdol to Syene" (Ezek. 29:10; 30:6 NRSV, NASB), that is from the northern extremity of the land, Migdol, to the southern extremity of the land, Syene.

Since "migdol" could be used as a proper name, "Migdol," or as a common noun, "tower," two questions remain unresolved. What is the exact location of the site of Migdol? Do all of the references to Migdol refer to the same site, or was there more than one site in Egypt named Migdol? More than one site may have borne the name Migdol, though the evidence we have at hand is inconclusive. The Amarna Letters from Egypt refer to an Egyptian city named Maagdali, but information about its location is not given. For instance, a papyrus manuscript mentions the Migdol of Pharoah Seti I. This Migdol was located near Tjeku, the location of which is still debated. Some prefer to identify Tjeku with Succoth, modern-day Tell el-Maskhutah, while others identify it with Tell el-

Her located further north near Pelusium. For this reason we may assume with some certainty that there were at least two sites named Migdol: the Migdol referred to by Jeremiah and Ezekiel located near Pelusium and the Migdol on the route of the exodus located near Succoth. Both may have been part of a line of border fortresses or migdols designed to provide protection for Egypt against invasion from the Sinai. See *Amarna, Tell el; Egypt; Watchtower.*

LaMoine DeVries

MIGHTY MEN Applied to the descendants of the Nephilim, "mighty men" likely indicates men of great size (Gen. 6:4; perhaps Josh. 10:2). Elsewhere mighty men refers to valiant warriors, especially to the elite groups of three and 30 who served David (2 Sam. 17:8,10; 23:8-39; 1 Kings 1:10,38). Many of David's elite forces were mercenaries.

MIGRON (Mĭg´ rŏn) Place-name meaning "precipice." Town (or towns) in Benjamin (1 Sam. 14:2; Isa. 10:28). The town of 1 Samuel is generally located near Gibeah south of Michmash. The town of Isaiah 10 is generally located between Aiath (Ai) and Michmash, that is, to the north of Michmash. Suggested sites include Makrun, Tell Miryam, and Tell el 'Askar.

MIJAMIN (Mĭj´ ȧ mĭn) Contracted form of the personal name Miniamin, meaning "lucky" (literally, "from the right hand"). The name is attested in Neo-Babylonian and Persian business documents. **1.** Priest in David's time (1 Chron. 24:9). **2.** Priest who returned from exile with Zerubbabel (Neh. 12:5). **3.** Priest witnessing Ezra's covenant renewal (Neh. 10:7). **4.** Layman with a foreign wife (Ezra 10:25). The KJV form of 2. and 4. is Miamin.

MIKLOTH (Mĭk´ lŏth) Personal name meaning "sticks." **1.** Descendant of Jeiel and resident of Gibeon (1 Chron. 8:32; 9:37-38). **2.** Officer in David's militia (1 Chron. 27:4). REB, RSV followed the early Greek translation in omitting the name.

MIKNEIAH (Mĭk nī´ ah) Personal name meaning "Yahweh acquires" or "Yahweh creates." Levitic musician in David's time (1 Chron. 15:18,21).

MIKTAM (Mĭk´ tăm) See *Michtam*.

MILALAI (Mĭl´ à lī) Personal name meaning "eloquent." Musician participating in Nehemiah's dedication of the wall (Neh. 12:36). The earliest Greek translation lacks the name, prompting some to suggest a scribal corruption due to repeating the following name (Gilalai). The shorter Greek text may, however, result from omission due to the scribe skipping to a word with a similar ending.

MILCAH (Mĭl´ cah) Personal name meaning "queen." **1.** Abraham's niece and the wife of Nahor, the patriarch's brother. She bore eight sons, one of whom was Bethuel, Rebekah's father (Gen. 11:29; 24:15). **2.** One of five daughters of Zelophehad (Num. 26:33), left without support after the death of their father. They pled their case before Moses for an inheritance as a son would receive. In a landmark ruling for Israel, God commanded Moses to give each of the daughters an inheritance from their father's estate (Num. 27:1-8; 36:11; Josh. 17:3).

MILCOM (Mĭl´ cŏm) Name of deity meaning "king" or "their king." Apparently a form created by Hebrew scribes to slander and avoid pronouncing the name of the national god of Ammon (1 Kings 11:5,7), who may have been identified with Chemosh, the god of Moab. From the inscription of Mesha there appears to have been a god, Athar, whose local titles were Chemosh and Milcom. This cult may have been practiced in Jerusalem before the Israelite conquest. "King" may have been the god's name or his title as king of the gods. David defeated Ammon and confiscated the crown (2 Sam. 12:30) of their king (KJV, NASB, NIV) or of the statue of the god Milcom (NRSV, REB; cp. TEV). Solomon built sanctuaries to Milcom on the Mount of Olives at the request of his foreign wives, reviving the ancient cult (1 Kings 11:5,33). The sites of Solomon's sanctuaries were destroyed and defiled during Josiah's reforms in 621 B.C. (2 Kings 23:13). Jeremiah described past accomplishments attributed to Milcom, but in a play on Judg. 11:24, he

announced destruction and captivity for Milcom (Jer. 49:1,3 NRSV, NASB, REB; cp. NIV, TEV). Worshiping Milcom was turning one's back on Yahweh (Zeph. 1:5-6). See *Chemosh; Gods, Pagan; Moab; Molech*.

MILDEW Fungus causing a whitish growth on plants. The Hebrew term rendered "mildew" means "paleness." The term may refer to the yellowing of leaves as a result of drought rather than to a fungus (Deut. 28:22-24; 1 Kings 8:37; 2 Chron. 6:28; Amos 4:9; Hag. 2:17). Mildew is one of the agricultural plagues God sent to encourage repentance.

MILE The Roman mile of Matt. 5:41 is about 4,848 feet (about 432 feet shorter than the modern statute mile).

MILETUM (Mĭ lē´ tŭm) (KJV) or **MILETUS** (Mĭ lē´ tŭs) Ancient city on the west coast of Asia Minor. Miletus had four natural harbors and was a major port for the Minoan and Mycenean cultures. After 700 B.C. the Ionians developed it into an even greater center of commerce. It served as the port for Ephesus. It featured a major school of philosophy; many artisans practiced there; and it was among the first cities to mint coins. This culture flour-

A Roman milestone. The inscriptions are in two languages—Palmyrene and Greek.

A view of the walkway underneath where the audience sat in the theater at Miletus.

Reconstruction of the Asian city of Miletus as it appeared in the first century A.D.

M

The theater at Miletus.

ished until 494 B.C. when the Persians sacked the city in answer to a revolt by the Ionians. Alexander captured Miletus on his way eastward in 334 B.C., and the city saw a revival of the arts under his Hellenistic regime. In particular the architectural beauty of the city increased. Rome's influence increased the pace of economic development.

Paul encountered a robust city when he sailed to Miletus. The people probably were open to the gospel he preached. He chose to meet with the elders of the church at Ephesus in Miletus (Acts 20:15-17). A second visit may have been made by the apostle a few years later (2 Tim. 4:20). The harbor began to silt up by A.D. 100, bringing a gradual halt to the city's usefulness and prominence. Today the ruins are over five miles inland. See *Asia Minor, Cities of; Ephesus.*   *Mike Mitchell*

MILK Nourishing liquid and its by-products, a staple of the Hebrew diet. The OT uses the term variously of sweet milk, soured milk, cheese, butter, and, symbolically, of blessing and abundance. The NT only has a symbolic use of what is first and basic in the Christian life. The word is used 43 times in the OT, with 20 being symbolic, and only five times in the NT.

Most often milk came from sheep and goats (Prov. 27:27; Deut. 32:14); cow's milk was also known (Isa. 7:21-22), as was milk from humans (Isa. 28:9). Butter and cheese were known among the ancients (1 Sam. 17:18) as well as curdled, sour milk which still forms, after bread, the chief food of the poorer classes in Arabia and Syria. This soured milk was carried by travelers who mixed it with meat, dried it, and then dissolved it in water to make a refreshing drink

such as that set by Abraham before the messengers (Gen. 18:8). After setting awhile, the drink would carry an intoxicating effect leading some to believe that the fermented variety is the drink that Jael gave to Sisera (Judg. 4:19).

The OT's most extensive use of milk is in conjunction with honey to symbolize abundance and blessing (Exod. 3:17; 13:5; 33:3; Lev. 20:24; Num. 13:27; Deut. 6:3; Josh. 5:6). Milk is also used to symbolize whiteness (Lam. 4:7) and in Song of Songs as a symbol of marital bliss (5:1).

Milk as a symbol prevails in the NT where the term is used only five times (1 Cor. 3:2; 9:7; Heb. 5:12-13; 1 Pet. 2:2). In each instance it speaks concerning what is basic to the Christian life but not all that is needed. The ancient Bedouins could live on milk for days but eventually had to have meat; so must the Christian.

One of the more perplexing sayings of Scripture is the repeated rule (Exod. 23:19; 34:26; Deut. 14:21) not to boil a kid in its mother's milk. The rabbis interpreted this command to mean that milk and meat should neither be cooked nor eaten together. Certain scholars have seen in the command a prohibition relating to Canaanite sacrificial customs though recent archaeological investigations lend little support to this view.   *G. Al Wright, Jr.*

MILL Two circular stones used to grind grain. Usually it was worked by two women facing each other. One woman fed the grain at the center, and the other guided the products into little piles. The grain to be ground is fed into the central hole in the upper stone and gradually works down between the stones. As the grain is reduced to flour, it flies out from between the stones onto a cloth or skin placed underneath the mill. To make fine flour, it is reground and sifted. The stone was made of basalt and was about a foot and a half in diameter and two to four inches thick.

It was forbidden to take millstones as a pledge because they were so important to sustaining life (Deut. 24:6). The manna which fell in the wilderness was tough enough so that people ground it in mills before cooking it (Num. 11:7-8).

In the NT our Lord prophesied that at His coming "two women will be grinding at the mill: one will be taken and one left" (Matt. 24:41 HCSB). In Rev. 18:21 the millstone was cast into

Rotary mills at Capernaum.

the sea as a symbol of absolute destruction. See *Manna.*   *Gary Bonner*

MILLENNIUM This expression, taken from Latin words, means 1,000 years. The Bible passage that mentions the "thousand years" is Rev. 20:1-7, where the word appears six times. The Latin Vulgate uses *mille anni* and its variant renderings to translate the Greek *chilia ete.*

Various theological proposals have been offered to explain this passage from Rev. 20 as well as various other Scriptures that might be taken to speak to the same issue. One's view on this text will be determined by one's approach to interpreting predictive prophecy and by one's view on symbolic and apocalyptic language.

Broadly there are three schools of thought: amillennialism, premillennialism, and postmillennialism. The prefixes "a," "pre," and "post" suggest the view of the timing of the Lord Jesus Christ's second advent in relation to the "thousand years." Hence, postmillennialists argue that Christ returns after the "thousand years." Premillennialists argue that Christ comes before the thousand years. Amillennialists also contend that the Lord comes after the thousand years much like postmillennialists, but they understand the thousand years differently. For the amillennialist, as the prefix suggests, there really is no literal thousand years. Instead, the whole interadvent period between the first and second comings of Christ is taken to be the "millennium." Some postmillennialists argue with the amillennialists that the millennium may not be a literal thousand years, yet they generally agree with the premillennialists that the millennium is yet future. There are many variations even among adherents to the same broad view of the millennium.

The amillennialist links the thousand years beginning with the binding of the devil (Rev. 20:2-3) which he interprets as having taken place at the first coming of Christ. In Mark 3:27 Jesus mentioned the binding of "the strong man." Amillennialists also believe in a single cataclysmic end, which leaves no room for a literal thousand-year reign of Christ on the earth. Ephesians 1:10 and Rom. 8:18-23 suggest one event. Jesus Himself spoke of "that day" in which resurrection takes place. In a classic passage the resurrection of the righteous and unrighteous appears to take place on the same day (John 5:24-29).

The main argument of the postmillennialist is that the gospel will advance victoriously in the world, Christianize the nations, and usher in a golden age (the thousand years: literal or symbolic of an extended period of time). In Matt. 16 Jesus promised the church victory in the world. Postmillennialists remind us that Jesus affirmed that the "gates of hell (Hades)" would not prevail against the church. Gates are not used in attack but in defense. As the church marches on, it will triumph. The defenses of Satan will fall under the mighty power of God's Word. Jesus promised as much in His parable of the mustard seed (Matt. 13:31-32; Mark 4:30-32; Luke 13:18-19). In Rev. 7:9-10 a great multitude is seen as redeemed. This is seen by postmillennialists as the great advance and victory of the gospel in the world.

Premillennialists contend that the millennium is actually begun only with the cataclysmic arrival of Jesus in His second coming as indicated by Rev. 19:11-21. Only then do we see the reign of Christ on the earth. By reading the book of Revelation in chronological progression, a premillennial scenario naturally unfolds. Premillennialists have appealed to the many OT prophecies given by God concerning the nation of Israel and the land of Canaan, such as Jer. 30–33; Ezek. 36–37; 40–48, Isa. 2; 11–12; Joel 2, and so forth. Many premillennialists argue that these texts await a future fulfillment. Some premillennialists further argue that OT prophecies should not be spiritualized or allegorized but allowed to stand as prophecies made to Israel. Just as prophecies concerning Christ's first coming were fulfilled literally, so will those of His second coming. Jesus spoke of inheriting the earth in His Sermon on the Mount (Matt. 5:5;

cp. Ps. 37). The Apostle Paul expected a future for Israel in Rom. 11:11-36 and very likely expected an intermediate phase of the kingdom between the coming of Christ and the end (1 Cor. 15:20-28).

Despite differences on the details, all evangelicals are firmly committed to the literal second coming of Jesus Christ. See *Eschatology; Rapture; Future Hope; Seventy Weeks; Tribulation.*

Doros Zachariades

MILLENNIAL PERSPECTIVES ON REVELATION See *Revelation, Book of.*

MILLET [*Panicum miliacum*] Smallest cereal grain. Millet makes a poor quality bread and is normally mixed with other grains (Ezek. 4:9). Some identify the Hebrew term with "sorghum" (*Sorghum vulgare*).

MILLO (Mĭl´ lō) Hebrew word meaning "filling" which describes a stone terrace system employed in ancient construction. **1.** The story of Abimelech in the book of Judges mentions Beth-millo, "The House of the Filling." Probably a suburb of Shechem, the Beth-millo most likely was a Canaanite sanctuary. The shrine was built upon an artificial platform or fill and thus received the name "House of the Filling." **2.** The extension of Jerusalem, beyond the original Jebusite city David captured, stretched northward to include the Hill of Moriah, the site of the future temple. A large open space between the hill and the main city below left ample room for added construction. To provide a level platform upon which to build, a series of retaining walls were raised along the slope of the hill. Loads of earth and rock were dumped behind the walls to form large terraces to support the royal halls and residences planned by Solomon. The area came to be called the Ophel, meaning "high" or "lofty." It is probable that additional supporting terraces were built on the southern slopes in the city proper to extend the area available for general construction. Joash's murder by his own men near the Beth-millo "on the road to Silla" may refer to terraces in this portion of the city.

MIND Center of intellectual activity, an English term translating several different Hebrew and Greek terms. The biblical languages possess no one word parallel to the English "mind." KJV translates at least six different Hebrew terms as mind. The primary word is *leb*, which means "heart." For example, Moses said, "Hereby ye shall know that the Lord hath sent me to do all these works; for I have not done them of mine own mind (Num. 16:28 KJV; cp. 1 Sam. 9:20; Neh. 4:6). In addition, the word *nephesh* (soul) is translated "mind" in Deut. 18:6 when it refers to the desire of a man's mind (soul) and in Gen. 23:8 where it refers to mind in the sense of a decision or judgment. The word *ruach* (spirit) is rendered "mind" in Gen. 26:35. It speaks of the "grief of mind" (spirit) which Isaac and Rebekah experienced because Esau married heathen wives. Also used are the words *lebbab* (heart) in Ezek. 38:10; *yetser* (imagination) in Isa. 26:3; and *peh* (mouth, speech) in Lev. 24:12.

The NT has a similar situation because of the large number of terms that are used to describe mankind's "faculty of cognition." As in the OT the term "heart" (*kardia*) is sometimes used to represent the concept "mind." Matthew 13:15 speaks of understanding with the "heart." Other words include *ennoia*, which means "mind" in the sense of "intent," "arm yourselves also with the same resolve" (1 Pet. 4:1 HCSB). *Gnome* refers to mind in the sense of "purpose" (Rev. 17:13) or "opinion" (Philem. 14). *Noema* is also used to denote the mind, especially the "thought process." Paul said that Israel's "minds were blinded" so that they could not understand the OT (2 Cor. 3:14; 4:4; 11:3). The word *phronema* refers to what one has in the mind, the "thought": "The mind-set of the flesh is death" (Rom. 8:6 HCSB).

The more common terms for mind, however, are *nous* and *dianoia*. *Dianoia* occurs 12 times in the NT. It refers to "thinking through" or "thinking over" of something or to the "understanding" or "sentiment" which results from that process of reflection. Paul said that in times past we all lived according to the flesh, "carrying out the inclinations of our flesh and thoughts" (those things we had already thought over, Eph. 2:3). *Nous* is the most prominent term for mind; it occurs 24 times. *Nous* represents the "seat of understanding," the place of "knowing and reasoning." It also includes feeling and deciding. Hence it sometimes includes the counsels and purposes of the mind. An example is Paul's statement: "Each one must be fully convinced in his own mind" (Rom. 14:5 HCSB). The meaning of purpose is found in Rom. 11:34, which says, "For who has known the mind of the Lord? Or who has been His counselor?"

Mind is sometimes associated with the human soul. Three times in the KJV the word *psuche* (soul or life) is rendered by the word "mind." Philippians 1:27 says believers are to be of "one mind (soul)." Hebrews 12:3 urges believers not to "faint in your minds (souls)" (Acts 14:2 also). These passages illustrate the fact that the mind is considered to be the center of the person. However, in Scripture the heart is more often considered to be the center of the human personality. In the OT especially this is true because of the lack of an exact equivalent for mind. The word "heart" fills this void, and the NT follows the practice of the OT very closely. Both mind and heart can be spoken of as the center of a person because in Hebrew thought a person is looked at as a single entity with no attempt to compartmentalize the person into separate parts which act more or less independently of one another. Therefore, the heart, mind, and soul, while in some ways different, are seen as one.

The mind is portrayed oftentimes, especially in the NT, as the center of a person's ethical nature. The mind can be evil. It is described as "reprobate" (Rom. 1:28 KJV), "fleshly" (Col. 2:18), "vain" (Eph. 4:17), "corrupt" (1 Tim. 6:5; 2 Tim. 3:8), and "defiled" (Titus 1:15). On the other hand, three Gospels command us to love God with "all" our mind (Matt. 22:37; Mark 12:30; Luke 10:27). This is possible because the mind can be revived and empowered by the Holy Spirit (Rom. 12:2) and because God's laws under the new covenant are put into our minds (Heb. 8:10; 10:16). See *Anthropology; Heart; Humanity; Soul.*   *Gerald Cowen*

MINERALS AND METALS Inorganic elements or compounds found naturally in nature. A number of minerals and metals are mentioned in the biblical record.

Precious Stones Stones are desirable because of rarity, hardness, and beauty, the latter expressed in terms of color, transparency, luster, and brilliance. The Bible has three main lists of precious stones: the 12 stones of Aaron's breastpiece (Exod. 28:17-20; 39:10-13), the treasures

of the king of Tyre (Ezek. 28:13), and the stones on the wall foundation of the new Jerusalem (Rev. 21:18-21). Other lists are found in Job 28:15-19; Isa. 54:11-12; and Ezek. 27:16. The precise identification of some of the terms is unclear, unfortunately, as can be seen by comparing these lists in various translations.

Adamant Appears in KJV, RSV, REB of Ezek. 3:9 and Zech. 7:12. The Hebrew word is sometimes translated "diamond" (Jer. 17:1 KJV, NRSV, REB, NASB). The stone was "harder than flint" (Ezek. 3:9) and may be emery (Ezek. 3:9 NASB) or an imaginary stone of impenetrable hardness. It is perhaps best translated "the hardest stone" (Ezek. 3:9 NRSV).

Agate Multicolored and banded form of chalcedony. It served on Aaron's breastpiece (Exod. 28:19) and by some translations is the third stone on the new Jerusalem foundation (Rev. 21:19 NRSV).

Amethyst (Exod. 28:19; 39:12; Rev. 21:20) Identical with modern amethyst, a blue-violet form of quartz.

Beryl (beryllium aluminum silicate) Most translations show beryl to be the first stone in the fourth row of the breastpiece (Exod. 28:20; 39:13; REB "topaz"; NIV "chrysolite"). The word also occurs in the list of the king of Tyre's jewels (Ezek. 28:13; RSV, NIV "chrysolite"; NRSV "beryl"; REB "topaz"). The RSV translates another and the NIV a third word in the list as "beryl." More certainty surrounds the use of beryl in Rev. 21:20.

Carbuncle In KJV, RSV the third stone of Aaron's breastpiece (Exod. 28:17; 39:10; REB "green feldspar;" NASB, NRSV "emerald"; TEV "garnet"; NIV "beryl") and material for the gates of the restored Jerusalem (Isa. 54:12; REB "garnet"; NIV "sparkling jewels"). RSV also appears to translate a third word as carbuncle in Ezek. 28:13 by reversing the KJV order of emerald and carbuncle. NRSV omits carbuncle.

Carnelian (KJV and sometimes RSV, NASB "sardius") A clear to brownish red variety of chalcedony. NRSV reading for one of the stones of the king of Tyre (Ezek. 28:13; NASB, TEV, NIV "ruby"; REB "sardin") and the sixth stone on the foundation of the new Jerusalem wall (Rev. 21:20; cp. 4:3).

Chalcedony Alternate translation for agate as the third stone decorating the new Jerusalem foundation (Rev. 21:19 HCSB, KJV, NASB, REB,

NIV). This noncrystalline form of quartz, or silicone dioxide, has many varieties including agate, carnelian, chrysoprase, flint, jasper, and onyx.

Chrysolite (Rev. 21:20) Represents various yellowish minerals. It replaces the KJV rendering "beryl" frequently in the RSV (Ezek. 1:16; 10:9; 28:13) and throughout the NIV but not in NRSV. REB reads "topaz."

Chrysoprase or **Chrysoprasus** (KJV) Apple-green variety of chalcedony, the tenth stone of the foundation for the new Jerusalem's wall (Rev. 21:20).

Coral (Job 28:18; Ezek. 27:16) Calcium carbonate formed by the action of marine animals. NRSV, REB, NASB translated a second word as coral (Lam. 4:7 KJV, NIV "rubies").

Crystal Refers to quartz, the two Hebrew words so translated being related to "ice." In Job 28:18 KJV has "pearls," the NIV "jasper," but NRSV, NASB read "crystal," while REB has "alabaster." The glassy sea (Rev. 4:6) and river of life (Rev. 22:1) are compared to crystal.

Diamond Third stone of the second row of the high priest's breastpiece (Exod. 28:18; 39:11; REB "jade"; NIV "emerald") and one of the jewels of the king of Tyre (Ezek. 28:13; NRSV, REB "jasper"; NIV "emerald"). It is not clear, however, if diamonds were known in the ancient Near East, and the translation is uncertain.

Emerald Bright green variety of beryl, readily available to the Israelites. It is the usual translation of the fourth stone of the high priest's breastpiece and one of the stones of the king of Tyre (Exod. 28:18; 39:11; Ezek. 28:13; REB "purple garnet"; NASB, NIV, NRSV "turquoise"), with NRSV translating another word as "emerald" in Ezek. 28:13. The rainbow around the throne is compared to an emerald (Rev. 4:3), which also served as the fourth stone in the foundations of the new Jerusalem wall (Rev. 21:19).

Jacinth Transparent red to brown form of zirconium silicate. It appears in Aaron's breastpiece (Exod. 28:19; 39:12; KJV "ligure"; REB, TEV "turquoise") and the new Jerusalem wall foundation (Rev. 21:20).

Jasper (Exod. 28:20; 39:13; Rev. 21:11,18-19) A red, yellow, brown, or green opaque variety of chalcedony. In the RSV for Ezekiel 28:13, "jasper" translates the word elsewhere rendered "diamond" (REB "jade"), but NRSV reads moon-

stone with the sixth stone jasper as in other translations.

Lapis Lazuli Not one mineral but a combination of minerals that yields an azure to green-blue stone popular in Egypt for jewelry. It is an alternate translation for sapphire (NASB in Ezek. 28:13; NIV marginal notes).

Onyx A flat-banded variety of chalcedony; sardonyx includes layers of carnelian. Onyx was used on the ephod (Exod. 25:7; 28:9; 35:27; 39:6) and in the high priest's breastpiece (Exod. 28:20; 39:13). It was provided for the settings of the temple (1 Chron. 29:2) and was one of the precious stones of the king of Tyre (Ezek. 28:13).

Pearl (Job 28:18 NASB, NRSV; KJV, NIV "rubies"; REB "red coral") Formed around foreign matter in some shellfish. In the NT, "pearl" serves as a simile for the kingdom of God (Matt. 13:46), a metaphor for truth (Matt. 7:6), and a symbol of immodesty (1 Tim. 2:9; Rev. 17:4; 18:16). Pearl is also material for the gates of the new Jerusalem (Rev. 21:21).

Ruby Red variety of corundum, or aluminum oxide. The first stone of Aaron's breastpiece is sometimes translated "ruby" (Exod. 28:17; 39:10 NASB, NIV; KJV, RSV, REB "sardius"; NRSV "carnelian"). It also appears as a stone of the king of Tyre (Ezek. 28:13 NASB, NIV; REB, KJV "sardius"; NRSV "carnelian").

Sapphire (Exod. 24:10; 28:18; 39:11; Job 28:6,16; Isa. 54:11; Lam. 4:7; Ezek. 1:26; 10:1; 28:13; Rev. 21:19) The Hebrew *sappir* is a blue variety of corundum. Despite the name, it is possible that *sappir* refers to lapis lazuli (NIV marginal notes) rather than true sapphire.

Topaz Second stone of Aaron's breastpiece (Exod. 28:17; 39:10); also mentioned in the wisdom list (Job 28:19) and the list of the king of Tyre's precious stones (Ezek. 28:13). True topaz is an aluminum floro silicate and quite hard, but the OT topaz may refer to peridot, a magnesium olivine. The ninth decorative stone of the new Jerusalem wall foundation is topaz (Rev. 21:20). See *Beryl, Chrysolite* above.

Turquoise Sky-blue to bluish-green base phosphate of copper and aluminum was mined in the Sinai by the Egyptians and was a highly valued stone in antiquity. Turquoise is sometimes substituted for emerald (Exod. 28:18 NASB, NIV); or jacinth (Exod. 28:19; 39:11 REB, TEV).

Common Minerals *Alabaster* In modern terms a fine-grained gypsum, but Egyptian alabaster was crystalline calcium carbonate with a similar appearance. Alabaster may be mentioned once in the Song of Songs (5:15 NRSV, NASB; KJV, REB, NIV "marble"). In the NT (Matt. 26:7; Mark 14:3; Luke 7:37) it refers to containers for precious ointment.

Brimstone Refers to sulfur (NRSV, NIV). Burning sulfur deposits created extreme heat, molten flows, and noxious fumes, providing a graphic picture of the destruction and suffering of divine judgment (Deut. 29:23; Job 18:15; Ps. 11:6; Isa. 30:33; Ezek. 38:22; Luke 17:29).

Salt Sodium chloride is an abundant mineral, used as a seasoning for food (Job 6:6) and offerings (Lev. 2:13; Ezek. 43:24). As a preservative, salt was symbolic of covenants (Num. 18:19; 2 Chron. 13:5). Both meanings are present in Jesus' comparison of the disciples to salt (Matt. 5:13). Salt was also a symbol of desolation and barrenness, perhaps because of the barrenness of the Dead Sea, the biblical Salt Sea. The "salt pits" of Zeph. 2:9 were probably located just south of the Dead Sea. Sodium chloride could leech out of the generally impure salt from this area, leaving a tasteless substance (Luke 14:34-35).

Soda (Prov. 25:20 NASB, NIV; Jer. 2:22 REB, NIV), or **Nitre** (KJV), is probably sodium or potassium carbonate. Other translations prefer lye (Jer. 2:22 NRSV, NASB). In Prov. 25:20 the Hebrew text refers to vinegar or lye or soda, but some modern translations follow the earliest Greek translation in reading "vinegar on a wound" (NRSV, REB; TEV "salt in a wound").

Metals Many metals occur naturally in compound with other elements as an ore which must be smelted to obtain a usable product. Biblical lists of metals (Num. 31:22; Ezek.

Mineral deposits from the hot mineral springs at Hierapolis.

22:18,20) mention gold, silver, bronze, iron, tin, and lead.

Brass Relatively modern alloy of copper and tin. Brass in the KJV should be rendered copper or bronze. RSV substitutes bronze, retaining brass only in a few places (Lev. 26:19, Deut. 28:23; Isa. 48:4; NRSV using brass only in Isa. 48:4). NIV does not use brass.

Bronze Usual translation of the Hebrew word that can indicate either copper or bronze. An alloy of copper and tin, and stronger than both, bronze was the most common metal used for utensils in the ancient Near East. The Bible mentions armor (1 Sam. 17:5-6), shackles (2 Kings 25:7), cymbals (1 Chron. 15:19), gates (Ps. 107:16; Isa. 45:2), and idols (Rev. 9:20), as well as other bronze objects.

Copper Usually alloyed with tin to make bronze which possessed greater strength. The KJV uses copper only in Ezra 8:27 (NRSV, NIV "bronze"). See *Ezion-geber.*

Gold Valued and used because of its rarity, beauty, and workability. It can be melted without harm and is extremely malleable. Thus it can be used for cast objects, inlays, or overlays. A number of Israel's worship objects were solid gold or gilded (Exod. 37). Gold occurs in the Bible more frequently than any other metal, being used for jewelry (Exod. 12:35; 1 Tim. 2:9), idols, scepters, worship utensils, and money (Matt. 10:9; Acts 3:6). The new Jerusalem is described as made of gold (Rev. 21:18,21).

Iron A more difficult metal to smelt than copper, it did not come into widespread use until about the time of Israel's conquest of Canaan. Prior to this time metal weapons and agricultural tools were of bronze. For some time thereafter iron technology was not widespread. The Canaanites' "chariots of iron" (Josh. 17:16,18; Judg. 1:19; 4:3) represent a technological advantage over Israel, while the Philistines may have enjoyed an iron-working monopoly (1 Sam. 17:7; 13:19-21). Iron was more widespread by the time of David (2 Sam. 12:31; 1 Chron. 20:3; 22:14), though it remained valuable (2 Kings 6:5-6). It was used where strength was essential and became a symbol of hardness and strength (Deut. 28:48; Ps. 2:9; Isa. 48:4; Jer. 17:1; Rev. 2:27). See *Iron.*

Lead Gray metal of extremely high density (Exod. 15:10) used for weights, heavy covers

(Zech. 5:7-8), and plumb lines (cp. Amos 7:7-8). Lead is quite pliable and useful for inlays such as lettering in rock (Job 19:24). It was also used in the refining of silver (Jer. 6:27-30).

Silver Used in the Near East from quite early times; though not occurring often in a natural state, silver is easily extracted from its ores. Silver was originally more valuable than gold, usually occurring before it in lists. It became a measure of wealth (Gen. 13:2; 24:35; Zeph. 1:18; Hag. 2:8). By Solomon's day it was common in Israel (1 Kings 10:27) and was the standard monetary unit, being weighed in shekels, talents, and minas (Gen. 23:15-16; 37:28; Exod. 21:32; Neh. 7:72; Isa. 7:23). Silver was used for objects in Israel's worship (Exod. 26:19; 36:24; Ezra 8:26,28), idols (Exod. 20:23; Judg. 17:4; Ps. 115:4; Isa. 40:19), and jewelry (Gen. 24:53; Song 1:11). See *Weights and Measures.*

Tin (Num. 31:22; Ezek. 22:18,20) Sometimes confused with lead; articles of pure tin were rare. It was principally used in making bronze, an alloy of tin and copper. See *Bdellium; Mines and Mining.*   *Daniel C. Browning, Jr.*

MINES AND MINING Extraction of minerals from the earth.

The Earliest Mines Early mining efforts in the Fertile Crescent sought to provide people with the stones necessary to make weapons and tools. While the earliest walled settlements in the region date back to before 6000 B.C., people had been mining stones for tools long before that. Before 10,000 B.C. people were using tools and weapons made of flint found on the surface of the ground. From exposed beds of obsidian (a black volcanic stone) and flint (chert) early people no doubt removed the stone necessary to produce the axes, knives, and scrapers used to kill and clean food. With the domestication of small animals, wheat, and barley, people found greater uses for stone tools. Sickle blades with serrated edges were chipped from flint, several pieces being fitted together in a bone or wood handle. Larger stone tools, such as the hand ax, were suitable for cutting and shaping wooden beams used in building. The greatest use of surface-mined stones was the making of weapons for hunting. Flake blades of all sizes served as knives. Finely worked arrowheads found alongside large quantities of animal bones indicated the dependence upon hunting by Neolithic man

in Palestine. Flint scrapers and borers were used in the tanning and sewing of hides.

Copper The use of mined minerals to form metals began sometime around 6500 B.C. near Catal Huyuk in Asia Minor. While making pigment from crushed malachite, a greenish carbonate of copper, human beings probably stumbled upon the knowledge for smelting, ushering in the Chalcolithic Period, about 4500–3200 B.C.

The Bible refers to Tubal-cain, a descendant of Cain, as the father of copper (bronze) and iron forging (Gen. 4:22). In the beginning copper ore was taken from deposits above the ground. Soon, however, mine shafts and tunnels were cut into areas where surface deposits hinted at the larger ore supplies below. In the Arabah and Sinai mining settlements were founded. Complex series of narrow shafts were bored into the mountains and hills of the Timna Valley to reach the valued copper deposits within the earth. Near the mines were constructed a series of huts, walls forming windbreaks, and areas for smelting to support the mining operations. The ruins of the mining center Khirbet en-Nahas, 17 miles south of the Dead Sea, possibly mark the location of biblical Irnahash, the "Copper City." Palestine, however, was relatively poor in copper ore. Much of what was used had to be imported from regions with greater ore concentrations. Trade relations were established with settlements in Asia Minor, Armenia, and the Island of Cyprus. Copper sheets and ingots were shipped by sea and land thousands of miles to meet the growing needs for metal tools, weapons, and jewelry. In later years these ingots served as a crude style of currency. Before 3000 B.C. people discovered that copper could be mixed with arsenic to form a stronger alloy. Copper tools last longer than stone implements and could withstand greater abuse. Men continued to mine the veins of minerals which ran into the earth often following the deposits with tunnels 50 yards long into the side of a hill. The widespread use of copper in the ancient Near East is highlighted from the magnificent copper hoard discovered at Nahal Mishmar near the Dead Sea. Among more than 400 copper artifacts were numerous mace heads, chisels and adzes, scepters, and small, heavy "crowns." The copper from Naham Mishmar was most likely imported from Armenia or Azerbaijan, hundreds of miles away.

Bronze Copper tools, however, were soon replaced. Around 3200 B.C. metalsmiths discovered that by combining nine parts copper with one part tin a much stronger metal—bronze—was formed. Easier to cast than copper, bronze became the most widely used metal of the period. The copper for bronze continued to be mined in the same manner it always had, although stone tools for digging out the ore were replaced with stronger bronze counterparts. Tin deposits in Mesopotamia made the growth of this new technology easier in the northern Fertile Crescent, while Palestine and Egypt, without local tin deposits and mines, were forced to import raw materials. The regions of modern-day Afghanistan exported the necessary tin throughout the ancient Near East.

Around 2500 B.C. Phoenicians established colonies in Spain and Portugal to mine the vast local supplies of copper and tin. These and other European tin supplies were shipped throughout the ancient Near East as late as the Roman period. Roman tin mines in Britain were worked by slave labor and had shafts cutting 350 feet deep into the ground. In Palestine the Timna copper mines came under the control of the Egyptians during the late Bronze period. Remains of a small open-air temple dedicated to Hathor, patron goddess of miners, have been discovered. The small enclosure has a small sacred area set with *matsevot*, standing stones dedicated to the deity. A central shrine with small niches carved into the overhanging face of a cliff was the focal point of the sanctuary, its "holy of holies." The entire shrine was covered with a woolen tent. The design of the desert temple is similar to the Israelite tabernacle or tent of meeting. Before 1100 B.C. Kenites and Midianites occupied Timna, but no remains from between 1000 and 900 have been identified. It is hard to imagine, however, that Israel during the period of the United Monarchy, especially during Solomon's reign, would not have exploited these rich deposits within its domain.

Iron The chaotic political climate after 1300 B.C. disrupted the trade routes and commercial structures of the ancient Near East. Copper supplies dwindled, and the import of tin and copper by Egypt and Palestine was disrupted, forcing metalsmiths to develop a new method for tool manufacture. Attention was turned to iron. Although small beads discovered in Egypt give

evidence of the early use of meteoric rocks for iron smelting around 4000 B.C., the much higher melting point of iron (400 degrees higher than that of copper) necessitated the development of new smelting methods. So great was the heat needed that the Bible compares the enslavement of Israel in Egypt to the ironsmith's furnace (Deut. 4:20). More efficient bellows were created to produce the high temperatures needed to melt the iron ore. Since iron deposits lay close to the surface, they were much easier to mine than those of copper had been.

The Hittites were among the earliest people to use iron on a large scale. They traded iron tools and weapons to Egypt. For the most part, however, the Hittites protected iron as a monopoly. Only after the fall of the Hittite kingdom about 1200 B.C. did iron become more widely used. Still, Israel made little use of it. The Bible describes Canaan as a land "whose stones are iron, and out of whose hills you can dig copper" (Deut. 8:9 NASB). Only small amounts of both ores were available. Iron mines located in the Gilead near 'Ajlun at Magharat Warda probably served as one of the earliest iron sources in Palestine, possibly providing for the iron bedstead of Og, king of Bashan.

The Bible speaks of the Philistines as controlling the iron-working skills in Palestine (1 Sam. 13:19-22), an ability that prevented Israelite domination over the Philistine settlements in the Coastal Plain and Shephelah. The domination of iron technology by these "Sea-Peoples" points to the early development and usage of iron in the Aegean region, homeland of the Philistines. At Beth-shemesh, a Philistine stronghold in the Jordan Valley, a large industrial area with bronze and ironworking facilities was discovered. Smelting ovens and flow pipes for the fires give evidence of the metalworking that occurred. Numerous iron weapons and pieces of jewelry were also found. However, excavation in other Philistine cities such as Ashdod and Tel Qasile (near modern Tel Aviv) give little evidence of the widespread use of iron. While the Philistines may have controlled the use of iron to some degree, theirs was not a monopoly. For the most part, tools in Palestine continued to be made of bronze. Common tools such as sickles were still chipped from flint even after 1000 B.C. Iron chariots, spear points, knives and swords, and common tools such as sickles and plows became more common after 900 B.C., replacing earlier bronze counterparts. During the United Monarchy, Israel gained increased control of bronze and metal exports across the ancient Near East, bringing great wealth to the empire of David and Solomon. Solomon created a virtual trade war between Israel and the Arameans to the north.

Other Minerals Other minerals were also mined in the ancient Near East but were more difficult to obtain and work. Lapis lazuli, a deep blue stone, was quarried for its beauty and used in jewelry. Egyptian faience was an attempt to produce a synthetic lapis. Lead was mined as early as 3000 B.C., but its soft nature made it unsuitable for tools or jewelry. Lead was later incorporated into bronze and, in the Roman period, was used in glassmaking. Silver was first mined in northeast Asia Minor and taken from a lead-silver alloy. Electrum, silver mixed with small amounts of gold, was also mined. Raw gold is found in veins of granite. These veins, however, were not mined in early periods. Rather, the weathering of gold-bearing rocks put pea-sized and larger bits of the metal into streams and rivers, mixing it with alluvial gravel. Found mostly at the upper reaches of rivers in areas of Egypt, the Nubian Desert, and the Caucasus, gold began to be mined rather late because of its more isolated location. Since the headwaters of rivers and streams were often in locales less accessible or desirable for pasturing flocks, gold mines only became widespread around 2500 B.C. Egyptian paintings depict the washing of river sand to extract nuggets, and authors such as Strabo and Pliny the Elder (60 B.C.) spoke in later periods of rich gold deposits in Spain. The rarity of gold made it synonymous with extravagant wealth and luxury. The Apostle John's description of heaven as a city with walls and streets of gold provided the believer with a glimpse of the grandeur and glory of an eternity with God. See *Minerals and Metals.*

David C. Maltsberger

MINGLED PEOPLE KJV term for foreigners who are perhaps of mixed race and are associated with a dominant population (Jer. 25:20,24; 50:37; Ezek. 30:5). Modern translations generally replace mingled people with foreigners or with foreign plus a noun suitable to the context (folk, tribes, troops). The underlying Hebrew consists of the same three consonants as the term for Arabia. Modern translations follow the alternate vocalization and read Arabia or Arabs at Ezek. 30:5.

MINIAMIN (Mĭ nī´ á mĭn) Personal name meaning "lucky" (literally "from the right hand"). **1.** Levite in the time of Hezekiah (2 Chron. 31:15). **2.** Priestly family in the time of the high priest Joiakim (Neh. 12:17). **3.** Priest who participated in Nehemiah's dedication of the wall (Neh. 12:41).

MINISTER, MINISTRY One who serves another. God's call to Abram (Gen. 12) contains the foundations of ministry. God's promise was to begin with Abram and Sarai and from them make a nation God would bless, which would be a blessing to all nations. The English words "minister" or "ministry" appear as translation of the Hebrew word *sharat* that literally means "to wait on" or "serve" as Joseph did for Potiphar (Gen. 39:4; Exod. 24:13; 1 Sam. 2:11). A related Hebrew word is *ebed* which has a more general meaning than *sharat. Ebed* can mean "work" or "work the ground." *Sharat* is used to describe what the priests do in serving as God's representatives to the people and the peoples' representatives to God. So while Israel was created and called to be a people of God through whom all nations would be blessed, God designated Moses' brother Aaron and his male heirs (Exod. 28:35,43; 39:1) and the Levites (Num. 18:2; Deut. 10:8) to perform specific functions in the worship and service of God within Israel.

For Christians Jesus is the supreme model of a minister. In His inaugural sermon in the synagogue at Nazareth, Jesus read from the Prophet Isaiah, summarizing the purpose and the many dimensions of His ministry (Luke 4:18-19). Although Jesus has all authority in heaven and on earth, His style of leadership and ministry was not one of dominating His followers (Mark 10:42) but one of service. On one occasion when James and John sought prominent places in Jesus' kingdom, He reminded them, "For even the Son of Man did not come to be served, but to serve, and to give His life—a ransom for many" (Mark 10:45 HCSB).

Jesus' ministry included teaching, preaching, evangelism, casting out demons, healing, providing for physical needs of people, and counseling.

His supreme act of ministry was His obedience to the Father in going to the cross where He gave His life to atone for the sins of the world.

Jesus' ministry did not end with His resurrection from death and ascension to the right hand of the Father. Luke introduces his history of the early church by reminding his reader, Theophilus, that in his first volume, he described "all that Jesus began to do and teach until the day He was taken up" (Acts 1:1-2 HCSB). Luke is saying in effect that Jesus continues to do what He was doing. Before He did this as a person; now He is doing these things through His people, the church.

Ministry in Christ's church looks like Jesus' ministry on earth. God the Holy Spirit, Christ's representative in the church gives a variety of roles and gifts to those in the church for the purpose of ministry. These include preaching, evangelism, teaching, pastoral care, and administration. Three principal Greek words translated "minister" all carry a connotation of service rather than domination. *Diakonos* (Mark 10:43; Eph. 3:7; 6:21), in some passages translated "deacon," has the connotation of one who waits on tables. *Huperetes* (Luke 1:2; 1 Cor. 4:1) originally designated the under-rowers who labored in a ship's belly. *Leitourgos* (Rom. 13:6; 15:16; Heb. 1:7) was used of a servant of the state or a temple. See *Offices in the New Testament; Ordination, Ordain; Pastor; Priests.*　　　　　　　　　*Steve Bond*

MINNI (Mĭn´ nī) People inhabiting the mountainous area south of Lake Urmia northeast of the Tigris-Euphrates valley (Jer. 51:27). The Minni are among the tribes summoned to punish the wickedness of Babylon. The Minni are known as the Manneans in Assyrian inscriptions from 800 to 600 B.C.

MINNITH (Mĭn´ nĭth) One of 20 cities involved in Jephthah's conquest of the Ammonites (Judg. 11:29-33). The site is unknown. The city likely lay between Rabbath-ammon and Heshbon. Suggested sites include Khirbet Hanizeh and Khirbet umm el-Hanafish.

MINSTREL KJV term for musician (Matt. 9:23). Modern translations have "flute players" or "musicians." These musicians were hired to assist in mourning the child's death. See *Grief and Mourning.*

MINT AND CUMIN Mint is a sweet-smelling herb used to season food. Cumin is a carawaylike herb Judaism also used in seasonings and in medicine. Jesus named mint, dill, and cumin as He criticized the Pharisees for requiring the tithe of the herbs while ignoring more important matters of the Law (Matt. 23:23). See *Cummin; Plants.*

MIPHKAD GATE (Mĭph´ kăd) KJV, TEV transliteration of the Hebrew name of a gate of Jerusalem or of the temple (Neh. 3:31), following the earliest Greek translation in taking Miphkad as a proper name. Other translations take "miphkad" as a common noun. Suggested meanings include: inspection (NASB, NIV); muster (REB, NRSV); or prison (cp. Jer. 52:11). If the Miphkad Gate is a city gate, it is perhaps identical with the Benjamin Gate (Jer. 37:13; 38:7; Zech. 14:10), located at the northernmost point on the east wall (perhaps identical with the Gate of the Guard, Neh. 12:39).

MIRACLES, SIGNS, WONDERS Events which unmistakably involve an immediate and powerful action of God designed to reveal His character or purposes. Words used in the Scriptures to describe the miraculous include sign, wonder, work, mighty work, portent, power. These point out the inspired authors' sense of God's pervasive activity in nature, history, and people.

Old Testament The two Hebrew words most frequently used for "miracle" are translated "sign" (*ot*) and "wonder" (*mophet*). They are synonyms and often occur together in the same text (Exod. 7:3; Deut. 4:34; 6:22; 7:19; 13:1; 26:8; 28:46; 34:11; Neh. 9:10; Ps. 105:27; Isa. 8:18; Jer. 32:20; Dan. 6:27). "Sign" may be an object or daily activity as well as an unexpected divine action (Gen. 1:14; Exod. 12:13 RSV; Josh. 4:6; Ezek. 24:24). The basic nature of a sign is that it points people to God. "Wonders" describe God's supernatural activity, a special manifestation of His power (Exod. 7:3), but false prophets can perform actions that people perceive as signs and wonders (Deut. 13:1-3). Wonders can serve as a sign of a future event. Signs seek to bring belief (Exod. 4:5; cp. 10:2), but they do not

M

compel a person to believe (Exod. 4:9). At times God invites people to ask for signs (Isa. 7:11). The signs He has done should make all peoples on earth stand in awe (Ps. 65:8). They should join the psalmist in confessing that the God of Israel "alone does wonders" (Ps. 72:18 HCSB).

New Testament The phrase "signs and wonders" is often used in the NT in the same sense as it is found in the OT and also in Hellenistic literature (Matt. 24:24; Mark 13:22; John 4:48; Acts 2:43; 4:30; 5:12; 6:8; 7:36; 14:3; 15:12; Rom. 15:19; 2 Cor. 12:12; 2 Thess. 2:9; Heb. 2:4).

"Sign" (*semeion*) in the NT is used of miracles taken as evidence of divine authority. Sometimes it is translated as "miracle" (Luke 23:8 NIV; Acts 4:16,22 NASB, NIV). John was particularly fond of using "sign" to denote miraculous activity (2:11,18,23; 3:2; 4:54; 6:2,14,26; 7:31; 9:16; 10:41; 11:47; 12:18; 37; 20:30; Rev. 12:1,3; 13:13-14; 15:1; 16:14; 19:20).

"Wonders" (*teras*) translates a Greek word from which the word "terror" comes. It denotes something unusual that causes the beholder to marvel. Although it usually follows "signs," it sometimes precedes it (Acts 2:22,43; 6:8) or occurs alone (as in Acts 2:19). Whereas a sign appeals to the understanding, a wonder appeals to the imagination. "Wonders" are usually presented as God's activity (Acts 2:19; 4:30; 5:12; 6:8; 7:36; 14:3; 15:12), though sometimes they refer to the work of Satan through human instruments (Matt. 24:24; Mark 13:22; 2 Thess. 2:9; Rev. 13:11-13).

New Testament writers also used *dunamis*, power or inherent ability, to refer to activity of supernatural origin or character (Mark 6:2; Acts 8:13; 19:11; Rom. 15:19; 1 Cor. 12:10,28-29; Gal. 3:5; 2 Thess. 2:9; Heb. 2:4).

"Work" (*ergon*) is also employed in the NT in the sense of "miracle." John the Baptist heard of the "works" of Jesus while he was in prison (Matt. 11:2). The Apostle John used the term frequently (5:20,36; 7:3; 10:38; 14:11-12; 15:24).

Worldview Considerations Contemporary philosophical and theological arguments over the possibility and definition of "miracle" reflect the altered worldview of the last several centuries—from a theistic to a nontheistic concept of the universe. The perceived tension between the natural and the miraculous as a by-product of a naturalism that is intent on squeezing out the supernatural realm of reality.

The people of the Bible did not face this problem. The biblical perspective on the universe is that it is created, sustained, and providentially governed by God. The Bible makes no clear-cut distinction between the natural and supernatural. In the "natural" event the Bible views God as working providentially; whereas, in the miraculous, God works in striking ways to call attention to Himself or His purposes.

Christian thinkers have responded in different ways throughout the centuries in saying how miracles relate to the natural order. Some hold that miracles are not contrary to nature (Augustine and C. S. Lewis, for instance). This harmony view contends that human knowledge with limited perspective does not fully understand or comprehend the higher laws that God employs in working the miraculous. Others (like Thomas Aquinas) have maintained miracles stand outside the laws of nature. This approach is called the intervention view, based on their belief that God intervenes in the natural order to do the miraculous.

One's view of the miraculous is related to one's view of the universe. A mechanistic perspective believes the world is controlled by unalterable natural laws and cannot allow for the possibility of miracles. Christians in every century have refused to have their universe so limited. They have affirmed the continuing miraculous work of God in the universe He created, continues to care for, uses to reveal Himself, and has promised to redeem. See *Sign*.

T. R. McNeal

MIRIAM (Mĭr´ ĭ ăm) Personal name of uncertain meaning, perhaps "bitter," "God's gift," "beloved," or "defiant." **1.** Sister of Moses and Aaron and the daughter of Jochebed and Amram. Miriam played a key role in the rescue of Moses (Exod. 2:4-8) and in the subsequent experience of the exodus and the wilderness community. After crossing the Red Sea, she assumed the role of prophetess and led the women in the song of victory that was steeped in faith and gratitude (Exod. 15:20-21). At Hazeroth Miriam sided with Aaron in an act of rebellion against Moses when he married an Ethiopian woman (Num. 12:1-15). Beneath her disapproval of Moses' choice of a wife lay a deeper problem of ambition and insubordination. Consequently God reminded her of Moses' divinely appointed leadership and chastened her with leprosy. She was healed following Moses' intercessory prayer and a seven-day quarantine (Num. 12:15). Miriam died at Kadesh (Num. 20:1). Later biblical writers remembered her as an example to Israel in cases of leprosy (Deut. 24:9) and as a leader sent by God (Mic. 6:4). See *Intercession; Leprosy; Poetry.* **2.** Member of the clan of Caleb (1 Chron. 4:17).

R. Dean Register

MIRMA or **MIRMAH** (Mĭr´ mà) Leader of tribe of Benjamin (1 Chron. 8:10).

MIRROR Polished or smooth surface that produces images by reflection. Throughout the biblical period mirrors were made of polished metal (bronze, Exod. 38:8; molten [metal], Job 37:18). Glass mirrors became available only in the late Roman period. Paul's readers could be expected to appreciate the illustration of the unclear image of a metal

Bronze mirror with a bone handle from the Etruscan culture (ca. 350 B.C.).

mirror (1 Cor. 13:12). See *Gauze, Garments of; Glass.*

MISGAB (Mĭs´ găb) KJV, REB transliteration of the Hebrew for "height" used as a proper place-name (Jer. 48:1). Other translations treat the term as a common noun and translate as "fortress" or a similar term.

MISHAEL (Mĭsh´ ā ĕl) Personal name, perhaps meaning "Who is what God is?" **1.** Cousin of Moses and Aaron (Exod. 6:22) who helped bury Nadab and Abihu (Lev. 10:4). **2.** One standing with Ezra at the public reading of the law (Neh. 8:4). **3.** One of Daniel's three friends (Dan. 1:6-7,11,19; 2:17), given the Babylonian name "Meshach."

MISHAL (Mī´ shăl) Personal name meaning "depression." Form of Misheal in modern translations.

MISHAM (Mī´ shăm) Benjaminite builder of Ono and Lod (1 Chron. 8:12). The name perhaps derives from the root meaning "to inspect."

MISHEAL (Mī´ shə ăl) Place-name meaning "place of questioning." Levitical town in the territory of Asher (Josh. 19:26). Elsewhere, the KJV used the form Mishal (Josh. 21:30) or Mashal (1 Chron. 6:74). The town appears in the list of towns conquered by Pharaoh Thutmose III. The site is unknown.

MISHMA (Mĭsh´ mà) Personal name meaning "fame." **1.** Arab tribe descended from a son of Ishmael (Gen. 25:14; 1 Chron. 1:30). **2.** Descendant of Simeon. Inclusion of the names Mibsam and Mishma in the genealogies of both Ishmael and Simeon suggest the incorporation of Arabs into that tribe as Simeon expanded southward (cp. 1 Chron. 4:38-43).

MISHMANNAH (Mĭsh măn´ nah) Personal name meaning "strength" or "tasty morsel." One of David's army officers (1 Chron. 12:10).

MISHNAH Hebrew term that means "to repeat" and eventually, in the rabbinic period (beginning about A.D. 100), "to learn."

Specifically, in rabbinic Judaism *mishnah* refers to the teaching or learning about the oral law (*halakah*) passed on by a particular teacher (rabbi). Today the Mishnah usually refers to the collected edition of rabbinic discussions of halakah compiled by Judah ha-Nasi (literally "the Prince," or Patriarch), head of the rabbinic academy at Javneh (or Jamnia) at about A.D. 220. In rabbinic tradition he is usually referred to simply as "Rabbi."

Organization The Mishnah has six major divisions:

1. *Zeraim* (seeds) deals with agricultural produce and proper tithing.

2. *Moed* (set feasts) deals with religious festivals.

3. *Nashim* (women) deals with laws regulating women.

4. *Nazikim* (damages) deals with property rights and legal proceedings.

5. *Kodashim* (holy things) deals with the temple.

6. *Tohoroth* (cleannesses) deals with laws of purity.

The six major divisions are each further subdivided into specific tractates. References to the Mishnah in scholarly writing are usually given according to tractate, not according to the major divisions. While these divisions appear clear and orderly, the modern reader of the Mishnah is frequently confused by the inclusion of what appears to be legal discussion unrelated to the major division in which they are found. For example, Benedictions (*Berakoth*) are treated in the first division on agricultural produce. To some extent these inconsistencies become more understandable when we look at the way in which the Mishnah was developed from earlier mishnoth of individual rabbis.

Development According to the Mishnah itself, oral tradition and its teachings go all the way back to Moses himself who received the halakah from God on Sinai and passed it on to subsequent generations. In rabbinic tradition this understanding seems to have functioned in at least two ways. First, the teachings of previous generations is regarded as important in setting oral law. Second, this understanding did not mean that oral law was seen as the literal passing on of particular words. Halakah was to some extent a spiritual ideal only imperfectly brought to concrete realization in the teaching of specific

rabbis. Therefore halakah was a matter of exceptional religious importance and heated debate. The Mishnah frequently preserved contrary opinions. While it usually resolves the matter on one side or the other, the preservation in the tradition also allows for reconsideration by later generations.

Modern scholars see the Mishnah as a collection and editing of Jewish case law whose traditions may go back to about 150 B.C. but primarily from the period of 50 B.C. to A.D. 220. The tradition of the Mishnah appears to begin with the sect of Judaism called the Pharisees, who sought to liberalize the legal system of Judaism by applying regulations for temple purity particularly with regard to food laws to the entirety of Judaism. This sect may be regarded as liberal since they argued that the entirety of the nation should be righteous before God in ways similar to the priesthood. The Pharisees were largely a lay movement. The major representatives of this party in the Mishnah are Hillel and Shammai who taught around A.D. 50.

After the Romans destroyed the Jerusalem temple in A.D. 70, Yohannan ben Zakkai founded the rabbinic movement at Javneh (Jamnia) in Galilee. This movement succeeded in eventually unifying the surviving elements of Judaism into a coherent traditional system that forms the core of Judaism into the modern era. Hence, one of their primary concerns was to set the boundaries of legal interpretation or "make a fence around the Law." The Mishnah primarily represents the collections of various teachers' opinions on halakah and seeks to establish the limits of normative interpretation through an examination of case law and Scripture. Rabbi Akiba (A.D. 50–135) is one of the towering figures who probably contributed to the present system of the organization of the Mishnah. He also sought to make explicit the scriptural basis of halakah. His student Rabbi Meir appears to be the connecting link between Akiba's Mishnah and the Mishnah of Rabbi.

The Mishnah of Rabbi is the basis of the Talmud that was written in Palestine about A.D. 360 and in Babylonia about A.D. 500. Those rabbis quoted in the Mishnah are referred to as the Tannaim while those in the Talmud are referred to as Amoraim. Scholars are somewhat divided on the issue to what extent Rabbi simply collected and systematized various rabbis' opinions or to what extent he functioned as an editor who left his own stamp upon the material. It is probably safe to conclude that Rabbi was a highly respected rabbi whose opinion was considered authoritative in his day. Nevertheless, the extent to which he could creatively edit the rabbinic traditions of halakah was probably limited by the community of rabbis who would not hesitate to challenge him if he misrepresented tradition. The Mishnah may therefore be seen as a compendium of the tradition of rabbinic Judaism for the first two centuries.

Rabbinical Oral Law Several principles seem to have been used to determine the oral law that would enter the Mishnah. First, the Mishnah presumes the written Mosaic law as given in Scripture as its fundamental underpinning. Rabbi Akiba sought to give explicit scriptural precedent for decisions in the oral law, sometimes in what appear to be exceptionally strained logic. The Mishnah preserves some legal debate based upon direct scriptural commentary (referred to as *midrash*). In most of the Mishnah, however, the oral law is developed by reference to precedent and the development of case law, much on the same order that British and American jurisprudence has developed. From generation to generation certain rabbis are considered to be of particular importance in establishing the halakah. For example, almost always the halakah is according to Hillel rather than Shammai, even though Shammai's opinion is also quoted. While much of the Mishnah concerns matters of pragmatic concern to the social and religious organization (the rabbis do not distinguish between the two) of Judaism, some segments seem to preserve tradition for its own sake. For example, the Mishnah preserves an entire section dealing with the temple organization and sacrifice, in spite of the fact that the temple no longer existed at the time of the writing of the Mishnah. Such discussion indicates that perhaps priests were part of the academy of Yohannan ben Zakkai and also reflects the continuing hope through the first two centuries that the temple would be rebuilt.

Mishnah and Understanding the Bible The Mishnah has proven helpful to an understanding of the Bible in two ways. First, it has helped in reconstructing specific elements in the Judaism of Palestine at the time of Jesus. Second, it has been helpful in understanding the development of Judaism during the same period that the early Christians were engaged in similar development.

1. An earlier generation of Christian scholars tended to see the Mishnah as descriptive of the practices of Judaism in Palestine during Jesus' life. More recent scholars are more cautious since they recognize the long history of development of the Mishnah and also since it has become more and more apparent that Judaism in Jesus' day was composed of many religious viewpoints and movements. Particularly, the practices of the Pharisaic sect may be reflected in some of the early traditions included in the Mishnah. For example, Jesus' saying in Matt. 7:12 is quite similar to rabbinic statements in the Mishnah. Also, certain Mishnaic evidence may be helpful in better understanding social relationships depicted in the Gospels. For example, evidence from Nashim (on women) helps us to reconstruct the social position of Palestinian Jewish women in the first century. In this context it appears that Jesus is certainly more liberal in His treatment of women than was rabbinic tradition. The evidence of the Mishnah should not be taken as representative of what all or most Jews believed in the first century. Rather, it should be taken as a clue to what some Jews believed and balanced with other historical data. See *Jewish Parties in the New Testament.*

2. Since the earliest Christians were also Jews, the Mishnah may give some indication of the development of early Christianity alongside of the development of rabbinic Judaism. At the same time that Yohannan ben Zakkai was founding the academy at Javneh, Christian Jews were coping with the loss of the temple and the development of their own religious communities. Understanding of the development of Judaism in this period alongside the development of Christianity may help in understanding the commonalities and strains between the two sibling religions. See *Pharisees; Talmud; Torah; Tosephta.* *Stephenson Humphries-Brooks*

MISHRAITES (Mĭsh´ rā ĭts) Family from Kiriath-jearim (1 Chron. 2:53). The name designates residents of Mishra, a place of which nothing is known.

MISPAR (Mĭs´ pär) Modern translation spelling of personal name meaning "writing."

Returning from exile with Zerubbabel (Ezra 2:2).

MISPERETH (Mĭs pĕr´ ĕth) Personal name meaning "court recorder" or "learned." Exile who returned with Zerubbabel (Neh. 7:7). Parallel list has Mizpar (Ezra 2:2).

MISREPHOTH-MAIM (Mĭs rə phŏth-mā´ ĭm) Limit of pursuit of the coalition of King Jabin of Hazor (Josh. 11:8; 13:6). The most likely site is Khirbet el-Mushreifeh at the north end of the plain of Acco. The meaning of the name is debated. Suggestions include: Mishrephoth on the west (REB); "eminence of the waters"; "hot springs"; "lime burning at the water."

MISSION(S) Task on which God sends a person that He has called, particularly a mission to introduce another group of people to salvation in Christ. In the Christian context the person sent is called a missionary. This person is charged with the task of spreading the gospel of Jesus Christ to people to whom he is sent. The mission of the churches is to send our missionaries to all parts of the world until everyone has had the opportunity to hear the message of Jesus and accept Him as Lord. Interestingly, the term mission is not found in the Scriptures, yet the concept of mission permeates the entire Bible.

Old Testament While some scholars insist that the OT has little, if anything, to say about mission, the more general understanding is that mission is an important OT concept. Its foundation lies in the understanding that the transcendent God is also the God who is involved in history. He is the God who acts. The record of His involvement in history indicates that His work is both revelatory and redemptive. People know who God is by what He has done. Since the fall (Gen. 3), God's primary activity has been redemptive, as the confessions in the OT reveal (Deut. 6:20-24; 26:5-9; Josh. 24:2-15). This redeeming activity of God is missionary because God sends His messengers to the house of Israel and His prophets as His spokesmen to all nations.

Clearly, God's mission concern is inclusive, not exclusive. As indicated in the listing of the nations in Gen. 10, God's interest has been in all people, not just in Israel. When God called Abraham and his descendants, they were chosen, not to be exclusive vessels, but rather to be a means of blessing "all families of the earth" (Gen. 12:1-3; 18:16-19; 22:9-19; 26:1-5; 28:10-14). Later God told Israel that they had been elected as God's chosen people (Exod. 19:3-6). They were to be the recipient and guardian of God's special revelation (Heb. 1:1-3) and the channel through which the Redeemer would enter the stream of human history (Isa. 49:1-10). Still, the election was not an end in itself. God called Israel to be holy, separate, or distinct from other nations, but they were also to be priests to the other nations. To live among them and lead them to God was their purpose for being.

This truth was kept before Israel in three ways. The message of the prophets served as the first important reminder. For instance, Jeremiah was called to be a prophet to all nations (Jer. 1:3-10) and spoke out in judgment against them (Jer. 48:47; 49:6,39). He also prophesied that all nations would be gathered in Jerusalem (Jer. 3:17). In like manner, Isaiah envisioned that all nations would be redeemed by coming to Jerusalem (Isa. 25; 66:18-24). Further, he warned them of God's judgment (Isa. 12–25) and called upon Israel to be a "light to the Gentiles" (Isa. 49:6).

The second reminder of Israel's responsibility in mission came through worship. The Psalms took into account that God was the Lord of all nations (Pss. 67:1-2; 72:8,17,19; 50; 96). The architecture of the temple provided a place for foreigners to worship in the court of the Gentiles (1 Kings 8:41-43), and the prayer of Solomon at the temple dedication mentioned this fact (2 Chron. 6:32-33).

Furthermore, the history of Israel reminded her of her mission responsibility through Rahab (Josh. 6:22-25) and Ruth (Ruth 1–4) becoming a part of Israel although they were foreigners.

The OT emphasized that the nations would have to come to Jerusalem to be saved. Jonah was shocked to receive a different kind of mission. God told him to go to Nineveh and call the people to repentance. He rebelled at helping the nation's oppressor escape judgment. Still, the book of Jonah became the major OT witness to God's love for and willingness to let foreigners relate to Him in worship.

New Testament The NT brings to a crescendo the Bible's symphonic theme of mission. The mission begins with Jesus who was sent to earth to reveal the Father (John 1:18; 14:9), to glorify Him (John 13:31; 14:13; 17:1,6), to bring the kingdom of God on earth (Matt. 12:22-32), and to make God's love and mercy known to a lost world. He came to seek and save the lost (Luke 19:10). His mission was also inclusive. While Jesus' ministry was primarily for the Jews, He also met the needs of non-Jews. He healed the daughter of a Canaanite woman and praised the woman for her faith (Matt. 15:21-29). He also healed the servant of the Roman centurion (Matt. 8:5-13). On another occasion, He initiated a conversation with a Samaritan woman that led both to her conversion and to that of the entire community (John 4).

Through His teachings Jesus made clear that His mission was to continue after He ascended. Each of the Gospels and Acts contains an account of His mandate to His followers, telling them to go to all the world, make disciples, baptize them, and preach the gospel (Matt. 28:19-20; Mark 16:15-16; Luke 24:46-49; John 20:21-22; Acts 1:8). Jesus assumed that the church would reach out beyond itself. This commission made a dramatic change in the emphasis of mission. Instead of looking to foreigners to come to Jerusalem as did the OT, the church's mission is to go into the entire world and not wait for the world to come to it. Not just selected prophets like Jonah but all the believers were to go and tell what they had seen with others.

The scope of mission was inclusive. The church was to cross all barriers—to reach out to all ethnic groups, clans, tribes, social classes, and cultures. The message of salvation was to be shared with all people everywhere.

The new disciples were to be baptized and taught. The purpose of the teaching was to do more than share information. It was to provide nourishment in the faith as well.

Since the Great Commission is a mandate, the church is expected to be obedient. Even so, it does not have to do the job alone. Christ has promised that He will be with the church until "the end of the world." With this assurance the church was obedient, for the gospel was presented first in Jerusalem (Acts 1–8), then in Samaria (Acts 8–12), and finally to all the world (Acts 13–28).

Jesus' presence would be felt through the Holy Spirit. In fact, the disciples were not to go out into the world until the Holy Spirit had come upon them (Acts 1:8). This is the only time in the Bible that a church is told not to be involved in mission. The reasons are clear. The Holy Spirit empowers the church. He also convicts and converts sinners (Acts 5:14; 11:21,24; 18:8), performs mighty works of grace in believers (Acts 4:8-10), disciplines the church (Acts 5:13-14), sends forth workers (Acts 8:26; 13:1-3), presides over the missionary council (Acts 15), restrains and contains workers (Acts 16:6-10), and exercises supreme ecclesiastical authority (Acts 20:28).

Empowered by the Holy Spirit, the church did mission by preaching Jesus (Acts 2; 8:35; 10:36-44; 1 Cor. 2:1-2). The church's mission to the world was strengthened through its intimate fellowship and unity (Acts 2:44), and every effort was made to maintain this characteristic (Acts 6:1-7; 15; and Paul's letters to the churches in Corinth and Galatia).

The missionaries Jesus sent out were instructed to go only to the house of Israel to preach and to meet human need. They were not to be overly concerned about their physical or material needs nor were they to spend an undue amount of time with those who willfully rejected their message (Matt. 10:1-15). After the resurrection missionaries were arrested (Acts 4–5), suffered (2 Cor. 4:7-10), and died (Acts 7).

The Apostle Paul was the most outstanding of these missionaries. God had called him as a missionary to the Gentiles (Acts 26:16-18; Rom. 1:5; Eph. 3:1), and he was sent out by the church in Antioch (Acts 13:1-3). The Holy Spirit led him in his ministry (Acts 16:6-10). He preached Jesus (1 Cor. 2:1-2), met people on their own level (Acts 17), established autonomous, indigenous churches (Acts 14:23), and worked with others—often training them to do the works of the ministry (Acts 16:1-3). Paul further refused to be dependent on the work he established for his own livelihood, yet he was grateful when churches responded to his needs (Phil. 4:14-18). Significantly, he identified with those with whom he worked (1 Cor. 9:19-23).

Mission was the heartbeat of the NT churches. See *Confession; Election; Evangelism; Gospel; Holy Spirit; Kingdom of God; Paul; Salvation.*   *Bob Compton*

MIST Translation of several Hebrew and Greek terms with a combined range of

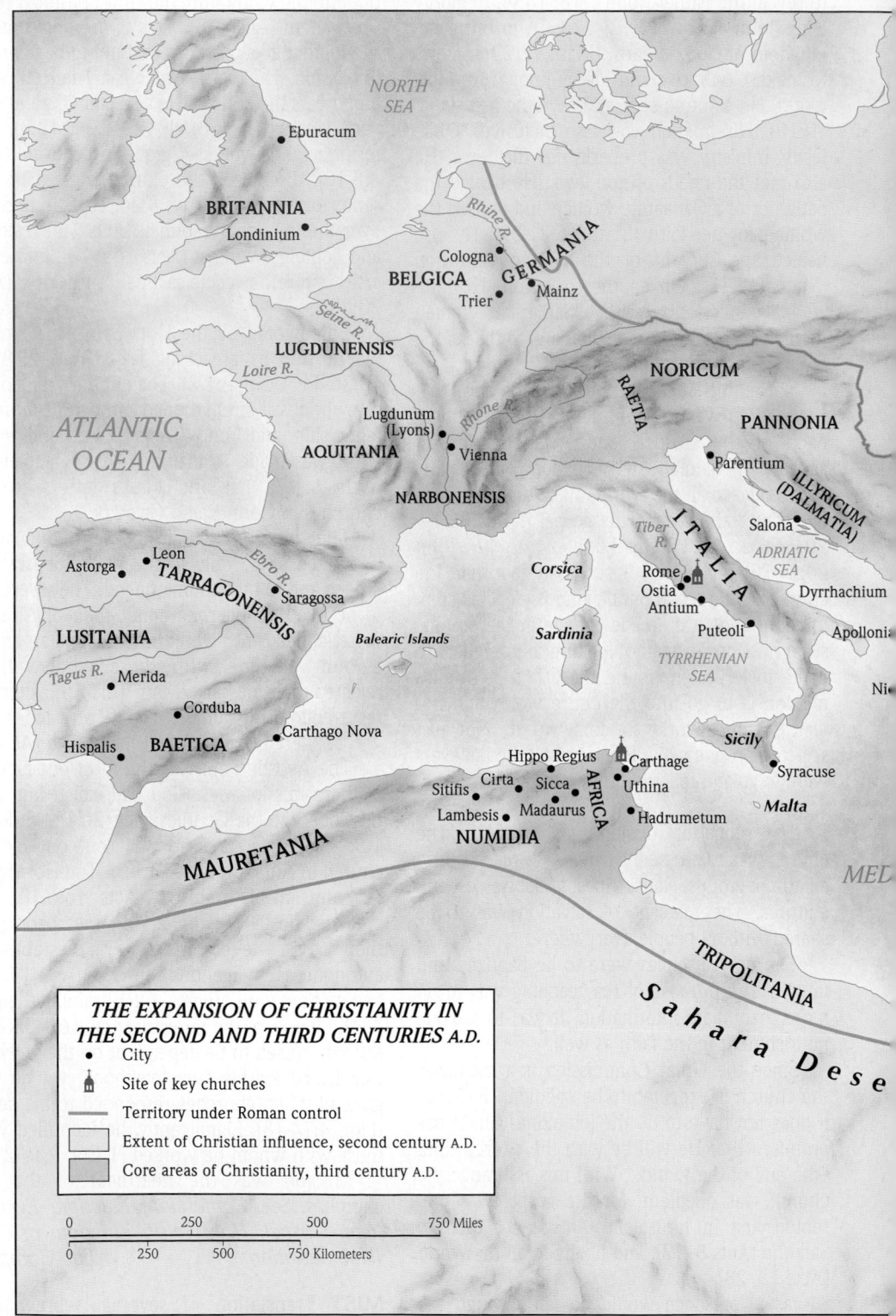

**THE EXPANSION OF CHRISTIANITY IN
THE SECOND AND THIRD CENTURIES** A.D.

- • City
- ⛪ Site of key churches
- ── Territory under Roman control
- ▢ Extent of Christian influence, second century A.D.
- ▢ Core areas of Christianity, third century A.D.

| 0 | 250 | 500 | 750 Miles |

| 0 | 250 | 500 | 750 Kilometers |

SARMATIA

Dniester R.

Dnieper R.

DACIA

Danube R.

BLACK SEA

BOSPORUS

CASPIAN SEA

COLCHIS

IBERIA

ALBANIA

Cyrus R.

Volga R.

THRACE

salonica

Philippi

Anchialus

Debeltum

Byzantium

(İstanbul)

Amastris

Ionopolis

Sinope

Amisus

BITHYNIA AND

PONTUS

Nicomedia

Neocaesarea

ARMENIA

Araxes R.

Apollonia

Troas

ASIA

Ancyra

Halys R.

Antioch

in Pisidia

Caesarea

(Mazaca)

CAPPADOCIA

ADIABENE

AEGEAN

SEA

Pergamum

Magnesia

1. 2. 3.

LYDIA

Larissa

Athens

IONIA

4. 5.

CARIA 6.

GALATIA

LYCAONIA

PHRYGIA

Iconium

Malatya

Samosata

Beit Zabde

L. Van

L. Urmia

inth

Cenchreae

Sparta

Miletus

Hierapolis

Lystra

Derbe

CILICIA

Edessa

Nisibis

on

LYCIA

Perga

Tarsus

Apamea

Euphrates R.

MESOPOTAMIA

Tigris R.

PARTHIA

*Cyclades
Islands*

Rhodes

Myra

Antioch

SYRIA

Laodicea

Orontes R.

Crete

Cnossus

Rhodes

Salamis

Dura-Europos

Palmyra

Gortyna

NEAN SEA

1. Thyatira
2. Sardis
3. Philadelphia
4. Ephesus
5. Laodicea
6. Colossae

Paphos

Cyprus

Tripolis

Beirut

PHOENICIA

Damascus

Ctesiphon

Babylon

Tyre

Bostra

YRENAICA

Alexandria

Ptolemais (Acco)

JUDEA

Philadelphia (Amman)

Jerusalem

Gaza

ARABIA (PETRAEA)

Naucratis

Petra

Heliopolis

Babylon

EGYPT

Sinai

*Syro-
Arabian
Desert*

Hermopolis

Antinoe

PATHROS

Nile R.

RED SEA

Syene

N

meaning including subterranean water, fog, and clouds. The KJV frequently has "vapor(s)" where modern translations have "mist." The mist of Gen. 2:6 refers to subterranean waters welling up and watering the ground. In Job 36:27 rain distills from the mist or fog rising from the earth. Mist often appears as a symbol for something which quickly passes away (Isa. 44:22; Hos. 13:3; James 4:14; 2 Pet. 2:17).

MITANNI (Mĭ tăn´ nī) Major kingdom between 1500 and 1300 B.C., located in what is now the northern parts of Turkey and Iran. Mitanni rivaled Egypt in its developed culture and control of the ancient Near East during this period. The people had many advanced technologies, including horse-drawn chariots. They also had fairly sophisticated laws for that day. Mitanni maintained considerable influence over Palestine for several centuries, affecting in particular the Jebusite culture of Jerusalem. See *Chariots; Egypt; Jebusites; Jerusalem.*

MITE See *Coins.*

MITHAN (Mĭth´ ăn) Place-name, perhaps meaning "gift." Town of unknown location; hometown of Joshaphat (1 Chron. 11:43). Greek translation understood this as Bethany.

MITHCAH (Mĭth´ cah) (KJV) or **MITHKAH** (Mĭth´ kah) Place-name meaning "sweetness." One of the wilderness stations (Num. 33:28-29).

MITHNITE (Mĭth´ nīt) Title given to Joshaphat, a member of David's army (1 Chron. 11:43). See *Mithan.*

MITHRA, MITHRAISM Persian god and the mystery religion devoted to his worship.
The God Mithra Originally a Persian deity considered to be the mediator between mankind and Ahura Mazda, god of light. This god overcame evil and brought life, both animal and vegetable, to mankind. Statues of Mithra characteristically show him holding a bull by the nostrils while plunging a knife into its neck. The Romans identified Mithra with the sun god. December 25 was celebrated as his birthday. Three traditions relate the birth of Mithra: (1) he was born of an incestuous relationship between

Ahura Mazda and his own mother; (2) he was born of an ordinary mortal; (3) Mithra was born from a rock. After his redemptive work on earth was finished, Mithra partook of a last supper with some of his devotees and then ascended to heaven where he continues to assist the faithful in their struggle against demons.
The Religion of Mithra Since Mithraism belongs to the general category known as mystery religions, our knowledge of its specific doctrines and rituals is very limited. Only devotees of the religion were allowed to witness its rituals or have access to its sacred doctrines. Most of our knowledge, therefore, consists of inferences drawn from artifacts and places of worship discovered by archaeologists.
Characteristics of Mithraism Mithraism was basically a religion of the common people, although at least one Roman emperor (Commodius, A.D. 180–192) was initiated into its mysteries. It was the only mystery religion that excluded women from membership. It had no professional clergy. Its seven stages of initiation prepared the initiate for ascent to the god of light. These stages corresponded to the seven planetary spheres through which one must ascend to reach the abode of the blessed: the Raven, the Occult, the Soldier, the Lion, the Persian, the Runner of the Sun, and the Father. Male children were allowed to participate in the lower stages.
Rituals In its ancient rural setting the actual slaying of a bull was part of the ritual. The initiate was placed in a pit covered by an iron grate. The bull was slain on the grate, and the initiate attempted to catch its sacred blood with his tongue. By the time the religion reached the Roman Empire, this act seems to have become mere symbolism. Beyond this, we know almost nothing except that bas-reliefs depict celebrants carrying counterfeit heads of animals, Persians, etc. This suggests the wearing of costumes corresponding to the stage of initiation.
Rival to Christianity Of all the mystery religions, Mithraism became the strongest rival to Christianity. Its rivalry with Christianity may be explained by common external features. Among the more prominent are: December 25, the god's birthday; Sunday, the holy day; baptism; a sacred meal; categorical ethics; belief in a final judgment with eternal life for the righteous and punishment for the wicked; and that the world

would finally be destroyed by fire. See *Mystery Religions.* *Joe E. Lunceford*

MITHREDATH (Mĭth´ rə dăth) Personal name meaning "gift of Mithra" (a Persian deity). **1.** Cyrus' treasurer who returned the temple vessels (Ezra 1:8). **2.** Syrian officer who protested Nehemiah's rebuilding of the walls of Jerusalem (Ezra 4:7).

MITRE KJV term for a type of headdress, probably a turban. The mitre formed part of the high priest's garments (Exod. 28:4,36-39) and was required dress on the Day of Atonement (Lev. 16:4). Priests were prohibited from showing signs of mourning such as disheveled hair (Ezek. 24:17; Lev. 21:10). They perhaps wore turbans whenever they went out. In Zech. 3:5 the high priest Joshua received a clean mitre as a sign of the restoration of the priesthood.

MITYLENE (Mĭt ə lē´ nə) Place-name meaning "purity." Chief city of the Aegean island of Lesbos southeast of Asia Minor. Paul stopped at Mitylene on his return trip to Syria from Achaia as part of his third missionary journey (Acts 20:14).

MIXED MULTITUDE Term for foreigners who associate themselves with a dominant ethnic group. The term is used for those foreigners who joined with the Israelites in the exodus from Egypt (Exod. 12:38), who became associated with the people of Judah during the exile (Neh. 13:3), or who were associated with the Egyptians (Jer. 25:20) or Babylonians (Jer. 50:37). See *Mingled People.*

MIZAR (Mĭ´ zär) Proper name meaning "littleness" or an adjective meaning "little" (Ps. 42:6). The context of the psalm suggests a site at the headwaters of the Jordan in the territory of Dan.

MIZPAH or **MIZPEH** (Mĭz´ päh, Mĭz´ pĕh) Place-name or common noun meaning "watchtower" or "lookout." A name commonly used in Palestine to refer to places used to provide security. The name appears in two different forms, Mizpah and Mizpeh, with the same basic meaning.

The name Mizpah was used for at least two different sites in the Transjordan, one located in the territory of Gilead, the other in Moab. In Gilead, Laban and Jacob made a covenant (Gen. 31:25-55), set up a pillar, and named it Mizpah (Gen. 31:49). Mizpah was also the name of the hometown of Jephthah, the Gileadite (Judg. 11). While the location of Mizpah of Gilead is not known, it was most likely located in the northern part of Gilead, perhaps a site like Ramoth-gilead. The location of Mizpeh in Moab has not been identified. In biblical history this was the site to which David took his parents (1 Sam. 22:3-5) when Saul sought his life.

At least two sites and one region west of the Jordan were named Mizpah. The account of Joshua's encounter with Jabin, king of Hazor (Josh. 11) refers to "the land of Mizpah" (v. 3) and "the valley of Mizpeh" (v. 8), a region in north Palestine, the location of which is unknown. A second Mizpeh west of the Jordan was located in the tribal territory of Judah (Josh. 15:38). While the exact location is unknown, this Mizpeh may have been near Lachish.

The town of Mizpeh located in the territory of Benjamin (Josh. 18:26) seems to be the most important of the Mizpeh's in the OT. In spite of the numerous references to this important OT site, its location is still debated. Two major sites have been suggested as possible locations: Nebi Samwil, located about five miles north of Jerusalem, and Tell en-Nasbeh, located about eight miles north of Jerusalem. While a major excavation has never been done at Nebi Samwil, the stories of Samuel seem to fit this location. On the other hand, Tell en-Nasbeh has been excavated, and the archaeological data fits well the history of Mizpeh of Benjamin.

The important role of Mizpah played in OT history is reflected in the many events associated with the site. Mizpah was a rallying point for Israel as they gathered against the tribe of Benjamin (Judg. 20). Samuel gathered Israel to Mizpah for prayer in the light of the Philistine threat (1 Sam. 7:5-11). Mizpah was a major site at which legal decisions were made (1 Sam. 7:15-17). One of the most interesting chapters in the history of Mizpah took place after the fall of Jerusalem. With Jerusalem in shambles following the Babylonian attack in 587 B.C., Mizpah became the administrative center of this Babylonian province. At Mizpah, Gedaliah, who had been appointed governor of the province, sought to encourage those who had remained behind (Jer. 40). See *Gedaliah; Jephthah; Ramoth-gilead; Samuel; Watchtower.*

LaMoine DeVries

MIZPAR (Mĭz´ pȧr) (KJV, Ezra 2:2) See *Mispar.*

MIZRAIM (Mĭz´ rā ĭm) Hebrew word for Egypt (Gen. 12:10; 13:10; 25:18). **1.** Son of Ham (Gen. 10:6,13). **2.** The Mushri, a people of Cilicia in southeastern Asia Minor (possibly 1 Kings 10:28; 2 Kings 7:6; 2 Chron. 1:16-17 TEV; NIV note). Mushri derives from the Assyrian word for "march" and possibly designates any people living outside their borders. Some scholars revocalize the Hebrew consonantal text to read Mushri, but they have no textual evidence for this. See *Egypt.*

MIZZAH (Mĭz´ zah) Personal and clan name meaning "from this" or "light ray." Edomite clan chief (Gen. 36:13,17; 1 Chron. 1:37).

MNASON (Mnā´ son) Personal name meaning "remembering," variant of Jason. Native of Cyprus, and Paul's host during his final trip to Jerusalem in about A.D. 60 (Acts 21:16).

MOAB AND THE MOABITE STONE (Mō´ ăb, Mō´ ȧ bĭt) Personal and national name and monument the nation left behind. The narrow strip of cultivable land directly east of the Dead Sea was known in biblical times as "Moab," and the people who lived there, as "Moabites." Moab is rolling plateau (averaging approximately 3,300 feet elevation), bounded on the west by the rugged escarpment which drops down to the Dead Sea (almost 1,300 feet below sea level), on the east by the desert, and running through it the steep Wadi al-Mojib canyon (the Arnon River of biblical times). The Mojib/Arnon, which flows essentially east-west and enters the Dead Sea approximately midway along the latter's western shore, separates northern Moab from Moab proper.

Relatively few springs appear on the Moabite plateau, and the waters of the Mojib/Arnon are virtually inaccessible because of the steepness of the river canyon. Still, the area is well watered by winter rains brought by winds from the Mediterranean. The porous soil holds enough of the moisture for the villagers to grow cereal crops and to find good pasturage for their sheep and goats. Moab's agricultural productivity is illustrated by the biblical passages pertaining to Ruth and King Mesha, surely the two best-known Moabites from the Bible. The book of Ruth opens with a time of famine in Judah; thus Elimelech, Naomi, and their two sons emigrated to Moab where food was still available (Ruth 1:1-5). King Mesha, we are told, "was a sheep breeder, and used to pay the king of Israel 100,000 lambs and the wool of 100,000 rams" (2 Kings 3:4 NASB).

The chief cities of northern Moab, the region north of the Arnon River to the Jabbok, were Heshbon, Medeba, and Dibon. Since this region was somewhat cut off from Moab proper by the Arnon, it was more vulnerable to international pressures and often changed hands during biblical times. According to Num. 21:25-30, sometime before the appearance of the Israelites in the region, the Amorites had taken it from Moab. Then the Amorites lost it to the Israelites and assigned it to the tribe of Reuben (Josh. 13:15-28). According to Judg. 11:13 Ammon (the region north of the Jabbok) claimed that the land belonged to them, even though they apparently had never occupied it. Moab finally reconquered the area, probably in the mid-ninth century B.C. (2 Kings 3; Isa. 15–16; Jer. 48).

Moab proper was more isolated from the outside world, bounded by the Dead Sea escarpment on the west, the desert on the east, the Mojib/Arnon on the north, and a second river canyon on the south—called today Wady el-Hesa, probably, but not certainly, the River Zered of biblical times (Num. 21:12). The chief cities of Moab proper were Kir-hareseth (present-day Kerak) and a place called Ar Moab (possibly to be identified with the present-day village of Rabbah approximately nine miles northeast of Kerak). Second Kings 3 describes a military campaign undertaken by King Jehoram of Israel and supported by King Jehoshaphat of Judah which penetrated Moab proper and culminated in a siege of Kir-hareseth. The siege was lifted when King Mesha of Moab sacrificed his oldest son on the city wall.

In addition to biblical passages such as those indicated above and occasional references in Assyrian texts, our major source of information about ancient Moab is the so-called Moabite Stone. This stone, which bears an inscription from the reign of the same King Mesha mentioned in 2 Kings 3, was discovered in 1868, near the ruins of ancient Dibon, by a German missionary. Known also as The Mesha Inscription, the monument reports the major accomplishments of King Mesha's reign. He boasts especially of having recovered Moabite independence from Israel and of having restored Moabite control over northern Moab.

Since they were neighbors, the history of the Moabites was intertwined with that of Israel. Moreover, the Israelites regarded the Moabites as close relatives, as implied by Gen. 19:30-38. We hear of peaceful interchange as well as conflicts between the Israelites and Moabites already during the time of the Judges. The story of Ruth illustrates peaceful relations, while the episode of Ehud and Eglon illustrates conflict (Judg. 3:12-30). Saul is reported to have fought against the Moabites (1 Sam. 14:47). David, a descendant of the Moabitess Ruth according to the biblical genealogies (Ruth 4:18-22), placed his parents under the protection of the king of Moab while he was on the run from Saul (1 Sam. 22:3-4). Yet he is reported to have defeated the Moabites in battle later on and to have executed two-thirds of the Moabite prisoners by arbitrary selection (2 Sam. 8:2). Moab was represented among Solomon's wives, and the worship of Chemosh, the Moabite god, accommodated in Solomon's Jerusalem (1 Kings 11:1-8).

Our most detailed information about Moabite-Israelite relations comes from the mid-ninth century B.C., the time of the Omri dynasty of Israel and King Mesha of Moab (1 Kings 16:15–2 Kings 10:18). At this point the inscription of the Moabite Stone supplements the biblical record. We learn that Omri conquered northern Moab and gained some degree of domination over Moab proper. Ahab continued Omri's policies. King Mesha ascended the throne of Moab approximately midway during Ahab's reign, however, and eventually succeeded in throwing off the Israelite yoke. Mesha apparently began the struggle for Moabite independence during the turbulent years following Ahab's death (2 Kings 1:1). Ahaziah, who succeeded Ahab to the throne of Israel, was unable to respond to Mesha's challenge because of an accident that led to his premature death (2 Kings 1). Later, when Jehoram followed Ahaziah to the throne of Israel and attempted to restore Israelite control over Mesha, he was unsuccessful (2 Kings 3).

Eventually by 700 B.C. Moab fell under the shadow of Assyria as did Israel, Judah, Ammon, and the other petty Syro-Palestinian kingdoms. Thus Moab and Moabite kings are mentioned in the records of Tiglath-pileser III, Sargon II, Sennacherib, and Esarhaddon. Also, prophetic oracles such as Amos 2:1-3; Isa. 15; and Jer. 48 pertain to these last waning years of the Moabite kingdom. See *Arnon; Jehoshaphat; Joram; Kir-hareseth; Mesha; Ruth; Transjordan.*

      Maxwell Miller and E. Ray Clendenen

MOABITE (Mō á bīt) Resident of Moab.

MOABITESS (Mō á bīt´ ĕs) Female resident of Moab. Prominent women from Moab include Ruth (Ruth 1:22; 2:2,21; 4:5,10), some of Solomon's wives (1 Kings 11:1), and the mother of Jehozabad (2 Chron. 24:26).

MOADIAH (Mō á dī´ ah) Personal name meaning "Yah promises" or "Yah's ornament." Priestly clan in the time of the high priest Joiakim (Neh. 12:17), perhaps to be identified with Maadiah (Neh. 12:5).

MODERATION Self-control; calmness; temperateness (Phil. 4:5). The underlying Greek term is used in parallel with kindness (2 Macc. 9:27). Modern translations read "forbearance" (RSV), "forbearing spirit" (NASB), "gentleness" (NIV, NRSV), and "consideration of others" (REB).

MODIOS See *Weights and Measures.*

MOLADAH (Mō lā´ dah) Place-name meaning "generation." City near Beersheba in southern Judah assigned both to Judah (Josh. 15:26) and to Simeon (Josh. 19:2), perhaps reflecting the political realities of different times or the dependence of Simeon on Judah. The similarity to the name Molid suggests that Moladah was a Jerahmeelite settlement (1 Sam. 27:10; 1 Chron. 2:29). The city was among those repopulated by Jews returning from exile (Neh. 11:26). Moladah is perhaps identical to the Edomite village of Malathah which served as a retreat for Herod Agrippa I. Various sites have been proposed: Khirbet Kuseifeh, 12 miles east of Beersheba; Tell el-Milh, southeast of Beersheba; and Khereibet el-Waten, east of Beersheba.

MOLE Large rodent, gray in color. In Lev. 11:30 some translate the Hebrew word as "chameleon" (NIV, NASB, RSV). Others translate "mole" in Lev. 11:29 (NASB, NEB), or in Isa. 2:20 (NASB, RSV, KJV). See *Rodents.*

MOLECH (Mō´ lĕk) Transliteration of Hebrew word related to word for "king" but describing a foreign god or a practice related to foreign worship. The meaning of "Molech" is debated. Two views generally are proposed. One suggestion is that "Molech" denotes a particular type of offering, a votive sacrifice made to confirm or fulfill a vow. This viewpoint is supported by the fact that some Carthaginian-Phoenician (Punic) inscriptions from the period 400–150 B.C. imply that the word *malak* is a general form for "sacrifice" or "offering." Such a meaning is possible in some passages (Lev. 18:21; 20:3-5; 2 Kings 23:10; Jer. 32:35).

A second suggestion is that "Molech" is the name of a pagan deity to whom human sacrifices were made. This deity often is associated with Ammon (cp. 1 Kings 11:7) "the abomination of the children of Ammon." Leviticus 20:5 condemns those who "commit whoredom with Molech" (Lev. 18:21; 20:3-5; 2 Kings 23:10; Jer. 32:35). Some recent archaeological evidence points to child sacrifice in ancient Ammon. Many scholars contend that all the biblical texts referring to Molech can be understood by interpreting it as a divine name.

The etymology of the term *Molech* is interesting. Scholars suggest that it is a deliberate mis-vocalization of the Hebrew word for king or for the related participle (*molek*), "ruler." They propose that the consonants for the Hebrew word for king (*mlk*) were combined with the vowels from the word for shame (*boshet*). Thus, this title was a divine epithet expressing contempt for the pagan god.

In times of apostasy some Israelites, apparently in desperation, made their children "go through the fire to Molech" (Lev. 18:21; 20:2-5; 2 Kings 23:10; cp. 2 Kings 17:31; Jer. 7:31; 19:5; 32:35). It generally is assumed that references

like these are to the sacrifices of children in the Valley of Hinnom at a site known as Topheth ("Topheth" probably means "fire pit" in Syriac). Precisely how this was done is unknown. Some contend that the children were thrown into a raging fire. Certain rabbinic writers describe a hollow bronze statue in the form of a human but with the head of an ox. According to the rabbis, children were placed in the structure that was then heated from below. Drums were pounded to drown out the cries of the children.

An alternate view contends that the expression "passed through Molech" refers not to human sacrifices but that parents gave up their children to grow up as temple prostitutes. Such a view appeals to Lev. 18 where throughout the chapter the writer is concerned with sexual intercourse (esp. vv. 19-23). Another view sees an original fire ceremony dedicating, but not harming children, that later was transformed into a burnt-offering ceremony.

The practice of offering children as human sacrifice was condemned in ancient Israel, but the implication is clear in the OT that child sacrifice was practiced by some in Israel (2 Kings 21:6; 23:10; 2 Chron. 28:3; Ps. 106:38; Jer. 7:31; 19:4-5; Ezek. 16:21; 23:37,39). The exile seems to have put an end to this type of worship in Israel. However it lingered on in North Africa and among the Carthaginian Phoenicians into the Christian era. See *Ashtaroth; Gods, Pagan; Hinnom, Valley of; Sacrifice.*

Paul E. Robertson

MOLID (Mō´ lĭd) Personal name meaning "begetter." Descendant of Judah (1 Chron. 2:29).

MOLOCH (Mō´ lŏk) Variant form of Molech used at Acts 7:3.

MOLTEN SEA Large cast bronze basin that stood in the courtyard to the southeast of Solomon's temple (1 Kings 7:23-26; 2 Chron. 4:2-5). The basin was cast by Hiram of Tyre who was responsible for all the bronze work in the temple (1 Kings 7:13-14). The bronze for the molten sea was supplied by the spoils from David's campaigns (1 Chron. 18:8). The basin was over 14 feet in diameter, over seven feet high, and over 43 feet in circumference. It was about three inches thick. The estimated weight is about 30 tons, and the estimated volume is about 12,000 gallons (U.S.). The brim was turned outward resembling a lily, and below the brim were two rows of gourds (cp. 1 Kings 7:24; 2 Chron. 4:3). The sea rested on the backs of 12 oxen. The oxen were arranged in groups of three, each group facing toward one of the four compass directions (1 Kings 7:25; 2 Chron. 4:4). The oxen were later removed by Ahaz and replaced with a stone base (2 Kings 16:17; cp. Jer. 52:20). After the fall of Jerusalem in 587 B.C., the basin was broken in pieces and taken to Babylon (2 Kings 25:13; Jer. 52:17). The basin was used for the purification of the priests (2 Chron. 4:6).   *Phil Logan*

MOMENT See *Instant.*

MONEY See *Coins.*

MONEY BELT Modern rendering of the term the KJV translated as purse (Matt. 10:9; Mark 6:8). See *Purse.*

MONEY CHANGERS Persons whose profession was to sell or exchange Roman or other moneys for Jewish money acceptable in the temple worship. In NT times regions and cities issued their own money. This caused Jews of the Dispersion, those who lived outside of Judea, to bring many kinds of money to Jerusalem. To help visitors change money into that acceptable in Jerusalem, money changers set up tables in the temple court of the Gentiles. Syrian silver coins were the money of Jerusalem then, and worshipers used them to pay their temple tax of a half shekel and to buy sacrifices for the altar.

Three words are translated "money changers": *kollubistes* (Matt. 21:12; Mark 11:15; John 2:15) of Semitic origin referred to the exchange rate or commission; *kermatistes* (John 2:14) referred to a dealer in small change; and *trapetzites* (Matt. 25:27) which Luke used in a slightly different form (*trapezan,* 19:23, or *shulhanim* in Hebrew) referred to a money agent who sat at a table.

Money changers were in the area with vendors who sold animals, birds, and other items used in temple worship and sacrifices. Such transactions were numerous and required the service of brokers who knew the value of foreign money. Some exchangers profited greatly and

loaned their money along with what others invested with them. Their interest rates ranged from 20 to 300 percent per year.

In anger at this corruption of the purpose of the temple, Jesus turned over the tables of the money changers and drove them and the sellers of animals out of the temple court (Matt. 21:12).
                                          Elmer L. Gray

MONITOR LIZARD See *Reptiles.*

MONKEY Small, long-tailed primate. TEV, REB include monkeys among the exotic animals brought as gifts to King Solomon (1 Kings 10:22; 2 Chron. 9:21). NIV, NRSV note read "baboons." KJV, NASB, NRSV render the Hebrew term "peacocks."

MONOTHEISM/POLYTHEISM See *Gods, Pagan.*

MONTH See *Calendar; Time.*

MOON Light in the night sky created by God and controlling the calendar (Gen. 1:14-19). Hebrew uses several words for moon, new moon, full moon, or bright, white moon. Two of Israel's greatest festivals were celebrated at the beginning of the full moon: the Passover in the spring and the Feast of Booths in the fall. Each month they celebrated the "new moon" with a little more festivity than a regular Sabbath (Num. 28:11-15 NIV).

Still the OT strongly teaches against worshiping the moon (Deut. 4:19; Job 31:26-28; Isa. 47:13-15) as did Israel's neighbors. The people of Israel were to remember that the moon was nothing more than an object created by Yahweh and had no power over people. Joel said in the last days the moon would become dark (Joel 2:10; 3:15) or turn to blood (Joel 2:31). The moon will not give its light on the "day of the LORD," the light of the sun and the moon being replaced by the everlasting light of the Lord (Isa. 13:10; 60:19-20).   *James Newell*

MOON, NEW See *Calendar; Festivals; Time.*

MORAL DECLINE The Bible teaches that in the latter days the world will be gripped by an unprecedented decline in morals. False teaching will allow wickedness to grow, resulting in apathy (Matt. 24:12) and open hostility (Matt.

24:9-11,24; 2 Tim. 3:1-5) toward the things of Christ. Religion will become a pretense for personal gain rather than an expression of true devotion to God (cp. 2 Tim. 3:5), and as a result the standards of moral behavior rooted in the Bible will be held to be irrelevant.

The NT lists the characteristics of persons who reject Christ (Gal. 5:19-21; Eph. 5:3-5; Col. 3:5-6; 1 Tim. 1:9-10; Rev. 21:8). These include all thoughts and actions that are less than Christlike. Today many who speak of morals often limit their discussion to sexual matters. The NT, however, is clear that sexuality is just one of many elements of human behavior to be judged by God's moral code.

Although at their root level the kinds of activities which will become rampant at the end of time will be the same kinds of activities that people have always done in opposition to God, their intensity will be much greater and their effect worldwide in scope.   *Paul H. Wright*

MORASTHITE (Mō răs´ thīt) Resident of Moresheth (Jer. 26:18; Mic. 1:1).

MORDECAI (Môr´ də kī) Personal name meaning "little man." **1.** Esther's cousin and the mastermind behind her rise to power and subsequent victory over the evil Haman. Haman, a descendant of the Amalekite king Agag, sought to destroy the Jewish race. Mordecai, a descendant of King Saul's family, led Esther to thwart the attempt. Haman was hanged on the gallows he had erected for Mordecai. See *Esther, Book of.* **2.** A man who returned from Babylon to Jerusalem with Zerubbabel (Ezra 2:2; Neh. 7:7).

MOREH (Mō´ rĕh) Place-name meaning "instruction" or "archers." **1.** Place where several important events in the lives of the patriarchs and the nation Israel occurred. An oak tree at the site near Shechem is mentioned several times as being the focal point. Abraham's first encampment in the land of Canaan was at Shechem by the oak of Moreh. There he built an altar after God had appeared to him and entered into covenant (Gen. 12:6-7). Jacob at Shechem buried the foreign gods his family had brought from Haran (Gen. 35:4). At Moreh God set forth the blessings and curses on Israel regarding their keeping the commandments (Deut. 11:26-30). Joshua set up a memorial stone under the oak as a reminder of the covenant made between God and the people (Josh. 24:26). **2.** Hill in tribal territory of Issachar where Gideon reduced his troops by testing the way they drank water (Judg. 7:1). Modern Nebi Dachi opposite Mount Gilboa.

MORESHETH or **MORESHETH-GATH** (Mō´ rə shĕth-Găth) Place-name meaning "inheritance of Gath." Home of the Prophet Micah (Mic. 1:1). The prophet pictured his home as a bride receiving a going away gift from Jerusalem, her father, a warning of exile for Jerusalem's leaders and thus separation from their neighbors (1:14). The city was apparently located near Philistine Gath and is usually identified with Tell ej-Judeideh about 22 miles southwest of Jerusalem and nine miles east of Gath. Recently, this identification has been questioned. This may be the Gath Rehoboam fortified (2 Chron. 11:8). It may be Muchrashti of the Amarna letters.

MORIAH (Mō rī´ ah) Place-name of uncertain meaning translated in various ways, including "Amorites" by earliest translators. The rocky outcropping in Jerusalem located just north of the ancient city of David. It was on this rock that Abraham would have sacrificed Isaac as a burnt offering, but God intervened and provided a ram (Gen. 22:2,13). Later the Jebusite city of Salem was built adjacent to the hill. After David captured the site, he purposed to build there a temple for the ark of the covenant. However, God gave that task to his son Solomon (1 Chron. 28:3-6). It may be modern Khirbet Beth-Lejj.

The hill of Moreh.

A stone mortar for grinding grain or other substances at Lachish.

MORNING First part of the day by modern reckoning. Morning can refer to the time before dawn (Mark 1:35; cp. Gen. 44:3), to dawn (Gen. 19:15; 29:25; Judg. 16:2), or to some time after sunrise. Morning is frequently paired with evening (Gen. 1:5,8) to indicate a complete day. The coming of morning serves as a figure for joy (Ps. 30:5) or vindication (Ps. 49:14) which comes quickly.

MORNING STAR See *Day Star*.

MORSEL See *Sop*.

MORTAR 1. Vessel in which substances are crushed with a pestle. Mortars were frequently fashioned from basalt or limestone. They were used to grind grain for flour, herbs for medicine, olives for oil (Num. 11:8). By extension, mortar designates a hollow place (pestle) (Josh. 15:19). Mortar is used as a proper name for a district of Jerusalem in Zeph. 1:11. **2.** Building material, usually clay (Exod. 1:14; Isa. 41:25; Nah. 3:14), though sometimes bitumen (Gen. 11:3; KJV "slime"), used to secure joints in brick or stone. Modern translations sometimes replace the mortar of the KJV with another term, for example, plaster (Lev. 14:42,45) or whitewash (Ezek. 13:10-11,14-15).

MOSERA, MOSERAH, or **MOSEROTH** (Mō sē´ rŏth) Place-name meaning "chastisements." A wilderness station (Num. 33:30-31). The singular form of the name (Mosera or Moserah) was the site of Aaron's burial (Deut. 10:6). Numbers 20:22-28 has prompted the location of Moseroth in the vicinity of Mount Hor.

MOSES (Mō´ zəs) Personal name meaning "drawn out of the water." Moses was the leader of the Israelites in their exodus from Egyptian slavery and oppression, their journey through the wilderness with its threats in the form of hunger, thirst, and unpredictable enemies, and finally in their audience with God at Mount Sinai/Horeb where the distinctive covenant, bonding Israel and God in a special treaty, became a reality. Nothing is known about Moses from sources outside the OT. To be sure, the name "Moses" doubtlessly appears in Egyptian dress in compound names such as Tuthmoses III, but none of these references gives information about the Moses of Israel.

The story about Moses in the OT, found in the extensive narratives from Exod. 1 through Deut. 34, is more than simply a biography of Moses. It is a covenant document that celebrates God's making of the redemptive people of Israel in fulfillment of His promises to the patriarchs and declares the glory of that God and the nature of His relationship to them.

The artistic narrative begins in Exod. 1, not with data about Moses, but with an account of events in Egypt that affected Moses' people. Since the Israelites had grown to be a large people, the Egyptian pharaoh feared their power. To control them he launched an official policy of oppression against them. When the oppression failed to curb the population growth of the Israelites, the pharaoh announced a new policy for limiting that growth. "You must throw every son born to the Hebrews into the Nile, but let every daughter live" (Exod. 1:22 HCSB). The next chapter announces the birth of Moses. Moses' life began under the pharaoh's judgment of death.

The mother, however, acted to protect the baby Moses from the pharaoh's death decree. When the baby could no longer be hidden, the mother constructed an ark, a basket of bulrushes made waterproof with bitumen and pitch. She placed the child in the basket and the basket in the river. A sister stood watch over the basket to know what might happen. She witnessed an apparently terrible twist of fate, however, when the pharaoh's own daughter came to the river. She found the ark, opened it, and recognized the child as a Hebrew. Rather than killing the child as her father had commanded, however, the

M

Stream in the Wilderness of Zin that local tradition says was formed when Moses and Aaron hit the rock.

woman showed compassion on the child, made the proper preparations, and, with the help of the baby's sister, established a procedure for adopting the baby as her own child. As a part of that process, the princess committed the child to a wet nurse suggested by the girl watching the ark. Of course, the wet nurse was the child's own mother.

After the baby had been weaned, the mother delivered the child to the princess. As a part of the adoption procedure, the princess named the child Moses. The young hero grew to maturity in the palace of the king who had sought to kill

Rock traditionally considered the Rock of Rephidim that Moses struck to get water for the Israelites.

him. The mature Moses became concerned about the oppression of his people. The story-teller emphasized the identity between the oppressed people and Moses. "He went out to his own people ... he saw an Egyptian beating a Hebrew, one of his people" (Exod. 2:11 HCSB). Moses responded to the particular act of oppression against his people by killing the Egyptian.

In the wake of his violent act against the Egyptian taskmaster, Moses fled from Egypt and from his own people to the land of Midian. Again he intervened in the face of oppression, inviting danger and risk. Sitting at a well, the typical meeting place for the culture (Gen. 29:2), Moses witnessed the violent aggression of male shepherds against female shepherds who had already drawn water for their sheep. Moses saved the oppressed shepherds, whose father, the priest of Midian, invited him to live and work under the protection of the Midianite's hospitality. Eventually one of the Midianite's daughters became Moses' wife. In the idyllic peace of the Midianite's hospitality, Moses took care of Jethro's sheep, fathered a child, and lived at a distance from his own people.

The event at the burning bush while Moses worked as a shepherd introduced him to the critical character of his heroic work. The burning bush caught Moses' attention. There Moses met the God of the fathers who offered Moses a distinctive name as the essential key for Moses' authority—"I am who I am." This strange formulation played on God's promise to Moses to be present with him in his special commission. God sent Moses back to the pharaoh to secure the release of his people from their oppression. The divine speech of commission has a double character. As the heroic leader of Israel, he would initiate events that would lead to Israel's exodus from Egypt. But as the man of God, he would represent God in delivering the people from their Egyptian slavery. With the authority of that double commission, Moses returned to the pharaoh to negotiate the freedom of his people.

The negotiation narratives depict Moses in one scene of failure after the other. Moses posed his demands to the pharaoh, announced a sign that undergirded the demand, secured some concession from the pharaoh on the basis of the negotiations, but failed to win the release of the people. The final scene is hardly a new stage in the negotiations. To the contrary, God killed the

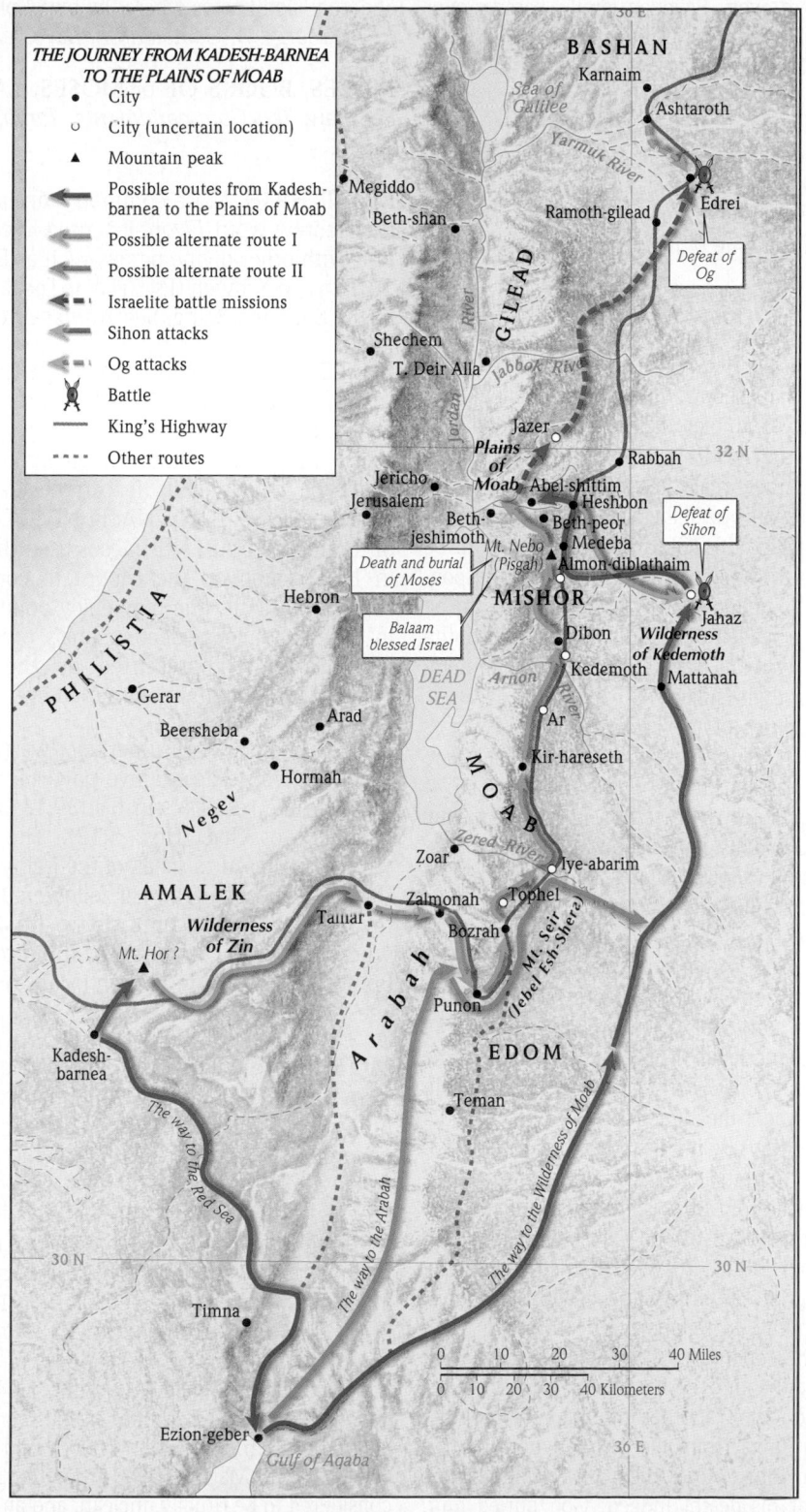

THE JOURNEY FROM KADESH-BARNEA
TO THE PLAINS OF MOAB

- • City
- ○ City (uncertain location)
- ▲ Mountain peak
- Possible routes from Kadesh-barnea to the Plains of Moab
- Possible alternate route I
- Possible alternate route II
- Israelite battle missions
- Sihon attacks
- Og attacks
- Battle
- King's Highway
- Other routes

BASHAN

Karnaim
Ashtaroth
Sea of Galilee
Yarmuk River
Edrei
Defeat of Og
Ramoth-gilead
Megiddo
Beth-shan
GILEAD
Shechem
T. Deir Alla
Jabbok River
Jazer
Plains of Moab
Rabbah
Jericho
Jerusalem
Abel-shittim
Heshbon
Beth-peor
Beth-jeshimoth
Medeba
Mt. Nebo (Pisgah)
Almon-diblathaim
Death and burial of Moses
Defeat of Sihon
Balaam blessed Israel
MISHOR
Hebron
Dibon
Wilderness of Kedemoth
Jahaz
Kedemoth
Mattanah
DEAD SEA
Arnon River
PHILISTIA
Gerar
Beersheba
Arad
Hormah
Ar
Kir-haresheth
MOAB
Negev
Zered River
Zoar
Iye-abarim
AMALEK
Zalmonah
Tophel
Wilderness of Zin
Tamar
Bozrah
Mt. Seir (Jebel Esh-Shera)
Mt. Hor ?
Punon
Arabah
EDOM
Kadesh-barnea
Teman
The way to the Red Sea
The way to the Arabah
The way to the Wilderness of Moab
Timna
30 N
Ezion-geber
Gulf of Aqaba

0 10 20 30 40 Miles
0 10 20 30 40 Kilometers

firstborn of every Egyptian family, passing over the Israelite families. In the agony of this death scene, the Egyptians drove the Israelites out of Egypt (Exod. 12:30-36). But they acquired silver, gold, and clothing from the Egyptians in preparation for the event. When they escaped, they took the silver, gold, and clothing. Thus in leaving Egypt, Israel robbed the most powerful nation at the time of its firstborn sons and of its wealth.

Moses led the people into the wilderness where the pursuing Egyptians trapped the Israelites at the Red Sea. God, who had promised to be with His people, defeated the enemy at the Sea. Then God met their needs for food and water in the hostile wilderness. Even the serpents and the Amalekites failed to frustrate the wilderness journey of the Israelites under Moses' leadership. Exodus 17:8-13 shows Moses to be faithful in the execution of his leadership responsibilities. Numbers 12:1-16 shows Moses to be humble, a leader of integrity who fulfilled the duties of his office despite opposition from members of his own family.

The center of the Moses account emerges with clarity in the events at Mount Sinai. The law at Sinai constitutes God's gift for Israel. It showed Israel how to respond to God's saving act in the exodus, and it showed each new generation how to follow Moses' teaching in a new setting in the life of the people. The laws carried the name of Moses as an affirmation of their authority. The law of Moses became a model for Israelite society. Indeed, Israel's historians told the entire story of Israel under the influence of the Moses model and suggested that the Davidic kings should have constructed their leadership for Israel under the influence of the Moses model (Joshua—Kings). Only the good king Josiah and, to a lesser extent, Hezekiah matched that model.

The death of Moses is marked by tragic loneliness yet graced with God's presence. Because of Moses' sin (Num. 20) God denied Moses the privilege of entering the promised land. Deuteronomy 34 reports the death scene. Central to the report is the presence of God with Moses at the time of his death. Moses left his people to climb another mountain. Atop that mountain, away from the people whom he had served so long, Moses died. God attended this servant at his death. Indeed, God buried him,

and only God knows where the burial place is.

George W. Coats and E. Ray Clendenen

MOSES, BOOKS OF or **MOSES, LAW OF** See *Law, Ten Commandments, Torah; Pentateuch.*

MOST HIGH Most common translation of the Hebrew word *Elyon.* It is used in conjunction with other divine names such as El (Gen. 14:18), and Yahweh (Ps. 7:17) to speak of God as the Supreme Being. See *Names of God.*

MOTE Archaic English word referring to a small particle or speck. It is found in the KJV in Matt. 7:3 for the Greek word *karphos,* which refers to a minute fragment of straw, chaff, or wood. Thus it can be translated "speck" (HCSB, NRSV, NASB, NIV, TEV, REB) or "splinter" (NAB, NJB). Jesus used the word in His Sermon on the Mount to contrast a slight moral fault one may enjoy pointing out in others, while neglecting one's own more heinous fault, represented by the "log," "plank," or "beam" in one's own eye.

MOTH Literally "consumer" or "waster," it is an insect whose destructive power is used to illustrate the result of sin (Ps. 39:11) and the judgment of God (Hos. 5:12). The moth's weakness is used to speak of the frailty of man (Job 4:19). Jesus urged His followers to avoid the temptation to accumulate wealth on earth where the moth could destroy it but to lay up immortal treasures in heaven (Matt. 6:19-20). See *Insects.*

MOTHER Female parent who carries, gives birth to, and cares for a child. Usually refers to humans but may refer to animals or even as a metaphor for deity. In the Bible a wife has two equally important roles: to love, support, and provide companionship and sexual satisfaction for her husband and to bear and rear children. So important was the latter that a stigma was attached to barrenness (Gen. 16:1-2; 18:9-15; 30:1; 1 Sam. 1:1-20; Luke 1:5-25, esp. v. 25).

The Bible refers to every aspect of motherhood: conception (Gen. 4:1; Luke 1:24), pregnancy (2 Sam. 11:5; Luke 1:24), the pain of childbirth (Gen. 3:16; John 16:21), and nursing (1 Sam. 1:23; Matt. 24:19). A new mother was considered to be ritually unclean, and an offering was prescribed for her purification (Lev. 12; cp. Luke 2:22-24). The book of Proverbs (1:8; 31:1) indicates that even in ancient times mothers shared with fathers the responsibility for instructing and disciplining children. Mothers have the same right to obedience and respect as fathers (Exod. 20:12; Lev. 19:3), and in OT times death could be the penalty for those who cursed or assaulted parents (Exod. 21:15; 17; Deut. 21:18-21). Jesus enforced the fifth commandment and protected it against scribal evasion (Matt. 15:3-6).

Motherly virtues are often extolled: compassion for children (Isa. 49:15), comfort of children (Isa. 66:13), and sorrow for children (Jer. 31:15, quoted in Matt. 2:18).

The fact that God would use a human mother to bring His Son into the world has bestowed upon motherhood its greatest honor. Jesus set an example for all to follow by the provision He made for His mother (John 19:25-27). Jesus made plain, however, that devotion to God must take precedence to that of a mother (Matt. 12:46-50). Even the OT (Gen. 2:24) indicated that a man's devotion to his wife supercedes that to his mother.

In addition to the literal sense, including that of animal mothers (Exod. 34:26; Lev. 22:27), the word is often used metaphorically. Israel is compared to an unfaithful mother (Hos. 2:2-5; Isa. 50:1). Revelation 17:5 calls Babylon (Rome) the mother of harlots (those who are unfaithful to God). A city is the "mother" of her people (2 Sam. 20:19). Deborah was the "mother" (or deliverer) of Israel. In a more positive vein, the heavenly Jerusalem is the "mother" of Christians (Gal. 4:26). Jesus spoke of His compassion for Jerusalem as being like that of a mother hen for her chicks (Matt. 23:37). Paul compared his ministry to a mother in labor (Gal. 4:19) and a nursing mother (1 Thess. 2:7).

James A. Brooks

MOULDY KJV spelling of moldy (Josh. 9:5,12). The underlying Hebrew term perhaps means "crumbled" (NASB, REB).

MOUNT BAAL-HERMON (Bā ȧl-hẽr´ mon) A variant name for Mount Hermon (Judg. 3:3), perhaps indicating its use as a worship place for Baal.

MOUNT CARMEL See *Carmel, Mount*.

MOUNT EPHRAIM See *Ephraim, Mount*.

MOUNT HERES See *Har-Heres; Heres*.

MOUNT HERMON See *Hermon, Mount*.

MOUNT HOR See *Hor*.

MOUNT OF ASSEMBLY See *Mount of the Congregation*.

MOUNT OF CORRUPTION See *Corruption, Mount of*.

MOUNT OF OLIVES See *Olives, Mount of*.

MOUNT OF THE AMALEKITES Mountainous region in the territory of Ephraim (Judg. 12:15; cp. the Hebrew "in Amalek" of 5:14). Some interpreters dispute a connection with the desert tribe of the same name.

MOUNT OF THE AMORITES KJV designation for the hill country of Judah and Ephraim (Deut. 1:7,20).

MOUNT OF THE BEATITUDES The "Horns of Hattin" near Capernaum which tradition identifies as the site of the Sermon on the Mount (Matt. 5:1–7:29). The reference to Jesus' ascending the mountain is perhaps meant to recall the story of Moses at Sinai (Exod. 19:3,20).

MOUNT OF THE CONGREGATION KJV expression generally rendered Mount of Assembly by modern translations. Part of Isaiah's exposure of the pride of the king of Babylon is the charge that he desired to ascend to the distant mountain where according to Babylonian myth the gods assembled (Isa. 14:13). The desire is tantamount to a claim to divinity.

MOUNT OF THE VALLEY KJV designation for an elevation in a valley in the territory of Reuben in Transjordan (Josh. 13:19). Modern translations render the phrase hill in/of the valley.

MOUNT SINAI See *Sinai, Mount*.

MOUNTAIN Elevated topographical feature formed by geological faulting and erosion. The

Jebel Musa, the traditional site of Mount Sinai, in the southern Sinai Peninsula.

geography of Palestine featured high mountains and deep rifts. The two usual words for mountain in the Bible are *har* (Hb.) and *oros* (Gr.). The simple definition for each is mountain or hill, though they may indicate hill country or a mountainous region.

Many important events in the Bible took place on or near mountains. God called Moses to His work at Mount Horeb, sometimes called "the mountain of God." A part of God's call was the promise that the Israelite people would worship there upon their escape from Egypt (Exod. 3:1-12). After the exodus God commanded Moses to gather the people at Mount Sinai (probably identical to Horeb). There God gave the law including the Ten Commandments to Moses.

Other OT mountain episodes include Aaron's death on Mount Hor (Num. 33:38), the death of Moses on Mount Nebo (Deut. 34:1-8), and Elijah's defeat of the prophets of Baal on Mount Carmel (1 Kings 18:15-40).

Much of Jesus' life and ministry also took place on mountains. One of the temptations took place on "a very high mountain" (Matt. 4:8 HCSB). Jesus' most famous teaching session is called the "Sermon on the Mount" (Matt. 5–7). Jesus went up to a mountain to pray (Luke 6:12).

Jesus was transfigured on a mountain (Matt. 17:1-8). There He was declared to be preeminent over both Moses and Elijah, the representatives of the Law and Prophets. Many of their greatest victories came on mountains.

The term "mountain" also is used symbolically. It is a natural image for stability (Ps. 30:7), obstacles (Zech. 4:7), and God's power (Ps. 121:1-2). God will remove all obstacles when His redemption is complete "and every mountain and hill be made low" (Isa. 40:4 NASB).

Mountains often have been called "holy places." Jerusalem (elevation 2,670 feet) often was called Mount Zion, the hill of the Lord (Pss. 2:6; 135:21: Isa. 8:18; Joel 3:21; Mic. 4:2). God met His people there in worship. The "new Jerusalem" is also known as Mount Zion (Rev. 14:1).

Some of the more famous biblical mountains with their feet elevations are: Ebal (3,084), Gerizim (2,890), Gilboa (1,630), Hermon (9,230), Nebo (2,630), Tabor (1,930), Sinai (7,500). See *Jerusalem; Palestine; Sermon on the Mount; Zion.*   *Bradley S. Butler*

MOUNTAIN SHEEP See *Chamois; Sheep.*

Church of the Beatitudes on the traditional site of the Sermon on the Mount by the Sea of Galilee.

MOURN, MOURNER, MOURNING See *Grief and Mourning.*

MOUSE Rodent with a pointed snout. As such, it is unclean (Lev. 11:29). Mice were apparently feared as carriers of the plague (1 Sam. 6:4). See *Rodents.*

MOUTH The external orifice used to ingest food and to communicate. **1.** Synonym for lips (1 Kings 19:18; 2 Kings 4:34; Job 31:27; Prov. 30:20; Song 1:2). **2.** Organ of eating and drinking (Judg. 7:6; 1 Sam. 14:26-27), sometimes used in figurative expressions such as when wickedness (Job 20:12) or God's word (Ps. 119:13) is described as sweet to the mouth. Anthropomorphic descriptions of the earth or Sheol speak of them opening their mouths to drink blood or swallow persons (Gen. 4:11; Num. 16:30,32; Isa. 5:14). **3.** Organ of speech (Gen. 45:12; Deut. 32:1) or laughter (Job 8:21; Ps. 126:2). The phrase "the mouth of the LORD has spoken" serves as a frequent reminder of the reliability of a prophetic message (Isa. 1:20; 40:5; Jer. 9:12; cp. Deut. 8:3; Matt. 4:4). Fire (2 Sam. 22:9) or a sword (Rev. 1:16) proceeding from the mouth of God pictures the effectiveness of God's word of judgment. **4.** Hebrew term for "mouth" is used for the openings of wells, caves, sacks, as well as for the edge of a sword.

MOZA (Mō´ ză) Personal name meaning "offspring." **1.** Descendant of Judah (1 Chron. 2:46). **2.** Descendant of King Saul (1 Chron. 8:36-37; 9:42-43).

MOZAH (Mō´ zah) Place-name meaning "unleavened." City in Benjamin (Josh. 18:26), later a center for pottery production as attested by numerous vessels recovered at Jericho and Tell-en-Nasbeh bearing the inscription Mozah on their handles. The site is likely that of modern Qaluniya, four miles northwest of Jerusalem on the Tel Aviv road.

MUFFLER KJV term for a scarf (NRSV) at Isa. 3:19. The item is part of the finery of the Jerusalem socialites. Other translations render the Hebrew term as veils (NASB, NIV, TEV) or coronets (REB).

MULE Hybrid animal produced by the union of a male ass and a female horse. Since the Mosaic law forbade crossbreeding (Lev. 19:19), the Israelites imported mules (Ezek. 27:14). They were used as war animals, for riding, and for carrying burdens (2 Kings 5:17). They were especially good for moving heavy burdens in mountainous areas, being better than the horse, ass, or camel. David chose a mule to symbolize royalty for Solomon's coronation (1 Kings 1:33), possibly because the Israelites did not have horses. However, this is not the donkey used in Zech. 9:9 and Matt. 21:5 for Jesus' entry to Jerusalem.

MUPPIM (Mŭp´ pĭm) Son of Benjamin (Gen. 46:21). The name perhaps is derived from the root "to wave." See *Shephupham.*

MURDER Intentional taking of human life. Human life is given great value in the Bible. Persons are created in the image of God; and persons are called to obey, serve, and glorify God. Human life is viewed as a sacred trust. It is because of this that taking human life is viewed as a serious crime in the Bible.

The prohibition against murder is found in the Ten Commandments, the heart of Hebrew law (Exod. 20:13; Deut. 5:17). Murder is the unlawful killing of a human being by another. Deliberately taking the life of a human being usurps the authority that belongs to God. The prohibition against murder is a hedge to protect human dignity. The OT (Gen. 9:6) prescribed that a murderer should be prepared to forfeit his own life. In Num. 35:16-31 careful attention is given to determining whether a killing is to be classified as murder.

Jesus removed the concept of murder from a physical act to the intention of one's heart (Matt. 5:21-22). According to Jesus, murder really begins when one loses respect for another human being. Spitting in the face of another, looking with contempt upon another, or unleashing one's anger are signs that a murderous spirit is present. Jesus forces us to move to the spirit behind the prohibition of murder. We are compelled to do all that we can do to protect the life of our neighbor and help it flourish. The writer of 1 John pushed Jesus' teaching to its ultimate: "Everyone who hates his brother is a murderer, and you know that no murderer has eternal life residing in him" (1 John 3:15 HCSB). See *Image of God; Law, Ten Commandments, Torah.*

D. Glenn Saul

MURRAIN (Mûr´ ĭn) KJV term derived from the French for "to die" (*morir*), referring to an infectious disease affecting livestock (Exod. 9:3). The earliest Greek translation used the term "death." Modern translations use either "disease" (TEV), "pestilence" (NASB, NRSV), or "plague" (NIV, RSV).

MUSE To ponder or reflect upon something, often without coming to conclusions (Ps. 143:5; Luke 3:15).

MUSHI (Mū´ shī) Personal name meaning "draw out." Son of Merari who gave his name to a family of priests, the Mushites (Exod. 6:19; Num. 3:20,33; 26:58; 1 Chron. 6:19,47; 23:21,23; 24:26,30).

MUSHITE (Mū´ shīt) Member of clan of Mushi.

MUSIC, INSTRUMENTS, DANCING Expression of the full range of human emotions vocally or instrumentally through music was as much a part of the lives of biblical people as it is of modern times. Workers bringing in the harvest might sing a vintage song (Isa. 16:10; Jer. 48:33). Those digging a well (Num. 21:17), as well, might be heard singing. Indeed all of life could be touched by song. The celebrations of a community, ritual practices of worship, even the act of warfare gave rise to song.

In such a musical climate, celebration through dance found a natural place in both the religious and secular life of ancient Israel. A variety of musical instruments was available to provide instrumental accompaniment to both song and dance.

Music Music as performed in early Near Eastern times has become better known through archaeological finds of descriptive texts and the remains of actual instruments.

The secular and religious music of ancient Israel found its home against this background of ancient Near Eastern music in which all of life could be brought under the spell of song. In reading the OT, Gen. 4:21 stands as the first reference to music. As one of Lamech's sons, Jubal

"was the father of all those who play the lyre and pipe" (NASB). Jubal brought the advent of music to the portrayal of cultural advance. The name Jubal itself is related to the Hebrew word for "ram" (*yovel*), the horns of which served as a signaling instrument in ancient Israel.

The joy taken in music is evidenced by its prominent role in the celebrations of life. A farewell might be said "with joy and with songs, with timbrel and with lyre" (Gen. 31:27 NASB); a homecoming welcomed "with tambourines and with dancing" (Judg. 11:34; cp. Luke 15:25). Work tasks of everyday living enjoyed the music evidenced by the songs or chants of the well diggers (Num. 21:17-18), those who tread grapes (Jer. 48:33), and possibly the watchman (Isa. 21:12).

Under certain circumstances musical celebration brought condemnation. The account of Moses' return from the mountain to be confronted by the singing and dancing of the people around the golden calf (Exod. 32:17-19) symbolized a condition of broken covenant. The Prophet Isaiah's rebuke of the idle rich who have "lyre and harp, tambourine and flute and wine" at their feasts is cast against their failure to take notice of the deeds of Yahweh (Isa. 5:12 NRSV). Both the scorn of mockers (Job 30:9) and the acclamation of heroes (1 Sam. 18:6-7) were expressed in song.

Victory in warfare provided impetus for numerous songs. The song of Miriam, one of the oldest poetic verses in the OT, celebrated the defeat of Pharaoh at the Sea (Exod. 15:21). Judges 5 stands as musical witness to Israel's victory over Jabin, the king of Canaan. Known as the "Song of Deborah," the verses are the musical celebration of a narrative event. Chants of victory on the lips of the victor (cp. Samson following his slaying of the Philistines recorded in Judg. 15:16) or those greeting the one successful in battle (cp. 1 Sam. 18:7) establish music as a medium for uncontainable joy. Celebration erupted into song. Emotions that might be limited by the restriction of prose, expressed themselves through the poetry of music as seen in David's moving lament at the death of Saul and Jonathan (2 Sam. 1:19-27).

In the early days of OT history, a special place seems to be accorded women in musical performance. The Prophetess Miriam and Deborah, a prophetess and judge, were among Israel's earliest musicians. Judges 11:34 pictures Jephthah's daughter greeting his victorious return from battle against the Ammonites "with tambourines and with dancing." David's reputation for valor spread through the singing of women's voices: "Saul has slain his thousands, and David his ten thousands" (1 Sam. 18:7). The depiction of dancing women entertaining at festive occasions found on Egyptian tomb paintings provides early Near Eastern background for the role of women in musical celebration.

The establishment of the monarchy about 1025 B.C. brought a new dimension to the musical tradition of ancient Israel with the appearance of professional musicians. Egypt and Assyria, neighboring countries to Israel, had known the tradition of professional musicians much earlier. Such musicians took their place both at court (1 Kings 1:34,39-40; 10:12; Eccles. 2:8) and in religious ritual. An Assyrian inscription, praising the victory of the Assyrian king Sennacherib over King Hezekiah of Judah, lists male and female musicians as part of the tribute carried off to Nineveh.

Although much uncertainty remains concerning the specifics of temple worship, biblical references offer clues to the role music played in cult observances. As a hymn proclaiming the future rule of God in all the earth, Ps. 98 calls for the employment of music in praise:

Shout to the LORD, all the earth;

be jubilant, shout for joy, and sing.

Sing to the LORD with the lyre,

with the lyre and melodious song.

With trumpets and the blast of the ram's horn

shout triumphantly in the presence of the LORD, our King (vv. 4-6 HCSB).

Worship featured trumpet calls (cp. Num. 10:10) and songs of thanksgiving, expressions of praise and petition sung after the offering of sacrifices (2 Chron. 29:20-30).

The psalms show not only the emotional range of music from lament to praise but also provide words for some of the songs used in temple worship. Guilds of musicians, known through reference to their founders in some psalm headings (for example, "the sons of Korah"), were evidently devoted to the discipline of liturgical music.

During the Babylonian exile the question, "How can we sing the LORD's song on foreign soil?" (Ps. 137:4), arose. Psalm 137 further alludes to the demand of the Babylonians for the Hebrew captives to "sing us one of the songs of Zion" (v. 3). The return from exile and reestablishment of the temple saw the descendants of the original Levitical musicians (cp. Ezra 2:40-41) reassume responsibility for liturgical music. Strabo's statement that the singing girls of Palestine were considered the most musical in the world shows that music continued in importance in Israel during Hellenistic times.

The structures of some psalms offer evidence for conjecturing the nature of vocal performance. Refrains (such as the "Lift up your heads, O gates! Rise up, O ancient doors!" of Ps. 24) and acclamations such as "Hallelujah" as well as divisions into strophes stand as performance clues. The common device of poetic parallelism, whereby a thought is balanced synonymously or antithetically with a second thought, provides further evidence for surmising the nature of musical performance, responsive and antiphonal performances being possibilities.

In light of the recognized obscurity in many of the headings, one can speak in general terms of five different types of information provided by the Psalm titles. Representatives of this classification are titles that identify psalms with persons or groups of persons (Pss. 3; 72; 90); titles purporting to indicate historical information concerning the psalm, particularly with respect to David (Pss. 18; 34); titles containing musical information (Pss. 4; 5); titles with liturgical information (Pss. 92; 100); and titles designating the "type" of psalm in question (Ps. 120, "a song of ascents"; Ps. 145, "a song of praise").

Nearly two-thirds of the psalms contain terms indicating collections, compilers, or authors in their headings: David, portrayed in biblical tradition as a composer, instrumentalist, court musician, and dancer, being most often mentioned. Others mentioned include the sons of Korah, Asaph, Solomon, Heman the Ezrahite, Ethan the Ezrahite, Moses, and Jeduthun.

Deriving from the Greek translation of the Hebrew *mizmor*, the word "psalm" is applied to some 57 songs. As a technical term appearing only in the Psalter, psalm refers to songs with instrumental accompaniment. Other terms indicating the type of psalm include *shiggaion* (Ps. 7), sometimes argued to indicate a lament; *miktam* (Pss. 16; 56–60) connected to the Akkadian meaning "to cover"; *maskil* (Ps. 78) whose meaning is still unknown. Some 30 psalms include in their heading the word "song" (Hb. *shir*), with "song of praise," "prayer," "a song of love," and "a song of ascent" also occurring. Headings may include as well terms which indicate the liturgical aim and usage of the particular psalm (for instance, "for the thank offering," "for the memorial offering," "for the Sabbath").

Some 55 psalms contain the expression "to the choirmaster" in their headings. Other technical musical expressions consisting of remarks that concern types or kinds of performances include "with stringed instruments" (*neginot*, Pss. 4; 6; 54, perhaps meant to exclude percussion and wind instruments) and "for the flutes" (*nehilot*), though both meanings are dubious. The terms *higgaion* (perhaps "musical flourish"), *shemini* ("on the eighth," perhaps an octave higher), and "the *gittith*" (Pss. 8; 81; 84) remain obscure as to meaning.

The singing of psalms to other tunes popular at the time is suggested by headings such as "Hind of the Dawn" in Ps. 22 (RSV) and "to Lilies" used in Pss. 45; 69; 80 (RSV).

Although found some 71 times in the Psalter, the interpretation of the term *Selah* remains uncertain. Suggestions range from understanding the term according to its earliest Greek translation, generally thought to indicate a type of musical interlude or change in singing, to a call for repetition of the verse, louder singing, or the kneeling and bowing down of worshipers.

Musical Instruments Pictorial representations as well as remains from instruments discovered through archaeology aid in our present knowledge of ancient musical instruments. A wide scope of literary remains gives further evidence. Descriptions and comments about musical instruments are to be found in both the OT and NT, their early translations, rabbinic and patristic literature, and the writings of Roman and Greek authors. Caution, however, must be applied in using the data available, leaving many identifications difficult and at best hypothetical.

The most frequently named musical instrument in the Bible is the "shofar" (ram's horn). Limited to two or three notes, the shofar (often translated "trumpet") served as a signaling instrument in times of peace and war (Judg. 3:27; 6:34; Neh. 4:18-20). Having as its chief function the making of noise, the shofar announced the new moons and Sabbaths,

warned of approaching danger, and signaled the death of nobility. As the only ancient instrument still used in the synagogue today, the shofar found a prominent place in the life of Israel, noted by its function in national celebration (1 Kings 1:34; 2 Kings 9:13).

Similar in function to the shofar was the trumpet, a straight metal instrument flared on the end and thought to have had a high, shrill tone. Sounded in pairs, the trumpet was known as the instrument of the priests (cp. Num. 10:2-10 for a description of uses; 2 Chron. 5:12-13 where some 20 trumpeters are mentioned). The sound of the trumpets introduced temple ceremony and sacrifice, the trumpet itself being counted among the sacred temple utensils (2 Kings 12:13; Num. 31:6).

As the instrument of David and the Levites, the lyre (Hb., *kinnor*, KJV "harp") was employed in both secular and sacred settings (cp. Isa. 23:16; 2 Sam. 6:5). A popular instrument throughout the ancient Near East, the lyre was often used to accompany singing. The number of strings on the lyre could vary; its basic shape was rectangular or trapezoidal.

The harp was a favorite instrument of the Egyptians. In Hebrew the designation *nebel*, though admittedly uncertain, may imply a type of angular harp with a vertical resonator or represent another type of lyre. Mainly a religious instrument in biblical tradition, the *nebel* is rarely mentioned in secular functions (cp. Isa. 5:12; 14:11). Like the lyre, the harp was often associated with aristocracy, thus being often made from precious woods and metals (1 Kings 10:12; 2 Chron. 9:11).

Chief among "flutes" and "pipes," woodwinds generally associated with secular uses, was the *chalil*, the most popular wind instrument in the ancient Near East and principal among the biblical wind instruments. Perhaps better described as a primitive clarinet, the *chalil* (NASB "flute" or KJV "pipe") was an instrument consisting of two separate pipes made of reed, metal, or ivory; each pipe having a mouthpiece with single or double reeds. Used in the expression of joy (1 Kings 1:39-40) or mourning (Jer. 48:36; Matt. 9:23), the *chalil* was primarily a secular instrument that could be played at funerals or feasts.

Other musical instruments mentioned in the biblical texts include the timbrel or tambourine

(Hb. *toph*, often symbolic of gladness, Gen. 31:27), cymbals, bells (presumably metal jingles without clappers; Exod. 28:33-34; 39:25-26 where they are attached to the high priest's robe), and a rattle-type noisemaker translated variously as castanets, rattles, sistrums, cymbals, or clappers (2 Sam. 6:5).

Mentioned in the NT are pipes (RSV "flute"), the lyre (RSV "harp"), cymbals, and the trumpet. The "sounding brass" of 1 Cor. 13:1 is perhaps understood through rabbinic literature in which it is seen as a characteristic instrument for weddings and joyous celebrations.

Dancing As rhythmic movement often performed to music, dancing enjoyed a prominent place in the life and worship of Israel. Various Hebrew words in the OT used to express the idea of dance seem to imply different types of movement: to skip about (*raqad*, Job 21:11), whirling about (*karar*, 2 Sam. 6:14,16), and perhaps twisting or writhing (*machol*, Ps. 30:11). Pictured in the homecoming welcome of victorious soldiers by women, dancing could be accompanied by song and instrument music (1 Sam. 18:6). See *Dancing; David; Levites; Psalms, Book of; Shiloh; Zither.*

Kandy Queen-Sutherland

MUSTARD Large annual plant which grows quite fast. Its seeds were once thought to be the smallest in the plant world. Jesus used the mustard plant in a parable to symbolize the rapid growth of the kingdom of God (Matt 13:31-32), and its seed as a simile for faith (Matt. 17:20). See *Plants.*

MUSTER GATE NRSV, REB designation for a Jerusalem city gate where troops were mustered, that is, gathered for enlistment (Neh. 3:31). See *Miphkad Gate.*

MUTENESS Inability to speak. In the OT muteness is traced to God (Exod. 4:11). God made Ezekiel mute (Ezek. 3:26) in response to Israel's failure to listen to his message. Later He restored Ezekiel's speech (24:27; 33:22) as a sign of the people's receptiveness to hear. Daniel became speechless in response to the appearance of a heavenly messenger (Dan. 10:15). The psalmist considered muteness an appropriate punishment for liars (Ps. 31:18). By extension, to be mute means to hold one's peace (Ps. 39:2,9; Isa. 53:7; Acts 8:32), espe-cially in the face of injustice. In Prov. 31:8 the mute are the symbol of all those who suffer without a voice. Isaiah 56:10 pictures Israel's leaders as mute dogs who cannot bark a warning. In Isa. 35:6 the singing of those once mute accompanies return from the exile. In Hab. 2:18-19 idols are mocked as mutes (1 Cor. 12:2).

In the NT muteness is either not explained (Mark 7:32,37) or else attributed to demons (Matt. 9:32; 12:22; Mark 9:17,25; Luke 11:14). An exception is Zechariah's muteness (Luke 1:20,22) which served as a sign of the truthfulness of Gabriel's message as well as a punishment for Zechariah's unbelief.

MUTH-LABBEN (Mŭth-lăb´ bĕn) Hebrew phrase in the title of Ps. 9 which means "death of the son." The phrase likely refers to the tune to which the psalm was performed.

MUTTER To utter words indistinctly or with a low voice. Muttering together with chirping characterized the speech of mediums (Isa. 8:19). See *Medium; Sheol.*

MUZZLE Leather or wire covering for an animal's mouth to prevent its eating or biting. Deuteronomy 25:4 is one of many laws in the Deuteronomic code concerned with humane treatment of others. Paul cited this prohibition of muzzling a treading ox to illustrate the principle that "the laborer is worthy of his pay" and specifically that "those who preach the gospel should earn their living by the gospel" (1 Cor. 9:9-14; 1 Tim. 5:17-18 HCSB).

MYRA (Mī´ rà) One of the six largest cities of Lysia in southeastern Asia Minor located on the River Andracus about two and one-half miles from the sea. The site of the ancient ruins is called Dembre today. Myra was a stopping point on Paul's voyage to Rome (Acts 27:5-6). Some manuscripts of the Western Text give Myra as port call after Patara in Acts 21:1.

MYRIAD (Mīr´ ĭ ăd) Greek term literally meaning 10,000 but frequently used to mean "countless or innumerable" (Jude 14; Rev. 5:11; 9:16; Luke 12:1; Acts 19:19; 21:20; Heb. 12:22).

MYRRH Aromatic resin having many uses in the ancient Near East. It was traded along with spices (Gen. 37:25), used as an ingredient in anointing oil (Exod. 30:23), applied as perfume (Esther 2:12), placed in clothes to deodorize them (Ps. 45:8), given as a gift (Matt. 2:11), and used to embalm bodies (John 19:39).

MYRTLE See *Plants.*

MYSIA (Mĭs´ ĭ à) Northwest region of Asia Minor (Acts 16:7). The NT mentions several cities in this region: Adramyttium (Acts 27:2); Assos (Acts 20:13-14); Pergamum (Rev. 1:11; 2:12); and Troas (Acts 16:8,11; 20:5,6; 2 Cor. 2:12; 2 Tim. 4:13). Hindered from mission work in Bythinia, Paul passed through Mysia before embarking on his Macedonian mission (Acts 16:6-11). Acts 20 records Paul's seven-day stay at Troas and an overland (mission) trip to Assos. On another occasion Paul found in Troas an open door of mission opportunity (2 Cor. 2:12).

MYSTERY Comes from the Greek noun *musterion*, though our English word does not do it justice. A *musterion* in the ancient world was any religious cult that demanded secrecy from its participants, who had to undergo sacred rites for membership. An element of this may lie behind *musterion* in the NT, but the word normally translated "mystery" in the book of Daniel is more likely the background for NT usage. In Daniel a mystery (Aramaic *raz*) was a revealed secret, something that could not be understood apart from divine revelation or explanation (Dan. 2:17-47; 4:9); this is certainly the force of the numerous instances of *musterion* in the NT. Jesus used *musterion* only once, and this was in reference to the mysteries or secrets about the kingdom that He revealed and explained to His disciples (Matt. 13:11; cp. Mark 4:11; Luke 8:10). Paul used *musterion* 21 times, and on each occasion the secret is already known from previous revelation (see Rom. 16:25; Eph. 1:9; 6:19; Col. 2:2; 4:3; 1 Tim. 3:16), or it is explained in the context (see Rom. 11:25; 1 Cor. 15:51; Eph. 3:1-13; 5:32; Col. 1:25-27)—that is, it is no longer a secret. The final four uses of *musterion* in the NT occur in Revelation, where the secret is a symbol that needs to be decoded (1:20; 10:7; 17:5,7).   *Stephen W. Carlson*

The Eleusinian Caves, center of worship for the Eleusinian mystery religion.

MYSTERY RELIGIONS Several different cults or societies characterized in part by elaborate initiation rituals and secret rites. Though attested in Greece before 600 B.C., the mystery religions flourished during the Hellenistic and Roman periods (after 333 B.C.) before dying out before A.D. 500. In particular the intermingling of religious concepts made possible by Alexander the Great's far-flung conquests accelerated the spread of some cults and facilitated the development of others. Knowledge of the mystery religions is fragmentary due to the strict secrecy imposed on those initiated; scattered references in ancient writers, some antagonistic to mystery religions, and archaeological data provide the most important evidence. Scholars often disagree about the interpretation of the data.

Many mystery religions emerged, but among the more important were those associated with the following deities: the Greek Demeter (the famous Eleusinian mysteries) and Dionysus, the Phyrgian Cybele (the Magna Mater) and Attis; the Syrian Adonis; the Egyptian Isis and Osiris (Sarapis); and Mithra, originally a Persian deity. Orphism and Sabazius both contributed to the mysteries of Dionysus while Samothrace was the home of the Cabiri mysteries. Many of the deities in the mystery religions were ancient and were worshiped in separate cults both before and after the development of the mystery cults.

The central feature of each mystery religion was the sacred rites, called mysteries, in which the cultic myth of the god or goddess worshiped in the cult was reenacted. Only those formally initiated into the cult could participate. The precise nature of these rites is unknown due to the vow of secrecy but probably involved a drama based upon the cult myth and the dramatic visual presentation of certain sacred objects. Mention is made of "things said," probably sacred formulas and secret love. References exist to eating and drinking, likely a form of communion. By participating in these rites the worshiper identified with the deity and shared in the deity's fate. These powerful symbols afforded those initiated the means to overcome the suffering and difficulties of life and promised a share in the life beyond.

Many, but not all, of the deities worshiped in the mysteries were originally associated with fertility. As such, their associated myths often referred to the natural cycle as it waxes and wanes (for instance, Demeter) or to the dying and rising of a god (Attis, Adonis, Osiris). Some scholars think that the mysteries used this feature of the myth to give symbolic expression of rising to immortality with the deity. However, not all scholars agree; some deities venerated in mystery religions did not die or rise; moreover, the exact use of the myth in the mysteries is often unclear, though some concept of immortality seems to be implied.

Public festivals were given in honor of some deities worshiped in the mystery religions, but their relationship to the secret rites is not clear. The spring festival of Cybele (March 15–27) involved processions, sacrifices, music, and frenzied dancing which led to castration. The public revelry, pantomimes, theatric productions, and excesses of drink associated with the worshipers of Dionysius/Bacchus (the Bacchanalia) are well-known.

Rites of initiation into the mystery religions included ritual cleansing in the sea, baptisms, and sacrifices. Mention should be made of the Taurobolium, used in the worship of Cybele, a rite in which a bull was slaughtered on a grill placed over a pit in which a priest stood; the person below eagerly covered himself with blood. Some have interpreted this as a rite of initiation, but it is more likely a purification ritual affording rebirth for a period of time, perhaps 20 years. The mystery religions dislodged religion from the traditional foundations of state and family and made it a matter of personal choice. With a few exceptions, for instance, Mithraism that was restricted to males, the mysteries were open to all classes and sexes. Those initiated formed an association bound together by secret rites and symbols peculiar to their cult. These associations met regularly with a designated leader in houses or specially built structures. The worshipers of Mithras met in a structure called a Mithraeum designed to imitate the cave in which Mithras killed the bull, the central act of the cult myth. Scenes of the slaying (tauroctony) appear prominently in several such structures.

At the meetings ritual acts or sacraments practiced by the particular cult were shared by the members. Mention is made of common meals or banquets. Members of the association were required to meet certain moral standards; some mention also is made of ascetic requirements. However, a word of caution is in order: generalizations about the mystery religions are difficult since each cult was individualistic. Exceptions to nearly all generalizations can be found.   *Thomas V. Brisco*

N

Sunrise over the Nile from Minia.

NAAM (Nā´ ăm) Personal name meaning "pleasantness." Descendant of Caleb (1 Chron. 4:15).

NAAMAH (Nā´ á mah) Name meaning "pleasant" or "delightful." **1.** Sister of Tubal-cain (Gen. 4:22). **2.** Ammonite wife of Solomon and mother of Rehoboam (1 Kings 14:21,31; 2 Chron. 12:13). **3.** Village in the Shephelah district of Judah (Josh. 15:41), likely Khirbet Farad about 22 miles west of Jerusalem between Timnah and Eltekeh.

NAAMAN (Nā´ á màn) Personal name meaning "pleasantness." Syrian general cured of leprosy under the direction of the Prophet Elisha (2 Kings 5). Naaman's leprosy apparently was not contagious, nor was it seen as the result of some moral sin. Following his cleansing, he professed faith in Israel's God. See *Leprosy.*

NAAMATHITE (Nā´ á mà thīt) Title meaning "resident of Na'ameh," given to Zophar, one of Job's three friends (Job 2:11; 11:1; 20:1; 42:9). Na'ameh is perhaps Djebel-el-Na'ameh in northwest Arabia.

NAAMITES (Nā´ á mīts) Family of Benjaminites descended from Naaman (Num. 26:40).

NAARAH (Nā´ á räh) Name meaning "girl" or "mill." **1.** Wife of Ashur (1 Chron. 4:5-6). **2.** Form of Naarath preferred by modern translations.

NAARAI (Nā´ á rī) Personal name meaning "attendant of Yah." One of David's 30 elite warriors (1 Chron. 11:37). The parallel account gives the name Paarai (2 Sam. 23:35).

NAARAN (Nā´ á răn) City allotted to Ephraim, likely identical with Naarah (1 Chron. 7:28; cp. Josh. 16:7).

NAARATH (Nā´ á räth) KJV form of Naarah, a city in the tribal territory of Ephraim just north of Jericho (Josh. 16:7). Suggested sites include 'Ain Duq, Khirbet el 'Nayash about five miles northeast of Jericho, and Tell el-Jishr. The city is perhaps identical to Naaran (1 Chron. 7:28).

NAASHON (Nā´ ăsh ŏn) or **NAASSON** (Nā ăs´ on) (KJV) See *Nahshon.*

Part of a large stable from the late Nabatean period at Kurnub (the ancient Nabatean town of Mampsis).

NABAL (Nā´ băl) Personal name meaning "fool" or "rude, ill-bred." See *Abigail.*

NABATEANS (Nă bá tē´ àns) Arabic people whose origins are unknown. Although not mentioned in the Bible, they greatly influenced Palestine during intertestamental and NT times. They appear to have infiltrated ancient Edom and Moab from a homeland southeast of Petra. That city later became their capital. From Petra they continued pushing northward as far as Madeba. In 85 B.C. Damascus requested a ruler of the Nabateans. The Arabs responded. Although

Excavations at the ancient Nabatean city of Mampsis.

The Treasury building of ancient Petra as seen from the only entranceway into the city.

overrun by Pompey in 63 B.C., they continued to influence Transjordan through a series of governors. Paul narrowly escaped being arrested in Damascus (2 Cor. 11:32). He spent time in Arabia following his conversion, probably preaching the gospel (Gal. 1:17).

NABONIDUS (Nă bō nī´ dŭs) Personal name meaning "Nabu is awe inspiring." Last king of the Neo-Babylonian Empire (555–539 B.C.). See *Babylon.*

NABOPOLASSAR (Nă bō pō lăs´ sàr) Personal name meaning "Nabu, protect the son." King (626–605 B.C.) who revolted from the Assyrians and established the Neo-Babylonian Empire. He rebelled in 627 B.C. and established his capital in Babylon. His reign was one of continual warfare as he slowly captured the cities of the Assyrian realm. He made an alliance with the Median

King Cyaxares in 614, and the two conquered Nineveh in 612 B.C. See *Babylon.*

NABOTH (Nā´ bŏth) Personal name, perhaps meaning "sprout." Owner of a vineyard in the Jezreel Valley adjacent to the country palace of King Ahab, who desired the property for a vegetable garden. Naboth refused to sell on the grounds that the property was a family inheritance (1 Kings 21:3-4). Hebrew law only allowed farmland to be leased for the number of crops until the Jubilee Year (Lev. 25:15-16). Farmland was not to be sold in perpetuity (Lev. 25:23). Jezebel, who had no regard for Israel's laws, plotted Naboth's judicial murder on the charge that he had blasphemed God and the king (1 Kings 21:8-14). Naboth's murder evoked God's judgment on Ahab and his family (1 Kings 21:17-24).

NACHON (Nā´ kŏn) (KJV) See *Nacon.*

NACHOR (Nā´ kôr) (KJV, Josh. 24:2; Luke 3:34) See *Nahor.*

NACON (Nā´ cŏn) Place-name meaning "firm" or "prepared." Threshing floor between Baal-judah (Kiriath-jearim) and Jerusalem (2 Sam. 6:6). The designation is either a place-name or the name of the owner. Chidon is given as the owner's name in the parallel account (1 Chron. 13:9).

NADAB (Nā´ dăb) Personal name meaning "willing" or "liberal." **1.** Aaron's eldest son (Exod. 6:23; Num. 3:2; 1 Chron. 6:3), who participated in the ratification of the covenant (Exod. 24:1,9), served as a priest (Exod. 28:1), and was consumed by fire along with his brother Abihu for offering unholy fire before the Lord (Lev. 10:1-7; Num. 26:61). Nadab died childless (Num. 3:4; 1 Chron. 24:2). **2.** Descendant of Judah and Tamar (1 Chron. 2:28,30). **3.** Descendant of Benjamin and great-uncle of Saul (1 Chron. 8:30; 9:36). **4.** Son of Jeroboam (1 Kings 14:20) and idolatrous king of Israel (901–900 B.C.). Baasha assassinated him during a siege of the Philistine city of Gibbethon (1 Kings 15:25-28). The extermination of the family of Jeroboam (15:29) was seen as fulfillment of the Ahijah's prophecy (14:10-11).

NAG HAMMADI (Nàg Hăm ma´ dē) Modern Egyptian village 300 miles south of Cairo and about 60 miles north of Luxor or ancient Thebes. Because of the close proximity of Nag Hammadi to the site of an important discovery of ancient documents relating to Gnosticism, the collection of documents is usually referred to as the Nag Hammadi Documents or Library. Another name occasionally associated with the documents is Chenoboskion, the name of an ancient Christian community that is also near the discovery site. Although the documents were found in an abandoned cemetery near Chenoboskion, they probably had no ancient association with that community.

Unlike the Dead Sea Scroll materials, which consisted primarily of scrolls, the documents found near Nag Hammadi are codices, books containing leaves. Each codex was formed of sheets of papyrus bound in leather, and measured from about 9½ inches to 11½ inches. Thirteen separate codices were found containing 51 smaller writings. While the documents are written in the Coptic language, an ancient language of Egypt, they are probably translations of Greek originals. The date of the present documents appears to be about A.D. 350. While there is debate as to the dates of the original texts, some were probably written before A.D. 200.

Discovery of the Nag Hammadi Documents
As in the case with many major archaeological discoveries, the find was something quite unexpected. In 1945 an Arab peasant, digging in an ancient cemetery for soft dirt to be used as fertilizer, found instead a large earthenware jar. At first he feared to open the jar due to his superstitious beliefs, but the prospect of valuable treasure inside prompted him to break open the container. He found the 13 leather-bound books or codices. Some of the documents may have been destroyed, but the discovery eventually came to the attention of those involved in antiquity studies.

Contents of the Nag Hammadi Documents
Practically all the materials reflect the religious outlook called "Gnosticism," an emerging worldview that caused considerable difficulty for early Christianity. Until the discovery of the Nag Hammadi Documents, our knowledge of Gnosticism came primarily from early Christian writers who wrote against the movement. Christian writers such as Irenaeus, Clement of Alexandria, Origen, and Tertullian not only gave descriptions of the teachings of Gnosticism, but they also quoted from gnostic writings. With the Nag Hammadi discovery, however, a small library of actual gnostic writings became available for study.

The Nag Hammadi Documents represent a rather wide diversity of content. Of special interest are several more clearly defined categories. The materials referred to as "Gospels" are especially important. In this category are such works as *The Gospel of Philip*, *The Gospel of Truth*, and perhaps the most important work found at Nag Hammadi, *The Gospel of Thomas*, which purports to be a collection of sayings of Jesus. Another category of documents concerns the work and circumstances of the apostles. *The Apocalypse of Paul* relates an account of the heavenly journey of Paul. *The Revelation of Peter* describes special revelations given to Peter by Jesus before Peter's imprisonment. *The Revelation of James* tells of the death of James.

An additional category of documents contains a wide variety of mythological speculations covering such topics as creation, redemption, and ultimate destiny. In this category are such works as *On the Origin of the World*, *Secret Book of the Great Invisible Spirit*, *Revelation of Adam*, *The Thought of Our Great Power*, *The Paraphrase of Shem*, *The Second Logos of the Great Seth*, and *The Trimorphic Protennoia*.

Although the Nag Hammadi Documents represent a diversity of gnostic systems, most of the materials do reflect the gnostic orientation. A possible exception is the work called *The Acts of Peter and the Twelve Apostles,* which is an apocryphal work about the 12 apostles.

Significance of the Nag Hammadi Documents (1) They provide primary source material enabling a greater understanding of Gnosticism. (2) They prove the existence of gnostic systems independent of the Christian framework. Some were primarily Jewish, and others existed as movements independent of either a Jewish or a Christian orientation. (3) They enhance the study of the NT, especially of the books that may have been written as reactions to Gnosticism, such as Colossians, John, and possibly 1 Corinthians. (4) They reflect the diversity of Gnosticism and point to the diversity of early Christianity and the resultant struggle for orthodoxy. (5) They reinforce an appreciation for the seriousness of the gnostic threat to early Christianity. Firsthand evidence now exists of the divergent gnostic views of creation, Christ, redemption, the doctrine of humanity, and the significance of the institutional church.

In conclusion, although not as well-known as the Dead Sea Scrolls, the discovery at Nag Hammadi represents an important milestone in the understanding of the struggles and developments of the early Christian church. See *Apocrypha, New Testament; Gnosticism.*

Bruce Tankersley

NAGGAI (Năg´ ī) or **NAGGE** (Năg´ gě) (KJV) Personal name, perhaps meaning "splendor of the sun." Ancestor of Jesus (Luke 3:25).

NAHALAL (Nȧ hăl´ ȧl) Place-name meaning "pasture" with alternate forms: Nahallal (Josh. 19:15 KJV); Nahalol (Judg. 1:30). Town Zebulun's territory allotted to the Levites (Josh. 19:15; 21:35). The Israelites did not drive out the Canaanite inhabitants of the city (Judg. 1:30). The site is uncertain. Tell en-Nahl north of the Kishon River at the southern end of the plain of Acco is possible as are modern Nahalal about six miles west of Nazareth and Tell el-Beida.

NAHALIEL (Nȧ hā´ lĭ ĕl) Place-name meaning "palm grove of God," "torrent valley of God," or less likely, "God is my inheritance." One of Israel's stopping places in Transjordan (Num. 21:19). The streambed is perhaps the Wadi Zerqa Ma'in or the Wadi Wala, a north tributary of the Arnon.

NAHALLAL (Na hăl´ lȧl) or **NAHALOL** (Nā´ hȧ lŏl) (KJV) See *Nahalal.*

NAHAM (Nā´ hăm) Personal name meaning "consolation." Either the brother (KJV, REB) or brother-in-law (NASB, NIV, NRSV) of Hodiah (1 Chron. 4:19).

NAHAMANI (Nā hȧ mā´ nī) Personal name meaning "comfort." Exile who returned with Zerubbabel (Neh. 7:7). The name does not appear in the parallel list (Ezra 2:2).

NAHARAI (Nā´ hȧ rī) or **NAHARI** (KJV) Personal name meaning "intelligent" or "snorting." One of David's 30 elite warriors who served as armor bearer to Joab (2 Sam. 23:37; 1 Chron. 11:39). The KJV used the alternate form Nahari in 2 Samuel.

NAHASH (Na´ hăsh) Personal name meaning "serpent" or perhaps "magnificence."

1. Ammonite ruler whose assault of Jabesh-Gilead set the stage for Saul's consolidation of power as king (1 Sam. 11:1-11). Saul's opponent was likely the Nahash who befriended David (2 Sam. 10:1-2). His son Hanun provoked David's anger (2 Sam. 10:3-5). Another son, Shobi, served as David's ally (2 Sam. 17:27). **2.** Parent of Abigal (2 Sam. 17:25). Various harmonizations of 2 Sam. 17:25 and 1 Chron. 2:16 have been offered: Nahash was a woman; Nahash is an alternate name for Jesse; the Amorite ruler Nahash and Jesse were at different times the husband of the same woman.

NAHATH (Nā´ hăth) Personal name meaning "descent," "rest," "quietness," or even "pure, clear." **1.** Edomite clan chief (Gen. 36:13,17; 1 Chron. 1:37). **2.** Levite (1 Chron. 6:26), possibly identical with Toah (1 Chron. 6:34) and Tohu (1 Sam. 1:1). **3.** Overseer in Hezekiah's time (2 Chron. 31:13).

NAHBI (Năh´ bī) Personal name meaning "hidden" or "timid." Naphtali's representative among the 12 spies sent to survey Canaan (Num. 13:14).

NAHOR (Nā´ hôr) Personal name meaning "snore, snort." **1.** Son of Serug, father of Terah, and grandfather of Abraham (Gen. 11:22-26). **2.** Son of Terah and brother of Abraham (Gen. 11:26). He married Milcah, his niece, who bore eight sons for him (11:29; 22:20-23). Nahor's genealogy shows the link between the Hebrews and other Semitic peoples of the ancient Near East. Of special interest is his relationship to the Arameans who dwelled in the region of modern Syria, probably descendants of his children born to Reumah (22:24), his concubine. **3.** City in Mesopotamia where Abraham's servant sought and found a wife for Isaac (Gen. 24:10); this was in keeping with the ancient custom of marrying within one's family. The city probably was located southeast of Haran. It is mentioned in the Mari Texts.

NAHSHON (Năh´ shŏn) Personal name meaning "serpent." Leader of the tribe of Judah during the wilderness years (Num. 1:7; 2:3; 7:12,17; 10:14), brother-in-law of Aaron (Exod. 6:23), and an ancestor of King David (Ruth 4:20-22) and of Jesus (Matt. 1:4; Luke 3:32).

NAHUM, BOOK OF (Nā´ hŭm) Personal name "Nahum" means "comfort, encourage." He was a Hebrew prophet and the OT book that bears his name contains some of his messages. Very little biographical information is known about the Prophet Nahum. He is called an Elkoshite (1:1), but the location of Elkosh is unknown.

The date of the prophet's ministry can be placed between 600 and 700 B.C. by two events mentioned in his book. Nahum 3:8 refers to the destruction of the Egyptian capital, No-amon or Thebes, in 663 B.C. and indicates that the prophet was active after this time. In chapter 2 he looked forward to the destruction of Nineveh which took place in 612 B.C. Nahum, therefore, prophesied after 650 B.C., probably close to the time of the fall of Nineveh.

Historical Background Since about 730 B.C. Israel and Judah had been Assyrian vassals. Almost a century later the Assyrian Empire began its decline. Many vassal nations revolted along with Josiah of Judah (2 Kings 22-23). A coalition of Medes, Babylonians, and Scythians attacked Assyrians and in 612 B.C. destroyed the capital, Nineveh. The Assyrians formed a coalition with the Egyptians, but in 605 B.C. they were defeated. See *Assyria.*

The Prophet's Message The Assyrian oppression caused the people to ask how God could allow such inhumanity to go unanswered. Nahum responded to Assyrian tyranny with a message marked by its vivid language. Assyria's might had been heavy upon Judah, but Nahum announced that God would destroy them.

The book opens with an affirmation of God as an avenging God. The fierceness of His wrath is pictured in terms of the destruction of nature. For over a century the Assyrians seemed to have had an uncontrolled reign, but now God was responding. His judgment is likened to an approaching storm. Perhaps the people of Judah doubted God's justness since Assyria seemed to have no restraints. Nahum, however, sought to dispel this notion.

The second chapter graphically portrays the future fall of Assyria's capital, Nineveh. Such an event must have been hard for the people to imagine. Nineveh was a massive city with a defensive wall that measured eight miles in circumference and ranged in height from 25 to 60 feet. A moat also surrounded it. Yet Nahum poetically affirmed the city's fall. The enemy would rush upon the city with their chariots (2:4), but the defenders would be unable to keep them out (2:5). The great city would be plundered (2:7-10).

The book of Nahum closes with more threats against Nineveh. Ironically, as Assyria had destroyed Thebes in 663 B.C., so the same fate would befall Nineveh (3:8-11). Preparations for a siege on the city are alluded to in 3:14. Water would be stored and fortifications strengthened by the addition of more mud bricks. Yet these preparations would not keep away God's devastating judgment.

While the book of Nahum is harsh and deals with the unpleasantness of war, it served to give hope to the people of Judah. They had been subjected to the cruel domination of Assyria for over a century, but now their faith in God to act on their behalf could be bolstered through God's response. God's justness was reaffirmed.

Outline

I. The Sovereign God Makes Himself Known (1:1-11).
   A. The jealous, patient Lord takes vengeance on His adversaries (1:1-3).
   B. The earth quakes at the arrival of God (1:4-5).
   C. God's anger is poured out (1:6).
   D. The Lord is a refuge for His troubled, trusting people (1:7).
   E. God protects those who seek Him but will destroy the enemy (1:8-9).
   F. The enemy must drink the cup of God's wrath (1:10-11).

II. In the Enemy's Fall, God Offers Hope for His Oppressed People (1:12-15).
   A. God can defeat the enemies no matter how strong and numerous they are (1:12-13).
   B. God judges the enemy because of its false gods (1:14).
   C. God calls His delivered people to celebrate (1:15).

III. God Will Bring Judgment upon His Wicked Enemy (2:1–3:19).
   A. The enemy will fall, but God's people will be restored (2:1-2).
   B. Armies and wealth cannot prevent God's judgment (2:3-12).
   C. When God declares war, the enemy is helpless (2:13).
   D. God humiliates wicked peoples (3:1-19).

Scott Langston

Nails from Roman times.

NAIL 1. Keratinous covering of the top ends of fingers and toes. If an Israelite desired to marry a prisoner of war, she was to cut her nails either as a sign of mourning for her parents or as part of her purification on entering the community of Israel (Deut. 21:12). **2.** Metal fasteners used in construction and for decoration (1 Chron. 22:3; 2 Chron. 3:9; Isa. 41:7; Jer. 10:4). The earliest nails were made of bronze. With the introduction of iron, larger nails were made of iron. Smaller nails continued to be made of bronze. Nails were sometimes plaited with precious metal and nail heads decorated with gold foil when used for ornament (cp. 2 Chron. 3:9). The nails used in the crucifixion of Jesus were likely iron spikes five to seven inches long (John 20:25). **3.** KJV used nail (pin) as an alternate translation for a Hebrew term modern translations consistently render "peg" (Exod. 35:18; Judg. 4:21-22; Zech. 10:4).

NAIN (Nān) Place-name meaning "pleasant." Village in southwest Galilee where Jesus raised a widow's son (Luke 7:11-15). The ancient town sat on a hillside overlooking the Plain of Esdraelon.

NAIOTH (Nā´ ŏth) Place-name meaning "dwelling." The name refers either to a building or district in the city of Ramah that housed the prophetic school that Samuel led (1 Sam. 19:18-24). David sought refuge from Saul at Naioth. Three groups of royal messengers and finally Saul himself fell victim to prophetic frenzy when they attempted to capture David there.

NAKED Being without clothes (Gen. 2:25; Job 1:21; Eccles. 5:15; Amos 2:16; Mic. 1:8) or else poorly clothed (Deut. 28:48; Matt. 25:36-44; James 2:15). The phrase "to uncover the nakedness of" means to have sexual intercourse (Lev. 18:6-19; 20:11,17-21). Nakedness frequently occurs in conjunction with shame (Gen. 3:7; 9:21-27; Isa. 47:3; Ezek. 16:8,36-37).

NAMES OF GOD The name of God holds an important key to understanding the doctrine of God and the doctrine of revelation. The name of God is a personal disclosure and reveals His relationship with His people. His name is known only because He chooses to make it known. To the Hebrew mind, God was both hidden and revealed, transcendent and immanent. Even though He was mysterious, lofty, and unapproachable, He bridged the gap with mankind by revealing His name. See *Naming*.

The truth of God's character is focused in His name. The divine name reveals God's power, authority, and holiness. This accounts for Israel's great reverence for God's name. The Ten Commandments prohibited the violation of God's name (Exod. 20:7; Deut. 5:11). Prophets spoke with authority when they uttered God's name. Oaths taken in God's name were considered binding, and battles fought in the name of God were victorious. Other nations would fear Israel not because it was a mighty nation but because it rallied under the Lord's name. In the NT God's name is manifested most clearly in Jesus Christ. He is called "the Word" (John 1:1), and Jesus Himself makes the claim that He has revealed the name of God (John 17:6). God's name is His promise to dwell with His people.

God of the Fathers Before Moses' encounter with God in the Midianite desert, God was known generally as the God of the Fathers. Various names were used for God under this conception, most of which were associated with the primitive Semitic word *El*.

El is a generic term for God or deity. It appears in ancient languages other than Hebrew. One can see the similarities to the modern Arabic word for God, *Al* or *Allah*. The word *El* refers to an awesome power that instills within mankind a mysterious dread or reverence.

Even though *El* was a term for God in pagan or polytheistic religions, it is not a designation for an impersonal force like one would find in animism. Pagans worshiped *El* as a high and lofty God. He was the chief God in the Canaanite pantheon. See *Canaan*.

The word *El* in the Bible is often a reference to deity as opposed to the particular historical revelation associated with the name "Yahweh" (see below). More often than not, however, it is used interchangeably as a synonym for Yahweh, the God of Israel, and translated God.

One of the most interesting uses of *El* is its alliance with other terms to reveal the character of God. Some of these combinations are:

El-Shaddai "God of the Mountains" or "The Almighty God." This term is more closely associated with the patriarchal period and can be found most frequently in the books of Genesis and Job. Exodus 6:3 underlines El-Shaddai as the name revealed to the patriarchs. God used it to make His covenant with Abraham (Gen. 17:1-2).

El-Elyon "The Most High God" or "The Exalted One" (Num. 24:16; 2 Sam. 22:14; Ps. 18:13). Melchizedek was a priest of El-Elyon and blessed Abraham in this name (Gen. 14:19-20), referring to El-Elyon as "Maker of heaven and earth." Canaanites at Ugarit also worshiped god as El-Elyon. El-Elyon seems to have had close ties to Jerusalem.

El-Olam "God of Eternity" or "God the Everlasting One" (Gen. 21:33; Isa. 26:4; Ps. 90:2). God's sovereignty extends through the passing of time and beyond our ability to see or understand.

El-Berith "God of the Covenant" (Judg. 9:46) transforms the Canaanite Baal Berith (8:33) to show God alone makes and keeps covenant.

El-Roi "God who sees me" or "God of vision" (Gen. 16:13). God sees needs of His people and responds.

Elohim Plural form for deity. It is a frequently used term and the most comprehensive of the "El" combinations. The plurality of this word is not a hint of polytheism. It is a plural of majesty. It is a revelation of the infinite nature of God. In the creation narrative we read: "Then Elohim said, "Let us make man in our image" (Gen. 1:26). This name suggests that there is a mystery to the Creator God which mankind cannot fully fathom. God is absolute, infinite Lord over creation and history. The Christian sees in this term a pointer to the Trinitarian reality of creation.

Other Uses The name *El* is frequently combined with other nouns or adjectives. Some examples are: Isra-el (One who is ruled by God), Beth-el (House of God), Peni-el (Face of God). In the crucifixion narrative (Mark 15:34) Jesus employed a form of *El* when he cried from the cross, "Eloi, Eloi," "My God, My God," quoting Ps. 22.

Covenant Name The covenant name for God was "Yahweh." Israel's faith was a new response to God based on His disclosure. This name was so unique and powerful that God formed a covenant with His people based upon His self-revelation. Yahweh titles appear in English translations as Jehovah. See *YHWH*.

Yahweh-Jireh "The LORD will provide" (Gen. 22:14). This was the name given to the location where God provided a ram for Abraham to sacrifice in the place of Isaac. This name is a testimony to God's deliverance.

Yahweh-Nissi "The LORD is my banner" (Exod. 17:15). Moses ascribed this name to God after a victory over the Amalekites. The name of God was considered a banner under which Israel could rally for victory. The Lord's name was the battle cry.

Yahweh-Mekaddesh "The LORD sanctifies" (Exod. 31:13). Holiness is the central revelation of God's character. God calls for a people who are set apart.

Yahweh-Shalom "The LORD is peace" (Judg. 6:24). This was the name of the altar that Gideon built at Ophrah signifying that God brings well-being not death to His people.

Yahweh-Sabaoth "The LORD of hosts" (1 Sam. 1:3; Jer. 11:20; cp. 1 Sam. 17:45). This can also be rendered "the LORD Almighty." It represents God's power over the nations and was closely tied to Shiloh, to the ark of the covenant, and to prophesy. The title designates God as King and Ruler of Israel, its armies, its temple, and of the entire universe.

Yahweh-Rohi "The LORD is my shepherd" (Ps. 23:1). God is the One who provides loving care for His people.

Yahweh-Tsidkenu "The LORD is our righteousness" (Jer. 23:5-6; 33:16). This was the name Jeremiah gave to God, the Righteous King, who would rule over Israel after the return from captivity. He would establish a new kingdom of justice.

Yahweh-Shammah "The LORD is there" (Ezek. 48:35). This is the name of God associated with the restoration of Jerusalem, God's dwelling place.

Other Names *Baal* This was the chief god of the Canaanite pantheon. In some ancient religions, Baal and El could be used interchangeably. There were tendencies within Israel to identify Baal with Yahweh, but Baal worship was incompatible with Hebrew monotheism. Prophets, such as Elijah and Hosea, called the people away from these tendencies and back to the covenant.

Adon or *Adonai* This is a title of authority and honor. It can be translated "Lord." It is not exclusively a title for deity because it is used in addressing a superior, such as a king or master. In this sense it is used to ascribe the highest honor and worship to God. Adon or Adonai was often used in conjunction with Yahweh. In time Adonai became a substitute for Yahweh. In the postexilic period it took on the connotation of God's absolute lordship.

Symbolic Titles A prominent characteristic of Scripture is its use of figurative language. Many of the names for God are symbolic, illustrative, or figurative.

Ancient of Days (Dan. 7:9,13,22) The picture presented is of an old man who lived for many years. This, of course, is not a literal description of God but a confession that He lives forever and His kingdom is everlasting. His rule encompasses the expanses of time. Unlike the portrait presented in other religions where the gods are bound within time, Yahweh is active in time and history. He gives history meaning and is drawing it to a conclusion. He is from "everlasting to everlasting" (Ps. 90:2).

Rock (Deut. 32:18; Ps. 19:14; Isa. 26:4) God is strong and permanent. Yahweh is sometimes identified as "The Rock of Israel."

Refuge (Ps. 9:9; Jer. 17:17) God is a haven from the enemy.

Fortress (Ps. 18:2; Nah. 1:7) God is a defense (stronghold) against the foe.

Shield (Gen. 15:1; Ps. 84:11) God is protection.

Sun (Ps. 84:11) God is the source of light and life.

Refiner (Mal. 3:2-3) God is purifier.

Political Names Many descriptions of God came from political life.

King In the ancient East it was common to address gods as king. Kingship was also ascribed to Yahweh. His covenant people were to obey Him as a Sovereign. This title is the key to understanding the kingdom of God, which is the most frequent title used in Scripture to describe God's rule.

Judge The judge was the political ruler during the time of tribal confederacy. Yahweh is the Judge who arbitrates disputes, sets things right, and intervenes for Israel in its military campaigns.

Shepherd God is frequently described as a Shepherd. This was a nurturing term to describe the care given to His covenantal people. It also had political or ruling connotations. Yahweh is the Shepherd King (Ezek. 34). In the NT the image of God as shepherd is continued in parables (Luke 15:4-7) and in John's portrayal of Christ as the Good Shepherd (John 10:1-18).

God the Father In the OT the word "father" is used for God to describe the close kinship that He enjoys with His worshipers. There are many figurative references to God's fatherhood. "As a father has compassion on his children, so the LORD has compassion on those who fear Him" (Ps. 103:13 HCSB). God is a "father to Israel" (Jer. 31:9) and speaks of Israel as His "son" (Exod. 4:22; Hos. 11:1).

Father is the distinguishing title for God in the NT. Jesus taught His disciples to use the Aramaic *Abba*, a term of affection that approximates our word "Daddy," to address the heavenly Father. See *Abba*.

Father takes on a richer meaning when it is joined with other designations:

Our Father (Jesus taught His disciples to address God in this manner when they prayed; Matt. 6:9);

Father of mercies (2 Cor. 1:3);

Father of lights (James 1:17);

Father of glory (Eph. 1:17).

When the Father title is juxtaposed with the word "Son," the significance of God's name in relation to Jesus Christ is understood. Christ's claim to have come in His Father's name reveals that He was God's unique representative (John 5:43). He shares the Father's essential authority and works done in His Father's name bear witness to this special relationship (John 10:25). Christ has provided a full revelation of God because He has clearly declared His name (John 12:28; 17:6). See *Jehovah*.   *Brad Creed*

NAMING In biblical tradition the task of naming a child generally fell to the mother (Gen. 29:31–30:24; 1 Sam. 1:20) but could be performed by the father (Gen. 16:15; Exod. 2:22) and in exceptional cases by nonparental figures (Exod. 2:10; Ruth 4:17). The last son of Jacob and Rachel received a name from each parent, Jacob altering the name Rachel gave (Gen. 35:18). Naming could be attributed to God originating through a divine birth announcement (Gen. 17:19; Luke 1:13). Naming took place near birth in the OT and on the eighth day accompanying circumcision in NT narratives (Luke 1:59; 2:21).

The biblical concept of naming was rooted in the ancient world's understanding that a name expressed essence. To know the name of a person was to know that person's total character and nature. Revealing character and destiny, personal names might express hopes for the child's future. Changing of name could occur at divine or human initiative, revealing a transformation in character or destiny (Gen. 17:5,15; 32:28; Matt. 16:17-18).

The knowing of a name implied a relationship between parties in which power to do harm or good was in force. That God knew Moses by name occasioned the granting of Moses' request for divine presence (Exod. 33:12,17). The act of naming implied the power of the namer over the named, evidenced in the naming of the animals in Gen. 2:19-20 or Pharaoh's renaming Joseph (Gen. 41:45; cp. Dan. 1:6-7; 2 Kings 24:17).

Proper names consisting of one or more terms consciously chosen by the namer conveyed a readily understandable meaning within the biblical world. Reflecting circumstances of birth Rachel, called the child of her death, Benoni, "son of my sorrow" (Gen. 35:18). Jacob was named "the supplanter" for he was "holding on to Esau's heel" (Gen. 25:26). Moses, the "stranger in a strange land," named his son Gershom (Exod. 2:22). Conditions of the times proved imaginative as well: Ichabod, "The glory has departed from Israel," came about by the ark of the covenant falling into Philistine hands (1 Sam. 4:21-22) and the symbolic names of Isaiah's sons: Shear-jashub, "a remnant shall return," (Isa. 7:3); Maher-shalal-hash-baz, "swift is the booty, speedy is the prey," (Isa. 8:3, NASB).

Personal characteristics: Esau means "hairy"; Careah means "bald" (Gen. 25:25; 2 Kings 25:23); and the use of animal names in early times; Deborah means "bee"; Jonah means "dove"; Rachel means "ewe." Less frequently occurring are names taken from plants: Tamar means "palm tree"; Susanna meaning "lily."

Simple names functioning as epithets, such as Nabal meaning "fool" and Sarah meaning "princess," gave way to compound names factual or wishful in nature, such as Mattaniah meaning "gift of Yahweh" and Ezekiel meaning "may God strengthen." Compound names in the main employ the divine names El and Yah (Elijah, Ishmael, Nathaniel). Titles and kinship terms (Abimelech, melech means "king"; Abigail, Ab(i) means "father") and foreign names occur: Aramaic, Greek, and Roman (Martha, Salome, Alexandra, John Mark).

The patronymic practice whereby a child received the name of a relative, especially the grandfather (Simon Bar-Jona is "son of Jona") was common by the Christian era. Geographical identities are attested as well (Goliath of Gath and Jesus of Nazareth). See *Family; Names of God.* *Kandy Queen-Sutherland*

NAOMI (Nā ō´ mǐ) Personal name meaning "my pleasantness." Wife of Elimelech and mother-in-law to Orpah and Ruth (Ruth 1:2,4). Naomi suffered the deaths of her husband and two sons while in Moab. Her matchmaking between Ruth and Boaz was successful, and she became a forebearer of David, Israel's greatest king (Ruth 4:21-22). See *Ruth, Book of.*

NAPHATH-DOR (Nā phăth-Dôr´) Designation of the region surrounding the coastal city of Dor about 15 miles west of Megiddo (Josh. 12:23; 1 Kings 4:11). The alternate form Naphoth-Dor is used at Joshua 11:2 (RSV). KJV translated the term *Naphath* variously (borders, coasts, regions). NASB rendered the term "height(s)," relegating the Hebrew to the margin; REB, "districts."

NAPHISH (Nā´ phĭsh) Personal name meaning "refreshed." A son of Ishmael and ancestor of a northwest Arabian tribe of the same name (Gen. 25:15; 1 Chron. 1:31). The tribe dwelt in Transjordan before being displaced by Reuben, Gad, and the half-tribe of Manasseh (1 Chron. 5:19).

NAPHOTH-DOR (Nā phŏth-Dôr´) RSV alternate form of Naphath-Dor (Josh. 11:2). The NIV consistently used the form Naphoth Dor (Josh. 11:2; 12:23; 1 Kings 4:11).

NAPHTALI (Năph´ tȧ lī) Personal name meaning "wrestler." Sixth son of Jacob and second son by his concubine Bilhah (Gen. 30:6-8). In blessing him Jacob likened Naphtali to a hind let loose (49:21), probably a reference to unbridled energy. The tribe which bears his name inhabited a territory north of the Sea of Galilee that extended along the northwest side of Jordan beyond Lake Huleh (Josh. 19:32-39).

Naphtali is praised in the Song of Deborah for placing itself in jeopardy on behalf of Israel (Judg. 5:18). The tribe joined with Asher and Manasseh to help drive the Midianites out of the land (7:23). During Solomon's reign the territory was designated a separate economic district (1 Kings 4:7,15) and produced Hiram, the king's chief brass worker (7:13-14). The Syrians invaded Naphtali during Baasha's reign and inflicted heavy losses (15:20). The territory finally succumbed to Tiglath-pileser III in 734 B.C. (2 Kings 15:29). See *Tribes of Israel.*

NAPHTUHIM (Năph´ tū hĭm) Residents of Naphtuh, an unidentified geographic area (Gen. 10:13; 1 Chron. 1:11; Naphtuhites, NIV and REB). The Naphtuhim were most likely residents of the Nile Delta or else inhabitants of the oases to the west of the Nile Valley. The term may come from Egyptian for Ptah, pointing to Middle Egypt.

NAPKIN See *Handkerchief.*

NARCISSUS (När sĭs´ sŭs) Common name among both slaves and freedmen meaning "daffodil." The Narcissus of Rom. 16:11 headed a household, perhaps including slaves and/or associated freedmen, which included some Christians. The most famous Narcissus was a freedman who served as an advisor to Emperor Claudius (A.D. 41–54). He committed suicide shortly after Nero's accession of the throne. It is possible, though not certain, that Paul had this Narcissus in mind.

NARD Expensive fragrance derived from the roots of the herb *Nardostachys jatamansi.* The term appears twice in the Song of Songs (1:12 ESV; 4:13-14) and in two of the Gospel accounts of the woman anointing Jesus at Simon's house in Bethany (Mark 14:3; John 12:3; "spikenard," KJV). The disciples rebuked her for this action, stating that the ointment could have been sold for a sizable sum and the proceeds donated to the poor.

NATHAN (Nā´ thăn) Personal name meaning "gift." **1.** Prophet in royal court during reign of David and early years of Solomon. David consulted Nathan about building a temple. Nathan responded favorably. That night the Lord spoke to Nathan with instructions for David that his successor would build the temple. Nathan included the words of the Lord that David would have a house, a great name, and a kingdom forever. David responded with gratitude to the Lord (2 Sam. 7; 1 Chron. 17).

David committed adultery with Bathsheba and had her husband, Uriah, slain in battle. The Lord was displeased and sent Nathan to rebuke the king. The prophet told a story in which a rich man took the only little ewe lamb that belonged to a poor man and prepared a meal for one of his guests. David said the rich man should die. Nathan responded, "You are the man!" David repented, but his first child born to Bathsheba died (2 Sam. 11–12).

Adonijah tried unsuccessfully to become king in the closing days of David's life. Nathan, along with Zadok, the priest, Benaiah the son of Jehoiada, Shimei, Rei, and David's mighty men, opposed Adonijah. Bathsheba and Nathan spoke to David about an earlier decision to appoint Solomon as the next king. David declared Solomon to be king (1 Kings 1:5-53).

Later references indicate that Nathan wrote the chronicles for David (1 Chron. 29:29) and a history of Solomon (2 Chron. 9:29). Nathan advised David in arranging the musical instruments played by the Levites (2 Chron. 29:25). **2.** Son of David, born in Jerusalem (2 Sam. 5:14; 1 Chron. 14:4). His mother was Bathsheba (Bath-shua) (1 Chron. 3:5). He is in the genealogy of Jesus Christ (Luke 3:31). **3.** Nathan of Zobah, father of Igal, one of David's mighty men (2 Sam. 23:36). He may be the same as Nathan the brother of Joel (1 Chron. 11:38), within another list of David's mighty men. **4.** The two Nathans mentioned as fathers of Azariah and Zabud may be the same man and identified as the Prophet Nathan (1 Kings 4:5) during Solomon's reign. If Zubad (1 Chron. 2:36) is the same as Zabud, his father Nathan may be the prophet; thus, the prophet's father was Attai, a descendant of Jerahmeel (1 Chron. 2:25). **5.** Returning exile whom Ezra sent on a mission to secure ministers for God's house (Ezra 8:15-17). He may be the same exile who had married a foreign wife and put her away (Ezra 10:39). *Omer J. Hancock, Jr.*

NATHANAEL (Nă thăn´ ā ĕl) Personal name meaning "giver of God." An Israelite whom Jesus complimented as being guileless (John 1:47) and who, in turn, confessed the Lord as being the Son of God and King of Israel (v. 49).

Nathanael was from Cana of Galilee (John 21:2) and apparently became one of the inner core of disciples who followed Jesus. Although Matthew, Mark, and Luke do not mention him by name, his two appearances in John point to his devotion to Christ. Some have equated him with Bartholomew.

Philip announced to Nathanael that Jesus was the promised Messiah (John 1:45). It was then that Nathanael made the infamous remark, "Can anything good come out of Nazareth?" (v. 46). See *Disciple.*

NATHAN-MELECH (Nă thăn-mē´ lĕk) Personal name meaning "the king has given" or perhaps "Melech [the god Molech] has given." Nathan-Melech served as an official of King Josiah (2 Kings 23:11). See *Eunuch.*

NATIONS See *Gentiles.*

NATIVES Term used by several modern translations (NASB, REB, NRSV) to designate the inhabitants of Malta (Acts 28:2). Barbarous people (KJV) reflects the Greek *barbaroi* which designates the islanders as non-Greek speaking. NIV reads "islanders," HCSB "local people."

NATIVITY OF CHRIST See *Jesus Christ; Jesus, Life and Ministry.*

The silver star marks the traditional site of Jesus' birth in the Grotto of the Nativity in Bethlehem.

Sunset over Bethlehem with the belfry of the Church of the Nativity silhouetted in the center right.

NATURAL According to nature. **1.** Natural use (Rom. 1:26-27 KJV; natural relations, RSV) refers to heterosexual relations, thus "natural intercourse," (NRSV, REB). **2.** Natural affection refers specifically to affection for family members. Those lacking natural affection (*astorgoi*) are unloving to their families or generally inhuman or unsociable (Rom. 1:31; 2 Tim. 3:3). **3.** Natural branches refer to original or native branches as opposed to engrafted ones (Rom. 11:21,24). **4.** Natural or unspiritual person (1 Cor. 2:14) is one not open to receiving gifts from God's Spirit or to discerning spiritual matters (contrast 2:15). This contrast between the spiritual and natural is also evidenced by James 3:15 (NASB) and Jude 19 (NIV). **5.** The natural face (James 1:23) is literally the face of one's birth. To see one's natural face is to see oneself as one actually is.

NATURAL REVELATION See *Revelation.*

NAUM (Nā´ ŭm) KJV form of Nahum, an ancestor of Christ (Luke 3:25).

NAVE 1. Term used by some modern translations (NASB, NRSV) for the main room of the temple between the vestibule and the holy of holies (1 Kings 6:3,5,17; 7:50; 2 Chron. 3:4-5,13; 4:22). KJV referred to this room as the temple or house. See *Temple of Jerusalem.* **2.** KJV used "nave" for the center of a wheel through which an axle passes (1 Kings 7:33). Modern translations render the underlying Hebrew as "rim."

NAVEL 1. Depression in the middle of the belly marking the place where the umbilical cord was formerly attached. Ezekiel 16:4 graphically portrays Jerusalem's hopeless state before God's adoption in the image of a child whose umbilical cord (navel string) is not cut. Modern translations often replace "navel" with another word more appropriate to the context, for example, "flesh" or "belly" (Job 40:16; Prov. 3:8; Song 7:2). See *Midwife*. **2.** Hebrew expression for "midst of the land" or "center of the earth" (NRSV) in Judg. 9:37; Ezek. 38:12. Israel's neighbors used the term to designate the earthly place, often a worship place or sacred city, linking heaven and earth. Some scholars use later Jewish references to Jerusalem as the cultic "navel of the earth" to interpret Gerazim and Jerusalem as places celebrated as the earth's linking point. However the two biblical passages seem to have only geographical meanings.

NAVY See *Fleet; Ships, Sailors, and Navigation.*

NAZARETH, NAZARENE (Năz´ à rĕth; Năz á rĕn´) Place-name meaning "branch." Nazareth did not enjoy a place of prominence until its association with Jesus. It does not appear in the OT. As He became known as "Jesus of Nazareth" (Matt. 26:71; Luke 18:37; 24:19; John 1:45; Acts 2:22; 3:6; 10:38), His hometown became fixed in Christian memory. Nazareth was located in lower Galilee about halfway between the Sea of Galilee and the Mediterranean Sea. It lay in the hill country north of the Plain of Esdraelon. The hills formed a natural basin with three sides but open toward the south. The city was on the slopes of the basin, facing east and southeast. Cana was about five miles to the northeast. A Roman road from Capernaum westward to the coast passed near Nazareth.

It was a small village in Jesus' day, having only one spring to supply fresh water to its inhabitants. Today the spring is referred to as "Mary's well." The modern city has about 20,000 citizens, mainly Moslems and Christians. The angel went to Nazareth to announce to Mary and Joseph the coming birth of Jesus (Luke 1:26-28). Following Jesus' birth in Bethlehem and the sojourn in Egypt, Joseph and Mary returned with Jesus to Nazareth (Matt. 2:19-23) where Jesus grew from boyhood to manhood (Luke 2:39-40; 4:16), being stamped as a Nazarene (Matt. 2:23), apparently a midrashic play on the Hebrew term *netser*, "shoot" in Isa. 11:1.

Nazareth did not possess a good reputation, as reflected in the question of Nathanael, himself a Galilean (John 1:46). The early church received similar scorn as the Nazarene sect (Acts 24:5). Such lack of respect was likely due to an

A religious service inside the Church of the Nativity in Bethlehem.

unpolished dialect, a lack of culture, and quite possibly a measure of irreligion and moral laxity. Jesus was rejected by His townspeople near the beginning of His public ministry, being cast out of the synagogue at Nazareth (Luke 4:16-30; Matt. 13:54-58; Mark 6:1-6). See *Galilee*.

Jerry W. Batson

NAZIRITE (Năz´ ĭ rīt) Member of a class of individuals especially devoted to God. The Hebrew term means consecration, devotion, and separation. Two traditional forms of the Nazirite are found. One was based on a vow by the individual for a specific period; the other was a life-long devotion following the revelatory experience of a parent that announced the impending birth of a child.

The Nazirite's outward signs—the growth of hair, abstention from wine and other alcoholic products, the avoidance of contact with the dead—are illustrative of devotion to God. Violation of these signs resulted in defilement and the need for purification so the vow could be completed. Numbers 6:1-21 regulated the practice and lined the phenomenon to cultic law and locality. Verses 1-8 show how the Nazirite's period was begun. In case of defilement, a method of purification was given (vv. 9-12). The

The Catholic Church of the Annunciation built over the caves where tradition says Mary and Joseph lived.

An overview of modern Nazareth from the southwest.

status was terminated (vv. 13-21) by the burning of shaven hair and the giving of various offerings. Parallels exist between the cultic purity of the high priest and the Nazirite.

The lifelong Nazirite in biblical tradition included Samson (Judg. 13), Samuel (1 Sam. 1), and John the Baptist (Luke 1:15-17). In the NT Paul took the Nazirite vow for a specific period of time (Acts 18:18; 21:22-26). Amos 2:12 shows an ethical concern for protecting the status of the Nazirite. See *Abstinence.*

NEAH (Nē´ ah) Place-name meaning "settlement." Border town in the tribal territory of Zebulun (Josh. 19:13). The site was perhaps that of modern Nimrin west of Kurn Hattin.

NEAPOLIS (Nə ăp´ o lĭs) Name meaning "new city," of the seaport of Philippi (Acts 16:11). Neapolis (modern Kavala) is located about 10 miles from Philippi in northeastern Macedonia. The city sits on a neck of land between two bays, each of which serve as harbors.

NEARIAH (Nē á rī´ ah) Personal name, perhaps meaning "Yah's young man." **1.** Descendant of David (1 Chron. 3:22-23). **2.** Commander of Hezekiah's forces who defeated the Amalekites (1 Chron. 4:42-43).

NEBAI (Nē´ bī) Personal name meaning "projecting" or "fruitful." One of the witnesses to Ezra's renewal of the covenant (Neh. 10:19).

NEBAIOTH (Nə bī´ ŏth) or **NEBAJOTH** (Nə bā´ jŏth) (KJV) Personal name meaning "fruitfulness." Son of Ishmael and ancestor of an Arab tribe of the same name (Gen. 25:13; 28:9; 36:3). KJV used the alternate form Nebajoth in 1 Chron. 1:29; Isa. 60:7.

NEBALLAT (Nə băl´ lăt) Place-name, perhaps meaning "blessed with life." The name perhaps derives from Nabu-uballit, the personal name of an Assyrian governor of Samaria. Neballat was resettled by Benjaminites after the exile (Neh. 11:34). The site is identical with modern Beit Nebala on the edge of the Plain of Sharon about four miles east of Lod.

NEBAT (Nē´ băt) Personal name meaning "God has regarded." Father of Jeroboam I (1 Kings 11:26; 12:2,15). Nebat was from Zeredah about 10 miles west of Shiloh.

The harbor, town, and acropolis of Neapolis (modern Kavala).

NEBO (Nē´ bō) Place and divine name meaning "height." **1.** Babylonian god of speech, writing, and water. Worship of Nebo was popular during the Neo-Babylonian era (612–539 B.C.). Isaiah mocked parades featuring the idol of Nebo (Isa. 46:1). **2.** Moabite city located southwest of Heshbon. The tribes Reuben and Gad requested the area around Nebo for their flocks (Num. 32:2-3). It was held by Israel until recaptured by King Mesha about 850 B.C. **3.** Town reinhabited by exiles returning from Babylon (Ezra 2:29). The site has been identified with Nob. **4.** Mountain about 12 miles east of the mouth of the Jordan River from which Moses viewed the promised land (Deut. 32:49). It rises over 4,000 feet above the Dead Sea and gives an excellent view of the southwest, west, and as far north as Mount Hermon. Israel captured the area around Mount Nebo as they marched toward Canaan. They camped in the area of Mount Nebo opposite Jericho when the Balaam incident occurred (Num. 22–24). During the period of the judges, it was the possession of Eglon of Moab. David recaptured the area (2 Sam. 8:2), and it remained a part of Israel until Mesha rebelled and took control about 850 B.C.

NEBO-SARSEKIM (Nē bō-Sär´ sĕ kĭm) NIV form of the name of a Babylonian official (Jer. 39:13). The NIV and similar REB readings result from dividing the present Hebrew text differently from the majority of English translators. See *Sarsechim.*

NEBUCHADNEZZAR (Nĕb ū kăd nĕz´ zår) Personal name meaning "Nabu protects." King of Babylon 605–562 B.C. He was the son of Nabopolassar and inherited the throne upon the death of his father. Nebuchadnezzar served as a general under his father and was a brilliant strategist. His victory over the Egyptian forces at Carchemish (605) signaled the completion of Babylon's conquest of Palestine (Jer. 46:1-2). See *Babylon.*

NEBUSHASBAN, NEBUSHAZBAN (Nĕ bū shǎs´ bǎn, Nĕ bū shǎz´ bǎn) Variant transliterations of personal name meaning "Nabu save me." High official of Nebuchadnezzar involved in the fall of Jerusalem (Jer. 39:13).

NEBUZARADAN (Nĕb´ ū zär´ å dǎn) Personal name meaning "Nebo has given offspring." An officer in the Babylonian army during King

The Jordan Valley from the top of Mount Nebo looking toward Jericho.

Nebuchadnezzar's reign. His title is given as "captain of the guard" (bodyguard, Jer. 39:13), a designation which is uncertain. He led his troops in a siege of Jerusalem in 587 B.C. (2 Kings 25:8-9), burned the city's buildings, tore down its walls, and carried away the people into exile. Four years later he returned and deported still more citizens (Jer. 52:30). See *Babylon.*

NECHO (Nē´ kō) KJV form of Neco (2 Chron. 35:20,22; 36:4). KJV used the hyphenated form Pharaoh-necho at Jer. 46:2. See *Neco.*

NECHOH (Nē´ kōh) KJV alternate form of Neco. This form always occurs in the hyphenated form Pharaoh-nechoh (2 Kings 23:29,33-35). See *Neco.*

NECK Portion of the body connecting the head to the torso. To put one's feet on the neck of an enemy is a sign of complete victory (Josh. 10:24). A yoke placed on the neck is a frequent emblem of servitude (Gen. 27:40; Deut. 28:48; Isa. 10:27). To fall upon someone's neck with weeping or kissing is a special sign of tenderness (Gen. 33:4; 45:14; cp. Luke 15:20). To be stiffnecked or to harden one's neck is a common picture of stubborn disobedience (Exod. 32:9; 33:3,5).

NECKLACE Ornament worn around the neck (Song 1:10; Ezek. 16:11). The gift of a gold necklace is sometimes the sign of installation to a high office (Gen. 41:42; Dan. 5:29).

NECO (Nē´ cō) Second Pharaoh (609–594 B.C.) of the 26th dynasty of Egypt whose forces killed Josiah in battle (2 Kings 23:29-35; 2 Chron. 35:20-24) and who installed Jehoiakim as king of Judah in his place (2 Kings 23:34-35). The Twenty-sixth Dynasty was established with Assyrian patronage. Neco began to reign three years after the fall of Nineveh, the Assyrian capital. The resulting power vacuum encouraged the ambitious Neco to seize Gaza as a base (Jer. 47:1) for a campaign to bring Syria under his control and to bring aid to the Assyrian remnant in their struggle with the rising force of Babylon. Josiah met Neco in battle as the latter was on route to Carchemish. There Neco was defeated by Nebuchadnezzar in 605 B.C. (Jer. 46:2). Later Nebuchadrezzar would extend his control as far as the Nile (2 Kings 24:7). See *Assyria; Egypt; Josiah.*

NECROMANCY Conjuring the spirits of the dead to predict or influence future events. See *Medium.*

NEDABIAH (Nĕd á bī´ ah) Personal name meaning "Yah is generous." Son of Jeconiah, the exiled king of Judah (1 Chron. 3:18).

NEEDLE Small slender instrument used in sewing with an eye at one end through which thread is passed. The needles of NT times were similar in size to modern needles with the exception of our smallest needles. Needles were most often made of bronze, though bone and ivory were also used. Jesus' teaching that "it is easier for a camel to go through the eye of a needle than for a rich person to enter the kingdom of God" (Matt. 19:24 HCSB; cp. Mark 10:25; Luke 18:25) illustrates the impossibility of a rich person's being saved apart from the intervention of God who does the impossible (Matt. 19:26). Some late Greek manuscripts read "rope" (*kamilos*) for camel (*kamelos*). This attempt to dull the sharp edge of Jesus' saying runs counter to the context. The use of the term "needle's eye" for a gate of Jerusalem is an interpretive fiction, again designed to make Jesus' word more palatable. No such gate exists.

NEEDLEWORK Decorative work sewn upon cloth. Needlework was used in the decoration of the screens for the tabernacle door (Exod. 26:36; 36:37) and for the gate to its court (Exod. 27:16; 38:18) as well as for Aaron's girdle (Exod. 28:39; 39:29). Needlework was included in the prize spoils of war (Judg. 5:30) and in lists of luxury items for trade (Ezek. 27:16,24). Embroidered garments were the clothing of royalty (Ezek. 16:10,13,18; 26:16). The mention of material of various colors suggests that some needlework may have involved applique.

NEESINGS (nēēz´ ĭngs) KJV term meaning "sneezings" or "sneezes" (Job 41:18).

NEGEB (Nĕg´ eb) or **NEGEV** (Nĕg´ ĕv) (preferred sp.) Place-name meaning "dry" referring to an arid region in southern Palestine and coming to mean "south." During biblical times it was more populated than today indicating either more rainfall then or better conservation of the resources. It was the land of the Amalekites during Abraham's day (Gen. 14:7). There he exiled Hagar (21:14). The Israelites wandered in the

Negev after a futile attempt to enter Canaan (Num. 14:44-45). David incorporated it into his kingdom, and Solomon established fortresses in the region. Daniel used the term, translated "south," to refer to Egypt (Dan. 11:15,29). After Judah fell in 586 B.C. Edom took the area into its kingdom. In NT times it was known as Nabatea. See *Directions; Nabateans; Palestine.*

NEGINAH, NEGINOTH (Nĕ gē´ nah, Nĕg´ ĭ nŏth) Neginoth, the plural form of neginah, is used as a technical term in the superscriptions of several psalms (Pss. 4; 6; 54–55; 61; 67; 76) and as the subscription of Hab. 3:19. The term is generally understood to specify the instrumentation needed for performance "with stringed instruments" (cp. Isa. 38:20; Lam. 5:14). Other references suggest that neginah designates a taunt song (Job 30:9; Ps. 69:12; Lam. 3:14).

NEHELAM, NEHELAMITE (Nĕ hĕl´ ăm, Nĕ hĕl´ ă mīt) Either a family name or a reference to the home of the false prophet Shemaiah (Jer. 29:24,31-32). The name is perhaps a play on the Hebrew word for dreamer (cp. Jer. 23:25,32).

NEHEMIAH (Nē hə mī´ ah) Personal name meaning "Yah comforts or encourages" and name of OT book featuring work of Nehemiah. **1.** Leader who was among the first to return with Zerubbabel from exile to Judah in about 538 B.C. (Ezra 2:2; Neh. 7:7). **2.** Son of Azbuk, "the ruler of the half part of Bethzur" (Neh. 3:16), one who helped Nehemiah son of Hachaliah with rebuilding the walls of Jerusalem. **3.** Nehemiah, the son of Hachaliah, is the main character in the book that bears his name. He was a contemporary of Ezra and Malachi, Socrates in Greece (470–399 B.C.), and only a few decades later than Gautama Buddha in India (560–480 B.C.) and Confucius in China (551–479 B.C.).

Nehemiah held the distinguished position of cupbearer to the king (1:11). This was an office of trust; tasting the king's wine and food, the cupbearer stood between the king and death. That Nehemiah, a Jew and a captive, served this Gentile king in such a strategic capacity was an unusual credit and honor to this man of strong character.

Nehemiah's memoirs include first-person accounts (1:1–7:5; 12:27-47; 13:4-31), and the other material uses the third person pronoun (chaps. 8–10). Thus his story is both autobiographical and biographical. Visitors to Susa informed him of the dilapidation of Jerusalem's walls. He was so upset that he cried and "mourned for days" (1:4); he prayed a confession (1:5-11). His grief became apparent to Artaxerxes who permitted him to go to Jerusalem.

Nehemiah's first act there was to inspect the walls at night (2:15). He then called an assembly and convinced the people of the need for a building program. He was an excellent leader who demonstrated engineering knowledge and brilliant organizing ability (chap. 3) so the work began.

Trouble arose from without and from within. Sanballat and his friends tried to stop the work but without success (chap. 4). Trouble from within was economic. Building the walls caused a labor shortage; farms were mortgaged and high rates of interest were charged. Nehemiah said, "The thing which you are doing is not good" (5:9 NASB). He corrected the problem and even gave financial aid to those in need (chap. 5). Again Sanballat and other non-Jews made several attempts to lure Nehemiah away from the job and shut it down, but they failed. Nehemiah proved to be a person of strong will and unusual boldness. "So the wall was completed … in fifty and two days" (6:15). The dedication of the wall is described later in 12:27-43.

The theological climax of the book of Nehemiah and of the life of Ezra is the Great Revival (Neh. 8–10). It was a grand experience. It warrants close study for revival attempts today. People assembled and requested Ezra to read from the book of the law of Moses (8:1). The book was probably the Pentateuch (Torah) or some part of it. Ezra read, and others helped by giving "the sense so that they understood the reading" (8:8 NASB). This probably included translating the Hebrew Scripture into Aramaic, the commonly spoken language.

A great celebration occurred, and they observed the Feast of Tabernacles. Results were impressive: "They confessed and worshiped the LORD their God" (9:3 NASB) and "separated themselves from all foreigners" (9:2) that is, they divorced their foreign spouses. They prayed a long prayer of confession (9:6-37). The people responded, "Now because of all this we are making an agreement in writing" (9:38). The signers and terms of the covenant were then recorded (chap. 10).

Nehemiah was dissatisfied with the small size of the population of Jerusalem. He made an ingenious proposal: to "cast lots to bring one out of ten to live in Jerusalem, the holy city, while nine-tenths remained in the other cities" (11:1 NASB). Nehemiah's last chapter cites his reforms made during his second visit to Jerusalem in 432 B.C. He threw out a Gentile who was permitted to live in the temple; he restored the practice of tithing to support the Levites; he corrected Sabbath wrongs by those who bought and sold on the Sabbath; and he dealt forthrightly with those who had married foreigners, those not in covenant relation with God.

Nehemiah was indeed an outstanding person. His theology was very practical; it affected every area of life. Note his prayers and how prac-

tical they were (1:4-11; 2:4; 4:4-5,9; 5:19; 6:9,14; 13:14,22,29,31). He boldly asked, "Remember me, O my God, for good, according to all that I have done for this people" (5:19 NASB; cp. 13:14,31). His faith was practical: "And the king granted them to me because the good hand of my God was on me" (2:8; cp. 2:18 for a practical application of this concept). He believed "the God of heaven will give us success" (2:20) and that "our God will fight for us" (4:20). He had respect for the Sabbath, the temple and its institutions, the Levites, and tithing.

Nehemiah was a man of action; he got things done. He knew how to use persuasion but also force. One may properly call him the father of Judaism. Because of Nehemiah, Judaism had a fortified city, a purified people, a dedicated and unified nation, renewed economic stability, and a new commitment to God's law.

D. C. Martin

N

NEHEMIAH, BOOK OF Nehemiah and Ezra were one book in the ancient Hebrew and Greek OT and probably were not divided until after the interbiblical period. Jewish tradition says Ezra or Nehemiah was the author. Because of the close connection between Chronicles and Ezra-Nehemiah, one person might have written or compiled all three books. Those who follow this argument refer to the author as the Chronicler.

The literary style of Nehemiah is similar to that in Ezra. There are many lists (chaps. 3; 10:1-27; 11; 12:1-26). The author/compiler wove Ezra's and Nehemiah's stories together, Ezra being featured in Neh. 8.

Nehemiah's Jerusalem.

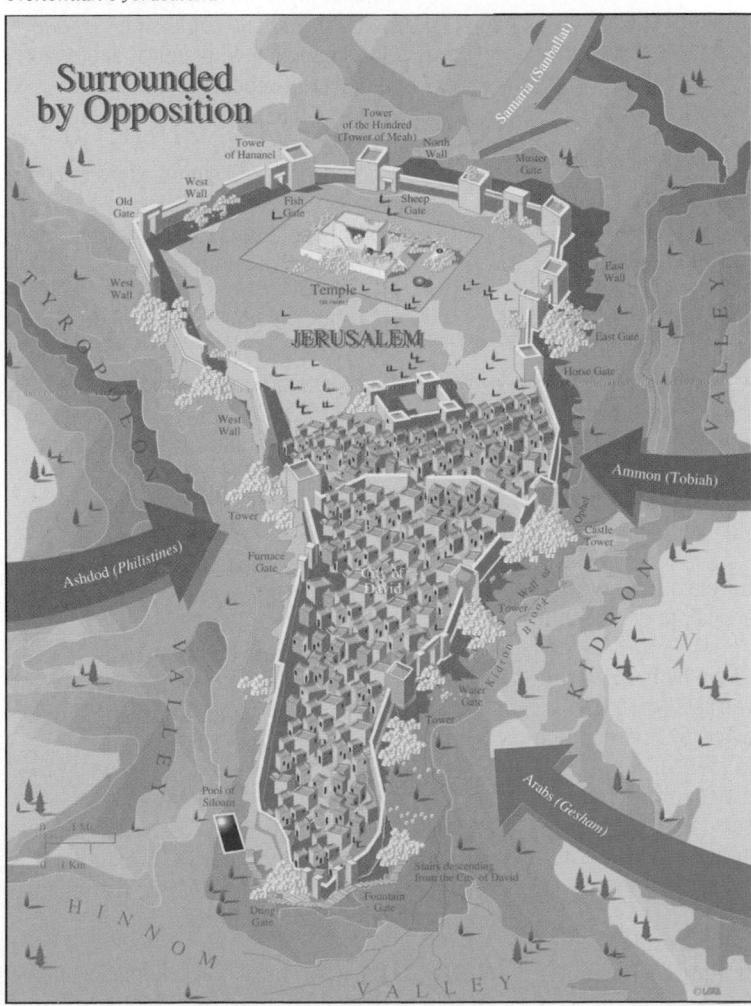

The book has four major sections: the rebuilding of Jerusalem's walls (chaps. 1–7), the Great Revival (chaps. 8–10), population and census information (chaps. 11–12), and the reforms of Nehemiah (chap. 13). Nehemiah made two visits from King Artaxerxes to Jerusalem (2:1-6; 13:6-7). His first, 445 B.C., was to repair the walls; they were in a state of disrepair almost a century after the first arrival from exile in 538 B.C. The second was a problem-solving trip in the 32nd year of Artaxerxes (13:6), 432 B.C. See *Ezra, Book of; Nehemiah 3.*

Outline

I. God's Work Must Be Done (1:1–7:33).
   A. God's leaders must be informed of needs in God's work (1:1-3).
   B. God's leaders must be responsive spiritually to needs in God's work and must pray (1:4-11).
   C. God's leaders must enlist the aid of others, sometimes outside the family of God (2:1-9).
   D. God's leaders likely will encounter opposition (2:10).
   E. God's leaders must exercise caution and discretion along with careful planning (2:11-16).
   F. God's leaders must inform and challenge God's people to work (2:17-20).
   G. God's work demands hard work, good organization, plenty of cooperation, and good records to give credit where credit is due (3:1-32).
   H. God's leaders will pray in the face of ridicule and insult (4:1-9).
   I. God's leaders may expect opposition from within as well as from without (4:10-12).
   J. God's leaders must encourage weary workers with practical, prayerful faith (4:13-15).
   K. God's work gets done by hard work and committed workers (4:16-23).
   L. God's work is slowed by internal problems of unfairness (5:1-5).
   M. God's leaders must confront profiteering problem causers (5:6-13).
   N. God's leaders at times can be sacrificially generous to meet a pressing need (5:14-19).
   O. God's leaders know opposition can be very personal and must deal with it head-on (6:1-14).
   P. God's help and the cooperation of many workers bring success (6:15-16).
   Q. God's work can have traitors within (6:17-19).
   R. God's leaders will enlist others and give them clear instructions (7:1-5).
   S. God's leaders need to keep and use good records (7:6-73).
II. God's Way Must Include Revival and Reformation (8:1–13:31).
   A. God's people want to hear God's Word (8:1-3).
   B. God's Word must be read and then interpreted (8:4-8).
   C. God's way calls for joyous celebration (8:9-12).
   D. God's way prescribes formal expressions of joyous worship (8:13-18).
   E. God's way elicits confession (9:1-5).
   F. God's people give practical expression to prayerful repentance (9:6-37).
   G. God's people are willing to commit themselves (9:38).
   H. God's people will sign pledges of commitment (10:1-27).
   I. God's people must give practical expressions of commitment (10:28-39).
   J. God's people must be willing to make some changes (11:1-2).
   K. God's work requires good records (11:3–12:26).
   L. God's work should be dedicated and celebrated (12:27-47).
   M. God's people must be a separated people (13:1-9).
   N. God's work, including His finance program, must not be neglected (13:10-14).
   O. God's day must be respected (13:15-22).
   P. God's way demands purity in marriage and in ministers (13:23-31).

D. C. Martin

NEHILOTH (Nē´ hǐ lŏth) Technical musical term in the superscription of Ps. 5. The term is generally understood to specify the instrumentation for the psalm, "with flutes."

NEHUSHTA (Nə hŭsh´ tà) Personal name meaning "serpent" or "bronze." Mother of King

Jehoiachin of Judah (2 Kings 24:8). As queen mother she was among those deported in the first exile (24:12,15).

NEHUSHTAN (Nə hŭsh´ tăn) Name of a "brazen serpent" destroyed by King Hezekiah as part of an attempt to reform Judah's life and worship (2 Kings 18:4). The object was believed to be the one Moses fashioned to relieve a plague in the Israelite camp during the exodus (Num. 21:8-9). The word "Nehushtan" probably is a play on words in the Hebrew, the word for bronze being very similar. Nehushtan probably was a serpentine nature god worshiped in connection with the Canaanite cults. King Jehoiachin's mother was Nehushta (2 Kings 24:8), probably in honor of this foreign deity. See *Bronze Serpent.*

NEIEL (Nə ī´ ĕl) Name meaning "dwelling place of God." Town assigned to Asher (Josh. 19:27). The site is probably that of Khirbet Ya'nin on the eastern edge of the plain of Acco about 18 miles southeast of that city.

NEIGH Loud, prolonged cry of a horse used as a figure of approaching battle (Jer. 8:16) or of unbridled sexual desire (Jer. 5:8; 13:27; 50:11).

NEIGHBOR The Bible records a number of directives concerning the treatment of a neighbor but little definition as to what or who a neighbor is. In Exodus the term is first used in a way which crosses ethnic or national bounds, when the Israelites were to borrow gold and silver jewelry from their Egyptian neighbors (Exod. 3:22; 12:36). In this instance it was the women of Israel who were to go to their Egyptian friends and neighbors and to ask them for the jewelry made of precious metals.

After those references, the remainder of OT texts concerning neighbors are either positive commands, "Share with your closest neighbor" regarding the Passover meal (Exod. 12:4) and "Love your neighbor as yourself" (Lev. 19:18) or negative injunctions. Such commandments include prohibition of false witness and coveting (Exod. 20:17-18), moving property lines, and otherwise defrauding one living in close proximity (Lev. 19:13). Several teachings in the book of Proverbs and in the writings of the prophets address proper attitudes and actions toward one's neighbors.

The fact that certain directives were national in nature gives a ready explanation for the later mind-set addressed by Jesus when dealing with or teaching about "undesirable" neighbors. Usury, for example, could not be charged on a loan to a neighbor but was allowable to foreigners.

Though the Samaritans lived in close proximity to the Jews in NT times, they were not socially recognized to be neighbors by the Jews. When Jesus spoke to a Samaritan woman at Sychar (John 4), both the woman and Jesus' disciples were initially uncomfortable with the contact.

The most important teaching to define a neighbor came from Jesus' answer to the question, "Who is my neighbor?" Jesus responded by giving the parable of the good Samaritan, which portrayed the Samaritan as the merciful neighbor. Jesus told the man to "go and do the same" (Luke 10:37).

Douglas K. Wilson, Jr.,
and Kimberly P. Wilson

NEKEB (Nē´ kĕb) KJV transliteration of a Hebrew term meaning tunnel, shaft, or mine (Josh. 19:33). Modern translations take Nekeb as a component of the place-name Adami-nekeb. If a separate site is intended, el-Bossa is possible.

NEKODA (Nə kō´ dà) Personal name meaning "speckled." **1.** Family of temple servants returning to Jerusalem after the exile (Ezra 2:48; Neh. 7:50). **2.** Family who returned from exile but were unable to establish their Israelite descent (Neh. 7:62).

NEMUEL (Nĕm´ ū ĕl) **1.** Ancestor of a family of Simeonites, the Nemuelites (Num. 26:12; 1 Chron. 4:24); this Nemuel is also called Jemuel (Gen. 46:10; Exod. 6:15) **2.** A Reubenite (Num. 26:9).

NEMUELITES (Nĕm ū ĕl īts) See *Nemuel.*

NEPHEG (Nē´ phĕg) Personal name meaning "boaster." **1.** A Levite (Exod. 6:21). **2.** Son born to David in Jerusalem (2 Sam. 5:15; 1 Chron. 3:7; 14:6).

NEPHEW 1. The son of one's brother or sister. KJV never used "nephew" in this sense, but NASB and NIV used it in this sense for Lot (Gen. 12:5; 14:12). **2.** When KJV was translated, "nephew" was used in the broader sense of a lineal descendant, especially a grandson (Judg. 12:14; Job 18:19; Isa. 14:22; 1 Tim. 5:4).

NEPHILIM Transliteration of a Hebrew word that designates a class of beings mentioned in Gen. 6:4 and Num. 13:33. Some interpreters believe the word is related to *naphal* meaning "to fall." In Gen. 6:4 the term refers to "heroes of old" (NRSV) so some have concluded that these are beings that have fallen from heaven and married the daughters of men. However, the text does not state that explicitly. At most it says that the Nephilim were on the earth during the days when the sons of God married the daughters of men. When the 12 spies were sent to Canaan, they saw giants whom they called the Nephilim, beside whom they seemed small, as "grasshoppers." There is no attempt to relate these people to the Nephilim of Gen. 6. See *Giants; Rephaim; Sons of God.*

NEPHISH (Nē´ phĭsh) (KJV, 1 Chron. 5:19) See *Naphish.*

NEPHISHESIM (Nĕ phĭsh´ ə sĭm) See *Nephisim.*

NEPHISIM (Nĕ phī´ sĭm) Family of temple servants who returned from exile (Ezra 2:50), probably identical with the Nephushesim (Nephishesim, KJV) of Neh. 7:52.

NEPHTHALIM (Nĕph´ thà lĭm) Greek form of Naphtali used by the KJV (Matt. 4:13,15; Rev. 7:6).

NEPHTOAH (Nĕph tō´ ah) Name meaning "opening," found only in the phrase "Waters of Nephtoah." Boundary marker for Judah and Benjamin (Josh. 15:9; 18:15). The site was formerly identified with Atam, south of Bethlehem. The most frequent identification is now Lifta, about three miles northwest of Jerusalem.

NEPHUSHESIM (Nĕ phūsh´ ə sĭm) See *Nephisim.*

NER (Nēr) Personal name meaning "light." Father of Saul's general Abner and grandfather of Saul (1 Sam. 14:51; 26:5,14; 2 Sam. 2:8; 1 Chron. 9:36).

NEREUS (Nē´ rūs) Personal name borrowed from Greek mythology where Nereus is the sea god who fathers the Nereids (sea nymphs). The NT Nereus was a Roman Christian, possibly the son of Philogus and Julia (Rom. 16:15).

NERGAL (Nēr´ găl) Name, perhaps a form of "Ne-uru-gal" (Lord of the great city), of the Mesopotamian god of the underworld whose cult was centered in the ancient city of Cuth (Cuthah, modern Tell Ibrahim). Following the fall of the Northern Kingdom of Israel, the Assyrians resettled Samaria with Mesopotamian peoples who brought their gods, including Nergal, with them (2 Kings 17:30). The name is also an element in the name of the Babylonian official Nergal-sharezar (Jer. 39:3,13). See *Assyria.*

NERGAL-SHAREZER (Nēr´ găl-shà rē´ zēr) A personal name meaning "Nergal, protect the king." Probably a different spelling of the name "Neriglissar." He is mentioned as being among the officers of Nebuchadnezzar's court who helped destroy Jerusalem in 586 B.C. (Jer. 39:3,13). He was a son-in-law of Nebuchadnezzar who usurped the Babylonian throne following the death of Evil-merodach. Nergal-sharezer quite possibly had something to do with the rebellion and the king's death. From the Babylonian Chronicle it is known that Nergal-sharezer mounted a military campaign across the Taurus Mountains to fight the Medes. He succeeded at first but was met with a bitter defeat later and soon died, perhaps at the hands of those who placed Nabonidus on the throne. See *Babylon.*

NERI (Nē´ rī) Personal name meaning "lamp." An ancestor of Jesus (Luke 3:27).

NERIAH (Nə rī´ ah) Personal name meaning "Yahweh is light." Father of two men who assisted Jeremiah: Baruch the scribe (Jer. 32:12; 36:4-19) and Seraiah the quartermaster (Jer. 51:59).

NERO (Nē´ rō) Personal name meaning "brave." Roman emperor A.D. 54–68. Nero became emperor in A.D. 54 at the age of 17. He succeeded his stepfather, Claudius, who was probably murdered at the request of Agrippina, Nero's mother.

For the first years of his reign, Nero was content to be dominated by his mother and his two mentors, Burrus and Seneca. The latter was a leading Stoic philosopher who was able, for a time, to moderate Nero's more excessive tendencies. As he grew older, Nero threw off these moderating influences and took control. To remove opposition he probably was involved in the death of his half brother Britannicus, and he had his mother murdered.

Nero was a complex personality. He could be extremely cruel, and his life was marked with debauchery and excess. Yet he was also a poet, an actor, a musician, and an athlete. He attempted to turn the crowds of Rome away from the brutal gladiatorial contests to an appreciation of the Greek-style Olympic games and other forms of cultural competition.

During Nero's rule the Great Fire broke out in Rome (A.D. 64). Much of the city was destroyed including Nero's palace. The story, probably true in part, goes that Nero fiddled while Rome burned.

Nero took measures to provide relief for those affected by the fire. Still he could not dispel the rumor that he had the fire set. People knew that he planned to build a much larger palace for himself, and they reasoned that he used the fire to clear off the land. Nero felt the need to divert suspicion to another group. He selected the Christians as his scapegoats. He claimed that they had set the fire. A systematic persecution of the Christians followed. Because of his lifestyle and the persecution, many Christians viewed him as the antichrist.

Nero neglected the army. This proved to be his downfall. He lost the loyalty of large segments of the army. Finally, several frontier armies revolted. Nero's support at home melted away. Realizing that the end was inevitable and near, he committed suicide by stabbing himself in A.D. 68. See *Rome and the Roman Empire.*

Gary Poulton

NEST Hollow container fashioned by a bird to contain its eggs and young. Nest is often used as a simile or metaphor for a human dwelling (Num. 24:21; Job 29:18; Hab. 2:9; Prov. 27:8). The term translated "nest" (Matt. 8:20; Luke 9:58) suggests a leafy "tent" rather than a nest.

NET 1. Loosely woven mesh of twine or cord used for catching birds, fish, or other prey. Fishing nets were of two basic types. The first was a cone-shaped net with leads around its wide mouth used for hand casting (Matt. 4:18-21; Mark 1:16-19). The second was the seine net, a large draw with floats at its head and lead sinkers at its foot. Such a net was often hauled ashore to empty (Isa. 19:8; Ezek. 26:5,14; 32:3; 47:10; Matt. 13:47). In the majority of OT cases the seine net is a figure for judgment at the hands of ruthless military forces. Fowling nets frequently had hinged mouths that could clamp shut when sprung (Prov. 1:17; Hos. 7:11-12). Nets of unspecified type are frequently used as figures of the Lord's chastisement (Job 19:6; Ps. 66:11; Lam. 1:13; Ezek. 12:13) or of the plots of the wicked (Pss. 9:15; 31:4; 35:7-8). **2.** Netting or network refers to grillwork used as part of the ornament of the altar of burnt offering (Exod. 27:4-5; 38:4) and of the capitals of the temple columns (1 Kings 7:17-20). The grillwork of the altar perhaps functioned as a vent.

NETAIM (Nə tā´ ĭm) Name meaning "plantings." Site of a royal pottery works (1 Chron. 4:23). The site has not been identified.

NETHANEEL (Nə thăn´ ə ĕl) or **NETHANEL** (Nə thăn´ ĕl) Personal name meaning "given by God." **1.** Leader of the tribe Issachar and a son of Zuar (Num. 1:8). He commanded an army of 54,400 men (2:5-6). **2.** Fourth son of Jesse and brother of King David (1 Chron. 2:14). **3.** One of several priests to blow the trumpet before the ark of God (1 Chron. 15:24). **4.** Prince of Judah whom King Jehoshaphat sent out with others to teach the law of God in the cities of Judah (2 Chron. 17:7-9). **5.** Levite and father of Shemaiah who recorded the names and order of the people who would minister in the temple (1 Chron. 24:6). **6.** Fifth son of Obed-edom who was a gatekeeper in the temple (1 Chron. 26:4). **7.** Levite who contributed to the Passover offering when Josiah was king (2 Chron. 35:9). **8.** Priest and son of Pashur who had married a foreign wife while exiled in Babylon (Ezra 10:22). He might have participated in the dedication of the wall around Jerusalem (Neh. 12:36). **9.** Head of the priestly family of Jedaiah when Joiakim was high priest (Neh. 12:21). **10.** Priest, one of Asaph's associates, who played a trumpet, in dedicating the rebuilding of Jerusalem's wall (Neh. 12:36). Some identify him with **8.**

NETHANIAH (Nĕth á nī´ ah) Personal name meaning "given of Yah." **1.** Son of Asaph who served in a company of prophets established by David. They issued their message with harps, psalteries, and cymbals (1 Chron. 25:1-2). **2.** Levite sent along with Jehoshaphat's princes to teach from the book of the law of God in all the cities of Judah (2 Chron. 17:7-9). **3.** Father of Jehudi sent to Baruch by the princes of Jehoiakim (Jer. 36:14). **4.** Father of Ishmael who killed Gedaliah (2 Kings 25:23-25; Jer. 40:8,14-16; 41).

NETHINIM (Nĕth´ ĭ nĭm) Name meaning "those given (to the priests and Levites)," which Ezra and Nehemiah apply to persons of foreign extraction who performed menial tasks in the temple. Moses assigned Midianite prisoners of war to the priests (32 servants; Num. 31:28,40) and the Levites (320 servants; Num. 31:30,47). Joshua forced the Gibeonites to serve as wood-cutters and water bearers for the sanctuary (Josh. 9:27). The servants which David gave to the Levites were also likely war prisoners (Ezra 8:20).

Representatives of the Nethinim returned from exile with Zerubbabel in 538 B.C. (Ezra 2:43-54; Neh. 7:46-56). The lists of returnees contain many foreign names suggesting their origin as prisoners of war. Despite their foreign origin, the Nethinim appear to be accepted as part of the people of Israel. They were prohibited from mixed marriages with the people of the land (Neh. 10:28-30) and shared in the responsibility for repair of the Jerusalem city walls (Neh. 3:26; contrast Ezra 4:1-3). The Nethinim resided in the Ophel district of Jerusalem, likely near the water gate (Neh. 3:26), a site conducive with their task as water bearers.

NETOPHAH (Nə tō´ phah) Name meaning "dropping." A village and surrounding district in the hill country of Judah (2 Sam. 23:28-29; 1 Chron. 11:30; 27:13; Neh. 7:26). Netophah is frequently associated with Bethlehem, suggesting a site near that town. The inference finds added support in the inclusion of two Netophites in David's elite circle of warriors. The site is most likely Khirbet Bedd Faluh, about three and a half miles southeast of Bethlehem. The nearby spring, Ain en-Natuf, preserves the name.

NETOPHATHITES (Nə tŏph´ á thīts) Residents of Netophah (1 Chron. 9:16; Neh. 12:27-28).

NETTLE Two different Hebrew words are sometimes translated "nettle" (other times "weeds," "thistles" [HCSB]). Nettles are coarse plants with stinging hairs belonging to the family *Urtica*; generally, any prickly or stinging plant (Job 30:7; Prov. 24:31; Isa. 34:13; Hos. 9:6; Zeph. 2:9). NIV frequently replaced "nettles" with "undergrowth," "weeds," or "briars." The Hebrew term used at Job 30:7 and Zeph. 2:9 perhaps refers to wild mustard. Nettles are used as a sign of desolation and judgment.

NEW Different from one of the same which existed before; made fresh. Scripture expresses God's concern for persons and the larger creation in the broad categories of a new act and a new relationship.

God's New Act Scripture often calls to mind past acts such as the creation and exodus that reveal God's care for God's world and people. Though rooted in God's acts in history, biblical faith does not relegate God to the distant past. Time and again writers of Scripture called God's people to anticipate God's new intervention in their lives. Isaiah 43:14-21 promised Babylonian exiles that God was now "doing a new thing" which paralleled God's acts saving Israel from Egyptian slavery. God again acted in a new way in Jesus Christ who offered a new teaching with authority (Mark 1:27) and whose ministry could be compared to new wine bursting old expectations of God's involvement in human salvation (Mark 2:22).

New Relationships God acted in the past to establish relationships, notably with the descendants of Abraham and the people of Israel at Sinai. Jeremiah anticipated God's establishing a new covenant with God's all-too-often faithless people, a covenant in which God would make knowledge of the law a matter of the heart (Jer. 31:31-34; Heb. 8:8-13). Luke 22:20 points to Christ's sacrificial death as the basis for this new covenant. In Christ the believer experiences newness of life (Rom. 6:4; 2 Cor. 5:17). This renewed life is characterized by new relationships with God and others (Eph. 2:15-16; Col. 3:10-11). See *New Birth*.

NEW AGE See *Age to Come*.

NEW BIRTH Term referring to God's imparta-tion of spiritual life to sinners. It is synonymous with regeneration and finds its origin in John 3:1-10. There Jesus told Nicodemus, "Unless someone is born again, he cannot see the king-dom of God" (v. 3 HCSB). Jesus indicated that the idea of the new birth is rooted in the OT when He chastised Nicodemus for his dismay at this teaching: "Are you a teacher of Israel and don't know these things?" (v. 10; cp. Ezek. 36:26-27). The new birth is caused by the gra-cious and sovereign act of God apart from man's cooperation (John 1:13; Eph. 2:4-5). God brings the new birth about through the preaching of the word of God (1 Pet. 1:23; James 1:18). The result of the new birth is a changed life (2 Cor. 5:17) which includes saving faith and repen-tance (Eph. 2:8; Acts 11:18; 16:14) and obedi-ence to God's law (1 John 3:9). See *Regeneration; Salvation.*   *Steven B. Cowan*

NEW COVENANT See *Covenant.*

NEW GATE A gate of the Jerusalem temple (Jer. 26:10; 36:10), which should perhaps be identi-fied with the Upper Gate that Jothan built (2 Kings 15:35) and/or with the Upper Ben-jamin Gate (Jer. 20:2).

NEW JERUSALEM See *Eschatology; Jerusalem.*

NEW MOON See *Calendar; Festivals.*

NEW TESTAMENT Second major division of the Christian Bible with 27 separate works (called "books") attributed to at least eight dif-ferent writers. Four accounts of Jesus' life are at the core. The first three Gospels (called "Synop-tic") are very similar in content and order. The Fourth Gospel has a completely different per-spective.

A history of selected events in the early church (Acts) is followed by 20 letters to churches and individuals and one apocalypse. The letters deal mainly with the interpretation of God's act of salvation in Jesus Christ. Matters of discipline, proper Christian behavior, and church polity also are included. The apocalypse is a coded message of hope to the church of the first century that has been reinterpreted by each suc-ceeding generation of Christians for their own situations.   *Mike Mitchell*

NEZIAH (Nə zī´ ah) Personal name meaning "faithful" or "illustrious." Head of a family of temple servants (Nethinim) who returned from exile (Ezra 2:54; Neh. 7:56).

NEZIB (Nē´ zĭb) Name meaning "garrison," "idol," "pillar," or "standing place." Village in the Shephelah district of Judah (Josh. 15:43). Site is identified with Beit Nesib east of Lachish about two miles from Khirbet Qila (Keilah).

NIBHAZ (Nĭb´ hăz) Deity worshiped by the res-idents of Avva whom the Assyrians used to reset-tle the area about Samaria after the fall of that city in 722 B.C. (2 Kings 17:31). The deity is oth-erwise unknown. The name is perhaps a delib-erate corruption of the term for altar (*Mizbeach*), which had possibly become an object of worship.

NIBSHAN (Nĭb´ shăn) Name meaning "proph-esy." Town assigned to the tribe of Judah (Josh. 15:62). Location of the site is uncertain, though its position in the list suggests a locale on the shore of the Dead Sea.

NICANOR (Nī cā´ nôr) Personal name mean-ing "conqueror." One of seven Hellenists "full of faith and the Holy Spirit" (HCSB) chosen to administer food to the Greek-speaking widows of the Jerusalem church (Acts 6:5).

NICODEMUS (Nic o de´ mŭs) Personal name meaning "innocent of blood." John identifies Nicodemus as a Pharisee, "a ruler of the Jews" (John 3:1), that is, a member of the Sanhedrin, the Jewish ruling council, and as "a teacher of Israel" (John 3:10), that is, an authority on the interpretation of the Hebrew Scriptures. Nicode-mus' coming at night suggests his timidity and his trek from the darkness of his own sin and ignorance to the light of Jesus (John 3:2). Nicodemus greeted Jesus with a title of respect, "Rabbi" (teacher), recognizing Him as a God-sent teacher whose signs bore witness to the presence of God (John 3:2). Jesus replied that Nicodemus could never see the kingdom of God without being "born again" (v. 3) or "born of water and the Spirit" (v. 5). Nicodemus could only marvel at the impossibility of such a thing (vv. 4,9), but the text does not indicate whether Jesus was finally able to make it clear to him.

True to his name, Nicodemus defended Christ before his peers (John 7:51) who were unaware that one of their number might have believed in Him (v. 48). Their response is a twofold rebuke that may be paraphrased, "Are you a Galilean peasant?" and, "Are you ignorant of the Scriptures?" (v. 52).

The reference to Nicodemus' initial coming at night highlights his later public participation in Jesus' burial (John 19:39-41). Nicodemus' contribution was enough aloes and spices to prepare a king for burial, and so he did. On one level the burial was a simple act of Pharisaic piety (cp. Tobit 1:17). On a deeper level it recognized that in His suffering and death Christ fulfilled His role as King of the Jews.

NICOLAITANS (Nĭc ō lā´ ĭ tăns) Heretical group in the early church who taught immorality and idolatry. They are condemned in Rev. 2:6,15 for their practices in Ephesus and Pergamum. Thyatira apparently had resisted the false prophecy they preached (Rev. 2:20-25). The Nicolaitans have been linked to the type of heresy taught by Balaam (Num. 25:1-2; 2 Pet. 2:15), especially the pagan feasts and orgies that they apparently propagated in the first-century church.

NICOLAS (Nĭc´ ō lȧs) Personal name meaning "conqueror of people." One of seven Hellenists "full of faith and the Holy Spirit" chosen to administer food to the Greek-speaking widows of the Jerusalem church (Acts 6:5). Nicolas was a proselyte, that is, a Gentile convert to Judaism, from Antioch. Some church fathers connect Nicolas with the heretical sect of the Nicolaitans (Rev. 2:6,15). The name, however, is common, and there is no other reason to associate this Nicolas with a sect active in Asia Minor.

NICOLAUS (Nĭc ō lā´ ŭs) NRSV and HCSB form of Nicolas (Acts 6:5), which more accurately transliterates the Greek *Nikolaus*.

NICOPOLIS (Nĭc ŏp´ ō lĭs) Place-name meaning "city of victory," shared by many cities in the ancient world. The site in which Paul most likely wintered (Titus 3:12) was Nicopolis in Epirus in northwest Greece on the north side of the Sinus Ambracicus. Octavius founded the city on the campsite from which he mounted his successful battle of Actium.

NIGER (Nī´ gēr) Latin nickname meaning "black." Surname of Simeon (KJV, Symeon), one of the teacher-prophets of the early church at Antioch. Blacks were a common sight among the populations of Egypt and North Africa in the Hellenistic period. Simeon's Latin nickname suggests that he originated from the Roman province of Africa, to the west of Cyrenica. His inclusion in Acts 13:1 demonstrates the multiracial and multinational leadership of the church at Antioch. Their concern for missions was likely rooted in their own ethnic diversity. Some have conjectured that Simeon Niger was identical to Simon of Cyrene (Mark 15:21). Acts 13:1, however, only designates Lucius as a resident of Cyrene.

NIGHT Period of darkness between sunset and dawn. Night occurs often in the simple temporal sense. Night forms part of God's ordering of time (Gen. 1:5,14; 8:22). Night is frequently a time of encounter with God, either through dreams or visions (Gen. 20:3; 31:24; 46:2; 1 Kings 3:5; Job 33:15; Dan. 2:19; 7:2,7,13; Acts 16:9; 18:9), appearances (Gen. 26:24; Num. 22:20; 1 Chron. 17:3; 2 Chron. 1:7; 7:12; Acts 23:11; 27:23), or by speech (Judg. 6:25; 7:9; 1 Sam. 15:16). Night is sometimes associated with danger (Ps. 91:5). The absence of night in the heavenly Jerusalem (Rev. 21:25; 22:5) points to the security of believers and the constant presence of God there. Night can also be associated with God's acts of deliverance (Deut. 16:1; 2 Kings 19:35; Job 34:25).

NIGHT MONSTER Translation (NASB, ASV) of the Hebrew term *lilit* (Isa. 34:14 NRSV). The term occurs only here in Scripture unless textual emendations are accepted (Job 18:15; Isa. 2:18). Interpreters divide over the natural (night creatures, NIV; nightjar, REB) or supernatural (night monster, KJV, NASB; night hag, RSV) nature of "Lilith" (English). Whatever Lilith's nature, the text stresses the great desolation which falls on God's enemies.

NIGHT WATCH Ancient division of time (Pss. 90:4; 119:148; Lam. 2:19; Matt. 14:25). According to the later Jewish system, the night was divided into three watches (evening, midnight, and morning). The Greco-Roman system added a fourth (crowing of the rooster, HCSB) between midnight and morning (Mark 13:35). The fourth watch (Matt. 14:25; Mark 6:48) designates the time just before dawn.

NILE RIVER Major river considered the "life" of ancient Egypt. Hebrew word usually used for the Nile in the OT is *y'or*. This is in fact borrowed from the Egyptian word *itrw* or *itr* by which the Egyptians referred to the Nile and the branches and canals that led from it.

The Egyptian Nile is formed by the union of the White Nile that flows out of Lake Victoria in Tanzania and the Blue Nile from Lake Tana in Ethiopia. These join at Khartum in the Sudan and are later fed by the Atbara. Thereafter the Nile flows 1,675 miles northward to the Mediterranean Sea without any further tributary. In antiquity six cataracts or falls prevented navigation at various points. The first of these, going upstream, is found at Aswan, generally recognized as the southern boundary of Egypt. From Aswan northwards the Nile flows between two lines of cliffs that sometimes come directly down to its edge but in other places are up to nine miles away. The shore land could be cultivated as far as Nile water could be brought. This cultivated area the Egyptians called the Black Land from the color of the rich soil. Beyond that lay the Red Land of the low desert stretching to the foot of the cliffs. At the cliff tops was the great inhospitable desert where few Egyptians ventured. Below the modern capital, Cairo, and the nearby ancient capital, Memphis, the Nile forms a huge delta. The many ancient cities in this area now lie below the water table. Little archaeological excavation has been done here, though this is the area where the closest links with Palestine are likely to have been located. The eastern edge of the Delta is the site of the land of Goshen where Jacob/Israel and his descendents were settled. See *Goshen*.

The Nile is the basis of Egypt's wealth, indeed of its very life. It is the only river to flow northwards across the Sahara. Egypt was unique as an agricultural community in not being dependent on rainfall. The secret was the black silt deposited on the fields by the annual flood caused when the Blue Nile was swollen by the runoff from the winter rains in Ethiopia. This silt was remarkably fertile. Irrigation waters, raised laboriously from the river, let the Egyptians produce many varieties of crops in large quantities (Num. 11:5; Gen. 42:1-2). If the winter rains failed, the consequent small or nonexistent inundation resulted in disastrous famine: some are recorded as lasting over a number of years (cp. Gen. 41).

Even today water is brought to the individual fields by small channels leading off the arterial ditches. These channels are closed off by earth

Sailboat on the Nile River.

dams which can be broken down with the foot when it is a particular farmer's turn to use the water (Deut. 11:10). Since life was concentrated in the valley, the river was also a natural highway. All major journeys in Egypt were undertaken by boat helped by the current when traveling north or by the prevailing wind when headed south. See *Egypt.*   *John Ruffle*

NIMRAH (Nĭm′ rah) Place-name meaning "clear (water)." Alternate form of Beth-nimrah (Num. 32:36) used at Num. 32:3.

NIMRIM (Nĭm′ rĭm) Place-name meaning "leopards" or "basins of clear waters." The name occurs in the phrase "Waters of Nimrim" (Isa. 15:6; Jer. 48:34), the stream upon which Moab's agricultural productivity depended. The stream is either the Wadi en-Numeirah which flows east into the Dead Sea about eight miles north of its lower end or the Wadi Nimrin which flows east into the Jordan eight miles north of its mouth.

NIMROD (Nĭm′ rŏd) Personal name meaning "we shall rebel." Son of Cush or Ethiopia (Gen. 10:8-10; 1 Chron. 1:10). A hunter and builder of the kingdom of Babel who some Bible students have linked to Tukulti-ninurta, an Assyrian king (about 1246–1206 B.C.). The Bible does not give sufficient information to connect him with any other known figure of history. Others think that Amenophis III of Egypt (about 1411–1375 B.C.) or the heroic Gilgamesh might have been the ancient Nimrod. Regardless, extremely popular legends involve Nimrod as a ruler in both Assyrian and Egyptian lore. The Prophet Micah called Assyria "the land of Nimrod" (5:6). Nimrod shows that the great Mesopotamian culture had its origin from the creative work of the God of Israel.

NIMSHI (Nĭm′ shī) Personal name meaning "weasel." Grandfather of Jehu (2 Kings 9:2,14). Elsewhere Jehu is called the son of Nimshi (1 Kings 19:16; 2 Kings 9:20; 2 Chron.

22:7). Either "son" is used loosely in the sense of descendant, or a variant tradition is involved.

NINEVE (Nĭn′ ə və) (KJV, Luke 11:32) or **NIN-EVEH** Greatest of the capitals of the ancient Assyrian Empire, which flourished from about 800 to 612 B.C. It was located on the left bank of the Tigris River in northeastern Mesopotamia (Iraq today). Its remains are represented by two mounds named *Quyundjiq* ("Many Sheep") and *Nebi Yunus* ("The Prophet Jonah").

Biblical References Nineveh is first mentioned in the OT as one of the cities established by Nimrod (Gen. 10:9-12). It was the enemy city to which God called the reluctant Prophet Jonah in the eighth century B.C. The book of Jonah calls it "that great city" (1:2; 4:11) and "an exceeding great city" (3:3). The additional phrase "of three days' journey" (3:3) has been rendered by the NIV: "a visit required three days." The phrase could be an idiom that would refer to the first day for travel to, the second for visiting, and the third day for the return from a site. The phrase "more than a hundred and twenty thousand people who cannot tell their right hand from their left" (4:11) has sometimes been taken to refer to children, which would yield a population of 600,000. The area within the city walls, however, would not have contained more than 175,000.

The final biblical references are from Nahum, who prophesied the overthrow of the "bloody city" by the attack of the allied Medes and Chaldeans in 612 B.C. By 500 B.C. the prophet's words (Nah. 3:7) "Nineveh is devastated" (NASB) were echoed by the Greek historian Herodotus who spoke of the Tigris as "the river on which the town of Nineveh formerly stood."

Excavations Muslim village and cemetery have occupied the site of Nebi Yunus preventing excavations there. The tell of Quyundjiq which rises 90 feet above the plain has attracted excavators after it was first accurately sketched by C. J. Rich in 1820.

In 1842 Paul Emile Botta, the French consul at the nearby city of Mosul, became the first excavator of the Near East when he began digging at Quyundjiq. In 1845 the Englishman, A. H. Layard, dug briefly at Quyundjiq for a month. Both moved to other sites that they mistakenly believed to be Nineveh. Layard later returned in

1849 to Quyundjiq and discovered Sennacherib's palace there.

Hormuz Rassam, a native of Mosul assisted Layard and then worked at the site of Quyundjiq 1852–54 and 1878–82. He found Ashurbanipal's palace and library in 1853. George Smith, who had deciphered the Babylonian flood story in the Gilgamesh Epic in 1872, was sent to the site by *The Daily Telegraph*. In 1873 he found a tablet which contained 17 further lines of the flood story. Iraqi scholars made some soundings in 1954 at Nebi Yunus that confirmed Layard's guess that Esarhaddon's palace lay here.

Palaces Sennacherib (704–681 B.C.) built the enormous southwest palace at Quyundjiq. We observe on his reliefs captive Philistines, Tyrians, Aramaeans, and others working under the supervision of the king himself. His "palace which has no equals" covered five acres and had 71 rooms, including two large halls 180 feet long and 40 feet wide. He boasted that the materials for the palace included "fragrant cedars, cypresses, doors banded with silver and copper … painted brick … curtain pegs of silver and copper, alabaster, breccia, marble, ivory." The rooms were embellished with 9,880 feet of sculptured reliefs depicting Assyrian victories over enemy cities, including the Judean city of Lachish captured in 701 B.C. Sennacherib's city was enclosed by eight miles of walls with 15 gates. It had gardens and parks watered by a 30-mile long aqueduct.

Ashurbanipal (669–627 B.C.), the last great Assyrian king, built the northern palace with its magnificent reliefs of royal lion hunts. He amassed a library of 20,000 tablets, which contained important literary epics, magical and omen collections, royal archives and letters. See *Assyria*.   *Edwin Yamauchi*

NINEVITES (Nĭn´ ə vīts) Residents of the Assyrian capital Nineveh (Luke 11:30,32). The Ninevites served as an example of Gentiles who repented and were accepted by God (Jon. 3). See *Assyria*.

NIPPUR (Nĭp´ pŭr) City located in Mesopotamia, approximately 50 miles southeast of the ancient city of Babylon and approximately 100 miles south of modern Baghdad, Iraq. Although it is never mentioned in the Bible, its history is important in the larger context of the biblical world. It is believed to have been the center of one of the first true civilizations, that of Sumer.

The city was founded approximately 4000 B.C. by a primitive group called the "Ubaidians."

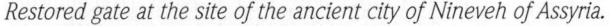

Restored gate at the site of the ancient city of Nineveh of Assyria.

N

Nippur was for more than 2,000 years the undisputed cultural and religious center, although it never was used as the capital city for any kingdom.

Nippur was a flourishing center of industry and scribal education. Documents discovered in the area describe a variety of commercial enterprises. Some of the tablets, dating back to 2500 B.C. and earlier, were found, as were records of a much later time. One of the most important later discoveries appeared in the ruins of a business house. The records, known as the Murashu documents after the banking family responsible for them, give some indication of the extent of Jewish involvement in the business world after the time of the Babylonian exile. Scribal education concerned the use of one of the earliest forms of writing called cuneiform. Also, part of education was an emphasis on mathematics.

Nippur was most important, however, for its religion. Various gods controlled every aspect of life. The chief deity was En-lil, also occasionally called Bel ("the lord"). He was thought of as god of the terrestrial world and the father of other gods. His significance made his home, Nippur, the place where people from peasants to kings came to offer gifts.

According to tradition, kingly authority descended from heaven after the flood. The several cities in the area, except for Nippur, took turns as the seat of government and often waged war against each other for political supremacy. The undisputed source of this supremacy, however, was En-lil, the principal deity. His authority was transmitted to the human kings through the priesthood of his temple, the *Ekur* ("mountain house"), the leading shrine in the area.

Nippur's influence and prominence began to wane with the rise of Babylonian power. By the time of Hammurabi, 1792–1750 B.C., Nippur had been replaced by Babylon as the religious and cultural center. It did, however, continue to be an influential city to about 250 B.C. See *Babylon; Cuneiform; Hammurabi; Mesopotamia; Sumer.*										*Hugh Tobias*

NISAN (Nē san´) Foreign term used after the exile for the first month of the Hebrew calendar (Neh. 2:1; Esther 3:7). This month that falls within March and April was formerly called Abib. See *Calendar.*

NISROCH (Nĭs´ rŏk) God worshiped by the Assyrian king Sennacherib (2 Kings 19:37; Isa. 37:38). No god of this name is otherwise known. The name is perhaps a corruption of the name Marduk, Nusku (the fire god), or Ashur (cp. early Greek readings Esdrach and Asorach).

NITER (Nī´ tẽr) (KJV, Prov. 25:20; Jer. 2:22) See *Lye.*

NO, NO-AMON (Nō, Nō-ā´ mŏn) Ancient name for Egyptian city of Thebes (modern Luxor). Inherent in its name is its reputation. "*No*" is a word for the best of cities and "Amon" was the name of the Egyptian god Amun-Re. Jeremiah (46:25), Ezekiel (30:14-16), and Nahum (3:8) were well aware of its prominence. To attack this capital city was to strike at the heart and spirit of Egypt.

Although Thebes existed before the Middle Kingdom (about 2040–1750 B.C.), it was not particularly noteworthy. In the new kingdom (about 1550–1070 B.C.) Thebes became the worship and cultural center of Egypt. Pharaoh after pharaoh added to the magnificent temples of Karnak and its "queen" just to the south, Luxor. These two edifices dominated the east side of the Nile while the funerary temples and the valleys of the kings (Biban el-Moluk) and queens occupied the west side. Deir el-Bahri (Hatshepsut), the Memnon Colossi (Amenhotep III), the Ramasseum (Rameses II), and Medinet Habu (Rameses III) are just a few sites still witnessing to the past glory of Thebes. As Nahum indicated, Thebes was not invincible. In 661 B.C. Ashurbanipal (of Assyria) sacked the sacred site. Mortally wounded, the city never fully recovered. See *Egypt.*										*Gary C. Huckabay*

NOADIAH (Nō á dī´ ah) Personal name meaning "Yah has met." **1.** Levite who returned from exile and served as a temple treasurer (Ezra 8:33). **2.** Prophetess who discouraged Nehemiah's building of the walls of Jerusalem (Neh. 6:14).

NOAH (Nō ah) Personal name of uncertain meaning, related to "rest." **1.** Son of Lamech, a descendant of Adam in the line of Seth, and a survivor of the flood. A good and righteous man, Noah was the father of Shem, Ham, and Japheth who were born when he was 500 years old. God warned Noah that He was going to wipe mankind from the face of the earth. Because Noah walked with God and stood blameless among the people of that time, God gave him specific instructions for building the ark by which Noah and his family would survive the coming flood. Noah followed the building instructions down to every detail. Then a week before the flood (Gen. 7:4), Noah led his family and all of the animals into the ark just as God directed. After seven days the rain began and lasted for 40 days. As he sought to know whether it was safe to leave the ark, he sent out first a raven and then a dove. When the dove returned with an olive leaf, Noah knew the water had receded.

Once out of the ark, Noah built an altar and sacrificed clean animals as burnt offerings on the altar. Then the Lord promised never again to destroy living creatures as He had done in the flood and established a covenant with Noah and his sons and sealed that covenant with a rainbow.

The sinful nature of humanity is one thing that remained preserved on the ark. Once on dry ground, Noah planted a vineyard, drank of its wine, became drunk, and exposed himself in his tent. Ham informed Shem and Japheth about their father's nakedness. The latter two showed respect for their father and covered him. As a result, they received rich blessings for their descendants from Noah. Ham in turn received a curse for his descendant: Canaan. Noah lived another 350 years after the flood and died at the age of 950 years.

Hebrews 11:7 affirms Noah's actions of faith in building the ark. The references to Noah in 1 Pet. 3:20 and 2 Pet. 2:5 speak of Noah and his family who were saved from the flood. See *Covenant; Flood.*

2. One of Zelophehad's five daughters (Num. 26:33). Of the tribe of Manasseh, these daughters received an inheritance in the land in their father's name even though he was dead with no male offspring (27:1-11). This was most unusual in that time.　　　　　　*Judith Wooldridge*

NOB (Nŏb) City in Benjamin likely situated between Anathoth and Jerusalem (Neh. 11:31-32; Isa. 10:32). Following the destruction of the Shiloh sanctuary in about 1000 B.C. (Jer. 7:14), the priesthood relocated to Nob. Because the priest Ahimelech gave aid to the fugitive David (1 Sam. 21:1-9), Saul exterminated 85 of the priests of Nob (1 Sam. 22:9-23). Only Abiathar escaped. The site of Nob was perhaps on Mount Scopas about one mile northeast of ancient Jerusalem, on the hill Qu'meh one mile further north, or Ras el-Mesharif about one mile north of Jerusalem. See *Ahimelech.*

NOBAH (Nō´ băh) Personal name meaning "barking" or "howling." **1.** Leader of the tribe of Manasseh who conquered Kenath in Gilead (Num. 32:42). **2.** Town in Gilead, formerly Kenath (Num. 32:42). Site is perhaps identical with Kanawat about 60 miles east of the Sea of Galilee. **3.** Town in Gilead (Judg. 8:10-11) to the east of Succoth and Penuel and west of the king's highway (KJV, "the way of them that dwell in tents"; NRSV, "caravan route").

NOD (Nŏd) Place-name meaning "wandering." After murdering his brother Abel, Cain was condemned to be "a fugitive and a wanderer on the earth" (Gen. 4:12,14 NRSV). Nod is located "away from the presence of the LORD" and "east of Eden" (Gen. 4:16). The text is not so much interested in fixing the physical location of Nod as in emphasizing the "lostness" of the wanderer Cain.

NODAB (Nō´ dăb) Name meaning "nobility." Tribe conquered by Reuben, Gad, and the half tribe of Manasseh (1 Chron. 5:19). The name is preserved by Nudebe in Hauran. The association of Nodab with Jetur and Naphish suggests its identification with Kedemah (Gen. 25:15; 1 Chron. 1:31).

NOE (Nō´ ĕ) (KJV, NT) See *Noah.*

NOGAH (Nō´ găh) Personal name meaning "brilliance" or "luster." Son born to David in Jerusalem (1 Chron. 3:7; 14:6). The omission of the name in the parallel list (2 Sam. 5:15) has suggested that the name results from dittography or copying twice of the following name, Nepheg.

NOHAH (Nō´ hăh) Personal name meaning "quiet." Son of Benjamin (1 Chron. 8:2). The name is omitted from the parallel list (Gen. 46:21).

NON (Nŏn) (KJV, NASB) Alternate form of the personal name "Nun" (1 Chron. 7:27).

N

N

NOON Middle of the day, specifically 12 o'clock noon. Noon is frequently associated with death and destruction (2 Sam. 4:5; 1 Kings 20:16; 2 Kings 4:20; Ps. 91:6; Jer. 6:4; 15:8; 20:16; Zeph. 2:4). Noon is also associated with blessings and vindication (Job 11:17; Ps. 37:6; Isa. 58:10).

NOOSE Loop of rope used as a trap (Job 18:10 NASB, NIV; Prov. 7:22 NIV). See *Fowler; Hunting.*

NOPH (Nŏph) Variant form of Moph, the Hebrew term for Memphis (Isa. 19:13; Jer. 2:16; 44:1; 46:14,19; Ezek. 30:13,16). See *Memphis.*

NOPHAH (Nō´ phah) Place-name meaning "blast." Nophah passed from Moabite to Ammonite to Israelite control (Num. 21:30). The REB and RSV by altering one letter of the Hebrew text read "fire spread," a reading supported by the earliest Greek translation and Samaritan Pentateuch. If Nophah was a place, it is perhaps Nobah (Num. 32:42).

NORTH See *Directions.*

NORTHEASTER See *Euroclydon.*

NORTH GATE Designation of two gates in Ezekiel's vision of the renewed temple, a gate entering the outer court (Ezek. 8:14; 44:4; 46:9; 47:2) and a gate entering the inner court (Ezek. 40:35,40,44).

NOSE Part of the face between the eye and mouth that bears the nostrils and covers the nasal cavity. Jewelry was worn in the nose (Gen. 24:47; Isa. 3:21; Ezek. 16:12). Prisoners of war were sometimes led captive with hooks in their noses (2 Kings 19:28; Isa. 37:29). The precise significance of placing a vine or branch to one's nose (Ezek. 8:17) is unknown. Suggestions include an act connected with idolatrous worship, a provocative gesture (cp. our turning up one's nose), or, if the text is emended, to a stench from the people which reaches God's nose. Cutting off the nose of an adulteress is a penalty known from Assyrian law (Ezek. 23:25,35).

Nostrils are often associated with the breath of life (Gen. 2:7; 7:22; Job 27:3; Isa. 2:22). The Lord's nostrils pile up the waters, allowing passage through the sea (Exod. 15:8; 2 Sam. 22:16) and are associated with judgment (2 Sam. 22:9; Job 41:20; Ps. 18:8; Isa. 65:5).

NOSE RINGS See *Jewels, Jewelry.*

NOSTRIL See *Nose.*

NUBIANS (Nū´ bĭ ȧnz) Residents of an ancient kingdom along the Nile River in southern Egypt and northern Sudan (Dan. 11:43 NIV; also NRSV margin). Cushites (REB) designates inhabitants of the same area. Other translations use Ethiopians,

Ivory cylinder seal showing a Nubian striking a kneeling figure.

Relief of the Nubian god Mandulis.

which formerly designated people of the same area. Modern Ethiopia lies further to the southeast. See *Ethiopia*.

NUCLEAR WEAPONS Description of the end of the world predicted in 2 Pet. 3:10,12 is interpreted by some as describing the effects of an atomic blast. In modern military arsenals only nuclear weapons can cause the elements "to burn and be dissolved" (2 Pet. 3:10 HCSB).

Nuclear weapons represent the best in mankind combined with the worst in mankind. People were created with the capacity for great intelligence and creativity. Nothing that people propose to do, said God in response to the Tower of Babel, will be impossible for them (Gen. 11:6). Yet by means of nuclear weapons, people now also hold the capacity to literally destroy creation.

Like all technological advances, nuclear weapons tempt those who control them into thinking that they can control their own lives. For this reason, Isaiah's warning to Hezekiah, who "depended on the weapons of the house of the forest" (Isa. 22:8b NASB) for security, is apropos: without first ordering one's life according to God's principles, even the best of human efforts is futile (Isa. 22:11; cp. Isa. 7:9), and quite possibly self-destructive.   *Paul H. Wright*

NUMBERS, BOOK OF Fourth in the chronological series of the Torah, Numbers carries the title *Bemidbar* ("in the wilderness") in the original Hebrew text. This is the initial word in the text, and it characterizes much of the ensuing history recorded in the book.

Though the descendants of Jacob were introduced to the covenant relationship with Yahweh, or the Lord, they chose their own way on many occasions. As a result, they faced God's judgment time and again. For their rebellion, disobedience, and lack of faith, the adults who left Egypt were sentenced to die in the wilderness, and their children took their place as the warriors and leaders who would later receive the promised land.

The book carries the title Numbers in English translations as a result of the early Greek title *Arithmoi* and the Latin title *Numeri*. In both instances, the title reflects a focus on the censuses taken to account for the number of fighting men in each tribe.

Numbers is a book of transition, in which the conditional nature of the Sinaitic covenant is most clearly demonstrated to the generation of adults who escaped Egyptian bondage. The older generation chose disobedience, which carried a death sentence in the wilderness. More time elapses historically in this book than the other books combined which relate to the exodus from Egypt (Exodus, Leviticus, Deuteronomy). The nearly 40 years of wandering take place in Numbers as a result of Israel's disobedience and lack of faith in the covenant God, Yahweh.

This book is essential for understanding the reasons for the second giving of the commandments (see Exod. 20 and Deut. 5). Were it not for the death sentence on the adults, it would not have been necessary for Moses to reintroduce the Law and the commandments to another generation who would take the promised land.

Numbers also records historical details which are only alluded to by other biblical writers. In Ps. 95, for example, the writer gives the command, "Do not harden your hearts as at Meribah, as on that day at Massah in the wilderness" (HCSB). The context indicates a reference to Israel's choice to accept the spies' majority report (Num. 14). Another incident found in Numbers is the fashioning of the bronze snake (Num. 21). Jesus refers to this event during His instruction of Nicodemus.

Many individuals hold to a multiple authorship scheme for the Torah. No legitimate grounds exist, however, for presupposing that Moses did not record most of the events of the Exodus (Exod., Lev., Num.) during the time covered in this book. The internal and external evidence of Numbers points to Moses as the original author. See *Aaron; Balaam; Eleazar; Joshua; Moses; Pentateuch; Tabernacle; Tribes of Israel.*

Outline

    I. Heading out from Sinai (chaps. 1–10)
        A. Separating the fighting men (chap.1)
        B. Separating the tribes for camp (chap. 2)
        C. Separating the priests & Levites (chap. 3–4)
        D. Separating from defilement (chap. 5)
        E. Separating of the Nazirite (chap. 6)
        F. Separating gifts of the leaders (chap. 7)
        G. Separating of the Levites (chap. 8)
        H. Separating for the Passover (9:1-14)
        I. Separating and moving the camp (9:15–10:36)

II. Heading Nowhere at Kadesh-barnea (chaps. 11–21)
   A. Rebellion/judgment of fire (11:1-3)
   B. Provision of quail (11:4-35)
   C. Rebellion/judgment of Aaron/Miriam (chap. 12)
   D. Provision of fruit from Canaan (13:1-25)
   E. Rebellion/judgment of spies & adults (13:26–14:43)
   F. Provision of miscellaneous instructions (chap. 15)
   G. Rebellion/judgment of Korah (chap. 16)
   H. Provision of miraculous work and further instructions (chaps. 17–19)
   I. Rebellion/judgment of Moses and Aaron (chap. 20)
   J. Provision of military victory (21:1-3)
   K. Rebellion/judgment by snakes (21:4-7)
   L. Provision of healing and victories (21:8-35)
III. Heading into Trouble at Moab (chaps. 22–25)
   A. Balaam's oracles (chaps. 22–24)
   B. Israel's idolatry, immorality, and judgment (chap. 25)
IV. Heading for the Promised Land (chaps. 26–36)
   A. Initiating a second census (chap. 26)
   B. Inheritance for Zelophehad's daughters (chap. 27)
   C. Instructions to the new generation (chaps. 28–30)
   D. Defeat of the Midianites and Balaam (chap. 31)
   E. Israel's Transjordan tribes (chap. 32)
   F. Moses' overview of the exodus (chap. 33)
   G. Division of the lands in Canaan (chaps. 34–36) *Douglas K. Wilson, Jr.*

NUMBER SYSTEMS AND NUMBER SYMBOLISM To understand properly the number systems of the biblical world, one must look to the neighbors of Israel. The Egyptians were already using relatively advanced mathematics by 3000 B.C. The construction of such structures as the pyramids required an understanding of complex mathematics. The Egyptian system was decimal. The Sumerians by that same time had developed their own number system. In fact, the Sumerians knew two systems, one based on 10 (a decimal system) and one based on six or 12 (usually designated as a duodecimal system). We still make use of remnants of the Sumerian system today in our reckoning of time—12 hours for day and 12 hours for night, 60 minutes and 60 seconds as divisions of time. We also divide a circle into 360 degrees. Our calendar was originally based on the same division with the year having 12 months of 30 days for a total of 360. Even our units of the dozen (12) and gross (144) and inches to the foot may have their origin in the Sumerian mathematical system.

The Hebrews did not develop the symbols to represent numbers until the postexilic period (after 539 B.C.). In all preexilic inscriptions, small numbers are represented by individual strokes (for example, //// for four). Larger numbers were either represented with Egyptian symbols, or the name of the number was written out ("four" for the number 4). The Arad inscriptions regularly used Egyptian symbols for numbers, individual strokes for the units and hieratic numbers for five, 10, and larger numbers. The Samaria ostraca more frequently wrote out the number. Letters of the Hebrew alphabet are first used to represent numbers on coins minted in the Maccabean period (after 167 B.C.).

With the coming of the Hellenistic and Roman periods to Palestine, Greek symbols for numbers and Roman numerals appeared. The Greeks used letters of their alphabet to represent numerals, while the Romans used the familiar symbols I, V ,X, L, C, M, and so on.

Biblical passages show that the Hebrews were well acquainted with the four basic mathematical operations of addition (Num. 1:20-46), subtraction (Gen. 18:28-33), multiplication (Num. 7:84-86), and division (Num. 31:27). The Hebrews also used fractions such as a half (Gen. 24:22), a third (Num. 15:6), and a fourth (Exod. 29:40).

In addition to their usage to designate specific numbers or quantities, many numbers in the Bible came to have a symbolic meaning. Thus seven came to symbolize completeness and perfection. God's work of creation was both complete and perfect, and it was completed in seven days. All of mankind's existence was related to God's creative activity. The seven-day week reflected God's first creative activity. The Sabbath was that day of rest following the workweek, reflective of God's rest (Gen. 1:1–2:4).

Israelites were to remember the land also and give it a sabbath, permitting it to lie fallow in the seventh year (Lev. 25:2-7). Seven was also important in cultic matters beyond the Sabbath: major festivals such as Passover and Tabernacles lasted seven days as did wedding festivals (Judg. 14:12,17). In Pharaoh's dream the seven good years followed by seven years of famine (Gen. 41:1-36) represented a complete cycle of plenty and famine. Jacob worked a complete cycle of years for Rachel; then, when he was given Leah instead, he worked an additional cycle of seven (Gen. 29:15-30).

A major Hebrew word for making an oath or swearing, *shaba*, was closely related to the word "seven," *sheba*. The original meaning of "swear an oath" may have been "to declare seven times" or "to bind oneself by seven things."

A similar use of the number seven can be seen in the NT. The seven churches (Rev. 2–3) perhaps symbolized all the churches by their number. Jesus taught that forgiveness is not to be limited, even to a full number or complete number of instances. We are to forgive, not merely seven times (already a generous number of forgivenesses) but 70 times seven (limitless forgiveness, beyond keeping count) (Matt. 18:21-22).

As the last example shows, multiples of seven frequently had symbolic meaning. The year of Jubilee came after the completion of every 49 years. In the year of Jubilee all Jewish bondslaves were released and land which had been sold reverted to its former owner (Lev. 25:8-55). Another multiple of seven used in the Bible is 70. Seventy elders are mentioned (Exod. 24:1,9). Jesus sent out the 70 (Luke 10:1-17). Seventy years is specified as the length of the exile (Jer. 25:12, 29:10; Dan. 9: 2). The messianic kingdom was to be inaugurated after a period of 70 weeks of years had passed (Dan. 9:24).

After seven the most significant number for the Bible is undoubtedly 12. The Sumerians used 12 as one base for their number system. Both the calendar and the signs of the zodiac reflect this 12-base number system. The tribes of Israel and Jesus' disciples numbered 12. The importance of the number 12 is evident in the effort to maintain that number. When Levi ceased to be counted among the tribes, the Joseph tribes, Ephraim and Manasseh, were counted separately to keep the number 12 intact. Similarly, in the NT when Judas Iscariot committed suicide, the

11 moved quickly to add another to keep their number at 12. Twelve seems to have been especially significant in the book of Revelation. New Jerusalem had 12 gates; its walls had 12 foundations (Rev. 21:12-14). The tree of life yielded 12 kinds of fruit (Rev. 22:2).

Multiples of 12 are also important. There were 24 divisions of priests (1 Chron. 24:4) and 24 elders around the heavenly throne (Rev. 4:4). Seventy-two elders, when one includes Eldad and Medad, were given a portion of God's spirit that rested on Moses, and they prophesied (Num. 11:24-26). An apocryphal tradition holds that 72 Jewish scholars, six from each of the 12 tribes, translated the OT into Greek, to give us the version we call today the Septuagint. The 144,000 servants of God (Rev. 7:4) were made up of 12,000 from each of the 12 tribes of Israel.

Three as a symbolic number often indicated completeness. The created cosmos had three elements: heaven, earth, and underworld. Three Persons make up the Godhead: Father, Son, and Holy Spirit. Prayer was to be lifted at least three times daily (Dan. 6:10; cp. Ps. 55: 17). The sanctuary had three main parts: vestibule, nave, inner sanctuary (1 Kings 6). Three-year-old animals were mature and were, therefore, prized for special sacrifices (1 Sam. 1:24; Gen. 15:9). Jesus said He would be in the grave for three days and three nights (Matt. 12:40), the same time Jonah was in the great fish (Jon. 1:17). Paul often used triads in his writings, the most famous being "faith, hope, and love" (1 Cor. 13:13). One must also remember Paul's benediction: "The grace of the Lord Jesus Christ, and the love of God, and the communion of the Holy Ghost be with you all" (2 Cor. 13:14).

Four was often used as a sacred number. Significant biblical references to four include the four corners of the earth (Isa. 11:12), the four winds (Jer. 49:36), four rivers which flowed out of Eden to water the world (Gen. 2:10-14), and four living creatures surrounding God (Ezek. 1; Rev. 4:6-7). God sent forth the four horsemen of the Apocalypse (Rev. 6:1-8) to bring devastation to the earth.

The most significant multiple of four is 40, which often represented a large number or a long period of time. Rain flooded the earth for 40 days (Gen. 7:12). For 40 days Jesus withstood Satan's temptations (Mark 1:13). Forty years represented approximately a generation. Thus all the adults who had rebelled against God at Sinai died during the 40 years of the Wilderness Wandering period. By age 40 a person had reached maturity (Exod. 2:11; Acts 7:23).

A special system of numerology known as *gematria* developed in later Judaism. Gematria is based on the idea that one may discover hidden meaning in the biblical text from a study of the numerical equivalence of the Hebrew letters. The first letter of the Hebrew alphabet, *aleph* represented one; *beth*, the second letter, represented two, and so on. With gematria one takes the sum of the letters of a Hebrew word and seeks to find some meaning. For example, the Hebrew letters of the name Eliezer, Abraham's servant, have a numerical value of 318. When Gen. 14:14 states that Abraham took 318 trained men to pursue the kings from the east, some Jewish commentaries interpret this to mean that Abraham had but one helper, Eliezer, since Eliezer has the numerical value of 318. Likewise, the number 666 in Revelation is often taken as a reverse gematria for the emperor Nero. The name Nero Caesar, put in Hebrew characters and added up following gematria, totals 666. Any interpretation based on gematria must be treated with care; such interpretation always remains speculative.

Joel F. Drinkard, Jr.

NUN 1. (Nūn) Father of Joshua (Exod. 33:11; Num. 11:28; 13:8,16). **2.** (Nŭn) Fourteenth letter of the Hebrew alphabet which serves as a heading for Ps. 119:105-112. Each verse of this section begins with "nun."

NUNC DIMITTIS Latin phrase meaning "you can now dismiss." The first words in Latin of Simeon's psalm of praise in Luke 2:29-32 and thus the title of the psalm. See *Benedictus; Magnificat.*

NURSE 1. Woman who breast-feeds an infant (Gen. 21:7; Exod. 2:7; 1 Sam. 1:23). In OT times children were often nursed as long as three years (1 Sam. 1:22-24). Weaning was often a time of celebration (Gen. 21:8). Generally a mother nursed her own child; though sometimes a wet nurse was employed (Exod. 2:7). A nurse might continue as an honored family member after the child was grown (Gen. 24:59; 35:8). Paul likened the gentleness of his missionary approach to a mother nursing her children (1 Thess. 2:7). **2.** Woman who cares for

a child such as a governess or nanny (Ruth 4:16; 2 Sam. 4:4). **3.** One who cares for the sick (1 Kings 1:2,4 NASB, RSV).

NURTURE KJV translation (Eph. 6:4) of the Greek *paideia* (disciple, instruction). The noun occurs elsewhere in the Pauline corpus only once (2 Tim. 3:16) which relates that all Scripture is profitable for "training (*paideia*) in righteousness." To bring up children "in the training and instruction of the Lord" (Eph. 6:4 HCSB) is to discipline and correct them as the Lord would.

NUTS See *Plants.*

NUZI (Nū´ zē) City located in the northeast section of the Fertile Crescent, and then named Gasur, that flourished under Sargon shortly before 2000 B.C. Few cities that are not mentioned in the OT contribute to its understanding as significantly as Nuzi (modern Yorghan Tepe). Its most relevant history, as far as the OT is concerned, is its revival as part of the Hurrian kingdom, situated in the state of Mitanni, about 1500 B.C., about the time of the Israelites' bondage in Egypt. Twenty thousand Akkadian documents have been found at Nuzi that reflect primarily the legal, social, and economic situation of Mesopotamian culture about 2000–1400 B.C. The sociological importance of this discovery is estimated differently among scholars. Most scholars accept the value for general Near Eastern studies and biblical background, and some use the information to determine the date of the patriarchs and the literature about them according to biblical parallels with Nuzi customs.

Some parallels are more exact than others, but the following examples can be cited as relevant to patriarchal and later Israelite culture. Marriage customs of Nuzi and the patriarchs converge when we hear Rachel and Leah complain how their father Laban unfairly hoarded their dowry and left them nothing, contrary to provisions they expected under Nuzilike marriage arrangements (Gen. 31:14-16). In spite of this injustice, Laban later relied on the honor of Jacob to conform to the custom of not marrying additional wives (Gen. 31:50). In the case of infertility, both Rachel and Leah offered their maids as surrogate mates that would bear sons to their husband Jacob, a custom seen also at Nuzi (Gen. 30:1-13). Jacob's grandmother, Sarah, had done the same for Abraham (Gen. 16:1-4), assuming as one would have in Nuzi that the child would be hers (v. 2). Up to that point Abraham had despaired that his servant Eliezer was his only legal heir, hinting that he had adopted Eliezer for this purpose, according to Nuzi custom (Gen. 15:2). Two further parallels in the area of inheritance are found in Jacob's verbally removing Reuben's privileges as the first born because of his sin against his father (Gen. 49:2-4), and the transfer of inheritance between the brothers Esau and Jacob (Gen. 25:27-34). Both cases indicate prerogatives provided in Nuzi law. Though the exact reason why Rachel stole her father's idols is not explained (Gen. 31:19,27-32), the importance of possessing one's father's idols appears at Nuzi as well. Nuzi parallels with Israelite law are also very interesting. The double portion granted to the firstborn on the basis of Deut. 21:15-17 (cp. Gen. 48:21-22), the occasional rights of daughters to be heirs (Num. 27:8), and cancellation of debts after so many years (Deut. 15:1-3) are examples.

The name "Hebrew" for an alien as Joseph was in Egypt (Gen. 39:13-14), and as the Israelites were in that country (Exod. 1:15-19) or while in Philistia (1 Sam. 14:21), is very similar to the same use of the term *habiru* found in the Nuzi documents and elsewhere. This sheds light on the perpetual discussion of the source and meaning of this significant name for the Israelites. See *Abraham; Archaeology and Biblical Study; Habiru; Hurriam; Mesopotamia; Patriarchs.*

Dan Fredricks

NYMPHA (Nĭm´ pha) or **NYMPHAS** (Nĭm´ phàs) Christian host of a house church, likely in Laodicea (Col. 4:15). Because the name occurs only in the accusative case, it is not possible to determine whether it is masculine or feminine. Modern translations follow the best Greek manuscripts in reading "her house" and using the feminine name Nympha. The KJV followed other manuscripts reading "his house" and thus used the masculine form Nymphas, an abbreviation of Nymphadorus meaning "gift of nymphs."

O

The Mount of Olives viewed through one of the arched eastern entryways at the Temple Mount.

OAK See *Plants*.

OAK, DIVINER'S See *Diviner's Oak*.

OARSMEN NIV term for those who row a galley (Ezek. 27:8,26). See *Ships, Sailors, and Navigation*.

OATHS Statements by which a person promises or guarantees that a vow will be kept or that a statement is, in fact, true. In the OT the name of God was invoked as the One who would guarantee the results or veracity of a statement. Oaths were often accompanied and evidenced by the raising of a hand or hands toward heaven or by placing the hand under the thigh (Gen. 14:22; 24:2-3; Dan. 12:7).
Old Testament In Israel oaths were often announced at a sacred place and a prophet or priest would preside over the oath ceremony. If someone violated the oath, it was considered a serious matter. Using the Lord's name in an oath directly appealed to Him for involvement in the oath. Thus He is established as the supreme Enforcer and Judge in the oath. Those who violated oaths were considered to have defiled the name of the Lord (Lev. 19:12; Ezek. 17:13-18). Often oaths included a curse intended to carry the conviction that the one taking the oath was making a true statement. The more serious the oath the more terrible the curse would be to enforce the oath.

A common formula for oaths is seen in the phrase, "May the LORD do so to me and worse, if" (Ruth 1:17; 1 Sam. 14:44). At times a ruler might use his name joined with an oath to enforce an oath's truthfulness (1 Sam. 20:13; 2 Sam. 3:8-10). Thus the oaths carried a curse that supported the veracity of the statement, and they called God to be the witness and judge of the oath.

An oath reinforced God's promises to His people (Gen. 26:3). There were boundaries clearly stated in the Law concerning vows and their disposition (Num. 30). Because of the risk of perjury or breaking an oath, there are a number of admonitions against oaths (Exod. 20:7; Lev. 19:12; Jer. 34:18-20). There are also examples of the consequences of making an oath in a rash manner (Judg. 11:30-36).
New Testament There appears to be a subtle difference in the NT when it comes to the issue of oaths. Jesus did not use oaths to confirm the authority of His teaching. He pointed to a higher ethic that rests upon the integrity of the child of God as one not needing to prove his veracity by affirming an oath. So in the Sermon on the Mount, Jesus exhorts His followers to refrain from oaths, and, "But let your word 'yes' be 'yes' and your 'no' be 'no.' Anything more than this is from the evil one" (Matt. 5:33-37 HCSB).

The admonition of Jesus to His followers to have honesty in their speech does not discount the use of oaths in the NT. Though Jesus did not use oaths when Caiaphas placed Him under oath, He accepted the challenge and declared Himself to be the promised Messiah of Israel (Matt. 26:63-64).

Paul, like Jesus, condemned lying and perjury (1 Tim. 1:10). Paul did use oaths of a type when he called upon God to be a witness to his holy, righteous, and blameless behavior (1 Thess. 2:10), his gentleness towards the believers (2 Cor. 1:23), and his service and love towards them (Rom. 1:9; Phil. 1:8).

Jesus emphasized the integrity and sincerity that should exist between people. Oaths should be rarely used and are left for serious cases. A current application of proper oath taking would be when a witness in a court of law takes an oath before God to tell the truth. *Brent R. Kelly*

OBADIAH (Ō bả dī´ ah) Personal name meaning "Yahweh's servant." **1.** Person in charge of Ahab's palace. He was devoted to Yahweh and saved Yahweh's prophets from Jezebel's wrath. He was the go-between for Elijah and Ahab (1 Kings 18:3-16). **2.** Descendant of David through Hananiah (1 Chron. 3:21). **3.** Son of Izrahiah of the tribe of Issachar (1 Chron. 7:3). **4.** Son of Azel of the tribe of Benjamin (1 Chron. 8:38; 9:44). **5.** Levite who returned to Jerusalem with the first of the Babylonian exiles (1 Chron. 9:16). **6.** Gadite who joined David, along with Ezer and Eliab. Obadiah was second in command behind Ezer (1 Chron. 12:8-9). **7.** Father of Ishmaiah, an officer from the tribe of Zebulun who served in David's army (1 Chron. 27:19). **8.** One of five officials Jehoshaphat sent throughout the cities of Judah to teach "the book of the law of the LORD" (2 Chron. 17:7-9). See *Jehoshaphat*. **9.** Levite descended from Merari appointed by Josiah to oversee the repairing of the temple (2 Chron. 34:12). See *Josiah*. **10.** Priest who returned from Babylonian exile to Jerusalem with Ezra (Ezra 8:9). He joined other priests along with princes and Levites in putting his seal upon the covenant (Neh. 9:38) made between the people and God (Neh. 10:5). **11.** Gatekeeper and guardian of "the ward" (KJV), "the storehouses of the gates" (NASB) during the leadership of Ezra and Nehemiah (Neh. 12:25).

OBADIAH, BOOK OF Shortest book of the Minor Prophets, preserving the message of the Prophet Obadiah.

The Prophet No source outside his book mentions Obadiah. "Obadiah" is a common name in the OT. Meaning "servant of Yahweh," it reflects his parents' faith and spiritual ambitions for their child. The title "The vision of Obadiah" turns attention to the divine author, "vision" being a technical term for a prophetic revelation received from God.

The Situation Historically, the book belongs to the early postexilic period at the end of the sixth century B.C. Its central section, verses 10-14, deals with the fall of Jerusalem to the Babylonians in 586 B.C., concentrating on the part the Edomites played in that tragic event. Edom was a state to the southeast of Judah. Despite treaty ties ("brother," v. 10) the Edomites, along with others, had failed to come to Judah's aid and had even helped Babylon by looting Jerusalem and handing over refugees. Moreover, the Edomites filled the vacuum caused by Judah's exile by moving west and annexing the Negev to the south of Judah and even its southern territory (cp. v. 19).

Judah reacted with a strong sense of grievance. Obadiah's oracle responded to an underlying impassioned prayer of lament, like Pss. 74; 79; or 137, in which Judah appealed to God to act as providential trial Judge and Savior to set right the situation.

The Message The response begins with a prophetic messenger formula which reinforces the thrust of the title that God is behind the message. Verses 2-9 give the divine verdict. Addressing Edom, God promised to defeat those supermen and topple the mountain capital which reflected their lofty self-conceit. Their allies would let them down, and neither their famed wisdom nor their warriors would be able to save them. This seems to look fearfully ahead to the Nabateans' infiltration from the eastern desert and their eventual takeover of Edom's traditional territory. The end of verse 1 appears to be a report from the prophet that already a coalition of neighboring groups was planning to attack Edom.

The catalog of Edom's crimes (vv. 10-14) functions as the accusation that warranted God's verdict of punishment. Repetition raises "day" to center stage. The underlying thought is that Judah had been the victim of "the day of the LORD" when God intervened in judgment and had drunk the cup of God's wrath (vv. 15-16; cp. Lam. 1:12; 2:21). In OT theology the concept of the day of the Lord embraces not only God's people but also their no-less-wicked neighbors. This wider dimension is reflected in verses 15-16 (cp. Lam. 1:21). The fall of Edom was to trigger this eschatological event in which order would be restored to an unruly world. Then would come the vindication of God's people, not for their own sakes but as earthly witnesses to His glory; and so "the kingdom will be the LORD's" (Obad. 21).

The Meaning Like the book of Revelation, which proclaims the downfall of the persecuting Roman Empire, the aim of Obadiah is to sustain faith in God's moral government and hope in the eventual triumph of His just will. It brings a pastoral message to aching hearts that God is on the throne and cares for His own.

Outline

I. God Knows and Will Judge the Sins of His People's Enemies (vv. 1-14).
   A. Pride deceives people into thinking they can escape God's judgment (vv. 1-4).
   B. Deceitful people will be deceived by their "friends" (vv. 5-7).
   C. Human wisdom cannot avoid divine judgment (vv. 8-9).
   D. Conspiracy against "brothers" will not go unpunished (vv. 10-14).
II. The Day of the Lord Offers Judgment for the Nations but Deliverance for God's People (vv. 15-21).
   A. Sinful people will receive just recompense (vv. 15-16).
   B. God will deliver His people in holiness (vv. 17-18).
   C. God's remnant will be restored (vv. 19-20).
   D. The kingdom belongs to God alone (vv. 21).   *Leslie C. Allen*

OBAL (Ō´ băl) Personal name meaning "stout." Son of Joktan and ancestor of an Arab tribe (Gen. 10:28). At 1 Chron. 1:22 the name takes the alternate form Ebal.

OBED (Ō´ bĕd) Personal name meaning "serving." **1.** Son of Boaz and Ruth (Ruth 4:13-17), father of Jesse, and grandfather of King David. He was an ancestor of Jesus Christ (Matt. 1:5; Luke 3:32). **2.** Son of Ephlal and father of Jehu (1 Chron. 2:37-38). **3.** One of David's mighty men (1 Chron. 11:47). **4.** Gatekeeper in Solomon's temple (1 Chron. 26:7). **5.** Father of Azariah, a commander assisting in coronation of King Josiah (2 Chron. 23). See *Athaliah.*

OBED-EDOM (Ō bĕd-ē´ dom) Personal name meaning "serving Edom." **1.** Philistine from Gath who apparently was loyal to David and Israel. At Obed-edom's house David left the ark of the covenant following the death of Uzzah at the hand of God (2 Sam. 6:6-11). Obed-edom was unusually blessed of God (probably a reference to prosperity) during the three months the ark was at his house. **2.** Levite who served as both gatekeeper and musician in the tabernacle in Jerusalem during David's reign (1 Chron. 15:18,24; 16:5). His duties related especially to the ark of the covenant. A guild of Levites may have adopted the name "Obed-edom" as their title as keepers of the ark. **3.** Member of the Korhites (1 Chron. 26:1,4-8) who kept the south of the temple (v. 15). **4.** Keeper of the sacred vessels of the temple. Joash of Israel took with him the sacred vessels to Samaria following his capture of Jerusalem and of Amaziah king of Judah (2 Chron. 25:23-24).

OBEDIENCE To hear God's Word and act accordingly. The word translated "obey" in the OT means "to hear" and is often so translated. In the NT several words describe obedience. One word means "to hear or to listen in a state of submission." Another NT word often translated "obey" means "to trust."

The person's obedient response to God's Word is a response of trust or faith. Thus, to really hear God's Word is to obey God's Word (Exod. 19:5; Jer. 7:23).

The Bible views disobedience as a failure to hear and do God's Word (Ps. 81:11). Israel's story was one of a nation who failed to hear or to

listen to God (Jer. 7:13; Hos. 9:17). Jesus warned: "Anyone who has ears should listen!" (Matt. 11:15 HCSB).

Obedience does affect one's spiritual life. It is essential for worship (1 Sam. 15:22; John 4:23-24). The obedience of faith brings about salvation (Rom. 1:5; 10:16-17). Obedience secures God's blessings (John 14:23; 1 John 2:17; Rev. 22:14). Spiritual insight is gained through obedience (John 7:17). A life of obedience to God is the fruit of faith (James 2:21-26).

True obedience means imitating God in holiness, humility, and love (1 Pet. 1:15; John 13:34; Phil. 2:5-8). True disciples do the will of God (Matt. 7:21). Facing clashing claims for one's allegiance, the Christian obeys God rather than other persons (Acts 5:29).

What motivates us to obey God? Obedience springs from gratitude for grace received (Rom. 12:2). Christians obey God as an expression of their spiritual freedom (Gal. 5:13; 1 Pet. 2:16). Jesus taught that our love for God motivates us to obey Him (John 14:21,23-24; 15:10).

How does obedience affect our relationships with others? The Bible speaks of obedience from the wife to the husband (Eph. 5:22), from children to their parents (Eph. 6:1), from slaves to masters (Col. 3:22). Obedience with joy should be shown to church leaders (1 Thess. 5:12-13). Obedience is expected from all Christians to persons in authority (1 Pet. 2:13-14).

The NT places special emphasis on Jesus' obedience. Christ's obedience stands in contrast to Adam's disobedience (Rom. 5:12-21). A desire to obey the will of God motivated Jesus' actions (Luke 4:43; John 5:30). Jesus acted and spoke only as the Father directed (John 3:34). By living a life of obedience, Jesus showed Himself to be the Savior (Heb. 5:7-10). Christ's work on the cross is viewed as a sacrifice of obedience (Rom. 5:19; Heb. 10:7-10).

God has spoken in the Scriptures. Disobedience to God's Word comes from a sinful heart— a heart that will not trust God. Obedience comes from a heart that trusts God. If God's people obey Him, they find the blessings He yearns to give. If they disobey, believers receive judgment and necessary discipline.   *Gary Hardin*

OBEISANCE To bow down with one's face to the ground as a sign of homage and submission. KJV and RSV translate the Hebrew *chavah* as "obeisance" when the object of homage is a person but as "worship" when the object of homage is God or other gods (84 times in the RSV). Most often persons did obeisance to the king (1 Sam. 24:8; 2 Sam. 1:2; 9:6-8; 14:4) or a royal official (Gen. 43:28; Esther 3:2,5). Moses did obeisance before his father-in-law (Exod. 18:7). Saul did obeisance before Samuel's ghost (1 Sam. 28:14).

OBELISK Stone pillar used in worship, especially of the Egyptian sun god Amun-Re. Four-sided and made from one stone, obelisks tapered to the top, where a pyramid rested. They apparently symbolized the rays of the rising sun and the hope of the pharaoh for rejuvenation and new vitality. At times they were used in tombs to represent hope for resurrection. A 4,000-year-old obelisk still stands in modern Matariyeh, ancient On. Another has been transplanted to Central Park in New York City. Many obelisks were built from about 1550 to about 1100 B.C. Some were more than 100 feet tall. The Hebrew term translated "obelisks" at Jer. 43:13 (NASB, NRSV, RSV) means pillar or standing stone ("sacred pillars," NIV, REB). The Egyptian context suggests the pillars were in fact obelisks, perhaps dedicated to the sun-god Re. See *On*.

OBESITY Because most people in the ancient world constantly lived on the edge of starvation, obesity was neither an option nor, for most, something to be avoided. Only the rich could afford the luxury of being fat, and for

this reason fatness became a mark of status and wealth.

Eglon, king of Moab, was "very fat" (Judg. 3:17,22) and Eli, high priest at Shiloh, was "heavy" (1 Sam. 4:18; cp. 2:29). Both men had attained a social position by which they could be "acceptably fat," yet in both cases their fatness is portrayed as a narrative symbol of extravagance and slothfulness. The book of Proverbs similarly cautions that excessive eating and drinking is the mark of a fool (Prov. 23:20-21; cp. Phil. 3:19) and urges restraint (Prov. 23:1-3; 25:16).

Paul H. Wright

OBIL (Ō´ bĭl) Personal name of uncertain meaning, perhaps "camel driver," "tender," or "mourner." Overseer in charge of David's camels (1 Chron. 27:30).

OBLATION Gift offered at an altar or shrine, especially a voluntary gift not involving blood. KJV used "oblation" to translate four Hebrew words. Modern translations often replace "oblation" with either "offering" (Lev. 7:38; Isa. 1:13; Ezek. 44:30) or "gifts," sometimes "contributions" (2 Chron. 31:14; Ezek. 20:40). RSV used "oblation" only at 1 Kings 18:29,36 where it replaced the "sacrifice" of the KJV, NIV, and NASB. See *Sacrifice and Offering*.

OBOTH (Ō´ bŏth) Place-name meaning "fathers" or "water skins." A wilderness station (Num. 21:10-11; 33:43-44), perhaps identical with 'Ain el-Weiba near Panon (modern Feinan).

Fallen Egyptian obelisk at Rameses (Tanis).

OBSCENE OBJECT REB translation for an object the queen mother Maacah erected for the worship of Asherah, a fertility goddess (1 Kings 15:13; 2 Chron. 15:16). The precise nature of the image is unclear. The Vulgate or early Latin translation took the image to be a phallic emblem. Some recent interpreters have suggested a stylized palm tree as a symbol of fertility. Alternate translations include: idol (KJV); abominable image (NRSV); repulsive Asherah pole (NIV); and horrid image for Asherah (NASB). See *Asherah; Fertility Cult.*

OBSCURITY KJV term for gloom or darkness (Isa. 29:18; 58:10; 59:9).

OBSERVER OF TIMES KJV term for a sooth-sayer (Deut. 18:10,14; cp. Lev. 19:26; 2 Kings 21:6; 2 Chron. 33:6). See *Divination and Magic.*

OCCUPATIONS AND PROFESSIONS
Occupations and professions of ancient civilizations were, as in modern times, related to the natural resources, commerce, and institutions of the nations. Israel was no exception.

In the course of time, occupations developed from the simple task to the more complex and from unskilled to skilled labor. This evolution was spurred by Israel's shift from a nomadic existence to a settled life and from a clan-type government to that of the monarchy. The development of secular occupations paralleled the settlement of the people into towns and villages and the evolution of their government from a loose-knit tribal group to a nation involved in international politics. In earliest biblical times the Hebrews followed their herds from pastureland to pastureland and water hole to water hole, though at times they lived for long periods near major cities (Gen. 13:18; 20:1; 26:6; 33:19). Their occupations were centered in the family enterprise.

When Israel entered into Canaan, the Hebrews moved toward a settled existence. As a settled people agricultural pursuits became extremely important for survival. As the monarchy developed, many new occupations appeared within the biblical text, mostly to maintain the royal house. Finally, as villages grew larger, and commerce between cities and nations expanded, various trades and crafts expanded with them.

A sampling of the most common occupations and professions of the Bible are briefly described

and grouped around the places where they were usually practiced: the home, the palace, the marketplace, and the religious occupations related to the church of Christianity and temple of Judaism.

Occupations around the Home The earliest occupations and professions mentioned in the Bible, as might be expected, are tasks and chores done at home. One of the principal duties around the home centered on food preparation. *Baker* (Gen. 40:5) is mentioned early in Scripture as a member of the Egyptian pharaoh's court. Baking bread was a frequent task performed in the Hebrew home long before it evolved into a specialized trade. *Butler* of the pharaoh's palace was also known as a *cup-bearer* (Neh. 1:11; cp. Gen. 40:5,21), one who was responsible for providing the king with drink. He, presumably, tasted each cup of wine before it was presented to the pharaoh as a precaution against poisoning. *Cooks* did the majority of the ancient people's food preparation (1 Sam. 9:23-24). Within the home female family members did the cooking. As cooking became an occupation outside of the home, men entered the trade. A related, and daily, chore of grinding grain fell to the *grinder* (Matt. 24:41) or *miller*, another trade which later entered the marketplace. See *Mill.*

The majority of persons in biblical times were involved in some form of food gathering or production. *Fishermen* (Isa. 19:8; Matt. 4:18) were one such group of food gatherers. The ancient fishermen's tools were not unlike his modern counterparts: fishing by hook and line, spears, and nets. The fisherman, and fishing, is mentioned often in Scripture, most notably as a metaphor as in Mark 1:17 when Jesus challenged Simon and Andrew to become "fishers of men." *Hunters* (Jer. 16:16) form the second major group of food gatherers. The ancient hunter's success depended upon proficiency in the use of a bow and arrow, spear, traps and snares, and his knowledge of his prey. Nimrod (Gen. 10:9) is the first person to be designated a hunter in the Bible. *Shepherds* (Luke 2:8) were also engaged in food production. Those persons who have rule over others are often described in terms of the shepherd's duties. They were to care for and feed the people for whom they were responsible. Psalm 23 identifies the Lord as a Shepherd and vividly describes the duties of the keeper of the sheep. Given the rugged terrain of Palestine, the constant threat from wild animals,

A Middle Eastern craftsman placing tiles into a mosaic inlaid box.

and the ceaseless search for water and pasture-land, the responsibilities and dangers of the shepherd were great. Abel is the first to be described as a "keeper of sheep" (Gen. 4:2). Closely akin to the shepherd was the **herds-man** (Gen. 4:20). Jabal is described as one "having cattle." The only distinction that might be made between a shepherd and herdsman is in their charges: the shepherd had sheep; the herdsman had cattle. Abel's brother Cain is identified as the first **farmer** (Gen. 4:2). The Bible calls the worker of land a "tiller" or "plower" (Ps. 129:3). He is closely associated with God in Scripture since it is God who instructs and works closely with him in producing the crops. Farm work involved the **gleaner** (Ruth 2:3), **harvestman** (Isa. 17:5), and **reaper** (Ruth 2:3). The harvestman and reaper are, apparently, two names for the same task. It is likely, also, that the farmer served as his own harvester. The gleaner is different. By gleaning what farmers left in the field, the poor and landless obtained food. See *Agriculture; Fish; Gleaning; Hunter.*

Nomadic existence does not require any complicated structure of government. Rule was in the hands of the leader of each tribe. Some form of government became necessary, however, when towns and villages began to form. Before the coming of the monarchy, with its more centralized system of government, God chose **judges** (Judg. 2:16) to lead His people, especially in times of crisis. Since the crises were generally wars, the judges were primarily military leaders, who rescued the Israelite tribes from destruction by their warring neighbors. These and later judges also settled disputes (cp. Luke 18:2) See *Judge.*

Occupations around the Palace People who worked around the home could be found doing multiple tasks on any given day. Outside the home skills became more specialized. In Israel with the development of the monarchy, some of the Hebrews found employment within the palace. The **king** (1 Sam. 8:5) held first place. Many kings, among Israel's neighbors, were held to be gods; not so in Israel. The Israelite king was the political ruler and spiritual example and leader to his people. The king determined, by his obedience or disobedience to Israel's God, the fortunes of the nation, but he was never god. (Note, however, the poetic designation in Ps. 45:6). See *King.*

Joseph was a **governor** (Gen. 42:6) of Egypt. His position was second only to Pharaoh. He was, in fact, ruler (Gen. 41:43) over all the land of Egypt. Daniel was another Hebrew who enjoyed rule in a foreign nation. He was one of three **administrators** or commissioners (Dan. 6:2) given rule over the Median Empire. No information is given regarding his duties.

In NT times the Roman government used a **deputy** (Acts 13:7), also called a **proconsul**, to oversee the administrative responsibilities of its provinces. The Romans had extended their empire beyond the limits of the emperor's ability to rule personally. Deputies were used where the Roman army was unnecessary. Where a military presence was necessary, a governor (Matt. 27:2), or **procurator**, was used. The NT names only three men employed as governors in Palestine, although there were more: Pontius Pilate, Felix, and Festus. See *Governor; Rome and the Roman Empire.*

Beyond the task of governing, the palace provided ample opportunity for military occupations to develop. The **armor-bearer** (Judg. 9:54) was one of the servants provided for a warrior as he went into battle. The army was made up of men of various ranks and responsibilities.

A Middle Eastern rug weaver operating his loom.

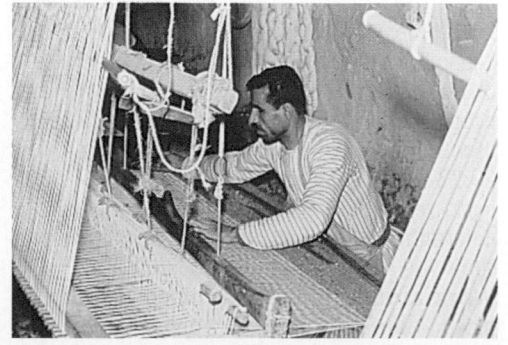

Many of the terms designating those in places of leadership are ambiguous and may refer to one and the same rank. The **commander** (Isa. 55:4) apparently referred to any leader among the people. It is possible that such ranks as captain, lieutenant, and prince, which could be included under the umbrella of "commander," were, in the first place, military ranks alone. **Soldiers** (1 Chron. 7:4) are mentioned frequently in connection with the many wars recorded in the Bible. The geographical location of Israel put it in constant danger of invading armies. Every adult male (over the age of 20) within the tribes of Israel was expected to serve in the military. The Mosaic law, especially in the book of Numbers, set forth the regulations for establishing an army. See *Arms and Armor*.

The government included a corps of service and judicial personnel, as well. The **jailer** (Acts 16:23) is prominent in several NT passages. He had charge of all prisoners—political or religious. Under Roman rule the jailer was strictly responsible for the safekeeping of the inmates. If one were to escape, or otherwise be unable to complete his sentence, the jailer was liable to fulfill the sentence of the prisoner.

In addition to providing government and a military presence, nations found it necessary to collect taxes from their citizens. The despised **publican** or **tax collector** (Matt. 9:10) is well-known from the NT. The principal duty was extorting as much in taxes as possible. It is believed, by some, that the publican was able to keep for himself any amount of monies collected beyond that levied by the government.

The **scribe** (Matt. 5:20), in addition to service in a religious fashion, served in an administrative capacity in the government as well. Scribes involved in the copying and interpretation of the law of Moses are known from the time of Ezra, who is identified as a "scribe skilled in the law of Moses" (Ezra 7:6). Within ancient governments scribes served the royal court, keeping records of the king's reign. Each king organized his government with advisors and people responsible for different areas. The Bible lists the organization of David (2 Sam. 8:16-18; 20:23-26) and Solomon (1 Kings 4:1-19). The exact responsibility of each official is difficult to determine as a look at different translations will show.

Work around the Marketplace The marketplace offered numerous opportunities for

A stonemason working at his craft.

employment outside the home. These opportunities may be grouped around the sale of goods, many of which could be classified as arts and crafts, and dispensing of services.

Among early craftsmen the **carpenter** (2 Sam. 5:11) had special meaning as the occupation of Jesus. Most of the biblical references to carpenters, however, are to foreign workers. Most notable are the workers of Hiram, king of Tyre, who labored on Solomon's temple. Associated with these craftsmen of wood are the **feller** (Isa. 14:8) and **hewers** (Josh. 9:21), both cutters of wood. The metalworkers identified in the Bible are the **coppersmith** (2 Tim. 4:14), the **goldsmith** (Neh. 3:8), and the **silversmith** (Acts 19:24) as workers in their respective metals. In more general terms metalworkers are identified as **founders** (Judg. 17:4) and **smiths** (1 Sam. 13:19). Oddly enough, miners are not directly mentioned in the biblical text, although craftsmen in various metals were numerous. The metals used by the craftsmen were often imported, though Israel may have controlled some mines near the Red Sea when they controlled those regions. See *Mines and Mining*.

In the sphere of salesmanship, the **merchant** (Gen. 23:16) or **seller** (Isa. 24:2) held a prominent position in commerce from the earliest biblical times. Their trade developed into one of international proportions. The **potter** (Jer. 18:2; Rom. 9:21) may have been one of the busiest men in the marketplace. The demands for his product would be great. Pottery was less expensive and more durable than other containers available to the Israelites, which accounts for its common use.

The **mason** sold his talent of cutting stone for building purposes (2 Kings 12:12), while the **tanner** (Acts 9:43) busied himself with preparing skins for use in clothing and as containers. **Tent-making** (Acts 18:3) must have been a craft learned from Israel's earliest days of semi-nomadic existence in the time of the patriarchs. This trade carried over into the NT period. Paul, Aquila, and Priscilla are said to have made their living by making tents (Acts 18:3).

Many services were offered in biblical times. The **apothecary** or **perfumer** (Neh. 3:8) has been characterized as the equivalent of a modern druggist. His main task involved the compounding of drugs and ointments for medical purposes. Jewish religious practices suggest that making perfume was also a part of the apothecary's craft (Exod. 30:35).

The **banker**, called a **lender** (Prov. 22:7), suffered a poor reputation among the Jews. Their religious law forbade the lending of money for interest. In the NT these bankers were the infamous "money changers" of the temple. See *Banking; Commerce.*

The **fuller** (Mal. 3:2) may be best described as an ancient laundryman. He worked with soiled clothing and with the material from the loom ready for weaving. His service entailed the cleaning of any fabric.

A **host** (Luke 10:35), often thought of as an "innkeeper," provided minimal accommodations for travelers, in some cases, little more than provision of space for erecting a tent or a place to lie down to sleep.

Among the most respected persons of Scripture was the **master** (James 3:1), more appropriately called an **instructor** or **teacher** (Rom. 2:20). Biblical references to this profession apply mainly to religious teaching, but the term suited anyone who offered instruction. See *Education in Bible Times.*

Prominent, throughout the Bible, are various occupations related to musical talents. Descriptive names include: **singers** and **players** (Ps. 68:25) in the OT, and **musicians**, **harpists**, **flutists** (**pipers**), and **trumpeters** (Rev. 18:22) in the NT. In both Testaments music played a significant part in the religious life and worship of the nation.

Occupations around the Church and Temple While "occupation" is not a technically accurate term when referring to the early church, there were "offices" filled by Christians, normally on a voluntary basis. See *Offices in the New Testament.*

The officers of the temple were much more authoritarian. The **priest** (Exod. 31:10) acted as an intermediary between God and the people who came to worship at the temple. In many cases priests sacrificed the offerings for the people and the nation, taking for themselves a share in the offering. Priests also served as advisers to the king (2 Sam. 20:25). Until recently the **prophet** (Gen. 20:7) was looked upon as the antithesis of priesthood. Many of the prophets were hostile toward the abuses of the priests and the excesses of the priesthood, but they did not condemn the priesthood, itself. In fact, some prophets were members of the temple personnel. The prophets functioned mainly as "messengers" of their God. Where the priest was a "ritual" intermediary, the prophet was a "speaking" one. Their message, at times, had a predictive element in it; generally, however, they addressed the historical situation facing their hearers. See *High Priest; Levite; Priests; Prophets; Temple.*

Conclusion Occupations during the entire span of biblical times were many and varied, as they are today. However, they were occupations suited to a nontechnological society. The nation of Israel remained an agriculturally oriented economy throughout its existence as recorded in the biblical text. *Phillip J. Swanson*

OCHRAN (Ok' răn) (NASB, REB, NRSV) or **OCRAN** (KJV, NIV) Personal name meaning "troubler." Father of Pagiel, a leader of the tribe of Asher (Num. 1:13; 2:27; 7:72,77; 10:26).

ODED (Ō' dĕd) Personal name of uncertain meaning, perhaps "counter," "restorer," or "timekeeper." **1.** Father of the Prophet Azariah (2 Chron. 15:1). **2.** Prophet in the time of Ahaz who urged the Israelites to release the people of Judah they had taken as prisoners of war (2 Chron. 28:8-15).

ODOR Scent or fragrance, usually in the phrase "pleasing odor" (KJV, "sweet savour"). A synonym for a burnt offering (Num. 28:1-2). See *Sacrifice and Offering.*

OFFAL NIV term for the waste remaining from the butchering of a sacrificial animal (Exod. 29:14; Lev. 4:11; 8:17; 16:27; Num. 19:5; Mal. 2:3). Other translations render the underlying Hebrew as "dung."

OFFENSE Translates several Hebrew and Greek terms. The following two senses predominate. **1.** That which causes indignation or disgust (Gen. 31:36). Here offense approximates crime (Deut. 19:15; 22:26), guilt (Hos. 5:15), trespass (Rom. 5:15,17-18,20), or sin (2 Cor. 11:7). Christ is said to be a rock of offense in this sense (Rom. 9:33; Gal. 5:11; 1 Pet. 2:8). What was especially offensive was the claim that an accursed one was the Messiah and that faith in this crucified one and not works was necessary for salvation. **2.** That which serves as a hindrance (Matt. 16:23) or obstacle (2 Cor. 6:3). This hindrance is often temptation to sin (Matt. 18:7; Luke 17:1).

OFFERINGS See *Sacrifice and Offering.*

OFFICES IN THE NEW TESTAMENT Although technical terms for "office" have been avoided in the NT, the concept of office is present. Formal characteristics in the NT associated with what we now call offices include permanency, recognition by others (possibly by a title), authority, payment, and appointment (including the laying on of hands). The first three elements are somewhat essential, the last two are not. Terms often associated with offices include apostles, prophets, evangelists, bishops, and deacons. The NT focus on these offices is usually on function or task more than status or position.

The term "apostle" occurs 80 times in the NT and has various referents. Most narrowly it applied to the 12 disciples. When Matthias replaced Judas, the requirement was one who had followed Jesus from His baptism to His ascension (Acts 1:21-22). Paul uses the term technically to refer to those who have seen the

risen Lord (1 Cor. 9:1; 15:7-9) and who have been personally commissioned by Christ (e.g., Acts 9:15; Rom. 1:1). Thus Paul claims to be the last of the apostles (1 Cor. 15:7-8) and regards this office as the most significant (1 Cor. 12:28; Eph. 4:11). Most believe that the apostolate ceased in the first century due to the qualification of being an eyewitness of Jesus' resurrection (cp. Eph. 2:20).

Some of Paul's coworkers are also given the title of apostle. Barnabas is called an apostle in Acts 14:14 (cp. Acts 14:4; 1 Cor. 9:5-6). Although not directly named apostles, Apollos is possibly included in Paul's references to "us apostles" in 1 Cor. 4:9 (cp. 1 Cor. 4:6) and Silas in Paul's mention of "apostles of Christ" in 1 Thess. 2:6 (cp. 1 Thess. 1:1). Whether Andronicus and Junias were well-known "among the apostles" or "by the apostles" (Rom. 16:7) is debated.

A few times Paul uses the term nontechnically meaning "messenger." Paul sent Titus and a brother as messengers (*apostoloi*) to the Corinthians in order to hasten their collection efforts (2 Cor. 8:23). Paul also states that Epaphroditus was a messenger (*apostolos*) sent by the Philippian church to bring him aid (Phil. 2:25). The term "apostle" is also applied to Jesus who is "the apostle and high priest of our confession" (Heb. 3:1).

Often closely tied to the office of apostle is that of prophet. Prophets were those who regularly proclaimed the divine word to the community (1 Cor. 13:2; 14:22,29; Eph. 3:5; 2 Pet. 1:19-21). Their message was given directly from God and was considered authoritative. Because of the importance of the prophetic word and the possibility of this gift being abused, it was necessary that prophetic utterances be tested. The most extensive passage is found in 1 Cor. 14. Paul provides some guidelines for how prophets and other gifted individuals should conduct themselves in worship. He states that those who prophesy do so for the edification, exhortation, and comfort of the body (1 Cor. 14:3-5,26,31). Consequently Paul prefers that the congregation focus on prophecy more than speaking in tongues (1 Cor. 14:5,12,19,22-26). The prophets are to conduct themselves in an orderly fashion and others are to pass judgment on the validity of their utterances (1 Cor. 14:29-33,40). The importance of the prophets is seen in 1 Cor. 12:28 and Eph. 4:11, where they are listed second after apostles. Prophets mentioned by name include Anna (Luke 2:36), Judas and Silas (Acts 15:32), and Agabus (Acts 21:10). Prophets were in Jerusalem (Acts 11:27), Antioch (Acts 13:1), and Corinth (1 Cor. 14). Some believe that the office of prophet ceased shortly after the completion of the canon (cp. Eph. 2:20; Heb. 1:1-2).

The term "evangelist" is a derivative of the verb *euangelizomai* ("to announce good news" or "preach the gospel"). Evangelists are mentioned only three times in the NT. In Acts 21:8 Philip, one of seven chosen in Acts 6, is called "the evangelist." Evangelists are named third in Eph. 4:11 after apostles and prophets. Finally, Timothy is exhorted by Paul to "do the work of an evangelist" (2 Tim. 4:5), which probably means to make known the truths of the gospel.

By the time the Pastoral Epistles were written, there appear to be two established offices in the local congregations, bishops and deacons. The terms "bishop" (or overseer) and "elder" (or presbyter) are used interchangeably, denoting the same office. Since the Greek word for bishop (*episkopos*) means "overseer," the main function of the bishop was to oversee the spiritual life of the congregation. The qualifications for a bishop are given in 1 Tim. 3:1-7 and Titus 1:5-9 and focus on character more than duties. One of the distinguishing requirements between a bishop and a deacon was the bishop's ability to teach (1 Tim. 3:2; 5:17; Titus 1:9). Pastors and teachers (Eph. 4:11) appear to be those whom Christ has given to shepherd and instruct the church. As such it is probable that these leaders can also be identified as bishops or elders.

Although the term "deacon" comes from a Greek word (*diakonos*) meaning "servant" or "minister," it is sometimes used technically referring to an office-holder in the church. In Phil. 1:1 Paul addresses the "bishops and deacons" and the qualifications for deacons are given in 1 Tim. 3:8-13. Another possible reference to official usage of the term is found in Rom. 16:1, where Paul mentions that Phoebe was a *diakonon* of the church at Cenchrea (cp. 1 Tim 3:11). The account of the appointing of seven men to aid in the distribution of food may provide the prototype for this office (Acts 6:1-6). The deacons' responsibility can probably be best described as a supporting role to the bishops (or elders). That is, they were responsible for taking care of those duties which would allow the bishops to devote themselves more freely to the word of God and prayer (1 Tim. 3:2; Titus 1:9; cp. Acts 6:2-4).

Other leaders are often mentioned without a specific office being named. In Gal. 6:6 Paul states that those who are taught the word should provide for the physical sustenance of their teachers. This text suggests that a class of teachers was giving formal Christian instruction and that they were teaching to such an extent as to need compensation for their labors. In 1 Thess. 5:12-13 Paul exhorts the congregation to respect and highly esteem those who diligently labor, lead, and admonish them. Although Paul does not use any formal title, it is possible that these leaders were, or later became known as, bishops or elders. Other leaders mentioned by Paul include Stephanas (1 Cor. 16:15-16), Epaphras (Col. 1:7; 4:12), and Archippus (Col. 4:17). Furthermore, in Heb. 13:17 the author instructs the congregation to obey their leaders and to submit to them. The reason for such respect is because these leaders keep watch over their souls and are accountable to God for such leadership.

Some have included the order of widows as an official "office" (1 Tim. 5:3-16). The reason for this is that Paul states that certain widows over 60 are to be "placed on the official support list" (1 Tim. 5:9 HCSB). It is difficult, however, to know how formal this "order" was and precisely what the widows' functions were.

Although offices are important in the church, the NT stresses that all believers share in the responsibility of ministry. Those who hold offices have been specially gifted by God. Yet all have gifts of service and all are expected to serve.

Ben L. Merkle

OFFSCOURING That which is removed by scouring: the dregs, filth, garbage, refuse, or scum (Lam. 3:45; 1 Cor. 4:13).

OG (Ōg) Amorite king of Bashan defeated by the Israelites before they crossed the Jordan (Num. 21:33-35; Deut. 1:4; 3:1-13). Og is identified as the last member of the Rephaim or giants (Deut. 3:11). The term translated "bed" (cp. Job 7:13; Amos 3:12) is perhaps better rendered "resting place" in the sense of burial place. Some interpreters suggest that this resting place was similar to black basalt sarcophagi found in Transjordan.

OHAD (Ō´ hăd) Personal name meaning "unity." Son of Simeon (Gen. 46:10; Exod.

6:15). The name is omitted in parallel lists (Num. 26:12-14; 1 Chron. 4:24).

OHEL (Ō´ hĕl) Personal name meaning "tent," "family (of God)," or "(God is) shelter." Descendant of David (1 Chron. 3:20).

OHOLAH (Ō hō´ lah) Personal name meaning "tent dweller." A woman's name Ezekiel used to portray Samaria (Ezek. 23:1-10). Oholah and her sister Oholibah (Jerusalem) are shown as whores who consorted with various men (other nations). The obvious meaning is their spiritual adultery against God. God declared through the prophet that Samaria eventually would be delivered into the hands of her "lover," Assyria (23:9).

OHOLIAB (Ō hō´ lĭ ăb) Personal name meaning "father's tent." Danite craftsman, designer, and embroiderer who assisted Bezalel in supervision of the construction of the tabernacle and its equipment (Exod. 31:6; 35:34; 36:1-2; esp. 38:23).

OHOLIBAH (Ō hōl´ ĭ bah) Personal name meaning "tent worshiper." Younger sister in the allegory of Ezek. 23 identified with Jerusalem (23:4,11-49). The sexual misconduct of these sisters represents Israel's and Judah's embrace of idolatry. See *Ohalah*.

OHOLIBAMAH (Ō´ hŏl ĭ bā´ mah) Personal name meaning "tent of the high place" or "tent dweller of the false cult." **1.** Hivite daughter of Anah and wife of Esau (Gen. 36:2). **2.** Edomite leader descended from Esau (Gen. 36:41).

OIL Indispensable commodity in the ancient Near East for food, medicine, fuel, and ritual. Oil was considered a blessing given by God (Deut. 11:14), and the olive tree was a characteristic of the land which God gave to Israel (Deut. 8:8).
Preparation In biblical times domestic oil was prepared from olives. Sometimes oil was combined with perfumes and used as a cosmetic (Esther 2:12). The extraction of oil from olives is abundantly confirmed by archaeological findings of stone presses found at several sites in Palestine. This oil, called "beaten oil," was lighter and considered the best oil. After the beaten oil was

Ancient oil lamp decorated with two human figures.

extracted, another grade of oil was produced by heating the pulp and pressing it again.

Domestic oil was stored in small cruses, pots, or jars (1 Kings 17:12; 2 Kings 4:2); oil used in religious ceremonies was also kept in horns (1 Sam. 16:13).
Use Oil was used in a variety of ways in biblical times; but, most often, oil was used in the preparation of food, taking the place of animal fat. Oil was used with meal in the preparation of cakes (Num. 11:8; 1 Kings 17:12-16) and with honey (Ezek. 16:13), flour (Lev. 2:1,4), and wine (Rev. 6:6).

Oil was used as fuel for lamps, both in homes (Matt. 25:3) and in the tabernacle (Exod. 25:6).

Oil was extensively used in religious ceremonies. The morning and evening sacrifices required, in addition to the lambs, a tenth of a measure of fine flour and a fourth of a hin of beaten oil. Other cereal offerings also required oil. Oil was used during the offering of purification from leprosy. In the NT oil was used to anoint a body in preparation for burial (Matt. 26:12; Mark 14:8). Several persons in the OT were anointed with oil: kings (1 Sam. 10:1; 16:13), priests (Lev. 8:30), and possibly prophets (1 Kings. 19:16; Isa. 61:1). Some objects were also anointed in dedication to God: the tabernacle and all its furniture (Exod. 40:9-11), the shields of soldiers (2 Sam. 1:21; Isa. 21:5), altars (Lev. 8:10-11), and pillars (Gen. 35:14).

As medicine oil or ointment was used in the treatment of wounds (Isa. 1:6; Luke 10:34).

James 5:14 may refer either to a symbolic use of oil or to its medicinal use.

Oil was used cosmetically as protection against the scorching sun or the dryness of the desert (Ruth 3:3; Eccles. 9:8). Since olives were found in abundance in Palestine, olive oil was also used as a commodity of trade (1 Kings 5:11; Ezek. 27:17; Hos. 12:1).

Oil was regarded as a symbol of honor (Judg. 9:9), while virtue was compared to perfumed oil (Song 1:3; Eccles. 7:1). The abundance of oil was a demonstration of blessing and prosperity (Job 29:6; Joel 2:24). However, as a symbol of affluence, oil was also associated with the arrogance of the rich (Hb. "valley of oil"; KJV "fat valley," Isa. 28:1,4). Oil was a symbol of joy and gladness (Ps. 45:7), and in time of sorrow, anointing with oil was not practiced (2 Sam. 14:2). See *Agriculture; Anoint; Commerce; Cosmetics.* *Claude F. Mariottini*

OINTMENT Perfumed unguents or salves of various kinds used as cosmetics, medicine, and in religious ceremonies. The use of ointments and perfumes appears to have been a common practice in the ancient Near East including the Hebrews.

Terminology The OT uses various words to describe ointment. The most common, *shemen*, simply means "oil" (Gen. 28:18; Hos. 2:8). The OT does not distinguish between oil and ointment. In the NT, *muron*, "ointment" (Matt. 26:7; Mark 14:3-4; Luke 7:37-38) was a perfumed ointment.

Manufacture The base for ointment was olive oil. Olives were very common in Palestine; however, perfumed salves were very expensive. A great demand arose for ointments as people attempted to protect themselves against the hot wind from the desert and the arid condition of the land.

The preparation of ointments was the job of skilled persons trained in the art of producing perfume. Bezaleel and Aholiab were appointed by God to prepare the sacred ointment and the incense used in worship (Exod. 31:1-11). While the blending of perfumes and ointment for secular use was probably done by women (1 Sam. 8:13), priestly families were responsible for the production of the large amount of ointments necessary for temple use (1 Chron. 9:30). In the postexilic period a group of professional people in Jerusalem were skilled in the manufacture of perfumed ointments (Neh. 3:8). These people were called "apothecaries" (KJV) or "perfumers" (HCSB, NASB, NRSV, NIV) (Exod. 30:25,35; 37:29; Eccles. 10:1). Their function was to take the many gums, resins, roots, and barks and combine them with oil to make the various ointments used for anointing purposes. In many cases, the formula for these ointments and perfumes was a professional secret, handed down from generation to generation. Egyptian and Ugaritic sources have shown that water mixed with oil was heated in large pots (Job 41:31). While the water was boiling, the spices were added. After the ingredients were blended, they were transferred to suitable containers. To preserve the special scents of the ointment, alabaster jars with long necks were sealed at the time the ointment was prepared and then broken just before use (Mark 14:3). Dry perfumes were kept in bags (Song 1:13) and in perfume boxes (Isa. 3:20 NRSV; NIV: "perfume bottles"; KJV: "tablets"). See *Vessels and Utensils.*

Ingredients Various spices were used in the manufacturing of ointments and perfumes: aloes (Ps. 45:8; John 19:39); balsam (Song 5:1,13; 6:21); galbanum (Exod. 30:34), myrrh, or more literally mastic or ladanum (Gen. 37:25; 43:11); myrrh (Esther 2:12; Matt. 2:11), nard (Song 4:13-14; Mark 14:3; KJV "spikenard"), frankincense (NIV "incense"; Isa. 60:6; Matt. 2:11); balsam or balm (Gen. 37:25; Jer. 8:22); cassia (Exod. 30:24; Ezek. 27:19), calamus (Exod. 30:23, NRSV "aromatic cane"; Song 4:14;), cinnamon (Exod. 30:23; Rev. 18:13), stacte (Exod. 30:34), and onycha (Exod. 30:34). Onycha, an ingredient derived from mollusks found in the Red Sea, was used in the mixture to be burned on the altar of incense. These spices were used as fragrant incense in worship. They were also mixed with oil to produce the holy anointing oil and to produce cosmetics and medicine.

Value Most of these spices were imported by the people who lived in Palestine. The great variety of spices used in the manufacture of ointments gave rise to merchants who traded in expensive spices and perfumes (Gen. 37:28; Ezek. 27:17-22). In biblical times Arabia was one of the principal traders in aromatic spices. Spices were also imported from Africa, India, and Persia. Perfumed ointments were highly prized. Solomon received an annual payment of perfume as tribute from his subjects (1 Kings 10:25); the queen of Sheba brought many costly

O

spices as gifts to Solomon (1 Kings 10:2). Hezekiah, king of Judah, included valuable perfumed ointment and spices as part of his treasure (2 Kings 20:13; Isa. 39:2). When Mary anointed Jesus with a pound of costly ointment, Judas Iscariot rebuked Jesus because the ointment was worth the equivalent of one year's salary (John 12:3-8).

Use Many personal things were perfumed with spiced ointment. The breath was perfumed (Song 7:8), probably with spiced wine (Song 8:2). The garments of the king were perfumed with myrrh, aloes, and cassia (Ps. 45:8), or myrrh, frankincense, and with "every fragrant powder of the merchant" (Song 3:6 HCSB). The bed of the prostitute was perfumed with myrrh, aloes, and cinnamon (Prov. 7:17).

One of the most important uses of ointment in the OT was in religious ceremonies. The manufacture of the anointing oil consisted of mixing olive oil with myrrh, sweet cinnamon, calamus, and cassia (Exod. 30:22-25). This ointment was considered to be holy; anyone who manufactured the sacred oil for use outside the worship place was to be cut off from the people (Exod. 30:33). Many individuals were anointed with the sacred ointment. The anointing of a person was viewed as an act of designation of that person to the service of God. The shield of a soldier was anointed with oil (2 Sam. 1:21) as a symbol of dedication to God. Jacob anointed the pillar at Bethel, and the site where God appeared to him became a holy place (Gen. 28:18; 35:14). Ointments were used also in burial rites.

Many people in the ancient Near East believed strongly in the curative power of oil. For this reason they used ointments as medicine in the treatment of some diseases (Jer. 8:22; Mark 6:13; James 5:14) and as unguents for wounds (Isa. 1:6; Luke 10:34). The law of Moses commanded the person healed of leprosy to be anointed with oil (Lev. 14:15-18,26-29).

Ointments were used as cosmetics for protection of the skin. Perfumes were used to counteract bodily odor. The whole body was usually anointed with perfume after bathing (Ruth 3:3; 2 Sam 12:20; Ezek. 16:9). Perfumes were used inside the clothes (Song 1:13) and by women who desired to be attractive to men (Esther 2:12). See *Anoint; Burial; Diseases; Oil.*

Claude F. Mariottini

OLD GATE KJV, NASB, NRSV designation for a Jerusalem city gate repaired in Nehemiah's time (Neh. 3:6; 12:39). This rendering is doubtful on grammatical grounds (the adjective and noun do not agree). Some interpreters thus propose gate of the old (city). Others take the Hebrew *Yeshanah* as a proper name (NIV, REB, TEV). A village named Jeshanah is located near Bethel. The gate may have pointed in this direction.

OLD TESTAMENT First part of the Christian Bible, taken over from Israel. It tells the history of the nation of Israel and God's dealings with them to the return from exile in Babylon. For Jews it is the complete Bible, sometimes called Tanak for its three parts (Torah or Law, Nebiim or Prophets, Kethubim or Writings). Christians see its complement in the NT, which reveals Jesus Christ as the fulfillment of OT prophecy. The OT has three major divisions: Law, Prophets (Former and Latter), and Writings. The Law (Genesis–Deuteronomy) begins with the creation of the world and concludes as Israel is about to enter the promised land. The Prophets—Joshua, Judges, Samuel, Kings, Isaiah, Jeremiah, Ezekiel, and the 12 Minor Prophets—continue with the nation in the land of Palestine until the exile and includes prophetic messages delivered to the nation. The Writings (all other books) contain the account of the return from exile, collected wisdom literature from throughout the nation's history, and selected stories about God's leading in individual lives. See *Bible Formation and Canon.*

OLD TESTAMENT QUOTATIONS IN THE NEW TESTAMENT Influence of the OT is seen throughout the NT. The NT writers included approximately 250 express OT quotations, and if one includes indirect or partial quotations, the number jumps to more than 1,000. It is clear that the writers of the NT were concerned with demonstrating the continuity between the OT Scriptures and the faith they proclaimed. They were convinced that in Jesus the OT promises had been fulfilled.

Types of Quotations *Formula quotations* are introduced by a typical introductory quotations formula that generally employ verbs of "saying" or "writing." The most common introductory formulas are: "as the Scripture has said" (John 7:38 HCSB); "what does the Scripture say?" (Gal. 4:30); "as it is written," emphasizing the permanent validity of the OT revelation (Mark 1:2; Rom. 1:17; 3:10); "this took place to fulfill," emphasizing the fulfillment of OT prophecies (Matt. 4:14; 12:17; 21:4); "as God said," "He also says," "the Holy Spirit says," which personify Scripture and reflect its divine dimension (Rom. 9:25; 2 Cor. 6:16; Heb. 3:7); "Moses," "David," or "Isaiah" says, which emphasize the human element in Scripture (Rom. 10:16,19-20; Heb. 4:7).

Composite quotations combine two or more OT texts drawn from one or more of the sections of the Hebrew OT canon (Law, Prophets, and Writings). For example, Rom. 11:8-10 quotes from the Law (Deut. 29:4), the Prophets (Isa. 29:10), and the Writings (Ps. 69:22-23). In some cases a series of OT texts may be used in a commentarylike fashion as in John 12:38-40 and Rom. 9–11. Composite quotes are often organized around thematic emphases or catchwords in keeping with a practice common to Judaism and based on the notion set forth in Deut. 19:15 that two or three witnesses establish the matter. The "stumbling stone" motif reflected in Rom. 9:33 (Isa. 8:14; 28:16) and 1 Pet. 2:6-9 (Isa. 8:14; 28:16; Ps. 118:22) is a good example of this method.

Unacknowledged quotations are often woven into the fabric of the NT text without acknowledgment or introduction. For example, Paul quoted Gen. 15:6 in his discussion of Abraham (Gal. 3:6) and Gen. 12:3 (Gal. 3:8) with no acknowledgment or introductory formula.

Indirect quotations or allusions form the most difficult type of OT quotation to identify. The gradation from quotation to allusion may be almost imperceptible. An allusion may be little more than a clause, phrase, or even a word drawn from an OT text that might easily escape the notice of the reader. For example, the reader might easily miss the fact that the words spoken from the cloud at the transfiguration of Jesus as recorded in Matt. 17:5 combine three separate OT texts: "You are My Son" (Ps. 2:7 HCSB), "in whom My soul delights" (Isa. 42:1 NASB), and "you must listen to him" (Deut. 18:15).

Sources of Old Testament Quotations Since the NT was written in Greek for predominantly Greek readers, it is not surprising that a large majority of OT quotes in the NT are drawn from the Greek translation of the OT known as the Septuagint (LXX). Of Paul's 93 quotes, 51 are in absolute or virtual agreement with the LXX, while only 4 agree with the Hebrew text. This means that 38 diverge from all known Greek or Hebrew OT texts. Of Matthew's 43 quotes, 11 agree with the LXX, while the other 32 differ from all known sources. How then are these quotes to be explained? The NT writers may have used a version of the OT that is unknown to us, or they may have been quoting from memory. It is also possible that the NT writers were more concerned with meaning and interpretation. It has also been suggested that the OT quotations may have been drawn from "testimony books," collections of selected, combined, and interpreted OT texts gathered by the early Christian community for proclamation and apologetics. The frequent use of certain OT texts, such as Ps. 110, Isa. 43, and so forth, in the preaching and writing of the early church and the discovery of such collections at Qumran seem to support such a possibility.

Uses of Old Testament Quotations The NT writers used OT quotations for at least four reasons: (1) to demonstrate that Jesus is the fulfillment of God's purposes and of the prophetic witness of the OT Scriptures (Rom. 1:2; Matt. 4:14; 12:17-21; 21:4-5); (2) as a source for ethical instruction and edification of the church (Rom. 13:8-10; 2 Cor. 13:1); (3) to interpret contemporary events (Rom. 9–11; 15:8-12); (4) to prove a point on the assumption that the Scripture is God's Word (1 Cor. 10:26; 14:21; 15:55). The approaches employed in the use of the OT are reflective of first-century Judaism as represented in the Dead Sea Scrolls, Philo of Alexandra, and later rabbinic Judaism. Some OT quotations are used in their literal historical sense and, therefore, have the same meaning in the NT as they had in the OT. The quotation of Ps. 78:24 in John 6:31 is a good example of such usage. Some quotations reflect a typical approach to interpreting the OT in first-century Judaism known as midrash. Midrash is an exposition of a text that aims at bringing out its contemporary relevance. The OT text is quoted and explained so as to make it apply to or be meaningful for the current situation. The use of Gen. 15:6 in Rom. 4:3-25 and the use of Ps. 78:24 in John 6:31-58 reflect such an approach.

Some OT texts are interpreted typologically. In this approach the NT writer sees a correspondence between persons, events, or things in the

OT and persons, events, or things in their contemporary setting. The correspondence with the past is not found in the written text but within the historical event. Underlying typology is the conviction that certain events in the past history of Israel as recorded in earlier Scriptures revealed God's ways and purposes with persons in a typical way. Matthew's use of Hos. 11:1 (2:15) suggests that the Gospel writer saw a correspondence between Jesus' journey into Egypt and the Egyptian sojourn of the people of Israel. Jesus recapitulated or reexperienced the sacred history of Israel. The redemptive purposes of God demonstrated in the exodus (reflected by the prophet Hosea) were being demonstrated in Jesus' life. In some cases the understanding and application of the OT quotation is dependent on an awareness of the quotation's wider context in the OT. The use of the quotation is intended to call the reader's attention to the wider OT context or theme and might be referred to as a "pointer quotation." In first-century Judaism where large portions of Scripture were known by heart, it was customary to quote only the beginning of a passage even if its continuation was to be kept in mind. A good example of this use may be seen in Rom. 1–3. Paul had discussed both

The olive tree has always been one of the most important trees in Israel's culture and economy. It provided food, and the oil extracted was used for cooking, medicinal purposes, and light.

the faithfulness of God and the sinfulness of humanity. In Rom. 3:4 Paul quoted Ps. 51:4 to support his first point. He continued his argument with a further reference to human wickedness which is, in fact, the subject of Ps. 51:5; but he did not feel the need to quote the verse since it was already suggested to those familiar with the biblical text. Finally, there is a limited allegorical use of the OT text in which the text is seen as a kind of code having two meanings—the literal, superficial level of meaning, and a deeper, underlying meaning such as in Gal. 4:22-31.

Despite similarities with contemporary Jewish use(s) of the OT, the NT writers interpreted the OT in a radically new way. New Testament writers did not deliberately use a different exegetical method. They wrote from a different theological perspective. The writers of the NT were convinced that the true meaning of the OT is Jesus Christ and that He alone provides the means of understanding it. True interpretation of the OT is achieved by reading OT passages or incidents in light of the event of Christ. While many of the OT texts quoted in the NT had already been accepted as messianic (e.g., Ps. 110:1) or could in light of Jesus' actual life claim to be messianic (Ps. 22; Isa. 53), for the early Christians, all Scripture was to be interpreted by the fact of Christ because it is to Him that the OT Scripture points (John 5:39). In summary, the NT writer quoted or alluded to the OT in order to demonstrate how God's purposes have been fulfilled and are being fulfilled in Jesus.

Hulitt Gloer

An ancient olive press. Olives have been an export of Canaan for as many as 3,000 years before Christ.

OLIVES See *Agriculture; Ointment; Plants.*

OLIVES, MOUNT OF Two-and-a-half mile-long mountain ridge that towers over the eastern side of Jerusalem, or more precisely, the middle of the three peaks forming the ridge. Heavily covered with olive trees, the ridge juts out in a north-south direction (like a spur) from the range of mountains running down the center of the region. Both the central Mount of Olives and Mount Scopus, the peak on its northern side, rise over 200 feet above the Temple Mount across the Kidron Valley. It provided a lookout base and signaling point for armies defending Jerusalem.

The western slope of the Mount of Olives on which Jesus gave His Olivet discourse.

David crossed the Mount of Olives when fleeing Absalom (2 Sam. 15:30). Ezekiel saw the cherubim chariot land there (Ezek. 11:22-23). Zechariah described how the Mount of Olives would move to form a huge valley on the Day of the Lord (Zech. 14:3-5). Many crucial events in Jesus' life occurred on the Mount of Olives (Matt. 26:30; Mark 11:1-2; Luke 4:5; 22:39-46; Acts 1:9-12).   *Robert O. Byrd*

OLIVET DISCOURSE (Ŏlʹ ĭ vĕt) Jesus' major sermon preached on the Mount of Olives; Jesus gave instructions concerning the end of the age and the destruction of Jerusalem. The discourse (Matt. 24–25; Mark 13) is in part an apocalypse because it uses symbolic, visionary language that makes it a difficult passage to understand. Parts of it appear scattered throughout Luke 12–21.

Meaning of the Signs (Matt. 24:4-8) The opening remarks warn against misplaced belief in deceptive signs which do not in any way signal the end of the world. These signs occurred in Jesus' day and preceded the destruction of Jerusalem, the event uppermost in Jesus' mind and for which He sought to prepare His disciples. They are still operative after 2,000 years, a further indication that they do not herald the end time.

Time of Persecution (Matt. 24:9-14) These verses suggest a time of severe distress. Many

View of the Kidron Valley to the northeast toward the Mount of Olives.

would say that the reference is to a period of ultimate suffering that is to take place just before the Parousia (Christ's return or second coming; 24:14). Jesus' assertion that the gospel must be preached worldwide seems to strengthen this view. "The one who endures to the end" (24:13 HCSB) could refer to the period immediately prior to the Parousia. It could also pertain to the end of some other event such as the destruction of Jerusalem. Oppression of Christians and family betrayal were common. That Christians were despised and subjected to great suffering is an accurate description of the situation in Judea before the Jewish War, A.D. 66–70, when Titus destroyed the city.

Abomination that Makes Desolate (Matt. 24:15-22) Extrabiblical histories describe the desecration of the Jerusalem temple in 167 B.C. by Antiochus Epiphanes, who built an altar there to Zeus. That event is usually seen as having fulfilled Daniel's prophecy (Dan. 11:31). However, Jesus applied the prophecy to a future overthrow of Jerusalem by Titus' armies. The horror of this siege was unprecedented. Temple and city were utterly demolished. See *Intertestamental History and Literature.*

Second Coming of Christ (Matt. 24:26–25:46) Jesus spoke in veiled language about His coming. Unnatural occurrences in the heavens were commonly used in apocalyptic writings to describe the indescribable but also to screen deliberately from view those things meant to remain hidden. Much of God's plans are mystery, but Jesus disclosed enough. The coming of the Son of Man will be entirely public and "at an hour you do not expect" (Matt. 24:44 HCSB). He will come in the clouds with great power (Acts 1:9-11). The sign of His Parousia is obscure in its meaning. The sermon is interrupted by the statement, "This generation will certainly not pass away until all these things take place" (Matt. 24:34). Jesus was not confused or in error concerning these events. He referred to the destruction of Jerusalem that took place in that generation as a foretaste of the final coming. Concluding parables teach the necessity of remaining watchful. A description of final judgment ends the discourse. Its basic message is a call to be prepared when Jesus does return.

Diane Cross

OLYMPAS (Ō lĭm´ pàs) Perhaps a shortened form of Olympiodorus (gift of Olympus).

Christian whom Paul greeted in Rom. 16:15. Olympas was apparently a member of a house church including the others mentioned in 16:15.

OMAR (Ō´ mar) Personal name meaning "talkative." Son of Eliphaz and ancestor of an Edomite clan of the same name (Gen. 36:11,15; 1 Chron. 1:36).

OMEGA (Ō mā´ gà) Last letter in the Greek alphabet. Together with the first letter, alpha, omega designates God and Christ as the all-encompassing "Reality" (Rev. 1:8; 21:6; 22:13). See *Alpha.*

OMEN 1. Sign used by diviners to predict the future. The Israelites were prohibited from interpreting omens (Deut. 18:10 NASB, NIV). Pagan prophesy employed reading of omens (Num. 24:1 NASB, NRSV; Ezek. 21:21 NIV). As Lord of history God frustrates the plans of "liars" who interpret omens (Isa. 44:25 NASB, NRSV). See *Divination and Magic.* **2.** Sign indicating a future event. Ahab's reference to Ben-hadad as "my brother" was understood as an omen or sign of Ahab's favor (1 Kings 20:33 NASB, NRSV). Companions of the high priest Joshua were a good omen (NRSV) or a symbol (NASB) of hope for a restored people of God (Zech. 3:8). The faithful witness of Christians in the face of opposition is likewise an omen or sign pointing to the salvation of believers and the destruction of God's enemies (Phil. 1:28).

OMER (Ō´ mĕr) **1.** Unit of dry measure equal to one tenth of an ephah or a little more than two quarts (Exod. 16:13-36). See *Weights and Measures.* **2.** First sheaf (omer) of the barley harvest that was elevated as an offering (Lev. 23:9-15). See *Sacrifice and Offering.*

OMNIPOTENCE State of being all-powerful, which theology ascribes to God. Scripture often affirms that all power belongs to God (Ps. 147:5), that all things are possible for God (Luke 1:37; Matt. 19:26), and that God's power exceeds what humans can ask or think (Eph. 3:20). For Scripture God's omnipotence is not a matter of abstract speculation but a force to be reckoned with. God's power is revealed in God's creating and sustaining the universe (Ps. 65:6; Jer. 32:17; Heb. 1:3), in God's deliverance of Israel from Pharaoh's forces (Exod. 15:1-18), in the conquest of Canaan (Deut. 3:21-24), in the incarnation (Luke 1:35), in Christ's death on the cross (1 Cor. 1:17-18,23-24), and in the ongoing ministry of the church (1 Cor. 2:5; Eph. 3:20). See *God.*

OMNIPRESENCE Being present everywhere at once; one of God's unique attributes. One of the characteristics of created objects is that they are limited by space. An object or person can occupy only one place at a time. Because God created the heavens and the earth (Gen. 1:1) and through His Son continually sustains all that is (Heb. 1:3), He is present to the whole of creation and to its parts. King David realized that there was nowhere he could go to escape God's presence (Ps. 139:7-12), and no conditions such as darkness could hide him from God. Even though God is present everywhere, He is not perceived everywhere. He can be fully present and yet hidden from the eyes of creatures, or He can make His presence felt either in blessing or judgment. See *God.*

Steve Bond

OMNISCIENCE State of being all knowing, which theology ascribes to God. Though Scripture affirms God's immeasurable understanding (Ps. 147:5), God's omniscience is not a matter of abstract speculation. Rather,

God's knowing is a matter of personal experience. God knows us intimately (Ps. 139:1-6; Matt. 6:4,6,8). Such knowledge is cause for alarm for the unrighteous but for confidence for God's saints (Job 23:10; Pss. 34:15-16; 90:8; Prov. 15:3; 1 Pet. 3:12). See *God.*

OMRI (Ŏm´ rĭ) Personal name meaning "pilgrim" or "life." **1.** King of Israel 885–874 B.C. and founder of the Omride dynasty, which ruled until 842. Omri came to the throne in a

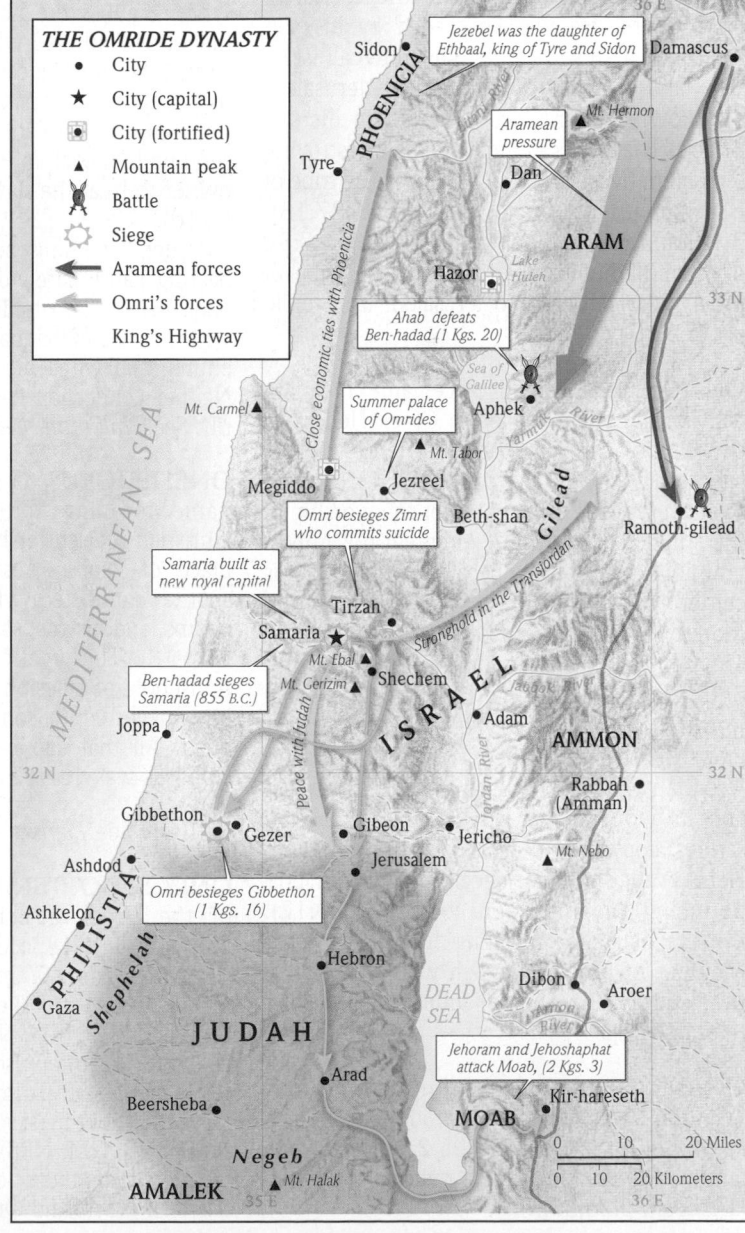

THE OMRIDE DYNASTY

- • City
- ★ City (capital)
- ▣ City (fortified)
- ▲ Mountain peak
- Battle
- Siege
- ← Aramean forces
- ← Omri's forces
- King's Highway

Jezebel was the daughter of Ethbaal, king of Tyre and Sidon

Aramean pressure

Ahab defeats Ben-hadad (1 Kgs. 20)

Summer palace of Omrides

Omri besieges Zimri who commits suicide

Samaria built as new royal capital

Ben-hadad sieges Samaria (855 B.C.)

Omri besieges Gibbethon (1 Kgs. 16)

Jehoram and Jehoshaphat attack Moab, (2 Kgs. 3)

MEDITERRANEAN SEA · PHOENICIA · Sidon · Damascus · Mt. Hermon · Tyre · Dan · ARAM · Close economic ties with Phoenicia · Hazor · Lake Huleh · Sea of Galilee · Mt. Carmel · Aphek · Yarmuk River · Mt. Tabor · Megiddo · Jezreel · Beth-shan · Gilead · Ramoth-gilead · Tirzah · Samaria · Stronghold in the Transjordan · Mt. Ebal · Mt. Gerizim · Shechem · ISRAEL · Adam · AMMON · Joppa · Jordan River · Peace with Judah · Rabbah (Amman) · Gibbethon · Gezer · Gibeon · Jericho · Mt. Nebo · Ashdod · Jerusalem · Ashkelon · PHILISTIA · Shephelah · Gaza · Hebron · Dibon · Aroer · DEAD SEA · Arnon River · JUDAH · Arad · Kir-hareseth · Beersheba · MOAB · Negeb · AMALEK · Mt. Halak

0　　10　　20 Miles
0　　10　　20 Kilometers

very odd manner. Zimri, a chariot captain in Israel's army, assassinated King Elah and took control of the palace of Tirzah (1 Kings 16:8-15). Half of the people rebelled and installed Omri ("commander of the army," v. 16 NASB) as king. When Zimri realized his situation was hopeless, he burned the palace down upon himself. Omri became king only after successfully opposing another rebellion in the person of Tibni (vv. 21-22). In his reign of 11 years, Omri's greatest accomplishment was to buy the hill of Samaria and build the capital of Israel there. He was succeeded by his son Ahab. Assyrian sources continued to call Israel "the land of Omri." Micah accused Jerusalem of following Omri's actions and also his son Ahab's. That was grounds for God's destroying Jerusalem (Mic. 6:16). **2.** Officer of the tribe of Issachar under David (1 Chron. 27:18). **3.** Grandson of Benjamin (1 Chron. 7:8). **4.** Grandfather of a member of the tribe of Judah who returned to Jerusalem from exile about 537 B.C.

ON (Ŏn) **1.** Egyptian place-name meaning "city of the pillar," called in Greek Heliopolis or "city of the sun" and in Hebrew Beth-shemesh, "city of the sun" (Jer. 43:13) and Aven. It was the cult center for the worship of the sun-god, Re (Atum). Although not important politically, the city became a vital religious center very early in Egypt's history. Located at Matariyeh about five miles northeast of modern Cairo, the city endured as a cult center until very late. Joseph's Egyptian wife came from On (Gen. 41:45), her father serving as priest in the temple there. Speaking in Egypt, Jeremiah warned that God would destroy On and its worship (Jer. 43:13). Ezekiel or the scribes copying his work substituted Aven, Hebrew for "trouble, deceit," for On in pronouncing judgment on it (Ezek. 30:17). **2.** Personal name meaning "powerful, rich." Member of tribe of Reuben who was one of the leaders challenging authority of Moses (Num. 16:1).

ONAM (Ō´ năm) Personal name meaning "vigorous." **1.** Ancestor of an Edomite subclan (Gen. 36:23; 1 Chron. 1:40). **2.** Ancestor of a family of Jerahmeelites, a subclan of Judah (1 Chron. 2:26,28).

ONAN (Ō´ năn) Personal name meaning "power." A son of Judah and his Canaanite wife, Shuah (Gen. 38:2-8). Following the death of his older brother, Er, Onan was to have married the widow and produced a son who would carry on Er's name. Onan repeatedly failed to complete the responsibilities of the marriage and thus God killed him (38:8-10). See *Levirate Law, Levirate Marriage.*

ONESIMUS (Ō nĕs´ ĭ mŭs) Personal name that may mean "profitable." The slave for whom Paul wrote his letter to Philemon. In his letter Paul pled with Philemon to free the servant because Onesimus had been so helpful to the apostle. Onesimus had robbed his master, escaped, met Paul, and accepted Christ. In sending him back to Philemon, Paul urged the owner to treat the slave as a Christian brother (v. 16).

Later, Onesimus accompanied Thychius in bearing Paul's letter to the church at Colossae (Col. 4:7-9). Two traditions connect Onesimus with a bishop of that name in the second-century church and with Onesiphorus in 2 Tim. 1:16. Neither connection has been proven satisfactorily. See *Philemon, Letter to.*

ONESIPHORUS (Ō nĕ sĭph´ ō rŭs) Personal name meaning "profit bearing." Ephesian Christian praised for his effort to seek out the place of Paul's arrest, his disregard of the shame connected with befriending one in chains, and his past service in Ephesus (2 Tim. 1:16-18). The greeting of and prayer for the household of Onesiphorus (2 Tim. 1:16; 4:19) has suggested to some that he was already dead. All that can be assumed is that Onesiphorus was not at Ephesus.

ONION See *Plants.*

ONLY BEGOTTEN KJV alternate rendering of the Greek adjective *monogenes* (John 1:14,18; 3:16,18; Heb. 11:17; 1 John 4:9). Elsewhere the KJV rendered the term "only [child]" (a son in Luke 7:12; 9:38; a daughter in 8:42). KJV, NKJV, NASB render *monogenes* as "only begotten [son]" when referring to Jesus (cp. NASB margin, "unique, only one of His kind"), but most modern translations (ESV, NAB, NJB, NLT, NRSV, REB, TEV) render the term consistently as "only." NIV, HCSB render the term "One and Only [Son]."

The term *monogenes* is related to Greek *monos,* "only," and *genes,* "offspring, race, kind," suggesting the meaning "only one of its kind, unique" for *monogenes.* Four times the Septuagint (Greek translation of the Hebrew Old Testament) uses *monogenes* to translate Hebrew *yachid,* "only" (Judg. 11:34 ["only child"]; Pss. 22:20 ["my very life"]; 25:16 ["alone"]; 35:17 ["my very life"]). In Gen. 22 referring to Isaac as Abraham's "only son" (vv. 2,12,16) and a few other places, the Septuagint rendered *yachid* with *agapetos,* "beloved."

Although *unicus,* "only," had been used in the Old Latin to translate *monogenes,* Jerome (A.D. 340?-420) replaced it with *unigenitus,* "only begotten," in the Latin Vulgate, from which derives the traditional English rendering. Jerome's concern was to refute the Arian doctrine that claimed the Son was not begotten but made. This led Jerome to impose the terminology of the Nicene Creed (A.D. 325) onto the NT.

Monogenes is used for an only child (Luke 7:12; 8:42; 9:38), but the writer of Hebrews used *monogenes* of Isaac with full knowledge that Isaac was not Abraham's only child (Heb. 11:17-18). Here *monogenes* designates Isaac as Abraham's son in a unique sense, the special child of promise through whom Abraham's descendants would be named.

Believers are rightly called *huioi,* "sons" of God by adoption in Christ (Matt. 5:9; Luke 20:36; Rom. 8:14,19; 9:26; Gal. 3:26; 4:6-7; Rev. 21:7), but John used *monogenes* to designate the unique relationship of eternal Sonship that Jesus has with God. Being fully God and of the same nature as God the Father, Jesus the Son alone can make God's glory known (John 1:14,18; cp. Heb. 1:1-3). As the "One and Only Son," Jesus is the unique gift of God, the giving of God's own self for salvation (John 3:16; 1 John 4:9). Because Jesus is the unique representative of God, rejection of Jesus means rejection of God, resulting in swift condemnation (John 3:18).

Chris Church and E. Ray Clendenen

ONO (Ō´ nō) Name meaning "grief." Benjaminite town about seven miles southeast of Joppa. The town appears in a list of Pharaoh Thutmose III (1490–1436 B.C.). The Mishnah regarded Ono as fortified since the time of Joshua. The city was rebuilt by Shemed, a descendant of Benjamin (1 Chron. 8:12). Ono was home to some of those who returned from exile (Ezra 2:33; Neh. 7:37; 11:35). Ono is identified with Kefr' Ana in the Wadi Musrara. This broad wadi is called the valley of craftsmen (Neh. 11:35) and the Plain of Ono (Neh. 6:2).

ONYCHA (Ŏn´ ĭ ká) Spice probably derived from the closing flaps or the shell of a Red Sea mollusk which was used in the incense reserved for the worship of Yahweh (Exod. 30:34).

ONYX See *Minerals and Metals.*

OPEN FIELDS See *Suburbs.*

OPHEL (Ō´ phĕl) Place-name meaning "swelling," "fat," "bulge," or "mound." It became the proper name of a portion of the hill on which the city of David was built (2 Chron. 27:3). The Ophel was just south of Mount Moriah, on which the temple was constructed, joining the old city with the area of Solomon's palace and temple. The hill has been inhabited since pre-Israelite times by peoples such as the Jebusites from whom David took the site. David and later kings further fortified Ophel. It served as the living quarters for those who rebuilt the ramparts following the exile (Neh. 3:26-27). This may reflect a gradual extension of the name to an ever-larger area. Micah used the Hebrew term to name "the strong hold of the daughter of Zion" (4:8 KJV). Isaiah warned that the "forts" or "hill" (NASB) would be destroyed (32:14). The Hebrew term is used with an uncertain meaning in 2 Kings 5:24 for "tower," "hill," (NASB), "citadel" (NRSV). The term also occurs on the Moabite stone.

OPHIR (O´ phīr) Placename and personal name meaning "dusty." Place famous in the ancient Near East for its trade, especially in gold. Solomon's ships with help from Phoenician sailors brought precious goods from Ophir (1 Kings 9:28; 10:11; cp. 1 Kings 22:48). Gold from Ophir was apparently highly valued, the phrase becoming a stock descriptive term in ancient Near Eastern commercial language (Isa. 13:12; Job 22:24; 28:16; Ps. 45:9). Ophir is mentioned outside the Bible on a piece of broken pottery found at Tell el-Qasileh, north of Tel Aviv on the Plain of Sharon. This inscription reads, "Gold of Ophir for Beth-horon, 30 shekels."

The geographical location of Ophir is disputed among biblical scholars. Three regions have been suggested: India, Arabia, and Africa. Scholars who support an Indian location do so because of the resemblance of the Septuagint (the Greek translation of the OT) form of Ophir to the Egyptian name for India. The available evidence with regard to trade practices indicates that Egyptian, Phoenician, and Greek fleets obtained eastern goods indirectly through ports in South Arabia and East Africa.

Other scholars have suggested that Ophir was located on the Arabian Peninsula. At least five areas have been identified, but the evidence for certainty with regard to any of them is lacking. The strongest argument for an Arabian location is the occurrence of the name Ophir among the names of Arabian tribes, descendants of Joktan, in the Table of Nations in Gen. 10.

Finally, one location in Africa has been suggested: the East African coast in the general vicinity of Somaliland. This location is supported because of its distance from Palestine and the products that are characteristic of Africa that are mentioned in biblical texts (1 Kings 9:28; 10:11,22).

The location of Ophir will remain a matter of uncertainty. A knowledge of ancient trade routes and practices, maritime ventures in the ancient Near East, and economic policies in ancient Israel will be helpful in determining the cite of Ophir. See *Aphek; Commerce; Economic Life.*

James Newell

OPHNI (Ŏph´ nĭ) Name meaning "high place." Town allotted to Benjamin (Josh. 18:24). Ophni was likely in the vicinity of Geba and is perhaps Jifna, three miles northwest of Bethel near the intersection of the road between Jerusalem and Shechem and the road leading from the Plain of Sharon to Bethel.

OPHRAH (Ŏph´ rah) Name meaning "fawn." **1.** Descendant of Judah (1 Chron. 4:14). **2.** City in Benjamin (Josh. 18:23), likely north of Michmash (1 Sam. 13:17-18). This Ophrah is perhaps identical with Ephron (2 Chron. 13:19) and Ephraim (2 Sam. 13:23; John 11:54). Jerome located Ophrah five Roman miles east of Bethel. This site is likely et-Taiyibeh five miles north of Michmash and four

miles northeast of Bethel. **3.** Town associated with the Abiezer clan of Manasseh who settled west of the Jordan (Judg. 6:11,24; 8:32). This Ophrah was the home of Gideon. Suggested sites include et-Taiyibeh south of modern Tulkarm, et-Taiyibeh (Afula) on the Plain of Esdraelon west of Mount Moreh, and Fer-'ata west of Mount Gerazim near Shechem. The latter site is better identified with Tizrah.

ORACLES Communications from God. The term refers both to divine responses to a question asked of God and to pronouncements made by God without His being asked. In one sense oracles were prophecies since they often referred to the future; but oracles sometimes dealt with decisions to be made in the present. Usually in the Bible the communication was from Yahweh, the God of Israel. In times of idol worship, however, Israelites did seek a word or pronouncement from false gods (Hos. 4:12). Many of Israel's neighbors sought oracles from their gods.

Although the word "oracle" is not used very frequently in the OT, oracles were common in that period. This difference occurs because the Hebrew words translated "oracle" may also be translated as "burden," "saying," "word," and such. Translations are not consistent in how they render these Hebrew words. Both the NRSV and the NASB translate the same Hebrew word as "oracle" in Num. 24:3, but it is rendered "declare" in 1 Sam. 2:30. Jeremiah 23:33-34 makes a play on a Hebrew word that may be translated either "burden" or "oracle." The NASB and NIV use "oracle," but the NRSV and KJV use "burden." Moreover, in the KJV the English word "oracle" is used to refer to the holy of holies in the temple.

Concordance study shows the following meaning and use of "oracle." Sometimes "oracle" refers to the whole of a prophetic book (Mal. 1:1 NRSV, NASB, NIV) or a major portion of one (Hab. 1:1 NRSV). In Isaiah several smaller prophecies of judgment or punishment are called "oracles" (13:1 NRSV; 14:28). The NRSV also entitles Zech. 9 and 12 "An Oracle." Specific sayings about God's judgment on Joram (2 Kings 9:25) and Joash (2 Chron. 24:27) are also called oracles. Other examples, although the word "oracle" is not used, include Elijah's word to Ahab (1 Kings 21:17-19) and Elisha's word to Jehoram (2 Kings 3:13-20). On the basis of these kinds of usages, many Bible students understand oracles to be divine words of punishment or judgment. However, Balaam's oracle (Num. 24:3-9) is a blessing. Also references to Ahithophel's counsel (2 Sam. 16:23) and to oracles in Jerusalem which were pleasing but false (Lam. 2:14) show us that prophetic pronouncements were not always negative.

The NT does not reflect quite the same use of oracles or the word "oracle" as does the OT. The early church did have prophets like Agabus (Acts 21:10-11), who expressed God's word regarding what was to come. The word "oracles" in the NT most often refers to the teachings of God in the OT (Acts 7:38; Rom. 3:2). It may refer to Christian teachings too (Heb. 5:12).

Why Were Oracles Given? We must distinguish between oracles that were sought and those that came without any request. The first kind might be called "decision oracles." The second kind will be referred to as "pronouncement oracles." Decision oracles came when people asked God a question or sought His counsel. For example, David needed to know the right time to attack the Philistines, so he asked God. The answers he received were oracles (2 Sam. 5:19,23-24). Saul, the first king of Israel, was chosen through an oracle (1 Sam. 10:20-24). In that case, the communication from God was through the casting of lots. The falling of the lots was considered an oracle from God. Decision oracles, then, were God's response to questions and concerns in the present. They did not condemn sin or predict the future in any specific sense.

Pronouncement oracles were God's word to a situation or a person even though no word from God had been sought (but see comments below on Balaam's oracle). The pronouncement oracles were sometimes brief as when Elijah foretold a drought in Israel (1 Kings 17:1). The message could be long; thus the whole book of Malachi is a pronouncement oracle. This kind of oracle usually told what was going to happen. It also frequently condemned sin. It expressed God's view of present acts or circumstances. In that sense, many of the prophecies in the OT were pronouncement oracles. Because they were God's word, these pronouncements were true, even though they could be changed as in the case of Jonah's pronouncement over Nineveh (Jon. 3:4-9).

Pronouncement oracles were given to produce an effect. People were to hear and to change their ways. With that in mind, the pronouncement oracles against foreign nations form a special group. Many of the writing prophets have pronouncements against (or concerning) nations surrounding Israel (Amos 1; Isa. 13–19; Jer. 46–51). These foreign nations had little chance to hear and heed the word of an Israelite prophet. Other nations had their own gods and their own prophets. Apparently, the pronouncements over foreign nations were intended to have an effect on the people of Israel as well as bring about the events described. At times Israel or Judah heard their name included among foreign nations (e.g., Amos 2:4-16). God cared for the other nations even though they cared little for Him. God's expression of concern by pronouncing judgment (or salvation as in Isa. 19:19-22) was intended to remind Israel of her mission to share God with others. At least these words reminded the hearers of God's international, even universal, power and expectations.

Balaam's oracle (Num. 24) is a special case. Balak sought a pronouncement through the prophet Balaam. Balak's intention was to curse or to pronounce judgment on the Israelites. God did not allow this but gave Balaam an oracle of blessing to pronounce. Balaam's oracle, then, was positive and sought—a positive pronouncement oracle. The seeking of a pronouncement like this may have been more common than we know. Oracles came either in response to human questions or when God wished to make His views known to produce a change.

How Were Oracles Given or Received? Oracles were given through special people. Although anyone could seek a word from God, and many, such as Gideon or Abraham, received an oracle directly, these divine communications usually came through priests, prophets, or prophetesses. These groups seemed to have their own specific ways of receiving oracles. In the earlier period priests were more often sought out to receive a word from God. Later the prophets were more prominent. Of course, for a long period both functioned as intermediaries. One caution about prophets and their pronouncements must be made. Often the prophets were not prophets until they received God's word (consider Amos' experience in Amos 7:14-15). The word came to some reluctantly as in the case of Jeremiah. God's giving of an oracle to a man or woman made them a prophet; for, when the divine word came, the prophet had to speak (Amos 3:8b).

Different methods were used by priests and prophets to receive the two forms of oracles although we should not try to make too rigid a distinction. Decision oracles often came through the use of objects. Examples of such objects include the High Priest's Urim and Thummim and the ephod. Lots, too, were used. See *Ephod; Lots; Urim and Thummim.*

Decision oracles could also come through a person without the use of any objects. David sought the Lord's will at the point of building a temple. His answer came through Nathan, the prophet (2 Sam. 7). In 1 Kings 22 a dramatic conflict arose while the kings of Judah and Israel together sought a decision oracle. No objects were used in this case. The drama came from a true prophet receiving one answer regarding the decision and a large number of false prophets giving a different answer. Prophets did sometimes use music as a means of receiving a decision oracle as did Elisha (2 Kings 3:15). However the exact way music was used is unclear to us.

Frequently the OT gives no indication as to how God communicated His pronouncement oracles to His prophet or priest. Careful reading of the OT shows a variety of methods in use. Audition—the actual hearing of a voice—and visions undoubtedly played a part in the receiving of God's words. We cannot know how much of God's revelation came through the actual ear or eye or how much came through the mind. Balaam spoke when the Spirit came upon him (Num. 24:2-3). He described himself as one whose eye was opened, one who heard God's word and saw His vision. Nahum and Habakkuk wrote of a vision or of seeing their oracles (Nah. 1:1; Hab. 1:1). Through Jeremiah God condemned those prophets who relied on dreams to receive an oracle (Jer. 23:23-32). However, Solomon earlier had received God's pronouncement in a dream (1 Kings 3:5-15). Several times God used scenes that the prophet saw as a means of giving a pronouncement oracle. Some of the scenes were external (Jer. 18:1-12), and some were visionary (Ezek. 37:1-14). The frequent use of sights in pronouncements has led some to believe that the prophets had encounters with God that later they had to interpret and communicate to others.

Regardless of how the oracle came, it was to be expressed to others. This expression seems most often to have been oral. The priest or prophet told the oracle to either the individual or a group. The place may have been in a field or a king's throne room. The pronouncement oracles were often proclaimed in the city, even in a temple (Amos in Bethel and Jeremiah in Jerusalem). Many of the oracles, though, give us no indication of where or when they were spoken.

Oracles which were not simply yes or no seem most often to have been given in poetic form. This is especially true of the pronouncements of the writings of the prophets, which have been preserved for us. Though given orally in the beginning, at some time the pronouncement oracles were written down. They may have been written by disciples of the prophet or by others who heard. They may have been written when they were first told or at a later time. Whatever the case, the oracles were given by God and preserved for us.

How Did People Respond to the Oracles? Again, a distinction should be made between the decision and the pronouncement oracles. Those who were seeking God's help or counsel in a decision-making process undoubtedly acted on what they learned. Others, who heard oracles they had neither sought nor welcomed, may not have been as quick to accept the pronouncement (consider Elijah's words to Ahab, 1 Kings 21:20-24). Most often the response of those who heard or read the oracles of God can be guessed at. Two points should be recognized. First, oracles were remembered long after their pronouncement. When Jehu killed Joram (2 Kings 9:24-25), he had the body taken to Naboth's vineyard in order that an oracle pronounced in Ahab's day might be fulfilled. Second, though we do not know the response of the original hearers, God's pronouncements are still being read and are producing change in people in our day. Thus, the oracles are still functioning. See *Divination and Magic; Inspiration; Priest; Prophet; Spirit.*

Albert F. Bean

ORATION, ORATOR Elaborate speech delivered in a formal and dignified manner and designed to persuade an audience. An orator is one distinguished for skill and persuasiveness as a public speaker. HCSB uses "oration" in Prov. 30:1 while KJV and RSV use the term only once in Acts 12:21; NRSV, HCSB, and

NIV used "public address." Herod Agrippa's oration was praised for the rhetorical skill (12:22), but Herod was judged for failure to give God the glory (12:23). A similar antipathy between skill in oratory and reliance on God's power is often found in Paul (1 Cor. 2:1-2,4,13; 4:19-20).

Paul spoke of "the debater of this age" (1 Cor. 1:20 HCSB). Paul disclaimed "brilliance of speech" and claimed to be "untrained in public speaking" (1 Cor. 2:1; 2 Cor. 11:6) but elsewhere compared his preaching to a skilled builder laying a foundation (1 Cor. 3:10) and spoke of destroying arguments and obstacles to knowledge of God (2 Cor. 10:5). Acts often presents Paul as a persuasive speaker (Acts 18:4,13;19:26; 26:28-29). Festus, in fact, recognized Paul as a man of great learning from his speech (Acts 26:24). Acts also portrays Apollos as an eloquent speaker (Acts 18:24).

The Greeks classified oratory into three modes. (1) The judicial mode, the speech of the law court, concerns guilt and innocence. Examples of judicial rhetoric include the cases involving Paul which were brought before Gallio, Felix, and Festus (Acts 18:12-16; 24:1-21; 25:15,18-19; 26:1-29). (2) The deliberative mode is concerned with the expediency of a course of future action. Examples include the Sanhedrin's debate over Jesus' growing following which culminated in Caiaphas's suggestion that the expedient course was to seek Jesus' death (John 11:47-50) and Demetrius's discourse on what action was necessary to save the business of the silversmiths in Ephesus (Acts 19:23-27). (3) The epideictic (demonstrative) mode concerns praise and blame. Examples include Paul's praise of love (1 Cor. 13) and his censure of the Galatians (Gal. 1:6-9; 3:1-5). Broadly speaking, this mode includes any exhortation to virtuous action (as in James). See *Rhetoric.*   *Chris Church*

ORCHARD Grove of fruit (Neh. 9:25; Eccles. 2:5) or nut trees (Song 6:11). An enclosed orchard is sometimes called a garden or park.

ORDINANCES Christians agree universally that baptism and the Lord's Supper were instituted by Christ and should be observed as "ordinances" or "sacraments" by His followers. Jesus doesn't use "ordinance" in connection with baptism or the Lord's Supper. Some interpreters believe sacrament conveys the concept that God's grace is dispersed almost automatically through participation in the Lord's Supper. Others believe ordinance stresses obedience in doing that which Christ explicitly commanded. Extreme dangers involved in the terms range from superstition to legalism.

The "sacraments" varied in number for a thousand years in the church's early history. Peter Lombard (about A.D. 1150) defended seven, and Thomas Aquinas (about A.D. 1250) argued that all were instituted by Christ. After A.D. 1500 Martin Luther and other Protestant reformers rejected five of these, insisting that only baptism and the Lord's Supper have a biblical basis. Most Protestants agree with their assessment.

Not only the name and number but the practice and meaning of the ordinances have been matters of continuing debate. Who should receive baptism or participate in observing the Lord's Supper? What are essential elements in the observances that ensure validity? What do they accomplish in the life of the individual and the church? Definitive answers acceptable to all Christians have not been forthcoming for these or many other questions, but a survey of biblical evidence should be helpful in reaching some conclusions.

Baptism Biblical references to baptism abound in the Gospels, Acts, Pauline Epistles, and other NT books. John the Baptist preached and practiced a baptism of repentance (Matt. 3:11-12; Mark 1:2-8; Luke 3:2-17). His proclamation looked forward to the coming kingdom. "Repent, because the kingdom of heaven has come near!" (Matt. 3:2 HCSB). Multitudes responded. Confessing their sins, they "were baptized by him in the Jordan River" (Mark 1:5). Apparently not everyone who came received baptism because John challenged some to "produce fruit consistent with repentance" (Matt. 3:8). John regarded his role as a transitional one to prepare the way (Matt. 3:11). The coming One would baptize with the Holy Spirit and with fire.

All the Gospel writers record that Jesus was baptized by John (Matt. 3:13-17; Mark 1:9-11; Luke 3:21-22; John 1:32-34). Matthew noted that John hesitated to baptize Jesus but finally consented "to fulfill all righteousness" (3:15). The identification of Jesus as Messiah followed as the heavens opened, the Spirit descended on Him like a dove, and a voice proclaimed Him the beloved Son. This event inaugurated His public ministry and set the stage for Christian baptism.

The coming age prophesied by John the Baptist arrived in Jesus. Jesus affirmed the ministry of John by submitting to baptism and adopted the rite for His own ministry, giving it new meaning for the new age. The Gospel of John indicates that Jesus gained and baptized more followers than John the Baptist (John 4:1-2) but notes that the actual baptizing was done by His disciples. Jesus referred to His impending death as a baptism (Luke 12:50), linking the meaning of baptism with the cross. These and other scattered references to baptism in the Gospels are evaluated and interpreted in a variety of ways by Bible students, but the total impact of evidence favors the view that Jesus practiced and commanded baptism. Central in this evidence is the Great Commission (Matt. 28:19-20).

The Acts of the Apostles reflects the practice of the earliest Christian churches regarding baptism, referring to baptism far more frequently than any other NT book. At Pentecost after Peter's sermon, "those who accepted His message were baptized, and that day about 3,000 people were added to them" (Acts 2:41 HCSB). They had been exhorted by the apostle to "repent, ... and be baptized, each of you, in the name of Jesus the Messiah for the forgiveness of your sins, and you will receive the gift of the Holy Spirit" (2:38). At other times baptism was "in the name of the Lord Jesus" (8:16; 19:5). Sometimes the gift of the Spirit followed baptism; at other times, the spirit preceded baptism (10:44-48). These were apparently regarded as separate experiences.

Baptism "for" the forgiveness of sins may be translated "on the basis of." Many NT passages stress that forgiveness is based on repentance and trust in what Jesus had done, not on a rite—baptism or otherwise (John 3:16; Acts 16:31). The gospel is for everyone; baptism is for disciples. Salvation is provided by Christ and not through baptism. References to Jesus' blessing little children contain no indications of baptism (Mark 10:13-16), and baptism of "households" described in Acts (16:31-33) should not be utilized to defend a later Christian practice.

If baptism is for believers only and does not convey salvation, then why do Christians universally baptize? It is highly unlikely that the early Christians would have adopted this practice without hesitation unless they were convinced strongly that Christ had intended that they do so. Further reflection upon what Christ had done enabled them to understand baptism in relation to the gospel. No NT writer contributed more to a fuller theological interpretation of baptism than Paul.

Paul (Saul) encountered the living Christ while on a journey to Damascus to persecute Christians. This led to a meeting in Damascus with Ananias, where Paul's sight was restored and where he was also baptized (Acts 9:17-18). What Paul had known about baptism previously must have been largely negative, but from this time baptism became a part of his missionary message and practice among both Jews and Gentiles.

Paul's basic message declared that a right relationship with God is based exclusively on faith in Jesus Christ. "For in it [the gospel] God's righteousness is revealed from faith to faith, just as it is written: 'The righteous will live by faith'" (Rom. 1:17 HCSB). Throughout Romans Paul stressed the primacy of grace over law. Access to this grace is through faith in Jesus Christ (5:2). Where sin (breaking the law) abounds, grace much more abounds. This poses the question (6:1), "What should we say then? Should we continue in sin in order that grace may multiply?" Paul denied emphatically that this is the case, for one dead to sin lives no longer in it. This fact is clearly illustrated in Christian baptism. "Are you unaware that all of us who were baptized into Christ Jesus were baptized into His death? Therefore we were buried with Him by baptism into death, in order that, just as Christ was raised from the dead by the glory of the Father, so we too may walk in a new way of life" (vv. 3-4).

Paul assumed here the universal Christian practice of baptism and a common understanding that it symbolizes death, burial, and resurrection of the believer with Christ. The mode of immersion most clearly preserves this symbolism along with the added emphasis of death to sin and resurrection to a new life in Christ. The stress is on what Christ has done more than what the believer does. Through faith in Him grace is received and makes baptism meaningful.

Paul in 1 Corinthians related unity in Christ to baptism. "For we were all baptized by one Spirit into one body" (12:13). The body of Christ encompasses Jews and Greeks, slave and free, each with a diversity of gifts; but they are bound together in a unity of spirit and symbolized in baptism. Galatians 3:26-29 stresses identification with Christ and unity in Him also, using the figure of putting on clothing. "For as many of you as have been baptized into Christ have put on Christ" (3:27). However, the preceding verse should be noted also. "You are all sons of God through faith in Christ Jesus." For those who belong to Christ, earthly distinctions disappear; and all are one in Christ, heirs according to the promise.

The subjective aspect of baptism for the believer and the objective aspect in Christ are brought together in Col. 2:9-12. In a circumcision not by hands of men but by Christ, the sinful nature is put off. The Colossians have been buried with Christ in baptism and raised with Him through faith in the power of God, who raised Him from the dead. Consequently, they are to set their hearts on things above and put to death the earthly nature (3:1,5).

It is evident from the above and other passages that, for Paul, baptism portrayed the gospel message of the death and resurrection of Christ, affirmed the death of the believer to sin and the rising to walk in newness of life, and signified a union of the believer with Christ and a unity with other believers. The rite itself does not effect these, for they are based on what Christ has done and is doing. Baptism serves as the effective public symbol and declaration for those who trust in Christ as Savior and Lord.

The Lord's Supper The earliest written account of the institution of the Lord's Supper is in 1 Cor. 11:23-26. The Corinthian church was divided, and many of its members were selfish and self-indulgent. In their fellowship meal, therefore, they did not eat "the Lord's Supper" (v. 20), for some overindulged while others were left hungry and humiliated. In response to this abuse, Paul reminded them of the tradition that he had received and passed on to them regarding the Supper of the Lord with His disciples the night He was betrayed.

On the night when He was betrayed,
the Lord Jesus took bread, gave thanks,
broke it, and said, "This is My body,
which is for you. Do this in remembrance of Me."
In the same way He also took the cup, after supper,
and said, "This cup is the new covenant in My blood.

Do this, as often as you drink it, in remembrance of Me." (HCSB)

The terms "eucharist" or "thanksgiving" and "communion" or "fellowship" are often applied to the Supper, and each highlights a significant aspect of this ordinance. "The Lord's Supper" appears more satisfactory for the overall designation, reminding Christians that they share the loaf and cup at His table, not their own.

The account of the Last Supper in Mark 14:22-26 is roughly parallel to Paul's account but with some differences (Matt. 26:26-30; Luke 22:17-20). Both accounts (Mark's and Paul's) record the blessing (thanksgiving) and breaking of bread. Both refer to covenant in connection with the cup as His blood, though only Paul called this a new covenant (Jer. 31:31-34). Both contain a future emphasis, though in different forms. Mark indicated that Jesus said He would not drink again of the fruit of the vine until He drank it anew in the kingdom of God. Paul related that "as often as you eat this bread and drink the cup, you proclaim the Lord's death until He comes" (1 Cor. 11:26 HCSB).

Paul stressed the memorial aspect of the Supper. "Do this in remembrance of Me." Christians were to remember that the body of Christ was broken and His blood shed for them. As in baptism sharing the Supper is a proclamation of the gospel in hope, "until He comes." As the Passover was a symbol of the old covenant, the Lord's Supper is a symbol of the new. Christians remember the sacrifice provided for their deliverance from bondage and look forward to the ultimate consummation in the land of promise, the kingdom of God.

The Supper shared in remembrance of the past and hope for the future is fulfilled in fellowship for the present. Time and again the phrase "in Christ" is repeated in the writings of Paul. Union in Christ and unity with Christians is a recurring theme. Not surprisingly, therefore, one finds these emphases related to the Lord's Supper. "The cup of blessing that we bless, is it not a sharing in the blood of Christ? The bread that we break, is it not a sharing in the body of Christ?" (1 Cor. 10:16 HCSB). Paul was not talking about a repetition of the sacrifice of Christ, but a genuine sharing of fellowship (*koinonia*) with the living Lord. Fellowship in Christ is basic for fellowship in His body (v. 17).

All Christians are unworthy to share the Lord's Supper, but His grace has provided for them in their unworthiness. The tragedy is that some partake in an unworthy manner, not discerning the Lord's body. Paul addressed this matter for the Corinthians and for us, urging that Christians examine themselves and respect the corporate body of Christ as they share the Supper of the Lord.

Conclusions Christ instituted both ordinances. Both portray publicly and visibly the essential elements of the gospel, and both symbolize realities involving divine activity and human experience. Baptism is a once-for-all experience, but the Lord's Supper is repeated many times. Baptism follows closely one's profession of faith in Christ and actually in the NT was the declaration of that faith. The Lord's Supper declares one's continuing dependence upon the Christ proclaimed in the gospel, who died, was buried, and rose for our salvation.

The significance of baptism and the Lord's Supper will increase as churches and people commit themselves anew to the Christ proclaimed by the gospel. This commitment will recognize that, in observing the ordinances, they are presenting in a unique way the gospel of Christ and committing themselves fully to its demands. Calling upon Christ the Savior and Lord to provide strength and leadership for the people of God individually and collectively, believers will leave the observance of the ordinances to give faithful service in His world.

Claude L. Howe, Jr.

ORDINATION, ORDAIN Appointing, consecrating, or commissioning of persons for special service to the Lord and His people.

English Translations KJV uses "ordain" to translate over 20 Hebrew and Greek words. These words relate to a variety of ideas such as God's work and providence; the appointment to an office or a task; and the establishment of laws, principles, places, or observances. While all these ideas do not relate directly to ordination, they contain basic concepts of divine purpose, choice, appointment, and institution that undergird the practice.

Old Testament Four primary examples provide OT precedents for ordination: the consecration of Aaron and his sons as priests to God (Exod. 28–29; Lev. 8–9), the dedication of the Levites as servants of God (Num. 8:5-14), the appointment of 70 elders to assist Moses (Num. 11:16-17,24-25), and the commissioning of Joshua as

Moses' successor (Num. 27:18-23). The variety in these examples helps explain the various contemporary understandings of ordination.

The ordination of the priest was based on God's choice of Aaron and his sons "to minister as priest to Me" (Exod. 28:1 NASB). The ordination itself was a seven-day act of consecration accompanied by washing, donning vestments, anointing, sacrificing, and eating (Lev. 8). The basic Hebrew term for "ordination" literally means to "fill the hands" and may refer to filling the priest's hands with the offerings (Lev. 8:27). The ordination of the Levites also was based on God's choice of them "to serve the tent of meeting" (Num. 8:15 NASB). The ordination involved cleansing, presentation before the Lord, laying on of hands by the whole congregation, offering the Levites as a wave offering, and sacrifices.

The appointment of the 70 to assist Moses in bearing "the burden of the people" (Num. 11:17) was at God's initiative, but Moses selected persons who were known as elders and leaders. Their ordination involved standing with Moses and receiving from the Lord the Spirit who previously was upon Moses. When the Spirit rested on them, they prophesied (11:25). The ordination of a successor for Moses was at Moses' initiative (27:15-17), but Joshua was chosen by God because he was "a man in whom is the Spirit" (v. 18). Joshua's ordination involved standing before the priest and the entire congregation and being commissioned in their sight. Moses laid his hand on Joshua, and Moses placed some of his authority on Joshua, including the role of inquiring of the judgment of the Urim.

New Testament The NT practice of ordination is generally associated with the laying on of hands, but other appointments, consecrations, and commissionings must be considered even if they lack formal investiture.

Jesus' appointment of the Twelve "that they might be with Him and that He might send them out to preach" (Mark 3:14 HCSB) was based on prayer (Luke 6:12), His choice and call (Mark 3:13), and the apostles' responses. When He sent them out, He gave them "power and authority" (Luke 9:1) but no formal ordination. The same was true of the 70 (Luke 10:1). The Great Commission was given solely on the basis of Jesus' "power" (KJV) (or authority, Matt. 28:18). The Holy Spirit was given directly without the laying on of hands (John 20:22). The disciples were chosen and appointed by Jesus for their task of bearing fruit (John 15:16).

Several other NT passages describe appointments without reference to ordination. Having been chosen by lot, Matthias was installed as one of the Twelve (Acts 1:21-26). Barnabas and Paul appointed elders "in every church" after prayer and fasting (14:23). Titus was left in Crete to perform the same function (Titus 1:5).

Several passages describe ordination accompanied by the laying on of hands. Acts 6:1-6 tells of the appointment of seven men to the daily ministry to widows in the Jerusalem congregation. Barnabas and Paul were set apart for the work to which God had called them (Acts 13:1-3). Timothy was chosen by prophecy, recommended by Paul, and ordained to his task by the laying on of hands by Paul and the assembly of elders (1 Tim. 4:14; 2 Tim. 1:6). References to laying on of hands in 1 Tim. 5:22 and Heb. 6:2 likely deal with other practices than ordination. See *Laying on of Hands; Minister, Ministry.*

Michael Fink

OREB AND ZEEB (Ō´ rĕb and Zē´ ĕb) Personal names meaning "raven" and "wolf." Two Midianite princes captured and executed by the Ephraimites following Gideon's rout of their forces (Judg. 7:24–8:3). The Midianite nobles gave their names to the sites of their deaths, the rock of Oreb near Beth-barah on the Jordan and the winepress of Zeeb. Israel's deliverance from Midian became proverbial for God's deliverance of His people (Ps. 83:11; Isa. 9:4; 10:26).

OREN (Ō´ rĕn) Personal name meaning "cedar." Member of the Jerahmeelite clan of Judah (1 Chron. 2:25).

ORGAN KJV term for a musical instrument which modern translations identify as a pipe or shrill flute (Gen. 4:21; Job 21:12; 30:31; Ps. 150:4). At the time of the KJV translation, "organ" designated any wind instrument. The modern pipe organ was not known in the biblical period, though primitive organs were used in the Jerusalem temple after 100 B.C. and provided music for Roman games and combats. The organ came into the church after A.D. 600.

ORION Constellation bearing the name of a giant Greek hunter who, according to myth,

was bound and placed in the heavens. Job 38:31 perhaps alludes to this myth. God is consistently portrayed as the creator of the Orion constellation (Job 9:9; Amos 5:8). The plural of the Hebrew term for Orion is rendered constellations at Isa. 13:10.

ORNAMENT See *Amulets; Anklet; Breastpiece; Cloth, Clothing; Jewels, Jewelry; Necklace.*

ORNAMENT OF THE LEGS (KJV, Isa. 3:20) See *Anklet.*

ORNAN (Ôr´ năn) Personal name meaning "prince." Alternate name of Araunah (1 Chron. 21:15,18,20-25,28; 2 Chron. 3:1). See *Araunah.*

ORONTES RIVER (Ō rŏn´ tĕz) Principal river of Syria which originates east of the Lebanon ridge (modern Asi [Turkish], Nahr el-'Asi [Arabic]), rises near Heliopolis (Bealbek) in the Beka Valley of Lebanon, and flows north some 250 miles through Syria and Turkey before turning southwest into the Mediterranean south of Antioch-on-the-Orontes (Antakya) to reach the coast just south of ancient Seleucia, the seaport of Antioch. This river is never actually mentioned in the Bible but was famous for its association with Antioch, which owed to the river the fertility of its district. Cities of the Orontes Valley include Antioch (Acts 11:19; 13:1), Hamath (2 Sam. 8:9; 2 Kings 17:24; 2 Chron. 8:4; Isa. 11:11), Qarqar, where King Ahab of Israel joined a coalition of Syrian kings warring against Shalmaneser III, and Riblah (2 Kings 23:33; 25:6,21). Nahr el-'Asi (rebellious river) is the modern name of the Orontes. See *Antioch; Rivers and Waterways.*   *Colin J. Hemer*

ORPAH (Ôr´ pah) Personal name meaning "neck," "girl with a full mane," or "rain cloud." Daughter-in-law of Naomi who returned to her people and gods after Naomi twice requested that she go (Ruth 1:4-15). See *Ruth.*

ORPHANS See *Fatherless.*

ORYX (Ôr´ ĭks) Large, straight-horned antelope. See *Antelope.*

OSEE (Ō´ zē) Greek form of Hosea used by KJV (Rom. 9:25).

OSHEA (Ō´ shē å) KJV alternate form of Hoshea (Joshua) at Num. 13:8,16.

OSNAPPAR (Ŏs nap´ pər) or **OSNAPPER** Assyrian king who repopulated Samaria with foreigners following its capture in 722 B.C. (Ezra 4:10). Osnappar is most often identified with Ashurbanipal. KJV used the form Asnapper. See *Assyria.*

OSPRAY, OSPREY Large, flesh-eating hawk included in lists of unclean birds (Lev. 11:13; Deut. 14:12 KJV, NRSV). The identity of the bird is questionable. Other possibilities include: black vulture (NASB margin, NIV); black eagle, (KJV margin); bearded vulture (REB); and buzzard (NASB).

OSSIFRAGE English applies "ossifrage" to three birds: the bearded vulture, the osprey, and the giant petrel. The KJV included the ossifrage among the unclean birds (Lev. 11:13; Deut. 14:12). Other translations identify the bird as a black vulture (REB) or vulture (NASB, NIV, NRSV).

OSTIA (Ŏs´ tē å) Roman city at the mouth of the Tiber about 15 miles from Rome which, following construction of an artificial harbor by Claudius (A.D. 41–54), served as the principle harbor for Rome. Before this construction silt prohibited seagoing vessels from using the port. Such vessels were forced to use the port of Puteoli about 138 miles to the south of Rome (Acts 28:13).

OSTRACA (Ŏs´ trå ca) Potsherds (pottery fragments), especially fragments used as an inexpensive writing material. See *Archaeology and Biblical Study; Pottery; Writing.*

OSTRICH The ostrich, the largest of birds, is a swift, flightless fowl. One passage in Job (39:13-18) describes some of the characteristic habits of the ostrich. The female lays her eggs in the sand. The male does most of the incubating, mainly at night. Unhatched eggs serve as food for the young. Although the parent bird leaves the nest when it senses danger, this diversionary tactic actually is a protective measure. However, such habits may have cre-

ated the impression that the ostrich was indifferent to its young (Lam. 4:3). The ostrich is listed as unclean (Lev. 11:16; Deut. 14:15), probably because of its eating habits.

Janice Meier

OTHNI (Ŏth´ nī) Personal name, perhaps meaning "force" or "power." Levitic gatekeeper (1 Chron. 26:7).

OTHNIEL (Ŏth´ nĭ ĕl) Name meaning "God is powerful." **1.** First of Israel's judges or deliverers. Othniel received Caleb's daughter Achsah as his wife as a reward for his capture of Kiriath-sepher (Debir) (Josh. 15:15-19; Judg. 1:11-15). As the first judge Othniel rescued Israel from the Mesopotamian king Cushan-rishathaim (Judg. 3:7-11). Othniel was the only judge to come from the southern tribes. See *Judges, Book of.* **2.** Clan name associated with a resident of Netophah (1 Chron. 27:15).

OUCHES KJV term for (filigree) settings for precious stones (Exod. 28:11,13-14,25; 39:6,13,16, 18). See *Jewels, Jewelry; High Priest.*

OUTCAST Scripture never employs outcast in the now common sense of one rejected by society. Outcast rather designates one banished from court (2 Sam. 14:14 NRSV) or more often dispersed persons, exiles, or refugees (Deut. 30:4; Ps. 147:2: Isa. 11:12; 56:8; Jer. 30:17; Mic. 4:6-7). "Outcasts" often has the technical sense of Diaspora. NASB employs outcast for one excommunicated from the synagogue (John 16:2).

OUTER SPACE The Bible teaches that outer space was created by God (Gen. 1:1,14-19; Job 9:7-10; 26:7; Pss. 8:3; 136:7-9; Amos 5:8). God made the sun, moon, and stars to provide light for the earth and indicate the passage of time through seasons, days, and years (Gen. 1:14-15).

Long before recorded history people began to worship the heavenly bodies. The deities of the sun, moon, and stars held prominent places in the pantheons of the ancient Near East. The Babylonians developed a sophisticated system of causation based in part on the movement of the stars. These ideas penetrated ancient Israel (e.g., 2 Kings 23:5; Jer. 8:1-2) where they were roundly condemned as idolatrous by the writers of the Bible (Deut. 4:19; 17:3; Job 31:26-28; Isa. 47:13; Jer. 10:2).

The biblical poets were awestruck by the vastness and mystery of outer space. They often referred to the sun, moon, and stars as witnesses to the power of God and permanence of His work. For instance, Job recognized that the earth "hangs on nothing" (Job 26:7) and that the movements of the constellations were known only to God (Job 38:31-33). The psalmist likened the permanence of the Davidic monarchy to the sun and moon (Pss. 72:5; 89:37). It is only at the end of time, when the creation process will be reversed by the day of the Lord, that the sun, moon, and stars will be darkened (Isa. 13:10; Joel 2:31; Matt. 24:29; Rev. 6:12-13; 8:12).

The Bible gives no indication that there is life on other planets, and strongly supports the uniqueness of life on Earth.

OUTER TUNIC (Gk. *chiton*) See *Cloth, Clothing.*

OUTLANDISH KJV term meaning "foreign" (Neh. 13:26).

OVEN Device used for baking food, especially bread (Lev. 2:4; Exod. 8:3). Ancient ovens were cylindrical structures of burnt clay two to three feet in diameter. A fire was built on pebbles in the oven bottom. Bread was baked by either placing the dough against the oven walls or upon the heated pebbles. Dried grass (Matt. 6:30; Luke 12:28), thorny shrubs, and animal dung were often used as fuels. See *Cooking and Heating.*

OVENS, TOWER OF THE See *Furnaces, Tower of.*

OVERLIVE KJV term meaning "outlive" (Josh. 24:31).

OVERPASS KJV term (Jer. 5:28) meaning either "surpass" previous limits or bounds (NASB, NIV, RSV, TEV) or else "pass over" in the sense of overlook (NASB margin, REB).

OVERRUN Term meaning "outrun" (2 Sam. 18:23; Ps. 105:30 HCSB).

Large domed oven.

OVERSEER Superintendent or supervisor. Various translations use overseer for a variety of secular positions (household manager, Gen. 39:4-5; prime minister, Gen. 41:34; foreman or supervisor, 2 Chron. 2:18) and ecclesiastical (Acts 20:28) offices. HCSB, NASB, and NIV employ overseer for the bishop of the KJV, NRSV (Phil. 1:1; 1 Tim. 3:1-2; Titus 1:7).

OVERSHADOW To cast a shadow over; to envelop. The cloud which overshadowed the mount of transfiguration (Matt. 17:5; Mark 9:7; Luke 9:34) recalls the cloud "overshadowing" the tabernacle (Exod. 40:35 according to earliest Gk. translation) when it was filled with God's glory. Luke 1:35 describes the mystery of the virginal conception in terms of Mary's being "overshadowed" by the power of God. Luke's picture does not involve sexual intercourse of a god and human woman as was common in pagan myth. The Spirit is Creator, not consort (Gen. 1:2; Ps. 33:6; and especially Job 33:4; Ps. 104:30 where the Spirit's roll is life-giver). The Spirit which brought power and life to the church at Pentecost (Acts 1:8) and is the source of resurrection life (Ezek. 37:5-14) brought life to Mary's womb.

OWL Bird of prey belonging to the order *Strigiformes* which are generally nocturnal. Hebrew terms for various bird species cannot be identified precisely with English terms. NRSV mentions two species of owl, the little and great owls (Deut. 14:16). KJV mentions these as well as the owl of the desert (Deut. 14:16; Ps. 102:6) and screech owl (Isa. 34:14). NIV mentions six species: the horned owl; screech owl (Lev. 11:16; Deut. 14:15); little owl (Lev. 11:17; Deut. 14:16); great owl; white owl; and desert owl (Lev. 11:18; Deut. 14:16). Owls, like other predatory birds, were classed as unclean. Owls nesting in ruins are a common image of desolation (Ps. 102:6; Isa. 34:11,15; Zeph. 2:14).

OWNERSHIP Possession of property. Two general principles guided Israelite laws of ownership: (1) all things ultimately belong to God, and (2) land possession is purely a business matter. After the division of the land among the 12 tribes, individual plots were given to family groups or clans. If the occasion demanded it, the land could be redivided at a later time. Land sales and transfers were recorded by scribes on leather or papyrus scrolls, on clay tablets, or in the presence of witnesses with the symbolic removal of a sandal (Ruth 4:7) or the stepping onto the land by the new owner. Land passed from father to son but could be given to a daughter. Private lands ultimately reverted to the king if not used for several years (2 Kings 8). The law of the kinsman-redeemer (Lev. 25:25) was developed to assure that land belonging to a particular clan did not pass out of its hands despite the death of an heirless husband. The next-of-kin was required to purchase the land and provide an heir to the name of the deceased. The impoverished widow would not be forced to sell her land to outsiders, thus diminishing the tribal area of the clan.

While it is true that the king did purchase lands from his subjects, private lands were subject to seizure by the ruler. Royal land was given as revenue-producing gifts by the ruler to members of his family or men who gained his favor. Often the land was tenant farmed for the king who continued to hold the ultimate right of its disposal. When economic times were difficult, kings exchanged their lands for other services, such as Solomon's gift of land to Hiram of Tyre for gold and laborers in the building of the temple (1 Kings 9:11). Priestly families and local shrines also owned land, especially that surrounding the Levitical cities, where the priests farmed their own fields (Josh. 21). With the consolidation of worship in the Jerusalem temple, many of the priestly lands were sold.

Private ownership continued in much the same fashion during the NT era. Bills of sale and land deeds written on papyrus scrolls from this period have been discovered, attesting to the exchange of private lands. Often the sale of private land was subject to royal approval. The Romans oversaw the control of lands in Palestine, requiring heavy taxes from owners. The early Christian community existed through the generosity of those members who sold many of their possessions to help poorer believers. See *Economic Life.*   *David Maltzberger*

OX Large, often domesticated, bovine. In the OT it was extremely valuable as a work animal. Important in the economy of Israel, oxen were essential for farm work. They were often yoked in pairs to do farm work and were used to transport burdens. Permitted as food, they were also offered as sacrifices (Deut. 14:4-6; Lev. 17:3-4).

The wild ox was a large beast believed to be the ancestor of domestic cattle. It symbolized ferocious strength. The Hebrew word translated "unicorn" in Num. 23:22 (KJV) has been identified as the word for wild ox (NASB, NIV, NRSV; cp. Pss. 22:21; 92:10). See *Cattle.*

OXGOAD See *Goad.*

OZEM (Ō´ zĕm) Personal name meaning "irritable" or "strength." **1.** Sixth son of Jesse (1 Chron. 2:15). **2.** Fourth son of Jerahmeel (1 Chron. 2:25).

OZIAS (Ō zī´ ás) Greek form of Uzziah used by KJV (Matt. 1:8-9).

OZNI (Ŏz´ nī) Personal name meaning "my hearing" or "attentive." Ancestor of a Gadite family, the Oznites (Num. 26:16).

OZNITES (Ŏz´ nīts) See *Ozni.*

PQ

The lush green fronds of a date palm tree in Haifa, Israel.

PAARAI (Pā´ á·rī) Personal name meaning "revelation of Yahweh." One of David's 30 elite warriors (2 Sam. 23:35) designated an Arbite, a resident of Arbah (Josh. 15:52). The parallel list has the name "Naarai" (1 Chron. 11:37).

PADAN-ARAM (KJV) or **PADDAN-ARAM** (Pād dan-ā´ răm) Place-name, perhaps meaning "way of Syria," "field of Syria," or "plow of Syria." The land from where Abraham journeyed to Canaan. One of the principal cities was Haran. Later Abraham sent his steward to Paddan-aram (Gen. 25:20) to seek a wife for Isaac (Gen. 24:1-9), and Jacob fled there and married into Laban and Rebekah's branch of the patriarchal family (28:2-5). It may be modern Tell Feddan near Carrhae. Hosea 12:13 calls it the field or country of Syria.

PADDLE KJV term for a digging tool (Deut. 23:13). Modern translations render the term as something to dig with (NIV), spade (NASB), stick (RSV, TEV), or trowel (NRSV, REB). The Israelites were required to respect God's presence in their camp by burying their excrement.

PADON (Pā´ dŏn) Personal name meaning "redemption." Ancestor of a family of postexilic temple servants (Ezra 2:44; Neh. 7:47). See *Nethinim*.

PAGANS Those who worship a god or gods other than the living God to whom the Bible witnesses. NIV, REB, and RSV sometimes use pagans as the translation of the Greek *ethnoi* (1 Cor. 5:1; 10:20), which is generally translated "Gentiles" (so KJV, NASB). In English,

The altar of Zeus, the highest god in the Greek pantheon.

Gentile relates to ethnic background while pagan refers to religious affiliation. See *Gentiles; Gods, Pagan.*

PAGIEL (Pā´ gĭ ĕl) Personal name meaning "fortune of God." "God is entreated," or "God meets." Wilderness leader of the tribe of Asher (Num. 1:13; 2:27; 7:72,77; 10:26).

PAHATH-MOAB (Pā hăth-Mō´ ăb) Title meaning "governor of Moab." A family of returned exiles likely descended from the Hebrew governor of Moab in the time of David (2 Sam. 8:2; Ezra 2:6; 8:4; 10:30; Neh. 7:11; 10:14).

PAI (Pā´ ī) Place-name meaning "groaning." Alternate form of Pau used at 1 Chron. 1:50 (cp. Gen. 36:39). See *Pau.*

PAINT Mixture of pigment and liquid used to apply a closely adhering, colorful coat to a surface. Most scriptural references are to painting the eyes. The sole exception is Jer. 22:14 which refers to Jehoiakim's plans to paint his palace vermilion. The prohibition of making images (Exod. 20:4) perhaps curtailed development of painting in Israel. Archaeologists have uncovered numerous tomb and palace paintings in both Egypt and Mesopotamia. See *Cosmetics.*

PALACE Residence of a monarch or noble. KJV often used "palace" in passages where modern translations have substituted a term more appropriate to the context. Terms designating a strongly fortified section of the king's residence often replaced "palace": citadel (1 Kings 16:18; 2 Kings 15:25); tower (Ps. 122:7 NRSV; Song 8:9 NIV); stronghold (Isa. 34:13; Amos 1:4 NRSV); fortress (Amos 1:4 NIV); battlement (Song 8:9 NRSV; parapet, REB). At Amos 4:3 modern translations replace "palace" with the proper name Harmon. The KJV uses "palace" twice for the Greek *aule* (Matt. 26:3; Luke 11:21). The crowd in Matt. 26 gathered in the courtyard of the high priest's residence. Modern translations rendered *aule* variously: palace (NIV, NRSV, TEV); court (NASB); house (REB). The strong man of Luke 11 guarded the open courtyard of his home. Modern translations are again divided on the translation of *aule*: castle (NRSV); homestead (NASB); house

(NIV, TEV); palace (REB, RSV). The KJV also used "palace" to translate the Latin loanword *praetorium* (Phil. 1:13). Modern translations replaced "palace" with "praetorian guard" (NASB, RSV) or an equivalent expression (imperial guard, NRSV, REB; palace guard, NIV, TEV).

Palaces served not only as royal residences but as a means of displaying the wealth of a kingdom. Esther 1:6-7 describes the palace of King Ahasuerus (Xerxes I) of Assyria which featured fine curtains, marble pillars, and ornate mosaic floors. David's palace was built by workers sent by King Hiram of Tyre and featured cedar woodwork (2 Sam. 5:11). The palace must have been large to accommodate David's growing number of wives, concubines, and children (2 Sam. 3:2-5; 5:13-16), as well as store booty, such as the golden shields which David seized (2 Sam. 8:7). Solomon's palace complex required 13 years for completion (1 Kings 7:1). His palace complex included the "house of the forest of Lebanon" (7:2), an immense hall featuring 45 cedar pillars and Solomon's golden shields (10:16-18), the "porch of pillars" (7:6), the "Hall of Justice" (7:7

An example of a wall fresco, a major art form of the Roman period that utilized types of paints.

NRSV), featuring an ivory and gold throne (10:18-20), and private dwellings for both king and Pharaoh's daughter (7:8). Builders used costly hewn stone and cedar throughout the palace (7:9,11). Portions of this palace complex survived the destruction of Jerusalem by the Babylonians (Neh. 3:25). King Ahab's palace in Samaria was decorated with ivory panels, some of which have been recovered by archaeologists (1 Kings 22:39).

The prophets, particularly Amos, condemned the rich for building palaces at the expense of the poor. Amos' announcements of doom refer to summer and winter residences, ivory furniture and palaces, and great houses of hewn stone (Amos 3:15; 5:11; 6:4,11). Jeremiah offered a similar critique of Jeroboam's building program in Jerusalem (22:13-15)

Chris Church

PALAL (Pā´ lăl) Personal name meaning "God comes to judge." One of those assisting in Nehemiah's repair of the wall (Neh. 3:25).

PALANQUIN (Păl ən kēn´) REB, RSV term for an enclosed seat or couch carried on servants' shoulders (Song 3:9). Other translations include: carriage (NIV), chariot (KJV), and sedan chair (NASB).

PALESTINA (Păl əs tī´ nà) KJV alternate name for Philistia (Exod. 15:14; Isa. 14:29,31). See *Palestine; Philistines*.

PALESTINE (Păl´ ĕs tīne) Geographical designation for the land of the Bible, particularly land west of Jordan River that God allotted to Israel for an inheritance (Josh. 13–19). Various terms have been used to designate that small but significant land known in the early OT era as "Canaan" (Gen. 12:5) and often referred to as the promised land (Deut. 9:28). The area was designated "Israel" and "Judah" at the division of the kingdoms in 931 B.C. By NT times the land had been divided into provincial designations: Judea, Samaria, Galilee, and others. Generally the region was considered to be a part of Syria.

Palestine is derived from the name *Pelishtim* or "Philistines." The Greeks, familiar primarily with the coastal area, applied the name "Palestine" to the entire southeastern Mediterranean region. Although the word "Palestine" (or "Palestina") is found four times in the KJV

(Exod. 15:14; Isa. 14:29,31; Joel 3:4), these are references to the territory of the Philistines and so properly designate only the strip of coastland occupied by that people. See *Philistines.*

For the purposes of this article, Palestine extends to the north 10 to 15 miles beyond the ancient site of Dan and NT Caesarea Philippi into the gorges and mountains just south of Mount Hermon. To the east it extends to the Arabian steppe. To the south Palestine extends 10 to 15 miles beyond Beer-sheba. On the west is the Mediterranean Sea. It therefore includes western Palestine—between the Jordan River and the Sea, and eastern Palestine—between the Jordan and the Arabian steppe.

Palestine west of the Jordan covers approximately 6,000 square miles. East of the Jordan an area of about 4,000 square miles was included in the land of Israel.

Geographical Features Palestine is naturally divided into four narrow strips of land running north and south.

Coastal Plain This very fertile plain begins 10 to 12 miles south of Gaza, just north of the Egyptian border, and stretches northward to the Sidon-Tyre area. Usually it is divided into three sections: the Plain of Philistia, roughly from south of Gaza to Joppa (Tel Aviv); the Plain of Sharon, from Joppa north to the promontory of the Carmel chain; and the detached Plain of Acco, which merges with the Plain of Esdraelon, the historic gateway inland and to the regions to the north and east. The Plain of Sharon varies from a width of a few hundred yards just south of Carmel to more than 12 miles wide near Joppa. Covered with fertile alluvial soil and well watered by springs, the area was once covered with extensive forests.

Further south is the Plain of Philistia. Here were located the Philistine strongholds of Gaza, Ashkelon, Ashdod, Ekron, and Gath. Salt marshes—the Serbonian bog—located at the southern end of the Philistine plain have been known as breeding grounds of disease.

Forming the southwestern end of the Fertile Crescent, the coastal plain has been the highway of commerce and conquest for centuries. This was the route followed by the Hittites and the Egyptians, by Cambyses, Alexander, Pompey, and Napoleon.

The coastal plain lacked an outstanding natural harbor. Joppa had roughly semicircular reefs that formed a breakwater 300 to 400 feet offshore and, consequently, was used as a port. Entrance from the south was impossible, however, and the north entrance was shallow and treacherous.

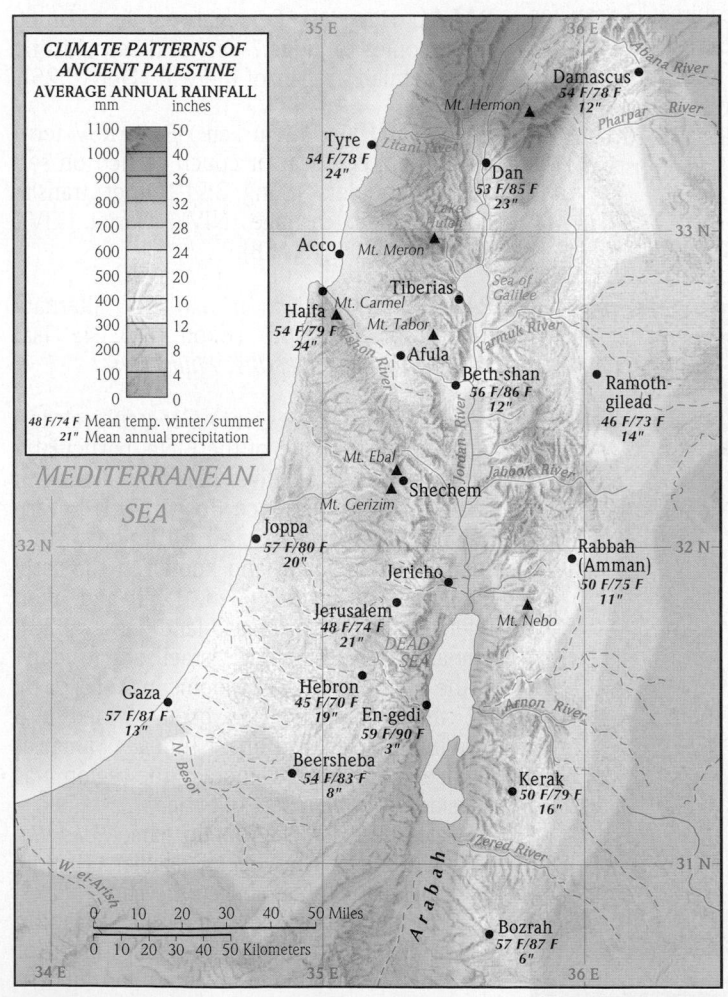

CLIMATE PATTERNS OF ANCIENT PALESTINE
AVERAGE ANNUAL RAINFALL

mm	inches
1100	50
1000	40
900	36
800	32
700	28
600	24
500	20
400	16
300	12
200	8
100	4
0	0

48 F/74 F Mean temp. winter/summer
21" Mean annual precipitation

Herod the Great developed Caesarea Maritima into an artificial port of considerable efficiency. See *Caesarea*.

Central Hill Country The second strip of land is the mountainous ridge beginning just north of Beer-sheba and extending through all of Judea and Samaria into upper Galilee. Actually, the rugged terrain running the length of the land is a continuation of the more clearly defined Lebanon Mountains to the north. The only major break in the mountain range is the Plain of Esdraelon also called the Valley of Jezreel. Three divisions are evident: Judea, Samaria, and Galilee.

Judea Rising from the parched Negev (Negev means "parched" or "dry land"), the Judean hills reach their highest point, 3,370 feet, near Hebron. Jerusalem is located in the Judean hills at an elevation of 2,600 feet. The eastern slopes form the barren and rugged "wilderness of Judea," then fall abruptly to the floor of the Jordan Valley. The wilderness is treeless and waterless. Deep gorges and canyons cut into the soft sedimentary formations. See *Negeb or Negev*.

The western foothills of Judea are called the "Shephelah," meaning "valley" or "lowland." The name has been inaccurately applied to the Plain of Philistia, but the towns assigned by the OT to the Shephelah are all situated in the low hills rather than the plain. The Shephelah is a belt of gently rolling hills between 500 and 1,000 feet in height. Five valleys divide the region, from the Wadi el Hesy in the south to the Valley of Ajalon in northern Judea. These passes have witnessed the conflicts between Saul and the Philistines, the Maccabees and the Syrians, the Jews and the Romans, Richard I and Saladin. Here Samson grew to manhood. Here David encountered Goliath.

The Shephelah had great military importance. It formed a buffer between Judea and the enemies of the Hebrew people—Philistines, Egyptians, Syrians. Formerly heavily wooded with sycamores, the region served to impede an attack from the west.

Samaria The hills of Samaria descend gently from the Judean mountains, averaging just over 1,000 feet in height. Several notable mountains such as Gerizim (2,890 feet), Ebal (3,083), and Gilboa (1,640 feet) dominate the area. This land of mountains is marked by wide and fertile valleys. Here the majority of the people lived during the OT era, and here significant events of Hebrew history took place. The openness of Samaria is a prominent feature of the land, making movement much easier than in Judea and thus inviting armies and chariots from the north.

The valley between Mount Ebal and Mount Gerizim was a central location, apparently providing the perfect point from which a united nation could have been governed. Roads went in all directions—to Galilee, the Jordan Valley, south to Jerusalem. Here Shechem was located, important to the patriarchs and in the day of the judges. Shechem, however, had no natural defenses and was consequently rejected by the kings of Israel as their capital.

From this region the main range of mountains sends out an arm to the northwest that reaches the coast at Mount Carmel. Carmel reaches a height of only 1,791 feet, but it seems loftier because it rises directly from the coastline. It receives abundant rainfall, an average of 28 to 32 inches per year, and consequently is rather densely covered with vegetation, including some woodland.

The Carmel range divides the Plain of Sharon from the narrow coastal plain of Phoenicia. It forms the southern side of the Plain of Esdraelon, with the ancient fortress of Megiddo standing as one of its key cities. This natural barrier caused the passes in the Carmel chain to achieve unusual importance, lying as it does on the historic route between Egypt and Mesopotamia.

Galilee North of the Plain of Esdraelon and south of the Leontes River lies the region called Galilee. The name comes from the Hebrew *galil*, meaning literally "circle" or "ring." In Isa. 9:1 the prophet refers to it as "Galilee of the Gentiles." The tribes of Asher, Naphtali, and Zebulun were assigned to this area. There is evidence of mixed population and racial variety from early times. In the day of Jesus, many Gentiles were in Galilee.

The region is divided into upper Galilee and lower Galilee. Lower Galilee is a land of limestone hills and fertile valleys. Most of the region is approximately 500 feet above sea level—but with mountains like Tabor reaching a height of 1,929 feet. Grain, grass, olives, and grapes were abundant. Fish, oil, and wine were common exports. Several major international roads crossed the area, and caravan traffic from Damascus through Capernaum to the south was heavy. Josephus spoke of Galilee as "universally rich and fruitful."

Some of the most important cities of Galilee were on the shore of the Sea of Galilee. Those on the northwestern shore, such as Capernaum, were more Jewish than those to the south. Tiberias, built in A.D. 25 by Herod Antipas and named after the reigning Caesar, became the capital and the most important city during the NT era.

The terrain of upper Galilee is much more rugged than lower Galilee, an area of deeply fissured and roughly eroded tableland with high peaks and many wadis. The highest peak is Mount Meron at 3,963 feet, the highest point in Palestine. The basic rock is limestone, in the eastern sections often covered with volcanic rock. In the east Galilee drops off abruptly to the Jordan, while farther south, near the Sea of Galilee, the slopes become much more gradual and gentle.

Jordan Rift Valley As a result of crustal faulting, the hills of Palestine drop into the deepest split on the surface of the earth. The fault is part of a system that extends north to form the valley between the Lebanon and the Anti-Lebanon chains, also extending south to form the Dead Sea, the dry Arabah Valley, the Gulf of Aqaba, and, eventually, the chain of lakes on the African continent.

The Jordan River has its source in several springs, primarily on the western and southern slopes of Mount Hermon. Several small streams come together near Dan, then flow into shallow, reedy Lake Hula, (Huleh). From its sources to Hula the Jordan drops somewhat less than 1,000 feet over a distance of 12 miles, entering Lake Hula at 230 feet above sea level (not seven feet, as reported by some older publications). In recent years the Jordan bed has been straightened after it leaves Hula, the swamps of the valley have been drained, and the size of the lake has been greatly reduced. Most of the area is now excellent farmland. Over the 11 miles from Hula to the Sea of Galilee, the Jordan drops 926 feet, flowing in part through a narrow canyon. From Galilee to the Dead Sea there is an additional drop of 600 feet.

The Sea of Galilee is a significant part of the upper Rift Valley and is formed by a widening of it. It has several names—Lake of Gennesaret, Sea of Tiberias, Lake Chinnereth—but it is best known as the Sea of Galilee. Around it most of the ministry of Jesus took place. Here He could rest, escape crowds, find cool relief from the heat. Shaped much like a harp, it is 13 miles long and seven miles wide. The hard basalt environment has given the lake an almost constant level and size. In NT days the lake was the center of a thriving fishing industry. The towns around the lake testify to this fact: Bethsaida means "fishing place," and Tarichea is from a Greek term meaning "preserved fish."

As the Jordan flows south out of the Sea of Galilee, it enters a gorge called the Ghor, or "depression." The meandering Jordan and its periodic overflows have created the Zor, or "jungle," a thick growth of entangled semitropical plants and trees. Although the distance from the lower end of the Sea of Galilee to the upper end of the Dead Sea is only 65 miles, the winding Jordan twists 200 miles to cover that distance. The Ghor is about 12 miles wide at Jericho.

Seven miles south of Jericho the Jordan flows into the Dead Sea, one of the world's most unique bodies of water. The surface of the water is 1,296 feet below sea level, the lowest point on the surface of the earth. Forty-seven miles long and eight miles wide, the Dead Sea has no outlet. It has been calculated that an average of 6.5 million tons of water enters the sea each day. The result of centuries of evaporation is that now 25 percent of the weight of the water is mineral salts. Magnesium chloride gives the water a bitter taste, and calcium chloride gives it an oily touch. Fish cannot live in Dead Sea water. Indeed, it destroys almost all organic life in it and around it.

Thirty miles down the eastern side, a peninsula, the Lisan, or the "Tongue," juts into the sea. North of it the sea is deep, reaching a maximum depth of 1,319 feet to 2,650 feet below sea level. South of the peninsula the sea is very shallow with a maximum depth of 13 feet. It is thought that this area is the location of "the cities of the Plain" (Gen. 13:12), Sodom and Gomorrah.

Transjordan Plateau East of the Jordan is an area where the tribes of Reuben, Gad, and the half-tribe of Manasseh settled. In NT times Decapolis and Perea were located there. The ministry of Jesus took Him to limited parts of these provinces. Transjordan is divided into sections by several rivers—the Yarmuk, the Jabbok, the Arnon, and the Zered.

Across from Galilee and north of the Yarmuk River is Bashan (Hauron), an area of rich volcanic soil with rainfall in excess of 16 inches per year. The plateau averages 1,500 feet above sea level. To the east of Bashan lies only desert that begins to slope toward the Euphrates. In the NT era it was a part of the territory of Philip, the Tetrarch, son of Herod the Great.

South of the Yarmuk, reaching to the Jabbok River, was Gilead. During the Persian rule the boundaries were rather rigid. Both before and after Persian domination, Gilead reached as far south as Rabbah (Philadelphia, modern Amman). Formerly heavily wooded with many springs and with gently rounded hills, Gilead is one of the most picturesque regions of Palestine. Olive groves and vineyards are found on the hillsides. Jerash and Amman, the capital of the Heshemite Kingdom of Jordan, are located here.

South of Gilead lies Moab. Originally, its northern border was the Arnon River, but the Moabites pushed north, giving their name to the plains east of the spot where the Jordan enters the Dead Sea (Ammon attempted to establish herself between Gilead and Moab using Rabbath-ammon as her stronghold. This succeeded only under the infamous Tobiah during the years of the exile.) Moab's southern border was the Zered River, Wadi al Hasa.

Still farther south is Edom, with the highest mountains of the region. The area is arid and barren. Fifty miles south of the Dead Sea lies the ancient fortress of Petra, "rose-red ... half as old as time."

Climate Palestine lies in the semitropical belt between 30 degrees 15 feet and 33 degrees 15 feet north latitude. Temperatures are normally high in the summer and mild in the winter, but these generalizations are modified by both elevation and distance from the coast. Variety is the necessary word in describing Palestinian weather, for in spite of its relatively small size, the geographical configuration of the area produces a diversity of conditions. Because of the Mediterranean influence, the coastal plain has an average annual temperature of 57 degrees at Joppa. Jerusalem, only 35 miles away, has an annual average of 63 degrees. Its elevation of 2,500 feet above sea level causes the difference. Jericho is only 17 miles further east, but it is 3,400 feet lower (900 feet below sea level), consequently having a tropical climate and very low humidity. Here bitterly cold desert nights offset

rather warm desert days. Similarly, much of the area around the Sea of Galilee experiences temperate conditions, while the Dead Sea region is known for its strings of 100 degrees-plus summer days.

Palestine is a land of two seasons, a dry season and a rainy season, with intervening transitional periods. The dry season lasts from mid-May to mid-October. From June through August no rain falls except in the extreme north. Moderate, regular winds blow usually from the west or southwest. The breezes reach Jerusalem by noon, Jericho in early afternoon, and the Transjordan plateau by mid afternoon. The air carries much moisture, but atmospheric conditions are such that precipitation does not occur. However, the humidity is evident from the extremely heavy dew that forms five nights out of six in July.

With late October the "early rain" so often mentioned in Scripture begins to fall. November is punctuated with heavy thunderstorms. The months of December through February are marked by heavy showers, but it is not a time of unrelenting rain. Rainy days alternate with fair days and beautiful sunshine. The cold is not severe, with occasional frost in the higher elevations from December to February. In Jerusalem snow may fall twice during the course of the winter months.

All of Palestine experiences extremely disagreeable warm conditions occasionally. The sirocco wind (the "east wind" of Gen. 41:6 and Ezek. 19:12) blowing from the southeast during the transition months (May—June, September—October) brings dust-laden clouds across the land. It dries vegetation and has a withering effect on people and animals. On occasion the temperature may rise 30 degrees Fahrenheit and the humidity fall to less than 10 percent.

Along the coastal plain, the daily temperature fluctuation is rather limited because of the Mediterranean breezes. In the mountains and in Rift Valley the daily fluctuation is much greater.

Timothy Trammel

PALLET Small, usually straw-filled, mattress light enough to be carried. All biblical references are found in accounts or summaries of the healing of invalids (Mark 2:4-12; John 5:8-12; Acts 5:15). The "bedridden" man of Acts 9:33 was one who had lain on a pallet for eight years.

P
Q

PALLU (Păl´ lū) Personal name meaning "conspicuous," "wonder," or "distinguished." Second son of Reuben (Gen. 46:9; Exod. 6:14; Num. 26:5,8; 1 Chron. 5:3). KJV used the alternate spelling Phallu in Genesis.

PALLUITES (Păl´ lū īts) Descendants of Pallu (Num. 26:5).

PALMERWORM Caterpillar stage of a species of locust (Joel 1:4; 2:25; Amos 4:9). See *Insects.*

PALMS Date palm (*Phoenix dactylifera*) was among the earliest cultivated trees. Five thousand-year-old inscriptions from Mesopotamia give instruction for their cultivation. Palms are characteristic of oases and watered places (Exod. 15:27; Num. 33:9). The fruit of the date palm is highly valued by desert travelers since it may be consumed fresh or else dried or made into cakes for a portable and easily storable food. Jericho was known as the city of palms (Deut. 34:3; Judg. 1:16; 3:13). The judge Deborah rendered her decisions under a palm bearing her name (Judg. 4:5). The palm was a symbol of both beauty (Song 7:7) and prosperity (Ps. 92:12). Thus, images of palms

were used in the decoration of the temple (1 Kings 6:29,35; 7:36) and were part of Ezekiel's vision of the new temple (Ezek. 40:16,22,26). Palms were used in the construction of the booths for the festival of booths (Lev. 23:40; Neh. 8:15). In John 12:13 the crowd used palm branches to welcome Jesus to Jerusalem. See *Dates; Plants.*

PALMS, CITY OF Alternate name for Jericho (Deut. 34:3; Judg. 1:16; 3:13; 2 Chron. 28:15). See *Jericho.*

PALSY KJV term for paralysis (Matt. 4:24; 9:2; Luke 5:18; Acts 8:7). The descriptions of the Gospel writers do not permit identifications with specific forms of paralysis. The Gospel writers were rather concerned to present Jesus as the One to whom God had entrusted the authority to forgive sins (Matt. 9:6) and whose healing ministry was a cause for glorifying God (Matt. 9:8).

PALTI (Păl´ tī) Personal name meaning "my deliverance." **1.** Benjamin's representative among the 12 spies sent to survey Canaan (Num. 13:9). **2.** Second husband of Michal, King Saul's daughter who had previously been

Palm trees in the Wadi Feiran on the Sinai Peninsula.

The road north from Antalia to Isparta in the Roman province of Pamphylia (modern Turkey).

given in marriage to David (1 Sam. 25:44; KJV, Phalti). Michal was later returned to David in consequence of Abner's defection from Ishbosheth (2 Sam. 3:15-16). The fuller form Paltiel, meaning "God delivers," is used in 2 Samuel (KJV, Phaltiel).

PALTIEL (Păl´ tĭ ĕl) Personal name meaning "God is (my) deliverance." **1.** Leader of Issachar whom Moses appointed to assist Joshua and Eliezer in distribution of land to the tribes west of the Jordan (Num. 34:26). **2.** Fuller form of the name of Saul's son-in-law (2 Sam. 3:15-16). See *Palti.*

PALTITE (Păl´ tīt) Title meaning "resident of Beth-pelet," given to Helez, one of David's 30 elite warriors (2 Sam. 23:26). The parallels in 1 Chronicles read Pelonite (11:27; 27:10).

PAMPHYLIA (Păm phĭl´ ĭ à) One of the provinces of Asia Minor. Located in what is now southern Turkey, Pamphylia was a small district on the coast. It measured about 80 miles long and 20 miles wide. One of the chief cities was Perga, where John Mark left Paul and Barnabas during the first missionary journey (Acts 13:13). Other important cities were the ports of Side and Attalia. The NT records no other significant events for the early church in Pamphylia, perhaps because of the concentration of non-Hellenized people in the region. This would make the spread of the gospel slower and harder to achieve.

PAN Shallow, metal cooking utensil. Pans were used for baking bread for family use (2 Sam. 13:9) or as an offering (Lev. 2:5; 6:21; 1 Chron. 23:29). Deeper pans were used for boiling meat (1 Sam. 2:14). NASB used pans to refer to dishes for incense (Num. 7:14,20,26). NIV mentioned silver pans among Cyrus' gifts for rebuilding the Jerusalem temple (Ezra 1:9). In the KJV an iron pan (NRSV plate) serves as symbol of the coming siege of Jerusalem (Ezek. 4:3).

PANNAG (Păn´ ag) Hebrew term, perhaps meaning "pastry," which the KJV took as a place-name (Ezek. 27:17). NASB, NIV readings (cakes, confection) are supported by an Akkadian cognate and the Targum. RSV follows variant manuscripts in reading "early figs." REB, NRSV read "millet." TEV reads "wheat." The Greek term *chartes,* translated "paper" in 2 John 12, designates a sheet of papyrus.

PAPER, PAPYRUS (Pȧ pī´ rŭs) Popular writing material invented by the Egyptians and used by scribes from 2500 B.C. to A.D. 700.

The English word "paper" is derived from the word *papyrus.* The papyrus plant once grew in abundance along the Nile delta ("Can the papyrus grow tall where there is no marsh?" [Job 8:11 NIV]), providing the Egyptians with an inexpensive writing material which was exported throughout the Mediterranean world. The papyrus plant is a tall, aquatic reed that grows as high as 15 feet and becomes as thick as a person's wrist. Its triangular stalk was cut into 12-inch sections. The center section of each stick of papyrus, the pith, would be sliced into thin one-inch strips. A sheet of paper was made by arranging these one-by-twelve-inch strips vertically and overlaying them with another layer of strips horizontally. The two layers of green

A modern variety of the ancient papyrus plant from whose stalks writing material was made.

P
Q

fibrous strips were then mashed together and dried by the sun, which bonded the double-layered sheet of papyrus. The horizontally lined side of the papyrus sheet was scraped smooth, obviously providing the best writing surface for horizontal script. Several sheets were glued together to form a papyrus roll, which was called a *biblos* (Gk. for "scroll" or "book").

By A.D. 100 papyrus was used to make a codex (Latin for "book"). The codex—a stack of papyrus sheets, bound at one end—proved to be more economical than the roll since a scribe could write on both sides of the paper. A codex was also less cumbersome, considering the transportation of rolls and the difficulty of cross-referencing. Eventually, papyrus was replaced by the more expensive and yet more durable "parchment" (animal skins). Aged papyrus became brittle, literally causing words to fall off the page. Furthermore, unlike papyrus, parchment could be erased and used again. The only biblical reference to papyrus paper is found in 2 John 12, where the Elder writes: "Though I have many things to write to you, I don't want to do so with paper (Gk. *chartes*) and ink" (HCSB).

New Testament manuscripts produced before the fourth century were written exclusively on papyrus; after the fourth century almost all NT documents were preserved on parchment. See *Bible Texts and Versions; Library; Writing.*

Rodney Reeves

PAPHOS (Pā′ phŏs) Town on the southwest side of Cyprus and capital of the island during NT times. Paul, Barnabas, and John Mark came to the city on their first missionary journey and possibly led the proconsul, Sergius Paulus, to Christ (Acts 13:6-12). See *Cyprus.*

The ruins of ancient Paphos on the island of Cyprus.

PAPS KJV term used for a woman's breasts (Ezek. 23:21; Luke 11:27) or a man's chest (Rev. 1:13).

PARABLES Stories, especially those of Jesus, told to provide a vision of life, especially life in God's kingdom. Parable means a putting alongside for purposes of comparison and new understanding. Parables utilize pictures such as metaphors or similes and frequently extend them into a brief story to make a point or disclosure. Nevertheless, a parable is not synonymous with an allegory.

The difference between a parable and an allegory turns on the number of comparisons. A parable may convey other images and implications, but it has only one main point established by a basic comparison or internal juxtaposition. For example, the parable of the mustard seed (Mark 4:30-32; Matt. 13:31-32; Luke 13:18-19) compares or juxtaposes a microscopically small seed initially with a large bush eventually.

An allegory makes many comparisons through a kind of coded message. It correlates two areas of discourse, providing a series of pictures symbolizing a series of truths in another sphere. Each detail is a separate metaphor or what some call a "cryptogram." If you are an insider who knows, you receive the second or intended message. Otherwise, you can follow only the surface story. Jonathan Swift's *Gulliver's Travels* is an allegory as is John Bunyan's *Pilgrim's Progress.* In the OT Ezekiel recounts an incident in nature about great eagles and vines (17:3-8) and then assigns a very allegorical application to each of the details (17:9-18).

The word "allegory" never appears in the Gospels. Parable is the basic figure Jesus used. Though no parable in the Synoptic Gospels is a pure allegory, some parables contain subordinated allegorical aspects, such as the parable of the wicked tenants (Mark 12:1-12; Matt. 21:36-46; Luke 20:9-19). Even in the parable of the mustard seed the passing reference to the birds of heaven nesting in the branches (Mark 4:32) may be an allegorical detail, but the distinction of the parable establishing a basic, single comparison remains and aids interpretation. See *Allegory.*

Parables Prior to Jesus Though Jesus perfected the oral art of telling parables, their background can be found in the OT and in secular sources. The OT employs the broader category of *mashal*, which refers to all expressions that contain a comparison. A *mashal* can be a proverb (1 Sam. 10:12), a taunt (Mic. 2:4), a dark riddle (Ps. 78:2), an allegory (Ezek. 24:3-4), or a parable. The stories of Jesus are linked with the heritage of the prophetic parables in the OT (Isa. 28:23-29; 5:1-7; 1 Kings 20:39-43; Eccles. 9:13-16; 2 Sam. 12:1-4).

Perhaps the most interesting antecedent of the parables of Jesus comes from Nathan's word to David. Nathan told the unsuspecting David the seemingly harmless story of a rich man and a poor man living in the same city (2 Sam. 12:1-4). The poor man owned only a single little ewe lamb he loved as a household pet while the rich man possessed large flocks; yet when the wealthy farmer had a guest to serve, he seized the poor man's single lamb for the dinner! The teller of the story was living dangerously as he seized a teachable moment to confront the life of the most famous king of Israel. He sought to get inside David's guard and cut the iron bonds of his self-deception to strike a moral blindness from his eyes. In a sense it was a well-laid trap since David responded with moral outrage, thus condemning himself. Nathan then applied the parable to the king's affair with Bathsheba (2 Sam. 12:5-14). This eventful parable and others in the OT belong to the same tradition in which our Lord stood.

The parable was also recognized as a literary type before the time of Jesus in the writings of the Greeks concerning rhetoric. The famous writer Homer included 189 parables in *The Illiad* and 39 more in *The Odyssey*. Plato's poetic speech was rich in similitudes interwoven into his speech but not so much independent unities like those of Jesus. Some of the illustrations of Socrates were parabolic. Aristotle recognized the place of parable in his writings.

Bible students disagree about whether the rabbis prior to Jesus used parables. Scholars like C. A. Bugge and Paul Fiebig pointed to numerous rabbinic parables derived from the beginning of the first century A.D. Others, such as Jeremias, found almost none until after the days of Jesus. We do know of parables from the rabbis soon after the time of Jesus, and we do recognize that the parables of Jesus are not only far more compelling but center in the coming kingdom of God rather than in exposition of the Law or Torah as the rabbinic parables.

Jesus' Special Use of Parables Many of the parables grew out of the conflict situations when Jesus answered His religious critics. These answering parables, usually for Pharisees and sinners simultaneously, expose and extol. Jesus exposed the self-righteousness of His critics and extolled the kingdom of God. When John the Baptizer was accosted for being too serious and Jesus for being too frivolous, Jesus came back with the parable of the playing children (Matt 11:16-19; Luke 7:31-35) to expose the inconsistency of the criticism. In His most famous parable He extolled the forgiving love of the father and exposed the hostile criticism of the unforgiving elder brother (Luke 15:11-32).

In fact Jesus interpreted His ministry and its place in salvation history by means of parable. He addressed different audiences such as the crowds, the disciples, and the critics with definite purposes. Indeed, the teller as well as the tale is important. That is, the fact that Jesus was the author affects the meaning. As Jesus interpreted His ministry through parables, these sometimes have a "Christological penetration." Jesus Himself appears indirectly in the story (Mark 3:23-27). The parables are not merely clever stories but proclamation of the gospel. The hearer must respond and is invited by the story to make a decision about the kingdom and the King. The parable of the wicked tenants (Mark 12:1-12) represented a blatant confrontation.

These stories got Jesus in trouble as He made veiled claims of kingliness and exposed the hypocrisy regnant in the religious hierarchy. One of the reasons they crucified Jesus was because of His challenging parables and the claims of His kingdom.

Jesus' Different Kinds of Parables Jesus could turn people's ears into eyes, sometimes with a still picture and then again with a moving picture. He uttered parabolic sayings referring to the salt of the earth (Matt. 5:13) or throwing pearls before swine (Matt. 7:6). These parable germs or incipient parables were generally one liners with a picturesque appeal to the imagination. Remarkably, the Gospel of John has no parables as such; it does include 13 parabolic sayings.

Jesus also spoke simple parables that represent a picture elaborated into a story. These extended pictures portray a general situation growing out of a typical experience and appealing to common sense. They are often specifically concerning the kingdom of God and are introduced with the saying, "The kingdom of God is like.... " Examples are the paired parables of the treasure and the pearl (Matt. 13:44-46), the tower builder and the warring king (Luke 14:28-32), and the lost sheep and lost coin (Luke 15:3-10). They are extended similes.

Additionally, Jesus told His famous narrative parables that represent a specific situation and often include in the first sentence reference to a certain person. While Matthew reported a great many parabolic sayings, Luke contains numerous narrative parables, such as the parable of the unjust steward (16:1-8), the compassionate Samaritan (10:30-37), and the rich fool (12:16-21). A narrative parable is a dramatic story composed of one or more scenes, drawn from daily life yet focused on an unusual, decisive circumstance.

Special Literary Considerations Narrative parables and the simple parables total more than 40 examples. Certain metaphors recur in the different parables. For example, seed parables such as those of the sower, the seed growing of itself, and the mustard seed in Mark 4 focus on the nature of the coming kingdom. Master/servant parables reflect a time of critical reckoning. Kingly parables, especially in Matthew, portray the sovereignty of the divine judgment and grace. Householder parables feature an authoritative figure whose purpose is resisted or rejected yet whose will is finally achieved. This latter category points to the realism of rejection of the will of God fully allowable on the one hand by the divine provision of freedom while on the other hand the divine insistence of the eventual triumph of His loving purpose.

Attention to parable form also brings up the prominence of the question format, the refusal parables, and the place of direct discourse. Jesus intended to involve His hearers, and so He constructed many parables that amount to one big question. The parable of the servant and his wages moves by means of two questions (Luke 17:7-10). The parable of the unjust steward (Luke 16:1-8) includes four questions. These interrogatives within parables often define a dilemma (Luke 12:20; Mark 12:9) or call for an agreeing nod in one area of life that carries over to another.

The refusal parables are those that express the intention of a character not to do what is requested. The elder brother refused to enter the festivities in honor of the prodigal son (Luke 15:28), and wedding guests rejected the invitation to attend the festivities of a wedding (Matt. 22:3). These and other examples of the refusal to do the will of God recognize the reality of human pride, stubbornness, hypocrisy, and rejection that Jesus encountered during His proclaiming ministry.

Direct discourse is also immensely important in many of the parables because it brings the stories to life. Through the human conversation the parable often makes its point, especially in the last speech. Surely Jesus delivered these lines from each of the parabolic characters in a most animated fashion and even interpreted His parables by the tone of His voice.

Common Theme of Jesus' Parables Jesus' great thesis centers on the kingdom of God (Mark 1:15). Each parable explores and expands the theme. The kingship of God or Yahweh may be found first in the OT (Ps. 24:9-10; Isa. 6:5). Daniel 4 proclaims the divine sovereignty over the secular kingdoms, and the Ten Commandments require full obedience to God.

Jesus lifted the theme to new heights and through His parables portrayed the nature of the kingdom (Mark 4:26-29), the grace of the kingdom (Luke 18:9-17), the crisis of the kingdom (Luke 12:54-56), and the conditions of the kingdom such as commitment (Luke 14:28-30), forgiveness (Matt. 18:23-35), and compassion (Luke 10:25-37).

The parables further proclaim the kingdom as ethical, experiential or existential, eschatological, and evangelistic. Several parables accentuate ethical concerns such as attitude toward one's fellows (Luke 18:9-14; 15:25-32; Matt. 18:23-35). Jesus insisted on being religious through relationships. The rousing call to repentance embodied in many parables requires a moral and spiritual reorientation of life around the kingdom.

Many parables reach the water table of common experience and illumine existence or life. Jesus could expose a pale or petrified life. He could convey the moving experience of being lost in the far country and then to come to oneself and go home (Luke 15:17). His parables exposed the inauthentic life aggressively as self-centered and greedy (Luke 12:13-21; 16:19-31).

As Jesus proclaimed through parables, God was bursting into history, the hinge of history had arrived. He announced it with urgency. He brought an otherworldly perspective to bear in the parable of the rich fool (Luke 12:13-21). He foresaw the full future coming of the kingdom (Matt. 13:8,30,32,39).

The parables are evangelistic because they sought to stimulate a decision and change a life. They invited the audience to repent and believe. The parables intended to awaken faith. The teller's faith was contagious. The segment about the elder brother (Luke 15:25-32) is unfinished and open-ended. He could choose to swallow his pride, activate his own forgiving spirit, put on his dancing shoes, and join the party.

Unspoken Parables Like the prophets, Jesus enacted some of His intended message. His parabolic acts were boldly done. For example, He chose from His larger following a special group of 12 disciples (Mark 3:13-19), symbolizing His creation of a new Israel. Throughout His ministry Jesus graciously received spiritual and social outcasts as the friend of sinners, indicating the Father's loving grace. He cursed the fig tree (Mark 11:12-14,20-21), pointing to the divine judgment on Israel. He rode into Jerusalem in regal humility on the first Palm Sunday, calling forth Zechariah's expectation. He cleansed the temple (Mark 11:15-19), enacting God's will for Israel to be a light to the nations. At the Last Supper as He broke the bread and poured the wine, He enacted with mini parables the loving sacrifice of Calvary.

Parables' Perspective on Life Some of the stories carry a pastoral and others a prophetic relevance. They have both sugar and steel. The parable of the mustard seed speaks pastorally about ending despair, and the parable of the persistent widow (Luke 18:1-8) encourages one to hang in there. The parable of the barren fig tree (Luke 13:6-9) speaks prophetically concerning national priorities; the parable of the wicked tenants accosts arrogant religious leaders; and the parable of the rich fool confronts false confidence in materialism. Through the parable of the Pharisee and the tax collector, grace peers down on two people praying in the temple, and appearances take a pounding. Grace shines on worship, and revelation happens! See *Jesus Christ; Kingdom of God.*   *Peter Rhea Jones*

PARACLETE Transliteration of the Greek word literally meaning "called beside or alongside to help." John exclusively used the term in the NT. He described the Spirit as another "Paraclete" who teaches (John 14:16), reminds the disciples of what Jesus taught (John 14:26), testifies (John 15:26), and convicts of sin (John 16:7-8). John also described Jesus as the first "Paraclete" (John 14:16) or advocate (1 John 2:1). See *Advocate; Comforter; Counselor; Holy Spirit.*
Thomas Strong

PARADISE Old Persian term which means literally "enclosure" or "wooded park," used in the OT to speak of King Artaxerxes' forest (Neh. 2:8) and twice of orchards (Eccles. 2:5; Song 4:13). All three NT occurrences (Luke 23:43; 2 Cor. 12:4; Rev. 2:7) refer to the abode of the righteous dead (heaven). The Greek OT (Septuagint) used "paradise" to translate the Hebrew words for the garden of Eden in Gen. 2–3. Over the years the terms became synonymous, and eventually paradise came to refer to heaven. Jewish theology then developed an opposite place for wicked persons, *gehenna*, a burning furnace. See *Future Hope; Heaven.*

PARAH (Pā´ rah) Place-name meaning "heifer" or "young cow." Village in territory of Benjamin about five miles northeast of Jerusalem, identified with modern Khirbet el-Farah (Josh. 18:23). The Hebrew *parat*, often translated Euphrates (KJV, NASB, NRSV), may refer to the spring 'Ain Farah at Jer. 13:4-7 (cp. NASB, NRSV margin, "Parah"). NIV, REB simply transliterate the term.

PARALLELISM See *Poetry.*

PARALYSIS See *Disabilities and Deformities; Palsy.*

PARAMOUR Illicit sexual partner (Ezek. 23:20 KJV, NASB, NRSV; Hos. 3:1 RSV). Other translations read: lovers (NIV); male prostitutes (REB); and oversexed men (TEV).

PARAN (Pā´ rȧn) **1.** Wilderness area south of Judah, west of Edom, and north of Sinai. Israel camped there after leaving Sinai during the exodus and sent spies to scout out the promised land from Kadesh, a location in Paran (Num. 10:11-12; 13:3,26). Chedorlaomer turned back his military campaign at El-paran (Gen. 14:5-7). Ishmael made his home there

P
Q

after Abraham was forced to send Hagar and him away (Gen. 21:21). King Hadad of Edom eluded Joab by going through Paran to Egypt (1 Kings 11:17-18). **2.** Mount Paran appears as a poetic parallel to Mount Sinai (Deut. 33:2; cp. Hab. 3:3) as the place of revelation. If not the same place as Sinai, the location is unknown.

PARBAR (Pär´ bär) Hebrew term of uncertain meaning used only at 1 Chron. 26:18. Some translations (KJV, NASB, RSV) merely transliterate the term. Others offer plausible translations: (western) colonnade (NRSV, REB), western pavilion (TEV), and court to the west (NIV). Suggested renderings of the plural of *parvar* (or a related term) in 2 Kings 23:11 include: precincts (NASB, NRSV), court (NIV), and suburbs (KJV). It was apparently a road, an open area, or a room near the temple.

PARCHED GRAIN Common food prepared by roasting grains in a pan or by holding heads of grain over a fire (Lev. 23:14; Josh. 5:11; Ruth 2:14; 1 Sam. 17:17; 25:18; 2 Sam. 17:28). Parched grain served as food for harvest workers, soldiers, and refugees. Mosaic law prohibited the eating of parched grain before the firstfruits of the grain had been offered to God. The exact type of grain is not indicated by the Hebrew term; probably barley or wheat was meant.

PARCHED PLACES Expression some translations (KJV, NIV, NRSV) use for "arid land" (Jer. 17:6). Other translations include "stony wastes" (NASB) and "among the rocks" (REB).

PARCHMENT See *Paper, Papyrus.*

The parched land and places of the Wadi Arabah south of the Dead Sea.

PARDON Authoritative act reversing a sentence given under a guilty verdict. Prayer for God's pardon for sin is based on the greatness of God's covenant love and on the long history of God's acts of forgiveness (Num. 14:19; Mic. 7:18). The OT believers were already aware that the condition for seeking pardon was a repentant heart rather than ritual exactness (1 Chron. 29:18). God's willingness to abundantly pardon serves as an incentive to repentance (Isa. 55:7). See *Atonement; Forgiveness; Reconciliation.*

PARE To trim or shave off. The paring of nails served as a sign of mourning for lost parents (Deut. 21:12 KJV, REB, NRSV). An Israelite desiring to marry a female prisoner of war was required to allow her to cut her hair and pare her nails first. These actions perhaps symbolized purification on entering the covenant community.

PARENTS, PARENTING See *Family.*

PARLOUR British variant of "parlor." The KJV used "parlour" in three passages. In each case modern translations replace parlor with a term more suitable to the context: (1) inner chambers (NRSV), courts (REB), or rooms (NIV) of the temple (1 Chron. 28:11); (2) dining hall (REB) or hall (NIV, NRSV) in which Saul shared a sacred meal with Samuel (1 Sam. 9:22); (3) the upper room (NIV) or roof chamber (NRSV, REB) of a palace (Judg. 3:20,23-25).

PARMASHTA (Pär mäsh´ tà) Personal name, probably of Persian origin, possibly meaning "strong-fisted" or "the very first." One of Haman's 10 sons (Esther 9:9).

PARMENAS (Pär´ mə nås) Personal name meaning "faithful" or "constant." One of the seven chosen by the Jerusalem congregation to distribute food to the Greek-speaking widows of that church (Acts 6:5).

PARNACH (Pär´ năk) Persian personal name of uncertain meaning. Father of Elizaphan (Num. 34:25).

PAROSH (Pā´ rŏsh) Personal name meaning "flea." **1.** Ancestor of a postexilic family (Ezra 2:3; 8:3; KJV, Pharosh; 10:25; Neh. 7:8).

2. One of the witnesses to Ezra's renewal of the covenant (Neh. 10:14), possibly the father of Pedaiah (Neh. 3:25). This Parosh was likely the chief member of the family above.

PAROUSIA (Pär ū sē´ å) Transliteration of Greek word which means "presence" or "coming." In NT theology it encompasses the events surrounding the second coming of Christ. See *Day of the Lord; Eschatology; Future Hope; Kingdom of God.*

PARSHANDATHA (Pär shăn dā´ thá) Personal name, probably of Persian origin, possibly meaning "inquisitive." One of Haman's 10 sons (Esther 9:7).

PARSIN (Pär´ sĭn) See *Mene, Mene, Tekel, Upharsin.*

PARTHIANS (Pär´ thĭ åns) Tribal people who migrated from Central Asia into what is now Iran. Their homeland was an area southeast of the Caspian Sea. They spoke an Aryan dialect very close to Persian and worshiped the Persian god, Ahura Mazda. The Parthians adopted Greek culture following their fall to Alexander the Great. About 250 B.C. they revolted against the Seleucid rule and reached a height of power under King Mithradates who ruled from 171 to 138 B.C. In 53 B.C. the Romans invaded but were defeated on several occasions. They did not gain control of Parthia until A.D. 114. Some Parthians were among those in Jerusalem on the Day of Pentecost who heard the gospel in their own language (Acts 2:9-11).

PARTIES, JEWISH See *Jewish Parties in the New Testament.*

PARTRIDGE Stout-bodied, medium-size game bird with variegated plumage. David likened his life as a fugitive from Saul to a hunted partridge (1 Sam. 26:20). The translation of the proverb of the partridge (Jer. 17:11) is difficult; the Hebrew is extremely terse, and one of the verbs is of uncertain meaning (brood, gather, or lay). Various translations understand the action in the following ways: a partridge sits on eggs which will not hatch (KJV); a partridge gathers chicks it did not hatch (RSV); a partridge sits on eggs it did not lay (REB); a partridge hatches eggs it did not lay (NASB, NIV, NRSV TEV). The KJV interpretation is an apt picture of riches that come to nothing. In other interpretations the partridge that steals eggs or chicks is no less fortunate than any bird whose chicks grow and leave the nest.

PARUAH (Pá rū´ ah) Personal name meaning "blossoming," "joyous," or "increase." Father of Jehoshaphat (1 Kings 4:17).

PARVAIM (Pär vä´ ĭm) Source of gold for Solomon's decoration of the temple (2 Chron. 3:6). The place is perhaps el Farwaim (Farwa) in Yemen, or else a general term for the East.

PASACH (Pā´ săk) Personal name, perhaps meaning "divider." Member of the tribe of Asher (1 Chron. 7:33).

PASCHAL Adjective expressing relation to the Passover. From the Greek *pascha*, which is the Hellenized spelling of the Aramaic *pascha* (or *pischa*) for the Hebrew *pesach,* "Passover." The paschal meal was the supper prepared and eaten during the Passover celebration (Exod. 12; Matt. 26:17,19; Mark 14:14,16; Luke 22:8,11,13; John 18:28, where the "Passover" meal is specifically in view). By metonymy, *pascha* is sometimes used in particular of the paschal lamb found at the center of the paschal meal's observance and significance (Exod. 12:21; Ezra 6:20; Mark 14:12; Luke 22:7, e.g., where the literal "Passover" lamb is in view). Paul rightly sees in Christ the completion and fulfillment of the paschal sacrifice (1 Cor. 5:7)—the unblemished Lamb of God slain "by" the people and yet "for" the people, whose blood protects everyone under it from the avenging hand of God's wrath and opens the way for God's full redemption (Rom. 3:25; 5:9; Eph. 1:7; Rev. 1:5). Interestingly, most translations simply use the word "Passover" both as a noun and as an adjective, though "paschal" is found, for example, once in the RSV and NRSV (1 Cor. 5:7).

B. Spencer Haygood

PASDAMMIN (Păs dăm´ mĭn) Place-name meaning "boundary of blood." Scene of David's victory over the Philistines (1 Chron.

11:13). The site is probably between Socoh and Azekah, the same as Ephes-dammin (1 Sam. 17:1).

PASEAH (Pă sē´ ah) Personal name meaning "lame." **1.** Member of the tribe of Judah (1 Chron. 4:12). **2.** Ancestor of a family of temple servants (Neh. 7:51; KJV "Phaseah"). **3.** Father of Joiada (Neh. 3:6).

PASHHUR (Păsh´ ŭr) Personal name meaning "son of (the god) Horus." **1.** Chief officer in the Jerusalem temple in the last years before Nebuchadnezzar's victory over the city. He had Jeremiah beaten and imprisoned (Jer. 20:1-2). He or another Pashhur was the father of Gedaliah (Jer. 38:1). **2.** Man in Zedekiah's court in Jerusalem (Jer. 21:1). As the Babylonian army approached, Pashhur asked Jeremiah for a word from the Lord. Jeremiah prophesied the destruction of the city (21:1-7; cp. 38:1-3). **3.** Forebear of a priestly family (1 Chron. 9:12) who returned from the exile (Ezra 2:38) and who later gave up their foreign wives (10:22; cp. Neh. 10:3; 11:12).

PASSION 1. Any bodily desire which leads to sin (Rom. 6:12; Gal. 5:24; Eph. 2:3). Passion is especially used for strong sexual desire (Rom. 1:26-27; 1 Cor. 7:9; 1 Thess. 4:5). Unregenerate life is characterized by slavery to passions (Eph. 2:3; Titus 3:3; 1 Pet. 1:14). Those who belong to Christ have crucified fleshly passions (Gal. 5:24; cp. Rom. 6:5-14). In their frequent appeals to renounce passions, NT letters likely echo charges to baptismal candidates (Col. 3:5; 2 Tim. 2:22; Titus 2:12). **2.** KJV twice used the phrase "like passions" (Acts 14:15; James 5:17) to mean "shared human nature." **3.** The suffering of Jesus during the last two days of His life. Luke uses a word translated "passion" only in Acts 1:3 (KJV, after His passion). The root is the Greek verb *pascho*, "to suffer." Acts 17:3 and 26:23 use *pathein* to speak specifically of Christ's suffering—Jesus foretold His sufferings a number of times, and yet His disciples rejected this possibility (Matt. 16:21; Mark 9:12; Luke 17:25). His passion is reflective of the prophetic portrait of the Suffering Servant (Isa. 53).

Jesus was not presented as a victim. He suffered and died willingly in accordance with God's purpose (Matt. 20:28; Heb. 9:26). The suf-

ferings of Jesus were for a specific purpose—the salvation of all who would believe. His passion became an atoning act for the sins of the world. KJV and RSV used "passion" once (Acts 1:3). HCSB, NASB, NIV, and NRSV replace "passion" with "suffering." REB and TEV read "death."

W. Dan Parker

PASSOVER (Păss´ ō vĕr) Most important Hebrew feast, commemorating their deliverance from Egyptian bondage. See *Festivals*.

PASTOR Common translation of the Greek noun *poimen* (Eph. 4:11) and its verb form; also the Hebrew *ra'ah* (Jer. 3:15; 10:21; 12:10; 22:22 KJV). Literally, a shepherd or one who keeps animals (Gen. 4:2; 13:7; 46:32,34; Exod. 2:17; Isa. 13:20; Jer. 6:3; Luke 2:8,15,18,20) but used figuratively of those called by God to feed (Jer. 3:15; John 21:16), care for (Acts 20:28), and lead (1 Pet. 5:2) His people, who are His "flock" (Num. 27:17; 1 Kings 22:17; Jer. 3:15; 10:21; 12:10; 22:22; Ezek. 34:2,5,7-10; Zech. 10:3; John 21:16; Acts 20:28; Eph. 4:11; 1 Pet. 5:2). Much instruction directed toward such church leaders can be found in the Pastoral Epistles (1 and 2 Tim. and Titus). Preeminently, the idea is applied to and fulfilled in Christ (Isa. 40:11; Mic. 5:2; Zech. 13:7; Matt. 2:6; 25:32; 26:31; Mark 14:27; John 10:11,14; Heb. 13:20; 1 Pet. 2:25; Rev. 7:17) and God Himself (Pss. 23:1; 27:9; 47:5; Jer. 23:3; 31:10; Ezek. 34:12,23-24; Hos. 13:5). In the NT pastor (shepherd) appears to depict aspects, or functions, of the responsibilities of the overseer/elder (1 Pet. 2:25, where the two are put together in Christ). See *Minister, Ministry*.

B. Spencer Haygood

PASTORALS First and Second Timothy and Titus are called the Pastoral Epistles, a title first used by Anton in 1753. Paul wrote these letters to coworkers he had left in charge of the churches in Ephesus and Crete, respectively.

A theme of entrustment and stewardship of the gospel runs throughout these epistles. Paul composed 1 Timothy to instruct his young associate to stop the false teaching in Ephesus (1:3) and to inform Timothy how persons should conduct themselves within the church (3:14-15). The apostle directed Titus to set the Cretian churches in order (1:5). Paul penned 2 Timothy to "pass on the mantle" and encourage Timothy to remain a faithful steward of the gospel.

Only since the 19th century have scholars seriously questioned the authorship and setting of these letters. Defenders of the Pastorals' authenticity argue that Paul was released from his two-year imprisonment in Acts 28, traveled back to the East, engaged in further missionary work, and was later arrested and imprisoned in Rome again, from where he wrote 2 Timothy. Accordingly, the apostle wrote the Pastorals sometime after his first imprisonment around A.D. 62 and before A.D. 68. Many scholars argue that an admirer or associate of Paul composed these epistles in the second century.

Critics support the latter theory using these criteria. First, they stress that the vocabulary and style differ from the other Paulines. Such arguments are subjective. Variations in subject matter, occasion, purpose, and addressees may account for these differences. The use of a secretary by Paul may also explain the presence of many words in the Pastorals.

Second, defenders of pseudonymity contend that church structure is too advanced for Paul's time, and reflects a monarchial bishopric. Such objections overlook that the same type of church structure found in the Pastorals also is found in Paul's ministry (cp. Acts 20:17-28; Phil. 1:1).

Third, they date the heresy opposed in these letters later than Paul's lifetime and contend for a developed, second-century Gnosticism. An incipient first-century Gnosticism probably operated in Paul's day. The false teaching addressed also contained many Jewish elements (1 Tim. 1:7; Titus 1:10,14; 3:9).

Fourth, they contend that the Pastorals do not emphasize characteristic Pauline doctrines like the believer's union with Christ and the work of the Holy Spirit. Many also suggest that a concern for "sound teaching" and tradition reflects the end of the first century. However, the absence of typical themes is overstated. Moreover, the emphasis on doctrine does not require a later date. Paul stressed tradition (cp. 1 Cor. 11:2) and cited creedal sayings and hymns in his letters (cp. 1 Cor. 15:3-5; Phil. 2:6-8; Col. 1:15-17).

Finally, opponents of Pauline authorship argue that these letters contain historical allusions to Paul's life which cannot be placed within the book of Acts (cp. 1 Tim. 1:3; Titus 1:5; 2 Tim. 1:8,16-17; 4:16). Traditionally, defenders of authenticity have responded with the theory of a second Pauline imprisonment in Rome. A study of Acts 28 does indicate that Paul was likely released. Under this view references in the Pastorals cannot be placed within Acts because they happened at a later date. Also, the book of Acts does not record some details of Paul's life (cp. 2 Cor. 11).

A resort to pseudonymity and a date in the second century is not necessary for the Pastoral Epistles. These letters can be wholly relied upon as authentic and trustworthy. See *Timothy, First Letter to; Timothy, Second Letter to; Titus, Letter to.* *Terry Wilder*

PASTURE Open land surrounding towns and villages, regarded as common property to be freely used by village shepherds and herdsmen (Num. 35:2,7; Josh. 14:4; 21:11). The same Hebrew term designates open space around a city or the sanctuary (Ezek. 27:28; 45:2; 48:17). See *Suburbs.*

PATARA (Păt´ à rà) See *Asia Minor, Cities of.*

PATH A walkway. Two contrasting paths are a common image for rival ways of life in Hebrew wisdom literature. The path of the wicked (Prov. 4:14) who forget God (Job 8:13) is crooked (Prov. 2:15). This approach to life contrasts with the path of righteousness (Ps. 23:3; Prov. 2:13,20). This alternate path is called the path of God (cp. Pss. 17:5; 25:4,10) and of light (Job 24:13). This life-path entails living by the commands or instruction of the Lord (Ps. 119:35,105; Prov. 10:17). The reward for following this path is life (Prov. 10:17; 12:28; cp. Ps. 16:11; Prov. 2:19; 5:6). The wise are those who follow this way (Prov. 15:24). The paths of justice (Prov. 2:8; 8:20), peace (Prov. 3:17), and righteousness refer to the practice of these qualities.

PATHROS (Păth´ rŏs) Hebrew transliteration of Egyptian term for Upper (southern) Egypt. Upper Egypt included the territory between modern Cairo and Aswan. The NIV translates the term; other translations transliterate (Isa. 11:11; Jer. 44:1,15; Ezek. 29:14; 30:14).

PATHRUSIM (Păth rū´ sĭm) Son of Mizraim (Egypt) and ancestor of the inhabitants of upper (southern) Egypt who bore his name (1 Chron. 1:12).

PATHRUSITES (Păth rū′ sĭts) (NIV, 1 Chron. 1:12) See *Pathrusim.*

PATIENCE Active endurance of opposition, not a passive resignation. Patience and patient are used to translate several Hebrew and Greek words. Patience is endurance, steadfastness, long-suffering, and forbearance.

God is patient (Rom. 15:5). He is slow to anger in relation to the Hebrews (Exod. 34:6; Num. 14:18; Neh. 9:17; Ps. 86:15; Isa. 48:9; Hos. 11:8-9). The Hebrews were frequently rebellious, but God patiently dealt with them. Jesus' parable of the tenants depicted God's patience with His people (Mark 12:1-11). God's patience with sinners allows time for them to repent (Rom. 2:4), especially in the apparent delay of the return of Christ (2 Pet. 3:9-10).

God's people are to be patient. The psalmist learned to be patient when confronted with the prosperity of the wicked (Ps. 37:1-3,9-13,34-38). Christians should face adversity patiently (Rom. 5:3-5). Patience is a fruit of the Spirit (Gal. 5:22). Christian love is patient (1 Cor. 13:4,7). Ministers are to be patient (2 Cor. 6:6).

Christians need patient endurance in the face of persecution. Hebrews stressed endurance as the alternative to shrinking back during adversity (Heb. 6:9-15; 10:32-39). Jesus is the great example of endurance (Heb. 12:1-3). Perseverance is part of maturity (James 1:2-4). Job's perseverance is another example for suffering Christians (James 5:11). John frequently highlighted the patient endurance of Christians (Rev. 2:2,19; 3:10; 13:10; 14:12). Christian patience is ultimately a gift from God (Rom. 15:5-6; 2 Thess. 3:5). See *Perseverence; Steadfast.*

Warren McWilliams

PATMOS (Păt′ mos) Small island (10 miles by six miles) in the Aegean Sea located about 37 miles southwest of Miletus. The Romans used such places for political exiles. John's mention of the island in Rev. 1:9 probably means that he was such a prisoner, having been sent there for preaching the gospel. Eusebius (an early church father) wrote that John was sent to Patmos by Emperor Domitian in A.D. 95 and released after one and one-half years. See *Revelation, Book of.*

PATRIARCHS Israel's founding fathers— Abraham, Isaac, Jacob, and the 12 sons of Jacob (Israel). The word "patriarch" comes from a combination of the Latin word *pater,* "father," and the Greek verb *archo,* "to rule."

The island of Patmos on which John was probably exiled by the Romans.

A patriarch is thus a ruling ancestor who may have been the founding father of a family, a clan, or a nation.

The idea of a binding agreement between God and mankind antedated the patriarchs, being first expressed in the time of Noah (Gen. 6:18; 9:8-17). The growth of the Hebrew nation was promised specifically to Abraham in the patriarchal covenant (Gen. 15; 17), along with the provision of a land in which Abraham's off-spring would dwell. Since several generations elapsed before this situation developed, the covenant with Abraham must be regarded as promissory. The promises made to Abraham established the concept of a people descended through Abraham, Isaac, and Jacob, who would be in a special historical and spiritual relationship with God. See *Covenant*.

Abraham, or Abram as he was called in the earlier chapters of Genesis, was a ninth-generation descendant of Shem, son of Noah. Abram's father Terah was born in Ur of the Chaldees, as were his brothers Nahor and Haran (Gen. 11:26,28). See *Shem; Terah; Ur*.

At an early period Abraham had testified that God was the Most High God (Gen. 14:22), the righteous Judge of mankind (Gen. 15:14), and the Guarantor of the covenant of promise. He experienced close communion with God (Gen. 18:33; 24:40) and worshiped Him consistently to the exclusion of all other gods. His fidelity and obedience were characteristic features of his personality and made this renowned forefather of Israel (cp. Rom. 4:1-4) an example of the way in which men and women are justified before God. See *Abraham; Nuzi*.

The line of descent by which the covenant was to be perpetuated consisted solely of Abraham's son Isaac; through him the covenant promises were continued. Isaac's name is generally thought to mean "laughter," but it possibly also conveys the more subtle sense of "joker." It commemorated the occasion when both Abraham and Sarah laughed at God's promise to provide them with a son in their old age (Gen. 17:17-19; 18:9-15).

We have very little information about the maturing years of Isaac except that he was used as the supreme test of Abraham's faith in the covenant promises. Under the patriarchal system the father had the power of life or death over every living person and thing in his household. At the very moment that Isaac's life was about to

be taken, his position as covenant heir was safeguarded by the provision of an alternative sacrificial offering (Gen. 22:9-13). The circumstances attending his marriage to Rebekah afforded Isaac great comfort after the death of his mother (Gen. 24:67). Isaac prayed earnestly to God for covenant heirs, and in due time Rebekah became pregnant with twins when Isaac was 60 years old. Esau grew up to be a hunter, while Jacob followed the more sedentary lifestyle of his father by supervising the family's flocks and herds, moving with them when it was necessary to find fresh pasture (Gen. 25:27). Isaac unfortunately provoked sibling rivalry by favoring Esau above Jacob. The former brought his father tasty venison, whereas Jacob's culinary expertise seems only to have extended to preparing lentil soup (Gen. 25:28-29). In a moment of desperate hunger, Esau traded his birthright for some of Jacob's soup, thereby transferring to his brother a double portion of Isaac's estate as well as other rights.

In old age Isaac's sight failed, and, when it became apparent that Esau might inherit the extra birthright provision after all, Rebekah conspired with her favorite son Jacob to deceive Isaac into blessing him rather than Esau. The success of the scheme made Esau extremely angry. To escape his vengeance Jacob fled to Mesopotamia on his father's instructions. Before he arrived he received a revelation from God which confirmed his inheritance in the covenant. Jacob later encountered the family of Laban, son of Nahor, and in due course married two of Laban's daughters. After some years absence Jacob finally returned to Mamre, where his father was living, and along with Esau buried him when he died at the age of 180 years.

Isaac's life, though less spectacular than Abraham's, was nevertheless marked by divine favor. He was circumcised as a sign of covenant membership and owed his life to timely divine intervention when a youth (Gen. 22:12-14). He was obedient to God's will (Gen. 22:6,9), a man of devotion and prayer (Gen. 26:25), and a follower of peace (Gen. 26:20-23). He fulfilled his role as a child of promise (Gal. 4:22-23). See *Isaac*.

The life of Jacob, the last of the three great patriarchs, was marked by migrations, as had been the case with his ancestors. Although he lived successively at Shechem (Gen. 33:18-20), Bethel Gen. 35:6-7), and Hebron (Gen. 35:27),

P
Q

Jacob was basically a resident alien who did not have a capital city.

Just before Isaac's death, God appeared again to Jacob (Gen. 35:9) and renewed the promise of his new name. Jacob resided in Canaan thereafter and only left when a famine overtook the land. Jacob and his sons were invited to live in Egypt by Joseph. As his life drew to a close, Jacob, like his father Isaac, became blind, but he blessed his sons by means of a spoken last will and testament, after which he died peacefully. His body was embalmed in the Egyptian manner, and he was buried subsequently in the cave of Machpelah along with his ancestors (Gen. 49:30–50:13). Despite his apparent materialism, Jacob was a person of deep spirituality who, like Abraham, was esteemed highly by his pagan neighbors. Despite his fears he behaved honorably and correctly in dealing with his avaricious father-in-law Laban and was equally consistent in fulfilling his vow to return to Bethel. Jacob trusted the God whom he had seen at Peniel to implement the covenant promises through him; and when he died, he left behind a clearly burgeoning nation. See *Jacob*.

The date of the patriarchal period has been much discussed. A time before 2000 B.C. (early Bronze Age) seems too early and cannot be supported easily by reference to current archaeological evidence. The middle Bronze period (2000–1500 B.C.) seems more promising because of contemporary archaeological parallels and also because many of the Negev irrigation systems date from that period. Some scholars have suggested the Amarna period (1500–1300 B.C.) as the one in which the patriarchs lived, but this presents problems for any dating for the exodus. The same objection applies to a late Bronze Age (1500–1200 B.C.) period for the patriarchs. The least likely date is in the Judges period or the time of King David. All such dates do not allow time for the patriarchal traditions to have developed and make it impossible for Abraham, Isaac, and Jacob to be fitted realistically into an already known chronology. A date in the middle Bronze Age seems to offer the most suitable solution to a complex problem of dating.   *R. K. Harrison*

PATRIARCHS, TESTAMENT OF THE TWELVE See *Pseudepigrapha*.

PATROBAS (Păt´ rō băs) Personal name meaning "life of (or from) father." Member of

a Roman house church whom Paul greeted (Rom.16:14).

PAU (Pā´ ū) Edomite city meaning "they cry out." Hadar's (Hadad) capital (Gen. 36:39). The parallel in 1 Chron. 1:50 gives the name as Pai. It may be Wadi Fai west of the southern end of the Dead Sea.

PAUL Outstanding missionary, theologian, and writer of the early church. Paul is a very important figure in the NT and in the history of Christianity. He wrote 13 epistles that comprise almost one-fourth of the NT. Approximately 16 chapters of the book of Acts (13–28) focus on his missionary labors. Thus Paul is the author or subject of nearly one-third of the NT and the most important interpreter of the teachings of Christ and of the significance of His life, death, and resurrection.

Early Life and Training (A.D. 1–35) *Birth and Family Background* Paul was born in a Jewish family in Tarsus of Cilicia (Acts 22:3), probably sometime during the first decade of the first century. According to Jerome, Paul's family moved to Tarsus from Gischala in Galilee. Paul's family was of the tribe of Benjamin (Phil. 3:5), and he was named for the most prominent member of the tribe—King Saul. Paul probably came from a family of tentmakers or leatherworkers and, according to Jewish custom, was taught this trade by his father. Apparently the business thrived and Paul's family became moderately wealthy. Paul was a citizen of the city of Tarsus, "an important city" (Acts 21:39). According to one ancient writer, the property qualification for Tarsian citizenship was 500 drachmae, a year and a half's wages.

Roman Citizenship More importantly, Paul was born a Roman citizen. Many speculate that Paul's father or grandfather was honored with citizenship because of some special service rendered to a military proconsul. However, early Christian tradition preserved by Jerome and Photius stated that Paul's parents had been carried as prisoners of war from Gischala to Tarsus, enslaved to a Roman citizen, then freed and granted citizenship. Regardless of how Paul's parents received their citizenship, the book of Acts states three times that he possessed it, and his citizenship was accompanied by important rights that would benefit him in his missionary labors.

The colonnaded Arcadian Way of Ephesus, the city that became Paul's home for over two years.

The Roman citizen had the right of appeal after a trial, exemption from imperial service, right to choose between a local or Roman trial, and protection from degrading forms of punishment like scourging. Paul might have carried a wax tablet that functioned as a birth certificate or certificate of citizenship in order to prove his Roman citizenship. However, most people who claimed citizenship were trusted since the penalty for impersonating a Roman citizen was death.

Rabbinic Training Acts 22:3 shows that Paul grew up in Jerusalem. Paul used this fact to prove that he was no Diaspora Jew who was more influenced by Gentile culture than Jewish ways. He was educated in Jerusalem in the Jewish religion according to the traditions of his ancestors (Acts 22:3). The Mishnah taught: "At five years old [one is fit] for the Scripture, at ten years for the Mishnah, at thirteen [for the fulfilling of] the commandments, at fifteen for the Talmud, at eighteen for the bride-chamber, at twenty for pursuing a calling, at thirty for authority." This is probably a fairly accurate description of the regimen of training that Paul experienced. Acts 22 says that Paul was trained by Rabbi Gamaliel I, the member of the Sanhedrin mentioned in Acts 5:33-39. Gamaliel was a leading Jewish teacher in Paul's day. The Mishnah mentions Gamaliel I frequently and expresses many of his opinions. Gamaliel was listed among 13 great rabbis whose deaths marked the decline of Judaism: "When Rabbi Gamaliel the Elder died, the glory of the Law ceased and purity and abstinence died." The passage implies that Gamaliel was as renowned for his high moral standards as for his interpretation of the Scriptures. Paul quickly excelled as a Jewish rabbinical student. As Paul says in Gal. 1:14, "I advanced in Judaism beyond many contem-

poraries among my people, because I was extremely zealous for the traditions of my ancestors." In Phil. 3 Paul describes himself as "circumcised the eighth day; of the people of Israel, of the tribe of Benjamin, a Hebrew born of Hebrews; as to the law, a Pharisee; as to zeal, persecuting the church; as to the righteousness that is in the law, blameless" (HCSB). In Acts 26:5 Paul again identifies himself with the sect of the Pharisees. His father had also been a Pharisee (Acts 23:6).

Persecution of Christians As an ideal Pharisee Paul was probably active as a Jewish missionary winning Gentiles as proselytes. He may have been like the Pharisees Jesus described who traveled "over land and sea to make one convert" (Matt. 23:15 HCSB). Paul's words "If I still preach circumcision" may allude to his past as a Jewish missionary (Gal. 5:11). Paul, more than his mentor Gamaliel (Acts 5:34-39), recognized the serious threat that the followers of Jesus posed to the traditional Jewish religion. The Mishnah taught that a Jewish male was ready for a position of authority at age 30. Thus Paul was probably in his thirties when he, with authorization from the chief priest, began to imprison believers first in the synagogues of Jerusalem and then later in Damascus. Perhaps Paul's clearest description of persecution is found in Acts 26:9-11, "I myself supposed it was necessary to do many things in opposition to the name of Jesus the Nazarene. This I actually did in Jerusalem, and I locked up many of the saints in prison, since I had received authority for that from the chief priests. When they were put to death, I cast my vote against them. In all the synagogues I often tried to make them blaspheme by punishing them. Being greatly enraged at them, I even pursued them to foreign cities" (HCSB). Some believe this reference to casting a vote (literally "casting a pebble"—black for no or white for yes) implies that Paul was a member of the Sanhedrin. However, it is difficult to imagine that Paul would not have explicitly stated this especially on those occasions in which he highlights his devout Jewish pedigree. Most commentators thus take the statement as a metaphor implying that Paul consented to the execution of believers or suggest that he was a member of a committee appointed by the Sanhedrin and vested with this authority. Paul's initial and adamant rejection of Jesus as the Messiah may largely have been motivated by

Jesus' ignoble death. Death by crucifixion was indicative of divine curse (Deut. 21:23). Certainly the Messiah could not have died under the curse of God. But when Paul wrote his first epistle, this death curse was recognized as the grounds for substitutionary atonement (Gal. 3:10-14). In 1 Cor. 1 Paul explained that the idea of a crucified Messiah was a stumbling block to the Jews. Probably Paul was speaking from his own past experience.

Paul's Conversion (A.D. 35) While Saul was on his way to Damascus to arrest and imprison believers there, the resurrected and glorified Christ appeared to him with blinding radiance. Christ's words "It is hard for you to kick against the goads" indicate that God had already begun His convicting work earlier. Like an ox kicking against a goad in the hand of the ox driver, Paul had been resisting divine guidance and leadership resulting in his own harm and pain. At the appearance of Christ, Saul immediately surrendered to His authority and went into the city to await further orders. There his blindness was healed and he received the Holy Spirit and accepted believer's baptism. No doubt Ananias shared with Paul the message that the Lord had given him in a vision: "This man is My chosen instrument to carry My name before Gentiles, kings, and the sons of Israel. I will certainly show him how much he must suffer for My name!" Paul spent a few days with the disciples in Damascus.

Paul's Missionary Travels (A.D. 35–61)
Early Travels Soon after his conversion, Paul traveled to Arabia where he began evangelization of the Nabatean Arabs (Gal. 1:17; 2 Cor. 11:32-33) and probably experienced his first opposition to the gospel from political authorities. He then returned to Damascus where he began to go into the synagogues to preach the message that had been revealed to him on the Damascus road: Jesus is the Son of God and the promised Messiah. The Jews in Damascus watched the city gates in order to kill Paul, and he had to escape through a window in the wall by being lowered in a basket (Acts 9:22-25).

Paul then traveled to Jerusalem. Church leaders were initially suspicious of Paul, but Barnabas intervened in his behalf (Acts 9:26-30 and

PAUL'S CONVERSION AND EARLY MINISTRY

- • City
- ▲ Mountain peak
- ✕ Pass
- ⬅ Paul sent to Damascus
- ⬅··· Paul spends time in Arabia
- ⬅ Paul returns to Jerusalem
- ⬅ Paul flees from Hellenists
- ⬅ Paul and Barnabas travel to Antioch
- ⬅ Paul and Barnabas sent to Jerusalem
- ⬅ Paul and Barnabas return to Antioch
- ▨ Kingdom of Agrippa I

COMMAGENE

Cilician Gates

Tarsus

Issus

Syrian Gates

Amanus Mts.

Amanus Mts.

6. Paul and Barnabas establish a strong church where believers were first called Christians

Antioch

Seleucia Pieria

Aleppo

Euphrates R.

7. Paul and Barnabas travel to Jerusalem with aid for famine

SYRIA

Cyprus

Paphos

Hamath

Emesa

8. Paul and Barnabas return to Antioch

Palmyra (Tadmor) •

Tripolis

Orontes R.

Byblos

MEDITERRANEAN SEA

Litani R.

Sidon

COELE-SYRIA

3. Paul baptized and preaches about his newfound faith

5. Paul returns to his hometown of Tarsus

Tyre

Mt. Hermon

Damascus

2. Paul has a vision of Jesus and converts

PHOENICIA

Caesarea-Philippi

Ptolemais (Acco)

Capernaum

Canatha (Kenath)

Tiberias

Gamala

▲ Mt. Hauran

Caesarea Maritima

Scythopolis

Bostra

Antipatris

Pella

4. Paul flees to Arabia then returns to Jerusalem

Joppa

Jabbok R.

Azotus (Ashdod)

JUDEA

Jericho

Philadelphia (Amman)

Gaza

Jerusalem

Raphia

IDUMEA

DEAD SEA

Syro-Arabian Desert

1. Paul sanctioned to arrest followers in Damascus

Arabah

NABATEA

N

0   25   50   75   100 Miles

0 25 50 75 100 Kilometers

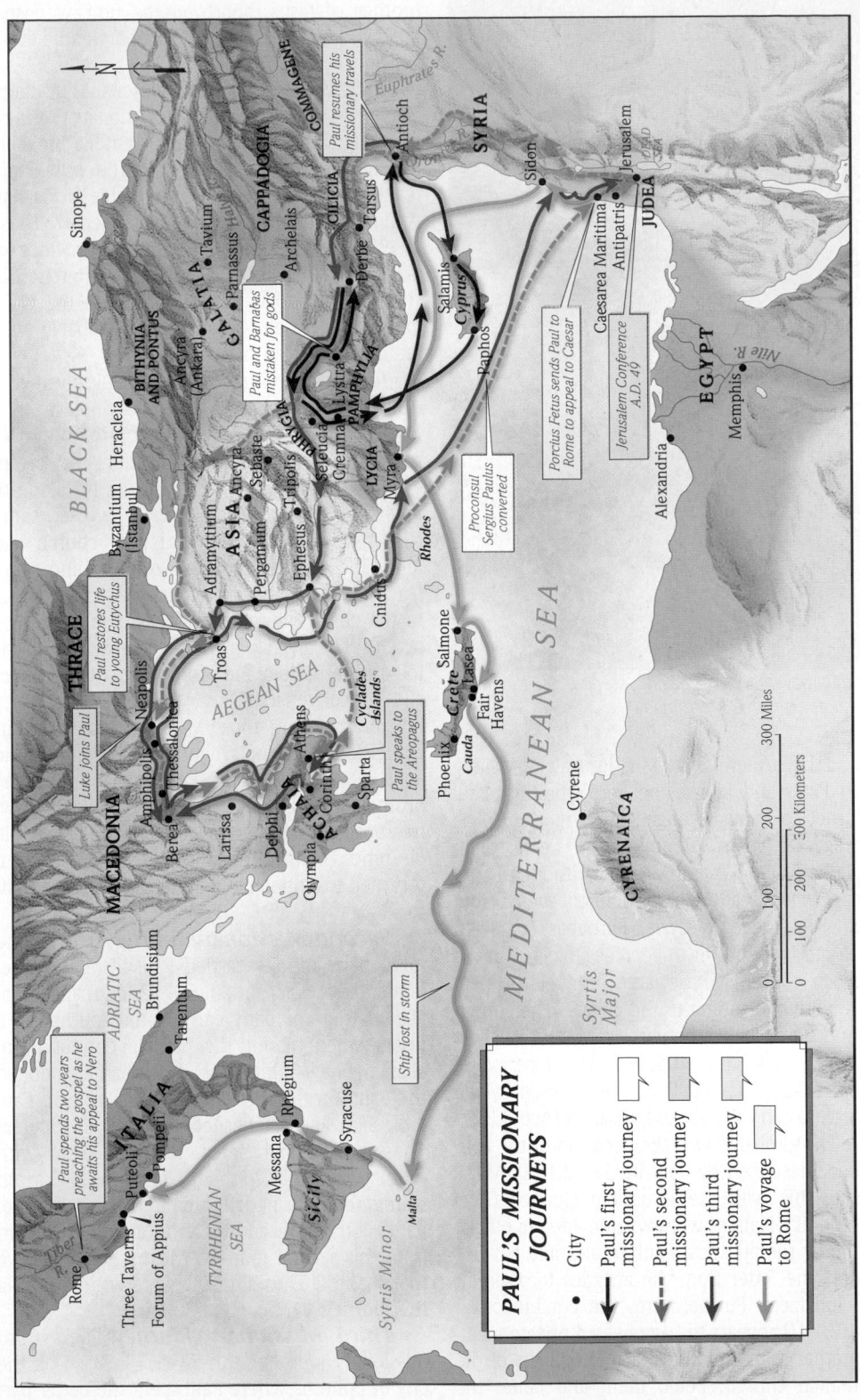

PAUL'S MISSIONARY JOURNEYS

- City
- Paul's first missionary journey
- Paul's second missionary journey
- Paul's third missionary journey
- Paul's voyage to Rome

Paul resumes his missionary travels

Paul and Barnabas mistaken for gods

Proconsul Sergius Paulus converted

Porcius Festus sends Paul to Rome to appeal to Caesar

Jerusalem Conference A.D. 49

Paul restores life to young Eutychus

Luke joins Paul

Paul speaks to the Areopagus

Ship lost in storm

Paul spends two years preaching the gospel as he awaits his appeal to Nero

Roman pavement, or paving stones, on the main street at Caesarea Maritima.

Gal. 1:18). After 15 days in Jerusalem, visiting with Peter and James, the Lord's brother, Paul returned to Tarsus, evangelizing Syria and Cilicia for several years. Doubtless he heard them describe Jesus' life and teachings, though Paul's gospel was already clearly defined even before this visit. While in Syria, Barnabas contacted Paul and invited him to become involved in the Antioch church, where large numbers of Gentiles were responding to the gospel. The church at Antioch collected money to carry to the believers who suffered in Judea during a period of famine. Barnabas and Paul were chosen by the church to carry the gift to Jerusalem (Acts 11:27-30). This probably was the occasion of the conference described by Paul in Gal. 2:1-10. Many equate this with the Jerusalem Council (Acts 15), but if Galatians were written after an official ruling by the apostles, Paul would only have to display the letter from the apostles to discredit the Judaizers. Furthermore, the conference in Gal. 2:1-10 appears to have been a private meeting rather than a public affair. The pillars of the Jerusalem church, Peter, John, and James the

brother of Jesus, approved the no-Law gospel preached by Paul and his focus on Gentile evangelism.

First Missionary Journey Paul and Barnabas soon began their first missionary journey, traveling through Cyprus and Anatolia probably during the years A.D. 47–48. The missionary team carried the gospel to the cities of Pisidian Antioch, Iconium, Lystra, and Derbe. These cities were located in the Roman province of Galatia, and it is probably these churches in south Galatia to which the epistle to the Galatians is addressed. Galatians was probably written during this journey.

Jerusalem Council When Paul returned to Antioch from the first missionary journey, he found himself embroiled in controversy over requirements for Gentile salvation. Peter and even Barnabas were vacillating on the issue of Jew-Gentile relationships. Even worse, some false teachers from the Jerusalem church had infiltrated congregations in Antioch and were teaching, "Unless you are circumcised according to the custom taught by Moses, you cannot be saved." The church appointed Paul and Barnabas to go to Jerusalem and settle the matter. A council was convened in A.D. 49 that included the missionary team, those who insisted upon circumcision as a requirement for salvation, and the apostles. The Apostle Peter and James the brother of Jesus spoke in defense of Paul's Law-free gospel, and a letter was sent to the Gentile churches confirming the official view. Paul returned to Antioch and remained there from 49 to 51.

Second Missionary Journey The second missionary journey carried Paul through Macedonia and Achaia in A.D. 50–52. Paul and Barnabas parted company early in this journey in a disagreement about the participation of Barnabas' nephew John Mark. Mark had abandoned the team on the first journey (Acts 15:38). Paul took Silas and established churches in Philippi, Thessalonica, and Berea. Barnabas went with John Mark. Paul also spent 18 months in Corinth strengthening a fledgling church there. Four of Paul's letters are addressed to churches known from this second journey. Most scholars believe that 1 and 2 Thessalonians were written during this journey.

Third Missionary Journey Paul's third missionary journey (A.D. 53–57) focused on the city of Ephesus where Paul spent the better part of three years. Toward the end of this journey, Paul worked hard to collect another relief offering for Jerusalem believers. Paul wrote 1 and 2 Corinthians and Romans during this journey.

Final Years Paul carried the relief offering to Jerusalem. While in the temple performing a ritual to demonstrate his Jewish faithfulness to some of the Jerusalem believers, Jewish opponents incited a riot, and Paul was arrested (A.D. 57). Paul was sent to Caesarea to stand trial before the procurator Felix. After two years of procrastination on the part of his detainers, Paul finally appealed to the Roman emperor for trial. After arriving in Rome, Paul spent two years under house arrest awaiting his trial. Paul wrote Philemon, Colossians, Ephesians, and Philippians during this first Roman imprisonment.

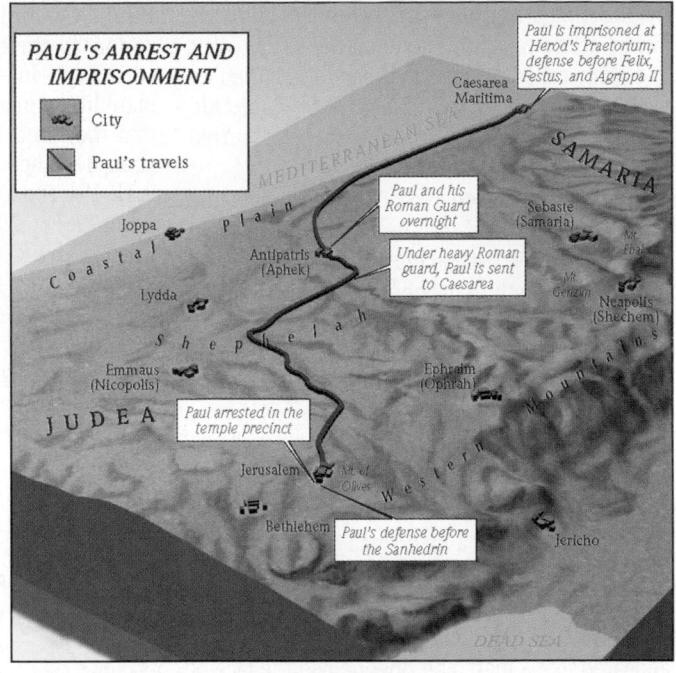

The record of Acts ends at this point, so information as to the outcome of the trial is sketchy. Early church tradition suggests that Paul was acquitted (ca. A.D. 63) or exiled and fulfilled the dream expressed in Rom. 15:23-29 of carrying the gospel to Spain (A.D. 63–67). Paul probably wrote 1 and 2 Timothy and Titus during the period between his acquittal and a second Roman imprisonment. According to church tradition Paul was arrested again and subjected to a harsher imprisonment. He was condemned

Reconstruction of Caesarea Maritima where Paul was imprisoned for two years (Acts 23:31–26:32).

by the Emperor Nero and beheaded with the sword at the third milestone on the Ostian Way, at a place called Aquae Salviae and lies buried on the site covered by the basilica of St. Paul Outside the Walls. His execution probably occurred in A.D. 67.

Paul's Appearance No biblical record of the appearance of Paul or his physical condition exists. We know that he must have been a hearty individual to endure the abuses and trials that he suffered as an apostle (2 Cor. 11:23-29). He was evidently the victim of some serious eye disease (Gal. 4:12-16). This may account for his characteristically large signature appended to letters which were penned by a secretary (Gal 6:11). The earliest description of Paul's appearance appears in a book from the NT Apocrypha which says that Paul was "a man small of stature, with a bald head and crooked legs, in a good state of body, with eyebrows meeting and nose somewhat hooked, full of friendliness; for now he appeared like a man, and now he had the face of an angel." The writer attributes the description of Paul to Titus, and it may have some historical basis. Although it sounds unflattering to moderns, several of the physical features mentioned were considered to be traits of the ideal Roman.

Paul's Gospel Paul's gospel indicted all humanity for the crime of rejecting God and His rightful authority. Under the influence of Adam's sin, mankind plunged into the depths of depravity so that they were utterly unable to fulfill the righteous demands of God (Rom. 1:18-32; 3:9-20; 9:12-19) and deserved only the wrath of God (Rom. 1:18; 2:5-16). The sinner was alienated from God and at enmity with Him (Col. 1:21). Consequently, the sinner's only hope was the gospel which embodied God's power to save those who had faith in Christ (Rom. 1:16). The focus of Paul's gospel was Jesus Christ (Rom. 1:3-4). Paul affirmed Jesus' humanity and His deity. Christ was a physical descendent from the line of David (Rom. 1:2), came in the likeness of sinful man (Rom. 8:3), and had assumed the form of a humble obedient servant (Phil. 2:7-8). Yet He was the visible form of the invisible God (Col. 1:15), all the fullness of deity living in bodily form (Col. 2:9), the very nature of God (Phil. 1:6), and possessed the title "Lord" (Greek title for the God of the OT), the name above all names (Phil. 2:9-11). Paul believed that by virtue of His sinlessness, Jesus was qualified to be the sacrifice which would make sinners right with God (2 Cor. 5:21). In His death on the cross, Jesus became the curse for sin (Gal. 3:10-14),

Roman-age columns on the agora in Tarsus, the place of Paul's birth and early life.

and the righteous died for the unrighteous (Rom. 5:6-8). Salvation is a free gift granted to believers and grounded solely in God's grace. Salvation is not dependent upon human merit, activity, or effort, but only upon God's undeserved love (Eph. 2:8-10; Rom. 6:23). Those who trust Jesus for their salvation, confess Him as Lord, and believe that God raised Him from the dead (Rom. 10:9) will be saved from God's wrath, become righteous in God's sight (Rom. 5:9), adopted as God's children (Rom. 8:15-17), and transformed by the Spirit's power (Gal. 5:22-24). At the coming of Christ believers will be resurrected (1 Cor. 15:12-57), will partake fully of the Son's righteous character (Phil. 3:20-21), and will live forever with their Lord (1 Thess. 4:17). By his union with Christ through faith, the believer participated spiritually in Christ's death, resurrection, and ascension (Rom. 6:1-7:6; Eph. 2:4-5). Consequently, the believer has been liberated from the power of sin, death, and the Law. He is a new, though imperfect, creation that is continually being made more Christlike (Col. 3:9-10; 2 Cor. 5:17). Although the believer is no longer under the authority of the written Law, the Holy Spirit functions as a new internal law which leads him naturally and spontaneously to fulfill the Law's righteous demands (Rom. 8:1-4). As a result, the Law-free gospel does not encourage unrighteous behavior in believers. Such behavior is contrary to their new identity in Christ. The union of believers with Christ brings them into union with other believers in the body of Christ, the church. Believers exercise their spiritual gifts in order to help one another mature, to serve Christ, and glorify Him, which is the church's highest purpose (Eph. 3:21; 4:11-13). Christ now rules over the church as its Head, its highest authority (Eph. 1:22). When Christ comes again, His reign over the world will be consummated, and all that exists will be placed under His absolute authority (Phil. 2:10-11; 4:20; Eph. 1:10). He will raise the dead: unbelievers for judgment and punishment; believers for glorification and reward (2 Thess. 1:5-10). *Charles L. Quarles*

PAULUS, SERGIUS See *Sergius Paulus.*

PAVILION Large, often richly decorated tent. KJV used "pavilion" seven times: three times in the literal sense of tents used in military campaigns (1 Kings 20:12,16; Jer. 43:10), twice of the thick canopy of clouds surrounding God (2 Sam. 22:12; Ps. 18:11) which illustrates the mystery of God, and twice as an image of God's protection (Pss. 27:5; 31:20). NASB, NIV, and NRSV substituted various terms (booths, canopy, shelter, tabernacle, tent) in each of these passages. The NASB used "pavilion" in the literal sense of tent in Dan. 11:45. Elsewhere in modern translations "pavilion" appears in poetic passages: a pavilion for the sun (Ps. 19:4-5 NIV), God's pavilion of clouds (Job 36:29 NASB, REB, NIV, NRSV), and a pavilion protecting Jerusalem from heat and rain (Isa. 4:5, RSV).

PEACE OFFERING See *Sacrifice and Offering.*

PEACE A condition or sense of harmony, well-being, and prosperity. The biblical concept means more than the absence of hostility, and it is more than a psychological state.

Old Testament The Hebrew word *shalom* and its derivatives have been said to represent "one of the most prominent theological concepts in the OT." (The word group occurs about 180 times in the OT.) It was not a negative or passive concept but involved wholeness and completeness. The related verb could mean to "repay" or "fulfill a vow" and so referred to completing or repairing a relationship. A related adjective could be used to describe something as "uninjured, safe, complete, peaceable." Peace could refer to harmony between friends or allies, triumph in war, success in one's endeavors, good health, and security. The Hebrew equivalent of the English greeting "How are you?" is "Do you have 'peace'?" (cp. Gen. 29:6; 2 Sam. 18:29; 2 Kings 4:26; Esther 2:11).

A bilateral "treaty of peace" (Josh. 9:15; 10:1) would mean that both parties promised to refrain from hostilities against the other and furthermore would seek the other's welfare, including a pledge of aid if the treaty partner were attacked. To "go in peace" meant to go with an assurance of friendship and favor (Gen. 26:31; Exod. 4:18; 1 Sam. 20:42; Mark 5:34; Luke 7:50). God's "covenant of peace" with His people would involve the assurance of an enduring relationship with the One who is our peace (Isa. 9:6; Mic. 5:5) and a pledge to protect their welfare and to abundantly bless them by His divine

P
Q

grace, wisdom, and power (Num. 25:12; Isa. 54:10; Ezek. 34:25; 37:26; Mal. 2:5).

Walking with the Lord "in peace and uprightness" (Mal. 2:6 NIV) means to maintain harmony with Him by faith and obedience and so to enjoy His peace (cp. Num. 6:26; Job 21:25; Ps. 125:5; Prov. 3:17; Isa. 48:18; 57:2; 59:8; cp. Luke 1:79). Peace is the opposite of the ultimate experience of the wicked (Isa. 48:22; 57:21; 59:8).

The *shelem* offering, traditionally translated "peace offering" but more often today "communion" or "fellowship offering," was an offering which celebrated the joy of having "peace" with God and all it involved. Finally, the term "peace" can refer to the sense of confident awareness that all is well (Gen. 15:15; 2 Kings 22:20; Ps. 4:8; Isa. 26:3).

In view of this it is not surprising that the term *shalom* is so often associated with the Davidic covenant and the prophetic promises of a coming messianic kingdom. The salvation of the Lord, spoken of so often in the OT, essentially amounts to a bringing of peace (1 Kings 2:33— "for David, his descendants, his house, and his throne, there will be peace forever from the LORD"; Isa. 9:7—"Of the increase of his government and peace there will be no end. He will reign on David's throne and over his kingdom, establishing and upholding it with justice and righteousness from that time on and forever"). That peace will be the result of God's coming and ruling in righteousness (Isa. 32:17; 60:17).

New Testament The term translated "peace" in the NT is *eirene.* It occurs in every NT book except 1 John (most frequently in Luke, 14 times; followed by Rom. 10; then Eph. 8). Outside the Bible the Greek word was likely to mean just the opposite of war, but its use to translate *shalom* in the Septuagint may have been what broadened its usage. Like *shalom,* the term in the NT could refer not only to the absence of hostility, strife, and disorder (1 Cor. 14:33) but also to the condition and sense of being safe and secure (Acts 9:31). Christ made peace between believing Jew and Gentile by making them into one new man in Him (Eph. 2:14-15). The term could also describe a state of either physical or spiritual well-being. When Jesus used it as a blessing (Luke 24:36; John 14:27; 16:33; 20:19,21,26; cp. Col. 3:15) and the Apostle Paul used it at the beginning of his letters, they referred to more than a sense of confidence in

God. The term brought to mind all that Christ would do or had done through the cross and the resurrection to end the dominion of sin and to make peace between God and man (Rom. 5:1; Col. 1:20), peace between all who are in Christ (2 Cor. 13:11; Eph. 4:3), and a state of being spiritually whole again (Rom. 14:17; Gal. 5:22). The gospel message was called "the gospel of peace" (Eph. 6:15). "Peace" was the angelic promise at Jesus' birth in Luke 2:14, "peace on earth to people He favors!" (HCSB; cp. Luke 19:38). The world cannot achieve or provide peace (Jer. 6:14; John 14:27; 1 Thess. 3:5) because it cannot deal with the problem of sin. Thus God's peace that guards the Christian's heart and mind "surpasses every thought" (Phil. 4:7; cp. 2 Thess. 3:16).

E. Ray Clendenen

PEACEMAKERS Those who actively work to bring about peace and reconciliation where there is hatred and enmity. God blesses peacemakers and declares them to be His children (Matt. 5:9). Those who work for peace share in Christ's ministry of bringing peace and reconciliation (2 Cor. 5:18-19; Eph. 2:14-15; Col. 1:20).

PEACOCK Male of any of several species of large pheasants, native to southeastern Asia and the East Indies, which are raised as ornamental birds. KJV translated two Hebrew words as "peacock." Modern translations replaced "peacock" with "ostrich" at Job 39:13. NASB, NRSV read "peacock" with KJV at 1 Kings 10:22 and 2 Chron. 9:21. Other translations read "monkey" (REB, RSV) or "baboon" (NIV, NRSV margin).

PEARL See *Jewels, Jewelry; Minerals and Metals.*

PEASANTRY NASB and RSV translation of an obscure Hebrew term used only in Deborah's song of victory (Judg. 5:7,11). KJV, NIV, TEV followed the Targum (Aramaic paraphrase) and Syriac version in reading "villages." REB reads "champion." Various commentators have suggested "leading class," "warriors," and "strength" as possible meanings.

PEDAHEL (Pěd´ á hěl) Personal name meaning "God delivers." Leader of the tribe of Naphtali whom Moses appointed to assist Joshua and Eliezer in the distribution of land to the tribes living west of the Jordan (Num. 34:28).

PEDAHZUR (Pə dăh´ zŭr) Personal name meaning "(the) Rock redeems." Father of Gamaliel (Num. 1:10; 2:20; 7:54,59; 10:23).

PEDAIAH (Pə dī´ ah) Personal name meaning "Yah redeems." **1.** Maternal grandfather of King Jehoiakim (2 Kings 23:36). **2.** Father (1 Chron. 3:18-19) or uncle (Ezra 3:2,8; 5:2; Neh. 12:1; Hag. 1:1,12,14; 2:2,23) of Zerubbabel. First Chronicles presents Pedaiah and Shealtiel as brothers. **3.** Manassite father of Joel (1 Chron. 27:20). **4.** Son of Parosh assisting in Nehemiah's repair of the wall (Neh. 3:25). **5.** Witness to Ezra's renewal of the covenant (Neh. 8:4), perhaps identical with 4. **6.** Benjaminite father of Joed (Neh. 11:7). **7.** Levite whom Nehemiah appointed as temple treasurer (Neh. 13:13).

PEDDLER One who sells goods, usually on the street or door-to-door. Paul denied being a peddler of God's word (2 Cor. 2:17). Here Paul either emphasized that he did not preach for pay (1 Cor. 9:12,15) or that he did not use tricks to gain converts (2 Cor. 4:2; 12:16).

PEDIMENT NRSV term for the stone base upon which Ahab set the bronze sea after removing it from the 12 bronze oxen (2 Kings 16:17). Other translations for pediment include: base (NIV), foundation (TEV), pavement (KJV, NASB). Ahab's changes in the temple equipment were an attempt to gain favor with the Assyrians.

PEER PRESSURE Feeling need to follow course of action because friends and colleagues advise it or follow it; usually works negatively rather than positively (Prov. 18:24; Rom. 12:2; 1 Cor. 15:33; Heb. 3:13; 12:1). Instead of listening to the elder advisors of his father, Rehoboam submitted to pressure from his peers, "the young men who had grown up with him" (1 Kings 12:8; cp. 2 Chron. 13:7). In contrast, Solomon asked God for wisdom and knowledge so that he might reign well (2 Chron. 1:10).

PEG Small, cylindrical, or tapered piece of wood (or some other material). Pegs were used: to secure tents (Judg. 4:21-22; 5:26); to

hang articles (Isa. 22:23,25; Ezek. 15:3); to weave cloth (Judg. 16:14); even to dig latrines (Deut. 23:13). Isaiah 22:23-25 used the image of a peg that gives way to picture false security in a leader. Zechariah 10:4 used the peg as one of several images for rulers. In Isa. 33:22 secure tent pegs symbolize that God keeps Jerusalem secure. The enlarged tent and strengthened tent pegs of Isa. 54:2 illustrate God's restoration of Jerusalem.

PEKAH (Pē´ kah) Personal name meaning "open-eyed." Officer in Israel's army who became king in a bloody coup by murdering King Pekahiah (2 Kings 15:25). His reign of 20 years (15:27) probably is the total time he held military control in Gilead and Samaria. Pekah appeared to be the leader in Gilead during Menahem's reign but surrendered control there when Tiglath-pileser III of Assyria confirmed Menahem's rule. Pekah then was given a high office in the army, and the coup followed shortly after Pekahiah succeeded Menahem. Pekah reigned in Samaria 752–732 B.C. and was in turn assassinated by Hoshea (15:30). See *Menahem*.

PEKAHIAH (Pĕk á hī´ ah) Personal name meaning "Yah has opened his eyes." King of Israel 742–740 B.C. He succeeded his father, Menahem, as a vassal of the Assyrian throne (2 Kings 15:23). The tense political situation he inherited was very hostile, as the loyalists and rebel zealots vied for control. Pehakiah's uneventful reign ended when he was assassinated by an army officer, Pekah (15:25), who was supported by Syria and opposed to the Assyrian domination. See *Pekah*.

PEKOD (Pē´ kŏd) Hebrew for "punishment" or "judgment" which plays on the name Puqadu, an Aramean tribe inhabiting the area east of the mouth of the Tigris (Jer. 50:21; Ezek. 23:23). Sargon II (722–705 B.C.) incorporated Pekod into the Assyrian Empire. Pekod formed part of the Babylonian Empire in the time of Jeremiah and Ezekiel.

PELAIAH (Pē la´ yah) Personal name meaning "Yahweh is wonderful (or performs wonders)." **1.** Descendant of David (1 Chron. 3:24). **2.** Levite assisting in Ezra's public reading of the Law (Neh. 8:7). **3.** Levite witnessing Nehemiah's covenant (Neh. 10:10), perhaps identical to 2.

PELALIAH (Pĕ lä lī´ ah) Personal name meaning "Yahweh intercedes." Ancestor of a priest in Ezra's time (Neh. 11:12).

PELATIAH (Pĕl à tī´ ah) Personal name meaning "Yahweh delivers." **1.** Descendant of David (1 Chron. 3:21). **2.** One of the Simeonites destroying the remaining Amalekites at Mount Seir (1 Chron. 4:42). **3.** Judean prince who offered "wicked counsel," perhaps appealing to Egypt for help in a revolt against the Babylonians (Ezek. 11:1,13; cp. Jer. 27:1-3; 37:5,7,11). **4.** Witness to Nehemiah's covenant (Neh. 10:22).

PELEG (Pē´ lĕg) Personal name meaning "division" or "watercourse." Descendant of Shem (Gen. 10:25), ancestor of Abraham (Gen. 11:16-19; 1 Chron. 1:19,25) and Jesus (Luke 3:35). Peleg's name is attributed to one of the many firsts recorded in Genesis, the "division" of the earth or land. Tradition associates this division with the confusing of languages and the consequent scattering of peoples from Babel (Gen. 11:8-9). Noting that *peleg* often refers to a stream of water (Job 29:6; Pss. 1:3; 46:4; 119:136; Prov. 5:16; 21:1; Isa. 30:25; 32:2), some suggest that the "division" of the land refers to irrigation ditches crisscrossing the landscape. According to this interpretation, Peleg's name commemorates the beginnings of organized agriculture. Though Peleg's descendants are only traced through Abraham, Peleg is recognized as the ancestor of all the Semitic peoples of Mesopotamia, while his brother Joktan was ancestor of the Arabian Semites. See *Table of Nations*.

PELET (Pē´ lĕt) Personal name derived from a root meaning "escape." **1.** Descendant of Caleb (1 Chron. 2:47). **2.** Benjaminite warrior who defected from Saul to David (1 Chron. 12:3).

PELETH (Pē´ lĕth) Personal name meaning "swift." **1.** Father of On (Num. 16:1). The name is possibly a textual corruption of Pallu (Gen. 46:9; Num. 26:5,8), whose descendants are also associated with the Korah rebellion

(Num. 26:9-10). **2.** A Jerahmeelite (1 Chron. 2:33).

PELETHITES (Pē´ lĕth īts) Family name meaning "courier." Foreign mercenaries King David employed as bodyguards and special forces. Their leader was Benaiah (2 Sam. 8:18). The Pelethites are mentioned in conjunction with the Cherethites. These two groups probably were sea peoples who formed a loyalty to David during his days in the Philistine country while evading Saul. They remained with him until his death, fighting for him during the rebellions against his throne. Following his death they helped Solomon purge the kingdom of David's enemies. See *Cherethites*.

PELICAN Any member of a family of large, web-footed birds with gigantic bills having expandable pouches attached to the lower jaw. Pelicans are found in Palestine. The Hebrew term translated "pelican" in Lev. 11:18; Deut. 14:17, however, suggests a bird which regurgitates its food to feed its young. Other passages (Ps. 102:6; Isa. 34:11; Zeph. 2:14) associate the same Hebrew term with deserted ruins, an unlikely habitat for the pelican. Suggested identifications include the jackdaw (NASB margin), owl (NASB margin, NRSV), and vulture (RSV).

PELLA (Pĕl´ là) City just east of the Jordan River and southeast of the Sea of Galilee. It received a large part of the Jerusalem church when they fled there before the Roman destruction of the Holy City in A.D. 66. Pella became an important link in the church structure from that time. The site was inhabited as early as 1900 B.C. and is mentioned in the Egyptian Execration Texts (1850 B.C.) and the Amarna Letters (about 1400 B.C.). Pella was destroyed shortly before the Israelite conquest and not rebuilt until about 350 B.C. Alexander the Great settled the city with Macedonians. In the early years of the first century B.C., it was destroyed again but rebuilt and greatly enhanced by Pompey.

PELONITE (Pē´ lō nīt) Resident of Pelon, an unknown site. The title belongs to two of David's 30 elite warriors (1 Chron. 11:27,36; 27:10). Pelonite is perhaps a textual corruption for Paltite, the title of Helez in the parallel in 2 Sam. 23:26.

PELUSIUM (Pĕ luz´ ĭ ŭm) Egyptian military outpost near the mouth of the easternmost branch of the Nile, about 18 miles west of the Suez Canal, identified with modern el Farama. Some modern translations follow the Vulgate in reading "Pelusium" at Ezek. 30:15-16 (NIV, NRSV, TEV; also KJV and NASB margins). Pelusium was the site of the defeat of Pharaoh Psammetichus III by Cambyses of Persia in 525 B.C. KJV, NASB follow the Hebrew in reading "Sin." Some Greek and Latin witnesses read "Sais," the capital of the Twenty-sixth (Saite) Dynasty (663–525 B.C.), at 30:15. Sais was located on the westernmost branch of the Nile. The REB follows the earliest Greek translation in reading Syene (modern Aswan) at 30:16. See *Sin, Wilderness of.*

PEN or **PENCIL** See *Writing.*

PENDANT See *Jewels, Jewelry.*

PENIEL (Pə nī´ ĕl) (Gen. 32:30) See *Penuel.*

PENINNAH (Pə nĭn´ nah) Personal name, perhaps meaning "woman with rich hair," "coral," or "pearl." It may be an intentional word play meaning "fruitful." Elkanah's second wife and rival of barren Hannah (1 Sam. 1:2,4).

PENKNIFE Another name for a scribe's knife. See *Writing.*

PENNY See *Coins.*

PENTAPOLIS League of five Philistine city-states which banded together to oppose the Israelite occupation of Canaan. See *Philistines.*

PENTATEUCH The expression derives from two Greek words *penta*, "five," and *teuchos*, "vessel, container," and refers to the first five books of OT. This designation dates to the time of Tertullian (ca. 200 A.D.), but Jewish canons label these books collectively as the Torah, which means "Teaching, Instruction." In English Bibles these first five books are commonly called "Law." This designation is misleading because it misrepresents the con-

tent of the Pentateuch. Large portions are not law at all; they are actually inspiring narratives (virtually all of Genesis; Exod. 1–11; 14–20; 32–34; Lev. 8–10; Num. 9–14; 16–17; 20–25; 27; 31–32; 36). Although *Deuteronomium* means "second law," the book presents itself as preaching, Moses' final pastoral addresses.

The Structure and Contents of the Pentateuch The Pentateuch is one continuous narrative. For example, the first verb in Lev. 1:1 ("And He called") lacks a subject, which must be supplied from the last verse of Exodus. Because of the physical limitations of scrolls, it was necessary, probably from the outset, to divide the narrative into five segments more easily manageable on leather or vellum scrolls. This division dates at least to the second century B.C. in the Septuagint. The partitioning creates the unfortunate impression that these are distinct compositions to be interpreted separately. This is wrong. The story that begins in Gen. 1:1 climaxes with the making of the covenant at Sinai and ends with Moses' theological exposition of the covenant in Deuteronomy.

In the Hebrew text the names derive primarily from the opening words of each scroll. Genesis is called *bere'shith*, "In [the] Beginning"; Exodus, *we'elleh shemoth*, "These are the Names"; Leviticus, *wayyiqra*, "And He Called"; Numbers, *bemidbar*, "In the Desert" [the fifth word]; and Deuteronomy, *elleh haddebarim*, "These are the Words." The names of the books in our English Bibles came via the Latin Vulgate, which followed the Greek Septuagint. They are descriptive of the contents: Genesis, "generation, origin," derives from the formula that occurs 11 times in the book, "These are the generations of" (Gk. *geneseos*; e.g., 2:4; 5:1; etc.); Exodus, "going out"; Leviticus reflects the Levitical cultic system; Numbers refers to the numbering of the tribes; and Deuteronomy means "second law" (cp. 17:18). Following Martin Luther, Germans and Scandinavians call them 1st Moses, 2nd Moses, 3rd Moses, 4th Moses, and 5th Moses, reflecting the Mosaic authorship of each book.

We do not know when the divisions originated, but the lines between the books are logical and substantive. The division between Genesis and Exodus occurs where the family history of the Patriarchs ends. The division between Exodus and Leviticus occurs where the narrative describing the construction of the

P
Q

Tabernacle ends (Exod. 35:1–40:18). The book of Numbers begins with the registration of Israel's fighting forces (Num. 1:1–2:34) and Levites (3:1–4:49) as Israel prepares to leave Sinai. Deuteronomy is most obviously a self-contained literary unit, consisting of Moses' final speeches prior to his death. However it may be argued that Deut. 32:48–34:12 represents a natural narrative conclusion to Numbers and that the speeches of Moses (Deut. 1:1–32:47) are a series of sermonic insertions.

In any case, the division of the Pentateuch is artificial. On the basis of style and content, it divides naturally into a series of smaller literary blocks: Gen. 1–11:26, primeval history from creation to Abraham; Gen. 11:27–50:26, the Patriarchal narratives; Exod. 1:1–18:27, Israel's exodus from Egypt; Exod. 20:1–Num. 10:10; Israel at Sinai; Num. 10:11–21:35, Israel in the desert; and Num. 22:1–Deut. 34:12, Israel on the Plains of Moab. Each of these sections consists of easily identifiable literary subdivisions.

It is conceivable that before the present form was cast the materials were preserved on a series of smaller scrolls. Genesis, for example, is punctuated by the formula "These are the generations of …," which occurs 11 times and divides the book formally into 12 sections (2:4; 5:1; 6:9; 10:1; 11:10; 11:27; 25:12; 25:19; 36:1; 36:9; 37:2). The Joseph cycle (Gen. 37; 39–48; 50) has its own literary style and may have been preserved separately as perhaps was the narrative of Israel's exodus from Egypt (Exod. 1:1–18:27). We know that the Decalogue (Exod. 20:2-17) was preserved from the outset as a separate document, "written by the finger of God" (Exod. 24:12; 31:18; cp. 32:15-16; 34:1,28; Deut. 4:13; 5:22; 10:2-4). Exod. 24:7 mentions "the covenant document" (Hb. *seper berith,* usually

The Samaritan Pentateuch at Nablus. Samaritans consider only the Pentateuch as canonical.

rendered "the book of the covenant," preserved in Exod. 21:1–23:3 (if not beginning in 20:22). It appears likely Yahweh's speeches at Mount Sinai (e.g., the prescriptions for construction of the Tabernacle and the dressing of priests [Exod. 25:1–31:17]; instructions concerning the sacrifices [Lev. 1:1–7:38]; the so-called "Holiness Code" [Lev. 17–27]; etc.) were written down immediately, perhaps on separate scrolls and, that when Israel left Sinai, they carried the documents with them. The archaic flavor of the poetry in the pentateuchal narratives (the blessing of Jacob, Gen. 49; the Song of the Sea, Exod. 15:2-18; the Balaam Oracles in Num. 22–24; the Song of Yahweh, Deut. 32:1-43 [intended as Israel's "national anthem"]; Moses' blessing of the tribes, Deut. 33:2-33), suggests these were preserved in written form from the beginning. According to Num. 21:14 Israel possessed a "Book of the Wars of Yahweh," apparently containing records of and poems commemorating his triumphs over Israel's enemies (cp. Exod. 17:14). Numbers 33:1-3 reports that Israel kept a diary of their experiences wandering from place to place (the stopping places listed in 33:5-49. Deuteronomy contains numerous references to "the Torah" that Moses preached as a written text (e.g., 17:18; 27:3; 28:58; 29:21; 30:10). In fact, 31:9 suggests Moses wrote down his final speeches himself. It is plausible that genealogies and other statistical material derive from separate written documents. However the Pentateuch was composed, these documents represent the true origin of the Pentateuch.

The Plot of the Pentateuch The pivotal event of the Pentateuch is God's revelation of himself at Sinai. Everything before is prologue, and all that comes after is epilogue. This is evident from the redundant highlighting of the place in Deut. 19:1-3, and also from the explicit anticipation of Exod. 3:12, where Yahweh told Moses that Israel's service to God at Mount Sinai would prove Yahweh had sent him. This is confirmed by Moses' demands to Pharaoh that he let Israel go to serve Yahweh in the desert (4:23; 5:1,3; 6:11; 7:16; 8:1,25-28; 9:13; 10:3,7,9,24-26). The Patriarchal narratives also look forward to Sinai. In Gen. 12:2 God promises Abraham that he would be a blessing to the whole world. Later we learn that this would involve being the recipient of the divine revelation (cp. Deut. 4:5-8), being a kingdom of priests, a holy nation, a special treasure "among all the peoples, for all the earth is mine" (Exod. 19:5-6). The narrative invites the reader to anticipate the Exodus to Sinai by Yahweh's self-identification in Gen. 15:7: "I am Yahweh who brought you up from Ur of the Chaldees," which echoes a phrase appearing dozens of times later, "I am Yahweh, who brought you up out of Egypt" (cp. Lev. 11:45); by citing God's prediction of Israel's enslavement, deliverance, and emergence with wealth (15:13-14), wealth needed to build the tabernacle; by citing Yahweh's promise to give Abraham's descendants the land of Canaan (Gen. 15:18-21), which becomes the expressed reason for the exodus (Exod. 3:7-8; 6:6-8); and by citing God's (El Shaddai's) announcement that He would be God to Abraham *and his descendants after him* (Gen. 17:7), with whom He would establish His covenant. At Sinai the God of Abraham, Isaac, and Jacob formally became the God of Israel, binding Abraham's descendants to him by confirming the eternal covenant (Exod. 31:16-17; Lev. 24:8; cp. Judg. 2:1). Finally, Sinai is anticipated in Gen. 26:5, where Yahweh recognizes that Abraham "obeyed Me and kept My charge, My commandments, My statutes and My laws" (Gen. 26:5). The expressions echo the Sinai revelation; apparently Abraham fulfilled the requirements of the Sinai covenant without the benefit of the Sinai revelation.

The narratives describing Israel's journey from Sinai to the Plains of Moab are told against the backdrop of Yahweh's covenant with Israel and Israel's promise to do "all that Yahweh had told them." Numbers 28:6 explicitly refers to the Sinai revelation. But the book of Deuteronomy, virtually in its entirety, represents Moses' exposition of the Sinai covenant. However, remember that the primary character is not human; this is a record of God's relationship with those He created in His own image, whom He elected, redeemed, and commissioned to be His agents on the earth.

The Themes of the Pentateuch The theological themes developed in the Pentateuch are virtually innumerable. These represent the theological skeleton of the narratives: God as Creator (Gen. 1–2); God as Judge of sinful humanity, who spared Noah (Gen. 3–11:26); God as the one who elected His agents of blessing the world, entered into covenant relationship with them, and promised to give the land of Canaan to their descendants as an eternal possession

(Gen. 11:37–50:26); God as one who redeemed His people from slavery (Exod. 1–15:21); God as one Who accompanied His people during their desert travels, providing for their physical needs and punishing the faithless (Exod. 15:22–17:7; 18:1-27; Num. 10:11–20:29); God as one who entered into covenant relationship with and revealed His will comprehensively to Israel at Sinai (Exod. 19:1–Num. 10:10); God as one who fights for Israel against their enemies (Exod. 17:8-16; Num. 22:1–25:18); God as one who will give Israel their land and promises to be with then after the death of Moses (Num. 26:1–Deut. 34:12).

Literary Forms and Genres in the Pentateuch Although the Pentateuch is commonly called "The Law," formal legislative material is limited. In fact this designation is misleading, as even a cursory reading of Ps. 1 suggests. If the Pentateuch were primarily "law," it would scarcely be the psalmist's delight or a source of light and life (Ps. 1:2-3). The Pentateuch is dominated by "gospel," good news of God's grace demonstrated through election, salvation, and the providential care of His people. Those who doubt this need only to read Exod. 34:6-7, where Yahweh defines His glory in immanent and gracious terms (ESV): "The LORD, the LORD, a God merciful and gracious, slow to anger, and abounding in steadfast love and faithfulness, keeping steadfast love for thousands, forgiving iniquity and transgression and sin, but who will by no means clear the guilty, visiting the iniquity of the fathers on the children and the children's children, to the third and the fourth generation."

The Pentateuch is dominated by narratives developing this theme. In Gen. 1–4 God graciously spared a race that alienated itself from Him through sin and promised to solve the problem at its root; in Gen. 6–9 God graciously (6:8; 8:1) rescued Noah and his family from the fury of His own wrath; in Gen. 11:26–50:26 God graciously called Abraham and preserved His family to be the agent of blessing to a world under the curse of sin and death; in Exod. 1–18 God graciously redeemed His people from bondage; in Exod. 19–24 God graciously entered into covenant relationship with Israel; in Exod. 25–40 God graciously provided a way He might reside among His people; in Exod. 20–23, most of Leviticus, and large sections of Numbers, God graciously revealed His will to Israel (cp. Deut. 4:6-8); during Israel's desert wanderings God graciously cared for His people, feeding them and defending them against their enemies, ensuring they would enter the promised land; in Deuteronomy God graciously provided Israel with Moses to explain His will. Most of the prescriptive material of Exodus–Leviticus is divine speeches framed by narrative comments, "Then God/Yahweh said/spoke." Even Deuteronomy is narrative with inserted addresses and poems by Moses. Narrative, not "law," is the dominant genre of the Pentateuch.

"Law" is present, if by "law" we mean commandments prescribing human behavior. The Pentateuch contains hundreds of such prescriptions (Jewish Rabbis counted 613), referred to variously as *tora* ("teaching"), *miswoth* ("commands"), *huqqoth* ("statutes, ordinances, decrees"), *mispatim* ("judgments, regulations, laws"), *edot* ("covenant stipulations"), which may be characterized as constitutional regulations. With respect to form, the regulations tend to be of two types. "Apodictic" commands, cast in the second person ("You shall" or "You shall not"), are generally without qualification, condition, or motivation (most of the Decalogue). "Casuistic" regulations are cast in the third person, beginning with a conditional clause ("If a person"), and ending with a declaration of the consequences ("If A, then B"). Christians tend to divide the laws into moral, civil, and ceremonial, but the Pentateuch offers no such distinctions. On the contrary, texts like Lev. 19, mixing all three types, assume that all of life is sacred and that it is wrong to "compartmentalize" behavior.

Although prescriptive material is found elsewhere, for the sake of convenience we refer specifically to six prescriptive sections: the Decalogue (Exod. 20:1-17; Deut. 5:6-21); the "Book of the Covenant" (Exod. 21:1–23:33); the Tabernacle Prescriptions (Exod. 25–31); the "Manual on Ritual Worship" (Lev. 1–7); the so-called "Holiness Code" (Lev. 17–25); and the so-called "Deuteronomic Code" (Deut. 12–26). Leviticus and Numbers contain much additional prescriptive material, but the above are commonly recognized as self-contained units.

The Decalogue (Exod. 20:1-17; Deut. 5:6-21) Although the Decalogue contains divine commands, the Pentateuch never refers to "the Ten Commandments." They are consistently identified as "the Ten Words" (Exod. 34:28; Deut. 4:13; 10:4), captured in the precise Greek term *decalogos*, "ten words." As "words," the

Decalogue encapsulates the principles of covenant relationship with easily memorized statements (one for each finger). That this is the fundamental covenant document is clear because Yahweh Himself provided the first copy (Exod. 24:12; 34:1-24; Deut. 4:13; 5:22; 10:1-5) and from Moses' use of them in Deuteronomy. The Decalogue is more a worship document than a legal code, as confirmed by the fundamental opening statement: "I am Yahweh your God Who brought you out of the land of Egypt, out of the house of slavery." Obedience to these 10 principles represents the worship response to salvation received as a gift from Yahweh (cp. Lev. 19:6). The preamble provides background and motivation for worship. Without it the call for obedience is a legalistic demand.

The "Book of the Covenant" (Exod. 21:1–23:33; some add 20:22-26) The name derives from 24:7, according to which Moses read the *seper habberit* ("covenant document") in the hearing of all the people assembled prior to the ratification ritual. The Book of the Covenant subdivides into six parts arranged chiastically:

(a) Introduction (20:22) Placing Israel's response to covenant in the present context of divine revelation

(b) Principles of Worship (20:23-26) Highlighting Israel's cultic expression of devotion to Yahweh

(c) Casuistic Laws (21:1–22:20) Highlighting Israel's ethical expression of devotion to Yahweh

(c') Apodictic Laws (22:21–23:9) Highlighting Israel's ethical expression of devotion to Yahweh

(b') Principles of Worship (23:10-19) Highlighting Israel's cultic expression of devotion to Yahweh

(a') Conclusion (23:20-33) Placing Israel's response to covenant in the future context of divine action

Prescriptions for Israel's worship frame prescriptions governing daily life. The purpose of worship is to inspire devotion to Yahweh and to create an ethical community of faith

The Tabernacle Prescriptions (Exod. 25–31) Patterned after the days of creation are seven divine speeches, climaxing in the provision of the Sabbath as a sign of the eternality of God's covenant with Israel. Although the instructions have long-range implications, for the most part they concern one event: the construction of the tabernacle as a sacred residence for Yahweh. Through the tabernacle God graciously provided a means of constant communion with His people. This communion was severely threatened by the apostasy of worshiping the golden calf, but Yahweh graciously renewed the covenant (Exod. 32–34). Exodus 35–40 is a narrative description of the construction of the tabernacle according to God's specifications, climaxing in His visible affirmation by the movement of His radiant glory into the structure.

The "Manual on Ritual Worship" (Lev. 1–7) This material prescribes permanent practices "throughout your generations" (Lev. 3:17) and is in imperative form like legislation. However it is motivated not only by God's desire for obedience but by human well being, that Israelites "may be forgiven" (4:35) and may enjoy communion with God.

The "Holiness Code" (Lev. 17–25; some add 26–27) This section derives its name from the statement, "You shall be holy; for I the LORD your God am holy" (19:2; 20:7,26), and from the overall emphasis. The Lord identified Himself as the Holy One (19:2; 20;26; 21:8); the one who makes Israel holy (20:8; 21:8,15,23; 22:9,16,32), and separates her from the other people (20:24,26); He challenges the Israelites to sanctify themselves (20:7) and "be holy" (19:2; 20:7,26; 21:6; cp. vv. 7-8). Many articles and persons are described as holy—the Lord's name (20:3; 22:3,32), sacrificial food (19:8), ordinary food (19:24), sacred bread (21:22; 24:9), food dedicated to the Lord (22:1-6,10-16); convocations (23:2-8,21-27,35-37); a place (tabernacle, 24:9); and a time (year of jubilee, 25:12).

Outline: Instructions in Holy Living (The "Holiness Code") (17:1–25:55)

1. The Sanctity of Life (17:1–18:30)
2. The Sanctity of the Community (19:1–20:27)
3. The Sanctity of Worship (21:1–24:23)
   a. The Sanctity of the Priesthood (21:1-24)
   b. The Sanctity of Gifts for God (22:1-33)
   c. The Sanctity of Holy Days (23:1-44)
   d. The Sanctity of the Tabernacle (24:1-9)
   e. The Sanctity of the Divine Name (24:10-23)
4. The Sanctity of the Land (25:1-55)

The "Deuteronomic Code" (Deut. 12–26) This section begins with the announcement, "These are the ordinances and laws that you shall be careful to obey in the land which the LORD, the God of your fathers has given you to possess as long as you live on the earth" (12:1). However, Deut. 12–26 represent a part of Moses' second address to the tribes just before they crossed the Jordan to go into Canaan. He set the stage with an extended presentation of the nature of covenant relationship and by repeated appeals to exclusive love and service for Yahweh (5:1–11:32). The commandments in chapters 12–26 derive from the revelation at Sinai but have a pronounced sermonic (cp. 26:16-19), as opposed to legal, flavor. So the designation of this section as a legal "code" is misleading. Moses' role is pastoral rather than legislative, applying laws given at Sinai to the new situation facing the Israelites. Accordingly, the instructions are laced with motive clauses, warnings of divine judgment for disobedience and promises of blessing and long life for covenant fidelity. This difference accounts for the Deuteronomic instructions' divergence from those in the "Book of the Covenant" or the "Holiness Code." In keeping with Moses' concern for exclusive allegiance to Yahweh (as formalized in the Shema, "Hear O Israel, Yahweh is our God, Yahweh alone" [6:4]) and total, unreserved love for him (6:5), he declared that once established in the land, Yahweh would identify the place He has chosen to establish His name, the place where all Israel would come to worship (e.g. 12:1-14).

General Theme: The Specific Stipulations of the Covenant (12:1–26:15)

1. The Religious Life of the Holy People (12:1–16:17)
   a. The Unity and Purity of Worship (12:1–14:21)
   b. Institutional Regulations (14:22–16:17)
2. The Government of the Holy People (16:18–21:9)
   a. The Structures of Theocratic Government (16:18–18:22)
   b. The Conduct of Government (19:1–21:9)
3. Family Law (21:10–22:30)
   a. Female Prisoners of War (21:10-14)
   b. The Rights of Firstborn (21:15-17)
   c. Rebellious Sons (21:18-21)

Although generally interpreted as law codes, one should realize that none are legislation simply for the sake of legislation. Nor is the obedience demanded simply for the sake of obedience. Each involves conduct to be followed by God's people in response to His gracious salvation and as an expression of fidelity to Him. In no case should the laws be viewed as a way of salvation; on the contrary, grateful and willing obedience is the expression of love for God in response to His provided salvation and the privilege of covenant relationship with Him. God's primary expectation was always a disposition of love (covenant commitment) and fear to be demonstrated by observable ethical behavior (Deut. 10:12–11:1).

In addition to historiographic narrative and constitutional prescriptions, other literary genres are represented in the Pentateuch. These include poetic texts in the narrative (including "Jacob's Blessing of His Sons," Gen. 49:1-27; The "Song of the Sea," Exod. 15:1-18; "Balaam's Oracles," Num. 23:7-10,18-24, and 24:3-9, 15-24; Israel's "National Anthem," Deut. 32:1-43; and "Moses' Blessing of the Tribes," Deut. 33:2-29; statistical material (genealogies, Gen. 5; 10; 11:1-26; 25:1-4; 36; 46:8-27; Exod. 6:14-27; military registration lists, Num. 1:1–3:51; 26:1-65; booty lists, Num. 31:32-47; a journey itinerary, Num. 33:1-49; boundary descriptions, Num. 34:1-12; and personnel lists, Num. 34:16-29), proverbial sayings (Gen. 2:23; 3:19; 10:9; Exod. 33:19), aetiologies (explanations of the origins of practices or names, Gen. 2:25; 21:31, and 26:33 [Beersheba]; Exod. 2:10 [Moses]; etc.) and treaty/covenantal forms. The Decalogue itself is presented as a covenant document, complete with preamble, historical prologue, and stipulations. Covenantal forms extend to Numbers and Leviticus as well (note especially the covenant curses in Lev. 26) and in particular to the book of Deuteronomy. Although Deuteronomy consists of Moses' farewell addresses, they are arranged to reflect ancient near eastern (second millennium B.C. Hittite) treaty forms.

The Historical Significance of the Pentateuchal Narratives Prior to the enlightenment the historicity of the patriarchal and exodus narratives was not questioned. However, this changed dramatically in the past centuries. The first casualty to higher critical scholarship was the opening chapters of Genesis. Because creation in Gen. 1–3 apparently disagrees with some modern scientific conclusions, because events of Gen. 4–11 involve prehistoric and preliterate events, and because texts like 2:7 and 6:1-8 describe divine and semi-divine beings relating directly to human beings, these texts are interpreted as mythological, akin to Babylonian creation and flood accounts rather than as a historical record. The second casualty was the patriarchs. Because these stories present idealized pictures of Israel's ancestors and deal with preliterate times, they are largely dismissed as legendary retrojections of later Israel, created to explain the existence and unity of Israel. The third casualty was Moses and the exodus. Although until recently many critical scholars recognized a historical core in the exodus narratives (the memory of a handful of slaves who escaped from Egypt to Palestine, now even this reduction is rejected as theological historicizing. The fact that archaeology has failed to give evidence validating the characters or events in the Pentateuch is accepted as proof that none of this is true.

However, the issue is not that simple. Concerning the archaeological record, we accept the axiom, "Absence of evidence is not evidence of absence." Furthermore, while doubtful that archaeology can prove the Bible, the discoveries of the past century allow us to reconstruct patterns of life and a "skeleton" of ancient Near Eastern history, in which the events described in the Pentateuch are quite at home. As for the historicity of the exodus, just as it is impossible to explain the existence of the church without reference to the historical incarnation and resurrection of Christ, so it is impossible to explain the existence of Israel without the dramatic intervention of God on her behalf, the memory of which underlies the entire OT. With respect to the patriarchal narratives, the authors of these texts did not consider themselves to be writing fiction. Based upon ancient stories handed down in oral or written form, these narratives preserve the ancient memory of God's gracious intervention for the purpose of bringing blessing and life to a world under the curse of death. Genesis 1:1–2:4a is composed in a lofty and elegant style, appropriate for text to be used in worship, but this does not mean that it is the product of human imagination. This text not only celebrates God as the Creator of all things, but humanity as the climax of His creation. The generic, stylistic, and substantive links between the early chapters of Genesis and the later narratives, including Joshua, Judges, Samuel, and Kings, suggest a continuous historical story line from the creation of the universe to the rise and fall of Israel.

The Date and Authorship of the Pentateuch Although Jewish and Christian tradition almost unanimously recognize Moses as author of the Pentateuch, few issues relating to the OT now are debated as hotly, and in few is the gulf between critical and evangelical scholarship so wide. Many conservative scholars continue to believe that Moses wrote virtually all of the Pentateuch with his own hand. So long as critical scholars recognized Moses as a historical figure, in principle his involvement in the composition of the Pentateuch was not excluded—unless, of course literacy was denied him. However, from the middle of the 19th century A.D., especially following Julius Wellhausen, most critical scholars have rejected Moses having a significant role in the origin of the Pentateuch.

The questioning began early with doubts whether Moses recorded his own death and burial (Deut. 34), or knew of a place in northern Israel called Dan (Gen. 14:14; cp. Josh. 19:47; Judg. 18:28b-29), or referred to the conquest of Canaan as past (Deut. 2:12). Thus scholars developed an alternative explanation for the origins of the Pentateuch known as the Documentary Hypothesis. According to the classical form of the theory, the Pentateuch is the product of a long and complex literary evolution, specifically incorporating at least four major literary strands composed independently over several centuries and not combined in the present form until the time of Ezra (fifth century B.C.). These sources are identified as J, E, D, and P. J represents a ninth-century B.C. (ca. 850) document that originated in Judah, distinguished by its preference for the name Yahweh (Jehovah). The E source preferred the divine title Elohim and theoreti-

cally was composed in Israel in the eighth century B.C. D stands for Deuteronomy, supposedly written around 621 B.C. to lend support to Josiah's reforms. The priestly document, P, assumedly was composed about 500 B.C. by priests seeking to preserve their own version of Israel's history. According to the theory, these sources were compiled and combined in the middle of the fifth century B.C. Nehemiah 8 recounts the moment when Ezra publicly read the Pentateuch as a unit for the first time. Because Joshua describes the fulfillment of the promises of land to the patriarchs and because of stylistic links to Deuteronomy, Gerhard von Rad added Joshua to the pentateuchal corpus, calling the six books the Hexateuch.

Variations of the Documentary Hypothesis prevailed for more than a century. However, due to advances in literary studies, today the state of pentateuchal scholarship is confused, with new theories or radical modifications appearing often. The new theories push the dates for pentateuchal origin ever later. Martin Noth created the term Tetrateuch ("four books"), arguing that Deuteronomy was originally composed as a theological foreword to the "Deuteronomistic History," consisting of Joshua, Judges, 1–2 Samuel, and 1–2 Kings. However many scholars now are going in the opposite direction, recognizing more Deuteronomistic features in Genesis–Numbers. Because of the link between Deuteronomy and Josiah's reform, some assert that the earliest sources underlying the Pentateuch were composed in the sixth century B.C. during the exile. It is commonly recognized that some of the law "codes" may be earlier, but as literary documents, they are said to be late. R. N. Whybray argued that the Pentateuch is a unitary composition written in the fourth century B.C., inspired perhaps by the Greek *Histories* of Herodotus.

The bewildering variety of theories fosters little confidence in critical scholarship. However the fact remains that nowhere does the Pentateuch specifically name its author. As was common in the ancient Semitic world, it is anonymous. On the other hand, the internal evidence suggests that Moses kept a record of Israel's experiences in the desert (Exod. 17:14; 24:4,7; 34:27; Num. 33:1–2; Deut. 31:9,11). Furthermore, many statements in the OT credit the Pentateuch to Moses (e.g., Josh. 1:8; 8:31-32; 1 Kings 2:3; 2 Kings 14:6; Ezra 6:18; Neh.

P
Q

13:1; Dan. 9:11-13; Mal. 4:4), and the NT identifies the Torah very closely with him (Matt. 19:8; John 5:46-47; 7:19; Acts 3:22; Rom. 10:5). A series of additional features within the text point to an early date for its composition: (1) the forms of the names and many of the actions of the patriarchs make best sense in a second millennium B.C. environment; (2) the narratives suggest a thorough acquaintance with Egypt; (3) Egyptian loanwords appear with greater frequency in the Pentateuch than anywhere else in the OT; (4) the name Moses itself suggests an Egyptian provenance for the story; (5) the general viewpoint of the narrative is foreign to Canaan; (6) the seasons are Egyptian; the flora and fauna are Egyptian and Sinaitic; (7) in some instances the geography reflects a foreign viewpoint (e.g., a comment like that found in Gen. 33:18, "a city of Shechem, which is in the land of Canaan," is unlikely after the exile because by then Israel had been in the land for 900 years); (8) and archaisms in the language (like the use of the third-person singular pronoun, *hîʾ*, for both genders), all point to an early date.

Moses could very well have written most of the Pentateuch himself. Having been raised in the court of Pharaoh, and given the new 22-letter alphabet, Moses' own literary qualifications for writing should not be dismissed.

It is unlikely that all these considerations establish that Moses wrote all the Pentateuch as we have it. It is doubtful he wrote the account of his death in Deut. 34. Frequently the text provides explanatory notes updating facts for a later audience (e.g., "Esau, that is Edom," Gen. 36:1; the aboriginal inhabitants of the Transjordan, Deut. 2:10-12). Furthermore, the form of the cursive Canaanite script that Moses probably used was still in its infancy and was replaced with the square Aramaic script in the postexilic period, and the vowels were added a millennium later. The archaic qualities of the poems (Gen. 49; Exod. 15; etc.) in contrast to the surrounding narrative suggests the latter may have been updated periodically in accordance with the evolution of the Hebrew language. This may explain why the grammar and syntax of Deuteronomy in its present form reads much like Jeremiah, who lived long after Moses. At the same time Moses could have used a scribe or secretary.

There is no reason to doubt that Moses wrote down the speeches he delivered (Deut. 31:9-13),

or that when he came down from Mount Sinai, he arranged for the transcription of the revelation he had received on the mountain, if he did not write it all himself. It is equally plausible that he authorized the written composition of many of the stories and genealogies of the patriarchs that had been transmitted orally or in rudimentary written form. Just as the pieces of the tabernacle were constructed and woven by skilled craftsmen and finally assembled by Moses (Exod. 35–40) so literary craftsmen may have composed some bits and pieces of the Pentateuch, submitted them to Moses, who then approved them. When exactly the pieces were put together in their present form we may only speculate (Deuteronomy suggests some time after the death of Moses), but it seems likely that by the time David organized for temple worship, the contents of the Torah were fixed. The Pentateuch is fundamentally and substantially Mosaic, and later Israelites accepted it as bearing the full force of his authority.

The Pentateuch was the Torah that priests were to teach and model (Deut. 33:10; 2 Chron. 15:3; 19:8; Mal. 2:6,9; cp. Jer. 18:18; Ezek. 7:26; Ezra 7:10), that psalmists praised (Pss. 19:7-14; 119; etc.), to which the prophets appealed (Isa. 1:10; 5:24; 8:20; 30:9; 51:7), by which faithful kings ruled (1 Kings 2:2-4; 2 Kings 14:6; 22:11; 23:25), and the righteous lived (Ps. 1). See *Authority; Inspiration; Revelation, Book of.*   *Daniel I. Block*

PENTATEUCH, SAMARITAN See *Bible Texts and Versions; Samaritan Pentateuch.*

PENTECOST One of three major Jewish feasts also called the Feast of Weeks. The name "Pentecost" is derived from the Greek word meaning "fifty." Pentecost occurs in the month of Sivan (May/June), 50 days after Passover, and celebrates the end of the grain harvest. The Pentecost that followed Jesus' death and resurrection was the occasion on which the Holy Spirit was given to believers in Jerusalem.

Believers were together celebrating Pentecost when suddenly unusual sights and sounds signaled an event that would have far-reaching implications. They heard the sound of "a violent rushing wind" (Acts 2:2 HCSB). They saw tongues of fire resting on believers, and each believer was able to communicate in languages they had never before spoken. They were able to speak with Jewish pilgrims of many languages from all over the Mediterranean world.

These phenomena got the attention of the Jewish faithful gathered in Jerusalem. Many thought the disciples were intoxicated. But Simon Peter got up and pointed out that it was too early in the day for people to be drunk. Peter then took this unusual opportunity to proclaim that this event was the fulfillment of Joel's prophecy that God would pour out His Spirit on all people. Peter linked the gift of the Spirit with the life, death, resurrection, and ascension of Jesus.

Peter's message found its way into the hearts of over 3,000 who responded by repenting and being baptized in the name of Jesus and receiving the gift of the Holy Spirit. See *Festivals; Spirit.*   *Steve Bond*

PENUEL (Pə nū′ ĕl) Name meaning "face of God." **1.** Descendant of Judah and founder (father) of Gedor (1 Chron. 4:4). **2.** A Benjaminite (1 Chron. 8:25). **3.** Site on Jabbok River northeast of Succoth where Jacob wrestled with the stranger (Gen. 32:24-32; cp. Hos. 12:4). The city was destroyed by Gideon because its inhabitants refused him provisions while he pursued the Midianites (Judg. 8:8-9,17). Jeroboam I built (perhaps rebuilt or fortified) the city (1 Kings 12:25). The site is identified with the easternmost of two mounds called Tulul edh-Dhahab, which commands the entrance to the Jordan Valley from the Jabbok gorge, about seven miles east of the Jordan.

PEOPLE OF GOD Group elected by God and committed to be His covenant people. Scripture repeatedly defines who is included in the people of God. The history of revelation shows God electing Israel by grace.
Election and Covenant The election of Israel as the people of God may be traced from Abraham (Gen. 12; cp. Gal. 3:29; Rom. 9:7-8). However, the relationship between Yahweh and Israel began in the exodus. Exodus 19 represents a special covenant form with both conditions (v. 5) and promises of the covenant (vv. 5b-6). The condition of the covenant was obedience; the promise was that "you shall be My own possession out of all the peoples." This promise involves a God-people and people-God

relationship that is the center of the OT. This promise was inherited by the church as the true Israel or the new Israel (Rom. 9:6-8; 1 Cor. 10:18-21; Gal. 6:16). Here is the unique position of the church as the people of God in the divine order (Rom. 9:25-26; 1 Cor. 6:14-17; Titus 2:14; Heb. 8:10; 1 Pet. 2:9-10; Rev. 21:3). See *Church; Covenant; Election; Israel, Spiritual.*

The faith of Israel became more concrete when the remnant idea was developed from corporate salvation out of the divine wrath and judgment. To the remnant fell the status and condition of God's long purpose for His people. Jesus explained the remnant as the chosen one in Matt. 22:14. Most of all, Jesus Himself is the remnant. Truly, the church carries the ideas from the OT that the remnant in the figure of the Servant is the witness of universal salvation and the agent of a final revelation. The servant of Yahweh represented by Israel would be a light to the nations. The universal character of Israel's vocation is most clearly expressed here. The idea of God's people in the OT culminates in the person of the Servant who is the idea of the remnant personified as an individual.

Christ claimed His servant-messiahship, for He is the Son of David, fulfilling the promise of God in the OT. Jesus is the King but rejected every political interpretation of His messianic vocation. His kingdom is not of this world (John 18:36). He is the Suffering Servant who gave His life as a ransom for many and thereby inaugurated the New Covenant.

The role of servant-messiah developed another dimension in its collectivity, that is, church. The servant idea is determinative for an understanding of the priesthood of the whole church. Christology (Christ) is related to ecclesiology (church) (2 Cor. 4:5). Christians are servants sharing that servanthood that the Servant par excellence creates. The call into peoplehood is a call into servanthood. The church is truly the people of God.   *Samuel Tang*

PEOPLE OF THE EAST See *Kadmonites.*

PEOPLE OF THE LAND Translation of the technical Hebrew term *am ha'arets,* used primarily in Jeremiah, Ezekiel, 2 Kings, and 2 Chronicles (Gen. 23:7; Exod. 5:5; Lev. 20:2; Num. 14:9; Hag. 2:4; Zech. 7:5; Dan. 9:6). In most cases, the term apparently refers to the male citizens who lived upon their own land and who had the responsibility as citizens to participate in judicial activities, cultic festivals, and army service. Nonetheless, the references are so diverse that we cannot be sure the same people were in mind each time the term appears. Some scholars think the "people of the land" represented a particular influential element in society such as a national council, influential aristocrats, free citizens and property owners, landless poor, or non-Jerusalemites. Such theories cannot be proven.

In preexilic Judah the "people of the land" first appear in association with the coronation of Joash (2 Kings 11:4-20). They appear slightly later in the avenging of Amon's murder and the elevation of Josiah to the kingship (2 Kings 21:24). They are depicted as being capable of liberating slaves (Jer. 34, especially vv. 18-20, where the "people of the land" both participated in the covenant making and were held responsible for breaking the same). They could also be agents of oppression (Ezek. 22:29). Second Kings 25:18-21 records that Nebuchadnezzar put to death at Riblah "sixty men of the people of the land," along with others held responsible for the revolt against Babylon resulting in the fall of Jerusalem in 587 B.C. Clearly, in these situations these are people who have social, economic, political, and religious significance.

The "people of the land" are also portrayed as "the poor of the land" who remained in Jerusalem during the Babylonian exile (2 Kings 24:14; 25:12). It is notable that when the exiles returned they distanced themselves from those who had remained in Judah by using "people of Judah" to characterize the returning exiles (Ezra 4:4). Disapproval is expressed in Ezra and Nehemiah for the pagan half-Jew and half-Gentile, essentially nonobservant Jews (Ezra 10:2,11; Neh. 10:28-31). In Ezra 9:1-2,11 the plural, the "people of those lands," is used to designate the groupings with whom intermarriage had occurred, "the Canaanites, the Hittites, the Perizzites, the Jebusites, the Ammonites, the Moabites, the Egyptians, and the Amorites" (9:1).

There was considerable bad feelings between the "people of the land" and the Pharisees. In the Synoptic Gospels Jesus is portrayed as supporting the "people of the land" (Mark 7:1-5; Luke 6:1-5). The later postexilic use as witnessed in Ezra

and Nehemiah as well as in the Synoptic Gospels (John 7:49) is further reflected in the rabbinical classification of the "people of the land" as those ignorant of the law and non-observant in their daily lives. Because their condition was not dependent upon birth, however, the deficiencies could be remedied by a greater awareness of and adherence to the Torah.   *Frank E. Eakin, Jr.*

PEOR (Pē´ ôr) Name, perhaps meaning "opening." **1.** Mountain in Moab opposite the wilderness of Judah. Balak brought Balaam there to curse the camp of the Israelites which was visible from the site (Num. 23:28; 24:2). **2.** Abbreviated form of Baal-Peor (lord of Peor), a god whom the Israelites were led to worship (Num. 25:18; 31:16; Josh. 22:17). See *Baal-Peor.* **3.** Site in Judah identified with modern Khirbet Faghur southwest of Bethlehem (Josh. 15:59 REB, following the earliest Greek translation).

PERATH (Pē´ răth) See *Parah.*

PERAZIM (Pĕr´ å zĭm) See *Baal-Perazim.*

PERDITION Describes the eternal state of death, destruction, annihilation, or ruin.
Old Testament Words of the family from which perdition is derived usually relate to a state of physical rather than moral or religious destruction. Perdition is held in contrast to the blessing of God. It is the penalty for disobedience (Deut. 22:24; 28:20). The OT sometimes links this term to the concept of Sheol (2 Sam. 22:5; Ps. 18:4).
New Testament Perdition is the fate of all that do not come to repentance. The way that leads to this destruction is broad in contrast to the narrow road which leads to life (Matt. 7:13). Perdition, as used in the NT, does not convey the idea of simple extinction or annihilation. Set into the context of eternity, the Gospel writers used it to mean an everlasting state of death and judgment. Just as surely as salvation expresses the idea of eternal life, so perdition designates a hopeless eternity of destruction. The phrase "son of perdition" describes the person who has fallen victim to this destruction (cp. Judas in John 17:12). The "man of lawlessness" is doomed to perdition (2 Thess. 2:3). A form of this word is used in Rev. 9:11 to describe the ultimate enemy of God—

the Destroyer. See *Death; Devil; Eternal Life; Everlasting Punishment; Hell; Sheol.*

Ken Massey

PEREA (Pě rē´ ȧ) Roman district in Transjordan which became a part of Herod the Great's kingdom. The capital was Gadara where Jesus drove demons out of a man. (Modern translations follow other manuscripts reading "Gerasenes.") Other important sites in the province were the fortress of Machaerus, where John the Baptist was beheaded, and Pella, where Christians from Jerusalem fled just before the Roman destruction of the Holy City in A.D. 66. Perea was the area through which the Jews traveled to avoid going through Samaria. Although not referred to by name in the NT, it is mentioned as "Judea beyond the Jordan" in several texts (Matt. 19:1; Mark 10:1 RSV). See *Gadarene; Machaerus; Pella; Transjordan.*

PERESH (Pē´ rěsh) Personal name meaning "separate." A Manassite (1 Chron. 7:16).

PEREZ (Pē´ rěz) Personal name meaning "breach." One of the twins born to the illicit affair between Judah and his daughter-in-law, Tamar (Gen. 38). After she was widowed and her brother-in-law, Onan, refused to fulfill his duties in levirate marriage (designed to carry on the name of the deceased through a son), she tricked her father-in-law, Judah, into an affair (vv. 13-30). "His descendents were called Perezites" (Num. 26:20).

PEREZ-UZZA (Pē´ rěz-Ŭz´ zȧ) (NASB, RSV) or **PEREZ-UZZAH** Place-name meaning "breach of Uzzah." Site of the threshing floor of Nacon (or Chidon) west of Jerusalem on the Kiriath-jearim road where the anger of the Lord "broke out" against Uzzah, who touched the ark to steady it (2 Sam. 6:8; 1 Chron. 13:11). The site is perhaps that of Khirbet el-Uz about two miles east of Kiriath-jearim.

PERFECT To be whole or complete; also referred to as "mature." Throughout the Bible, especially in the OT, God is referred to as being "perfect" (Ps. 18:32). He is complete and lacks nothing. In addition, the "ways" of God are perfect, implying that not only is God perfect in His essence, but He is perfect in His actions (2 Sam. 22:31). God's law is also

described as being perfect, indicating that it is complete and able to accomplish its purpose (Ps. 19:7). In the NT James reminded his readers that "every generous act and every perfect gift" originates from God (James 1:17 HCSB). Therefore, God also becomes the source of all that is "perfect" within this world.

God, in His perfection, likewise desires for His children to be "perfect." In the Sermon on the Mount, Jesus commanded, "Be perfect, therefore, as your heavenly Father is perfect" (Matt. 5:48). The perfection demanded of Christians is a state of spiritual maturity or completeness. Jesus was commanding His followers to strive towards a state of moral and spiritual Godlikeness in their lives. Specifically, He was encouraging His disciples to love their enemies in the same way that God loved them. By so doing they were demonstrating the perfection or maturity that He desired. Because of sin within the world, Christians will only realize true perfection in heaven, but the exhortations given in Scripture encourage all to continue to strive towards it in this life.

The journey towards perfection is not an individual accomplishment. First, and foremost, it is a gift from God. Isaiah reminded his readers that God is the one who provides "perfect peace" for those who remain committed to Him (Isa. 26:3). In addition, Paul revealed his understanding of the necessity of working together towards perfection when he stated that the goal of his ministry was to be able to "present everyone mature" (Col. 1:28 HCSB; NASB, complete). Therefore, all Christians are reminded that the goal is to help one another reach completeness as Paul was striving to do in his ministry. See *Holy.*   *Thomas Strong*

PERFUME, PERFUMER Modern translation of a word translated as "apothecary" by the KJV (Exod. 30:25,35; 37:29; 2 Chron. 16:14; Neh. 3:8; Eccles. 10:1). Perfumes mentioned in the Bible include aloes, balsam (or balm), bdellium, calamus (or sweet or fragment cane), camel's thorn, cinnamon (or cassia), frankincense, galbanum, gum, henna, myrrh, nard (or spikenard), onycha, saffron, and stacte. See *Cosmetics; Occupations and Professions; Oil; Ointment.*

P
Q

Carved reliefs found among the ruins of the stadium at ancient Perga.

A portion of the Roman theater located at ancient Pergamum.

PERGA (Pĕr´ gà) Ancient city in the province of Pamphylia, about eight miles from the Mediterranean Sea. Settlement at Perga dates to prehistory. Alexander the Great passed through the town during his campaigns and used guides from there. A temple to Artemis was one of the prominent buildings. Paul, Barnabas, and John Mark came to Perga from Paphos (Acts 13:13). There young John left the team to return home.

PERGAMOS (Pĕr´ gà mŏs) (KJV, Rev. 1:11; 2:12) or **PERGAMUM** (Pĕr´ gà mŭm) Place-name meaning "citadel." A wealthy ancient city in the district of Mysia in Asia Minor. See *Asia Minor, Cities of.*

PERIDA (Pə rī´ dà) Personal name meaning "unique" or "separated." Head of a family of Solomon's servants, some of whom returned from exile (Neh. 7:57; cp. Peruda, Ezra 2:55).

PERISHABLE Term some translations (KJV, REB, NRSV) use to describe the present, mortal body (1 Cor. 15:42,50,53-54), which is subject to death and decay. Other translations render the underlying Greek as corruptible (NASB, NIV) or mortal (TEV). Paul contrasted

The south Hellenistic gate of the ancient city of Perga in Pamphylia (modern Turkey).

the perishable reward champion athletes receive with the lasting reward for which Christians compete (1 Cor. 9:25). First Peter 1:7 compares the testing of lasting faith with that of perishable gold.

PERIZZITES (Pĕr´ ĭz zīts) Group name meaning "rustic." One of the groups of people who opposed the Israelite occupation of Canaan (Josh. 9:1-2). They dwelled in the land as early as Abraham's time (Gen. 13:7). The name implies that the Perizzites probably dwelled in the open country while the Canaanites walled up their encampments.

PERJURY False statement given voluntarily under oath. Perjury involves either false witness to past facts or the neglect of what has been previously vowed. Mosaic law prohibited false swearing (Lev. 19:12; Exod. 20:7) and giving false witness (Exod. 20:16). False witness was punishable with the sentence that would have gone to the one falsely accused of guilt (Deut. 19:16-21). Vows and oaths to perform an act were to be fulfilled (Num. 30:2). See *Oaths*.

PERSECUTION Harassment and suffering which people and institutions inflict upon others for being different in their faith, worldview, culture, or race. Persecution seeks to intimidate, silence, punish, or even to kill people.

Old Testament Israel was the agent of persecution of nations (Judg. 2:11-23; Lev. 26:7-8). The Bible gives special attention to Israel's fate in Egypt (Exod. 1–3) and in the exile (Ps. 137). On an individual level Saul persecuted David (1 Sam. 19:9-12), and Shadrach, Meshach, and Abednego were persecuted because they refused to worship the image of the king (Dan. 3). Jezebel persecuted the prophets of the Lord, and the Prophet Elijah persecuted and killed the prophets of Baal (1 Kings 18). Job felt persecuted by God himself (7:11-21). The Prophets—Amos (7:10-12), Jeremiah (Jer. 1:19; 15:15; 37–38), and Urijah (Jer. 26:20-23)—suffered persecution because they lived out the will of God in adverse circumstances. The Psalms speak of the righteous sufferer who felt persecuted as a result of faith in God, and who prayed to God for deliverance (7; 35; 37; 79; 119:84-87).

Intertestamental period This era witnessed the concerted attempt to make the Jewish

P
Q

The temple of Athena at ancient Pergamum.

people renounce their faith in God. In this conflict, persecution took place on both sides (1 and 2 Maccabees). See *Intertestamental History and Literature.*

New Testament Jesus was persecuted and finally killed by the religious and political establishments of His day (Mark 3:6; Luke 4:29; John 5:16; Acts 3:13-15; 7:52; passion stories). He lived out the liberating passion of God (Luke 4:16-29) and came into conflict with the religious institutions of the cult by healing on the Sabbath (Mark 3:1-6), criticizing the temple activities (Mark 11:15-18), and the law (Matt. 5:21-48).

Jesus pronounced God's salvation upon those who are persecuted for righteousness sake (Matt. 5:10-12). In an evil world disciples are to expect persecution (Matt. 10:16-23), just as was the case with the prophets in the OT (Matt. 5:12; Heb. 11:32-38). Paul (1 Cor. 4:11-13; 2 Cor. 4:8-12; 6:4-10; 11:24-27; Gal. 5:11; 1 Thess. 2:2; 3:4; Acts 17:5-10; 18:12-17; 21:30-36; 23:12-35), as well as Stephen (Acts 6:8–7:60), James (Acts 12:2), and Peter (Acts 12:3-5), together with many anonymous martyrs experienced the truth of the Johannine saying: "If they persecuted Me, they will also persecute you" (John 15:20 HCSB; Acts 4:3; 5:17-42; 8:1; 12:1; Rev. 2:3,9-10,13,19; 3:8-10; 6:9; 16:6; 17:6; 18:24; 20:4).

Whole epistles and books like 1 Peter, Hebrews, and Revelation were written to encourage Christians in a situation of persecution (1 Pet. 3:13-18; 4:12-19; 5:6-14; Heb. 10:32-39; 12:3; Rev. 2–3). Something like a theology of persecution emerged, which emphasized patience, endurance, and steadfastness (Rom. 12:12; 1 Thess. 2:14-16; James 5:7-11); prayer (Matt. 5:44; Rom. 12:14; 1 Cor. 4:12); thanksgiving (2 Thess. 1:4); testing (Mark 4:17) and the strengthening of faith (1 Thess. 3:2-3); experiencing the grace of God (Rom. 8:35; 2 Cor. 4:9; 12:10), and being blessed through suffering (Matt. 5:10-12; 1 Pet. 3:14; 4:12-14). For Paul, persecuting Christians could be a living and visible testimony to the crucified and risen Christ (2 Cor. 4:7-12).

There seems to be an element in religious fanaticism (Paul before his conversion: 1 Cor. 15:9; Gal. 1:13,23; Phil. 3:6; Acts 8:3; 9:1-2; 22:4), which breeds intolerance and can lead to persecution. Christians should repent of this element in their own history and must be radically committed to the abolition of all persecution. See *Apocrypha; Disciple; Martyr; Prophecy, Prophets; Suffering.*   *Thorwald Lorenzen*

PERSEVERANCE Maintaining Christian faith through the trying times of life. As a noun the term "perseverance" occurs in the NT only at Eph. 6:18 (*proskarteresis*) and Heb. 12:1 (*hupomone*). The idea is inherent throughout the NT in the great interplay of the themes of assurance and warning.

The background setting for the idea of perseverance blossomed out of the context of persecution and temptation. The believer was expected faithfully to endure and to remain steadfast in the face of opposition, attack, and discouragement. The NT writers were forthright in advising believers to be consistent in prayer (Eph. 6:18; Phil. 4:6), and they employed athletic imagery to remind Christians to be effectual as they trained in the ways of God (1 Cor. 9:24-27; Rom. 12:11-12; Heb. 12:1-12). Israel's failure of faithfulness in the exodus was also a haunting picture for Christians, and the inspired NT writers found it to be an important basis for warning (1 Cor. 10:1-14; Heb. 3:7-19). They were committed to making absolutely clear that the requirements of Christian living were recognized as an essential element of Christian believing. Authentic life and true belief are both necessary parts of being a Christian.

While the warnings are very stern, especially in Hebrews (2:3; 6:1-8; 10:26-31), the NT writers were firmly convinced that those who truly committed themselves to Christ should persevere to the end because they had gained a new perspective and become a people who would not treat lightly the biblical admonitions (cp. Heb. 6:9-12; 10:39). They believed Christians would finish the race because Christians would focus their attention on Jesus, the lead runner and model finisher of their faith (Heb. 2:10; 12:1-2).

In the early church Christians wrestled with the problem of the renouncers during and after periods of persecution. Christians found in the model of Peter's restoration (John 21) an important clue. Restoration for Peter was possible, but restoration still meant his death. Restoration for Christians, therefore, could be possible, but it demanded absolute seriousness for defectors. They would be expected to persevere thereafter, even in the face of death. As time passed, however, baptism became regarded by some Christians as a bath that would provide cleansing from all types of sin, including renunciation. Some would thus delay baptism almost to the time of death to guarantee that all sins in life would be expunged. The need was seen by these Christians for a final rite to care for such post-baptismal, unconfessed sins. Others found such views of baptism and extreme unction to be foreign to NT perspectives.

However, the perseverance of the saints is one of the great theological ideas that needs to be reaffirmed in this era. It is the human side of the salvation equation, and it deals with faithfulness of Christians in matters of God's will (James 1:25). It encompasses the taking seriously of human weakness, without denying the mysterious nature of God's patience with His people. It permits judgment concerning the way people live in this world, but it does not exclude God's abundant graciousness.

Persevering Christians take prayer seriously as a reflection of life. They recognize the way of love and forgiveness because they understand the nature of human weakness and divine help. They know they have experienced grace beyond their human capacities. Persevering Christians recognize that the warnings of the Bible are meant for them to obey and that Christ gave His life to transform their lives. Perseverance is thus a call to faithfulness, but it is also an affirmation that somehow, in spite of our failures, God will bring His committed people through the difficulties and concerns of life to their promised destiny in Christ.   *Gerald L. Borchert*

PERSIA As a nation Persia corresponds to the modern state of Iran. As an empire Persia was a vast collection of states and kingdoms reaching from the shores of Asia Minor in the west to the Indus River Valley in the east. It reached northward to southern Russia and in the south included Egypt and the regions bordering the Persian Gulf and the Gulf of Oman. In history the empire defeated the Babylonians and then fell finally to Alexander the Great.

The nation was named for the southernmost region of the area called Parsis or Persis. It was a harsh land of deserts, mountains, plateaus, and valleys. The climate was arid and showed extremes of cold and heat. Gold and silver and wheat and barley were native to the area.

The region was settled shortly after 3000 B.C. by people from the north. An Elamite culture developed which, at its peak in 1200 B.C., dominated the whole Tigris River Valley. It lasted until 1050 B.C. After its destruction other northern groups entered the area. Among these groups were tribesmen who formed a small kingdom in the region of Anshan around 700 B.C. It was ruled by Achaemenes, the great, great-grandfather of Cyrus II, the Great. (Thus, the period from Achaemenes to Alexander is called the Achaemenid Period.) This small kingdom was the seed of the Persian Empire.

When Cyrus II came to his father's throne in 559 B.C., his kingdom was part of a larger Median kingdom. The Medes controlled the territory northeast and east of the Babylonians. In 550 B.C. Cyrus rebelled against Astyages, the Median king. His rebellion led to the capture of the king and gave Cyrus control over a kingdom stretching from Media to the Halys River in Asia Minor. Soon Cyrus challenged the king of Lydia. Victory there gave Cyrus the western portion of Asia Minor. Then in 539 B.C. Babylon fell to Cyrus due to his skill and internal dissension in the Babylonian Empire. See *Babylon.*

Cyrus died in 530 B.C.; however, the Persian Empire continued to grow. Cambyses II, Cyrus' son, conquered Egypt in 525 B.C. Cambyses' successor Darius I expanded the empire eastward to the Indus and attempted to conquer or control the Greeks. Darius lost to the Greeks at Marathon in 490 B.C. This was the greatest extension of the empire. Later emperors did little to expand the empire. They even had difficulty holding such a far-flung empire together.

The Persian Empire is important to the history and development of civilization. It had major effects on religion, law, politics, and economics. The impact came through the Jews, the Bible, contacts with the Greeks, and through Alexander the Great's incorporation of ideas and architecture from the Persians.

Politically the Persian Empire was the best organized the world had ever seen. By the time of Darius I, 522–486 B.C., the empire was divided into 20 satrapies (political units of varying size and population). Satrapies were subdivided into provinces. Initially Judah was a province in the satrapy of Babylon. Later Judah was in one named "Beyond the River." The satrapies were governed by Persians who were directly responsible to the emperor. Good administration required good communications that called for good roads. These roads did more than speed administration, though. They encouraged contacts between peoples within the empire. Ideas and goods could move hundreds of miles with little restriction. The empire became wealthy and also gave its inhabitants a sense that they were part of a larger world. A kind of "universal awareness" developed. The use of minted coins and the development of a money economy aided this identification with a larger world. The emperor's coins were handy reminders of the power and privileges of being part of the empire. Also the Persians were committed to rule by law. Instead of imposing an imperial law from above, however, the emperor and his satraps gave their authority and support to local law. For the Jews this meant official support for keeping Jewish law in the land of the Jews.

The Persian Empire affected the Jews and biblical history a great deal. Babylon had conquered Jerusalem and destroyed the temple in 586 B.C. When Cyrus conquered Babylon, he allowed the Jews to return to Judah and encouraged the rebuilding of the temple (Ezra 1:1-4). The work was begun but not completed. Then, under Darius I, Zerubbabel and the high priest, Joshua, led the restored community with the support and encouragement of the Persians. (Ezra 3–6 tells of some of the events while Haggai's and Zechariah's prophecies were made during the days of the restoration.) Despite some local opposition Darius supported the rebuilding of the temple, which was rededicated in his sixth year (Ezra 6:15). In addition, both Ezra and Nehemiah were official representatives of the Persian government. Ezra was to teach and to appoint judges (Ezra 7). Nehemiah may have been the first governor of the province of Yehud (Judah). He undoubtedly had official support for his rebuilding of the walls of Jerusalem.

The Jews had trouble under Persian rule, too. Although Daniel was taken into exile by the Babylonians (Dan. 1), his ministry continued through the fall of the Babylonians (Dan. 5) into the time of the Persians (Dan. 6). His visions projected even further. Daniel 6 shows a stable government but one in which Jews could still be at risk. His visions in a time of tranquillity remind readers that human kingdoms come and go. Esther is a story of God's rescue of His people during the rule of the Persian emperor, Ahasuerus (also known as Xerxes I). The story shows

an empire where law was used and misused. Jews were already, apparently, hated by some. Malachi, too, was probably from the Persian period. His book shows an awareness of the world at large and is positive toward the Gentiles and the government.

Throughout the period the Jews kept looking for the kind of restoration promised by prophets such as Isaiah (chaps. 40–66) and Ezekiel (chaps. 40–48). Prophets such as Haggai and Zechariah and Malachi helped the Jews to hope, but these men of God also reminded their hearers of the importance of present faithfulness and obedience to God. See *Artaxerxes; Cyrus; Daniel; Darius; Esther; Ezra, Book of; Mithra; Nehemiah, Book of; Temple.* *Albert F. Bean*

PERSIS (Pĕr´ sĭs) Personal name meaning "Persian woman." Leader in the Roman church whom Paul greeted and commended for diligent service (Rom. 16:12).

PERSON OF CHRIST See *Christ, Christology; Jesus Christ.*

PERSONALITY See *Anthropology; Heart; Humanity; Mind.*

PERVERSE Translation of one Greek and several Hebrew terms with the literal meaning "bent," "crooked," or "twisted," applied to persons involved in moral error. Most biblical references are in the book of Proverbs which mentions "perverse": persons (Prov. 3:32; 14:14); minds (11:20; 12:8; 23:33); tongues (10:31; 17:20); words or speech (10:32; 19:1); and perverse ways (28:6). Paul urged Christians to be moral "lights" witnessing to their "crooked and perverse generation" (Phil. 2:15; cp. Deut. 32:5). Jesus accused His generation of both faithlessness and perversity (Matt. 17:17; Luke 9:41; cp. Deut. 32:20).

PESHITTA (Pĕ shĕt´ tä) Common Syriac version of the Scriptures. The OT was likely translated between A.D. 100 and 300. The NT translation dates from before A.D. 400. The Peshitta lacked those books rejected by the Syriac-speaking churches (2 Pet.; 2 and 3 John; Jude; Rev.). See *Bible Texts and Versions.*

PESTILENCE Devastating epidemic that OT writers understood to be sent by God (Exod.

9:15; Jer. 15:2; Hab. 3:5; Amos 4:10), sometimes by means of a destroying angel (2 Sam. 24:16; 1 Chron. 21:15). God sent pestilence as punishment for persistent unbelief (Num. 14:12) and failure to fulfill covenant obligations (Deut. 28:21) as well as to encourage repentance (Amos 4:10). God withheld pestilence from Egypt to allow for survivors to witness to His acts of liberation (Exod. 9:16). Earnest prayer averted pestilence (1 Kings 8:37); fasting and sacrifice without repentance did not (Jer. 14:12). Pestilence is often associated with war and siege conditions (Exod. 5:3; Lev. 26:25; Amos 4:10; Luke 21:11).

PESTLE Small, club-shaped tool used to grind in a mortar (Prov. 27:22).

PETER Derived from the Greek *petros*, meaning "rock." The name occurs 159 times in the NT. Simon was his personal name; Peter was given to him by Jesus (Matt. 16:18). Though Peter is dominant, there are three other names: the Hebrew Simeon (Acts 15:14), Simon, and Cephas (Aramaic for rock), used mostly by Paul (1 Cor. 1:12; 3:22; 9:5; 15:5; Gal. 1:18; 2:9,11,14) and one other time (John 1:42).

Peter's Family The Gospels provide information about Peter and his family. He was called Barjona (Aramaic for "son of Jona," Matt. 16:17) or son of John (Gk. for Barjona, Luke 1:42). Peter and his brother Andrew came from Bethsaida (John 1:44) and were Galilean fishermen (Mark 1:16; Luke 5:2-3; John 21:3) in business with James and John (Luke 5:10). Peter was married (Mark 1:30) and lived in Capernaum (Mark 1:21-31). Peter and Andrew were associated with John the Baptist prior to becoming disciples of Jesus (John 1:40).

Peter's Role Among the Disciples Peter was leader and spokesman for the 12 disciples (Mark 8:29; Matt. 17:24). Peter often posed questions to Jesus representing concerns of the others (Matt. 15:15; 18:21; Mark 11:21; Luke 12:41). Peter's name occurred first in listing the names of the Twelve (Matt. 10:2; Mark 3:16; Luke 6:14) and the inner circle (Peter, James, and John, in Mark 5:35-41; 9:2-8; 14:33,43-50).

Peter sometimes had little faith. He was sometimes presumptuous (Matt. 16:22; John 13:8; 18:10) and timid (Matt. 14:30; 26:69-72). Sometimes he was self-seeking (Matt. 19:27), while at other times he was self-sacrificing (Mark 1:18). Sometimes he was spiritually perceptive (Matt. 16:16; John 6:68) and other times slow to understand spiritual matters (Matt.

P
Q

Church of St. Peter in Gallicantu that honors the traditional site of Peter's weeping after his denial of Jesus.

15:15-16). Once he walked on water with Jesus, but his faith waned and he began to sink (Matt. 14:28-31). The greatest example of Peter's inconsistency was his confession, "You are the Messiah" (Matt. 16:16 HCSB), opposed to his denial, "I don't know this man" (Mark 14:71). After Pentecost (Acts 2:1) Peter was bold when persecuted. On two occasions Peter was arrested and warned to refrain from preaching about Jesus (Acts 4:1-22; 5:12-40). Herod imprisoned Peter with intent to execute him (Acts 12:3-5). Peter, however, was freed and delivered by an angel (Acts 12:6-11).

Peter's Role in the Early Church and His Legacy Though Peter led the disciples and took a prominent role in the early church (Acts 1–5), he did not emerge as the leader. Peter helped establish the Jerusalem church, but James the brother of Jesus assumed the leadership of the Jerusalem church (Acts 15). Though active in the spread of the gospel to the Gentiles (Acts 11–12), Paul became "the apostle to the Gentiles" (Acts 14; 16–28). Peter served as a bridge to hold together the diverse people of the early church (Acts 15). Peter became the "apostle to the Jews," preaching throughout Palestine. Peter died as a martyr in Rome under Nero, probably in A.D. 64 or 65 (1 Clement 5:1–6:1). Tradition holds that Peter was crucified upside down because he felt unworthy to die in the same manner as Jesus.

Conservative scholarship maintains that Peter wrote 1 and 2 Peter with scribal assistance. Eusebius held that John Mark wrote the Gospel of Mark to preserve the preaching of Peter. Apparently devotees of Peter produced pseudonymously the noncanonical books, the Acts of Peter and the Gospel of Peter, assigning Peter's name to them. See *Peter, First Letter from; Peter, Second Letter from.* *Steven L. Cox*

PETER, FIRST LETTER FROM First Peter is addressed to churches in Asia Minor experiencing persecution. Peter reminded them of their heavenly hope and eternal inheritance so that they would be strengthened to persevere in the midst of suffering. He emphasized that believers are called to holiness and a life of love. Believers are called upon to glorify God in their daily lives and to imitate Christ who suffered on the cross for the sake of His people. Peter sketched what it means to live as a Christian, how believers relate to governing authorities, to cruel masters, and unbelieving husbands. He warned believers that suffering may be intense, but believers should rely upon God's grace, knowing there is a heavenly reward.

Author The letter claims to be written by the Apostle Peter (1:1), and there is no good reason to doubt Petrine authorship. The early church fathers also supported Petrine authorship, and there is wide and early evidence in the fathers to support such a view. Nevertheless, scholars raised a number of objections to Petrine authorship. (1) A Galilean fisherman could not have written the cultivated Greek. (2) The OT quotations stem from the Septuagint, and Peter, since he did not know Greek, would not have used the LXX. (3) The theology of 1 Peter is remarkably Pauline in character, demonstrating that it is not authentically Petrine. (4) The letter says very little about the historical Jesus. (5) The persecution in the letter is empire-wide and would be dated in the time of Domitian (A.D. 81–96) or Trajan (A.D. 98–117).

None of these arguments are compelling, and Petrine authorship is solidly established. (1) Significant evidence exists that Greek was spoken in Palestine and especially in Galilee. As a fisherman in Galilee, Peter would have engaged in business with other Greek speakers. The notion that Peter was uneducated or illiterate is a myth. Acts 4:13 merely means that he was not trained rabbinically and should not be used to say he was unable to read. (2) Since Peter knew Greek, it is not surprising that he used the Septuagint. In particular Peter quoted from the Bible that his readers used, like any good pastor. (3) The old Tübingen notion that the theology of Peter and Paul was at loggerheads should be laid to rest. Paul himself argued that the apostles agreed upon the gospel (Gal. 2:1-10; 1 Cor. 15:11). (4) More allusions to the teaching of Jesus exist in the letter than some claim. In any case, there is no reason to insist that Peter was compelled to refer to the historical Jesus often in an occasional letter written for a specific purpose. (5) The notion that the persecution is empire-wide and state sponsored is hardly clear from 1 Peter, and most scholars now reject such a theory. Instead, 1 Peter indicates that sporadic persecution was breaking out against believers. Indeed the letter says nothing about believers being put to death, though the latter is a possibility. Hence, there is no compelling reason to doubt that the letter was written while Nero was emperor (A.D. 54–68) and Peter was still alive. It should be noted that not even Nero instituted an empire-wide persecution of Christians. His punishment of Christians in Rome after the fire that destroyed much of Rome was not the beginning of a policy that reached to the edges of the empire. (6) It is also possible that Peter used a secretary (amanuensis) to write the letter. Many have argued that the secretary was Silvanus (1 Pet. 5:12), though the language used in the verse denotes the carrier of the letter rather than the secretary. Still it is possible that Silvanus or some other person functioned as a secretary.

Date/Destination If we accept Petrine authorship, the letter was likely written in the early 60s, before the composition of 2 Peter. The first verse of the letter indicates that the letter was written to various churches in the northern part of Asia Minor (present-day Turkey). The courier of the letter, presumably Silvanus, probably traveled in a circle in reading the letter to the various churches. The purpose of the letter was to fortify the churches and give them hope as they experienced persecution. We already noted that the persecution was sporadic and not state sponsored. Nor is there a clear indication that believers were being executed. Most likely, believers were being discriminated against in society and the work place and were subject to various forms of harassment.

Outline

I.   Opening (1:1-2)
II. Called to Salvation as Exiles (1:3–2:10)
     A. Praise for Salvation (1:3-12)
        1. A Promised Inheritance (1:3-5)
        2. Result: Joy in Suffering (1:6-9)
        3. The Privilege of Revelation (1:10-12)
     B. The Future Inheritance as an Incentive to Holiness (1:13-21)
        1. Setting One's Hope on the Inheritance (1:13-16)
        2. A Call to Fear (1:17-21)
     C. Living as the New People of God (1:22–2:10)
        1. A Call to Love (1:22-25)
        2. Longing for the Pure Milk (2:1-3)
        3. The Living Stone and Living Stones (2:4-10)
III. Living as Aliens to Bring Glory to God in a Hostile World (2:11–4:11)

A. The Christian Life as a Battle and Witness (2:11-12)
B. Testifying to the Gospel in the Social Order (2:13–3:12)
   1. Submit to the Government (2:13-17)
   2. Slaves submit to masters (2:18-25)
      a. To Receive a Reward (2:18-20)
      b. To Imitate Christ (2:21-25)
   3. Wives Submit to Husbands (3:1-6)
   4. Husbands Live Knowledgeably with Your Wives (3:7)
   5. Conclusion: Live a Godly Life to Obtain an Inheritance (3:8-12)
C. Responding in a Godly Way to Suffering (3:13–4:11)
   1. The Blessing of Suffering for Christ (3:13-17)
   2. Christ's Suffering as the Pathway to Exaltation (3:18-22)
   3. Preparing to Suffer as Christ Did (4:1-6)
   4. Living in the Light of the End (4:7-11)
IV. Persevering in Suffering (4:12–5:11)
    A. Suffer Joyfully in accord with God's Will (4:12-19)
    B. Exhortations to Elders and the Community (5:1-11)
       1. Exhortations for Elders and Younger Ones (5:1-5)
       2. Closing Exhortations and Assurance (5:6-11)
V. Concluding Words (5:12-14)

Thomas R. Schreiner

PETER, SECOND LETTER FROM In his second epistle Peter wrote in response to false teachers who denied the second coming of the Lord Jesus Christ and advocated a libertine lifestyle. Peter maintained that God's grace is the foundation for a godly life and that living a life of godliness is necessary to obtain an eternal reward. Such a claim does not amount to works righteousness, for such works do not merit salvation but are a result of God's transforming grace. Peter also vigorously defended the truth of Christ's second coming, which was anticipated in the transfiguration and promised in God's word. Those who reject Christ's coming deny God's sovereignty. They reject God's intervention in the world and remove any basis for ethical living. Peter urged his readers to grow in grace and knowledge until the day of salvation arrives.

Author Many scholars deny that 2 Peter was written by the Apostle Peter, claiming the letter is pseudonymous. This view is defended by the following arguments: (1) Peter used Jude as a source in his second chapter, and the letter of Jude is too late to have been used by the historic Peter who died in the 60s. Further, some insist that Peter would have never borrowed from a writer like Jude. (2) The Hellenistic vocabulary and theology in the letter show that Peter, a Galilean fisherman, could not be the author. The style and syntax are quite different from 1 Peter, demonstrating a different author from the first epistle. (3) The false teachers in the letter are second-century gnostics, and obviously Peter could not have written the letter in the second century. (4) Paul's letters are considered to be Scripture (2 Pet. 3:15-16), but it is impossible that Paul's letters could have been collected together and viewed as Scripture while Peter was alive. (5) The letter lacks clear attestation in the second century, and even in the fourth century its canonicity was questioned. Some evangelicals, such as Richard Bauckham, argue that 2 Peter fits a testament genre, but the letter was a "transparent fiction," and hence none of the original readers thought the letter was genuinely written by Peter. It follows, then, that the original readers were not deceived by the inclusion of Peter's name.

Despite the objections of many, Petrine authorship is still the most convincing view. (1) Most important, the letter claims to be written by Peter (1:1). He claimed that his death is imminent (1:14). Even more striking, he claims to have heard and seen Jesus' transfiguration (1:16-18). The author is obviously open to a charge of deception and fraud if he was not Peter. (2) The use of Jude as a source is not certain but only a theory. Furthermore, even if Peter used Jude, there is no problem. Jude likely wrote before Peter died. Nothing in Jude demands a late date, and there is no reason why an apostle would not use another source. (3) The idea that the opponents were second-century gnostics is not verified by the data of the letter. No evidence exists of the cosmological dualism that was typical of Gnosticism. Nor is it clear that the opponents rejected the material world. (4) It is unnecessary to conclude from 2 Pet. 3:15-16

that all of Paul's letters were collected and stamped as canonical. Peter obviously knows some of the Pauline letters and considers them to be authoritative, but that is not the same thing as a collected canon of Pauline writings. Those who think that such a commendation of Paul by Peter is impossible are overly influenced by the old Tübingen hypothesis. (5) The vocabulary and style of 2 Peter are distinct from 1 Peter, and the language has a Hellenistic flavor. But this is not an insuperable problem. We need to observe firstly that the corpus of Petrine writings is incredibly small. Hence, judgments about "Petrine style" should be made with humility. Second, Peter may have adapted his style to speak to the situation of his readers, just as Paul did in Athens (Acts 17:16-34). Finally, Peter may have instructed a secretary (amanuensis) to compose the writing, and this may account for some of the stylistic differences. (6) The argument that Peter uses a different theology does not stand either. We need to recall that the letter is occasional and hence is not a summary of all of Peter's theology. Furthermore, the differences between 1 and 2 Peter theologically have often been overemphasized. (7) Second Peter is not as strongly attested by external evidence as many other letters. Still, some evidence for the letter's use exists even in the second century, and we ought to remember that the letter was ultimately judged to be authentic and canonical. (8) The "transparent fiction" hypothesis of Richard Bauckham is an interesting attempt to solve the problem of authorship. But Bauckham's view ultimately fails. No historical evidence exists that the letter was viewed as "transparent fiction." If it was transparent, how could it be forgotten so quickly, so that any trace of such a fictional device has vanished from the historical record? Furthermore, there is no good evidence that pseudonymous letters were accepted as canonical. Indeed, they were rejected because they were fraudulent.

Date/Destination/Opponents The date of 2 Peter depends upon one's view of authorship. Probably Peter wrote the letter shortly before his death in the mid 60s. The letter was most likely written to the same readers who received 1 Peter (cp. 3:2), and hence it was probably sent to churches in Asia Minor. We have already noted that the opponents cannot legitimately be identified as gnostics. Jerome Neyrey suggests some affinities to the Epicureans, but no specific identification has been successful. We do know that the opponents were libertines and denied Christ's second coming. Both of these features are eminently possible in Peter's lifetime.

Outline

   I. Greeting (1:1-2)

  II. God's Grace the Foundation for a Life of Godliness (1:3-11)

     A. Divine Provision (1:3-4)

     B. Pursue a Godly Life Diligently (1:5-7)

     C. Godly Virtues Necessary for Entrance into the Kingdom (1:8-11)

 III. Peter's Apostolic Reminder (1:12-21)

     A. The Function of the Reminder: To Stir them for Action: (1:12-15)

     B. The Truth of Jesus' Coming is Based on Eyewitness Testimony (1:16-18)

     C. The Truth of Jesus' Coming is Based on the Prophetic Word (1:19-21)

 IV. The Arrival, Character, and Judgment of False Teachers (2:1-22)

     A. The Impact of False Teachers (2:1-3)

     B. The Certain Judgment of the Ungodly and the Preservation of the Godly (2:4-10a)

     C. False Teachers Judged for Their Rebellion and Sensuality (2:10b-16)

     D. The Adverse Impact of the False Teachers upon Others (2:17-22)

  V. Reminder: The Day of the Lord Will Come (3:1-18)

     A. Scoffers Doubt the Coming Day (3:1-7)

     B. The Lord's Timing is Different from Ours (3:8-10)

     C. Living Righteously because of the Future Day (3:11-18)

Thomas R. Schreiner

PETHAHIAH (Pĕ thȧ hī´ ah) Personal name meaning "Yahweh opens." **1.** Ancestor of a postexilic priestly family (1 Chron. 24:16). **2.** Royal advisor to the Persian king, either at his court or as his representative in Jerusalem (Neh. 11:24). **3.** Levite participating in Ezra's covenant renewal (Neh. 9:5). **4.** Levite with a foreign wife (Ezra 10:23), perhaps identical with 3.

PETHOR (Pĕ´ thôr) Place-name meaning "soothsayer." City in upper Mesopotamia identified with Tell Ahmar, 12 miles south of Carchemish near the confluence of the Sajur

and Euphrates Rivers. Home of Balaam (Num. 22:5; Deut. 23:4).

PETHUEL (Pȧ thū´ ĕl) Personal name meaning "vision of God" or "youth of God." Father of the Prophet Joel (1:1).

PETITION See *Prayer.*

PETRA (Pĕ´ tra) Capital city of the Nabatean Arabs located about 60 miles north of the Gulf of Aqaba. Petra is sometimes identified with Sela (Judg. 1:36; 2 Kings 14:7; Isa. 16:1; 42:11) because both names mean "rock." Lack of archaeological evidence of Edomite settlement in the basin suggests that Sela is better identified with Um el Bayyarah on the mountain plateau overlooking Petra. The Nabatean king Aretas IV (2 Cor. 11:32-33) reigned from Petra.

PEULLETHAI (Pȧ ŭl´ lē thī) or **PEULTHAI** (Pȧ ŭl thī) (KJV) Personal name meaning "recompense." A Levitical gatekeeper (1 Chron. 26:5).

PHALEC (Phā´ lĕc) (KJV, Luke 3:35) See *Peleg.*

PHALLU (Phăl´ lū) (KJV, Gen. 46:9) See *Pallu.*

PHALTI (Phăl´ tī) (KJV, 1 Sam. 25:44) See *Palti.*

PHALTIEL (Phăl´ tĭ ĕl) (KJV, 2 Sam. 3:15) See *Paltiel.*

PHANUEL (Phȧ nū´ ĕl) Alternate form of the personal name Penuel meaning "face of God." Father of the Prophetess Anna (Luke 2:36).

PHARAOH Title meaning "great house" for the ancient kings of Egypt. Every ancient pharaoh had five "great names" which he assumed on the day of his accession. Since it was not deemed proper to use such powerful names in direct fashion, a polite circumlocution developed; he came to be called Pharaoh.

Egyptians applied "pharaoh" to the royal palace and grounds in the fourth dynasty (about 2500 B.C.). The title Pharaoh came to be applied to the king from about 1500 B.C. until the Persian domination, about 550 B.C.

A view from the front of the Treasury building of the narrow entryway into the Nabatean city of Petra.

The funerary mask of King Tut (Pharaoh Tutankhamun) of Egypt.

An ancient pharaoh was an absolute monarch, supreme commander of the armies, chief justice of the royal court, and high priest of all religion. His absolute power may be seen in that justice was defined as "what Pharaoh loves"; wrongdoing as "what Pharaoh hates." An example of his divine power was that he daily conducted "the Rite of the House of the Morning," an early morning ritual in which he broke the seal to the statue of the sun god, waking him up with a prayer. This act brought the sun up and started every day for the people.

References to 10 pharaohs can be clearly distinguished in the OT: the pharaoh of Abraham, Gen. 12:10-20; of Joseph, Gen. 39–50; of the oppression, Exod. 1; of the exodus, Exod. 2:23–15:19; of 1 Chron. 4:18; of Solomon, 1 Kings 3–11; of Rehoboam, called Shishak, king of Egypt, 1 Kings 14:25; of Hezekiah and Isaiah, 2 Kings 18:21; Isa. 36; of Josiah, 2 Kings 23:29; of Jer. 44:30 and Ezek. 29:1-16. See *Egypt; Exodus, Book of.*

Valley of the Kings, containing tombs of pharaohs, across the Nile River from Luxor at ancient Thebes.

PHARES (Phā´ rēz) (KJV, NASB, Matt. 1:3; Luke 3:33) See *Perez.*

PHAREZ (Phā´ rĕz) (KJV, NASB, Gen. 38:29; 46:12; Num. 26:20-21; Ruth 4:12,18; 1 Chron. 2:4-5; 4:1; 9:4) See *Perez.*

PHARISEES Largest and most influential religious-political party during NT times. See *Jewish Parties in the New Testament.*

PHAROSH (Phā´ rŏsh) (KJV, Ezra 8:3) See *Parosh.*

PHARPAR (Phär´ pär) River associated with Damascus (2 Kings 5:12). The river is perhaps the Nahr el 'A'waj, which flows from Mount Hermon, passing about 10 miles south of Damascus, or else the Nahr Taura.

PHARZITES (Phär´ zīts) (KJV, Num. 26:20) See *Perez.*

PHASEAH (Phà sē´ ah) (KJV, Neh. 7:51) See *Paseah.*

PHEBE (Phē´ bē) (KJV, Rom. 16:1-2) See *Phoebe.*

PHENICE, PHENICIA (Phǝ nī´ sǝ, Phě nĭsh´ ĭ à) KJV alternate forms of Phoenicia (Phenice, Acts 11:19; 15:3; 27:12; Phenicia, Acts 21:2).

PHIBESETH (Phī´ bǝ sĕth) Place-name derived from the Egyptian, "house of Bastet," a goddess represented as a cat (Ezek. 30:17). Bastet (Gk. *Boubastos*) was located on the right shore of the old Tanite branch of the Nile about 45 miles northeast of Cairo. Bastet served as capital of the 18th nome (administrative district) and, during the Twenty-second and Twenty-third Dynasties (940–745 B.C.), as capital of a fragmented Egyptian Empire. The site is identified with modern Tell Basta.

PHICHOL (Phī´ kŏl) (KJV) or **PHICOL** Personal name meaning "mighty." The chief captain of the Philistine army under King Abimelech (Gen. 21:22). He witnessed covenants between his commander and Abraham (21:32) and Isaac (26:26-28). See *Abimelech; Abraham; Covenant; Isaac.*

P
Q

Temple ruins at the site of the ancient city of Philadelphia in Asia Minor (modern Turkey).

PHILADELPHIA (Phĭl à dĕl´ phĭ à) Place-name meaning "love of brother." A Hellenistic city in the province of Lydia in western Asia Minor. See *Asia Minor, Cities of; Revelation, Book of.*

PHILEMON, LETTER TO (Phī lē´ mon) Personal name meaning "affectionate" and 18th book of the NT. Philemon owed his conversion to the Christian faith to the Apostle Paul (v. 19). This conversion took place during Paul's extended ministry in Ephesus (Acts 19:10). There is no evidence that Paul ever visited Colossae where Philemon lived. Paul and Philemon became devoted friends. Paul referred to Philemon as a "dear friend and co-worker" (v. 1 HCSB).

Paul's only letter of a private and personal nature included in the NT was written to Philemon in A.D. 61. This letter concerned a runaway slave. The slave Onesimus had robbed Philemon and escaped to Rome. There Onesimus found the Apostle Paul who was imprisoned. Paul wrote to Philemon concerning Onesimus. Paul sent both the letter and Onesimus back to Colossae. The letter states that Onesimus was now a Christian. Paul requested that Philemon forgive and receive Onesimus not as a slave but as a brother (v. 16). This request was not made from Paul's apostolic authority but tenderly as a Christian friend. Paul wrote, "Accept him as you would me" (v. 17 HCSB).

Paul also stated that he was willing to pay any damages caused by Onesimus. Some scholars indicate that Paul may have been asking subtly that Philemon release Onesimus so that he could return and aid Paul in his evangelistic endeavors. Philemon had a judicial right to pun-

ish severely or even kill Onesimus. Paul's short epistle of some 355 Greek words challenged Philemon to apply Christian love in dealing with Onesimus. Paul's approach eventually caused the end of slavery. See *Onesimus; Paul; Slave, Servant.*

Outline

I. Greetings of Grace and Peace (1-3)
II. Commendation for Philemon's Love, Faith, and Example (4-7)
III. Plea for Onesimus on Basis of Friendship (8-22)
IV. Closing Salutation (23-25)

Kenneth Hubbard

PHILETUS (Phī lē´ tŭs) Personal name meaning "beloved." Heretical teacher who asserted that the (general) resurrection had already occurred (2 Tim. 2:17-18), perhaps in a purely spiritual sense.

PHILIP (Phĭl´ ĭp) Personal name meaning "fond of horses." **1.** A respected member of the church at Jerusalem who was chosen as one of the seven first deacons (Acts 6:5). Following Stephen's martyrdom, Philip took the gospel to Samaria, where his ministry was blessed (Acts 8:5-13). Subsequently, he was led south to the Jerusalem-Gaza road where he introduced the Ethiopian eunuch to Christ and baptized him (Acts 8:26-38). He was then transported by the Spirit to Azotus (Ashdod) and from there conducted an itinerant ministry until he took up residence in Caesarea (Acts 8:39-40). Then, for nearly 20 years, we lose sight of him. He is last seen in Scripture when Paul lodged in his home on his last journey to Jerusalem (Acts 21:8). He had four unmarried daughters who were prophetesses (Acts 21:9). See *Acts of the Apostles; Deacon; Evangelism.* **2.** One of 12 apostles (Matt. 10:3). From Bethsaida he called Nathanael to "come and see" Jesus (John 1:43-51). Jesus tested Philip concerning how to feed the multitude (John 6:5-7). He and Andrew took inquiring Gentiles to Jesus (John 12:21-22). Philip asked Jesus to show them the father (John 14:8-9), opening the way for Jesus' teaching that to see Him is to see the Father. See *Disciple.* **3.** Tetrarch of Ituraea and Trachonitis (Luke 3:1). See *Herod.*   *Paul Powell*

PHILIP, HEROD See *Herod.*

PHILIPPI (Phĭl´ ĭp pī) City in the Roman province of Macedonia. Paul did missionary work in Philippi (Acts 16:12) and later wrote a letter to the church there (Phil. 1:1).

History In ancient times the site was in a gold mining area. After 400 B.C. Philip II of Macedon seized the mines, fortified the city, and named it for himself. Philippi, along with the rest of Macedonia, came under Roman control after 200 B.C. In 42 B.C. Philippi was the site of a decisive battle that sealed the fate of Rome as a republic and set the stage for the establishment of an empire. The forces of Octavian (later to be Augustus Caesar, the first emperor) and Antony defeated the army of Brutus and Cassius. In honor of the victory Antony settled some Roman soldiers there and made Philippi a Roman colony. After defeating Antony at the Battle of Actium in 31 B.C., the victorious Octavian dispossessed the supporters of Antony from Italy, but he allowed him to settle in places like Philippi. Octavian refounded Philippi as a Roman colony.

Paul and Philippi Paul first visited Philippi on his second missionary journey in response to his Macedonian vision (Acts 16:9). They and his companions sailed from Troas across the Aegean Sea to Neapolis, on the eastern shore of Macedonia (Acts 16:11). Then they journeyed a few

miles inland to "Philippi, a Roman colony, which is a leading city of that district of Macedonia" (Acts 16:12 HCSB).

On the Sabbath Paul went to a prayer meeting on the riverbank. When Paul spoke, Lydia and others opened their hearts to the Lord (Acts 16:13-15). As a rule, Paul first went to the Jewish synagogue when he came to a new city. The fact that he did not do this in Philippi probably shows that Philippi had no synagogue.

The Roman character of the city is apparent from Paul's other experiences in Philippi. He healed a possessed slave girl whose owners charged that Jews troubled the city by teaching customs unlawful for Romans to observe (Acts 16:20-21). The city magistrates ordered Paul and Silas to be beaten and turned over to the jailer (Acts 16:20,22-23). After Paul's miraculous deliverance and the jailer's conversion, the magistrates sent the jailer word to release Paul (Acts 16:35-36). Paul informed the messengers that he was a Roman citizen. Since he had been beaten and imprisoned unlawfully, Paul insisted that the magistrates themselves come and release him (Acts 16:37). The very nervous magistrates went to the jail. They pled with Paul not only to leave the jail but also to leave town (Acts

P
Q

Philip's Martyrium at Hierapolis built to commemorate the tradtion that Philip the Apostle was martytred there.

16:38-40). See *Paul; Philippians, Letter to the; Roman Law.*   *Robert J. Dean*

PHILIPPIANS, LETTER TO THE (Phĭ lĭp´ pĭ ăns)

Eleventh book of the NT, written by Paul to the church at Philippi, the first church he established in Europe. It is one of the Prison Epistles (along with Eph., Col., and Phil.). The authenticity of the letter generally is accepted. The terminology and theology are thoroughly Pauline.

In spite of the negative circumstances from which Paul wrote, Philippians is a warm, personal, positive letter (except for chap. 3). Paul wrote to thank the church for a gift it had recently sent to Paul in prison and to inform them of his circumstances and of Timothy's and Epaphroditus' travel plans. The underlying theme that holds the letter together is a call for unity in the church.

The date of the letter depends on which imprisonment Paul was enduring. The traditional date and place of writing is A.D. 61/62 from Rome. If Philippians was written from Caesarea,

The agora (marketplace) in the ancient city of Philippi in Macedonia.

we would assign a date in the late 50s; if from Ephesus, the mid 50s. See below.

Origin of Philippians Where was Paul when he wrote Philippians? The letter itself reveals only that he was in prison. Acts records Pauline imprisonments in Caesarea and in Rome. Some evidence indicates that Paul was also in prison in Ephesus (Acts 19; 2 Cor. 11:23; 1 Cor. 15:30-32).

Philippians is traditionally assigned to Rome. Reference to Caesar's household (Phil. 4:22), the praetorium or palace guard (1:13 NIV), as well as the ability to receive visitors (Acts 28:16,30-31) like Epaphroditus and the possibility of execution (Phil. 1:20-26) seem to mesh well with the imprisonment described in the closing verses of Acts.

An Ephesian origin for Philippians also has much in its favor. Ephesus was the capitol of Asia. A provincial governor's guard occupied a "praetorium," and the governor's residence was termed "Caesar's household." An Ephesian imprisonment and origin for Philippians makes sense of Paul's stated intent to visit Philippi upon his release (Phil. 2:24; from Rome Paul intended to go to Spain, Rom. 15:23-24). In addition, Phil. 2:25-30 implies that several trips, bearing news, had been made between Paul's locale and Philippi. A trip from Rome to Philippi took several weeks; from Ephesus to Philippi required only several days. The large number of trips implied in Philippians is difficult to fit into a two-year Roman imprisonment but is less problematic even in a much shorter Ephesian imprisonment.

A Caesarean origin for Philippians has had fewer supporters over the years. Its detractors point out Paul's intent to go to Rome (not visit Philippi) upon his release and doubt that Paul ever feared execution in Caesarea, as Philippians implies, since he always had the option of appealing to Caesar.

Content of the Letter Philippians is structured much like a typical personal letter of that day. The introduction identifies the sender(s): Paul and Timothy, and the recipients: the saints, overseers, and deacons. This typical letter form, however, is filled with Christian content. The usual secular greeting and wish for good health is transformed into a blessing (v. 2), a thanksgiving for the Philippian church's faithful participation in the work of the gospel (1:3-8), and a prayer that they may be blessed with an ever growing, enlightened, Christian love (1:9-11). See *Letter Form and Function.*

The body of the letter begins with Paul explaining his current situation (1:12-26). In verses 12-18 Paul revealed that his primary concern (the proclamation of the gospel) was being accomplished in spite of his difficult circumstances. His captors were being evangelized (vv. 12-13). His compatriots have gained confidence through his bold example (v. 14). Even the brethren who were working with wrong motives were sharing the good news actively. (There is no hint that these were preaching a false gospel; Paul rejoiced in their work, vv. 15-18.) The severity of Paul's imprisonment is reflected in 1:19-26. His death appears to be a real possibility. Death would unite him with Christ. Life would give him the joys of continued productive ministry. He found cause for genuine rejoicing in both. Paul seemed confident, however, that he would eventually be released and reunited with the Philippians.

When Paul returned to Philippi, he hoped to find a church united in Christ. Philippians 1:27–4:9 is a multifaceted call for unity in the church. The great cause of the proclamation of the gospel calls for them to be united in spirit, in task, and in confidence (1:27-30). Their common Christian experience (2:1) and purpose (2:2) should also rule out a self-centered, self-serving attitude (2:3-4). Those who follow Christ must follow him in selfless service to others (2:5-11).

Philippians 2:6-11 is known as the *kenosis* passage (from the Greek word translated "emptied" in 2:7 RSV). The language and structure of the passage have convinced most commentators that Paul was quoting a hymn that was already in use in the church. The purpose of the pre-Pauline hymn was probably to teach the believer about the nature and work of Christ. Preexistence, incarnation, passion, resurrection, and exaltation are all summarized in a masterful fashion. In the context of Philippians, however, the *kenosis* passage is used to highlight the humility and selfless service demonstrated by Jesus, whose example the Christian is to follow. See *Kenosis.*

Paul was concerned that the Philippians demonstrate the reality of their Christian profession in action. Neither the grumbling so characteristic of Israel in the wilderness or the perversity of a world that does not know God

An inscription from the Roman period at ancient Philippi.

should characterize the church. Paul had sacrificed himself to engender true faith in the Philippians. His desire for them and for himself was that he be able to rejoice that his sacrifice was not in vain (2:12-18).

Philippians 2:25-30 explained to the church why Epaphroditus was returning to Philippi. The church has sent him to take a gift to Paul (Phil. 4:10-20) and minister to him in his imprisonment. Paul probably feared that some would criticize Epaphroditus for returning earlier than planned.

The tone of the letter changes in chapter 3. The encouragement to rejoice (3:1) unexpectedly becomes a stern warning (3:2). (The change is so marked that some scholars think chap. 3 is a later addition to the letter.) A problem was threatening the church at Philippi that had the potential of destroying the foundation of unity and the basis of joy.

The exact nature of the problem is unclear. Jewish legalism (3:2-11), Christian or gnostic perfectionism (3:12-16), and pagan libertinism (3:17-21) are all attacked. What is clear, however, is that Paul countered the heretical teachings with Christian truths: Jesus Christ is the only avenue to righteousness (3:2-11); the stature of Christ is the goal of Christian maturity (3:12-16); and the nature of Christ and His kingdom is the standard by which the Christian must live (3:17-21).

Chapter 4 returns to a more positive instruction and affirmation of the church. Two women, Euodia and Syntyche (4:2-3), were exhorted to end their conflict, for personal disagreements may be as damaging to the unity of the church as false doctrine.

General exhortations to rejoice and to remain faithful (4:4-9) led to Paul's expression of gratitude for the Philippians' faithful support of him and of the ministry (4:10-20). The letter closes in typical Pauline fashion, with an exchange of greetings and a prayer for grace.

Outline

I. Salutation (1:1-2)
II. Introduction (1:3-26)
    A. Thanksgiving prayer (1:3-11)
    B. Adverse personal circumstances may advance the gospel (1:12-26)
III. Pastoral Admonitions (1:27–2:18)
    A. Admonition to consistency (1:27)
    B. Admonition to courage (1:28-30)
    C. Admonition to unity (2:1-11)
    D. Admonition to responsibility and obedience (2:12-13)
    E. Admonition to a blameless life of rejoicing (2:14-18)
IV. Pastoral Concerns (2:19-30)
    A. Pastoral concern for the church's welfare (2:19-24)
    B. Pastoral concern for a distressed minister (2:25-30)
V. Pastoral Warning and Encouragement (3:1–4:1)
    A. Warning against legalistic zealots: glory only in Christ (3:1-3)
    B. Warning against confidence in the flesh: place confidence only in Christ and the resurrection hope (3:4-11)
    C. Warning against satisfaction with the past: press onward to the heavenly prize (3:12-16)
    D. Warning against enemies of the cross: stand firm as citizens of heaven (3:17–4:1)
VI. Final Exhortation (4:2-9)
    A. To personal reconciliation (4:2-3)
    B. To joy and gentleness (4:4-5)
    C. To peace of mind (4:6-7)
    D. To noble thoughts (4:8-9)
VII. Conclusion (4:10-23)
    A. The apostle's contentment in Christ's strength (4:10-13)
    B. The apostle's appreciation for the church's stewardship (4:14-20)
    C. The apostle's final greetings and benediction (4:21-23)   *Michael Martin*

PHILISTIA (Phĭ lĭs´ tĭ à) Coastal plain of southwestern Palestine that was under the control of the Philistines (Exod. 15:14; Pss. 60:8; 87:4; 108:9; Isa. 14:29-31). KJV sometimes referred to Philistia as Palestina (Exod. 15:14; Isa. 14:29-31). See *Philistim or Philistines.*

PHILISTIM (Phĭ lĭs´ tĭm) (KJV, Gen. 10:14) or **PHILISTINES** (Phĭ lĭs´ tēns) One of the rival groups the Israelites encountered as they settled the land of Canaan. References to the Philistines appear in the OT as well as other ancient Near Eastern writings. Philistine refers to a group of people who occupied and gave their name to the southwest part of Palestine. Ancient Egyptian records from the time of Merneptah and Ramses III referred to them as the *prst.* Ancient Assyrian records include references to the Philistines in the terms *Philisti* and *Palastu.*

The origin and background of the Philistines has not been completely clarified. Ancient Egyptian records include the *prst* as part of a larger movement of people known as the Sea Peoples, who invaded Egypt about 1188 B.C. by land and by sea, battling the forces of Ramses III, who, according to Egyptian records, defeated them. The Sea Peoples, a massive group that originated in the Aegean area, included the Tjeker, the Skekelesh, the Denyen, the Sherden, and the Weshwesh as well as the *prst* or Pelesti, the biblical Philistines. As they moved eastward from the Aegean region, the Sea Peoples made war with people in their path including the Hittites in Anatolia and the inhabitants at sites in North Syria such as those at the site of Ugarit. According to biblical references, the homeland of the Philistines was Caphtor (Amos 9:7; Jer. 47:4). See *Caphtor.*

Philistines are first mentioned in the patriarchal stories (Gen. 21:32,34), a reference that some suggest is anachronistic and others suggest refers to the migrations of an Aegean colony in the patriarchal period. The most dramatic phase of Philistine history begins in the period of the Judges when the Philistines were the principal enemy of and the major political threat to Israel. This threat is first seen in the stories of Samson (Judg. 13–16). The threat intensified as the Philistines encroached on the territory of the tribe of Dan ultimately forcing Dan to move north (Judg. 18:11,29). The threat reached crisis proportions in the battle of Ebenezer (1 Sam. 4:1-18), when the Israelites were soundly defeated and the ark of the covenant, brought over from Shiloh (1 Sam. 4:3-4), was captured.

During the time of Samuel, the Israelites defeated the Philistines at times (1 Sam. 7:5-11; 14:16-23), but, generally speaking, their advance against the Israelites continued. Saul not only failed to check their intrusion into Israelite territory but in the end lost his life fighting the Philistines at Mount Gilboa (1 Sam. 31:1-13). David finally checked the Philistine advance at Baal-perazim (2 Sam. 5:17-25).

Several features of Philistine life and culture are reflected in the OT. Politically, the Philistines had a highly organized city-state system comprised of five towns in southwest Palestine: Ashdod, Gaza, Ashkelon, Gath, and Ekron (1 Sam. 6:17). Each of the city-states was ruled by a "lord" (1 Sam. 6:18), a kinglike figure. Gath was perhaps the major city of this Philistine Pentapolis and, as such, served as the hub of the city-state system.

The Philistines were experts in metallurgy, the skill of processing metals (1 Sam. 13:19-23). Philistine expertise in this area put the Israelites at a decided disadvantage in their struggles with the Philistines (1 Sam. 13:22). See *Minerals and Metals*.

The Philistines had a highly trained military organization. Sea and land battles between the Egyptians and Sea Peoples are depicted on large panels at the temple of Ramses III at Medinet Habu in Thebes. The Philistines were in ships designed with a curved keel and the head of a bird on the bow. Philistine warriors wore a plumed or feathered headdress, a feature that added height to their physical appearance. On land the Philistines were equipped with horses and chariots, numerous foot soldiers, and archers (1 Sam. 13:5; 31:3). The armor of Philistine soldiers included bronze helmets, coats of mail, leg protectors, spears, and shields (1 Sam. 17:5-7). The story of Goliath indicates that at times the Philistines used individual combat (1 Sam. 17). Most likely the Philistine warrior went through a cursing ritual just prior to the confrontation (1 Sam. 17:43). David, who recognized the military expertise of the Philistines, selected Cherethites (Cretans) and Pelethites (Philistines) (2 Sam. 20:23) for his palace guard or mercenary army. This segment of the army provided protection for David and his family during times of revolt. See *Arms and Armor*.

While our information on Philistine religion is limited, three Philistine gods are mentioned in the OT—Dagon, Ashtoreth, and Baalzebub.

Dagon appears to be the chief god of the Philistines. Temples of Dagon were located at Gaza (Judg. 16:21-30) and Ashdod (1 Sam. 5:1-7). Ashtoreth, the fertility goddess of the Canaanites, was most likely adopted by the Philistines. Apparently, the Philistines had Ashtoreth temples at Beth-shan (1 Sam. 31:10) and, according to Herodotus, at Ashkelon (Herodotus I.105). Baalzebub, the Philistine god whose name means "lord of the flies," was the god of Ekron (2 Kings 1:1-16). Most likely the Philistines worshiped Baalzebub as a god who averted pestilence or plagues.

Archaeological excavations have brought to light many features of the material culture of the Philistines. The distinctive Philistine pottery that reflects styles and designs adopted and adapted from other cultures has been found at many sites. The major types of Philistine pottery are the so-called beer jugs with a spouted strainer on the side, the crater bowl, the stirrup jar, and the horn-shaped vessel. The pottery was often decorated with red and black painted designs including geometric designs often consisting of circles and cross-halving and stylized birds. Clay coffins were used by the Philistines for burials. These distinctive coffins, called "anthropoid coffins" because they were made in the shape of a human body, had lids decorated with the physical features of the upper part of a human being, features such as a head, arms, and hands.

Recent excavations especially at the sites of Ashdod, Tel-Qasile, Tel Jemmeh, and Tel Mor have added significantly to our understanding of the Philistine culture. The excavations at Tel Qasile revealed a Philistine iron smeltery, a Philistine temple, offering stands, and other vessels used in religious rituals as well as many other artifacts and installations. A new series of excavations is under way at Ashkelon. The current excavations will add yet a new dimension to our understanding of the Philistines. The political influence of the Philistines was most prominent between 1200 and 1000 B.C., but their influence continues through the use of the name Palestine, a name derived from "Philistine." See *Ashdod; Ashkelon; Ekron; Gath; Gaza; Palestine*.   LaMoine DeVries

PHILO JUDAEUS (Phī´ lō Jū dē ŭs) Early Jewish interpreter of Scripture known for use of allegory. Also known as Philo of Alexandria, he lived about the same time as Jesus (about

20 B.C. to A.D. 50). A member of a wealthy Jewish family in Alexandria, Egypt, He was well educated in Greek schools and used the Greek OT, the Septuagint, as his Bible.

Philo's writings—particularly his commentaries on the Scriptures—influenced the early church. A literal interpretation was all right for the average scholar, but for the enlightened ones such as himself, he advocated an allegorical interpretation. See *Bible Hermeneutics*.

James Taulman

PHILOLOGUS (Phĭ lŏ´ lō gŭs) Personal name meaning "lover of words," either in the sense of "talkative" or of "lover of learning." Member, perhaps the head, of a Roman house church whom Paul greeted (Rom. 16:15). Philologus was perhaps the husband of Julia and father of Nereus and Olympas.

PHILOSOPHY IN THE NEW TESTAMENT Greek thinkers called themselves philosophers ("lovers of wisdom") centuries before the NT era. Rejecting the myths of their culture, philosophers examined the world by means of reason, not religion. A. N. Whitehead recognized that philosophy's golden era had passed after Plato, thus since then philosophy has been "a series of footnotes." By the NT period philosophy had sunk to its nadir. Christian thinkers recognize, however, that with the passing of philosophy's best but inadequate theories, God was providentially preparing the way for Christ and the gospel.

Major Philosophical Systems in the New Testament Era Two major philosophical systems (mentioned in Acts 17:18) vied for allegiance in the NT era. The Epicureans were essentially materialists, viewing reality as a random configuration of indivisible atoms. If gods exist, they are of no consequence. Life should be spent on simple pleasures. Stoicism was essentially pantheistic and stressed strength of character. Matter is animated and organized by the Logos or universal word, of which all humans are children.

Philosophy in the New Testament Two NT passages specifically use the words philosophy and philosopher. In Col. 2:8 Paul warns against being taken captive by "philosophy and empty deceit." The specific heresy drawing this warning is still the subject of debate. But the apostle's readers would know that "philosophy" applies to

all theories about God, the world, and life's meaning—and a Christian cannot surrender the gospel to any philosophy.

Few passages in Acts have been analyzed more than Acts 17:16-34, which details Paul's encounter with Epicurean and Stoic philosophers (v. 18). Paul quotes two Greek thinkers (v. 28) in his speech to the intellectuals at Athens. Paul takes ideas that originally allude to God as Zeus, the principal deity in Stoic tradition, only to illustrate that the true God is Father of all life and cannot be contained in temples. The apostle quickly moves from this point of contact to a presentation of the gospel. He likely would have told them more had they listened. Apparently Paul's evangelistic methodology was to establish contact with Jews via the OT but with Gentiles via creation. For example, in Acts 14:15-17, Paul had to stop the Lystrans from worshiping him and Barnabas as an incarnation of gods after they healed a lame man. Paul pointed them to the one, true God who left Himself a witness by blessing them with good gifts (rains, seasons, food, and gladness—cp. also Rom. 1:18-21). Students of Scripture should pause before assuming Paul was wrong in his approach at Athens.

Other NT passages are sometimes viewed as dependent upon Greek philosophy. The Gospel of John is often accused of allegorizing the OT by way of the first-century Jewish philosopher, Philo. Or else, John is charged with importing Stoic ideas (such as the Logos). But biblical scholars are increasingly recognizing that John is primarily based upon the first chapter of Genesis. If the Gospel makes any use of current philosophical ideas, they are not primary, only secondary points of contact. The book of Hebrews is also viewed by some as a handbook of Platonism, but this misses the mark. Hebrews does not posit the unreality of the material world as does Plato but instead emphasizes the transience of the OT priestly system and its final fulfillment in Jesus Christ. The early church was not afraid to think carefully but did shun speculative theorizing when it came at the expense of God's revelation. They were aware that the world knew not God through wisdom (1 Cor. 1:21).　　*Ted Cabal*

PHINEHAS (Phĭn´ ə hăs) Personal name meaning "dark-skinned" or "mouth of brass." **1.** Grandson of Aaron and high priest who, on several occasions, aided Moses and Joshua. See *High Priest*. **2.** One of Eli the priest's worthless sons. He engaged in religious prostitution (1 Sam. 2:22) and led the people to follow. He and Hophni died in a battle with the Philistines while attempting to keep the ark from being captured (4:11). When his pregnant wife heard of his death, she immediately delivered, naming the child Ichabod ("the glory has departed").

PHLEGON (Phlē´ gŏn) Personal name meaning "burning," perhaps in the sense of "zealous." Member of a Roman house church whom Paul greeted (Rom. 16:14).

PHOEBE (Phē´ bē) Personal name meaning "bright." "Servant," "minister" (REB), "deaconess" (NASB, NIV note), or "deacon" (NRSV) of church at Cenchrea whom Paul recommended to church at Rome (Rom. 16:1-2). See *Deacon.*

PHOENICIA (Phə nĭsh´ ĭ à) Place-name meaning "purple" or "crimson," translation of Hebrew *Canaan,* "land of purple." The narrow land between the Mediterranean Sea and the Lebanon Mountains between Tyre in the south and Arvad in the north. New Testament Phoenicia reached south to Dor. Great forestland enabled the people to build ships and become the dominant seafaring nation. The forests also provided timber for export, Phoenician cedars being the featured material of Solomon's temple (1 Kings 5:8-10).

Culture Phoenician religion was akin to that of the Canaanites, featuring fertility rites of Baal. Later Baal's Greek counterpart Adonis ("my lord") was worshiped in similar fashion to Tammuz. The Phoenician princess Jezebel imported devotion to Baal to Israel. Phoenicia introduced the alphabet to the western world but little of their literature survived. See *Canaan; Elijah; Fertility Cult; Jezebel.*

History City-states rather than central government dominated Phoenicia. Leading cities were Tyre, Sidon, Byblos (Gebal), and Berytos (Beirut). An early Neolithic race disappeared about 3000 B.C., being replaced by Semitic colonizers from the east. Invading armies from north (Hittites), east (Amorites and Assyrians), and south (Egyptians) dominated history until 1000 B.C. when King Hiram of Tyre established local rule (981–947 B.C.). They were able to take advantage of their location on the sea with nat-

A relief depicting a Phoenician shepherd.

ural harbors and their forests to establish far-flung trade (cp. Ezek. 27). Their sailors established trading colonies to the west and south all along the Mediterranean coast. The most notable colony was Carthage on the North African coast.

Growth of Assyrian power about 750 B.C. led to Phoenicia's decline. The Persian Empire gave virtual independence to Phoenicia, using the Phoenician fleet against Egypt and Greece. Alexander the Great put an end to Phoenician political power, but the great cities retained economic power. See *Hiram.*

New Testament Jesus' ministry reached Tyre and Sidon (Matt. 15:21). Persecution, beginning with Stephen's death, led the church to spread into Phoenicia (Acts 11:19; cp. 15:3; 21:2-3). See *Sidon; Tyre.*   *Timothy Trammel*

PHOENIX (Phē´ nĭx) Place-name, perhaps meaning "date palm." Port on the southeast coast of Crete where Paul and the ship's crew hoped to reach for winter harbor (Acts 27:12). Phoenix is often identified with Port Loutro, which, however, faces the wrong direction to offer shelter from winter storms. Phoenix is better identified with some point on Phinika Bay to the west of Loutro.

PHRYGIA (Phrĭj´ ē à) Place-name meaning "parched." In very ancient times the area immediately west of the Hellespont. Later the people migrated into Asia Minor. During Roman times Phrygia was a subregion of Galatia, and her people often were slaves or servants. The area remained relatively undefined but contained Antioch of Pisidia, Laodicea, and at times, Iconium. Some of the Phrygians were present in Jerusalem on the Day of Pentecost and heard the gospel in their native language (Acts 2:10; cp. 16:6; 18:23). See *Asia Minor, Cities of.*

PHURAH (Phū´ rah) (KJV) See *Purah.*

PHUT (Phŭt) (KJV, Gen. 10:6; Ezek. 27:10) See *Put.*

PHUVAH (Phū´ vah) (KJV, Gen. 46:13) See *Puvah.*

PHYGELUS (Phĭ ġĕl´ us) Personal name meaning "fugitive." Christian who deserted Paul (2 Tim. 1:15). The contrast with Onesiphorus, who was not ashamed of the imprisoned Paul (1:16-17), suggests that Phygelus abandoned Paul in prison.

PHYLACTERY See *Frontlet.*

PHYSICIAN See *Diseases.*

PI-BESETH (Pī-bē´ sĕth) Egyptian city, name meaning "house of Bastet," located on the shore of the old Tanite branch of the Nile about 45 miles northeast of Cairo; served as capital of the 18th nome (administrative district) and, during the 22nd and 23rd Dynasties (940–745 B.C.), as capital of a fragmented Egyptian Empire. The site is tell Basta. Ezekiel mentions this city in his oracle against Egypt (Ezek. 30:17).

PICK See *Tools.*

PICTURE KJV term in three passages where modern translations use a term better suited to the context. **1.** Carved stone figures (Num. 33:52). **2.** Settings (NASB, NIV, NRSV) or fili-

A copper or bronze bucket in the form of a ram's head dating to the Phrygian period from Gordion.

An orthodox Jewish man wearing the traditional phylactery (frontlet) on his forehead.

gree (REB) (Prov. 25:11). **3.** Sailing craft or vessel (Isa. 2:16).

PIECE OF MONEY 1. Translation of the Hebrew *qesitah,* a coin of uncertain weight and value (Gen. 33:19; Job 42:11 KJV, NASB, NRSV). NIV reads "pieces of silver." **2.** KJV translation of the Greek term *stater* (Matt. 17:27). Modern translations read: stater (NASB); four drachma coin (NIV); shekel (RSV); coin (NRSV, REB). See *Coins.*

PIETY Translation of a Hebrew expression and several Greek terms. **1.** NIV used "piety" to translate the Hebrew idiom "the fear [or reverence] of the Lord" (Job 4:6; 15:4; 22:4; cp. REB). **2.** NRSV used piety to translate the Greek term meaning "righteousness" (Matt. 6:1), where the concern was with an external show of religion (Matt. 6:2-6). **3.** Piety translates two Greek terms for fear or reverence for God (Acts 3:12 NASB, NRSV; Heb. 5:7 NASB). **4.** Piety represents the religious duty of caring for the physical needs of elderly family members (1 Tim. 5:4 KJV, NASB).

PIG See *Swine.*

PIGEON "Pigeon" is a general term referring to any of a widely distributed subfamily of fowl (*Columbinae*). The term "pigeon" basically is employed when referring to the use of these birds for sacrificial offerings. In Leviticus pigeons serve as burnt offerings and as sin offerings (Lev. 1:14; 5:7,11). They also play a role in the rituals for purification following childbirth (Lev. 12:6,8) and for the cleansing of a healed leper (Lev. 14:22,30). Along with turtledoves, pigeons are the least expensive animal offerings. Mary offered a pigeon and two turtledoves after Jesus' birth (Luke 2:24). See *Dove.*   *Janice Meier*

PIHAHIROTH (Pī hả hī´ rŏth) Hebrew placename derived from the Egyptian, "house of Hathor" and interpreted in Hebrew as "mouth of canals." Pihahiroth lay in the eastern Nile Delta to the east of Baal-zephon. The site is unknown. The Israelites encamped at Pihahiroth in the early days of the exodus (Exod. 14:2,9; Num. 33:7). The alternate form Hahiroth appears at Num. 33:8.

PILATE, PONTIUS (Pī´ lăt, Pŏn´ shŭs) Roman governor of Judea remembered in history as a notorious anti-Semite and in Christian creeds as the magistrate under whom Jesus Christ "suffered" (1 Tim 6:13). The NT refers to him as "governor," while other sources call him "procurator" or "prefect" (an inscription found in Caesarea in 1961). Pilate came to power about A.D. 26, close to the time when two of his contemporaries, Sejanus in Rome and Flaccus in Egypt, were pursuing policies apparently aimed at the destruction of the Jewish people. Pilate's policies were much the same. His procuratorship consisted of one provocation of Jewish sensibilities after another. He broke all precedent by bringing into Jerusalem military insignia bearing the image of Caesar in flagrant defiance of Jewish law. He removed them only when the Jews offered to die at the hands of his soldiers rather than consent to such blasphemy. He brutally suppressed protest by planting armed soldiers, disguised as civilians, among the Jewish crowds. Against such a backdrop it is not hard to understand the reference in Luke 13:1 to "the Galileans whose blood Pilate had

The only known extrabiblical mention of Pilate's name is shown here in a Latin dedicatory inscription on a stone slab found at Caesarea Maritima.

mixed with their sacrifices" (HCSB). Pilate was finally removed from office as the result of a similar outrage against Samaritan worshipers who had gathered on Mount Gerizim, their holy mountain, to view some sacred vessels that they believed Moses had buried there. When the Samaritans complained to Vitellius, the governor of Syria, Pilate was ordered to Rome to account for his actions to the emperor and is not mentioned again in reliable contemporary sources.

In view of his record it is surprising that Pilate allowed himself to be pressured by a group of Jewish religious authorities into allowing Jesus to be executed. A possible explanation is that he already felt his position in the empire to be in jeopardy (note the threat implicit in John 19:12). Pilate seems to have had no personal inclination to put Jesus to death, and the NT writers are eager to show that he did not (Luke 23:4,14,22; John 18:38; 19:4,6; cp. Matt. 27:19). The Gospel writers sought to demonstrate that Jesus was innocent from the standpoint of Roman law and that consequently Christianity in their day

was not a threat to the Roman political and social order. The fact that Jesus was brought to Pilate at all probably means that He had not been formally tried and convicted by the Sanhedrin, or Jewish ruling Council (if he had, he would probably have been stoned to death like Stephen, or like James the Just in A.D. 62). Instead a relatively small group of Jerusalem priests, including the high priest, wanted to forestall any kind of a messianic movement by the people because of the repression it would provoke from the Romans (John 11:47-50,53). They maneuvered Pilate into doing their work for them (cp. Luke 23:2). Pilate is represented in all the Gospels as questioning Jesus, especially on the subject of kingship, but he remained unconvinced that Jesus was in any way a serious claimant to Jewish or Roman political power. See *Cross.*

J. Ramsey Michaels

PILDASH (Pĭl´ dăsh) Personal and clan name, perhaps meaning "powerful." Sixth son of Nahor (Gen. 22:22), probably the ancestor of an otherwise unknown north Arabian tribe.

PILEHA (Pĭ´ lə hă) (KJV) See *Pilha.*

PILFER To steal secretly, usually little by little (John 12:6 NASB, REB; Titus 2:10 NASB, REB, NRSV).

PILGRIMAGE A journey, especially a religious trek to a site at which God has revealed Himself in the past. KJV used "pilgrimage" in the nontechnical sense of journeys (Exod. 6:4). KJV, NASB, RSV used pilgrimage in a figurative sense for life journey (Gen. 47:9 KJV; Ps. 119:54). The only explicit mention of religious pilgrimage occurs in the NIV of Ps. 84:5 (cp. REB).

In Israel's early history numerous local shrines were the goals of religious pilgrimage: Bethel (Gen. 28:10-22; 31:13; 35:9-15; Amos 4:4; 5:5); Gilgal (Josh. 4:19-24; Hos. 4:15; Amos 4:4; 5:5); Shiloh (Judg. 20:26-27; 1 Sam. 1:3,19); Beersheba (Amos 5:5; 8:14); Gibeon (1 Kings 3:3-5); even Horeb (1 Kings 19:8). Jerusalem was not the goal of religious pilgrims until David relocated the ark there (2 Sam. 6:12-19). Hezekiah's and Josiah's reforms attempted to destroy the pagan sites of pilgrimage and idol worship (2 Kings 18:4; 23:8) and make Jerusalem the exclusive focus of pilgrimage. Mosaic law required adult male Israelites to appear before the Lord (where the ark of the covenant rested) three times a year (Exod. 23:14-17; 34:18-23; Deut. 16:16). Crowds of pilgrims (Pss. 42:4; 55:14; Luke 2:44) sang on the way to Jerusalem (Isa. 30:29). The Psalms of Ascent (Pss. 24; 84; 118; 120-134) were likely sung as pilgrims climbed the ascent to the temple mount in Jerusalem. The prophets condemned the celebration of religious pilgrimages and feasts when not accompanied by genuine devotion to the Lord expressed in righteous lives (Isa. 1:12-13; Amos 4:4-5; 5:5-6,21-24).

The NT witnessed the continuing popularity of pilgrimage to Jerusalem (Matt. 21:8-11; Luke 2:41; John 2:13; 5:1; 7:2,10; 12:12,20; Acts 2:5-10; 20:16). *Chris Church*

PILHA (Pĭl´ hȧ) Personal name meaning "millstone." Lay leader witnessing Ezra's covenant renewal (Neh. 10:24).

PILLAR Stone monuments (Hb. *matstsevah*) or standing architectural structures (Hb. *amudim*). **1.** Stones set up as memorials to persons. Jacob set up a pillar on Rachel's grave as a memorial to her (Gen. 35:20). Because Absalom had no son to carry on his name, he set up a pillar and carved his name in it (2 Sam. 18:18). **2.** Shrines both to the Lord and to false gods. Graven images often were pillars set up as gods. God commanded Israel to break down such "images" (Hb. *matstsebot*, Exod. 23:24). The Canaanites erected pillars at their places of worship and probably influenced Israelite practice. Archaeologists found pillars at Gezer. Jacob set up a pillar following his dream (Gen. 28:18) and again when God spoke to him at Bethel (35:9-15) as memorials of God's revelation. Moses set up 12 pillars to commemorate the giving of the law to the tribes of Israel (Exod. 24:4). **3.** As structural supports pillars were used extensively. The tabernacle used pillars for the veil (Exod. 26:31-32), the courts (27:9-15), and the gate (27:16). The temple in Jerusalem used pillars for its support (1 Kings 7:2-3), and the porch had pillars (7:6). Figuratively, pillars were believed to hold up heaven (Job 26:11) and earth (1 Sam. 2:8). **4.** God led Israel through the wilderness with a pillar of cloud by day and a pillar of fire by night (Exod. 13:21; cp. 14:19-20). These pillars were symbols of God's presence with Israel as much as

signs of where they were to go. **5.** Solomon's temple had two freestanding brass pillars (1 Kings 7:15). See *Jachin and Boaz*.
Mike Mitchell

PILLAR OF FIRE AND CLOUD Visible evidence of God's presence with Israel during the exodus and wilderness wanderings (Exod. 14:24; 33:9-10; Num. 12:5; Deut. 31:15). As a sign of God's presence, the pillar of fire and cloud was associated with divine actions: salvation (Exod. 14:19-20); revelation (Exod. 33:9-10; Ps. 99:7); judgment (Num. 12:5); commissioning (Deut. 31:15). Nehemiah used the pillar as a sign of God's faithfulness (Neh. 9:12,19). Psalm 99:7 reflects an otherwise unknown tradition that the pillar abided with Israel until the time of Samuel. Jesus' self-presentation as the incarnate Light of the World (John 8:12) recalls the guiding light of the wilderness wanderings. In Jesus' day the celebration of the Feast of Tabernacles (John 7:2) included the lighting of great, golden lamps in the temple court as a reminder of the pillar of fire and cloud. Jesus as the living Light challenged persons to follow Him as Israel had followed God's earlier light.

PILLOW A support for the head. KJV and REB described the rock on which Jacob rested his head as a pillow (Gen. 28:11,18). The Hebrew term translated "pillow" at 1 Sam. 19:13,16 (KJV, RSV, TEV) is of uncertain meaning. Possible translations include "quilt" (NASB), "net" (NRSV), and "rug" (REB). KJV followed the earliest Greek translation in reading "pillows" at Ezek. 13:18,20. Modern translations render the underlying Hebrew as "magic bands" (NASB, REB, NRSV), "charms" (NIV), or "wristbands" (TEV). Jesus demonstrated His absolute trust in God by sleeping through a storm with his head on a pillow (Mark 4:38 KJV, TEV) or cushion (HCSB, NASB, NIV, REB, NRSV). See *Magic Bands.*

PILOT Helmsman. Ancient pilots steered by positioning a side rudder which was an oversized oar pivoted in a slanting position near the vessel's stern (James 3:4; KJV "governor"). Most translations used "pilot" in Ezek. 27:8,27-29 in parallel to terms translated "mariners," "rowers," or "sailors." The NIV

P
Q

rendered the underlying Hebrew as "seaman." See *Ships, Sailors, and Navigation.*

PILTAI (Pĭl´ tī) Short form of personal name meaning "(Yah is) my deliverance." Head of a family of postexilic priests (Neh. 12:17).

PIM See *Weights and Measures.*

PIN See *Peg.*

PINE TREE See *Plants.*

PINNACLE Highest point of a structure. NRSV referred to the pinnacles of the temple or the city of Jerusalem (Isa. 54:12). The underlying Hebrew suggests a structure catching the sun's rays. Other translations include battlements (NASB, NIV, REB), towers (TEV), and windows (KJV). The pinnacle (literally, "little wing") of the temple (Matt. 4:5; Luke 4:9) is not mentioned in the OT, intertestamental literature, or rabbinic sources. Possible identifications include the southeastern corner of the royal colonnade that overlooked the Kidron Valley and a lintel or balcony above one of the temple gates. The account of the martyrdom of James the Lord's brother by

The traditional "pinnacle of the temple."

Hegesippus relates that James was thrown from the pinnacle of the temple and then stoned and clubbed. This (likely conflated) account suggests a high structure overlooking the temple court. See *Temple.*

PINON (Pī´ nŏn) Edomite clan chief (Gen. 36:41; 1 Chron. 1:52), whose descendants perhaps settled Punon (Num. 33:42-43).

PINT See *Weights and Measures.*

PIONEER See *Prince of Life.*

PIPE See *Music, Instruments, Dancing.*

PIRAM (Pī´ răm) Personal name, perhaps meaning "wild ass." King of Jarmuth southwest of Jerusalem and member of a coalition of five Amorite kings who battled Joshua unsuccessfully (Josh. 10:3,23).

PIRATHON, PIRATHONITE (Pī rā´ thŏn, Pī rā´ thŏn īt) Place-name meaning "princely" or "height, summit" and its inhabitants. The town in the hill country of Ephraim was the home of the judge Abdon (Judg. 12:13,15) and of Benaiah, one of David's elite warriors (2 Sam. 23:30; 1 Chron. 11:31). The site is identified with Far'ata about five miles southwest of Shechem.

PISGAH (Pĭs´ gah) Place-name, perhaps meaning "the divided one." Mountain in the Abarim range across the Jordan River from Jericho. Some Bible scholars believe it was part of Mount Nebo; others think it could have been a separate rise, either en-Neba or near modern Khirbet Tsijaga. God allowed Moses to view the promised land from the heights of Pisgah (Deut. 34:1) but would not let him cross into Canaan. Israel had camped near Pisgah (Num. 21:20). Balak took Balaam to its height so the prophet could see Israel and curse them (Num. 23:14). It was a limit of Sihon's kingdom (Josh. 12:23; Ashdoth-pisgah in KJV) and also for the tribe of Reuben (13:20).

PISHON (Pī´ shŏn) Name meaning "free-flowing," designating one of the rivers of Eden (Gen. 2:11). The identity of the river is unknown. Some suggest the "river" was a canal connecting the Tigris and Euphrates or

The snow-capped mountains of the ancient Roman province of Pisidia in Asia Minor (modern Turkey).

another body of water, such as the Persian Gulf.

PISIDIA (Pĭ sĭd´ ĭ á) Small area in the province of Galatia in southern Asia Minor bounded by Pamphylia, Phrygia, and Lyconia. The territory lay within the Taurus Mountain range and therefore resisted invasion by ancient peoples. Only in 25 B.C. did the Romans gain control over the region through economic diplomacy. Antioch was made the capital, although some historians contend that the city was not actually in Pisidia. Paul and Barnabas came through Antioch (Acts 13:14) after John Mark left them in Perga (v. 13). The NT does not record any missionary activity in Pisidia itself, probably because there were few Jews there with which to start a congregation. See *Asia Minor, Cities of.*

PISPA, PISPAH (Pĭs´ pá,) Personal name of unknown meaning. Member of the tribe of Asher (1 Chron. 7:38).

PISTACHIO NUTS See *Plants.*

PIT Translation of 12 Hebrew and two Greek words in KJV for water reservoir, ditch, or place of destruction. The most common use of "pit" is to refer to a well or cistern (Gen. 37:20-29; Exod. 21:33-34; Pss. 7:15; 55:23; Prov. 26:27; 28:10). See *Cistern; Well.*

Sometimes "pit" refers to a ditch or a marsh (Jer. 14:3; Isa. 30:14). Many times the word was used as a synonym for a place of destruction (Ps. 55:23), corruption (Pss. 16:10; 49:9; Isa. 38:17), or death (Isa. 14:15; Jon. 2:6). Three times KJV translated the word *Sheol* as "pit" (Num. 16:30,33; Job 17:16). One Greek word is

translated "bottomless pit" in Rev. 9:1,2 (cp. Ps. 88:6). See *Everlasting Punishment; Hell; Sheol.*   *Ralph L. Smith*

PITCH 1. Dark-colored, viscous mixture of hydrocarbons used for waterproofing sailing vessels (Gen. 6:14; cp. Exod. 2:3). Mineral pitch occurs naturally and is highly flammable (Isa. 34:9). **2.** KJV used "pitch" as a verb meaning "to coat or cover with pitch" (Gen. 6:14).

PITCHER Vessel with a handle and either a molded lip or a spout. Clay pitchers served as symbols of mortality (Eccles. 12:6) and of the commonplace (Lam. 4:2). For literal uses, see *Pottery.*

PITFALL Trap or snare, especially a roughly camouflaged pit. RSV used "pitfall" four times (Job 18:8; Ps. 119:85; Lam. 3:47; Rom. 11:9; the latter changed by NRSV to "stumbling block"). All uses are figurative. "Pitfall" in the OT suggests hidden or unrecognized dangers.

PITHOM AND RAMESES (Pī´ thŏm, Răm´ ə sēz) Egyptian cities located in northern Egypt (Nile Delta) in or near the Wadi Tumilat. They were built by the Israelites while in Egypt (Exod. 1:11) as supply hubs for royal, military, and religious purposes and were located near palaces, fortresses, and temples. Pithom (Temple of Atum) has been identified with Tell er-Retaba, Tell el-Maskhutah, or Heliopolis, and Rameses has been identified with Qantir. However, neither of the first two sites for Pithom has produced evidence from the 15th century B.C. and evidence for its identification with Heliopolis is lacking.

Rameses (Qantir) was first mentioned in Gen. 47:11 (as a synonym for Goshen) as the region where Joseph settled his father Jacob and his brothers. It was later the starting point for the Israelites' exodus from Egypt (Exod. 12:37; Num. 33:3,5). Rameses was the site of the Hyksos capital called Avaris (1638–1530 B.C.) before they were driven out by the Theban pharaoh Ahmose I (1540–1515 B.C.), the first pharaoh of the Eighteenth Dynasty, who established a fortress and settlement on the site. Ahmose I's successors, down to Thutmose III, built and used a large royal compound just south of this site, which was in use until the reign of Amenhotep II. However, Pharaoh Raamses II (pharaoh

P
Q

for the late-date exodus) also built near this site. See *Egypt; Exodus.* *Eric Mitchell*

PITHON (Pī´ thŏn) Personal name of unknown meaning. Descendant of Saul (1 Chron. 8:35; 9:41).

PITY Sympathetic sorrow toward one facing suffering or distress. Pity was expected of friends (Job 19:21), kin (Amos 1:11), and God (Ps. 90:13). Enemies lacked pity (Pss. 17:10; 69:20; Isa. 13:18; Jer. 21:7). Those guilty of idolatry, murder, or false witness were to be denied pity (Deut. 7:16; 13:8; 19:13). The images of the father and shepherd illustrate God's pity (Ps. 103:13; Isa. 49:10). God pities the penitent (Judg. 2:18), the weak and needy (Ps. 72:13), Jerusalem in ruins (Ps. 102:13), those who fear God (Ps. 103:13), and the exiles (Isa. 49:10). In judgment God withholds pity from God's people (Jer. 13:14; 20:16; Lam. 2:17; 3:43; Ezek. 5:11). Ezekiel pictured Jerusalem as an unpitied child denied the most basic postnatal care (Ezek. 16:5). Hosea illustrated the fate of Israel with *Loruchamah*, a child's name meaning "not pitied" (1:6; 2:23).

Pleas for pity are a common feature of healing narratives (Mark 9:22; Luke 17:13). Pity moved Jesus to heal (Matt. 20:34). Jesus used a compassionate Samaritan as an unexpected example of active pity (Luke 10:33). Such active concern for those in need serves as evidence that one is a child of God (1 John 3:17).

PLACE OF THEM THAT BOIL See *Kitchen.*

PLAGUES Disease interpreted as divine judgment, translation of several Hebrew words. The 10 plagues in the book of Exodus were the mighty works of God that gained Israel's release and demonstrated God's sovereignty and were called "plagues" (Exod. 9:14; 11:1), "signs" (Exod. 7:3), and "wonders" (Exod. 7:3; 11:9). They showed the God of Moses was sovereign over the gods of Egypt, including Pharaoh who was considered a god by the Egyptians.

The primary reference to the plagues in the Bible is in Exod. 7:1–13:15 (cp. Deut. 4:34; 7:19; 11:3; Jer. 32:20). Two psalms (78; 105) contain detailed accounts of the plagues but neither includes all 10. Paul used the plagues to stress the sovereignty of God in the hardening of Pharaoh's heart (Rom. 9:17-18). The plagues of the book of Revelation reflect OT influence (Rev. 8; 16).

Natural or Supernatural Modern distinctions between the natural and the supernatural were not allowable considerations for the Israelites. For them, whatever happened, God did it. Everything was under God's immediate control. For the inspired writer the plagues were nothing more or less than the Lord's judgment upon the Egyptians and His saving actions for Israel. Most interpreters point out that the plagues depict events of nature that might occur in Egypt. Clearly the author of Exodus saw them as the product of a purposive, divine will. Since Egypt's magicians duplicated the first two events, the uniqueness of the plagues may rest in their timing, locale, intensity, and theological interpretation.

Purpose The plagues resulted in Israel's freedom. However, the central purpose was the revelation of God. Pharaoh and the Egyptians, as well as Moses and the Israelites, would come to know the Lord through the events of the plagues (Exod. 7:17; 8:10,22; 9:14,16,29). Paul acknowledged this purpose: "that My name may be proclaimed in all the earth" (Rom. 9:17 HCSB). See *Exodus, Book of; Miracles, Signs, Wonders.* *Billy K. Smith*

PLAIN See *Palestine.*

PLAISTER KJV variant form of plaster (Isa. 38:21). Here plaster refers to a fig poultice (cp. NIV, REB, NASB, NRSV).

PLAIT KJV term meaning "to braid" (1 Pet. 3:3). See *Hair.*

PLANE TREE See *Plants.*

PLANKS Long, flat pieces of timber, thicker than boards, used in shipbuilding (Ezek. 27:5; Acts 27:44) and for the flooring of Solomon's temple (1 Kings 6:15 KJV). The "thick planks upon the face of the porch" in Ezekiel's vision of the renewed temple (Ezek. 41:25 KJV) likely refers to some type of canopy (NRSV; overhang, NIV; covering, TEV; cornice, REB) or to a threshold (NASB).

PLANTATION KJV term (Ezek. 17:7) to designate a bed (NASB, REB, NRSV) or plot (NIV) where plants are planted.

PLANTS On the third day of creation, recorded in Genesis, God spoke to the land to produce vegetation: the seed-bearing plants and trees (Gen. 1:11-12; cp. 2:4-6). In Gen. 1:29-30 He gave the plants and trees to man and to the creatures He had created, every plant for food. Genesis 2:9 tells that the trees were "pleasing to the eye and good for food." Trees, vines, shrubs, herbs, and even grasses are referenced throughout OT and NT. Adam and Eve "sewed fig leaves together" for their first clothing (Gen. 3:7). After the fall God cursed the ground that man would have to contend with unwanted plants that corrupted the fields he had to tend (Gen. 3:17-18).

Some of the plant life included in Scripture is not easily translated into familiar names; therefore categories of plants have been devised. Similarities in appearance and use have been noted. See *Flowers*.

Lily and Rose Red lips of Song 5:13 indicate a red-flowered "lily," such as scarlet tulip or anemone. Other references, such as Song 2:1-2, may refer to the actual white madonna lily (*Lilium candidum*), now very rare in the area, or wild hyacinth (*Hyacinthus orientalis*), wild crocus (*Crocus* species), the rose of Isa. 35:1-2 (see NASB). It is impossible to be sure to which "lilies" Jesus referred (Matt. 6:28; Luke 12:27). It may have been the anemone or any of the conspicuous wild flowers such as crown daisy (*Chrysanthemum coronarium*).

The biblical "rose" is similarly difficult to identify. The "rose of Sharon" (Song 2:1) has been equated with anemone, rockrose, narcissus, tulip, and crocus.

Reeds Certain water plants may be distinguished from the several Hebrew words used. The following species are likely to be the ones referred to:

Common reed (*Phragmites communis*) forms great stands in shallow water or wet salty sand. The plumed flower head may have been given to Jesus in mockery (Matt. 27:29). Pens (3 John 13) were made from the bamboolike stems.

Papyrus sedge (*Cyperus papyrus*) also grows in shallow water in hot places such as in Lake Huleh and along the Nile, but it is now extinct in Egypt except in cultivation. Its tall, triangular, spongy stems were used for rafts (Isa. 18:1-2) and for making baskets (Exod. 2:3) and papyrus paper on which much of the Bible may have been written.

Cattail or reed mace (*Typha domingensis*) is often associated with the above-mentioned reeds, and it seems to have been the one among which Moses was hidden (Exod. 2:3). This is often referred to as bulrush, but the tree bulrush (*Scirpus lacustris*) is a sedge with slender stems, which also occurs in lakes and pools.

Thorns Jesus' crown of thorns has led to two shrubs known as Christ's-thorn (*Ziziphus spina-christ, Paliurus spina-christi*). The former grows near the Dead Sea not far from Jerusalem (Matt. 27:29; Mark 15:17; John 19:5), while the latter does not grow nearer than Syria. However it may have occurred on the Judean hills in biblical times. Some authors consider the common spiny burnet (*Poterium* or *Sarcopoterium spinosum*) to be the species concerned.

Even today nobody can walk far in the Holy Land without seeing prickly weeds. The ground is cursed with them (Gen. 3:18; Num. 33:55). Many different Hebrew words have been used to distinguish them, and some are identifiable. Thorns are usually woody plants, such as Acacia, Lycium, Ononis, Prosopis, Rubus, Sarcopoterium, while thistles are herbaceous, such as Centaurea, Notobasis, Silybum. The latter could have been the "thorns' that suffocated the grain in Jesus' parable (Matt. 13:7).

Fragrant Plants In biblical times strong-smelling plants included the following kinds:

Cassia and cinnamon are traditionally identified with the Far Eastern trees *Cinnamomum cassia* and *C. zeylanicum*. The ground bark was used in the holy anointing oil for priests (Exod. 30:24), and cinnamon was used for perfumery (Prov. 7:17; Rev. 18:13).

Calamus or sweet cane (*Acorus calamus*) was the dry rhizome of this water plant imported from temperate Asia used for perfume (Isa. 43:24 NRSV).

Galbanum, a very strong-smelling resin burnt as incense (Exod. 30:34), was obtained from the stem of *Ferula galbaniflua*, a relative of parsley growing on dry hills in Iran.

Henna (*Lawsonia inermis*) leaves were crushed and used both as a perfume (Song 1:14 NASB) and as a yellow dye for skin, nails, and hair. It is a subtropical shrub with white flowers.

Hyssop used for ritual cleansing (Lev. 14:4,49) and sprinkling of blood in the tabernacle (Exod. 12:22) was the white marjoram

(*Origanum syriacum* or *Majorana syriacu*) which grows commonly in rocky places and is related to the mint. See *Hyssop.*

Myrtle (*Myrtus communis*) is a shrub with fragrant leaves and white flowers frequent in bushy places. It was especially favored for temporary shelters in the fields at the Feast of Tabernacles (Lev. 23:40; Neh. 8:15).

Rue (*Ruta chalepensis*) grows on the hills of the Holy Land as a low straggling shrub with pungent smelling leaves. Jesus referred to it being tithed (Luke 11:42).

Spikenard or nard, an expensive perfumed oil (Song 4:13-14; John 12:3), obtained either from the leaves of a desert grass (*Cymhybopogon schoenanthus*) or, traditionally, the valerian relative *Nardostachys jatamansi* from the Himalayas.

Stacte, one of the spices referred to in Exod. 30:34 to be used in the incense, may be the resin of the balm of Gilead (*Commiphora gileadensis*) from southern Arabia.

Culinary Herbs Bitter herbs for Passover are certain wild plants with sharp-tasting leaves. The desert plant wormwood (*Artemisia*) was also bitter and depicted sorrow and suffering (Prov. 5:4; Lam. 3:15,19).

Coriander (*Coriandrum sativum*) provides both salad leaves and spicy seeds (Exod. 16:31) which were likened by the Israelites to the manna in the desert (Num. 11:7).

Cummin (*Cuminum cyminum*) and **dill** (*Anethum graveolens*), like coriander, are members of the parsley family with spicy seeds (Isa. 28:25-27; Matt. 23:23).

Fitches or black cummin (*Nigella sativa*) is an annual plant with black oily seeds easily damaged in harvesting (Isa. 28:25-27).

Mint (*Mentha longifolia*), a popular seasoning herb, was tithed by Jewish leaders (Luke 11:42).

Mustard (*Brassica nigra*), well-known for its hot-flavored seeds, is referred to by Jesus for having small seeds which grow into a tree (Matt. 13:31-32).

Saffron (*Crocus sativus*), a yellow powder prepared from the stigmas, is used as a subtle flavor (Song 4:14) and also as a food coloring and a medicine.

Frankincense and Myrrh are resins produced by certain trees that grow in dry country in southern Arabia and northern Africa.

This large thistle plant is one of many varieties that grow in Israel.

Frankincense is a white or colorless resin yielded by several species of *Boswellia*, chiefly *B. sacra*, which is a shrub or small tree growing on both sides of the Red Sea. The resin is obtained by cutting the branches and collecting the exuding "tears' that are burnt as incense in religious rites or as a personal fumigant. In the Bible frankincense was prescribed for holy incense mixture (Exod. 30:31,34; Luke 1:9). It was also brought by the wise men to the infant Jesus, together with gold and myrrh (Matt. 2:11).

Myrrh is a reddish-colored resin obtained from a spiny shrub, *Commiphora myrrha,* in a similar manner to frankincense. This resin was not usually burnt but dissolved in oil and either eaten or used as a medicine and cosmetically (Ps. 45:8; Matt. 2:11).

Medicinal Plants Many medicinal herbs were gathered from the hills and valleys where the wild plants grew. Local people were well versed in plant lore, but these common weeds are not specially mentioned in the Bible. Some special imported medicines are referred to. See *Frankincense and Myrrh* above.

Aloes of the NT (*Aloe vera*) were succulent plants with long swordlike leaves with serrations and erect flower heads up to three feet high imported from Yemen. The bitter pith was used as a medicine and for embalming (John 19:39). In the OT, aloes refers to an expensive fragrant timber obtained from a tropical Indian eaglewood tree (*Aquilaria agallocha*).

Balm (Gen. 37:25) is a general term for medicinal ointment prepared from resin-bearing plants such as the rockrose (*Cistus laurifolius*) which produces ladanum. The balm of Gilead or opobalsam is yielded by *Commiphora gileadensis*, a nonspiny shrub of dry country in Southern Arabia and said to have been cultivated by Solomon at En-Gedi near the Dead Sea (Song 5:1, "spice"). Gum was imported with balm by the Ishmaelites (Gen. 37:25). It is extruded from cut roots of a spiny undershrub (*Astragalus tragacanth*) grown on dry Iranian hillsides.

Some plants, such as the gourd *Citrullus colocynthis*, could be medicinal purges in very small quantities but bitter poisons otherwise (2 Kings 4:39-40).

Cereal Grains for Bread Well-to-do citizens made bread primarily from wheat, but the poor man had to make do with coarse barley (2 Kings 4:42; John 6:9). No other cereals were grown, these being the OT "corn." About NT times, however, sorghum was introduced. Rice came later still, and maize, not until America was opened up.

Wheat (emmer wheat *Triticum dicoccum;* bread wheat *T. aestivum*) is an annual crop that grows about three feet, though the primitive varieties were taller in rich soil, and with bearded ears.

Grains of wheat are hard and dry and easily kept in storehouses as Joseph did in Egypt before the time of famine (Gen. 41:49; KJV "corn"). It was important to retain seed for sowing (Gen. 47:24), but ancient tomb grain will not germinate. See *Bread*.

Barley (*Hordeum vulgare*) tolerates poorer soil than wheat, is shorter, has bearded ears, and ripens sooner (Exod. 9:31-32). It was also used for brewing beer and as horse and cattle fodder

(1 Kings 4:28). Sometimes barley was eaten roasted as parched grain (Ruth 2:14).

Wheat and barley straw remaining after threshing was used for fuel (Isa. 47:14), and the fine chaff for instant heat in the oven.

Fruits Olive trees (*Olea europaea*) are small rounded orchard trees with narrow gray-green leaves and small cream-colored flowers in May. The stone fruits ripen toward the end of summer and are pickled in brine either unripe as green olives or ripe as black olives. However, the bulk of the crop was gathered for the sake of the olive oil. See *Oil.*

Grape vines (*Vitis vinifera*), grown either in vineyards or singly as shady bowers around houses and courtyards, have long flexible stems with tendrils and lobed leaves. Short flower heads grow among the new leaves in early summer, and the numerous tiny flowers develop into a cluster of round sweet grapes that ripen either as green or black fruits. The fruits are eaten fresh as grapes, or dried and stored as raisins (1 Sam. 30:12). Wine was prepared from the fermented juice. See *Wine.*

The common **fig tree** (*Ficus carica*) has a short stout trunk and thick branches and twigs bearing coarsely lobed rough leaves (Gen. 3:7). Rounded fruits ripen during the summer. These sweet fig fruits have numerous small seeds in their interior cavity. Fresh figs were favored as first fruits (Isa. 28:4; Jer. 24:2). Figs dry very well and were stored as cakes for future use (1 Sam. 25:18; 30:12). Jesus referred to figs and fig trees several times (Matt. 7:16; Luke 21:29-31).

Another kind of fig tree, the **sycamore** (*Ficus sycomorus*) grew in Egypt and in the warmer areas of the Holy Land. This large tree usually has low-growing branches such as would have enabled the short Zacchaeus to climb one to see Jesus passing along the streets of Jericho (Luke 19:4).

The juicy fruit of the **pomegranate** (*Punica granatum*), about the size of a tennis ball, is full of seeds and sweet pulp. It develops from beautiful scarlet flowers that cover the twiggy bush in spring. Pomegranate bushes were often grown in gardens and beside houses (Deut. 8:8; Song 6:11). Moses was instructed to embroider pomegranate fruits on the hem of the priests' robes (Exod. 28:33), and their form ornamented the columns of Solomon's temple in Jerusalem (1 Kings 7:18; 2 Chron. 3:16).

P
Q

Only one palm, the **date palm** (*Phoenix dactylifera*), yielded fruit in biblical times. This very tall tree with a rough unbranched trunk bearing a terminal tuft of huge feather leaves, fruits best in hot conditions of the Dead Sea oases. Hence, Jericho was known as the city of palm trees (Judg. 1:16). The wandering Israelites reached Elim where there were 70 palm trees (Exod. 15:27). The psalmist considered it to be such a fine tree that he compared the righteous flourishing to one (Ps. 92:12). Revelation 7:9 refers to the symbolic use of palm leaves (as "branches") denoting victory, as when Jesus entered Jerusalem and the people strewed the way with leaves (John 12:13).

It is doubtful whether the **black mulberry** (*Morus niger*) was present in the Holy Land until NT times as it originated in the Caspian Sea region. The only probable reference to it (as "sycamine") is when Jesus spoke of believers having enough faith to destroy one (Luke 17:6)—perhaps because old trees are stout, gnarled, and long-lived.

Another questionable fruit is that referred to as "apple" (Prov. 25:11; Song 2:3,5; 7:8; 8:5; Joel 1:12), although some versions translate the word as "apricot." Either could be possible, but it is unlikely that fine varieties of apples were available so early.

Nuts Popularly considered to be hard dry fruits and seeds, as distinct from the more succulent fruits described above.

The most important biblical nut was the **almond** (*Prunus dulcis*), which is a small tree with delightful whitish flowers in early spring before the leaves have sprouted. The nuts are well-known today either fresh or as marzipan; the kernel is contained in a very hard thick casing. Almonds were carried to Egypt by Joseph's brothers (Gen. 43:11). Aaron's walking stick budded and produced almonds overnight and proved that Aaron was God's man to assist Moses (Num. 17:8). The holy lampstand had cups like almond flowers (Exod. 25:33; 37:19).

The **walnut** tree (*Juglans regia*) originated in the Caspian region and may not have been commonly planted in the Eastern Mediterranean region until after the biblical period. However, it is possible that Solomon grew it in his garden (Song 6:11). The tree grows to a considerable size. The leaves are compound, and the oily edible nuts look like a miniature brain—hence the

ancient name *Jovis glans* and the scientific adaptation *Juglans.*

True **pistachio** nuts (*Pistacia vera*) also arrived late. The pistachio nuts referred to in the Bible (Gen. 43:11 NIV) would be from the native terebinth trees (*Pistachia terebinthus*, *P. atlantica*) of the hillsides. One is a small shrubby tree, while the other is as large as an oak. Both yield small round edible fruits.

Vegetables The wandering Israelites longed for vegetables in the desert after they had left Egypt (Num. 11:5). Onions, leeks, and garlic are mentioned, as well as cucumbers and melons. Elsewhere, we read of lentils and other pulses (2 Sam. 17:28; Dan. 1:12).

Onions (*Allium cepa*) are the bulbs familiar to us today. They are white or purple and grow quickly from seeds in one season. Leeks (*Allium porrum*) do not form such a distinct bulb. They are cooked, or the leaves were chopped up. Garlic (*Allium sativum*) is a strongly flavored onion that produces a bulb composed of separate scales.

The **cucumbers** of biblical Egypt were most likely the snake- or muskmelon *Cucumis melo*, which has longitudinal lines on its exterior. The melons were the watermelon (*Citrullus lanatus*) and not the squash or honeydew melon which are of American origin and now widely grown in the Middle East.

Several **beans** or pulses were grown in biblical times, especially lentils (*Lens culinaris*) in the more arid areas. The red pottage or soup made of lentils enabled Jacob to obtain Esau's birthright (Gen. 25:29-34). Lentil plants are small and slender with pealike flowers and small flat pods containing two seeds. Of the other pulses the broad bean (*Vicia faba*) and the chickpea (*Cicer arietinum*) were important and may have been the vegetables Daniel and his friends ate in Babylon (Dan. 1:12).

Trees From Genesis to Revelation trees have a special place, both factually and symbolically. We can divide them into groups according to their natural habitats.

Trees of dry and desert areas Rainfall is erratic, and trees may be restricted to dry watercourses where residual water remains.

Several species of acacia (KJV *shittim*, using the Hb. word) occur in Sinai. Their timber was used for the construction of the tabernacle, the tent of meeting (Exod. 25). Acacias are usually flat-topped trees that possess strong thorns.

Tamarisk (*Tamarix* species) is a shrub or small tree with fine branchlets, scale leaves, and pink or white flowers, inhabiting salty places in the desert. Abraham planted one at Beersheba (Gen. 21:33 NIV).

Trees of streams, rivers and lakes Water is usually available throughout the year in these habitats.

Oleander (*Nerium oleander*) is an erect shrub with long, narrow poisonous evergreen leaves and beautiful pink flowers in summer. Although it may be found in streambeds in dry country, it is also in the marshes and streams such as those of Mount Carmel. It may be the "roses" at Jericho and the "roses" planted by the brook (Ecclesiasticus 24:14; 39:13). Even some of the references to willow trees may mean oleanders.

Plane (*Platanus orientalis*) is a large tree with flaking bark and digitate leaves. Its minute flowers are clustered in several hanging balls. The plane tree inhabits rocky streambeds. It was one of the rods Jacob peeled (Gen. 30:37; also Ezek. 31:8, KJV, "chestnut").

Poplar (*Populus euphratica*) is another of the trees Jacob peeled (Gen. 30:37). It grows beside water, especially the rivers Euphrates and Jordan. It is a tall tree with shaking leaves and numerous suckering shoots around its base. The white poplar (*P. alba*) or the storax (*Styrax officinalis*) were more likely to be the trees upon the mountains (Hos. 4:13).

Willows (*Salix acynophylla*), like poplars, root easily in wet places, but they are not as tall and usually have long narrow leaves (Job 40:22; Isa. 44:4; Ezek. 17:5).

Trees of hills and plains In biblical times certainly before the Israelite conquest of Canaan, the hills of the Holy Land were well wooded, while Lebanon was famous for its dense forests. Agriculture, terracing, sheep and goat grazing, and the constant demand for fuel and timber has left little woodland at the present day. Only isolated trees remain in many places. Even the plains between the Mediterranean and the hills were covered with oaks until recent times.

Cypress (*Cypressus sempervirens*) is a dense coniferous forest tree typically with spreading branches although often seen as a tall narrow tree planted beside cemeteries. References in the Bible to coniferous trees are confus-ing, but the cypress is evidently intended in Isa. 40:20; 60:13, among others.

Cedar (*Cedrus libani*), the famous cedar of Lebanon, grew in extensive coniferous forests which are now sadly depleted. The stout flat-topped trees provide excellent timber which was used for David's house (2 Sam. 5:11) and Solomon's temple (1 Kings 5:6-10), as well as the later one (Ezra 3:7).

Oak (*Quercus species*) trees provide excellent timber for ships (Ezek. 27:6) and other construction, although the evergreen kermes oak often grows no more than a shrub. The deciduous oak still forms woodland on some hills of Palestine, such as Carmel, Naphtali, and Bashan (Isa. 2:13). Oaks were used to mark graves (Gen. 35:8) or as landmarks (1 Sam. 10:3) or for sacrilegious ceremonies (Hos. 4:13).

Pine (*Pinus halepensis*), especially the Aleppo pine, is a tall coniferous tree with long needle-leaves and cones containing winged seeds. Its timber is workable and used for construction; probably the tree referred to in Isa. 44:14 (KJV, ash; NRSV, cedar).

Terebinth (*Pistacia terebinthus*, *P. atlantica*) produced fruits used as nuts, but the timber of the large oaklike *P. atlantica* is also useful. The shade of terebinths was used for pagan sacrifices and offerings (Hos. 4:13 NIV).

Foreign trees Expeditions brought back rare timbers during the OT period, and, in NT times, foreign timbers entered through normal trade routes.

Almug wood, traditionally identified as sandal wood (*Pterocarpus santalinus*), was imported from Ophir to Judah by Hiram's fleet for Solomon (1 Kings 10:10-11). Whether algum and almug are synonymous is a matter of dispute, since algum is clearly stated to be from Lebanon (2 Chron. 2:8), in which case it could have been the Cilician fir (*Abies cilicia*) or the Grecian juniper (*Juniperus excelsa*).

Ezekiel 27:15 links ebony with imported ivory tusks. The black-red ebony of ancient Egypt was an African leguminous tree *Dalbergia melanoxylon*, while later the name was transferred to the tropical Asian *Diospyros ebenum* that has jet-black timber.

Thyine wood is timber from the North African sandarac tree (*Tetraclinis articulata*), a coniferlike cypress, which was used by the Greeks and Romans for cabinetmaking. It is dark, hard, and fragrant (Rev. 18:12).

P
Q

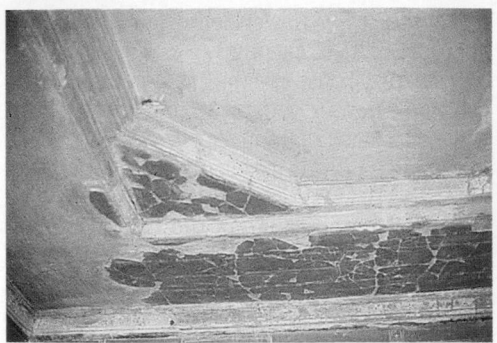

Ceiling of a room in Pompeii showing the decorative way in which plaster was used in the first century.

See *Broom Tree; Gall; Heath; Juniper; Palm.*   *F. Nigel Hepper*

PLASTER Pastelike mixture, usually of water, lime, and sand, which hardens on drying and is used for coating walls and ceilings. Mosaic law included regulations for treating homes in which mold or rot appeared in the plaster (Lev. 14:41-48). Writing was easy on a surface of wet plaster (Deut. 27:2-4).

PLATE 1. Shallow vessel from which food is eaten or served. See *Pottery.* **2.** Sheet of metal (Exod. 28:36; Num. 16:38).

PLATTER Large plate. The platter bearing the head of John the Baptist was likely of gold or silver (Matt. 14:8,11 and parallels). Ceramic platters were in common use (Luke 11:39 NASB). See *Pottery.*

PLAY See *Games.*

PLEDGE Something given as down payment on a debt. The OT regulated this practice. An outer garment given in pledge was to be returned before night since it was the only protection the poor had from the cold (Exod. 22:26; Deut. 24:12-13). One was not permitted to take as a pledge what was required for someone to earn a living (Deut. 24:6). Creditors were prohibited from entering a house to seize a pledge (Deut. 24:10). Job denounced abuses in the taking of pledges from family (22:6), from orphans and widows (24:3), as well as the practice of taking children as pledges (24:9). Ezekiel warned repeatedly against failing to restore pledges. Amos rebuked those who coupled idolatry with holding garments in pledge (2:8).

PLEIADES (Plē´ ə dēz) Brilliant grouping of six or seven visible stars located in the shoulder of the constellation Taurus (Job 9:9; 38:31; Amos 5:8). The derivation of the name has been traced to the seven daughters of Atlas and Pleione in Greek mythology, the adjective *pleos*, suggesting the "fullness" of the cluster, or to the verb *pleo* (to sail) from the cluster's usefulness in navigation.

PLOW To break up the ground to prepare it for sowing seed. Biblical writers often appealed to the image of a farmer plowing. Plowing served as an image of sin (Prov. 21:4; Hos. 10:13) and of repentance (Jer. 4:3; Hos. 10:11). Plowing served as a picture of oppression (Ps. 129:3) and destruction (Jer. 26:18; Mic. 3:12) but also of expectation of reward (1 Cor. 9:10). To plow with another's heifer meant to commit adultery with his wife (Judg. 14:18). To have one's hands on the plow and look back was to have reservations about discipleship (Luke 9:62). For literal uses of plow, see *Agriculture.*

PLUMB LINE Cord with a weight (usually metal or stone) attached to one end. The plumb line would be dangled beside a wall during its construction to assure vertical accuracy. Prophets spoke of the measurement God would use on the nation (Isa. 28:17; Amos 7:7-8). Israel had been built straight, but, because it was out of line, it would be destroyed.

POCHERETH-HAZZEBAIM (Pŏk´ ə rĕth-hăz zə bā´ ĭm) Personal name signifying an official office, "binder (or hunter) of Gazelles." Head of a family of Solomon's servants included in those returning from exile (Ezra 2:57; Neh. 7:59). KJV takes "Zebaim" as a place-name.

PODS Dry coverings split in the shelling of beans and similar plants. The pods of Luke 15:16 (NASB, NIV, REB, NRSV; husks, KJV; bean pods, TEV) were likely the pods of the carob tree which served as a common feed for livestock. These sweet-tasting pods may reach one foot in length.

POET One who composes poetry or verse. In ancient times poets passed on the history and wisdom of their cultures. In witnessing to a sophisticated Greek audience at Athens, Paul appealed to poets familiar to his bearers. The line "For in Him we live and move and exist" (Acts 17:28 HCSB) is sometimes attributed to Epimenides of Crete (around 500 B.C.). The line "For we are also His offspring" is traced to the Phaenomena of Arastus (around 310 B.C.) or to Cleanthes' Hymn to Zeus.

POETRY "Poetry" calls to mind a Western pattern of balanced lines, regular stress, and rhyme. Hebrew manuscripts do not distinguish poetry from prose in such a clear-cut way. Hebrew poetry has three primary characteristics—parallelism, meter, and the grouping of lines into larger units called stanzas. Parallelism appears as two or three short lines connected in different ways. Meter may be reckoned in various ways. The most straightforward is a word count of the individual parallel lines. Stanzas may be recognized by a change of theme or the presence of a refrain. The distinction in Hebrew between poetry and prose is not so much a difference in kind as a difference in degree. Each of the three elements mentioned may be found to a lesser extent in prose.

One third of the OT is cast in poetry. Every OT book except Nehemiah, Esther, Haggai, and Malachi contains at least some poetry, though in some cases it is confined to a few verses or one or two chapters (Exod. 15:1-18,21; Lev. 10:3; Deut. 32:1-43; 33:2-29; Josh. 10:12-13; Ruth 1:16-17,20-21; 2 Kings 19:21-28; 1 Chron. 16:8-36; Ezra 3:11; Jonah 2:2-9). Some books are almost all poetry (Job, Psalms, Proverbs, Song, Isaiah, Lamentations, Hosea, Joel, Amos, Obadiah, Micah, Nahum, Habakkuk, Zephaniah).

Parallelism The predominant feature of Hebrew poetry is parallelism. In parallelism two or three short lines stand in one of three relationships to one another: synonymous, antithetic, or synthetic.

In synonymous parallelism the succeeding line expresses an identical or nearly identical thought:
"My mouth speaks wisdom;
my heart's meditation [brings] understanding."
(Ps. 49:3 HCSB).

The lines are not synonymous in the sense that they express exactly the same meaning. To the contrary slight differences color the parallel lines expanding or narrowing the theme brought forward in the first line.

In antithetic parallelism succeeding lines express opposing thoughts:
"The wicked borrows and does not repay,
but the righteous is gracious and giving."
(Ps. 37:21 HCSB).
Line two is a positive expression of line one, but the psalmist's choice of words does more than reflect a pair of mirrored images. Each line means something more as it is linked with the other.

In synthetic parallelism succeeding lines display little or no repetition:
"How good and pleasant it is
when brothers can live together!"
(Ps. 133:1 HCSB).
There is no one-to-one correspondence between the word groups. Continuity joins the parallel lines. Synthetic parallel lines may describe an order of events, list characteristics of a person or thing, or simply modify a common theme.

Meter Various methods for determining meter have been developed. Attempts to establish a classical system of meter (iambic feet, for example) have failed. Other theories use letter counts, vowel counts, stress counts, and word counts. The last mentioned is one of the most effective methods. Hebrew word units may be illustrated by the use of hyphens:
"As-a-deer longs for-streams-of-water,
so-I long for-you, God."
(Ps. 42:1 HCSB).
This example shows a 3+4 meter. Particles and other words which play minor roles in the syntax of Hebrew are generally excluded from the count. Individual lines range from two to four words each, even though these "words" may be translated as two or three words in English. 3+2 and 2+3 meter is common. Parallel lines may also be 3+3. Groups of three parallel lines may express a 2+2+2 pattern or 3+3+3. Numerous metrical systems are possible. Consequently Hebrew meter is described in terms of general patterns rather than absolute uniformity. Systems of meter, unlike parallelism, are apparent only in the Hebrew language and not in English translations.

Stanzas Sets of parallel lines are often, but not always, divided into larger units. Such stanzas may be set off by identical lines or by parallel lines expressing similar thoughts. These introductions may take the form of a refrain not unlike a musical refrain. Sections separated in this way may be dissimilar in theme, form, and vocabulary. Psalms 42–43 present a good example of clear-cut stanzas. The two psalms together form a single poem. A refrain is repeated three times: 42:5,11; 43:5. The refrain subdivides the poem into three sections.

Poetry provides imagery and tone for inspired writers to bring God's word home to His people. Awareness of poetic form alerts the reader to listen for the images and moods of a passage.

Donald K. Berry

POISON Chemical agent causing ill health or death when in contact with or ingested by an organism. Poison served as a frequent image for wickedness, especially lying speech (Deut. 32:32-33; Job 20:16; Pss. 58:4; 140:3). Poisonous weeds illustrated lawsuits springing up from broken oaths and covenants (Hos. 10:4). In Amos 6:12 poison served as an image of injustice. Poisoned water pictured God's judgment on sin (Jer. 8:14).

POKERETH-HAZZEBAIM (Pŏk´ ə rĕth-Hăz zə bā´ ĭm) (NIV) See *Pochereth-Hazzebaim.*

POLICE, POLICEMEN NASB, NRSV used police (HCSB) and policemen to refer to those Roman officials who attended the chief magistrates (Acts 16:35,38).

POLL 1. KJV term for "to cut off" or "to trim" hair (2 Sam. 14:26; Ezek. 44:20; Mic. 1:16). Priests were permitted to "poll" their hair but not to shave their heads. Polling one's hair could be understood as a sign of mourning. **2.** KJV term for "the head," especially that part on which hair grows. To count every male "by their polls" (Num. 1:2; cp. 1 Chron. 23:3,24) is to count "heads."

POLL TAX Tax levied on a person, usually as a prerequisite for voting. NASB used poll tax sometimes when other translations read either taxes or tribute (Matt. 17:25; 22:17; Mark 12:14). Poll tax is perhaps misleading. The Roman Empire was not a democracy in which the Jewish people participated by voting. "Head tax" is the meaning the NASB translators had hoped to convey. See *Poll.*

POLLUTE See *Clean, Cleanness.*

POLLUTION Things of an inferior quality (Mal. 1:7, 12) or things fouled by sin (Ezra 6:21; Acts 15:20; Rev. 21:8). In modern parlance pollution refers to things that befoul the natural environment. As a result of the fall, the environment, which was created clean and pure, has become subject to all manner of pollution, making the land (Deut. 29:22-28; cp. Jer. 4:23), rivers and streams (Exod. 7:20-24; Prov. 25:26; Ezek. 32:2; 34:18-19; Rev. 8:9-10; 16:4), and the sea (Rev. 8:8-9; 16:3) unfit for life as God intended it. The earth and its resources belong to God (Ps. 24:1) yet have been entrusted to people (Gen. 1:28-29; 9:1-4), who have a sacred responsibility to care for the earth with the same diligence that God cares for it (Deut. 11:12).   *Paul H. Wright*

POLLUX (Pŏl´ lŭx) One of the twin brothers in the constellation Gemini (Acts 28:11). See *Castor and Pollux; Figurehead.*

POMEGRANATE Small tree, the fruit of which has a thick shell, many seeds, and a red pulp. See *Plants.*

POMMELS KJV term for the bowl-shaped capitals topping the temple pillars (2 Chron. 4:12-13).

The pomegranate is one of the many fruits found in the Middle East.

POND At Exod. 7:19; 8:5, "pond" renders the Hebrew *agam* meaning "marsh" or "muddy pool." The term is usually translated "pool." The Hebrew underlying "ponds for fish" (Isa. 19:10) is rendered grieved (in soul) or sick at heart by modern translations, based on a Hebrew homonym apparently occurring only in this passage.

PONTIUS PILATE See *Pilate, Pontius.*

PONTUS (Pŏn´tŭs) Province just south of the Black Sea in Asia Minor. The terrain varies from fertile plains along the shore to rugged mountains farther inland. The Greeks colonized the plains shortly after 700 B.C., but the mountains remained free of their influence. Mithradates founded the kingdom of Pontus in about 302 B.C., and it remained in his dynasty until 63 B.C. when Rome took over. Christianity spread to Pontus early. First Peter was addressed to the elect there (1:1-2). Citizens of Pontus were in Jerusalem on the Day of Pentecost (Acts 2:9). See *Asia Minor, Cities of.*

POOL Collection of water, natural or artificial. Small pools were commonly seen as a place to collect rainwater from the roof that was used for irrigation or drinking. These reservoirs were important sources of water supply in the arid climate of the Middle East.

The following are some of the principal pools mentioned in Scripture: pool of Hezekiah (2 Kings 20:20), upper and lower pools of Gihon (Isa. 7:3; 22:9), old pool (Isa. 22:11), King's pool at Jerusalem (Neh. 2:14), pool of Bethesda (John 5:2,4,7), and pool of Siloam (John 9:7,11). Solomon also made pools to water his nursery (Eccles. 2:6).

Most of the pools near the cities were carved from stone, fed by rainwater channeled into them by channels cut in the rock. Pools were natural meeting places (John 9:7). Pools are used metaphorically to illustrate God's power to transform the barren into something fruitful (Isa. 41:18), judgment (Isa. 42:15), and the beauty of a woman's eyes (Song 7:4). See *Cistern; Pond; Reservoir.*   *C. Dale Hill*

POOR IN SPIRIT Not those who are spiritually poor, that is, lacking in faith or love, but those who have a humble spirit and thus depend on God (Matt. 5:3). Luke's parallel

A pool in the Baths of Faustina from the Roman ruins of Miletus (in modern Turkey).

speaks simply of the poor (Luke 6:20). That God has "chosen those who are poor in the eyes of the world to be rich in faith and to possess the kingdom" was regarded as a well-established fact (James 2:5 REB).

POOR, ORPHAN, WIDOW Three groups of people of the lower social classes in need of legal protection from the rich and powerful who sometimes abused them (Job 24:3-4). God's promise of care for the poor, the fatherless, and the widows was a tremendous source of hope during times of severe difficulty.

Condition and Hope of the Poor The words used to describe the poor have the underlying meaning of "humble, oppressed, needy, weak, dependent." The contexts where these words are used suggest that the poor were those who had been wrongfully oppressed and impoverished (Job 24:14; 29:12; Ps. 10:9; Isa. 3:14); those who begged for food (Deut. 15:7-11; Job 31:16-21); or those who had no economic or social status (2 Sam. 12:1-4; Prov. 14:20; Eccles. 9:13-18). Ideally, there should be no poor people among the covenant people of God because of the blessings of God and the generosity of the people toward those in need (Deut. 15:7-11). In actuality, God's blessings did not always come to His sinful people, and the rich did not always share with the poor. To provide for the poor God allowed them to glean the remains of the fields and vineyards and harvest the corners (Lev. 19:10; 23:22). If poor people were forced into slavery, they were to be treated like hired servants (Lev. 25:39-43). The courts were to see that the poor received just, not favorable or unfavorable, treatment (Exod. 23:3,6-7).

The hope of the poor was based on their status before God. Because they were part of the people God redeemed from the slavery of Egypt, they inherited God's blessings of freedom, protection, and a portion of the land (Lev. 25:38,42,55). The psalms picture God as the refuge and deliverer of the poor (Pss. 12:5; 14:6; 70:5). In some passages the poor are identified as the righteous (Ps. 14:5-6). The prophets predicted the destruction of Judah and Israel in part because of the oppression of the poor by fellow Israelites (Amos 2:6-8; 4:1-3; 5:10-13; 8:4-6). The prophets encouraged the people to defend the poor and instructed the kings to rule with equity (Prov. 29:7,14; Isa. 1:17; Jer. 22:3). God brought judgment on Sodom (Gen. 18:16–19:29) and on Judah because the people did not care for the poor (Ezek. 16:46-50).

Jesus was particularly concerned with the poor, and He preached a message of good news to the poor (Matt. 11:5; Luke 4:18) and told parables that encouraged generosity toward the poor (Luke 14:13-24). The first Christians provided for the needs of poor widows (Acts 6:1-6), and Paul exerted great effort to collect funds for the poor in Jerusalem (Rom. 15:26). This positive attitude toward the poor was not present among all the early believers (James 2:1-6).

Condition and Hope of the Orphan and Widow Among the poor, the fatherless, and the widow were the most vulnerable. The Hebrew word (*yatom*) often translated "orphan" (NASB, NIV, NLT, NRSV) refers more precisely to a fatherless child (the mother could still be alive; cp. Ps. 109:9). The widow, of course, was a woman whose husband had died. In both cases no mature male figure could defend against unscrupulous persons who would wish to defraud these individuals out of their inheritance. Consequently biblical (and nonbiblical) legal codes provide for the protection of the rights of the fatherless and the widow (Exod. 22:22; Deut. 10:18; 24:17-22). The prophets were particularly concerned with the injustice done to the fatherless and widow (Isa. 1:17; Jer. 5:28; Mic. 2:9; Mal. 3:5). God declared that He would be a Father to the fatherless and provide justice for the widow (Deut. 10:18; Ps. 68:5).

The NT measured true religious character by a person's care for the fatherless and the widow (James 1:27). The early Christians cared for the widows (Acts 6:1-8), but Paul limited these provisions because of abuses on the part of some (1 Tim. 5:3-16). Jesus condemned the Pharisees for devouring widows' houses (Matt. 23:40). See *Ethics; Family; Fatherless; Humble; Inheritance; Oppressed.* Gary V. Smith

POPLAR See *Plants.*

PORATHA (Pō rā´ thǎ) Persian personal name meaning "bounteous." One of Haman's 10 sons (Esther 9:8).

PORCH In English "porch" designates a covered entrance to a building, usually having a separate roof. English translations vary greatly in their use of "porch" for several Hebrew and Greek terms. KJV and NASB used "porch" freely (41 and 40 times, respectively); NIV and RSV used "porch" sparingly (2 and 3 times, respectively). The vast majority of OT references concern the "porch" of the Jerusalem temple as in 1 Kings 6:3. This reflects a view of a two-room temple with an attached porch. REB and NRSV translation, "vestibule," reflects a view of a three-room temple. The terms translated "porch" in Matt. 26:71 and Mark 14:68 can refer to a gateway or forecourt. The "porches" in John 5:2 and Acts 3:11 were likely freestanding porticoes or colonnades. See *Arch.*

PORCIUS FESTUS (Pôr´ shǔs Fěs´ tǔs) See *Festus.*

PORCUPINE Large rodent, sometimes called a hedgehog, that has stiff, sharp bristles mixed with its hair. Disagreement exists about the translation of the Hebrew word. Some feel "porcupine" is the correct translation (Isa. 14:23; 34:11 NKJV, NLT). NASB uses "hedgehog" in Isaiah and Zeph. 2:14. Others have various translations (NIV, owl; KJV, bittern; NEB, bustard).

PORPHYRY Rock composed of feldspar crystals embedded in a dark red or purple groundmass (Esther 1:6; KJV, "red marble").

PORPOISE Any of several species of small-toothed whales. NASB uses porpoise skins for a covering over the tabernacle (Exod. 25:5; Num. 4:6; KJV, NKJV, badger; NIV, sea cow) and "sandals of porpoise skin" in Ezek. 16:10. See *Sea Cow.*

PORTER KJV term for a gate or doorkeeper. Such persons served at city gates (2 Sam. 18:26; 2 Kings 7:10), temple gates (1 Chron. 9:22,24,26), the doors of private homes (Mark 13:34), and even the gate of a sheepfold (John 10:3). See *Doorkeeper*.

PORTICO See *Arch.*

PORTION Allotment, allowance, ration, share. Portion is frequently used in the literal sense of a share in food, clothing, or property as well as in a variety of figurative senses. Wisdom writings often designate one's lot in life as one's portion (Job 20:29; 27:13; Eccles. 9:9). God's chosen people are termed God's portion (Deut. 32:9; Jer. 21:10). The Levites did not receive tribal territory with the other tribes but had the Lord for their special portion (Num. 18:20). To have a portion in the Lord is to share the right of joining the community in worship of God (Josh. 22:25,27; cp. Neh. 2:20). The psalms often speak of the Lord as the portion of the faithful (Pss. 16:5; 73:26; 119:57).

POSSESSION, DEMON See *Demon Possession.*

POSTEXILIC Time in Israel's history between the return from exile in Babylon in 538 B.C. and the Roman occupation in 63 B.C. During this period the Jews returned to Jerusalem and Palestine to rebuild what the Assyrians and Babylonians had destroyed. See *Israel, Land of; Intertestamental History and Literature.*

POT See *Pottery; Vessels and Utensils.*

POTENTATE KJV term in 1 Tim. 6:15 meaning "ruler" (NIV) or "sovereign" (NASB, NRSV, REB), used as a title for God.

POTIPHAR (Pŏt´ ĭ phár) Personal name meaning "belonging to the sun." Egyptian captain of the guard who purchased Joseph from the Midianite traders (Gen. 37:36; 39:1). He saw great potential in Joseph's abilities and appointed him as steward over his household. Potiphar's wife tried to seduce Joseph, but he refused her advances. Because of this rejection, she told her husband that Joseph tried to rape her. Potiphar had Joseph thrown in prison.

POTIPHERA or **POTIPHERAH** (Pō tĭ´ phĕr ah) Priest in the Egyptian city of On (Heliopolis) where the sun god, Re, was worshiped. Joseph married his daughter, Asenath, at the pharaoh's command (Gen. 41:45). Potipherah and Potiphar are the same in Egyptian, leading some to believe that one name was slightly changed in Hebrew to distinguish between the captain of the guard and the priest.

POTSHERD (Pŏt´ shĕrd) Fragment of a baked, clay vessel, "potsherd" (more commonly called a "sherd" by archaeologists) is used in the OT with both a literal and symbolic or figurative meaning. Job used a potsherd (2:8) to scrape the sores that covered his body; the underparts of the mythological monster Leviathan are said to be "jagged potsherds" (41:30 NIV). The latter is a particularly arresting image for anyone familiar with the jagged, sharp sherds always encountered in archaeological excavations where clay vessels were in use, as in the Near East.

Isaiah (30:14) used the image of a sherd as a sign of the worthlessness of ancient Judah. The psalmist (22:15) used the image of a dry

Pile of pottery sherds at Banias.

potsherd as a simile for some physical illness he was experiencing.

Since the Hebrew word translated "potsherd" in the above passages can also mean "earthen vessel" in other contexts (cp. Lev. 14:5,50; Num. 5:17), it is not always clear as to which meaning is to be preferred. Such is the case in Prov. 26:23 where a comparison of the NRSV translation ("earthen vessel") with the KJV ("potsherd") highlights the problem. Elsewhere, textual confusion compounds the problem. In Isa. 45:9, the Hebrew text literally reads: "a potsherd (or "earthen vessel") with potsherds (or "earthen vessels") of ground." In neither case is the text clear, though the symbolism of the futility of a person striving with God is obviously intended.

Finally, the obscure text in Ezek. 23:24 assigned Judah the same fate as her sister, Samaria. She would not only drink the cup of wrath but also "gnaw its sherds" (NRSV). See *Archaeology and Biblical Study; Pottery.*

John C. H. Laughlin

POTSHERD GATE See *East Gate 1.*

POTTAGE Thick soup usually made from lentils and vegetables and spiced with various herbs. Jacob served pottage and bread to the famished Esau in return for the birthright (Gen. 25:29-34). Elisha added meal to a tainted recipe of pottage at Gilgal (2 Kings 4:38-41).

POTTER'S FIELD Tract of land in the Hinnom Valley outside Jerusalem used as a cemetery for pilgrims to the Holy City since the interbiblical era. The field was bought with the money paid for betraying Jesus (Acts 1:18). Matthew 27:3-10 records that the priests bought the field with the money Judas returned. Their reasoning was that the money had been used to bring about bloodshed and could not be returned to the temple treasury.

POTTERY Everyday household utensils whose remains form the basis for modern dating of ancient archaeological remains. Relatively few Bible texts refer to the methods and products of the potter even though the industry formed a vital part of the economic structure of the ancient world. The few statements about the preparation of the clay, "the potter treads clay" (Isa. 41:25), and the potter's fail-

ure and success on the wheel (Jer. 18:3-4) hardly hint at the importance and abundance in antiquity of "earthen vessels" (Lev. 6:21; Num. 5:17; Jer. 32:14), the common collective term for pottery in the Bible. However, the work of the potter in shaping the worthless clay provided the imagery the biblical writers and prophets used in describing God's creative relationship to human beings (Job 10:8-9; Isa. 45:9).

The pottery sherds (Job 2:8), those indestructible remnants of the potters' skill, are recovered in abundance at every archaeological site. They have not only clarified the pottery industries but have also shed light on the migration of peoples, their trade, and commerce. They have become the key to establishing a firmer chronological framework for other cultural data, especially in those periods for which few or no written remains are available. This begins in the Neolithic period, before 5000 B.C. when pottery first appeared.

The Bible specifically identifies only two vessels as pottery: earthen pitchers (Lam. 4:2) and earthen bottles (Jer. 19:1). An additional series of vessels probably came from the potter's workshop: "jar" for water (Gen. 24:14 NRSV); "pot" (Exod. 16:3); "bowl" (Num. 7:85); "bowl" (Judg. 6:38); "vial" (1 Sam. 10:1); "cruse" for oil and "jar" for flour (1 Kings 17:14 NRSV); another type of "jar" (2 Kings 4:2 NRSV); "bowl" and "cup" (Song 7:2; Isa. 22:24); "cup" (Isa. 51:17,22); and "cup" and "pitcher" (Jer. 35:5 NRSV). Similar English words represent different Hebrew terms.

Pottery Production Two factors appear to have contributed to the late appearance of fired pottery: early nomads found pottery too cumbersome to transport and a lengthy trial-and-error process in discovering and understanding the firing process.

Clay for the production of pottery may be divided into two types: pure aluminum silicate ("clean" clay), not found in Israel, and aluminum silicate mixed with iron oxides, carbon compounds, and other ingredients (sometimes referred to as "rich" clay). The potter prepared the dry clay by sifting and removing foreign matter and letting it stand in water to achieve uniform granules. Having achieved the desired texture, the potter mixed it by treading on it or hand-kneading it. Then the potter was ready to shape the vessel.

The earliest pottery from the Neolithic period was handmade. Clay was coiled into the desired shape on a base or stand. These earliest efforts of the potter's trade were coarse and badly fired. Other vessels were hand shaped from a clay ball. Innovations soon led to refinement of method and technique. During the Chalcolithic and early Bronze periods (5000–2000 B.C.), turning boards or stones ("tournettes") formed the prototypes of the potter's wheel. A refinement of the wheel came with the production of two horizontal stone disks with corresponding cone and fitting socket lubricated with water or oil. While the lower stone with the socket served as a stationary base, the upper stone allowed for easy, smooth rotation to enhance the quality and productivity of the potter. Extensive use of the wheel came during the middle Bronze Age (about 1900–1550 B.C.), though a few examples have been identified belonging to the early Bronze Age.

The potter rotated the wheel and used both hands to "draw" the moist clay from base to rim into the shape of desired curvature, diameter, and height. The vessel was set aside to dry to a leather-hard consistency. At this point the vessel received its distinctive modifications such as base, handles, projecting decorations, and spout adjustment. Coloration and ornamentation followed with a variety of options such as slips and paint, burnishing, incisions, impressions, and reliefs. A second drying period further reduced water content to about three percent. Then the vessel was fired in an open or closed kiln at temperatures between 450 and 950 degrees Celsius.

The best wares obviously were achieved at the highest and most consistent temperatures, a result determined by the nature of the kiln. Firing may have begun by accident when people noticed the quality of clay vessels left near or in a fireplace or recovered after a building or town burned. First combustible materials were burned over the pottery in open pits. Later the pottery appears to have been stacked above the firebox. Ultimately the need to equalize the distribution of heat led to the closed kiln. The introduction of bellows and forced air firing provided the desirable higher temperatures.

Importance of Pottery Analysis for Historical Studies Each culture produced its own distinctive, durable pottery. That distinctiveness has enabled archaeologists to trace each culture's "fingerprints" through time. The archaeologist can describe the movement of a race from one place to another, the influence of new people in a particular region or area, and the

P
Q

A modern Middle Eastern potter fashioning pottery in the same manner used in biblical times.

commercial activity of the people. Archaeologists have used changes in pottery forms, shapes, decorations, and materials from one period to the next to establish a relative chronological framework for dating purposes. The type pottery in an excavated layer or strata provides the key for dating, at least in a relative way, all other cultural artifacts and architectural remains within the strata.

Developments in Pottery Production in Palestine The significance of pottery analysis may be highlighted in a general way by recognizing the major developments of pottery production in Palestine throughout biblical history period by period.

Neolithic Period (7000–5000 B.C.) Neolithic pottery, the earliest attempts at this important industry, were poorly handmade and badly fired, although some types including bowls and storage jars were decorated elaborately with red slip, burnished, painted (triangular and zigzag lines, herringbone design), and incised (herringbone). Jericho, Sha'ar ha-Golan, and other sites in the Jordan Valley have provided the best examples of these early cultural developments.

Chalcolithic Period (5000–3000 B.C.) The Ghassulian (in the Jordan Valley) and Beersheba (in the Negev) cultures have provided the best assemblages for this period of pottery advancement. Rope ornamentation on this handmade pottery clearly suggests the practical strengthening of the clay vessels with various rope netting or binding. A wide variety of shapes and sizes suggests the proliferation of household and commercial uses for storage and transport of both dry and liquid products and merchandise.

Early Bronze Age (3000–2000 B.C.) This period has been divided into three and pos-

Fourteenth-century B.C. pottery found at Hazor in Israel.

sibly four distinct cultural periods on the basis of the distinctive pottery. The first period (EB I) is characterized by grey burnished ware, band-slip ware, and burnished red-slip ware. The second period (EB II) is identified with "Abydos" ware (pitchers and storage jars with burnished red-slips on the lower half and brown-and-black-painted triangles and dots on the upper half), first found in Egyptian royal tombs of the First Dynasty at Abydos in Upper Egypt and most important in the chronological correlation of Egyptian and Palestinian history. The third period (EB III) includes kraters (large storage or mixing bowls), bowls, pitchers, and stands, first identified at Khirbet Kerak (Beth Yerak) at the southern end of the Sea of Galilee, which has a distinctive combination of highly burnished red and black slip. This culture appears to have originated in eastern Anatolia. The fourth period (EB IV) with innovations may be a cultural continuation of the previous period.

Middle Bronze Age (about 2000–1500 B.C.) A transitional phase (first identified MB I, and now mostly EB-MB) resulted from nomadic or seminomadic tribes who destroyed the final phase of EB culture. They produced a distinctive pottery with globular and cylindrical shapes. These combined hand-shaped bodies and wheelmade necks and out-flared rims. The period introduced the pinching of the rim of a small bowl to produce a four-wicked lamp. The patriarchal period usually is identified with the next period (MB IIa). The pottery reflects the arrival of a highly developed culture that results in a prosperous, urbanized, sedentary population with rich cultural ties to the upper Euphrates region from which Abraham migrated, according to the biblical text. The pottery exhibits excellent workmanship and, in many instances, suggests metal prototypes. Possibly the earliest Semitic wheelmade vessels were the beautiful carinated bowls and vessels of this period. Skilled potters, with the advent of the new fast wheel, were able to produce elegant new shapes with wide bodies, narrow bases, and flaring rims, all with refined details. During the MB IIb an unusual group of juglets indicate pottery exchange with Egypt which during this period was politically joined to Syria-Palestine.

Late Bronze Age (about 1550–1200 B.C.) This period generally coincides with the vibrant New Kingdom period in Egypt when Palestine primarily was under Egyptian control, a rule that became more concentrated and demanding toward the end of the period. Canaan also maintained extensive trade connections with Aegean and northeastern Mediterranean powers. Cypriot pitchers called "bilbils" and shaped as poppyseed heads (upside-down), were among the most popular Palestinian imports. They may have been used to transport opium in wine or water from Cyprus to other Mediterranean sites.

Clear pottery distinctives again suggest a three-period division. The late Bronze I (about 1550–1400) reflects a continuation of the vitality of the earlier middle Bronze culture. The pottery of the late Bronze IIa (about 1400–1300) shows a deterioration of forms and quality during a period of political instability associated with the el-Amarna Period. That deterioration becomes more evident during the late Bronze IIb (about 1300–1200) as Egypt's Nineteenth Dynasty established a firmer control over the affairs of the economy and urban centers of Canaan. An abundance of Mycenaean and Cypriot pottery throughout the country would seem to suggest a growing commercial interest in the Levant for export and trade.

Iron Age (about 1200–587/6 B.C.) The Iron Age basically runs from the conquest of Canaan to the demise of the Judean Kingdom and usually is divided into two distinct periods. The distinguishing elements in pottery and other cultural elements for making the archaeological divisions of this period are not overly clear. Iron Age I (1200–925) pottery from the settlement to the division of the kingdom begins with a continuation of late Bronze traditions, as Israel borrowed industrial techniques from the local Canaanite population.

The arrival of the Philistines after 1200 B.C. brought a distinctively decorated pottery with Mycenaean shapes and motifs. The deterioration of the quality and design of this pottery tends to reflect the eclectic nature of these "Sea Peoples." By 1000 B.C. the distinctive nature of the pottery in the Philistine plain had basically disappeared.

Philistine ware made its debut during this period. Some of the liquid containers had strainers in the spouts to prevent the dregs (pulp and debris that usually settled to the bottom) from coming out with the liquid. Philistine ware is an amalgamation of Mycenaean types with clear influences from Egypt and Canaan. Red and

Storage jars from the palace complex of Knossos on the island of Crete.

black decorations, especially people and animals, are typical of this type pottery.

During the Iron II period (925–587/6), from the division of the United Monarchy to the fall of the Judean Kingdom to the Babylonians, the political separation produced clear distinctions in the regional pottery types, generally known as "Samaria" and "Judean" ware. During most of this period the northern pottery exhibits the higher standard of workmanship. Most prominent in imported ware up to 700 B.C. is the Cypro-Phoenician ware. From 700 to 500 B.C. imports of Assyrian origin resulted in local potters copying Assyrian prototypes.

Persian Period (586–330 B.C.) The deterioration of the pottery with inferior clay, firing, and general workmanship appears to reflect the general economy disruption throughout the region, a situation that seems to prevail throughout the Near East. In Palestine a growing number of Greek imports appeared, especially toward the end of the period.

Hellenistic Period (330–63 B.C.) While the local pottery was basically crude and uninspired, imported wares include a wide range of luxury items from molded Megarian bowls to impressed and roulette decorated black-glazed and red-glazed ware. The maritime trade connections further are evident, for example, in widespread appearance of Rhodian amorphae.

Alexander the Great brought to the Middle East the Hellenistic culture and its large variety of ceramic ware. Large, heavy vessels mark this period. They show a uniformity of style owing to the Greek dominance of all major production centers.

Roman Period (63 B.C.–A.D. 325) Only Herodian pottery is of particular interest for an understanding of the biblical period. Local pottery basically followed earlier traditions with the dominant innovation a ribbing of many vessel surfaces. The most common imported ware is both eastern and western red-glazed terra sigillata, noted for its outstanding finish and general workmanship. The Nabateans who controlled the trade routes of the Negev/Sinai and the Transjordan produced the finest local varieties, emulating the skills and export products of the Roman potters of the period.

By the time Rome conquered Palestine in 63 B.C., a new type of cylindrical jar with angular to rounded shoulders appeared. It had a ring base and a rim made to receive a lid. This type vessel made an excellent storage jar for solids, especially scrolls. The famous Dead Sea Scrolls were kept in these finely crafted containers for almost 2,000 years.

See *Archaeology and Biblical Study; Bottle; Cruse; Flagon; Flask; Jug; Lamps, Lighting, Lampstand; Vessels and Utensils.*

George L. Kelm and Mike Mitchell

POUND See *Coins; Weights and Measures.*

POVERTY See *Poor, Orphan, Widow.*

POWDERS, FRAGRANT Pulverized spices used as a fragrance (Song 3:6). See *Spices.*

POWER Ability to act or produce an effect; the possession of authority over others. These two aspects of power are often related in Scripture. Because God has revealed His power in the act of creation, He has authority to assign dominion to whomever He wills (Jer. 10:12; 27:5). God revealed His power by miraculously delivering Israel from Egyptian slavery (Exod. 4:21; 9:16; 15:6; 32:11) and in the conquest of Canaan (Ps. 111:6). God's acts are foundational for His claim on Israel. God's power includes not only the power to judge

but also the power to forgive sin (Num. 14:15-19; Jer. 32:17-18). Second Kings 3:15 links the onrush of the power of God with prophecy. Here power approximates God's Spirit (cp. Mic. 3:8; Luke 1:35).

Christ's miracles evidenced the power of God at work in His ministry (Matt. 14:2; Mark 5:30; 9:1; Luke 4:36; 5:17). Luke highlighted the role of the Holy Spirit in empowering the ministry of Jesus (Luke 4:14; Acts 10:38) and the ongoing ministry of the church (Acts 1:8; 3:12; 4:7,33; 6:8). Paul stressed the paradox that the cross—what is apparently Jesus' greatest moment of weakness—is the event in which God's power to save is realized (1 Cor. 1:17-18; cp. Rom. 1:16). This scandal of God's power revealed in Christ's death continues in God's choice to work through the powerless (1 Cor. 1:26-29; 2:3-4; 2 Cor. 12:9). In some texts "powers" refer to angelic powers (Rom. 8:38; Eph. 3:10; Col. 2:15; 1 Pet. 3:22).   *Chris Church*

PRAETORIAN GUARD Roman military branch assigned to personal security for the imperial family and to represent and protect the emperor's interests in the imperial provinces. A related Greek term (*praetorion*) may refer to the imperial high court. "Praetorium" referred to the residence of a Roman governor in the Gospels and Acts. The term is used in Phil. 1:13 with regard to a unit of the Praetorian guard. Greetings from "those from Caesar's household" (Phil. 4:22 HCSB) do not prove Paul was in Rome when he wrote Philippians. The term "Caesar's household" was applied often to the Praetorian guard, and units were dispersed throughout the Roman Empire. Paul may have been in Caesarea, Ephesus, or Antioch, though Rome seems most likely. *Praetorion* is used in Mark 15:16 in reference to the headquarters where Jesus was taken and subsequently mocked by Roman soldiers prior to His crucifixion. The NT locates the praetorium in Jerusalem as the palace of the Roman governor, the Tower of Antonia, located adjacent to the temple on the northwestern corner (Matt. 27:27; Mark 15:16; John 18:28,33; 19:9) of Temple Mount.

Charles W. Draper and Steven L. Cox

PRAETORIUM This term is used in reference to the emperor's palace in noncanonical literature. Herod's praetorium in Caesarea (Acts 23:35 NASB, RSV; judgment hall, KJV) was the residence of Felix, the Roman procurator of Judea, though the Greek praetorium does not occur in this verse.

Praetorium was formerly the headquarters or barracks of a Roman camp; however, in the provinces as well as in Rome, praetorium came to be used in reference to the governor's or emperor's official residences. The Romans accommodated themselves with such buildings by seizing and appropriating the palaces of conquered royalty of the local area. See *Praetorian Guard*.   *Steven L. Cox*

PRAISE One of humanity's many responses to God's revelation of Himself. The Bible recognizes that men and women may also be the objects of praise, either from other people (Prov. 27:21; 31:30) or from God Himself (Rom. 2:29), and that angels and the natural world are likewise capable of praising God (Ps. 148). Nevertheless, human praise of God is one of Scripture's major themes.

"Praise" comes from a Latin word meaning "value" or "price." Thus, to give praise to God is to proclaim His merit or worth. Many terms are used to express this in the Bible, including "glory," "blessing," "thanksgiving," and "hallelujah," the last named being a transliteration of the Hebrew for "Praise the Lord." The Hebrew title of the book of Psalms ("Praises") comes from the same root as "hallelujah" and Pss. 113–118 have been specially designated the "Hallel" ("praise") psalms.

The modes of praise are many, including the offering of sacrifices (Lev. 7:13), physical movement (2 Sam. 6:14), silence and meditation (Ps. 77:11-12), testimony (Ps. 66:16), prayer (Phil. 4:6), and a holy life (1 Pet. 1:3-9). However, praise is almost invariably linked to music, both instrumental (Ps. 150:3-5) and, especially, vocal. Biblical songs of praise range from personal, more or less spontaneous outbursts of thanksgiving for some redemptive act of God (Exod. 15; Judg. 5; 1 Sam. 2; Luke 1:46-55,67-79) to formal psalms and hymns adapted for corporate worship in the temple (2 Chron. 29:30) and church (Col. 3:16).

While the Bible contains frequent injunctions for people to praise God, there are also occasional warnings about the quality of this praise. Praise is to originate in the heart and not become mere outward show (Matt. 15:8).

The front of the praetorium at the palace of the Roman emperor Hadrian.

Corporate praise is to be carried on in an orderly manner (1 Cor. 14:40). Praise is also firmly linked to an individual's everyday life (Amos 5:21-24). *See Music, Instruments, Dancing; Psalms, Book of; Worship.*   *David W. Music*

PRAYER Dialogue between God and people, especially His covenant partners.

Old Testament Israel is a nation born of prayer. Abraham heard God's call (Gen. 12:1-3), and God heard the cries of the Hebrew children (Exod. 3:7). Moses conversed with God (Exod. 3:1–4:17) and interceded for Israel (Exod. 32:11-13; Num. 11:11-15). By prayer Joshua discerned sin in the conquest community (Josh. 7:6-9) but was tricked when he did not discern God's opinion by prayer (Josh. 9). God also spoke to the judges to deliver His people when the people called out to Him for deliverance. David's spiritual acumen is seen in his prayers of confession (2 Sam. 12:13; Ps. 51). Solomon fulfilled the promises made to David after praying for wisdom (1 Kings 3:5-9) and dedicated the temple in prayer (1 Kings 8). God worked miracles through the prayers of Elijah and Elisha (1 Kings 17:19-22; 18:20-40). The writing prophets noted that genuine prayer calls for accompanying moral and social accountability (Hos. 7:14; Amos 4:4-5).

Isaiah's call reflected the intense cleansing and commitment involved in prayer (Isa. 6). Jeremiah's dialogue and intercession frequently voiced reservation and frustration (Jer. 1; 20:7-18), teaching honesty in prayer. The book of Psalms teaches that variety and honesty in prayer are permissible; the psalms proclaim praise, ask pardon, seek such things as communion (63), protection (57), vindication (107), and healing (6). Psalm 86 provides an excellent pattern for prayer. Daily patterned prayer becomes very important to exiles denied access to the temple (Dan. 6:10).

New Testament Jesus' example and teaching inspire prayer. Mark emphasized that Jesus prayed in crucial moments, including the disciples' appointment (3:13), their mission (6:30-32), and the transfiguration (9:2). Jesus displayed a regular and intense prayer life (Matt. 6:5; 14:23; Mark 1:35). Luke taught that Jesus was guided by the Holy Spirit (Luke 3:22; 4:1,14,18; 10:21; Acts 10:38). John reported that Jesus sometimes prayed aloud for the benefit of those present (John 11:41-42). He also reported Jesus' prayer of intercession for the first disciples and future believers (John 17). Both prayers display Jesus' unity with the Father and desire to give Him glory (John 11:4; 17:1).

Modern orthodox Jews pray in old Jerusalem in a manner similar to the Hebrews of the OT.

The Lord's Prayer (Matt. 6:9-13; Luke 11:2-4) is taught to disciples who realize the kingdom is present but still to come in all its fullness. Significantly the disciples asked Jesus to teach them to pray after watching Him pray (Luke 11:1). The prayer also provides a contrast to hypocritical prayers (Matt. 6:5). Although it is permissible to repeat this prayer, it may be well to remember Jesus was emphasizing how to pray, not what to pray. See *Lord's Prayer*.

Jesus also corrected some abuses and misunderstandings regarding prayer. First, prayer is not to be offered to impress others. Disciples should rather seek a storage closet or a shed and pray in private. Jesus did not reject group prayer, but his warning might apply to a believer who prays to impress a congregation (Matt. 6:5-6). Second, Jesus also prohibited long-winded attempts that try to manipulate God. While Jesus prayed for long periods of time (Luke 6:12; Mark 1:35) and repeated Himself (Mark 14:36-42), He called for people to trust their Father and not their own eloquence or fervor.

Jesus' teaching on persistence in prayer is linked to the inbreaking kingdom (Luke 11:5-28; 18:1-8). God is not like the reluctant neighbor, even though Christians may have to wait for answers (Luke 11:13; 18:6-8). The ironies of prayer are evident: God knows our needs, yet we must ask; God is ready to answer, yet we must patiently persist. Children of the kingdom will have their requests heard (Matt. 6:8; 7:7-11; 21:22; John 14:13; 15:7,16; 16:23; cp. 1 John 3:22; 5:14; James 1:5), particularly believers gathered in Jesus' name (Matt. 18:19).

In Hebrew thought the name was mysteriously linked to the person's character and prerogatives. Thus prayer in Jesus' name is prayer that is seeking His will and submissive to His authority (John 14:13; 1 John 5:14).

The church remembered Jesus' teaching regarding the Spirit, prayer, and the kingdom mission. The disciples prayed awaiting the Holy Spirit's outpouring (Acts 1:14). The early church is characterized by prayer (Acts 2:42). They prayed regarding selection of leaders (Acts 1:24; 6:6; 13:3), during persecution (Acts 4:24-30; 12:5,12), and in preparing to heal (Acts 9:40; 28:8). Calling upon God's name—prayer—is the first act and true mark of a believer (Acts 2:21; 9:14,21; 22:16).

Paul's ministry reflected his constant prayer of intercession and thanksgiving (1 Tim. 2:1;

Jewish men praying at the Wailing Wall—a point close to the probable site of the ancient temple.

Eph. 1:16; 5:4; Acts 9:11). The Lord spoke to Paul in prayer (Acts 22:17). Prayer is crucial to continuing in the Christian life (Rom. 12:12). The indwelling Spirit enables a believer to call God "Abba" (Rom. 8:15); that is, the Spirit's work within the believer prompts him or her to address God with the confidence of a child (Rom. 8:14). The Spirit must intercede because our prayers are weak; apart from the Spirit Christians pray without discernment. He takes up our petitions with an earnest pleading beyond words (Rom. 8:26-27; Gal. 4:6).

Answered Prayers—Unanswered Petitions Not every petition is granted. Job's demand for answers from God was eclipsed by the awesome privilege of encountering Him (Job 38–41). Modern believers must also cherish communion with the Father more than their petitions.

Jesus, with His soul sorrowful to the point of death, prayed three times that His cup of suffering might pass, but He was nevertheless submissive to God's will (Matt. 26:38-39,42,45). Both the boldness of the petition to alter God's will and the submission to this "hard" path of suffering are significant.

Paul asked three times for deliverance from his "thorn in the flesh." God's answer to Paul directed him to find comfort in God's sufficient grace. In addition, God declared that His power is best seen in Paul's weakness (2 Cor. 12:8-9). God gave him the problem to hinder his pride. Ironically, Paul claimed that God gave the problem, and yet he called it a messenger of Satan. Paul learned that petitions are sometimes denied in light of an eventual greater good: God's power displayed in Paul's humility.

Faith is a condition for answered petitions (Mark 11:24). Two extremes must be avoided concerning faith. (1) With Jesus' example in mind we must not think that faith will always cause our wishes to be granted. (2) We must not go through the motions of prayer without faith. Believers do not receive what they pray for because they pray from selfish motives (James 4:2-3). Prayers are also hindered by corrupted character (James 4:7) or injured relationships (Matt. 5:23-24; 1 Pet. 3:7).

Theological Insights Dialogue is what is essential to prayer. Prayer makes a difference in what happens (James 4:2). Our understanding of prayer will correspond to our understanding of God. When God is seen as desiring to bless (James 1:5) and sovereignly free to respond to persons (Jon. 3:9), then prayer will be seen as dialogue with God. God will respond when we faithfully pursue this dialogue. Prayer will lead to a greater communion with God and a greater understanding of His will.   *Randy Hatchett*

PREACHING Human presentation, through the Holy Spirit's power, of God's acts of salvation through Jesus Christ. This proclamation of God's revelation functions as God's chosen instrument for bringing us to salvation by grace, although its message of a crucified Messiah seems to be foolishness to people of worldly wisdom and a scandalous offense to Jews (1 Cor. 1:21-23). True Christian preaching interprets the meaning of God's acts into contemporary contexts. A sermon becomes God's word to us only as God's servant reconstitutes the past realities of the biblical revelation into vital present experience.

Old Testament Traditions The great prophets of the OT heralded God's direct messages against the sins of the people, told of coming judgments, and held out future hope of the great Day of the Lord. God's revelation to families, regularly shared as private instruction (Deut. 11:19), became the foundation of the public reading of the law every seven years to all the people (Deut. 31:9-13). During periods of special revival, natural leaders traveled about sharing the revelation in great assemblies (2 Chron. 15:1-2; 17:7-9; 35:3). Nehemiah 8:7-9 records that Ezra and his associates interpreted the "sense" of what was read in such gatherings. The continuing need for such public interpretation and instruction led in the faith gave rise to an expository tradition of OT revelation. This continued after the exile in the regular services of the local synagogues that arose in dispersed Judaism as substitutes for temple worship.

New Testament Practice Jesus began His ministry in the synagogue by announcing He was the Herald who fulfilled Isaiah's prophecy concerning the preaching of the kingdom and its blessings (Luke 4:16-21). By the time Peter and the other apostles preached, their emphasis focused on the person and work of Christ as the central point of history certifying the presence of God's kingdom on earth today. In the NT this message concerned a summation of the basic facts about the life, character, death, burial, resurrection, and coming again of Christ. It continues today as the main word of revelation to the world through the church. Although the NT uses some 30 different terms to describe the preaching of John the Baptist, Jesus, and the apostles, those most commonly used can be grouped under either proclamation (to herald, to evangelize) or doctrine (to teach). Many scholars define these emphases as either gospel preaching (proclaiming salvation in Christ) or pastoral teaching (instructing, admonishing, and exhorting believers in doctrine and lifestyle). In practice each function melds into the other. Thus 1 Cor. 15:1-7 not only represents the "irreducible core" of the gospel message, but it also includes clear doctrinal teaching on the substitutionary atonement and the fulfillment of messianic prophecies. The same passage forms a foundation for the exposition of the extensive doctrine of general resurrection and its Christian dimensions taught in the following verses. Stephen's address in Acts 7:1-53 represents the best of the OT tradition, weaving narrative and historical portions of Scripture together with contemporary interpretation and application to the present situation.

Peter's sermon in Acts 2 affirms the atoning nature of Jesus' death and the reality of His resurrection together with a clear call to faith and repentance forming a balanced argument framed around the central proposition that "Jesus Christ is Lord."

Special Perspectives Paul firmly believed that proclaiming the full glory of Christ not only warns men and women of the need for salvation but that through this preaching believers can grow towards spiritual maturity (Col. 1:28). He wrote that the ministry of God-called leaders equips believers in each local assembly for service through mutual ministries to one another and leads to the healthy up building of Christ's body (Eph. 4:11-16). He defined his content as including "the whole plan of God" and his practice as being "to Jews and Greeks," and "from house to house," as well as "publicly," and "in all seasons" (Acts 20:17-21,27).

Homiletics Paul underlined the need for careful attention to principles of communication in preaching. While he refused to adopt some of the cunning word craftiness of the secular rhetoricians of his day (2 Cor. 4:2; 1 Thess. 2:3,5), nevertheless, he adapted his preaching well to a variety of audiences and needs. In the synagogue Paul spoke to Jews about the special dealings God has with His people (Acts 13:16-41) but to the Greek philosophers he presented a living God as a challenge to their love for fresh ideas, quoting from their own writers as he did so (Acts 17:22-31). To Agrippa and Festus Paul molded the gospel message in lofty and legal terms (Acts 26:2-23). When meeting a charge of apostasy from the Jewish faith, he addressed the people in their own tongue concerning his origins and his experiences in Christ (Acts 21:40–22:21). Paul also counseled young pastor Timothy to be conscientious about himself as well as his teaching (1 Tim. 4:16). Paul advised the need for diligent practice to improve Timothy's skills in the public reading of the Scriptures and in motivational teaching (1 Tim. 4:13-15). Paul noted that such responsibilities involved "hard labor" (1 Tim. 5:17).   *Craig Skinner*

PRECIOUS STONES See *Jewels, Jewelry; Minerals and Metals.*

PREDESTINATION God's purposes in grace directed toward those whom He will ultimately save to the uttermost.

The word "predestine" as a verb with God as its subject is used six times in the NT (Acts 4:28; Rom. 8:29, 30; 1 Cor. 2:7; Eph. 1:5, 11). The English word comes from the Latin *praedestino,* which is used in the Vulgate to translate the Greek word *proorizo,* which means essentially, "to decide upon beforehand." Other words convey a similar idea: to determine, to elect, to foreknow. ("Election" and "Foreknowledge" are treated as separate articles in this volume.)

Major Texts In both Rom. 8 and Eph. 1 Paul makes strong claims about the priority of God's grace in salvation. "For those He foreknew He also predestined to be conformed to the image of His Son, so that He would be the firstborn among many brothers" (Rom. 8:29 HCSB). The Father determined that He would fashion those whom He foreknew into the image of Christ. He predestined them fully sanctified. To make clear just how this predestination fits into God's overall plan of salvation, Paul then lists a sort of "chain of grace": "And those He predestined, He also called; and those He called, He also justified; and those He justified, He also glorified" (v. 30 HCSB). In each link in the chain, God is the one acting, and persons are the objects of the action. God foreknew persons, not, incidentally, something about those persons, i.e., that they would believe; rather He foreknew the persons themselves. The ones He foreknew are the same ones He predestined, and the same ones He called, and the same ones He justified, and the same ones He glorified. There is no break in the link at any point. That is, there is no possibility that someone initially predestined would fail to be finally glorified. In this Paul is in full agreement with Jesus, who in John 6:37-40 makes clear that all of the ones given to Him by the Father (predestination) will believe on Him and will finally be raised up on the last day (glorification). None will fail to be saved to the uttermost.

In Eph. 1:3-6,11 Paul takes up the issue of predestination again. Here he makes several points that are easily seen in the text. He uses both the term "predestine" and the term "chosen" (*eklegomai*) here, in a synonymous fashion. First, in verse 4 he notes that God chose "us" (believers) before the foundation of the world. Second, Paul says this election was "in Him" (Christ). Third, this election has the goal "to be holy and blameless in His sight." Fourth,

He predestined us "in love" (vv. 4-5). Fifth, this predestination was unto our adoption as children. Sixth, the predestining was "according to His favor and will" (v. 5 HCSB). Seventh, it causes us to praise "His glorious grace" (v. 6). In verse 11 the apostle reemphasizes one or two points he made in the earlier verses: "In Him we were also made His inheritance, predestined according to the purpose of the One who works out everything in agreement with the decision of His will." Here Paul links believers' predestination with their being adopted children (hence, the inheritance), and he notes again that this election was done according to God's own purposes, who does everything in accordance with His own will. These are strong statements to the effect that God is a gracious God and that the only hope anyone has in this world is that God would bestow that grace on him.

Two final texts use the word *proorizo*. In 1 Cor. 2:7 Paul tells his readers that God "predestined" the mystery of His hidden wisdom. This mystery is God's purpose in salvation through Christ, which is given to both Jew and Gentile, based on God's grace and received through faith alone (cp. 1 Cor. 2:1; 4:7; Rom. 11:25; 16:25; Eph. 1:9; 3:3,4,9; 6:19-20; Col. 1:25,27; 2:2; 4:3). Here Paul tells us that God has predestined Christ and His atoning work as the only hope for salvation. In Acts 4:27-28 the Jerusalem church prays, "For, in fact, in this city both Herod and Pontius Pilate, with the Gentiles and the peoples of Israel, assembled together against Your holy Servant Jesus, whom You anointed, to do whatever Your hand and Your plan had predestined to take place" (HCSB). These believers are affirming that wicked men were used by God to carry out His plan of salvation, for by crucifying Jesus, they were putting into action the predestined plan of God.

The reader of Scripture ought not to be surprised that it presents a God who is truly sovereign and powerful. His plans will always be fulfilled (Ps. 33:10-11; Job 9:12; Dan. 4:35). He is in control of all of history so that even minor details are part of His work (Prov. 21:1; 16:1,9,33). Nothing can prevent the fulfillment of His predictions (Isa. 14:24-27; 44:24-45; Prov. 19:21).

Theological Considerations Theologically this teaching presents a challenge for some Christians. Along with these passages which emphasize God's priority in grace, there are many texts which affirm the importance of repentance and faith (Rom. 10:9-14; Acts 2:38), and the need of the sinner to "come" to Christ (Rev. 22:17). Though the concept of predestination seems to conflict with the responsibility of the individual to answer the Gospel call, the two must be compatible, since the same inspired teachers in Scripture emphasize both. Paul can say that Christians are predestined by God, and yet on the next page or so urge, "If you confess with your mouth, 'Jesus is Lord,' and believe in your heart that God raised Him from the dead, you will be saved. With the heart one believes, resulting in righteousness, and with the mouth one confesses, resulting in salvation. Now the Scripture says, 'No one who believes on Him will be put to shame,' for there is no distinction between Jew and Greek, since the same Lord of all is rich to all who call on Him. For 'everyone who calls on the name of the LORD will be saved'" (Rom. 10:9-13 HCSB). He who wrote that we are predestined according to the good pleasure of God's will, a few sentences later noted, "For by grace you are saved through faith, and this is not from yourselves; it is God's gift" (Eph. 2:8 HCSB). For Jesus and Paul the two ideas are complementary, not contradictory (cp. John 10:25-30).

Various attempts have been made to "reconcile" God's sovereignty in predestination with the human response. Some have claimed that God predestines believers based on His foreknowledge of who will one day believe the gospel. The problem is that no text teaches this. The passage in Rom. 8:29 does not say, "Whom He foreknew would believe, these He predestined to salvation." As noted earlier, the word "foreknew" refers to the people whom God foreknew, not something about those people (that they would one day believe). In addition, Eph. 1:11 makes clear that predestination is not based on something God sees in those persons. That is, it is not based on foreseen works, foreseen faith, foreseen perseverance, or anything else. It says predestination is based on God's purposes, though it does not specify just what that might mean. On the other end of the spectrum, some have argued that God began by planning to save some, then reprobate others, to His own glory, and then set about to create the world in order to make that happen. Both of these "solutions" to the logical difficulty share something in common—they are philosophical solutions, not based on sound study of the text.

It is important to adhere to the Bible and its teachings on this subject. It says this about predestination: God predestined persons out of His love to adoption in Christ before the world was made that those persons might become holy and blameless, conformed to the image of Christ, that they might be about the task of praising Him for His grace and serving Him out of gratitude. He did this not based on anything He saw in them, but according to His own purposes, unknown to human wisdom, so that a great multitude might be in His eternal kingdom (Rom. 8:29-30; Eph. 1:3-6,11). God planned this redemption through the preordained work of Christ on Calvary, whom the Father determined to have crucified from before time. Though it was His will for Christ to be so killed, those who killed Him did it of their own free and wicked purposes, not constrained by God, and so are culpable before Him for their crime (Acts 4:28; 2:22-23; Rev. 13:8). We also know that the God who predestines also sends out His laborers into the harvest to carry out His purposes in mission. There is not one iota of reason for the church to grow slack in evangelism, for without one preaching to them, sinners will never be saved. It is the church's task to testify to the truth and believe that the Lord will open the hearts of unbelievers (Acts 16:14), so as in the case of the Gentiles who heard Paul and Barnabas, "all who had been appointed to eternal life believed" (Acts 13:48 HCSB).

Though Christians today may not be able to understand how all of that works, they can affirm it as true, and they certainly must obey the call of God to the work of ministry. See *Anthropomorphism; Election; Foreknowledge; Salvation; Sovereignty of God.*

Chad Brand

PREEXILIC Period in Israel's history before the exile in Babylon (586–538 B.C.). See *Israel Land of.*

PREEXISTENCE OF SOULS The idea that the immaterial human soul exists prior to the body. As the Bible teaches physical death is not the end of personal existence, some have suggested that conception is not the beginning.

Plato maintained historical events are realization of preexisting realities within an ideal world of the divine mind. He taught that the soul exists prior to its bodily incarnation in this ideal world. Other thinkers similarly have explanations.

Pagan ideas of preexistence of the soul were introduced into Christian thought at certain points in church history. The arguments of early Christian theologian Origen (ca. A.D. 185–254) suggested that human bodies are inhabited by souls who sinned in some prior incorporeal state and have been consigned to the material realm as punishment. Christian orthodoxy, however, has consistently repudiated such a doctrine. Instead, the soul is created directly by God and united with the body at conception or birth (creationism) or that the soul is begotten along with the body through the reproductive process (traducianism).

The concept of the soul's preexistence is alien to the Bible. From the moment God "breathed the breath of life into his (Adam's) nostrils" (Gen. 2:7 HCSB), Scripture never severs the creation of material and spiritual parts of any individual. Indeed, the Bible allows no concept of a disembodied existence, except the intermediate state between death and the resurrection of the body (Phil. 1:21-23).

David references the beginning of his existence as taking place in his mother's womb (Pss. 51:5-6; 139:13-16). God declares that He knew Jeremiah before he was formed in the womb (Jer. 1:5), but this points not to spiritual antiquity, but to God's sovereign omniscience and foreknowledge. The NT speaks of God knowing believers before the foundation of the world but always in the context of His kind intention to save them in Christ (Rom. 8:29).

The preexistence of Jesus (John 1:1-2) in no way argues for preexistence of human souls. Scripture ties Jesus' preexistence not to human experience but to His identity as the eternal, uncreated, and self-existent God (John 8:58), who took on human nature to serve as Mediator between God and sinners.

The Bible, unlike philosophy and mysticism, does not dismiss the body as a container for the soul. Instead, the Bible speaks of both creation and redemption of the whole person, body and soul (Rom. 8:11). The Bible affirms creation of the body by God as integral to human existence, as is bodily resurrection from the dead (John 6:39). The purposes of God do not end in restoring humanity to some preexistent state but in redeeming the material cosmos into a glorious new creation (2 Pet. 3:13).   *Russell D. Moore*

PREMARITAL SEX Engaging in sexual intercourse prior to marriage. The Song of Songs is an extended poem extolling the virtue of sexual fidelity between a king and his chosen bride. Sexual desire runs strong throughout the song as the king and his beloved anticipate their union together. At intervals the poet repeats a refrain counseling sexual restraint: "Young women of Jerusalem, I charge you, by the gazelles and the wild does of the field: do not stir up or awaken love until the appropriate time" (Song 2:7 HCSB; 3:5; 8:4). To the church in Corinth, a city well-known for profligate sexual activity, Paul wrote that Christians must control their sexual desires and that those who cannot do so ought to marry (1 Cor. 7:2,8-9,36-37). Paul counseled Timothy to flee youthful passions and pursue instead things that make for pure living (2 Tim. 2:22). Although the temptation to gratify one's passions can be strong, Paul taught that God promises strength to overcome greater than the temptation (1 Cor. 10:12-13).

God chose the marriage relationship as a means to express to people the intimacy He shares with believers (Hos. 1–3; 2 Cor. 11:2; Rev. 21:2). Anything that cheapens or lessens the union of a husband and wife in marriage, such as pre- or extramarital sex, also tarnishes God's relationship with His people. See *Fornication; Sex, Biblical Teaching on.*   *Paul H. Wright*

PREPARATION DAY Sixth day of week in which Jews prepared life's necessities to avoid work on the Sabbath (cp. Exod. 20:8-11; Matt. 12:1-14; John 9:14-16). Preparation of food, completing work, and spiritual purification were included. The Hebrew day began and ended at 6:00 p.m., so the day of preparation extended from 6:00 p.m. on Thursday until the beginning of the Sabbath at 6:00 p.m. Friday.

The Feast of Passover was immediately followed by the holy convocation of the Feast of Unleavened Bread (Lev. 23:1-7). No one worked on either of these holy days, so a day of preparation was set aside to prepare for the holiday period (John 19:14). John explicitly identified the day of preparation as the day of Jesus' execution (John 19:14,31,42) and placed the Last Supper before Passover (John 13:1). The Synoptic Gospels, however, dated the Last Supper on the day of Passover (Matt. 26:17; Mark 14:12; Luke 22:7). This apparent contradiction in dating may depend on whether the Gospel writers were referring to the preparation day for the Sabbath or to the preparation day for the Passover.

Steve W. Lemke

PRESBYTER See *Elder.*

PRESENCE OF GOD God's initiative in encountering people. Biblical words for the presence of God usually relate to the "face" of God.

Old Testament During the patriarchal period God used a variety of means of revelation to communicate with the people (Gen. 15:1; 32:24-30). These are often described as theophanies, appearances of God to humanity. Moses had a close relationship with God. He encountered God in the burning bush and knew God "face to face" (Deut. 34:10). The presence of God was also closely related to the tabernacle, the place for ancient Israel to encounter God in worship. The tabernacle was the place of the Lord's name or glory, a manifestation of God's presence and activity in the world (Exod. 40:34,38). The cloud and fire symbolized the presence of God leading on the journey to Canaan.

Perhaps the primary tangible symbol of God's presence with the people was the ark of the covenant, the container for the tablet of the law and the seat of God's throne. It led the people in the journey to Canaan and into battle (Josh. 3:1-6). The ark was associated with the sanctuary and eventually came to rest in the temple, the place of the presence of God. Here Isaiah had a powerful vision of the holy God (Isa. 6).

God also manifested Himself in other ways: in fire (1 Kings 18) and in a still small voice (1 Kings 19), both to Elijah. The Psalms speak of God's presence with the worshiping community (Ps. 139) and of the apparent absence of this present God (Ps. 13). In either case, God is still addressed. Ezekiel spoke of the exile in terms of the glory (presence) of God leaving ancient Israel but then returning at the end of the exile in Babylon (Ezek. 43:1-5). Much of the OT discussion of the presence of God centers on the fact that God is utterly free to be where God wills but constantly chooses to be with His people to give them life.

New Testament The primary NT manifestation of the presence of God is in Jesus Christ, Immanuel, "God with us" (Matt. 1:23; John 1:14; Heb. 1:1-3). This presence did not end with the death of Christ. The risen Christ appeared to the disciples (John 21:1-14) and to Paul. Through the apostles, Paul, and the disciples, Christ's work continued (Acts 1:8; 26:12-18). The Holy Spirit is an important manifestation of the presence of God and continues the redemptive work of God. The return of Christ will bring permanence to the presence of God with His people.

The church is called to be a manifestation of God's presence. That community is fed by the presence of God found in communion between worshiper and God.   *W. H. Bellinger, Jr.*

PRESENTATION OFFERING. See *Sacrifice and Offering.*

PRESERVATION OF THE SAINTS See *Perseverance; Security of the Believer.*

PRESSFAT KJV term for a wine vat (Hag. 2:16). See *Wine; Winepress.*

PRESUMPTION See *Pride.*

PRICK See *Goad.*

PRIDE Undue confidence in and attention to one's own skills, accomplishments, state, possessions, or position. Pride is easier to recognize than to define, easier to recognize in others than in oneself. Many biblical words describe this concept, each with its own emphasis. Some of the synonyms for pride include arrogance, presumption, conceit, self-satisfaction, boasting, and high-mindedness. It is the opposite of humility, the proper attitude one should have in relation to God. Pride is rebellion against God because it attributes to oneself the honor and glory due to God alone. Proud persons do not think it necessary to ask forgiveness because they do not admit their sinful condition. This attitude toward God finds expression in one's attitude toward others, often causing people to have a low estimate of the ability and worth of others and therefore to treat them with either contempt or cruelty. Some have considered pride to be the root and essence of

sin. Others consider it to be sin in its final form. In either case, it is a grievous sin.

"Boasting" can be committed only in the presence of other persons (1 John 2:16; James 4:16). "Haughtiness" or "arrogance" measures self as above others (Mark 7:23; Luke 1:51; Rom. 1:30; 2 Tim. 3:2; James 4:6; 1 Pet. 5:5). This word refers primarily to the attitude of one's heart. First Timothy 3:6; 6:4; and 2 Tim. 3:4 use a word literally meaning "to wrap in smoke." It emphasizes the plight of the one who has been blinded by personal pride.

Pride may appear in many forms. Some of the more common are pride of race, spiritual pride, and pride of riches. Jesus denounced pride of race (Luke 3:8). The parable of the Pharisee and the publican was directed at those guilty of spiritual pride, the ones "who trusted in themselves that they were righteous and looked down on everyone else" (Luke 18:9 HCSB). James 1:10 warns the rich against the temptation to be lifted up with pride because of their wealth.   *Gerald Cowen*

PRIESTHOOD OF BELIEVERS Christian belief that every believer has direct access to God through Jesus Christ and that the church is a fellowship of priests serving together under the lordship of Christ.

The concept of priesthood is integral to both the OT and the NT and is fulfilled in Christ as Mediator and great high priest. The foundation of the priestly ministry is found in the OT where the priestly ministry is assigned to the Aaronic line of descent and the tribe of Levi (Exod. 40:13, Num. 1:47-54). According to the OT model, the priest fulfilled a representative function—entering the Holy of Holies on the Day of Atonement and making a sacrificial offering on behalf of the people.

This representational role was fulfilled by Christ, whose offices as Prophet, Priest, and King describe His accomplished and continuing work. As mediator, Christ fulfilled the representational role to which the Aaronic priesthood pointed. The letter to the Hebrews explains this fulfillment by describing Jesus Christ as the "great high priest" who, having accomplished His mediatorial work of substitutionary atonement, has now passed through the heavens (Heb. 4:14).

Christ's death on the cross is described as a priestly act that once for all paid the penalty for our sin. As priest, Christ did not take the blood of a representative animal into the Holy of Holies but instead entered "the greater and more perfect tabernacle" and shed His own blood to obtain "eternal redemption" (Heb. 9:11-12 HCSB).

Now that Christ has fulfilled the representational role of the priesthood, and since He is the one mediator between God and men (1 Tim. 2:5), there is no continuing need or role for a human priest. No longer does a human priest stand to represent other humans before God.

As the people of God, the church is now a "royal priesthood" (1 Pet. 2:9), ministering together in the name of Christ. Though we do not represent one another before the Father, believers are called to pray for one another, to encourage each other to good works, and to call one another to holiness.

Central to the doctrine of the priesthood of believers is the concept of the gathered church, or congregationalism. Each church is comprised of believers who have been redeemed by Jesus Christ and now serve as priests together. In its purest sense this doctrine refers to believers gathered together under the lordship of Christ, not to individual believers standing alone. The doctrine does, however, rightly affirm that we need no human priest to stand between the individual believer and God. As mediator, Jesus Christ alone fulfills that role.

A graphic illustration of this was provided when the great veil in the temple separating the holy of holies from the larger temple was torn from top to bottom. Similarly, the Apostle Paul described Christ's atonement as breaking down the barriers that had separated and segregated persons by race and gender in the temple (Eph. 2:14-16).

As priests together, Christians are to offer "spiritual sacrifices acceptable to God through Jesus Christ" (1 Pet. 2:5). These spiritual sacrifices replace any notion of representational or sacramental ministrations. The doctrine of the priesthood of believers thus affirms the right of every believer to fellowship with God through Christ, and the obligation of every believer to be a fully functioning member of a congregation, exercising Christian discipleship among the fellowship of other believer-priests.

R. Albert Mohler, Jr.

PRIESTHOOD OF CHRIST That work of Christ in which He offers Himself as the supreme sacrifice for the sins of humankind

and continually intercedes on their behalf. See *Atonement; Christ, Christology; Jesus Christ; High Priest.*

PRIESTS Personnel in charge of sacrifice and offering at worship places, particularly the tabernacle and temple.

Functions Priesthood in the OT primarily involved sacrificing at the altar and worship in the shrine. Other functions were blessing the people (Num. 6:22-26), determining the will of God (Exod. 28:30), and instructing the people in the law of God (Deut. 31:9-12). This instruction included the application of the laws of cleanness (Lev. 11–15). Some of these functions, like blessing and teaching, would not be reserved for priests alone, but sacrificing and the use of the Urim and Thummim were theirs exclusively.

If the main characteristic of priesthood was sacrificing, the office is as old as Abel. Noah sacrificed and so did Abraham and the patriarchs. We may say that they were family priests. Jethro, the priest of Midian, brought sacrifices to God and worshiped with Moses, Aaron, and the elders of Israel (Exod. 18:12). God promised that Israel, if it were faithful, would be "a kingdom of priests and a holy nation" (Exod. 19:6). This may have meant that Israel was called to mediate God's word and work to the world—to be a light to the nations (Isa. 42:6).

Later, when God purposed to establish the nation, He chose Moses to organize the army, to set up a system of judges, to build a house of worship, and to ordain priests to serve therein. The formal priesthood goes with the formal worship of an organized nation of considerable size. On Mount Sinai God gave Moses instructions to build the tabernacle. On the mount God told Moses to appoint Aaron and his four sons to serve as priests, that is, to serve at the altar and in the sanctuary (Exod. 28:1,41). Their holy garments are prescribed in detail, and their consecration ritual is given in chapters 28–29. As to the work of these priests, most of Leviticus and some of Numbers and Deuteronomy give details. Aaron and his descendants of the tribe of Levi served in the tabernacle and temple as priests. Members of the tribe of Levi not related to Aaron assisted the priests but did not offer sacrifices. Priests were supported by offerings, and Levites were supported by tithes (Num. 18:20-24). See *Aaron; High Priest; Levites; Urim and Thummim.*

R. Laird Harris

PRINCE More frequently designates the position and authority of a ruler, not just the limited sense of a male heir of a sovereign or noble birth (see Zeph. 1:8, which distinguishes princes and king's sons). KJV used "prince" as a title for Israel's king (1 Sam. 13:14), a leading priest (1 Chron. 12:27), a Midianite tribal chief (Num. 25:18), the leading men of a city or province (Gen. 34:2; 1 Kings 20:15; Jer. 34:19), and for rulers in general (Matt. 20:25; 1 Cor. 2:6,8). By extension "prince" applies to supernatural beings. "Prince of Peace" (Isa. 9:6), "Prince of life" (Acts 3:15 KJV), and "Prince and a Savior" (Acts 5:31) are messianic titles. Daniel 8:25 refers to God as "Prince of princes." Daniel 12:1 gives Michael, the angelic advocate of Israel, the title "prince." Satan is often described as "the prince of this world" (John 12:31; 14:30; 16:11; cp. Matt. 9:34; 12:24; Eph. 2:2).

PRINCE OF LIFE Word translated as "prince" (Acts 3:15; 5:31, "author" and "leader" respectively in some modern versions) is also translated as "captain" (Heb. 2:10; "pioneer" or "author" in some modern versions) and "author" (Heb. 12:2; "pioneer" in modern versions). All of these references are to Jesus as the founder of a new life that His followers now share with Him.

PRINCESS Two Hebrew constructions are translated "princess." **1.** "Daughter of a king." Solomon's 700 wives were princesses married to seal political ties with their fathers (1 Kings 11:3). Lamentations 1:1 pictures the reversal of Jerusalem's fortune in the image of a princess turned servant. **2.** Feminine form of the common word for leader or ruler applied to a king's wife (Ps. 45:13 NIV, NRSV) and to the leading women of Judah (Jer. 43:6 NRSV). See *Prince*.

PRINCIPALITIES Supernatural spiritual powers, whether good or evil. Principalities were created by and are thus subject to Christ (Col. 1:16). Neither principalities nor any other force can separate a believer from God's love found in Christ (Rom. 8:38).

PRISCA (Prĭs´ cȧ) or **PRISCILLA** (Prĭs sĭl´ lȧ) See *Aquila and Priscilla*.

PRISON GATE KJV designation for a gate in Jerusalem (Neh. 12:39). Modern translations refer to the Gate of the Guard or Guardhouse Gate. The gate is perhaps identical with the Miphkad (Muster) Gate (Neh. 3:31).

PRISON, PRISONERS Any place where persons accused and/or convicted of criminal activity are confined and the persons so confined or captured in war.
Old Testament Imprisonment as a legal punishment is not a feature of ancient law codes. The Mosaic law allowed for a place of custody until the case was decided (Lev. 24:12; Num. 15:34), but beginning only in the Persian period the Bible mentions incarceration as a penalty for breaking the religious law (Ezra. 7:26).

Prisons mentioned in the OT were under the control of the crown. Joseph was put in a royal prison in Egypt (Gen. 39:20), apparently attached to the house of the captain of the guard (40:3). Asa of Judah (2 Chron. 16:10) and Ahab of Israel (1 Kings 22:26-27) made use of prisons, probably associated with the palace. The experience of Jeremiah, however, provides the most interesting glimpses of prisons and prison life. The royal prisons were apparently not large, as the one in which Jeremiah was initially placed was a converted private house (Jer. 37:15). He was confined to an underground dungeon (Jer. 37:16), perhaps a converted cistern. Jeremiah later was placed under house arrest in the "court of the guard" (Jer. 37:20-21). There he was available for consultation with the king (Jer. 38:14,28), able to conduct business (Jer. 32:2-3,6-12), and able to speak freely (Jer. 38:1-4). Because the latter enraged the princes, Jeremiah was confined for a time to a muddy cistern in the "court of the guard" (Jer. 38:4-13).

Persons were confined in royal prisons for offending the king (Gen. 40:1-3), perhaps by political intrigue. In Israel prophets were jailed for denouncing royal policy (2 Chron. 16:10), predicting ill of the king (1 Kings 22:26-27), and suspected collaboration with the enemy (Jer. 37:11-15). Political prisoners in Assyrian and Babylonian prisons included former kings of rebellious nations (2 Kings 17:4; 24:15; 25:27; Jer. 52:11). Samson became a prisoner in a Philistine prison (Judg. 16:21). Prisoners of war were usually either killed or enslaved.

The lot of prisoners was pitiable, sometimes consisting of meager rations (1 Kings 22:27) and hard labor (Judg. 16:21). In some cases prisoners were restrained and tortured by the stocks or collar (2 Chron. 16:10; Jer. 29:26). Jehoiachin was clothed in special prison garments in Babylon (2 Kings 25:29). Prison life became a symbol of oppression and suffering (Ps. 79:11), and release from prison provided a picture of restoration or salvation (Pss. 102:20; 142:7; 146:7; Isa. 61:1; Zech. 9:11-12).

New Testament In NT times persons could be imprisoned for nonpayment of debt (Matt. 5:25-26; Luke 12:58-59), political insurrection and criminal acts (Luke 23:19,25), as well as for certain religious practices (Luke 21:12; Acts 8:3). For some of these offenses, public prisons were also employed (Acts 5:18-19). John the Baptist was arrested for criticizing the king (Luke 3:19-20) and seems to have been held in a royal prison attached to the palace (Mark 6:17-29). Later Peter was held under heavy security, consisting of chains, multiple guards, and iron doors (Acts 12:5-11).

Paul, who imprisoned others (Acts 8:3; 22:4; 26:10), was often in prison himself (2 Cor. 11:23). His experiences provide the most detail on prisons in the NT world. In Philippi he and Silas were placed under the charge of a lone jailer, who "put them into the inner prison and secured their feet in the stocks" (Acts 16:23-24 HCSB). Excavations at Philippi have uncovered a crypt revered by early Christians as the prison and adorned with frescoes depicting Paul and Silas in Philippi. If the identification is correct, the crypt's small size eliminates any doubt that when Paul and Silas sang hymns, "the prisoners were listening to them" (Acts 16:25 HCSB). Perhaps the crypt, originally a cistern, served only as the "innermost cell" (Acts 16:24) for maximum security or solitary confinement. In Jerusalem Paul was held in the barracks of the Roman cohort (Acts 23:16-18). After his transfer to Caesarea, he was confined with some freedom in the headquarters of Roman procurators and was allowed to receive visitors (Acts 23:35; 24:23). As he and other prisoners were transferred to Rome by ship, Paul was again given some freedom (Acts 27:1,3); but when shipwreck became imminent, the soldiers resolved to kill them all lest they should escape (27:42-43). While awaiting trial in Rome, Paul remained under constant guard in a kind of house arrest (28:16-17,30), met his own expenses, and was free to receive visitors and preach the gospel "with full boldness and without hindrance" (28:31 HCSB). Paul

Interior of the Mamertinum in Rome, the prison where tradition says both Peter and Paul were held prior to their executions.

considered his imprisonment as for Christ (Eph. 3:1; 4:1; Phil. 1:13-14; Philem. 1,9).

The situation for prisoners remained dismal in NT times, and concern for such persons is a virtue expected by Christ of every disciple (Matt. 25:36,39,43-44). It is Satan who will be imprisoned during the millennium (Rev. 20:1-3,7).

Daniel C. Browning, Jr.

PRIZE Award in an athletic competition. Paul used the image to illustrate the goal of the Christian life (Phil. 3:14; cp. 1 Cor. 9:24). The prize is sometimes identified as Paul's heavenly destination. More likely the "upward call" designates the total call to Christian maturity. The larger context uses multiple expressions (know Christ, 1 Cor. 2:8,10; gain Christ, 2:8; know the power of Christ's resurrection; share Christ's suffering and death, 2:10) to define the goal of Christian living. Though Paul used a competitive image, he was aware that the righteousness which matters was not the result of his own efforts but is God's gift through faith (3:9).

PROCHORUS (Prŏk´ o rŭs) Personal name meaning "leader of the chorus (or dance)." One of the seven selected to assist in distribution of food to the Greek-speaking widows of the Jerusalem church (Acts 6:5).

PROCLAMATION See *Kerygma; Preaching.*

PROCONSUL Office in the Roman system of government. Proconsuls oversaw the administration of civil and military matters in a province. They were responsible to the senate in Rome. The NT refers to two proconsuls: Sergius Paulus in Cyprus (Acts 13:7) and Gallio in Achaia (Acts 18:12; cp. Acts 19:38). See *Rome and the Roman Empire.*

PROCORUS (Prŏk´ o rŭs) (NIV) See *Prochorus.*

PROCURATOR Roman military office that developed into a powerful position by NT times. They had control over entire countries under the Roman system. The procurator could issue death warrants (a privilege often withheld from subject peoples) and have coins struck in his name. Three procurators are named in the NT: Pilate (Matt. 27:2; some question whether Pilate was a procurator),

Felix (Acts 23:24), and Festus (Acts 24:27). See *Rome and the Roman Empire.*

PRODIGAL SON This term is used both as the title of Jesus' parable in Luke 15:11-32 and a description of the younger son's lifestyle. English translations do not use the term prodigal to describe this lifestyle but describe it by saying that he "wasted" or "squandered" his inheritance in "wild" or "loose" living. Unfortunately this title, focusing on the younger son, causes one to miss the point that both Jesus and Luke are making. The parable should be called "The Parable of the Gracious Father," for he is the character who occurs in both halves of the story and is the main character of the parable. In addition, the parable's main point comes from the conversation between the older son and the father, through which Jesus defends the offer of salvation that God makes to the tax collectors and sinners (and other prodigals like them) and condemns the Pharisees and scribes for their opposition to this offer of mercy (Luke 15:1-2).   *Donny Mathis*

PROFANE To treat that which is holy as common. Profane often approximates defile in meaning. See *Clean, Cleanness; Holy.*

PROGNOSTICATORS KJV term for those predicting the future by astrology (Isa. 47:13). See *Divination and Magic.*

PROGRESSIVE REVELATION See *Revelation of God.*

PROMISE God's announcement of His plan of salvation and blessing to His people, one of the unifying themes integrating the message and the deeds of the OT and NT.

Promise Embraces Both Declaration and Deed God's promise begins with a declaration by God; it covers God's future plan for not just one race but all the nations of the earth. It focuses on the gifts and deeds that God will bestow on a few to benefit the many. We may define God's promise this way: the divine declaration or assurance made at first to Eve, Shem, Abraham, Isaac, and Jacob and then to the whole nation of Israel that: (1) He would be their God, (2) they would be His people, and (3) He would dwell in their midst. The blessing of land and of growth as a nation as well as the call to bless the nations was part of the promise to Abraham. Added to these words of assurance were a series of divine actions in history. These words and deeds of God began to constitute the continuously unfolding divine plan by which all the peoples and nations of the earth would benefit from that day to this.

The OT did not use a specific Hebrew word for "promise." It used quite ordinary words to encapsulate the pivotal promise of God: speak, say, swear. However the NT does use both the noun "promise" (51 times) and the verb (11 times).

"Promise" in these references can denote either the form or the content of those words. They could refer either to the words themselves as promissory notes on which to base one's confidence for the future, or they could refer to the things themselves which were promised. Since God's one promise-plan was made up of many specifications, the plural form of "promises" appears 11 times in the NT. Nevertheless, the singular form was greatly predominant.

Varying Formulations of the Promise in the Old Testament
In Gen. 1–11 the promise of God is represented by the successive "blessings" announced both in the creative order and on the human family—even in spite of their sin. The promise of blessing, therefore, was both introductory to the promise and part of the promise itself.

The Promise and the Patriarchs For the fathers of Israel (Abraham, Isaac, and Jacob), we may speak of the promise in the singular even though it announced three significant elements. Each of the three elements is incomplete without the support of each other and without being interlocked into one promise-plan.

This triple promise included: (1) the promise of a seed or offspring (an heir; Gen. 12:7; 15:4; 17:16,19; 21:12; 22:16-18; 26:3-4,24; 28:13-14; 35:11-12), (2) the promise of land (an inheritance; Gen. 12:1,7; 13:17; 15:18; 17:8; 24:7; 26:3-5; 28:13,15; 35:12; 48:4; 50:24) (3) the promise of blessing on all the nations (a heritage of the gospel; Gen. 12:3; 18:18; 22:17-18; 26:4; 28:14).

To demonstrate the eternality and one-sidedness in the gracious offer of God, only God passed between the pieces in Gen. 15:9-21 thus obligating Himself to fulfill His promises without simultaneously and similarly obligating Abraham and the subsequent beneficiaries of the promise.

The Promise and the Law The promise was eternal, Abraham's descendants had to transmit the promise to subsequent generations until the final Seed, even Jesus the Messiah, came. They had to do more. God expected them to participate personally by faith. Where faith was present, already demands and commands were likewise present. Thus Abraham obeyed God and left Ur (Gen. 12:1-4) and walked before God in a blameless way (Gen. 17:1). His obedience to God's "requirements," "commands," "decrees," and "laws" (Gen. 26:5 NIV) was exemplary.

The law extended these demands to the entire life of the people all the while presupposing the earlier promises as the very basis, indeed, as the lever by which such demands could be made (Exod. 2:23-25; 6:2-8; 19:3-8; 20:2). The Apostle Paul will later ask whether the promises have nullified the law (Rom. 3:31). He answered, "Absolutely not! On the contrary, we uphold the law" (Rom. 3:31 HCSB).

The Promises and David The monarchy, prematurely founded by the whims of a people who wished to be like the other nations, received a distinctive role through God's promise. A lad taken "from the pasture" (2 Sam. 7:8 NIV) would be given a name equal to "the greatest men of the earth" (2 Sam. 7:9 NIV); indeed, his offspring would be seated at God's "right hand" (Ps. 110:1) and inherit the nations (Ps. 2:8).

The Promise and the New Covenant The new covenant of Jer. 31:31-34 both repeats many of the elements and formulas already contained in the previously announced promise-plan of God and adds several new features. The new promise still contains the law of God, only now it will be internalized. It still pledges that God will be their God, and they will be His people. It still declares that He will forgive their sins and remember them no more. However, it also adds that it will no longer be necessary to teach one's neighbor or brother; for everyone, no matter what their station in life, will know the Lord.

In spite of Israel's future loss of its king, its capital, its temple, and its former glory, God would fulfill His ancient promises by founding new promises on "the former things [foretold] long ago" (Isa. 48:3). He would send His new David, new temple, new Elijah, new heavens and new earth—but all in continuity with what He had pledged long ago.

The New Testament Enlarges the Ancient Promises The NT promises may be gathered into these groups. The first, and most frequent, are the references to God's promises to Abraham about the heir he was to receive, even Jesus Christ (Rom. 4:13-16,20; 9:7-9; 15:8; Gal. 3:16-22; 4:23; Heb. 6:13-17; 7:6; 11:9,11,17). A second major grouping may be made around David's seed and the sending of Jesus as a Savior "according to the promise" (Acts 13:23,32-33 HCSB; 26:6). Perhaps we should connect with this group the gift of "the promise of life in Christ Jesus" (2 Tim. 1:1 HCSB), the "promise of the eternal inheritance" (Heb. 9:15), and the promise that "He Himself made to us: eternal life" (1 John 2:25). This promise is what was promised "by faith in Jesus Christ" (Gal. 3:22).

The third major group is the gift of the Holy Spirit. The promises appear after our Lord's resurrection (Luke 24:49; Acts 2:33,38-39).

There are other subjects related to God's promise: rest (Heb. 4:1); the new covenant with its prospect of an eternal inheritance (9:15); the new heavens and new earth (2 Pet. 3:13); the resurrection (Acts 26:6); the blessing of numerous descendants (Heb. 6:14); the emergence of an unshakable kingdom (12:28); and Gentiles as recipients of the same promise (Eph. 2:11-13).

The Promise Has Some Notable Differences from Prophecy While much of the promise doctrine is also prophetic in that it relates to the future, there are some notable differences between promise and prophecy. (1) Promises relate to what is good, desirable, and that which blesses and enriches. Prophecy, however, also may contain notes of judgment, destruction, and calamity when people and nations fail to repent. (2) Promises ordinarily implicate the entire human race in their provisions whereas prophecies more typically are aimed at specific nations, cultures, or peoples. (3) Promises deliberately have a continuous fulfillment for generation after generation while prophecies invoke promise when they wish to speak to the distant future. (4) The promise of God is unconditional while most prophecies are conditional and have a suppressed "unless" or "if" you repent attached to their predictions of judgment. (5) The promise of God embraces many declarations of God ("very great and precious promises," 2 Pet. 1:4), whereas prophecies are usually directed to more specific events and particular individuals.

The promise-plan of God, then, is indeed His own Word and plan, both in His person and His works, to communicate a blessing to Israel and thereby to bless all the nations of the earth.

Walter C. Kaiser, Jr.

PROPERTY See *Inheritance; Ownership.*

PROPHECY, PROPHETS Reception and declaration of a word from the Lord through a direct prompting of the Holy Spirit and the human instrument thereof.

Old Testament Three key terms are used of the prophet. *Ro'eh* and *hozeh* are translated as "seer." The most important term, *navi'*, is usually translated "prophet." It probably meant "one who is called to speak."

History Moses, perhaps Israel's greatest leader, was a prophetic prototype (Acts 3:21-24). He appeared with Elijah in the transfiguration (Matt. 17:1-8). Israel looked for a prophet like Moses (Deut. 34:10).

Prophets also played a role in the conquest and settlement of the promised land. The prophetess Deborah predicted victory, pronounced judgment on doubting Barak, and even identified the right time to attack (Judg. 4:6-7,9,14). Samuel, who led Israel during its transition to monarchy, was a prophet, priest, and judge (1 Sam. 3:20; 7:6,15). He was able to see into the future by vision (3:11-14) and to ask God for thunder and rain (12:18). Samuel led in victory over the Philistines (1 Sam. 7), and God used him to anoint kings. Gad and Nathan served as prophets to the king. Elijah and Elisha offered critique and advice for the kings. The prophets did more than predict the future; their messages called Israel to honor God. Their prophecies were not general principles but specific words corresponding to Israel's historical context.

Similarly the classical or writing prophets were joined to history. Israel's political turmoil provided the context for the writing prophets. The Assyrian rise to power after 750 B.C. furnished the focus of the ministries of Amos, Hosea, Isaiah, and Micah. The Babylonian threat was the background and motive for much of the ministry of Jeremiah and Ezekiel. The advent of the Persian Empire in the latter part of the sixth century set the stage for prophets such as Obadiah, Haggai, Zechariah, and Malachi. Thus the prophets spoke for God throughout Israel's history.

The prophets influenced almost every institution of Israel, despite the fact that they were often viewed with contempt; they were locked up (Jer. 37), ignored (Isa. 6:9-13), and persecuted (1 Kings 19:1-2). In addition to serving judges and kings, the prophets also addressed Israel's worship. They criticized vain worship (Amos 5:23-24) and priestly failures (Amos 7:10; Mal. 2). The word of the Lord was also spoken in worship (Pss. 50:5; 60:6; 81:6-10; 91:14-16; 95:8-11). The prophets' call to covenant faithfulness revealed an awareness of the law (Isa. 58:6-9; Ezek. 18; Mic. 6:6-8; Hos. 6:6; Amos 2:4; 5:21-24).

Prophets formed guilds or schools (2 Kings 4:38; 1 Sam. 10:5; 19:20). While most references to prophetic schools belong to the period of the monarchy, there is some evidence to believe the schools continued (Jer. 23:13-14). The mere existence of the books of prophecy is probably due in part to the prophets' helpers (Jer. 36:4). Perhaps their words were recorded because they provided a moral challenge to the entire nation and not merely to a king or individual. Surely once the prophet's words were written, they were not ignored but continually studied and reapplied.

The Experience of the Prophet Prophets generally shared several key experiences and characteristics. (1) An essential mark of a prophet was a call from God. Attempting to prophesy without such a commission was false prophecy (Jer. 14:14). The prophets were at times allowed to see into the throne room or heavenly court (Isa. 6:1-7; 1 Kings 22:19-23; Jer. 23:18-22; cp. Amos 3:7; Job 1:6-12; 2:1-6; 2 Cor. 12:1-4; Rev. 1:1-3; 22:18-19). (2) Prophets received a word from God through many means—direct declarations, visions, dreams, or an appearance of God. The great variety in prophetic experience prohibits any oversimplification; ecstatic experiences were not mandatory for receiving God's word. (3) Prophets spoke the word of God. They were primarily spokespersons who called His people to obedience by appealing to Israel's past and future. For example, God's past blessing and future judgment should provoke social justice and mercy for the disadvantaged. (4) Prophets relayed God's message by deed as well as by word. They worked symbolic acts that served as dramatic, living parables. Hosea's marriage taught about God's relationship with Israel (Hos. 2:1-13; Isa. 20:1-3; Ezek. 4:1-3; Jer. 19:10-11). (5) The prophets also performed miracles that confirmed their message. While some prophets like Moses (Exod. 4:1-9) and Elijah (1 Kings 17) worked many miracles, virtually all prophets occasionally saw a miraculous fulfillment of God's word (Isa. 38:8). This miracle-working capacity also included healing (1 Kings 17:17-22; 2 Kings 5; Matt. 12:22-29). (6) Prophets also conveyed the word of God by writing (Isa. 8:1; Ezek. 43:11). (7) Prophets were to minister to their people. They were to test God's peoples' lives (Jer. 6:27) and be watchmen for moral compromise (Ezek. 3:17). Particularly important was the role of intercessor—sometimes even for the prophet's enemy (1 Kings 13:6; 17:17-24; 2 Kings 4:18-37; Amos 7:2; Jer. 14:17-20,21; Isa. 59:16). (8) Throughout Israel's history genuine prophets had ecstatic experiences.

False Prophets Distinguishing between false and true prophets was very difficult, though several tests of authenticity emerge in the OT. The true prophet must be loyal to the biblical faith directing one to worship Yahweh alone (Deut. 13:1-3). A second test required that the words of a true prophet be fulfilled (Deut. 18:22; Jer. 42:1-6; Ezek. 33:30-33). We must remember that this is a difficult test to apply. There were often long lapses between predictions and fulfillment (Mic. 3:12; Jer. 26:16-19). Some predictions seemed very unlikely, and others were conditional—based upon the hearer's response (Jon. 3:4-5). Furthermore, prophets could behave inappropriately (Num. 12:1-2; 20:1-12; Jer. 15:19-21; 38:24-27). Prophets appeared ambivalent at times when simply delivering the word of God as it was given (2 Kings 20:1-6). Also one could predict correctly while not being loyal to Yahweh (Deut. 13:1-3). Accurate prediction was not a final test. Other tests included agreement with previous prophets' words (Jer. 28:8), good character (Mic. 3:11), and a willingness to suffer because of faithfulness (1 Kings 22:27-28; Jer. 38:3-13). Similarly, the NT believers had to distinguish true prophecy (1 John 4:1; 1 Cor. 14:29). See *False Prophet.*

Hints for Interpretation Prophets intended to evoke faith by proclamation, not merely to predict the future. Thus reading the prophets with a lustful curiosity is inappropriate. Our primary desire must be to know God, not just the facts of the future.

The interpreter must remember the limited perspective of the prophet. The prophets were not all knowing but all telling—that is, they told what God had told them to tell. Prophecy has a progressive character. One must seek to read prophecy in light of its whole, deriving partial insight from different prophets. Prophecy must also be read in its historical context. Particular attention must be paid to the intention of the prophet. For example, a prophet may rebuke another country to offer assistance to Israel (Isa. 46–47), make Israel examine its own conduct (Amos 1–2), or bring a nation to repentance (Jon. 3:4,8-9).

Caution must be exercised when reading predictive prophecy because prophecy often has more than one fulfillment. Many prophecies have an immediate application to their own situation and are also applicable to another context. Thus the prediction that Christ is born of a virgin (Matt. 1:23) also had a fulfillment in Isaiah's day (Isa. 8:3). Similarly prophecies of "the day of the Lord" had several fulfillments (partial) which also foreshadowed a final fulfillment (Obad. 15; Joel 1:15; 2:1; Zeph. 1:7,14; Ezek. 30:3; cp. 2 Pet. 3:10).

Modern evangelicals understand predictive prophecies in several ways. (1) Some prophecies seem to have a direct, literal fulfillment: the Messiah was to be born in Bethlehem (Matt. 2:5-6; Mic. 5:2). (2) Not all predictions were fulfilled literally. Jesus taught that the prediction about Elijah's return was fulfilled by John the Baptist and not a literal Elijah (Matt. 11:13-15; Mal. 3:1-4). Similarly, Paul applied prophecies about literal, national Israel to the church (Rom. 9:25-26; Hos. 1:9-10; 2:23). The literal father of Israel, Abraham, was seen to be the father of the believing church (Rom. 4:11,16; Gal. 3:7). This distinctively Christian reading was thought to be legitimate because of Christ's fulfillment and interpretation of the OT (Luke 4:17-21). (3) This Christian reading of the OT often takes the form of typological interpretation. The NT authors believed OT events, persons, or things foreshadowed the later Christian story. Thus they used the images of the OT to understand the NT realities. Christ can be compared to Adam (1 Cor. 15:22-23; 10:11). (4) Some readers believe that OT words take on a "fuller sense" or meaning. Old Testament expressions may have a divine significance, unforeseen by the OT author, which comes to light only after God's later word or deed. See *Typology.*

New Testament The word *prophetes* means "to speak before" or "to speak for." Thus it refers to one who speaks for God or Christ. Prophets were also called "pneumatics" (*pneumatikos*), "spiritual ones" (1 Cor. 14:37). The prophets played a foundational role in the early church (1 Cor. 12:28-31; Eph. 4:11; 2:20). Due to the presumed prophetic silence in the time between the Testaments, the coming of Jesus is seen as an inbreaking of the Spirit's work especially visible in prophecy. For example, in Luke the angel's visitation and prediction (1:11,26-27) provoked Mary and Zechariah to prophesy (1:46-79). After an angelic visitation to the shepherds, the prophet and prophetess declared Jesus to be the redemption Israel awaited (2:10-12,25,36-38). John the Baptist also predicted that Jesus would baptize in the Spirit (Matt. 3:11).

Jesus called Himself a prophet (Luke 13:33). His miracles and discernment were rightly understood as prophetic (John 4:19). He taught not by citing expert rabbis but with His own prophetic authority (Mark 1:22; Luke 4:24).

The early believers saw the outpouring of the Spirit (Acts 2:17) as a fulfillment of Joel's prediction that all God's people, young and old, male and female, would prophesy. These gifts may intensify at the end of time as will evil. While any Christian might occasionally receive a prophecy, some seem to have a special gift of prophecy (1 Cor. 12:29; 13:2). Prophets function primarily in the worship of the church (Acts 13:2). They predict (Acts 11:28; 20:23; 27:22-26), announce judgments (Acts 13:11; 28:25-28), act symbolically (Acts 21:10-11), and receive visions (Acts 9:10-11; 2 Cor. 12:1). Prophetic insights led to missionary efforts (Acts 13:1-3; 10:10-17; 15:28,32). While teaching and prophecy are different, they also can be related (Acts 13:1-2; Rev. 2:20). Some prophets "preached" lengthy messages (Acts 15:32) and gave exposition to biblical texts (Luke 1:67-79; Eph. 3:5; Rom. 11:25-36).

The prophets used phrases such as "the Lord says" or "the Holy Spirit says" as introductory formulas for prophetic insight into the future (Acts 21:11) or for inspired adaptation of an OT text (Heb. 3:7).

New Testament prophecy was limited (1 Cor. 13:9); it was to be evaluated by the congregation (1 Cor. 14:29; 1 Thess. 5:20-21). One may even respond inappropriately to prophecy (Acts 21:12). The supreme test for prophecy is loyalty to Christ (1 Cor. 12:3; Rev. 19:10). Some Christians have the gift of discernment (1 Cor. 12:10). Jesus said prophets could be known by their fruit (Matt. 7:15-20). Paul demanded orderly, Christ-honoring, upbuilding prophecy that submits to apostolic authority (1 Cor. 14:26-40). Thus prophecy is not without restraint. Circumstance may even demand that the dress of men and women prophets be stipulated (1 Cor. 11:5-7). Prophecy outside of apostolic authority can be safely ignored; thus prophecy is not a threat to Scripture's special authority (1 Cor. 14:38-39; 2 Tim. 3:16; 2 Pet. 1:20-21). *Randy Hatchett*

PROPHETESS 1. Female prophet; women serving as God's spokesperson. Five women are explicitly identified as prophetesses: Miriam (Exod. 15:20), Deborah (Judg. 4:4), Huldah (2 Kings 22:14), Noadiah, a "false" prophetess (Neh. 6:14), and Anna (Luke 2:36). Jezebel claimed to be a prophetess (Rev. 2:20). The ministries of prophetesses varied greatly. Miriam called upon Israel to celebrate God's deliverance. Deborah combined the offices of prophetess and judge, even accompanying Barak into battle. Huldah spoke God's words of judgment (2 Kings 22:16-17) and forgiveness (22:18-20) to King Josiah. Anna shared the good news of Jesus' birth with the temple crowds. The false prophetess Noadiah sought to frighten Nehemiah. Jezebel attempted to involve the church of Thyatira in idolatry. The Prophet Joel anticipated a time when all God's people, "male servants and female servants," would be filled with God's Spirit and prophecy (Joel 2:28-29). This prophetic hope was fulfilled at Pentecost (Acts 2:17-18) and in the ongoing life of the early church (Acts 21:9). Paul encouraged all believers to desire to prophesy (1 Cor. 14:1), that is, to offer speech which builds up the church (14:5). First Corinthians 11:5 presumes women were involved in prophesying and prayer in public worship. **2.** The wife of a prophet (Isa. 8:3). See *Prophet*.

PROPITIATION See *Expiation*.

PROSELYTES Converts to a religion; non-Jews who accepted the Jewish faith and completed the rituals to become Jews. The NT attests to the zeal of the first-century Pharisees in proselytizing Gentiles (Matt. 23:15). The success of the Jewish missionary efforts is indicated by synagogue and grave inscriptions referring to proselytes and by Roman and Jewish literary references. Tacitus (History V.5) complains, for example, that proselytes despised the gods, disdained their kindred, and abjured their fatherland.

Gentiles were impressed by three features of Judaism. First, the concept of one God who created, sustains, and rules all things was clearly superior to polytheistic views. Second, Judaism stressed a lifestyle of moral responsibility with its monotheism. Third, it was a religion of ancient and stable tradition in contrast to the faddish cults of the time.

Proselytes usually embraced Judaism gradually because much needed to be learned, such as the proper observance of the Sabbath and the careful following of the dietary rules, before one could win acceptance into the Jewish community. Persons attracted to Judaism and keeping the Sabbath and food laws were termed fearers or worshipers of God. These terms appear in the NT where Cornelius (Acts 10:1-2) and Lydia (Acts 16:14) are so described (John 12:20; Acts 17:4; 18:7). Many God fearers went on to become proselytes or fully accepted and integrated members of the Jewish community. This involved fulfilling the Jewish demands of circumcision (males) which related one to the covenant (see Gal. 5:3), baptism (males and females) which made one ritually clean, and an offering (males and females) in the Jerusalem temple which atoned for sin. See *God Fearer*. *Harold S. Songer*

PROSTITUTION Trading of sexual services for pay. It is the result of a double standard whereby men insist on the sexual purity of their wives and daughters, while desiring access to other women. This dynamic is seen clearly in Gen. 38. Judah, thinking that his daughter-in-law Tamar was a prostitute, had intercourse with her; but upon hearing that she was pregnant as the result of "playing the harlot," he demanded that she be burned. Hosea criticized the attitude which called for the punishment of prostitutes (and women

P
Q

committing adultery) while tolerating the men with whom these acts were committed (Hos. 4:14). Because of this double standard, the prostitute or harlot, as she is also called, has had an ambiguous status in society. She was tolerated in ancient Israel—as long as she was not married—but her profession was not socially acceptable. The children of harlots suffered from social biases against them (Judg. 11:2).

Although the OT records no laws prohibiting men from visiting prostitutes and making use of their services, there are strong counsels against such behavior (Prov. 23:27-28; 29:3). The apocryphal book of Ecclesiasticus gives similar warnings (9:3-9; 19:2).

The Holiness Code prohibited Israelite fathers from turning their daughters into prostitutes (Lev. 19:29), which might have been a temptation during times when poverty was widespread. It may be that most prostitutes in Israel were foreign or Canaanite women. That would help explain why the book of Proverbs speaks of the harlot literally as a "strange" and "foreign" woman (translated in the RSV as "loose woman," "evil woman") (Prov. 2:16; 5:3; 6:24).

Jesus told the religious leaders of His day that harlots would go into the kingdom before they would (Matt. 21:31) not because He condoned prostitution but because harlots did not have the self-righteousness which kept the religious leaders from repentance. Paul reminded Corinthian Christians that their bodies were the temple of the Holy Spirit; therefore, they should refrain from immorality, including sexual relations with prostitutes (1 Cor. 6:15-20).

The term "cult prostitution" is frequently used to refer to certain practices in Canaanite fertility cults, including the cult of Baal. This practice and the beliefs on which it was based were incompatible with monotheism and with the nature of Israel's God. The terms *qadash* (masc.) and *qedeshah* (fem.), from the word meaning "holy," are generally translated "cult prostitute" (or "sodomite"). The masculine term is probably also used in a generic sense to refer to both male and female cult prostitutes. Such prostitutes functioned in the temple in Jerusalem at various times in Israel's history and were removed during periods of religious reform (1 Kings 14:24; 15:12; 22:46; 2 Kings 23:7). Cult prostitution is outlawed by the Deutero-

nomic law code (Deut. 23:17-18). See *Fertility Cult.*

The presence of both "secular" and "cult prostitutes" provided the prophets with a powerful metaphor for the unfaithfulness of the people toward God. The covenant was imaged as a marriage between the Lord and the people; their continual interest in other gods, especially Baal, was seen as a form of harlotry. This idea is graphically presented in Ezek. 16 (cp. Ezek. 23). Because the Lord's bride has become a harlot, she will be punished as a harlot. Hosea also attacked the Israelite attraction to the fertility religion of Canaan as harlotry. He felt called of God to marry a harlot (Hos. 1:2), a symbolic action (or object lesson) representing God's relationship with Israel. Hosea's love for his unfaithful and harlotrous wife was analogous to God's love for unfaithful Israel.

The book of Revelation applies the image of harlot to Rome, which is likened to a woman in scarlet and jewels, to whom the kings of the earth go (Rev. 17:1-6). See *Harlot.*

Wilda W. Morris

PROVENDER Grains and grasses used as animal feed (Isa. 30:24 KJV, RSV). Other translations use fodder or silage.

PROVERBS, BOOK OF The book of Proverbs contains the essence of Israel's wisdom. It provides a godly worldview and offers insight for living. Proverbs 1:7 provides the perspective for understanding all the proverbs: "The fear of the LORD is the beginning of knowledge; fools despise wisdom and instruction." "Fear of the LORD" is biblical shorthand for an entire life in love, worship, and obedience to God.

Date and Composition Though the title of Proverbs (1:1) seems to ascribe the entire book to Solomon, closer inspection reveals that the book is composed of parts and that it was formed over a period of several hundred years. It is difficult to know precisely the role Solomon and his court may have had in starting the process that culminated in the book of Proverbs. This process may be compared to the way psalms of Davidic authorship eventually led to the book of Psalms. In Israel wisdom was considered Solomonic almost by definition. Thus the titles in 1:1 and 10:1 are not strictly statements of authorship in the modern sense. See *Apocrypha, Wisdom of*

Solomon; Ecclesiastes, Book of; Song of Songs.

Proverbs as a collection of collections that grew over time is best seen from its variety of content and from its titles. These titles introduce the book's major subcollections and are found in 1:1; 10:1; 22:17 ("words of the wise"); 24:23; 25:1; 30:1; 31:1. For dating, 25:1 places the copying or editing of chapters 25–29 in the court of Hezekiah, thus about 700 B.C., some 250 years after Solomon. The process of compilation probably extended into the postexilic period.

Because wisdom writings have almost no historical references, they are very difficult to date. Most scholars place chapters 10–29 sometime in the period of kings. Chapters 1–9 are in a different genre (see below) from the Solomonic sayings of chapters 10:1–22:16, and their date is disputed. Some say it may be as early as Solomon. Others say it is postexilic, that chapters 1–9 were added to 10–29 to give later readers a context from which to understand the short sayings in the latter chapters. The date of chapters 30–31 is also uncertain. One scholar has argued there is a play on the Greek word for wisdom (*sophia*) in 31:26. This would date chapter 31 after the conquest of Palestine by Alexander the Great in 332 B.C.

Literary Character and Forms The book of Proverbs uses a variety of wisdom forms or genres. The Hebrew word for proverb (*mashal*), found in the book's title, can refer to a variety of literary forms beside the proverb: prophetic "discourse" (Num. 23:7,18), "allegory" (Ezek. 17:2; 24:3), "taunt song" (Mic. 2:4). Different sections of the book specialize in characteristic forms. Long wisdom poems, which scholars call "Instructions" after their Egyptian counterpart, dominate 1:8–9:18. These usually begin with a direct address to "son/children" and contain imperatives or prohibitions, motive clauses (reasons for actions), and sometimes narrative development (7:6-23). The setting of these instructions may be a school for young aristocrats. This section also contains public speeches by personified Wisdom (1:20-33; 8:1-36; 9:1-6).

"Sayings" which express wise insights about reality are the primary forms in 10:1–22:16 and 25:1–29:27. Sayings are characterized by extreme brevity. In Hebrew they usually have two lines with only six to eight words in contrast to their much longer English translations. These sayings may simply "tell it like it is," and let read-ers draw their own conclusions (11:24; 17:27-28; 18:16). They can also make clear value judgments (10:17; 14:31; 15:33; 19:17). Mostly "antithetical sayings," which contrast opposites, appear in 10:1–15:33, but mixed in are a few "better ... than" sayings ("Better is a meal with vegetables where there is love than a fattened calf with hatred," 15:17 HCSB; cp. v. 16) which are also scattered in other sections (16:8,19; 17:1; 19:1; 21:9; 25:24; 27:5,10b; 28:6). The section 25:1–25:27 is especially rich in comparative proverbs which set two things beside one another for comparison: "Good news from a distant land is like cold water to a parched throat," (25:25 HCSB; cp. 25:12-14,26,28; 26:1-3,6-11,14,20 among others). Such sayings also occur elsewhere, "A beautiful woman who rejects good sense is like a gold ring in a pig's snout" (11:22).

"Admonitions" characterize 22:17–24:22. Similarity with Egyptian wisdom marks this section. These short wisdom forms contain imperatives or prohibitions, usually followed by a motive clause which gives a reason or two for doing that which is being urged: "Don't move an ancient property line, and don't encroach on the fields of the fatherless, for their Redeemer is strong, and He will take up their case against you" (23:10-11 HCSB). Admonitions are a shorter relative of the instruction.

The words of Agur (chap. 30) specialize in numerical sayings (30:15-31). The epilogue of the book (31:10-31) presents an alphabetic poem on wisdom embodied in the "valiant woman." This brief sketch of wisdom forms presents only the basic types. Even within the types here presented, a great deal of subtle variation occurs.

Themes and Worldview In spite of being a collection of collections, Proverbs displays a unified, richly complex worldview. Proverbs 1–9 introduces this worldview and lays out its main themes. The short sayings of Proverbs 10–31 are to be understood in light of the first nine chapters.

The beginning and end of wisdom is to fear God and avoid evil (1:7; 8:13; 9:10; 15:33). The world is a battleground between wisdom and folly, righteousness and wickedness, good and evil. This conflict is personified in Lady Wisdom (1:20-33; 4:5-9; 8; 9:1-6) and Harlot Folly (5:1-6; 6:23-35; 7; 9:13-18). Both "women" offer love and invite simple young men (like those in the royal school) to their homes to sample their wares. Wisdom's invitation is to life (8:34-36); the seduction of Folly leads to death (5:3-6; 7:22-27; 9:18).

Mysteriously Lady Wisdom speaks in public places, offering wisdom to everyone who will listen (1:20-22; 8:1-5; 9:3). Wisdom does not hide but stands there for all who seek her. Some scholars consider Wisdom to be an attribute of God, especially shown in creation (3:19-20; 8:22-31). More accurately stated, however, Wisdom is "the self-revelation of creation." That is, God has placed in creation a wise order that speaks to mankind of good and evil, urging humans toward good and away from evil. This is not just the "voice of experience" but God's general revelation that speaks to all people with authority. The world is not silent but speaks of the Creator and His will (Pss. 19:1-2; 97:6; 145:10; 148; Job 12:7-9; Acts 14:15-17; Rom. 1:18-23; 2:14-15).

This perspective eliminates any split between faith and reason, between sacred and secular. The person who knows God also knows that every inch of life is created by God and belongs to Him. Experiences of God come only from experiences in God's world. Experiences in the world point the person of faith to God.

Thus the wise person "fears God" and also lives in harmony with God's order for creation. The sluggard must learn from the ant because the ant's work is in tune with the order of the seasons (Prov. 6:6-11; cp. 10:5).

Thinking Proverbially The short proverbs in chapters 10–29 cover a wealth of topics from wives (11:22; 18:22; 25:24) to friends (14:20; 17:17-18; 18:17; 27:6), strong drink (23:29-35; 31:4-7), wealth and poverty, justice and injustice, table manners and social status (23:1-8; cp. 25:6-7; Luke 14:7-11).

One cannot just use any proverb on any topic, for proverbs can be misused: "A proverb in the mouth of a fool is like lame legs that hang limp" (Prov. 26:7 HCSB; cp. v. 9). Proverbs are designed to make one wise, but they require wisdom to be used correctly. Proverbs are true, but their truth is realized only when they are fitly applied in the right situation. Job's friends misapplied proverbs about the wicked to righteous Job. Many things have more than one side to them, and the wise person will know which is which. Wives can be a gift from the Lord (18:22), but sometimes singleness seems better (21:9,19). Silence can be a sign of wisdom

(17:27) or a cover-up (17:28). A "friend" (Hb. *rea*ʿ) can be trusted (17:17) but not always (17:18; "neighbor" = *rea*ʿ)!

Wealth can be a sign of God's blessing (3:9-10), but some saints suffer (3:11-12). Wealth can result from wickedness (13:23; 17:23; 28:11; cp. 26:12). It is better to be poor and godly: "Better a little with righteousness than great income with injustice" (16:8 HCSB; cp. 15:16-17; 17:1; 19:1; 28:6). In the end God will judge: "The one who shuts his ears to the cry of the poor will himself also call out and not be answered" (21:13 HCSB; cp. 3:27-28; 22:16; 24:11-12; 10:2; 11:4).

The problem of fittingness is most sharply put in 26:4-5:

"Don't answer a fool according to his foolishness,

or you'll be like him yourself.

Answer a fool according to his foolishness,

or he'll become wise in his own eyes" (HCSB).

Such dilemmas force us to confront the limits of our wisdom (26:12) and to rely upon God (3:5-8).

Proverbs generally operate on the principle that consequences follow acts: you reap what you sow. In a fallen world, however, God's justice is sometimes delayed. The "better ... than" proverbs, in particular, show the disorder of the present world, the "exceptions to the rule." The righteous thus works and prays, like the psalmist, for the day when God will make all things right.

Outline

I. Proverbs Is Designed to Impart Divine Wisdom Concerning Life (1:1-6).

II. Wisdom's Contribution to Life Is to Be Praised (1:7–9:18).

A. The goal of all wisdom is that people "fear ... the LORD" (1:7).

B. Wisdom identifies sin and calls sinners to repentance (1:8-33).

C. Wisdom enables the sinner to be set free and experience meaningful life (2:1-22).

D. Wisdom produces a sense of divine presence, joy, and peace in the believer (3:1-26).

E. Wisdom admonishes believers to share God's love with others (3:27-35).

P
Q

F. Wisdom helps a father instruct his son how to obtain a meaningful life (4:1-27).

G. Wisdom calls for purity and honesty in all marriage relationships (5:1-23).

H. Wisdom admonishes the believer to work hard and spend wisely (6:1-19).

I. Wisdom warns against the peril of adultery (6:20–7:27).

J. Through divine wisdom God offers Himself to humankind (8:1-36).

K. Wisdom presents us with two choices, life or death (9:1-18).

III. One's Response to Wisdom Brings about Earthly Consequences (10:1–22:16).

A. The righteous find blessings, but the wicked suffer greatly (10:1-32).

B. The deceitful pay a terrible price, but the honest find God's favor (11:1-31).

C. The righteous are open to instruction, but the wicked are not (12:1-28).

D. The righteous are obedient to God's will; however, the wicked rebel (13:1-25).

E. The foolish will be judged, but the righteous will be accepted by God (14:1-35).

F. The Lord watches over all humankind and judges each accordingly (15:1-33).

G. The Lord is the fountain of life for the faithful (16:1-33).

H. The foolish thrive on bribery, but the wise are honest yet merciful (17:1-28).

I. The foolish are haughty, but the righteous are humble (18:1-24).

J. The poor are to be pitied, but the wealthy are honored by God (19:1-29).

K. The wise work hard and treat both friend and foe with love (20:1-30).

L. God requires holy lives and not just holy rituals (21:1-31).

M. The wise discipline themselves to follow God in everything (22:1-16).

IV. Wisdom Provides Prudent Counsel for Both the Present and the Future (22:17–34).

A. Wisdom tells one when to speak and when to be silent (22:17-21).

B. The wise ones care for and protect the poor (22:22-29).

C. Wisdom warns one not to fall into the trap of another's craftiness (23:1-11).

D. Youth need instruction and correction to become what they should be (23:12-28).

E. The drunkard destroys his life and that of others (23:29-35).

F. Wisdom leads to a meaningful life, but wickedness leads to destruction (24:1-9).

G. The wise ones steadfastly trust God in both the good and bad times (24:10-22).

H. Wisdom promotes true justice (24:23-34).

V. Wisdom Constantly Reminds People of Their Past Heritage (25:1–29:27).

A. The king shares in the responsibility for promoting wisdom (25:1-14).

B. The righteous exercise self-discipline and love in all of life (25:15-28).

C. The foolish fail the test of life and face God's judgment (26:1-28).

D. Life's quest for meaning is brief and frustrating at times (27:1-22).

E. People should learn to live as responsible stewards (27:23-27).

F. God expects justice from His followers (28:1-28).

G. Discipline is an essential part of life (29:1-27).

VI. The True Source of Meaningful Existence Can Be Found Only in God (30:1–31:31).

A. Human beings cannot fully discover or understand God's wisdom (30:1-33).

B. Humans can practice righteousness and show loving-kindness (31:1-9).

C. The key to meaningful existence is found in one's faith relationship to God (31:10-31).

Raymond C. Van Leeuwen

PROVIDENCE God's benevolent and wise superintendence of His creation. Of this superintendence, the Westminster Confession of Faith (1647) states, "God, the great Creator of all things, doth uphold, direct, dispose, and govern all creatures, actions, and things, from the greatest even to the least, by his most wise and holy providence, according to his infallible foreknowledge and the free and immutable counsel of his own will, to the praise of the glory of his wisdom, power, justice, goodness, and mercy." As this indicates, God—from whom nothing is hidden (cp. Pss. 33:13-15; 139:1-16; Isa. 40:27-28) and whose power is surpassingly great (cp. Job 42:2; Jer. 32:17)—wisely oversees and sovereignly controls all creation. In so doing He attends not only to apparently momentous events and people but also to those that seem both mundane and trivial. Thus, while He holds the lives of both kings and nations in His hand (cp. Isa. 40:21-26; Jer. 18:1-6), God also concerns Himself with the welfare of the lowly and meek (cp. Pss. 104:10-30; 107:39-43). Indeed, so all encompassing is God's attention to events within creation that nothing—not even the casting of lots—happens by chance (cp. Prov. 16:33).

With regard to God's role in the course of earthly events, one must avoid the error of Deism on the one hand and that of fatalism on the other. Deism is the view that God created the universe as a sort of colossal machine, set it in motion according to various natural laws (which, perhaps, He Himself established), and now simply sits back and watches events unfold in accordance with those laws. The view that God occasionally intervenes in earthly affairs is itself a version of Deism. And, since God involves Himself in everything that happens, Deism is false.

Fatalism is the view that every event that happens had to happen. So, on the fatalist's view, anything that happens is unavoidable in the sense that it could not have failed to happen. Since it implies that one could do nothing other than what one actually does and thus that one has no real choice—or control—over what one does, such a view undermines personal responsibility. And, since Scripture clearly indicates that humans do face real choices and are in general responsible for their actions (cp. Deut. 30:11-20), fatalism is false.

So, while Deism unbiblically minimizes God's role in the course of history, fatalism unbiblically minimizes human responsibility for human actions. To be true to the biblical witness, one's account of providence must provide both for the very active role which God plays in directing events toward ends which He chooses and for the responsibility which humans have for the way in which they contribute toward those ends. So, for instance, God uses the actions of Joseph's brothers to bring him to Egypt (cp. Gen. 37:12-28; 45:1-8; 50:15-21) as well as the actions of the religious leaders in Jerusalem to bring about Christ's death (cp. Matt. 26:1-5,47-68; 27:1-26; John 18:1–19:16; Acts 2:22-24). But, while God worked through their actions for His own purposes, this does not negate the responsibility of either Joseph's brothers or those religious leaders for those actions.

An important corollary of providence is divine foreknowledge. Since He sovereignly directs whatever happens, God has complete knowledge of those events yet to occur (cp. Isa. 42:8-9). In short, God never need revise His plans in light of some surprising or unexpected event. His knowledge of the future extends even to what His creatures will choose to do in ages yet to come. Of course, this raises two potentially troubling questions: First, if God foreknows what a creature will choose to do at some point in the future, does it not follow that the creature could not have failed to make that choice and thus is not responsible for making it? Second, if God controls history to such an extent that He foreknows the future in every detail, does this not mean that He could have foreseen—and thus could have forestalled—the evil in the world? The former question gives rise to what is known as the problem of freedom and foreknowledge, the second to the problem of evil.

Perhaps the best known response to the problem of freedom and foreknowledge involves the suggestion—made by Augustine, Boethius, and others—that God exists timelessly (i.e., He exists "outside" of time) and thus suffers no temporal limitations. On this suggestion, what is future from a merely human point of view is present from the divine point of view. Thus, for those who take this suggestion seriously, God's timeless knowledge of one's future actions does not make one any less able to refrain from doing them than does the knowledge of an observer in the present time.

In response to the problem of evil, a couple of points deserve mention. First, given God's character, it must be that He has good reasons for allowing the evil that He allows. Second, in response to Job's questions about his own suffering, God points out to Job that he is in no position to understand His reasons for allowing him to suffer (cp. Job 38:1-7; 40:6-14). Job resembles a baby in need of surgery who faces suffering for which he cannot understand the reasons. So, while God presumably has good reasons to allow evil, no mere human can presume even to be able—let alone actually—to understand those reasons. Even so, like the parent of the baby needing surgery, God can—and does—make His love evident even in the midst of evil and suffering. Of course, in making Himself known, He has promised one day to conquer evil (cp. 1 Cor. 15:24-28) and to eliminate pain and sorrow (cp. Rev. 21:3-4). Thus, in His providence, God ultimately will deliver His people from evil.

Still, it would be a mistake to think that the only comfort to be found in providence involves the blessed hope of the new heaven and earth. For, of course, God now works for the good of those who love Him (cp. Rom. 8:28) and invites them to cast their cares upon Him (cp. 1 Pet. 5:6-7) in faith that He will provide (cp. Matt 6:26-33). See *Election; Evil; Foreknowledge; Freedom; God; Predestination.*

Douglas Blount

PROVINCE Roman political region. During NT times there were three types of provinces. Imperial districts were governed directly by the emperor. Senatorial provinces answered to the senate. Special type provinces were those composed of rugged terrain or newly conquered people. These demanded more strict control and were under the control of an imperial procurator. Judea was a special province because the Jews so fiercely hated the Roman domination.

Israel practiced a type of provincial system during Ahab's reign (1 Kings 20:14-15). Later the Babylonians and Persians used such districts in Palestine (Esther 4:11). The Romans refined the system dramatically and used it to maintain control over their vast empire. See *Government; Rome and the Roman Empire.*

PROVOCATION In Heb. 3:8,15 that which aroused God's anger. Provocation corresponds to the place-name "Meribah," meaning "contention" (Exod. 17:1-7; Num. 20:1-13; Ps. 95:7-11; Heb. 3:7-11). See *Massah.*

PRUDENCE See *Wisdom and Wise Men.*

PRUNING HOOK See *Tools.*

PSALMIST Writer of psalms or hymns. Second Samuel 23:1 calls David the "sweet psalmist of Israel." Superscriptions ascribe about one half of the psalms to David. See *David; Psalms, Book of.*

PSALMS OF SOLOMON See *Pseudepigrapha.*

PSALMS, BOOK OF The Hebrew title of the book means "praises." The English title (Psalms) comes from the Septuagint, the ancient Greek translation of the Hebrew Old Testament. The Greek word *psalmoi* means "songs," from which comes the idea, "songs of praises" or "praise songs."

The individual psalms of the book came from several authors. David, the sweet psalmist of Israel (2 Sam. 23:1), wrote approximately half of the 150 psalms in the book. David's psalms became the standard followed by others, thereby, imprinting a Davidic character to the entire book. Other authors include Asaph (12), the sons of Korah (10), Solomon (two), Moses (one), Heman (one), and Ethan (one). Approximately 48 psalms are anonymous.

The book of Psalms contains individual psalms covering a thousand-year period from the time of Moses (15th century B.C.) to the postexilic period (fifth century B.C.). Most of the psalms were written in the time of David and Solomon (1010–930). The final editor of the work was probably Ezra (450).

The titles or superscriptions to the psalms are very old, and the author of the psalm, in many cases, may have written the title. The obscure words and phrases of the titles and the absence of titles with certain psalms (the rabbis refer to these psalms as "orphan" psalms) strongly suggest the reliability and antiquity of the titles. If later scribes were arbitrarily adding these, why not add them to all without obscurities?

Outline Traditionally the book has been divided into five sections corresponding to the five books of Moses, each section ending with a doxology (Book 1, Psalms 1–41; Book 2, Psalms 42–72; Book 3, Psalms 73–89; Book 4, Psalms 90–106; Book 5, Psalms 107–150). These divisions may suggest that the "books" were independent for a time. (Note that Pss. 14 and 53 are very similar and occur in different "books.") Some psalms also may be grouped according to their function; for example, the Songs of Ascent (120–134) were probably sung by Israelites on their way to the three required feasts in Jerusalem. Another group of psalms (93; 96–99) celebrate the Lord's divine sovereignty over the universe.

Scholars have debated the forms and classifications of individual psalms for centuries. The book of Psalms contains hymns (145–150), laments (38–39), songs of thanksgiving (30–32), royal psalms (2; 110), enthronement psalms (96,98), penitential psalms (32; 38; 51), and wisdom or didactic psalms (19; 119).

A *lament* can be expressed by the community (e.g., 44; 74; 79) or the individual (22; 38; 39; 41; 54). Both types of laments are prayers or cries to God on the occasion of distressful situations. Differences are related to the types of trouble and the experiences of salvation. For the community the trouble may be an enemy; with an individual it may be an illness. The basic pattern includes an invocation of God, a description of the petitioner's complaint(s), a recalling of past salvation experiences (usually community laments), petitions, a divine response (or oracle), and a concluding vow of praise.

The *thanksgiving psalms* are also spoken by the community (106; 124; 129) and the individual (9; 18; 30). These psalms are related to the laments as they are responses to liberation occurring after distress. They are expressions of joy and are fuller forms of the lament's vow of praise.

The *hymn* (8; 19; 29) is closest in form to a song of praise as sung in modern forms of worship. These psalms are uniquely liturgical and could be sung antiphonally; some have repeating refrains (Ps. 8; 136). The hymn normally includes a call to praise. Then the psalm describes the reasons for praising God. The structure is not as clear-cut as other types of psalms.

Some psalms are considered *royal psalms* (2; 18; 20). These psalms are concerned with the earthly king of Israel. Again, these are usually understood as mixed psalms. They were used to celebrate the king's enthronement. They may have included an oracle for the king. In some cases (such as Ps. 72), prayers were made to intercede on behalf of the king.

Another mixed type is the *enthronement psalms* that celebrate Yahweh's kingship (Pss. 96–99). They are closely related to the hymns; the main difference is a celebration of Yahweh as king over all creation.

Penitential psalms are expressions of contrition and repentance. The psalmist pleads to be restored to a right relationship with God (Pss. 38; 51).

A final type of psalm is the *wisdom psalm*. This type has poetic form and style but is distinguished because of content and a tendency toward the proverbial. These psalms contemplate questions of theodicy (73), celebrate God's Word (the Torah, Ps. 119), or deal with two different ways of living—that of the godly person or the evil person (Ps. 1).

As the mixed psalms indicate, the psalms are not neatly or easily categorized,. However, identification helps the reader to know what type of psalm is being read, with a possible original context or a fitting present context in worship. See *Music, Instruments, Dancing*.

These classifications, however, should not be taken too strictly. They are not rigid molds. The genuine religious feelings and expressions found in the Psalms may at times intersect with many of these classifications, or even transcend these classifications. A few psalms (25; 34; 37; 111; 112; 119; 145) are acrostically arranged according to the Hebrew alphabet, probably to aid in memorizing the psalm.

Interpreting the Psalms The Psalms represent the devout and inspired meditations of the heart upon God's law and His providential works. In fact, they are the religion of the OT internalized in the heart and life of the believer. They have always been, as divinely intended, the model and pattern of acceptable worship and devotion to God, both privately and publicly. Although other psalms or songs are found in the Bible (for example, the Song of Moses in Deut. 32:1-43), they were not intended for Israel's permanent worship in the temple. The book of Psalms, therefore, has appropriately been known as the hymnbook of Israel and, of course, the church for many centuries. As the inspired hymnbook, the Psalms expand and develop the OT. The law is expanded by bringing forth the true spiritual application of the law to the heart of the individual and, at times, by interpreting significant events and practices in the law. Similarly, the Psalms at times interpret events in the historical books, furnishing spiritual insights and responses to many situations of life. The book of Psalms illuminates the writings of the prophets by showing the dangers of separating outward

P
Q

ritual (such as sacrifice) from true inward devotion and worship.

The book of Psalms covers a wide range of theological topics. Monotheism is clearly affirmed: idols are man's creation without power (115; 96). God's existence and attributes are frequently affirmed (omniscience and omnipotence, 139; righteousness and truth, 86; goodness, 103; holiness, 99): atheism, theoretical, and practical, is wickedness and foolishness (14; 53). The revelation of God in nature and in His Word is the theme of 19 and 119. The Lord's covenant relationship with His people is stressed in 89; 105; and 68. Man's natural sinfulness is affirmed in 51. The importance of repentance and restoration is the subject of 51; 32; 6; 143; 38. Although the evildoer may prosper at times, the righteous will be with God here and hereafter (37; 1). Moreover, the Lord will fulfill His promises, and, as the refuge of His people, He will deliver His people (40; 2). Perhaps one of the more controversial theological topics of the Psalter is the imprecatory prayer (35; 69; 109; 137). These prayers seek divine justice against the enemies of God (who are also the enemies of the writer) for wrongs and crimes committed. These prayers are not expressing individual revenge and vindictiveness; they are pleas for God to execute righteous justice, similar to certain prayers of the NT (Matt. 11:25; 2 Tim. 4:16; Rev. 6:10).

Most importantly, the Psalms focus on the Messiah, the hope and fulfillment of all Israelite history and religion. The Messianic teachings of the psalms are woven throughout the book. Messiah is often found, therefore, when human limits are removed or when man is represented in an ideal state (2; 8). When the Lord appears or comes in relations to man, He does so in the person of the Son (102; 97). Moreover, Messiah is often seen typologically through the experiences of David and Solomon (22), with the language sometimes going beyond the types and applying directly and exclusively to Messiah (Pss. 16:10; 110). The Psalms refer to Messiah's incarnation (Ps. 40; Heb. 10:5), His humiliation and exaltation (Ps. 8; Heb. 2:5-10), His eternal throne (Ps. 45; Heb. 1:8-9), His sufferings (Ps. 22; Matt. 27), His resurrection (Ps. 16; Acts 2:24-31), and His offices as prophet, priest, and king (Ps. 110). See *Typology*.

The book of Psalms has been a source of instruction, comfort, and blessing for the people of God by teaching His people how to worship, serve, and glorify God forever.

David M. Fleming and Russell Fuller

PSALTER 1. Alternate name for the book of Psalms. **2.** Any collection of psalms used in worship.

PSEUDEPIGRAPHA (sū dĕ pĭ´ gră phá) Intertestamental literature not accepted into the Christian or Jewish canon of Scripture and often attributed to an ancient hero of faith. Ongoing discovery and research provide differing lists of contents. A recent publication listed 52 writings. They give much information about the development of Jewish religion and culture.

Pseudepigraphal Books Pseudepigrapha means "writings falsely attributed." This is based on those books claiming to be written by Adam, Enoch, Moses, and other famous OT people. Some of the writings are anonymous; thus some scholars prefer the name "outside books" for all of these writings, emphasizing that they did not become part of canon. Some ancient Christians and the Roman church have used the term "Apocrypha," since for them what Protestants call "Apocrypha" is part of their canon. See *Apocrypha*.

Both Palestinian and Hellenistic Jews authored books in the Pseudepigrapha. They used a variety of styles and literary types—legend, poetry, history, philosophy—but apocalypse was the dominant literary type. A review of the most important and representative books will show the significance of the Pseudepigrapha in understanding the background of the NT. See *Apocalyptic*.

First Enoch has been preserved in the Ethiopic language. It is a composite work of five sections, written at different times. The first section (chaps. 1–36) tells how Enoch was taken up into heaven and shown its secrets. The sons of God of Gen. 6 were seen as angels. They committed sin, and the children born to them were evil giants. Emphasis is placed upon judgment and punishment. Even the realm of the dead is divided into separate places for the righteous and the wicked. The second section (chaps. 37–71) is the most important for its relation to the Bible. It is the Parables or Similitudes. These chapters refer to the Son of Man. Opinions differ as to how such references form part of the background to the NT teachings about Jesus as the Son of Man. There is uncertainty about the date of this section and of chapters. The rest of the book comes from between 200 and 1 B.C., but the Similitudes may have been written later, shortly before A.D. 100. Fragments of all the other sections have been found in the caves of Qumran, but no fragments of this section have been discovered yet. The third section (chaps. 78–82) deals with the heavenly bodies. The author argues for a calendar based on the movement of the sun in distinction to the standard Jewish lunar calendar. The fourth section (chaps. 83–90) contains two dream visions dealing with the flood and the history of Israel from Adam to the Maccabean revolt. The final section (chaps. 91–108) gives religious instruction concerning the end time. The entire book is apocalyptic.

Second Enoch is also an apocalypse preserved primarily in the Slavonic language. It was written between 100 B.C. and A.D. 100. In it Enoch was taken up into heaven and commanded to write 366 books. He was allowed to return to earth for 30 days to teach his sons, after which he returned to heaven. This writing describes the contents of the seven heavens and divides time into seven one-thousand-year periods.

Second Baruch is apocalyptic and shows how some Jews responded to the destruction of Jerusalem by the Romans in A.D. 70. It was written shortly before A.D. 100. Three visions seek to console the people by showing that even though destruction has come, God has prepared something better for them. The writings teach that the Messiah will be revealed to bring in a time of great plenty. Emphasis is placed on obedience to the Law.

The *Sibylline Oracles* were very popular apocalyptic writings in the ancient world. The Jews took over the originally pagan writings and modified them by inserting ideas about monotheism, Mosaic requirements, and Jewish history. Three of the 15 books in the collection are missing. Book 3, from between 200 and 100 B.C., is the most important and the most Jewish. It traces Jewish history from the time of Abraham to the building of the second temple. It pronounces God's judgment upon pagan nations but holds out hope that they may turn to God.

The *Testament of Moses* (sometimes called the *Assumption of Moses*) is also apocalyptic. The manuscripts are incomplete, and the miss-

ing portion may have contained an account of Moses' death and his being taken to heaven. Early Christian writers state that Jude 9 was to be found in the *Assumption of Moses* known to them. This book is a rewriting of Deut. 31–34. Moses is the chosen mediator of God, prepared from the beginning of time. The book traces the history of the people from their beginning to the author's own time. Since chapters 6 and 7 seem to refer to Herod the Great, the book was probably written shortly after A.D. 1. It emphasized that God has planned all things and keeps them under His control.

The *Testaments of the Twelve Patriarchs* are patterned after Gen. 49, the closing instructions of Jacob to his sons. Each of the sons of Jacob addressed his descendants, giving a brief survey of his life, with special attention to some sin or failure. For example, Reuben stressed his adultery with Bilhah (Gen. 35:22), and Simeon told of his jealousy of Joseph. Joseph, however, emphasized the maintaining of his purity. Using the confessed sin as a background, patriarchs urged their children to live in an upright manner. Special emphasis is given to love for the neighbor and sexual purity. In most of the testaments, the children are told to give honor to Levi and Judah. The book refers to two messiahs: one from Levi, one from Judah. The earliest portions of the testaments come from after 200 B.C.

The *Book of Jubilees* is a rewriting of Genesis and the opening chapters of Exodus from after 200 B.C. It traces the history of Israel from creation to the time of Moses, dividing time into jubilee periods, 49 years each. The calendar is based on the sun, not the moon. The writer strongly opposed the Gentile influences he found coming into Judaism urging Jews to keep separate from the Gentiles. In the *Book of Jubilees*, Abraham was the ideal righteous man. The book shows how a conservative, priestly Jew about 150 B.C. viewed the world.

The *Psalms of Solomon* is a collection of 18 psalms written about 50 B.C. They reflect the situation of the people in Jerusalem following its capture by the Romans under Pompey in 63 B.C. *Psalms of Solomon* 17 and 18 are of special importance because of their references to the Messiah. According to these psalms, the Messiah was to be a human figure, a descendant of David, wise and righteous, and without sin. The titles Son of David and Lord Messiah are used of Him.

P
Q

Third Maccabees, written after 200 B.C., has nothing to do with the Maccabees. It tells about the attempt of Ptolemy IV to kill the Jews in Egypt. God foiled his efforts resulting in the advancement of the Jews. This book shows the vindication of the righteous.

Fourth Maccabees is based to some extent upon material found in 2 Maccabees 6–7. It is a philosophical writing stressing that pious reason can be the master of the passions. Reason is derived from obedience to the law. In the account of the seven sons who are martyred, the author greatly expanded the account but left out all references to resurrection. The book comes from the time shortly after A.D. 1.

The *Life of Adam and Eve* has been preserved in both Latin and Greek. The two versions are different in length and content. Blame for the fall is placed upon Eve. Sin entered human experience through her. This writing refers to Satan being transformed into the brightness of angels (9:1; 2 Cor. 11:14), and states that paradise is in the third heaven (cp. 2 Cor. 12:2-3). The *Life of Adam and Eve* was written after A.D. 1.

The *Letter of Aristeas* was composed after 200 B.C., telling how the OT law was translated into Greek. Actually, it is more concerned about the table conversation at banquets in Alexandria than it is about the translation of the Septuagint. It seeks to show that the Jewish law was in conformity with the highest ideals of Greek thought and life. It indicates that it is possible for Jew and Greek to live together in peace. So far as its account of the translation of the Law into Greek is concerned, its only historical validity is that it was at this time (during the reign of Ptolemy Philadelphus, 285–246 B.C.) that this translation was begun. See *Apocalyptic; Apocrypha; Bible Texts and Versions.*   *Clayton Harrop*

PSEUDONYMITY Text is pseudonymous when it is not authored by the person whose name it bears. Such works are written after the purported author's death by another person or during his life by someone who is not commissioned to do so. Pseudonymous writings are not the same as anonymous texts. The former works make definite claims to authorship; the latter do not.

Many critical scholars believe that pseudonymity exists in the OT (e.g., Daniel) and the NT (e.g., the Pastoral Epistles). Several pseudonymous writings are certainly present outside the canon of Scripture (e.g., 1 Enoch, 4 Ezra, 3 Corinthians, the Epistle to the Laodiceans, and the Gospel of Peter). Evidence is lacking, however, to support the presence of such works in the Scriptures.

To promote the idea that pseudonymity exists within the canon, critics appeal to Greco-Roman (the Pythagorean and Cynic schools) and Jewish sources. Some pseudonymity seems to have been customary in such settings (cp. Iamblichus, *de Vita Pythagorica* § 198, 158). Authors of no reputation would often write using the pseudonym of an older, reputable figure in order to secure a hearing for their own works.

Specific attributions of authorship were not typically found within ancient Jewish writings. Nonetheless, pseudonymity can be found among the Jews. The phenomenon occurred mostly in apocalyptic writings after 200 B.C. and arguably was due to a general belief that prophetic inspiration had ceased (cp. Josephus, Against Apion 1.41; Babylonian Talmud, Sanhedrin 11a).

Jewish literature is generally not very helpful to a study of pseudepigrapha in early Christianity. The NT writings most often classified by critical scholars as pseudonymous are epistles. Thus, one should look to Jewish epistolary literature to establish a precedent. Only two pseudonymous letters have come down to us from Jewish sources: the Letter of Aristeas and the Epistle of Jeremiah. The former work, strictly speaking, is not a letter because it does not occur in epistolary form. It is an apologetic narrative providing an account of the translation of the Hebrew OT into Greek. The latter writing, a sermon warning the Jews against pagan idolatry, calls itself a letter and identifies its senders and addressees, but purports to be a copy of an epistle. Thus, it is not entirely comparable to NT epistles. Other pseudonymous Jewish letters exist (e.g., 1 Baruch, 2 Baruch 78–87, 1 Enoch 92–105, and some letters contained in 1 and 2 Maccabees), but such writings occur within composite, apocalyptic, or narrative frameworks. These letters had a different form and function than NT epistles and are not relevant to the latter.

Nonetheless, some pseudonymous letters can be found within Christian circles, though these are few in number and unremarkable (e.g., the Letters of Christ and Abgarus, the Letter of Lentulus, the Correspondence of Paul and Seneca, the Epistle of Titus, the Epistle to the

Laodiceans, the Epistle of the Apostles, 3 Corinthians, and the pseudo-Ignatian letters). They also do not closely resemble any NT epistles and were written at a much later date.

The NT contains passages that have a tremendous bearing on the question of pseudonymity in early Christianity. For example, in 2 Thess. 2:2 Paul warned the church against accepting the false teaching that "the Day of the Lord has come." He cautioned his readers that, no matter through what agency they had received this heresy—whether through "spirit, word, or letter"—he and his missionary associates had nothing to do with it. Paul would have objected to a pseudonymous letter being attributed to him that contained falsehood, wrong teaching, or material that he did not write. The apostle clearly puts a moratorium on pseudonymity in his name (cp. 2 Thess. 3:17).

The Pauline signatures in the NT (1 Cor. 16:21; Gal. 6:11; Col. 4:18; 2 Thess. 3:17; Philem. 19) indicated the apostle's use of a secretary and provided readers with a sign of his letters' authenticity and authority. Surely Paul would have frowned upon someone using a facsimile of his signature in a pseudonymous letter which purported to be his.

In Rev. 22:18-19 John warned that no one was to tamper with what he had written in the book by rewriting it in any way. One can extrapolate from this interpretation of these verses to somebody writing another book and falsely attributing it to him by means of pseudonymity. John would have objected to a pseudonymous letter being attributed to him that contained falsehood or material that he did not write. To write a pseudonymous work and attribute it to somebody is a sort of extension of tampering with an existing document. Thus, to enlarge pseudonymously an existing body of literature—for example, the Pauline corpus—by adding a few inauthentic works is to tamper with an author's actual corpus.

The NT also contains several appeals for truth that are difficult to reconcile with the thinking of an author who had deliberately used pseudonymity. For example, in 1 Tim. 4:1-2 Paul warned his readers not to embrace the doctrine of "deceitful spirits" and "the hypocrisy of liars." In Eph. 4:15 he instructed his readers to speak "the truth in love." In Eph. 4:25 he exhorted the church to "put away lying" and "speak the truth." In Col. 3:9 he admonished his readers:

"Do not lie to one another." Furthermore, the Holy Spirit, who indwells every believer (1 Cor. 6:19; 12:13) and is described as the "Spirit of truth" (John 14:17; 16:3), created an ethos in the Christian community in which pseudonymity would have been frowned upon and could not have flourished. A careful study of the terms for "deception" reveals that a concept of legitimate deception for the NT is difficult to support.

Known early Christian responses to pseudepigrapha do not affirm the practice as acceptable (cp. Tertullian's comments in *de Baptismo* 17 on the Acts of Paul; Serapion's remarks on the Gospel of Peter recorded in Eusebius' Ecclesiastical History 6.12; the reference in the Muratorian Canon to "forged" Pauline letters, etc.). The language used by early church leaders in reference to pseudonymous works clearly describes them as fraudulent and deceptive. Early Christians simply did not embrace pseudonymous works they viewed in such a pejorative manner. If discovered, they firmly rejected such writings.

Not all critics agree. Some scholars argue that the early church was really only concerned about the content of works and not pseudonymity. However this theory does not explain the exclusion from the church's canon of several pseudonymous writings which were orthodox in their content (e.g., the Preaching of Peter, the Apocalypse of Peter, the Epistle of the Apostles, the Correspondence of Paul and Seneca, the extant Epistle to the Laodiceans, etc.).

Other critics object that the evidence of later Gentile Christian attitudes towards pseudepigrapha is anachronistic and should not be used to judge the first-century Jewish-Christian phenomenon of pseudonymity. However, the fact that the Jews themselves rejected pseudonymous works like 1 Enoch and 4 Ezra from the Hebrew canon helps render the latter theory untenable. Undeniably, second-century orthodox Christians strongly disapproved of pseudonymity, and it is improbable that first-century Christians had a different opinion on the matter.

Even more scholars note that the church's rejection of pseudonymity took place in a period when a great deal of heretical literature attributed to the apostles was circulating. Thus, the latter phenomenon possibly colored the way that orthodox churchmen, who were concerned about heresy, looked at all pseudonymity. However, the early church could conceivably have responded differently—for example, by only screening the content of documents and not their authorship. Notably, the early Christians did no such thing; instead they utilized both standards when recognizing books as inspired of God and canonical.

To be sure, the inspired and inerrant books of the Holy Bible are accurate. They can be trusted to have been written by whom they say they are.

Terry Wilder

PTOLEMIES (tŏl´ ə mēz) Dynastic powers which emerged in Egypt in the aftermath of the conquests of Alexander the Great.

Ptolemy I Soter (323–283 B.C.) established the dynasty which bears his name and moved the capital of Egypt from Memphis to Alexandria, the city Alexander founded. He and his successors ruled an empire that included at times Cyrenaica, Palestine, Phoenicia, Cyprus, and some parts of western Asia Minor and the Aegean. Ptolemaic policies brought great wealth to the state through taxation and trade. The Ptolemies did not force Hellenization upon native populations, but the obvious commercial, cultural, and social benefits of Ptolemaic policies led to greater acceptance of Hellenistic ideas and customs. Land was farmed out under state control, and the reserves funneled to the central government. Payment of heavy yearly taxes, however, assured a measure of local autonomy. The Ptolemies introduced a ruler cult, but permitted native religions to continue unimpeded. In addition to Ptolemy I, the most energetic of these rulers were Ptolemy II Philadelphus (282–246 B.C.) and Ptolemy III Euergetes (246–221 B.C.).

The Ptolemies made Alexandria a center of learning and commerce. In particular the early Ptolemies supported a large group of scholars at the famous museum and developed the nucleus of the great library. The Ptolemies founded or refurbished several cities in Palestine and Transjordan giving them Greek names and often endowing them with Greek features. Examples included Acco renamed Ptolemais, Bethshan now termed Scythopolis, and ancient Rabboth-Ammon refounded as Philadelphia.

Ptolemaic rule directly impacted Jews both inside and outside of Palestine. During the campaigns to secure Palestine for Egypt, Ptolemy I transported large numbers of Jews from Palestine to Alexandria for settlement. This was the begin-

The forecourt of Ptolemy IX in the temple of Horus, the Egyptian falcon-god, at Edfu in Upper Egypt.

ning of a large and influential Jewish community that prospered by maintaining good relations with the Ptolemies, frequently serving as mercenaries and merchants. Soon Alexandria became a major center of world Jewry. The Alexandrian Jews imbibed Hellenism much more deeply than their counterparts in Judea as evidenced by the need to translate the OT writings into Greek. This translation, known as the Septuagint, probably was begun in the reign of Ptolemy II but was not completed until about 100 B.C.

The Ptolemies treated Judea as a temple state given over by the king in trust to the high priest at Jerusalem. Authority in religious and most civil matters was granted the high priest in lieu of a yearly tax.

During the reign of Ptolemy II the first of five wars with the Seleucids over possession of Pales-

A wall relief showing Ptolemy I Soter (pictured twice) making offerings.

line broke out. Egypt successfully resisted the Seleucid challenge under the first three Ptolemaic rulers. However Ptolemaic power began to wane under Ptolemy IV Philopator (221–204 B.C.), a notorious womanizer. In 200 B.C. Antiochus III defeated the Egyptian army at Banyas (later Caesarea Philippi) and seized control of Palestine. Subsequently the Ptolemaic kingdom declined and increasingly came under the influence of Rome. Cleopatra VII was the last Ptolemaic ruler prior to the annexation of Egypt to Rome in 30 B.C. See *Egypt; Intertestamental History and Literature.*   *Thomas V. Brisco*

PUA (Pū´ à) (KJV, REB, Num. 26:23) See *Puvah.*

PUAH (Pū´ ah) **1.** Personal name meaning "girl." Hebrew midwife who disobeyed Pharaoh's orders to kill male Hebrew infants (Exod. 1:15). **2.** Personal name meaning "red dye." Father of the judge Tola (Judg. 10:1) and an alternate form of Puvah (1 Chron. 7:1).

PUBLICAN Political office created by the Romans to help collect taxes in the provinces. Actually, the title "tax collector" is more correct than the older term "publican" in referring to the lowest rank in the structure. Zacchaeus is called a "chief tax collector" (Luke 19:2 HCSB), probably indicating one who contracted with the government to collect taxes, and who in turn hired others to do the actual work. In NT times people bid for the job of chief tax collector and then exacted the tax plus a profit from the citizens. Most of the offices were filled by Romans, although some natives got the bids. Publicans were held in the lowest esteem because of their excessive profits, being placed in the same category as harlots (Matt. 21:32). Jesus was accused of eating with and befriending them (Matt. 9:11).

PUBLIUS (Pŭb´ lĭ ŭs) Personal name meaning "pertaining to the people." The highest official, either Roman or local, on Malta (Acts 28:7-8).

PUDENS (Pū´ dĕnz) Personal name meaning "modest." Roman Christian who greeted Timothy (2 Tim. 4:21). This Pudens is sometimes

identified with the friend of the Roman poet Martial.

PUHITES (Pū´ hĭts) (KJV) See *Puthites.*

PUITES (Pū´ ĭts) (NIV) See *Punites.*

PUL (Pŭl) **1.** Alternate name of the Assyrian king Tiglath-Pileser III (2 Kings 15:19; 1 Chron. 5:26). The name is perhaps a contraction of Pileser. See *Assyria.* **2.** The Hebrew Pul in Isa. 66:19 is likely a textual corruption of Put.

PULPIT KJV, RSV term for a raised platform (NRSV, REB, NIV, TEV) on which a speaker stood (Neh. 8:4); not a lectern or high reading desk behind which a reader stands.

PULSE General term for peas, beans, and lentils (Dan. 1:12,16). Modern translations read "vegetables." The Hebrew is literally "things which have been sown," a designation including grains in addition to vegetables.

PUNITES (Pū nīts) Descendants of Puvah (Num. 26:23). Some manuscripts read "Puvanites" or "Puvites."

PUNON (Pū´ nŏn) Place-name meaning "ore pit." Edomite mining center located at the junction of the Wadi el-Gheweil and Wadi esh-Sheqer on the east side of the Arabah about 25 miles south of the Dead Sea. The site was first occupied about 2200 B.C. The second occupation began shortly before the Israelites encamped there about 1200 B.C. (Num. 33:42-43). The site was perhaps home to descendants of the clan chief Pinon (Gen. 36:41). The site is identified with modern Feinan. Two ancient smelting sites, Khirbet en-Nahas and Khirbet Nqeib Aseimer, lie to the north-northeast.

PUR (Pŭr) or **PURIM** (Pū´ rĭm) See *Festivals.*

PURAH (Pū´ rah) Personal name meaning "beauty" or nickname meaning "metal container." Gideon's servant (Judg. 7:10-11). KJV used the form Phurah.

PURGATORY Centuries-old dogma of the Roman Catholic Church. The term itself is derived from the Latin *purgare*, which means "to cleanse" or "to purify." Several early Christian writers endorse the idea of purgatory, or prayers for the dead (which may not necessarily imply purgatory) to one degree or another (Origen, Cyprian, Ambrose, Tertullian, Jerome, and Augustine). The Council of Lyons in 1274 articulated the doctrine. The Council of Florence in 1439 defined it as both penal and purificatory in nature. In 1563 the Council of Trent recognized the validity of suffrages performed for the benefit of those in purgatory.

According to Roman Catholicism, souls of Christians who die burdened by venial or remitted mortal sins are translated to purgatory, where they undergo a process of cleansing for those sins. It is unclear whether purgatory is a place or a state. The sufferings of those in purgatory vary tremendously in intensity and duration, depending upon the degree to which the baptized but not fully cleansed Christian has sinned. Most agree that those in purgatory are purged by fire, but there is no consensus as to whether the fire is literal or figurative. Regardless of the intensity or duration of one's suffering, purgatory is temporary in nature, until the general resurrection of the dead, although individuals may be delivered from purgatory before then. This is accomplished through the actions of living Christians who perform good works on behalf of the dead. Such works include the Mass, prayers (for the dead), and the giving of alms. Those who are in a state of perfect grace will not need to go to purgatory—they will go immediately to heaven. Others will go immediately to hell. But the majority of the just will spend some time in purgatory, being purified. Related to purgatory there are two additional specialized abodes for the dead. *Limbus infantium* is reserved for infants who die before baptism. While they do not suffer in purgatory, they are forever denied the beatific vision. Old Testament saints were consigned to *Limbus patrum* prior to Christ's atoning work, after which they were translated to heaven.

Roman Catholics appeal to Matt. 12:32; 1 Pet. 3:18-20; 4:6; and 1 Cor. 3:15 for biblical support of the dogma. They also appeal to 2 Maccabees 12:38-45 in the OT Apocrypha for support. None of these texts explicitly articulates a doctrine of Purgatory; the doctrine is formed from extrabiblical tradition.   *Robert Stewart*

PURGE To cleanse from impurity, frequently in the figurative sense of cleansing from evil

(Deut. 13:5), guilt (Deut. 19:13), idolatrous worship (2 Chron. 34:3), and sin (Ps. 51:7). See *Clean, Cleanness.*

PURITY, PURIFICATION State of being or process of becoming free of inferior elements or ritual uncleanness. A basic goal of religion is to attain purity before the deity.

Old Testament *Flawless* The primary Hebrew root word for pure (*tahar*) often refers to pure or flawless gold (1 Kings 10:21; Job 28:19; Ps. 12:6). *Tahar* and other Hebrew words for "pure" are used to describe other objects such as salt (Exod. 30:35), oil (Exod. 27:20), and incense (Exod. 37:29). Thus, a basic OT meaning is that of "refined, purified, without flaw, perfect, clean" (cp. Lam. 4:7).

Ritual Purity To be ritually pure means to be free of some flaw or uncleanness which would bar one from contact with holy objects or places, especially from contact with the holy presence of God in worship. God is the ideal of purity, and those who are to come in contact with God's presence are also to be pure. Hab. 1:13 indicates that God's eyes are too pure to look upon evil.

The altar for sacrifice was purified so that it would be prepared for worship (Lev. 8:15; Ezek. 43:26). The objects of gold used in the tabernacle and temple were also pure in this sense; this would be true of the incense in Exod. 37:29. The Levites were to purify themselves for service in the tabernacle (Num. 8:21). When that which was unclean or impure came into contact with that which was holy, danger resulted and could even lead to death. This is probably the background for the preparation made for the theophany, a manifestation of God's presence, in Exod. 19 and for the death of Uzzah when he was unprepared (not purified) to touch the ark of the covenant, a most holy object (2 Sam. 6:1-11). Malachi 1:11-12 contrasts the pure offerings of Gentiles with blemished offerings given by God's people; such a state necessitated purification (Mal. 3:3-4).

Purity qualified one to participate in worship, an activity central to the life of ancient Israel. Breaking that purity was a serious matter. Ritual impurity came as a result of bodily emissions (Lev. 15) by way of disease or menstrual flow or discharge of semen. This chapter also shows that such impurity could be spread by contact, for anything coming into contact with the unclean person had to be purified. Leviticus 12 also discusses impurity associated with childbirth, probably because of the discharge of blood. Blood related to the mysterious power of life, and any loss of blood called for purification. Ritual impurity also came as a result of contact with a corpse since death was an enemy of God (Num. 19). Participation in war could thus cause impurity. Also impurity was brought on by contact with foreign gods. This was probably the background of the need for purification when the people returned from exile in Babylon. The priests and Levites purified themselves first and then the people and then the city gates and wall (Isa. 52:11; Ezra 6:20; Neh. 12:30). This also prepared them for worship.

Ethical Purity Thought and behavior befitting the people of God are pure (Pss. 24:4; 73:1; Prov. 15:26; 22:11; 30:12). Such purity of thought is to result in conduct which is appropriate for people (Ps. 119:9; Prov. 16:2; 20:9,11; 21:8). Notice also the pure prayer of Job 16:17.

Since Pss. 15 and 24 speak of qualifications for worship in terms of ethical purity, it is important not to distinguish sharply between ritual and ethical purity in the OT. God expects ethical purity, and sin results in uncleanness. Thus sin and ritual uncleanness stand together in the OT as unacceptable to the Lord. Their counterparts—ethical and ritual purity—also stand together.

Purification Rituals Since the OT assumes that the people would encounter sin and uncleanness, it provides a way to return to cleanness.

The purification ritual usually started with a waiting period beginning when the cause of the impurity stopped. Less serious causes brought a waiting period of one day. Contact with a corpse (Num. 19:11,14), birth of a male child (Lev. 12:2), the cure of leprosy (Lev. 14:8-9), and other discharges (Lev. 15:13,19,28) brought about a waiting period of seven days. The waiting period after the birth of a girl was 14 days (Lev. 12:5). The same period applied to the quarantine of a suspected leper (Lev. 13:4-6).

A cleansing agent was required: water, blood, or fire (Num. 31:23). Water, the most common purifying agent, symbolized cleansing and was used in the rituals related to a waiting period. The person was to wash the clothes and bathe the body (Lev. 15:7). Blood was used to cleanse the altar and the holy place (Lev. 16:14-

19). It was mixed with other ingredients for cleansing from leprosy (Lev. 14) and contact with the dead (Num. 19).

The final element of the ritual of purification is sacrifice. Purification from discharges required two pigeons or turtledoves, one for a sin offering and one for a burnt offering (Lev. 15:14-15,29-30). A lamb and pigeon or turtledove were offered after childbirth (Lev. 12:6). Sacrifice in the purification ritual for lepers was quite complicated, indicating the seriousness of leprosy as a cause of impurity (Lev. 14). The priest also touched the person's extremities with blood from the offering and with oil, cleansing and life-renewing agents. The poor were allowed to substitute less valuable animals for use in their sacrifices.

New Testament Most NT uses of words for purity relate to cleanness of some type. Old Testament meanings are often reflected. Perfection is the meaning in Mark 14:3; this is mixed with religious purity in Heb. 10:22; 1 John 3:3.

Ethical purity dominates in the NT. The person who is in right relationship with God is to live a life of purity (2 Tim. 2:21-22; Titus 1:15 and references to a pure heart—Matt. 5:8; 1 Tim. 1:5; Heb. 9:14; James 4:8; 1 Pet. 1:22). Purity is also listed among virtues (2 Cor. 6:6; Phil. 4:8; 1 Tim. 4:12; cp. Mark 7:15).

Purification through sacrifice is also mentioned in the NT and applied to the death of Christ, a purification which does not need repeating and thus is on a higher level than OT sacrifices (Heb. 9:13-14). The sacrifice of Christ brings purification; Christ cleansed as a part of the work of the high priest, and His blood cleanses from sin (1 John 1:7). See *Atonement; Clean, Cleanness; Ethics; Holiness; Levite; Priest; Sacrifice.*   *W. H. Bellinger, Jr.*

PURLOIN KJV term meaning "to misappropriate" (Titus 2:10). Modern translations use "pilfer" or "steal." See *Pilfer.*

PURPLE See *Blue; Colors.*

PURPLE GARNET REB designation of a precious stone (Exod. 28:18; 39:11) which other translations identify as an emerald or turquoise. See *Minerals and Metals.*

PURSE KJV translation of a Greek term for a belt, girdle, or waistband (Matt. 10:9; Mark 6:8). Travelers could tuck the loose ends of their garments into such a belt to allow freer movement. The folds of such waistbands were frequently used for storing money. Jesus encouraged His disciples to trust God and depend on the generosity of others as they shared the gospel. See *Girdle*.

PURSLANE Fleshy-leafed, trailing plant used as a potherb or in salads, which the RSV of Job 6:6 used as an illustration of tasteless food. Other translations follow the Targum in reading "white of an egg" (KJV, NASB, NIV) or find reference to another plant, the mallow (NRSV, REB).

PUT (Pŭt) Personal name and a geographic designation, perhaps derived from the Egyptian *pdty* meaning "foreign bowman." **1.** Son of Ham (Gen. 10:6; 1 Chron. 1:8) in "Table of Nations" and thus ancestor of inhabitants of Put. **2.** Designation for a region of Africa bordering Egypt (Jer. 46:9; Ezek. 27:10; 30:5; 38:5; Nah. 3:9; and, by emendation, Isa. 66:19). Put is generally identified with Libya, perhaps with the city of Cyrene. All references to the men of Put involve mercenaries, that is, soldiers for hire.

PUTHITES (Pū´ thīts) Family of Judahites (1 Chron. 2:53; KJV, Puhites).

PUTIEL (Pū´ tĭ ĕl) Personal name meaning "he whom God gives" or "afflicted by God." Father-in-law of the priest Eleazar (Exod. 6:25).

PUVAH (Pū´ vah) Personal name spelled differently in Hebrew text and in various manuscripts and versions; thus rendered differently by translators. NASB (Num. 26:23) and NRSV (Gen. 46:13; Num. 26:23) form of the name of a son of Issachar. Other renderings include: Pua (KJV, REB); Puah (NIV, TEV); and Phuvah (KJV).

PUVVAH (Pūv vah) (NASB, Gen. 46:13) See *Puvah*.

PYGARG KJV term for a white-rumped antelope (Deut. 14:5). Most modern translations identify the underlying Hebrew term with the ibex. The REB has "white-rumped deer." See *Antelope; Deer; Ibex*.

PYRAMIDS Four-sided structures have captivated visitors to Egypt for centuries. The pres-

The smallest of the three pyramids at Giza, built by Mycerinus (Menkaure).

A large stone quarry in the area of Baalbak (in modern Lebanon) on the Orontes River.

ent name apparently originated with some ancient Greek tourists who jokingly called the monuments "wheat cakes." This may describe the first "step pyramid," built by Djoser (Zoser) at Saqqara, but it was an injustice to those erected at Giza which represent one of the Seven Wonders of the World. The fourth dynasty (about 2520–2480 B.C.)

reflected the zenith of pyramid construction.

The best known of these artificial mountains rises majestically on the edge of the Nile near Cairo (at Giza). The "Great Pyramid" stands 481 feet high with a base of 755 feet. This was constructed by Cheops (Khufu) about 2580 B.C. His son, Chephren (Khafre), and grandson, Mycerinus (Menkaure), followed in their father's

The step-pyramid of King Djoser (Zoser) of the Third Dynasty located at Saqqara.

The famous Sphinx of Giza, built by Chephren (Khafre), measures 240 feet from front to back.

footsteps literally building in his shadow. Although not as grand, pyramids were constructed at various other places along the Nile including the distinctive "Bent Pyramid" at Dashur.

The purpose of these edifices was to entomb and immortalize the rulers. They actually act as focal points for a whole complex of buildings including a funerary temple, a causeway to a valley building near the Nile, and buried barges to carry the deceased to their eternal abode. They were not meant to be, however, astro-observatories or generators of mystical power. See *Archaeology and Biblical Study; Egypt.*

Gary C. Huckabay

PYRE Pile of material to be burned, especially that used in burning a body as part of funeral rites (Isa. 30:33 NASB, NRSV; pile, KJV; fire pit, NIV, REB). God's preparation of a funeral pyre for the Assyrian king highlights the certainty of God's judgment.

PYRRHUS (Pĭr´ ŭs) Personal name meaning "fiery red." Father of Paul's companion Sopater (Acts 20:4).

PYTHON 1. Large constricting snake. **2.** A spirit of divination (*python*, Gk., Acts 16:16). The word "Python" is not used in the Bible, but the Greek word does occur. Greeks believed the Python was first the dragon guarding the oracle at Delphi, later slain by Apollo. The dragon's spirit influenced the shrine's priestess who gave revelations. Those who possessed the diviner's or soothsayer's spirit (ventriloquists) exhibited what many called demon possession as noted in Mark 1:23-26. Paul encountered this in Acts 16:16-26 where he cast the spirit out of a slave girl. See *Divination and Magic.*

Q Abbreviation of the German *Quelle*, meaning "source," used to designate the hypothetical common source of over 200 verses found in Matthew and Luke but not in Mark. According to the two-document hypothesis, Matthew and Luke inserted sayings of Jesus stemming from Q into Mark's narrative framework of the Jesus story (cp. Luke 1:1 for evidence of previous sources). Verbatim agreements in the double tradition (material shared by Matthew and Luke but not Mark), common sequence of sayings within blocks of materials, and doublets (repetition) of sayings found but once in Mark point to the common source. A common version of the Q hypothesis regards Q as written in Greek in Palestine, perhaps Caesarea, between A.D. 50–60. Luke is held to have preserved the overall order of the Q sayings better, while Matthew felt free to rearrange much of the shared material to form his five major discourses. Some scholars are so confident in their ability to decipher Q that they have written commentaries and theologies of the alleged source. Others prefer to think of Q as an "oral" source. Still others remove any need for a common source for the double tradition by arguing for the priority of Matthew. See *Harmony of the Gospels.*

QOHELETH (kō hěl´ ěth) See *Koheleth.*

QUAIL The Hebrew term translated "quail" in the OT is found only in connection with God's provision of food for Israel in the wilderness (Exod. 16:13; Num. 11:31-32; Ps. 105:40).

The quails mentioned in the OT differ from the North American bobwhite quails. Besides being migratory, the quails of the Bible are mottled brown in color and are smaller than the bobwhite quails. The quails mentioned in the OT have short wings and weak powers of flight.

Janice Meier

QUARRY Area of land where stones were extracted for building various objects and buildings. Good stone lay close to the surface. In most places it was broken out of its bed by cracking the stones along lines of cleavage. Cutting these stones was obviously a dangerous business (Eccles. 10:9). KJV refers to quarries in Judg. 3:19–26. The Hebrew term *pesalim* usually refers to images of gods. Thus most modern translations read "idols" or "sculpted stones," the latter possibly referring to Joshua's stones of commemoration (Josh. 4). Modern translations use "quarry" in 1 Kings 6:7 to make explicit the intention of the more literal KJV reading. See *Masons*.

QUARTERMASTER Officer charged with receipt and distribution of rations and supplies (Jer. 51:59 NASB, NRSV, REB). Quartermaster reflects the Hebrew "tribute-prince." The KJV reading "quiet prince" reflects a different vocalization of the Masoretic text. The NIV reading "staff-officer" likely reflects a slight change in the consonantal text to read "prince of the camp." See *Prince*.

QUARTUS (kwär´ tŭs) Latin personal name meaning "fourth." Christian, most likely from Corinth, who sent greetings to the Roman church through Paul (Rom. 16:23). Quartus and Tertius, whose name means "third" (Rom. 16:22), were possibly the third and fourth sons of the same family.

QUATERNION (kwə tĕr´ nĭ ŏn) KJV term for a squad composed of four soldiers (Acts 12:4; cp. John 19:23). By translating the underlying Greek as simply "squad," NASB and RSV failed to convey the size of the guard.

QUEEN Wife or widow of a monarch and the female monarch reigning in her own right.

Queen mother refers to the mother of a reigning monarch. Female regents were known in the ancient Near East (1 Kings 10:1-13, the queen of Sheba; Acts 8:27, the Ethiopian Candace). No queen ruled Israel or Judah in her own right, though Athaliah usurped power (2 Kings 11:1-3). The wives of monarchs varied in their influence. Since marriages often sealed political alliances (2 Sam. 3:3; 1 Kings 3:1; 16:31; 2 Kings 8:25-27), daughters of more powerful allies such as the Egyptian pharaoh or king of Tyre enjoyed special privileges (1 Kings 7:8) and influence (1 Kings 16:32-33; 18:19; 21:7-14). The mother of the designated heir also enjoyed special status. Nathan enlisted Bathsheba rather than Solomon in his plan to have Solomon confirmed as king (1 Kings 1:11-40). Queen mother was an official position in Israel and Judah. Great care was taken in preserving the names of the queen mothers (1 Kings 14:21; 15:2,13; 22:42; 2 Kings 8:26). Asa's removal of his mother from the office for idolatry (1 Kings 15:13) points to its official character.

P
Q

Famous bust of Queen Nefertiti (from about 1356 B.C.), wife of Pharaoh Akhenaton of Egypt.

On her son's death Athaliah murdered her own grandsons, the legitimate heirs, in order to retain the power she had enjoyed as queen mother (2 Kings 11:1-2). The queen mother likely served as a trusted counsel for her son (Prov. 31:1). As queen mother, Jezebel continued as a negative force after the death of Ahab (1 Kings 22:52; 2 Kings 3:2,13; 9:22).

QUEEN OF HEAVEN Goddess that women in Judah worshiped to ensure fertility and material stability (Jer. 7:18; 44:17). Forms of worship included making cakes (possibly in her image as in molds found at Mari), offering drink offerings, and burning incense (Jer. 44:25). Exactly which goddess was worshiped is not certain. The words could be translated "stars of heaven" or "heavenly host." However, "queen of heaven" appears to be the best rendering. The major influence could have been Ishtar, the Mesopotamian goddess called there the "queen of heaven" (imported to Israel by Manasseh), or the Canaanite Ashtarte. Archaeologists have uncovered many images of nude goddesses from Israelite sites, showing why Jeremiah protested against such worship.

QUEEN OF SHEBA See *Sabean.*

QUICK, QUICKEN KJV terms meaning "living, alive" and "make alive, revive, refresh" (Pss. 55:15; 119:25; John 5:21; Acts 10:42).

QUICKSANDS KJV translation of the Greek *surtis* meaning "sandbar" (Acts 27:17). Modern translations take *surtis* as a proper name for the great sandbars off the west coast of Cyrene (modern Libya). NIV and REB paraphrase "sandbars of Syrtis" which conveys the sense. See *Syrtis.*

QUILT NASB translation of a Hebrew term in 1 Sam. 19:13,16. Other possible translations include net (NRSV), pillow (KJV, RSV), and rug (REB).

QUIRINIUS (Kwĭ rĭn´ ĭ ŭs) Latin proper name which the KJV transliterated as Cyrenius. Modern versions prefer the Latin spelling. See *Cyrenius.*

QUIVER Leather case, hung over one's shoulder, for carrying arrows. See *Arms and Armor.*

Excavations at the site of the Qumran community on the northwestern edge of the Dead Sea.

QUMRAN (Qŭm´ răn) Archeological site near the caves where Dead Sea Scrolls were discovered and center of Jewish Essene community.

Location The ruins called Khirbet Qumran are located eight miles south of Jericho and three-fourths of a mile west of the northwestern edge of the Dead Sea. After the first discovery of the Dead Sea Scrolls in 1947, Qumran became the focus of archaeological investigation and was thoroughly excavated between 1953 and 1956. Among the areas excavated (a cemetery, extensive water system, refectory, kitchen, and prayer and study rooms), a room was discovered complete with the ruins of plaster benches and inkwells from the Roman period demonstrating that this was probably the "scriptorium" where the scrolls were copied.

Qumran Community The Qumran site was inhabited from about 130 B.C. to A.D. 70 by a sect so similar in nature, theology, and practice to a Jewish sect known as Essenes that most scholars believe it was one variety of this sect. Ritual baptism, monastic life, and manual labor characterized the life of the Qumran Essenes. Although they allowed marriage, they shunned any contact with the outside world. Their main concern in life was complete and strict devotion to God. They expressed this through their scribal activity, the copying and studying of Scripture. In A.D. 70, with the Roman army posing a major threat to their existence, the Essenes of Qumran made a hasty exit, hiding their manuscripts in the surrounding caves as they left.

Scrolls and Their Value In 1947 a young Bedouin shepherd boy found an ancient scroll in a cave on the face of one of the sandstone cliffs in the Qumran area. In the following weeks and

A close-up view of one of the caves in which the Essenes hid their sacred scrolls from the Romans.

Ritual bath used for purification rites for the sect members at the site of the Qumran community.

The limestone cliffs of the Qumran region showing the caves in which the Dead Sea Scrolls were discovered.

months a careful search of the area yielded 40,000 fragments of ancient manuscripts from 11 caves. Some 800 manuscripts are represented, of which 170 are fragments of OT books (including manuscripts of each OT book except Esther). The most important may be a nearly complete text of Isaiah. The rest of the scrolls include commentaries on Habakkuk and Micah, Jewish extrabiblical documents from the inter-biblical and NT time periods, and extrabiblical writings specifically related to the community at Qumran such as the *Genesis Apocryphon, Temple Scroll,* and *Manual of Discipline.* Scrolls were found in Hebrew, Aramaic, and Greek, and the scroll material included both parchment and papyrus. (Two copper scrolls were also discovered.) While the content of many of the scrolls extends to a much earlier date, the scrolls themselves have been dated to about 200 B.C. to A.D. 70.

The value of the Dead Sea Scrolls to biblical studies is twofold. First, they provide OT Hebrew manuscripts that are one thousand years older than any other extant OT manuscripts. Before 1947 the earliest Hebrew OT manuscripts known to exist dated to the late ninth century A.D. With the discovery of the Dead Sea Scrolls, biblical scholarship now has access to OT manuscripts dating from about 200–100 B.C. The significance of this is heightened by the fact that these are copies, which presuppose originals, thus offering another verification of an early date for the actual writing of the OT. Second, the scrolls provide a glimpse into the Jewish theological and cultural milieu of the time of Christ and also provide examples of verbal expressions contemporary with the NT time period. See *Dead Sea Scrolls; Essenes.*

Marsha A. Ellis Smith

QUOTATIONS IN THE NEW TESTAMENT See *Old Testament Quotations in the New Testament.*

R

Colossal statue of Ramses the Great at Karnak in Egypt.

RAAMA or **RAAMAH** (Rā´ à m̀a) Son of Cush (Gen. 10:7) and ancestor of Sheba and Dedan. Arab tribes occupying southwest and west-central Arabia (1 Chron. 1:9). Raamah and Sheba were trading partners of Tyre (Ezek. 27:22). Raama is likely modern Negran in Yemen, though the earliest Greek translation identified Raamah with Regmah on the Persian Gulf.

RAAMIAH (Rā à mī´ ah) Returning exile (Neh. 7:7). Variant form of Reelaiah (Ezra 2:2).

RAAMSES (Rā ăm´ sēz) Alternate form of place-name "Rameses" (Exod. 1:11).

RAB-MAG (Răb´-măg) Title of the Babylonian official Nergal sharezer (Jer. 39:3,13). The name derives from the Akkadian *rab mugi*. The first element (*rab*) means "chief." Unfortunately the meaning of the second element is unknown. If associated with the root for "magi," the Rab-mag was likely the officer in charge of divination (cp. Ezek. 21:21).

RABBAH (Răb´ bah) Place-name meaning "greatness." **1.** Village near Jerusalem (Josh. 15:60) assigned to tribe of Judah but apparently in territory of Benjamin. Its location is uncertain. **2.** Capital of Ammon that Moses apparently did not conquer (Deut. 3:11; Josh. 13:25), located about 23 miles east of the Jordan River. Inhabited in prehistoric times and again before 1500 B.C., the city became a fortified settlement early in its history. David besieged the city (2 Sam. 11:1) and captured it (12:28-29). It remained under Israelite control throughout the period of the united monarchy but regained its independence shortly after the Israelite division. Rabbah was destroyed during the Babylonian sweep through the area (590–580 B.C.) and not rebuilt for several hundred years. Rabbah was renamed Philadelphia by the Hellenists and later became Amman, the modern capital of Jordan. See *Philadelphia*.

RABBATH (Răb´ bàth) (KJV, Deut. 3:11; Ezek. 21:20) See *Rabbah*.

RABBI (Răb´ bī) Title meaning "my master," applied to teachers and others of an exalted and revered position. During the NT period the term "rabbi" came to be more narrowly applied to one learned in the law of Moses, without signifying an official office. In the NT the title "rabbi" is used in only three of the Gospels. In Matt. 23:7-8 scribes generally are addressed. In John 3:26 John the Baptist is called "Rabbi" by his disciples. In all other occurrences "rabbi" and an alternate form "rabboni" apply to Jesus in direct address (Mark 9:5; 11:21; Mark 14:45, John 1:49; 3:2; 4:31; 6:25; 9:2; 11:8; 20:16).

Luke never used the term "rabbi" but the word *epistates*, the equivalent of "school-master," a term more meaningful to his predominantly Greek readers (Luke 17:13). A unique relationship existed between Jesus and His disciples, compared to the typical rabbi and his pupils. They were forbidden to call one another "rabbi" (Matt. 23:8), and in Matthew, particularly, Jesus' disciples call Him "Lord" (*Kurie*). For Matthew Jesus was not just a teacher to His followers; He was their Lord.   *Robert Stagg*

RABBIT (*Oractolagus cuniculus*) Small, long-eared furry mammal related to the hare but differing in giving birth to naked young. NASB, NIV, and TEV use "rabbit" for an unclean animal in Lev. 11:6; Deut. 14:7 where other English translations use "hare." See *Hare*.

RABBITH (Răb´ bĭth) Unidentified site in territory of Issachar (Josh. 19:20). Rabbith is possibly a corruption of Daberath, a site included in other lists of Issachar's territory (Josh. 21:28; 1 Chron. 6:72) but missing in Josh. 19.

RABBONI (Răb bō´ nī) An Aramaic honorary title, and variant spelling of "rabbi," meaning "teacher" that was used by blind Bartimaeus and Mary Magdalene to address Jesus (Mark 10:51; John 20:16). The term "Rabboni" possibly connotes heightened emphasis or greater honor than the almost synonymous expression "rabbi." "Rabboni" is a more personal term, signifying a relationship between the teacher and the one speaking to the teacher. The force of the term is, "My teacher," and it was used by Mary Magdalene to address Jesus after the resurrection (John 20:16). See *Rabbi*.

Robert L. Plummer and Charles W. Draper

RABSARIS (Răb´ sȧ rĭs) Assyrian court position with strong military and diplomatic powers. The Hebrew *saris* means "eunuch," but the term here is a transliteration of Akkadian and should not be taken literally. The title literally means "he who stands by the king." The OT records that the rabsaris was sent on two occasions to deal with the Israelite kings (2 Kings 18:17; Jer. 39:3). Hezekiah and Zedekiah each rebelled against the Assyrian rule and withheld tribute payment. The rabsaris was among the ambassadors who called on the kings to demand payment. See *Eunuch.*

RABSHAKEH (Răb´ shȧ kə) Assyrian title, literally, "chief cupbearer." The position probably began as a mere butler but developed into a highly influential post by the time of its mention in the Bible. The official who dealt with Hezekiah spoke for the Assyrian king much as an ambassador would. He urged the people of Jerusalem to make peace with Assyria rather than believing King Hezekiah that God would protect Judah (2 Kings 18:17-32).

Mike Mitchell

RACA (Ra´ cȧ) Word of reproach, meaning "empty" or "ignorant," that the Hebrew writers borrowed from the Aramaic language. Jesus used it in Matt. 5:22 as a strong term of derision, second only to "fool." He placed it in the context of anger and strongly condemned one who would use it of another person.

RACAL (Rā´ cal) Unidentified site in southern Judah (1 Sam. 30:29). Most commentators follow the reading of the earliest Greek translation, "Carmel," and regard Racal as a textual corruption.

RACHAB (Rā´ kăb) (KJV, Matt. 1:5) See *Rahab.*

RACHAL (Ra´ kȧl) (KJV, REB, 1 Sam. 30:29) See *Racal.*

RACHEL (Rā´ chĕl) Personal name meaning "ewe." Younger daughter of Laban, the second wife and cousin of Jacob, and the mother of Joseph and Benjamin. In flight from his brother Esau, Jacob met Rachel when she

The traditional location of Rachel's tomb in Bethlehem.

brought the sheep to water. She immediately became the object of his attention. See *Jacob.*

Two OT passages outside Genesis mention Rachel. Ruth 4:11 calls her one who built up the house of Israel. Jeremiah 31:15 refers to her weeping over children being taken in exile. In the NT Matthew (2:18) cited Jeremiah's reference of weeping in connection with Herod's order to kill male children under two.

RACIAL TENSION Unrest and division among people caused by differing racial origins. Personal identity in the ancient world was not primarily based on race but on family, tribal, city, national, ethnic, or religious ties.

Shepherds (who were typically Semitic) were an abomination to the (non-Semitic) Egyptians (Gen. 46:34). When the Jews lived outside Palestine, racial differences became more significant (Esther 3:1-6; cp. Luke 4:25-28). Paul reports an accepted Greek maxim stigmatizing the Cretans as always being "liars, evil beasts, slow bellies" (Titus 1:12-13; "lazy gluttons" NIV). Because there is no racial distinction in Christ (Gal. 3:28-29; Eph. 2:19), the church was able to spread rapidly to the Gentile world to encompass persons of all races. Divisions and prejudice based on race are unacceptable for Christians.

Paul H. Wright

RADDAI (Răd´ dā ī) Personal name meaning "Yahweh rules." Son of Jesse and brother of David (1 Chron. 2:14).

RAFT King Hiram's means of transporting timber for the temple by lashing logs together and floating them down the coast from Tyre to

Joppa (1 Kings 5:9; 2 Chron. 2:16). See *Ships, Sailors, and Navigation.*

RAGAU (Rā´ gau) (KJV, Luke 3:35) See *Reu.*

RAGUEL (Rȧ gū´ĕl) (KJV, Num. 10:29) See *Reuel.*

RAHAB (Rā´ hăb) Name meaning "arrogant, raging, turbulent, afflicter." **1.** Primeval sea monster representing the forces of chaos that God overcame in creation (Job 9:13; 26:12; Ps. 89:10; Isa. 51:9; cp. Ps. 74:12-17). **2.** Symbolic name for Egypt (Ps. 87:4). Isaiah 30:7 includes a compound name Rahab-hem-shebeth. Translations vary: "Rahab who sits still" (NRSV); "Rahab who has been extermi-nated" (NASB); "Rahab the Do-Nothing" (NIV); "Rahab the Subdued" (REB). **3.** The plural appears in Ps. 40:4 for the proud, arro-gant enemies. **4.** Personal name meaning "broad." Harlot in Jericho who hid two Hebrew spies that Joshua sent there to deter-mine the strength of the city (Josh. 2:1). When the king of Jericho learned of the spies' pres-ence, he sent men to arrest them. Rahab out-smarted the king and hid the men on her roof, sending the arresting officers on a false chase toward the Jordan River. In return for her help Joshua spared her and her clan when the Hebrews destroyed Jericho (Josh. 6:17-25). Matthew named Rahab as Boaz's mother (1:5) in his genealogy of Christ, making her one of the Lord's ancestors. Some interpreters think, however, that the Rahab in Matthew was a dif-ferent woman. Hebrews 11:31 lists Rahab among the heroes of faith.

RAHAM (Rā´ hăm) Personal name meaning "mercy, love." Descendant of Judah (1 Chron. 2:44).

RAHEL (Rā hĕl) (KJV, Jer. 31:15) See *Rachel.*

RAIL KJV term meaning "revile," "deride," "cast contempt upon," or "scold using harsh and abusive language" (1 Sam. 25:14; 2 Chron. 32:17; Mark 15:29; Luke 23:39).

RAIMENT See *Cloth, Clothing.*

RAIN Moisture from heaven providing nour-ishment for plant and animal life. Palestine was a land dependent upon the yearly rains to ensure an abundant harvest and an ample food supply for the coming year. Thus, the presence or absence of rain became a symbol of God's continued blessing or displeasure with the land and its inhabitants. Rain fell in two sea-sons: the early rains during October and November, and the later rains in February and March (James 5:7). Rarely did rain of any sig-nificance fall outside these two periods. West-erly winds from the Mediterranean Sea brought wet storms during the winter, most of the rain falling along the coastal plain, in the north, and in the central hills. Lower eleva-tions, the Jordan Valley, and the south received less rain during the year. Long droughts often were followed by flash floods that quickly filled the seasonal creeks and riverbeds. The runoff was captured in cisterns for drinking water. In the Negev farmers plowed during the rains to allow the fine desert dust to absorb the little rain that was available. The coming of the rain was viewed as God's continued pleasure with His people. The lack of rain in spring proclaimed His judg-ment for sin and disobedience. The Canaan-ites worshiped Baal as the god of rain and thunder, and sexual orgies were enacted to provoke his presence in the land.

RAINBOW Caused by the reflection and refraction of sunlight by droplets of rain, a rainbow often appears after the passing of thunderstorms, marking its end. The bow is colored by the division of sunlight into its pri-mary colors. The rainbow served to remind Israel and her God of His covenant with Noah never again to destroy the earth by flooding (Gen. 9:8-17). The Mesopotamian epic of Gil-gamesh, another ancient flood account, does not include the sign of the rainbow. The rain-bow and its beauty became a symbol of the majesty and beauty of God. While having a vision, Ezekiel compared the brightness of the glory of God with the colors of the rainbow (1:28). Habakkuk also used the bow to describe the scene of God's final deliverance of His people (3:9). The book of Revelation records John's vision of the throne of Christ as surrounded by "a rainbow that looked like an emerald" (4:3 HCSB). Later Revelation 10:1 pictures a descending angel with the rainbow shining upon his head and having a face as the sun.

RAISIN CAKES Food prepared by pressing dried grapes together. David gave raisin cakes ("flagon," KJV) to those who accompanied the ark to Jerusalem (2 Sam. 6:19; 1 Chron. 16:3 NRSV). Hosea 3:1 (NRSV) links raisin cakes with the worship of pagan deities (cp. Jer. 7:18).

RAKEM (Rā´ kĕm) Personal name meaning "variegated, multicolored." Grandson of Manasseh (1 Chron. 7:16).

RAKKATH (Răk´ käth) Place-name meaning "spit," "narrow," or "swamp." Fortified town in the territory of Naphtali (Josh. 19:35), either at Tiberias or else at Tell Eqlatiyeh about one and one-half miles northwest of Tiberias. Artifacts spanning the Bronze Age have been recovered from the latter site.

RAKKON (Răk kon) Place-name possibly meaning "swamp" or "narrow place." Village in the vicinity of Joppa allotted to Dan (Josh. 19:46). The site is perhaps Tell er-Reqqeit, two miles north of the mouth of the Jarkon River (Nahr el-'Auja). The omission of the name in the earliest Greek translation suggests that Rakkon may result from a scribe having copied Me-jarkon and then started over in the middle of the word, copying the last half twice.

RAM (Răm) Personal name meaning "high, exalted." **1.** Ancestor of David (Ruth 4:19; 1 Chron. 2:9) and Jesus (Matt. 1:3-4). **2.** Jerahmeel's eldest son (1 Chron. 2:25,27), the nephew of 1. **3.** Head of the family to which Job's friend Elihu belonged (Job 32:2).

RAM, BATTERING See *Arms and Armor.*

RAM'S HORN See *Shophar.*

RAMA (Rā´ mȧ) (KJV, Matt. 2:18) or **RAMAH** Place-name meaning "high," applied to several cities located on heights, especially military strongholds. **1.** Border town in tribal territory of Asher (Josh. 19:29). The precise location of the city is unknown, although most scholars would place it in the vicinity of Tyre. **2.** Fortified city of tribal territory of Naphtali (Josh. 19:36); this town is probably to be identified with present-day er-Rameh. Ramah of Asher and Ramah of Naph-

tali could have been the same community since the boundaries of Asher and Naphtali join. **3.** Ramah of Gilead usually called Ramoth-gilead (cp. 2 Kings 8:28-29; 2 Chron. 22:6). See *Ramoth-gilead.* **4.** City in the inheritance of Benjamin listed along with Gibeon, Beeroth, Jerusalem, and others (Josh. 18:25). It is to be identified with modern er-Ram five miles north of Jerusalem. In ancient times this location placed the city between the rival kingdoms of Israel and Judah, which led to dire consequences (1 Kings 15:16-22; 2 Chron. 16:1,5-6). The traditional site of Rachel's tomb was connected with Ramah (1 Sam. 10:2; Jer. 31:15). Deborah, the prophetess, lived in and judged Israel from the Ramah vicinity (Judg. 4:4-5). Hosea mentioned Ramah (Hos. 5:8), and Isaiah prophesied that the approaching Assyrian army would march through Ramah (Isa. 10:29). The Babylonians apparently used Ramah as a prisoner-of-war camp from which captives of Jerusalem were processed and sent into Babylonian exile. There Jeremiah was released from his chains and allowed to remain in Judah (Jer. 40:1-6). People returning from captivity settled there (Ezra 2:26; Neh. 7:30). **5.** City of the Negev, the arid desert south of Judea, in the tribal inheritance of Simeon (Josh. 19:8). David once gave presents to this town following his successful battle with the Amalekites (1 Sam. 30:27). **6.** Birthplace, home, and burial place of Samuel (1 Sam. 1:19; 2:11; 7:17; 8:4; 15:34; 25:1). In 1 Sam. 1:1 the long form, Ramathaim-zophim, is used. Samuel built an altar to the Lord at Ramah. From there he "judged" Israel and went on a yearly circuit to other cities (1 Sam. 7:15-17). Some have argued that Ramathaim-zophim is identical with Ramah of Benjamin. It may also be the town, Arimathea, hometown of Joseph, in whose tomb Jesus was buried (Matt. 27:57-60).   *J. Randall O'Brien*

RAMATH (Rā´ mäth) Place-name meaning "height, elevated place." An element of several names: Ramath-lehi meaning "height of the jawbone," site of Samson's victory over the Philistines (Judg. 15:17); Ramath-mizpeh (alternately Ramath-mizpah) meaning "height of lookout or watchtower" (Josh. 13:26); Ramath-negev meaning "Ramath of the South" (Josh. 19:8; 1 Sam. 30:27). See *Rama.*

RAMATH-LEHI (Rā măth-lē´ hī) See *Ramath*.

RAMATH-MIZPAH (Rā măth-mĭz´ pah) See *Ramath*.

RAMATH-MIZPEH (Rā măth-mĭz´ pĕh) See *Ramath*.

RAMATH-NEGEV (Rā măth-nĕg´ ev) See *Rama; Ramath*.

RAMATH OF THE SOUTH See *Rama; Ramath*.

RAMATHAIM (Rā mȧ thā´ ĭm) (NIV) or **RAMATHAIM-ZOPHIM** Birthplace of Samuel (1 Sam. 1:1). The first element in the name means "twin peaks." The final element distinguishes this Ramath from others. Zophim is perhaps a corruption of Zuph, the home district of Samuel (1 Sam. 9:5).

RAMATHITE (Rā´ măth īt) Resident of Ramah (1 Chron. 27:27).

RAMESES (Răm´ ĕ sēz) Egyptian capital city and royal residence during the 19th and 20th Dynasties (about 1320–1085 B.C.). See *Pithom and Rameses*.

The head of a monumental statue of Ramesses the Great, builder of the store-city of Rameses.

RAMIAH (Rȧ mī´ ah) Personal name meaning "Yahweh is exalted." Israelite having a foreign wife (Ezra 10:25).

RAMOTH (Rā´ mŏth) See *Remeth*.

RAMOTH-GILEAD (Rā mŏth-gĭl´ ə ȧd) Place-name meaning "heights of Gilead." One of the cities of refuge Moses appointed for unintentional killers (Deut. 4:43; cp. Josh. 20:8) and Levitical cities (Josh. 21:38). It probably was located in northeastern Gilead, east of the Jordan. Solomon made Ramoth-gilead a district capital (1 Kings 4:13). After the division of the kingdom about 922 B.C., the city

The gateway to the city of Rameses (Tanis).

fell to Syria (1 Kings 22:3) and remained there for almost 70 years. Ahab attempted to retake the city but was mortally wounded in the battle (1 Kings 22:29-40). Joram did recapture the city (2 Kings 9:14; cp. 8:28). In Ramoth-gilead Elisha anointed Jehu as king over Israel (2 Kings 9:1-6). In 722 B.C. the region was taken by Assyria.   *Mike Mitchell*

RAMOTH-NEGEV (Rā mŏth-nĕg´ ĕv) See *Rama; Ramath.*

RAMPART Outer ring of fortifications, usually earthworks. The underlying Hebrew term is literally "encirclement" and can be applied to moats and walls as well as earthworks (2 Sam. 20:15; Ps. 122:7; Lam. 2:8). Because Jerusalem was ringed by steep valleys, only its north side had extensive ramparts.

RANGE KJV term for a rank or row of soldiers (2 Kings 11:8,15; 2 Chron. 23:14).

RANSOM Payment, usually of money, required to release someone from punishment or slavery.
Old Testament The term is used to translate words related to the concept of redemption or atonement, as in Exod. 21:30; 30:12; Num. 35:31; Job 33:24; Ps. 49:7; Prov. 6:35 (Hb. *kopher*); Lev. 27:29; Ps. 69:18 (Hb. *padah*). Sometimes the deliverance is in view more than the price paid, as when God is said to have "ransomed" Israel in delivering the nation from foreign domination (Jer. 31:11; Hos. 13:14).
New Testament The word "ransom" is used in the NT to translate various words related to the Greek verb *lutroo,* which means "to ransom, redeem." These words occur about 20 times in the NT (though they occur over a hundred times in the Gk. translation of the OT). The three main passages in which the term "ransom" is found in many English translations are Mark 10:45, "For even the Son of Man did not come to be served, but to serve, and to give His life— a ransom for many" (HCSB), with the parallel in Matt. 20:28, and 1 Tim. 2:5-6, "For there is one God and one mediator between God and man, a man, Christ Jesus, who gave Himself—a ransom for all, a testimony at the proper time." The point of these passages is that Jesus' sacrificial death on the cross was the price paid to secure the release from the guilt and bondage of sin for

all who would believe. The term was metaphorical, perhaps intended as an analogy to the ancient practice of paying for the release of slaves or prisoners. Although Heb. 2:14 says the devil held the power of death, nowhere does the Bible say that Jesus' death was a ransom paid to him. It rather was the price paid to satisfy divine justice (Rom. 3:25-26). See *Atonement; Expiation, Propitiation; Redeem, Redemption, Redeemer; Salvation.*   *E. Ray Clendenen*

RAPE Crime of engaging in sexual intercourse with another without consent, by force and/or deception. Mosaic law required a man who had seduced a virgin to pay the bride price and offer to marry her (Exod. 22:16-17). The rape of an engaged woman was a capital offense (Deut. 22:25-27). In other cases of rape, the offender was required to marry his victim and was not permitted to divorce her (Deut. 22:28-29). Lot's daughters made their father drunk and then raped him (Gen. 19:30-35). Shechem raped Dinah by force (Gen. 34:1-2). The men of Gibeah gang raped a Levite's concubine and so brutalized her that she died (Judg. 19:25). Amnon's rape of his half sister Tamar was a premeditated act involving both deception and force (2 Sam. 13:1-22). This account reveals the mind of the rapist whose uncontrolled desire quickly turned to fierce hatred for his victim (13:15). Rape was one horror associated with the fall of Jerusalem (Lam. 5:11; Zech. 14:2).

The Mosaic code highlighted the victim's rights, both to monetary compensation and to recovery of dignity. This quest for dignity was a driving force behind acts of retaliatory violence recorded in the narrative texts. These texts, however, suggest the ease with which the victim is forgotten in the spiral of vengeful violence. See *Sex, Biblical Teaching on.   Chris Church*

RAPHA (Rā´ phà) Personal name meaning "He has healed." **1.** Fifth son of Benjamin (1 Chron. 8:2). The parallel in Gen. 46:21 gives the name "Naaman." **2.** KJV form of Raphah (1 Chron. 8:37).

RAPHAH (Rā phah) Personal name from a root meaning "heal." A descendant of Saul (1 Chron. 8:37). Raphah is identified with Rephaiah of 1 Chron. 9:43.

RAPHU (Rā´ phū) Personal name meaning "healed." Father of the Benjaminite representative among the 12 spies sent to survey Canaan (Num. 13:9).

RAPTURE God's taking the church out of the world instantaneously. The Latin term *rapio*, which means to "snatch away" or "carry off," is the source of the English word. While there are differing views of the millennium (Rev. 20:2-7) in relation to Christ's second coming (e.g., premillennial, postmillennial, and amillennial), nevertheless, all evangelicals affirm a literal return of Christ to the earth preceding the eternal state. In premillennialism, however, the distinct event of the rapture is often emphasized.

The main biblical passage for the rapture (Gk. *harpazo*) of the church is 1 Thess. 4:15-17. Other texts often used to support the doctrine of the rapture are John 14:1-3 and 1 Cor. 15:51-52. There are three main approaches to understanding the rapture in premillennialism: (1) In the *pretribulational* view Christ raptures the church before any part of the seven-year tribulation begins (Dan. 9:24-27; Matt. 24:3-28; Rev. 11:2; 12:14). Upon Christ's coming in the air, which is distinct from and that precedes His coming to the earth, believers will be "caught up together ... in the clouds to meet the Lord in the air" (1 Thess. 4:17 HCSB). In this view believers are delivered "from the coming wrath" (1 Thess. 1:10; Rev. 3:10) by being taken out of the world. (2) A *midtribulational* view also sees the rapture as a distinct event that precedes Christ's second coming and delivers believers from the last half of the seven-year period, the "great tribulation" (Matt. 24:15-28; Rev. 16-18). (3) A *posttribulational* view holds that the rapture and the second coming occur at the same time. Therefore, the church remains on earth during "the time of Jacob's distress" (Jer. 30:7 NASB). Unlike the world, however, believers who go through the tribulation will be protected from the devastating outpouring of God's wrath and judgment (1 Thess. 5:9). See *Eschatology; Future Hope; Millennium; Second Coming; Tribulation.*

Pete Schemm

RAS SHAMRA See *Ugarit.*

RAT Large rodent listed among the unclean animals (Lev. 11:29), but they were eaten by a disobedient people (Isa. 66:17). See *Rodents.*

RAVEN The raven, conspicuous because of its black color (Song 5:11), is a member of the crow family. The raven acts as a scavenger and is listed among the unclean birds (Lev. 11:15; Deut. 14:14). Biblical writers cite the raven as an example of God's care for His creation (Job 38:41; Ps. 147:9; Luke 12:24).

The raven was the first bird Noah sent forth from the ark following the flood (Gen. 8:7). He may have selected the raven for several reasons. It can fly without rest for long spans of time. Also the raven makes its home in the rocky crags, and thus it would scout out mountain peaks emerging from the flooded earth. Finally, the raven is a resourceful bird with a remarkable memory.

God sent ravens to sustain Elijah by the brook Cherith (1 Kings 17:4-6). Ravens often store surplus food beneath leaves or in rocky crevices. Although ravens often have been viewed as birds of evil omen, in the Elijah story they serve as symbols of God's love for His servant and of His mighty sovereignty over nature.

Janice Meier

RAVEN, RAVIN KJV term for "prowl for food" or "feed greedily" (Ps. 22:13; Ezek. 22:25,27). KJV used "ravin" both as a verb meaning "to prowl for food" (Gen. 49:27) and as a noun meaning "something taken as prey" (Nah. 2:12).

RAVINE OF THE POPLARS or **RAVINE OF THE WILLOWS** See *Arabim; Brook of the Willows; Brook of Zered.*

RAZORS Shaving instruments used in the process of removing facial hair. The customs of ancient nations regarding facial hair varied greatly. The availability of inscriptional and pictorial evidence as to these customs shows that nations had their own individual practices. Egyptians were known for their fastidious attention to personal cleanliness. Their normal custom was to shave both their heads and beards except in times of mourning. The pictures and statues of pharaohs show them with beards that we now know were fake.

The custom of shaving the face and head was less common among the Hebrews. Among them, in parallel with most Western Asiatics including the Assyrians, the beard was considered as an ornament and point of pride and was not shaven, only trimmed (2 Sam. 19:24; Ezek. 44:20). The beard was cherished as the badge of dignity of manhood. Shaving was done with a sharp cutting instrument (made from a variety of materials, usually flint, obsidian, or iron; Isa. 7:20; Ezek. 5:1), but only in unusual circumstances. The razor could be a simple knife, probably elongated with a rounded end, or an elaborate instrument, sometimes decorated. Shaving was practiced as a sign of mourning (Job 1:20; Jer. 7:29), as a sign of subservience to a superior (Num. 8:7; Gen. 41:14), and as a treatment for a person with leprosy (Lev. 14:9).

Jimmy Albright

RE (Rā) Chief Egyptian god, worshiped at his temple in Thebes, credited with creating the universe and believed to have been the first pharaoh. In images he is depicted usually as the sun disc. See *Egypt; Gods, Pagan.*

REAIA (Rə ī′ a) (KJV, 1 Chron. 5:5) or **REAIAH** Personal name meaning "Yahweh has seen." **1.** Member of the tribe of Judah (1 Chron. 4:1-2). **2.** Member of the tribe of Reuben (1 Chron. 5:5). **3.** Head of a family of temple servants returning from exile (Ezra 2:47; Neh. 7:50).

REAP To harvest grain using a sickle (Ruth 2:3-9). Reaping is used as a symbol of recompense for good (Hos. 10:12; Gal. 6:7-10) and evil (Job 4:8; Prov. 22:8; Hos. 8:7; 10:13), of evangelism (Matt. 9:37-38; Luke 10:2; John 4:35-38), and of final judgment (Matt. 13:30,39; Rev. 14:14-16).

REBA (Rē′ bà) Personal name from a root meaning "lie down." Midianite king whom Israel defeated in the time of Moses (Num. 31:8). Joshua 13:21 connects the defeat of the Midianite kings with that of the Amorite king Sihon (Num. 21:21-35).

REBECCA (Rĕ bĕk′ à) New Testament form of "Rebekah," Rom. 9:10; Greek transliteration used by KJV, NKJV, NRSV, RSV, REB, NJB, TEV.

REBEKAH (Rĕ bĕk′ à) Personal name, perhaps meaning "cow." Daughter of Bethuel, Abraham's nephew (Gen. 24:15); Isaac's wife (24:67); and mother of Jacob and Esau (25:25-26). Rebekah was a complex character. She is introduced as a beautiful virgin (24:16), willing servant (24:19), and as hospitable to strangers (24:25). In obedience to God's will, she left her home in Paddan-aram to be Isaac's wife (24:58). Rebekah comforted Isaac after the death of Sarah (24:67). When distressed by her problem pregnancy, she turned to God for counsel (25:22-23). Less favorable is Rebekah's favoritism towards Jacob (25:28), especially as evidenced in the plan she concocted to enable Jacob to steal Esau's blessing (27:5-17). Rebekah was forced to send her favorite son to her brother's household to save Jacob from Esau's vengeance (27:42-46).

RECAB, RECABITES (Rē′ căb) NIV form of Rechab, Rechabites.

RECAH (Rē′ cah) Unidentified site in Judah (1 Chron. 4:12). Early Greek manuscript has Rechab in place of Recah.

RECHAB (Rē′ kăb) Personal name meaning "rider" or "charioteer." **1.** Leader, together with his brother, of a band of Benjaminite raiders. He and his brother murdered Saul's son Ish-bosheth, thinking to court David's favor. His response was their execution (2 Sam. 4:1-12). **2.** Father or ancestor of Jehonadab, a supporter of Jehu's purge of the family of Ahab and other worshipers of Baal (2 Kings 10:15,23). **3.** Father or ancestor of Malchijah, who assisted in Nehemiah's repair of Jerusalem's walls (Neh. 3:14), possibly identical with 2.

RECHABITES (Rē′ kă bīts) Descendants of Jehonadab ben Rechab, who supported Jehu when he overthrew the house of Ahab (2 Kings 10:15-17). About 599 B.C. the Rechabites took refuge from Nebuchadnezzar in Jerusalem (Jer. 35). At that point the Lord commanded Jeremiah to take them to the temple and give them wine to drink. When he did so, they refused, saying that their father Jonadab (Jehonadab) had commanded them not to drink wine, or to live in houses, or to

R

engage in agriculture. These regulations may have been intended as a protest against Canaanite religion or settled life in general, but more likely they protected the Rechabites' lifestyle and trade secrets as itinerant metalworkers. Jeremiah contrasted their faithfulness to the commandments of their ancestor with the faithlessness of the people of Judah to the Lord. *Ricky L. Johnson*

RECHAH (Rē´ kah) (KJV) See *Recah*.

RECONCILIATION Bringing together of two parties that are estranged or in dispute. Jesus Christ is the one who brings together God and man, with salvation as the result of the union. Reconciliation basically means "change" or "exchange." The idea is of a change of relationship, an exchange of antagonism for goodwill, enmity for friendship. Attitudes are transformed and hostility ceases.

In the ancient world the initiative for reconciliation was usually made in one of two ways. A third party could seek reconciliation, or an alienated party could take the first step. The latter is what is found in the Bible. The NT has two instances of person-to-person reconciliation. In each case the person who caused the break of relationship took the initiative, the brother who wronged another (Matt. 5:24) and the woman who left her husband (1 Cor. 7:11). The person seeking reconciliation is said to "be reconciled" to the other person—the effects of the reconciliation are upon the injured party. In these instances the offenders can only confess their fault, offer reparation, and seek forgiveness. The final decision rests with the injured party, who will either grant a reprieve or continue the estrangement.

In the restoration of relationship between God and humanity, reconciliation occurs with an unexpected twist. God, the injured party, takes the initiative (2 Cor. 5:19). This initiating, reconciling action from God is contrary to expectations. The removal of alienation, created by man's sin, is the work of God. The Bible never portrays man as reconciling himself to God or God being influenced by humans to reconciliation. When Paul admonishes his readers in 2 Cor. 5:20 to "be reconciled to God," he is telling them to receive humbly and gratefully the reconciliation that God has already achieved in Christ.

A debated issue is whether reconciliation is double; that is, in some sense, are human beings only reconciled to God or is God also reconciled to human beings? Those reconciled to God were "once alienated and hostile in mind because of your evil actions" (Col. 1:21 HCSB). Paul elsewhere asserts, "The mind-set of the flesh is hostile to God" (Rom. 8:7). Sinful man is opposed to God and to everything that is of God. The sinful nature disobeys God's law and disbelieves the gospel. Unredeemed human beings are in rebellion against God; they are at enmity with their Creator. Although human beings are hostile toward God, is God likewise at enmity with humanity? The Bible seems to indicate that, to some degree, God is at enmity with sinners. Paul states in Rom. 5:10 that Christ died for sinners "while we were enemies." The word "enemies" is not a mere description of moral character. It is also a statement of the relation of sinners to God. They are objects both of God's love and His displeasure (Matt. 5:43-48). Sinners work contrary to God's purposes, and He works contrary to their purposes. God not only extends His grace, mercy, and patience to sinners, but He also expresses His displeasure through His wrath (Rom. 1:18-32). As Paul reminded the Ephesians, "We too all previously lived among them in our fleshly desires, carrying out the inclinations of our flesh and thoughts, and by nature we were children under wrath" (Eph. 2:3).

Several themes are essential to a biblical understanding of reconciliation. First is a recognition of the need for reconciliation (Rom. 5:10; Eph. 2:12; Col. 1:21). Sin has created the separation and alienation between God and man. Reconciliation assumes there is a need for separation to be bridged and for God and humanity to be restored in right relationship. Second, God is the Reconciler; reconciliation is His work. The incarnation is God's declaration that the initiative for reconciliation resides exclusively with Him (2 Cor. 5:19). Third, the death of Jesus Christ is the means by which God accomplishes reconciliation (Rom. 5:10). Fourth, reconciliation is a completed work but is still being fulfilled. Although the substitutionary sacrifice of Christ has already procured reconciliation, human beings still receive God's reconciling work and gracious gift by grace through faith in Jesus Christ. Fifth, the divine-human act of reconciliation serves as the basis for authentic person-to-person reconciliation. Finally, God's reconciling work is in large measure the ministry of the church. Believers have been commissioned by the resurrected Lord to have a message and ministry of reconciliation. In this sense reconciliation is not only a reality of life for believers, but it is also a purpose of their kingdom ministry. See *Atonement; Cross, Crucifixion; Jesus Christ; Salvation.*   *Stan Norman*

RECORDER Government post with unidentified responsibilities (as in 2 Sam. 8:16; 20:24). The REB identified the recorder as the secretary of state. The TEV identified the recorder as the official in charge of [court] records. The term possibly refers to a court herald or court historian. Most translations use "recorder," thus leaving the function open.

RED KJV used "red" as the translation of several Hebrew terms where modern translations substitute another meaning: "foaming" or "blended" (Ps. 75:8); "pleasant" or "delight" (Isa. 27:2); and "porphyry" (Esther 1:6). See *Colors.*

RED HEIFER Function of the red heifer ceremony was production of ash for the water used to remove ritual impurity contracted through contact with a corpse, bones, or a grave (Num. 19). The rite involved: slaughter of a sacrificially acceptable heifer outside the camp; sprinkling blood toward the tent of meeting seven times; burning the entire heifer, including its blood and dung, together with cedarwood, hyssop, and scarlet thread (cp. Lev. 14:4); and storing the ash in a clean place outside the camp. The water for removing the impurity contracted through contact with the dead was prepared by mixing running water with the ash. Impure persons and objects were sprinkled on the third and seventh days after contamination to remove uncleanness. Hebrews 9:14 uses the image of the red heifer ceremony to picture Christ's cleansing believers of the effect of "dead works." Dead works refer either to acts that lead to death (NIV), "useless rituals" in view of salvation (TEV), or works produced prior to being made alive in Christ (cp. Heb. 6:1).

RED SEA (REED SEA) Body of water God divided in the exodus. Red Sea is a common translation of two Hebrew words *yam suph.* *Yam* means "sea," but *suph* does not normally mean "red." *Suph* often means "reeds" (Exod. 2:3,5; Isa. 19:6) or "end," "hinder part" (Joel 2:20; 2 Chron. 20:16; Eccles. 3:11). *Yam*

The Red Sea.

suph could be translated "Sea of Reeds" or "Sea at the end of the world." The earliest known translation of the Hebrew Bible (the Gk. Septuagint about 200 B.C.) translated *yam suph* consistently with *Erthra Thalassa* "Red Sea." Jerome continued the process in the Latin Vulgate (A.D. 400) by using *Mare Rubrum* "Red Sea" for *yam suph*. Most English translations have followed the Vulgate and use "Red Sea" in the text with a footnote indicating the literal translation is "Reed Sea." TEV uses various terms to translate *yam suph*: "Gulf of Suez" (Exod. 10:19); "Red Sea"; and "Gulf of Aqaba" (1 Kings 9:26).

We do not know who first suggested the translation "Reed Sea." In the 11th century the French Jewish scholar Rashi spoke of *yam suph* in terms of a marsh overgrown with weeds. In the 12th century Ibn Ezra, a Spanish Jew, commented that *yam suph* in Exod. 13:18 may be so named because reeds grow around it. Martin Luther translated *yam suph* as *Schilfmeer*, "Reed Sea." Although the name "Reed Sea" has been widely accepted by many scholars, there have been many recent attempts to prove the term "Sea of Reeds" is not a legitimate reading for *yam suph*.

The OT uses the term *yam suph* to refer to more than one location. In Exod. 10:19 it refers to the Gulf of Suez as the place where the locusts were driven and destroyed. In 1 Kings 9:26 it refers to the Gulf of Aqaba where the ships of Solomon's navy were stationed. The same location may be indicated in Jer. 49:21 where the cries of Edom could be heard. The "Way of the Red Sea" (*yam suph*) is part of the name of a highway out of Egypt (Exod. 13:18; Num. 21:4; Deut. 1:40; 2:1; Judg. 11:16). The "Red Sea" was the name of a camp along the way from Egypt (Num. 33:10-11). *Yam suph* marked the ideal southern border of Israel (Exod. 23:31), but the most significant reference of "Red Sea" in the OT was to the place where God delivered Israel from Pharaoh's army (Exod. 15:4,22; Num. 21:14; Deut. 11:4; Josh. 2:10; 4:23; 24:6; Neh. 9:9; Pss. 106:7,9-11,22; 136:13-15).

No one knows the exact location of the place where Israel crossed the "Red Sea" on the way out of Egypt. Four primary theories have been suggested as to the place of the actual crossing of the isthmus of Suez: (1) the northern edge of the Gulf of Suez; (2) a site in the center of the isthmus near Lake Timsah; (3) a site at the northern edge of the isthmus and the southern edge of Lake Menzaleh; and (4) across a narrow stretch of sandy land which separates Lake Sirbonis from the Mediterranean Sea. Although no one knows the exact site of the crossing, the weight of the biblical evidence is on the side of suggested site number two. See *Exodus*.   *Ralph L. Smith*

REDEEM, REDEMPTION, REDEEMER To pay a price in order to secure the release of something or someone. It connotes the idea of paying what is required in order to liberate from oppression, enslavement, or another type of binding obligation. The redemptive procedure may be legal, commercial, or religious.

In the OT two word groups convey the idea of redemption. The verb *ga'al* and its cognates mean "to buy back" or "to redeem." In the book of Ruth (Ruth 2:20), Boaz acts as kinsman-redeemer to secure the freedom of Ruth from poverty and widowhood. Boaz purchases the land of Elimelech and, in so doing, "redeems" Ruth and takes her to be his wife (Ruth 4:1-12). In another account God commands the Prophet Jeremiah to buy family land; he redeems the family estate by paying the redemption price (Jer. 32:6-15). Jeremiah depicts that God will one day redeem Israel from oppression of the Babylonians (Jer. 32:16-44).

When *ga'al* is used of God, the idea is redemption from bondage or oppression, typically from one's enemies. In the Exodus account Yahweh declares to Moses: "I am the LORD ... and I will redeem you with an outstretched arm and with mighty acts of judgment" (Exod. 6:6 NIV). Some uses of *ga'al* and its cognates speak of redemption from oppression by enemies (Pss. 69:18; 72:14; 106:10; 107:2; Isa. 48:20). *Ga'al* rarely refers to redemption from sin (Isa. 44:22) or from death (Ps. 103:4; Hos. 13:14).

Padah is primarily used with regard to the redemption of persons or of living things. Since God spared the firstborn Israelites when the last plague was sent upon Egypt, God required that all firstborn sons or animals be redeemed (Exod. 13:13-15; 34:20; Num. 18:15). If a negligent owner did not properly secure an ox, and the ox gored the child of a neighbor, both ox and owner would be stoned. The father of the slain person could, however, accept a redemption price for the lost child, thereby permitting the owner of the ox to live (Exod. 21:29-30). *Padah* and its cognates could refer to a general deliverance from trouble or distress (2 Sam. 4:9; 1 Kings 1:29; Ps. 25:22), or they could speak of redemption from sin (Pss. 26:11; 49:7; 103:8; 130:8; Isa. 1:27; 59:20) or from death (Job 4:20; Pss. 44:26; 49:15).

The notion of redemption from sin is also implicitly revealed in the OT. The sacrificial system was a constant reminder to the Israelites that a price had to be paid in order to have redemption from their sins. Every offering sacrificed depicted the notion of the price of sin and the need for the price to be paid. Additionally, the Israelites viewed liberation from oppressive circumstances, such as the Babylonian captivity, essentially as redemption from sin, since it was their sin that brought about their captivity (Isa. 40:2).

In the NT two word groups convey the concept. The first consists of *lutron* and its cognates. They mean "to redeem," "to liberate," or "to ransom." The idea of ransom suggests the heart of Jesus' mission (Mark 10:45). His life and ministry culminated in His sacrificial death. His death served as the ransom to liberate sinners from their enslaved condition.

Another word family, *agorazein*, means "to buy at the market," or "to redeem." This group is used several times to express God's redemptive activity in Christ. For example, God's redemption of fallen humanity is costly (1 Cor. 6:20). Believers are liberated from the enslaving curse of the law (Gal. 3:13, 4:5). God's redemptive mission among the nations is cause for eschatological worship (Rev. 5:9; 14:3-4).

Paul provides the fullest explanation in the NT, connecting the redemptive work of Christ with the legal declaration of the sinner's pardon (justification) and the appeasement of God's wrath against sin (propitiation, Rom. 3:24; 1 Cor. 1:30). Paul also interpreted the redeeming activity of Christ from two perspectives. Based on the ransom price paid by Christ's shed blood, forgiveness can be presently applied to the believer (Eph. 1:7). This redeeming work of Christ also has a future aspect. There will be a final deliverance of the physical body from the present decay and corruption (Rom. 8:23). This final redemptive act will occur at the resurrection of the body. This is not, however, as the first expression of redemption of believers. Rather, the earlier "redeeming" that occurred within the believer will culminate in the final redemption

of the body from sin and the grave (Eph. 4:30). See *Christ, Christology; Jesus Christ; Atonement; Reconciliation.*   *Stan Norman*

REED PIPE See *Music, Instruments, Dancing.*

REED, VESSELS OF See *Ships, Sailors, and Navigation.*

REEDS See *Plants.*

REELAIAH (Rē ə lī´ ā) Personal name meaning "Yahweh has caused trembling." Exile who returned with Zerubbabel (Ezra 2:2); identical to Raamiah (Neh. 7:7).

REFINE To reduce to a pure state; often used figuratively of moral cleansing. See *Crucible; Ezion-Geber; Furnace; Minerals and Metals; Mines and Mining.*

REFINING POT See *Crucible; Fining Pot.*

REFORMATION Translation of the Greek *diorthosis* (Heb. 9:10). The term refers either to the new order for relating to God established by Christ (NIV) or else to the process of establishing the new order (NRSV, TEV). See *Covenant.*

REFUGE, CITIES OF See *Cities of Refuge.*

REFUSE GATE See *Dung Gate.*

REGEM (Rē´ gĕm) Personal name meaning "friend." Descendant of Caleb (1 Chron. 2:47).

REGEM-MELECH (Rē gĕm-mē´ lĕk) Personal name meaning "friend of the king." Delegate whom the people of Bethel sent to Jerusalem to inquire about continuing to fast in commemoration of the destruction of the Jerusalem temple (Zech. 7:2). The prophet repeated the word of previous prophets: God desires moral lives rather than fasts (7:9-10).

REGENERATION Special act of God in which the recipient is passive. God alone awakens the person spiritually through the power of His Holy Spirit. Both the OT and NT also speak of the renewing of the individual. In a technical sense the act of regeneration

R

takes place at the moment of conversion as the individual is spiritually awakened.

The term "regeneration" is the Greek word *palingenesia* (used only in Matt. 19:28 of creation and Titus 3:5). The Titus text refers to the regeneration of the individual, "He saved us—not by works of righteousness that we had done, but according to His mercy, through the washing of regeneration and renewal by the Holy Spirit" (HCSB). The Bible expresses the concept in numerous places with other terms like born again, renewed, remade, and born of God. For instance, in John 3:3-8 Jesus tells Nicodemus that in order to enter the kingdom of God, he must be born again. This thought is echoed in 1 Pet. 1:23, "Since you have been born again—not of perishable seed but of imperishable—through the living and enduring word of God." The Bible clearly teaches that man must undergo a spiritual re-creation in order to have a relationship with God or enter His kingdom.

Paul provides further explanation in Eph. 2:1: "You were dead in your trespasses and sins." Clearly Paul does not mean physical death but instead is referring to man's spiritual state. Sin has left man dead spiritually, unable to respond to God. However, regeneration reawakens or resurrects man's spiritual capacity so that he can have relationship with God. Paul explained in Eph. 2:4-5, "Because of His great love that He had for us, [God] made us alive with the Messiah even though we were dead in trespasses" (HCSB). Regeneration gives man the ability to commune with God, thus making man "a new creation" (2 Cor. 5:17).

This same idea is expressed in the OT. For example, God told Israel in Ezek. 36:26, "I will give you a new heart and put a new spirit within you; and I will remove the heart of stone from your flesh and give you a heart of flesh" (NASB). This need for a new heart was expressed by the psalmist: "God, create a clean heart for me and renew a steadfast spirit within me" (Ps. 51:10 HCSB). Jeremiah 31:31-34 also speaks of God establishing a new covenant where His law will be written on men's hearts. These verses clearly speak of a change in man's heart resulting in an improved response to God and His will, which is reflective of the NT concept of regeneration.

Several church traditions, like the Roman Catholic, have associated the regenerative act with the baptism. However, the Bible clearly teaches that baptism is a testimony that regeneration has taken place and not a means to attain it. The Bible is clear that regeneration is brought about by the Holy Spirit alone (Titus 3:5; 1 Cor. 2:6-16).

Regeneration is the catalyst that allows the Christian to interact with his creator. It is the beginning step of an eternal walk with God. Regeneration allows the individual to have a relationship with God and thus stands at the beginning of the Christian life. *Scott Drumm*

REGIMENT NIV term for "cohort," a tenth of a legion (Acts 10:1; 27:1). See *Cohort*.

REGISTER KJV term for a record of names, a genealogical registry (Ezra 2:62; Neh. 7:5,64). Modern translations use "register" more often in the verbal sense, to record in formal records (NASB: Num. 1:18; 11:26; 2 Sam. 24:2,4; Neh. 12:22-23; Ps. 87:6). See *Census*.

REHABIAH (Rē há bī´ ah) Personal name meaning "Yahweh has made wide." Son of Eliezer and ancestor of a group of Levites (1 Chron. 23:17; 24:21; 26:25).

REHOB (Rē´ hŏb) Personal and place-name meaning "broad or open place." **1.** Father of a king of Zobah, an Aramean city north of Damascus (2 Sam. 8:3,12). **2.** Witness to Nehemiah's covenant (Neh. 10:11). **3.** Town in the vicinity of Laish in upper Galilee (Num. 13:21) See *Beth-rehob*. **4.** Town in the territory of Asher (Josh. 19:28,30). Asher was not able to drive out the Canaanite inhabitants (Judg. 1:31). Elsewhere, Rehob in Asher is assigned to the Levites (Josh. 21:31; 1 Chron. 6:75). The site is perhaps Tell el-Gharbi about seven miles east-southeast of Acco.

REHOBOAM (Rē hŏ bō´ ám) Personal name meaning "he enlarges the people." One of Solomon's sons and his successor to the throne of the united monarchy (1 Kings 11:43). He reigned about 931–913 B.C. While at Shechem for his crowning ceremony as king over Israel (1 Kings 12), the people asked Rehoboam if he would remove some of the tax burden and labor laws which his father had placed on them. Instead of taking the advice of the older men, he acted on the counsel of those who wanted to increase the burden further. The Northern tribes revolted and made the rebel Jeroboam their king. Rehoboam was left with only the tribes of Judah and Benjamin. He continued the pagan ways which Solomon had allowed (14:21-24) and fought against Jeroboam and Shishak of Egypt. Some of his fortifications may be those at Lachish and Azekah.

REHOBOTH (Rē hō´ bŏth) Place-name meaning "broad places." **1.** Rehoboth-Ir, "broad places of the city," likely denotes an open space within Nineveh or its suburbs (Gen. 10:11) rather than a separate city between Nineveh and Calah. **2.** Site of a well dug and retained by Isaac's men in the valley of Gerar (Gen. 26:22). The name affirms that God had made room for them following confrontations over rights to two previous wells. **3.** Unidentified Edomite city (Gen. 36:37; 1 Chron. 1:48). KJV, NIV, and TEV distinguish this city as Rehoboth by the river. NASB, NRSV, and REB identify the river as the Euphrates. Edomite dominion reaching the Euphrates is improbable. Thus some suggest the Zered Brook, the principal stream in Edom, as the site of Rehoboth.

REHUM (Rē´ hŭm) Personal name meaning "merciful, compassionate." **1.** One returning from exile with Zerubbabel (Ezra 2:2); the parallel (Neh. 7:7) reads "Nehum." **2.** Persian official with oversight of the Trans-Euphrates territory, including Judah. His protest of the rebuilding of the Jerusalem temple and city walls resulted in suspension of the project (Ezra 4:8-24). **3.** Levite engaged in Nehemiah's repair of the wall (Neh. 3:17). **4.** Witness to Nehemiah's covenant (Neh. 10:25). **5.** Priest or priestly clan (Neh. 12:3), perhaps a corruption of Harim.

REI (Rē´ ī) Personal name meaning "friendly." David's officer who sided with Solomon in his succession struggle with Adonijah (1 Kings 1:8).

REINS KJV term for kidneys, used both in a literal anatomical sense and in a figurative sense for the seat of the emotions. The substitutions made by the NRSV are illustrative of those of other modern translations: literal sense as "kidneys" (Job 16:13), "inward parts" (Ps. 139:13), and "loins" (Isa. 11:5);

figurative sense as "heart" (Job 19:27; Pss. 7:9; 16:7; 26:2; 73:21; Jer. 11:20) with the exception of Prov. 23:16 ("soul").

REKEM (Rē´ kĕm) Personal and place-name meaning "maker of multicolored cloth." **1.** One of five Midianite kings whom Israel defeated in Moses' time (Num. 31:8; Josh. 13:21). Rekem was apparently the earlier name of Petra. See *Reba.* **2.** Descendant of Caleb (1 Chron. 2:43-44). **3.** Ancestor of a family living in Gilead (1 Chron. 7:16). **4.** Unidentified site in Benjamin (Josh. 18:27).

RELEASE, YEAR OF Hebrew expression that occurs only twice (Deut. 15:9; 31:10 KJV, RSV), both times in reference to the Sabbatical Year as a year of release from debt. Some confusion results from modern translations using the verb "release" in connection with both the Sabbatical Year and the Year of Jubilee. See *Jubilee, Year of; Sabbatical Year.*

RELIGION Relationship of devotion or fear of God or gods. **1.** The cognate terms translated "religious" and "religion" (Acts 17:22; 25:19) can indicate positive reverence for the gods or else negative fear of the gods. The pejorative translations "superstitious" (KJV) and "superstition" (KJV, RSV) is unfortunate. Paul hardly alienated the Athenians at the outset of his speech. He rather pointed to their outward expressions of piety (Acts 17:22). Though a monotheist (believer in one God) would not use "fear of the gods" to describe Judaism, the expression is natural on pagan Roman lips (Acts 25:19). **2.** The cognate terms translated "religion" and "religious" in Acts 26:5 and James 1:26-27 point to the "fear of God" as evidenced in religious conduct, particularly ritual practice. In Acts 26:5 Paul referred to Judaism as "our" way of evidencing reverence for God. According to James 1:26-27, one who thinks himself religiously observant but who cannot control the tongue will find religious observance worthless. James continued that the religious observance God cares about is not a cultic matter but an ethical matter, care of the helpless of society. **3.** Several terms derived from *sebomai* (to fear) are translated religious or religion. The term in Acts 13:43 is rendered "religious" (KJV), "devout" (HCSB, NRSV),

R

and "God-fearing" (NASB). The term RSV translated "religion" in 1 Tim. 2:10 is literally "God-fearing," here in the sense of obedient to God's commands (cp. John 9:31). The NIV translation "who profess to worship God" highlights the connection between fear and reverence. The KJV and NASB translation "godliness" accentuates the linkage of fear with an obedient life. The term RSV translated as "religion" (1 Tim. 3:16; 2 Tim. 3:5) and "religious duty" in 1 Tim. 5:4 is generally translated "godliness" or "piety." The emphasis is again on conduct. **4.** The meaning of the term the NASB translated as "self-made religion" is uncertain (Col. 2:23). The Greek roots suggest freely chosen worship (KJV, "will worship"; NIV, "self-imposed worship"; RSV, "promoting rigor of devotion"). Similar constructions with *thelo* suggest the meaning "alleged worship." **5.** KJV translated *Ioudaism* (Judaism) as the "Jews' religion" (Gal. 1:13-14). **6.** NIV frequently inserts the adjective "religious" into its paraphrase to clarify the nature of feasts (Amos 5:21; 8:10; Col. 2:16) or service (Heb. 10:11) when there is no corresponding term in the Greek or Hebrew text.

Chris Church

REMALIAH (Rĕm á lī´ ah) Personal name meaning "may Yahweh be exalted" or "Yahweh adorned." Father of Pekah who murdered King Pekahiah of Israel and reigned in his stead (2 Kings 15:25; Isa. 7:1).

REMETH (Rē´ mĕth) Place-name meaning "height." Town in Issachar's territory (Josh. 19:21), likely identical with Ramoth (1 Chron. 6:73) and Jarmuth (Josh. 21:29).

REMISSION Release, forgiveness. RSV used "remission" only in the sense of refraining from exacting a tax (Esther 2:18). Other modern translations avoided the term. KJV frequently used the expression, "remission of sins," to mean release from the guilt or penalty of sins. Modern translations generally substitute the term "forgiveness." With the exception of Rom. 3:25, the underlying Greek term is *aphesis*. Remission of sins is often linked with repentance, both in the preaching of John the Baptist (Mark 1:4; Luke 3:3) and the early church (Luke 24:47; Acts 2:38; 5:31). Remission of sins results from Christ's sacrificial death (Matt. 26:28; cp. Heb. 10:17-18) and from Christ's exaltation (Acts 5:31). Remission of sins is available to all who believe in the name of Jesus (Acts 10:43; cp. Luke 24:47; Acts 2:38). Because Christ's sacrifice has freed believers from the guilt and penalty of sin, no additional sacrifices are needed (Heb. 10:18). The term rendered "remission" in Rom. 3:25 (*paresis*) refers to God's letting sin go unpunished in anticipation of the work of Christ. See *Forgiveness.*

REMMON (Rĕm mŏn) KJV variant of Rimmon (Josh. 19:7). RSV reads "En-rimmon." Other modern translations follow the KJV in understanding two cities: Ain and Rimmon.

REMMON-METHOAR (Rĕm´ mŏn-mĕ thō´ är) KJV took Remmon-methoar as a proper name (Josh. 19:13). Modern translations take the second element (Methoar) to mean "bends toward" (NRSV), "stretches to" (NASB), or a similar expression. See *Rimmon.*

REMNANT Something left over, especially the righteous people of God after divine judgment. Several Hebrew words express the remnant idea: *yeter*, "that which is left over"; *she'ar*, "that which remains"; *she'rit*, "residue"; *pelitah*, "one who escapes"; *sarid*, "a survivor"; and, *sherut*, "one loosed from bonds." In the NT "remnant" or left over is the equivalent of the Greek words: *kataleimma*, *leimma*, and *loipos*.

Several activities of everyday life are associated with these words. Objects or people may be separated from a larger group by selection, assignment, consumption (eating food), or by destruction. What is left over is the residue, or, in the case of people, those who remain after an epidemic, famine, drought, or war.

Noah and his family may be understood as survivors, or a remnant, of a divine judgment in the flood (Gen. 6:5-8; 7:1-23). The same could be said of Lot when Sodom was destroyed (Gen. 18:17-33; 19:1-29), Jacob's family in Egypt (Gen. 45:7), Elijah and the 7,000 faithful followers of the Lord (1 Kings 19:17-18), and the Israelites going into captivity (Ezek. 12:1-16). They were survivors because the Lord chose to show mercy to those who had believed steadfastly in Him and had been righteous in their lives.

About 750 B.C. Amos found that many people in Israel believed that God would protect all of them and their institutions. With strong language he tore down their mistaken ideas (3:12-15; 5:2-3,18-20; 6:1-7; 9:1-6). Divine judgment would be poured out on all Israel. He corrected the tenet that everyone would live happily and prosper (9:10) with the doctrine that only a few would survive and rebuild the nation (9:8b-9,11-15). This new life could be realized if one and all would repent, turn to the Lord, and be saved (5:4b-6a,14-15).

Hosea's book does not use the remnant terminology, but the concept of the Lord's mercy extended to those experiencing judgment is present in several places (2:14-23; 3:4-5; 6:1-3; 11:8-11; 13:14; 14:1-9) including calls to repentance and descriptions of what the remnant may enjoy in life.

The book of Micah has much the same emphasis. After announcements of judgment, the Lord proclaimed that people would be assembled like sheep and led by the Lord (2:12-13) as their king (4:6-8). The Messiah would give special attention to them (5:2-5,7-9). The climax of the book is an exaltation of God as the one who pardons and removes sin from their lives after the judgment had passed (7:7-20).

The remnant doctrine was so important to Isaiah that he named one of his sons Shear-jashub, meaning "a remnant shall return" (7:3). The faithful would survive the onslaughts of the Assyrian army (4:2-6; 12:1-6) as illustrated by the remarkable deliverance of the few people in Jerusalem from the siege of the city by the Assyrians (chaps. 36–38).

Many remnant passages are closely tied with the future king, the Messiah, who would be the majestic ruler of those who seek his mercies (9:1-7; 11:1-16; 32:1-8; 33:17-24). These passages have a strong eschatological thrust, expecting future generations to be the remnant. Other passages looked to the generation of Isaiah's day to provide the remnant. Numerous statements in the latter part of the book have an evident futuristic orientation. In that future there would be a new people, a new community, a new nation, and a strong faith in one God. This remnant would be personified in the Suffering Servant (chap. 53).

Amos, Hosea, Micah, and Isaiah thus raised a chorus. Only a few would survive judgment events, basically because they repented and rested their future on the compassion of their Lord. An important segment of the remnant would be those who were afflicted (Isa. 14:32). Later, Zephaniah spoke of the humble and the lowly as the ones who would find refuge among the remnant (2:3; 3:12-13).

Jeremiah announced that Judah would be destroyed for rebelling against the Lord of the covenant. The political, religious, and social institutions of the state would be eliminated; many would lose their lives; others would be taken into exile for 70 years. In the exile those who believed in the one true God would be gathered for a return to the promised land. God would create a new community. Statements of hope and promise for the remnant are concentrated in chapters 30–33.

Ezekiel agreed with Jeremiah that the remnant of Judah taken to Babylon would be the source of people fit for the Lord's new community. These few would participate in a new exodus and settle in the promised land around a new temple (chaps. 40–48).

Zechariah spoke in glowing terms of how the remnant, the returned exiles to Jerusalem, would prosper (8:6-17; 9:9-17; 14:1-21). Ezra recognized the people who had returned to Jerusalem as members of the remnant, in danger of reenacting the sins of the past (9:7-15).

In the NT Paul quoted (Rom. 9:25-33) from Hosea and from Isaiah to demonstrate that the saving of a remnant from among the Jewish people was still part of the Lord's method of redeeming His people. There would always be a future for anyone among the covenant people who would truly turn to the Lord for salvation (chaps. 9–11).   *George Herbert Livingston*

REMPHAN (Rĕm´ phăn) (KJV) See *Rephan.*

RENDING OF GARMENTS Tearing or pulling garments apart, often as a sign of mourning (Gen. 37:34; Lev. 10:6; 21:10; 1 Sam. 4:12; 2 Sam. 3:31), repentance (Gen. 37:29; Josh. 7:6; 2 Chron. 34:27; Joel 2:13), or as a response to the rejection of God's plan (Num. 14:6) or (perceived) blasphemy (Matt. 26:65; Mark 14:63; Acts 14:14). See *Blasphemy; Grief and Mourning.*

REPENTANCE Change of mind; also can refer to regret or remorse accompanying a realization that wrong has been done or to any shift or reversal of thought. In its biblical sense repentance refers to a deeply seated and thorough turning from self to God. It occurs when a radical turning to God takes place, an experience in which God is recognized as the most important fact of one's existence.

Old Testament The concept of a wholehearted turning to God is widespread in the preaching of the OT prophets. Terms such as "return," turn," or "seek" are used to express the idea of repentance.

In Amos 4–5 the Lord sends judgment in order for the nation to return to Him. Corporate repentance of the nation is a theme in Hosea (Hos. 6:1; 14:2) and the result of Jonah's preaching to Nineveh (Jon. 3:10). Classic calls to repentance are found in Ezek. 18 and 33 as well as Isa. 55. The shift toward an emphasis on individual repentance can be seen in Ezek. 18.

New Testament Repentance was the keynote of the preaching of John the Baptist, referring to a complete turn from self to God. A note of urgency is attached to the message, "The kingdom of heaven has come near!" (Matt. 3:2 HCSB). Those who were prepared to make such a radical reorientation of their lives demonstrated that by being baptized (Mark 1:4). This complete redirection of their lives was to be demonstrated by profound changes in lifestyle and relationships (Luke 3:8-14).

The emphasis upon a total life change continues in the ministry of Jesus. The message of repentance was at the heart of His preaching (Mark 1:15). When describing the focus of His mission, Jesus said, "I have not come to call the righteous, but sinners to repentance"(Luke 5:32 HCSB).

The call to repentance is a call to absolute surrender to the purposes of God and to live in this awareness. This radical turning to God is required of all people: "Unless you repent, you will all perish" (Luke 13:3). Those who had witnessed the ministry of Jesus, the reality of God, and His claims on their lives faced serious jeopardy if they failed to repent. Jesus warned of serious consequences for those where His ministry had been rejected: "He proceeded to denounce the towns where most of His miracles were done, because they did not repent" (Matt. 11:20 HCSB). On the other hand, for the one sinner who repents, there is great "joy in heaven" (Luke 15:7). In His final words to the disciples, Jesus demanded that the same message of repentance He had preached would be preached to all nations (Luke 24:47).

The term remained in use as the early church began to take shape. The preaching in the book of Acts contains the call to repentance (Acts 2:38; 3:19; 8:22). On the one hand, Paul's discourse at Athens reveals God as the one who "commands all people everywhere to repent" (17:30 HCSB). On the other hand, repentance is shown to be the result of the initiative of God: "God has granted repentance resulting in life to even the Gentiles" (Acts 11:18; 2 Tim. 2:24-26). The abundance of NT references makes clear that repentance is an essential element in the salvation experience. In response to the call of God in one's life, there must be repentance, that is, the willful determination to turn from a life of sin and self-rule to a life ruled by God and lived in His righteousness. Repentance can be said to have occurred when someone has been convicted of the reality of their personal sinfulness, rejects and renounces that life of sin, and turns to God through faith in Jesus Christ. Repentance is so central that when Paul summarized his ministry he could say, "I testified to both Jews and Greeks about repentance toward God and faith in our Lord Jesus" (Acts 20:21 HCSB). The experience of repentance precedes salvation (2 Pet. 3:9).

While the majority of calls to repentance are directed to unbelievers, repentance sometimes refers to believers. Paul wrote of a letter sent to the Corinthians which caused them grief but which ultimately led them to repentance (2 Cor. 7:8-13). Several times in the letters to the churches in Revelation, repentance is called for (Rev. 2:5,16,21-22; 3:3,19), in order that these believers and churches might bring their lives into greater conformity to the will of God. Individual believers, as well as churches, must constantly engage in self-examination, allowing the Spirit of God to point out areas where change is needed. Repentance is more than just remorse. See *Confession; Conversion; Faith; Kingdom of God; Sackcloth.* *Clark Palmer*

REPENTANCE OF GOD Old Testament description of God's reaction to human situations. The Hebrew verb (*nacham*) expresses a strong emotional content, perhaps with a reference to deep breathing of distress or relief. It should be noted that "repent" is not always the best translation for *nacham* but was the translation used by the KJV. The scope of possible translations includes "repent" (Jer. 18:8,10 RSV), "grieve" (Gen. 6:7 NIV), "pity" (Judg. 2:18 NASB), "change of mind" (Ps. 110:4 REB), and "relent" (Ps. 106:45 NASB). Therefore, the concept of the repentance of God would also include God's grieving, pitying, changing His mind, and relenting.

The concept of God's repentance is not limited to one section of the OT but can be found throughout the Law, the Prophets, and the Writings. The repentance of God became Israel's creed alongside other attributes of God like "gracious," "merciful," "slow to anger," and "great in covenant-love" (cp. Joel 2:13; Jon. 4:2).

The repentance of God was usually in response to His creation, such as human disobedience (Gen. 6:6-7), intercessory prayer (Amos 7:1-6), or repentance (Jon. 3:6-10). In many instances God is said to have changed His mind about some evil that He had planned to do (Exod. 32:12,14; Jon. 3:10). In one instance God is said to change His mind (Jer. 18:10) about His good intentions.

God's repentance plays an important role in our understanding about the role of prayer and about certain attributes of God, such as immutability, timelessness, and impassability. The God who repents is free to answer prayer and to interact with people. This freedom is part of His being the same forever.

M. Stephen Davis

REPHAEL (Rĕph´ ā ĕl) Personal name meaning "God heals." Temple gatekeeper (1 Chron. 26:7).

REPHAH (Rē´ phah) Personal name meaning "overflow." An Ephraimite (1 Chron. 7:25).

REPHAIAH (Rə phī´ ah) Personal name meaning "God healed." **1.** Descendant of David (1 Chron. 3:21). **2.** Simeonite living at Mount Seir (1 Chron. 4:42). **3.** Warrior from the tribe of Issachar (1 Chron. 7:2). **4.** Descendant of Saul (1 Chron. 9:43). **5.** One helping with Nehemiah's repair of the wall who had oversight of one-half of the administrative district embracing Jerusalem (Neh. 3:9).

REPHAIM (Rĕph´ a ĭm) **1.** Residents of Sheol, often translated, "shades" or "the dead" (Job 26:5 NRSV; Ps. 88:10; Prov. 9:18; 21:16; Isa. 14:9; 26:14,19). See *Sheol*. **2.** Ethnic designation of the pre-Israelite inhabitants of Palestine, equivalent to the Anakim, the Moabite term *Emim* (Deut. 2:10-11), and the Ammonite term *Zanzummim* (2:20-21). Despite their reputation for might and height, the Rephaim were defeated by a coalition of eastern kings (Gen. 14:5) and were later displaced by the Israelites (Deut. 3:11,13; cp. Gen. 15:20) and their distant kin, the Moabites (Deut. 2:10-11) and the Ammonites (2:20-21). KJV regularly translated Rephaim as "giants" (except Gen. 14:5; 15:20, and some references to the valley or land of the Rephaim). NASB and RSV used the translation "giants" only in reference to individual giants in 2 Samuel and 1 Chronicles. NIV avoided the translation "giant" completely, using "Rephaim" when referring to the valley or land, "Rephaites" when referring to the pre-Israelite inhabitants, and "descendant of Rapha" for individuals in 2 Samuel and 1 Chronicles. The artificial distinction between Rephaites and descendant of Rapha apparently attempts to ease the tension between the designation of King Og of Bashan as the last of the Rephaim (Deut. 3:11; Josh. 12:4) and the mention of later descendants in 2 Sam. 21:16,18,20,22; 1 Chron. 20:6,8. See *Giants; Nephilim*.

REPHAITES (Rĕph´ ā īts) NIV alternate translation for the Hebrew *Rephaim* when applied to the pre-Israelite inhabitants of Canaan. See *Rephaim*.

REPHAN (Rē´ phăn) Term for a foreign, astral deity (Acts 7:43; NASB, Rompha). Acts 7 follows the earliest Greek OT translation reading at Amos 5:26. The Hebrew Masoretic text reads "Kaiwan," the Babylonian name for Saturn.

REPHIDIM (Rĕph´ ĭ dĭm) Site in the wilderness where the Hebrews stopped on their way to Canaan just prior to reaching Sinai (Exod. 17:1; 19:2). There the people complained of thirst, and God commanded Moses to strike the rock out of which would come water. While the Hebrews were encamped at

Rephidim, the Amalekites came against them and were defeated by Israel under Joshua's leadership. Moses' father-in-law, Jethro, came to Rephidim and helped the leader delegate his authority over the people (18:13-26). The exact location is unknown.

REPROACH Term used to indicate disgrace or dishonor, or to discredit someone or something. In the KJV the word or its derivative occurs more than 130 times. Reproach can be incurred in various circumstances. Its sources include a woman's barren condition (Gen. 30:23; 1 Sam. 1:6-10; Luke 1:25), rape (Gen. 34:14), singleness (Isa. 4:1), uncircumcision (Josh. 5:9), physical mutilation (1 Sam. 11:2), widowhood (Isa. 54:4), fasting (Ps. 69:10), mistreatment of parents (Prov. 19:26), famine (Ezek. 36:30), sin (Prov. 14:34), military defeat (Ps. 79:4), illness (Ps. 31:11), or the destruction of Jerusalem (Neh. 2:17; Ps. 89:41). Second, it can refer to a state of shame, disgrace, or humiliation (Neh. 1:3; Job 19:5; 27:6; Ps. 15:3). Third, it can be an expression of blame, taunt, or disapproval (1 Sam. 11:2; 2 Kings 19:4,16; Neh. 4:4; 5:9; Jer. 23:40). Fourth, it expresses an upbraid or rebuke (1 Sam. 17:26; Job 19:3; Zeph. 2:8; Luke 11:45). Fifth, it can indicate scorn or disappointment (Ruth 2:5; Neh. 6:13; Jer. 6:10; 29:18; 42:18; 44:8). Christ Himself suffered reproach in His earthly ministry (Rom. 5:13; Heb. 13:13). Christians are called upon to suffer reproach for God's name (Pss. 69:7; 89:50) or for the sake of Christ (Luke 6:22; 2 Cor. 12:10; Heb. 10:33; 11:26; 1 Pet. 4:14). See *Shame and Honor.*   *William Chandler*

REPROBATE KJV term used in two senses: that which fails to meet a test and is thus rejected as unworthy or unacceptable, as impure silver (Jer. 6:30) or persons (2 Cor. 13:5-7; Titus 1:16); and that which is depraved or without morals (Rom. 1:28; 2 Tim. 3:8). NASB and RSV used "reprobate" to mean "one rejected by God" (Ps. 15:4; cp. HCSB, REB, TEV).

REPTILES Animals that crawl or move on the belly or on small short legs. This category of animals includes alligators, crocodiles, lizards, snakes, and turtles. It is generally agreed that in many instances the reptiles in the Bible can-

not be specifically determined. Many times the same Hebrew word is translated in different ways. Leviticus 11:30 is a case in point. The same Hebrew word translated "lizard" in a number of translations is translated "crocodile" here in the RSV. There does, however, seem to be a grouping of reptiles in this verse, even though the specific names may be difficult to determine. See *Creeping Things.*

Adder Venomous snake. See *Serpent* below.

Asp Venomous snake. Modern translations often use "cobra." See Isa. 11:8 in various translations. See *Serpent* below.

Chameleon Kind of lizard that changes color according to its surroundings. The unique design of its eyes characterizes the chameleon. Each eyeball moves independently; thus, it can look two ways at the same time. Feeding mostly on insects, the chameleon is harmless. In Palestine it lives in trees and bushes and hangs onto branches with its long tail.

Cobra Deadly poisonous snake with loose skin on its neck that forms a hood when the cobra is excited. See *Asp.*

Cockatrice Venomous snake. Cockatrice is the name for a legendary serpent. As used in the KJV, however, it is a venomous snake. Later versions translate the Hebrew word "adder" (RSV) and "viper" or "venomous snake" (NIV).

Crocodile Large, thick-skinned, aquatic reptile. See *Lizard* below.

Gecko Wall lizard, a common type of lizard in the Holy Land. Sucking-disc toes enable it to run over walls and ceilings. Early versions translated the Hebrew word "ferret," while later scholars believe "gecko" is the correct translation (NASB, RSV, NIV). It is chiefly nocturnal and harmless.

Lizard Long-bodied reptile that is distinguished from the snake by two sets of short legs. Several kinds of lizards are mentioned in Lev. 11:30: gecko, monitor lizard, wall lizard, skink, and chameleon (NIV). One traveler identified as many as 44 different species in Palestine.

Serpent General name for long-bodied reptiles, specifically snakes such as the adder and viper. The serpent is mentioned numerous times. At least 33 different species may be found in Palestine. Translators use various terms to translate the eight Hebrew terms. The serpent—usual name for snake—has been a continuing symbol of evil and of the evil one.

Skink Small lizard listed among the unclean animals (Lev. 11:30 NIV). Other translations render

Large cistern (water reservoir) with column in center at ancient Pergamum.

"sand reptile" (NASB), "snail" (KJV), "sand lizard" (NRSV).

Snake See *Serpent* above.

Tortoise Land turtle listed among the unclean animals (Lev. 11:29 KJV). Other versions have "great lizard" (RSV; NASB; NIV) instead of tortoise.

Viper Venomous snake. See *Serpent* above.

Shirley Stephens

REPUTATION Term used in the KJV to indicate "an opinion" (*dokeo*) of someone or something. It can be used as a term of great esteem or regard such as was attributed to Gamaliel (Acts 5:34), the Jerusalem apostles (Gal. 2:2), and Epaphroditus (Phil. 2:29). It can, however, carry negative implications in reference to individual character (Eccles. 10:1). In Phil. 2:7 the word is translated as "emptied Himself" (HCSB, NASB, NRSV) in reference to Christ's taking on the human form of a bondservant. See *Kenosis*.

William Chandler

RESEN (Rē´ sən) Place-name meaning "fountain head." City that Nimrod founded between Nineveh and Calah (Gen. 10:12). Probably modern Salemijeh (in Iraq), two and a half miles northwest of Nimrud.

RESERVOIR Place for catching and storing water for later use, either agricultural (2 Chron. 26:10; Eccles. 2:6) or as an urban supply in anticipation of a siege (2 Kings 20:20; Isa. 22:8b-11). Reservoirs were a necessity in most of Palestine where seasonal rains were the major water source. See *Water*.

RESH (Rāsh) Twentieth letter in the Hebrew alphabet, which the KJV used as heading for the eight verses of Ps. 119:153-160 that each begin with this letter.

RESHEPH (Rē´ shĕph) Personal name meaning "flame." An Ephraimite (1 Chron. 7:25).

RESIN NIV translation of "bdellium" (Gen. 2:12; cp. Num. 11:7). See *Bdellium*.

RESPECT OF PERSONS Honor and partiality. Respect or honor is to be shown to older men (Lev. 19:32; cp. Lam. 5:12), public officials (Rom. 13:7), parents (1 Tim. 3:4), masters (1 Pet. 2:18), and Christian leaders (1 Thess. 5:12). Christians are to live in such a way that they command the respect of neighbors and thus serve as effective witnesses (1 Thess. 4:12). Scripture repeatedly affirms that God is no respecter of persons, that is, that God does not show partiality; thus God's people are to refrain from prejudice.

RESTITUTION Act of returning what has wrongfully been taken or replacing what has been lost or damaged and the divine restoration of all things to their original order.

Human Restitution The Law required "trespass offerings" to be made for sins against a neighbor (theft, deception, dishonesty, extortion, keeping lost property, or damaging property). Such crimes involved "unfaithfulness" toward God and disrupted fellowship and peace among the people. They were to be atoned for by a guilt offering to God and restitution to the wronged neighbor. Atonement and forgiveness of the sin were received after restitution had been made to the victim. The sin offering to God always followed the act of restitution. Old Testament law established a principle of "punishment to fit the crime" (life for life, eye for eye, tooth for tooth, wound for wound). Restitution was consistent with this concept of equity. The stolen property was to be returned, or "full" compensation was to be made. The guidelines for making complete restitution also included a provision for punitive damages (up to five times what had been lost), justice that moved beyond "an eye for an eye." Provisions were made for complications in this process (Exod. 22:3). The act of making restitution to a victim was so closely identified with the atoning sacrifice made to God that the two expressions could be seen as elements of the same command. Neither could stand alone. Specific examples of this law in operation are not found, but the principle in action is found (1 Kings 20:34; 2 Kings 8:6; Neh. 5:10-12). There is no legal or ritual application of this command in the NT; however, the principle of restitution is clearly pictured in the story of Zacchaeus (Luke 19:1-10). Jesus implicitly validated the practice when He admonished followers to "be reconciled" to a brother before offering a gift to God (Matt. 5:23-24).

Divine Restitution The NT (Gk.) word is found only once (Acts 3:21) and is sometimes translated "restoration." It describes the future work of God that will reestablish all "things" to their pristine order and purpose. The implication here is not the restoration of persons but of the created order, that is, the universal renewal of the earth. This divine restoration will accompany the return and triumph of Christ (1 Cor. 15:25-28).   *Ken Massey*

RESURRECTION Future, bodily rising from the dead of all persons. Believers in Christ rise to eternal life and bliss with God; unbelievers to eternal torment and separation from God.

Old Testament Though not prominent, OT passages demonstrate belief in bodily resurrection. Prophets used the idea to express hope of national rebirth for Israel (Ezek. 37; Isa. 26:19). Psalm 16:10 views resurrection in a messianic framework; God will not abandon His "Holy One" to the grave. Believers may be confident facing death because God will not leave them destitute; He will "redeem" them from the grave and take them to Himself (Ps. 49:14-15). Death was not final; God would renew the body and the individual could "see God" (Job 19:26). Daniel 12:2 provides the clearest OT statement on resurrection: "Multitudes who sleep in the dust of the earth will awake: some to everlasting life, others to shame and everlasting contempt" (NIV). Both righteous and wicked will be resurrected. Thus eternal consequences are tied to actions and decisions made in life.

New Testament The NT provides clear and extensive treatment of the resurrection. The Gospels foreshadow a future, bodily resurrection. In the Synoptic Gospels Jesus twice resuscitates deceased persons: the son of a widow (Luke 7:11-17) and the daughter of Jairus (Mark 5:22-43). Further, Jesus instructed the Twelve to

"raise the dead" (Matt. 10:8). These revealed that the kingdom of God had come in the person and mission of Jesus and pointed forward to the raising from the dead of Jesus' followers, never to die again. Jesus taught the resurrection and reward of the righteous in the parable of a dinner (Luke 14:12-14). The resurrection provides background for a discussion with the Sadducees. Answering their question of the woman with seven husbands, Jesus replied that resurrection life is different; marriage will no longer be needed (Mark 12:18-23). Jesus used the occasion to assert that the patriarchs still lived (Mark 12:26-27).

Resurrection is prominent in John, who portrays resurrection as a present, spiritual reality and a future eschatological event. The dead will be raised to eternal life; resurrection life also can now be experienced in part. Jesus' underscored this at the death of Lazarus: "I am the resurrection and the life. The one who believes in Me, even if he dies, will live. Everyone who lives and believes in Me will never die" (John 11:25-26 HCSB). The resurrection life is a present reality of life in the Son (John 5:25-26). The resurrection of the body is a future promise awaiting fulfillment (John 6:35-40). John also connects the believer's bodily resurrection to the reality of Jesus' bodily resurrection (John 20:17).

The concept of resurrection was pivotal in the early church. The message of the apostles was closely tied to the resurrection of Jesus (Acts 3:14). Because of Jesus' resurrection, the apostles were able to do mighty works (Acts 4:10). The persistent witness to the resurrection of Jesus and the promise of believers' resurrection produced hostility, opposition, and persecution (Acts 4:1-21; 5:29-32; 23:6).

For Paul the resurrection was a historical event and a supernatural act of God. The goal of salvation is full possession of the inheritance (a resurrection body) at the resurrection (Eph. 1:14). Christ will descend with all believers who have died, the immaterial will be reunited with the material, and souls will be joined to resurrected, glorified bodies (1 Thess. 4:13-18). The resurrection will provide a resurrection body suitable for life in the consummated kingdom of God (1 Cor. 15:35-56). For Paul the resurrection was of such paramount importance that to deny the resurrection of the believer was essentially to deny the resurrection of Christ. Without the resurrection of Christ, believers had no hope, and their faith is vain (1 Cor. 15:12-34). To deny the reality of the resurrection (1 Cor. 15) or to teach that the resurrection had already occurred (2 Tim. 2:17-18) was destructive of the faith.

Biblical Teaching First, resurrection is different from resuscitation. A resuscitation, like that of Lazarus, is a return to life, but eventually physical death comes again. Those resurrected will not die again. Resurrection is to eternal life, perfect peace, joy, and bliss in God's kingdom forever. Second, resurrection is bodily. Bodily resurrection is essential to receive the full redemptive, atoning work of God. Salvation is not complete until the body experiences full redemption. Conversely, eternal damnation is not complete until unbelievers experience the pain and anguish of hell in body and soul. The resurrection of the body re-proclaims the Edenic pronouncement of the goodness of Creation (Gen. 1:31) and underscores the importance of the body in the purposes of God. Third, the nature of the resurrection body remains somewhat mysterious. Some aspects, such as personal identity, carry over to the resurrected state. But life in a resurrected body will be different from that previously known (1 Cor. 15:37-44). "For we know that if our earthly house, a tent, is destroyed, we have a building from God, a house not made with hands, eternal in the heavens" (2 Cor. 5:1 HCSB).   *Stan Norman*

RESURRECTION OF JESUS THE CHRIST

Historical event whereby Jesus came back from physical death to newness of life with a glorified body, never to die again. The bodily resurrection of Jesus is one of the central tenets of the Christian faith. His bodily resurrection validates the claim that He is both Lord and Christ. It substantiates the proposition that His life and death were not just the life and death of a good man but that He indeed was God incarnate and that by His death we have forgiveness of sin.

The four Gospels are selective in the events they report surrounding the resurrection. Each emphasizes the empty tomb, but each is somewhat different in the postresurrection appearances recounted.

Mark's Gospel Mark's account is the briefest, containing only eight verses, if the shorter ending of Mark is accepted as authentic. The focus of his account is on the women's discovery of the empty tomb (Mark 16:1-4), the announcement of the resurrection by a young man wearing a white robe, and Jesus' promise to meet them in Galilee (16:5-7). The women's response is one of fear and awe (16:8).

Matthew's Gospel Matthew's report is 20 verses long. He emphasizes three aspects: the empty tomb, his answer to the false accusation that the disciples stole the body, and the Great Commission. Matthew recounts only two resurrection appearances: first, to the women as they fled the empty tomb, and then to the Eleven in Galilee. His account is in four scenes. The first takes place at the empty tomb and involves Mary Magdalene, the "other Mary," a violent earthquake, the appearance of an angel, the paralyzing fear of the guards, and an admonition to tell the disciples that Jesus is alive (Matt. 28:1-7). The second describes Jesus' encounter with the women after they fled the tomb (28:8-10). The third is a description of the religious leaders' attempt to cover up the events at the tomb (28:11-15). The fourth takes place in Galilee and concludes with Jesus giving the Great Commission (28:16-20).

Luke's Gospel Luke's record is 53 verses in length. His account consists of a series of resurrection appearances of Jesus ending with Jesus' ascension. All resurrection appearances in Luke are in Jerusalem. Luke has at least three aims: first, presenting the historical facts (cp. Luke 1:1-4), describing how the unbelieving disciples came to believe in the resurrection by emphasizing the physical nature of Jesus' resurrected body (24:30,37-43); second, to show that Jesus' death and resurrection fulfill OT prophecy (24:25-27,32); and third, to show that the disciples are to preach the gospel in the power of the Spirit to all the nations (24:46-49). The material is in four vignettes. The first involves the women's discovery of the empty tomb and the investigation of the tomb by Peter and John (24:1-12). The second, the longest, is Jesus' appearance to two disciples on the road to Emmaus. The third is Jesus' appearance to the disciples during the evening of resurrection Sunday. The fourth is Jesus' final instructions to His followers at His ascension (24:50-53; cp. Acts 1:9-11).

John's Gospel John's resurrection account is the longest, extending two full chapters. John records three appearances in Jerusalem: the first to Mary Magdalene at the empty tomb (20:1-18) and the other two appearances to the disciples, once with Thomas absent (John 20:19-25) and once with Thomas present (20:26-29). Jesus' Jerusalem appearances conclude with Thomas' great confession, "My Lord and my God" (John 20:28). Like Luke, John focuses on the corporeality of Jesus (20:17,20,25-27). The appearance in chapter 21 takes place in Galilee. His purpose seems to be to describe the reestablishing of Peter's leadership (21:15-19) and to expel the rumor that John, the disciple "whom Jesus loved" (13:23 HCSB) would not die before Jesus' return.

A cursory reading of the resurrection accounts in the four Gospels reveals a wide variety of material. Admittedly, any attempt at harmonization of the accounts is speculative, and dogmatism must be avoided. It is impossible to know which, if any, of them is correct, but each shows a possible arrangement of events in a credible sequence. The problem of varying accounts, however, is not confined to events surrounding the resurrection; problems arising from differences in details from various sources have attended almost every event in history. The variances in the scriptural accounts suggest independent witnesses rather than the repetition of an "official" party line.

Paul's Account The oldest account of the resurrection is found in 1 Cor. 15. In that passage Paul recounted a number of postresurrection appearances. He established that the believer's future resurrection is based on the historicity of Christ's bodily resurrection. However, the authenticity of Christ's resurrection is greatly debated.

Response of Critics Since the 19th century scholars have questioned the historicity of the resurrection of Jesus. Some have argued that the women and disciples went to the wrong tomb. The problem with this argument is that the Jewish leadership could have presented the corpse of Jesus in response to the proclamation of the resurrection. Surely they knew the location of the tomb. Another proposed alternative is that the disciples stole the body of Jesus. It is unlikely that the disciples would have stolen the body and thereby invented a story for which they were willing to suffer persecution and martyrdom. Still others contend that Jesus never really died on the cross but He merely "swooned" and later in the coolness of the tomb revived enough to escape. This proposal fails to take seriously the severe beatings Jesus endured, the horrific process of crucifixion, the recognition by a centurion that He was dead (Mark 15:39), as well as the piercing of His side to confirm His death (John 19:32-34). Another suggestion by skeptics is that Jesus continued to live after His crucifixion in some "spiritual" sense but that this did not involve a bodily resurrection. However, the biblical evidence for corporeality is very strong (Luke 24:40-43; John 20:27). Finally, some scholars have compared the resurrection appearances to hallucinations. However, the NT gives evidence of appearances in various places to numerous people, even 500 at one time (1 Cor. 15:6). This proposal also fails to acknowledge that the disciples were psychologically unprepared for the resurrection and actually disbelieved the initial reports.

The evidence in favor of the historicity of the bodily resurrection of Jesus is very strong. The evidence for the empty tomb is weighty. First, the story of the empty tomb is found in all four Gospels and is implicit in the early church's proclamation of the resurrection. How could they preach the bodily resurrection of Jesus if everyone in Jerusalem knew that His body was still in the tomb? Second, it is difficult to believe that the early church would have fabricated the story of the resurrection and then made women the first witnesses to the empty tomb and the resurrection, since women were not considered reliable witnesses in Jewish culture (illustrated by the disciple's response to them). Third, something incredible must have taken place on that Sunday to cause Jewish believers to begin worshiping on the first day of the week instead of the Sabbath (Acts 20:7; 1 Cor. 16:2; Rev. 1:10). Finally, nothing short of the miracle of the resurrection can explain the postresurrection transformation in the disciples. The biblical record indicates that at the time of Jesus' arrest they all fled (Mark 14:50). When the women reported that they had seen Jesus, the men did not believe (Luke 24:11), yet these same men were later willing to suffer persecution and martyrdom in order to preach Jesus as the resurrected Lord. See *Ascension; Christ, Christology; Jesus Christ; Resurrection.*   *Bill Cook*

RETINUE NASB, REB, NRSV, REB term for the attendants of the queen of Sheba (1 Kings 10:2; KJV, train; NIV, caravan). See *Caravan.*

RETURN OF CHRIST See *Eschatology; Future Hope; Millennium; Parousia; Second Coming.*

REU (Rē´ ū) Personal name meaning "friend, companion." Descendant of Shem (Gen. 11:18-21; 1 Chron. 1:25), possibly the ancestor of a Semitic tribe associated with Ra'ilu, an island in the Euphrates below Anat.

REUBEN, REUBENITES (Rū´ bĕn [īts]) Eldest son of Jacob, born to Leah (Gen. 29:32) while the couple was living with her father, Laban, in Paddan-aram, and the clan or tribe descended from him. Among his acts recorded in the Bible, Reuben found mandrakes (out of which a love potion probably was made for his mother to use with Jacob, 30:14,16-17) and had sexual relations with one of his father's concubines (35:22), for which he later was chastised (49:4). Reuben felt compassion for young Joseph when his brothers wanted to kill the brash dreamer (37:21-22) and was willing to be responsible to his father for Benjamin's welfare when the unknown Joseph commanded that the youngest brother be brought to Egypt (42:37).

The tribe that was named for Reuben held a place of honor among the other tribes. The territory the tribe inherited was just east of the Dead Sea and was the first parcel of land to be bestowed (Num. 32).

REUEL (Rū´ ĕl) Personal name meaning "friend of God." **1.** Son of Esau and ancestor of several Edomite clans (Gen. 36:4,10,13,17; 1 Chron. 1:35,37). **2.** Exodus 2:18 identifies Reuel as the "father" of Zipporah, Moses' wife. Numbers 10:29 presents Reuel as the father of Hobab, Moses' father-in-law. Elsewhere Moses' father-in-law is called Jethro. The tradition is also divided regarding the background of Moses' father-in-law, either Midianite (Exod. 2:16; 3:1) or Kenite (Judg. 1:16; 4:11). See *Jethro.* **3.** A Gadite (Num. 2:14). **4.** A Benjaminite (1 Chron. 9:8).

REUMAH (Rū´ mah) Personal name meaning "coral." Nahor's concubine, an ancestress of several Aramean tribes living northwest of Damascus (Gen. 22:24).

REVELATION OF GOD Content and process of God's making Himself known to people. All knowledge of God comes by way of revelation. Human knowledge of God is revealed knowledge, since God, and He alone, gives it. He bridges the gap between Himself and His creatures, disclosing Himself and His will to them. By God alone can God be known.

Modern thought often questions the possibility and/or reality of revelation. Biblical faith affirms revelation is real because the personal Creator God has chosen to let His human creatures know Him. The question remains, "How can a person know God?" The Bible appears to distinguish two ways of knowing God, general and special revelation.

Biblical emphasis points to Jesus Christ as God's final revelation. God has provided ongoing generations of believers a source of knowledge about Himself and His Son. That source is the Bible.

Definition The word "revelation" means an uncovering, a removal of the veil, a disclosure of what was previously unknown. Revelation of God is God's manifestation of Himself to mankind in such a way that men and women can know and fellowship with Him. Jesus explained to Peter: "Blessed are you, Simon son of Jonah, because flesh and blood did not reveal this to you, but My Father in heaven" (Matt. 16:17 HCSB). The knowledge of Jesus' sonship was not attained by human discovery, nor could it have been; it came from God alone.

All Christians recognize that God has acted and spoken in history, revealing Himself to His creatures. Yet a variety of opinions seek to define what constitutes revelation.

General Revelation God and His creation are distinct. Yet God might reveal Himself through His actions in that world. Besides saying or writing things, persons may reveal facts about themselves in other ways, such as physical gestures or facial expressions. Sometimes persons' actions communicate whether they are selfish or generous, clumsy or skillful. A grimace, a smile, or a frown can often be telling. Transferring these things to a theological context is not simple because God is not visible. He does not have facial features or bodily parts with which to gesture. To say God reveals Himself through nature means that through the events of the physical world God communicates to us things about Himself that we would otherwise not know.

What sort of things might God tell us in this manner? Paul explained, "From the creation of the world His invisible attributes, that is, His eternal power and divine nature, have been clearly seen, being understood through what He has made. As a result, people are without excuse" (Rom. 1:20 HCSB). The psalmist (Ps. 19:1) saw the glory of God through the spectacles of special revelation. What the psalmist saw was objectively and genuinely there. We can rephrase these observations to say that all that can be known about God in a natural sense has been revealed in nature. This is what we call natural or general revelation. General revelation is universal in the sense that it is God's self-disclosure of Himself in a general way to all people at all times in all places. General revelation occurs (1) through nature, (2) in our experience and in our conscience, and (3) in history.

In the wonders of the heavens and in the beauty of the earth, God manifests Himself. Jesus taught that God "causes His sun to rise on the evil and the good, and sends rain on the righteous and the unrighteous" (Matt. 5:45 HCSB), thus revealing His goodness to all. "The living God, who made the heaven, the earth, the sea, and everything in them ... did not leave Himself without a witness, since He did good: giving you rain from heaven and fruitful seasons, and satisfying your hearts with food and happiness" (Acts 14:15-17 HCSB). God makes Himself known in the continuing care and provision for mankind. The universe as a whole serves the Creator's purposes as a vehicle of God's self-manifestation.

God also reveals himself in men and women. They are made in the "image" and "likeness" of God (Gen. 1:26-27). Humans, as a direct creation of God, are a mirror or reflection of God. People are God's unique workmanship evidenced by their place of dominion over the rest of creation; in their capacity to reason, feel, and imagine; in their freedom to act and respond; and in their sense of right and wrong (Gen. 1:28; Rom. 2:14-15). Especially through this moral sense, God reveals Himself in the consciences of men and women. The fact that religious belief and practice is universal confirms the apostle's statements in Rom. 2. Yet the creatures who worship, pray, build temples, idols and shrines, and seek after God in diverse ways do not glorify God as God or give Him thanks (Rom. 1:21-23).

Nevertheless, because each person has been given the capacity for receiving God's general revelation, they are responsible for their actions.

God manifests Himself in the workings of history. All of history, rightly understood, bears the imprint of God's activity and thus has a theological character. Primarily, God is revealed in history through the rise and fall of peoples and nations (cp. Acts 17:22-31).

God's general revelation is plain, whether in nature, in human conscience, or in history. Even though it is plain, it is often misinterpreted because sinful and finite humans are trying to understand a perfect and infinite God. What we have seen so far is compatible with the following:

(1) Religious belief is a nearly universal human phenomenon.

(2) Such religious belief is implanted by God.

(3) All people ought to acknowledge God on the basis of what they learned from the world around them.

(4) All people believe in God and show their belief even though they do not admit it.

(5) No one, no matter how seemingly insignificant or weak-minded, can be excused for missing God's revelation.

The light of nature is not sufficient to give the knowledge of God necessary for salvation. For God's power (Rom. 1:20), goodness (Matt. 5:45), and righteousness (Rom. 2:14-15) have been revealed but not His salvific grace. That is revealed only through special revelation. Special revelation is necessary to instruct people how to worship God rightly. God in His general revelation reveals Himself, but, because of our sinfulness, humans pervert the reception of His general revelation, a revelation so plain it leaves all without excuse. It is as if a lawyer were offered the information necessary to solve a case yet chose perversely to ignore it.

In summary, humans lack the willingness to come to a pure and clear knowledge of God. Men and women suppress God's truth because they do not like the truth about God. They do not like the God to whom the truth leads them, so they invent substitute gods and religions instead. The universality of religion on earth is evidence of truths discussed above. According to Paul, the act of suppressing the awareness of God and His demands warps our reason and conscience. Because of this rejection of God, He righteously reveals His wrath against mankind. God's general revelation does not bring one into a saving relationship with God; it does reveal God to His creatures, and they are, therefore, responsible for their response. This view of general revelation can only be accepted through special revelation.

Special Revelation God has revealed Himself in nature, human experience, and history, but sin's entrance into the world has changed the revelation as well as the interpretation of it. What is needed to understand God's self-disclosure fully is His special revelation. Divine truth exists outside of special revelation, but it is consistent with and supplemental to, not a substitute for, special revelation.

In contrast to God's general revelation, which is available to all people, God's special revelation is available to specific people at specific times in specific places; it is available now only by consultation of sacred Scripture. Special revelation is first of all particular. God reveals Himself to His people. These people of God are the children of Abraham, whether by natural (Gen. 12:1-3) or spiritual descent (Gal. 3:16,29). Does this mean that God confines knowledge of Himself to a particular people? Not necessarily, because God's general revelation has been given to all, though perverted and rejected by the universal wickedness of mankind. He now chooses to whom and through whom He will make Himself known. As with Abraham, God said: "All the peoples on earth will be blessed through you" (Gen. 12:3 HCSB). God manifests Himself in a particular manner to His people so they will be a channel of blessing to all others.

Special revelation is also progressive. Biblical history witnesses to a developing disclosure of God, His will, and His truth in the OT and NT. The development is not contradictory in any fashion. It is complementary and supplementary to what had been previously revealed. We should not think of the progress from untruth to truth but from a lesser to a fuller revelation (Heb. 1:1-3). The revelation of the law in the OT is not superseded by the gospel but is fulfilled in it.

Special revelation is primarily redemptive and personal. In recognition of the human predicament, God chose at the very beginning to disclose Himself in a more direct way. Within time and space God has acted and spoken to redeem the human race from its own self-imposed evil. Through calling people, miracles,

the exodus, covenant making, and ultimately through Jesus Christ, God has revealed Himself in history.

The ultimate point of God's personal revelation is in Jesus Christ. In Him the Word became flesh (John 1:1,14; 14:9). The OT promise of salvation as a divine gift to people who cannot save themselves has been fulfilled in the gift of His Son. The redemptive revelation of God is that Jesus Christ has borne the sins of fallen humanity, has died in their place, and has been raised to assure justification. This is the fixed center of special revelation.

Special revelation is also propositional. It includes not only those personal, redemptive acts in history but also the prophetic-apostolic interpretation of those events. God's self-disclosure is propositional in that it made known truths about Him to His people. Knowledge about someone precedes intimate knowledge of someone. The primary purpose of revelation is not necessarily to enlarge the scope of one's knowledge. Yet propositional knowledge is for the purpose of personal knowledge.

We can thus affirm that special revelation has three stages: (1) redemption in history, ultimately centering in the work of the Lord Jesus Christ; (2) the Bible, written revelation interpreting what He has done for the redemption of men and women; (3) the work of the Holy Spirit in the lives of individuals and the corporate life of the church, applying God's revelation to the minds and hearts of His people. As a result, men and women receive Jesus Christ as Lord and Savior and are enabled to follow Him faithfully in a believing, covenant community until life's end.

The content of special revelation is primarily God Himself. Mystery remains even in God's self-revelation. God does not fully reveal Himself to any person. God does, however, reveal Himself to persons to the degree they can receive it. Special revelation is the declaration of truth about God, His character, and His action and relationship with His creation to bring all creation under Christ, the one head (Eph. 1:9-10).

The proper setting of special revelation is Christian faith. God makes Himself known to those who receive His revelation in faith (Heb. 11:1,6). Faith is the glad recognition of truth, the reception of God's revelation without reservation or hesitation (Rom. 10:17).

R

For today the Bible is of crucial importance. Through the Bible the Spirit witnesses to individuals of God's grace and the need of faith response. In the Bible we learn of God's redemption of sinners in Christ Jesus. Our faith response to God's Word and acts, recorded and interpreted by the prophets and apostles, calls for us to embrace with humility and teachableness, without finding fault, whatever is taught in Holy Scripture.

In summary we can say that God has initiated the revelation of Himself to men and women. This revelation is understandable to mankind and makes it possible to know God and grow in relationship with Him. God's self-manifestation provides information about Himself for the purpose of leading men and women into God's presence. For believers today the Bible is the source of God's revelation. In the written word we can identify God, know and understand something about Him, His will, and His work, and point others to Him. Special revelation is not generally speculative. The Bible primarily speaks on matters of cosmology and history where these issues touch the nature of faith. God has manifested Himself incarnately through human language, human thought, and human action as ultimately demonstrated in the incarnation of Jesus Christ.   *David S. Dockery*

REVELATION, BOOK OF Last book in the Bible. Its title is from its first word, *apokalupsis*, meaning to "unveil," "disclose," or "reveal." Revelation 1:1 gives the theme of the book: it is a revelation "of," "from," and "about" Jesus Christ. Revelation is apocalyptic literature, though actually a combination of three literary types: (1) *apocalyptic*—a heightened or intensified form of prophecy which uses cryptic, richly symbolic language to portray the dramatic end-time vindication and victory of God and his people (1:1); (2) *prophecy*—God's direct word of proclamation to his people through his servants, both foretelling and forth telling (1:3); (3) *epistle*—a letter addressing needs of particular churches (1:4-7; 2–3; 22:21). Revelation points to future hope and calls for present faithfulness and perseverance.

To encourage faithfulness Revelation points to the glorious world to come, a world where "death will exist no longer; grief, crying, and pain will exist no longer" (21:4 HCSB; cp. 7:16)

at the reappearing of the crucified and risen Jesus. The enthroned Lord will return to conclude world history with the destruction of God's enemies, the final salvation of His people, and creation of a new heaven and a new earth (21–22). The intensity of John's experience is matched only by the richness of the apocalyptic symbolism employed to warn his readers of impending disasters and temptations that would require steadfast allegiance to the risen Lord. To be sure, the Lord will come in power and glory but not before His enemies have exercised a terrible but limited (by divine mercy) attack on those who "hold to the testimony of Jesus" (cp. 1:9; 6:9; 12:11).

Author Four times the author identifies himself as John (1:1,4,9; 22:8). Early Christian traditions attribute the Gospel, the three letters, and the book of Revelation to the Apostle John. Revelation is the only one claiming to be written by someone named John. Though the author does not claim to be the Apostle John, it seems unlikely that any other first-century Christian leader would have had the authority or was associated closely enough with the churches of Asia Minor to have referred to himself simply as John. There are some differences in style and language between the Gospel, the Johannine epistles, and the Revelation, but there are also significant similarities. For example, only the Gospel and Revelation refer to Jesus as the Word of God (John 1:1; Rev. 19:13) and the Lamb. The theme of "witness" is also particularly prominent in all five books. The best view is that the John of the Revelation was in fact John the apostle, brother of James, son of Zebedee. See *John*.

Setting The author's situation was one of suffering. He was a "brother and partner in the tribulation" which is "in Jesus" and, because of his testimony to Jesus, was exiled to the island of Patmos (1:9 HCSB). The situations of the recipients varied, though all were experiencing difficulties. A faithful Christian in Pergamum suffered death (2:12-13), and the church in Smyrna was warned of impending persecution (2:10). Ephesus had left its first love (2:4), Pergamum and Thyatira tolerated false teaching (2:14-15; 20), Sardis was spiritually dead (3:1), Philadelphia faced Jewish opposition (3:9), and Laodicea was lukewarm (3:16). These seven churches are the immediate destination of the book. The representative character of the seven churches and the prophetic message of the book indicates, however, that it was for a much wider audience, the church at large.

Date Revelation was written late in the first century. Early tradition dated the book during the reign of the Roman emperor Domitian (A.D. 81–96). An alternative view dates it shortly after the reign of Nero (A.D. 54–68). Scholars who favor the time of Nero argue that the repeated references to persecution in the book (1:9; 2:2-3,10,13; 3:9-10; 6:10-11; 7:14-17; 11:7; 12:13–13:17; 14:12-20; 19:2; 21:4) fit better during his reign, when persecutions clearly took place. The allusion to the temple in 11:1 seems to imply it is still standing, requiring a pre A.D. 70 date. Those who argue for the time of Domitian note that this was the view of Irenaeus, Victorinus, Eusebius, and Jerome. The letters to the seven churches presuppose development and decline, while these churches (not founded until the late 50s) seem to be doing well when Paul was imprisoned in the 60s. By the time of Domitian, a second generation might not exhibit the convictions of the first, especially facing intensified opposition and challenges to compromise (cp. the background to the letters from John). Most scholars affirm the time of Domitian as better and set the date ca. A.D. 90 to 96. Whichever date is correct, it was a time of growing persecution, doctrinal challenge, and moral compromise.

Literary Structure of the Book Several approaches have been offered, of which two have special appeal. First, the book may be outlined around the phrase "in the Spirit" used at four strategic locations when John moves to a different location (1:10; 4:2; 17:3; 21:10). A second approach sees 1:19 as the interpretive key. John is told to write "what you have seen" (chap. 1), "what is" (chaps. 2–3), "and what will take place after this" (chaps. 4–22) (HCSB).

Interpretive Approaches to Revelation Interpreters can usually be placed in one of four categories:

1. Preterist The book is about and for the first century. Most, if not all, of the events described in the book were fulfilled in John's day.

2. Historicists The book is a panorama of church history with attention focusing on its development in the West.

3. Idealist The book is symbolic of timeless truth and the conflict between good and evil. No specific persons or events are in view. The message to be proclaimed and received is that in the end God is victorious.

4. Futurist Beginning with chapter 4 (or 6) the book describes what will take place at the end of history just before the second coming of Jesus Christ and the establishment of His kingdom.

Introduction (1:1-8) Written to "the seven churches" of the Roman province of Asia Minor, John's work is a "revelation" about and from Jesus Christ of "what must quickly take place." The theme is clear: the Lord God Himself has guaranteed the final vindication of the crucified Jesus (1:7-8). A blessing (the first of seven) is promised to those who hear and heed its message (1:3).

John's Vision on the Island of Patmos (1:9-20) While in exile on Patmos, John saw the risen Lord (1:9-20). Appearing clothed in power and majesty (1:9-20), the Living One revealed Himself as the Lord of the churches and instructed John to send not only the seven letters but also an account of the things which he had seen and would see, a revelation of "what will take place after this" (1:19 HCSB).

Letters to the Seven Churches (2:1–3:22) The letters to the churches of Ephesus, Smyrna, Pergamum, Thyatira, Sardis, Philadelphia, and Laodicea have a fairly consistent format. First, after designating the recipients, the risen Lord describes Himself using a portion of the description in 1:9-20. Then follows an "I know" section of commendation and/or criticism. Next, typically, is some form of exhortation: to those receiving criticism, an exhortation to repent; however, to the churches of Smyrna and Philadelphia, for whom the Lord had only praise, the exhortation is one of assurance (2:10; 3:10-13). Each letter concludes with both an exhortation to "listen to what the Spirit says to the churches" and a promise of reward to the "victor," the one who conquers by persevering in the cause of Christ. Each promise finds its source in the glorious consummation (Rev. 19–22). The church at Ephesus (2:1-7) is told to return to her first love; the church at Smyrna (2:8-11) to be faithful unto death; the churches of Pergamum (2:12-17) and Thyatira (2:18-29) must beware of false teaching and immoral deeds accompanying erroneous theology. The church at Sardis (3:1-6) is told to wake up and

Millennial Perspectives on Revelation

Point of Interpretation	Amillennial	Historical (Post-tribulation) Premillennial	*Pretribulation Premillennial	Preterist Postmillennialism
Description of View	Viewpoint that the present rule of Christ in heaven or the present age of Christ's rule in the church is the millennium; holds to one resurrection and judgment marking the end of history as we know it and the beginning of the eternal state	Viewpoint that Christ will reign on earth for 1,000 years following His second coming; saints will be resurrected at the beginning of the millennium, nonbelievers at the end, followed by the judgment	Viewpoint that Christ will reign on earth for 1,000 years, following His second coming; saints will be resurrected at the rapture prior to the tribulation and those who die during the tribulation at the beginning of the millennium	"Millennial" kingdom of Christ established in first century and will continue to spread and increase until the time of final resurrection and judgment
Book of Revelation	Current history written in code to confound enemies and encourage Asian Christians; message applies to all Christians	Immediate application to Asian Christians; applies to all Christians throughout the ages, but the visions also apply to a great future event	Immediate application to Asian Christians; applies to all Christians throughout the ages, but the visions also apply to a great future event	A history of events now past with consequences extending into the present time. Seven Churches of John's day
Seven candlesticks (1:13)	Seven Churches of John's day	Seven Churches of John's day	Seven Churches of John's day	Seven Churches of John's day
Seven stars (1:16,20)	Pastors	Symbolizes heavenly or supernatural character of the church (some believe refers to pastor)	Pastors or angels	Pastors
Churches addressed (chaps. 2–3)	Specific historical situations, truth apply to churches throughout the ages; do not represent periods of church history	Specific historical situations, truth apply to churches throughout the ages; do not represent periods of church history	Specific historical situations, truth apply to churches throughout the ages; do not represent periods of church history	Specific historical situations, truth apply to churches throughout the ages; do not represent periods of church history
Twenty-four elders (4:4, 10; 5:8, 14)	Twelve patriarchs and twelve apostles; together symbolize all the redeemed	Company of angels who help execute God's rule (or elders represent twenty-four priestly and Levitical orders, or symbolizes all the redeemed)	The rewarded church; or represents twelve patriarchs and twelve apostles (the redeemed of all the ages)	?
Sealed book (5:1-9)	Scroll of history; shows God carrying out His redemptive purpose in history	Contains prophecy of end events of chapters 6–22; related to Ezekiel's book of woes (2:9-10) and Daniel's sealed book (12:4, 9-10).	Contains prophecy of end events of chapters 6–22; related to Ezekiel's book of woes (2:9-10) and Daniel's sealed book (12:4, 9-10).	God's decree of His divorce from Israel and of judgment upon Israel
144,000 (7:4-8)	Redeemed on earth who will be protected against God's wrath	Church on threshold of great tribulation (some see as Jewish converts)	Jewish converts of tribulation period who witness for Jesus (same as 14:1)	Jewish Christians

Millennial Perspectives on Revelation

Point of Interpretation	Amillennial	Historical (Post-tribulation) Premillennial	*Pretribulation Premillennial	Preterist Postmillennialism
Great Multitude (7:9-10)	Uncountable multitude in heaven praising God for their salvation	Church, having gone through great tribulation, seen in heaven	Redeemed during tribulation period (possibly martyrs)	The church as a whole?
Great tribulation (first reference in 7:14)	Persecution faced by Asian Christians of John's time; symbolic of tribulation that occurs throughout history	Period at end time of unexplained trouble, before Christ's return; church will go through it; begins with seventh seal (8:1), which contains trumpets 1–6 (8:2 to 14:20)	Period at end-time of unexplained trouble referred to in 7:14 and described in chapters 11–18; latter half of seven-year period between rapture and millennium	Persecution of Asian Christians of John's time
"Star" 9:1	Personified evil	Represents an angelic figure divinely commissioned to carry out God's purpose		Satan
Forty-two months (11:2); 1,260 days (11:3)	Indefinite duration of pagan desolation	A symbolic number representing period of evil with reference to last days of the age	Half of seven-year tribulation period	Time from the beginning of the Jewish revolt in spring of A.D. 66 to penetration of the inner wall of Jerusalem in August A.D. 70
Two witnesses (11:3-10)	Spread of gospel in first century	Symbolic of the church and its witness	Two actual historical persons who witness for Jesus	?
Sodom and Egypt (11:8)	Rome as seat of Empire	Earthly Jerusalem	Earthly Jerusalem	Earthly Jerusalem
Woman (12:1-6)	True people of God under old and new covenants (true Israel)	True people of God under old and new covenants (true Israel)	Indicates Israel, not church; key is comparison with Gen. 37:9	?
Great red dragon (12:3)	All views identify as Satan	All views identify as Satan	All views identify as Satan	All views identify as Satan
Manchild (12:4-5)	Christ at His birth, life events, and crucifixion, whom Satan sought to kill	Christ, whose work Satan seeks to destroy	Christ, whose work Satan seeks to destroy	(probably Christ)?
1,260 days (12:6)	Indefinite time	Symbolic number representing period of evil with special reference to last days of the age	Half of great tribulation after church is raptured	Same as 42 months?
Sea beast (13:1)	Emperor Domitian, personification of Roman Empire (same as in chap. 17)	Antichrist and his kingdom, here shown as embodiment of the four beasts in Dan. 7	Antichrist and his kingdom, here shown as embodiment of the four beasts in Dan. 7	Roman empire generally and Nero specifically

Millennial Perspectives on Revelation

Point of Interpretation	Amillennial	Historical (Post-tribulation) Premillennial	*Pretribulation Premillennial	Preterist Postmillennialism
Seven heads (13:1)	Roman emperors	Great power, shows kinship with dragon	Seven secular empires and revived Roman Empire	The city of Rome generally and Roman emperors specifically from Julius to Galba
Ten horns (13:1)	Symbolic power	Kings represent limited crowns (10) against Christ's many	Ten nations that will serve the beast	?
Earth beast (13:11)	*Concilia,* Roman body in cities responsible for emperor worship	Organized religion as servant of first beast during great tribulation period; headed by a false prophet	Organized religion as servant of first beast during great tribulation period; headed by a false prophet	?
666 (13:18)	Imperfection, evil; personified as Domitian	Symbolic of evil, short of 777; if a personage meant, he is unknown but will be known at the proper time	Symbolic of evil, short of 777; if a personage meant, he is unknown but will be known at the proper time	The numerical value of "Nero Caesar"
144,000 on Mount Zion (14:1)	Total body of redeemed in heaven	Total body of redeemed in heaven	Redeemed Jews gathered in earthly Jerusalem during millennial kingdom	Jewish Christians?
River of blood (14:20)	Symbol of infinite punishment for the wicked	Means God's radical judgment crushes evil thoroughly	Scene of wrath and carnage that will occur in Palestine	Symbol of blood shed in Israel during the Jewish war
Babylon (women, 17:5)	Historical Rome	Symbol of evil opposition to God	?	Jerusalem
Beast	Domitian	Antichrist		Roman Empire
Seven mountains (17:9)	Pagan Rome, which was built on seven hills	Indicate power, so here means a succession of empires, last of which is end time Babylon	Rome, revived at end time	?
Seven heads (17:7) and seven kings (17:10)	Roman emperors from Augustus to Titus, excluding three brief rules	Five past godless kingdoms; sixth was Rome; seventh will arise in end time	Five past godless kingdoms; sixth was Rome; seventh will arise in end time	?
Ten horns (17:7) and ten kings (17:12)	Vassal kings who ruled with Rome's permission	Symbolic of earthly powers that will be subservient to antichrist	Ten kingdoms arising in future, who will serve the antichrist	?
Bride, wife (19:7)	The church			
Marriage supper (19:9)	Climax of the age; symbolizes complete union of Christ with His people	Union of Christ with His people at His coming	Union of Christ with His people at His coming	Symbolizes the new relation of God with the church as opposed to His divorce from Israel
One on white horse (19:11-16)	Vision of Christ's victory over pagan Rome; return of Christ occurs in connection with events of 20:7-10	Second coming of Christ	Second coming of Christ	Christ comes to destroy Jerusalem and judge Israel while taking a new bride, the church

Millennial Perspectives on Revelation

Point of Interpretation	Amillennial	Historical (Post-tribulation) Premillennial	*Pretribulation Premillennial	Preterist Postmillennialism
Battle of Armageddon (19:19-21; see 16:16)	Not literally at end of time but symbolizes power of God's word overcoming evil; principle applies to all ages	Literal event of some kind at end time but not literal battle with military weapons; occurs at Christ's return at beginning of millennium	Literal bloody battle at Armageddon (valley of Megiddo) at end of great tribulation between Christ and the armies of the beast; they are all defeated by Christ and then the millennium begins; stands in contrast to marriage supper	?
Great supper (19:7)	Stands in contrast to marriage supper	Stands in contrast to marriage supper		
Binding of Satan (20:2)	Symbolic of Christ's resurrection victory over Satan	Removal of Satan's power during the millennium		The limitations of Satan's power that began in the first century and continues to the present
Millennium (20:2-6)	Symbolic reference to period from Christ's first coming to His second	A historical event, though length of one thousand years may be symbolic, after Armageddon during which Christ rules with His people	A one-thousand-year period during which Christ rules with His people	Symbolic of the time of Christ's kingdom from the judgment of Israel in the first century to the final judgment
Those on thrones (20:4)	Martyrs in heaven; their presence with God is a judgment on those who killed them	Saints and martyrs who rule with Christ in the millennium	Saints and martyrs who rule with Christ in the millennium	The church, ruling with Christ in His present kingdom
First resurrection (20:5-6)	The spiritual presence with Christ of the redeemed that occurs after physical death	Resurrection of saints at beginning of millennium when Christ returns	Includes two groups: (1) those raptured; (2) tribulation saints martyred during tribulation	Salvation
Second death (20:6)	Spiritual death, eternal separation from God	Spiritual death, eternal separation from God	Spiritual death, eternal separation from God	Spiritual death, eternal separation from God
Second resurrection (implied)	All persons, lost and redeemed, rise when Christ returns in only resurrection that takes place	Nonbelievers, resurrected at end of millennium for the great white throne judgment		Spiritual death, eternal separation from God Physical resurrection of all from their graves
New heavens and earth (21:1)	A new order; redeemed earth and heaven	A new order; redeemed earth and heaven	A new order; redeemed earth and heaven	
New Jerusalem (21:2-5)	God dwelling with His saints (the church) in the new age after all other end-time events	God dwelling with His saints (the church) in the new age after all other end-time events	God dwelling with His saints (the church) in the new age after all other end-time events	The church in the glory of salvation which is already present in the world.
New Jerusalem (21:10–22:5)	Same as 21:2-5	Same as 21:2-5	Same as 21:2-5	Same as 21:2-5

Series in Revelation

Point of Interpretation	Amillennial	Historical (Post-tribulation) Premillennial	*Pretribulation Premillennial	Preterist Postmillennialism
Seal 1 (6:1-2)	Earthly conqueror or Christ	Proclamation of gospel; others believe is earthly conqueror	Spirit of conquest; possibly counterfeit Christ	The Roman march toward Jerusalem in A.D. 67
Seals 2-4 (6:3-8)	Also with seal 1, suffering that must be endured throughout history	Constant problems of war, scarcity, and death	Sequence of disasters brought about by sinful humanity	The Jewish war and its consequences of famine and death
Seal 5 (6:9-11)	Assurance for faithful (all ages) that God will judge evil	Martyrs throughout history	Martyrs of tribulation period	Martyr vindication
Seal 6 (6:12-17)	End of time; God's final judgment	Real cosmic catastrophe at end of age	Real cosmic catastrophe at end of age	Climax of judgment on Israel
Seal 7 (8:1)	The seven trumpets to follow	The seven trumpets to follow	The seven trumpets	The seven trumpets
Trumpets 1-4 (chap. 8)	Fall of Roman Empire through natural calamities	God's wrath falls on a civilization that gives allegiance to antichrist when choice is very clear; first four trumpets involve natural catastrophes	God's wrath falls on a civilization that gives allegiance to antichrist when choice is very clear; first four trumpets involve natural catastrophes	More symbolism of effects of the Jewish war
Locusts, fifth trumpet (9:3-4)	Internal decay bringing fall of Roman Empire	Symbolic of actual demonic forces released during great tribulation, inflict torture	Symbolic of actual demonic forces released during great tribulation, inflict torture	The siege of Jerusalem
Army from East, sixth trumpet (9:13-19)	External attack bringing fall of Roman Empire	Symbolic of actual divine judgment on corrupt civilization, inflicts death	Invasion of army from the East	Other Roman legions joining the war
Seventh trumpet (11:15)	God will one day claim His victory	Announces victorious outcome	The seven bowls	Victory over Jerusalem
First bowl (16:2)	Judgment on adherents of false religion, including Domitian worshipers	Inflicted specifically on followers of antichrist	Plague of physical suffering	Further description of the judgment of Jerusalem
Second bowl (16:3)	Destruction of sources of physical sustenance	Death of everything in sea	Death of everything in sea	?
Third bowl (16:4-7)	Those who shed blood of saints will receive a curse of blood	Affects fresh water	Affects fresh water	?
Fourth bowl (16:8-9)	Even when people recognize that source of all life fights against them for God, they blaspheme and refuse to repent	God overrules processes of nature to bring judgment, but people still refuse to repent	God overrules processes of nature to bring judgment, but people still refuse to repent	?
Fifth bowl (16:10-11)	God's judgment on seat of beast's authority; darkness indicates confused and evil plotting	Directed against the demonic civilization of end-time	Directed against the demonic civilization of end-time	?
Sixth bowl (16:12-16)	Forces against God will ultimately be destroyed; here refers specifically to Parthians	Serves as preparation for great battle of end time; a coalition of demonically inspired rulers	Refers to great world conflict of many nations at Armageddon in Palestine	?
Seventh bowl (16:17-21)	Poured in the air all must breathe; strikes note of final judgment on Roman Empire	Describes fall of end-time Babylon (dealt with more fully later)	Utter destruction of everything built without God; the overthrow of sinful human civilization	?

*Dispensationalism is a popular form of Pretribulation Premillennialism.

Chart by: Daniel L. Akin, Robert B. Sloan, and Craig Blaising.

complete her works of obedience. The church at Philadelphia (3:7-13) is promised, in the face of persecution, that faith in Jesus assures access to the eternal kingdom; and the church at Laodicea (3:14-22) is told to turn from self-deception and repent of lukewarmness.

The Sovereignty of the Creator God Committed to the Crucified and Now Enthroned Lamb (4:1–5:14) Chapters 4 and 5 are pivotal, tying the risen Lord's exhortations to the churches (chaps. 2–3) and to the judgments and final triumph of the Lamb (chaps. 6–22). These chapters provide the historical and theological basis of the risen Lord's authority over both the church and the world by depicting His enthronement and power to carry out the judging and saving purposes of God. Chapter 4 asserts the sovereign authority of God the Father as Creator. Chapter 5 depicts the sovereign authority of God the Son as Redeemer. By creation and redemption God is righteous in exercising authority over all things. In Rev. 5 is a book of retribution, redemption, and restoration. This book, containing the remainder of the revelation (chaps. 6–22), is related to Ezekiel's book of woes (2:9-10) and the sealed book of Daniel (12:4,9-10). The crucified Lord Jesus is the risen and exalted Lion and Lamb of God who is all-powerful, all knowing, and present everywhere (5:6). He and He alone is worthy to take the book and open its seven seals. When the Lamb begins to break the seals, the climactic events of history begin to unfold.

The Enthroned Lamb's Judgments via the Seven Seals (6:1–8:5) The breaking of the first four seals brings forth the four horsemen (6:1-8). These riders, paralleling the chaos predicted in Matt. 24 (cp. Mark 13; Luke 21), represent God's judgments through war and its devastating consequences (violence, famine, pestilence, and death). The fifth seal (Rev. 6:9-11) is the plea of martyred saints for divine justice upon their oppressors. For now they must wait.

The sixth seal is important for understanding the literary structure and episodic sequence of Revelation. When broken, it brings forth the typical signs of the end: a great earthquake, blackening of the sun, ensanguining of the moon, and falling of the stars of heaven (cp. Matt. 24:29). At this point we are at the end of world history. The mighty and the lowly of the earth realize that the great day of God's (and the Lamb's) wrath has come, and nothing can save them (6:14-17). The description of the judgments initiated by the first six seals would overwhelm John's audience, so he interrupted the sequence, leading to the seventh seal to remind them that the people of God need not despair, for as the "slaves of our God" (7:3 HCSB), they have the promise of heaven.

A careful reading of Revelation shows that both the seventh seal and the seventh trumpet are empty of content. Some suggest that the three series of judgments (seals, trumpets, and bowls) have a telescopic relationship, so that the seventh seal contains the seven trumpets, and the seventh trumpet contains the seven bowls, accounting for the intensity and rapidity of the judgments toward the end. This also explains being brought to the close of history at the end of each series of judgments, at least in some respect.

Chapter 7 is two visions (7:1-8,9-17) and is something like a parenthesis. The sealing of the 144,000 (7:1-8) is understood by many to be a reference to actual Jewish persons who come to Christ and perform a unique and special service during the tribulation period (cp. Rom. 11:25-29). Others believe John employs Jewish symbolism to represent all believers who have put their trust in Christ. The latter view is unlikely because in the second vision (7:9-17) John sees a great multitude and makes no distinctions among them. Using descriptions of heaven (21:3-4,23; 22:1-5), John tells us they are "coming out of the great tribulation," now to experience the joys of heaven and relief from tribulations (cp. 7:14-17 with 21:1-6; 22:1-5). To come "out of the great tribulation" (7:14) indicates these are most likely martyred saints who suffered death as witnesses to Jesus (cp. 6:9-11; 12:10-12; 20:4-6). In heaven they now enjoy the presence of God (7:15; 21:3). Christians ("the slaves of our God," 7:3) have the seal of God. Refusing the mark of the beast (13:16-17; 14:11), they bear testimony to Jesus (14:12) in spite of persecution (12:17; 13:7) and therefore have the promise of final deliverance from great tribulation (7:14).

Revelation 8:1-5 gives the seventh seal and the sign of the very end of human history and the coming of the Lord, but the prophet is not yet ready to describe the Lord's return. Still more must be fulfilled, additional judgments of God, the mission of God's people, and the persecution of the beast. The seventh seal contains the seven trumpets. Using this symbolic vehicle, John reveals the second major series of judgments that move ever closer to the end.

The Enthroned Lamb's Judgments via the Seven Trumpets (8:6–11:19) The first four trumpets describe partial judgments ("one-third") upon the earth's vegetation, the oceans, fresh waters, and the heavenly lights (8:6-13). The last three trumpets are grouped together and are described as three "woes" upon the earth, emphasizing God's judgment. These judgments have no redemptive effect, for the "rest of the people" not killed by plagues do not repent of their immoralities (9:20-21).

The interlude between the sixth and seventh seals reminded us that the people of God are safe from the eternally destructive effects of God's wrath, so also between the sixth and seventh trumpets we are reminded of God's protective hand on His people (10:1–11:14). In the trumpet interlude we learn also that God's protection during days of tribulation does not mean isolation, for the people of God must bear a prophetic witness to the world.

In 10:1-8 John's call (cp. Ezek. 2:1–3:11) is reaffirmed. The note of God's providence, protection, and witness is again struck in 11:1-13 with the measuring of the tribulation temple (11:1-2). Persecutions will last "42 months," but His people cannot be destroyed, for the "two witnesses" (11:3-13) must bear witness to the mercy and judgment of God. The "two witnesses" (two suggests confirmed, legal testimony) are also called "two lampstands" (11:4). Some believe they symbolize testifying believers (cp. 1:20). Others think they are two actual persons who will bear witness and be martyred. Like Moses and Elijah, they maintain a faithful prophetic witness to the world, even unto death. Though the earth rejoices when their testimony is brought apparently to an end, the temporary triumph of evil ("three-and-a-half days," 11:9,11) will turn to heavenly vindication as the two witnesses are raised from the dead (11:11-12).

With the seventh trumpet (and third woe) comes the end of history again, the time "for the dead to be judged," and the saints to be rewarded (11:18). Yet John is not ready to describe the actual coming of the Lord. Sadly, he has more to relate regarding "the beast that comes up out of the abyss" to "make war" with the people of God (11:7). John now unfolds the

"42 months," the period of persecution, protection, and witness.

The Dragon's Persecution of the Righteous (12:1–13:18) Chapter 12 is crucial for understanding John's view of the sequence of history. Christians and Jews associated the number "three and a half" with times of evil and judgment. John variously referred to the three and a half years as either "42 months," or "1,260 days," or "a time, times, and half a time." During this time, a period when the powers of evil will do their works, God will protect His people (12:6,14) while they bear witness to their faith (11:3) and simultaneously suffer at the hands of evil powers (11:2,7; 12:13-17; 13:5-7). This terrible period of tribulation will end with the coming of the Lord. The critical question, however, is when the three-and-a-half-year period of persecution and witness begins. Some scholars locate the "three-and-a-half years" to some time in the future. Others pinpoint its beginning with the ascension and enthronement of Christ (12:5). When the woman's (Israel's) offspring is "caught up to God and to His throne" (12:5), there is war in heaven, and the dragon is cast down to the earth.

Heaven rejoices because the offspring has been rescued from Satan, but the earth must mourn because the devil has been cast down to earth, and his anger is great. He knows he has been defeated by the risen and exalted Christ and that he has but a short time (12:12). The woman, who (as Israel) brought forth the Christ (12:1-2) and also other "offspring," those who "have the testimony about Jesus," now receives the brunt of the frustrated dragon's wrath (12:17). As the enraged dragon seeks to vent his wrath upon the woman, she is nonetheless nourished and protected for "1,260 days" (12:6), for a "time, times, and half a time" (12:14).

The dragon then brings forth two henchmen (chap. 13) to help in pursuit of those who believe in Jesus. Satan is embodied in a political ruler, the beast from the sea (13:1), who will blaspheme for "42 months" (13:5). This is Paul's man of lawlessness (2 Thess. 2:3-12) and the antichrist of John (1 John 2:18,22; 4:3; 2 John 7). He is both a person and the head of a political power. He will "wage war against the saints" (13:7), while the second beast (or false prophet, 19:20) who comes up from the earth (13:11), seeks to deceive the earth so that its inhabitants worship the first beast.

Chapter 12 may be viewed as something of a panorama of redemptive history. Chapter 13 is to be understood in connection with Dan. 7 at the coming of the eschatological antichrist. In the dragon (Satan), the beast and the false prophet will encounter nothing less than a counterfeit trinity, as well as a counterfeit resurrection (13:3). Revelation is clear that Satan is the master deceiver and counterfeiter.

Summary of Triumph, Warning, and Judgment (14:1-20) After depressing news of ongoing persecutions by the unholy trinity, John's readers need another word of encouragement and warning. Chapter 14 employs seven "voices" to relate again the hopes and warnings of heaven. First is another vision of the 144,000, the Jewish remnant. Faithful in their worship of the one true God through Jesus Christ and not seduced by the satanic deceptions of the first beast and his ally, the false prophet, they will be rescued and taken to heaven's throne (14:15).

An angel announces the eternal gospel and warns the earth of coming judgment (14:6-7). The remaining "voices" (or oracles) follow in rapid succession. The fall of "Babylon the Great," an OT symbol for a nation opposed to the people of God, is announced (14:8). The people of God are warned not to follow the beast lest those who follow him suffer separation from God (14:9-12). Finally, two voices call for harvest (14:14-20).

The Enthroned Lamb's Judgments via the Seven Bowls (15:1–16:21) Another dimension of His judgment is the seven bowls of wrath, similar to the seven trumpets and the seven seals but also different. The wrath of God is no longer partial or temporary but complete and everlasting, final and irrevocable. The partial judgments ("one-third") of the trumpets suggest that God uses sufferings and evil to draw mankind toward repentance and faith; but such tribulations also foreshadow the final hour of judgment when God's wrath is finished.

The seven bowls have no break between the sixth and seventh outpourings of judgment. Only wrath is left with no more delay. Babylon the Great, the symbol for all who have vaunted themselves against the most high God, will fall. The end has come (16:17).

The Fall and Ruin of Babylon (17:1–18:24) Chapter 17 retells the sixth bowl, the fall of Babylon the Great, and chapter 18 gives a moving lament for the great city.

The Marriage Supper of the Lamb (19:1-10) Although John has withheld a description of the coming of the Lord on at least three earlier occasions (8:5; 11:15-19; 16:17-21; cp. 14:14-16), he is now prepared to describe the glories of the Lord's appearance. All of heaven rejoices over the righteous judgment of God upon evil (19:16). The Lamb's bride, the people of God, has made herself ready by her faithfulness to her Lord through the hour of suffering (19:7-8).

The Second Coming of the Lord Jesus (19:11-21) Heaven is opened, and the One whose coming has been faithfully anticipated from ages past appears to battle the enemies of God, a conflict whose outcome is not in doubt (19:11-16). The first beast (the antichrist) and the second beast (the false prophet) are thrown into the lake of fire from which there is no return (19:20), a place of everlasting punishment and torment, not annihilation.

The Millennial Kingdom (20:1-6) The dragon (Satan) is cast into the abyss, a prison for the demonic, which is shut and sealed for a thousand years (20:1-3). Christ will reign for a thousand years on the earth as King of kings and Lord of lords. The dead in Christ are raised to govern with Him (20:4-6), and God's rightful rule over the earth is vindicated.

Satan's Final Rebellion and the Great White Throne Judgment (20:7-15) At the end of the thousand years, the final disposition of Satan will occur (20:7-10). Though Satan will have one last deception, his final insurrection will be short. In one final battle Satan and his followers are overcome, and the devil joins the beast and the false prophet in the lake of fire where "they will be tormented day and night forever and ever" (20:10). Then the final judgment takes place, at which all not included in "the book of life" are thrown into the lake of fire (20:11-15).

The Rejoicing of Heaven, the Revelation of the Lamb, and the Advent of the Bride, the Holy City (21:1–22:5) Chapter 21 refers to the eternal state ushered in by the great white throne judgment and describes the new heaven, new earth, and in particular, the new Jerusalem. It describes the glorification of the bride of the Lamb (21:1-22:5). To be the bride is to be the holy city, the new Jerusalem, to live in the

R

presence of God and the Lamb, and to experience protection, joy, and the everlasting, life-giving light of God (21:9-27). The throne of God and of the Lamb is there, and there His bond-servants shall serve Him and reign with Him forever and ever (22:1-5). The new Jerusalem is both a people and a place.

Conclusion (22:6-21) John concluded his prophecy by declaring the utter faithfulness of his words. Those who heed his prophecy will receive the blessings of God. Those who ignore the warnings will be left outside the gates of God's presence (22:6-15). Solemnly and hopefully praying for the Lord to come, John closed his book (22:17,20). The churches must have ears to hear what the Spirit has said (22:16). The people of God must, by His grace (22:21), persevere in the hour of tribulation, knowing their enthroned Lord will return in triumph.

Outline

I. Introduction (1:1-8)
II. John's Vision on the Island of Patmos (1:9-20)
III. Letters to the Seven Churches (2:1–3:22)
IV. The Sovereignty of the Creator God Committed to the Crucified and Now Enthroned Lamb (4:1–5:14)
V. The Enthroned Lamb's Judgments via the Seven Seals (6:1–8:5)
VI. The Enthroned Lamb's Judgments via the Seven Trumpets (8:6–11:19)
VII. The Dragon's Persecution of the Righteous (12:1–13:18)
VIII. A Summary of Triumph, Warning, and Judgment (14:1-20)
IX. The Enthroned Lamb's Judgments via the Seven Bowls (15:1–16:21)
X. The Fall and Ruin of Babylon (17:1–18:24)
XI. The Marriage Supper of the Lamb (19:1-10)
XII. The Second Coming of Jesus Christ (19:11-21)
XIII. The Millennial Kingdom (20:1-6)
XIV. Satan's Final Rebellion and the Great White Throne Judgment (20:7-15)
XV. The Rejoicing of Heaven, the Revelation of the Lamb, and the Advent of the Bride, the Holy City (21:1–22:5)
XVI. Conclusion (22:6-21)

Daniel L. Akin and Robert B. Sloan

REVELRY Noisy partying or merrymaking. English translations vary greatly in use of revel and its cognates (revelers, reveling, revelry). KJV used "revellings" twice, as a work of the flesh (Gal. 5:21) and as behavior associated with Gentiles (1 Pet. 4:3). RSV used "revelry" once, as a characterization of the behavior of the rich of Samaria (Amos 6:7). NASB and NIV used cognates of "revel" more often (four and eleven times, respectively). In their use "revel" often means little more than rejoice or exult. Of special interest is the association of revelry and idolatry (Exod. 32:6; 1 Cor. 10:7).

REVENGE, REVENGER See *Avenger.*

REVERENCE Respect or honor paid to a worthy object. In Scripture reverence is paid: to father and mother (Lev. 19:3; Heb. 12:9); to God (1 Kings 18:3,12; Heb. 12:28); to God's sanctuary (Lev. 19:30; 26:2); and to God's commandments (Ps. 119:48). The failure to revere God (Deut. 32:51) and the act of revering other gods (Judg. 6:10) have dire consequences. Reverence for Christ is expressed in mutual submission within the Christian community (Eph. 5:21). Christian persecution takes on new meaning as suffering becomes an opportunity for revering Christ (1 Pet. 3:14-15). See *Awe, Awesome; Fear.*

REZEPH (Rē´ zĕph) Place-name meaning "glowing coal." Town the Assyrians conquered, most likely under Shalmaneser III (about 838 B.C.), and which the Assyrians used as a warning to King Hezekiah of Judah in 701 B.C. against relying on God to deliver him from them (2 Kings 19:12; Isa. 37:12). The site is possibly Rezzafeh about 100 miles southeast of Aleppo.

REZIA (Rē zī´ à) (KJV) See *Rizia.*

REZIN (Rē´ zĭn) King of Syria about 735 B.C. during the reigns of Pekah in Israel and Ahaz in Judah. When Ahaz refused to join Rezin and Pekah in fighting against Assyria, Rezin persuaded Pekah to ally with him against the Judean king (2 Kings 15:37; 16:5). Ahaz appealed for help to Tiglath-pileser of Assyria, who came against Rezin and Pekah and destroyed their kingdoms. Rezin died in 732 B.C. when Damascus fell to the Assyrians.

REZON (Rē´ zŏn) Personal name meaning "prince." An Aramean leader who led a successful revolt against Solomon and established an independent state with its capital at Damascus (1 Kings 11:23-25). See *Damascus*.

RHEGIUM (Rē´ ġĭ ŭm) Place-name either derived from the Greek *rhegnumi* (rent, torn) or from the Latin *regium* (royal). Port located at the southwestern tip of the Italian boot about seven miles across the Strait of Messina from Sicily. Paul stopped there en route to Rome (Acts 28:13). Rhegium was settled by Greek colonists and retained Greek language and institutions into the first century.

RHESA (Rē´ sȧ) Ancestor of Jesus (Luke 3:27).

RHETORIC Art of communicating persuasively and memorably. Scriptural authors employed various rhetorical devices to communicate effectively. Understanding these methods of expression enables students of the Bible to understand their messages more clearly and to share them more effectively with others.

Some rhetorical devices connect words, ideas, or events because of some similarity. Sometimes the similarity was a shared concept. In Heb. 1:5-13 the author used six OT passages that demonstrated the supremacy of the Messiah using a method the rabbis called "pearl-stringing." Sometimes words or ideas were placed together to highlight differences. Matthew 7:24-27 offers an illustration of what an obedient hearer is like and then contrasts him with a disobedient hearer.

Sometimes the similarity between words is due to sound or spelling rather than meaning. The Greek text of Rom. 1:31 is an example of alliteration, each word begins with the same letter. The first two words are an example of assonance. They rhyme and differ in spelling by only one letter. Similarly, in Rom. 1:29 the words envy and murder differ in spelling by only one letter. Psalm 119 is an acrostic in which the verses of each stanza begin with the same letter of the Hebrew alphabet. Each new stanza begins the next consecutive letter of the Hebrew alphabet. These devices were interesting and made the text easier to remember.

Sometimes ideas were linked because of logical relationships such as cause and effect, problem and resolution, or question and answer. Paul proceeded from cause to effect in Rom. 1:18-32 by showing how sin results in greater corruption and eventually death. Throughout Romans he introduced rhetorical questions, then provided answers and supporting evidences (Rom. 2:21-24; 3:1-4; 6:1-2).

Rhetoric includes literary devices like hyperbole, an intentional exaggeration used to make a powerful point (Matt. 5:29-30), and simile, a comparison using "like" or "as" ("the kingdom of heaven is like"). Rhetoric also involves carefully organizing speech or writing to have a greater impact. Sometimes an account or argument is organized so as to build to a climax. In Phil. 3:2, for example, Paul repeats three times the warning to beware of opponents to the gospel of grace. With each repetition description of his opponents becomes more severe. In a chiasm words were arranged to correspond to one another in the order A B C followed by a reversal C B A (Isa. 6:10).

In the late 20th century a new tool for biblical study developed called rhetorical criticism. The approach was based upon recognition that an understanding of the use of rhetoric in Scripture may provide a useful guide for interpretation. This approach involves studying ancient handbooks on rhetoric in order to understand the models that educated people, particularly during the NT era, used to communicate. Then one compares these models to sections or entire books of Scripture. The method may help one understand the writer's message, its structure and purpose, and even how the original readers might have responded.   *Charles L. Quarles*

RHODA (Rō´ dȧ) Personal name meaning "rose." Rhoda's relationship to the household of Mary, the mother of John Mark, is not clear. She was most likely a servant, though it is possible that she was a family member or a guest at the prayer service. In her great joy at finding Peter at the door, Rhoda failed to let him in. Her joy in rushing to tell the disciples and their response accusing her of madness recall details of Luke's resurrection narrative (Acts 12:13; cp. Luke 24:9-11).

RHODES (Rōdz) Island off the southwest coast of Asia Minor in the Mediterranean Sea associated with the Dodanim (NASB, KJV; Gen. 10:4; Ezek. 27:15). Rhodes was founded as a Minoan trading colony about 1500 B.C. and came under the control of a single government around 407 B.C. A wealthy shipping center, Rhodes developed navies that controlled the eastern Mediterranean. Standing with one foot on either side of the harbor entrance was the 105-foot-tall brass Colossus, one of the "Seven Wonders of the World." Set up in 288 B.C., it fell during an earthquake about 64 years later. Disloyalty to Roman rule met with stiff economic sanctions against the city and threw it into decline. While enjoying some popularity as the center of the cult of Helios, the sun god, Rhodes could not rise above Roman economic pressure. When the Apostle Paul stopped over on his voyage from Troas to Caesarea (Acts 21:1), Rhodes was only a minor provincial city. See *Dodanim.*

RIBAI (Rĭ´ bā ī) Personal name meaning "Yahweh contends." Father of Ittai, one of David's 30 elite warriors (2 Sam. 23:29; 1 Chron. 11:31).

RIBBAND KJV form of ribbon (Num. 15:38). Modern translations read "cord" (NASB, NIV, NRSV) or "thread" (REB).

RIBLAH (Rĭb´ lah) **1.** Syrian town located near Kadesh on the Orontes near the border with Babylonia. There Pharaoh Neco imprisoned King Jehoahaz of Judah after the young monarch had reigned only three months (2 Kings 23:31-33). Later, when Zedekiah rebelled against Nebuchadnezzar of Babylon, he was taken to Riblah as a prisoner and viewed the execution of his sons before having his eyes put out (25:4-7). See *Diblah.* **2.** Otherwise unknown town on eastern border of Canaan (Num. 34:11). Earliest translations read "Arbelah."

RICHES See *Wealth and Materialism.*

RIDDLE Enigmatic or puzzling statement, often based on the clever use of the ambiguities of language. The classic biblical example of a riddle is that posed by Samson to the Philistines. The riddle is in poetic form (Judg. 14:12-14), and the question, "What is it?" is implied. The Philistines reply is in the form of another riddle (v. 18a) whose original answer

The city and harbor area of the island of Rhodes.

Temple ruins in the area of Lindos on the island of Rhodes.

was probably "love." Samson's retort may reflect yet another commonly known, and rather risqué, riddle (v. 18b).

The Hebrew word for "riddle" also appears elsewhere in the OT. The Lord spoke with Moses directly, not in "riddles" (Num. 12:8 NIV, REB, NRSV) or "dark speech" (KJV, NASB). The Queen of Sheba tested Solomon with "hard questions" or riddles (1 Kings 10:1-13). Riddles were a form of poetic expression (Ps. 49:4); a mark of wisdom was the ability to solve them (Prov. 1:6). Daniel had such wisdom (Dan. 5:12).   *Daniel C. Browning, Jr.*

The streets of Rhodes have remained basically unchanged for centuries.

RIGHT MIND Sound mind, mentally healthy (Mark 5:15; Luke 8:35). Elsewhere, the underlying Greek term is rendered "sober judgment" (Rom. 12:3 NRSV) or "self-controlled" (Titus 2:6 NRSV).

RIGHTEOUSNESS Biblical terminology used to denote the term "righteousness" is from one basic word group. The Hebrew *tsadiq* is translated by the Greek *dikaiosune* and its various forms in both the LXX and the NT.

Old Testament Objects are considered righteous in the Torah. Leviticus 19:36 and Deut. 25:15 speak of "just weights and measures." Similarly, Deut. 4:8 and 33:19 speak respectively of right statues and sacrifices. Persons are often referred to as righteous. Noah (Gen. 6:9), Jezreel (1 Kings 10:9), and with some qualifications Ish Bosheth (2 Sam. 4:11-12) are all considered righteous. Abraham (Gen. 15:6) and Phinehas (Ps. 106:31) are both credited righteous by God. In the OT righteousness is used in a comparative moral sense (Gen. 38:26: 1 Sam. 24:17). The individuals (Tamar and David) are not righteous because of innocence but in comparative virtue to their counter-parts (Judah and Saul).

Righteous as a forensic theme is present in the OT. Absalom seeks to usurp his father's authority by becoming a seditious judge (2 Sam. 15:4), while his father is seemingly fulfilling the obligations of a righteous king (2 Sam. 8:5). The phrase "just and right" that describe David's actions in 2 Sam. 8:5 is used elsewhere (Isa. 9:7; 32:16; Jer. 4:2; 9:24; 33:15; Ezek. 18:5,19,21,27; 45:9; Amos 5:7,24).

In the Prophets righteousness often represents the idea of socio-covenantal justice. Amos 5:24 sets forth the Day of the Lord as bringing about "justice" and "righteousness." In Isaiah the presence of righteousness results in peace (Isa. 9:2-7; 32:16-17; 60:17). Isaiah also describes righteous in an eschatologically salvific sense (56:1; 59:4; 62:1-2; 64:5). Hosea views righteousness in the context of Israel's lack of faithfulness to God (2:19; 10:12; cp. 14:9). Jeremiah, Habakkuk, and Ezekiel all speak of righteousness as covenant obligation, whether to the king (Jer. 22:15; 23:5) or any Israelite (Ezek. 3:20-21; 14:12-20; 18:5-32; 33:12-20). Habakkuk 2:4 asserts the just will live by faith (cp. Rom. 1:16-17). Malachi and Zechariah picture righteousness as an eschatological theme (Mal. 3:17-18; Zech. 3:7-8).

Wisdom literature presents a multifaceted picture of righteousness. The driving question for Job 3–41 is "Can a mortal be more righteous than God?" (Job 4:17 NIV). This question gives the context for the ensuing discussion. In Proverbs the righteous person is characterized as honest (10:11; 31:32), generous (21:26), steadfast and courageous (11:8-10; 12:7; 18:10), merciful and just (12:10; 29:7; cp. 31:9), and his ways lead to life (10:16; 11:19; 12:28; 21:21). While neither Proverbs nor Job articulates a specific standard of righteousness, the righteous person is pictured as the quintessential covenant keeper; one committed to God and living justly among His people.

In Psalms righteousness sometimes denotes what is right (4:5; 23:3; 52:3). The righteous person might experience God's blessing (Ps. 18:20,24) or afflictions, some of which are divine in their origin (34:19; 69:26; 119:75; 146:8). Psalms 111–112 provide a holistic picture of the righteousness of God and the righteous man. Righteousness itself is grounded in the character of God (Exod. 9:27; Deut. 32:4; Judg. 5:11; 1 Sam. 12:7; Mic. 6:4; cp. Ps. 103:6; Dan. 9:16; 2 Chron. 12:6; Ezra 9:15; Neh. 9:8; Pss. 119:137; 129:4). He is righteous, His law is righteous, and He alone credits righteousness to man.

New Testament In the NT, like the OT, God and all that comes from Him is righteous. His judgments are righteous (2 Thess. 1:5-6; Rev. 16:7; 19:2; 2 Tim. 4:8), as He Himself is as a judge (John 5:30). All God's revealed will in Jesus' teachings is righteousness (Matt. 6:33; John 16:8-10).

In the Gospels and Acts, the idea of righteousness is applied to Christ (Matt. 27:19,24; Luke 23:47; Acts 3:14; 7:52; 22:14). Mark describes John the Baptist as righteous (6:20). The Holy Spirit is described as righteous in John 16:8.

Paul utilizes the idea of righteousness more than other writers in the NT. God demonstrates His righteousness perfectly in the propitiatory death of His Son (Rom. 3:21,25-26). Jesus' death on the cross was ordained by God, is in conformity with His character, and accomplishes God's righteous purposes with sinners (Rom. 5:16,18). Righteousness is revealed clearly in the gospel (Rom. 1:16-17). Therefore God's indignation towards sin and His covenant love in justifying sinners are both realized in Jesus' death. Romans 3:6 parallels God's righteousness with His love and faithfulness (cp. Pss. 116:5; 145:17). The resurrection of Christ vindicates Christ (Act. 3:14-15; 1 Pet. 2:23; 3:18; 1 Tim. 3:16) and completes God's transaction between fallen humanity and Jesus. "He made the One who did not know sin to be sin for us, so that we might become the righteousness of God in Him" (2 Cor. 5:21 HCSB). God is shown to be both just and the justifier of those who believe in Christ (Rom. 3:26). Thus, the righteous live no other way but by faith (Hab. 2:4; cp. Rom. 1:16-17), for through faith they are granted the righteousness of God.

Man is not naturally righteous (Pss. 14:1; 53:1, cp. Rom. 3:10-18). Righteousness is not native to him but to God. In Jesus' teaching the righteousness of the Pharisees is not enough to gain entrance into the kingdom of God (Matt. 5:20; cp. 3:13,21,32). Paul argues in Rom. 3 that no man is naturally righteous. Even after conversion Paul speaks of the struggle to follow the law of righteousness and not the law he finds in his "body of death" (Rom. 7:14–8:1). God credits righteousness to those who exercise faith in Him (Rom. 4:15). In Christ one becomes all that God requires (2 Cor. 5:21; cp. Rom. 4:6,14). The result of becoming the righteousness of God is a life of righteousness before God. Paul urges believers to continue to offer up the members of their bodies as instruments of righteousness to God (Rom. 6:13). The Christian is urged to put on the breastplate of righteousness (Eph. 6:14). Timothy is exhorted to flee youthful lusts, call on God from a pure heart, and pursue righteousness (2 Tim. 4:8). Those trained through discipline produce the peaceful fruit of righteousness (Heb. 12:9-11).

In James the anger of man does not achieve the righteousness of God (1:2), but the prayer of a righteous man does achieve much (5:16). In Revelation Jesus comes back to judge in righteousness (Rev. 16:7; 19:2). See *Ethics; Grace; Law; Mercy; Salvation.* *Jeff Mooney*

RIMMON (Rĭm´ mon) Place-name and divine name meaning "pomegranate." **1.** Chief god of Syria, also called Hadad. Naaman worshiped Rimmon in Damascus (2 Kings 5:18). **2.** Town allotted to tribe of Judah (Josh. 15:32) but then given to Simeon (19:7; cp. 1 Chron. 4:32). Early translations and many modern interpreters read En-rimmon in all occurrences. It is modern Khirbet er-Ramamin two miles south of Lahav. Zechariah 14:10 described it as the southern boundary of God's new exalted kingdom. See *En-rimmon.* **3.** Levitical city in Zebulun (Josh. 19:13; 1 Chron. 6:77), probably the original reading for present Dimnah (Josh. 21:35). It is present Rummaneh, six miles northeast of Nazareth. See *Dimnah.* **4.** Rock near Gibeah to where the people of Benjamin fled from vengeful Israelites (Judg. 20:45-47), modern Rammun four miles east of Bethel. **5.** Father of Rechab and Baanah, who killed Saul's son Ish-Bosheth (2 Sam. 4:2,9).

RIMMON-PAREZ (Rĭm mon-Pā´ rĕz) (KJV) or **RIMMON-PEREZ** (Rĭm mon-Pē´ rĕz) Place-name meaning "pomegranate of the pass." Campsite during Israel's wilderness wanderings (Num. 33: 19-20).

RIMMONO (Rĭm mōn´ ō) Place-name meaning "his Rimmon." NIV, NASB, NRSV reading of Rimmon in 1 Chron. 6:77 (cp. Josh. 19:13; 21:25).

RING See *Jewels, Jewelry.*

RINNAH (Rĭn´ nah) Personal name meaning "ringing cry." Descendant of Judah (1 Chron. 4:20).

RIPHATH (Rī´ phăth) Personal name of foreign origin. Son of Gomer, likely the ancestor of an Anatolian tribe (Gen. 10:3). The name is likely a scribal corruption of Diphath (1 Chron. 1:6).

RISHATHAIM (Rĭsh à thā´ ĭm) Mesopotamian king, Cushan-rishathaim, who conquered and oppressed Israel (Judg. 3:8). Cushan may relate to Guzana or Tell Halaf. KJV uses Chushan-rishathaim. See *Cushan-Rishathaim.*

RISSAH (Rĭs´ sah) Place-name possibly meaning "dewdrop," "rain," or "ruins." Campsite during Israel's wilderness wanderings (Num. 33:21-22), modern Sharma, east of Gulf of Aqaba.

RITHMAH (Rĭth´ mah) Place-name meaning "broom plant." Campsite during Israel's wilderness wanderings (Num. 33:18-19), possibly valley called er-Retame, east of Gulf of Aqaba.

RITUAL See *Sacrifice and Offering; Worship.*

RIVER OF EGYPT See *Brook of Egypt.*

RIVERS AND WATERWAYS From the earliest efforts at permanent settlement in the ancient Near East, people were attracted to the rivers and streams that ultimately would dictate population distribution between the mountains, deserts, and the seas. The flood plains of many of these rivers originally were inhospitable with thick, tangled jungles, wild beasts, and unpredictable flooding and disease. However, within the areas of plain and lowland that provided a more constant food supply and ease of movement, the need for a permanent water source attracted settlers to the riverbanks. Thus the early river civilizations of the Nile, the Tigris, and Euphrates starting about 3000 B.C., and the Indus civilization slightly later, resulted in response to the challenges and benefits these important waterways presented. Flood control, social and economic organization, and invention of writing as a means of communication developed. Trade was facilitated by means of navigable waterways. Since roads followed the lines of least resistance, the pattern of early trade routes conformed closely, especially in more rugged terrain, to channels and courses of the rivers and streams, and along the shoreline where the earliest fishing villages developed.

Rivers and Streams Each of the biblical rivers was developed to meet distinct human needs. A study of rivers helps understand the culture near the river.

Nile River The name "Nile" is not explicitly mentioned in KJV, but modern translations most often translated the Hebrew *ye'or* as the Nile. The Nile plays a prominent role in the early events in the life of Moses in Exodus (Moses, Exod. 2:3; the 10 plagues, Exod. 7:15,20). The Nile is alluded to in many other passages as "the river" (Gen. 41:1), the "river of Egypt" (Gen. 15:18), the "flood of Egypt" (Amos 8:8), Shihor (Josh. 13:3), river of Cush among other names. The "brook of Egypt" mostly is a reference to Wadi el-Arish, the drainage system of the central Sinai. The Prophets Amos (8:8; 9:5) and Jeremiah (46:8) used the Nile as the symbol of Egypt, a concept that is readily understood in terms of the river's historical importance to the survival and well-being of the country.

For the Egyptians the predictable annual flooding of the Nile with the depositing of the fertile black alluvial soil meant the enrichment of the flood plain and the difference between food and famine. From the central highlands of East Africa, the Nile with a watershed of over one million square miles is formed by the union of the White and Blue Niles and flows a distance of nearly 3,500 miles. From its low ebb at the end of May, the flow of the river gradually rises to its maximum flood stage at the beginning of September. Historically, approximately 95 percent of Egypt's population depended upon the productivity of the 5 percent of the country's land area within the flood plain of the Nile. In the Delta at least three major branches facilitated irrigation in the extensive fan north of Memphis, the ancient capital of lower Egypt. See *Egypt; Nile River*.

Euphrates First mentioned in Gen. 2:14 as one of the four branches of the river that watered the garden of Eden, the Euphrates flows 1,700 miles to become the longest river in Western Asia. From the mountainous region of northeast-ern Turkey (Armenia), it flows southward into northern Syria and turns southeasterly to join the Tigris and flows into the Persian Gulf. On the Middle Euphrates, Carchemish, originally the center of a small city-state, became the important provincial capital of the Mitanni kingdom, later of the Hittite and Assyrian Empires. At Carchemish in 605 B.C., Nebuchadnezzar II defeated Pharaoh Necho as he began his successful drive to claim the former Assyrian Empire for Babylon (2 Kings 24:7; Jer. 46). Two important tributaries, the Belikh and Khabur, flow into the Euphrates from the north before it continues on to the ancient trade center at Mari. The Lower Euphrates generally formed the western limits of the city-states that made up the early Sumerian civilization. From the river plain to the delta, both the Tigris and Euphrates Rivers regularly have formed new branches and changed their courses. About 90 percent of their flow mysteriously is lost to irrigation, evaporation, pools and lakes, and the swamps and never reaches the Persian Gulf. Lost as well in this region are the vast amounts of sediment that the Tigris and Euphrates bring from the mountainous regions. Sediment deposits along the lower courses of these rivers average 16 to 23 feet with 36-foot deposits in some regions. It has been calculated that the Tigris alone removes as much as three million tons of eroded highland materials in a single day. In the extreme south the two rivers join in a combined stream that today is known as the Shatt el-Arab.

The flooding of the Mesopotamian rivers in March and April differs from the Nile schedule, which during that season is at its low ebb. The melting snows and rains at their sources create sudden, disastrous torrents that, along the Tigris especially, must be controlled by dams during such periods before they can supply a beneficial irrigation system. See *Euphrates and Tigris Rivers*.

The course of the Upper Euphrates was described as the northern border of the promised land (Gen. 15:18; Deut. 1:7; 11:24; Josh. 1:4). David, in fact, extended his military influence to its banks during the height of his power (2 Sam. 8:3; 10:16-18; 1 Kings 4:24). The terms "the river," "the flood," "the great river," and "beyond the river" (Josh. 24:2-3; Ezra 4:10-13; Neh. 2:7-9) refer to the Euphrates, historically a significant political and geographical boundary.

Tigris From its source in a small lake (Hazar Golu), about 100 miles west of Lake Van, in Armenia, the Tigris flows in a southeasterly direction for about 1,150 miles before joining the Euphrates and emptying into the Persian Gulf. It achieves flood stage during March and April from the melting mountain snows and subsides after mid-May. While its upper flow is swift within narrow gorges, from Mosul and Nineveh southward its course was navigable and was extensively used in antiquity for transport. A series of tributaries from the slopes of the Zagros emptied into the Tigris from the east, including the Greater and Lesser Zab and the Diyala. The Diyala flows into the Tigris near Baghdad. In antiquity its banks were inhabited by a dense population maintained and made prosperous by an excellent irrigation system. The Euphrates, flowing at a level nine meters higher than the Tigris, permitted the construction of a sequence of irrigation canals between the two rivers that resulted in unusual productivity. South of Baghdad where their courses again separated, a more complicated system of canals and diversions were necessary.

The banks of the Tigris were dotted by some of the most important cities of antiquity: Nineveh, the capital of Assyria during the Assyrian Empire; Asshur, the original capital of Assyria; Opis (in the vicinity of Baghdad), the important commercial center of Neo-Babylonian and later times; Ctesiphon, the capital of the Parthians and Sassanians; and Seleucia, capital of the Seleucid rulers of Mesopotamia.

Rivers of Anatolia Several rivers water this part of modern Turkey. See *Asia Minor, Cities of.*

Halys River From its sources in the Armenian mountains, the Halys begins its 714-mile flow to the southwest only to be diverted by a secondary ridge into a broad loop until its direction is completely reversed into a northeasterly direction through the mountainous regions bordering the southern shore of the Black Sea. As the longest river in Anatolia, the Halys, like the other principal rivers in Turkey, is the result of heavy rainfall in the Pontic zone. Because of their winding courses within the coastal mountain chains, none of these rivers is navigable. Within this loop of the Halys in the northern Anatolian plateau, the Hittites established their capital Boghazkoy. The course of the Halys generally formed the borders of the district of Pontus.

Rivers of the Aegean Coast The broken Aegean coastline boasted a series of sheltered havens and inlets that prompted Greek colonization and the establishment the great harbor cities of the later Greek and Roman periods. The mouths of the Aegean rivers deemed ideal for maritime centers during colonization ultimately proved disastrous. The lower courses of these rivers, relatively short and following a meandering course over their respective plains, are very shallow and sluggish during the summer months. Their upper courses, however, of recent formation, carry enormous quantities of alluvium from the highlands that tended to fill the estuaries and gulfs. Constant dredging was required to maintain the harbor's access to the sea and to avoid the formation of malaria-infested swamps. Thus the Hermus (155 miles) was diverted to prevent the destruction of the harbor of Smyrna (Izmir). To the south at Ephesus, the original town site on the disease-ridden marshlands was abandoned about A.D. 400 for the construction of a new harbor on the Cayster River. During the days of Ephesus' prosperity, the constant dredging was adequately maintained. However, with the decline of the Roman Empire after A.D. 200, the silting of the harbor brought the rapid decline of the city. Miletus, on the alluvial plain of the Maeander River (236 miles), was originally established on a deep gulf well sheltered from the prevailing winds. The great Ionian city had possessed four harbors, but the silting of the harbors by the alluvial deposits of the Maeander ultimately brought about the decline and abandonment of the city. Though these Aegean rivers were not navigable, the alluvial plains that bordered them provided convenient and vital access and communications to the interior.

Rivers of Syro-Palestine In Syria and Palestine rivers often separated peoples rather than providing economic power.

Orontes and Litani High within the Beqa Valley that forms the rift between the Lebanon and Anti-Lebanon mountain ranges, a watershed (about 3,770 feet above sea level) forms the headwaters of the Orontes and Litani Rivers. The rains and snow on the mountain summits at heights of over 11,000 feet course down into the six- to 10-mile-wide Beqa which is a part of the great Rift ("Valley of Lebanon," Josh. 11:17). From the watershed the Orontes flows northward and bends westward to empty into the Mediterranean near Antioch. The Litani flows southward and ultimately escapes to the sea north of Tyre. Unfortunately its lower course has formed such a deep, narrow gorge that it is useless for communication. See *Palestine.*

Jordan River A series of springs and tributaries, resulting from the rains and snows on the heights of Mount Hermon (up to 9,100 feet above sea level) at the southern end of the Anti-Lebanon mountains east of the Rift Valley, converge in Lake Huleh to form the headwaters of the Jordan River. Along the eastern edge of the Huleh Valley, it flows southward into Lake Kinnereth (the Sea of Galilee). Only about eight miles wide and 14 miles long, the fresh waters of the Galilee and its fishing industry sustained a dense population during most historical periods. At the Galilee's southern end the Jordan exits and flows 65 miles on to the Dead Sea (about 1,300 feet below sea level). The Jordan flows 127 miles with a drainage area of about 6,380 square miles. The Yarmuk River joins the Jordan five miles south of the Sea of Galilee. The Jabbok River reaches the Jordan from the east 25 miles north of the Dead Sea.

At the Jordan's end the Dead Sea extends another 45 miles between high, rugged cliffs of Nubian sandstone and limestone between the arid wilderness bordering the Judean watershed on the west and the Transjordanian plateau on the east. The sea and the inhospitable terrain along its shoreline discouraged regular travel and transport within the area.

The Jordan appears never to have served as a waterway for travel or transport but rather as a natural barrier and a political boundary that because of its steep banks and the densely wooded fringe that lined its devious route ("thickets of the Jordan," Jer. 49:19, NASB, NRSV; cp. 2 Kings 6:4) could be crossed without difficulty only at its fords (Josh. 3). Control of the fords during military confrontations in biblical times constituted a critical advantage (Judg. 3:28; 12:5-6). The Jordan's role as a political boundary appears to have been established already shortly after 2000 B.C. when the eastern frontier of the Egyptian province of Canaan followed the Jordan. Even though Israelite tribes were given special permission to settle in the Transjordan, it was always clear that, beyond the

Jordan, they actually were residing outside the promised land (Josh. 22). Even in postbiblical times the eastern boundary of the Persian and Hellenistic province of Judea followed the Jordan. Apart from the fertile oases that dotted the Jordan Valley, agricultural prosperity was assured during the Hellenistic and Roman times when irrigation was developed along the gradual slopes on either side of the Jordan within the Rift Valley. See *Jordan.*

Kishon River The Kishon River forms the drainage system of the Jezreel Plain and the southern portion of the Accho Plain. While a number of its small tributaries have their sources in springs at the base of Mount Tabor, in southern Galilee and in the extension of the Carmel in the vicinity of Taanach and Megiddo, the Kishon is rarely more than a brook within relatively shallow and narrow banks except during the heavy rains of the winter months. During those times its course becomes a marshy bog and impassable. From the Jezreel it passes along the base of Mount Carmel through the narrow pass formed by a spur of the Galilean hills and into the Accho Plain, where some additional tributaries join before it empties into the Mediterranean. Its total length from the springs to the sea is only 23 miles. In biblical history it is best known for its role in the Barak-Deborah victory over the Canaanite forces of Sisera (Judg. 4–5) and Elijah's contest with the prophets of Baal on Mount Carmel (1 Kings 18:40).

Yarkon River The Yarkon is formed by the seasonal runoff from the western slopes of the Samaritan and Judean hills that flows into the Brook Kanah, its major tributary, and the rich springs at the base of Aphek about eight miles inland from the Mediterranean shoreline. Though anchorages and small harbors, such as Tel Qasile, a Philistine town, were established along its course and the cedar timbers from Lebanon were floated inland to Aphek for transport to Jerusalem for the construction of Solomon's palace and temple, the Yarkon historically formed a major barrier to north-south traffic because of the extensive swamps that formed along its course. The profuse vegetation that bordered its banks probably suggested its name that was derived from the Hebrew *yaroq*, meaning "green." The Yarkon, in biblical times, formed the border between the tribes of Dan and Ephraim to the north. Farther inland the Brook

Kanah formed the boundary between Ephraim and Manasseh (Josh. 16:8; 17:9).

Major Bodies of Water Two major seas heavily influenced Israel's political, economic, and cultural history.

Mediterranean Sea The Mediterranean Sea had a width of 100 to 600 miles and stretched over 2,000 miles from the Straits of Gibraltar to the Palestinian coast.

Formed by the movement of the European and North African continental plates, the greater Mediterranean consists of a series of basins and extended shoreline that historically contributed to the vitality of maritime commerce and trade. The unusually straight coast along the south portion of its eastern shoreline and the lack of natural coves and harbor facilities limited Israelite opportunities for direct involvement in Mediterranean maritime commerce. While limited port facilities existed at coastal towns such as Joppa, Dor, and Accho, they were hardly adequate to facilitate more than a local fishing fleet and an occasional refuge during a storm for the larger merchant ships that frequented the great harbors established farther to the north along the Phoenician coast. As a result the treaties established between the Israelite kings and the Phoenicians provided for an exchange of agricultural and horticultural produce in exchange for lumber and imports (2 Chron. 2:16), and a mutually beneficial cooperation in maintaining a monopoly on both land and sea routes of commerce and trade (1 Kings 9:26-27). The Mediterranean became the "Roman" sea when the peaceful conditions of Roman control of land masses along most of the Mediterranean shoreline fostered a dramatic movement of products, merchandise, and people to satisfy the diverse needs of the provinces and Roman policy in them. See *Mediterranean Sea.*

Red Sea The Red Sea (Hb. *yam suph*, lit. "Sea of Reeds") is a long narrow body of water separating the Arabian Peninsula from the northeastern coast of Africa (Egypt, Sudan, and Ethiopia). At its southern end its narrow straits (21 miles wide) open to the Indian Ocean. With a length of about 1,240 miles and a width that varies from 124 to 223 miles, the total surface area is just over 176,000 square miles. While its average depth is about 1,640 feet, as a part of the great rift or fault that runs northward from Lake Victoria to the base of the Caucasus Moun-

tains in southern Russia, the Red Sea plunges to 7,741 feet near Port Sudan. It is the warmest and most saline of all the open seas. Though the shores of the Red Sea historically have been sparsely settled and its ports have been few, its waterway provided access to the distant ports of the Indian Ocean and the eastern shoreline of Africa where the Phoenician merchant fleets under lease to Solomon bartered for the luxury goods that graced the royal courts of the Levant (1 Kings 9:26).

In the north the Gulf of Suez and the Gulf of Elath (Aqaba) form the western and eastern arms making up the shorelines of the Sinai Peninsula. The Egyptian pharaohs used the Gulf of Suez as the shortest route to the Mediterranean. It was linked with the Bitter Lakes and the Nile by a canal that existed before 600 B.C. and was maintained by the Persians, the Ptolemies, and the Romans.

With the expansion of David's empire, the Gulf of Elath (Aqaba) provided the vital maritime trade outlet that the kings of Israel and Judah and the Phoenician allies exploited to fill the coffers of Jerusalem. After the demise of the Judean kingdom, the Nabateans established a similar monopoly over the same marine commerce and the overland caravan routes through Petra to Damascus and Gaza for transshipment on the Mediterranean. Again in Hellenistic times, the Indian trade routes were reestablished and maintained throughout Roman times. See *Red Sea.*

Conclusion Apart from the significant roles played by the Nile in Egypt and the Tigris and Euphrates in Mesopotamia, the rivers of the biblical world were small and mostly unnavigable. As a result, apart from the alluvial plains that bordered their banks, these rivers played a more meaningful role as barriers and boundaries than as waterways for travel and transport. In terms of early biblical history, the Mediterranean and the Red Seas played the more dominant roles in intercultural and commercial exchange. As the Greek and Roman Empires developed, the western seas—the Aegean, Ionian, Adriatic, and Tyrrhenian—grew in importance. In the north and east, the Black Sea, the Caspian Sea, and the Persian Gulf with the mountain ranges that linked them basically formed the limits of the biblical world.   *George L. Kelm*

RIZIA (Rĭ´ zĭ á) Personal name meaning "delight." Head of a family within the tribe of

Asher who was a renowned warrior (1 Chron. 7:39-40).

RIZPAH (Rĭz´ pah) Personal name meaning "glowing coals" or "bread heated over coals or ashes." Saul's concubine whom Abner took as wife in what amounted to a claim to the throne (2 Sam. 3:7; cp. 1 Kings 2:22). Rizpah is best known for her faithful vigil over the bodies of her executed sons (2 Sam. 21:10-14) until David commanded their burial.

ROAD KJV term for "raid" (1 Sam. 27:10). See *King's Highway; Transportation and Travel.*

ROASTED GRAIN See *Parched Grain.*

ROBBERY Taking another person's property without the person's consent. The basic biblical law concerning robbery is the prohibition of the Ten Commandments, "You shall not steal" (Exod. 20:15; Deut. 5:19). Such an absolute statement makes it irrelevant whether the robber acquires property by force, duplicity, or oppression (Gen. 31:31; Lev. 19:13; Deut. 24:14-15; Mal. 3:5; John 10:1). Remarkably little concerning robbery is written in the law of Moses. Unlike Assyrian and Babylonian law, no specific penalty is prescribed. Instead, the emphasis is upon restoration of the stolen property to its lawful owner (Exod. 22:1,4,7,9; Lev. 6:1-7; Num. 5:5-8). If a thief could not return or replace it, the thief could be sold into slavery until restitution was made (Exod. 22:3).

During the NT period robbery was the jurisdiction of Roman law. Captured robbers, on occasion, were crucified (Matt. 27:38; Mark 15:27). Robbery could be political. Palestine contained various groups called Zealots, famous for zeal in Judaism and opposition to Rome. The more militant groups, such as the Sicarii, resorted to murder and robbery.

First-century robbers frequently operated together in bands, attacking travelers (Luke 10:30). The surprise of such an attack is analogous to the suddenness of Christ's return (Rev. 3:3). Robbery threatens material possessions; therefore, Jesus commanded faith in spiritual things (Matt. 6:19-20).   *LeBron Matthews*

ROBE See *Cloth, Clothing.*

ROBOAM (Rō bō´ am) (KJV, Matt. 1:7) See *Rehoboam.*

ROCK Use of rocky sites as places of refuge (Num. 24:21; Judg. 15:8; 20:47) led to the frequent image of God as a rock, that is, a source of protection. Titles of God include: the "Stone of Israel" (Gen. 49:24 NASB); the Rock (Deut. 32:4); the Rock of salvation (32:15); the Rock who begot Israel (32:18); "a rock that is high above me" (Ps. 61:2 HCSB). Isaiah 8:13-14 pictures the Lord of Hosts as a "rock to stumble over" (NASB) to the unholy people of Israel and Judah. Paul identified Christ as the spiritual Rock which nourished Israel in the wilderness (1 Cor. 10:4). Other texts apply to Christ, the Isaiah image of a rock which causes persons to fall (Rom. 9:33; 1 Pet. 2:8). Jesus' teaching is the rock-solid foundation for life (Matt. 7:24-25). The identity of the rock upon which Christ promised to build the church (Matt. 16:18) is disputed. Possible identifications include: Peter (whose name means "rock"), the larger group of disciples, Christ Himself, and Peter's confession of faith. The different Greek terms employed (*Petros* and *petra*) argue against a quick identification of Peter as the foundation. Both Christ (1 Cor. 3:11) and the larger circle of apostles (Eph. 2:20; Rev. 21:14) are pictured as the foundation of the church elsewhere. It seems unlikely that Matthew presents Christ as both builder and foundation of the church. Application of the foundation image to evangelistic work (Rom. 15:20; 1 Cor. 3:10) suggests that Peter's God-revealed confession of faith in Jesus as the Christ, the Son of the living God (Matt. 16:16), is the foundation of the church which lays siege to the gates of Hades. See *Keys of the Kingdom; Peter.*   *Chris Church*

ROCK BADGER (NRSV) Maybe the hyrax, a mammal somewhat resembling a shrew (Lev. 11:5; Ps. 104:18; Prov. 30:26). See *Badger; Coney.*

ROCK OF ESCAPE See *Selah-Hammahlekoth.*

ROD, STAFF "Rod" designates a straight, slender stick growing on (Jer. 1:11) or cut from (Gen. 30:37-41) a tree. "Rod" is sometimes used interchangeably with "staff" (Isa. 10:5;

Rev. 11:1). Elsewhere, rod designates a shorter, clublike stick (Ps. 23:4). Rods and staffs were used as walking sticks (Gen. 32:10), for defense (Ps. 23:4), for punishment (Exod. 21:20; Num. 22:27; Prov. 13:24; 1 Cor. 4:21), and for measurement (Rev. 11:1). Rods and staffs were also used as symbols of prophetic (Exod. 4:2-4; 7:8-24; Judg. 6:21), priestly (Num. 17:1-10), and royal (Gen. 49:10 NRSV; Judg. 5:14 NRSV; Jer. 48:17; Rev. 2:27) offices.

RODANIM (Rŏd´ à nĭm) Inhabitants of Rhodes (1 Chron. 1:7 NRSV). The parallel in Gen. 10:4 (KJV) reads "Dodanim" which should be preferred as the more difficult reading. Rhodians, however, fits well in the general geographic context.

RODENTS All small rodents are designated by the Hebrew *akbar,* a generic word including both mice and rats. The Mosaic prohibition against eating rodents (Lev. 11:29) reveals their presence in the Holy Land. As a guilt offering for stealing the ark of the covenant, the Philistines were advised to send "five golden mice" to the Israelites when they returned the ark to them (1 Sam. 6:4, KJV; rats, NIV). More than 20 varieties of small rodents have been identified in the Holy Land today.

ROE, ROEBUCK (*Capreolus capreolus*) One of the smallest species of deer, measuring about 26 inches at the shoulder (2 Sam. 2:18; Deut. 12:15 KJV). Other translations use "gazelle" or "deer." See *Deer; Gazelle.*

ROGELIM (Rō´ gĕ lĭm) Place-name meaning "[place of] the fullers." City on the Jabbok River in Gilead (2 Sam. 17:27-29; 19:31). The site is perhaps Zaharet's Soq'ah. Tell Barsina lacks evidence of occupation in David's time.

ROHGAH (Rōh´ gah) Personal name, perhaps meaning "cry out." Leader of the tribe of Asher (1 Chron. 7:34).

ROLL See *Scroll.*

ROLLER KJV term for something wrapped around the arm (Ezek. 30:21) as a bandage (NASB, REB, NRSV) or splint (NIV).

ROMAMTI-EZER (Rō măm tī-ē´ zĕr) Personal name meaning "I have exalted help." Temple musician (1 Chron. 25:4,31). Some scholars recognize a prayer of praise behind the names of the temple musicians Hananiah through Mahazioth (25:4).

ROMAN LAW The Roman Empire dominated the first-century A.D. Mediterranean world, including Palestine. Roman law developed over a period of 1,000 years, from the publication of the XII Tables in 451 to 450 B.C., to Justinian's codification in A.D. 529 to 534. The major points of the relevance of Roman law were for interpreting the parts of the NT centered on Roman criminal jurisprudence, Roman citizenship, and adoption. The sources of Roman law were the laws and statutes passed by the citizens of Rome in legal assembly, resolutions made by the senate, edicts of magistrates and governors, legal interpretations made by jurists, edicts, and judicial decisions of emperors, and the consultation of jurists. Provincial laws and customs also contributed to the codification of laws during the Roman era. Imperial decisions could have been invalidated (for example, those laws of crazed rulers such as Caligula and Nero), unless these laws were renewed by the emperor's successor. Beginning in the second century, jurists collected and organized the laws, judicial decisions, and other components of the legal system of various venues that served as guides for future jurisprudence. The collection and organization of laws reached its climax in the codes of Theodosius and Justinian in the fourth and sixth centuries respectively.

By the early part of the first century A.D., a considerable legal system, known as *ordo,* had developed which covered offenses against persons, society, and the government and applied to all citizens. The *ordo* contained a list of crimes and punishments with the maximum and minimum penalties that could be exacted against Roman citizens. The *ordo* referred to prescribed procedures and punishments for breaking certain statutes and was binding in Rome. Crimes not covered in the *ordo* were left to the jurisdiction of governors and magistrates. Public law in Rome and Italy did not automatically apply to subjects in the provinces. Offenses of noncitizens were left to the local magistrate (a chief judicial official of a city) to judge based on his own discretion whether to follow local law, to follow the regular Roman law, or to delegate the judgment to others. The magistrate was free to adopt the guidelines of the *ordo*, if appropriate, but he was also free to be as harsh and arbitrary as he desired. In most circumstances governors would leave matters to local law and local jurisdiction. The exceptions would be crimes involving Roman citizens and crimes that posed a threat to Rome itself.

The governor was not a legal expert; therefore, this placed great importance on those who were experts in the law for their consultation. Those who argued a case were rhetoricians. Minor cases were usually left to local courts; whereas governors became involved primarily in matters affecting public order (e.g., Acts 18:12-16; 19:40; 21:31-40). A Roman governor could enforce public order at his own discretion without reference to specific legislation. On different levels both governors and magistrates took whatever action they deemed just and proper. Though Roman citizens possessed the right of appeal to Caesar, provincial subjects had little to protect them against abuses of life-and-death power.

The judicial process was initiated by the drawing up of charges, penalties, and the formal act of accusation by an interested party. The enforcement of the law depended on private initiative, for the Roman system had no public prosecutor. Magistrates functioned in the roles of prosecuting attorney, judge, and jury. In a trial heard by a magistrate, the case would be heard by the magistrate in person (John 19:13; Acts 18:12), perhaps assisted by his council of friends and/or officials. The principle of the accused meeting the accusers face-to-face (Acts 25:16) was a deterrent of false charges being made. Roman law held those who made charges and then abandoned them (false accusations) responsible to pay the penalty that the charged would face.

Governors were Roman "knights" of nonsenatorial rank and were invested with the same powers as higher officials. The Roman provincial governors had almost unlimited power of life and death over provincials and were restricted only by cases concerning extortion and treason. The governor could not delegate this power of life and death. The governor was accountable only to the emperor and senate. The administration of justice was highly personal, and major cases were heard wherever the governor was.

The provincial governor held the total power of Roman administration, jurisdiction, defense, and maintenance of law and order in the province he ruled over. The governor's primary responsibility was to maintain public order; whereas the execution of justice was his secondary role. The governor's authority extended over both the Roman and non-Roman citizens living in an occupied province.

The Roman system of criminal justice distinguished between public and private penalties. Private penalties consisted of the sum of money a person paid to the victim of his actions or public beatings for minor crimes. In the later empire banishment to hard labor appeared as a penalty for breaking the law, usually associated with confiscation of one's property. The Apostle John was sentenced to exile on the island of Patmos (to work in mines) because of his Christian faith (Rev. 1:9). The death penalty was rarely given to a citizen unless found guilty of treason. The customary manner of execution for citizens was decapitation, though some chose to commit suicide. Roman law prescribed more cruel methods for those who were not Roman citizens, such as burning, being thrown to beasts, crucifixion, or drowning. The long-term incarceration of a prisoner for a crime was not common during the Roman era.

The NT describes the trials of both Jesus and Paul before Roman governors and magistrates. Roman trial proceedings were normally public and before a tribune. As noted above, interested parties brought formal charges, which had to be specific (Matt. 27:12). The Jewish Sanhedrin lacked the authority to condemn a person to death, as John 18:31 indicates. Jesus was charged before Pilate with a political crime (Matt. 27:12); the Romans would never execute Jesus or anyone else simply on the basis of religious grounds.

It was not uncommon for governors to transfer cases to the local authorities as Pilate did by sending Jesus to Herod (Luke 23:6-7). The trial of Jesus took place early in the day, at the time of day when ancient Roman officials were normally extremely busy (John 18:28). Roman criminal trials included the questioning of the accused. After A.D. 50 it was common for the accused person to receive three opportunities to respond to charges made against them. Pilate apparently did this in the trial of Jesus (John 18:33-37), following the judicial rules of the day. The failure of the accused to respond to the charges resulted in conviction by default. When Jesus remained silent and made no defense, Pilate had no other option but to pronounce judgment on Him. Following the questioning, the governor would then render his verdict and sentence to a particular punishment. According to Matt. 27:19 Pilate received a message from his wife concerning the trial of Jesus. Roman women normally assisted their husbands by serving as career diplomats or advisors.

Chapters 24–26 of Acts demonstrate some aspects of Roman law and trials. Since Paul was a Roman citizen, procedure and custom allowed that he could be tried only in a Roman court. In Acts 24:18-19 a group of Jews made charges against Paul, but they subsequently disappeared from the trial scene. Roman law required that formal accusations be made, as Tertullus did (Acts 24:5-8); however, later Paul objected to Felix that his accusers should be present to bring their charges before the defendant face-to-face (Acts 25:16-19). Paul's appeal to Caesar demonstrated the right of appeal that every Roman citizen possessed. The right of appeal went back to the laws of the Roman Republic, where a citizen had the guarantee of a trial by a jury of peers. During imperial times the emperor replaced the jury as this court of appeal. However, emperors probably did not personally hear all cases, but they often delegated this responsibility. Acts closes (28:30) with Paul under "house arrest" in Rome, and some speculate that there was some delay in Paul's trial. Such an apparent delay in a trial could be explained by a variety of things, including a congested court list, the failure of his accusers to appear to file their charges, or the political chaos that was typical of Nero's reign.

The book of Acts identifies Paul as a Roman citizen from birth (Acts 16:39; 22:28), whose citizenship proved beneficial during his missionary travels. The NT does not reveal how Paul's family had acquired citizenship; however, Roman citizenship could be obtained by several means: by inheriting it at birth from parents who were citizens; it could be bought (Acts 22:28); it could be attained by doing one of several types of service to the empire, either civil or military; or by being a citizen of a captive city that was pronounced as an imperial city by the emperor.

It is not clear as to how citizens documented their citizenship, but it is probable that Roman citizens carried credentials that certified their citizenship, made either of small metal or wooden diptychs, which were normally kept in the family archives. False claims to citizenship resulted in the death penalty. Paul's claim of citizenship appears to have sufficed without having to produce official documents (Acts 22:27).

Citizenship granted rights that include: the right to vote for magistrates or be elected as a magistrate; the right of legal marriage; the right to own property; and the right to appeal a case to the emperor (Acts 25:10-12), seeking to reverse the verdict of officials of lower rank. Likewise, citizens could not be legally bound or scourged (cp. Acts 22:24-29).

Adoption was recognized by Roman law and was a common practice in Roman society (cp. the law of adoption with Rom. 8:15,23; 9:4; Gal. 4:5; Eph. 1:5). Adoption was more common in Roman society than it is today. The person adopted was taken out of his previous condition to begin a new life, with all old relations and debts cancelled. He started a new life in the relation with the new father and family in which he received the new family name and inheritance. The new father took possession of the adoptee's property and controlled his personal relationships. The new father had the right of discipline, while assuming responsibility for the adoptee's support and liability for his actions. See *Adoption; Citizen, Citizenship; Family; Governor; Magistrate.*   *Steven L. Cox*

ROMANS, LETTER TO THE Longest and most intensely theological of the 13 NT letters written by Paul. This letter is also the most significant in the history of the church. Martin Luther was studying Romans when he concluded that a person becomes righteous in the sight of God through faith alone. His discovery led to the Reformation battle cry, *sola fide,* "by faith alone."

Who Wrote the Book of Romans? Although Paul's authorship of several letters has been contested, the evidence for his authorship of Romans is so strong that only the most radical have challenged it. Contemporary scholars do debate, however, the role of Tertius in penning the letter (Rom. 16:22). Some suspect that Paul communicated only general themes to Tertius, but that Tertius was responsible for the town near Corinth. Third, Paul sent greetings from Gaius and Erastus (Rom. 16:23) who were probably residents at Corinth (1 Cor. 1:14; 2 Tim. 4:20).

Most significant for dating is his appearance before Gallio, the proconsul of Achaia (Acts 18:12-17), during his stay in Corinth on the second missionary journey. Ancient inscriptions indicate that Gallio was proconsul of Achaia from July 51 to July 52. This suggests that the second missionary journey ended in late summer or autumn of A.D. 51. Paul's third missionary journey included a three-year stay in Ephesus, which probably extended from mid or late 52 to mid or late 55. We cannot determine the precise amount of time that Paul spent in Macedonia between departing from Ephesus and beginning his three-month stay in Greece (Acts 20:1-3). However, we may reasonably estimate that Paul penned Romans from Greece in 56 or 57. Tacitus described unrest in Rome over excessive taxation early in Nero's reign (A.D. 56–58), and Rom. 13:1-7 may indicate that Paul was aware of this, confirming the proposed date.

Why Did Paul Write Romans? Some interpreters have felt that Romans was a "theological treatise." While Romans is intensely theological, it is still written to address the particular situation of a particular church. The letter does not present some important aspects of Paul's theology such as his doctrine of the Lord's Supper (1 Cor. 11:17-24) or the second coming (1 Thess. 4:13-5:11). Paul also gives much attention to matters like the wrath of God (Rom. 1:18-32) and the Jews' rejection of Jesus (Rom. 9-11), which are not discussed extensively in other letters. Several aspects of Romans, like the discussion of the weak and the strong (Rom. 14:1-15:6) and the discussion about how believers should relate to the government, seem to reflect the struggles that this particular congregation faced. Thus Romans was not a textbook of theology written to strangers.

Paul had several reasons for writing Romans. First, Paul wanted to remind the Roman believers of some fundamental truths of the gospel, fulfilling his duty of proclaiming the gospel to the Gentiles (Rom. 15:14-16). Paul was well aware of many ways his message might be misunderstood or misapplied. He wrote to clarify important aspects of his message to people who had only heard about him. Romans 16:17-20 shows that Paul was concerned about false teachers

The interior of the Colosseum at Rome showing the area beneath the arena.

composition of the letter. However, Romans is so similar to other letters written by Paul without Tertius' involvement, Paul probably dictated the letter.

Where and When Did Paul Write Romans? Romans 15:25-29 indicates Paul wrote Romans shortly before a trip to Jerusalem. He went to Jerusalem to present money collected by Gentile churches in Macedonia and Achaia for poor believers in Jerusalem (15:26). Paul hoped to travel from Jerusalem through Rome to Spain to "evangelize where Christ has not been named" (HCSB). This fits well with Luke's description of Paul's travels at the close of the third missionary journey (Acts 19:21; 20:16). Acts 20:3 shows that Paul spent three months in Greece during his trip from Macedonia to Jerusalem. Paul wrote Romans at this time. Although Luke did not specify the location, several clues suggest Corinth. First, 1 Cor. 16:5-6 shows that Paul intended to visit Corinth after leaving Ephesus and possibly to winter there. Second, Rom. 16 serves as a commendation to the Roman church for Phoebe from Cenchrea, a infiltrating the church. In the face of this danger, an articulation of the essentials of Paul's gospel was needed particularly.

Second, Paul wanted to address several problems the Roman church was facing. In particular he wanted to call the church to unity. He was aware that some of the differences in outlook between Gentile and Jewish believers had produced disunity in the congregation. These differences emerged in arguments about diet and observance of Jewish holy days. Perhaps at the heart of the debate was the larger question, "Did the inclusion of the Gentiles in the people of God mean that God had abandoned His promises to Israel?" (see especially Rom. 9–11). Paul stresses the equality between Jewish and Gentiles believers. Jews and Gentiles alike are condemned as sinners (Rom. 2:9; 3:9,23) and are saved by grace through faith apart from the works of the Law (Rom. 3:22,28-30).

Third, Paul wanted to formally introduce himself to the Roman church and solicit support for his Spanish mission. Paul had fully proclaimed the gospel through the eastern half of the Roman Empire, "from Jerusalem all the way around to Illyricum." Now he was planning to introduce the gospel in Spain in the extreme west of the empire. After Paul left Jerusalem, he would travel to Spain by way of Rome. Paul hoped to receive a gift from the Roman church to assist his endeavors in Spain (Rom. 15:21).

What Is the Key Concept in Romans? Interpreters of Romans have searched for a single theme that unifies the epistle. During the Reformation the tendency was to focus on the first section of the book and single out "justification by faith" as the theme of the letter. Later interpreters argued that Rom. 6–8 was the heart of the epistle and the central theme was the believer's union with Christ and the work of the Spirit. Others replied that Rom. 9–11 was the centerpiece of the letter and that the real focus was the relationship of Jews and Gentiles in God's saving plan. Still others insisted that the practical section, Rom. 12–15, expressed the central theme of the book. Paul's main intention was to call the church to unity and promote harmony between Jewish and Gentile believers. Each of these views tends to emphasize one section of the letter and neglect the rest.

Recent scholars generally agree that the one theme that may encapsulate the entire book is

"the righteousness of God." Unfortunately, the precise meaning of this phrase is disputed. First, traditionally Protestant interpreters have argued that the phrase refers to a gift that God grants. God judges sinners to be righteous if they believe in Christ (Rom. 3:21-22; 4:1-8; 10:3). Catholic interpreters, still acknowledging that righteousness is a gift, have argued that it refers to an actual righteousness that God produces in believers by His transforming power (Rom. 6–8). Perhaps the most commonly held view today is that "righteousness of God" refers to a power that God exercises, God's saving power. This interpretation emphasizes the OT concept of divine righteousness (Ps. 98:2; Isa. 46:13; 51:8). Finally, others see the phrase as expressing a quality that God possesses. God is righteous. This righteousness is expressed both in His just condemnation of sinners and in His declaring and then actually making believers righteous (Rom. 3:3-5,25-26). The fact is one cannot isolate any of these definitions as the single meaning of the phrase. Each definition is applicable in various contexts. The fourth and final definition, however, is probably the one that Paul has in mind in Rom. 1:17.

"The righteousness of God" is probably too narrow to serve as a theme for the entire book. A better approach recognizes "the gospel" or "the gospel of the righteousness of God" to be the theme of the book. The word "gospel" and related terms appear frequently in the introduction and conclusion to the letter. The word is also most prominent when Paul announces the theme in Rom. 1:16-17.

What Is the Message of Romans? The introduction includes a brief summary of the gospel that highlights its foundation in the OT and its focus on Christ. Christ's Davidic lineage confirms His right to rule as Messiah-King. By virtue of His resurrection, Jesus is also "Son of God in power." Since the next occurrence of "power" in Romans refers to God's saving power (Rom. 1:16), the title signifies that Jesus possesses the power to save because of His resurrection (Rom. 4:25; 1 Cor. 15:14,17,20). Finally, Jesus is called "our Lord," a title that clearly denotes deity (Rom. 10:9,13; Joel 2:32).

Romans 1:16-17 expresses the theme of the letter. Paul is not ashamed to proclaim the gospel because the gospel is God's saving power that accomplishes salvation for all who believe whether they are Jews or Gentiles. The gospel reveals God's righteousness, both His justice and His activity of justifying sinners (Rom. 3:21-26). Salvation by faith was not new but was the message of the OT prophets (Rom. 1:17; Hab. 2:4).

Gentiles deserve God's wrath because their sins are not committed in ignorance but involve suppression of the truths about God that are apparent to all. Man's chief sin is failure to give God the glory that He deserves. God has expressed His wrath by releasing humanity to the corrupting power of sin so that man's sinful behavior is progressively more heinous and repulsive despite his clear understanding that sin results in death.

Condemning others does not prevent God from noticing our own guilt. God will judge each person fairly and give him either the punishment or reward that his deeds deserve. God will judge both Jews and Gentiles equally, fairly, and justly, because God's judgment is not based on favoritism.

Jews as well as Gentiles deserve God's wrath. Though they preach and teach the law, they have failed to obey the law, thereby dishonoring God and blaspheming His name. Circumcision grants no protection against divine judgment. The true Jew whom God will praise is a person who has been internally transformed. Jews do possess certain advantages. God chose to grant them the OT Scriptures, and God remains faithful to His promises to Israel. Still, God's justice is not compromised by His punishment of the sins of Jews but would be compromised if He failed to punish their sins. The Law that Israel possessed was not a means of salvation. Rather it demonstrated man's sinfulness so that he would despair of trying to save himself by his own righteousness.

The famous Colosseum at Rome was built in the latter years of the first century A.D.

Both the Law and the Prophets testify that God declares sinners who have failed to keep the law to be righteous in His sight if they believe in Jesus Christ. This righteous standing is granted freely by divine grace and based on the atoning sacrifice of Christ. This gracious declaration of righteousness eliminates all human boasting and places both Gentiles and Jews on equal footing. Righteousness through faith rather than law-keeping does not dispense with the Law. On the contrary, it affirms what the Law said about salvation all along. The Law says plainly that Abraham, the father of the Jews, was declared righteous in God's sight through faith (Gen. 15:6). This righteousness was a gift that he received. Thus God credits this righteousness to a person based on faith alone, apart from circumcision.

This righteousness was also credited to Abraham before the Mosaic law was given, further demonstrating that God grants this righteousness on the basis of faith and not law-keeping. The promises to Abraham's offspring (which include receiving a righteous standing and life in the world to come) are granted to believers, both Jews and Gentiles, fulfilling the promise that Abraham would be the father of many nations. Abraham believed God could bring life out of death, a little child out of aged people as good as dead. Christians likewise believe that God raised Jesus from the dead, thereby exhibiting Abraham's faith and receiving the promise of imputed righteousness.

Because of justification, believers are at peace with God and joyfully anticipate full and final transformation. Through Jesus' sacrificial and substitutionary death, believers who were formerly God's enemies and deserved His wrath have been reconciled to God. The impact of Adam's disobedience on the human race offers a negative parallel to the impact of Christ's obedience on believers. Due to Adam's sin, all people die. Even those who lived before the giving of the law and who had no explicit commandment to defy died. Clearly a single act by one person can have a universal and eternal impact. However, the obedience of Jesus Christ has the power to cancel the consequences of Adam's disobedience. If the disobedience of one man can cause the death of many, Christ's obedience can likewise grant righteousness and life to many. Just as the effects of Adam's disobedience were universal, the effects of Christ's obedience are also universal. The law did not introduce death into the world. It did offer Adam's descendants explicit commandments to defy just as Adam had done. This made sin more rampant and more heinous. This only served to magnify the abundance and greatness of God's grace.

One should not conclude from this that sin should be continued. The believer's union with Christ in His death, burial, and resurrection is inconsistent with a sinful lifestyle. The old person that the believer was died with Christ. Now the believer has been liberated from sin's mastery. Eventually, the believer's union with Christ will result in his resurrection and complete liberation from sin. Believers should live now in light of the fact that sin's mastery has been broken. They should offer themselves to God as instruments for righteousness. The believer has a new spiritual master, righteousness. Slavery to sin granted no benefits to the sinner and condemned him to die. Slavery to righteousness produces holiness and results in eternal life.

The believer has been liberated from the law. Death nullifies covenants so that they are no longer legally binding. When a spouse dies, the surviving spouse is liberated from the law of marriage and free to marry. In a similar way, death nullifies the power of the law. By union with Christ in His death, the believer is liberated from the law and free to devote himself to God. Liberation from the law, union with God in Christ, and empowerment by the Spirit enable the believer to live a righteous life, which the law could not accomplish.

The law aggravates and arouses sin in unbelievers, but this does not mean the law is bad. The law is holy, righteous, and good, but the sinful nature used the law to destroy sinners. The law still served a positive function. It demonstrated man's utter corruption and slavery to sin. However, it could not liberate him from that slavery. Paul illustrated this by describing his own frustration in trying to fulfill the law's demands. Paul had been caught in a tug-of-war between delighting in God's law and being dominated by sin. Paul confessed that this conflict would end only through the bodily resurrection.

Yet the believer can enjoy victory over sin. The Spirit accomplishes for the believer what the Law could not. The Spirit liberates the believer from slavery to sin and moves him to fulfill naturally and spontaneously the law's righteous demands. The Spirit exercises the same power that He used to raise Jesus from the dead in order to produce new life in the believer. Those who live by God's Spirit are God's children and thus heirs who will share in God's glory. The whole creation longs for this glory. The believer longs for their adoption through the redemption of the body.

God presently works through every circumstance for the spiritual good of the believer. God's eternal purpose will not be thwarted, and he will unfailingly make those whom He loved from eternity past become like His Son. The completion of the believer's salvation through justification at final judgment and his glorification is certain because it is grounded in God's undying love.

The rejection of Christ by Israel, God's chosen people, might seem to contradict the infallibility of God's promises and shake the believer's hopes. However, God's promises to Israel have not failed. Not all physical descendants of Abraham are true Israelites. God's promises apply to those whom He has chosen. This choice is based not on human character or behavior but God's mysterious purpose.

One cannot charge God with injustice. God is free to show mercy to whomever He wills because the Creator has complete authority over His creatures. One cannot challenge God's character if He glorifies Himself by expressing wrath against some and lavishing mercy on others. God would have been just if He had saved no one. He is certainly just if He chooses to save a great portion of humanity.

Still, Israel is fully responsible for its spiritual condition. Gentiles obtained true righteousness by faith. Israel sought righteousness but attempted to establish her own righteousness through obedience to the law rather than faith in Christ. Israel did not find true righteousness despite all her efforts because the law is fulfilled only through faith in Christ. Salvation comes only through faith in Christ as the OT demonstrates.

Israel did not fail to confess faith in Christ because she was uninformed. All Israel heard the message about Christ, but most rejected the message in stubborn disobedience. Yet God has not rejected Israel entirely. God has chosen a portion of Israel by His grace for salvation. This

R

remnant will obtain the righteousness that Israel sought. God hardened the rest.

God used Israel's rejection of the gospel for gracious purposes, to bring salvation to the Gentiles. Now God will use the Gentiles' reception of the gospel to make them envious and move some of them to faith in Christ. The Gentiles should not boast over Israel. Their salvation rests in God's promises to Israel and upon faith. God is ready to accept the rest of Israel when they repent of unbelief.

Gentiles should not assume they have favored status with God. After all elect Gentiles have been saved, God will shift His focus to national Israel again. Great masses of Jews will be saved because God's gifts and call are irrevocable. God has displayed His mysterious wisdom by using Gentiles and Jews to prompt one another to believe in Christ.

Believers respond to God's mercy by devoting themselves completely to Him and by renewed minds that know God's will. The renewed mind recognizes the interdependency of the members of the church and does not establish a hierarchy based on spiritual gifts. The renewed mind is characterized by love. This love expresses itself through forgiveness, sympathy, harmony, humility, and kindness.

Believers should submit themselves to governing authorities. Governmental authority is appointed by God, preserves order, and thwarts lawlessness. For this reason, believers pay their taxes and show respect for political leaders.

Believers should fulfill the law by expressing love for others. Expressing love to others and living righteously are especially important since we are approaching Christ's return. Believers should accept one another in love even when they disagree over issues of conscience, even as they follow their own consciences. They should be careful not to allow their behavior to disturb other believers who hold different convictions. They should be especially careful not to encourage other believers to do something they do not believe is right. It is wrong to eat, drink, or do anything that disturbs one's conscience.

Jewish and Gentile believers, the weak and the strong, should live in unity and try to build up one another. They should learn to glorify God with one heart and one voice. Jesus Himself came into the world as a servant to the Jews, fulfilling the promises to the Jews, and yet including Gentiles in God's plan so that they might glorify God like the OT foretold. See *Ethics; Righteousness; Salvation.*

Outline

I. Introduction (1:1-15).
   A. Jesus Christ is the focus of the gospel, and Paul is qualified to proclaim the gospel (1:1-7).
   B. Paul thanks God for the Roman Christians and expresses his love for them (1:8-15).

II. Theme: The Gospel Reveals God's Power for Salvation and His Righteousness (1:16-17).

III. The Promise Offered by the Gospel: Justification by Faith (1:18-4:25).
   A. Man's need for justification (1:18–3:20).
      1. All Gentiles are sinners (1:18-32).
      2. All Jews are sinners (2:1–3:8).
      3. All people are sinners (3:9-20).
   B. God's gift of justification (3:21–4:25).
      1. God provides justification through Christ by faith (3:21-26).
      2. Justification of both Jews and Gentiles is based upon faith rather than works (3:27–4:25).

This bas-relief of Rome's symbol of power, the Roman imperial eagle, was found at Jerusalem.

IV. The Benefits Conferred by the Gospel (5:1–8:39).
   A. The believer has peace, righteousness, and joy (5:1-11).
   B. The believer escapes the consequences of Adam's transgression, the reign of sin in death (5:12-21).
   C. The believer is liberated from slavery to sin (6:1-23).
   D. The believer is liberated from bondage to the Law (7:1-25).
   E. The believer lives a righteous life through the power of the Spirit (8:1-17).
   F. The believer will ultimately enjoy complete victory over corruption (8:18-39).
V. Israel's Rejection of the Gospel (9:1–11:36).
   A. Israel has rejected Christ (9:1-5).
   B. Israel's temporary rejection of Christ is consistent with God's eternal plan (9:6-29).
   C. Israel's temporary rejection of Christ is due to her own stubborn pursuit of self-righteousness (9:30–10:21).
   D. God has chosen a present remnant of the Jews for salvation and has hardened the rest (11:1-10).
   E. God will ultimately save the nation of Israel (11:11-32).
   F. God's plan is mysterious and wise (11:33-36).
VI. The Practical Implications of the Gospel (12:1–15:13).
   A. Christians should respond to God's mercy by living transformed lives (12:1-2).
   B. Transformed living will impact relationships within the church (12:3-21).
   C. Transformed living will affect relationships with political authorities (13:1-7).
   D. Transformed living is urgent because of the nearness of Christ's return (13:8-14).
   E. Transformed living will lead to mutual acceptance of stronger and weaker Christians (14:1–15:13).
VII. Conclusion (15:14–16:27).

Charles L. Quarles

ROME AND THE ROMAN EMPIRE International rule that the government in Rome, Italy, exercised after 27 B.C. when the Republic of Rome died and the Roman Empire was born. The reasons for the fall of the republic are not anymore clearly demonstrable than those surrounding the later fall of the empire. They were the product of a complicated interaction of numerous components that included: changes in the values, wealth, and education of the upper classes; innovations in finances, agriculture, and commerce; expansion of the senate; enormous increases in citizenship; unrest among the classes; problems in maintaining order in the districts in and around Rome, and difficulty in recruiting sufficient personnel for the army. The major factor in its demise seems to have been political. The senate lost political control of the state, and into that vacuum Julius Caesar stepped with ambitions of control that the senate found intolerable. His declaration of himself in early 44 B.C. as perpetual dictator provoked his assassination on the Ides of March by a group of senatorial assassins led by Brutus and Cassius. Caesar's generals, Antony and Lepidus along with Caesar's heir Octavian, formed a temporary ruling triumvirate. They defeated Caesar's assassins in the battle at Philippi in 42 B.C. This finally resulted in the exclusion of Lepidus and the division of the empire into the West, controlled by Octavian, and the East, controlled by Antony. Antony's military failure against the Parthians led to his excessive reliance on Egyptian resources and created a correspondingly inordinate influence of Egypt's Queen Cleopatra on the Roman ruler. Octavian was able to use Antony's reliance on Egypt against him, persuading the senate that Antony wanted to make Alexandria the capital of the empire. The two led their armies against each other in 31 B.C. at Actium in Greece, resulting in the defeat of Antony and the eventual suicide of both Antony and Cleopatra. Octavian became sole ruler and in 27 B.C. took the name Augustus Caesar. The republic became the empire, and Octavian became what Julius had only dreamed of becoming—the first emperor of Rome.

Augustus was extremely efficient as an administrator and corrected many of the

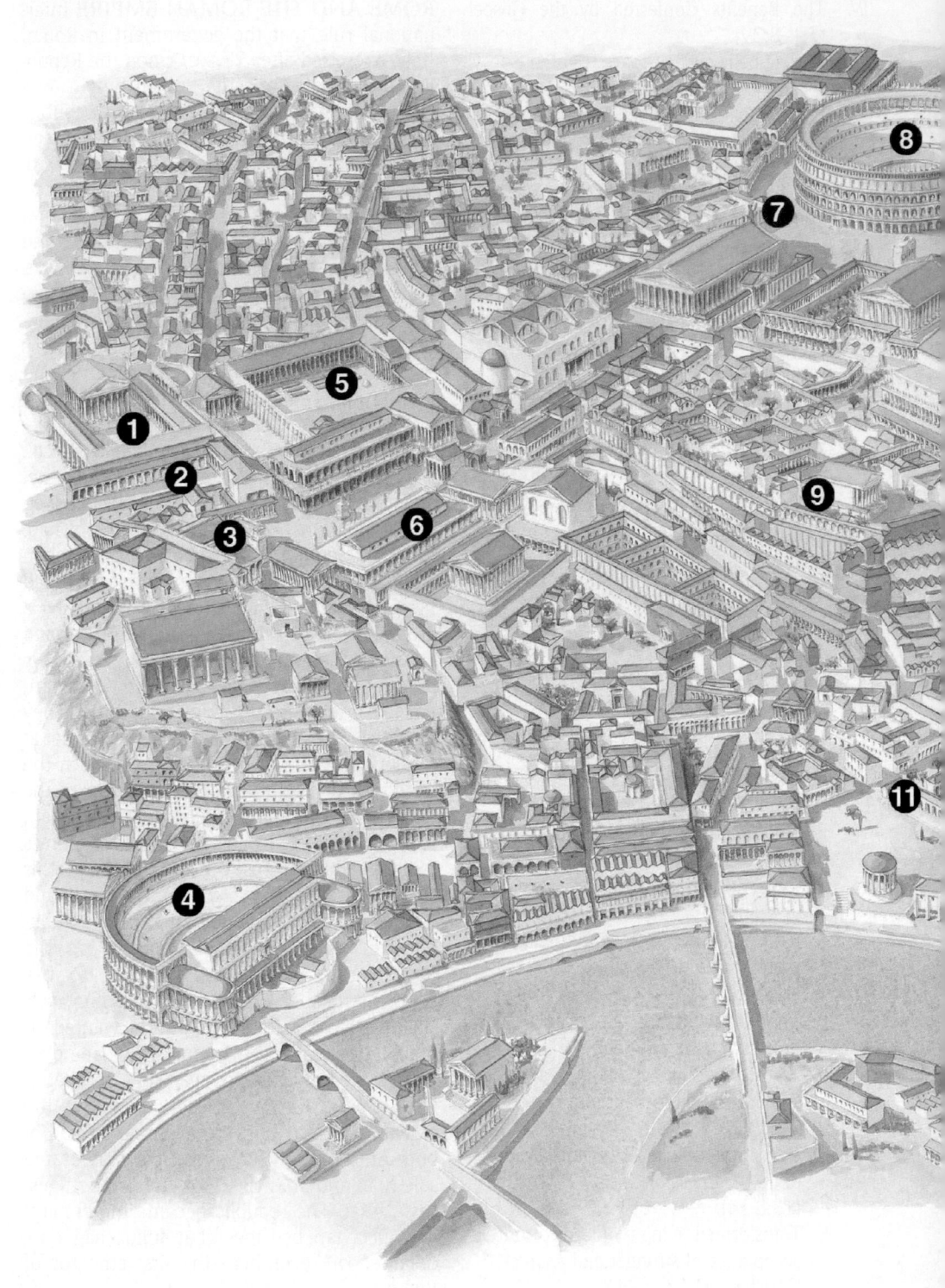

Reconstruction of Rome

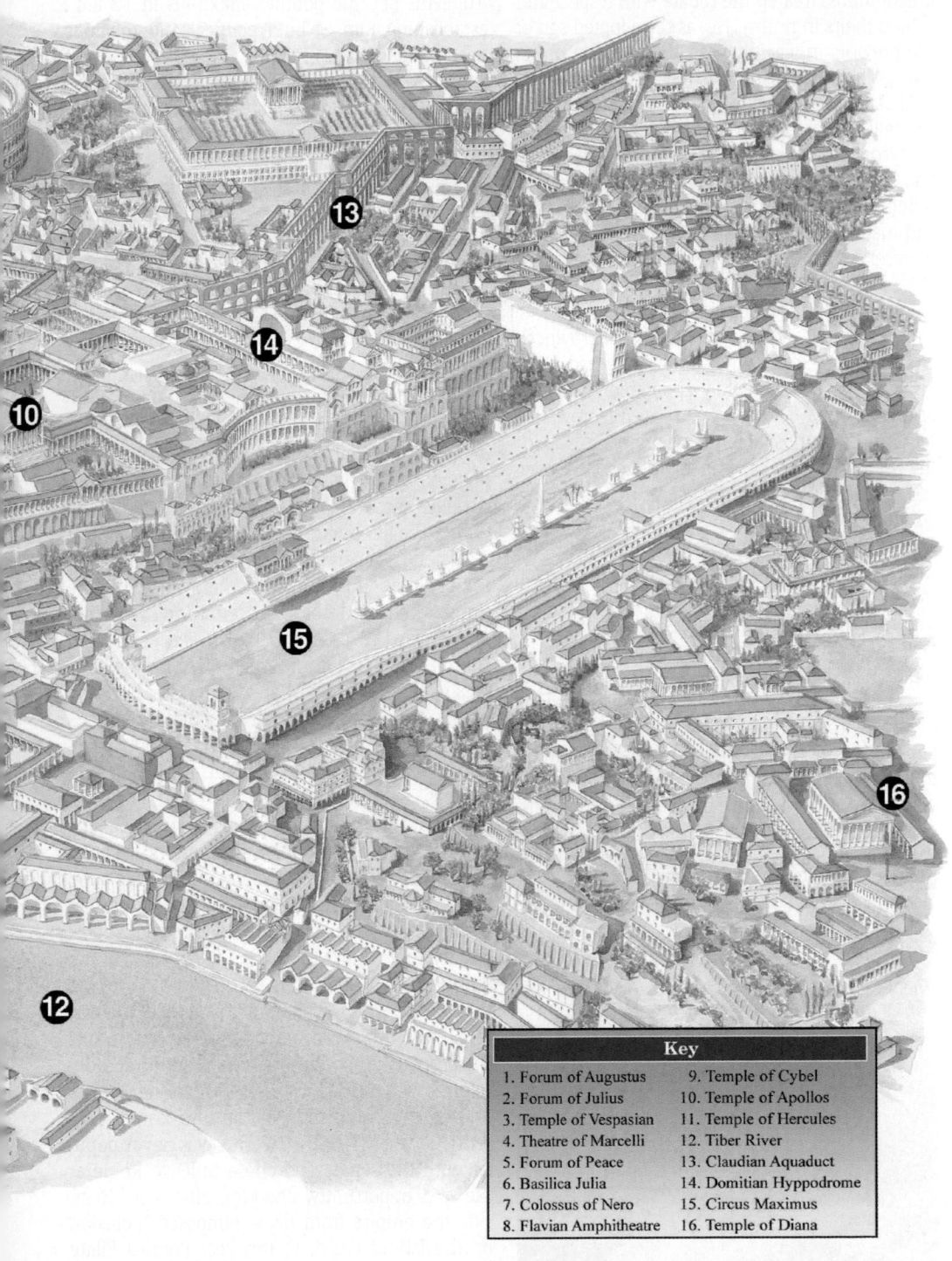

Key	
1. Forum of Augustus	9. Temple of Cybel
2. Forum of Julius	10. Temple of Apollos
3. Temple of Vespasian	11. Temple of Hercules
4. Theatre of Marcelli	12. Tiber River
5. Forum of Peace	13. Claudian Aquaduct
6. Basilica Julia	14. Domitian Hyppodrome
7. Colossus of Nero	15. Circus Maximus
8. Flavian Amphitheatre	16. Temple of Diana

R

problems that plagued the old republic. He, unlike Julius, treated the senate with respect and gained theirs in return. He, as the adopted son of the previous ruler, inherited the affection of his army. The relationship proved so popular that, after Augustus, every emperor had to be either the real son or the adopted son of the previous emperor to command the allegiance of the army and of the people of the empire. Augustus reduced the senate gradually from 1,000 to 600 and made membership in it hereditary, although he reserved the privilege of nominating new senators.

A major achievement involved sharing power over the empire's provinces. Senatorial provinces were created, over which the senate had jurisdiction and to which they appointed governors or proconsuls. These were peaceful provinces requiring no unusual military presence. Gallio, the brother of Seneca, was made proconsul over the southern Grecian province of Achaia in A.D. 51 during the time Paul was in Corinth (Acts 18:12). Imperial provinces were controlled by the emperor. He appointed procurators over these potentially volatile areas, where the Roman legions or armies were stationed. Pontius Pilate was such a procurator or governor over Judea (Luke 3:1).

Augustus inaugurated an extensive program of social, religious, and moral reform. Special benefits were given to those couples who agreed to have children. Adultery, which previously was widely condoned, was made a public crime entailing severe penalties. Traditional religion was stressed, and 82 pagan temples were renovated. Many ancient cults were revived, further accentuating the time-honored view that the peace and prosperity of the republic was depend-

The Egnatian Way shown here near Neapolis was part of the extensive Roman road system.

ent upon the proper observance of religious duty. Augustus became pontifex maximus in 12 B.C., establishing him as both political and religious head of state.

An extensive building program was undertaken. Augustus added another forum to the already existing Roman Forum and Forum of (Julius) Caesar. The forum served as a judicial, religious, and commercial center for the city, containing basilicas, temples, and porticoes. Later, other fora were built by Vespasian, Nerva, and Trajan, all of them just north of the old Roman Forum. The great variety of other new structures included theaters, libraries, temples, baths, basilicas, arches, and warehouses. For entertainment purposes the first permanent amphitheater in Rome's history was built. Extensive water systems were constructed that included artificial lakes, canals, aqueducts, and flood control. The sewage system was renovated. A police force of 3,000 men was created along with a fire-fighting force that numbered 7,000.

The first several emperors ruled at the time of the beginning of the Christian movement in the Roman Empire. Jesus was born during the reign of Augustus (27 B.C. to A.D. 14) and conducted His ministry during the reign of Augustus' successor, Tiberius (A.D. 14 to 37; cp. Luke 3:1). The latter's image was stamped on a silver denarius that Jesus referred to in a discussion about taxation (Luke 20:20-26). In about A.D. 18 Herod Antipas, the son of Herod the Great, built his capital on the western shore of the Sea of Galilee and named it Tiberias after the emperor. Tiberius was an extremely able military commander and a good administrator, leaving a large surplus in the treasury when he died. He followed Augustus' example of not expanding the borders of the empire and thus avoiding war. The *pax Romana* (peace of Rome) which Augustus had inaugurated was preserved, providing easy, safe travel throughout the empire. Paul undoubtedly referred to this in Gal. 4:4 when he wrote: "When the completion of the time came, God sent His Son" (HCSB). Tiberius was never popular with the senate and chose to leave Rome at the first opportunity, choosing after A.D. 26 to rule the empire from his self-imposed seclusion on the Isle of Capri. In this year Pontius Pilate was appointed governor of Judea, a post he held until A.D. 36, just prior to the death of Tiberius in A.D. 37.

Tiberius was succeeded by his mentally unbalanced grandnephew, Gaius (Caligula), who proved to be a disaster. During his reign (A.D. 37 to 41) and that of his successor, his aging uncle Claudius (A.D. 41 to 54), most of the ministry of the Apostle Paul took place. Claudius is reported to have expelled from Rome Jews who were creating disturbances because of Christ (cp. Acts 18:2). Initially, his contemporaries viewed Claudius as inept, but he proved to have considerable hidden talents of administration and turned out to be one of Rome's more proficient emperors. He was responsible for the conquest of southern Britain in A.D. 43–47, although it took another 30 years to subjugate northern Britain and Wales. His fourth wife, Agrippina, is mentioned on a recently discovered sarcophagus in the Goliath family cemetery on the western edge of Jericho. She poisoned Claudius in A.D. 54 to speed up the succession of Nero, her son by a previous marriage.

Nero (A.D. 54–68) was in some respects worse than Caligula. He was a man without moral scruples or interest in the Roman populace except for exploitation of them. Both Paul and Peter seem to have been martyred during Nero's reign, perhaps in connection with the burning of Rome by Nero in A.D. 64, an event that he blamed on Christians. The Roman historian Tacitus wrote that when the fire subsided, only four of Rome's 14 districts remained intact. Yet Paul wrote, "All the saints greet you, but especially those from Caesar's household" (Phil. 4:22 HCSB). Nero's hedonism and utter irresponsibility led inevitably to his death. The revolt of Galba, one of his generals, led to Nero's suicide.

Galba, Otho, and Vitellius, three successive emperor-generals, died within the year of civil war (A.D. 68–69) that followed Nero's death. Vitellius's successor was Vespasian, one of the commanders who had taken Britain for Claudius and who was in Judea squelching the first Jewish revolt. He was declared emperor by the Syrian and Danube legions and returned to Rome to assume the post, leaving his son Titus to finish the destruction of Jerusalem with its holy temple in the next year (A.D. 70). This event was prophesied by Jesus toward the end of His life when He said: "When you see Jerusalem surrounded by armies, then know that its desolation has come near" (Luke 21:20 HCSB).

The aristocratic Julio-Claudian dynasties that had reigned until the death of Nero were happily replaced by the Flavian dynasty, which issued from the rural middle class of Italy and reflected a more modest and responsible approach to the use of power. Vespasian's reign (A.D. 69–79) was succeeded by the brief tenure of his son Titus (A.D. 79–81), who at his death gave way to the rule of his brother Domitian (A.D. 81–96). The fourth century historian Eusebius reported that the Apostle John was exiled to Patmos (cp. Rev. 1:9) in the reign of Domitian. Eusebius also claimed that in Nerva's reign the senate took away Domitian's honors and freed exiles to return home, thus letting John return to Ephesus.

Nerva's reign was brief, lasting little more than a year (A.D. 96–98). He was succeeded by Trajan (A.D. 98–117), who bathed the empire

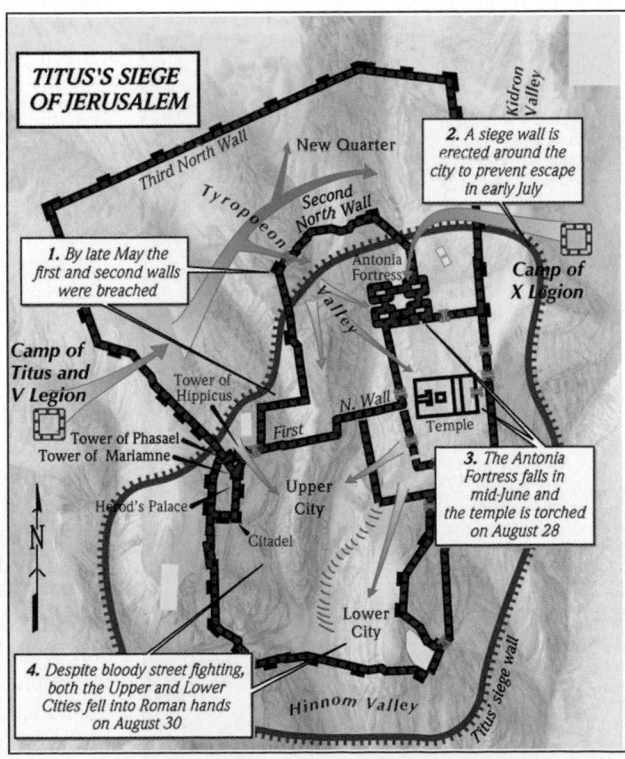

TITUS'S SIEGE OF JERUSALEM

Kidron Valley

Third North Wall

New Quarter

Tyropoeon

Second North Wall

2. A siege wall is erected around the city to prevent escape in early July

1. By late May the first and second walls were breached

Antonia Fortress

Camp of X Legion

Valley

Camp of Titus and V Legion

Tower of Hippicus

N. Wall

Temple

Tower of Phasael
Tower of Mariamne

First

3. The Antonia Fortress falls in mid-June and the temple is torched on August 28

Herod's Palace

Upper City

Citadel

N

Lower City

4. Despite bloody street fighting, both the Upper and Lower Cities fell into Roman hands on August 30

Hinnom Valley

Titus's siege wall

red in the blood of Christians. His persecution was more severe than that instituted by Domitian. Irenaeus wrote in the second century that John died in Ephesus in the reign of Trajan. The persecution of the church, depicted in the book of Revelation, probably reflects the ones initiated by Trajan and Domitian. Trajan, the adopted son of Nerva, was the first emperor of provincial origin. His family roots were in the area of Seville, Spain. Marcus Aurelius, a later emperor of Spanish descent (A.D. 161–180), also persecuted the church.

Trajan adopted Hadrian, his nephew by marriage, who succeeded him (A.D. 117–138) and quickly abandoned his predecessor's only partially successful attempts to conquer the East. More than half of Hadrian's reign was spent in traveling throughout the empire and involving himself deeply in the administration of the provinces, an activity for which he was especially talented. He left evidence of his propensity for building all over the Mediterranean world including the arch at the entrance to the precincts of the Athenian temple of Jupiter, the

A Roman milestone with Latin inscription at Caesarea Maritima.

Ecce Homo Arch in Jerusalem, his villa near Rome, and the magnificent Pantheon in Rome, whose perfectly preserved construction continually awes the visitor. Hadrian will be best remembered by those of the Judeo-Christian tradition, however, because of his attempt to Hellenize Jerusalem by changing the name of the city to Aelia Capitolina, by erecting a temple to himself and Zeus on the site of the previous temple of Solomon and by prohibiting circumcision. The brutal way in which he put down the unavoidable revolt from A.D. 132–135 was consistent with Hadrian's declaration of himself as another Antiochus Ephiphanes (the second-century B.C. Hellenizer who, while king of Syria, also desecrated the Jewish temple and precipitated the Maccabean Revolt). See *Intertestamental History and Literature.*

The success of the Roman Empire depended upon the ability of the legions to keep peace throughout the world. *Pax Romana* was the key to prosperity and success. Greek and Latin were universal languages; nevertheless, most of the conquered countries retained their own languages as well, including Celtic, Germanic, Semitic, Hamitic, and Berber. Not since that time has the world been able to so effectively communicate in common languages. If the Mediterranean Sea is included, the Roman Empire was roughly the size of the continental United States, reaching from Britain to Arabia and from Germany to Morocco. One could go from one end of the Mediterranean to the other by boat in three weeks. Less effectively, one could travel 90 miles a day on the fine network of roads that interlaced the empire, including the Appian Way and the Egnatian Way.

The quality of the Greco-Roman culture disseminated by Rome was strongest in the areas bordering the Mediterranean and weakest in those farthest removed from major routes of communication. The most effective resistance to the culture was, as might be expected, among the eastern countries such as Egypt, Syria, Mesopotamia, and the Levant (Syria-Palestine) which had the longest history of civilization. Western Europe, with a comparatively recent and uncivilized history, was no opposition and was soon thoroughly and permanently immersed in the phenomenon of western civilization.

Education in the empire was the prerogative of the wealthy. The poor had neither the time, the money, nor the need for an education that was designed to prepare the upper classes for positions of public service. The goal of education was to master the spoken word. Successful civic life was tied to proficiency in the language. Oratory was indispensable. Grammar and rhetoric were the primary subjects of study with emphasis on style over content. Among Latin authors, Virgil, Terence, Sallust, and Cicero were studied most while Homer, Thucydides, Demosthenes, and the Attic tragedians were the favorite Greek writers.

In the beginning of the empire, religion was diverse and almost chaotic. Both politicians and philosophers attempted to bring the same order to religion that they achieved in other aspects of Roman life. The Roman emperor was the head of the state religion, which included worship of the emperor and the traditional gods of Rome. The emperor functioned as semidivine while alive and as a god after his death. John may refer to emperor worship in Pergamum, where the first Asian temple to a Roman emperor was erected, in his references to the place "where Satan's throne is" (perhaps meaning the altar of Zeus; Rev. 2:13 HCSB). Mystery religions such as Mithraism, and the worship of Cybele and Isis were abundant. Philosophical systems, such as Epicureanism and Stoicism, functioned virtually as religions for agnostic intellectuals. Judaism, with its monotheistic emphasis, and Christianity, with its Judaistic origin and equally high code of ethics and morals, were anomalies. The inevitable clash between Judeo-Christians and the Romans was a clash between monotheism and polytheism, between morality and immorality.   *John McRay*

ROOF See *Architecture; House.*

ROOF CHAMBER See *Architecture; Chamber.*

ROOSTER See *Cock.*

ROOT Part of a plant buried in and gaining nourishment through the ground. In Scripture "root" generally appears in a figurative sense. Root indicates source as when the unrighteous are pictured as a root bearing bitter and poisonous fruit (Deut. 29:18; Heb. 12:15) or when the love of money is described as the root of all kinds of evil (1 Tim. 6:10). Deep-sinking roots picture stability (Ps. 80:9; Prov.

12:3) and prosperity (Prov. 12:12; cp. Ps. 1:3). Exile is termed being uprooted (1 Kings 14:15; Jer. 24:6), while taking root again pictures return from exile and the renewal of God's blessing (2 Kings 19:30; Isa. 27:6; 37:31).

Seed that fails to take root pictures those whose commitment to Christ is not firm enough to withstand trouble or persecution (Matt. 13:6,21). To be rooted in Christ is to be established in faith (Col. 2:6). Root of Jesse (Isa. 11:10; Rom. 15:12) and root of David (Rev. 5:5; 22:16) serve as titles of the Messiah. In Paul's allegory of the grapevine, Israel is the root of the plant, the church is the branches (Rom. 11:16-18).

ROSE See *Plants.*

ROSETTA STONE Stone monument engraved with a trilingual text (Egyptian hieroglyphic, Demotic, and Greek), honoring Ptolemy V Epiphanes (196 B.C.), which provided the necessary clues for deciphering the two dead languages (Egyptian hieroglyphic and Demotic). The name stems from the site of the stone's discovery in the Nile Delta in 1799. See *Archaeology and Biblical Study; Egypt.*

ROSETTES See *Filigree.*

ROSH (Rōsh) Personal name meaning "head" or "chief." Seventh son of Benjamin (Gen. 46:21). The earliest Greek translation regards Rosh as a son of Bela, hence Benjamin's grandson. The name is absent in parallel lists of Benjamin's sons (Num. 26:38-39; 1 Chron. 8:1-5).

ROUND TIRES KJV translation of a Hebrew term which modern translations render as "crescent necklaces" or "ornaments" (Isa. 3:18). The KJV rendered the same Hebrew term as "ornaments" at Judg. 8:21,26. See *Jewels, Jewelry.*

ROWERS, ROW See *Ships, Sailors, and Navigation.*

ROYAL CITY City having a monarchical government. Gibeon (Josh. 10:2) was compared in size and strength to cities with kings, such as Ai and Jericho. Gath (1 Sam. 27:5) was one of five Philistine cities ruled by kings or lords. Rabbah (2 Sam. 12:26) served as capital of the Ammonite kingdom.

RUBY See *Jewels, Jewelry; Minerals and Metals.*

RUDDER See *Ships, Sailors, and Navigation.*

RUDDY Having a healthy, reddish color (1 Sam. 16:12; 17:42; Song 5:10; Lam. 4:7; cp. Gen. 25:25).

RUDIMENTS See *Elements, Elemental Spirits.*

RUE (*Ruta graveolens*) Strong-smelling shrub used as a condiment, in medicines, and in charms (Luke 11:42). Dill appears in the Matthean parallel (Matt. 23:23).

RUFUS (Rū´ fŭs) Personal name meaning "red haired." **1.** Son of Simon of Cyrene and brother of Alexander (Mark 15:21). **2.** Recipient of Paul's greetings in Rom. 16:13. If Mark was written from Rome, both references likely refer to the same person.

RUHAMAH (Rū hā´ mah) Personal name meaning "pitied." Name Hosea used to symbolize the change in Israel's status before God following God's judgment (2:1; cp. 1:6). First Peter 2:10 applies Hosea's image to Christians who have experienced God's mercy in Christ.

RULER OF THE SYNAGOGUE See *Synagogue.*

RUMAH (Rū´ mah) Place-name meaning "elevated place." Home of Jehoiakim's mother (2 Kings 23:36), possibly identified with Khirbet Rumeh near Rimmon in Galilee or with Arumah.

RUN, RUNNING Serves as common metaphor for the struggle to live out the Christian life (1 Cor. 9:24-26; Gal. 5:7; Heb. 12:1). At Gal. 2:2 "running" applies specifically to Paul's struggle to evangelize.

RUNNERS Messengers (2 Chron. 30:6,10; Esther 3:13; Jer. 51:31) and royal bodyguards (1 Sam. 8:11; 22:17; 2 Sam. 15:1; 1 Kings 1:5; 2 Kings 10:25; 11:4).

RUNNING SORES Disqualified a man from service as a priest (Lev. 21:20 NIV) and animals from serving as sacrifices (Lev. 22:22 NASB, NIV). The curse placed on Joab's descendants included affliction with running sores (2 Sam. 3:29 NIV).

RUSH, RUSHES English terms used to translate several types of reedlike plants. See *Plants.*

RUST Coating produced by the corrosive effects of air and water on metal, especially iron. Rust on a copper cooking pot symbolized Jerusalem's persistent wickedness in Ezek. 24:6,12-13. Jesus highlighted the folly of relying on earthly treasures subject to rust (Matt. 6:19-20). In the style of an OT prophet, James outlined God's future judgment on the wealth-reliant rich as if it were already accomplished (James 5:1-6). James' mention of riches, moths, and rust (vv. 2-3) suggests that he was applying Jesus' words. The scientific observation that gold and silver do not rust should not obscure James' primary emphasis: one is a fool to rely on riches that will not survive God's coming judgment. Ill-gotten riches will serve as evidence and witness for God's prosecution. The very riches relied on for security will provide the corrosive rust effecting God's judgment.

RUTH, BOOK OF OT book whose principal character is a Moabite woman named Ruth, an ancestor of David and Jesus. Given the nature of later Judaism with its denigration of women and its contempt for outsiders, it is remarkable that a biblical book was named for a Moabite woman. This is all the more striking since Ruth is not as important as Boaz and Naomi, and that the book's significance is linked directly to Boaz, as shown in the concluding genealogy.

In the liturgical canon represented by the *Leningrad Codex*, the book of Ruth is the first of the five Megilloth (scrolls read at Jewish festivals) and is placed immediately after Proverbs. Those responsible for this probably viewed Ruth as the supreme example of a virtuous woman, as described in Prov. 31, a conclusion reinforced by Boaz's characterization of Ruth as an *eseth hayil* ("noble woman," Ruth 3:11), the same epithet found in Prov. 31:10 (the heading to the acrostic description of the noble woman in 31:10-31).

The placement of the book in English Bibles follows the Septuagint. This placement was based on a concern to locate the events described in the book in their historical and chronological contexts. In another Jewish tradition Ruth precedes Psalms, recognizing its significance as a testimony to the role of David in Israelite history.

After reading the book of Judges, which paints a dark and depressing picture of Israel, the reader is relieved to encounter Ruth. One learns that while Israel was in a state of severe moral and spiritual decline, Bethlehem represented an oasis of covenant loyalty in an otherwise barren landscape. Many have recognized in Ruth a supreme literary masterpiece, a delightful short story with a classical plot that moves from crisis (famine and death threaten the existence of a family), to complication (the introduction of a primary but less desirable candidate to resolve the crisis), to resolution (the desirable candidate rescues the family line). With great skill the narrator draws the reader into the minds of the characters (successively Naomi, Ruth, and Boaz), inviting us to identify with their personal anxieties and joys and in the end to celebrate the movement from emptiness and frustration to fulfillment and joy. In the course of the narrative, each of the main characters proves to be a person of extraordinary courage and covenant love (*chesed,* "lovingkindness, faithfulness, loyalty," is the key word in the book: 1:8; 2:20; 3:10). These are people whose spiritual commitment is demonstrated clearly in godly living.

As admirable and psychologically fascinating as the characters appear, Ruth is not primarily a tale of interesting human personalities. In the end this book is a glorious statement of the providence of God. Although the narrator attributes events to the direct action of God only twice (1:6; 4:13), the human characters repeatedly express their faith in God through their accusations (1:13,20-21), but especially through the blessings they pronounce on one another and their pleas for divine favor (1:8-9; 2:4,12,19-20; 3:10; 4:11-12,14-15). The hand of God is evident to all who read the book with the eyes of faith: (1) in apparently natural meteorological events (Famine, in light of the covenant curses of Lev. 26:19-20 and Deut. 28:23-24, must be interpreted as a divine act. When there is bread in Bethlehem, people attribute this to God); (2) in apparently random events (Ruth's arrival

at the field of a man who "just happened" to be both gracious and related. The key phrase in 2:3 translates literally "her chance chanced upon," or in contemporary English, by "a stroke of luck" she came to the field of Boaz); (3) the delicate and daring schemes of humans (Naomi's ethically questionable scheme in 3:1-7); (4) the legal procedures of the court (the disposition of Elimelech's estate in 4:1-10); (5) natural biological events (a woman who unable to conceive in 10 years of marriage immediately gets pregnant with Boaz, 4:13). In every one of these cases, the outcome could and perhaps from a natural perspective should have been different. But God's hand superintends everything so that in the end peoples' needs are met, and, more importantly, His goals are accomplished.

What are those goals? Although many dismiss the genealogy in 4:18-22 as secondary and virtually irrelevant, these verses are the key to the book. From the perspective of the author, these events have significance, primarily because of the critical place these events have in the history of the Davidic line. One of the questions the book answers is, "How can David, the man after God's own heart, emerge from the dark and demoralized period of the judges (cp. 1:1)?" The answer is, "Because of the providential hand of God on this family in Bethlehem." Like the genealogies in Gen. 5 and 11, this genealogy consists of 10 names in linear relationship. And like those genealogies, a critical moment occurs in the seventh generation (Boaz compares with Enoch (Gen. 5:21-24), who walked with God, and with Peleg (Gen. 11:16-17), in whose time the earth was divided (Gen. 10:25).

Primarily Ruth is about David. With this story the author declares not only that God set His sights on David from the beginning but also that David is an unlikely candidate for the most significant position in Israel's history, that of the divinely anointed king. In his veins flows the blood of Moabites (hence the significance of the eightfold reference to Ruth as a Moabite), who were despised by the Israelites because of their incestuous origin (Gen. 1:30-38), their hostility to the Israelites when they came out of Egypt (Num. 22–24; cp. Deut. 23:3-6), and their seduction of the Israelites into physical and spiritual adultery (Num. 25:1-9). No alert reader will miss the irony: at a time when the Israelites were behaving more like Canaanites than like

R

the people of Yahweh (the period of the judges), a despised Moabite provides the model of covenantal loyalty and kindness (see Boaz' testimony concerning Ruth in 3:10-11).

But ultimately the book of Ruth is about the Messiah. Although the author may not have recognized the full significance of these events, when Matthew begins his Gospel with a long genealogy of Jesus the Messiah, the son of David and Abraham, the names of Boaz and Ruth appear (Matt. 1:5). Three other women in this genealogy (Tamar, v. 3; Rahab, v. 5; Bathsheba, v. 6) are also tainted. The theological significance of these women in this list of men is obvious: Jesus the Messiah represents all the peoples of the earth, and if God can accept Gentiles like Ruth, and incorporate them into His plan of salvation, then there is hope for all (cp. Matt. 28:18-20). Through Boaz and Ruth not only was a threatened family rescued from extinction, but through them God prepared the way for David, and ultimately David's greatest son, Jesus the Messiah.

Although the book of Ruth is generally classified as a short story, it is helpful also to interpret it as a drama in four acts, whose flow may be captured with an outline like the following:

Theme: The Preservation of Israel's Royal Line

Outline

    Act I: The Crisis for the Line (1:1-21)
        1. The setting for the crisis (1:1-2)
        2. The nature of the crisis (1:3-5)
        3. The response to the crisis (1:6-18)
        4. The interpretation of the crisis (1:19-21)
    Act II: The Ray of Hope for the Line (1:22–2:23)
        1. The new setting (1:22–2:1)
        2. The initiative of Ruth (2:2-3)
        3. The grace of Boaz (2:4-16)
        4. The results (2:17-23)
    Act III: The Complication for the Line (3:1-18)
        1. The scheme of Naomi (3:1-5)
        2. The implementation of the scheme (3:6-15)
        3. The results of the scheme (3:16-18)
    Act IV: The Rescue of the Line (4:1-17)
        1. The legal resolution (4:1-12)
        2. The genealogical resolution (4:13-17)
    Epilogue: The Royal Genealogy (4:18-22)

Daniel I. Block

RYE (*Secale cereale*) Hardy grass grown as a cereal (Exod. 9:32 KJV) and cover crop (Isa. 28:25 KJV, NASB). Other translations render the underlying Hebrew as "spelt." See *Agriculture; Grain; Plants.*

S

A young Jewish boy at his bar mitzvah with the Torah scroll opened before him.

SABAOTH (Sä bā´ ōth) Transliteration of Hebrew, meaning "hosts, armies, heavenly bodies." Part of a divine title, "Lord of Hosts," variously interpreted as Lord of Israel's armies (cp. 1 Sam. 17:45); the stars; members of Yahweh's heavenly court or council; a comprehensive title for all beings, heavenly and earthly; an intensive title describing God as all powerful. Interestingly, the title does not appear in Genesis through Judges. The earliest Greek translation at times translated "Sabaoth" as a proper name, sometimes as "Almighty," and sometimes not at all. The title was apparently closely tied to Shiloh and the ark of the covenant (1 Sam. 1:3,11; 4:4; 6:2). When David brought the ark to Jerusalem, he also introduced the title "Yahweh of Hosts" to Jerusalem worship (2 Sam. 6:2). Yahweh Sabaoth seems to have emphasized God's place as divine king enthroned on the cherubim with the ark as His footstool ruling over the nation, the earth, and the heavens (Ps. 24:10). He is the God without equal (Ps. 89:8) who is present with His people (Ps. 46:7,11; cp. 2 Sam. 5:10). See *Army; Lord of Hosts; Names of God.*

SABBATH Day of rest, considered holy to God by His rest on the seventh day after creation and viewed as a sign of the covenant relation between God and His people and of the eternal rest He has promised them.

Old Testament The word "sabbath" comes from the Hebrew *shabbat*, meaning "to cease" or "desist." The primary meaning is that of cessation from all work. Some persons have traced the origin of the concept to the Babylonian calendar that contained certain days, corresponding to phases of the moon, in which kings and priests could not perform their official functions. Such days bore an evil connotation, and work performed on them would have harmful effects. The 15th of the month, the time of the full moon in their lunar calendar, was *shapattu*, the "day of pacifying the heart" (of the god) by certain ceremonies.

Although one can show similarities to the Babylonian concept, the Hebrew Sabbath did not follow a lunar cycle. It was celebrated every seven days and became basic to the recognition and worship of the God of creation and redemption. Regulations concerning the Sabbath are a main feature of the Mosaic laws. Both reports of the Ten Commandments stated that the Sabbath belonged to the Lord. On six days the Israelites should work, but on the seventh, they, as well as all slaves, foreigners, and beasts, must rest. Two reasons are given. The first is that God rested on the seventh day after creation, thereby making the day holy (Exod. 29:8-11). The second was a reminder of their redemption from slavery in Egypt (Deut. 5:12-15).

The day became a time for sacred assembly and worship (Lev. 23:1-3), a token of their covenant with God (Exod. 31:12-17; Ezek. 20:12-20). Death was the penalty for desecration (Exod. 35:1-3). The true observance of not following one's own pursuits on that day would lift a person to God's holy mountain and bring spiritual nourishment (Isa. 56:1-7; 58:13-14), but failure to keep the Sabbath would bring destruction to their earthly kingdom (Neh. 13:15-22; Jer. 17:21-27).

Interbiblical The Sabbath became the heart of the law, and the prohibitions were expanded. Thirty-nine tasks were banned, such as tying or untying a knot. These in turn were extended until ingenious evasions were devised that lost the spirit but satisfied the legal requirement.

New Testament The habit of Jesus was to observe the Sabbath as a day of worship in the synagogues (Luke 4:16), but His failure to comply with the minute restrictions brought conflict (Mark 2:23-28; 3:1-6; Luke 13:10-17; John 5:1-18). At first, Christians also met on the Sabbath with the Jews in the synagogues to proclaim Christ (Acts 13:14). Their holy day, the day that belonged especially to the Lord, was the first day of the week, the day of resurrection (Matt. 28:1; Acts 20:7; Rev. 1:10). They viewed the Sabbath and other matters of the law as a shadow of the reality which had now been revealed (Col. 2:16-23), and the Sabbath became a symbol of the heavenly rest to come (Heb. 4:1-11). See *Lord's Day.*   *Barbara J. Bruce*

SABBATH DAY'S JOURNEY Distance a Jew in Jesus' day considered ritually legal to walk on the seventh day. This phrase appears only once in the Bible (Acts 1:12), describing the distance from the Mount of Olives to Jerusalem. Scholars have surmised that the expression came from God's instruction to the children of Israel as they prepared to cross the Jordan into Canaan (Josh. 3:4). As they followed the priests bearing the ark of the covenant, they were to maintain a distance of 2,000 cubits from it. Earlier, while in the wilderness, they had been told not to leave home on the Sabbath (Exod. 16:29). Rabbis eventually interpreted these commands as limiting Sabbath travel to 2,000 cubits. That was the farthest that a loyal Jew should be from his center of worship on the Sabbath. The length of the cubit depended on who was counting. Greeks said it was one foot, six inches; but Romans claimed it was one foot, nine inches. Thus, 2,000 cubits could be from 3,000 to 3,600 feet, somewhat more than a half mile. Anyone who wanted to "bend" the rule could carry a lunch sometime before the Sabbath to a place about half a mile from his home. Then, by eating it on the Sabbath, he could claim that place as a "legal" home and go another Sabbath day's journey. See *Sabbath* W. J. Fallis

SABBATICAL YEAR Every seventh year when farmers rested their land from bearing crops to renew the land and people of Israel. Mosaic law directed that every seventh year the land would not be planted in crops; food would come from what grew wild (Exod. 23:10-11; Lev. 25:1-7). Just as the law reserved the seventh day as holy unto God, so too was the seventh year set aside as a time of rest and renewal. This not only assured the continued fertility of the land by allowing it to lie fallow but also protected the rights of the poor. Peasants were allowed to eat from the natural abundance of the untended fields. It may be that only a portion of the land was allowed to rest each Sabbath year, the remainder farmed as usual. Hebrews sold into slavery were to be released in that year (Exod. 21:2). Loans and debts to Israelites were also to be forgiven (Deut. 15:1-3). It is doubtful that the Sabbath year was celebrated in early Israel. Jeremiah reminded the people that their fathers had ignored the observance of the law (Jer. 34:13-14; cp. Lev. 26:35). Although Israel renewed her dedication to practice the Sabbath year during Nehemiah's time, it is unclear whether it was carried out (Neh. 10:31). During the intertestamental period an attempt was made by Israel to observe the Sabbath year despite the political turmoil of the times (1 Macc. 6:49). The Sabbath year laws consistently pointed to helping the poor. David Maltsberger

SABEAN (Să bē´ an) Transliteration of two Hebrew national names. **1.** Descendants of Seba, son of Cush (Gen. 10:7a), expected to bring gifts signifying loyalty to Jerusalem (Ps. 72:10; Isa. 45:14; cp. Ezek. 23:42). God could use the Sabeans to "pay for" Israel's ransom from captivity (Isa. 43:3). These are often identified with people of Meroe in Upper Egypt between the White and Blue Nile, thus the capital of Ethiopia. Other scholars locate it much further south, the territory east and southeast of Cush bordering on the Red Sea. Other scholars would identify at least some references here as identical with 2. following. **2.** Descendants of Sheba, the son of Raamah (Gen. 10:7b) or Joktan (Gen. 10:28; cp. 25:3). The rich queen of Sheba visited Solomon (1 Kings 10). Sabeans destroyed Job's flocks and herds and servants (Job 1:15). They were known as "travelling merchants" (Job 6:19 REB; cp. Ps. 72:10,15; Isa. 60:6; Jer. 6:20; Ezek. 27:22; 38:13; Joel 3:8). This is usually equated with the city in southern Arabia, modern Marib in Yemen. Some scholars think this is too far south and seek biblical Sheba in northern Arabia near Medina on the Wadi esh-Shaba. Sabeans could have become a general term for foreign or nomadic merchants. Sheba in southern Arabia gained riches through trade with nearby Africa and with India, whose goods they transported and sold to the empires to the north. Sheba produced and traded incense.

SABTA or **SABTAH** (Săb´ tà) Son of Cush and apparently the ancestor of citizens of Sabota, capital of Hadramaut about 270 miles north of Aden. Others identify it with an Ethiopian ruler about 700 B.C. Josephus identified it with Astaboras, modern Abare.

SABTECA or **SABTECAH** (Săb´ tē kà) Place-name of uncertain meaning. Sometimes equated with Ethiopian ruler Sabataka (700–689 B.C.) but more probably with an Arabian city-state such as Ashshabbak near Medina or Sembrachate in northern Yemen.

SABTECHA (KJV, REB) or **SABTECHAH** See *Sabteca.*

SACAR or **SACHAR** (Să´ kär) (NRSV, TEV) Personal name meaning "salary." **1.** Man from Harar and father of one of David's heroes (1 Chron. 11:35), called "Sharar" in 2 Sam. 23:33. **2.** Temple gatekeeper (1 Chron. 26:4).

SACHIA (NASB, NRSV) or **SACHIAH** (REB) (Să kī´ à) See *Shachia.*

SACK See *Bag 5.*

SACKBUT KJV term for musical instrument (Dan. 3:5), identified in modern translations as zither (TEV), lyre (NIV), trigon (NASB, NRSV), or triangle (REB). It is apparently an instrument of Asian origin, a triangular harp with four or more strings. The related Hebrew and Aramaic term refers to lattice work. Along with the other instruments in the list, it apparently was not used in worship but only in more popular settings, possibly representing a rebuke from the biblical writer for a pagan musical setting for worship.

SACKCLOTH Garment of coarse material fashioned from goat or camel hair worn as a sign of mourning or anguish, also marked by fasting and sitting on an ash heap (Isa. 58:5). Jonah 3:8 notes even animals mourned in sackcloth. The shape of the garment could have been either a loose fitting sack placed over the shoulders or a loincloth. The word "sack" is a transliteration of the Hebrew word rather than a translation. See *Grief and Mourning.*

SACRAMENT Religious rite or ceremony regarded as an outward sign of an inward, spiritual grace. The rite or ceremony was instituted by Jesus Christ. The Latin term *sacramentum* means an "oath of allegiance" and may have originally referred to a vow taken by soldiers entering the Roman army. Christian use apparently began with Tertullian and was the Latin translation of the Greek word "mystery" (1 Cor. 2:7; Eph. 3:3; Col. 1:26).

The number of sacraments has varied in Christianity. Early Christians used the term to designate baptism. Later, this concept was extended to include the Lord's Supper. The Roman Catholic Church practices seven sacraments: confirmation, penance, ordination, marriage, last rites, baptism, and the Eucharist. Protestant churches recognize only two: baptism and the Lord's Supper.

The exact meaning of sacrament has varied in Christian history. Roman Catholic theology taught that the sacraments actually convey what they represent, saving grace. In Lutheran theology the promise of the word of God is conveyed through the sacraments. Reformed theologians underscore the significance of the sacraments in terms of "signs and seals" of the covenant. In all these confessional traditions, the ritual is connected with the spiritual truth and reality conveyed through the act.

Some sacramental rituals are considered by various Christian denominations to be ordinances. Ordinances, like sacraments, are considered established by Jesus Christ and are observed in obedience to His command. Unlike sacraments, ordinances are not understood to convey some type of grace. Ordinances are rites that commemorate the death, burial, and resurrection of Christ. Ordinances are performed as expressions of loving obedience to Christ. Two ordinances underscore various aspects of the Christian's life. The ordinance of baptism is a person's public profession of faith and serves as an initiatory rite of entrance into the community of faith. The Lord's Supper is a continuing ordinance denoting the person's ongoing commitment of the life to Christ.

The idea that outward signs convey spiritual realities is taught in the Bible. For example, believer's baptism is an outward, public demonstration of the believer's spiritual union with Christ. Non-sacramentalists would do well to emphasize the spiritual realities represented in the ritual as well as the commemoration of Christ's sufferings and death. The notion that sacraments convey grace, however, is contrary to Scripture. In its entirety the thrust of the Bible is that grace comes through faith, not works (Rom. 4:3; Gal. 3:6). The understanding that sacraments convey grace implies that a person can, through the performance of some ritual, receive grace as reward for effort. The biblical perspective is that genuine faith produces works. Sacraments are not the automatic or mechanical transmission of divine grace. Genuine faith issues forth in works of faith, but works do not result in the reception of grace.   *Stan Norman*

SACRIFICE AND OFFERING Physical elements the worshiper brings to the Deity to express devotion, thanksgiving, or the need for forgiveness.
Ancient Near East Israel was not unique among the nations of the ancient Near East in their use of sacrifices and offerings as a means of religious expression. Some type of sacrificial system characterized the many religious methodologies that the nations employed in their attempts to honor their gods. The presence of sacrifices and offerings in Israel, therefore, was not unique to Israel.

Many references to the offering of sacrifices exist in extrabiblical literature. The primary approach to the gods was through the sacrificial system. In Babylon part of the ritual of purifying the temple of Bel for the New Year festival involved the slaughter of a ram. The animal was decapitated and the priest, in turn, used the body in the purification ceremony. The ram's body then was thrown into the river. The ritual accompanying the replacing of the head of the kettledrum that was used in the temple required that a black bull be selected for sacrifice. After an elaborate ceremony that culminated in the sacrifice of the bull, its hide was dipped in and rubbed with two separate mixtures and then used to cover the kettledrum.

While the above sacrifices were performed on special occasions, a variety of rams, bulls, and birds were offered as meals to the idols on a daily basis. Barley beer, mixed beer, milk, and wine also were placed before the deities, as well as loaves of bread.

The sacrifices and offerings were designed to serve the gods by meeting any physical need that they might have had. The sacrifices were the food and drink of the gods. Faithfulness to the preparation and presentation of them was an act of devotion.

Old Testament From the earliest times of the OT, sacrifice was practiced. Cain and Abel brought offerings to the Lord from the produce of the land and from the first born of the flock (Gen. 4). Upon disembarking from the ark after the great flood, Noah immediately built an altar and offered burnt sacrifices. These were a soothing aroma to the Lord (Gen. 8). Other ancient Near Eastern flood stories have parallels to this act by Noah. The patriarchal stories in Gen. 12–50 are filled with instances of sacrifice to God. The most famous is that of Abraham and Isaac (Gen. 22).

An organized system of sacrifice does not appear in the OT until after the exodus of Israel from Egypt. In the instructions given for the building of the tabernacle and the establishment of a priestly organization, sacrifices were to be used in the consecration or ordination of the priests (Exod. 29). A bull was slaughtered as a sin offering. Other sacrifices provided Aaron and his sons a holy meal. These sacrifices were repeated each day for a week as a part of the "ordination" of the priests. The altar itself was consecrated through the offering of two lambs

Iron Age sacrificial altar located at the site of ancient Arad.

and a grain offering and a libation or "drink offering" (a misnomer, since it was never drunk but poured) of wine. This sacrifice also was carried out each day for a week.

The sacrifices that constituted much of the worship of Israel at this time were burned on an altar that was made from acacia wood and overlaid with copper (Exod. 27). In addition to the sacrifices offered on this altar, incense was burned on a smaller altar (Exod. 30). While the sacrificial altar was placed in the courtyard, just before the door of the tabernacle, the incense altar was positioned inside the tabernacle, just before the ark of the covenant. See *Altar.*

Leviticus 1–7 gives the most detailed description of Israel's sacrificial system, including five types of sacrifices. The sacrifices and offerings that were brought by the people were to be the physical expression of their inward devotion.

1. Burnt offering (olah) Offered in the morning and in the evening, as well as on special days such as the Sabbath, the new moon, and the yearly feasts (Num. 28–29; 2 Kings 16:15; 2 Chron. 2:4; 31:3; Ezra 3:3-6). Rituals performed after childbirth (Lev. 12:6-8), for an unclean discharge (Lev. 15:14-15) or hemorrhage (Lev. 15:29-30), or after a person who was keeping a Nazirite vow was defiled (Num. 6:10-11) required a burnt offering, as well as a sin offering.

The animal for this sacrifice could be a young bull, lamb, goat, turtledove, or young pigeon, but it had to be a perfect and complete specimen. The type of animal chosen for this sacrifice seems to be dependent on the financial ability of the one who brings the offering. The one bringing the offering was to lay a hand on the animal, indicating that the animal was taking the person's place, and then he was to kill it. The priest then collected the blood and sprinkled it around the altar and the sanctuary, and the worshiper cut up and skinned the animal. If a bird was brought, the priest killed it. After the priest arranged the various parts on the altar, the entire animal was burned as a sacrifice. The only portion that remained was the hide, and the priest received it (Lev. 7:8). The one who made this sacrifice did so to restore the relationship with God and to atone for some sin. When Araunah offered to David his threshing floor, oxen, and wood without cost so that David could sacrifice, David refused. His explanation was that he could not offer burnt offerings that cost him nothing (2 Sam. 24:18-25).

2. Grain offering (*minchah;* "meat offering," KJV) Offering from the harvest of the land; the only type that required no bloodshed. It was composed of fine flour mixed with oil and frankincense. Sometimes this offering was cooked into cakes prior to taking it to the priest. These cakes, however, had to be made without leaven. Every grain offering had to have salt in it (Lev. 2:13), perhaps as a symbol of the covenant (Num.18:19; 2 Chron. 13:5). Only a portion of this offering was burned on the altar, with the remainder going to the priests. While no reason is given for the grain offering, it may have symbolized the recognition of God's blessing in the harvest by a society based to a large degree on agriculture. The bringing of a representative portion of the grain harvest was another outward expression of devotion. Grain offerings as well as "drink offerings" or libations of wine accompanied all burnt offerings and peace offerings (Num.15:3-4).

3. Peace offering (*zebach shelamim;* "well-being," NRSV; "shared," REB; "fellowship," NIV) Consisting of the sacrifice of a bull, cow, lamb, or goat that had no defect. As with the burnt offering, the individual laid a hand on the animal and killed it. The priests, in turn, sprinkled the blood around the altar. Only certain parts of the internal organs were burned. The priest received the breast and the right thigh (Lev. 7:28-36), but the one who offered the sacrifice was given much of the meat to have a meal of celebration (Lev. 7:11-21). As part of the meal, various kinds of bread were offered (and ultimately kept by the priest). A "peace offering" was to be brought in response to an unexpected blessing (a "thank offering") or an answer to prayer (a "vow offering"), or for general thankfulness (a "freewill offering"). The idea of thanksgiving was associated with the peace offering. It often accompanied other sacrifices in celebration of events such as the dedication of the temple (1 Kings 8:63) or spiritual renewal (2 Chron. 29:31-36). The "wave offerings" (*tenuphah,* "consecrated gift") and the "heave offerings" (*terumah,* "contribution") were associated with the peace offerings. They were portions presented or lifted up before the Lord, mentioned first as part of the priestly ordination ceremony (Exod. 29:24-27). Whereas the wave offering was always offered in the sanctuary, the heave offering could be presented anywhere.

4. Sin offering (*chatta't;* "purification," REB) This was designed to purify the sanctuary from sin that was committed unintentionally, and thereby allow God to continue dwelling with His people. Its nature varied according to who committed the sin. If the priest or the congregation of Israel sinned, then a bull was required. A leader of the people had to bring a male goat, while anyone else sacrificed a female goat or a lamb. The poor were allowed to bring two turtledoves or two young pigeons. The one bringing the offering placed a hand on the animal and then slaughtered it. When the priest or the congregation sinned, the blood was sprinkled seven times before the veil in the sanctuary, and some of it was placed on the horns of the incense altar. The rest of the blood was poured out at the base of the sacrificial altar. For others who sinned, the sprinkling of the blood before the veil was omitted. The same internal organs that were designated for burning in the peace offering were likewise designated in this sacrifice. The rest of the animal was taken outside of the camp to the place where the ashes of the sacrifices were disposed, and there it was burned. These disposal procedures were not followed when the sin offering was made on behalf of a non-priestly person (Lev. 6:24-30). In this case, the priest was allowed to eat some of the meat.

5. Guilt offering (*asham,* "trespass," KJV; "reparation," REB) This offering seems to overlap somewhat with the sin offering (Lev. 4–5). In Lev. 5:6-7 the guilt offering is called a sin offering. The guilt offering was concerned supremely with restitution. Someone who took something illegally was expected to repay it in full plus 20 percent of the value and then bring a ram for the guilt offering. Other instances in which the guilt offering was prescribed included the cleansing of a leper (Lev. 14), having sexual relations with the female slave of another person (Lev. 19:20-22), and for the renewing of a Nazirite vow that had been broken (Num. 6:11-12).

The burnt, grain, peace, sin, and guilt offerings composed the basic sacrificial system of Israel. These sacrifices were commonly used in conjunction with each other and were carried out on both an individual and a corporate basis. The sacrificial system taught the necessity of dealing with sin and, at the same time, demonstrated that God had provided a way for dealing with sin.

Prophets' Attitude toward the Sacrificial System The prophets spoke harshly about the people's concept of sacrifice. They tended to ignore faith, confession, and devotion, thinking the mere act of sacrifice ensured forgiveness. Isaiah contended that the sacrifices were worthless when they were not accompanied by repentance and an obedient life (Isa. 1:10-17). Micah reflected the same sentiments when he proclaimed that God was not interested in the physical act of sacrifice by itself but in the life and heart of the one making the sacrifice (Mic. 6:4-6). Jeremiah condemned the belief that as long as the temple was in Jerusalem and the people were faithful to perform the sacrifices, then God would protect them. The symbol of the sacrifice must be reflected in the individual's life (Jer. 7:1-26). Malachi chastised the people for offering the lame and sick animals to God instead of the best, as the Levitical law required. In doing this, the people were defiling the altar and despising God (Mal. 1:7-14).

The prophets did not want to abolish the sacrificial system. They, instead, denounced the people's misuse of it. God wanted more than the physical performance of meaningless sacrifices. He desired the offerings to exemplify the heart of the worshiper.

New Testament During the time of the NT the people sacrificed according to the guidelines in the OT. In keeping with the Levitical law (Lev. 12), Mary brought the baby Jesus to the temple and offered a sacrifice for her purification. She sacrificed turtledoves or pigeons, indicating the family's low financial status. When Jesus healed the leper (Luke 5:12-14), He told him to go to the priest and make a sacrifice (cp. Lev. 14). The cleansing of the temple (John 2) came about because people were selling animals and birds for the various sacrifices within the temple precincts. These people had allowed the "business" of sacrifice to overwhelm the spiritual nature of the offerings. Jesus chided the Pharisees for neglecting family responsibilities by claiming that something was "corban," or offered to God, and thus unavailable for the care of their parents (Mark 7). *Corban* is the most common and general Hebrew word for sacrificial offering (Lev. 1:2). See *Corban*.

The NT consistently describes Christ's death in sacrificial terms. Hebrews portrays Christ as the sinless high priest who offered Himself up as a sacrifice for sinners (7:27). The superiority of Christ's sacrifice over the Levitical sacrificial system is seen in that His sacrifice had to be offered only once. The book ends with an encouragement to offer sacrifices of praise to God through Christ. This thought is reflected in 1 Pet. 2 where believers are called a holy and royal priesthood who offer up spiritual sacrifices.

Paul used the terminology of the OT sacrifices in teaching about the death of Jesus. His death was an offering and sacrifice to God and, as such, a fragrant aroma (Eph. 5:2). He associated Jesus with the Passover sacrifice (1 Cor. 5:7).

The first-century church lived in a culture that sacrificed to their gods. Paul and Barnabas at Lystra were thought to be the gods Zeus and Hermes. The priest of Zeus sought to offer sacrifices to them (Acts 14). The church at Corinth was embroiled in a controversy over whether or not it was permissible for Christians to eat meat offered to idols (1 Cor. 8–10). Paul's preaching of the gospel at Ephesus disrupted the business and worship of the goddess Artemis (Acts 19).

When the temple in Jerusalem was destroyed in A.D. 70, the Jews' sacrificial system ceased. By this time, however, the church had begun to distance itself from Judaism. The biblical view of sacrifice changed as well. In the OT and in the beginning years of the NT, sacrifice was the accepted mode of worship. With the death of Christ, however, animal sacrifice became unnecessary. As the temple and priest of God, the believer now has the responsibility for offering acceptable spiritual sacrifices (Rom. 12:1-2; 1 Pet.2:5; Heb. 13:15). Paul also spoke of himself as a libation poured out (Phil. 2:17). He called the Philippians' gift a fragrant aroma

S

and an acceptable sacrifice to God (Phil. 4:18; Rom. 15:16).

Scott Langston and E. Ray Clendenen

SADDUCEES (Săd´ ū sēz) Religious group which formed during the period between the Testaments when the Maccabees ruled Judah. They took their name from one of David's co-priests, Zadok, and claimed descent from him. Their name meant "righteous ones." See *Jewish Parties in the New Testament.* *Mike Mitchell*

SADOC (Sā´ dŏc) KJV spelling of Zadok (Matt. 1:14) following Greek.

SAFFRON See *Spices.*

SAILOR See *Ships, Sailors, and Navigation.*

SAINTS Holy people, a title for all God's people but applied in some contexts to a small group seen as the most dedicated ones.

Old Testament Two words are used for saints: *qaddish* and *chasid.* *Qaddish* comes from the *qadosh* and means "holy." To be holy is to separate oneself from evil and dedicate oneself to God. This separation and union is seen both with things and people. All the items of worship are separated for the Lord's use: altar (Exod. 29:37), oil (Exod. 30:25), garments (Exod. 31:10), and even the people are to be holy (Exod. 22:31). This separation reflects God's very character, for He is holy (Lev. 19:2). Holiness is clearly portrayed as an encounter with the living God, which results in a holiness of lifestyle (Isa. 6). Therefore, holiness is more than a onetime separating and uniting activity. It is a way of life. "Be holy because I, the LORD your God, am holy" (Lev. 19:2 HCSB). Saints are people who try to live holy lives (Dan. 7:18-28). See *God; Holy.*

Chasid means "to be kind or merciful." These are qualities of God. Thus, *chasid* people are godly people because they reflect His character. Saints praise the Lord for His lifelong favor (Ps. 30:4), rejoice in goodness (2 Chron. 6:41), and know that God keeps their paths (1 Sam. 2:9). God's encounter with His people through the covenant enables them to walk as His saints.

New Testament One word, *hagios*, is used for saints in the NT. This word, like *qadosh*, means "holy." Consequently, saints are the holy ones. There is only one reference to saints in the Gospels (Matt. 27:52). In this verse dead saints

are resurrected at the Lord's crucifixion. The death of the Holy One provides life for those who believe in God. In Acts, three of the four references occur in chapter 9 (vv. 13,32,41). First Ananias and then Peter talk of the saints as simply believers in Christ. Paul continues this use in his Epistles to the Romans, Corinthians, Ephesians, Philippians, Colossians, Thessalonians, and Philemon. In each case, saints seem simply to be people who name Jesus as Lord. In the book of Revelation, however, where the word "saints" occurs more times than in any other single book (13 times), the meaning is further defined. Saints not only name Jesus as Lord, but they are faithful and true witnesses for Jesus.

Little wonder then that the early church considered witnesses who were martyred for their testimonies to be saints. In fact, soon these saints were accorded special honor and then even worship. Unfortunately, the term "saints" came to be applied only to such special people.

Biblically, though, the term "saint" is correctly applied to anyone who believes Jesus Christ is Lord. To believe in Jesus demands obedience and conformity to His will. A saint bears true and faithful witness to Christ in speech and lifestyle. To be a saint is a present reality when a believer seeks to let the Spirit form Christ within (Rom. 8:29; Gal. 4:19; Eph. 4:13). See *Spirit; Witness, Martyr.* *William Vermillion*

SAKIA (Sȧ kī´ȧ) (NIV) See *Shachia.*

SAKKUTH (Săk´ ŭth) NRSV transliteration of Assyrian divine name applied to god Ninurta (or Ninib), apparently an Assyrian name for Saturn or another astral deity. Some translators take the name as a common noun meaning "shrine" (REB, NIV), "tabernacle" (KJV), since the Hebrew term resembles the word for "tent." Amos condemned Israel for such false worship (Amos 5:26). See *Succoth-benoth.*

SALA or **SALAH** (Sā´ lȧ) Personal name meaning "sprout." Father of Eber (Gen. 10:24; 11:12-15; 1 Chron. 1:18,24). See *Shelah.*

SALAMIS (Săl´ ȧ mǐs) Most important city of Cyprus, located on its east coast and containing more than one Jewish synagogue (Acts 13:5). See *Cyprus.*

SALATHIEL (Sȧ lā´ thǐ ĕl) See *Shealtiel.*

SALCAH or **SALCHAH** (Săl´ kah) Territory and/or city on extreme eastern border of Bashan, possibly modern Salkhad, the defensive center of the Jebel el-Druze, 63 miles east of the Jordan (Deut. 3:10; Josh. 12:5). See *Bashan.*

SALECAH (Săl´ ə kah) (NASB, NRSV, NIV, TEV) See *Salcah.*

SALEM (Sā´ ləm) Abbreviated form of Jerusalem (Gen. 14:18; Ps. 76:2; Heb. 7:1-2). See *Jerusalem; Melchizedek.*

SALIM (Sā´ lĭm) Place-name meaning "peace." Town near which John the Baptist baptized (John 3:23). Its site is disputed: northeast of Dead Sea near Bethabara; west bank of northern Jordan Valley, eight miles south of Scythopolis; in Samaria four miles south-southeast of Shechem. The third site would identify John as well as Jesus with Samaritan ministry. The second and third sites would have John leaving for the north, allowing Jesus to minister near Jerusalem. See *Aenon; Samaria.*

SALLAI (Săl´ lā ī) Personal name, perhaps meaning "the restored one." **1.** Benjaminite who lived in Jerusalem after exile (Neh. 11:8). Commentators often emend the Hebrew text to read "and his brothers, men of valor." Others read "Sallu." **2.** Priestly family after the exile (Neh. 12:20), apparently the same as Sallu (v. 7).

SALLU (Săl´ lū) Personal name, perhaps meaning "the restored one." **1.** A Benjaminite (1 Chron. 9:7; Neh. 11:7). **2.** Leading priest after the exile (Neh. 12:7). See *Sallai.*

SALMA (Săl´ mà) Personal name meaning "coat." **1.** Father of Boaz and ancestor of David (1 Chron. 2:11). **2.** Descendant of Caleb and father of Bethlehem (1 Chron. 2:51).

SALMON (Săl´ mŏn) Personal name and place-name meaning "coat." **1.** Father of Boaz (Ruth 4:21; Matt. 1:5; Luke 3:32). See *Salma.* **2.** KJV spelling of Zalmon (Ps. 68:14). See *Zalmon.*

SALMONE (Săl mō´ nə) Promontory on northeast coast of Crete; modern Cape Sidero. Temple to Athena Salmonia stood there. Paul sailed by there on the way to Rome (Acts 27:7).

SALOME (Sà lō´ mə) Personal name meaning "pacific." Wife of Zebedee and mother of James and John (if one combines Mark 16:1 and Matt. 27:56; cp. John 19:25). She became a disciple of Jesus and was among the women at the crucifixion who helped prepare the Lord's body for burial. Some believe that she is mentioned in John 19:25 as Mary's sister, and thus she would have been Jesus' aunt with James and John His cousins. See *Mary.*

SALT Common crystalline compound used in seasoning food and in sacrifices. See *Minerals and Metals.*

SALT SEA See *Dead Sea.*

SALT, CITY OF See *City of Salt.*

SALT, COVENANT OF See *Covenant; Covenant of Salt.*

SALT, VALLEY OF Geographical passageway south and east of the Dead Sea, often identified with Wadi el-Milch south of Beersheba, but this location is not accepted by modern commentators. David killed 18,000 Edomites there (2 Sam. 8:13; cp. 1 Chron. 18:12; Ps. 60). King Amaziah (796–767 B.C.) killed 10,000 Edomites (2 Kings 14:7).

SALTWORT (REB, Job 30:4). See *Mallow.*

SALU (Sā´ lū) Personal name meaning "the restored one." Father of Zimri (Num. 25:14) and tribal leader in Simeon.

SALUTATION Act of greeting, addressing, blessing, or welcoming by gestures or words; a specific form of words serving as a greeting, especially in the opening and closing of letters.

In the ancient Near East a salutation covered a wide range of social practices: exchanging a greeting ("Hail"), asking politely about another's welfare, expressing personal regard, and the speaking of a parting blessing ("Go in peace"). Physical actions, such as kneeling, kissing, and embracing, were also involved. The salutation functioned to maintain close, personal contact and to foster good relations. Though the practice continued into the first century, Jesus and early Christians transformed the act of saluting. Jesus critiqued the Pharisees for practicing long, protracted deferential salutations (Mark 12:37b-40;

S

Luke 20:45-47; cp. Matt. 23:1-36) and forbade His disciples from practicing such public displays (Luke 10:4). Instead, Jesus endorsed a salutation when it signified the long-awaited presence of messianic "peace" (Hb. *shalom*), that is the "peace" of the kingdom of God (Luke 10:5-13; 19:42; John 14:27; 20:21; cp. Luke 2:14,29). Paul, as do other NT authors, also transformed the salutation to speak of newness brought on by the cross and resurrection. The typical greeting in Greek letters was the infinitive "to rejoice" (*chairein*). Paul never opened his letters with this greeting; instead, the apostle fused the Greek word for the typical Hebrew blessing, "Peace" (*eirene*), with the noun form of the Greek blessing, "Grace" (*charis*), to yield the distinctly Christian salutation: "Grace and peace" (*charis kai eirene*). By such a subtle change in the form of Greek letter writing, Paul was able to invoke the range of apostolic blessings found in Jesus: mercy from God ("grace") and eternal well-being from God's presence ("peace"). See *Letter Form and Function. Carey C. Newman*

SALVATION One of the key concepts of God's revelation to humanity. The biblical idea of salvation involves three notions. First is the rescue from danger, harm, or even death of an individual, group, or nation. Most specifically salvation is the rescue from sin and death. Second is the renewing of the spirit. Scripture explains that humanity fell from the original condition of moral purity into the state of sin. God's salvation always renews the spirit of a person to lead a life that is morally pleasing to Him. Third is the restoration of a right relationship with God. One of the effects of sin is separation from God. The written word of God makes clear that salvation restores one's relationship with God, as Rom. 5:10 says, "For if, while we were enemies, we were reconciled to God through the death of His Son." In both the OT and NT God's salvation includes rescue, renewal, and restoration and is accomplished through the person and work of His Son, our Lord and Savior Jesus Christ.

Old Testament The OT gives many examples of a type of physical salvation to teach about the more important spiritual salvation. This teaching about salvation begins in the first three chapters of Genesis. The first two chapters tell how God created the heavens and the earth, the fish of the sea, the birds of the air, the animals of the land, and the first man and woman. All that God cre-

ated was very good (Gen. 1:31). Chapter three explains how sin entered into God's created order and God's promise of salvation through the seed of the woman (Gen. 3:15). Even though male and female were created in the image of God, now God's image is marred in all mankind. The results of sin include death and separation from God.

The eroding of human nature into godlessness is clearly evident in the story of Noah. Since God is holy, He cannot abide with or condone that which is unholy. God's judgment against sin and sinners is real and demonstrated by a worldwide flood. However, God revealed His grace and mercy by providing an ark of salvation for Noah and his family (Gen. 6–9). This is a living picture of the salvation God brought about for sinners in and through Jesus.

The Lord made a covenant with Abraham promising to bless all the nations of the earth through him (Gen. 12:1-3). This promise is another illustration of God's intent to provide salvation. Later in Israel's history Moses led the nation out of bondage into the promised land. God proved Himself stronger than the false gods of Egypt, wiser than the wisdom of Pharaoh, and more powerful than the Egyptian army. God provided salvation for His people.

Moses further instructed God's people in the need of blood sacrifices to atone for sin. The book of Leviticus gives the proper method and means of sacrifices and chapter 16 explains the Day of Atonement. The high priest enters the holy of holies with the blood of a bull to make atonement first for himself and then for the people. The lesson further illustrated God's holiness and the need for a sacrifice to experience His salvation.

While much of the OT deals with the salvation of the nation of Israel, the Psalms focus more on the salvation of the individual and the prophets extend God's plan of salvation to the nations (Pss. 13; 18; 51; Isa. 2:2-4; Mic. 4:1-4; Zech. 8:20-23). The OT lays the foundation for a biblical understanding of salvation. God is holy and cannot tolerate sin, human beings are fallen and sinful creatures, God initiates and provides a way of salvation, and finally people respond to God's offer of salvation. God is always the One who saves and redeems His people, and redemption usually comes with a blood sacrifice.

New Testament In the NT salvation by grace alone through faith in the person and work of

Jesus Christ is the dominant theme. Salvation begins with the initiating love of God (John 3:16; Eph. 1:3-6). God's eternal purpose is to save sinners through Jesus' atoning death on the cross. Thus, Christology is a vital component of the NT and relates directly to the doctrine of salvation. Specifically Jesus' nature as the God-man and His substitutionary death on the cross are the key elements. The NT cannot be properly understood apart from a right view of who Jesus is and what Jesus did. As John says, "Jesus performed many other signs in the presence of His disciples that are not written in this book. But these are written so that you may believe Jesus is the Messiah, the Son of God, and by believing you may have life in His name" (John 20:30-31 HCSB).

All the NT writers witness to the importance of the death, burial, and resurrection of Jesus for salvation (Rom. 1:6; 1 Cor. 15:3-11; 1 Pet. 2:21-25). The preaching of both Peter and Paul in the book of Acts further attests to the centrality of the atonement and resurrection as the Gospel message (Acts 2:14-39; 3:11-26; 10:34-48; 13:26-43; 17:22-34; 24:2-21). In the NT salvation is found in no other name but the name of Jesus (Acts 4:12).

The NT identifies several other key doctrines or elements as part of a complete understanding of salvation. One is the work of the Holy Spirit in convicting of sin and bringing about the new birth. In the Gospel of John, Jesus explains that the ministry of the Holy Spirit involves conviction of sin, righteousness, and judgment (John 16:5-11). Earlier in John's Gospel Jesus has a conversation with Nicodemus in which Jesus instructs the Pharisee on the necessity of the new birth (John 3:3-8). Paul calls this new birth regeneration (Titus 3:5). He writes of the work of the Holy Spirit in convicting and convincing persons of their sin and need for a Savior in terms of "calling" (Rom. 11:29; 1 Cor. 1:26).

"Conversion" is often the term used to describe when someone actually receives salvation. This is the point when a person repents and believes. Faith and repentance are the conditions of salvation, according to the NT (Mark 1:15). Repentance means turning from self and sin to God and holiness while faith is believing the historic facts about Jesus and trusting Him alone to forgive one of sins and to grant eternal salvation (Heb. 11:1-6). The promise of salvation

is eternal life with Jesus in heaven (John 3:16; 1 John 2:25).

The NT teaches that believing in the gospel results in justification before God. The doctrine of justification by faith is central to Pauline theology and has been very influential in the history of the Church. In Romans, Galatians, and Philippians Paul discusses justification by faith alone at length (Rom. 3:21–5:21; Gal. 3:1–4:31; Phil. 3:2-16). The essential point in relation to salvation is that at the moment of conversion the sinner is declared not guilty before God through the blood of Jesus. By trusting in Jesus alone for salvation, the righteousness of Jesus Christ is imputed to the sinner so that God now treats the sinner in light of the righteousness of Jesus (Rom. 3:21-26).

At the moment of conversion, the sinner becomes a saint, not free from actual sin in this life but free from the death penalty of sin. The Bible teaches that the Holy Spirit actually indwells the sinner at the moment of conversion. A lifelong process of growth in Christlikeness now begins an is called "sanctification." Since salvation is a gift of God, the believer can never lose the gift of salvation. This is a testimony to the fullness of God's grace. The Christian's eternal future is secure because, not only does God initiate salvation, He also preserves the Christian through the indwelling presence of the Holy Spirit. Salvation is a free gift from God that rescues the believer from sin and its consequences, renews the believer to a holy life, and restores the believer to a right relationship with God for all eternity. See *Atonement; Conversion; Election; Eschatology; Forgiveness; Future Hope; Grace; Justification; New Birth; Predestination; Reconciliation; Redeem, Redemption, Redeemer; Repentance; Sanctification; Security of the Believer.*   *Douglas C. Walker*

SAMARIA, SAMARITANS (Sȧ mā´ rǐ ȧ; Sȧ mâr´ ĭ tȧns) Place-name of mountain, city, and region, meaning "mountain of watching," and the residents thereof. Forty-two miles north of Jerusalem and nine miles northwest of Nablus, a hill protrudes from the broad valley that cuts across the central highlands of Israel. There lie ruins of ancient Samaria near a small village called Sebastiya. Samaria was the capital, residence, and burial place of the kings of Israel (1 Kings 16:23-28; 22:37; 2 Kings 6:24-30). Following the Northern Kingdom's fall to Assyria

(721 B.C.), exiles from many nations settled Samaria (Ezra 4:9-10). Later, the Greeks conquered the region (331 B.C.) and Hellenized the area with Greek inhabitants and culture. Then the Hasmoneans, under John Hyrcanus, destroyed the city (119 B.C.). After a long period without inhabitants, Samaria lived again under Pompey and the Romans (63 B.C.). Finally, Herod the Great obtained control of Samaria in 30 B.C. and made it one of the chief cities of his territory. Again, the city was resettled with people from distant places, this time mercenaries from Europe. Herod renamed the city Sebaste, using the Greek word for Augustus, the emperor. When the Jews revolted in A.D. 66, the Romans reconquered the city and destroyed it. The Romans later rebuilt Samaria, but the city never regained the prestige it once had.

Samaria is the only major city founded by Israel, the Northern Kingdom. Omri, the sixth king of Israel (885–874 B.C.), purchased the hill of Samaria for his royal residence. Shechem had been the capital of the Northern Kingdom until Jeroboam relocated it at Tirzah.

When Ahab, Omri's son, became king of Israel, he built an ivory palace at Samaria. Amos denounced him for doing this (Amos 6:1,4; 1 Kings 22:39). Jezebel influenced Ahab, her husband, to make the city the center for Baal worship (1 Kings 16:29-33). Jezebel also had many prophets of Yahweh killed in Samaria (1 Kings 18:2-4).

On two occasions Ben-hadad, the king of Syria, besieged the city of Samaria. However, both times he was unsuccessful (1 Kings 20; 2 Kings 6). Naaman, a Syrian leper, had come to Samaria to be healed by Elisha a short time prior to Ben-hadad's attack (2 Kings 5).

Long colonnaded street built by the emperor Severus at NT Sebaste, which was the OT city of Samaria.

Here Elijah destroyed the messengers of King Ahaziah, who were seeking the consultation of Baal-zebub. He, likewise, prophesied of King Ahaziah's death (2 Kings 1). Later, Jehu killed Ahab's 70 sons in Samaria (2 Kings 10). Finally, Samaria fell to Assyria in 721 B.C. after a three-year siege (2 Kings 17:5, 18:9-12). This destruction came after many prophecies concerning its sins and many warnings about its doom (Isa. 8:4; 9:8-14; 10:9; 28:1-13; 36:19; Jer. 23:13; Ezek. 23:1-4; Hos. 7; 13:16; Amos 3:12; Mic. 1:6). See *Assyria.*

While the term "Samaria" was first identified with the city founded by Omri, it soon became associated with the entire region surrounding the city, the tribal territory of Manasseh and Ephraim. Finally, the name "Samaria" became synonymous with the entire Northern Kingdom (1 Kings 13:32; Jer. 31:5). After the Assyrian conquest Samaria began to shrink in size. By NT times it became identified with the central region of Palestine, with Galilee to the north and Judea to the south.

The name "Samaritans" originally was identified with the Israelites of the Northern Kingdom (2 Kings 17:29). When the Assyrians conquered Israel and exiled 27,290 Israelites, a "remnant of Israel" remained in the land. Assyrian captives from distant places also settled there (2 Kings 17:24). This led to the intermarriage of some, though not all, Jews with Gentiles and to widespread worship of foreign gods. By the time the Jews returned to Jerusalem to rebuild the temple and the walls of Jerusalem, Ezra and Nehemiah refused to let the Samaritans share in the experience (Ezra 4:1-3; Neh. 4:7). The old antagonism between Israel to the north and Judah to the south intensified the quarrel.

The Jewish inhabitants of Samaria identified Mount Gerizim as the chosen place of God and the only center of worship, calling it the "navel of the earth" because of a tradition that Adam sacrificed there. Their Scriptures were limited to the Pentateuch, the first five books of the Bible. Moses was regarded as the only prophet and intercessor in the final judgment. They also believed that 6,000 years after creation, a Restorer would arise and would live on earth for 110 years. On the judgment day the righteous would be resurrected in paradise and the wicked roasted in eternal fire.

In the days of Christ, the relationship between the Jews and the Samaritans was

Byzantine church at Sebaste (Samaria) built over the traditional site of John the Baptist's burial place.

greatly strained (Luke 9:52-54; 10:25-37; 17:11-19; John 8:48). The animosity was so great that the Jews bypassed Samaria as they traveled between Galilee and Judea. They went an extra distance through the barren land of Perea on the eastern side of the Jordan to avoid going through Samaria. Yet Jesus rebuked His disciples for their hostility to the Samaritans (Luke 9:55-56), healed a Samaritan leper (Luke 17:16), honored a Samaritan for his neighborliness (Luke 10:30-37), praised a Samaritan for his gratitude (Luke 17:11-18), asked a drink of a Samaritan woman (John 4:7), and preached to the Samaritans (John 4:40-42). Then in Acts 1:8 Jesus challenged His disciples to witness in Samaria. Philip, a deacon, opened a mission in Samaria (Acts 8:5).

A small Samaritan community continues to this day to follow the traditional worship near Shechem. See *Israel, Land of; Sanballat.*

Donald R. Potts

SAMARITAN PENTATEUCH Canon or "Bible" of the Samaritans, who revere the Torah as God's revelation to Moses on Mount Sinai and do not regard the rest of the Hebrew Bible as canon. The Samaritans regarded themselves as the true heirs (rather than Judahites) to the Mosaic tradition. Their Scripture includes Genesis through Deuteronomy with many variant readings from the Masoretic Text or Hebrew text currently used by scholars. See *Bible Texts and Versions; Samaria, Samaritans.*

SAMGAR-NEBO (Săm gär-nē´ bō) or **SAMGAR-NEBU** (Săm gär-nē´ bū) (NASB) Personal name of Babylonian official who accompanied Nebuchadnezzar of Babylon in capturing Jerusalem in 587 B.C., according to Hebrew text (Jer. 39:3). Many modern scholars seek to

Samaritans of the 20th century celebrating their Passover on Mount Gerizim.

Samaritan priests with a copy of their scripture—the Samaritan Pentateuch.

Roman period additions to the Heraion (great sanctuary of Hera of Samos) on the island of Samos.

reconstruct the original Akkadian name. Such reconstructions relate the name to a city—Simmagir—known from other Babylonian records. This would mean the previous person in the list—Nergal-sharezer—was from the city (REB, cp. NIV). Other scholars see Samgar-Nebo as a title describing the position Nergal-sharezer held.

SAMLAH (Săm´ lah) Personal name, perhaps meaning "coat." Ruler of Edom (Gen. 36:36).

SAMOS (Sā´ mŏs) Place-name meaning "height." Small island (only 27 miles long) located in the Aegean Sea about a mile off the coast of Asia Minor near the peninsula of Trogyllium. In the strait between Samos and the mainland, the Greeks defeated the Persian fleet about 479 B.C. and turned the tide of power in the ancient Near East. Traveling from Jerusalem to Rome, Paul's ship either put in at Samos or anchored just offshore (Acts 20:15).

SAMOTHRACE (Săm´ ō thrās) or **SAMOTHRACIA** (Săm ō thrā´ shȧ) (KJV, TEV) Place-name, perhaps meaning "height of Thrace." Mountainous island in northern Aegean Sea 38 miles south of coast of Thrace with peaks rising 5,000 feet above sea level. Paul spent a night there on his second missionary journey as he headed to Philippi (Acts 16:11). A famous mystery cult was practiced there.

SAMSON (Săm´ son) Personal name meaning "of the sun." Last of the major judges over Israel about 1100 B.C. (Judg. 13:1–16:31). The son of Manoah of the tribe of Dan, Samson was a legendary hero who frequently did battle against the Philistines, who at that time "were ruling over Israel" (14:4 HCSB).

Before his conception, Samson was dedicated by his parents to be a lifelong Nazirite (13:3-7), a person especially devoted or consecrated. Part of the vow included letting the hair grow and abstaining from wine and strong drink. Samson's legendary strength did not come from his long hair. Rather, it came through the "Spirit of the LORD" who would take control of him to enable him to perform amazing feats of physical strength (14:6,19; 15:14; cp. 16:28-29). Although a Nazirite, Samson did not live a devoted life. More frequently, he was careless in his vow. He secretly disobeyed the prohibition of approaching a dead body (14:8-9) and had immoral relations with a Gaza harlot (16:1) and with Delilah (16:4-20).

Samson is portrayed as a headstrong young man with little or no self-control. None of his exploits show him as a religious enthusiast. In fact, every major crisis in his life resulting in clashes against the Philistines was brought on by his relationships with Philistine women. Samson's fascination with Delilah finally wrought his downfall. The lords of the Philistines offered her 1,100 pieces of silver from each of them to find out the source of Samson's strength. In her first three attempts, Samson gave her false answers. However, he did not seem to equate the Philistines binding him each time with betrayal by Delilah. Finally, she coaxed the truth from him, and Samson was captured.

Ultimately, Samson proved little more than a thorn in the flesh to the Philistines. He never really freed Israel from the dominion of the Philistines. In his death he killed more Philistines than the total he had killed during his life (16:30). He is listed with the heroes of faith in Heb. 11:32 because his strength came from God

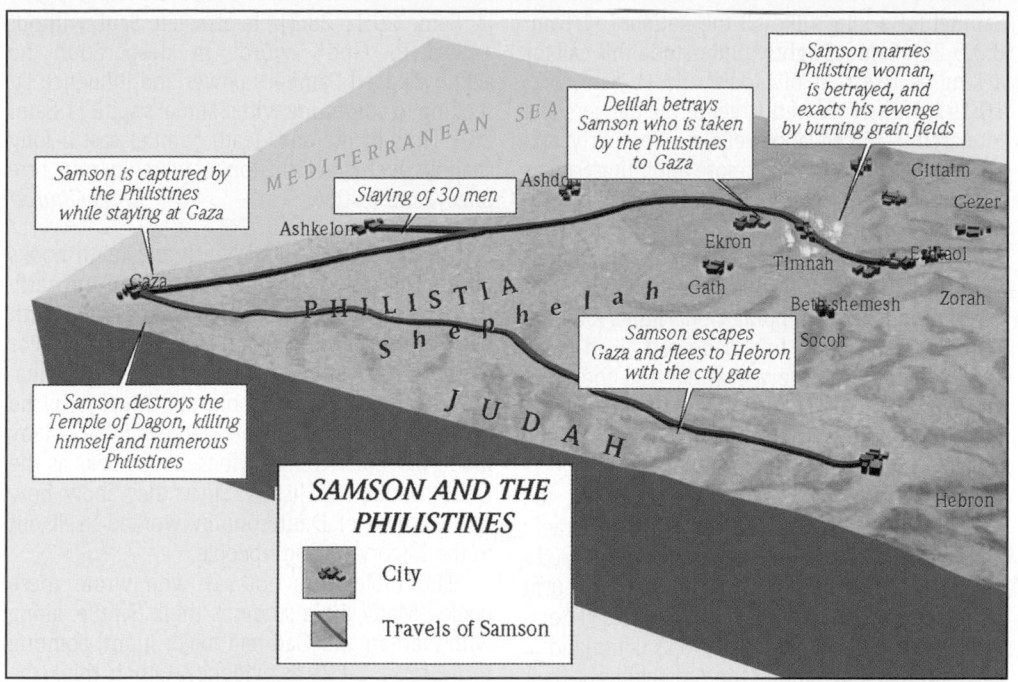

Samson marries Philistine woman, is betrayed, and exacts his revenge by burning grain fields

Delilah betrays Samson who is taken by the Philistines to Gaza

Samson is captured by the Philistines while staying at Gaza

Slaying of 30 men

Samson escapes Gaza and flees to Hebron with the city gate

Samson destroys the Temple of Dagon, killing himself and numerous Philistines

SAMSON AND THE PHILISTINES

City

Travels of Samson

MEDITERRANEAN SEA · *PHILISTIA* · *Shephelah* · *JUDAH*

Gaza · Ashkelon · Ashdod · Ekron · Gath · Timnah · Beth-shemesh · Socoh · Gittaim · Gezer · Eshtaol · Zorah · Hebron

and because in his dying act, he demonstrated his faith. See *Judge; Judges, Book of; Nazirite; Spirit.*   *Darlene R. Gautsch*

SAMUEL (Săm´ ū ĕl) Personal name in the ancient Near East meaning "Sumu is God" but understood in Israel as "his name is God," or "name of God." The last judge, first kingmaker, priest, and prophet who linked the period of the judges with the monarchy (about 1066–1000 B.C.). Born in answer to barren Hannah's tearful prayer (1 Sam. 1:10), Samuel was dedicated to the Lord before his birth (1:11); as the firstborn male to open Hannah's womb, he was "given to the LORD" for all his life (1:28 HCSB; 2:20). Eli raised Samuel at the Shiloh sanctuary (1 Sam. 2:11). As a child Samuel grew "in stature and in favor with the LORD and with men" (1 Sam. 2:26 HCSB; cp. Luke 2:52). Samuel met God and received his first prophetic mission as a young lad (1 Sam. 3:1,11-14). God's initial word to Samuel concerned God's rejection of Eli's family from service as priests as punishment for the sins of Eli's sons.

Samuel was responsible for a revival of the Shiloh sanctuary (1 Sam. 3:21). Psalm 99:6-7 relates that God spoke with Samuel from out of the pillar of cloud as God had previously with Moses and Aaron. God "was with him and let

nothing he said prove false" (1 Sam. 3:19; 9:6). Jeremiah regarded Samuel and Moses as the two great intercessors of Israel (Jer. 15:1).

Following the deaths of Eli and his sons, Israel experienced 20 years (1 Sam. 7:2) of national sin and Philistine oppression. Samuel reemerged in the role of judge, calling Israel to repentance and delivering them from foreign domination. Samuel also exercised the judicial role of judge, administering justice at Bethel, Gilgal, Mizpah, and Ramah (1 Sam. 7:15-17).

Samuel served as the prototype for future prophets in tension with the kings of Israel and Judah. The sins of Samuel's sons and the Philistine threat led the elders of Israel to appeal to

Tel Rama (Ramah)—birthplace of Samuel the prophet.

Samuel for a king "like all the nations" (1 Sam. 8:3,5,20). Samuel rightly understood this call for a king as rejection of God's rule (1 Sam. 8:7; 10:19). Samuel warned Israel of the dangers of a monarchy—forced labor, seizure of property, taxation (1 Sam. 8:10-18)—before anointing Saul as Israel's first king (1 Sam. 10:1). Samuel's recording of the rights and duties of kingship (1 Sam. 10:25) set the stage for later prophets to call their monarchs to task for disobedience to God's commands and for overstepping God's limits for kingship in Israel. Samuel foreshadowed Elijah in his call for rain during the wheat harvest, the usual dry season, as vindication of his word of judgment concerning Israel's demand for a king (1 Sam. 12:17-18).

Samuel's relations with Saul highlight the conditional nature of kingship in Israel. Israel's king was designated by God and served at God's pleasure. Saul's presumption in offering burnt sacrifice before battle with the Philistines (1 Sam. 13:8-15) and his disregard of God's command to leave no survivors among the Amalekites or their flocks (1 Sam. 15) occasioned Samuel's declaration of God's rejection of Saul's kingship. Obeying God's call to anoint another king amounted to treason in Saul's eyes, and Samuel had concerns for his life. Samuel was, however, obedient in anointing David as king over Israel (1 Sam. 16:13). Later when Saul sought David's life, David took refuge with Samuel and his band of prophets at Ramah (1 Sam. 19:18-24). Finally, Samuel's death brought national mourning

(1 Sam. 25:1; 28:3). It also left Saul without access to God's word. In desperation he acknowledged Samuel's power and influence by seeking to commune with Samuel's spirit (1 Sam. 28). Thus in life and death Samuel cast a long shadow over Israel's history of worship, rule, prophecy, and justice.   *Chris Church*

SAMUEL, BOOKS OF Ninth and tenth books of English Bible following the order of the earliest Greek translation but combined as the eighth book of the Hebrew canon named for the major figure of its opening section. Along with Joshua, Judges, and Kings, the books of Samuel form the "Former Prophets" in the Hebrew Bible. Many modern scholars refer to these four books as the Deuteronomistic History, since they show how the teaching of Deuteronomy worked itself out in the history of God's people.

The Bible does not say who wrote these books. Many Bible students think Samuel along with Nathan and Gad had major input, pointing to 1 Chron. 29:29 as evidence. Others think the books had a long history of composition with various narratives or narrative sources being composed from the time of the events until the time of the exile, when the "Former Prophets" were gathered into one collection. Such individual narratives would include Shiloh (1 Sam. 1–3), the Ark (1 Sam. 4:1–7:1), the Rise of Kingship (1 Sam. 9:1–11:15), Battles of Saul (1 Sam. 13–15), the History of David's Rise to Power (1 Sam. 16:14–2 Sam. 5:25), David's Reign (2 Sam. 9–20), and the Succession to the Throne of David (1 Kings 1–2). See *Chronicles, Books of.*

The books of Samuel arose as a reflection upon the nature of human kingship in light of Israel's tradition that Yahweh was their king. They answered a first generation's burning questions. Had God rejected David as He had rejected Saul? Why was the young Solomon named king

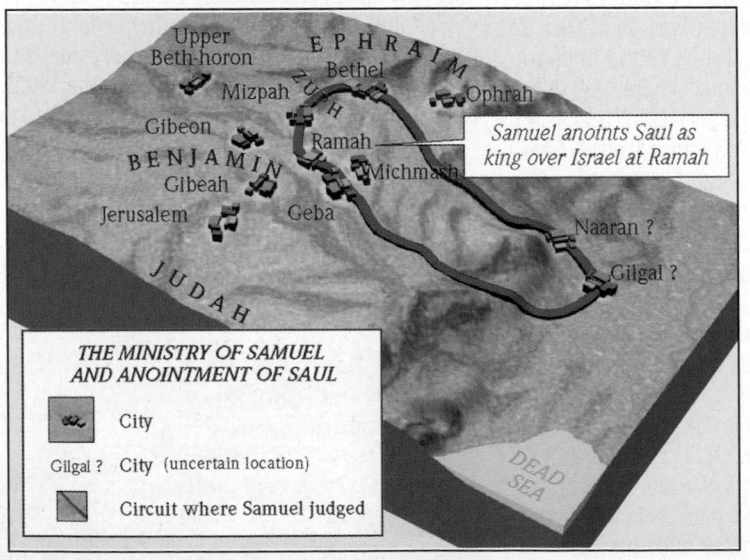

Samuel anoints Saul as king over Israel at Ramah

THE MINISTRY OF SAMUEL AND ANOINTMENT OF SAUL

City

Gilgal ? City (uncertain location)

Circuit where Samuel judged

rather than his older brothers? Could the violent measures Solomon undertook when he assumed the throne be justified? To answer the questions, the books tell the narrative of three major figures: Samuel, Saul, and David. The story of each combines tragedy, despair, and direction toward future hope. The dangers of kingship (1 Sam. 8) and the hope for kingship (2 Sam. 7) form the narrative tension for the books. The final chapter (2 Sam. 24) does not solve the tension. It points further ahead to the building of the temple, where God's presence and Israel's worship can be at the center of life leading the king to be God's humble, forgiven servant. See *David; King, Kingship; Kingdom of God; Samuel; Saul.*

The books of Samuel thus point to several theological themes that can guide God's people through the generations. Leadership is the guiding theme. Can God's people continue with a loosely knit organization as in the days of the judges, or must they have a king "to judge us the same as all the other nations have" (1 Sam. 8:5 HCSB)? Samuel does not explicitly answer the question. God does not wholeheartedly accept kingship as the only alternative. Kingship means the people have rejected God (1 Sam. 8:7; 10:19). Still, kingship can flourish if the people and the king follow God (1 Sam. 12:14-15, 20-25). Saul showed God's threats could be realized soon (1 Sam. 13:13-14). A new family from a new tribe would rule. This did not mean eternal war among tribes and families. A covenant could bind the two families together (1 Sam. 20; 23:16-18). Anger on one side does not require anger from the other as David's reactions to Saul continually show, summarized in 1 Sam. 24:17: "You are more righteous than I, for you have done good to me though I have done evil to you" (HCSB). David neither planned the demise of Saul and his family nor rewarded those who did (2 Sam. 4:9-12). David established his kingdom and sought to establish a house for God (2 Sam. 7:2). The king, however, gave in to God's plan to establish David's house and let his son build the house for God (2 Sam. 7:13). The king's response shows the nature of true leadership. He expresses praise for God, not pride in personal achievement (2 Sam. 7:18-29).

Working through His promise to David, God then worked to establish His own kingdom among His people. He could work through an imperfect king who committed the outlandish sin with Bathsheba (2 Sam. 11) because the king

was willing to confess his sin (2 Sam. 12:13). The rule of God's king does not promise perfect peace. Even David's own household revolted against him. Human pride and ego did not determine history. God's promise to David could not be overthrown.

Other themes are subordinate to that of leadership for Israel. The call for covenant commitment and obedience, the forgiveness and mercy of God, the sovereignty of God in human history, the significance of prayer and praise, the faithfulness of God to fulfill prophecy, the need for faithfulness to human leaders, the holy presence of God among His people, the nature of human friendship, and the importance of family relationships all echo from these books.

1 Samuel
Outline
I. God Gives His People an Example of Dedicated Leadership (1:1–7:17).
  A. A dedicated leader is the answer to parental prayers (1:1-28).
  B. A dedicated leader comes from grateful, sacrificial parents who worship the incomparable God (2:1-10).
  C. A dedicated leader is a priest who faithfully serves God rather than seeking selfish interests (2:11-36).
  D. A dedicated leader is a prophet who is called by the word of God and who faithfully delivers the word of God (3:1–4:15).
  E. Superstitious use of religious relics is not a substitute for dedicated leadership (4:16-22).
  F. Only a dedicated priest, not foreign gods or disobedient persons, can stand before God (5:1–7:2).
  G. A dedicated political leader is a man of prayer (7:3-17).
II. Human Kingship Represents a Compromise with God by a People Who Have Rejected the Kingship of God (8:1–15:35).
  A. Hereditary kingship is a rejection of God which hurts His people and separates them from God (8:1-22; cp. Judg. 8:22–9:57).
  B. A dedicated king is a humble person from a humble family who knows he owes his position to God's choice (9:1–10:27).

S

C. The dedicated king is a Spirit-filled deliverer (11:1-15).

D. The dedicated leader is morally pure and uses the history of God's people to call them to obedience (12:1-25).

E. Kingship depends on obedience to God, not human wisdom (13:1-23).

F. A dedicated leader is used by God to unify and deliver His people (14:1-23).

G. God delivers His dedicated leader from inadvertent sins (14:24-46).

H. The king is responsible to defeat the enemies of the people of God (14:47-52).

I. A disobedient king is rejected by God (15:1-35).

III. God Raises Up New Leadership for His People (16:1–31:13).

A. God gives His Spirit to the chosen person meeting His leadership qualifications (16:1-13).

B. God provides unexpected opportunities of service for His chosen king (16:14-23).

C. God uses the skills and faith of His leader to defeat those who would defy God (17:1-58).

D. God provides His presence and the loyalty of friends to protect His chosen one from the jealous plots of an evil leader (18:1–20:42).

E. God's priests affirm the special position of God's chosen leader (21:1-9).

F. God protects His benevolent and faithful leader from the vengeance of evil enemies (21:10–22:23).

G. God heeds the prayer of His chosen and delivers him from treacherous enemies (23:1-29).

H. God honors the righteousness of His chosen leader (24:1-22).

I. God avenges His chosen against the insults of foolish enemies (25:1-39a).

J. God provides family for His chosen (25:39b-44).

K. God rewards the righteousness and faithfulness of His chosen leader (26:1-25).

L. The chosen leader cunningly begins building his kingdom even under adverse circumstances (27:1-12).

M. God fulfills His prophecy and destroys disobedient leaders (28:1-25).

N. God protects His chosen leader from compromising situations (29:1-11).

O. God restores the property taken from His chosen leader (30:1-20).

P. God's chosen leader shares his goods with the needy and with colleagues (30:21-31).

Q. God destroys disobedient leaders (31:1-7).

R. God honors people who express loyalty to their chosen leaders (31:8-13).

2 Samuel
Outline

I. To Achieve His Purposes, God Honors Obedience, Not Treachery (1:1–6:23).

A. Those who dishonor God's chosen leaders are punished (1:1-16).

B. God's leader honors the memory of his predecessors (1:17-27).

C. God leads people to honor His obedient leader (2:1-4a).

D. God honors loyal, obedient people (2:4b-7).

E. God blesses efforts for peace (2:8-28).

F. God strengthens His obedient leader (2:29–3:19).

G. God's leader refuses to honor treachery and revenge (3:20–4:12).

H. God fulfills His promises to His patient servant (5:1-16).

I. God provides victory for His people (5:17-25).

J. God's people must honor His holy presence (6:1-23).

II. God Establishes His Purposes through His Faithful Yet Fallible Servant (7:1–12:31).

A. God promises to bless the house of David forever (7:1-17).

B. God's servant praises the incomparable God (7:18-29).

C. God gives victory to His faithful servant (8:1-18).

D. God's servant shows kindness in memory of his departed friends (9:1-13).

E. Enemy coalitions cannot prevent God from taking vengeance (10:1-19).

F. Disobedience from God's leader displeases the Lord and brings judgment but also mercy (11:1–12:14a).

G. God brings honor to His penitent servant (12:14b-31).

III. Lack of Attention to Family Relations Leads to National Problems for God's Leader (13:1–20:26).
   A. The inattention of a godly father can lead to family feuds, shame, and vengeance (13:1-39).
   B. Reconciliation, not anger and judgments, should mark the family life of God's servants (14:1-33).
   C. Unhealed family wounds lead to revolt (15:1-37).
   D. Leaders need advisors whom God can use to accomplish His purposes (16:1–17:29).
   E. The time of sorrow is too late to set family relationships right (18:1-33).
   F. God's victorious servant deals kindly with those who helped and those who opposed him (19:1-40).
   G. Victory cannot remove rivalries among God's people (19:41–20:26).

IV. God's People Learn from the Experience and Example of God's Leader (21:1–24:25).
   A. God blesses the leader who is faithful to the tradition of His people (21:1-22).
   B. God's leader praises God for His deliverance (22:1-51; cp. Ps. 18).
   C. God's leader teaches what he has learned—his experiences with God (23:1-7).
   D. God's leader depends on brave, faithful associates (23:8-39).
   E. The leader's foolish decisions bring punishment, even on a repentant leader (24:1-17).
   F. Proper worship brings God's mercy for His people (24:18-25).

SANBALLAT (Săn băl´ lăt) Akkadian personal name meaning "Sin (the god) has healed." According to the Elephantine Papyri from the reign of Darius I, Sanballat was governor of Samaria around 407 B.C. He had sons whose names included the term "Yahweh," for the God of Israel. Although addressed by his Babylonian name (probably acquired during the exile), Sanballat was a practicing Jew. His daughter was married to the grandson of Jerusalem's high priest (Neh. 13:28), indicating harmonious rela-

tions between Judah and Samaria at that time. Nehemiah referred to Sanballat as the "Horonite," suggesting a connection with Upper or Lower Beth-horon. (Neh. 2:10). These cities controlled the major highway between Jerusalem and the Mediterranean Sea. If Sanballat had influence with these towns, he could greatly affect Jerusalem's economy. Sanballat, in league with Tobiah and Shemaiah, opposed Nehemiah's rebuilding of Jerusalem. If the Holy City regained prominence, it would erode the powers of the surrounding cities. The struggle appears to have been more political than racial or religious. Papyri from Wadi Daliyeh appear to indicate two later Sanballats also served as governors of Samaria.

SANCTIFICATION Process of being made holy resulting in a changed lifestyle for the believer. The English word "sanctification" comes from the Latin *sanctificatio*, meaning the act or process of making holy, consecrated. In the Greek NT the root *hag-* is the basis of *hagiasmos*, "holiness," "consecration," "sanctification"; *hagiosune*, "holiness"; *hagiotes*, "holiness"; *hagiazo,* "to sanctify," "consecrate," "treat as holy," "purify"; and *hagios,* "holy," "saint." The root idea of the Greek stem is to stand in awe of something or someone. The NT usage is greatly dependent upon the Greek translation of the OT, the Septuagint, for meaning. The *hag-* words in the Septuagint mostly translated the Hebrew *qadosh,* "separate, contrasting with the profane." Thus, God is separate; things and people dedicated to Him and to His use are separate. The moral implications of this word came into focus with the prophets and became a major emphasis in the NT. See *Holy.*

Old Testament In OT thought the focus of holiness (*qadosh*) is upon God. He is holy (Ps. 99:9); His name is holy (Pss. 99:3; 111:9) and may not be profaned (Lev. 20:3). Since God exists in the realm of the holy rather than the profane, all that pertains to Him must come into that same realm of holiness. This involves time, space, objects, and people.

Certain times are sanctified in that they are set apart especially to the Lord: the Sabbath (Gen. 2:3), the various festivals (Lev. 23:4-44), the Year of Jubilee (Lev. 25:12). By strictly observing the regulations governing each, Israel sanctified (or treated as holy) these special times of the year. Also the land of Canaan (Exod.

S

15:13), as well as Jerusalem (Isa. 11:9), was holy to the Lord and was not to be polluted by sinful conduct (Lev. 18:27-28). The tabernacle/temple and all the objects related to it were holy (Exod. 28:38; Ezek. 40–48). The various gifts brought in worship were sanctified. These fall into three groupings: those whose sanctity was inherent (e.g., firstborn males of female animals and human beings, Exod. 13:2,11-13; Lev. 27:26); objects whose sanctification was required (e.g., tithes of crops and pure animals, Lev. 27:30-33; Deut. 26:13); and gifts whose sanctification was voluntary (see partial list in Lev. 27). The dedication of these objects mostly occurred not at some ritual in the sanctuary but at a prior declaration of dedication (Judg. 17:3; Lev. 27:30-33).

Of course, the priests and Levites who functioned in the sanctuary, beginning with Aaron, were sanctified to the Lord by the anointing of oil (Exod. 30:30-32; 40:12-15). Additionally, the Nazirite was consecrated (Num. 6:8), although only for a specified period of time. Finally, the nation of Israel was sanctified to the Lord as a holy people (Exod. 19:6; Deut. 7:6; 14:2,21; 26:19). This holiness was closely identified with obedience to the Law of Holiness in Lev. 17–26, which includes both ritual and ethical commands. In the prophets especially, the ethical responsibility of being holy in conduct came to the forefront (Isa. 5; Jer. 5–7; Amos 4–5; Hos. 11).

New Testament The same range of meanings reflected by the Septuagint usage is preserved in the NT but with extension of meaning in certain cases. Objects may be made holy (Matt. 23:17,19; 1 Tim. 4:4-5) or treated as holy (Matt. 6:9; Luke 11:2), but, mostly, the word group stresses the personal dimension of holiness. Here, the two streams of OT meaning are significant: the cultic and the ethical. Sanctification is vitally linked to the salvation experience and is concerned with the moral/spiritual obligations assumed in that experience. We were set apart to God in conversion, and we are living out that dedication to God in holiness.

The link of NT thought to OT antecedents in the cultic aspect of sanctification is most clearly seen in Hebrews. Christ's crucifixion makes possible the moving of the sinner from the profane to the holy (that is, sanctifies, makes holy) so that the believer can become a part of the temple where God dwells and is worshiped (Heb. 13:11-16; 2:9-11; 10:10,14,29). Paul (Rom. 15:16;

1 Cor. 1:2; 6:11; Eph. 5:26-27; 2 Thess. 2:13) and Peter (1 Pet. 1:2) both affirmed the work of the Holy Spirit in conversion as a sanctification, making the believer holy so as to come before God in acceptance. Especially in Paul, justification and sanctification are closely related concepts. See *Justification*.

Hebrews also emphasizes the ethical aspect of sanctification. Sanctification/holiness is to be pursued as an essential aspect of the believer's life (Heb. 12:14); the blood of sanctification must not be defiled by sinful conduct (10:26-31). Paul stressed both the individual's commitment to holy living (Rom. 6:19-22; 1 Thess. 4:3-8; 2 Cor. 7:1) and the enabling power of God for it (1 Thess. 3:13; 4:8). The summation of the ethical imperative is seen in Peter's use (1 Pet. 1:15-16) of Lev. 11:44; 19:2; 20:7: "Be holy, because I am holy" (HCSB). See *Ethics; Hebrews; Salvation*. *Lorin L. Cranford*

SANCTUARY Place set aside as sacred and holy, especially a place of worship. On sites where the patriarchs had erected altars, the people of Israel later built shrines and temples to commemorate the encounters with God. Specifically, the tabernacle and the temple in Jerusalem were revered as sanctuaries.

SANDALS, SHOES Items worn to protect the feet. Ancient shoes are well-known from paintings, sculptures, and carved reliefs. The shoe was considered the humblest article of clothing and could be bought cheaply. Two types of shoes existed: slippers of soft leather and the more popular sandals with a hard leather sole. Thongs secured the sandal across the insole and between the toes. Although shoes could be bought at a low price, they were often repaired by the poor. Shoes were removed at the doorway of the tent or house, or during a period of mourning. Shoes were also removed as evidence of humility in the presence of kings. The removal of the guest's sandals was the job of the lowliest servant who was also required to wash the dusty and soiled feet of the visitor. In early Israel legal contracts and oaths were often sealed with the removal and giving of a shoe by one party (Ruth 4:7). Going barefoot was a sign of poverty and reproach. Isaiah walked barefooted to symbolize the impending poverty of Israel before the judgment of God (Isa. 20:2). During NT times Jewish practice forbade the wearing of sandals with multilayered

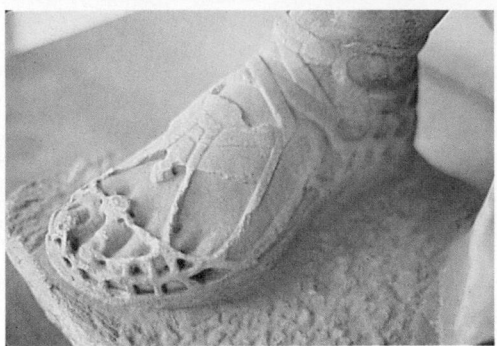

The sandaled foot on a Roman statue.

leather soles nailed together, as this was the shoe worn by Roman soldiers. See *Footwashing.*

David Maltsberger

SANDBAR See *Quicksands; Syrtis.*

SAND LIZARD See *Reptiles; Snail.*

SAND REPTILE See *Reptiles; Snail.*

SANHEDRIN (Săn hē´ drĭn) Highest Jewish council in the first century. The council had 71 members and was presided over by the high priest. The Sanhedrin included both of the main

Leather thong sandals from the Roman period.

Jewish parties among its membership. Since the high priest presided, the Sadducean priestly party seems to have predominated, but some leading Pharisees also were members (Acts 5:34; 23:1-9).

The word "Sanhedrin" is usually translated "council" in the English translations of the Bible. Because of the predominance of the chief priests in the Sanhedrin, at times the words "chief priests" seem to refer to the action of the Sanhedrin, even though the name itself is not used.

According to Jewish tradition, the Sanhedrin began with the 70 elders appointed by Moses in Num. 11:16 and was reorganized by Ezra after the exile. However, the OT provides no evidence of a council that functioned like the Sanhedrin of later times. Thus, the Sanhedrin had its origin sometime during the centuries between the Testaments. See *Intertestamental History and Literature; Jewish Parties in the New Testament.*

During the first century the Sanhedrin exerted authority under the watchful eye of the Romans. Generally, the Roman governor allowed the Sanhedrin considerable autonomy and authority. The trial of Jesus, however, shows that the Sanhedrin did not have the authority to condemn people to death (John 18:31). Later, Stephen was stoned to death after a hearing before the Sanhedrin, but this may have been more of a mob action than a legal execution authorized by the Sanhedrin (Acts 6:12-15; 7:54-60).

The Gospels describe the role of the Sanhedrin in the arrest, trials, and condemnation of Jesus. The Sanhedrin, under the leadership of Caiaphas the high priest, plotted to have Jesus killed (John 11:47-53). The chief priests conspired with Judas to betray Jesus (Matt. 26:14-16). After His arrest they brought Jesus into the council (Luke 22:66). They used false witnesses to condemn Jesus (Matt. 26:59-60; Mark 14:55-56). They sent Him to Pilate and pressured Pilate into pronouncing the death sentence (Mark 15:1-15).

The book of Acts describes how the Sanhedrin harassed and threatened the apostles. The healing of the man at the temple and Peter's sermon attracted the attention of the chief priests. Peter and John were called before the council and warned not to preach anymore in the name of Jesus (Acts 4:5-21). When the

S

apostles continued to preach, the council had them arrested (Acts 5:21,27). The wise counsel of Gamaliel caused the council to release the apostles with a beating and a warning (Acts 5:34-42). Stephen had to appear before the Sanhedrin on charges that sounded like the false charges against Jesus (Acts 6:12-15).

After Paul was arrested in Jerusalem, the Roman commander asked the council to examine Paul to decide what was Paul's crime (Acts 22:30; 23:28). Paul identified himself as a Pharisee who was on trial for his hope of resurrection. This involved the council in a debate of the divisive issue of the resurrection (Acts 23:1-9). The chief priests and elders were part of a plot to have Paul assassinated as he was led to another hearing before the council (Acts 23:13-15,20).

Robert J. Dean

SANSANNAH (Săn săn´ nah) Place-name, perhaps meaning "branch of the date palm." Town in tribal territory of Judah (Josh. 15:31). Modern Khirbet esh-Shamshaniyat, nine miles northwest of Beersheba. Apparently the same as Hazar-susah (Josh. 19:5) and Hazar-susim (1 Chron. 4:31), thus assigned to the tribe of Simeon.

SAPH (Săph) Personal name, perhaps meaning "threshold." A giant the men of David killed (2 Sam. 21:18). See *Giants; Rapha; Rephaim; Sibbechai.*

SAPHIR (Sā´ phĭr) Place-name meaning "beautiful town." Town that Micah lamented over (Mic. 1:11). Location is unknown; suggestions include Khirbet el-Kom or Tell Eitun. It must be near Lachish.

SAPPHIRA (Să phī´ ră) Personal name meaning "beautiful" or "sapphire." See *Ananias.*

SAPPHIRE See *Minerals and Metals.*

SARA or **SARAH** (Sĕr´ ă) Variant Hebrew form of name Sarai. See *Sarai.*

SARAI (Sĕr´ ī) Personal name meaning "princess." Wife and half sister of Abraham (Gen. 11:29–25:10). Sarah, first called Sarai, had the same father as Abraham. Marriages with half brothers were not uncommon in her time. Sarah traveled with Abraham from Ur to Haran. Then at the age of 65 she accompanied him to Canaan as Abraham followed God's leadership in moving

The building of the Cheops Pyramid at Giza, Egypt, predates Abram's and Sarai's Egyptian sojourn.

to the land God had promised. During a famine in Canaan, Abraham and Sarah fled to Egypt. This was Abraham's first attempt to pass off Sarah as his sister rather than wife because he feared that he would be killed when the Egyptians saw Sarah's beauty. Consequently, the Pharaoh thought Sarah was Abraham's sister, took Sarah into court, and treated Abraham well. When the Lord sent serious disease on Pharaoh's household, he saw the deception and sent them away. The second trick about Abraham's relationship with Sarah was in the court of Abimelech, king of Gerar, who also took in Sarah. God intervened in Abimelech's dream and protected Sarah. He sent them away with the right to live there and with a gift for Sarah.

In her grief over her barrenness, Sarah gave her maid Hagar to Abraham in the hope of an heir, but she expressed resentment when Hagar conceived. When Sarah was almost 90 years old, God changed her name and promised her a son. A year later she bore Isaac.

At the age of 127, Sarah died at Hebron, where she was buried in the cave in the field of Machpelah near Mamre.

In the NT Rom. 4:19 refers to Sarah's barrenness as evidence of Abraham's faith; Rom. 9:9

cites her conception of Isaac as an example of God's power in fulfilling a promise. Galatians 4:21-31 contrasts her with Hagar without naming her, Heb. 11:11 lauds her faith, and 1 Pet. 3:6 describes her relationship with Abraham.

Judith Wooldridge

SARAPH (Sā´ răph) Personal name meaning "burning." Member of tribe of Judah who exercised power in Moab (1 Chron. 4:22).

SARDIS (Sär´ dĭs) City of one of the seven churches addressed in Rev. 3:1-6. The church was condemned as being "dead," perhaps a reference to its ineffectiveness in the world. However, some of its members were commended (v. 4). The city of the same name was the capital of the province of Lydia and was located in the Hermus River Valley northeast of Ephesus. An impressive acropolis overlooks the site. One of the major features there in NT times was a temple to Artemis, the goddess of love and fertility. See *Asia Minor, Cities of.*

SARDITE (Sär´ dīt) Descendant of or member of clan of Sered (Num. 26:26).

SARDIUS (Sär´ dĭ ŭs) Precious stone sometimes used to translate Hebrew *odem,* "red," and Greek *sardion.* Other translators use "carnelian" or "ruby." See "ruby" under *Minerals and Metals.*

SARDONYX Precious stone (Rev. 21:20), a form of agate. See "Onyx" under *Minerals and Metals.*

SAREPTA (Sá rĕp´ tá) Greek transliteration of Hebrew Zarephath (Luke 4:26). See *Zarephath.*

SARGON (Sär´ gŏn) Akkadian royal name meaning "the king is legitimate." An ancient throne name first taken by the king of Akkad about 2100 B.C. In 722 B.C. Sargon II of Assyria succeeded his brother, Shalmaneser V. His father was the famous king Tiglath-pileser III. Sargon finished the destruction of Samaria begun by his brother (Isa. 20:1). He deported the people of Israel to Media and other parts of the Middle East. Sargon then launched military campaigns against King Midas of Muski in southeast Asia Minor and against the kingdom of Urartu. He conquered both. Sargon was succeeded by his son, Sennacherib. See *Assyria; Israel, Land of.*

Ruins of the Roman gymnasium at the ancient city of Sardis in Asia Minor (modern Turkey).

Columns of the temple of Artemis at Sardis (modern Turkey).

SARID (Sā´ rĭd) Place-name meaning "survivor." Border town of tribe of Zebulun (Josh. 19:10). Spelled "Sedud" by some early versions, Sarid is probably modern Tell Shadud at the northern edge of the Jezreel Valley about six miles northeast of Megiddo and five miles southeast of Nazareth.

SARON (Sā´ rŏn) Greek transliteration of Sharon (Acts 9:35). See *Sharon*.

SARSECHIM (Sär´ sə kĭm) or **SARSEKIM** (NASB) Babylonian personal name or title, possibly meaning "overseer of black slaves" or "overseer of the mercenary troops." Often seen as copyist's change from Nebushasban (Jer. 39:13). A Babylonian leader during capture of Jerusalem in 587 B.C. (Jer. 39:3). Compare translations. See *Rab-saris*.

SARUCH (Sā´ rŭk) Greek transliteration of Serug (Luke 3:35).

SATAN (Sā´ tǎn) Transliteration of Hebrew word meaning "adversary." The Hebrew term appears in Num. 22:22,32; 1 Sam. 29:4; 2 Sam. 19:22; 1 Kings 5:4; 11:14,23,25; Ps. 109:6, nor-

mally translated in English as adversary or accuser. In Job 1–2; Zech. 3:2; and 1 Chron. 21:1 the same term is translated as a proper name. See *Devil, Satan, Evil, Demonic.*

SATAN, SYNAGOGUE OF Term used in Revelation (2:9; 3:9) to describe Jewish worshipers who persecuted the church.

SATISFACTION Theory explaining Christ's atonement as satisfying demands of God's holy law and thus satisfying demands of God's wrath. See *Atonement; Expiation, Propitiation.*

SATRAP (Sā´ trăp), **SATRAPY** (Sā´ trăp ē) Political office in the Persian Empire comparable to governor. A satrap's territory was called a satrapy. KJV translated the office "lieutenants" (Ezra 8:36). These officials aided the people of Israel in rebuilding Jerusalem and the temple. At the height of the Persian rule, there were at least 20 satrapies. See *Persia.*

SATYR Hairy, demonic figure with the appearance of a goat, translating a Hebrew term otherwise translated "hairy" or "male goat." Bible students differ in interpreting passages as to whether a demonic figure or a normal animal is meant. Israelites apparently sacrificed to such desert-dwelling demons, since they had to have a law forbidding such sacrifice (Lev. 17:7). Some have even interpreted the scapegoat rites (Lev. 16:20-22) as sending Israel's sins back to their author, a desert demon with a different name from that translated "satyr." Jeroboam I (926–909 B.C.) appointed priests to serve these demons (2 Chron. 11:15). Here idols in the forms of goats may be intended as parallel to the famous calves Jeroboam built. Isaiah promised that Babylon would become so desolate that the desert-dwelling demons would live in the ruins (Isa. 13:21; cp. 34:14). Some commentators read 2 Kings 23:8 to refer to worship places for these demons at a gate in Jerusalem (cp. REB). A similar reality is expressed by a different Hebrew word in Deut. 32:17 and Ps. 106:37 (cp. Matt. 12:43; Mark 5:13; Luke 11:24; Rev. 18:2). "Lilith" (Isa. 34:14 NRSV) may also be a name for the desert demons.

SAUL Personal name meaning "asked for." First king of Israel and the Hebrew name of Paul, the apostle. See *Paul.*

Old Testament The Hebrew name *Sha'ul* is used of four persons in the OT. It is usually rendered "Shaul" for a king of Edom (Gen. 36:37-38), the last son of Simeon (Gen. 46:10), and a Levite of the Kohathites (1 Chron. 6:24). Saul, however, primarily refers to the first king of a united Israel, a tall and handsome son of Kish from the tribe of Benjamin (1 Sam. 9:1-2,21). Chosen by God (1 Sam. 9:15-17) and secretly anointed by Samuel (10:1), Saul was later selected publicly by lot (10:17-24). Despite some people's skepticism (10:27), he proved himself an able leader by delivering the city of Jabesh-gilead and was acclaimed king at Gilgal (11:1-15).

The numbers in 1 Sam. 13:1 are incomplete in the Hebrew text, but Saul's reign is generally dated about 1020–1000 B.C. He made his capital at "Gibeah of Saul" ("Saul's hill," 1 Sam. 11:4), probably Tell el-Ful, three miles north of Jerusalem where excavations have uncovered contemporary foundations of a modest fortress-like palace. From Gibeah Saul drove the Philistines from the hill country (13:19–14:23) and fought other enemies of Israel (14:47-48).

A tragic figure, Saul's heart was initially changed; he had even prophesied (1 Sam. 10:9-13). His presumptuous offering (13:8-14), however, and violation of a holy war ban led to his break with Samuel and rejection by God (15:7-23). The Spirit of the Lord left Saul and was replaced by an evil spirit that tormented him. David is introduced as a musician who soothed him by playing the lyre (16:14-23). After the Goliath episode, Saul became jealous and fearful of David (18:6-9,12), eventually making several spontaneous and indirect attempts on David's life (18:10-11,25; 19:1,9-11). Saul's fits of rage, his obsession with David, and the slaughter of the priests at Nob (22:17-19) make it appear as though he suffered from some sort of psychotic state. His final wretched condition is betrayed by his consultation of the witch at En-dor (28:7-8). The following day Saul and three sons were killed at the hands of the Philistines on Mount Gilboa (1 Sam. 31). Saul's body was beheaded and hung on the walls of Beth-shan; it was rescued and buried by the grateful inhabitants of Jabesh-gilead (31:8-13).

The enigma of Saul was sensed by David who refused to lift his hand against "the LORD's anointed" (1 Sam. 26:9-11,23) and at his death

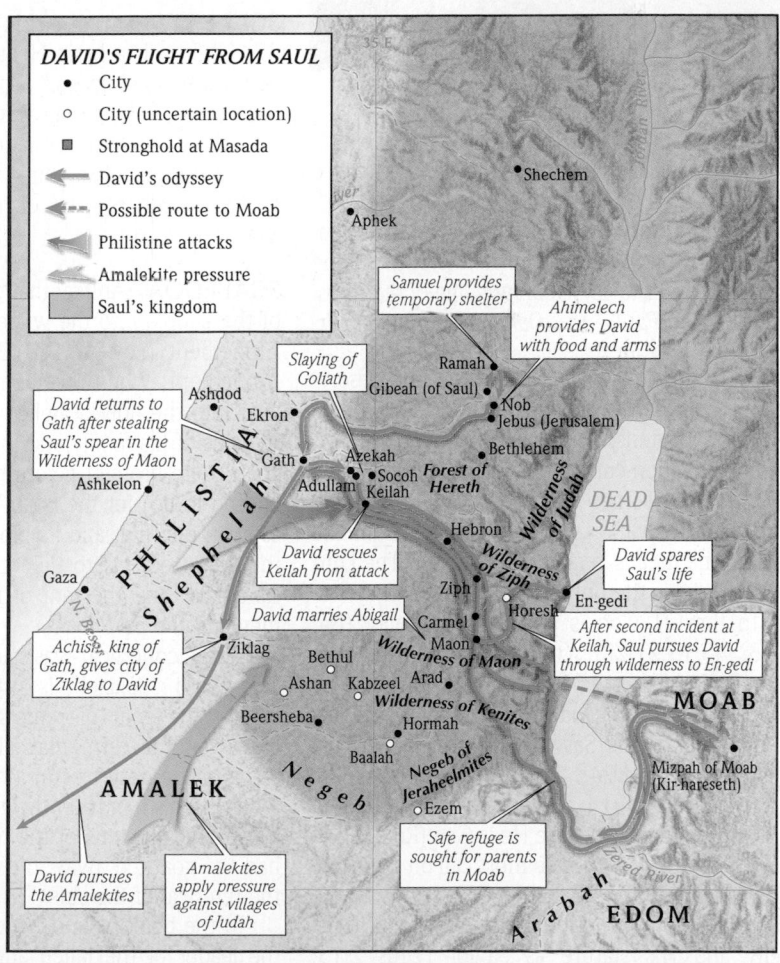

DAVID'S FLIGHT FROM SAUL

- • City
- ○ City (uncertain location)
- ■ Stronghold at Masada
- ← David's odyssey
- ← - - Possible route to Moab
- ◄ Philistine attacks
- ◄ Amalekite pressure
- ☐ Saul's kingdom

Shechem

Aphek

Samuel provides temporary shelter

Ahimelech provides David with food and arms

Slaying of Goliath

Ramah

Gibeah (of Saul)

David returns to Gath after stealing Saul's spear in the Wilderness of Maon

Ashdod

Ekron

Nob

Jebus (Jerusalem)

Bethlehem

Gath

Azekah

Forest of Hereth

Ashkelon

Adullam

Socoh

Keilah

PHILISTIA

Shephelah

Hebron

DEAD SEA

David rescues Keilah from attack

Wilderness of Ziph

David spares Saul's life

Gaza

Ziph

En-gedi

Horesh

David marries Abigail

Carmel

After second incident at Keilah, Saul pursues David through wilderness to En-gedi

Achish, king of Gath, gives city of Ziklag to David

Ziklag

Bethul

Maon

Wilderness of Maon

Ashan

Kabzeel

Arad

Beersheba

Wilderness of Kenites

MOAB

Hormah

Baalah

Negeb of Jeraheelmites

Mizpah of Moab (Kir-hareseth)

AMALEK

Negeb

Ezem

Safe refuge is sought for parents in Moab

David pursues the Amalekites

Amalekites apply pressure against villages of Judah

Arabah

EDOM

Zered River

S

Sunset over the site of ancient Azekah near the location of a battle between Saul and the Philistines.

provided a fitting elegy (2 Sam. 1:17-27). See *Prophets*.

New Testament Though the king Saul is mentioned in passing, most occurrences of the name in the NT refer to the Hebrew name of the Apostle Paul. See *Paul*.   *Daniel C. Browning, Jr.*

SAVIOR One who saves by delivering, preserving, healing, or providing (2 Sam. 22:2-7). Unlike all other religions, Christianity is unique in portraying salvation completely by the grace of a savior. Salvation comes exclusively and completely from God. Salvation's source is grace from the savior. The means is faith in the savior. The Lord Jesus Christ is the only Savior (John 4:42).

In the OT God is portrayed as Savior (Isa. 43:3; 45:15,21-22). Categorically, God is the only Savior (Isa. 43:11; Hos. 13:4). This is the NT teaching also (Jude 25; James 4:12; Acts 4:12). Jesus is the Savior who provides eternal life (John 3:16; Matt. 1:21; Rom. 3:21-26; 5:1-11; 1 John 2:2; 4:14; 5:13).

Jesus is Savior because He is God (Rom. 10:9-10,13; cp. Joel 2:32). One must call on the name of the Lord (*Yahweh* in the OT, *Kurios* in the NT). Also note the close affinity between Jesus' deity and His stature as Savior (Titus 2:13;

2 Peter 1:1). Jesus is the Savior also because He is God incarnate, fully human and fully divine. Jesus stated, "If you do not believe that I am He, you will die in your sins" (John 8:24 HCSB). The phrase "I am He" is "I am" in Greek and is similar to "Before Abraham was, I am" (John 8:58). Clearly this is a self-attestation of Jesus Christ's essential deity, an appropriation of the personal name of God as His own. See *Salvation*.

Doros Zachariades

SAW Tool for cutting wood or stone. See *Tools*.

SCAB See *Diseases; Scurvy*.

SCALE Skin disease involving flaking of the scalp. See *Itch; Scall*.

SCALES Instrument for weighing materials. See *Balances; Weights and Measures*.

SCALL KJV term for a skin disease (Lev. 13:30-37; 14:54). The basic Hebrew term means "to tear away, pull loose." The disease produced head sores, itching, hair thinning, and hair turning yellow. Modern translations refer to a scale or itch. Some scholars think favus is the disease described; others speak of ringworm or eczema. See *Itch*.

SCAPEGOAT Animal that carried away the sins of the people into the wilderness on the Day of Atonement (Lev. 16:8,10,26). On the Day of Atonement, when the high priest went once a year into the holy of holies to offer sacrifices for the sins of his family and for all the people, two goats were brought before him. By lot, one was chosen to be "for the LORD." This goat was slain as a sin offering, and its blood was sprinkled on the cultic objects to help cleanse the altar, the sanctuary, and the tent of meeting from defilements of the past year.

The second goat was said to be "for Azazel." The word "Azazel" is usually interpreted to mean "the goat of removal," or "scapegoat." However, the term may also refer to a rocky place in the desert or to a demon of the desert. By laying his hands on the goat's head, the priest transferred the sins of the people to it and then had the goat led away into the desert, picturing the removal of the sins.

In the book of Enoch, Azazel is identified as the leader of the fallen angels who lies bound beneath rocks in the desert awaiting judgment. The goat is led to that area and thrown to its death from a cliff. See *Intertestamental History and Literature; Pseudepigrapha; Sacrifice and Offering.*

Although the scapegoat is not mentioned by name in the NT, Heb. 10:3-17 contrasts sanctification through the sacrifice of Christ with the blood of bulls and goats which can never take away sins. See *Sanctification.*

SCARLET Color used especially in clothing, often designating royal honor (Dan. 5:7,16,29). See *Cloth, Clothing; Colors; Crimson; Dyeing.*

SCEPTER Official staff or baton of a king, symbolic of his authority. It probably was descended from the ancient club carried by the prehistoric rulers. Ancient Middle Eastern scepters were depicted in Scripture as the striking power of the king (Num. 24:17). As part of the royal regalia, the scepter was extended to a visitor or dignitary (Esther 5:2) to signal approval of the visit and allow the person to approach the throne. Scepters were decorated elaborately with gold and precious stones. The shapes varied from wide short maces to long slender poles, usually with ornate heads. The type of scepter usually differed from one kingdom to the next.

SCEVA (Sē´ và) Jewish "high priest" in Ephesus with seven sons who tried unsuccessfully to exorcise demons in Jesus' name as Paul had done (Acts 19:14). The evil spirit jumped on them instead. No such Jewish high priest is known from other sources, particularly not one living in Ephesus. The title may be the result of a copyist or a title Sceva took upon himself to impress leaders of other religions in Ephesus.

SCHOOL Place and agency for education, particularly of children. The word "school" is not mentioned in the OT and only once in the NT where the reference is to a Greek school (Acts 19:9). Until the exile in Babylon (586 B.C.), the education of children was like that of all ancient peoples: it was centered in the home. The main concern of the Jewish people was for religious education in the home.

A new stage in Jewish education came about due to the catastrophe of the Babylonian exile when the upper classes of Judea were transported to Babylon. The exiles assembled on the Sabbath for prayer and worship. As time went by, buildings were erected where the people could meet. These little gatherings were the origin of the synagogue, which ultimately became the center of Jewish religious life after the exile. In the synagogue the scribes taught the law to the people. Children were not taught in the synagogue until much later times. The father was responsible for transmitting what he had learned to his children.

The attempt of Antiochus Epiphanes to eradicate Judaism by force brought about the fierce nationalistic revolt of the Maccabees (Jewish patriots) in 168 B.C. The Jews who had remained faithful learned a lesson. They saw that they needed schools for the young as well as adult classes for their fathers. Simon ben Shetah, the leader of the Pharisees, founded schools for boys of 16 and 17 to promote the study of the Scriptures. A century later, as an inevitable consequence, private schools for younger children appeared. After the destruction of Herod's temple by Titus in A.D. 70 and the disappearance of the Jewish state after the revolt of Bar-Kochba in A.D. 135, public instruction was instituted for all children. See *Intertestamental History and Literature.*

The elementary school, significantly called Beth-hasepher, the "house of the book," was originally housed in some easily available room; but by A.D. 200, it had become firmly established in the synagogue. Boys entered at the age of six or seven and continued until 13. Here, study was wholly devoted to the written law. This involved the learning of Hebrew, since Aramaic had long before replaced Hebrew as the everyday language of the people. Knowledge of the written word, in school as in the home, had the religious goal of bringing about obedience to the law.

The school was not only a place of learning but also a house of prayer; its aims were not cultural but religious. A strong sense of community responsibility, evidenced by an education tax on all parents, had by A.D. 200 opened all schools to the children of the poor. However, the Jewish school, like the Greek school, remained an independent, fee-paying institution. See *Education in Bible Times; Scribes; Synagogue; Torah.*

Jeff Cranford

SCHOOLMASTER Law's role until coming of Christ (Gal. 3:24-25 KJV). Other translations use "guardian" (HCSB), "disciplinarian" (NRSV), "supervision" (NIV), "tutor" (NASB), "charge" (REB; TEV; cp. NIV), or "custodian" (RSV). See *Custodian; Guardian.*

SCIENCE KJV term (Dan. 1:4; 1 Tim. 6:20) for knowledge. Scripture describes Daniel's knowledge with admiration and approval but warns against meaningless debate of issues for the sake of human pride not leading to useful knowledge. See *Gnosticism.*

SCOFFER Person who shows contempt for others. Habakkuk predicted the Babylonians would be scoffers as they conquered the Near East (Hab. 1:10). Second Peter 3:3 warns that the last days will see scoffers laughing at the idea of Christ's return (cp. Jude 18). The wisdom writers repeatedly warned their students not to become scoffers (Job 11:3; Prov. 9:7-12; 13:1; 14:6; 15:12; 19:25; 21:24; 22:10; 24:9; cp. Ps. 1:1; Isa. 28:14,22). Still, God is a scoffer, jeering at the feeble efforts of those who oppose Him (Ps. 2:4; Prov. 3:34). Jesus endured scoffing (Luke 16:14; cp. Acts 13:41).

SCORN, SCORNFUL Dislike that turns to contempt and derision. "Scorn" often appears in some Bible translations where "scoff" appears in others. Scorn is often expressed by laughter (2 Kings 19:21; 2 Chron. 30:10). In deep trouble psalmists often felt themselves scorned (Pss. 22:6; 31:11; 39:8; 44:13; 80:6; 89:41; 119:22; 123:4). God scorns the wicked (Prov. 3:34), who, in turn, scorn Him (2 Sam. 12:14). When His people refuse to be faithful, God can scorn them and their worship, expressed in destruction (Lam. 2:7). See *Scoffer.*

SCORPION An order of arachnids known for the venom and sting in their narrow segmented tails. In the wilderness God protected Israel from scorpions (Deut. 8:15) and could protect His prophet from them (Ezek. 2:6). Scorpions gave their names to an insidious instrument of punishment with lashes and spikes. Rehoboam chose to use these to enforce his harsh policies (1 Kings 12:11,14).

SCORPION PASS See *Akrabbim.*

SCOURGE Severe form of corporal punishment involving whipping and beating, usually was done with the victim tied to a post or bench and administered by a servant of the synagogue (if for religious reasons) or by a slave or soldier. John 19:1 uses this word for the beating given Jesus before His crucifixion. Matthew and Mark use a word meaning "flog" (a lesser punishment), while Luke says that Pilate offered to have Jesus "whipped" (23:16 HCSB), which was a still lighter punishment. The number of blows was set in Deut. 25:3 at 40 but later reduced to 39. There were to be 13 strokes on the chest and 26 on the back. Often the victim died from the beating.

SCREECH OWL English translation used for different Hebrew terms by different translations. KJV uses it for "Lilith" (Isa. 34:14). NIV uses it for Hebrew *qippod* (Isa. 34:11; Zeph. 2:14) but simply "owls" at Isa. 14:23. NRSV used "screech owl" at Zeph. 2:14. NIV also uses "screech owl" for Hebrew *tachmas* (Lev. 11:16; Deut. 14:15). REB uses "screech owl" for Hebrew *yanshuph* (Lev. 11:17; Deut. 14:16; Isa. 34:11). *Qippod* may be *Syrnium aluco* or *Scops giu.* Others suggest the Arabian Desert fowl (*Ammoperdrix heyi*). *Tachmas* cannot be identified with any certainty. *Yanshoph* may be the eared owl (*Asiootus*) or the *Merops apiaster.* See *Owl; Satyr.*

SCRIBE Person trained in writing skills and used to record events and decisions (Jer. 36:26; 1 Chron. 24:6; Esther 3:12). During the exile in Babylon educated scribes apparently became the experts in God's written word, copying, preserving, and teaching it. Ezra was a scribe in this sense of expert in teaching God's word (Ezra 7:6). A professional group of such scribes developed by NT times, most being Pharisees (Mark 2:16). They interpreted the law, taught it to disciples, and were experts in cases where people were accused of breaking the law of Moses. They led in plans to kill Jesus (Luke 19:47) and heard His stern rebuke (Matt. 23). See *Government; Jewish Parties in the New Testament; Sanhedrin; Secretary.*

SCRIP See *Bag 4.*

SCRIPTURE Historic Judeo-Christian name for the specific literature that the church receives as divine instruction. Scripture means "a writing," rendering the Latin *scriptura* and the Greek *graphe.* The term is used some 50 times in the NT for some or all of the OT.

In the history of the church, the divine character of Scripture has been the great presupposition for the whole of Christian preaching and theology. This is apparent in the way the NT speaks about the OT. New Testament writers often used formulas like "God says" and "the Holy Spirit says" to introduce OT passages. For the NT authors Scripture was the record of God speaking and revealing Himself to His people. Thus Scripture and God are so closely joined together that these writers could speak of Scripture doing what it records God as doing (Gal. 3:8; Rom. 9:17).

Because of their belief in the Scripture's divine origin and content, the NT writers described it as "strongly confirmed" (2 Pet. 1:19 HCSB), trustworthy "deserving of full acceptance" (1 Tim. 1:15), and "confirmed" (Heb. 2:3). Its word "endures forever" (1 Pet. 1:24-25). Those who build their lives on Scripture "will not be put to shame" (Rom. 9:33 HCSB). The Bible was written for "instruction" and "encouragement" (Rom. 15:4), to lead to "salvation through faith" (2 Tim. 3:15), to guide people toward godliness (2 Tim. 3:16b), and to equip believers for good works (2 Tim. 3:17).

The purpose of Scripture is to place men and women in right standing before God and to enable believers to seek God's glory in all of life's activities and efforts. It is above all a book of redemptive history.

Scripture is not only a divine book but also a divine-human book. It is important to recognize that the biblical writers employed the linguistic resources available to them as they wrote to specific people with particular needs at particular times. The human authors were not lifted out of their culture or removed from their contexts. They functioned as members of believing communities, aware of God's leadership in their lives.

Scripture, comprised of 66 books, written by over 40 authors spanning almost 1,500 years, reveals to God's people the unifying history of His redeeming words and acts. The ultimate focus of Scripture is the incarnation and redemptive work of Jesus Christ. He is the center to which everything in Scripture is united and bound together—beginning and end, creation and redemption, humanity, the world, the fall,

A Torah scroll being held in its wooden case at a celebration in Jerusalem.

history, and the future. See *Bible Formation and Canon; Inspiration of Scripture.*

David S. Dockery

SCROLL Roll of papyrus (a paperlike material made of the papyrus plant) or parchment (specially treated leather) used as a medium for writing (Ezra 6:2; Jer. 36:2; Ezek. 2:9; Zech. 5:1-2; Luke 4:17; Rev. 5:1). One of the most famous and best-preserved ancient scrolls is the "Isaiah scroll," a complete copy of the book of Isaiah written on a parchment roll, dated to the second century B.C. Early books or "codices" were not widely used until the third century A.D. See *Paper; Papyrus; Writing.*   *Robert L. Plummer*

SCURVY Disease of the gums resulting in loosening of and/or loss of teeth. KJV translation of Hebrew term for festering eruption (Lev. 21:20; 22:22), but in Deut. 28:27 KJV and NASB used "scab," while only there did NRSV and RSV use "scurvy." NIV used "festering sores." HCSB uses "festering rash." NASB used "eczema" in Leviticus. See *Diseases.*

SCYTHIANS (Sĭ´ thē ənz) Nomadic, Indo-European people, speaking an Iranian dialect, who migrated from central Asia into southern Russia between 800 and 600 B.C. They were skilled horsemen who excelled in barbaric attack and plunder. Archaeologists have discovered abundant evidence of Scythian artistry in metalwork. Their forces, in pursuit of the Cimmerians, drove south through or around the Caucasus Mountains to the borders of Assyria. A Scytho-Assyrian alliance was formed about 680 to 670 B.C.

According to the Greek historian Herodotus, a Scythian attack forced the Medes to withdraw from an assault against Nineveh (apparently 626–620 B.C.). Later, the Scythians advanced southward along the Palestinian coast to the Egyptian border (611 B.C.), where the Egyptian Pharaoh bought them off. They were eventually driven back northward into southern Russia by the Medes.

Scythian power was dominant in the area northwest of the Black Sea until about 350 B.C. Eventually, new invaders, the Sarmatians, having confined them to the Crimean area, destroyed the Scythian remnants after A.D. 100.

The OT refers to Scythians as Ashchenaz (Gen. 10:3; Jer. 51:27). Earlier scholars identified the Scythians as Jeremiah's foe from the north and Zephaniah's threatened invader of Judah, but such theories rest on weak evidence. Colossians 3:11 uses Scythians to represent the most repugnant barbarian and slave, saying they, too, are accepted in Christ, all social and cultural barriers being abolished in His church. See *Ashchenaz.* *Charles Graham*

SEA COW NIV translation, explained in text note as "dugong" (Exod. 25:5; 26:14; 35:7,23; Num. 4). Aquatic herbivorous mammal related to the manatee. The male has short tusklike teeth. The skin is mentioned as a covering for the tabernacle (HCSB, manatee; KJV, badger's skins; NASB, porpoise; REB, dugong; RSV, goat; NRSV, fine leather). See *Badger Skins.*

SEA GULL See *Cuckow.*

SEA MONSTER (KJV, Lam. 4:3) See *Dragon.*

SEA OF GALILEE See *Galilee, Sea of; Palestine.*

SEA OF GLASS See *Glass.*

SEA OF JAZER Body of water connected with town of Jazer (Jer. 48:32) but unknown to modern Bible students. Some commentators use

The Sea of Galilee as viewed from Mount Arbel.

A calm Sea of Galilee at dusk with snow-capped Mount Hermon in the distance.

manuscript and Isa. 16:8 evidence to eliminate "sea of" from the text (NRSV, REB). See *Jazer.*

SEA OF THE PLAIN See *Dead Sea.*

SEA, MOLTEN See *Molten Sea.*

SEAL Signet containing a distinctive mark that represented the individual who owned it. The earliest seals found so far date before 3000 B.C. Seals varied in shapes and sizes. Some were round and were worn around the neck. Others were rings worn on the finger. The mark was made by stamping the seal into soft clay. Many cylinder seals have been found which contain scenes that communicate a message. These were rolled in the clay to form the impression. Tamar asked for Judah's signet as collateral on a pledge he made (Gen. 38:18). Joseph was given pharaoh's ring when he was placed in command of the country (Gen. 41:42), symbolizing Joseph's right to act with the ruler's authority. Jezebel used Ahab's seal to sign letters asking

that Naboth be tried and stoned to death (1 Kings 21:8).

SEASON KJV translation of several Hebrew and Greek terms with different meanings. **1.** Indefinite but somewhat extended period of time (Gen. 40:4; Josh. 24:7; Luke 4:13). **2.** A regularly scheduled, recurring time (Exod. 13:10; Num. 9:2; John 5:4). **3.** To add ingredients to food to improve the flavor (Lev. 2:13; Mark 9:50). See *Salt; Spices.* **4.** A particular part of a year (Gen. 1:14; 2 Kings 4:16). **5.** An indefinite part of a day (Job 30:17; Ps. 22:2). **6.** Time appointed by God (Ps. 104:27; Matt. 24:45). **7.** The proper time for an action (Isa. 50:4). See *Time.*

SEBA See *Sabean.*

SEBAM (Sē´ băm) Place-name probably meaning "high" or "cold." Town east of the Jordan that the tribes of Reuben and Gad wanted to settle after God conquered it for them (Num. 32:3). Early versions agree with verse 38 in reading "Sibmah," which the tribes rebuilt. Its location is not certain.

SEBAT (Sē´ băt) Eleventh month in Babylonian calendar used to date Zechariah's vision (1:7). This would be February–March. See *Calendars.*

SECACAH (Sə kā´ kah) Place-name meaning "covered." Town in tribal territory of Judah in the Judean wilderness (Josh. 15:61). It is modern Khirbet es-Samrah in the central Buqeia. Some would equate it with the site of Qumran.

SECHU (Sē´ kū) Place-name, perhaps meaning "lookout." Otherwise unknown site where Saul

North Syrian and Hittite stamp-type seals.

searched for David (1 Sam. 19:22). Many commentators follow the earliest Greek translation and change the Hebrew text to read "on the bare height" (NRSV note).

SECOND COMING Biblical teaching that Christ will return visibly and bodily to the earth to render judgment and complete His redemptive plan.

Old Testament The concept of the second coming originally derived from the OT teachings about a coming Messiah. Therein, the prophets foretold the Lord would send One from within the nation of Israel (Num. 24:17; Jer. 23:5-6) who would not only be God's anointed but would in fact be God Himself (Isa. 9:6; Mic. 5:2). As various descriptions of this Messiah developed, two portraits emerged. One described Him as a mighty redeemer who would destroy Israel's enemies, bring salvation, and restore peace (Jer. 33:15; Zech. 9:9-10) while the other portrayed Him as a servant who would suffer and be rejected (Isa. 53; Zech. 13:7). These contrasting descriptions of Messiah, however, would not be delineated into two separate comings until the NT.

New Testament The NT clearly distinguishes between two comings of Jesus Christ, the Messiah: the first in the incarnation and the second at the end of this present age. The earliest instructions of this second coming are recounted in the Gospels where Christ Himself explicitly claimed He would come again. For example, He urged people to be prepared because He would come unexpectedly, like a thief (Matt. 25:1-13; Mark 13:35-36; Luke 21:34-36). He also promised to return in order to claim His own and reward them (Matt. 25:31-46; John 14:1-3). Furthermore, at His ascension angels declared that He would return to the earth in the same manner in which He left (Acts 1:10-11).

Later, other NT writers explained Christ's teachings even further. They taught that He would come in glory to judge unbelievers, Satan, his hoards, and even the earth itself (2 Thess. 1:6-10; 2:8; 2 Pet. 3:10-12; Rev. 19:20–20:3). Likewise, He would come in the heavens to gather all believers unto Himself forever by resurrecting the dead, catching them up along with the living into the air to meet Him on His return, and then reward them all for their faithfulness (1 Cor. 15:51-57; 2 Cor. 5:10; 1 Thess. 4:13-17). Because the second coming promised both vin-

dication and salvation, it acted as a motivation for godly living and became the blessed hope of the early church (Titus 2:13; 1 John 3:2-3).

The Time of His Coming Historically, Christians have differed on two major issues pertinent to the second coming. The first relates to the millennial era mentioned in Rev. 20:1-10. Many equate the millennium with the current church age or the time between Pentecost and Christ's return. Consequently, some propose that Christ's return will occur at the close of the church age to either bring an end to wickedness and sinful rebellion (i.e., Amillennialism) or as a climax to a gradual development of universal righteousness and peace on the earth (i.e., Postmillennialism). Others, who do not view the millennium as the present church age, believe it will be a period after Christ's return wherein He will establish a literal kingdom on earth (i.e., Premillennialism).

The second issue, which is a concern primarily among Premillennialists, regards the sequential relationship between the catching up of believers (i.e., the "rapture") and a future time of worldwide judgment known as the Tribulation period (Jer. 30:7; Dan. 9:23-27; 2 Thess. 2:3-7). Many believe the rapture will occur prior to the Tribulation while Christ's return to the earth will occur afterwards (i.e., Pretribulationism). Others think the rapture will occur midway or towards the latter end of the Tribulation (i.e., Midtribulationism). Finally, some are convinced the rapture and His coming to the earth will both occur consecutively after the Tribulation (i.e., Posttribulationism). This latter group generally disdains the word "rapture," since the "catching up" is at the same moment as the second coming.

All of the above interpretations affirm that there will be a literal, physical return of Jesus at the end of time as a prelude to final judgment and the redemption of creation. Although Christians embrace diverse views on many of the details, in the end the certainty of the second coming should bring hope and comfort to all believers (1 Thess. 4:18; Heb. 9:28; Rev. 22:20). See *Christ, Christology; Future Hope; Eschatology; Jesus Christ; Judgment; Millennium; Rapture; Tribulation.*   *Everett Berry*

SECOND DEATH Eternal separation from God. The concept is referred to in Rev. 2:11; 20:6,14; and 21:8. According to Rev. 20:15 it includes being "thrown into the lake of fire." The first death would be physical death (see Matt. 10:28).

Although the expression "first death" does not occur, the concept is implied in Rev. 20:6 which states that "the second death has no power" over "the one who shares in the first resurrection." Sharing in the first resurrection would be impossible unless they had previously died. See *Death; Resurrection.*

SECOND QUARTER Northern part of Jerusalem whose boundaries were extended during the monarchy. This part of the city was most open to enemy attack. See *College.*

SECOND SABBATH Chronological notation in some manuscripts of Luke 6:1 believed by many commentators to be a later addition to the text (NRSV, NIV, NASB, REB).

SECRETARY Royal official in charge of state records (2 Sam. 8:17 in modern translations; REB, "adjutant-general"). See *Government; Scribe.*

SECT Group having established their own identity and teachings over against the larger group to which they belong, especially the different parties making up Judaism in NT times. See *Jewish Parties in the New Testament.*

SECU (Sē´ cū) Modern translations' transliteration of Sechu.

SECUNDUS (Sə kŭn´ dŭs) Latin personal name meaning "second." Representative of church of Thessalonica who accompanied Paul on his journey as he took the churches' contributions to the Jerusalem church (Acts 20:4).

SECURITY OF THE BELIEVER Teaching that God protects believers for the completion of their salvation. Contemporary Christianity needs to deal forthrightly with the universal human problem of insecurity. The natural gulf between the invisible, infinite God and finite, fallible humanity makes the quest for assurance and security a very significant theological issue. Slogans such as "once saved, always saved" and "eternal security" often easily gain a reverential status normally reserved only for biblical texts and become symbols of "evangelical orthodoxy." Indeed, it comes as a shock to some when they discover that their symbols are not actually biblical terms.

The Bible does teach that salvation does not depend merely upon human effort. God is the author of salvation (2 Cor. 5:18-19; John 3:16). God justifies or treats as acceptable sinners who receive Christ in faith (Rom. 3:21-26). The great message of the Reformation says: No one can earn assurance or security with God. Assurance of salvation is God's gift! Security does not come by absolutions, church attendance, good works, reciting Scripture, or performances of penance. God who has begun the work of salvation in Christians also provides the necessary assurance to bring His work to its completion in the day of Christ (Phil. 1:6). God in Christ protects and keeps Christians (John 10:27-29; 2 Thess. 3:3) just as Jesus took seriously the task of preserving the disciples while He was on earth (John 17:12-15). We do not possess the strength to secure ourselves.

The biblical view of security, however, is probably best epitomized in the Christian doctrine of perseverance (Eph. 6:18; Heb. 12:1; James 1:25). Christians must realize that their security does not lie in a fairy-tale approach to life where once a person becomes a Christian everything is a bed of roses forever and ever. Such a view fails to take seriously the traumas of human life. See *Perseverance.*

The biblical view of assurance or security is rooted in the conviction that when Jesus departed from the disciples, the Lord did not orphan them or leave them without support. He promised Christians that He would come to them and would provide them with a companion Spirit (the Comforter or Paraclete) who would not only be at their side but would be within them, as much a part of them as their very breath (John 14:16-18). The Spirit would be their sense of peace and security, their witness concerning Jesus, their attorney with the world, and their guide or teacher into all truth (John 14:25-30; 15:26-27; 16:8-15). See *Advocate; Comforter; Helper.*

Along with great promises of assurance, the Bible contains strong warnings that call Christians to consistent living, even as they have yielded to temptations and sin and capitulated to the hostile forces of evil (1 Cor. 10:1-12; Heb. 2:1-3; 3:12-19; 6:1-8; 10:26-31; James 5:19-20). These and many other warnings are not merely phantom warnings unrelated to Christian life. They are meant to be taken with great

S

seriousness. They are no more a game with God than was the death of Christ.

These warnings appear in the NT within clear statements reminding believers that temptation is accompanied by God's presence. Christians are expected to resist temptations and flee ungodly activity (1 Cor. 10:13-14). Evil patterns of life are inconsistent with Christian transformation. The writers of the NT were convinced that Christians would heed these warnings and resist the devil (James 4:7; 1 Pet. 5:8-9). It is virtually unthinkable for a Christian to do otherwise. The Christian is anchored to the person of God. Evil has to be dealt with. The Christian can find in God an enduring security for the soul. Such is the meaning of Heb. 6:17-20. God's consistency is the basis for a Christian's security in the midst of the world's traumas.

The security of the believer is not merely focused upon this life on earth. It has a dynamic focus on the life to come. The NT writers are convinced that a Christian will take very seriously the warnings in this life because this life is related to the life with Christ in heaven. The Christian, therefore, is expected to persevere to the end (1 Pet. 1:5; 1 John 5:18; Rev. 3:10).

The confidence or secure sense of the believer with respect to the life hereafter is rooted in the united witness of the NT writers that the resurrection of Jesus Christ is the hinge point of the Christian faith. In raising His Son Jesus, God provided Christians with the sign of the destinies and the basis for their security. Without the resurrection the Christian proclamation would be empty (1 Cor. 15:14). Moreover, in the coming of the Holy Spirit, God provided the guarantee of our marvelous relationship with God (2 Cor. 1:22). In our identity with Adam, humanity experienced sin and, consequently, death. However, as we identify with the ultimate power of Christ in the resurrection, we, too, shall experience the effective meaning of the security of the believer in the triumph of God (1 Cor. 15:20-28).   *Gerald L. Borchert*

SEDITION Rebellion against lawful authority. Government officials in Persia's province headquartered in Samaria accused the Jews in Jerusalem of a history of rebellion as evidence against allowing Jerusalem and its temple to be rebuilt (Ezra 4:15). Barabbas had been imprisoned for sedition (Luke 23:19). Jewish leaders tried to convince Felix, the governor, that Paul

had incited sedition (Acts 24:5). KJV uses "seditions" in Gal. 5:20 for one of the works of the flesh, but modern translations are more accurate in using "dissensions." Relationships among believers rather than to governments is the apparent meaning. See *Barabbas*.

SEER See *Divination and Magic; Prophecy, Prophets*.

SEGUB (Sē´ gŭb) Personal name meaning "He has revealed Himself as exalted" or "He has protected." **1.** Second son of Hiel, whose death during rebuilding of Jericho showed power of God's prophesy through the centuries (1 Kings 16:34). **2.** Son of Judahite father and Machirite or Manassehite mother (1 Chron. 2:21-22).

SEIR, MOUNT (Sā´ īr) Place-name meaning "hairy" and thus "thicket" or "small forested region." A mountain range that runs the length of biblical Edom, leading at times to an equation of Edom and Seir. Parts of the range are almost impassable. The highest peak is about 5,600 feet above sea level. The region was home to Esau and his descendants (Gen. 32:3; Josh. 24:4). Some documents found in Egypt seem to make Seir and Edom two different tribal habitats, and it is possible that at times in its history the area was ruled over simultaneously by several local clans. The "sons of Seir" represented an early Horite clan from the region. See *Edom; Horim or Horites*.

SEIRAH (Sā´ ĭ rah) Place-name meaning "toward Seir." Modern translations' reading for KJV "Seirath" (Judg. 3:26). The name would seem to point to Mount Seir in Edom, but the context seems to make that location impossible. Otherwise, the location is not known. It must be a forested place in the tribal territory of Benjamin.

SEIRATH (Sā ī´ răth) KJV transliteration of place-name in Judg. 3:26. See *Seirah*.

SELA (Sē´ là) Place-name meaning "rock." Major fortified city in Edom. The biblical references lend themselves to varying interpretations, since Sela may also be read as a common noun referring to rocky country or wilderness. Judges 1:36 refers to a border of the Amorites, though some commentators change this to Edomites

(REB). Amaziah of Judah (796–767 B.C.) captured Sela and renamed it Joktheel (2 Kings 14:7; cp. 2 Chron. 25:12 NRSV). Isaiah's oracle against Moab calls for action from Sela, which many commentators take to be the rocky wilderness bordering Moab rather than the more distant town of Sela (Isa. 16:1). Traditionally from the earliest Greek translation on, Sela has been identified with Petra, the capital of Edom, or the nearby umm-Bayyara in the Wadi Musa. More recent study has placed it at es-Sela, two and a half miles northwest of Bozrah and five miles southwest of Tafileh. Modern translations include Sela in Isa. 42:11, God's call to joy at the coming salvation.

SELAH (Sē´ lah) Term of unknown meaning appearing in psalms, outside the book of Psalms only in Hab. 3. Scholars have advanced various unprovable theories: a pause either for silence or musical interlude; a signal for the congregation to sing, recite, or fall prostrate on the ground; a cue for the cymbals to crash; a word to be shouted by the congregation; or a sign to the choir to sing a higher pitch or louder. The earliest Jewish traditions thought it meant "forever."

Mike Mitchell

SELAH-HAMMAHLEKOTH (Sē lå-håm mäh´ lə kŏth) Place-name meaning "rock of hiding, haunt, refuge." David's hiding place in the wilderness of Maon while Saul pursued him (1 Sam. 23:28 KJV). Modern translations often translate the name rather than transliterate it: "Rock of Separation" (HCSB), "Dividing Rock" (REB), "Rock of Escape" (NRSV, NASB).

SELED (Sē´ lĕd) Personal name meaning "jumping." Member of tribe of Judah (1 Chron. 2:30).

SELEUCIA (Sə lū´ shĭ å) Syrian city on Mediterranean coast, five miles north of the Orontes River and 15 miles from Antioch. Paul stopped there on his first missionary journey (Acts 13:4). It was founded by Seleucus Nicator, the first Seleucid king, in 301 B.C. See *Seleucids.*

SELEUCIDS (Sē lū´ sĭds) Descendants of Seleucus, one of the generals of Alexander the Great. Following the death of Alexander, 323 B.C., his kingdom was divided among five of his leading commanders. Seleucus chose for himself the eastern part of the empire around the city of Babylon. During the next several years much confusion prevailed. Seleucus was forced to leave Babylon for a time and take refuge with his friend Ptolemy, ruler of Egypt. Later, with the help of Ptolemy, he was able to control Babylon again. The important date is 312 B.C. The Syrian calendar has its beginning at this time.

The overall situation remained unchanged until the battle of Ipsus, 301 B.C. In that battle four of the generals, including Seleucus, fought against Antigonus who had become the most powerful of the generals and claimed to be king over much of Asia Minor and northern Syria. Antigonus was slain in the battle, and his territory was given to Seleucus along with title to the land of Palestine. However, Ptolemy took control of Palestine, and his successors retained it for over a hundred years. This was a serious point of contention between the two empires throughout this period of time.

Seleucus was assassinated in 281 B.C. Antiochus I, his son, became ruler and made peace with the Egyptians. He sought throughout his reign to consolidate his rule, but the years were for the most part a time of intense struggle and warfare. At his death in 262 or early 261 B.C., his son Antiochus II became king (261–246 B.C.). During the early years of Antiochus II, conflict continued with Egypt. When peace between the two nations was reached in 253 B.C., Ptolemy offered his daughter to Antiochus as wife with the understanding that he would desert his first wife. The goal was that a son born to this marriage would become the ruler of the Seleucid Empire and cement relations between the two. However, it did not work out in this way, and Antiochus died in 246 B.C., perhaps murdered by his first wife.

The eldest son of Antiochus, Seleucus II, was named king. He ruled until his death in 226 B.C. However, some Syrians, along with Egypt, supported the infant son of the second wife of Antiochus. The Egyptian army could not reach the area quickly enough to defend the child, and Seleucus was able to regain control of the territory ruled by his father, some of which had been lost at the time of his father's death. In 241 B.C. peace was again reached between the Seleucids and Egypt. When Seleucus died as the result of falling from his horse, his son Alexander became king as Seleucus III. He was assassinated in 223

S

B.C. and was succeeded by his son Antiochus III, known as Antiochus the Great (223–187 B.C.).

With the death of Antiochus Epiphanes, the situation of the Seleucids fell into disarray. From this time on it seems that more than one strong individual was contending for the crown at all times. Lysias had been left with responsibility for the care of the young son of Epiphanes. He assumed that upon the death of the king the son would become king. However, before his death the king had evidently appointed Philip, a close friend with him in the East, to be king. Philip returned to Antioch, the capital in Syria, and this forced Lysias to cut off his efforts to quell the Jewish revolt. In his effort to bring peace, he granted religious freedom to the Jews. Lysias was able to thwart the effort of Philip, and the son, Antiochus V, reigned as king for a brief time (164–162 B.C.).

Demetrius, the young son of Seleucus IV, was a hostage in Rome. His desire to return home at the death of his father was denied. When Antiochus IV died, he managed to escape from Rome and fled to Syria, 162 B.C. He had himself proclaimed as king and had Lysias and Antiochus V put to death. He remained as king until 150 B.C. These years were involved in attempts to put down the Jewish revolt and to consolidate and expand his position in the East.

A strong rival appeared—Alexander Balas. He claimed to be the illegitimate son of Antiochus Epiphanes. In 153 B.C. the Roman senate acknowledged him as king of Syria although the senate was probably aware that his claim was false. The two rivals both made extensive offers to the Jews for their support. Jonathan, the Jewish leader, supported Alexander, who, in 150 B.C., gained victory over Demetrius, who was killed in battle. Alexander reigned until 145 B.C., supported at first by the ruler of Egypt, who gave Alexander his daughter in marriage. When Ptolemy learned that Alexander was plotting to kill him, he turned against Alexander, brought his daughter back, and offered her in marriage to the young son of Demetrius. Defeated in battle by Ptolemy, Alexander fled to Arabia, where he was killed. The young son of Demetrius, Demetrius II, was made king (reigning twice, 145–139 and 129–125 B.C.).

Needing their support, Demetrius granted political freedom to the Jews during the early years of his reign. One of his generals, Tryphon, supported Alexander Balas' young son, who

claimed the throne as Antiochus VI (145–142 B.C.). Tryphon had Antiochus murdered and had himself proclaimed as king (142–139 B.C.). Demetrius II was taken prisoner in a campaign against the Parthians, and his brother Antiochus VII (139–128 B.C.) became king. He defeated Tryphon, who then committed suicide. Antiochus made one last effort to interfere in the life of the Jews. In 133 B.C. he invaded Judea and began a siege of Jerusalem that lasted for almost a year. Finally, peace was made between him and John Hyrcanus, guaranteeing the independence of the Jews from Syrian intervention. Antiochus made a campaign against the Parthians where he died.

With the death of Antiochus VII, the Seleucids ceased to be a major factor in the political life of the eastern Mediterranean world. Although Demetrius was released by the Parthians and resumed his role as king, neither he nor any other person was able to gain firm control of the empire. The following years were filled with internal conflict that drained the resources of the empire and saw at least 10 persons claim rule in less than 50 years. In 83 B.C. the king of Armenia took possession of Syria, and the rule of the Seleucids came to an end. See *Intertestamental History and Literature.*   *Clayton Harrop*

SELF-CONTROL Modern translations' term for several Greek words indicating a sober, temperate, calm, and dispassionate approach to life, having mastered personal desires and passions. Biblical admonitions expect God's people to exercise self-control (Prov. 25:28; 1 Cor. 7:5; 1 Thess. 5:6; 1 Tim. 3:2; 2 Tim. 3:3; Gal. 5:23; 2 Tim. 1:7; Titus 1:8; 2 Pet. 1:6). Freedom in Christ does not give believers liberty to cast off all moral restraint as some members in Galatia and other churches apparently believed. Nor does it call for a withdrawal from life and its temptations. It calls for a self-disciplined life following Christ's example of being in the world but not of the world. See *Ethics; Freedom.*

SELF-ESTEEM Respect for and confident acceptance of oneself as a person created by and useful to God. Self-esteem must be based on an understanding that people are created by God to be highly exalted (Ps. 8:3-8; cp. Gen. 1:26-27) yet are miserably fallen sinners (Rom. 3:23; 7:24). Every person, no matter how sinful, is of inestimable value to God (Luke 15:11-32; 1 Cor.

6:20) and supremely loved by Him (1 John 4:10; cp. Rom. 8:35-39). Christians possess a new nature that allows them to be self-confident, but only through Christ (1 Cor. 9:24; 2 Cor. 3:5; 10:7; Phil. 3:4-7; 4:13). Both self-elation and self-abasement ignore the work of Christ in a believer (2 Cor. 12:7-10; Col. 2:18,23). Paul taught that Christians should strive for a balanced self-esteem that is able to minister to the needs of others (Rom. 12:3; 2 Cor. 10:7-13; Gal. 6:1-3; Phil. 2:3).

SELF-WILLED To do something arbitrarily without divine permission; to act on one's own decision rather than considering the needs of others and the purpose of God. Jacob rebuked Simeon and Levi for wanton, undisciplined actions (Gen. 49:6). Titus 1:7 teaches that a bishop cannot be self-willed, that is, stubborn and arrogant. Such activity is presumptuous and marks the fleshly person (2 Pet. 2:10).

SELVEDGE KJV translation of Hebrew term for the end, edge, border, or corner (Exod. 26:4; 36:11), apparently referring to the outermost curtain of the tabernacle.

SEM (Sĕm) KJV spelling of Shem, following the Greek (Luke 3:36).

SEMACHIAH (Sĕm á kī´ ah) or **SEMAKIAH** (NIV) Personal name meaning "Yahweh supports." Levitical gatekeeper (1 Chron. 26:7), described as a valiant man or warrior, possibly a title of honor for public service.

SEMEI (Sĕ´ mə ī) or **SEMEIN** (Sĕ´ mē ĭn) Greek form of Hebrew personal name, Shimei, among Jesus' ancestors (Luke 3:26).

SEMEN See *Discharge.*

SEMITE (Sĕm´ īt) A person who claims descent from Noah's son Shem (Gen. 5:32; 10:21-31) or, more precisely as a linguistic term, those people speaking one of the Semitic languages. The racial list of Genesis and the list of linguists do not always include the same people groups.

Genesis 10:21-31 lists five sons and 21 descendants/people derived from Shem. These people spread geographically from Lydia to Syria, to Assyria, to Persia. Armenia formed the northern boundary while the Red Sea and Persian Gulf formed the southern boundary. The Elamites, Assyrians, Lydians, Arameans, and numerous Arab tribes are said to have been descendants of Shem.

The place of origin for the Semites is difficult to determine. The Fertile Crescent contains evidence of Semitic influence at the dawn of civilization. One unproven theory is that they migrated from northern Arabia in waves of nomadic movements into the Fertile Crescent.

Three major divisions exist in the Semitic family of languages. East Semitic would include Akkadian used in ancient Babylon and Assyria. Northwest Semitic involves Hebrew, Aramaic, Syrian, Phoenician, Samaritan, Palmyrene, Nabatean, Canaanite, and Moabite. South Semitic includes Arabic, Sabean, Minean, and Ethiopic. Approximately 70 distinct forms of Semitic languages are known. Some have large libraries of literature while others remain entirely unwritten or only small collections of literature exist. See *Assyria; Babylon; Canaan; Languages of the Bible.* Steve Wyrick

SENAAH (Sə nā´ ah) Personal name of uncertain meaning, perhaps "thorny" or "hatred." Clan head or hometown of people who returned with Zerubbabel from Babylonian exile about 537 B.C. (Ezra 2:35).

SENATE (KJV, NASB, Acts 5:21). See *Sanhedrin.*

SENEH (Sē´ nĕh) Place-name meaning "shiny" or "slippery." A "cliff" (NIV) or "sharp column of rock" (REB) between Michmash and Geba (1 Sam. 14:4). See *Bozez.*

SENIR (Sē´ nĭr) Mountain name meaning "pointed." Amorite name for Mount Hermon (Deut. 3:9). Song of Songs 4:8 may indicate that Senir was a different peak than Hermon in the Anti-Lebanon range or that it indicated the entire range (cp. 1 Chron. 5:23). See *Hermon, Mount.*

SENNACHERIB (Sə năk´ ə rĭb) Assyrian royal name meaning "Sin (the god) has replaced my brother." King of Assyria (704–681 B.C.). See *Assyria; Israel, Land of.*

SENSUAL Activities or appearances characterized by or motivated by physical lust or luxury. God condemned Babylon for their sensual

Ahab's palace in Samaria. Sennacherib conquered Samaria in 722 B.C. (See page 1471.)

desires for pleasure and luxury (Isa. 47:8). It is part of the evil of the human heart (Mark 7:22; cp. Rom. 13:13), calling for repentance (2 Cor. 12:21). See *Lasciviousness; Sex, Biblical Teaching on; Wantonness.*

SENTRY Government official with responsibility for guarding a prison (Acts 5:23; 12:6) or possibly a captain over such a guard (Jer. 37:13).

SEORIM (Sē ō´ rĭm) Personal name, perhaps meaning "the shaggy-haired." Head of fourth division of priests appointed under David (1 Chron. 24:8).

SEPARATION Term used for period when a person is ritually unclean during menstruation (Lev. 12:2,5; 15:20,25-26) or for time of refraining from certain activities because of a vow (Num. 6). KJV term for water used to make one ritually pure or clean (Num. 19).

SEPHAR (Sē´ phăr) Place-name, perhaps meaning "numbering, census." Eastern border of sons of Joktan (Gen. 10:30). The site is apparently in southern Arabia, perhaps the coastal town of Tsaphar in Oman or Itsphar south of Hadramaut.

SEPHARAD (Sĕph´ à răd) Place-name of uncertain meaning. Place where Jerusalem's exiles lived. Obadiah promised them new possessions in the Negev (v. 20). The location is disputed: possibly a country south of Lake Urmia and north and west of Media, beyond the Babylonian Empire, but more likely the capital city of the Persian satrapy of Sepharad or Sardis in Lydia near the Aegean Sea. Early Syriac (Peshitta) and Aramaic (Targum) evidence points to Spain, but this is improbable.

SEPHARVAIM (Sĕph är vā´ ĭm) Racial name of foreign origin. Peoples the Assyrians conquered and resettled in Israel to replace the Israelites they deported in 722 B.C. (2 Kings 17:24). The name may represent the two Sippars on the Euphrates River or Shabarain in Syria. It may be the same as Sibraim in Syria (Ezek. 47:16), a border in Ezekiel's promised restoration of Israel. Despite Assyria's claims, Sepharvaim's gods could not compare with Yahweh, the God of Israel (2 Kings 19:12-13; cp. 17:31).

SEPHARVITES (Sĕph´ är vīts) Citizens of Sepharvaim (2 Kings 17:31).

SEPPHORIS Town in Galilee that served as the Roman capital of the region during Jesus' time. Four miles from Nazareth, Jesus probably knew it well and perhaps Jesus plied His trade as a carpenter there. Excavation has revealed Sepphoris to be a cosmopolitan Roman city with beautiful buildings, temples, an amphitheater, and other marks of sophistication. The character of Sepphoris contradicts the image of Galilee as a rural, unsophisticated environment and the image of Jesus as unsophisticated and ill at ease in an urban setting like Jerusalem. *Charles W. Draper*

SEPTUAGINT (Sĕp tū´ à gĭnt) Title meaning "the 70." Oldest Greek translation of the Hebrew OT. It also contains several apocryphal books. Most NT quotations of the OT are from the Septuagint. See *Apocrypha; Bible Texts and Versions.*

SEPULCHRE (Sĕ´ pəl kər) Tomb or grave (Gen. 23:6). It translates a Hebrew word that refers to a niche hewn out of a rock in which bodies were placed. In ancient Palestine sepulchres usually were carved out of the walls in existing caves. Families were buried together on the carved slabs of stone. After a body had decayed to the bones, the remains were placed in a hole farther back in the cave so that the next body could be placed in the sepulchre (tomb, HCSB). Jesus was buried in such a cave (Mark 15:46). See *Burial.*

SERAH (Sē´ rah) Personal name meaning "progress, develop, overflow" or "splendor, pride." Daughter of Asher (Gen. 46:17; Num. 26:46, where KJV reads Sarah).

Inside the Church of the Holy Sepulchre, traditional site of Jesus' burial (tomb of Joseph of Arimathea).

SERAIAH (Sə rī´ ah) Personal name meaning "Yah has proved Himself ruler." **1.** David's royal "scribe" and thus probably functioning as a modern secretary of state (2 Sam. 8:17). The Hebrew tradition has various spellings of the name: Sheva, Sheya (2 Sam. 20:25); Shisha (1 Kings 4:3) if this is not a Hebraic spelling of the Egyptian word for "scribe"; Shavsha (1 Chron. 18:16). **2.** Chief priest taken into Babylonian exile in 587 B.C. (2 Kings 25:18; 1 Chron. 16:14; Jer. 52:24). **3.** "Quiet prince" (KJV), "quartermaster" (REB, NASB, NRSV) that Zedekiah

A worshiper kneels at the Stone of Unction inside the Church of the Holy Sepulchre in Jerusalem.

(597–586 B.C.) sent to Babylon with instructions from himself and from Jeremiah (Jer. 51:59-64). **4.** Priest and father of Ezra (Ezra 7:1). **5.** Army officer who reported to Gedaliah when he was named governor immediately after the fall of Jerusalem in 586 B.C. (2 Kings 25:23; cp. Jer. 40:8). He may have been involved in rebellion Ishmael led. **6.** Leader in tribe of Judah (1 Chron. 4:13). **7.** Member of tribe of Simeon (1 Chron. 4:35). **8.** Leader of returning exiles under Zerubbabel (Ezra 2:2); apparently the same as Azariah (Neh. 7:7). **9.** Priestly family (Neh. 10:2; 12:12).

SERAPHIM (Sĕr´ á phĭm) Literally, "the burning ones," seraphim (a plural word) were winged serpents whose images decorated many of the thrones of the Egyptian pharaohs. In some cases, they wore the crowns of the Egyptian kingdoms and were thought to act as guardians over the king. Isaiah envisioned the seraphim as agents of God who prepared him to proclaim the Lord's message to Judah (Isa. 6:2). See *Angels*.

SERAPIS (Sə rā´ pəs) Also known as Sarapis, this Egyptian-Greek sun deity was worshiped first at Memphis along with the bull-god, Apis. Serapis was introduced to Egypt by the Greeks and was worshiped originally as a god of the underworld. The temple to him at Alexandria was the largest and best known among several. Serapis came to be revered also as a god of healing and fertility, and his worship spread throughout the Roman Empire via the trade routes.

SERED (Sē´ rĕd) Personal name meaning "baggage master." Clan leader in tribe of Zebulun (Gen. 46:14; Num. 26:26).

SEREDITE (Sē´ rə dīt) Member of clan of Sered in modern translations (Num. 26:26).

SERGIUS PAULUS (Sĕr´ gĭ us Pŏ´ lŭs) Personal name of proconsul of Cyprus when Paul visited the capital of Paphos on his first missionary journey (Acts 13:6-12). Sergius Paulus was under the influence of a sorcerer named Barjesus when Paul and Barnabas arrived. Sergius Paulus asked to hear the gospel that the two missionaries were preaching, but the sorcerer tried to keep him from the appointment. Paul spoke directly to the sorcerer, who became blinded

The bronze bust of the Egyptian-Greek god Serapis dates from the first century A.D. (See page 1473.)

temporarily, and Sergius Paulus, seeing what had happened, was converted to Christ.

SERJEANT KJV term for Roman "lictor," a constable or policeman (Acts 16:35). See *Prison, Prisoners.*

SERMON ON THE MOUNT Matthew 5–7 is commonly known as the Sermon on the Mount, the first of five major discourses by Jesus in the Gospel of Matthew. An astute exposition of the law and how it meshes with the new covenant in Christ, the sermon also offers a stinging indictment of Pharisaic legalism and cold, formal self-righteousness. Jesus stresses His demands for disciples and issues a call to demonstrate true righteousness, a righteousness of heart that the law cannot produce.

Interpretations Few passages of Scripture have such divergent interpretations. The sermon contains such lofty ethics and uncompromising demands that scholars have always differed greatly on its intent and application. No one can perfectly meet the strict demands of the sermon, and the disparity between expectations and behavior creates a perplexing problem. The following are some of the major approaches to the passage.

One common interpretation is the "interim ethic" view, that Jesus advocated such radical ethics in the sermon because He expected the consummated kingdom to begin immediately. The breaking in of that kingdom was so imminent that the disciples were to practice these rigid requirements for the brief period of time until it arrived. Because, however, the consummated kingdom did not arrive, the demands of the "interim" sermon must be dismissed. This view is not widely held.

Another approach, that of classic liberalism, was popular at the turn of the 1900s, and dismissed the need for personal redemption through the atoning work of Christ. Adherents said the sermon is essentially a roadmap to building a better, more progressive, society. Optimistic faith in the inherent goodness of mankind led them to replace the gospel with a secular philosophy. Major world conflicts and the continual unraveling of society have shown them to be wrong.

Another interpretation, one with more merit than the previous two, is the view of Lutheran orthodoxy. It holds that the sermon is an impossibly high ethic designed to show us the hopelessness of achieving on our own the righteousness that God demands. The sermon is really evangelistic, showing the need to turn to God for righteousness. The weakness is that it applies systematic theology to the sermon rather than interpreting it.

The "existential" approach views the sermon as a call to personal decision rather than as concrete ethical principles. The purpose of the sermon is to orient life to a heavenly perspective. These existentialists do not emphasize a literal, coming kingdom. Rather, the present life is compared with the ideal, "heavenly" conduct of what ought to be. The view fosters an attitude of self-reflection and openness to make the future better. This view has glaring weaknesses.

Another interpretation, most popular in North America, is the dispensational approach. In its classic form dispensationalism rigidly distinguished the period of law from the period of grace. It was the epitome of a "discontinuity" view of Scripture—that is, that God dealt with people differently during different periods. The extreme form of this system even held that people were saved by a different method in the OT than in the NT. It should be noted that dispensationalism has radically altered in recent years and reflects a more moderate theology. Dispensationalism still holds that when Jesus preached the sermon He was offering a millennial kingdom to the Jews. He offered to usher it in immediately after His death if the nation embraced Him. The Jews did not receive Him as their Messiah and King, and so the offer is temporarily rescinded. Rather than inaugurating the kingdom, Jesus resorted to "Plan B," as it were, and ushered in the present age of grace. The sermon, in this model, has no immediate relevance for the "church age" but is reserved for the still future millennial kingdom when Christ returns. Many conservative Christians hold this view, but it is not the best interpretation.

Though several of the approaches above contain truth, it seems best to interpret the sermon in the straightforward way in which Jesus preached it. "Straightforward" does not necessarily mean "literal." Some passages present real problems if taken literally rather than recognizing figurative language. Reading in a straightforward manner means recognizing the context and Jesus' intent. This discourse was to people who followed Him right then, people living in a sinful world waiting for the King to return and establish the kingdom. The sermon is the standard toward which disciples should strive. It describes the kind of life we should live because He owns us and we want to be like Him. He wants His followers to live a new kind of life, even though we will never fully attain this standard until He comes again.

Content The sermon opens with the beatitudes (Matt. 5:3-12) and then moves to describe the witness Christ's disciples are to bear in the world (5:13-16). Jesus' relationship to and interpretation of the law follows (5:17-48); then He enumerated some specific acts of righteousness—including the model prayer (6:1-18). The heart attitudes Jesus requires of His disciples comes next (6:19–7:12), and the sermon closes with a challenge to live as true disciples (7:13-27).

The introduction to the sermon (5:1-2) reveals that Jesus preached to a "mixed" congregation. Some were on the fringe, some were leaning toward Jesus, and others were committed to following Him. The sermon was addressed directly and primarily to His disciples, but the rest of the crowd heard it with much interest. They marveled at His teaching because,

unlike their teachers of the law, He spoke with great authority (Matt. 7:28-29). See *Beatitudes; Ethics; Jesus, Life and Ministry.*

Dale Ellenburg

SERPENT English translation of several biblical words for snakes. A symbol for evil and Satan. God gave Moses a sign showing His control of the feared serpents (Exod. 4:3; 7:9-10; cp. Job 26:13). Jesus accused the Pharisees of being as evil and deadly as serpents (Matt. 23:33). He gave the 70 power over serpents (Luke 10:19). See *Devil, Evil, Satan, Demonic; Reptiles.*

SERPENT CHARMERS See *Charm.*

SERPENT OF BRASS See *Bronze Serpent.*

SERPENT, BRONZE See *Bronze Serpent.*

SERUG (Sē´ rŭg) Personal name and place-name, perhaps meaning "offshoot, descendant." Ancestor of Abraham (Gen. 11:20), and thus of Jesus (Luke 3:35), and city 20 miles northwest of Harran mentioned in Assyrian texts.

SERVANT OF THE LORD Title Jesus took up from the OT, especially Isa. 40–55. The term "the servant of the Lord" ("My servant" or "His servant" where the pronouns refer to God) is applied to many leaders of God's people: to Moses over 30 times, to David over 70 times, and to Israel as a nation a number of times.

In Isaiah the idea is introduced almost incidentally. Chapter 41 pictures a great crisis, as a powerful army moves westward from Persia, conquering many nations and filling all with terror. In contrast, God told Israel not to fear. "But you, Israel, My servant, Jacob whom I have chosen, descendant of Abraham My friend, ... 'You are My servant, I have chosen you and not rejected you'" (Isa. 41:8-9b NASB). Israel had to be preserved because it was God's instrument to perform a task of worldwide importance.

Isaiah 42 gives a remarkable picture of the ideal Servant of the Lord and the great work that God intends Him to accomplish. He is to "bring forth judgment to the nations" (v. 1), "until He has established judgment in the earth," and the "coastlands will wait expectantly for His law" (v. 4). The tasks He is destined to accomplish are almost beyond belief. He is to bring God's justice to all the nations (vv. 1,4).

Almost more remarkable than the immensity of the task that the Servant must perform is the description of the way He is to do it. He will move forward with absolute confidence, but nothing indicates strenuous effort will be needed. He will have such an understanding of His overwhelming power that He can be absolutely gentle as He does His work (vv. 2-4) even toward those whose efforts have failed. This first part of chapter 42 pictures the ideal Servant—the goal for which Israel was to be preserved.

As an Israelite read this prediction, he would think: "How can Israel even think of performing this great task that God's Servant must do?" Soon the Lord Himself called attention to the inability of the natural Israelite to fulfill the picture of the ideal Servant. In verse 19 He says, "Who is blind but My servant, or so deaf as My messenger whom I send?" Israel had a responsibility to fulfill this ideal, but to do so was far beyond its power. Still, the Lord says: "You are My witnesses, and My servant whom I have chosen" (43:10; cp. 44:1-2,21).

Israel had responsibility to do the work of the Servant. Yet not all Israel could be meant, for some were blasphemers and idolaters. Could part of Israel be the real Servant? Or might it really point to One who must come out of Israel—One who could represent Israel in accomplishing the task? Matthew 12:17-21 quotes Isa. 42:1-4 as fulfilled in Jesus Christ.

Chapter 49 presents the work of the Servant in more detail. The Servant tells the "islands" and the "peoples from afar" that God called Him before His birth, even mentioning His name: Israel (Isa. 49:3). Verse 4 describes the godly in Israel who know what God wants but feel their own inadequacy and provides assurance that the work belongs to God, and He will bring it to pass. Verses 5 and 6 distinguish between the One who will fulfill the work of the Servant and the nation of Israel, to which this One belongs and which He represents. Not only is He to bring judgment to all the world—He is "to bring Jacob back to Him" (v. 5) and "to restore the preserved ones of Israel" (v. 6). He is to be "a light of the nations" so "that My salvation may reach to the end of the earth" (v. 6). In 50:4-10 we hear of the sufferings to which He will voluntarily submit.

All this leads up to the triumphal picture in Isa. 52:13–53:12, showing the sufferings of the Servant (52:14; 53:2-5,7-8,10), their vicarious and redemptive nature (52:15; 53:4-6,8,10-12; cp. 1 Pet. 1:1-2). Chapter 54 shows the outreach of the Servant's work, and chapter 55 gives the glorious call to receive the salvation won by the Servant's redemptive work, "without money and without cost" (v. 1).

After chapter 53 Isaiah never again used "servant" in the singular; rather he spoke of the blessings that the followers of the Servant will receive, calling them "the servants of the LORD" (54:17); "His servants" (56:6; 65:15; 66:14); and "My servants" (65:8-9,13-14).

The NT pictures Jesus as the Suffering Servant fulfilling the glorious descriptions of Isaiah. In refusing to let disciples reveal His true identity, Jesus was the pleasing Servant who did not strive or cry out (Matt. 12:14-21). In the resurrection and ascension, God glorified Jesus the Servant (Acts 3:13; cp. v. 26 where the same Greek word for "servant" appears though KJV translates "Son."). Gentile and Jewish leaders conspired to make Jesus, "Your holy Servant," suffer as God "had predestined to take place" (Acts 4:27-28 HCSB). This led the early church to pray that as God's servants they would speak with boldness and perform miracles through the name of "Your holy Servant Jesus" (Acts 4:29-30). Jesus saw His mission as that of the Servant (Luke 4:18-19; cp. 22:37) and symbolized it for His disciples, calling on them to serve one another and the world (John 13:4-17). See *Christ, Christology; Isaiah; Jesus Christ; Slave, Servant; Son of God.*   *Allan A. MacRae*

SERVICE Work done for other people or for God and the worship of God. Jacob worked for Laban seven years for each of his wives (Gen. 29:15-30). Service could be slave labor (Exod. 5:11; Lev. 25:39; 1 Kings 12:4; Isa. 14:3; cp. Lam. 1:3), farm work (1 Chron. 27:26), or daily labor on the job (Ps. 104:23). It could be service of earthly kingdoms (2 Chron. 12:8; cp. 1 Chron. 26:30), of God's place of worship (Exod. 30:16; cp. Num. 4:47; 1 Chron. 23:24), of God's ministers (Ezra 8:20), and of God (Josh. 22:27). Not only people do service; God also does service (Isa. 28:21). Even righteousness has a service (Isa. 32:17).

Service at its best is worship. This involves the service of temple vessels (1 Chron. 9:28), of worship actions (2 Chron. 35:10; cp. Exod. 12:25-26), of bringing offerings (Josh. 22:27), of priestly work (Num. 8:11). Interestingly, the OT never ascribes service to other gods.

The NT similarly speaks of forced service (Matt. 27:32), sacrificial living (Rom. 12:1; Phil. 2:17 with a play on words also indicating an offering), slave labor done for Christ's sake (Eph. 6:7; Col. 3:22; cp. Phil. 2:30), worship (Rom. 9:4; Heb. 12:28), offerings (Rom. 15:31; 2 Cor. 9:12), and personal ministry (Rom. 12:7; 1 Tim. 1:12; 2 Tim. 4:11). Hebrews 1:14 talks of the ministry of angels. Being in an army is also service (2 Tim. 2:4), and those who persecute Christ's followers think they do service for God (John 16:2).

SERVITUDE Hard labor done by servants or conscripted workers (Gen. 47:21; 2 Chron. 10:4; Neh. 5:18; Jer. 28:14; Lam. 1:3). The same Hebrew term is also translated "service."

SETH (Sĕth) Personal name meaning "He set or appointed" or "replacement." Third son of Adam and Eve, born after Cain murdered Abel (Gen. 4:25; 5:3). He was an ancestor of Jesus (Luke 3:38).

SETHUR (Sē´ thŭr) Personal name meaning "hidden." Spy representing tribe of Asher in scouting out the promised land (Num. 13:13).

SEVEN CHURCHES OF ASIA Original recipients of book of Revelation (Rev. 1:4). See *Asia Minor, Cities of.*

SEVEN WORDS FROM THE CROSS Statements that Jesus made during six agonizing hours of His crucifixion. Being made during the central act of redemption gives these words great weight and significance. No single Gospel records all seven sayings but fit the remarks into a commonly accepted order.

Jesus' first three remarks were made between 9:00 a.m. and noon (Mark 15:25). First, He asked forgiveness for those who crucified Him (Luke 23:34). On the cross Jesus made forgiveness possible not only for those involved in His crucifixion, but also for all who would put their trust in Him. Second, Jesus promised the penitent thief he would meet the Lord in paradise that very day (Luke 23:43), giving us insight into what happens following believers' deaths.

The Church of St. John in Pergamum, a city where one of the seven churches of Asia was located.

CHURCHES OF THE REVELATION

- • City
- ♣ ◦ Cities of the Seven Churches
- —— Major road

28 E

30 E

Heraclea

Byzantium
(Istanbul)

Bosporus

Chalcedon

MARMARA SEA

Nicomedia

Dardanelles

Cyzicus

BITHYNIA AND PONTUS

Imbros

Abydos

Nicaea

Prusa

Troas

MYSIA

Simav R.

40 N

Assos

Adramyttium

Dorylaeum

Lesbos

Mitylene

Cotiaeum

A S I A

Nacoleia

Pergamum

Ancyra

Appia

Thyatira

Hermus R.

Chios

Temenothyrae/
Flaviopolis

Smyrna

Sardis

Philadelphia

Sebaste

LYDIA

Tripolis

PHRYGIA

Ephesus

Hierapolis

Apamea

38 N

Tralles

Laodicea

Samos

Magnesia

Maeander R.

Colossae

PISIDIA

Ikaria

Samos

Alabanda

Trogyllium

Aphrodisias

Patmos

Heraclea

Miletus

John writes Revelation
encouraging Christians
to remain faithful.

CARIA

Cibyra

*Dalaman R.
(Indus R.)*

PAMPHYLIA

*Cestrus R.
(Aksu R.)*

Idyma

Cos

Halicarnassus

Cos

Perga

Cnidus

LYCIA

Rhodes

Rhodes

Xanthus

Patara

Myra

36 N

MEDITERRANEAN SEA

S

Third, Jesus made provision for the care of His mother by John (John 19:26-27).

Jesus' last four statements were spoken between noon and 3:00 p.m., the final hours before His death (Matt. 27:45; Mark 15:33; Luke 23:44). His fourth statement was a cry of isolation, quoting Ps. 22:1 in Aramaic (Matt. 27:46; Mark 15:34). This statement arose not so much from His own physical pain, but the anguish of solitarily taking upon Himself the sin of the world. His physical agony is expressed in the fifth statement, when Jesus acknowledged His thirst (John 19:28). After being given a sour drink, Jesus made His sixth statement, "It is finished" (John 19:30), a cry of victory, not defeat. Jesus was not finished, but redemption was complete. In His final words Jesus quoted Ps. 31:5 as He committed His spirit to God (Luke 23:46). See *Crucifixion.*   *Steve W. Lemke*

SEVEN, SEVENTH Number of completeness. See *Number Systems and Number Symbolism.*

SEVENTY WEEKS Time spoken of in Dan. 9:24-27, usually understood as 70 weeks of years or 490 years. The passage groups the weeks in three parts: seven weeks (49 years), 62 weeks (434 years), and one week (seven years). The 49 years are associated with rebuilding Jerusalem in "times of trouble" (v. 25 HCSB). The 434 years relate to the intervening time before a cutting off of the Anointed One (v. 26). The seven years are connected with the period of a covenant between a ruler and Jerusalem, which is violated in the middle of the seven years (v. 27).

The significance of the 70 weeks is variously understood. A historical approach relates these years to the period of history between the fall of Jerusalem and the restoration of the temple in 164 B.C. following the atrocities of Antiochus Epiphanes. See *Intertestamental History and Literature.*

A prophetic approach sees the reference to reach to the birth of Christ, His subsequent crucifixion (the cutting off of the Anointed One), and the destruction of Jerusalem by the Romans in A.D. 70. At that time sacrifices under the old covenant ceased. The same dating without reference to Jesus has been the usual Jewish understanding since Josephus. They focus on the destruction of the temple.

The dispensational approach makes the 70 weeks a prophetic framework for end time events, rather than a prophecy of what took place in the work of Christ at His first coming. The 69th week is seen as completed at Christ's death, while the 70th week is yet to be fulfilled at a future Great Tribulation period. The interval between the two is seen as a parenthesis in the prophetic pattern that contains the present church age, a period said not to be revealed in OT prophecy. See *Dispensation; Eschatology; Millennium, Tribulation.*   *Jerry W. Batson*

SEVENTY YEARS Prophetic and apocalyptic figure pointing to time of Israel's exile in Babylon and to the end of tribulation in Daniel's vision. Seventy years represented an even number of the normal human life span (Ps. 90:10). Isaiah 23:15 and the Babylonian Black Stone of Esarhaddon may indicate that 70 years was an expected time of punishment and desolation for a defeated city. Jeremiah predicted that Judah would serve Babylon 70 years (Jer. 25:11; cp. 29:10). Second Chronicles 36:21 saw the completion of the 70 years in the coming of Cyrus (538 B.C.). This apparently sees the years as from the first deporting of Judeans into Babylon (about 605 B.C.) until Cyrus came. Zechariah seems to have seen the 70 years ending in his own day with the rebuilding of the temple (Zech. 1:12). This would span the period from the destruction of the temple (586 B.C.) to the dedication in 516 B.C. Some interpreters see in the Chronicler's references to Sabbaths an indication of a second meaning for 70 years, that is, 70 Sabbatical Years (Lev. 25:1-7; 26:34-35) or 490 years. By this reckoning Israel had not kept the Sabbatical Year commandment since the period of the Judges, so God gave the land 70 consecutive Sabbatical Years during the exile. Daniel meditated on Jeremiah's prophecy (Dan. 9:2) and learned that 70 weeks of years were intended (v. 24). See *Sabbatical Year; Seventy Weeks.*

SEX, BIBLICAL TEACHING ON The Bible addresses human sexuality from a holistic perspective of God's intention and design. In contrast to both pagan sex rituals and modern obsession with sex, the Bible places sex within the total context of human nature, happiness, and holiness.

S

Gender and Relation God created human beings as male and female, both in His own image (Gen. 1:27). Thus, gender is not a mere biological accident or social construction. The contrast and complementarity between the man and the woman reveal that gender is part of the goodness of God's creation. Modern efforts to redefine or redesign gender are directly contrary to the Bible's affirmation of maleness and femaleness as proper distinctions. This pattern of distinction is affirmed and enforced by liturgical orders and restrictions on dress, hair length, etc. Any effort to confuse or deny gender differences is expressly forbidden and opposed by Scripture, especially as seen in OT legal codes.

Throughout the Bible a complementary pattern of relation between man and woman, particularly within the institution of marriage, is presented as the divine intention. Both are equal in dignity and status, but a pattern of male leadership in the home and in the church is enforced by both descriptive and prescriptive passages (1 Tim. 2:8–3:7; 1 Cor. 11:2-16; 14:34-38).

Sex as Gift and Responsibility The Bible places sex and sexual activity within the larger context of holiness and faithfulness. In this regard, the Bible presents an honest and often detailed explanation of God's design for sex and its place in human life and happiness.

First, the biblical writers affirm the goodness of sexuality as God's gift. The Song of Songs is an extended love poem with explicit erotic imagery and language. Sex is affirmed as a source of pleasure and shared intimacy between husband and wife.

Second, the gift of sexual activity is consistently located only within the context of the marital covenant. Joined to each other within this monogamous covenant, the man and the woman may be naked and not ashamed (Gen. 2:25). The consistent witness of the biblical writers is that sexual relations are limited to this covenant relationship. All forms of extramarital sexual activity are condemned, including premarital sex (fornication) and adultery (Exod. 20:14; Deut. 22:22; 1 Cor. 6:9-10). At the same time, the husband and wife are ordered to fulfill their marital duties to each other and not to refrain from sexual union (1 Cor. 7:2-5).

Third, though pleasure is one of the goods biblically associated with sexual union (Prov. 5:15-19), the Bible consistently links procreation with the marital act (Ps. 128:3). Sexual pleasure and procreation are linked in a healthy and natural approach that avoids the denial of either. Modern contraceptive technologies were unknown in the Bible, and the contemporary "contraceptive mentality" that champions sexual pleasure completely severed from procreation is foreign to the biblical worldview.

Fourth, the biblical writers address human sexuality honestly. Paul acknowledged the reality of sexual passions (1 Cor. 7:9) and admonished those who have not been given the gift of celibacy to marry, rather than to allow their passions to turn into sinful lust.

The reality of sexual brokenness is also addressed. The pain and shame of adultery, for example, are demonstrated in the account of David's sin with Bathsheba. Paul's horror in learning of sexual sin among the Corinthians occasioned some of his clearest teachings on sexuality and holiness.

Sex, Holiness, and Happiness The biblical writers affirm sexuality as a part of our embodied existence. As human beings we are sexual creatures, and as sexual creatures we are called to honor God with our bodies (1 Cor. 6:15-20). Within the context of the marital covenant, the husband and wife are free to express love for each other, experience pleasure, and join in the procreative act of sexual union. This is pleasing to God and is not to be a source of shame.

The biblical writers link holiness to happiness. True human happiness comes in the fulfillment of sexual holiness. The attempt to enjoy sexual happiness without holiness is the root of sexual deviance.

Sexual Deviance Just as the biblical writers present marital sex as holy and natural, all other forms of sexual activity are presented as condemned and sinful. In addition to adultery and fornication, the Bible expressly forbids homosexuality, bestiality, incest, prostitution, rape, pederasty, and all other forms of sexual deviance (Exod. 22:16-17,19; Lev. 18:6-18,22-23; Prov. 7:1-27; Rom. 1:26-27; 1 Cor. 5:1-13).

The Bible presents sexual deviance as intentional rejection of God's authority as Creator and Lord (Rom. 1:18-25). As Paul warns, those who practice such sins will not inherit the kingdom of God (1 Cor. 6:9-10). Both OT and NT writers warn that the people of God are to remain untainted and uncorrupted by such sins. Interestingly, the sexual practices of the various pagan nations described in the OT and the sexual mores of the Roman Empire of the first century are remarkably like the obsessions of our own day.

Sexuality is one of God's good gifts, and the source of much human happiness. At the same time, once expressed outside its intended context of marital fidelity, it can become one of the most destructive forces in human existence.

Marital sexual love is expressed in the intimacy of sexual union and the marital act of conjugal union is the source of both pleasure and procreation. Both are goods of the marital act and relationship that are to be welcomed and accepted with thankfulness. The biblical writers instruct that true sexual happiness is inextricably linked to sexual holiness as believers live their lives before God.   *R. Albert Mohler, Jr.*

SHAALABBIN (Shā á lăb´ bĭn) Place-name meaning "place of foxes." Town in tribal territory of Dan (Josh. 19:42); apparently the same as Shaalbim.

SHAALBIM (Shā ăl´ bĭm) Place-name meaning "place of foxes." Spelled and interpreted differently in different texts and early Greek versions. Amorite stronghold eventually controlled by Manasseh and Ephraim (Judg. 1:35). Part of Solomon's second district for supplying provisions for the royal household (1 Kings 4:9). Its location is probably modern Selbit seven miles southeast of Lydda and three miles northwest of Ajalon. David's military hero Eliahba came from Shaalbim (2 Sam. 23:32). See *Shaalabbin.*

SHAALBON (Shā´ ăl´ bŏn) RSV, NRSV, TEV, REB rendering of Shaalbonite, representing an alternative Hebrew spelling of Shaalbim.

SHAALBONITE (Shā ăl´ bō nīt) See *Shaalbon.*

SHAALIM (Shā´ á lĭm) Place-name, perhaps meaning "caves, cavities." Place where Saul sought his father's lost donkeys (1 Sam. 9:4). The place is sometimes equated with Shaalbim or the land of Shual.

SHAAPH (Shā´ ăph) Clan name meaning "balsam." Apparently two persons in Caleb's line, though some interpreters identify the two (1 Chron. 2:47,49). See *Madmannah.*

SHAARAIM (Shā á rā´ ĭm) Place-name meaning "double doors." **1.** City in tribal territory of Judah (Josh. 15:36). Place where David's soldiers pursued Philistine army (1 Sam. 17:52). Some would locate it at Khirbet esh-Sharia a mile northeast of Azekah. **2.** Town where tribe of Simeon lived (1 Chron. 4:31), but the parallel texts read Shilhim (Josh. 15:32) and Sharuhen (Josh. 19:6). Many scholars think Sharuhen is meant in Chronicles.

SHAASHGAZ (Shā ăsh´ găz) Hebrew transliteration of Persian name of uncertain meaning. Eunuch in charge of Xerxes's harem of which Esther became a member before she was chosen queen (Esther 2:14).

SHABBETHAI (Shăb´ bə thī) Personal name meaning "belonging to the Sabbath." Levite who explained the law to the people as Ezra read it (Neh. 8:7). He or a namesake opposed Ezra's plan of divorce for foreign wives (Ezra 10:15). He was in charge of "external business of the house of God" (Neh. 11:16 REB), either maintaining outward appearance of the temple or collecting the tithes.

SHACHIA (Shá kī´ á) Personal name meaning "Yahweh fenced in or protected." Clan leader in tribe of Benjamin (1 Chron. 8:10), following different manuscripts than modern translations which read Sachia. Many manuscripts and early versions read "Shabia."

SHACKLES See *Bond; Fetter.*

SHADDAI (Shă´ dī) Transliteration of Hebrew name for God, often translated "Almighty" following the earliest Greek translation. See *Almighty; God of the Fathers; Names of God.*

SHADES See *Sheol; Rephaim.*

SHADOW Dark image of an object created when the object interrupts rays of light. The Bible uses the term in both literal and figurative senses.

Old Testament The Hebrew *tsel* speaks of "shadow" as protection and as transitory, short-lived, and changing. The intensive heat, particularly in the summer, made shade and shadows important in Palestine. Travelers sought rest under a tree (Gen. 18:4; cp. Job 40:22) or in a house (Gen. 19:8). Especially at midday when shade virtually vanished, people looked for a shadow (Isa. 16:3; cp. Gen. 21:15; Jon. 4; Job

S

7:2). In the afternoon shadows lengthen (Jer. 6:4; cp. Neh. 13:19 NIV). In the evening cool, shadows disappear (Song 2:17). In the desert wilderness the traveler found little hope for shade but looked for shade or shadow from hills (Judg. 9:36), large rocks (Isa. 32:2), a cave (Exod. 33: 22; 1 Kings 19:9), or a cloud (Isa. 25:5).

Powerful people offer the shadow of protection and security (Song 2:3). So does a king (Lam. 4:20; Ezek. 31:6). Still, Israel knew the false claims of kings to provide such protection (Judg. 9:15; cp. Isa. 30:2; Ezek. 31). Biblical writers looked to the Messiah for needed shade or shadow (Isa. 32:2; Ezek. 17:23). God was the ultimate shadow of protection for His people (Pss. 36:7; 91:1; 121:5; Isa. 25:4; 49:2; 51:16).

Human life itself is only a brief shadow (Job 8:9; 14:2; Pss. 102:11; 144:4; Eccles. 6:12; 8:13).

New Testament The Greek *skia* can refer to a literal shadow (Mark 4:32; Acts 5:15). More often it refers to death or to an indication of something to come, a foreshadowing. References to death come from OT prophecy—Matt. 4:16 and Luke 1:79, picking up Isa. 9:2. Dietary laws and religious festivals were only a shadow preparing Israel for the reality made known in Christ (Col. 2:17; Heb. 8:5; 10:1). James used a related Greek word to say that God is not a fleeting, changing shadow (1:17)   *Trent C. Butler*

SHADRACH (Shăd´ răk) Babylonian name meaning "circuit of the sun." One of Daniel's three friends taken to Babylon during the exile (Dan. 1:6-7). His Hebrew name was Hananiah. The three were cast into a fiery furnace for refusing to worship a graven image set up by King Nebuchadnezzar. The Lord miraculously delivered them, and they were given places of honor in the kingdom (Dan. 3:30). See *Abednego; Daniel; Meshach.*

SHAGE (Shā gə) or **SHAGEE** (Shā´ gē) Father of one of David's military heroes (1 Chron. 11:34). The parallel text in 2 Sam. 23 has two similar names: verse 11, Shammah the son of Agee; verse 33, Shammah the Hararite. Shage may represent a combination of the two Hebrew words Shammah and Agee.

SHAHAR (Shā´ här) Transliteration of Hebrew word meaning "dawn." Part of title of Ps. 22,

translated by most modern translations. NASB transliterates "Hashshahar," including the Hebrew definite article. See *Aijeleth Shahar.*

SHAHARAIM (Shā hȧ rā´ ĭm) Personal name meaning "double dawns." Benjaminite who divorced his wives and lived in Moab (1 Chron. 8:8).

SHAHAZIMAH (Shā hȧ zī´ mah) Place-name meaning "double peak." Town or mountain marking tribal boundary of Issachar (Josh. 19:22). Its location is not known. Some have suggested it is a combination of two town names: Shahaz and Yammah.

SHAHAZUMAH (Shā hȧ zū´ mah) Modern translation spelling of Shahazimah following the written Hebrew text rather than the notes of the earliest Hebrew scribes.

SHALEM (Shā´ ləm) Place-name meaning "peace, safety," according to KJV translation (Gen. 33:18; cp. NIV text note). Modern translations read "safely."

SHALIM (Shā´ lĭm) (KJV) See *Shaalim.*

SHALISHA (Shăl´ ĭ shä) or **SHALISHAH** Place-name meaning "the third." Territory where Saul sought his father's lost donkeys (1 Sam. 9:4); probably the same as Baal-shalishah. Its location has recently been questioned. See *Baal-shalishah.*

SHALLECHETH (Shăl´ lə kěth) or **SHAL-LEKETH** (NIV) Place-name of uncertain meaning, sometimes thought on basis of earliest translations to have resulted from scribe's transposition of first two letters and thus to have read originally "chamber." Jerusalem gate mentioned only in 1 Chron. 26:16.

SHALLUM (Shăl´ lŭm) Personal name meaning "replacer" or "the replaced." **1.** King of Israel (752 B.C.). He assassinated Zechariah and was, in turn, assassinated by Menahem a month later (2 Kings 15:10-15). **2.** See *Jehoahaz 3.* **3.** Husband of Huldah (2 Kings 22:14). **4.** A gatekeeper (1 Chron. 9:17,19,31; cp. Ezra 2:42; Neh. 7:45). This may be the same as Shelemiah (1 Chron. 26:14) and Meshelemiah (1 Chron. 9:21; 26:1-14), since these names are closely related in Hebrew. **5.** A chief priest (1 Chron. 6:13; Ezra

7:2). **6.** Descendant of Judah (1 Chron. 2:40). **7.** Jeremiah's uncle (Jer. 32:7). **8.** Temple door-keeper (Jer. 35:4). **9.** Descendant of Simeon (1 Chron. 4:25). **10.** Descendant of Naphtali (1 Chron. 7:13). **11.** Father of Jehizkiah (2 Chron. 28:12). **12.** Porter who agreed to divorce his foreign wife (Ezra 10:24). **13.** Israelite with a foreign wife (Ezra 10:42). **14.** Supervisor of half of Jerusalem who helped Nehemiah rebuild the walls (Neh. 3:12).

SHALLUN (Shăl´ lŭn) Personal name, perhaps meaning "peaceful, carefree." Man who helped Nehemiah by repairing the Fountain Gate (Neh. 3:15). NRSV, NASB, TEV follow some early version evidence and read "Shallum."

SHALMAI (Shăl´ mā ī) Personal name meaning "coat." Manuscripts have several variant spellings. Servant (Nethanim) in temple (Ezra 2:46; Neh. 7:48).

SHALMAN (Shăl´ măn) Personal name meaning "complete, peace." Mysterious figure in Hos. 10:14, sometimes identified by scholars as an abbreviation of Shalmaneser V of Assyria and sometimes as a ruler of Moab listed by Tiglath-pileser III among kings paying him tribute. His name became synonymous with violence and ruthlessness.

SHALMANESER (Shăl mà nē´ zĕr) Personal name meaning "Shalmanu (the god) is the highest ranking one." **1.** Assyrian king who ruled 1274–1245 B.C. Records of his military exploits set a precedent which succeeding kings followed. **2.** Shalmaneser III ruled Assyria 858–824 B.C. He fought a group of small kingdoms, including Israel, in the battle of Qarqar in 853 B.C. Despite claiming victory, Shalmaneser proceeded no farther. **3.** Shalmaneser V ruled Assyria 726–722 B.C. He completed the attack on Samaria begun by his predecessor, Tiglath-pileser III. In 722 Israel fell to Shalmaneser (2 Kings 17:6), thus ending the Northern Kingdom forever. See *Assyria; Israel, Land of.*

SHAMA (Shā´ mà) Personal name meaning "he has heard." Military hero under David (1 Chron. 11:44).

SHAMARIAH (Shăm à rī´ ah) KJV spelling of Shemariah (2 Chron. 11:19).

SHAME AND HONOR Honor and shame were values that shaped everyday life in biblical times. Honor, the primary measure of social

Replica of the Black Obelisk of Shalmaneser III (858–824 B.C.). The obelisk was found in 1846 during excavations at Nimrud, an ancient site south of Baghdad, Iraq.

S

status, was based upon ascribed honor and acquired honor. Inherited or ascribed honor was social standing due to being part of a social unit, principally the family. Those born to rulers and leaders were held in high esteem due to family honor. Jewish preoccupation with genealogies ensured inherited honor was secure. Matthew (Matt. 1:1-17) and Luke (Luke 3:23-38) give genealogies for Jesus that highlight the high status claimed for Him. In Matthew, Jesus' pedigree is right both as to Jewishness (direct link to Abraham) and His right to be king of the Jews (descended from David). Luke traces Jesus' lineage through Adam to God, claiming Jesus' right to be Savior of all of mankind.

Acquired honor was gained through meritorious deeds or public performance. Family social position provided the honor base from which males launched out with hope of increasing family and personal honor. The public forum provided challenges for gaining or losing honor. A challenge might show the superiority of one person or group over another. A challenge could be ignored if not worthy of response due to social distance between the parties, but a true honor challenge required response. The party recognized as winning gained honor and the other lost honor or social standing. For example, when the Pharisees and Herodians observed Jesus to see if He would heal the man with the withered hand (Mark 3:1-6), an honor challenge took place. If Jesus violated Sabbath law, He would lose honor. If He did not heal the man, He also would lose honor. The trap looked perfect. In response to this unethical challenge, Jesus clarified the Sabbath's intent so He could lawfully heal the man. When the trap failed, they decided to collaborate to destroy Jesus and His rising social status (which came at their expense).

Constant competition in public for honor infected even religion. In both Testaments the tendency to use religion for gaining personal honor based upon a show of piety is denounced. In Matt. 6:1-18 Jesus decried misuse of religious acts (almsgiving, prayer, and fasting) for gaining personal honor.

Shame was not simply the opposite of honor, both positive and negative shame existed. Shame could be handled positively by knowing how to keep matters out of public awareness. For example, a woman could bear shame well by remaining covered in public and by avoiding male dominated arenas. Shame could also designate dishonor or loss of honor. When people claimed an undeserved place of honor, shame resulted (Luke 14:7-11).

Perhaps the most vivid honor/shame text is Phil. 2:5-11. Jesus had unquestionable inherited, ascribed honor; yet He gave it all up and took the most humble of all honor bases (a slave) and died the most shaming of all deaths, crucifixion. However, God gave Him the highest of all honor positions and a name above all names on the honor scale, causing all to bow before Him. The honor code is thus defined by God instead of men.

Women especially bore shame and were expected to do so in a positive manner. Women were also seen as threats to honor. An immoral woman tainted the honor of the entire family, and so women generally were kept away from things tending to dishonorable behavior. The veiling of women related to this concern.

"Shamelessness" described one who refused to abide by honor and shame codes. Such people did not respect social norms nor care about public opinion of their social status. In Luke 18:1-8 the unjust judge is a classic example of a shameless person, one who "didn't fear God or respect man" (HCSB). In the OT the "fool" is a "shameless" person who likewise neither feared God or respected social wisdom and norms.

Bill Warren

SHAMED (Shā´ mĕd) Personal name meaning "destroyed, ruin." KJV, REB reading following Hebrew of Benjaminite's name (1 Chron. 8:12). Other modern translations read "Shemed." Many commentators follow early manuscripts and versions in reading "Shemer."

SHAMER (Shā´ mĕr) Variant spelling of Shomer or Shemer (1 Chron. 6:46; 7:34).

SHAMGAR (Shăm´ gär) Hurrian name meaning "Shimig (the god) has given." A mysterious warrior who slew 600 Philistines with an oxgoad, a long metal-tipped pole (Judg. 3:31). His name is Hurrian, but whether that was his lineage is uncertain. In the song of Deborah (Judg. 5), Shamgar (the "son of Anath") is praised for clearing the highways of robbers, making travel once again possible. See *Anath; Judges, Book of.*

SHAMHUTH (Shăm´ hŭth) Head of fifth division of David's army, serving during the fifth month (1 Chron. 27:8). Many commentators consider the name a scribal combination of Shammah (2 Sam. 23:25) and Shammoth (1 Chron. 11:27).

SHAMIR (Shā´ mīr) Personal name and place-name meaning "thorn" or "diamond." **1.** Levite (1 Chron. 24:24), written Shamur in some manuscripts. **2.** Town in hill country of Judah assigned to tribe of Judah (Josh. 15:48). Located either at modern el-Bireh near Khirbet Somera northeast of en-Rimmon or Khirbet es-Sumara about 12 miles west-southwest of Hebron. **3.** Home of Tola, the judge from the tribe of Issachar, in Mount Ephraim (Judg. 10:1). Located possibly at Khirbet es-Sumara about seven miles south of Shechem. Some commentators would equate it with Samaria.

SHAMLAI (Shăm´ lī) Written form of personal name in Hebrew text of Ezra 2:46. Scribal note has Shalmai and is followed by many translations. See *Shalmai*.

SHAMMA (Shăm´ mà) Personal name of uncertain meaning. Leader of clan of Asher (1 Chron. 7:37).

SHAMMAH (Shăm´ ah) Personal name of uncertain meaning, perhaps "frightful" or "astonishing" or "he heard." **1.** Edomite tribe descended from Esau (Gen. 36:13). **2.** Older brother of David (1 Sam. 16:9; 17:13) and father of Jonadab (2 Sam. 13:3,32) and Jonathan (2 Sam. 21:21) if the similar Hebrew spellings in 2 Samuel point to the same person mentioned in 1 Samuel. See *Shimea; Shimei.* **3.** David's military hero (2 Sam. 23:11,25; spelled Shammoth in 1 Chron. 11:27). **4.** Another of David's military heroes (2 Sam. 23:33) or, with a slight change of the Hebrew text suggested by many commentators, the father of Jonathan, the military hero (REB, NRSV, NIV). **5.** See *Shamhuth.*

SHAMMAI (Shăm´ mā ī) Abbreviated form of personal name, perhaps meaning "He heard." **1.** Member of tribe of Judah and clan of Jerahmeel (1 Chron. 2:28,32). **2.** Descendant of Caleb (1 Chron. 2:44). **3.** Another descendant of Caleb (1 Chron. 4:17).

SHAMMOTH (Shăm´ ŏth) Variant spelling (1 Chron. 11:27) for Shammah (2 Sam. 23:25).

SHAMMUA (Shăm´ mū à) or **SHAMMUAH** Personal name meaning "one who was heard." **1.** Spy representing tribe of Reuben (Num. 13:4). **2.** Son of David (2 Sam. 5:14; spelled "Shimea" in 1 Chron. 3:5). **3.** Father of a Levite (Neh. 11:17; spelled "Shemaiah" in 1 Chron. 9:16). **4.** Priest in days of Joiakim about 600 B.C. (Neh. 12:18).

SHAMSHERAI (Shăm´ shə rī) Personal name of uncertain meaning; some commentators regard it as a combination of Shimshai and Shimri. Benjaminite living in Jerusalem (1 Chron. 8:26).

SHAPHAM (Shā´ phăm) Personal name of unknown meaning. Leader of tribe of Gad (1 Chron. 5:12).

SHAPHAN (Shā´ phăn) Personal name meaning "coney." Prominent court official during King Josiah's reign in Judah (2 Kings 22). Shaphan served as scribe and treasurer. During Josiah's religious reforms and refurbishment of the temple, Shaphan delivered the newfound book of the law (probably Deuteronomy) from Hilkiah the priest to the king's palace. He also was sent to Huldah the prophetess to confer concerning the book (22:14). Shaphan and his sons befriended Jeremiah on several occasions. See *Ahikam; Elasah; Gedeliah; Jaazaniah.*

SHAPHAT (Shā´ phăt) Personal name meaning "He has established justice." **1.** Spy from tribe of Simeon (Num. 13:5). **2.** Father of Elisha (2 Kings 6:31). **3.** Descendant of David and Zerubbabel (1 Chron. 3:22). **4.** Supervisor of David's cattle herds (1 Chron. 27:29). **5.** Member of tribe of Gad (1 Chron. 5:12).

SHAPHER (Shā´ phēr) KJV for Mount Shepher. Place-name, perhaps meaning "lovely." Stop on Israel's wilderness journey (Num. 33:23), somewhere on east of the Gulf of Aqaba.

SHAPHIR (Shā´ phīr) Modern translations' spelling of Saphir.

SHARAI (Shā´ rī) Personal name, perhaps meaning "he loosed or redeemed." Man with a foreign wife (Ezra 10:40).

SHARAIM (Shà·rā´ ĭm) (KJV, Josh. 15:36) See *Shaaraim.*

S

SHARAR (Shā´ rår) Personal name, perhaps meaning "he is healthy." See *Sacar*.

SHARD Pottery fragment found in archaeological excavations and used for dating. See *Archaeology and Biblical Study; Chronology of the Biblical Period; Potsherd; Pottery; Writing*.

SHAREZER (Shá rē´ zĕr) Abbreviated form of Akkadian name meaning "may (god's name) protect the king." **1.** Son of Sennacherib who helped murder his father (2 Kings 19:37). Assyrian records report the death as occurring in 681 B.C. See *Assyria*. **2.** Name open to several interpretations in Zech. 7:2. The full name may be Bethel-sharezer, meaning "may the god Bethel protect the king" (REB). Sharezer may be a man sent to the house of God (Hb. *beth-el*) to pray (KJV). The town of Bethel may have sent Sharezer to pray (NASB, NIV, NRSV, TEV). The name probably indicates the person was born in Babylonian exile. He may have come with his questions from Babylon and have come as a representative of the people of Bethel.

SHARON, PLAIN OF (Shâr´ ón) Geographical name meaning "flat land" or "wetlands." **1.** Coastal plain which runs from near modern Tel Aviv to just south of Mount Carmel (about 50 miles). The area had abundant marshes, forests, and sand dunes, but few settlements during biblical days. Because of its fertility and low risk of flooding, the plain was used more by migrant herdsmen than settled farmers. Isaiah 35:2 parallels Sharon with Lebanon, which was known for its trees. Isaiah 65:10 speaks of the area as an excellent pasture for flocks, symbolic of the peace that God would one day grant to His people. See *Palestine*. **2.** Area of uncertain location east of the Jordan inhabited by the tribe of Gad (1 Chron. 5:16) and mentioned by King Mesha of Moab. See *Mesha*.

SHARONITE (Shâr´ ó nīt) Person who lived in Plain of Sharon.

SHARUHEN (Shá rū´ hĕn) Place-name, perhaps meaning "free pasture land." Town assigned to tribe of Simeon (Josh. 19:6) located in the territory of Judah (Josh. 15:32, spelling is Shilhim; 1 Chron. 4:31 spelling is Shaaraim; Egyptian spelling is apparently Shurahuna). The Hyksos withdrew there after the Egyptians defeated

them about 1540 B.C. The traditional location is Tell el-Farah, but recent study has favored Tell el-Ajjul about four miles south of Gaza, though this has often been identified as Beth Eglayim. Excavations have shown this to have been a large, well-fortified, wealthy city. See *Hyksos*.

SHASHAI (Shā´ shī) Personal name of uncertain meaning. Man married to a foreign wife (Ezra 10:40).

SHASHAK (Shā´ shăk) Personal name of uncertain meaning, perhaps of Egyptian origin. Leader of tribe of Benjamin living in Jerusalem (1 Chron. 8:14,25).

SHAUL (Shā´ ūl) Personal name meaning "asked of." **1.** Transliteration of Hebrew name of King Saul. **2.** Grandson of Jacob and son of Simeon with a Canaanite mother (Gen. 46:10). **3.** Early king of Edom from Rehoboth (Gen. 36:37; 1 Chron. 1:48). **4.** Levite (1 Chron. 6:24).

SHAULITE (Shā´ ūl īt) Member of clan of tribe of Simeon descended from Shaul (Num. 26:13).

SHAVEH (Shā´ vĕh) Place-name meaning "valley," "plain," or "ruler." Place where the king of Sodom met Abraham on the latter's return from defeating the coalition of kings (Gen. 14:17). It is also called the king's valley or dale. There Absalom raised a monument to himself (2 Sam. 18:18). The Genesis Apocryphon locates it in Beth-hakkerem, which is two and a half miles south of Jerusalem where the Kidron and Hinnom Valleys join. It has also been located north, east, and west of Jerusalem.

SHAVEH-KIRIATHAIM (Shā vĕh-kĭr ĭ á thā´ ĭm) Place-name meaning "waste land of Kiriathaim." This valley is the high plain above the Arnon River. There Chedorlaomer and his coalition of kings defeated the Emim (Gen. 14:5). See *Chedorlaomer; Emim; Kiriathaim*.

SHAVING See *Razors*.

SHAVSHA (Shăv´ shá) Spelling of Shisha (1 Kings 4:3) in 1 Chron. 18:16. See *Shisha*.

SHEAF Harvested grain bound together into a bundle. English translation of three Hebrew terms. Joseph's dream featured sheaves still in

An ancient shaving razor with a goat's leg handle.

the field (Gen. 37:7). Laws of sacrifice called for the first harvested sheaves to be sacrificed (Lev. 23:10-15). Some sheaves were for gleaners (Deut. 24:19; Ruth 2:7). The prophets used sheaves as figures of judgment (Jer. 9:22; Amos 2:13; Mic. 4:12; Zech. 12:6). See *Agriculture; Gleaning; Grain; Harvest; Sacrifice and Offering.*

SHEAL (Shē´ ăl) Personal name meaning "ask." Many commentators change the Hebrew text slightly to read "Yishal" or "Jishal," meaning "he asks." Israelite who married a foreign wife (Ezra 10:29).

SHEALTIEL (Shə ăl´ tĭ ĕl) Personal name meaning "I have asked of God." Father of Zerubbabel, the governor of Jerusalem under the Persian regime following the exile (Ezra 3:2, Neh. 12:1; Hag. 1:1). First Chronicles 3:17 makes him Zerubbabel's uncle. This could involve the practice of Levirate marriage (Deut. 25:5-10). He was included in the genealogy of Christ (Matt. 1:12; Luke 3:27).

SHEARIAH (Shē á rī´ ah) Personal name, perhaps meaning "Yah has honored" or "Yah knows." Descendant of Saul (1 Chron. 8:38).

SHEARING HOUSE KJV translation (2 Kings 10:12,14) of what many modern translators take as place-name. REB reads, "shepherds' shelter." See *Beth-eked.*

SHEAR-JASHUB (Shē är-jā´ shŭb) Symbolic personal name meaning "a remnant shall return." First son of the Prophet Isaiah, born probably around 737 B.C., near the beginning of his father's ministry in Jerusalem. Isaiah apparently named him (and his brother, Mahershalalhashbaz) as an embodiment of prophecy, that Judah would fall, but a remnant would survive.

On one occasion Shear-jashub accompanied his father on a trip to assure King Ahaz that the alliance of Syria and Israel would not be allowed to harm Judah (Isa. 7:3-7). See *Isaiah.*

SHEATH Protective holder for sword attached to a belt. See *Arms and Armor; Sword.*

SHEBA (Shē´ bá) **1.** See *Sabean.* **2.** Personal name meaning "fullness, completeness." Name of a Benjaminite who led a revolt against David (2 Sam. 20) and of a member of the tribe of Gad (1 Chron. 5:13). **3.** Personal name spelled in Hebrew like the nation of 1. above. The name of a son of Joktan (Gen. 10:28) and of Jokshan (Gen. 25:3).

SHEBA, QUEEN OF Ruler of Sabeans who visited Solomon (1 Kings 10) to test his wisdom, learn of his God, and enhance trade relations. See *Sabean.*

SHEBAH (Shē´ bah) Place-name meaning "overflow" or "oath." Name Isaac gave Beersheba (Gen. 26:33). See *Beer-sheba.*

SHEBAM (Shē´ băm) (KJV) See *Sebam.*

SHEBANIAH (Shĕb á nī´ ah) Personal name appearing in short and long forms in Hebrew meaning "Yahweh came near." A clan of Levites in which the name was used for several individuals (1 Chron. 15:24; Neh. 9:4-5; 10:4,10,12; 12:14).

SHEBARIM (Shĕb´ á rĭm) Place-name meaning "the breaking points." Place with symbolic name and uncertain location near Ai (Josh. 7:5), translated as "stone quarries" (NIV; cp. REB). Commentators have suggested "breaks" or "ravines."

SHEBAT (Shē´ băt) See *Sebat.*

SHEBER (Shē´ bēr) Personal name, perhaps meaning "foolish one," "lion," or "fracture." Son of Caleb (1 Chron. 2:48).

SHEBNA (Shĕb´ ná) or **SHEBNAH** Personal name meaning "He came near." Royal scribe (2 Kings 18:18,37; 19:2; Isa. 36:3,22; 37:2) and "comptroller of the household" (Isa. 22:15 REB) under King Hezekiah about 715 B.C. See *Scribe.*

S

SHEBUEL (Shĕ bū´ əl) Personal name meaning "return, O God." **1.** Grandson of Moses and head of a clan of Levites (1 Chron. 23:16; 26:24; sometimes equated with Shubael of 1 Chron. 24:20). **2.** Levite, son of Heman (1 Chron. 25:4); apparently the same as Shubael (1 Chron. 25:20).

SHECANIAH (Shĕk á nī´ ah) Personal name meaning "Yahweh has taken up dwelling." Both long and short forms appear in the Hebrew text. **1.** Clan leader (Ezra 8:3). **2.** Leader of another clan (Ezra 8:5). **3.** Israelite with a foreign wife (Ezra 10:2). **4.** Father of man who helped Nehemiah repair Jerusalem wall and keeper of the east gate (Neh. 3:29). **5.** Father-in-law of Nehemiah's enemy, Tobiah (Neh. 6:18). **6.** Priest who returned to Jerusalem with Zerubbabel about 537 B.C. (Neh. 12:3). **7.** Descendant of David and Zerubbabel (1 Chron. 3:21). **8.** Leader of priestly division under David (1 Chron. 24:11; may be equated with founder of priestly clan of Neh. 10:4; 12:14 spelling is Shebaniah). **9.** Priest in time of Hezekiah (2 Chron. 31: 15).

SHECHANIAH (Shĕk á nī´ ah) Abbreviated Hebrew form of personal name, Shecaniah.

SHECHEM (Shĕk´ əm) Personal name and place-name meaning "shoulder, back." District and city in the hill country of Ephraim in north central Palestine. The first capital of the Northern Kingdom of Israel, the city was built mainly on the slope, or shoulder, of Mount Ebal. Situated where main highways and ancient trade routes converged, Shechem was an important city long before the Israelites occupied Canaan.

The city makes its earliest appearance in biblical history in connection with Abram's arrival in the land (Gen. 12:6-7). When Jacob returned from Paddan-aram, he settled down at Shechem and purchased land from the sons of Hamor (33:18-19). In Gen. 33–34 Shechem was the name of the city and also of the prince of the city. While Jacob was at Shechem, the unfortunate incident of Dinah occurred. Simeon and Levi, her full brothers, destroyed the city (Gen. 34). Later, the brothers of Joseph were herding Jacob's flock at Shechem when Joseph was sent to check on their welfare. Joseph was buried in the plot of ground that his father Jacob had purchased here (Josh. 24:32).

As the Israelites conquered Canaan, they turned unexpectedly to Shechem. Joshua built an altar on Mount Ebal and led the people in its building, renewing their commitment to the law of Moses (Josh. 8:30-35; cp. Deut. 27:12-13). Shechem lay in the tribal territory of Ephraim near their border with Manasseh (Josh. 17:7). It was a city of refuge (Josh. 20:7) and a Levitical city (21:21). Joshua led Israel to renew its covenant with God there (Josh. 24:1-17). Gideon's son Abimelech fought the leaders of Shechem (Judg. 8:31–9:49).

Rehoboam, successor to King Solomon, went to Shechem to be crowned king over all Israel (1 Kings 12:1). Later, when the nation divided into two kingdoms, Shechem became the first capital of the Northern Kingdom of Israel (1 Kings 12:25). Samaria eventually became the permanent political capital of the Northern Kingdom, but Shechem retained its religious importance. It apparently was a sanctuary for worship of God in Hosea's time about 750 B.C. (6:9).

The name "Shechem" occurs in historical records and other sources outside Palestine. It is mentioned as a city captured by Senusert III of Egypt (before 1800 B.C.) and appears in the Egyptian cursing texts of about the same time. "The mountain of Shechem" is referred to in a satirical letter of the 19th Dynasty of Egypt. Shechem also figures in the Amarna Letters; its ruler, Lab'ayu, and his sons were accused of acting against Egypt, though the ruler protested that he was absolutely loyal to the pharaoh.

At Shechem (sometimes identified with Sychar), Jesus visited with the Samaritan woman at Jacob's well (John 4). The Samaritans had built their temple on Mount Gerizim, where they practiced their form of religion. See *Cities of Refuge; Levitical Cities.*   *Rich Murrell*

SHECHEMITE (Shĕk´ əm īt) Resident of or native of Shechem.

SHEDEUR (Shĕd´ ĕ ŭr) Dialectical spelling (pronunciation) of a personal name meaning "Shaddai is light." Father of a leader of the tribe of Reuben (Num. 1:5; 2:10; 7:30,35; 10:18).

SHEEP Stocky mammal, larger than a goat but has no beard. A prominent animal in the sacrificial system of Israel, sheep are first mentioned in Gen. 4:2 where Abel is identified as a keeper of sheep. They were the primary wealth of pastoral people.

The sheep found in the Bible usually are the broad-tailed variety. The tail, weighing as much as 15 pounds, was sometimes offered as a sacrifice (Exod. 29:22; Lev. 3:9). Of this species only the male had horns; females of other species did have horns. Rams' horns were used as trumpets (shophars) (Josh. 6:4) and as oil containers (1 Sam. 16:1). Sheep were also a source for food and clothing. The Bible contains hundreds of references to sheep. Often, they are referred to as small cattle. These animals were important to the economy of ancient Israel and her neighbors.

Seven different Hebrew words and expressions are translated as sheep. *Tso'n* is a collective term for small domesticated animals, particularly sheep and goats. *Seh* is an individual member of the collective *tso'n*, one sheep or goat. *Kebes* is a young ram, as is the apparently related word *keseb*. *Kibsah* and *kisbah* are young lambs. *Tsoneh* is either a variant spelling of or the feminine of *tso'n*. The male sheep or ram is *ayil*, which served as a symbol of authority and rule (Exod. 15:15; Ezek. 17:13; 31:11).

Sheep symbolized people without leadership and unity, scattered like sheep without a shepherd (1 Kings 22:17), innocent people not deserving of punishment (1 Chron. 21:17), helpless, facing slaughter (Ps. 44:11,22) and death (Ps. 49:14). God's people are His sheep enjoying His protection and listening to His voice (Pss. 78:52; 95:7; 100:3; cp. Ps. 23). Sheep represent economic prosperity (Ps. 144:13) or poverty (Isa. 7:21). Straying sheep illustrate human sin (Isa. 53:6), but the silent lamb at the slaughter prepares the way for Christ's sacrifice (Isa. 53:7). Ezekiel 34 uses the life of sheep and shepherds to picture God's relationship with His people and their rulers. Human value is contrasted to that of sheep (Matt. 12:12). The shepherd's separating his *tso'n* into sheep and goats illustrates the final judgment (Matt. 25). The search for one lost sheep depicts God's love for His people (Luke 15). Jesus contrasted His care for His flock with other religious leaders, especially the Pharisees who behaved as thieves and robbers (John 10). His commission to Peter was to take care of the sheep (John 21). See *Agriculture; Cattle; Economic Life; Lamb of God; Shepherd.*

Trent C. Butler

SHEEP BREEDER See *Herdsman.*

SHEEP GATE Entrance in northeastern corner of Jerusalem's city wall (Neh. 3:1,32; 12:39). Apparently sheep for temple sacrifice entered the city through it. It was close to the Pool of Bethesda (John 5:2). See *Gates of Jerusalem and the Temple.*

SHEEP MARKET KJV translation of Greek term meaning "pertaining to sheep" and referring to the Sheep Gate (John 5:2). See *Sheep Gate.*

SHEEPCOTE KJV translation of Hebrew term meaning "home." Modern translations usually use "pasture" as the sheep's home (2 Sam. 7:8; 1 Chron. 17:7). In 1 Sam. 24:3 the Hebrew term refers to an enclosure and is usually translated "sheepfolds" or "sheep pens."

SHEEPFOLD English translation of several Hebrew terms and one Greek term referring to a place where sheep were kept. The basic meanings range from "stone wall," to "place of confinement," and "home." Related words appearing in Gen. 49:14; Judg. 5:16; Ezek. 40:43; and Ps. 68:13 are variously interpreted from the context and translated: "saddlebags," "double-pronged hooks," and "campfires" (NIV), "sheepfolds" and "pegs" (NRSV), "sheepfolds" and "double hooks" (NASB), "cattle pens," "sheepfolds," and "rims" (REB), "burdens," "sheepfolds," "pots," and "hooks" (KJV), "saddlebags," "sheep," "sheep pens," and "ledges" (TEV). The latest Hebrew dictionary completed in 2000 but published in parts over two decades gives differing meanings for the two related terms: "saddlebaskets" and "sheepfolds," separating the Ezekiel passage out as a meaning unto itself.

Asian sheep grazing on the site of what was once the ancient city of Laodicea.

SHEEPSHEARERS Persons who cut wool from the sheep. Evidently, these are not professionals but the owners of the sheep (Gen. 31:19) or persons working for the owner (Gen. 38:12). The Hebrew does not distinguish between "sheepshearers" and "sheepshearing," so that both translations are possible in several passages. The time of shearing sheep was a festive time of parties and inviting friends (1 Sam. 25; 2 Sam. 13). The word for shearing sheep was also used for cutting human hair (Jer. 7:29; Mic. 1:16).

SHEERAH (Shē´ ə rah) Personal name, perhaps meaning "blood kin." Female member of tribe of Ephraim who established the two cities of Beth-horon and Uzzen-sheerah (1 Chron. 7:24).

SHEET English translation of Greek word meaning "a linen cloth" and usually used for ships' sails. Such a cloth held all the clean and unclean animals in the vision that taught Peter that God loved and offered salvation to people who were not Jews (Acts 10:11; 11:5).

SHEHARIAH (Shē hȧ rī´ ah) Personal name meaning "Yah is the dawn." Leader of tribe of Benjamin who lived in Jerusalem (1 Chron. 8:26).

SHEKEL (Shĕk´ ĕl) Hebrew weight of about four tenths of an ounce. This became the name of a silver coin with that weight. See *Coins; Weights and Measures*.

SHEKINAH (Shĕ kī´ nah) Transliteration of Hebrew word not found in the Bible but used in many of the Jewish writings to speak of God's presence. The term means "that which dwells," and is implied throughout the Bible whenever it refers to God's nearness either in a person, object, or His glory. It is often used in combination with glory to speak of the presence of God's shekinah glory. See *Glory*.

SHELAH (Shē´ lah) Personal name meaning "please" or "be still, rest." Son of Judah and original ancestor of clan in tribe of Judah (Gen. 10:25; 46:12; Num. 26:20; 1 Chron. 2:3; 4:21). At times Shelah is the transliteration for the Hebrew name otherwise transliterated Salah. See *Sala or Salah*.

SHELANITE (Shē´ lȧn īt) Member of clan of Shelah.

SHELEMIAH (Shĕ lĕ mī´ ah) Personal name appearing in longer and shorter Hebrew forms meaning "Yahweh restored, replaced, repaid." **1.** Father of a messenger of King Zedekiah about 590 B.C. (Jer. 37:3). **2.** Father of the captain of the guard who arrested Jeremiah (Jer. 37:13). **3.** Ancestor of an official of King Jehoiakim (Jer. 36:14). **4.** Court official whom King Jehoiakim (609–597 B.C.) ordered to arrest Jeremiah and from whom God hid Jeremiah (Jer. 36:26). **5.** Temple gatekeeper (1 Chron. 26:14) and apparently called Meshelemiah in 1 Chron. 26:1,9. **6. and 7.** Two Jews who married foreign women (Ezra 10:39,41). **8.** Father of man who helped Nehemiah rebuild Jerusalem's wall (Neh. 3:30). **9.** Priest whom Nehemiah made treasurer (Neh. 13:13).

SHELEPH (Shē´ lĕph) Tribal name, perhaps meaning "remove, take out of." Son of Joktan and original ancestor of Yemenite tribes living near Aden (Gen. 10:26).

SHELESH (Shē´ lĕsh) Personal name, perhaps meaning "triplet." Leader of a clan in the tribe of Asher (1 Chron. 7:35).

SHELOMI (Shə lō´ mī) Personal name meaning "my peace." Father of a leader of tribe of Asher (Num. 34:27).

SHELOMITH (Shə lō´ mĭth) Feminine form of Shelomoth. **1.** Head of a family which returned from Babylonian exile with Ezra about 458 B.C. (Ezra 8:10). **2.** Son of King Rehoboam (2 Chron. 11:20). **3.** Cousin of Moses and head of a Levitical group (1 Chron. 23:18); apparently the same as Shelomoth (1 Chron. 24:22). **4.** Priest over the cultic treasury under David (1 Chron. 26:25-28, Hebrew scribes have interchanged Shelomith and Shelomoth). **5.** Woman of tribe of Dan whose son cursed the divine name, thus being guilty of blasphemy. The Israelites followed God's orders and stoned him to death (Lev. 24:10-23). **6.** Daughter of Zerubbabel (1 Chron. 3:19).

SHELOMOTH (Shə lō´ mŏth) Personal name meaning "peaces." Levitical leader under David (1 Chron. 23:9; Hb. scribal note has "Shelomith"). See *Shelomith*.

SHELUMIEL (Shə lū´ mĭ ĕl) Personal name meaning "God is my wholeness or health." Leader in tribe of Simeon (Num. 1:6; 2:12; 7:36,41; 10:19).

SHEM (Shĕm) Personal name meaning "name." Noah's oldest son and original ancestor of Semitic peoples including Israel (Gen. 5:32; 6:10; 7:13; 9:18-27; 10:1,21-22,31; 11:10-11). He carried God's blessing (9:26-27). Through his line came Abraham and the covenant of blessing.

SHEMA (Shə mä´) Transliteration of Hebrew imperative meaning "hear" (Deut. 6:4) and applied to 6:4-9 as the basic statement of the Jewish law. The Shema became for the people of God a confession of faith by which they acknowledged the one true God and His commandments for them. Later worship practice combined Deut. 6:4-9; 11:13-21; Num. 15:37-41 into the larger Shema as the summary of Jewish confession. When Jesus was asked about the "greatest commandment," He answered by quoting the Shema (Mark 12:29).

SHEMA (Shē´ mä) Personal name meaning "a hearing" and place-name, perhaps meaning "hyena." **1.** Son of Hebron and grandson of Caleb (1 Chron. 2:43). **2.** Member and clan ancestor of tribe of Reuben (1 Chron. 5:8); possibly the same as Shemaiah (1 Chron. 5:4). **3.** Benjaminite clan leader in Aijalon (1 Chron. 8:13); apparently the same as Shimhi (1 Chron. 8:21). **4.** Man who helped Ezra teach the law (Neh. 8:4). **5.** Town in tribal territory of Judah (Josh. 15:26) and apparently occupied by Simeon (Josh. 19:2; Sheba may be a scribe's repetition of previous word instead of similar sounding Shema). It may be the same as Jeshua (Neh. 11:26). See *Jeshua 9.*

SHEMAAH (Shə mä´ ah) Personal name, perhaps meaning "a hearing." Father of Benjaminite military leaders who deserted Saul to join David at Ziklag (1 Chron. 12:3).

SHEMAIAH (Shə mä´ yä) Personal name meaning "Yahweh heard," with both long and short forms in Hebrew. **1.** Prophet in the days of Rehoboam whose message from God prevented war between Israel and Judah about 930 B.C. (1 Kings 12:22). His preaching humbled Rehoboam and the leaders of Judah, leading God not to permit Shishak of Egypt to destroy Jerusalem (2 Chron. 12). **2.** False prophet among Babylonian exiles who opposed Jeremiah's word (Jer. 29:24-32). **3.** Descendant of David and Zerubbabel (1 Chron. 3:22). **4.** Member of tribe of Simeon (1 Chron. 4:37). **5.** Member of tribe of Reuben (1 Chron. 5:4); perhaps identical with Shema 2. (1 Chron. 5:8). **6.** A Levite (Neh. 11:15; cp. 1 Chron. 9:14). **7.** A Levite (1 Chron. 9:16) probably identical with Shammua 3. (Neh. 11:17). **8.** Head of one of the six Levitical families under David (1 Chron. 15:8,11). **9.** Levitical scribe who recorded the priestly divisions under David (1 Chron. 24:6). **10.** Head of an important family of gatekeepers (1 Chron. 24:4-8). **11.** Levite in time of Hezekiah about 715 B.C. (2 Chron. 29:14); possibly identical with the Levite of 2 Chron. 31:15. **12.** Head of a family that returned with Ezra from Babylonian exile about 458 B.C. (Ezra 8:13). He may be the same man Ezra sent to get more ministers for the temple (Ezra 8:16). **13.** Priest married to a foreign woman (Ezra 10:21). **14.** Man married to a foreign woman (Ezra 10:31). **15.** Keeper of east gate who helped Nehemiah repair Jerusalem's wall about 445 B.C. (Neh. 3:29). **16.** Prophet Tobiah and Sanballat hired against Nehemiah (Neh. 6:10-12). **17.** Original ancestor of a priestly family (Neh. 10:8; 12:6,18). **18.** Leader of Judah who participated with Nehemiah in dedicating the rebuilt walls of Jerusalem (Neh. 12:34). **19.** Priest who helped Nehemiah dedicate the walls (Neh. 12:42). **20.** Priest whose grandson helped Nehemiah dedicate the walls (Neh. 12:35). **21.** Levitical musician who helped Nehemiah dedicate the walls (Neh. 12:36). **22.** Father of the Prophet Urijah (Jer. 26:20). **23.** Father of an official at Jehoikim's court about 600 B.C. (Jer. 36:12). **24.** Levite in days of Jehoshaphat (873–848 B.C.) who taught God's law to the people (2 Chron. 17:8). **25.** Levite in days of Josiah about 621 B.C. (2 Chron. 35:9).

SHEMARIAH (Shĕm à rī´ ah) Personal name in longer and shorter Hebrew forms meaning "Yahweh protected." **1.** Benjaminite who deserted Saul to join David's army at Ziklag (1 Chron. 12:5). **2.** Son of King Rehoboam (2 Chron. 11:19). **3. and 4.** Men with foreign wives under Ezra (Ezra 10:32,41).

S

SHEMEBER (Shĕm ē´ bēr) Royal name meaning "powerful name." King of Zeboiim who rebelled against Chedorlaomer, leading to Abraham's rescue mission of Lot (Gen. 14:2). The Genesis Apocryphon and Samaritan Pentateuch read his name as Shemiabad, "the name is lost." See *Zeboiim*.

SHEMED (Shē´ mĕd) Personal name meaning "destruction." Benjaminite credited with building or rebuilding Ono and Lod (1 Chron. 8:12). See *Shamed*.

SHEMER (Shē´ mēr) Personal name meaning "protection, preservation." See *Shamed*. **1.** Modern translations' spelling of Shamer, the father of a temple musician under David (1 Chron. 6:46). **2.** Head of clan of tribe of Asher (1 Chron. 7:34) with variant spelling Shomer (v. 32). **3.** Original owner of the mount of Samaria for whom Samaria was named (1 Kings 16:24). See *Samaria*.

SHEMIDA (Shə mī´ dà) or **SHEMIDAH** Personal name meaning "the Name has known" or "the Name troubles Himself for." Clan head among the Gileadites in tribe of Manasseh (Num. 26:32; cp. Josh. 17:2; 1 Chron. 7:19). The Samaritan Ostraca lists Shemida as a territorial name in territory of Manasseh.

SHEMIDAITE (Shə mī´ dà īt) Member of clan of Shemida.

SHEMINITH (Shĕm´ ə nǐth) Musical direction meaning "the eighth" used in titles of Pss. 6; 12; and 1 Chron. 15:21. It may mean on an eight-stringed instrument, on the eighth string of an instrument, on a deeper octave than the Alamoth (1 Chron. 15:20), for the eighth and concluding rite of the fall New Year festival, or it may be referring to the tuning of the instrument or the scale of the melody.

SHEMIRAMOTH (Shə mǐr´ à mŏth) Personal name of uncertain meaning. **1.** Temple Levitical musician in David's time (1 Chron. 15:18,20; 16:5). **2.** Levite under King Jehoshaphat (873–848 B.C.) who taught the law (2 Chron. 17:8).

SHEMUEL (Shĕm´ ū ĕl) Personal name meaning "Sumu is god," "the name is God," "God is

exalted," or "Son of God." **1.** Precise transliteration of Hebrew for Samuel. See *Samuel*. **2.** Leader of tribe of Simeon (Num. 34:20). **3.** Clan chief in tribe of Issachar (1 Chron. 7:2).

SHEN (Shān) Place-name meaning "the tooth." Locality used to locate Eben-ezer (1 Sam. 7:12), translated and interpreted variously since the earliest translations. It may refer to a prominent hill or mountain shaped like a tooth. Early translations read it as "Jeshanah" (REB, NRSV), but that appears to be too far east for the context. Some early translators read "Beth-shan." The exact location is debated and uncertain.

SHENAZAR (Shə nā´ zər) or **SHENAZZAR** Babylonian personal name meaning "Sin (a god) protects" or "may Sin protect." Son of King Jehoiachin (1 Chron. 3:18). He is often identified with Sheshbazzar as an alternate transliteration of a Babylonian name, but this has been denied recently. See *Sheshbazzar*.

SHENIR (Shē´ nǐr) (KJV, Deut. 3:9; Song 4:8) See *Senir*.

SHEOL (Shē´ ōl) Place of the dead, or more specifically, the place of the unrighteous dead according to the Hebrew Bible. It is one of a constellation of words and phrases that designate death, the dead, and the destiny of those who have passed beyond this life. Scripture speaks of God as the One who brings about a man's death (Job 30:23). Some of the patriarchs are said to have gone to their fathers (Gen. 15:15) or rested with their fathers (Deut. 31:16) at death. Old Testament persons were reminded that they were dust and would return to dust at death (Gen. 3:19; Eccles. 3:20).

The origins of the word *she'ol* are unknown, though some have linked it to a similarly named Akkadian deity of the underworld. Whether this is the case or not, biblical usage has no connection with Akkadian mythology. In a number of texts persons are spoken of as descending to Sheol or of going into a pit (Ps. 88:6,10; Amos 9:2). This likely indicates that the Hebrews saw Sheol as something beneath their feet. The dead, of course, were buried in graves or tombs, often in family ossuaries, so the language concerning a realm of the dead beneath the earth is easily understood. That is not to say that the OT writers simply borrowed their view from surrounding peoples. Though many other ancient Near Eastern cultures professed belief in some kind of underworld, the OT understanding is unique both in the language it employs and in the content of its teaching. It does not imply that the Hebrews believed in a three-decked universe, with gods above, demons under the ground, and humans on the surface of the earth. It is likely that they used language in a metonymic fashion, that is, where a word is substituted for the reality to which it points. It is not likely that they believed there existed some set of deep underground caverns in which the departed dead dwelled as denizens of some nether kingdom.

Sheol occurs 21 times in "psalmodic" type literature (Pss. 6:5; 9:17; 16:10; 18:5; 30:13; 31:17; 49:14-15; 55:15; 86:13; 88:3; 89:48; 116:3; 139:8; 141:7; 1 Sam. 2:6; 2 Sam. 22:6; Isa. 38:10,18; Jon. 2:2), 20 times in "reflective" literature (Job 7:9; 11:8; 14:13; 17:13,16; 21:13; 24:19; 26:6; Prov. 1:12; 5:5; 7:27; 9:18; 15:11,24; 23:14; 27:20; 30:16), 17 times in prophetic literature (Isa. 5:14; 7:11; 14:9,11,15; 28:15,18; 57:9; Ezek. 31:15-17; 32:21,27; Hos. 13:14; Amos 9:2; Hab. 2:5), and 8 times in narrative literature (Gen. 37:35; 42:38; 44:29,31; Num. 16:30,33; 1 Kings 2:6,9). From this list it seems clear that the word was used primarily in poetic contexts (whether prophecy, psalmody, or wisdom) and in speeches about death. It was a word that indicated a serious engagement with the reality of death, mortality, and the way one's life impacted one's destiny.

The Hebrew word is translated in various ways. The KJV often translated it as "hell," presumably because it is "in the earth," and because the wicked are the general inhabitants. But this is surely a bad translation, since hell as the "lake of fire" is no one's dwelling place until final judgment (Rev. 20:14). In other places the KJV translates the word as "the grave" or "the pit." Recent translations often leave the word untranslated, and simply transliterate the Hebrew, "Sheol." That is probably the best approach, as the word sometimes demands a literal interpretation and sometimes a metaphorical one.

Sheol is a place that is set over against the work of Yahweh. Those who dwell there are separated from Yahweh spiritually and morally (Isa. 38:18; Ps. 6:5-6), though not physically, since there can be no real escape from God, even in Sheol (Ps. 139:8; Amos 9:2). It is a place

in which one is captive (Pss. 18:5; 116:3). It is a place of darkness (Ps. 88:6) and of silence (Ps. 115:17). It is also a place of demotion from rank and privilege. In Isa. 14 the prophet speaks of one who was a king but who has now been brought down to Sheol where others say to him, "Even you have been made weak as we, you have become like us. Your pomp and the music of your harps have been brought down to Sheol. Maggots are spread out as your bed beneath you and worms for your covering" (Isa. 14:10-11 NASB). Sheol is the leveler of men, especially those who exalted themselves in this life rather than humbling themselves before the true King (see also Ezek. 32).

Sheol is the destiny of those who end their lives in impenitence. The foolish rich will find themselves in Sheol (Ps. 49:14), as will the immoral (Prov. 5:5) and the ungodly (Isa. 5:14). The Egyptians will be there (Ezek. 31:15-17), as will some specific persons, such as Korah (Num. 16:30). Some texts seem to indicate that even the righteous will find themselves in Sheol. So Job laments that he is headed for that dread destination (Job 17:13-16), as do Jacob (Gen. 37:35) and Hezekiah (Isa. 38:10). If one carefully examines these texts, though, one will find that these persons were in the depth of sorrowful or tragic circumstances. In these texts Sheol takes on more of a metaphorical meaning, as if a modern person were to say, "I have been deep in a pit these past days."

Two texts (Ps. 89:48-49 and Eccles. 9:7-10) seem on the surface to teach that all persons will end up in Sheol. But the former passage really teaches that humanity under sinful judgment is destined for Sheol. The latter text is in the section of Ecclesiastes where Solomon is lamenting the absurdity of all life, but of course, that is not his final word (see 12:14). It is simply inconceivable that Sheol is the abode of the righteous dead for several reasons. The fact that in Sheol there is no praise of Yahweh (Pss. 6:5; 115:17) indicates that it is not the abode of the righteous. It is a place of pain and distress (Ps. 116:3), of weakness (Isa. 14:10), helplessness (Ps. 88:4), hopelessness (Isa. 38:10), and destruction (Isa. 38:17).

The righteous had a different expectation. Though the OT does not speak with the clarity of the NT on the subject of life after death, it does speak in a complementary fashion. One scholar noted that the OT is like a room richly

S

furnished but dimly lit. Many OT figures expected that after death they would remain in fellowship with God and not simply be consigned to darkness and emptiness. "For You will not abandon me to Sheol; ... in Your right hand are eternal pleasures" (Ps. 16:10-11 HCSB). "Only goodness and faithful love will pursue me all the days of my life, and I will dwell in the house of the LORD (Beth Yahweh) as long as I live" (Ps. 23:6). Concerning the foolish rich, "Like sheep they are headed for Sheol; Death will shepherd them" (Ps. 49:14), but not so the righteous: "But God will redeem my life from the power of Sheol, for He will take me" (Ps. 49:15 HCSB). Other texts speak of the expectation of resurrection of the righteous unto eternal life (Deut. 32:39; Dan. 12:2; Isa. 26:19).

Sheol in the OT is roughly analogous to hades in the NT. Jesus spoke of the rich man as being tormented in hades, while Lazarus was in the bosom of Abraham, dwelling in joy and peace (Luke 16:19-31). Jesus told His disciples that the gates of hades would not prevail against His church (Matt. 16:18). Hades here again is that realm set over against God and His righteous kingdom—the dwelling place of the unrighteous and their "king." Then we find at the end that death and hades are cast into the lake of fire (Rev. 20:14). The final destiny of those who dwell in Sheol/hades is eternal separation from God's righteousness and love. As they sought to be separate from Him in life, so will they be in death and in eternity.   *Chad Brand*

SHEPHAM (Shē´ phăm) Place-name of uncertain meaning and location in northeastern Transjordan forming the northeastern border of the promised land (Num. 34:10).

SHEPHATIAH (Shĕph á tī´ ah) Personal name in longer and shorter Hebrew forms meaning "Yahweh has created justice." **1.** David's fifth son (2 Sam. 3:4). **2.** King Zedekiah's (597–586 B.C.) official (Jer. 38:1). **3.** A Benjaminite (1 Chron. 9:8). **4.** Head of a family of exiles who returned with Ezra about 458 B.C. (Ezra 2:4; 8:8; Neh. 7:9). **5.** Ancestor of family included among "Solomon's servants," that is royal officials, perhaps with temple responsibilities (Ezra 2:57; Neh. 7:59). **6.** Member of tribe of Judah (Neh. 11:4). **7.** Benjaminite who deserted Saul to join David's army at Ziklag (1 Chron. 12:5). **8.** Leader of Simeon's tribe under David

(1 Chron. 27:16). **9.** Son of King Jehoshaphat (2 Chron. 21:2).

SHEPHELAH (Shĕ´ phə läh) Transliteration of Hebrew geographical term referring to the Judean foothills between the Philistine coastal plain and the highlands of Judah farther inland. It served as a battleground for Israel and Philistia during the period of the judges and early monarchy. Joshua 15:33-41 lists about 30 villages and towns located in the region. See *Palestine.*

SHEPHER, MOUNT (Shē´ phēr) Place-name, perhaps meaning "beauty." Stop on Israel's wilderness journey whose location is not known (Num. 33:23).

SHEPHERD Keeper of sheep. The first keeper of sheep was Adam's son Abel (Gen. 4:2). Shepherding was the chief occupation of the Israelites in the early days of the patriarchs: Abraham (Gen. 12:16); Rachel (Gen. 29:9); Jacob (Gen. 30:31-40); Moses (Exod. 3:1).

As cultivation of crops increased, shepherding fell from favor and was assigned to younger sons, hirelings, and slaves (cp. David in 1 Sam. 16:11-13). Farmers, such as in Egypt, even hated shepherds (Gen. 46:34).

The Bible mentions shepherds and shepherding over 200 times. However, the Hebrew word for shepherding is often translated "feeding." Shepherds led sheep to pasture and water (Ps. 23) and protected them from wild animals (1 Sam. 17:34-35). Shepherds guarded their flocks at night whether in the open (Luke 2:8) or in sheepfolds (Zeph. 2:6) where they counted the sheep as they entered (Jer. 33:13). They took care of the sheep and even carried weak lambs in their arms (Isa. 40:11).

"Shepherd" came to designate not only persons who herded sheep but also kings (2 Sam. 5:2) and God Himself (Ps. 23; Isa. 40:11). Later prophets referred to Israel's leaders as shepherds (Jer. 23; Ezek. 34).

In Bible times the sheep cared for by shepherds represented wealth. They provided food (1 Sam. 14:32), milk to drink (Isa. 7:21-22), wool for clothing (Job 31:20), hides for rough clothing (Matt. 7:15), and leather for tents (Exod. 26:14). Furthermore, sheep were major offerings in the sacrificial system (Exod. 20:24). They were offered as burnt offerings (Lev. 1:10), sin offerings (Lev. 4:32), guilt offerings (Lev. 5:15), and peace offerings (Lev. 22:21).

The NT mentions shepherds 16 times. They were among the first to visit Jesus at His birth (Luke 2:8-20). Some NT references used a shepherd and the sheep to illustrate Christ's relationship to His followers who referred to Him as "our Lord Jesus—the great Shepherd of the sheep" (Heb. 13:20 HCSB). Jesus spoke of Himself as "the good shepherd" who knew His sheep and would lay down His life for them (John 10:7-18). Jesus commissioned Peter to feed His sheep (John 21). Paul likened the church and its leaders to a flock with shepherds (Acts 20:28). The Latin word transliterated "pastor" means shepherd.   *Elmer Gray*

SHEPHERD'S BAG See *Bag 4.*

SHEPHI (Shē´ phī) (1 Chron. 1:40) or **SHEPHO** (Shē´ phō) Tribal name, perhaps meaning "male sheep, ram." Edomite tribe or clan (Gen. 36:23).

SHEPHUPHAM (Shə phū´ phăm) Personal name of uncertain meaning. Leader of Benjaminite clan according to Hebrew text (Num. 26:39) but probably a scribe repeated a letter in Shupham (KJV, REB, NIV).

SHEPHUPHAN (Shə phū´ phăn) Personal name of uncertain meaning. Member of tribe of Benjamin (1 Chron. 8:5). Some commentators read "Shupham" on basis of early translations.

SHERAH (Shē´ rah) (REB, KJV) See *Sheerah.*

SHERD Alternate spelling for "shard" often used by archaeologists. See *Shard.*

SHEREBIAH (Shĕr ə bī´ ah) Personal name, perhaps meaning "Yah gave a new generation," "Yah understands," or "Yah made it hot." Ancestor of a family of Levites (Ezra 8:18,24; Neh. 8:7; 9:4-5; 10:12; 12:8,24). He had responsibility for the temple gold that Ezra took back to Jerusalem from exile and helped Ezra teach the people the law.

SHERESH (Shē´ rĕsh) Personal name meaning "sprout" or "sly, clever." Descendant of Manasseh (1 Chron. 7:16) as well as the name of a city in the kingdom of Ugarit.

SHEREZER (Shĕ rē´ zĕr) (KJV, Zech. 7:2) See *Sharezer.*

SHESHACH (Shē´ shăk) Code word Jeremiah used to indicate Babylon (25:26; 51:41). The code uses the first word of the alphabet for the last, the second for the next to last, and so on. In English *a* would stand for *z*, *b* for *y*, and so on.

SHESHAI (Shē´ shī) Probably a Hurrian name of uncertain meaning. A man or clan living near Hebron descended from the Anakim (Num. 13:22) and driven out by Caleb (Josh. 15:14) and the tribe of Judah (Judg. 1:10). They may have entered Palestine with the Sea Peoples to whom the Philistines are related. See *Anak, Anakim.*

SHESHAK (Shē´ shăk) (NASB, Jer. 51:41) See *Sheshach.*

SHESHAN (Shē´ shăn) Personal name of uncertain meaning. Member of clan of Jerahmeel from tribe of Judah (1 Chron. 2:31-35).

SHESHBAZZAR (Shĕsh băz´ zăr) Babylonian name probably meaning "may Shamash (sun god) protect the father." Jewish leader who accompanied the first group of exiles from Babylon to Jerusalem in 538 B.C. (Ezra 1:8). King Cyrus of Persia apparently appointed Sheshbazzar governor of restored Judah and supplied his company of people with provisions and many of the treasures that the Babylonians had taken from Jerusalem. He attempted to rebuild the temple (Ezra 5:16) but got no farther than the foundation when he was replaced by Zerubbabel. His genealogy is not clear, but some believe the Shenazar of 1 Chron. 3:17 may be Sheshbazzar. If so, he was a son of Jehoiachin and uncle of Zerubbabel.

SHETH (Shĕth) Personal and tribal name of uncertain meaning. Moabite clan whose destruction Balaam prophesied (Num. 24:17). The Hebrew spelling is the same as Seth (Gen. 4:25). Egyptian and Babylonian texts point to a people called Sutu, seminomads in the Syrian and Arabian Deserts. Rather than a proper name, some commentators think the translation should be "sons of tumult."

S

SHETHAR (Shē' thär) Persian name of uncertain meaning. Advisor of King Ahasuerus of Persia, an expert in the "law and custom" of Persia and possibly in astrology (Esther 1:13-14 NRSV).

SHETHAR-BOZENAI (Shē thär-bŏz' ə nī) or **SHETHAR-BOZNAI** (KJV) Persian name, perhaps meaning "Mithra is deliverer." Persian provincial official who questioned Zerubbabel's right to begin rebuilding the temple (Ezra 5:3,6) but responded to King Darius' answer by helping the Jews build (Ezra 6:13). The name appears in the Elephantine papyri.

SHETHITES (Shĕth' īts) NRSV reading of "sons of Sheth" (Num. 24:17). See *Sheth.*

SHEVA (Shē' và) Personal name meaning "similarity." **1.** Scribe for David (2 Sam. 20:25), perhaps the transliteration of an Egyptian title meaning "writer of letters." The name is Seraiah in 2 Sam. 8:17; Shavsha in 1 Chron. 18:16. See *Scribe.* **2.** Descendant of Caleb and original ancestor of a clan (1 Chron. 2:49).

SHEWBREAD Sacred loaf made probably of barley or wheat that was set before the Lord as a continual sacrifice (Exod. 25:30). The old bread was then eaten by the priests (Lev. 24:5-9). David requested the bread for his hungry men as they fled from King Saul (1 Sam. 21:4-6). Jesus used this account to illustrate His teaching on the Sabbath, that the day was made to benefit people (Mark 2:23-28). See *Bread of the Presence.*

SHIBAH (Shīb' ah) Modern translation spelling of Shebah (Gen. 26:33; HCSB, "Oath").

SHIBBOLETH (Shīb' ō lĕth) Transliteration of Hebrew password meaning "ears," "twigs" or "brook." People of Gilead east of the Jordan used it to detect people of Ephraim from west of the Jordan since the Ephraimite dialect evidently did not include the *sh* sound, so Ephraimites always said, "Sibboleth," a word not used elsewhere in Hebrew (Judg. 12:6).

SHIBMAH (Shīb' mah) (KJV, Num. 32:38) See *Sibmah.*

SHICRON (Shīk' rŏn) Place-name meaning "henbane" (a type of nightshade plant). Border town of tribe of Judah (Josh. 15:11). It may be located at Tell el-Ful north of the Soreq River and three and a half miles northwest of Ekron.

SHIELD Protective device used in battle. See *Arms and Armor.*

SHIGGAION (Shī gā' ŏn) Transliteration of a Hebrew technical term used in psalm titles (Ps. 7; Hab. 3). Suggested translations include "frenzied" or "emotional." Some think the basic meaning is "to wander" in reference to a wandering style of thought or melody or to the unconnected expressions of a lament.

SHIGIONOTH (Shīg ĭ ō' nŏth) Hebrew plural of Shiggaion. See *Shiggaion.*

SHIHON (Shī' hŏn) Place-name of uncertain meaning, perhaps "worthless." Some would locate it at modern Sirim, about 13 miles southeast of Mount Tabor. It was a border town of Issachar (Josh. 19:19).

SHIHOR (Shī' hôr) Egyptian place-name meaning "pool of Horus (a god)." It formed the border of the promised land (Josh. 13:3), marking the widest extent of Israel's territorial claims (1 Chron. 13:5). In Isa. 23:3 and Jer. 2:18 the term apparently refers to one of the branches of the Nile River inside Egypt, but the border point places it outside Egypt, identical with the Brook of Egypt or extending Israel's claim to the Nile. The earliest translators did not understand the term in Josh. 13. See *Brook of Egypt; Palestine.*

SHIHOR-LIBNATH (Shī hôr-līb' năth) Place-name, perhaps meaning "swamp of Libnath." Border of tribal territory of Asher (Josh. 19:26), variously identified as the Nahr ez-Zerqa on the southern border of Asher; the swampy territory between the rivers Nahr ed-Difleh and Nahr ez-Zerqa, and Tell Abu Hawam at the mouth of the Kishon.

SHIKKERON (Shīk' ə rŏn) Modern translations' spelling of Shicron (Josh. 15:11). See *Shicron.*

SHILHI (Shīl' hī) Personal name meaning "he sent me," "Salach (underworld god or river) has me," or "my offshoot." A similar formation has been found at Tell Arad. Maternal grandfather of King Jehoshaphat (1 Kings 22:42).

SHILHIM (Shĭl´ hĭm) Alternative Hebrew spelling of Sharuhen. See *Sharuhen.*

SHILLEM (Shĭl´ lĕm) Personal name meaning "he has replaced or repaid." Son of Naphtali and original ancestor of clan in that tribe (Gen. 46:24). First Chronicles 7:13 has "Shallum."

SHILLEMITE (Shĭl´ lĕm ĭt) Member of clan of Shillem (Num. 26:49).

SHILOAH, WATERS OF (Shī lō´ ah) Place-name meaning "being sent." Waters supplying Jerusalem diverted from the Gihon spring and representing God's supply making reliance on foreign kings unnecessary (Isa. 8:6). It differs from the Siloam Tunnel Hezekiah built (2 Kings 20:20). The background may be anointing of kings at the Gihon (1 Kings 1:33-40), thus implying rejection of God's kingship represented through His anointed king.

SHILOH (Shī´ lōh) Place-name, perhaps meaning "tranquil, secure." About 30 miles north of Jerusalem sat the city which would be Israel's religious center for over a century after the conquest, being the home of Israel's tabernacle (Josh. 18:1). See *Tabernacle.*

Judges 21:19 described Shiloh's location as "north of Bethel, east of the highway that goes up from Bethel to Shechem, and south of Lebonah." Twelve miles south of Shechem, Shiloh was in a fertile plain at 2,000 feet elevation. This is apparently modern Seilun, where archaeologists have unearthed evidence of Canaanite settlement by 1700 B.C. Perhaps when Israel chose a spot for the tabernacle, Shiloh was available for Joshua to use as the place to allot land to the tribes (Josh. 18).

Tribal annual pilgrimages to the tabernacle set the scene for another incident in Shiloh. The tribe of Benjamin had a dilemma in that no other tribe would give them their daughters for wives (Judg. 21). Because of this, the men of Benjamin waited in the vineyards (v. 20) until the dancing women went out of Shiloh where they were then captured and taken as wives.

Samuel's early years provided another connection with Shiloh (1 Sam. 1–4). At the tabernacle Hannah vowed to the Lord that if He would give her a son she would give him back to God (1 Sam. 1). After the birth of Samuel, Hannah brought him to Shiloh in gratitude to God (1 Sam. 1:24-28). Thus, Shiloh became home for Samuel as he lived under the care of Eli, the high priest, and his two wicked sons,

Ruins of an ancient synagogue at the site of the city of Shiloh.

Hophni and Phinehas. Later, Samuel received the Lord's message that the priesthood would be taken from Eli's family (1 Sam. 3). Years later, following a defeat at Aphek, the Israelite army sent for the ark of the covenant from Shiloh. Mistakenly thinking that the ark would bring victory, the Israelites lost the second battle of Aphek to the Philistines. Results included losing the ark; the deaths of Hophni, Phinehas, and Eli; and the apparent conquering of Shiloh (1 Sam. 4).

No explicit biblical reference was made to Shiloh's final fate. According to archaeological evidence, Shiloh apparently was destroyed about 1050 B.C. by the Philistines. Supporting this was the fact that when the Philistines finally returned the ark of the covenant, it was housed at Kiriath-jearim rather than Shiloh (1 Sam. 7:1). Also, Jeremiah warned Jerusalem that it might suffer the same destructive fate as Shiloh (7:12).

Centuries later, Jeremiah used Shiloh and the tabernacle as illustrations to warn Jerusalem that it was not safe merely because it housed the temple (7:12-14). Hearing the same message again, the people sought to kill Jeremiah (26:6-9). Jeremiah mentioned some men from Shiloh as late as 585 B.C. (41:5), indicating some occupation at that time. See *Eli; Joshua; Samuel.*

Larry McGraw

SHILONI (Shī lō´ nī) Transliteration of Hebrew for Shilonite, taken by KJV as personal name (Neh. 11:5).

SHILONITE (Shī´ lō nīt) Resident of or native of Shiloh.

SHILSHAH (Shĭl´ shäh) Personal name, perhaps meaning "little triplet." Original ancestor of clan in tribe of Asher (1 Chron. 7:37).

SHIMEA (Shĭm´ ə à) Personal name meaning "hearing." **1.** Son of David (1 Chron. 3:5; 2 Sam. 5:14, "Shammuah"). **2.** A Levite (1 Chron. 6:30). **3.** Levite ancestor of Asaph (1 Chron. 6:39). **4.** Older brother of David (1 Chron. 2:13; 20:7; 1 Sam. 16:9 and 17:13, "Shammah"). See *Shammah 2.* **5.** See *Shimeam.*

SHIMEAH (Shĭm´ ə ah) Alternate Hebrew spelling of Shammah. See *Shammah 2.; Shimea 4.*

SHIMEAM (Shĭm´ ə ăm) Personal name, perhaps meaning "their hearing." Benjaminite who lived in Jerusalem (1 Chron. 9:38; 8:32, "Shimeah").

SHIMEATH (Shĭm´ ə äth) Personal name meaning "hearing." Parent of court official who murdered King Joash about 796 B.C. (2 Kings 12:21). Second Chronicles 24:26 takes the apparently feminine form of the Hebrew name and identifies the parent as an Ammonite woman.

SHIMEATHITE (Shĭm´ ə à thīt) Either a descendant of a person named Shimeath or, more likely, a native of the town of Shema (Josh. 15:26), perhaps settled by the clan of Shema (1 Chron. 2:43). See *Shema 1. and 5.*

SHIMEI (Shĭm´ ə ī) Personal name meaning "my being heard." **1.** Grandson of Levi and head of Levitical family (Exod. 6:17; Num. 3:18; cp. 1 Chron. 6:42). **2.** A Levite (1 Chron. 23:9 if the text does not represent duplication in copying as some commentators suggest; cp. v. 10). **3.** Relative of King Saul who cursed and opposed David as he fled from Absalom (2 Sam. 16). When David returned after Absalom's death, Shimei met him and pleaded for forgiveness and mercy, which David granted because of the festive occasion (2 Sam. 19). Solomon followed David's advice and had Shimei slain (1 Kings 2). **4.** Court personality who refused to support Adonijah against Solomon (1 Kings 1:8). **5.** District supervisor in territory of Benjamin responsible for supplying Solomon's court one month each year (1 Kings 4:18); he could be identical with 4. above. **6.** Ancestor of Mordecai, the cousin of Esther (Esther 2:5). **7.** Brother of Zerubbabel (1 Chron. 3:19). **8.** Member of tribe of Simeon (1 Chron. 4:26). **9.** Member of tribe of Reuben (1 Chron. 5:4). **10.** A Levite (1 Chron. 6:29). **11.** A Benjaminite (1 Chron. 8:21; apparently identical with Shema in v. 13). **12.** Temple musician under David (1 Chron. 25:17; perhaps also in v. 3 with a Hebrew manuscript and some Greek manuscripts as in NRSV, REB, NASB, NIV, TEV). **13.** Supervisor of David's vineyards (1 Chron. 27:27). **14. and 15.** Two Levites under Hezekiah (2 Chron. 29:14; 31:12-13). **16.** Levite married to a foreign woman under Ezra (Ezra 10:23). **17. and 18.** Two Jews married to foreign women under Ezra (Ezra 10:33,38).

SHIMEITES (Shī´ mē īts) Members of the clan descending from Shimei (Num. 3:21; Zech. 12:13).

SHIMEON (Shĭm ə ŏn) Alternate English transliteration of Hebrew Simeon. Israelite with foreign wife (Ezra 10:31).

SHIMHI (Shĭm´ hī) Alternate English transliteration of Shimei (1 Chron. 8:21). See *Shimei 11.*

SHIMI (Shĭm´ ī) (KJV, Exod. 6:17). See *Shimei 1.*

SHIMITE (Shĭm´ īt) (KJV, Num. 3:21) See *Shimeites.*

SHIMMA (Shĭm´ ma) (KJV, 1 Chron. 2:13) See *Shimea 4.*

SHIMON (Shī´ mŏn) Personal name of uncertain meaning. Original ancestor of clan in tribe of Judah (1 Chron. 4:20).

SHIMRATH (Shĭm´ răth) Personal name meaning "protection." Member of tribe of Benjamin (1 Chron. 8:21).

SHIMRI (Shĭm´ rī) Personal name meaning "my protection." **1.** Member of tribe of Simeon (1 Chron. 4:37). **2.** Father of one of David's military heroes (1 Chron. 11:45). **3.** Levitical gatekeeper (1 Chron. 26:10). **4.** Levite in time of Hezekiah (2 Chron. 29:13).

SHIMRITH (Shĭm´ rĭth) Personal name meaning "protection." Moabite mother whose son murdered King Joash in 796 B.C. (2 Chron. 24:26). In the parallel passage Shomer is the parent and appears to be the father (2 Kings 12:21).

SHIMROM (Shĭm´ rŏm) (KJV, 1 Chron. 7:1) or **SHIMRON** (Shĭm´ rŏn) Personal name and place-name probably meaning "protection." **1.** Son of Issachar and original ancestor of clan in that tribe (Gen. 46:13). **2.** Canaanite city-state which joined Hazor's northern coalition against Joshua and met defeat (Josh. 11:1). Some commentators think the original name was Shimon and identify it with modern Khirbet Sammuniyeh five miles west of Nazareth in the Esdraelon Valley. Others have suggested Marun er-Ras, 10 miles northwest of modern Safed above the Sea of Chinnereth, that is the Sea of Galilee. It was allotted to the tribe of Zebulun (Josh. 19:15).

SHIMRON-MERON (Shĭm rŏn-mē´ rŏn) Town in list of cities Joshua defeated (Josh. 12:20). Apparently a longer name of Shimron (11:1), though the earliest Greek translation and some commentators see two separate cities here.

SHIMRONITE (Shĭm´ rŏn īt) Member of clan of Shimron (Num. 26:24).

SHIMSHAI (Shĭm´ shī) Personal name meaning "little sunshine." Scribe who penned letter of Samaritan officials opposing rebuilding of Jerusalem and the temple about 537 B.C. (Ezra 4).

SHIN (Shēn) Next to last letter of Hebrew alphabet used as title for Ps. 119:161-168 since each verse of the section begins with that letter.

SHINAB (Shī´ năb) Akkadian name meaning "Sin (a god) is father." King of Admah who joined coalition against Chedorlaomer (Gen. 14:2), leading eventually to Abraham's rescue of Lot.

SHINAR, PLAIN OF (Shī´ när) Place-name of uncertain meaning used in various ancient Near Eastern documents apparently with somewhat different localities in mind. Some evidence points to a Syrian district cited as Sanhara in the Amarna letters. Some scholars equate Shinar in Assyrian texts with modern Sinjar west of Mosul in Iraq. Others think a Kassite tribe was meant originally. Whatever its meaning outside the Bible, biblical texts use Shinar as a designation for Mesopotamia (Gen. 10:10). See *Mesopotamia.*

The tower of Babel was built in Shinar (Gen. 11:2-9). The king of Shinar opposed Abraham (Gen. 14:1). Isaiah prophesied that God would bring out a remnant of His people from Shinar (11:11). Daniel 1:1-2 and probably Zech. 5:11 equate Babylon and Shinar, thus limiting Shinar to its major city in the writers' day.

SHION (Shī´ ŏn) Modern translations' spelling of Shihon.

SHIPBUILDER See *Ships, Sailors, and Navigation.*

A felucca (Egyptian boat) on the Nile River near the city of Cairo, Egypt.

SHIPHI (Shī´ phī) Personal name meaning "my overflow." Member of tribe of Simeon (1 Chron. 4:37).

SHIPHMITE (Shĭph´ mīt) Noun indicating either the hometown, native land, or clan from which Zabdi came. Some have suggested town of Shepham (Num. 34:10), but this is far from certain.

SHIPHRAH (Shĭph´ rah) Personal name meaning "beauty." Midwife for Israel in Egypt who disobeyed Pharaoh because they feared God (Exod. 1:15-21).

SHIPHTAN (Shĭph´ tȧn) Personal name meaning "process of justice." Father of a leader from tribe of Ephraim (Num. 34:24).

SHIPMASTER Captain in charge of a ship (Jon. 1:6; Rev. 18:17).

SHIPS, SAILORS, AND NAVIGATION Travel by sea in biblical times. People first went down to the sea in anything that would keep them afloat. The early development of the two major centers of civilization along the major river systems of the Near Eastern world, the Tigris/Euphrates and the Nile, was not coincidental. Even though the first boats were punted or towed along the shore, such waterborne transportation and movement of goods facilitated the exchange of local products in more distant markets, first along the riverbanks and then beyond the open seas. From very basic, crude beginnings before 3000 B.C., ship technology and seamanship persistently developed as people strove to overcome the barriers that rivers and seas

imposed. Thus Assyrian reliefs depict fishermen afloat on inflated bladders and soldiers lying on them to paddle across the water. In wooded areas the single log or bundle of reeds to support one person soon developed into the raft of bound logs that could support additional personnel and produce. Along the marshy stretches of the Nile, Tigris, and Euphrates, rafts of reed bundles were refined into the reed canoe. The special requirements of rapids and swift waters of the Upper Tigris and Euphrates prompted the development of the buoyed raft, a wooden platform supported on inflated skins that continued in use until very recent times. At the destination downstream, the wooden parts could be disassembled and sold while the deflated skins were easily transported upstream for reuse.

True boats, in their earliest forms, probably consisted of sewn leather stretched and sewn over light frames of branches for ease of transport when necessary. Such boats, essential for river travel, are depicted in detail in Assyrian reliefs between 1000 and 600 B.C. In water free from rocks, such as the Nile Delta where adequate materials for branch frames were lacking, clay tublike boats made their appearance. Where wood was available, the bark canoe (a troughlike strip of bark with clay ends) was followed by the dugout that required a cutting tool or controlled use of fire in its production. Wherever forests supplied the logs from Europe to India, the dugout was familiar to waterways from the Stone Age into the late Roman period. Modified dugouts with heightened sides and interior reinforcements were the prototypes of the planked boats with keel, ribs, and strakes.

Inland Waterways Civilization arose along the two waterways that connected territories in major political units and provided internal transportation.

Boats on Egypt's Nile The Nile provided 750 miles of unobstructed waterway with a current that carried boats from Aswan and the First Cataract to its mouth and prevailing north winds that brought those boats under sail back again. Such ideal conditions that obviously contributed to the development of water travel and transport unfortunately were offset by a lack of lumber. Thus, the Egyptians turned to the abundant reeds along the Nile to create simple rafts. Before 3000 B.C. those Nile rafts had become long slender and pointed vessels outfitted with paddles and steering oars. Modifications included cabins

S

and a growing number of oarsmen. The shape was bowed, or sickle-shaped, with squared prow and stern rising almost vertically from the water. A square sail was set well forward above the reed platform that served its passengers and cargo. The lightweight and shallow draft made such craft most useful in the canals and marshes of the Nile River system.

Shortly after 3000 B.C. these fragile reed boats, reinforced with planks, ferried the massive granite and stone blocks used for the impressive stone architecture that began to grace the Nile's banks. These planked reed boats provided the forms for Egypt's first true boats— flat-bottomed and square-ended. Soon, however, relieved of the bulky reed bundles, Egyptian boats were outfitted with rounded bottom, pointed prow, and rounded stern. Pictorial representations in paintings, reliefs, and models indicate that Nile River craft, primarily constructed of Asia Minor and Lebanon cedar, dramatically grew in size and diversity. Cargo boats 150 feet in length requiring 40 to 50 rowers, and, later, massive 200-by-70-foot barges towed by a fleet of oar-powered tugs, shuttled up and down the Nile to the massive building operations between Aswan and the Delta. Smaller vessels were poled, paddled, or rowed, with some also equipped with a sail.

For international maritime trade, Egypt enjoyed a distinct advantage as the only nation with direct access to both the Mediterranean and the Red Seas. As a result, two long-distance maritime routes to Syria and Punt (East Africa) already were established during the Old Kingdom period. The earliest route to Byblos soon was extended to Cyprus, Crete, and possibly other Aegean sites. The earliest seagoing vessel depicted in a relief dated about 2450 B.C. had a spoon-shaped hull with a long, slender overhanging bow and stern and a rope truss that could be tightened by twisting to compensate for any sagging of bow or stern. The ships of Queen Hatshepsut's fleet trading with the East African coast reflect considerable refinement of the general lines. A two-legged forward mast with a tall, narrow rectangular sail had been replaced by a low, wide sail on a pole mast amidships. A single, massive steering oar had replaced smaller steering oars on each quarter. Fifteen rowers a side (requiring a space of not less than 45 feet) would suggest a vessel about 90 feet in length. By the end of the New Kingdom period, the

ships used by Ramses III against the invading Sea Peoples (about 1170 B.C.), as depicted in his reliefs, indicate radical changes in construction. See *Egypt*.

Mesopotamian Shipping Mesopotamian kings and merchants also operated long-distance maritime routes in the Red Sea and Indian Ocean from several inland cities that were accessible along the Tigris and Euphrates Rivers. By 3000 B.C. overseas trade was a thriving aspect of regional economy. Maritime ventures included royal and private efforts at supplying metals, timber, and luxury items that the Mesopotamian economy lacked.

A clay model of a bowl-like boat, with slight evidence of prow and stern, possibly made of skins and dated about 3400 B.C., is our earliest evidence of Mesopotamian vessels. The existence of a mast and use of sails was possible, though firm evidence of sailing boats comes much later. Earliest representations on seals suggest the use of squared reed crafts similar to Egyptian types. A prevailing north wind and rapids in the Upper Tigris and Euphrates Rivers diminished the development of commercial shipping and the need for larger vessels. As a result, early light craft propelled by paddles or oars gradually evolved into wooden craft with sail as well as oars. The largest vessels appear to carry less than 11 tons with most half that size, usually constructed of edge-joined planks with framing inserted for stability. Square-ended, these boats carried a single sail of cloth or reed matting with the largest powered by 11 oarsmen.

Phoenician trader (merchant).

S

Between 3000 and 2000 B.C. overseas trade with East Africa and India flowed through the Persian Gulf on relatively small seagoing vessels, the largest known with a capacity of only about 28 tons.

International Travel and Trade Sea routes opened opportunities for evolving nations to gain wealth and explore the mysteries of far-off lands.

The Eastern Mediterranean: 3000–1000 B.C. Major developments of maritime travel between 2000 and 1500 B.C. must be attributed to the island world of the Aegean and the coastlines of the eastern Mediterranean. There the Minoans of Crete especially developed an impressive naval fleet and a merchant marine that linked their island world. Ultimately, however, the Mycenaeans—Greeks from the mainland—overpowered Crete, forming an Aegean confederacy. From 1500 to 1200 B.C. they claimed control over the waters of the Eastern Mediterranean.

Cretan ships with their rounded hulls, portrayed on seals about 1500 B.C., were quite distinct from the Aegean straight-lined angular-ended vessels. Though the engravings obviously are stylized, the slender rounded hull, in some cases almost crescent-shaped, supported a pole mast with stays fore and aft and a high square sail. These Cretan vessels with 10 or 15 oars to the side were about 50 and 75 feet in length, respectively. Passenger vessels were outfitted with a cabin or shelter on deck.

An Egyptian wall painting in a 1400 B.C. tomb depicts a Syrian fleet of merchant ships with spoon-shaped hulls, with straight stem-post, deck beams through the sides, and a broad square sail very much like Egyptian vessels of the period. (The Egyptian vessels were braced with a rope truss.) The representation of the sailors (their beards, profile, and clothing) clearly suggests their Syrian origin. (It is unlikely, though the evidence comes from Egypt, that these are Egyptian vessels manned by Syrians.) The rounded hulls are best related to Crete from about 1600 B.C. onwards. These merchantmen with their deck and roomy hold grew in size. By about 1200 B.C. an Ugaritic tablet suggests their size in referring to a single shipment of grain of 450 tons.

The war fleets of the Levant in 1200 B.C. were impressive in number and design. The fighting craft lost their spoon-shaped hull that was elongated and rounded. They were undecked with the oarsmen protected behind a high bulwark. The mast with an adjustable sail was crowned with a lookout. The naval battle (depicted on the Medinet Habu temple walls) between Aegean ("Sea Peoples") and Egyptian ships indicates the clear similarity of construction and design apart from ornamental or cultic aspects. The only offensive weapon appears to be the grappling irons for boarding enemy vessels. Aside from the tactical maneuvering of the vessels, sea battles were fought with bow, sword, and pike as on land. The modification of the bow for ramming appears to have been a later development.

The Eastern Mediterranean: 1000–500 B.C. During this period the Phoenicians gained a reputation as the ablest of seamen and maritime traders. Their primary challenge came from the Greek world where merchantmen and war vessels controlled the northern Mediterranean shoreline and the Black Sea. The low sleek "hollow" hull, with only a scant deck forward for the outlook and a slightly larger one aft for the captain and passengers, was constructed low and long primarily for speed. Several standard-sized galleys included the 20-oared dispatch and local transport, the 30-oared "triaconter" galley, the 50-oared "penteconter" for troop transport, and the 100-oared large transport. They were constructed of oak, poplar, pine, and fir, with the oars and masts of fir. A single, large-bladed steering car was replaced after 800 B.C. by double-steering oars that became standard thereafter. A single square sail on a mast amidships could be raised and lowered. Sails of sewn patches of woven linen were controlled with lines of twisted papyrus and leather. Other equipment included stern-mooring lines, stone anchors, punting poles, long pikes for fighting, and bags and jars for holding provisions. Screens along the sides could be closed during heavy weather.

The introduction of the ram was a dramatic innovation that revolutionized ship construction. The pointed cutwater for puncturing the hull of the enemy vessel required construction with heavier materials to withstand contact, especially in the bow area. The open or latticed bow area gave way to a cumbersome superstructure for sustaining the ram. This represented the first period of specialization in the construction and class of vessel—the open galley with a lighter hull for carrying dispatches and personnel and the galley with superstructure, including relatively high platforms as fighting stations at bow and stern, for combat. The invention of the two-banked galley soon followed to increase the number of rowers and the speed of the vessel without increasing the length and reducing the seaworthiness of its hull. The Phoenician ship-wrights should be credited with many of these important innovations.

The rigging for most war galleys during this period was standard—a single square sail amidships with a retractable mast. After 600 B.C. single-banked and double-banked galleys appear in all sizes up to 100 oars.

The first Mediterranean merchant ships probably were oar driven. Plagued by calm waters during the summer months when maritime activity probably was at its peak, only oared ships could have provided the reliability and speed required for prompt delivery of merchandise. Later, as the volume of cargo grew, larger seaworthy sailing ships came into use. The merchantman was only slightly modified from the warship design to include a roomier and stronger hull and a sturdier mast for a bigger sail. Ultimately, however, the sailing ship with a rounded hull and a single square sail became the primary cargo ship from Phoenicia to Italy.

The Age of the Trireme: 500–323 B.C.
The galley rowed by three more or less superimposed banks of oarsmen came into vogue after 500 B.C. and maintained its prominence into the later Roman Empire. The additional power and speed required by the ram seemed to outweigh the relatively unseaworthy hull of this oar arrangement. As a result, sea battles were carefully scheduled near land during the mild summer months to avoid adverse weather conditions. While the first two lines of rowers worked their oars through ports in the hull and on a second line on or just below the gunwale, the third line worked from an outrigger projecting laterally above and beyond the gunwale. Corinth appears to have been the first to launch such a fleet sometime after 700 B.C., and a century later it appears to have been accepted generally. Athenian naval records suggest that such ships were built with great care and, despite their fragile construction, remained in service for an average of 20 years. The Phoenician ship-wrights increased the height of their vessels to accommodate three-level rowing.

Warships of the Hellenistic Period: 323–31 B.C. In both Phoenician and Greek

A second- or third-century A.D. drawing of a ship inscribed in Latin, found in Jerusalem excavations.

navies of the period, the primary innovation was the construction of larger and larger vessels, though the exact nature of oaring is not clearly understood. Generally, the greater power and speed were achieved with longer oars and a double banking of the rowers, while the oversized ships relied on a variety of oaring arrangements. Ramming remained a standard naval tactic, though gradually subordinated to the firing of missiles, the heaving of grapnels, and boarding. Darts and grapnels were fired from catapults at longer range, while short-range battles included archers and the slinging of javelins and stones. Shortly after 200 B.C. the Rhodians introduced the fire pot, slung from long poles (extending over the bow) onto the enemy vessel.

To complement these larger ships, light vessels such as skiffs with speed and maneuverability made their appearance for express transport and the carrying of dispatches. Some were equipped with rams, while others were intended to disrupt the tactics and break the oars of the larger vessels. Later, the Roman imperial navy would not only add to the variety of vessels, but their architects would introduce significant defensive innovations.

Greek and Roman Shipbuilding The Greco-Roman shipwrights, aware of the ancient Egyptian method of edge-joining planks in the construction of the hull, created their own form of ship carpentry in which they locked the shell of planks together with mortises and then reinforced that hull with interior framing. This method was consistently used in the construction of all vessels from the smallest lake skiff to the largest seaworthy freighters. In larger vessels massive cables for undergirding the ship during emergencies were kept on board. It was usual to smear seams and sometimes the whole hull with pitch or pitch and wax as a protective coating.

S

Though fir, cedar, and pine appear to have been preferred for planking and frames, local availability of lumbers finally determined the choice.

The ancient Mediterranean sailor knew only the side rudder, an oversized oar pivoted in a slanting position near the stern. The pushing or pulling of a tiller bar socketed into the upper part of the loom adjusted the blade of the oar at an angle to the hull and thus maneuvered the ship. A series of ropes with individual functions fitted the mast and sail. Navigational aids were limited and simple. Handbooks with brief notes on distances, landmarks, harbors, and anchorages were available. There are no historical references to the use of charts. Soundings were taken (see Acts 27:28-29). Flags and lights were used for signaling. Anchors were large and numerous.

The ideal sailing season in the Mediterranean was from May 27 to September 14 with an extension to outside limits from March 10 to November 10. As a result, sailing during the late fall and winter was reduced to bare essentials such as the carrying of vital dispatches, the transport of essential supplies, and urgent military movement. The severity of winter storms and the poor visibility due to fog and cloudiness made navigation before the compass most difficult (see Acts 27:12-20).

Mediterranean currents generally are too weak seriously to affect sea travel. However, prevailing wind direction produced a definite pattern with ships traveling in most southerly directions, from Italy or Greece to Asia Minor, Syria, Egypt, and Africa, anticipating a quick and easy voyage with the aid of northerly winds. The return, on the other hand, was difficult against the prevailing winds, and thus a course near the coastline at times provided quieter waters and periodic shelter. The ancient square-riggers were designed for traveling with the wind astern or on the quarters. Roman ships appear to have logged four and a half to six knots with the wind. Tacking, or using the familiar zigzag course, at best was difficult and slow. When rowing was unavoidable, the oarsmen were divided into squads for rotation or given regular short rest periods.

Organizational structure and rank on the earlier, smaller vessels of the Greek and Roman navy was limited to the commanding officer who manned the helm, the rowing officer who maintained the oarsmen's beat, and the bow officer ("lookout") who was responsible for the course

and well-being of the ship. Around 400 B.C., when the Athenian trireme had a crew of 200, the officers numbered five: the executive officer or captain; the commanding officer; the rowing officer, responsible for the training and morale of the oarsmen; subordinate officer, with important administrative duties such as paymaster, purchasing, and recruiting officer; and officer of the bow. Other personnel included the ship's carpenter, flutist (to time the rowers' stroke) or time beater, side chiefs (to set the stroke), deckhands, oar tenders, and ship's doctor, among others. The number of fighting personnel (marines) varied according to strategy: the Athenian ships that relied primarily on the ram had as few as 10; others intent on boarding tactics had as many as 40. A few archers (four to six) usually were on board, together with some catapult operators.

A seagoing merchantman was controlled by its owner or charter, usually with a hired professional captain with total authority over the vessel and its crew (see Acts 27:11). Under way the "sailing master" was usually in command. Two officers were in charge of operations (first mate) and administration (maintenance). The large merchantmen also had quartermasters, carpenters, guards, rowers to man the ship's boats, and others. The sailors generally wore limited or no clothing when aboard ship and wore a tunic but no sandals when ashore.

A wide variety of smaller craft, usually driven by oars and a small auxiliary sail, were prevalent in every harbor to provide various services. River and coastal craft provided towing services and transfer of cargo and merchandise to harbor warehouses and points inaccessible to the larger ships. Man-made harbors with artificial sea walls to create protected anchorage appear before 700 B.C. Gradually, quays, warehouses, and defensive towers were added to create a secure commercial port. By 400 B.C. the Piraeus harbor was surrounded by an extensive covered emporium to facilitate the handling of import and export merchandise. By Roman times both sea and river were well endowed with harbors, with smaller ports benefiting from coastal shipping by becoming distribution centers for inland areas removed from major land routes. Unfortunately the decline of the late Roman Empire and political weakness with a recurrence of piracy on the high seas led to a marked decline of commercial shipping in the Mediterranean. With the ultimate fragmentation of the Roman Empire, barbarian invasions in the east, and the shift of the economic center to the west, the Mediterranean, devoid of large ships, slowly was reduced to small local craft with minimal economic impact beyond the patron port.   *George L. Kelm*

SHIRT Modern translation of "coat" in some passages, reflecting Greek *chiton*, garment that both sexes wore next to the skin. See *Cloth, Clothing*.

SHISHA (Shī´ sha) Personal name or, more likely, an official title borrowed from Egyptian: royal scribe who writes letters. Apparently, "sons of Shisha" (1 Kings 4:3) refers to members of a scribal guild. Sheva (2 Sam. 20:25) and Shavsha (1 Chron. 18:16) may represent other ways to transliterate the Egyptian title into Hebrew.

SHISHAK (Shī´ shăk) Egyptian royal name of unknown meaning. A pharaoh of Egypt known also as Sheshonk I. He ruled about 945–924 B.C. and founded the 22nd Dynasty. Just after Rehoboam began to reign in Judah, Shishak invaded Jerusalem and carted off the temple treasures (1 Kings 14:25-26). According to inscriptions on the walls of a temple to the god Amon in Karnak, Shishak captured over 150 towns in Palestine including Megiddo, Taanash, and Gibeon. Some equate him with the pharaoh whose daughter married Solomon (3:1) and who later burned Gezer and gave it to his daughter (9:16). See *Egypt*.

SHITRAI (Shĭt´ rā ī) Personal name, perhaps meaning "minor official." Official in charge of David's grazing animals in Sharon (1 Chron. 27:29). Early Hebrew scribes noted the spelling as "Shirtai."

SHITTAH TREE KJV spelling of Shittim tree (Isa. 41:19). See *Shittim*.

SHITTIM (Shĭt´ tĭm) Transliteration of Hebrew word for acacia trees. **1.** Name of a large area in Moab directly across the Jordan from Jericho and northeast of the Dead Sea. Israel camped there for a long period before crossing into the promised land. While at Shittim, they were blessed by Balaam (whom Balak had hired to curse Israel; Num. 22–24; cp. Mic. 6:5), committed sin with the Moabite and Midianite women (Num. 25), and Joshua was announced

The yellow blooms of a modern variety of the acacia (shittim) tree in Israel.

as Moses' successor (Deut. 34:9). Joshua sent spies out from Shittim (Josh. 2:1; cp. 3:1). It is modern Tell el-Hammam es Samri about eight miles east of the Jordan. **2.** In Joel 3:18 the symbolic meaning of acacias (note NASB) comes to the fore in the messianic picture of fertility for the Kidron Valley with a stream flowing from the temple.

SHITTIM TREE, WOOD See *Acacia; Plants*.

SHIZA (Shī´ za) Abbreviated personal name of uncertain meaning. Member of tribe of Reuben in time of David (1 Chron. 11:42).

SHOA (Shō´ a) National name meaning "help!" Nation God used to punish His people (Ezek. 23:23). They are usually identified with the Sutu, a nomadic people from the Syrian and Arabian Deserts known from documents from Mari, Amarna, and Assyria. Some commentators see them mentioned in Isa. 22:5, where most translate "crying."

SHOBAB (Shō´ băb) Personal name meaning "one brought back" or "fallen away, rebel." **1.** Son of David (2 Sam. 5:14). **2.** Son of Caleb and ancestor of clan in tribe of Judah (1 Chron. 2:18).

SHOBACH (Shō´ băk) Personal name of uncertain meaning. Commander of Syrian army under Hadad-ezer killed by David's troops in battle (2 Sam. 10:16,18). The name appears as Shophak in 1 Chron. 19:16,18.

SHOBAI (Shō´ bā ī) Personal name of uncertain meaning. Head of family of gatekeepers (Ezra 2:42).

S

SHOBAL (Shō´ băl) Personal name probably meaning "lion." **1.** Son of Seir and ruler in Edom (Gen. 36:20,23,29). **2.** Son of Caleb and founder of Kirjath-jearim (1 Chron. 2:50), listed under sons of Judah (1 Chron. 4:1), possibly an indication of "son of" denoting belonging to a tribe.

SHOBEK (Shō´ běk) Personal name meaning "victor." Jewish leader who signed Nehemiah's covenant (Neh. 10:24).

SHOBI (Shō´ bī) Personal name of uncertain meaning. Ammonite who helped David as he fled across Jordan from Absalom (2 Sam. 17:27).

SHOCHO or **SHOCHOH** Alternate spelling of Soco or Socoh.

SHOHAM (Shō´ hăm) Personal name meaning "gem." Levite in time of David (1 Chron. 24:27).

SHOMER (Shō´ měr) Personal name meaning "protector." **1.** Father of one of the murderers of King Joash (2 Kings 12:21). See *Shimrith.* **2.** See *Shemer 2.*

SHOPHACH (Shō´ phăk) See *Shobach.*

SHOPHAN (Shō´ phăn) KJV interpretation of separate town. Modern translations have compound name. See *Atroth-shophan.*

SHOPHAR (Shō´ phàr) Hebrew word for the ceremonial ram's horn used to call the people of Israel together (Exod. 19:16). The shophar was to be blown on the Day of Atonement in the Jubilee Year to signal the release of slaves and debt. It also was used as a trumpet of war as the Israelites were campaigning against their enemies. See *Music, Instruments, Dancing.*

Mike Mitchell

SHOSHANNIM (Shō shăn´ nĭm) Transliteration of Hebrew word meaning "lotuses." Technical term used in titles of Pss. 45; 60; 69; 80. It may be the title of a melody, a flower used in a ceremony seeking a word from God, designation of a love song later expanded in meaning, or indication of a six-stringed instrument. See *Lily of the Covenant.*

SHOSHANNIM-EDUTH (Shō´ shăn´ nĭm-ē´ dŭth) Term in tiles of Pss. 60; 80. "Eduth" means "witness" or "laws." Its implication in the psalm titles is not clear. See *Shoshannim; Lily of the Covenant.*

SHOULDERPIECE Translation of Hebrew word meaning "shoulder, upper arm, side." The straps were going over the shoulder so the high priest could wear the ephod (Exod. 28:7).

SHOVEL Instrument used to remove ashes from the altar (Exod. 27:3).

SHRINE Small building devoted to the worship of a particular deity, usually with an image of that god. Sometimes shrines were located in larger temples, set apart by a partition or niche in a wall. An Ephraimite, Micah, had a shrine in Israel during the days of the judges (Judg. 17:5). He hired a Levite to administer worship at the site. Later, shrines were seen as pagan (2 Kings 17:29). King Josiah had them demolished during his reign (2 Kings 23:19). The Apostle Paul confronted the silversmith Demetrius with his sin of selling shrines of the goddess Artemis (Acts 19:21-27). See *Artemis; High Place.*

SHRINE OF HIS OWN IDOL NIV translation in Ezek. 8:12. See *Chambers of Imagery.*

SHROUD Linen burial cloth. Shrouds usually were very long pieces of cloth that were wound around the body. As the winding was done, spices were placed within the folds of the shroud. After His crucifixion, Jesus' body was so buried by Joseph of Arimathea and the women disciples (Matt. 27:59-61). In one recorded instance, a shroud was worn as a garment (Mark 14:51-52).

SHUA (Shū´ à) Personal name meaning "help!" **1.** Father-in-law of Judah (Gen. 38:2; 1 Chron. 2:3). **2.** Woman descended from Asher (1 Chron. 7:32), with slightly different Hebrew spelling.

SHUAH (Shū´ ah) Personal name, perhaps meaning "sunken." **1.** Son of Abraham (Gen. 25:2) and possibly thought of as original ancestor of the Suhu mentioned in Assyrian sources as living on the Euphrates River below the mouth of the Chabur. **2.** Home of Job's friend Bildad (Job 2:11), possibly to be identified with people mentioned in 1. or with an otherwise unknown tribe in the Syrian and Arabian Deserts, perhaps an offshoot of 1.

S

SHUAL (Shū´ ăl) Personal name and place-name meaning "jackal." **1.** Descendant of Asher (1 Chron. 7:36). **2.** Territory that a biblical writer used to describe the path that a group of Philistines took against Saul (1 Sam. 13:17). Some would identify it with the land of Shaalim (1 Sam. 9:4). The location is uncertain.

SHUBAEL (Shū´ bā ĕl) See *Shebuel.*

SHUHAH (Shū´ häh) Personal name of uncertain meaning. Brother or, according to some manuscript evidence, the son of Caleb (1 Chron. 4:11). Some commentators connect the name to Suchati known from Egyptian sources and think of a forefather of a nomadic clan who lived in the Negev.

SHUHAM (Shū´ hăm) Personal name of uncertain meaning. Son of Dan (Num. 26:42). See *Hushim.*

SHUHAMITE (Shū´ hăm īt) Member of clan of Shuham (Num. 26:42).

SHUHITE (Shū´ hīt) Person from Shuah.

SHULAMITE (Shŭ´ lăm īt) or **SHULAMMITE** Description of woman in Song 6:13, either as from Shunem through a copying change; or from Shulam, an otherwise unknown town; or Solomonite, referring to a relationship to Solomon; or a common noun meaning "the replaced one."

SHUMATHITE (Shū´ măth īt) Clan name of uncertain meaning descended from Caleb (1 Chron. 2:53).

SHUNEM, SHUNAMMITE (Shū´ něm, Shū´ năm mīt) Place-name and clan name of uncertain meaning. Town in tribe of Issachar located southeast of Mount Carmel. The site was captured by the Egyptian pharaoh Thutmose III about 1450 B.C., again by Labayu of Shechem about 1350 B.C., and rebuilt by Biridya of Megiddo. The Israelites controlled it under Joshua (Josh. 19:18). The Philistines camped at Shunem while fighting with Saul (1 Sam. 28:4,7). About 920 B.C. the Egyptian pharaoh Shishak captured the town. See *Shishak.* As David lay dying, Abishag the Shunammite was hired to minister to the king (1 Kings 1:3; cp. 2:17). The Prophet Elisha stayed often at the home of a Shunammite couple, prophesied that a son would be born to them, and raised the boy from the dead after an accident in the field (2 Kings 4). It is modern Solem, about eight miles north of Jenin and three miles east of Affulah. See *Abishag.*

SHUNI (Shū´ nī) Personal name of uncertain meaning. Son of Gad and head of a clan in that tribe (Gen. 46:16).

SHUNITE (Shū´ nīt) Member of clan of Shuni (Num. 26:15).

SHUPHAM (Shū´ phăm) Personal name of uncertain meaning reconstructed by scholars as son of Benjamin on basis of the clan name Shuphamite (Num. 26:39). The personal name in Hebrew is "Muppim" in Genesis and "Shephupham" in Numbers. In 1 Chron. 7:6 the name is absent, but in 7:12,15 "Shupim" occurs.

SHUPHAMITE (Shŭ´ phăm īt) Member of Benjaminite clan of Shupham or Shephupham. See *Shephupham; Shupham.*

SHUPPIM (Shŭp´ pĭm) Personal name of uncertain meaning and plural form in Hebrew. Apparently a son of Benjamin (1 Chron. 7:12) but related to Machir in verse 15. The Chronicles texts apparently have experienced loss of words through copying. REB emends the text so that Shuppim is not included. See *Shupham.*

SHUR, WILDERNESS OF (Shūr) Place-name meaning "wall." Region on Egypt's northeastern border, perhaps named after wall that Egyptians built to protect their border, where Moses made first stop after crossing the Red Sea (Exod. 15:22). Earlier, Sarah's handmaid, Hagar, had

The Wilderness of Shur.

come toward Shur after her expulsion from the clan of Abraham (Gen. 16:7). Abraham lived near Shur (Gen. 20:1). Saul smote the Amalekites in that area (1 Sam. 15:7). David and his men made forays as far as Shur while eluding King Saul (1 Sam. 27:8). Shur may be modern Tell el-Fara.

SHUSHAN (Shū´ shăn) Persian place-name transcribed in Hebrew with word borrowed from Egyptian meaning "lily" or "lotus." City in southwestern Iran which served as the ancient capital of the nation Elam. The site was inhabited as early as 3000 B.C. It was located on the caravan routes between Arabia and points north and west, and therefore it became a very rich city. Archaeological evidence indicates that Shushan traded heavily with nations in Mesopotamia. In Esther 1:2 the city is identified as the throne city of Ahasuerus and called Susa by modern translations. The Achaemenean Dynasty between 500 and 300 B.C. took Shushan to its height politically and economically. It served as the king's winter residence; they moved to Ecbatana in summer. During periods of Seleucid and Parthian rule, it declined and finally was destroyed in the fourth century A.D. See *Elam; Persia.*

SHUSHAN-EDUTH (Shū shăn-ē´ dŭth) See *Shoshannim; Shoshannim-eduth; Lily of the Covenant.*

SHUTHALHITE (Shū thăl´ hīt) Member of clan of Shuthelah (Num. 26:35).

SHUTHELA(H)ITE (Shū thē´ lă hīt) Modern translations' spelling of Shuthalhite.

SHUTHELAH (Shū´ thə lah) Personal name of uncertain meaning. Original ancestor of clan in tribe of Ephraim (Num. 26:35).

SHUTTLE See *Loom.*

SIA (Sī´ à) Personal name meaning "helper." Family of temple servants or Nethinim (KJV, Nethinims) (Ezra 2:44; Neh. 7:47). See *Nethinim.*

SIAHA (Sī´ à hà) Personal name meaning "helpers of God." Temple servants (Ezra 2:44). This is apparently a variant spelling of Sia.

SIBBECAI (Sĭb´ ə kī) or **SIBBECHAI** Personal name of uncertain meaning. Member of David's army who killed a giant or, more literally, a descendant of the Rephaim (2 Sam. 21:18 REB). First Chronicles 11:29 lists him among David's military heroes, leading many commentators to see Sibbecai as the original reading for Mebunnai in 2 Sam. 23:27 resulting from a confusion of Hebrew letters by early scribes. Sibbecai commanded David's forces for the eighth month (1 Chron. 27:11).

SIBBOLETH (Sĭb´ bō lĕth) See *Shibboleth.*

SIBLING RIVALRY Tensions and fighting among brothers or sisters including Cain and Abel (Gen. 4:1-16); Shem, Ham, and Japheth (Gen. 9:20-27); Jacob and Esau (Gen. 25:22–28:9; 32:1–33:17; Mal. 1:2-3); Leah and Rachel (Gen. 29:16–30:24); Joseph and his brothers (Gen. 37; 39–45); Er and Onan (Gen. 38:1-10); Moses, Aaron, and Miriam (Num. 12:1-15); Abimelech and Jotham (Judg. 9:1-57); David and Eliab (1 Sam. 17:28-30); Absalom and Amnon (2 Sam. 13:1-39); and Solomon and Adonijah (1 Kings 1:5-53). In each case one, or usually both, of the siblings attempts to gain status or favor over the other.

Families are given by God (Ps. 127:3) and are not, like friends, chosen by their members. The physical and emotional proximity of family members is characteristic quite close. The potential for sibling rivalry is built into the family dynamic, as the writer of Proverbs understood: "A friend loves at all times, and a brother is born for a difficult time" (Prov. 17:17 HCSB; 18:24; Matt. 10:21). The psalmist praised the goodness and pleasantness of brothers who are able to dwell together in unity (Ps. 133:1-3).

Paul H. Wright

SIBMAH (Sĭb´ mah) Place-name meaning "cold" or "high." City tribe of Reuben rebuilt in Transjordan (Num. 32:38). It became part of their tribal inheritance (Josh. 13:19). Isaiah mentioned it in his lament over Moab (16:8-9; cp. Jer. 48:32). "Sebam" (Num. 32:3) is often seen as a copyist's change from Sibmah. It may be located at Khirbet al-qibsh about three miles east-north-east of Mount Nebo and three miles southwest of Hesban.

SIBRAIM (Sĭb´ rā ĭm) Place-name of uncertain meaning. Apparently the northern border between Damascus and Hamath. Some would identify it with Sepharvaim (2 Kings 17:24). The precise location is not known.

SIBYLLINE ORACLES See *Pseudepigrapha.*

SICARII (Sĭ cär´ ē ī) See *Assassins.*

SICHEM (Sī´ kĕm) (KJV, Gen. 12:6) See *Shechem.*

SICK See *Diseases.*

SICKLE Curved blade of flint or metal used to cut stalks of grain. Sickles varied in size and handle length but usually had a short wooden handle that required the user to bend near the ground to harvest the crop. They are among the oldest tools known by humans, dating to 8500 B.C. Biblical texts often used the sickle symbolically to speak of coming judgment. Revelation 14 uses the analogy of Christ reaping the harvest of mankind at the great judgment. See *Agriculture.*

SIDDIM (Sĭd´ dĭm) Place-name, perhaps meaning "flats" or "fields." A variant name for the Dead Sea where the coalition faced Chedorlaomer and his allies, leading to Abraham's rescue of Lot (Gen. 14). The reference is apparently to the land bordering the Dead Sea. Some think the Hebrew should be read "Shadim" and interpreted as a reference to the Valley of Demons.

SIDON AND TYRE (Sī´ dŏn, Tīr) Phoenician cities located on the coastal plain between the mountains of Lebanon and the Mediterranean Sea (Gen. 10:15). Sidon and Tyre were ancient cities, having been founded long before the Israelites entered the land of Canaan. Extrabiblical sources first mention Sidon before 2000 B.C. and Tyre just after 2000 B.C. While Sidon seems to have been the more dominant of the two cities during the early part of their histories, Tyre assumed this role in the latter times. Both cities were known for their maritime exploits and as centers of trade. One of Tyre's most coveted exports was purple dye. Joshua could not conquer the territory (Josh. 13:3-4).

Israel had relations with the two cities, but especially with Tyre. David employed Tyrian

Inside the main tunnel at the Cumae Shrine of the Sibyl, the primary Sibylline sanctuary.

stonemasons and carpenters and used cedars from that area in building a palace (2 Sam. 5:11). The construction of the temple in Jerusalem during Solomon's reign depended heavily on the materials and craftsmen from Tyre. About 870 B.C. Ahab married Jezebel, the daughter of the Phoenician king, bringing Baal worship to Israel's court. Ezekiel 28 characterizes the king of Tyre as the ultimate example of pride. Under Roman rule the two cities were important ports of trade, but they did not enjoy the dominance they previously held. Jesus spent time in Tyre and Sidon and, differing with the prophets' attitude toward the cities, He contrasted them with the Jews as examples of faith (Matt. 11:20-22). Paul spent seven days in Tyre after his third missionary journey (Acts 21:3-4). See *Phoenicia.*

Scott Langston

SIEGE Battle tactic in which an army surrounds a city and cuts off all supplies so that the enemy army is forced to surrender for lack of food and water. Deuteronomy 28:53-57 described the horrible actions to which siege leads (cp. Jer. 19:9). Ezekiel 4 describes the prophet's symbolic act of building a miniature city of Jerusalem under siege. Preparing for siege, a city stored

S

Hippodrome at Tyre, the largest hippodrome in the Roman Empire.

The harbor at Sidon in the modern state of Lebanon.

water inside the city walls and repaired the walls (Nah. 3:14). One response was to "gather up your goods and flee the country" (Jer. 10:17 REB). To remain under siege was to "give yourselves over to die by hunger and by thirst" (2 Chron. 32:11 NASB). This was the major tactic used in Near Eastern wars. Judah suffered siege from Sennacherib (2 Kings 18–19) and from Nebuchadnezzar (2 Kings 24–25).

SIEGEWORKS Platforms or towers an army built around and above the city walls of a city under siege. This allowed the besieging army to shoot arrows and throw missiles of war down into the city. Israel's law did not allow fruit trees to be cut down to build such platforms (Deut. 20:19-20). Ramps built up to the city walls allowed soldiers to attack the walls and to shoot fire arrows and other weapons into the city. Scaling ladders lifted armies over the walls into the city. Battering rams destroyed city gates. Fires at the base of the walls weakened the sandstone bricks. Tunnels dug under the walls further weakened them. Thus the population's emotions were drained, its supplies were exhausted, and its defenses destroyed.

SIEVE Instrument used to remove unwanted materials from sand or grain. Pebbles or straw remain in the sieve, while the sand or grain passes through. God warned Israel He would place them in a sieve of judgment and none would fall through, for none of them were good grain (Amos 9:9). Another Hebrew word traditionally translated "sieve" in Isa. 30:28 refers to a swinging action. Precisely what is swung is not clear, the noun coming from the same root as the verb. In some manner Isaiah proclaimed God's judgment would swing over His people.

SIGN Symbol, action, or occurrence that points to something beyond itself. In the OT signs occasionally refer to celestial phenomena such as the lights God spoke into existence as "signs for festivals and for days and years" (Gen. 1:14 HCSB). Often signs refer to miraculous intervention by God. They can point observers to knowledge of God, such as the events of the exodus (Deut. 4:34). Signs can reinforce faith through remembrance of His mighty deeds, such as memorial stones from the Jordan that were to be "a sign among you" (Josh. 4:6). Signs can also point to God's covenant with His people. These include the rainbow (Gen. 9:12), circumcision (Gen. 17:11), the Sabbath (Exod. 31:13), and the wearing of phylacteries on the wrist and forehead (Deut. 6:8; 11:18).

One of the most significant OT uses of "sign" is an attestation that a prophetic message was from God. One example is the staff of Moses becoming a serpent and his hand becoming leprous, then whole again (Exod. 4:8-9). In Ezek. 12:6 the prophet himself is a sign to the house of Israel by carrying his baggage as a symbol of the prophesied exile. The presence of signs alone is not sufficient to guarantee that a prophet speaks God's word. Deuteronomy 13:1-5 states that after a sign is given, the prophet could still prophesy falsely. His message must be tested by its truth.

Of particular interest is the sign of the virgin's conception in Isa. 7:14. The fulfillment of this prophecy is apparently double, the first occurring with a conception and birth in Isaiah's time as a symbol of God's deliverance of Judah. The ultimate fulfillment is in the coming virgin-born Messiah, Jesus Christ (Matt. 1:20-23).

In the NT "sign" is usually translated from the Greek word *semeion*. *Semeion* occurs over 70 times in the NT, mostly in the Gospels and Acts, seven times in Paul's letters, two in Hebrews, and six in Revelation. *Semeion* can refer to a natural event, but more often it refers either to a miraculous act authenticating God's activity or to an eschatological sign pointing to the final culmination of history.

Luke records signs at the birth of Jesus. The "baby wrapped snugly in cloth" (HCSB) was a sign to the shepherds that verified the angels' announcement (Luke 2:12), and Simeon prophesied that Jesus Himself was a sign, one to be opposed by many (Luke 2:34).

While signs can point to God's work, Jesus condemned the demand for signs to prove God was working through Him. When the scribes and Pharisees requested a sign from Jesus, He responded that signs were craved by "an evil and adulterous generation" (Matt. 12:39 HCSB). The only sign they would be given was the sign of Jonah, a reference to His death and resurrection. In the Gospel of John, Jesus tells those following Him after the feeding of the 5,000, "You are looking for Me, not because you saw signs, but because you ate the loaves and were filled" (John 6:26). They physically saw the signs Jesus performed but did not perceive their significance that He was the Son of God.

In John's Gospel *semeion* is used for the miracles of Jesus as well as other attestations of His deity. John's use of "sign" for miracle puts the focus on what the miracle signifies rather than upon the supernatural act itself. That significance is the identity of Jesus and the work of God through Him.

In Acts "sign" is used to refer to God's activity in the OT (Acts 7:36) and in Jesus (2:22; 4:30). Additionally, signs occur to attest God's activity in and through the apostles. After Pentecost "many wonders and signs were being performed through the apostles" (2:43, HCSB; 5:12; Heb. 2:4). The ministries of Philip (Acts 8:6; 8:13) and Paul (14:3; 15:12) were authenticated by signs.

Paul refers to Abraham's circumcision as a sign and seal of the righteousness of his faith (Rom. 4:11). Signs were also an indicator of God's presence in Paul's ministry (Rom. 15:19; 2 Cor. 12:12). He echoed Jesus: "Jews ask for signs and the Greeks seek wisdom, but we preach Christ crucified" (1 Cor. 1:22-23 HCSB). Tongues were identified as a sign to unbelievers (1 Cor. 14:22). He told the Philippians their firmness in persecution was a sign of destruction to persecutors and a sign of their salvation (Phil. 1:27-28). Paul warned that the "lawless one" will come "based on Satan's working, with all kinds of false miracles, signs, and wonders" (2 Thess. 2:9; cp. Deut. 13:2).

Jesus warned against signs produced by false prophets preceding His second coming (Matt. 24:24) but also spoke of signs of His coming and the end of the age (Matt. 24:30; Luke 21:11,25). Similarly, Peter quoted Joel at Pentecost, "I will display wonders in the heaven above and signs on the earth below" (Acts 2:19 HCSB). Revelation 12 includes the eschatological signs of the "woman clothed with the sun" (Rev. 12:1) and the "great fiery red dragon" (12:3). Over half the references to signs in Revelation are referring to those performed by the beast who comes out of the earth and the false prophet (13:13-14; 16:14; 19:20).

Signs can be a verification of the presence and power of God at work in circumstances or in His people. Signs can point to the second coming of Christ. Signs can also be counterfeited and be present with those who deceive. While signs can and do point to God and to Christ, they are inadequate to bring anyone to saving faith.

David R. Beck

SIGNET Usually a ring with a seal carefully crafted upon it that an important or rich person used to authenticate a document. It was used much like a signature on a document today. The ring of kings would carry the highest authority in a land and empowered subordinates to act for the king. Examples of such rings in the Bible are: Pharaoh's ring given to Joseph (Gen. 41:42); Ahasuerus' ring given to Haman and then to Mordecai after Haman was hanged (Esther 3:10,12; 8:2); King Darius's sealing the den of lions after Daniel was thrown into it (Dan. 6:17). The signet could be worn on a chain around the neck. In an unusual use of the word, Zerubbabel is said to be "a signet" because the Lord had chosen him (Hag. 2:23). Zerubbabel was granted Yahweh's authority, and thus completion of the temple was guaranteed. Another unusual use of the word was the special engraving of the stones on the ephod of the high priest "as a gem cutter engraves a seal" (Exod. 28:11 HCSB). See *Seal.*

SIHON (Sī´ hŏn) Amorite personal name of unknown meaning. Amorite king whose capital was Heshbon (Deut. 2:26). He opposed Israel's passage through his country as they journeyed toward the promised land (Num. 21:23). Although he allied with Og, king of Bashan, neither could withstand the Hebrew migration. The tribes of Reuben and Gad settled in the area formerly held by Sihon, just east of the Jordan River.

SIHOR (Sī´ hôr) (KJV) See *Shihor.*

SIKKUTH (Sĭk´ ŭth) NASB spelling of Sakkuth. See *Kaiwan; Rephan; Sakkuth.*

SILAS, SILVANUS (Sī´ làs, Sĭl vā´ nŭs) Apparently, the Greek and Latin forms of the same name, possibly derived from Aramaic or Hebrew name "Saul." Leader in the early Jerusalem church. He accompanied both Peter and Paul on separate missionary journeys. One of his first missions was to carry news of the Jerusalem conference to the believers at Antioch (Acts 15:22). He and Paul left Antioch together on a mission to Asia Minor (15:40-41) and later to Macedonia. In Philippi the two were imprisoned (16:19-24), but they later won the jailer and his family to the Lord after God delivered them from prison. Later in his ministry Silas teamed with Peter on missions in Pontus and Cappadocia. He also served as Peter's scribe, writing the first letter from Peter and perhaps other letters. Many believe that he composed and arranged most of the letter since Peter probably had little education. See *Paul; Peter, First Letter from.*

SILENCE Absence of sound. The Bible uses silence in several ways: as reverence to God (Hab. 2:20), as a symbol of death (Ps. 94:17), as a symbol of Sheol (Ps. 115:17), and as an expression of despair (Lam. 2:10). It is a way to shut up the opposition (Matt. 22:34). It is also used as a dramatic pause following the opening of the seventh seal in Rev. 8:1.

SILK Cloth made from thread that came from the Chinese silkworm. Very early China and India traded silk, and India also traded with Mesopotamia. Some think that Solomon may have gotten silk from India. Some feel that the Hebrew word translated "silk" should rather be "fine linen" or "expensive material" (Ezek. 16:10; Prov. 31:22), the Hebrew indicating something glistening white. Revelation 18:12

indicates that the rich in Babylon bought silk from merchants.

SILLA (Sĭl´ lå) House of Millo in which King Joash was murdered by his servants was said to be "on the way that goes down to Silla" (2 Kings 12:20 NRSV). Silla is an unknown place, perhaps near Jerusalem. See *Millo.*

SILOAM (Sĭ lō´ ŭm) Greek place-name possibly derived from Hebrew "Shiloah," meaning "sending." Place easily confused with the waters of Shiloah mentioned in Isa. 8:6 through similarity of spelling. Siloam was the pool created by Hezekiah's tunnel that diverted the waters of Shiloah from the Siloam spring to a point less vulnerable to the Assyrian enemy. It was located on the southern end of the old Jebusite city of Jerusalem. Thus, Siloam is to be distinguished from the King's Pool mentioned in Neh. 3:15. Hezekiah's inscription preserved on the tunnel wall describes the meeting of tunnel builders boring through rock from each end of the tunnel.

John 9:7,11 uses the etymological significance of the term "Siloam" for a play on words to press the point that the blind man was "sent" to Siloam by one who was Himself the One who was "sent." To gain his sight, the blind man went to and obeyed the One who was sent. Luke 13:4 is a reference more to an unknown tower at Siloam than to Siloam. The tower may have been an aborted effort to protect the water supply. The theological issue of Luke 13 does not hinge on the geographical issue of Siloam. The pool, created by Hezekiah and known by Jesus, is still a source of water today. See *Jerusalem; King's Pool.* *John R. Drayer*

SILVANUS (Sĭl vā´ nŭs) See *Silas, Silvanus.*

SILVER Comparatively scarce precious metal with a brilliant white color and remarkably resistant to oxidation. It melts at 960.8° C (1,861° F). Biblical references often refer to the process of refining silver (1 Chron. 29:4; Ps. 12:6; Prov. 17:3; Ezek. 22:20-22). It is so malleable that it is beaten into sheets as thin as 0.00025 mm. Until about 500 B.C., silver was the most valuable metal in the Near East. Thus, in most of the OT it is given a priority over gold. Only in Chronicles and Daniel is gold considered to have more worth. Hence the analogy that in

The Siloam Pool in Jerusalem.

The solid silver case of a Torah scroll.

S

Jerusalem silver was as common as stone (1 Kings 10:27; 2 Chron. 9:27) is reflective of the lavish wealth of Solomon's empire. Coins were first minted after 700 B.C., but weight continued to be the most common standard of determining value. In the NT period, the drachma, a silver coin, was required for the temple tax. Figuratively, refining silver is used in the Bible for testing human hearts (Ps. 66:10; Isa. 48:10; cp. 1 Cor. 3:10-15) and the purity of God's word (Ps. 12:6). Wisdom is declared to be of more value than silver (Job 28:10-15; Prov. 3:13-14; 8:10,19; 16:16). See *Coins; Gold; Minerials and Metals; Money.*   *LeBron Matthews*

SILVERSMITH Person who works with silver. It could be in refining the silver from the ore or the making of the refined silver into the finished product. Silver was used for money and religious images (Judg. 17:4). It was used in making many of the utensils used in the tabernacle and temple (Num. 7:13). The only mention of silversmiths in the NT was a dispute with Paul where his preaching was threatening their livelihood (Acts 19:23-41). See *Occupations and Professions.*

SIMEON (Sĭm´ ə ŏn) Personal name meaning "hearing" or possibly, "little hyena beast." **1.** One of Jacob's 12 sons, the second by Leah (Gen. 29:33). He joined Levi in avenging Dinah's rape by Shechem (Gen. 34:25-31). Joseph kept Simeon bound in Egypt to ensure that he would see Benjamin (Gen. 42:24). See *Jacob; Tribes of Israel.* **2.** Devout Jew who lived in Jerusalem during the time of Jesus' birth. He was seeking the fulfillment of messianic prophecy when Israel would be restored (Luke 2:25). God promised Simeon that he would not die before seeing the Christ. When Joseph and Mary brought Jesus to the temple for the purification rites, Simeon announced to them God's plan for the boy (2:34). **3.** Ancestor of Jesus (Luke 3:30). **4.** Prophet and teacher in church at Antioch (Acts 13:1). **5.** Alternate form in Greek for Simon, original Greek name of Peter. See *Peter; Simon.*

SIMEONITES (Sĭm´ ē ŏ nīts) People of the tribe of Simeon, the second son of Jacob and Leah (Gen. 29:33).

SIMILITUDE "Likeness" or "similarity." **1.** The OT used it of things being like God. Three words

are translated "similitude" in the OT: *demut* (2 Chron. 4:3; Dan. 10:16), *tabnit* (Pss. 106:20; 144:12), and *temunah* (Num. 12:8; Deut. 4:12). **2.** In the NT it is used to translate *homoios* or its derivative three times (Rom. 5:14; Heb. 7:15; James 3:9: "likeness" or "like," HCSB).

SIMMAGIR See *Samgar-Nebo.*

SIMON (Sī´ mŏn) Greek personal name meaning "flat-nosed." Used in NT as Greek alternative for Hebrew "Simeon." **1.** The father of Judas Iscariot (John 6:71). **2.** One of Jesus' disciples; a son of Jonah (Matt. 16:17) and brother of Andrew. After he confessed Jesus as the Christ, the Lord changed his name to Peter (v. 18). See *Peter; Simeon.* **3.** Pharisee who hosted Jesus at a dinner (Luke 7:36-50). Simon learned valuable lessons about love, courtesy, and forgiveness after a sinful woman anointed Jesus at this event. **4.** Native of Cyrene who was forced to carry Jesus' cross to Golgotha (Mark 15:21). See *Cyrene.* **5.** Tanner of animal skins who lived in the seaport of Joppa. Peter stayed at his house (Acts 9:43) and there received a visionary message from God declaring all foods to be fit for consumption (10:9-16). **6.** Jesus' disciple also called "the Canaanite" (Matt. 10:4) or the Zealot (Luke 6:15). **7.** Brother of Jesus (Matt. 13:55). **8.** Leper who hosted Jesus and saw a woman anoint Jesus with costly ointment (Matt. 26:6-13; cp. 3. above). **9.** Magician from Samaria who believed Philip's preaching, was baptized, and then tried to buy the power of laying on hands and giving the Holy Spirit to people (Acts 8:9-24).

SIMPLE, SIMPLICITY Very similar to sincerity. A simple person is one who is open, honest, and direct, without hypocrisy. Sometimes there is the idea of uneducated, inexperienced, or unsophisticated. Simplicity is associated with ideas like integrity (2 Sam. 15:11), without evil (Rom. 16:18), generosity (Rom. 12:8), a life of devotion to God (2 Cor. 1:12), and simply believing the gospel truth (2 Cor. 11:3). God is said to "preserve" the simple (Ps. 116:6). Proverbs is filled with sayings about the simple, both good and bad (1:22; 14:15,18; 21:11). See *Sincerity.*

SIMRI (Sĭm´ rī) See *Shimri.*

The traditional area of the home of Simon the tanner in ancient Joppa (modern Jaffa near Tel Aviv).

SIN Actions by which humans rebel against God, miss His purpose for their life, and surrender to the power of evil rather than to God.

Sin as Rebellion One of the central affirmations throughout the Bible is humanity's estrangement from God. The cause for this estrangement is sin, the root cause of all the problems of humanity. The Bible, however, gives no formal definition for sin. It describes sin as an attitude that personifies sin as rebellion against God. Rebellion was at the root of the problem for Adam and Eve (Gen. 3) and has been at the root of humanity's plight ever since.

Sin is universal—we all sin. The Bible does not give a complete account of the origin of sin. God is in no way responsible for sin. Satan introduced sin when he beguiled Eve, but the Bible does not teach that sin had its origin with him either. Sin's origin is to be found in humanity's rebellious nature. Since Adam and Eve rebelled against the clear command of God, sin has infected humanity like a dread malignancy.

Some passages such as Ps. 51:5 and Eph. 2:3 could be interpreted to mean that this sinful nature is inherited. Other passages seem to affirm that sin is due to human choice (Ezek. 18:4,19-20; Rom. 1:18-20; 5:12). Humanity both inherits a sinful nature and every person is indeed responsible for his/her choice of sin.

Another possibility for understanding how sin has infected all of humanity may be found in the biblical understanding of the solidarity of the human race. This understanding of the human situation would say that when Adam rebelled against God, he incorporated all of his descendants in his action (Heb. 7:9-10 for a similar analogy). This view certainly does not eliminate the necessity for each individual to accept full responsibility for sinful acts.

Adam and Eve introduced sin into human history by their rebellious actions. The Bible affirms that every person who has lived since has followed their example. Whatever else one may say about sin's origin, this much is surely affirmed throughout the Bible.

The Bible Views Sin from Various Perspectives One concept of sin in the OT is that of transgression of the law. God established the law as a standard of righteousness; any violation of this standard is defined as sin. Deuteronomy 6:24-25 is a statement of this principle from the perspective that a person who keeps the law is righteous. The implication is that the person who does not keep the law is not righteous, that is, is sinful.

Another concept of sin in the OT is as breach of the covenant. God made a covenant with the nation of Israel; they were bound by this covenant as a people (Exod. 19; 24; Josh. 24). Each year on the Day of Atonement, the nation went through a covenant renewal. When the high priest consecrated the people by sprinkling them with the blood of the atoning sacrifice, they renewed their vows to the Lord to be a covenant-keeping people. Any breach of this covenant was viewed as sin (Deut. 29:19-21.)

The OT also pictures sin as a violation of the righteous nature of God. As the righteous and holy God, He sets forth as a criterion for His people a righteousness like His own (Lev. 11:45). Any deviation from God's own righteousness is viewed as sin.

The OT has a rich vocabulary for sin. *Chata'* means "to miss the mark," as does the Greek *hamartia*. The word could be used to describe a person shooting a bow and arrow and missing the target with the arrow. When it is used to

S

describe sin, it means that the person has missed the mark that God has established for the person's life.

Aven describes the crooked or perverse spirit associated with sin. Sinful persons have perverted their spirits and become crooked rather than straight. *Ra'* describes the violence associated with sin. It also has the connotation of the breaking out of evil. Sin is the opposite of righteousness or moral straightness in the OT.

The New Testament Perspective of Sin The NT picture is much like that of the OT. Several of the words used for sin in the NT have almost the same meaning as some of the Hebrew words used in the OT. The most notable advancement in the NT view of sin is the fact that sin is defined against the backdrop of Jesus as the standard for righteousness. His life exemplifies perfection. The exalted purity of His life creates the norm for judging what is sinful.

In the NT sin also is viewed as a lack of fellowship with God. The ideal life is one of fellowship with God. Anything that disturbs or distorts this fellowship is sin.

The NT view of sin is somewhat more subjective than objective. Jesus taught quite forcefully that sin is a condition of the heart. He traced sin directly to inner motives stating that the sinful thought leading to the overt act is the real sin. The outward deed is actually the fruit of sin. Anger in the heart is the same as murder (Matt. 5:21-22). The impure look is tantamount to adultery (Matt. 5:27-28). The real defilement in a person stems from the inner person (heart) which is sinful (Matt. 15:18-20). Sin, therefore, is understood as involving the essential being of a person, that is, the essential essence of human nature.

The NT interprets sin as "unbelief." However, unbelief is not just the rejection of a dogma or a creed. Rather, it is the rejection of that spiritual light which has been revealed in Jesus Christ. Or, from another perspective, unbelief is the rejection of the supreme revelation as it is found in the person of Jesus Christ. Unbelief is resistance to the truth of God revealed by the Spirit of God and produces moral and spiritual blindness. The outcome of such rejection is judgment. The only criterion for judgment is whether or not one has accepted or rejected the revelation of God as found in Jesus Christ (John 3:18-19; 16:8-16).

The NT further pictures sin as being revealed by the law of Moses. The law was preparatory, and its function was to point to Christ. The law revealed sin in its true character, but this only aroused in humanity a desire to experience the forbidden fruit of sin. The law as such is not bad, but humanity simply does not have the ability to keep the law. Therefore, the law offers no means of salvation; rather, it leaves humanity with a deep sense of sin and guilt (Rom. 7). The law, therefore, serves to bring sin into bold relief, so that it is clearly perceptible.

The most common NT word for sin is *hamartia* (see above). *Parabasis*, "trespass" or "transgression," literally, means to step across the line. One who steps over a property line has trespassed on another person's land; the person who steps across God's standard of righteousness has committed a trespass or transgression.

Anomia means "lawlessness" or "iniquity" and is a rather general description of sinful acts, referring to almost any action in opposition to God's standard of righteousness. *Poneria*, "evil" or "wickedness," is even more inclusive than *anomia*. *Adikia*, "unrighteousness," is just the opposite of righteous. In forensic contexts outside the NT, it described one who was on the wrong side of the law.

Akatharsia, "uncleanness" or "impurity," was a cultic word used to describe anything which could cause cultic impurity. It was used quite often to describe vicious acts or sexual sins. *Apistia*, "unbelief," literally refers to a lack of faith. To refuse to accept the truth of God by faith is to sin. Hence any action which can be construed as unfaithful or any disposition which is marked by a lack of faith is sinful.

Epithumia, often translated "lust," is actually a neutral word. Only the context can determine if the desire is good or evil. Jesus said, "I have fervently desired to eat this Passover with you before I suffer" (Luke 22:15 HCSB). Paul used this word with a modifier meaning "evil," in Col. 3:5, where it is translated "evil concupiscence" or "evil desire." When used in this way, the word could refer to almost any evil desire but was most often used to describe sexual sins (Matt. 5:28).

Sin's Consequences The Bible looks upon sin in any form as the most serious of humanity's problems. Though sinful acts may be directed against another person, ultimately every sin is against God, the Creator of all things. Perfect in righteousness, God cannot tolerate that which violates His righteous character. Therefore, sin creates a barrier between God and persons.

Sin also necessitates God's intervention in human affairs. Since humanity could not extricate itself from the entanglements of sin, it was necessary for God to intervene if humanity was ever to be freed from these entanglements. See *Salvation.*

The consequences of sin both personally and in society are far reaching. That person who constantly and consistently follows a sinful course will become so enmeshed in sin that for all practical purposes he or she is enslaved to sin (Rom. 6).

Another of the awful consequences of sin is spiritual depravity in society in general as well as in the lives of individuals. Some will argue that depravity is the cause of sin, and this surely is a valid consideration. However, there can be no escaping the fact that a continuance in sin adds to this personal depravity, a moral crookedness or corruption, eventually making it impossible to reject sin. Sin also produces spiritual blindness. Spiritual truths simply are not visible to that person who has been blinded by sin.

Moral ineptitude is another devastating consequence of sin. The more people practice sin, the more inept they become as far as moral and spiritual values are concerned. Eventually, sin blurs the distinction between right and wrong.

Guilt is certainly a consequence of sin. No person can blame another person for a sin problem. Each person must accept responsibility for sin and face the guilt associated with it (Rom. 1–3).

In the Bible sin and death are corollaries. One of the terrible by-products of sin is death. Continual, consistent sin will bring spiritual death to that person who has not come under the lordship of Christ through repentance and faith (Rom. 6:23; Rev. 20:14.) For those who have trusted Christ Jesus for salvation, death no longer holds this dread. Christ has negated the power of Satan in making death horrible and has freed the person from slavery to this awful fear (Heb. 2:14-15). See *Death.*

Another serious consequence of sin is that it brings separation from God, estrangement, and a lack of fellowship with God. This need not be permanent, but if a person dies not having corrected this problem by trusting Christ, then the separation does become permanent (Rom. 6:23). See *Hell.*

Sin produces estrangement from other persons just as surely as it produces an estrangement from God. All interpersonal problems have sin as their root cause (James 4:1-3). The only hope for peace to be achieved on either the personal or national level is through the Prince of peace. *Billy E. Simmons*

SIN, WILDERNESS OF Barren region somewhere west of the Sinai plateau on the Sinai Peninsula. The Hebrew people stopped here on their journey from Egypt to the promised land (Exod. 16:1). It was here that God first provided manna and quail for them to eat. The place sometimes has been confused with the Wilderness of Zin, which is located on the northwestern side of Sinai. See *Zin, Wilderness of.*

SINAI, MOUNT (Sī´ nī) Mountain in the south central part of a peninsula in the northwestern end of Arabia. God made many significant revelations of Himself and His purposes to Israel there. The meaning of the name is unclear, but it probably means "shining" and was likely derived from the word *sin*, a Babylonian moon god.

The entire peninsula takes the shape of an inverted triangle whose base is 150 miles long and is bounded on the east by the north end of the Red Sea and on the west by the Gulf of Aqaba. The Gaza Strip lies directly north. This peninsula contains 23,442 square miles and has a population of approximately 270,000 at time of publication. The central and southern parts are extremely mountainous, ranging from 5,000 to about 9,000 feet, and the land today is valued for its oil fields and manganese deposits.

The desolate country of the Wilderness of Sin.

![Jebel Musa, the traditional site of Mount Sinai, in the southern Sinai Peninsula.]

Jebel Musa, the traditional site of Mount Sinai, in the southern Sinai Peninsula.

The Bible uses the term "Sinai" for both the mountain and the entire wilderness area (Lev. 7:38). Sometimes Sinai is called "the mount" (Exod. 19:2), sometimes "the mountain of God" (Exod. 3:1), sometimes "the mount of the LORD" (Num. 10:33).

The term *Horeb* is often used to refer to Sinai in such a way as to make the names synonymous (Exod. 3:1). Since Horeb means "waste" or "wilderness area," it seems best to think of Horeb as the general term for the area and Sinai as the specific peak where God manifested Himself to Moses.

The modern name for the traditional site of Sinai is Jebel Musa (the mount of Moses). *Jebel* is the Arabic word for "hill," sometimes written Jabal or Gabel (French has Djebel).

Jebel Musa (7,500 ft.) is one of three granite peaks near the southern tip of the peninsula. The highest peak, Jebel Katarin (Mount Catherine, 8,652 ft.), lies immediately on the southwest, and Ras es-Safsafeh (6,540 ft.) on the north-northeast of Jebel Musa. Many explorers think Ras es-Safsafeh is the biblical Sinai because it has a plain, *er Rahah*, on its northwest base, which is two miles long and about two thirds of a mile

View from Jebel Musa (the probable location of Mount Sinai) of the surrounding rugged landscape.

wide. This plain was certainly large enough to accommodate the camp of the Israelites.

Another suggested location for Mount Sinai is far north and east of Jebel Musa, near the top of the Gulf of Aqaba. The major argument for this view is that Sinai's phenomena indicate volcanic action—fire, smoke, quaking earth (Exod. 19:16-18)—and no volcano is found on the Sinai Peninsula. The nearest volcano lies far east of the Gulf. However, the phenomena that appeared at Sinai were undoubtedly supernatural in origin, for they were accompanied by the sounds of a trumpet and the voice of God (Exod. 19:19).

Another location for Sinai is sought far north of Jebel Musa, primarily because of historical references such as the battle with the Amalekites (Exod. 17:8-16). The Amalekites lived in Canaan proper (Num. 14:42-45) and would not, it is claimed, have met the Israelites in the Sinai Peninsula. However, the Amalekites could have followed the recently delivered Israelites to the south of their territory for the purpose of preying on the poorly organized refugees (Deut. 25:17-19). See *Exodus; Palestine; Wilderness.*

James L. Travis

SINCERITY Personal quality of living life from a pure motive without deceit. Associated with words or ideas like "truth" (1 Cor. 5:8), "genuineness" (2 Cor. 8:8), "godliness" (2 Cor. 1:12), and preaching the gospel sincerely (2 Cor. 2:17). It is also contrasted with words like hypocrisy, deceit, and wickedness. See *Holy; Truth.*

SINEW Tendons and connective tissue that connect muscles to bone in the body. The literal use is seen in Scripture (Job 10:11; 30:17; Ezek. 37:6,8). Isaiah 48:4 uses it in a figurative way to show rebellion against God. Because of Jacob's wrestling with the angel that resulted in the angel's striking the sinew of his thigh, the Jews cut away this sinew and did not eat it (Gen. 32:24-32). See *Body.*

SINGING, SINGERS See *Hymn; Levites; Music, Instruments, Dancing.*

SINIM (Sī´ nĭm) Land from which God promised to gather the Babylonian exiles (Isa. 49:12). Traditionally translated as China and treated variously by early translators as Persia or the south, the term received clarification from an Isaiah

manuscript among the Dead Sea Scrolls, which reads "Syenites," a reference to modern Aswan (cp. NIV, REB, NRSV).

SINITE (Sī´ nīt) People from a city-state controlled by Ugarit, the Hittites, and the Assyrians whose inhabitants descended from Canaan (Gen. 10:17). It is in northern Phoenicia near Arqa, either Siyanu, two and a half miles east of Gebala, or Shen, south-southeast of Halba.

SINNER Person who has missed God's mark for life, rebelling against Him. The Bible considers every person a sinner (Rom. 3:23). In the OT people who did not live by the law were considered sinners (Ps. 1). The NT uses *anomia* in a similar way (1 Tim 1:9). Jews regarded Gentiles as sinners (Gal. 2:15) as well as people who did not keep the tradition of the Pharisees, including Jesus (Matt. 11:19; Luke 15). Paul spoke of sinners as those separated from God (Rom. 5:8). See *Law; Salvation; Sin.*

SION (Sī´ ŏn) **1.** KJV spelling of Sirion (Deut. 4:48). **2.** KJV spelling of Zion (Ps. 65:1; Matt. 21:5; Rom. 11:26; Rev. 14:1). See *Zion.*

SIPHMOTH (Sĭph´ mŏth) Town in southern Judah that received booty of war from David for befriending him (1 Sam. 30:26,28). The location of Siphmoth is unknown. A man named Zabdi may have been a resident of the town (1 Chron. 27:27). See *Shiphmite.*

SIPPAI (Sĭp´ pā ī) Alternate rendering (1 Chron. 20:4) of the name "Saph" (2 Sam. 21:18), a son of a giant killed by Sibbechai the Hushathite. See *Saph.*

SIRAH (Sī´ rah) Place-name meaning "thorn." A well ("cistern of Sirah" NRSV) where Joab and Abishai murdered Abner for killing their brother Asahel (2 Sam. 3:26-30). This well is probably the well named Ain Sarah, a little over a mile northwest of Hebron. See *Wells.*

SIRION (Sĭr´ ĭ ŏn) Sidonian name for Mount Hermon (Deut. 3:9). See *Hermon, Mount.*

SISAMAI (Sĭs´ ă mī) (KJV) See *Sismai.*

SISERA (Sĭs´ ə rä) Personal name meaning "mediation." **1.** Military leader of Jabin, king of Canaan (Judg. 4:2) who was killed by Heber's

S

wife, Jael (v. 21). **2.** Nethinim descendant who returned to Palestine with Zerubbabel (Ezra 2:53; Neh. 7:55). See *Jabin.*

SISMAI (Sĭs´ mī) Personal name of uncertain meaning. Son of Eleasah and father of Shallum (1 Chron. 2:40; "Sisamai" KJV).

SISTER Female sibling counterpart to brother (Gen. 29:13; 30:1,8). In patriarchal times it was permissible to marry a sister (Gen. 20:12). "Sister" was also used of people held in special esteem as a counterpart to brotherly affection (Song 4:9; 8:8). Christian women who proved helpful and assisted the church to live like family were called "sister" (Rom. 16:1-2). Martha and Mary, sisters of Lazarus, were well-known as friends and supporters of Jesus. Jesus said, "Whoever does the will of God, the same is my brother, and my sister, and mother" (Mark 3:35 HCSB). See *Family; Women.*

SITHRI (Sĭth´ rī) Personal name probably meaning "He is my protection." A son of Uzziel in the genealogy of Levi (Exod. 6:22; "Zithri" KJV).

SITNAH (Sĭt´ nah) Well that Isaac's servants dug in the area of Gerar (Gen. 26:21). The well was seized by the servants of Abimelech, therefore, the name means "hatred" or "opponent." See *Well.*

SIVAN (Sī´ văn) Third month (May–June) of the Hebrew calendar, time of wheat harvest and Pentecost. See *Calendars.*

SKIN Outer part of the human body and of the body of animals. **1.** The mention of human skin is often in relation to disease (Lev. 13). Human skin is also mentioned in relationship to hairiness (Gen. 27:11-12,16,22-23), to sickness (Job 7:5; Lam. 5:10), and to the color (Jer. 13:23). **2.** Genesis 3:21 is the first mention of animal skins in the Bible; this is where God made garments of skin for Adam and Eve as clothing. Animal skins were used to make containers for various kinds of liquids: water, milk, wine (Judg. 4:19; Matt. 9:17). The most used hides probably came from the animals most in use: sheep, goats, oxen, and donkeys, although other animal skins certainly were used when available. **3.** The sacrifice of animals sometimes called for the destruction of the entire animal (Lev. 4:11-12). At other times the

skins were the property of the priests for their use (Lev. 7:8). **4.** The skin was also used in several proverbial sayings: "Skin for skin" (Job 2:4), "the skin of my teeth" (Job 19:20), and "Can the Ethiopian change his skin or the leopard his spots?" (Jer. 13:23). See *Diseases; Leprosy; Vessels and Utensils.*

SKINK See *Reptiles; Snail.*

SKIRT Article of clothing. Three Hebrew words are translated "skirt." **1.** *Kanaph* refers to the four loose corners of a garment. David cut off one of these corners of Saul's robe to show he meant Saul no harm (1 Sam. 24:4,11). "To reveal a skirt" (literal reading of Deut. 22:30; 27:20) is a euphemism for sexual relationships, since placing the skirt over a woman of marriageable age was the same as claiming her for marriage (Ruth 3:7-14). **2.** *Peh,* meaning "mouth," is translated "skirts" in Ps. 133:2 ("collar" NIV, NRSV; "edge" NASB). **3.** *Shul* refers to the part of a garment that hangs the closest to the ground. In some passages it refers to the loose garment of a woman. Several references to Jerusalem use this word figuratively to show her sin (Jer. 13:22,26; Lam. 1:9; Nah. 3:5). The lifting of the skirt brought shame because the nakedness of a person was seen (Isa. 47:1-3; Nah. 3:5). See *Cloth, Clothing.*

SKULL See *Calvary.*

SKY See *Heaven.*

SLANDER To speak critically of another person with the intent to hurt (Lev. 19:16). In a court of law it means to falsely accuse another (Exod. 20:16; Deut. 5:20). Jesus said, "I tell you that on the day of judgment people will have to account for every careless word they speak" (Matt. 12:36 HCSB). This should cause each person to be very careful what they say about others (Eph. 4:31; 1 Pet. 2:1). The Bible shows that slander is a mark of the unregenerate world (James 4:11-12; 1 Pet. 2:12; 3:16). Jesus spoke of Satan as one who "has not stood in the truth, because there is no truth in him. When he tells a lie, he speaks from his own nature, because he is a liar and the father of liars" (John 8:44 HCSB). *Diabolos* can mean "slanderous" or "the slanderer" (the devil). See *Devil, Satan, Evil, Demonic; Ethics.*

SLAVE, SERVANT Person totally responsible to and dependent upon another person.

Slavery was prevalent and widely accepted in the ancient world. The economy of Egypt, Greece, and Rome was based on slave labor. In the first Christian century, one out of three persons in Italy and one out of five elsewhere was a slave. Huge gangs toiled in the fields and mines and on building projects. Many were domestic and civil servants. Some were temple slaves and others were craftsmen. Some were forced to become gladiators. Some were highly intelligent and held responsible positions. Legally, a slave had no rights; but, except for the gangs, most were treated humanely and were better off than many free persons. Domestics were considered part of the family, and some were greatly loved by their masters. Canaan, Aram, Assyria, Babylonia, and Persia had fewer slaves because it proved less expensive to hire free persons. Still, the institution of slavery was unquestioned. The Stoics insisted that slaves were humans and should be treated accordingly. Israel's law protected slaves in various ways. Christian preachers called upon masters to be kind, but only the Essenes opposed slavery. See *Essenes; Freedom; Jewish Parties in the New Testament.*

A person could become a slave as a result of capture in war, default on a debt, inability to support and "voluntarily" selling oneself, being sold as a child by destitute parents, birth to slave parents, conviction of a crime, or kidnapping and piracy. Slavery cut across races and nationalities.

Manumission or freeing of slaves was possible and common in Roman times. Masters in their wills often freed their slaves, and sometimes they did so during their lifetimes. Industrious slaves could make and save money and purchase their own freedom. By the first Christian century, a large class of freedmen had developed. There was even a synagogue of the Freedmen in Jerusalem (Acts 6:9).

Old Testament Slavery laws appear in Exod. 21:1-11; Lev. 25:39-55; and Deut. 15:12-18. Most of these concern humane treatment and manumission. A Hebrew sold to another Hebrew or a resident alien because of insolvency was to be released after six years of service and given provisions to start over. If he had come with a wife, she and any children were also released. If the master had given him a wife, she and the children were to remain. If, however, the slave wanted to stay with his wife and chil-

dren rather than be free, he could enroll himself as a slave for life. A Hebrew who sold himself to another Hebrew or resident alien was to be released during the Jubilee Year. A slave could be redeemed at any time by a relative. A Hebrew girl sold by her father to another Hebrew to become his wife was to be released if that man or his son did not marry her. A slave permanently maimed by his or her master was to be freed (Exod. 21:26-27). A fugitive slave—presumably one who had escaped from a foreign owner—was not to be extradited (Deut. 23:15-16). Foreigners could be enslaved permanently, but they had the right to circumcision (Exod. 12:44-48), Sabbath rest (Exod. 20:10), and holidays (Deut. 16:11,14). One was to be punished for beating a slave to death (Exod 21:20-21). See *Year of Jubilee.*

New Testament Paul and Peter insisted that Christian slaves be obedient to their masters (Eph. 6:5-8; Col. 3:22-25; 1 Tim. 6:1-2; 1 Pet. 2:18-21) and not seek freedom just because of conversion (1 Cor. 7:20-22). Masters were urged to be kind (Eph. 6:9; Col. 4:1). Slave trading was condemned (1 Tim. 1:10). Paul claimed that in Christ human status was unimportant (Gal. 3:28). But neither Jesus nor the apostles condemned slavery. Slavery was so much a part of their society that to call for abolition would have resulted in violence and bloodshed. Rather, Jesus and the apostles set forth principles of human dignity and equality that eventually led to abolition.

Metaphorical Uses of Slavery In most ancient societies few things were more despicable than to be a slave. In Israel, however, the idea emerged that it was a great privilege to be a servant or slave of God (the various Hebrew and Greek words could be translated either). Many of the heroes of the OT are so called (Exod. 32:13; Deut. 34:5; 2 Sam. 7:5; 2 Kings 21:10). Very significant are the Servant Songs of Isa. 42:1-4; 49:1-6; 50:4-9; and 52:13–53:12, which originally referred to Israel but were reinterpreted by the early church to refer to Jesus. See *Servant of the Lord.*

Jesus adopted a servant's role (John 13:4-5; Mark 10:45; cp. Phil. 2:7) and indicated that His disciples should also (Matt. 6:24; 10:24; 24:45-46; Luke 17:10; John 13:12-16). Paul referred to himself as a slave or servant of Jesus Christ (Rom. 1:1; Gal. 1:10; Phil. 1:1), as did James (1:1), Peter (2 Pet. 1:1), and Jude (1).

S

There are three other metaphorical uses of slavery in the NT. A life of sin is spoken of as slavery to sin (John 8:34; Rom. 6:6,16-20; Heb. 2:15). Legalism is a kind of slavery (Gal. 4:24-25; 5:1). Paradoxically, however, there is also a blessed slavery to righteousness (Rom. 6:16-22). See *Servant of the Lord.* James A. Brooks

SLEEP Natural state of rest for human beings and animals (Ps. 4:8). God causes "deep sleep," sometimes for revelation (Gen. 2:21; 15:12; Job 4:13), and sometimes to prevent prophetic vision (Isa. 29:10; cp. 1 Sam. 26:12). It is also used as a sign of laziness (Prov. 19:15). Sleep is a figure of physical death (John 11:11-14; 1 Cor. 15:51). See *Death; Eternal Life.*

SLIME See *Bitumen.*

SLING, SLINGERS, SLINGSTONES Weapon of two long straps with a piece between them at the end to hold the stone. Shepherds and professional soldiers used slings, dating back to at least 4500 B.C. See *Arms and Armor.*

SLOTHFUL Loose, undisciplined. Hebrew term can refer to a bow not strung or equipped with an arrow for action (Ps. 78:57; Hos. 7:16). A similar or related Hebrew root describes a loose tongue or mind as deceitful (Job 13:7; 27:4; Pss. 32:2; 52:4; Mic. 6:12). The slothful person cannot lead but becomes subjected to another's rule (Prov. 12:24; cp. 10:4; 19:15). God's work must not be done in such a spirit (Jer. 48:10). A second Hebrew term refers to that which is difficult, heavy, or hindered and indicates foolish laziness or sluggishness. The tribe of Dan was encouraged to take the new territory and not be slothful or reluctant (Judg. 18:9). The wise, hardworking ant illustrates the opposite of sloth (Prov. 6:6), while the sloth wants only to sleep (Prov. 6:9; cp. 10:26; 13:4; 15:19; 19:24; 20:4; 21:25; 22:13; 24:30; 26:16). The virtuous woman is the opposite of slothful, not having to live with the results of idle slothfulness (Prov. 31:27). Ecclesiastes 10:18 says, "Because of utter laziness, the roof caves in, because of idle hands, the house leaks" (HCSB). Jesus condemned an evil, lazy slave (Matt. 25:26) but praised and rewarded the "good and faithful slave" (Matt. 25:23 HCSB). See *Ethics.*

Ruins of the forum at the site of the ancient city of Smyrna in Asia Minor (modern Turkey).

SMELTING POT REB for crucible. See *Crucible; Pottery.*

SMYRNA (Smĕr´ nȧ) Major city on the west coast of Asia Minor, the modern city of Izmir, Turkey. It had good harbor facilities, was at the end of a major road, and was surrounded by rich farmland. It is the second of the seven churches addressed in Rev. 2:8-11, one of two churches of which the Lord spoke no negative word (Philadelphia was the other). Smyrna gave its loyalty to the Romans at an early stage (about 195 B.C.) and never wavered. The Romans often rewarded Smyrna for its loyalty. The city was headquarters for the imperial cult of emperor worship in that area of the empire. Christians were persecuted by Jews and Romans. Polycarp was a famous Christian martyr who was burned at the stake in Smyrna about A.D. 156. See *Asia Minor, Cities of.*

SNAIL Animal whose name apparently means "moist one." It illustrates the quick end to life (Ps. 58:8; HCSB, "slug"). Attempts to translate

Statues found in the ruins of Smyrna (modern Izmir, Turkey).

"miscarriage" instead of "snail" do not seem to be based on good linguistic evidence. KJV translated the unclean reptile of Lev. 11:30 as "snail." Other suggestions include "sand reptile" (NASB), "skink" (HCSB, NIV), "sand lizard" (NRSV), and "great lizard" (REB).

SNARE Trap to catch birds and animals. There were basically two kinds of snares. One used rope or cord. Either the animal stepped in the trap and was snared by the feet, or the rope fell from above and caught the animal by the neck. The most common was a trap with a net. The animal would be attracted by the bait. When the baited trigger was released, the net covered the animal and captured it. Also the opening of a pit would be camouflaged with cover. The animal would fall into the pit and be captured. Figuratively, snares spoke of peril or death and the destruction of persons (Job 22:10; Ps. 18:5; cp. 1 Sam. 28:9). See *Fowler; Hunt, Hunter.*

SNOW Being basically in a hot climate, Palestine rarely has snow. Yet Mount Hermon has a snowcap that can be seen throughout much of Palestine. Snow is used in the Bible figuratively: whiteness (Isa. 1:18), cleanness (Job 9:30), refreshing coolness (Prov. 25:13). See *Weather.*

SNUFFERS Two different instruments used to tend the lamps in the tabernacle and the temple. One instrument seems to be a cutting tool used for trimming the wicks of the lamps. The other word is often translated "tongs" (Isa. 6:6), meaning that it consisted in two parts working together. Exodus 25:38 speaks of "tongs" and "snuffdishes." Evidently these instruments were used to trim the wicks of the lamps and dispose of the waste.

SOAP Cleaner made by mixing olive oil and alkali from burning certain salt-producing plants. It was used of washing the body (Jer. 2:22) and of washing clothes (Mal. 3:2). Perhaps the scant references to soap are due to the fact that people in the Near East use oil for cleansing the body and pound clothes on rocks while wet to cleanse them. See *Fuller.*

SOBER Characterized by self-control, seriousness, and sound moral judgment (1 Thess. 5:6,8; 1 Tim. 3:2,11; Titus 1:8; 2:2,6; 1 Pet. 1:13; 5:8). The KJV employed "sober" to mean in one's right mind at 2 Cor. 5:13.

SOCO, SOCOH (Sō´ cō) Place-name meaning "thorns." **1.** Town in southern Judah hill country used as a fortification against people approaching from the south (Josh. 15:35). It is modern Khirbet Abbad. Philistines gathered to battle Saul there (1 Sam. 17:1). Rehoboam fortified it (2 Chron. 11:7). **2.** Town in the southern hill country of Judah about ten miles southwest of Hebron (Josh. 15:48) at Khirbet Shuweikeh. **3.** Town belonging to Ben-hesed (1 Kings 4:10 NRSV), one of the 12 officials who provided food for Solomon and his household. It is as-Shuweikeh, west of Nablus and two miles north of Tulkarm. **4.** Native of Judah, the son of Heber (1 Chron. 4:18). Some interpreters feel that this is a place-name rather than personal name. May be the same as 2.

SODI (Sō´ dī) Personal name meaning "my counsel." Father of Gaddiel of Zebulun, one of the spies Moses sent to spy out Canaan (Num. 13:10).

SODOM AND GOMORRAH (Sŏ´ dom, Go môr´ rà) Place-names of uncertain meaning. Two cities in Palestine at the time of Abraham. Sodom and Gomorrah were among the five "cities of the valley" (Gen. 13:12; 19:29; KJV, NIV, "plain") of Abraham's time. Exact locations are unknown, but they were probably situated in the Valley of Siddim (Gen. 14:3,8,10-11) near the Dead Sea, perhaps the area now covered by the Sea's shallow southern end. Lot moved to this area, eventually settling in Sodom (Gen. 13:10-12; 14:12; 19:1).

Sodom and Gomorrah were renowned for their wickedness (Gen. 18:20). Despite Abraham's successful plea (18:22-32) not even 10 righteous men could be found in Sodom, and the cities were judged by the Lord, then destroyed by "brimstone and fire" (19:24; HCSB, NIV, "burning sulfur").

The unnatural lusts of the men of Sodom (Gen. 19:4-8; Jude 7) have given us the modern term "sodomy," but the city was guilty of a full spectrum of sins including pride, oppression of the poor, haughtiness, and "abominable things" (Ezek. 16:49-50). Together, Sodom and Gomorrah provided a point of comparison for the sinfulness of Israel and other nations (Deut. 32:32;

S

Reconstruction of Solomon's temple in Jerusalem showing the Holy Place and the Holy of Holies.

Isa. 1:10; Jer. 23:14). The memory of their destruction provided a picture of God's judgment (Isa. 13:19; Jer. 49:18; Matt. 10:14-15; 11:23-24) and made them an example to be avoided (Deut. 29:23-25; 2 Pet. 2:6).

Daniel C. Browning, Jr.

SODOMITE Originally a citizen of the town of Sodom, one of the cities of the valley near the Dead Sea (Gen. 13:12). The term came to mean a male who has sexual relations with another male. The wickedness of Sodom became proverbial (Gen. 19:1-11). See *Homosexuality; Sex, Biblical Teaching on.*

SOLDIER Person trained to fight, usually on active military duty. In early Israelite history every male was called on to fight when the tribes were threatened. David was the first to put together a national army made up of professional soldiers. Kings often had a personal group of soldiers to guard them. The NT soldier was usually the Roman soldier. John the Baptist indicated that the average Roman soldier extorted money from civilians by threatening them (Luke 3:14). On the other hand, the centurion (leader of 100 men) is held in esteem in the NT (Acts 10). See *Army; Centurion.*

SOLEMN ASSEMBLY See *Festivals.*

SOLOMON (Sŏl´ o mon) Personal name whose meaning is variously interpreted as "his peace," "(God) is peace," "Salem (a god)," "intact," or "his replacement." Tenth son of David and the second son of Bathsheba, Solomon became the third king of Israel and reigned 40 years about 1000 B.C.

Old Testament Solomon was born to David and Bathsheba after the death of their first son (2 Sam. 12:24). Although not the oldest living son of David, he was crowned king after his mother and Nathan the prophet intervened with David and secured David's decision to have Solomon succeed him (1 Kings 1–2). Solomon is remembered most for his wisdom, his building program, and his wealth generated through trade and administrative reorganization.

Solomon was remembered as having 3,000 proverbs and 1,005 songs in his repertoire (1 Kings 4:32). Thus, it is not surprising that Proverbs and Song of Songs are attributed to Solomon (Prov. 1:1; Song 1:1) as are several apocryphal and pseudepigraphal books. His wisdom is also illustrated in the Bible by the accounts of the two harlots who claimed the single surviving child (1 Kings 3:16) and by the visit of the queen of Sheba (1 Kings 10). See *Apocrypha; Pseudepigrapha.*

While Solomon's temple was the most famous of his building projects (1 Kings 5–8), it was by no means the only one. Solomon fortified

Model of Solomon's Porch in first-century Jerusalem (Holyland Hotel, Jerusalem).

a number of cities that helped provide protection to Jerusalem, built "store-cities" for stockpiling the materials required in his kingdom, and established military bases for contingents of charioteers (1 Kings 9:15-19). The temple complex in Jerusalem was composed of several buildings including Solomon's palace, the "house of the forest of Lebanon," the "hall [or porch] of pillars," the "hall [or porch] of the throne," and a

Reconstruction of Solomon's temple (957–587 B.C.) in Jerusalem. Shown is the temple (center) flanked on the north and south by ten lavers (five on each side of the temple), the molten sea (lower center), and the altar of burnt offerings (right).

S

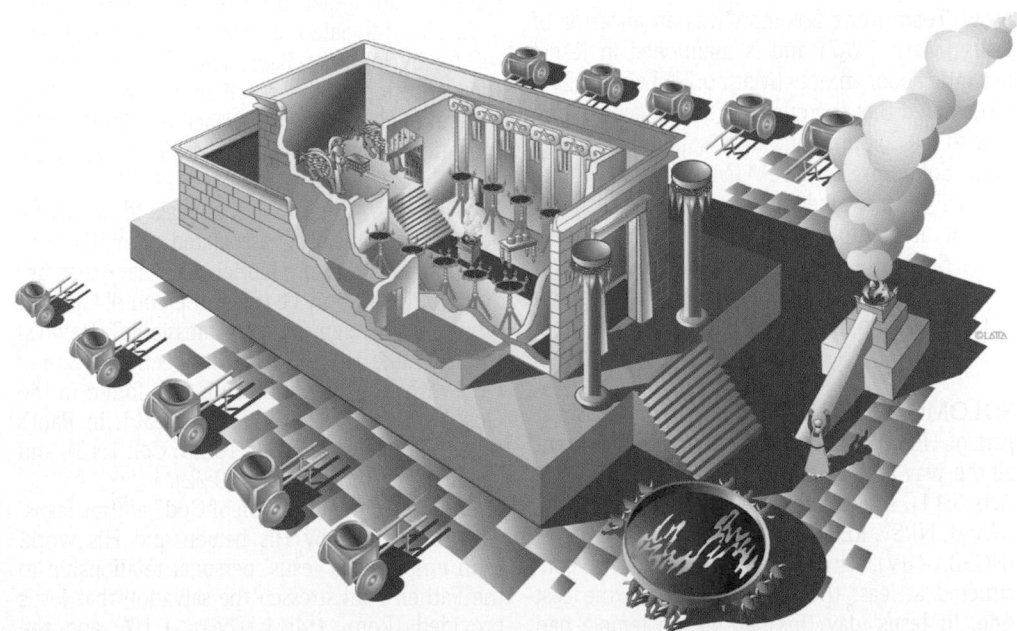

palace for one of his wives, the daughter of the pharaoh of Egypt (1 Kings 7). See *Archaeology; Gezer; Hazor; Megiddo; Temple.*

Solomon divided the country into administrative districts that did not correspond to the old tribal boundaries (1 Kings 4:7-19) and had the districts provide provisions for the central government. This system, combined with control of vital north/south trade routes between the Red Sea and what was later known as Asia Minor, made it possible for Solomon to accumulate vast wealth. This wealth was supplemented both from trading in horses and chariots and from trade carried on by a fleet of ships (1 Kings 9:26-28; 10:26-29). See *Eloth; Ezion-geber.*

The Bible clearly notes that Solomon had faults as well as elements of greatness. The "seven hundred wives, princesses, and three hundred concubines" came from many of the kingdoms with which Solomon had treaties (1 Kings 11:1,3). He apparently allowed his wives to worship their native gods and even had altars to those gods constructed in Jerusalem (1 Kings 11:7-8). This kind of compromise indicated to the historian a weakness in Solomon not found in David. Rebellions led by the king of Edom, Rezon of Damascus, and Jeroboam, one of Solomon's own officers, indicate that Solomon's long reign was not without its turmoil.

New Testament Solomon was an ancestor of Jesus (Matt. 1:6-7) and is mentioned in Jesus' teaching about anxiety (Matt. 6:29; Luke 12:27). Jesus noted that the queen of Sheba came a long way to see Solomon and that "something greater than Solomon is here" (Matt. 12:42; Luke 11:31). Jesus walked in "Solomon's porch," a part of the temple area (John 10:23; cp. Acts 3:11; 5:12). Stephen noted that though David sought to find a place for God, it was Solomon who "built Him a house" (Acts 7:47).

Joe O. Lewis

SOLOMON'S PORCH The raised outermost part of Herod's temple with columns that went all the way around the outer court (John 10:23; Acts 3:11). It is called "the portico of Solomon" (NASB, NRSV, REB) and "Solomon's Colonnade" (HCSB, NIV), since Solomon's workers constructed at least the oldest portico on the east side. In Jesus' day this part of the temple had been built by Herod's laborers. See *Temple.*

SON OF GOD Term used to express the deity of Jesus of Nazareth as the one, unique Son of God. In the OT certain men and angels (Gen. 6:1-4; Pss. 29:1; 82:6; 89:6) are called "sons of God" (note text notes in modern translations). The people of Israel were corporately considered the son of God (Exod. 4:22; Jer. 31:20; Hos. 11:1). The concept also is employed in the OT with reference to the king as God's son (Ps. 2:7). The promises found in the Davidic covenant (2 Sam. 7:14) are the source for this special filial relationship. The title can be found occasionally in intertestamental literature (Wisd. of Sol. 2:18; 4 Ezra 7:28-29; 13:32,37,52; 14:9; Book of Enoch 105:2).

Jesus' own assertions and intimations indicate that references to Him as Son of God can be traced to Jesus Himself. At the center of Jesus' identity in the Fourth Gospel is His divine Sonship (John 10:36). Jesus conceived of His divine Sonship as unique as indicated by such assertions as "the Father and I are one" (John 10:30 HCSB) and the "Father is in Me and I in the Father" (John 10:38). Elsewhere, He frequently referred to God as "My Father" (John 5:17; 6:32; 8:54; 10:18; 15:15; Matt. 7:21; 10:32-33; 20:23; 26:29,53; Mark 8:38; Luke 2:49; 10:21-22).

At Jesus' baptism and transfiguration, God the Father identified Jesus as His Son, in passages reflecting Ps. 2:7. He was identified as Son of God by an angel prior to His birth (Luke 1:32,35), by Satan at His temptation (Matt. 4:3,6), by John the Baptist (John 1:34), and by the centurion at the crucifixion (Matt. 27:54). Several of His followers ascribed to Him this title in various contexts (Matt. 14:33; 16:16; John 1:49; 11:27).

The term "Son of God" reveals Jesus' divine Sonship and is closely associated with His royal position as Messiah. Gabriel told Mary that her Son would not only be called the Son of God but would also reign on the messianic (David's) throne (Luke 1:32-33). The connection of Son of God with Jesus' royal office is also found in the Gospel of John (1:49; 11:27; 20:30), in Paul's letters (Rom. 1:3-4; 1 Cor. 15:28; Col. 1:13), and in Luke's writings (Acts 9:20-22).

Primarily, the title "Son of God" affirms Jesus' deity evidenced by His person and His work. John emphasized Jesus' personal relationship to the Father. Paul stressed the salvation that Jesus provided (Rom. 1:4; 1 Thess. 1:10), and the author of Hebrews focused on Jesus' priesthood

(5:5). All of these are vitally related to His position as Son of God.   *David S. Dockery*

SON OF MAN Expression found in both the OT and the NT. "Son of Man" is used in these ways: (1) as a poetic synonym for "man" or "human," as in Pss. 8:4 and 80:17; (2) in Ezekiel as the title by which God regularly addresses the prophet (2:1,3; 3:1,3); and (3) in Dan. 7 as the identity of the glorious person whom the prophet sees coming with the clouds of heaven to approach the Ancient of Days. "The Son of Man" is a designation of Christ found frequently in the NT. It was Jesus' favorite designation of himself to imply both his messianic mission and his full humanity.

In the Old Testament "Son of Man" appears often in the OT as a synonym for "man" or "humankind." In fact, outside Ezekiel and Daniel it is always used in this way (Job 25:6; Isa. 56:2; Jer. 50:40).

The book of Ezekiel used "Son of Man" more than 90 times to refer to the prophet. His meaning is debated. Some believe the expression simply serves as an editorial convention. Others say it points to his identification with his people or is used to distinguish Ezekiel from other men. In any case, Ezekiel exhibited a profound sense of the holiness and majesty of God, and the phrase is at least intended to mark the distance that separated the prophet, as human, from Jehovah.

The most important occurrence of the title "Son of Man" in the OT is in Dan. 7:13. The context is the slaying of the terrifying fourth beast of Dan. 7, whereupon "one like the Son of Man" appears before the Ancient of Days and receives everlasting dominion and glory. While some have interpreted this divine being as a symbol for faithful Jews or "saints of the Most High," it is best to see this as a clear reference to Messiah. Jesus often designated Himself as such and the clouds of heaven appear again in association with the second coming of Christ (Rev. 1:7). Here the Lord Jesus is distinct from God the Father, the Ancient of Days, who will give to Christ a kingdom that will never be destroyed (Dan. 2:44).

In the Gospels The phrase is used 32 times by Matthew, 14 times by Mark, 26 times by Luke, and 12 times by John, for a total of 84 occurrences in the Gospels. Adding the occurrences mentioned below in Acts, Hebrews, and Revelation brings the total to 88 in the NT. Of those occurrences, the phrase is always in the mouth of Jesus except for five times: John 12:34; Acts 7:56; Heb. 2:6; Rev. 1:13; 14:14.

In the Gospels the "Son of Man" sayings fall into three general categories, all of which are found on the lips of Jesus. *Eschatological* or *apocalyptic* sayings are those in which Jesus refers to His coming in the future on the clouds of heaven with great power and majesty (Mark 8:38; 13:26; Matt. 24:27; 25:31). This use is most frequent. These references are clearly reminiscent of Dan. 7. The references to the future coming yield the following important insights: (1) The Son of Man will come in glory with angels and bring about end-time judgment (Matt. 16:27; 25:31; 26:64; John 5:27). (2) This glorious coming will be a time of renewal and regeneration. Christ will be enthroned and His apostles will be given special places of honor (Matt. 19:28). (3) This coming will be sudden and unexpected, like a flash of lightning (Matt. 24:27; Luke 12:40; 17:24). (4) When Christ comes in His glory, He will gather to Himself His elect (Luke 21:36; Mark 13:27). (5) This sudden and unexpected coming (Matt. 10:23; 24:44) will usher in the time when He takes His seat on the promised messianic throne (Matt. 25:31).

Passion or suffering "Son of Man" sayings are those that Jesus spoke with reference to His imminent suffering, death, and resurrection. The passion sayings are the second largest group. Mark records three occasions when Jesus plainly foretold the rejection, crucifixion, and resurrection of the Son of Man (Mark 8:31; 9:31; 10:33-34). This anticipation was difficult for the Jews of Jesus' day because messianic expectation did not connect the Son of Man with suffering and death. Jesus clearly understood these predictions to refer to Himself.

Finally, there are sayings connected with the *present ministry* of Jesus. These references usually illustrate the lowly estate of Jesus, the glorious Lord who humbled Himself to become human. Matthew 8:20 shows that He didn't have a permanent home. His purpose was to seek and to save those who are lost (Luke 19:10) and to give His life as a ransom for many (Matt. 20:28). He is the one who sows the seed of God's kingdom (Matt. 13:37) and in so doing was misunderstood and rejected (Luke 7:34). He warned that His disciples might be called on to suffer in the same way for His sake (Luke 6:22). This

S

humble Son of Man is no ordinary person, however. He claims authority to forgive sins (Mark 2:10) and He assumes lordship over the Sabbath (Matt. 12:8).

Another aspect of the "Son of Man" concept emerges in John. While he uses the term sparingly, he blends the elements of the first three Gospels together in a beautiful way. The ascending/descending theme of the Son of Man is John's primary emphasis. There is a constant interplay between humiliation and exaltation of the Son of Man in John. The Son of Man who descended from heaven is the same one who is now on earth (John 3:13). He was to be lifted up on a cross (the ultimate humiliation) so that He might be exalted (3:14). He is the Bread who came down out of heaven but who ascended back to heaven when His work was completed (6:62). One must accept the humanity of the Son of Man to find true life (6:53), but this one is also Son of God who came from above and who links heaven to earth (1:51). Even Judas' betrayal of Him (13:32) served the purpose that He might be glorified. In the Gospels, but especially in John, "Son of Man" means humanity and humiliation, but "Son of Man" also means exaltation and glory.

In the Rest of the New Testament Outside the Gospels the title "Son of Man" is found only four times. In Acts 7:56 Stephen saw the Son of Man standing in heaven beside God's throne to receive him after his stoning. Hebrews 2:6 quotes Ps. 8, a passage that originally referred to mankind in general. The writer of Hebrews, however, used it to ascribe uniqueness to Jesus as the perfect representative of humanity. Revelation 1:13 and 14:14 follow the Dan. 7 imagery of the Son of Man as exalted Judge. The title is noticeably absent from Paul's writings, but many Bible students have suggested that Paul's idea of Christ as the heavenly man or second Adam can be related to the "Son of Man" concept. Paul's theology certainly built on the reality of Christ's sacrificial work as the God/man, as 1 Cor. 15:3-7 clearly shows.

Conclusion Saint Augustine wrote, "The Son of God became the Son of man that you who were sons of men might be made sons of God." Jesus became one of us, yet He was distinct from us. Only Jesus is Son of Man and Son of God united in one person. In Matt. 16:13-17 Jesus asked the disciples, "Who do people say that the Son of Man is?" Simon Peter answered, "You are the Messiah, the Son of the living God!"

Dale Ellenburg and John B. Polhill

SONG OF SONGS, SONG OF SOLOMON
Collection of romantic poetry comprising the 22nd book of the English OT. The Hebrew title, "Solomon's Song of Songs," means that this is the best of songs and that it in some way concerns Solomon.

Author and Date While the title appears to name Solomon as the author, the Hebrew phrase can also mean for or about Solomon. Solomon or "king" is mentioned in the book several times (1:1,4-5,12; 3:7,9,11; 7:5; 8:11-12), but scholars remain uncertain about its author. An ancient rabbinic tradition (Baba Bathra 15a) attributes the Song to Hezekiah and his scribes (cp. Prov. 25:1).

Similarly, it is hard to establish the date of the book from internal evidence. Some scholars argue on linguistic grounds for authorship much later than Solomon. Such grounds include the use of expressions akin to Aramaic and the presence of certain foreign loan words (Persian: *pardes* "orchard," Song 4:13; *appiryon* from Greek *phoreion* "carriage" or [by way of Aramaic] "canopied bed," 3:9). Others argue that such linguistic usages and borrowings can go back to the time of Solomon or merely reflect the date of the book's final editing.

Canon and Interpretation Because of its erotic language and the difficulty of its interpretation, the rabbis questioned the place of the Song of Songs in the canon. The positive resolution of that debate is reflected in the famous declaration of Rabbi Akiva, "The whole world is not worth the day on which the Song of Songs was given to Israel; all the Writings are holy, but the Song of Songs is the holy of holies."

The problems of the book's place in the canon and its interpretation are closely related. Under the influence of Greek views, which denigrated the body, and with the loss of a biblical view of the created goodness of the body and human love, many interpreters felt compelled to find in the Song an allegory of sacred love between God and Israel, Christ and the church, or Christ and the soul. With few exceptions, allegorical readings of the Song have prevailed for most of church history.

In the modern period most scholars have returned to a literal reading of the Song. Conflict remains even about the literal sense of the text. Some compare Egyptian and Mesopotamian poems and see the Song as a mere collection of secular love ditties. Another view tries to see it as an adaptation of pagan fertility rituals. (This view is in reality a modern allegorical reading.) Others see the Song as a drama in which the pure love of the Shulammite maid and her shepherd prevails over Solomon's callous attempt to bring the girl into his harem. This view tries to do justice to the alteration of speakers in the Song in its various dialogues. (These shifts are indicated in Hebrew by shifts in grammatical person and number.)

A recent, promising approach is aware of parallels to Egyptian love poetry but shows that the Song itself gives expression to a uniquely biblical perspective on sexual love. While containing a number of smaller love poems, the Song is unified by patterns of dialogue, repetition, the use of catchwords, and above all, a consistent vision of love. Like Gen. 2:23-25, the Song celebrates God's gift of bodily love between man and woman. Here the Creator's wisdom and bounty are displayed. Thus, the Song is best taken as an example of Israel's wisdom poetry (cp. Prov. 5:15-20; 6:24-29; 7:6-27; 30:18-20). Like many psalms that praise God and also teach, the Song's main purpose is to celebrate rather than to instruct. Yet one can overhear in it biblical wisdom on love. "Love is as strong as death ... Mighty waters cannot extinguish love ... If a man were to give all his wealth for love, it would be utterly scorned" (8:6-7 HCSB). Moreover, there is a right time and place for love: "Young women of Jerusalem, I charge you ... do not stir up or awaken love until the appropriate time" (3:5). In these poems love is portrayed in its power and splendor, its freshness and devotion to the beloved. Love in all its variety parades before us: moments of union and separation, ecstasy and anguish, longing and fulfillment.

Finally, a certain validity remains in the long history of interpretation, which saw in the pure love of the Song a reflection of divine-human love (cp. Eph. 5:21-32; Song 3:6-11; and the messianic typology of Ps. 45). Nonetheless, this parallel should not be pushed to the point of allegorizing details of the poem.

See also *Allegory; Wisdom and the Wise Men.*

Outline
   I.   Longing Is a Part of Love (1:1-8).

  II.   Love Will Not Be Silent (1:9–2:7).
 III.   Spring and Love Go Together (2:8-17).
 IV.   Love Is Exclusive (3:1-5).
  V.   Love Is Enhanced by Friendship (3:6-11).
 VI.   Love Sees Only the Beautiful (4:1-7).
VII.   Love Involves Giving and Receiving (4:8–5:1).
VIII.   Love Means Risking the Possibility of Pain (5:2–6:3).
 IX.   Words Fail for Expressing Love (6:4–7:9).
  X.   Love Must Be Given Freely (7:10-13).
 XI.   True Love Is Priceless (8:1-14).

Raymond C. Van Leeuwen

SONS OF GOD The literal rendering of a phrase that refers to a class of beings in some relationship to God. Its meaning and translation vary according to context.

Old Testament The Hebrew phrase *beney ha'elohim* is found in Gen. 6:2,4 and Job 1:6; 2:1; 38:7. In the Job passages, "the sons of God" are the angels (Job 38:7, in poetic parallel with "the morning stars") or heavenly court (1:6 and 2:1).

The Genesis text (6:1-4) historically has been one of the most difficult passages in the OT to interpret. The crux of the interpretative question is how to understand the distinction between the two groups mentioned in this text: "the sons of God" and "the daughters of men." Three views have been proposed.

The first position is that "the sons of God" were princes or civil rulers, and "the daughters of men" were commoners or socially inferior women. The principal support for this view is a comparison with the Babylonian Gilgamesh Epic in which the king, Gilgamesh, has the first right to have sexual relations with a new bride. Only then may her husband take her as his wife. The primary objection to this position is that nowhere else in the OT does the phrase "sons of God" refer to royalty.

A second position is that "the sons of God" should be translated as "godly sons" and thus refers to the godly descendants of Seth. By this view, "the daughters of men" are "worldly women," the ungodly descendants of Cain. The argument is that these intermarriages would have diluted the line of Seth, spiritually and physically. However, good exegetical principles require that "men/mankind" has the same meaning in 6:2 as in 6:1 *Ha'adam* (the same word in both verses) is understood generically as "humanity/mankind" in 6:1, thus referring to the entire human race, including both the descendants of Seth and Cain. If "the daughters of men" is understood to refer only to the ungodly descendants of Cain, then *ha'adam* must therefore have a more restricted meaning in 6:2. This more restricted meaning would violate good exegetical principles.

The final position is that "the sons of God" were angels or supernatural beings, and thus the "daughters of men" were human women. Two objections have been raised regarding this interpretation. Both are based on presuppositions about the nature of angels, which are not supported by Scripture: (1) that angels are without gender and therefore incapable of cohabiting with human beings, and (2) that understanding "sons of God" as angels requires the narrative to be understood as a mythological rather than a historical event.

Several lines of support have been proposed in defense of this interpretation. (1) The phrase "the sons of God" is elsewhere in the OT understood as "angels" (Job 1:6; 2:1; 38:7). (2) The third century b.c. Greek translation of the OT (the Septuagint, Alexandrine text) reads "angels of God" for the Hebrew "the sons of God." (3) If 6:4 is connected to what precedes and follows, then the offspring of the union between the angels and women are the Nephilim (giants), the renowned mighty men of old. (4) Finally, it is this sexual union that prompts God to judge the world by flood. This sin was such a terrible act of rebellion against God's standards that complete destruction of the world by flood was the only response of a holy God. Would the cohabitation between godly Sethites and ungodly Cainites or between kings and commoners have warranted this complete and utter destruction? The unholy sexual union between angels and women appears to be the best explanation for the heinous sin that resulted in judgment by flood.

New Testament Israel was the adopted son of God in the OT because of God's sovereign choice and covenant (Exod. 4:22-23; Hos. 11:1; cp. Matt. 2:13-15; Rom. 9:4; 2 Cor. 6:18). Even more personally, and closer to God's heart, He adopted David and his royal seed (2 Sam. 7:14; 1 Chron. 17:13; 28:6; Ps. 2:7-8), ultimately the divine King in His role as Savior of Israel (Luke 1:32; Acts 2:29-36; 13:32-37; Rom. 1:3-4; Heb. 1:3-5). Likewise, Christians are said to be sons of God and therefore heirs of God and heirs of the kingdom

(Matt. 5:9) by adoption, chosen in Christ, having the Holy Spirit live within, and destined to be conformed to Christ's image (Luke 20:36; Rom. 8:14-17,29; Gal. 3:26; 4:4-7; Eph. 1:5). "Angels" is the usual NT term for heavenly beings/messengers. See *Angels; Council, Heavenly; Nephilim.* *Francis Kimmitt*

SONS OF THE PROPHETS Members of a band or guild of prophets. "Sons of" refers to membership in a group or class and does not imply a family relationship. "Sons of the prophets" suggests a community or guild of prophets. The most extensive use of the expression occurs in the Elisha stories where the prophet is portrayed as the leader of the prophetic guild. In that capacity Elisha cared for the needs of a prophet's widow (2 Kings 4:1-7), agreed to the building of a common dwelling (2 Kings 6:1-7), and presided at a common meal (2 Kings 4:38-44). The sons of the prophets functioned either as witnesses (2 Kings 2:3,5,7,15) or as agents of Elisha's ministry (2 Kings 9:1-3).

The single reference outside the Elisha cycle to the sons of the prophets is to someone identified as "a certain man of the sons of the prophets" who condemned Ahab's release of Ben-Hadad (1 Kings 20:35-42). The "company of prophets" (1 Sam. 10:5,10; 19:20) are groups of prophets whose charismatic spirit involved Saul in prophecy (1 Sam. 10:10) and, later, both Saul and his messengers (1 Sam. 19:20).

Amos's famous declaration, "I am not a prophet, nor am I the son of a prophet" (7:14 NASB), is probably a declaration of independence from the prophetic guilds of his day. Similarly, Jeremiah's claim that God made him a prophet even before conception (Jer. 1:5) may obliquely represent a rejection of association with the prophetic schools of Judah. See *Prophet.* *Fred L. Horton, Jr.*

SOOTHSAYER'S TREE See *Diviner's Oak; Terebinth.*

SOP KJV translation of *psomion,* meaning a small piece of bread that could be dipped in a dish or wine. It appears only in John 13:26-30 (cp. Ruth 2:14). Most translators today use "morsel" (NASB) or "piece of bread" (HCSB, NIV, NRSV). Today in Bible lands a host honors a guest by dipping a piece of bread into the sauce of the main dish and handing it to the guest.

Most interpreters feel that Jesus was making His last appeal to Judas to change his mind. Then Jesus would accept him. Although Judas accepted the bread signifying friendship, John said, "Satan entered him" (v. 27). At that moment Judas gave himself over to the will of Satan and left to betray Jesus. See *Judas*.

SOPATER (Sŏp´ á tẽr) Personal name meaning "sound parentage." This man accompanied Paul on his final trip to Jerusalem (Acts 20:4). Some feel he is the same as "Sosipater" in Rom. 16:21.

SOPHERETH (Sōph´ ə rĕth) Personal name meaning "learning." One of Solomon's servants whose descendants returned to Jerusalem with Zerubbabel (Ezra 2:55; Neh. 7:57). Modern translations translate it "Hassophereth" in Ezra 2:55 and "Sophereth" in Neh. 7:57 (NASB, NIV, NRSV).

SORCERER Person who practices sorcery or divination. See *Divination and Magic*.

SORE Translation of six Hebrew words and a Greek word in RSV and of at least 10 Hebrew and 10 Greek words in KJV. **1.** Adverb meaning "very, extremely" as in "sore afraid" (Gen. 20:8 KJV). **2.** Adverb meaning "severely, insistently, with urgent pressure" as in "they pressed sore" (Gen. 19:9). **3.** To experience pain (Gen. 34:25). **4.** "Strong, severe" as in "the famine was sore" (Gen. 43:1). **5.** A wounded or diseased spot or a plague (Lev. 13:42). **6.** Something evil or bad (Deut. 6:22; 28:35). **7.** A great amount as in "wept sore" (Judg. 21:2). **8.** With vexation or anger (1 Sam. 1:6). **9.** Cruel, tough, obstinate (1 Sam. 5:7). **10.** Fully, greatly (Neh. 2:2). **11.** Hand (Ps. 77:2). **12.** Weakness or sickness (Eccles. 5:13). **13.** Horrible, terrible (Ezek. 27:35). **14.** Large, exceeding (Dan. 6:14). **15.** Pressing, irritating (Mic. 2:10). **16.** An ulcer (Rev. 16:2). **17.** Blisters or boils (Exod. 9:9). See *Boils*. **18.** An inflamed spot sometimes interpreted as smallpox or a skin disease akin to leprosy (Exod. 9:9-11; Lev. 13:18-20; 2 Kings 20:7; Isa. 38:21). **19.** A wound (Gen. 4:23; Isa. 53:5).

SOREK (Sō´ rĕk) Place-name meaning "red grape." A valley on the western side of Palestine. It runs from near Jerusalem toward the Mediterranean Sea. Beth-shemesh guarded the eastern end, while the Philistines controlled the western

portion during the era of the judges. Delilah, Samson's mistress, lived in the valley of Sorek (Judg. 16:4). See *Palestine*.

SORROW Emotional, mental, or physical pain or stress. Hebrew does not have a general word for sorrow. Rather it uses about 15 different words to express the different dimensions of sorrow. Some speak to emotional pain (Ps. 13:2). Trouble and sorrow were not meant to be part of the human experience. Humanity's sin brought sorrow to them (Gen. 3:16-19). Sometimes God was seen as chastising His people for their sin (Amos 4:6-12). To remove sorrow, the prophets urged repentance that led to obedience (Joel 2:12-13; Hos. 6:6).

The Greek word for sorrow is usually *lupe*. It means "grief, sorrow, pain of mind or spirit, affliction." Paul distinguished between godly and worldly sorrow (2 Cor. 7:8-11). Sorrow can lead a person to a deeper faith in God; or it can cause a person to live with regret, centered on the experience that caused the sorrow. Jesus gave believers words of hope to overcome trouble, distress, and sorrow: "I have told you these things so that in Me you may have peace. In the world you have suffering. Be courageous! I have conquered the world" (John 16:33 HCSB). See *Grief and Mourning*.

SOSIPATER (Sō sĭp´ á tẽr) Personal name meaning "to save one's father." He is said to be a kinsman (a Jew) of Paul who sent greetings to Rome (Rom. 16:21). "Sopater ... from Beroea" (Acts 20:4 HCSB) may be the same.

SOSTHENES (Sŏs´ thə nēz) Personal name meaning "of safe strength." A ruler of a synagogue in Corinth (Acts 18:17). He apparently assumed the post after Crispus, the former chief ruler, became a Christian under Paul's preaching (18:8). When an attempt to prosecute Paul legally failed, the citizens of the city took revenge and beat Sosthenes. Tradition holds that Sosthenes later was converted and became one of Paul's helpers (1 Cor. 1:1). Whether the two are one person cannot be determined from existing evidence.

SOTAI (Sō´ tā ī) One of Solomon's servants whose descendants returned to Jerusalem with Zerubbabel (Ezra 2:55; Neh. 7:57).

S

SOUL In Scripture and in the history of theology and philosophy, the word "soul" has had a varied and complex constellation of meanings. Though it is often used in popular theology to refer only to the inner part of the person, the non-physical aspect of each human being, it is used in other ways in Scripture, as well.

Old Testament In the Hebrew OT the word generally translated "soul" is *nephesh*. The word occurs over 750 times, and it means primarily "life" or "possessing life." It is used of both animals (Gen. 9:12; Ezek. 47:9) and humans (Gen. 2:7). The word sometimes indicates the whole person, as for instance in Gen. 2:7 where God breathes breath (*neshamah*) into the dust and thus makes a "soul" (*nephesh*). A similar usage is found in Gen. 12:5 where Abram takes all the "souls" (persons) who were with him in Haran and moves on to Canaan. Similarly in Num. 6:6 it is used as a synonym for the body—the Nazirite is not to go near a dead *nephesh* (Lev. 7:21; Hag. 2:13).

The word is also used in the OT to refer to the inner life, psychological or spiritual states of the human person. In Ps. 42, for instance, the soul longs to know God. "As a deer longs for streams of water, so I [my soul] long for You, God" (Ps. 42:1 HCSB). The rest of this psalm echoes this inner desire for God (vv. 2,4-6,11). In 2 Kings 4:27 the Shunammite woman's "soul is troubled within her" (NASB). In 2 Sam. 17:8 Hushai spoke to Absalom and told him, "You know your father and his men, that they are mighty men and they are fierce (literally, chafed in soul, *nephesh*), like a bear robbed of her cubs in the field." The word also refers to the source of emotion in Job 30:25, "Was not my soul grieved for the needy?" In Ps. 107:26 it is used of courage: "their courage [*nephesh*] melting away in anguish" (HCSB; cp. 1 Sam. 1:10; Ps. 86:4; Song 1:7). It can even refer to the attitudes of God: "I [my soul] hate your new moon festivals and your appointed feasts" (Isa. 1:14 NASB).

"Soul" in the OT can also point to the physical appetite. "You may slaughter your animals ... and eat as much ... as you (lit., the *nephesh* of you) want" (Deut. 12:15 NIV; cp. verses 20,23; Mic. 7:1). The term sometimes is simply another way of indicating oneself. So in Judg. 16:16 we find that Samson was tired "to the death of his *nephesh*" of Delilah's nagging. Likewise, Jonathan is said to love David "as himself

[*nephesh*]" (1 Sam. 18:1 NASB). Similar passages are in Ps. 120:6 and Ezek. 18:4.

New Testament Greek word *psuche* carries many of the same meanings as the Hebrew *nephesh*. Often the soul is equated with the total person. Romans 13:1 says, "Everyone [soul] must submit to the governing authorities" equating "soul" (one) with "person" (cp. Acts 2:41; 3:23). There will be "affliction and distress for every human being [soul] who does evil, first to the Jew, and also to the Greek" (Rom. 2:9 HCSB). Soul in the NT also indicates the emotions or passions: "But the Jews who refused to believe stirred up and poisoned the minds [*psuche*] of the Gentiles against the brothers" (Acts 14:2 HCSB). In John 10:24 the Jews asked Jesus, "How long are You going to keep us [our souls] in suspense?" Jesus also told the disciples that they should love God with all of their souls (Mark 12:30), indicating something of the energy and passion that ought to go into loving Him.

It is also the case that the NT speaks of the soul as something that is distinguishable from the physical existence of a person. Jesus made this point when He observed, "Don't fear those who kill the body but are not able to kill the soul; but rather, fear Him who is able to destroy both soul and body in hell" (Matt. 10:28 HCSB). James seems to have the same thing in mind when he concludes his letter, "He should know that whoever turns a sinner from the error of his way will save his life [soul] from death" (James 5:20 HCSB; cp. Rev. 6:9; 20:4). This may be the idea found in Mark 8:36, "For what does it benefit a man to gain the whole world yet lose his life [soul]?" (HCSB). Scripture clearly teaches that persons continue to exist consciously after physical death. Jesus pointed out that as the God of Abraham, Isaac, and Jacob, He is the God of the living. These still live, their souls having returned to God (Eccles. 12:7). In addition, Paul equated being absent from the body with being present with Christ. Whether it is the "immaterial" aspect of the soul which is consciously alive with God after death, awaiting resurrection completeness, or whether believers exist in some kind of physical form, uninterrupted existence is certain (Phil. 1:23; 2 Cor. 5:1-10; Luke 23:43).

The NT often uses "soul" (*psuche*) in a manner interchangeable with "spirit" (*pneuma*). John 10:17 speaks of laying down one's life (*psuche*), and in John 19:30 Jesus gave up the spirit in the act of laying down His life. Acts 27:10,22 speak of loss of one's life in the sense of losing the soul out of the body. Matthew 11:29 speaks of rest for the soul while 2 Cor. 7:13 speaks of Titus's spirit having rest. James 5:20 speaks of salvation of the soul while 1 Cor. 5:5 speaks of salvation of the spirit. In Hebrew parallel fashion, Mary sings, "My soul proclaims the greatness of the Lord, and my spirit has rejoiced in God my Savior" (Luke 1:46-47 HCSB). Spirit and soul are not different parts of the human here but are the same. Though some interpreters appeal to Heb. 4:12 and 1 Thess. 5:23 in an attempt to distinguish these two components, the vast majority of texts demonstrate that they are not distinct. The NT does not make a fundamental distinction between soul and spirit in the person but sees the terms as interchangeable.

Theological Consideration Christians have generally taken one of two approaches to understanding the relationship between body and soul. Most have held to holistic dualism—that there is a difference between body and soul, but the two are linked together by God such that humans are not complete when the two are separated. Some have held to a monistic view that the soul is not separable from the body at all. Nearly all who have held the second view have also believed that after death Christians "go to sleep" and await the resurrection. In light of the texts listed above, this view does not seem tenable. An even more serious error, though, is the Gnostic idea that the body is inferior to the soul because the body is made up of matter. Such persons teach salvation by releasing the soul from the body. This idea is found nowhere in Scripture. See *Anthropology; Intermediate State; Salvation; Spirit.* *Fred Smith and Chad Brand*

SOUTH See *Directions; Negev.*

SOVEREIGNTY OF GOD Biblical teaching that God possesses all power and is the ruler of all things (Ps. 135:6; Dan. 4:34-35). God rules and works according to His eternal purpose, even through events that seem to contradict or oppose His rule.

Biblical Teaching Scripture emphasizes God's rule in three areas: creation, human history, and redemption. Scripture testifies clearly to God's rule over His creation (Gen. 1; Mark 4:35-41; Rom. 8:20-21), including Christ's sustaining and governing of all things (Heb. 1:3, Col. 1:15-17). The Bible affirms also that God rules human history according to His purpose, from ordinary events in the lives of individuals (Judg. 14:1-4; Prov. 16:9,33) to the rise, affairs, and fall of nations (Ps. 22:28; Hab. 1:6; Acts 17:26). Scripture depicts redemption as the work of God alone. God, according to His eternal purpose, takes the initiative in the provision and application of salvation and in enabling man's willing acceptance (John 17:2; Rom. 8:29-30; Eph. 1:3-14; 2 Thess. 2:13-14; 2 Tim. 1:9-10).

Five issues seem to be at odds with the claim of God's absolute rule: evil, free will, human responsibility, evangelism, and prayer.

Sovereignty and Evil The Bible does not explain the relationship between divine sovereignty and evil. Scripture does teach that God neither does evil nor approves of evil (Hab. 1:13; James 1:13); rather, though He allows it, He also restrains it (Job 1:12-2:7), judges it (Isa. 66:3-4; Acts 12:19-23; Rev. 20:11-15), uses it for the good of His children, and the fulfillment of His purposes (Gen. 50:20; Rom. 8:28-29).

Sovereignty and Free Will Some see contradiction between divine sovereignty and human free will, an often misunderstood term. Man's will is free in that he makes willing choices that have actual consequences. Yet man's will is not morally neutral; rather, it is in bondage to sin, and without divine grace he chooses freely and consistently to reject God (Rom. 3:10-11; Eph. 2:1-3; 2 Tim. 2:25-26). Scripture affirms both divine sovereignty and man's willing activity. Pharaoh's rise to power was entirely in accordance with his own will; it was also entirely by the hand of God (Exod. 9:16). The crucifixion of Christ was fully the free act of sinful men, and at the same time fully the purpose of God (Acts 2:23; 4:27-28). Conversions are reported in Acts in a manner consistent with both concepts (Acts 13:48; 16:14).

Sovereignty and Human Responsibility Though God is sovereign, man is still accountable to God for his actions (Rom. 2:5-11; 3:19). The relationship between these two concepts is mysterious but not contradictory. Paul raises the issue but, rather than resolving the tension, simply affirms both (Rom. 9:19-29).

Sovereignty and Evangelism Jesus affirmed the absolute sovereignty of God and in the same context invited sinners to Himself for salvation (Matt. 11:25-30). Paul began his profound treatment of divine sovereignty by expressing his burden for his lost kinsmen (Rom. 9:1-5); in the same context he expressed his heartfelt prayer for their salvation (Rom. 10:1), and affirmed the promise of salvation to "everyone who calls on the name of the Lord" (Rom. 10:12-13 HCSB). Thus an affirmation of divine sovereignty is consistent with evangelism, with missionary labors (2 Tim. 1:12; 2:10), and with desiring and praying for the salvation of any lost person or people. **Sovereignty and Prayer** God's sovereignty means for the believer that "if God is for us, who is against us?" (Rom. 8:31 HCSB). Scripture declares abundantly God's willingness to grant the believer's requests (Rom. 8:32; 1 John 5:14-15). The believer can pray with confidence that his prayers will be heard and answered. See *God; Providence.* *T. Preston Pearce*

SOW 1. To scatter seeds on the ground (field). **2.** The female counterpart of the boar. The mature female swine. See *Swine.*

SOWER Person who held a vessel filled with seed in the left hand and scattered the seed with a practiced motion with the right hand. The seed was usually scattered on untilled ground. Then with a plow or harrow, the ground would be scratched or turned to cover the seed. It seems that any seed to be sowed had to be ceremonially clean (Lev. 11:37). Mixed seed could not be sowed together (Lev. 19:19). Purity reached into the far corners of Hebrew life. Jesus used the sower for a parable about life and illustrated the everyday hardships farmers faced (Matt. 13:3-9; Mark 4:3-9; Luke 8:4-8). See *Agriculture; Plow.*

SPAIN Country still known by that name in the southwest corner of Europe. It was opened to the Romans just before 200 B.C. Paul wanted to go to Spain (Rom. 15:24,28). According to Clement (about A.D. 95–96) and the Muratorian Fragment (about A.D. 195–196), he did just that. See *Tarshish.*

SPAN Half a cubit. A cubit is the length of the forearm, about 18 inches. The span is measured from the thumb to the little finger both extended, about eight or nine inches. See *Weights and Measures.*

SPARK Literal flame of fire (Job 18:5) used in a figurative sense of a person's dying. Also used fig-

An Arab farmer near Bethlehem sowing seeds on his land.

uratively to show that humanity lives a troubled life (Job 5:7). Leviathan is pictured with a flaming mouth (Job 41:19-21). It is used of sparks from a fire (or "torches" NIV) in Isa. 50:11. See *Fire.*

SPARROW Often translated "bird" (*tsippor*) as representative of all birds (Ps. 8:8; Ezek. 17:23 NASB, NIV, NRSV). It was ceremonially clean and sometimes eaten as food by the poor. The sparrow belongs to the finch family. The translation "sparrow" occurs in the HCSB, NIV, NRSV, and RSV in Ps. 84:3 and in Prov. 26:2. The KJV also translates *tsippor* "sparrow" in Ps. 102:7, but the translation "sparrow" may be inappropriate because the verse refers to a bird "alone upon the house top," and the most common sparrows always appeared in flocks. On the other hand, the psalmist may have intended this contradiction to emphasize the depth of loneliness and utter desolation that he was experiencing.

Jesus used the sparrows (Matt. 10:31; Luke 12:7) to show their lack of worth as contrasted with human beings. In these parallel passages Jesus taught His disciples to have confidence in God's love. The God who cares for all of His creation, even the insignificant sparrow, certainly cares for people. *Janice Meier*

SPECK Modern translation of KJV "mote." See *Mote.*

SPECTACLE Theatre or play. Paul felt that he was on display before the world. The world did not appreciate the commitment of Paul to Christ but saw Paul as a spectacle, one to watch and perhaps laugh at (1 Cor. 4:9).

SPELT Wheat of an inferior quality (*Triticum spelta*). Egyptians made bread from it. It had not sprouted when the plagues struck Egypt (Exod. 9:32). Spelt illustrates the farmer's planning, placing it on the outer edge of the field to retard the intrusion of weeds (Isa. 28:25; cp. Ezek. 4:9). See *Agriculture.*

SPICES Aromatic, pungent substances used in the preparation of foods, sacred oils for anointings, incense, perfumes, and ointments used for personal hygiene and for burial of the dead.

Spices were very expensive and highly prized in antiquity. They were brought into Palestine from India, Arabia, Persia, Mesopotamia, and Egypt. Solomon had an extensive commercial venture with Hiram, king of Tyre, dealing in spices and other commodities. His fleet of ships brought much needed revenue into the Israelite economy (1 Kings 10:15). Solomon also taxed the caravan groups that passed through his lands. The land of Sheba, present-day Yemen, had an extensive commerce in spices. The queen of Sheba made a long journey of 1,200 miles because she was afraid that her caravan spice business would be hurt by Solomon's merchant fleet. In her visit she gave to Solomon "a very great amount of spices" (2 Chron. 9:9 NASB).

Spices were widely used in the worship service of the temple and in the lives of the people. Several spices, which the Talmud called "food improvers," were used in the preparation of foods. These included cumin, dill, cinnamon, and mint. Frankincense, stacte, galbanum, and onycha were used in the preparation of the incense to be used in the worship of Israel (Exod. 30:34-35). Balsam, myrrh, cinnamon, cassia, and calamus were used in the preparation of the holy anointing oil (Exod. 30:23-25). Cassia, aloes, and spikenard were some of the spices used in the preparation of cosmetics (Song 4:14; Mark 14:3; John 12:3). Myrrh and aloes were used in ointments for burial (Luke 23:56; John 19:39). See *Ointment.*

Some of the most important spices were:

Aloe (*Aloexyllon agallochum* and *Aquilaria agallocha*) Spice used to perfume garments and beds (Prov. 7:17; Ps. 45:8;). The aloe mentioned in John 19:39 was a different plant. The extract from its leaves was mixed with water and other spices to make ointment for the anointing of the dead.

Balsam (*Pistacia lentiscus*) This product of Gilead was exported to Egypt and to Tyre. The resin from this desert plant was used for medicinal and cosmetic purposes (Jer. 46:11).

Cassia (*Flores cassiae*) Two Hebrew words are used to translate cassia (Exod. 30:24; Ps. 45:8). The dried bark or blooms were used in the preparation of the anointing oil; the pods and leaves were used as medicine.

Cinnamon Highly prized plant, used as a condiment, in the preparation of perfumes (Prov. 7:17) and in the holy oil for anointing (Exod. 30:23). The NT lists cinnamon as one of the commodities found in Babylon (Rev. 18:13).

Coriander (*Coriandrum sativum*) Aromatic seed used as a spice in food; its oil was used in the manufacture of perfume. The Israelites compared the manna to the coriander seed (Exod. 16:31; Num. 11:7).

Cumin (*Cuminum cyminum*) This seed was used as a spice in bread. Its dry seed was beaten with a stick, for it was too soft to be threshed with a sledge (Isa. 28:23-28).

Dill Seed and leaves were used to flavor foods and as medicine to wash skin wounds (Matt. 23:23; KJV, "anise").

Frankincense (*Boswellia carteri* and *frereana*) Resin of a tree which, when burned, produced a strong aromatic scent. Frankincense was used in the preparation of the sacred oil for anointing of kings and priests and for the sacrifices in the temple. The men from the East brought frankincense to Jesus (Matt. 2:11).

Galbanum Fragrant resin which gave a pleasant scent when burned; it was one of the ingredients of the holy incense (Exod. 30:34).

Henna Plant used as a cosmetic; its leaves produced a dye women used (Song 1:14; 4:13). KJV translates the word as "camphire," but camphire was not native to Palestine and may not have been known in biblical times.

Mint Leaves were used as a condiment (Matt. 23:23; Luke 11:42).

Myrrh (*Commiphora abessinica*) Resinous gum of a plant which was included in the preparation of the holy anointing oil (Exod. 30:23). It was also used for its aromatic properties (Ps. 45:8) and used for female purification (Esther 2:12). Myrrh was given to Jesus at His birth as a gift (Matt. 2:11) and as a drink when He was on the cross (Mark 15:23).

Onycha Traditionally taken as the aromatic crushed shell of a mollusk but in light of Ugaritic

S

plant lists probably a type of cress (*Lepidium sativum*). It was used in holy incense (Exod. 30:34).

Rue *(Ruta graveolens)* Herb used as a condiment. It was valued for its medicinal properties. Its leaves were used in the healing of insect bites (Luke 11:42).

Saffron *(Curcuma longa, Crocus sativus)* Substance of a plant that produced a yellow dye and was used to color foods. When mixed with oil, it was used as medicine and perfume (Song 4:14).

Spices The Hebrew word should be translated "balsam" (*Balsamodendrium opolbalsamum*). Shrub with a resin that gave a pleasant odor. Balsam was used as perfume and as medicine. The balsam was one of the ingredients of the anointing oil (Exod. 30:23).

Spikenard *(Nardos tacs jatamansi)* Very expensive fragrant oil used in the manufacture of perfumes and ointments (Song 1:12; 4:13; Mark 14:3; John 12:3).Also translated as "perfume" and "nard." The Gospels of Mark and John record that a woman anointed Jesus with this expensive perfume.

Stacte *(Pistacia lentiscus)* Small tree which produced a resin used in the sacred incense (Exod. 30:34).   *Claude F. Mariottini*

SPIDER Animal in Palestine known for spinning a web (Job 8:14; Isa. 59:5). The spider's web is usually used as a sign of frailty.

SPIKENARD See *Spices*.

SPINDLE Used only in Prov. 31:19, KJV translates "spindle" in the first line and "distaff" in the second line. Modern translations (NASB, NIV, NRSV) reverse the words in their translations (HCSB uses "spinning staff" and "spindle"). The distaff was a stick that held the fibers from which thread was spun. The spindle was a round stick with a round disk fastened closer to one end. The spun thread was wound around the spindle. See *Cloth, Clothing*.

SPINNING AND WEAVING Major elements involved in making cloth and were familiar processes in biblical times.

Spinning Threads woven into cloth were produced from raw fibers by spinning (Matt. 6:28; Luke 12:27). Flax, or linen (Lev. 13:47-48; Prov. 31:13; Jer. 13:1; Ezek. 40:3; 44:17; Hos. 2:5), and wool (Lev. 13:47) were the major fibers used in the biblical world.

In spinning, raw fibers were pulled into a loose strand and twisted to form a continuous thread. A spindle (2 Sam. 3:29; Prov. 31:19 NRSV) was a slender stick which could be twirled to twist drawn out fibers caught in a hook or slot at the top. A spindle whorl acted as a flywheel for more efficient twisting. Spun thread was wound onto the stick. Sometimes it was plied or twined, two or three threads being twisted together (Exod. 26:1; 36:8,35). The finished product could then be used for weaving (Exod. 35:25-26).

Weaving Interlacing of threads to form fabric. Weaving was conducted on looms, devices designed to create openings (sheds) between alternating vertical warp threads through which the horizontal weft threads were passed. After each weft thread was placed, it was beaten against the previous one with a flat stick, thus firming up the fabric.

Three main loom designs were used in the biblical world. On a horizontal ground loom, the warp threads were stretched between beams pegged to the ground. This type is apparently referred to in the Samson story (Judg. 16:13-14), as it would have enabled Delilah to weave his locks while he slept. When Samson jumped up, he pulled away the pin(s) of the loom (v. 14b) that secured the beams to the ground. In some vertical looms the warp was stretched between two beams fixed in a rectangular frame. Work proceeded from the bottom of the loom, and the woven cloth could be rolled onto the bottom beam (Isa. 38:12). This permitted the weaver to remain seated and to produce much longer finished products. Another type of vertical loom had the warp threads attached to an upper beam and held taut in groups by a series of stone or clay weights. Weaving was done from the top to the bottom, and the weft beaten upwards. Large numbers of excavated loom weights testify to the popularity of warp weighted looms in OT Israel.

Stripes or bands of color were made by using dyed threads for portions of the warp or weft threads. Warp weighted looms allowed portions of the shed to be opened at a time, so intricate patterns could be made in the weft by covering small areas with different colors. It was forbidden, however, to wear clothes made of linen and wool woven together (Deut. 22:11). Weavers apparently were professionals who specialized in

A bedouin woman spinning wool into yarn.

particular types of work. The OT differentiates between ordinary weavers, designers, and embroiderers (Exod. 35:35).

Daniel C. Browning, Jr.

SPIRIT Empowering perspective of human life and the Holy Spirit bringing God's presence and power to bear in the world. A translation of the Hebrew word *ruach* and the Greek work *pneuma,* which can be translated as "wind," "breath," or "spirit" depending upon the context.

In both Testaments "spirit" is used of both God and human beings. Spirit, whether used of God or of human beings, is difficult to define. The kinship of spirit, breath, and wind is a helpful clue in beginning to understand spirit. In His conversation with Nicodemus (John 3), Jesus said that the Spirit is like the wind in that one cannot see it but one can see its effects. This is true of both the Spirit of God and the spirit of a human being.

Spirit of God At the beginning of creation, the Spirit of God hovered over the waters (Gen. 1:3). Elihu acknowledged to Job that the Spirit

of God had made him and was the source of his life (Job 33:4). The animals were created when God sent out His "breath" (Ps. 104:30 HCSB, NRSV note).

The Spirit of God is present everywhere. The psalmist sensed that no matter where he was, God's Spirit was there (Ps. 139:7). The Pharaoh saw the Spirit of God in Joseph (Gen. 41:38). Moses realized that the Spirit of God was on him, and he desired that God's Spirit be on all of His people (Num. 11:29). During the period of the judges, the Spirit of the Lord came to individuals and empowered them to accomplish specific tasks (Judg. 3:10; 6:34; 11:29; 13:25; 14:6; 14:19). When Samuel, the last of the judges, anointed Saul, Israel's first king, he told Saul that the Spirit of the Lord would come upon him. The result was that Saul prophesied and was changed into a different person (1 Sam. 10:6). Later, the Spirit departed from Saul (1 Sam. 16:14). Likewise, the Spirit came upon David when Samuel anointed him (1 Sam. 16:13). In his last words David said that the Spirit of the Lord had spoken through him (2 Sam. 23:2).

Isaiah spoke of one who is to come from the line of Jesse, one on whom the Spirit of the Lord would rest. This person would have the Spirit of wisdom, understanding, counsel, power, knowledge, and the fear of the Lord (Isa. 11:1-3). Ezekiel prophesied that God would put His Spirit within His people, removing from them hearts of stone and putting within them hearts of flesh that would be obedient to God's way (Ezek. 36:26-27).

New Testament Teaching Each of the four Gospels has numerous references to the Spirit of God or the Holy Spirit. The Spirit was the agent of Jesus' miraculous conception (Matt. 1:18,20), came down on Jesus at His baptism (Matt. 3:16), led Him into the wilderness where He was tempted by the devil (Matt. 4:1), and enabled Him to heal diseases and cast out demons (Matt. 12:28). Jesus promised the Spirit to His followers as He prepared to leave the world. The Spirit would serve as Comforter and Counselor, continuing to teach Jesus' followers and reminding them of what He had said to them (John 14:25-26). Not many days after Jesus' ascension, the promised Spirit came upon His followers during the Feast of Pentecost. The advent of the Spirit was accompanied by a sound that was like a mighty wind. Those who witnessed this event saw what seemed to be tongues of fire resting on

S

the believers. Moreover, these disciples were empowered to speak in tongues other than their native language (Acts 2:1-3). Throughout Luke's account of the early church, the Holy Spirit empowered and guided the followers of Jesus in their mission to the world surrounding the Mediterranean (Acts 11:12; 13:2; 15:28; 16:6-7; 20:22; 21:11).

The Spirit is important in Paul's understanding of the believer's relationship to God. The Spirit is a gracious personal presence who lives in one who has confessed that Jesus Christ is Lord. Relationship to God through Christ by the Spirit is revolutionary. In Galatians, Paul argued that legalism and the way of faith are incompatible. God's Spirit comes to us as a gift based on our faith in Christ and His grace (Gal. 3:1-5). God's Spirit comes into a believer's life with assurance that we are God's children (Rom. 8:16). The Spirit is God's pledge to us that we will be fully transformed and conformed to the image of Christ (Rom. 8:1-29; 2 Cor. 1:22). Paul identified the Spirit with the Lord (the risen Christ) and asserted that where the Spirit of the Lord is, there is freedom, a growing freedom from the law of sin and death (2 Cor. 3:18; cp. Rom. 8:2).

The Spirit distributes gifts in the church that are designed to equip God's people for serving and building up the body of Christ (1 Cor. 12; Eph. 4:7-13). Evidence that the Spirit of God is at work in a person or group of persons is love, joy, patience, kindness, goodness, faithfulness, gentleness, and self-control (Gal. 5:22-23).

At the beginning of Scripture we see the Spirit at work in creation. As Scripture closes, the Spirit and the bride, the church, issue an invitation for all who are thirsty to come and drink of the water of life (Rev. 22:17).

Human Spirits In both the OT and NT, "spirit" is used of humans and of other beings. When used of humans, spirit is associated with a wide range of functions including thinking and understanding, emotions, attitudes, and intentions. Elihu told Job it was spirit in a person, the breath of God, which gave understanding (Job 32:8). When Jesus healed the paralytic, He perceived in His "spirit" that the religious leaders present were questioning His forgiving the man's sins (Mark 2:8).

"Spirit" is used extensively with human emotions including sorrow (Prov. 15:4,13), anguish (Exod. 6:9; John 13:21), anger (Prov. 14:29;

16:32), vexation (Eccles. 1:14), fear (2 Tim. 1:7), and joy (Luke 1:47).

A variety of attitudes and intentions are associated with "spirit." Caleb had a different spirit than most of his contemporaries in that he followed the Lord wholeheartedly (Num. 14:24). Sihon, king of Heshbon, had a stubborn spirit (Deut. 2:30). First Kings 22 refers to a lying spirit. The psalmist called persons who have no deceit in their spirits, "blessed" (Ps. 32:2). A person's spirit can be contrite (Ps. 34:18), steadfast (Ps. 51:10), willing (Ps. 51:12), broken (Ps. 51:17), and haughty (Prov. 16:18). The Gospel of Mark has numerous references to Jesus healing persons with unclean or foul spirits.

Spirit is used of nonphysical beings, both good and evil. Satan is called the ruler of the kingdom of the air, the spirit who is at work in those who are disobedient (Eph. 2:2).

One of the perennial points of conflict between the Sadducees and the Pharisees was over whether there are angels and spirits. The latter believed that there were such while the former denied that such existed. When the risen Christ appeared to the disciples, they were startled and frightened, thinking they were seeing a spirit. Jesus invited them to touch Him. He then reminded them that a spirit does not have flesh and bones (Luke 24:37-39). See *Anthropology; God; Holy Spirit; Humanity.*   Steve Bond

SPIRITIST See *Medium.*

SPIRITS IN PRISON In 1 Pet. 3:19 the text says that Christ "went and made a proclamation to the spirits in prison" (HCSB). Peter further says that they "in the past were disobedient, when God patiently waited in the days of Noah." Several interpretations have been offered concerning these curious words. One is that these spirits are fallen angels who tried God's patience in the antediluvian era. On this view, Christ descended into hades after His crucifixion to preach either a message of salvation or a message of triumph. This interpretation is, however, unacceptable. Scripture never suggests that demons are given the opportunity for salvation.

The better interpretation sees them as those people whom God destroyed in the flood and who are now in hell or hades.

There are differing views on when and what Christ did preach to them. One view holds that Christ descended into the lower realm after His crucifixion to preach either a message of salvation or a message of triumph. Again, this is unlikely. The idea that Christ offers sinners a postmortem opportunity for salvation contradicts Heb. 9:27 and Luke 16:19-31. A better approach is that Christ preached to these persons "in the spirit" through Noah while they were still alive. This interpretation is confirmed by 1 Pet. 1:11 where Peter indicates that Christ spoke through the OT prophets and in 2 Pet. 2:5 where Noah is called a "preacher of righteousness." See *Descent to Hades*. *Steven B. Cowan*

SPIRITUAL GIFTS The phrase, "spiritual gifts," does not appear as such in the NT. It has gained common usage, though, in referring to what Scripture identifies as the God-granted empowerment for ministry on the part of believers. Scripture specifically employs these terms: "gifts" (Gk. *domata*, Eph. 4:8), "spiritual things" (*pneumatika*, 1 Cor. 12:1), "graces" (*charismata*, Rom. 12:6; 1 Cor. 12:4,9,28,30-31; 1 Pet. 4:10), "workings" (*energemata*, 1 Cor. 12:6), and "manifestation" (*phanerosis*, 1 Cor. 12:7). These terms point to that which God grants to believers for the carrying out of the work of ministry in the church. It seems appropriate to use the phrase "spiritual gifts," to refer to these, since they do come from the Holy Spirit (though they could also be said to come from the Father through the redemptive work of the Son—Eph. 4:8-11; 1 Cor. 12:5-7,11), and since they are given by God according to His own sovereign purposes (1 Cor. 12:11).

In the two lengthiest discussions of these *charismata*, Paul emphasizes the diversity that is to be found in the church, the body of Christ, as reflected in the various spiritual gifts (1 Cor. 12:1-31; Rom. 12:3-8). Indeed, the variety of types of gifts is remarkable. Scholars have made various attempts to classify the types of gifts, but none of these schemes is compelling. One such classification (James D. G. Dunn) makes these distinctions:

(1) Activities (miracles, healing, faith)

(2) Manifestations (revelation of Christ, vision and ecstasy, knowledge and wisdom, guidance)

(3) Inspired utterance (proclamation, prophecy, discerning of spirits, teaching, singing, prayer, tongues, interpretation)

(4) Service (giving and caring, helping and guiding)

Another (Bridge and Phypers) follows this pattern:

(1) Recognized church officers (apostles, prophets, evangelists, pastors and teachers, service, administrators, helpers)

(2) The whole church (wisdom, knowledge, faith, healing, miracles, prophecy, discernment, tongues, interpretation, voluntary poverty, martyrdom, celibacy, contribution, acts of mercy)

There may be other, better ways to classify the gifts. The point is that the various gifts need to be seen in the context of ministries, but that those ministries can be understood in more than one way. Just what are these gifts in the NT? There is considerable disagreement among scholars concerning the interpretation of some of the gifts, but it will be helpful to make some comments on the various gifts.

Some gifts seem to be very spectacular in their manifestation. Gifts of miracles (1 Cor. 12:28-29) refer to a gift of power by which the lordship of Christ over all of reality is made manifest. Nothing is outside His lordship. "Message of wisdom" (1 Cor. 12:8 HCSB) has to do with the ability to speak a word of wise counsel in any difficult situation. Many have experienced that in church situations in which someone had the ability to know the mind of the Spirit and say just the right thing. The healing ministry of the church comes next. Many in the NT demonstrated remarkable gifts of healing, and these manifestations were among "the signs of an apostle" (2 Cor. 12:12). There were some, though, who were not healed, as Paul makes clear: "Trophimus I left sick at Miletus" (2 Tim. 4:20), and to Timothy he urged, "Use a little wine because of your stomach and your frequent illnesses" (1 Tim. 5:23). Though Paul had a gift to heal (Acts 14:6-10), it is clear that he could only heal those whom God willed to be healed in such a manner. It may also be significant that Paul calls this gift, "gifts of healings" (1 Cor. 12:28, lit. Gk.). The plural may indicate that such a gift can be manifested in more than one way—miraculous healing may only be one form that it takes. Other forms might be found in the prayers of the elders for the sick (James 5:13-16) or even in the use of medicine and medical technology (see Paul's words of instruction to Timothy noted above). Certainly this gift points to the fact that God will ultimately effect the complete healing of the body in glorification. However, as in other areas of the Christian experience, what we have is in some measure ours already, but not yet completely, as the final redemption of the body awaits the return of the Lord (Rom. 8:23; 1 Cor. 15:42-44). "Distinguishing between spirits" (1 Cor. 12:10) may refer either to the ability to detect evil spirits (Acts 16:16-18) or the ability to have a discerning heart in dealing with human spiritual needs (Jer. 17:9-10; 1 Cor. 2:14). See *Prophecy, Prophets; Tongues, Gift of.*

Other gifts appear to be more "normal" and might not even seem to come directly from God. Teaching, service, administrations helping, mercy appear to be rather mundane, yet these are listed among the spiritual gifts with no indication that they are of inferior importance in the church. Rather Paul makes it clear in his analogy of the body that the "less honorable" (1 Cor. 12:23) gifts are just as important as the more visible and frequently honored gifts. No church could function if everyone wanted to have only the roles of pastor, teacher, and evangelist. These are charismatic (grace) gifts in the same way that prophecy and miracles are.

Interpreters sometimes ask whether the gifts listed in the NT are the only spiritual gifts that God grants. That question may be impossible to answer with any authority. It does seem safe to say that these were the representative gifts in the church of the first century, and, since the real needs of people and the church do not change, they are probably representative for the church of today as well. These gifts can of course be transferable to a variety of specific ministry contexts.

Others ask whether all of the gifts listed in these texts are still operative in the church today. It is not an easy question to answer. One must recognize first that the gifts are given according to the sovereignty of the Spirit (1 Cor. 12:11). Second, there is nothing within any of these texts that would demand that merely because God has granted a special gift or ministry in the past that He is thereby obligated to give the same gift or ministry to people in every generation. It might be the case, though again it might not be, that God would wish to give some gift which has a temporary purpose, and once that purpose is accomplished, that there would not be the need for that gift in all later generations. In some periods of biblical history, miracles and wonders were not prominent, even in the lives of some of the heroes of Scripture. Moses, for instance, witnessed many signs and wonders, but David

apparently did not. This question is especially relevant to the gifts of prophecy and apostleship. Paul reminded the Ephesians that these two gifts constituted the foundation of the church (Eph. 2:20), and Jesus demonstrates to John that the names of the apostles are on the foundation of the heavenly city (Rev. 21:14). If that is so, it does not seem that those gifts would need to be operative, at least not in the same way, as they were in the first generation of the Christian church. Otherwise, the foundation would be in the process of being laid again in every generation, and that does not appear to be consistent with these and other texts. That is not to say that these gifts "ceased," as though the church of later days lost its power and focus. Rather, it may be that God's intention for some of the gifts was that they were needed for a specific intention, and once that goal had been attained, they were no longer needed. If prophecy and apostleship had to do with the formation of the Christian Scriptures and the revelation of the NT message, then we would not expect those gifts to be needed (at least in the same manner) as they were during the early days of the church.

Though the gifts are many, the Spirit who grants them is one. God has given a diverse number of gifts to the church since the needs of the Christian community are broad and complex. The church needs instruction, exhortation, ministries of mercy, administration of its program, encouragement and healing in times of illness, wise counsel in dark days, and many other things besides. So, God has given to His people a wide diversity of empowerments and enablements, and each person should find his or her own area of giftedness and be happy with that (1 Cor. 12:15-25). But this diversity ought not to result in schisms and quarrels, since all are gifted by the same Holy Spirit, who also indwells them (Rom. 8:9-11; 1 Cor. 12:4-7).

God gives spiritual gifts to His people so that they might be effective and enabled for ministry. All Christians have spiritual gifts (1 Cor. 12:7; Eph. 4:7). These gifts are never given to believers that they might profit by them or that they might somehow use the gifts for themselves. They are given, as the apostle says, "to produce what is beneficial" (1 Cor. 12:7 HCSB). Gifts entail ministry. This means that all Christians are ministers. All Christians have tasks to perform in the service of the Lord in the church. No one is ever meant merely to be a receiver of ministry;

all of God's people both give and receive ministry. Churches will never achieve the level of maturity that Christ means for them to have until all members are actively demonstrating their giftedness by engaging in the ministries which their gifts entail (Eph. 4:12-16). When churches discover the importance of an every-member ministry, they will truly experience the growth of the body, for the edifying of itself in love (Eph. 4:16). See *Holy Spirit.* *Chad Brand*

SPIT, SPITTLE Spitting at or on someone is the strongest sign of contempt. The brother who refused to perform levirate marriage (have a child by his brother's wife to carry on the name of the brother, Deut. 25:5-6) would have his face spit in by the spurned wife of the brother (Deut. 25:7-9). The soldiers that mocked Jesus before His crucifixion spat on Him (Matt. 27:30). The religious leaders who tried Jesus before taking Him to Pilate spat in His face (Matt. 26:67). Spittle was used to heal (Mark 8:23; John 9:6). Mixing spittle with clay (John 9:6) may have been to deliberately break the Sabbath laws of the Jewish religious leaders.

SPOIL Anything taken by a victorious soldier. In ancient warfare a soldier could take anything he could carry that had belonged to a foe. This plunder could be precious metals, clothes, cattle, or the vanquished people themselves. Holy war laws dedicated all such booty to God (Deut. 20). The battles of Joshua illustrated this.

SPONGE Skeleton of a marine animal whose structure retains water. It was especially useful in bathing. The only instances of its use in the Bible involve giving Jesus a drink while upon the cross (Matt. 27:48; Mark 15:36; John 19:29). See *Cross.*

SPOON KJV translation for the dish in which incense was burned in the tabernacle and temple (Num. 7:14). Other translations are "gold bowl" (HCSB), "gold pan" (NASB), "golden dish" (NRSV), and "gold dish" (NIV). The 12 dishes were made of 10 shekels of gold (vv. 84-86). See *Incense; Vessels and Utensils.*

SPORT To laugh at, to mock, to play with, and in one place to live in luxury. The versions do not agree on how to translate this word. For instance, Isa. 57:4 (KJV) is translated, "Against

whom do ye sport yourselves?" ("jest" NASB; "mocking" NIV, NRSV). Samson is said to have made sport for the Philistines (Judg. 16:25). Modern translations use "perform" and "entertain." Second Peter 2:13 (KJV) speaks of the unrighteous as "sporting themselves with their own deceivings while they feast with you." Modern translations translate "reveling."

SPORTS The Hebrew verb "make sport" is used to indicate ridicule (e.g., Gen. 21:9) but also sport in the sense of entertainment (Judg. 16:25,27) or play (Exod. 32:6; Ps. 104:26; Zech. 8:5).

Several games of skill are alluded to in the Bible. Jacob's single-handed combat at Peniel seems to have been a wrestling match between two skilled fighters (Gen. 32:24-32). The fight at the pool of Gibeon between the soldiers of Abner and the soldiers of Joab may have begun as a show of strength through wrestling (2 Sam. 2:12-17). Job 16:12-13 speaks of archery, a sport depicted on Assyrian reliefs. Isaiah 22:18 suggests a game of ball. Foot races are alluded to in Ps. 19:5. Paul mentions Greco-Roman gladiatorial bouts, surely the most gruesome of all entertainment events (1 Cor. 4:9; 15:32).

The NT uses various games as figures of the Christian life. Paul often spoke of his work on behalf of the Gospel as "running" (Gal. 2:2; 5:7; Phil. 2:16; 3:13-14; cp. Heb. 12:1) and likened the spiritual discipline required for successful living to that required for winning foot races and boxing matches (1 Cor. 9:24-27; cp. 2 Tim. 2:5; 4:7). "Racing" was a natural metaphor for Paul to adopt, not only because of the popularity of foot races in the Greco-Roman world, but also because from the earliest days of the OT a believer's relationship with God was described as "walking" or "running" with Him (Gen. 3:8; 5:24; Ps. 119:32; Isa. 40:31). *Paul H. Wright*

SPOT Skin blemishes of differing kinds indicating sickness that made a person ceremonially unclean (Lev. 13:1-8). The priest declared such persons clean or unclean. Only animals "without spot" (Num. 28:3 KJV) could be used for an offering to Yahweh. Jesus Himself was spoken of by Peter as "a lamb without defect or blemish [spot]" (1 Pet. 1:19 HCSB). The faithful are urged "to keep the commandment without spot" (1 Tim. 6:14). In this sense it means to be

S

morally pure and obedient to God's will. See *Sacrifice and Offering*.

SPOUSAL ABUSE Physical, emotional, and sexual mistreatment of a marriage partner. Spousal abuse is a particularly serious matter in the eyes of God because it fractures the marriage relationship established as the foundation of society (Gen. 2:24). Biblical stories such as Abraham passing off his wife as his sister in Egypt (Gen. 12:10-20; cp. 20:2-14; 26:6-11) portray the consequences of spousal abuse.

The Bible describes traits that characteristically appear in persons who abuse their spouses. Jealous men act beyond the bounds of control (Prov. 6:34). Sometimes kind and gentle speech, "buttery words," masks violence (Ps. 55:20-21 HCSB). The effects of sins committed by one person are felt in successive generations (Exod. 34:7), a pattern well-known in abused families.

Although the husband is head of his wife, his actions toward her must be like those of Christ to the church (1 Cor. 11:3; Eph. 5:23-24). Every husband must love his wife as he loves himself (Eph. 5:25-33), showing her great consideration (1 Pet. 3:7), honor (1 Thess. 4:4), and gentleness (Col. 3:19). A husband must provide for his family, for not to do so would make him worse than an unbeliever (1 Tim. 5:8).

God chose the marriage relationship as a picture of His relationship with both Israel and the church. Any action that tarnishes the marriage relationship, such as spousal abuse, cheapens a believer's relationship with God. See *Marriage*.

SPRING Place where water bubbles up freely from the ground (NASB, NIV, NRSV). KJV usually translates "fountain." See *Fountain; Water; Well*.

SQUAD Modern translation of "quaternion" (KJV) (Acts 12:4; HCSB, "squads of four soldiers each"). See *Quaternion*.

STABLE Place where animals are kept either by enclosing them or tying them. Animals were usually kept in numbers rather than one animal in a stable or stall, as is often the case today. It could be a simple enclosure, a cave, or a building. Solomon kept large numbers of horses in stalls (1 Kings 4:26). Most people just kept their animals together. Some kept them in a lower part of their homes. Jesus was born in a stable possibly

belonging to an inn for He was put in a manger (trough where animals were fed) after being wrapped snugly in cloth. See *Manger; Solomon*.

STACHYS (Stā´ kĭs) Personal name meaning "head of grain." Man that Paul called "my dear friend" (Rom. 16:9 HCSB).

STACTE Gum of the storax tree which was combined with onycha, galbanum, and frankincense to make the incense to be burned in the tabernacle (Exod. 30:34). It is a small tree plentiful in rocky places in most of Palestine. See *Incense*.

STAFF See *Rod*.

STAG Modern translation of "hart," an adult male deer. See *Deer*.

STAIRS Series of steps whereby a person can climb easily to another level. Houses in Palestine usually had stairs on the outside going up to the roof. Many activities were on the roof of the average house. Sometimes the steepness of city streets would make stairs from one level to another necessary. Also wells and cisterns in many cities in Palestine would have stairs leading down to the water. There were stairs in two visions in the OT: Jacob's ladder may have been stairs (Gen. 28:12); Ezekiel's temple had stairs (steps) (Ezek. 43:17). See *Architecture; House*.

STAKE Instrument used with cords to anchor a tent. Sometimes translated "pegs." It was used figuratively of Jerusalem (Isa. 33:20; 54:2). See *Peg*.

An area at Megiddo thought to be a stable complex (or possibly storehouses) from the time of Ahab.

STALL Place where animals were kept and fed. See *Stable*.

STANDARD Flag or banner usually used by the military to identify groups of soldiers or a central flag to rally all the soldiers at one time (Num. 1:52; 2:2; 10:14,18). It is also used figuratively of God (Isa. 59:19). See *Banner*.

STARGAZER See *Astrologer*.

STARS Constellations, planets, and all heavenly bodies except the sun and the moon. God is acknowledged to be the Creator of all such (Gen. 1:16) as well as the One who knows their names and numbers (Ps. 147:4). Biblical writers knew many of the constellations. The Lord asked Job, "Can you bind the chains of the Pleiades, or loose the cords of Orion?" (Job 38:31 NASB).

Individual stars are mentioned (Amos 5:26; Acts 7:43). Probably the most famous and intriguing of all the stars mentioned in Scripture is the star of Bethlehem (Matt. 2). Many theories have been posited regarding its identity. Suffice it to say that Scripture does not name the star. It is one of many miracles that attest to the power of our God and is similar to the pillar of fire used to demonstrate God's presence and might to the children of Israel as they made their way to the land of Canaan. In the final book of the Bible, the Lord Jesus is called "the Bright Morning Star" (Rev. 22:16 HCSB).   *C. Dale Hill*

STATURE Usually refers to the height of a person, sometimes used figuratively (Ezek. 17:6; 19:11). Jesus "increased in wisdom and stature" (Luke 2:52). It was used to show the weakness of humanity and the need to rely on God (Matt. 6:27; Luke 12:25). It was also used as a measure of the maturity of the Christian (Eph. 4:13).

STATUTE Law or commandment; could be from God or an earthly ruler. Different statutes of God were given by Moses to God's people (Exod. 15:25-26). Joseph was able to create laws as a ruler in Egypt (Gen. 47:26).

STEADFASTNESS Word meaning to endure patiently. A steadfast person is one who is reliable, faithful, and true to the end. Paul said Jesus was a person of steadfastness (Rom. 15:3-5). The NASB translates steadfastness with "persever-ance" (2 Thess. 1:4). James said that trials that test our faith produce steadfastness (1:3 KJV "patience"; HCSB, NRSV, NASB "endurance"; NIV "perseverance").

STEAL See *Robbery*.

STEEL KJV translation of a word that most modern versions translate "bronze" (2 Sam. 22:35). See *Minerals and Metals*.

STEPHANAS (Stĕph´ à nàs) Greek name meaning "crown." One of Paul's first converts ("firstfruits") in the Roman province of Achaia (Greece). Paul reports that he baptized Stephanas and his household, who have now "devoted themselves to serving the saints" (HCSB)—apparently meaning that they are now serving the Corinthian church as recognized leaders (1 Cor. 1:16; 16:15; cp. 1 Clement 42.4. Stephanas served as a member of the Corinthian delegation that visited Paul during the apostle's ministry in Ephesus (1 Cor. 16:17-18).
                                           Robert L. Plummer

STEPHEN (Stē´ vən) Personal name meaning "crown." The first Christian martyr; foremost of those chosen to bring peace to the quarreling church (Acts 6:1-7) and so mighty in the Scriptures that his Jewish opponents in debate could not refute him (Acts 6:10) as he argued that Jesus was the Messiah. Saul of Tarsus heard Stephen's speech to the Jewish Sanhedrin accusing the Jewish leaders of rejecting God's way as their forefathers had (Acts 6:12–7:53). Saul held the clothes of those who stoned Stephen to death; he saw him die a victorious death. Stephen may well have been the human agency that God used to conquer him who would become the great Christian missionary.

St. Stephen's Gate (Lion's Gate) at Jerusalem.

Stephen was in the forefront of those who saw Christianity as much more than a Jewish sect. They took seriously the commission of Jesus to carry the gospel to the whole world and led to the founding of the world mission movement that took the gospel to the whole Roman Empire in the first century. The believers had to flee Jerusalem after Stephen's death while the apostles alone remained there (Acts 8:1).

Fred L. Fisher

STEWARDSHIP Responsibility to manage all the resources of life for the glory of God, acknowledging God as provider.

Old Testament *Asher al bayit* is translated "steward" (HCSB, KJV, NIV, and NKJV) or "house steward" (NASB) (Gen. 43:19; 44:1,4; 1 Kings 16:9). The Genesis references are to Joseph and in 1 Kings, the reference is to Arza as steward of Elah, son of Baasha, who reigned over Israel for two years. The expression is literally "one over a house," one charged with oversight of household operations. An added term, *ha'ish* (the man), appears in Gen. 43:19. Thus the literal translation is "the man over a house."

Ben mesheq (Gen. 15:2) is translated "steward" (KJV), "the one who will inherit my estate" (NIV), and "the heir of my house" (HCSB, NASB, NKJV). The expression literally means "son of acquisition." Eliezer was a servant/slave in the house of Abram, who in the absence of a son of Abraham stood to inherit his estate.

Sar is used infrequently in this regard, and may mean also "prince," "head," "chief," or "captain," or "ruler." The term is translated in 1 Chron. 28:1 as "officials" in charge of property (NIV) and as "overseers" (NASB).

New Testament *Epitropos* is the first of two primary Greek terms translated "steward" in the NT (Matt. 20:8; Luke 8:3). In Matthew reference is to a "lord" who speaks to his "steward." In Luke Chuza (HCSB, NRSB, KJV, NASB) or Cuza (NIV) is identified as the steward of Herod.

Oikonomos, the second Greek term, deals with the person, task, or place of "stewardship." The word first appears in Luke 12:42, a "faithful and wise steward" (KJV; HCSB, "faithful and sensible manager"). This masculine noun focuses on the person, not the task. The feminine form of the noun, two words later, is usually translated "stewardship," highlighting the task, the responsibility granted such a person.

This term is used mostly in the NT. Other occurrences include Luke 16:1,3,8; 1 Cor. 4:1-2; Titus 1:7; and 1 Pet. 4:10. Each text illumines a little more the meaning of stewardship and frames the NT picture of the believer as a "house manager" for God in this world.

The biblical concept of stewardship, beginning with Adam and Eve and developed more fully in the NT, is that God is owner and provider of all that any of us possess. Since all belongs to Him, it is incumbent that all be used for His purposes and glory. A collective responsibility was given to mankind to have dominion over the earth, care for it, and manage it for His glory. Individually, whether financial resources, real property, other valuable items, time, influence, or opportunity, the believer is to seek the mind and will of God for every decision. God not only expects that we return a portion of what He gives us as tithes and offerings, He expects for all that we have to be used in ways which please and honor Him. He expects that we, regardless of vocation, will exercise responsible stewardship, on His behalf, of every day that we live. One day His eternal kingdom will come. In the meantime, we are to live as if it has already come. See *Tithe*.

Don H. Stewart and Charles W. Draper

STOCKS Instrument that secured the feet (and sometimes the neck and hands) of a prisoner (Job 13:27; Jer. 29:26; Acts 16:24). They were usually made of wood with holes to secure the feet. They could also be an instrument of torture by stretching the legs apart and causing the prisoner to sit in unnatural positions. The Romans often added chains along with the stocks.

STONE Hardened mineral matter comprising much of the earth. Palestine is a stony country. Often it was necessary to clear a field of stone in preparation for its cultivation (Isa. 5:2). An enemy's fields were marred by throwing stones on them, and his wells were choked with stones (2 Kings 3:19,25). Stones were used for various purposes: city walls (Neh. 4:3), dwellings (Lev. 14:38-40), palaces (1 Kings 7:1,9), temples (1 Kings 6:7), pavement in courtyards and columns (Esther 1:6), and in Herodian times, at least, for paving streets. The Israelites used unhewn stones for building their altars. They often heaped stones to commemorate some great spiritual event or encounter with God (Gen.

Intricate stone carving on a column piece at ancient Baalbek (Heliopolis).

31:46; Josh. 4). They marked the grave of notorious offenders with stones (Josh. 7:26). One of the most popular uses of stone was the building of the walls of the temple and the building of the walls of the city of Jerusalem (1 Kings 7:9-12).

Single stones were used to close the mouth of cisterns, wells, and tombs (Gen. 29:2; Matt. 27:60; John 11:38). They were also used to mark boundaries (Deut. 19:14). The Israelites sometimes consecrated a single stone as a memorial to God (Gen. 28:18-22; 1 Sam. 7:12).

The OT and NT refer to stones being used as lethal weapons. Two popular stories about the

use of stones for weapons are those about David killing Goliath (1 Sam. 17:49) and about the enemies of the Christian faith stoning Stephen (Acts 7:58). See *Arms and Armor*.

Stones were often used for weights on scales. They were employed for writing documents. The most obvious example is the writing of the Ten Commandments on stone by the Spirit of God when Moses went up on Mount Sinai.

Symbolically, a stone denotes hardness or insensibility (1 Sam. 25:37; Ezek. 36:26). It could also mean firmness and strength. The followers of Christ were called living stones that were built up into the spiritual temple of Christ. Christ Himself became the chief cornerstone (Eph. 2:20-22; 1 Pet. 2:4-8). See *Minerals and Metals*. 　　　　　　　　　　　　*Gary Bonner*

STONE QUARRIES See *Shebarim*.

STONES OF FAIR COLORS See *Antimony*.

STOOL Simply made object for a person to sit on (2 Kings 4:10). Some translate "chair" (NASB, NRSV, NIV). It is also mentioned in Exod. 1:16 ("birthstool" NASB, NRSV; "delivery stool" NIV). God is said to have a footstool where the faithful worship Him (Ps. 99:5 HCSB). James speaks of a footstool being in the assembly of the early church (2:3).

STOREHOUSE, STORAGE CITY Storehouses were built early in human history to protect harvested crops from vermin and extreme weather. The typical storehouse during the Israelite period was a rectangular building with a double row of columns that divided the building into three narrow aisles. Large, thick walls supported the roof, and small side rooms led off of the main

Roman marble column shafts in secondary use to reinforce a crusader sea wall at Caesarea Maritima.

Storage rooms, or storehouse, excavated at Tel Beersheba in the Negev.

hall. Storerooms at Herod's fortress of Masada had walls 11 feet high constructed of stones weighing over 400 pounds. Community storehouses could also be used as public markets. In large cities certain sections of the town were designated as storage areas, with several storehouses lining the streets. During the divided kingdom period, royal storage facilities were established in regional capitals to collect tax payments made in flour, oil, grain, or wine. Specially marked jars held these royal stores which later could be distributed to the army or royal palaces. The temple complex included special storage areas, both for the utensils of worship and to serve as a sort of bank where valuables might be placed. The picture of a full storehouse served as an image of God's blessing and was often used by the prophets (Mal. 3:10; cp. Job 38:22; Jer. 10:13).

David Maltsberger

STORK One of a number of large, long-legged birds that usually wade for their food. They eat fish and an assortment of animals that live around water. They are known for the care they take of their young and for returning each year to the same nesting area. The stork migrates from Africa in the winter to Europe in the spring. It stops in Palestine during its migration. It was ceremonially unclean (Lev. 11:19). It is related to the heron. See *Birds*.

STRAIGHT STREET A street in Damascus where Paul was staying after being struck blind in his experience with the risen Christ (Acts 9:10-12). This street still exists today called Darb al-Mustaqim. See *Damascus*.

STRANGE WOMAN See *Adventuress*.

STRANGER See *Alien*.

STRAW Usually barley or wheat stalks after they have been cut (sometimes translated "chaff"). It was usually used as bedding for animals, much as many farmers use it today. The Israelites were forced to use straw in the making of bricks (Exod. 5:6-13). See *Stubble*.

STREETS Pathways established and constructed for transportation via animals and vehicles. The layout of city streets often was established by the shape of the outer city walls. In some cities a wide street encircled the city, following the line of the outer wall. In other towns streets radiated

The street called Straight in Damascus, Syria.

from a main plaza or thoroughfare. The doors of shops, storehouses, and private homes opened onto the street. Often household wastes were thrown out into the street. Small, crooked lanes and alleyways led off from main streets, ending at a central courtyard serving several homes or shops. Streets were often paved with large, flat stones, although dirt paths were not uncommon. Larger towns constructed drainage canals beneath city streets, some to carry away wastewater and others to trap the runoff from winter rains, which was channeled into cisterns. During the NT era Roman engineers designed cities throughout the empire with wide, straight, and well-constructed streets, usually leading to a central plaza or temple. Sidewalks with raised curbs bordered streets set with large polygonal paving stones. Drains below the pavement carried away sewage and rainwater. The constant traffic of carts and pedestrians often wore ruts into the streets, necessitating repair.

David Maltsberger

STRIPES See *Scourge.*

STRONG DRINK Intoxicating drink made from grain. It may have at first been used of beer made from barley. Wine is usually included along with strong drink but is separate from it (1 Sam. 1:15; Judg. 13:4,7,14; Luke 1:15). It was usually denied to priests (Lev. 10:8-9) and those who took the Nazirite vow (Num. 6:3). Isaiah warned against drinking too much (5:11). The Bible warns against drunkenness. The NT says that the drunkard will have no place in the kingdom of God (1 Cor. 6:9-10). See *Drunkenness; Wine.*

STUBBLE Stalks of grain dried out in the field or left on the threshing floor. It is sometimes translated "straw" or "chaff." Stubble burns quickly and can be blown away by the wind. Figuratively it is used of God's judgment (Joel 2:5; Isa. 5:24). Stubble was used by God's people to make bricks while they were slaves in Egypt (Exod. 5:12).

STUMBLING BLOCK Anything that causes a person to stumble or to fall. It is used literally (Lev. 19:14), but most often it is used as a metaphor. It is used of idols (Ezek. 7:19), of God's work with faithless people (Jer. 6:21), and of God Himself in relation to His people (Isa.

The Street of Curetes looking toward the Library of Celsus in the ruins of ancient Ephesus.

8:14). Paul warned Christians not to let their freedom result in a stumbling block to other believers (Rom. 14:13; 1 Cor. 8:9). The disobedient are warned that Jesus Himself could be a stumbling block (Rom. 9:32-33; 1 Cor. 1:23; 1 Pet. 2:8). The Greek word *skandalon* was the bait stick in a trap. It was also used symbolically for the trap itself. It came to mean a temptation to sin or to have false faith.

SUAH (Sū´ ah) Personal name meaning "sweepings." Son of Zophah of the tribe of Asher (1 Chron. 7:36).

SUBMISSION, SUBORDINATION Voluntary placement of oneself under the authority and leadership of another (Gk. *hupotasso*). Submission is taught in the context of various relationships. In divinely ordained relationships, submission enables a unique Christian harmony, based on God's good design.

Husbands and Wives The Bible's teaching about the submission of wives to husbands begins in Genesis, which declares that God made man in His own image as male and female

(1:27). The equality of men and women is the necessary foundation from which to begin the discussion of headship and submission in marriage. Adam's headship and authority in marriage were established before the fall. First, Adam was created (Gen. 2:7; cp. 1 Cor. 11:8; 1 Tim. 2:13). Second, the command to leave and cleave is addressed to the man, thus giving him the responsibility to establish the home (Gen. 2:24). Third, the woman is designated as the helper for the man (Gen. 2:18; cp. 1 Cor. 11:9). Fourth, Adam's authority is seen in that he named Eve (Gen. 2:23). Fifth, man was designated "Adam," which was the term used to describe the whole human race (Gen. 1:26-27; 5:2). In the NT 1 Cor. 11:3-10 teaches the headship of the man in marriage and bases this instruction on the creation account. Ephesians 5:22-33 instructs wives to submit to the authority of their husbands as to the Lord (Col. 3:18; Titus 2:3-5; 1 Pet. 3:1-7), while husbands should love their wives. Peter also exhorts the wife to submit to her husband and cautions that the husband's authority should be exercised with understanding and honor toward his wife (1 Pet. 3:1-7). This structure, when balanced with Gen. 1:26-27, demonstrates that men and women are essentially equal before God but different in their role and function.

Some have suggested that, according to Eph. 5:21, submission in marriage is a two-way idea. That is, along with the wife submitting to the husband, the husband submits to the wife through his loving, sacrificial leadership. However, in Eph. 5:21 it is more accurate to speak of spheres of authority and submission to one another, not mutual submission.

Christ and the Church The relationship between Christ and the Church is a paradigm for submission and authority in marriage (Eph. 5:22-33). The Church willingly submits herself to Christ, her designated head (Eph. 5:23; Col. 1:18), while Christ, as head, is clearly the authority over the Church (Eph. 1:22-23). Christ loves the Church and gave Himself for her so as to present her spotless (Eph. 5:25-27).

The Trinity One aspect of submission in the Godhead is seen in the relationship between the Father and the Son. Although fully equal with God the Father (John 5:18), the Son freely submits Himself to the Father in eternity past (1 Cor. 8:6; 11:3), throughout His earthly ministry (Phil. 2:6-11), and in the eternal kingdom (1 Cor. 15:20-28). Within the Godhead there is equality of essence but difference in role and function, providing another possible paradigm for headship and submission in marriage.

Other Relationships There are several other relationships in the Bible that are structured based on authority and submission. First, all human beings are required to submit to God (Deut. 6:1-9; Isa. 45:23; 1 John 2:3-6). Second, the Bible teaches submission to God-appointed leaders as in the cases of Abraham and Moses or, in the NT, the chosen pastor and elders of a local church (Heb. 13:17; 1 Pet. 5:1-5). Third, human beings are required to submit to governmental authorities such as kings Saul, David, and Solomon or, in the NT, government in general (Rom. 13:1-7). Fourth, children are required to submit to, and obey, their parents (Deut. 5:16; 21:18-21; Eph. 6:1-4). See *Family; Marriage.*

Randy Stinson

SUBURBS Pastureland around cities that were used in common for the feeding of sheep, cattle, and other animals (Lev. 25:34 KJV). Other versions translate "open land" (NRSV); "pastureland" (HCSB, NIV); and "pasture fields" (NASB). See *Cities and Urban Life.*

SUCATHITE (Sū´ kȧ thīt) People who claimed ancestry from the Kenites and the Rechabites (1 Chron. 2:55). KJV has Suchathites.

SUCCOTH (Sŭk´ ŏth) **1.** Place-name meaning "booths." A city east of the Jordan in the tribal territory of Gad. Jacob dwelt there upon his return to Canaan (Gen. 33:17). It was an important town during the time of Gideon. Its leaders were punished by Gideon for not helping him in a campaign against the Midianites (Judg. 8:5-7,13-16). Near Succoth Hiram made vessels for Solomon's temple (1 Kings 7:45-46). It is usually located at Tell Deir Alla, but some excavation results have called this into question. **2.** Place where the Israelites camped upon leaving Egypt (Exod. 12:37; 13:20; Num. 33:5-6). It was near Pithom and is usually identified with Tell el-Maskhutah or Tell er-Retabah.

SUCCOTH-BENOTH (Sŭc cŏth-bē nŏth) Divine name meaning "booths of daughters." A pagan deity that people from Babylon brought with them to Israel when it was resettled by the Assyrians after the fall of Samaria in 722 B.C. (2 Kings 17:30). Interpreters disagree concerning the identification of this idol. Many feel that it is likely Sarpanitu, the consort of Marduk. See *Gods, Pagan; Sakkuth.*

SUFFERING Causes of Human Suffering Scripture asserts suffering is inevitable in a fallen world (Gen. 3:14-19; Pss. 10:1-18; 22:1-31; 38:1-22; 90:1-17; Mark 13:12-13; John 16:33; Acts 14:22). Indeed, Christians may suffer more than do unbelievers (Rom. 6:1-14; 8:35-39; 1 Cor. 12:26; 1 Thess. 2:14; 2 Tim. 3:10-12; 1 Pet. 4:1-14; Rev. 2:10). Experiences of suffering fall into three categories: suffering caused by physical limitations (disease, physical and psychological pain, depression, and mental illness), by natural disasters (storms, fire, flood, and earthquake), and by human actions (harming oneself or others, individually or corporately).

Confronted with suffering, biblical individuals raise important questions. One is, "Why does the one true God allow evil and suffering?" The Bible teaches much about causes of suffering and articulates some explanations. However, some instances are left unexplained, and Scripture gives no comprehensive explanation. God's reasons and purposes transcend human finite knowledge, and we cannot always understand suffering. Some events remain a mystery. At times we must trust God without understanding (Job 42:2-3; Isa. 55:8-9; Hab. 2:2-4). We will not have complete answers until eternity (John 14:1-3; Rom. 8:18; 1 Cor. 2:9; 15:1-58; 2 Cor. 4:16-18; 1 Thess. 4:13-18; Rev. 21:4-5).

One cause of suffering is sinfulness (Ps. 7:12-16; Hos. 8:7; Rom. 2:3-6; Gal. 6:7-8; James 1:13-15). Misuse of God's gift of freedom, beginning with the fall of Adam and Eve and continuing in all persons, brings devastating consequences (Gen. 3:14-19; Rom. 3:23; 5:12-21; 6:23). Sin may result in suffering (Ps. 1:1-6; Jer. 31:29-30; Ezek. 18:2-4), whether by individuals or corporate groups (Josh. 7:1-12; 2 Kings 17:7-24; Amos 1:3-2:16). However, the assumption that suffering is always the direct result of sin is wrong (Job 4:1-5:27; 42:7-8; Luke 13:1-5; John 9:1-3). Some evil and suffering transcend human depravity and are caused by Satan and demonic forces (Job 1:9-12; 2:6; Luke 9:38-42; 13:16; Acts 10:38; 2 Cor. 12:7-9; Eph. 6:10-13). Though suffering intrudes into God's good creation, twisting good into evil, nothing is ever beyond God's sovereign control (2 Sam. 14:14; Amos 3:6; 4:10-13; Isa. 45:7; Rom. 8:28-39).

A second reason is that God either sends or allows suffering to teach, discipline, and mature us. Suffering reminds us of our finitude and teaches us to trust patiently in God (Judg. 2:21-3:6; Job 1:9-12; Ps. 66:10; Mal. 3:3; Rom. 5:3-5; 8:28; 1 Pet. 5:10; 1 Cor. 9:24-27; 2 Cor. 12:7-10). God disciplines those He loves. His discipline is a sign of love rather than wrath (Ps. 94:12; Prov. 3:11-12; 1 Cor. 11:32; Heb.12:3-13). Suffering should not be received with sadness or defeat, but with rejoicing because it leads to maturity and godly character (James 1:2-12; 1 Pet. 1:6-9).

Suffering of Believers A goal of human existence is not to avoid suffering but become godly. Suffering can be redemptive or vicarious (Hos. 1:1-3:5; Isa. 53:1-12; 2 Cor. 1:3-12; 1 Pet. 3:18). Joseph realized his suffering led to blessing his people, so although suffering is not good in and of itself, it may lead to greater good (Gen. 50:15-21; Rom. 8:28). Christ exemplified vicarious suffering in the crucifixion (Matt. 16:21; Luke 24:44-48; 1 Cor. 15:1-4; Heb. 2:9-10; 9:24-28). Believers may participate in His suffering (Matt. 5:11-12; Mark 13:7-9; Luke 9:22-26; Acts 5:38-41; Rom. 8:17-18; 2 Cor. 1:5-11; 4:7-18; Phil. 1:19-29; 3:8-11; 1 Thess. 1:4-8; 1 Pet. 4:12-14).

Another question is, "Why does God allow the righteous to suffer?" The unrighteous do sometimes prosper, and the righteous sometimes suffer (Ps. 73:2-12; Jer. 12:1-4; Mal. 3:13-15). Job was a righteous man, but he suffered great disaster. Yet through all his suffering, Job continued to serve God (Job 1:21). At a national level Habakkuk asks why God allows an unrighteous nation to defeat a more righteous nation (Hab. 1:12-13). When David realized the eternal consequences of unrighteousness, he reaffirmed the goodness and justice of God (Ps. 73:1-28).

Believers should not suffer with resignation but with hope (Pss. 39:7-13; 73:15-28; 1 Cor. 15:57-58; 2 Cor. 4:16-18; 1 Thess. 4:16-18; 1 Pet. 5:8-11). Through hope in the resurrection, Christians can endure victoriously, not in defeat or despair (John 16:33; Rom. 5:1-6; 8:17-39). The promises and presence of God turn the sufferer toward the future with confidence God will redeem even the worst suffering. The ultimate solution to suffering comes in heaven (Rev. 21:4-5). Even amid suffering, Christians

S

experience God's care. He hears and answers prayers for strength in suffering (Pss. 23:1-6; 66:13-20; 102:1-17; Mark 11:22-24; Heb. 4:14-16). However painful suffering is, it is a shadow compared to the glory yet to come (Rom. 8:17-18).   *Steve W. Lemke*

SUICIDE The Bible records several instances of suicide (Abimelech—Judg. 9:54; Samson—Judg. 16:29-30; Saul—1 Sam. 31:4; Saul's armor-bearer—1 Sam. 31:5; Ahithophel—2 Sam. 17:23; Zimri—1 Kings 16:18; and Judas—Matt. 27:5; cp. Acts 16:27). Of these, the deaths of Abimelech and Saul could be called "assisted" suicide. With the possible exception of Samson (whose death may be better termed "martyrdom"), the Bible presents each person who committed suicide as an individual whose behavior is clearly not to be emulated.

While the Bible nowhere specifically prohibits suicide, it does proclaim the sanctity of life (Gen. 1:26-27; 2:7; Ps. 8:5) and assuredly declares that God's people should choose life over death (Deut. 30:15,19). The right to give life and take it away is reserved by God for Himself (Job 1:21; cp. Exod. 20:13). Christians are called to steadfastness in the midst of trial (2 Cor. 12:7-10; Phil. 4:11-13; James 1:2-4), but John saw that in the latter days men facing difficulties would instead seek death (Rev. 9:6).

Moses (Num. 11:14-15), Elijah (1 Kings 19:4), Job (Job 6:8-11), and Jonah (Jon. 4:3) each asked God to take their lives, but in every case God refused. Simeon (Luke 2:29) and Paul (2 Cor. 5:2,8; Phil. 1:20-23) longed to be in heaven yet were content to remain alive, all the while waiting for God to act in His own time. Such instances provide ample biblical evidence that suicide is never the proper choice.

SUKKIIMS (Sŭk´ ĭ ĭms) Mentioned only in 2 Chron. 12:3, these people were part of Shishak's (king of Egypt) army when he fought against Rehoboam of Judah. They may have been desert-dwelling mercenaries out of Libya, known in Egyptian sources as Tjukten from 1300 to 1100 B.C.

SULFUR HCSB, NRSV, NIV, REB translate Rev. 9:17-18 "sulfur" rather than the usual "brimstone." The Near East has large deposits of this mineral. See *Brimstone; Minerals and Metals.*

SUMER (Sū´ mēr) One of the two political divisions originally comprising what came to be Babylonia. Its principal cities were Nippur, Adab, Lagash, Umma, Larsa, Erech, Ur, and Eridu, most of which were on or near the Euphrates. The area consists primarily of the fertile plain between the Tigris and Euphrates Rivers and is now the southern part of modern Iraq.

In the OT Sumer is the territory referred to as Shinar (Gen. 10:10) or Chaldea (Jer. 50:10). See *Shinar.*

Archaeologists believe the inhabitants of ancient Sumer developed humanity's first high civilization about 3000 B.C. Perhaps the most important Sumerian contribution to civilization was the invention of cuneiform writing, a wedge-shaped script formed by pressing a reed stylus into wet clay tablets, which were later dried, baked, and stored in libraries. The Babylonians and other surrounding peoples adapted the cuneiform script to their own languages, so that for centuries cuneiform was the dominant mode of writing in ancient Mesopotamia. Most Sumerian tablets contain economic and administrative records, but others include mythology, history, hymns, wisdom texts, law, and much more. Of special interest to biblical scholars are: the law code of Ur-nammu, the Sumerian king list, the flood story of Zuisudra, the paradise myth of Enki and Ninhursag, early forms of the Gilgamesh epic, and the descent of Inanna to the underworld.

Originally Sumer consisted of a number of city-states, each with its own protective god. Political power was held by the free citizens of the city and a governor called *ensi.* As the city-states vied with one another for power and as pressures from outside invaders increased, the institution of kingship emerged, whereby the ruler of one city-state dominated others.

About 2100 B.C. Sumer was conquered by invading tribesmen from the west and north. A mighty warrior named Sargon (later known as Sargon I, Sargon the Great, and Sargon of Akkad) conquered this area and extended his empire from the Persian Gulf to the Mediterranean Sea. He founded a new capital city, Agade, which was, for more than half a century, the richest and most powerful capital in the world.

Sumer enjoyed a brief revival at Ur (about 2050 B.C.) only to decline before the rise of the Elamites, a people to their east. Finally, in about

1720 B.C., Hammurabi of Babylon united Sumer (the southern division of ancient Babylon) into one empire. This conquest by Hammurabi marked the end of ancient Sumer, but the cultural and intellectual impact of the Sumerians continued until after the Persians became the dominant force in this part of the ancient world.

Rich Murrell

SUN Source of light for earth. Ancient people considered the sun as a necessary part of the cycle of the seasons. Thus, it was often viewed as a god. Ancient Egyptians worshiped the sun as the god Re, and the Greeks as Helios. The Canaanite city of Beth-shemesh, "House of the Sun," probably referred to a temple in the city. The Bible simply views the sun as the "greater light" God created to rule the day (Gen. 1:16). In Israel the new day began with sunset. The Psalms compared the sun's brightness to God's glory by which it will one day be replaced (Ps. 84:11). Zacharias described Christ's coming as a new sunrise ("Dawn," HCSB) for mankind (Luke 1:78). The darkening or eclipse of the sun was often interpreted as a sign of God's displeasure with humans. See *Gods, Pagan.*

David Maltsberger

SUNDAY See *Lord's Day.*

SUNDIAL Device, generally a flat disk with numbers around its edge, used to measure time by the position of a shadow cast by the sun. The root of the Hebrew word translated "dial" (2 Kings 20:11; Isa. 38:8) means "to go up" and usually refers to stairs. Most interpreters thus understand Ahab's dial to be a staircase on which a shadow went up as the day progressed. The sign involved the shadow's moving back down 10 steps.

SUPERSCRIPTION Usually the Romans identified a person's crime by writing it on a wooden sign, carrying it before the condemned person, and finally nailing it to the person's cross. All four Gospels mention such a superscription (Matt. 27:37; Mark 15:26; Luke 23:38; John 19:19) being nailed over Jesus' head. However, they do not speak of the sign being carried before Jesus as He walked to the place of crucifixion. Superscription is also used for the titles of some psalms giving information concerning the

writer and the context of the psalm. See *Cross, Crucifixion; Psalms, Book of; Trial of Jesus.*

SUPERSTITIOUS KJV translation of Greek word *deisidaimon* signifies a reverence or fear for a "deity," "demon," or other "pagan" gods. NASB and NIV translate the same word as "religious in all respects" and "religious," respectively; HCSB has "extremely religious." The word has both positive and negative connotations. In Acts 17:22 Paul uses this word to describe the religious affections of the philosophers at Athens. The term is also used in Acts 25:19 by Festus in his conversation with King Agrippa to describe religious accusations against Paul by the Jewish authorities.

William Chandler

SUPERVISION See *Schoolmaster.*

SUPH (Sūph) Place-name meaning "reed." **1.** Hebrew name for Red Sea. See *Red Sea.* **2.** A place named in order to help locate where Moses was when he delivered the speech found in the book of Deuteronomy (Deut. 1:1). It may be Khirbet Safe just southeast of Medeba in the mountains of Moab, but this is uncertain.

SUPHAH (Sūph´ ah) Apparently a place-name, perhaps meaning "toward the reeds." The Hebrew text of Num. 21:14 has no verb and has been translated and emended in many ways to achieve one (cp. translations). KJV created "Yam-Suph," or "Red Sea." Others find a compound place-name, "Waheb in Suphah," indicating two locations in Moab.

SUR, GATE OF Gate in Jerusalem. Some feel that it may be the gate leading from the king's palace to the temple spoken of in the account of the murder of Queen Athaliah (2 Kings 11). In the parallel account (2 Chron. 23) the gate is called "the gate of the foundation" (v. 5).

SURETY Person who is legally responsible for the debt of another or the money or thing of value put down to guarantee the debt. Should there be a default, the surety would have to pay the debt or even be enslaved until the debt was paid. Judah became surety for Benjamin to Joseph (Gen. 43:9; 44:32). God was asked by a faithful psalmist to be his surety (119:121-122). Proverbs warns against being surety for someone

S

you do not know well (11:15). In a positive sense Jesus is said to be surety for the faithful under the new covenant (Heb. 7:22). See *Loan; Pledge; Slave, Servant.*

SUSA (Sū´ sà) Winter capital of the ancient Persian Empire. The territory is now in modern Iran. Cyrus made Susa a capital city along with Ecbatana and Babylon. When Alexander the Great captured Susa, he found a large treasure that he confiscated. Archaeologists have excavated Susa largely around four areas: the royal palace, the acropolis, the royal city, and an artisan tell. Some believe Susa to be the place where Queen Esther and King Ahasuerus ruled. See *Esther, Book of; Nehemiah, Book of; Persia.*

SUSANCHITES (Sū´ săn kīts) Citizens of the city of Susa. See *Susa.*

SUSANNA (Sū zăn´ nà) Personal name meaning "lily." One of several women who followed Jesus and supported Him financially (Luke 8:2-3).

SUSI (Sū´ sī) Personal name meaning "my horse." The father of Gaddi, one of the spies Moses sent from the wilderness of Paran to spy out the land of Canaan (Num. 13:11).

SWADDLING CLOTHES A long piece of linen used in ancient times to wrap babies and broken limbs. The cloth or band of cloth was wrapped tightly around the body to prohibit movement. Mary wrapped Jesus in swaddling clothes just after His birth (Luke 2:7,12).

SWALLOW Bird that migrates to Palestine from March until winter. It made nests in the temple (Ps. 84:3) and was often seen with the common sparrow. It was sometimes confused with the swift. See *Birds.*

SWAN KJV rendering of the Hebrew *tinshemet* (Lev. 11:18; Deut. 14:16). Other versions translate "the desert owl" or "pelican" (NRSV) or "the white owl" (HCSB, NIV, NASB). See *Owl.*

SWEAR See *Oaths.*

SWEET CANE See *Calamus.*

SWIFT Bird similar to a swallow but unrelated to swallows. Jeremiah mentions the swift (8:7

NASB, NIV). Other versions translate "swallow" (KJV, NRSV). Some commentators think a bulbul or wryneck is meant. Perhaps "bulbul" (*Pycnonotus reichenovi*) is the best linguistic guess.

SWINE Stout-bodied animals that have a large snout and thick skin. The swine of the Bible, in most instances, probably were the wild pig, still common in Palestine. While Canaanite pagans kept herds of swine, the Mosaic law classified this animal as "unclean" and thus forbade the eating of its flesh (Lev. 11:7; Deut. 14:8). Isaiah condemned the eating of swine, dogs, and mice (65:4; 66:3,17). One who tended swine was barred from the temple. A scavenger in ancient times, this animal became a symbol for baseness and paganism. They were used as metaphors for uncleanness (Prov. 11:22; Matt. 7:6; 2 Pet. 2:22). Interestingly, Hezir, a proper Jewish name, is the same word as that translated "swine" (1 Chron. 24:15; Neh. 10:20).

The fact that the prodigal son resorted to tending swine points to the extreme humiliation he experienced. Mark 5:11-17 speaks of a large herd of swine in the Decapolis area where Jesus saw them as fit bearers of demons. Many ancient people ate swine and used swine for sacrifice to idols.

SWORD Close-range weapon. The Hebrew word *cherev* and the Greek word *machaira* designate either a dagger or a sword. The Hebrew word also designates an iron tool ("axes," Ezek. 26:9) or a chisel ("tool," Exod. 20:25). In Josh. 5:2 the word designates stone knives used in the circumcision of the people of Israel.

Archaeology has shown that different kinds of swords were used in the ancient Near East. The sickle or curved sword was used throughout

An Arab mother watches her baby who is wrapped in swaddling clothes.

Mesopotamia, Egypt, and in Palestine. The earlier swords were straight, relatively short, and made of bronze. Ehud's sword was the two-edged short dagger; it measured about 18 inches (Judg. 3:16). The sword used by the Israelites in the conquest of Canaan probably was the long-bladed, curved sword (Josh. 6:21).

The Sea Peoples introduced to Canaan the two-edged long sword made of iron. This type of iron sword was kept out of the hands of the Israelites by the Philistines for military and economic reasons until the times of David (1 Sam. 13:19). The OT gives witness that in the wars between the Israelites and the Philistines, the Israelites did not possess this new weapon (1 Sam. 13:22). The sword was kept in a sheath (1 Sam. 17:51; Matt. 26:52). It hung from a belt (1 Sam 25:13) and was generally put on the left hip (2 Sam. 20:8).

There are many symbolic uses for the word "sword" in the Bible. The word was used as a metaphor for war (Jer. 14:15; Matt. 10:34); the sword was an instrument of divine justice (Ezek. 21:3; Rev. 1:16). Rash words are compared to a sword that pierces (Prov. 12:18); the tongue is like a sharp sword (Ps. 57:4); malicious words are "drawn swords" (Ps. 55:21). The word of God is sharper than a "two-edged sword" (Heb. 4:12); the sword of the Spirit, which is the word of God, is part of the Christian's armament in the fight against evil (Eph. 6:17). See *Arms and Armor.*　　　　　*Claude F. Mariottini*

SYCAMORE Combination "fig" and "mulberry" tree (*Ficus sycomorus*) indicating the fig tree in the Jordan Valley that had leaves like our mulberry tree. Its fruit was inferior to the fig tree and had to be punctured to make the fruit edible. Amos was employed as "one who took care of sycamore-fig trees" (7:14 NIV; cp. Ps. 78:47). This tree has no relation to the American sycamore tree. It was used as food for the poor and bore fruit several times a year (1 Kings 10:27; 2 Chron. 1:15; 9:27). It was often planted along roadways for its shade (Luke 19:4). Poor people used its wood rather than expensive cedar (Isa. 9:10).

SYCHAR (Sī´ kär) Place-name intended to note "falsehood," though perhaps originally derived from "Shechem." A village in Samaria where Jacob's well is located (John 4:5-6). Jesus rested by the well and there ministered to a Samaritan woman. Jacob bought the parcel of land from "the children of Hamor, Shechem's father" (Gen. 33:19). The site has been identified variously with Shechem and a village just north of there called Askar. Archaeological excavations have revealed that Sychar and Shechem are part of the same ancient settlement.

SYENE (Sī ē´ nǐ) Egyptian sister settlement of Elephantine, island in the Nile. It bears some commercial and military significance. Syenite, a rose granite stone, was quarried there. Syene (Assuan) is the location of the dam completed in 1902 to control the irrigation of the Nile. Isaiah 49:12 in the NRSV uses "Syene," although it is usually read as "Sinim."

SYMBOL Token or sign. While the word "symbol" does not appear in the Bible, both the OT

Sword dating from the Middle Kingdom of Egypt.

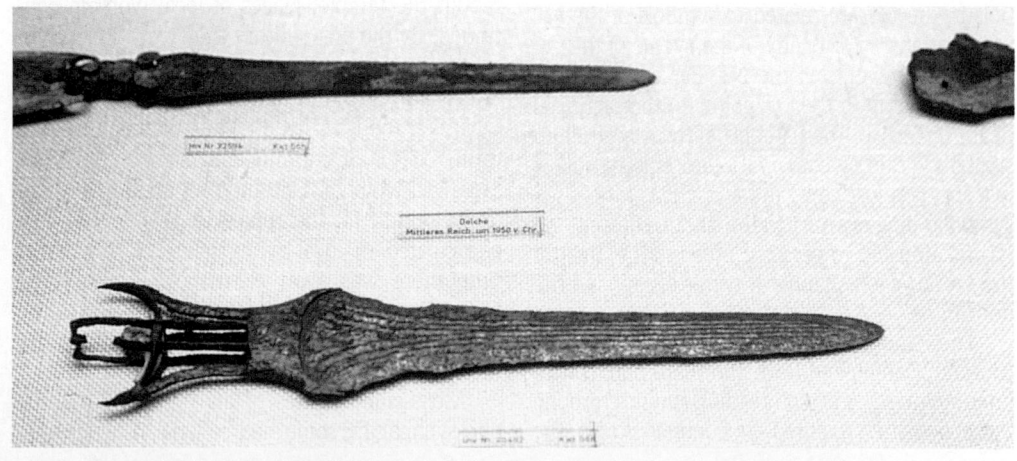

and NT are rich in symbolism and symbolic language.

Symbols, whether objects, gestures, or rituals, convey meaning to the rational, emotional, and intuitive dimensions of human beings. The universal and supreme symbol of Christian faith is the cross, an instrument of execution. For Christians this hideous object comes to be a sign of God's love for human beings.

The meaning of symbols grows and even changes over time. For the Apostle Paul the meaning conveyed by the cross changed radically as did his view of Jesus of Nazareth. As a rabbi, zealous to keep the Mosaic law and to bring others to do so, Paul believed that anyone hung on a tree was cursed by God (Deut. 21:23). For this reason and others he strongly resisted the claims that Jesus was Messiah. Only when the risen Lord appeared to Saul did he realize that what appeared to be a curse had been transformed into a source of the greatest blessing. Christ's death seen through the resurrection is at the center of the two major symbolic rituals of Christian faith—baptism and the Lord's Supper or the Eucharist. See *Ordinances; Sacrament.*

Baptism is a picture of the death, burial, and resurrection of Christ. In being baptized, a person says to the world that the baptismal candidate is identifying with the saving act being pictured. That means the new believer is dying to sin and is rising to walk in new life, living now for God and with God as the center of life.

The Lord's Supper employs the ordinary elements of bread and wine to picture Christ's broken body and His blood shed for humanity's sin.

While the cross, the water, the bread, and wine are symbols at the center of Christian faith and practice, they are not the only symbols. Symbols in the OT are related to symbols of the NT in important ways. Many of the events of the OT foreshadow events of the NT. For example, the sacrificial lamb in the OT points to the sacrificial death of Christ. The parables of Jesus are rich in symbols: grain, weeds, various kinds of soil, a lost sheep, a lost coin, and a lost son. Jesus used symbolic language in talking about Himself and His relationship to persons: bread of life, light of the world, good shepherd, water of life, and the door.

The apocalyptic writings of the Bible (Ezekiel, Daniel, and Revelation) are rich in symbolic language. A person reading and interpreting these books is required to come to know the

The excavated remains of a third-century synagogue at the site of ancient Chorazin (Korazin), Israel.

symbolic meaning of the terms being used in almost the same way as a person trying to break a code. See *Apocalyptic.* Steve Bond

SYNAGOGUE (Sĭn´ ȧ gŏg) Local meeting place and assembly of the Jewish people during late intertestamental and NT times.

Origin Jewish tradition claimed that the synagogue was begun by Moses, but the OT does not support this claim. Local worship was discouraged during most of the OT because it often was associated with pagan practices. Worship centered on the temple in Jerusalem. Psalm 74:8, written late in OT times, may refer to local places of worship destroyed when the temple was destroyed. Some translations use the word "synagogue" of these places, but we have no other certain knowledge about them.

The synagogue of the NT era had its roots in the time after Solomon's temple was destroyed and the people of Judah went into Babylonian exile. Local worship and instruction became necessary. Even after Jews returned to Jerusalem and rebuilt the temple, places of local worship continued. By the first century they were called synagogues.

Facts about Synagogues Synagogues existed wherever the Jews lived. While the temple stood until A.D. 70, it continued to be the center for sacrificial worship. Faithful Jews continued to go to the temple for the appointed feasts. They also participated in local synagogues. During Jesus' time there was even a synagogue within the temple itself. This was probably the place in the temple where the 12-year-old Jesus talked with the teachers (Luke 2:46).

Most communities of any size had at least one synagogue; some had several. A synagogue was to be established wherever there were as many as 10 Jewish men. A synagogue had to be located close enough for faithful Jews to attend without breaking the Sabbath by exceeding the distance the rabbis allowed one to walk on the Sabbath day. A typical service consisted of recitation of the Shema ("Listen, Israel: The LORD our God, the LORD is One."), prayers, Scripture readings from the Law and the Prophets, a sermon, and a benediction. Luke 4:16-21 is a good example of a first-century synagogue service. See *Shema.*

Local elders had oversight of the synagogue. They appointed a ruler of the synagogue, a layman who cared for the building and selected participants in Sabbath services. The ruler had an attendant, one of whose duties was to deliver the sacred scrolls to those reading the Scriptures and return them to their special keeping place (Luke 4:17,20).

Jesus and Synagogues Jesus customarily went to the synagogue in His hometown of Nazareth on the Sabbath (Luke 4:16). After beginning His public ministry, Jesus frequently taught and preached in synagogues (Matt. 4:23; 9:35; Mark 1:39; Luke 4:44). Early in His ministry, Jesus healed a man in the synagogue in Capernaum (Mark 1:21-28; Luke 4:31-37).

Jesus often encountered opposition in synagogues. Luke 4:16-30 tells what happened in the synagogue of Nazareth (cp. Matt. 13:54-58; Mark 6:1-6). Jesus' preaching and teaching aroused strong negative reactions. Luke 13:10-16 tells of Jesus healing a woman in a synagogue on the Sabbath, bringing an angry reaction from the ruler of the synagogue. Jesus, in turn, rebuked the man for his hypocrisy.

Jesus warned against the hypocrisy of those who paraded their righteousness in the synagogue. He warned against giving and praying in order to be seen and praised (Matt. 6:2,5). He also rebuked those who sought the chief seats (Matt. 23:6; Mark 12:39; Luke 11:43; 20:46).

As opposition to Jesus increased, He warned His disciples of a future time when they would be persecuted in their own synagogues (Matt. 10:17; 23:34; Mark 13:9; Luke 12:11; 21:12).

Reconstruction of a typical synagogue of the first century A.D. showing the large inner room where the men gathered and its loft above where the women gathered. This particular drawing is patterned after the synagogue at Capernaum.

S

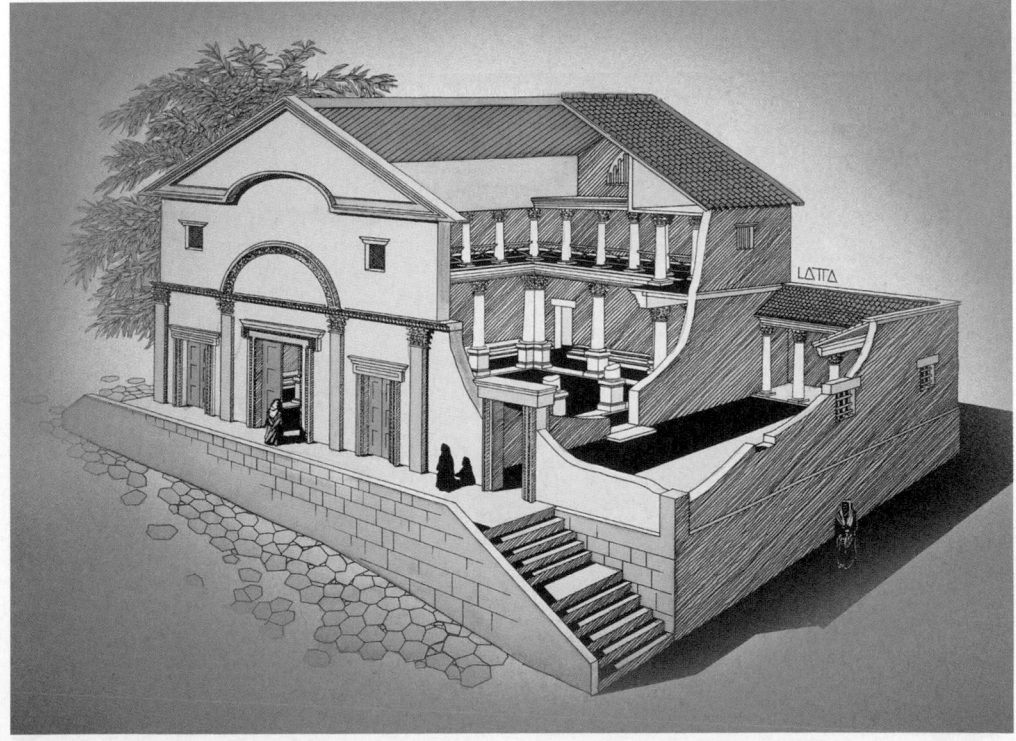

Synagogues in Acts The early part of Acts shows that Palestinian Jewish believers continued to worship in the synagogues. Saul went into synagogues to find and persecute believers (Acts 9:2; 22:19; 26:11). As persecution developed, believers were forced out of some synagogues. See *Freedmen, Synagogue of the.*

After Saul's conversion, he immediately preached Christ in synagogues in Damascus (Acts 9:20). Believing Jews were still in synagogues outside Palestine, as the ministry of Paul demonstrates. During Paul's missionary journeys, he began his work in a new city by going to the synagogue (Acts 13:5,14; 14:1; 17:1,10,17; 18:4; 19:8). The exception in Philippi was probably because there were not enough Jews there to have a synagogue, so Paul went to a place where faithful Jews met to pray on the Sabbath (Acts 16:13).

Generally, Paul, as a good Pharisaic rabbi, was welcomed and given opportunity to present his views. He found receptivity especially among Gentiles who attended synagogues, but some Jews also believed (Acts 13:42-43). Others strongly opposed Paul. Often he was forced to leave the synagogue and worship elsewhere with believers (Acts 18:6-8; 19:8-10). The church and

synagogue finally separated permanently in the first third of the second century.

Synagogues in the General Epistles The letter from James is one of the earliest books in the NT, written possibly around A.D. 50 to believers in Palestine. In James 2:2 the writer cautions the believers not to show favoritism to a wealthy person who comes to worship. The Greek word used is *sunagoge* (synagogue). Obviously, 20 years after the crucifixion, believers in Palestine were still worshiping in synagogues that accepted Jesus as Messiah.

The letter to the Hebrews probably was written to Jewish believers in Rome in the mid-60s. The situation seems to be that under persecution some believers were leaving their messianic synagogues and going back to synagogues where Jesus was not accepted as Messiah, because those synagogues were not being persecuted.

Influence of the Synagogue The synagogue was the means of preserving Jewish faith and worship. Jews all over the ancient world maintained their distinctive faith. Synagogues were a seedbed for Christian faith as missionaries spread the message of the gospel. Synagogue worshipers believed in the one true God, studied the Scriptures, and looked for the coming Messiah. Syna-

The synagogue at the site of ancient Capernaum.

gogues were the obvious starting place for the evangelistic thrust of the earliest church.

Robert J. Dean and Charles W. Draper

SYNOPTIC GOSPELS See *Gospel; Harmony of the Gospels.*

SYNTYCHE (Sĭn´ tĭ kē) Personal name meaning "pleasant acquaintance" or "good luck." Woman in the church at Philippi addressed by Paul concerning an argument with Euodia (Phil. 4:2).

SYRACUSE (Sĭr´ à cūz) Major city on the island of Sicily. Paul stayed in the Syracuse harbor three days on his way to Rome (Acts 28:12). The city was strong enough to defeat an attack from Athens in 413 B.C. but was defeated by Rome in 212 B.C. It became the residence of the governor of Sicily under Roman government and enjoyed great prosperity during the Roman years.

SYRIA (Sĭr´ ĭ à) Region or nation directly north of Palestine in the northeast corner of the Mediterranean Sea.

Name and Geography Syria is most properly a geographical term for the northeastern Mediterranean region situated between Palestine and Mesopotamia, roughly equal to the modern states of Syria and Lebanon with small portions of Turkey and Iraq. The name may come from a Greek shortening of Assyria and was only accidentally applied to the area. There is no geographical connection between Assyria and Syria.

Syria, like Palestine, has four basic geographical features as one moves from the Mediterranean eastward: (1) a narrow coastal plain; (2) a line of mountains; (3) the rift valley; and (4) the fertile steppe fading into desert. The two main rivers rise near one another in the rift valley. The Orontes flows north before abruptly turning west to the sea in the plain of Antioch, while the Leontes flows south then turns west through a narrow gorge and empties into the sea. See *Palestine; Rivers and Waterways.*

Old Testament *Early History* During the early Bronze Age (about 3200–2200 B.C.), Syria was home to large city-states similar to those found in Mesopotamia. The latter part of this period has been illuminated by the recent discovery of cuneiform tablets in the state archive at Ebla, the capital of a small empire in northern Syria. Many of these tablets are in Eblaite, an ancient language similar to Hebrew, and promise to aid in biblical study. See *Ebla.*

In the middle Bronze Age (2200–1550 B.C.), the time of the Hebrew patriarchs, north Syria was home to the kingdoms of Yamhad, with its capital at Aleppo, and Qatna. The area south of Qatna was known as Amurru (the Akkadian word for Amorite). Further south, Damascus was probably in existence (Gen. 15:2), though it is unknown from contemporary records. In the late Bronze Age (about 1550–1200 B.C.), Syria became the frontier and sometimes battlefield between the empires of the new kingdom Egypt in the south and initially Mitanni, then the Hittites to the north. Important cities in this period included Qadesh and Ugarit. The former led a number of rebellions against Egyptian authority. Excavations at the latter yielded alphabetic cuneiform tablets in Ugaritic (a language similar to Hebrew), which have shed much light on the nature of Canaanite religion. See *Archaeology; Canaan; Ugarit.*

Aramean Kingdoms Some English versions of the OT (KJV, NKJV) use the modern designation Syria. Most versions (HCSB, NIV, NRSV, NASB) refer to the country as Aram and the people as Arameans, based on the Hebrew word *Aram* (Deut. 26:5). The Arameans began to settle in Syria and northern Mesopotamia around the beginning of the Iron Age (about 1200 B.C.), establishing a number of independent states. The OT mentions the Aramean kingdoms of Beth-eden in north Syria, Zobah in south central Syria, and Damascus in the south.

By the beginning of Israel's monarchy, the kingdom of Zobah held sway in Syria and was encountered by Saul (1 Sam. 14:47). David decisively defeated Aram-Zobah (2 Sam. 10:6-19) whose king, Hadadezer, had enlisted help from his Aramean subject states (10:16,19). As a result Zobah and its vassals, apparently including Damascus, became subject to David (2 Sam. 8:3-8; 10:19). Hamath, a neo-Hittite state in north Syria that had been at war with Zobah, also established friendly relations with David (2 Sam. 8:9-10). Meanwhile, a certain Rezon broke from Hadadezer of Zobah following David's victory and became the leader of a marauding band. Late in Solomon's reign, he established himself as king in Damascus (1 Kings 11:23-25), taking southern Syria out of Israelite control. Subsequent occurrences of "Aram" or "Arameans"

("Syria" or "Syrians") in the OT refer to this Aramean kingdom of Damascus.

The rise of Aram-Damascus' power was facilitated by the division of Israel following the death of Solomon. When Baasha of Israel built a fort at Ramah threatening Jerusalem, Asa of Judah enticed the king of Damascus, "Ben-hadad son of Tabrimmon son of Hezion" (NRSV), to break his league with Israel and come to Judah's aid (1 Kings 15:18-19). Ben-hadad responded by conquering a number of cities and territory in the north of Israel (v. 20). The genealogy given in this passage has been confirmed by a stele, found near Aleppo, dedicated to the god Melqart by Ben-hadad. Rezon is not mentioned, however, and it has been suggested that he is identical to Hezion. See *Damascus.*

Syrian Culture Aramean culture was essentially borrowed from their neighbors. Typical Semitic gods were worshiped, the most important of which was the storm god, Hadad, often called by the epithet Rimmon (2 Kings 5:18; Zech. 12:11), meaning "thunder." The most enduring contribution of the Arameans was their language that became the language of commerce and diplomacy by the Persian period. Portions of Daniel and Ezra are written in Aramaic, which is similar to Hebrew. By NT times Aramaic was the language commonly spoken in Palestine and probably used by Jesus. The Aramaic script was adopted and slightly modified for writing Hebrew. See *Aramaic; Canaan; Gods, Pagan.*

The Intertestamental Period In 331 B.C. Syria, with the rest of the Persian Empire, fell to the advances of Alexander the Great. At his death the area formed the nucleus of the Hellenistic Seleucid kingdom with its capital at Antioch. It is in this period that the term "Syria" became widespread. The Seleucid kingdom oppressed Judaism, causing the Maccabean Revolt in 167 B.C. that resulted in Jewish independence. Syria continued to decline until the arrival of the Romans who made it a province in 64 B.C. See *Intertestamental History and Literature; Seleucids.*

New Testament In NT times Judea was made part of a procuratorship within the larger Roman province of Syria (Matt. 4:24), the latter being ruled by a governor (Luke 2:2). Syria played an important role in the early spread of Christianity. Paul was converted on the road to Damascus (Acts 9:1-9) and subsequently evangelized in the province (Acts 15:41; Gal. 1:21). Antioch, where believers were first called "Christians" (Acts 11:26), became the base for his missionary journeys (Acts 13:1-3). *Daniel C. Browning, Jr.*

SYROPHENICIAN (KJV) or **SYROPHOENI-CIAN** (Sī rō phĭ nē´ shŭn) Combination of Syria and Phoenicia. The word reflects the joining of the two areas into one district under Roman rule. Prior to this era, Phoenicia was the coastal area of northern Palestine, and Syria was a separate country located farther inland. Jesus encountered in the Syrophoenician district a woman whose daughter was possessed by a devil (Mark 7:26). The parallel account calls her "a Canaanite woman" (Matt. 15:22), the ancient name for these people. After she repeatedly asked for her daughter's healing, the Lord granted her request.

SYRTIS (Sĭr´ tĭs) Translated "quicksands" in Acts 27:17 (KJV). Probably what is now known as the Gulf of Sidra, a place of shallow water with hidden rocks, sandbanks, and quicksands off the African coast west of Cyrene. See *Quicksands.*

T

The Mount of Temptation as seen from the top of Old Testament Jericho.

TAANACH (Tā´ à năk) Place-name of uncertain meaning. One of the sites along the northern slope of the Mount Carmel range protecting the accesses from the Plain of Esdraelon to the region of Samaria. Irbid, Megiddo, and Taanach each protect strategic passes through the Carmel range. Taanach thus sat along one fork of the major north-south road of antiquity that went through Palestine, usually called the Via Maris. It also sat on an east-west road that led from the Jordan Valley to the Mediterranean Sea near modern Haifa.

In the Bible Taanach is only mentioned seven times, usually in lists such as tribal allotments (Josh. 17:11; 1 Chron. 7:29), administrative districts (1 Kings 4:12), Levitical towns (Josh. 21:25), or conquered cities (Josh. 12:21; Judg. 1:27). The most famous biblical reference to Taanach is that of the battle fought at "Taanach near the waters of Megiddo" (NASB) where the Hebrew forces under Deborah and Barak defeated the Canaanites under Sisera (Judg. 5:19).

Taanach was a town of about 13 acres, about the same size as the better known Megiddo. Its history runs through the Bronze Ages and into the Iron Age, from about 2700 B.C. to about 918 B.C. when the Egyptian Pharaoh Shishak destroyed it. A large fortress was built on the site during the early Islamic period, and that fortress may well have continued in use during the Crusades.

While Megiddo was apparently a major Canaanite administrative center, Taanach seems to have been less heavily populated and perhaps the home for the farmers of the surrounding area and their tenants. Excavations have shown a number of cultic objects and installations at Taanach, suggesting that it was a religious center as well. *Joel F. Drinkard, Jr.*

TAANATH-SHILOH (Tā à năth-Shī´ lōh) Place-name likely meaning "approach to Shiloh." Village located about seven miles southeast of Shechem between Michmethath and Janoah (Josh. 16:6), identified with the modern Khirbet Ta'nah el Foqa.

TABBAOTH (Tăb´ bā ŏth) Personal name meaning "signet ring." Head of a family of temple servants (Nethinim) returning from exile (Ezra 2:43; Neh. 7:46).

TABBATH (Tăb´ bàth) Place-name, perhaps meaning "sunken." Site in the mountains of Gilead east of the Jordan where Gideon ended his pursuit of the Midianites (Judg. 7:22), identified with modern Ras Abu Tabat northwest of Pakoris.

TABEEL (Tăb´ ə ĕl) Aramaic personal name meaning "God is good." **1.** Father of a man whom King Rezin of Damascus and King Pekah of Israel hoped to install as puppet king of Judah rather than Ahaz (Isa. 7:6). Alternately, Tabeel designates a region in northern Transjordan and home of the potential puppet. Spelling has been slightly changed in Hebrew to mean "good for nothing." **2.** Persian official in Samaria who joined in a letter protesting the reconstruction of the Jerusalem temple (Ezra 4:7).

TABERAH (Tăb´ ə rà) Place-name meaning "burning." Unidentified site in the wilderness wandering. The name commemorates God's "burning anger," which broke out in fire against the ever-complaining Israelites (Num. 11:3; Deut. 9:22). The name does not appear in the itinerary of Num. 33.

TABERING KJV term meaning "beating" (Nah. 2:7). See *Grief and Mourning.*

TABERNACLE (Tăb´ ẽr năk əl), **TENT OF MEETING** Sacred tent, portable and provisional sanctuary, where God met His people (Exod. 33:7-10). A tent was the dwelling place of a nomadic person. When the sacred tent was meant, it was usually used with some distinguishing epithet. Two compound phrases (*ohel mo'ed* and *ohel ha'eduth*) are used to designate this tent: "the tabernacle of the congregation" (Exod. 29:42,44), literally the "tent of meeting" (NRSV, NIV, NASB, REB) and "the tabernacle of witness" (Num. 17:7) or "tent of witness." In both cases it was the place where the God of Israel revealed Himself to and dwelled among His people. The basic Hebrew term (*mishkan*) translated as "tabernacle" (Exod. 25:9) comes from a verb which means "to dwell." In this sense it is correctly translated in some instances as "dwelling," "dwelling place," "habitation," and "abode."

The OT mentions three tents or tabernacles. First, after the sin of the golden calf at Mount Sinai, the "provisional" tabernacle was established outside the camp and called the "tent of meeting" (Exod. 33:7). Second, the "Sinaitic" tabernacle was built in accordance with directions given to Moses by God (Exod. 25–40). Unlike the tent of meeting, it stood at the center of the camp (Num. 2). Third, the "Davidic" tabernacle was erected in Jerusalem for the reception of the ark (2 Sam. 6:17).

The original "tent of meeting" was a provisional edifice where God met with His people (Exod. 33:7-11; 34:34-35). Apparently, only Moses actually entered the tent to meet God. Joshua, Moses' "servant" (Exod. 33:11), protected and cared for the tent. After the golden calf was made, God refused any longer to acknowledge Israel as His people and to dwell in their midst. Estrangement brought distance between God and the people because of their sin. Because of this situation and to symbolize it, Moses pitched this "tent of meeting" outside the camp (Exod. 33:7). Ultimately, God promised again to go into the midst of Israel (Exod. 34:9).

The exact nature of this tent is uncertain. It apparently formed the headquarters of the camp until the building of the Sinaitic tabernacle. Joshua guarded the tent in Moses' absence (Exod. 33:11). Since the earliest Greek translation, some would equate Moses' tent in Exod. 18:7 with the tent of meeting, but Scripture does not explicitly make this connection. The people could all go to the tent of meeting to seek the Lord (Exod. 33:7) either in looking for God's answer to a judicial case, in petition, in worship, or for a prophetic word. Apparently, Moses acted as the prophet who took the people's questions to God and received an answer, since "to seek Yahweh" usually appears in prophetic contexts. Prophetic content appears with the tent also in Num. 11:16-29. Moses installed Joshua as his successor at the tent (Deut. 31:14-15).

Moses called it the tent of meeting because it was the place of revelation. There God met His people when the pillar of cloud descended to the door of the tent (Exod. 33:9). It may have borne

Reconstruction of the Israelite tabernacle and its court. The court was formed by curtains attached to erect poles. In front of the tent was placed the altar of burnt offerings and the laver. The tabernacle was always erected to face the east, so this view is from the northeast.

its appropriate name from the first, or perhaps Moses used the name from the instructions which he received regarding the permanent tabernacle (Exod. 27:21).

Apparently, the tent did not become a national sanctuary. It did not contain an ark or those items necessary for worship nor did it possess a priesthood. This tent was cared for by Joshua (Exod. 33:11), while Aaron was responsible for the tabernacle (Lev. 10:7). The cloud descended on this tent when Moses came to inquire of God, but the cloud stayed on the permanent tabernacle and the glory of the Lord filled it so Moses could not enter it (Exod. 40:34-35,38).

The center of attention in the wilderness narratives is the tabernacle with rich decorations, curtains, bread of the presence, ark, lights, and altar. This is the portable sanctuary Israel carefully delegates to the priests and Levites for transportation (Num. 3). The camp of Israel has this tabernacle as its center (Num. 2). This, too, is the tent of meeting (Exod. 27:21), where holy God comes to sinful people. Here the sacrifices and atonement procedures of the book of Leviticus were carried out. "I will also meet with the Israelites there, and that place will be consecrated by My glory. I will dwell among the Israelites and be their God" (Exod. 29:43,45 HCSB). *Jimmy Albright*

TABERNACLES, FEAST OF See *Festivals.*

TABITHA (Tăb´ ĭ thá) Aramaic personal name meaning "gazelle," which serves as the counterpart to the Greek name Dorcas (Acts 9:36). See *Dorcas.*

TABLE Flat surface supported by legs. **1.** Dinner tables. The earliest "tables" were simply skins spread on the ground (cp. the expressions "spread a table" and "a fine spread"). Representations of tables are rare in Egyptian art before the new kingdom (1300–1100 B.C.). The earliest scriptural mention (Judg. 1:7) falls within this same time frame. Most references concern a sovereign's table (Judg. 1:7; 2 Sam. 9:7; 1 Kings 2:7; 4:27; 10:5; 18:19; cp. 1 Kings 13:20). Tables generally sat on short legs, allowing one to eat sitting or reclined on a rug (Isa. 21:5). Judges 1:7, however, reflects a table high enough for kings to rummage underneath (cp. Mark 7:28). In NT times guests ate while reclining on couches, supporting their heads with their left hands and eating from a common bowl with their right. This practice explains a woman's standing at Jesus' feet (Luke 7:38) and the beloved disciple's position at Jesus' breast (John 13:23) during meals. See *Furniture.* **2.** Ritual tables. A table for the bread of the presence formed part of the furnishings for both the tabernacle (Exod. 25:23-30; 26:35; Lev. 24:5-7) and temple (1 Kings 7:48). Other tables were used in the sacrificial cult (1 Chron. 28:14-16; 2 Chron. 4:7-8; Ezek. 40:38-43). Malachi 1:7,12 describes the altar itself as a table. To share in a god's table was an act of worship. Isaiah 65:11 and 1 Cor. 10:21 refer to idolatrous worship. The "Lord's table" (1 Cor. 10:21) refers to the observance of the Lord's Supper. **3.** Money tables. The money changers' tables were likely small trays on stands (Matt. 21:12; Mark 11:15; John 2:15). **4.** Tables of law. Some translations use table in the sense of a tablet (Exod. 24:12; 31:18; Deut. 9:9). See *Tablet.* *Chris Church*

TABLE OF NATIONS Genesis 10 lists the descendants of Noah's sons to explain the origin of the nations and peoples of the known world. The account is unique for several reasons. First, a new chapter begins in biblical history at this point; humanity has a new beginning through Noah and his three sons. Second, the account highlights the ethnic makeup of the ancient world, listing some 70 different ethnic groups that formed the basis of the known world. Third, despite our lack of knowledge about many of the groups listed in the chapter, Gen. 10 underlines the fact that the Bible is based on historical events. Fourth, Gen. 10 provides the basis for understanding Abraham, introducing his world and his relationship to that world. The account of the Table of Nations, with a few variations, also appears in 1 Chron. 1:5-23.

The Table of Nations has three basic divisions. The people and lands of the known world fit into one of three families, the family of Shem, Ham, or Japheth. The names which appear in each of the families are names which come from several different categories: racial descent, geographical location, language differences, or political units.

Japheth's descendants (Gen. 10:2-5) inhabited the Aegean region and Anatolia or Asia Minor. The descendants of Ham (Gen. 10:6-20) were located especially in the regions of North

Africa and the coastal regions of Canaan and Syria. The descendants of Shem (Gen. 10:21-31) are especially important because Abraham comes from the line of Shem. Thus Abraham is a Shemite or Semite. Because he is also a descendant of Eber, he is called a Hebrew (Gen. 11:14-32). The descendants of Shem were located generally in north Syria, that is, the region of the upper part of the Euphrates River and Mesopotamia, especially the eastern part. See *Assyria; Babylon; Canaan; Habiru; Israel; Mesopotamia; Semites.*   *LaMoine DeVries*

TABLET Usually a flat surface used for writing. **1.** Law tablets. Scripture names the stone objects bearing the Ten Commandments the tablets (or tables) of the law (Exod. 24:12), testimony (Exod. 31:18), and covenant (Deut. 9:9). These tablets were perhaps small steles such as those other nations used to publicize their laws. **2.** Writing tablets. Writing was often done on clay tablets (Ezek. 4:1) or wood tablets covered with wax (Luke 1:63). The heart is often described as a tablet upon which God writes His law (Prov. 3:3; Jer. 17:1; 2 Cor. 3:3). **3.** KJV translation in Exod. 35:22 for part of the jewelry brought to the Lord for constructing the tent of meeting.

TABOR (Tā´ bôr) Place-name of uncertain meaning, perhaps "height." **1.** Mountain in the valley of Jezreel. About six miles east of Nazareth, it has played an important role in Israel's history since the period of the conquest. It served as a boundary point for the tribes of Naphtali, Issachar, and Zebulun (Josh. 19:12,22), where the tribes worshiped early (Deut. 33:18-19). Barak gathered an army at Tabor to defend against Sisera (Judg. 4:6). Apparently, it was the site of false worship (Hos. 5:1). Tradition holds that Tabor was the site of Jesus' transfiguration (Mark 9:2), although no evidence exists to validate the claim. **2.** Levitical city (1 Chron. 6:77), apparently replacing Nahalal in the earlier list (Josh. 21:35). It may be Khirbet Dabura. **3.** The "Plain of Tabor" (1 Sam. 10:3) was apparently near Gibea.

TABOR, OAK OF NASB, NRSV designation of a site between Rachel's tomb (near Bethlehem) and Gibeah of Saul (1 Sam. 10:3). Other translations read "plain" (KJV), "great tree" (NIV), or "terebinth" (REB) of Tabor.

TABRET KJV term for tambourine. Scripture associates the tambourine with occasions of strong emotion: farewells (Gen. 31:27);

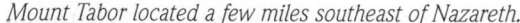

Mount Tabor located a few miles southeast of Nazareth.

T

prophetic ecstasy (1 Sam. 10:5); a victory procession (1 Sam. 18:6); the procession of the ark to Jerusalem (2 Sam. 6:5). Tambourine music often accompanied festive occasions of drinking and merrymaking (Isa. 5:12; 24:8; 30:32; Jer. 31:4). Often women were the musicians (1 Sam. 18:6; 2 Sam. 6:5; Ps. 68:25). See *Music, Instruments, Dancing.*

TABRIMMON (Tăb rĭm´ mŏn) Personal name meaning "Rimmon is good." Father of King Ben-hadad of Damascus (1 Kings 15:18). Rimmon was the Akkadian god of thunder. See *Hadad; Hadad-rimmon; Rimmon.*

TACHES KJV term meaning "hooks" or "clasps" (Exod. 26:6,11,33) used to connect the individual curtains of the tabernacle into one tent.

TACHMONITE (Tăk´ mŏ nīt) (KJV, TEV) See *Tahchemonite.*

TACKLING KJV form of tackle, that is, gear used to handle cargo and rigging to work a ship's sails (Isa. 33:23; Acts 27:19). See *Ships, Sailors, and Navigation.*

TADMOR (Tăd´ môr) Place-name of uncertain meaning. A city in northern Palestine built by Solomon (2 Chron. 8:4), probably to control a caravan route. Early Hebrew scribes read Tadmor as the city instead of Tamar of the written text in 1 Kings 9:18. The city enjoyed prosperity at various periods, especially during Solomon's reign and again in the third century A.D., shortly before it was destroyed. The site has been identified with Palmyra, a great Arabian city, located about 120 miles northeast of Damascus.

TAHAN (Tā´ hăn) Personal name meaning "graciousness." **1.** Third son of Ephraim (Num. 26:35). The parallel list gives Tahath as Ephraim's third son (1 Chron. 7:20). **2.** Ephraimite ancestor of Joshua (1 Chron. 7:25).

TAHANITES (Tā´ hăn īts) Member of the Ephraimite clan descended from Tahan (Num. 26:35).

TAHAPANES (Tā hă´ pả nēz) (KJV, Jer. 2:16) See *Tahpanhes.*

TAHASH (Tā´ hăsh) Personal name meaning "porpoise" or "dugong." Third son of Nahor and Reumah (Gen. 22:24) and ancestor of an Arab tribe, perhaps associated with Tahshi north of Damascus. The Tell el-Amarna letters and the records of Thutmose III mention Tahash.

TAHATH (Tā´ hăth) Personal name and place-name meaning "beneath, low" or "substitute, compensation." **1.** A Levite (1 Chron. 6:24,37). **2.** Two descendants of Ephraim (1 Chron. 7:20). See *Tahan.* **3.** Stopping place during the wilderness wandering (Num. 33:26-27).

TAHCHEMONITE (Tā kē´ mon īt) or **TAHKE-MONITE** (NIV) Title of one of David's 30 elite warriors (2 Sam. 23:8), likely a scribal altering of the Hebrew *ha Hachmonite* (REB), which occurs in the parallel list (1 Chron. 11:11).

TAHPANHES (Tăh´ pŭn hēz) Hebrew transliteration of an Egyptian place-name meaning "fortress of Penhase" or "house of the Nubian." City in the Nile Delta near the eastern border of Egypt (Jer. 2:16). The site, identified with Daphnai (Tell Defneh), shows little evidence of heavy occupation before the Saite dynasty (663 B.C.), which garrisoned Greek mercenaries there to hedge against Assyrian advances. In 605 B.C. then crown prince Nebuchadnezzar defeated the Egyptian forces at Carchemish on the northern Euphrates and pursued them to the border of Egypt. In 601 B.C. Nebuchadnezzar and Pharaoh Neco again fought to a stalemate at the Egyptian border. Jeremiah 46:14 perhaps relates to one of these incidents. Following the destruction of Jerusalem and continuing unrest in Judah, a large group of Jews took Jeremiah with them and fled to Tahpanhes (Jer. 43:7; 44:1). Jeremiah argued against the move (Jer. 42:19), warning that Nebuchadnezzar would again reach Tahpanhes (Jer. 46:14).

TAHPENES (Tăh´ pả nēz) Egyptian royal consort; title for queen of Egypt in 1 Kings 11:19-20. Her sister was given in marriage to Hadad the Edomite, an enemy of David and later of Solomon.

TAHREA (Tăh rē´ ả) Alternate form of Tarea (1 Chron. 9:41).

TAHTIM-HODSHI (Tăh tĭm-hŏd´ shī) Site in northern Israel which David's census takers visited (2 Sam. 24:6). The name is not attested elsewhere, prompting various emendations: Kadesh in the land of the Hittites (REB, NRSV, TEV) and the land below Hermon.

TALENT See *Weights and Measures.*

TALITHA CUMI (Tăl´ ĭ thà cū´ mĭ) Transliteration of Aramaic phrase meaning "damsel, arise." Jesus' words to Jairus's daughter (Mark 5:41). The girl's relatives thought she was dead by the time the Lord arrived, but He pronounced it only as sleep (5:39). The Aramaic reflects Mark's attempt to preserve the actual words of Jesus, who probably spoke Aramaic rather than Greek, in which most of the NT is written. See *Jairus.*

TALMAI (Tăl´ mī) Personal name meaning "plowman" or else derived from the Hurrian word for "big." **1.** One of three Anakim (giant, pre-Israelite inhabitants of Canaan) residing in Hebron (Num. 13:22). Caleb (Josh. 15:14) and Judah (Judg. 1:10) are credited with driving the Anakim from Hebron. **2.** King of Geshur, father of David's wife Maacah and grandfather of Absalom (2 Sam. 3:3; 1 Chron. 3:2). After Absalom murdered his half brother Amnon, he took refuge with his grandfather (2 Sam. 13:37).

TALMON (Tăl´ mŏn) Personal name meaning "brightness." **1.** Levite whom David and Samuel appointed as a gatekeeper (1 Chron. 9:17), ancestor of a family of temple gatekeepers who returned from exile (Ezra 2:42; Neh. 7:45). **2.** Leader of the postexilic gatekeepers (Neh. 11:19; 12:25).

TALMUD Jewish commentaries. Talmud means "study" or "learning" and refers in rabbinic Judaism to the opinions and teachings that disciples learn from their predecessors particularly with regard to the development of oral legal teachings (*halakah*). The word "Talmud" is most commonly used in Judaism to refer specifically to the digest of commentary on the Mishnah. The Mishnah (a codification of oral legal teachings on the written law of Moses) was probably written down at Javneh in Galilee at about A.D. 220. Between A.D. 220 and 500 the rabbinic schools in Palestine and Babylonia amplified and

applied the teachings of the Mishnah for their Jewish communities. Two documents came to embody a large part of this teaching: the Jerusalem Talmud and the Babylonian Talmud.

Those scholars represented in the Mishnah are referred to as the *Tannaim.* Generally, they lived from the first through the second centuries A.D. The Talmud gives the opinions of a new generation of scholars referred to as the *Amoraim* (A.D. 200–500). Various teachers became famous and attracted students from a variety of locales in the ancient world. By this means, the decisions of rabbis resident in Babylon became normative for a broad cross section of ancient Jewish life. How strongly rabbinic decisions influenced the average Jew we cannot know. Passages from the Talmud reflect the great concern of some rabbis that their advice was not being followed by the people.

The Talmud represents a continuation of the application of the oral law (*halakah*) to every sphere of Jewish life. This process probably began with the early Jewish sect known as the Pharisees. Many of the discussions in the Talmud, however, seem to have no direct practical application but are theoretical in nature.

The passing on of the tradition and the remembering of the specific decisions and reasoning of the teachers by their disciples was apparently emphasized in the rabbinic schools. There is some evidence that both Mishnah and Talmud were remembered according to chants or musical melodies.

The Babylonian Talmud became the more authoritative of the two written Talmuds due both to the political fortunes of the Jewish communities in Palestine and Babylon in the first four centuries A.D. and also to its more sophisticated style. Later generations of Jewish scholars also recognized that the Babylonian Talmud was completed later and so supposed that it absorbed or superseded the Jerusalem one.

Apart from haggadic passages that are mostly Hebrew, it was written in Eastern Aramaic, the language of Babylon at the time. The Babylonian Talmud reflects a highly developed system for settling disputed questions of halakah (oral law). It includes commentary on all six major divisions of the Mishnah but deletes certain subsections. For example, discussion of the segments of Mishnah that deal with the temple service are omitted, presumably because the Jewish community in Babylon did not anticipate the rebuild-

T

ing of the temple in the near future (interestingly, the Jerusalem Talmud does discuss these sections).

The Babylonian Talmud also contains theoretical legal discussion as well as information on the daily life of Jewish people in the first six centuries, history, medicine, astronomy, commerce, agriculture, demonology, magic, botany, zoology, and other sciences. It also incorporates a large measure of haggadah (illustrative stories and poetry) in addition to legal discussion.

The Jerusalem Talmud was not compiled in Jerusalem but in the centers of Tiberias, Caesarea, and Sepphoris in Palestine, since Jerusalem ceased to be a major center of Jewish learning after the destruction of the second temple in A.D. 70. It uses Western Aramaic, the dialect of Palestine. It is succinct and concise in its presentation of legal arguments and does not contain the considerable body of haggadah included in the Babylonian Talmud. The Jerusalem Talmud was completed about A.D. 400, approximately a century before the Babylonian Talmud.

The importance of the Talmud to Jewish life until the modern period can hardly be overestimated. Talmud and commentary on it became a major focus of religious action in the medieval period. The Talmud became the central document for Jewish education during the medieval period.

New Testament scholars are especially interested in the Talmud. Some of the halakah embodied in the Talmud is attributed to early rabbis and may reflect Jewish practice in the time of the writers of the NT or of Jesus. This material must be used judiciously in historical reconstruction, however, since it was compiled five centuries after the fact. See *Haggadah or Halakah; Mishnah.*   *Stephenson Humphries-Brooks*

TAMAH (Tā´ mah) (KJV, Neh. 7:55) See *Temah.*

TAMAR (Tā´ mär) Personal name meaning "date palm." **1.** Daughter-in-law of Judah, wife of his eldest son, Er (Gen. 38:6). After her wicked husband died without fathering a child, Tamar was given to Er's brother, Onan, for the purpose of bearing a child in the name of the dead man. Onan refused to impregnate Tamar, for which God killed him. She then tricked her father-in-law into fathering her child (38:18). See *Levirate Marriage.* **2.** Daughter of David raped

by her half brother, Amnon (2 Sam. 13:14). The act was avenged by her full brother, Absalom, when he had Amnon murdered (13:28-29). These acts were part of Nathan's prophecy that the sword would never depart from David's house (2 Sam. 12:10). **3.** Absalom named his only daughter Tamar. She is called "a beautiful woman" (2 Sam. 14:27). **4.** City built by Solomon "in the wilderness" (1 Kings 9:18). The text should perhaps read Tadmor (2 Chron. 8:4), since the Hebrew lacks the qualifying phrase "of Judah" and the Masoretic vowel points correspond with Tadmor. See *Tadmor.* **5.** Fortified city at the southern end of the Dead Sea, marking the ideal limit of Israel (Ezek. 47:19; 48:28). If identical with 4., this Tamar likely served as a supply depot for Solomon's mines in the Arabah and as a frontier post to guard the border with Edom.

TAMARISK Shrublike tree (*Tamarix syriaca*) common to the Sinai and southern Palestine with small white or pink flowers. Many varieties of the tree exist. Abraham planted a tamarisk at Beer-sheba (Gen. 21:33), and Saul was buried beneath one at Jabesh-gilead (1 Sam. 31:13). Saul convened his court under one (1 Sam. 22:6). KJV translated "grave" and "tree." Some believe the resin that the tamarisk produces may have been the manna eaten by the Hebrews during the wilderness wanderings.

TAMBOURINE See *Music, Instruments, Dancing; Tabret.*

TAMMUZ (Tăm´ mŭz) Sumerian god of vegetation. The worship of Tammuz by women in Jerusalem was revealed as one of the abominations in Ezekiel (8:14-15). According to the pagan religion, Tammuz was betrayed by his lover, Ishtar, and as a result dies each autumn. The wilting of the vegetation at that time of year is seen as a sign of his death. This caused great mourning in the ancient world and was why the women in Jerusalem wept. See *Fertility Cult; Gods, Pagan.*

TANACH (Tā´ näk) (KJV, Josh. 21:25) See *Taanach.*

TANHUMETH (Tăn hū´ mĕth) Personal name meaning "comforting." Father of Seraiah, a captain of forces remaining with Gedaliah in Judah following the deportation of Babylon (2 Kings

25:23; Jer. 40:8). A Lachish stamp witnesses to the name as does an Arad inscription.

TANIS (Tăn´ ĭs) See *Zoan.*

TAPHATH (Tā´ phăth) Personal name meaning "droplet." Daughter of Solomon and wife of Ben-abinadab, a Solomonic official (1 Kings 4:11).

TAPPUAH (Tăp´ pū ah) Personal name meaning "apple" or "quince." **1.** A Calebite, likely a resident of a town near Hebron (1 Chron. 2:43). **2.** City in the Shephelah district of Judah (Josh. 15:34), possibly Beit Nettif about 12 miles west of Bethlehem. **3.** City of the north border of Ephraim (Josh. 16:8) whose environs were allotted to Manasseh (17:7-8), likely the Tappuah of Josh. 12:17 and 2 Kings 15:16. The site is perhaps Sheikh Abu Zarod about eight miles southwest of Shechem. Some scholars read "Tappuah" for "Tiphsah" in 2 Kings 15:16 (REB). See *Beth-tappuah; En-tappuah.*

TAR See *Bitumen.*

TARAH (Tā´ rah) KJV form of "Terah," the wilderness campsite (Num. 33:27-28).

TARALAH (Tär´ à lah) Place-name meaning "strength." Unidentified site in Benjamin, likely northwest of Jerusalem (Josh. 18:27).

TAREA (Tā´ rə à) Personal name of unknown derivation. Descendant of Saul (1 Chron. 8:35; "Tahrea" 1 Chron. 9:41).

TARES KJV term for grassy weeds resembling wheat, generally identified as darnel (*genus Lolium*) (Matt. 13:25-30,36-40).

TARGUM (Tär´ gŭm) Early translations of the Bible into Aramaic, the native language of Palestine and Babylon in the first century A.D. Targum, in its verbal Hebrew form, means "to explain, to translate." The most important of these translations still in existence is Targum Onkelos, which was probably read weekly in synagogue services from a relatively early date. The Targums are not simply translations but seem to include a large amount of biblical commentary that perhaps reflects sermons in Jewish Palestinian synagogues. Therefore, the material is of interest to NT scholars who attempt to

understand the Judaism of which Jesus was a part. See *Aramaic.*

Stephenson Humphries-Brooks

TARPELITES (Tär´ pĕ līts) KJV transliteration of an Aramaic title in Ezra 4:9. Most modern translations render the term "officials" (NIV, "men of Tripolis").

TARSHISH (Tär´ shĭsh) Personal name and place-name of uncertain derivation, either meaning "yellow jasper," as in the Hebrew of Exod. 28:20; Ezek. 28:13, or else derived from an Akkadian term meaning "smelting plant." **1.** Son of Javan (Gen. 10:4; 1 Chron. 1:7) and ancestor of an Aegean people. **2.** Benjaminite warrior (1 Chron. 7:10). **3.** One of seven leading officials of King Ahasuerus of Persia (Esther 1:14). This name possibly means "greedy one" in Old Persian. **4.** Geographic designation, most likely of Tartessus at the southern tip of Spain but possibly of Tarsus in Cilicia. Jonah sailed for Tarshish, the far limit of the western world, from the Mediterranean port of Joppa in his futile attempt to escape God's call (Jon. 1:3). Tarshish traded in precious metals with Tyre, another Mediterranean port (Isa. 23:1; Jer. 10:9; Ezek. 27:12). **5.** References to Tarshish in 1 Kings and 2 Chronicles suggest a non-geographic meaning. Solomon's (1 Kings 10:22; 2 Chron. 9:21) and Jehoshaphat's (1 Kings 22:48; 2 Chron. 20:36) fleets were based at Ezion-geber on the Red Sea. Solomon's cargo suggests east African trading partners. Thus "ships of Tarshish" may designate seagoing vessels like those of Tarshish or else ships bearing metal cargo like those of Tarshish (cp. Isa. 2:16, where "ships of Tarshish" parallels "beautiful crafts").

TARSUS (Tär´ sŭs) Birthplace of Paul (Acts 9:11) and capital of Roman province of Cilicia. See *Asia Minor, Cities of; Paul.*

TARTAK (Tär´ tăk) Deity worshiped by the Avvites, whom the Assyrians made to settle in Samaria after 722 B.C. (2 Kings 17:31). The name is otherwise unattested and is likely a deliberate corruption of Atargatis, the Syrian high goddess and wife of Hadad.

TARTAN (Tär´ tăn) Title of the highest ranking Assyrian officer under the king; commander in chief; supreme commander (2 Kings 18:17;

T

The Cleopatra Gate at Tarsus commemorating Mark Antony's meeting of Cleopatra at this ancient city.

Isa. 20:1). First mention of the office occurred under Adad-nirari II (911–891 B.C.).

TARTARUS See *Hell.*

TASKMASTER Oppressive overseers of forced labor gangs employed by monarchies for large public works projects (Egyptian: Exod. 1:11; 3:7; 5:6-14; Israelite: 2 Sam. 20:24; 1 Kings 4:6; 5:16; 12:18; 2 Chron. 10:18).

TASSEL See *Fringe.*

TATNAI (Tăt´ nī) (KJV) or **TATTENAI** (Tăt´ tĕ nī) Contemporary of Zerubbabel, governor of the Persian province "across the (Euphrates) River," which included Palestine (Ezra 5:3,6; 6:6,13).

TAW (Täv) Twenty-second and final letter of the Hebrew alphabet, which the KJV (Tau) used as a heading for Ps. 119:169-176, each verse of which begins with the letter.

TAX COLLECTOR See *Publican.*

TAXES Regular payments to rulers. Early Israel only paid taxes to support the tabernacle and the priests. Terms in the OT that refer to taxes were: "assessment," "forced labor," "tribute," and "toll." Before Israel established a king, worship taxes were the only ones levied from within the nation. Tribute had to be paid, of course, to invaders such as the Philistines. During David's reign an army was maintained by tribute paid by conquered tribes. Taxes increased under Solomon's rule. Tradesmen and merchants paid duties; subject peoples paid tribute; farmers paid taxes in kind—oil and wine; and many Israelites did forced labor on the temple. The burden of

taxation contributed to the rebellion following Solomon's death (1 Kings 12). Soon Israel became a vassal state, paying tribute—a compulsory tax—to Assyria and eventually to Rome.

In the NT era Herod the Great levied a tax on the produce of the field and a tax on items bought and sold. Other duties owed to foreign powers were a land tax, a poll tax, a kind of progressive income tax (about which the Pharisees tested Jesus, Matt. 22:17), and a tax on personal property. In Jerusalem a house tax was levied. These taxes were paid directly to Roman officials.

Export and import customs paid at seaports and city gates were farmed out to private contractors who paid a sum in advance for the right to collect taxes in a certain area. Such were Zacchaeus (Luke 19) and Matthew (Matt. 9). Rome apparently placed little restriction on how much profit the collector could take. An enrollment for the purposes of taxation under the Roman emperor brought Joseph and Mary to Bethlehem where Jesus was born (Luke 2:1-7). In addition to the taxes owed occupying powers, the Jewish people also had to pay religious duties. A *didrachma* (half shekel) was owed to the temple by all Jewish males throughout the world (Matt. 17:24). The second tax was a tithe, 10 percent of everything the soil produced, collected by the Levites.

The Israelites resented most deeply the duties paid to the occupying powers. Many zealous Jews considered it treason to God to pay taxes to Rome. When questioned about paying the poll tax, Jesus surprised His questioners by saying that the law should be obeyed (Mark 12:13).

Gary K. Halbrook

TEACHING See *Education in Bible Times; Instruction.*

TEARS See *Grief and Mourning.*

TEBAH (Tē´ bah) Personal name meaning "slaughter." Son of Nahor and ancestor of an Aramaean tribe (Gen. 22:24). Tebah is perhaps associated with Tubihi, a site somewhere between Damascus and Kadesh.

TEBALIAH (Tĕb á lī´ ah) Personal name meaning "Yahweh has dipped, that is, purified," or "loved by Yahweh," or "good for Yahweh." Postexilic Levitic gatekeeper (1 Chron. 26:11).

TEBETH (Tē´ bĕth) Tenth month (December–January) of the Hebrew calendar (Esther 2:16). The name derives from an Akkadian term meaning "sinking" and refers to the rainy month. See *Calendars.*

TEETH Hard bony structures in the jaws of persons and animals used to cut and grind food. In OT thinking, the loss of a tooth was a serious matter subject to the law of retaliation (Exod. 21:23-25; Lev. 24:19-20; Deut. 19:21; cp. Matt. 5:38-42). Teeth set on edge, that is made dull or insensitive, illustrates the concept of corporate or inherited guilt challenged by the prophets (Jer. 31:29-30; Ezek. 18:2-3). Gnashing of teeth displays the raging despair of those excluded from Christ's kingdom (Matt. 8:12; 13:42).

TEHAPHNEHES (Tə hăph´ nĕ hēz) Alternate form of Tahpanhes (Ezek. 30:18).

TEHINNAH (Tə hĭn´ nah) Personal name meaning "supplication" or "graciousness." Descendant of Judah responsible for founding Irnahash (1 Chron. 4:12).

TEIL TREE KJV term meaning "lime" or "linden tree," used to translate a Hebrew term generally rendered oak or terebinth (Isa. 6:13). See *Plants; Terebinth.*

TEKEL (Tĕk´ əl) See *Mene, Mene, Tekel, Upharsin.*

TEKOA (Tə kō´ ȧ) Place-name meaning "place of setting up a tent." A city in the highlands of Judah six miles south of Bethlehem and 10 miles south of Jerusalem; home of the Prophet Amos. God called Amos from among the shepherds of Tekoa to preach to the Northern Kingdom of Israel (Amos 1:1). The priest tried to send him back to Tekoa (7:12).

One of David's chief fighting men was Ira, the son of Ikkesh from Tekoa (2 Sam. 23:26). Sometime between 922 B.C. and 915 B.C. Rehoboam cited Tekoa as one of the cities whose fortifications were to be strengthened (2 Chron. 11:5-6). Approximately 50 years later, Jehoshaphat defeated a force of Ammonite, Meunite, and Moabite invaders in the wilderness between Tekoa and En-gedi (2 Chron.

20:20-22). After the return from exile, Tekoa remained occupied (Neh. 3:5). See *Amos.*
Kenneth Craig

TEKOITE (Tə kō´ īt) Resident of Tekoa (2 Sam. 23:26; Neh. 3:5).

TEL-ABIB (Tĕl-ȧ´ bēb) Place-name meaning "mound of the flood" or "mound of grain." Tel-abib on the Chebar Canal near Nippur in Babylon was home to Ezekiel and other exiles (Ezek. 3:15). The Babylonians may have thought it was the ruined site of the original flood.

TELAH (Tē´ lah) Personal name meaning "breach" or "fracture." An ancestor of Joshua (1 Chron. 7:25).

TELAIM (Tə lā´ ĭm) Place-name meaning "young speckled lambs." City in southern Judah where Saul gathered forces to battle the Amalekites (1 Sam. 15:4). Suggested sites include Khirbet Umm es-Salafeh southwest of Kurnub and Khirbet Abu Tulul 12 miles southeast of Beer-sheba. The earliest Greek translation of 1 Sam. 27:8 reads "from Telem" rather than "from old." See *Telem.*

TEL-ASSAR (Tĕl-ăs´ sȧr) Place-name meaning "mound of Asshur." City in northern Mesopotamia which the Assyrians conquered (2 Kings 19:12; KJV, "Thelasar"; Isa. 37:12). Its location is not known.

TEL-AVIV (Tĕl-ȧ vēv´) See *Tel-abib.*

TELEM (Tē´ lĕm) Personal name and place-name meaning "brightness" or "lamb." **1.** Levite with a foreign wife (Ezra 10:24). **2.** City in

Excavations at the site of ancient Tekoa, hometown of Amos the prophet.

southern Judah (Josh. 15:24), a variant form of Telaim.

TEL-HARESHA (Tĕl-hả rē´ shả) KJV, NIV alternate form of Tel-harsha (Neh. 7:61).

TEL-HARSA (Tĕl-här´ sả) (KJV, Ezra 2:59) or **TEL-HARSHA** (Tĕl-här´ shả) Place-name meaning "mound of the forest" or "mound of magic." Home of Babylonian Jews unable to demonstrate their lineage (Ezra 2:59; Neh. 7:61). Tel-harsha was likely located in the flatlands near the Persian Gulf.

TELL Semitic term meaning "mound," applied to areas built up by successive settlement at a single site. "Tell" or "tel" is a common element in Near Eastern place-names. See *Archaeology*.

TELL EL-AMARNA See *Amarna, Tell el*.

TEL-MELAH (Tĕl-mē´ lah) Place-name meaning "mound of salt." Babylonian home of a group of Jews unable to demonstrate their lineage (Ezra 2:59; Neh. 7:61). Tel-melah is perhaps Thelma of Ptolemy in the low salt tracts near the Persian Gulf.

TEMA (Tē´ mả) Personal name and place-name meaning "south country." Tema, a son of Ishmael (Gen. 25:15; 1 Chron. 1:30), is associated with Tema (modern Teima), a strategic oasis located on the Arabian Peninsula 250 miles southeast of Aqaba and 200 miles north-north-east of Medina. Job 6:19 alludes to Tema's importance as a caravan stop. Isaiah 21:14 likely refers to the campaign of the Assyrian king Tiglath-pileser III (738 B.C.) when Tema escaped destruction by paying tribute. Jeremiah 25:23 perhaps refers to a campaign of Nebuchadnezzar. Having conquered and rebuilt Tema, Nabonidus, the last king of Babylon, remained there 10 years, leaving his son Belshazzar as vice-regent in Babylon (Dan. 5).

TEMAH (Tē´ mah) Family of temple servants (Nethinim) returning from exile (Ezra 2:53; Neh. 7:55).

TEMAN (Tē´ măn) Personal name and place-name meaning "right side," that is, "southern." **1.** Edomite clan descended from Esau (Gen. 36:11,15; 1 Chron. 1:36). **2.** City of area associated with this clan (Jer. 49:7,20; Ezek. 25:13;

Amos 1:12; Obad. 1:9; Hab. 3:3). Teman has often been identified with Tawilan, 50 miles south of the Dead Sea just east of Petra, though archaeological evidence does not confirm the site as the principal city of southern Edom. Others understand Teman to designate southern Edom in general. To others the linkage with Dedan (Jer. 49:7; Ezek. 25:13) suggests Tema on the Arabian Peninsula. See *Tema*.

TEMANI (Tē´ măn ī) (KJV) or **TEMANITES** (Tē´ măn īts) Descendants of Teman or residents of Teman, the southern area of Edom. The land of the Temanites designates (southern) Edom (Gen. 36:34 KJV "Temani"; 1 Chron. 1:45). The Temanites were renowned for their wisdom (Job 2:11; cp. Jer. 49:7).

TEMENI (Tē´ mě nī) Personal name, perhaps meaning "on the right hand," that is, "to the south." Descendant of Judah (1 Chron. 4:6).

TEMPERANCE See *Self-control*.

TEMPLE OF JERUSALEM Place of worship, especially the temple of Solomon built in Jerusalem for national worship of Yahweh. Sacred or holy space is the meaning of our word "temple," very like the two Greek words, *hieron* (temple area) and *naos* (sanctuary itself) which are translated "temple" in the NT. In the OT the language is usually beth Yahweh or beth Elohim, "house of the Yahweh" or "house of God," because He is said to have dwelt there. The other Hebrew expression for temple is *hekal*, "palace, great house," deriving from the Sumerian word for "great house," whether meant for God or the earthly king. So David, when he had built for himself a cedar palace, thought it only proper he should build one for Yahweh, too (2 Sam. 7:1-2). Nathan at first approved his plan, but the Lord Himself said He had been used to living in a tent since the exodus from Egypt. He would allow David's son to build Him a house (temple), but He would build for David a house (dynasty, 2 Sam. 7:3-16). This covenant promise became exceedingly significant to the messianic hope fulfilled in the coming of the ideal king of the line of David. See *Tabernacle, Tent of Meeting*.

Chronicles makes clear that David planned the temple and accumulated great wealth and gifts for it, though Solomon was the one who actually built it. Solomon's temple may not have actually been the first temple which housed the ark of the covenant, since there was a house of Yahweh, also called a temple, at Shiloh (1 Sam. 1:7,9,24; 3:3), but in 1 Sam. 2:22 (NIV) it is called "tent of meeting," whether the wilderness tabernacle or not. Jeremiah in his great temple sermon warned all who came into the Lord's house in Jerusalem that if they trusted primarily in the temple instead of the Lord, He could destroy Solomon's temple just as He had the previous one at Shiloh (Jer. 7:1-15; 26:1-6).

Israel knew other worship places with history far older than the Jerusalem temple. Former patriarchal holy places near Shechem or Bethel (Gen. 12:6-8; 28:10-22; cp. Deut. 11:29-30; 27:1-26; Josh. 8:30-35; 24:1-28; Judg. 20:26-27), these are not called temples in Scripture though local inhabitants may have called them temples. It cannot be determined what kind of sanctuaries were at Ophrah, Gilgal, Nob, Mizpah, Ramah, or other "high places" where Yahweh was worshiped, but "the temple" is the one at Jerusalem from Solomon's time.

Solomon's Temple There were three historical temples in succession, those of Solomon, Zerubbabel, and Herod in the preexilic, postexilic, and NT periods. Herod's temple was really a massive rebuilding of the Zerubbabel temple, so both are called the "second temple" by Judaism. All three were located on a prominent hill north of David's capital city, which he conquered from the Jebusites (2 Sam. 5:6-7). David had acquired the temple hill from Araunah the Jebusite at the advice of the Prophet Gad to stay a pestilence from the Lord by building an altar and offering sacrifices on the threshing floor (2 Sam. 24:18-25). Chronicles identifies this hill with Mount Moriah, where Abraham had been willing to offer Isaac (2 Chron. 3:1; Gen. 22:1-14). So the temple mount today in Jerusalem is called Mount Moriah, and the threshing floor of Araunah is undoubtedly the large rock enshrined within the Dome of the Rock, center of the Muslim enclosure called Haram es-Sharif (the third holiest place in Islam, after Mecca and Medina). This enclosure is basically what is left of Herod's enlarged temple platform, the masonry of which

Reconstruction of Herod's temple (20 B.C.–A.D. 70) at Jerusalem as viewed from the southeast. The drawing reflects archaeological discoveries made since excavations began in 1967 along the south end of the Temple Mount platform gateway.

T

Modern Orthodox Jews praying at the Wailing Wall of the Temple Mount in Jerusalem.

may best be seen in its Western Wall, the holiest place within Judaism since the Roman destruction of Herod's temple.

No stone is left that archaeologists can confidently say belonged to the Solomonic temple. We do have the detailed literary account of its building preserved in Kings (1 Kings 5:1–9:10) and Chronicles (2 Chron. 2–7). Ezekiel's vision of the new Jerusalem temple after the exile (Ezek. 40–43) is idealistic and was perhaps never realized in Zerubbabel's rebuilding of the temple, but many of its details would have reflected Solomon's temple in which Ezekiel probably ministered as a priest before being deported to Babylon in 597 B.C. The treaty with Hiram, the king of Tyre, and the employment of the metalworker Hiram (or Huram-abi, a different person from the king), which he provided, show that considerable Phoenician influence, expertise, craftsmanship, and artistic design went into the building of the temple.

The primary meaning of the temple was the same as that of the ark it was constructed to enshrine—a symbol of God's presence in the midst of His people (Exod. 25:21-22). Because it was God's house, the worshipers could not enter the holy place, reserved only for priests and other worship leaders, much less the holiest place (holy of holies) to be entered by the high priest only once a year (Lev. 16). The worshipers could gather for prayer and sacrifice in the temple courtyard(s) where they could sing psalms as they saw their offerings presented to Yahweh on His great altar. The spirit of Israel's prayer and praise is to be found in the Psalms and in the worship experiences such as that of Isaiah when he surrendered to his prophetic call experience in the forecourt of the temple (Isa. 6:1-8).

The account of Isaiah's experience makes it clear that the earthly temple was viewed as a microcosm of the heavenly temple where the King of the universe really dwelt. The quaking and smoke of the Lord's presence at Sinai were now manifested in Zion (Isa. 6:4). Israel understood that it was only by God's grace that He consented to dwell with His people. So Deuteronomy represents the central sanctuary as the place where Yahweh caused His name to dwell (Deut. 12:5; cp. 1 Kings 8:13), and priestly thinkers viewed it as filled with His glory (cp. the tabernacle, Exod. 40:34). Obviously, no one can house God: "But will God really live on earth? Indeed, heaven, even the highest heaven, cannot contain You, much less this temple I have built!" (1 Kings 8:27 HCSB).

Solomon's temple was shaped as a "long house" of three successive rooms from east to west, a vestibule of only 15-feet depth, a nave (the holy place) of 60 feet and an inner sanctuary (the most holy place) of 30 feet (1 Kings 6:2-3,16-17). It was approximately 30 feet wide and 45 feet high by its interior measurements for the "house" proper, not counting the porch, which was sort of an open entryway. This is similar to, though not precisely the same as, the shape of several Syrian and Canaanite temples excavated in the past few decades (at Hazor, Lachish, Tell Tainat). There is even one Israelite "temple" at the southeast border of Judah in the Iron Age fortress of Arad that some have compared with Solomon's temple. None was so symmetrical or ornately decorated, or even as large as the Jerusalem temple, even though Solomon's palace complex of which the temple was only a part (1 Kings 7:1-12) was much larger and took longer to build (Tell Tainat, in northern Syria, is the closest analogy). Around the outside of the house proper was constructed three stories of side chambers for temple storehouses, above which were recessed windows in the walls of the holy place (1 Kings 6:4-6,8-10).

The inside of the house proper was paneled with cedar, floored with cypress, and inlaid with gold throughout. It was decorated with well-known Phoenician artistic ornamentation, floral designs with cherubim, flowers, and palm trees. The most holy place, a windowless cube of about 30 feet, housed the ark of the covenant and was dominated by two guardian cherubim 15 feet tall with outstretched wings spanning 15 feet to touch in the middle and at each side wall (1 Kings 6:15-28). One of the interesting results of archaeological research is the recovery of the form of these ancient cherubim. They are Egyptian-type sphinxes (human-headed winged lions) such as are pictured as the arms of a throne chair of a Canaanite king on one of the Megiddo ivories. The ark, the mercy-seat lid of which had its own guardian cherubim (Exod. 25:18-20), was Yahweh's "footstool." Beneath these awesome cherubim God was invisibly enthroned.

The double doors of the inner sanctuary and the nave were similarly carved and inlaid of finest wood and gold (1 Kings 6:31-35). The arrangement prescribed for the wall of the inner court, "three rows of cut stone and a row of cedar beams" (NASB), was followed in Solomonic buildings excavated at Megiddo (1 Kings 6:36; 7:12). This arrangement is also known from the Tell Tainat temple. This exquisite sanctuary took seven years to build (about 960 B.C.; 1 Kings 6:37-38). The marvelous furnishings of the holy place and the courtyard require another chapter to describe (1 Kings 7:9-51).

The most mysterious creations were two huge free-standing bronze pillars about 35 feet tall, including their beautifully ornamented capitals of lily-work netting and rows of pomegranates (1 Kings 7:15-20). They were nearly six feet in diameter, hollow, with a thickness of bronze about three inches. The pillars were named Jachin ("He shall establish") and Boaz ("in the strength of"), perhaps to signify the visible symbolism of the temple as a testimony to the stability of the Davidic dynasty to which it was intimately related.

The reader at this point expects an account of the bronze altar, included in Chronicles (2 Chron. 4:1), but only presumed in Kings (1 Kings 8:22,54,64; 9:25). This altar is large,

The southeast quadrant of the upper court of the Temple Mount in Jerusalem.

35 feet square and 15 feet tall, presumably with steps.

The molten sea, which may have had some kind of cosmic symbolism, stood in the south-central quadrant of the inner courtyard opposite the bronze altar. It was round with a cup-shaped brim, 15 feet in diameter, 7 and a half feet tall, with a circumference of 45 feet. It was cast of heavy bronze, ornately decorated, and resting on the back of 12 bronze oxen in four sets of three, facing each point of the compass. Since it held about 10,000 gallons of water, it must have been for supplying water to the lavers by some sort of siphoning mechanism.

The third great engineering feat was the crafting of 10 ornate, rolling stands for 10 lavers, five on either side of the courtyard. These were six feet square and four and a half feet tall, each containing some 200 gallons of water, quite heavy objects to be rolled about on chariot wheels. Chronicles says they were used to wash the utensils for sacrificial worship (2 Chron. 4:6).

At the Feast of Tabernacles, Solomon conducted an elaborate dedication festival for the temple (1 Kings 8:1–9:9). The story begins with a procession of the ark containing the two tables of the Decalogue. God's glory in the shining cloud of His presence filled the sanctuary (1 Kings 8:1-11). Then the king blessed the assembly, praised God for His covenant mercies in fulfilling Nathan's promise to David, and gave a long, fervent prayer on behalf of seven different situations in which the prayers of His people should arise to the heavenly throne of God from His earthly temple, closing with a benediction. Solomon provided myriads of sacrifices for the seven days of the great dedication festival. God

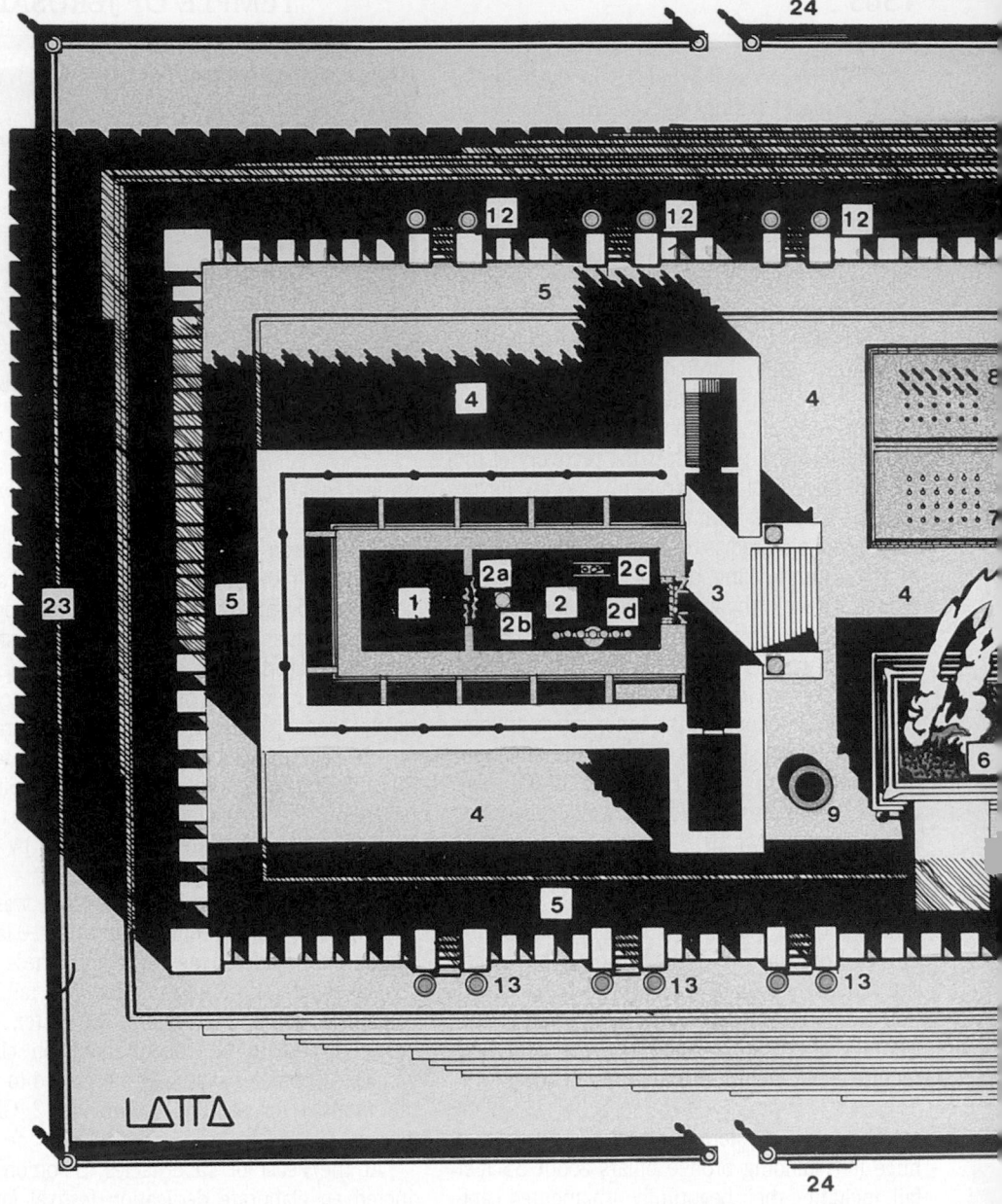

LATTA

24

Herod's temple (20 B.C.–A.D. 70) was begun in the 18th year of King Herod the Great's reign (37–4 B.C.). According to Josephus, the first-century Jewish historian, Herod's temple was constructed after removing the old foundations. The old edifice, Zerubbabel's temple, was a modest restoration of the temple of Solomon destroyed by the Babylonian conquest. The central building was completed in just two years—without any interruption of the temple services. The surrounding buildings and spacious courts, considerably enlarged, were not completed until A.D. 64. The Temple was destroyed by the Romans under the command of Titus during the second Jewish revolt in A.D. 70.

1. Holy of holies (where the ark of the covenant and the giant cherubim were once enshrined).
2. Holy place.
2a. Veil (actually two giant tapestries hung before the entrance of the holy of holies to allow the high priest entry between them without exposing the sacred shrine. It was this veil that was "split in two" upon the death of Jesus).
2b. Altar of Incense.
2c. Table of Shewbread.
2d. Seven-branched Lampstand (Great Menorah).

3. Temple porch.
4. Court of priests.
5. Court of Israel (men).
6. Altar of burnt offerings.
7. Animal tethering area.
8. Slaughtering and skinning area.
9. Laver.
10. Chamber of Phineas (storage of vestments).
11. Chamber of the bread maker.
12. North gates of the inner courts.
13. South gates of the inner courts.
14. East (Nicanor) Gate.
15. Court of women.
16. Court of Nazirites.
17. Court of woodshed.
18. Lepers' Chamber.
19. Shemanyah (possible meaning "oil of Yah").
20. Women's Balconies (for viewing Temple activities).
21. Gate Beautiful (?).
22. Terrace.
23. Soreg (three-cubit high partition).
24. Warning Inscriptions to Gentiles.

Notes containing prayer requests are still placed between the massive stones of the Wailing Wall.

had consecrated this house of prayer, but He required covenant obedience of Solomon and each of his successors, lest He have to destroy this magnificent sanctuary because of the apostasy of His people (1 Kings 9:1-9). The consistent emphasis of Solomon's prayer and God's answer is the awareness of sin and the necessity for wholehearted repentance to keep the temple a ceremonial and meaningful symbol of worship and devotion (2 Chron. 7:13-14). The great prophets preached that, in their temple worship, Israel was not able to avoid syncretism with pagan religious impulses or the hypocritical irrelevance of meaningless overemphasis upon ritual without righteous obedience to their sovereign overlord (Isa. 1:10-17; Mic. 6:6-8; Jer. 7:1-26).

The history of Solomon's temple has many ups and downs through its almost 400 years of existence. Its treasures of gold were often plundered by foreign invaders like Shishak of Egypt (1 Kings 14:25-26). At the division of the kingdoms, Jeroboam set up rival sanctuaries at Bethel and Dan that drew worshipers away from Jerusalem for 200 years. King Asa plundered his own temple treasuries to buy a military ally, Ben-

hadad of Syria against Baasha, king of North Israel (1 Kings 15:18-19), though he had previously repaired the temple altar and carried out limited worship reforms (2 Chron. 15:8-18). Temple repairs were carried out by Jehoash (Joash) of Judah after the murder of wicked Queen Athaliah, but even he had to strip the temple treasuries to buy off Hazael, king of Syria (2 Kings 12). Jehoash (Joash), king of Israel, when foolishly challenged to battle by Amaziah, king of Judah, not only defeated him, but also came to Jerusalem and plundered the temple (1 Kings 14:12-14). King Ahaz plundered his own temple for tribute to Assyria during the Syro-Ephraimitic war of 735 B.C., even stripping some of the bronze furnishings in the courtyard (2 Kings 16:8-9,17). Good King Hezekiah raised a huge tribute for Sennacherib, king of Assyria, in his 701 B.C. invasion, even stripping gold off the temple doors (2 Kings 18:13-16). During the long and disastrous reign of King Manasseh many abominable idols and pagan cult objects were placed in the temple that good King Josiah had to remove during his reform (2 Kings 23:4-6,11-12). Both Hezekiah and Josiah were able to centralize worship in the Jerusalem temple during their reforms and even recover some worshipers from the north for the Jerusalem sanctuary, but Josiah's successor, Jehoiakim, reversed all of Josiah's reforms and filled up the temple with pagan abominations (Ezek. 8). Despite the warnings of Jeremiah and Ezekiel, the people refused to repent of their political and religious folly, and their temple and holy city were first plundered by Nebuchadnezzar in 597 B.C., then burned by Nebuzaradan, his general, in 587/586 B.C.

For both groups of Judah, those in Babylon and those still in Jerusalem, the loss of the temple and city were a grievous blow (Ps. 137; Lam. 1–5). But Jeremiah and Ezekiel had prepared a remnant in their prophecies for a return and rebuilding of the temple.

Zerubbabel's Temple The decree of Cyrus in 538 B.C. permitted the Jews to return from the Babylonian exile with the temple vessels that had been taken. It charged them to rebuild the temple of Jerusalem with Persian financial aid and freewill offerings from Jews who remained in Babylon (Ezra 1:1-4). Sheshbazzar, the governor, laid the foundation. The project was halted when the people of the land discouraged the builders (Ezra 1:8,11; 4:1-5). Then in the second year of Darius, 520 B.C., the work was renewed by the new governor Zerubbabel and Jeshua the high priest at the urging of the prophets Haggai and Zechariah (Ezra 5:1-2).

When local Persian officials tried to stop the rebuilding, Darius found a record of Cyrus' decree that included the overall dimensions (Ezra 6:1-6). The size seems to have been approximately that of Solomon's temple. Ezekiel's temple vision had considerable influence on the new temple (Ezek. 40–42), so that Zerubbabel's temple perhaps was mounted on a platform and measured about 100 feet by 100 feet with the interior dimensions being virtually the same as those of Solomon's temple. It was probably not as ornately decorated (Ezra 3:12-13; Hag. 2:3).

The differences between the two sanctuaries have to do with furniture and courtyard arrangements or gates. As Jeremiah had foreseen, the ark of the covenant was never replaced (Jer. 3:16). Josephus said the holy of holies was empty. It was now separated from the holy place by a veil instead of a door. There was only one seven-branched lampstand, as had been true of the tabernacle, probably the one pictured by Titus in his triumphal arch at Rome as having been carried off when Herod's temple was plundered. The importance of the new temple was that it became a symbol of the Lord's holiness and the religious center of life for the new community. It was completed in 515 B.C. and dedicated with great joy (Ezra 6:14-16). Priesthood had replaced kingship as the authority of the postexilic community.

The Maccabean revolt changed this, and Judas Maccabeus rededicated the temple in 164 B.C. after Antiochus had profaned it in December 167 B.C. This joyous event is still remembered in the Jewish celebration of Hanukkah. Judas' successors appointed themselves as high priests, and the temple became more like a political institution. Pompey captured the temple in 63 B.C. but did not plunder it. See *Intertestamental History and Literature.*

Herod's Temple Herod the Great came to power in 37 B.C. and determined that he would please his Jewish subjects and show off his style of kingship to the Romans by making the Jerusalem temple bigger and better than it had ever been. His most notable contribution was the magnificent stonework of the temple platform that was greatly enlarged. The descriptions

The Muslim Dome of the Rock on the Temple Mount in Jerusalem with the Wailing Wall in the foreground.

in Josephus and the Mishnah have been fleshed out by recent archaeological discoveries.

Herod surrounded the whole enclosure with magnificent porches, particularly the royal stoa along the southern wall. Through the Huldah gates, where double and triple arches can still be seen, worshipers went up through enclosed passageways into the court of the Gentiles. Greek inscriptions separating this court from the court of the women and the holier inner courts of Israel (men) and the priests have been found. The steps south of the temple, where Jesus may have taught on several occasions, have been excavated and reconstructed. An inscription: "To the place of trumpeting" was found below the southwest corner where there was a monumental staircase ascending into the temple from the main street below. Perhaps this was the "temple pinnacle" from which Satan tempted Jesus to throw Himself.

The Jerusalem temple is the focus of many NT events. The birth of John the Baptist was announced there (Luke 1:11-20). The offering by Joseph and Mary at the circumcision of the baby Jesus was brought there. Simeon and Anna greeted Jesus there (2:22-38). Jesus came there as a boy of 12 (2:42-51) and later taught there during His ministry (John 7:14). His cleansing of the temple was instrumental in precipitating His death. He knew no earthly temple was necessary to the worship of God (4:21-24). He predicted the temple's destruction by the Romans, and His warnings to His followers to flee when this happened actually saved many Christians' lives (Mark 13:2,14-23). Early Christians continued to worship there, and Paul was arrested there (Acts 3; 21:27-33).

T

After the Jewish revolt in A.D. 66, Vespasian and then his son Titus crushed all resistance. The temple was destroyed in A.D. 70. Stephen's preaching tended to liberate Christian thinking from the necessity of a temple (Acts 7:46-50), and Paul thought of the church and Christians as the new temple (1 Cor. 3:16-17; 6:19-20). For John, the ideal that the temple represented will ultimately be realized in a "new Jerusalem" (Rev. 21:2). See *Ark of the Covenant; Herod; Holy of Holies; Moriah; Shiloh; Solomon; Tabernacle, Tent of Meeting; Zerubbabel.*

M. Pierce Matheney

TEMPLES, PAGAN See *Canaan; Egypt; Fertility Cult; Gods, Pagan; High Place; Mystery Religions.*

TEMPTATION Broadly defined, temptation is the enticement to do evil. Satan is the tempter (Matt. 4:3; 1 Thess. 3:5). Beginning with Eve, Satan successfully tempted Adam, Cain, Abraham, and David to sin. He was less successful with Job, and Jesus was "tested in every way as we are, yet without sin" (Heb. 4:15 HCSB). James explains that God cannot be tempted by evil, and He does not tempt anyone (James 1:13). Temptation may be for the purpose of destroying a person through sin leading to death and hell. This is Satan's intent. God may allow testing for the purpose of bringing forth faith and patience, which ultimately honor Him, as in the case of Job. James further explains that a blessing awaits the one who endures temptation (James 1:12).

James describes the mechanism of temptation. "Each person is tempted when he is drawn away and enticed by his own evil desires" (James 1:14 HCSB). The origin of the temptation is attributed to fallen human nature (Rom. 6:6; Eph. 4:22; Col. 3:9; and 2 Cor. 5:17). On the other hand, God does not desire His children to be ensnared by evil but to overcome evil with good (Rom. 12:21).

Next James uses a metaphor, that of a woman bearing children, to paint a terrible picture. Once a person has been drawn away by his own desire, desire becomes pregnant and gives birth to sin. Temptation is not sin; yielding to temptation is. Jesus said that cherishing adultery in thought is to commit adultery (Matt. 5:28).

When the full cycle is completed, sin in turn brings forth death. For the unbeliever, spiritual

Ruins of the Roman temple of Apollo at Hierapolis, Turkey.

death is to be separated from God forever in the lake of fire (Rev. 20:10,15). For the believer, "sin that brings death" may mean that he or she is disciplined by dying early (Acts 5:1-5; 1 John 5:16; Gal. 6:8).

Paul explains that "no temptation has overtaken you except what is common to humanity. God is faithful and He will not allow you to be tempted beyond what you are able, but with the temptation He will provide the way of escape, so

The temple of Apollo at Didyma near ancient Miletus (modern Turkey).

The pylon entrance to the Luxor temple complex at ancient Thebes was built by Ramses II of Egypt.

that you are able to bear it" (1 Cor. 10:13 HCSB). He desires us to withstand the temptation and glorify Him in our bodies, which have been purchased by His blood (1 Cor. 6:20). See *Devil, Satan, Evil, Demonic; Temptation of Jesus.*   *David Lanier*

TEMPTATION OF JESUS Jesus was tempted by the devil in the wilderness subsequent to His baptism by John. These are the only two events described by the synoptic evangelists between Jesus' childhood and the beginning of His min-

The Parthenon, a temple dedicated to Athena, dominates the Acropolis in Athens, Greece.

istry. While no reason for the temptations is given, each of the Synoptics associates Jesus' temptations closely with His baptism. The references to sonship, "You are My beloved Son; in You I take delight!" (Mark 1:11 HCSB; Matt. 3:17; Luke 3:22) and "If You are the Son of God" (Matt. 4:3,6; Luke 4:3,9) suggest that one aspect of the purpose was a test to determine what kind of Messiah Jesus would be.

The brevity of Mark's account (1:13-14) is striking. He reports only that the Spirit drove Jesus into the wilderness, He remained there 40 days, wild animals were present, and angels ministered to Him. The unique feature is the reference to the presence of wild animals.

Matthew and Luke describe in some detail three encounters between Jesus and Satan. The foremost difference between the accounts is the reversal of the order of the final two temptations. Matthew connects the first two with a connective particle that can have chronological implications. Luke's interest in Jerusalem and the temple (1:9; 2:22,25,37,41-50) make it more likely that he used the third temptation as a climax to the temptations.

Forty days in the wilderness is reminiscent of the fasts of Moses (Exod. 34:28; Deut. 9:9) and

Elijah (1 Kings 9:8) and the 40 years of the Israelites in the desert (Num. 14:33; 32:13). The only parallel developed, however, is the wilderness wanderings of Israel. As God led Israel in the wilderness, likewise the Spirit led Jesus into the wilderness. God tested Israel in the wilderness and they failed. God allowed Jesus to be tempted by the devil and He succeeded in resisting.

The first temptation (Matt. 4:3-4) was an attempt to get Jesus to doubt God's providential care. If Jesus had turned the stones into bread, He would have been acting independently from His heavenly Father. The devil did not try to get Jesus to doubt His sonship, which was announced from heaven at His baptism (Matt. 3:17). Rather, the devil argued that since Jesus is the Son of God, He should use His powers to meet His own needs. Jesus' response (Deut. 8:3) teaches that spiritual nourishment is more significant than physical nourishment.

In the second temptation (Matt. 4:5-7) Satan misapplied Scripture (Ps. 91:11-12) in an attempt to get Jesus to jump from the highest point of the temple to test God's promise to pro-

A Christian monastery on the Mount of Temptation marks the traditional site of Jesus' temptation.

tect Jesus from physical harm. Jesus' quote of Deut. 6:16 alludes to Israel's rebellion at Massah (Exod. 17:1-7). Jesus refused to test the faithfulness and protection of God. He trusted the Father and needed no tests.

The third temptation was an opportunity for Jesus to seize a kingdom and avoid the cross. Satan first presented Jesus the "bait" ("all the kingdoms of the world and their splendor") before the compromising stipulation ("if You will fall down and worship me"). Jesus response to the devil (Deut. 6:13) emphasized the close relationship between worship and service. While Israel had a tendency to chase false gods (Deut. 6:10-15), Jesus maintained total allegiance to God. Angels ministered to Jesus after the temptations.

Luke's placement of the genealogy (3:23-38) between Jesus' baptism (3:21-22) and temptation (4:1-13) may suggest that Jesus, "My beloved Son" (3:22 HCSB), is beginning to reverse what Adam, "son of God" (3:38), did in the fall. Whereas the first Adam fell in the idyllic setting of Eden, the second Adam withstood the enemy in the barren wilderness. Another unique feature in Luke's account is the role of the Spirit. He comments (4:1) that the Spirit led Jesus to the wilderness. After the temptation Jesus "returned to Galilee in the power of the Spirit" (4:14). Luke is the only evangelist to note that Satan's departure was not the end of the conflict (4:13), but the intensity was not repeated until Gethsemane (22:40,46,53) and Golgotha (23:35-36,39).

Several significant features stand out as one contemplates Jesus' temptation in the wilderness. His encounter with the devil in the wilderness is a source of encouragement and instruction to believers as they battle temptation (Heb. 2:18; 4:15). His commitment to the Father's will, use of Scripture, and resolve to resist the devil (James 4:7) are helpful examples for battling temptation. See *Devil, Satan, Evil, Demonic; Jesus, Life and Ministry.*   *Bill Cook*

TEN See *Numbers Systems and Number Symbolism.*

TEN COMMANDMENTS Although many people refer to the "Decalogue" as "the Ten Commandments," this is unfortunate for several reasons. First, it obscures the fact that this is not what the OT calls them. Wherever it is referred to by title it is identified as *aseret haddebarim,* "the Ten Words" (Exod. 34:28; Deut. 4:13; 10:4). This sense is captured precisely in the Greek word decalogos. Second, in both the original context in which the Decalogue was given (Exod. 20:1) and Moses' remembrance of the event in Deut. 4:12 and 5:22, the Decalogue is presented as a set of spoken words rather than a written set of laws. Third, "Ten Commandments" obscures the fact that the Decalogue is a covenant document whose form follows ancient Near Eastern treaty tradition. Fourth, as a code of laws the Decalogue is virtually unenforceable. For all these reasons, although the 10 statements are in the form of commands, we should follow the lead of the biblical texts and refer to them as the "Ten Words/Declarations," the 10 fundamental principles of covenant relationship. The stipulations revealed in the "Book of the Covenant," the "Holiness Code," and other parts of the Pentateuch represent clarifications and applications of these principles. Presumably the stipulations of the covenant were reduced to 10 principles so they could be easily memorized.

Apart from Moses' citation of the Decalogue in Deut. 5, the OT gives little if any evidence of giving the Decalogue greater authority than any of the other laws revealed at Sinai. This does not mean that these tablets were not treated as special. On the contrary, Moses notes that the Decalogue contained the only revelation that was communicated by God directly to the people (Deut. 4:12-13; 5:22) and committed to writing on tablets of stone by God's own hand (Exod. 24:12; 31:18; 34:1; Deut. 4:13; 5:22; 10:1-4). All subsequent revelation at Sinai was communicated indirectly through Moses, the covenant mediator. The special status of the tablets is reflected in the fact that these tablets (and these alone) were deposited inside the ark of the covenant (Deut. 10:5; 1 Kings 8:9).

Two forms dominate Israelite covenant law. *Casuistic law* is framed in the third person, usually deals with specific situations, often cites consequences for compliance/non-compliance, and is cast in the following form: "If a person does X, then Y will/shall be the consequence." *Apodictic law* by contrast is framed in the second person, usually deals with general principles, rarely sets conditions or cites consequences, and is cast in the following form: "You shall/shall not do X." The Decalogue belongs to the latter category.

The Decalogue may be interpreted legitimately as a Bill of Rights, perhaps the world's first Bill of Rights. Yet unlike modern bills of

St. Catherine's Monastery as seen from atop Mount Sinai where Moses received the Ten Commandments.

rights, this document seeks not to secure my rights but to protect the rights of others. I am perceived as a potential violator of the other person's rights. Understood this way, the significance of the 10 declarations may be summarized as follows:

(1) God's right to exclusive allegiance (Exod. 20:3; Deut. 5:7).

(2) God's right to self-definition (Exod. 20:4-6; Deut. 5:8-10).

(3) God's right to proper representation by His people (Exod. 20:7; Deut. 5:11).

(4) God's right to His people's time (Exod. 20:8-11); a household's right to humane treatment by the head of the house (Deut. 5:12-15).

(5) My parents' right to respect (Exod. 20:12; Deut. 5:16).

(6) My neighbor's right to life (Exod. 20:13; Deut. 5:17).

(7) My neighbor's right to a secure marriage (Exod. 20:14; Deut. 5:18).

(8) My neighbor's right to personal property (Exod. 20:15; Deut. 5:19).

(9) My neighbor's right to an honest hearing in court (Exod. 20:16; Deut. 5:20).

(10) My neighbor's right to secure existence in the community (Exod. 20:17; Deut. 5:21).

The first four statements protect the rights of the covenant Lord; the last six protect the rights of the covenant community. The Decalogue calls on the redeemed to respond to the grace they have experienced in salvation with covenant commitment, first to God, and then to others. This is the essence of "love" (*'ahab*) as understood in both the OT and NT. See *Law, Ten Commandments, Torah.*   *Daniel I. Block*

TENDERHEARTED KJV used "tenderhearted" in two senses: of timidity (2 Chron. 13:7) and of compassion (Eph. 4:32). See *Bowels; Compassion.*

TENON KJV, NASB, REB, RSV translation of a Hebrew term meaning "hands," applied to projections designed to fit into a mortise or socket to form a joint (Exod. 26:17,19; 36:22,24). Other translations employ "projections" (NIV, TEV) or "pegs" (NRSV).

TERAH (Tĕr´ ă) Personal name, perhaps meaning "ibex." **1.** The father of Abraham, Nahor, and Haran (Gen. 11:26). Along with a migration of people from Ur of the Chaldees, Terah moved his family, following the Euphrates River to Haran (11:31). He intended to continue from Haran into Canaan but died in Mesopotamia at the age of 205 (11:32). A debate has centered on Terah's religious practices, for Josh. 24:2 apparently points to his family when it claims records that the father worshiped gods other than Yahweh. **2.** Wilderness campsite (Num. 33: 27-28).

TERAPHIM (Tĕr´ ă phĭm) Transliteration of a Hebrew word for household idols of indeterminate size and shape. They were also referred to as "gods" (cp. Gen. 31: 19,30-35; 1 Sam. 19:13). Some scholars have understood ancient Near Eastern rights of inheritance as being based on the possession of these images as shown in Nuzi inheritance documents. However, the evidence is ambiguous in determining the motive of Rachel's theft or their overall meaning. Jacob (Gen. 35:2) disposed of such religious artifacts before returning to Bethel. Teraphim were sometimes used for divination (Judg. 17:5; 18:14-20; 1 Sam. 15:23; 2 Kings 23:24; Hos. 3:4; Ezek. 21:21; Zech. 10:2). The Bible condemns such idolatrous practices, however. Translations used different words in different passages to translate "teraphim." See *Divination and Magic.*

David M. Fleming

TEREBINTH (Tĕr´ ə bĭnth) Large, spreading tree whose species is uncertain so that translations vary in reading the Hebrew *'elah* into English (cp. 2 Sam. 18:9; Isa. 1:30; 6:13). The tree had religious connections as a place under which pagan gods were worshiped (Hos. 4:13; Ezek. 6:13) which were at times taken up in Israel's religion (Gen. 35:4; Josh. 24:26; Judg. 6:11; 1 Kings 13:14). See *Diviner's Oak.*

TERESH (Tĕ´ rĕsh) Personal name meaning "firm, solid," or derived from an Old Persian term meaning "desire." One of two royal eunuchs who plotted an unsuccessful assassination of the Persian king Ahasuerus. Following their exposure by Mordecai, the two were hung (Esther 2:21-23).

TERRACE KJV translation of a Hebrew term of uncertain meaning (2 Chron. 9:11). Most modern translations follow the earliest Greek and Latin versions in reading "steps" (NASB, NIV, RSV) or "stairs" (TEV). REB reads "stands."

TERROR See *Fear; Fear of Isaac.*

TERTIUS (Tẽr´ shĭ ŭs) Latin personal name meaning "third [son]." Paul's amanuensis (secretary) for the writing of Romans who included his own greeting at Rom. 16:22. Some suggest that Quartus, whose name means "fourth," is perhaps Tertius' younger brother (Rom. 16:23).

TERTULLUS (Tẽr tŭl´ lŭs) Diminutive of the personal name Tertius, meaning "third" (Acts 24:1-8). Tertullus was the prosecutor opposing Paul before Felix, the Roman governor of Judea. Tertullus accused Paul of being a political agitator and of attempting to defile the temple. According to the longer Western text (24:7), Tertullus was a Jew. The shorter text allows for his being a Roman. Whatever his ethnic origin, he was skilled in judicial oratory and was familiar with Roman legal conventions.

TESTAMENT See *Covenant.*

TETH (Tãth) Ninth letter of the Hebrew alphabet which KJV used as a heading for Ps. 119:65-72, each verse of which begins with this letter.

TETRARCH Political position in the early Roman Empire. It designated the size of the territory ruled (literally the "fourth part") and the amount of dependence on Roman authority. Luke 3:1 names one of the tetrarchs who served in the year of Jesus' birth. The position became less powerful with time, and the limits of authority narrowed. When Herod the Great died, his kingdom was divided among his three sons, one of whom was called "ethnarch" while the other two were named tetrarchs. See *Roman Law.*

TETRATEUCH See *Pentateuch.*

TEXTUAL CRITICISM, NEW TESTAMENT
Textual Criticism (sometimes called Lower Criticism) is the art and science of reconstructing the text of a work that no longer exists in its original form. We should note that the word "criticism" is not a negative term. It refers to methods of careful study and analysis. When applied to the NT, the ultimate purpose is to determine the original text of each book with the greatest possible degree of detail and accuracy through the careful study and comparison of all extant manuscripts. This is accomplished primarily by the collation of manuscripts and evaluation of the data derived from collation. To collate is to compare the text of a manuscript with a base text, letter by letter, and to record each and every difference from the base text. By the comparison of the collations of as many manuscripts as possible, at all places where manuscripts differ (called variant readings or variants), the original text is sought. This process of comparison and evaluation is the primary element of the reconstruction of the original text.

Other objectives include following the historical transmission of the text (determining the text that was used at particular times and places) and determining relationships between and among manuscripts (allowing them to be grouped into groups, families, and text-types). This allows many insights into the theological situations and controversies that occurred during the early centuries of Christian history and into the historical development of Christian doctrine.

It is important to remember that prior to the printing press every copy of Scripture was made by hand, and all hand-copied documents of substantial length of the same document differ from one another. No two handwritten NT manuscripts of any NT book or group of books are identical. But we have every reason to believe that every original reading has survived in some manuscripts. That is why textual critics study as many manuscripts as possible.

Manuscripts of the Greek NT generally contain a group of books: Gospels, Pauline Epistles, Acts and the General Epistles, or Revelation (which generally circulated alone). Fewer than 60 manuscripts once contained the entire text of the Greek NT. Manuscripts useful for establishing the original text of the Greek NT are of six types. The very oldest and best are written on papyrus. About 115 Papyri have been identified, many of them from the second century. Most of the Papyri have a small amount of text, but some are extensive. Uncial manuscripts are written in large letters similar to capital letters. The great early Codexes Sinaiticus, Vaticanus, and Alexandrinus are among the Uncials. Over 300 Uncials have been identified, dating from the fourth through the 10th centuries. The Papyri and the Uncials are our most important sources. Minuscule manuscripts are written in a cursive style of handwriting that developed after the eighth century. Over 2,800 Minuscules are known, dating from the ninth through the 16th centuries.

Lectionaries are NT texts arranged according to a reading schedule through the year for public worship. These date from the eighth through the 16th centuries, but some are valuable as they are copied from a much older exemplar. Over 2,400 lectionaries have been classified. The texts used by the early church fathers may be determined by studying their quotations of the Bible. As some of these are quite early, this is a valuable type of resource. Early translations of the Greek NT into other languages (versions) can be very useful, as they were translated from early manuscripts that no longer exist. Among the important early versions are the Latin, Syriac, Coptic, Armenian, Georgian, Ethiopic, and Slavonic. See *Bible Texts and Versions.*

A family, or group, of manuscripts is relatively tight knit, exhibiting striking similarities analogous to a family resemblance. A text-type is more broadly based, with definite patterns of common readings. Text-types developed in particular regions where similar exemplars were repeatedly used for copying the NT. Four text-types are identified.

The Alexandrian (Egyptian) text-type, accepted as the earliest and best by most scholars, originated with well-trained scribes in the vicinity of Alexandria, Egypt, in the second century. The oldest and best papyrus and early parchment manuscripts are of this type. The Western text-type also originated in the second century and was widely distributed. The Western text is characterized by additions to the text and paraphrase, indicating a freer and less disciplined copy process. The Western text of Acts is about 10 percent longer than the Alexandrian. The Caesarean text-type is thought to have originated when the church father Origen (third century) took early Egyptian texts with him from Alexandria to Caesarea in Palestine, and later on to Jerusalem, where they were used as exemplars for copying the Greek NT. The Caesarean tends to mix readings that are distinctively Alexandrian and Western. The Caesarean is the least homogenous of the text-types, and some scholars dispute its existence.

The latest text-type is the Byzantine (also called Koine, Syrian, or Antiochean), which did not appear until late in the fourth century. The earliest extant Byzantine manuscripts are from the fifth century. Based on a late third-century edition of the Greek NT by Lucian of Antioch in Syria, the Byzantine deliberately combined ele-

ments of the earlier text-types (called conflation of readings). Lucian and later editors wanted to produce a complete, smooth, and easy-to-read text. By the time the Byzantine text-type originated, all the others were established, as is demonstrated by the absence of distinctively Byzantine readings in earlier manuscripts. Thus the Byzantine is secondary in nature. Only very rarely (two times) does a distinctively Byzantine reading preserve an original reading in preference to the other text-types. The Byzantine is represented in the great majority of surviving NT manuscripts and became the standard text of the Greek Orthodox churches. This standardization and the preponderance of Byzantine manuscripts occurred primarily because the church in the West abandoned Greek in favor of Latin, and Greek continued to be used and the Greek NT continued to be copied in Greek only in the Eastern churches. The large number of these manuscripts does not mean that they are the best or that they represent the original text. Clearly they are not and do not. Manuscripts must be weighed as to their value, not just counted. A great number of inferior manuscripts does not somehow make theirs the best text. See *Textus Receptus.*

Variant readings occur only in about 5 percent of the Greek NT text, and so all the manuscripts agree about 95 percent of the time. Only about 2,100 variant readings may be considered "significant" and in no instance is any point of Christian doctrine challenged or questioned by a variant reading. Only about 1.67 percent of the entire Greek NT text still is questioned at all. We may be confident that our current eclectic, or critical, Greek NT text (an eclectic, or critical text is one based on the study of as many manuscripts as possible), is far beyond 99 percent established. In fact, there is more variation among some English translations of the Bible than there is among the manuscripts of the Greek NT. God's Word is infallible and inerrant in its original copies (autographs), all of which have perished. Textual critics of the Greek NT will continue their work until, if possible, the original of every questioned reading is firmly established.

Textual critics operate by certain procedures called the "Canons of Textual Criticism." Variant readings are categorized as intentional or unintentional and as significant or insignificant. The overwhelming majority of all variants are unintentional and insignificant, involving spelling. The significant variant readings in manuscripts are evaluated by study of internal (literary) evidence, related to the particular manuscript itself (like scribal practices and stylistic matters), and external (historical) evidence (like the date, geographic distribution, and relationships to other manuscripts). Unintentional variants may be the result of errors of sight, hearing, lack of concentration, or poor judgment, on the part of the scribe. Intentional variants generally occurred when the scribe thought he was improving the text by making spelling or grammar changes, changes for liturgical (worship) use, correcting geography or history, or harmonizing parallel passages (especially in the Synoptic Gospels). Old Testament quotations were sometimes expanded and natural complements were added (such as changing Jesus to Lord Jesus or to Lord Jesus Christ). Occasionally changes were made for doctrinal reasons. Most of these were intended to make the text more orthodox (as the scribe understood orthodoxy). This explanation may not sound like it, but on the whole scribes were remarkably scrupulous and careful to be faithful to the text they were copying.

When evaluating internal evidence, perhaps the key consideration is determining which reading best accounts for the rise of the other readings. The more difficult reading is usually preferred, as scribes were more likely to make a reading easier rather than harder to understand. The shorter reading is generally preferred, as additions to the text are far more common than exclusions. When considering external evidence, earlier manuscripts are generally preferred because they were the result of a shorter copy process and thus are closer to the original. Place of origin, if known, is important, as are textual affinities to the various manuscript families and text-types. The wider a particular reading was distributed geographically at an early date, the more likely it is to be original. All the evidence is considered, readings from manuscripts of all text-types are evaluated, and a decision is made as to which reading is most likely original. Textual Criticism is a science, but it is also an art, and the subjective element can never be completely eliminated. This is why textual critics work together in cooperative efforts, so that all perspectives are considered and obvious biases are not allowed to determine the outcome.

There are two commonly used critical Greek NTs, the Nestle/Aland (currently in its 27th edition—N/A27) and the United Bible Societies (currently in its 4th Revised Edition—UBS4). The Nestle/Aland began with the work of Erwin Nestle late in the 19th century, which was later taken over by his son, Eberhard. Still later, Kurt Aland and a committee became responsible for it. In 1966 the United Bible Societies produced an edition of the Greek NT primarily for the use of students and translators. Since 1979 the text of these two Greek NTs has been the same, being under the supervision of the same committee. The difference is in the accompanying critical apparatuses. In a critical apparatus, significant variant readings and the evidence supporting them are placed at the bottom of each page, so that each student of the Greek NT may evaluate each variant for himself or herself. The critical apparatus of the N/A27 contains more variants and is thus more useful to scholars. The apparatus in the UBS4 contains fewer variants, but more evidence is given for each one, making it more useful to students and translators. Readings in the text at places of variation in the UBS4 are graded as to their certainty (A, B, C, D) by vote of the editorial committee.

As more and more manuscripts are collated and compared, these data are entered into databases for consideration of inclusion in future editions of the Greek NT. A major international effort, the International Greek New Testament Project, is at work on a new critical edition of the Greek NT. The Gospel of Luke is complete, the Gospel of John is nearing completion, and work is under way on the book of Acts. The work is coordinated by many leading scholars, such as Dr. Bill Warren, Director of the Center for New Testament Textual Studies at New Orleans Baptist Theological Seminary. The New Orleans Center figures prominently in the effort, annually collating more manuscripts than all other North American institutions combined.

We have more copies of all or part of the Greek NT than of any other ancient text, approximately 5,700. Scholars of other ancient literature wish they could establish the texts they study as completely as the text of the Greek NT, but they cannot because their ancient documents survive in only a few, or in rare instances, a few hundred copies. Thus the Greek text of the NT is the best attested and most accurate of any ancient document. We may have confidence that the Bibles we use, based on the critical texts of the Greek NT and Hebrew OT, are the pure Word of God. See *Bible Texts and Versions; Textual Criticism, Old Testament.*

Charles W. Draper

TEXTUAL CRITICISM, OLD TESTAMENT

Textual criticism (sometimes called lower criticism) is the study of copies of any work whose original no longer survives. We should note that "criticism" is not a negative word in this context. It is rather careful study and analysis. When applied to the OT it refers to the ongoing effort to study the ancient Hebrew text of the OT as thoroughly as possible. Thousands of copies of all or part of the Hebrew OT have survived, but until recent decades nearly all of them represented a fairly uniform and stabilized text. Since the middle of the 20th century exciting discoveries have been made that expand our knowledge of the development of the original Hebrew text and its history of transmission.

The Dead Sea Scrolls are the most famous finds, containing about 40,000 fragments representing some 600 documents, 200 of them biblical texts. These predate our next oldest manuscripts of the OT by about 1,000 years, and their importance can scarcely be overstated. But also, manuscripts have been found at the Jewish fortress of Masada, at Muraba'at near the Dead Sea, at a Cairo synagogue Genizah (a storage room for worn texts awaiting proper disposal), and two tiny silver amulets have surfaced that contain a quotation from Numbers. These demonstrate that a process of development did indeed occur, but they also show that the later, stabilized text (the Masoretic text) is highly accurate. Far beyond 90 percent of the text is firmly established, and serious questions remain at only a very small percentage of variants. Old Testament textual critics are therefore more thoroughly equipped today to tackle difficult textual issues than at any time in the past. See *Bible Texts and Versions.*

As in NT textual criticism, manuscripts may be studied and evaluated through the data derived from the collation of manuscripts. To collate is to compare the text of a manuscript to a base, or standard, text and to note each and every difference from the base text. Places where manuscripts differ are called variant readings, or variants. The ultimate purpose is to establish the original reading at each place of variation.

Unlike NT textual criticism, OT textual criticism deals with some items other than the words of the text, because Hebrew manuscripts contain marginal readings pertaining to the text which are the product of an ancient practice of textual criticism. These shed light on the transmission of the text and aid the textual critic in making decisions about which reading is most likely to be the original.

Textual critics of the Hebrew OT are guided by "canons," as are NT textual critics, but these are somewhat different from those for the study of the NT. The task is both science and art, and a degree of subjectivity cannot be avoided. Because the text is so thoroughly standard, OT textual criticism affects mostly relatively insignificant details and inconsistencies. Manuscripts must be evaluated ("weighed") as to their significance and not just counted. Internal (literary) evidence of the manuscript being studied (like scribal tendencies, literary structures, grammar, syntax, chiasmic structures, acrostic patterns, and sentence structure) is considered. External (historical) evidence (like date and place of writing, and relationships to other manuscripts) is considered also. The identity of the reading most appropriate for the immediate context is sought. The reading that is most likely to account for the other variants is generally preferred, as are the most distinct reading and the shortest reading. Early translations of the Hebrew OT (early Greek and the Greek Septuagint, Aramaic Targums, Syriac Peshitta, and Latin) also are valuable, as they may sometimes represent an early Hebrew exemplar. See *Textual Criticism, New Testament.*

More OT textual critics are active currently than ever before. The current scholarly text, *Biblia Hebraica Stuttgartensia*, is based on the Leningrad Codex (A.D. 1009) and is under revision. The new edition, *Biblia Hebraica Quinta*, will be completed in the near future. A sample of it has been published (Ruth). A new edition, also based on the Leningrad Codex, *Biblia Hebraica Leningradensia*, has been prepared by Tel Aviv University. The long awaited *Hebrew University Bible*, based on the Aleppo Codex (A.D. 930), has been in development since 1955. Isaiah and Jeremiah have been published. All these editions are "diplomatic," that is, they are based on a single manuscript. Though they have critical apparatuses that record variant readings, they are not true eclectic, or critical, texts (based on the study of many manuscripts). The editors' choices of the earliest recoverable readings remain in one of the several accompanying critical apparatuses. Various textual traditions are extant in the many manuscripts of the Hebrew Bible, and these are being studied, yet all the current texts retain the priority of one branch of the Masoretic text, that of the ben Asher family of Tiberian Masoretes. Admittedly, it became the standardized text and is best preserved, but it is itself a critical text produced long ago and far away without all the resources available to scholars today. A Hebrew text could be produced that is truly eclectic, a true *editio critica maior*, utilizing all available manuscript sources. The proposed *Oxford Hebrew Bible* of Oxford University Press appears to have an eclectic text as its goal. Regardless, the next generation will see in print richer resources for the careful study of the Hebrew text of the OT than have ever been available before.

Some argue for the priority of the ben Chayim text of the Hebrew OT over that of the traditional Masoretic text, considering it the *textus receptus* of the OT. The arguments for this are unconvincing, as the stated objective of Jacob ben Chayim was to recover the Masoretic text of Aaron ben Moses ben Asher, which is exactly what we have in the Leningrad and Aleppo Codexes. See *Textus Receptus*.

Charles W. Draper

TEXTUS RECEPTUS Term that is generally applied to certain printed editions of the Greek NT, but sometimes extended to refer also to the ben Chayim edition of the Hebrew OT.

The first Greek NT to be printed (1514), in preparation for 12 years, was edited by James Lopez de Stunica and sponsored by Spanish Cardinal Ximenes as part of the great Complutensian Polyglot Bible (a polyglot contains multiple translations or versions). The Complutensian contained Latin, Aramaic, Hebrew, and Greek versions. Formal Papal approval for its distribution did not come until 1521, and it was not distributed until 1522. The massive volume was not often reproduced in later years. In 1515 the Dutch Roman Catholic humanist NT scholar, Desiderius Erasmus of Rotterdam, was hired by a printer in Basel, Switzerland, Johann Froben, to produce an edition of the Greek NT. Wanting to beat Ximenes' edition into print, Froben gave Erasmus less than six months to complete his

work on a critical text (a critical text is one based on comparison of more than one manuscript). The work extended to 10 months and Erasmus's Greek NT (a diglot, with Greek and Latin text on facing pages) was released in 1516.

According to Erasmus, he had access to only six manuscripts, none of them complete. His oldest and best manuscript (Codex 1) was from the 10th century, but he did not use it much because for some reason he did not trust it. The Gospels were in four of the manuscripts, the oldest from the 15th century. Acts and the General Epistles were in three, the oldest from the 13th century. The Paulines were in four of these late manuscripts. For Revelation he had only one manuscript (from the 12th century), and it was missing the last page, so Erasmus had to translate the last six verses of Revelation from the Latin Vulgate into Greek. Where his manuscripts were unclear or defective, Erasmus consulted the Vulgate, resulting in at least a dozen places where his reading is supported by no Greek manuscript. Due to the rush to get it into print, there were many printing errors in the first edition. Erasmus himself said that this work was "precipitated rather than edited." His second edition (1522) contained over 400 corrections and changes. Luther made his German translation from the second edition. The third edition was again somewhat changed but not enough to correct its massive deficiencies. This third edition was the basis for the "Textus Receptus" and was published by various people with little change over the next four centuries. Recognizing the superiority of the Ximenes text, Erasmus drew on it to make hundreds of changes in his fourth (1527) and fifth (1535) editions, but these were not reproduced often. Thus, primarily because it was distributed first, cost less, and was smaller in size, Erasmus's work became the standard text for hundreds of years.

Erasmus's work essentially was reproduced in four editions by the French printer Robert Estienne (latinized as Stephanus) and in nine editions (1565–1604) by Reformation scholar Theodore Beza. Stephanus's fourth edition (1551) and Beza's text differed somewhat from Erasmus's, and it is these editions which are most commonly referred to as the Textus Receptus (even though the term did not originate until 1633). Stephanus, for his fourth edition (1551), included some readings from the Complutensian Polyglot and Codex Bezae (fifth century). Beza, though he followed Erasmus and Stephanus closely, did employ in some readings Codex Claromontanus (sixth century), which he owned, in his later editions. Both of these early manuscripts were used only infrequently because they differed from Erasmus so much. The texts of Beza and Stephanus underlie the NT of the King James Version of 1611.

Dutch printers, the Elzivirs, produced seven editions of the Greek NT, mainly taken from Beza's 1565 edition, beginning in 1624. There were two Elzivir brothers, Bonaventure and Matthew, and Matthew's son Abraham. Their first edition was heavily criticized for numerous errors. Having carefully corrected the first edition, in their second edition (1633) they wrote in the preface the Latin statement, "Textum ergo habes, nunc ab omnibus receptum: in quo nihil immutatum aut corruptum damus" ("You have therefore the text now received by all: in which we give nothing altered or corrupt.") Two words were extracted from this sentence, Receptum (Received) and Textum (Text), placed in their nominative forms, Textus Receptus (Received Text), and became the common way to refer to this and other editions of the Greek NT, even to some editions originating decades before the term arose. Thus, from what Bruce Metzger called a "more or less casual phrase advertising the edition," and J. K. Elliott termed "meaningless advertising," and Eldon Epp described as an "arrogant generalization," came a term of monumental import. The preface statement was the equivalent of a modern publisher's promotional "blurb." No authority figure of any kind beyond a printer ever anointed this text as superior to other texts, much less as "original." The Textus Receptus is itself a critical text, but unlike modern critical editions based on at least hundreds of manuscripts, it was based in total on fewer than 10.

Sometimes the Textus Receptus is confused with the Majority Text, a recent critical Greek NT based on the study of hundreds of the Byzantine manuscripts. They are not the same, as the Majority Text differs from the Textus Receptus at about 1,800 places, including some places where the Textus Receptus reading is not the majority reading. See *Textual Criticism, New Testament.*

Though the underlying textual traditions of the Hebrew OT are obviously different, the arguments for the priority of the ben Chayim text of the Hebrew OT over the Masoretic Text of the ben Asher family are similarly weak and yield the same kind of conclusion. The Masoretic text is earlier and more reliable. See *Textual Criticism, Old Testament.*

Erasmus would be the first to applaud the study of as many manuscripts as possible and would be horrified to know that his tentative work achieved such a revered status. Until the end of his life, he continued to improve his Greek NT whenever better manuscripts and editions became available to him.

Charles W. Draper

THADDAEUS (Thăd´ ĭ ŭs) Personal name, perhaps meaning "gift of God" in Greek but derived from Hebrew or Aramaic meaning "breast." See *Disciple; Judas; Lebbeus.*

THAHASH (Thā´ hăsh) (KJV) See *Tahash.*

THAMAH (Thā´ mah) (KJV, Ezra 2:53) See *Temah.*

THAMAR (Thā´ mär) (KJV, Matt. 1:3) See *Tamar.*

THANKSGIVING 1. Gratitude directed towards God (except Luke 17:9; Acts 24:3; Rom. 16:4), generally in response to God's concrete acts in history. Thanksgiving was central to OT worship. Sacrifice and offerings were to be made not grudgingly but with thanksgiving (Ps. 54:6; Jon. 2:9). The psalmist valued a song of thanksgiving more than sacrifice (Ps. 69:30-31). David employed Levites "to commemorate the LORD God of Israel, and to give Him thanks and praise." (1 Chron. 16:4 HCSB; 23:30; Neh. 12:46). Pilgrimage to the temple and temple worship were characterized by thanksgiving (Pss. 42:4; 95:2; 100:4; 122:4). Thankfulness was expressed: for personal (Ps. 35:18) and national deliverance (Ps. 44:7-8); for God's faithfulness to the covenant (Ps. 100:5); and for forgiveness (Ps. 30:4-5; Isa. 12:1). All creation joins in offering thanks to God (Ps. 145:10). See *Psalms, Book of.*

Thanksgiving is a natural element of Christian worship (1 Cor. 14:16-17) and is to characterize all of Christian life (Col. 2:7; 4:2). Early Christians expressed thanks: for Christ's healing ministry (Luke 17:16); for Christ's deliverance of the believer from sin (Rom. 6:17-18; 7:25); for God's indescribable gift of grace in Christ (2 Cor.

9:14-15; 1 Cor. 15:57; cp. Rom. 1:21); and for the faith of fellow Christians (Rom. 1:8).

2. Epistolary thanksgiving: an element in the opening of a typical Greek letter. All of the Pauline Letters with the exception of Galatians begin with a thanksgiving. See *Letter.*

THARA (Thā´ rá) (KJV, Luke 3:34) See *Terah.*

THARSHISH (Thär´ shĭsh) (KJV, 1 Kings 10:22; 22:48; 1 Chron. 7:10) See *Tarshish.*

THEATER Public drama was apparently unknown in OT Israel except for possible worship activities and only arrived with the Greeks after 400 B.C. As a symbol of Greco-Roman culture, the presence of theaters in Palestine was a constant reminder of Greek and Roman control of the Jewish state. Herod I built numerous theaters in the Greek cities during his reign in Palestine (37–4 B.C.). Their presence, especially near the temple in Jerusalem, continually infuriated the Jews. Outside of Israel and across the Roman Empire, theaters flourished. Public performances began with a sacrifice to a pagan deity, usually the patron god of the city. Dramas and comedies included historical or political themes and were often lewd and suggestive. The semicircular seats of the theater rose step fashion, either up a natural hillside or on artificial tiers. A facade of several stories (as high as the uppermost seats) was decorated with sculptures and stood behind the stage. The general public sat in the higher seats, farther back, but wealthier patrons were given seats lower and closer to the stage. A large central area was reserved for the local governor or ruler. Theaters varied in size. Those in small towns held approximately 4,000 persons, while

The Roman Theater at the site of ancient Aspendos located in southern Turkey.

A tomb painting from the Valley of the Kings, the mortuary area across the Nile River from Thebes.

larger theaters, such as that in Ephesus where Paul was denounced (Acts 19:29), were capable of holding 25,000 or more. See *Greece; Rome and the Roman Empire.*

David Maltsberger

THEBES (Thēbz) Capital of Egypt's Upper Kingdom for most of its history (about 2000–661 B.C.). The city waned only during the brief Hyksos period (about 1750–1550 B.C.). Thebes (called "No" in KJV) was the center of worship

The Hypostyle Hall of Amun-Re's Temple at Karnak in the northern part of ancient Thebes in Egypt.

T

for the god Amon, a chief deity in Egyptian religion. Majestic temples remain as monuments to the city's dedication to Amon. See *Egypt*.

THEBEZ (Thē´ bĕz) Likely Tubas, 13 miles northeast of Shechem where the roads from Shechem and Dothan converge to lead down to the Jordan Valley. During the siege of Thebez, a woman of the city fatally wounded Abimelech by throwing an upper millstone on his head (Judg. 9:50-53; 2 Sam. 11:21).

THEFT See *Crimes and Punishment; Ethics; Law, Ten Commandments, Torah*.

THELASAR (Thə lā´ sär) (KJV) See *Tel-assar*.

THEOCRACY Form of government in which God directly rules. As the Sovereign King, God may rule directly through unmediated means, or He may choose to use various mediators to manifest His rule. In either case, God Himself is the Sovereign Ruler.

The theocracy of God is revealed progressively in the Scripture. A case could be made that the earliest forms of God's governing were His direct encounters with Adam in the garden of Eden. It was not until the call of Abram in Ur of the Chaldees (Gen. 12), however, that the plan of God to establish a national theocracy upon the earth was revealed.

The giving of the Mosaic law by God to the Israelites gave the Hebrew people a unique theocratic structure. The civil and moral laws provided the guidance for governance of the state and personal relationships within the theocracy. These laws would establish the basic social structures of the theocratic state: judicial decision-making, processes of adjudication, marital guidelines, parental responsibilities, regard for human life, property rights, and so forth. The ceremonial law addressed the issues of religious observances and practice.

The next step in the development of the theocratic state was the taking of promised land (the conquest) and the period of the judges (conflict). Under Joshua's capable leadership, the Israelites were able to enter and conquer Canaan according to the promises of God. In this act the people of God were provided a land in which to build a theocratic state.

The people soon asked for a king. The existence of a human king, however, did not ideally conflict with the theocracy. The king, as chosen by God, would not be a despotic, selfish dictator,

Ram-headed sphinxes line the processional avenue before the temple of Amun-Re at Thebes.

but rather a man who would walk in the light of the Lord and seek God's guidance in all matters. Thus, the rule of the human monarch would glorify God and manifest the theocratic ideal.

The theocratic ideal experience declined among the Israelites following the division of the monarchy and the exilic/postexilic periods. There is a sense, however, in which the ideal of a theocracy is resumed in the NT. Christ, as the Messiah and the Davidic King, is the person in whom the kingdom of God resides. With His preaching and earthly ministry, He gave evidence that "the kingdom of God is at hand." Further, following His resurrection, He declared to His followers: "All authority has been given to Me in heaven and on earth. Go, therefore, and make disciples of all nations" (Matt. 28:18-20, HCSB). With this declaration the risen King commissioned His followers to go and to proclaim the existence of His kingdom. As Christians individually and corporately submit and propagate the Lordship of Christ, in a sense they experience and express the theocratic ideal of God's direct governance. Thus, a NT church should endeavor to realize and appropriate the direct rule of the Sovereign King in all areas

Stan Norman

THEOLOGY, BIBLICAL Discussion of what the Bible itself teaches about God and His dealings with human beings and the rest of creation. Biblical theology has existed since the Bible was written. For instance, in Deut. 1–11 Moses describes and interprets God's past acts on Israel's behalf recorded in Exodus–Numbers even as he discloses more divine revelation. Samuel interprets Israel's past theologically in 1 Sam. 8–12, Stephen does the same in Acts 7, and the list of examples could be extended.

Though biblical theology originated in biblical times, its formal modern academic origins are generally traced to 1787, when J. P. Gabler asserted the need for biblical theology to stand over against systematic theology so that church doctrine would not predetermine the meaning of biblical texts. This declaration began the practice of defining biblical theology by contrasting it with systematic theology, historical theology, and pastoral theology. This method of defining biblical theology usually follows similar lines. Whereas systematic theology uses categories drawn from philosophy as well as from the Bible, biblical theology uses categories drawn solely from Scripture. Historical theology traces the history of doctrinal development, but biblical theology describes the actual elements of those doctrines. Pastoral theology applies the contents of the Bible, while biblical theology describes them, and so forth.

These distinctions are not always useful, however, since biblical theology must organize its findings. Christians have wrestled with the Bible's theology throughout church history, and theological research should aid church ministry. Also, biblical theology has the potential to aid systematic theology by providing biblically accurate data and to help pastoral theology by providing data that is both theologically and pastorally sound. When practiced appropriately, biblical theology works in conjunction with other theological disciplines, not strictly in contrast to them.

Foundational Principles Because it takes its subject matter from the Bible, biblical theology asserts some foundational principles. First, Ps. 19:7-11 claims that the OT's law is "perfect," its testimonies "trustworthy," its precepts "right," its commandments "radiant," and its rules "reliable and altogether righteous" (HCSB). Paul summarizes his opinions on the scriptures (holy writings) by asserting that they are all "inspired by God and profitable for teaching, for rebuking, for correcting, for training in righteousness" (2 Tim. 3:16). Therefore, the Bible claims that the whole Bible is God's breathed out (inspired) word written down for permanent preservation and, as a result, is authoritative and useful for godly living for every successive generation. Second, the Bible reflects the character of the one whose word it reports. Deuteronomy 6:4-9 states that "God, the LORD is One," or a unified, whole person. Thus, His word and its message are also a unified whole. As Jesus says, "The Scripture cannot be broken" (John 10:35). Further, since God never lies (Heb. 6:18), this unified word is truthful. Third, the Bible unfolds in a particular order, which is reflected in Luke 24:44, when Jesus taught two disciples the things written about Himself in the Law, Prophets, and Psalms. This order follows the order commonly accepted in first-century Palestinian Judaism and is reflected in the OT itself (Josh. 1:1-9; Ps. 1). The NT also has three clear segments, the Gospels and Acts, the Pauline epistles, and the General epistles and Revelation. Thus, biblical theology has a clear order in which to work that is evident in the text of Scripture. Fourth, God works in history to redeem human beings, so human history has significance. This fact is evident in passages like Pss. 78; 89; and 104–106 that survey God's past actions. It is also evident from the many biblical books that highlight Israelite and church history. Fifth, the life, death, resurrection, and second coming of Jesus Christ are the literary and thematic heart of the Bible. God's saving work in history culminates in these deeds. Sixth, God's people are redeemed by God and exist to glorify God in the world by being holy people (Exod. 19:5-6; 1 Peter 2:5-9). Seventh, within the unity of the Bible, there is obvious diversity. But this diversity operates in complementary, not contradictory, ways.

Methodology Even if one accepts these foundational principles, the Bible does not state exactly how to report what the Bible says about God and His relationship with the human race. Therefore, scholars have approached biblical theology from a variety of ways. Some have sought a central theme that helps hold the Bible's message together, such as creation, covenant, kingdom, salvation (or redemptive) history, the messianic promise, the gospel, new creation, God's presence, or some other important biblical idea. They then use that theme to integrate related ideas. Others order their study by examining major historical eras in the Bible and the themes that arose within them. Still others have focused on the NT's preaching of the gospel and how that message pulls together the Bible's major themes. Each of these methods is valid in its own way, and each one contributes to an understanding of biblical theology.

The description of biblical theology below utilizes the order of the Bible, major themes, and historical eras to make its points. It also highlights the character of God. This somewhat eclectic approach attempts to use the best elements of methods proven effective over the past several decades.

Biblical Theology: The Law (Genesis– Deuteronomy) Genesis begins with the assertion that God, not the gods, created the heavens and earth. This claim of one God making everything sets the Bible apart from other ancient creation accounts, all of which are polytheistic in theology. This one sovereign God rules everything yet commands human beings, who are made in His image, to rule the earth as His appointed stewards (Gen. 1:26-31). God situates man and woman in a garden, establishes a relationship with them, commands them not to eat of two trees, and places them in a committed relationship with one another (Gen. 2:4-25). Unfortunately, the woman and the man believed the word of the serpent instead of the word of God. Because of this lack of faith in their creator and His word, they sinned by eating the forbidden fruit (3:1-6). This sin led to shame and loss of perfect relationship with one another and with God (3:7-13). It also led to specific consequences, such as pain in childbirth and in her relationship with her husband for the woman and pain in his labor for the man (3:14-19). Still, all is not lost, for God disclosed that a child born in the future would defeat the serpent, and He also promised to protect the man and woman from harm (3:15,20-24). In many ways the rest of the Bible works out these basic themes. The Creator works to redeem a struggling, sinful humanity from lack of trust in Him. Only through God's redemptive work can human beings recover their lost relationship with God and one another.

As sin spread on earth from the first persons to their children and each successive generation, the Creator decided to destroy the creation by water, sparing only Noah and his family (4:1–8:19). Thus, the Creator and Deliverer is also the Judge of creation. But this Judge is also determined to redeem. Therefore, He makes a covenant, a binding agreement between a greater and a lesser party that includes responsibilities, benefits, and consequences, with Noah and the human race, not to destroy the earth by water again. This covenant is significant in its own right, yet even more important is the first explicit making of such an agreement between God and people.

God made another essential covenant in Gen. 12:1-9, when He promised Abram that a great nation would come from his descendants, that this nation would be given Canaan as their homeland, and that all the world would be blessed by him. The Creator determined to help the whole of sinful humanity through this family, which became the Jewish people. Abraham was counted righteous because of his faith (15:6) and lived in a faithful, though imperfect, manner because of this relationship with God.

After centuries passed and the family grew into a nation of enslaved refugees in Egypt

(Exod. 1–4), God determined to deliver them from bondage through great miracles administered by Moses. This "exodus" (Exod. 5–18) demonstrated God's power over creation, God's witness to Egypt, God's faithfulness to promises made to Abraham, and God's desire to deliver His people. A mixed racial group (Exod. 12:38), the chosen people traveled to Mount Sinai, where God revealed another covenant through Moses. The purpose of this covenant was to make Israel a "kingdom of priests and a holy nation" (19:5-6).

Clearly, this covenant was based on an already existing relationship; it did not create a relationship between God and Israel. Only faith can create a relationship with God (Gen. 15:6). This covenant was intended to reflect the relationship between God and Israel so that a kingdom of priests could minister to the world God created and so bless all nations through Abraham (Gen. 12:1-9). Every law in the Mosaic covenant was intended to make Israel unique enough among the nations to glorify God in His own creation. Sadly, the whole newly delivered nation was not faithful even in its infancy (Exod. 32–34), so God's grace and mercy (Exod. 34:6-7) compelled Him to judge for the purpose of redemption.

This covenant expressed high standards yet understood that people sin. Thus, the covenant included forgiveness for sin based on sacrifices and prayer (Lev. 1–7; 16). These sacrifices were annual, seasonal, or daily in nature. They were not permanent. Still, they were effective (4:26,31; 16:21-22). God included in this covenant laws regulating a just, fair, kind, and protective society (Lev. 11–15; 17–27).

Despite all God did for Israel, the nation did not believe God sufficiently to enter the promised land when ordered to do so (Num. 14:11-12). Unbelief continued to be the root cause of sin. Thus, God judged the incipient generation and gave the land to their children (Num. 15–36). God renewed and expanded the covenant with this new generation, setting standards for the people, kings, and prophets (Deut. 1–12; 17:14-20; 18:15-22). As the capstone to the covenant, God offered the people the choice between benefits or punishments, life or death (Deut. 27–28). The supreme punishment was loss of the promised land. If God sent this punishment, the people could still find renewal by repenting of sin and returning to the Lord (Deut.

30:1-10). Grace continued to characterize God's work, and love was the motive for God's work with Israel and their response to Him (Deut. 6–7).

Biblical Theology: The Prophets The Hebrew Bible divides the Prophets into the Former and Latter Prophets, with Joshua–Kings comprising the first group and Isaiah–Malachi comprising the second. Joshua recounts God giving the promised land to Abraham's descendants, just as was pledged some six centuries earlier, while Judges demonstrates how far Israel was able to stray from the covenant's principles and to what lengths God would go to restore the people. First and Second Samuel stress the rise of the Israelite monarchy. It particularly focuses on David's slow rise to power and subsequent successes and failures. Now the Bible begins a long process of stating ways in which God's kingdom is or is not evident on earth.

Most importantly, 2 Sam. 7:1-17 relates God's covenant with David. God promised that David's son (Solomon) would succeed him, that this son would build a temple, and that David's kingdom would be eternal. This final promise led to future prophetic passages about a coming savior, a messiah, or anointed one of God. So the child mentioned in Gen. 3:15 would come through Abraham and David's line, thereby blessing all nations and providing David with an endless kingdom. This promise to David became difficult to understand when the nation divided in 930 B.C. and had its parts destroyed in 722 and 587 B.C. respectively.

Isaiah 1–12 emphasizes Israel's pattern of covenant breaking and God's two-fold response to that sin. God will send the Davidic heir to be Israel's savior and righteous leader, and God will punish all sin on judgment day, which is called "the Day of the LORD" here and elsewhere in the Bible. Isaiah 40–55 describes a servant of the Lord who ministers to God's servant Israel and to the nations (42:1-9; 49:1-7). He will die for the people's sin, make many of them righteous, and share spoils even after death (52:13–53:12). In this way He will deal with Israel and the nations' sins. At the end of time, the Lord will defeat death (25:6-12), create a new heavens and earth and a new Jerusalem (65:17-25), and judge the wicked (66:18-24).

Jeremiah and Ezekiel agree with Isaiah's assessment of the messiah and of Israel and the nation's sin. They also highlight God's future acts. Jeremiah envisions a "new covenant," one in which all those associated with it know the Lord and have His law written directly on their hearts. The problem with the old covenant was that the people broke it, not that God failed in any way (31:31-34). In the new covenant God will finally have a faithful partner. Ezekiel states that God will change Israel's hearts by placing His Spirit on their hearts (36:22-32). Again, there will be no unfaithful covenant partners. Ezekiel envisions a vast new Jerusalem where the Lord lives with His people in the absence of sin (40–48).

While they also agree with the concept of messiah and a glorious future, the Minor Prophets stress the threat of judgment, the need for repentance, and the many ways that judgment will vindicate the righteous and punish the wicked. The Day of the Lord is a constant theme; though after Israel is destroyed, the books highlight the renewal of Jerusalem and the coming of the savior. These books end with Malachi promising a new Elijah coming to prepare the people for the Day of the Lord.

Biblical Theology: The Writings This section of the OT underscores life lived in light of the covenantal history and theology introduced in the previous two sections. For instance, Psalms offers theologically driven ways to worship in the midst of Israel's history. Job and Proverbs explain living wisely in extreme and normal circumstances, as do Ruth, Ecclesiastes, Esther, and Daniel. Ezra, Nehemiah, and 1–2 Chronicles demonstrate God's determination to restore Israel to the land before the coming of the messiah. Each book contributes examples of serving God or the opposite in the midst of suffering, judgment, or renewal.

These books also contribute to the messianic promise. In particular, Psalms states that the Davidic heir will rule the nations (Pss. 2; 110), overcome death (Ps. 16), and be rejected by many (Ps. 118:22). Daniel 7:13-14 describes "one like a son of man" to whom God gives the kingdoms of the world, and this figure shares His kingdom with the holy ones.

By NT times the OT was considered God's word. Those who believed in and served God did not doubt its authority for living even when they misinterpreted it. Any new candidate for acceptance as Scripture had to prove itself the equal of the OT, not the other way around.

Biblical Theology: The Gospels and Acts The Gospels and Acts proclaim that the promised Messiah has come. Jesus of Nazareth, a Davidic descendant (Matt. 1:1-17) and a descendant of Adam (Luke 3:23-38; Gen. 3:15) is the One promised in the OT. His appearing indicates that the "kingdom of God is near," which means the Day of the Lord, God's judgment day, has come. Those who believe in Him protect themselves from the coming wrath (Matt. 3:1-12; Mark 1:14-15), and those who do not may expect certain judgment (Matt. 24; Mark 13). He is the new Moses (Matt. 5–7), the Son of Man to whom God gives the kingdom (Mark 14:62), and the Servant who dies for the people (Matt. 27:57; Luke 22:37). He is the Creator and the Word of God (John 1:1-18) and is therefore God. His life and teaching affirm and supplements the law (Matt. 5:17-20), yet also set aside its sacrifices (Matthew 27:51) and table laws (Mark 7:19).

His death is the heart of the Bible's message, and it is the means by which the new covenant with the new people of God is instituted (Luke 22:14-23). His resurrection from the dead means that He is the Lord (John 20:18). In short, He fulfills the Scriptures' specific predictions and broader patterns of the Messiah, or Christ. He also teaches how one may do God's will and glorify God on earth. His last command to His disciples is to go into all the earth with the message they have learned (Matt. 28:16-20). In this way the whole earth will be blessed through Abraham.

When John the Baptist, Jesus, and the early church preached and taught these themes, they called the sum total of this message "the gospel." The details of the gospel expand or contract depending on whether the audience knows much or little about the Bible's promises and rules (cp. Acts 2:14-41; 7:2-53; 13:13-48; 17:22-34), though the resurrection is a staple in these sermons. For the early believers the preaching of the gospel meant that the great themes of the OT were related to the life, teachings, death, resurrection, and service of Jesus Christ.

Acts introduces readers to Paul, the missionary apostle who dominates the next section of the NT. A convert from Pharisaic Judaism, Paul becomes the seminal force in early Christianity, especially in the Gentile churches. His preaching and teaching of the gospel may well be the most influential writings in the church to this day.

Biblical Theology: The Pauline Epistles
Paul's ministry lasted long enough and was diverse enough to make his epistles difficult to systematize. For the sake of this article, however, his letters may be divided into letters dealing with difficult specific church problems, letters that are more introductory or general in nature, and letters that deal with the organization and ordering of churches.

His general and introductory letters set forth his own understanding of the gospel. In Romans he stresses that people become right with God (are justified) the same way Abraham did—by faith (Rom. 1–4; Gen. 15:6). As people of faith, they live to glorify God (Rom. 5–8). Such living reflects God's gifts to human beings and results in a godly witness in the world (Rom. 12–16). Similarly, in Ephesians Paul stresses that God the Creator planned believers' salvation in Christ from the foundation of the world and sealed that salvation with the Holy Spirit (1:3-14; Ezek. 36:22-32). God has placed all of creation under Jesus' authority (1:15-22). Salvation is by grace through faith, which is God's gift, so that no one can boast. God saved believers so that they might do good works He prepared for them to do at the same time He planned their salvation—at the beginning of time (2:1-10). Jews and Gentiles share in this salvation, so God the Creator is worshiped and served throughout the world (2:11-22). The church, God's people, demonstrate God's wisdom in the world (3:1-13), for they have Christ's gifts (4:1-16), new life (4:17-32), and a new order for living in a sinful world (5:1–6:24). For Paul the gospel means that Christ is the Creator (Col. 1:15-20; John 1:1-18) and that Christ's salvation transforms people into witnesses of God's kingdom.

Paul's letters to troubled churches also provide connections to biblical theology. For example, as he deals with the Galatians, he teaches that one cannot be saved by doing "works of the law" because the Bible teaches salvation by faith (Gal. 3–4; Gen. 15:6). To proclaim the opposite pits the Law and Prophets against their own teachings. As he corrects the Corinthians, he stresses the Lord's Supper as a new covenant service (1 Cor. 11:17-34) and the reality of the resurrection as the capstone of the gospel (1 Cor. 15). As he corrects the Thessalonians' misconceptions concerning the final judgment, he asserts the coming of Christ and the Day of the Lord (1 Thess. 5:1-11). Paul fiercely defends the validity of the OT for believers (Rom. 7:1-12; 1 Cor. 10:1-13), even as he corrects misconceptions about what the law does or does not teach and examines Christian faithfulness that flows from faith in Christ (Rom. 1:16-17).

Paul's letters to his associates about the ordering of churches highlights the need for sound doctrine. False teachers will arise and pervert the true meaning of the law (1 Tim. 1:3-11), and in the last days false teachers will gain hearers (2 Tim. 3:1-10). Thus, teachers must guard the deposit of true doctrine until the Day of the Lord (2 Tim. 1:3-18). This deposit is found in God's breathed-out word, which is what Paul calls "all Scripture" (2 Tim. 3:14-17). It is this true deposit that the church leaders described must pass on to each successive generation.

Biblical Theology: The General Epistles and Revelation As a whole these books are written to churches under persecution, or at least under a great deal of pressure. Thus, they apply the great themes of biblical theology to difficult circumstances.

For instance, Hebrews proclaims Christ's superiority to the great truths and symbols of the old covenant. Christ has instituted the new covenant. He is greater than Moses, greater than angels, greater than Aaron, and greater than the OT sacrifices. Indeed, His death was the final sacrifice, the one in which all others found their fulfillment (Heb. 1–10). Therefore, the persecuted church should have faith in Him and live out that faith as they look for God's kingdom (Heb. 11–13). James teaches that they should consider persecution proof of their faith (1:2-4) and urges readers to live an active faith, for "faith, if it doesn't have works, is dead by itself" (2:14-26 HCSB).

Similarly, Peter tells his readers that they are, like Israel of old, a kingdom of priests and a holy nation (1 Pet. 2:5,9; Exod. 19:5-6). The persecuted church must glorify the Lord until the Day of the Lord comes (2 Pet. 3:1-13). John's readers have endured defections from their ranks, and the apostle helps them understand the need for confession of sin, love for one another, and an ability to forgive one another. Jude stresses contending for the faith in the last days.

The book of Revelation concludes the Bible on a triumphant note. The church is persecuted (Rev. 1–3), yet it will persevere and triumph. Judgment awaits the wicked (Rev. 20), but those who love Christ, the King of kings (19:16), will

T

inhabit the new Jerusalem promised in Isaiah, where death and sorrow have ceased (Rev. 21:1-27; Isa. 65:17-25; Ezek. 40–48).

By the end of Revelation, then, the Bible has completed a journey from creation to new creation, a journey made possible by the death and resurrection of Jesus Christ, who was sent to redeem sinful men and women from judgment on the Day of the Lord. Revelation is a colorful rendering of the gospel within biblical theology, but it is a presentation of the gospel, nonetheless. **Conclusion** Biblical theology opens up the unity of the Bible by exposing and collecting its major themes. It demonstrates the many ways in which diverse books and material are united by the character of God the Father, Son, and Holy Spirit. Without neglecting ways, the Bible declares new divine works and reapplies old truths to new situations; it highlights the wholeness of divine revelation.   *Paul House*

THEOPHANY (Thē ŏph´ á nē) Physical appearance or personal manifestation of a god to a person.
Need for a Theophany The basic postulate here is that to see God could be fatal. "He said, 'You cannot see My face, for no one can see Me and live!'" (Exod. 33:20 HCSB; cp. Gen. 16:13; Exod. 3:2-6; 19:20-21; Judg. 6:22-23; 13:20-22). Yet the record is unmistakable that people did see God, such as Moses and others at Sinai (Exod. 24:9-10); the Lord's rebuke of Aaron and Miriam (Num. 12:4-8); and the majestic vision to Isaiah (Isa. 6:1,5). Customarily, God is not revealed to ordinary sight, but at times chooses to reveal Himself in theophanies.
Kinds of Theophanies There are some five forms of theophanies.

In human form Without question the theophany in Exod. 24:10 involved the appearance of a human being, for the text clearly states that a pavement of sapphire appeared "under His feet." At Peniel, Jacob testified that he had seen God face to face (Gen. 32:30). On Mount Horeb it was the experience of Moses to speak to God "face to face, just as a man speaks with his friend" (Exod. 33:11 HCSB). In the same passage when Moses begged God to show him His glory (v. 18), the Lord graciously granted Moses a vision of Himself, saying, "I will take My hand away, and you will see My back, but My face will not be seen" (v. 23). If it is protested that the subject is enveloped in mystery, it needs to be

remembered that theology without mystery is sheer nonsense. God in His wisdom does not restrict Himself to one method of self-revelation. Notice God's pronouncement in Num. 12:6-8, which was quite unlike that of Deut. 4:12-15 where only a voice was granted.

In vision Even self-seeking Balaam was allowed by God to see the Lord in a vision (Num. 24:3-4). Isaiah, Ezekiel, and Daniel, giants among the prophets, saw God in visions (Isa. 6; Ezek. 1; Dan. 7:9). Jacob, sent off by Isaac to Paddan-aram, was granted a dream in which he saw the Lord (Gen. 28:12-13).

By the "Angel of the Lord" This is the most usual form of theophany, called the "angel of the Lord" or "angel of God." Observe it is not an "angel of God," which could include any of the angelic hosts created by God. The "angel of the Lord" is identified in the accounts with Yahweh Himself. He appears only occasionally in human form. The encounter of the angel of the Lord with Hagar is of significance in this connection (Gen. 16:7-13). See *Angels.*

Not in human form In some instances the theophany came as at the burning bush (Exod. 3:2–4:17) and in the guidance through the wilderness (13:21; cp. Acts 7:30). The glory of the Lord appears to people in numerous passages. God's presence is in a cloud (Exod. 16:10; 33:9-10; Ezek. 10:4). God was also manifest in nature and history (Isa. 6:3; Ezek. 1:28; 43:2). See *Glory.*

As the name of the Lord God's sacred name represented His presence (Deut. 12:5; Isa. 30:27; 59:19).
Contrast with the Incarnation The incarnate Christ was not, and indeed is not, a theophany. The phenomena of theophanies were temporary, for the occasion that required them and then disappeared. On the other hand, in the incarnate Christ His deity and humanity were joined, not for time alone, but for eternity. See *Incarnation; Jesus Christ.*
The Time Factor Only in the OT economy did God's people need a theophany; since the incarnation, there is no such necessity. The NT doctrine of God is final and complete. God is always present in the risen Christ and the Holy Spirit. Still, at times, God's people are more aware of that presence than at others.

Charles Lee Feinberg

THEOPHILUS (Thə ŏph´ ĭ lŭs) Personal name meaning "friend of God"; the person to whom the books of Luke and Acts were written (Luke 1:3; Acts 1:1). However, his exact identity is unknown. Speculation has ranged from the generic "friend of God" intended to all Christians to a specific benefactor, perhaps in high social and/or political standing. If the latter is true, the name may be a pseudonym to protect the individual from persecution. One conjecture holds that Theophilus was unsaved and that Luke wrote the letter to persuade his belief in Christ.

THESSALONIANS, FIRST LETTER TO THE
(Thĕs sả lō´ nĭ áns) Thessalonica was the largest city in first-century Macedonia and the capital of the province. It was a free city. Paul, Silas, and Timothy evangelized the city against the strong opposition of the Jews; but, though their stay was short, they were successful in establishing a church (Acts 17:4). There was not time to give much instruction to the new converts, so it is not surprising that questions arose as to the meaning of some aspects of the Christian faith and of the conduct demanded of believers. See *Macedonia.*

To help the new church, Paul wrote 1 Thessalonians not long after Timothy came to him (1 Thess. 3:6). This probably means not long after Timothy's arrival at Corinth (Acts 18:5) rather than his being with Paul in Athens (1 Thess. 3:1-2), for the shorter period scarcely allows enough time for the problems with which the apostle deals in the letter to have arisen. An inscription referring to Gallio (Acts 18:12) enables us to date that proconsul's time in Corinth as the early 50s. Scholars reason from this that Paul probably wrote 1 Thessalonians early in A.D. 50 (though in view of the uncertainties this must be regarded as no more than approximate). Plainly, this is one of the earliest of Paul's letters and one of the earliest Christian documents surviving.

The authenticity of 1 Thessalonians is almost universally accepted. It is Pauline in style and is mentioned in early Christian writings such as the lists of NT books given by Marcion in the first half of the second century and by the Muratorian Canon a little later. Some of the problems with which it deals must have arisen quite early in the life of the church (for instance, what will

happen to believers who die before Christ returns?).

Among the problems the Thessalonian church faced was persecution by pagans (2:14) and a temptation for believers to accept pagan sexual standards (4:4-8). Some of the Christians seem to have given up working and to have relied on the others to supply their needs (4:11-12). There was uncertainty about the fate of believers who had died, and some of the Thessalonians appear to have thought that Christ would come back soon and take them all to be with Him. What would happen to those who had died before the great event (4:13-18)? Paul's reply to this gives us information about Christ's return that we find nowhere else. Again, some of the believers seem to have been concerned about the time of Jesus' return (5:1-11). So Paul wrote this pastoral letter to meet the needs of inexperienced Christians and to bring them closer to Christ. See *Paul.*

Outline

I. The Church Is Founded on Past Faithfulness (1:1-10).
   A. Signature, address, and greeting (1:1).
   B. Past faith, love, and hope inspire thanksgiving (1:2-3).
   C. Election, power, conviction, and the Spirit brought the gospel (1:4-5).
   D. Model Christian living resulted from the gospel (1:6-7).
   E. Zealous witness and far-reaching Christian influence spread the gospel (1:8-9).
   F. Earnest hope in the resurrection marked the church's life (1:10).

II. Opposition and Persecution Cannot Halt the Gospel (2:1-20).
   A. Suffering and insult do not deter Christian witness (2:1-2).
   B. Sincerity of method and purpose stand behind gospel witness (2:3-6a).
   C. Love, not personal greed, motivates witness (2:6b-12).
   D. Steadfastness and endurance mark Christian converts (2:13-16).
   E. The gospel creates enduring fellowship and love (2:17-18).
   F. A new church becomes the reward for a Christian witness (2:19-20).

III. Concern for the Church Dominates the Minister's Heart (3:1–4:12).

T

A. Sacrificial love leads the minister to show concern even under personal persecution (3:1-5).
B. The church's faithfulness gives the minister encouragement and joy (3:6-10).
C. The concerned minister prays for the church's future (3:11-13).
D. The concerned minister teaches the church righteous living (4:1-8).
E. The concerned minister leads the church to grow in brotherly love (4:9-12).
IV. Problems Related to the Lord's Return (4:13–5:11).
A. Living and deceased believers have equal hope (4:13-18).
B. The time is uncertain (5:1-3).
C. The church needs to be alert (5:4-8).
D. Believers have assurance (5:9-11).
V. Concluding Exhortations (5:12-28).
A. Respect Christian leaders (5:12-13).
B. Care for fellow Christians (5:14-15).
C. Always be thankful (5:16-18).
D. Test prophetic utterances to God (5:19-22).
E. Commit yourself to God, who is faithful (5:23-24).
F. Closing requests and benediction (5:25-28). *Leon Morris*

THESSALONIANS, SECOND LETTER TO THE (Thĕs sả lō´ nĭ ảns) This letter claims to have been written by Paul (1:1), and the style, the language, and the theology fit in with this claim. Early writers like Polycarp and Ignatius seem to have known it, and it is included in the lists of NT books given by Marcion and the Muratorian Canon. The letter claims to have Paul's signature (3:17). Most scholars agree that this is a genuine letter of Paul written to the Thessalonian church not long after the first letter. The situation presupposed by this writing is so similar that there could not have been a long time between the two writings, perhaps only a matter of weeks.

In recent times some have argued that this is not a genuine letter of Paul. They argue that in 1 Thessalonians the second coming of Christ is seen as very near, whereas here it is to be preceded by the appearance of the man of lawlessness and other signs. This is not a serious objection, for Christians have often held both these points of view; there is no reason why Paul should not have done so. That the teaching about the man of lawlessness is unlike anything else in Paul is of no greater force, for nowhere else does Paul face the contention that "the Day of the Lord has come" (2 Thess. 2:2 HCSB).

The exact date of Paul's mission to Thessalonica is not known, and the same is true of his letters to the very young church there. Most scholars agree that 2 Thessalonians must have been written not more than a year or two after Paul and Silas left the city. The church was apparently enthusiastic, but clearly the believers had not as yet matured in their faith. Paul wrote to committed Christians who had not progressed very far in the Christian life.

The Greeks of the first century were not a stolid race. We see their enthusiasm and excitement expressed in the riots when the first Christian preachers visited them. Such a riot broke out in Thessalonica (Acts 17:5-8,13). Those who became Christians during this time did so with verve and enthusiasm. However, they had not yet had the time to come to grips with all that being a Christian meant.

The opening salutation spoke of grace and peace as coming from God the Father and the Lord Jesus Christ (2 Thess. 1:2). Throughout the whole letter Christ is seen in the closest relationship to the Father. This is indicated by the fact that we are sometimes uncertain whether "Lord" means the Father or the Son, as in the expression "the Lord of peace" (3:16). The greatness of Christ is seen in the description of His majestic return with the angels when He comes in judgment (1:7-10). There is not a great deal in this letter about salvation through Christ, though there are references to the gospel (1:8, 2:14), to salvation (2:13), and to the "testimony" of the preachers (1:10). It is plain enough that Paul had preached the good news of the salvation Christ had brought about by His death for sinners, and that the Thessalonians were so clear on this that Paul had no need to go over it again.

They were not allowed to study the meaning of their new faith in peace and quietness (1:4). While they exulted in what the new relationship to God meant, they apparently did not take seriously enough the demands of Christian teaching, particularly in two areas. These areas included the second coming of our Lord and that of daily living. Some of them had come to believe that "the Day of our Lord" was at hand, or had even come (2:2). Some of them had given up working for their living (3:6-13), perhaps because they held the view that the Lord's coming was so close that there was no point in it. Paul wrote to settle them down a little, while not restraining their enthusiasm.

The letter is not a long one and does not give us a definitive outline of the whole Christian faith. Paul wrote to meet a present need, and the arrangement of his letter focuses on local circumstances.

Perhaps we can say that there are four great teachings in this letter:

(1) the greatness of God,

(2) the wonder of salvation in Christ,

(3) the second coming, and

(4) the importance of life and work each day.

God loves people like the Thessalonians and has brought them into the church (1:4). He has elected them (2:13), called them (1:11; 2:14), and saved them. His purposes last through to the end when they will be brought to their climax with the return of Christ and judgment of all. It is interesting to see so clearly expressed in this early letter these great doctrines of election and call, which meant so much to Paul. We may see also his doctrine of justification behind the references to God counting the believers worthy (1:5,11) and, of course, in his teaching on faith (1:3; 4:11; 2:13; 3:2).

Salvation in Christ is proclaimed in the gospel and will be consummated when Christ comes again to overthrow all evil and bring rest and glory to His own. This great God loves His people and has given them comfort and hope, two important qualities for persecuted people (2:16). The apostle prayed that the hearts of his converts would be directed to "God's love" (3:5), which may mean God's love for them or their love for God. Probably it is God's love for them that is the primary thought, but Paul also notes an answering love from the new believers. There are repeated references to Revelation (1:7; 2:6,8). While the term is not used in quite the same way as in some other places, it reminds us that God has not left us to our own devices. He has revealed what is necessary and has further revelations for the last days.

The second coming is seen here in terms of the overthrow of all evil, especially the man of lawlessness. Paul made it clear that Christ's coming will be majestic, that it will mean punishment for people who refuse to know God and who reject the gospel, and that it will bring rest and glory to believers (1:7-10). In the end it is God and good that will be triumphant, not evil.

In view of God's love issuing in election and call, it is interesting to see Paul's stress on God's judgment. He spoke of God's righteous judgment (1:5) and felt that God will in due course punish those who persecute the believers and will give the believers rest (1:6-7). Others will suffer in the judgment. Those who refuse to know God and those who reject the gospel will receive the consequences of their actions (1:8-9). Eternal issues are involved when the gospel is preached, and Paul would not allow the Thessalonians to miss these.

Some of the converts believed Christ's second coming was imminent (2:2). They had misunderstood either a "spirit" (i.e., a prophecy or a revelation) or a "message" (oral communication) or a "letter" (which may mean a genuine letter from Paul that was not understood correctly, or a letter that claimed to be from Paul and was not). In fact, they thought Christ had already returned. Of course, the glorious appearing of Christ had not taken place yet, but "the Day of the Lord" was a complex event, with quite a number of features. They evidently felt "the day" had dawned, the events had begun to unfold, and all that the coming of Christ involved would very soon be accomplished.

Paul made clear that this was not so. There were several things that must happen first, for example, "the rebellion" (HCSB, "apostasy") that occurs and the revelation of "the man of lawlessness" (2:3). He did not explain either. He was probably referring to what he had told the Thessalonians while he had been among them. Unfortunately, we do not know what he said then, so we are left to do some guessing. That a rebellion against the faith will precede the Lord's return is clearly a well-known part of Christian teaching (Matt. 24:10-14; 1 Tim. 4:1-3; 2 Tim. 3:1-9; 4:3-4). Some manuscripts read "man of sin" (instead of "lawlessness"), but there is no real difference in meaning for "sin is the breaking of law" (1 John 3:4 HCSB). The Bible does not use the term "man of lawlessness" elsewhere, but clearly he is the same as the one called "antichrist" (1 John 2:18). Paul was saying that in the end time one would appear who will do the work of Satan in a special way. He will oppose the true God and claim divine honors for himself (2:4).

The identity of the "restrainer" in 2:6-7 is unclear. There is a neuter participle "restrainer" in v. 6 and a masculine one in v. 7. An ancient interpretation still held by some today is that the restrainer in v. 6 is the Roman Empire and in v. 7 the emperor. Paul was relying on Rome to maintain law and order. A more recent interpretation is that v. 6 refers to the preaching of the gospel and v. 7 to either the Apostle Paul or an angel. Another quite different view is that v. 6 refers to the principle (or mystery) of rebellion and v. 7 to Satan or again the Roman emperor. In this case, the verb is understood to mean not "restrain" but "hold sway," "rule," or "prevail." Perhaps the most popular interpretation is that the restrainer is the Holy Spirit. A common dispensational interpretation is that the restraint will be removed when the church will be taken up by God at the rapture (1 Thess. 4:17).

However, Paul's important point is that believers should not be rushing into premature expectations. In due course these things will take place, and God will do away with all the forces of evil (2:8-10).

Paul had a good deal to say about people he calls "disorderly" and who appear to be idle, not working at all (3:6-12). This may have been because they thought the Lord's coming was so close there was no point in it, or perhaps they were so "spiritual minded" that they concentrated on higher things and let other people provide for their needs. Paul counseled all to work for their living (3:12). No doctrinal emphasis, not even that of Christ's return, should lead Christians away from work. People able to work should earn their daily bread. Believers are to work for their living and not grow weary in doing good.

Timothy had just come to Paul from Thessalonica with fresh news (1 Thess. 3:2). Paul saw that the troubles he dealt with in the first letter were still present. So he wrote once more to rebuke the lazy (2 Thess. 3:10) and to encourage the downhearted. There was a new error about the second coming, with some saying that the Day of the Lord had already come. Paul set these people right, teaching them that evil will flourish when the man of lawlessness appears, but that they should look beyond that to the certainty that in due time Christ will return and defeat every force of evil. Christians have been heartened by such teaching from that day to this.

Outline

I. Salutation (1:1-2).
II. Church Leaders Pray for the Church (1:3-12).
   A. Growth in Christian faith, love, and perseverance inspire thanksgiving (1:3-4).
   B. God is just and will help His people who suffer injustice (1:5-7a).
   C. Christ's return will provide ultimate justice (1:7b-10).
   D. Prayer helps God's people fulfill their purposes and glorify Christ (1:11-12).
III. Christ's Return Will Defeat Satanic Forces (2:1-12).
   A. Despite deceptive reports, Christ has not returned (2:1-2).
   B. The man of lawlessness must appear before Christ returns (2:3-8).
   C. Deceived followers of lawlessness will perish (2:9-12).
IV. Election Leads to Thanksgiving (2:13-17).
   A. God chose us to share Christ's glory (2:13-14).
   B. God calls you to firm commitment to His teachings (2:15).
   C. Encouragement and hope come from God's grace (2:16-17).
V. God Is Faithful (3:1-5).
   A. God's evangelists need our prayers (3:1-2).
   B. God is faithful to protect His people (3:3).
   C. God's people are faithful to follow His will (3:4-5).
VI. God Disciplines His People (3:6-15).
   A. God's people must not become lazy busybodies (3:6-13).
   B. Disobedient people must receive brotherly discipline (3:14-15).
VII. Concluding Greetings (3:16-18).

Leon Morris

THESSALONICA (Thĕs să lō nī´ că) Name of modern Thessaloniki, given to the city about 315 B.C. by Cassander, a general of Alexander the Great. He founded the city in that year, naming it after his wife who was the daughter of Philip II and half sister of Alexander. Located on the Thermaic Gulf (Gulf of Salonika) with an excellent harbor—and at the termination of a major trade route from the Danube—it became, with Corinth, one of the two most important commercial centers in Greece. In the Roman period it retained its Greek cultural orientation and functioned as the capital of Macedonia after 146 B.C. See *Macedonia.*

When the Apostle Paul visited the city, it was larger than Philippi and reflected a predominantly Roman culture. Thessalonica was a free city, having no Roman garrison within its walls and maintaining the privilege of minting its own coins. Like Corinth, it had a cosmopolitan population due to the commercial prowess of the city. The recent discovery of a marble inscription, written partly in Greek and partly in a Samaritan form of Hebrew and Aramaic, testifies to the presence of Samaritans in Thessalonica. The book of Acts testifies to the presence of a Jewish synagogue there (17:1).

Since most of the ancient city still lies under modern Thessaloniki, it has been impossible to excavate it. However, in the center of town, a large open area has been excavated revealing a Roman forum (marketplace), about 70 by 110 yards, which dates from about A.D. 100 to 300. An inscription found in the general area, dating to 60 B.C., mentions an *agora* (Gk. for the Roman "forum") and opens the possibility that a Hellenistic marketplace was located here just prior to the construction of this Roman one. In Hellenistic times there was a stadium, a gymnasium, and a temple of Serapis in the city. A third-century odeum (small theater) is preserved on the east side of the forum.

The authenticity of Acts has been questioned due to Luke's mention of Roman officials in Thessalonica by the name of politarchs (Acts 17:6), who are otherwise unknown in extant Greek literature. However, a Roman arch at the western end of ancient Vardar Street contained an inscription from before A.D. 100 that began, "In the time of the Politarchs." Several other inscriptions from Thessalonica, one of them dating from the reign of Augustus Caesar, mention politarchs. See *Thessalonians, First Letter to the; Thessalonians, Second Letter to the.*

John McRay

THEUDAS (Thū´ dȧs) Personal name meaning "gift of God." Acts 5:36 refers to a Theudas who was slain after leading an unsuccessful rebellion of 400 men prior to the census (A.D. 6). Josephus knew a Theudas who led an unsuccessful rebellion during the consulate of Cuspius Fadus (about A.D. 44). Either two rebels are involved, or one of the historians incorporated an inaccurate source into his narrative.

The Triumphal Arch of the Emperor Galerius built over the Egnatian Way in Thessalonica.

THIEF See *Crimes and Punishment; Law, Ten Commandments, Torah.*

THIGH Side of the lower torso and the upper part of the leg. Sometimes the reference is simply physical (Judg. 3:16; Ps. 45:3; Song 3:8; 7:1). More often Scripture regards the thigh as the seat of vital functions, especially procreation. English translations often obscure this connection. The Hebrew text of Gen. 46:26; Exod. 1:5; and Judg. 8:30 gives the thighs (HCSB, "direct descendants"; KJV "loins") as the source of offspring. Marital infidelity was punishable by making the "thigh shrivel" (HCSB), that is, by failure of the reproductive system (Num. 5:16-21). In the patriarchal period oaths were taken by placing a hand "under the thigh," a veiled reference to the reproductive organs. (The English terms "testify" and "testes" witness a similar relation.) The action perhaps represents the calling of one's descendants as witnesses of the oath. When the "stranger" at Peniel did not prevail against Jacob, he touched Jacob at the hip socket of his thigh, leaving him limping (Gen. 32:25-32). Jacob escaped the struggle broken but unbowed. Slapping the thigh indicated sorrow, shame, or remorse (Jer. 31:19; Ezek. 21:12). The thigh was among the portions of the sacrifice going to the priests (Lev. 7:32-34; 10:14; cp. 1 Sam. 9:24 where Samuel honored Saul with this portion).

THIMNATHAH (Thĭm´ nà thah) (KJV, Josh. 19:43) See *Timnah.*

THIN WORK See *Beveled Work.*

THOMAS Personal name from Hebrew meaning "a twin." One of the first 12 disciples of Jesus (Mark 3:18). The apocryphal book, *The Acts of Thomas*, uses the literal meaning of his name ("twin") in making him the twin of Jesus Himself! His personality was complex, revealing a skepticism mixed with loyalty and faith (John 11:16). Thomas sought evidence of Jesus' resurrection (John 20:25) but, when convinced of the miracle, made a historic confession of faith (20:28). See *Apocrypha, New Testament; Didymus; Disciple.*

THORN IN THE FLESH Greek word *skolops* occurred in classical Greek as a stake or sharp wooden shaft used to impale. In Hellenistic Greek the variations "thorn" and "splinter" are found. The majority of references in the LXX, the NT, and papyri are translated as thorn, splinter, or sliver. Origen's theological opponents Ceisus and Eustathius used *skolops* as a derogatory reference to the cross.

Because false teachers in Corinth claimed receiving divine revelation, Paul shared his vision of the "third heaven" as miraculous evidence of his apostolic calling. Paul's revelation was balanced by a "thorn in the flesh" (2 Cor. 12:7). During this era physical ailments were a constant problem. As a result, most patristic writers perceived Paul's affliction as either a painful, chronic physical problem or ongoing persecution.

In the Middle Ages the "thorn" was taken as carnal temptation. The Vulgate encouraged the perception of the thorn as a sexual temptation. In the Reformation Luther and Calvin rejected the idea of sexual temptation. Calvin interpreted the "thorn in the flesh" as a variety of physical and spiritual temptations. Luther interpreted the thorn as physical illness.

Four modern theories concern Paul's thorn in the flesh. The most common theory is some sort of recurring physical illness, possibly malaria, based on a perceived relationship to Paul's bodily illness of Gal. 4:13. Some hold that Paul suffered from an eye disease (*ophthalmia*), pointing to Gal. 4:13-15, where Paul confirmed that the Galatians would have given him, if possible, their eyes. Further, in Gal. 6:11 Paul indicates he wrote in large script, which is logical for a person with eye trouble. A third common theory was sorrow and pain because of Jewish unbelief (Rom. 9:1-3). A fourth theory is that of a "messenger of Satan," rather than a physical ailment, given as a redemptive judgment of God on Paul for the purpose of humility.

Other theories were hysteria, hypochondria, gallstones, gout, rheumatism, sciatica, gastritis, leprosy, lice, deafness, dental infection, neurasthenia, a speech impediment, and remorse for persecuting the Church.   *Steven L. Cox*

THREE TAVERNS Rest stop on the Appian Way, 33 miles southeast of Rome and 10 miles northwest of the Forum of Appius, where Roman Christians met Paul on his trip to Rome (Acts 28:15).

THUMMIM See *Urim and Thummim.*

THUTMOSE (Thüt mō´ sə) Egyptian royal name meaning "Thoth the moon god is born." Four pharaohs of the Egyptian 18th Dynasty (about 1550–1310 B.C.). Their combined efforts, especially those of Thutmose I and III, did much to expand Egyptian wealth and influence.

Thutmose I rose to power through his skills as a general and by marrying the daughter of his predecessor, Amenhotep I. His military exploits expanded Egypt to include Nubia to the south and Syria, north to the Euphrates River. The tribute from his conquests allowed Eneni, his architect, to restore and add to the temples of Thebes. Eneni was also instructed to initiate the work at Biban el-Moluk (gates of the kings) known today as the Valley of the Kings. Thutmose I had no clear heir to the throne when he died.

Thutmose II succeeded in gaining the throne by marrying his ambitious half sister Hatshepsut. His reign lasted only a few years and was obscured by the shadow of this queen.

Thutmose III marched in the steps of his grandfather Thutmose I but only after about 20 years of "co-rule" with Hatshepsut. His hatred of her must have smoldered all those years, for he removed much of the evidence of her reign as soon as she was dead. Thutmose III conducted 14 military campaigns in 17 years, continuing his rule another 15 years. The Theban temple of Karnak contains displays of his exploits. He especially enjoyed hunting and was devoted to the god Amun. Some scholars believe him to be the pharaoh of the Israelite oppression. Amenhotep II became co-regent with his father for about three years at the conclusion of his reign.

Thutmose IV, like Thutmose II, seized his position by marriage. He seemed content to maintain the status quo and clear the sand from the Sphinx where he had dreamed of becoming Pharaoh according to a stela, an ancient stone bearing some inscription. That he was not the firstborn son of the previous pharaoh is considered by some to be evidence that Amenhotep II was the pharaoh of the exodus. See *Egypt; Thebes.*   *Gary C. Huckabay*

THYATIRA (Thī à tī´ rá) City in the Lycus River Valley. Although never a magnificent city, Thyatira was the center of a number of trade guilds that used the natural resources of the area to make it a very profitable site. Thyatira had a Jewish contingent out of which grew a NT church. One of Paul's first converts from the European

The ruins of Thyatira in ancient Asia Minor (modern Turkey).

continent, Lydia, was a native of Thyatira (Acts 16:14). She probably was a member of a guild there that dealt in purple dye. The church at Thyatira was praised for its works of charity, service, and faith (Rev. 2:19), but criticized for allowing the followers of Jezebel to prosper in its midst (2:20). See *Asia Minor, Cites of; Revelation, Book of.*

TIAMAT (Tē ä´ mät) Sumerian-Akkadian goddess viewed by the Babylonians as one of the major gods of their pantheon. She controlled the salt waters and was seen as a capricious goddess because of the destructive yet beneficial nature of the rivers and seas. In the creation epic, *Enuma Elish*, Tiamat and her consort, Apsu, gave birth to Anshar and Kishar, the universe above and below. According to the epic, the creation of the earth was the result of Tiamat's defeat by the god Marduk, who split Tiamat in two to form heaven and earth, a picture of the primordial sea being driven back and giving way to the land.

TIBERIAS (Tī bĭr´ ĭ ás) Mentioned only in John 6:23 (cp. 6:1; 21:1), Tiberias is a city located on the western shore of the Sea of Galilee encompassing today what was in ancient times two separate cities, Tiberias and Hammath, each surrounded by its own wall. Once a mile apart (Palestinian Talmud, *Megillah* 2.2), they were combined into a single city, apparently in the first century after Christ (Tosefta, *'Erubin* 7.2,146). At this time, about A.D. 18, Herod Antipas (Luke 3:1) built the larger city on a major trade route connecting Egypt with Syria, to replace Sepphoris as the capital of Galilee (Josephus, *Antiquities* 18.36). It remained the

T

capital until A.D. 61 when it was given to Agrippa II by Nero (*Antiquities* 20.159). It was paganized by Hadrian after the second Jewish revolt in A.D. 132–135 but became the center of Jewish learning after A.D. 200. The Mishnah, which was compiled in Sepphoris by Judah haNasi, took its final shape in Tiberias as did the Talmud and the Masoretic Text of the Hebrew Bible.

Excavations by N. Slouschz in 1921 and M. Dothan in 1961 at Hammath-Tiberias, near the warm baths, revealed several superimposed synagogues dating from about 300 to 800, some having beautiful mosaic floors. In 1973 and 1974 G. Foerster, digging just south of this area, found the southern gate of the city, having two round towers and dating to the founding of Tiberias before A.D. 100.   *John McRay*

TIBERIUS CAESAR (Tī bĭr´ ĭ ŭs Çē´ zăr) Person who had the unenviable task of following Augustus as Roman emperor. He ruled the empire from A.D. 14–37. Tiberius was especially ill suited to follow Augustus. A solid, taciturn man, he lacked the public relations ability of Augustus.

Tiberius was 54 when he ascended to the throne. He was a republican at heart, so he must have felt very uncomfortable with the system of government that Augustus left him. He had a deep respect for the Senate, and he took great pains to preserve the dignity of that body. Yet even Tiberius came to realize that it was too late to make the Senate an equal partner in government.

During the reign of Tiberius, Jesus began His ministry, and He was crucified. This event was probably not noted at the emperor's court. Tiberius died in A.D. 37. He was 79 years old. See *Rome and the Roman Empire.*   *Gary Poulton*

TIBHATH (Tĭb´ hăth) Place-name meaning "place of slaughter." City from which David took spoils (or received tribute) of bronze (1 Chron. 18:8). The site is likely in the vicinity of Zobah north of Damascus. The parallel in 2 Sam. 8:8 reads "Betah."

TIBNI (Tĭb´ nī) Personal name meaning "intelligent" or "straw." Likely an army officer who struggled with Omri over succession to the throne of Israel following Zimri's suicide (1 Kings 16:21-22).

TIDAL (Tī´ dăl) One of four kings allied against five in Gen. 14:1,9. The name is similar to Tud'alia, the name of several Hittite kings, sug-

Modern Tiberias, built over the ancient city of Tiberias, overlooks the Sea of Galilee.

T

gesting the king's origin in eastern Asia Minor. The king is perhaps Tudhalia I (about 1700–1650 B.C.).

TIGLATH-PILESER (Tĭğ lăth-pĭ lē´ zẽr) Personal name meaning "My trust is the son of Esarra (the temple of Asshur)." King of Assyria from 745 to 727 B.C. (2 Kings 16:7), also known as Tilgath-pilneser (1 Chron. 5:6; 2 Chron. 28:20) and Pul (2 Kings 15:19; 1 Chron. 5:26). See *Assyria.*

TIGRIS RIVER See *Euphrates and Tigris Rivers; Rivers and Waterways.*

The Tigris River flows through the country of Iraq (ancient Mesopotamia).

TIKVAH (Tĭk´ vah) Personal name meaning "hope, expectation." **1.** Father-in-law of Huldah, the prophetess (2 Kings 22:14; 2 Chron. 34:22). **2.** Father of Jahaziah who opposed Ezra's call for Israelites to divorce their foreign wives (Ezra 10:15).

TIKVATH (Tĭk´ văth) KJV alternate form of Tikvah (2 Chron. 34:22), perhaps representing original form of foreign name written in Hebrew as Tikvah.

TILGATH-PILNESER (Tĭl ğăth-pĭl nē´ zẽr) Alternate form of Tiglath-pileser (1 Chron. 5:6; 2 Chron. 28:20).

TILON (Tĭ´ lŏn) Personal name of uncertain meaning. Descendant of Judah (1 Chron. 4:20).

TIMAEUS (Tĭ mē´ ŭs) Personal name meaning "highly prized" (Mark 10:46). Bartimaeus is Aramaic for "son of Timaeus."

TIMBREL KJV term for a tambourine. See *Tabret; Music, Instruments, Dancing.*

TIME, MEANING OF **God and Time** God is Lord over time because He created and ordained time (Gen. 1:4-5,14-19). God Himself is timeless and eternal, not bound by space or time (Exod. 3:14-15; 1 Chron. 16:36; Pss. 41:13; 90:1-2; 93:2; 146:10; Isa. 9:6; John 1:1-18; 8:58; Heb. 13:8; 2 Pet. 3:8; Jude 25). On the other hand, God is not removed from time. Through His providential care and especially in the incarnation of Jesus Christ, God enters into time without being limited by the constraints of time.

Because of His foreknowledge, only God knows and foreordains events in time (Dan. 2:20-22; Mark 13:31-32; Acts 1:7; 2:22-23). God sees all things in time from a perspective of eternity, sees the end from the beginning. Humans, however, are trapped in time, and sometimes cannot discern the meaning and significance of time in their own day (Eccles. 3:1-11; 9:12; Ps. 90:9-10; Luke 12:54-56; James 4:13-16). Being bound by the remorseless march of time is a telling reminder of human finitude and temporality.

Structure of Time The agricultural societies surrounding the Hebrew people had a cyclical view of time tied to the annual cycle of the sun. Israel's economy was also agricultural, and thus the Israelite calendar took account of the cycles of the moon and the sun (Num. 10:10; 1 Sam. 20:5,18,24; 1 Kings 4:23; Ps. 81:2; Isa. 1:13-14; Col. 2:16). Scripture sometimes hints at a cyclical view of history, such as in the life cycles described in Ecclesiastes (1:3-12; 3:1-8), and in the repeated pattern in the book of Judges (Israel sins, a crisis arises, the people cry out for God's help, and God's delivers them). However, the Bible affirms a distinctively different view of time than that of the surrounding cultures. Scripture frames history with a linear view of time, beginning with creation, continuing through history directed by the providence of God, and culminating in the Day of the Lord. Time begins at a decisive moment by the creation of God (Gen. 1:14-19). The history of God's interaction with humanity is recorded in Scripture in chronological order in narrative books in both the OT and NT. Whereas the overarching theme of the Bible is God's actions in history, the scriptural writers were careful to document the date of their narratives very specifically. For example, there are over 180 references in the Bible translated "month," usually in reference to a specific holy day, to an event in the life of Israel, or to the reception by prophets of the Word of the Lord. All the Gospel writers had concern for chronology, but Luke was most careful to date biblical events intentionally by well-known public events (Luke 1:1-4; 2:1-3; 3:1-2). The specific dating of these events underscores that these are real events in time and space, not merely mystical or mythological stories.

Measuring Time God ordained the day and night (Gen. 1:14-19) and weeks (Gen. 1:1-2:3; Exod. 16:25-26; 20:9-11) as measures of time. At the time that Scripture was written, Jews viewed the day as beginning the evening before (Gen. 1:5,8,13,19, 23,31; Mark 13:35). The daytime hours were counted as 12 hours, with noon being the sixth hour (Mark 15:25; John 11:9). The days were divided into three or four "watches," evidently tied to the watch hours of military sentries (Exod. 14:34; 1 Sam 11:11; Judg. 7:19; Lam. 2:19; Matt. 14:25; Mark 6:48; Luke 12:38). The only time instrument mentioned in the Bible is a sundial owned by King Ahaz (2 Kings 20:8-11; Isa. 38:7-8).

There were 12 months in the Hebrew year. These months were counted on the lunar calendar as about 30 days each, and thus adjustments were made periodically to make the year 365 days and correspond to the solar calendar. The first month was called Abib (Exod. 13:4; 23:15; 34:18; Deut. 16:1) or Nisan (Neh. 2:1; Esther 3:7). The second month was Ziv (1 Kings 6:1,37); the third month was Sivan (Esther 8:9); and the names of the fourth and fifth months are not given in Scripture. The sixth month is Elul (Neh. 6:15); the seventh is Ethanim (1 Kings 8:2); the eighth is Bul (1 Kings 6:38); the ninth is Chislev (Neh. 1:1; Zech. 7:11); the tenth is Tebeth (Esther 2:16); the eleventh is Shebat (Zech. 1:7); and the twelfth is Adar (Ezra 6:15; Esther 3:7,13; 8:12; 9:1,15,17,19,21). The annual Israelite calendar was framed by a series of feast days, holy days, and religious festivals. There was no systematic dating system for years, but years were usually stated in reference to other historical events. In the books of 1 and 2 Kings and 1 and 2 Chronicles, the date a king began his reign in one kingdom was measured by the date the king in another kingdom began his reign (1 Kings 15:1,9,15,28,33; 16:8,10,15, 23,29). The coronation of kings and other dramatic events became the measuring rods for dating other events (Isa. 6:1; 20:1; Amos 1:1; Luke 2:1-3; 3:1-2).

Discerning Time Apart from the chronological measurement of time, another sense of time is emphasized in Scripture as divinely appointed times. Although the distinction is not absolute, there are two words in the NT that emphasize these two dimensions of time. *Chronos* is the Greek term usually referring simply to the chronological measurement of time (Luke 20:9; John 7:33; Acts 14:38), while *kairos* usually refers to the spiritual significance of an era (Mark 1:15; Luke 19:44; Rom. 5:6; Titus 1:3; Rev. 1:3). Some times are divinely appointed, especially in carrying out God's will for a specific mission at a specific time (Acts 17:26; Heb. 9:27), or in events appropriate to each season of life (Deut. 11:14; Ps. 145:15; Eccles. 3:1-11; Jer. 18:23). It was of vital importance that Jesus' incarnation occurred in the *kairos* moment, in the fullness of time (John 7:8; Gal. 4:4). Sometimes the spirit of the age may be characterized as evil or good (Isa. 49:8; Eph. 5:15; 4:2-3). It is incumbent on all believers to look beyond the surface things of life to discern the spiritual significance of their own day, the deeper spiritual issues which give life meaning (Ps. 90:9-10; Luke 12:54-56). For example, John portrays the miracles of Jesus as not merely a series of unusual events, but as signs pointing to the divinity of Christ (John 2:11,23; 4:54; 6:2,14,26; 9:16; 11:47; 12:37; 20:30). With spiritual discernment, there is more to the events of an era than meets the eye. Each moment of this life is an arena for decisions with eternal consequences (2 Cor. 6:2; Eph. 5:15-16). Therefore, Christians should be careful to discern the meaning and significance of their time, comprehending both the reality of evil and the movement of God in history.

Time and Eternity A Christian lives in time but looks forward to the day when the sting of time shall be no more. In the present we participate in the kingdom of God. There is a sense in which we already have a foretaste of eternity within time. John particularly emphasized this "realized eschatology" in his Gospel—that eternal life is a present possession of the believer (John 3:16,36; 5:24). The kingdom of God is realized in us as we acknowledge Jesus' lordship in our lives. Yet we also look toward an age to come, the Day of the Lord (Amos 5:18-20; Obad. 1:15; Zeph. 1:7-14; 2 Thess. 2:1-12). The Bible draws a clear distinction between the present age and the age to come (Mark 10:30; Rom. 8:18; Eph. 1:21; 2:4-7; Titus 2:12-13). The present age is the time of

The modern name Timna refers to a large copper-mining area north of the Gulf of Aqaba.

Overview of Tell Batash (site of the ancient city of Timnah).

decision and service in the kingdom of God; the age to come is the full realization of God's provision of eternal life. Christians thus live in the tension between "already" (that eternity has invaded time through Jesus Christ) and the "not yet" (that our salvation awaits completion in heaven). Time will cease being meaningful when we enter into eternity, believers with God in heaven and unbelievers with Satan in hell (Dan. 7:18,27; Matt. 25:41-46; Rev. 14:11; 20:5,10-15). Human finitude and death give time its significance. In eternity time will be redeemed. See *History.*   *Steve W. Lemke*

TIMNA (Tĭm´ nà) Personal name meaning "holding in check" or "she protects." **1.** Sister of the Horite clan chief Lotan (Gen. 36:22; 1 Chron. 1:39), concubine of Esau's son Eliphaz, and mother of Amalek (Gen. 36:12). **2.** Son of Eliphaz (1 Chron. 1:36; Gen. 36:16 "Teman") and Edomite clan chief (Gen. 36:40; 1 Chron. 1:51). Timna is associated with either Timna in southern Arabia or, following Gen. 36:16, Teman in southern Edom. It is the name of the capitol of Qataban. **3.** Modern name for an ancient copper mining site 14 miles north of Elath.

TIMNAH (Tĭm´ nah) Place-name meaning "allotted portion." **1.** Town assigned to Dan (Josh. 19:43), located on the southern border with Judah (Josh. 15:10). The site is likely Tell el-Batashi about four miles northwest of Beth-shemesh in Judah. Philistines occupied the site at the time of Samson (Judg. 14:1-5). Uzziah likely took the site as part of his conquest of Philistine cities (2 Chron. 26:6). His grandson Ahaz lost the city to the Philistines again

(2 Chron. 28:18). The city fell to the Assyrian king Sennacherib in 701 B.C. **2.** Village in the hill country of Judah (Josh. 15:57). This Timnah was the likely scene of Judah's encounter with Tamar (Gen. 38:12-14). The probable site lies south of Hebron about four miles east of Beit Nettif.

TIMNATH (Tĭm´ năth) (KJV, Gen. 38:12-14) See *Timnah 2.*

TIMNATH-HERES or **TIMNATH-SERAH** (Tĭm năth-hē´ rēz, Tĭm năth-sē´ rah) Place of Joshua's inheritance and burial (Judg. 2:9; Josh. 19:50; 24:30). Timnath-heres means "portion of the sun," suggesting a site dedicated to sun worship (Judg. 2:9). Timnath-serah means "remaining portion," pointing to land given to Joshua following distribution of land to the tribes (Josh. 19:50; 24:30). The site is identified with Khirbet Tibneh about 17 miles southwest of Shechem.

TIMNITE (Tĭm´ nīt) Resident of Timnah (Judg. 15:6).

TIMON (Tī´ mŏn) Personal name meaning "honorable." One of seven chosen to supervise distribution of food to the Greek-speaking widows of the Jerusalem church (Acts 6:5).

TIMOTHY Personal name meaning "honoring God." Friend and trusted coworker of Paul. When Timothy was a child, his mother Eunice and his grandmother Lois taught him the Scriptures (2 Tim. 1:5; 3:15). A native of Lystra, he may have been converted on Paul's first missionary journey (Acts 14:6-23). Paul referred to Timothy as his child in the faith (1 Cor. 4:17; 1 Tim. 1:2; 2 Tim. 1:2). This probably means

T

that Paul was instrumental in Timothy's conversion. When Paul came to Lystra on his second journey, Timothy was a disciple who was well respected by the believers (Acts 16:1-2). Paul asked Timothy to accompany him. Timothy's father was a Greek, and Timothy had not been circumcised. Because they would be ministering to many Jews and because Timothy's mother was Jewish, Paul had Timothy circumcised (Acts 16:3).

Timothy not only accompanied Paul but also was sent on many crucial missions by Paul (Acts 17:14-15; 18:5; 19:22; 20:4; Rom. 16:21; 1 Cor. 16:10; 2 Cor. 1:19; 1 Thess. 3:2,6). For example, when Paul was unable to go to Corinth, he sent Timothy to represent Paul and his teachings (1 Cor. 4:17). Later when Paul was in prison, he sent Timothy to Philippi (Phil. 2:19). Paul felt that no one had any more compassion and commitment than Timothy (Phil. 2:20-22).

So close were Paul and Timothy that both names are listed as the authors of six of Paul's letters (2 Cor. 1:1; Phil. 1:1; Col. 1:1; 1 Thess. 1:1; 2 Thess. 1:1; Philem. 1). In addition, Paul wrote two letters to Timothy (1 Tim. 1:2; 2 Tim. 1:2). As Paul's ministry neared the end, he challenged Timothy to remain true to his calling (1 Tim. 1:18). As Paul faced death, he asked Timothy to come to be with him (2 Tim. 4:9). At some point in his life, Timothy was imprisoned, but he was released (Heb. 13:23). See *Paul; Timothy, First Letter to; Timothy, Second Letter to.*

Robert J. Dean

TIMOTHY, FIRST LETTER TO First of two letters Paul wrote to Timothy. The letter was written in approximately A.D. 63, following Paul's first imprisonment in Rome. It is likely that Paul left Rome and traveled to Ephesus. There is some debate concerning the place of writing. Rome and Macedonia have been offered as possibilities. Perhaps, in light of 1 Tim. 1:3, Macedonia could be the better choice. The letter was addressed to Timothy in Ephesus. Paul had urged Timothy to remain in Ephesus and lead this important church as its pastor (1:3).

Purpose Paul had hoped to visit Timothy in Ephesus but was fearful of a delay. If he were delayed, he wanted Timothy to "know how people ought to act in God's household" (3:14-15 HCSB). The epistle contains instructions concerning order and structure in the church and practical advice for the young pastor. One impor-

tant theme in this and the other two Pastoral Epistles (2 Timothy and Titus) is sound teaching. Paul urged Timothy and Titus to confront the false teaching by sound or healthy teaching. This word occurs eight times in these three letters (1 Tim. 1:10; 6:3; 2 Tim. 1:13; 4:3; Titus 1:9,13; 2:1-2). See *Letters; Paul; Timothy.*

Overview *Chapter One* Paul wrote as an apostle of Jesus Christ. He was writing with the authority of Jesus Himself. The error described in verses 3-4 was Jewish in nature. Some were falsely teaching a mythological treatment of OT genealogies. This teaching was both meaningless and controversial. Timothy was urged to teach "sound teaching" in its place (1:10-11 HCSB). Two leaders among the false teachers were Hymenaeus and Alexander; Paul said he "delivered them to Satan, so that they may be taught not to blaspheme" (1:20; cp. 1 Cor. 5:5). The purpose of this and all Christian discipline was the eventual restoration of the offender.

Chapter Two Prayer is given priority in the worship services in the church. Seven different Greek words appear in the NT for prayer, and four of them occur in verse 1. One of the most significant statements in the entire NT is found in verse 5. Paul wrote there is "one God" and "one mediator between God and man, a man, Christ Jesus" (HCSB). Monotheism is clearly taught as opposed to the polytheism of the first-century religious world. Mediator is a word that means "go-between." Jesus is humanity's "go-between" to God. He is also called our "ransom" in verse 6. A ransom was paid to a slave owner to purchase the freedom of the slave. Jesus paid for our redemption with His death on the cross.

Chapter Three Qualifications for church leadership are discussed in this chapter. Fifteen moral and ethical requirements are mentioned in verses 2-7. See *Offices in the New Testament.*

Chapter Four Paul affirmed that "everything created by God is good" (4:4 HCSB). Some false teachers maintained that marriage and certain foods were wrong. Paul drew from the message of Genesis in which God affirmed everything He created was good! Mankind takes God's good creation and corrupts it. The apostle reminded Timothy to be a "good servant of Christ Jesus" (4:6) and to "be an example to the believers in speech, in conduct, in love, in faith, in purity" (4:12).

Chapter Five Paul gave practical instructions concerning the ministry of the church to various groups that comprise its membership.

Chapter Six The teachers of false doctrine were motivated by "material gain" (6:5 HCSB). Paul warned in light of this fact and others that "the love of money is a root of all kinds of evil" (6:10).

Outline

I. Greetings (1:1-2)
II. Introductory Remarks (1:3-20)
    A. False doctrine and misuse of the law (1:3-11)
    B. Paul's testimony (1:12-17)
    C. Engage in battle (1:18-20)
III. The Worship of the Church (2:1-15)
    A. Instructions on prayer (2:1-7)
    B. Instructions to men and women (2:8-15)
IV. Qualifications of Church Leaders (3:1-13)
V. The Mystery of Godliness (3:14-16)
VI. The Ministry of the Church (4:1–6:10)
    A. Demonic influence (4:1-5)
    B. A good servant of Jesus Christ (4:6-10)
    C. Instructions for ministry (4:11–5:2)
    D. Support of widows (5:3-16)
    E. Honoring the elders (5:17-25)
    F. Honoring the masters (6:1-2a)
    G. False doctrine and human greed (6:2b-10)
VII. Concluding Remarks (6:11-21)
    A. Compete for the faith (6:11-16)
    B. Instructions to the rich (6:17-19)
    C. Guard the heritage (6:20-21)

Mark E. Matheson

TIMOTHY, SECOND LETTER TO Second of Paul's letters to Timothy, pastor of the church in Ephesus. The letter was the last letter of which we have a record written by Paul. He wrote this letter from his jail cell during his second imprisonment in Rome. He was awaiting trial for his faith. It is clear that he felt he would not be released (4:6). If Nero executed Paul and if Nero was killed in A.D. 68, then Paul had to have been executed sometime before. The letter can be dated between A.D. 63 and A.D. 67. Timothy was the recipient of Paul's letter. He had been the apostle's representative in the city of Ephesus for sometime.

Purpose The letter contains Paul's stirring words of encouragement and instruction to his young disciple. Paul longed to see Timothy (1:4) and asked him to come to Rome for a visit. It is generally believed that Timothy went. Paul asked him to come before winter (4:21) and bring the winter coat Paul left in Troas (4:13). Timothy was also asked to bring the scrolls and the parchments so Paul could read and study (4:13). See *Letters; Paul; Timothy.*

Overview *Chapter One* Paul was reminded that Timothy's faith first lived in his grandmother Lois and in his mother Eunice (1:5). Paul had in reality become Timothy's father (1:2). Timothy may have been a naturally timid person. Because of this, Paul told him to minister with a spirit of power (1:7). The Holy Spirit empowers believers, but we should be careful to exercise this power in a spirit of "love and sound judgment" (1:7 HCSB). Two men, Phygelus and Hermogenes, deserted Paul (1:15). Onesiphorus was a refreshing friend and not ashamed of Paul's chains (1:16).

Chapter Two Paul urged Timothy to be strong in Jesus Christ. Paul used the metaphors of a good soldier, athlete, and a hardworking farmer when describing the Christian's calling. The purpose of that calling is so all "may obtain salvation, which is in Christ Jesus" (2:10 HCSB). Timothy was to be one who would be "correctly teaching the word of truth" (2:15) in the face of those who mishandled it. Hymenaeus (1 Tim. 1:20) and Philetus were singled out. They were teaching that the resurrection had already taken place and were destroying the faith of some (2:18).

Chapter Three "The last days" are a reference to the second coming of Jesus. The days preceding His return will be "difficult." Characteristics of these last days have appeared in many different ages, but the times before Jesus' actual return will be even more intense. Paul listed 18 characteristics of evil men in verses 2-5. He compared them to Jannes and Jambres who opposed Moses (3:8). Although these two individuals are not mentioned in the OT, Jewish tradition maintains that these men were two Egyptian magicians who opposed Moses and Aaron. The evil and false teaching is to be overcome by the holy Scripture (3:16-17).

Chapter Four Paul further instructed Timothy to be prepared to "proclaim the message" (HCSB) at all times. The need is paramount, for people will not always adhere to "sound doctrine" (4:3). Paul, drawing on the imagery of

T

Num. 28:24, compared his life to that of a "drink offering." This was poured on a sacrifice before it was offered. He was ready to depart this life and go to be with the Lord. He anticipated the "crown of righteousness" that awaited him (4:8). The letter closes with practical instructions and pastoral remarks for Timothy.

Outline

    I.   Greeting (1:1-2)
    II. Thanksgiving (1:3-7)
   III. Not Ashamed of the Gospel (1:8-12)
   IV. Be Loyal to the Faith (1:13-18)
    V. Be Strong in Grace (2:1-13)
   VI. An Approved Worker (2:14-26)
  VII. Difficult Times Ahead (3:1-9)
 VIII. The Sacred Scriptures (3:10-17)
   IX. Fulfill Your Ministry (4:1-8)
    X. Final Instructions (4:9-18)
   XI. Benediction (4:19-22)

Mark E. Matheson

TIN See *Minerals and Metals.*

TINKLING ORNAMENTS (KJV) Anklets making a tinkling noise as one walked. Part of the finery of the affluent women of Jerusalem (Isa. 3:16,18). See *Anklet.*

TIPHSAH (Tĭph´ sah) Place-name meaning "passage, ford." **1.** City on the west bank of the Euphrates about 75 miles south of Carchemish, representing the northeastern limit of Solomon's kingdom (1 Kings 4:24). **2.** Site near Tirzah in Samaria (2 Kings 15:16), possibly a corruption of Tappuah, the reading of the earliest Greek translation which REB, RSV, TEV follow.

TIRAS (Tī´ răs) Division of the descendants of Japheth who are all seagoing peoples (Gen. 10:2; 1 Chron. 1:5). Traditionally, they have been related to Turscha, part of the sea peoples Rameses III (1198–1166 B.C.) fought. Some have identified them with the Etruscans of Italy.

TIRATHITES (Tī´ răth īts) Family of Kenite scribes (1 Chron.2:55).

TIRE KJV term meaning "turban" (Ezek. 24:17,23).

TIRHAKAH (Tĭr hā´ kah) Egyptian pharaoh of the 25th Dynasty (689–664 B.C.) who supported Hezekiah's revolt against the Assyrian king Sennacherib (2 Kings 19:8-9; Isa. 37:9).

TIRHANAH (Tĭr hā´ nah) Personal name of uncertain meaning. Son of Caleb and Maacah (1 Chron. 2:48).

TIRIA (Tĭr´ ĭ à) Personal name meaning "fear." Descendant and family of Judah (1 Chron. 4:16).

TIRSHATHA (Tĭr shä´ thà) Title of honor designating respect for an official, sometimes translated "your excellence" (Ezra 2:63; Neh. 7:65,70; 8:9; 10:1).

TIRZAH (Tĭr´ zah) Personal name and place-name meaning "she is friendly." **1.** Daughter of Zelophehad who inherited part of tribal land allotment of Manasseh since her father had no sons. **2.** Originally a Canaanite city noted for its beauty (Song 6:4) but captured in the conquest of the promised land (Josh. 12:24). It became one of the early capitals of Israel when Jeroboam I established his residence there (1 Kings 14:17) and continued as the capital until Omri built Samaria (1 Kings 16:23-24). Archaeological discoveries, coupled with biblical references, suggest that Tirzah is to be identified with modern Tell el-Fara, a tell of extraordinary size about seven miles northeast of Shechem. The area evidently was first occupied before 3000 B.C. and flourished, off and on, as a Canaanite city until its capture by Joshua between 1550 and 1200 B.C. It remained an Israelite city until the Assyrian conquest of 722 B.C. By 600 B.C. Tirzah was completely abandoned.   *Hugh Tobias*

TISHBITE (Tĭsh´ bīt) Resident of an unidentified village, Tishbe, used as a title of Elijah (1 Kings 17:1; 21:17,28; 2 Kings 1:3,8; 9:36). Tishbite is possibly a corruption of Jabeshite or a class designation (cp. the Hebrew *toshab* which designates a resident alien, Lev. 25:6). See *Elijah.*

TITHE Tenth part, especially as offered to God. Abraham presented a tithe of war booty to the priest-king of Jerusalem, Melchizedek (Gen. 14:18-20). Jacob pledged to offer God a tithe of all his possessions upon his safe return (Gen. 28:22). The tithe was subject to a variety of legislation. Numbers 18:20-32 provides for support of the Levites and the priests through the tithe. The Deuteronomic code stipulated that the tithe of agricultural produce be used for a family feast at the sanctuary celebrating God's provision (Deut. 14:22-27). The same code stipulated the third year's tithe for care of the Levites, orphans, widows, and foreigners (Deut. 14:28-29). Some scholars think the differences in legislation reflect different uses of the tithe at various stages of Israel's history. The rabbis of the NT period, however, understood the laws as referring to three separate tithes: a Levitical tithe, a tithe spent celebrating in Jerusalem, and a charity tithe. Malachi 3:8 equates neglect of the tithe with robbing God. Jesus, however, warned that strict tithing must be accompanied by concern for the more important demands of the law, namely, for just and merciful living (Matt. 23:23; Luke 11:42). See *Stewardship.*

TITIUS JUSTUS See *Justus.*

TITTLE See *Dot.*

TITUS (Tī´ tŭs) Gentile companion of Paul (Gal. 2:3) and recipient of the NT letter bearing his name. Titus may have been converted by Paul who called him "my true child in our common faith" (Titus 1:4 HCSB). As one of Paul's early associates, Titus accompanied the apostle and Barnabas to Jerusalem (Gal. 2:1), probably on the famine relief visit (Acts 11:28-30).

Though Acts does not mention Titus, he was quite involved in Paul's missionary activities as shown in the Pauline letters. He was evidently known to the Galatians (Gal. 2:1,3), possibly from the first missionary journey to that region. Titus also seems to have been a very capable person, called by Paul "my partner and coworker" (2 Cor. 8:23 HCSB). He was entrusted with the delicate task of delivering Paul's severe letter (2 Cor. 2:1-4) to Corinth and correcting problems within the church there (2 Cor. 7:13-15). Titus' genuine concern for and evenhanded dealing with the Corinthians (2 Cor. 8:16-17; 12:18) no doubt contributed to his success, which he reported in person to Paul, anxiously awaiting word in Macedonia (2 Cor. 2:13; 7:5-6,13-15). Paul responded by writing 2 Corinthians that Titus probably delivered (2 Cor. 8:6,16-18,23).

Paul apparently was released after his first Roman imprisonment and made additional journeys, unrecorded in Acts. One of these took him and Titus to Crete, where Titus remained behind to oversee and administer the church (Titus 1:5). It was to Crete that Paul wrote his letter, asking Titus to join him in Nicopolis on the west

The Arch of Titus, emperor of the Roman Empire and son of Vespasian, in the city of Rome, Italy.

coast of Greece (Titus 3:12). Following Paul's subsequent re-imprisonment, Titus was sent to Dalmatia (2 Tim. 4:10). According to church tradition, Titus was the first bishop of Crete. See *Crete.*   *Daniel C. Browning, Jr.*

TITUS, CAESAR (Tī´ tŭs) Roman emperor A.D. 79–81, eldest son of Vespasian. Titus, like his father, was a soldier. He served in Germany and Britain and later in the Middle East. When Vespasian left his Middle East command to become emperor in A.D. 69, he left Titus in charge of crushing the Jewish revolt. In A.D. 70 his troops captured the temple in Jerusalem. They took the last stronghold, Masada, in A.D. 73. His victory over the Jews was vividly depicted on the Triumphal Arch erected in Rome that still stands today.

Titus was deeply admired by his soldiers; when he later became emperor, the populace loved him. He was considered an honest ruler and an efficient administrator. An adherent of Stoic philosophy, he believed that the Roman emperor was the servant of the people. He and his father before him (the so-called Flavian emperors) struggled after the excesses of Nero to reestablish stability in the empire and in the government. They managed to return the empire to sound financial footing.

Titus was constantly plagued by the activities of his younger brother, Domitian. Even though he did not believe that Domitian was worthy to be his successor, he would not dispose of him. See *Jerusalem; Rome and the Roman Empire.*

Gary Poulton

TITUS, LETTER TO Paul the apostle wrote to Titus, a trusted Gentile co-worker. When Paul and Barnabas went to Jerusalem to discuss the gospel with the apostles, they took Titus along with them as an example of a believing Gentile who had not been circumcised (Gal. 2:1-3). The apostle also used Titus to deliver a difficult letter to the Corinthian church (2 Cor. 2:3-4,13; 7:6-16) and to collect the church's gift for the poor saints in Jerusalem (8:16-24).

The circumstances of the writing of Titus are similar to those of the first letter to Timothy. After his first Roman imprisonment (A.D. 60–62), Paul returned to the East for missionary work. Apparently after Paul and Titus had evangelized Crete, Titus was left behind to set the churches in order, appointing elders in every city (Titus 1:5). Paul probably wrote this letter on the way to Nicopolis from Crete around A.D. 63–65. Just as in the first letter to Timothy, Paul warned against false teachers and issued instructions to various groups regarding proper Christian behavior. Furthermore, he instructed Titus to join him in Nicopolis whenever a replacement arrived (3:12).

Paul described the gospel as a fixed set of beliefs, "godliness" (Titus 1:1), "the truth" (1:1), "sound teaching" (1:9; 2:1,8), and "the faith" (1:13). That the gospel is described in this way should not trouble us nor lead to a suspicion that Paul did not write Titus. Unlike his letters to churches, Paul wrote to a person he trusted with the ministry of the gospel, and we would expect him to describe the gospel in these ways. In other letters Paul referred to the gospel in similar ways, stressing holding firmly to tradition (1 Cor. 11:2), citing creedal statements which reflected the gospel's content (15:3-5), and designated the gospel as "the faith" (Gal. 1:23).

As in the other Pastorals, heresy was a problem, made up of myths (Titus 1:14) and genealo-

gies (3:9), as well as some Jewish elements (1:10,14). The false teachers enjoyed controversies and disputes (1:10; 3:9-10) and were deceptive (1:10), detestable, disobedient, and worthless (1:15-16). They also hoped for profit from their teaching (1:11). The false teaching may have been similar to the Colossian heresy.

Paul mentioned two offices of church leaders: elder (*presbuteros*, Titus 1:5), bishop/overseer (*episkopos*, 1:7), apparently used interchangeably, as in Acts 20:17,28. "Bishop" is more descriptive of function, while "elder" may refer to age and/or experience. These had spiritual oversight of the congregations. This does not necessarily reflect monarchical church structure later than Paul's lifetime. Paul did not discuss the duties of bishops and elders in detail, but elders/overseers must be of unimpeachable moral character (Titus 1:5-9) and are to manage their families well (1:6).

Because the term "elders" is plural (Titus 1:5) many hold that each congregation had a plurality of elders. However, this cannot be proven. The use of the plural is natural when more than one person is indicated. The plural could easily be because there were multiple churches, thus multiple elders. Though multiple elders may have led each congregation, it seems more likely that individual elders led each house church.

Paul viewed humanity as having a problem with sin (Titus 3:3), but salvation was provided graciously by God, based solely on His grace and mercy and not on works (3:4-7). Paul also explained that those saved by Christ should devote themselves to good works (2:11-14; 3:3-8). See *Apollos; Circumcision; Holy Spirit; Paul; Salvation.*

Outline

I. Greeting (1:1-4)
II. Titus's Ministry in Crete (1:5-16)
III. Sound Teaching (2:1-15)
IV. The Importance of Good Works (3:1-11)
V. Final Instructions and Closing (3:12-15)

Terry Wilder

TIZITE (Tī´ zīt) Title of Joha, one of David's 30 elite warriors (1 Chron. 11:45), designating his hometown or home region, which is otherwise unknown.

TOAH (Tō´ ah) Personal name, perhaps meaning "humility." A Kohathite Levite (1 Chron.

6:34). The parallel lists read Nahath (1 Chron. 6:26) and Tohu (1 Sam. 1:1).

TOB (Tŏb) Place-name meaning "good." Syrian city in southern Hauran to which Jephthah fled from his brothers (Judg. 11:3-5). Tob contributed troops to an unsuccessful alliance against David (2 Sam. 10:6-13). Tob is perhaps identical with Tabeel (Isa. 7:6). The site is perhaps et-Taiyibeh about 12 miles east of Ramoth-gilead near the source of the Yarmuk River.

TOBADONIJAH (Tŏb ăd o nī´ jah) Personal name meaning "Yah, my Lord, is good." Levite whom Jehoshaphat sent to teach the people of Judah (2 Chron. 17:8). The name is perhaps a combination of the two preceding names in the list.

TOBIAH (Tō bī´ ah) Personal name meaning "Yah is good." **1.** One of the major adversaries to Nehemiah's rebuilding efforts at Jerusalem, Tobiah was a practicing Jew who lived in a residence chamber in the temple. He is called an "Ammonite" (Neh. 2:10,19) probably because his family fled to that territory at the destruction of Jerusalem. He enjoyed aristocratic favor and had the title "servant" bestowed on him by the Persian ruler. He opposed the rebuilding of Jerusalem because it would weaken his political authority in the area. Tobiah allied with Sanballat and Geshem in trying to thwart Nehemiah. **2.** Ancestor of clan who returned from exile but could not show they were Israelites (Ezra 2:60).

TOBIJAH (Tō bī´ jah) Alternate form of Tobiah. **1.** Levite whom Jehoshaphat sent to teach the people (2 Chron. 17:8). **2.** Returned exile who apparently brought a gift of gold from Babylon for the Jerusalem community. Zechariah used him as a witness for his crowning of Joshua, the high priest, and to preserve the crowns in the temple (Zech. 6:9-14).

TOCHEN (Tō´ kĕn) Place-name meaning "measure." An unidentified village in Simeon (1 Chron. 4:32). The parallel lists in Josh. 15:42; 19:7 have "Ether."

TOGARMAH (Tō gár´ mah) Son of Gomer and name of a region of Asia Minor (Gen. 10:3; 1 Chron. 1:6; cp. Beth-togarmah, Ezek. 38:6) inhabited by his descendants. Togarmah was

famed for its horses (Ezek. 27:14). This site is likely modern Gurun, 70 miles west of Malatya, or an area in Armenia.

TOHU (Tō´ hū) Ancestor of Samuel (1 Sam. 1:1). Parallel lists read "Nahath" (1 Chron. 6:26) and "Toah" (6:34) in the corresponding position.

TOI (Tō´ ī) Personal name meaning "error." King of Hammath on the Orontes who sent tribute to David following his defeat of their mutual foe, Hadadezer of Zobah (2 Sam. 8:9-10; Tou, 1 Chron. 18:9-10).

TOKEN KJV term meaning "sign" (Gen. 9:12-17; Pss. 65:8; 135:9). See *Sign.*

TOKHATH (Tŏk´ hăth) Alternate form of Tikvah (2 Chron. 34:22).

TOLA (Tō´ lȧ) Personal name meaning "crimson worm." **1.** Issachar's firstborn son (Gen. 46:13; Num. 26:23; 1 Chron. 7:1-2). **2.** Judge who governed Israel for 23 years from Shamir, likely at or near Samaria (Judg. 10:1).

TOLAD (Tō´ lăd) Alternate form of Eltolad (1 Chron. 4:29).

TOLAITE (Tō´ lā īt) Division of Issachar descended from Tola (Num. 26:23-25).

TOLL See *Publican; Taxes; Tribute.*

TOMB OF JESUS According to the NT accounts, the tomb of Jesus was located in a garden in the place where Jesus was crucified (John 19:41) outside the city walls of Jerusalem (19:20). It was a "new tomb" which had been "cut into the rock" by Joseph of Arimathea (Matt. 27:60 HCSB; cp. Luke 23:50-56) who had apparently prepared it for his own family's use. It was not uncommon for the well-to-do to prepare such a tomb in advance because of the difficulty of digging graves in the rocky ground around Jerusalem. The tomb was large enough for someone to sit inside (Mark 16:5; cp. John 20:11-12) and required that one stoop down to look inside and enter (John 20:5-6,11; cp. Luke 24:12). A great rolling stone sealed the entrance (Matt. 27:60; Mark 15:46; 16:3).

This description suggests a typical Jewish tomb of the Herodian period consisting of (1) an antechamber, (2) a slow doorway that could be

T

sealed with a stone (in many cases a rolling stone fitted into a groove or track so that the tomb could be opened and closed by rolling the stone back and forth in front of the doorway), and (3) a passageway leading to a rectangular-shaped tomb chamber. Here the body (having been wrapped in a linen cloth) could be laid lengthwise in either a rectangular, horizontal, oven-shaped shaft driven back into the vertical rock face measuring 78x25x20 inches or laid on a simple rock shelf cut laterally into the rock with a vaulted arch over it. The sequence of events narrated in the Gospel accounts (esp. John 20:5-6) would seem to indicate that Jesus' tomb had this vaulted arch.

The traditional site of the tomb of Jesus is marked by the Church of the Holy Sepulchre, which stands over the site of a first-century rock quarry that in Jesus' day was outside the city walls of Jerusalem and in which other typical first-century tombs have been discovered. An alternative site known as the "Garden Tomb" (adjacent to "Gordon's Calvary") was identified in 1883.   *Hulitt Gloer*

TONGS Pinchers for holding coals (1 Kings 7:49; 2 Chron. 4:21; Isa. 6:6). KJV used "tongs" at Exod. 25:38; Num. 4:9 where modern trans-

lations read "snuffers" (HCSB, NASB, NRSV) or "wick trimmers" (NIV).

TONGUE The tongue (Hb. *lashon*, Gk. *glossa*) is the organ of speech. In both the OT and NT the word is also used for languages spoken (Isa. 28:11-12; Acts 2:4,11) as well as for the people who are represented by those languages (Isa. 66:18; Rev. 5:9). The word is also used of the tongues of animals, especially when humans are said to take on some animal-like quality related to the tongue, such as having a poisonous tongue like an asp (Job 20:16).

Because the tongue is the instrument of speech, many passages use the word metaphorically (or metonymically) to praise or criticize the kinds of speech in which humans engage. The speech that comes from the tongue can be either good or evil (Ps. 120:2; Prov. 6:17; 10:20; James 3:7-12). Proverbs addresses these matters in picturesque language. "The tongue of the righteous is pure silver" (10:20 HCSB). "The tongue of the wise [brings] healing, … but a lying tongue [is for] only a moment" (12:18-19). "The tongue that heals is a tree of life" (15:4). "A ruler can be persuaded through patience, and a gentle tongue can break a bone" (25:15). Finally, for the "capa-

The Garden Tomb is one site offered by tradition as the burial place of Jesus' body.

T

ble wife," "loving instruction is on her tongue" (31:26).

The tongue can be a window into the human heart. It pronounces the thoughts and intents contained in the heart, which could be good (Ps. 34:30) or evil (Pss. 34:13; 52:2; 109:2; 120:2-3; Isa. 59:3). The tongue is important in demonstrating one's true relationship to God. For the unbeliever the tongue is an instrument of deceit, showing man's true nature (Rom. 3:13). Jesus said that it is by men's words that they are justified or condemned (Matt. 12:37).

Controlling the tongue is one of the keys to a successful life (Prov.21:23; James 3:2; 1 Pet. 3:10). It is so potent that both death and life are in its power (Prov. 18:21). The tongue is sharp, even as sharp as a sword (Ps. 64:3) or an arrow (Jer. 9:3,8).

Genesis 11 refers to the confusion of "tongues" that resulted from God's judgment on human pride at the building of the tower. That judgment brought about a division in human life exemplified in the diversity of languages. That diversity was symbolically broken down at Pentecost (Acts 2:4-12), though that diversity of tongues will not be realized finally until the fulfillment of the kingdom expectations (Rev. 5:9). In addition, though not all persons will ultimately be saved, it is the case that one day every tongue shall confess that Jesus Christ is Lord (Phil. 2:11). See *Spiritual Gifts; Tongues, Gift of.*

Chad Brand

TONGUES, GIFT OF The NT deals with the practice of speaking in tongues both by example and instruction in Acts and the first letter to the Corinthians. There is also a brief mention of it in the long ending of Mark. There is no specific presentation of the practice in the OT, though some interpreters see the prophetic activities of Saul and the elders to be precursors (1 Sam. 10:9-13; 19:18-24) of "tongues" speech. There is no clear evidence in the text, though, that this prophesying involved speaking in tongues.

Three passages in Acts treat this phenomenon. In Acts 2 the disciples are baptized in the Spirit on the day of Pentecost, and, as a witness to this event, they speak with other tongues (*heterais glossais*—Acts 2:4). These tongues are known languages, as is clear from the following verses, where the pilgrims from Cappadocia, Phrygia, Egypt, etc., heard them speaking of the wonders of God in their own languages (*dialek-*

toi—Acts 2:8), or tongues (*glossais*—Acts 2:11). Here Luke uses the two words, *dialektos* (language) and *glossa* (tongue, language), interchangeably. In other NT literature the terms are likewise both used to mean "known language" (cp. Acts 1:19; 22:2; 26:14 for examples of *dialektos* and Rev. 7:9; 10:11; 11:9; 13:7; 14:6; 17:15 for examples of *glossa*), though the word *glossa* also refers to the tongue as a part of the anatomy (Acts 2:26; James 3:5; Rev. 16:10). *Glossa* is used as well in identifying the tongue with a person in the act of speech (*metonymy*): "Every tongue should confess" (Phil. 2:11 HCSB; Rom. 14:11, "will give praise"). *Glossa* carries the same range of meaning in other Greek literature.

Speaking in tongues in Acts 2 is evidentiary. The unique speech is demonstrable proof that something supernatural has happened to the 120 disciples of Jesus. Tongues are the sign that these people have received the promise given by Jesus in Acts 1:5, "You will be baptized with the Holy Spirit not many days from now." This sign was clear enough so that all of those present for the Feast of Weeks were able to see that an impossible event was actually happening. The language speech in this chapter has a second, though subordinate, purpose—the communication of the gospel to people of a foreign tongue. It is likely that the pilgrims present could speak Greek, but the text does indicate that the communication of the gospel in their languages was still important.

In Acts 10 Peter was sent by God to preach to Cornelius, a centurion of the Roman guard, with his family and associates. While Simon was preaching, the Spirit fell upon the assembly (v. 44), and the Gentiles spoke with tongues, demonstrating to the Jews there that these persons had "received the Holy Spirit just as we [the Jews] have" (v. 47 HCSB). Immediately Peter returned to Jerusalem to report to the believers there on the outpouring of salvation to the Gentiles. When the Jerusalem Christians heard about the gift of the Spirit, evidenced by tongues, they responded, "So God has granted repentance resulting in life to even the Gentiles" (11:18). In chapter 19 Paul encountered a group of 12 disciples of John the Baptist. He showed them that John had taught the people "that they should believe in the One who would come after him, that is, in Jesus" (19:4 HCSB). When they believed in Christ, the Spirit came upon them,

T

and "they began to speak with [other] languages and to prophesy" (v. 6). This was significant since John still had many disciples in the world of that day, and since John himself had first predicted the coming Spirit baptism that would be given by Jesus (Matt. 3:11).

The book of Acts features these three texts as occasions of what scholars call "glossolalia." It is possible that the evangelization of the Samaritans in Acts 8 also featured "tongues" speech, since Simon Magus witnessed an unusual phenomenon when the Spirit was given (8:17-18), though the text makes no specific mention of tongues. In each case the experience is linked to the reception of the Spirit. However, it is important to note that each case represents the movement of the gospel to include a new group: Jews, Samaritans (possibly), Gentiles, disciples of John. There are no other examples of glossolalia in Acts.

The other extended treatment of this gift is found in the first letter to the Corinthians. There Paul lists it as a spiritual gift (1 Cor. 12:7-10), gives instructions about its nature, suggests qualifications for its use, and contrasts it with prophecy (14:1-40). He who speaks in tongues speaks mysteries (*musteria*—14:2). This word is used by Paul, John, and Jesus to refer to the giving of new revelations to the new covenant community (Matt. 13:11; Rom. 11:25; 16:25; 1 Cor. 2:1,7; 4:1; 15:51; Eph. 1:9; 3:3-4,9; 6:19-20; Col. 1:25-27; 2:2; 4:3; 1 Tim. 3:9,16; Rev. 10:7; 17:5-7). Among other things, then, tongues constituted one of the ways in which God revealed the content of the NT revelation to the early church. The apostle also noted that unless tongues speech is interpreted, it ought not to be employed in public worship, since the purpose of spiritual gifts is the edification of the body (1 Cor. 14:3-6). But interpreted tongues speech might have the same function as prophecy. Further, tongues speech, like all public expressions in worship, needs to be done in an orderly manner (14:26-33). Some interpreters have postulated that the tongues speech at Corinth differed from that in Acts in that it was not languages, but "ecstatic speech." This cannot be proven from the linguistic evidence, since both Luke and Paul use the word *glossa* predominately. Nor can it be proven contextually, as there is no evidence in the text that this was a different kind of speech than that in Acts. One would not be likely to come to such a conclusion simply from looking at the text of Corinthians. This interpretation

likely arises out of experience in communities that practice glossolalia, since they rarely attest to actual languages being spoken.

Several key questions have been voiced concerning this practice. One, is this a gift only for NT times or is it also for the church all through history? As noted above, tongues in the NT has three functions—to show the progress of the gift of the Spirit to the various people groups in the book of Acts in a salvation-history context, as a way of revealing the content of the NT revelation, and as a means of communicating cross-linguistically. The first two purposes would no longer be applicable, since the gospel has now gone out to the entire world and the NT revelation has been given. The third possibility will be addressed shortly. Two, is tongues speech the sign of Spirit baptism? It was in Acts, but only among the people groups that constituted the process of salvation history: Jews, Samaritans, Gentiles, and finally the disciples of John, who first predicted the gift of the Spirit. Spirit baptism occurs at conversion, and its evidence is the fruit of the Spirit (Gal. 5:22-23), not tongues. Three, ought all persons to speak in tongues? Paul answers this clearly in the negative (1 Cor. 12:30). Four, is modern tongues supposed to be languages or ecstatic utterance? This article has argued that there is no compelling reason to believe that "ecstatic utterance" is the same thing as the biblical gift of tongues. Five, is there such a thing as a private prayer language? People certainly do pray in tongues, but nothing in the text authorizes a private prayer language. Though Paul mentions praying with reference to tongues in 1 Cor. 14:2,14-15, the entire context is one of public worship, not private prayer. Such tongues speech comes under the guidance of the entire chapter in the governing of public tongues. Six, might tongues speech be demonic? It might. The enemy can counterfeit God's good gifts. But even in cases where someone's "tongues" does not match the biblical criteria, the experience might not be demonic; it is possible for persons to tap into a basic ability that all have to engage in such linguistic-free discourse. It would not be the same thing as the biblical gift of tongues and would not be miraculous, but it might still be done reverently. Seven, is it possible for one to receive a gift of languages for the purpose of evangelism? No one would wish to limit God's ability to grant such a gift. There are even stories of such events from the mission field, though undoubtedly some of them have been embellished. It is also the case that all Pentecostal groups that send missionaries send them for language training first. See *Baptism in the Holy Spirit; Holy Spirit; Pentecost; Spiritual Gifts.* *Chad Brand*

TOOLS Implements or instruments used with the hands for agricultural, construction, commercial, or craft purposes. In the earliest periods tools were made of stone, especially flint. An effective cutting surface was achieved by chipping off flakes along the edge of the shaped stone. The first metal tools were of copper, which proved to be too soft for most applications. It was soon found that much harder tools could be made from bronze, an alloy of copper and tin. Bronze, like copper, could be melted and poured into molds before final shaping by a smith. The hardest tools were made of iron (Deut. 27:5; 1 Kings 6:5-7), which required much higher temperatures to smelt. Iron only came into use in Canaan around 1200 B.C., about the time of the Israelite settlement. Handles and other parts of certain tools were made of wood, leather, bone, or ivory. See *Minerals and Metals.*

Knives One of the most common of tools is the knife. The flint knives of earlier periods continued in use even after metal became widespread. It has been suggested that the command to use flint knives for circumcision (Josh. 5:2 NIV) reflects a taboo on using new technology for ancient rites. The real reason, however, is probably more practical: flint knives kept a sharp edge longer than metal blades. Nevertheless, bronze knives became the standard for general use prior to the Israelite monarchy. The blade was cast in a stone mold, and handles of wood were usually attached by a tang or rivets. Iron knives, which became popular during the Israelite monarchy, were made in a similar fashion.

The knife served various purposes and was known in different forms. The average knife in Palestine was between 6 and 10 inches, but a mold has been found to produce 16-inch blades. These would have been used for general cutting and butchering (Gen. 22:6; Judg. 19:29). A smaller version used by Jehoiakim to cut up Jeremiah's scroll (Jer. 36:23; KJV, NRSV, "penknife"; NIV, "scribe's knife") is represented by a Hebrew word elsewhere used for razors

A winnowing fork was a tool to aid the farmer in separating chaff from the grains of wheat.

(Num. 6:5; Ezek. 5:1). The latter (Judg. 13:5; 16:17; 1 Sam. 1:11) were evidently quite sharp, as they are used as symbols of God's judgment (Isa. 7:20) and the cutting power of the tongue (Ps. 52:2).

Agricultural Tools Plows had basically the same design from the earliest models known down to those used in the present day in the Near East. The handles, crossbar, and other structural parts were of wood, while the plow point, or plowshare, needed to be of harder material to penetrate the ground. The earliest plowshares were of bronze, which was only slowly replaced by iron following the Israelite settlement of Canaan. Early Iron Age levels at several archaeological sites in Palestine have produced examples of both types. Plowshares were elongated blades with a pointed end for cutting into the ground and the other end rolled like a pipe to fit on the wooden shaft. Plows were pulled by animals which were prodded with a goad, a wooden stick fitted with a metal tip (Judg. 3:31; 1 Sam. 13:21; Eccles. 12:11). On hilly or rocky terrain which was difficult to plow, the ground was broken using a hoe (Isa. 7:25 NRSV, NIV; KJV, "mattock"). A similar tool, the mattock (1 Sam. 13:21), was also used for digging chores. It is probably incorrectly translated as "plowshares" in the famous prophetic passages about the tools of war and peace (Isa. 2:4; Mic. 4:3; Joel 3:10). Just prior to the monarchy, the Philistines, perhaps holding a monopoly on iron technology, forced the Israelites to come to them for sharpening of agricultural tools. The charge in silver was a pim, two-thirds of a shekel, for sharpening plowshares and mattocks and one-third of a shekel for smaller tools (1 Sam. 13:19-22). See *Weights and Measures.*

The reaping of standing grain was done with a sickle (Deut. 16:9; 23:25; Jer. 50:16), a small tool with a handle and curved blade. Sickles consisting of several serrated flint segments fitted into a shaft of bone or hollowed-out wood were typical of the Canaanite culture. In Israelite and NT times sickles had metal blades and short wooden handles. The sickle is used as a symbol of God's judgment (Joel 3:13) and the ingathering of the saints (Mark 4:29; Rev. 14:14-19). A tool, which resembled the sickle but with a broader and shorter blade, was the "pruning hook" (Isa. 2:4; Mic. 4:3; Joel 3:10). It was a type of knife used for pruning and harvesting grapevines (Isa. 18:5).

Building Tools The OT mentions several different types of axes used in various hewing chores. The largest ax (Isa. 10:15) was used for felling trees (Deut. 19:5; 20:19) and quarrying stone (1 Kings 6:7). This type of ax was mentioned as a stone cutting tool in the Siloam Tunnel inscription in Jerusalem. A smaller ax was used for lighter jobs (Judg. 9:48; 1 Sam. 13:20-21; Ps. 74:5; Jer. 46:22). The Hebrew word used for ax head literally means "iron," indicating its material (Deut. 19:5; 2 Kings 6:5; Isa. 10:34). Trimming was done with a different tool (Jer. 10:3 REB; NIV, "chisel"), perhaps an adze with its cutting edge perpendicular to the handle. Small hand axes or hatchets were also known (Ps. 74:6 KJV; NRSV, "hammers"; REB, "pick"). A single word is used for axes in the NT (Matt. 3:10; Luke 3:9). See *Siloam*.

Wood and stone were also cut using saws (2 Sam. 12:31; 1 Kings 7:9; 1 Chron. 20:3; Isa. 10:15). Single and double-handled varieties are pictured in Egyptian tomb paintings. Bronze was used for the blades in the earlier periods and iron in the later. According to an apocryphal work (the Ascension of Isaiah), the Prophet Isaiah was martyred by being sawn in two (cp. Heb. 11:37).

Detail work was marked out using a "line" and "compass" (Isa. 44:13; NIV, "chisels" and "compasses"). Various types of measuring tools, lines, and chisels have been found in Egyptian tombs. Plumb lines were used quite early in Egypt and Palestine for determining verticality and levels in construction. The true levels determined by the measuring line and the plumb line are compared to the justice and righteousness God required of Israel and Judah (2 Kings 21:13; KJV, "plummet"; Isa. 28:17; Amos 7:7-8).

Hammers (Isa. 44:12; Jer. 10:4) were originally stone pounders, but in the Bronze Age holes were often bored for the insertion of a handle. Egyptian paintings show the use of broad wooden mallets not unlike those still used today in sculpture work. The "planes" used in shaping (Isa. 44:13) were probably chisels (as in the NIV). Chisels were used for rough and detail work in both wood and stone. Holes were made with awls (Exod. 21:6; Deut. 15:17) or drills.

Industrial Tools Special tools were used in the work of various industries. Early potters used wooden tools to help shape their handmade vessels. A considerable advance came with the invention of the pottery wheel (Jer. 18:3). See *Pottery*.

Weavers conducted their craft on devices called looms. A number of tools were used to assist in the weaving process. In some types of weaving, the horizontal weft threads were "beaten" in with a flat wooden stick. The weaving of patterns required picks and combs to manipulate and press up the threads. These were usually made of bone, less often of ivory or wood. See *Spinning and Weaving*.

Metalworking required unique tools as well. A bellows was needed to bring a fire to the high temperatures required for smelting ore. Hand operated bellows are shown in an Egyptian tomb painting of Semitic nomads from about the time of Abraham. These were used in small furnaces equipped with nozzles of clay to withstand the extreme heat. Molds were used to shape molten metal into tools, weapons, and other items. Metal smiths also used a variety of tongs, clamps, and hammers (Isa. 44:12), and the like.

Daniel C. Browning, Jr.

TOPAZ See *Minerals and Metals*.

TOPHEL (Tō´ phĕl) Place near the site of Moses' farewell speech to Israel (Deut. 1:1), identified with et-Tafileh about 15 miles southeast of the Dead Sea between Kerak and Petra. It may represent the name of a territory rather than a city.

TOPHET (Tō´ phĕt) or **TOPHETH** (Tō´ pheth) Name for a place in the Hinnom Valley outside Jerusalem derived from Aramaic or Hebrew meaning "fireplace" but altered by Hebrew scribes to mean "shameful thing" because of the illicit worship carried on there (Jer. 7:31-32; KJV,

"Tophet"). Child sacrifice was practiced at Topheth, leading the prophet to declare a slaughter of people there when God would come in vengeance (Jer. 19:6-11). See *Hinnom, Valley of.*

TORAH (Tō´ rah) Hebrew word normally translated "law," which eventually became a title for the Pentateuch, the first five books of the OT.
Old Testament Though universally translated "law" in the KJV, *torah* also carries the sense of "teaching" or "instruction," as reflected in more recent translations (Job 22:22; Ps. 78:1; Prov. 1:8; 4:2; 13:14; Isa. 30:9). The meaning, law, is certainly present in the OT. *Torah*, for example, is used in connection with terms for requirements, commands, and decrees (Gen. 26:5; Exod. 18:16). The Torah was given to Moses (Exod. 24:12) and commanded to be kept (Exod. 16:28; Deut. 17:19; Ezek. 44:24).

Within the book of Deuteronomy, *Torah* is used to represent the body of the Deuteronomic Code (Deut. 4:8; 30:10; 32:46), that is, the essence of Israel's responsibilities under the covenant. Subsequent OT writings continue to speak of *Torah* as "The Law" in this sense (Isa. 5:24; Jer. 32:23; 44:10; Dan. 9:11), often as "the book of the law," the "law of Moses," or a combination (Josh. 1:8; 8:31-32,34; 2 Kings 14:6). The "book of the law" found in the temple which fueled Josiah's reforms (2 Kings 22:8-13) is often regarded to be roughly equivalent to the book of Deuteronomy. By the time of Ezra and Nehemiah "the book of the law of Moses" (Neh. 8:1) included more material than the Deuteronomic Code. Ezra cited "the law of Moses that the LORD had commanded Israel" (HCSB) concerning the feast of booths, which is prescribed in Leviticus (22:33-43). Eventually the name *Torah* came to be applied to the entire Pentateuch, the five books traditionally ascribed to Moses: Genesis, Exodus, Leviticus, Numbers, and Deuteronomy. In rabbinical Judaism the scope of the Torah is sometimes expanded to include all of the Scriptures or even the entirety of God's revelation.
New Testament During NT times the limits on the OT canon were being finalized. The Jews began to think of their Scriptures as consisting of three sections: the Torah (Law), the Prophets, and the Writings (cp. Luke 24:44). The books of Moses were considered "law" despite the fact that a considerable amount of their material is not legalistic in nature. The Torah was unques-

tionably considered the most important division of the Scriptures. The Sadducees, in fact, accepted only the Torah as inspired Scripture. The same is true of the Samaritans who considered themselves God's true chosen people.

In the NT period the Torah was more than merely a section of the Scriptures; it became central to Judaism. The will of God was seen as embodied in the observance of the law. Pious Jews, therefore, needed some elaboration on the commands contained in the Torah to determine more precisely their obligation, and the interpretation of various passages became the subject of much debate. The traditions of the Pharisees went far beyond the bounds of the law as spelled out in the Torah. These traditions became for them the oral Torah, considered given to Moses at Mount Sinai to accompany the written law. Jesus scathingly denounced the Pharisees' placing their tradition above the intent of the law (Mark 7:8-13). Jesus never denied the authority of the Torah but denounced the elevation of ritual concerns above "more important matters of the law—justice, mercy and faith" (Matt. 23:23 HCSB). Some of the precepts of the law,

Jewish rabbis conversing in front of an elaborately decorated scroll of the Torah.

T

according to Jesus, were provided because of humanity's nature and fall short of God's perfect will (Matt. 5:33-37; 19:8-9). For true believers Jesus demanded a commitment that went far beyond the supposed righteousness gained by keeping the law (Luke 18:18-23).

The Apostle Paul preached justification by faith rather than by the keeping of the law. Thus, he had much to say about Torah. Torah, according to Paul, would lead to life if it were actually practiced (Rom. 10:5), but such practice is impossible (Rom. 3:20). The effect of the law has been to manifest a knowledge of sin and bring about its increase (Rom. 3:20; 5:20; 7:5,7-11; 1 Cor. 15:56). Mankind was thus consigned to sin and God's resulting wrath (Rom. 4:14; Gal. 3:22), which set the stage for the revelation of God's grace through Christ (Rom. 3:21-26; Gal. 3:22-25). For Paul the Torah epitomized the old covenant, with the law written on stone (2 Cor. 3:7). In the superior new covenant, the law is in the Spirit (2 Cor. 3:6), written on the hearts of believers (cp. Jer. 31:33). Believers are not subject to the Torah (Gal. 5:18), but by walking "according to the Spirit" (Rom. 8:4 HCSB; Gal. 5:16) they produce fruits which transcend (Gal. 5:22-25) and fulfill the essence of the law (Rom. 13:8-10; Gal. 5:14; cp. Matt. 22:37-40). See *Law, Ten Commandments, Torah; Pentateuch.*

Daniel C. Browning, Jr.

TORCH Long pole with cloths dipped in oil wrapped around one end used as a light. The Greek *lampas* is generally rendered "torch" (John 18:3; Rev. 4:5; 8:10), unless the context suggests the translation "lamp" (Acts 20:8). The lamps of the wise and foolish virgins (Matt. 25:1-8) were perhaps torches.

TORTOISE See *Reptiles.*

TOSEPHTA Hebrew term *tosaphah* and its Aramaic parallel *tosephta* denote a collection of additional rabbinic opinion arranged in the order of the Mishnah of Judah ha-Nasi. It may be regarded as a collected appendix to the Mishnah. In its current form the Tosephta was probably edited about the end of the fourth century A.D. It was compiled in Palestine at about the same time as the Jerusalem Talmud. The intent of the editor seems to have been to "update" or further supplement the Mishnah with reference to new case law developed over the two centuries that sepa-

Ruins of the city walls of the ancient city of Perga showing the remains of a defense tower.

rated the two works. Its existence shows the development in the legal system of the rabbis of Palestine as they sought to adapt the law orally to new and changing social and religious conditions. See *Mishnah; Talmud.*

Stephenson Humphries-Brooks

TOU (Tō´ ū) Alternate form of Toi (1 Chron. 18:9-10).

TOW Short, broken fibers of flax, known to be easily broken and highly flammable, used as a figure for weakness and transience (Judg. 16:9; Isa. 1:31; 43:17).

TOWER Tall edifice erected so watchmen could guard pastures, vineyards, and cities. Towers ranged from small one-room structures to entire fortresses. Archaeological remains confirm the wide usage of towers from the earliest times. Most were made of stones, although some wooden towers have been unearthed. The word is used figuratively of God's salvation in 2 Sam. 22:51, indicating the strength of the Lord's action. See *Assayer.*

TOWN See *Cities and Urban Life.*

TRACHONITIS (Trăk o nī´ tĭs) Place-name meaning "heap of stones." A political and geographic district in northern Palestine on the east side of the Jordan River (Luke 3:1). Its terrain was rugged and best suited to raising sheep and goats. The area was almost totally devoid of timber. During John the Baptist's ministry Trachonitis was ruled by Philip, the brother of Herod Antipas. Known as Bashan in the OT (Amos 4:1), it was just south of Damascus. See *Bashan; Herod.*

TRADE See *Commerce*.

TRADITION Teaching or ritual which is handed down. The term "tradition" has several usages. The term is often used to speak of denominations or distinct theological viewpoints, such as the Baptist tradition or the Reformed tradition. The term is also commonly used to refer to liturgical consistency or to historical practice, as in a tradition of the church. Tradition also is used to speak of legend material, such as the tradition of Peter asking to be crucified upside-down. From a technical standpoint, the term is used to describe two distinct groups of theological material: Biblical material prior to its being written down as Scripture and writings which are not part of the Bible but are still esteemed by the church.

Scriptural Tradition Scholars use the word "tradition" to describe the existence of biblical material before it reached its biblical form. It is necessary to talk of tradition given the gap in time between the occurrence of biblical events and the biblical recording of those events. The term "tradition" describes the knowledge of the event during the time between the event and its recording in Scripture. Certain parts of the Bible, such as Revelation, did not have an existence prior to their writing, yet much of the biblical material did exist in some form. For example, when Paul ministered to the churches in Asia, he taught numerous things about Jesus, living a Christian life, and the ministry of the church. Many of these same teachings were reiterated in his epistles. Thus elements of Paul's teaching existed before he physically wrote his teaching down in the epistles, even though those elements were not written down anywhere.

Traditional material may have taken a number of forms. Tradition may have been in a written form. Luke implies that he used written sources to help him write his Gospel (Luke 1:1-4). The writer of the book of 1 Kings also mentions that he has utilized written documents when writing his work (1 Kings 14:19; 15:7; 16:5; 22:39). In addition, tradition may have been orally transmitted. In ancient cultures accounts were often ritualistically repeated around a campfire or as part of a religious service. Thus everyone in the community became a repository of the tradition. Whatever form it took, the existence of tradition is true of both OT and NT material.

The OT describes events that occurred over a period of thousands of years. Thus when Moses wrote the book of Genesis, he was writing about some events that had occurred some 2,500 years before he was born. Yet, Moses was able to write Genesis under the inspiration of the Holy Spirit, in part, because the teaching of how God had created the world, how He had saved Noah, and how He had made a covenant with Abraham had been passed down to Moses as tradition. Deuteronomy 6 clearly teaches that subsequent generations must be told of God's works. Thus the Bible itself contains a command to continue to pass on the tradition. In addition, most of the prophetic material was originally delivered as sermons. The prophets would quite literally preach to the people. These sermons existed as tradition until they were finally written down. In fact, the Bible describes Jeremiah's effort to hire Baruch to help him record his sermons (Jer. 36). Thus the OT was the product of tradition, preserving the memory of God's deeds in the consciousness of man.

This same process was at work in the formation of the NT. The Gospels, which describe the life and work of Jesus Christ, were not written immediately after His resurrection but were written some years later. Yet that does not mean that the church did not know what Jesus had done and what He had taught. Jesus' deeds and teachings were orally transmitted to new converts. Acts 2:42 records that the church "devoted themselves to the apostles' teaching" (HCSB). Elements of this teaching undoubtedly included information about Jesus' acts and teachings given to the disciples. Peter himself, when confronted by the Jewish religious leaders, proclaimed, "We are unable to stop speaking about what we have seen and heard" (Acts 4:20). This oral testimony of Christ was tradition. Paul alluded to this process in 1 Cor. 15:3 when he said, "For I passed on to you as most important what I also received" (cp. 1 Cor. 11:2). In fact, the pluralistic form of tradition is shown in 2 Thess. 2:15 where Paul stated, "Therefore, brothers, stand firm and hold to the traditions you were taught, either by our message or by our letter." Paul recognized the existence of tradition and understood that it may have been contained in several different forms.

Biblical scholars have dealt with tradition in different ways at different times. In the past OT scholars worked to separate the biblical texts into the traditions that lay behind the text. The most famous of these types of works was the Documentary Hypothesis, popularized by Julius Wellhausen, which separated the Pentateuch into four distinct traditions (Yahwist, Elohist, Priestly, and Deuteronomistic). The end result tended to be the fragmentation of both the text and its message. Modern OT scholarship has tended to preserve the literary integrity of the biblical text while recognizing the existence of tradition behind the text.

New Testament scholars have also been interested in identifying the traditions that lay behind the text. This is especially true of the Gospel materials. The similarities and differences between the Synoptic Gospels (Matthew, Mark, and Luke) have birthed an effort to discover the traditions which are the foundation to all three. Indeed, NT scholarship has spent over 200 years trying to explain the relationship of the Synoptic Gospels and their use of tradition. In recent NT studies in America, a non-evangelical group has begun to try and actually reconstruct the traditions that lay behind the Gospels. This group, selfentitled the Jesus Seminar, has gone so far as to edit Jesus' teaching and remove those elements which they believe to be additions to the original traditions. However, evangelical scholars have rejected the group's methodology, presuppositions, and findings.

Extrabiblical Tradition This refers to writings that are not included in the NT canon but are esteemed by the church. There are two primary factors that contributed to the continued usage of tradition in the church. The first factor relates to early church practice using non-canonical materials. Initially, before the canon was constructed, churches used both documents that were later accepted as part of the NT and material not accepted later into the NT. The formation of the canon was a gradual process that occurred over a long period of decades, during which non-canonical documents continued to be used. Even after the formation of the canon, the church continued to use some of these documents, which they recognized as tradition, meaning something other than canonical literature.

The second factor relates to the church's response to heretical groups. Various heretical groups, which arose within the church often, reinterpreted Scripture to support their particular viewpoint. Rather than address the hermeneutical methodologies of the heretics, the church argued that the new heretical interpretations were not what the church had always believed. In other words, these new ideas were not in keeping with church tradition, as expressed in these non-canonical writings. Thus the church began to elevate the traditional material, which supported their biblical interpretations and stood as a witness against the heretics. This practice eventually evolved into what the church called the rule of faith. The rule of faith is what the church has always believed as expressed in the various tradition materials.

Tradition, whether it be canonical antecedents or non-canonical writings, can be very useful to the modern student. Tradition shows the development and evolution of theology and church structure. It is also extremely helpful in explaining the development of the Roman Catholic Church. See *Bible Formation and Canon; Inspiration of Scripture.*

Scott Drumm

TRAIN Used to refer to the part of a robe that trails behind the wearer (Isa. 6:1 KJV, NASB, NIV). See *Caravan; Retinue.*

TRANCE Translation of the Greek term that literally means a change of place. The term came to mean a mental state of a person who experienced an intense emotional reaction to stimuli that were perceived as originating outside the person, the results of which were visual or auditory sensations or other impressions of the senses.

Trance is descriptive of an experience in which a person received a revelation by supernatural means (Acts 10:10; 11:5; 22:17; HCSB, "visionary state"). In these instances, the author of Acts, in reference to the experiences of Peter and Paul, seemed to be interested in showing that the trance was only a vehicle for a revelation from God. Luke illustrated that the trances that Peter and Paul experienced "happened" to them and were not self-induced. The distinctions between "trance," "dream," and "vision" are not always clear. See *Ecstasy; Prophets.*

James Newell

TRANSFIGURATION Transformation of Jesus in His appearance with Moses and Elijah before Peter, James, and John (Matt. 17:1-13; Mark 9:1-13; Luke 9:28-36; cp. 2 Pet. 1:16-18). This event took place shortly after the confession at Caesarea Philippi, the first passion prediction, and a discourse on the cost of discipleship. Jesus took Peter, James, and John to a mountain where the event took place. Jesus' personal appearance and that of His garments were changed. Moses and Elijah appeared and talked with Jesus. Peter said it was good to be there, and they should build three booths. A cloud came over them, and God spoke from the cloud identifying Jesus as His Son (cp. the voice at the baptism) and commanding the disciples to hear Him. When the cloud lifted, Jesus was alone with the disciples, who were afraid. Jesus told the disciples to tell no one.

Aside from minor differences in wording, Mark alone states that Jesus' garments became so white that "no launderer could whiten them" (HCSB) and that Peter did not know what to say. Also Mark alone has no reference to a change in Jesus' face. Matthew alone indicates that God expressed His pleasure with Jesus, that the disciples fell on their faces, and that Jesus touched them to get them up. Instead of the "six days" of Matthew and Mark, Luke has "about eight days." He alone indicated that Jesus and the disciples were praying, that Moses and Elijah conversed with Jesus about His coming death, that the disciples were sleepy, and that they saw Jesus' glory. Luke alone has "Chosen One" rather than "beloved Son." In Matthew, Jesus is addressed as Lord, in Mark as Rabbi, and in Luke as Master.

The Nature of the Event It has often been claimed that the story is a misplaced resurrection appearance; but it is Moses and Elijah, not Jesus, who appear, and there is no reference to them or a voice from heaven in any other resurrection account. Others have claimed that the transfiguration was not an objective but a visionary experience. This is possible, but there is no more of the miraculous in three different disciples actually having similar visions than in a historical event, which is certainly what the writers described.

The Place The traditional site is Mount Tabor in lower Galilee, but it is not a high mountain (only 1,850 feet) and was probably fortified and inaccessible in Jesus' day. Much more likely is Mount Hermon (9,100 feet) to the north of Caesarea Philippi. See *Hermon, Mount.*

Meaning A mountain in the Bible is often a place of revelation. Moses and Elijah represented the law and the prophets respectively, which testify to but must give way to Jesus. (The

latter is the reason why Peter's suggestion was improper.) Moses and Elijah themselves were heralds of the Messiah (Deut. 18:15; Mal. 4:5-6). The three booths suggest the Feast of Tabernacles which symbolizes a new situation, a new age. Clouds represent divine presence. The close connection of the transfiguration with the confession and passion prediction is significant. The Messiah must suffer, but glorification and enthronement, not suffering, are His ultimate fate. These involve resurrection, ascension, and return in glory. The disciples needed the reassurance of the transfiguration as they contemplated Jesus' death and their future sufferings. See *Jesus, Life and Ministry.*   *James Brooks*

TRANSGRESSION Image of sin as overstepping the limits of God's law. See *Evil; Forgiveness; Repentance; Salvation; Sin.*

TRANSJORDAN Area immediately east of the Jordan River settled by Reuben, Gad, half of Manasseh, Edom, Moab, and Amon. The most prominent topographical feature of Palestine is the Jordan River Valley, referred to in the OT as the "Arabah" and called today, in Arabic, the *Ghor.* This valley represents a huge geographical fault line which is prominent also in Lebanon, where it creates the Beqa'a Valley, continues southward from Palestine to form the Red Sea, and extends even as far as Mozambique in east Africa. Center stage of the biblical narrative is the hill country west of the Jordan where most of the Israelite tribes were settled and where the famous cities of Samaria, Shechem, Jerusalem, and Hebron were sited. See *Jordan River; Palestine.*

The highlands east of the Jordan also played a significant role, especially during OT times. Transjordan included the River Jabbok, scene of the account of Jacob's wrestling on his return from Aram (Gen. 32:22-32); the Plains of Moab, where the Israelites are said to have camped following their exodus from Egypt and where Balaam prophesied; and Mount Nebo from which Moses viewed the promised land (Num. 22:1–24:25; Deut. 34). Three Transjordanian kingdoms (Ammon, Moab, and Edom) were contemporary with the two Hebrew kingdoms (Israel and Judah), sometimes as allies, sometimes as enemies (1 Sam. 11; 14:47; 2 Sam. 8:12; 10; 2 Kings 3; Amos 1:11–2:3). The Prophet Elijah was from Tishbe, a town in the

Transjordanian territory of Gilead (1 Kings 17:1). Other Israelite prophets and poets often referred to the territories and peoples of the Transjordan. See, for example, the allusions in Amos 4:1 and Ps. 22:12 to the cows and bulls of Bashan.

The vast Arabian Desert stretches southeastward from the geological fault line described above. The Transjordan, which figures in the biblical narratives, is not the whole desert expanse but rather the north-south strip of highlands sandwiched between the Jordan Valley and the desert. This strip of highlands receives abundant rainfall from the Mediterranean winds during the winter months, which allows farming and cattle grazing. The rainfall fades rapidly as one moves eastward, however, so that the generally rugged and cultivable land gives way to rocky desert approximately 30 to 35 miles east of the Jordan.

Four major rivers, along with numerous smaller and intermittently active streambeds, drain the Transjordanian highlands into the Jordan Valley. (1) The Yarmuk River, not mentioned in the Bible, drains the area known in OT times as Bashan. Bashan, good cattle country as indicated above, was situated roughly east of the Sea of Galilee. Main biblical cities in the Bashan region were Ashtaroth and Karnaim (Josh. 9:10; 12:4; Amos 6:13). (2) Nahr ex-Zerqa, the Jabbok River of OT times, drains the area known then as Gilead. Gilead, situated east of that portion of the Jordan which connects the Sea of Galilee with the Dead Sea, produces grapes, olives, vegetables, cereals, and also is mentioned in the Bible as a source of balm (Gen. 37:25; Jer. 8:22). Among Gileadite cities which appear in the biblical narratives were Mizpah, Jabesh, and Ramoth (Judg. 10:17; 1 Sam. 11:1; 31:12; 1 Kings 22:3, 2 Kings 8:28). (3) Wadi el-Mujib, the Arnon River of ancient times, bisected the ancient land of Moab and enters the Dead Sea approximately midway along its eastern shore. (4) Wadi Hesa— probably the ancient Zered but not absolutely certain—would have separated Moab from Edom and enters the Arabah at the southern end of the Dead Sea.

An important trade route passed through the Transjordan during biblical times, connecting Damascus and Bostra of Syria with the Gulf of Aqaba and western Arabia. Some scholars prefer to translate the term *derek hamelek* (Num. 20:17; 21:22) as a proper noun ("the King's Highway") and identify it with this ancient route. Others interpret the term as a common,

appellative noun ("royal road") and doubt that it referred to a specific route, in the same sense that present-day terms such as "freeway" and "state road" refer to categories of roads rather than to specific highways. In either case, we know that the old trade route which traversed the Transjordan would have played an important role in the economy of ancient Palestine and was refurbished by the Romans who named it the *Via Nova Traiana*.

The Israelite tribes of Reuben and Gad along with certain Manassite clans settled in the Transjordan—primarily in Gilead, it seems, although with some spillover into Bashan and into the traditionally Moabite territory immediately north of the Arnon (Num. 32). Later, after the establishment of the Hebrew monarchy, several Israelite and Judean kings attempted, some more successfully than others, to rule this portion of the Transjordan with which Israelite tribes were associated. David, Omri, Ahab, and Jeroboam II were the more successful ones. Weaker kings, such as Rehoboam and Jehoash of Judah for example, had little or no influence in the Transjordan. Of course, one reads of occasional Moabite and Edomite military campaigns which threatened even Jerusalem (2 Chron. 20).

With the rise of Assyria, especially during and following the reign of Tiglath-pileser III (744–727 B.C.), the various regions of Syria-Palestine fell under Assyrian domination. The Transjordan was no different. Several of the kings of Ammon, Moab, and Edom are mentioned in Assyrian records—usually listed among those paying tribute or providing other forms of involuntary support to the Assyrian monarch. When the Assyrian Empire collapsed and was superseded by the Babylonian Empire, presumably the Babylonians also controlled the Transjordan.

By NT times a cluster of Greco-Roman-oriented cities with primarily Gentile populations (the so-called "Decapolis" cities) had emerged in the northern Transjordan (earlier Bashan, Gilead, and Ammon). The southern Transjordan (earlier Moab and Edom) was dominated, on the other hand, by the Nabateans, a people of Arab origin who established a commercial empire along the desert fringe with its capital at Petra. Eventually, the whole of the Transjordan was incorporated into the Roman Empire. Domitian annexed the northern Transjordan in A.D. 90, forming the administrative province of Arabia. Trajan added the Nabatean territory in A.D. 106 and renamed the province Arabia Petraea. See *Ammon; Arnon; Bashan; Decapolis; Edom; Gilead; Jabbok; Moab; Tribes of Israel.*

J. Maxwell Miller

TRANSLATE 1. KJV term meaning "to transfer," used of the transfer of Saul's kingdom to David (2 Sam. 3:10) and the transfer of believers from the power of darkness to the sphere of Christ's control (Col. 1:13). **2.** KJV term meaning "to take up," used of Enoch's being taken up into God's presence without experiencing death (Heb. 11:5). See *Death; Future Hope; Resurrection.* **3.** Converting text from one language to another, retaining the original meaning or putting words in simpler terms.

TRANSPORTATION AND TRAVEL Means and ways of commercial and private movement among towns and nations in the biblical period. Travel in the ancient, as well as the modern world, is the result of economic, political, social, and religious factors. For the most part, transportation and travel in the biblical world was on foot (Judg. 16:3; Josh. 9:3-5; 1 Kings 18:46). At first this meant following the paths animals made through the hills and valleys of Palestine. However, as the economic and political demands of the region increased, so did the traffic. Better-marked and smoother roads were needed for travelers and for the transport of larger amounts of goods from place to place. Large draft animals of various types also had to be domesticated and harnessed to this work (Exod. 23:5).

As trade began to expand beyond the local area, international highways and trade routes such as the coastal road, the *Via Maris,* and the Transjordanian king's highway were developed. Heavily traveled routes such as these were a factor in the founding of many cities. They also functioned as the principle link from which branched lesser roads connecting cities and towns in Palestine to the rest of the Near East (Prov. 8:2-3). These highways promoted the movement of businessmen, religious pilgrims, government officials, and armies between regions of the country and foreign nations. The resulting blend of cultures and economies created the society described in biblical and extrabiblical texts.

Geographical Factors in Travel Perhaps the greatest obstacle that travelers and road builders had to overcome was the rugged geographical character of Palestine. The desert regions of the Negev and Judean highlands in the south required the identification of wells and pasturage for the draft animals. The hilly spine of central Palestine forced the traveler to zigzag around steep ascents (such as that between Jericho and Jerusalem) or follow ridges along the hilltops (the Beth-horon route northwest of Jerusalem), or go along watersheds (Bethlehem to Mizpah). Numerous streams as well as the Jordan River had to be forded by travelers (2 Sam. 19:18), sometimes at the expense of baggage and animals.

Where valleys, such as the Jezreel, had to be traversed, roads generally followed the higher ground along the base of the hills so as to bypass marshy areas and stay away from the raging torrents that sometimes filled streambeds in the rainy season. Narrow, twisting valleys, as in the Judean desert, often provided perfect areas for ambushes by bandits. Along the coastal plain sandy dunes required a detour further inland into the foothills of the Shephelah plateau.

The rough coastline of Palestine lacked a good, deep-water port for shipping. As a result, an additional journey overland was required to transport agricultural and other trade goods to and from the ports of Ezion-geber (1 Kings 9:26-28) on the Red Sea and the Phoenician ports of Tyre and Sidon to the cities of Israel. Solomon kept a fleet of ships operating in the Red Sea to ply the African trade. Another group of Solomon's ocean-going vessels (Hb. "ships of Tarshish") joined forces with the fleets of Hiram of Tyre in the Mediterranean (1 Kings 10:22). Despite this activity, Israel's kings had a general lack of experience with the sea. This sometimes made them reluctant to rely on shipping. For instance, King Jehoshaphat of Judah rejected further attempts to obtain gold from Ophir after his first fleet of ships was sunk off Ezion-geber (1 Kings 22:48-49). See *Ships, Sailors, and Navigation.*

Despite these difficulties, the desire to travel and the commercial needs of nations motivated the identification of routes that were relatively safe from attack by bandits and allowed free transport of goods by pack animals and carts to every region in the land. The roads that carried this traffic varied in size from two land thoroughfares about ten feet wide to simple tracks through fields barely wide enough for a man and donkey to pass single file. The determining factor in each case was the usage each received. Roads carrying two- and four-wheeled carts and wagons pulled by oxen required more room and a smoother roadbed (Isa. 62:10) than a lane crossing a vineyard.

Kings of the ancient Near East (Shulgi of Ur III, Mesopotamia, and Mesha, king of Moab) often boasted in their official inscriptions of their road-building activities. These roadways, so important to the maintenance of political and economic control of the nation, were probably kept in shape by government-sponsored corvée workers (2 Sam. 20:24; 1 Kings 9:15) or by the army. Since bridges were unknown in the biblical period, fords were identified (Judg. 12:5-6 NASB, NRSV, NIV) for general use, and, in the Roman period, were smoothed by the placement of flat stones in the riverbed. Where no river crossing could be found, boats were lashed together to form temporary ferries or large transports.

Political and Military Factors in Transportation While terrain had a great deal to do with the building of roads, another important factor was the political situation in the region. In ancient Israel roads not only linked trading and religious centers, they also protected population centers and speeded the nation's armies to war. The vast network of roads in the difficult area of the Judean hill country speaks eloquently of the importance of Jerusalem, which was the hub of activities in that region. It functioned as the political center of the Davidic monarchy as well as the religious focus of the nation with many pilgrims making the ascent to Zion (Ps. 122:1). An even more elaborate system of highways was built by the Roman legions to help them dominate the country and forestall organized rebellion after the revolts of A.D. 69–70 and 135.

Throughout the monarchy, military campaigns required well-kept roadways to facilitate the movement of troops about the country. Protecting the valleys and highways that led to the capital at Jerusalem were a series of fortresses including Gezer, Beth-horon, Baalath, and Tamar (Tadmor) (1 Kings 9:17-19). Royal entourages also traveled these guarded roads in peacetime to conduct governmental business (1 Kings 12:1; 18:16).

To help with the constant flow of government travelers, way stations (every 10 to 15 miles in the Persian Empire) and administrative outposts were constructed. In a time before inns,

these stations provided supplies to traveling officials and fresh mounts to couriers. The private traveler had to rely on the hospitality of towns or friends along the way (Judg. 19:10-15; 2 Kings 4:8).

The road systems and port facilities of the kings of Israel and Judah were expanded in times of prosperity and contested for in times of war (2 Kings 16:6). Megiddo, which commanded the western entrance into the Jezreel Valley, controlled the traffic along the Via Maris as it moved inland and then north to Damascus. Solomon demonstrated his awareness of its strategic importance for fortifying the site, along with Hazor and Gezer, to protect the borders of Israel (1 Kings 9:15). Foreign rulers also fought to hold the city (which was destroyed over a dozen times during its period of occupation), and King Josiah of Judah died here defending the pass against the army of Pharaoh Neco II in 609 B.C. (2 Kings 23:29).

Religious Factors in Travel One of the chief reasons given for travel in the biblical text was to visit a religious shrine and make sacrifices. Throughout much of Israel's history the people are described as making journeys to places like Shechem (Josh. 24), Shiloh (1 Sam. 1:3), Ophrah (Judg. 8:27), Dan (Judg. 18:30), and Bethel (1 Kings 12:26-33). Here they would make their devotions before a sacred image or the ark of the covenant. High places (*bamot*) were also popular sites for religious pilgrims. In the period before Jerusalem's ascendancy as the religious focal point of the nation, prophets like Samuel regularly visited these local shrines to officiate at sacrifices (1 Sam. 9:12). Local religious rites sometimes also included an ingathering of family from across the nation as well as part of the yearly celebration (1 Sam. 20:6).

Animals Used in Travel Most of what is known about the animals used to transport people and materials in the ancient world is based on textual evidence and art. The Bible mentions several different types of draft animals: donkeys, mules, camels, and oxen. Among these, donkeys appear to have been the most popular means of transport in the Near East. They are described in Old Assyrian texts (about 2100 B.C.) transporting copper ingots from Cappadocia in Turkey. The Beni-hasan tomb paintings from Egypt dating to 1900 B.C. graphically portray Semitic caravanners with their donkeys laden with baggage and trade goods.

A traveler along the Jericho road to Jerusalem riding one donkey while his other donkey leads the way.

In the biblical narrative the donkey was the chief means of private and commercial transport throughout the history of the nation of Israel. Jacob's sons carried their grain purchases from Egypt to Canaan on donkey back (Gen. 42:26); Jesse sent David and a donkey loaded with provisions to Saul's court (1 Sam. 16:20); and Nehemiah became incensed when he saw Judeans transporting grain on donkeys during the Sabbath (Neh. 13:15).

Mules are less commonly mentioned. This may be due to a shortage of horses for breeding or to a custom restricting the use of mules to the upper classes (2 Sam. 13:29). For instance, David's sons Absalom (2 Sam. 18:9) and Solomon (1 Kings 1:33) are described as riding mules. One passage (Isa. 66:20) pictures the caravan of returning exiles riding on horses, mules, and dromedaries, as well as in chariots and litters. Each of these means of transport, however, fits the prophet's vision of a glorious procession on its way to Jerusalem rather than the normal groupings of travelers along the international route.

Camels appear several times in the text carrying huge loads (five times that of a donkey). One clear example of this is found in 2 Kings

8:9. Ben-hadad, the king of Syria, sent 40 camels loaded with goods to Elisha in an attempt to learn if he would recover from an illness. In another case Isaiah denounced the leaders of Judah for sending camel loads of gifts to Egypt to buy their aid against Assyria (30:6). Because of its broad but tender hoofs, best fit for desert travel, the camel was of little use in the hill country. These beasts were probably used only on the major routes such as the Via Maris, along the coast, or on the smoother valley roads of the Shephelah and the Negev.

Oxen are exclusively associated with travel by wheeled vehicle and will be discussed below in that context. Israelite use of horses does not appear in the text before 1000 B.C. when David began to incorporate them into his forces (2 Sam. 8:3-4). They are mentioned primarily in military contexts: ridden into battle (Job 39:18-25) and harnessed to chariots (1 Kings 12:18). Official messengers also rode horses (2 Kings 9:18-19), as did scouts for the army (2 Kings 7:13-15).

Wheeled Vehicles The most commonly mentioned wheeled vehicle in the biblical narrative is the chariot. It was used first by Israel's enemies during the conquest period (Judg. 1:19; 4:3). However, it could not be used effectively in the rough hill country where the tribes first settled (Josh. 17:16). Once the monarchy was established, chariots became an integral part of the kings' battle strategy (1 Kings 10:26; 22:31-34). They were also used as a standard means of travel by kings (2 Kings 9:16) and nobles (2 Kings 5:9). Private ownership of chariots is found in Isa. 22:18. In this passage the prophet condemns Shebna, the king's household steward ,for his extravagance and pride. His chariots, like his rock-cut tomb, were status symbols for high-ranking members of the royal bureaucracy in Hezekiah's time (cp. Acts 8:26-38).

No physical remains of chariots have been found in Palestine, although a magnificent example of a royal Egyptian chariot was discovered in the tomb of Pharaoh Tutankhamen (about 1300 B.C.). A three-man Judean battle chariot is depicted in the Assyrian relief (about 701 B.C.) of Sennacherib's siege of Lachish. It was fitted with a yoke for four horses. Estimates of the chariot's size in this period are based on the width of ruts in the roadways in Mesopotamian and Roman cities. If these are used, the standard width of chariots was 1.23

T

meters between the wheels and 1.53 meters overall.

The use of large-wheeled vehicles apparently originated in Sumer where models, dating to 2500 B.C., of large covered wagons drawn by oxen have been found. These bulky vehicles, carrying heavy loads, required well-kept, broad roadways. Neglected paths could become overgrown (Prov. 15:19) or filled with stones from eroded hillsides. Thus, for traffic to be maintained, teams of workmen must have traveled the roads making necessary repairs. Gateways also had to be widened to permit the entrance of wheeled vehicles. Those excavated in Israel range in width from 2.5 to 4.5 meters. Some, like those at Gezer and Megiddo, had a cobblestone or crushed-stone roadbed within the heavily traveled gate complex.

Large two- and four-wheeled carts and wagons were also commonly used in biblical times for transporting heavy loads and people. In the patriarchal period Joseph sent carts to Canaan to carry his father and the households of his brothers to Goshen (Gen. 45:19-27). After the completion of the wilderness tabernacle, six covered wagons, each pulled by two oxen, were donated by the tribal leaders to the Levites to transport holy items along the line of march (Num. 7:1-8).

Once the people had settled into Canaan, carts became an everyday aid to farmers who had to transport sheaves of grain to the threshing floor (Amos 2:13). A similar two-wheeled cart was used by David to carry the ark of the covenant from Kiriath-jearim (also called Baale of Judah) to his new capital in Jerusalem (2 Sam. 6:2-17). The somewhat clumsy nature of these carts can be seen in its almost overturning as it came to the threshing floor of Nacon. Several men walked beside the cart to guide the oxen and prevent the cargo from shifting.

The broader roads and heavy-wheeled vehicles of Palestine were also used, in the period of the Assyrian conquest, to transport the people into exile. Sennacherib's stone relief of his siege of Lachish includes a picture of Judeans being taken away in two-wheeled carts drawn by a team of oxen. The new exiles sit atop bundles containing their belongings while a man walks alongside the left-hand ox guiding it with a sharpened stick. Isaiah's vision of the return (66:20) must have struck a poignant note for the exiles who had seen their ancestors depicted in the Assyrian relief. See *Economic Life.*

Victor H. Matthews

TRAPPER See *Fowler.*

TREASURE, TREASURY What one values, whether silver and gold or something intangible, and the storage place of what is valuable. In OT times treasure might be stored in the king's palace (2 Kings 20:13) or in the temple (1 Kings 7:51). In Jesus' day the term also applied to 13 trumpet-shaped offering receptacles in the temple court of the women where Jesus watched people make their offerings (Mark 12:41). "Treasure" and "treasury" are also used as illustrations or figures of speech. Israel was God's treasure (Exod. 19:5). This is reflected in the idea of Christians as God's own people (1 Pet. 2:9). A person's memory is a treasure (Prov. 2:1; 7:1). Fear (awe) of the Lord was Israel's treasure (Isa. 33:6).

Jesus Himself used the term frequently. He contrasted earthly treasures to those of heaven (Matt. 6:19-20). What a person treasures or values determines one's loyalty and priorities (Matt. 6:21). Paul marveled that the treasure of God's revelation of Himself in Christ had been deposited in an earthen vessel such as Paul himself (2 Cor. 4:7). See *Temple.*   *Elmer Gray*

TREATY See *Covenant.*

TREE OF KNOWLEDGE Plant in the midst of the garden of Eden whose fruit was forbidden to Adam and Eve (Gen. 2:17). Reference to "the tree of the knowledge of good and evil" is in a context concerned with the fall. In Gen. 3:3 the tree is designated as "the tree in the middle of the garden" (HCSB). Eating from the tree brought the knowledge of good and evil (Gen. 3:5,22).

The tree of knowledge was Adam and Eve's opportunity to demonstrate obedience and loyalty to God, but the serpent used it to tempt Eve to eat and to become like God "knowing good and evil" (Gen. 3:5). When Adam joined Eve in eating the forbidden fruit, the result was shame, guilt, exclusion from the garden, and separation from the tree of life and from God. The Bible's primary interest about the tree of knowledge is not what kind of knowledge it represented— moral judgment, secular knowledge, sexual knowledge, universal knowledge, or some other kind—but how it served as God's test and Satan's temptation. The result for mankind was disaster as they failed the test and fell to the temptation. See *Adam and Eve; Eden; Tree of Life.*   *Billy K. Smith*

TREE OF LIFE Plant in the garden of Eden symbolizing access to eternal life. Also, a metaphor used in Proverbs. For the biblical writer the tree of life was an important consideration only after Adam and Eve disobeyed. Sin interrupted the quality of life God intended for them. They were to obey God (Gen. 2:17) in a family setting (Gen. 2:18-25) and perform their assigned tasks (Gen. 2:15). The implication is that they had access to all the trees in the garden, including the tree of life, but God gave an explicit command not to eat of the tree of knowledge. Their relationship to God changed radically when they disobeyed that command. Chief among the radical changes was that they no longer had access to the tree of life (Gen. 3:22-24).

The "tree of life" appears in Proverbs four times (Prov. 3:18; 11:30; 13:12; 15:4) and in Rev. 2:7; 22:2,14. To lay hold of wisdom is to lay hold on "a tree of life" (Prov. 3:18). "The fruit of the righteous is a tree of life" (11:30). Yet another proverb has this comparison: "Fulfilled desire is a tree of life" (13:12 HCSB). The author of another proverb wrote, "The tongue that heals is a tree of life" (15:4). None of these proverbs seems to refer to "the tree of life" mentioned in Genesis. All of the references in Revelation do. See *Adam and Eve; Eden; Tree of Knowledge.*   *Billy K. Smith*

TRIAL OF JESUS Two systems of justice combined to produce a sentence of death for Jesus. Jewish religious leaders accused Jesus of blasphemy, a capital offense under Jewish law (Lev. 24:16). The Jewish leaders at Jesus' trial manipulated procedures to coerce Jesus into an admission that He was God's Son (Luke 22:66-71). For them this constituted blasphemy.

Roman leaders allowed conquered people such as the Jews to follow their own legal system so long as they did not abuse their privileges. The Romans did not give the Jews the right of capital punishment for the accusation of blasphemy. The Jews had to convince a Roman judge that their demand for capital punishment was justified.

The Jewish Trial Jewish leaders were determined to seek Jesus' death when they put Him on trial (Luke 22:2; Mark 14:1). They held the Jewish trial at night hoping that Jesus' supporters would be asleep and unable to protest His arrest. The Jewish portion of the trial had three separate phases: an appearance before Annas, an informal investigation by Caiaphas, and a condemnation by the Sanhedrin. Annas was father-in-law of the high priest Caiaphas. He had been high priest himself from A.D. 7–15. He was the most influential member of the Sanhedrin. The details of the interview before Annas are meager (John 18:12-14,19-24). The high priest mentioned in John 18:19 may have been Annas. If so, he held a brief interrogation of Jesus and sent Him to his son-in-law Caiaphas (John 18:24).

The meeting with Caiaphas took place in his residence (Luke 22:54). Some members of the Sanhedrin worked frantically to locate and train witnesses against Jesus (Matt. 26:59-60). The carefully prepared witnesses could not agree in their testimony (Mark 14:56; cp. Deut. 19:15).

During this circuslike activity Caiaphas talked with Jesus and put Him under oath (Matt. 26:63-64). He charged Jesus to tell if He were God's Son. Perhaps Jesus felt that silence under this oath would be a denial of His divine origin. He affirmed that He was God's Son (Mark 14:62), knowing that this would lead to death. The Sanhedrin condemned Him but did not pronounce a sentence (Mark 14:64). After the condemnation the group broke up into wild disorder. Some began to slap and spit upon Jesus (Mark 14:65).

Shortly after dawn the Sanhedrin convened again to bring a formal condemnation against Jesus (Luke 22:66). Jewish law stipulated that a guilty verdict in a capital crime had to be delayed until the next day. The vote for condemnation after dawn gave the semblance of following this requirement.

The procedure at this session was similar to that of the night trial. No witnesses came forward to accuse Christ. Jesus again claimed that He was God's Son (Luke 22:66-71). The Sanhedrin again approved the death sentence and took Jesus to Pilate for sentencing (Luke 23:1).

The procedures of the Jewish leaders during Jesus' trial were illegal. Jewish law required that trial for a capital crime begin during the daytime and adjourn by nightfall if incomplete. Sanhedrin members were supposed to be impartial

T

judges. Jewish rules prohibited convicting the accused on His own testimony.

The Roman Trial The Roman trial of Jesus also had three phases: first appearance before Pilate, appearance before Herod Antipas, and second appearance before Pilate. The Jews asked Pilate to accept their verdict against Jesus without investigation (John 18:29-31). Pilate refused this, but he offered to let them carry out the maximum punishment under their law, probably beating with rods or imprisonment. They insisted that they wanted death.

The Jews knew that Pilate would laugh at their charge of blasphemy. They fabricated three additional charges against Jesus which would be of concern to a Roman governor (Luke 23:2). Pilate concerned himself only with the charge that Jesus had claimed to be a king. This charge sounded like treason. The Romans knew no greater crime than treason.

Pilate interrogated Jesus long enough to be convinced that He was no political rival to Caesar (John 18:33-37). He returned to the Jews to announce that he found Jesus no threat to Rome and hence not deserving of death (John 18:38). The Jews responded with vehement accusations against Jesus' actions in Judea and Galilee (Luke 23:5). When Pilate learned that Jesus was from Galilee, he sent Jesus to Herod Antipas of Galilee who was then in Jerusalem (Luke 23:6-12). Herod wanted Jesus to entertain him with a miracle. Jesus did not even speak a word to Herod. The king and his soldiers mocked and ridiculed Jesus, finally sending Him back to Pilate.

When Herod returned Jesus to Pilate, the Roman governor announced that he still found Jesus innocent of charges of treason. Three times Pilate tried to release Jesus. First, Pilate offered to chastise or beat Jesus and then to release Him (Luke 23:16). Second, he offered to release either Jesus or Barabbas, a radical revolutionary. To Pilate's surprise the crowd chanted for Barabbas' release (Luke 23:17-19). Third, he scourged Jesus. Soldiers flailed at Jesus' bare back with a leather whip. The whip had pieces of iron or bone tied to the ends of the thongs. Pilate then presented the bleeding Jesus, who was wearing a crown of thorns and a purple robe, to the crowd as their king. He hoped that this spectacle would lead them to release Jesus out of pity. Again they chanted for crucifixion (John 19:4-6).

When Pilate seemed to waver one more time concerning crucifixion, the Jews threatened to report his conduct to Caesar (John 19:12). That threat triggered Pilate's action. After symbolically washing his hands of the entire affair (Matt. 27:24), he delivered Jesus for crucifixion (John 19:16). See *Annas; Caiaphas; Pilate, Pontius; Roman Law; Sanhedrin.*   *Thomas D. Lea*

TRIBES OF ISRAEL Social and political groups in Israel claiming descent from one of the 12 sons of Jacob.

Tribal Unit The tribal unit played an important role in the history of the formation of the nation of Israel. In ancient times a nation was referred to as "a people," an *am*; in Israel's case it was the "people of Israel." The nation in turn was made up of "tribes." The "tribe," a *shevet* or *matteh*, was the major social unit that comprised the makeup of the nation. The tribe was comprised of "clans." The "clan," a *mishpachah*, was a family of families or a cluster of households that had a common ancestry. The clan was comprised then of the individual households or families referred to as the "father's house," the *beth av*. Actually, the family in ancient times might be made up of several families living together and forming one household (Num. 3:24). See *Family.*

Tribal Origins The ancestral background of "the tribes of Israel" went back to the patriarch Jacob, whose name was changed to "Israel." The nation of Israel was identified as "the children of Israel," or more literally "the sons of Israel." According to the biblical account, the family of Jacob, from which the tribes came, originated in north Syria during Jacob's stay at Haran with Laban his uncle. Eleven of the 12 sons were born at Haran, while the 12th, Benjamin, was born after Jacob returned to Canaan. The birth of the sons came through Jacob's wives Leah and Rachel and their maids Zilpah and Bilhah. The sons of Leah included Reuben, Simeon, Levi, Judah (Gen. 29:31-35), Issachar, and Zebulun, as well as one daughter named Dinah (Gen. 30:19-21). Rachel's sons were Joseph (Gen. 30:22-24), who became the father of Ephraim and Manasseh (Gen. 41:50-52), and Benjamin (Gen. 35:16-18). Jacob's sons through Zilpah, Leah's maid, were Gad and Asher (Gen. 30:9-13), while Bilhah, the maid of Rachel, bore Dan and Naphtali (Gen. 30:1-8).

This family of families or family of tribes occupied the focal point in the history of the development of Israel as a nation. While there are details of that history that we do not clearly understand and other groups simply referred to as "an ethnically diverse crowd" (Exod. 12:38 HCSB) that were perhaps incorporated into the nation, the central focus is always on the "tribes of Israel," the descendants of Jacob. For that reason lists of the 12 sons of Jacob or of the tribes appear in several places in the OT, though the lists vary somewhat. Some of the major lists include that of Jacob's blessing of the 12 (Gen. 49), the review of the households as the period of oppression in Egypt is introduced (Exod. 1:1-10), Moses' blessing of the tribes (Deut. 33), and the song of Deborah (Judg. 5).

Tribes of Israel Each tribe had its own history in its allotment of land. We know few details about the individual tribes.

1. Reuben, the firstborn son of Jacob by his wife Leah, was in line to assume a leadership role in the family, but he forfeited that right because of an illicit affair he had with his father's concubine Bilhah (Gen. 35:22). The impact of this reflected in Jacob's blessing where Reuben is addressed as "turbulent as water, you will no longer excel, because you got into your father's bed" (Gen. 49:4 HCSB). At the time of the migration of Jacob's family to Egypt, Reuben had four sons (Gen. 46:8-9).

In some of the lists of the tribes of Israel, Reuben is mentioned first (Exod. 1:1-4; Num. 1:5-15), while in other lists Reuben appears further down (Num. 2:1-11). During the journey through the wilderness, the tribes of Reuben, Simeon, and Gad formed the second unit of the procession with the tribe of Reuben in the lead position (Num. 10:17-20). This cluster of tribes headed by the tribe of Reuben was next in line after the tabernacle (Num. 10:17-18). As the tribes approached the land of Canaan and allotments were made to each tribe, the tribe of Reuben along with Gad and the half-tribe of Manasseh occupied the Transjordan, that is the highland plateau region east of the Jordan River (Josh. 13:8-31; cp. Num. 32:1-5,33-42). The tribe of Reuben occupied the southern region extending roughly from the Arnon River to the site of Heshbon (Josh. 13:15-23). Formerly, this territory was the homeland of the kingdom of Sihon. While we know little about the tribe of Reuben during the period of the settlement, the song of Deborah suggests that the tribe was criticized by some of the other tribes for not taking a more active role in the conquest (Judg. 5:15-16). See *Transjordan*.

2. Simeon was Jacob's second son by Leah and played a key role in the encounter Dinah had with Shechem. Because Simeon and Levi were full brothers of Dinah, they sought to avenge her (Gen. 34:25-26) for Shechem's actions (34:1-4). The radical response of the two brothers, in which they "took their swords, went into the unsuspecting city, and killed every male" (Gen. 34:25 HCSB), is reflected in Jacob's blessing of the two: "their knives are vicious weapons … Their anger is cursed, for it is strong, and their fury, for it is cruel! I will disperse them throughout Jacob and scatter them throughout Israel" (Gen. 49:5-7 HCSB). During the years of famine as the sons of Jacob traveled back and forth between Egypt and Canaan, Simeon was held hostage by Joseph at one point (Gen. 42:24).

In the lists of the tribes, Simeon is listed in second place, that is, next after Reuben (Exod. 1:2; 6:14-15; Num. 1:5-6,22-23; 13:5; 26:12-14). Generally, the tribe of Simeon seems to be characterized by weakness. Its status is best reflected in the final statement of Jacob's blessing of Simeon and Levi: "I will disperse them throughout Jacob and scatter them throughout Israel" (Gen. 49:7 HCSB). Perhaps because of its weak status, the tribe of Simeon apparently was not given a separate inheritance in the land (Josh. 19:1-9). Rather, "their inheritance was within the portion of the descendents of Judah" (Josh. 19:1 HCSB), in the southern Negev.

3. Levi was the third son of Jacob and Leah (see *Simeon* above). During the journey from Egypt to Canaan, the sons of Levi slaughtered 3,000 rebellious Hebrew males (Exod. 32:25-29). They became the landless priestly tribe. See *Levites; Levitical Cities; Priests*.

4. Judah, the fourth son of Jacob by his wife Leah (Gen. 29:35), appears as a leader and a spokesman among his brothers (Gen. 37:26; 43:3; 44:16; cp. 46:28). Judah was promised preeminence over the other tribes in Jacob's blessing (Gen. 49:8-12).

In the journey from Egypt to Canaan, Judah had the lead position (Num. 2:9). As the tribes entered the land, it was Achan of the tribe of Judah who was guilty of taking some of the forbidden booty or loot from Jericho (Josh. 7). The tribe of Judah occupied the southern part of Palestine, basically the territory between the Dead Sea on the east and the Mediterranean on the west (Josh. 15). The northern boundary of

T

Judah was marked by the territories of Benjamin and Dan. The territory of Jerusalem may have formed something of a barrier between Judah and the tribes of the north because it was not finally secured until the time of David (2 Sam. 5:6-10). The capture of Jerusalem by David paved the way for the tribes to have a kind of unity they had not previously experienced. The territory of the tribe of Judah constituted the major portion of the Southern Kingdom, thus forming the kingdom of Judah with its capital Jerusalem.

5. Issachar was the ninth son born to Jacob, but the first of a second family he had by Leah (Gen. 30:18). Beyond his birth little else is known about his life or that of the tribe. During the journey from Mount Sinai to Canaan the tribe of Issachar followed the tribe of Judah; that is, it was a part of the first cluster of tribes located on the east side of the tabernacle (Num. 2:5). The territory occupied by the tribe of Issachar is difficult to outline precisely (Josh. 19:17-23). They were located west of the Jordan in the region just south of the Sea of Galilee stretching on down to the Valley of Jezreel. Because the blessing of Moses says that Zebulun and Issachar "summon the peoples to a mountain; there they offer acceptable sacrifices" (Deut. 33:19 HCSB), some have speculated that the two tribes perhaps had a center of worship on Mount Tabor, a mountain located on the border between the two tribes. Because the blessing of Jacob speaks of Issachar as a beast of burden and as "a forced laborer" (Gen. 49:14-15 HCSB), the tribe of Issachar may have faced a variety of hardships. For instance, there may have been a time during the tribal period when the people of Issachar served as slaves in the forced labor projects of their neighbors, the Canaanites.

6. Zebulun was the tenth son of Jacob and the sixth and final son by his wife Leah (Gen. 30:19-20). Little else is known about Zebulun's life. The territory allotted to the tribe of Zebulun was in the north in the region of southern Galilee bounded by Issachar on the south-southeast, Naphtali on the east, and Asher on the west (Josh. 19:10-16). The blessing of Jacob speaks of Zebulun's territory including "the seashore," presumably the Mediterranean Sea, and "his territory will be next to Sidon" (Gen. 49:13 HCSB) a city on the coast north of Mount Carmel. While this territory was traditionally occupied by the tribe of Asher, it is quite possible that at some point Zebulun occupied a part of this region and, therefore, would have had access to the sea. The blessing of Moses further states that Zebulun along with Issachar would benefit from "the wealth of the seas and the hidden treasures of the sand" (Deut. 33:19 HCSB). During the period that the tribes were settling in the land of Canaan, Zebulun apparently went beyond the call of duty in providing support. It is the only tribe in the song of Deborah to be mentioned twice (Judg. 5:14,18).

7. Joseph was the first son born to Jacob by Rachel, Jacob's favorite wife (Gen. 30:22-24). Two of the tribes of Israel came from Joseph, namely, Ephraim and Manasseh.

The story of Joseph is the most eventful of the sons of Jacob. Joseph had two sons, Manasseh and Ephraim (Gen. 41:50-52), who were born in Egypt. Jacob adopted Ephraim and Manasseh and therefore each became the father of a tribe in Israel (Gen. 48:8-20). While Manasseh was the older of the two, Jacob gave preference to Ephraim (v. 14; cp. Deut. 33:17). The blessing of Jacob (Gen. 49:22-26) mentions only Joseph; the blessing of Moses (Deut. 33:13-17) begins with Joseph and notes Ephraim and Manasseh; the song of Deborah (Judg. 5:14) speaks of Ephraim and Machir. See *Joseph; Machir*.

Ephraim occupied a major portion of the central hill country with Manasseh during the tribal period. Ephraim's territory consisted of the region just north of Dan and Benjamin and ran from the Jordan River on the east to the Mediterranean Sea on the west. That Ephraim played a major leadership role among the tribes is reflected in the tribal history. Joshua, one of the 12 spies and a member of the tribe of Ephraim, became the successor of Moses (Num. 13:8,16; Josh. 1:1-11). Ephraim demanded leadership in the period of the judges (Judg. 3:27; 4:5; 7:24; 8:1; 10:1; 12:1-6; 17:1; 18:2,13; 19:1). Shiloh, located in the territory of the tribe of Ephraim, became the major center of worship during the tribal period (Josh. 18:1; 1 Sam. 1:1-18). Samuel, the leader of the tribes (1 Sam 7:15-17) near the end of the period of the judges and just prior to the beginning of the kingship, came from Ephraim (1 Sam. 1:1-20).

Ephraim's influence is seen not only during the tribal period but in Israel's later history as well. For instance, as the nation Israel divided into two kingdoms following the death of Solomon in 922 B.C., it was an Ephraimite named Jeroboam who led the northern tribes in their plea for leniency (1 Kings 12:1-5). When Rehoboam rejected their plea, the northern tribes broke their ties with the south, formed a separate kingdom (1 Kings 12:16-19), and selected Jeroboam as their king (1 Kings 12:20). Ephraim's influence is seen also during the time of the prophets. For instance, Hosea refers to Israel some three dozen times using the name Ephraim as being synonymous with Israel.

Manasseh was the oldest son of Joseph and Asenath. The tribe of Manasseh occupied territory both east and west of the Jordan River. Manasseh's territory east of the Jordan included the regions of Gilead and Bashan and most likely extended from the Jabbok River to near Mount Hermon. Manasseh's territory west of the Jordan was located north of Ephraim. Apparently the tribe of Manasseh played an important role in the conquest. For instance, the sons of Machir, Manasseh's son, took the land of Gilead and drove out the Amorites who occupied it (Num. 32:39; cp. Judg. 5:14) while other descendants of Manasseh engaged in the activities of the conquest elsewhere (Num. 32:41-42). Perhaps Gideon is the most familiar of the descendants of Manasseh (Judg. 6:12-15). Gideon defeated the Midianites with a small band of men (Judg. 6–7).

8. Benjamin was Jacob's youngest son, born to him by Rachel, and the only son born after returning to Palestine from Haran (Gen. 35:16-20). He was the only full-blooded brother of Joseph. Therefore, the tribes of Benjamin, Ephraim, and Manasseh formed a special group. Benjamin's tribal territory was a small area west of the Jordan, sandwiched between Ephraim to the north and Judah to the south (Josh. 18:11-28). The Benjaminites had a reputation as men of war. The blessing of Jacob refers to them as "a wolf" who "tears his prey" (Gen. 49:27 HCSB). The book of Judges notes their activities as warriors during the tribal period (Judg. 5:14; 20:12-16). They were referred to as those "who were left-handed" and experts with the sling (Judg. 20:16). The story of the Levite and his concubine reflects the inhumane acts for which the Benjaminites were responsible (Judg. 19). The second judge, Ehud (Judg. 3:12-30), and the first king, Saul (1 Sam. 9:15-17; 10:1), came from the tribe of Benjamin.

9. Dan was the fifth son of Jacob and the first of two sons by Bilhah, Rachel's maid (Gen. 30:5-8). Therefore, Dan and Naphtali were full-blooded brothers and are often mentioned together (Gen. 46:23-24; Exod. 1:4). The tribe of Dan originally occupied the territory just west of Benjamin with Ephraim on the north and Judah and the Philistines on the south (Josh. 19:40-48). Shortly after settling in this area, the Amorites and the Philistines apparently attempted to drive them out of the region (Judg. 1:34-36). The pressure and harassment the people of Dan experienced from the Philistines is reflected in the stories of Samson, the Danite, and his encounters with them (Judg. 13–16). The Philistine pressure resulted in the migration of the tribe to an area north of Lake Hula, to the city of Laish and its territory (Judg. 18:14-27). The people of Dan captured the city and renamed it Dan (Judg. 18:29). See *Dan*.

10. Naphtali was the sixth son of Jacob and younger full-blooded brother of Dan (Gen. 30:6-8). The name, Naphtali, which conveys the idea of "wrestling" was selected because of the personal struggles between Rachel and Leah (Gen. 30:7-8). The Bible provides little information concerning Naphtali the person or tribe. During the tribal period the tribe of Naphtali occupied the broad strip of land west of the Jordan in the area of Lake Hula and the Sea of Chinnereth (Galilee). This band of land ran from Issachar and Zebulun in the south to near Dan in the north (Josh. 19:32-39). Apparently the tribe of Naphtali provided forces during the conquest of the land (Judg. 5:18) and during the Midianite threat (Judg. 6:35; 7:23).

11. Gad was the seventh son of Jacob and the first of two sons by Zilpah, the maid of Leah (Gen. 30:9-11). Because Leah saw this birth as a sign of "good fortune," especially in light of the fact that she had ceased having children, she named him "Gad" which means "fortune" (Gen. 30:11). We know very little about Gad the patriarch beyond the brief details about his birth. The tribe's territory was the east side of the Jordan River and the Dead Sea, including a part of the region called Gilead (Num. 32:34-36; Josh. 13:24-28), extending from the region of the Jabbok River in the north to the region of the Arnon River in the south. According to the blessing of Jacob, the tribe of Gad perhaps experienced numerous raids (Gen. 49:19) especially from groups like the Ammonites as reflected in the story of Jephthah (Judg. 11). Perhaps such raids were prompted by the fact that Gad occupied some of the best land in the Transjordan

T

(Deut. 33:20-21). Apparently the men of Gad achieved great expertise as warriors (1 Chron. 12:8).

12. Asher was the eighth son of Jacob, the second son by Zilpah and the younger full-blooded brother of Gad (Gen. 30:9-13). Like Gad, little information is shared about the patriarch Asher. The tribe of Asher occupied the region west of Zebulun and Naphtali, that is, the northern coastal region of Palestine. The territory extended from near Mount Carmel in the south to near Tyre in the north (Josh. 19:24-31). Asher is the only tribe not recognized as providing a judge during the tribal period. While Asher occupied choice territory (Gen. 49:20), it apparently was reproached and perhaps failed to gain the respect of some of the other tribes (Judg. 5:17b). **Conclusion** While discussion and research will continue concerning the history of the tribes and the territory they occupied, the tribal period will always be recognized as an important though enigmatic period in the development of the history of Israel. With the development of the monarchy, the tribal period came to an end. However, tribal ties and traditions may have continued to be quite strong. Many scholars suggest that tribal jealousies and traditions played a major role in bringing about the division of the kingdom and the formation of two kingdoms, the Northern Kingdom and the Southern Kingdom in 922 B.C. *LaMoine DeVries*

TRIBULATION Generally refers to the suffering and anguish of the people of God. According to the NT, tribulations are an expected reality among the followers of Christ.

The Hebrew word commonly rendered tribulation is *tsara*, which literally means "narrow" (Num. 22:26) or "compressed" (Job 41:15). A figurative understanding means "affliction, distress, or tribulation" (Deut. 4:30; Job 15:24; Ps. 32:7; Isa. 63:9; Jon. 2:2). The Greek word *thlipsis* conveys the idea of "severe constriction," "narrowing," or "pressing together" (Matt. 7:14; Mark 3:9). Similar notions underlie the Latin term *tribulum* (a threshing sledge), from which the English word comes.

The Bible teaches several important truths concerning the tribulations of believers. First, the tribulations of Christ are the pattern for the sufferings of believers. As tribulation was inevitable and expected in the messianic ministry of Jesus, so tribulation will be present among His followers (Matt. 13:21; John 16:33; Acts 14:22; Rom. 8:35; 12:12; 1 Thess. 3:3; 2 Thess. 1:4; Rev. 1:9). Second, the tribulations of believers are in a sense participation in the sufferings of Christ (Col. 1:24; 2 Cor. 1:5; 4:10; Phil. 3:10; 1 Pet. 4:13). Third, the tribulations of believers promote transformation into the likeness of Christ (Rom. 5:3; 2 Cor. 3:18; 4:8-12,16). Tribulation teaches Christ's followers to comfort and encourage others in similar situations, enabling those suffering to persevere and persist (2 Cor. 1:4; 4:10; Col. 1:24; 1 Thess. 1:6).

Another biblical understanding of tribulation is eschatological. The expression "great tribulation" refers to the time of trouble that will usher in the second coming of Christ (Matt. 24:21; Rev. 2:22; 7:14). Jesus warned that the great tribulation would be so intense that its calamities will nearly decimate all of life (Matt. 24:15-22). Jesus' words in Matt. 24:29 may refer to Dan. 12:1, "a time of distress such as never occurred since there was a nation until that time" (NASB). This allusion suggests an eschatological view of the great tribulation.

One's millennial view usually determines the interpretation of the time and nature of this period of intense tribulation. Postmillennialists and amillennialists consider the great tribulation as a brief, indefinite period at the end of this age, usually identifying it with the revolt of Gog and Magog in Rev. 20:8-9. Dispensational premillennialists identify the tribulation with the 70th week of Daniel's prophecy (Dan. 9:27), a period of seven years whose latter half is the great tribulation. The rapture of the church precedes a literal, seven-year tribulation, which is followed by the second coming of Christ. Historical premillennialists (posttribulationalists) assert that the tribulation is a horrific period of trouble immediately preceding the millennium and typically teach that believers and unbelievers will both undergo this tribulation.

Although this event should rightly be regarded as a future occurrence, attempts to connect the time of tribulation with specific events or persons have proved futile. Believers are exhorted to watch for Christ and fix their hope on Him, not upon events surrounding His coming (1 John 3:3). *Stan Norman*

TRIBUNE Commander of an ancient Roman cohort, a military unit ideally comprising 1,000 men. Some English versions use this term for the

Greek word *chiliarchos*, which is also rendered "commander." The Greek word for "cohort" is *speires*, which is sometimes rendered "regiment" (cp. Acts 21:31-33; 22:24-29; 23:10-22; 24:22; 25:23). According to Josephus, the Romans stationed a cohort in Jerusalem at the Antonia Fortress to suppress disturbances in the city. *E. Ray Clendenen*

TRIBUTE Any payment exacted by a superior power, usually a state, from an inferior one. The weaker state, called a vassal state, normally contributed a specified amount of gold, silver, or other commodities on a yearly basis. The imposition of tribute demonstrated the subservient status of the vassal state, thus undermining political autonomy and often causing financial weakness. Powerful nations collected tribute from both hostile states and allies. Refusal to render tribute by either was regarded as rebellion and normally resulted in military reprisals.

Imposing tribute was practiced widely and can be tracked back to before 2000 B.C. The Tell el Amarna Letters from Canaanite kings after 1400 B.C. clearly reveal their vassal status to Egypt. During a few periods of strength, Israel took tribute from neighboring peoples. David and Solomon exacted tribute from several smaller states (2 Sam. 8:14; 1 Kings 4:21). Later, Moab paid a tribute of 100,000 lambs and the wool of 100,000 rams to Ahab of Israel (2 Kings 3:4).

After the division of Solomon's kingdom in 922 B.C., the relatively weaker states of Judah and Israel more often were forced to pay tribute to the large powers which increasingly dominated the Near East. This was especially true of the Assyrian period (850–600 B.C.) as both biblical and archaeological evidence attest. The Black Obelisk of Shalmaneser III (about 841 B.C.) shows Jehu of Israel paying tribute prostrate before the Assyrian king. Menahem of Israel (2 Kings 15:19) and Ahaz of Judah (2 Kings 16:7-9) rendered tribute to Tiglath-pileser III (Pul) for different reasons. The heavy tribute paid by Hezekiah to Sennacherib about 701 B.C. was recorded in both biblical and Assyrian texts (2 Kings 18:13-16).

The Jews later paid tribute in one form or another to Babylon, Persia, the Ptolemies and Seleucids, and Rome. The Roman *tributum* was a form of taxes. In effect the famous question posed to Jesus by the Pharisees about taxes

(Matt. 22:15-22) was about tribute. See *Assyria; Babylon; Egypt; Rome and the Roman Empire.*

Thomas V. Brisco

TRIGON (Trī´ gŏn) Small, three cornered harp with four strings (Dan. 3:5,7,10; KJV "sackbut"; HCSB, "lyre").

TRINITY Theological term used to define God as an undivided unity expressed in the threefold nature of God the Father, God the Son, and God the Holy Spirit. As a distinctive Christian doctrine, the Trinity is considered as a divine mystery beyond human comprehension to be reflected upon only through scriptural revelation. The Trinity is a biblical concept that expresses the dynamic character of God, not a Greek idea pressed into Scripture from philosophical or religious speculation. While the term "trinity" does not appear in Scripture, the trinitarian structure appears throughout the NT to affirm that God Himself is manifested through Jesus Christ by means of the Spirit.

A proper biblical view of the Trinity balances the concepts of unity and distinctiveness. Two errors that appear in the history of the consideration of the doctrine are tritheism and unitarianism. In tritheism error is made in emphasizing the distinctiveness of the Godhead to the point that the Trinity is seen as three separate Gods, or a Christian polytheism. On the other hand, unitarianism excludes the concept of distinctiveness while focusing solely on the aspect of God the Father. In this way Christ and the Holy Spirit are placed in lower categories and made less than divine. Both errors compromise the effectiveness and contribution of the activity of God in redemptive history.

The biblical concept of the Trinity developed through progressive revelation. The OT consistently affirms the unity of God through such statements as "Listen, Israel: The LORD our God, the LORD is One" (Deut. 6:4 HCSB). God's oneness is stressed to caution the Israelites against the polytheism and practical atheism of their heathen neighbors. See *Revelation, Book of; Shema.*

The OT does feature implications of the trinitarian idea. This does not mean that the Trinity was fully knowable from the OT, but that a vocabulary was established through the events of God's nearness and creativity; both receive developed meaning from NT writers. For

T

example, the word of God is recognized as the agent of creation (Ps. 33:6,9; cp. Prov. 3:19; 8:27), revelation, and salvation (Ps. 107:20). This same vocabulary is given distinct personality in John's prologue (John 1:1-4) in the person of Jesus Christ. Other vocabulary categories include the wisdom of God (Prov. 8) and the Spirit of God (Gen. 1:2; Ps. 104:30; Zech. 4:6).

A distinguishing feature of the NT is the doctrine of the Trinity. It is remarkable that NT writers present the doctrine in such a manner that it does not violate the OT concept of the oneness of God. In fact, they unanimously affirm the Hebrew monotheistic faith, but they extend it to include the coming of Jesus and the outpouring of the Holy Spirit. The early Christian church experienced the God of Abraham in a new and dramatic way without abandoning the oneness of God that permeates the OT. As a fresh expression of God, the concept of the Trinity—rooted in the God of the past and consistent with the God of the past—absorbs the idea of the God of the past but goes beyond the God of the past in a more personal encounter.

The NT does not present a systematic presentation of the Trinity. The scattered segments from various writers that appear throughout the NT reflect a seemingly accepted understanding that exists without a full-length discussion. It is embedded in the framework of the Christian experience and simply assumed as true. The NT writers focus on statements drawn from the obvious existence of the trinitarian experience as opposed to a detailed exposition.

The NT evidence for the Trinity can be grouped into four types of passages. The first is the trinitarian formula of Matt. 28:19; 2 Cor. 13:13/14; 1 Pet. 1:2; Rev. 1:4-6. In each passage a trinitarian formula, repeated in summation fashion, registers a distinctive contribution of each person of the Godhead. Matthew 28:19, for example, follows the triple formula of Father, Son, and Holy Spirit that distinguishes Christian baptism. The risen Lord commissioned the disciples to baptize converts with a trinitarian emphasis that carries the distinctiveness of each person of the Godhead while associating their inner relationship. This passage is the clearest scriptural reference to a systematic presentation of the doctrine of the Trinity.

Paul, in 2 Cor. 13:13/14, finalized his thoughts to the Corinthian church with a pastoral appeal that is grounded in "the grace of the Lord Jesus Christ, and the love of God, and the fellowship of the Holy Spirit." The formulation is designed to have the practical impact of bringing that divided church together through their personal experience of the Trinity in their daily lives. Significantly, in the trinitarian order Christ is mentioned first. This reflects the actual process of Christian salvation, since Christ is the key to opening insight into the work of the Godhead. Paul was calling attention to the trinitarian consciousness, not in the initial work of salvation that has already been accomplished at Corinth, but in the sustaining work that enables divisive Christians to achieve unity.

In 1 Pet. 1:2 the trinitarian formula is followed with reference to each person of the Godhead. The scattered Christians are reminded through reference to the Trinity that their election (foreknowledge of the Father) and redemption (the sanctifying work of the Spirit) should lead to holy living in obedience to the Son.

John addressed the readers of the book of Revelation with an expanded trinitarian formula that includes references to the persons of the Godhead (Rev. 1:4-6). The focus on the triumph of Christianity crystallizes the trinitarian greeting into a doxology that acknowledges the accomplished work and the future return of Christ. This elongated presentation serves as an encouragement to churches facing persecution.

A second type of NT passage is the triadic form. Two passages cast in this structure are Eph. 4:4-6 and 1 Cor. 12:3-6. Both passages refer to the three persons of the Trinity, but not in the definitive formula of the previous passage. Each Scripture balances the unity of the church. Emphasis is placed on the administration of gifts by the Godhead.

A third category of passages mentions the three persons of the Godhead but without a clear triadic structure. In the accounts of the baptism of Jesus (Matt. 3:13-17; Mark 1:9-11; and Luke 3:21-22), the three Synoptic writers recorded the presence of the Trinity when the Son was baptized, the Spirit descended, and the Father spoke with approval. Paul, in Gal. 4:4-6, outlined the work of the Trinity in the aspect of the sending Father. Other representative passages in this category (2 Thess. 2:13-15; Titus 3:4-6; Jude 20–21) portray each member of the Trinity in relation to a particular redemptive function.

The fourth category of trinitarian passages includes those presented in the farewell discourse of Jesus to His disciples (John 14:16; 15:26; 16:13-15). In the context of these passages, Jesus expounded the work and ministry of the third person of the Godhead as the Agent of God in the continuing ministry of the Son. The Spirit is a Teacher who facilitates understanding on the disciples' part and, in being sent from the Father and the Son, is one in nature with the other persons of the Trinity. Jesus said the Spirit takes what is His and declares it to believers (John 16:15). The discourse emphasizes the interrelatedness of the Trinity in equality and operational significance.

All of these passages are embryonic efforts by the early church to express its awareness of the Trinity. The NT is christological in its approach, but it involves the fullness of God being made available to the individual believer through Jesus and by the Spirit. The consistent trinitarian expression is not a formulation of the doctrine, as such, but reveals an experiencing of God's persistent self-revelation.

In the postbiblical era the Christian church tried to express its doctrine in terms that were philosophically acceptable and logically coherent. Greek categories of understanding began to appear in explanation efforts. Discussion shifted from the NT emphasis on the function of the Trinity in redemptive history to an analysis of the unity of essence of the Godhead.

A major question during those early centuries focused on the oneness of God. The Sabelians described the Godhead in terms of modes that existed only one at a time. This theory upheld the unity of God but excluded His permanent distinctiveness. The Docetists understood Christ as an appearance of God in human form, while Ebonites described Jesus as an ordinary man with God's power existing within Him at baptism. Arius was also an influential theologian who viewed Jesus as subordinate to God. To Arius, Jesus was a being created by God, higher than man, but less than God. This idea, as well as the others, was challenged by Athanasius at Nicea (A.D. 325), and the council decided for the position of Jesus as "of the exact same substance as the Father."

Probably the most outstanding thinker of the early centuries was Augustine of Hippo (A.D. 354–430). He began with the idea of God as one substance and sought explanation of the Godhead in psychological analogy: a person exists as one being with three dimensions of memory, understanding, and will; so also the Godhead exists as a unity of Father, Son, and Holy Spirit. While this explanation is helpful and contains the concept of three persons in one, it does not resolve the complex nature of God.

Perhaps four statements can summarize and clarify this study.

1. God is One. The God of the OT is the same God of the NT. His offer of salvation in the OT receives a fuller revelation in the NT in a way that is not different but more complete. The doctrine of the Trinity does not abandon the monotheistic faith of Israel.

2. God has three distinct ways of being in the redemptive event, yet He remains an undivided unity. That God the Father imparts Himself to mankind through Son and Spirit without ceasing to be Himself is at the very heart of the Christian faith. A compromise in either the absolute sameness of the Godhead or the true diversity reduces the reality of salvation.

3. The primary way of grasping the concept of the Trinity is through the threefold participation in salvation. The approach of the NT is not to discuss the essence of the Godhead, but the particular aspects of the revelatory event that includes the definitive presence of the Father in the person of Jesus Christ through the Holy Spirit.

4. The doctrine of the Trinity is an absolute mystery. It is primarily known, not through speculation, but through experiencing the act of grace through personal faith. See *God; Holy Spirit; Jesus Christ.*   *Jerry M. Henry*

TRIPOLIS (Trĭ´ pŭ lĭs) (Ezra 4:9 HCSB, NIV) See *Tarpelites.*

TRIUMPHAL ENTRY Term used for the entry of Jesus into the city of Jerusalem on the Sunday prior to His crucifixion. Due to the fact that palm branches were placed before Him, this day is often called "Palm Sunday." The event is recorded in Matt. 21:1-9; Mark 11:1-10; Luke 19:28-38; John 12:12-15. All accounts agree in substance with each adding certain detail. Whether by prearrangement or by divine foreknowledge, the disciples found a colt in Bethphage as Jesus had described. (Matthew ties the account closely to Zechariah's prophesy [9:9], mentioning the colt and its mother.) It is possible that Christ rode the donkey for the more difficult part of the journey, transferring to the colt upon

To Emmaus

To Samaria

Golgatha

Tower Gate

Damascus Gate

Tomb

Gennath Gate

Herod's Palace

Theater

House of Caiaphas

Upper City

Upper Room

Lower City

Siloam Pool

Aqueduct

©LATTA

HINNOM VA

Jesus' path from Bethany to the East Gate of Jerusalem

actually entering Jerusalem. There a large crowd applauded Him, spreading the road with their garments and with branches. They acknowledged Him as the son of David.

The triumphal entry is of vital significance in understanding the messianic mission of Jesus. Prior to this moment, Jesus had refused to allow any public acknowledgement of His being the Messiah. By conducting His ministry outside Jerusalem, He had avoided further intensification of conflict with the Jewish religious leaders. Now, however, the time was at hand. The opponents of Jesus understood the strong messianic implications of the manner of His entry into Jerusalem. The riding upon the colt, the garments and palm branches in the road, and the shouts of the multitude—all of these pointed to Jesus as the Messiah. When He was urged to quiet the people, Jesus replied, "If they were to keep silent, the stones would cry out!" (Luke 19:40 HCSB).

Ironically, though the triumphal entry was a public acceptance of Jesus being the Messiah and presented a direct challenge to His enemies, it must have been a disappointment to many of His followers. Christ did not enter Jerusalem upon a warhorse of conquest but upon a colt representing humility. As a result, the religious leaders demanded His crucifixion, while the multitudes ultimately turned away with indifference. See *Jesus, Life and Ministry; Messiah.*

Steve Echols

TROAS (Trō ăz) City in northwest Asia Minor visited by Paul during his second and third missionary journeys (Acts 16:8,11; 20:5-6; 2 Cor. 2:12; 2 Tim. 4:13). Troas was founded before 300 B.C. by Antigonus, a successor of Alexander the Great, and was located about 10 miles south of the city of Troy. The emperor Augustus (31 B.C.–A.D. 14) made it a Roman colony. It served as an important seaport in the Roman Empire for those traveling between Asia Minor and Macedonia. Today ruins of the city wall (about six miles in circumference), a theater, and an aqueduct remain. See *Asia Minor, Cities of; Paul.*

Scott Langston

TROGYLLIUM (Trō ğĭl´ lĭ ŭm) Promontory on the west coast of Asia Minor less than one mile across the strait from Samos, a stopping place on Paul's return to Jerusalem according to the Western text of Acts 20:15.

TROPHIMUS (Trŏph´ ĭ mŭs) Personal name meaning "nutritious." Gentile Christian from Ephesus who accompanied Paul to Jerusalem for the presentation of the collection (Acts 20:4;

A section of the ruins of the theater at Troas.

21:29). Paul's free association with Trophimus led to the false charge that Paul had defiled the temple by bringing a Gentile within the Court of Israel (Acts 21:19). The Trophimus whom Paul left in Miletus (2 Tim. 4:20) is either another Trophimus or else evidence for a second Roman imprisonment. According to Acts, Paul did not pass by Miletus on his way to Rome.

TRUMPET See *Music, Instruments, Dancing; Shophar.*

TRUST See *Faith, Faithfulness.*

TRUTH Past biblical scholars often overgeneralized about distinctions between Greek and Hebrew conceptions of truth, claiming Greek philosophical tradition understood truth to be static, timeless, and theoretical, in contrast to the Hebrew view of truth as practical and experiential. They maintain that, though Hebrew understanding predominates in the Bible, the contrasting Greek view is represented in the NT, especially in Johannine literature.

The tide has turned against this idea (see A. Thiselton, "Truth" in *The New International Dictionary of New Testament Theology*). Increasingly, scholars now recognize that major biblical words translated "truth" (Hb. *emet;* Gk. *aletheia*) have a wide range of meaning, as propositional, personal, moral, and historical truth. *Emet* frequently does mean "faithfulness," OT writers using it to describe God's word and deeds. His word can be trusted because He is faithful and because it is true. The genius of biblical teaching is that all truth is unified and grounded in the faithful and true God.

Truth as Truth Telling The most common meaning of biblical words refers to statements accurately reflecting facts, such as accurate and trustworthy witnesses (Prov. 12:17; cp. 1 John 2:21). Lying is the opposite of truth (Jer. 9:3; cp. Gen. 42:16). The people of God are to speak truth to one another (Zech. 8:16; Eph. 4:25). Jesus stresses the authority and certainty of His message in saying, "I tell you the truth" (Luke 9:27 HCSB; cp. Luke 4:24; John 16:7). John stresses he is telling the truth about Jesus (John 19:35), and Paul emphasizes he is not lying (Rom. 9:1; cp. 2 Cor. 7:14; 1 Tim. 2:7; Acts 26:25).

For Moses the covenant God abounds in truth (Exod. 34:6). His truth is eternal (Ps.

117:2). Human testimony can swear to truth by nothing higher than God (1 Kings 22:16; Isa. 65:16). Since God is true, so is His word (Ps. 119:160; cp. John 17:17; 2 Sam. 7:28; Pss. 43:3; 119:142,151). Scripture is this very word of truth and thus should be handled carefully (2 Tim. 2:15). The gospel is equated with the truth (Gal. 2:5,14; Eph.1:13), and the truth is equated with the gospel (Gal. 5:7).

Other Uses of "Truth" Because God's word is truth, it is ultimately real and not ephemeral, as opposed to all else, and liberates men (John 8:32). Satan and men lie (John 8:44; Rom. 1:25) and enslave. Jesus is Savior because He is Truth incarnate (John 14:6; cp. 1:14,17; Eph. 4:21). Now the Holy Spirit indwells believers, guiding them into all truth (John 14:17; 15:26; 16:13; cp. 1 John 5:6).

Yet people resist truth. Jesus implied this, "Because I tell the truth, you do not believe Me" (John 8:46 HCSB). The Bible teaches that believing truth is not a mechanical psychological function but is related to the human will. People choose the lie rather than God's truth (Rom. 1:25; 2 Tim. 3:8; 4:4; Titus 1:14).

More than half the uses of *aletheia* and cognates occur in Johannine writings (John 16:7; 1 John 2:4,21,27). John uses it to refer to reality in contrast to falsehood or appearance but does not reject OT teaching on truth. Nor does John have a Greek mind-set. In fact, John 1:14 describes Jesus in His incarnation as "full of grace and truth," a reference to the OT concept of covenant loyalty/faithfulness (*chesed*), now seen firsthand in the Logos as the genuine reality of God. In John 14:6 Jesus describes Himself as "the way, the truth, and the life," combining a number of concepts. Jesus is the true way leading to life, and men should not come to Him seeking truth but, because He is the end of the search, the revealed reality of God. *Ted Cabal*

TRYPHAENA AND TRYPHOSA (Trī phē´ nà, Trī phō´ sà) Personal names meaning "dainty" and "delicate." Two women whom Paul greeted as those "who have worked hard in the Lord" (Rom. 16:12 HCSB). The two were perhaps deacons serving the Roman church (cp. Phoebe in Rom. 16:1) or else "marketplace" evangelists like Priscilla (Acts 18:26; Rom. 16:3). The similarity of their names suggests the two were perhaps (twin) sisters.

TUBAL (Tū´ bàl) Son of Japheth (Gen. 10:2; 1 Chron. 1:5) and ancestor of a people, likely of Cappadocia or Cilicia in Asia Minor (Isa. 66:19; Ezek. 27:13; 32:26; 38:2-3; 39:1).

TUBAL-CAIN (Tū´ bàl-cān) Son of Lamech, associated with the origin of metalworking (Gen. 4:22). The two elements in his name mean "producer" and "smith."

TUNIC Loose-fitting, knee-length garment worn next to the skin (Matt. 10:10; Mark 6:9). See *Cloth, Clothing.*

TURBAN Headdress formed by wrapping long strips of cloth around the head. A distinctive headdress formed part of the garb of the high priest (Exod. 28:4,37,39; 29:6; 39:28,31; Lev. 8:9; 16:4). Removal of one's turban was a sign of mourning or shame (Isa. 3:18-23; Ezek. 24:17,23). See *Cloth, Clothing; Headband, Headdress.*

TURNING OF THE WALL Expression used in the KJV, elsewhere translated as "the corner buttress" (NASB), "the Angle" (NRSV), "the escarpment" (REB), and "the angle of the wall" (NIV). One segment of the Jerusalem ramparts probably located near the palace. It was fortified by Uzziah (2 Chron. 26:9) and rebuilt by Nehemiah

Relief of two Roman men wearing tunics partially visible beneath their outer togas.

(Neh. 3:19-20,24). Not to be confused with "the corner" (Neh. 3:31) nor associated with the corner gate. See *Corner Gate.*

TURQUOISE See *Minerals and Metals; Antimony.*

TURTLEDOVE See *Dove.*

TUTOR See *Custodian; Guardian.*

TWELVE, THE See *Apostle; Disciple.*

TYCHICUS (Tĭk´ ĭ cŭs) Personal name meaning "fortunate." One of Paul's fellow workers in the ministry. A native of Asia Minor (Acts 20:4), he traveled with the apostle on the third missionary journey. Tychicus and Onesimus carried the Colossian letter from Paul (Col. 4:7-9) and were to relate to the church Paul's condition. Paul also sent Tychicus to Ephesus on one occasion (2 Tim. 4:12) and possibly to Crete on another (Titus 3:12). Tradition holds that he died a martyr.

TYPOLOGY Method of interpreting some parts of Scripture by seeing a pattern which an earlier statement sets up by which a later is explained. The Greek words that help us understand typology come under a verbal root that means "to beat, strike, or smite." In building construction, what is "beaten out" can become a pattern. This article will examine how various words in the family are used and how typology functions in interpreting the OT.

Foundational Words and Meanings All of these related words show the effects of an imprint.

1. Blow, strike, mark A literal meaning *tupos* is found in the narrative about Thomas' skepticism: "If I don't see the mark (*tupos*) of the nails in His hands, put my finger into the mark of the nails, and put my hand into His side, I will never believe!" (John 20:25 HCSB). Jesus invited Thomas to examine His hands and side. Then Jesus urged: "Don't be an unbeliever, but a believer" (John 20:27). Thomas showed he did just that when he exclaimed, "My Lord and my God!" (John 20:28).

2. Technical model or pattern Both Heb. 8:5 and Acts 7:44 use *tupos* to refer to Exod. 25:40, where the Lord commanded Moses to make the furniture and utensils of the tabernacle "according to the model of them you have been shown on the mountain" (HCSB). The Hebrew word for pattern is *tabnit*, from a Hebrew root meaning "to build." The noun means "construction, pattern, or figure." The writer of Hebrews stressed that Christ could not be an earthly priest, for such priests served in the copy and shadow of heavenly things. Moses saw an earthly copy of the heavenly reality. Jesus became a high priest and a minister of the holy places and true tent, which the Lord pitched (Heb. 8:2). Even this earthly language shows the superiority of Christ's heavenly priesthood to that of the earthly priests.

In Acts 7:44 Stephen said that the whole tabernacle, which he called "the tabernacle of the testimony" (HCSB), was made "according to the pattern" that Moses had seen. The word *tupos* means a model or pattern.

3. Image or status In Acts 7 Stephen said that Israel "took up the tent of Moloch and the star of your god Rephan, the images that you made to worship" (Acts 7:43 HCSB). Here what is stamped or beaten out is an idol. The imprint became an object of worship.

4. Pattern as a mold or norm While Stephen pointed out a bad pattern in the case of idolatry, Paul emphasized a good pattern in Rom. 6:17. Paul thanked God that, although the Romans were once slaves of sin, they became subject to the gospel. He described the gospel as the "pattern of teaching you were entrusted to" (HCSB). The gospel is a norm or pattern showing how we should live (cp. Rom. 1:16-17).

5. Persons as examples or patterns When people internalize the gospel, their lives begin a process of transformation. Paul spoke of himself and his fellow workers as examples or patterns. He urged the Philippians to become imitators of himself: "observe those who live according to the example you have in us" (Phil. 3:17 HCSB). He said to the Thessalonians, "We did it to make ourselves an example to you so that you would imitate us" (2 Thess. 3:9). Paul obtained mercy and God showed His forbearance to Paul "as an example to those who would believe in Him" (1 Tim. 1:16).

The Thessalonians, by their faith during tribulation, became models or patterns for believers in Macedonia and Achaia, "in every place that your faith in God has gone out" (1 Thess. 1:7-8 HCSB). Paul commanded Timo-

thy to be a pattern or model for believers "in speech, in conduct, in love, in faith, in purity" (1 Tim. 4:12). At the same time, Timothy had his own standard to guide him: "Hold on to the pattern of sound teaching that you have heard from me, in the faith and love that are in Christ Jesus" (2 Tim. 1:13). Titus likewise was to be a model or pattern of good works, soundness in teaching, respectfulness, sound preaching that is beyond reproach (Titus 2:7-8). Peter urged all the elders to become examples or patterns for the flock rather than "lording it over" the flock (1 Pet. 5:3). Christians, and especially Christian leaders, are being watched and often imitated. The pattern or model they exhibit is crucial.

Typology as a Method of Interpreting the Old Testament Sometimes the NT explicitly refers to its method of interpreting the OT as "type," or "typically." Usually, however, the NT uses typology as a method of interpreting the OT without explicitly saying so. Typology involves a correspondence, usually in one particular matter between a person, event, or thing in the OT with a person, event, or thing in the NT. All elements except this one may be quite different, but the one element selected for comparison has a genuine similarity in the two different historical contexts.

1. Old Testament warnings Paul used this kind of typology in 1 Cor. 10:1-11. He rehearsed the experiences of the people of Israel in the exodus and in their 40 years in the desert: the destruction of Pharaoh's army in the sea (Exod. 14–15); the eating of manna (Exod. 16); their conduct when thirsty—Rephidim—striking the rock (Exod. 17); Kadesh—speaking to the rock (Num. 20); sin of the gold calf (Exod. 32); fornication with the daughters of Moab at Baal of Peor (Num. 25); murmuring when going from Mount Hor around the land of Edom (Num. 21). Paul stressed one point of correspondence between the OT events and the NT message: All the people participated in these experiences, but God was not pleased with most of them; the majority died in the desert and could not enter the promised land (1 Cor. 10:5). Paul pointed to this conduct of the majority who angered God as types or warning patterns, models, examples for Christians (1 Cor. 10:6). Christians are not to desire evil things, as in the golden calf incident and as at Baal-Peor (1 Cor. 10:7-8). They were not to complain or murmur as the Israelites did when they were bitten by fiery serpents or in the

T

judgment of the sons of Korah (1 Cor. 10:9-10; cp. Num. 16; 21). Paul concluded, "Now these things happened to them as examples, and they were written as a warning to us, on whom the ends of the ages have come" (1 Cor. 10:11 HCSB).

2. Adam as a type of Christ Paul compared Adam and Christ in Rom. 5:12-21. He argued that Christ's deed is much more powerful than Adam's transgression. Paul said specifically that Adam "is a prototype of the Coming One" (v. 14 HCSB). Certainly, huge differences separate Adam and Christ. The one point of correspondence in the passage is the effect of influence upon mankind. Adam affected mankind adversely; Christ affects the same mankind for the good. Adam's trespass brought a verdict of condemnation of all people; Christ's righteous deed brought the gracious benefit to all people for the acquittal that brings life (vv. 16,18). Where sin abounded, grace was overflowing in greater abundance (v. 20). To make Christ's deed effective, people must receive the abundance of God's grace and the gift of righteousness (v. 17).

3. Baptism as a fulfillment Peter, after discussing Christ's work in preaching in the spiritual realm to spirits in prison, mentioned Noah's ark and the flood: "In it [the ark], a few—that is, eight people—were saved through water. Baptism, which corresponds to this, now saves you (not the removal of the filth of the flesh, but the pledge of a good conscience toward God) through the resurrection of Jesus Christ" (1 Pet. 3:20-21 HCSB). Baptism is a drama of faith. Here it is called a "pledge"—an acted-out pledge of a good conscience. We are saved by faith expressed in water baptism. What is the one point of correspondence with the flood? The flood was a type of baptism because people of faith (and recipients of God's favor) experienced deliverance. Noah and his family were delivered by the ark and the water. Christians expressing in baptism genuine faith are delivered from bondage to sin.

One point of correspondence between an OT event and a NT event shows the same God at work in both covenants. Typology, a comparison stressing one point of similarity, helps us see the NT person, event, or institution as the fulfillment of that which was only hinted at in the OT.

Berkeley Mickelson

TYRANNUS (Tĭ răn´ nŭs) Latin form of the Greek term *turannos,* a ruler with absolute authority. After Paul withdrew from the synagogue in Ephesus, he preached for two years at the lecture hall of Tyrannus (Acts 19:9). Tyrannus was either the owner of the hall or a prominent philosopher associated with it. According to some Western texts, Paul preached from 11:00 until 4:00 p.m., the time of the afternoon break from work. If accurate, this tradition explains the availability of the hall (schools generally met in the morning) and the freedom of "all Asia" to hear Paul during their "siesta."

TYRE (Tĭr) See *Sidon and Tyre.*

TYRIAN (Tĭr´ ĭ án) Person from Tyre.

TYROPOEON VALLEY (Tĭ rō´ pĭ ŏn) Narrow depression between Jerusalem's Ophel (Hill of David) and the western or upper hill of the city. It was much deeper in ancient times but has been filled up with debris through the centuries, especially since the destruction of the city by the Romans in A.D. 70. When David captured the city, the valley served as one of the natural defensive barriers. During Hellenistic times it was included within the city walls. During Herod's building campaign, he constructed bridges across the valley to connect the palace area with the temple complex.

TYRUS (Tĭr´ ŭs) (KJV) See *Sidon and Tyre.*

Looking at the west side of the Temple Mount from the west with the Tyropoeon Valley in the foreground.

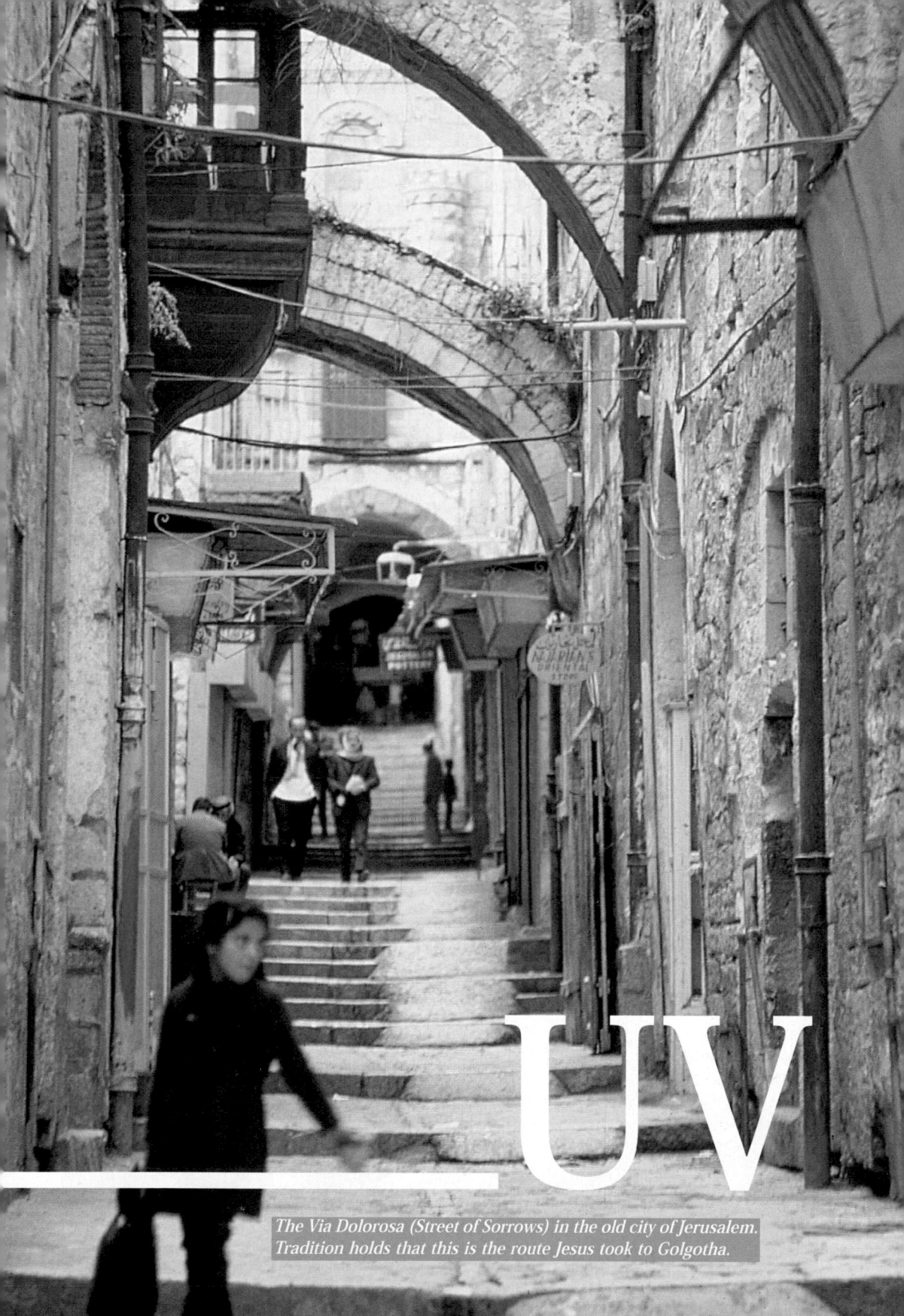

UV

The Via Dolorosa (Street of Sorrows) in the old city of Jerusalem. Tradition holds that this is the route Jesus took to Golgotha.

UCAL (Ū´ căl) Personal name meaning "I am strong" or "I am consumed." Pupil of Agur, the wisdom teacher responsible for Prov. 30 (v. 1). REB followed the earliest Greek translation in rendering the proper names Ithiel and Ucal as "I am weary, God, I am weary and worn out" (cp. HCSB, NRSV).

UEL (Ū´ ĕl) Personal name meaning "will of God," or a contraction of Abiel meaning "God is father." Contemporary of Ezra with a foreign wife (Ezra 10:34).

UGARIT (Ū gă´ rĭt)Important city in Syria whose excavation has provided tablets giving the closest primary evidence available for reconstructing the Canaanite religion Israel faced.

Location Ruins of the ancient city of Ugarit lie on the Mediterranean coast about nine miles north of Latakia. The contemporary name is Ras Shamra, "head [land] of fennel." Located at the juncture of major trade routes from Anatolia, northwest Mesopotamia, and Egypt, and possessing a harbor (modern Minet el-Beida) which accommodated vessels from Cyprus, the Aegean, and Egypt, Ugarit was an important commercial center in most periods until the Sea Peoples destroyed it in 1180 B.C. Its culture was cosmo-

politan, so much so that it is difficult to identify those elements that were uniquely Ugaritic. Although it was the capital of a city-state, it was most often under the power or dominating influence of larger states.

The Excavations Although the existence of Ugarit had been known from Mesopotamian and Egyptian documents, its location was uncertain. In 1928 a farmer's discovery of what turned out to be an extensive cemetery just north of Minet el-Beida led in 1929 to excavations in the cemetery and on the tell nearby (Ras Shamra). In that first season of excavations, important texts written in a previously unknown cuneiform script were discovered, one of which mentioned that the document was written during the time of Niqmaddu, king of Ugarit. This was the first indication that the site was indeed ancient Ugarit.

Excavations were carried out annually, 1929–1939, under the direction of C. F. A. Schaeffer. After the hiatus caused by World War II, excavations were resumed and continued on a regular basis through 1976. In addition, adjacent sites have either been surveyed or excavated. The history of the city may now be traced from its earliest beginnings in the pre-pottery Neolithic period (about 6500 B.C.), through the Chalcolithic, early Bronze, and middle Bronze

An overview of the ruins of Ugarit at Ras Shamra on the Syrian coast near the Orontes River.

U
V

periods, to its complete and final destruction in the late Bronze period soon after 1200 by the Sea Peoples. We have no evidence that the site of Ugarit was ever occupied again, although artifacts from as late as Roman times have been found.

The late-Bronze city of Ugarit, covering about 70 acres, contained the remains of palaces, temples, private dwellings, workshops, storage areas, and fortifications. Temples were found dedicated to Baal and to El; between these buildings was located the house of the high priest and scriptorium. The palaces were located on the northwestern side of the tell. The material culture of late Bronze Ugarit was of the highest order, showing cultural influences from all the surrounding areas.

The most significant discoveries at Ugarit for the study of both history and religion are the discoveries of the epigraphic materials. Clay tablets and other inscriptions representing eight languages have come to light. The majority of these documents consist of economic and administrative texts, private correspondence, and liturgical-religious texts that represent major mythological themes.

From the first season of excavation, a large number of clay tablets emerged that were written in an unknown script. The new script, used to inscribe texts in the Ugaritic language, was in alphabetic cuneiform consisting of 31 signs, 28 of which were consonants and three of which indicated the letter *aleph* as used with three different vowels. For the student of the Bible, the religious and mythological texts present a rather full picture of Canaanite religious practice and belief already known from the Bible. The study and evaluation of all the material remains from Ugarit and contiguous sites will continue until the archaeological history can be clarified, until the fullest possible social and political history can be written, and until the full yield of information from the Ugaritic texts has been achieved. See *Canaan*.

The Religious Texts The poetic mythological texts and poetic legends have elicited the greatest interest because of the information they provide about Canaanite religion. Foremost is the Baal-Anath cycle that has survived in a number of large tablets and smaller fragments. It is difficult to determine the exact story line because there is little agreement on the order of the tablets. The central figure was Baal, the god of

The excavated areas of Ugarit that have yielded much material about Canaan and Canaanite religion.

storm cloud and rain or the giver of life and fertility, who struggled against his foes in order to gain a dominant position in the pantheon. The head of the pantheon was El who appears in the epic as far removed, almost a god emeritus, although nothing could be accomplished without his approval. Asherah and Anath were the consorts of El and Baal, respectively. Baal's antagonists were Prince Sea (Yam) and Mot (god of the dry season and underworld). Having received permission to build a house (temple), Prince Sea struck fear into the hearts of the gods by demanding that Baal be surrendered to him. Yet Baal defeated Prince Sea in an episode reminiscent of Marduk's defeat of the sea monster, Tiamat, in the *Enuma Elish*. Then Baal was permitted to build a palace (temple) as a symbol of his new status among the gods. However, Baal's mightiest foe, Mot, defeated Baal, crushing him like a kid in his gullet and taking him down to the netherworld. The world went into mourning. El wept piteously at the news, gashing his back, chest, and arms, while Anath, having found Baal's corpse, put on sackcloth and bewailed the death of the lord of life. Mot boasted of his victory to Anath, whereupon she slew Mot, ground him up, and scattered his remains over the fields. Then came the joyous cry that Baal was alive; the rains came, and the world returned to life. See *Babylon*.

The myth was closely related to the cycle of the year and described the ongoing struggles between life and death. While Baal ruled half the year, giving rain and crops, Mot held dominion over the other half—the dry season. Fertility religion consisted in part of various magical and ritual practices designed to bring Baal back to life. Hints of these practices are given in the

U
V

Baal-Anath cycle. El, upon hearing that Baal was dead, gashed his body: "He harrows the roll of his arm, he plows his chest like a garden, harrows his back like a plain." Like the prophets of Baal on Mount Carmel (1 Kings 18), he was practicing imitative magic as though preparing the fields to receive the rain. For her part, Anath wept for Baal, the falling tears intended to encourage the rain to fall. In addition to these acts, in actual practice the Canaanites employed sacred prostitution and other imitative practices to restore fertility to the world. See *Fertility Cult.*

The legend of King Keret and the legend of Aqhat are also related in some way to the fertility cycle. King Keret, having lost his seven wives to various tragedies before they could give him an heir, bewailed his fate. In a dream El told him to attack another kingdom to obtain another wife who could produce an heir. Keret succeeded in this, and eight sons and eight daughters were born to him. However, apparently because of an unfulfilled vow, Keret fell sick; his impending death seemed to affect the fertility of the land. El intervened, death was shattered, and Keret returned to normal life. The full significance of the Keret legend is difficult to determine, whether it is a cultic myth or a social myth with a historical basis, but it does seem to affirm the central role of the king in the fertility of land and people.

The legend of Aqhat also treats the typical elements of the birth of a long-awaited son, the tragedy of death, and the possibility of immortality. Danel's son, Aqhat, was given a composite bow which the goddess Anath coveted. Anath promised Aqhat immortality if he would give her the bow, but Aqhat refused and was killed. The rains then failed for seven years. Aqhat's sister was sent to avenge his death, but the text broke off before the story was completed, leaving unanswered the question whether Aqhat was restored to life and the drought ended. While the connection of the legend with fertility is clear enough, there is no clear consensus on how to interpret the legend.

These myths and legends, together with others like Shachar and Shalim and Nikkal and the Kathirat, may have been used as the spoken parts of annual or periodic rituals. In any case these texts, together with other artifacts, provide a more complete picture of Canaanite religious practice that proved such a temptation to the Israelites (cp. the book of Judges) and against which the prophets protested.

Importance for Old Testament Study The Ugaritic texts and material remains offer OT scholars primary resources for much of their study.

1. Lexicography The Ugaritic texts have provided a welcome resource for clarifying the meanings and nuances of unknown and obscure words and phrases in the OT. Although we must use due caution because of the chronological, geographical, and cultural factors that separate the Ugaritic texts from the OT texts, no scholar today would neglect the linguistic data provided by Ugarit. New readings of biblical texts in the light of Ugaritic grammar, syntax, and lexicon open up innumerable possibilities for new or revised interpretations and translations. Translators now do not hasten so quickly to emend the Hebrew text on the basis of early translations. They look first to Ugaritic evidence.

2. Poetic studies Poetic parallelism, the chief characteristic of Hebrew poetry, is characteristic of Ugaritic poetry as well. Indeed, the study of Ugaritic poetic texts makes one more sensitive to the sophisticated techniques of the psalmists and other poets. Clear Ugaritic cases of chiastic construction, composite divine names separated within a verse, nouns and verbs serving a double-duty function, characteristic word-pairs, and the analysis of meter by the counting of syllables are helpful in the analysis of Hebrew poetry, especially the Psalms.

3. Religion While about 250 deity names occur in the texts from Ugarit, a much smaller number actually comprised the pantheon. Many of these names are known in the OT: El, Baal, Asherah, Anath, Yarih (moon), Shahar, Shalim, Mot, Dagon, for example. The existence of the divine assembly (Ps. 82; Job 1–2) is attested at Ugarit, especially in the Baal-Anath cycle. The practice of imitative magic in order to manipulate deity and the natural order is mentioned often (cp. 1 Kings 18:28; Jer. 41:5). So too was religious prostitution (cp. Deut. 23:18; Hos. 4:14). All in all, the texts from Ugarit give a rather full picture of the type of fertility religion, characteristic of an agricultural people, which many Israelites adopted in most periods of Israelite history. A comparative study of Hebrew and Ugaritic texts allows one to see the common cultural and religious possessions as well as the distinctive characteristics of each.

Thomas Smothers

U
V

ULAI (Ū´ lā ī) Canal connecting the Kerkha and Abdizful Rivers just north of Susa (Dan. 8:2,16).

ULAM (Ū´ lăm) Personal name meaning "first" or "leader." **1.** Descendant of Manasseh (1 Chron. 7:16-17). **2.** Leader of a family of Benjaminite archers (1 Chron. 8:39-40).

ULLA (Ŭl´ là) Personal name meaning "burden" or "yoke." Descendant of Asher (1 Chron. 7:39). Scholars suggest a variety of emendations.

UMMAH (Ŭm´ mah) Place-name meaning "kin." Town in Asher (Josh. 19:30). The name is perhaps a copyist's change from Acco as may be indicated by Greek manuscript evidence.

UNCIRCUMCISED See *Circumcision.*

UNCTION KJV term meaning "anointing" (1 John 2:20,27). See *Anoint.*

UNDEFILED Ritually clean, frequently used for moral cleanness. See *Clean, Cleanness.*

UNICORN KJV word for several related Hebrew terms which modern translations render as "wild ox" (Num. 23:22; 24:8; Deut. 33:17).

UNITY State of being undivided; having oneness; a condition of harmony.
Old Testament Central to the faith of Israel is the confession of the unity of God: "Listen, Israel: The LORD our God, the LORD is One" (Deut. 6:4 HCSB). Because God is one, one set of laws was to apply to both Israelites and foreigners (Num. 15:16). Human history is a story of sin's disruption of God's ordained unity. God's ideal for marriage is for husband and wife to experience unity of life, "one flesh" (Gen. 2:24). Sin in the garden bred mistrust and accusation (3:12). Stubbornness of will ("hardness" of heart, Mark 10:5) continues to disrupt God's desired unity in marriage. God's ideal for the larger human family is again unity. The primeval unity of humanity ("same language" Gen. 11:1) was likewise disrupted as a result of sinful pride (11:4-8). The prophetic vision of God's future anticipates the day when God will reunite the divided kingdoms of Israel and Judah, bringing back all the scattered exiles (Ezek. 37:15-23). Indeed, the prophetic hope includes the reunit

ing of all the peoples of the world under the sovereignty of the one Lord (Zech. 14:9).
New Testament Jesus prayed that His disciples would experience unity modeled on the unity that Jesus experienced with the Father (John 17:11,21-23). Such unity verifies Jesus' God-sent mission and the Father's love for the world. Jesus' prayer for unity was realized in the life of the earliest church. The first believers were together in one place; they shared their possessions and were of one heart and soul (Acts 2:1,43; 4:32). As in the OT, sin threatened the God-ordained unity. The selfishness of Ananias and Sapphira (Acts 5:1-11), the prejudice of those who neglected the Greek-speaking widows (6:1), the rigidness of those who demanded that Gentiles become Jews before becoming disciples (15:1)—all threatened the unity of the church. In every circumstance, however, the Holy Spirit led the church in working out creative solutions that challenged the church to go beyond dissension to ministry (Acts 6:2-7; 15:6-35). Paul spoke repeatedly of believers as "one body in Christ," which transcends varieties of giftedness (Rom. 12:5-8; 1 Cor. 12:13,27-30) and human labels (Gal. 3:28; Eph. 2:14-15; 3:6). For Paul the unity of the church reflects the unity of the Godhead: one God (1 Cor. 12:6), one Lord (Rom. 10:12; 1 Cor. 12:5; Eph. 4:5), and one Spirit (1 Cor. 12:4,11; Acts 11:17). Christian unity has various aspects: the shared experience of Christ as Lord and confession of Christ in baptism (Eph. 4:5,13); the shared sense of mission ("thinking the same way," Phil. 2:2 HCSB); the shared concern for one another (1 Cor. 12:25; "same love," Phil. 2:2; 1 Pet. 3:8); and the shared experience of suffering for Jesus' sake (2 Cor. 1:6; Phil. 1:29-30; 1 Thess. 2:14; 1 Pet. 5:9).   *Chris Church*

UNLEAVENED BREAD Bread baked without using leaven, a substance such as yeast that produces fermentation in dough. Unleavened bread was often served to guests (Gen. 19:3; Judg. 6:19; 1 Sam. 28:24). The eating of unleavened bread took on special significance through the Feast of Unleavened Bread celebrated in connection with Passover (Exod. 12:8,15,20; 13:3,6-7). See *Exodus; Festivals; Passover.*

UNNI (Ŭn´ nī) or **UNNO** (Ŭn´ nō) Personal name, perhaps meaning "afflicted" or "answered." **1.** Levitical harpist in David's time

U
V

(1 Chron. 15:18,20). **2.** Levite returning from exile with Zerubbabel (Neh. 12:9). The Hebrew Masoretic text reads *Unno;* the scribal marginal notes (*Qere*) read *Unni.*

UNPARDONABLE SIN All three Synoptic Gospels (Matt. 12:31-32; Mark 3:28-29; Luke 12:10) refer to this concept. The context is identical in Matthew and Mark, following an exorcism by Jesus, including the accusation that Jesus casts out demons by Beelzebub's (Satan's) authority. Luke records the saying together with a warning about confessing and denying Jesus before men (Luke 12:8-9). It would be a mistake to equate the "unpardonable sin" with unbelief and equally wrong to interpret it as rejection of the work of the Holy Spirit. Both were true of Paul prior to his conversion. Luke's context is of controversy with the Pharisees (Luke 11:15), with the accusation that Jesus' authority for exorcism came from Beelzebub.

The warning includes the statement that blasphemy against the Son of Man, while a sin, can be forgiven. This would be a rejection of the gospel, the good news of God's salvation in Jesus. In light of the context, the unpardonable sin can be defined as rejecting the power and authority of the Holy Spirit working in Jesus and crediting that authority to Satan. The Pharisee's false accusation prompts the warning, but Jesus never explicitly says that they have crossed the line and committed the unpardonable sin. Perhaps this indicates that the unpardonable sin occurs when one knowingly credits the power and authority of the Holy Spirit to Satan. If so, some Pharisees may or may not have been guilty of making a charge against Jesus that they knew was false.

People could only knowingly give Satan the credit for the working of the Holy Spirit if their hearts were so hardened that they had already irrevocably rejected God's offer of salvation in Jesus Christ. A genuine believer in Christ could never commit this sin. See *Blasphemy; Devil, Satan, Evil, Demonic; Holy Spirit; Sin.*

David R. Beck

UPHARSIN (Ū phär´ sĭn) See *Mene, Mene, Tekel Upharsin.*

UPHAZ (Ū´ phăz) Unidentified source of fine gold (Jer. 10:9; Dan. 10:5) or else a term for fine gold. A related Hebrew term is translated "best gold" (1 Kings 10:18; Isa. 13:12). "Uphaz" is

The traditional site of the upper room, or Hall of the Coenaculum, in Jerusalem.

possibly a copyist's change for "Ophir" at Jer. 10:9 as indicated by early versions.

UPPER CHAMBER or **UPPER ROOM** Upstairs room chosen by Jesus in which to hold a final meal with His disciples before His arrest (Mark 14:14-15). Jesus commanded two of His followers to prepare the room and the meal. Tradition holds that the disciples gathered in this room following Jesus' ascension (Acts 1:13). More than a century after Christ's ministry on earth the room believed to be the one in which the meal was eaten was made into a shrine and still is commemorated today. See *Chamber.*

UR (Ûr) Place-name meaning "fire oven." An ancient city in lower Mesopotamia that is mentioned as Abraham's birthplace. Ur, Kish, and Uruk were three important population centers in Sumerian and Babylonian civilization. Abraham's family home is alluded to in Gen. 12:1 and Acts 7:2. The site associated with Ur is located in present-day Iraq, in the lower eastern portion of the Fertile Crescent. It is identified with Tell el-Muqayyar some 350 kilometers (220 miles) southeast of Baghdad. The site had an oval shape with harbor facilities on the Euphrates River, until its course shifted 12 miles east from the city's western limit. With the river's shift the city lost both its population and prominence. Other sites have been proposed for the biblical Ur, such as Urartu (Turkey) or Urfa (northwest of Haran). Occupation of Tell el-Muqayyar began about 4000 B.C. and was important in Sumerian, Babylonian, and Neo-Babylonian cultures. The third dynasty of Ur was its most prosperous and highly developed period. Important remains discovered were a ziggurat (a three-stage, stepped pyramid) and royal tombs. This Sumerian site is most prob-

The belltower of the Church of the Dormition adjacent to the traditional upper room in Jerusalem.

The excavations at Ur showing the palace foundations in the foreground with the ziggurat in the distance.

The outer wall of the ziggurat, or temple tower, at Ur in ancient Mesopotamia (modern Iraq).

ably to be identified as Abraham's city of origin. Yet, as with most identifications, such can be questioned. See *Abraham; Babylon; Chaldees; Mesopotamia; Sumeria.*   *David M. Fleming*

URBANE (Ûr´ bān)(KJV) or **URBANUS** (Ûr bā´ nŭs) Personal name meaning "of the city," that is, "elegant, refined." Roman Christian whom Paul greeted as a "co-worker in Christ" (Rom. 16:9 HCSB).

URI (Ū´ rī) Personal name meaning "fiery." **1.** Father of the tabernacle artisan Bezalel (Exod. 31:2; 35:30). **2.** Father of Geber, one of Solomon's officers charged with providing the royal household food for a month (1 Kings 4:19). **3.** Postexilic, Levitical singer with a foreign wife (Ezra 10:24).

URIAH (Ū rī´ ah) Personal name meaning "fire of Yah." **1.** Hittite mercenary or native, perhaps noble Israelite of Hittite ancestry, in David's army (2 Sam. 11), a member of David's elite warriors (23:39). He was the husband of Bathsheba, the woman with whom David committed adultery. The sin led to the eventual murder of Uriah after the king could cover the affair no longer. The Dead Sea Scrolls and Josephus report that Uriah was Joab's weapon-bearer. Uriah displayed more character and morality than did the king. See *Bathsheba; David.* **2.** High priest in Jerusalem temple under King Ahaz who followed the king's instructions in setting up an altar in the temple according to a Syrian pattern (2 Kings 16:10-16). He apparently served as a witness for Isaiah (8:2). **3.** Priest in time of Ezra and Nehemiah (Ezra 8:33; Neh. 3:4,21). **4.** Person who helped Ezra in informing the people of God's word (Neh. 8:4).

URIEL (Ū´ rĭ ĕl) Personal name meaning "God is light" or "flame of God." **1.** Chief of the Levites assisting in David's transport of the ark to Jerusalem (1 Chron. 6:24; 15:5,11). **2.** Grandfather of King Abijah of Judah (2 Chron. 13:2).

URIJAH (Ū rī´ jah) Personal name meaning "flame of Yahweh." Variant spelling of Uriah. **1.** Chief priest who complied with Ahab's order to build an Assyrian-style altar for the Jerusalem temple (2 Kings 16:10-16). Ahab likely hoped the incorporation of foreign elements into Israel's worship would impress the Assyrian king Tiglath-pileser with his loyalty. **2.** Prophet who joined Jeremiah in preaching against Jerusalem. When King Jehoiakim ordered his execution, Urijah fled to Egypt. He was, however, captured, returned to Jerusalem, and executed (Jer. 26:20-23).

URIM AND THUMMIM (Ū´ rĭm and Thŭm´ mĭm) Objects Israel, and especially the high priest, used to determine God's will. Little is known about the Urim and Thummim. They are first mentioned in Exodus as being kept by the high priest in a "breastplate of judgment" (Exod. 28:15-30). Later on, Moses gave the tribe of Levi special responsibility for their care (Deut. 33:8). After Aaron's and Moses' death, Eleazar was to carry and to use the lots to inquire of the Lord (Num. 27:18-23). They apparently were two objects that served as sacred lots. That is, they were used to determine God's will or to receive a divine answer to a question. Saul called for their use, for instance, in determining who had broken Saul's vow in a battle with the Philistines (1 Sam. 14:41-45). This text also hints as to how the objects were used. They were "given," perhaps drawn or shaken, from a bag. One object

gave one answer. The other lot gave another answer. Probably, whichever lot came out first, that was understood to be God's answer. The Urim and Thummim were not, however, automatic or mechanical. God could refuse to answer. Saul sought the spirit of Samuel through a witch because God would not answer Saul through the Urim or dreams or prophets (1 Sam. 28:6-25).

The ultimate fate of the Urim and Thummim is unknown. In Nehemiah's time expectation continued that someday a priest would arise with the Urim and Thummim (Ezra 2:63; Neh. 7:65). This probably refers to the ability to receive an answer from the Lord, however, rather than a return of the lots given to Aaron. See *High Priest; Inquire of God; Lots; Oracles.*

Albert F. Bean

USURY Sum of money charged for a loan. OT laws prohibited a Jew from charging another Jew usury but permitted it when money was loaned to a Gentile (Deut. 23:19-20). Although the word has negative connotations today, it was not so in biblical days when usury simply was the interest charged for a loan. Excessive usury was condemned.

UTHAI (Ū´ thī) Personal name meaning "Yahweh is help" or "He has shown Himself supreme." **1.** Postexilic descendant of Judah (1 Chron. 9:4). **2.** Head of a family of those returning from exile (Ezra 8:14).

UZ (Ŭz) Personal name and place-name, perhaps meaning "replacement." **1.** Unspecified territory, most likely in Hauran south of Damascus (Jer. 25:20) or else between Edom and northern Arabia (Job 1:1; Lam. 4:21). **2.** Descendant of Shem's son Aram (Gen. 10:23; 1 Chron. 1:17) and progenitor of an Aramaean tribe. **3.** Descendant of Abraham's brother Nahor (Gen. 22:21). **4.** Descendant of Esau (Gen. 36:28) and member of the Horite branch of Edomites.

UZAI (Ū´ zī) Personal name meaning "hoped for" or "he has heard." Father of one helping with Nehemiah's repair of the wall (Neh. 3:25).

UZAL (Ū´ zăl) Son of Joktan and ancestor of an Arabian tribe (Gen. 10:27; 1 Chron. 1:21). Scholars have linked the tribe with Izalla in northeastern Syria and Azalla near Medina.

Ezekiel 27:19 includes them among Tyre's trading partners.

UZZA (Ŭz´ zȧ) Personal name meaning "strength." **1.** Descendant of Benjamin (1 Chron. 8:7). **2.** Descendant of Levi (1 Chron. 6:29). **3.** Head of a family of postexilic temple servants or Nethinims (Ezra 2:49). **4.** Owner of the garden in which Manasseh and Amon were buried (2 Kings 21:18,26). **5.** Variant English spelling of "Uzzah."

UZZAH (Ŭz´ zah) Personal name meaning "he is strong." **1.** One of the drivers of the cart carrying the ark of the covenant when David began moving it from the house of Abinadab in Gibeah to Jerusalem (2 Sam. 6:3). When the ark started to slip from the cart, Uzzah put out his hand to steady it, and God struck him dead for touching the holy object (6:6-7). **2.** Ancestor of exiles who returned to Jerusalem from Babylon (Ezra 2:49). **3.** Name of garden in which kings Manasseh and Ammon were buried. This distinguished them from other kings who "slept with their fathers," that is, were buried in the royal tomb. Uzzah may have been a noble who owned the garden burial plot or may have been a variant spelling of the Canaanite god Attar-melek. **4.** Member of tribe of Benjamin (1 Chron. 8:7). **5.** Family of temple servants who returned from exile with Zerubbabel (Ezra 2:49). **6.** A Levite (1 Chron. 6:29).

UZZEN-SHEERAH (Ŭz zən-shē´ ə rah) Place-name meaning "ear of Sheerah." Village which Ephraim's daughter, Sheerah, founded (1 Chron. 7:24). The site is perhaps Beit Sira, three miles south of lower Beth-horon.

UZZI (Ŭz´ zī) Personal name; an abbreviated form of "Yahweh is my strength." **1.** Aaronic priest (1 Chron. 6:5-6,51; Ezra 7:4). **2.** Family of the tribe of Issachar (1 Chron. 7:2-3). **3.** Descendant of Benjamin (1 Chron. 7:7; 9:8). **4.** Overseer of Jerusalem Levites after the exile (Neh. 11:22). **5.** Postexilic priest (Neh. 12:19). **6.** Musician involved in Nehemiah's dedication of Jerusalem's walls (Neh. 12:42).

UZZIA (Ŭz zī´ ȧ) Personal name meaning "Yahweh is strong." One of 16 whom the Chronicler added to the list of David's 30 elite warriors (1 Chron. 11:44).

UZZIAH (Ŭz zī´ ah) Personal name meaning "Yahweh is [my] strength." **1.** Descendant of Levi (1 Chron. 6:24). **2.** Father of one of David's treasurers (1 Chron. 27:25). **3.** Also known as Azariah (2 Kings 15:1,6-8,17,23,27); son and successor of King Amaziah of Judah. "All the people of Judah" declared Uzziah king when he was 16 (2 Kings 14:21; 2 Chron. 26:1). Some conjecture that the Judeans, rather than have King Joash of Israel install a puppet king, put Uzziah forward as king following Amaziah's defeat and subsequent imprisonment by Joash (2 Chron. 25:21-24). According to this reconstruction, Uzziah began his reign about 792 B.C. and continued as joint regent after his father's release upon the death of Joash (2 Chron. 25:25). Uzziah's reign was a time of great material prosperity for Judah. Uzziah mounted a successful campaign against the Philistines, destroying the walls of some of their chief cities, Gath, Jabneh, and Ashdod. To secure the caravan route along the Mediterranean coast (Via Maris), Uzziah built cities, perhaps military outposts, in the vicinity of Ashdod and at other sites on the Philistine plain (2 Chron. 26:6). To secure the eastern caravan route (the King's Highway), Uzziah rebuilt Elat (Eloth), the strategic port on the Gulf of Aqaba (26:2) and campaigned against the Arabs of Gurbaal (possibly Gur east of Beer-sheba), the Meunites (a branch of Edomites), and the Ammonites (2 Chron. 26:7-8). Uzziah refortified the walls of Jerusalem with towers (2 Chron. 26:9; cp. 25:23). His construction of numerous cisterns and military outposts in the wilderness (the Arad Negev) made widespread settlement possible. Archaeological evidence confirms that construction in the Negev flourished during Uzziah's reign. Uzziah was a lover of the soil who promoted agriculture (2 Chron. 26:10). Unlike his predecessors who relied on the troops to supply their own arms, Uzziah armed his troops with the most advanced weapons (2 Chron. 26:11-15). Uzziah is not so much remembered as the leader who brought Judah to a golden age rivaling David's and Solomon's empires but as the "leper king." The brief account of Uzziah's reign in 2 Kings 15:1-7 portrays the king as one who did what "was right in the Lord's eyes" (15:3 HCSB). No explanation for the king's affliction is given in Kings other than "the LORD afflicted the king" (15:5). The Chronicler traced Uzziah's leprosy to his prideful attempt to usurp the priestly prerogative of offering incense in the temple (2 Chron. 26:16-20; cp. Num. 16:1-40; 1 Sam. 13:8-15). Thereafter, his son Jotham reigned in his stead, though Uzziah likely remained the power behind the throne (26:21). As a leper, Uzziah was denied burial in the royal tombs at Jerusalem. Rather, he was buried in a field (26:23). **4.** Postexilic priest with a foreign wife (Ezra 10:21). **5.** Descendant of Judah and father of a postexilic resident of Jerusalem (Neh. 11:4).   *Chris Church*

UZZIEL (Ŭz´ zĭ ĕl) Personal name meaning "God is strength." **1.** Descendant of Levi (Exod. 6:18; Num. 3:19; 1 Chron. 6:2,18) and ancestor of a subdivision of Levites, the Uzzielites (Num. 3:27; 1 Chron. 15:10; 26:23). **2.** One captain in the successful Simeonite attack on the Amalekites of Mount Seir (1 Chron. 4:42). **3.** Descendant of Benjamin (1 Chron. 7:7). **4.** Levitical musician (1 Chron. 25:4). **5.** Levite involved in Hezekiah's reform (2 Chron. 29:14). **6.** Goldsmith assisting in Nehemiah's repair of the Jerusalem walls (Neh. 3:8).

UZZIELITE (Ŭz zē´ ə līt) Member of Levitical clan of Uzziel.

VAIN Self-conceit, usually a translation of a number of words that mean "nothingness" or "unreliability." In relation to God, trying to thwart His will is vain (Ps. 2:1; Acts 4:25). Trying to do things without God's help is vain (Ps. 127:1). We are warned not to take God's name in vain (as though it were nothing) in the Ten Commandments (Exod. 20: 7; Deut. 5:11). Mark warned that believers are not to give God vain lip service but obedience from the heart (Mark 7:6-7; Isa. 1:13; 29:13; James 1:26).

VAIZATHA (Vī´ zȧ thȧ) or **VAJEZATHA** (Vȧ jĕz´ ȧ thȧ) Persian personal name, perhaps meaning "the son of the atmosphere." One of Haman's 10 sons the Jews killed after Esther gained permission to retaliate against Haman's deadly plan (Esther 9:9).

VALLEY Depression between mountains, a broad plain or plateau, a narrow ravine, or a low terrain. "Valleys" of varying shapes and sizes mark Palestine's landscape.

Five Hebrew terms are designated "valley" in the OT. *Biqe‘ah* is a broad plain (Gen. 11:2; Isa. 41:18). *Gaye'* is a deep ravine, gorge, or

The western edge of the Jordan Valley from the top of OT Jericho.

valley (Isa. 40:4; Zech. 14:4). *Nachal* is a wadi, that is, the bed of a stream that is often dry (Num. 34:5; Ezek. 48:28). *Emeq* is a long, broad sweep between parallel ranges of hills (Num. 14:25; Josh. 8:13; Jer. 21:13). *Shephelah* is the low land, plain, or slope sweeping gently down from mountains (Deut. 10:1; Josh. 9:1; Jer. 17:26). One Greek term, *pharanx*, is used in the NT for each of these.

"Valley" is often used symbolically to refer to the difficulties of life. The classic example of this is Ps. 23:4. All people go through these trials, but God is present with His people, protecting them during these times. See *Palestine*.

Bradley S. Butler

VALLEY OF CRAFTSMEN See *Geharashim*.

VALLEY OF ZERED See *Brook of Zered*.

VANIAH (Vă nī´ ah) Personal name possibly meaning "worthy of love." Man who married a foreign wife (Ezra 10:36).

VASHNI (Văsh´ nī) Personal name, perhaps meaning "weak." Samuel's son according to Hebrew text of 1 Chron. 6:28 (KJV), which reads literally, "And sons of Samuel the firstborn Vashni and Abiah." Modern translations and commentators follow 1 Sam. 8:2 and manuscripts of early versions, taking Vashni as a copyist's change from the similar Hebrew word for "the second" and inserting "Joel."

VASHTI (Văsh´ tī) Personal name meaning "the once desired, the beloved." Wife of King Ahasuerus and queen of Persia and Media (Esther 1:9). The king called for her to show off her beauty to a group he was entertaining, but she refused. Vashti was deposed as queen (1:19), and a beauty contest was arranged to select a new queen. Esther was chosen as the new queen (2:16). No records yet have been recovered that name Vashti as the queen of any king of the Medo-Persian Empire, leading some to speculate whether she was a historical person. The only other queen with Ahasuerus (also called Xerxes) was named Amestris. See *Ahasuerus; Esther; Persia; Xerxes*.

VEIL (KJV "vail") Cloth covering. **1.** *Womens' veils* Rebekah veiled herself before meeting Isaac (Gen. 24:65). Her veil was perhaps the sign that she was a marriageable maiden. Tamar used her

veil to conceal her identity from Judah (Gen. 38:14,19). Another Hebrew term renders "veil" at Isa. 3:23. Here veils are but one of the items of finery which the elite women of Jerusalem would lose in the coming siege. The same Hebrew term is rendered "shawl" (NASB), "cloak" (HCSB, NIV, REB), and "mantle" (KJV, NRSV) at Song 5:7. There, removal of the shawl was part of a humiliating assault on the king's beloved. At Isa. 47:2 the removal of one's veil is again a sign of shamelessness. Paul regarded the wearing of veils as necessary for women praying or preaching ("prophesying") in public (1 Cor. 11:4-16). **2.** *Moses' veil* Moses spoke to God with his face unveiled and then delivered God's message to the people with his face still unveiled. Afterwards Moses veiled his face (Exod. 34:33-35). For Paul, Moses' practice illustrated the superiority of the new covenant: Christians see the abiding splendor of the era of the Spirit and God-given righteousness; Israel saw the fading splendor of the era of death reflected in Moses' face (2 Cor. 3:7-11). Moses' veil further illustrated the mental barrier preventing Israel from recognizing Christ in the OT (3:12-15). Through faith in Christ the veil is removed, and believers enjoy free access to God who transforms life (3:15-18). **3.** *Imagery* The "veil which is stretched over the nations" (Isa. 25:7 NASB) is likely an image for death which is also swallowed up (25:8). The veil possibly includes reproach as well. **4.** *Temple veil* This curtain separated the most holy place from the holy place (2 Chron. 3:14). Only the high priest was allowed to pass through the veil and then only on the Day of Atonement (Lev. 16:2). At Jesus' death the temple veil was ripped from top to bottom, illustrating that in Christ God had abolished the barrier separating humanity from the presence of God (Matt. 27:51; Mark 15:38; cp. Luke 23:45). Hebrews 10:20 uses the tabernacle veil, not as the image of a barrier but of access. Access to God is gained through the flesh of the historical Jesus (cp. John 10:7). *Chris Church*

VEILS Referenced in Ezek. 13:18,20. See *Kerchiefs*.

VENGEANCE English word used principally to translate several Hebrew words in the OT, which are constructed on the stem *nqm*, from which the most recurring form, *naqam*, means "to avenge," "to take vengeance," "to be avenged," or "to be punished." The English word "vengeance" also translates the Greek word *ekdikeo* and its cognate forms. This Greek term was used to translate the Hebrew words for "vengeance" in the Septuagint, the earliest Greek rendering of the Hebrew OT. The Law (Pentateuch) was translated around 250 B.C. The other parts of the OT were translated later.

Old Testament Behind the Hebrew usage of *naqam* stood the awareness that Israel's sense of community solidarity and integrity had been damaged by the nation's enemies. The restoration of community integrity seems to have expected some deed(s) of retaliation or punishment by God. The range of meanings in this community motif go beyond "vengeance" as punishment. They include the positive side as well, "vengeance" as "deliverance" for the people of God.

Human revenge against one's enemies is expressed in a variety of situations in the OT (Gen. 4:23-24; Jer. 20:10). Thus, Samson's reaction to his enemies was described as "vengeance" in Judg. 15:7. Such "vengeance" was a just punishment directed at an adulterer (Prov. 6:32-34). It might also be directed against a whole ethnic group like the Philistines (1 Sam. 18:25). Sometimes, this human "vengeance" is sought against Israel by her enemies (Ezek. 25:12,15,17).

In the context of loving one's neighbor, human revenge toward a fellow Hebrew was strictly forbidden (Lev. 19:17-18; Deut. 32:35). On occasion, however, the word *naqam* was used of legitimate punishment administered by humans on humans for wrongs having been done (Exod. 21:20,23-25; Lev. 24:19; Deut. 19:21). As an act of God on behalf of His people, the term is best understood as just retribution (Judg. 11:36) rather than emotion-driven vengeance.

In support of this usage, David was often the recipient of such favor (2 Sam. 4:48; 22:48; Ps. 18:47). Vengeance is used in this same manner in the prayers of Jeremiah (Jer. 11:20; 15:15; 20:12) and of the psalmist (Pss. 58:10; 79:10; 94:1). In several of these passages deliverance is the apparent intent, a positive motivation for vengeance. Ultimately, the intended deliverance has an eschatological dimension. God is preserving Israel for an eternal reason, an eschatological deliverance to be made available to all people. The equating of the "day of vengeance" and the

"year of (His) redemption" in Isa. 34:8 seems to support that conclusion.

New Testament Primary Greek word translated "vengeance" in the NT is *ekdikeo*, a verb (used five times in cognate forms). Its noun form, *ekdikesis*, is used nine times, *ekdikos*, an adjective/pronoun form, meaning "one who is vengeful," twice. The motif of "vengeance" in the NT occurs infrequently and is kept in perspective by a strong emphasis on "compassion" and "forgiveness."

Interestingly, Luke is the only Gospel writer who used both the verb and noun forms. He used them in Jesus' parable of the unjust judge/persistent widow. Vengeance against her enemies was reluctantly granted (Luke 18:1-8). Another Lukan use of this word is found in Luke 21:22, reflexive of Isa. 63:4, where the eschatological dimension is in focus. Luke finally used the term for God's vengeance in Stephen's speech in Acts 7:34.

Paul forbade human "vengeance" much like Deut. 32:35 (cp. Lev. 19:18), asserting that God is the one who avenges wrong (Rom. 12:19; 1 Thess. 4:6-7). He utilized both the noun and verb forms in the Corinthian correspondence to speak of a "punishment" designed to bring about repentance (2 Cor. 7:10-11; 10:5-6). He also wrote of the eschatological wrath (vengeance/judgment) of God (2 Thess. 1:7-8; cp. Isa. 66:15; Ps. 79:6). See *Avenger; Wrath, Wrath of God*.   *Don Stewart*

VENISON Flesh of a wild animal taken by hunting (Gen. 25:28; "game," NASB, NRSV; "wild game," NIV, HCSB). The word is only used in the narrative of Jacob's stealing Esau's birthright. Isaac preferred Esau because of his love of wild game.

VENOM Poisonous secretion from an animal such as a snake, spider, or scorpion that is released into its victim by a bite or sting. Venom is a translation of *ro'sh* (Deut. 32:33; Job 20:16). The same Hebrew term is used for a dangerous, poisonous plant (Deut. 29:18; Hos. 10:4, among others). See *Poison*.

VESPASIAN (Vĕs pā´ zhǎn) Emperor of Rome A.D. 69–79. He was born into a wealthy family and became a military hero as commander of a legion under Emperor Claudius. After becoming commander of three legions, he was ordered to

U
V

quell the Jewish revolt in Palestine in A.D. 66. Three years into the war, he answered the call of the army to become emperor. Vespasian left his command to his son, Titus, and went to Rome. He sought to establish a dynasty, but it lasted only through his two sons, Titus and Domitian. See *Caesar; Rome and the Roman Empire; Titus, Caesar.*

VESSELS AND UTENSILS Implements or containers ordinarily used in, for example, the temple service or household activities. Vessels are utensils designed for holding dry or liquid products. A number of vessels and other utensils are mentioned in the Bible.

Vessel Materials Vessels in biblical times were made of a variety of materials. As early as 3000 B.C. cups and goblets of precious metals were made by silversmiths and goldsmiths throughout the Near East. These were used for religious service (Num. 7:13,19; 1 Chron. 28:17; 2 Chron. 4:8; Ezra 1:9-10; 8:27) or by persons of great wealth or authority (Gen. 44:2). Copper and bronze vessels were also known (Exod. 27:3; Lev. 6:28).

Metalware has been found in abundance in the lands of the Bible. Although palaces and temples often had vessels made of gold or silver, by far the most common material for metalware was an alloy of copper and tin called bronze. Pure copper rarely was used.

Many containers, both large and small, were made of stone. Alabaster was easily carved and polished. It was especially prized for storage of perfumes (Matt. 26:7; Mark 14:3-4; Luke 7:37). According to rabbinical writings, stone containers were not susceptible to ritual uncleanness. Thus, a sizable industry existed in Jerusalem of NT times for making a variety of stone vessels. Excavations there have produced examples of all sizes and types, from large stone jars (John 2:6) turned on a lathe to cups carved by hand. By NT times glass was becoming widely used for juglets and bottles.

Baskets, made from reeds, were inexpensive containers that could be used for transportation and sometimes storage. Water or wine bottles were frequently made from animal skins (Josh. 9:4,13; Judg. 4:19; 1 Sam. 1:24; 10:3; 2 Sam. 16:1; Neh. 5:18; Job 32:19; Ps. 119:83; Matt. 9:17; Mark 2:22; Luke 5:37). Such leather vessels were popular among nomadic peoples for their durability.

Wood was used to produce storage boxes and bowls. Boxes were made by nailing together planks, whereas bowls usually were hollowed from single pieces of wood. More wooden containers have been found in Egypt partly because the climate is more conducive to their preservation than other parts of the Middle East.

By far the most widely used material for vessels was clay, which was cheap and readily available. Indeed, pottery or "earthenware vessels" (Num. 5:17; Jer. 32:14) were among the most common objects made in antiquity. The earliest ceramics, beginning before 5000 B.C., were handmade and somewhat crude. Though making pottery by hand continued, wheel-made pottery was predominant by Israelite times.

The abundance of pottery and widespread familiarity with the process of its manufacture provided object lessons for understanding spiritual truths. Isaiah referred several times to potters and their products. He likened the fury of God's chosen instruments to a potter treading clay (Isa. 41:25). Israel is compared to a potter's vessel that, when broken, will not yield a single useful fragment (Isa. 30:14). For Isaiah the potter's work demonstrated the sovereignty of the Creator (Isa. 45:9). Paul took up the same analogy to make a point about election (Rom. 9:20-21): the potter can make any sort of vessel he chooses. Jeremiah also allegorically related a potter and his work to God, who molded His people Israel (the clay) and is able to rework a spoiled product (Jer. 18:1-6). A completed clay vessel was used by the prophet to announce the fate of Jerusalem, which like the vessel would be irreparably smashed (Jer. 19:1-2,10-11).

The fragments, or sherds, of a broken pottery vessel are extremely hard (cp. Job 41:30) and thus remain forever. They are found in enormous quantities at every Near Eastern archaeological mound or tell and were quite familiar to biblical persons. Job, for example, used a handy potsherd to scrape his sores (2:8). The ubiquitous sherds served as symbols of dryness (Ps. 22:15) and useless remnants (Isa. 30:14). See *Glass; Pottery; Potsherd.*

Types of Vessels The OT sometimes refers to pottery by a generic term translated "earthen(ware) vessel" (Lev. 6:28; 11:33; 14:5,50; Num. 5:17; Jer. 32:14; NIV "clay jar"). Only two types of vessels are specifically designated as pottery, "earthen pitchers" (Lam. 4:2) and "earthen bottle" (Jer. 19:1). Nevertheless, other common vessels mentioned in the Bible were presumably made of clay as well. The terms, especially for the OT, are not entirely clear and are variously rendered even within the same English translation.

One of the most common and basic pottery forms was the bowl. Large mixing and serving bowls or basins (Exod. 24:6 HCSB, NRSV, "basins"; Song 7:2 NIV, "goblet"; Isa. 22:24 NRSV, "cups"), called "kraters" by archaeologists, generally had handles in the Israelite period. A different Hebrew word identifies similar, perhaps smaller, serving bowls (Judg. 5:25; 6:38). Sprinkling bowls (Num. 7:84-85; HCSB, NRSV, "basins") were usually of metal. A generic word for bowl designates the silver vessels used in the dedication of the altar (Num. 7:84; NASB, "dishes"; NRSV, NIV, "plates"). The main "dish" (2 Kings 21:13; Prov. 19:24; 26:15 NRSV; Matt. 26:23) at meals was actually a medium-sized handleless bowl. It was evidently large enough to use for boiling (2 Chron. 35:13; NRSV, NIV, "pans"). Smaller versions were used for other purposes (2 Kings 2:20). Plates did not become common until NT times. Cups in the modern sense also were virtually unknown in OT times. Three Hebrew words so translated (Gen. 40:11; Isa. 51:17,22; Jer. 35:5; Zech. 12:2) refer to small bowls. Joseph's silver "cup" (Gen. 44:2,12,16-17) was probably a goblet or chalice. NT cups (Luke 11:39) remained bowl-like and varied in size.

A special bowl-like trough was used for kneading dough in bread making (Exod. 8:3; 12:34; Deut. 28:5,17). Other special bowls served as firepots for holding coals (Zech. 12:6). Lamps in the OT were essentially bowls for oil whose rims were pinched in to hold a wick. By NT times lamps (Matt. 25:1; Mark 4:21) were molded in two parts forming a covered bowl with central opening to which a handmade spout was added. See *Lamps, Lighting, Lampstand.*

"Pot" in the OT (Exod. 16:3; Num. 11:8; 2 Kings 4:38-41; Job 41:20,31; NIV, "caldron") generally translates several Hebrew words which designate cooking pots. In pre-Israelite times these were similar to deep bowls without handles. Israelite cooking pots of the monarchy period usually had two handles and were more closed. A more globular shape with a short neck and smaller mouth also developed. NT cooking pots were similar but smaller and more delicate

with thin straplike handles. Cooking pots required clay tempered with various grit materials to withstand the expansion of extreme heating and cooling. They were produced in graduated sizes much like their modern counterparts.

Another basic vessel type in antiquity was the storejar, a tall oval or pear-shaped jar usually having two or four handles. The top was closed with an appropriately shaped potsherd or by a clay stopper. Jars were used for storage of flour or meal (1 Kings 17:14) or for transport and storage of liquid rations such as water (Mark 14:13; HCSB, "water jug"; KJV, "pitcher"; John 4:28 KJV, "waterpot"). A smaller jar was used for storing oil (2 Kings 4:2; KJV, "pot"; NIV, "a little"). Storejars were often designed to hold standard measures, a common size in the OT period being two baths, averaging 25 inches high and 16 inches in diameter. Typical storejars had rounded, almost pointed bases and were placed in stands, holes in wood planks, or pressed into soft ground. A special type was shaped like a cylinder with no handles and a ribbed rim.

Jugs or pitchers (1 Kings 14:3; KJV, "cruse"; Jer. 19:1,10; KJV, "bottle"; 35:5; KJV, "pots") were smaller than storejars and generally had a single handle attached to the neck and shoulder. There were wide and narrow-necked varieties, the former being more likely to have a pinched rim forming a slight spout. A variation on the jug was the pilgrim flask, a flattened bottle with twin handles around a thin neck that functioned like a canteen. Saul may have used one of these (1 Sam. 26:11-12; NRSV, "jar"), but the same Hebrew word (1 Kings 17:14) can refer to the smaller juglet. Juglets with round or oblong bodies, a single handle, and small necks and openings are well-known to archaeologists who work in the Holy Land. They were used for dipping liquids out of large jars and keeping oil (1 Sam. 10:1; NRSV, "vial"; NIV, "flask"; 2 Kings 9:3; NRSV, NIV, "flask"). NT versions (variously translated) are mentioned as containers for oil (Matt. 25:4) and, in alabaster, for perfume (Matt. 26:7).

By the time Rome conquered Palestine in 63 B.C., a new type of cylindrical jar with angular to rounded shoulders appeared. It had a ring base and a rim made to receive a lid. This type vessel made an excellent storage jar for solids, especially scrolls. The famous Dead Sea Scrolls were

U V

kept in these finely crafted containers for almost 2,000 years.

Utensils A general word for utensils (KJV, "vessels" or "furniture") is often used in the OT as a collective term for the gold and bronze articles used in the tabernacle service (Exod. 25:39; 27:3,19; 30:27-28; NIV, "accessories," "utensils," or "articles"). These included snuffers, trays, shovels, pots, basins, forks, firepans, hooks, and the like. The same word is used of utensils used in the temple service (1 Chron. 9:28-29; 2 Chron. 24:14-19; Jer. 27:18-21; NIV, "articles" or "furnishings") and for household articles (1 Kings 10:21; 2 Chron. 9:20; NRSV, "vessels").

Common household utensils included items for cooking. In OT times grain was ground by hand (Exod. 11:5; Isa. 47:2) using grindstones usually made of basalt, a hard volcanic stone with many cavities that made natural cutting edges. In the Roman world of the NT, large examples of millstones were common; the heavy upper stones (Matt. 18:6; Mark 9:42; Luke 17:2; Rev. 18:21) required animals or two persons (Matt. 24:41) to operate. Smaller grinding and crushing chores were done with a mortar and pestle (Num. 11:8; Prov. 27:22). See *Cooking and Heating.*

Eating utensils are not usually found in excavations and were probably made of wood. Knives (Gen. 22:6; Judg. 19:29; Prov. 30:14) for various purposes were made of flint (Josh. 5:2-3), copper, bronze, or iron. See *Archaeology; Tools.*

Daniel C. Browning, Jr., and Mike Mitchell

VESTIBULE See *Arch.*

VIA DOLOROSA (Vĭ´ä Dō lŏ rō´ sà) Literally, "way of suffering." Christian pilgrims from the

One of the stations on the Via Dolorosa ("the Way of Suffering," or "the Way of the Cross") in Jerusalem.

time of the Crusaders have retraced the alleged path of Jesus from the Fortress of Antonia to the cross. This journey assumes the trial took place at the Antonian Fortress, which is debatable. Even if the fortress was the location of Jesus' trial before Pilate, the centuries of remains have filled in and changed the streets from Jesus' time. Thus, the 14 "stations" of the cross are traditional rather than authentic. Franciscan monks follow the "way of suffering" in an organized procession on Friday afternoons, stopping at each of the 14 stations. Several of the stations are based on "legend" and have no foundation in the biblical accounts. The final five stations of the Via Dolorosa are located inside the Church of the Holy Sepulcher.

The 14 stations are: (1) Jesus is condemned to death, (2) Jesus receives the cross, (3) Jesus falls for the first time, (4) He meets His mother Mary, (5) Simon is enlisted to carry the cross, (6) Jesus' face is wiped by Veronica, (7) Jesus falls for a second time, (8) Jesus speaks to the women of Jerusalem, (9) He falls for a third time, (10) He is stripped of His clothing, (11) Jesus is nailed to the cross, (12) Jesus dies on the cross, (13) He is taken down from the cross, (14) Jesus is placed in the tomb of Joseph of Arimathea.

Bill Cook

VIAL Vessel that held oil, usually for anointing purposes (1 Sam. 10:1 KJV, NRSV; NASB, NIV, "flask"). The same word is used a number of times in the book of Revelation (5:8; 15:7; 16:1-4,8,10,12,17; 17:1; 21:9; HCSB, NASB, NIV, NRSV, "bowls"). See *Anoint; Oil; Vessels and Utensils.*

VILLAGE OT distinguishes between city and village. The city was usually walled and much larger, while the village was characterized by no wall and usually homes consisting of one room (Lev. 25:29,31). The village had little or no organized government. Archaeology shows Israelite villages built around the circumference with house walls joining to form the only defense system and open community space left in the middle. Many villages had 20 to 30 houses. The cattle were kept in the inner open space where grain was stored. The main job in the villages was farming. Small craft manufacturing was practiced. Usually a common threshing floor was available. Shepherds often gathered around villages. The pastureland was seen as the possession of the village (1 Chron. 6:54-60). See *Agriculture; Cities and Urban Life; House.*

VINE Any plant having a flexible stem supported by creeping along a surface or by climbing a natural or artificial support. While ancient Israel grew different types of plants that produced vines, such as cucumbers and melons (Num. 11:5; Isa. 1:8), the word "vine" almost always refers to the grapevine or vineyard. The climate of Palestine was well suited for growing vineyards. Along with the olive and fig trees, the grapevine is used throughout the OT to symbolize the fertility of the land (Deut. 6:11; Josh. 24:13; 1 Sam. 8:14; 2 Kings 5:26; Jer. 5:17; 40:10; Hos. 2:12).

The origin of viticulture lies in the antiquity of the unknown past. The Bible traces the origin of caring for vineyards to the time of Noah (Gen. 9:20-21). Such knowledge seems to have been an indigenous undertaking known in many regions of the ancient world. References to vineyards appear from the time of Gudea (a ruler in ancient Sumer before 2100 B.C.). A wall painting found in a tomb at Thebes in Egypt, dating from before 1400 B.C., depicts the entire process of wine making from the gathering and treading of the grapes to the storing of the wine in jars.

The planting and care of a vineyard required constant and intensive care. The most detailed description of the work involved is found in Isa. 5:1-6. Hillsides are frequently mentioned as the most desirable locations for the vines, especially since they were less suitable for other forms of agriculture (cp. Ps. 80:8-10; Jer. 31:5; Amos 9:13). However, vineyards were also grown in the plains and valleys; the Hebron area was particularly noted for its grapes (Num. 13:22-24).

Stone walls and/or hedges were usually built around the vineyard to protect the grapes from thirsty animals and from thieves (Song 2:15; Jer. 49:9). Watchtowers were also built to provide further protection. The hewing out of a winepress or vat completed the vineyard installation (Isa. 5:2). During the harvesting season the owner of the vineyard might live in a booth to stay close to his valuable crop (Isa. 1:8).

After the grapes had set on the branches, the vines were pruned (Lev. 25:4; Isa. 18:5; John 15:1-2). This process produced stronger branches and a greater fruit yield. The pruned branches were useless except to be used as fuel (Ezek. 15:2-8). The vines for the most part were allowed to run on the ground, though occasionally they might climb a nearby tree (cp. Ps. 80:8-10; Ezek. 15:2; 19:11). Perhaps it was this latter

Grapes growing on the vine.

U
V

occurrence that made it possible for a man to "sit under" his vine (1 Kings 4:25). Only in the Roman period were artificial trellises introduced.

The harvest of the grapes took place in August or September. How many grapes an average vineyard produced is unknown (cp. Isa. 5:10), but a vineyard was considered so important that a man who had planted one was exempt from military service (Deut. 20:6). Some of the harvested grapes were eaten fresh (Jer. 31:29) and others dried into raisins (1 Sam. 25:18). Most were squeezed for their juice to make wine.

Several laws governed the use of vineyards in OT times. Vineyards could not be stripped totally of their grapes; the owner was to allow gleanings for the poor and the sojourner (Lev. 19:10), as well as the fatherless and the widow (Deut. 24:21). Vineyards were to lie fallow every seventh year (Exod. 23:10-11; Lev. 25:3-5), and other plants could not be sown in them (Deut. 22:9). This latter law apparently was not followed by NT times (cp. Luke 13:6). Vineyards were cultivated by their owner or hired laborers (Matt. 20:1-16), or rented out to others (Song 8:11; Matt. 21:33-43). See *Gleaning*.

The Bible frequently uses vine or vineyard as a symbol. Vine is often used in speaking of Israel. Thus Israel is said to have been brought out of Egypt and planted as a vine on the land but was forsaken (Ps. 80:8-13; cp. Isa. 5:1-7). Israel was planted a "choice vine" but became a "wild vine" (Jer. 2:21; cp. Hos. 10:1). As the dead wood of a vine is good for nothing but fuel, so the inhabitants of Jerusalem would be consumed (Ezek. 15:1-8; 19:10-14).

On the other hand, the abundance of vines and vineyards was seen as an expression of God's favor. The fruit of the vine gladdens the heart of mankind (Ps. 104:15; Eccles. 10:19) and suppresses pain and misery (Prov. 31:6-7). Israel was "like grapes in the wilderness" when God found them (Hos. 9:10), and the remnant surviving the exile is compared to a cluster of grapes (Isa. 65:8). Finally, an abundance of the vine symbolizes the glorious age to come when the treader of the grapes will overtake the one who sows the seed (Amos 9:13-15; cp. Gen. 49:10-12).

In the NT Jesus often used the vineyard as an analogy for the kingdom of God (Matt. 20:1-16). Those who hope to enter the kingdom must be like the son who at first refused to work in his father's vineyard but later repented and went

(Matt. 21:28-32 and parallels). Ultimately, Jesus Himself is described as the "true vine" and His disciples (Christians) as the branches (John 15:1-11). See *Agriculture; Eschatology; Israel; Wine, Winepress.*   *John C. H. Laughlin*

VINEGAR Literally, "that which is soured," related to Hebrew term for "that which is leavened" and referring to a drink that has soured, either wine or beer from barley (Num. 6:3). In biblical times vinegar was most commonly produced by pouring water over the skins and stalks of grapes after the juice had been pressed out and allowing the whole to ferment. However, any fruit could be used for making wine or vinegar. Vinegar in two forms was forbidden to the Nazirite because of its association with strong drink (Num. 6:3). It irritates the teeth (Prov. 10:26) and neutralizes soda (Prov. 25:20). It was an unpleasant drink (Ps. 69:21), though some sopped bread in it (Ruth 2:14); some see this as the common Near Eastern chickpea paste called *chimmuts*. In the NT it is mentioned only in connection with the crucifixion. The first instance, which Jesus refused, was a mixture used to deaden the sense of the victim and nullify the pain. Possibly the vinegar mentioned in the second instance, which Christ accepted, was the customary drink of a peasant or soldier called *posca*, a mixture of vinegar, water, and eggs.

Vinegar was most commonly used as a seasoning for food or as a condiment on bread (Ruth 2:14). Solomon figuratively used vinegar to describe the irritation caused by a lazy man's attitude. See *Wine.*   *C. Dale Hill*

VIOLENCE One of many terms for sin in the OT. The Hebrew word often translated "violence" *(chamas)* occurs 60 times in the OT. All such "violence" is ultimately directed against God (Ezek. 22:26; Zeph. 3:4). But it usually also involves what has been described as "cold-blooded and unscrupulous infringement of the personal rights of others, motivated by greed and hate and often making use of physical violence and brutality." It sometimes includes false accusation (Ps. 27:12) and usually describes those who are strong doing wrong or injury to the weak (Ps. 72:14; Isa. 53:9; Jer. 22:3; Mic. 6:12). So it can often be equated with oppression and does not necessarily involve physical action.

The word is also one of many in the OT used to describe human wickedness in a somewhat

U
V

general sense and is the sin charged against corrupt mankind before the flood (Gen. 6:11,13). There and almost everywhere the Greek translation of the OT rendered *chamas* with terms meaning "unrighteousness," "lawlessness," or "ungodliness." *Chamas* is the charge against the Edomites, who were arch villains of Israel and of God (Joel 3:19; Obad. 10), the people of Nineveh (Jon. 3:8), and even Israel when they were ripe for judgment (Hab. 1:3,9). As such it is found closely related to words such as sin, iniquity, pride, malice, wickedness, and especially oppression (Pss. 12:5; 55:11; 73:8; Isa. 59:6-7; 60:18; Jer. 6:6-7; 20:8; Ezek. 45:9; Amos 3:9-10; Hab. 2:17). "Violent men" are also described (HCSB) as "wicked" (Ps. 140:4; Prov. 3:33), "evil" (Ps. 140:1), "worthless" (Prov. 16:27), and "contrary" (16:28).

The opposite of committing "violence" would be bestowing "blessings," "good," "salvation," "praise," "right," and especially "peace" and "justice" (Prov. 10:6; 13:2; Isa. 59:6,8; 60:18; Amos 3:10; Hab. 1:2-3). The word in Mal. 2:16 should probably be translated "unrighteousness" or "injustice." In Ps. 73:6 the arrogant and wicked are said to be clothed with violence like a garment, which means it is a characteristic of their lives and they practice it shamelessly (cp. also Jer. 2:34).

The term "violence" is less frequent in the NT. Matthew 11:12 ("From the days of John the Baptist until now, the kingdom of heaven has been suffering violence, and the violent have been seizing it by force," HCSB) is difficult to translate. It seems to speak of the world's opposition to Jesus and the kingdom of God (also Luke 16:16). Those who are citizens of the kingdom, on the other hand, are commanded to avoid unnecessary conflict (1 Tim. 3:3; 2 Tim. 2:24; Titus 3:2; James 4:1).

E. Ray Clendenen

VIOLET See *Blue; Colors.*

VIPER Poisonous snake. Several species of snakes are called vipers, and the various words used in the Bible for them probably do not designate specific types. Some scholars take the OT references to refer to the *Echis colorata.* Jesus spoke of the wicked religious leaders as vipers (Matt. 3:7) because of their venomous attacks on Him and their evil character in leading the people astray. Paul was bitten by a viper (Acts 28:3) but suffered no ill effect from it.

VIRGIN, VIRGIN BIRTH The event that initiated the incarnation of Christ whereby He was supernaturally conceived in the womb of a virgin without the participation of a human father. **Old Testament** Among the few OT prophecies that allude to Christ's birth (e.g., Mic. 5:2), the only one that the NT interprets as a reference to a virginal conception is in Isaiah (Isa. 7:14; Matt. 1:23). During the reign of Ahaz over the Southern Kingdom of Judah, Isaiah foretold that a virgin would conceive and give birth to a son whose name would be Immanuel (Isa. 7:14). There are questions concerning the way this prophecy was initially fulfilled in Ahaz's day, as well as debate about the meaning of the Hebrew word translated as "virgin." The word used in Isa. 7:14 is one of two words in the OT that refer to young women. The more generic *betulah* (approximately 60 times) was used to refer to virgins (Gen. 24:16; Deut. 22:16-17), maidens who may not have been virgins (Esther 2:17-19), and symbolically to Israel (Jer. 14:17). The less common *almah* (approximately 9 times),

A viper partially hidden in the surrounding grass and wildflowers.

U
V

which is used in Isa. 7:14, likewise referred to virgins (Gen. 24:43), but some translators argue that it was also used to refer to maidens who were not necessarily virgins (Prov. 30:19). The semantic versatility of *almah* does not, however, conclusively eliminate the possibility that a virginal conception was being conveyed in Isa. 7:14, though of course the reference to Isaiah's wife would preclude that she was a virgin. *Almah* certainly could be translated "virgin," and in Matthew's use of the text, "virgin" would be the appropriate translation.

New Testament The NT texts that deal with the virgin birth are Matt. 1:18-25 and Luke 1:26-35. Matthew recounts that after discovering Mary was pregnant, Joseph contemplated whether he should dissolve their betrothal. While struggling with this decision, an angel informed Joseph that Mary was still a virgin and the child she had conceived was the Messiah. Matthew then gives a parenthetical summary of this event by stating that Isa. 7:14 had herein found its fulfillment (Matt. 1:23). This interpretation of Isaiah has raised serious questions, one being that Matthew quotes from the Septuagint rather than the original Hebrew text, thereby translating the original *almah* with the Greek word *parthenos*. In the Septuagint *parthenos* is occasionally used to describe females who were not virgins (Gen. 34:4), but in the NT it is only used with reference to virgins or spiritual purity (approximately 15 times). Consequently, Matthew's choice of words displays his belief that Isaiah's prophecy included a promise that a virgin would supernaturally conceive. In addition, Isa. 7:14 must be read in light of the entire context of 7:1–9:7. This requires the interpretation that Isaiah's words do not find their primary fulfillment in the birth of his own son, but in the birth of the Messianic "Son," who will be called, "Wonderful Counselor, Mighty God, Eternal Father, Prince of Peace" (Isa. 9:6 HCSB).

In Luke's Gospel the story is told with Mary as the emphasis. He begins by mentioning that Mary was a virgin (*parthenos*, Luke 1:27) and to clarify the meaning of the term, the following dialogue is explicitly clear. After the angel Gabriel's announcement that Mary would conceive, she asks how this can occur "since I have not been intimate with a man?" (HCSB); or as some translations render it, "since I am a virgin?" (NASB, NIV). Mary was obviously uncertain about the possibility of conceiving because she had never experienced sexual union. Gabriel then answers that the Holy Spirit would bring about the conception supernaturally (1:36). It is, therefore, unquestionable in Luke's account that Mary was indeed a virgin prior to her conceiving.

Other references that implicitly support the virginal conception are found in instances where the maternal relationship is emphasized almost to the exclusion of the paternal. For example, in the genealogies of Christ, it is stated that Jesus was born of Mary, not Mary and Joseph (Matt. 1:16), and that Jesus was only the "supposed" son of Joseph (Luke 3:23; KJV, NIV, NASV). Throughout His life Jesus was also socially identified with His mother and siblings instead of His "father" (Mark 6:3). There was even a tone of scandal during His ministry because of accusations that He was born illegitimately (John 8:41).

Theological Relevance The virginal conception affects two major areas of theology. First, it relates to the truthfulness of Scripture. The NT clearly states that Jesus was born of a virgin, and to deny this is to question the veracity and authenticity of the text. Second, the virgin conception is linked to the deity of Christ, for through this event He simultaneously retained His divine nature and received a sinless human nature. Furthermore, Scripture reveals it as a critical aspect of the incarnation.   *Everett Berry*

VISION Experience in the life of a person whereby a special revelation from God was received. The revelation from God had two purposes. First, a vision was given for immediate direction, as with Abram in Gen. 12:1-3; Lot, Gen. 19:15; Balaam, Num. 22:22-40; and Peter, Acts 12:7. Second, a vision was given to develop the kingdom of God by revealing the moral and spiritual deficiencies of the people of God in light of God's requirements for maintaining a proper relationship with Him. The vision of prophets such as Isaiah, Amos, Hosea, Micah, Ezekiel, Daniel, and John are representative of this aspect of revelation.

Several Greek and Hebrew terms are translated by the English word "vision." In some references the literal sense of perception with the physical organs of sight is the intended meaning of the word (Job 27:11-12; Prov. 22:29). In 2 Sam. 7:17; Isa. 22:1,5; Joel 3:1; and Zech. 13:4, the Hebrew word refers to the prophetic function of receiving and delivering the word of God by the prophet.

"Vision" in varying forms occurs approximately 30 times in the book of Daniel. The term denotes the mysterious revelation of that which the prophet described as knowledge of the future. In Ezekiel the words are used literally and metaphorically.

Among the classical prophets (Amos, Hosea, Isaiah, Micah, Obadiah, etc.) the vision was the primary means of communication between God and the prophet. By this avenue the prophets interpreted the meaning of immediate events in the history of Israel. "Vision" and "Word of Yahweh" became synonymous in these prophetic writings (Obad. 1:1). See *Prophecy, Prophets; Revelation of God.*   *James Newell*

VOCATION See *Call, Calling.*

VOLUNTEERS Persons who ask God to use them to accomplish His work. The spirit of volunteerism, prompted by devotion to God, arose at crucial times in biblical history, enabling daunting tasks to be accomplished. Moses received voluntary contributions of precious goods from the Israelites sufficient to construct the tabernacle (Exod. 25:1-9). Israelites voluntarily contributed their wealth so Solomon could build the temple (1 Chron. 29:6-9). Under Josiah Israel's leaders again made a voluntarily contribution so that the people of Israel and the priests could have lambs for Passover (2 Chron. 35:7-9). When Sheshbazzar led the returnees from exile in Babylon back to Jerusalem, they carried great wealth voluntarily given by "all those about them" (Ezra 1:5-6 NASB), including the Persian king (Ezra 7:14-15).

In financial giving the lead in volunteerism was normally taken by persons who had the means by which to give. However, even the widow without means willingly gave (Luke 21:1-4), thus providing an example of selfless giving adopted by the early church (2 Cor. 8:1-4; 9:7).

Others contributed their time and skills. Deborah led volunteer military commanders (Judg. 5:9) and fighters (Judg. 5:2) who delivered to Israel Jabin, king of Canaan (Judg. 4:23-25). Those who volunteered to move to Jerusalem during the days of Nehemiah were blessed for doing so (Neh. 11:1-2). Amasiah served as a volunteer in the temple during the reign of Jehoshaphat (2 Chron. 17:16).

Paul H. Wright

VOPHSI (Vŏph´ sī) Personal name of uncertain meaning. Father of Nahbi of the tribe of Naphtali (Num. 13:14). Nahbi was one of the spies Moses sent into Canaan.

VOWS Voluntary expressions of devotion usually fulfilled after some condition had been met. Vows in the OT usually were conditional. A common formula for vows was the "if ... then" phrase (Gen. 28:20; Num. 21:2; Judg. 11:30). The one making the religious vow proposed that if God did something (such as give protection or victory), then he or she in return would make some act of devotion. Not all vows, however, were conditional. Some, such as the Nazirite vow (Num. 6), were made out of devotion to God with no request placed upon God. Whether conditional or not, the emphasis in the Bible is on keeping the vow. A vow unfulfilled is worse than a vow never made. While vows do not appear often in the NT, Paul made one that involved shaving his head (Acts 18:18).

Scott Langston

VOYEURISM Seeking sexual stimulation by visual means. In the culture of the Bible, having one's nakedness exposed and viewed publicly was normally done to indicate shame for previous sin not for sexual titillation (e.g., Gen. 9:20-23; Isa. 3:17; 20:2-4; 47:2-3; Jer. 13:22,26; Lam. 1:8; Hos. 1:10; Rev. 3:17-18). Before the fall, because there was neither shame nor voyeurism, nakedness and sexuality were undefiled (Gen. 2:25).

Voyeurism was the prelude to further sexual sin by David (2 Sam. 11:2) and evidently played a part in the desirous affections of Pharaoh toward Sarah (Gen. 12:14-15) and Potiphar's wife toward Joseph (Gen. 39:6-7). The beauty contest sponsored by Ahasuerus had voyeuristic overtones (Esther 2:2-4).

Job recognized that voyeurism, an act of the heart, breaks God's laws (Job 31:1-4). This was confirmed by Jesus, who equated voyeurism with adultery (Matt. 5:28). Paul's injunctions to avoid youthful lusts (2 Tim. 2:22; cp. 1 Thess. 5:22) in favor of pure thoughts (Phil. 4:8) speak against voyeurism.   *Paul H. Wright*

U
V

A mosaic in the chapel of Jerome's Room, the traditional site where Jerome translated the Latin Vulgate, located under the Church of the Nativity in Bethlehem.

VULGATE Latin translation of the Bible by Jerome about A.D. 400. See *Bible Texts and Versions.*

VULTURE Both carrion vulture and vulture are listed in the unclean bird lists (Lev. 11:13-19; Deut. 14:12-18 RSV). The English word "vulture" is used to translate several different Hebrew terms. The Bible does not permit a positive identification of the types of vultures known during the biblical period. In contrast to eagles and hawks, which usually kill living prey, vultures feed on dead animals.

The Hebrew term *nesher*, sometimes translated "eagle," is translated "vulture" in Hosea's threat to Israel (8:1). Lack of a proper burial was viewed as a great horror in biblical times. The common belief was that as long as a body remained unburied, the person could not be gathered to the fathers and experience rest in Sheol. Goliath and David threatened one another with this fate (1 Sam. 17:44,46). The curses in Deuteronomy warned the disobedient of this horrible consequence (Deut. 28:26). Ultimately the author of Revelation used the image of the birds of prey to picture the defeat of evil before the reign of Christ (Rev. 19:17-21; cp. Ezek. 29:5; 32:4; 39:4, 17-20).   *Janice K. Meier*

W

Young woman carrying a can of water on her head from a village well near Jerusalem.

The wadi through the limestone cliffs at Qumran near the Dead Sea.

WADI (Wä´ dī) Transliteration of Arabic word for a rocky watercourse that is dry except during rainy seasons. These creek beds can become raging torrents when especially heavy rains fall. Wadis are numerous in the Middle East.

WADI OF THE WILLOWS See *Arabim.*

WAGES Terms of employment or compensation for services rendered encompass the meaning of the Hebrew and Greek words. Their usage in the text applies to commercial activities and labor service, as well as judgmental recompense for one's actions in life.

In a mixed economy of agriculture and pastoralism without coined money, wages often included little more than meals and a place of employment (cp. Job 7:2; John 10:12). Still, a skilled shepherd, like Jacob, might receive a portion of the flock and thus begin his own herd (Gen. 30:32-33; 31:8; and legal texts from both Assyria and Babylonia). No fixed wage was set for farm laborers. They may have received a portion of the harvest (John 4:36), or, as in Matt. 20:1-8, an agreed upon daily wage. By law these landless workers were to be paid at the end of each day for their efforts (Lev. 19:13; Deut. 24:14-15). Texts mention enough instances of fraud, however, to suggest that this group was often cheated out of their wages (Jer. 22:13; Mal. 3:5; James 5:4).

Kings hired mercenary troops to fight their wars (Judg. 9:4; 2 Sam. 10:6) and employed skilled laborers, along with slaves and unpaid draftees, to build and decorate their palaces and temples (1 Kings 5:6-17; Isa. 46:6; 2 Chron. 24:11-12). The services of priests (Judg. 18:4; Mal. 1:10) and the advice of elders (Ezra 4:5; 1 Tim. 5:17-18) were obtained for gold or silver

at fees to match their abilities. The authority of prophets could also be purchased. Balaam, for example, was paid "fees for divination" in exchange for his cursing of Israel (Num. 22:7), and Shemaiah was hired by Sanballat to trap Nehemiah with a false prophecy (Neh. 6:10-13).

Theological usage of these terms promises God's reward for the faithful (Gen. 15:1) and proper recompense for His people Israel (Isa. 40:10; 62:11). His justice also ensured that the reward of the unrighteous was equal to their crimes (Ps. 109:20; Rom. 6:23; 2 Pet. 2:15). See *Commerce; Economic Life; Slave, Servant.*

Victor H. Matthews

WAGON Vehicle of transportation with two or four wooden wheels. The two-wheeler was usually called a cart. Wagons were used to transport people and goods (Gen. 45:17-21). Sometimes wagons were used as instruments of war (Ezek. 23:24). Wagons were usually pulled by oxen. The use of the wagon was quite different from that of the chariot. See *Transportation and Travel.*

WAIL See *Grief and Mourning; Repentance.*

WALK Slower pace contrasted with running. It is used literally (Exod. 2:5; Matt. 4:18) and figuratively to mean a person's conduct or way of life (Gen. 5:24; Rom. 8:4; 1 John 1:6-7).

WALK TO AND FRO KJV translation (Zech. 1:10-11) of a military term meaning "patrol" (NASB, NRSV) or "go and inspect" (TEV).

WALLS Outside vertical structures of houses and the fortifications surrounding cities. In ancient times the walls of cities and houses were constructed of bricks made of clay mixed with reed and hardened in the sun. Archaeologists estimate that the walls of Nineveh were wide enough to drive three chariots abreast and the walls of Babylon were wide enough to drive six chariots abreast on the top.

In scriptural language a wall is a symbol of salvation (Isa. 26:1; 60:18), of the protection of God (Zech. 2:5), of those who afford protection (1 Sam. 25:16; Isa. 2:15), and of wealth of the rich in their own conceit (Prov. 18:11). A "fortified wall of bronze" (NRSV) is symbolic of prophets and their testimony against the wicked (Jer. 15:20). The "wall of partition" (Eph. 2:14 KJV; HCSB, dividing wall of hostility) represented temple worship and Jewish practice separating Jew from Gentile. *See Architecture; Fort, Fortification.*

WANDERINGS IN THE WILDERNESS

Israel's movements from Egypt to the promised land under Moses, including the placenames along the routes. A reconstruction of the Israelites' wilderness wanderings is more complex than a casual reading of the biblical account at first would seem to indicate. The "wanderings" refer to that difficult period in Israel's history between their departure from the area of Egyptian enslavement in the land of Goshen and arrival in the Jordan Valley to claim their long-standing inheritance of the promised land (Exod. 12:31–Num. 33:49). The sequence of that extended event is complicated by the nature of the biblical data.

The itinerary from the border of Egypt to the oasis of Kadesh-barnea is relatively clear. Only three established trade routes across the northern Sinai were viable options for the movement of such a large contingent of people and livestock. Decisions in Egypt during the early stages of their migration reduced those options to only one. The shortest, most northerly route along the Mediterranean shoreline was not taken because of a possible encounter with Egyptian military guarding oasis forts or returning from regular incursions and punitive raids in Canaan (Exod. 13:17). A second relatively direct route to Kadesh-barnea appears to have been avoided by divine plan when they approached the border at Etham and then were instructed to turn back to the seemingly impossible situation "by the Sea" where God miraculously delivered them from the pharaoh's forces (Exod. 13:20–14:2). This route is identified with Marah (15:23), Elim (15:27), the Wilderness of Sin (16:1), Rephidim (17:1), the Wilderness of Sinai (18:5; 19:1), Sinai (19:2), the Wilderness of Paran (Num. 10:12), Taberah (11:3) or Kibroth-hattaavah ("the cemetery of the lusters," 11:34), Hazeroth ("corrals," 11:35; 12:16) where the mention of enclosures for the livestock and a series of events in the biblical account suggest an extended stay, and, ultimately, Kadesh (Num. 20:1). A later reference to the distance between Mount Sinai (Horeb) and Kadesh-barnea (Deut. 1:2) seems to suggest that the early itinerary took them basically along the major trade route used by the Amalekites between modern Suez at the northern end of the Gulf of Suez and the northern end

of the Gulf of Aqaba (Elath and Ezion-geber) and then northward into the extensive clustering of oases at Kadesh that would become their tribal center and the location of the tabernacle during the next 38 years.

The negative response to an immediate conquest following the spies' report resulted in the additional 38 years in the Sinai wilderness. When that generation of military died, the camp of Israel again was mobilized for the assault on Canaan. Their request to pass through Edomite territory and to proceed along the King's Highway through Moab and into the Jordan Valley opposite Jericho was blocked by a show of military force by the king of Edom. Their attempt to enter Canaan from the south was stopped by the king of Arad, and so a very difficult detour southward to the head of the Gulf of Aqaba and northeastward around Edomite and Moabite lands (Num. 20:14; Deut. 2) brought them finally to Mount Nebo overlooking the Jordan Valley north of the Dead Sea.

This itinerary is complicated by a comprehensive list of place-names in Num. 33 related to the exodus and wanderings that includes many more locations seemingly playing a part in this extended event. Obviously many of these places naturally may be related to the 38 years of the wanderings. More important is the fact that Num. 33 indicates that in fact the Israelite itinerary from Egypt to the Jordan Valley did include passage through Edomite and Moabite territory along the King's Highway. This route cannot be associated with the Moses/Joshua-led exodus because of the specific statements in Num. 20–21. Many scholars therefore conclude that Num. 33 is a combined compilation of place-names that are related to pre-Mosaic infiltration from Egypt to Canaan by way of the King's Highway, the place along the second route around Edomite-Moabite territory followed by the Moses/Joshua-led contingent and all those places visited by the Israelites during those 38 punitive years of desert wanderings when like the nomads of every generation they sought water and pasturage for their flocks within that hostile arid environment of the Sinai. *See Exodus; Kadesh-barnea; Moses; Sinai.*

George L. Kelm

WAR CRIMES Illegal actions by nations, armies, and individuals in time of battle and fighting. Clearly some of the practices of warfare—ancient and modern—exceed all

W

sensibilities (e.g., 2 Sam. 8:2; Ps. 137:9). It may be helpful to label such acts with modern terminology such as "war crimes" or "ethnic cleansing." Amos declared that waging war in order to deport whole populations as slaves or massacring Israelite women and children in warfare deserved the judgment of God (Amos 1:6,9). Similarly, Moses recognized that Amalek's ambush of the Israelites from behind when they were tired and helpless should not go unpunished (Deut. 25:17-19). More problematic is God's response that Israel similarly wipe out Amalek, including its helpless women and children (1 Sam. 15:1-3; cp. Ps. 137:9) or His command to annihilate the Canaanites (Deut. 7:2). In some ways God's election of Israel as a nation (Gen. 12:1-3; Exod. 19:5-6) superseded the right of other nations to harm Israel. The Mosaic law included rules of warfare intended to allow the enemies of Israel room to surrender (Deut. 20:1-20) and to safeguard the rights of captive women (Deut. 21:10-14). *Paul H. Wright*

WASHING See *Ablutions; Bathing.*

WASP See *Insects.*

WATCH Division of time in which soldiers or others were on duty to guard something. They are listed as "evening," "midnight," "crowing of the rooster," and "morning" (Mark 13:35 HCSB). Nehemiah set watches that may mean armed persons or just citizens on guard (4:9; 7:3). The OT seems to have had three watches rather than four. There was the "beginning of the night watches" (Lam. 2:19), the "middle watch" (Judg. 7:19), and the "morning watch" (Exod. 14:24). See *Time, Meaning of.*

WATCHMAN One who stands guard. Ancient cities had watchmen stationed on the walls. Their responsibility was to sound a warning if an enemy approached (2 Kings 9:17; Ezek. 33:2-3). Israel's prophets saw themselves as watchmen warning the nation of God's approaching judgment if the people did not repent. Vineyards and fields also had watchmen, especially during harvest. Their responsibility was to guard the produce from animals and thieves.

WATCHTOWER Tower on a high place or built high enough to afford a person tthe ability to see for some distance. The person doing the watch-

An ancient watchtower remains relatively unchanged in an open field in Israel.

ing might be a soldier or a servant (2 Kings 9:17; Isa. 5:2; Mark 12:1). See *Tower.*

WATER The Bible speaks of water in three different ways: as a material resource, as a symbol, and as a metaphor.

A Material Necessity that God Provides Water as a material resource is necessary for life. God made water a part of His good creation, and He exercises sovereignty over it (Gen. 1–2; Isa. 40:12). He controls the natural processes of precipitation and evaporation, as well as the courses of bodies of water (Job 5:10; 36:27; 37:10; Pss. 33:7; 107:33; Prov. 8:29). God normally assures the provision of water for human needs (Deut. 11:14). However, water is sometimes used in punishment for sin, as with the flood of Noah's day (Gen. 6:17) or the drought proclaimed by Elijah (1 Kings 17:1). The divine control of water teaches people obedience to and dependency upon God.

Many of the great acts of God in history have involved water, such as the parting of the sea (Exod. 14:21), the provision of water for the Israelites in the wilderness (Exod. 15:25; 17:6),

An Arab man drinks from the spout of a multi-spouted waterpot as he would have done in biblical times.

and the crossing of the Jordan River (Josh. 3:14-17). Water was also involved in several of Jesus' miracles (Matt. 14:25; Luke 8:24-25; John 2:1-11).

Water was a crucial element in God's gift of the promised land to Israel (Deut. 8:7). Palestine contains several natural sources of water: rain, springs, wells, and a few short, perennial streams. The average annual rainfall in Palestine is about 25 inches, all of which normally falls between November and April. The dry months of May to October made necessary the use of cisterns and pools for water storage. Several famous biblical cities had pools, such as Gibeon (2 Sam. 2:13), Hebron (2 Sam. 4:12), Samaria (1 Kings 22:38), and Jerusalem (2 Kings 20:20).

A Theological Symbol and Metaphor The OT contains laws for the use of water in rituals as a symbol of purification. Priests, sacrificial meat, and ritual utensils were washed before involvement in rituals (Lev. 1:9; 6:28; 8:6). Unclean people and things were also washed as a symbol of ritual cleansing (Lev. 11:32-38; 14:1-9; 15:1-30; Num. 31:23). The book of Genesis uses water as a symbol of instability before the completion of creation (1:2), and Ezekiel spoke of water as a symbol of renewal in the age to come (47:1-12).

The Bible contains dozens of metaphorical usages of water. For example, in the OT, water is a metaphor or simile for fear (Josh. 7:5), death (2 Sam. 14:14), sin (Job 15:16), God's presence (Ps. 72:6), marital fidelity (Prov. 5:15-16), the knowledge of God (Isa. 11:9), salvation (Isa. 12:3), the Spirit (Isa. 44:3-4), God's blessings (Isa. 58:11), God's voice (Ezek. 43:2), God's wrath (Hos. 5:10), and justice (Amos 5:24). Among the metaphorical uses of water in the NT are references to birth (John 3:5), the Spirit (John 4:10), spiritual training (1 Cor. 3:6), and life (Rev. 7:17). See *Creation; Famine and Drought; Flood; Rain.*   *Bob R. Ellis*

WATERPOT Vessel made for carrying water, usually made of clay although some were made of stone (John 2:6). Large pots stored water (1 Kings 18:33; John 2:6); a woman could carry smaller pots on her shoulder (John 4:28). Small pitchers were used for pouring water (Luke 22:10; Jer. 19). Water was also carried in animal skins. See *Pottery; Skin; Vessels and Utensils.*

WAVE OFFERING See *Sacrifice and Offering.*

WAW (Väv) Sixth letter in the Hebrew alphabet. Heading of Ps. 119:41-48 (KJV, Vau) in which each verse begins with the letter.

WEALTH AND MATERIALISM Physical possessions having significant value, such as land, livestock, money, and precious metals, and the practice of valuing such possessions more highly than they ought to be valued, especially when this results in the misalignment of ones' priorities and undermines one's devotion to God.

Wealth To understand the biblical view of wealth, one must understand the biblical account of creation. On that account God created the universe—and everything therein— "out of nothing" (Gen. 1:1-27). This means that while He created the entire universe, God used no preexisting materials in doing so. So, unlike painters who use things that already exist (brushes, canvases, paints) in creating their works, God created the universe without using anything which already existed. Here the psalmist instructs: "For the LORD is a great God, a great King above all gods. The depths of the earth are in His hand, and the mountain peaks are His. The sea is His; He made it. His hands formed the dry land" (Ps. 95:3-5 HCSB). Thus, in virtue of being the absolute Creator, God's claim on the universe and everything therein is absolute—everything ultimately belongs to Him and to Him alone (cp. Ps. 50:10-12).

Of course, in His wisdom, God gave humanity dominion over the earth (Gen. 1:26-28), thus entrusting His wealth to humans. In so entrusting them, God appointed them stewards over creation. However, from this fact several consequences follow. First, since everything belongs ultimately to God, whatever one possesses—and thus owns—comes as a trust from Him; for this reason, one's right of ownership is never absolute—one's property always belongs first and foremost to God Himself. Second, since it comes as a trust from God, ownership of property carries with it significant responsibilities. For instance, God holds those to whom He has entrusted wealth responsible for giving to His work (cp. Num. 18:20-32; Deut. 14:28-29; Mal. 3:8-10; 2 Cor. 9:6-14; 1 Tim. 5:18-18) and for caring for the poor among them (cp. Prov. 29:7; Amos 5:11-12; Matt. 19:21; 1 Tim. 5:3-5). It is important to note that while God calls His children to underwrite the ministries of the church through sacrificial giving, the responsibility to handle wisely what God has given extends

W

further. So one dare not think that once a certain percentage of one's income has been given to the church that it does not matter what one does with the rest.

God has blessed some with abundant wealth. Abram, Isaac, Solomon, and Job were each blessed with great riches (cp. Gen. 13:2; 26:12-14; 1 Kings 3:13; Job 42:12). This does not mean, however, that poverty is a sign of God's disfavor. According to Scripture, God takes special interest in the poor (Ps. 72:12-15). Moreover, Job was righteous when God allowed him to become impoverished (Job 1:1,13-19). Job's righteousness is evident even as he reacts to his misfortune: "He said, 'Naked I came from my mothers womb, and naked I shall return there. The LORD gave and the LORD has taken away. Blessed be the name of the LORD'" (Job 1:21 NASB). Therefore it would be a mistake to conclude that Job's impoverishment indicates God's displeasure with him. Still, from those whom He has blessed abundantly, God expects much. Jesus' own words underscore this: "Much will be required of everyone who has been given much" (Luke 12:48 HCSB).

Materialism Scripture warns against valuing one's wealth too highly. Riches can prevent one from bearing spiritual fruit (cp. Luke 8:14). Perhaps awareness of this lies behind Agur's plea that he not be given riches lest he deny God (Prov. 30:8-9). That riches can hinder spiritual growth receives eloquent expression from Jesus: "Again I tell you, it is easier for a camel to go through the eye of a needle than for a rich person to enter the kingdom of God" (Matt. 19:24 HCSB). Elsewhere Jesus warns against splitting one's allegiance: "No one can be a slave of two masters, since either he will hate one and love the other, or he will be devoted to one and despise the other. You cannot be slaves of God and of money" (Matt. 6:24 HCSB). Moreover, as Paul tells Timothy, the love of money has led to many evils—even leading some to wander from the faith (1 Tim. 6:10). So, then, one ought to be content with one's possessions and seek righteousness rather than wealth (Matt. 6:33; Luke 12:15-21; Heb. 13:5).

A generous spirit accompanies righteousness. Zacchaeus responds to Jesus not only by restoring fourfold what he had gained dishonestly, but also by giving freely to the poor (Luke 19:8), and the members of the church in Jerusalem shared their possessions with one another (Acts 2:44-45; 4:32-35). Such generosity characterizes

those who have been freed from the love of money and have sought to store up for themselves treasure in heaven rather than on earth (Matt 6:19-21). See *Creation; Sacrifice and Offering; Stewardship; Tithe.* Douglas Blount

WEAPONS Since mankind's beginnings, the desire to impose one's will upon another person or being has led to active conflict using many types of weapons. Human history shows marked means by which the implements were advanced technologically through the past six millennia.

The implements of warfare and defense are known from three sources: excavations; pictorial representations in murals, reliefs, and models; and written documents. Tombs of Egypt contained actual weapons and models. Assyrian reliefs depicted great battles in detail. Excavations have uncovered numerous examples of stone and metal weapons; and biblical and inscriptional sources provide names of objects, strategy and tactics, and methods of construction.

Military action has been defined in terms of ability to achieve supremacy over the enemy in

Reconstruction of a Roman siege tower with battering ram (first century A.D.).

Reconstruction of a Roman battering ram (first century A.D.).

three fields: mobility, firepower, and security. Mobility is exemplified by the chariot and cavalry; firepower by bow, sling, spear, ax and sword; and security by shield, armor, and helmet. See *Arms and Armor; Chariots; Horse.*

R. Dennis Cole

WEASEL Unclean animal (Lev. 11:29); a small mammal related to the mink. Some translations see this animal as the "mole" (NASB) or "mole-rat" (REB). It may be a member of the mole family (*Spalax ehrenbergi*) found in many countries, including Palestine. The weasel was common in the Holy Land, although mentioned only once in the Bible.

WEATHER Climatic conditions in Palestine, including geographical factors and seasonal changes. The weather patterns of Palestine result from the clash between the extreme heat of the Arabian Desert and the cooler Mediterranean winds from the west. The climate is subtropical with humid, cold winters and hot, dry summers. From October to April the days range from cool and sunny to overcast, cold, and rainy. The rains fill the seasonal brooks and streams, which provide the majority of water for the coming year. The elevation of the land, dropping from 3,900 feet in upper Galilee to 1,296 feet below sea level at the Dead Sea, provides natural barriers that influence the weather. Rain generally diminishes as one travels farther south and inland. Thus, the coastal plain and Galilee receive more rain than the central hill country

and Negev desert. Snow covers the higher elevations of Mount Hermon throughout most of the winter and occasionally falls on Jerusalem and the surrounding hills. The Jordan Valley, particularly in the area of the Dead Sea, remains mild in the winter, making it the traditional site of the winter palaces of kings and rulers. The Mediterranean Sea becomes windy and cold, making travel dangerous.

In April and May the climate changes dramatically. Hot desert winds blow across the land from the east in the early morning hours. The land and seasonal rivers begin to dry, and the vegetation turns brown. Near noon each day, the air turns to the west, bringing with it slightly cooler air from the sea. The difference is minimal, however, and the heat remains intense. The central hill country is cooler than the foothills and coastal areas, but the Judean wilderness and Negev become fiercely hot. Temperatures along the Dead Sea and Arabah remain above 90 degrees Fahrenheit for weeks on end. Once across the Jordan Valley atop the Transjordan plateau to the east, the temperature moderates once more. Rain is uncommon in the summer months, usually falling in October, November, February, and March.

The Bible hints at the influence that the weather imposed on life in Palestine. The winds and rain were considered to be under God's personal direction. Thus, Christ's control of the elements demonstrated to the disciples His heavenly calling. The hot east wind was often viewed as the wrath of God, bringing infertility and death. Rain signified the continued blessings of God; its absence, His judgment. See *Fertility Cults; Palestine; Rain; Wind.*

David Maltsberger

WEAVER, WEAVING See *Cloth, Clothing; Loom.*

A Middle Eastern weaver operating his loom.

W

WEB 1. A fabric usually woven on a loom (Judg. 16:13-14). See *Loom.* **2.** The weaving of a spider that looks like thread. The spider's web is used figuratively to represent that which is impermanent and untrustworthy (Job 8:14). See *Spider.*

WEDDINGS In biblical times the father selected the bride for his sons. Abraham sent his servant to Haran to find a wife for his son Isaac (Gen. 24). In arranging a marriage, the bridegroom's family paid a price (Hb. *mohar*) for the bride (cp. Gen. 34:12; Exod. 22:16; 1 Sam. 28:25). When the marriage had been arranged, the couple entered the betrothal period, usually lasting a year and much more binding than the engagement of today. During that year the man prepared the home for his bride. The betrothal was established in one of two ways: a pledge in the presence of witnesses together with a sum of money or a written statement and a ceremony with a concluding benediction. Before Israel's exile the betrothal was ratified by a verbal promise (Ezek. 16:8); after the exile the bride and groom's parents signed a covenant binding the couple together. In NT times the parents of the bride and groom met, along with others as witnesses, while the groom gave the bride a gold ring or other valuable item. To the bride he spoke this promise: "See by this ring you are set apart for me, according to the law of Moses and of Israel."

The serious nature of the betrothal is evident. If a man had sexual relations with a woman betrothed to another man, they were both subject to the death penalty (Deut. 22:23-24). Had she not been betrothed, the man would have paid 50 shekels to the woman's father as a dowry, and she would have become his wife (Deut. 22:28-29).

The wedding was largely a social event during which a blessing was pronounced on the bride: "May you, our sister, become thousands of ten thousands, and may your descendants possess the gate of those who hate them" (Gen. 24:60). The blessing reflected the concept of God's blessing, namely, a large family and victory over one's enemies. The marriage itself was secured by the formalizing of a marriage contract.

The parable of the 10 virgins is rich with explanation of the Jewish wedding (Matt. 25:1-13). The wedding ceremony began with the bridegroom bringing home the bride from her parents' house to his parental home. The bride-groom, accompanied by his friends and amid singing and music, led a procession through the streets of the town to the bride's home (cp. Jer. 16:9). Along the way friends who were ready and waiting with their lamps lit would join in the procession (Matt. 25:7-10). Veiled and dressed in beautifully embroidered clothes and adorned with jewels, the bride, accompanied by her attendants, joined the bridegroom for the procession to his father's house (Ps. 45:13-15). Isaiah 61:10 describes the bridegroom decked out with a garland and the bride adorned with jewels. The bride's beauty would be forever remembered (Jer. 2:32). The bride and groom were considered king and queen for the week. Sometimes the groom even wore a gold crown.

Once at the home, the bridal couple sat under a canopy amid the festivities of games and dancing which lasted an entire week—sometimes longer (Song 2:4). Guests praised the newly married couple; songs of love for the couple graced the festival. Sumptuous meals and wine filled the home or banquet hall (John 2:1-11). Ample provision for an elaborate feast was essential—failure could bring a lawsuit (John 2:3). The bridal couple wore their wedding clothes throughout the week; guests also wore their finery, which was sometimes supplied by wealthy families (Matt. 22:12).

On the first night, when the marriage was to be consummated, the father escorted his daughter to the bridal chamber (Gen. 29:21-23; cp. Judg. 15:1). The bride's parents retained the bloodstained bed sheet to prove their daughter's virginity at marriage in case the husband attempted any recourse by charging that his bride was not a virgin (Deut. 22:13-21; cp. v. 15).

In some cases the bride did not remove the veil from her face until the following morning. When Jacob thought he was marrying Rachel, in the morning he discovered his wife was Leah (Gen. 29:25). At other times the veil was removed during the feast and laid on the groom's shoulder and the pronouncement made, "the government shall be on his shoulders" (cp. Isa. 9:6). See *Family; Marriage.*   *Paul P. Enns*

WEEK For the Jews, any seven consecutive days ending with the Sabbath (Gen. 2:1-3). The Sabbath began at sunset Friday and lasted until sunset Saturday. The Christians moved their day of worship to Sunday, the first day of the week. In this way they called attention to the resurrection of their Lord Jesus Christ (Luke 24:1-7). The week is of ancient Semitic origin. It was shared with the ancient world through the Bible and the religious practice of both Jews and Christians. See *Calendar; Time, Meaning of.*

WEEPING See *Grief and Mourning.*

WEIGHTS AND MEASURES Systems of measurement. In the ancient Near East weights and measures varied. The prophets spoke against merchants who used deceitful weights (Mic. 6:11).

Weights Considering first the OT evidence, Hebrew weights were never an exact system. An abundance of archaeological evidence demonstrates that not even inscribed weights of the same inscription weighed the same. Weights were used in a balance to weigh out silver and gold, since there was no coinage until the Persian period after 500 B.C. This medium of exchange replaced bartering early in the biblical period.

The *shekel* is the basic unit of weight in the Hebrew as well as the Babylonian and Canaanite systems, though the exact weight varied from region to region and sometimes also according to the kind of goods for sale. The Mesopotamian system was sexagesimal, based on sixes and sixties. So, for example, the Babylonian system used a *talent* of 60 *minas*, a *mina* of 60 *shekels*, and a *shekel* of 24 *gerahs*.

The Hebrew system was decimal like the Egyptian, though the weights were not the same. Variations in the weights of the shekel may be attributed to several factors other than the dishonesty condemned in the Law (Deut. 25:13-16) and the Prophets (Amos 8:5; Mic. 6:11). There could have been variation between official and unofficial weights, including the setting of new standards by reform administrations such as that of good King Josiah. There might have been a depreciation of standards with passage of time, or a use of different standards to weigh different goods (a heavy standard was used at Ugarit to weigh purple linen), or the influence of foreign systems. There seems to have been three kinds of shekel current in Israel: (1) a temple shekel of about 10 grams (.351 ounces) which depreciated to about 9.8 grams (.345 ounces); (2) the common shekel of about 11.7 grams (.408 ounces), which depreciated to about 11.4 grams (.401 ounces); and (3) the

heavy ("royal"?) shekel of about 13 grams (.457 ounces).

The smallest portion of the shekel was the *gerah*, which was 1/20 of a shekel (Exod. 30:13; Ezek. 45:12). The *gerah* has been estimated to weigh .571 grams. There were larger portions of the shekel, the most familiar of which was the *beqaʿ* or half shekel (Exod. 38:26), known also from Egypt. Inscribed examples recovered by archaeologists average over six grams and may have been half of the heavy shekel mentioned above. The *pim*, if it is 2/3 of a shekel as most scholars suppose, is also related to the heavy shekel and weighs about eight grams. It may have been a Philistine weight, since it is mentioned as the price the Philistines charged Israelite farmers to sharpen their agricultural tools when the Philistines enjoyed an iron monopoly over Israel (1 Sam. 13:19-21).

Multiples of the shekel were the *mina* and the *talent.* According to the account of the sanctuary tax (Exod. 38:25-26), 3,000 shekels were in a talent, probably 60 minas of 50 shekels each. This talent may have been the same as the Assyrian weight, since both 2 Kings 18:14 and Sennacherib's inscriptions mention the tribute of King Hezekiah as 30 talents of silver and of gold. This was 28.38 to 30.27 kilograms (about 70 pounds). The mina was probably 50 shekels (as the Canaanite system), though Ezekiel 45:12 calls for a mina of 60 shekels, and the early Greek translation reads "50." The mina has been estimated at 550 to 600 grams (1.213 to 1.323 lbs.). One table of OT weights, based on a shekel of 11.424 grams, is as follows:

1 talent (3,000 shekels)	34.272	kilograms	75.6 lbs.
1 mina (50 shekels)	571.2	grams	1.26 lbs.
1 shekel	11.424	grams	.403 oz.
1 pim (2/3 shekel?)	7.616	grams	.258 oz.
1 beqaʿ (1/2 shekel)	5.712	grams	.201 oz.
1 gerah (1/20 shekel)	.571	grams	.02 oz.

We should remember, however, that this is misleading, for OT weights were never so precise as this. The Lord's ideal was "just" weights and measures (Lev. 19:36; Prov. 16:11; Ezek. 45:10), but dishonest manipulations were all too common (Prov. 11:1; 20:23; Hos. 12:7). Archaeologists have discovered weights that have been altered by chiseling the bottom. Interesting things weighed in the OT were Goliath's armor (1 Sam. 17:5-7) and Absalom's annual haircut (2 Sam. 14:26). In the NT the talent and mina were large sums of money (Matt. 25:15-28; cp. Luke 19:13-25), and the "pound of

Table of Weights and Measures

WEIGHTS

BIBLICAL UNIT	LANGUAGE	BIBLICAL MEASURE	U.S. EQUIVALENT	METRIC EQUIVALENT	VARIOUS TRANSLATIONS
Gerah	Hebrew	1/20 shekel	1/50 ounce	.6 gram	gerah; oboli
Beqa'	Hebrew	1/2 shekel or 10 gerahs	1/5 ounce	5.7 grams	bekah; half a shekel; quarter ounce; fifty cents
Pim	Hebrew	2/3 shekel	1/3 ounce	7.6 grams	2/3 of a shekel; quarter
Shekel	Hebrew	2 bekahs	2/5 ounce	11.5 grams	shekel; piece; dollar; fifty dollars
Litra (pound)	Greco-Roman	30 shekels	12 ounces	.4 kilogram	pound; pounds
Mina	Hebrew/Greek	50 shekels	1¼ pounds	.6 kilogram	mina; pound
Talent	Hebrew/Greek	"3,000 shekels or 60 minas"	75 pounds/ 88 pounds	34 kilograms/ 40 kilograms	talent/talents; 100 pounds

LENGTH

BIBLICAL UNIT	LANGUAGE	BIBLICAL MEASURE	U.S. EQUIVALENT	METRIC EQUIVALENT	VARIOUS TRANSLATIONS
Handbreadth	Hebrew	1/6 cubit or 1/3 span	3 inches	8 centimeters	handbreadth; three inches; four inches
Span	Hebrew	1/2 cubit or 3 handbreadths	9 inches	23 centimeters	span
Cubit/Pechys	Hebrew/Greek	2 spans	18 inches	.5 meter	cubit/cubits; yard; half a yard; foot
Fathom	Greco-Roman	4 cubits	2 yards	2 meters	fathom; six feet
Kalamos	Greco-Roman	6 cubits	3 yards	3 meters	rod; reed; measuring rod
Stadion	Greco-Roman	1/8 milion or 400 cubits	1/8 mile	185 meters	miles; furlongs; race
Milion	Greco-Roman	8 stadia	"1,620 yards"	1.5 kilometer	mile

DRY MEASURE

BIBLICAL UNIT	LANGUAGE	BIBLICAL MEASURE	U.S. EQUIVALENT	METRIC EQUIVALENT	VARIOUS TRANSLATIONS
Xestes	Greco-Roman	½ cab	1 1/6 pints	.5 liter	pots; pitchers; kettles; copper pots; copper bowls; vessels of bronze
Cab	Hebrew	1/18 ephah	1 quart	1 liter	cab; kab
Choinix	Greco-Roman	1/18 ephah	1 quart	1 liter	measure; quart
Omer	Hebrew	1/10 ephah	2 quarts	2 liters	omer; tenth of a deal; tenth of an ephah; six pints
Seah/Saton	Hebrew/Greek	1/3 ephah	7 quarts	7.3 liters	measures; pecks; large amounts
Modios	Greco-Roman	4 omers	1 peck or ¼ bushel	9 liters	bushel; bowl; peck-measure;corn-measure; meal-tub
Ephah [Bath]	Hebrew	10 omers	⅗ bushel	22 liters	bushel; peck; deal; part; meas ure; six pints; seven pints
Letek	Hebrew	5 ephahs	3 bushels	110 liters	half homer; half sack
Kor [Homer]/ Koros	Hebrew/Greek	10 ephahs	6 bushels or 200 quarts/14.9	220 liters/525 liters	cor; homer; sack; measures; bushels/sacks; measures; bushels or 500 quartsous

LIQUID MEASURE

BIBLICAL UNIT	LANGUAGE	BIBLICAL MEASURE	U.S. EQUIVALENT	METRIC EQUIVALENT	VARIOUS TRANSLATIONS
Log	Hebrew	1/72 bath	⅓ quart	.3 liter	log; pint; cotulus
Xestes	Greco-Roman	⅛ hin	1⅙ pints	.5 liter	pots; pitchers; kettles; copper pots; copper bowls; vessels of bronze
Hin	Hebrew	⅙ bath	1 gallon or 4 quarts	4 liters	hin; pints
Bath/Batos	Hebrew/Greek	1 ephah	6 gallons	22 liters	gallon(s); barrels; liquid meas ure/gallons; barrels; measures
Metretes	Greco-Roman	10 hins	10 gallons	39 liters	firkins; gallons

fragrant oil" (John 12:3 HCSB) is probably the Roman standard of 12 ounces.

Measures Measures of capacity, like the weights, were used from earliest times in the market place. These were also only approximate and varied from time to time and place to place. Sometimes different names were used to designate the same unit. Some names were used to describe both liquid and dry measures as the modern liter. The basic unit of dry measure was the *ephah* that means basket. The *homer*, "ass's load," was a dry measure, the same size as the *kor*, both a dry and a liquid measure. Each contained 10 ephahs or baths, an equivalent liquid measure (Ezek. 45:10-14). The ephah is estimated at 1.52 to 2.42 pecks, about ⅜ to ⅔ of a bushel.

The *bath* is estimated from two fragments of vessels so labeled from Tell Beit Mirsim and Lachish to have contained 21 to 23 liters or about 5 ½ gallons, which would correspond roughly to an ephah of ⅜ to ⅔ of a bushel. *Letek*, which may mean half a homer (or cor), would be five ephahs. *Seah* was a dry measure that may be a third of a ephah. *Hin*, an Egyptian liquid measure, which means "jar," was approximately a sixth of a bath. The *omer*, used only in the manna story (Exod. 16:13-36), was a daily ration and is calculated as a tenth of an ephah (also called issaron, "tenth"). A little less than half an omer is the *kab* (only 2 Kings 6:25 NRSV), which was four times the smallest unit, log (only Lev. 14:10-20 NRSV), which is variously estimated according to its Greek or Latin translation, as a half pint or ⅔ pint.

Although OT measures of capacity varied as much as the difference between the American and English gallon, the following table at least represents the assumptions of the above discussion:

Dry Measures

kab	1.16 quarts
omer, issaron ¹⁄₁₀ ephah	
2.09 quarts	
seah, ⅓ ephah	⅔ peck
ephah	½ bushel
letek, ½ homer	2.68 bushels
homer, kor	5.16 bushels

Liquid Measures

log	0.67 pint
hin	1 gallon
bath	5 ½ gallons
cor, homer	55 gallons

In the NT measures of capacity are Greek or Roman measures. The sextarius or "pot" (Mark 7:4) was about a pint. The measure of John 2:6 (*metretas*) is perhaps 10 gallons. The bushel (*modios*) of Matt. 5:15 and parallels is a vessel large enough to cover a light, perhaps about a fourth of an American bushel. As remarked before, the amount of ointment Mary used to anoint Jesus (John 12:3) was a Roman pound of 12 ounces (a measure of both weight and capacity), and Nicodemus brought a hundred such pounds of mixed spices to anoint Jesus' body (John 19:39).

In measures of length, all over the ancient Near East, the standard was the *cubit*, the length of the forearm from the elbow to the tip of the middle finger. Israel knew two different lengths for the cubit just as did Egypt. The common cubit, mentioned in connection with the description of the bed of Og, king of Bashan (Deut. 3:11), was about 17 ½ inches. This may be deduced from the 1,200 cubit length mentioned in the Siloam inscription for King Hezekiah's tunnel that has been measured to yield a cubit of this length. Ezekiel (40:5) mentions a long cubit consisting of a common cubit plus a handbreadth which would yield a "royal" cubit of about 20 ½ inches, similar to the Egyptian short and long cubits.

Even figuring with the common cubit, Goliath's height was truly gigantic at six cubits and a span (1 Sam. 17:4), about nine and a half feet tall. If Solomon's temple is figured with the common cubit, it was about 90 feet long, 30 feet wide, and 45 feet high (1 Kings 6:2). The span is half a cubit (Ezek. 43:13,17), or the distance between the extended thumb and little finger. If it is half the long cubit, the span would be about 10 ½ inches; if half the common cubit, it was about 8 ¾ inches.

The *handbreadth* or palm is a sixth of a cubit, consisting of the breadth of the hand at the base of the four fingers. This measure is a little less than three inches. The smallest Israelite measure of length was the finger, a fourth of a handbreadth (Jer. 52:21) and was about three-fourths inch. Larger than a cubit was the *reed*, probably consisting of six common cubits. Archaeologists have noticed several monumental buildings whose size can be calculated in round numbers of such cubits or reeds. Summarizing on the basis of the common cubit, linear measurements of the OT were:

Common Cubit

1 reed	6 cubits	8 ft. 9 in.
1 cubit	6 handbreadths	17.5 in.
1 handbreadth	4 fingers	2.9 in.
1 finger		.73 in.

Ezekiel's Cubit

| 1 reed | 6 cubits | 10 ft. 2.4 in. |
| 1 cubit | 7 handbreadths | 20.4 in. |

There were indefinite measures of great length, such as a day's journey or three day's journey or seven day's journey, the calculation of which would depend on the mode of transportation and the kind of terrain. Shorter indefinite distances were the bowshot (Gen. 21:16) and the furrow's length (1 Sam. 14:14 NRSV; HCSB, about a half-acre).

In the NT measures of length were Greek or Roman units. The cubit was probably the same as the common cubit, since the Romans reckoned it as one and one-half times the Roman foot. The *fathom* (Acts 27:28) was about six feet of water in depth. The *stadion* or furlong was a Roman measure of 400 cubits or one eighth Roman mile. The Roman mile (Matt. 5:41) was 1,620 yards. Josephus calculated this as six stadia or 1,237.8 yards.

Measures of area were indefinite in the OT. An "acre" was roughly what a yoke of oxen could plow in one day. Land could be measured by the amount of grain required to sow it. In NT times a Roman measure of land was the Latin *jugerum*, related to what a yoke of oxen could plow, figured at 28,000 square feet or ⅝ of an acre. Another was the furrow, 120 Roman feet in length.

In conclusion, weights and measures in biblical times are seldom precise enough to enable one to calculate exact metric equivalents, but the Lord set forth an ideal for "just" balances, weights, and measures. Different standards in surrounding Near Eastern countries affected biblical standards. Sometimes there were two standards operating at the same time, such as short and long, light and heavy, common and royal. There is enough evidence to figure approximate metrological values for the biblical weights and measures.   *M. Pierce Matheney*

WELFARE PROGRAMS Governmental attempts to assist people in economic need. God expects people to work for a living (Prov. 10:4; 19:5; 20:4; Eph. 4:28; 1 Thess. 4:11; 2 Thess. 3:6-13). Yet the Bible also recognizes that in every society there will be poor people in need

of assistance (Deut. 15:11; John 12:8). For this reason God commands His people to be willing, free, and generous in helping others (Deut. 15:10-14; Acts 11:29; 1 Cor. 16:2-3; 2 Cor. 8:1-4; 9:5-7).

The Mosaic law provided for those who could not adequately care for themselves: sojourners, widows, fatherless, and Levites; the latter did not receive a landed tribal inheritance. Each was to receive assistance paid by other Israelites in the form of a tithe (Deut. 14:28-29). These poor were to be allowed to glean in the fields, orchards, and vineyards of those who were able to earn a productive living (Exod. 23:10-11; Lev. 19:9-10; 25:1-7; Deut. 24:19-22; Ruth 2:2-3; 15-17). Every seventh year was a year of release in which all debts were forgiven, thus allowing the poor a fresh start (Deut. 15:1-18). To neglect the poor in ancient Israel was to close oneself to God's blessing (Job 31:16-22; Prov. 25:21-22; 28:27). Yet the prophetic denunciation regarding the lack of social justice in ancient Israel suggests that these welfare programs were not practiced (e.g., Isa. 58:6-7; Ezek. 18:5-9).

Jesus taught the necessary union of true spirituality and personal social responsibility (Matt. 5:42; 19:21; 25:31-46; Mark 9:41; Luke 10:32-37), a connection stressed by James (2:14-17) and the other apostles (Gal. 2:9-10; Eph. 4:28; 1 Tim. 6:18; 1 John 3:17-18). The early church provided for the physical needs of its members (Acts 2:43-47; 4:32 35; 6:1-4; 10:1-2; 11:27-30; Rom. 15:25-27; 2 Cor. 8:1-4; Phil. 4:15-18). See *Poor, Orphan, Widow.*   *Paul H. Wright*

WELL Source of water created by digging in the earth to find available water. In the semiarid climate of ancient Israel, the availability of water was a constant concern; the Bible contains many references to the sources used for obtaining it. Several Hebrew words are used in different contexts to denote these sources, making it sometimes difficult to know which English word to use in translation.

The Hebrew word most commonly translated "well" is *be'er* (Gen. 21:30-31; Num. 21:16-18). *Be'er* also occurs in several place-names indicating the location of important wells: Beer (Num. 21:16); Beer-elim (Isa. 15:8); Beeroth (Deut. 10:6); Beer-lahai-roi (Gen. 16:14); Beer-sheba (Gen. 21:31).

The digging of a well could be a time for celebration (Num. 21:17-18), but wells were also fought over as different people tried to control the precious resource (Gen. 21:25-26; 26:15-22; Exod. 2:16-17). Wells were located wherever a water source could be found. This included fields (Gen. 29:2), towns (2 Sam. 23:15), and the wilderness (Gen. 16:7,14).

"Well" is also used figuratively of a "forbidden woman" (Prov. 23:27 HCSB) and of a wicked city (Jer. 6:7). Elsewhere it is used as a metaphor for sexual pleasure (Prov. 5:15; Song 4:15). See *Cistern; Fountain; Pit; Spring; Water.*

John C. H. Laughlin

WEST See *Directions.*

WHALE Large aquatic mammal that resembles a large fish (Ezek. 32:2; Jon. 1:17; Matt. 12:40).

The Greek word translated "whale" in Matt. 12:40 (KJV) is also called "a great fish" (Jon. 1:17), "great creature" (Gen. 1:21; Ps. 148:7 NIV), "monster" (Job 7;12; Ezek. 32:2 NIV). The exact identification of the animal is impossible with present knowledge.

KJV translation (Gen. 1:21; Job 7:12; Ezek. 32:2; and in Matt. 12:40 with reference to Jonah) for Hebrew *tannin.* The Hebrew term can refer to a primeval sea monster or dragon (Isa. 27:1; 51:9), to a serpent (Exod. 7:9; Ps. 91:13), or possibly a crocodile (Ezek. 29:3; 32:2). Matthew used the Greek *ketos,* indicating a great sea monster rather than indicating a particular species.

WHEAT Staple grain of the ancient Near East (Num. 18:12). Wheat has been raised in this region since at least Neolithic times (8300–4500 B.C.). Many species exist, and exact types cannot be determined from the biblical words. It became the major crop after the nomads began

A chaduf for raising well water near ancient Lystra in south central Asia Minor (modern Turkey).

settling into agrarian societies. It is used as an analogy to speak of God's judgment (Matt. 3:12) and His care (Ps. 81:16). Wheat was used to make bread and was also parched (Lev. 23:14). KJV often translated "wheat" by the word "corn" (Mark 4:28). Wheat harvest was an ancient time reference (Exod. 34:22) and was celebrated by the Feast of Weeks. Wheat is said to have been harvested (1 Sam. 6:13), threshed (Judg. 6:11), and winnowed (Matt. 3:12). See *Agriculture; Bread; Harvest; Plants.*

WHEEL Disk or circular object capable of turning on a central axis. Archaeologists and historians believe that the wheel was probably invented in Mesopotamia before 3000 B.C.

The Bible describes both a functional use and symbolic meaning for the wheel. The wheel was indispensable for transportation. It was used on wagons, carts, and chariots, and the word "wheel" could be a synonym for any of these vehicles (Ezek. 23:24; 26:10; Nah. 3:2). In Solomon's temple there were 10 stands upon which rested 10 lavers. Each of the stands was adorned with four wheels (1 Kings 7:30-33).

Ezekiel's vision of the great wheel in the sky (1:4-28; 10) was a symbol of God's presence. There were four cherubim around the throne. Beside each there was a wheel which "sparkled like chrysolite" (1:16 NIV). Ezekiel described the rims of the wheel as "high and awesome" and "full of eyes" (v. 18). The exact meaning of these mysterious images is unknown. Perhaps they represented the wheels of God's invisible chariot moving across the sky ("chariots of the sun," 2 Kings 23:11) or the wheels of God's throne (Dan. 7:9).

Other symbolic uses of the wheel are a whirlwind (Ps. 77:18 HCSB, NIV, NRSV, NASB) and God's judgment, as a wheel is driven over the wicked (Prov. 20:26). Jeremiah described God's redemption as the reshaping of marred clay on a potter's wheel (18:13). See *Chariots.*

Brad Creed

WHELP Lion's cub, used figuratively in the OT (Gen. 49:9; Jer. 51:38; Nah. 2:11). See *Lion.*

WHIRLWIND English translation of four Hebrew words that designate any windstorm that is destructive. Only Ps. 77:18 uses a term indicating circular motion. True whirlwinds and tornadoes are rare in Palestine. They usually occur near the coast where the cool breezes of

A burned Roman wagon wheel.

the Mediterranean Sea collide with the hot wind from the desert. Lesser whirlwinds are seen as whirling dust is thrown up into the air. The Lord used the raging wind to take Elijah to heaven (2 Kings 2:1,11) and to talk with Job (38:1; 40:6). The prophets used the "storm wind" as a figure for judgment (Isa. 5:28; Jer. 4:13; Hos. 8:7; Amos 1:14; Zech. 7:14). God comes to deliver His people riding the stormy winds (Zech. 9:14).

WHITE See *Colors*.

WIDOW Special consideration for widows is first mentioned in Exod. 22:22 (fatherless are also mentioned in v. 22, and foreigners are mentioned in v. 21; see Ps. 94:6). Since God has compassion on widows (Pss. 68:5; 146:9; Prov. 15:25), we should do the same (Isa. 1:17; 1 Tim. 5:3; James 1:27). When a nation and its leaders do so, they are promised a blessing (Deut. 14:29; Jer. 7:5-7); the person or nation that does not is cursed (Deut. 27:19; Job 22:9-11; Jer. 22:3-5; Ezek. 22:7,15-16; Mal. 3:5; Mark 12:40). Joab appealed to David's compassion for childless widows when he sent the woman of Tekoa to tell a story in order to get David to restore Absalom (2 Sam. 14:1-21).

Widows and orphans lacked the economic, legal, and physical protection a man provided in that society.

To be both a widow and childless is a double hardship. Such a woman has no husband to be provider and protector and also has no son or even prospects for a son to carry on the family name and to support her in her old age (Ruth 4:10; 2 Sam. 14:7; 1 Kings 17:8-24; 1 Tim. 5:4). For this reason, God is sometimes doubly gracious to such a person (Ruth 4:13-17; Luke

7:11-15). In the biblical accounts the bereaved widow was given a son either by miraculous restoration (the widow of Zeraphath, the widow of Nain) or by marriage (Naomi). See *Levirate Law, Levirate Marriage*.

A high priest was not allowed to marry a widow or a divorced woman (Lev. 21:14).

Sometimes nations were threatened or cursed by saying that the women would become widows (Exod. 22:24; Ps. 109:9). This is another way of saying that the men would be killed (Ezek. 22:25; Jer. 15:8; 18:21). In a similar image, a city or country can be called a "widow" figuratively (Isa. 47:5-9; Lam. 1:1; Rev. 18:7), meaning that it would be destitute and not under anyone's protection. Babylon is depicted as a widow in denial (Isa. 47:5-9; Rev. 18:7). God can restore a "widowed" city (Isa. 54:4).

The law provided for widows through a special tithe (Deut. 14:28-29; 26:12-13) and a policy of leaving gleanings during harvest (Deut. 24:19-21). The early church also had a policy of supporting its widows (Acts 6:1). Paul instructed Timothy to withhold this support from those widows who had other family who should support them, those who lived an ungodly lifestyle, and those young enough to support themselves or to remarry (1 Tim. 5:3-16). See *Poor, Orphan, Widow; Woman*.   *David K. Stabnow*

WIFE Female marriage partner. See *Family; Marriage; Woman*.

WILD ASS See *Ass*.

WILD BEASTS Designation of any wild animal in contrast to domesticated animals, translating different Hebrew words. Most often the Hebrew

A small whirlwind in the desert of the Wadi Arabah.

W

is *chayyah* indicating living creatures (Gen. 1:24) including wild animals (Gen. 1:25). The same Hebrew form indicates humans as "living" beings (Gen. 2:7). The context shows the precise type creature meant.

WILD BEASTS OF THE ISLAND KJV phrase for a beast identified by modern translations as the hyena or jackal. See *Hyena.*

WILD DONKEY See *Ass.*

WILD GOAT See *Goat; Ibex.*

WILD GOURD Poisonous plant, probably *Citrillus colocynths* (2 Kings 4:39).

WILD OX See *Ox.*

WILDERNESS Holy Land areas, particularly in the southern part, with little rainfall and few people. The words for "wilderness" in the OT come close to our word "desert" because they usually mean a rocky, dry wasteland. Desert in the lands of the Bible is usually rocks instead of sand dunes. These have been called "tame" deserts because they have infrequent rainfall and wells or oases enough to accommodate some nomadic or seminomadic human occupancy. It was the land that neighbored inhabited land to which shepherds could drive their sheep and goats for pasture. David's older brother Eliab taunted him: "With whom have you left those few sheep in the wilderness?" (1 Sam. 17:28 NRSV). The wilderness could also have the forbidding sense of uninhabitable land, as Jeremiah described it: "a land of deserts and pits ... a land of drought and deep darkness ... a land that no one passes through, where no one dwells" (Jer. 2:6 NRSV). It was a fearful place in which to get lost (Ps. 107:4-9).

Geographically the wilderness lay south, east, and southwest of the inhabited land of Israel in the Negev, Transjordan, and the Sinai. A particular wilderness, closer to home, lay on the eastern slopes of the Judean mountains in the rain shadow leading down to the Dead Sea. This particular wilderness, sometimes called Jeshimon, became a refuge for David when he fled from Saul and was the locale of the temptation of Jesus.

Historically the wilderness was particularly connected with the wandering of the Hebrews after their miraculous escape from Egypt and just prior to the conquest of Transjordan. This was remembered in their retelling of the story as "the great and terrible wilderness" (Deut. 1:19 HCSB; 8:15). There was good news and bad news about this period of the nation's existence. The good news was that God had provided manna, quail, and water from the rock. He had led them in the wilderness and revealed Himself and His covenant laws to them at Sinai/Horeb, the mountain of revelation. The bad news was they had rebelled against the Lord and murmured against Moses again and again in the wilderness. The book of Numbers is called in the Hebrew Bible *bemidbar*, "in the desert." It tells the tragic story of Kadesh-barnea in the Wilderness of Paran and the spy committee who persuaded the people not to attack the promised land from the south, so that a whole generation died in the desert (Num. 13–14). In the book of Psalms the worshiping Israelites confessed these ancient sins (78:40; 106:26), and NT preachers used them as a warning to "wilderness Christians" not to make the same mistakes (1 Cor. 10:1-13; Heb. 3:16-19). There were several specific wilderness areas mentioned, such as those of Sin, Shur, Sinai, Paran, and Zin on the way of wilderness wanderings. Some specific locales were connected with David's outlaw years, such as Wilderness of En-gedi, of Judah, of Maon, of Ziph. Jeremiah once yearned for a desert lodge as a place of escape from his rebellious audience (9:2). People in biblical times mostly feared the desert as a place inhabited by beasts of prey, snakes, and scorpions (even demons) to which one might drive out the scapegoat (Lev. 16:10,22,26; Isa. 13:21-22; 34:13-14). So it was appropriate as a place for Jesus' temptation (Matt. 4:1-11; Mark 1:12-13; Luke 4:1-13).

The prophets felt that most of Israel's religious troubles began with the settlement of

The Wilderness of Judea.

Canaan and apostasy to Canaanite idolatry, but they also looked forward to a renewed pilgrimage in the wilderness (Hos. 2:14-15; 9:10, cp. Deut. 32:10; Jer. 2:2-3; 31:2-3). There would be a new exodus after the Babylonian exile through the north Syrian Desert to make the Lord their king and "prepare his way" (Ezek. 20:30-38; Isa. 40:3-5). John the Baptist appeared in the wilderness of Judea as the promised prophetic forerunner (Matt. 3:1-3; Mark 1:2-4; Luke 3:2-6; John 1:23). Not only did Jesus overcome the tempter in the wilderness, but He fed the 4,000 in a desolate place east of the Sea of Galilee (Mark 8:1-9). See *Desert; Mount Sinai; Paran; Shur, Wilderness of; Sin, Wilderness of; Wanderings in the Wilderness.*   *M. Pierce Matheney*

WILL See *Free Will.*

WILL OF GOD God's plan and purpose for His creation and for each individual. God does whatever He pleases (Ps. 135:6) and desires that all people do His will. Only people fully mature in Christ are able to do God's will consistently (Col. 4:12; cp. Ps. 40:8). God's will is always good, acceptable, and perfect (Rom. 12:2). Doing God's will sustained Jesus for life (John 4:34). Sometimes, however, the will of God leads to suffering (Rom. 8:28; James 1:2-4; 1 Pet. 3:17), as it did for Jesus (Isa. 53:10; Matt. 26:39,42).

Christians are to strive to know the will of God for their lives (Ps. 143:10; Eph. 5:17; Col. 1:9; cp. Rom. 1:10). Christians are to discern God's will through prayer (Col. 1:9) and also pray that God's will for the world be done (Matt. 6:10). Jesus counted those who did God's will as His own family members (Matt. 12:50). They, like Jesus, will live forever (1 John 2:17).

WILLOW Tree usually found where water is plentiful, particularly along the Jordan River. Often the willow and the poplar are found together. The willow can grow up to 40 feet high. Willow branches were used to make the booths for the Feast of Tabernacles (Lev. 23:40). In Babylonian captivity the Jews hung their harps on willow trees because they did not feel like singing about Jerusalem in a foreign land (Ps. 137:1-4). NIV often translated willow as "poplar." See *Plants.*

WILLOW CREEK See *Arabim.*

WILLOWS, BROOK OF See *Arabim.*

WILLOWS, RAVINE OF See *Arabim.*

WILLOWS, WADI OF See *Arabim.*

WIMPLE Covering that women wore around their head and neck (Isa. 3:22). Other translations use "cloaks." See *Cloth, Clothing.*

WIND Natural force that represents in its extended meaning the breath of life in human beings and the creative, infilling power of God and His Spirit.

Early Concepts Two words in the Bible—the Hebrew *ruach* and the Greek *pneuma*—bear the basic meaning of wind but are often translated as spirit. Some understanding of the development of the latter word clarifies this transfer in meaning and enriches the concept.

Pneuma originally represented an elemental, vital, dynamic wind or breath. It was an effective power, but it belonged wholly to the realm of nature. This force denoted any type of wind and ranged from a soft breeze to a raging storm or fatal vapor. It was the wind in persons and animals as the breath they inhaled and exhaled. It was life, since breath was the sign of life. It was soul, since the animating force left when breathing ceased.

Metaphorically speaking, *pneuma* could be extended to mean a kind of breath that blew from the invisible realms; thus, it could designate spirit, a sign of the influence of the gods upon persons, and the source of a relationship between mankind and the divine. In primitive mythology this cosmic wind possessed a life-creating power, and a god could beget a son by his breath. The divine breath also inspired poets and granted ecstatic speech to prophets.

In all of these reflections, wind remained an impersonal, natural force. When we come to the Judeo-Christian understanding, however, the concept and terms retain their dynamic characteristics but rise from cosmic power to personal being.

Old Testament In the OT the primary meaning of the word *ruach* is wind. There is the slight breeze (Ps. 78:39), the storm wind (Isa. 32:2), the whirlwind (2 Kings 2:11), and the scorching wind (Ps. 11:6). Winds from the mountains and sea to the north and west brought rain and storm (1 Kings 18:43-45; Exod. 10:19; Ezek. 1:4); those coming from the deserts of the south and east could at times be balmy but more often would sear the land and dry up the vegetation

(Gen. 41:6; Job 37:1-2). Coming from different directions, wind was identified with those directions, referring to the four corners or quarters of the earth or of heaven (Jer. 49:36; Ezek. 37:9).

Theophanies, or manifestations of God, were often associated with the wind. God answered Job out of the whirlwind (Job 38:1), and the four living creatures appeared to Ezekiel in a strong wind from the north (1:4).

Wind was a symbol of transience (Ps. 78:39), fruitless striving (Eccles. 1:14), and desperateness (Job 6:26). More importantly, it was a mighty force which only God could command (Jer. 10:13). The wind did God's bidding (Ps. 104:4). So closely is the wind connected with God's will that it is called His breath that He blew on the sea to cover the chariots of Pharaoh (Exod. 15:10), or by which He froze rivers (Job 37:10) and withered grass (Isa. 40:7).

The wind is also breath in humans as the breath of life (Gen. 6:17). The entry of breath gives life (Ezek. 37:5-7); and, when it is taken away, the person dies (Ps. 104:29). The breath that brings death when it is withdrawn is identified as God's breath (Job 34:14-15). This same breath of the Almighty is the spirit of wisdom and understanding in a person (Job 32:8). When *ruach* is used of the will, intellect, and emotions, or related to God, the meaning often expands from the wind to spirit (Isa. 40:13). Thus Psalm 51 uses *ruach* three times when referring to the steadfast, willing, and broken spirit of the psalmist and once when speaking of God's Holy Spirit (vv. 10-12,17). Sometimes opinions differ whether the meaning is best served by translating the word as "wind" (breath) or "spirit" when it is specifically designated the *ruach* of God. Thus NRSV translates Gen. 1:2, "a wind from God," to mean that a wind was moving over the primordial waters; other translations speak of God's Spirit hovering there.

New Testament God makes His angels winds (Heb. 1:7), and "with the breath of His mouth" the Lord Jesus will destroy the wicked one (2 Thess. 2:8).

The extended meaning, after the experience of Pentecost, has become dominant, and *pneuma* usually refers to a person's inner being (in distinctions from the body) with which the personal Spirit of God communicates and blends as it generates and sanctifies Christians and forms them into the body of Christ (John 3:5-8; Rom. 8:14-16; 1 Cor. 12:7-13; Gal. 5:16-23). In each of these extended meanings, we can still

A limestone window grill from Tel el-Amarna in Egypt dating from the Eighteenth Dynasty, 1570 to 1320 B.C.

detect in their foundation the image of the wind (*pneuma*) which blows where it wills (John 3:8). See *Spirit*.

WINDOW English translation of several Hebrew and Greek terms indicating holes in a house. Such holes served several purposes: as a chimney for smoke to escape (Hos. 13:3); holes in places where doves live (Isa. 60:8); holes in heaven through which rain falls (Gen. 7:11; 8:2; Mal. 3:10; cp. 2 Kings 7:2). The Hebrew term indicates holes in the wall for air and light (Gen. 8:6; Josh. 2:15; Judg. 5:28). Recessed windows with lattice work marked elaborate public buildings such as the temple (1 Kings 6:4) and the royal palace (2 Kings 9:30). A third Hebrew term related to enabling something to be seen (1 Kings 7:4). See *Architecture; House*.

WINE Beverage made from fermented grapes. Grapes grew throughout ancient Palestine. Even in areas with limited rainfall, enough dew fell at

An ancient Pompeii wine shop where wine was served from pottery containers sunk into the bar counter.